OXFORD EU LAW LIBR

General Editors:

ROBERT SCHÜTZE

Professor of European and Global Law, Durham Law School and Co-Director, Global Policy Institute, Durham Law School

PIET EECKHOUT

Professor of EU Law and Dean of the Faculty of Laws, UCL; Academic Director of the European Institute

EU CONSTITUTIONAL LAW

OXFORD EU LAW LIBRARY

The aim of the series is to publish important and original studies of the various branches of EU law. Each work provides a clear, concise, and critical exposition of the law in its social, economic, and political context, at a level which will interest the advanced student, the practitioner, the academic, and government officials.

OTHER TITLES IN THE LIBRARY

EU Customs Law
Third Edition
Timothy Lyons

Principles and Practice in EU Sports Law
Stephen Weatherill

EU Justice and Home Affairs Law
Fourth Edition
Steve Peers

EU Procedural Law
Koen Lenaerts, Ignace Maselis, Kathleen Gutman, Janek Tomasz Nowak

EU Anti-Discrimination Law
Second Edition
Evelyn Ellis and Philippa Watson

EU Securities and Financial Markets Regulation
Third Edition
Niamh Moloney

The EU Common Security and Defence Policy
Panos Koutrakos

EU External Relations Law
Second Edition
Piet Eeckhout

EU Employment Law
Fourth Edition
Catherine Barnard

The EU Common Fisheries Policy
Robin Churchill and Daniel Owen

EU Constitutional Law

KOEN LENAERTS
PIET VAN NUFFEL

Edited by
Tim Corthaut

OXFORD
UNIVERSITY PRESS

OXFORD
UNIVERSITY PRESS

Great Clarendon Street, Oxford, OX2 6DP,
United Kingdom

Oxford University Press is a department of the University of Oxford.
It furthers the University's objective of excellence in research, scholarship,
and education by publishing worldwide. Oxford is a registered trade mark of
Oxford University Press in the UK and in certain other countries

© Koen Lenaerts, Piet Van Nuffel, Tim Corthaut 2021

The moral rights of the authors have been asserted

First published 2021
First published in paperback 2022

All rights reserved. No part of this publication may be reproduced, stored in
a retrieval system, or transmitted, in any form or by any means, without the
prior permission in writing of Oxford University Press, or as expressly permitted
by law, by licence or under terms agreed with the appropriate reprographics
rights organization. Enquiries concerning reproduction outside the scope of the
above should be sent to the Rights Department, Oxford University Press, at the
address above

You must not circulate this work in any other form
and you must impose this same condition on any acquirer

Public sector information reproduced under Open Government Licence v3.0
(http://www.nationalarchives.gov.uk/doc/open-government-licence/open-government-licence.htm)

Published in the United States of America by Oxford University Press
198 Madison Avenue, New York, NY 10016, United States of America

British Library Cataloguing in Publication Data
Data available

Library of Congress Cataloging in Publication Data
Data available

ISBN 978–0–19–885159–2 (Hbk.)
ISBN 978–0–19–886652–7 (Pbk.)

DOI: 10.1093/oso/9780198851592.001.0001

Links to third party websites are provided by Oxford in good faith and
for information only. Oxford disclaims any responsibility for the materials
contained in any third party website referenced in this work.

Preface

When this book was published in its first edition as *Constitutional Law of the European Union* (1999), it was rather innovative, and even controversial, to have the European Union presented from a constitutional perspective. More than twenty years later, the Union has radically expanded in geographical terms – after the withdrawal of the United Kingdom, now encompassing 27 Member States – but also saw its constitutional foundations reinforced with the entry into force of the Treaty on European Union, the Treaty on the Functioning of the European Union and the Charter of Fundamental Rights of the European Union. These are the texts that now determine the competences and govern the functioning of the Union and that define the fundamental rights enjoyed by the Union's citizens and other subjects of Union law. They operate as a self-referential system of norms whose observance conditions the legality of the operation of the Union as a common governance structure for the Member States and their citizens. That is why Union law is said to be autonomous, as the "law of the land" common to the Member States. In order to keep its common character that law is to be uniformly interpreted, applied and enforced. This is the main thrust of the constitutionalization of the Union underpinning the contents of the present book.

Our book seeks to provide practitioners, academics and students with a comprehensive and systematic analysis of the Union's constitutional law, in the broadest sense of that expression. We deal not only with the Union's competences, institutional structure, decision-making procedures, legal instruments and remedies in law, but also with the main substantive provisions of Union law.

Our work opens with a historical survey covering the successive steps taken towards the 'constitution' of the European Union, setting out the structure of its constituent Treaties, the procedure for amending them and the conditions for accession to and withdrawal from the Union (Part I). This is followed by an outline of the Union's competences (Part II). The starting point is a reminder of the values and objectives of the Union – amongst which democracy, the rule of law and respect for fundamental rights - followed by an examination of the principles of conferral of competences, subsidiarity, proportionality, sincere cooperation and equal treatment, which together constitute the overarching legal framework within which the Union exercises its competences in order to achieve those objectives. Part II goes on to provide an extensive overview of substantive Union law, which places particular emphasis on citizenship of the Union, the internal market and the area of freedom, security and justice. Due to space constraints, certain discrete fields of Union law that are worthy of study in their own right (such as competition law), are dealt with only in outline, but those sections are accompanied by numerous references to scholarly articles and textbooks, should readers wish to learn more.

Part III identifies the institutional actors that shape the European Union and its democratic life, that is, on the one hand, the institutions and bodies of the Union and, on the other, the Member States, with particular reference to the role played by national parliaments in monitoring the Union's activities. Part IV sets out the decision-making process in the Union, which includes the adoption of legislative acts and the implementation of legislation, but also the budgetary processes and negotiation of international agreements.

In our survey of the sources of Union law (Part V), efforts have been made not only to describe the principles of primacy and direct effect of that law, but also to provide clear and practical guidance concerning their application, for each of the different legal instruments of the Union. Particular attention is paid to the role played by the rights and principles enshrined in the Charter of Fundamental Rights.

The final part (Part VI) sets out the avenues available to citizens, companies and public authorities to have Union law enforced. It discusses the effective judicial protection available before the Court of Justice of the European Union and through Member State courts, both in situations of non-compliance with Union law by Member States or individuals and in situations where judicial review is being sought of the Union's action.

We would like to express our gratitude to those who have been assisting us with the successive versions of this book, starting with Robert Bray, without whom its first edition would never have seen the light, and Nathan Cambien, whose assistance was invaluable for the changes needed after the Lisbon Treaty. For this edition, we are especially grateful to our colleague Tim Corthaut, who has spared no efforts to assist us with the adaptation of the text to recent legal developments. We also thank Roel De Meu, Fien Van Reempts and Enrico Nadbath, as well as the editing team at Oxford University Press, for all support provided. This book reflects the state of the law on 21 May 2021.

All views expressed are our own and should not be ascribed to the institutions to which we belong.

Koen Lenaerts
Piet Van Nuffel
Luxembourg and Brussels
21 May 2021

Summary Contents

Introduction to the Source Material	xxi
Table of Cases	xxix
Table of Treaties Protocols and Declarations	lxxxiii
Table of Conventions and Agreements Concluded by the EU or the Former EC	cv
Table of Interinstitutional Agreements	cxi
Table of European Union Acts	cxiii
Table of Rules of Procedure	clxvii
Table of National Legislation	clxxi
List of Abbreviations	clxxiii
Overview of Differentiated Integration among European States	clxxxi

PART I CONSTITUTING THE EUROPEAN UNION

1. The Development from European Communities to European Union	3
2. The Treaty of Lisbon and the Current Treaties	40
3. Amendment of the Treaties	50
4. Accession to and Withdrawal from the European Union	58

PART II COMPETENCES OF THE EUROPEAN UNION

5. Values, Objectives, and Principles Governing the Union Competences	77
6. Citizenship of the Union	132
7. The Internal Market	153
8. The Area of Freedom, Security, and Justice	243
9. Other Areas of Union policy	275
10. External Action of the Union	336
11. Limitations and Exceptions to the Application of the Treaties	375

PART III INSTITUTIONAL ACTORS OF THE EUROPEAN UNION

12. The Political Institutions of the Union	391
13. Other Institutions and Bodies of the Union	441
14. The Union as an International Organization	474
15. The Member States of the Union	501
16. The Relationships between the Institutional Actors	517

PART IV DECISION-MAKING IN THE EUROPEAN UNION

17. The Legislative Procedures	529
18. The Implementation of Union Legislation	565
19. CFSP Decision-making	587
20. The Budgetary Procedures	594
21. The Procedure for Concluding International Agreements	604
22. Decision-making Restricted to Particular Member States	616

PART V SOURCES OF LAW OF THE EUROPEAN UNION

23. Union Law and its Effects in the National Legal Systems	629
24. The Treaties: Primary Union Law	654
25. Fundamental Rights and General Principles of Union Law	659
26. International Law	695
27. Acts Adopted by the Institutions and Bodies of the Union	713
28. Other Sources of Union Law	749

PART VI JUDICIAL PROTECTION IN THE EUROPEAN UNION

29. Judicial Protection vis-à-vis Member States and Private Parties	765
30. Judicial Protection vis-à-vis the Institutions and Bodies of the Union	791
The Authors	811
Index	813

Contents

Introduction to the Source Material	xxi
Table of Cases	xxix
Table of Treaties Protocols and Declarations	lxxxiii
Table of Conventions and Agreements Concluded by the EU or the Former EC	cv
Table of Interinstitutional Agreements	cxi
Table of European Union Acts	cxiii
Table of Rules of Procedure	clxvii
Table of National Legislation	clxxi
List of Abbreviations	clxxiii
Overview of Differentiated Integration among European States	clxxxi

PART I CONSTITUTING THE EUROPEAN UNION

1. The Development from European Communities to European Union — 3
    I. The Establishment of the European Communities — 3
        A. Post-war initiatives for European Integration — 3
        B. The ECSC Treaty — 7
        C. Proposals for political cooperation — 8
        D. The EEC Treaty and the EAEC Treaty — 9
        E. The supranational character of Community law — 13
    II. Intergovernmental Cooperation between EC Member States — 19
        A. European political cooperation — 19
        B. European monetary cooperation — 21
        C. Police and judicial cooperation — 22
    III. Bringing Together the Paths of Integration into the European Union — 25
        A. Steps towards a European Union — 25
        B. The establishment of the European Union — 27
        C. Subsequent amendments — 32
            1. The Treaty of Amsterdam — 32
            2. The Treaty of Nice — 34
        D. The Constitution for Europe — 36

2. The Treaty of Lisbon and the Current Treaties — 40
    I. The Treaty of Lisbon — 40
        A. Negotiation and ratification of the Treaty of Lisbon — 40
        B. New structure of the basic Treaties — 42
        C. Constitutional innovations — 43
        D. Amending the institutional framework — 45
    II. Union Law and its Relationship to Previous Community and Non-Community Law — 45
    III. New Intergovernmental Systems — 48
    IV. Future of the Union — 49

3. Amendment of the Treaties — 50
    I. Ordinary Revision Procedure — 50

x CONTENTS

  II. Simplified Procedures for Specific Treaty Amendments   52
  III. Limits to the Possibility to Amend the Treaties   55

4. Accession to and Withdrawal from the European Union   58
  I. Member States of the European Union   58
  II. Accession of Member States   61
   A. Conditions for accession to the European Union   62
   B. Procedure for acceding to the European Union   64
   C. Pending applications   65
  III. Member States Leaving the Union   66
  IV. Suspension of Treaty Rights and Obligations   71

PART II COMPETENCES OF THE EUROPEAN UNION

5. Values, Objectives, and Principles Governing the Union Competences   77
  I. Values of the Union   77
  II. Objectives of the European Union   81
  III. The Principle of Conferral of Competences   84
   A. Need for a legal basis   84
   B. Competences distinguished according to the legal basis   90
    1. Competences conferred expressly or impliedly by the Treaties   90
    2. Supplementary competence to achieve Union objectives (Article 352 TFEU)   92
   C. Exclusive and non-exclusive competence   94
  IV. The Principle of Subsidiarity   98
   A. Role played by the principle   98
   B. The requirements of subsidiarity   99
   C. Application of the principle of subsidiarity   100
  V. The Principle of Proportionality   104
   A. Role played by the principle   104
   B. The requirements of proportionality   105
   C. Application of the principle of proportionality   107
  VI. The Principle of Sincere Cooperation   109
   A. Role played by the principle   109
   B. The requirements of the principle of sincere cooperation   111
    1. Supplementary requirements   111
    2. Derogatory requirements   114
  VII. The Principle of Equal Treatment   116
   A. Field of application   116
    1. Prohibition of discrimination on grounds of the nationality of a Member State   117
    2. Prohibition of discrimination on grounds of sex/gender   123
    3. Other prohibited forms of discrimination   125
   B. Content   129
    1. Substantive discrimination   129
    2. Direct and indirect discrimination   129
    3. Reverse discrimination   130

6. Citizenship of the Union   132
  I. Creation of Citizenship of the Union   132

II.	Granting Citizenship	134
III.	Substance of Citizenship	136
	A. Free movement and residence rights	137
	B. Right to equal treatment and prohibition on obstacles to the right to move and reside	147
	C. Political rights	149
	D. Right to protection	151

7. The Internal Market 153
  I. The Establishment of the Internal Market 153
    A. Scope of the internal market 153
    B. From common market to internal market 156
  II. The Treaty Provisions on Free Movement 158
    A. Free movement of goods 160
      1. The customs union 161
        a. Prohibition of customs duties and charges having equivalent effect 162
        b. Permissible charges 163
        c. The Common Customs Tariff 165
      2. Prohibition of non-tariff restrictions 166
        a. Prohibition of quantitative restrictions and measures having equivalent effect 167
        b. Exceptions 170
    B. Free movement of workers and self-employed persons 178
      1. General scope 178
      2. Beneficiaries 179
        a. Nationals of a Member State 179
        b. Qualifying workers 180
        c. Self-employed persons and companies 183
        d. Connection with Union law 183
      3. Substance 185
        a. Right to enter, leave, and reside 185
        b. Prohibition of discriminatory and non-discriminatory obstacles 185
        c. Primary and secondary right of establishment 192
      4. Permitted restrictions 195
        a. Restrictions on grounds of public policy, public security, and public health 195
        b. Employment in the public service and exercise of public authority 196
        c. Restrictions based on the rule of reason 199
      5. Harmonization and recognition of professional rules 202
      6. Social security and the free movement of persons 207
    C. Freedom to provide services 211
      1. Definition and beneficiaries 212
      2. Substance of the freedom to provide services 215
      3. Permitted restrictions on freedom to provide services 218
        a. Restrictions on grounds of Articles 51 and 52 TFEU 218
        b. Restrictions based on the rule of reason 218
      4. The Services Directive 223
    D. Free movement of capital and payments 227
      1. Definition and substance 227
      2. Permitted restrictions on the free movement of capital and payments 228

III.	Harmonization of National Legislation	232
	A. The impact of Union harmonization measures	233
	B. Harmonization under Articles 114 and 115 TFEU	237

8. The Area of Freedom, Security, and Justice   243

I.	The Gradual Integration of Member States' Action in Matters of Justice and Home Affairs	243
II.	Policies on Border Checks, Asylum, and Immigration with respect to Third-country Nationals	248
	A. Border checks and visa policy	248
	B. Asylum and other international regimes of protection	250
	C. Immigration policy	254
	D. Rights derived from agreements with third countries	256
III.	Judicial Cooperation in Civil Matters	257
IV.	Judicial Cooperation in Criminal Matters	262
V.	Police Cooperation	269
VI.	Exceptional Status of Denmark and Ireland	271

9. Other Areas of Union Policy   275

I.	Protection of Personal Data	275
II.	Agriculture and Fisheries	276
III.	Transport	280
IV.	Competition	283
	A. Rules for undertakings	284
	1. Article 101 TFEU	284
	2. Article 102 TFEU	288
	3. Control of concentrations	289
	4. Public undertakings and services of general interest	290
	B. State aid	292
V.	Economic and Monetary Policy	300
	A. Introduction of the Economic and Monetary Union	300
	B. Economic policy	305
	C. Monetary Policy	311
VI.	Social Policy and Employment	313
VII.	Education, Vocational Training, Youth, and Sport	318
VIII.	Culture	320
IX.	Public Health and Consumer Protection	322
X.	Economic, Social, and Territorial Cohesion and Trans-European Networks	326
XI.	Industry	328
XII.	Research and Technological Development and Space	329
XIII.	Environment and Energy	330
XIV.	Tourism and Civil Protection	333
XV.	Administrative Cooperation	334
XVI.	Implementation of the Solidarity Clause	335

10. External Action of the Union   336

I.	General Provisions on the Union's External Action	336
II.	The Common Commercial Policy	338
	A. Scope	338

B. Autonomous measures	341
C. Trade agreements and cooperation agreements	343
D. Participation in GATT and the World Trade Organization	344
III. Association	346
A. Association of overseas countries and territories	347
B. Association agreements pursuant to Article 217 TFEU	348
IV. Development Cooperation and Humanitarian Aid	354
V. Economic, Financial, and Technical Cooperation with Third Countries and Neighbourhood Policy	357
VI. The Common Foreign and Security Policy (CFSP)	358
VII. Other External Competences of the Union	368
VIII. Relationship to the Member States' International Powers	371
11. Limitations and Exceptions to the Application of the Treaties	375
I. Personal Scope of the Treaties	375
II. Temporal Scope of the Treaties	376
A. Entry into force of the Treaties	376
B. Duration of the Treaties	377
III. Territorial Scope of the Treaties	378
IV. Exceptions to the Application of the Treaties	384

PART III INSTITUTIONAL ACTORS OF THE EUROPEAN UNION

12. The Political Institutions of the Union	391
I. The European Parliament	391
A. Powers	391
1. Nature	391
2. Survey of powers	392
a. Participation in decision-making	392
b. Budgetary authority	393
c. Supervision of other institutions and bodies	393
B. Composition	396
C. Operation	402
D. Internal organization	403
II. The European Council	405
A. Powers	405
B. Composition	408
C. Operation	410
D. Internal organization	411
III. The Council	412
A. Powers	412
1. Decision-making	412
2. Coordination	413
3. Implementation	413
4. Relationship to other institutions and bodies	413
B. Composition	414
C. Operation	418
D. Internal organization	425

IV. The European Commission	428
A. Powers	428
1. Supervision	428
2. Participation in decision-making	430
3. Implementation	431
4. Representation	431
B. Composition	431
C. Operation	438
D. Internal organization	439
13. Other Institutions and Bodies of the Union	441
I. The Court of Justice of the European Union	441
A. Jurisdiction	442
B. Composition	448
C. Procedure	450
D. Internal organization	450
II. The European Central Bank	451
A. Powers	451
B. Composition	453
C. Operation	454
D. Internal organization	454
III. The European Court of Auditors	455
A. Powers	455
B. Composition	456
C. Operation	456
D. Internal organization	457
IV. Advisory Bodies	457
A. The European Economic and Social Committee	457
B. The Committee of the Regions	458
C. Other committees	460
V. The European Investment Bank	461
VI. The European Ombudsman	462
VIII. Other Union Bodies, Offices, and Agencies	464
14. The Union as an International Organization	474
I. Legal Personality and Representation	475
II. Privileges and Immunities	478
III. The Budget of the Union	480
A. General principles	480
B. Revenue	482
C. Expenditure	485
IV. The Seats of the Institutions and Bodies	486
V. Status of Officials and Other Servants	488
VI. Rules Governing Languages	490
VII. Transparency and Access to Documents	495
15. The Member States of the Union	501
I. The Member States as Constituent Authority	501

II.	The Member States as Actors in Decision-making	504
	A. The role of the national governments	504
	B. The role of the national parliaments	505
III.	The Member States' Role in Implementing Union Law	512
IV.	The Member States' Role in Connection with the Judicial Implementation and Enforcement of Union Law	513
V.	The Role Played by Decentralized Authorities of the Member States	513

16. The Relationships between the Institutional Actors — 517
   - I. Relationship between the Institutions of the Union and the Member States — 517
   - II. Representation of Interests through Institutions and Member States — 518
   - III. Balance between the Institutions — 519
   - IV. The Allocation of the Classical Functions of a State — 523

PART IV DECISION-MAKING IN THE EUROPEAN UNION

17. The Legislative Procedures — 529
   - I. General Principles — 529
     - A. Definition of legislation — 529
     - B. Basic outline of legislative process — 530
     - C. Decision-making power — 533
       1. Participation of the Council — 533
       2. Participation of the European Parliament — 533
     - D. Right of initiative — 536
   - II. The Ordinary Legislative Procedure — 544
   - III. Special Legislative Procedures — 552
     - A. Participation of the Council — 552
     - B. Participation of the European Parliament — 553
       1. Consultation — 553
       2. Consent — 555
   - IV. Other Procedures — 556
     - A. Other involvement of the European Parliament — 557
     - B. Interinstitutional agreements — 557
     - C. Involvement of the social partners — 558
     - D. Involvement of other bodies and groups — 560
   - V. Democratic Content of Decision-Making — 562

18. The Implementation of Union Legislation — 565
   - I. Implementation by the Member States — 565
   - II. Implementation by Institutions, Bodies, Offices, or Agencies of the Union — 571
     - A. Relation between legislation and implementation — 571
     - B. Implementation by the Commission or the Council — 573
       1. Delegation to the Commission — 573
       2. Implementation by the Commission (or the Council) — 575
         a. General principles — 575
         b. Control over the implementation by the Commission: 'comitology' — 577
     - C. Implementation by other bodies, offices, or agencies — 583

19. CFSP Decision-making 587
    I. Policy-making under the CFSP 587
    II. Implementation of the CFSP 590

20. The Budgetary Procedures 594
    I. Adoption of the Budget 594
    II. Implementation of the Budget and Audit 597

21. The Procedure for Concluding International Agreements 604
    I. Field of Application of the Procedure 604
    II. Procedure for the Negotiation and Conclusion of Agreements 605
        A. Negotiations 605
        B. Conclusion of agreements 607
            1. Initialling and signature 607
            2. Power to conclude agreements 608
            3. Involvement of the European Parliament 609
                a. Consultation 610
                b. Consent 610
    III. Mixed Agreements 612
    IV. Opinion of the Court of Justice 613

22. Decision-making Restricted to Particular Member States 616
    I. Area of Freedom, Security, and Justice 616
    II. Economic and Monetary Union 619
    III. Enhanced Cooperation between Member States 620

PART V SOURCES OF LAW OF THE EUROPEAN UNION

23. Union Law and its Effects in the National Legal Systems 629
    I. Forms of Union Law 629
    II. Sources of Law and their Hierarchy 630
    III. The Principles of Primacy and Direct Effect of Union Law 631
        A. Requirements flowing from the primacy of Union law 632
            1. The principle of primacy of Union law 632
            2. The principle of interpretation in conformity with Union law 634
            3. Duty to set aside conflicting national rules 635
            4. Liability of the Member State for damage arising out of a breach of Union law 640
        B. Incorporation in the Member States' legal systems 644
        C. The direct effect of Union law 651

24. The Treaties: Primary Union Law 654
    I. Status of Primary Union Law 654
    II. Survey of the Treaties as Primary Union Law 655

25. Fundamental Rights and General Principles of Union Law 659
    I. Fundamental Rights 659
        A. Status of fundamental rights 659
            1. Fundamental rights as general principles of Union law 660

	2. The Charter of Fundamental Rights of the European Union	662
	B. Scope of fundamental rights' protection	664
	1. Protection vis-à-vis institutions and bodies of the Union	664
	2. Protection vis-à-vis Member States implementing Union law	665
	3. Limitations to the application of the Charter	669
	4. Relationship with the protection offered by the European Convention of Human Rights	671
	C. Survey of rights protected	676
II.	General Principles of Union law	684
	A. Status of general principles of Union law	684
	B. Survey of general principles of Union law	687
26. International Law		695
I.	International Agreements Concluded by the Union	695
	A. Legal force and direct effect of international agreements	695
	B. Legal force and direct effect of decisions adopted by organs set up by international agreements	699
	C. Status of agreements concluded within the framework of the GATT/WTO	700
	D. Interpretation and reviewing the legality of international agreements	702
II.	International Agreements Concluded by Member States with Third Countries	704
	A. Agreements concluded after the Treaties entered into force	704
	B. Agreements concluded before the Treaties entered into force	705
III.	Other Rules of International Law	708
	A. Customary international law and general principles of law	708
	B. Obligations in connection with the United Nations	710
27. Acts Adopted by the Institutions and Bodies of the Union		713
I.	Autonomous Measures Adopted by Institutions and Bodies	713
	A. Formal requirements and status	713
	1. Choice between different instruments	713
	2. Distinction between legislative acts and non-legislative acts	714
	3. Manner in which acts come into being	716
	4. Statement of reasons	717
	5. Publication or notification—entry into effect	718
	6. Enforcement	720
	7. Judicial review	720
	B. Regulations	721
	C. Directives	723
	1. The transposition of directives into national law	723
	2. The direct effect of provisions of an unimplemented or incorrectly implemented directive	727
	a. Expiry of the time-limit	727
	b. Direct effect only against a Member State	728
	3. Other effects of an unimplemented or incorrectly implemented directive	731
	a. Interpretation in conformity with the directive	731
	b. Disapplication of conflicting national law.	734
	c. State liability for damages	736
	D. Decisions	739

	E. Recommendations and opinions	741
	F. Other acts	742
II.	Interinstitutional Agreements	745

28. Other Sources of Union Law — 749
   I. Acts of Member State Governments and Conventions between the Member States — 749
   II. Collective Agreements — 752
   III. The Case Law of the Union Courts — 753
   IV. Non-Community Acts Adopted before the Entry into Force of the Lisbon Treaty — 754
      A. Distinguishing non-Community from Community law — 754
      B. Acts of the European Council and the Council pursuant to the CFSP and PJCC — 755
      C. International agreements concluded by the Union in connection with the CFSP and PJCC — 759
      D. Conventions concluded between the Member States — 760

PART VI JUDICIAL PROTECTION IN THE EUROPEAN UNION

29. Judicial Protection Vis-à-Vis Member States and Private Parties — 765
   I. Enforcement of Union Law in the National Courts — 765
      A. Guarantees for ensuring effective legal protection — 765
      B. Interpretation and application of Union law by national courts — 768
      C. Questions for a preliminary ruling on the interpretation of Union law — 773
         1. Possibility and obligation to refer questions for a preliminary ruling — 774
            a. Courts that may refer questions — 774
            b. Possibility to ask questions — 774
            c. Obligation to ask questions — 775
         2. Subject matter of questions referred for a preliminary ruling — 776
         3. Procedure for asking and answering questions referred for a preliminary ruling — 778
            a. Formulation of the reference for a preliminary ruling — 778
            b. Consideration by the Court of Justice — 780
         4. Consequences of preliminary rulings — 783
   II. Action for Failure by a Member State to Fulfil its Obligations — 784
      A. Initiative — 784
      B. Procedure — 785
      C. Consequences of a finding of non-compliance — 788

30. Judicial Protection Vis-à-Vis the Institutions and Bodies of the Union — 791
   I. Legal Remedies before the Court of Justice — 791
      A. Action for annulment — 792
         1. Possible defendants — 792
         2. Possible applicants — 793
            a. Institutions and Member States — 793
            b. Natural and legal persons — 793

	3. Reviewable acts	797
	4. Grounds for annulment	798
	5. Time-limit	798
	6. Effect of annulment	799
B.	Action for failure to act	799
C.	Action for damages	800
D.	Plea of illegality	801
E.	Procedure for direct actions	802
II. Judicial Protection through National Courts		804
A.	Possibility and Obligation to Ask a Question for a Preliminary Ruling on Validity	804
B.	Subject Matter of the Question Referred for a Preliminary Ruling on Validity	805
C.	Consideration of the Question for a Preliminary Ruling on Validity	806
III. Complete System of Judicial Protection?		807

The Authors   811
Index   813

Introduction to the Source Material

I. Official Publications

http://europa.eu
The internet is the easiest way to find information about the European Union. The 'europa' website is a source of news and information about the history and activities of the Union and leads visitors to the websites of the various institutions and to several databases containing official information, including 'EUR-Lex'.

http://eur-lex.europa.eu
The 'EUR-Lex' site is the starting point for any enquiry for legal information about the European Union. This site provides access in all official languages to the Treaties on which the Union is based, to Union legislation, and to the case law of the Union Courts. It is also a conduit to a number of other official documents, including the *Official Journal of the European Union*.

A. Treaties

Under the heading 'Treaties' of EUR-Lex can be found the text of the Treaty on European Union (TEU) and the Treaty on the Functioning of the European Union (TFEU); the Charter of Fundamental Rights of the European Union; as well as the original EC Treaty, EU Treaty, and the amending treaties, including the Treaty of Lisbon.

B. Legislation

EUR-Lex provides access to the *Official Journal of the European Union*, which is the official source for acts of the European Union.[1] The *Official Journal* is published in all of the official languages (before 1 May 2004 with linguistic versions in different colours, the English version being recognizable by its mauve-coloured spine[2]). While only the electronic version is authentic, a paper version can be purchased through the website.

---

[1] Before 1 February 2003, its official name was *Official Journal of the European Communities*.
[2] The secondary law in force before the accession of the United Kingdom and Ireland to the Communities (until the end of 1972) has been covered in *English Special Editions of the Official Journal*. If no English version of an acts exists, the practice is to cite the French *Journal Officiel* reference. Also for other accession of Member States, Special Editions of the Official Journal contain the secondary law in force on the date of accession of the Member State concerned.

Before 1968, the *Official Journal* appeared in one part.[3] Since 1968, the *Official Journal* has been published in two series. The *Official Journals* whose numbers are preceded by the letter L (*législation*, Legislation, cited as OJ 2021 L1/1) contain decisions of the institutions and bodies, divided into 'legislative acts' (regulations, directives, and decisions) and 'non-legislative acts' (international agreements, other regulations, directives and decisions, recommendations, guidelines, rules of procedure, acts adopted by bodies created by international agreements and interinstitutional agreements). The *Official Journals* whose numbers are preceded by the letter C (*communications*, Information and Notices, cited as OJ 2021 C1/1) publish resolutions, recommendations and opinions; information; preparatory acts (initiatives or proposals from the Member States or the institutions); notices from the institutions, bodies, offices, and agencies and announcements (such as summaries of judgments of the Union Courts and notices of cases brought before the Union Courts). The C-series issues indicated with a terminal 'A' (e.g. OJ 2020 C444A/1) contain administrative notices (such as competitions organized for recruitment of staff).[4] In 2016, a new subseries with terminal 'I' was introduced for both the L and C series, allowing for greater flexibility in the event of a change in publication planning (e.g. OJ 2020 L433I/1).

There is a Supplement to the *Official Journal* (numbers preceded by the letter S) which publishes public procurement contracts exceeding specified limits. Since July 1998 this supplement may be consulted only electronically through the TED (Tenders Electronic Daily) database: https://ted.europa.eu/.

On the EUR-Lex site, the heading 'Legal acts' leads to the *Directory of European Union legislation in force*, a list of all legislation in force including consolidated legislation, which is available in full. The link to 'Preparatory documents' leads to proposals for legislation of the Commission and to opinions provided by other institutions and bodies in the legislative process. Documents originating with the Commission are classified as 'COM' documents or—when not adopted by the College of Commissioners—as 'SEC' (Secretariat-General) or 'SWD' (Staff Working Document) documents; 'JOIN' documents are issued by the High Representative for Foreign Affairs and Security Policy and the Commission jointly. In order to find out where matters stand with a given proposal for legislation, the heading 'Lawmaking Procedures' leads to a useful search screen.

C. Case law

Since June 1997 the most important decisions of the Court of Justice of the European Union (Court of Justice and General Court) are available on the day of pronouncement from the

---

[3] Initially, its page numbers ran on from one volume to the next. Since 1 July 1967, the pagination of each volume starts from page 1 (*e.g.* OJ 1967 100/1).
[4] C-series issues indicated with a terminal 'E' (e.g. OJ 2002 C228E/1) existed only in electronic form and contained, *inter alia*, minutes of the sittings of the European Parliament, preparatory acts (such as positions adopted by the Parliament or the Council in the course of the ordinary legislative procedure), and written questions by members of the Parliament and their answers.

'curia' website: http://curia.europa.eu/. A search form allows users to search for cases, *inter alia*, by case number, date or name of the parties, fields, and words in the text.

The case number is preceded by the letter C (*Cour*) for proceedings brought before the Court of Justice; by the letter T (*Tribunal*) for proceedings brought before the General Court; and by the letter F (*Fonction publique*) for proceedings brought before the Civil Service Tribunal (from 2006 to 2016). Where the case number is followed by '- P' (*pourvoi*), the case is an appeal against a decision of the General Court; where it is followed by '- R' (*référé*), the decision relates to an application for interim measures. Cases treated under the urgent preliminary ruling procedure have a case number followed by 'PPU' (*procédure préjudicielle d'urgence*). A European Case Law Identifier (ECLI) is assigned to all decisions delivered by the Court of Justice and the General Court as well as the Opinions of the Advocates General. This ECLI is composed of the prefix 'ECLI', 'EU', 'C', or 'T' (depending on whether the decisions emanates from the Court of Justice or the General Court), the year of the decision, and an ordinal number, all separated by a semi-colon (e.g. ECLI:EU:C:2020:1033 for the judgment of the Court of Justice of 17 December 2020, *L and P*, Joined Cases C-354/20 PPU and C-412/20 PPU).

The case law of the Court of Justice and the General Court is published in all the official languages in the *Reports of Cases before the Court of Justice of the European Union* (*European Court Reports* or ECR). Until 2011 the European Court Reports were published in paper form (with linguistic versions in different colours, the English version being mauve). They can be found on the 'curia' website or on the EUR-Lex website under the heading 'Case law'.

The 'curia' website is also a source of other useful information. Under the heading 'Case-law' links are provided, *inter alia*, to the Digest of case law (systematic summaries of judgments and orders) and a useful survey of annotations of judgments. Under the heading 'Judicial Network of the European Union', access is given to references for a preliminary ruling submitted as from July 2018, in the language of the case and other available languages; to a selection of decisions of national courts and tribunals; and to notes, studies, or fact sheets on case law carried out by the member courts of the Judicial Network of the European Union, which consists of the Court of Justice of the European Union and the Constitutional and Supreme Courts of the Member States.

D. Other documents

The 'europa.eu' portal guides the site visitor under the heading 'Documents and publications' to a number of official documents, such as the document registers of the European Parliament, the European Council, the Council, and the Commission; minutes, reports. and resolutions from the European Parliament; minutes of the Council and of the weekly meetings of the Commission; and annual reports of the various Union institutions and bodies. This includes the *General Report on the Activities of the European Union* (available in electronic form since 1997), which the Commission issues every year, together with other reports, including the *Report on Competition Policy*, which is available from the website of the Commission's Competition Directorate General: http://ec.europa.eu/competition/.

An interesting feature is the catalogue of the Commission's library, which contains references to more than 200,000 publications and gives access to a search engine: https://ec.europa.eu/libraries/.

Until 2009, the Commission each month published the *Bulletin of the European Union* (EU Bull., prior to 1994: *Bulletin of the European Communities*, EC Bull.), which provided an overview of major events at Union level and described the activities of the institutions. Additionally, there were regular supplements to the *Bulletin* dealing with specific subjects. Issues of the *Bulletin* since 1996 are available in electronic form. The publication ended in 2009, but its archives are available online: https://ec.europa.eu/archives/bulletin/en/bullset.htm.

The historical archives of the Union institutions may be consulted (partially also via the internet) at the European University Institute in Florence: https://www.eui.eu/Research/HistoricalArchivesOfEU. Interesting historic documents are also to be found at the University of Luxembourg's CVCE.eu research infrastructure (cvce.eu).

II. Further Information

In most of the Member States there are a number of learned journals specializing in European Union law. Those published in English include *Common Market Law Review* (CMLRev.), *European Law Review* (ELRev), *Columbia Journal of European Law* (Col JEL), *European Papers* (electronic and open access journal) and the *Maastricht Journal of European and Comparative Law* (MJECL). Among other journals, there are *Cahiers de droit européen* (CDE), *Europarecht* (EuR), *Journal de droit européen* (JDE), *Revue du Marché Commun et de l'Union européenne* (RMCUE), *Revue trimestrielle de droit européen* (RTDE), and *SEW—Tijdschrift voor Europees en economisch recht* (SEW). Major European Union and national judicial decisions are reported in many of those journals. Moreover, general and specialist law journals increasingly contain articles on European Union law.

There are several useful blogs covering developments on European Union law, such as European Law Blog (europeanlawblog.eu), EU Law Analysis (eulawanalysis.blogspot.com) and the European Parliamentary Research Service Blog (epthinktank.eu/category/blog/).

Up-to-date information on the activities of the European Union can be found in *Europe*, a daily publication in several languages (including English) of the press agency *Agence Europe*. Also https://www.euractiv.com/ and https://eulawlive.com/ offer daily updates on European affairs. An excellent insight into current events on the European scene is given by *Politico Europe* (https://www.politico.eu). The very latest news can be found on the web page *EU news*, which publishes press releases from the institutions as they are issued. This web page also provides links to the press services of the institutions and bodies: https://europa.eu/newsroom/home_en.

III. Sources cited in abbreviated form

Accession Treaty 1972	Treaty of 22 January 1972 between the Member States of the European Communities, the Kingdom of Denmark, Ireland, the Kingdom of Norway and the United Kingdom of Great Britain and Northern Ireland concerning the accession of the Kingdom of Denmark, Ireland, the Kingdom of Norway and the United Kingdom of Great Britain and Northern Ireland to the European Economic Community and to the European Atomic Energy Community (see para. 4-002)
Accession Treaty 1979	Treaty of 28 May 1979 between the Member States of the European Communities and the Hellenic Republic concerning the accession of the Hellenic Republic to the European Economic Community and to the European Atomic Energy Community (see para. 4-003)
Accession Treaty 1985	Treaty of 12 June 1985 between the Member States of the European Communities and the Kingdom of Spain and the Portuguese Republic concerning the accession of the Kingdom of Spain and the Portuguese Republic to the European Economic Community and to the European Atomic Energy Community (see para. 4-004)
Accession Treaty 1994	Treaty of 24 June 1994 between the Member States of the European Union and the Kingdom of Norway, the Republic of Austria, the Republic of Finland and the Kingdom of Sweden concerning the accession of the Kingdom of Norway, the Republic of Austria, the Republic of Finland and the Kingdom of Sweden to the European Union (see para. 4-005)
Accession Treaty 2003	Treaty of 16 April 2003 between the Member States of the European Union and the Czech Republic, the Republic of Estonia, the Republic of Cyprus, the Republic of Latvia, the Republic of Lithuania, the Republic of Hungary, the Republic of Malta, the Republic of Poland, the Republic of Slovenia, the Slovak Republic, concerning the accession of the Czech Republic, the Republic of Estonia, the Republic of Cyprus, the Republic of Latvia, the Republic of Lithuania, the Republic of Hungary, the Republic of Malta, the Republic of Poland, the Republic of Slovenia and the Slovak Republic to the European Union (see para. 4-006)
Accession Treaty 2005	Treaty of 25 April 2005 between the Kingdom of Belgium, the Czech Republic, the Kingdom of Denmark, the Federal Republic of Germany, the Republic of Estonia, the Hellenic Republic, the Kingdom of Spain, the French Republic, Ireland, the Italian Republic, the Republic of Cyprus, the Republic of Latvia, the Republic of Lithuania, the Grand Duchy of Luxembourg, the Republic of Hungary, the Republic of Malta, the Kingdom of the Netherlands, the Republic of Austria, the Republic of Poland, the Portuguese Republic, the Republic of Slovenia, the Slovak Republic, the Republic of Finland, the Kingdom of Sweden, the United Kingdom of Great Britain and Northern Ireland (Member States of the European Union) and the Republic of Bulgaria and Romania, concerning the accession of the Republic of Bulgaria and Romania to the European Union, OJ 2005 L157/11 (see para. 4-007)

Accession Treaty 2011	Treaty between the Kingdom of Belgium, the Republic of Bulgaria, the Czech Republic, the Kingdom of Denmark, the Federal Republic of Germany, the Republic of Estonia, Ireland, the Hellenic Republic, the Kingdom of Spain, the French Republic, the Italian Republic, the Republic of Cyprus, the Republic of Latvia, the Republic of Lithuania, the Grand Duchy of Luxembourg, the Republic of Hungary, the Republic of Malta, the Kingdom of the Netherlands, the Republic of Austria, the Republic of Poland, the Portuguese Republic, Romania, the Republic of Slovenia, the Slovak Republic, the Republic of Finland, the Kingdom of Sweden, the United Kingdom of Great Britain and Northern Ireland (Member States of the European Union) and the Republic of Croatia concerning the accession of the Republic of Croatia to the European Union, OJ 2012 L112/10 (see para. 4-008)
Act of Accession 1972	Act appended to the 1972 Accession Treaty (see para. 4-002)
Act of Accession 1979	Act appended to the 1979 Accession Treaty (see para. 4-003)
Act of Accession 1985	Act appended to the 1985 Accession Treaty (see para. 4-004)
Act of Accession 1994	Act concerning the conditions of accession of the Republic of Austria, the Republic of Finland and the Kingdom of Sweden and the adjustments to the Treaties on which the Union is founded (see para. 4-005)
Act of Accession 2003	Act concerning the conditions of accession of the Czech Republic, the Republic of Estonia, the Republic of Cyprus, the Republic of Latvia, the Republic of Lithuania, the Republic of Hungary, the Republic of Malta, the Republic of Poland, the Republic of Slovenia and the Slovak Republic and the adjustments to the Treaties on which the European Union is founded (see para. 4-006)
Act of Accession 2005	Act concerning the conditions of accession of the Republic of Bulgaria and Romania and the adjustments to the Treaties on which the European Union is founded (see para. 4-007)
Act of Accession 2011	Act concerning the conditions of accession of the Republic of Croatia and the adjustments to the Treaty on European Union, the Treaty on the Functioning of the European Union and to the Treaty establishing the European Atomic Energy Community (see para. 4-008)
Act on the Direct Election of the European Parliament	Act concerning the election of the European Parliament by direct universal suffrage (see para. 12-014)
Amsterdam Treaty	Treaty of Amsterdam of 2 October 1997 amending the Treaty on European Union, the Treaties establishing the European Communities and certain related acts (see para. 1-050)
Charter of Fundamental Rights	Charter of Fundamental Rights of the European Union of 7 December 2000 (see para. 25-005)
CJ Rules of Procedure	Rules of Procedure of the Court of Justice (see para. 13-017)
Comitology Decision	Council Decision 1999/468/EC of 28 June 1999 laying down the procedures for the implementing powers conferred on the Commission (see para. 18-014)
Comitology Regulation	Regulation (EU) No 182/2011 of the European Parliament and of the Council of 16 February 2011 laying down the rules and general principles concerning mechanisms for control by Member States of the Commission's exercise of implementing powers, OJ 2011 L55/13 (see para. 18-014)
Commission Rules of Procedure	Rules of Procedure of the Commission (see para. 12-070)

INTRODUCTION TO THE SOURCE MATERIAL   xxvii

Conditions of Employment	Conditions of employment of other servants of the European Union (see para. 14-022)
Council Rules of Procedure	Rules of Procedure of the Council (see para. 12-044)
Decision on Provisional Location	Decision of the Representatives of the Governments of the Member States on the provisional location of certain institutions and departments of the Communities (see para. 14-019)
EAEC Treaty	Treaty establishing the European Atomic Energy Community (see para. 1-015)
EC Treaty	Treaty establishing the European Community (see para. 1-045)
ECHR	European Convention for the Protection of Human Rights and Fundamental Freedoms (see para. 1-007)
ECJ Statute	Protocol on the Statute of the Court of Justice of the European Union (see para. 13-002)
ECSC Treaty	Treaty establishing the European Coal and Steel Community (see para. 1-009)
EEA Agreement	Agreement on the European Economic Area (see para. 10-020)
EEC Treaty	Treaty establishing the European Economic Community (see para. 1-014)
EIB Statute	Protocol on the Statute of the European Investment Bank (see para. 13-037)
Eight Decision on Own Resources	Council Decision (EU, Euratom) 2020/2053 of 14 December 2020 on the system of own resources of the European Union, OJ 2020 L424/1 (see para. 14-013)
EP Rules of Procedure	Rules of Procedure of the European Parliament (see para. 12-017)
ESC Rules of Procedure	Rules of Procedure of the European Economic and Social Committee (see para. 13-032)
ESCB Statute	Protocol on the Statute of the European System of Central Banks and of the European Central Bank (see para. 13-019)
ESM Treaty	Treaty establishing the European Stability Mechanism (see para. 9-037)
EU Constitution	Treaty establishing a Constitution for Europe (see para. 1-059)
EU Treaty	Treaty on European Union, as applicable until the entry into force of the Lisbon Treaty (see para. 1-042; 'TEU' is used for references to the Treaty on European Union as amended by the Lisbon Treaty)
European Council Rules of Procedure	Rules of Procedure of the European Council (see para. 12-030)
Financial Regulation	Financial Regulation applicable to the general budget of the European Communities (see para. 14-010)
First Decision on Own Resources	Council Decision 70/243 of 21 April 1970 on the replacement of financial contributions from Member States by the Communities' own resources (see para. 14-013)
First Decision on the Seats of the Institutions	Decision of 12 December 1992 taken by common agreement between the Representatives of the Governments of the Member States on the location of the seats of the institutions and of certain bodies and departments of the European Communities (see para. 14-020)
First Treaty on Budgetary Provisions	Treaty of 22 April 1970 amending certain Budgetary Provisions of the Treaties establishing the European Communities and of the Treaty establishing a Single Council and a Single Commission of the European Communities (see para. 20-001)
GC Rules of Procedure	Rules of Procedure of the General Court (see para. 13-017)

Lisbon Treaty	Treaty of 13 December 2007 amending the Treaty on European Union and the Treaty establishing the European Community (see para. 2-002)
Merger Treaty	Treaty establishing a Single Council and a Single Commission of the European Communities (see para. 1-017)
Nice Treaty	Treaty of Nice of 26 February 2001 amending the Treaty on European Union, the Treaties establishing the European Communities and certain related acts (see para. 1-053)
Ombudsman Regulations	Decision of the European Parliament of 9 March 1994 on the regulations and general conditions governing the performance of the Ombudsman's duties (see para. 13-039)
Protocol on Privileges and Immunities	Protocol on the Privileges and Immunities of the European Union (see para. 14-007)
Protocol on Seats	Protocol on the location of the seats of the institutions and of certain bodies, offices, agencies and departments of the European Union (see para. 14-020)
Rules of Procedure — Court of Auditors	Rules of Procedure of the Court of Auditors (see para. 13-028)
Schengen Protocol	Protocol integrating the Schengen *acquis* into the framework of the European Union (see para. 8-004)
Second Decision on the Seats of the Institutions	Decision of 29 October 1993 taken by common agreement between the Representatives of the Governments of the Member States, meeting at Head of State and Government level, on the location of the seats of certain bodies and departments of the European Communities and of Europol (see para. 14-020)
Second Treaty on Budgetary Provisions	Treaty of 22 July 1975 amending Certain Budgetary Provisions of the Treaties establishing the European Communities and of the Treaty establishing a Single Council and a Single Commission of the European Communities (see para. 20-001)
Seventh Decision on Own Resources	Council Decision 2014/335/EU, Euratom of 26 May 2014 on the system of own resources of the European Union, OJ 2014 L 168/105 (see para. 14-013)
Single European Act	Single European act (para. 1-041)
Social Agreement	Agreement on social policy concluded between the Member States of the European Community with the exception of the United Kingdom of Great Britain and Northern Ireland (see para. 9-046)
Social Protocol	Protocol on social policy (see para. 9-046)
Staff Regulations	Staff Regulations of Officials of the European Union (see para. 14-022)
TEU	Treaty on European Union as amended by the Lisbon Treaty (see para. 2-003)
TFEU	Treaty on the Functioning of the European Union (see para. 2-003)
Third Decision on the Seats of the Institutions	Decision taken by common agreement between the Representatives of the Member States, meeting at Head of State or Government level, of 13 December 2003 on the location of the seats of certain offices and agencies of the European Union (see para. 14-020)
TSCG	Treaty on Stability, Coordination and Governance in the Economic and Monetary Union (see para. 9-041)
Withdrawal Agreement	Agreement on the withdrawal of the United Kingdom of Great Britain and Northern Ireland from the European Union and the European Atomic Energy Community, OJ 2020 L29/7 (see para. 4-016)

Table of Cases

COURT OF JUSTICE

4/54 ISA v High Authority EU:C:1955:3 . . . . 27.008
7/56 and 3–7/57 Algera and Others v Common Assembly EU:C:1957:7 . . . . 25.022
9/56 Meroni v High Authority EU:C:1958:7 . . . . 16.009, 18.022, 18.023, 18.024, 24.004, 30.005
10/56 Meroni v High Authority EU:C:1958:8 . . . . 18.022, 24.004
15/57 Compagnie des Hauts Fourneaux de Chasse v High Authority EU:C:1958:6 . . . . 24.004
18/57 Nold v High Authority EU:C:1959:6 . . . . 27.007
1/58 Stork v High Authority EU:C:1959:4 . . . . 25.003
27–29/58 Compagnie des Hauts Fourneaux et Fonderies de Givors and Others v
    High Authority EU:C:1960:20 . . . . 24.004
Opinion 1/59 Procedure for amendment to the third and fourth paras of Article 95 of
    the ECSC Treaty [EU:C:1959:30 . . . . 16.010
30/59 De Gezamenlijke Steenkolenmijnen in Limburg v High Authority EU:C:1961:2 . . . . .9.022
43/59, 45/59 and 48/59 Von Lachmüller and Others v Commission EU:C:1960:37 . . . . 14.002
44/59 Fiddelaar v Commission EU:C:1960:47 . . . . 14.002
6/60 Humblet EU:C:1960:48 . . . . 23.017
13/60 Geitling v High Authority EU:C:1962:15 . . . . 24.004
7/61 Commission v Italy EU:C:1961:31 . . . . .7.032
10/61 Commission v Italy EU:C:1962:2 . . . . 26.009, 26.013
24/62 Germany v Commission EU:C:1963:14 . . . . 27.007
26/62 Van Gend & Loos EU:C:1963:1 . . . . 1.025, 1.026, 7.016, 23.008, 23.031, 23.032
13/63 Italy v Commission EU:C:1963:20 . . . . 5.061, 11.012
73/63–74/63 Handelsvereniging Rotterdam EU:C:1964:8 . . . . 11.012
75/63 Hoekstra (née Unger) EU:C:1964:19 . . . . .7.050
90/63–91/63 Commission v Luxembourg and Belgium EU:C:1964:80 . . . . 1.024, 27.046, 29.049
101/63 Wagner EU:C:1964:28 . . . . 24.004
6/64 Costa v ENEL EU:C:1964:66 . . . . 1.025, 1.027, 9.026, 11.005, 23.010, 23.011
16/65 Schwarze EU:C:1965:117 . . . . 1.026, 27.007
18/65 and 35/65 Gutmann v Commission EU:C:1967:6 . . . . 25.024
32/65 Italy v Council and Commission EU:C:1966:42 . . . . .7.005
57/65 Lütticke EU:C:1966:34 . . . . .7.021
5/67 Beus EU:C:1968:13 . . . . 27.007
19/67 Bestuur van de Sociale Verzekeringsbank EU:C:1967:49 . . . . 14.025
27/67 Fink Frucht EU:C:1968:22 . . . . .7.021
28/67 Molkerei–Zentrale Westfalen EU:C:1968:17 . . . . 23.032
6/68 Zuckerfabrik Watenstedt v Council EU:C:1968:43 . . . . 27.013
7/68 Commission v Italy EU:C:1968:51 . . . . .7.014
13/68 Salgoil EU:C:1968:54 . . . . 7.032, 11.011, 23.032
14/68 Wilhelm EU:C:1969:4 . . . . 23.010, 25.024
24/68 Commission v Italy EU:C:1969:29 . . . . .7.017
2–3/69 Sociaal Fonds voor de DiamantarbeidersEU:C:1969:30 . . . . .7.017
29/69 Stauder EU:C:1969:57 . . . . 25.001
38/69 Commission v Italy EU:C:1970:11 . . . . 1.023, 27.047
40/69 Bollmann EU:C:1970:12 . . . . 23.012
41/69 ACF Chemiefarma v Commission EU:C:1970:71 . . . . 17.036
48/69 ICI v Commission EU:C:1972:70 . . . . 12.070, 25.022
52/69 Geigy v Commission EU:C:1972:73 . . . . 12.070
77/69 Commission v Belgium EU:C:1970:34 . . . . 18.003, 29.041
8/70 Commission v Italy EU:C:1970:94 . . . . 18.003

9/70 Grad EU:C:1970:78 .... 23.034, 27.022, 27.041
11/70 Internationale Handelsgesellschaft EU:C:1970:114......23.010, 23.011, 23.029, 25.001, 25.003
14/70 Bakels EU:C:1970:102 .... 26.013
20/70 Lesage EU:C:1970:84 .... 27.041
22/70 Commission v Council EU:C:1971:32 .... 3.009, 5.008, 5.019, 5.020, 5.026, 5.049,
 10.005, 10.037, 10.038, 10.039, 14.005, 27.044, 27.045
23/70 Haselhorst EU:C:1970:85 .... 27.041
25/70 Köster EU:C:1970:115 .... 16.010, 18.009, 18.012, 18.013
30/70 Scheer EU:C:1970:117 .... 18.002
33/70 SACE EU:C:1970:118 .... 7.016, 27.022
37/70 Rewe-Zentrale EU:C:1971:15 .... 11.012
38/70 Tradax EU:C:1971:24 .... 18.009
78/70 Deutsche Grammophon EU:C:1971:59 .... 7.036
5/71 Zuckerfabrik Schöppenstedt v Council EU:C:1971:116 .... 23.020, 27.035
7/71 Commission v France EU:C:1971:121 .... 3.008
12/71 Henck EU:C:1971:86 .... 25.022
18/71 Eunomia di Porro EU:C:1971:99 .... 7.016
20/71 Sabbatini v European Parliament EU:C:1972:48 .... 5.052
43/71 Politi EU:C:1971:122 .... 27.016
48/71 Commission v Italy EU:C:1972:65 .... 23.014, 29.048
92/71 Interfood EU:C:1972:30 .... 26.013
93/71 Leonesio EU:C:1972:39 .... 27.016
6/72 Europemballage and Continental Can v Commission EU:C:1973:22 .... 24.004
8/72 Cementhandelaren v Commission EU:C:1972:84 .... 9.014, 12.070
21–24/72 International Fruit Company and Others EU:C:1972:115 .... 26.001, 26.002,
 26.003, 26.005, 26.012
29/72 Marimex EU:C:1972:126 .... 7.017
30/72 Commission v Italy EU:C:1973:16 .... 18.003, 23.011
39/72 Commission v Italy EU:C:1973:13 .... 27.015, 29.046
40/72 Schroeder EU:C:1973:14 .... 5.037
72/72 Einfuhr- und Vorratsstelle Getreide EU:C:1973:36 .... 11.012
81/72 Commission v Council EU:C:1973:60 .... 27.045
2/73 Geddo EU:C:1973:89 .... 7.027
4/73 Nold v Commission EU:C:1974:51; EU:C:1975:114 .... 25.003, 25.018
9/73 Schlüter EU:C:1973:110 .... 25.023, 26.005, 27.016, 27.046
34/73 Variola EU:C:1973:101 .... 27.015, 27.016
39/73 Rewe-Zentralfinanz EU:C:1973:105 .... 7.019
40–48, 54–56, 111 and 113–114/73 Suiker Unie and Others v Commission EU:C:1975:174 ... 14.025
120/73 Lorenz EU:C:1973:152 .... 9.026
127/73 BRT EU:C:1974:25 .... 9.015
130/73 Vandeweghe EU:C:1973:131 .... 26.007
148/73 Louwage v Commission EU:C:1974:7 .... 27.045
152/73 Sotgiu EU:C:1974:13 .... 5.062, 7.059, 7.068
155/73 Sacchi EU:C:1974:40 .... 7.083, 9.017, 9.019
167/73 Commission v France EU:C:1974:35 .... 9.009
175/73 Union Syndicale v Council EU:C:1974:95 .... 25.018
181/73 Haegeman EU:C:1974:41 .... 21.006, 26.001, 26.006
192/73 Van Zuylen EU:C:1974:72 .... 7.036
2/74 Reyners EU:C:1974:68 .... 7.044, 7.061, 7.069
8/74 Dassonville EU:C:1974:82 .... 7.011, 7.028
9/74 Casagrande EU:C:1974:74 .... 5.019
14/74 Norddeutsches Vieh- und Fleischkontor EU:C:1974:92 .... 11.008
15/74 Centrafarm EU:C:1974:114 .... 7.036
16/74 Centrafarm EU:C:1974:115 .... 7.036
17/74 Transocean Marine Paint v Commission EU:C:1974:106 .... 25.024

33/74 Van Binsbergen EU:C:1974:131 .... 7.087, 7.090, 7.095
36/74 Walrave EU:C:1974:140 .... 7.044, 7.051, 11.006, 23.033, 27.027
41/74 Van Duyn EU:C:1974:133................................. 7.044, 23.032, 26.013, 27.022
48/74 Charmasson EU:C:1974:137 .... 9.003
63/74 Cadsky EU:C:1975:33 .... 7.017
92/74 Van den Berg EU:C:1975:63 .... 26.013
94/74 IGAV EU:C:1975:81 .... 7.021
100/74 C.A.M. v Commission EU:C:1975:152 .... 18.009
Opinion 1/75 Draft Understanding on a Local Cost Standard drawn up under the auspices
    of the OECD EU:C:1975:145 .... 5.023, 10.005, 21.001, 21.016, 21.017, 26.006
23/75 Rey Soda EU:C:1975:142 .... 18.013
24/75 Petroni EU:C:1975:129 .... 7.078
31/75 Costacurta v Commission EU:C:1975:167 .... 25.023
36/75 Rutili EU:C:1975:137............................... 6.016, 7.067, 25.018, 25.019, 27.032
38/75 Nederlandse Spoorwegen EU:C:1975:154 .... 26.001, 26.002
43/75 Defrenne EU:C:1976:56 .... 3.009, 5.058, 9.048, 23.033, 25.022, 28.003, 28.006
52/75 Commission v Italy EU:C:1976:29.. 27.020
59/75 Manghera EU:C:1976:14....................................... 3.009, 7.013, 27.046
87/75 Bresciani EU:C:1976:18.. 7.017, 10.014, 26.003
94/75 Süddeutsche Zucker EU:C:1976:20 .... 25.023
104/75 De Peijper EU:C:1976:67 .... 7.034
110/75 Mills v European Investment Bank EU:C:1976:152............................... 13.037
118/75 Watson and Belmann EU:C:1976:106 .... 7.010
119/75 Terrapin EU:C:1976:94 .... 7.036
130/75 Prais v Council EU:C:1976:142 .... 25.018
Opinion 1/76 Draft Agreement establishing a European laying-up fund for inland
    waterway vessels EU:C:1977:63 .... 5.019, 10.037, 14.005, 18.023
3–4/76 and 6/76 Kramer EU:C:1976:114................... 5.023, 10.005, 10.037, 11.009, 14.005
13/76 Donà EU:C:1976:115.. 7.051, 7.059
33/76 Rewe EU:C:1976:188................................... 5.046, 5.049, 23.018, 29.009
40/76 Kermaschek EU:C:1976:157 .... 7.049
41/76 Donckerwolcke EU:C:1976:182................................. 5.023, 5.024, 7.014
45/76 Comet EU:C:1976:191................................... 5.046, 5.049, 23.018, 29.009
46/76 Bauhuis EU:C:1977:6... 7.020
50/76 Amsterdam Bulb EU:C:1977:13............................... 18.007, 23.012, 27.015
51/76 Verbond van Nederlandse Ondernemingen EU:C:1977:12 .... 27.032
66/76 CFDT v Council EU:C:1977:31 .... 13.003
71/76 Thieffry EU:C:1977:65.. 5.047, 7.061, 7.072
74/76 Iannelli EU:C:1977:51 .... 7.026
78/76 Steinike & Weinlig EU:C:1977:52 .... 9.024, 9.026
85/76 Hoffmann-La Roche v Commission EU:C:1979:36 1 .... 25.024
101/76 Koninklijke Scholten Honig v Council and Commission EU:C:1977:70 .... 27.013
111/76 Van den Hazel EU:C:1977:83 .... 23.012
117/76 and 16/77 Ruckdeschel EU:C:1977:160....................................... 5.051, 5.061
121/76 Moli v Commission EU:C:1977:170 .... 25.024
11/77 Patrick EU:C:1977:113 .... 7.061
13/77 INNO EU:C:1977:185... 9.012
30/77 Bouchereau EU:C:1977:172 .... 6.016, 14.025
38/77 Enka EU:C:1977:190 .... 7.067, 26.013, 27.032
61/77 Commission v Ireland EU:C:1978:29 .... 11.009, 27.046
65/77 Razanatsimba EU:C:1977:193 .... 10.019
68/77 IFG v Commission EU:C:1978:23 .... 25.023
80–81/77 Commissionnaires Réunis EU:C:1978:87 .... 7.013, 9.003
100/77 Commission v Italy EU:C:1978:78... 27.020
102/77 Hoffmann-La Roche EU:C:1978:108 .... 7.036

xxxii   TABLE OF CASES

106/77 Simmenthal (Simmenthal II) EU:C:1978:49 .... 5.049, 23.014, 23.015, 29.016
112/77 Töpfer v Commission EU:C:1978:94 .... 25.020, 25.022
113/77 NTN Toyo Bearing Company v Council EU:C:1979:91 .... 18.009
148/77 Hansen EU:C:1978:173 .... 11.007
149/77 Defrenne EU:C:1978:130 .... 25.004
156/77 Commission v Belgium EU:C:1978:180 .... 9.009, 9.028, 29.049
Opinion 1/78 International Agreement on Natural Rubber EU:C:1979:224 .... 5.023, 10.003, 10.005, 21.013, 21.017
Ruling 1/78 Draft Convention of the International Atomic Energy Agency on the Physical Protection of Nuclear Materials, Facilities and Transport EU:C:1978:202 .... 14.006, 21.016, 21.017
3/78 Centrafarm EU:C:1978:174 .... 7.036
15/78 Société Générale Alsacienne de Banque EU:C:1978:184 .... 7.092, 7.095
21/78 Delkvist EU:C:1978:213 .... 27.032
83/78 Pigs Marketing Board EU:C:1978:214 .... 7.026
84/78 Tomadini EU:C:1979:129 .... 25.022
86/78 Peureux EU:C:1979:64 .... 7.021
93/78 Mattheus EU:C:1978:206 .... 4.010
98/78 Racke EU:C:1979:14 .... 27.008, 27.009
99/78 Decker EU:C:1979:15 .... 27.008
110–111/78 Van Wesemael EU:C:1979:8 .... 7.092, 7.094
115/78 Knoors EU:C:1979:31 .... 7.055, 7.072, 7.095
120/78 Rewe-Zentral (Cassis de Dijon) EU:C:1979:42 .... 7.037, 7.040, 7.042
136/78 Auer EU:C:1979:34 .... 27.047
141/78 France v United Kingdom EU:C:1979:225 .... 27.046, 29.042
148/78 Ratti EU:C:1979:110 .... 7.033, 27.023, 27.024
159/78 Commission v Italy EU:C:1979:243 .... 23.014
170/78 Commission v United Kingdom EU:C:1983:202 .... 7.022
175/78 Saunders EU:C:1979:88 .... 7.055
207/78 Even EU:C:1979:144 .... 7.060
209–215/78 and 218/78 Van Landewyck v Commission EU:C:1980:248 .... 25.008
230/78 Eridania EU:C:1979:216 .... 5.061, 18.009, 25.018, 27.015
231/78 Commission v United Kingdom EU:C:1979:101 .... 24.007
240/78 Atalanta EU:C:1979:160 .... 25.023
15/79 Groenveld EU:C:1979:253 .... 7.030
32/79 Commission v United Kingdom EU:C:1980:189 .... 27.044
44/79 Hauer EU:C:1979:290 .... 5.035, 5.039, 23.029, 25.018, 25.019, 27.050
62/79 Coditel EU:C:1980:84 .... 7.036, 7.092
68/79 Just EU:C:1980:57 .... 23.018
73/79 Commission v Italy EU:C:1980:129 .... 7.023
98/79 Pecastaing EU:C:1980:69 .... 25.018
102/79 Commission v Belgium EU:C:1980:120 .... 27.018, 27.019, 27.020
131/79 Santillo EU:C:1980:131 .... 6.016
133/79 Sucrimex and Westzucker v Commission EU:C:1980:104 .... 27.042
136/79 National Panasonic v Commission EU:C:1980:169 .... 25.018, 25.019
138/79 Roquette Frères v Council EU:C:1980:249 .... 12.001, 12.003, 12.036, 16.010, 17.010, 17.011, 17.035, 30.010
139/79 Maïzena v Council EU:C:1980:250 .... 12.001, 12.003, 16.010, 17.010, 17.011, 17.035
149/79 Commission v Belgium EU:C:1982:195 .... 6.006, 7.068
155/79 AM & S v Commission EU:C:1982:157 .... 25.021, 25.024
730/79 Philip Morris v Commission EU:C:1980:209 .... 9.022, 9.028, 30.008, 30.010
804/79 Commission v United Kingdom EU:C:1981:93 .... 5.023, 5.024, 5.049, 27.046
812/79 Burgoa EU:C:1980:231 .... 26.009, 26.011
817/79 Buyl v Commission EU:C:1982:36 .... 17.036
823/79 Carciati EU:C:1980:230 .... 7.040

828/79 Adam v Commission EU:C:1982:37 .... 17.036
1253/79 Battaglia v Commission EU:C:1982:38 .... 17.036
27/80 Fietje EU:C:1980:293 .... 7.040
35/80 Denkavit Nederland EU:C:1981:3 .... 5.061
55/80 and 57/80 Musik-Vertrieb membran EU:C:1981:10 .... 7.036
96/80 Jenkins EU:C:1981:80 .... 5.063
98/80 Romano EU:C:1981:104 .... 18.023
113/80 Commission v Ireland EU:C:1981:139 .... 7.032
115/80 Demont v Commission EU:C:1981:308 .... 25.024
137/80 Commission v Belgium EU:C:1981:237 .... 18.002
155/80 Oebel EU:C:1981:177 .... 7.028, 7.030
187/80 Merck EU:C:1981:180 .... 7.036
188–190/80 France, Italy and United Kingdom v Commission EU:C:1982:257 ..... 9.020, 17.004, 24.004
208/80 Lord Bruce of Donington EU:C:1981:194 .... 5.050, 12.016, 16.008
211/80 Advernier v Commission EU:C:1984:15 .... 27.050
212–217/80 Meridionale Industria Salumi and Others EU:C:1981:270 .... 2.007, 11.003, 27.009
270/80 Polydor EU:C:1982:43 .... 1.020, 5.008
272/80 Frans-Nederlandse Maatschappij voor Biologische Producten EU:C:1981:312 .... 7.034
279/80 Webb EU:C:1981:314 .... 7.092, 7.094
6/81 Industrie Diensten Groep EU:C:1982:72 .... 7.040
8/81 Becker EU:C:1982:7 .... 27.020, 27.022, 27.025
12/81 Garland EU:C:1982:44 .... 23.032
14/81 Alpha Steel v Commission EU:C:1982:76 .... 25.022
15/81 Schul EU:C:1982:135 .... 7.003
16/81 Alaimo v Commission EU:C:1982:154 .... 13.046
17/81 Pabst & Richarz EU:C:1982:129 .... 26.003
21/81 Bout EU:C:1982:47 .... 27.009
53/81 Levin EU:C:1982:105 .... 7.050, 7.051
62–63/81 Seco EU:C:1982:34 .... 7.088, 7.092
75/81 Blesgen EU:C:1982:117 .... 7.028
96/81 Commission v Netherlands EU:C:1982:192 .... 15.017, 18.003, 18.005
104/81 Kupferberg EU:C:1982:362 .... 26.001–26.003
106/81 Kind v EEC EU:C:1982:291 .... 7.020, 30.023
115–116/81 Adoui and Cornuaille EU:C:1982:183 .... 6.016, 7.067
144/81 Keurkoop EU:C:1982:289 .... 7.036
230/81 Luxembourg v European Parliament EU:C:1983:32 .... 3.011, 5.044, 5.050, 12.002,
                                                                    14.019, 16.008, 16.013, 24.004
261/81 Rau EU:C:1982:382 .... 7.029, 7.041, 7.042
266/81 SIOT EU:C:1983:77 .... 7.016
267–269/81 SPI and SAMI EU:C:1983:78 .... 26.005, 26.007
270/81 Felicitas Rickmers-Linie EU:C:1982:281 .... 27.023
283/81 CILFIT EU:C:1982:335 .... 29.005, 29.006, 29.019
301/81 Commission v Belgium EU:C:1983:51 .... 27.020
314–316/81 and 83/82 Waterkeyn [EU:C:1982:430 .... 18.003, 29.050
322/81 Michelin v Commission EU:C:1983:313 .... 25.024
8/82 Wagner EU:C:1983:41 .... 5.061
35–36/82 Morson and Jhanjan EU:C:1982:368 .... 29.018
43/82 and 63/82 VBVB and VBBB v Commission EU:C:1984:9 .... 12.070, 25.019
158/82 Commission v Denmark EU:C:1983:317 .... 7.022
159/82 Verli-Wallace v Commission EU:C:1983:242 .... 25.022
165/82 Commission v United Kingdom EU:C:1983:311 .... 25.019
199/82 San Giorgio EU:C:1983:311 .... 23.018, 29.011
205–215/82 Deutsche Milchkontor EU:C:1983:233 .... 18.007
237/82 Jongeneel Kaas EU:C:1984:44 .... 7.030
238/82 Duphar EU:C:1984:45 .... 7.032

xxxiv   TABLE OF CASES

266/82 Turner v Commission EU:C:1984:3 .... 24.004
286/82 and 26/83 Luisi and Carbone EU:C:1984:35 .... 7.102
320/82 D'Amario EU:C:1983:346 .... 7.078
324/82 Commission v Belgium EU:C:1984:152 .... 27.047
13/83 European Parliament v Council EU:C:1985:220 .... 7.004, 9.010, 12.009, 12.036, 17.005
14/83 Von Colson and Kamann EU:C:1984:153 .... 5.043, 18.007, 27.029
15/83 Denkavit Nederland EU:C:1984:183 .... 7.030
37/83 Rewe-Zentrale EU:C:1984:89 .... 7.013, 7.056, 11.006
63/83 Kirk EU:C:1984:255 .... 25.018, 25.022
72/83 Campus Oil EU:C:1984:256 .... 7.032
79/83 Harz EU:C:1984:155 .... 27.029
105/83 Pavkries EU:C:1984:178 .... 26.008
107/83 Klopp EU:C:1984:270 .... 7.064
108/83 Luxembourg v European Parliament EU:C:1984:156 .... 14.019
117/83 Könecke EU:C:1984:288 .... 25.022
143/83 Commission v Denmark EU:C:1985:34 .... 1.023, 18.006, 27.047
180/83 Moser EU:C:1984:233 .... 7.055
229/83 Leclerc EU:C:1985:1 .... 5.049
237/83 Prodest EU:C:1984:277 .... 11.006
238/83 Meade EU:C:1984:250 .... 7.048
240/83 ADBHU EU:C:1985:59 .... 25.018
242/83 Patteri EU:C:1984:278 .... 7.078
248/83 Commission v Germany EU:C:1985:214 .... 27.019
271/83, 15/84, 36/84, 113/84, 158/84 and 203/84 and 13/85 Ainsworth and Others v
    Commission and Council EU:C:1987:7 .... 13.045
288/83 Commission v Ireland EU:C:1985:251 .... 7.032
293/83 Gravier EU:C:1985:69 .... 5.055, 9.050, 27.046
294/83 Les Verts v European Parliament EU:C:1986:166 .... 1.026, 1.028, 13.003, 13.006,
                16.007, 16.008, 16.013, 24.001, 24.004, 27.011, 30.001, 30.004, 30.041
19/84 Pharmon EU:C:1985:304 .... 7.036
29/84 Commission v Germany EU:C:1985:229 .... 27.019
41/84 Pinna EU:C:1986:1 .... 5.062
44/84 Hurd EU:C:1986:2 .... 5.043
52/84 Commission v Belgium EU:C:1986:3 .... 5.043, 5.046
56/84 Von Gallera EU:C:1984:136 .... 28.018
60–61/84 Cinéthèque EU:C:1985:329 .... 7.040
112/84 Humblot EU:C:1985:185 .... 7.022
137/84 Mutsch EU:C:1985:335 .... 7.060
152/84 Marshall (Marshall I) EU:C:1986:84 .... 23.018, 27.022, 27.024–27.027
170/84 Bilka EU:C:1986:204 .... 5.063
174/84 Bulk Oil EU:C:1986:60 .... 5.024
178/84 Commission v Germany EU:C:1987:126 .... 26.013
205/84 Commission v Germany EU:C:1986:463 .... 7.086, 7.090, 7.092
209–213/84 Asjes and Others EU:C:1986:188 .... 9.009, 9.012
222/84 Johnston EU:C:1986:206 .... 11.011, 25.004, 25.009, 25.019, 27.025
237/84 Commission v Belgium EU:C:1986:149 .... 27.047
239/84 Gerlach EU:C:1985:443 .... 24.004
270/84 Licata v Economic and Social Committee EU:C:1986:304 .... 27.009
307/84 Commission v France EU:C:1986:222 .... 7.068
311/84 CBEM EU:C:1985:394 .... 9.019
5/85 AKZO Chemie v Commission ECLI:EU:C:1986:328 .... 12.070, 16.008, 25.019
15/85 Consorzio Cooperative d'Abbruzzo v Commission EU:C:1987:111 .... 25.022
59/85 Reed EU:C:1986:157 .... 7.060
66/85 Lawrie-Blum EU:C:1986:284 .... 7.051, 7.068
85/85 Commission v Belgium EU:C:1986:129 .... 5.043, 5.050

C-89, 104, 114, 116–117 and 125–129/85 Åhlström and Others v Commission
   EU:C:1988:447 .... 9.014, 26.013
96/85 Commission v France EU:C:1986:189 .... 7.070, 7.072
121/85 Conegate EU:C:1986:114 .... 26.009
139/85 Kempf EU:C:1986:223 .... 7.051
149/85 Wybot EU:C:1986:310 .... 16.010
186/85 Commission v Belgium EU:C:1987:208 .... 5.047
194/85 and 241/85 Commission v Greece EU:C:1988:95 .... 26.002
201–202/85 Klensch EU:C:1986:439 .... 18.007
225/85 Commission v Italy EU:C:1987:284 .... 7.068
227–230/85 Commission v Belgium EU:C:1988:6 .... 15.017, 18.005
249/85 Albako EU:C:1987:245 .... 23.010, 23.014, 27.040, 27.041
281, 283–285 and 287/85 Germany, France, Netherlands, Denmark and
   United Kingdom v Commission EU:C:1987:351 .... 5.019, 27.046
311/85 VVR EU:C:1987:418 .... 5.008
314/85 Foto-Frost EU:C:1987:452 .... 13.003, 13.006, 17.049, 24.004, 30.001, 30.032
316/85 Lebon EU:C:1987:302 .... 6.014
352/85 Bond van Adverteerders and Others EU:C:1988:196 .... 7.082, 7.085, 7.089
356/85 Commission v Belgium EU:C:1987:353 .... 7.022
358/85 and 51/86 France v European Parliament EU:C:1988:431 .... 14.019
363/85 Commission v Italy EU:C:1987:196 .... 27.019
372–374/85 Traen EU:C:1987:222 .... 27.026
12/86 Demirel EU:C:1987:400 .... 10.014, 25.019, 26.003, 26.006
14/86 Pretore di Salò EU:C:1987:275 .... 27.026, 27.030, 27.031
24/86 Blaizot EU:C:1988:43 .... 5.055
31 and 35/86 LAISA and Others v Council EU:C:1988:211 .... 4.013
34/86 Council v European Parliament EU:C:1986:291 .... 27.050
39/86 Lair EU:C:1988:322 .... 5.055, 7.060
45/86 Commission v Council EU:C:1987:163 .... 5.012, 5.013, 5.016, 5.020
46/86 Romkes EU:C:1987:287 .... 18.021
60/86 Commission v United Kingdom EU:C:1988:382 .... 23.012
63/86 Commission v Italy EU:C:1988:9 .... 7.087
66/86 Ahmed Saeed Flugreisen and Others EU:C:1989:140 .... 9.019
68/86 United Kingdom v Council EU:C:1988:85 .... 3.009, 5.012, 5.014, 9.004, 12.043, 27.048
74/86 Commission v Germany EU:C:1988:198 .... 5.046
80/86 Kolpinghuis Nijmegen EU:C:1987:431 .... 5.043
85/86 Commission v European Investment Bank EU:C:1988:110 .... 13.037, 14.009
120/86 Mulder EU:C:1988:213 .... 25.022
131/86 United Kingdom v Council EU:C:1988:86 .... 5.012
147/86 Commission v Greece EU:C:1988:150 .... 7.068, 7.069
158/86 Warner Brothers and Others EU:C:1988:242 .... 7.036
170/86 Von Deetzen EU:C:1988:214 .... 25.022
197/86 Brown EU:C:1988:323 .... 5.055
204/86 Greece v Council EU:C:1988:450 .... 5.048
222/86 Heylens EU:C:1987:442 .... 7.061
249/86 Commission v Germany EU:C:1989:204 .... 7.067
255/86 Commission v Belgium EU:C:1988:63 .... 23.012
263/86 Humbel EU:C:1988:451 .... 9.050
267/86 Van Eycke EU:C:1988:427 .... 5.008, 9.012
286/86 Deserbais EU:C:1988:434 .... 26.009
291/86 Central-Import Münster EU:C:1988:361 .... 18.013
297/86 CIDA v Council EU:C:1988:351 .... 17.045
302/86 Commission v Denmark EU:C:1988:421 .... 7.037, 7.040, 7.041
1/87 SA Universal Tankship EU:C:1987:298 .... 14.008
C-3/87 Agegate EU:C:1989:650 .... 7.051

42/87 Commission v Belgium EU:C:1988:454 ....5.055
46/87 and 227/88 Hoechst v Commission EU:C:1989:337 ....25.015, 25.019, 25.021
53/87 CICRA and Maxicar EU:C:1988:472..7.036
70/87 Fediol v Commission EU:C:1989:254 ....26.005
81/87 Daily Mail and General Trust EU:C:1988:456 ....7.065
85/87 Dow Benelux v Commission EU:C:1989:379.......................................25.021
94/87 Commission v Germany EU:C:1989:46 ....5.046
97–99/87 Dow Chemical Ibérica and Others v Commission EU:C:1989:380..........12.070, 25.021
143/87 Stanton EU:C:1988:378..7.044, 7.062
154–155/87 Wolf and Microtherm Europe EU:C:1988:379 ....7.044, 7.062
165/87 Commission v Council EU:C:1988:458 ....5.015, 5.016
186/87 Cowan EU:C:1989:47 ....5.053, 5.055, 5.056
187/87 Saarland and Others EU:C:1988:439..29.006
190/87 Oberkreisdirektor des Kreises Borken and Others (Moormann)
 EU:C:1988:424 ....5.046
C-193–194/87 Maurissen v Court of Auditors EU:C:1990:18............................25.019
196/87 Steymann EU:C:1988:475..7.051
235/87 Matteucci EU:C:1988:460 ....5.047
238/87 Volvo EU:C:1988:477 ....7.036
242/87 Commission v Council EU:C:1989:217 ....5.018, 5.020, 6.003
265/87 Schräder EU:C:1989:303..5.035, 5.037
302/87 European Parliament v Council EU:C:1988:461 ....12.009, 16.010
C-339/87 Commission v Netherlands EU:C:1990:119 ....27.019
340/87 Commission v Italy EU:C:1989:219..7.017
344/87 Bettray EU:C:1989:226 ....7.051
355/87 Commission v Council EU:C:1989:220 ....17.017
374/87 Orkem v Commission EU:C:1989:387 ....25.004, 25.021
379/87 Groener EU:C:1989:599 ....7.072, 9.054
1/88 SA Générale de Banque v Commission EU:C:1989:142 ....14.008
C-2/88 Imm. Zwartveld and Others EU:C:1990:315 ....5.047
C-3/88 Commission v Italy EU:C:1989:606 ....7.069
5/88 Wachauf EU:C:1989:321 ....25.009
C-16/88 Commission v Council EU:C:1989:397 ....18.008, 18.012, 18.014, 20.007
C-18/88 GB-INNO-BM EU:C:1991:474 ....9.019
22/88 Vreugdenhil and Others EU:C:1989:277.. 18.009
25/88 Wurmser and Others EU:C:1989:187 ....5.047, 7.034
27/88 Solvay v Commission EU:C:1989:388..25.021
30/88 Greece v Commission EU:C:1989:422 ....26.004
33/88 Allué and Others EU:C:1989:222...................................5.062, 7.059, 7.068
C-62/88 Greece v Council EU:C:1990:153 ....27.007
68/88 Commission v Greece EU:C:1989:339 ....18.007
C-69/88 Krantz EU:C:1990:97 ....7.028
C-70/88 European Parliament v Council EU:C:1990:217 ....5.014
C-70/88 European Parliament v Council EU:C:1991:373 ....5.014
C-100/88 Oyowe and Traore v Commission EU:C:1989:638 ....25.019
C-103/88 Fratelli Costanzo EU:C:1989:256 ....18.005, 23.014, 27.022, 27.025, 27.032
125/88 Nijman EU:C:1989:401 ....7.014
C-131/88 Commission v Germany EU:C:1991:87 ....27.019
C-143/88 and C-92/89 Zuckerfabrik Süderdithmarschen and Zuckerfabrik
 Soest EU:C:1991:65 .... 30.038
C-145/88 Torfaen Borough Council EU:C:1989:593 ....7.043
151/88 Italy v Commission EU:C:1989:201...27.042
171/88 Rinner-Kühn EU:C:1989:328 ....5.063
C-175/88 Biehl EU:C:1990:186..7.059
C-202/88 France v Commission EU:C:1991:120 ....9.020
C-213/88 and C-39/89 Luxembourg v European Parliament EU:C:1991:449 ....14.019

C-217/88 Commission v Germany EU:C:1990:290 ....5.046
C-221/88 Busseni EU:C:1990:84..1.026
C-262/88 Barber EU:C:1990:209 ....5.058
C-297/88 and C-197/89 Dzodzi EU:C:1990:360..................................6.016, 7.055
C-302/88 Hennen Olie EU:C:1990:455 ....7.030
C-322/88 Grimaldi EU:C:1989:646 ....27.042, 27.043, 30.035
C-326/88 Hansen EU:C:1990:291...18.007
C-331/88 Fedesa and Others EU:C:1990:391 ....5.038
C-347/88 Commission v Greece EU:C:1990:470 ....7.013
C-350/88 Delacre and Others v Commission EU:C:1990:71 ....27.007
C-361/88 Commission v Germany EU:C:1991:224...................................27.019
C-362/88 GB-INNO-BM EU:C:1990:102..7.029
C-366/88 France v Commission EU:C:1990:348 ....18.021
C-5/89 Commission v Germany EU:C:1990:320.....................................9.028
C-6/89 Commission v Belgium EU:C:1990:166.....................................13.048
C-10/89 Hag GF EU:C:1990:359...7.036
C-23/89 Quietlynn and Richards EU:C:1990:300....................................7.028
C-28/89 Germany v Commission EU:C:1991:67 ....5.046
C-34/89 Italy v Commission EU:C:1990:353 ....5.046
C-48/89 Commission v Italy EU:C:1990:255 ....5.045
C-51/89, 90/89 and 94/89 United Kingdom, France and Germany v Council EU:C:1991:241......5.020
C-61/89 Bouchoucha EU:C:1990:343..7.055, 7.072
C-68/89 Commission v Netherlands EU:C:1991:226 ....6.010
C-69/89 Nakajima v Council EU:C:1991:186..26.005
C-93/89 Commission v Ireland EU:C:1991:374.......................................7.061
C-100–101/89 Kaefer and Procacci EU:C:1990:456..................................11.009
C-106/89 Marleasing EU:C:1990:395..5.046
C-113/89 Rush Portuguesa EU:C:1990:142.....................................7.049, 7.052
C-154/89 Commission v France EU:C:1991:76 ....7.085, 7.090, 7.092, 7.094, 7.095
C-180/89 Commission v Italy EU:C:1991:78 ....7.085, 7.090, 7.092
C-188/89 Foster and Others EU:C:1990:313...27.025
C-192/89 Sevince EU:C:1990:322...8.013, 26.003, 26.004, 26.006
C-198/89 Commission v Greece EU:C:1991:79 ....7.085, 7.090, 7.092
C-213/89 Factortame and Others (Factortame I) EU:C:1990:257 ....5.049
C-221/89 Factortame and Others (Factortame II) EU:C:1991:320 ....7.054, 7.061, 7.066, 26.013
C-229/89 Commission v Belgium EU:C:1991:187....................................5.063
C-234/89 Delimitis EU:C:1991:91..5.047
C-246/89 Commission v United Kingdom EU:C:1991:375 ....7.061
C-251/89 Athanasopoulos and Others EU:C:1991:242.................................5.047
C-260/89 ERT EU:C:1991:254 ....9.019, 25.009, 25.011, 25.019, 25.021
C-288/89 Collectieve Antennevoorziening Gouda EU:C:1991:323...................7.090, 7.092
C-292/89 Antonissen EU:C:1991:80 ....7.052
C-300/89 Commission v Council EU:C:1991:2449 ....5.013, 5.015
C-306/89 Commission v Greece EU:C:1991:463.....................................7.069
C-312/89 Conforama and Others EU:C:1991:93.....................................7.043
C-332/89 Marchandise and Others EU:C:1991:94...............................7.030, 7.043
C-339/89 Alsthom Atlantique EU:C:1991:28 ....5.008, 7.030
C-340/89 Vlassopoulou EU:C:1991:193 ....5.047, 7.072
C-345/89 Stoeckel EU:C:1991:324 ....5.058
C-353/89 Commission v Netherlands EU:C:1991:325 ....7.090, 7.092
C-355/89 Barr and Montrose Holdings EU:C:1991:287 ....11.009
C-357/89 Raulin EU:C:1992:87 ....5.055
C-363/89 Roux EU:C:1991:41..7.067
C-370/89 SGEEM v European Investment Bank EU:C:1992:482..................13.036, 30.022
C-374/89 Commission v Belgium EU:C:1991:60.....................................5.045
C-377/89 Cotter and McDermott EU:C:1991:116 ....23.018

C-2/90 Commission v Belgium EU:C:1992:310 .... 7.014, 7.041
C-3/90 Bernini EU:C:1992:89 .... .7.051
C-6/90 and 9/90 Francovich and Others EU:C:1991:428 .... .5.046
C-18/90 Kziber EU:C:1991:36 .... 8.013, 26.003
C-41/90 Höfner and Elser EU:C:1991:161 .... 9.013, 9.019
C-47/90 Delhaize Frères EU:C:1992:250 .... .7.030
C-48/90 and 66/90 Netherlands and Others v Commission EU:C:1992:63 .... 9.020, 27.039
C-62/90 Commission v Germany EU:C:1992:169 .... 25.019
C-63/90 and 67/90 Portugal and Spain v Council EU:C:1992:381 .... .5.044
C-65/90 European Parliament v Council EU:C:1992:325 .... 17.036
C-69/90 Commission v Italy EU:C:1991:478 .... 6.006, 27.007
C-76/90 Säger EU:C:1991:331 .... 7.088, 7.095, 26.013
C-78–83/90 Compagnie commerciale de l'Ouest and Others EU:C:1992:118 .... .7.023
C-159/90 Society for the Protection of Unborn Children Ireland (Grogan)
    EU:C:1991:378 .... 7.082, 7.085, 25.011, 25.019
C-163/90 Legros and Others EU:C:1992:326 .... .7.017
C-179/90 Merci convenzionali porto di Genova EU:C:1991:464 .... .9.019
C-204/90 Bachmann EU:C:1992:35 .... 7.070, 7.072
C-208/90 Emmott EU:C:1991:333 .... 23.018, 27.020
C-213/90 ASTI EU:C:1991:291 .... .7.068
C-237/90 Commission v Germany EU:C:1992:452 .... 18.005
C-240/90 Germany v Commission EU:C:1992:408 .... 18.009, 18.013
C-269/90 Technische Universität München EU:C:1991:438 .... 27.007
C-271/90, 281/90 and 289/90 Spain v Commission EU:C:1992:440 .... .9.020
C-284/90 Council v European Parliament EU:C:1992:154 .... 14.012, 20.004, 24.009
C-286/90 Poulsen and Diva Navigation EU:C:1992:453 .... 11.006, 26.012-26.013
C-294/90 British Aerospace and Rover v Commission EU:C:1992:55 .... .9.026
C-295/90 European Parliament v Council EU:C:1992:294 .... 5.019, 5.057
C-300/90 Commission v Belgium EU:C:1992:37 .... .7.072
C-303/90 France v Commission EU:C:1991:424 .... 18.021, 27.045
C-310/90 Egle EU:C:1992:27 .... 27.047
C-313/90 CIRFS and Others v Commission EU:C:1993:111 .... 18.009, 27.045
C-351/90 Commission v Luxembourg EU:C:1992:266 .... .7.064
C-354/90 FNCE EU:C:1991:440 .... .9.026
C-369/90 Micheletti and Others EU:C:1992:295 .... .6.006
C-370/90 Surinder Singh EU:C:1992:296 .... .7.055
C-376/90 Commission v Belgium EU:C:1992:457 .... 26.013
Opinion 1/91 Draft Agreement relating to the creation of the European
    Economic Area EU:C:1991:490 .... 1.020, 1.025, 1.028, 3.010
Opinion 2/91 Convention No. 170 of the International Labour Organisation
    concerning safety in the use of chemicals at work EU:C:1993:106 .... 5.023, 5.026
C-2/91 Meng EU:C:1993:885 .... .9.012
C-3/91 Exportur EU:C:1992:420 .... .7.036
C-4/91 Bleis EU:C:1991:448 .... .7.068
C-72–73/91 Sloman Neptun EU:C:1993:97 .... .9.022
C-97/91 Oleificio Borelli v Commission EU:C:1992:491 .... 25.009, 25.019, 25.021
C-101/91 Commission v Italy EU:C:1993:16 .... 23.014
C-106/91 Ramrath EU:C:1992:230 .... 7.064, 7.072, 7.074
C-109/91 Ten Oever EU:C:1993:833 .... 28.006
C-111/91 Commission v Luxembourg EU:C:1993:92 .... 7.059, 7.061
C-140–141 and 278–279/91 Suffritti and Others EU:C:1992:492 .... 27.023
C-148/91 Veronica Omroep Organisatie EU:C:1993:45 .... 7.092, 7.095
C-149–150/91 Sanders Adour SNC and Guyomarc'h Orthez Nutrition Animale
    EU:C:1992:261 .... .7.021
C-152/91 Neath EU:C:1993:949 .... 28.006
C-156/91 Hansa Fleisch Ernst Mundt EU:C:1992:423 .... 27.041

C-158/91 Levy EU:C:1993:332 .... 5.058
C-159–160/91 Poucet and Pistre EU:C:1993:63 .... 9.013
C-165/91 Van Munster EU:C:1994:359 .... 5.047
C-168/91 Konstantinidis EU:C:1993:115 .... 7.061
C-169/91 Council of the City of Stoke-on-Trent and Norwich City Council EU:C:1992:519 .... 7.043
C-181/91 and 248/91 European Parliament v Council and Commission
   EU:C:1993:27 .... 2.010, 28.003–28.004
C-183/91 Commission v Greece EU:C:1993:233 .... 9.028
C-184/91 and 221/91 Oorburg and van Messem EU:C:1993:121 .... 9.011
C-185/91 Reiff EU:C:1993:886 .... 9.012
C-188/91 Deutsche Shell EU:C:1993:24 .... 26.006
C-197/91 FAC EU:C:1993:204 .... 25.021
C-200/91 Coloroll Pension Trustees EU:C:1994:348 .... 5.058
C-211/91 Commission v Belgium EU:C:1992:526 .... 7.089, 7.095
C-212/91 Angelopharm EU:C:1994:21 .... 18.009, 18.020, 29.006
C-219/91 Ter Voort EU:C:1992:414 .... 25.019, 25.020
C-225/91R Matra v Commission EU:C:1991:460 .... 9.026
C-237/91 Kus EU:C:1992:527 .... 8.013, 26.004
C-245/91 Ohra EU:C:1993:887 .... 9.012
C-267–268/91 Keck and Mithouard EU:C:1993:905 .... 7.029
C-271/91 Marshall (Marshall II) EU:C:1993:335 .... 23.018
C-272/91 Commission v Italy EU:C:1994:167 .... 7.069
C-316/91 European Parliament v Council EU:C:1994:76 .... 2.010
C-320/91 Corbeau EU:C:1993:198 .... 9.019
C-325/91 France v Commission EU:C:1993:245 .... 25.022
C-327/91 France v Commission EU:C:1994:305 .... 14.005
C-330/91 Commerzbank EU:C:1993:303 .... 7.061
C-338/91 Steenhorst-Neerings EU:C:1993:857 .... 29.011
Opinion 1/92 Draft Agreement relating to the creation of the European
   Economic Area EU:C:1992:189 .... 3.009, 10.020, 10.037
Opinion 2/92 Third Revised Decision of the OECD on national treatment
   EU:C:1995:83 .... 5.026, 10.037, 10.039, 21.017
C-2/92 Bostock EU:C:1994:116 .... 25.009, 25.011
C-13–16/92 Driessen and Others EU:C:1993:828 .... 17.036, 25.023
C-17/92 Distribuidores Cinematográficos EU:C:1993:172 .... 7.089
C-19/92 Kraus EU:C:1993:125 ....7.055, 7.062, 7.070, 7.072
C-25/92 Miethke v European Parliament EU:C:1993:32 .... 12.013
C-34/92 GruSa Fleisch EU:C:1993:317 .... 27.009
C-42/92 Thijssen EU:C:1993:304 .... 7.069
C-60/92 Otto EU:C:1993:876 .... 25.025
C-91/92 Faccini Dori EU:C:1994:292 .... 7.112, 27.024, 27.026, 27.027, 27.034, 27.035
C-92/92 and 326/92 Phil Collins and Others EU:C:1993:847 .... 5.056
C-93/92 CMC Motorradcenter EU:C:1993:838 .... 7.028
C-128/92 Banks EU:C:1994:130 .... 23.032
C-135/92 Fiskano v Commission EU:C:1994:267 .... 25.025
C-137/92P Commission v BASF and Others EU:C:1994:247 .... 12.070–12.071, 27.006
C-188/92 TWD Textilwerke Deggendorf EU:C:1994:90 .... 9.028, 30.033
C-199/92P Hüls v Commission EU:C:1999:358 .... 25.019
C-235/92P Montecatini v Commission EU:C:1999:362 .... 25.019
C-275/92 Schindler EU:C:1994:119 .... 7.012
C-292/92 Hünermund and Others EU:C:1993:932 .... 7.043
C-315/92 Verband Sozialer Wettbewerb EU:C:1994:34 .... 7.043
C-317/92 Commission v Germany EU:C:1994:212 .... 25.023
C-334/92 Wagner Miret EU:C:1993:945 .... 27.030, 27.034
C-350/92 Spain v Council EU:C:1995:237 .... 7.109
C-359/92 Germany v Council EU:C:1994:306 .... 18.013

xl   TABLE OF CASES

C-364/92 Eurocontrol EU:C:1994:7 .... 9.013
C-373/92 Commission v Belgium EU:C:1993:227 .... 7.034
C-379/92 Peralta EU:C:1994:296 .... 5.053, 7.028
C-382/92 Commission v United Kingdom EU:C:1994:233 .... 27.019
C-387/92 Banco Exterior de Espana EU:C:1994:100 .... 9.022
C-388/92 European Parliament v Council EU:C:1994:213 .... 17.036
C-391/92 Commission v Greece EU:C:1995:199 .... 7.043
C-396/92 Bund Naturschutz in Bayern and Others EU:C:1994:307 .... 27.020
C-398/92 Mund & Fester EU:C:1994:52 .... 28.018
C-401–402/92 Tankstation 't Heukske and Boermans EU:C:1994:220 .... 7.043
C-404/92P X v Commission EU:C:1994:361 .... 25.008, 25.019
C-405/92 Mondiet EU:C:1993:906 .... 11.006
C-408/92 Avdel Systems EU:C:1994:349 .... 5.058
C-410/92 Johnson EU:C:1994:401 .... 29.011
C-419/92 Scholz EU:C:1994:62 .... 7.055, 7.074
C-421/92 Hebermann-Beltermann EU:C:1994:187 .... 27.031
C-430/92 Netherlands v Commission EU:C:1994:373 .... 10.013
C-432/92 Anastasiou and Others EU:C:1994:277 .... 26.003, 26.013, 26.016
C-9/93 IHT Internationale Heiztechnik and Danzinger EU:C:1994:261 .... 7.036
C-23/93 TV10 EU:C:1994:362 .... 7.092, 7.095, 25.019
C-28/93 van den Akker EU:C:1994:351 .... 5.058
C-37/93 Commission v Belgium EU:C:1993:911 .... 7.068
C-41/93 France v Commission EU:C:1994:196 .... 7.115
C-43/93 Vander Elst EU:C:1994:310 .... 7.049, 7.052
C-44/93 Namur-Les Assurances du Crédit EU:C:1994:311 .... 9.024, 9.026
C-45/93 Commission v Spain EU:C:1994:101 .... 5.055
C-46/93 and 48/93 Brasserie du Pêcheur and Factortame (Factortame IV)]
    EU:C:1996:79 .... 16.010, 16.013, 23.017, 23.019–23.022, 23.024,
                                                    25.001, 25.022, 29.012, 30.023
C-47/93 Commission v Belgium EU:C:1994:181 .... 5.055
C-51/93 Meyhui EU:C:1994:312 .... 7.013
C-55/93 Van Schaik EU:C:1994:363 .... 7.092
C-57/93 Vroege EU:C:1994:352 .... 28.006
C-58/93 Yousfi EU:C:1994:160 .... 26.003
C-60/93 Aldewereld EU:C:1994:271 .... 7.056
C-65/93 European Parliament v Council EU:C:1995:91 .... 5.043, 5.048
C-69/93 and 258/93 Punto Casa and PPV EU:C:1994:226 .... 7.043
C-128/93 Fisscher EU:C:1994:353 .... 28.006
C-132/93 Steen EU:C:1994:254 .... 5.064
C-133/93, 300/93 and 362/93 Crispoltoni EU:C:1994:364 .... 5.037
C-143/93 Van Es Douane Agenten EU:C:1996:45 .... 25.022
C-154/93 Tawil-Albertini EU:C:1994:51 .... 7.076
C-156/93 European Parliament v Commission EU:C:1995:238 .... 18.021
C-279/93 Schumacker EU:C:1995:31 .... 7.059
C-280/93 Germany v Council EU:C:1994:367 .... 5.037, 5.061
C-296/93 and 307/93 France and Ireland v Commission EU:C:1996:65 .... 18.021
C-312/93 Peterbroeck EU:C:1995:437 .... 29.009, 29.013
C-316/93 Vaneetveld EU:C:1994:82 .... 27.023, 27.027
C-317/93 Deutsche Renault EU:C:1995:438 .... 7.036
C-319/93 and C-40/94 and 224/94 Dijkstra and Others EU:C:1995:433 .... 9.003, 9.015
C-320/93 Ortscheit EU:C:1994:379 .... 7.033, 7.043
C-324/93 Evans Medical EU:C:1995:84 .... 26.009
C-345/93 Fazenda Pública EU:C:1995:66 .... 7.022
C-347/93 Boterlux EU:C:1994:314 .... 25.024
C-355/93 Eroglu EU:C:1994:369 .... 26.004
C-358/93 and 416/93 Bordessa and Others EU:C:1995:54 .... 7.106

C-360/93 European Parliament v Council EU:C:1996:84 .... 26.006
C-363/93 and 407–411/93 Lancry and Others EU:C:1994:315............................7.017
C-381/93 Commission v France EU:C:1994:370 ....7.088
C-384/93 Alpine Investments EU:C:1995:126 ....7.085, 7.090, 7.092, 7.094
C-387/93 Banchero EU:C:1995:439..7.013, 7.043
C-392/93 British Telecommunications [EU:C:1996:131 .... 23.020, 23.022, 27.035
C-412/93 Leclerc-Siplec EU:C:1995:26 ....7.043
C-415/93 Bosman EU:C:1995:463 .... 7.044, 7.051, 7.059, 7.062, 7.067, 7.072
C-417/93 European Parliament v Council EU:C:1995:127 .... 17.035, 18.019, 18.021
C-418–421/93, 460–462/93 and 464/93 and C-9–11/94, 14–15/94, 23–24/94 and
    332/94 Semeraro Casa Uno and Others EU:C:1996:242 ....7.043
C-427/93, 429/93 and 436/93 Bristol-Myers Squibb and Others EU:C:1996:282...............7.036
C-430–431/93 Van Schijndel and Van Veen EU:C:1995:441................. 29.009, 29.011, 29.013
andandC-441/93 Pafitis and Others EU:C:1996:92 .... 27.033
C-443/93 Vougioukas EU:C:1995:394..7.055
C-450/93 Kalanke EU:C:1995:322 ....5.059
C-469/93 Chiquita Italia EU:C:1995:435............................... 26.002-26.003, 26.005
C-470/93 Mars EU:C:1995:224..7.043
C-472/93 Spano and Others EU:C:1995:421... 27.031
C-473/93 Commission v Luxembourg EU:C:1996:263 ....7.068
C-475/93 Thévenon EU:C:1995:371.. 26.009
C-476/93P Nutral v Commission EU:C:1995:401 .... 18.002
C-484/93 Svensson and Gustavsson EU:C:1995:379 ....7.089, 7.101
C-485–486/93 Simitzi EU:C:1995:281...7.017
Opinion 1/94 Agreement establishing the World Trade Organisation
    EU:C:1994:384 .... 5.026, 10.004, 10.011, 10.036, 10.037, 10.039, 21.017
Opinion 2/94 Accession by the Community to the European Convention for the
    Protection of Human Rights and Fundamental Freedoms
    EU:C:1996:140 ....3.009, 5.010, 5.020, 10.037
Opinion 3/94 Framework Agreement on Bananas EU:C:1995:436 .... 21.017
C-5/94 Hedley Lomas EU:C:1996:205...1.024, 7.033
C-13/94 P EU:C:1996:170 ....5.058
C-16/94 Dubois and Général Cargo Services EU:C:1995:268 ....7.017
C-18/94 Hopkins and Others EU:C:1996:180....................................24.004, 27.017
C-21/94 European Parliament v Council EU:C:1995:220 .... 17.036
C-25/94 Commission v Council EU:C:1996:114 .... 11.006
C-29–35/94 Aubertin EU:C:1995:39 ....7.085
C-39/94 SFEI and Others EU:C:1996:285 ....9.022, 9.026
C-45/94 Cámara de Comercio, Industria y Navegación, Ceuta (Ayuntamiento de Ceuta)
    EU:C:1995:425 .... 11.007
C-51/94 Commission v Germany EU:C:1995:352 ....7.042
C-55/94 Gebhard EU:C:1995:411............................... 7.063, 7.064, 7.070, 7.072, 7.086
C-58/94 Netherlands v Council EU:C:1996:171................. 14.030, 16.008, 25.026, 27.050
C-61/94 Commission v Germany EU:C:1996:313 ....26.002, 26.005
C-63/94 Belgapom EU:C:1995:270 ....7.043
C-68/94 and C-30/95 France and Others v Commission EU:C:1998:148 ....9.018
C-70/94 Werner EU:C:1995:328.. 10.006
C-71–73/94 Eurim-Pharm Arzneimittel EU:C:1996:286 ....7.036
C-80/94 Wielockx EU:C:1995:271 ....7.059
C-83/94 Leifer EU:C:1995:329.. 10.006
C-84/94 United Kingdom v Council EU:C:1996:431....................................5.033
C-85/94 Piageme and Others EU:C:1995:312 .... 27.033
C-101/94 Commission v Italy EU:C:1996:221 .... 6.016, 7.061, 7.067, 7.072, 7.094
C-103/94 Krid EU:C:1995:97 ....8.013
C-107/94 Asscher EU:C:1996:251 .... 7.046, 7.055, 7.059
C-113/94 Casarin EU:C:1995:413 ....7.022

C-120/94 Commission v Greece EU:C:1996:116 .... 11.011
C-120/94R Commission v Greece EU:C:1994:275 .... 11.011
C-122/94 Commission v Council EU:C:1996:68 .... 9.004, 9.027
C-129/94 Ruiz Bernáldez EU:C:1996:143 .... 27.031
C-134/94 Esso Española EU:C:1995:414 .... 7.028, 7.055
C-140–142/94 DIP and Others EU:C:1995:330 .... 7.028
C-151/94 Commission v Luxembourg EU:C:1995:357 .... 7.059
C-152/94 Van Buynder EU:C:1995:388 .... 7.055
C-157/94 Commission v Netherlands EU:C:1997:499 .... 7.013, 9.019
C-158/94 Commission v Italy EU:C:1997:500 .... 9.018
C-159/94 Commission v France EU:C:1997:501 .... 9.018
C-163/94, C-165/94 and C-250/94 Sanz de Lera and Others EU:C:1995:451 .... 7.100,
                                                              7.101, 7.106, 7.107
C-167/94R Gomis EU:C:1995:113 .... 1.049
C-175/94 Gallagher EU:C:1995:415 .... 6.016
C-178–179/94 and 188–190/94 Dillenkofer and Others EU:C:1996:375 ...... 23.022, 23.024, 27.035
C-192/94 El Corte Inglés EU:C:1996:88 .... 27.026, 27.034
C-193/94 Skanavi and Chryssanthakopoulos EU:C:1996:70 .... 5.054
C-194/94 CIA Security International EU:C:1996:172 .... 7.111
C-201/94 Smith & Nephew and Primecrown EU:C:1996:432 .... 27.033
C-214/94 Boukhalfa EU:C:1996:174 .... 7.056, 11.006
C-232/94 MPA Pharma EU:C:1996:289 .... 7.036
C-233/94 Germany v European Parliament and Council EU:C:1997:231 .... 5.033, 5.037, 7.013
C-237/94 O'Flynn EU:C:1996:206 .... 7.041, 7.060, 7.073
C-244/94 Fédération française des sociétés d'assurance and Others EU:C:1995:392 .... 9.013
C-246–249/94 Cooperativa Agricola Zootecnica S. Antonio and Others EU:C:1996:329 ..... 18.009
C-253/94P Roujansky v Council EU:C:1995:4 .... 1.041, 1.049
C-268/94 Portugal v Council EU:C:1996:461 .... 5.016, 10.021, 10.022
C-271/94 European Parliament v Council EU:C:1996:133 .... 9.058
C-272/94 Guiot EU:C:1996:147 .... 7.094
C-277/94 Taflan-Met EU:C:1996:315 .... 8.013
C-278/94 Commission v Belgium EU:C:1996:321 .... 7.052, 7.060
C-283/94 and 291–292/94 Denkavit and Others EU:C:1996:387 .... 27.047
C-285/94 Italy v Commission EU:C:1997:313 .... 18.021
C-290/94 Commission v Greece EU:C:1996:265 .... 7.068
C-293/94 Brandsma EU:C:1996:254 .... 7.034
C-303/94 European Parliament v Council EU:C:1996:238 .... 18.021
C-321–324/94 Pistre and Others EU:C:1997:229 .... 7.028
C-333/94P Tetra Pak v Commission EU:C:1996:436 .... 9.017
C-334/94 Commission v France EU:C:1996:90 .... 7.061, 7.066
C-336/94 Dafeki EU:C:1997:579 .... 8.015
C-341/94 Allain EU:C:1996:356 .... 5.043, 18.007
C-3/95 Reisebüro Broede EU:C:1996:487 .... 7.092, 7.094
C-9/95, 23/95 and 156/95 Belgium and Germany v Commission EU:C:1997:50 ...... 18.021
C-11/95 Commission v Belgium EU:C:1996:316 .... 1.024
C-13/95 Süzen EU:C:1997:141 .... 10.020, 26.004
C-18/95 Terhoeve EU:C:1999:22 .... 7.055, 7.062, 7.072
C-24/95 Alcan Deutschland EU:C:1997:163 .... 9.024
C-29/95 Pastoors and Trans-Cap EU:C:1997:28 .... 5.056, 5.061, 5.062
C-34–36/95 De Agostini and TV Shop EU:C:1997:344 .... 7.043
C-43/95 Data Delecta and Forsberg EU:C:1996:3571 .... 5.056
C-53/95 Kemmler EU:C:1996:58 .... 7.064
C-57/95 France v Commission EU:C:1997:164 .... 27.045
C-65 and 111/95 Shingara and Radiom EU:C:1997:300 .... 6.016
C-66/95 Sutton EU:C:1997:207 .... 23.024

C-70/95 Sodemare and Others EU:C:1997:301 ....7.086
C-72/95 Kraaijveld EU:C:1996:404 ....14.025, 27.032
C-74/95 and 129/95 Criminal Proceedings against X EU:C:1996:491......... 25.019, 27.030-27.031
C-84/95 Bosphorus EU:C:1996:312....................................... 18.007, 25.020, 26.016
C-94–95/95 Bonifaci and Others and Berto and Others EU:C:1997:348 ....23.022, 27.036
C-96/95 Commission v Germany EU:C:1997:165 .... 27.019
C-120/95 Decker EU:C:1998:167 ....7.040
C-122/95 Germany v Council EU:C:1998:94 ....5.052
C-124/95 Centro-Com EU:C:1997:8 .... 11.011
C-126/95 Hallouzi–Choho EU:C:1996:368...8.013, 26.003
C-127/95 Norbrook Laboratories EU:C:1998:151 .... 23.024
C-142/95P Associazione Agricoltori della Provincia di Rovigo and Others v
   Commission EU:C:1996:493 .... 27.046
C-147/95 Evrenopoulos EU:C:1997:201 .... 28.006
C-168/95 Arcaro EU:C:1996:363 .... 27.026, 27.031, 27.033
C-169/95 Spain v Commission EU:C:1997:10 ....9.024
C-171/95 Tetik EU:C:1997:31..7.052
C-177/95 Ebony Maritime and Loten Navigation EU:C:1997:89....................11.010, 26.015
C-180/95 Draehmpaehl EU:C:1997:208 .... 27.033
C-185/95P Baustahlgewebe v Commission EU:C:1998:608 .... 25.019
C-188/95 Fantask and Others EU:C:1997:580 .... 29.011
C-189/95 Franzén EU:C:1997:504 ....7.013, 7.043
C-191/95 Commission v Germany EU:C:1998:441 .... 12.070
C-225–227/95 Kapasakalis and Others EU:C:1997:345...................................7.055
C-240/95 Schmit EU:C:1996:259 ....7.029
C-244/95 Moskof EU:C:1997:551.. 18.009
C-261/95 Palmisani EU:C:1997:351... 27.036
C-263/95 Germany v Commission EU:C:1998:47 .... 18.020
C-265/95 Commission v France EU:C:1997:595 .... 5.046, 7.013, 7.026
C-267–268/95 Merck and Beecham EU:C:1996:468 ....7.036
C-284/95 Safety Hi-Tech EU:C:1998:352 .... 26.002
C-296/95 EMU Tabac and Others EU:C:1998:152.. 14.025
C-300/95 Commission v United Kingdom EU:C:1997:255 .... 27.019
C-310/95 Road Air EU:C:1997:209 .... 10.013
C-323/95 Hayes EU:C:1997:169 ....5.056, 5.061
C-337/95 Parfums Christian Dior EU:C:1997:517..1.004
C-341/95 Bettati EU:C:1998:353 .... 26.002
C-343/95 Diego Cali & Figli EU:C:1997:160..9.013
C-344/95 Commission v Belgium EU:C:1997:81..7.052
C-345/95 France v European Parliament EU:C:1997:450 ....5.050
C-367/95P Commission v Sytraval and Brink's France EU:C:1998:154.......... 9.026, 9.028, 30.011
C-368/95 Familiapress EU:C:1997:325 ....7.040, 7.043
C-373/95 Maso and Others EU:C:1997:353 .... 27.036
C-388/95 Belgium v Spain EU:C:2000:244 ....7.030, 7.036
C-390/95P Antillean Rice Mills and Others v Commission EU:C:1999:66.................. 10.013
C-392/95 European Parliament v Council EU:C:1997:289 .... 17.036
C-398/95 SETTG EU:C:1997:282...7.087, 7.092
C-408/95 Eurotunnel and Others EU:C:1997:532 ....17.017, 17.036
C-409/95 Marschall EU:C:1997:533..5.059
C-1/96 Compassion in World Farming EU:C:1998:113 ....7.033
C-9/96P Zanone v Council of Europe and France, not reported 25.013
C-14/96 Denuit EU:C:1997:260 ....1.024
C-15/96 Schöning-Kougebetopoulou EU:C:1998:3................................7.068, 7.074
C-22/96 European Parliament v Council EU:C:1998:258 ....9.058
C-27/96 Danisco Sugar EU:C:1997:563..4.011

C-35/96 Commission v Italy EU:C:1998:303 .... 9.012
andandandandC-50/96 Schröder EU:C:2000:72 .... 9.048, 28.006
C-51/96 and C-191/97 Deliège EU:C:2000:199 .... 7.081–7.082
C-53/96 Hermès International EU:C:1998:292 .... 26.002, 26.006
C-55/96 Job Centre EU:C:1997:603 .... 9.019
C-56/96 VT4 EU:C:1997:284 .... 7.095
C-57/96 Meints EU:C:1997:564 .... 7.060
C-62/96 Commission v Greece EU:C:1997:565 .... 7.061
C-64/96 and C-65/96 Uecker and Jacquet EU:C:1997:285 .... 5.064, 6.014
C-67/96 Albany EU:C:1999:430 .... 9.014, 9.019
C-85/96 Martínez Sala EU:C:1998:217 .... 5.053, 5.055, 6.018
C-89/96 Portugal v Commission EU:C:1999:573 .... 18.021
C-90/96 Petrie and Others EU:C:1997:553 .... 7.059
C-97/96 Daihatsu Deutschland EU:C:1997:581 .... 27.026, 27.034
C-106/96 United Kingdom v Commission EU:C:1998:218 .... 16.010
C-108/96 Mac Quen and Others EU:C:2001:67 .... 7.074
C-114/96 Kieffer and Thill EU:C:1997:316 .... 7.040, 7.042
C-122/96 Saldanha and MTS EU:C:1997:458 .... 5.056
C-129/96 Inter-Environnement Wallonie EU:C:1997:628 .... 5.049
C-131/96 Mora Romero EU:C:1997:317 .... 5.054
C-149/96 Portugal v Council EU:C:1999:574 .... 5.008
C-151/96 Commission v Ireland EU:C:1997:294 .... 7.061
C-157/96 National Farmers' Union and Others EU:C:1998:191 .... 5.037
C-158/96 Kohll EU:C:1998:171 .... 7.072, 7.080, 7.094
C-162/96 Racke EU:C:1998:293 .... 21.006, 26.003, 26.013, 26.016
C-163/96 Raso and Others EU:C:1998:54 .... 9.019
C-170/96 Commission v Council EU:C:1998:219 .... 1.049
C-171/96 Pereira Roque EU:C:1998:368 .... 11.007
C-177/96 Banque Indosuez and Others EU:C:1997:494
C-180/96 United Kingdom v Commission EU:C:1998:192 .... 25.022
C-184/96 Commission v France EU:C:1998:495 .... 7.040
C-187/96 Commission v Greece EU:C:1998:101 .... 7.074
C-197/96 Commission v France EU:C:1997:155 .... 27.021
C-200/96 Metronome Musik EU:C:1998:172 .... 25.019–25.020
C-203/96 Dusseldorp and Others EU:C:1998:316 .... 7.041
C-207/96 Commission v Italy EU:C:1997:583 .... 27.020
C-212/96 Chevassus-Marche EU:C:1998:68 .... 11.007
C-213/96 Outokumpu EU:C:1998:155 .... 7.023
C-234–235/96 Vick and Conze EU:C:2000:73 .... 28.006
C-239–240/96R United Kingdom v Commission EU:C:1996:347 .... 20.007
C-246/96 Magorrian and Cunningham EU:C:1997:605 .... 29.011
C-248/96 Grahame and Hollanders EU:C:1997:543 .... 7.056
C-249/96 Grant EU:C:1998:63 .... 5.058, 5.060
C-253–258/96 Kampelmann and Others EU:C:1997:585 .... 27.023, 27.025, 27.034
C-262/96 Sürül EU:C:1999:228 .... 8.013, 26.004
C-264/96 ICI EU:C:1998:370 .... 5.049, 7.066, 7.072
C-274/96 Bickel and Franz EU:C:1998:563 .... 5.055, 7.060
C-288/96 Germany v Commission EU:C:2000:537 .... 27.045
C-289/96, 293/96 and 299/96 Denmark, Germany and France v Commission
 EU:C:1999:141 .... 18.021
C-291/96 Grado and Bashir EU:C:1997:479 .... 5.056
C-319/96 Brinkmann Tabakfabriken EU:C:1998:429 .... 27.035
C-323/96 Commission v Belgium EU:C:1998:411 .... 18.005
C-336/96 Gilly EU:C:1998:221 .... 7.055, 7.059
C-343/96 Dilexport EU:C:1999:59 .... 29.011
C-348/96 Calfa EU:C:1999:6 .... 6.016

C-350/96 Clean Car Autoservice EU:C:1998:205 . . . . 7.053, 7.059, 7.067
C-355/96 Silhouette International Schmied EU:C:1998:374 . . . . .7.036
C-368/96 Generics EU:C:1998:583 . . . . 27.047
C-369/96 and 376/96 Arblade and Others EU:C:1999:575 . . . . .7.094
C-389/96 Aher-Waggon EU:C:1998:357 . . . . .7.041
C-416/96 El-Yassini EU:C:1999:107 . . . . 8.013, 26.003
C-33/97 Colim and Bigg's Continent Noord EU:C:1999:274 . . . . 24.007-24.008
C-75/97 Belgium v Commission EU:C:1999:311 . . . . .5.046
C-93/97 Fédération Belge des Chambres Syndicales de Médecins EU:C:1998:375 . . . . .9.061
C-95/97 Région Wallonne v Commission EU:C:1997:184 . . . . 18.005
C-104/97P Atlanta v Council and Commission EU:C:1999:498 . . . . 12.006, 25.008, 26.005
C-106/97 Dutch Antillean Dairy Industry EU:C:1999:433 . . . . 18.009
C-110/97 Netherlands v Council EU:C:2001:620 . . . . 27.009
C-111/97 Evobus Austria EU:C:1998:434 . . . . 27.034
C-113/97 Babahenini EU:C:1998:13 . . . . 8.013, 26.003
C-114/97 Commission v Spain EU:C:1998:519 . . . . 7.067, 7.068, 7.069
C-115–117/97 Brentjens' Handelsonderneming and Others
    EU:C:1999:434 . . . . .9.014
C-126/97 Eco Swiss China Time EU:C:1999:269 . . . . 29.014
C-131/97 Carbonari and Others EU:C:1999:98 . . . . 27.029
C-140/97 Rechberger and Others EU:C:1999:306 . . . . 26.006, 27.035
C-158/97 Badeck and Others EU:C:2000:163 . . . . .5.059
C-176–177/97 Commission v Belgium and Luxembourg EU:C:1998:285 . . . . 26.007
C-178/97 Banks and Others EU:C:2000:169 . . . . .5.047
C-181/97 van der Kooy EU:C:1999:32 . . . . 10.013
C-185/97 Coote EU:C:1998:424 . . . . .5.058
C-189/97 European Parliament v Council EU:C:1999:366 . . . . 21.011
C-202/97 Fitzwilliam Executive Search EU:C:2000:75 . . . . .5.047
C-212/97 Centros EU:C:1999:126 . . . . .7.066
C-215/97 Bellone EU:C:1998:189 . . . . 27.027, 27.033, 29.007
C-219/97 Drijvende Bokken EU:C:1999:437 . . . . .9.014
C-222/97 Trummer and Mayer EU:C:1999:143 . . . . .7.101
C-224/97 Ciola EU:C:1999:212 . . . . 7.085, 7.089
C-226/97 Lemmens EU:C:1998:296 . . . . 23.014
C-230/97 Awoyemi EU:C:1998:521 . . . . 27.029
C-233/97 KappAhl Oy EU:C:1998:585 . . . . 24.007, 24.008
C-234/97 Fernández de Bobadilla EU:C:1999:367 . . . . .7.077
C-254/97 Baxter EU:C:1999:368 . . . . .7.066
C-262/97 Engelbrecht EU:C:2000:492 . . . . .5.046
C-270–271/97 Sievers and Schrage EU:C:2000:76 . . . . 9.048, 28.006
C-273/97 Sirdar EU:C:1999:523 . . . . 5.058, 11.011
C-293/97 Standley, Metson and Others EU:C:1999:215 . . . . .9.061
C-295/97 Industrie Aeronautiche e Meccaniche Rinaldo Piaggio EU:C:1999:313 . . . . .9.026
C-302/97 Konle EU:C:1999:271 . . . . 7.101, 7.105, 18.005
C-307/97 Saint-Gobain ZN EU:C:1999:438 . . . . 26.007
C-311/97 Royal Bank of Scotland EU:C:1999:216 . . . . .7.061
C-319/97 Kortas EU:C:1999:272 . . . . 5.043, 5.047
C-321/97 Andersson and Andersson EU:C:1999:307 . . . . 11.003, 26.006
C-323/97 Commission v Belgium EU:C:1998:347 . . . . .6.021
C-337/97 Meeusen EU:C:1999:284 . . . . 7.051, 7.060, 7.061
C-340/97 Nazli EU:C:2000:77 . . . . .6.016
C-360/97 Nijhuis EU:C:1999:180 . . . . .7.079
C-378/97 Wijsenbeek EU:C:1999:439 . . . . .7.055
C-387/97 Commission v Greece EU:C:2000:356 . . . . 29.053
C-391/97 Gschwind EU:C:1999:409 . . . . .7.059
C-404/97 Commission v Portugal EU:C:2000:345 . . . . .5.046

C-412/97 ED EU:C:1999:324 ....7.030
C-414/97 Commission v Spain EU:C:1999:417 .... 11.011
C-421/97 Tarantik EU:C:1999:309..7.022
C-424/97 Haim EU:C:2000:357 ....7.072
C-430/97 Johannes EU:C:1999:293 ....5.056
C-434/97 Commission v France EU:C:2000:98 .... 29.006
C-435/97 WWF and Others EU:C:1999:418.. 27.032
C-437/97 EKW and Wein & Co EU:C:2000:110... 28.006
C-439/97 Sandoz EU:C:1999:499 ....7.101
C-6/98 ARD EU:C:1999:532 ....7.092
C-7/98 Krombach EU:C:2000:164 .... 25.019
C-17/98 Emesa Sugar EU:C:2000:70 .... 10.013, 13.013, 25.019, 29.032
C-35/98 Verkooijen EU:C:2000:294....................................... 7.101, 7.104-7.105
C-36/98 Spain v Council EU:C:2001:64..9.062
C-37/98 Savas EU:C:2000:224..8.013, 26.003
C-49–50, 52–54 and 68–71/98 Finalarte Sociedade de Construcao Civil and
    Others EU:C:2001:564...7.052
C-61/98 De Haan EU:C:1999:393..11.003, 27.009
C-62/98 Commission v Portugal EU:C:2000:358...................................... 26.010
C-84/98 Commission v Portugal EU:C:2000:359...................................... 26.010
C-99/98 Austria v Commission EU:C:2001:94...9.026
C-102 and 211/98 Kocak and Örs EU:C:2000:119.....................................8.013
C-150/98P Economic and Social Committee v E EU:C:1999:616 .... 25.019
C-151/98 P Pharos v Commission EU:C:1999:563 .... 18.019
C-165/98 Mazzoleni EU:C:2001:162 ....7.094
C-168/98 Luxembourg v European Parliament and Council EU:C:2000:598...........7.076, 27.007
C-173/98 Sebago and Maison Dubois EU:C:1999:347...................................7.036
C-174/98 and 189/98P Netherlands and Van der Wal v Commission EU:C:2000:1 .... 14.031
C-175/98 and 177/98 Lirussi and Bizarro EU:C:1999:486..............................9.061
C-179/98 Mesbah EU:C:1999:549 ....6.006
C-180–184/98 Pavlov and Others EU:C:2000:428 ....9.014
C-190/98 Graf EU:C:2000:49 ....7.062
C-195/98 Österreichischer Gewerkschaftsbund EU:C:2000:655 ....7.074
C-200/98 X and Y EU:C:1999:566 ....7.066
C-203/98 Commission v Belgium EU:C:1999:380.......................................7.066
C-209/98 Sydenhavnens Sten & Grus EU:C:2000:279 ....7.041
C-222/98 van der Woude EU:C:2000:475 ....9.014
C-224/98 D'Hoop EU:C:2002:432 ....5.055, 7.055
C-238/98 Hocsman EU:C:2000:440 ....7.077
C-240–244/98 Océano Grupo Editorial and Others EU:C:2000:346......................7.052
C-251/98 Baars EU:C:2000:205 ....7.066
C-254/98 TK-Heimdienst Sass EU:C:2000:12 ....7.043
C-274/98 Commission v Spain EU:C:2000:206 .... 18.005
C-277/98 France v Commission EU:C:2001:603 ....5.046
C-281/98 Angonese EU:C:2000:296...5.053, 7.044, 7.055, 7.062
C-285/98 Kreil EU:C:2000:2 ....5.058, 11.011
C-287/98 Linster and Others EU:C:2000:468 .... 27.032
C-300/98 and 392/98 Parfums Christian Dior and Others EU:C:2000:688 ....26.005-26.006
C-314/98 Snellers Auto's EU:C:2000:557 ....7.040
C-318/98 Fornasar and Others EU:C:2000:337 ....9.061
C-343/98 Collino and Chiaperro EU:C:2000:441 27.031
C-344/98 Masterfoods EU:C:2000:689 ....9.015
C-352/98P Laboratoires Pharmaceutiques Bergaderm and Goupil v Commission
    EU:C:2000:361 .... 23.020, 27.035, 30.023
C-355/98 Commission v Belgium EU:C:2000:113................................7.067, 7.069

TABLE OF CASES   xlvii

C-357/98 Yiadom EU:C:2000:604 ....6.016
C-367/98 Commission v Portugal EU:C:2002:326........................... 7.101, 7.104-7.106
C-368/98 Vanbraekel and Others EU:C:2001:400 ....7.080
C-369/98 Fisher and Fisher EU:C:2000:443 .... 25.019
C-376/98 Germany v European Parliament and Council EU:C:2000:544 1175......... 5.013, 5.018,
    7.113, 9.055, 16.013
C-377/98 Netherlands v European Parliament and Council EU:C:2001:523 .... 5.014, 5.033,
    7.113, 25.019, 26.003, 26.005, 27.007
C-378/98 Commission v Belgium EU:C:2001:370..5.046
C-393/98 Gomez Valente EU:C:2001:109 ....7.022
C-397/98 and 410/98 Metallgesellschaft and Others EU:C:2001:134 ....7.061, 7.066
C-403/98 Azienda Agricola Monte Arcosu EU:C:2001:6 ....27.015-27.016
C-405/98 Gourmet International Products EU:C:2001:135 ....7.043
C-407/98 Abrahamsson and Anderson EU:C:2000:367 ....5.059
C-411/98 Ferlini EU:C:2000:530 .... 5.053, 7.044, 7.051
C-423/98 Albore EU:C:2000:401 ....7.104
C-424/98 Commission v Italy EU:C:2000:287 ....6.010
C-434/98P Council v Busaca and Court of Auditors EU:C:2000:546 ....5.052
C-443/98 Unilever Italia EU:C:2000:496..23.014, 27.033
C-448/98 Guimont EU:C:2000:663 ....7.028
C-456/98 Centrosteel EU:C:2000:402 .... 23.013, 27.027, 27.029, 27.031
C-466/98 Commission v United Kingdom EU:C:2002:624 ....10.039, 26.013
C-467/98 Commission v Denmark EU:C:2002:625..............................10.037, 10.039
C-468/98 Commission v Sweden EU:C:2002:626 .... 10.037
C-469/98 Commission v Finland EU:C:2002:627 ....10.037, 10.039
C-471/98 Commission v Belgium EU:C:2002:628.. 10.039
C-472/98 Commission v Luxembourg EU:C:2002:629...........................10.037, 10.039
C-475/98 Commission v Austria EU:C:2002:630................................10.037, 10.039
C-476/98 Commission v Germany EU:C:2002:631 ....10.037, 10.039
C-478/98 Commission v Belgium EU:C:2000:497...................................7.101, 7.104
C-9/99 Echirolles Distribution EU:C:2000:532 ....5.008
C-29/99 Commission v Council EU:C:2002:734 ....5.043
C-35/99 Arduino EU:C:2002:97 25 ....10.037, 10.039
C-36/99 Idéal tourisme EU:C:2000:405.. 18.007
C-54/99 Eglise de scientologie EU:C:2000:124.......................................7.101, 7.104
C-63/99 Gloszczuk and Gloszczuk EU:C:2001:488 .... 26.003
C-95–98/99 and 180/99 Khalil and Others EU:C:2001:532 ....7.055
C-107/99 Italy v Commission EU:C:2002:59 .... 27.006
C-110/99 Emsland-Stärke EU:C:2000:695 .... 25.024
C-122/99 and 125/99P D and Sweden v Council EU:C:2001:304.........................5.060
C-135/99 Elsen EU:C:2000:647 ....6.008
C-141/99 AMID EU:C:2000:696 ....7.066
C-143/99 Adria-Wien Pipeline and Wietersdorfer & Peggauer Zementwerke
    EU:C:2001:598 ....9.022
C-144/99 Commission v Netherlands EU:C:2001:257 .... 27.019
C-145/99 Commission v Italy EU:C:2002:142 ....7.086, 23.014
C-150/99 Stockholm Lindöpark EU:C:2001:34 .... 27.035
C-157/99 Smits and Peerbooms EU:C:2001:404 ....7.080, 7.082, 7.092, 7.094
C-159/99 Commission v Italy EU:C:2001:278 .... 27.019
C-162/99 Commission v Italy EU:C:2001:35 .... 18.007
C-172/99 Liikenne EU:C:2001:59..10.020, 26.005
C-184/99 Grzelczyk EU:C:2001:458...6.005, 6.010, 6.012, 6.018
C-192/99 Kaur EU:C:2001:106..6.006
C-205/99 Analir and Others EU:C:2001:107 ....7.094
C-232/99 Commission v Spain EU:C:2002:291 ....7.077

xlviii TABLE OF CASES

C-234/99 Nygård EU:C:2002:244 .... 7.021, 7.023
C-235/99 Kondova EU:C:2001:489 .... 26.003
C-236/99 Commission v Belgium EU:C:2000:374 .... 5.046
C-238/99, 244–245/99, 247/99, 250–252/99 and 254/99P Limburgse Vinyl
   Maatschappij NV and Others v Commission EU:C:2002:582 .... 25.019, 25.025
C-257/99 Barkoci and Malil EU:C:2001:491 .... 26.003
C-261/99 Commission v France EU:C:2001:179 .... 5.046
C-262/99 Louloudakis EU:C:2001:407 .... 18.007
C-265/99 Commission v France EU:C:2001:169 .... 7.022
C-268/99 Jany and Others EU:C:2001:616 .... 7.054, 7.067
C-269/99 Carl Kühne and Others EU:C:2001:659 .... 25.009, 25.019
C-274/99P Connolly v Commission EU:C:2001:127 .... 25.019
C-283/99 Commission v Italy EU:C:2001:307 .... 7.068, 7.069
C-290/99 Council v Bangemann, removed from the register 12.067
C-307/99 OGT Fruchthandelsgesellschaft EU:C:2001:228 .... 26.005, 26.009
C-309/99 Wouters and Others EU:C:2002:98 .... 9.013–9.014
C-313/99 Mulligan EU:C:2002:386 .... 18.007
C-315/99P Ismeri Europa v Court of Auditors EU:C:2001:391 .... 20.011
C-319/99 Commission v France EU:C:2000:649 .... 27.020
C-334/99 Germany v Commission EU:C:2003:55 .... 12.067
C-340/99 TNT Traco EU:C:2001:281 .... 9.019
C-353/99P Council v Hautala EU:C:2001:661 .... 14.031
C-366/99 Griesmar EU:C:2001:648 .... 5.059
C-372/99 Commission v Italy EU:C:2002:42 .... 27.019
C-385/99 Müller-Fauré and van Riet EU:C:2003:270 .... 7.080
C-390/99 Canal Satélite Digital EU:C:2002:34 .... 7.011, 7.012
C-413/99 Baumbast and R EU:C:2002:493 .... 6.007, 6.008, 6.010, 6.014
C-414–416/99 Zino Davidoff and Others EU:C:2001:617 .... 7.036
C-439/99 Commission v Italy EU:C:2002:14 .... 7.011
C-451/99 Cura Anlagen EU:C:2002:195 .... 7.094
C-453/99 Courage EU:C:2001:465 .... 9.015
C-459/99 MRAX EU:C:2002:461 .... 6.010, 6.016
C-462/99 Connect Austria Gesellschaft für Telekommunikation EU:C:2003:297 .... 29.009
C-475/99 Firma Ambulanz Glöckner EU:C:2001:577 .... 9.019
C-476/99 Lommers EU:C:2002:183 .... 5.059
C-478/99 Commission v Sweden EU:C:2002:281 .... 27.019
C-481/99 Heininger and Heininger EU:C:2001:684 .... 23.006
C-482/99 France v Commission EU:C:2002:294 .... 9.021
C-483/99 Commission v France EU:C:2002:327 .... 7.101, 7.104, 7.105–7.106
C-499/99 Commission v Spain EU:C:2002:408 .... 5.046
C-503/99 Commission v Belgium EU:C:2002:328 .... 7.104, 7.105-7.106
C-512/99 Germany v Commission EU:C:2003:40 .... 7.115, 11.003
C-515/99, 519–524/99 and 526–540/99 Reisch and Others EU:C:2002:135 .... 7.101, 7.105-7.106
Opinion 1/00 Proposed Agreement on the establishment of a European Common
   Aviation Area EU:C:2002:231 .... 3.010
C-1/00 Commission v France EU:C:2001:687 .... 21.017
Opinion 2/00 Cartagena Protocol EU:C:2001:664 .... 5.010, 5.013, 5.014
C-3/00 Denmark v Commission EU:C:2003:167 .... 7.115, 25.023, 25.025
C-11/00 Commission v European Central Bank EU:C:2003:395 .... 13.019-13.020,
                                                          16.008, 18.025, 20.013, 30.025
C-12/00 Commission v Spain EU:C:2003:21 .... 7.043
C-13/00 Commission v Ireland EU:C:2002:184 .... 26.002
C-15/00 Commission v European Investment Bank EU:C:2003:396 .... 13.037, 13.038,
                                                                 16.008, 18.025, 20.013
C-17/00 De Coster EU:C:2001:651 .... 7.088, 12.016, 29.015
C-18/00 Perino (order) not published 27.026

C-20/00 and 64/00 Booker Aquaculture and Hydro Seafood GSP EU:C:2003:397 . . . . 25.009
C-27/00 and 122/00 Omega Air EU:C:2002:161. . . . . 26.005
C-31/00 Dreessen EU:C:2002:35 . . . . .7.077
C-41/00P Interporc v Commission EU:C:2003:125. . . . . 14.030
C-50/00P Unión de Pequeños Agricultores v Council and Commission
    EU:C:2002:462 . . . . 13.003, 13.006, 25.019, 30.010, 30.043
C-52/00 Commission v France EU:C:2002:252 . . . . .7.110
C-53/00 Ferring EU:C:2001:627. . . . . .9.023
C-55/00 Gottardo EU:C:2002:16 . . . . 26.007
C-60/00 Carpenter EU:C:2002:434 . . . . 7.085, 25.019, 27.018
C-62/00 Marks & Spencer EU:C:2002:435 . . . . 26.003, 27.023, 29.011
C-76/00P Petrotub and Republica v Council EU:C:2003:4 . . . . 26.005
C-93/00 European Parliament v Council EU:C:2001:689 . . . . 18.009, 18.021
C-94/00 Roquette Frères EU:C:2002:603. . . . . .5.047
C-112/00 Schmidberger EU:C:2003:333 . . . . 7.013, 7.040, 7.072
C-118/00 Larsy EU:C:2001:368 . . . . 23.018, 23.022
C-129/00 Commission v Italy EU:C:2003:656 . . . . 15.013, 18.007, 29.041
C-137/00 Milk Marque and National Farmers' Union EU:C:2003:429 . . . . .9.003
C-154/00 Commission v Greece EU:C:2002:254 . . . . .7.110
C-159/00 Sapod Audic EU:C:2002:343 . . . . .7.013
C-162/00 Pokrzeptowicz-Meyer EU:C:2002:57 . . . . 11.003, 26.001
C-183/00 González Sánchez EU:C:2002:255. . . . . .7.110
C-188/00 Kurz EU:C:2002:694 . . . . .7.051
C-206/00 Mouflin EU:C:2001:695 . . . . .5.058
C-208/00 Überseering EU:C:2002:632 . . . . 7.065, 7.072
C-218/00 Cisal di Battistello Venanzio EU:C:2002:36 . . . . .9.013
C-221/00 Commission v Austria EU:C:2003:44 . . . . .7.039
C-224/00 Commission v Italy EU:C:2002:185 . . . . .5.053
C-233/00 Commission v France EU:C:2003:371 . . . . 27.019
C-246/00 Commission v Netherlands EU:C:2003:398 . . . . .7.072
C-253/00 Muñoz and Superior Fruiticola EU:C:2002:497 . . . . 27.016
C-257/00 Givane and Others EU:C:2003:8 . . . . 14.025
C-275/00 Frist and Franex EU:C:2002:711 . . . . .5.047
C-279/00 Commission v Italy EU:C:2002:89 . . . . .7.094
C-280/00 Altmark Trans and Regierungsprasident Magdeburg EU:C:2003:415 . . . . .9.023
C-294/00 Deutsche Paracelsus Schulen für Naturheilverfahren EU:C:2002:442 . . . . 6.016, 7.011,
    7.067, 7.074
C-340/00P Commission v Cwik EU:C:2001:7013 . . . . 25.019
C-347/00 Barreira Pérez EU:C:2002:560 . . . . 28.006
C-355/00 Freskot EU:C:2003:298. . . . . 23.012
C-360/00 Ricordi & Co Buhnen- und Musikverlag EU:C:2002:346 . . . . .5.056
C-372/00 Commission v Ireland EU:C:2001:702 . . . . 27.019
C-378/00 Commission v European Parliament and Council EU:C:2003:42. . . . . 18.015, 23.005
C-383/00 Commission v Germany EU:C:2002:289 . . . . 18.005
C-388/00 and 429/00 Radiosistemi EU:C:2002:390. . . . . 7.040, 7.042
C-409/00 Spain v Commission EU:C:2003:92 . . . . 9.022, 27.045
C-423/00 Commission v Belgium EU:C:2002:32 . . . . 18.003
C-435/00 Geha Naftiliaki EPE and Others EU:C:2002:661 . . . . .9.009
C-438/00 Kolpak EU:C:2003:255. . . . . .7.059
C-441/00 Commission v United Kingdom EU:C:2002:318 . . . . 27.019
C-444/00 Mayer Parry Recycling EU:C:2003:356 . . . . 23.006
C-445/00R Austria v Council EU:C:2001:123. . . . . 24.001
C-445/00 Austria v Council EU:C:2003:445 . . . . 17.017, 24.002, 24.006
C-453/00 Kühne & Heitz EU:C:2004:17 . . . . 25.022, 28.006, 29.038
C-465/00 and C-138–139/01 Österreichischer Rundfunk and Others
    EU:C:2003:294 . . . . 25.009, 25.019, 27.022

TABLE OF CASES

C-469/00 Ravil and Others EU:C:2003:295. . . . . .7.030
C-470/00P European Parliament v Ripa di Meana and Others EU:C:2004:241 . . . . 25.022
C-30/01 Commission v United Kingdom EU:C:2003:489 . . . . 11.007
C-58/01 Océ van der Grinten EU:C:2003:495. . . . . 17.035
C-83/01 and 93-94/01P Chronopost EU:C:2003:388 . . . . .9.022
C-91/01 Italy v Commission EU:C:2004:244 . . . . 27.045
C-95/01 Greenham and Abel EU:C:2004:71. . . . . .7.034
C-98/01 Commission v United Kingdom EU:C:2003:273 . . . . .7.101
C-100/01 Oteiza Olazabal EU:C:2002:712 . . . . .7.067
C-103/01 Commission v Germany EU:C:2003:301 . . . . .5.033
C-108/01 Consorzio del Prosciutto di Parma and Others EU:C:2003:296 . . . . 7.013, 7.030
C-109/01 Akrich EU:C:2003:491 . . . . .6.014
C-110/01 Tennah-Durez EU:C:2003:357 . . . . .7.076
C-114/01 AvestaPolarit Chrome Oy EU:C:2003:448 . . . . .5.033
C-117/01 K.B. EU:C:2004:7. . . . . .5.058
C-147/01 Weber's Wine World and Others EU:C:2003:533 . . . . 29.010
C-167/01 Inspire Art EU:C:2003:512. . . . . .7.066
C-171/01 Wählergruppe Gemeinsam EU:C:2003:260. . . . . .7.068
C-186/01 Dory EU:C:2003:146. . . . . .5.058, 11.011
C-187/01 and 385/01 Gozütok and Brügge EU:C:2003:87 . . . . 25.025
C-189/01 Jippes and Others EU:C:2001:420. . . . . 5.007, 5.038
C-198/01 Consorzio Industrie Fiammiferi EU:C:2003:430 . . . . .9.012
C-209/01 Schilling and Fleck-Schilling EU:C:2003:610 . . . . .7.062
C-211/01 Commission v Council EU:C:2003:452 . . . . .5.012
C-215/01 Schnitzer EU:C:2003:662 . . . . .7.086
C-216/01 Bude˘jovicky´ Budvar EU:C:2003:618 . . . . 26.009-26.010, 26.013
C-224/01 Köbler EU:C:2003:513 . . . . .7.074
C-232/01 Van Lent EU:C:2003:535 . . . . .7.062
C-233/01 Riunione Adriatica di Securtà EU:C:2002:621 . . . . 27.033
C-234/01 Gerritse EU:C:2003:340 . . . . .7.087
C-236/01 Monsanto Agricoltura Italia and Others EU:C:2003:431 . . . . 25.023
C-239/01 Germany v Commission EU:C:2003:514 . . . . 18.021
C-243/01 Gambelli and Others EU:C:2003:597 . . . . 7.085, 7.091-7.092, 7.094
C-257/01 Commission v Council EU:C:2005:25 . . . . 18.012
C-261-262/01 van Calster and Others EU:C:2003:571 . . . . .9.026
C-264/01, 306/01 and 354-355/01 AOK Bundesverband and EU:C:2004:150. . . . . .9.013
C-285/01 Burbaud EU:C:2003:432. . . . . .7.077
C-300/01 Salzmann EU:C:2003:283. . . . . 7.105, 26.006
C-308/01 GIL Insurance and Others EU:C:2004:252. . . . . .9.022
C-313/01 Morgenbesser EU:C:2003:612 . . . . 7.076-7.077
C-317/01 and 369/01 Abatay and Others EU:C:2003:572 . . . . 7.084, 8.013
C-322/01 Deutscher Apothekerverband EU:C:2003:664 . . . . 7.040, 7.043, 7.072
C-338/01 Commission v Council EU:C:2004:253 . . . . 5.014, 5.015
C-353/01P Mattila v Council and Commission EU:C:2004:42. . . . . 14.031
C-361/01P Kik v Office for Harmonisation in the Internal Market EU:C:2003:434. . . . . 14.025, 14.029
C-383/01 De Danske Bilimportorer EU:C:2003:352 . . . . .7.022
C-387/01 Weigel and Weigel EU:C:2004:256 . . . . .5.054
C-388/01 Commission v Italy EU:C:2003:30 . . . . 7.089, 7.092, 18.005
C-393/01 France v Commission EU:C:2003:307 . . . . .18.009, 18.021
C-397-403/01 Pfeiffer EU:C:2004:584. . . . . .27.029-27.031, 27.033
C-405/01 Colegio de Oficiales de la Marina Mercante Española EU:C:2003:515. . . . . .7.068
C-415/01 Commission v Belgium EU:C:2003:118 . . . . 27.019
C-416/01 ACOR EU:C:2003:631 . . . . 23.012
C-422/01 Skandia and Ramstedt EU:C:2003:380. . . . . .5.054
C-439/01 Cipra and Kvasnicka EU:C:2003:31 . . . . 23.006, 26.007
C-465/01 Commission v Austria EU:C:2004:530. . . . . 26.002

C-482/01 and 493/01 Orfanopoulos and Others EU:C:2004:262 . . . . 6.016, 7.067
C-486/01P Front National v European Parliament EU:C:2004:394 . . . . 12.021
C-488/01P Martinez v European Parliament EU:C:2003:608 . . . . 12.021, 25.019
C-491/01 British American Tobacco (Investments) and Imperial Tobacco
  EU:C:2002:741 . . . . 5.014, 5.015, 5.016, 5.026, 5.033
C-8/02 Leichtle EU:C:2004:161 . . . . 7.094
C-14/02 ATRAL EU:C:2003:265. . . . . 27.021
C-25/02 Rinke EU:C:2003:435 . . . . 5.052, 5.063
C-36/02 Omega Spielhallen EU:C:2004:614 . . . . 7.012
C-47/02 Anker and Others EU:C:2003:516. . . . . 7.068
C-60/02 Criminal Proceedings against X EU:C:2004:373 . . . . 23.013, 25.019, 27.016, 29.017
C-71/02 Herbert Karner Industrie-Auktionen EU:C:2004:181 . . . . 7.012, 7.043
C-110/02 Commission v Council EU:C:2004:395 . . . . 9.027
C-138/02 Collins EU:C:2004:172 . . . . 5.053, 5.055, 6.018, 7.052
C-141/02P Commission v T-Mobile Austria EU:C:2005:98 . . . . 9.020
C-148/02 Garcia Avello EU:C:2003:539. . . . . 5.055, 6.006
C-157/02 Rieser Internationale Transporte and Asfinag EU:C:2004:76. . . . . . 27.021-27.022, 27.025, 27.032
C-167/02P Rothley and Others v European Parliament EU:C:2004:193 . . . . 12.016
C-171/02 Commission v Portugal EU:C:2004:270 . . . . 7.086
C-184/02 and 223/02 Spain and Finland v European Parliament and Council
  EU:C:2004:497 . . . . 5.016
C-189/02, 202/02, 205–208/02 and 213/02P Dansk Rørindustri and Others v
  Commission EU:C:2005:408 . . . . 25.004, 25.019, 27.045
C-200/02 Zhu and Chen EU:C:2004:639 . . . . 5.055, 6.006, 6.010, 6.014
C-201/02 Wells EU:C:2004:12 . . . . 23.017, 27.026, 27.033, 29.038
C-224/02 Pusa EU:C:2004:273 . . . . 5.055, 5.056, 7.055
C-233/02 France v Commission EU:C:2004:173 . . . . 21.001
C-234/02P European Ombudsman v Lamberts EU:C:2004:174 . . . . 6.022
C-245/02 Anheuser-Busch EU:C:2004:717. . . . . 26.005, 26.006, 27.047
C-255/02 Halifax and Others EU:C:2006:121 . . . . 25.024
C-263/02P Commission v Jégo-Quéré EU:C:2004:210 . . . . 25.019, 30.010-30.011, 30.043
C-275/02 Ayaz EU:C:2004:570 . . . . 8.013
C-278/02 Handelbauer EU:C:2004:388 . . . . 27.015
C-286/02 Bellio Fratelli EU:C:2004:212 . . . . 10.020, 26.002, 26.004
C-293/02 Jersey Produce Marketing Organisation EU:C:2005:664 . . . . 7.017
C-299/02 Commission v Netherlands EU:C:2004:620 . . . . 7.061, 7.071
C-304/02 Commission v France EU:C:2005:444 . . . . 29.053
C-309/02 Radlberger Getrankegesellschaft EU:C:2004:799 . . . . 7.041
C-315/02 Lenz EU:C:2004:446 . . . . 7.104
C-319/02 Manninen EU:C:2004:484 . . . . 7.101, 7.104
C-327/02 Panayotova EU:C:2004:718 . . . . 10.017
C-345/02 Pearle and Others EU:C:2004:448 . . . . 9.021
C-365/02 Lindfors EU:C:2004:449 . . . . 6.019
C-377/02 Léon Van Parys EU:C:2005:121 . . . . 26.005
C-387/02, 391/02 and 403/02 Berlusconi and Others EU:C:2005:270 . . . . 18.007, 23.013,
  25.019, 27.031, 27.033
C-428/02 Fonden Marselisborg Lystbadehavn EU:C:2005:126 . . . . 14.025
C-429/02 Bacardi France EU:C:2004:432 . . . . 7.091
C-434/02 Arnold André EU:C:2004:800 . . . . 7.113
C-438/02 Hanner EU:C:2005:332 . . . . 7.013
C-441/02 Commission v Germany EU:C:2006:253 . . . . 6.016
C-442/02 CaixaBank France EU:C:2004:586 . . . . 7.062
C-453/02 and 462/02 Linneweber and Akritidis EU:C:2005:92 . . . . 28.006
C-456/02 Trojani EU:C:2004:488 . . . . 6.008, 7.051
C-464/02 Commission v Denmark EU:C:2005:546 . . . . 7.062
C-465–466/02 Germany and Denmark v Commission EU:C:2005:636 . . . . 14.025

lii   TABLE OF CASES

C-467/02 Cetinkaya EU:C:2004:708 .... 26.004
Opinion 1/03 New Lugano Convention on jurisdiction and the recognition and
    enforcement of judgments in civil and commercial matters EU:C:2006:81 .... 5.026, 5.049
C-12/03P Commission v Tetra Laval EU:C:2005:87 ....9.019
C-39/03P Commission v Artegodan and Others EU:C:2003:418 .... 25.023
C-61/03 Commission v United Kingdom EU:C:2005:210 .... 24.004
C-65/03 Commission v Belgium EU:C:2004:402...5.055
C-72/03 Carbonati Apuani EU:C:2004:506...7.017
C-88/03 Portugal v Commission EU:C:2006:511.................................9.022, 18.005
C-105/03 Pupino EU:C:2005:386..........................8.020, 25.004, 28.011, 28.014
C-110/03 Belgium v Commission EU:C:2005:223................................... 27.045
C-136/03 Dörr and Ünal EU:C:2005:340..6.016
C-147/03 Commission v Austria EU:C:2005:427...5.055
C-152/03 Ritter-Coulais EU:C:2006:123...7.055
C-160/03 Spain v Eurojust EU:C:2005:168....................................14.029, 30.005
C-172/03 Heiser EU:C:2005:130..9.022
C-173/03 Traghetti del Mediterraneo EU:C:2006:391..........................23.020, 23.022
C-176/03 Commission v Council EU:C:2005:542................................. 1.049, 5.019
C-178/03 Commission v European Parliament and Council EU:C:2006:4..................5.015
C-182/03 and 217/03 Belgium and Forum 187 v Commission EU:C:2006:416 ....25.022, 27.046
C-203/03 Commission v Austria EU:C:2005:76...5.058
C-205/03P FENIN v Commission EU:C:2006:453...9.013
C-208/03P Le Pen v European Parliament EU:C:2005:429............................. 12.014
C-209/03 Bidar EU:C:2005:169 ....5.055, 6.015, 6.020
C-210/03 Swedish Match EU:C:2004:802..5.037, 5.052
C-213/03 Pêcheurs de l'Etang de Berre EU:C:2004:464.............................. 23.035
C-227/03 van Pommeren-Bourgondien EU:C:2005:431................................7.055
C-231/03 Coname EU:C:2005:487...7.061
C-234/03 Contse EU:C:2005:644...7.093
C-239/03 Commission v France EU:C:2004:598 .... 26.002
C-265/03 Simutenkov EU:C:2005:213.. 26.003
C-266/03 Commission v Luxembourg EU:C:2005:341.................................5.049
C-320/03 Commission v Austria EU:C:2005:684...7.040
C-330/03 Colegio de Ingenieros de Caminos, Canales y Puertos EU:C:2006:45 ....7.076
C-347/03 Regione autonoma Friuli–Venezia Giulia EU:C:2005:285........................5.023
C-349/03 Commission v United Kingdom EU:C:2005:488 .... 11.007
C-357/03 Commission v Austria EU:C:2004:681..................................... 18.005
C-358/03 Commission v Austria EU:C:2004:824..................................... 18.005
C-371/03 Aulinger EU:C:2006:160.. 26.015
C-373/03 Aydinli EU:C:2005:434.. 26.004
C-374/03 Gürol EU:C:2005:435... 26.004
C-376/03 D EU:C:2005:424..7.101, 7.104, 26.007
C-380/03 Germany v European Parliament and Council EU:C:2006:772..............7.113, 9.055
C-383/03 Dogan EU:C:2005:436..8.013
C-399/03 Commission v Council EU:C:2006:417 ....9.027
C-402/03 Skov EU:C:2006:6...7.110, 29.007
C-403/03 Schempp EU:C:2005:446 ....5.055, 6.019
C-408/03 Commission v Belgium EU:C:2006:192.......................................6.010
C-411/03 SEVIC Systems EU:C:2005:762..7.066
C-432/03 Commission v Portugal EU:C:2005:669.......................................7.034
C-433/03 Commission v Germany EU:C:2005:462 ....5.049
C-436/03 European Parliament v Council EU:C:2006:277................................5.020
C-446/03 Marks & Spencer EU:C:2005:763....................................7.066, 7.072
C-451/03 Servizi Ausiliari Dottori Commercialisti EU:C:2006:208 ....7.069, 7.073
C-453/03 and C-11-12 and 194/04 ABNA and Others EU:C:2005:741 ....5.038, 5.042
C-459/03 Commission v Ireland EU:C:2006:345..1.024

C-461/03 Gaston Schul Douane-expediteur EU:C:2005:742 .... 30.032
C-469/03 Miraglia EU:C:2005:156... 25.025
C-470/03 A.G.M.-COS.MET EU:C:2007:213............................... 7.110, 27.035, 29.012
C-503/03 Commission v Spain EU:C:2006:74 ....6.016
C-513/03 van Hilten-van der Heijden EU:C:2006:131 ....7.101
C-533/03 Commission v Council EU:C:2006:64 ....7.114
C-540/03 European Parliament v Council EU:C:2006:429......................... 8.012, 12.009,
    25.004, 25.007-25.008, 25.019
C-27/04 Commission v Council EU:C:2004:436 .... 17.017
C-28/04 Tod's EU:C:2005:418...5.056
C-36/04 Spain v Council EU:C:2006:209.. 24.007
C-39/04 Laboratoires Fournier EU:C:2005:161 ....7.092
C-65/04 Commission v United Kingdom EU:C:2006:161 .... 24.004
C-66/04 United Kingdom v European Parliament and Council EU:C:2005:743 ....7.113
C-94/04 and C-202/04 Cipolla and Others EU:C:2006:758 ....7.088, 9.012
C-105/04P Nederlandse Federatieve Vereniging voor de Groothandel op
    Elektrotechnisch Gebied v Commission EU:C:2006:592 .... 25.024
C-109/04 Kranemann EU:C:2005:187...7.051, 7.068
C-113/04P Technische Unie v Commission EU:C:2006:593....................... ..... 25.024
C-119/04 Commission v Italy EU:C:2006:489 .... 29.053
C-136/04 Deutsches Milch-Kontor EU:C:2005:716................................... 29.007
C-144/04 Mangold EU:C:2005:709 ....5.060
C-145/04 Spain v United Kingdom EU:C:2006:543...................................6.021
C-150/04 Commission v Denmark EU:C:2007:69.....................................7.092
C-154-155/04 Alliance for Natural Health EU:C:2005:449 ....5.033, 7.113
C-158-159/04 Alfa Vita Vissilopoulos EU:C:2006:562 ....7.043
C-170/04 Rosengren EU:C:2007:313...7.013
C-196/04 Cadbury Schweppes EU:C:2006:544......................... 7.012, 7.066, 7.072
C-201/04 Molenbergnatie EU:C:2006:136 .... 27.010
C-212/04 Adeneler and Others EU:C:2006:443 .... 27.029
C-217/04 United Kingdom v European Parliament and Council
    EU:C:2006:279 ....7.113
C-234/04 Kapferer EU:C:2006:178...5.049
C-237/04 Enirisorse EU:C:2006:197 ....9.022
C-244/04 Commission v Germany EU:C:2006:49 ....7.049
C-266-270/04, 276/04 and 321-325/04 Distribution Casino France and Others
    EU:C:2005:657 ....9.026
C-273/04 Poland v Council EU:C:2007:622 ....4.013
C-280/04 Jyske Finans EU:C:2005:753 .... 29.006
C-282-283/04 Commission v Netherlands EU:C:2006:608 ....7.101
C-289/04P Showa Denko v Commission EU:C:2006:431............................. 25.024
C-290/04 FKP Scorpio Konzertproduktionen EU:C:2006:630..........................7.084
C-292/04 Meilicke and Others EU:C:2007:132......................... 7.101, 7.104, 28.006
C-295-298/04 Manfredi EU:C:2006:461........................... ...... 9.014, 9.015, 29.013
C-300/04 Eman and Sevinger EU:C:2006:545 ....11.007, 12.015
C-302/04 Ynos EU:C:2006:9..11.003, 29.020
C-308/04P SGL Carbon v Commission EU:C:2006:433 .... 25.024
C-316/04 Stichting Zuid-Hollandse Milieufederatie EU:C:2005:678 .... 27.021
C-317-318/04 European Parliament v Council and Commission
    EU:C:2006:346.. 7.113, 21.009, 28.017
C-338/04 and 359-360/04 Placanica and Others EU:C:2007:133 ....7.074
C-344/04 IATA and ELFAA EU:C:2006:10 ....5.052
C-347/04 Rewe Zentralfinanz EU:C:2007:194 ....7.072
C-351/04 Ikea Wholesale EU:C:2007:547 .... 26.005
C-354/04P Gestoras Pro Amnistía and Others v Council EU:C:2007:115 ....1.049
C-355/04P Segi and Others v Council EU:C:2007:1163 ....1.049

liv TABLE OF CASES

C-368/04 Transalpine Ölleitung in Österreich EU:C:2006:644 . . . . .9.026
C-372/04 Watts EU:C:2006:325 . . . . .7.080
C-392/04 i-21 Germany and Arcor EU:C:2006:586. . . . . 29.010
C-393/04 and C-41/05 Air Liquide Industries and Others EU:C:2006:403. . . . . .7.021
C-406/04 De Cuyper EU:C:2006:491. . . . . 6.020, 7.055
C-413/04 European Parliament v Council EU:C:2006:741 . . . . .4.013
C-414/04 European Parliament v Council EU:C:2006:742 . . . . .4.013
C-423/04 Richards EU:C:2006:256. . . . . .5.058
C-432/04 Commission v Cresson EU:C:2006:455 . . . . 12.067
C-436/04 Van Esbroeck EU:C:2006:165 . . . . 25.024
C-437/04 Commission v Belgium EU:C:2007:178. . . . . 14.008-14.009
C-441/04 A-Punkt Schmuckhandels EU:C:2006:141 . . . . .7.043
C-446/04 Test Claimants in the FII Group Litigation EU:C:2006:774. .7.012
C-452/04 Fidium Finanz EU:C:2006:631 . . . . .7.012
C-467/04 Gasparini EU:C:2006:610. . . . . 25.024
C-470/04 N. EU:C:2006:525 . . . . .7.055
C-479/04 Laserdisken EU:C:2006:549. . . . . .7.036
C-490/04 Commission v Germany EU:C:2007:430 . . . . .7.072
C-506/04 Wilson EU:C:2006:587. . . . . 25.019
C-513/04 Kerckhaert and Morres EU:C:2006:713 . . . . .7.104
C-519/04P Meca-Medina and Majcen v Commission EU:C:2006:492 . . . . 7.081, 9.014
C-520/04 Turpeinen EU:C:2006:703 . . . . .7.055
C-522/04 Commission v Belgium EU:C:2007:405. . . . . .7.062
C-523/04 Commission v Netherlands EU:C:2007:244 . . . . 10.039, 29.046
C-524/04 Test Claimants in the Thin Cap Group Litigation EU:C:2007:161 . . . . .7.012
C-1/05 Jia EU:C:2007:1 . . . . .6.014
C-10/05 Mattern EU:C:2006:220 . . . . .7.049
C-13/05 Chacón Navas EU:C:2006:456. . . . . .5.060
C-32/05 Commission v Luxembourg EU:C:2006:749 . . . . 27.018
C-39/05 and 52/05P Sweden and Turco v Council EU:C:2008:374 . . . . 14.031
C-40/05 Lyyski EU:C:2007:10. . . . . .7.072
C-64/05P Sweden v Commission EU:C:2007:802 . . . . 14.031
C-76/05 Schwarz and Gootjes-Schwarz EU:C:2007:492 . . . . 6.018, 7.055
C-77/05 United Kingdom v Council EU:C:2007:803. . . . . 8.028, 22.003, 24.008
C-81/05 Cordero Alonso EU:C:2006:529 . . . . 27.029
C-91/05 Commission v Council EU:C:2008:288 . . . . .1.049, 5.014, 10.021,
 13.012, 27.046, 28.016, 30.013
C-97/05 Gattoussi EU:C:2006:780 . . . . 26.003
C-101/05 A EU:C:2007:804. . . . . .7.107
C-110/05 Commission v Italy EU:C:2009:66 . . . . 7.029, 7.043
C-112/05 Commission v Germany EU:C:2007:623. . . . . .7.101
C-119/05 Lucchini EU:C:2007:4348. . . . . 9.027-9.028, 30.033
C-137/05 United Kingdom v Council EU:C:2007:805. . . . . 8.028, 22.003
C-138/05 Stichting Zuid-Hollandse Milieufederatie EU:C:2006:577 . . . . 27.021
C-140/05 Valeško EU:C:2006:647 . . . . 24.007
C-142/05 Mickelsson and Roos EU:C:2009:336. . . . . 7.029, 7.043
C-150/05 Van Straaten EU:C:2006:614 . . . . 25.024
C-152/05 Commission v Germany EU:C:2008:17. . . . . 6.019, 7.062
C-167/05 Commission v Sweden EU:C:2008:202 . . . . .7.022
C-170/05 Denkavit EU:C:2006:783 . . . . .7.066
C-173/05 Commission v Italy EU:C:2007:362 . . . . .7.017
C-192/05 Tas-Hagen and Tas EU:C:2006:676. . . . . 6.020, 7.055
C-199/05 European Community v Belgian State EU:C:2006:678. . . . . 14.008
C-208/05 ITC EU:C:2007:16. . . . . 7.053, 7.055, 7.072
C-212/05 Hartmann EU:C:2007:437 . . . . .7.055

C-213/05 Geven EU:C:2007:438. . . . . .7.060
C-222–225/05 van der Weerd and Others EU:C:2007:318 . . . . 29.009
C-229/05P PKK and KNK v Council EU:C:2007:32 . . . . 25.004
C-231/05 AA Oy EU:C:2007:439 . . . . .7.066, 7.072
C-266/05P Sison v Council EU:C:2007:75 . . . . .14.031, 29.007
C-278/05 Robins and Others EU:C:2007:56 . . . . 27.035
C-284/05 Commission v Finland EU:C:2009:778 . . . . 11.011
C-287/05 Hendrix EU:C:2007:494 . . . . .7.060
C-291/05 Eind EU:C:2007:771 . . . . .6.014
C-294/05 Commission v Sweden EU:C:2009:779 . . . . 11.011
C-303/05 Advocaten voor de Wereld EU:C:2007:261 . . . . 8.020, 26.016, 28.007, 30.037
C-305/05 Ordre des barreaux francophones et germanophone and
    Others EU:C:2007:383. . . . . 25.002, 25.008, 25.019, 29.006
C-318/05 Commission v Germany EU:C:2007:495 . . . . .7.062, 7.088
C-321/05 Kofoed EU:C:2007:408 . . . . 25.024
C-325/05 Derin EU:C:2007:442 . . . . 26.004
C-335/05 Řízení EU:C:2007:321. . . . . 26.002
C-337/05 Commission v Italy EU:C:2008:203 . . . . 11.011
C-341/05 Laval un Partneri EU:C:2007:809 . . . 7.075, 7.081, 7.089, 7.092, 7.094, 9.047, 25.004, 25.019
C-345/05 Commission v Portugal EU:C:2006:685. . . . . .7.062
C-356/05 Farrell EU:C:2007:229. . . . . 27.025
C-366/05 Optimus EU:C:2007:366 . . . . 11.003
C-370/05 Festersen EU:C:2007:59 . . . . .7.105, 25.019
C-372/05 Commission v Germany EU:C:2009:780 . . . . 11.011
C-379/05 Amurta EU:C:2007:655 . . . . .7.104
C-387/05 Commission v Italy, EU:C:2009:781 . . . . 11.011
C-392/05 Alevizos EU:C:2007:251 . . . . .7.068
C-393/05 Commission v Austria EU:C:2007:722. . . . . 7.069, 9.006
C-396/05 Habelt and Others EU:C:2007:810 . . . . .7.079
C-402/05 and 415/05P Kadi and Al Barakaat International Foundation v Council
    and Commission EU:C:2008:461 . . . . 3.010, 5.020, 10.031, 11.011, 24.001,
            25.002, 25.004, 25.008, 25.019, 25.020, 25.025, 26.002, 26.009, 26.012, 26.015
C-403/05 European Parliament v Commission EU:C:2007:624. . . . . 18.021
C-404/05 Commission v Germany EU:C:2007:723 . . . . 7.069, 9.006
C-409/05 Commission v Greece, EU:C:2009:782. . . . . 11.011
C-411/05 Palacios de la Villa EU:C:2007:604 . . . . .5.060
C-422/05 Commission v Belgium EU:C:2007:342. . . . . 27.021
C-431/05 Merck Genéricos EU:C:2007:496 . . . . 26.005-26.006
C-432/05 Unibet EU:C:2007:163 . . . . 30.044
C-438/05 International Transport Workers' Federation and Finnish Seamen's Union
    EU:C:2007:772 . . . . 7.044, 7.072, 9.047, 25.004, 25.018, 25.019
C-439/05 and 454/05P Land Oberösterreich v Commission [EU:C:2007:510 . . . . .7.115
C-440/05 Commission v Council EU:C:2007:625 . . . . .5.014, 5.019, 8.021, 28.016
C-444/05 Stamatelaki EU:C:2007:231 . . . . 7.080, 7.092, 7.094
C-446/05 Doulamis EU:C:2008:157. . . . . .9.012
C-451/05 ELISA EU:C:2007:594. . . . . .7.106
C-456/05 Commission v Germany EU:C:2007:755 . . . . .7.062, 7.072
C-460/05 Poland v European Parliament and Council EU:C:2007:447. .7.076
C-461/05 Commission v Denmark EU:C:2009:783. . . . . 11.011
C-464/05 Geurts and Vogten EU:C:2007:631 . . . . 7.061, 7.072
C-7/06P Garcia v Commission EU:C:2007:724 . . . . 15.016
C-8/06 Romeu v Commission EU:C:2007:725. . . . . 15.016
C-9/06P Brier v Commission EU:C:2007:726. . . . . 15.016
C-10/06P de Bustamante Tello v Council EU:C:2007:727. . . . . 15.016
C-11–12/06 Morgan and Bucher EU:C:2007:626. . . . . .6.018, 6.020, 7.055, 9.050

lvi   TABLE OF CASES

C-14/06 and 295/06 European Parliament and Denmark v Commission
    EU:C:2008:176 ....18.009, 18.021
C-38/06 Commission v Portugal EU:C:2010:108......................................11.011
C-50/06 Commission v Netherlands EU:C:2007:325 ....6.008
C-80/06 Carp EU:C:2007:327...27.041, 29.020
C-104/06 Commission v Sweden EU:C:2007:40..7.062
C-120–121/06P FIAMM and Others v Council and Commission
    EU:C:2008:476 ....26.003, 26.005, 30.023
C-133/06 European Parliament v Council EU:C:2008:257.................17.003, 18.012, 18.021
C-143/06 Ludwigs-Apotheke EU:C:2007:656...7.043
C-157/06 Commission v Italy EU:C:2008:530..11.011
C-158/06 ROM-projecten EU:C:2007:370..............................25.023, 27.008, 27.040
C-161/06 Skoma-Lux EU:C:2007:773..14.025, 27.008
C-199/06 CELF (CELF I) EU:C:2008:79...9.024, 9.028
C-205/06 Commission v Austria EU:C:2009:118......................................26.010
C-206/06 Essent Netwerk Noord EU:C:2008:413......................................7.021
C-210/06 Cartesio EU:C:2008:723..7.065, 29.028
C-212/06 Government of the French Community and Walloon Government v
    Flemish Government EU:C:2008:178..5.064, 7.055
C-221/06 Stadtgemeinde Frohnleiten and Gemeindebetriebe Frohnleiten
    EU:C:2007:657 ....7.021, 7.041
C-228/06 Soysal and Savatli EU:C:2009:101..26.002
C-231/06 to C-233/06 Jonkman EU:C:2007:373.......................................5.046
C-239/06 Commission v Italy EU:C:2009:784...11.011
C-244/06 Dynamic Medien EU:C:2008:85......................................25.004, 25.018
C-249/06 Commission v Sweden EU:C:2009:119....................................26.010
C-250/06 United Pan-Europe Communications Belgium and Others
    EU:C:2007:783 ....7.085, 7.088, 7.092, 29.026
C-256/06 Jäger EU:C:2008:20..7.104-7.105
C-266/06P Evonik Degussa v Commission EU:C:2008:295.............................25.019
C-267/06 Maruko EU:C:2008:179...5.060
C-268/06 Impact EU:C:2008:223...............................23.018, 25.004, 28.005, 29.011
C-275/06 Promusicae EU:C:2008:54..25.018-25.020
C-281/06 Jundt EU:C:2007:816...7.092
C-301/06 Ireland v European Parliament and Council EU:C:2009:68......................7.113
C-303/06 Coleman EU:C:2008:415 ....5.060
C-308/06 Intertanko and Others EU:C:2008:312......11.006, 25.023, 26.001-26.003, 26.007, 26.013
C-341–342/06P Chronopost EU:C:2008:375.....................................9.022, 25.019
C-345/06 Heinrich EU:C:2009:140...27.008
C-353/06 Grunkin and Paul EU:C:2008:559.......................................6.019, 7.055
C-372/06 Asda Stores EU:C:2007:787..26.004
C-409/06 Winner Wetten EU:C:2010:503...23.014
C-411/06 Commission v European Parliament EU:C:2009:518..........................10.003
C-413/06P Bertelsmann and Sony Corporation of America EU:C:2008:392................9.018
C-427/06 Bartsch EU:C:2008:517...5.060, 23.029
C-428–434/06 Unión General de Trabajadores de La Rioja EU:C:2008:488...........9.022, 18.005
C-445/06 Danske Slagterier EU:C:2009:178...................7.033, 7.110, 23.021, 23.024, 27.035
C-450/06 Varec EU:C:2008:91..25.016, 25.019
C-452/06 Synthon EU:C:2008:565..23.022, 27.035
C-468–478/06 Sot Lélos kai Sia EE and Others EU:C:2008:504...........................7.005
C-499/06 Nerkowska EU:C:2008:300...6.020, 7.055
C-518/06 Commission v Italy EU:C:2009:270.........................7.062, 7.072, 7.074, 7.088
C-524/06 Huber EU:C:2008:724..5.055
C-531/06 Commission v Italy EU:C:2009:315........................7.062, 7.072, 7.074, 9.055
C-42/07 Liga Portuguesa de Futebol Profissional and Bwin International EU:C:2009:519......7.074, 7.094
C-45/07 Commission v Greece EU:C:2009:81....................................1.024, 10.039

TABLE OF CASES　lvii

C-47/07P Masdar v Commission EU:C:2008:726 . . . . 13.003, 25.017, 25.023, 30.023
C-54/07 Feryn ECLI:EU:C:2008:397 . . . . .5.060
C-94/07 Raccanelli EU:C:2008:425 . . . . .5.053, 7.044
C-113/07P SELEX Sistemi Integrati v Commission EU:C:2009:191 . . . . .9.013
C-118/07 Commission v Finland EU:C:2009:715 . . . . .1.024, 26.010
C-127/07 Arcelor Atlantique et Lorraine and Others EU:C:2008:728. . . . . 5.052, 9.062, 17.015
C-139/07P Commission v Technische Glaswerke Ilmenau EU:C:2010:376 . . . . 14.031
C-141/07 Commission v Germany EU:C:2008:492 . . . . .7.043
C-152–154/07 Arcor and Others EU:C:2008:426. . . . . 27.026
C-155/07 European Parliament v Council EU:C:2008:605 . . . . .5.015
C-158/07 Förster EU:C:2008:630 . . . . .5.055, 6.015
C-166/07 European Parliament v Council [2009] E.C.R. I-7135 . . . 5.015, 5.020, 5.021, 17.033, 17.037
C-169/07 Hartlauer EU:C:2009:141. . . . . 5.037, 7.072, 7.074, 7.080, 9.055
C-171–172/07 Apothekerkammer des Saarlandes and Others EU:C:2009:316 . . . . 7.072, 9.055
C-186/07 Club Náutico de Gran Canaria EU:C:2008:227. . . . . 11.007
C-188/07 Commune de Mesquer EU:C:2008:359 . . . . .9.061, 27.029
C-200–201/07 Marra EU:C:2008:579 . . . . 12.016
C-203/07P Greece v Commission EU:C:2008:606 . . . . 26.013
C-205/07 Gysbrechts EU:C:2008:730. . . . . .7.030
C-208/07 von Chamier-Glisczinski EU:C:2009:455 . . . . .6.019
C-221/07 Zablocka-Weyhermüller EU:C:2008:681. . . . . .6.020, 7.055
C-222/07 UTECA EU:C:2009:124 . . . . 7.072, 7.092, 7.105, 9.054
C-228/07 Petersen EU:C:2008:494 . . . . .7.079
C-239/07 Sabatauskas and Others EU:C:2008:551 . . . . 14.025
C-246/07 Commission v Sweden EU:C:2010:203 . . . . 5.049, 10.039, 14.006, 26.007
C-249/07 Commission v Netherlands EU:C:2008:683 . . . . .7.032
C-269/07 Commission v Germany EU:C:2009:527 . . . . .7.060
C-292/07 Commission v Belgium EU:C:2009:246. . . . . 27.019
C-297/07 Bourquain EU:C:2008:708 . . . . 25.024
C-306/07 Andersen EU:C:2008:743. . . . . 18.006
C-308/07P Gorostiaga Atxalandbaso EU:C:2009:103 . . . . 25.019
C-318/07 Persche EU:C:2009:33. . . . . 7.101, 7.104, 7.106
C-334/07P Commission v Freistaat Sachsen EU:C:2008:709 . . . . .9.026
C-337/07 Altun EU:C:2008:744 . . . . .8.013
C-349/07 Sopropé EU:C:2008:746 . . . . 25.019
C-350/07 Kattner Stahlbau EU:C:2009:127. . . . . .9.013
C-364/07 Vassilakis and Others EU:C:2008:346. . . . . 27.029
C-370/07 Commission v Council EU:C:2009:590 . . . . 5.010, 5.011, 5.012, 5.013, 5.016
C-378–380/07 Angelidaki and Others EU:C:2009:250 . . . . 27.021, 27.029, 28.005
C-384/07 Wienstrom EU:C:2008:747 . . . . .9.028
C-385/07P Der Grüne Punkt–Duales System Deutschland v Commission
　EU:C:2009:456 . . . . 25.018-25.019
C-388/07 Age Concern England EU:C:2009:128 . . . . 27.019
C-393/07 and C-9/08 Italy and Donnici v European Parliament EU:C:2009:275. . . . . 12.014
C-402/07 and 432/07 Sturgeon EU:C:2009:716 . . . . .5.052, 9.010, 25.021, 29.006
C-404/07 Katz EU:C:2008:553 . . . . 28.011
C-414/07 Magoora EU:C:2008:766 . . . . 11.003
C-420/07 Apostolides EU:C:2009:271 . . . . 4.011, 11.003, 11.006
C-421/07 Damgaard EU:C:2009:222 . . . . 25.019
C-428/07 Horvath EU:C:2009:458 . . . . 5.041, 9.006, 18.005
C-471/07 AGIM and Others EU:C:2010:9 . . . . 27.022
C-478/07 Budějovický Budvar EU:C:2009:521 . . . . .9.006, 26.009
C-491/07 Turanský EU:C:2008:768 . . . . 25.024
C-514/07, 528/07 and 532/07P Sweden v API and Commission EU:C:2010:541. . . . . 14.031
C-518/07 Commission v Germany EU:C:2010:125 . . . . .5.041, 7.113, 16.012,
　　　　　　　　　　　　　　　　　　　　　　　　　　　　　　　　　　　　　　　17.046, 25.004, 25.018

lviii   TABLE OF CASES

C-531/07 LIBRO EU:C:2009:276 .... 7.040, 7.041, 9.054
C-546/07 Commission v Germany EU:C:2010:25 .... 7.093, 26.007
C-550/07P Akzo Nobel Chemicals and Akcros Chemicals v Commission EU:C:2010:512 .... 25.024
C-555/07 Kücükdeveci EU:C:2010:21 .... 2.007, 5.060, 23.029, 25.018, 25.021, 27.028, 27.033
C-560/07 Balbino EU:C:2009:341 .... 27.008
C-567/07 Woningstichting Sint Servatius EU:C:2009:593 .... 7.105
C-570–571/07 Blanco Pérez and Chao Gómez EU:C:2010:300 .... 7.072, 7.092, 9.055
Opinion 1/08 General Agreement on Trade in Services EU:C:2009:739 ...... 5.013, 10.004, 10.005, 21.017
C-2/08 Fallimento Olimpiclub EU:C:2009:506. .... 25.023, 29.011
C-3/08 Leyman EU:C:2009:595 .... 7.079
C-12/08 Mono Car Styling EU:C:2009:466 .... 27.029, 27.031
C-22/08 and C-23/08 Vatsouras and Koupatantze EU:C:2009:344 .... 5.053, 6.015, 7.051
C-28/08P Commission v Bavarian Lager EU:C:2010:378 .... 14.031, 25.021, 25.025
C-45/08 Spector Photo Group and Van Raemdonck EU:C:2009:806 .... 25.004, 25.019
C-47/08 Commission v Belgium EU:C:2011:334 .... 7.069
C-50/08 Commission v France EU:C:2011:335 .... 7.069
C-51/08 Commission v Luxembourg EU:C:2011:336 .... 7.069
C-58/08 Vodafone and Others EU:C:2010:321 .... 5.029, 5.033, 5.037, 5.038, 7.113, 17.015, 29.007
C-66/08 Kozłowski EU:C:2008:437 .... 8.020, 28.011
C-73/08 Bressol and Others EU:C:2010:181 .... 5.053, 5.055, 5.062, 9.050
C-88/08 Hütter EU:C:2009:381 .... 5.060
C-89/08P Commission v Ireland and Others EU:C:2009:742. .... 25.004, 25.025
C-96/08 CIBA EU:C:2010:185 .... 11.003
C-101/08 Audiolux and Others EU:C:2009:626 .... 25.021
C-102/08 SALIX EU:C:2009:345 .... 27.019
C-103/08 Gottwald EU:C:2009:597 .... 5.053, 5.062
C-115/08 ČEZ EU:C:2009:660 .... 5.051, 5.053, 5.062, 24.004
C-116/08 Meerts EU:C:2009:645 .... 25.004
C-118/08 Transportes Urbanos y Servicios Generales EU:C:2010:39 .... 29.010
C-123/08 Wolzenburg EU:C:2009:616. .... 5.053, 8.020
C-127/08 Metock and Others EU:C:2008:449 .... 6.014
C-133/08 ICF EU:C:2009:617 .... 8.016, 28.018
C-135/08 Rottmann EU:C:2010:104 .... 6.006, 25.004, 26.013
C-140/08 Rakvere Lihakombinaat EU:C:2009:667 .... 27.008
C-147/08 Römer EU:C:2011:286 .... 5.060
C-153/08 Commission v Spain EU:C:2009:618 .... 7.089, 7.093
C-154/08 Commission v Spain EU:C:2009:695 .... 15.013
C-160/08 Commission v Germany EU:C:2010:230 .... 7.069
C-169/08 Regione Sardegna EU:C:2009:709. .... 7.087, 7.094, 9.022
C-171/08 Commission v Portugal EU:C:2010:412. .... 7.101
C-174/08 NCC Construction Danmark EU:C:2009:669 .... 25.021
C-175–176/08 and 178–179/08 Salahadin Abdulla and Others
  EU:C:2010:105 .... 8.008, 25.002, 25.012, 26.001
C-197/08 Commission v France EU:C:2010:111 .... 7.032, 9.055
C-198/08 Commission v Austria EU:C:2010:112. .... 7.032
C-211/08 Commission v Spain EU:C:2010:340 .... 7.080
C-221/08 Commission v Ireland EU:C:2010:113 .... 7.032
C-227/08 Martín Martín EU:C:2009:792. .... 29.013
C-243/08 Pannon EU:C:2009:350 .... 29.013
C-250/08 Commission v Belgium EU:C:2011:793 .... 5.064
C-261/08 and 348/08 Zurita García and Choque Cabrera EU:C:2009:648 .... 14.025, 7.104
C-265/08 Federutility and Others EU:C:2010:205 .... 9.019
C-271/08 Commission v Germany EU:C:2010:426 .... 7.044, 25.004
C-301/08 Bogiatzi EU:C:2009:649 .... 26.001, 26.009
C-304/08 Zentrale zur Bekämpfung unlauteren Wettbewerbs EU:C:2010:12 .... 7.110, 27.029

C-310/08 Ibrahim EU:C:2010:80 . . . . 6.014, 29.007
C-314/08 Filipiak EU:C:2009:719. . . . . 23.014
C-317–320/08 Alassini and Others EU:C:2010:146. . . . . 23.018, 25.019, 27.043, 29.009
C-325/08 Olympique Lyonnais EU:C:2010:143 . . . . .7.044, 7.062, 7.072, 9.051
C-333/08 Commission v France EU:C:2010:44 . . . . 7.034, 7.042, 25.023
C-340/08 M and Others EU:C:2010:232 . . . . 14.025, 25.021
C-341/08 Petersen EU:C:2010:4 . . . . .9.055
C-343/08 Commission v Czech Republic EU:C:2010:14. . . . . 9.047, 27.019
C-344/08 Rubach EU:C:2009:482. . . . . 25.019
C-345/08 Peśla EU:C:2009:771 . . . . .7.068, 7.069
C-351/08 Grimme EU:C:2009:697. . . . . 26.006
C-360/09 Pfleiderer EU:C:2011:389. . . . . 9.015, 29.011
C-362/08P Internationaler Hilfsfonds v Commission EU:C:2010:40 . . . . 14.031
C-378/08 Raffinerie Mediterranee (ERG) and Others EU:C:2010:126 . . . . 8.013, 9.061
C-379–380/08 Raffinerie Mediterranee (ERG) and Others EU:C:2010:127 . . . . 5.038, 25.019
C-384/08 Attanasio Group EU:C:2010:133. . . . . .7.062
C-386/08 Brita EU:C:2010:91 . . . . 10.018, 26.012-26.013
C-403/08 and C-429/08 Football Association Premier League Ltd and Others
    EU:C:2011:631 . . . . 7.012, 9.051
C-405/08 Ingeniorforeningen i Danmark EU:C:2010:69 . . . . .7.069
C-438/08 Commission v Portugal EU:C:2009:651. . . . . .7.069
C-441/08 Elektrownia Patnów EU:C:2009:698. . . . . 11.003
C-480/08 Teixeira EU:C:2010:83 . . . . .6.014
C-484/08 Caja de Ahorros y Monte de Piedad de Madrid EU:C:2010:309 . . . . .5.008
C-485/08P Gualtieri v Commission EU:C:2010:188 . . . . .5.060
C-486/08 Zentralbeҭriebsrat der Landeskrankenhäuser Tirols EU:C:2010:215 . . . . 23.034
C-526/08 Commission v Luxembourg EU:C:2010:379 . . . . 25.023, 25.025
C-533/08 TNT Express Nederland EU:C:2010:243 . . . . .8.015
C-542/08 Barth EU:C:2010:193 . . . . 29.010
C-562/08 Müller Fleisch EU:C:2010:93 . . . . .5.038
C-578/08 Chakroun EU:C:2010:117 . . . . 6.010, 25.002, 25.007, 25.019
Opinion 1/09, Draft Agreement on the European and Community Patents
    Court EU:C:2011:123 . . . . 7.109, 18.023, 21.017, 25.018, 29.015
C-1/09 CELF (CELF II) EU:C:2010:136 . . . . 9.026-9.028
C-14/09 Genc EU:C:2010:57. . . . . 7.051, 8.013
C-31/09 Bolbol EU:C:2010:351. . . . . 14.025
C-34/09 Ruiz Zambrano EU:C:2011:124. . . . . .6.017
C-56/09 Zanotti EU:C:2010:288 . . . . .7.082, 25.008
C-63/09 Walz EU:C:2010:251 . . . . 26.002
C-98/09 Sorge EU:C:2010:369 . . . . 28.005
C-108/09 Ker-Optika EU:C:2010:725 . . . . .7.032
C-132/09 Commission v Belgium EU:C:2010:562. . . . . 13.048, 28.004
C-137/09 Josemans EU:C:2010:774 . . . . 7.012, 7.092
C-145/09 Tsakouridis EU:C:2010:708 . . . . .6.016
C-162/09 Lassal EU:C:2010:592 . . . . 6.008, 6.013, 25.018
C-173/09 Elchinov EU:C:2010:581 . . . . 27.040, 29.028
C-176/09 Luxemburg v European Parliament and Council EU:C:2011:290. . . . . .5.038
C-197/09 RX–II EMEA EU:C:2009:804 . . . . 13.009, 25.025
C-208/09 Sayn-Wittgenstein EU:C:2010:806 . . . . 5.041, 6.019, 6.020, 25.018
C-212/09 Commission v Portugal EU:C:2011:717. . . . . 7.012, 7.101
C-221/09 AJD Tuna EU:C:2011:153. . . . . 5.052, 25.018, 25.023
C-263/09 Association belge des Consommateurs Test-Achats EU:C:2011:452 . . . . 5.058, 23.007
C-291/09 Guarnieri EU:C:2011:217. . . . . .5.053
C-338/09 Yellow Cab Verkehrsbetriebs EU:C:2010:814 . . . . .7.061
C-348/09 PI EU:C:2012:300 . . . . .6.016

C-367/09 SGS Belgium and Others EU:C:2010:648.................................... 25.023
C-379/09 Casteels EU:C:2011:131 ....7.044
C-391/09 Runevic- Vardyn and Wardyn EU:C:2011:291 .... 5.041, 6.019, 6.020
C-403/09PPU Detiček EU:C:2009:810 .... 25.007
C-434/09 McCarthy EU:C:2011:277 ....6.017
C-503/09 Stewart EU:C:2011:500...6.018
C-539/09 Commission v Germany EU:C:2011:733.........................5.029, 5.045
C-550/09 E and F EU:C:2010:382... 25.019
C-4/10 and C-27/10 Bureau national interprofessionel du Cognac EU:C:2011:484 .... 27.015
C-7/10 and C-9/10 Kahveci and Inan EU:C:2012:180....................................8.013
C-17/10 Toshiba Corporation EU:C:2012:72 ....11.003, 25.016
C-29/10 Koelzsch EU:C:2011:151 ....8.016
C-42/10, C-45/10 and C-57/10 Vlaamse Dierenartsvereniging and Janssens
    EU:C:2011:253 ....27.015, 27.040
C-53/10 Mücksch EU:C:2011:585 ....23.013, 27.031
C-69/10 Samba Diouf EU:C:2011:524.. 25.016
C-72/10 Criminal Proceedings against Costa EU:C:2012:80 .... 25.022
C-107/10 Enel Maritsa Iztok 3 EU:C:2011:298.. 25.022
C-109/10P Solvay v Commission EU:C:2011:686 .... 25.016
C-110/10P Solvay v Commission EU:C:2011:687 .... 25.024
C-111/10 Commission v Council EU:C:2013:785 ....9.003, 9.027
C-117/10 Commission v Council EU:C:2013:786 ....9.003
C-118/10 Commission v Council EU:C:2013:787 ....9.003
C-121/10 Commission v Council EU:C:2013:784 ....9.003
C-123/10 Brachner EU:C:2011:675 ....5.063
C-124/10P Commission v EDF EU:C:2012:318 ....9.022
C-130/10 European Parliament v Council EU:C:2012:472....... 5.015, 7.107, 10.031, 25.008, 28.012
C-135/10 SCF EU:C:2012:140.. 26.003
C-155/10 Williams and Others EU:C:2011:588 .... 25.016
C-163/10 Patriciello EU:C:2011:543 .... 12.016, 25.016
C-177/10 Rosado Santana EU:C:2011:557 .... 27.030
C-187/10 Unal EU:C:2011:623 ....8.013
C-188/10 and C-189/10 Melki and Abdeli EU:C:2010:363......................23.015, 29.016
C-210/10 Urbán EU:C:2012:64..5.035
C-211/10PPU Povse EU:C:2010:400 .... 25.016
C-214/10 KHS EU:C:2011:761 ....25.004, 25.016
C-227/10 Luksan EU:C:2011:142..25.016, 26.009
C-252/10P Evropaïki Dynamiki v European Maritime Safety Agency EU:C:2011:512........ 18.024
C-282/10 Dominguez EU:C:2012:33....................23.014, 25.012, 27.029, 27.032, 27.034
C-292/10 G EU:C:2012:142.. 25.016
C-297/10 and C-298/10 Hennigs and Mai EU:C:2011:560......................... 25.016
C-316/10 Danske Svineproducenter EU:C:2011:863............................... 27.015
C-347/10 Salemink EU:C:2012:17 .... 11.006
C 355/10 European Parliament v Council EU:C:2012:516 ....18.009, 18.010
C-357/10 to C-359/10 Duomo Gpa EU:C:2012:283.....................................7.054
C-360/10 SABAM..EU:C:2012:85 25.016
C-364/10 Hungary v Slovak Republic EU:C:2012:630............... 6.008, 25.023, 26.013, 29.042
C-366/10 Air Transport Association of America and Others EU:C:2011:864 .. 21.006, 26.003, 26.013
C-371/10 National Grid Indus EU:C:2011:785..7.065
C-384/10 Voosgeerd EU:C:2011:842 ....8.016
C-385/10 Elenca EU:C:2012:634 ....7.028
C-387/10 Commission v Austria EU:C:2011:625.......................................7.086
C-393/10 O'Brien EU:C:2012:110 .... 25.016
C-399/10P and C-401/10P Bouygues and Bouygues Télécom v Commission EU:C:2013:175...... 9.022
C-400/10PPU McB EU:C:2010:582 ....25.012, 25.016

TABLE OF CASES lxi

C-404/10P Commission v Éditions Odile Jacob EU:C:2012:393 . . . . 14.031
C-411/10 and C-493/10 NS EU:C:2011:865 . . . . . .8.001, 8.010, 25.004, 25.007, 25.014, 25.016, 25.019
C-412/10 Homawoo EU:C:2011:747 . . . . .8.016, 29.006
C-416/10 Križan and Others EU:C:2013:8 . . . . .25.016, 25.019
C-419/10 Hofmann EU:C:2012:240. . . . . 14.025
C-430/10 Gaydarov EU:C:2011:749. . . . . .6.019
C-434/10 Aladzhov EU:C:2011:750. . . . . .6.019
C-468/10 and C-469/10 ASNEF and FECEMD EU:C:2011:777. . . . . 25.016
C-477/10P Commission v Agrofert Holding EU:C:2012:394. . . . . 14.031
C-482/10 Cicala EU:C:2011:868. . . . . 25.022
C-490/10 European Parliament v Council EU:C:2012:525. . . . . .5.014
C-510/10 DR and TV2 Danmark EU:C:2012:244 . . . . .26.001, 29.008
C-533/10 CIVAD EU:C:2012:347. . . . . 25.023
C-539/10P and C-550/10P Stichting Al Aqsa v Council EU:C:2012:711. . . . . 25.022
C-544/10 Deutsches Weintor EU:C:2012:526. . . . . 25.016
C-547/10P Confédération suisse v Commission EU:C:2013:139. . . . . 26.006
C-566/10P Italy v Commission EU:C:2012:752 . . . . 5.060, 14.028, 25.018
C-571/10 Kamberaj EU:C:2012:233. . . . . 8.012, 25.004, 25.012, 25.016
C-577/10 Commission v Belgium EU:C:2012:814. . . . . .7.098
C-578/10 to 580/10 Van Putten EU:C:2012:246 . . . . .7.101
C-581/10 and C-629/10 Nelson and TUI Travel EU:C:2012:657 .5.052, 29.008
C-584/10P, C-593/10P, and C-595/10P Commission United Kingdom and Council v
    Kadi EU:C:2013:518. . . . . .3.010, 10.001, 10.031, 25.002, 25.008, 25.016, 25.024, 29.032
C-589/10 Wencel EU:C:2013:303. . . . . .7.079
C-602/10 SC Volksbank România EU:C:2012:443. . . . . .7.083
C-606/10 ANAFE EU:C:2012:348 . . . . .8.007, 25.022
C-610/10 Commission v Spain EU:C:2012:781 . . . . 5.006, 11.003, 29.048
C-615/10 Insinööritoimisto InsTiimi EU:C:2012:324. . . . . 11.011
C-617/10 Åkerberg Fransson EU:C:2013:105. . . . . .23.029, 25.009, 25.012, 25.016, 25.024
C-619/10 EU:C:2012:531 Trade Agency 25.016
C-4/11 Puid EU:C:2013:740 . . . . 25.014
C-12/11 McDonagh EU:C:2013:43 . . . . .25.016, 25.019
C-27/11 Vinkov EU:C:2012:326. . . . . 25.011
C-40/11 Iida EU:C:2012:691. . . . . 6.014, 8.012, 25.009
C-41/11 Inter-Environnement Wallonie en Terre wallonne EU:C:2012:103 . . . . .23.014, 27.033
C-42/11 Lopes Da Silva Jorge EU:C:2012:517. . . . . .5.052, 8.020, 27.029, 28.014
C-62/11 Feyerbacher EU:C:2012:486. . . . . 14.009
C-75/11 Commission v Austria EU:C:2012:605. . . . . .5.055
C-77/11 Council v European Parliament EU:C:2013:559 . . . . .17.003, 20.005
C-97/11 Amia EU:C:2012:306 . . . . .23.014, 27.032
C-135/11P IFAW Internationaler Tierschutz-Fonds v Commission EU:C:2012:376 . . . . 14.031
C-141/11 Hörnfeldt EU:C:2012:421. . . . . 25.016
C-146/11 AS Pimix EU:C:2012:450 . . . . 27.008
C-154/11 Mahamdia EU:C:2012:491. . . . . 26.013
C-170/11 Lippens EU:C:2012:540 . . . . .8.015
C-171/11 Fra.bo EU:C:2012:453. . . . . .7.013
C-190/11 Mühlleitner EU:C:2012:542. . . . . 29.007
C-197/11 and C-203/11 Libert and Others EU:C:2013:288 . . . . 7.012, 7.072, 7.074, 7.097, 7.105
C-199/11 Otis EU:C:2012:684. . . . . 14.002
C-202/11 Las EU:C:2013:239 . . . . 5.041, 7.053, 7.072
C-212/11 Jyske Bank Gibraltar EU:C:2013:270 . . . . .7.092
C-221/11 Demirkan EU:C:2013:583 . . . . .8.013, 26.006
C-226/11 Expedia EU:C:2012:795 . . . . .9.016
C-237/11 and C-238/11 France v European Parliament EU:C:2012:796. . . . . . . 12.005, 12.018, 14.020
C-241/11 Commission v Czech Republic EU:C:2013:423. . . . . .29.048, 29.053

lxii   TABLE OF CASES

C-256/11 Dereci EU:C:2011:734 ....6.017, 8.013, 25.004, 25.011
C-267/11P Commission v Latvia EU:C:2013:624. .... 29.007
C-268/11 Gülbahce EU:C:2012:695 ....8.013
C-274/11 and C-295/11 Spain and Italy v Council EU:C:2013:240 ....7.109, 22.009
C-277/11 M EU:C:2012:744 .... 25.021
C-280/11P Council v Access Info Europe EU:C:2013:671 ....14.031, 15.009
C-283/11 Sky Österreich EU:C:2013:28. ....25.016, 25.023
C-300/11 ZZ EU:C:2013:363. .... 25.024
C-325/11 Alder EU:C:2012:824 ....8.015
C-332/11 ProRail EU:C:2013:87. ....8.015
C-335/11 HK Danmark EU:C:2013:222 .... 26.001
C-356/11 and C-357/11 O and S EU:C:2012:776 .... 25.017
C-364/11 El Karem El Kott EU:C:2012:826. .... 26.016
C-379/11 Caves Krier EU:C:2012:798 ....7.053
C-396/11 Radu EU:C:2013:39. ....8.020
C-399/11 Melloni EU:C:2013:107 .... 8.001, 8.020, 23.011, 23.029, 25.004, 25.007, 25.012
C-401/11 Soukupová EU:C:2013:223 ....5.052
C-410/11 Espada Sánchez EU:C:2012:747 .... 26.013
C-414/11 Daiichi Sankyo EU:C:2013:520 .... 10.004, 10.005, 10.011
C-420/11 Leth EU:C:2013:166 .... 23.023
C-439/11P Ziegler v Commission EU:C:2013:513. .... 25.017
C-443/11 Jeltes EU:C:2013:224. .... 29.007
C-451/11 Dülger EU:C:2012:504 ....8.013
C-476/11 HK Danmark EU:C:2013:590 .... 27.033
C-487/11 Laimonis Treimanis EU:C:2012:556. .... 29.007
C-501/11P Schindler Holding v Commission EU:C:2013:522. .... 25.008, 25.016, 25.022
C-509/11 ÖBB-Personenverkehr EU:C:2013:613 .... 27.015
C 510/11P Kone and Others v Commission EU:C:2013:696. .... 25.008
C-514/11P and C-605/11P LPN and Finland v Commission EU:C:2013:738 .... 14.031, 25.025
C-523/11 and C-585/11 Prinz and Seeberger EU:C:2013:524 .... 5.055, 6.018, 6.020
C-530/11 Commission v United Kingdom EU:C:2014:67 .... 27.019
C-533/11 Commission v Belgium EU:C:2013:659. .... 18.004, 18.005
C-537/11 Manzi and Compagnia Naviera Orchestra EU:C:2014:19 .... 26.007
and C-544/11 Petersen and Petersen EU:C:2013:124. ....7.056
C-545/11 Agrargenossenschaft Neuzelle EU:C:2013:169 .... 27.047
C-548/11 Mulders EU:C:2013:249. ....7.079
C-583/11P Inuit Tapiriit Kanatami v European Parliament and Council 13.003, 13.006,
      29.007, 30.001, 30.007, 30.011, 30.044
C-592/11 Ketelä EU:C:2012:673. .... 27.015
C-604/11 Genil 48 EU:C:2013:344. .... 14.025
C-614/11 Kuso EU:C:2013:544. .... 27.025
C-628/11 International Jet Management EU:C:2014:171 ....5.053
C-658/11 European Parliament v Council EU:C:2014:2025 ....12.004, 12.009, 17.041,
      21.002, 21.003, 21.008, 30.013
C-7/12 Riežniece EU:C:2013:410 ....5.063
C-20/12 Giersch EU:C:2013:411. ....7.072, 7.074
C-24/12 and C-27/12 X and TBG EU:C:2014:1385 .... 11.007
C-28/12 Commission v Council EU:C:2015:282 .... 12.046, 28.003
C-40/12P Gascogne Sack Deutschland v Commission EU:C:2013:768 .... 25.024
C-45/12 Hadj Ahmed EU:C:2013:390. ....5.053
C-49/12 Sunico EU:C:2013:545 ....8.015
C-50/12P Kendrion v Commission EU:C:2013:771. .... 25.016
C-57/12 Femarbel EU:C:2013:517 ....7.097, 27.046
C-58/12P Groupe Gascogne v Commission EU:C:2013:770 .... 25.008
C-60/12 Baláž EU:C:2013:733. ....8.020

C-64/12 Schlecker EU:C:2013:551 .... 8.016
C-81/12 Accept EU:C:2013:275 .... 5.060
C-86/12 Alokpa and Moudoulou EU:C:2013:645 .... 6.017
C-87/12 Ymeraga and Ymeraga-Tafarshiku EU:C:2013:291 .... 6.014, 25.009
C-89/12 Bark EU:C:2013:276 .... 29.007
C-93/12 ET Agrokonsulting-04-Velko Stoyanov EU:C:2013:432 .... 25.016
C-99/12 Eurofit EU:C:2013:487 .... 25.023
C-101/12 Schaible EU:C:2013:661 .... 25.016
C-103/12 and C-165/12 European Parliament and Commission v Council
    EU:C:2014:2400 .... 9.005, 17.038
C-105/12 to C-107/12 Essent EU:C:2013:677 .... 7.040, 7.101
C-111/12 Ordine degli Ingegneri di Verona e Provincia EU:C:2013:100 .... 7.085
C-114/12 Commission v Council EU:C:2014:2151 .... 10.039
C-131/12 Google Spain and Google EU:C:2014:317 .... 9.002, 25.002, 25.016
C-136/12 Consiglio Nazionale dei Geologi EU:C:2013:489 .... 29.016
C-137/12 Commission v Council EU:C:2013:675 .... 10.005
C-139/12 Caixa d'Estalvis i Pensions de Barcelona EU:C:2014:174 .... 7.055
C-140/12 Brey EU:C:2013:565 .... 6.010
C-141/12 and C-372/12 YS EU:C:2014:2081 .... 25.016, 25.022
C-151/12 Commission v Spain EU:C:2013:690 .... 18.005, 27.019
C-176/12 AMS EU:C:2014:2 .... 23.033, 25.010, 25.012, 25.016, 25.021, 27.030, 27.033
C-180/12 Stoilov EU:C:2013:693 .... 29.028
C-184/12 Unamar EU:C:2013:663 .... 8.016
C-195/12 Industrie du bois de Vielsalm & Cie EU:C:2013:598 .... 5.052
C-199/12 to C-201/12 X, Y and Z EU:C:2013:720 .... 25.016
C-203/12 Billerud Karlsborg and Billerud Skärblacka EU:C:2013:664 .... 5.037
C-204/12 to C-208/12 Essent Belgium EU:C:2014:2192 .... 7.041
C-220/12 Menenes EU:C:2013:683 .... 6.020
C-225/12 Demir EU:C:2013:725 .... 8.013
C-233/12 Gardella EU:C:2013:449 .... 7.051, 25.016
C-234/12 Sky Italia EU:C:2013:496 .... 5.052
C-244/12 Salzburger Flughafen EU:C:2013:203 .... 27.026
C-246/12P Ellinika Nafpigeia v Commission EU:C:2013:133 .... 11.011
C-262/12 Vent de Colère EU:C:2013:851 .... 9.022
C-267/12 Hay EU:C:2013:823 .... 5.060
C-270/12 United Kingdom v European Parliament and Council
    EU:C:2014:18 .... 7.113, 18.022, 18.023
C-274/12P Telefónica v Commission EU:C:2013:852 .... 13.006, 30.011
C-276/12 Sabou EU:C:2013:678 .... 25.011
C-284/12 Deutsche Lufthansa EU:C:2013:755 .... 9.024
C-290/12 Della Rocca EU:C:2013:235 .... 29.007
C-291/12 Schwarz EU:C:2013:670 .... 25.016
C-293/12 and C-594/12 Digital Rights Ireland EU:C:2014:238 ..... 9.002, 16.013, 25.004, 25.016, 25.019
C-295/12P Telefónica and Telefónica de España v Commission EU:C:2014:2062 .... 25.008
C-314/12 UPC Telekabel Wien EU:C:2014:192 .... 25.016, 25.019
C-327/12 SOA Nazionale Costruttori EU:C:2013:827 .... 7.069
C-334/12RX-II Arango Jaramillo and Others v EIB EU:C:2013:134 .... 25.018
C-343/12 Euronics Belgium EU:C:2013:154 .... 7.110
C-350/12P Council v in 't Veld EU:C:2014:2039 .... 14.031
C-351/12 OSA EU:C:2014:110 .... 7.096
C-355/12 Nintendo EU:C:2014:25 .... 23.006
C-356/12 Glatzel EU:C:2014:350 .... 25.012, 25.018
C-362/12 Test Claimants in the Franked Investment Income Group Litigation
    EU:C:2013:834 .... 25.022
C-363/12 Z EU:C:2014:159 .... 5.060, 26.003

C-365/12P Commission v EnBW Energie Baden-Württemberg EU:C:2014:112 .... 14.031
C-370/12 Pringle EU:C:2012:756.............2.010, 3.001, 3.006, 3.011, 5.020, 5.023, 9.036, 9.037,
            9.044, 12.023, 13.008, 16.007, 24.003, 26.007, 28.004, 29.007, 29.035, 30.035
C-375/12 Bouanich EU:C:2014:138..7.083
C-377/12 Commission v Council EU:C:2014:1903 .... 5.014, 10.001, 10.021
C-378/12 Onuekwere EU:C:2014:13 .... 6.013, 6.016
C-385/12 Hervis Sport- és Divatkereskedelmi EU:C:2014:47.............................7.012
C-390/12 Pfleger EU:C:2014:281 ....25.009, 25.011
C-394/12 Abdullahi EU:C:2013:813 .... 25.014
C-399/12 Germany v Council EU:C:2014:2258 .... 21.006
C-400/12 MG EU:C:2014:9..6.016
C-401/12P to C-403/12P Council, European Parliament and Commission v Vereniging
    Milieudefensie and Stichting Stop Luchtverontreiniging (Utrecht) EU:C:2015:4 .... 26.003
C-421/12 Commission v Belgium EU:C:2014:2064......................................7.110
C-425/12 Portgás EU:C:2013:829..27.025, 27.026
C-427/12 Commission v European Parliament and Council EU:C:2014:170..........18.010, 18.011
C-428/12 Commission v Spain EU:C:2014:218 ....7.029
C-456/12 O and B EU:C:2014:135 ....6.014
C-470/12 Pohotovosť EU:C:2014:101 ....25.012, 25.018
C-474/12 Schiebel Aircraft EU:C:2014:2139... 11.011
C-483/12 Pelckmans Turnhout EU:C:2014:304 ....7.088
C-501/12 to C-506/12, C-540/12, and C-541/12 Specht EU:C:2014:2005................... 27.035
C-507/12 Saint-Prix EU:C:2014:2007 ....7.052
C-508/12 Vapenik EU:C:2013:790 ....8.015
C-530/12P OHIM v National Lottery Commission EU:C:2014:186 .... 25.018
C-543/12 Zeman EU:C:2014:2143... 25.018
C-557/12 Kone EU:C:2014:1317..9.015
C-573/12 Ålands Vindkraft EU:C:2014:2037 .... 7.033, 7.039, 7.040, 7.041, 7.042, 25.022
C-576/12P Jurašinović EU:C:2013:777 .... 14.031
C-579/12RX- II Commission v Strack EU:C:2013:570 ....25.018, 30.030
C-599/12 Jetair and Travel4you EU:C:2014:144.. 27.021
Opinion 2/13 Accession of the EU to the ECHR EU:C:2014:2454............... 1.020, 3.010, 5.003,
                                                    8.001, 21.017, 25.016, 30.045
C-28/13P Thesing and Bloomberg Finance v ECB EU:C:2014:230 .... 14.031
C-58/13 and C-59/13 Torresi EU:C:2014:2088... 25.024
C-65/13 European Parliament v Commission EU:C:2014:2289..................18.011, 18.012
C-66/13 Green Network EU:C:2014:2399.. 10.039
C-79/13 Saciri EU:C:2014:103 .... 25.018
C-81/13 United Kingdom v Council EU:C:2014:2449..............................5.013, 5.016
C-91/13 Essent Energie Productie EU:C:2014:2206 ....7.085, 8.013
C-119/13 and C-120/13 eco cosmetics and Raiffeisenbank St. Georgen EU:C:2014:2144 ....8.015
C-124/13 and C-125/13 European Parliament and Commission v Council
    EU:C:2015:790 .... 9.005, 17.038, 18.012
C-127/13P Strack v Commission EU:C:2014:2250 .... 25.019
C-129/13 and C-130/13 Kamino International Logistics and Datema Hellmann
    Worldwide Logistics EU:C:2014:2041............................... 25.002, 25.019, 25.024
C-133/13 Spezzino EU:C:2014:2460 ....9.055
C-146/13 Spain v European Parliament and Council EU:C:2015:298.......... 7.109, 22.013, 27.015
C-147/13 Spain v Council EU:C:2015:299................................ 7.109, 14.025, 14.029
C-156/13 Digibet and Albers EU:C:2014:1756 .... 5.041, 7.094, 18.005
C-166/13 Mukarubega EU:C:2014:2336 .... 25.018, 25.022, 25.023
C-168/13PPU Jeremy F EU:C:2013:358. .... 25.018
C-170/13 Huawei Technologies EU:C:2015:477...9.017
C-171/13 Demirci EU:C:2015:8 ....8.013
C 184/13 to C 187/13, C 194/13, C 195/13, and C 208/13 API and Others
    EU:C:2014:2147 ....9.012, 9.014

C-198/13 Julián Hernández and Others EU:C:2014:2055............................... 25.009
C-202/13 McCarthy and Others EU:C:2014:2450 ....8.028
C-206/13 Siragusa EU:C:2014:126..25.009, 25.021
C-209/13 United Kingdom v Council EU:C:2014:283.................................. 22.013
C-213/13 Impresa Pizzarotti EU:C:2014:2067 ....25.023, 29.011
C-220/13P Nicolaou v Court of Auditors EU:C:2014:2057.............................. 25.018
C-226/13, C-245/13, C-247/13, and C-578/13 Fahnenbock EU:C:2015:383 ....8.015
C-244/13 Ogieriakhi EU:C:2014:2068...6.013, 23.022
C-249/13 Boudjlida EU:C:2014:2431.. 25.022
C-254/13 Orgacom EU:C:2014:2251...7.017, 7.023
C-261/13P Schönberger v European Parliament EU:C:2014:2423.............. 6.022, 12.011, 25.018
C-303/13P Commission v Andersen EU:C:2015:647 ....2.007
C-305/13 Haeger & Schmidt EU:C:2014:2320 ....8.015
C-317/13 and C-679/13 European Parliament v Council EU:C:2015:223...... 17.003, 23.004, 28.010
C-318/13 X EU:C:2014:2133.. 27.035
C-322/13 Grauel Rüffer EU:C:2014:189 ....5.055
C-333/13 Dano EU:C:2014:2358 .... 6.010, 6.012, 6.015
C-341/13 Cruz & Companhia EU:C:2014:2230 .... 25.023
C-359/13 Martens EU:C:2015:118 .... 5.055, 6.018, 6.020
C-377/13 Ascendi Beiras Litoral e Alta, Auto Estradas das Beiras Litoral e
    Alta EU:C:2014:1754 .... 29.015
C-378/13 Commission v Greece EU:C:2014:2405 ....29.049, 29.053
C-383/13 G and R EU:C:2013:533 .... 25.018
C-396/13 Sähköalojen ammattiliitto EU:C:2015:86...................................... 25.010
C-398/13P Inuit Tapiriit Kanatami v Commission EU:C:2015:535..................25.017, 25.018
C-400/13 and C-408/13 Sanders and Verhagen EU:C:2014:2461..........................8.015
C-409/13 Council v Commission EU:C:2015:217 ....5.048, 12.060, 16.007, 16.010, 17.017
C-413/13 FNV Kunsten EU:C:2014:2411 ....9.014
C-425/13 Commission v Council EU:C:2015:483 ....16.010, 21.003
C-437/13 Unitrading EU:C:2014:2318 .... 25.019
C-439/13P Elitaliana v Eulex Kosovo EU:C:2015:753 .... 13.012, 25.008, 30.013
C-456/13P T & L Sugars v Commission EU:C:2015:284 .... 13.006
C-498/13 Agrooikosystimata EU:C:2015:61.. 14.025
C-508/13 Estonia v Parliament and Council EU:C:2015:403 ....5.029, 5.033
C-518/13 Eventech EU:C:2015:9..9.022
C-519/13 Alpha Bank Cyprus EU:C:2015:603 ....8.015
C-528/13 Léger EU:C:2015:288 .... 25.018
C-540/13 European Parliament v Council EU:C:2015:224 ....17.003, 23.004
C-543/13 Fipa Group and Others EU:C:2015:359 ....9.061
C-562/13 Abdida EU:C:2014:2453..25.012, 25.018
C-583/13P Deutsche Bahn EU:C:2015:404..25.018, 25.019
C-585/13P Europäisch- Iranische Handelsbank v Council EU:C:2015:145 .... 25.023
C-593/13 Rina Services EU:C:2015:399..7.067, 7.098
C-596/13P Commission v Moravia Gas Storage and Czech Republic EU:C:2015:203 ....2.007
C 608/13P CEPSA v Commission EU:C:2016:414...................................... 14.025
C-640/13 Commission v United Kingdom EU:C:2014:2457 .... 29.011
C-647/13 Melchior EU:C:2015:54 ....5.050
C-650/13 Delvigne EU:C:2015:648 .... 6.021, 12.012, 25.009, 25.018
C-660/13 Council v Commission EU:C:2016:616 .... 16.010
C-667/13 Banco Privado Português EU:C:2015:151 .... 30.034
C-673/13P Commission v Stichting Greenpeace Nederland and Pesticide Action
    Network Europe (PAN Europe) EU:C:2016:889 .... 14.031
C-689/13 PFE EU:C:2016:199........................... 23.015, 23.018, 29.016, 29.037
and 25.018C-5/14 Kernkraftwerke Lippe-Ems EU:C:2015:354 .... 29.016
C-23/14 Post Danmark EU:C:2015:651...9.017
C-25/14 and C-26/14 UNIS and Others EU:C:2015:821................................ 28.006

lxvi   TABLE OF CASES

C-44/14 Spain v European Parliament and Council EU:C:2015:554 . . . . 22.003
C-48/14 European Parliament v Council EU:C:2015:91 . . . . 5.014, 17.011
C-62/14 Gauweiler and Others EU:C:2015:400 . . . . 5.037, 9.036, 9.044, 23.029, 29.007
C-67/14 Alimanovic EU:C:2015:597 . . . . 6.010, 6.012
C-69/14 Târşia EU:C:2015:662 . . . . 25.023
C-72/14 X and van Dijk EU:C:2015:564 . . . . 29.019
C-73/14 Council v Commission EU:C:2015:663 . . . . 12.062, 14.002, 14.006, 16.010
C-74/14 Eturas and Others EU:C:2016:42 . . . . 25.018
C-83/14 CHEZ Razpredelenie Bulgaria EU:C:2015:480 . . . . .5.060
C-88/14 Commission v European Parliament and Council EU:C:2015:499. . . . . 18.011
C-98/14 Berlington Hungary Tanácsadó és Szolgáltató and Others EU:C:2015:386 . . . . . 7.012, 25.023
C-105/14 Taricco EU:C:2015:555 . . . . 18.007, 20.013, 25.012, 25.018
C-113/14 Germany v European Parliament and Council EU:C:2016:635. . . . . 9.005, 17.038
C-117/14 Nisttahuz Poclava EU:C:2015:60 . . . . 25.011
C-129/14PPU Spasic EU:C:2014:586 . . . . 25.011, 25.012, 25.018, 25.020, 25.025
C-132/14 to C-136/14 European Parliament and Commission v Council
   EU:C:2015:813 . . . . 11.006, 11.007, 11.008, 11.009, 17.011, 27.003
C-157/14 Neptune Distribution EU:C:2015:823 . . . . 25.018, 25.023
C-158/14 A and Others EU:C:2017:202 . . . . 30.033
C-160/14 Ferreira da Silva e Brito EU:C:2015:565 . . . . 16.013, 23.019, 29.012, 29.019
C-163/14 Commission v. Belgium EU:C:2016:4. . . . . 14.008
C-165/14 Rendon Marín EU:C:2016:675 . . . . .6.017
C-168/14 Grupo Itevelesa EU:C:2015:685 . . . . .7.097
C-179/14 Commission v Hungary EU:C:2016:108 . . . . 7.082, 7.086, 7.098, 7.099
C-198/14 Visnapuu EU:C:2015:751 . . . . 7.021, 7.043
C-200/14 Câmpean EU:C:2016:494 . . . . .5.049
C-216/14 Covaci EU:C:2015:686 . . . . .8.020
C-218/14 Singh EU:C:2015:476 . . . . .6.014
C-220/14P Ezz v Council EU:C:2015:147 . . . . 10.001
C-222/14 Maïstrellis EU:C:2015:473 . . . . 25.004, 25.018
C-223/14 Tecom Mical EU:C:2015:744 . . . . .8.015
C-235/14 Safe Interenvíos EU:C:2016:154 . . . . .7.110
C-241/14 Bukovansky EU:C:2015:766 . . . . .5.056
C-245/14 Thomas Cook Belgium EU:C:2015:715 . . . . .8.015
C-258/14 Florescu and Others EU:C:2017:448 . . . . 25.018, 27.044, 27.045
C-263/14 Parliament v Council EU:C:2016:435 . . . . 5.013, 5.014, 10.001,
                                                                           12.004, 12.009, 17.041, 21.003, 21.008
C-274/14 Banco de Santander EU:C:2020:17 . . . . 29.015
C-286/14 European Parliament v Commission EU:C:2016:183 . . . . 18.010
C-293/14 Hiebler EU:C:2015:843 . . . . 7.069, 7.097, 7.098
C-298/14 Brouillard EU:C:2015:652 . . . . .7.068
C-299/14 García Nieto EU:C:2016:114 . . . . 6.010, 6.011, 6.015
C-300/14 Imtech Marine Belgium EU:C:2015:825 . . . . .8.015
C-304/14 CS EU:C:2016:674 . . . . 6.016, 6.017
C-308/14 Commission v United Kingdom EU:C:2016:436 . . . . 6.012, 7.079
C-317/14 Commission v Belgium EU:C:2015:63 . . . . .7.062
C-333/14 Scotch Whisky Association EU:C:2015:845 . . . . 7.029, 7.034
C-340/14 and C-341/14 Trijber and Harmsen EU:C:2015:641 . . . . 7.072, 7.097, 7.098
C-342/14 X-Steuerberatungsgesellschaft EU:C:2015:827 . . . . .7.092
C-350/14 Lazar EU:C:2015:802 . . . . .8.016
C-354/14 Capoda Import-Export EU:C:2015:658 . . . . 7.028, 7.040, 8.015
C-358/14 Poland v European Parliament and Council EU:C:2016:323 . . . . 5.029, 5.033, 7.113
C-362/14 Schrems EU:C:2015:650 . . . . 9.002, 16.013, 25.018, 25.020, 27.040
C-363/14 European Parliament v Council EU:C:2015:579 . . . . 17.003, 17.011, 18.009, 18.010
C-377/14 Radlinger EU:C:2016:283 . . . . 29.013

TABLE OF CASES   lxvii

C-402/14 Viamar EU:C:2015:830. . . . . .7.021
C-413/14P Intel v Commission EU:C:2017:632 . . . . .9.017
C-419/14 WebMindLicenses EU:C:2015:832 . . . . 25.018
C-438/14 Bogendorff von Wolffersdorff EU:C:2016:401. 5.041, 5.055, 6.020
C-439/14 and C-488/14 SC Star Storage and Others EU:C:2016:688. 25.018
C-440/14P National Iranian Oil Co v Council EU:C:2016:128. . . . . 18.008, 18.012
C-441/14 Dansk Industri EU:C:2016:278 . . . . 23.013, 27.033
C-443/14 and C-444/14 Alo and Osso EU:C:2016:127 . . . . 8.009, 26.001
and C-455/14P H v Council EU:C:2016:569. . . . . 10.001, 13.012, 30.013
C-458/14 and C-67/15 Promoimpresa and Melis EU:C:2016:558 . . . . .7.098
C-464/14 SECIL EU:C:2016:896. . . . . 26.003
C-477/14 Pillbox 38 EU:C:2016:324. . . . . 17.015, 25.018, 25.023
C-485/14 Commission v France EU:C:2015:506 . . . . .7.101
C-486/14 Kossowski EU:C:2016:483 . . . . 25.018
C-492/14 Essent Belgium EU:C:2016:732. . . . . .7.041
C-505/14 Klausner Holz Niedersachsen EU:C:2015:742. . . . . 25.023
C-508/14 Český telekomunikační EU:C:2015:657 . . . . 27.026
C-511/14 Pebros Servizi EU:C:2016:448 . . . . .8.015
C-515/14 Commission v Cyprus EU:C:2016:30 . . . . 5.050, 7.072
C-524/14P Commission v Hansestadt Lübeck EU:C:2016:971 . . . . 5.041, 9.022, 18.005
C-525/14 Commission v Czech Republic EU:C:2016:714. . . . . 29.032
C-526/14 Kotnik EU:C:2016:767 . . . . 9.024, 25.023, 27.045
C-540/14P DK Recycling und Roheisen v Commission EU:C:2016:469 . . . . . . 18.009, 18.010, 18.011
C-542/14 Commission v Czech RepublicEU:C:2016:578 . . . . .7.040
C-543/14 Ordre des barreaux francophones et germanophones EU:C:2016:605. . . . . . .25.018, 26.003
C-547/14 Philip Morris Brands EU:C:2016:325 . . . . .5.033, 5.038, 7.115,
                                                                                            17.015, 23.004, 25.018, 29.006
C-554/14 Ognyanov EU:C:2016:835 . . . . 23.013, 28.014
C-557/14 Commission v Portugal EU:C:2016:471. . . . . 29.053
C-561/14 Genc EU:C:2016:247. . . . . 7.072, 8.012, 8.013
C-562/14P Sweden v Commission EU:C:2017:356 . . . . 14.031
C-566/14 Marchiani v European Parliament EU:C:2016:437 . . . . 25.025
C-573/14 Lounani EU:C:2017:71 . . . . 26.016
C-595/14 European Parliament v Council EU:C:2015:847 . . . . 28.010
C-600/14 Germany v Council EU:C:2017:935 . . . . 10.036, 10.037, 21.006, 21.014
C-601/14 Commission v Italy EU:C:2016:759 . . . . 29.047, 29.049, 30.025
C-614/14 Ognyanov EU:C:2016:514 . . . . 23.014, 25.018, 29.017
Opinion 1/15 EU-Canada PNR Agreement EU:C:2016:656. . . . . 5.010, 5.015, 21.017
Opinion 2/15 Free Trade Agreement between the European Union and the Republic
  of Singapore EU:C:2017:376 . . . . 10.001, 10.002, 10.003, 10.004, 10.005,
                                                                                            10.010, 10.011, 10.037, 10.039, 21.017, 26.011
Opinion 3/15 Marrakesh Treaty to Facilitate Access to Published Works for Persons
  who are Blind, Visually Impaired or Otherwise Print Disabled
  EU:C:2016:657 . . . . 10.005, 10.037, 10.039, 21.017
C-8/15P to C-10/15P Ledra Advertising v Commission and ECB EU:C:2016:701 . . . . . . 9.037, 30.021
C-14/15 and C-116/15 European Parliament v Council EU:C:2016:715. . . . . 17.011
C-15/15 New Valmar EU:C:2016:464 . . . . 5.041, 7.030
C-18/15 Brisal EU:C:2016:549 . . . . .7.087
C-19/15 Verband Sozialer Wettbewerb EU:C:2016:563 . . . . .7.096
and C-20/15P and C-21/15P Commission v World Duty Free Group EU:C:2016:981 . . . . .9.022
C-25/15 Balogh EU:C:2016:423 . . . . .8.020
C-47/15 Affum EU:C:2016:408. . . . . .8.012
C-51/15 Remondis EU:C:2016:985 . . . . .5.041
C-60/15P Saint-Gobain Glass Deutschland v Commission EU:C:2017:540 . . . . 14.031
C-63/15 Ghezelbash EU:C:2016:409 . . . . .8.010

C-72/15 PJSC Rosneft Oil Co EU:C:2017:236. . . . . 5.004, 10.001, 10.031, 13.003,
13.012, 25.008, 25.024, 29.023, 30.013, 30.036, 30.045
C-76/15 Vervloet EU:C:2016:975. . . . . .9.022
C-105/15P to C-109/15P Mallis v Commission and ECB EU:C:2016:702 . . . . 12.040
C-115/15 NA EU:C:2016:487 . . . . 6.014, 29.007
C-121/15 ANODE EU:C:2016:637. . . . . 25.018
C-133/15 Chavez-Vilchez EU:C:2017:354. . . . . .6.017
C-135/15 Nikiforidis EU:C:2016:774. . . . . .8.016
C-148/15 Deutsche Parkinson Verein EU:C:2016:776. . . . . 7.032, 7.043
C-155/15 Karim EU:C:2016:410. . . . . .8.010
C-157/15 Achbita EU:C:2017:203 . . . . 5.060, 5.062
C-168/15 Tomášová EU:C:2016:602 . . . . 23.020, 27.035
C-174/15 Vereniging Openbare Bibliotheken EU:C:2016:856 . . . . 26.002
C-182/15 Petruhhin EU:C:2016:630 . . . . 5.055, 6.020, 8.020
C-188/15 Bougnaoui EU:C:2017:204. . . . . .5.060
C-201/15 AGET Iraklis EU:C:2016:972. . . . . 5.007, 7.062, 7.072, 25.009, 25.018, 25.019
C-203/15 and C-698/15 Tele2 Sverige and Others EU:C:2016:970 . . . . 25.018
C-213/15P Commission v Breyer EU:C:2017:563 . . . . 14.031
C-221/15 Etablissements Fr. Dolruyt EU:C:2016:704 . . . . .7.043
C-230/15 Brite Strike Technologies EU:C:2016:560. . . . . 26.008
C-237/15PPU Lanigan EU:C:2015:474 . . . . .8.020
C-249/15 Wind 1014 EU:C:2018:21. . . . . .7.092
C-256/15 Nemec EU:C:2016:954 . . . . 11.003
C-258/15 Salaberria Sorondo EU:C:2016:873. . . . . .5.060
C-268/15 Ullens de Schooten EU:C:2016:874. . . . . 5.064, 7.055, 29.017
C-284/15 M EU:C:2016:220 . . . . .7.078
C-296/15 Medisanus EU:C:2017:431. . . . . .5.054
C-316/15 Hemming EU:C:2016:879 . . . . .7.098
C-331/15P France v Schlyter EU:C:2017:639 . . . . 14.031
C-337/15P European Ombudsman v Staelen EU:C:2017:256 . . . . 6.022, 13.041, 30.023
C-339/15 Vanderborght EU:C:2017:335 . . . . 7.088, 7.092
C-342/15 Piringer EU:C:2017:196 . . . . 7.069, 7.092
C-360/15 and C-31/16 X and Visser EU:C:2018:44 . . . . 7.082, 7.096, 7.097, 7.098
C-375/15 BAWAG PSK Bank für Arbeit und Wirtschaft und Österreichische
Postsparkasse EU:C:2017:38. . . . . 10.020
C-379/15 Association France Nature Environnement EU:C:2016:603 . . . . 23.014
C-389/15 Commission v Council EU:C:2017:798 . . . . 10.004, 10.005
C-390/15 RPO EU:C:2017:174 . . . . .5.061
C-392/15 Commission v Hungary EU:C:2017:73 . . . . .7.069
C-394/15P Dalli v Commission EU:C:2016:262. . . . . 12.068
C-395/15 Daouidi EU:C:2016:917 . . . . 25.011, 26.002, 26.003
C-401/15 and C-403/15 Depesme and Others EU:C:2016:955. . . . . .6.014
C-404/15 and C-659/15PPU Aranyosi and Căldăraru EU:C:2016:198 . . . . 5.003, 8.020, 25.018
C-406/15 Milkova EU:C:2017:198 . . . . .5.052
C-413/15 Farrell EU:C:2017:745. . . . . 27.025
C-420/15 U EU:C:2017:408. . . . . .5.054
C-429/15 Danqua EU:C:2016:789 . . . . 29.011
C-434/15 Asociación Profesional Élite Taxi EU:C:2017:981. . . . . . . 7.004, 7.083, 7.085, 7.097, 9.009, 9.056
C-443/15 Parris EU:C:2016:897 . . . . .5.060
C-444/15 Associazione Italia Nostra Onlus EU:C:2016:978. . . . . 25.011, 25.018
C-466/15 Adrien EU:C:2016:749 . . . . .7.078
C-491/15P Typke v Commission EU:C:2017:5 . . . . 14.030
C-497/15 and C-498/15 Euro-Team and Spirál-Gép EU:C:2017:229 . . . . .5.035
C-507/15 Agro Foreign Trade & Agency EU:C:2017:129 . . . . .8.013

C-508/15 and C-509/15 Ucar and Kilic EU:C:2016:986 ....8.013
C-521/15 Spain v Council EU:C:2017:982. ....9.038, 18.012
C-549/15 E.ON Biofor Sverige EU:C:2017:490. .... 7.039, 7.040
C-552/15 Commission v Ireland EU:C:2017:698 ....7.092
C-566/15 Erzberger EU:C:2017:562. ....7.059
C-572/15 F. Hoffmann-La Roche EU:C:2016:739 .... 24.003
C-574/15 Scialdone EU:C:2018:295. .... 23.018
C-579/15 Popławski EU:C:2017:503 .... 23.013
C-582/15 van Vemde EU:C:2017:37. ....8.020
C-589/15P Anagnostakis v Commission EU:C:2017:663 ....9.036, 17.013
C-591/15 Gibraltar Betting and Gaming Association EU:C:2017:449. ....7.085
C-593/15P and C-594/15P Slovak Republic v Commission EU:C:2017:800 .... 27.042
C-601/15PPU JN EU:C:2016:84. .... 8.011, 8.012, 29.007
C-612/15 Kolev EU:C:2018:392 ....8.020, 20.013
C-617/15 Hummel Holding EU:C:2017:390. .... 23.006
C-620/15 A-Rosa Flussschiff EU:C:2017:309 ....7.078
C-626/15 and C-659/16 Commission v Council EU:C:2018:925. .... 9.008, 10.039, 21.014
and C-628/15 The Trustees of the BT Pension Scheme EU:C:2017:687. .... 23.017
C-643/15 and C-647/15 Slovakia and Hungary v Council EU:C:2017:631 .... 5.037, 8.010,
10.011, 12.024, 17.002, 17.003, 17.017, 17.038
C-648/15 Austria v Germany EU:C:2017:664. ....13.008, 28.004
C-652/15 Tekdemir EU:C:2017:239. ....8.013
C-668/15 Jyske Finans EU:C:2017:278 ....5.060
C-671/15 Association des producteurs vendeurs d'endives (APVE) EU:C:2017:860 ....9.004
C-687/15 Commission v Council EU:C:2017:803 .... 5.010, 27.007
C-696/15P Czech Republic v Commission EU:C:2017:595 ....18.009, 18.010
C-5/16 Poland v European Parliament and Council EU:C:2018:483. .....5.037, 9.062, 17.015, 27.046
C-16/16P Belgium v Commission EU:C:2018:79. .... 30.012
C-44/16P Dyson v Commission EU:C:2017:357 .... 18.010
C-49/16 Unibet International EU:C:2017:491 .... 25.023
C-52/16 and C-113/16 SEGRO and Horvath EU:C:2018:157. ....7.105
C-57/16P ClientEarth v Commission EU:C:2018:660. .... 14.030
C-64/16 Associação Sindical dos Juízes Portugueses EU:C:2018:117 .....3.010, 5.003, 13.013, 15.013
C-74/16 Congregación de Escuelas Pías Provincia Betania EU:C:2017:496. ....9.013
C-78/16 and C-79/16 Pesce EU:C:2016:428 .... 5.037, 18.013, 25.023
C-82/16 KA EU:C:2018:308 .... 6.005, 6.014, 6.017, 8.012, 25.018
C-99/16 Lahorgue EU:C:2017:391 ....7.092
C-104/16P Council v Front Polisario EU:C:2016:973 ....26.013, 26.016
C-106/16 Polbud–Wykonawstwo EU:C:2017:804 .... 7.054, 7.065
C-111/16 Fidenato EU:C:2017:676. .... 25.023
C-115/16, C-118/16, C-119/16, and C-299/16 N Luxembourg 1 EU:C:2019:134 .... 25.024
C-116/16 and C-117/16 T Danmark EU:C:2019:135. .... 25.024
C-135/16 Georgsmarienhütte EU:C:2018:582 ....9.028, 30.033
C-165/16 Lounes EU:C:2017:862. ....6.008, 6.014
C-171/16 Beshkov EU:C:2017:710. ....8.020
C-174/16 H EU:C:2017:637. .... 25.018
C-179/16 F. Hoffmann-La Roche EU:C:2018:25 ....9.014
C-181/16 Gnandi EU:C:2018:465. ....8.012, 25.018
C-183/16P Tilly-SabcoSAS v Commission EU:C:2017:704 ....18.014, 18.015
C-187/16 Commission v Austria EU:C:2018:194. .... 11.011
C-191/16 Piscotti EU:C:2018:222. ....6.008, 6.020
C-196/16 and C-197/16 Comune di Corridonia and Others EU:C:2017:589. ....5.046
C-201/16 Shiri EU:C:2017:805 ....8.010
C-207/16 Ministerio Fiscal EU:C:2018:788. .... 25.018

TABLE OF CASES

C-218/16 Kubicka EU:C:2017:755 ....8.015
and C-236/16 and C-237/16 Asociación Nacional de Grandes Empresas de
    Distribución (ANGED) EU:C:2018:291 .... 18.005
C-243/16 Miravitlles Ciurana EU:C:2017:969 .... 25.009
C-244/16P Industrias Químicas del Vallés v Commission EU:C:2018:177.................. 30.011
C-251/16 Cussens EU:C:2017:881 .... 25.024
C-266/16 Western Sahara Campaign UK EU:C:2018:118............................... 26.013
C-278/16 Sleutjes EU:C:2017:757...8.020
C-284/16 Achmea EU:C:2018:158..................................1.020, 1.024, 13.008, 26.009
C-297/16 Colegiul Medicilor Veterinari din România EU:C:2018:141............... 7.097, 7.098
C-306/16 Maio Marques da Rosa EU:C:2017:844 .... 25.004
C-316/16 and C-424/16 B and Vomero EU:C:2018:256 ....6.016
C-320/16 Uber France EU:C:2018:221 .... 7.004, 7.097, 7.111, 9.009, 9.056
C-331/16 and C-366/16 K and HF EU:C:2018:296 ....6.016
C-353/16 MP EU:C:2018:276... 8.009, 25.018
C-359/16 Altun EU:C:2018:63 ....5.047, 7.078, 7.083, 25.023
C-367/16 Piotrowski EU:C:2018:27..8.020
C-368/16 Assens Havn EU:C:2017:546 ....8.015
C-372/16 Sahyouni EU:C:2017:988 .... 8.016, 22.013
C-377/16 Spain v European Parliament EU:C:2019:249 .... 14.025, 25.023
C-390/16 Lada EU:C:2018:532..8.020
C-391/16 C-77/17, and C-78/17 M EU:C:2019:403 ....8.008, 8.009, 23.004, 25.018
C-405/16P Germany v Commission EU:C:2019:268.......................................9.022
C-414/16 Egenberger EU:C:2018:257 .... 5.007, 5.060, 25.009
C-420/16P Izsák and Dabis v Commission EU:C:2019:177 .... 17.013
C-426/16 Liga van Moskeeën en Islamitische Organisaties Provincie Antwerpen
    EU:C:2018:335 ....5.007, 25.018
C-442/16 Gusa EU:C:2017:1004...5.055
C-451/16 MB EU:C:2018:492 ....5.058
C-452/16PPU Poltorak EU:C:2016:858... 16.013
C-477/16PPU Kovalkovas EU:C:2016:861 .... 16.013
C-490/16 AS EU:C:2017:585...8.010, 25.004
C-516/16 Erzeugerorganisation Tiefkühlgemüse EU:C:2017:1011 .... 25.023
C-528/16 Confédération paysanne EU:C:2018:583 .... 7.109, 25.023
C-537/16 Garlsson Real Estate EU:C:2018:193..................................25.018, 25.020
C-540/16 Spika and Others EU:C:2018:565 .... 25.009
C-554/16 EP Agrarhandel EU:C:2018:406 .... 14.025
C-558/16 Mahnkopf EU:C:2018:138..8.015, 22.013
C-569/16 and C-570/16 Bauer and Willmeroth EU:C:2018:871 ....23.014, 25.004, 25.007, 25.022, 27.033
C-578/16PPU CK EU:C:2017:127 .... 25.018
C-579/16 Commission v FIH Holding A/S and FIH Erhvervsbank A/S EU:C:2018:159 ....9.022
C-585/16 Alheto EU:C:2018:584 ....8.009, 27.022
C-590/16 Commission v Greece EU:C:2018:77 .... 29.047
C-599/16P Yanukovych v Council EU:C:2017:785 .... 10.001
C-619/16 Kreuziger EU:C:2018:872... 25.018
C-620/16 Commission v Germany EU:C:2019:256 .... 21.006
C-622/16P to C-624/16P Scuola Elementare Maria Montessori v Commission
    EU:C:2018:873 .... 30.008
C-626/16 Commission v Slovak Republic EU:C:2018:525 .... 29.047
C-638/16PPU X and X EU:C:2017:173 ....5.026, 8.007, 23.012, 25.004, 25.011
C-646/16 Jafari EU:C:2017:586...8.010
C-650/16 A/S Bevola EU:C:2018:424....................................... 7.066, 7.072
C-651/16 DW EU:C:2018:162..7.078
C-673/16 Coman EU:C:2018:385.........................5.041, 5.060, 6.010, 6.014
C-680/16P August Wolff and Remedia v Commission EU:C:2019:257..................... 25.023

C-684/16 Max-Planck-Gesellschaft zur Förderung der Wissenschaften
   EU:C:2018:874 .... 23.033, 25.010
Opinion 1/17 EU–Canada CET Agreement EU:C:2019:341 .... 1.028, 3.010, 10.001,
   10.004, 21.006, 21.016, 21.017, 25.008, 25.018
C-12/17 Dicu EU:C:2018:799 .... 25.018
C-17/17 Hampshire EU:C:2018:674.. 27.035
C-25/17 Jehovan todistajat—uskonnollinen yhdyskunta EU:C:2018:551............. 25.018, 29.032
C-33/17 Čepelnik EU:C:2018:896 .... 7.084, 7.085, 7.092, 7.094, 7.097
C-34/17 Donnellan EU:C:2018:282 .... 20.013
C-39/17 Lubrizol France SAS 7.017, 7.021
C-42/17 MAS EU:C:2017:936... 18.007, 20.013, 25.018
C-68/17 IR EU:C:2018:696 .... 5.007, 5.060, 27.033
C-73/17 France v European Parliament EU:C:2018:787 .... 12.005, 12.018,
   14.020, 16.008, 20.003, 27.050
and 25.018C-93/17 Commission v Greece EU:C:2018:903........................ 11.011, 29.053
C-97/17 Commission v Bulgaria EU:C:2018:285.. 29.047
C-105/17 Kamenova EU:C:2018:808.. 25.018
C-115/17 Clergeau EU:C:2018:651 .... 25.018
C-120/17 Ministru kabinets EU:C:2018:638.. 25.023
C-122/17 Smith EU:C:2018:631............................. 27.026, 27.030, 27.032, 27.033
C-123/17 Yön EU:C:2018:632... 26.004
C-128/17 Poland v European Parliament and Council EU:C:2019:194......... 5.048, 17.016, 27.050
C-135/17 X EU:C:2019:136... 7.107
C-136/17 GC EU:C:2019:773 .... 25.010, 25.018
C-137/17 Van Gennip EU:C:2018:771... 7.097
C-147/17 Sindicatul Familia Constanţa EU:C:2018:926 .... 25.018
C-151/17 Swedish Match EU:C:2018:938 .... 25.023
C-152/17 Consorzio Italian Management and Catania Multiservizi EU:C:2018:264 .... 25.009
C-161/17 Renckhoff EU:C:2018:634 .... 25.018
C-163/17 Jawo EU:C:2019:218 .... 8.001, 25.014
C-167/17 Klohn EU:C:2018:833... 25.023
C-169/17 Asociación Nacional de Productores de Ganado Porcino EU:C:2018:440...... 7.028, 7.030
C-171/17 Commission v Hungary EU:C:2018:881 .... 7.097, 7.098
C-177/17 and C-178/17 Demarchi Gino and Garavaldi EU:C:2017:656.................... 25.009
C-193/17 Cresco EU:C:2019:43 .... 5.052, 5.060, 23.033, 25.010, 25.018, 27.033
C-207/17 Rotho Blaas EU:C:2018:840 .... 26.005
C-208/17P to C-210/17P NF, NG and NM v European Council EU:C:2018:705 .... 28.003
C-219/17 Berlusconi and Fininvest EU:C:2018:1023.................. 5.050, 9.042, 23.007, 30.005
C-221/17 Tjebbes EU:C:2019:189 .... 6.006, 25.018
C-234/17 XC EU:C:2018:853 ....23.018, 25.018
C-235/17 Commission v Hungary EU:C:2019:432 .... 7.012, 7.104, 7.105, 11.003, 25.009, 25.018
C-242/17 LEGO EU:C:2018:804.. 7.039, 7.040
C-244/17 Commission v Council EU:C:2018:662 .... 5.012, 21.006
C-247/17 Raugevicius EU:C:2018:898............................... 5.055, 6.020, 25.018
C-258/17 EB EU:C:2019:17... 5.060
C-297/17, C-318/17, C-319/17, and C-438/17 Ibrahim EU:C:2019:219 ...... 8.001, 8.008, 25.014, 25.018
C-298/17 France Télévisions EU:C:2018:1017 .... 7.085
C-299/17 VG Media EU:C:2019:716 .... 7.111
C-305/17 FENS EU:C:2018:986 .... 7.017, 10.005, 10.006
C-312/17 Bedi EU:C:2018:734 .... 25.018
C-324/17 Gavanozov EU:C:2019:892 .... 8.020
C-342/17 Memoria EU:C:2018:906 .... 7.086, 7.097
25.018C-349/17 Eesti Pagar EU:C:2019:172...................................... 9.028, 23.017
C-374/17 A-Brauerei EU:C:2018:1024... 9.022
C-377/17 Commission v Germany EU:C:2019:562 .... 7.098

C-378/17 The Minister for Justice and Equality and The Commissioner of the
    Garda Síochána EU:C:2018:979 . . . . 23.014, 27.032, 29.009
C-384/17 Dooel Uvoz-Izvoz Skopje Link Logistic N&N 25.018
C-387/17 Fallimento Traghetti del Mediterraneo EU:C:2019:51 . . . . .9.026
C-391/17 Commission v United Kingdom EU:C:2019:919 . . . . 5.050, 10.013, 11.007
C-393/17 Kirschstein EU:C:2019:563 . . . . 7.096, 7.097, 7.098
C-395/17 Commission v Netherlands EU:C:2019:918 . . . . .5.046, 5.050, 10.013, 11.007
C-411/17 Inter-Environnement Wallonnie and Bond Beter Leefmilieu
    Vlaanderen EU:C:2019:622. . . . . .23.014, 28.006
C-416/17 Commission v France EU:C:2018:811 . . . . 29.041
C-430/17 Walbusch Walter Busch EU:C:2019:47 . . . . 25.018
C-431/17 Monachos Eirinaios EU:C:2019:368 . . . . .7.076, 7.109
C-437/17 Gemeinsamer Betriebsrat EurothermenResort Bad Schallerbach EU:C:2019:193. . . . .7.062
C-441/17 Commission v Poland EU:C:2018:255 . . . . .5.046
C-469/17 Funke Medien NRW EU:C:2019:623 . . . . 25.018
C-473/17 and C-546/17 Repsol Butano EU:C:2019:308 . . . . .7.098
C-476/17 Pelham EU:C:2019:624. . . . . 25.020
C-482/17 Czech Republic v European Parliament and Council
    EU:C:2019:1035 . . . . 5.013, 5.036, 5.037, 7.113, 17.015, 25.018, 25.022, 27.050
C-493/17 Weiss EU:C:2018:1000 . . . . 5.039, 9.036, 9.044, 23.029, 27.007, 29.005
C-497/17 Œuvre d'assistance aux bêtes d'abattoirs (OABA) EU:C:2019:137 . . . . .5.007, 9.006
C-507/17 Google EU:C:2019:772. 5.026, 23.012, 25.002, 25.010, 25.012, 25.020
C-511/17 Lintner EU:C:2020:188. . . . . 29.013
C-515/17P and C-561/17P Uniwersytet Wrocławski and Republic of Poland v
    Research Executive Agency EU:C:2020:73 . . . . 18.024, 23.007, 30.026
C-516/17 Spiegel Online EU:C:2019:625. . . . . 25.018
C-543/17 Commission v Belgium EU:C:2019:573. . . . . 12.058, 18.003, 18.004, 18.005, 29.052, 29.053
C-556/17 Torubarov EU:C:2019:626 . . . . .8.009, 25.018
C-573/17 Popławski EU:C:2019:530 . . . . 5.049, 8.020, 23.010, 23.013, 23.014, 23.032, 23.033,
        23.034, 27.014, 27.016, 27.022, 27.026, 27.028, 27.029, 27.032, 27.034, 28.014, 29.008
C-591/17 Austria v Germany EU:C:2019:504. . . . . .5.054, 5.056, 7.028, 7.043, 7.088, 9.011, 29.042
C-597/17 Belgisch Syndicaat van Chiropraxie EU:C:2019:544. . . . . .5.046
C-609/17 and C-610/17 TSN EU:C:2019:981 . . . . 9.047, 25.009, 25.011
C-611/17 Italy v Council EU:C:2019:332. . . . . 5.036, 5.037, 9.008, 25.022, 27.007, 27.009
C-616/17 Blaise EU:C:2019:800 . . . . 17.015, 25.023
C-620/17 Hochtief Solutions AG Magyarországi Fióktelepe EU:C:2019:630. . . . . 25.023
C-623/17 Privacy International EU:C:2020:790. . . . . 5.041, 9.002, 25.018
C-625/17 Vorarlberger Landes- und Hypothekenbank EU:C:2018:939 .7.083
C-637/17 Cogeco Communications EU:C:2019:263 . . . . .9.015
C-679/17 Huijbrechts EU:C:2018:940 . . . . 7.103, 7.104, 7.105
C-699/17 Allianz Vorsorgekasse EU:C:2019:290 . . . . 25.018
C-703/17 Krah EU:C:2019:850. . . . . 5.053, 7.062, 7.074
C-706/17 Achema EU:C:2019:407 . . . . .9.022
C-715/17, C-718/17, and C-719/17 Commission v Poland, Hungary and
    Czech Republic EU:C:2020:257 . . . . 5.041, 11.011, 29.049
C-724/17 Skanska Industrial Solutions EU:C:2019:204. . . . . .9.015
C-729/17 Commission v Greece EU:C:2019:534 . . . . .7.098
C-16/18 Dobersberger EU:C:2019:1110 . . . . .7.083
C-21/18 Textilis EU:C:2019:199 . . . . 10.020
C-22/18 TopFit and Biffi EU:C:2019:497. . . . . 6.015, 6.018, 9.051
C-28/18 Kerr EU:C:2019:673 . . . . .8.016
C-38/18 Gambino EU:C:2019:628. . . . . .8.020
C-55/18 Federación de Servicios de Comisiones Obreras (CCOO) EU:C:2019:402. . . .23.013, 25.018
C-59/18 Italy v Council, pending 28.002
C-64/18, C-140/18, C-146/18 and C-148/18 Maksimovic EU:C:2019:723 . . . . .7.092, 7.097

TABLE OF CASES   lxxiii

C-66/18 Commission v Hungary EU:C:2020:792 . . . . .7.065, 7.067, 7.072, 7.096, 9.050,
                        10.010, 10.011, 21.006, 25.009, 25.018, 26.002, 29.039
C-70/18 A, B, and P EU:C:2019:823 . . . . .8.013
C-75/18 Vodafone Magyarország Mobil Távközlési EU:C:2020:139 . . . . .7.061, 9.024
C-78/18 Commission v Hungary EU:C:2020:476 . . . . 7.101, 7.104, 7.105, 7.107, 25.018
C-89/18 A EU:C:2019:580 . . . . .8.013
C-92/18 France v European Parliament EU:C:2020:506 . . . . 12.018, 14.020, 16.008
C-93/18 Bajrati EU:C:2019:809. . . . . .6.010
C-94/18 Chenchooliah EU:C:2019:693 . . . . 6.014, 6.016, 6.017
C-102/18 Brisch EU:C:2019:34. . . . . .8.015
C-122/18 Commission v Italy EU:C:2020:41 . . . . .5.046
C-123/18P HTTS Hanseatic Trade Trust & Shipping v Council EU:C:2019:694 . . . . 10.001, 27.007
C-128/18 Dorobantu EU:C:2019:857. . . . . 5.003, 8.001, 8.020, 25.012, 25.019
C-129/18 SM EU:C:2019:248 . . . . 6.014, 25.018
C-134/18 Vester EU:C:2019:212 . . . . .7.079
C-149/18 da Silva Martins EU:C:2019:84 . . . . .8.016
C-171/18 Safeway EU:C:2019:839 . . . . 5.058, 25.023
C-178/18P MSD Animal Health Innovation v European Medicines Agency EU:C:2020:24 . . . 14.031
C-182/18 Comune di Milano v Council, pending 28.002
C-183/18 Bank BGZ BNP Paribas EU:C:2020:153. . . . . .8.020
C-192/18 Commission v Poland EU:C:2019:924 . . . . .5.003, 5.058, 13.003, 29.003
C-202/18 and C-238/18 Rimšēvičs v Latvia EU:C:2019:139 . . . . 9.043, 13.006, 30.005
C-209/18 Commission v Austria EU:C:2019:632 . . . . 7.094, 7.096, 7.098
C-216/18PPU LM EU:C:2018:586 . . . . 5.003, 5.005, 8.020, 13.003, 15.013,
                                            25.009, 25.018, 29.004, 29.035
C-220/18PPU Generalstaatsanwaltschaft EU:C:2018:589 . . . . 25.004, 25.012, 25.019
C-230/18 PI EU:C:2019:383 . . . . .7.072
C-233/18 Haqbin EU:C:2019:956. . . . . 8.011, 25.018
25.018C-236/18 GRDF EU:C:2019:1120 . . . . 25.023, 27.026
C-261/18 Commission v Ireland EU:C:2019:955 . . . . 5.046, 29.049
C-262/18P and C-271/18P Commission v Dôvera zdravotná poisťovňa EU:C:2020:450 . . . .9.013, 9.022
C-307/18 Generics (UK) EU:C:2020:52 . . . . .9.017
C-311/18 Schrems EU:C:2020:559. . . . . 9.002, 16.013, 27.040
C-314/18 SF EU:C:2020:191 . . . . .8.020
C-323/18 Tesco-Global Áruházak EU:C:2020:140 . . . . 7.012, 7.061, 7.066
C-325/18PPU and C-375/18PPU CE and NE EU:C:2018:739 . . . . .8.015
C-363/18 Organisation juive européenne EU:C:2019:954 . . . . 10.001, 26.013
C-384/18 Commission v Belgium EU:C:2020:124 . . . . 7.062, 7.096
C-387/18 Delfarma EU:C:2019:556 . . . . .7.034
C-390/18 X EU:C:2019:1112 . . . . .7.085, 7.097, 7.111, 27.033
C-393/18PPU UD EU:C:2018:835 . . . . .8.015
C-398/18 and C-428/18 Torrico and Bode EU:C:2019:1050 . . . . 7.078, 7.079
C-414/18 Iccrea Banca EU:C:2019:1036 . . . . 5.050, 30.006
C-417/18 AW and Others EU:C:2019:671 . . . . 29.012
C-418/18P Puppinck v Commission EU:C:2019:1113 . . . . 5.004, 12.011, 17.013, 17.015
C-435/18 Otis EU:C:2019:1069 . . . . .9.015
C-442/18P ECB v Espírito Santo Financial (Portugal) EU:C:2019:1117 . . . . 13.023, 14.031
C-443/18 Commission v Italy EU:C:2019:676 . . . . .5.046
C-447/18 UB EU:C:2019:1098 . . . . .7.060
C-451/18 Tibor-Trans Fuvarozó és Kereskedelmi EU:C:2019:635. . . . . .8.015
C-453/18 and C-494/18 Bondora EU:C:2019:1118 . . . . .8.015
C-457/18 Slovenia v Croatia EU:C:2020:65 . . . . 11.006, 26.007, 28.004
C-460/18P HK v Commission EU:C:2019:1119 . . . . .5.060
C-464/18 ZX EU:C:2019:311. . . . . .8.015
C-467/18 EP EU:C:2019:765 . . . . .8.020

lxxiv TABLE OF CASES

C-468/18 R EU:C:2019:666 .... 8.015
C-469/18 and C-470/18 JN and JM EU:C:2019:895 .... 25.011
C-482/18 Google Ireland EU:C:2020:141 .... 7.085, 7.087, 7.088
C-507/18 NH EU:C:2020:289 .... 5.060
C-508/18 and C-82/19PPU OG and PI EU:C:2019:456 .... 8.001, 8.020, 16.013
C-509/19 PF EU:C:2019:457 .... 8.001, 8.020, 16.013, 25.018
C-511/18, C-512/18, and C-520/18 La Quadrature du Net and Others
    EU:C:2020:791 .... 5.041, 9.002, 25.004, 25.018, 25.019, 29.006
C-518/18 RD EU:C:2019:546 .... 8.015
C-542/18 RX-II Simpson v Council EU:C:2020:232 .... 10.020
C-548/18 BGL BNP Paribas EU:C:2019:848 .... 8.016
C-549/18 Commission v Romania EU:C:2020:563 .... 12.058, 18.004, 27.027, 29.052, 29.053
C-550/18 Commission v Ireland EU:C:2020:564 .... 12.058, 18.004, 27.027, 29.052, 29.053
C-558/18 and C-563/18 Miasto Łowicz EU:C:2020:234 .... 5.005, 29.017, 29.025
C-575/18P Czech Republic v Commission EU:C:2020:530 .... 25.012, 25.024, 27.042, 29.040
C-581/18 RB EU:C:2020:453 .... 5.053, 5.054, 7.097
C-585/18, C-624/18, and C-625/18 AK and Others EU:C:2019:982 .... 5.003, 5.005, 13.003,
                                     15.013, 16.013, 23.018, 25.018, 29.003, 29.004
C-594/18P Austria v Commission EU:C:2020:742 .... 2.006, 9.021, 9.024, 9.063, 24.003, 27.045
C-597/18P, C-598/18P, C-603/18P, and C-604/18P Council v Dr K Chrysostomides &
    Co and Others EU:C:2020:1028 .... 12.040, 22.005
C-610/18 AFMB EU:C:2020:565 .... 7.051, 25.024
C-619/18 Commission v Poland EU:C:2019:531 .. 5.003, 5.005, 13.003, 15.013, 25.004, 29.003, 29.004
C-619/18R Commission v Poland (order) EU:C:2019:575 .... 5.005, 30.028
C-620/18 Hungary v European Parliament and Council EU:C:2020:1001 ..... 5.007, 5.013, 5.040, 7.075
C-621/18 Wightman EU:C:2018:999 .... 4.015, 4.016, 5.003, 11.005, 24.001, 29.035
C-626/18 Poland v European Parliament and Council EU:C:2020:1000 .... 5.007, 5.013, 7.075
C-634/18 JI EU:C:2020:455 .... 8.021, 25.018
C-641/18 Rina EU:C:2020:349 .... 8.015, 26.002, 26.003, 26.005
C-644/18 Commission v Italy EU:C:2020:895 .... 29.049
C-650/18 Hungary v European Parliament EU:C:2021:426 .... 4.020, 12.019
C-663/18 BS and CA EU:C:2020:938 .... 7.034
C-671/18 ZP EU:C:2019:1054 .... 8.020
C-688/18 TX and UW EU:C:2020:94 .... 25.012
C-717/18 X EU:C:2020:142 .... 8.020
C-719/18 Vivendi EU:C:2020:627 .... 7.012
C-724/18 and C-727/18 Cali Appartments SCI EU:C:2020:743 .... 7.096, 7.097, 7.098
C-752/18 Deutsche Umwelthilfe EU:C:2019:1114 .... 5.035, 23.014, 23.018,
                                                  23.019, 25.018, 25.019, 25.020
C-788/18 Stanleyparma Sas di Cantarelli Pietro & Co EU:C:2020:110 .... 7.085, 7.088
C-802/18 Caisse pour l'avenir des enfants EU:C:2020:269 .... 7.059
C-808/18 Commission v Hungary EU:C:2020:1029 .... 8.009
C-830/18 PF and Others EU:C:2020:275 .... 25.018
C-836/18 RH EU:C:2020:119 .... 6.010
Opinion 1/19 Istanbul Convention 21.017
C-5/19 Overgas Mrezhi and Balgarska gazova asotsiatsia EU:C:2020:343 .... 25.018
C-24/19 A and Others EU:C:2020:503 .... 9.061, 27.033, 28.006, 29.006, 29.007
C-32/19 AT EU:C:2020:25 .... 6.013
C-41/19 FX EU:C:2020:425 .... 8.015, 23.006
C-59/19 Wikingerhof EU:C:2020:950 .... 8.015
C-73/19 Movic EU:C:2020:568 .... 8.015
and C-87/19 TV Play Baltic EU:C:2019:1063 .... 7.085, 7.092
C-113/19 Luxaviation EU:C:2020:228 .... 25.018
C-119/19P and C-126/19P Commission and Council v Carreras Sequeros
    EU:C:2020:676 .... 25.004, 25.008, 25.012, 25.018, 25.019, 25.023, 27.017, 30.025

C-129/19 BV EU:C:2020:566 . . . . 27.036
C-134/19P Bank Refah Kargaran v Council EU:C:2020:793. . . . . 30.045
C-212/19 Compagnie des pêches de Saint-Malo EU:C:2020:726. . . . . 30.033
C-223/19 YS EU:C:2020:753 . . . . 25.018
C-130/19 Court of Auditors v Pinxten 13.027
C-134/19P Bank Refah Kargaran v Council EU:C:2020:793. . . . . 30.021, 30.023
C-168/19 and C-169/19 HB and IC EU:C:2020:338. . . . . .5.056
C-181/19 Jobcenter Krefeld–Widerspruchsstelle EU:C:2020:794 . . . . 6.014, 7.060
C-186/19 Supreme Site Services EU:C:2020:638 . . . . 29.032
C-223/19 YS EU:C:2020:753 . . . . .5.060, 25.018
C-225/19 and C-226/19 RNNS and KA EU:C:2020:951 . . . . 8.007, 25.018, 25.023
C-243/19 A EU:C:2020:872. . . . . .7.080
C-245/19 and C-246/19 Etat luxembourgeois EU:C:2020:795 . . . . 25.004, 25.018, 25.020
C-249/19 JE EU:C:2020:570 . . . . .8.017, 22.013
C-253/19 MH EU:C:2020:585. . . . . .8.015
C-265/19 Recorded Artists Actors Performers EU:C:2020:677 . . . . 10.039, 25.018, 26.003, 26.013
C-272/19 Land Hessen EU:C:2020:535 . . . . 29.015
C-311/19 BONVER WIN EU:C:2020:981. . . . . 7.084, 7.085, 7.090
C-316/19 Commission v Slovenia :EU:C:2020:1030 . . . . 5.045, 5.047, 14.008, 16.008, 29.005
C-336/19 Centraal Israëlitisch Consistorie van België EU:C:2020:1031 . . . . 5.007, 25.009, 25.018
C-343/19 Verein für Konsumenteninformation EU:C:2020:534 . . . . .8.015
C-396/19P ECB v Insolvent Estate of Espírito Santo Financial Group EU:C:2020:845 . . . . 13.023
C-398/19 BY EU:C:2020:1032. . . . . .6.008, 6.020
C-445/19 Viasat Broadcasting UK EU:C:2020:952 . . . . 9.019, 9.024, 9.028
C-481/19 DB, EU:C:2021:84 . . . . 25.025
C-489/19PPU NJ EU:C:2019:849. . . . . 16.013
C-502/19 Junqueras Vies EU:C:2019:1115 . . . . 5.004, 5.050, 6.021, 12.001,
                                                                                                12.012, 12.014, 12.016, 25.018
C-508/19 Prokurator Generalny, pending. 29.004
C-510/19 AZ EU:C:2020:953 . . . . .8.020
C-566/19PPU and C-626/19PPU JR and YC EU:C:2019:1077. . . . . 16.013
C-584/19 A EU:C:2020:1002. . . . . .8.020
C-625/19PPU XD EU:C:2019:1078 . . . . 16.013
C-627/19PPU ZB EU:C:2019:1079. . . . . 16.013
C-743/19 European Parliament v Council, pending 14.021, 28.002
C-791/19R Commission v Poland EU:C:2020:277. . . . . .5.005, 30.028
C-879/19 IN EU:C:2021:409 . . . . .5.055
C-896/19 Repubblika EU:C:2021:311 . . . . 29.004
C-897/19PPU IN EU:C:2020:262. . . . . 6.020, 7.085, 7.087, 8.020, 25.018, 29.035
C-924/19PPU and C-925/19PPU FMS and Others EU:C:2020:367 . . . . 8.009, 8.011,
                                                                                                          8.012, 25.018, 29.017
C-928/19P European Federation of Public Service Unions (EPSU) v
    Commission EU:C:2021:656 . . . . .17.044, 18.006
C-354/20PPU and C-412/20PPU L and P EU:C:2020:1033 . . . . .5.005, 8.020

GENERAL COURT

T-1–4/89 and 6–15/89 Rhône-Poulenc and Others v Commission EU:T:1991:56. . . . . .5.035
T-30/89 Hilti v Commission EU:T:1991:70. . . . . 25.024
T-51/89 Tetra Pak v Commission EU:T:1990:41. . . . . .9.017
T-79/89, 84–86/89, 89/89, 91–92/89, 94/89, 96/89, 98/89, 102/89 and 104/89 BASF
    and Others v Commission EU:T:1992:26 357. . . . . .12.070, 27.006
T-80–81/89, 83/89, 87–88/89, 90/89, 93/89, 95/89, 97/89, 99–101/89, 103/89, 105/89,
    107/89 and 112/89 BASF and Others v Commission EU:T:1995:61 . . . . .12.070, 27.006
T-123/89 Chomel v Commission EU:T:1990:24. . . . . 25.022

TABLE OF CASES

T-148/89 Tréfilunion v Commission EU:T:1995:68 .... 14.025
T-43/90 Díaz Garcia v European Parliament T:1992:120 .... 23.007
T-32/91 Solvay v Commission EU:T:1995:117 .... 27.006
T-36/91 ICI v Commission EU:T:1995:118 .... 25.024
T-37/91 ICI v Commission EU:T:1995:119 ....25.024, 27.006
T-47/91 Auzat v Commission EU:T:1992:116 .... 5.061
T-75/91 Scaramuzza v Commission EU:T:1992:117 .... 5.061
T-83/91 Tetra Pak v Commission EU:T:1994:246 .... 9.017
T-38/92 AWS Benelux v Commission EU:T:1994:43 .... 27.007
T-39–40/92 CB and Europay v Commission EU:T:1994:20 .... 25.024
T-77/92 Parker Pen v Commission EU:T:1994:85 .... 14.025
T-10/93 A v Commission EU:T:1994:39 .... 25.004
T-32/93 Ladbroke Racing v Commission EU:T:1994:261 .... 9.020
T-435/93 ASPEC and Others v Commission EU:T:1995:79 .... 12.070
T-442/93 AAC and Others v Commission EU:T:1995:80 .... 12.070
T-480/93 and T-483/93 Antillean Rice Mills and Others v Commission EU:T:1995:162 ...... 10.013
T-492/93 and T-492/93R Nutral v Commission EU:T:1993:85 .... 18.002
T-535/93 F v Council EU:T:1995:40 .... 25.018
T-571/93 Lefebvre and Others v Commission EU:T:1995:163 .... 17.015
T-584/93 Roujansky v Council EU:T:1994:87 .... 1.041, 1.049, 3.011
T-115/94 Opel Austria v Council EU:T:1997:3 .... 25.022
T-162/94 NMB France and Others v Commission EU:T:1996:71 .... 26.005
T-176/94 K v Commission EU:T:1995:139 ....25.018, 25.019
T-179/94 Bonnamy v Council, not reported 1.049
T-194/94 Carvel and Guardian Newspapers v Council EU:T:1995:183 ....27.047, 27.050
T-230/94 Farrugia v Commission EU:T:1996:40 .... 6.006
T-305/94–T-307/94, T-313/94–T-316/94, T-318/94, T-325/94, T-328/94–T-329/94
    and T-335/94 Limburgse Vinyl Maatschappij NV and Others v
    Commission (PVC II) EU:T:1999:80 .... 25.024
T-346/94 France-aviation v Commission EU:T:1995:187 .... 25.024
T-369/94 and T-85/95 DIR International Film and Others v Commission EU:T:1998:39 ..... 18.024
T-380/94 AIUFFASS and AKT v Commission EU:T:1996:195 .... 27.045
T-66/95 Kuchlenz-Winter v Commission EU:T:1997:56 .... 6.010
T-105/95 WWF UK v Commission EU:T:1997:26 .... 14.031, 27.045, 27.050
T-146/95 Bernardi v European Parliament EU:T:1996:105 .... 13.040
T-149/95 Ducros and Others v Commission EU:T:1997:165 .... 27.045
T-184/95 Dorsch Consult v Council and Commission EU:T:1998:74 .... 26.015
T-201/95 Zanone v Council of Europe and France, not reported 25.013
T-213/95 and T-18/96 SCK and FNK v Commission EU:T:1997:157 ....25.018, 25.024
T-42/96 Eyckeler & Malt v Commission EU:T:1998:40 .... 25.024
T-48/96 Acme Industry v Council EU:T:1999:251 .... 25.004
T-83/96 van der Wal v Commission EU:T:1998:59 .... 25.018
T-102/96 Gencor v Commission EU:T:1999:65 .... 9.018, 11.006, 26.013
T-124/96 Interporc v Commission EU:T:1998:25 .... 14.031
T-125/96 and T-152/96 Boehringer Ingelheim Vetmedica v Council and
    Commission EU:T:1999:302 .... 17.036
T-135/96 UEAPME v Council EU:T:1998:128 .... 17.044
T-175/96 Berthu v Commission EU:T:1997:72 .... 9.032
T-192/96 Lebedef v Commission EU:T:1998:162 .... 26.013
T-202/96 and T-204/96 Von Löwis and Alvarez-Cotera v Commission EU:T:1998:177 .... 14.009
T-203/96 Embassy Limousines & Services v European Parliament EU:T:1998:302 .... 25.022
T-148/97 Keeling v Office for Harmonisation in the Internal Market EU:T:1998:114 .... 18.024
T-164/97 Busaca and Others v Court of Auditors EU:T:1998:233 .... 5.052
T-188/97 Rothmans v Commission EU:T:1999:156 .... 18.014
T-254/97 Fruchthandelsgesellschaft Chemnitz v Commission EU:T:1999:178 .... 26.005

T-264/97 D v Council EU:T:1999:13 ....5.060
T-266/97 VTM v Commission EU:T:1999:144..9.019
T-309/97 Bavarian Lager Company v Commission EU:T:1999:257 .... 14.031
T-610/97R Carlsen v Council EU:T:1998:48... 14.031
T-14/98 Hautala v Council EU:T:1999:157 .... 14.031
T-92/98 Interporc v Commission EU:T:1999:308 ....14.030, 14.031
T-172/98 and 175–176/98 Salamander and Others v European Parliament and
    Council EU:T:2000:168.. 27.021
T-2/99 T. Port v Council EU:T:2001:186 .... 26.005
T-3/99 Banatrading v Council EU:T:2001:187 .... 26.005
T-6/99 ESF Elbe-Stahlwerke Feralpi v Commission EU:T:2001:145 .... 23.006
T-13/99 Pfizer Animal Health v Council EU:T:2002:209 .... 25.022
T-18/99 Cordis Obst und Gemuse Groβhandel v Commission EU:T:2001:95................ 26.005
T-20/99 Denkavit Nederland v Commission EU:T:2000:209............................. 14.031
T-30/99 Bocchi Food Trade International v Commission EU:T:2001:96 .... 26.005
T-54/99 max.mobil Telekommunikation Service v Commission EU:T:2002:20 .... 25.021
T-70/99 Alpharma v Council EU:T:2002:210 ....5.016, 25.022
T-103/99 Associazione delle cantine sociali Venete v European Ombudsman and
    European Parliament EU:T:2000:135 .... 13.041
T-106/99 Meyer v Commission EU:T:1999:272....................................... 14.030
T-120/99 Kik v Office for Harmonisation in the Internal Market EU:T:2001:189 .... 14.029
T-144/99 Institute of Professional Representatives before the European Patent Office v
    Commission EU:T:2001:105... 24.001
T-164/99, T-37/00 and T-38/00 Leroy and Others v Council EU:T:2001:170.............. 24.006
T-191/99 Petrie and Others v Commission EU:T:2001:284 ....14.030, 14.031
T-192/99 Dunnett and Others v European Investment Bank EU:T:2001:72................ 25.023
T-219/99 British Airways v Commission EU:T:2003:343 .... 12.068
T-222/99, T-327/99 and T-329/99 Martinez and Others v European Parliament
    EU:T:2001:242 ....12.021, 25.018
T-227/99 and T-134/00 Kvaerner Warnow Werft v Commission EU:T:2002:54 .... 12.067
T-228/99 and T-233/99 Westdeutsche Landesbank Girozentrale v Commission
    EU:T:2003:57 .... 12.068
T-333/99 X v European Central Bank EU:T:2001:251 .... 24.006
T-17/00 Rothley and Others v European Parliament EU:T:2002:39 .... 12.016
T-74/00, 76/00, 83–85/00, 132/00, 137/00 and 141/00 Artegodan and Others v
    Commission EU:T:2002:283... 25.022
T-111/00 British American Tobacco International v Commission EU:T:2001:250........... 14.031
T-209/00 Lamberts v European Ombudsman EU:T:2002:94 .... 13.041
T-211/00 Kuijer v Council EU:T:2002:30 .... 14.031
T-251/00 Lagardère and Canal+ v Commission EU:T:2002:278 .... 25.022
T-307/00 C v Commission EU:T:2003:21 ....5.060
T-19/01 Chiquita Brands and Others v Commission EU:T:2005:31 .... 26.005
T-26/01 Fiocchi munizioni v Commission EU:T:2003:248.............................. 11.011
T-45/01 Sanders and Others v Commission EU:T:2007:221............................ 13.045
T-64–65/01 Afrikanische Frucht-Compagnie and Internationale Fruchtimport
    Gesellschaft Weichert v Council and Commission EU:T:2004:37 .... 26.005
T-94/01, 125/01 and 286/01 Hirsch and Others v European Central Bank EU:T:2003:3 ....5.052
T-172/01 M v Court of Justice EU:T:2004:108 .... 23.007
T-177/01 Jégo-Quéré v Commission EU:T:2002:112...............................30.010, 30.043
T-195/01 and 207/01 Government of Gibraltar v Commission EU:T:2002:111............. 11.007
T-203/01 Michelin v Commission EU:T:2003:250.......................................9.017
T-315/01 Kadi v Council and Commission EU:T:2005:332 .... 26.015
T-127/02 Concept—Anlagen u. Gerate nach "GMP" für Produktion u. Labor v Office for
    Harmonisation in the Internal Market EU:T:2004:110 .... 14.001
T-144/02 Eagle and Others EU:T:2007:222... 13.045

lxxviii TABLE OF CASES

T-228/02 Organisation des Modjahedines du peuple d'Iran v Council EU:T:2006:384 .... 25.024
T-2/04 Korkmaz EU:T:2006:97.. 17.018
T-25/04 González y Díez EU:T:2007:257.. 25.022
T-201/04 Microsoft v Commission EU:T:2007:289 ....9.017
T-219/04 Spain v Commission EU:T:2007:121....................................... 14.025
T-234/04 Netherlands v Commission EU:T:2007:335...................................7.115
T-240/04 France v Commission EU:T:2007:290.......................................5.019
T-264/04 WWF European Policy Programme EU:T:2007:114.......................... 14.031
T-348/04 SIDE v Commission EU:T:2008:109 .... 11.003
T-355/04 and 446/04 Co-Frutta v Commission EU:T:2010:15........................ 14.031
T-374/04 Germany v Commission EU:T:2007:332................................... 27.045
T-406/04 Bonnet v Court of Justice EU:T:2006:322.................................. 13.018
T-474/04 Pergan Hilfsstoffe für Industrielle Prozesse v Commission EU:T:2007:306......... 25.016
T-70/05 Evropaïki Dynamiki v European Maritime Safety Agency EU:T:2010:55 .... 18.024
T-237/05 Editions Odile Jacob v Commission EU:T:2010:224......................... 14.031
T-300/05 and 316/05 Cyprus v Commission EU:T:2009:380 .... 12.070
T-324/05 Estonia v Commission EU:T:2009:381 .... 24.007
T-345/05 Mote v European Parliament EU:T:2008:440............................. 12.016
T-403/05 My Travel v Commission EU:T:2008:316 .... 14.031
T-42/06 Gollnisch v European Parliament EU:T:2010:102........................... 12.016
T-143/06 MTZ Polyfilms v Council EU:T:2009:441...................................5.019
T-405/06 ArcelorMittal Luxembourg v Commission EU:T:2009:90 .... 11.004
T-411/06 Sogelma v European Agency for Reconstruction EU:T:2008:419 .... 18.024
T-24/07 ThyssenKrupp Stainless v Commission EU:T:2009:236............. 1.009, 11.003, 11.004
T-256/07 People's Mojahedin Organization of Iran v Council EU:T:2008:461.............. 10.031
T-334/07 Denka International v Commission EU:T:2009:453............... 11.003, 25.020, 27.009
T-341/07 Sison v Council EU:T:2011:687 .... 10.031
T-407/07 CMB Maschinenbau & Handels GmbH and J Chrisof v Commission
    EU:T:2011:477 .... 18.024
T-58/08P Roodhuijzen EU:T:2009:385 ....5.060
T-439/08 Joséphidès v Commission and EACEA EU:T:2010:442 .... 18.024
T-173/09R Z v Commission EU:T:2009:180.. 27.039
T-224/10 Association belge des consommateurs test-achats v Commission
    EU:T:2011:588 .... 5.007, 25.018
T-240/10 Hungary v Commission EU:T:2013:645................................... 18.014
T-339/10 and T 532/10 Cosepuri v EFSA EU:T:2013:38............................. 14.031
T-406/10 Emesa-Trefilería and Industrias Galycas v Commission EU:T:2015:499 .... 25.008
T-590/10 Thesing and Bloomberg Finance v ECB EU:T:2012:635..................... 14.031
and T-256/11 Ezz v Council EU:T:2014:93... 10.001
T-331/11 Besselink v Council EU:T:2013:419...................................... 14.031
T-496/11 United Kingdom v ECB EU:T:2015:133..............................5.019, 13.020
T-306/12 Spirlea v Commission EU:T:2014:816.................................... 14.031
T-402/12 Schlyter v Commission EU:T:2015:209 .... 14.031
T-450/12 Anagnostakis v Commission EU:T:2015:739.............................. 17.013
T-512/12 Front populaire pour la libération de la saguia-el-hamra et du rio de oro
    (Front Polisario) v Council of the EU EU:T:2015:953 ....25.008, 25.018
T-562/12 Dalli v Commission EU:T:2015:270 .... 12.068
T-337/13 CSF v Commission EU:T:2015:502..7.115
T-529/13 Izsák and Dabis v Commission EU:T:2016:282 .... 17.013
T-623/13 Unión de Almacenistas de Hierros de España v Commission EU:T:2015:268....... 14.031
T-646/13 Bürgerausschuss für die Bürgerinitiative Minority SafePack–one million
    signatures for diversity in Europe v Commission EU:T:2017:59 .... 17.013
T-44/14 Costantini v Commission EU:T:2016:223 .... 17.013
T-54/14 Goldfish and Others v Commission EU:T:2016:455......................25.004, 25.018
T-138/14 Chart v European External Action Service EU:T:2015:981 .... 25.018

T-348/14 Yanukovych v Council EU:T:2016:508 .... 10.001
T-353/14 and T-17/15 Italy v Commission EU:T:2016:495 .... 14.025
T-561/14 European Citizens' Initiative One of Us v Commission EU:T:2018:210 .... 17.013
T-577/14 Gascogne Sack Deutschland and Gascogne v Commission EU:T:2017:1 .... 30.022
T-716/14 Tweedale v European Food Safety Authority EU:T:2019:141 .... 18.024
T-754/14 Efler and Others v Commission EU:T:2017:323 .... 17.013
T-47/15 Germany v Commission EU:T:2016:281 ....9.022
T-110/15 International Management Group v Commission EU:T:2016:322 .... 14.031
T-216/15 Dôvera zdravotná poisťovňa v Commission EU:T:2018:64 ....9.013
T-540/15 De Capitani v European Parliament EU:T:2018:167 ....14.031, 15.009
T-729/15 MSD Animal Health Innovation v European Medicines Agency EU:T:2018:67 ..... 14.029
T-192/16 NF v European Council EU:T:2017:128 ....12.023, 28.003
T-323/16 Banco Cooperativo Español v Single Resolution Board EU:T:2019:822 .... 27.006
T-339/16, T-352/16, and T-391/16 Ville de Paris v Commission EU:T:2018:927 ....7.115
T-518/16 Carreras Sequeros v Commission EU:T:2018:873 .... 27.017
T-770/16 Korwin- Mikke v Parliament EU:T:2018:320 .... 25.018
T-851/16 Access Info Europe v Commission EU:T:2018:69 .... 14.031
T-852/16 Access Info Europe v Commission EU:T:2018:71 .... 14.031
T-48/17 ADDE v European Parliament EU:T:2019:780 .... 25.018
T-329/17 Hautala v European Food Safety Authority EU:T:2019:142 .... 14.031
T-310/18 European Federation of Public Service Unions (EPSU) v Commission
  EU:T:2019:757 ....17.044, 18.006
T-180/20 Sharpston v Council and Conference of Representatives of the
  Governments of the Member States EU:T:2020:473 .... 28.002
T-550/20 Sharpston v Council and Representatives of the Governments of the
  Member States EU:T:2020:475 .... 28.002

CIVIL SERVICE TRIBUNAL

F-65/07 Aayhan and Others v European Parliament EU:F:2009:43 .... 5.047
F-83/07 Zangerl-Posselt v Commission EU:F:2009:158 .... 5.060
F-46/09, V v European Parliament EU:F:2011:101 .... 25.008

EFTA COURT

E-1/94 Restamark [1994-1995] EFTA Court Report 15; [1995] 1 C.M.L.R. 161 .... 10.020
E-3/00 EFTA Surveillance Authority v Norway [2000–2001] EFTA Court Report 73 .... 25.022
E-1/02 EFTA Surveillance Authority v Norway [2003] EFTA Court Report 1 .... 5.059
E-9/07 and 10/07 L'Oréal [2008] EFTA Court Report 261 .... 10.020
E-10/17 Nye Kystlink 10.020
E-8/19 Scanteam 2020 .... 10.020

EUROPEAN COURT OF HUMAN RIGHTS

8030/77 CFDT v EEC [1979] 2 C.M.L.R. 229 .... 25.013
13258/87 M & Co. v Germany, not reported 25.013
13710/88 Niemietz v Germany [1993] 16 E.H.R.R. 97 .... 25.015
17862/91 Cantoni v France, 1996 .... 25.014
24833/94 Matthews v United Kingdom [1999] 28 E.H.R.R. 361 .... 12.003, 24.009, 25.013, 25.014
28957/95 Goodwin v United Kingdom [2002] 35 E.H.R.R. 18 .... 25.007, 25.012
37971/97 Colas Est and Others v France [2004] 39 E.H.R.R. 17 .... 25.015
45036/98 Bosphorus v Ireland [2006] 42 E.H.R.R. 25.014
51717/99 Guérin Automobiles v Belgium and Others, not reported 25.013
56672/00 Senator Lines v Belgium and Others [2004] 39 E.H.R.R. SE3 .... 25.013
6422/02 and 9916/02 Segi and Gestoras Pro-Amnistía v Belgium and Others, not reported ... 25.013

lxxx   TABLE OF CASES

13645/05 Coöperatieve producentenorganisatie van de Nederlandse Kokkelvisserij v
   Netherlands [2009] 48 E.H.R.R. SE18 .... 13.013, 25.013, 25.014
17502/07, Avotins v Latvia, 2016 .... 25.014
30696/09, M.S.S. v Belgium and Greece, 2011 .... 25.014
12323/11, Michaud v France, 2012 .... 25.014
47287/15, Ilias and Ahmed v Hungary, 2019 .... 25.014

DOMESTIC COURTS BY JURISDICTION

Belgium

Grondwettelijk Hof/cour constitutionnelle, October 16, 1991, No. 26/91, B.S./M.B.,
   November 23, 1991, A.A., 1991, 271 .... 23.030
Grondwettelijk Hof/cour constitutionnelle, February 13, 1994, No. 12/94, B.S./M.B.,
   March 11, 1994, A.A., 1994, 211 .... 23.030
Grondwettelijk Hof/cour constitutionnelle, April 26, 1994, No. 33/94, B.S./M.B., June 23,
   1994, A.A., 1994, 419 .... 23.030
Grondwettelijk Hof/cour constitutionnelle, Judgment of 14 January 2004, No. 3/ 2004,
   MB 9 March 2004 .... 23.030
Grondwettelijk Hof/cour constitutionnelle, Judgment of 28 April 2016, No. 62/ 2016 .... 23.030
Hof van Cassatie/Cour de Cassation, judgment of May 27, 1971 (Franco-Suisse Le Ski) 23.025
Hof van Cassatie/Cour de Cassation, judgment of December 8, 1994,
   Arr. Cass. 1994, No. 541 .... 23.020
Hof van Cassatie/Cour de Cassation, judgment of January 14, 2000,
   Arr. Cass., 2000, No. 33 .... 23.020
Raad van State/Conseil d'Etat, November 5, 1996, No. 62.621 (Goosse) 23.027
Raad van State/Conseil d'Etat, November 5, 1996, No. 69.922 (Orfinger) 23.027

Czech Republic

Ústavní soud, judgment of November 26, 2008, Pl.ÚS 19/08 .... 2.002
Ústavní soud, judgment of November 3, 2009, Pl.ÚS 29/09 .... 2.002

Denmark

Judgment of the Danish Supreme Court (Højesteret) of 6 December 2016 in
   Case No. 15/ 2014 Dansk Industri (DI) acting for Ajos A/ S vs. The estate left by A 23.026

Germany

Bundesgerichthof, judgment of October 24, 1996, III ZR 127/91 Eu.Z.W. 761 .... 23.024
Bundesverfassungsgericht, judgment of October 23, 1986 (Solange II), (1986) BverfGE 73 ... 20.029
Bundesverfassungsgericht, judgment of October 12, 1993 (Maastricht-Urteil), (1993)
   Eu.GR.Z. 429; (1993) EuR. 294 .... 20.029
Bundesverfassungsgericht, judgment of June 30, 2009 (2009) BVerfGE, 2 BvE 2/08,
   2 BvE 5/08, 2 BvR 1010/08, 2 BvR 1022/08, 2 BvR 1259/08 and 2 BvR 182/09 ..... 2.002, 15.003,
                                                                                                                            15.008, 23.029
Bundesverfassungsgericht, Judgment of 6 July 2010, 2 BvR 2661/ 06 .... 23.029
Bundesverfassungsgericht, Judgment of 14 January 2014, 2 BvR 2728/ 13, 2 BvR 2729/ 13,
   2 BvR 2730/ 13, 2 BvR 2731/ 13, 2 BvE 13/ 13 .... 23.029
Bundesverfassungsgericht, Judgment of 21 June 2016, 2 BvR 2728/ 13, 2 BvE 13/ 13,
   2 BvR 2731/ 13, 2 BvR 2730/ 13, 2 BvR 2729/ 13 .... 23.029
Bundesverfassungsgericht, Judgment of 18 July 2017, 2 BvR 859/ 15; 2 BvR 1651/ 15;
   2 BvR 2006/ 15; 2 BvR 980/ 16 .... 23.029
Bundesverfassungsgericht, Judgment of 5 May 2020, 2 BvR 859/ 15 .... 23.029, 29.005

Ireland

Supreme Ct, Meagher v Minister for Agriculture and Food [1994] 2 C.M.L.R. 654. . . . . 15.012

Italy

Corte costituzionale, Judgment No. 170/84 of June 8, 1984, Granital 23.027

United Kingdom

R. v Secretary of State for Transport Ex p. Factortame and Others (No. 5) [1997]
    T.L.R. 482 QBD. 23.024
R (on the application of Miller) v Secretary of State for Exiting the European Union [2017]
    UKSC 5; [2018] AC 61; [2017] 1 WLUK 387 (SC) 4.016

Table of Treaties, Protocols and Declarations

1951 European Coal and Steel
 Community Treaty (ECSC
 Treaty) 1.002, 1.008–1.011,
  1.015, 1.017–1.018, 1.022,
  1.041, 1.043, 3.009, 4.001, 4.005,
  6.022, 9.063, 11.003–11.004,
  12.005, 12.010, 12.034, 12.042,
  12.056, 12.063, 12.068, 13.002,
  13.009, 13.018, 13.024, 13.030,
  13.032, 13.043, 13.048, 14.001,
  14.009, 14.011, 14.013–14.014, 1
  4.019, 14.022, 17.010, 20.013,
  21.001, 21.007, 23.006,
  24.004, 27.002, 27.026, 27.042
 Preamble 1.008
 Art 3 .... 16.009
 Art 6 .... 14.002
 Art 8 .... 1.010
 Art 9 .... 1.021
 Art 14 .... 1.010, 27.002, 27.017
 Art 15 .... 27.007
 Art 20 .... 12.001
 Art 21 .... 12.014
 Art 24 .... 1.010
 Art 26 .... 1.010
 Art 31 .... 1.010
 Art 32d 13.002
 Art 34 .... 24.004
 Art 36 .... 24.004
 Art 38 .... 24.004
 Art 41 .... 24.004
 Art 59(2) 17.012
 Art 59(5) 17.012
 Art 65 .... 24.004
 Art 66 .... 24.004
 Art 85 .... 1.010
 Art 86 .... 5.043, 18.007, 23.017
 Art 95 .... 1.010, 13.048, 16.010
 Art 96 .... 3.003, 3.009
 Art 97 .... 1.009, 11.004
 Art 98 .... 4.009, 4.012
 Art 99 .... 11.003
 Art 100 .... 14.024
1952 European Defence Community
 Treaty (EDC Treaty)
 Art 1 .... 1.011
 Art 38 .... 1.011
 Art 38(1) 1.011
1957 Convention on certain institutions
 common to the European
 Communities 1.017

European Atomic
 Energy Community Treaty
 (EAEC Treaty or Euratom
 Treaty) 1.004, 1.015, 1.017,
  1.020, 1.022, 1.041, 1.043,
  2.003, 2.006, 2.008, 5.001, 5.051,
  5.053, 5.062, 9.063, 11.003,
  13.024, 13.030, 13.045,
  14.024, 21.016, 24.004
 Art 3(2) 13.030
 Art 8 .... 13.043
 Art 9 .... 13.048
 Art 9, first para 13.030
 Art 31, first para 13.030
 Art 32, first para 13.030
 Art 40 .... 13.030
 Art 41, second para 13.030
 Art 45 .... 13.045
 Arts 52–56 .... 13.045
 Art 76 .... 3.008
 Art 85 .... 3.008
 Art 90 .... 3.008
 Art 96 .... 24.004
 Art 96, second para 13.030
 Art 98, second para 13.030
 Art 101, first para 10.002
 Art 102 .... 21.013
 Art 103 .... 21.016
 Arts 105–106 .... 21.001, 26.008
 Art 106a(3) 2.006, 24.004
 Art 108 .... 3.007
 Art 122 .... 12.039
 Art 136 .... 25.001
 Art 140a 13.002
 Art 146 .... 23.003
 Art 150 .... 24.004
 Art 156 .... 24.004
 Art 159 .... 27.010
 Art 164 .... 27.010
 Art 165 .... 13.030
 Art 173 .... 14.013
 Art 183 .... 14.010
 Art 184 .... 1.043, 14.002
 Art 185 .... 14.002
 Art 188 .... 25.021
 Art 189 .... 14.019
 Art 190 .... 14.025
 Art 192 .... 5.043
 Art 198 .... 11.006
 Art 198, second para 11.007
 Art 198, third para 11.007

Art 198, fourth para,
   indent (a) 11.007
Art 198, fourth para,
   indent (c) 11.007
Art 200. . . . . 1.006
Art 203. . . . . 5.001, 13.048
Art 204. . . . . 24.006
Art 205. . . . . 4.009, 4.012
Art 206. . . . . 10.014, 10.016
Art 207. . . . . 13.002
Art 224. . . . . 11.003
Art 225. . . . . 14.024
Art 240. . . . . 11.005
European Economic Community
   Treaty (EEC Treaty) . . . 1.013–1.019,
   1.025–1.027, 1.042, 1.045, 2.011, 5.020,
   5.033, 6.006, 7.002, 7.027–7.028, 7.101,
      9.062, 10.013, 10.020, 11.005,
         11.007–11.008, 11.012, 12.014,
      13.024, 17.010, 24.002, 30.006, 30.041
   Pt Two 1.014
   Pt Four. 10.013, 11.007
   Preamble 4.010
   Art 2. . . . . 1.014
   Art 3. . . . . 1.014
   Art 4. . . . . 7.027, 24.050
   Art 5(2) 1.027
   Art 8a. 7.009
   Art 8b. 7.009
   Art 8c. 7.009
   Art 12. . . . . 23.025
   Art 30. . . . . 7.043
   Art 173. . . . . 30.004
   Art 236. . . . . 1.041
   Art 247. . . . . 11.003
European Community Treaty, as
   applicable until the entry into
   force of the Treaty of Lisbon
   (EC Treaty) (as amended) 1.009,
   1.020, 1.051–1.054, 1.059, 2.001, 2.007,
   3.010, 5.007, 5.014, 5.028, 6.001, 7.001–
   7.005, 7.015, 7.081, 7.109, 8.004, 8.008,
   8.028, 9.009, 9.032, 9.046, 9.054, 9.057,
   10.021, 10.034, 10.039, 11.002, 11.004,
   11.007, 11.011, 12.049, 13.002, 13.019,
   14.007, 16.010, 21.016, 24.001, 24.004,
   26.001, 26.009–26.010, 27.045, 27.049,
      28.006, 28.007, 28.018, 30.013
   Preamble 1.051
   Pt Two 6.004
   Title III. 12.040
   Pt Three, Title IV 1.038, 1.047, 2.003,
         3.007, 8.002, 8.004–8.005,
            12.040, 13.011, 17.018
   Pt Four. 10.019, 10.021
   Title VII. 12.040
   Title VIII 1.051
   Title X 1.051
   Art 2. . . . . 9.047
   Art 3(g) 9.012
   Art 10. . . . . 5.043, 5.044, 27.049
   Arts 61–69. . . . . 1.051
   Art 80(2) 8.021
   Art 81. . . . . 9.015
   Art 81(3) 9.016
   Art 82. . . . . 9.015
   Art 86(3) 9.020
   Art 93. . . . . 9.024
   Art 95. . . . . 7.115
   Art 121(4) 9.033
   Arts 125–130. . . . . 1.051
   Art 135. . . . . 1.051
   Art 139(2) 17.044
   Art 175(1) 8.021
   Art 190(4) 12.014
   Art 228(4) 17.045
   Art 205(2) 19.002
   Art 251. . . . . 17.020, 17.023, 17.028
   Art 281. . . . . 1.043
   Art 299(1) 11.004
   Art 299(2) 11.007
   Art 308. . . . . 9.063, 10.031

**PROTOCOLS ANNEXED TO THE
EC TREATY (AS AMENDED)**

Protocol (No.14) on social policy
   (1992) (Social Protocol) . . . 1.045, 1.052
Protocol (No.17) concerning Art
   119 (later Art 141) of the EC
   Treaty (1992) 28.006
Protocol (No.19) on the Statute of
   the European Monetary
   Institute (1992) 13.019
   Art 5(1) 22.002
Protocol (No.29) on asylum for
   nationals of Member States of
   the European Union (1997) . . . 8.008
Protocol (No.30) on the application
   of the principles of subsidiarity
   and proportionality (1997) . . . 5.028
Protocol (No.31) on external
   relations of the Member States
   with regard to the crossing of
   external borders (1997)
Protocol (No.33) on protection and
   welfare of animals (1997) 5.007
Protocol (No.34) on the financial
   consequences of the expiry of
   the ECSC Treaty and on the
   Research Fund for Coal and
   Steel (2001). 1.009

PROTOCOLS ANNEXED TO THE EC AND EU TREATIES (AS AMENDED)

Protocol (No.2) integrating the Schengen acquis into the framework of the European Union (1997) (Schengen Protocol) 8.004, 8.006, 8.028, 22.003
- Art 2 .... 8.006
- Art 3 .... 8.026
- Art 4 .... 22.003
- Art 5 .... 8.028
- Art 5(1) 8.028, 22.003
- Art 5(3) 22.003
- Art 7 .... 8.006

Protocol (No.4) on the position of the United Kingdom and Ireland (1997)
- Art 1 .... 22.002
- Art 8 .... 22.002

Protocol (No. 22) on the position of Denmark ... 8.027, 22.004, 24.006
- Art 1 .... 22.002
- Art 4 .... 22.002
- Art 7 .... 22.002
- Art 8 .... 22.004

PROTOCOLS ANNEXED TO THE EAEC, EC, ECSC AND EU TREATIES (AS AMENDED)

Protocol (No.7) on the institutions with the prospect of enlargement of the European Union (1997) 1.053

Protocol (No.8) on the location of the seats of the institutions and of certain bodies and departments of the European Communities and Europol (1997) 14.020

Protocol (No.9) on the role of national Parliaments in the European Union (1997) 15.008

Protocol (No.10) on the enlargement of the European Union (2001) .. 12.049
- Art 4 .... 12.063

1967 Treaty establishing a Single Council and a Single Commission of the European Communities (Merger Treaty) 1.017, 12.034, 13.024, 14.019
- Art 2 .... 12.041
- Art 9 .... 12.056
- Art 14 .... 12.064
- Art 16 .... 12.068
- Art 19 .... 1.022
- Art 20 .... 1.017
- Art 20(1) 14.010
- Art 24 .... 1.017
- Art 28 .... 14.007
- Art 32 .... 12.063
- Art 37 .... 14.019

1970 Treaty amending certain budgetary provisions of the Treaties establishing the European Communities and of the Treaty establishing a Single Council and a Single Commission (First Treaty on Budgetary Provisions) 20.001

1972 Accession Treaty (Accession Treaty 1972) (Denmark, Ireland and United Kingdom)
Act of Accession (Denmark, Ireland and the United Kingdom) 28.018
- Art 2 .... 4.013

PROTOCOLS ANNEXED TO THE 1972 ACT OF ACCESSION

Protocol (No.3) on the Channel Islands and the Isle of Man ... 11.007

1975 Treaty amending certain financial provisions of the Treaties establishing the European Communities and of the Treaty establishing a Single Council and a Single Commission of the European Communities (Second Treaty on Budgetary Provisions) 20.001

1979 Accession Treaty (Greece) (Accession Treaty 1979) 4.003
Act of Accession 1979 (Greece) ... 12.063
- Art 130 .... 11.012
- Art 147 .... 14.025

1984 Treaty amending, with regard to Greenland, the Treaties establishing the European Communities 11.007

1985 Accession Treaty (Portugal and Spain) (Accession Treaty 1985) 4.004, 4.009
Act of Accession 1985 (Portugal and Spain)
- Art 3(2) 28.018

Art 6 . . . . 24.002
Art 15 . . . . 12.063
Art 25 . . . . 11.007
Art 379 . . . . 11.012
Art 397 . . . . 14.025

PROTOCOLS ANNEXED TO THE 1985 ACT OF ACCESSION

Protocol (No.2) concerning the Canary Islands and Ceuta and Melilla 11.007

1986 Single European Act (SEA) 1.018, 1.033, 1.041–1.042, 3.001, 4.012, 5.028, 6.003, 7.001, 7.009, 7.112, 9.031, 9.046, 9.060, 9.061, 12.001, 12.048, 15.003, 17.010, 17.037, 18.014, 24.005
Title III 1.032, 1.046
Art 1 . . . . 1.032
Art 2 . . . . . 1.032, 1.046, 12.022, 12.026
Art 3(1) 12.001
Art 3(2) 1.032, 1.046
Art 27 . . . . 1.045
Art 30 . . . . 1.032
Art 33 . . . . 11.003
Art 34 . . . . 14.024
Art 127 . . . . 1.045
Arts 130a-e 1.045
Arts 130f-p 1.045
Arts 130r-t. 1.045
Art 150 . . . . 1.045
Arts 158–62. . . . . 1.045
Arts 163–173. . . . . 1.045

DECLARATIONS ANNEXED TO THE SINGLE EUROPEAN ACT

1992 Treaty on European Union, as applicable until the entry into force of the Treaty of Lisbon (EU Treaty) (as amended) 1.018, 1.033, 1.036, 1.042–1.045, 1.049, 1.059, 2.001, 3.001, 3.005, 3.007, 4.005, 4.009, 4.012, 4.019, 5.028, 6.003–6.004, 6.006–6.007, 7.009, 7.082, 8.002–8.003, 8.028, 9.032–9.033, 9.050, 9.053, 9.055, 9.058–9.059, 9.062, 10.021, 10.031, 11.007, 12.006, 12.009, 12.011, 12.014, 12.016, 12.023, 12.026, 12.034, 12.040, 12.042, 12.056, 12.064, 12.066, 13.002, 13.024, 13.033–13.034, 13.045–13.046, 14.011, 15.003, 15.006–15.007, 16.010, 17.007, 17.010, 17.022, 17.032, 17.045, 21.001, 21.016, 22.005, 23.027, 23.029, 24.005, 25.003, 27.008, 28.007–28.008, 28.011, 28.015, 29.024, 30.006, 30.037
Preamble 1.051
Title II 1.044
Title III. 1.044
Title IV 1.044, 1.051
Title V 1.032, 1.046, 1.051, 5.014, 6.022, 10.026, 28.009, 28.011, 28.016, 30.013
Title VI 1.038, 1.044, 1.046–1.047, 1.051–1.052, 2.003, 2.008, 5.014, 6.022, 7.025, 8.003–8.004, 8.021, 8.027, 20.013, 28.009, 28.011, 28.012, 28.016
Title VII. 1.052
Art 6 . . . . 5.007
Art 8(83) 4.009
Art 9(2) 1.022
Art 9(21) 4.009
Art 10(28) 4.009
Arts 14–16. . . . . 1.048
Art 34. . . . . 1.048
Art 34(2) 1.048
Art 36(2) 1.048
Art 39. . . . . 1.048
Arts 43–45. . . . . 1.054
Art 48. . . . . 1.043, 1.057
Art 49. . . . . 1.043
Art 50. . . . . 12.041
Art 51 . . . . 11.005
Art 52. . . . . 11.003
Art 52(2) 11.003
Art 53. . . . . 14.024
Art J.5(3) 12.042
Art K.3 . . . . 1.038, 8.020–8.021, 20.013, 28.019
Art K.4. 12.053

DECLARATIONS ANNEXED TO THE EU TREATY

Declaration (No.2) on nationality of a Member State (1992) 6.006
Declaration (No.3) on Part Three, Titles III and VI (later Titles III and VII) of the EC Treaty (1992) 12.040
Declaration (No.4) on Part Three, Title VI (later Title VII) of the EC Treaty (1992) 12.026, 12.040
Declaration (No.5) on monetary cooperation with non-Community countries (1992) 21.001

Declaration (No.7) on Art 73d
(later Art 58) of the EC Treaty
(1992) 7.104
Declaration (No.16) on the
hierarchy of Community
acts 27.005
Declaration (No.17) on the right
of access to information
(1992) 14.030
Declaration (No.29) on the use
of languages in the field of the
common foreign and security
policy (1992)................ 14.028
1994 Accession Treaty (Austria, Finland
and Sweden) (Accession Treaty
1994)................4.013, 12.042
Act of Accession 1994 (Austria,
Finland and Sweden) 12.063
Arts 2–5..................... 4.011
Art 3........................ 28.019
Art 4(1) 28.003
Art 4(2) 28.018
Art 4(3) 28.003
Art 5(2) 28.004, 28.018
Art 5(3) 28.004
Art 12....................... 12.042
Art 16....................... 12.063
Art 152...................... 11.012
Art 170...................... 14.025

PROTOCOLS ANNEXED TO THE 1994 ACT OF ACCESSION

Protocol (No. 2) to the 1994
Act of Accession 11.007
1997 Treaty of Amsterdam (Amsterdam
Treaty) ...1.018, 1.033, 1.038–1.039,
1.044–1.045, 1.047–1.053, 3.001, 3.007,
4.010, 4.020, 5.007, 5.028, 5.058, 6.006,
7.004, 7.010, 7.013, 7.016, 7.081, 7.115,
8.002–8.004, 8.006, 8.008, 8.014, 8.020,
8.027–8.028, 9.003, 9.009, 9.046, 9.019,
9.051, 9.055, 9.062, 10.028, 10.034, 10.039,
11.002, 12.013, 12.018, 12.023, 12.039,
12.064, 14.002, 14.007, 14.010, 14.020,
14.030, 15.003, 15.007, 17.010, 17.012,
17.020, 17.022, 17.025, 18.006, 19.002,
22.007, 24.005, 28.009, 28.019
Arts 1(1)-(3) 1.051
Art 2(1) 1.051
Art 6........................ 17.005
Art 7........................ 17.005
Art 8........................ 17.005
Art 9.................1.017, 12.034
Art 9(1) 1.017
Art 9(2) 1.017
Art 9(3) 1.017
Art 12....................... 1.051
Art 13....................... 11.005
Art 14................1.050, 11.003
Art 15....................... 14.024

DECLARATIONS ANNEXED TO THE TREATY OF AMSTERDAM

Declaration (No.13) on Art 7d
(later Art 16) of the EC Treaty
(1997) 9.019
Declaration (No.17) on Art 73k
(later Art 63) of the EC Treaty
(1997) 8.008
Declaration (No.22) regarding
persons with a disability (1997) 7.115
Declaration (No.27) on Art
118b(2) (later Art 139(2)) of
the EC Treaty (1997)........ 18.006
Declaration (No.29) on sport
(1997) 9.051
Declaration (No.37) on public
credit institutions in Germany
(1997) 9.019
Declaration (No.41) on the
provisions relating to
transparency, access to
documents and the fight
against fraud (1997) 14.030
Declaration (No.48) relating to
the Protocol integrating the
Schengen acquis into the
framework of the European
Union (1997) 8.008
Declaration by Belgium, France
and Italy on the Protocol
annexed to the EAEC, EC,
ECSC and EU Treaties on the
institutions with the prospect
of enlargement of the European
Union (1997) 1.053
Declaration by Denmark on Art
K.14 (later Art 42) of the EU
Treaty (1997) 3.007
2000 Charter of Fundamental
Rights of the European Union
(as amended).......... 1.001, 1.028,
1.055, 1.056, 1.059, 1.060, 2.001, 2.002,
2.004, 5.004, 5.051, 6.007, 8.008, 8.010,
8.013, 9.046, 23.004, 23.011, 23.029,
23.033, 25.001, 25.002, 25.004, 25.005,
25.006, 25.007, 25.008, 25.009, 25.010,
25.012, 25.017, 25.018, 25.019, 25.020,
25.022, 25.023

Preamble	25.012
Title II	5.004
Title III	5.004
Title IV	5.004
Title VI	5.004
Title VII	25.007, 25.012
Art 1	5.004
Arts 1–4	25.020
Art 4	8.010, 8.020, 25.012, 25.014
Art 6	5.035
Art 7	6.014, 25.010
Art 8	9.002, 13.043, 25.010
Art 9	25.012
Art 11	25.010
Art 12(2)	12.021
Art 15(2)	7.046
Art 15(3)	8.013
Art 17	25.012
Art 18	8.008
Art 19	6.020, 8.008
Art 20	5.051, 16.002, 23.029
Art 21	5.051, 5.060, 23.033, 27.033
Art 21(1)	5.060, 25.010
Art 21(2)	5.053
Art 22	5.051
Art 23	5.051, 5.058
Art 24	5.051, 6.017
Art 24(2)	6.014
Art 25	5.051
Art 26	5.051
Art 27	27.033
Art 31(2)	23.033, 25.009, 25.010, 27.033
Art 39	5.004, 12.012
Art 39(1)	6.021
Art 39(2)	6.021
Arts 39–46	6.007
Art 40	5.004
Art 41	25.023
Art 41(1)	25.023
Art 41(2)	25.022
Art 42	14.030, 16.013, 25.023
Art 44	12.011
Art 45(1)	6.008
Art 47	5.005, 8.020, 25.008, 25.010, 25.018, 25.023, 25.025, 29.002, 29.004, 29.015, 30.045
Art 47(1)	23.014
Art 48	25.023, 29.004
Art 49	25.023
Art 50	25.023
Art 51	25.012
Art 51(1)	5.060, 25.009, 25.010, 29.002
Art 52(1)	5.038, 25.020
Art 52(2)	25.012
Art 52(3)	25.012
Art 52(4)	25.012
Art 52(5)	25.012
Art 52(6)	25.012
Art 52(7)	25.012
Art 53	25.012

2001	Treaty of Nice (Nice Treaty)	1.018, 1.053–1.054, 1.056, 3.001, 3.005, 4.020, 9.062, 10.004, 10.024, 10.035, 12.009, 12.013, 12.048, 12.049, 12.063–12.064, 13.002, 13.009, 13.018, 13.026, 13.028, 13.034, 15.003, 15.007, 21.016, 22.007, 24.005, 25.006, 30.006
	Art 11	11.005
	Art 12	11.003
	Art 13	14.024

DECLARATIONS ANNEXED TO THE TREATY OF NICE

Declaration (No.3) on Art 10 of the EC Treaty (2001)	5.044, 27.049
Declaration (No.4) on the third para. of Art 21 of the EC Treaty (2001)	6.022
Declaration (No.16) on Art 225a of the EC Treaty (2001)	13.002
Declaration (No.20) on the enlargement of the European Union (2001)	12.049
Declaration (No.21) on the qualified majority threshold and the number of votes for a blocking minority in an enlarged Union (2001)	12.049
Declaration (No.22) on the venue for European Councils (2001)	12.030
Declaration (No.23) on the future of the Union (2001)	5.011, 25.007

2002	Act on the Direct Election of the European Parliament	12.013, 16.008, 24.009, 25.014
	Art 6(1)	12.016
	Art 11(3)	12.017
	Art 14	17.012, 17.045
2003	Accession Treaty (Czech Republic, Estonia, Cyprus, Latvia, Lithuania, Hungary, Malta, Poland, Slovenia and the Slovak Republic) (Accession Treaty 2003)	
	Art 2(2)	4.013
	Act of Accession 2003 (Czech Republic, Estonia, Cyprus, Latvia, Lithuania, Hungary,	

Malta, Poland, Slovenia and the
Slovak Republic) 7.082, 7.103,
10.035, 11.006, 11.008, 12.048–12.049
Arts 2–6..................... 4.011
Art 3........................ 8.006
Art 3(1) 4.011
Art 4........................ 8.006
Art 5(1) 28.003
Art 5(2) 28.018
Art 5(3) 28.003
Art 6........................ 26.008
Art 6(2)-(6).................. 28.004
Art 6(11) 28.004
Art 12(2) 12.049
Art 18....................... 7.107
Art 25....................... 12.013
Art 37....................... 11.012
Art 42(2)(a)................. 12.063
Art 45(2)(a)................. 12.064
Art 58....................... 14.025
Annex IV.................... 9.024

**PROTOCOLS ANNEXED TO THE
2003 ACT OF ACCESSION**

Protocol (No.6) on the acquisition
of secondary residences in
Malta..................... 7.103
Protocol (No.7) on abortion in
Malta..................... 7.082
Protocol (No.10) on Cyprus..... 11.006
Art 1....................... 11.006

2004 Draft Treaty establishing a
Constitution for Europe (EU
Constitution)... 1.028, 1.058–1.061,
2.001, 2.003–2.005, 3.002, 3.005, 4.007,
5.003, 9.066, 12.063, 12.065, 14.001,
17.002, 17.046, 17.050, 23.010, 25.006–
25.007, 25.012, 27.004–27.005
Art I-33(1).................. 27.005
Art I-42 .... 9.066
Art IV-437.................. 1.059

2005 Accession Treaty (Bulgaria
and Romania) (Accession
Treaty 2005) 4.014
Art 4(2) 4.013
Act of Accession 2005 (Bulgaria
and Romania) 26.008
Art 2....................... 28.010
Arts 2–6.................... 4.011
Art 3....................... 8.006
Art 3(1) 28.003
Art 3(3) 28.018
Art 3(4) 28.018
Art 4....................... 8.006
Art 4(1) 4.011

Art 5(2) 28.003
Art 6(2)-(6).................. 28.004
Art 6(11) 28.004
Art 10....................... 12.049
Art 16....................... 7.107
Art 21....................... 9.024
Art 36....................... 11.012
Art 58....................... 14.025
Art 60....................... 14.024
Annex V 9.024

2007 Treaty of Lisbon (Lisbon
Treaty) 1.001–1.002, 1.012,
1.018, 1.020, 1.028, 1.032–1.033, 1.038,
2.001–2.010, 3.001–3.007, 3.010, 4.009–
4.010, 4.015, 5.001, 5.007–5.008, 5.011,
5.014, 5.019–5.023, 5.026, 5.028–5.029,
5.032, 5.041, 5.044, 5.051, 5.053, 6.001,
6.004, 6.006, 6.009, 6.021–6.022, 7.001–
7.002, 7.005, 7.025, 7.045, 7.078, 7.108–
7.109, 7.112–7.113, 8.001, 8.003, 8.005–
8.008, 8.012, 8.014, 8.017–8.018, 8.021,
8.024–8.028, 9.002, 9.005, 9.009,
9.019, 9.021, 9.035, 9.050–9.051,
9.055, 9.059–9.060, 9.063–9.066,
10.002, 10.004–10.005, 10.023,
10.025–10.026, 10.028–10.032, 10.035–
10.037, 10.039, 11.002, 11.006–11.008,
12.003, 12.006, 12.008, 12.010, 12.012–
12.013, 12.022, 12.023, 12.025–12.027,
12.030, 12.034, 12.040, 12.042, 12.046,
12.048–12.049, 12.054, 12.057–12.058,
12.060, 12.063–12.064, 12.066, 12.068,
13.002–13.003, 13.009, 13.011–13.012,
13.014, 13.019, 13.030, 13.031, 13.033,
13.034, 13.042, 13.045–13.046, 14.002,
14.005–14.006, 14.011, 14.017–14.018,
14.020, 14.026, 15.001, 15.003–15.005,
15.007–15.008, 15.010, 15.013, 15.015,
16.003, 17.001–17.003, 17.005–17.007,
17.010, 17.012–17.013, 17.015, 17.018,
17.024, 17.029, 17.033, 17.037, 17.038,
17.042, 17.045–17.046, 17.050, 18.001–
18.002, 18.008, 18.010, 18.011–18.012,
18.015, 18.019, 18.021, 18.025, 19.002,
19.004–19.005, 20.001, 20.013, 21.001,
21.003, 21.010–21.011, 21.016, 22.004,
22.005, 22.007–22.010, 22.013, 23.002,
23.005, 23.010–23.011, 23.014, 23.029,
24.004–24.005, 25.001, 25.006–25.007,
25.015, 26.012, 27.003–27.005, 27.038,
27.049, 28.001, 28.004,-28.005, 28.007,
28.010, 28.020, 29.024, 30.005–30.007,
30.010–30.011, 30.013, 30.014,
30.019, 30.041–30.044
Art 3....................... 11.005
Art 5....................... 2.003

Art 6 .... 11.003
Art 6(2) 2.002, 11.003
Art 7 .... 14.024
Annex I 2.002

PROTOCOLS ANNEXED TO THE TREATY OF LISBON

Protocol (No.2) amending the
  EAEC Treaty (2007) ... 1.002, 24.004

DECLARATIONS ANNEXED TO THE TREATY OF LISBON

Declaration (No.6) on
  Art 15(5) and (6), Art 17(6)
  and (7) and Art 18 of the TEU
  (2010) 12.027, 12.064, 12.065
Declaration (No.7) on Art 16(4) of
  the TEU and Art 238(2) of the
  TFEU (2010) 12.047
Declaration (No.9) on Art 16(9)
  of the TEU concerning the
  European Council decision on
  the exercise of the Presidency
  of the Council (2010) 12.042
Declaration (No.17) concerning
  primacy (2010) 16.002, 23.010
Declaration (No.23) on the second
  paragraph of Art 48 of the
  TFEU (2010) 7.078, 17.033
Declaration (No.36) on Art 218
  of the TFEU concerning the
  negotiation and conclusion of
  international agreements by
  Member States relating to the
  Area of Freedom, Security and
  Justice (2010) 21.001
Declaration (No.41) on Art 352 of
  the TFEU (2010) 5.020
Declaration (No.42) on Art 352 of
  the TFEU (2010) 5.020
Declaration (No.51) by the
  Kingdom of Belgium
  on national Parliaments
  (2010) 15.003, 15.010
Declaration (No.52) by the
  Kingdom of Belgium, the
  Republic of Bulgaria, the
  Federal Republic of Germany,
  the Hellenic Republic, the
  Kingdom of Spain, the Italian
  Republic, the Republic of
  Cyprus, the Republic of
  Lithuania, the Grand-Duchy
  of Luxembourg, the Republic
  of Hungary, the Republic of
  Malta, the Republic of Austria,
  the Portuguese Republic,
  Romania, the Republic of
  Slovenia and the Slovak
  Republic on the symbols
  of the European
  Union (2010) 2.004, 14.001
Declaration (No.63) by the United
  Kingdom on the definition of
  the term "nationals" (2010) ... 6.006

2011 Accession Treaty (Croatia)
  (Accession Treaty 2011) 4.008
  Arts 2–6 .... 4.011
Act of Accession 2011 (Croatia)
  Art 3(4) 28.004, 28.018
  Art 4(1) 4.011
  Art 4(2) 8.006
  Art 6 26-008
  Art 6(2)-(5) 28.004
  Art 6(10) 28.004
  Art 12 .... 7.107
  Art 16 .... 9.024
  Art 37 .... 11.012
  Art 52 .... 14.025
  Annex IV 9.024
Art 2010 Treaty on European
  Union, as amended by the Treaty
  of Lisbon (TEU) (consolidated
  version) 1.001, 1.002,
    2.003, 2.006, 2.007, 2.008, 2.010,
    3.007, 5.006, 10.027, 11.005,
    15.014, 17.004, 24.004
  Preamble 5.003
  Title I 5.001, 5.004, 5.009, 10.002
  Title II 23.029
  Title III 5.004
  Title IV 22.007
  Title V 3.006, 5.009, 10.032
  Title V, Ch.2 ...10.002, 10.026, 19.001,
    19.002, 28.012, 29.023
  Art 1, first subpara 5.001
  Art 1, second para 14.030, 15.014
  Art 1, third para 2.003, 14.002
  Art 2 .... 1.028, 2.004, 3.010, 4.020,
    4.021, 5.001, 5.002, 5.003, 5.004,
    5.005, 5.051, 10.001, 12.012, 12.025,
    15.013, 17.046, 23.011, 23.029,
    25.002, 29.001, 29.003
  Art 3 .... 2.004, 5.001, 5.006,
    5.007, 9.036, 9.043
  Art 3(1) 5.006
  Art 3(2) 5.006, 7.010
  Art 3(3) 1.027, 5.006, 5.051,
    5.058, 7.001, 9.057
  Art 3(4) 5.004, 5.006, 9.029

Art 3(5) 5.006, 10.001, 25.002	Art 10(3) 6.021, 12.011,
Art 4. . . . . 5.009, 9.019	14.030, 17.013
Art 4(1) 5.009, 5.011, 17.017	Art 10(4) 12.021
Art 4(2) 5.004, 5.041, 5.051, 6.020,	Art 11(1) 17.045, 17.046
7.067, 9.054, 15.001, 15.015,	Art 11(2) 16.004, 17.045, 17.046
16.002, 17.049, 23.029, 30.001	Art 11(3) 17.015, 17.046
Art 4(3) 5.008, 5.043, 5.045,	Art 11(4) 6.022, 16.004,
5.046, 5.047, 5.049, 5.050, 7.013,	17.013, 17.018, 17.046
9.012, 10.039, 11.007, 13.048,	Art 12. . . . . 15.001, 15.003, 15.005
14.020, 15.012, 15.015, 16.003,	Art 12(a) 15.005
16.007, 16.008, 16.013, 18.002,	Art 12(b) 15.005
18.004, 19.003, 23.010, 23.013,	Art 12(c) 15.011
23.017, 23.019, 25.021,	Art 12(f) 15.005
26.007, 27.021, 27.029,	Art 13. . . . . 24.003
27.043, 27.046, 27.050	Art 13(1) 12.022, 12.034, 12.056,
Art 4(3), first subpara 5.043	13.024, 18.025, 30.022
Art 4(3), second subpara 5.043,	Art 13(1), second subpara. 1.033
5.046, 18.001	Art 13(2) 5.012, 5.044, 16.007,
Art 4(3), third subpara. 5.043	16.008, 17.017, 17.020, 25.021
Art 5. . . . . 5.009, 5.031, 12.024, 16.003	Art 13(2), second sentence 16.003
Art 5(1) 5.010, 5.019, 5.028	Art 13(4) 13.030
Art 5(2) 5.009, 5.010, 5.011,	Art 14(1) 12.002, 17.004
5.017, 17.017, 25.021	Art 14(2) 12.012, 12.013
Art 5(3) 5.028, 5.029, 5.030,	Art 14(2), first subpara 12.013
5.033, 25.021, 27.007	Art 14(2), second subpara. 12.013,
Art 5(3), first subpara 5.029,	12.025, 12.031, 17.037
5.030, 5.040	Art 14(3) 6.021, 12.012
Art 5(3), second subpara 5.031,	Art 14(4) 12.020
5.032, 5.042	Art 15(1) 12.024, 17.004
Art 5(4) 5.030, 5.039, 5.040,	Art 15(2) 12.026
23.029, 25.021, 29.005	Art 15(3) 12.026, 12.030
Art 6(1) 2.004, 5.001, 5.004,	Art 15(4) 12.031, 17.033
25.001, 25.002,	Art 15(5) 12.027
25.007, 25.021	Art 15(6) 12.027
Art 6(1), third	Art 15(6)(d) 12.007, 12.032
subpara. 25.007, 25.012	Art 15(6), second subpara. 14.006
Art 6(2) 5.004, 25.013,	Art 16(1) 12.035, 12.037, 17.004
25.015, 25.016	Art 16(2) 12.040, 12.041, 15.016
Art 6(3) 5.004, 25.001,	Art 16(3) 12.046, 17.007
25.002, 25.021	Art 16(4) 12.031, 12.046,
Art 7. . . . . 4.020, 4.021,	12.047, 12.049
5.005, 8.008, 25.002	Art 16(4), first subpara 12.047
Art 7(1) 4.020, 4.021, 5.005,	Art 16(5) 12.049
17.012, 17.037	Art 16(6) 12.025, 12.040
Art 7(2) 4.020, 12.025,	Art 16(6), first subpara 12.040
12.031, 17.037	Art 16(6), second subpara. 12.040
Art 7(3) 4.020, 5.003, 17.013	Art 16(6), third subpara 12.040
Art 7(4) 4.020	Art 16(7) 12.051
Art 7(5) 4.020, 17.037	Art 16(8) 12.044, 15.009, 17.002
Art 8(1) 10.025	Art 16(9) 12.025, 12.042
Art 8(2) 10.025, 21.001	Art 17(1) 12.057, 12.058, 12.060,
Art 9. . . . . 5.004, 5.060, 6.001, 6.006	12.062, 17.044, 21.003
Art 9C(4). 12.047	Art 17(2) 12.060, 17.004, 17.012
Art 10(1) 12.012, 17.046	Art 17(3) 12.066
Art 10(2) 12.007, 15.009,	Art 17(3), second subpara. 12.064
16.010, 17.046	Art 17(3), third subpara 12.066

Art 17(4) 12.014, 12.063	Art 24(1) 10.032, 12.024, 30.013
Art 17(5) 12.025, 12.031, 12.063	Art 24(1), first subpara 17.002
Art 17(6) 12.006, 12.065	Art 24(1), second subpara 12.004, 12.031, 13.012, 17.019, 19.001, 19.006, 27.004, 29.023, 30.013
Art 17(6), second subpara 12.068	
Art 17(6)(a) 12.071	
Art 17(6)(b) 12.071	
Art 17(6)(c) 12.064	Art 24(2) 10.027
Art 17(7) 12.006, 12.019, 12.025, 12.039, 12.065, 12.068	Art 24(3) 19.005
	Art 24(3), third subpara 19.006
Art 17(7), first subpara . . . 12.031, 12.064	Art 25 . . . . 27.003
Art 17(7), second subpara 12.064	Art 25(a) 27.044
Art 17(7), third subpara 12.031, 17.037	Art 25(3)(b) 28.009
	Art 26 . . . . 12.038, 18.012
Art 17(8) 12.065	Art 26(1) 10.027, 10.028, 12.024, 19.002, 27.044
Art 18 . . . . 12.031	
Art 18(1) 12.025, 12.065, 12.068	Art 26(2) 10.028
Art 18(2) 12.065	Art 26(2), first subpara 19.002
Art 18(2)–(4) 13.042	Art 26(2), second subpara 19.002
Art 18(3) 12.042	Art 26(3) 10.028, 19.005
Art 18(4) 12.065	Art 27(2) 14.006
Art 19 . . . . 13.012, 23.004, 26.004, 30.013	Art 27(3) 13.042, 14.022
	Art 28(1) 10.027, 10.030, 19.005
Art 19(1) 4.021, 5.005, 25.001, 25.016, 25.020, 29.001, 29.003, 29.015	Art 28(1), second subpara 28.013
	Art 28(2) 28.013
	Art 28(3) 19.005
Art 19(1), first subpara 13.002, 13.003	Art 28(4) 19.005
	Art 29 . . . . 10.029, 10.031, 19.005, 28.012
Art 19(1), second subpara 5.004, 5.005, 13.003, 15.013, 29.002, 30.044	
	Art 30(1) 19.003
	Art 30(2) 12.043, 19.003
Art 19(2) 13.013	Art 31(1) 9.066, 10.034, 17.002, 19.002
Art 19(2), second subpara 13.013	
Art 19(2), third subpara 13.014, 28.002	Art 31(1), first subpara 10.028, 17.019, 19.002, 27.004
Art 19(3) 13.004, 13.015	Art 31(1), second subpara 22.006
Art 20 . . . . 22.007	Art 31(2) 19.002
Art 20(1), first subpara 22.011	Art 31(2), first subpara 19.002
Art 20(1), second subpara 22.008, 22.009	Art 31(2), second subpara 12.024, 19.002
Art 20(2) 17.033, 22.010	Art 31(3) 3.001, 3.008, 12.025, 12.031, 15.008, 19.002
Art 20(3) 22.011	
Art 20(4) 22.007	Art 31(4) 3.008, 19.002
Art 21 . . . . 10.001, 10.021	Art 31(5) 19.002
Art 21(1) 5.004, 5.006, 10.001, 10.002, 25.002	Art 32 . . . . 12.024, 12.037
	Art 33 . . . . 10.030, 19.002, 19.005
Art 21(1), first subpara 26.012	Art 34(1) 19.005, 28.012
Art 21(2) 5.006, 10.001	Art 35 . . . . 19.005
Art 21(2)(b) 25.002	Art 36, first para 12.004, 12.007, 19.004
Art 21(3), second subpara 10.002, 12.036	
	Art 36, second para 12.004, 12.007, 19.004
Art 22(1) 12.024	
Art 22(1), third subpara 12.031	Art 37 . . . . 10.028, 21.001
Art 22(2) 19.003	Art 38 . . . . 18.025
Arts 23–46 . . . . 2.008, 10.002	Art 38, first para 12.053, 19.003, 19.006
Art 24 . . . . 12.038, 18.012	
Art 24, fourth para 14.025	Art 38, second para 12.053, 19.007
	Art 38, third para 12.053, 19.007

Art 39..................... 9.002	Art 48(7), third subpara 3.006
Art 40........... 2.003, 5.014, 5.020,	Art 48(7), fourth
13.012, 22.013, 29.023,	subpara............ 3.006, 12.019,
30.013, 30.045	12.031, 17.037
Art 41(1) 14.011	Art 49...... 4.009, 4.010, 4.015, 5.003,
Art 41(2) 14.011	11.008, 12.004, 12.019,
Art 41(2), first subpara 14.011	15.002, 15.003, 17.037
Art 41(2), second subpara..... 14.011	Art 49, first para . 4.012, 12.025, 17.045
Art 42..................... 10.035	Art 49, second para 4.012
Art 42(1) 10.032	Art 50.... 4.015, 4.016, 11.005, 12.054
Art 42(2) 12.031	Art 50(1) 4.015
Art 42(2), first subpara 3.007,	Art 50(2) 4.015, 12.025, 17.037
10.032, 12.025	Art 50(3) 4.015, 11.005,
Art 42(2), second subpara..... 10.033,	12.025, 12.031
10.034, 19.007	Art 50(4) 4.015
Art 42(3) 10.032, 19.007	Art 50(4), second subpara..... 12.047
Art 42(3), second	Art 50(5) 4.015
subpara............10.032, 19.007	Art 51......... 13.002, 13.020, 24.006
Art 42(5) 10.032, 19.007	Art 51(2) 11.006
Art 42(6) 22.007	Art 52(1) 11.006
Art 42(7) 1.012, 10.032, 10.033	Art 53..................... 11.005
Art 43...............10.027, 19.007	Art 55..................... 14.024
Art 43(1) 10.032	Art 55(2) 14.026
Art 43(3) 18.012	Treaty on the Functioning of the
Art 44(1) 10.032, 19.007	European Union (TFEU)
Art 44(2) 19.007	(consolidated version) 1.001,
Art 45..................... 10.032	2.003, 2.006, 2.007, 2.008, 2.010,
Art 46..................... 10.035	3.006, 5.009, 5.010, 5.013, 5.025,
Art 46(1) 10.035	5.026, 5.033, 6.017, 7.003,
Art 46(2) 10.035	7.004, 9.055, 10.029,
Art 46(3) 10.035	10.031, 11.004
Art 46(3), third subpara 12.047	Preamble................... 9.050
Art 46(4) 10.035	Pt Two 5.009, 6.001
Art 46(4), third subpara 12.047	Pt Three 3.006, 3.011,
Art 46(5) 10.035	5.009, 9.001, 12.025
Art 46(6) 10.035	Pt Three, Title II 7.003, 7.026
Art 47..................... 14.002	Pt Three, Title III 7.004
Art 48............3.006, 3.007, 3.009,	Pt Three, Title IV 7.003
12.025, 15.003, 15.004, 24.002	Pt Three, Title V 1.038, 2.003,
Art 48(2) 3.003, 15.003	8.001, 8.005, 8.006, 8.027, 8.028
Art 48(2)–(5) 12.003	Pt Three, Title V, Ch.1 .... 11.002
Art 48(2)–(6) 15.002	Pt Three, Title VI 10.004
Art 48(3) 3.002, 3.004,	Pt Three, Title VII............. 7.005
15.003, 17.045	Pt Four.............. 5.009, 10.013,
Art 48(3), first subpara 12.031	10.019, 11.007, 11.008
Art 48(3), second subpara...... 3.004,	Pt Five 5.009, 9.066
12.031, 17.037	Pt Five, Title II 10.003
Art 48(4) 15.003, 28.002	Art 1(1) 5.009
Art 48(4), second subpara...... 3.005	Art 1(2) 2.003
Art 48(6) 3.006, 3.011, 12.025,	Art 2....................... 5.022
15.003, 24.003, 30.035	Art 2(1) 5.011, 5.022, 5.024, 5.026
Art 48(6), second subpara..... 12.031	Art 2(2) 5.022, 5.026, 5.027
Art 48(7) 3.006, 12.025, 15.002,	Art 2(3) 5.025
15.003, 15.007, 15.008, 17.003	Art 2(4) 5.025
Art 48(7), first subpara 3.006	Art 2(5) 5.022, 5.027
Art 48(7), second subpara...... 3.006	Art 2(6) 5.009

Arts 2–4	5.022	Art 20(2)(b)	6.021
Arts 2–6	5.009	Art 21	5.055, 5.064, 6.007, 6.008, 6.010, 6.014, 6.017, 6.018, 6.019, 7.057
Art 3	5.023, 5.025, 9.012		
Art 3(1)	5.023, 10.005, 10.037		
Art 3(1)(a)	7.024	Art 21(1)	6.008, 6.010, 6.014, 6.016, 6.019
Art 3(1)(b)	5.023		
Art 3(1)(d)	9.008	Art 21(2)	6.009
Art 3(1)(e)	5.023	Art 21(3)	6.009
Art 3(2)	5.023, 10.037, 10.039	Arts 21–24	6.007
Arts 3–6	5.022	Art 22	6.021, 12.015
Art 4	5.022	Art 22(1)	6.021
Art 4(1)	5.022, 5.025, 5.027	Art 22(2)	6.021
Art 4(2)	5.025	Art 23	6.022
Art 4(2)(k)	9.055	Art 23, first para	6.022, 12.060
Art 4(3)	5.025, 5.026, 7.026, 9.060, 10.039	Art 23, second para	6.022
		Art 24	6.022, 10.026
Art 4(4)	5.025, 5.026, 10.039	Art 24, first para	6.022
Art 5(1)	5.025	Art 24, second para	12.011
Art 5(2)	5.025	Art 25	3.007, 11.011
Art 5(3)	5.025	Art 25, second para	6.007
Art 6	5.022, 5.025, 5.027, 9.053	Art 26	1.041, 7.113, 8.028
Art 6(a)	9.055	Art 26(2)	7.001, 7.003, 7.009
Art 6(b)	9.059	Art 28	7.013, 7.017, 7.021
Art 6(e)	6.018	Art 28(2)	7.014, 10.002
Art 6(g)	9.065	Arts 28–37	7.011
Art 7	5.007	Art 29	7.014, 10.002
Art 8	5.007	Art 30	7.013, 7.016, 7.017, 7.021
Art 9	5.007, 7.075	Art 31	7.013, 7.024, 7.025, 9.055, 10.003
Art 10	5.007, 5.058, 5.060		
Art 11	5.007, 9.004, 9.061	Art 31, first subpara	12.046
Art 12	5.007, 9.056	Art 32	7.013
Art 13	5.007	Art 33	5.018, 7.025
Art 14	5.007, 9.019	Art 34	7.026, 7.028, 7.030, 7.031, 7.037, 7.038, 7.042, 7.043, 7.116
Art 15	5.007		
Art 15(2)	12.043		
Art 16	5.007, 9.001, 9.002	Arts 34–36	7.013
Art 16(1)	9.002	Art 35	7.026, 7.030
Art 16(2)	9.002	Art 36	7.013, 7.026, 7.031, 7.032, 7.033, 7.034, 7.035, 7.036, 7.037, 7.041, 7.042, 7.043, 7.106, 7.115, 7.116, 10.006
Art 16(2), first subpara	9.002		
Art 16(2), second subpara	9.002		
Art 17	5.007		
Art 17(1)	5.007, 10.020	Art 36, last sentence	5.054
Art 17(2)	5.007	Art 37	7.013, 10.033
Art 17(3)	5.007	Art 37(1)	5.054
Art 18	1.027, 5.019, 5.051, 5.053, 5.054, 5.055, 5.056, 5.057, 5.064, 6.010, 6.015, 6.018, 6.019, 7.003, 7.044, 7.057, 9.019	Art 38 et seq	5.018
		Art 38(1)	9.003
		Art 38(2)	9.003
		Art 38(3)	9.003
Art 18, second para	5.019	Art 38(4)	9.003
Arts 18–25	6.001	Art 39(1)	9.004
Art 19	3.010, 5.058, 5.060	Art 39(1)(b)	9.046
Art 19(2)	5.018, 5.060	Art 39(2)	9.004
Art 20	6.007, 6.017	Arts 39–44	9.003
Art 20(1)	6.005, 6.006	Art 40	7.108
Art 20(2)	3.007, 6.005, 6.006, 6.007	Art 40(2)	5.051

Art 40(2), second subpara...... 5.051
Art 40(3) 9.005
Arts 40–43................... 9.008
Art 41....................... 7.108
Art 42....................... 9.003
Art 43...................... 10.037
Art 43(2) 9.005, 10.008
Art 43(3) 9.005
Art 45...... 6.008, 7.044, 7.051, 7.053,
            7.055, 7.059, 7.062
Art 45(1)–(3) 7.044, 7.068
Art 45(2) 5.054, 7.047,
            7.050, 7.058, 7.059
Art 45(3) 6.016, 7.044,
            7.067, 11.011
Art 45(3)(b) 7.057
Art 45(3)(c).................. 7.057
Art 45(3)(d) 7.044, 7.057, 12.060
Art 45(4) 7.044, 7.068, 11.011
Arts 45–48.............. 7.050, 7.079
Arts 45–66................... 7.011
Art 46............ 6.010, 7.045, 7.057,
            7.076, 7.108, 9.046
Art 48...... 6.008, 7.045, 7.078, 7.079,
            7.080, 7.108, 9.046, 12.024
Art 48, second para 7.078
Art 49............ 7.044, 7.047, 7.057,
            7.058, 7.061, 7.062, 7.064,
            7.065, 7.066, 7.086, 7.096,
            7.097, 7.098, 9.019, 10.039
Art 49, first para 7.054
Art 49, second para 5.054, 7.063
Art 50............ 7.057, 7.075, 7.108
Art 50(2) 7.045
Art 50(2)(g)............. 7.075, 7.108
Art 51................. 7.069, 7.081,
            7.089, 7.093, 7.099
Arts 51–52................... 11.011
Arts 51–54................... 7.081
Art 52................ 6.010, 6.016,
            7.044, 7.081, 7.089,
            7.092, 7.093, 7.099, 7.108
Art 52(1) 7.067
Art 52(2) 7.044
Art 53............ 7.045, 7.075, 7.081,
            7.096, 7.108, 9.050, 9.055
Art 53(1) 7.075, 7.076, 7.097
Art 54........ 7.054, 7.063, 7.065, 7.075
Art 55....................... 7.084
Art 56............ 7.081, 7.084, 7.085,
            7.087, 7.088, 7.097
Art 57........... 7.082, 7.083, 7.096
Art 57, second para 7.082
Art 57, third para 5.054, 7.085, 7.087
Art 58(1) 7.004, 7.083, 9.009

Art 59........... 6.010, 7.057, 7.108
Art 60, second para 12.060
Art 61....................... 5.054
Art 62........... 6.016, 7.075, 7.081,
            7.084, 7.096, 7.097, 9.055
Art 63.... 7.100, 7.101, 10.004, 10.039
Art 63(1) 7.100
Art 64................... 7.100, 7.103
Art 64(1) 7.107
Art 64(2) 7.107
Art 64(3) 7.107
Art 65......7.103, 7.104, 7.105, 11.011
Art 65(1) 7.105, 7.106
Art 65(1)(a)............. 7.103, 7.104
Art 65(1)(b) 7.100, 7.104
Art 65(2) 7.106
Art 65(3) 5.054, 7.103, 7.104, 7.106
Art 65(4) 7.107
Art 66................... 7.103, 7.107
Art 67................... 7.107, 8.005
Art 67(1) 8.001
Art 67(2) 7.010, 8.005
Art 67(3) 8.005
Art 67(4) 8.005
Art 68...................... 12.024
Art 71...................... 12.053
Art 72...................... 11.011
Art 75...... 7.103, 7.107, 8.028, 10.031
Art 75(1) 7.107
Art 76.................. 5.032, 8.021
Art 77.................. 7.010, 8.028
Art 77(1) 8.007
Art 77(1)(a).................. 8.007
Art 77(1)(b) 8.007
Art 77(1)(c).................. 8.007
Art 77(2)(a).................. 8.007
Art 77(2)(a)–(c) 8.007
Art 77(2)(d) 8.007
Art 77(2)(e).................. 8.007
Art 77(3) 6.009, 8.007
Art 77(4) 8.007, 11.006
Arts 77–80................... 10.002
Art 78(1) 8.008
Art 78(2) 8.009, 8.010
Art 78(2)(a).................. 8.009
Art 78(2)(b) 8.009
Art 78(2)(c).................. 8.010
Art 78(2)(d) 8.009
Art 78(2)(e).................. 8.010
Art 78(2)(f).................. 8.011
Art 78(2)(g)............. 8.011, 8.012
Art 78(3) 8.010
Art 79(1) 8.012
Art 79(2) 8.012
Art 79(3) 8.012, 10.036

Art 79(4)	8.012
Art 79(5)	8.012
Art 80	8.005, 8.010
Art 81	8.014
Art 81(1)	8.014
Art 81(2)	8.014
Art 81(2)(a)	8.015
Art 81(2)(b)	8.015
Art 81(2)(c)	8.016
Art 81(2)(d)	8.015
Art 81(2)(e)	8.017
Art 81(2)(f)	8.017
Art 81(2)(g)	8.017
Art 81(2)(h)	8.018
Art 81(3), first subpara	8.014
Art 81(3), second subpara	8.014
Art 81(3), third subpara	3.008, 8.014
Art 82(1)	8.019, 8.020, 8.025
Art 82(1), second subpara, sub (c)	8.020
Art 82(2)	8.019, 8.020
Art 82(2)(d)	3.008
Art 82(3)	8.019, 12.024
Arts 82–86	2.008
Art 83(1)	8.019
Art 83(1), first subpara	8.021
Art 83(1), second subpara	8.021
Art 83(1), third subpara	3.008, 8.021
Art 83(2)	5.019, 8.019, 8.021
Art 83(3)	8.019, 12.024
Art 84	8.022
Art 85(1), first subpara	8.023
Art 85(1), second subpara	8.023
Art 85(1), third subpara	8.023
Art 86(1)	8.024
Art 86(1), second subpara	8.024, 12.024
Art 86(1), third subpara	8.024
Art 86(2)	8.024
Art 86(4)	3.008, 8.024, 12.025
Art 87(1)	8.025
Art 87(2)	8.025
Art 87(2)(a)	8.025
Art 87(3)	8.025, 12.024
Arts 87–89	2.008
Art 88	8.026
Art 88(1)	8.026
Art 88(2)	8.026
Art 88(3)	8.026
Art 89	2.008, 8.025
Art 90	5.018, 9.009
Art 91	7.108, 10.008, 10.037
Art 91(1)	9.010
Art 92	5.054, 9.011
Art 93	9.011, 9.019
Art 94	9.010
Art 95(1)	5.054, 9.011
Art 95(3)	9.011
Art 96	9.011
Art 96(1)	9.011
Art 96(2)	9.011
Art 97, third para	12.060
Art 100(1)	9.009
Art 100(2)	10.008
Art 101	5.008, 5.023, 5.049, 7.001, 9.012, 9.014, 9.015, 9.016, 9.017, 12.058
Art 101(1)	9.013, 9.014, 9.015
Art 101(1)(d)	5.051
Art 101(2)	9.009, 9.014
Art 101(3)	9.014, 9.015, 9.016
Arts 101–105	7.005
Arts 101–106	9.012
Art 102	5.008, 5.023, 7.001, 9.012, 9.015, 9.016, 9.017, 9.019, 12.058
Art 102, second para, indent (c)	5.0514
Art 103	9.015
Art 104	9.015, 9.033
Art 105	9.015
Art 106	7.005, 9.019, 9.020
Art 106(1)	9.019
Art 106(2)	9.019, 9.023
Art 106(3)	9.020, 9.023, 12.060
Art 107	7.001, 9.003, 9.011, 9.012, 9.019, 9.023, 9.025, 9.026
Art 107(1)	9.021, 9.022, 9.024
Art 107(2)	9.021
Art 107(3)	9.021
Art 107(3)(e)	9.021
Arts 107–109	7.005
Art 108	7.001, 9.003, 9.011, 9.012, 9.024, 9.028, 11.011
Art 108(1)	9.025
Art 108(2)	9.021, 9.026, 9.027, 9.028
Art 108(2), first subpara	9.025
Art 108(2), second subpara	9.025
Art 108(2), third subpara	9.027
Art 108(2), fourth subpara	9.027
Art 108(3)	7.115, 9.023, 9.024, 9.026, 9.028
Art 108(4)	9.021
Art 109	9.003, 9.011, 9.012, 9.021
Art 110	7.021, 7.022, 7.023
Art 110, first para	5.054, 7.021
Art 113	5.015, 7.108, 7.114, 9.055
Arts 113–117	7.006

Art 114............5.014, 5.015, 5.026, 5.060, 7.009, 7.025, 7.033, 7.037, 7.075, 7.109, 7.112, 7.113, 7.115, 9.002, 9.020, 9.055, 9.056, 9.064	
Art 114(1).....5.018, 7.112, 7.113, 7.114	
Art 114(2)...............7.009, 7.114	
Art 114(3)...............7.113, 7.115	
Art 114(4)........ 5.047, 7.039, 7.115	
Art 114(4)–(7)................ 7.033	
Art 114(5)........ 5.047, 7.039, 7.115	
Art 114(6).................... 7.115	
Art 114(7).................... 7.115	
Art 114(9).................... 7.115	
Art 114(10)................... 7.115	
Arts 114–118.................. 7.108	
Art 115...........5.015, 5.018, 7.075, 7.112, 7.114, 9.056	
Art 116...................... 7.116	
Art 117...................... 7.116	
Art 117(1).................. 12.060	
Art 118................7.108, 7.109	
Art 118, first para............. 7.109	
Art 118, second para 7.109	
Art 119......5.006, 5.008, 9.029, 9.036	
Art 119(1)................... 9.012	
Art 119(2)........ 9.012, 9.029, 9.035	
Art 119(3)................... 9.029	
Art 120.......... 9.012, 9.036, 9.043	
Art 121...........7.108, 9.036, 9.038, 12.024, 12.037	
Art 121(2)................... 9.036	
Art 121(2), second subpara.... 12.024	
Art 121(3).................. 12.038	
Art 121(4).............9.039, 12.007	
Art 121(4), third subpara 12.047	
Art 121(5)............12.007, 12.060	
Art 121(6).............9.036, 9.038	
Art 121(14)................. 9.038	
Art 122................9.036, 9.037	
Art 123..................... 9.036	
Art 125................9.036, 9.037	
Art 126.....9.036, 9.041, 9.057, 12.038	
Art 126(1)................... 9.034	
Art 126(2)................... 9.036	
Art 126(3)–(5) 9.036	
Art 126(6)................... 9.036	
Art 126(7)................... 9.036	
Art 126(9).............9.036, 12.037	
Art 126(11)............ 4.019, 9.040, 12.007, 12.037	
Art 126(13), third subpara 12.047	
Art 126(14).................. 9.036	
Art 126(14), second subpara.... 9.036	
Art 126(14), third subpara 9.036	
Art 127(1).............9.012, 9.043	
Art 127(2)................... 9.044	
Art 127(5)................... 9.044	
Art 127(6).............3.008, 9.044	
Art 128(1)................... 9.045	
Art 128(2)................... 9.045	
Art 129(3)................... 5.019	
Art 130..................... 9.043	
Art 133..................... 9.044	
Art 133(2).................. 10.005	
Art 134(2), second indent..... 12.053	
Art 136................9.036, 9.038	
Art 136(2), second subpara.... 12.047	
Art 136(3)................... 9.037	
Art 138(3), second subpara.... 12.047	
Art 139(2)................... 9.034	
Art 139(4), second subpara.... 12.047	
Art 140................9.033, 9.035	
Art 140(1)................... 9.034	
Art 140(1), first subpara 9.033	
Art 140(2)................... 9.034	
Art 140(2), third subpara 12.047	
Art 140(3).............3.010, 9.034	
Art 141(1).................. 11.012	
Art 143(1), first subpara 12.060	
Art 145................5.018, 9.049	
Arts 145–150................. 9.046	
Art 146(1)................... 9.049	
Art 146(2)................... 9.049	
Art 147..................... 5.033	
Art 147(1)................... 9.049	
Art 147(2)................... 9.049	
Art 148(1)....... 9.039, 9.049, 12.024	
Art 148(2)................... 9.049	
Art 148(4)................... 9.049	
Art 148(5)............12.024, 12.060	
Art 149................5.018, 9.049	
Art 150.................... 12.053	
Art 151, first para............. 9.047	
Art 151, second para 9.047	
Art 151, third para 9.046	
Arts 151–164................. 9.046	
Art 153................7.108, 9.047	
Art 153(1)................... 9.047	
Art 153(1)(i)................. 5.058	
Art 153(2).............7.114, 10.008	
Art 153(2)(a)................. 9.047	
Art 153(2), fourth subpara 3.008	
Art 153(4).............5.018, 9.047	
Art 153(5)................... 9.047	
Art 154..................... 12.060	
Art 154(1)................... 9.047	
Art 156................9.047, 12.060	
Art 156, second para 7.108	
Art 157......5.051, 5.058, 5.063, 9.048	

Art 157(1)	5.058	Art 173(3), first subpara	9.059
Art 157(3)	5.058	Art 173(3), second subpara	5.018
Art 157(3), second subpara	9.059	Art 174	9.004, 9.057
Art 157(4)	5.059	Art 175	5.021, 9.057
Art 159	12.060	Art 175, first para	9.004, 9.057
Art 160	12.053	Art 175, second para	12.060
Art 162	9.047	Art 175, third para	9.057
Art 163	9.047	Art 176	9.057
Art 165	5.018, 10.038	Art 177, first para	9.057
Art 165(1)	5.018, 5.033, 9.050, 9.051	Art 177, second para	9.057
Art 165(2)	9.050	Art 178, first para	9.057
Art 165(2), first indent	9.050	Art 179	9.060
Art 165(2), second indent	6.018	Art 180	9.060
Art 165(2), last indent	9.051	Art 181	9.060
Art 165(3)	9.051, 10.037	Art 181, second para	7.108
Art 165(4)	5.018, 9.050, 9.051, 9.052	Art 181(2)	9.060, 12.060
Art 166	9.046, 9.047, 10.038	Art 182(1)	9.060
Art 166(1)	5.018, 9.052	Art 182(3)	9.060
Art 166(3)	5.018, 10.037	Art 182(4)	9.060
Art 166(4)	9.052	Art 184	9.060
Art 167	5.018, 9.054	Art 185	9.060
Art 167(1)	9.053	Art 186	9.060
Art 167(2)	5.033, 9.053	Art 186, second para	10.002, 10.036
Art 167(3)	10.037	Art 187	9.060
Art 167(5)	5.018, 9.053	Art 188, first para	9.060
Art 168	5.018	Art 188, second para	9.060
Art 168(1)	9.055	Art 189	9.060
Art 168(1), first subpara	9.004	Art 189(1)	9.060
Art 168(1), second subpara	9.055	Art 189(2)	9.060
Art 168(2)	5.033, 12.060	Art 190	12.060
Art 168(2), second para	7.108	Art 191	9.061
Art 168(3)	10.037	Art 191(1)	9.061
Art 168(4)	9.055	Art 191(2), first subpara	9.061, 9.062
Art 168(4)(b)	9.055	Art 191(2), second subpara	9.062
Art 168(4)(c)	9.055	Art 191(3)	9.061
Art 168(5)	5.018, 7.113, 9.055	Art 191(4)	9.062, 10.039
Art 168(6)	9.055	Art 191(4), first subpara	10.002, 10.036
Art 168(7)	9.055	Art 192	5.015
Art 169(1)	9.056	Art 192(1)	9.062, 10.008
Art 169(2)	9.056	Art 192(2)	9.062
Art 169(3)	9.056	Art 192(2), second subpara	3.008, 9.062
Art 169(4)	9.056	Art 192(3)	9.062
Art 170	9.058	Art 192(3), second subpara	9.062
Art 171	9.058	Art 192(4)	9.062
Art 171(1)	9.058	Art 192(5)	9.062
Art 171(2)	9.058, 12.060	Art 193	9.062
Art 171(3)	10.037	Art 194	7.109
Art 172	9.058, 10.037	Art 194(1)	9.063
Art 172, first para	9.058	Art 194(2), second subpara	9.063
Art 172, second para	9.058	Arts 194–197	7.108
Art 173(1)	9.059	Art 195	9.064
Art 173(2)	7.108, 9.059, 12.060	Art 195(2)	5.018, 9.064
Art 173(3)	5.018		

Art 196	7.109, 9.064
Art 196(2)	5.018, 9.064
Art 197	9.065
Art 197(2)	5.018, 9.065
Art 198, second para	10.013
Arts 198–204	10.013, 11.007
Art 199(1)	10.013
Art 199(2)	10.013
Art 199(3)	10.013
Art 200	10.013
Art 200(5)	5.054
Art 203	10.012, 10.013
Art 205(2)	12.047
Art 206	5.018, 7.015
Arts 206–214	10.002
Art 207	7.024, 7.025, 9.055, 10.003, 10.005, 10.008, 12.052
Art 207(1)	10.003, 10.004
Art 207(2)	10.005
Art 207(4), first subpara	10.008
Art 207(4), second subpara	10.005
Art 207(5)	10.004
Art 207(6)	5.018
Art 208, first subpara	10.022
Art 208(1), second subpara	10.021
Art 208(2)	10.021
Arts 208–211	10.021
Art 209	10.008, 10.021
Art 209(1)	10.022
Art 209(2)	10.022, 10.039
Art 209(3)	10.022
Arts 209–211	10.003
Art 210(1)	10.022
Art 210(2)	10.022, 12.060
Art 211	10.021
Art 212	10.008, 10.025
Art 212(2)	10.024
Art 212(3), second subpara	10.024
Art 213	10.024
Art 213(3)	10.039
Art 214(1)	10.023
Art 214(2)	10.023
Art 214(4)	10.023
Art 214(5)	10.023
Art 214(7)	10.023
Art 215	7.107, 10.002, 10.031
Art 215(1)	10.031
Art 215(2)	10.031
Art 216	10.002
Art 216(1)	10.036, 10.037, 10.039
Art 217	4.018, 10.008, 10.012, 10.013, 10.014, 10.016, 10.020
Art 218	5.012, 10.004, 10.022, 10.024
Art 218(5)	4.018
Art 218(6)	12.004
Art 218(8), second subpara	3.007, 4.018
Art 218(10)	12.004, 12.009
Art 219(1)	9.045, 10.036
Art 219(3)	9.045
Art 219(4)	10.039
Art 220(1)	1.004, 1.006
Art 222	9.066, 10.002
Art 222(1)	9.066
Art 222(2)	9.066
Art 222(3), first subpara	9.066
Art 222(4)	12.024
Art 223	12.015
Art 223(1)	12.014
Art 223(1), second subpara	3.007, 12.019
Art 223(2)	12.016, 12.039
Art 224	12.021
Art 225	12.003, 12.004, 12.019
Art 226	12.010
Art 226, first para	12.010
Art 226, third para	12.010
Art 227	6.022, 12.011
Art 228	6.022
Art 229, first para	12.017
Art 229, second para	12.019
Art 230, first para	12.017
Art 230, second para	12.006, 12.017
Art 230, third para	12.007, 12.017, 12.032
Art 231, first para	12.019
Art 232, first para	12.017, 12.019
Art 233	12.060
Art 234, second para	12.019
Art 235(1), first subpara	12.031
Art 235(1), second subpara	12.031
Art 235(1), third subpara	12.031
Art 235(2)	12.032
Art 235(3)	12.029, 12.031
Art 235(4)	12.033
Art 236	12.025
Art 236(a)	12.040
Art 236(b)	12.042
Art 237	12.043
Art 238(1)	12.046
Art 238(2)	12.031, 12.047, 12.048
Art 238(3)	12.047
Art 238(3)(a)	10.035, 12.047
Art 238(3)(b)	12.047
Art 238(4)	12.046
Art 239	12.045
Art 240(1)	12.051
Art 240(2)	12.055
Art 240(2), first subpara	12.055

Art 240(3)	12.043
Art 241	12.039
Art 242	12.039
Art 243	12.039
Art 244	12.025
Art 249(2)	12.060
Art 252	12.039
Art 252, first para	12.046
Art 253	9.046
Art 253, sixth para	12.039
Art 254, fifth para	12.039
Art 258	1.026, 2.008, 7.115, 9.020, 9.025, 11.011, 12.058
Arts 258–260	4.019
Art 259	1.026, 7.078, 7.115, 9.025, 11.011
Art 260	9.041
Art 260(1)	12.058
Art 260(2)	12.058
Art 260(3)	12.058
Art 262	3.007
Art 263	9.028, 10.031, 12.009, 12.058
Art 263, first para	12.023
Art 263, second para	12.039, 12.043
Art 263, third para	5.033
Art 263, fourth para	11.002
Art 265, first para	12.009, 12.039
Art 265, third para	11.002
Art 267	1.004, 1.026, 1.027, 5.047, 9.015, 10.031
Art 267(1)(b)	3.011
Art 269	4.020
Art 275, second para	10.031
Art 281, second para	12.039
Art 282	9.043
Art 282(1)	9.043
Art 283(2), second subpara	12.025
Art 284(1)	12.039
Art 284(2)	12.043
Art 284(3)	12.008, 12.039, 12.058
Art 284(3), first subpara	12.024
Art 286(2)	12.039
Art 287(1)	12.008
Art 287(4)	12.008
Art 287(4), first subpara	12.058
Art 287(4), second subpara	12.039, 12.060
Art 287(4), fifth subpara	12.039
Art 288	1.027, 5.012, 5.046
Art 290	12.061
Art 291(2)	12.038, 12.061
Art 291(3)	12.061
Art 292	12.060
Art 294	1.045
Art 294(7)(b)	12.019
Art 294(7)(c)	12.019
Art 304	12.039, 12.060
Art 305, third para	12.016
Art 307	12.039, 12.060
Art 308, third para	12.046
Art 311, third para	3.006, 3.007
Art 311, fourth para	3.006
Art 312(2)	12.025
Art 312(2), first subpara	3.006
Art 312(2), second subpara	3.006
Art 314(2)	12.058
Art 314(4)(c)	12.019
Art 314(7)(b)	12.019
Art 314(7)(c)	12.019
Art 317	12.061
Art 319(1)	12.008
Art 322	12.045
Art 329(1)	5.023
Art 330	3.008
Art 330, third para	12.047
Art 333(1)	3.008
Art 333(2)	3.008
Art 333(3)	3.008
Art 337	5.060
Art 341	12.018
Art 344	1.024
Art 345	7.036
Art 346	11.011
Art 346(1)	11.011
Art 346(1)(a)	11.011
Art 346(1)(b)	11.011
Arts 346–348	4.019, 11.011
Art 347	11.011
Art 348	11.011
Art 348, first para	11.011
Art 348, second para	11.011
Art 349	11.007, 11.008
Art 350	1.004
Art 352	3.006, 3.009, 5.001, 5.011, 5.015, 5.017, 5.020, 5.021, 5.032, 5.060, 6.004, 7.006, 7.057, 7.075, 7.108, 7.109, 9.047, 9.052, 9.057, 9.058, 9.061, 9.063, 9.064, 10.008, 10.031, 10.038
Art 352(1)	5.021
Art 352(2)	5.032
Art 352(3)	5.020, 10.038
Art 352(4)	5.020, 10.038
Art 353	3.006
Art 354	3.006
Art 354, first para	4.020
Art 354, second para	12.047

TABLE OF TREATIES, PROTOCOLS AND DECLARATIONS ci

Art 354, third para 12.047
Art 354, fourth para 4.020, 12.019
Art 355. 11.006
Art 355(1) 11.007, 11.008
Art 355(2) 11.007
Art 355(3) 11.007
Art 355(4) 11.007
Art 355(5)(a). 11.007
Art 355(5)(b) 11.007
Art 355(5)(c). 11.007
Art 355(6) 11.008, 12.025
Art 356. 11.005

PROTOCOLS ANNEXED TO THE TEU AND TFEU

Protocol (No.2) on the
 application of the principles
 of subsidiarity and
 proportionality (2010) 5.028,
  15.007, 15.010, 17.015, 24.004
Art 3. . . . . 17.012
Art 8. . . . . 13.033
Art 9. . . . . 12.024, 12.060
Protocol (No.4) on the Statute of
 the European System of Central
 Banks and of the European
 Central Bank (2010) (ESCB
 Statute) 3.008,
  9.043, 13.020
Art 4. . . . . 27.039
Art 6. . . . . 10.036
Art 9.2 . . . . 13.020
Art 10.1 . . . . 22.005
Art 10.2 . . . . 13.022
Art 10.3 . . . . 13.022
Art 10.4 . . . . 13.023
Art 11.1 . . . . 13.021
Art 11.2 . . . . 22.005
Art 11.4 . . . . 13.021
Art 11.5 . . . . 13.022
Art 12.1 . . . . 13.021
Art 12.3 . . . . 13.023
Art 14.2 . . . . 9.043, 13.004,
  13.020, 30.005
Art 14.3 . . . . 9.044, 27.045
Art 22. . . . . 14.009
Art 26. . . . . 14.011
Art 27. . . . . 14.011
Art 28.2 . . . . 13.019
Art 29.1 . . . . 13.019
Art 35.3 . . . . 14.003
Art 35.6 . . . . 13.020
Art 36. . . . . 13.020
Art 36(1) 14.022

Art 37. . . . . 13.021
Art 39. . . . . 14.007, 14.009
Art 40. . . . . 13.020
Art 40.2 . . . . 12.040, 13.022
Art 42. . . . . 22.005
Arts 44–46. . . . . 22.005
Art 46. . . . . 13.021
Art 49. . . . . 3.010
Protocol (No.5) on the Statute of
 the European Investment Bank
 (2010) (EIB Statute) 13.037
Art 4. . . . . 13.037
Art 5. . . . . 13.037
Art 7(1) 13.038
Art 7(2) 13.038
Art 7(3)(f) 14.011
Art 7(3)(h) 13.038
Art 8. . . . . 13.038
Art 9(1) 13.038
Art 9(2) 13.038
Art 9(3) 13.038
Art 10. . . . . 13.038
Art 11. . . . . 13.038
Art 11(2) 13.038
Art 11(8) 13.038
Art 12. . . . . 14.011, 20.011
Art 13(7) 14.022
Art 16(1) 13.037
Protocol (No.8) relating to Art 6(2)
 of the TEU on the accession
 of the Union to the European
 Convention on the Protection
 of Human Rights
 and Fundamental Freedoms
 (2010) 25.018
Protocol (No.9) on the decision
 of the Council relating to the
 implementation of Art 16(4) of
 the TEU and Art 238(2) of the
 TFEU between November 1,
 2014 and March 31, 2017 on the
 one hand, and as from April 1,
 2007 on the other (2010). 12.048
Protocol (No.10) on permanent
 structured cooperation
 established by Art 42 of the
 TEU (2010) 10.035
Protocol (No.11) on Art 42 of the
 TEU (2010) 10.039
Protocol (No.12) on the
 excessive deficit procedure
 (2010) 3.008, 9.036
Protocol (No.13) on the
 convergence criteria
 (2010) 9.033

cii TABLE OF TREATIES, PROTOCOLS AND DECLARATIONS

Protocol (No.14) on the Euro
  Group (2010) 12.040
  Art 1 .... 22.005
Protocol (No.15) on
  certain provisions relating
  to the United Kingdom
  (2010) 9.035, 22.005
Protocol (No.16) on certain
  provisions relating to Denmark
  (2010) 9.035,
                      22.005, 24.006
Protocol (No.18) on
  France (2010).............. 10.013
Protocol (No.19) on the Schengen
  acquis integrated into the
  framework of the European
  Union (2010) 8.006, 13.019,
                              22.002
Protocol (No.20) on the
  application of certain aspects
  of Art 26 of the TFEU to the
  United Kingdom and Ireland (2010)
Protocol (No.21) on the position
  of the United Kingdom and
  Ireland in respect of the Area of
  Freedom, Security and Justice
  (2010) 8.028,
              14.011, 22.001, 22.006
  Art 1 .... 8.028
  Art 2 .... 8.028, 22.002
  Art 3 .... 8.028
  Art 4a....................... 8.028
  Art 5 .... 8.028, 14.011
  Art 8 .... 8.028
  Art 9 .... 8.028
Protocol (No.22) on the position of
  Denmark (2010) 8.027, 22.002,
                              24.006
  Art 1 .... 8.027
  Art 2 .... 8.027
  Art 4 .... 8.027
  Art 5 .... 10.034, 14.011, 19.007
  Art 6 .... 8.027
  Art 7 .... 8.027
  Art 8 .... 8.027
Protocol (No.23) on
  external relations of the
  Member States with regard to
  the crossing of external borders
  (2010) 8.007, 10.039
Protocol (No.24) on asylum for
  nationals of Member States of
  the European Union (2010) ... 8.008
Protocol (No.25) on the exercise of
  shared competence (2010) 5.027

Protocol (No.26) on services of
  general interest (2010) 9.019
Protocol (No.27) on the internal
  market and competition
  (2010) 2.004, 5.006,
                          7.005, 9.012
Protocol (No.28) on economic,
  social and territorial cohesion
  (2010) 9.057
Protocol (No.29) on the system
  of public broadcasting in the
  Member States (2010).... 8.008, 9.019
Protocol (No.30) on the
  application of the Charter
  of Fundamental Rights of
  the European Union to Poland
  and to the United Kingdom
  (2010) 5.029, 25.007,
                              29.003
  Art 1 .... 25.007
Protocol (No.31) concerning
  imports into the European
  Union of petroleum products
  refined in the Netherlands
  Antilles (2010)............. 11.008
Protocol (No.32) on the
  acquisition of property in
  Denmark (2010) 7.103

PROTOCOLS ANNEXED
TO THE TEU, TFEU AND
THE EAEC TREATY

Protocol (No.1) on the role of
  National Parliaments in the
  European Union (2010) 5.032,
                      15.005, 17.016
  Art 1 .... 15.007
  Art 2 .... 15.007, 17.002, 17.012
  Art 5 .... 15.009
  Art 6 .... 3.006, 15.007
  Art 7 .... 15.007
  Art 8 .... 15.007
  Art 10....................... 15.005
Protocol (No.3) on the Statute
  of the Court of Justice of the
  European Union (2010) 3.008,
                      11.007, 13.002, 13.009
Protocol (No.6) on the
  location of the seats of the
  institutions and of certain
  bodies, offices, agencies and
  departments of the European
  Union (2010) 7.103, 12.018,
                      13.002, 13.032, 14.020

Protocol (No.7) on the Privileges
and Immunities of the
European Union (2010) 7.082,
14.007, 24.008
   Art 6 .... 21.007
   Art 7 .... 12.016
   Art 9 .... 12.016
   Art 10 .... 14.009
   Art 12 .... 14.014
   Art 19 .... 14.009
   Art 20 .... 14.009
Protocol (No.35) on Art 40.3.3 of the
Constitution of Ireland (2010) ... 7.082

Protocol (No.36) on Transitional
Provisions (2010) 2.008,
8.027, 13.011,
14.007, 29.024
   Art 3(2) 12.049
   Art 3(3) 12.049
   Art 4 .... 12.040
   Art 9 .... 2.008, 8.028
   Art 10 .... 29.024, 30.014
   Arts 10(1)-(3) 28.007
   Art 10(2) 2.008
   Art 10(4) 13.011
   Art 10(5) 8.028, 13.011

Table of Conventions and Agreements Concluded by the EU or the Former EC

1961	Association agreement with Greece 4.003		Trade and cooperation agreement with Hungary (26 September 1988, OJ 1988 L327/2) 10.008
	Art 53(1) 26.003	1989	Trade and cooperation agreement with Poland (19 September 1989, OJ 1989 L339/2) 10.008
1963	Yaoundé (Cameroon) association agreements with African States . . . 10.019		
1969	Association agreements with African States 10.019		Trade and cooperation agreement with the Soviet Union (19 December 1989, OJ 1990 L68/3) 10.008
1970	Agreement of 5 December 1970 with Malta, OJ 1971 L61/1 . . . . . . 10.017–10.018		
1973	Agreement with Cyprus, OJ 1973 L133/1 . . . . . . 10.017–10.018, 26.003	1990	Trade and cooperation agreement with Bulgaria (8 May 1990, OJ 1990 L291/8) 10.008
1975	ACP–EC Partnership Agreement 10.014, 10.019		Trade and cooperation agreement with Czechoslovakia (7 May 1990, OJ 1990 L291/29) 10.008
	Art 13(3) 10.019		
	Art 13(5)(c) 10.019		Trade and cooperation agreement with Romania (22 October 1990, OJ 1991 L79/13) 10.008
	Art 35 . . . . 10.019		
	Association agreement with Israel . . . 26.013		
1976	Association agreement with Algeria 8.013, 10.018	1991	Cooperation Agreement with the Socialist Federal Republic of Yugoslavia, OJ 1991 L325/23 . . . . 10.016, 21.001, 21.006, 26.013
1978	Cooperation agreement with Morocco 8.013, 10.018		
1980	Cooperation agreements of 7 March 1980 with the member countries of the Association of South-East Asian Nations (ASEAN: Indonesia, Malaysia, the Philippines, Singapore, and Thailand), OJ 1980 L144/2 . . . . 10.008	1992	Agreement on the European Economic Area (EEA Agreement) 4.005, 7.085, 10.020, 21.005, 26.002, 26.004, 26.006, 29.029
			Art 10 . . . . 26.003
			Art 99(1) 10.020
1982	United Nations Convention on the Law of the Sea, signed at Montego Bay on 10 December 1982, OJ 1998 L179/1 . . . . . . 11.006, 26.003		Art 99(3) 10.020
			Art 109 . . . . 10.020
			Art 109(1) 10.020
1985	Cooperation agreement with Brunei (OJ 1985 L81/2) 10.008		Art 111(1) 10.021
			Art 111(3) 10.021
1988	Cooperation agreement of 15 June 1988 with the countries party to the Charter of the Cooperation Council for the Arab States of the Gulf (United Arab Emirates, Bahrein, Saudi Arabia, Oman, Qatar, and Kuwait), OJ 1989 L54/3) 10.008		Cooperation agreement of 15 June 1992 with Macao (OJ 1992 L404/27) 10.008
			Trade and cooperation agreement with Albania (11 May 1992, OJ 1992 L343/1) 10.008
			Trade and cooperation agreement with Estonia (11 May 1992, OJ 1992 L403/2) 10.008
	Lugano Convention on jurisdiction and the enforcement of judgments in civil and commercial matters . . 5.026, 8.014–8.015		Trade and cooperation agreement with Latvia (11 May 1992, OJ 1992 L403/11) 10.008

Trade and cooperation agreement with Lithuania (11 May 1992, OJ 1992 L403/2) 10.008

1993 Cooperation agreement with of 20 December 1993 with India (OJ 1994 L223/24) 10.008

Framework cooperation agreement concluded on 22 February 1993 with the Republics of Costa Rica, El Salvador, Guatemala, Honduras, Nicaragua, and Panama (OJ 1999 L63/38) 10.008

1994 Agreement between the EFTA States on the establishment of a Surveillance Authority and a Court of Justice
Art 5 .... 10.020
Art 22 .... 10.020
Art 31 .... 10.020
Art 32 .... 10.020
Art 34 .... 10.020

Agreement establishing the World Trade Organisation (WTO) 10.010–10.011, 21.011, 26.003
Art IX(1) 10.011
Annex 2 .... 10.011

Agreement on Trade-Related Aspects of Intellectual Property Rights (TRIPs) 10.004, 10.010, 26.003

Cooperation Agreement with the Republic of South Africa of 10 October 1994, OJ 1994 L341 .... 10.008

Cooperation agreement of 18 July 1994 with Sri Lanka (OJ 1995 L85/33) 10.008

General Agreement on Tariffs and Trade (GATT) 10.010, 26.001, 26.005
Art I 7.015
Art XXIV(8) 1.019

1995 Cooperation agreement of 17 July 1995 with Vietnam (OJ 1996 L136/29) 10.008

Cooperation agreement of 20 November 1995 with Nepal (OJ 1996 L137/15) 10.008

Euro-Mediterranean association agreement with Tunisia 10.018, 26.003

1996 Association agreement with Turkey 10.017, 26.006

Framework agreement with Korea of 28 October 1996, OJ 2001 L90/45 .... 10.008

Framework cooperation agreement with Chile of 21 June 1996, OJ 1999 L42/46).

1997 Cooperation agreement of 29 April 1997 with Laos (OJ 1997 L334/14) and Cambodia (OJ 1997 C107/7) 10.008

Cooperation agreement of 25 November 1997 with Yemen (OJ 1998 L72/18, replacing the agreement of 9 October 1984, OJ 1985 L26/2) 10.008

EC–PLO Association Agreement 26.013

Economic partnership, political coordination, and cooperation agreement of 8 December 1997 with Mexico (OJ 2000 L276/45) 10.008

Euro-Mediterranean Interim Association Agreement of 24 February 1997 with the Palestine Liberation Organization (PLO) for the benefit of the Palestine Authority of the West Bank and the Gaza Strip (OJ 1997 L187/1) 10.018, 10-025

Partnership and cooperation agreement with Russia (OJ 1997 L327/3) 10.008

Trade and cooperation agreement with former Yugoslav Republic of Macedonia (29 April 1997, OJ 1997 L348/2) 10.008

1998 Framework agreement concluded on 23 April 1993 with the Cartagena Agreement and its member countries, namely Bolivia, Colombia, Ecuador, Peru, and Venezuela (OJ 1998 L127/10) 10.008

Partnership and cooperation agreement with Moldova (OJ 1998 L181/3) 10.008

Partnership and cooperation agreement with Ukraine (OJ 1998 L49/3) 10.008

1999 Agreement with Iceland and Norway on 30 June 1999 on the establishment of rights and obligations between Ireland and the United Kingdom of Great Britain and Northern Ireland... 8.006

Agreement between Republic of Iceland and the Kingdom of Norway, on the other, in areas

of the Schengen acquis which
apply to these States, OJ 2000
L15/2..................... 8.006
Association agreement with
South Africa.............. 10.008
Cooperation agreement with
Vietnam (OJ 1999 L117/30) ... 10.008
Interregional framework
cooperation agreement
concluded on 15 December
1995 with the Southern
Common Market ('Mercado
Común del Sur' or 'Mercosur')
and its Party States (Argentina,
Brazil, Paraguay, and Uruguay)
(OJ 1999 L112/65) 10.008
Partnership and cooperation
agreement with
Armenia............10.008, 10.025
Partnership and cooperation
agreement with
Azerbaijan 10.008, 10.025
Partnership and cooperation
agreement with Georgia (OJ
1999 L205/3) 10.008
Partnership and cooperation
agreement with Kazakhstan
(OJ 1999 L196/3)........... 10.008
Partnership and cooperation
agreement with Kyrgyzstan
(OJ 1999 L196/48).......... 10.008
Partnership and cooperation
agreement with Uzbekistan
(OJ 1999 L229/3)........... 10.008

2001 Cooperation agreement of 24
November 2001 with Pakistan
(OJ 2004 L378/22), replacing
the agreement of 23 July 1985,
OJ 1986 L108/2)............ 10.008
International Cocoa Agreement
2001, OJ 2002 L342/1 .... 10.009
Stabilisation and association
agreement with Croatia 10.017

2002 Association agreement with
Chile of 18 November 2002
(OJ 2002 L352/1............ 10.008
Euro-Mediterranean association
agreement with Lebanon 26.003

2003 Agreement with the North Atlantic
Treaty Organisation on the
security of information...... 10.033,
28.017
Agreements with the USA on
extradition and mutual legal
assistance in criminal matters... 28.017

2004 Agreement of 9 June 2004 between
Europol and Eurojust on
information exchange (Europe,
No. 8722, 10 June 2004, 10) ... 27.049
Association agreement with the
Former Yugoslav Republic of
Macedonia 10.017
Cooperation agreement of 29
March 2004 between the ECB
and the International Criminal
Police Organisation (Interpol),
OJ 2004 C134/9 .... 27.049

2005 Agreement with Denmark
on jurisdiction and the
recognition and enforcement
of judgments in civil and
commercial matters 22.004
Agreement with Denmark on
the service of judicial and
extrajudicial documents in civil
or commercial matters 8.015
Cooperation Agreement with the
Principality of Andorra,
OJ 2005 L135/14 .... 11.009
Hague Convention on Choice of
Court Agreements of 30 June
2005, approved on 26 February
2009, OJ 2009 L133/1
Art 29..................... 10.040
Art 30..................... 10.040

2006 Stabilisation and association
agreement with Albania 10.017
United Nations Convention of 13
December 2006 on the Rights
of Persons with Disabilities
Art 44..................... 10.040

2007 Agreement with the United States
of America on the processing
and transfer of Passenger
Name Record (PNR) data by
air carriers to the United States
Department of Homeland
Security (DHS) 28.017
International coffee
agreement................. 28.017
Stabilisation and association
agreement with
Montenegro 10.017

2008 Stabilisation and association
agreement with Bosnia and
Herzegovina............... 10.017
Stabilisation and association
agreement with Serbia 10.017

2009 Partnership and Cooperation
Agreement with Indonesia (OJ
2014 L125/17) 10.008
Partnership and cooperation
agreement with Tadjikistan
(OJ 2009 L350/3)........... 10.008

2010	Lugano Convention on jurisdiction and the recognition and enforcement of judgments in civil and commercial matters (OJ 2007 L339/3) 8.015		**CONVENTIONS AND AGREEMENTS CONCLUDED AMONG EU MEMBER STATES**
2011	Free trade agreements with South Korea (OJ 2011 L127/6 ...... 10.008 Partnership and cooperation agreement with Turkmenistan (OJ 2011 L80/1) 10.008	1968	Brussels Convention on jurisdiction and the enforcement of judgments in civil and commercial matters .... 1.037–1.038, 8.015, 28.018 Art 293..................... 28.018
2012	Trade agreement with Colombia and Peru (OJ 2012 L354/3)... 10.008	1972	Convention setting up a European University Institute .... 13.048 Art 6(3) .... 13.048 Art 19(2) 13.048
2013	Framework agreement with South Korea (OJ 2013 L20/2) 10.008	1976	Convention for the European patent for the common market (Community Patent Convention) Art 5...................... 28.018 Art 73..................... 28.018
2014	Cooperation agreement with the Republics of Costa Rica, El Salvador, Guatemala, Honduras, Nicaragua, and Panama (OJ 2014 L111) 10.008	1980	Rome Convention on the law applicable to contractual obligations 8.016, 28.018
2016	Association agreement with Georgia (OJ 2014 L261/4, concluded on 23 May 2016, ... 10.008, 10.018, 10.025 Association agreement with Moldova (OJ 2014 L269/4), concluded on 23 May 2016, ... 10.008, 10.018, 10.025 Association agreement with Ukraine (OJ 2014 L161/1) ...... 10.008, 10.018, 10.025 Trade agreement with Ecuador (OJ 2016 L356/3) 10.008	1987	Brussels Convention abolishing the legalisation of documents in the Member States of the European Communities...... 1.037
		1990	Brussels Convention on the elimination of double taxation in connection with the adjustment of profits of associated enterprises....... 28.018 Dublin Convention determining State responsibility for examining applications for asylum lodged in one of the Member States of the European Communities.... 1.038, 8.010, 8.027 Rome Convention on the simplification of procedures for the enforcement of maintenance payments....... 1.037
2017	Economic Partnership Agreement with Japan (OJ 2018 L330/3)........... 10.008 Strategic Partnership Agreement with Japan (OJ 2018 L2016/4).......... 10.008	1994	Convention defining the Statute of the European Schools....... 13.048
		1995	Convention on the protection of the European Communities' financial interests .... 8.021 Convention on simplified extradition procedure between the EU Member States .... 8.020 Convention on the establishment of a European Police Office (Europol Convention).......... 8.026, 13.045
2019	Cooperation agreement of 28 June 2019 between the Union and Mercosur states (Argentina, Brazil Paraguay, and Uruguay) Framework agreement with Singapore (OJ 2019 L294/1).................. 10.008		
2020	Framework agreement with Vietnam (OJ 2020 L186/6.... 10.008 Withdrawal Agreement with the United Kingdom........ 4.016–4.018, 6.006, 11.007, 12.025 Art 3(1)(b)................. 11.007 Art 38(2) .... 8.028 Art 185.................... 11.007	1997	Convention on the fight against corruption involving officials of

	the European Communities or officials of EU Member States............... 11.007, 20.013		Convention on the Nomenclature for the Classification of Goods in Customs Tariffs.......... 26.001
	Convention on the service in the EU Member States of judicial and extrajudicial documents in civil or commercial matters ... 8.015		European Convention for the Protection of Human Rights and Fundamental Freedoms (ECHR) 1.007, 3.007,
1998	Convention on jurisdiction and the recognition and enforcement of judgments in matrimonial matters (Second Brussels Convention) ... 1.038, 8.015		5.004, 12.004, 23.018, 25.001–25.004, 25.006, 25.009, 25.013, 25.014–25.019, 25.022
2000	Convention on mutual assistance in criminal matters between the EU Member States.... 28.017, 28.019		Art 3.......... 25.012, 25.014, 25.019 Art 6.......... 13.013, 25.008, 25.014, 25.019, 25.022, 25.025
2012	ESM Treaty.................... 2.010, 9.036–9.037, 28.004		Art 7................ 25.019, 27.031 Art 8................ 25.015, 25.019
	Art 13...................... 9.037		s 2...................... 25.020 Art 9..................... 25.019
2013	TSCG Treaty 2.010, 9.041		s 2...................... 25.020
	Title III..................... 9.041		Art 10.................... 25.019
	Art 3(2) 9.041		s 2...................... 25.020
			Art 10(1) 25.012
	OTHER INTERNATIONAL TREATIES AND CONVENTIONS		Art 11.................... 25.019
			s 2...................... 25.020
1929	Convention for the Unification of Certain Rules Relating to International Carriage by Air (Warsaw Convention)......... 26.001, 26.009		Art 12.................... 25.012
			Art 13.................... 25.019
			Art 14..................... 5.053
			Art 15..................... 8.008
			Art 28..................... 1.007
			Art 29..................... 1.007
1930	Hague Convention on certain questions relating to the conflict of nationality laws.... 6.006		Art 30..................... 1.007
			Art 33..................... 1.007
			Art 34..................... 1.007
1945	United Nations Charter 5.006, 10.001, 10.032, 26.012, 26.014, 26.016		Art 43(1) 1.007
			Art 43(2) 1.007
	Ch VII 26.014–26.015		Art 44..................... 1.007
	Art 2(6) 26.015		Art 46..................... 1.007
	Art 3...................... 26.014		Art 59(1) 1.007
	Art 4...................... 26.014		Protocol (No. 1)
	Art 27(1) 26.014		Art 1..................... 25.019
	Art 27(3) 26.014		Art 3................... 12.003, 24.009, 25.012
	Art 103.................... 26.014		Protocol (No. 4)
1947	General Agreement on Tariffs and Trade (GATT) 7.024, 7.026, 10.007, 10.010, 26.001, 26.003, 26.005, 26.014		Art 2..................... 25.019
			Protocol (No. 7)
			Art 4..................... 25.019
			Protocol (No. 11) 1.007
	Art 1....................... 7.015	1951	Geneva Convention relating to the Status of Refugees 8.008, 8.010, 26.001
	Art XXIV............... 7.015, 10.010		
	Art XXIV(8) 1.019		
1948	Brussels Treaty............ 1.004, 1.012		Art 1....................... 8.008
	Convention on European Economic Cooperation 1.004		Art 1F...................... 6.016
1949	North Atlantic Treaty 1.004, 10.033		Art 18...................... 8.008
1950	Convention establishing a Customs Cooperation Council 26.001		Art 33(1) 8.008
		1954	Paris Protocol.................. 1.012

	Treaty establishing the Western European Union 1.012, 10.032	1965	Treaty on the establishment and statute of the Benelux Court of Justice 1.004
1958	Treaty establishing a Benelux Economic Union............ 1.004	1966	International Covenant on Civil and Political Rights (ICCPR) 25.004, 25.017
1960	Benelux Treaty on the displacement of checks on persons to the external frontiers of the Benelux area 1.039		Art 14................25.022, 25.025 Art 14(3)(g)................. 25.019 Art 25..................... 25.019
	Convention establishing the European Free Trade Association (EFTA) 1.019	1969	Vienna Convention on the Law of Treaties. 3.005, 26.005, 26.013
		1973	Convention for the Prevention of Pollution from Ships........ 26.001
	Convention on the Organisation for Economic Cooperation and Development............... 1.004	1986	Vienna Convention on the Law of Treaties between States and International Organisations or between International Organisations 26.013
1961	European Social Charter 25.002, 25.004, 26.013		
1962	Convention on the Reduction of Statelessness............... 25.004	1989	United Nations Convention on the Rights of the Child 25.004

Table of Interinstitutional Agreements

1988 Interinstitutional Agreement of 29 June 1988 on budgetary discipline and improvement of the budgetary procedure (OJ 1988 L185/33) 14.017, 27.049

1993 Interinstitutional Agreement on procedures for implementing the principle of subsidiarity (OJ 1993 C329/135) 27.049

Interinstitutional Agreement of 29 October 1993 on budgetary discipline and improvement of the budgetary procedure (OJ 1993 C331/1) 14.017, 27.049

1994 Interinstitutional Agreement of 20 December 1994 on the official codification of legislative texts (OJ 1996 C102/2) 27.049

1997 Interinstitutional Agreement concluded by the European Parliament, the Council, and the Commission on 16 July 1997 on provisions regarding the financing of the CFSP (1997) 7/8 EU Bull. point 2.3.1 . . . . . 14.011, 19.006, 27.049

1998 Interinstitutional Agreement on legal bases and implementation of the budget (OJ 1998 C344/1; (1998) 7/8 EU Bull. point 1.6.1 . . . . 20.007, 27.049

Interinstitutional Agreement of 22 December 1998 on common guidelines for the quality of drafting of Community legislation (OJ 1999 C73/1). 27.049

1999 Interinstitutional Agreement of 6 May 1999 on budgetary discipline and improvement of the budgetary procedure (OJ 1999 C172/1) 14.017, 19.006

Interinstitutional Agreement of 25 May 1999 between the European Parliament, the Council and the Commission concerning internal investigations by the European Anti–Fraud Office (OLAF) (OJ 1999 L136/15) 20.013, 27.049

2001 Interinstitutional Agreement of 28 November 2001 on a more structured use of the recasting technique for legal acts (OJ 2002 C77/1) 27.049

2002 Interinstitutional Agreement of 28 February 2002 on the financing of the Convention on the future of the European Union (OJ 2002 C54/1) 27.049

Interinstitutional Agreement of 7 November 2002 on budgetary discipline and improvement of the budgetary procedure (OJ 2002 C283/1) 14.017, 27.049

Interinstitutional Agreement of 20 November 2002 between the European Parliament and the Council concerning access by the European Parliament to sensitive information of the Council in the field of security and defence policy, OJ 2002 C298/1 . . . . . . 19.004, 27.049

Interinstitutional Agreement of 12 December 2002 on budgetary discipline and improvement of the budgetary procedure, OJ 2002 C320/1 . . . . 27.049

2003 Interinstitutional Agreement between the European Parliament, the Council, and the Commission of 16 December 2003 on Better Law–making, point 3 et seq. (OJ 2003 C321/1) 17.015, 17.018, 27.049

2006 Interinstitutional Agreement of 17 May 2006 between the European Parliament, the Council, and the Commission on budgetary discipline and sound financial management, OJ 2006 C139/1 . . . . . 14.017, 19.004, 19.006, 27.049

2013 Interinstitutional Agreement of 2 December 2013 between the European Parliament, the Council, and the Commission on budgetary discipline, on cooperation in budgetary matters, and on sound financial management, OJ 2013 C373/1 . . . . 14.017, 19.004, 19.006, 27.049–27.050

2014 Interinstitutional Agreement between the European Parliament and the Council of 12 March 2014 concerning the forwarding to and handling by the European Parliament of classified information held by the Council on matters other than those in the area of the common foreign and security policy (OJ 2014, C95/1) 12.007

2016 Commission's proposal of 28 September 2016 for an Interinstitutional Agreement on a mandatory Transparency Register, COM(2016)627 final. 16.004

Interinstitutional Agreement between the European Parliament, the Council, and the Commission on Better Law-making, OJ 2016 L123/1 . . . . . 17.014–17.015, 17.017–17.018, 17.042, 18.010, 27.020, 27.049

2020 Interinstitutional Agreement of 16 December 2020 between the European Parliament, the Council, and the Commission on budgetary discipline, on cooperation in budgetary matters and on sound financial management, as well as on new own resources, including a roadmap towards the introduction of new own resources, OJ 2020 L433I/28 . . . . 14.016–14.017, 20.001, 27.049

Table of European Union Acts

REGULATIONS

1958 EEC Council: Regulation No 1 determining the languages to be used by the European Economic Community, OJ English special edition: Series I Volume 1952-1958 P. 59 ...... 14.025, 14.026
    Art 2 .... 14.025
    Art 6 .... 14.028
    Art 7 .... 14.027

1960 EEC Council: Regulation No 11 concerning the abolition of discrimination in transport rates and conditions, in implementation of Article 79 (3) of the Treaty establishing the European Economic Community, OJ 1960 English special edition: Series I Volume 1959-1962 P. 60 .... 9.011
    Art 17-18 .... 14.014

1962 EEC Council: Regulation No 17: First Regulation implementing Articles 85 and 86 of the Treaty, OJ 1962 English special edition: Series I Volume 1959-1962 P. 87 .... 9.014
    EEC Council: Regulation No 26 applying certain rules of competition to production of and trade in agricultural products, OJ 1962 English special edition: Series I Volume 1959-1962 P. 129 .... 9.003

1965 Regulation No 19/65/EEC of 2 March of the Council on application of Article 85 (3) of the Treaty to certain categories of agreements and concerted practices, OJ English special edition: Series I Volume 1965-1966 P. 35 .... 9.016

1968 Regulation (EEC, Euratom, ECSC) No 259/68 of the Council of 29 February 1968 laying down the Staff Regulations of Officials and the Conditions of Employment of Other Servants of the European Communities and instituting special measures temporarily applicable to officials of the Commission (Staff Regulations of Officials), OJ 1968 English special edition: Series I Volume 1968(I) P. 30 .... 14.022
    Regulation (EEC, Euratom, ECSC) No 260/68 of the Council of 29 February 1968 laying down the conditions and procedure for applying the tax for the benefit of the European Communities, OJ English special edition: Series I Volume 1968(I) P. 37 .... 14.010, 14.014
    Regulation (EEC) No 950/68 of the Council of 28 June 1968 on the common customs tariff, OJ 1968 English Special Edition (I), 275 .... 7.024
    Regulation (EEC) No. 1612/68 of the Council of 15 October 1968 on freedom of movement for workers within the Community, OJ 1968 English special edition: Series I Volume 1968(II) P. 475 .... 6.010, 7.049, 7.060

1969 Regulation (EEC) No 543/69 of the Council of 25 March 1969 on the harmonisation of certain social legislation relating to road transport, OJ 1969 L77/49 .... 5.019
    Regulation (EEC) No. 2603/69 of 20 December 1969 of the Council establishing common rules for exports, OJ 1969 English Special Edition (II) 590 .... 10.006

1970 Regulation (EEC) No. 1251/70 of the Commission of 29 June 1970 on the right of workers to remain in the territory of a Member State after having been employed in that State, OJ 1970 English Special Edition (II) 402 .... 7.057

1971 Regulation (EEC) No. 1408/71 of the Council of 14 June 1971 on the application of social security schemes to employed persons and their families moving within the Community, OJ 1971 English Special Edition (II) 416 ....7.078, 26.009

Regulation (EEC) No 2821/71 of the Council of 20 December 1971 on application of Article 85 (3) of the Treaty to categories of agreements, decisions and concerted practices, OJ English special edition: Series I Volume 1971(III) P. 1032 .... 9.016

1972 Regulation (EEC) No 574/72 of the Council of 21 March 1972 fixing the procedure for implementing Regulation (EEC) No 1408/71 on the application of social security schemes to employed persons and their families moving within the Community, OJ 1972 English Special Edition (I) 159 .... 7.078

1973 Regulation (EEC) No. 907/73 of the Council of 3 April 1973 establishing a European Monetary Cooperation Fund, OJ 1973 L89/2 .... 1.034

1975 Regulation (EC) No. 337/75 of the Council of 10 February 1975 establishing a European Centre for the Development of Vocational Training, OJ 1975 L39/1...............9.052, 13.046

Regulation (EC) No. 1365/75 of the Council of 26 May 1975 on the creation of a European Foundation for the improvement of living and working conditions, OJ 1975 L139/1..............9.047, 13.046

1978 Council Regulation (EEC) No. 3180/78 of 18 December 1978 changing the value of the unit of account used by the European Monetary Cooperation Fund, OJ 1978 L379/ 1) 1.035

Council Regulation (EEC) No. 3181/78 of 18 December 1978 relating to the European Monetary System, OJ 1978 L379/2............... 1.035

1980 Council Regulation (EEC, Euratom) No 3308/80 of 16 December 1980 on the replacement of the European unit of account by the ECU in Community legal instruments, OJ 1980 L 345/1............. 1.036

1981 Council Regulation (EEC) No. 3245/81 of 26 October 1981 setting up a European Agency for Cooperation, OJ 1981 L328/1................... 13.046

1983 Council Regulation (EEC, Euratom) No 354/83 of 1 February 1983 concerning the opening to the public of the historical archives of the European Economic Community and the European Atomic Energy Community, OJ 1983 L43/1 .... 14.031

1986 Regulation (EC) No. 4055/86 of 22 December 1986 applying the principle of freedom to provide services to maritime transport between Member States and between Member States and third countries, OJ 1986 L378/1....... 9.009

1987 Council Regulation (EEC) No. 2658/87 of 23 July 1987 on the tariff and statistical nomenclature and on the Common Customs Tariff, OJ 1987 L256/1 .... 7.024

1988 Council Regulation (EC) No. 2052/88 of 24 June 1988 on the tasks of the Structural Funds and their effectiveness and on the coordination of their activities between themselves and with the operations of the European Investment Bank and the other existing financial instruments, OJ 1988 L185/9 .... 9.031

1989 Council Regulation (EEC) No 4064/89 of 21 December 1989 on the control of concentrations between undertakings, OJ 1989 L395/1 .... 9.018

1990 Council Regulation (EEC) No. 1210/90 of 7 May 1990 on the establishment of the European Environment Agency and the European Environment Information and Observation Network, OJ 1990 L120/1.... 13.046

	Council Regulation (EEC) No. 1360/90 of 7 May 1990 establishing a European Training Foundation, OJ 1990 L131/1 ....13.046		(EEC) No 3831/90, (EEC) No 3832/90, (EEC) No 3833/90, (EEC) No 3834/90, (EEC) No 3835/90 and (EEC) No 3900/91 applying generalized tariff preferences for 1991 in respect of certain products originating in developing countries, and adding to the list of beneficiaries of such preferences, OJ 1992 L396/1 .... 17.035
1991	Council Regulation (EEC) No 1534/91 of 31 May 1991 on the application of Article 85 (3) of the Treaty to certain categories of agreements, decisions and concerted practices in the insurance sector, OJ 1991 L143/1..................... 9.016		
	Council Regulation (EEC) No. 1911/91 of 26 June 1991 on the application of the provisions of Community law to the Canary Islands, OJ 1991 L171/1 ..... 11.007	1993	Council Regulation (EEC) No. 1608/93 of 24 June 1993 introducing an embargo concerning certain trade between the European Economic Community and Haiti, OJ 1993 L155/2 .... 21.006
	Council Regulation (EC) No. 3921/91 of 16 December 1991 laying down the conditions under which non-resident carriers may transport goods or passengers by inland waterway within a Member State, OJ 1991 L373/1..................... 9.010		Council Regulation (EEC) No. 2309/93 of 22 July 1993 laying down Community procedures for the authorization and supervision of medicinal products for human and veterinary use and establishing a European Agency for the Evaluation of Medicinal Products, OJ 1993 L214/1.... 13.046
	Council Regulation (EEC) No. 3300/91 of 11 November 1991 suspending the trade concessions provided for by the Cooperation Agreement between the European Economic Community and the Socialist Federal Republic of Yugoslavia, OJ 1991 L315/1.... 21.006	1994	Council Regulation (EC) 40/94 of 20 December 1993 on the Community trademark (OJ 1994 L11/1) .... 7.109, 13.046 Art 115(2) 14.029
1992	Council Regulation (EEC) No. 1768/92 of 18 June 1992 concerning the creation of a supplementary protection certificate for medicinal products, OJ 1992 L182/1..... 7.109		Council Regulation (EC) No. 1131/94 of 16 May 1994 amending Regulation (EEC) No 337/75 establishing a European Centre for the Development of Vocational Training, OJ 1994 L127/1.................... 13.046
	Council Regulation (EEC) No. 2913/92 of 12 October 1992 establishing the Community Customs Code, OJ 1992 L302/1 7.025		Council Regulation (EC) No. 2062/94 of 18 July 1994 establishing a European Agency for Safety and Health at Work, OJ 1994 L216/1...............9.047, 13.046
	Council Regulation (EC) No. 3577/92 of 7 December 1992 applying the principle of freedom to provide sevices to maritime transport within Member States (maritime cabotage), OJ 1992 L364/7 .... 9.009		Council Regulation (EC) No. 2100/94 of 27 July 1994 on Community plant variety rights, OJ 1994 L227/1 ....7.109, 13.046 Art 34(2) .... 14.029 Art 34(3) 14.029
	Council Regulation (EEC) No 3917/92 of 21 December 1992 extending into 1993 the application of Regulations		Council Regulation (EC) No. 2965/94 of 28 November 1994 setting up a Translation Centre for

bodies of the European Union, OJ 1994 L314/1 .... 13.046
Council Regulation (EC) No. 3285/94 of 22 December 1994 on the common rules for imports and repealing Regulation (EC) No 518/94, OJ 1994 L349/53 ...... 10.006
Council Regulation (EC) No. 3381/94 of 19 December 1994 setting up a Community regime for the control of exports of dual-use goods, OJ 1994 L367/1 ...... 10.006

1995 Council Regulation (EC) No. 1683/95 of 29 May 1995 laying down a uniform format for visas, OJ 1995 L164/1 .... 8.007
Council Regulation (EC) No 2506/95 of 25 October 1995 amending Regulation (EC) No 2100/94 on Community plant variety rights, OJ 1995 L258/3 ...... 13.046
Council Regulation (EC, Euratom) No 2988/95 of 18 December 1995 on the protection of the European Communities financial interests, OJ 1995 L312/1 .... 20.013

1996 Council Regulation (EC) No. 384/96 of 22 December 1995 on protection against dumped imports from countries not members of the European Community, OJ 2009 L323/48
    Art 11(2) 27.004
Council Regulation (EC) No. 1356/96 of 8 July 1996 on protection against dumped imports from countries not members of the European Community, OJ 1996 L175/7 .... 9.010
Council Regulation (EC) No. 1488/96 of 23 July 1996 on financial and technical measures to accompany the reform of economic and social structures in the framework of the Euro-Mediterranean partnership (MEDA), OJ 1996 L189/1 .... 10.018
Regulation (EC) No. 1610/96 of the European Parliament and of the Council of 23 July 1996 concerning the creation of a supplementary protection certificate for plant protection products, OJ 1996 L198/30 ..... 7.109

1997 Council Regulation (EC) No. 552/97 of 24 March 1997 temporarily withdrawing access to generalized tariff preferences from the Union of Myanmar, OJ 1997 L85/8 .... 10.006
Council Regulation (EC) No. 1466/97 of 7 July 1997 on the strengthening of the surveillance of budgetary positions and the surveillance and coordination of economic policies, OJ 1997 L209/1
    Art 2a 9.039
    Art 5 .... 9.038
    Art 5(2) 9.039
    Art 6 .... 9.039
    Art 10 .... 9.039
Council Regulation (EC) No. 1035/97 of 2 June 1997 establishing a European Monitoring Centre on Racism and Xenophobia, OJ 1997 L151/1 .... 13.046
Council Regulation (EC) No 1466/97 of 7 July 1997 on the strengthening of the surveillance of budgetary positions and the surveillance and coordination of economic policies, OJ 1997 L209/1 ...... 9.038
Council Regulation (EC) No. 1467/97 of 7 July 1997 on speeding up and clarifying the implementation of the excessive deficit procedure, OJ 1997 L209/6 .... 9.038
    Art 11 .... 9.040
    Art 12 .... 9.040

1998 Council Regulation (EC) No. 974/98 of 3 May 1998 on the introduction of the euro, OJ 1998 L139/1
    Art 10 .... 9.045
Commission Regulation (EC) No. 975/98 of 3 May 1998 establishing the standard import values for determining the entry price of certain fruit and vegetables, OJ 1998 L139/6 .... 9.045
Council Regulation (EC) No. 2532/98 of 23 November 1998 concerning the powers of the European Central Bank to impose sanctions, OJ 1998 L318/4 .... 13.020

Council Regulation (EC) No. 2679/98 of 7 December 1998 on the functioning of the internal market in relation to the free movement of goods among the Member States, OJ 1998 L337/8 .... 7.013

Council Regulation (EC) No. 2866/98 of 31 December 1998 on the conversion rates between the euro and the currencies of the Member States adopting the euro, OJ 1998 L359/1 ... 1.036, 9.033

1999 Council Regulation (EC) No. 659/1999 of 22 March 1999 laying down detailed rules for the application of Article 93 EC Treaty, OJ 1999 L83/1 .... 9.024, 9.026

Regulation (EC) No. 1073/1999 of the European Parliament and the Council of 25 May 1999 concerning investigations conducted by the European Anti-Fraud Office (OLAF), OJ 1999 L136/1 .... 20.013

Council Regulation (EC) No. 1215/1999, OJ 1999 L148/1 of 10 June 1999 amending Regulation No 19/65/EEC on the application of Article 81(3) of the Treaty to certain categories of agreements and concerted practices 9.016

European Central Bank Regulation (EC) No. 2157/1999 of 23 September 1999 on the powers of the European Central Bank to impose sanctions, OJ 1999 L264/21 .... 13.020

Council Regulation (EC) No. 2454/1999 of 15 November 1999 amending Regulation (EC) No 1628/96 relating to aid for Bosnia and Herzegovina, Croatia, the Federal Republic of Yugoslavia and the former Yugoslav Republic of Macedonia, in particular by the setting up of a European Agency for Reconstruction, OJ 1999 L299/1 .... 13.046

2000 Council Regulation (EC) No. 1009/2000 of 8 May 2000 concerning capital increases of the European Central Bank, OJ 2000 L115/1 .... 13.019

Council Regulation (EC) No. 1334/2000 of 22 June 2000 setting up a Community regime for the control of exports of dual-use items and technology, OJ 2000 L159/1 .... 10.006, 13.019

Council Regulation (EC) No. 1346/2000 of 29 May 2000 on insolvency proceedings, OJ 2000 L160/1 .... 8.015

Council Regulation (EC) No. 1347/2000 of 29 May 2000 on jurisdiction and the recognition and enforcement of judgments in matrimonial matters and in matters of parental responsibility for children of both spouses, OJ 2000 L160/19; corrigendum in OJ 2000 C219/6 .... 8.015

Council Regulation (EC) No. 1348/2000 of 29 May 2000 on the service in the Member States of judicial and extrajudicial documents in civil or commercial matters, OJ 2000 L160/37 .... 8.015

Council Regulation (EC) No. 1478/2000 of 19 June 2000 amending Regulation (EC) No 2866/98 on the conversion rates between the euro and the currencies of the Member States adopting the euro, OJ 2000 L167/1 .... 9.033

Council Regulation (EC) No. 2667/2000 of 5 December 2000 on the European Agency for Reconstruction, OJ 2000 L306/7 .... 13.046

Council Regulation (EC) No. 2725/2000 of 11 December 2000 concerning the establishment of 'Eurodac' for the comparison of fingerprints for the effective application of the Dublin Convention, OJ 2000 L316/1 ... 8.010

2001 Council Regulation (EC) No. 44/2001 of 22 December 2000 on jurisdiction and the recognition and enforcement of judgments in civil and commercial matters, OJ 2001 L12/1 .... 8.015, 28.018

Regulation (EC) No. 45/2001 of the European Parliament and the Council of 18 December 2000 on the protection of

individuals with regard to the processing of personal data by the Community institutions and bodies and on the free movement of such data, OJ 2001 L8/1 ....9.002, 13.043
Council Regulation (EC) No. 539/2001 of 15 March 2001 listing the third countries whose nationals must be in possession of visas when crossing the external borders and those whose nationals are exempt from that requirement, OJ 2001 L81/1.......... 8.007, 8.027–8.028
Regulation (EC) No. 1049/2001 of the European Parliament and of the Council of 30 May 2001 regarding public access to European Parliament, Council and Commission documents, OJ 2001 L145/43 .... 14.030
   Art 4................14.031, 21.006
   Art 6(1) 14.031
   Art 9................14.030, 21.006
Council Regulation (EC) No. 1206/2001 of 28 May 2001 on cooperation between the courts of the Member States in the taking of evidence in civil or commercial matters, OJ 2001 L174/1 .... 8.015
Council Regulation (EC) No. 1338/2001 of 28 June 2001 laying down measures necessary for the protection of the euro against counterfeiting, OJ 2001 L181/6 .... 9.045
Council Regulation (EC) No. 1339/2001 of 28 June 2001 extending the effects of Regulation (EC) No 1338/2001 laying down measures necessary for the protection of the euro against counterfeiting to those Member States which have not adopted the euro as their single currency, OJ 2001 L181/11.... 9.045
Council Regulation (EC) No. 1515/2001 of 23 July 2001 on the measures that may be taken by the Community following a report adopted by the WTO Dispute Settlement Body concerning anti-dumping and anti-subsidy matters, OJ 2001 L201/10.................. 10.011
Council Regulation (EC) No. 2157/2001 of 8 October 2001 on the Statute for a European company (SE), OJ 2001 L294/1 .... 7.075
Council Regulation (EC) No. 2424/2001 of 6 December 2001 on the Schengen Information System, OJ 2001 L328/4..... 8.028

2002 Council Regulation (EC) No. 6/2002 of 12 December 2001 on Community designs, OJ 2002 L3/1 .... 7.109
   Art 98..................... 14.029
Regulation (EC) No. 178/2002 of the European Parliament and of the Council of 28 January 2002 laying down the general principles and requirements of food law, establishing the European Food Safety Authority, and laying down procedures in matters of food safety, OJ 2002 L31/1................ 9.055, 13.046
Regulation (EC) No. 733/2002 of the European Parliament and of the Council of 22 April 2002 on the implementation of the .eu Top Level Domain, OJ 2002 L113/1.................... 9.058
Council Regulation (EC) No. 743/2002 of 25 April 2002 established a general Community framework of activities to facilitate the implementation of judicial cooperation in civil matters, OJ 2002 L115/1 .... 8.018
Council Regulation (EC) No. 1030/2002 of 13 June 2002 laying down a uniform format for residence permits for third-country nationals, OJ 2002 L157/1.................... 8.012
Regulation (EC) No. 1406/2002 of the European Parliament and of the Council of 27 June 2002 establishing a European Maritime Safety Agency, OJ 2002 L208/1 .... 13.046
Regulation (EC) No. 1592/2002 of the European Parliament and

TABLE OF EUROPEAN UNION ACTS cxix

of the Council of 15 July 2002
on common rules in the field of
civil aviation and establishing
a European Aviation Safety
Agency, OJ 2002 L240/1 . . . . . 13.046
Regulation (EC) No. 2012/2002 of
11 November 2002 establishing
the European Union Solidarity
Fund, OJ 2002 L311/3 . . . . 9.057

2003 Council Regulation (EC) No. 1/
2003 of 16 December 2002 on
the implementation of the rules
on competition laid down in
Articles 81 and 82 of the Treaty,
OJ 2003 L1/1 . . . . 9.015, 17.038
Art 7(1) 9.016, 12.058
Art 11(4) 14.031
Art 11(6) 9.016
Art 16. . . . . 9.016
Art 17 to 21 . . . . 9.016
Art 23. . . . . 9.016, 14.014
Art 24. . . . . 9.016, 14.014
Art 27. . . . . 9.016
Art 31. . . . . 9.016
Council Regulation (EC) No.
58/2003 of 19 December
2002 laying down the statute
for executive agencies to
be entrusted with certain
tasks in the management of
Community programmes, OJ
2003 L11/1 . . . . 13.047, 18.022
Recitals 4-5 . . . . 18.023
Art 6(1) 18.023
Art 17. . . . . 14.022
Art 22. . . . . 18.024
Council Regulation (EC) No. 343/
2003 of 18 February 2003
establishing the criteria and
mechanisms for determining the
Member State responsible for
examining an asylum application
lodged in one of the Member
States by a third-country national
('Dublin II Regulation), OJ 2003
L50/1. . . . . 8.010, 25.014
Council Regulation (EC) No.
1435/2003 of 22 July 2003 on
the Statute for a European
Cooperative Society (SCE), OJ
2003 L207/1 . . . . 7.075
Regulation (EC) No. 2004/2003 of
the European Parliament and
of the Council of 4 November
2003 on the regulations
governing political parties at
European level and the rules
regarding their funding,
OJ 2003 L297/1 . . . . 12.021
Council Regulation (EC) No. 2201/
2003 of 27 November 2003
concerning jurisdiction and the
recognition and enforcement
of judgments in matrimonial
matters and the matters of
parental responsibility,
OJ 2003 L338/1 . . . . 8.015

2004 Council Regulation (EC) No. 139/
2004 of 20 January 2004 on
the control of concentrations
between undertakings (the EC
Merger Regulation), OJ 2004
L24/1. . . . . 9.018, 9.019
Art 14-15. . . . . 14.014
Regulation (EC) No. 261/2004 of
the European Parliament and
of the Council of 11 February
2004 establishing common
rules on compensation and
assistance to passengers in the
event of denied boarding and
of cancellation or long delay of
flights, OJ 2004 L46/1 . . . . 9.010
Regulation (EC) No. 460/2004 of
the European Parliament and
of the Council of 10 March
2004 establishing the European
Network and Information
Security Agency, OJ 2004
L77/1. . . . . 13.046
Council Regulation (EC,
Euratom) No 723/2004 of 22
March 2004 amending the Staff
Regulations of officials of the
European Communities and
the Conditions of Employment
of other servants of the
European Communities, OJ
2004 L 124/1. . . . . 5.060, 14.023
Regulation (EC) No. 726/2004
of the European Parliament
and of the Council of 31
March 2004 laying down
Community procedures for the
authorisation and supervision
of medicinal products for
human and veterinary use
and establishing a European
Medicines Agency,
OJ 2004 L136/1 . . . . 9.055, 13.046

Commission Regulation (EC)
No. 773/2004 of 7 April 2004
relating to the conduct of
proceedings by the Commission
pursuant to Articles 81 and 82 EC
Treaty, OJ 2004 L123/1 .... 9.016
Commission Regulation (EC)
No, 794/2004 of 21 April
2004 implementing Council
Regulation (EC) No. 659/1999,
OJ 2004 L140/1 .... 9.026
Commission Regulation (EC)
No. 802/2004 of 7 April
2004 implementing Council
Regulation (EC) No. 139/2004
on the control of concentrations
between undertakings, OJ 2004
L133/1 .... 9.018
Regulation (EC) No. 805/2004 of the
European Parliament and of the
Council of 21 April 2004 creating
a European Enforcement Order
for uncontested claims,
OJ 2004 L143/15 .... 8.015
Regulation (EC) No. 851/2004 of
the European Parliament and
of the Council of 21 April
2004 establishing a European
Centre for disease
prevention and control, OJ
2004 L142/1 ....9.055, 13.046
Art 28..................... 18.024
Council Regulation (EC) No. 866/
2004 of 29 April 2004 on a regime
under Article 2 of Protocol (No.
10) of the Act of Accession, OJ
2004 L161/128 (republished with
corrigendum:
OJ 2004 L206/51) 11.008
Regulation (EC) No. 881/2004
of the European Parliament
and of the Council of 29 April
2004 (establishing a European
Railway Agency), OJ 2004
L164/1................... 13.046
Regulation (EC) No. 883/2004 of
the European Parliament and
the Council of 29 April 2004
on the coordination of social
security systems, OJ 2004
L166/1 (republished with
corrigendum: OJ 2004
L200/1)...............7.051, 7.078
Art 4........................ 7.078
Art 11....................... 7.078

Council Regulation (EC)
No. 2007/2004 of 26 October
2004 establishing a European
Agency for the Management
of Operational Cooperation
at the External Borders of
the Member States of the
European Union, OJ 2004
L349/1 .... 8.007, 13.046
Council Regulation (EC) No. 2073/
2004 of 16 November 2004 on
administrative cooperation
in the field of excise duties, OJ
2004 L359/1 .... 7.114

2005 Council Regulation (EC) No
768/2005 of 26 April 2005
establishing a Community
Fisheries Control Agency and
amending Regulation (EEC)
No 2847/93 establishing a
control system applicable to the
common fisheries policy,
OJ 2005 L128/1 .... 13.046
Council Regulation (EC) No. 920/
2005 of 13 June 2005 amending
Regulation No 1 of 15 April 1958
determining the language to be
used by the European Economic
Community and Regulation No
1 of 15 April 1958 determining
the language to be used by
the European Atomic Energy
Community and introducing
temporary derogation measures
from those Regulations, OJ 2005
L156/3..................... 14.025
Council Regulation (EC) No 1055/
2005 of 27 June 2005 amending
Regulation (EC) No 1466/
97 on the strengthening of
the surveillance of budgetary
positions and the surveillance
and coordination of economic
policies, OJ 2005 L174/1....... 9.038
Council Regulation No. 1056/
2005 of 27 June 2005 amending
Regulation (EC) No 1467/97
on speeding up and clarifying
the implementation of the
excessive deficit procedure, OJ
2005 L174/5 .... 9.038

2006 Council Regulation (EC) No. 510/
2006 of 20 March 2006 on the
protection of geographical
indications and designations

of origin for agricultural products and foodstuffs, OJ 2006 L93/12 .... 9.006

Regulation (EC) No. 562/2006 of the European Parliament and of the Council of 15 March 2006 establishing a Community Code on the rules governing the movement of persons across borders (Schengen Borders Code), OJ 2006 L105/1 .... 8.007

Regulation (EC) No. 640/2006 of 10 April 2006 repealing Regulations (EEC) No 3181/78 and (EEC) No 1736/79 concerning the European Monetary System, OJ 2006 L115/1 .... 1.035

Regulation (EC) No. 1081/2006 of the European Parliament and of the Council of 5 July 2006 on the European Social Fund OJ 2006 L210/12 .... 9.047

Regulation (EC) No 1082/2006 of the European Parliament and of the Council of 5 July 2006 on a European grouping of territorial cooperation (EGTC), OJ 2006 L210/19 .... 9.057

Council Regulation (EC) No. 1086/2006 of 11 July 2006 amending Regulation (EC) No 2866/98 on the conversion rates between the euro and the currencies of the Member States adopting the euro, OJ 2006 L195/1 .... 9.033

Council Regulation (EC) No. 1184/2006 of 24 July 2006 applying certain rules of competition to the production of, and trade in, certain agricultural products, OJ 2006 L214/7 .... 9.003

Regulation (EC) No. 1367/2006 of the European Parliament and of the Council of 6 September 2006 on the application of the provisions of the Aarhus Convention on Access to Information, Public Participation in Decision-making and Access to Justice in Environmental Matters to Community institutions and bodies, OJ 2006 L264/13 .... 10.036, 14.031

Regulation (EC) No 1419/2006 of 25 September 2006 repealing Regulation (EEC) No 4056/86 laying down detailed rules for the application of Articles 85 and 86 of the Treaty to maritime transport, and amending Regulation (EC) No 1/2003 as regards the extension of its scope to include cabotage and international tramp services OJ 2006 L269/1 ...... 9.016

Regulation (EC) No. 1638/2006 of the European Parliament and of the Council of 24 October 2006 laying down general provisions establishing a European Neighbourhood and Partnership Instrument, OJ 2006 L310/1 ...... 10.018, 10.025

Council Regulation (EC) No. 1756/2006 of 28 November 2006 amending Regulation (EC) No 2667/2000 on the European Agency for Reconstruction, OJ 2006 L332/18 .... 13.046

Regulation (EC) No. 1896/2006 of the European Parliament and of the Council of 12 December 2006 creating a European order for payment procedure, OJ 2006 L399/1 .... 8.015

Regulation (EC) No. 1907/2006 of the European Parliament and of the Council of 18 December 2006 concerning the Registration, Evaluation, Authorisation and Restriction of Chemicals (REACH), establishing a European Chemicals Agency, OJ 2006 L396/1 .... 13.046
Art 94 .... 18.024

Regulation (EC) No. 1920/2006 of the European Parliament and of the Council of 12 December 2006 on the European Monitoring Centre for Drugs and Drug Addiction, OJ 2006 L376/1 .... 13.046

Regulation (EC) No. 1922/2006 of the European Parliament and of the Council of 20 December 2006 on establishing a European Institute for Gender Equality, OJ 2006 L403/9 .... 13.046

Regulation (EC) No. 1927/2006 of the European Parliament and of the Council of 20 December 2006 on establishing the European Globalisation Adjustment Fund, OJ 2006 L48/82 .... 9.047

Council Regulation (EC) No. 1933/2006 of 21 December 2006 temporarily withdrawing access to the generalized tariff preferences from the Republic of Belarus, OJ 2006 L405/35 ..... 10.006

Regulation (EC) No. 1987/2006 of the European Parliament and of the Council of 20 December 2006 on the establishment, operation, and use of the second generation Schengen Information System (SIS II), OJ 2006 L381/4 .... 8.006

Commission Regulation (EC) No. 1998/2006 of 15 December 2006 on the application of Articles 87 and 88 of the Treaty to de minimis aid, OJ 2006 L379/5.................... 9.021

2007 Council Regulation (EC) No. 168/2007 of 15 February 2007 establishing a European Union Agency for Fundamental Rights, OJ 2007 L53/1 .... 13.047

Council Regulation (EC) No. 834/2007 of 28 June 2007 on organic production and labelling of organic products and repealing Regulation (EC) No. 2092/91, OJ 2007 L189/1 .... 9.006

Regulation (EC) No. 861/2007 of the European Parliament and of the Council of 11 July 2007 establishing a European Small Claims Procedure, OJ 2007 L199/1.................... 8.015

Regulation (EC) No. 864/2007 of the European Parliament and of the Council of 11 July 2007 on the law applicable to non-contractual obligations (Rome II), OJ 2007 L199/40 .... 8.016

Council Regulation (EC) No. 1134/2007 of 10 July 2007 amending Regulation (EC) No 2866/98 as regards the conversion rate to the euro for Malta, OJ 2007 L256/1.................... 9.033

Council Regulation (EC) No. 1135/2007 of 10 July 2007 amending Regulation (EC) No 2866/98 as regards the conversion rate to the euro for Cyprus, OJ 2007 L256/2.................... 9.033

Regulation (EC) No. 1371/2007 of the European Parliament and of the Council of 23 October 2007 on rail passengers' rights and obligations, OJ 2007 L315/14................... 9.010

Regulation (EC) No. 1393/2007 of the European Parliament and of the Council of 13 November 2007 on the service in the Member States of judicial and extrajudicial documents in civil or commercial matters, OJ 2007 L324/79 .... 8.015

2008 Regulation (EC) No. 294/2008 of the European Parliament and of the Council of 11 March 2008, OJ 2008 L97/1 .... 13.046

Regulation (EC) No. 593/2008 of the European Parliament and of the Council of 17 June 2008 on the law applicable to contractual obligations (Rome I), OJ 2008 L177/6 ..... 8.016, 28.018

Council Regulation (EC) No. 694/2008 of 8 July 2008 amending Regulation (EC) No 2866/98 as regards the conversion rate to the euro for Slovakia, OJ 2008 L195/3.................... 9.033

Council Regulation (EC) No. 732/2008 applying a scheme of generalised tariff preferences for the period from 1 January 2009 to 31 December 2011 and amending Regulations (EC) No 552/97, (EC) No 1933/2006 and Commission Regulations (EC) No 1100/2006 and (EC) No 964/2007, OJ 2012 L303/1 ... 10.019

Commission Regulation (EC) No. 800/2008 of 6 August 2008 declaring certain categories of aid compatible with the common market in application of Articles 87 and 88 of the Treaty (General block exemption Regulation), OJ 2008 L214/3 .... 9.021

2009 Regulation (EC) No. 1008/2008 of the European Parliament and of the Council of 24 September 2008 on common rules for the operation of air services in the Community, OJ 2008 L293/3 ... 9.009
Regulation (EC) No. 1339/2008 of the European Parliament and of the Council of 16 December 2008 establishing a European Training Foundation, OJ 2008 L354/82 .... 9.052, 13.046
Regulation (EC) No. 4/2009 of 18 December 2008 on jurisdiction, applicable law, recognition and enforcement of decisions and cooperation in matters relating to maintenance obligations, OJ 2009 L7/1 .... 1.037, 8.015
Council Regulation (EC) No. 169/2009 of 26 February 2009 applying rules of competition to transport by rail, road and inland waterway, OJ 2009 L61/1 .... 9.006
Council Regulation (EC) No. 207/2009 on the European Union trademark, OJ 2009 L78/1 Art 119(3) 14.029
Council Regulation (EC) 246/2009 of 26 February 2006 on the application of Article 81(3) of the Treaty to certain categories of agreements, decisions and concerted practices between liner shipping companies (consortia) OJ 2009 L79/1 .... 9.009, 9.016
Council Regulation (EC) No. 260/2009 of 26 February 2009 on the common rules for imports, OJ 2009 L84/1 ...... 10.006
Regulation (EC) No. 401/2009 of the European Parliament and of the Council of 23 April 2009 on the European Environment Agency and the European Environment Information and Observation Network, OJ 2009 L126/13 .... 9.062, 13.046
Council Regulation (EC) No. 428/2009 of 5 May 2009 setting up a Community regime for the control of exports, transfer, brokering, and transit of dual-use items, OJ 2009 L134/1 ... 10.006
Art 26 .... 11.011

Regulation (EC) No. 469/2009 of the European Parliament and of the Council of 6 May 2009 concerning the supplementary protection certificate for medicinal products, OJ 2009 L152/1 .... 7.109
Council Regulation (EC) No. 487/2009 of 25 May 2009 on the application of Article 81(3) of the Treaty to certain categories of agreements and concerted practices in the air transport sector, OJ 2009 L1481 .... 9.016
Council Regulation (EC) No. 597/2009 of 11 June 2009 on protection against subsidized imports from countries not members of the European Community, OJ 2009 L188/93 .... 10.007
Regulation (EC) No. 662/2009 of the European Parliament and of the Council establishing a procedure for the negotiation and conclusion of agreements between Member States and third countries on particular matters concerning the law applicable to contractual and non-contractual obligations, OJ 2009 L200/25 .... 8.014
Council Regulation (EC) No. 664/2009 of 7 July 2009 establishing a procedure for the negotiation and conclusion of agreements between Member States and third countries concerning jurisdiction, recognition, and enforcement of judgments and decisions in matrimonial matters, matters of parental responsibility, and matters relating to maintenance obligations, and the law applicable to matters relating to maintenance obligations, OJ 2009 L200/46 .... 8.014
Regulation (EC) No. 810/2009 of the European Parliament and of the Council of 13 July 2009 establishing a Community Code on Visas (Visa Code), OJ 2009 L243/1 .... 8.007
Commission Regulation (EC) No. 906/2009 on the application of

Article 81(3) of the Treaty to certain categories of agreements, decisions and concerted practices between liner shipping companies (consortia), OJ 2009 L256/31 .... 9.016

Regulation (EC) No. 987/2009 of the European Parliament and of the Council of 16 September 2009 laying down the procedure for implementing Regulation (EC) No 883/2004 on the coordination of social security systems, OJ 2009 L284/1 .... 7.078

Council Regulation (EC) No.1061/2009 of 19 October 2009 establishing common rules for exports, OJ 2009 L291/1 ..... 10.006

Regulation (EC) No. 1072/2009 of the European Parliament and of the Council of 21 October 2009 on common rules for access to the international road haulage market, OJ 2009 L300/72 .... 9.009–9.010

Regulation (EC) No. 1073/2009 of the European Parliament and of the Council of 21 October 2009 on common rules for access to the international market for coach and bus services, and amending Regulation (EC) No 561/2006, OJ 2009 L300/88. .... 9.009–9.010

Council Implementing Regulation (EU) No. 1202/2009 of 7 December 2009 imposing a definitive anti- dumping duty on imports of furfuryl alcohol originating in the People's Republic of China following an expiry review pursuant to Article 11(2) of Regulation (EC) No. 384/96, OJ 2009 L323/48 .... 27.004

Council Regulation (EC) No. 1225/2009 of 30 November 2009 on protection against dumped imports from countries not members of the European Community, OJ 2009 L343/51 .... 10.007

Council Regulation (EU) No. 1286/2009 of 22 December 2009 amending Regulation (EC) No. 881/2002 imposing certain specific restrictive measures directed against certain persons and entities associated with Usama bin Laden, the Al-Qaida network and the Taliban, OJ 2009 L346/42 .... 19.003

2010 Commission Regulation (EU) No. 267/2010 of 24 March 2010 on the application of Article 101(3) of the Treaty on the Functioning of the European Union to certain categories of agreements, decisions and concerted practices in the insurance sector, OJ 2010 L83/1 .... 9.016

Commission Regulation (EU) No. 330/2010 of 20 April 2010 on the application of Article 101(3) of the Treaty on the Functioning of the European Union to categories of vertical agreements and concerted practices, OJ 2010 L102/1..... 9.016

Council Regulation (EU) No. 407/2010 of 11 May 2010 establishing a European financial stabilisation mechanism, OJ 2010 L118/1 ... 9.037

Regulation (EU) No. 439/2010 of the European Parliament and the Council of 19 May 2010 establishing a European Asylum Support Office, OJ 2010 L132/11 .... 13.046

Commission Regulation (EU) No. 461/2010 of 27 May 2010 on the application of Article 101(3) of the Treaty on the Functioning of the European Union to categories of vertical agreements and concerted practices in the motor vehicle sector, OJ 2010 L129/52 ...... 9.016

Council Regulation (EU) No. 671/2010 of 13 July 2010 amending Regulation (EC) No 2866/98 as regards the conversion rate to the euro for Estonia, OJ 2010 L196/4..................... 9.033

Regulation (EU) No 912/2010 of the European Parliament and of the Council of 22 September

TABLE OF EUROPEAN UNION ACTS   cxxv

2010 setting up the European
  GNSS Agency, repealing Council
  Regulation (EC) No 1321/2004
  on the establishment of structures
  for the management of the
  European satellite radio navigation
  programmes and amending
  Regulation (EC) No 683/2008 of
  the European Parliament and of the
  Council, OJ 2010 L276/11 . . . . . 13.046
Regulation (EU) No. 1093/2010
  of the European Parliament
  and of the Council of 24
  November 2010 establishing
  a European Supervisory
  Authority (European Banking
  Authority), amending Decision
  No 716/2009/EC and repealing
  Commission Decision
  2009/78/EC, OJ 2010
  L331/12. . . . . 9.042, 13.046
    Art 58. . . . . 18.024
Regulation (EU) No. 1094/2010
  of the European Parliament
  and of the Council of 24
  November 2010 establishing
  a European Supervisory
  Authority (European Insurance
  and Occupational Pensions
  Authority), amending Decision
  No 716/2009/EC and repealing
  Commission Decision
  2009/79/EC, OJ 2010
  L 331/48 . . . . .9.042, 13.046
Regulation (EU) No. 1095/2010 of
  the European Parliament and
  of the Council of 24 November
  2010 establishing a European
  Supervisory Authority
  (European Securities and
  Markets Authority), amending
  Decision No 716/2009/EC
  and repealing Commission
  Decision 2009/77/EC, OJ 2010
  L331 . . . . 9.042
Regulation (EU) No. 1177/2010 of
  the European Parliament and
  of the Council of 24 November
  2010 concerning the rights of
  passengers when travelling by
  sea and inland waterway, OJ
  2010 L334/1 . . . . 9.010
Commission Regulation (EU) No
  1217/2010 of 14 December
  2010 on the application of
  Article 101(3) of the Treaty
  on the Functioning of the
  European Union to certain
  categories of research and
  development agreements, OJ
  2010 L335/36 . . . . 9.016
Commission Regulation (EU) No
  1218/2010 of 14 December 2010
  on the application of Article
  101(3) of the Treaty on the
  Functioning of the European
  Union to certain categories of
  specialisation agreements, OJ
  2010 L335/43 . . . . 9.016
Council Regulation (EU) No.
  1259/2010 of 20 December
  2010 implementing enhanced
  cooperation in the area of the
  law applicable to divorce and
  legal separation, OJ 2010
  L343/10 . . . . . . 8.016, 22.007, 22.013

2011 Regulation (EU) No. 181/2011 of
  the European Parliament and
  of the Council of 16 February
  2011 concerning the rights of
  passengers in bus and coach
  transport, OJ 2011
  L55/1 . . . . 9.010
Regulation (EU) No 182/2011
  of the European Parliament
  and of the Council of 16
  February 2011 laying down the
  rules and general principles
  concerning mechanisms for
  control by Member States of
  the Commission's exercise
  of implementing powers
  (Comitology Regulation), OJ
  2011 L55/13 . . . . 18.010,
                    18.012, 18.014–18.015
    Art 2. . . . . 18.015
    Art 2(3) 18.015
    Art 3. . . . . 18.015
    Art 3(3) 18.015
    Art 4. . . . . 18.016
    Art 5(2) 18.017
    Art 5(3) 18.017
    Art 5(4) 18.017
    Art 5(5) 18.017
    Art 6(3) 18.017
    Art 8. . . . . 18.014
    Art 9(2) 18.014
    Art 10. . . . . 18.014
    Art 10(4) 18.018
    Art 11. . . . . 18.018

TABLE OF EUROPEAN UNION ACTS

Art 12.................... 18.019
Art 13.............. 18.011, 18.019
Regulation (EU) No. 211/2011 of the European Parliament and of the Council of 16 February 2011 on the citizens' initiative, OJ 2011 L65/1
   Art 4..................... 17.013
   Art 7..................... 17.013
   Art 10.................... 17.013
   Annex I 17.013
Regulation 492/2011 of 5 April 2011 on freedom of movement for workers within the Union OJ 2011 L141/1 ....7.060, 7.061
   Art 7(1) 7.060
   Art 7(2) 7.060
   Art 7(3) 7.060
   Art 8(1) 7.060
   Art 9 .... 7.060
   Art 10 6.014, 7.060
Regulation (EU) No 1173/2011 of the European Parliament and of the Council of 16 November 2011 on the effective enforcement of budgetary surveillance in the euro area, OJ 2011 L306/1
   Arts 4–6.................... 9.040
Council Regulation (EU) No. 1177/2011 of 8 November 2011 amending Regulation (EC) No 1467/97 on speeding up and clarifying the implementation of the excessive deficit procedure.................. 9.038
Council Regulation (EU) No. 1295/2011 of 13 December 2011 amending Regulation (EU) No. 1284/2009 imposing certain specific restrictive measures in respect of the Republic of Guinea, OJ 2011 L330/1 ..... 19.003

2012 Commission Delegated Regulation (EU) No. 268/2012 of 25 January 2012 amending Annex I of Regulation (EU) No. 211/2011 of the European Parliament and of the Council on the citizens' initiative, OJ 2012 L89/1 .... 17.013
Regulation (EU) No. 650/2012 of the European Parliament and of the Council of 4 July 2012 on jurisdiction, applicable law, recognition, and enforcement of decisions and acceptance and enforcement of authentic instruments in matters of succession and on the creation of a European Certificate of Succession, OJ 2012 L201/107 .....8.015
Regulation (EU) No. 651/2012 of the European Parliament and of the Council of 4 July 2012 on the issuance of euro coins, OJ 2012 L201/135.............. 9.045
Regulation (EU) No. 978/2012 of the European Parliament and of the Council of 25 October 2012 applying a scheme of generalized tariff preferences, OJ 2012 L303/1 .... 10.006
   Art 17..................... 10.019
   Art 18..................... 10.019
Regulation (EU, Euratom) No 966/2012 of the European Parliament and of the Council of 25 October 2012 on the financial rules applicable to the general budget of the Union and repealing Council Regulation (EC, Euratom) No 1605/2002, OJ 2012 L298/1..............13.028, 14.010
Regulation (EU) No. 1151/2012 of the European Parliament and of the Council of 21 November 2012 on quality schemes for agricultural products and foodstuffs, OJ 2012 L343/1.... 9.006
Regulation (EU) No. 1215/2012 of the European Parliament and of the Council of 12 December 2012 on jurisdiction and the recognition and enforcement of judgments in civil and commercial matters, OJ 2012L351/1 ....1.037, 8.015
Regulation (EU) No. 1219/2012 of the European Parliament and of the Council of 12 December 2012 establishing transitional arrangements for bilateral investment agreements between Member States and third countries, OJ 2012 L351/40.............. 10.005
Regulation (EU) No. 1257/2012 of the European Parliament and

of the Council of 17 December 2012 implementing enhanced cooperation in the area of the creation of unitary patent protection, OJ 2012 L361/1..............7.109, 22.007
Regulation (EU) No. 1260/2012 of 17 December 2012 implementing enhanced cooperation in the area of the creation of unitary patent protection with regard to the applicable translation arrangements, OJ 2012 L361/89.........7.109, 22.007

2013 Regulation (EU) No. 347/2013 of the European Parliament and of the Council of 17 April 2013 on guidelines for trans-European energy infrastructure and repealing Decision No 1364/2006/EC and amending Regulations (EC) No 713/2009, (EC) No 714/2009 and (EC) No 715/2009, OJ 2013 L115/39.... 9.058
Council Regulation (EU) No 401/2013 of 2 May 2013 concerning restrictive measures in respect of Myanmar/Burma and repealing Regulation (EC) No 194/2008, OJ 2013 L121/1 ... 19.003
Regulation No. 472/2013 of the European Parliament and the Council of 21 May 2013 on the strengthening of economic and budgetary surveillance of Member States in the euro area experiencing or threatened with serious difficulties with respect to their financial stability, OJ 2013 L140/1...... 9.039
Regulation (EU) No 473/2013 of the European Parliament and of the Council of 21 May 2013 on common provisions for monitoring and assessing draft budgetary plans and ensuring the correction of excessive deficit of the Member States in the euro area, OJ L 141/11 .... 9.039
Arts 4-7 .... 9.039
Regulation (EU) No. 524/2013 of the European Parliament and of the Council of 21 May 2013 on online dispute resolution for consumer disputes ('Regulation on consumer ODR'), OJ 2013 L165/1.................... 9.056
Regulation (EU) No. 575/2013 of 26 June 2013 of the European Parliament and of the Council on prudential requirements for credit institutions and investment firms, OJ 2013L176/338........... 7.075
Regulation (EU) No. 603/2013 of the European Parliament and of the Council of 26 June 2013 on the establishment of 'Eurodac' for the comparison of fingerprints for the effective application of Regulation (EU) No. 604/2013 and on requests for the comparison with Eurodac data by Member States' law enforcement authorities and Europol for law enforcement purposes, OJ 2013 L180/1 .... 8.010
Regulation (EU) No. 604/2013 of the European Parliament and of the Council of 26 June 2013 establishing the criteria and mechanisms for determining the Member State responsible for examining an application for international protection lodged in one of the Member States by a third-country national or a stateless person ('Dublin III Regulation'), OJ 2013 L180/31................ 8.010
Preamble, Recital 41.......... 8.028
Art 3(2) 8.010
Regulation (EU) No. 606/2013 of the European Parliament and of the Council of 12 June 2013 on mutual recognition of protection measures in civil matters, OJ 2013 L181/4...... 8.015
Regulation (EU) No. 607/2013 of the European Parliament and of the Council of 12 June 2013 repealing Council Regulation (EC) No 552/97 temporarily withdrawing access to generalised tariff preferences from Myanmar/Burma, OJ L181/13.................. 10.006
Regulation (EU) No. 870/2013 of 9 July 2013 amending Regulation

(EC) No 2866/98 as regards the conversion rate to the euro for Latvia, OJ 2013 L243/1 .... 9.033
Regulation (EU, Euratom) No 883/2013 of the European Parliament and of the Council of 11 September 2013 concerning investigations conducted by the European Anti-Fraud Office (OLAF) and repealing Regulation (EC) No 1073/1999 of the European Parliament and of the Council and Council Regulation (Euratom) No 1074/1999, OJ 2013 L248/1 .... 13.043, 20.013
  Art 15(2) 13.043
  Art 17(2) 13.043
Regulation 952/2013 of 9 October 2013 laying down the Union Customs Code, OJ 2013 L269/1 .... 7.025
  Art 4 .... 11.009
  Art 4(2) 11.009
Regulation (EU) No. 1024/2013 of 15 October 2013 conferring specific tasks on the European Central Bank concerning policies relating to the prudential supervision of credit institutions, OJ 2013 L287/63 .... 9.042, 13.020
  Art 26 .... 13.021
Regulation (EU) No. 1052/2013 of the European Parliament and of the Council of 22 October 2013 establishing the European Border Surveillance System (Eurosur), OJ 2013 L295/11 ... 8.007
Regulation (EU) No. 1285/2013 of the European Parliament and of the Council of 11 December 2013, OJ 2013 L347/1 .... 13.045
Regulation (EU) No. 1287/2013 of the European Parliament and of the Council of 11 December 2013 establishing a Programme for the Competitiveness of Enterprises and small and medium-sized enterprises (COSME) (2014–2020), OJ 2013 L347/33 .... 9.059
Regulation (EU) No. 1288/2013 of the European Parliament and of the Council of 11 December 2013 establishing 'Erasmus+': the Union programme for education, training, youth, and sport, OJ 2013 L347/50 .... 9.050
Regulation (EU) No. 1291/2013 of the European Parliament and of the Council of 11 December 2013 establishing Horizon 2020—the Framework Programme for Research and Innovation (2014–2020), OJ 2013 L347/104 .... 9.060
Regulation (EU) No. 1293/2013 of the European Parliament and of the Council of 11 December 2013 on the establishment of a Programme for the Environment and Climate Action (LIFE), OJ 2013 L347/185. .... 9.062
Regulation (EU) No. 1295/2013 of the European Parliament and of the Council of 11 December 2013 establishing the Creative Europe Programme (2014 to 2020), OJ 2013 L347/221 ..... 9.054
Regulation (EU) No. 1300/2013 of the European Parliament and of the Council of 17 December 2013 on the Cohesion Fund, OJ 2013 L347/281 .... 9.057
Regulation (EU) No. 1301/2013 of the European Parliament and of the Council of 17 December 2013 on the European Regional Development Fund and on specific provisions concerning the Investment for growth and jobs goal, OJ 2013 L347/ 289 .... 9.051
Regulation (EU) No. 1303/2013 of the European Parliament and of the Council of 17 December 2013 laying down common provisions on the European Regional Development Fund, the European Social Fund, the Cohesion Fund, the European Agricultural Fund for Rural Development, and the European Maritime and Fisheries Fund and laying down general provisions on the European Regional Development Fund, the European Social Fund, the

Cohesion Fund, and the European Maritime and Fisheries Fund, OJ 2013 L347/320. . . . . 9.057
Regulation (EU) No. 1305/2013 of the European Parliament and of the Council of 17 December 2013 on support for rural development by the European Agricultural Fund for Rural Development (EAFRD), OJ 2013 L347/487 . . . . 9.007
Regulation (EU) No. 1306/2013 of the European Parliament and of the Council of 17 December 2013 on the financing, management, and monitoring of the common agricultural policy, OJ 2013 L347/549
    Art 3(2) 9.005
Regulation (EU) No. 1308/2013 of the European Parliament and of the Council of 17 December 2013 establishing a common organisation of the markets in agricultural products and repealing Council Regulations (EEC) No 922/72, (EEC) No 234/79, (EC) No 1037/2001 and (EC) No 1234/2007, OJ 2013, L347/671. . . . . 9.006
    Arts 206–218. . . . . 9.003
    Art 222. . . . . 9.003
Regulation (EU) No. 1309/2013 of the European Parliament and of the Council of 17 December 2013 on the European Globalisation Adjustment Fund (2014–2020), OJ L2013 L34/855. . . . . 9.057
Council Regulation (EU, Euratom) No 1311/2013 of 2 December 2013 laying down the multiannual financial framework for the years 2014-2020, OJ 2013 L347/884 . . . . . 14.018
Regulation (EU) No. 1315/2013 of the European Parliament and of the Council of 11 December 2013 on Union guidelines for the development of the trans-European transport network and repealing Decision No 661/2010/EU, OJ 2013 L348/1 . . . . . 9.058
Regulation (EU) No. 1316/2013 of the European Parliament and of the Council of 11 December 2013 establishing the Connecting Europe Facility, OJ 2013 L348/129 . . . . 9.059
Regulation (EU) No. 1380/2013 of the European Parliament and of the Council of 11 December 2013 on the Common Fisheries Policy, OJ 2013 L354/22 . . . . . . 9.008
Commission Regulation (EU) No. 1407/2013 of 18 December 2013 on the application of Articles 107 and 108 of the Treaty on the Functioning of the European Union to de minimis aid, OJ 2013 L352/1 . . . . 9.021
Commission Regulation (EU) No. 1408/2013 of 18 December 2013 on the application of Articles 107 and 108 of the Treaty on the Functioning of the European Union to de minimis aid in the agriculture sector, OJ 2013 L352/9 . . . . 9.021

2014 Regulation (EU) No. 230/2014 of the European Parliament and of the Council of 11 March 2014 establishing an instrument contributing to stability and peace, OJ 2014 L77/1. . . . . 10.022
Regulation (EU) No. 232/2014 of the European Parliament and of the Council of 11 March 2014 establishing a European Neighbourhood Instrument, OJ 2014 L77/27 . . . . 10.025
Regulation (EU) No. 233/2014 of the European Parliament and of the Council of 11 March 2014 establishing a financing instrument for development cooperation for the period 2014–2020, OJ 2014 L77/44 . . . 10.022
    Art 2. . . . . 10.022
Regulation (EU) No 250/2014 of the European Parliament and of the Council of 26 February 2014 establishing a programme to promote activities in the field of the protection of the financial interests of the European Union (Hercule III programme), OJ 2014 L84/6 . . . . 20.013
Regulation (EU) No. 254/2014 of the European Parliament and of the Council of 26 February

Regulation (EU) No. 282/2014 of the European Parliament and of the Council of 11 March 2014 on the establishment of a third Programme for the Union's action in the field of health (2014–2020), OJ 2014 L86/1 .... 9.055

Regulation (EU) No. 283/2014 of the European Parliament and of the Council of 11 March 2014 on guidelines for trans-European networks in the area of telecommunications infrastructure and repealing Decision No 1336/97/EC, OJ 2014 L86/14 .... 9.058

Commission Regulation (EU) No. 316/2014 of 21 March 2014 on the application of Article 101(3) of the Treaty on the Functioning of the European Union to categories of technology transfer agreements, OJ 2014 L93/17 .... 9.016

Regulation (EU) No. 375/2014 of the European Parliament and of the Council of 3 April 2014 establishing the European Voluntary Humanitarian Aid Corps ('EU Aid Volunteers initiative'), OJ 2014 L122/1.... 10.023

Regulation (EU) No. 377/2014 of the European Parliament and of the Council of 3 April 2014 establishing the Copernicus Programme, OJ 2014 L122/44 .... 9.060

Council Regulation 390/2014 (EU) of 14 April 2014 establishing the 'Europe for Citizens' programme for the period 2014–2020, OJ 2014L115/3......... 6.004, 9.054

Regulation (EU) No. 468/2014 of the European Central Bank of 16 April 2014 establishing the framework for cooperation within the Single Supervisory Mechanism between the European Central Bank and national competent authorities and with national designated authorities (SSM Framework Regulation), OJ 2014 L141/1 .. 9.042

Regulation (EU) No. 508/2014 of the European Parliament and of the Council of 15 May 2014 on the European Maritime and Fisheries Fund, OJ 2014 L149/1 .... 9.008, 9.057

Regulation (EU) No. 543/2014 of the European Parliament and of the Council of 15 May 2014 amending Council Decision 2005/681/JHA establishing the European Police College (CEPOL), OJ 2014 L163/5 ..... 14.021

Regulation (EU) No 596/2014 of the European Parliament and of the Council of 16 April 2014on market abuse (market abuse regulation) and repealing Directive 2003/6/EC of the European Parliament and of the Council and Commission Directives 2003/124/EC, 2003/125/EC and 2004/72/EC, OJ 2014L173/1 .... 7.075

Commission Regulation (EU) No. 651/2014 of 17 June 2014 declaring certain categories of aid compatible with the internal market in application of Articles 107 and 108 of the Treaty, OJ 2014 L187/1 .... 9.021

Regulation (EU) No. 654/2014 of the European Parliament and of the Council of 15 May 2014 concerning the exercise of the Union's rights for the application and enforcement of international trade rules, OJ 2014 L189/50 .... 10.011

Commission Regulation (EU) No. 702/2014 of 25 June 2014 declaring certain categories of aid in the agricultural and forestry sectors and in rural areas compatible with the internal market in application of Articles 107 and 108 of the Treaty on the Functioning of the European Union, OJ 2014 L193/1..................... 9.021

Commission Regulation (EU) No. 717/2014 of 27 June 2014 on the application of Articles 107 and 108 of the Treaty on the

Functioning of the European
Union to de minimis aid in the
fishery and aquaculture sector,
OJ 2014 L190/45 . . . . 9.021
Council Regulation (EU) No.
729/2014 of 24 June 2014 on
denominations and technical
specifications of euro coins
intended for circulation, OJ
2014 L194/1 . . . . 9.045
Regulation (EU) No. 806/2014 of
the European Parliament and
of the Council of 15 July 2014
establishing uniform rules and
a uniform procedure for the
resolution of credit institutions
and certain investment firms
in the framework of a Single
Resolution Mechanism and a
Single Resolution Fund and
amending Regulation (EU)
No 1093/2010, OJ 2014
L225/1. . . . . .9.042, 13.046
Art 86. . . . . 18.024
Regulation (EU) No. 851/2014
of 23 July 2014 amending
Regulation (EC) No 2866/98 as
regards the conversion rate to
the euro for Lithuania, OJ 2014
L233/21. 9.033
Regulation (EU, Euratom) No
1141/2014 of the European
Parliament and of the
Council of 22 October 2014
on the statute and funding of
European political parties and
European political foundations,
OJ 2014 L317/1 . . . . 12.021
Art 6. . . . . 13.044

2015 Regulation (EU) 2015/476 of the
European Parliament and of the
Council of 11 March 2015 on the
measures that the Union may
take following a report adopted
by the WTO Dispute Settlement
Body concerning anti-dumping
and anti-subsidy matters, OJ
2015 L83/6, replacing Council
Regulation (EC) No. 1515/2001
of 23 July 2001, OJ 2001
L201/10 . . . . 10.011
Regulation (EU) 2015/477 of the
European Parliament and of the
Council of 11 March 2015 on
measures that the Union may
take in relation to the combined
effect of anti-dumping or
anti-subsidy measures with
safeguard measures,
OJ 2015 L83/11 . . . . 10.007
Regulation (EU) 2015/478 of the
European Parliament and of
the Council of 11 March 2015
on common rules for imports,
OJ 2018 L83/16 . . . . . 10.006–10.007
Art 1. . . . . 10.006
Art 24(2) 10.006
Regulation (EU) 2015/479 of the
European Parliament and of
the Council of 11 March 2015
on common rules for exports,
2015 OJ L83/34 . . . . 10.006
Council Regulation (EU) 2015/496
of 17 March 2015 amending
Regulation (EEC, Euratom) No
354/83 as regards the deposit
of the historical archives of the
institutions at the European
University Institute in Florence,
OJ 2015 L79/1 . . . . 14.031
Regulation (EU) 2015/755 of the
European Parliament and of
the Council of 29 April 2015
on common rules for imports
from certain third countries, OJ
2015 L123/33. . . . . 10.007
Regulation (EU) 2015/848 of the
European Parliament and of
the Council of 20 May 2015
on insolvency proceedings, OJ
2015 L141/19. . . . . 8.015
Regulation (EU) 2015/936 of the
European Parliament and of
the Council of 9 June 2015 on
common rules for imports of
textile products from certain
third countries not covered by
bilateral agreements, protocols,
or other arrangements, or by
other specific Union import
rules, OJ 2015 L160/1 . . . . 10.006
Regulation (EU) 2015/1017 of the
European Parliament and of the
Council of 25 June 2015 on the
European Fund for Strategic
Investments, the European
Investment Advisory Hub, and
the European Investment Project
Portal ('European Fund for Strategic
Investments') OJ 2015 L169/1 . . . 9.057
Commission Implementing
Regulation (EU) 2015/1472 of

26 August 2015 on amending
Annex I to Council Regulation
(EC) No 866/2004 on a regime
under Article 2 of Protocol No
10 to the Act of Accession, OJ
2015 L225/3 .... 11.008
Council Regulation (EU) 2015/
1588 of 13 July 2015 on the
application of Articles 107
and 108 of the Treaty on the
Functioning of the European
Union to certain categories of
horizontal State aid, OJ 2015
L248/1 .... 9.021
Council Regulation (EU) 2015/
1589 of 13 July 2015 laying
down detailed rules for the
application of Article 108
TFEU, OJ 2015 L248/9 .... 9.024
Art 1(f) 9.026
Art 4(7) 9.026
Council Regulation (EU) 2015/1755
of 1 October 2015 concerning
restrictive measures in view of
the situation in Burundi,
OJ 2015 L257/1 .... 19.003
Regulation (EU) 2015/2219 of the
European Parliament and of the
Council of 25 November 2015
on the European Union Agency
for Law Enforcement Training
(CEPOL) and replacing and
repealing Council Decision
2005/681/JHA,
OJ 2015 L319/1 ....8.025, 13.046
Council Regulation (EU, Euratom)
2015/2264 of 3 December
2015 extending and phasing
out the temporary derogation
measures from Regulation No
1 of 15 April 1958 determining
the languages to be used by
the European Economic
Community and Regulation No
1 of 15 April 1958 determining
the languages to be used by
the European Atomic Energy
Community introduced by
Regulation (EC) No 920/2005,
OJ 2021 L322/1 .... 14.025
Commission Delegated Regulation
(EU, Euratom) 2015/2401 of 2
October 2015 on the content
and functioning of the Register
of European political parties
and foundations, OJ 2015
L333/50. .... 12.021

2016 Regulation (EU) 2016/399 of the
European Parliament and of
the Council of 9 March 2016
on a Union Code on the rules
governing the movement
of persons across borders
(Schengen Borders Code),
OJ 2016 L77/1 .... 8.007
Regulation (EU) 2016/679 of the
European Parliament and of the
Council of 27 April 2016 on the
protection of natural persons
with regard to the processing
of personal data and on the free
movement of such data
(General Data Protection
Regulation), OJ 2016 L119/1 .. 9.002
Arts 68–76. .... 13.044
Regulation (EU) 2016/793 of the
European Parliament and of
the Council of 11 May 2016 to
avoid trade diversion into the
European Union of certain key
medicines, OJ 2016 L135/39 .. 10.006
Regulation (EU) 2016/794 of the
European Parliament and of the
Council of 11 May 2016 on the
European Union Agency for
Law Enforcement Cooperation
(Europol), OJ 2016
L135/53. .... 8.026, 13.045
Art 64. .... 14.029
Regulation (EU) 2016/796 of the
European Parliament and of
the Council of 11 May 2016 on
the European Union Agency
for Railways and repealing
Regulation (EC) No 881/2004,
OJ 2016 L138/1 .... 13.046
Regulation (EU) 2016/1036 of the
European Parliament and of
the Council of 8 June 2016 on
protection against dumped
imports from countries not
members of the European
Union, OJ 2016 L176/21. .... 10.007
Art 7. .... 10.007
Art 9. .... 10.007
Regulation (EU) 2016/1037 of the
European Parliament and of
the Council of 8 June 2016 on
protection against subsidized
imports from countries not

members of the European Union, OJ 2016 L176/55..... 10.007
Council Regulation (EU) 2016/1103 of 24 June 2016 implementing enhanced cooperation in the area of jurisdiction, applicable law, and the recognition and enforcement of decisions in matters of matrimonial property regimes, OJ 2016 L183/1........ 8.015, 22.007, 22.013
Council Regulation (EU) 2016/1104 of 24 June 2016 implementing enhanced cooperation in the area of jurisdiction, applicable law, and the recognition and enforcement of decisions in matters of the property consequences of registered partnerships, OJ 2016 L183/30 ....8.015, 22.007
Regulation (EU, Euratom) 2016/1192 of the European Parliament and of the Council of 6 July 2016 on the transfer to the General Court of jurisdiction at first instance in disputes between the European Union and its servants, OJ 2016 L200/137.................. 13.002
Regulation (EU) 2016/1624 of the European Parliament and of the Council of 14 September 2016 on the European Border and Coast Guard, OJ 2016 L251/1...............8.007, 13.046

2017 Regulation (EU) 2017/745 of the European Parliament and of the Council of 5 April 2017 on medical devices, OJ 2017 L117/1..................... 9.045
Regulation (EU) 2017/746 of the European Parliament and of the Council of 5 April 2017 on in vitro diagnostic medical devices, OJ 2017 L117/176..... 9.045
Regulation (EU) 2017/825 of the European Parliament and of the Council of 17 May 2017 on the establishment of the Structural Reform Support Programme for the period 2017 to 2020, OJ 2017 L129/1 .... 9.065

Regulation (EU) 2017/1001 of the European Parliament and of the Council of 14 June 2017 on the European Union trade mark, OJ 2017 L154/1 ....7.109, 13.046
Arts 105–114................ 18.024
Art 146..................... 14.029
Art 165..................... 18.024
Regulation (EU) 2017/1129 of the European Parliament and of the Council of 14 June 2017 on the prospectus to be published when securities are offered to the public or admitted to trading on a regulated market, and repealing Directive 2003/71/EC, OJ 2017 L168/12...... 7.075
Council Regulation(EU) 2017/1939 of 12 October 2017 implementing enhanced cooperation on the establishment of the European, Public Prosecutor's Office ('the EPPO') OJ 2017 L283/1 ...... 5.032, 8.024, 13.045, 20.008, 20.013, 22.007, 22.010
Art 5....................... 8.024
Regulation (EU) 2017/1954 of the European Parliament and of the Council of 25 October 2017 amending Council Regulation (EC) No 1030/2002 laying down a uniform format for residence permits for third-country national, OJ 2017 L286/9 .... 8.012
Council Regulation (EU) 2017/2063 of 13 November 2017 concerning restrictive measures in view of the situation in Venezuela, OJ 2017 L295/21.................... 19.003

2018 Regulation (EU, Euratom) 2018/1046 of the European Parliament and of the Council of 18 July 2018 on the financial rules applicable to the general budget of the Union, amending Regulations (EU) No 1296/2013, (EU) No 1301/2013, (EU) No 1303/2013, (EU) No 1304/2013, (EU) No 1309/2013, (EU) No 1316/2013, (EU) No 223/2014, (EU) No 283/2014, and Decision No 541/2014/EU

and repealing Regulation (EU, Euratom) No 966/2012, OJ 2018 L193/1 . . . . 13.028, 14.010, 14.012, 20.007, 20.008, 20.010, 25.021
Art 2(67) 14.012
Art 16(2) 20.006
Art 18 . . . . 14.012
Art 19 . . . . 14.012
Art 39 . . . . 20.002
Art 42 . . . . 20.006
Art 46-45 . . . . 14.012
Art 58 . . . . 20.007
Art 63(1) 20.008
Art 73-74 . . . . 20.010
Art 117-118 . . . . 20.010
Art 255(1) 20.011
Regulation (EU) 2018/1139 of the European Parliament and of the Council of 4 July 2018 on common rules in the field of civil aviation and establishing a European Union Aviation Safety Agency, and amending Regulations (EC) No 2111/2005, (EC) No 1008/2008, (EU) No 996/2010, (EU) No 376/2014 and Directives 2014/30/EU and 2014/53/EU of the European Parliament and of the Council, and repealing Regulations (EC) No 552/2004 and (EC) No 216/2008 of the European Parliament and of the Council and Council Regulation (EEC) No 3922/91, OJ 2018 L212/1 . . . . . . 13.046, 18.024
Council Regulation (EU) 2018/1542 of 15 October 2018 concerning restrictive measures against the proliferation and use of chemical weapons, OJ 2018 L259/12 . . . . 10.031
Regulation (EU) 2018/1717 of the European Parliament and of the Council of 14 November 2018 amending Regulation (EU) No 1093/2010 as regards the location of the seat of the European Banking Authority, OJ 2018 L291/1 . . . . 13.046
Regulation (EU) 2018/1718 of the European Parliament and of the Council of 14 November 2018 103, OJ 2018 L291/3 . . . . 13.046

Regulation (EU) 2018/1725 of the European Parliament and of the Council of 23 October 2018 on the protection of natural persons with regard to the processing of personal data by the Union institutions, bodies, offices, and agencies and on the free movement of such data, OJ 2018 L295/39 . . . . 9.002, 14.031
Arts 52 et seq. 13.043
Art 64 . . . . 18.024
Regulation (EU) 2018/1726 of the European Parliament and of the Council of 14 November 2018 on the European Union Agency for the Operational Management of Large-Scale IT Systems in the Area of Freedom, Security and Justice (eu-LISA), OJ 2018 L295/99 . . . . 8.007, 13.046
Regulation (EU) 2018/1727 of the European Parliament and of the Council of 14 November 2018 on the European Union Agency for Criminal Justice Cooperation (Eurojust), OJ 2018 L295/138 . . . . 8.023, 8.024, 13.045
Art 65 . . . . 14.022
Art 71 . . . . 14.029
Regulation (EU) 2018/1806 of the European Parliament and of the Council of 14 November 2018 listing the third countries whose nationals must be in possession of visas when crossing the external borders and those whose nationals are exempt from that requirement, OJ 2018 L303/39 . . . . 8.007, 8.027
Regulation (EU) 2018/1861 of the European Parliament and of the Council of 28 November 2018 on the establishment, operation, and use of the Schengen Information System (SIS) in the field of border checks, and amending the Convention implementing the Schengen Agreement, OJ 2018 L312/4 . . . . 8.006
Regulation (EU) 2018/1862 of the European Parliament and of

the Council of 28 November 2018 on the establishment, operation, and use of the Schengen Information System (SIS) in the field of police cooperation and judicial cooperation in criminal matters, OJ 2018 L312/56 . . . . . 8.006

Regulation (EU) 2018/1971 of the European Parliament and of the Council of 11 December 2018 establishing the Body of European Regulators for Electronic Communications (BEREC) and the Agency for Support for BEREC (BEREC Office), OJ 2018 L321/1 . . . . . 13.046

2019 Regulation (EU) 2019/6 of the European Parliament and of the Council of 11 December 2018 on veterinary medicinal products, OJ 2019 L4/43 . . . . . . 9.055

Regulation (EU) 2019/126 of the European Parliament and of the Council of 16 January 2019 establishing the European Agency for Safety and Health at Work (EU-OSHA), and repealing Council Regulation (EC) No. 2062/94, OJ 2019 L30/ 58 . . . . 9.047, 13.046

Regulation (EU) 2019/127 of the European Parliament and of the Council of 16 January 2019 establishing the European Foundation for the improvement of living and working conditions (Eurofound), and repealing Council Regulation (EEC) No. 1365/75, OJ 2019 L30/74 . . . . 9.047, 13.046

Regulation (EU) 2019/128 of the European Parliament and of the Council of 16 January 2019 establishing a European Centre for the Development of Vocational Training (Cedefop), OJ 2018 L30/90 . . . . 9.052, 13.046

Regulation (EU) 2019/452 of the European Parliament and of the Council of 19 March 2019 establishing a framework for the screening of foreign direct investments into the Union, OJ 2019 L79I/1 . . . . 10.007

Regulation (EU) 2019/473 of the European Parliament and of the Council of 19 March 2019 on the European Fisheries Control Agency, OJ 2019 L83/18 . . . . . 13.046

Regulation (EU) 2019/515 of the European Parliament and of the Council of 19 March 2019 on the mutual recognition of goods lawfully marketed in another Member State, OJ 2019 L91/1 . . . . 7.116

Regulation (EU, Euratom) 2019/ 629 of the European Parliament and of the Council of 17 April 2019 amending Protocol No 3 on the Statute of the Court of Justice of the European Union, OJ 2021 L111/1 . . . . 13.009

Regulation (EU) 2019/818 of the European Parliament and of the Council of 20 May 2019 on establishing a framework for interoperability between EU information systems in the field of police and judicial cooperation, asylum, and migration, OJ 2019 L135/85. . . . 8.010

Regulation (EU) 2019/881 of the European Parliament and of the Council of 17 April 2019 on ENISA (the European Union Agency for Cybersecurity) and on information and communications technology cybersecurity certification, OJ 2019 L151/15 . . . . 13.045

Regulation (EU) 2019/1240 of the European Parliament and of the Council of 20 June 2019 on the creation of a European network of immigration liaison officers, OJ 2019 L198/88 . . . . 8.012

Regulation (EU) 2019/942 of the European Parliament and of the Council of 5 June 2019 establishing a European Union Agency for the Cooperation of Energy Regulators, OJ 2019, L158/22. . . . . 13.046

Regulation (EU) 2019/1149 of the European Parliament and of the Council of 20 June 2019 establishing a European Labour Authority, OJ 2019 L186/21 . . . 13.046

Regulation (EU) 2019/1381 of the European Parliament and of the Council of 20 June 2019 on the transparency and sustainability of the EU risk assessment in the food chain, OJ 2019 L231/1 . . . . 9.055, 17.013
Regulation (EU) 2019/1896 of the European Parliament and of the Council of 13 November 2019 on the European Border and Coast Guard, OJ 2019 L295/1 . . . . 8.007
Regulation (EU) No. 2019/2175 of the European Parliament and of the Council, OJ L334/1 . . . . . 9.042

2020 Regulation (EU) 2020/672 of 19 May 2020 on the establishment of a European instrument for temporary support to mitigate unemployment risks in an emergency (SURE) following the COVID-19 outbreak, OJ 2020 L159/1 . . . . 9.036
Regulation (EU) 2020/1043 of the European Parliament and of the Council of 15 July 2020 on the conduct of clinical trials with and supply of medicinal products for human use containing or consisting of genetically modified organisms intended to treat or prevent coronavirus disease (COVID-19), OJ 2020 L231/12 . . . . 9.055
Regulation (EU) 2020/1783 of the European Parliament and of the Council of 25 November 2020 on cooperation between the courts of the Member States in the taking of evidence in civil or commercial matters (taking of evidence) (recast), OJ 2020 L405/1. . . . . 8.015
Regulation (EU) 2020/1784 of the European Parliament and of the Council of 25 November 2020 on the service in the Member States of judicial and extrajudicial documents in civil or commercial matters (service of documents) (recast) OJ 2020 L405/40. . . . . 8.015
Council Regulation (EU) 2020/1998 of 7 December 2020 concerning restrictive measures against serious human rights violations and abuses, OJ 2020 L410I/1 . . . . . 10.031
Regulation (EU, Euratom) 2020/2092 of the European Parliament and of the Council of 16 December 2020 on a general regime of conditionality for the protection of the Union budget, OJ 2020 L433I/1. . . . . 5.005, 14.015, 20.009
Council Regulation (EU, Euratom) 2020/2093 of 17 December 2020 laying down the multiannual financial framework for the years 2021 to 2027, OJ 2020 L443I/11 . . . . . 14.018
Council Regulation (EU) 2020/2094 of 14 December 2020 establishing a European Union Recovery Instrument to support the recovery in the aftermath of the COVID-19 crisis, OJ 2020 L433I/23 . . . . . 14.015

2021 Regulation (EU) 2021/241 of the European Parliament and of the Council of 12 February 2021 establishing the Recovery and Resilience Facility, OJ 2021 L57/17. 9.036
Regulation (EU) 2021/522 of the European Parliament and of the Council of 24 March 2021 establishing a Programme for the Union's action in the field of health ('EU4Health Programme') for the period 2021-2027, and repealing Regulation (EU) No 282/2014, OJ 2021 L107/1 . . . . 9.055
Regulation (EU) 2021/690 of the European Parliament and of the Council of 28 April 2021 establishing a programme for the internal market, competitiveness of enterprises, including small and medium-sized enterprises, the area of plants, animals, food and feed, and European statistics (Single Market Programme) and repealing Regulations (EU) No 99/2013, (EU) No 1287/2013, (EU) No 254/2014 and (EU) No 652/2014, OJ 2021 L153/1. . . . . 9.056, 9.058

Regulation (EU) 2021/691 of the European Parliament and of the Council of 28 April 2021 on the European Globalisation Adjustment Fund for Displaced Workers (EGF) and repealing Regulation (EU) No 1309/2013, OJ 2021 L153/48 .... 9.057

Regulation (EU) 2021/692 of the European Parliament and of the Council of 28 April 2021 establishing the Citizens, Equality, Rights and Values Programme and repealing Regulation (EU) No 1381/2013 of the European Parliament and of the Council and Council Regulation (EU) No 390/2014, OJ 2021 L156/1 .... 6.004, 9.053

Regulation (EU) 2021/695 of the European Parliament and of the Council of 28 April 2021 establishing Horizon Europe– the Framework Programme for Research and Innovation, laying down its rules for participation and dissemination, and repealing Regulations (EU) No 1290/2013 and (EU) No 1291/2013, OJ 2021 L170/1 .... 9.060

Regulation (EU) 2021/783 of the European Parliament and of the Council of 29 April 2021 establishing a Programme for the Environment and Climate Action (LIFE), and repealing Regulation (EU) No 1293/2013, OJ 2021 L172/53 .... 9.062

Regulation (EU) 2021/785 of the European Parliament and of the Council of 29 April 2021 establishing the Union Anti-Fraud Programme and repealing Regulation (EU) No 250/2014, OJ 2021 L172/110 .... 20.013

Regulation (EU) 2021/817 of the European Parliament and of the Council of 20 May 2021 establishing Erasmus+: the Union Programme for education and training, youth and sport and repealing Regulation (EU) No 1288/2013, OJ 2021 L189/1 .... 9.050

Regulation (EU) 2021/818 of the European Parliament and of the Council of 20 May 2021 establishing the Creative Europe Programme (2021 to 2027) and repealing Regulation (EU) No 1295/2013, OJ 2021 L189/34. .... 9.053

Regulation (EU) 2021/1153 of the European Parliament and of the Council of 7 July 2021 establishing the Connecting Europe Facility and repealing Regulations (EU) No 1316/2013 and (EU) No 283/2014, OJ 2021 L249/38 .... 9.058

DIRECTIVES

1962 Second Council Directive 63/21 adding to and amending the First Directive for the implementation of Art 67 of the Treaty [1963–1964] O.J. English Spec. Ed. 5 .... 7.101

1964 Council Directive 64/221 on the coordination of special measures concerning the movement or residence of foreign nationals which are justified on grounds of public policy, public security or public health [1963–1964] O.J. English Spec. Ed. (I) 117............. 6.016
Art 3(1) 6.016, 7.067
Art 3(2) 6.016

1968 Council Directive 68/360 on the abolition of restrictions on movement and residence for workers of Member States and their families [1968] O.J. English Spec. Ed. (II) 485 .... 7.049, 7.057

1970 Council Directive 70/50 on the abolition of measures which have an effect equivalent to quantitative restrictions on imports and are not covered by other provisions adopted in pursuance of the EEC Treaty [1970] O.J. English Spec. Ed. (I) 17 .... 7.028, 7.031

1973 Council Directive 73/148 on the abolition of restrictions on movement and residence within the Community for nationals of Member States with regard to establishment

and the provision of services OJ 1973 L172/14..........7.049, 7.057
Art 4(2).....................7.087

1975 Council Directive 75/34 concerning the right of nationals of a Member State to remain in the territory of another Member State after having pursued therein an activity in a self-employed category OJ 1975 L14/10..7.049, 7.057

Council Directive 75/117 on the approximation of the laws of the Member States relating to the application of the principle of equal pay for men and women OJ 1975 L45/19 ...... 5.058

Council Directive 75/362 concerning the mutual recognition of diplomas, certificates and other evidence of formal qualifications in medicine, including measures to facilitate the effective exercise of the right of establishment and freedom to provide services OJ 1975 L167/1..................... 7.076

Council Directive 75/363 concerning the coordination of provisions laid down by law, regulation or administrative action in respect of activities of doctors OJ 1975 L167/14 ..... 7.076

1976 Council Directive 76/207 on the implementation of the principle of equal treatment for men and women as regards access to employment, vocational training and promotion, and working conditions OJ 1976 L39/40...............5.058–5.059
Art 2(4) 5.059

Council Directive 79/409 on the conservation of wild birds OJ 1979 L103/1 .... 9.061

1983 Council Directive 83/189/EEC of 18 March 1983 requiring Member States to notify any draft technical regulations and standards to the Commission, OJ 1983 L109/8 .... 23.014

1985 Council Directive 85/374/EEC of 25 July 1985 on the approximation of the laws, regulations and administrative provisions of the Member States concerning liability for defective products, OJ 1985 L210/29................... 9.056

Council Directive 85/384/EEC of 10 June 1985 on the mutual recognition of diplomas, certificates and other evidence of formal qualifications in architecture, including measures to facilitate the effective exercise of the right of establishment and freedom to provide services, OJ 1985 L223/15................... 7.076

Council Directive 85/577/EEC of 20 December 1985 to protect the consumer in respect of contracts negotiated away from business premises, OJ 1985 L372/31....... 9.056, 27.026, 29.014

1986 Council Directive 84/457/EEC of 15 September 1986 on specific training in general medical practice, OJ 1986 L267/26 .... 7.076

Council Directive 86/378 on the implementation of the principle of equal treatment for men and women in occupational social security schemes OJ 1986 L225/40 .... 5.058

Council Directive 86/613 on the application of the principle of equal treatment between men and women engaged in an activity, including agriculture, in a self-employed capacity, and on the protection of self-employed women during pregnancy and motherhood OJ 1986 L359/56 .... 5.058

1987 Council Directive 87/54/EEC of 16 December 1986 on the legal protection of topographies of semiconductor products, OJ 1987 L24/36 .... 7.109

1988 Council Directive 88/361/EEC of 24 June 1988 for the implementation of [the former] Article 67 of the Treaty, OJ 1988 L178/5.......... 7.101, 7.106, 9.031
Art 1....................... 7.101
Art 7(1) 7.101

1989 Council Directive 89/48/EEC of 21 December 1988 on a general system for the recognition of higher education diplomas awarded on completion of professional education and training of at least three years' duration, OJ 1989 L19/16. . . . . .7.076–7.077

First Council Directive 89/104/EEC of 21 December 1988 to approximate the laws of the Member States relating to trade marks, OJ 1989 L40/1 . . . . 7.109

Council Directive 89/391/EEC of 12 June 1989 on the introduction of measures to encourage improvements in the safety and health of workers at work, OJ 1989 L183/1 ('framework' Directive) 9.047

Council Directive 89/665/EEC of 21 December 1989 on the application of review procedures to the award of public supply and public works contracts, OJ 1989 L395/33 . . . 7.109

1990 Council Directive 90/387/EEC of 28 June 1990 on the establishment of the internal market for telecommunications services through the implementation of open network provision, OJ 1990 L192/1. . . . . 9.020

1991 Council Directive 91/173/EEC of 21 March 1991 amending for the ninth time Directive 76/769/EEC on the approximation of the laws, regulations and administrative provisions of the Member States relating to restrictions on the marketing and use of certain dangerous substances and preparations, OJ 1991 L85/34 . . . . 7.115

Council Directive 91/250/EEC of 14 May 1991 on the legal protection of computer programs, OJ 1991 L122/42 . . . 7.109

Council Directive 91/439/EEC of 29 July 1991 on driving licences, OJ 1991 L237/1. . . . . 14.001

Council Directive 91/477/EEC of 18 June 1991 on control of the acquisition and possession of weapons, OJ 1991 L256/51 . . . 11.007

1992 Council Directive 92/13/EEC of 25 February 1992 on the application of Community rules on procurement procedures, OJ 1992 L76/14 . . . . 7.109

Council Directive 92/51/EEC of 18 June 1992 on a second general system for the recognition of professional education and training, OJ 1992 L209/25 . . . . 7.076

Directive 92/100 . . . . 7.109

1993 Council Directive 93/13/EEC of 5 April 1993 on unfair terms in consumer contracts, OJ 1993, L95/29 . . . . 9.056, 29.013

Council Directive 93/16/EEC of 5 April 1993 to facilitate the free movement of doctors and the mutual recognition of their diplomas, certificates and other evidence of formal qualifications, OJ 1993 L165/1. . . . . 7.076

Council Directive 93/83/EEC of 27 September 1993 on the coordination of certain rules concerning copyright and rights related to copyright applicable to satellite broadcasting and cable retransmission, OJ 1993 L248/15. . . . . 7.109

Council Directive 93/109/EC laying down detailed arrangements for the exercise of the right to vote and to stand as a candidate in elections to the European Parliament for citizens of the Union residing in a Member State of which they are not nationals OJ 1993 L329/34. . . . . 6.021, 12.015

Art 3. . . . . 12.015
Art 4. . . . . 12.015
Art 5. . . . . 12.015
Art 8(1) 6.021
Art 8(2) 6.021
Art 9(4) 6.021
Art 14. . . . . 12.015

1994 Directive 94/19 of the European Parliament and the Council on deposit–guarantee schemes OJ 1994 L135/5 . . . . 7.075

Council Directive 94/80 laying down detailed arrangements for the exercise of the right to vote and to stand as a candidate in municipal elections by

citizens of the Union residing in a Member State of which they are not nationals OJ 1994 L368/38. .... 6.021
Art 5. .... 6.021
Art 7(1) 6.021
Art 7(2) 6.021
Art 8(3) 6.021
Art 12(2) 6.021

1995 Directive 95/46/EC of the European Parliament and of the Council of 24 October 1995 on the protection of individuals with regard to the processing of personal data and on the free movement of such data, OJ 1995 L281/31 .... 9.002

1996 Directive 96/9/EC of the European Parliament and of the Council of 11 March 1996 on the legal protection of databases, OJ 1996 L77/20 .... 7.109

Council Directive 96/34/EC of 3 June 1996 on the Framework Agreement on parental leave concluded by UNICE, CEEP, and the ETUC, OJ 1996 L145/4 .... 17.044

Directive 96/71/EC of The European Parliament and of the Council of 16 December 1996 concerning the posting of workers in the framework of the provision of services OJ 1997 L18/1 .... 5.032, 7.075

1997 Council Directive 97/80/EC on the burden of proof in cases of discrimination based on sex, OJ 1998 L14/6 .... 5.058

Council Directive 97/81/EC of 15 December 1997 concerning the Framework Agreement on part-time work concluded by UNICE, CEEP, and the ETUC, OJ 1998 L14/9 .... 9.047, 17.044

1998 Directive 98/5/EC of the European Parliament and of the Council of 16 February 1998 to facilitate practice of the profession of lawyer on a permanent basis in a Member State other than that in which the qualification was obtained, OJ 1998 L77/36 .... 7.076, 7.109

Directive 98/34/EC of the European Parliament and of the Council of 22 June 1998 laying down a procedure for the provision of information in the field of technical standards and regulations and of rules on Information Society services, OJ 1998 L204/ 37 ...... 7.111, 23.014

Directive 98/44/EC of the European Parliament and of the Council of 6 July 1998 on the legal protection of biotechnological inventions, OJ 1998 L213/13 .... 7.109

Directive 98/71/EC of the European Parliament and of the Council of 13 October 1998 on the legal protection of designs, OJ 1998 L289/28 .... 7.109

1999 Directive 1999/34/EC of the European Parliament and of the Council of 10 May 1999, OJ 1999 L141/20 .... 9.056

Council Directive 1999/63/EC of 21 June 1999 concerning the Agreement on the organization of working time of seafarers concluded by the European Community Shipowners' Association (ECSA) and the Federation of Transport Workers' Unions in the European Union (FST), OJ 1999 L167/33 .... 17.044

Council Directive 1999/70/EC of 28 June 1999 concerning the framework agreement on fixed-term work concluded by ETUC, UNICE, and CEEP, OJ 1999 L175/43 .... 17.044

2000 Directive 2000/12 of the European Parliament and the Council relating to the taking up and pursuit of the business of credit institutions OJ 2000 L126/1 ... 7.075

Council Directive 2000/43 implementing the principle of equal treatment between persons irrespective of racial or ethnic origin OJ 2000 L180/22......... 5.060
Art 2(2) 5.060

Directive 2000/46 of the European Parliament and of the Council on the taking up, pursuit of and prudential supervision of the business of electronic money institutions OJ 2000 L275/39 ... 7.075

	Council Directive 2000/78 establishing a general framework for equal treatment in employment and occupation OJ 2000 L303/16 .... 5.060	2002	Directive 2002/8/EC of 27 January 2003 to improve access to justice in cross-border disputes by establishing minimum common rules relating to legal aid for such disputes, OJ 2003 L26/41..................... 8.017
2001	Directive 2001/29/EC of the European Parliament and of the Council of 22 May 2001 on the harmonization of certain aspects of copyright and related rights in the information society, OJ 2001 L167/10 ..... 7.109		Directive 2002/14/EC of the European Parliament and of the Council of 11 March 2002 establishing a general framework for informing and consulting employees in the European Community, OJ 2002 L80/29..................... 9.047
	Directive 2001/34 of the European Parliament and of the Council on the admission of securities to official stock exchange listing and on information to be published on those securities OJ 2001 L184/1 .... 7.075		Directive 2002/15/EC of the European Parliament and of the Council of 11 March 2002 on the organization of the working time of persons performing mobile road transport activities, OJ 2002 L80/35..... 9.047
	Council Directive 2001/40/EC of 28 May 2001 on the mutual recognition of decisions on the expulsion of third-country nationals, OJ 2001 L149/34 .... 8.012		Directive 2002/20/EC of the European Parliament and of the Council of 7 March 2002 on the authorization of electronic communications networks and services ('Authorization Directive'),OJ 2002 L108/21 ....7.097, 9.020
	Directive 2001/42/EC of the European Parliament and of the Council of 27 June 2001 on the assessment of the effects of certain plans and programmes on the environment, OJ 2001 L197/30 .... 9.061		Framework Directive 2002/21/EC and Directive 2002/19/EC (access), OJ 2002 L108/7...... 9.020
	Directive 2001/55/EC of 20 July 2001 on minimum standards for giving temporary protection in the event of a mass influx of displaced persons and on measures promoting a balance of efforts between Member States in receiving such persons and bearing the consequences thereof, OJ 2001 L212/12 .... 8.010		Directive 2002/22/EC of the European Parliament and of the Council of 7 March 2002 on universal service and users' rights relating to electronic communications networks and services (Universal Service Directive), OJ 2002 L108/51.... 9.020
	Directive 2001/84/EC of the European Parliament and of the Council of 27 September 2001 on the resale right for the benefit of the author of an original work of art, OJ 2001 L275/32 .... 7.109		Directive 2002/58/EC of the European Parliament and of the Council of 12 July 2002 concerning the processing of personal data and the protection of privacy in the electronic communications sector (Directive on privacy and electronic communications), OJ 2002 L201/37 .... 9.002
	Directive 2001/86/EC of 8 October 2001 with regard to the involvement of employees, OJ 2001 L294/22 .... 7.075		
	Directive 2001/95/EC of the European Parliament and of the Council of 3 December 2001 on general product safety, OJ 2002 L11/4...................... 9.055		Commission Directive 2002/77/EC of 16 September 2002 on competition in the markets for electronic communications networks and services, OJ 2002 L249/21.................... 9.020

2003

Directive 2002/87 of the European Parliament and of the Council of 16 December 2002 on the supplementary supervision of credit institutions, insurance undertakings and investment firms in a financial conglomerate OJ 2003 L35/1 .. 7.075

Council Directive 2002/90/EC of 28 November 2002 defining the facilitation of unauthorized entry, transit, and residence, OJ 2002 L328/17 .... 8.012

Council Directive 2003/9/EC of 27 January 2003 laying down minimum standards for the reception of asylum seekers, OJ 2013 L31/18 .... 8.011

Directive 2003/33/EC of the European Parliament and the Council of 26 May 2003 on the approximation of the laws, regulations and administrative provisions of the Member States relating to the advertising and sponsorship of tobacco products, OJ 2003 L152/16 .... 9.055

Council Directive 2003/48/EC of 3 June 2003 on taxation of savings income in the form of interest payments, OJ 2003 L157/38 .... 7.114

Council Directive 2003/72 supplementing the Statute for a European Cooperative Society with regard to the involvement of employees OJ 2003 L207/25..... 7.075

Council Directive 2003/86 on the right to family reunification OJ 2003 L251/12......... 6.010, 8.012, 12.009

Directive 2003/87/EC of the European Parliament and of the Council of 13 October 2003 establishing a scheme for greenhouse gas emission allowance trading within the Community, OJ 2003 L275/3.... 9.062

Directive 2003/88/EC of the European Parliament and of the Council of 4 November 2003 concerning certain aspects of the organization of working time, OJ 2003 L299/9 .... 9.047, 25.009

Council Directive 2003/109/EC of 25 November 2003 concerning the status of third-country nationals who are long-term residents 8.012
Art 6(1) 8.012
Art 11(1) 8.012
Arts 14–23................... 8.012

2004

Directive 2004/35/EC of the European Parliament and of the Council of 21 April 2004 on environmental liability with regard to the prevention and remedying of environmental damage, OJ 2004 L143/56..... 9.061

Directive 2004/38 of the European Parliament and of the Council on the right of citizens of the Union and their family members to move and reside freely within the territory of the Member States amending Reg. 1612/68 and repealing Dirs 64/221, 68/360, 72/194, 73/148, 75/34, 75/35, 90/364, 90/365 and 93/96 OJ 2004 L158/77.............. 5.055, 5.060, 6.010–6.016, 7.049, 7.057, 7.067, 7.079, 7.087
Preamble, Recital 16........... 6.012
Art 2....................... 7.057
Art 2(2) 6.014
Art 3(1) 6.014
Art 5(1) 6.010
Art 5(4) 6.010
Art 6....................... 6.010
Art 6(1) 6.011
Art 7.................... 6.010, 6.012
Art 7(1) 6.012, 6.014
Art 7(1)(a).................. 6.012
Art 7(1)(b).................. 6.012
Art 7(1)(c).................. 6.012
Art 7(2) 6.014
Art 7(3) 6.012
Art 7(4) 6.012
Art 8....................... 6.012
Art 9....................... 6.012
Art 13...................... 6.014
Art 14(1) 6.011
Art 14(2) 6.012
Art 14(3) 6.012
Art 14(4) 6.012
Art 15(3) 6.016
Art 16...... 6.010, 6.013–6.014, 6.016
Art 17.................. 6.013, 7.057

Art 23	7.060
Art 24	6.015
Art 24(1)	6.015
Art 24(2)	5.055, 6.011, 6.015
Art 27	6.016
Art 27(1)	7.067
Art 27(2)	6.016, 7.067
Art 28	6.016
Art 28(2)	6.016
Art 28(3)(a)	6.016
Arts 30–33	6.016
Art 32	6.016
Art 33	6.016

Directive 2004/48/EC of the European Parliament and of the Council on the enforcement of intellectual property rights, OJ 2004 L157/45 .... 7.109

Council Directive 2004/83/EC of 29 April 2004 on minimum standards for the qualification and status of third country nationals or stateless persons as refugees or as persons who otherwise need international protection and the content of the protection granted, OJ 2004 L304/12 .... 8.009

Council Directive 2004/113 implementing the principle of equal treatment between men and women in the access to and supply of goods and services OJ 2004 L373/37 .... 5.058

2005 Directive 2005/29/EC of the European Parliament and of the Council of 11 May 2005 concerning unfair business-to-consumer commercial practices in the internal market ('Unfair Commercial Practices Directive'), OJ 2005 L149/22 .... 7.110, 9.056

Directive 2005/35/EC of the European Parliament and of the Council on ship-source pollution and on the introduction of penalties for infringements, OJ 2009 L280/52 .... 8.021

Directive 2005/36/EC of the European Parliament and of the Council of 7 September 2005 on the recognition of professional qualifications, OJ 2005 L255/22 .... 7.076

Title III, Ch I	7.076
Title III, Ch II	7.076
Title III, Ch III	7.076

Directive 2005/60/EC of the European Parliament and of the Council of 26 October 2005 on the prevention of the use of the financial system for the purpose of money laundering and terrorist financing, OJ 2005 L309/15 .... 7.110

Council Directive 2005/85/EC of 1 December 2005 on minimum standards on procedures in Member States for granting and withdrawing refugee status, OJ 2005 L326/13 .... 8.009

2006 Directive 2006/54 of the European Parliament and of the Council of 5 July 2006 on the implementation of the principle of equal opportunities and equal treatment of men and women in matters of employment and occupation, OJ 2006 L203/23 .... 5.058, 9.048

Commission Directive 2006/111/EC of 16 November 2006 on the transparency of financial relations between Member States and public undertakings as well as on financial transparency within certain undertakings, OJ 2006 L318/17 .... 9.020

Council Directive 2006/112/EC of 28 November 2006 on the common system of value added tax, OJ 2006 L347/1 .... 14.015

Directive 2006/114/EC of the European Parliament and of the Council of 12 December 2006 concerning misleading and comparative advertising, OJ 2006 L376/21 .... 9.056

Directive 2006/115/EC of the European Parliament and of the Council of 12 December 2006 on rental right and lending right and on certain rights related to copyright in the field of intellectual property, OJ 2006 L376/28 .... 7.109

Art 8(2) 26.004

Directive 2006/116/EC of the European Parliament and of

the Council of 12 December 2006 on the term of protection of copyright and certain related rights, OJ 2006 L372/12 ...... 7.109

Directive 2006/123 of the European Parliament and of the Council on services in the internal market ('Services Directive'), OJ 2006 L376/36 ...... 7.067, 7.075, 7.081–7.082, 7.091, 7.096–7.099
- Ch II 7.096
- Ch IV 7.096
- Ch V 7.096
- Ch VI 7.096
- Art 1 .... 7.097
- Art 1(1) 7.096
- Art 2(1) 7.097
- Art 2(2) 7.097
- Art 2(2)(j) 7.097
- Art 2(3) 7.097
- Art 3(1) 7.097
- Art 4(1) 7.096
- Art 4(5) 7.096
- Art 4(6) 7.098
- Art 4(7) 7.098
- Art 6 .... 7.096
- Art 9 .... 7.098
- Arts 9–13 .... 7.098
- Art 10(2) 7.098
- Arts 11–13 .... 7.098
- Art 14 .... 7.067, 7.071, 7.098
- Art 14(1) 7.098
- Art 14(1)(b) 7.098
- Art 15 .... 7.094
- Art 15(2)(a) 7.098
- Art 15(2)(b) 7.098
- Art 15(2)(c) 7.098
- Art 15(2)(d) 7.098
- Art 15(2)(g) 7.098
- Art 15(4) 7.098
- Art 16(1) 7.099
- Art 16(2) 7.099
- Art 16(2)(a) 7.099

2008 Directive 2008/48/EC of the European Parliament and of the Council of 23 April 2008 on credit agreements for consumers, OJ 2008 L133/66 .... 9.056, 29.013

Directive 2008/52/EC of the European Parliament and of the Council of 21 May 2008 on certain aspects of mediation in civil and commercial matters, OJ 2008 L136/ 3 .... 8.017

Directive 2008/95/EC of the European Parliament and of the Council of 22 October 2008 to approximate the laws of the Member States relating to trademarks, OJ 2008 L299/25 .... 7.109

Directive 2008/99 on the protection of the environment through criminal law OJ 2008 L328/28 .... 5.019, 8.021

Directive 2008/104/EC of the European Parliament and of the Council of 19 November 2008 on temporary agency work, OJ 2008 L327/9 .... 9.047

Directive 2008/115/EC of the European Parliament and of the Council of 16 December 2008 on common standards and procedures in Member States for returning illegally staying third-country nationals, OJ 2008 L348/98 .... 8.012

2009 Directive 2009/24/EC of the European Parliament and of the Council of 23 April 2009 on the legal protection of computer programs, OJ 2009 L111/16 .... 7.109

Directive 2009/38/EC of the European Parliament and of the Council of 6 May 2009 on the establishment of a European Works Council or a procedure in Community-scale undertakings and Community-scale groups of undertakings for the purposes of informing and consulting employees, OJ 2009 L122/28 .... 9.047

Council Directive 2009/50/EC of 25 May 2009 on the conditions of entry and residence of third-country nationals for the purposes of highly qualified employment, OJ 2009 L155/17 .... 8.012

Directive 2009/65/EC of the European Parliament and of the Council on the coordination of law, regulations, and administrative provisions relating to undertakings for collective investment in transferable securities (UCITS), OJ 2009 L302/32 .... 7.075

Council Directive 2009/119/EC imposing an obligation on Member States to maintain minimum stocks of crude oil and/or petroleum products, OJ 2018 L263/57 .... 18.011

Directive 2009/123/EC of the European Parliament and of the Council of 21 October 2009 amending Directive 2005/35/EC on ship-source pollution and on the introduction of penalties for infringements, OJ 2009 L280/52 .... 8.021

Directive 2009/138/EC of the European Parliament and of the Council of 25 November 2009 on the taking-up and pursuit of the business of Insurance and Reinsurance (Solvency II), OJ 2009 L335/1 .... 7.075

2010 Council Directive 2010/18/EU of 8 March 2010 implementing the revised Framework Agreement on parental leave concluded by BUSINESSEUROPE, UEAPME, CEEP, and ETUC, OJ 2010 L68/13 .... 9.047, 17.044

Council Directive 2010/24/EU of 16 March 2010 concerning mutual assistance for the recovery of claims relating to taxes, duties, and other measures, OJ 2010 L84/ 1 .... 20.013

Directive 2010/41/EU of the European Parliament and of the Council of 7 July 2010 on the application of the principle of equal treatment between men and women engaged in an activity in a self-employed capacity, OJ 2010 L180/1 .... 5.058, 9.048

Directive 2010/64/EU of the European Parliament and of the Council of 20 October 2010 on the right to interpretation and translation in criminal proceedings, OJ 2010 L280/1 .... 8.020

2011 Council Directive 2011/16/EU of 15 February 2011 on administrative cooperation in the field of taxation, OJ 2011 L64/1 .... 7.114

Directive 2011/24/EU of the European Parliament and of the Council of 9 March 2011 on the application of patients' rights in cross-border healthcare, OJ 2011 L88/45 .... 7.080

Directive 2011/36/EU of the European Parliament and of the Council of 5 April 2011 on preventing and combating trafficking in human beings and protecting its victims, OJ 2011 L101/1 .... 8.021

Directive 2011/83/EU of the European Parliament and of the Council of 25 October 2011 on consumer rights, OJ 2011 L304/64. .... 9.056

Directive 2011/85/EU of the Council of 8 November 2011 on requirements for budgetary frameworks of the Member States, OJ 2011 L306 .... 9.038

Directive 2011/93/EU of the European Parliament and of the Council of 13 December 2011 on combating the sexual abuse and sexual exploitation of children and child pornography, OJ 2011 L335/1 .... 8.021

Directive 2011/95/EU of the European Parliament and of the Council of 13 December 2011 on standards for the qualification of third-country nationals or stateless persons as beneficiaries of international protection, for a uniform status for refugees or for persons eligible for subsidiary protection, and for the content of the protection granted, OJ 2011 L337/9 .... 8.009
Art 12(2) 6.016

Directive 2011/99/EU of the European Parliament and of the Council of 13 December 2011 on the European protection order, OJ 2011 L338/2 .... 8.020

2012 Directive 2012/13/EU of the European Parliament and of the Council of 22 May 2012 on the right to information in criminal proceedings, OJ 2012 L142/1 .. 8.020

Directive 2012/29/EU of the European Parliament and of the Council of 25 October 2012 establishing minimum standards on the rights, support, and protection of victims of crime, and replacing Council Framework Decision 2001/220/JHA, OJ 2012 L315/57. . . . . 8.020

Directive 2012/30/EU on coordination of safeguards which, for the protection of the interests of members and others, are required by Member States of companies within the meaning of the second para. of Article 54 TFEU, in respect of the formation of public limited liability companies and the maintenance and alteration of their capital, with a view to making such safeguards equivalent, OJ 2012 L315/74 . . . 7.075

Directive 2012/34/EU of the European Parliament and of the Council of 21 November 2012 establishing a single European railway area, OJ 2012 L343/3 . . . . 9.010

2013 Directive 2013/11/EU of the European Parliament and of the Council of 21 May 2013 on alternative dispute resolution for consumer disputes ('Directive on consumer ADR'), OJ 2013 L165/63. . . . . . 9.056

Directive 2013/32/EU of the European Parliament and the Council of 26 June 2013 on common procedures for granting and withdrawing international protection, OJ 2013 L180/249 . . . . 8.009

Directive 2013/33/EU of the European Parliament and of the Council of 26 June 2013 laying down standards for the reception of applicants for international protection, OJ 2013 L180/96 . . . . 8.011

Directive 2013/36/EU of the European Parliament and of the Council of 26 June 2013 on access to the activity of credit institutions and the prudential supervision of credit institutions and investment firms, OJ 2013 L176/338. . . . . 7.075, 9.042

Directive 2013/40/EU of the European Parliament and of the Council of 12 August 2013 on attacks against information systems, OJ 2013 L218/8. . . . . . 8.021

Directive 2013/48/EU of the European Parliament and of the Council of 22 October 2013 on the right of access to a lawyer in criminal proceedings and in European arrest warrant proceedings, and on the right to have a third party informed upon deprivation of liberty and to communicate with third persons and with consular authorities while deprived of liberty, OJ 2013 L294/1 . . . . 8.020

2014 Directive 2014/23/EU of the European Parliament and of the Council of 26 February 2014 on the award of concession contracts, OJ 2014 L94/1 . . . . . 7.109

Directive 2014/24/EU of the European Parliament and of the Council of 26 February 2014 on public procurement, OJ 2014 L94/65. 7.109

Directive 2014/25/EU of the European Parliament and of the Council of 26 February 2014 on procurement by entities operating in the water, energy, transport and postal services sectors, OJ 2014 L94/243 . . . . . 7.109

Directive 2014/41/EU of the European Parliament and of the Council of 3 April 2014 regarding the European Investigation Order in criminal matters, OJ 2014 L130/1. . . . . . 8.020

Directive 2014/49/EU on deposit guarantee schemes, OJ 2014 L173/149 . . . . . . 7.075, 9.042

Directive 2014/57/EU of the European Parliament and of the Council of 16 April 2014 on criminal sanctions for market abuse (market abuse directive), OJ 2014 L173/ 179. . . . . 8.021

Directive 2014/59/EU of the European Parliament and of the Council of 15 May 2014 establishing a framework for the recovery and resolution of credit institutions and investment

firms and amending Council
Directive 82/891/EEC, and
Directives 2001/24/EC, 2002/47/
EC, 2004/25/EC, 2005/56/EC,
2007/36/EC, 2011/35/EU, 2012/
30/EU and 2013/36/EU, and
Regulations (EU) No 1093/2010
and (EU) No 648/2012, of the
European Parliament and of the
Council, OJ 2014
L173/190.................. 9.042
Directive 2014/62/EU of the
European Parliament and of
the Council of 15 May 2014
on the protection of the euro
and other currencies against
counterfeiting by criminal law,
OJ 2014 L151/1 .... 8.021
Directive 2014/65/EU on markets
in financial instrumentsOJ
2014 L173/349............. 7.075
Directive 2014/66/EU of the
European Parliament and of
the Council of 15 May2014 on
the conditions of entry and
residence of third-country
nationals in the framework of
an intra-corporate transfer, OJ
2014 L157/1 .... 8.012
Directive 2014/104/EU of 26
November 2014 on certain
rules governing actions for
damages under national
law for infringements of the
competition law provisions
of the Member States and of
the European Union, OJ 2014
L349/1..................... 9.015

2015 Council Directive (EU) 2015/
637 on the coordination and
cooperation measures to
facilitate consular protection
for unrepresented citizens of
the Union in third countries
and repealing Decision 95/553/
EC, OJ 2015 L106/1.......... 6.022
Directive (EU) 2015/1535 of the
European Parliament and of the
Council of 9 September 2015
laying down a procedure for the
provision of information in the
field of technical regulations
and of rules on Information
Society services, OJ 2015
L241/1...............7.111, 23.014
Art 1(1)(b)................... 7.085

Directive (EU) 2015/2060 of
10 November 2015 repealing
Directive 2003/48/EC on
taxation of savings income in
the form of interest payments,
OJ 2015 L301/1 .... 7.114
Directive (EU) 2015/2436 of the
European Parliament and of
the Council of 16 December
2015 to approximate the laws of
the Member States relating to
trademarks, OJ 2015 L336/1 .... 7.109

2016 Directive (EU) 2016/97 of the
European Parliament and of
the Council of 20 January 2016
on insurance distribution,
OJ 2016 L26/19 .... 7.075
Directive (EU) 2016/680 of the
European Parliament and of the
Council of 27 April 2016 on the
protection of natural persons
with regard to the processing
of personal data by competent
authorities for the purposes of
the prevention, investigation,
detection, or prosecution
of criminal offences or the
execution of criminal penalties,
and on the free movement of
such data, OJ 2016 L119/89 ... 9.002
Directive (EU) 2016/681 of the
European Parliament and of the
Council of 27 April 2016 on the
use of passenger name record
(PNR) data for the prevention,
detection, investigation,
and prosecution of terrorist
offences and serious crime, OJ
2016 L119/132.............. 8.025
Directive (EU) 2016/797 of the
European Parliament and of
the Council of 11 May 2016 on
the interoperability of the rail
system within the European
Union, OJ 2016 L138/44...... 9.058
Directive (EU) 2016/801 of the
European Parliament and
of the Council of 11 May
2016 on the conditions of
entry and residence of third-
country nationals for the
purposes of research, studies,
training, voluntary service,
pupil exchange schemes, or
educational projects and au
pairing, OJ 2016 L132/21 ..... 8.012

TABLE OF EUROPEAN UNION ACTS

	Directive (EU) 2016/1919 of the European Parliament and of the Council of 26 October 2016 on legal aid for suspects and accused persons in criminal proceedings and for requested persons in European arrest warrant proceedings, OJ 2016 L297/1 ... 8.020		Directive (EU) 2019/770 of the European Parliament and of the Council of 20 May 2019 on certain aspects concerning contracts for the supply of digital content and digital services, OJ 2019 L136/1 ..... 9.056
2017	Directive (EU) 2017/541 of the European Parliament and of the Council of 15 March 2017 on combating terrorism, OJ 2017 L88/6 .... 8.021		Directive (EU) 2019/771 of the European Parliament and of the Council of 20 May 2019 on certain aspects concerning contracts for the sale of goods, OJ 2019 L136/28 .... 9.056
	Directive (EU) 2017/1132 of the European Parliament and of the Council relating to certain aspects of company law, OJ 2017 L169/46 .... 7.075		Directive (EU) 2019/882 of the European Parliament and of the Council of 17 April 2019 on the accessibility requirements for products and services OJ 2019 L151/70.................... 5.060
	Directive (EU) 2017/1371 of the European Parliament and of the Council of 5 July 2017 on the fight against fraud to the Union's financial interests by means of criminal law, OJ 2017 L198/29........ 8.021, 8.024, 20.013 Art 16..................... 20.013		Directive (EU) 2019/1152 of the European Parliament and of the Council of 20 June 2019 on transparent and predictable working conditions in the European Union, OJ 2019 L186/105 .... 9.047
2018	Directive (EU) 2018/957 amending Directive 96/71/EC concerning the posting of workers in the framework of the provision of services, OJ 2018 L173/26.............. 5.032, 7.075		Directive (EU) 2019/1158 of the European Parliament and of the Council of 20 June 2019 on work-life balance for parents and carers and repealing Council Directive 2010/18/EU, OJ 2019 L188/79 .... 9.047
	Commission Implementing Directive (EU) 2018/1581 of 19 October 2018 amending Council Directive 2009/119/EC as regards the methods for calculating stockholding obligations, OJ 2018 L263/57 .... 18.011		Directive (EU) 2019/1937 of the European Parliament and of the Council of 23 October 2019 on the protection of persons who report breaches of Union law, OJ 2019 L305/17 .... 20.013
2019	Directive (EU) 2019/1 of the European Parliament and of the Council of 11 December 2018 to empower the competition authorities of the Member States to be more effective enforcers and to ensure the proper functioning of the internal market, OJ 2019 L11/3 9.015	2020	Directive (EU) 2020/1828 of the European Parliament and of the Council of 25 November 2020 on representative actions for the protection of the collective interests of consumers, OJ 2020 L409/1..................... 9.056
	Directive (EU) 2019/713 of the European Parliament and of the Council of 17 April 2019 on combating fraud and counterfeiting of non-cash means of payment, OJ 2019 L123/18................... 8.021		**DECISIONS AND FRAMEWORK DECISIONS**
		1964	Dec. 64/300 on cooperation between the Central Banks of the Member States of the EEC [1963–1964] O.J. English Spec. Ed.141..................... 1.035

1965	Decision of the Representatives of the Governments of the Member States on the provisional location of certain institutions and departments of the Communities of 8 April 1965 (Decision on Provisional Location) 12.071, 14.019, 14.021			development of the Association (unpublished) .... 8.013, 10.017 Decision 3/80 of the EEC-Turkey Association Council of 19 September 1980 on the application of the social security schemes of the Member States of the European Communities to Turkish workers and members of their families , OJ 1983 C110/60 .... 8.013
	Art 3....................... 13.019			
	Art 5....................... 13.038			
	Art 8....................... 13.043	1983	Council Decision 83/516/EEC of 17 October 1983 on the tasks of the European Social Fund, OJ 1983 L289/38............... 9.047
	Art 9(a) 13.043		
1966	Council Decision 66/532/EEC of 26 July 1966 concerning the abolition of customs duties and the prohibition of quantitative restrictions as between Member States and the application of the common customs tariff duties to products not mentioned in Annex II [now Annex I] to the Treaty, JO 2971/66...... 7.007, 7.016		
		1985	Decision of the Council of 11 June 1985on the accession of Spain and Portugal to the ECSC [OJ 1985 L302/5....... 4.004
		1987	Council Decision 87/327/EEC of 15 June 1987 adopting the European Community Action Scheme for the Mobility of University Students (Erasmus), OJ 1987 L166/20 adopted on the basis of Articles 128 and 235 EEC 9.050
1970	Council Decision 70/243 of 21 April 1970 on the replacement of financial contributions from Member States by the Communities' own resources (First Decision on Own Resources) 14.013		
			Council Decision 87/373/EEC of 13 July 1987 laying down the conditions for the exercise of implementing powers conferred on the Commission, OJ 1987 L197/33 .... 18.014
1973	Dec. adjusting the documents concerning the accession of the new Member States to European Communities OJ 1973. L2/1................. 4.002		
		1988	Council Decision 88/591/ ECSC, EEC, Euratom of 24 October 1988 establishing a Court of First Instance of the European Communities [CFI Decision], OJ 1988 L319/ 1, and L241 .... 13.002
1976	Decisions 2/76 of the EEC-Turkey Association Council of 20 December 1976 (unpublished) 8.013, 10.017		
	Decision 76/787/ECSC, EEC, Euratom of the representatives of the Member States meeting in the council relating to the Act concerning the election of the representatives of the Assembly by direct universal suffrage OJ 1976 L278/1 ...... 3.007, 6.021, 12.014		Art 3...................... 13.009
		1989	Decision 89/663/EEC of 14 December 1989 amending Decision 87/327/EEC adopting the European Community action scheme for the mobility of university students (Erasmus), OJ 1989 L395 ..... 9.050
		1991	Council Decision 91/482/EEC of 25 July 1991 on the association of the overseas countries and territories with the European Economic Community, OJ 1991 L263/1 .... 10.013
1979	Decision of the Council of 24 May 1979on the accession of the Hellenic Republic to the ECSC OJ 1979 L291/5........ 4.003		
1980	Decision No 1/80 of the EEC-Turkey Association Council of 19 September 1980 on the		Council Decision 91/602/EEC of 25 November 1991 denouncing

the Cooperation Agreement between the European Economic Community and the Socialist Federal Republic of Yugoslavia, OJ 1991 L325/2.............10.016, 21.001

1992 Decision of 12 December 1992 taken by common agreement between the Representatives of the Governments of the Member States on the location of the seats of the institutions and of certain bodies and departments of the European Communities (First Decision on the Seats of the Institutions).............. 12.018
Art 1(a) 12.018
Council Decision 92/421/EEC of 31 July 1992 on a Community action plan to assist tourism, OJ 1992 L231/26.............. 7.109

1993 Decision 93/81/Euratom, ECSC, EEC amending the Act concerning the election of the representatives of the European Parliament by direct universal suffrage, annexed to Council Decision 76/787/ECSC, EEC, Euratom of 20 September 1976 OJ 1993 L33/15 .... 3.007
Decision of 29 October 1993 taken by common agreement between the Representatives of the Governments of the Member States, meeting at Head of State and Government level, on the location of the seats of certain bodies and departments of the European Communities and of Europol (Second Decision on the Seats of the Institutions), OJ 1993 C323/1 ......13.043, 13.045–13.046
Art (i).................... 13.022
Council Decision 93/350 of 8 June 1993 amending Council Decision 88/591/ECSC, EEC, Euratom establishing a Court of First Instance of the European Communities, OJ 1993 L144/21............. 13.009
Council Decision 93/591/EU, Euratom, ECSC, EC of 8 November 1993 concerning the name to be given to the Council following the entry into force of the Treaty on European Union, OJ 1993 L281/18 (corrigendum L285/41)................. 12.034
Council Decision 93/603/CFSP of 8 November 1993 concerning the joint action decided on by the Council on the basis of Article J.3 of the Treaty on European Union on support for the convoying of humanitarian aid in Bosnia and Herzegovina, OJ 1993 L286/1 .... 10.029
Council Decision 93/604/CFSP of 9 November 1993 concerning the joint action decided on by the Council on the basis of Article J.3 of the Treaty on European Union concerning the dispatch of a team of observers for the Parliamentary elections in the Russian Federation, OJ 1993 L286/3 .... 10.029
Council Decision 93/678/CFSP of 6 December 1993 on a joint action adopted by the Council on the basis of Article J.3 of the Treaty on European Union concerning support for the transition towards a democratic and multi-racial South Africa, OJ 1993 L316/45 .... 10.028

1994 Decision of the European Parliament of 9 March 1994 on the regulations and general conditions governing the performance of the Ombudsman's duties (Ombudsman Regulations) 17.014, 17.034, 17.045
Council Decision 94/149 of 7 March 1994 amending Decision 93/350/Euratom, ECSC, EEC amending Decision 88/591/ECSC, EEC, Euratom establishing a Court of First Instance of the European Communities, OJ 1994 L66/29 10.030
Council Decision 94/276/CFSP of 19 April 1994 on a joint action adopted by the Council on the basis of Article J (3) of the Treaty on European Union,

in support of the Middle East peace process, OJ 1994 L119/1 10.030

Decision 94/282 of 27 April 1994 of the Representatives of the Governments of the Member States of 27 April 1994 appointing a member of the Commission of the European Communities, OJ 1994 L121/41.................. 15.004

Council Decision 94/308/CFSP of 16 May 1994 adapting and extending the application of Decision 93/603/CFSP concerning the joint action decided on by the Council on the basis of Article J.3 of the Treaty on European Union on support for the convoying of humanitarian aid in Bosnia and Herzegovina, OJ 1994 L134/1 .... 10.030

Commission Decision 94/783/EC of 14 September 1994 concerning the prohibition of PCP notified by the Federal Republic of Germany, OJ L316/43................... 7.115

Council Decision 94/942/CFSP of 19 December 1994 on the joint action adopted by the Council concerning the control of exports of dual-use goods, OJ 1994 L367/8 .... 10.006

1995 Council Decision 95/1 adjusting the instruments concerning the accession of new Member States to the EU OJ 1995 L1/1 .... 4.005

Council Decision 95/2/EC, Euratom, ECSC of J January 1995 determining the order in which the office of President of the Council shall be held, OJ 1995 L1/220 .... 12.042

Council and Commission Decision 95/145/EC, ECSC of 10 April 1995 concerning the conclusion of the Agreement between the European Communities and the Government of the United States of America regarding the application of their competition laws, OJ 1995 L95/45................... 21.007

Decision 95/167/EC, Euratom, ECSC of the European Parliament, the Council, and the Commission of 19 April 1995 on the detailed provisions governing the exercise of the European Parliament's right of inquiry, OJ 1995 L113/2 ..... 12.010

Decision 95/553/EC of the Representatives of the Governments of the Member States meeting within the Council of 19 December 1995 regarding protection for citizens of the European Union by diplomatic and consular representations, OJ 1995 L314/73................... 6.022

1996 Commission Decision 96/282/Euratom of 10 April 1996 on the reorganization of the Joint Research Centre, OJ 1996 L107/12.................. 13.043

Decision 96/409/CFSP of the Representatives of the Governments of the Member States, meeting within the Council of 25 June 1996 on the establishment of an emergency travel document, OJ 1996 L168/4.................... 6.022

Council Decision 96/736/EC of 13 December 1996 in accordance with Article 109j of the Treaty establishing the European Community, on entry into the third stage of economic and monetary union, OJ 1996 L335/48.............9.033, 12.040

1997 Decision 97/803/EEC of 24 November 1997 amending at mid-term, Decision 91/482/EEC on the association of the overseas countries and territories with the European Economic Community, OJ 1997 L329/50 .... 10.013

1998 Council Decision 98/317/EC of 3 May 1998 in accordance with Article 109j (4) of the Treaty, OJ 1998 L139/30 Art 1....................... 9.033

Decision 98/345/EC taken by common accord of the Governments of the Member States adopting the single currency at the level of Heads of

State or Government of 26 May 1998 appointing the President, the Vice-President, and the other members of the Executive Board of the European Central Bank, OJ 1998 L154/33 . . . . 9.032

Council and Commission Decision 98/386/EC, ECSC of 29 May 1998, OJ 1998 L173/26 . . . . . . 21.007

Council Decision 98/392/EC of 23 March 1998 concerning the conclusion by the European Community of the United Nations Convention of 10 December 1982 on the Law of the Sea and the Agreement of 28 July 1994 relating to the implementation of Part XI thereof, OJ 1998 L179/1 . . . . . 11.006

Council Decision 98/415/EC of 29 June 1998 on the consultation of the European Central Bank by the national authorities on draft legislative provisions, OJ 1998 L189/ 42. . . . . 27.039

1999 Council Decision 1999/21/EC, Euratom of 14 December 1998 adopting a multiannual framework programme for actions in the energy sector (1998–2002) and connected measures, OJ 1999 L7/16 . . . . . 9.063

Council Decision 1999/291/EC, ECSC, Euratom of 26 April 1999 amending Decision 88/591/ECSC, EEC, Euratom establishing a Court of First Instance of the European Communities to enable it to give decisions in cases when constituted by a single judge, OJ 1999 L114/52 . . . . 13.009

Decision 1999/352/EC, ECSC, Euratom of 28 April 1999 establishing the European Anti-Fraud Office (OLAF), OJ 1999 L136/20 . . . . 13.043

Art 5(1) 13.043

Council Decision 1999/382/EC of 26 April 1999 establishing the second phase of the Community vocational training action programme 'Leonardo da Vinci', OJ 1999 L146/33. . . . . 9.052

Council Decision 1999/394/EC, Euratom of 25 May 1999 concerning the terms and conditions for internal investigations in relation to the prevention of fraud, corruption and any illegal activity detrimental to the Communities' interests, OJ 1999 L149/36 . . . . 20.013

Commission Decision 1999/396/EC, ECSC, Euratom of 2 June 1999 concerning the terms and conditions for internal investigations in relation to the prevention of fraud, corruption and any illegal activity detrimental to the Communities' interests, OJ 1999 L149/57 . . . . 20.013

Council Decision 1999/405/EC of 10 June 1999 authorizing the Kingdom of Spain to accede to the Convention establishing the Inter-American Tropical Tuna Commission on a temporary basis (IATTC), OJ 1999 L155/37. . . . . 5.024

Council Decision 1999/435/EC of 20 May 1999 concerning the definition of the Schengen acquis for the purpose of determining, in conformity with the relevant provisions of the Treaty establishing the European Community and the Treaty on European Union, the legal basis for each of the provisions or decisions which constitute the acquis, OJ 1999 L176/1 . . . . 8.004

Council Decision 1999/436/EC of 20 May 1999 determining, in conformity with the relevant provisions of the Treaty establishing the European Community and the Treaty on European Union, the legal basis for each of the provisions or decisions which constitute the Schengen acquis, OJ 1999 L176/17. . . . . 8.004

Council and Commission Decision 1999/445/EC, ECSC of 29 April

TABLE OF EUROPEAN UNION ACTS   cliii

1999 concerning the conclusion of the Agreement between the European Communities and the Government of Canada regarding the application of their competition laws, OJ 1999 L175/49. . . . . 21.007
Council Decision 1999/468/EC of 28 June 1999 laying down the procedures for the exercise of implementing powers conferred on the Commission, OJ 1999 L184/23. (Comitology Decision) . . . 18.010, 18.013–18.014, 18.019, 23.004, 27.049
    Art 4. . . . . 18.019
    Art 5. . . . . 18.011
    Art 5(a) 18.010
    Art 5(a)(3). 18.019
    Art 5(a)(4). 18.019
    Art 5(6) 18.019
    Art 6. . . . . 18.015
Council Decision 1999/493/EC, ECSC, Euratom of 9 July 1999 on the composition of the Commission, OJ 1999 L192/53. . . . . 12.068
Council Decision 1999/847/EC of 9 December 1999 establishing a Community action programme in the field of civil protection, OJ 1999 L327/53 . . . . 9.064
Dec. 1999/848 on the full application of the Schengen acquis in Greece OJ 1999 L327/58. 1.039

2000 Council Decision 2000/143/CFSP of 14 February 2000 setting up the Interim Political and Security Committee, OJ 2000 L49/1. . . . . 12.053
Council Decision 2000/144/CFSP of 14 February 2000 setting up the Interim Military Body, OJ 2000 L49/2 . . . . 12.053
Council Decision 2000/261/JHA of 27 March 2000 on the improved exchange of information to combat counterfeit travel documents, OJ 2000 L81/1. . . . 8.025
Council Decision 2000/354/CFSP of 22 May 2000 setting up a Committee for civilian aspects of crisis management, OJ 2000 L127/1. 12.053

Council Decision 2000/375/JHA of 29 May 2000 to combat child pornography on the Internet, OJ 200 L138/1 . . . . 8.021
Council Framework Decision 2000/383/JHA of 29 May 2000 on increasing protection by criminal penalties and other sanctions against counterfeiting in connection with the introduction of the euro, OJ 2000 L140/1 . . . . 8.021
Council Decision 2000/427/EC of 19 June 2000 in accordance with Article 122(2) of the Treaty on the adoption by Greece of the single currency on 1 January 2001, OJ L167/7 . . . . 9.033
Council Decision 2000/642/JHA of 17 October 2000 concerning arrangements for cooperation between financial intelligence units of the Member States in respect of exchanging information, OJ 2000 L271/4 . . . 8.025
Dec. 2000/777 on the application of the Schengen acquis in Denmark, Finland and Sweden, and in Iceland and Norway OJ 2000 L309/24 . . . . 1.039, 8.006
Council Decision 2000/799/JHA of 14 December 2000 setting up a Provisional Judicial Cooperation Unit, OJ 2000 L324/2. . . . . 8.023

2001 Council Decision 2001/78/CFSP of 22 January 2001 setting up the Political and Security Committee, OJ 2001 L27/1 . . . . 12.053, 19.003
Council Decision 2001/79/CFSP of 22 January 2001 setting up the Military Committee of the European Union, OJ 2001 L127/4. . . . . . . 12.053, 19.003, 19.007
Council Decision 2001/80/CFSP of 22 January 2001 on the establishment of the Military Staff of the European Union, OJ 2001 L27/7 . . . . 19.003, 19.007
Council Decision 2001/196/EC of 26 February 2001 concerning the conclusion of an Agreement between the European Community and the United

States of America renewing a programme of cooperation in higher education and vocational education and training, OJ 2001 L17/7 ..... 10.037

Council Framework Decision 2001/220/JHA on the standing of victims in criminal proceedings, OJ 2012 L315/57. 8.020

Council Framework Decision 2001/413/JHA of 28 May 2001 combating fraud and counterfeiting of non-cash means of payment, OJ 2001 L149/1.................... 8.021

Council Decision 2001/470/EC of 28 May 2001 establishing a European Judicial Network in civil and commercial matters, OJ 2001 L174/25 .... 8.018

Council Framework Decision 2001/500/JHA of 26 June 2001 on money laundering, the identification, tracing, freezing, seizing, and confiscation of instrumentalities and the proceeds of crime, OJ 2001 L182/1..................... 8.021

Commission Decision 2001/527/EC of 6 June 2001 establishing the Committee of European Securities Regulators, OJ 2001 L191/43..................... 7.075

Commission Decision 2001/528/EC of 6 June 2001 establishing the European Securities Committee, OJ 2001 L191/45.................... 7.075

Council Decision 2001/822/EC of 27 November 2001 on the association of the overseas countries and territories with the European Community, OJ 2001 L314/1 .... 10.013

Council Decision 2001/840/EC amending the Council's Rules of Procedure, OJ 2001 L313/40 14.030

Council Decision 2001/886/JHA of 6 December 2001 on the secondgeneration Schengen Information System, OJ 2001 L328/1..................... 8.025

2002 Decision 2002/187/JHA of 28 February 2002 setting up Eurojust with a view to reinforcing the fight against serious crime, OJ 2002 L63/1................8.023, 13.045

Council Decision 2002/192/EC of 28 February 2002 concerning Ireland's request to take part in some of the provisions of the Schengen acquis, OJ 2002 L64/20 .... 8.028

Dec. 2002/234 on the financial consequences of the expiry of the ECSC Treaty and on the research fund for coal and steel OJ 2002 L79/42 .... 1.009

Council Decision 2002/348/JHA of 25 April 2002 concerning security in connection with football matches with an international dimension, OJ 2002 L121/1 .... 8.025

Council Decisions 2002/361/EC, 2002/362/EC, and 2002/363/EC of 3 May 2002 on the granting of a national aid in favour of road transport undertakings by the authorities of the Netherlands, Italy, and France, respectively, OJ 2002 L131/12, L131/14, and L131/15 .... 9.027

Council Framework Decision 2002/465/JHA of 13 June 2002 on joint investigation teams, OJ 2002 L162/1 .... 8.025

Council Framework Decision 2002/475/JHA of 13 June 2002 on combating terrorism, OJ 2002 L164/3 .... 8.021

Council Framework Decision 2002/584/JHA of 13 June 2002 on the European arrest warrant and the surrender procedures between Member States, OJ 2002 L190/1 ....8.020, 16.013, 25.009

Decision 2002/620/EC of the European Parliament, the Council, the Commission, the Court of Justice, the Court of Auditors, the Economic and Social Committee, the Committee of the Regions, and the European Ombudsman of 25 July 2002, OJ 2002 L197/53 ..... 13.043

Decision 2002/621/EC of the Secretaries-General of those

institutions and committees
and of the Representative of the
European Ombudsman of 25
July 2002, OJ 2002 L197/56 . . . 13.043
Council Framework Decision 2002/
629/JHA of 19 July 2002 on
combating trafficking in human
beings, OJ 2002 L203/1 . . . . 8.021
Council Decision 2002/772/EC,
Euratom of 25 June 2002 and
23 September 2002 amending
the Act concerning the election
of the representatives of the
European Parliament by direct
universal suffrage, annexed to
Decision 76/787/ECSC, EEC,
Euratom, OJ 2002
L283/1 . . . . 3.007, 6.021, 12.014
Art 3. . . . . 12.014
Council Framework Decision
2002/946/JHA of 28 November
2002 on the strengthening of
the penal framework to prevent
the facilitation of unauthorised
entry, transit, and residence, OJ
2002 L328/1 . . . . 8.021
Council Decision 2002/956/JHA
of 28 November 2002 setting
up a European Network for the
Protection of Public Figures, OJ
2002 L333/1 . . . . 8.025
Council Decision 2002/970/EC of
18 November 2002 concerning
the conclusion on behalf of
the European Community
of the International Cocoa
Agreement 2001, OJ 2002
L342/1. 10.009

2003   Council Decision 2003/48/JHA
of 19 December 2002 on the
implementation of specific
measures for police and
judicial cooperation to combat
terrorism in accordance with
Article 4 of Common Position
2001/931/CFSP, OJ 2003
L16/68. . . . . 10.031
Council Framework Decision
2003/80/JHA of 27 January
2003 on the protection of the
environment through criminal
law, OJ 2003 L29/55 . . . . 8.021
Council Decision 2003/159/
EC of 19 December 2002
concerning the conclusion of
the Partnership Agreement
between the African Caribbean
and Pacific Group of States, of
the one part, and the European
Community and its Member
States, of the other part, signed
in Cotonou on 23 June 2000, OJ
2003 L65/27 . . . . 10.019
Council Decision 2003/165/EC of
18 February 2003 concerning
the establishment of the
Financial Services Committee,
OJ 2003 L67/17 . . . . 12.052
Council Decision 2003/211/
CFSP of 24 February 2003
concerning the conclusion of
the Agreement between the
European Union and the North
Atlantic Treaty Organisation on
the Security of Information,
OJ 2003 L80/35 . . . . . . 10.033, 28.017
Decision 2003/223/EC of the
Council meeting in the
composition of the Heads of
State or Government of 21
March 2003 on an amendment
to Article 10.2 of the Statute
of the European System of
Central Banks and of the
European Central Bank, OJ
2003 L83/66. . . . . .13.022
Council Decision 2003/432/
CFSP of 12 June 2003 on the
launching of the European
Union military operation in the
Democratic Republic of Congo,
OJ 2013 L147/42 . . . . 10.032
Council Decision 2003/516/EC
of 6 June 2003 concerning the
signature of the Agreements
between the European Union
and the United States of
America on extradition and
mutual legal assistance in
criminal matters, OJ 2003
L181/25. . . . . 28.017
Council Decision 2003/520/EC of
16 June 2003 concluding the
Agreement between the European
Community and the Government
of Japan concerning cooperation
on anti-competitive activities, OJ
2003 L183/11 . . . . 21.007
Council Framework Decision
2003/568/JHA of 22 July 2003

on combating corruption in the private sector, OJ 2003 L192/54 ....8.020

Council Framework Decision 2003/577/JHA of 22 July 2003 on the execution in the European Union of orders freezing property or evidence, OJ 2003 L196/45 .... 8.020

Decision 2003/603/EC of the European Economic and Social Committee of 1 July 2003 on public access to European Economic and Social Committee documents, OJ 2003 L205/19 .... 14.030

Council Decision 2003/642/JHA of 22 July 2003 concerning the application to Gibraltar of the Convention on the fight against corruption involving officials of the European Communities or officials of Member States of the European Union, OJ 2003 L226/27................. 11.007

Council Decision 2003/885/EC of 17 November 2003 concerning the conclusion of the Agreement on the application of certain Community acts on the territory of the Principality of Monaco, OJ 2003 L332/41 .... 11.009

Decision taken by common agreement between the Representatives of the Member States, meeting at Head of State or Government level, of 13 December 2003 on the location of the seats of certain offices and agencies of the European Union (Third Decision on the Seats of the Institutions), OJ 2004 L29/15 .... 14.021

2004 Council Framework Decision 2004/68/JHA of 22 December 2003 on combating the sexual exploitation of children and child pornography, OJ 2004 L13/44 .... 8.021

Council Decision 2004/79/EC of 17 December 2003 on the signing of the Agreement between the European Union and the Republic of Iceland and the Kingdom of Norway on the application of certain provisions of the Convention of 29 May 2000 on Mutual Assistance in Criminal Matters between the Member States of the European Union and the 2001 Protocol thereto, OJ 2004 L26/1..................... 28.017

Council Decision 2004/80/EC of 17 December 2003 concerning the conclusion of the Agreement between the European Community and the Government of the Hong Kong Special Administrative Region of the People's Republic of China on the readmission of persons residing without authorisation, OJ 2004 L17/23 .... 10.036

Decision 2004/97/EC, Euratom taken by common agreement between the Representatives of the Member States, meeting at Head of State or Government level, of 13 December 2003 on the location of the seats of certain offices and agencies of the European Union, OJ 2004 L29/15.................... 14.021

Council Decision 2004/424/EC of 21 April 2004 concerning the conclusion of the Agreement between the European Community and the Macao Special Administrative Region of the People's Republic of China on the readmission of persons residing without authorisation, OJ 2004 L143/97.................. 10.036

Council Decision 2004/441/EC of 26 April 2004 concerning the conclusion of the Trade, Development and Cooperation Agreement between the European Community and its Member States, on the one part, and the Republic of South Africa, on the other part, OJ 2004 L127/109............ 10.008

Council Decision 2004/496/EC of 17 May 2004 on the conclusion of an Agreement between the European Community and the United States of America on the processing and transfer of

PNR data by Air Carriers to the United States Department of Homeland Security, Bureau of Customs and Border Protection, OJ 2004 L183/83 .... 21.009

Council Decision 2004/511/EC of 10 June 2004 concerning the representation of the people of Cyprus in the European Parliament in the case of a settlement of the Cyprus problem, OJ 2004 L211/22 ... 11.008

Council Decision 2004/576/EC of 29 April 2004 concerning the conclusion of the Agreement on Scientific and Technical Cooperation between the European Community and the State of Israel, OJ 2004 L261/47 .... 10.036

Council Framework Decision 2004/757/JHA of 25 October 2004 laying down minimum provisions on the constituent elements of criminal acts and penalties in the field of illicit drug trafficking, OJ 2004 L335/8..................... 8.021

Council Decision 2004/803/CFSP of 25 November 2004 on the launching of the European Union military operation in Bosnia and Herzegovina, OJ 2004 L353/21 .... 10.032

2005 Council Decision 2005/49/EC, Euratom of 18 January 2005 concerning the operating rules of the committee provided for in Article 3(3) of Annex I to the Protocol on the Statute of the Court of Justice, OJ 2005 L21/13 .... 13.014

Decision 2005/118/EC of the European Parliament, the Council, the Commission, the Court of Justice, the Court of Auditors, the European Economic and Social Committee, the Committee of the Regions, and the Ombudsman of 26 January 2005 setting up a European Administrative School, OJ 2005 L37/14.................... 13.043

Council Framework Decision 2005/214/JHA of 24 February 2005 on the application of the principle of mutual recognition to financial penalties OJ 2005 L76/16................5.053, 8.020

Council Framework Decision 2005/222/JHA of 24 February 2005 on attacks against information systems, OJ 2005 L69/67..................... 8.020

Council Decision 2005/358/EC of 26 April 2005 designating the seat of the European Agency for the Management of Operational Cooperation at the External Borders of the Member States of the European Union, OJ 2005 L114/13..............8.007, 13.046

Council Decision 2005/370/EC of 17 February 2005 on the conclusion of the Convention on access to information, public participation in decision-making, and access to justice in environmental matters, OJ 2005 L124/1..... 10.036

Council Framework Decision 2005/667/JHA of 12 July 2005 to strengthen the criminal-law framework for the enforcement of the law against ship-source pollution, OJ 2005 L255/164 .... 8.020

Council Decision 2005/681/JHA establishing the European Police College (CEPOL) and repealing Decision 2000/820/JHA, OJ 2015 L319/1......... 8.025, 13.047, 14.021

Council Decision 2005/876/JHA of 21 November 2005 on the exchange of information extracted from the criminal record, OJ 2005 L322/33..............8.020, 28.016

2006 Council Decision 2006/188/EC of 21 February 2006 on the conclusion of the Agreement between the European Community and the Kingdom of Denmark extending to Denmark the provisions of Council Regulation (EC) No 343/2003 establishing the criteria and mechanisms for determining the Member State responsible for examining an asylum application lodged in one of the Member States by a third-country national and Council Regulation (EC) No 2725/2000 concerning the establishment of Eurodac for the comparison of fingerprints for the effective application of the Dublin Convention, OJ 2006 L66/37 .... 8.010

Council Decision 2006/325/EC of 27 April 2006 concerning the conclusion of the Agreement between the European Community and the Kingdom of Denmark on jurisdiction and the recognition and enforcement of judgments in civil and commercial matters, OJ 2006 L120/22 .... 8.015

Council Decision 2006/326/EC of 27 April 2006 concerning the conclusion of the Agreement between the European Community and the Kingdom of Denmark on the service of judicial and extrajudicial documents in civil or commercial matters, OJ 2006 L120/23. . . . . 8.015

Council Decision 2006/495/EC of 11 July 2006 in accordance with Article 122(2) of the Treaty on the adoption by Slovenia of the single currency on 1 January 2007, OJ 2006 L195/25 .... 9.033

Council Decision 2006/500/EC of 29 May 2006 on the conclusion of the Energy Community Treaty, OJ 2006 L198/15 ..... 10.036

Council Decision 2006/512/EC of 17 July 2006 amending Decision 1999/468/EC laying down the procedures for the exercise of implementing powers conferred on the Commission, OJ 2006 L200/11. . . . . 18.014

Council Decision 2006/697/EC of 27 June 2006 on the signing of the Agreement between the European Union and the Republic of Iceland and the Kingdom of Norway on the surrender procedure between the Member States of the European Union and Iceland and Norway, OJ 2006 L292/1. . . . . 8.020

Council Decision 2006/719/ EC of 5 October 2006 on the accession of the Community to the Hague Conference on Private International Law, OJ 2006 L297/1 .... 8.016

Framework Decision 2006/783/ JHA on the application of the principle of mutual recognition to confiscation orders, OJ 2006 L328/59. . . . . 8.020

Council Decision 2006/910/EC of 4 December 2006 concerning the conclusion of the Agreement between the European Community and the United States of America renewing the cooperation programme in higher education and vocational education and training, OJ 2006 L346/33 ... 10.037

Decision 2006/966/EC taken by common agreement between the representatives of the Governments of Member States of 11 December 2006, OJ 2006 L403/61. . . . . 13.046

Council Decision 2006/1006/EC of 21 December 2006 on the conclusion of the Agreement in the form of an Exchange of Letters relating to the provisional application of the Fisheries Partnership Agreement between the European Community, on the one hand, and the Government of Denmark and the Home Rule Government of Greenland, on the other, OJ 2006 L411/27. . . . . 11.007

2007

Council Decision 2007/198/ Euratom of 27 March 2007 establishing the European Joint Undertaking for ITER and the Development of Fusion Energy and conferring advantages upon it, OJ 2007 L90/8 ...... 13.045

Council Decision 2007/503/EC of 10 July 2007 in accordance with Article 122(2) of the Treaty on the adoption by Cyprus of the single currency on 1 January 2008, OJ 2007 L186/29 .... 9.033

Council Decision 2007/504/EC of 10 July 2007 in accordance with Article 122(2) of the Treaty on the adoption by Malta of the single currency on 1 January 2008, OJ 2007 L186/32 .... 9.033

Council Decision 2007/551/CFSP/JHA of 23 July 2007 on the signing, on behalf of the European Union, of an Agreement between the European Union and the United States of America on the processing and transfer of Passenger Name Record (PNR) data by air carriers to the United States Department of Homeland Security (DHS) (2007 PNR Agreement), OJ 2007 L204/16 .... 7.113, 28.017

Council Decision 2007/533/JHA of 12 June 2007 on the establishment, operation, and use of the second generation Schengen Information System (SIS II), OJ 2007 L205/63 ..... 8.006

Dec. 2007/801 on the full application of the Schengen acquis in the Czech Republic, Estonia, Latvia, Lithuania, Hungary, Malta, Poland, Slovenia and the Slovak Republic OJ 2007 L323/34 .... 1.039, 8.006

Decision 2007/829/EC concerning the rules applicable to national experts and military staff on secondment to the General Secretariat of the Council and repealing Decision 2003/479/EC, OJ 2015 L163/40 .... 19.003

2008 Council Decision 2008/101/CFSP of 28 January 2008 on the launching of the European Union military operation in the Republic of Chad and in the Central African Republic (Operation EUFOR Tchad/RCA), OJ 2008 L39 .... 10.032

Council Decision 2008/114 (EC, Euratom) of 12 February 2008 establishing Statutes for the Euratom Supply Agency, OJ 2008 L41/15 .... 13.045

Council Decision 2008/261/EC of 28 February 2008 on the signature, on behalf of the European Community, and on the provisional application of certain provisions of this protocol, OJ 2008 L83/3 ...... 8.006

Council Decision 2008/373/EC of 28 April 2008 concerning the conclusion of the Agreement amending the Partnership Agreement between the members of the African, Caribbean and Pacific Group of States, of the one part, and the European Community and its Member States, of the other part, signed in Cotonou on 23 June 2000, OJ 2008 L129/44 .... 10.019

Council Decision 2008/579/EC of 16 June 2008 on the signing and conclusion on behalf of the European Community of the International Coffee Agreement 2007, OJ 2008 L186/12 .... 10.009

Council Decision 2008/608/EC of 8 July 2008 in accordance with Article 122(2) of the Treaty on the adoption by Slovakia of the single currency on 1 January 2009, OJ 2008 L195/24 .... 9.033

Decision 2008/634/EC taken by common agreement between the Representatives of the Governments of the Member States of 18 June 2008, OJ 2008 L206/16 .... 13.046

Council Framework Decision 2008/675/JHA of 24 July 2008 on taking account of convictions in the Member States of the European Union in the course of new criminal proceedings, OJ 2008 L220/32 .... 8.020

Council Decision 2008/783/CFSP of 15 September 2008 concerning the conclusion of the Agreement between the European Union and the Republic of Croatia on the participation of the Republic of Croatia in the European Union military operation in the Republic of Chad and in the Central African Republic (Operation EUFOR Tchad/RCA), OJ 2008 L268/32 ..... 10.033

clx TABLE OF EUROPEAN UNION ACTS

Council Decision 2008/814/CFSP of 13 October 2008 concerning the conclusion of an Agreement between the European Union and the United States of America on the participation of the United States of America in the European Union Rule of Law Mission in Kosovo, EULEX KOSOVO, OJ 2008 L282/32................... 10.033

Council Decision 2008/903/EC of 27 November 2008 on the full application of the provisions of the Schengen acquis in the Swiss Confederation, OJ 2008 L327/15.................... 8.006

Council Framework Decision 2008/909/JHA of 27 November 2008 on the application of the principle of mutual recognition to judgments in criminal matters imposing custodial sentences or measures involving deprivation of liberty for the purpose of their enforcement in the European Union, OJ 2008 L327/27...... 8.020

Council Framework Decision 2008/913/JHA of 28 November 2008 on combating certain forms and expressions of racism and xenophobia by means of criminal law, OJ 2008 L328/55.................... 5.060

Council Decision 2008/918/CFSP of 8 December 2008 on the launch of a European Union military operation to contribute to the deterrence, prevention, and repression of acts of piracy and armed robbery off the Somali coast (Atalanta), OJ 2008 L330/19.................... 10.032

Council Framework Decision 2008/947/JHA on the application of the principle of mutual recognition to judgments and probation decisions with a view to the supervision of probation measures and alternative sanctions, OJ 2008 L337/102.... 8.020

Council Decision 2008/976/JHA of 16 December 2008 on the European Judicial Network, OJ 2008 L348/130 .... 8.023

Council Framework Decision 2008/977/JHA of 27 November 2008 on the protection of personal data processed in the framework of police and judicial cooperation in criminal matters, OJ 2008 L350/60..... 9.002

Council Decision 2008/783/CFSP of 15 September 2008 concerning the conclusion of the Agreement between the European Union and the Republic of Croatia on the participation of the Republic of Croatia in the European Union military operation in the Republic of Chad and in the Central African Republic (Operation EUFOR Tchad/RCA), OJ 2008 L268/32................... 10.033

2009 Council Framework Decision 2009/299/JHA of 26 February 2009 amending Framework Decisions 2002/584/JHA, 2005/214/JHA, 2006/783/JHA, 2008/909/JHA and 2008/947/JHA, thereby enhancing the procedural rights of persons and fostering the application of the principle of mutual recognition to decisions rendered in the absence of the person concerned at the trial, OJ 2009 L81/24 .... 8.020

Council Framework Decision 2009/315/JHA of 26 February 2009 on the organization and content of the exchange of information extracted from the criminal record between Member States, OJ 2009 L93/23 (replacing Council Decision 2005/876/JHA of 21 November 2005, OJ 2005 L322/33) 8.020

Council Decision 2009/316/JHA of 6 April 2009 on the establishment of the European Criminal Records Information System (ECRIS) in application of Article 11 of Framework Decision 2009/315/JHA, OJ 2009 L93/33 .... 8.020

Council Decision 2009/371/JHA of 6 April 2009 establishing the European Police Office (Europol), OJ 2009 L121/37.. 13.045
Art (j)..................... 13.045
Art 1...................... 13.045

Council Decision 2009/397/EC of 26 February 2009 on the signing on behalf of the European Community of the Convention on Choice of Court Agreements, OJ 2009 L133/1 .... 10.040
Decision 2009/496/EC of the European Parliament, the European Council, the Council, the Commission, the Court of Justice of the European Union, the Court of Auditors, the European Economic and Social Committee, and the Committee of the Regions of 26 June 2009, OJ 2009 L168/41 .... 13.043
Council Decision 2009/586/EC of 16 February 2009 relating to the conclusion of the Agreement between the European Community and the Government of the Republic of Korea concerning cooperation on anti-competitive activities, OJ 2009 L202/35 .... 21.007
Council Decision 2009/820/CFSP of 23 October 2009 on the conclusion on behalf of the European Union of the Agreement on extradition between the European Union and the United States of America and the Agreement on mutual legal assistance between the European Union and the United States of America, OJ 2009 L291/40 ..... 10.028, 28.017
Council Framework Decision 2009/829/JHA of 23 October 2009 on the application, between Member States of the European Union, of the principle of mutual recognition to decisions on supervision measures as an alternative to provisional detention, OJ 2009 L294/20 .... 8.020
Council Decision 2009/857/EG of 13 December 2007 relating to the implementation of Article 9C(4) of the TEU and Article 205(2) of the TFEU between 1 November 2014 and 31 March 2017 on the one hand, and as from 1 April 2017 on the other, OJ 2009 L314/73 .... 12.048
Art 4 .... 12.047

Decision 2009/879/EU of the European Council of 1 December 2009 electing the President of the European Council, OJ 2009 L315/48 ... 12.027
Council Decision 2009/881/EU of 1 December 2009 on the exercise of the Presidency of the Council, OJ 2009 L315/50 .... 12.042
Art 1(1) 12.042
Art 1(2) 12.042
Art 2 .... 12.054
Art 3 .... 12.040
Council Decision 2009/882/EU of 1 December 2009 adopting its Rules of Procedure, OJ 2009 L315/51 .... 12.029
Council Decision 2009/904/EC of 26 November 2009 on the position to be taken by the European Community regarding the renegotiation of the Monetary Agreement with the Republic of San Marino, OJ 2009 L322/12 ... 9.045
Council Decision 2009/908/EU of 1 December 2009 laying down measures for the implementation of the European Council Decision on the exercise of the Presidency of the Council, and on the chairmanship of preparatory bodies of the Council, OJ 2009 L322/28 (corrigendum: OJ 2009 L344/56) 12.042
Art 2 .... 12.042
Decision 2009/913/EU taken by common agreement between the Representatives of the Governments of the Member States of 7 December 2009, OJ 2009 L322/39 .... 13.046
Council Decision 2009/937/EU of 1 December 2009 adopting the Council's Rules of Procedure, OJ 2009 L325/35 .... 12.043
Council Decision 2009/941/EC of 30 November 2009 on the conclusion by the European Community of the Hague Protocol of 23 November 2007 on the Law Applicable to Maintenance Obligations, OJ 2009 L331/17 .... 8.015
Council Decision 2009/942 of 30 November 2009 amending

Decision 2006/325/EC to provide for a procedure for the implementation of Article 5(2) of the Agreement between the European Community and the Kingdom of Denmark on jurisdiction and the recognition and enforcement of judgments in civil and commercial matters, OJ 2009 L331/24 .... 8.015

Council Decision 2009/943 of 30 November 2009 amending Decision 2006/326/EC to provide for a procedure for the implementation of Article 5(2) of the Agreement between the European Community and the Kingdom of Denmark on the service of judicial and extrajudicial documents in civil or commercial matters, OJ 2009 L331/26.................... 8.015

Council Framework Decision 2009/948/JHA of 30 November 2009 on prevention and settlement of conflicts of exercise of jurisdiction in criminal proceedings, OJ 2009 L328/42.................... 8.020

2010 Council Decision 2010/48/EC of 26 November 2009 concerning the conclusion, by the European Community, of the United Nations Convention on the Rights of Persons with Disabilities, OJ 2010 L23/35.... 10.040

Council Decision 2010/124/EU of 25 February 2010 relating to the operating rules of the panel provided for in Article 255 of the TFEU, OJ 2010 L50/18 ... 13.014
   Art 7....................... 13.014
   Art 8....................... 13.014

Council Decision 2010/125/EU of 25 February 2010 appointing the members of the Panel, OJ 2010 L50/20 .... 13.014

Council Decision 2010/128/CFSP of 1 March 2010 amending Common Position 2003/495/CFSP on Iraq, OJ 2010 L51/22 .... 10.029

Council Decision 2010/131/EU of 25 February 2010 on setting up the Standing Committee on operational coordination on internal security, OJ 2010 L52/50 .... 12.053

Council Decision 2010/329/CFSP of 14 June 2010 on the EUPM undertaken in the framework of reform of the security sector (SSR) and its interface with the system of justice in the Democratic Republic of the Congo (EUPOL RD Congo), OJ 2010 L149/ 11 .... 10.030

Council Decision 2010/330/CFSP of 14 June 2010 on the European Union Integrated Rule of Law Mission for Iraq (EUJUST LEX-IRAQ), OJ L149/12...........3.004, 10.030

Decision 2010/349/EU taken by common agreement between the Representatives of the Governments of the Member States of 31 May 2010 (OJ 2010 L156/12)................... 13.046

Dec. 2010/350 on the examination by a conference of representatives of the governments of the Member States of the amendments to the Treaties proposed by the Spanish Government concerning the composition of the European Parliament and not to convene a Convention OJ 2010 L160/ 5 3.004

Council Decision 2010/416/EU of 13 July 2010 in accordance with Article 140(2) of the Treaty on the adoption by Estonia of the euro on 1 January 2011, OJ 2010 L196/ 24............... 9.033

Council Decision 2010/427/EU of 26 July 2010 establishing the organization and the functioning of the European External Action Service, OJ 2010 L201/30 .... 13.042
   Art 5(2) 14.006
   Art 5(3) 14.006
   Art 6....................... 14.022

European Council Decision 2010/594/EU of 16 September 2010 amending the list of Council configurations, OJ 2010 L263/12................... 12.040

Decision 2010/762/EU taken by common agreement between the Representatives of the Governments of the Member States of 25 February 2010, OJ 2010 L324/47) 13.046

2011 Council Decision 2011/168/CFSP of 21 March 2011 on the International Criminal Court and repealing Common Position 2003/444/CFSP, OJ 2011 L76/56 .... 10.029

European Council Decision 2011/199/EU of 25 March 2011 amending Article 136 of the Treaty on the Functioning of the European Union with regard to a stability mechanism for Member States whose currency is the euro, OJ 2011 L91/1 .... 9.037

Council Decision 2011/292/EU of 31 March 2011 on the security rules for protecting EU classified information, OJ 2011, L141/17 .... 12.044

Council Decision 2011/411/CFSP of 12 July 2011 defining the statute, seat and operational rules of the European Defence Agency and repealing Joint Action 2004/551/CFSP, OJ 2011 L183/16 .... 13.046

Council Decision 2011/842 on the full application of the provisions of the Schengen acquis in the Principality of Liechtenstein, OJ 2011. L344/27 .... 1.039

2012 Commission Decision 2012/21/EU of 20 December 2011 on the application of Article 106(2) of the Treaty on the Functioning of the European Union to State aid in the form of public service compensation granted to certain undertakings entrusted with the operation of services of general economic interest, OJ 2012 L7/3 .... 9.023

European Council Decision 2012/151/EU electing the President of the European Council, OJ 2012 L77/17 .... 12.027

Council Decision 2012/245/EU of 26 April 2012 on a revision of the Statutes of the Economic and Financial Committee, OJ 2012 L121/22 .... 13.036

European Council Decision 2012/419/EU of 11 July 2012 amending the status of Mayotte with regard to the European Union, OJ 2012 L204/131.... 11.008

Commission Decision 2012/504/EU of 17 September 2012 on Eurostat, OJ 2012, L251/49.... 13.043

Council Decision 2012/712/CFSP of 19 November 2012 relating to the 2013 Review Conference of the Convention on the Prohibition of the Development, Production, Stockpiling and Use of Chemical Weapons and on their Destruction (CWC), OJ 2012 L321/68 .... 10.029

Council Decision 2012/738/EU of 13 November 2012 on the conclusion, on behalf of the European Union, of the Food Assistance Convention, OJ 2012 L330/1 .... 10.023

2013 European Council Decision 2013/272/EU of 22 May 2013 concerning the number of members of the European Commission, OJ 2013 L165/98 .... 12.063

European Council Decision 2013/312/EU of 28 June 2013 establishing the composition of the European Parliament, OJ 2013 L181/5 .... 12.013

Council Decision 2013/336/EU of 25 June 2013 increasing the number of Advocates-General of the Court of Justice of the European Union, OJ 2013 L179/92 .... 13.013

Council Decision 2013/387/EU of 9 July 2013 on the adoption by Latvia of the euro on 1 January 2014, OJ 2013 L195/24 .... 9.033

Council Decision 2013/743/EU of 3 December 2013 establishing the specific programme implementing Horizon 2020, OJ 2013 L347/965 .... 9.060

clxiv TABLE OF EUROPEAN UNION ACTS

Commission Implementing Decision 2013/770/EU of 17 December 2013 establishing the Consumers, Health and Food Executive Agency and repealing Decision 2004/858/EC, OJ 2013 L341/69........ 13.047
Commission Implementing Decision 2013/771/EU of 17 December 2013 establishing the 'Executive Agency for Small and Medium-sized Enterprises' and repealing Decisions 2004/20/EC and 2007/372/EC, OJ 2013 L341/73 .... 13.047
Council Decision 2013/755/EU of 25 November 2013 on the association of the overseas countries and territories with the European Union ('Overseas Association Decision'), OJ 2013 L344/4................... 10.013
Commission Implementing Decision 2013/776/EU of 18 December 2013 establishing the 'Education, Audiovisual and Culture Executive Agency' and repealing Decision 2009/336/EC, OJ 2013 L343/46.... 13.047
Commission Implementing Decision 2013/778/EU of 13 December 2013 establishing the Research Executive Agency and repealing Decision 2008/46/EC, OJ 2013 L346/54..... 13.047
Commission Implementing Decision 2013/779/EU of 17 December 2013 establishing the European Research Council Executive Agency and repealing Decision 2008/37/EC, OJ 2013 L346/58........ 13.047
Commission Implementing Decision 2013/801/EU of 23 December 2013 establishing the Innovation and Networks Executive Agency and repealing Decision 2007/60/EC as amended by Decision 2008/593/EC, OJ 2013 L352/65.... 13.047

2014 Council Decision 2014/75/CFSP of 10 February 2014 on the European Union Institute for Security Studies, OJ 2014 L41/13.............10.032, 13.046

Council Decision 2014/137/EU of 14 March 2014 on relations between the European Union on the one hand, and Greenland and the Kingdom of Denmark on the other, OJ 2014 L76/1.................... 11.007
Council Decision 2014/335/EU, Euratom of 26 May 2014 on the system of own resources of the European Union, OJ 2014 L 168/105 (Seventh Decision on Own Resources) 14.013
Art 7...................... 14.013
Council Decision 2014/401/CFSP of 26 June 2014 on the European Union Satellite Centre and repealing Joint Action 2001/555/CFSP on the establishment of a European Union Satellite Centre, OJ 2014 L188/73...... 10.032, 13.046, 14.011
Council Decision 2014/415/EU of 24 June 2014 on the arrangements for the implementation by the Union of the solidarity clause, OJ 2014 L192/53..................... 9.066
Council Decision 2014/486/CFSP of 22 July 2014 on the European Union Advisory Mission for Civilian Security Sector Reform Ukraine (EUAM Ukraine), OJ 2014 L217/42 .... 10.030
Council Decision 2014/509/EU of 23 July 2014 on the adoption by Lithuania of the euro on 1 January 2015, OJ 2014 L228/29 .... 9.033
European Council Decision 2014/638/EU of 30 August 2014 electing the President of the European Council, OJ 2014 L262/5.................... 12.027
Council Decision 2014/857/EU of 1 December 2014 concerning the notification of the United Kingdom of Great Britain and Northern Ireland of its wish to take part in some of the provisions of the Schengen acquis which are contained in acts of the Union in the field of police cooperation and judicial cooperation

TABLE OF EUROPEAN UNION ACTS clxv

2015 in criminal matters and amending Decisions 2000/365/EC and 2004/926/EC, OJ 2014 L345/1 .... 8.028

Commission Decision 2014/858/EU of 1 December 2014 on the notification by the United Kingdom of Great Britain and Northern Ireland of its wish to participate in acts of the Union in the field of police cooperation and judicial cooperation in criminal matters adopted before the entry into force of the Treaty of Lisbon and which are not part of the Schengen acquis, OJ 2014 L345/6 .... 8.028

2015 Council Decision (CFSP) 2015/528 of 27 March 2015 establishing a mechanism to administer the financing of the common costs of European Union operations having military or defence implications (Athena) and repealing Decision 2011/871/CFSP, OJ 2015 L84/39 .... 14.011

2016 Decision (EU) 2016/1316 of 26 July 2016 amending Decision 2009/908/EU, laying down measures for the implementation of the European Council Decision on the exercise of the Presidency of the Council, and on the chairmanship of preparatory bodies of the Council, OJ 2016 L208/42. .... 12.042

2017 Council Decision 2017/444/EU of 9 March 2017 electing the President of the European Council, OJ 2017 L67/87 .... 12.027

2018 European Council Decision (EU) 2018/937 of 28 June 2018 establishing the composition of the European Parliament, OJ 2018 L165I/1
Art 1 .... 12.013

2019 European Council Decision (EU) 2019/476 taken in agreement with the United Kingdom of 22 March 2019 extending the period under Article 50(3) TEU, OJ 2019 L80I/1 .... 4.016

European Council Decision (EU) 2019/584 taken in agreement with the United Kingdom of 11 April 2019 extending the period under Article 50(3) TEU, OJ 2019 L101/1 .... 4.016

European Council Decision (EU) 2019/1135 of 2 July 2019 electing the President of the European Council, OJ 2019 L179/1. .... 12.027

2020 Council Decision (EU, Euratom) 2020/2053 of 14 December 2020 on the system of own resources of the European Union, OJ 2020 L424/1 (Eighth Decision on Own Resources) 14.013–14.015
Art 2(1) 14.014
Art 2(1)(b). 14.015
Art 2(1)(c). 14.015
Art 2(2) 14.015
Art 2(4) 14.015
Art 3 .... 14.015
Art 8 .... 14.012

Table of Rules of Procedure

Rules of Procedure of the
European Parliament (EP Rules
of Procedure) 5.048, 12.011,
12.017, 13.040
Art 77(3) 17.029
Art 208. . . . . 12.010
Rules 5–7. . . . . 12.016
Rule 12. . . . . 20.013
Rules 15–19. . . . . 12.020
Rule 22. . . . . 12.020
Rule 24. . . . . 12.020
Rule 25. . . . . 12.020
Rule 26. . . . . 12.020
Rule 27. . . . . 12.020
Rule 28. . . . . 12.020
Rule 29. . . . . 12.020
Rule 33. . . . . 12.021
Rules 33–36. . . . . 12.021
Rule 33(2) 12.021
Rule 38. . . . . 17.015
Rules 39–43. . . . . 17.021
Rule 48. . . . . 17.021
Rule 51 . . . . 12.019, 17.021
Rule 52. . . . . 17.021
Rule 55. . . . . 12.019
Rule 59. . . . . 17.021
Rule 63(1) 17.024
Rule 63(2) 17.024
Rule 66(3) 17.026
Rule 67. . . . . 17.024
Rule 67(1) 17.024
Rule 68(2) 17.026
Rule 71(2) 17.020
Rule 84. . . . . 17.044
Art 84(1) 17.036
Rule 105(1) 17.037
Rule 114. 21.001
Rule 114(1) 21.003
Rule 114(2) 21.003
Rule 114(3) 21.003
Rule 114(4) 21.003
Rule 114(8) 21.009
Rule 115. 21.006
Rule 118(4) 14.028, 19.004
Rule 118(6) 19.004
Rule 119(4) 12.007
Rule 121(2) 12.017
Rule 122. 14.030
Rule 124(1) 12.064

Rule 125(1)–(2) 12.064
Rule 127(1) 12.006
Rule 129(1) 13.026
Rule 129(4) 13.026
Rule 130(1) 13.021
Rule 130(4) 13.021
Rule 132(1) 12.017
Rule 153. 12.017
Rule 158(1) 12.019
Rule 163. 17.021
Rule 167. 14.028
Rule 167(3) 14.028
Rule 167(4) 14.028
Rule 178(2) 12.019
Rule 206. 12.019
Rule 209. 12.019
Rules 226–229. . . . . 12.011
Rule 232. 13.041
Rule 234. 12.020
Annex VI. 20.012
Annex VII 12.064
Annex XX 17.028
Rules of Procedure of the European
Council (European Council
Rules of Procedure)
Art 1(2) 12.030
Art 2(4) 12.027
Art 4(1) 12.030
Art 4(3) 12.030
Art 5. . . . . 12.032
Art 6(3) 12.031
Art 7. . . . . 12.031
Art 9(1) 14.028
Art 10(1) 12.030
Art 12(1) 27.008
Art 13(1) 12.033
Art 13(2) 12.033
Rules of Procedure of the Council
(Council Rules of
Procedure) 12.040
Art 1(2) 12.043
Art 1(3) 12.043
Art 2(2) 12.040, 12.047
Art 2(5) 12.040
Art 3(3) 17.016
Art 3(6) 12.044, 12.050
Art 3(8) 12.050
Art 5(1) 12.044
Art 5(2) 12.043

clxviii TABLE OF RULES OF PROCEDURE

Art 5(3)	12.043	Art 13(3)	12.070
Art 7(1)	12.044	Art 17(1)	14.028
Art 7(2)	12.044	Arts 17(2)–(5)	14.028
Art 7(3)	12.044	Art 21	12.071
Art 7(4)	12.044	Arts 23(1)–(3)	12.071
Art 8(1)	12.044	Art 23(4)	12.071
Art 8(2)	12.044		
Art 8(3)	12.044		
Art 9(1)	12.044		

Rules of Procedure of the Court of Justice (CJ Rules of Procedure) 13.017, 23.007, 30.026

Art 9(2)	12.044
Art 9(2)(a)	12.044
Art 11(1)	12.048
Art 11(2)	12.045
Art 11(3)	12.045
Art 11(4)	12.045
Art 12(1)	12.050
Art 12(2)(d)	12.050, 19.003
Art 14(1)	14.028
Art 15	27.006
Art 16	12.040
Art 17(1)(b)	17.024
Art 17(1)(c)	17.016
Art 17(1)(d)	21.006, 28.010
Art 17(1)(e)	21.006, 28.010
Art 17(1)(h)	28.017
Art 17(2)(a)	17.016
Art 17(2)(b)	27.008
Art 17(3)	27.008
Art 17(4)	27.008
Art 17(4)(c)	27.008
Art 17(5)	27.008
Art 18(1)	27.007
Art 18(2)(a)	27.007
Art 19(1)	12.051
Art 19(3)	12.052
Art 19(4)	12.054
Art 20(2)	12.042
Art 21	12.052
Art 23	12.055
Art 24	12.044
Art 26	12.007
Annex I	12.040
Annex III	12.047
Annex V	12.044, 12.054
Annex VI	27.007

Art 27	13.018
Art 32(1)	29.033
Art 36	14.027
Art 37	30.026
Art 37(1)	14.027
Art 37(2)	29.033
Art 37(3)	14.027
Art 38(7)	14.027
Art 39	14.027
Art 40	14.027
Art 41	14.027
Arts 50–51	30.016
Art 59	29.031
Art 60	29.031
Art 60(1)	13.018
Art 62(1)	29.031
Art 76	30.026
Art 76(1)	29.029
Art 76(2)	29.031
Art 94(a)	29.026
Art 94(b)	29.026
Art 94(c)	29.026
Art 96	29.028
Art 97(3)	29.029
Art 99	29.031
Art 101	29.031
Art 105	29.035
Art 107–114	29.035
Arts 115–118	29.036
Art 124	30.026
Art 126	30.026
Arts 133–135	30.027
Art 160(3)	30.028
Art 161(1)	30.028
Art 162	30.028
Art 196(2)	21.017

Rules of Procedure of the Commission (Commission Rules of Procedure)

Art 3(2)	12.071
Art 5	12.069
Art 7	12.069
Art 9	12.069
Art 10	12.069
Art 12	12.069
Art 13(1)	12.070

Rules of Procedure of the General Court (GC Rules of Procedure) 23.007, 30.026

Art 13	13.018
Art 15	13.018
Art 29	13.018
Art 44	14.027
Art 45	30.025
Art 45(1)	14.027

Art 45(4)	14.029	Art 158	30.028
Art 46(6)	14.027	Rules of Procedure of the Court of Auditors (Rules of Procedure–Court of Auditors)	12.039
Art 47	14.027		
Arts 47–62b	13.017		
Art 48	14.027	Art 28(1)	14.028
Art 49	14.027	Art 287(4)	12.039, 16.008
Arts 59–60	30.016	Rules of Procedure of the European Economic and Social Committee (ESC Rules of Procedure)	
Art 81	30.025		
Art 83	30.025		
Art 106	30.025	Rule 3	13.032
Arts 151–155	30.027	Rule 17	13.032
Art 156(4)	30.028	Rule 32	13.032

Table of National Legislation

AUSTRIA

1920	Constitution	1.050

BELGIUM

1831	Constitution (as consolidated)	23.030
	Art 34	23.027
	Art 168	15.003
	Art 169	18.005
1980	Special law of August 8, 1980 on institutional reform	15.007
	Art 16(3)	18.005
	Art 16(4)	18.005
	Art 81(6)	15.016
	Art 92*bis*	15.016
	Art 92*quater*	15.007
1994	Cooperation agreement on 8 March 1994 pursuant to Article 92*bis* of the special Law of 8 August 1980 on the representation of the Kingdom of Belgium in the Council of Ministers of the European Union, Belgisch Staatsblad/Moniteur belge, 17 November 1994	15.016
	Art 5	18.005
2018	Cooperation agreement of 29 March 2017 on the exercise of the powers allotted by the Treaties to the national Parliaments, Belgisch Staatsblad/Moniteur belge 17 July 2018	15.010
	Art 7	15.010

CZECH REPUBLIC

1992	Constitution	
	Art 10b	15.007

DENMARK

1953	Constitution	3.007

FRANCE

1958	Constitution	1.050
	Art 34	15.012
	Art 37	15.012
	Art 88	23.027
	Art 88–4	15.003
	Art 88–6	15.010
	Art 88–8	15.003
1976	Law No. 76–664 of 19 July 1976	11.008
1985	Law No. 85–595 of 11 June 1985	11.008
1990	Law of 10 May 1990	15.007

GERMANY

1949	*Grundgesetz* (Basic Law)	7.089, 23.029
	Art 23(1)	15.003
	Art 23(1a)	15.010
	Art 23(3)	15.008
	Art 23(4)	15.008
	Art 23(5)	15.008
	Art 23(6)	15.008
	Art 24	23.027
	Art 45	15.006
	Art 52(3)(a)	15.006
	Art 79(3)	3.010
1993	*Gesetz über die Zusammenarbeit von Bund und Ländern in Angelegenheiten der Europäischen Union* (implementing law of March 12, 1993)	15.008

HUNGARY

1949	Constitution	
	Art 35/A	15.007

IRELAND

1937	Constitution	1.050
	Art 29.4.5	15.012
	Art 40.3.3	7.082

ITALY

1947	Constitution	23.015
	Art 11	23.027
1987	*Legge-Fabbri* of 16 April 1987	15.007

LITHUANIA

2004	Constitutional Act of July 13, 2004 on the Membership of the	

Republic of Lithuania in the
European Union
    Art 3 . . . . 15.007
    Art 4 . . . . 15.007

NETHERLANDS

1953	Constitution	23.025
1983	Constitution	23.025
	Art 92	23.027
1985	*Rijkswet van 20 juni* 1985	11.007
1987	Media Law	7.092
1992	*Rijkswet* of 17 December 1992 ratifying the EU Treaty	
	Art 3(1)	15.007
1998	*Rijkswet* of 24 December 1998 ratifying the Treaty of Amsterdam	
	Art 3	15.007
2001	*Rijkswet* of 19 December 2001 ratifying the Treaty of Nice	
	Art 3	15.007
	Art 4	15.007
2008	*Rijkswet* of 10 July 2008 ratifying the Lisbon Treaty	
	Art 3	15.007
	Art 3(2)	15.008

PORTUGAL

1994   Law No.20/94 . . . . 15.007

SLOVAKIA

1992   Constitution
        Art 3a 15.007

SPAIN

1978	Constitution	4.004
1985	Law No. 47/85 of 27 December 1985	15.012

UNITED KINGDOM

1972	European Communities Act	
	s 2(1)	23.026
	s 2(4)	23.026
	s 3(2)	15.012
1981	British Nationality Act	6.006
1986	European Communities (Amendment) Act	1.041
1986	Sex Discrimination Act	23.018
1988	Merchant Shipping Act	23.016
	Merchant Shipping (Registration of Fishing Vessels) Regulations	23.016
1998	Human Rights Act	
	Sch 1	1.007
2008	European Union (Amendment) Act	
	s 6	15.003

List of Abbreviations

A Völkerr	Archiv des Völkerrechts
AAe	Ars Aequi
ACER	European Union Agency for the Cooperation of Energy Regulators
ACP	African, Caribbean, Pacific
AD	Actualités du droit
AG	Advocate General
AJCL	American Journal of Comparative Law
AJDA	L'actualité juridique—droit administratif
AJIL	American Journal of International Law
AJT	Algemeen Juridisch Tijdschrift
Ann Dr Louv	Annales de droit de Louvain
Ann Dr Lux	Annales du droit luxembourgeois
Ann Fac Dr Liège	Annales de la Faculté de droit, d'économie et de sciences sociales de Liège
AöR	Archiv des öffentlichen Rechts
Arr Cass	Judgments of the Belgian *Hof van Cassatie/Cour de Cassation*
BEREC	Office of the Body of European Regulators for Electronic Communications
Brooklyn JIL	Brooklyn Journal of International Law
BS	Belgisch Staatsblad/Moniteur belge
BTIR	Belgisch Tijdschrift voor internationaal recht
BTSZ	Belgisch Tijdschrift voor Sociale Zekerheid
BVerfGE	Decisions of the *Bundesverfassungsgericht*
BYIL	British Yearbook of International Law
Cambridge LJ	Cambridge Law Journal
CAP	common agricultural policy
CDE	Cahiers de droit européen
CDPK	Chroniques de droit public – Publiekrechtelijke Kronieken
CdT	Translation Centre for Bodies of the European Union
CDSP	Common security and defence policy
CEN	European Committee for Standardization
Cedefop	European Centre for the Development of Vocational Training
Cenelec	European Committee for the Coordination of Electrical Standards
CEPOL	European Union Agency for Law Enforcement Training
CETA	Comprehensive Economic and Trade Agreement EU-Canada
CFI	Court of First Instance of the European Communities
CFSP	common foreign and security policy
CJEU	Court of Justice of the European Union
CHAFEA	Consumers, Health, Agriculture and Food Executive Agency
CMLRep.	Common Market Law Reports
CMLRev	Common Market Law Review
Cm	command paper
CMO	common market organization
Col JEL	Columbia Journal of European Law
Col LRev	Columbia Law Review

Comp Polit Stud	Comparative Political Studies
Coreper	Committee of Permanent Representatives
Cornell ILJ	Cornell International Law Journal
COSAC	Conference of European Affairs Committees
CPVO	Community Plant Variety Office
CSCE	Conference for Security and Cooperation in Europe
CYELP	Croatian Yearbook of European Law & Policy
CYELS	Cambridge Yearbook of European Legal Studie
DG	Directorate-General
DöV	Die öffentliche Verwaltung
DR	Decisions and Reports of the European Commission on Human Rights
DSB	Dispute Settlement Body
DUE	Il Diritto dell'Unione Europea
DVbl	Deutsches Verwaltungsblatt
EACEA	Education, Audiovisual and Culture Executive Agency
EAEC	European Atomic Energy Community
EAFRD	European Agricultural Fund for Rural Development
EAGF	European Agricultural Guarantee Fund
EASA	European Aviation Safety Agency
EASO	European Asylum Support Office
EBA	European Banking Authority
EBRD	European Bank for Reconstruction and Development
E Bus LRev	European Business Law Review
E Bus Org LR	European Business Organization Law Review
EC	European Community
ECB	European Central Bank
EC Bull.	Bulletin of the European Communities
ECDC	European Centre for Disease Prevention and Control
ECHA	European Chemicals Agency
ECHR	European Convention for the Protection of Human Rights and Fundamental Freedoms
E Comp J	European Competition Journal
ECSC	European Coal and Steel Community
ECTS	European Credit Transfer and Accumlation System
ECJ	Court of Justice of the European Union
E Comp LRev.	European Competition Law Review
ECSA	European Community Shipowners' Association
ECR	European Court Reports
EC Tax Rev	EC Tax Review
EDA	European Defence Agency
EDC	European Defence Community
EDU	European Drugs Unit
EEA	European Economic Area
EEAS	European External Action Service
EEC	European Economic Community
E.En.Env.L.Rev.	European Energy and Environmental Law Review
E.Env.L.Rev.	European Environmental Law Review
EFCA	European Fisheries Control Agency

EFSA	European Food Safety Authority
EFTA	European Free Trade Association
E For Aff Rev	European Foreign Affairs Review
EGTC	European groupings of territorial cooperation
EGF	European Globalization Adjustment Fund
EHRLR	European Human Rights Law Review
EIB	European Investment Bank
EIGE	European Institute for Gender Equality
EIOPA	European Insurance and Occupational Pensions Authority
EIT	European Institute of Innovation and Technology
EJCCL & CJ	European Journal of Crime, Criminal Law & Criminal Justice
ELA	European Labour Authority
EJ Consumer L	European Journal of Consumer Law
EJ Health L	European Journal of Health Law
EJIL	European Journal of International Law
EJ L Ref	European Journal of Law Reform
EJLS	European Journal of Legal Studies
EJML	European Journal on Migration and Law
EJ.Soc Sec	European Journal of Social Security
ELJ	European Law Journal
ELRev.	European Law Review
EMA	European Medicines Agency
EMCDDA	European Monitoring Centre for Drugs and Drug Addiction
EMFF	European Maritime and Fisheries Fund
EMI	European Monetary Institute
EMS	European Monetary System
EMSA	European Maritime Safety Agency
EMU	economic and monetary union
ENISA	European Union Agency for Cybersecurity
ENP	European Neighbourhood Policy
Env LRev	Environmental Law Review
EP	European Parliament
EPAs	Economic Partnership Agreements
EPC	European Political Cooperation
EPC Bulletin	European Political Cooperation Documentation Bulletin
EPPO	European Public Prosecutor's Office
EPSO	European Personnel Selection Office
E Pub L	European Public Law
ERA	European Union Agency for Railways
ERCEA	European Research Council Executive Agency
ERCL	European Review of Contract Law
ERDF	European Regional Development Fund
E Rev Priv L	European Review of Private Law
ERPL/REDP	European Review of Private Law / Revue européenne de droit privé
ERTA	European Agreement on Road Transport
ESCB	European System of Central Banks
ESDP	European Security and Defence Policy
ESF	European Social Fund

ESMA	European Securities and Markets Authority
EStALQ	European State Aid Law Quarterly
ETF	European Training Foundation
ETS	European Treaty Series
ETSI	European Telecommunications Standards Institute
EU	European Union
EU Bull.	Bulletin of the European Union
EuConst	European Constitutional Law Review
Eu GRZ	Europäische Grundrechte Zeitschrift
EUIPO	European Union Intellectual Property Office
EUISS	European Union Institute for Security Studies
EU-LISA	European Agency for the Operational Management of Large-Scale IT Systems in the Area of Freedom, Security and Justice
EUMC	Military Committee of the European Union
EUMS	Military Staff of the European Union
EU-OSHA	European Agency for Safety at Work
EuR	Europarecht
Euredia	Revue Européenne de Droit Bancaire et Financier/European Banking and Financial Law Journal
Eur. LF	European Legal Forum
EUROFOUND	European Foundation for the Improvement of Living and Working Conditions
Eurojust	European Union Agency for Criminal Justice Cooperation
Europe	Europe. Daily news bulletin
European J Risk Regul	European Journal of Risk Regulation
EuZW	Europäische Zeitschrift für Wirtschaftsrecht
EWS	Europäisches Wirtschafts- und Steuerrecht
FAO	Food and Agricultural Organization
FEAD	Fund for European Aid to the Most Deprived
Fordham ILJ	Fordham International Law Journal
FPI	Foreign Policy Instruments
FRA	European Union Agency for Fundamental Rights
FRONTEX	European Border and Coast Guard Agency
FST	Federation of Transport Workers' Unions in the European Union
FVO	Food and Veterinary Office
GAR	Global Antitrust Review
GATS	General Agreement on Trade in Services
GATT	General Agreement on Tariffs and Trade
GDP	gross domestic product
GDPR	General Data Protection Regulation
GJ	Gaceta Jurídica
GLJ	German Law Journal
Glob Trade Cust J	Global Trade and Customs Journal
GNI	Gross national income
GNP	gross national product
GNSS GSA	European Global Navigation Satellite System Supervisory Authority
GRI	Group on Interinstitutional Relations

GYIL	German Yearbook of International Law
Harv ILJ	Harvard International Law Journal
HJD	Hague Journal of Demoracy
HRLR	Human Rights Law Review
Human Rights LJ	Human Rights Law Journal
IAS	Internal Audit Service
ICCPR	International Covenant on Civil and Political Rights
ICLQ	International and Comparative Law Quarterly
IGC	Intergovernmental Conference
IJCL	International Journal of Constitutional Law
ILJ	Industrial Law Journal
IJNL	International Journal of Nuclear Law
ILM	International Legal Materials
ILO	International Labour Organisation
Intertax	: international tax review
Int'l J Baltic L	International Journal of Baltic Law
Int'l J Comp Lab L & Ind Rel	International Journal of Comparative Labour Law and Industrial Relations
Int'l J Soc Sci	International Journal of Social Sciences
Int'l Rev Law	International Review of Law & Economics & Econ
IMF	International Monetary Fund
IOLR	International Organizations Law Review
IPRax	Praxis des Internationalen Privat- und Verfahrensrechts
IPS	Irish Political Studies
Ir JEL	Irish Journal of European Law
J Antitrust Enforc	Journal of Antitrust Enforcement
JCER	Journal of Contemporary European Research
JCMS	Journal of Common Market Studies
JCP	Jurisclasseur périodique—La semaine juridique
JDE	Journal de droit européen
JDI	Journal de driot international
JEI	Journal of European Integration
JEPP	Journal of European Public Policy
JET	Joint European Torus
Jersey LRev	Jersey Law Review
J Eur Comp LP	Journal of European Competition Law & Practice
J Eur Soc Policy	Journal of European Social Policy
J Env L	Journal of Environmental Law
JFC	Journal of Financial Crime
JHA	justice and home affairs
JIEL	Journal of International Economic Law
J Legis Stud	Journal of Legislative Studies
JRC	Joint Research Centre
JT	Journal des tribunaux
JTDE	Journal des tribunaux—Droit européen
JTT	Journal des tribunaux de travail
Jura Falc	Jura Falconis
JWT	Journal of World Trade

JZ	Juristen-Zeitung
Kst	Kamerstukken (Netherlands Parliament)
LIEI	Legal Issues of European Integration (since 2000: Legal Issues of Economic Integration)
Leiden JIL	Leiden Journal of International Law
LQR	Law Quarterly Review
MEP	Member of the European Parliament
MFF	Multiannual Financial Framework
MJECL	Maastricht Journal of European and Comparative Law
Mich LRev	Michigan Law Review
MLR	Modern Law Review
NATO	North Atlantic Treaty Organisation
NILR	Netherlands International Law Review
NJ./AB	Nederlandse Jurisprudentie. Administratiefrechtelijke beslissingen
NJECL	New Journal of European Criminal Law
NJB	Nederlands Juristenblad
NJW	Neue Juristische Wochenschrift
NJWb	Nieuw Juridisch Weekblad
Nordic JIL	Nordic Journal of International Law
Not U Eur	Noticias de la Unión Europea
NTB	Nederlands Tijdschrift voor bestuursrecht
NTER	Nederlands Tijdschrift voor Europees Recht
NTIR	Nederlands Tijdschrift voor internationaal recht
OCTs	Overseas countries and territories
OECD	Organisation for Economic Cooperation and Development
OHIM	Office for Harmonization
OJ	Official Journal of the European Union
OJLS	Oxford Journal of Legal Studies
OLAF	European Anti-Fraud Office
OMT	Outright Monetary Transactions
OP	Publications Office of the European Union
OPN	Open network provision
OSCE	Organization for Security and Cooperation in Europe
OUP	Oxford University Press
Pas lux	Pasicrisie luxembourgeoise
Pecs J Int'l & Eur L	Pecs Journal of International and European Law
PESCO	permanent structured cooperation
Pet Aff	Les petites affiches
PF	Perspectives on Federalism
PJCC	police and judicial cooperation in criminal matters
PLO	Palestinian Liberation Organization
PMO	Paymaster Office
PNR	Passenger Name Record
Publ. ECHR	Publications of the European Court of Human Rights
Pub.L.	Public Law
PSC	Political and Security Committee
RabelsZ	Rabels Zeitschrift für ausländisches und internationales Privatrecht
RAE	Revue des affaires européennes

RBDC	Revue belge de droit constitutionnel
RCC	Revue de la concurrence et de la consommation
RCDIP	Revue critique de droit international privé
RDEtr	Revue de droit des étrangers
RDIDC	Revue de droit international et de droit comparé
RDUE	Revue du droit de l'Union européenne
RDULB	Revue du droit de l'Université Libre de Bruxelles
RDUnif	Revue de droit uniforme/Uniform Law Review
REA	Research Executive Agency
REALaw	Review of European Administrative Law
Rec CE	Recueil des décisions du Conseil d'Etat statuant au contentieux, du Tribunal des conflits et des jugements des Tribunaux administratifs
Rec Con const.	Conseil constitutionnel—Recueil des décisions
Rec Dalloz	Recueil Dalloz-Sirey
RDS/TSR	Revue de Droit Social/Tijdschrift voor Sociaal Recht
RECIEL	Review of European Community and International Environmental law
REDP	Revue européenne de droit public
Rev EDE	Revista española de Derecho Europeo
Rev IS	Review of International Studies
RFDA	Revue française de droit administratif
RFDC	Revue française de droit constitutionnel
RGDIP	Revue générale de droit international public
RIDC	Revue internationale de droit comparé
RIEJ	Revue interdisciplinaire d'études juridiques
Riv DE	Rivista di diritto europeo
RIW	Recht der internationalen Wirtschaft
RMC	Revue du Marché Commun
RMCUE	Revue du Marché Commun et de l'Union européenne
RMUE	Revue du Marché Unique européen
RTDE	Revue trimestrielle de droit européen
RTDF	Revue trimestrielle de droit familial
RTDH	Revue trimestrielle des droits de l'homme
RUDH	Revue universelle des droits de l'homme
RW	Rechtskundig Weekblad
SADC	Southern African Development Community
SATCEN	European Union Satellite Centre
SEW	SEW—Tijdschrift voor Europees en economisch recht
SMEs	Small and medium-sized enterprises
SRB	Single Resolution Board
SRM	Single Resolution Mechanism
SSM	Single Supervisory Mechanism
Stat LRev	Statute Law Review
Stb	Staatsblad van het Koninkrijk der Nederlanden
Stud Dipl	Studia Diplomatica
Swiss Rev I Comp L	Swiss Review of International Competition Law
TAgrR	Tijdschrift voor Agrarisch Recht
TBH	Tijdschrift voor Belgisch handelsrecht
TBP	Tijdschrift voor bestuurswetenschappen en publiekrecht

Tex Int'l LJ	Texas International Law Journal
Themis	Rechtsgeleerd Magazijn Themis
Tilburg For L Rev	Tilburg Foreign Law Review
TORB	Tijdschrift voor onderwijsrecht en onderwijsbeleid
TPR	Tijdschrift voor privaatrecht
Trb	Tractatenblad van het Koninkrijk der Nederlanden
TRIPS	Trade-related Aspects of Intellectual Property Rights
TRV	Tijdschrift voor rechtspersonen en vennootschappen
Tulane E & Civ LF	Tulane European and Civil Law Forum
TVVS	TVVS. Maandblad voor ondernemingsrecht en rechtspersonen
TVW	Tijdschrift voor Wetgeving
UEAPME	European Union of Crafts and Small and Medium-sized Enterprises
UN	United Nations
UNCTAD	United Nations Conference on Trade and Development
UNTS	United Nations - Treaty Series
ULR	Utrecht Law Review
VJTL	Vanderbilt Journal of Transnational Law
VAT	value added tax
VUWLR	Victoria University of Wellington Law Review
WEU	Western European Union
World Comp	World Competition
WPPT	WIPO Performances and Phonograms Treaty
WTO	World Trade Organization
WuW	Wirtschaft und Wettbewerb
YARS	Yearbook of Antitrust and Regulatory Studies
YECHR	Yearbook of the European Convention on Human Rights
YEL	Yearbook of European Law
YPIL	Yearbook of Private International Law
ZaöRV	Zeitschrift für ausländisches öffentliches Recht und Völkerrecht
ZEuP	Zeitschrift für Europäisches Privatrecht
ZEuS	Zeitschrift für Europarechtliche Studien
ZfRV	Zeitschrift für Rechtsvergleichung, internationales Privatrecht und Europarecht
ZHW	Zeitschrift für das gesamte Handelsrecht und Wirtschaftsrecht
ZöR	Zeitschrift für öffentliches Recht
ZVglRW	Zeitschrift für vergleichende Rechtswissenschaft

Overview of Differentiated Integration among European States

		EEA (para. 10-020)	Euro area (para. 9-033)	Schengen *acquis* (para. 8-006)			ESDP (para. 10-032)	EU accession negotiation (para. 4-014)
				Schengen area	Integration existing acquis	Further development acquis		
EU Member States	Austria	X	X	X	X	X	X	
	Belgium	X	X	X	X	X	X	
	Bulgaria	X			X	X	X	
	Cyprus	X	X		X	X	X	
	Croatia	X			X	X	X	
	Czech Rep.	X		X	X	X	X	
	Denmark	X	(opt-out)	X	X	(opt-in)		
	Estonia	X	X	X	X	X	X	
	Finland	X	X	X	X	X	X	
	France	X	X	X	X	X	X	
	Germany	X	X	X	X	X	X	
	Greece	X	X	X	X	X	X	
	Hungary	X		X	X	X	X	
	Ireland	X	X		(opt-in)		X	
	Italy	X	X	X	X	X	X	
	Latvia	X	X	X	X	X	X	
	Lithuania	X	X	X	X	X	X	
	Luxembourg	X	X	X	X	X	X	
	Malta	X	X	X	X	X	X	
	Netherlands	X	X	X	X	X	X	
	Poland	X		X	X	X	X	
	Portugal	X	X	X	X	X	X	
	Romania	X			X	X	X	
	Slovak Rep.	X	X	X	X	X	X	
	Slovenia	X	X	X	X	X	X	
	Spain	X	X	X	X	X	X	
	Sweden	X		X	X	X	X	
Candidate Member States	Albania							X
	Montenegro							X
	North Macedonia							X
	Serbia							X
	Turkey							X
EFTA	Iceland	X		X	X	X		
	Liechtenstein	X		X	X	X		
	Norway	X		X	X	X		
	Switzerland			X	X	X		

PART I
CONSTITUTING THE EUROPEAN UNION

The European Union constitutes a legal order based on two treaties, the Treaty on European Union (TEU) and the Treaty on the Functioning of the European Union (TFEU) and on the Charter of Fundamental Rights of the European Union. As the 'constitutional' foundation of the European Union, the rules they contain structure the interaction of the Union's institutions and the relationship of the Union with its Member States and its citizens. Against that background, this book defines EU constitutional law as the rules of Union law relating to the general objectives, the allocation of competences, and the way in which legislative, executive, and judicial functions are performed within the European Union.

The origin of the European Union goes back to the European Communities established in 1951 and 1957. The first part of this book describes the parallel emergence of the Communities and the various forms of cooperation that the Member States set up outside the Communities, explaining how the European Union has combined these two paths towards integration (Chapter 1). It explains how successive Treaty amendments, most recently the Lisbon Treaty, have led to the current TEU and TFEU (Chapter 2) and sets out the procedures for amending these Treaties (Chapter 3) and for the accession to and withdrawal from the Union (Chapter 4).

1
The Development from European Communities to European Union

I. The Establishment of the European Communities

Communities. The starting point of the European Union was the three European Communities, which were established by treaty: the European Coal and Steel Community (ECSC), the European Economic Community (EEC, later the European Community, EC), and the European Atomic Energy Community (Euratom or EAEC). The legal provisions that were brought about in the framework of these Communities have been generally referred to as 'Community law'. Prior to this 'Community' integration process and in parallel thereto, European States have engaged in other forms of cooperation. Indeed, the Member States of the European Union have concluded agreements amongst themselves concerning cooperation in areas falling outside the Communities' sphere of operation to which they did not attach the same legal consequences as to Community action. **1.001**

Union. In 1992 the link which existed in practice between the two integration paths was institutionalized by packaging them into the European Union, yet without altering the specific legal character of either path. As a result, the distinction remained between Community and non-Community action, whereby only acts of the institutions based on one of the Community Treaties constituted a source of 'Community law'. This distinction largely disappeared with the entry into force on 1 December 2009 of the Lisbon Treaty, which merged both Community and non-Community provisions into one European Union based on the two aforementioned treaties (TEU and TFEU). As a result, the EC was replaced by the European Union (only Euratom continued to exist separately).[1] **1.002**

A. Post-war initiatives for European Integration

European integration. Europe's history is punctuated by attempts to bring peoples and States together in larger entities. At various times, powerful leaders have tried to establish a pan-European State by conquering and annexing neighbouring territories. The common factor in all these attempts was that they tried to unify peoples or States by force. Gradually, however, the idea emerged that European States could benefit from a process of peaceful cooperation. In the first half of the twentieth century, prominent politicians and intellectuals developed concrete proposals to achieve 'European integration' by step-by-step voluntary cooperation. The chaos of Europe in the aftermath of the Second World War turned out to be the ideal setting to turn this political idea into reality. **1.003**

---

[1] See Protocol (No. 2) annexed to the Treaty of Lisbon amending the Treaty establishing the European Atomic Energy Community, OJ 2007 C306/199.

1.004 **Economic and military cooperation.** The idea of 'European integration' was brought back to the attention of the public on 19 September 1946 by a speech made by Winston Churchill at the University of Zürich in which he called for the establishment of 'a kind of United States of Europe' on the continent. This call was in line with the desire on the part of the United States and the United Kingdom to establish cooperation between Western European States as a counterweight to the Soviet Union's increasing power; a cooperation, however, in which the United Kingdom was not to participate, in the view of Churchill.[2]

On a more limited scale, the Benelux countries (Belgium, Luxembourg, and the Netherlands) had already set an example by founding a customs union in 1948, which was later converted into an economic union in which their economic, financial, and social policies were coordinated.[3] The Committee of Ministers of the Benelux Union is assisted by a general secretariat and advisory bodies, including the Advisory Benelux Interparliamentary Council. A Benelux Court of Justice is responsible for ensuring the uniform interpretation of agreements concluded between the Benelux countries.[4] A first step towards economic cooperation was taken on 16 April 1948, when the Organisation for European Economic Cooperation (OEEC) was set up to coordinate economic recovery in Europe and in particular to distribute aid granted under the Marshall Plan.[5] Military cooperation was also initiated when France, the United Kingdom, and the Benelux countries signed the Brussels Treaty of 17 March 1948.[6] This was followed by the establishment of the North Atlantic Treaty Organization (NATO), set up by the North Atlantic Treaty of 4 April 1949.[7]

1.005 **Congress of Europe.** In May 1948 prominent persons from different social, cultural, and political circles meeting at the 'Congress of Europe' held in The Hague passed a number of resolutions working out the idea of European integration in two ways. First, they called for a European organization to be set up to safeguard the democratic systems of the European

---

[2] For the text of the speech, see https://www.cvce.eu.

[3] Treaty of The Hague of 3 February 1958 establishing a Benelux Economic Union (UNTS 5471) which succeeded the Customs Convention between Belgium, Luxembourg, and the Netherlands signed in London on 5 September 1944. The Treaty of 1958 was replaced in 2010 by a renewed Benelux Treaty signed at The Hague on 17 June 2008, which changed the official name from Benelux Economic Union to Benelux Union. The leading role played by Benelux (recognized in Article 350 TFEU, para. 26-008, *infra*), has now been largely assumed by the EU. For an analysis, see Rood, 'Een nieuw Benelux-verdrag: een nieuw élan voor de samenwerking? (2010) SEW 186–91; Wouters, Van Langenhove, Vidal, De Lombaerde, and De Vriendt, *De Benelux: tijd voor een wedergeboorte?* (Intersentia, 2007); Wouters and Vidal, 'Towards a Rebirth of Benelux?' (2007) BTIR 533–68; Leclercq, 'Le droit Benelux sous un jour nouveau, droit inconnu?' (2006) JT 613–24; Oosterkamp, 'Is er naast de Europese Unie nog toekomst voor de Benelux?' (2002) SEW 237–40; Mortelmans, 'Benelux 50 jaar: voorlopen, gelijklopen of doodlopen?' (1995) SEW 399–403.

[4] Treaty on the establishment and statute of the Benelux Court of Justice, signed at Brussels on 31 March 1965, as supplemented by the Protocol of 29 April 1969. It has been in force since 1 January 1974. The Benelux Court of Justice—composed of judges of the highest courts of each of the three countries—is itself a court against whose decisions there is no remedy under national law and hence is required by the third para. of Article 267 TFEU to make a reference for a preliminary ruling to the Court of Justice of the EC whenever a question of Union law is raised before it: C-337/95, *Parfums Christian Dior*, 1997, paras 15–31.

[5] Convention on European Economic Cooperation, signed in Paris on 16 April 1948, UNTS 59 (Cmd 7796). The OEEC was replaced on 30 September 1961 by the Organization for Economic Cooperation and Development (OECD), which also seeks to promote, alongside economic growth, employment, and rising living standards in member countries, the well-being of developing countries and other States. The Convention on the Organisation for Economic Cooperation and Development was signed in Paris on 14 December 1960 (1961) UNTS 21 (Cmd 1646). Its website is http://www.oecd.org. Article 220(1) TFEU makes provision for cooperation between the European Union and the OECD. See also Article 202 EAEC.

[6] Treaty between Belgium, France, Luxembourg, the Netherlands, and the United Kingdom (1949) UNTS 1 (Cmd. 7599).

[7] North Atlantic Treaty (1949) UNTS 56 (Cmd 7789). NATO's website is http://www.nato.int.

countries through multilateral supervision of compliance with human rights. Second, they called for a pooling of the crucial components of economic, industrial, and—hence also to some extent—political life with a view to forestalling the threat of war in Western Europe.

The Council of Europe. With the signature of the Statute of the Council of Europe on 5 May 1949, the ideas formulated at the Congress of Europe gave rise to an international organization.[8] The Council of Europe, which is based in Strasbourg, has, at present, forty-six member countries.[9] It may deal with all political, economic, and social matters of European interest and thus has a more extensive field of activity than the European Union.[10] The organization has a Committee of Ministers, which is advised by the Parliamentary Assembly (formerly the Consultative Assembly). Although the Assembly has been made up of delegates from the national parliaments since 1951, the Council of Europe is still organized on an intergovernmental model. It does not have any actual power to make laws. The two instruments employed in the context of the Council of Europe are non-binding resolutions and draft conventions, which take effect only between States which have ratified them. Whilst it has evolved into a valuable forum for discussion, providing interesting ideas for European cooperation, its structure does not afford any genuine prospects of realizing them.

1.006

European Convention on Human Rights. The most important convention which has come into being under the auspices of the Council of Europe is the European Convention for the Protection of Human Rights and Fundamental Freedoms (ECHR) of 4 November 1950.[11] The distinct place occupied by the ECHR within the Council of Europe is clear from two special characteristics.

1.007

First and foremost, the Council of Europe is identified with the ECHR. No State can join the Council of Europe unless it agrees to accede to the ECHR. At the same time, States may accede to the ECHR only if they are members of the Council of Europe (Article 59(1) ECHR). The preamble to the ECHR states that the central aim of the Council of Europe is 'the collective enforcement of certain of the rights stated in the Universal Declaration' of Human

---

[8] (1949) UNTS 61 (Cmd 7778). The Council of Europe's website is http://www.coe.int.

[9] The founder members were Belgium, Denmark, France, Greece (which withdrew from the Council of Europe in 1970 to be readmitted in 1974), Ireland, Italy, Luxembourg, the Netherlands, Norway, Sweden, and the United Kingdom. The Federal Republic of Germany, Iceland, and Turkey joined in 1950; Austria in 1956; Cyprus in 1961; Switzerland in 1963; Malta in 1965; Portugal in 1976; Spain in 1977; Liechtenstein in 1978; San Marino in 1988; Finland in 1989; Hungary in 1990; Poland in 1991; Bulgaria in 1992; the Czech Republic, Estonia, Lithuania, Romania, Slovakia, and Slovenia in 1993 (Czechoslovakia had already joined as a unitary State in 1991); Andorra in 1994; Albania, Latvia, Macedonia, Moldova, the Ukraine, and North Macedonia (previously named the Former Yugoslav Republic of Macedonia) in 1995; Croatia and Russia in 1996; Georgia in 1999; Armenia and Azerbaijan in 2001; Bosnia and Herzegovina in 2002; Serbia in 2003 (originally joined as Serbia and Montenegro); Monaco in 2004; and Montenegro in 2007. Russia ceased to be a member following its exclusion on 16 March 2022.

[10] Article 220(1) TFEU makes provision for cooperation between the European Union and the Council of Europe. See also Article 200 EAEC. See already Ouchterlony, 'The European Communities and the Council of Europe' (1984) LIEI 59–74.

[11] Cmd 8969. The ECHR and Protocols (Nos 1 and 6) thereto are set out in Schedule 1 to the Human Rights Act 1998. For an exhaustive discussion of the rights set out in the ECHR, see Reid, *A Practitioner's Guide to the European Convention on Human Rights* (Sweet & Maxwell, 2019); van Dijk, Van Hoof, van Rijn, and Zwaak, *Theory and Practice of the European Convention on Human Rights* (Intersentia, 2018); Schabas, *The European Convention on Human Rights: A Commentary* (OUP, 2017); Harris, O'Boyle, Bates, and Buckley, *Harris, O'Boyle & Warbrick: Law of the European Convention on Human Rights* (OUP, 2014); Mowbray, *Cases, Materials and Commentary on the European Convention on Human Rights* (OUP, 2012); Ovey and White, *Jacobs, White & Ovey: The European Convention on Human Rights* (OUP, 2010); Grabenwarter, *Europäische Menschenrechtskonvention: ein Studienbuch* (Beck, 2008).

Rights proclaimed by the General Assembly of the United Nations on 10 December 1948'. Accordingly, every person within the jurisdiction of the Contracting States is *ipso facto* protected by the ECHR, irrespective of his or her nationality or place of residence.

The ECHR constitutes a first expression of supranationalism in the European integration process. With the creation of the European Court of Human Rights, the ECHR provides an enforcement structure which subjects the States to 'European' supervision of their compliance with the provisions of the Convention. Ratification of the ECHR has the result that any Contracting Party may refer to the European Court of Human Rights any alleged breach of the provisions of the ECHR and the protocols thereto (Article 33 ECHR). More importantly, any person, non-governmental organization, or group of individuals claiming to be the victim of a violation by one of the Contracting Parties of the rights set forth in the ECHR may submit an application to the European Court of Human Rights (Article 34 ECHR). The procedure for dealing with individual applications has been radically altered by Protocol (No. 11) to the ECHR, which has been in force since 1 November 1998.[12] If an individual application is not declared inadmissible by a committee of the Court consisting of three judges, it will be referred to a Chamber of seven judges which decides on its admissibility and merits (Articles 28 and 29 ECHR).[13] After the Chamber has given judgment, any party may request that the case be referred to the Grand Chamber of seventeen judges (Article 43(1) ECHR). The Grand Chamber will accept such a request only if a panel of five judges determines that the case raises a serious question affecting the interpretation or application of the Convention or the Protocols thereto, or a serious issue of general importance (Article 43(2) ECHR). Judgments of the Grand Chamber and—in so far as no request is made to refer the case to the Grand Chamber or such a request is refused—of the Chambers are final and the Contracting Parties have to abide by them (Articles 44 and 46 ECHR).

As a result of Protocol No. 11 the Strasbourg procedure has come a long way from the original enforcement procedure, which severely limited direct access to the European Court of Human Rights by individual victims of violations. Originally, persons or groups of individuals lodged a complaint with the European Commission of Human Rights, which had to decide whether to consider the petition admissible and whether to remit the case to the Court of Human Rights. It could only do so if the Contracting State against which the petition was lodged had made a separate declaration that it recognized the competence of the Commission to receive such complaints and accepted the Court's jurisdiction. Under the present system, the jurisdiction of the Strasbourg Court and the individual right to submit applications are accepted by all the Contracting States.

---

[12] Protocol (No. 11) to the European Convention for the Protection of Human Rights and Fundamental Freedoms restructuring the control machinery established thereby, signed on 11 May 1994. For the position of the United Kingdom, see the Human Rights Act 1998. The Protocol is discussed in Wachsmann, Eissen, and Flauss (eds), *Le Protocole N° 11 à la Convention européenne des droits de l'homme* (Bruylant, 1995); Verrijdt, 'De gevolgen van het Elfde Protocol bij het E.V.R.M. Dilemma tussen de kwaliteit en de kwantiteit van de (grond)rechtsbedeling' (2002–2003) Jura Falc 571–651; Drzemczewski, 'The European Human Rights Convention: Protocol No. 11— Entry into Force and First Year of Application' (2000) Human Rights LJ 1–17; De Schutter, 'La nouvelle Cour européenne des droits de l'homme' (1998) CDE 319–52; Schermers, 'The Eleventh Protocol to the European Convention on Human Rights' (1994) ELRev 367–84.

[13] In certain cases, the Chamber may, before it has rendered its judgment, relinquish jurisdiction in favour of the Grand Chamber of seventeen judges, see Article 30 ECHR.

B. The ECSC Treaty

Schuman plan. The most successful initiative for European integration, which would lead to the establishment of the European Communities and, eventually, the European Union, was tabled on 9 May 1950, when the French Foreign Minister Robert Schuman launched a proposal to bring the coal and steel sectors of European States under one common policy. This proposal, which had earlier been conceived by Jean Monnet, a senior French civil servant, satisfied the French Government's concern to avoid a third resurgence of the German war machine and, at the same time, sought to reinforce the political clout of the Western European States in the face of Soviet expansionism in Central and Eastern Europe. The solemn declaration by Schuman on 9 May 1950 made clear that this initiative was a first step in a process of integration which would develop further and was open to other States. Schuman deliberately opted to start that process of integration by concrete cooperation in a defined field. He famously stated that 'Europe will not be made all at once, or according to a single plan. It will be built upon concrete achievements which first create a de facto solidarity'.[14] The aim was to transfer the administration of two basic industries to an independent supranational institution, the High Authority, which would be empowered to take decisions binding on both the Member States and coal and steel undertakings. Accordingly, the Schuman plan was based on a functional approach to the process of European integration which set specific aims and conferred genuine decision-making power on common institutions in designated fields to achieve them.

1.008

European Coal and Steel Community. Only five States responded to the French invitation to participate in the Schuman plan by attending the preparatory conference which opened in Paris on 20 June 1950. On 18 April 1951 in Paris, Belgium, France, Germany, Italy, Luxembourg, and the Netherlands signed the Treaty establishing the European Coal and Steel Community (ECSC Treaty) for a period of fifty years (the ECSC entered into force on 23 July 1952 and came to an end on 23 July 2002).[15] Since the tasks of the ECSC could be taken over by the European Community, the ECSC Treaty was not extended.[16] The ECSC Treaty established a common market in coal and steel by abolishing and prohibiting within the Community all import and export duties and charges having equivalent effect and, likewise, all quantitative restrictions on the movement of products, together with all measures discriminating between producers, purchasers, or consumers or interfering with the purchaser's free choice of supplier. Under the provisions of the Treaty, State aid and restrictive practices were prohibited. The ECSC institutions were given the task of ensuring an orderly supply to the market, equal access to sources of production, the lowest possible

1.009

---

[14] The text of the declaration is available at http:www.cvce.eu. This declaration was echoed in the preamble to the ECSC Treaty: 'recognising that Europe can be built only through practical achievements which will first of all create real solidarity, and through the establishment of common bases for economic development'.

[15] See Article 97 ECSC. Upon the expiry of the Treaty, the net assets of the ECSC were earmarked for research in sectors related to the coal and steel industry; see the Protocol annexed to the EC Treaty by the Treaty of Nice (OJ 2001 C80/67) and Decision 2002/234/ECSC of the Representatives of the governments of the Member States, meeting within the Council, of 27 February 2002 on the financial consequences of the expiry of the ECSC Treaty and on the research fund for coal and steel (OJ 2002 L79/42). See Obwexer, 'Das Ende der Europäischen Gemeinschaft für Kohle und Stahl' (2002) EuZW 517–24.

[16] See the Resolution of the Council of the European Union and the representatives of the governments of the Member States, meeting within the Council of 20 July 1998 concerning the expiry of the Treaty establishing the European Coal and Steel Community, OJ 1998 C247/5. For the continuity of the Community legal order and the succession of the ECSC, see T-24/07, *ThyssenKrupp Stainless*, 2009, paras 75–80 and 83.

prices, the encouragement of more efficient and modernized production and resource utilization, improved working conditions, and the growth of international trade.[17]

By accepting joint administration of sectors of their national economies, the founding States went further than the international consultation which had previously taken place within the Council of Europe (see para. 1-006, *supra*). This new form of cooperation was referred to from the outset as 'supranational' (see para. 1-020 *et seq.*, *infra*).

1.010 **ECSC Institutions.** The ECSC Treaty was a textbook example of a *traité-loi*. It contained virtually all the rules that the Member States deemed necessary for the smooth operation of a common market in the coal and steel sector. Since the Member States considered that their interests were sufficiently protected by the detailed Treaty provisions, they were prepared to place their confidence in an expert authority responsible for ensuring that those provisions were implemented. The Treaty therefore empowered a High Authority, composed of experts required to be independent vis-à-vis both the Member States and industry, to take binding decisions and make recommendations.[18]

The High Authority's autonomous power to take decisions was limited to matters already extensively regulated by the Treaty. More fundamental political and economic options required regulatory interaction between the High Authority and the Special Council of Ministers, an organ composed of representatives of the Member States.[19]

The ECSC Treaty also set up two supervisory institutions: a Common Assembly, composed of representatives from the national parliaments; and a Court of Justice, tasked with ensuring that 'in the interpretation and application of this Treaty, and of the rules laid down for the implementation thereof, the law is observed'.[20]

C. Proposals for political cooperation

1.011 **European Defence Community.** The success of the ECSC initially led to plans to bring political matters, such as defence and foreign policy, also under the umbrella of a supranational organization. On 27 May 1952 the ECSC Member States signed the Treaty establishing the European Defence Community (EDC).[21] The Member States of the EDC were to make army divisions available to the European Defence Forces under a Commissariat. The EDC was also to have a Council, a Parliamentary Assembly (the ECSC Common Assembly plus nine delegates) and to use the Court of Justice of the ECSC. The EDC was based on a plan put forward by the French Minister of Defence René Pleven which offered a solution enabling a military security structure to be put in place in continental Europe as a counterweight to the expansion of communism—a present threat in view of the Korean War—yet without ignoring French resistance to German rearmament.

---

[17] For an evaluation of the extent to which these objectives were achieved, see Hosman, 'Bij het afscheid van het EGKS-Verdrag: Droom en werkelijkheid' (2002) SEW 134–44.
[18] Articles 8 and 14 ECSC.
[19] See, on the one hand, Article 26 and, on the other, Articles 85 and 95, first para. ECSC. For a retrospective look at the application of those provisions, see Meunier, 'La Communauté européenne du charbon et de l'acier est morte, vive la fédération européenne!' (2001) RMCUE 509–15.
[20] See Articles 24 and 31 ECSC.
[21] See Fursdon, *The European Defence Community: A History* (Macmillan, 1980).

Prior to the entry into force of the EDC Treaty, the Ministers of Foreign Affairs of the ECSC decided to implement Article 38 of the EDC Treaty, which charged the Common Assembly with considering any changes eventually to be made to the Treaty, having regard to the principle that 'the final organisation which will replace the present provisional organisation should be so conceived as to be able to constitute one of the elements in a federal or confederal structure'. The aim of the changes was to coordinate the agencies for European cooperation, already existing or which might be established, within the framework of a federal or confederal structure (Article 38(1) EDC Treaty). The Common Assembly of the ECSC—meeting as the '*Ad Hoc* Assembly'—proposed that a European Political Community should be set up to coordinate Member States' foreign policy and establish a common market. The institutional structure of the ECSC was to be taken over and more extensive powers were to be given to the 'supranational' institutions, namely the independent policy institution and the Parliamentary Assembly.[22] Both the EDC Treaty and the draft Statute of the European Political Community expressly set out to establish a Community of a 'supranational character'.[23]

The whole plan fell through when, on 29 August 1954, the French National Assembly voted to postpone ratification of the EDC Treaty *sine die*. The Gaullists and Communists had opposed the EDC, the former fearful of surrendering French sovereignty, the latter shrinking from German rearmament.

Defence cooperation. In October 1954, a solution was found to the problem of growing German strength. NATO accepted the Federal Republic of Germany as a member. In addition, the Paris Protocol of 23 October 1954 amended the Brussels Treaty (see para. 1-004, *supra*) and set up the Western European Union (WEU),[24] which was joined by Germany, together with Italy. That organization continued into being until it was decided on 31 March 2010 to have it dismantled, as the Lisbon Treaty nowadays imposes a duty of mutual military assistance on the Member States.[25]

1.012

D. The EEC Treaty and the EAEC Treaty

Spaak Report. Following the failure of the EDC, the advocates of European integration switched to a more realistic economic and social approach. Encouraged by the Benelux countries and the influential Action Committee for the United States of Europe, the way was open to a *relance européenne*. Starting from a plan which had been put forward by the Dutch Foreign Minister Johan Willem Beyen, the Benelux countries proposed establishing a common market and coordinating policy decisions relating to market support. By the

1.013

---

[22] For the draft text, see http:www.cvce.eu.
[23] Article 1 EDC Treaty; Article 1 of the Draft Statute. See von Lindeiner-Wildau, *La supranationalité en tant que principe de droit* (Sijthoff, 1970), 9.
[24] The Treaty establishing the Western European Union and Protocols thereto, signed in Paris on 23 October 1954 (1955) UNTS 39 (Cmd 9498). See Dumoulin and Remacle, *L'Union de l'Europe occidentale. Phénix de la défense européenne* (Bruylant, 1998).
[25] See the Statement of 31 March 2010 of the Presidency of the Permanent Council of the WEU on behalf of the High Contracting Parties to the modified Brussels Treaty (Belgium, France, Germany, Greece, Italy, Luxembourg, The Netherlands, Portugal, Spain, and the United Kingdom), recalling that, since the entry into force of the Lisbon Treaty, Article 42(7) of the TEU commits the Member States to mutual aid and assistance in case of armed aggression.

Resolution of Messina of 2 June 1955, the Member States subscribed to these proposals and charged an intergovernmental committee, chaired by the Belgian Foreign Minister Paul-Henri Spaak, with working out the still embryonic ideas. The Spaak Report amounted to an all-embracing programme for the establishment of a common market, which was too detailed to be enshrined in a treaty. The resultant broad substantive approach made it necessary to rethink the regulatory process capable of reacting to economic and social developments.

1.014 **European Economic Community.** The Treaty establishing the European Economic Community (EEC Treaty, commonly referred to as the Treaty of Rome), which was signed in Rome on 25 March 1957 and entered into force on 1 January 1958,[26] took over the substantive aims and institutional structure proposed in the Spaak Report. The preamble and Articles 2 and 3 EEC set forth the objectives contemplated by the Contracting Parties. Article 2 EEC announced ambitious aims to be achieved through the establishment of a common market and the progressive approximation of the Member States' economic policies.[27] Article 3 EEC specified those objectives by listing the tasks of the Community. First, Article 3 EEC looked forward to the achievement of four economic freedoms. Free movement of goods, persons, services, and capital (including payments) formed the pillars on which the common market was based.[28] The 'activities of the Community' also included 'the approximation of the laws of Member States to the extent required for the proper functioning of the common market'[29] and 'the establishment of a common customs tariff and of a common commercial policy towards third countries'.[30] In order to prevent undertakings and Member States from frustrating the common market, free competition was to be secured.[31] Article 3 further provided for the adoption of common policies in the spheres of agriculture and transport. Lastly, Article 3 made provision for the coordination of the Member States' economic policies.[32]

1.015 **European Atomic Energy Community.** At the same time as the EEC Treaty, the Treaty establishing a European Atomic Energy Community (EAEC also known as Euratom) was signed. It also entered into force on 1 January 1958. Its aim was to create the conditions necessary for the speedy establishment and growth of nuclear industries. To this end, Article 2

---

[26] Article 8 of the Treaty on European Union of 7 February 1992 amended the Treaty establishing the European Economic Community so as to establish a European Community (EC). The abbreviation 'EEC' is therefore used in this work only where express reference is made to the original EEC Treaty.

[27] Four of the dynamically formulated aims were of an economic and social nature—(1) harmonious development of economic activities throughout the Community, (2) continuous and balanced expansion, (3) an increase in stability, and (4) an accelerated raising of the standard of living— whilst the fifth was simply a policy of seeking 'closer relations between the States belonging to [the Community]'.

[28] Free movement of goods (Articles 9 to 37 EEC), together with free movement of persons, services, and capital (Articles 48 to 73 EEC), the common agricultural policy (Articles 38 to 47 EEC) and the common transport policy (Articles 74 to 84 EEC), formed the 'foundations of the Community' (Part Two of the EEC Treaty).

[29] See Articles 99 to 102 EEC.

[30] See the section entitled 'Setting up of the common customs tariff' (Articles 18 to 29 EEC) in the title on the free movement of goods and the chapter entitled 'Commercial policy' (Articles 110 to 116 EEC) in the title on the economic policy of the Community.

[31] See Articles 85 to 98 EEC.

[32] This related to conjunctural policy (Article 103 EEC) and balance of payments (Articles 104 to 109 EEC). 'Social policy' (Articles 117 to 122 EEC) was not mentioned as such in Article 3, although it did refer to the 'creation of a European Social Fund' (Articles 123 to 128 EEC) and to the 'establishment of a European Investment Bank' (Articles 129 and 130 EEC). The last 'activity of the Community' set out in Article 3 is 'association of the overseas countries and territories' (Articles 131 to 136 EEC).

EAEC provided for common policies on research, safety standards, investment and installations, supplies of ores and fuels, application of the nuclear industry, right of ownership in fissile materials and international relations in the field of nuclear energy, and introduced a common market.[33] The EAEC Treaty does not embody the detailed market rules of the ECSC Treaty, but does share that Treaty's sectoral approach.

Traité-cadre. Since, in principle, the EEC Treaty covered all sectors of the economy and sought to attain the chosen policy objectives progressively, it was impossible to lay down the requisite rules of law exhaustively in the Treaty itself. Accordingly, it was not a *traité-loi* but a *traité-cadre* containing provisions relating to the functioning of the institutions and decision-making, alongside basic substantive rules which had to be complied with by the Community and the Member States. Within the framework of the EEC Treaty—and pursuant thereto—a substantial corpus of rules had been formulated, with the result that it could be said to be a *traité-fondation*[34] or a *traité-constitution* (see para. 1-028, *supra*).

1.016

Institutions. The EEC Treaty and EAEC Treaty built on the institutional structure of the ECSC Treaty. The institutional set up of the EEC and the EAEC also consisted of a Commission (the equivalent of the ECSC High Authority), a Council, an Assembly, and a Court of Justice. The parallels with the ECSC Treaty, however, did not extend any further than the organizational level, since the extensive programme to be achieved by the establishment of the EEC and the EAEC necessitated other roles for the institutions with decision-making powers.

1.017

The hub of the decision-making process was located in the Council. The Member States did not wish to vest any legislative powers in the Commission, because substantive policy choices had often been deliberately left open in the EEC Treaty. The ultimate policy choices were therefore to be determined by the Member States, within the Council. For those reasons, too, the role of the Assembly (which later became the European Parliament) was not extended either. The Commission's task, in principle at least, was confined to making proposals, implementing legislation, and supervising compliance with Community law.

The three Treaties (ECSC, EEC, and EAEC) provided for different powers for the institutions, although this was not reflected at the organizational level, since the institutions which each Treaty brought into being in parallel were merged. Already in 1957, when the EEC Treaty and the EAEC Treaty came into being, the Member States concluded the Convention on certain institutions common to the European Communities.[35] That Convention provided that there should be one Parliament and one Court of Justice serving the three Communities in accordance with the powers conferred on those institutions by the different Treaties (Convention, Articles 1–2 and 3–4). At the same time, it was provided that one Economic and Social Committee was to perform such tasks as the EEC Treaty and

---

[33] For a good description of the EAEC Treaty, see Cusak, 'A Tale of Two Treaties: An Assessment of the Euratom Treaty in Relation to the EC Treaty' (2003) CMLRev 117–42; 'Legislative Competences of Euratom and the European Community in the Energy Sector: The "Nuclear Package" of the Commission' (2003) ELRev 664–85. See also, X, *Euratom: 50 Years of Nuclear Energy Serving Europe* (Office for Official Publications of the European Communities, 2007). For a call for the integration of Euratom into a comprehensive European Union, see Trüe, 'The Euratom Community Treaty's prospects at the start of the new millennium' (2006) IJNL 247–60.

[34] Lesguillons, *L'application d'un traité-fondation: le traité instituant la C.E.E.* (Librairie Générale de Droit et de Jurisprudence, 1968).

[35] For the English text, see http:www.cvce.eu.

the EAEC Treaty conferred on it (Article 5 Convention). The Treaty establishing a Single Council and a Single Commission of the European Communities, known as the Merger Treaty, which was concluded on 8 April 1965 and entered into effect on 1 July 1967, was a further step in that direction.[36] It provided that one Council and one Commission would play the roles specifically ascribed to them by the various treaties. In addition, the Merger Treaty unified the Staff Regulations (Article 24) and laid down the principle that there should be a single budget of the European Communities (Article 20).

The Convention and the Merger Treaty were repealed by Article 9 of the Treaty of Amsterdam, which, however, confirmed the rule that the same institutions would act under each of the Treaties on the basis of the specific powers that such Treaty conferred to them.[37]

1.018 **Community method.** The Community's objectives and competences laid down in the EEC Treaty were supplemented by the Single European Act (SEA), the EU Treaty, the Treaty of Amsterdam, and the Treaty of Nice (see para. 1-051 *et seq.*, *infra*). In contrast, the objectives and competences of the ECSC and the EAEC remained unchanged. At the institutional level, the initial Treaty structure was largely preserved, although significant changes have been made to the respective roles of the institutions by subsequent amending Treaties, most recently by the Lisbon Treaty (13 December 2007). Throughout these changes the foundations of the institutional set-up of the EEC were maintained: the representatives of the Member States may only act within the Council on a proposal from the Commission by majority decision—according to later Treaty amendments, in principle, jointly with the European Parliament—and the Court of Justice is competent to interpret and enforce the rules that were adopted in this way. This system is commonly referred to as 'the Community method'.

1.019 **Reaction to the EEC.** Shortly after the EEC Treaty was signed, seven other Western European countries, Austria, Denmark, Norway, Portugal, the United Kingdom, Sweden, and Switzerland decided to cooperate economically. They were unwilling to go as far as the cooperation established by the EEC Treaty, which set up a customs union. Instead, they preferred to set up a free-trade area, without common external tariffs or supplementary harmonization of economic and social legislation.[38] On 4 January 1960, those seven States concluded the Convention establishing the European Free Trade Association (EFTA).[39]

---

[36] OJ 1967 152/5. See further Linthorst Homan, 'The Merger of the European Communities' (1965–66) CMLRev 397–419; Bleckmann, 'Die Einheit der Europäischen Gemeinschaftsrechtsordnung. Einheit oder Mehrheit der Europäischen Gemeinschaften' (1978) EuR 95–104. As regards the merger idea, see also: Van Stempel, 'Die Fusion der Organe der Europäischen Gemeinschaften', in Hallstein and Schlochauer (eds), *Zur Integration Europas. Festschrift für C.F. Ophüls* (Müller, 1965), 229–41.
[37] Amsterdam Treaty, Article 9(1), (2), and (3).
[38] According to Article XXIV(8) of the General Agreement on Tariffs and Trade (GATT, para. 10-010, *infra*), a free-trade area is a group of two or more customs territories in which the duties and other restrictive regulations of trade are eliminated on substantially all the trade between the constituent territories in products originating in such territories. A free-trade area differs from a customs union, in which the reciprocal abolition of restrictions on trade is coupled with a common external tariff; see the discussion in para. 7-015, *infra*.
[39] Convention establishing the European Free Trade Association, signed in Stockholm on 4 January 1960 (1960) UNTS 30, Cmnd 1026. EFTA's website is http://www.efta.int/. The EFTA States did not only aim at removing barriers to trade between themselves, but also referred expressly to the EEC Member States as potential members of a future multilateral economic cooperation association: see Jacot-Guillarmod, 'Expressions juridiques, au sein du système européen de libre-échange, du rapprochement de l'AELE et de la Communauté', in Capotorti et al., *Du droit international au droit de l'intégration. Liber Amicorum P. Pescatore* (Nomos, 1987), 317–18.

Finland, Iceland, and Liechtenstein joined later,[40] but first Denmark and the United Kingdom, then Portugal, and finally Austria, Finland, and Sweden left the organization to accede to the Communities and the Union (see para. 4-005, *infra*). EFTA's Council of Ministers and Committee of Parliamentarians have been supplemented—as far as the EFTA States belonging to the European Economic Area (Iceland, Liechtenstein, and Norway) are concerned—by a Standing Committee, a Joint Parliamentary Committee, a Surveillance Authority, and a Court of Justice (see para. 10-020, *infra*).

E. The supranational character of Community law

Community law. The EC Treaty and the EAEC Treaty constituted the foundation of 'Community law', which additionally consisted of the legislative and implementing measures adopted on the basis of the Treaties and the judicial interpretation of those Treaties and measures, supplemented by the unwritten general principles of law. Since the entry into force of the Lisbon Treaty on 1 December 2009, the EC has been replaced by the European Union and Community law—with its specific characteristics—has become Union law (see chapter 2). Community/Union law has its origin in international law, since the European Communities/Union constitute an 'international' organization based on treaties concluded between sovereign States. As a subject of law, the Community/Union acts vis-à-vis third countries in accordance with the rules of international law (see para. 14-005, *infra*). In contrast, relations between Member States (within the field of application of Community/Union law) and between Member States and the Communities/Union are no longer governed by international law.[41] Those relations are governed by Community/Union law. This is illustrated by the fact that the Court of Justice has given a different interpretation to provisions of the EC Treaty, on the one hand, and to corresponding provisions of international agreements concluded by the Community on the basis of the EC Treaty, on the other. The Court bases itself in this connection on the more extensive objectives of the EC Treaty, the specific characteristics of decision-making within the Community, and the possibilities of enforcing Community law.[42] The same reasoning holds good with regard to Union law since the entry into force of the Lisbon Treaty.

1.020

Supranational. With a view to distinguishing the Communities/Union and the Community/Union legal order more clearly from other forms of international organizations and from general international law, they are commonly referred to as a 'supranational' organization and as 'supranational' law. It is generally accepted that the term 'supranational'[43] refers to the particular set of relationships between Member States, Community/Union institutions, and individuals, of which the principal characteristics are as follows:

1.021

---

[40] Iceland became a member of EFTA on 1 March 1970, Finland (having been an associate member since 1961) on 1 January 1986, and Liechtenstein on 1 September 1991.
[41] See also Opinion 2/13, *Accession of the EU to the ECHR*, 2013, paras 155–77; C-284/16, *Achmea*, 2018, para. 33.
[42] See 270/80 *Polydor*, 1982, paras 14–20; Opinion 1/91, *Draft agreement between the Community, on the one hand, and the countries of the European Free Trade Association, on the other, relating to the creation of the European Economic Area*, 1991, paras 13–21. See para. 26-006, *infra*.
[43] The origin, meaning, and application of the term 'supranationality' are discussed extensively in von Lindeiner-Wildau, *La supranationalité en tant que principe de droit* (Sijthoff, 1970).

(a) the Community/Union has institutions which act independently of the Member States in terms of their composition and manner of operation;

(b) the Community/Union may take decisions by a majority, yet they will bind all the Member States;

(c) the institutions of the Community/Union implement those decisions or are responsible for supervising that they are properly implemented by the Member States;

(d) the founding Treaties and decisions of the Community/Union may give rise to rights and obligations on the part of individuals which are directly enforceable by courts in the Member States, even in the presence of conflicting provisions of national law.[44]

Consequently, the term 'supranationalism' fits the *sui generis* nature of the European Communities/Union perfectly. In addition, those characteristics express the dynamic nature of the integration process which has been taking place within the Communities/Union.[45]

1.022 (a) **Independent institutions**. The authentic French version of the ECSC Treaty used the term '*supranational*' in referring to the independent status of the High Authority (the Commission).[46] Indeed, the Commission is not made up of representatives of the governments of the Member States in the traditional manner of international institutions, as is still the case with the Council and the European Council. Members of the European Parliament, the Court of Justice, and the Court of Auditors are also independent from the governments of the Member States. In addition, the European Parliament is the only institution whose members are not appointed by the national governments (or the Council/European Council) but directly elected.[47]

1.023 (b) **Autonomous decision-making**. In international law, there is a principle of decision-making that States cannot be bound against their will. Although that principle is reflected in the contractual nature of the Treaties underlying the Communities/Union and in the requirement that certain votes in the Council have to be unanimous, in many respects it does not apply in the Community/Union legal order. In numerous cases a majority decision of the Council binds all Member States. In addition, the Court rejects the technique of international law whereby a State may enter a 'reservation' when a decision is taken and so avoid being bound by a provision of a treaty or a decision. The Court stresses that measures of the Communities/Union cannot be regarded as international agreements because of the independent institutional framework within which they are drawn up.[48] It further emphasizes that the rules laid down by the common institutions must be interpreted in a uniform

---

[44] cf. ibid., 45–61; Schermers and Blokker, *International Institutional Law* (Martinus Nijhoff, 1995), § 61, 41–2 (who mention, as additional requirements for supranational organizations, that the organization should be financially independent and that participating States must have the approval of all the States and the supranational institutions in order to leave the organization, wind it up, or change its powers); Hay, *Federalism and Supranational Organisations, Patterns for New Legal Structures* (University of Illinois Press, 1966), 30–4 (who sets out additional political qualifications, such as the compass of the organization's powers).

[45] Weiler, 'The Community System: the Dual Character of Supranationalism' (1981) YEL 267–306.

[46] See the original fifth and sixth paras of Article 9 ECSC (removed by Article 19 of the Merger Treaty and replaced by Article 10 of that Treaty, the wording of which was introduced as the new Article 9 ECSC by Article 9(2) of the EU Treaty). For an earlier use of the term and for its intentional omission from the EEC and EAEC Treaties, see Hay (n. 44, *supra*), 29–30; Jaenicke, 'Die Supranationalität der Europäischen Gemeinschaften', in Hallstein and Schlochauer (n. 36, *supra*), 85, 88.

[47] See para. 12-012, *infra*.

[48] 38/69, *Commission v Italy*, 1970, paras 10–11.

manner. That requirement would be detracted from if Community/Union law were to take account of reservations or objections entered by Member States at the preparatory stage.[49]

(c) **Implementation of decisions.** Member States of the Communities/Union must take all necessary measures to ensure fulfilment of the obligations arising for them under Community/Union law (see para. 5-043, *infra*). They are generally charged with implementing Community/Union law, unless implementation is specifically entrusted to an institution of the Communities/Union (see para. 18-001, *infra*). Under Community/Union law, Member States are subject to more far-reaching supervision than is generally the case under international law. Thus, the *exceptio non adimpleti contractus* (the retaliatory defence against a material breach of a treaty)[50] used in international law is not employed as a mechanism for enforcing reciprocal obligations; Community/Union law has procedures of its own for determining infringements and imposing sanctions therefor.[51] Under Article 344 TFEU Member States must submit any dispute concerning the interpretation or application of the Treaty to the methods of resolution provided for therein.[52] The jurisdiction of the Court of Justice is compulsory, and its judgments are binding throughout the Community/Union. In contrast, within the international legal order, the International Court of Justice adjudicates only if there is voluntary—general or specific—acceptance of the Court's jurisdiction on the part of the parties.

1.024

(d) **Separate legal order.** The Communities/Union constitute a legal order in their own right, which is different from the legal regimes commonly created by international agreements. The essential characteristics of the Community/Union legal order include the fact that individuals can rely in legal proceedings on a series of provisions of Community/Union law and the primacy of Community/Union law over the law of the Member States.[53] The Court of Justice established those basic principles in 1963 and 1964 in two ground-breaking judgments: *Van Gend & Loos* and *Costa v ENEL*.[54] In the latter judgment, the Court observed that 'the EEC Treaty has created its own legal system which, on the entry into force of the treaty, became an integral part of the legal systems of the Member States and which their courts are bound to apply'. The Court considered that the Member States had brought that legal order into being and at the same time had limited their sovereignty, albeit within limited fields, '[b]y creating a Community of unlimited duration, having its own institutions, its own personality, its own legal capacity and capacity of representation on the international plane and, more particularly, real powers [as a result of the Member States' having limited their own powers or transferred them to the Communities]'.[55] Whereas that judgment and the judgment in *Van Gend & Loos* (para. 1-026, *infra*) refer to a limitation of

1.025

---

[49] Case 143/83, *Commission v Denmark*, 1985, paras 12–13 (para. 27-047, *infra*).
[50] See Article 60 of the Vienna Convention of 23 May 1969 on the Law of Treaties (for that Convention, see para. 26-013, *infra*).
[51] 90 and 91/63, *Commission v Luxembourg and Belgium*, 1964, 631–2; C-5/94, *Hedley Lomas*, 1996, para. 20; C-11/95, *Commission v Belgium*, 1996, paras 37–9; C-14/96, *Denuit*, 1997, paras 34–35; C-45/07 *Commission v Greece*, 2009, para. 26; C-118/07, *Commission v Finland*, 2009, para. 48.
[52] C-459/03, *Commission v Ireland*, 2006, paras 123 and 132; C-284/16, *Achmea*, 2018, para. 32.
[53] Opinion 1/91, *Draft agreement between the Community, on the one hand, and the countries of the European Free Trade Association, on the other, relating to the creation of the European Economic Area*, 1991, para. 21.
[54] 26/62, *Van Gend & Loos*, 1963, 1; 6/64, *Costa v ENEL*, 1964, 585. See, among others, Lecourt, 'Quel eût été le droit des Communautés sans les arrêts de 1963 et 1964?', *L'Europe et le Droit, Mélanges en hommage à J. Boulouis* (Dalloz, 1991), 349–61.
[55] Case 6/64, *Costa*, 1964, at 593.

16   FROM EUROPEAN COMMUNITIES TO EUROPEAN UNION

sovereignty 'within limited fields', more recent case law speaks of a limitation of sovereign rights 'in ever wider fields'.[56]

1.026 **Rights for individuals.** In *Van Gend & Loos*, the Court held for the first time that Community law not only imposes obligations on individuals but is also intended to confer upon them 'rights which become part of their legal heritage'.[57] In so doing, it referred to 'the spirit, the general scheme and the wording' of the EEC Treaty. The Court first considered that '[t]he objective of the EEC Treaty, which is to establish a Common Market, the functioning of which is of direct concern to interested parties in the Community, implies that this Treaty is more than an agreement which merely creates mutual obligations between the contracting States'. The Court averred that this 'view' was 'confirmed' by 'the preamble to the Treaty which refers not only to governments but to peoples' and 'more specifically by the establishment of institutions endowed with sovereign rights, the exercise of which affects Member States and also their citizens'. Two further *indicia* led the Court to conclude that 'the Community constitutes a new legal order of international law for the benefit of which the States have limited their sovereign rights, albeit within limited fields, and the subjects of which comprise not only Member States but also their nationals'. The first was the fact that 'the nationals of the States brought together in the Community are called upon to co-operate in the functioning of this Community through the intermediary of the European Parliament and the Economic and Social Committee'. The second was that 'the task assigned to the Court of Justice under Article 177 [*now Article 267 TFEU*], the object of which is to secure uniform interpretation of the Treaty by national courts and tribunals, confirms that the States have acknowledged that Community law has an authority which can be invoked by their nationals before those courts and tribunals'.

Van Gend & Loos had to come to terms with the view then held by the Member States that Community law constituted a form of international law and, accordingly, that only subjects of that law could take the initiative of seeking a declaration that the agreed rules had been breached. Van Gend & Loos, a Dutch company, had brought an action in the competent national court in which it sought to recover an import duty which it considered the Netherlands tax authorities had charged contrary to Article 12 EEC. The national court made a reference for a preliminary ruling on the interpretation of Article 12, pursuant to what is now Article 267 TFEU. The Belgian, Netherlands, and German Governments argued before the Court that the reference was not concerned with the interpretation of the Treaty but with a Member State's compliance therewith. They contended that the Court could declare that national legislation was contrary to the Treaty only through the proper procedures provided for in Articles 169 and 170 EEC [*now Articles 258 and 259 TFEU*]. The Court's response was to hold that the fact that Articles 169 and 170 EEC enabled the Commission and the Member States to bring an action did not mean that individuals could not plead a Member State's infringement of Community law before a national court, which might result in a question being referred for an interpretation of Community law. The Court held that: '[t]he vigilance of individuals concerned to protect their rights amounts to an

---

[56] Opinion 1/91, *Draft agreement between the Community, on the one hand, and the countries of the European Free Trade Association, on the other, relating to the creation of the European Economic Area*, 1991, para. 21.
[57] 26/62, *Van Gend & Loos*, 1963, 12–13.

effective supervision in addition to the supervision entrusted by Articles 169 and 170 [*now Articles 258 and 259 TFEU*] to the diligence of the Commission and the Member States'.

Consequently, the individual legal subject enforces the rights that he or she draws from Union law through the national courts which, in accordance with Article 267 TFEU, 'cooperate' with the Court of Justice with the aim of ensuring that Union law is applied in a uniform manner in all the Member States.[58] In this way, the Treaties establish a complete system of legal remedies in order to secure compliance with Union law by Union institutions, Member States, and individuals.[59]

Primacy of Community/Union law. Among the various legal regimes which have been established by treaty, the Community/Union legal order is special inasmuch as it takes away from Member States the freedom to determine the position of Community/Union law vis-à-vis domestic law. Member States' courts and tribunals are automatically required to apply Community/Union law in the context of the domestic legal system. In the leading case of *Costa v ENEL* the Court inferred from 'the integration into the laws of each Member State of provisions which derive from the Community, and more generally the terms and the spirit of the Treaty' that it is 'impossible for the States, as a corollary, to accord precedence to a unilateral and subsequent measure over a legal system accepted by them on a basis of reciprocity'.[60]

1.027

The Court was answering a preliminary question from an Italian court concerning the compatibility with the EEC Treaty of an Italian law of 6 December 1962 nationalizing the electricity industry. The Italian Government submitted written observations to the Court in which it argued that the national court had no jurisdiction to make a reference under Article 177 EEC [*now Article 267 TFEU*], because it was obliged to apply the national law. The Court rejected that argument because accepting it would deprive the law stemming from the Treaty of its character as Community law and call into question the legal basis of the Community itself. 'The executive force of Community law cannot vary from one State to another in deference to subsequent domestic laws, without jeopardising the attainment of the objectives of the Treaty set out in Article 5(2) [*EEC Treaty, now Article 3(3) TEU*] and giving rise to the discrimination prohibited by Article 7 [*now Article 18 TFEU*].' The Court concluded that, if Member States were entitled to renounce their obligations unilaterally, those obligations would be merely contingent and the authorization provisions which enable a Member State to derogate from the Treaty in particular cases would lose their purpose. Lastly, the Court expressed the view that 'the precedence of Community law is confirmed by Article 189 [*now Article 288 TFEU*], whereby a regulation "shall be binding" and "directly applicable in the Member States"'.

Constitutional basis. As a result of its complete system of legal remedies, the Community has been called a community based on the rule of law, whose foundation is the 'constitutional

1.028

---

[58] 16/65, *Schwarze*, 1965, 886; C-221/88, *Busseni*, 1990, para. 13. See, in addition, Lenaerts, 'Form and Substance of the Preliminary Rulings Procedure', in Curtin and Heukels (eds), *Institutional Dynamics of European Integration. Essays in Honour of Henry G. Schermers*, Vol. II (Martinus Nijhoff, 1994), 355–80.

[59] 294/83, *Les Verts v European Parliament*, 1986, para. 23. See Lenaerts, 'Case 294/83 Parti écologiste 'Les Verts' v European Parliament [1986] ECR 1339; 'The Basic Constitutional Charter of a Community Based on the Rule of Law', in Poiares Maduro and Azoulai (eds), *The Past and Future of EU Law. The Classics of EU Law Revisited on the 50th Anniversary of the Rome Treaty* (Hart Publishing, 2009), 295–342.

[60] 6/64, *Costa*, 1964, 593–4.

charter' constituted by the Treaties.[61] For this reason, the texts of the Treaties have been described as the constitution of the Communities[62] and the Court of Justice as a constitutional court.[63] Even before the entry into force of the Lisbon Treaty, this work and other commentators referred to the 'constitutional law of the European Union', thereby extending the analysis to cover the areas in which the Union does not act as the Community.[64] The 'constitutional law' of the European Union consists of all the rules of Union law relating to the general objectives, the allocation of competences, and the way in which the legislative, executive, and judicial functions are performed within the Union. In view of the supranational character of the Union, Union law employs concepts taken from international law[65] and national constitutional law,[66] in particular the constitutional law of federal States.[67] The Court of Justice considers that 'the Union possesses a constitutional framework that is unique to it', encompassing the founding values set out in Article 2 TEU, the general principles of Union law, the provisions of the Charter, and the Treaty provisions containing, *inter alia*, rules on the conferral and division of competences, rules governing how the Union institutions and its judicial system are to operate, and fundamental rules in specific areas, structured in such a way as to contribute to the implementation of the process of integration.[68]

---

[61] 294/83, *Les Verts v European Parliament*, 1986, para. 23; Opinion 1/91, *Draft agreement between the Community, on the one hand, and the countries of the European Free Trade Association, on the other, relating to the creation of the European Economic Area*, 1991, para. 21 ('the EEC Treaty, albeit concluded in the form of an international agreement, none the less constitutes the constitutional charter of a Community based on the rule of law').

[62] Gerkrath, *L'émergence d'un droit constitutionnel pour l'Europe*, (Editions de l'Université de Bruxelles, 1997); Lenaerts, 'Constitutionalism and the Many Faces of Federalism' (1990) AJCL 205–63; Mancini, 'The Making of a Constitution for Europe' (1989) CMLRev 595; Ipsen, 'Europäische Verfassung—Nationale Verfassung' (1987) EuR 195–213; Lenaerts, *Le juge et la constitution aux Etats-Unis d'Amérique et dans l'ordre juridique européen* (Bruylant, 1988), §§ 243–5, 257–63; Hartley, 'Federalism, Courts and Legal Systems: The Emerging Constitution of the European Community' (1986) AJCL 229–47; Stein, 'Lawyers, Judges, and the Making of a Transnational Constitution' (1981) AJIL 1–27.

[63] See Lenaerts, Gutman, and Nowak, *EU Procedural Law* (2nd edn, OUP, 2022), Chapter 1.

[64] See, e.g., Lenaerts and Van Nuffel (Bray, ed.), *Constitutional Law of the European Union*, (Sweet & Maxwell, 1999); Weiler, *The Constitution of Europe* (Cambridge University Press, 1999); Rossi, '"Constitutionalisation" de l'Union européenne et des droits fondamentaux' (2002) RTDE 27–52; Arnold, 'European Constitutional Law: Some Reflections on a Concept that Emerged in the Second Half of the Twentieth Century' (1999) Tulane E & Civ LF 49–64; Piris, 'Does the European Union have a Constitution? Does it need one?' (1999) ELRev 557–85; Snyder, 'General Course on Constitutional Law of the European Union', in European University Institute, *Collected Courses of the Academy of European Law (1995—Volume VI-1)* (Nijhoff, 1998), 41–155; Favret, 'Le traité d'Amsterdam: une révision *a minima* de la "charte constitutionnelle" de l'Union européenne' (1997) CDE 555–605; Curtin, 'The Constitutional Structure of the Union: A Europe of Bits and Pieces' (1993) CMLRev 17–69; Pliakos, 'La nature juridique de l'Union européenne' (1993) RTDE 187–224; VerLoren van Themaat, 'De constitutionele problematiek van een Europese politieke Unie' (1991) SEW 436–54.

[65] See, the privileges and immunities of the Union in the national systems (para. 14-007, *infra*); the legal concept of the direct effect of Treaty provisions (para. 23-031, *infra*); the status of international law in the Union legal order (para. 26-001 *et seq.*, *infra*); the position in international law of the Union (para. 14-005 *et seq.*, *infra*).

[66] See, for instance, the allocation of the three classic functions of a State (paras 16-011–16-013); the distinction between legislation and the implementation of legislation (para. 18-008, *infra*); democratic legitimacy (paras 17-046 and 17-050, *infra*), and the role of the Parliament (para. 17-047, *infra*); citizenship (para. 6-001 *et seq.*, *infra*); the principle of equal treatment (paras 5-051–5-064, *infra*) and other general principles of law (paras 25-020–25-024, *infra*) and fundamental rights (paras 25-002–25-019, *infra*); the rules on public funding (paras 14-010–14-018, *infra*); the procedure for concluding international agreements (para. 21-001 *et seq.*, *infra*).

[67] See the discussion of exclusive and non-exclusive competence (paras 5-022–5-027); the principles of subsidiarity (paras 5-028–5-033, *infra*) and proportionality (paras 5-034–5-042); the duty of sincere cooperation (paras 5-043 *et seq.*, *infra*); the allocation of powers of implementation (para. 16-001 *et seq.*, *infra*); the primacy of Union law (para. 23-008 *et seq.*, *infra*); the relationship between the external powers of the Union and those of the Member States (paras 10-039–10-040, *infra* and paras 21-013–21-015, *infra*).

[68] Opinion 1/17, *EU-Canada CET Agreement*, 2019, para. 110.

A number of initiatives have been undertaken to provide the European Union with a true constitution in its own right in order to clarify the constitutional elements of the supranational legal order and confer greater democratic legitimacy on them. The European Parliament prepared on its own motion a formal Constitution of the European Union.[69] Constitutional questions were also raised in the Declaration adopted by the European Council of 14 and 15 December 2001 at Laeken. That declaration led to the convening of a 'Convention', which ultimately produced a Draft Treaty establishing a Constitution for Europe, which was later approved in the Intergovernmental Conference (see para. 1-056, *infra*). However, it proved unfeasible for this 'EU Constitution' to be ratified by all the Member States. Hence, the 2007 Intergovernmental Conference (IGC) chose to abandon the Constitutional Treaty and to incorporate many of the changes it would have introduced in a new treaty, the Treaty of Lisbon, which modified the existing treaties on which the Union was based, while leaving out any references to the constitutional character of the Treaties (see para. 2-001 *et seq.*, *infra*).

II. Intergovernmental Cooperation between EC Member States

Intergovernmental cooperation. From the outset, the momentum of supranational integration led the Member States to become involved in cooperation in areas which did not (as yet) fall within the competence of the Communities. The adjective 'intergovernmental' appropriately describes those forms of international cooperation: the international agreements involved were generally made between representatives of the executives or of the 'governments' (hence 'governmental') of the States party to them. By having recourse to such 'intergovernmental' cooperation, the EC Member States succeeded in cooperating amongst all or part of them in fields where they were not (yet) willing to act under the 'supranational' decision-making procedures provided for in the Community Treaties. In contradistinction to decisions taken within supranational organizations, intergovernmental decisions do not, in principle, have the force of law within national legal systems unless they are specifically adopted therein, and generally do not confer any rights on individuals.[70]

1.029

A. European political cooperation

Fouchet Plan. After the first years that the EEC and the EAEC were in operation, plans began to emerge anew to extend integration to less socio-economically oriented areas.[71] The French President de Gaulle presented plans for forming a Political Union, which were discussed in 1961 and 1962 first at summit conferences and subsequently in the Fouchet

1.030

---

[69] Draft Constitution of the European Union, not approved by the European Parliament, but published as an annex to a resolution of 10 February 1994, OJ 1994 C61/155. See Petersmann, 'Proposals for a New Constitution for the European Union: Building-Blocks for a Constitutional Theory and Constitutional Law of the EU' (1995) CMLRev 1123–75; Gouad, 'Le projet de Constitution européenne' (1995) RFDC 287–318.

[70] Schermers and Blokker, *International Institutional Law* (Martinus Nijhoff, 1995), §§ 58–9, 39–40, and §§ 1330–31, 819–20.

[71] Lang, 'Die Bemühungen um die politische Einigung Europas seit dem Scheitern der Europäischen Verteidigungsgemeinschaft', in Hallstein and Schlochauer (n. 36, *supra*), 125–41.

Committee.[72] Under the structure proposed by de Gaulle, the Heads of State or Government meeting within the Council of the Union would conduct common foreign and defence policies by unanimous vote and cooperate on culture, science, and safeguarding human rights, fundamental freedoms, and democracy. The Union was also to have a Political Commission and a Parliamentary Assembly, but no Court of Justice. Made up of national civil servants, the Political Commission was to confine itself to preparing and, where necessary, carrying out the decisions of the Council. The Parliamentary Assembly was to play an advisory role. Under the first proposal of November 1961, this *Union d'États* was to operate alongside the existing Communities. Under a subsequent proposal, this organization was also to have powers in the economic field and was to foresee the institutions of the Communities being bound by decisions of the Heads of State or Government. The 'Fouchet Plan' ultimately came to grief because of the fears of the smaller Member States that this would erode the powers and supranational character that the Communities had acquired. A further decisive factor was de Gaulle's refusal to have the United Kingdom (which applied in 1961 for membership of the Communities) involved in the negotiations.

1.031 **European Political Cooperation.** The field in which Member States agreed to coordinate their policies outside the sphere of competence of the Communities was foreign policy, resulting in the emergence of European Political Cooperation (EPC).[73] At a meeting of the Council held in Luxembourg on 27 October 1970, the Foreign Ministers gave their approval to the Davignon Report, which proposed that there should be half-yearly meetings of the Foreign Ministers, to which a member of the Commission could also be invited.[74] It was in this way that EPC came about.

Initially, the Foreign Ministers deliberately kept their EPC meetings separate from meetings of the Council of the European Communities.[75] But gradually a link grew between them.[76] Because having a special body for EPC was still reminiscent of the Political Committee proposed in the Fouchet Plan, the EPC secretariat was given purely administrative functions under the authority of the Presidency.

1.032 **Legal status.** All EPC decisions were taken by consensus, and the Court of Justice had no jurisdiction to supervise the fulfilment by Member States of the obligations which they assumed in the context of EPC. Accordingly, the rules of conduct governing EPC constituted a species of soft law influencing the international action of the Member States. It was not until 1986 that the Member States gave EPC practice a legal basis under a treaty by means of the Single European Act (Articles 1, 3(2), 30, or Title III Single European Act). In 1992, the EU Treaty converted EPC into the non-Community 'second pillar' of the Union, the Common Foreign and Security Policy based on Title V of the EU Treaty (CFSP; see paras 10-026–10-035).[77] As of 1 December 2009, the Lisbon Treaty abolished the pillar structure on which

---

[72] These plans are annexed to Bloes, *Le 'Plan Fouchet' et le problème de l'Europe politique* (College of Europe, 1970), 487–510; see also http://www.cvce.eu.
[73] de Schoutheete, *La coopération politique européenne* (Nathan/Labor, 1986); Ifestos, *European Political Cooperation—Towards a Framework of Supranational Diplomacy?* (Avebury, 1987).
[74] Report of the Ministers of Foreign Affairs of the Member States on the question of political integration (1970) 11 EC Bull. 9–14.
[75] The most striking example is one day in 1973 when the Foreign Ministers met in the morning in Copenhagen under EPC auspices and in the afternoon in Brussels as the Council of the European Communities.
[76] See Nuttall, 'Interaction between European Political Co-operation and the European Community' (1987) YEL 211–49.
[77] Title V EU. Article 50(2) EU repealed Articles 2, 3(2), and 30 (Title III) Single European Act.

the Union had been organized, although special provisions remain in place concerning the former 'second pillar'. The EPC thus formed the basis of the CFSP, which continues to have intergovernmental features, even though it has been integrated into the institutional framework of the European Union.

European Council. From 1961 onwards, the Heads of State or Government of the Member States held regular meetings in order to discuss political sticking points in Community policy.[78] At the Paris summit conference on 9 and 10 December 1974, they decided to hold such meetings from then on at least three times a year, accompanied by the Foreign Ministers.[79] The institution created thereby, the European Council, was intended not only to give impetus to European Political Cooperation, but also to matters coming within the sphere of competence of the Communities.[80] Although the European Council thus made pronouncements about matters for which the Communities were competent, it did not play a formal role in Community decision-making and did not constitute an institution hierarchically superior to the Community institutions. The Single European Act mentioned the European Council for the first time in the Treaties. The EU Treaty conferred a number of tasks on it in the context of the Community decision-making process and the CFSP. Consequently, since the EU Treaty and the Treaty of Amsterdam, the European Council has acted as a specific organ of the Union alongside the Community institutions (see para. 12-022, *infra*). The Treaty of Lisbon included the European Council among the institutions of the Union (see Article 13(1), second subpara. TEU).

1.033

B. European monetary cooperation

Initial steps. The initial successes of the Communities prompted the Heads of State or Government in December 1969 to investigate transforming the customs union, which had only just been introduced, into an economic and monetary union (EMU).[81] The Council set up the Werner Committee, which put forward proposals in October 1970 for achieving EMU in stages.[82] With a view to achieving the first stage, a resolution of 22 March 1971 of the Council and the representatives of the governments of the Member States looked forward to increased coordination of economic and monetary policies and limitation of the fluctuation margins between the Member States' currencies.[83] Since not all the measures seemed feasible—the economic climate became more unfavourable after the oil crisis— EMU remained at the starting block. In the monetary sphere, the Council nevertheless set up the European Monetary Cooperation Fund as planned.[84] Following the collapse of

1.034

---

[78] Such summit conferences took place twice in 1961 (Paris and Bonn) and thereafter in 1967 (Rome), 1969 (The Hague), 1972 (Paris), and 1973 (Copenhagen), each time at the prompting of the French President.

[79] Communiqué of the Heads of State or Government meeting in Paris on 9 and 10 December 1974 (1974) 12 EC Bull. point 1104(3).

[80] See Tindemans, 'Le Conseil européen: un premier bilan, quelques réflexions', *Mélanges Fernand Dehousse. II. La construction européenne* (Nathan/Labor, 1979), 167–73; Wessels, *Der Europäische Rat* (Europa Union, 1980).

[81] Final communiqué of the Conference (2 December 1969), EC Bull., 1-1970, point 8.

[82] The final report of the Werner Committee of 8 October 1970 was published in (1970) EC Bull. Suppl. 11, and in OJ 1970 C136.

[83] Resolution of the Council and of the Representatives of the Governments of the Member States of 22 March 1971 on the attainment by stages of economic and monetary union in the Community, OJ January 1974 English Special Edition, Second Series, IX. Resolutions of the Council and of the Representatives of the Member States, 40.

[84] Regulation (EEC) No. 907/73 of the Council of 3 April 1973 establishing a European Monetary Cooperation Fund, OJ 1973 L89/2.

the international system of fixed exchange rates (the Bretton Woods system), the Member States endeavoured, with varying degrees of success, to coordinate their intervention on the currency markets (the 'Snake').

1.035 **European Monetary System.** Monetary cooperation as between the Member States came into being on the basis of the resolution of the European Council of 5 December 1978 on the establishment of the European Monetary System (EMS).[85] Within the EMS, bilateral exchange rates were set between the various currencies. Initially, the EMS operated on the basis of the intergovernmental agreements contained in the resolution of the European Council and in agreements between the central banks. For the coordination of their general monetary policy, representatives of the central banks also met in institutions of the Communities, such as the Monetary Committee and the Committee of Governors of the central banks.[86] By a regulation, the Council subsequently entrusted the management of the EMS to the Monetary Cooperation Fund.[87] In 1978 the Council had adopted, in connection with monetary cooperation, a regulation introducing the ECU (European Currency Unit) as a unit of account for the exchange rate mechanism and a means of settling transactions between national authorities and the Fund.[88] The ECU was a basket of currencies whose value was determined by the value of the national currencies, weighted according to their share of the basket. That share was fixed commensurately with each Member State's share of the Union's Gross National Product and of internal Community trade. By means of a regulation, the Council introduced the ECU as the means of account for the Communities' budget.[89]

1.036 **Economic and Monetary Union.** The EU Treaty laid the foundations for the introduction of economic and monetary Union, thereby bringing monetary cooperation within the ambit of 'supranational' Community decision-making. On 31 December 1998 the conversion rates between the common currency—now named the euro—and the currencies of the Member States taking part in EMU were irrevocably fixed.[90] Since 1 January 1999 the euro has been the currency of the Member States participating in EMU (see para. 9-033 *et seq.*, *infra*).

C. Police and judicial cooperation

1.037 **First cooperation and agreements.** Equally outside the ambit of the Communities, forms of cooperation grew up between ministerial departments of the Member States with regard

---

[85] Resolution of the European Council of 5 December 1978 on the establishment of the European Monetary System (EMS) and related matters (1978) 12 EC Bull. point 1.1.11.
[86] For these bodies, see the Rules governing the Monetary Committee, OJ 1952–58 English Special Edition, 60; Council Decision 64/300/EEC of 8 May 1964 on cooperation between the Central Banks of the Member States of the European Economic Community, OJ 1963–1964 English Special Edition, 141.
[87] Council Regulation (EEC) No. 3181/78 of 18 December 1978 relating to the European Monetary System, OJ 1978 L379/2 (repealed by Council Regulation (EC) No. 640/2006 of 10 April 2006, OJ 2006 L115/1).
[88] Council Regulation (EEC) No. 3180/78 of 18 December 1978 changing the value of the unit of account used by the European Monetary Cooperation Fund, OJ 1978 L379/1).
[89] Council Regulation (EEC, Euratom) No. 3308/80 of 16 December 1980 on the replacement of the European unit of account by the ECU in Community legal instruments, OJ 1980 L345/1.
[90] Council Regulation (EC) No. 2866/98 of 31 December 1998 on the conversion rates between the euro and the currencies of the Member States adopting the euro, OJ 1998 L359/1.

to trans-frontier aspects of justice and home affairs. In December 1975, meeting in Rome, the European Council approved the initiative of ministers from the Member States meeting twice a year in order to discuss questions of law and order, such as terrorism and other forms of international lawlessness.[91] Various other intergovernmental bodies coordinated and studied national police policy.[92] Agreements were also concluded between the Member States on police and judicial cooperation in criminal matters and on judicial cooperation in civil matters, including the Brussels Convention.[93] Similar conventions are also concluded under the auspices of the Council of Europe.[94]

Cooperation extended to migration issues. The internal-market programme (see para. 7-008, *infra*) looked forward to the abolition of checks on persons at the internal frontiers of the Community by the end of 1992. Cooperation between the Member States in the sphere of customs controls and combating criminality therefore became essential. Free movement of persons meant that non-EC nationals could move freely within the Community once they had crossed the external borders. The Member States accordingly sought to arrive at forms of cooperation enabling a common control policy at the external borders and a uniform policy with regards access to, and movement and residence of nationals of, third countries in the Community. The European Council meeting at Rhodes on 2 and 3 December 1988 set up a Coordinators Group to coordinate the various activities in the sphere of the free movement of persons.[95] The activities of an *ad hoc* working group on immigration[96] resulted in agreements which were submitted to the Member States for ratification. The Dublin Convention of 15 June 1990, which determined which Member State should examine applications for asylum, entered into force on 1 September 1997 (see para. 8-010, *infra*). A draft Convention on the crossing of external borders of the Member States failed to

1.038

---

[91] (1975) 11 EC Bull. point 1104. These meetings were known as the Trevi Group. 'Trevi' refers to the Roman fountain and has been turned into an acronym for *Terrorisme, Radicalisme, Extrémisme et Violence Internationale*. For the structure and operation of Trevi, see Le Jeune, *La coopération policière européenne contre le terrorisme* (Bruylant, 1992), 105–48.

[92] For example, Celad (*Comité européen pour la lutte anti-drogue*), which was set up on the initiative of the French to coordinate national anti-drugs policies (1989) 12 EC Bull. point 1.1.9, and Interpol, an intergovernmental cooperative association which has been operating since 1923 not on the basis of a treaty. See Fijnaut, 'The "Communitisation" of Police Cooperation in Western Europe', in Schermers et al. (eds), *Free Movement of Persons in Europe. Legal Problems and Experiences*, (Martinus Nijhoff, 1993), 75–92.

[93] Brussels Convention of 27 September 1968 on jurisdiction and the enforcement of judgments in civil and commercial matters (Accession Convention for Denmark, Ireland, and the United Kingdom: OJ 1978 L304/77). The Brussels Convention has since been replaced, except as far as Denmark is concerned, by Regulation (EU) No. 1215/2012 of the European Parliament and of the Council of 12 December 2012 on jurisdiction and the recognition and enforcement of judgments in civil and commercial matters, OJ 2012 L351/1; see para. 8-015, *infra*, and for the interpretation of the Brussels Convention by the Court of Justice, para. 28-018, *infra*. See also the Brussels Convention of 25 May 1987 abolishing the Legalisation of Documents in the Member States of the European Communities, (1987) 5 EC Bull. point 3.4.3, which never entered into force, and the Rome Convention of 6 November 1990 between the Member States of the European Communities on the Simplification of Procedures for the Enforcement of Maintenance Payments (1990) Trb 54, which equally never entered into force but has since been overtaken by Council Regulation (EC) No. 4/2009 of 18 December 2008 on jurisdiction, applicable law, recognition and enforcement of decisions and cooperation in matters relating to maintenance obligations, OJ 2009 L7/1.

[94] For an overview of those conventions, see Oschinsky and Jenard, *L'espace juridique et judiciaire européen* (Bruylant, 1993).

[95] (1988) 12 EC Bull. point 1.1.3. The Coordinators Group drew a distinction as regards the various areas of cooperation between priority and ancillary measures. This resulted in the Palma document of June 1989, which was approved by the European Council held in Madrid in June 1989 (1989) 6 EC Bull. point 1.1.7.

[96] The *ad hoc* group consisted of national officials meeting in various working parties: policy on asylum, external borders, admission/deportation, visa policy, and forged papers. See (1986) 10 EC Bull. point 2.4.7.

get signed on account of differences between Spain and the United Kingdom relating to the application of the Convention to Gibraltar.[97]

After the EU Treaty entered into force, on 1 November 1993, intergovernmental cooperation between the Member States in the fields of the police and justice was conducted on the basis of the non-Community third pillar of the Union, namely Title VI of the EU Treaty. In this way, a convention was drawn up pursuant to the EU Treaty to supplement the Brussels Convention as regards jurisdiction and the recognition and enforcement of judgments in matrimonial matters.[98] In 1999, the Treaty of Amsterdam brought judicial cooperation in civil matters and immigration and asylum policy within the sphere of the EC Treaty, while retaining police and judicial cooperation in criminal matters in Title VI of the EU Treaty (see para. 8-014 *et seq.*, *infra*). As of 1 December 2009, the Lisbon Treaty brought the provisions of Title VI of the EU Treaty and the Community competence on 'visa, asylum, immigration and other policies related to the free movement of persons' (Part Three, Title IV of the EC Treaty) together in a single title (Part Three, Title V of the TFEU) on the 'area of freedom, security and justice' (see para. 8-001, *infra*).

1.039 **Schengen Agreements.** Some Member States had already taken the decision to replace border controls amongst themselves by a common policy at their external borders. The Benelux Treaty of 11 April 1960 obtained that outcome with effect from 1 July 1960.[99] National courts in the Benelux countries may refer questions on the interpretation of that Treaty to the Benelux Court of Justice (see para. 1-004, *infra*).

On 19 June 1990, France, Germany, and the Benelux countries concluded the Convention on the application of the Schengen Agreement of 14 June 1985 on the gradual abolition of checks at the common borders.[100] The Schengen Convention established free movement of persons without checks at internal frontiers and stepped up checks at the external borders of the Schengen countries. It introduced common rules on the grant of visas and a uniform visa for nationals of third States (i.e. non-EC nationals) intending to stay in the Schengen area for less than three months. In order to offset the disappearance of internal frontiers, the Convention introduced a system for the exchange of information and cooperation between police forces and the judicial authorities, together with the Schengen Information System (SIS), which enables authorities to consult personal data held by authorities in other States via a central computer in Strasbourg. Upon the entry into effect of the Amsterdam Treaty, in May 1999, all EU Member States at that time, with the exception of Ireland and the United Kingdom, were parties to the Schengen Convention and the agreements concluded

---

[97] See the discussion at para. 8-002, *infra*.
[98] Convention of 28 May 1998, drawn up on the basis of the former Article K.3 of the EU Treaty, on Jurisdiction and the Recognition and Enforcement of Judgments in Matrimonial Matters, OJ 1998 C221/2; the 'Brussels II Convention', see para. 8-015, *infra*).
[99] Agreement between the Kingdom of Belgium, the Grand Duchy of Luxembourg, and the Kingdom of the Netherlands on the displacement of checks on persons to the external frontiers of the Benelux area, signed at Brussels on 11 April 1960 (BS, July 1, 1960, Trb, 1960, 40).
[100] Schengen Convention of 19 June 1990 implementing the Schengen Agreement of 14 June 1985 between the Governments of the States of the Benelux Economic Union, the Federal Republic of Germany and the French Republic on the gradual abolition of checks at their common borders (OJ 2000 L239/19; for the Schengen Agreement of 14 June 1985: ibid., 13). See the discussion in Fijnaut, Stuyck, and Wytinck (eds), *Schengen: Proeftuin voor de Europese Gemeenschap?* (Kluwer/Gouda Quint, 1992); Schutte, 'Schengen: Its Meaning for the Free Movement of Persons in Europe' (1991) CMLRev 549–70.

pursuant to it.[101] The Treaty of Amsterdam then incorporated the Schengen *acquis* into the European Union (see para. 8-004, *infra*). The 'Schengen *acquis*' did not, however, enter into effect in all the States at the same time.[102] Since Denmark, Finland, and Sweden, together with Iceland and Norway, had already abolished checks on persons moving between them under the auspices of the Nordic Council, the Schengen *acquis* could not be applied until Iceland and Norway were able to take part in the Schengen cooperation by means of an agreement concluded with the Community.[103] Also, Switzerland and Liechtenstein have since acceded to the Schengen Agreement (see para. 8-006, *infra*). Within the European Union, the Schengen agreement currently applies to most of the Member States, except for Bulgaria, Croatia, Cyprus, Ireland, and Romania (see para. 8-006, *infra*).

III. Bringing Together the Paths of Integration into the European Union

A. Steps towards a European Union

Proposals. Ten years after the Fouchet Plan, there was a resurgence of the idea of expanding the area of activity of the Communities and, at the same time, of unifying the existing Community and non-Community integration paths. Several proposals suggested creating a 'European Union', whatever its legal status as the future framework. At the request of the December 1974 Paris Summit, then Prime Minister of Belgium, Leo Tindemans drew up a report on European Union on the basis of reports to be prepared by the European Parliament, the Commission, and the Court of Justice and after consulting 'with the governments and a wide range of public opinion in the Community'.[104] More radical was the Draft Treaty establishing the European Union which was approved by the European Parliament on 14 February 1984.[105] Although the Draft Treaty was never formally considered in view of a Treaty change, it did set in motion a political debate on amending the existing Treaties.

1.040

---

[101] Italy signed the convention on 27 November 1990; Portugal and Spain on 25 June 1991; Greece on 6 November 1992; Austria on 28 April 1995; and Denmark, Finland, and Sweden on 19 December 1996.

[102] For the last States, see Council Decision 1999/848/EC of 13 December 1999 on the full application of the Schengen *acquis* in Greece, OJ 1999 L327/58 (entry into force on 1 January 2000), and Council Decision 2000/777/EC of 1 December 2000 on the application of the Schengen *acquis* in Denmark, Finland, and Sweden, and in Iceland and Norway, OJ 2000 L309/24 (entry into force on 25 March 2001). As to the States that became full Members of the Schengen area long after the Treaty of Amsterdam, see Council Decision 2007/801/EC of 6 December 2007 on the full application of the provisions of the Schengen *acquis* in the Czech Republic, the Republic of Estonia, the Republic of Latvia, the Republic of Lithuania, the Republic of Hungary, the Republic of Malta, the Republic of Poland, the Republic of Slovenia, and the Slovak Republic, OJ 2007 L 323/34 (entry into force on 21 December 2007); Council Decision of 27 November 2008 on the full application of the provisions of the Schengen *acquis* in the Swiss Confederation, OJ 2008 L327/5 (entry into force on 12 December 2008); Council Decision 2011/842/EU of 13 December 2011 on the full application of the provisions of the Schengen *acquis* in the Principality of Liechtenstein, OJ 2011 L 334/27 (entry into force on 19 December 2011).

[103] See para. 8-006, *infra*.

[104] (1974) 12 EC Bull. point 1104, No. 13 (adoption of a resolution on the draft Treaty).

[105] OJ 1984 C77/33, and (1984) 2 EC Bull. point 1.1.2. For commentaries on the Draft Treaty, see Bieber, Jacqué, and Weiler, *An Ever Closer Union—A Critical Analysis of the Draft Treaty Establishing the European Union* (Commission of the EC, 1985); Capotorti et al., *Le Traité d'Union européenne—Commentaire du project adopté par le Parlement européen* (Editions de l'Université de Bruxelles, 1985); Nickel, 'Le projet de traité instituant l'Union européenne élaboré par le Parlement européen' (1984) CDE 511–42.

1.041 **Single European Act.** In June 1985, the Milan European Council decided to convene a conference of representatives of the governments of the Member States within the meaning of Article 236 EEC Treaty to discuss amendments to the Treaties.[106] In September 1985 the proceedings of the Intergovernmental Conference began. On 17 February 1986, nine Member States signed the Single European Act (SEA),[107] followed by Denmark, Greece, and Italy on 28 February 1986. The Danish Government wished first to hold a referendum and both Greece and Italy decided to await the outcome of that referendum before signing. Although the Danish Parliament voted to reject the Single European Act on 21 January 1986, the Danish people voted in a referendum on 27 February 1986 by 56.2 per cent to accept the results of the negotiations. On the following day, Denmark, Greece, and Italy signed the SEA. Although in Ireland the Parliament (the Dail) had voted in favour of the Single European Act, the Government could not deposit the instrument of ratification because an action was brought challenging the constitutionality of the new Treaty. As the Supreme Court ruled that the SEA necessitated a change in the Constitution, the latter was amended after a referendum held on 26 May 1987.[108] As a result, the Single European Act did not enter into force until 1 July 1987.[109] The SEA brought the Community and non-Community paths together into one text for the first time,[110] hence its name.

First, the Single European Act made major changes to the ECSC, EEC, and EAEC Treaties. It conferred new competences on the Community,[111] but did not alter the general objectives of the Community (Article 2 EEC) or the list of the Community's tasks (Article 3 EEC). In addition, the SEA looked forward to the completion of the common market by adding an Article 8a, which heralded the achievement by 31 December 1992 of an 'internal market', defined as 'an area without internal frontiers in which the free movement of goods, persons, services and capital is ensured in accordance with the provisions of this Treaty' (see now Article 26 TFEU). At the institutional level, the SEA made decision-taking more flexible by introducing qualified majority voting in the Council. The introduction of the cooperation procedure (Article 149, second para. EEC; now repealed) made for increased involvement of the Assembly, henceforward referred to in the Treaty as the European Parliament.

Second, the SEA codified for the first time existing practice in the matter of European Political Cooperation (see para. 1-030, *supra*). The Council could thus consider EPC

---

[106] (1985) 6 EC Bull. point I.2.2.
[107] For a general discussion, see De Ruyt, *L'Acte unique européen* (Editions de l'Université de Bruxelles, 1987); Bosco, 'Commentaire de l'Acte unique européen des 17-28 février 1986' (1987) CDE 355–82; VerLoren van Themaat, 'De Europese Akte' (1986) SEW 464–83; Krenzler, 'Die Einheitliche Europäische Akte als Schritt auf dem Wege zu einer Gemeinsamen Europäischen Außenpolitik' (1986) EuR 384–91; Jacqué, 'L'Acte unique européen' (1986) RTDE 575–612; Pescatore, 'Some Critical Remarks on the Single European Act' (1986) CMLRev 9–18; Edward, 'The Impact of the Single European Act on the Institutions' (1986) CMLRev 19–30; De Zwaan, 'The Single European Act: Conclusion of a Unique Document' (1986) 747–65; Glaesner, 'L'Acte unique européen' (1986) RMC 307–21; Nuttall, 'European Political Cooperation and the Single European Act' (1985) YEL 203–32.
[108] Murphy and Cras, 'L'affaire Crotty: la Cour Suprême d'Irlande rejette l'Acte Unique Européen' (1988) CDE 276–305; McCutcheon, 'The Irish Supreme Court, European Political Co-operation and the Single European Act' (1988) LIEI 93–100; Temple Lang, 'The Irish Court Case Which Delayed the Single European Act: *Crotty* v *An Taoiseach and others*' (1987) CMLRev 709–18.
[109] Implemented in the United Kingdom by the European Communities (Amendment) Act 1986.
[110] Hence its title 'Single European Act' (*Acte unique européen, Einheitliche Europäische Akte*).
[111] The most important areas entrusted to the Community by the SEA were: (1) increased Community competence with regard to social policy (Articles 118a and b EEC); (2) economic and social cohesion (Articles 130a to e EEC); (3) research and technological development (Articles 130f to q EEC) and (4) the environment (Articles 130r to t EEC).

matters alongside the decision-making relating to Community matters, at the initiative of the Member State holding the rotating presidency, with structural involvement of both the European Commission and the European Parliament. Nevertheless, the Intergovernmental Conference made sure that EPC would not interfere with Community action. In order to give Member States the last word on any further integration in the context of EPC, Article 31 of the SEA denied any jurisdiction to the Court of Justice to rule on acts taken by EPC institutions or bodies or by Member States within the framework of EPC.[112]

B. The establishment of the European Union

The Maastricht Treaty. In December 1989 the European Council held in Strasbourg decided to convene 'a conference of representatives of the governments of the Member States' within the meaning of Article 236 EEC.[113] This intergovernmental conference was to determine the changes which needed to be made to the EEC Treaty in order to achieve economic and monetary union. The unification of Germany and political developments in Central and Eastern Europe, however, triggered debate about the further development of the Community's political dimension, both internally and externally. The proceedings were eventually rounded off at the European Council held in Maastricht on 9–10 December 1991.[114] The two texts on which the European Council had reached agreement, namely provisions on Economic and Monetary Union and provisions on Political Union, were brought together in one Treaty on European Union, which was signed on 7 February 1992 by all the Member States. Just as in the case of the Single European Act, the entry into force of the EU Treaty was delayed by complications in national ratification procedures.[115] In Denmark, 50.7 per cent of the votes cast in the referendum held on 2 June 1992 were against the Treaty, although the Danish Parliament had voted in favour on 12 May 1992.[116] The Treaty was approved, however, by a referendum on 18 June 1992 in Ireland (by 69.05 per cent), and on 20 September 1992 in France, albeit narrowly (51.05 per cent). In many other Member States the ratification required prior amendment to the national constitution, primarily in order

1.042

---

[112] Article 31 provided that the provisions of the ECSC Treaty, the EEC Treaty, and the EAEC Treaty concerning the powers of the Court of Justice and the exercise of those powers applied only to the provisions of Title II and to Article 32. Consequently, that article ruled out the common provisions (Title I), the provisions on European cooperation in the sphere of foreign policy (Title III), and the general and final provisions (Title IV), with the exception of Article 32, which provided that, apart from Article 31 and the provisions of the Community Treaties, nothing in the Single European Act was to affect the Community Treaties. For the lack of jurisdiction of the ECJ to rule on an act of the European Council, see T-584/93, *Roujansky v Council* (order), 1994, paras 12–14, confirmed by C-253/94 P, *Roujansky v Council*, 1995.

[113] (1989) 12 EC Bull. point I.1.11.

[114] For commentaries on the negotiations, see Corbett, 'The Intergovernmental Conference on Political Union' (1992) JCMS 271–98; VerLoren van Themaat, 'De constitutionele problematiek van een Europese politieke Unie' (1991) SEW 436–54; VerLoren van Themaat, 'Some Preliminary Observations on the Intergovernmental Conferences: The Relations between the Concepts of a Common Market, a Monetary Union, an Economic Union, a Political Union and Sovereignty' (1991) CMLRev 291–318; Vignes, 'Le project de la Présidence luxembourgeoise d'un Traité sur l'Union' (1991) RMC 504–17; Reich, 'Le développement de l'Union européenne dans le cadre des conférences intergouvernementales' (1991) 704–9.

[115] For a survey of the national ratification procedures, see (1993) 10 EC Bull. point 2.3.1. See the discussion in Rideau, 'Les procédures de ratification du traité sur l'Union Européenne' (1992) RFDC 611–24; Arts et al., 'Ratification Process of the Treaty on European Union' (1993) ELRev 228–53, 356–60, 448–51, and 541–4.

[116] For the situation after the referendum, see Kapteyn, 'Denemarken en het Verdrag van Maastricht' (1992) NJB 781–3. Without Danish ratification, the EU Treaty could not enter into force (see Article 52 EU). Cf Rideau, 'La ratification et l'entrée en vigueur du Traité de Maastricht. Aspects internationaux' (1992) RFDC 479–91.

to allow those states to participate in the Economic and Monetary Union and to extend the franchise to citizens of other Member States. In order to enable the Treaty to be ratified in Denmark, the European Council, held in Edinburgh on 11–12 December 1992, laid down a number of special rules which would apply only to Denmark and enter into force at the same time as the Treaty itself.[117] Those rules were embodied partly in a decision of the Heads of State or Government meeting within the European Council,[118] and partly in unilateral 'declarations' of the European Council and Denmark itself.[119] The provisions helped to ease Denmark's obligations, yet without encroaching upon the EU Treaty. In a second referendum held on 18 May 1993, 56.8 per cent of Danes voted in favour of ratifying the EU Treaty.[120] Eventually, the Treaty on European Union entered into force on 1 November 1993.

1.043 **European Union.** By the EU Treaty, the Contracting Parties established a European Union, founded on the European Communities and supplemented by the policies and forms of cooperation established by the new Treaty (Article 1, first and third paras EU). The EU Treaty left the European Communities in place, but supplemented them with a new, overarching structure—the European Union.

Henceforward, there was to be one procedure for acceding to the Union, supplanting the various accession procedures provided for in the ECSC, EEC, and EAEC Treaties (Article 49 EU Treaty) and one procedure for amending the various Treaties on which the Union was founded (Article 48 EU Treaty). Yet, contrary to the regime applicable to the Communities, which had been given explicit legal personality (Article 281 EC Treaty and Article 184 EAEC Treaty), the EU Treaty did not confer legal personality on the Union as a whole.

1.044 **Three pillars.** The legal structure of the European Union was best understood as an entity supported by three pillars. The first pillar of the Union consisted of the Community Treaties, as significantly modified by Titles II, III, and IV of the EU Treaty. Community action under the first pillar was subject to the provisions of these Treaties. The second pillar of the Union consisted of the provisions on a CFSP laid down in Title V of the EU Treaty. The third pillar of the Union (Title VI of the EU Treaty) consisted initially of the provisions on 'cooperation in the fields of justice and home affairs' (JHA cooperation). A later treaty amendment, the Treaty of Amsterdam, would confer on the Community competence to adopt measures in various fields falling under JHA cooperation, thereby reducing the scope of application of Title VI of the EU Treaty to police and judicial cooperation in criminal matters (PJCC).

1.045 **Amendments to Community Treaties.** As regards the first pillar, the EU Treaty extended the sphere of action of the Community to such an extent that the title 'European Economic Community' was replaced by 'European Community'. New competences were conferred on

---

[117] (1992) 12 EC Bull. points I.33–I.44.
[118] Decision of the Heads of State or Government, meeting within the European Council, concerning certain problems raised by Denmark on the Treaty on European Union, OJ 1992 C348/2.
[119] Declarations of the European Council, OJ 1992 C348/3; Unilateral Declarations of Denmark, to be associated to the Danish instrument of ratification of the Treaty on European Union and of which the eleven other Member States will take cognizance, OJ 1992 C348/4.
[120] Glistrup, 'Le traité sur l'Union européenne: la ratification du Danemark' (1994) RMCUE 9–16; Howarth, 'The Compromise on Denmark and the Treaty on European Union: A Legal and Political Analysis' (1994) CMLRev 765–805. Gjørtler, 'Ratifying the Treaty on European Union: An Interim Report' (1993) ELRev 356–60. For this and other Danish referendums concerning European integration, see Simoulin, 'L'Europe au miroir danois' (2002) RMCUE 83–8.

the Community, also outside the economic sphere.[121] In addition, the EU Treaty clarified and extended the scope of existing Community competences under the original EEC Treaty and as added by the Single European Act.[122] What attracted the most attention was the decision to introduce, starting in 1997 and by no later than 1 January 1999, an economic and monetary union between Member States fulfilling the necessary conditions for the adoption of a single currency.[123] At the institutional level, the EU Treaty advanced further into the territory opened up by the Single European Act. On the one hand, the EU Treaty again extended the scope of qualified majority voting in the Council.[124] On the other, new steps were taken to give the European Parliament a greater say in the legislative process, in particular through the introduction of a co-decision procedure (Article 189b EC, now replaced by the ordinary legislative procedure (see Article 294 TFEU)) and more extensive application of the cooperation procedure and procedures requiring the Parliament to give its assent or to deliver advisory opinions.[125]

CFSP. Title V of the EU Treaty constituted the legal basis for the Union's CFSP, the Union's 'second pillar'. That policy replaced European Political Cooperation between the Member States (EPC; see para. 1-030, *supra*).[126] Title V of the EU Treaty did not determine how the CFSP was to take substantive shape, but elaborated the procedures and instruments pursuant to which the institutions and the Member States were to conduct a foreign and security policy (Articles 12 to 15). Pursuant to general guidelines and common strategies determined by the European Council, the Council was to adopt 'joint actions', 'common positions', or other decisions. The CFSP covered all matters bearing on the security of the Union and could lead to a 'common defence', should the European Council so decide (Article 17(1) EU; see para. 10-032, *infra*).

1.046

PJCC. Title VI of the EU Treaty provided the framework for police and judicial cooperation in criminal matters between Member States (PJCC); the third 'pillar'.[127] The area originally

1.047

---

[121] The EU Treaty conferred competence on the European Community with regards to: (1) citizenship of the Union (Articles 8 to 8e EC, later—with the Treaty of Amsterdam—renumbered into Articles 17 to 22); (2) the common policy on visas (Article 100c EC, later repealed); (3) economic and monetary policy (Articles 102a to 109m, later Articles 98 to 124 EC); (4) education (Article 126, later Article 149 EC); (5) culture (Article 128, later Article 151 EC); (6) public health (Article 129, later Article 152 EC); (7) consumer protection (Article 129a, later Article 153 EC); (8) trans-European networks (Articles 129b to 129d, later Articles 154 to 156 EC); (9) industry (Article 130, later Article 157 EC); (10) development cooperation (Articles 130u to 130y, later Articles 177 to 181 EC) and (11) extended powers in the social policy sphere as a result of the 'Protocol on social policy', with the same status as the EC Treaty, and the 'Agreement on social policy concluded between the Member States of the European Community with the exception of the United Kingdom of Great Britain and Northern Ireland' to which the Social Protocol refers. See Lane, 'New Community Competences under the Maastricht Treaty' (1993) CMLRev 939–79.

[122] See Article 127 (vocational training, later Article 150), Articles 130a to e (economic and social cohesion, later Articles 158 to 162), Article 130f to p (research and technological development, later Articles 163 to 173) and Article 130r to t (environment, later Articles 174 to 176) EC.

[123] Article 109j [later *Article 121*] (3) and (4) EC.

[124] See para. 17-007, *infra*.

[125] See Article 192, first para. EC for this enumeration. It is also noteworthy that the practice by which the nominated President and other Members of the Commission collectively are to be subject to a vote of approval by the European Parliament was enshrined in the Treaty (Article 214(2) EC).

[126] Article 50(2) EU repealed Articles 2 and 3(2) and Title III of the Single European Act.

[127] In decisions adopted pursuant to Title VI of the EU Treaty, the—less precise—abbreviation 'JHA' was used even after the Treaty of Amsterdam. For a discussion of the PJCC provisions, see the relevant sections in Peers, *EU Justice and Home Affairs Law* (2nd edn, OUP, 2006); Anderson and Apap, *Police and Justice Co-operation and the New European Borders* (Kluwer Law International, 2002); Monar, 'Justice and Home Affairs in the Treaty of Amsterdam: Reform at the Price of Fragmentation' (1998) ELRev 320–35; Margue, 'La coopération européenne en matière de lutte contre la criminalité organisée dans le contexte du traité d'Amsterdam' (1997) 3 RMUE 91–117.

covered by Title VI, 'cooperation in the fields of justice and home affairs' ('JHA cooperation'),[128] contemplated primarily such police and judicial cooperation as was necessary to accompany the liberalization of the movement of persons in the internal market.[129] Since the Treaty of Amsterdam, cooperation under Title VI of the EU Treaty was aimed at preventing and combating crime, organized or otherwise. Pursuant to Article 29 EU, the Council could act in various ways in order to prevent and combat crime, organized or otherwise, in particular terrorism, trafficking in persons and offences against children, illicit drug trafficking and illicit arms trafficking, corruption, and fraud (see Article 29, second para. EU).[130] As a result, the European Union became the pre-eminent forum for bringing Member States' criminal law policy closer together and to make a start with European criminal law.[131] Title VI of the EU Treaty constituted part of the legal basis for integrating the Schengen *acquis* into the European Union and its further development (see para. 8-004, *infra*).

1.048 **Single institutional framework.** According to the EU Treaty, the Union had for its action in the three pillars a 'single institutional framework' encompassing the European Council and the institutions of the Communities (the European Parliament, the Council, the Commission, the Court of Justice, and the Court of Auditors). The European Council was given the task of providing the Union with the necessary impetus for its development and of defining the general political guidelines. As far as the CFSP and PJCC were concerned, it was the Council, the most 'intergovernmental' institution of the Communities, that was to organize consultations among the Member States, adopt common positions and joint actions (in the context of the CFSP), and adopt common positions, framework decisions, and decisions.[132]

The fact that there was a 'single' institutional framework did not signify, however, that the institutions performed the same functions within each of the two integration paths.[133]

For the implementation of these provisions in the various legal orders of the Member States, see Moore and Chiavario (eds), *Police and Judicial Co-operation in the European Union* (Cambridge University Press, 2004).

[128] Ever since the Treaty of Amsterdam, cooperation in the fields of justice and home affairs under Title VI of the EU Treaty has been confined to police and judicial cooperation in criminal matters. Since the expression 'justice and home affairs' (JHA) bears on both the 'communitarized' competences (Title IV EC Treaty,) and on non-Community cooperation in criminal matters (Title VI EU Treaty), the authors have elected in this work to refer to cooperation pursuant to Title VI of the EU Treaty as police and judicial cooperation in criminal matters (PJCC) in line with the wording of the Treaty.

[129] See Müller-Graff, 'The Legal Base of the Third Pillar and its Position in the Framework of the Union Treaty' (1994) CMLRev 493–503. For the first results and the need to reform the third pillar, see Labayle, 'La coopération européenne en matière de justice et d'affaires intérieures et la Conférence intergouvernementale (1997) RTDE 1–35; Den Boer, 'Police Cooperation in the TEU: Tiger in a Trojan Horse?' (1995) CMLRev 555–78; Lepoivre, 'Le domaine de la justice et des affaires intérieures dans la perspective de la Conférence intergouvernementale' (1995) CDE 323–49; O'Keeffe, 'Recasting the Third Pillar' (1995) CMLRev 893–920. Compare Vignes, 'Plaidoyer pour le IIIème pilier' (1996) RMCUE 273–81 with Dehousse and Van den Hende, 'Plaidoyer pour la réforme du troisième pilier' (1996) RMCUE 714–18.

[130] Mitsilegas, 'Defining Organised Crime in the European Union: The Limits of European Criminal law in an Area of "Freedom, Security and Justice"' (2001) ELRev 565–81; Margue, 'La coopération en matière de prévention et de lutte contre le crime dans le cadre du nouveau troisième pilier' (2000) RDUE 729–47.

[131] See also Mitsilegas, *EU Criminal Law* (Hart Publishing, 2009); Barents, 'De denationalisering van het strafrecht' (2006) SEW 358–74; Guild, 'Crime and the EU's Constitutional Future in an Area of Freedom, Security and Justice' (2004) ELJ 218–34; von Bubnoff, 'Institutionelle Kriminalitätsbekämpfung in der EU—Schritte auf dem Weg zu einem europäischen Ermittlungs- und Strafverfolgungsraum' (2002) ZEuS 185–237; Harding, 'Exploring the Intersection of European Law and National Criminal Law' (2000) ELRev 374–90.

[132] Articles 14–to 16 EU Treaty (CFSP) and Article 34 EU Treaty (PJCC).

[133] cf. Curtin (n. 64, *supra*), 27–30, who referred to the single institutional framework as a 'fiction' and as 'being given the lie'. As regards the logistical support provided by the Community for the non-Community forms of co-operation, see Isaac, 'Le "pilier" communautaire de l'Union européenne, un "pilier" pas comme les autres' (2001)

Article 5 EU stated that the Community institutions were to exercise their powers under the conditions provided for and in order to achieve the objectives laid down, on the one hand, in the Community Treaties and, on the other, in the other provisions of the EU Treaty. Consequently, in the context of Title V (CFSP) and Title VI (PJCC) the institutions were to operate in accordance with the procedural rules laid down therein. As a result, in principle, for CFSP and PJCC matters the requirement that the Council must take decisions by a unanimous vote applied, unlike the voting rules applicable to the Community pillar. Furthermore, under the second and third pillars, the Commission did not have an exclusive right of initiative and exercised no supervision as to the Member States' compliance with the obligations they entered into. The European Parliament, for its part, was entitled only to be consulted and kept informed.[134] Yet, in principle, the Community budget procedure applied to all administrative and policy expenses related to Union action pursuant to Title V or Title VI. Accordingly, the European Parliament could also supervise the non-Community Union action (see para. 14-011, *infra*).

Community and non-Community provisions. The different decision-making procedures clearly demonstrate that the second and third pillars did not satisfy the criteria of the definition of supranational cooperation set out above. They exhibited the characteristics of an intergovernmental form of cooperation, with decision-making in the hands of the Council, and hence of the national governments collectively, although the European Parliament had the right to be consulted on PJCC measures adopted by the Council. In view of the task conferred on the Court of Justice with regard to police and judicial cooperation in criminal matters (PJCC), which was introduced by the Treaty of Amsterdam, this was less true of that form of cooperation. As far as Union action under the CFSP was concerned, any supervision by the Court of Justice was ruled out.[135] This also took acts of the European Council, which as such did not adopt acts of Community law (see para. 12-025, *infra*), outside the scope of judicial review.[136] As far as PJCC (Title VI) was concerned, although the Court of Justice was not empowered to review whether Member States fulfilled their Treaty obligations, Article 35 EU conferred jurisdiction on it to review, under certain conditions, acts adopted by the Union under Title VI (see para. 13-011, *infra*).[137]

1.049

Since the non-Community provisions of the EU Treaty were not to affect the Community Treaties or the Treaties and acts modifying or supplementing them (Article 47 EU), the Union had always to respect the *acquis communautaire*. The Court of Justice could enforce compliance with that obligation using the proper procedures against institutions of the

---

CDE 45, 49–63. With regard to the heterogeneous structure perpetuated by the Treaty of Amsterdam, see the commentaries in (1998) EuR Beiheft 2: Zuleeg, 'Die Organisationsstruktur der Europäischen Union—Eine Analyse der Klammerbestimmungen des Vertrags von Amsterdam', 151–63; von Bogdandy, 'Die Europäische Union als einheitlicher Verband', 165–83See also von Bogandy, 'The Legal Case for Unity: The European Union as a Single Organisation with a Single Legal System' (1999) CMLRev 887–910.

[134] Articles 18(4), 21, 22, and 27 (CFSP) and Articles 34(2), 36(2), and 39 (PJCC) EU Treaty.

[135] cf. the preliminary ruling procedure under Article 234 EC. See C-167/94 *Grau Gomis and Others* (order), 1995, para. 6, where the Court held that it had no jurisdiction to interpret Article 2 EU.

[136] See T-584/93, *Roujansky v Council* (order), 1994, paras 12–14 (and the parallel order given on the same day in T-179/94, *Bonnamy v Council* (order), 1994, paras 10–12), upheld by C-235/94 P, *Roujansky v Council* (order), 1995.

[137] See C-354/04 P, *Gestoras Pro Amnistía and Others*, 2007, paras 44–57; C-355/04 P, *Segi and Others*, 2007, paras 44–57.

32   FROM EUROPEAN COMMUNITIES TO EUROPEAN UNION

Communities acting for the Union and against Member States (Article 47 was among the final provisions of the EU Treaty which were enforceable by the Court).[138]

C. Subsequent amendments

1. The Treaty of Amsterdam

1.050 **Treaty of Amsterdam.** When the accession negotiations were being rounded off in 1994, the Member State governments committed themselves to discussing at an intergovernmental conference (IGC) scheduled for 1996 how the institutions should be adapted in order to operate effectively after the forthcoming and subsequent enlargements of the Union.[139] On 29 March 1996 the IGC opened, resulting in the Treaty on which the Heads of State or Government reached agreement in Amsterdam on 16 and 17 June 1997.[140]

On 2 October 1997 the Treaty of Amsterdam was signed, amending the Treaty on European Union, the Treaties establishing the European Communities, and certain related acts.[141] The Treaty of Amsterdam was the subject of a referendum in Ireland on 22 May 1998 (61.7 per cent in favour) and in Denmark on 28 May 1998 (55.1 per cent in favour) and prompted an amendment of the Constitution in Austria, France, and Ireland.[142] The Treaty entered into force on 1 May 1999.[143]

---

[138] See, to that effect, C-170/96, *Commission v Council*, 1998, paras 12–18; C-176/03, *Commission v Council*, 2005, paras 37–8; C-91/05, *Commission v Council*, 2008, paras 32–4. See Isaac, 'Le "pilier" communautaire de l'Union européenne, un "pilier" pas comme les autres' (2001) CDE 45–89.

[139] (1993) 12 EU Bull. point I.18 and (1994) 3 EU Bull. point I.3.28. For the challenges facing the IGC, see Dashwood, *Reviewing Maastricht issues for the 1996 IGC: Seminar series organised by the Centre for European Legal Studies Cambridge* (Sweet & Maxwell, 1996); Louis, 'La réforme des institutions' (1995) RMUE 233–42; Justus Lipsius, 'The 1996 Intergovernmental Conference' (1995) ELRev 235–42; Chaltiel, 'Enjeux et perspectives de la conférence intergouvernementale de 1996' (1995) RMCUE 625–36. Earlier, members of the European Parliament had produced a proposal for consolidating the texts of the Treaties into a Draft Constitution of the European Union, which was not approved by the Parliament, but published as an annex to a resolution of 10 February 1994, OJ 1994 C61/155.

[140] (1997) 6 EU Bull. points I.3 and II.4. For further discussion of the IGC, see Lenaerts and De Smijter, 'La conférence intergouvernementale de 1996' (1996) JTDE 217–29; Dehousse, 'Evolution ou révolution des institutions européennes: le débat fondamental de la Conférence intergouvernementale de 1996' (1996) JT 593–6; Kortenberg, 'Le Traité d'Amsterdam. La négotiation du Traité. Une vue cavalière' (1997) RTDE 709–19.

[141] OJ 1997 C340/1. For commentaries, see Barents, *Het Verdrag van Amsterdam in werking* (Kluwer, 1999); Hummer, Obwexer and Schweitzer, 'Die Europäische Union nach dem Vertrag von Amsterdam. Gegenwärtige Stand und künftige Entwicklung' (1999) ZfRV 132–46; De Zwaan, 'Het Verdrag van Amsterdam. Etappe in het proces van Europese integratie' (1999) NJB 492–500; Hilf and Pache, 'Der Vertrag von Amsterdam' (1998) NJW 705–13; Lenaerts and De Smijter, 'Le traité d'Amsterdam' (1998) JTDE 25–36; Manin, 'The Treaty of Amsterdam' (1998) Col JEL 1–26; Sauron, 'Le traité d'Amsterdam: une réforme inachevée?' (1998) Rec Dalloz 69–78; Timmermans, 'Het Verdrag van Amsterdam. Enkele inleidende kanttekeningen' (1997) SEW 344–51; Blumann, 'Le traité d'Amsterdam. Aspects institutionnels' (1997) RTDE 721–49; Petite, 'Le traité d'Amsterdam: ambition et réalisme' (1997) RMUE 17–52; Favret, 'Le traité d'Amsterdam: une révision *a minima* de la "charte constitutionnelle" de l'Union européenne' (1997) CDE 555–605.

[142] See the survey in Lepka and Terrebus, 'Les ratifications nationales, manifestations d'un projet politique européen—la face cachée du Traité d'Amsterdam' (2003) RTDE 365–88; Hoffmeister, 'Europäisches Verfassungsrecht nach Amsterdam' (1999) EuR 280–8. In France, the *Conseil constitutionnel* held, on 31 December 1997, that some provisions of Title IV of the EU Treaty introduced by the Amsterdam Treaty conflicted with the Constitution: see Chaltiel, 'Commentaire de la décision du Conseil constitutionnel relative au traité d'Amsterdam' (1998) RMCUE 73–84. For the French law ratifying the Amsterdam Treaty, see Karagiannis, 'Observations sur la loi française n° 99-229 du 23 mars 1999 autorisant la ratification du traité d'Amsterdam' (2001) RTDE 19–47. For the constitutional situation in Germany, see Bothe and Lohmann, 'Verfahrensfragen der deutschen Zustimmung zum Vertrag von Amsterdam' (1998) ZaöRV 1–44.

[143] Under Article 14 Amsterdam Treaty, it entered into force on the first day of the second month following that in which the instrument of ratification was deposited by the last signatory State to fulfil that formality. See information about the date of entry into force of the Treaty of Amsterdam, OJ 1999 L114/56.

Amendments to the Treaties. The Treaty of Amsterdam did not interfere with the structure **1.051** of the European Union as described above, yet it amended each of the three Community Treaties, it restructured the CFSP (EU Treaty, Title V) and it radically reformed Title VI of the EU Treaty (covering police and judicial cooperation in criminal matters).[144] The most conspicuous change introduced by the Amsterdam Treaty for practitioners and students was the renumbering of the articles, titles, and sections of the EU Treaty and the EC Treaty in order to reduce their complexity and make them more accessible.[145]

The most important change made by the Amsterdam Treaty with regard to the Community Treaties was the introduction in the EC Treaty of competences relating to visas, asylum, immigration, and other policies related to free movement of persons, to employment, and to customs cooperation.[146] On the institutional level, the Amsterdam Treaty refined the co-decision procedure.

The provisions on the CFSP (EU Treaty, Title V) were completely redrafted. Primarily, the procedure and instruments for determining and implementing the CFSP were clarified. As a result of the incorporation into the EC Treaty of a number of fields relating to justice and home affairs, which have to do with free movement of persons and customs, only police and judicial cooperation in criminal matters fell within the field of application of Title VI of the EU Treaty (PJCC). However, the Amsterdam Treaty did not confine such cooperation to that which was necessary in connection with the abolition of frontier checks, but placed it in the broader context of the Union's objective of providing 'citizens with a high level of safety within an area of freedom, security and justice'.[147] At the same time, maintaining and developing the Union as an area of freedom, security, and justice continued to be an objective of the Union itself (Article 2, fourth indent EU), which was to be pursued both by Community policy and by action in the context of PJCC.[148] The Treaty of Amsterdam cautiously subjected action on the part of the Union to achieve this objective to review by the Court of Justice, which was given jurisdiction to rule on the validity and interpretation of acts of the institutions in connection with PJCC.

Closer cooperation. In addition, the Treaty of Amsterdam provided general mechanisms **1.052** for Member States wishing to cooperate more closely with each other in Community matters or in matters covered by Title VI of the EU Treaty (PJCC), where not all the Member States showed the same readiness to cooperate (EU Treaty, Title VII). These mechanisms enabled Member States to cooperate more closely with each other, under certain conditions, while using the institutions, procedures, and mechanisms laid down by the EU Treaty and the EC Treaty (see para. 8-002, *infra*).

---

[144] Bardenhewer, 'Die Einheitlichkeit der Organisationsstruktur der Europäischen Union' (1998) EuR Beiheft 2, 125–38. See also Vedder, 'Die Unterscheidung von Unionsrecht und Gemeinschaftsrecht nach dem Vertrag von Amsterdam' (1999) EuR Beiheft 1, 7–44; Isaac, 'Le "pilier" communautaire de l'Union européenne, un "pilier" pas comme les autres' (2001) CDE 45–89. For the first time, a Treaty also amended the preamble to the EU Treaty (references to fundamental social rights, sustainable development, and the establishment of an area of freedom, security, and justice; see Article 1(1) to (3) of the Treaty of Amsterdam) and the preamble to the EC Treaty (reference to access to education; see Article 2(1) of the Treaty of Amsterdam).
[145] Article 12 of the Amsterdam Treaty, which refers to the tables of equivalences set out in the Annex thereto. A consolidated version of the EU Treaty and the EC Treaty was published together with the Treaty of Amsterdam, OJ 1997 C340/145 (EU Treaty) and p. 173 (EC Treaty).
[146] EC Treaty, Title IV (Articles 61 to 69); Title VIII (Articles 125 to 130); and Title X (Article 135), respectively.
[147] See Article 29, first para. EU.
[148] See Article 61 EC; para. 8-002, *infra*.

Forms of cooperation in which not all the Member States take part had already materialized before (see para. 22-001 *et seq.*, *infra*) both outside the context of the EU Treaty (e.g. Schengen) and within it, particularly pursuant to the EC Treaty (EMU) or a protocol to that Treaty authorizing Member States to engage in cooperation while using the Community institutions (Social Protocol). The Amsterdam Treaty reordered some of these forms of cooperation. It incorporated the Schengen cooperation into the European Union by introducing Community competences in this sphere, enlarging the scope of Title VI of the EU Treaty and adopting the Schengen *acquis*, partly as Community law and partly as Union law (with Denmark being given a special status and with exceptions being provided for Ireland and the United Kingdom; see para. 8-006, *et seq., infra*). Furthermore, the Treaty repealed the Social Protocol and transformed the corresponding cooperation entirely into Community competence (see para. 9-046, *infra*).

2. The Treaty of Nice

1.053 **Treaty of Nice.** The Protocol on the institutions with the prospect of enlargement of the European Union annexed to the Treaty of Amsterdam already signalled that it was necessary to reform the institutions with a view to the further enlargement of the Union.[149] The European Council held in Cologne on 3 and 4 June 1999 announced that a new Intergovernmental Conference (IGC) would be convened in early 2000 '[i]n order to ensure that the European Union's institutions can continue to work efficiently after enlargement'. This IGC concluded on 10 December 2000 in Nice when the Heads of State or Government reached agreement on a new treaty.[150] On 26 February 2001 the Treaty of Nice amending the Treaty on European Union, the Treaties establishing the European Communities, and certain related acts was signed.[151] The Treaty was put to a first referendum in Ireland on 7 June 2001 and rejected by 53.87 per cent of the votes. Following this, the Irish Government launched a national debate, culminating in a second referendum on 19 October 2002 in which 62.89 per cent voted in favour.[152] The Treaty entered into force on 1 February 2003.

1.054 **Amendments to the Treaties.** The Nice Treaty did not result in the comprehensive reform sought in some quarters, but was limited primarily to adjustments in the composition and

---

[149] For that protocol, see n. 81, *supra*. See also the Declaration by Belgium, France, and Italy on the Protocol annexed to the EU Treaty and the Community Treaties on the institutions with the prospect of enlargement of the European Union, OJ 1997 C340/144, in which those Member States stated that the Treaty of Amsterdam did not meet the need for substantial progress towards reinforcing the institutions, this being an indispensable condition for the conclusion of the first accession negotiations.

[150] (2000) 12 EU Bull. point 1.1.3. As to how the Treaty came about, see Wiedmann, 'Der Vertrag von Nizza— Genesis einer Reform' (2001) EuR 185–215.

[151] OJ 2001 C80/1. For general commentaries, see Lenaerts and Desomer, 'Het Verdrag van Nice en het "post-Nice"-debat over de toekomst van de Europese Unie' (2001–2002) RW 73–90; Bradley, 'Institutional Design in the Treaty of Nice' (2001) CMLRev 1095–124; Favret, 'Le traité de Nice du 26 février 2001: vers un affaiblissement irréversible de la capacité d'action de l'Union européenne?' (2001) RDE 271–304; Van Nuffel, 'Le Traité de Nice. Un commentaire' (2001) RDUE 329–87; Louis, 'Le Traité de Nice' (2001) JTDE 25–34; Hatje, 'Die institutionelle Reform der Europäischen Union—der Vertrag von Nizza auf dem Prüfstand' (2001) EuR 143–84; Shaw, 'The Treaty of Nice: Legal and Constitutional Implications' (2001) EPubL 195–215. For critical commentaries, see Pescatore, 'Nice—Aftermath' (2001) CMLRev 265–71; De Zwaan, 'Het Verdrag van Nice' (2001) SEW 42–52.

[152] For these referendums, see Gilland, 'Ireland's (First) Referendum on the Treaty of Nice' (2002) JCMS 527–35; Kämmerer, 'Das Déjà-vu von Dublin—Gedanken zum Ausgang des zweiten irischen Referendums über den Vertrag von Nizza' (2002) NJW 3596–8. For ratification in France, see Chaltiel, 'La ratification du Traité de Nice par la France' (2001) RMCUE 442–6; for ratification in Germany, see Streinz, '(EG)-Verfassungsrechtliche Aspekte des Vertrags von Nizza' (2003) ZöR 137–61.

operation of the European Parliament, the Council, and the Commission following the accession of new Member States and to a reform of the Community judicature.[153]

First, the Treaty provided that the Council was to nominate the President of the Commission by a qualified majority vote.[154] In addition, the Treaty provided that from 2005 the number of members of the Commission would be limited to one per Member State. At a later stage, the number of members of the Commission would be further limited insofar as the Member States having a national as a member would be chosen by rotation.[155] By way of compensation for losing their right to have a second national as member of the Commission, the large Member States demanded that the weighting of votes in the Council be adjusted. The upshot was a rather complex compromise for calculating whether the qualified majority was attained (see para. 12-047, *infra*). The number of members of the European Parliament would be gradually increased to 732, against the wishes of Parliament itself.[156]

Second, the Court of Justice and the Court of First Instance were radically reformed. Since the entry into force of the Treaty of Nice, in principle both courts were to sit as chambers. Institutions and Member States were still entitled to bring a case before the 'Grand Chamber' of the Court of Justice. The number of Advocates-General was still limited to eight, but they were to be involved only in cases where required by the Statute of the Court of Justice.[157] The possibility was created to set up specialized chambers ('judicial panels') for specific matters. An appeal would lie from those 'judicial panels' to the Court of First Instance.[158] The Court of First Instance could see its range of tasks expanded, since the Treaties allowed all direct actions to be concentrated in that court and enabled requests for preliminary rulings to be referred to it in respect of certain matters to be indicated in the Statute.[159]

Third, the Treaty of Nice increased the possibilities for 'enhanced cooperation'—although no use had been made of them up until then—whilst laying down more flexible conditions.[160] For instance, the minimum number of Member States required for enhanced cooperation was reduced to eight. Enhanced cooperation also became possible in the field of the CFSP, albeit on stricter conditions (see para. 22-006 *et seq.*, *infra*).

Charter of Fundamental Rights. In the margins of the Nice European Council, a Charter of Fundamental Rights of the European Union[161] was adopted. That list of fundamental rights was not incorporated in the Treaty itself, but jointly proclaimed by the European Parliament, the Council, and the Commission. Nevertheless, the Charter gained immediate acceptance as an authoritative description of the fundamental rights to which everyone in the European Union is entitled (see para. 22-005, *infra*).

1.055

---

[153] Furthermore, the Treaty of Nice modified the provisions of the EC Treaty on the common commercial policy (Article 133 EC) and introduced provisions on economic, financial, and technical cooperation with third countries (Article 181a EC).
[154] Article 214(2) EC.
[155] Article 4 of the Protocol, annexed to the EU Treaty and the Community Treaties by the Treaty of Nice, on the enlargement of the European Union.
[156] Article 189, second para. EC.
[157] Article 222 EC.
[158] Article 225a EC.
[159] Article 225 EC.
[160] 'Enhanced cooperation' being the new name for 'closer cooperation', see Articles 43–45 EU Treaty.
[161] (2000) EU Bull. 12, point 1.2.2; for the text of the Charter, see ibid., point 2.2.1 and OJ 2000 C364/1.

D. The Constitution for Europe

1.056 **Laeken Declaration.** When the Treaty of Nice was signed, it was clear that this text would be just another step in the ongoing process of reforming the European Union.[162] A declaration annexed to the Nice Treaty proposed that further discussion on the future of the Union should cover four areas: a more precise delimitation of competences between Member States and the Union, the status of the Charter of Fundamental Rights, simplification of the Treaties, and the role of national parliaments.

As announced at the Nice European Council, the European Council held in Laeken (Brussels) on 14 and 15 December 2001 adopted a Declaration on the future of the European Union.[163] The 'Laeken Declaration' convened a 'Convention' composed of representatives of the Heads of State or Government and the parliaments of the Member States and the candidate Member States, the European Parliament, and the Commission.[164] The terms of reference given to the Convention by the Laeken Declaration expanded upon the four issues mentioned above, whilst adding the question whether the simplification and reorganization of the Treaties might not lead to the adoption of a constitutional text for the Union in the long run.[165]

1.057 **Convention.** On 28 February 2002, the Convention on the future of Europe started its work, with Valéry Giscard d'Estaing acting as Chair and Giuliano Amato and Jean-Luc Dehaene as Vice-Chairs. Ultimately, a small steering committee, the Praesidium of the Convention, formulated a Draft Treaty establishing a Constitution for Europe on the basis of the conclusions and proposals drafted by the working parties, which obtained a broad consensus at the plenary session of the Convention held on 13 June 2003.[166] On 20 June 2003 the first two parts of the Draft Treaty establishing a Constitution for Europe were submitted to the European Council meeting in Thessaloniki;[167] the third and fourth parts of the Draft Constitution were adopted by the Convention on 10 July 2003. Given the fact that the Treaty establishing a Constitution for Europe intended to amend the existing Treaties, it had to be adopted in accordance with the procedure for the amendment of the Treaties laid down in then Article 48 of the EU Treaty. As a result, the changes needed to be approved by the representatives of the national governments meeting in an Intergovernmental Conference

---

[162] Brand, 'Quo vadis Europa? Thoughts on the Future of the Union' (2002) Tilburg For LRev 106–43; Prechal, 'Een constitutionele "post-Nice" agenda?' (2001) NJB 384–9; Touscoz, 'Un large débat. L'avenir de l'Europe après la conférence intergouvernementale de Nice (CIG-2000)' (2001) RMCUE 225–36.

[163] For the text of this Declaration, see (2001) 12 EU Bull. point I.27. See also Lenaerts, 'La déclaration de Laeken: premier jalon d'une Constitution européenne?' (2002) JTDE 29–43.

[164] (2001) 12 EU Bull. point I.1. See also the resolution of the European Parliament of 29 November 2001 on the constitutional process and the future of the Union, OJ 2002 C153E/310) and; Grawert, 'Wie soll Europa organisiert werden?—Zur konstitutionellen "Zukunft Europas" nach dem Vertrag von Nizza' (2003) EuR 971–91; Hobe, 'Bedingungen, Verfahren, und Chancen europäischer Verfassunggebung: Zur Arbeit des Brüsseler Verfassungskonvents' (2003) EuR 1–16; Rieder, 'Der Konvent zur Zukunft Europas' (2002) Zeitschrift für Rechtspolitik 241–80.

[165] See De Witte, 'Simplification and Reorganisation of the European Treaties' (2002) CMLRev 1255–87; Pache, 'Eine Verfassung für Europa—Krönung oder Kollaps der europäischen Integration?' (2002) EuR 767–84.

[166] A draft of the sixteen opening articles was presented in February 2003, see (2003) CMLRev 267–77.

[167] According to the European Council held in Thessaloniki on 19 and 20 June 2003, this marked 'a historic step in the direction of furthering the objectives of European integration'. Nevertheless, the European Council considered the text of the draft constitutional treaty to be no more than 'a good basis' for starting the intergovernmental conference: (2003) 6 EU Bull. points I.3.2–I.3.5.

(IGC) and the new text was to be ratified by all Member States in accordance with their respective constitutional requirements (see para. 3-002, *infra*).

IGC. On 18 July 2003 the Draft Constitution was submitted to the Italian Presidency of the Council in Rome. The Draft Constitution was further published in the *Official Journal*[168] and was widely debated by academics.[169] On 4 October 2003, the Italian Presidency of the Council convened an IGC.[170] Under the Irish Presidency, the IGC reached agreement on the Treaty establishing a Constitution for Europe (the 'EU Constitution') within the framework of the European Council held in Brussels on 18 June 2004. After signature by the representatives of the Member States on 29 October 2004, the Treaty establishing a Constitution for Europe was published in the *Official Journal*[171] and submitted for ratification to the Member States.[172]

1.058

Constitution for the EU. The Treaty establishing a Constitution for Europe sought to replace the EC Treaty and the EU Treaty by a new treaty.[173] It was proposed that the new Treaty would be the 'Constitution' of the new European Union, with legal personality, which would take the place of the European Community and the European Union. The EU Constitution was designed to simplify the legal structure of the Union by abolishing the pillar structure and by merging the Union's intergovernmental field of action with the field covered by the Community. Only the European Atomic Energy Community would continue to exist as a separate legal entity.

1.059

As mentioned earlier, the EU Constitution consisted of four parts. Part I set out the objectives of the Union, referred to fundamental rights and citizenship of the Union, catalogued the Union's competences, described its institutions and the way in which the Union's competences were to be exercised (institutionally and financially), and set forth the conditions

---

[168] OJ 2003 C169.
[169] For general comments, see Arnull, 'The Member States of the European Union and Giscard's Blueprint for its Future' (2004) Fordham ILJ 503–43; Temple Lang; 'The Main Issues After the Convention on the Constitutional Treaty for Europe' (2004) Fordham ILJ 544–89; Ruffert, 'Schlüsselfragen der Europäischen Verfassung der Zukunft: Grundrechte—Institutionen— Kompetenz—Ratifizierung' (2004) EuR 165–201; Kokott and Rüth, 'The European Convention and its Draft Treaty Establishing a Constitution for Europe: Appropriate Answers to the Laeken Questions?' (2003) CMLRev 1315–43; Dougan, 'The Convention's Draft Constitutional Treaty: Bringing Europe Closer to its Lawyers?' (2003) ELRev 763–93; Schwarze, 'Ein pragmatischer Verfassungsentwurf—Analyse und Bewertung des vom Europäischen Verfassungskonvent vorgelegten Entwurfs eines Vertrags über eine Verfassung für Europa' (2003) EuR 535–73; Epping, 'Die Verfassung Europas?' (2003) JZ 821–31; Geelhoed, 'Een Europawijde Europese Unie: een grondwet zonder staat?' (2003) SEW 284–310; Eijsbouts, 'Presidenten, parlementen, fundamenten—Europa's komende constitutie en het Hollands ongemak' (2003) NJB 662–73; Lenaerts, Binon, and Van Nuffel, 'L'Union européenne en quête d'une Constitution: bilan des travaux de la Convention sur l'avenir de l'Europe' (2003) JTDE 289–99.
[170] Pursuant to Article 48 EU, the IGC was convened following consultation of the European Parliament (Resolution of 24 September 2003 on the draft Treaty establishing a Constitution for Europe and on the convening of the Intergovernmental Conference), the Commission (Opinion of 17 September 2003 'A Constitution for the Union ', COM(2003)548 final), and the European Central Bank (Opinion of 19 September 2003, OJ 2003 C229/7), the Council having delivered an opinion in favour on 29 September 2003.
[171] OJ 2004 C310.
[172] For a discussion, see Closa, 'Constitution and Democracy in the Treaty Establishing a Constitution for Europe' (2005) 11 E Pub L 145–64; Lenaerts, 'The Constitution for Europe: Fiction or Reality?' (2005) Col JEL 465–79; Lenaerts and Gerard, 'The Structure of the Union According to the Constitution for Europe: The Emperor is Getting Dressed' (2004) ELRev 289–322; Lenaerts and Van Nuffel, 'La constitution pour l'Europe et l'Union comme entité politique et ordre juridique' (2005) CDE 13–125; Lever, 'The Treaty Establishing a Constitution for Europe' (2005) Fordham ILJ 1091–108; Toulemon, 'La Constitution européenne. Son origine, ses vertus, ses faiblesses' (2005) RMCUE 213–19; Ziller, 'National Constitutional Concepts in the New Constitution for Europe' (2005) EuConst 247–71.
[173] See the repeal of earlier Treaties envisaged by Article IV-437 EU Constitution.

for membership of the Union. Part II incorporated the Charter of Fundamental Rights of the Union, virtually unmodified. Part III entered at length into the policies and the functioning of the Union. It took over the various legal bases from the EC Treaty and the EU Treaty—with or without amendments and additions—and contained detailed provisions on the operation and internal organization of the institutions and bodies of the Union. The general and final provisions of Part IV determined the territorial scope of the Constitution, the procedure for amending it, and the conditions under which the Constitution would enter into force. Initially, the idea had been to give a different status to the various parts of the Constitution with the principal aim of enabling Part III to be more easily amended than Part I. Ultimately, however, the EU Constitution did not introduce any hierarchy between the various parts.

1.060 **Constitutional innovations.** The EU Constitution contained some remarkable innovations, such as the incorporation of the Charter of Fundamental Rights of the Union,[174] the fact that Member States would have the right to withdraw from the Union,[175] a clearer allocation of competences between the Union and the Member States,[176] the explicit statement of the principle of primacy of Union law over the law of the Member States, the fact that the co-decision procedure was to become the 'ordinary legislative procedure', and the introduction of new legislative instruments for the Union, such as 'European laws' and 'European framework laws' corresponding to the present regulations and directives respectively.[177] Moreover, the EU Constitution proposed to reinforce the arrangements on the basis of which the Union is to pursue its external policies,[178] *inter alia* by providing for the appointment of a Union Minister for Foreign Affairs who would conduct the CFSP and be responsible, at the same time, as Vice-President of the Commission, for handling external relations and coordinating other aspects of the Union's external action. On the institutional level, the EU Constitution proposed changes to the voting requirements in the Council and the composition of the Commission and formally recognized the European Council as an institution of the Union in its own right.[179] In order to strengthen the Union's identity, the EU Constitution expressly referred to the existing symbols of the Union, namely its flag, anthem, motto, the euro as its currency, and 9 May as Europe Day (see para. 6-003, *infra*).[180]

---

[174] See Arnull, 'Protecting Fundamental Rights in Europe's New Constitutional Order', in Tridimas and Nebbia (eds), *EU Law for the Twenty-First Century: Re-Thinking the New Legal Order* (Hart Publishing, 2004) 95–112; Young, 'The Charter, Constitution and Human Rights: Is This the Beginning or the End for Human Rights Protection by Community Law?' (2005) 11 E Pub L 219–39; Kapteyn, 'De reikwijdte van het Handvest van de grondrechten van de Europese Unie als onderdeel van een Grondwet voor Europa' (2004) Themis 111–19;.

[175] See De Witte, 'The European Constitutional Treaty: Towards an Exit Strategy for Recalcitrant Member States?' (2003) MJECL 3–8.

[176] See Goucha Soares, 'The Division of Competences in the European Constitution' (2005) E Pub L 603–21; Craig, 'Competence: Clarity, Conferral, Containment and Consideration' (2004) ELRev 323–44.

[177] See Lenaerts and Desomer, 'Towards a Hierarchy of legal acts in the European Union? Simplification of Legal Instruments and Procedures' (2005) ELJ 744–65; Blanchet, 'Les instruments juridiques de l'Union et la rédaction des bases juridiques: situation actuelle et rationalisation dans la Constitution' (2005) RTDE 319–43.

[178] See Bulterman, 'De externe betrekkingen van de Europese Unie in de Europese Grondwet' (2005) AAe 121–8; Cremona, 'The Draft Constitutional Treaty: External Relations and External Action' (2003) CMLRev 1347–66; Thym, 'Reforming Europe's Common Foreign and Security Policy' (2004) ELJ 5–22; Pernice and Thym, 'A New Institutional Balance for European Foreign Policy?' (2002) E For Aff Rev 369–400.

[179] See Blumann, 'Les institutions de l'Union dans le cadre du Traité établissant une Constitution pour l'Europe' (2005) RTDE 345–74; Dashwood and Johnston, 'The Institutions of the Enlarged EU under the Regime of the Constitutional Treaty' (2004) CMLRev 1481–518.

[180] For the EU Constitution as a step towards the building of a 'European' identity, see von Bogdandy, 'Europäische Verfassung und europäische Identität' (2004) JZ 53–104; for the link between the EU Constitution

No ratification by all Member States. As already mentioned, the EU Constitution was to replace the existing Treaties only if it was ratified by all the Member States in accordance with their respective constitutional requirements. In several Member States, ratification of the EU Constitution was made dependent on the positive outcome of a referendum. After the negative referenda in France (29 May 2005; 55 per cent against)[181] and the Netherlands (1 June 2005; 61.6 per cent against),[182] the fate of the EU Constitution became uncertain.[183] The European Council of 16 and 17 June 2005 announced a period of reflection, during which several of the Member States suspended the ratification process. It appeared that the EU Constitution would never be ratified by all Member States.[184] At the same time, most leaders agreed that there was a need to reform the existing institutional structure of the Union, especially because of the accession in 2004 of ten new Member States, followed by two more on 1 January 2007. The question became whether such a treaty amendment would give up the many constitutional innovations to which the Member States had already signed up in the Constitution for Europe.

1.061

and the citizens of Europe, see Schmitz, 'Das europäische Volk und seine Rolle bei einer Verfassunggebung in der Europäischen Union' (2003) EuR 217–43.
[181] Ziller, 'The End of Europe? A Flavour of Déjà-vu. Reflections on the French Referendum and its Aftermath', in Wouters, Verhey, and Kiiver (eds), *European Constitutionalism beyond Lisbon* (Intersentia, 2009) 17–31.
[182] Bursens and Meijer, 'Beyond First Order Versus Second Order Explanations of European Referendum Outcomes. Understanding the Dutch "Neen" and the Luxembourg "Jo"', in Wouters, Verhey, and Kiiver (eds), *European Constitutionalism beyond Lisbon* (Intersentia, 2009), 33–57; Besselink, 'Double Dutch: The Referendum on the European Constitution' (2006) E Pub L 345–51.
[183] By contrast, the consultative referenda in Spain on 20 February 2005 and in Luxembourg on 10 July 2005 had a positive outcome (76.7 per cent and 56.5 per cent in favour, respectively).
[184] See Hurrelmann, 'European Democracy, the Permissive Consensus and the Collapse of the EU Constitution' (2007) ELJ 343–59.

2
The Treaty of Lisbon and the Current Treaties

I. The Treaty of Lisbon

A. Negotiation and ratification of the Treaty of Lisbon

2.001 **New negotiations on a Reform Treaty.** In early 2007, the German Chancellor Angela Merkel initiated a new round of discussions on the reform of the Treaties. The German Presidency of the Council aimed at finding a consensus on the necessary amendments to the existing Treaties (EC and EU Treaties) that would sufficiently accommodate the political objections in certain Member States which had prevented the EU Constitution from entering into force. Eventually, the Brussels European Council of 21 and 22 June 2007 agreed to convene an Intergovernmental Conference, which was to draft a Reform Treaty amending the EU and EC Treaties and merging the Community and the EU into one European Union with legal personality, but without conferring on the Treaties a constitutional nature. The European Council adopted a precise and detailed mandate on the basis of which the IGC had to draft the amendments to the existing Treaties. The IGC started on 23 July 2007 and reached an agreement on 18 October 2007 about a number of important modifications to the EU Treaty and the EC Treaty, most of which were drawn from the text of the EU Constitution. This agreement could be reached only after certain derogations had been granted to Poland and the United Kingdom with respect to the application of the Charter of Fundamental Rights of the European Union and, again, to the United Kingdom on the judicial enforcement of measures in the field of police and judicial cooperation in criminal matters (see paras 1-058–1-059, *supra*). The resulting treaty text—the Treaty of Lisbon—forms the basis for the current framework of the European Union.

2.002 **Treaty of Lisbon.** On 13 December 2007, the Heads of State or Government of the Member States signed, in Lisbon, the Treaty amending the Treaty on European Union and the Treaty establishing the European Community (hereinafter, the Treaty of Lisbon or Lisbon Treaty).[1] The Treaty was set to enter into force on 1 January 2009, after ratification by all the Member States in accordance with their constitutional requirements, or—failing ratification by all

---

[1] OJ 2007 C306. For general discussions, see the contributions in Wouters, Verhey, and Kiiver (eds), *European Constitutionalism beyond Lisbon* (Intersentia, 2009); the contributions in Griller and Ziller (eds), *The Lisbon Treaty: EU Constitutionalism without a Constitutional Treaty?* (Springer Verlag, 2008); Cambien and Roes, 'Het Verdrag van Lissabon: *anywhere as long as it's forward?* Een overzicht voor de rechtspraktijk' (2010) TBP 195–206; Reh, 'The Lisbon Treaty: De-Constitutionalizing the European Union?' (2009) JCMS 625–50; Dougan, 'The Treaty of Lisbon 2007: Winning Minds, not Hearts' (2008) CMLRev 617–703; Craig, 'The Treaty of Lisbon: Process, Architecture and Substance' (2008) ELRev 137–66; Rood, 'De EU na het Verdrag van Lissabon: naar een nieuw politiek en institutioneel evenwicht?' (2008) SEW 132–5; Eijsbouts, 'Fundering en geleding. Opmerkingen over Lissabon en de institutionele evolutie van de Unie' (2008) SEW 82–8; T. Corthaut, 'Plus ça change, plus c'est la même chose? A comparison with the Constitutional Treaty' (2008) MJECL 21–34.

Member States by that date—on the first day of the month following the deposit of the instrument of ratification by the last signatory State to take this step (Article 6(2) Treaty of Lisbon). After the negative referendum in Ireland on 12 June 2008 (53.4 per cent against), it became clear that the Treaty would not enter into force on 1 January 2009. Cases brought before the constitutional courts of the Czech Republic[2] and Germany[3] also delayed ratification by those Member States. A new referendum in Ireland was organized on 2 October 2009, with a positive outcome this time (67.1 per cent in favour), which allowed Ireland to proceed with ratification.[4] The second referendum was only held after Ireland received guarantees on a number of specific Irish concerns.[5] To that end, the European Council agreed that, after the entry into force of the Lisbon Treaty, the Commission would continue to include one national of each Member State.[6] Furthermore, agreement was reached on a Decision of the Heads of State or Government of the Member States on the concerns of the Irish people on the Treaty of Lisbon and on a Solemn Declaration on Workers' Rights, Social Policy, and other issues.[7] It was agreed that this Decision would take effect on the date of entry into force of the Lisbon Treaty and that its provisions would be set out in a protocol to the TEU and the TFEU, to be adopted at the time of conclusion of the next accession treaty.[8] Poland, on 12 October 2009, and the Czech Republic, on 13 November 2009, were the last Member States to deposit their instruments of ratification. The Czech Republic only did so after receiving an assurance from the European Council that it would get the same exceptional treatment as Poland and the United Kingdom with respect to the application of the Charter of Fundamental Rights of the Union (even though that Member State did not insist on this in the end).[9] In accordance with Article 6(2), the Treaty of Lisbon entered into force on 1 December 2009.

---

[2] In a first judgment of 26 November 2008 (PL ÚS 19/08, available in English at http:www.usoud.cz), the Czech Constitutional Court ruled on the constitutionality of a number of specific articles of the Treaty of Lisbon and of the Charter of Fundamental Rights and found that these were compatible with the Czech constitutional order. In a second judgment of 3 November 2009 (PL ÚS 29/09, available in English at http://www.usoud.cz), the Czech Constitutional Court ruled on a challenge to the Treaty of Lisbon as a whole, and found that it was consistent with the Czech constitutional order. See the Editors, 'The Czech Constitutional Court's Second Decision on the Lisbon Treaty of 3 November 2009' (2009) EuConst 345–52.

[3] Judgment of 30 June 2009, (2009) BVerfGE, 2 BvE 2/08, 2 BvE 5/08, 2 BvR 1010/08, 2 BvR 1022/08, 2 BvR 1259/08, and 2 BvR 182/09, available at http://www.bundesverfassungsgericht.de/. See further, including for commentaries, para. 23-029, *infra*.

[4] See Carbone, 'From Paris to Dublin: Domestic Politics and the Treaty of Lisbon' (2009) JCER 43–60; Quinlan, 'The Lisbon Treaty Referendum 2008' (2009) IPS 107–21; Kingston, 'Ireland's Options after the Lisbon Referendum: Strategies, Implications and Competing Visions of Europe' (2009) ELRev 455–75; Cahill, 'Ireland's Constitutional Amendability and Europe's Constitutional Ambition: the Lisbon Referendum in Context' (2008) GLJ 1191–218.

[5] See the Statement of the Concerns of the Irish People on the Treaty of Lisbon as set out by the Taoiseach in Annex 1 to the European Council Presidency Conclusions of 11 and 12 December 2008 (17271/108 REV 1).

[6] See the European Council Presidency Conclusions of 11 and 12 December 2008 (17271/108 REV 1) and of 18 and 19 June 2009 (11225/2/09 REV 2). See also para. 12-063, *infra*.

[7] See the Decision of the Heads of State or Government of the twenty-seven Member States of the EU, meeting within the European Council on the concerns of the Irish people on the Treaty of Lisbon set out in Annex 1 and the Solemn Declaration on Workers' Rights, Social Policy and other issues set out in Annex 2 to the European Council Presidency Conclusions of 18 and 19 June 2009 (11225/2/09 REV 2).

[8] Point 5 of the European Council Presidency Conclusions of 18 and 19 June 2009 (11225/2/09 REV 2).

[9] See the Protocol on the Application of the Charter of Fundamental Rights of the European Union to the Czech Republic set out in Annex I to the European Council Presidency Conclusions of 29 and 30 October 2009 (15265/1/09 REV 1). The Protocol would be annexed to the TEU and the TFEU at the time of the conclusion of the next accession treaty (Point 2 of the Presidency Conclusions). Subsequently, the Czech Republic no longer insisted on obtaining any exceptional status regarding the application of the Charter, so that the draft Protocol was never submitted for ratification.

B. New structure of the basic Treaties

2.003 **New structure of the Treaties.** As the EU Constitution had proposed, the Treaty of Lisbon abolished the old pillar structure on which the European Union was based, and integrated the European Community into the European Union bestowed with legal personality, which henceforth exercises both the former Community and non-Community competences. Whereas the EU Constitution set out to replace the existing Treaties by one single Treaty, the Treaty of Lisbon maintained the existing Treaties, albeit in amended form. Union action continues to be based on the amended Treaty on European Union (TEU), on the one hand, and the amended Treaty establishing the European Community—renamed the Treaty on the Functioning of the European Union (TFEU)—on the other hand. Both Treaties were published in consolidated versions in the Official Journal.[10] The two Treaties have the same legal value.[11] The new European Union replaces and succeeds to the European Community (Article 1, third para. TEU). Only the European Atomic Energy Community continues to exist as a separate legal entity, based on the (amended) EAEC Treaty.[12]

A comparison of the Lisbon Treaty with the EU Constitution shows that most of the amendments proposed by the EU Constitution were taken over by the Treaty of Lisbon.[13] Some of them were introduced in the new Treaty on European Union, while others appear in the Treaty on the Functioning of the European Union. The Lisbon Treaty also provided for a new continuous numbering of the articles of the Treaty on European Union and the Treaty on the Functioning of the European Union.[14]

As the EU Constitution had proposed, the Treaty of Lisbon merged the Union's intergovernmental field of action with the field previously covered by the Community. The Union's competence in the field of police and judicial cooperation in criminal matters (PJCC), previously based on Title VI of the EU Treaty, was incorporated into the Treaty on the Functioning of the European Union, together with the existing Community competence on 'visa, asylum, immigration and other policies related to the free movement of persons' (Part Three, Title IV of the EC Treaty), resulting in a single Title of the TFEU (Part Three, Title V) on the 'area of freedom, security and justice' (see para. 8-001, *infra*). PJCC has thus become fully subject to the Community method—namely legislation is to be adopted by the European Parliament and the Council under the co-decision procedure (renamed as 'the ordinary legislative procedure'), whilst there is the possibility of judicial review by the Court of Justice, even though PJCC decision-making retains some specific characteristics of its own (see paras 17-012 and 17-034, *infra*). Transitional arrangements were in place with regard to the former third pillar (see paras 2-008–2-009, *infra*). Moreover, the United Kingdom negotiated a special status as regards the judicial enforcement of PJCC measures

---

[10] See OJ 2010 C83 (following up a first publication in OJ 2008 C115). For their latest, consolidated version, see OJ 2016 C202.
[11] Article 1, third para. TEU and Article 1(2) TFEU.
[12] For a consolidated version, see OJ 2016 C203. For an overview, see Popov, 'La Communauté Euratom: de la personnalité juridique distincte à la consécration d'un ordre juridique propre?'(2018) CDE 363–93.
[13] Barents, 'De Europese Grondwet is dood—leve de Europese Grondwet' (2007) NTER 174–84; Corthaut, 'Plus ça change, plus c'est la même chose? A Comparison with the Constitutional Treaty' (2008) MJECL 21–34; Jacobs, 'Het Verdrag van Lissabon en de Europese Grondwet. Is er een overtuigend onderscheid?' (2008) NJB 320–9. See also Lenaerts, 'De Rome à Lisbonne, la constitution européenne en marche?' (2008) CDE 229–53.
[14] Article 5 of the Lisbon Treaty.

(see para. 8-028, *infra*). The provisions on the common foreign and security policy (CFSP) remain to be found in Title V of the Treaty on European Union, but the Treaty of Lisbon added a number of general provisions, applicable to the whole of the Union's external action.[15] In the field of the CFSP, decision-making continues to exhibit significant features of intergovernmentalism (see para. 19-001 *et seq.*, *infra*). In this field, Union action is subject to judicial review by the Court of Justice solely as regards restrictive measures against natural or legal persons and the delimitation of Union competences as to CFSP and other competences (Article 40 TEU; see para. 13-012, *infra*).

C. Constitutional innovations

Constitutional innovations. The Treaty of Lisbon took up most of the innovations proposed by the EU Constitution, with the exception of the term 'Constitution' and a number of other elements considered by the IGC to be of a constitutional nature.[16]

2.004

In the first place, the Treaty of Lisbon updated the values and objectives of the Union (Articles 2 and 3 TEU; see para. 5-002 *et seq.*, *infra*). A major difference as compared with the EU Constitution is that the Lisbon Treaty did not incorporate the Charter of Fundamental Rights of the Union into the Treaties, although an explicit statement was introduced to confirm that the Union recognizes the rights, freedoms, and principles set out in the Charter, which has the same legal value as the Treaties (see Article 6(1) TEU). Here too, the United Kingdom, together with Poland, obtained exceptional arrangements (see para. 25-007, *infra*). The Treaty of Lisbon took over the democratic principles from the EU Constitution on which the functioning of the Union is based. A notable novelty, which also figured in the EU Constitution, lies in the fact that any Member State that no longer subscribes to the objectives and/or policies of the Union now has the right to withdraw from the Union (see para. 4-015, *infra*). This enabled the United Kingdom in 2016 to initiate the 'Brexit' process leading to its withdrawal (see para. 4-016, *infra*). The Treaty of Lisbon did not take over the express reference in the EU Constitution to the existing symbols of the Union, namely its flag, anthem, motto, the euro as its currency, and 9 May as Europe Day (see para. 6-003, *infra*).[17] Somewhat awkwardly, the Union objective of ensuring that competition in the internal market is not distorted was put out of sight into a protocol.[18]

Second, the Treaty of Lisbon clarified the allocation of competences between the Union and the Member States, as well as the extent to which the institutions of the Union can make use of the Union's competences. To this end, the Treaty of Lisbon classified the Union's competences largely on the basis of principles elaborated in the case law of the Court of Justice (see

---

[15] Articles 21–22.
[16] See the IGC mandate in Annex I to the Presidency Conclusions of the European Council of 21 and 22 June 2007 (11177/1/07 REV 1), 3.
[17] See, however, Declaration (No. 52), annexed to the Treaty of Lisbon OJ 2010 C83/355), in which sixteen of the Member States declare that these symbols will for them continue as symbols to express the sense of community of the people in the European Union and their allegiance to it.
[18] At the request of French President Sarkozy, the reference in the objectives to the principle of an open-market economy with free competition was removed, yet at the same time a Protocol (No. 27) on the internal market and competition was annexed to the Treaties as a reminder that the internal market encompasses a system ensuring that competition is not distorted.

para. 5-017 *et seq.*, *infra*). In contrast to the EU Constitution, the Treaty of Lisbon did not explicitly enshrine the principle of primacy of Union law over the law of the Member States (see para. 23-008, *infra*). As to the legal instruments of the Union, the Treaty of Lisbon made a clear distinction between legislative acts and other acts. All legislative acts are now adopted, in principle, by the European Parliament and the Council under the co-decision procedure—now called the 'ordinary legislative procedure' (see para. 17-019, *infra*).[19] The Treaty of Lisbon also extended the substantive scope of application of this procedure. However, it did not take up the new terminology proposed by the EU Constitution, which provided that legislative acts would take the form of a 'European law' or a 'European framework law', corresponding to the existing regulation and directive, respectively (see para. 27-005, *infra*). As regards other acts to be adopted by the Union for the implementation of the Treaties or for the implementation of legislative acts or other implementing acts, the Treaty of Lisbon reorganized the division of powers between the institutions (see para. 17-003 *et seq.*, *infra*). Also significant is the fact that for the first time national parliaments are formally involved in the decision-making procedure at Union level, as they are given the task of ensuring that the legislative action of the Union does not go against the principle of subsidiarity (see para. 5-032, *infra*).

Third, the Treaty of Lisbon reinforced the arrangements on the basis of which the Union is to pursue its external policies—in like manner to the EU Constitution.[20] As already mentioned, the Treaty of Lisbon brought together all external policies in one title on the Union's external action, for which specific objectives are formulated. In order to ensure consistency between the various external policies, the Treaty of Lisbon provided for the appointment of a High Representative of the Union for Foreign Affairs and Security Policy, who is to conduct the CFSP and will be responsible, at the same time, as Vice-President of the Commission, for handling external relations and coordinating other aspects of the Union's external action (see para. 12-065, *infra*). This means that the Lisbon Treaty takes over the functions of 'Union Minister of Foreign Affairs', as proposed in the EU Constitution, but with a title that no longer refers to a state-like entity. The High Representative is to chair the meetings of the Foreign Affairs Council. In addition, the Treaty of Lisbon created a single procedure for the negotiation and conclusion of international agreements which applies in the field of CFSP as well as in all other fields of external action (see para. 21-002, *infra*). Moreover, the Treaty of Lisbon took a number of significant steps towards a European security and defence policy. It extended the list of tasks that can be accomplished by the Union in this respect and consolidated the Member States' commitment to make civilian and military capabilities available to the Union. Furthermore, it provided for a species of 'structured cooperation' among those Member States that are capable of contributing thereto (see para. 10-035, *infra*).

Fourth, with respect to the procedure for future amendments of the Treaties, the Treaty of Lisbon determined that the intergovernmental stage of the amendment procedure is to be preceded by a Convention composed of representatives of the national governments,

---

[19] Best, 'Legislative Procedures after Lisbon: Fewer, Simpler, Clearer' (2008) MJECL 85–96.
[20] See Pernice and Thym, 'A New Institutional Balance for European Foreign Policy?' (2002) E For Aff Rev 369–400; Thym, 'Reforming Europe's Common Foreign and Security Policy' (2004) ELJ 5–22.

the national parliaments, the European Parliament, and the Commission (see para. 3-002, *infra*).

D. Amending the institutional framework

Institutional changes. The Treaty of Lisbon introduced a great number of amendments to the institutional framework of the Union, most of which were already set forth in the EU Constitution.[21] First of all, the Treaty of Lisbon stepped up the role played by the European Parliament in the legislative and budgetary process (see paras 12-003 and 20-001, *infra*). It is also important that for the first time the European Council was formally recognized as an institution of the Union in its own right, even though its function continues to be confined to issuing general policy guidelines without any participation in the legislative process (see para. 12-022, *infra*). A further novelty was that the European Council henceforth elects a permanent president (see para. 12-028, *infra*). The most controversial changes introduced by the Treaty of Lisbon were those directly affecting the balance of power between the Member States, in particular the number of seats allocated to each of the Member States in the European Parliament (see para. 12-013, *infra*), the arrangements relating to the presidency of the Council formations, the number of votes required for the Council to take decisions by a qualified majority (see para. 12-047 *et seq.*, *infra*), and the question as to whether or not the college of Commissioners should comprise at least one national of every Member State (see para. 12-063, *infra*). On 18 October 2007, the IGC managed to achieve a compromise on each of these items, although not without a number of last-minute concessions, such as the enlargement of the European Parliament by one seat and the special arrangements, set out in a Declaration annexed to the Treaties, under which a minority of the Member States in the Council is empowered to suspend the adoption of an act by a qualified majority (see paras 12-013 and 12-047, *infra*, respectively).

2.005

II. Union Law and its Relationship to Previous Community and Non-Community Law

New Union law. With the entry into force of the Treaty of Lisbon, the European Union no longer acts through either Community law measures or non-Community measures. The Union's action in each of its fields of competence now gives rise to measures of 'Union law'. Before the entry into force of the Lisbon Treaty, the expression 'Union law' was used ambiguously, either to refer to the whole body of law governing the European Union (Community and non-Community law) or to refer solely to those provisions of the Treaties that did not constitute Community law. Since 1 December 2009, Union law refers unambiguously to the

2.006

---

[21] For an overview, see Bribosia, 'The Main Institutional Innovations in the Lisbon Treaty', in Griller and Ziller (eds), *The Lisbon Treaty: EU Constitutionalism without a Constitutional Treaty?* (Springer Verlag, 2008), 57–78. On the amendments to the institutional framework proposed by the EU Constitution, see Moussis, 'For a Drastic Reform of European Institutions' (2003) ELRev 250–8; Huber, 'Das institutionelle Gleichgewicht zwischen Rat und Europäischem Parlament in der künftigen Verfassung für Europa' (2003) EuR 574–99; Chaltiel, 'Une Constitution pour l'Europe, an I de la République européenne' (2003) RMCUE 493–501; Smulders, 'Kritische kanttekeningen bij de gevolgen van het "ontwerp-Verdrag tot vaststelling van een grondwet voor Europa" voor het institutionele evenwicht' (2003) NTER 246–52.

Union's new legal order, that is to say, to all provisions of the TEU and the TFEU, all measures adopted pursuant to those provisions, and all other legal rules and principles that are applicable to the Member States and the Union institutions whenever they apply those provisions and measures.

Even where the Union institutions act within the framework of the EAEC—the only remaining 'Community'—one could say that their action also gives rise to acts of 'Union law' as the legal status of measures adopted pursuant to the EAEC Treaty is not any different from the status of previous Community law, which has now become Union law.[22]

2.007 **Continuity of previous Community law.** Although the Treaty of Lisbon has brought both previous Community law and non-Community law under the common denominator of 'Union law', it did not change the characteristics and legal effects that the Union Courts have attributed to previous Community law. Indeed, the reordering and renumbering of the provisions of the previous EC Treaty—now the TFEU—did not affect their legal status at all. Moreover, given the unity of the new Union legal order, the characteristics and legal effects of previous Community law now apply to all provisions of Union law. As a general rule, that goes for any provision of the Treaties and the measures adopted pursuant to them, irrespective of whether they are based upon the TEU or the TFEU, since both Treaties have the same legal value.[23] Hence, the general principles that the Union Courts have derived from the EC Treaty as principles of Community law (e.g. primacy of Community law) become principles of Union law (primacy of Union law).[24] The Union's current legal order thus replaces the pre-existing Community legal order while carrying over all its 'supranational' and 'constitutional' characteristics (see paras 1-025–1-028, *supra*). Likewise, the considerations on the basis of which the European Community could be called a 'supranational' organization continue to apply to the new European Union (see paras 1-021–1-024, *supra*).

In the absence of further transitional measures, the application of the provisions of the TEU and TFEU and the protocols attached thereto in areas that used to be governed by the EC Treaty must be done in accordance with the principles that govern the temporal application of the law. In order to uphold the principle of legal certainty and in order to protect legitimate expectations substantive provisions are only immediately applicable to the future effects of situations which arose under the earlier Treaty provisions; those new rules are in principle not applicable to situations existing before their entry into force.[25] By contrast, procedural rules are deemed to be applicable to all disputes pending at the time of entry into force of those rules.[26]

---

[22] The provisions of the Treaty on European Union and of the Treaty on the Functioning of the European Union shall not derogate from the provisions of this Treaty (Article 106a(3) EAEC). On this relationship between the EAEC Treaty on the one hand, and the TEU and TFEU on the other hand, see C-594/18 P, *Austria v Commission*, 2020, paras 30–3 and 39–45.

[23] However, the Court of Justice continues not to have jurisdiction in respect of most measures adopted within the framework of the CFSP (para. 13-012, *infra*). See also the transitional regime that applies to PJCC measures adopted prior to 1 December 2009 (see para. 2-008, *infra*).

[24] e.g. C-555/07, *Kücükdeveci*, 2010, paras 21 and 27 (principle of non-discrimination on grounds of age as a general principle of European Union law), 48 (duty to interpret national law in conformity with European Union law), and 54 (principle of primacy of European Union law). See the case note by Roes (2010) Col JEL 497–519.

[25] C-303/13 P, *Commission v Andersen*, 2015, paras 49–50; C-596/13 P, *Commission v Moravia Gas Storage and Czech Republic*, 2015, para. 33.

[26] 212-217/80, *Meridionale Industria Salumi*, 1981, para. 9; C-596/13 P, *Commission v Moravia Gas Storage and Czech Republic*, 2015, para. 34.

Status of previous non-Community law. With respect to those fields that, before 1 December 2009, did not form part of Community law, the Lisbon Treaty provides for some transitional arrangements laid down in Protocol (No. 36) on transitional provisions attached to the TEU, TFEU, and EAEC Treaty.[27] They concern acts adopted pursuant to the EU Treaty before 1 December 2009 (in practice, the pre-existing CFSP and PJCC measures).

2.008

According to Article 9 of that Protocol, the legal effects of the acts adopted by the institutions, bodies, offices, and agencies of the Union on the basis of the EU Treaty prior to the entry into force of the Lisbon Treaty, are preserved until those acts are repealed, annulled, or amended in implementation of the current Treaties. The same applies to agreements concluded by the Member States on the basis of the former Articles 24 and 38 EU.[28] Consequently, when applying and interpreting measures adopted on the basis of Title V and Title VI of the EU Treaty before 1 December 2009, account has to be taken of the specific legal status of these CFSP and PJCC instruments (see para. 28-007 *et seq.*, *infra*).

Moreover, with regard to non-Community acts adopted in the field of PJCC prior to the entry into force of the Lisbon Treaty, Article 10(1) of the Protocol provided for reduced powers for the Commission and the Court of Justice for a transitional period of five years. On the one hand, the Commission could not enforce the application of such acts by bringing infringement actions under Article 258 TFEU. On the other hand, with respect to those acts, the Court of Justice had only the powers that were attributed to it by Title VI of the EU Treaty before 1 December 2009, that is to say the powers attributed to the Court under Article 35 EU (see para. 13-010, *infra*). However, as soon as such PJCC acts were amended, the Commission and the Court started to enjoy the full scope of powers they now have under the Treaties with regard to current acts adopted in the field of PJCC (Article 10(2) of Protocol (No. 36)). The transitional period for PJCC acts adopted prior to 1 December 2009 expired on 1 December 2014. The UK also maintained a specific status regarding the application of such PJCC acts after that date.

In contrast, the Lisbon Treaty no longer provides for any different legal regime with respect to the current provisions of the Treaties on the CFSP (Articles 23 to 46 TEU), judicial cooperation in criminal matters (Articles 82 to 86 and 89 TFEU), and police cooperation (Articles 87 to 89 TFEU), nor with respect to the measures adopted by the Union institutions and bodies pursuant to those provisions. Consequently, Union law in those fields has the same legal effects as provisions of Community law before the entry into force of the Lisbon Treaty. Only with respect to the CFSP do the Treaties still not confer any general jurisdiction on the Court of Justice to rule on the interpretation and application of the relevant Treaty provisions and Union measures (see para. 13-011, *infra*).

Transitional provisions. Protocol No. 36 on transitional provisions contains some further institutional arrangements that were aimed at ensuring a smooth transition from the arrangements in place before the entry into force of the Lisbon Treaty to the ones contained in that Treaty. These applied in particular to the qualified majority voting requirement in the Council and the configurations of the Council (para. 12-040, *infra*) and the composition of

2.009

---

[27] Protocol (No. 36) on Transitional Provisions, OJ 2010 C83/349.
[28] Ibid., Article 9.

the European Parliament (para. 12-013, *infra*) and various advisory bodies (paras 13-031 and 13-034, *infra*).

III. New Intergovernmental Systems

2.010 **Intergovernmental instruments.** As indicated above, the Member States preferred to operate on the basis of intergovernmental arrangements in areas where the Union (or the Community at the time) did not yet have competence or where not all Member States were willing to apply the 'Community method', whereby the Commission and the European Parliament are involved in the decision-making process and the Court of Justice has jurisdiction to interpret and enforce the adopted rules (see para. 1-029, *supra*). Exceptionally the Member States opted to implement aspects of a Union regime by way of an intergovernmental agreement, for instance in respect of the financing of the aid given to third countries in the framework of the African, Caribbean, Pacific (ACP) agreement (see para. 10-019, *infra*). The Court of Justice has ruled that the Treaties do not prevent Member States, in areas that do not fall within the exclusive competences of the Union, from attributing tasks to the Union institutions—for instance entrusting the Commission with managing such funding—also in the framework of such an intergovernmental arrangement,[29] provided that those tasks do not alter the essential character of the powers conferred on those institutions by the TEU and TFEU.[30] The Member States may not go against rules of Union law by using intergovernmental arrangements or agreements (see para. 28-004, *infra*). Over time, many areas where Member States used to solely make use of intergovernmental arrangements or agreements, have become areas of Union competence that are governed by the Community method. As observed before, the CFSP remains, however, largely intergovernmental in nature (see para. 10-026, *infra*).

In addition, after the entry into force of the Treaty of Lisbon, Member States continue to make use of international agreements, even in respect of matters that fall within the scope of Union competence. In the context of the Economic and Monetary Union, the Member States that have the euro as their currency have turned to international agreements both for setting up stabilization mechanisms and for making stricter commitments as to budgetary discipline (see paras 9-037–9.042, *infra*). The decisive reason for opting for an international agreement was the fact that some Member States—in particular the United Kingdom—opposed a formal Treaty amendment in order to allow for the adoption of those measures within the Union framework. Both the ESM Treaty and the Treaty on Stability, Coordination and Governance in the Economic and Monetary Union (TSCG) do rely, however, on the Commission (and in the case of the ESM Treaty on the ECB as well) to put the agreed rules into operation; they also grant the Court of Justice jurisdiction in respect of the enforcement of some of their provisions. Accordingly, these agreements are intended

---

[29] C-181/91 and C-248/91, *European Parliament v Council and Commission*, 1993, para. 20; C-316/91, *European Parliament v Council*, 1993, para. 41.

[30] C-370/12, *Pringle*, 2012, para. 158. See de Witte and Beukers, 'The Court of Justice Approves the Creation of the European Stability Mechanism outside the EU Legal Order: Pringle' (2013) CMLRev 805–48; Craig, 'Pringle and Use of EU Institutions outside the EU Legal Framework: Foundations, Procedure and Substance' (2013) EuConst 263–84; Peers 'Towards a New Form of EU Law? The Use of EU Institutions outside the EU Legal Framework' (2013) EuConst 37–72.

to complement Union law, rather than undermine the Community method. Furthermore, they are often considered to be temporary arrangements that in time are to be replaced by a Union mechanism. In this respect the TSCG expressly states that 'the objective of the Heads of State or Government of the euro area Member States and of other Member States of the European Union is to incorporate the provisions of this Treaty as soon as possible into the Treaties on which the European Union is founded'.[31]

IV. Future of the Union

Conference on the Future of Europe. On the occasion of the sixtieth anniversary of the signing of the EEC Treaty, which was solemnly celebrated on 25 March 2017 in Rome, the Commission launched a debate on the future of the Union with a White Paper on the future of the Union, which used five possible scenarios to demonstrate that political choices on the intensity of the future integration process are crucial. In the months thereafter, the Commission adopted reflection documents on the social dimension of Europe, harnessing globalization, deepening of the Economic and Monetary Union, the future of European defence, and the future of EU finances.[32] The negotiations with the United Kingdom in respect of 'Brexit' (see para. 4-016, *infra*) gave a further impetus to the 'EU-27' to reflect on their future cooperation. Ahead of the 2019 elections for the European Parliament, both the Commission[33] and the Heads of State or government of the Member States[34] set out their ambitions for the Union. In her Political Guidelines presented to the European Parliament in July 2019, Ursula von der Leyen announced, as President-elect of the Commission, the idea of calling a Conference on the Future of Europe, which will bring together citizens, including young people and civil society, and Union institutions as equal partners.[35] The mandate for this Conference, was agreed in March 2020 between the European Parliament, the Council, and the Commission.[36]The Conference will be placed under the authority of the three institutions, represented by the President of the European Parliament, the President of the Council and the President of the European Commission, acting as its Joint Presidency. It seeks to give citizens a greater role in shaping the Union's future policies and ambitions, improving its resilience, through a multitude of Conference-events and debates organised across the Union, as well as through an interactive multilingual digital platform. An inaugural event took place on 9 May 2021 (Europe Day). It is to be seen whether the Conference on the Future of Europe will lead to concrete commitments requiring further institutional reforms in the upcoming decade.

2.011

---

[31] Treaty of 2 March 2012 on Stability, Coordination and Governance in the Economic and Monetary Union, 7th recital of the Preamble.
[32] https://ec.europa.eu/commission/white-paper-future-europe-reflections-and-scenarios-eu27_en.
[33] https://ec.europa.eu/commission/sites/beta-political/files/comm_sibiu_06-05_en.pdf.
[34] Sibiu Declaration of 9 May 2019, European Council, press release 335/19.
[35] von der Leyen, *A Union that Strives for More—My Agenda for Europe—Political Guidelines for the next European Commission 2019-2020*, available at https://ec.europa.eu/info/strategy/priorities-2019-2024_en#documents.
[36] Joint Declaration of the European Parliament, the Council and the European Commission on the Conference on the Future of Europe 'Engaging with citizens for democracy – Building a more resilient Europe' OJ 2021 C 91I/1.

3
Amendment of the Treaties

3.001 **Amendment.** An amendment to the Treaties enables amending or supplementing provisions to be adopted that have the same legal force as the original Treaty provisions.[1] In this way, the original Treaties were amended and supplemented by the Single European Act and the EU Treaty, the Treaty of Amsterdam, the Treaty of Nice, and the Treaty of Lisbon. Since the last Treaty amendment (the Treaty of Lisbon), the Treaties contain simplified procedures for amending specific provisions alongside the ordinary revision procedure.[2] After a discussion of these procedures, it will be considered whether the Treaties subject their amendment not only to procedural, but also to substantive constraints.

I. Ordinary Revision Procedure

3.002 **From two to three stages.** The ordinary revision procedure builds upon the revision procedure laid down in the initial Treaties. Amendments first required the Community institutions to act (the Community stage); subsequently, the amendments were determined by the conference of representatives of the Member State governments, the 'intergovernmental conference' or IGC (the intergovernmental stage). In December 2001, the European Council meeting in Laeken (Brussels) decided that the intergovernmental conference to be set up for the next amendment of the Treaties would be prepared by a 'Convention' consisting of representatives of the national governments, the national parliaments, the European Parliament, and the Commission (see para. 1-056 *et seq.*, *supra*). The discussions in the Convention resulted in the draft EU Constitution, which was submitted to the Intergovernmental Conference. Since the participants felt that the Convention constituted an improvement over the traditional procedure for amending the Treaties, an obligatory 'convention stage' was enshrined in the EU Constitution for every future amendment of the Constitution. This procedure was taken over in the Treaty of Lisbon in the provisions on the 'ordinary revision procedure' in respect of future changes to the Treaties. Accordingly, Article 48(3) TEU now provides for an initial phase during which the institutions can reflect on possible Treaty revisions, followed by the convening of a Convention, which will make recommendations as to the revisions that will, in a third stage, be decided by the IGC.

3.003 **Proposals for amendment.** Since the Lisbon Treaty, not only any Member State government and the European Commission, but also the European Parliament may submit proposals for amendment. These proposals may, *inter alia*, serve either to increase or to

---

[1] Para. 24-002, *infra*.
[2] For an overview, see Böttner, 'The Treaty Amendment Procedures and the Relationship between Article 31(3) TEU and the General Bridging Clause of Article 48(7)' (2016) EConstLRev 499; Peers, 'The Future of EU Treaty Amendments' (2012) YEL 17. See also C-370/12, *Pringle*, 2012, paras 30–7.

reduce the competences conferred on the Union in the Treaties. They are submitted to the European Council by the Council, which is also to notify the national parliaments (Article 48(2) TEU). The European Council has to consult the European Parliament[3] and the Commission. In the event that institutional changes in the monetary area are proposed, the European Central Bank must also be consulted by the Council.[4]

Negotiations. Proposals for amendment will be the subject of negotiations only if the European Council, by a simple majority, adopts a decision in favour of examining the proposed amendments (Article 48(3) TEU). In that event, the President of the European Council convenes a Convention composed of representatives of the national parliaments, the Heads of State or Government of the Member States, the European Parliament, and the Commission. The Convention is to adopt, by consensus, a recommendation to the intergovernmental conference. The European Council may, however, decide, after obtaining the consent of the European Parliament, that the extent of the proposed amendments does not justify convening a Convention. If so, the European Council refers the proposed amendments directly to the conference of representatives of the governments of the Member States (Article 48(3), second subpara. TEU). That was the case for the first amendment proposed after the Lisbon Treaty, which allowed the number of members of the European Parliament to be increased for a transitional period.[5]

3.004

Entry into force. The amendments do not enter into force until they have been ratified by all the Member States in accordance with their respective constitutional requirements (Article 48(4), second subpara. TEU). The consent of the European Parliament is therefore not required.[6] Member States' constitutions will normally require the national parliament to give its approval. Furthermore, in some Member States amendments must also be approved by parliaments of the federated entities or in a referendum. In any event, Member States only have a right to approve or reject the amendments, without any possibility of making changes to the amendments proposed.

3.005

Unless all the Member States ratify the amending Treaty, it cannot enter into force.[7] Consequently, the rejection of the EU Treaty by a referendum held in Denmark held up its

---

[3] Only Article 96 ECSC did not contain this requirement.

[4] The EU Treaty introduced that requirement into the revision procedure. Article 102a(2) EEC, however, already required the Monetary Committee and the Committee of Central Bank Governors to be consulted on such amendments.

[5] See European Council Decision 2010/350/EU of 17 June 2010 on the examination by a conference of representatives of the governments of the Member States of the amendments to the Treaties proposed by the Spanish Government concerning the composition of the European Parliament and not to convene a Convention, OJ 2010 L160/5 (see para. 12-013, *infra*).

[6] Article 84 of the European Parliament's Draft Treaty establishing the European Union (see para. 1-028, *supra*) proposed a revision procedure whereby the 'two arms of the legislative authority' (European Parliament and Council) had to approve any 'draft law amending one or more provisions of this Treaty'. Such amendments could be submitted by a representation in the Council or one-third of MEPs or the Commission. The draft law was to come into force when all the Member States had ratified it (OJ 1984 C77/52).

[7] Nevertheless, in theory, a treaty may enter into force between some of the parties if it allows for this possibility (Article 24(2) of the Vienna Convention on the Law of Treaties of 23 May 1969, para. 26-013, *infra*). The second para. of Article 82 of the Draft Treaty establishing the European Union (para. 1-028, *supra*) would have allowed the Treaty to enter into force as soon as it had been ratified by a majority of the Member States of the Communities whose population represented two-thirds of the total population of the Communities. In that case, the governments of the Member States that had ratified the Treaty were to meet in order to decide, by common accord, on the procedures by and the date on which the Treaty should enter into force and to decide on their relations with the other Member States (1984 OJ C77/52).

entry into force until that Member State proceeded to ratify it after a positive vote in a new referendum.[8] The problem recurred with the Treaty of Nice, which Ireland could not ratify until after the positive outcome of a second referendum.[9] Similarly, the EU Constitution never entered into force because of the negative outcome of the referenda in France and the Netherlands.[10] By the same token, the entry into force of the Treaty of Lisbon had to be delayed because of the negative outcome of the referendum in Ireland in June 2008, which made it impossible for Ireland to proceed with its ratification until after the positive outcome of the second referendum held in October 2009.[11]

The Treaty of Lisbon introduced a clause that seeks to avoid future amendments to the Treaties coming up against such impasse. Article 48(5) provides that if, two years after the signature of a treaty amending the Treaties, four-fifths of the Member States have ratified it and one or more Member States have encountered difficulties in proceeding with ratification, the matter 'shall be referred to the European Council'. In that event, consultations in the European Council may perhaps create the appropriate political climate for the Member States to proceed with ratification. However, it does not alter the fact that an amendment to the Treaties cannot enter into force unless it is ratified by all the Member States.

All the same, in order to increase the likelihood of ratification by each Member State, an amending Treaty will often contain opt-out provisions for particular Member States (see para. 22-001 *et seq.*, *infra*).

II. Simplified Procedures for Specific Treaty Amendments

3.006 **Simplified revision procedures.** The Treaty of Lisbon introduced a simplified revision procedure for amendments to the provisions of Part Three of the TFEU, relating to the internal policies and action of the Union, provided that they do not increase the competences of the Union (Article 48(6) TEU).[12] Under this procedure, the European Council is competent to take a decision to amend these provisions without having to convene an IGC. A proposal thereto is to emanate from a national government, the European Parliament, or the Commission. The European Council is to act by unanimity after consulting the European Parliament, the Commission, and the European Central Bank in the case of institutional changes in the monetary area.[13] However, such a European Council decision will not come into force until it has been approved by the Member States in accordance with their respective constitutional requirements.

Another simplified revision procedure introduced by the Treaty of Lisbon enables the European Council to adopt a decision authorizing the Council to act by a qualified majority

---

[8] Para. 1-042, *supra*. The procedure for Treaty amendment laid down in Article 236 EEC did not allow the EU Treaty to enter into force between the other Member States: Rideau, 'La ratification et l'entrée en vigueur du traité de Maastricht' (1992) RFDC 479–91.
[9] Para. 1-053, *supra*.
[10] Para. 1-061, *supra*.
[11] Para. 2-002, *supra*.
[12] See also C-370/12, *Pringle*, 2012, paras 45–75; Karagiannis, 'La révision du Traité sur le fonctionnement de l'union européenne selon la procédure spéciale de l'article 48, paragraphe 6, TUE' (2019) CDE 375–449.
[13] For the legal force of a decision of the European Council under Article 48 TEU, see paras 12-025 and 24-009, *infra*.

in an area or case where the TFEU or Title V of the TEU provides for the Council to act unanimously (Article 48(7), first subpara.).[14] Likewise, the European Council may adopt a decision allowing for the adoption of legislative acts according to the ordinary legislative procedure where the TFEU provides for such acts to be adopted by the Council according to a special legislative procedure (Article 48(7), second subpara.). These amendments can thus be undertaken without having to convene an IGC or having the amendments ratified within each of the Member States. However, the possibility of using Article 48(7) is explicitly excluded for a number of Treaty provisions (see Article 353 TFEU).[15] Moreover, any initiative taken by the European Council in this connection must be notified to the national parliaments. The European Council decision cannot be adopted if a national parliament makes known its opposition within six months of the date of notification of the initiative. This gives every national parliament *de facto* the same right to veto the adoption of decisions under Article 48(7) TEU as it would have if the constitutional system of the Member State concerned requires Treaty amendments to be approved by the national parliament.[16] In the absence of opposition, the European Council may adopt its decision, acting unanimously, after obtaining the consent of the European Parliament, which is to be given by a majority of its component members (Article 48(7), third and fourth subparas).

Other amendments without an intergovernmental conference. Alongside the procedures laid down in Article 48 TEU, some other Treaty articles may be amended without convening an intergovernmental conference. In such a case, it is not the European Council, but the Council which determines the amendment by a unanimous vote pursuant to an *ad hoc* decision-making procedure. Nevertheless, under the Treaty, the entry into force of the amendment in question is dependent upon its 'approval by the Member States in accordance with their constitutional requirements'.[17] There are five cases in which this may be done. First, the Council may, after obtaining the consent of the European Parliament, strengthen or add to the rights attaching to citizenship of the Union listed in Article 20(2) TFEU (Article 25, second para. TFEU). Second, the Council, after obtaining the consent of the European Parliament, is to adopt a decision on the accession of the Union to the European Convention for the Protection of Human Rights and Fundamental Freedoms (Article 218(8), second subpara. TFEU).[18] Third, the Council, after obtaining the consent of the European Parliament, which is to act by a majority of its component members, lays

3.007

---

[14] This possibility does not apply to decisions with military implications or those in the area of defence: Article 48(7), first subpara. TEU.

[15] According to Article 353 TFEU, the possibilities afforded by Article 48(7) TEU cannot be used with regard to Article 311, third and fourth paras TFEU (decisions on 'own resources'); Article 312(2), first subpara. TFEU (regulations laying down a multiannual framework), Article 352 TFEU (the 'flexibility clause'), and Article 354 TFEU (on the suspension of Treaty rights). However, Article 312(2), second subpara. TFEU does enable the European Council, acting unanimously, to authorize the Council to adopt regulations laying down a multiannual financial framework by a qualified majority.

[16] See also Article 6 of Protocol (No. 1) on the role of national parliaments in the European Union (OJ 2010 C83/203), which provides that national parliaments must be informed of an initiative of the European Council at least six months before any decision is adopted.

[17] For the legal force of such a Council decision, see para. 24-009, *infra*. Denmark has notified the constitutional procedure that has to be followed in the case of decisions taken under Article 22 EC [*now Article 25 TFEU*]. These decisions are seen as a 'case of a transfer of sovereignty, as defined in the Danish Constitution, [which requires] ... either a majority of 5/6 of Members of the Folketing or both a majority of Members of the Folketing and a majority of voters in a referendum'. See the Unilateral Declarations to be annexed to the Danish act of ratification of the EU Treaty of which the other Member States will take cognizance (1992 OJ C 348/4).

[18] This provision was added by the Lisbon Treaty.

down the provisions for the election of the European Parliament by direct universal suffrage in accordance with a uniform procedure or with principles common to all Member States (Article 223(1), second subpara. TFEU).[19] Fourth, the Council, after consulting the European Parliament, may adopt provisions to confer jurisdiction on the Court of Justice in disputes relating to European intellectual property rights (Article 262 TFEU). Fifth, the Council, after consulting the European Parliament, lays down provisions relating to the system of own resources of the Union (Article 311, third para. TFEU).[20]

The TEU provides for a similar procedure for the decision taken by the European Council for the realization of a common defence, whereby the European Council recommends to the Member States the adoption of such a decision in accordance with their respective constitutional requirements (Article 42(2), first subpara. TEU). In that case, however, the decision is only political in nature; it does not as such alter the Treaties.

3.008 Other amendments without national ratification. The Treaties also allow for some amendments to be fully implemented at Union level without ratification by the Member States. Mention has already been made of the general possibility for the European Council to extend qualified majority voting or the field of application of the ordinary legislative procedure (see para. 3-006, *supra*). In addition, the European Council has the power, acting unanimously, to extend the application of qualified majority voting in the field of the CFSP.[21] Furthermore, the Treaties permit the Council to extend the field of application of the ordinary legislative procedure into some areas by a unanimous vote and after consulting the European Parliament[22] or to extend qualified majority voting by a unanimous vote.[23] However, insofar as the extension of the ordinary legislative procedure to aspects of family law is concerned, the decision of the Council cannot be adopted if a national parliament makes known its opposition, just as the decision of the European Council to extend the scope of application of the ordinary legislative procedure and qualified majority voting can be blocked by such opposition emanating from a national parliament.[24] In addition, the

---

[19] On the basis of Article 108 EAEC and Article 190 EC, the Council adopted Decision 76/787/ECSC, EEC, Euratom of 20 September 1976 and the Act annexed to it concerning the election of the representatives of the Assembly by direct universal suffrage, OJ 1976 L278/1 and 278/5, respectively). This decision was approved in all the Member States. In accordance with the procedure laid down in the Treaty, the Act was amended by Council Decision of 1 February 1993 (OJ 1993 L33/15), which adjusted the number of seats of each Member State in the European Parliament (para. 12-013, *infra*) and by Council Decision of 25 June 2002 and 23 September 2002 laying down common principles for the election procedure in the Member States (OJ 2002 L283/1) (para. 12-014, *infra*).

[20] See the 'own-resources' decisions; para. 14-013, *infra*. Before the Lisbon Treaty, a Treaty amendment without an IGC was also possible if the Council, acting on the initiative of the Commission or a Member State, decided that action in areas of police and judicial cooperation in criminal matters was to fall under Title IV of the EC Treaty, rather than be the subject of non-Community cooperation (see ex Article 42 EU). See also the Declaration by Denmark on Article K.14 of the Treaty on European Union, annexed to the Treaty of Amsterdam (OJ 1997 C340/143).

[21] Article 31(3) TEU. This possibility does not exist for decisions having military or defence implications (Article 31(4) TEU).

[22] Article 81(3), second subpara. TFEU (judicial cooperation in civil matters—aspects of family law with cross-border implications, see para. 8-015, *infra*); Article 153(2), fourth subpara. TFEU (social policy, see para. 9-047, *infra*); Article 192(2), second subpara. TFEU (environment, see para. 9-061, *infra*); Article 333(2) TFEU (enhanced cooperation; see para. 22-006, *infra*). Unanimity under Article 333(2) refers to the votes of the participating Member States (see Article 330 TFEU). The article cannot be applied to decisions having military or defence implications (Article 333(3) TFEU).

[23] Article 333(1) TFEU (enhanced cooperation; see para. 22-006, *infra*). Unanimity is again calculated in accordance with Article 330 TFEU. Article 333(1) cannot be applied to decisions having military or defence implications (Article 333(3) TFEU).

[24] Article 81(3), third subpara. TFEU. See also para. 3-006, *supra*.

Treaties enable the Council, acting unanimously after obtaining the consent of the European Parliament, to enlarge the scope of action of the Union in the field of judicial cooperation in criminal matters.[25] The Council[26] or the Council and the European Parliament[27] may also amend provisions of a number of the Protocols annexed to the Treaty, acting in accordance with specific procedures, and confer new powers on the European Central Bank.[28]

Under the 'minor amendments procedure' laid down in Articles 76, 85, and 90 of the EAEC Treaty, the Council may amend the chapters 'Special provisions', 'Safeguards', and 'Property ownership', respectively, in exceptional circumstances on the initiative of a Member State or the Commission. Such an amendment has to be adopted unanimously by the Council on a proposal from the Commission and after consulting the European Parliament.[29]

III. Limits to the Possibility to Amend the Treaties

Procedural constraints. Under international law, a treaty may be amended at any time by agreement between the parties.[30] Some commentators have taken the view that it is implicit in the rules embodied in the Union legal order that the Member States as 'masters of the Treaties' may amend the Treaties without having to comply with the procedure set out in Article 48 TEU.[31] It is a fact that the ECSC Treaty has been amended on two occasions outwith Article 96 ECSC.[32] The amendments were made during the transitional period in which it was not possible to amend the Treaty pursuant to Article 96.[33] Nevertheless,

3.009

---

[25] Article 82(2)(d) TFEU (which allows the Council to add aspects of criminal procedure for which the European Parliament and the Council may establish minimum rules); Article 83(1), third subpara. TFEU (which allows the Council to add further areas of crime in respect of which the European Parliament and the Council may establish minimum rules concerning the definition of offences and sanctions). See also Article 86(4) TFEU (which enables the European Council, acting unanimously after obtaining the consent of the European Parliament and consulting the Commission, to extend the powers of the European Public Prosecutor's Office).

[26] See the second subpara. of Article 126(14) TFEU (Protocol (No. 12), annexed to the TEU, TFEU, and EAEC Treaty, on the excessive deficit procedure, OJ 2010 C83/279); Article 308, third para., TFEU (Protocol (No. 5), annexed to the TEU and TFEU, on the statute of the European Investment Bank, OJ 2010 C83/251).

[27] See Article 129(3) TFEU (Protocol (No. 4), annexed to the TEU and TFEU, on the statute of the European System of Central Banks and of the European Central Bank, OJ 2010 C83/230; para. 13-019, *infra*); Article 281 TFEU (Protocol (No. 3), annexed to the TEU, TFEU, and EAC Treaty, on the statute of Court of Justice of the European Union, OJ 2010 C83/210; para. 13-002, *infra*).

[28] Article 127(6) TFEU (the Council is to adopt regulations, acting unanimously and after consulting the European Parliament and the European Central Bank; para. 9-044, *infra*).

[29] The second para. of Article 76 EAEC further requires the Council to apply the provisions of Chapter VI in accordance with the same procedure in the event that it fails to confirm them within seven years of their entry into force. The fact that the Council did not proceed to confirm or amend the provisions in question does not mean that they must have lapsed: 7/71 *Commission v France*, 1971, paras 18–29.

[30] See Article 39 of the 1969 Vienna Convention (para. 26-013, *infra*).

[31] e.g. Deliège-Sequaris, 'Révision des traités européens en dehors des procédures prévues' (1980) CDE 539–52; Zuleeg, 'Der Bestand der Europäischen Gemeinschaft', in Bieber et al. (eds), *Das Europa der zweiten Generation. Gedächtnisschrift für C. Sasse* (Nomos, 1981), Vol. 2, 58–9. But see the commentary by Louis (1980) CDE 553–8; Everling, 'Sind die Mitgliedstaaten der Europäischen Gemeinschaften noch Herren der Verträge?', *Völkerrecht als Rechtsordnung. Internationale Gerichtsbarkeit. Menschenrechte. Festschrift H. Mosler* (Springer, 1983), 173, 186–90; König and Pechstein, 'Die EU-Vertragsänderung' (1998) EuR 130–50 (who argue that the resultant treaty would be valid only under international law).

[32] Treaty of 27 October 1956 amending the ECSC Treaty (change in the distribution of votes in Article 28 following the cession of the Saar to the Federal Republic of Germany) and the Convention of 25 March 1957 on certain institutions common to the European Communities (para. 1-009, *supra*).

[33] In the debate held in the Dutch Second Chamber prior to the law approving the Treaty of 27 October 1956, the Second Chamber passed a motion deploring the fact that it was possible for the Community Treaties to be amended otherwise than by recourse to the procedures provided for in the Treaties themselves to that end (*Handelingen*, Tweede Kamer, 1957–58, Annex I, 1957–58, 4763 No. 9) and the government stated that it would,

the Court of Justice has held that the Member States cannot amend provisions of primary Union law by means of Article 352 TFEU,[34] a joint resolution,[35] or an agreement jointly concluded with third countries,[36] and that the Treaty rules regarding the manner in which the Union institutions arrive at their decisions are not at the Member States' disposal.[37] The fact that the Member States are subject in their 'constituent' function to the rules governing the amendment of the Treaties ensues from the specific character of the Union legal order. The Court of Justice has ruled that, 'apart from any specific provisions, the Treaty can only be modified by means of the amendment procedure carried out in accordance with the Treaty'.[38]

3.010 **Substantive constraints.** A further question is whether there are also substantive, in addition to procedural, limits imposed by Union law on amendments to the Treaties. Where a Treaty article provides for a specific amendment procedure, the amendment remains confined to the content of that article. In addition, it appears from the Treaty articles, which refer to the 'irrevocable' fixing of exchange rates and of the value of the euro for the third stage of EMU,[39] that any later revision of the Treaty reversing that situation is precluded.

Under the EC Treaty, some commentators have taken the view that Community law debarred the Member States from introducing amendments detracting from the fundamental values of respect for human rights, democracy, and the rule of law or amendments affecting the identity and the very existence of the Community.[40] Although the Court of Justice has not ruled on any principles or specific Treaty articles which are purportedly not open to amendment, it nevertheless stressed the importance of the Court's function under Article 220 EC (now Article 19 TFEU) of guaranteeing the autonomy of the Community legal order, alongside other 'foundations of the Community'.[41] There is no reason why this would

---

in practice, comply with the motion (*Handelingen*, Tweede Kamer, 1957–58, 1092). See Van der Goes van Naters, 'La révision des traités supranationaux', in *N.T.I.R.* (*Varia Ius Gentium. Liber Amicorum J.P.A. François*) (Sijthoff, 1959), 120–31.

[34] Opinion 2/94, *Accession by the Communities to the Convention for the Protection of Human Rights and Fundamental Freedoms*, 1996, para. 30.

[35] 59/75, *Manghera*, 1976, paras 19–21; 43/75, *Defrenne*, 1976, paras 57–8.

[36] 22/70, *Commission v Council*, 1971, paras 17 and 22.

[37] 68/86, *United Kingdom v Council*, 1988, para. 38.

[38] 43/75, *Defrenne*, 1976, para. 58. In Opinion 1/92, the Court of Justice observed that '[t]he powers conferred on the Court by the Treaty may be modified pursuant only to the procedure provided for by Article 236 of the Treaty [*now Article 48 TEU*]', Opinion 1/92, *Draft Agreement between the Community, on the one hand, and the countries of the European Free Trade Association, on the other, relating to the creation of the European Economic Area*, 1992, para. 32.

[39] See Article 140(3) TFEU (see also ex Article 4(2), Article 118, second para., and Article 123(4) EC), and Article 49 of Protocol (No. 4), annexed to the TEU and TFEU, on the statute of the European System of Central Banks and of the European Central Bank, OJ 2010 C83/230.

[40] Bieber, 'Les limites matérielles et formelles à la révision des traités établissant la Communauté européenne' (1993) RMCUE 343–50; Da Cruz Vilaça and Piçarra, 'Y a-t-il des limites matérielles à la révision des traités instituant les Communautés européennes?' (1993) CDE 3–37; Curti Gialdino, 'Some Reflections on the *Acquis Communautaire*' (1995) CMLRev 1089, 1109–14. See also Heintzen, 'Hierarchisierungsprozesse innerhalb des Primärrechts der Europäischen Gemeinschaft' (1994) EuR 35–49 (who regards only the principles of democracy and the rule of law at Union level as inviolable on the ground that the Member States themselves are constituted on the basis thereof).

[41] Opinion 1/91, *Draft Agreement between the Community, on the one hand, and the countries of the European Free Trade Association, on the other, relating to the creation of the European Economic Area*, 1991, paras 35 and 69–72; see also Opinion 1/00, *Proposed Agreement between the European Community and non-Member States on the establishment of a European Common Aviation Area*, 2002, para. 5.

not also apply to the Union legal order after the entry into force of the Lisbon Treaty, especially in relation to values contained in Article 2 TEU.[42]

Judicial review. Since an amending Treaty concluded between the Member States is not an act of the institutions and has the same legal force as the Treaty sought to be amended, the Court of the Justice is not entitled to review the legality or validity of an amending Treaty.[43] However, the Commission is entitled to bring a Member State that has failed to fulfil its obligations under the Treaties before the Court of Justice. That Court also reviews the conduct of all the governments of the Member States for compliance with their Treaty obligations.[44] The commentators in question infer from this that the Court of Justice is entitled to act against the Member States as a whole in the event that they should disregard the procedural or substantive limits set with regard to amending the Treaties. They also argue that the Court would first attempt to construe any amending Treaty which were to transgress these substantive limits in such a way as to keep that Treaty within the bounds of Union law.[45]

3.011

Treaty amendments made through the simplified revision procedure of Article 48(6), however, involve a decision by the European Council, the validity of which can be reviewed by the Court pursuant to Article 267(1)(b) TFEU.[46] The Court is to verify, first, that the procedural rules laid down in Article 48(6) TEU were followed and, second, that the amendments decided upon concern only Part Three TFEU.[47] More generally, the Court has jurisdiction to assess the validity of decisions by the Council or the European Council in the light of the procedural and substantive requirements for relying on a simplified revision procedure.

---

[42] See already before Lisbon, C-402/05 P and C-415/05 P, *Kadi and Al Barakaat Foundation v Council and Commission*, 2008, paras 281–5 (see also C-584/10 P, C-593/10 P, and C-595/10 P, *Commission United Kingdom and Council v Kadi*, 2013); see after the Lisbon Treaty, Opinion 2/13, *Accession of the EU to the ECHR*, 2013, paras 155–77; C-64/16, *Associação Sindical dos Juízes Portugueses*, 2018, paras 30–6; Opinion 1/17, *Comprehensive Economic and Trade Agreement between Canada, of the one part, and the European Union and its Member States, of the other part (CETA)*, 2019, paras 109–11. All these cases hint at the existence of constitutional values of the European Union, similar to the *Ewigkeitsklausel* of Article 79(3) German Constitution (*Grundgesetz*).
[43] T-584/93, *Roujansky v Council* (order), 1994, para. 15 (para. 24-003, *infra*).
[44] 230/81, *Luxembourg v European Parliament*, 1983, paras 36–7.
[45] Bieber (n. 40, *supra*), 348–9; see also Da Cruz Vilaça and Piçarra (n. 40, *supra*), 17–18. See further König and Pechstein, 'Die EU-Vertragsänderung' (1998) EuR 130, 138–42 (who argue that such an amendment of the Treaties would be inapplicable).
[46] C-370/12, *Pringle*, 2012, para. 31.
[47] Ibid.

4
Accession to and Withdrawal from the European Union

I. Member States of the European Union

4.001 **Member States.** Seven waves of accession have enlarged the number of Member States from the original six (Belgium, France, Germany, Italy, Luxembourg, and the Netherlands) to twenty-eight. That number was reduced again to twenty-seven after the withdrawal of the United Kingdom from the Union. Since 1 February 2020, the European Union consists of the following twenty-seven Member States: Austria, Belgium, Bulgaria, Croatia, the Czech Republic, Cyprus, Denmark, Estonia, Finland, France, Germany, Greece, Hungary, Ireland, Italy, Latvia, Lithuania, Luxembourg, Malta, the Netherlands, Poland, Portugal, Romania, Slovakia, Slovenia, Spain, and Sweden.

4.002 **1 January 1973.** In 1961 Denmark, Ireland, Norway, and the United Kingdom applied for accession to the European Communities. After the UK accession negotiations foundered in January 1963 on the veto of the French President, General de Gaulle, it was not until June 1970 that accession negotiations started up again with Denmark, Ireland, Norway, and the United Kingdom. On 22 January 1972 the six Member States concluded with those four States an Accession Treaty and signed related documents setting out the conditions of accession.[1] France made ratification of the treaty conditional upon the result of a referendum, which was held on 23 April 1972. Accession was also approved by referendum in Ireland (10 May 1972) and Denmark (2 October 1972). Following the adverse outcome of a national referendum held on 24–25 May 1972 in Norway (53.6 per cent against accession), on 1 January 1973 only Denmark, Ireland, and the United Kingdom acceded to the three Communities.[2] EC membership was the subject of a referendum in the United Kingdom on 5 June 1975, where the result was in favour of that country remaining in the European Communities. In a referendum held on 23 February 1982 the population of Greenland expressed the wish to leave the European Communities. This wish was subsequently carried out by an amendment to the Treaties (see para. 11-007, *infra*).

---

[1] Treaty of 22 January 1972 between the Member States of the European Communities, the Kingdom of Denmark, Ireland, the Kingdom of Norway, and the United Kingdom of Great Britain and Northern Ireland concerning the accession of the Kingdom of Denmark, Ireland, the Kingdom of Norway, and the United Kingdom of Great Britain and Northern Ireland to the European Economic Community and to the European Atomic Energy Community, OJ 1972 English Special Edition (27 March) 5, and the appended Acts, Protocols, Exchanges of letters, Final Acts, and Declarations. For the accession to the ECSC, see the Decision of the Council of the European Communities of 22 January 1972 concerning the accession of the Kingdom of Denmark, Ireland, the Kingdom of Norway, and the United Kingdom of Great Britain and Northern Ireland to the European Coal and Steel Community OJ 1972 English Special Edition (27 March) 12.

[2] See the Decision of the Council of the European Communities of 1 January 1973 adjusting the documents concerning the accession of the new Member States to the European Communities, OJ 1973 L2/1.

1 January 1981. Greece was the first country to conclude an Association Agreement with **4.003**
the Communities, on 9 July 1961. The Agreement was considered as a precursor to accession
of Greece to the Communities. However, the military coup of 1967 rendered accession impossible. In 1975, after democracy was reinstated, Greece renewed its bid for accession. On
28 May 1979 the nine Member States concluded an Accession Treaty with Greece,[3] resulting
in the Hellenic Republic becoming a member of the Communities on 1 January 1981.

1 January 1986. Spain and Portugal applied for accession to the Communities after democracy was restored in these countries. In Spain, the death of Franco (1975) gave the impetus for democratic reforms resulting in the 1978 Constitution. In Portugal, the Carnation Revolution in 1974 opened the way to restoration of democracy. Portugal and Spain joined the Communities on 1 January 1986 following signature of the Accession Treaty on 12 June 1985.[4] **4.004**

1 January 1995. Following the entry into force of the EU Treaty, States have become **4.005**
members of the Communities by acceding to the European Union (see para. 6-009,
infra). Following the signature of the EU Treaty in 1991, it was agreed to deal with the
applications to accede made by the States which, as members of the European Free Trade
Area (EFTA), had signed the Agreement on the European Economic Area (EEA) (see
para. 10-020, *infra*). The negotiations, which started in February 1993 with Austria,
Finland, and Sweden, and in April 1993 with Norway, resulted in the Accession Treaty
signed in Corfu on 24 June 1994.[5] The accession was approved by referendum in Austria
on 12 June 1994 (66.36 per cent in favour), in Finland on 16 October 1994 (56.9 per cent
in favour), and in Sweden on 13 November 1994 (52.2 per cent in favour). Following
another adverse referendum in Norway on 27 and 28 November 1994 (52.5 per cent
against), on 1 January 1995 only Austria, Finland, and Sweden acceded to the European
Union (EU).[6]

---

[3] Treaty of 28 May 1979 between the Member States of the European Communities and the Hellenic Republic concerning the accession of the Hellenic Republic to the European Economic Community and the European Atomic Energy Community, OJ 1979 L291/9, and the appended Acts, Protocols, Final Acts, and Declarations; Decision of the Council of the European Communities of 24 May 1979 on the accession of the Hellenic Republic to the European Coal and Steel Community, OJ 1979 L291/5.

[4] Treaty of 12 June 1985 between the Member States of the European Communities and the Kingdom of Spain and the Portuguese Republic concerning the accession of the Kingdom of Spain and the Portuguese Republic to the European Economic Community and the European Atomic Energy Community, OJ 1985 L302/9, and the appended Acts, Protocols, Final Acts and Declarations; Decision of the Council of the European Communities of 11 June 1985 on the accession of the Kingdom of Spain and the Portuguese Republic to the European Coal and Steel Community, OJ 1985 L302/5.

[5] Treaty of 24 June 1994 between the Member States of the European Union and the Kingdom of Norway, the Republic of Austria, the Republic of Finland, and the Kingdom of Sweden concerning the accession of the Kingdom of Norway, the Republic of Austria, the Republic of Finland, and the Kingdom of Sweden to the European Union, OJ 1994 C241/9, and the Act concerning the conditions of accession of the Republic of Austria, the Republic of Finland, and the Kingdom of Sweden and the adjustments to the Treaties on which the European Union is founded, ibid. and the Final Act, OJ 1994 C241/371 (title amended by Decision 95/1 (see n. 6, *infra*).

[6] Decision 95/1/EC, Euratom, ECSC of the Council of the European Communities of 1 January 1995 adjusting the instruments concerning the accession of new Member States to the European Union, OJ 1995 L1/1. Further particulars may be found in Jorna, 'The Accession Negotiations with Austria, Sweden, Finland and Norway: A Guided Tour' (1995) ELRev 131–58; Goebel, 'The European Union Grows: The Constitutional Impact of the Accession of Austria, Finland and Sweden' (1995) Fordham ILJ 1092–190.

4.006 **1 May 2004.** The European Council considered that negotiations on additional accessions to the Union could not commence until after the conclusion of the Intergovernmental Conference scheduled to open in 1996.[7] In accordance with the decision taken by the European Council in Luxembourg on 12 and 13 December 1997, the enlargement process was started on 30 March 1998 with ten Central and Eastern European States and Cyprus.[8] On 31 March 1998 accession negotiations were commenced with Cyprus, the Czech Republic, Estonia, Hungary, Poland, and Slovenia, and on 15 February 2000 also with Bulgaria, Latvia, Lithuania, Malta, Romania, and Slovakia.[9] The negotiations resulted in the Accession Treaty signed in Athens on 16 April 2003 by the Member States and ten candidate Member States (Cyprus, the Czech Republic, Estonia, Hungary, Latvia, Lithuania, Malta, Poland, Slovenia, and the Slovak Republic).[10] Referendums were held on accession in nine of the candidate Member States. Each of them was in favour of joining the European Union: Malta on 8 March 2003 (53.6 per cent in favour), Slovenia on 23 March 2003 (89.6 per cent in favour), Hungary on 12 April 2003 (83.8 per cent in favour), Lithuania on 10 and 11 May 2003 (91.1 per cent in favour), the Slovak Republic on 16 and 17 May 2003 (92.5 per cent in favour), Poland on 7 and 8 June 2003 (77.4 per cent in favour), the Czech Republic on 13 and 14 June 2003 (77.3 per cent in favour), Estonia on 14 September 2003 (66.9 per cent in favour), and Latvia on 20 September 2003 (67 per cent in favour). On 1 May 2004 these States acceded to the European Union.

4.007 **1 January 2007.** As explained above, negotiations for the accession of Bulgaria and Romania were initiated in 2000, together with other candidate Member States. However, unlike the other candidate Member States, Bulgaria and Romania had not made sufficient progress in relation to the accession criteria in order to be able to accede to the EU in 2004. The European Council noted this backlog and proposed January 2007 as the date for their accession.[11] On 25 April 2005 an Accession Treaty was signed, in which it was agreed that Bulgaria and Romania would become parties to the EU Constitution unless it was not in force at the time of their accession, in which case they would become party to the existing

---

[7] See the European Council held in Corfu on 24–25 June 1994 ((1994) 6 EU Bull. point I.13), the European Council held in Essen on 9-10 December 1994 ((1994) 12 EU Bull. point I.13) and the European Council held in Cannes on 26–27 June 1995 ((1995) 6 EU Bull. point I.12).

[8] See (1997) 12 EU Bull. point I.2-6 (European Council) and (1998) 3 EU Bull. point 1.3.49. In Malta, the government formed after the elections on 26 October 1996 'froze' the Maltese application to accede; at the end of 1998 the application was 'reactivated'.

[9] For the negotiations, see Ott and Inglis (eds), *Handbook on European Enlargement—A Commentary on the Enlargement process* (TMC Asser Press, 2002).

[10] Treaty of 16 April 2003 between the Member States of the European Union and the Czech Republic, the Republic of Estonia, the Republic of Cyprus, the Republic of Latvia, the Republic of Lithuania, the Republic of Hungary, the Republic of Malta, the Republic of Poland, the Republic of Slovenia, the Slovak Republic, concerning the accession of the Czech Republic, the Republic of Estonia, the Republic of Cyprus, the Republic of Latvia, the Republic of Lithuania, the Republic of Hungary, the Republic of Malta, the Republic of Poland, the Republic of Slovenia, and the Slovak Republic to the European Union 2003 OJ L236/17, together with the Act concerning the conditions of accession of the Czech Republic, the Republic of Estonia, the Republic of Cyprus, the Republic of Latvia, the Republic of Lithuania, the Republic of Hungary, the Republic of Malta, the Republic of Poland, the Republic of Slovenia, and the Slovak Republic and the adjustments to the Treaties on which the European Union is founded, OJ 2003 L236/33, and the Final Act, OJ 2003 L236/959. For some rectifications to the Treaty, see OJ 2004 L126. For an appraisal, see the articles in Cremona (ed.), *The Enlargement of the European Union (Collected Courses of the Academy of European Law)* (OUP, 2003).

[11] See the conclusions of the European Council held in Brussels on 17 and 18 June 2004, points 20–24.

Treaties.[12] Since that was the case, the two countries acceded to the European Union on 1 January 2007 by becoming party to the existing Treaties. After their accession, the EU consisted of twenty-seven Member States.[13]

1 July 2013. On 21 February 2003, Croatia applied to accede to the EU. In October 2005 the Council opened accession negotiations. The Accession Treaty was signed on 9 December 2011.[14] After the deposit of the last ratification instrument on 21 June 2013, Croatia joined the European Union on 1 July 2013, which then consisted of twenty-eight Member States until the withdrawal of the United Kingdom on 1 February 2020, which brought the number back to the current twenty-seven Member States. 4.008

II. Accession of Member States

Accession. Article 49 TEU governs the accession of States to the European Union. That provision was introduced by the EU Treaty in 1992 and repealed the respective provisions of Article 98 ECSC, Article 237 EEC, and Article 205 EAEC.[15] As a result, the accessions to the Communities in 1973 (Denmark, Ireland, and the United Kingdom), 1981 (Greece), and 1985 (Portugal and Spain) were based on the specific rules contained in each of the Community Treaties, whereas the accessions to the European Union in 1995, 2004, and 2007 were based on ex Article 49 EU (which has not been renumbered by the Treaty of Lisbon). The 2013 accession of Croatia was based on Article 49 TEU. By becoming a member of the Union, a State accedes to all the Treaties on which the Union is based.[16] 4.009

---

[12] Treaty of 25 April 2005 between the Kingdom of Belgium, the Czech Republic, the Kingdom of Denmark, the Federal Republic of Germany, the Republic of Estonia, the Hellenic Republic, the Kingdom of Spain, the French Republic, Ireland, the Italian Republic, the Republic of Cyprus, the Republic of Latvia, the Republic of Lithuania, the Grand Duchy of Luxembourg, the Republic of Hungary, the Republic of Malta, the Kingdom of the Netherlands, the Republic of Austria, the Republic of Poland, the Portuguese Republic, the Republic of Slovenia, the Slovak Republic, the Republic of Finland, the Kingdom of Sweden, the United Kingdom of Great Britain and Northern Ireland (Member States of the European Union), and the Republic of Bulgaria and Romania, concerning the accession of the Republic of Bulgaria and Romania to the European Union, OJ 2005 L157/11; together with the Act concerning the conditions of accession of the Republic of Bulgaria and Romania and the adjustments to the Treaties on which the European Union is founded, OJ 2005 L157/203 and the Final Act, OJ 2005 L157/377. For an appraisal, see Lazowski, 'And Then They Were Twenty-Seven ... A Legal Appraisal of the Sixth Accession Treaty' (2007) CMLRev 401–30; van den Oosterkamp and Galama, 'De toetreding tot de Europese Unie van Bulgarije en Roemenië' (2007) SEW 8–22.

[13] For a general comment on the enlargement, see Falkner and Treib, 'Three Worlds of Compliance or Four? The EU-15 Compared to New Member States' (2008) JCMS 293–313; Petit, 'Quelques réflexions sur la capacité d'intégration de l'Union européenne' (2007) RMCUE 153–62; Rasmussen, 'Present and Future European Judicial Problems after Enlargement and the Post-2005 Ideological Revolt' (2007) CMLRev 1661–87.

[14] Treaty between the Kingdom of Belgium, the Republic of Bulgaria, the Czech Republic, the Kingdom of Denmark, the Federal Republic of Germany, the Republic of Estonia, Ireland, the Hellenic Republic, the Kingdom of Spain, the French Republic, the Italian Republic, the Republic of Cyprus, the Republic of Latvia, the Republic of Lithuania, the Grand Duchy of Luxembourg, the Republic of Hungary, the Republic of Malta, the Kingdom of the Netherlands, the Republic of Austria, the Republic of Poland, the Portuguese Republic, Romania, the Republic of Slovenia, the Slovak Republic, the Republic of Finland, the Kingdom of Sweden, the United Kingdom of Great Britain and Northern Ireland (Member States of the European Union), and the Republic of Croatia concerning the accession of the Republic of Croatia to the European Union, OJ 2012 L112/10 and the Final Act, OJ 2012 L112/95.

[15] Repealed by EU Treaty, Articles 9(21), 8(83), and 10(28), respectively.

[16] Likewise, before the EU Treaty, a would-be Member State always had to accede to all three Communities because of their institutional and political unity.

A. Conditions for accession to the European Union

4.010 **Essential conditions.** Article 49 TEU provides that '[a]ny European State which respects the values referred to in Article 2 and is committed to promoting them' may apply to become a member of the Union.

As far as what is meant by 'European' is concerned, it should be mentioned that in 1987 the Council did not accede to Morocco's request to join the Communities in all probability because Morocco was not regarded as a European State.[17] The Commission takes the view that not only geographical, but also historical factors contribute to the 'European identity' and that the essence of that notion is likely to be regarded differently by each succeeding generation.[18]

The requirement that a candidate Member State should respect 'the values referred to in Article 2' was introduced by the Treaty of Lisbon and refers to the values of respect for human dignity, freedom, democracy, equality, the rule of law, and respect for human rights, including the rights of persons belonging to minorities.[19] Even before such an explicit provision was added to the Treaties, respect for these values was deemed to be a fundamental requirement for accession to the Union.[20] The European Council, meeting in Copenhagen on 7 and 8 April 1978, associated itself with that declaration and affirmed that 'respect for and maintenance of representative democracy and human rights in each Member State are essential elements of membership of the European Communities'.[21] The European Council took over that requirement in Copenhagen on 21 and 22 June 1993 and coupled it with other criteria that candidate countries had to fulfil (the so-called 'Copenhagen criteria'). First, membership of the Union requires that the candidate Member State has achieved stability of institutions guaranteeing democracy, the rule of law, human rights, and respect for and protection of minorities. Second, there must be the existence of a functioning market economy as well as the capacity to cope with competitive pressures and market forces within

---

[17] See the wording of the application (1987) 7/8 EC Bull. point 2.2.35, and the Council's veiled answer (1987) 9 EC Bull. point 2.2.19. See also Dorau, 'Die Öffnung der Europäischen Union für europäische Staaten. "Europäisch" als Bedingung für einen EU-Beitritt nach Art. 49 EUV' (1999) EuR 736–53.

[18] Commission of the European Communities, *Europe and the Challenge of Enlargement* (1992) EC Bull., Suppl. 3, 11.

[19] This requirement replaces the requirement introduced by the Treaty of Amsterdam for respect for 'the principles set out in Article 6(1)', which already referred to the principles of liberty, democracy, respect for human rights and fundamental freedoms, and the rule of law (see Article 49 EU). As regards Bulgaria and Romania, pursuant to Articles 37 and 38 of the Act of Accession of 2005, a mechanism was set up before their accession to continue the monitoring of certain shortcomings in respect of the rule of law, requiring the Commission to regularly report on the situation. See the Commission decisions 2006/928/EC and 2006/929/EC of 13 December 2006 establishing a mechanism for cooperation and verification of progress in Romania to address specific benchmarks in the areas of judicial reform and the fight against corruption (OJ 2006 L354/56) and establishing a mechanism for cooperation and verification of progress in Bulgaria to address specific benchmarks in the areas of judicial reform and the fight against corruption and organized crime, OJ 2006 L354/58. On the legal nature and effects of this mechanism, see C-83/19, C-127/19, C-195/19, C-291/19, C-355/19 and C-397/19, *Asociaţia "Forumul Judecătorilor Din România" and Others*, 2021, paras 153–77.

[20] In the preamble to the EEC Treaty, the Contracting Parties called upon 'the other peoples of Europe who share their ideal' to join in their efforts towards integration. Admittedly, the Court of Justice held in 1978 that it had no jurisdiction to answer questions referred for a preliminary ruling on the form and content of the conditions for accession to the Community on the ground that 'the legal conditions for such accession remain to be defined in the context of [the procedure laid down by Article 237 EEC] without its being possible to determine the content judicially in advance' (93/78, *Mattheus*, 1978, para. 8).

[21] (1978) 3 EC Bull. 5–6.

the Union. Third, the candidate Member State must have the ability to take on the obligations of membership, including adherence to the aims of political, economic, and monetary union.[22]

Since the Treaty of Lisbon, Article 49 TEU states that 'the conditions of eligibility for accession agreed upon by the European Council shall be taken into account', which is a clear reference to the Copenhagen criteria.

Other requirements. Traditionally, membership of the European Union has always implied acceptance of the so-called *acquis communautaire*, which the Commission has defined as 'the rights and obligations, actual and potential, of the Community system and its institutional framework'.[23] Since the replacement of the Community by the Union, reference should be made in this connection to the 'Union *acquis*'.

4.011

The candidate Member State has to accept the provisions of the Treaties, the decisions taken by the institutions pursuant to the Treaties (including international agreements concluded by the Union), and the case law of the Court of Justice. It has to accede to the declarations, resolutions, decisions, and agreements made by the Member States meeting within the Council, in the European Council, or elsewhere that relate to the Communities or the Union. At the same time, it must undertake to accede to agreements concluded by the Member States which affect the functioning of the Union or are closely connected with action by the Union, international agreements concluded by the Member States jointly with the Union, and agreements concluded between the Member States relating to such agreements or implementing them.[24] Candidate Member States also accede to the provisions of the Schengen *acquis* as integrated into Union law and the acts building upon it or otherwise related to it.[25] Difficulties of adjustment are resolved by temporary derogations and transitional measures; only those derogations that have been expressly laid down can be validly invoked before the Court of Justice.[26]

---

[22] European Council meeting at Copenhagen on 21 and 22 June 1993 ((1993) 6 EC Bull. point I.13); *Europe and the Challenge of Enlargement*, (n. 18, *supra*), 12; Katz, 'Les critères de Copenhague' (2000) RMCUE 483–6. See also Tatham, *Enlargement of the European Union* (Kluwer law international, 2009), Chapter 8; Inglis, 'EU Enlargement: Membership Conditions Applied to Future and Potential Member States', in Blockmans and Łazowski, *The European Union and its Neighbours: A Legal Appraisal of the EU's Policies of Stabilisation, Partnership and Integration* (Cambridge University Press, 2006), 61–93; Cremona, 'EU Enlargement: Solidarity and Conditionality' (2005) ELRev 3–22; Nettesheim, 'EU-Beitritt und Unrechtsaufarbeitung' (2003) EuR 36–64; Hoffmeister, 'Changing Requirements for Membership', in Ott and Inglis (n. 9, *supra*), 90–102; Šarčević, 'EU-Erweiterung nach Art. 49 EUV: Ermessensentscheidungen und Beitrittsrecht' (2002) EuR 461–82; Williams, 'Enlargement of the Union and Human Rights Conditionality: A Policy of Distinction?' (2000) ELRev.601–17. For a recent application, see Cerruti, 'The Political Criteria for Accession to the EU in the Experience of Croatia' (2014) EPL 771. For a critical assessment of this conditionality requirement, see Kochenov, *EU Enlargement and the Failure of Conditionality* (Kluwer 2008), 358. See also Romanian rule of law cases (C-840/19 and others) Opinion of AG Bobek of 20 September 2020.

[23] *Europe and the Challenge of Enlargement*, (n. 18, *supra*), 12. For the origin and meaning of the term *acquis communautaire* in this context, see Goebel, 'The European Union Grows: The Constitutional Impact of the Accession of Austria, Finland and Sweden' (1995) Fordham ILJ 1092, 1140–1157.

[24] See Articles 2 to 4 of the 1972, 1979, and 1985 Acts of Accession, Articles 2 to 5 of the 1994 Act of Accession, Articles 2 to 6 of the 2003, 2005, and 2011 Acts of Accession. For further discussion of the legal force of the various instruments that new Member States must accept, see paras 27-045 and 28-007 *et seq.*, *infra*.

[25] See Article 3(1) of the 2003 Act of Accession and Article 4(1) of the 2005 and 2011 Acts of Accession (see para. 8-004).

[26] C-420/07, *Apostolides*, 2009, para. 33.

The establishment of the internal market means that transitional measures which might have the effect of maintaining the frontiers between established and new Member States must be kept to a strict minimum. Countries applying to accede to the Union are to take the necessary measures to satisfy the conditions of accession in good time.[27] After the Act of Accession has been signed, they must refrain from adopting measures interfering with the functioning of the Union.[28]

B. Procedure for acceding to the European Union

4.012 **Application and negotiations.** The accession procedure begins with an application to become a member of the Union. The request is to be addressed to the Council. At the same time, the European Parliament and national parliaments have to be notified of this application. Under Article 49 TEU, first para. the Council is to take its decision by a unanimous vote after consulting the Commission and receiving the consent of the European Parliament acting by a majority of its component members.[29] The Member States and the candidate Member State agree on the terms of accession and the resulting application of the Treaties (Article 49, second para. TEU).[30]

In practice, the Commission delivers an initial opinion and the Council takes an initial decision to open the procedure. The actual opinion of the Commission and the decisions of the European Parliament and the Council are adopted after the negotiations with the candidate Member State have been concluded. In accordance with the working procedure adopted by the Council on 8 and 9 June 1970, the candidate Member State in fact negotiates with the Union institutions (and therefore not with the Member States as such): the Council negotiates on the basis of common positions which it determines beforehand and, as far as some matters are concerned, it requires the Commission to negotiate with the candidate Member State.[31] The final agreement is concluded between the Member States and the candidate

---

[27] See Romanian rule of law cases (C-840/19 and others) Opinion of AG Bobek of 20 September 2020.
[28] C-27/96, *Danisco Sugar*, 1997, paras 24–31 (see also para. 26-013, *infra*).
[29] The Single European Act introduced the requirement for assent of the European Parliament in Article 237 EEC. The accession procedures laid down in Article 98 ECSC and Article 205 EAEC required the Council only to seek the opinion of the Commission. During the procedure for the accession of Portugal and Spain, the Economic and Social Committee delivered an own-initiative Opinion (OJ 1984 C23/51). Since the Council had consulted the European Parliament in accordance with point 2.3.7 of the Solemn Declaration of Stuttgart, the Parliament gave its views on the conclusion of the negotiations with Portugal and Spain in a resolution (OJ 1985 C141/130).
[30] Under the procedure laid down by Article 98 ECSC, the Council was to determine the terms of accession by a unanimous vote. As a result, the three rounds of accession negotiations prior to the entry into force of EU Treaty resulted in a Council decision on accession to the ECSC alongside a Treaty between the Member States and the applicant Member State regarding accession to the EC and the EAEC.
[31] For the procedure, see Puissochet, *L'élargissement des Communautés européennes: présentation et commentaire du Traité et des Actes relatifs à l'adhésion du Royaume-Uni, du Danemark et de l'Irlande* (Editions techniques et économiques, 1974), 21–22; for the application of the procedure during the more recent accession negotiations, see Tatham, *Enlargement of the European Union* (Kluwer law international, 2009), Chapter 9; Joly, 'Le processus de l'élargissement de l'Union européenne' (2002) RMCUE 239–46; Landaburu, 'The Fifth Enlargement of the European Union: The Power of Example' (2002) Fordham ILJ 1–11; Maurer, 'Negotiations in progress' and 'Progress of the Negotiations', in Ott and Inglis (eds), *Handbook on European Enlargement—A Commentary on the Enlargement Process* (TMC Asser Press, 2002) at 113–29.

Member States, and enters into force after ratification by all the States in accordance with their respective constitutional requirements (Article 49, second para. TEU).[32]

Accession Treaty. The conditions for accession and the resulting adjustments to the Treaties are laid down in an Act annexed to the Accession Treaty ('the Act of Accession'), as supplemented by Protocols, Declarations, and a Final Act.[33] The Court of Justice takes the view that the conditions of accession and the adjustments to the Treaties entailed thereby include adjustments to Union secondary legislation agreed by the Member States.[34] **4.013**

For every enlargement by which several countries accede, a single Accession Treaty has been drawn up which stipulates that the new Member States are to become members of the European Union subject to the conditions set out in an Act of Accession annexed to the Treaty.[35] In the course of ratification by each of the Member States, the national parliaments (and, in the event of a referendum, the people) cannot therefore confine their approval to only some of the new Member States mentioned in the Accession Treaty. Since, however, it is impossible to tell beforehand whether an Accession Treaty will be approved in all the candidate Member States, such a Treaty will generally contain a provision empowering the Council to make the necessary adjustments in the event that a smaller number of States actually join.[36]

C. Pending applications

Pending applications. Various countries have applied for membership. Following the last accession of new Member States, the following countries' applications remain outstanding: Turkey (14 April 1987), Switzerland (26 May 1992), North Macedonia (before 2019 known as the Former Yugoslav Republic of Macedonia, 22 March 2004), Montenegro (15 December 2008), Albania (28 April 2009), Iceland (16 July 2009), and Serbia (22 December 2009), Bosnia and Herzegovina (15 February 2016), Ukraine (28 February 2022) and Georgia and Moldova (3 March 2022). **4.014**

A request for accession of Norway has twice already led to negotiations resulting in an Accession Treaty (1972 and 1994) but in each case that Treaty was rejected in Norway by a majority of the population in a referendum.[37] In 2010 accession negotiations had also

---

[32] For where all the applicant States do not ratify the Treaty, see para. 3-005, *supra*. The European Parliament's draft Treaty (Article 2) would have made accession to the Union dependent on the conclusion of a treaty by the applicant State directly with the Union.

[33] For full references to the documents relating to preceding accessions, see para. 4-001 *et seq., supra*.

[34] 31-35/86, *LAISA and Another v Council*, 1988, paras 9–12, with a critical note by Vandersanden (1989) CMLRev 551–61. The Court has specified that the adaptation measures provided for by acts of accession, as a general rule, authorize only adaptations intended to render earlier Union measures applicable in the new Member States, to the exclusion of all other amendments (C-413/04, *European Parliament v Council*, 2006, paras 31–8, and C-414/04, *European Parliament v Council*, 2006, paras 29–36; C-273/04, *Poland v Council*, 2007, paras 45–51).

[35] See the Council's answer of 19 December 2002 and the Commission's answer of 20 August 2002 to questions E-2069/02 and E-2070/02, respectively (Van den Bos and Van der Laan), OJ 2003 C92 E/131 and C192 E/47, respectively.

[36] Pursuant to the third para. of Article 2 of the 1972 Accession Treaty and the second subpara. of Article 2(2) of the 1994 Accession Treaty, the Council adopted a decision each time Norway found it impossible, due to a negative referendum outcome, to ratify the Accession Treaty (on 1 January 1973 and 1 January 1995, respectively), adjusting the instruments concerning the accession of new Member States to the European Communities/European Union (OJ 1973 L2/1, and OJ 1995 L1/1). See also the second subpara. of Article 2(2) of the 1985 Accession Treaty, the second subpara. of Article 2(2) of the 2003 Accession Treaty, and the second subpara. of Article 4(2) of the 2005 Accession Treaty.

[37] Para. 4-005, *supra*. Norway had applied to join on 25 November 1992.

been opened with Iceland. However, in 2013 Iceland decided to put accession negotiations on hold. On 12 March 2015, the Government of Iceland informed the Presidency of the Council that it does not intend to resume these negotiations. As regards Switzerland, accession to the Union remains unlikely as long as there is no majority for joining the European Economic Area. The approval by referendum on 9 February 2014 of a proposal to reduce immigration into Switzerland—including that of Union citizens—has made a possible accession even less likely.

Turkey, North Macedonia, Montenegro, Albania, and Serbia have meanwhile been given the status of 'candidate Member State'. Accession negotiations have been launched with Turkey, Montenegro, and Serbia. As far as Turkey is concerned, the European Council of 12 and 13 December 1997 already confirmed Turkey's eligibility for accession to the European Union and that it would be judged on the basis of the same criteria as the other applicant States.[38] On 3 October 2005 accession negotiations were started with Turkey. However, given that country's backsliding on the rule of law, the independence of the judiciary, respect for human rights, and good relations with the Union and neighbouring countries, the accession negotiations with Turkey have come to a standstill.[39] Accession negotiations started with Montenegro on 29 June 2012 and with Serbia on 21 January 2014. Bosnia and Herzegovina and Kosovo (which has not yet applied for accession) are considered 'potential candidate Member States'. Whether they accede or not will depend on whether they comply with the general accession criteria and on the progress they make in the Stabilization and Association Process that the Union has established with those countries.

On the basis of the Instrument for Pre-Accession Assistance, the Union provides targeted support to both candidate and potential candidate Member States. Every year the Commission prepares progress reports on each country, which describe the political and economic developments in candidate and potential candidate Member States. The reports assess the ability of the candidate Member States to transpose EU legislation and the progress made by the potential candidate Member States to adopt EU legislation and comply with all the conditions for accession.

III. Member States Leaving the Union

4.015 **Possibility to withdraw.** Since the entry into force of the Treaty of Lisbon, the Treaties make it possible for any Member State to withdraw from the European Union (Article 50 TEU).[40] On 29 March 2017 the United Kingdom initiated the procedure set out in Article 50 TEU, which has led to its withdrawal from the Union as from 1 February 2020. The inclusion of a right of withdrawal in the Treaties initially had mainly a symbolic value. Even if, on the face

---

[38] (1997) 12 EU Bull. point I.6.31. See also the position expressed by the President of the Council at the meeting of the EC-Turkey Association Council of 29 April 1997 ((1997) 4 EU Bull. point 1.4.74).
[39] See the Council conclusions of 18 June 2019 on the enlargement and stabilization and association process.
[40] The Treaty of Lisbon takes over the rules proposed by the Constitution in this regard: see Article I-60. See Malathouni, 'Should I Stay or Should I Go: The Sunset Clause as Self-confidence or Suicide?' (2008) MJECL 115–24; Friel, 'Secession from the European Union: Checking out of the Proverbial "Cockroach Motel"' (2004) Fordham ILJ 590–641; Bruha and Nowak, 'Recht auf Austritt aus der Europäischen Union?' (2004) A Völkerr 1–25.

of it, the right of withdrawal may seem to endanger the internal cohesion of the Union, it also underscores the deliberate choice made by each Member State belonging to the Union.

The following rules apply to the withdrawal from the Union.[41] If a Member State has taken the decision to withdraw, in accordance with its own constitutional requirements, it has to notify the European Council of its intention to leave the Union. That notification may be revoked at any time during the entire period of negotiations, including any extensions.[42] The leaving Member State has to negotiate and conclude an agreement with the Union, setting out the arrangements for its withdrawal and taking account of the framework for its future relationship with the Union. That agreement is to be concluded on behalf of the Union by the Council, acting by a qualified majority after obtaining the consent of the European Parliament (Article 50(1) and (2) TEU).[43] In this connection, it will have to be determined to what extent rights and obligations stemming from Union law may continue to apply to citizens of the withdrawing Member State. However, a Member State cannot be forced to await the outcome of the negotiations on the conditions accompanying its withdrawal. In the absence of any agreement, the Treaties will cease to apply to the Member State in question two years after the notification of the intention to withdraw unless the European Council, in agreement with the Member State concerned, unanimously decides to extend this period (Article 50(3) TEU).

In the event that a State which has withdrawn from the Union should apply to rejoin, the procedure laid down in Article 49 TEU would apply (Article 50(5) TEU).

Towards Brexit. On 1 February 2020, the United Kingdom withdrew from the Union in accordance with Article 50 TEU (so-called Brexit). The withdrawal was prompted by the referendum of 23 June 2016 in which 51.9 per cent of the voters expressed their support for the United Kingdom leaving the Union. That referendum had been organized by then Prime Minister Cameron, who resigned after the result. His successor, Theresa May, announced in October 2016 her intention to trigger, in March 2017, the negotiations on the agreement to be concluded between the United Kingdom and the Union on the conditions of the withdrawal from the Union.

4.016

The new British Prime Minister needed to obtain the approval of the British Parliament[44] before she gave formal notice on 29 March 2017 with a letter to the President of the European

---

[41] For an overview, see Barnard, 'The Practicalities of Leaving the EU' (2016) ELRev 484; Hillion, 'Accession and Withdrawal in the Law of the European Union', in Arnull and Chalmers (eds), *Oxford Handbook of European Union Law* (OUP, 2015), chapter 6.

[42] C-621/18, *Wightman*, 2018, paras 37–75. See Popov, 'L'arrêt Wightman: de la consécration du droit de révocation unilatérale de la notification de retrait de l'Union européenne à la consolidation de la jurisprudence sur les actions et recours déclaratoires préventifs utilisés en vue de provoquer un renvoi préjudiciel' (2019) CDE 313–45. This right should not, however, be abused; see Benrath, 'Bona Fide and Revocation of Withdrawal: How Article 50 TEU Handles the Potential Abuse of a Unilateral Revocation of Withdrawal' (2018) ELRev 234–48; Sari, 'Reversing a Withdrawal Notification under Article 50 TEU: Can a Member State Change its Mind?' (2017) ELRev 451–73.

[43] The Council has to take into account the guidelines provided by the European Council (Article 50(2) TEU). The member of the European Council or of the Council representing the withdrawing Member State does not participate in the discussions of the European Council or Council or in decisions concerning it (Article 50(4) TEU).

[44] Following the judgment of the United Kingdom Supreme Court of 24 January 2017 in *R (on the application of Miller) v Secretary of State for Exiting the European Union* [2017] UKSC 5; [2018] AC 61; [2017] 1 WLUK 387 (SC). See also Young, 'R. (Miller) v Secretary of State for Exiting the European Union: Thriller or Vanilla?' (2017) EL Rev 280–95.

Council of the United Kingdom's intention to leave the Union. Based on the guidelines, which the European Council approved on 29 April 2017, and on the recommendation of the Commission, the Council subsequently determined the negotiation guidelines for the withdrawal agreement. The Commission enlisted former Commissioner Michel Barnier for these negotiations, who relied on a specific taskforce within the Commission. These negotiations touched upon the various areas in which a withdrawal from the Union would have immediate effects, such as the status of the citizens involved (rights of nationals of EU Member States in the United Kingdom and rights of British nationals in the twenty-seven Member States) and the financial settlement of the British membership, but did not determine the future relationship between the United Kingdom and the Union.

On 10 December 2018, the Court of Justice ruled in *Wightman* that the UK could unilaterally revoke its Article 50 notification. According to the Court, a Member State has a right to revoke the notification of its intention to withdraw from the EU as long as a withdrawal agreement has not entered into force or, if no such agreement has been concluded, as long as the two-year period, or any possible extension thereof, has not expired.[45]

Meanwhile, in November 2018, the Commission and the negotiators of the United Kingdom reached an agreement on a full draft withdrawal agreement as well as on an outline of a Joint Political Declaration on the framework of a future relationship.[46] The Withdrawal Agreement provided that, as from the date of withdrawal, a transitional period applied until 31 December 2020, during which matters stayed as they were with regard to the internal market, the customs union, and European policies, allowing citizens, administrations, and businesses to prepare and adapt to Brexit before the new 'future relationship' was in place. In order to avoid a hard border with border controls between Ireland and Northern Ireland, a Protocol to the Withdrawal Agreement initially provided for a 'backstop' solution that would kick in if, at the end of the transitional period, there was no future agreement resolving the issue. According to that 'backstop' there would be an EU–UK single customs territory, with Northern Ireland remaining aligned to the internal market and customs rules that are essential for avoiding a hard border.

However, the British government was unable to find enough support in the national parliament, with the House of Commons voting against the Withdrawal Agreement in January and March 2019. Pursuant to Article 50 TEU, in the absence of a withdrawal agreement, the United Kingdom would have been outside the Union from 30 March 2019 unless the European Council decided in advance to extend the negotiation period. Both the EU and the UK started preparing for a possible 'no deal' scenario in which the United Kingdom would exit the Union without any withdrawal agreement being ratified. Upon the request of the British Government, the European Council decided, on 22 March, to extend the Article 50 period until 22 May 2019 if the Withdrawal Agreement would pass by 29 March 2019 but, if it did not, then the UK would have until 12 April 2019 to indicate a way forward.[47] Since the Withdrawal Agreement was not ratified, Theresa May requested another extension of the Article 50 period. On 10 April 2019, the European Council decided to grant an

---

[45] C-621/18, *Wightman and Others*, 2018 (for commentaries, see n. 42, *supra*).
[46] 2019 OJ C66I/1.
[47] European Council Decision (EU) 2019/476 taken in agreement with the United Kingdom of 22 March 2019 extending the period under Article 50(3) TEU, OJ 2019 L80I/1.

extension until 31 October 2019, indicating that the UK would have to organize, in May 2019, elections to the European Parliament; otherwise it would leave the Union on 1 June 2019.[48] Following Theresa May's announcement that she would resign as Conservative Party leader as of 7 June 2019, Boris Johnson became UK Prime Minister on 24 July 2019, with the intention that the UK leave the Union on 31 October 2019 with or without 'a deal'. However, on 4 September 2019, the UK Parliament passed a bill requiring the Prime Minister to seek a third extension if the withdrawal agreement had not been approved by the European Council meeting on 17–18 October 2019.

On 17 October 2019, the Commission and the United Kingdom reached a deal on some amendments to the Protocol on Ireland/Northern Ireland in order to replace the 'backstop' with a new arrangement according to which, after Brexit, the UK will leave the EU customs territory entirely, with specific customs, sanitary and phytosanitary and VAT and excise rules of the Union still applying to Northern Ireland in order to avoid a hard border with border controls between Northern Ireland and Ireland.[49] On 19 October 2019, the British Government requested the European Council to agree to another extension of the Article 50 period, which the European Council granted until 31 January 2020.[50] Following new elections to the British Parliament on 12 December 2019, the British Parliament started preparing for the approval of the Withdrawal Agreement, which was eventually given Royal Assent on 23 January 2020. From the Union's side, the European Parliament then gave its consent to the Withdrawal Agreement on 29 January 2020, following which the Council approved it on 30 January 2020.[51]

Transition period. As from 1 February 2020, the United Kingdom is no longer a Member State of the Union. The United Kingdom therefore has no representatives anymore in the Union institutions, bodies, and agencies and no longer participates in Union decision-making. However, in accordance with the Withdrawal Agreement, Union law remained applicable during the transition period and the Union institutions maintained full competence in relation to the United Kingdom, including the Court of Justice's jurisdiction to deal with preliminary references from UK courts. The transition period expired on 31 December 2020, as no use was made of the possibility to extend the transition period once, for up to one or two years, by joint agreement. Meanwhile the negotiations had started on the future relationship between the United Kingdom and the Union, for which the groundwork was laid in in a revised political declaration agreed on 17 October 2019, in the margin

4.017

---

[48] European Council Decision (EU) 2019/584 taken in agreement with the United Kingdom of 11 April 2019 extending the period under Article 50(3) TEU, OJ 2019 L101/1.

[49] Agreement on the withdrawal of the United Kingdom of Great Britain and Northern Ireland from the European Union and the European Atomic Energy Community, OJ 2020 L29/7. For an analysis of the Protocol on Ireland/Northern Ireland, see Weatherill, 'The Protocol on Ireland/Northern Ireland: Protecting the EU's Internal Market at the Expense of the UK's' (2020) ELRev 222–36.

[50] European Council Decision (EU) 2019/1810 taken in agreement with the United Kingdom of 29 October 2019 extending the period under Article 50(3) TEU, OJ 2019 L278/I/1.

[51] Council Decision (EU) 2020/135 of 30 January 2020 on the conclusion of the Agreement on the withdrawal of the United Kingdom of Great Britain and Northern Ireland from the European Union and the European Atomic Energy Community, OJ 2020 L29/1. See, generally, Craig, 'Brexit, A Drama: The Endgame—Part I' (2020) ELRev 163–82. For an analysis of the content of the withdrawal agreement, see Dougan, 'So Long, Farewell, Auf Wiedersehen, Goodbye: The UK's Withdrawal Package' (2020) CMLRev 631–704; Dashwood, 'The Withdrawal Agreement: Common Provisions, Governance and Dispute Settlement' (2020) ELRev 183–92.

of the Withdrawal Agreement.[52] Union law ceased to be applicable in the United Kingdom on 1 January 2021.[53]

4.018 **Future Relationship with the UK.** On 24 December 2020 the United Kingdom and the European Union agreed on a set of three agreements to govern the relationship between the Union and the United Kingdom from 1 January 2021 onwards. The Council unanimously authorized the signing of the agreements on 29 December 2020,[54] whilst the House of Commons approved the agreements on 30 December 2020. The agreements are, in accordance with Article 218(5) TFEU, applied provisionally from 1 January 2021 onwards, pending their formal adoption by the Union, as the vote in the European Parliament could not be scheduled in a timely manner. They entered into force on 1 May 2021.

The key agreement is the Trade and Cooperation Agreement. Part One of the Agreement sets up an intricate institutional framework to govern the application of the Agreement and enable further developments. As to trade, Part Two of the Agreement provides for tariff-free and quota-free trade in goods between the Union and the United Kingdom, even though the United Kingdom has left the customs union (see para. 7-015, *infra*), but only limited access in respect of trade in services and other fields such as digital trade or energy. The minutiae of the trade relationship are developed in extensive annexes to the Agreement. The trade relationship is, moreover, subject to respect for a level playing field for open and fair competition, which may result in the imposition of so-called rebalancing measures—in essence tariffs—if significant divergences in respect to labour and social, environmental, or climate protection, or with respect to subsidy control, were to occur. The substantive cooperation also relates to transport—especially aviation and road transport—social security coordination, and visas for short-term visits and fisheries, with Union fishing vessels at least temporarily retaining access to United Kingdom waters, albeit subject to reduced quota. Part Three of the Agreement provides for a replication of a number of instruments in the field of law enforcement and judicial cooperation in criminal matters. Part Four of the Agreement creates a framework for cooperation in the fields of health security and cyber security. Part Five allows for the continued participation of the United Kingdom in a number

---

[52] Political declaration setting out the framework for the future relationship between the European Union and the United Kingdom, OJ 2019 C384I/178.
[53] A number of obligations however continue to apply in a more limited fashion on the basis of the Withdrawal Agreement, most notably in respect of citizenship, see Spaventa, 'The Rights of Citizens under the Withdrawal Agreement: A Critical Analysis' (2020) ELRev 193–206. On the effects of Brexit in various policy areas, see the many contributions in the Brexit Special (2020) SEW 257–391.
[54] Council Decision (EU) 2020/2252 of 29 December 2020 on the signing, on behalf of the Union, and on provisional application of the Trade and Cooperation Agreement between the European Union and the European Atomic Energy Community, of the one part, and the United Kingdom of Great Britain and Northern Ireland, of the other part, and of the Agreement between the European Union and the United Kingdom of Great Britain and Northern Ireland concerning security procedures for exchanging and protecting classified information (OJ 2020 L444/2). The decision is taken on the basis of Article 217 TFEU, which allows for the conclusion of association agreements. That choice of legal basis implies unanimity in the Council (Article 218(8), second para. TFEU). After the European Parliament gave its consent on 27 April 2021, agreements were concluded by the Council on 29 April 2021, see Council Decision (EU) 2021/689 of 29 April 2021 on the conclusion, on behalf of the Union, of the Trade and Cooperation Agreement between the European Union and the European Atomic Energy Community, of the one part, and the United Kingdom of Great Britain and Northern Ireland, of the other part, and of the Agreement between the European Union and the United Kingdom of Great Britain and Northern Ireland concerning security procedures for exchanging and protecting classified information (OJ 2021 L149/2). See also, *infra*, para. 10-014 *et seq.* and Chapter 21. For the Agreement between the Government of the United Kingdom of Great Britain and Northern Ireland and the European Atomic Energy Community for Cooperation on the Safe and Peaceful Uses of Nuclear Energy, see OJ 2021 L150/1.

of programmes. Part Six of the Agreement contains an elaborate framework for dispute settlement and governance. Part Seven of the Agreement contains the final provisions.

The Trade and Cooperation Agreement is complemented with two further agreements. One agreement provides for cooperation between the United Kingdom and the EAEC on the safe and peaceful uses of nuclear energy. The other agreement concerns security procedures for exchanging and protecting classified information.

It must also be recalled that the Withdrawal Agreement (see para. 4-016, *infra*) contains a series of provisions that continue to apply next to the new agreements, most notably in respect of the status of citizens who exercised their free movement rights before the end of the transition period, and in respect of Northern Ireland, which continues to have a far closer relationship to the Union than the other parts of the United Kingdom.

IV. Suspension of Treaty Rights and Obligations

No unilateral suspension. Member States may not suspend their own Treaty obligations vis-à-vis a Member State which is in persistent breach. Neither do the Treaties permit a Member State to be excluded or compelled to leave the Union.[55] A Member State which fails to fulfil its obligations may be brought before the Court of Justice by the Commission or another Member State and possibly fined (Articles 258 to 260 TFEU).[56] Commentators have been divided as to whether a unilateral suspension of Treaty obligations may be justified under international law where no solution can be found using the dispute-settlement procedures or the safeguard clauses of Articles 346–348 TFEU.[57] **4.019**

Article 7 TEU. The Treaty of Amsterdam introduced a mechanism allowing the Union to act when one of its Member States persistently disregards the values on which the Union is founded.[58] The values concerned are those referred to in Article 2 TEU, namely respect for human dignity, freedom, democracy, equality, the rule of law, and respect for human rights, **4.020**

---

[55] C-621/18, *Wightman and Others*, 2018, para. 68. See P. Pohjankoski, 'Expulsion of a Member State from the European Union: Ultimate remedy?', in Lenaerts et al. (eds), *An Ever-Changing Union? Perspectives on the Future of EU Law in Honour of Allan Rosas* (Hart Publishing, 2019), 321–37. Thus, when Denmark was unable to ratify the EU Treaty after a negative vote in a first referendum, the other Member States could not exclude it from the Community or replace the Community by some other organization: Rideau, 'La ratification et l'entrée en vigueur du traité de Maastricht' (1992) RFDC 479, 490–1; see to the same effect, Kapteyn, 'Denemarken en het Verdrag van Maastricht' (1992) NJB 781–3.

[56] For further details, see Lenaerts, Gutman, and Nowak *EU Procedural Law* (OUP, 2022), chapter 5. In the event of an excessive deficit, the Council, excluding the representative of the Member State concerned, may impose sanctions (Article 126(11) TFEU; para. 9-036, *infra*).

[57] For further literature and a number of scenarios for exceptional measures, see Ehlermann, 'Mitgliedschaft in der Europäischen Gemeinschaft—Rechtsproblem der Erweiterung, der Mitgliedschaft und der Verkleinerung' (1984) EuR 113, 120–1. The view that such measures would run counter to the Union legal order is discussed in Everling, 'Sind die Mitgliedstaaten der Europäischen Gemeinschaften noch Herren der Verträge?', Bernard, Geck, Jaenicke and Steinberger (eds), *Völkerrecht als Rechtsordnung. Internationale Gerichtsbarkeit. Menschenrechte. Festschrift H. Mosler* (Springer, 1983), 173–91.

[58] See, generally, Closa and Kochenov (eds), *Reinforcing Rule of Law Oversights in the EU* (Cambridge University Press, 2016); Schroeder (ed.), *Strengthening the Rule of Law in Europe: From a Common Concept to Mechanisms of Implementation* (Hart Publishing, 2016); Wilms, *Protecting Fundamental Values in the European Union through the Rule of Law—Articles 2 and 7 TEU from a Legal, Historical and Comparative Angle* (EU Publication Office, 2017); Kochenov, 'Article 7: Un commentaire de la fameuse disposition "morte"' (2019) RAE 33–50.

including the rights of persons belonging to minorities.[59] Pursuant to Article 7(3) TEU, if a Member State commits a 'serious and persistent breach' of the values referred to in Article 2 TEU,[60] the Council may decide to suspend certain of its rights deriving from the application of the Treaties. It is for the European Council to determine such a breach after inviting the Member State in question to submit its observations. The European Council makes that determination unanimously at the proposal of one-third of the Member States or the Commission, after obtaining the consent of the European Parliament (Article 7(2) TEU).

The Treaty of Nice supplemented this procedure with a 'first step' under which the Council may determine that there is a 'clear risk' of a serious breach by a Member State of the said values (Article 7(1) TEU). This requires a reasoned proposal by one-third of the Member States, by the European Parliament, or by the Commission which the Council must adopt by a majority of four-fifths of its members after obtaining the consent of the European Parliament. The Council must hear the Member State concerned and may address recommendations to it. It must regularly verify that the grounds on which such a determination was made continue to apply (Article 7(1) TEU). This 'first step' allows Member States to act where the political situation in a Member State is at risk of no longer affording the guarantees for the protection of the values set out in Article 2 TEU.[61]

The Treaties do not specify that there must have been a determination of a clear risk of a serious breach of the values under Article 7(1) before the European Council can determine under Article 7(2) that a serious and persistent breach exists. In the two instances where the Article 7 procedure has been triggered, a reasoned proposal has been submitted to the Council under Article 7(1), without the latter having taken a formal decision. On 20 December 2017 the Commission adopted a reasoned proposal requesting the Council to adopt a decision under Article 7(1) on the determination of a clear risk of a serious breach by Poland of the rule of law;[62] on 12 September 2018 the European Parliament adopted a resolution with a reasoned proposal calling on the Council to determine the existence of a

---

[59] On the Union's values, see para. 5-002. For the violation of fundamental rights, see already De Witte and Toggenburg, 'Human Rights and Membership of the European Union', in Peers and Ward (eds), *The EU Charter of Fundamental Rights* (Hart, 2004) 59–82; Wachsmann, 'Le traité d'Amsterdam. Les droits de l'homme' (1997) RTDE 883, 895–7; for breaches of the principle of democracy, see Verhoeven, 'How Democratic Need European Union Members Be? Some Thoughts after Amsterdam' (1998) ELRev 217–34. See also Sydow, 'Liberté, démocratie, droits fondamentaux et Etat de droit: analyses de l'article 7 du traité EU' (2001) RDUE 285–328.

[60] Before the Treaty of Lisbon, Article 7 EU referred to breach of the principles mentioned in Article 6(1) EU, namely the principles of liberty, democracy, respect for human rights and fundamental freedoms, and the rule of law.

[61] The need for introducing a warning procedure became clear when the existing procedure of determining a breach turned out to be inappropriate when Member States started reacting in January 2000 to the formation of a government including an extreme right-wing party in Austria, where bilateral contacts with members of the Austrian Government were broken off. See Gilliaux, 'L'Union européenne à l'épreuve de gouvernements liberticides?' (2000) JT 449–54; Schmahl, 'Die Reaktionen auf den Einzug der Freiheitlichen Partei Österreichs in das österreichische Regierungskabinett' (2000) EuR 819–35; Leidenmühler, 'Zur Legalität der Massnahmen gegen die österreichische Bundesregierung' (2000) ZöR 299–322; Regan, 'Are EU Sanctions Against Austria Legal?' (2000) ZüR 323–36. Following a situation report drawn up by a number of 'wise men', these 'sanctions' were lifted. See Adamovich, 'Juristische Aspekte der "Sanktionen" der EU-14 und des "Weisenberichtes"' (2001) Eu GRZ 89–92; Hummer, 'The End of EU Sanctions Against Austria—A Precedent for New Sanctions Procedures?' (2000–01) Eur LF 77–83; Burchill, 'The Promotion and Protection of Democracy by Regional Organisations in Europe: The Case of Austria' (2001) E Pub L 79–102.

[62] Reasoned Proposal in accordance with Article 7(1) TEU regarding the rule of law in Poland—Proposal of 20 December 2017 for a Council Decision on the determination of a clear risk of a serious breach by the Republic of Poland of the rule of law COM(2017)835 final.

clear risk of a serious breach by Hungary of the values on which the Union is founded[63] (see para. 4-021, *infra*).

When the European Council, acting unanimously, has determined under Article 7(2) TEU that there is a serious and persistent breach, the Council may decide by a qualified majority to suspend certain of the rights deriving from the application of the Treaties, including the voting rights of the representative of the government in question in the Council. The Council has to take into account the possible consequences of such a suspension on the rights and obligations of natural and legal persons. The obligations of the Member State in question under the Treaties continue in any case to be binding on that State (Article 7(3) TEU). Subsequently, the Council may decide by a qualified majority to vary or revoke the suspension of rights in response to changes in the situation which led to them being imposed (Article 7(4) TEU).

Throughout the procedure referred to in Article 7 TEU, decisions of the European Council or the Council are taken without taking into account the vote of the representative of the Member State concerned. By the same token, that Member State is not counted in the calculation of the one-third or four-fifths of Member States referred to in Article 7(1) and (2) TEU (see Article 7(5) TEU and Article 354, first para. TFEU).[64] The European Parliament is to act by a two-thirds majority of the votes cast, representing the majority of its component members (Article 7(5) TEU and Article 354, fourth para. TFEU).[65]

Within one month from the date of the determination that there is a 'serious and persistent breach' or a 'clear risk' of a serious breach, the Court of Justice may, at the request of the Member State concerned, rule on whether the purely procedural stipulations of Article 7 have been complied with. The Court is to decide within one month from the date of the request (Article 269 TFEU).

Triggering Article 7 TEU. In March 2014, the Commission adopted a 'new EU framework to strengthen the rule of law' with the aim of preventing situations in which a threat to the rule of law in a Member State could develop into a 'clear risk of a serious breach' of the values set out in Article 2 TEU within the meaning of Article 7 TEU.[66] This framework implies that where there are clear indications of a systemic threat to the rule of law in a Member State, the Commission will start up a process according to which it will, first, assess the situation in the Member State concerned, second, issue a recommendation, and third, monitor the measures taken by the Member State as a follow-up to the recommendation. If the Member State does not come up with a satisfactory follow-up, the Commission will then start up one of the mechanisms set out in Article 7 TEU.

4.021

---

[63] European Parliament resolution of 12 September 2018 on a proposal calling on the Council to determine, pursuant to Article 7(1) TEU, the existence of a clear risk of a serious breach by Hungary of the values on which the Union is founded (2017/2131(INL) (based on a report drafted by MEP Judith Sargentini).

[64] Abstentions by members present in person or represented do not prevent the adoption of decisions referred to in Article 7(2) TEU (Article 354, first para. TFEU).

[65] See C-650/18, *Hungary v European Parliament*, AG Bobek Opinion, 2020.

[66] Commission Communication of 11 March 2014 to the European Parliament and the Council—A new EU Framework to strengthen the Rule of Law, COM(2014) 158 final. See Pech and Kochenov, 'Better Late than Never? On the Commission's Rule of Law Framework and its First Activation' (2016) JCMS 1062–74.

In the context of this framework, the Commission adopted, on 27 July 2016 and on 21 December 2016, recommendations on the rule of law in Poland,[67] considering, *inter alia*, that the independence and legitimacy of the Constitutional Tribunal of Poland is seriously undermined and the constitutionality of Polish laws can no longer be effectively guaranteed. In subsequent recommendations to Poland, the Commission has been explaining how further legislative reforms in its view continue to endanger the independence of the Polish judiciary.[68] On 20 December 2017 the Commission not only issued a fourth recommendation in this sense, but also adopted the above-mentioned reasoned proposal under Article 7(1) TEU.[69]

From its side, the European Parliament adopted, on 12 September 2018, its reasoned proposal calling on the Council to determine, pursuant to Article 7(1) TEU, whether there exists a clear risk of a breach by Hungary of the values on which the Union is founded. This decision was based on a report listing several practices affecting the independence of the judiciary, freedom of expression, academic freedom, freedom of religion and association, equal treatment, and protection of minorities, migrants, asylum seekers, and refugees.[70]

Since the submission of the reasoned proposals, the Council has organized several hearings in respect of the situation in Poland and Hungary pursuant to Article 7(1) TEU.

Whereas the proceedings brought under Article 7(1) TEU have not led to any concrete results, many of the issues raised in that context have become the object of judicial proceedings before the Court of Justice. On the one hand, the Commission has started infringement proceedings for breaches of the duty under Article 19(1) TEU to ensure the independence of the judiciary; on the other, several national courts have put preliminary references to the Court requesting clarification of the obligations flowing from Union law in situations where the rule of law in one or the other Member State is considered under threat (see para. 5-004, *infra*).

---

[67] Commission Recommendation (EU) 2016/1374 of 27 July 2016 regarding the rule of law in Poland, OJ 2016 L217/53 and Commission Recommendation (EU) 2017/146 of 21 December 2016 regarding the rule of law in Poland, OJ 2017 L22/65.

[68] Commission Recommendation (EU) 2017/1520 of 26 July 2017 regarding the rule of law in Poland complementary to Recommendations (EU) 2016/1374 and (EU) 2017/146 OJ 2017 L228/19.

[69] Reasoned proposal mentioned in n. 62, *supra*; Commission Recommendation (EU) 2018/103 of 20 December 2017 regarding the rule of law in Poland complementary to Recommendations (EU) 2016/1374, (EU) 2017/146 and (EU) 2017/1520, OJ 2018 L17/50.

[70] See the Reasoned Proposal mentioned in n. 62, *supra*.

PART II
COMPETENCES OF THE EUROPEAN UNION

The competences of the Union, sometimes also called 'the jurisdiction of the Union', are laid down in the Treaty on European Union (TEU), as amended by the Lisbon Treaty, and in the Treaty on the Functioning of the European Union (TFEU), which is the new title of the EC Treaty as amended by the Lisbon Treaty. The fundamental principles governing the Union competences are set out in Title I of the TEU ('Common Provisions') and in Title I TFEU ('Categories and Areas of Union Competence'). Further details about these competences are to be found in the provisions of the TFEU relating to each area, which take over the provisions relating to the relevant areas that were set out in the EC Treaty, as amended by the Lisbon Treaty and supplemented with the provisions on police and judicial cooperation in criminal matters that were previously contained in Title VI of the EU Treaty. The common foreign and security policy (CFSP) is the only area set out in the TEU (Title V of the TEU, building upon Title V of the original EU Treaty). The EAEC Treaty remains relevant for the competences of the European Atomic Energy Community. After explaining the Union's values and objectives and the principles governing the Union competences (Chapter 5), this Part sets out the Union's competence and substantive rules relating to the citizenship of the Union (Chapter 6); the internal market (Chapter 7); the area of freedom, security, and justice (Chapter 8); other internal policies (Chapter 9); the external competences of the Union (Chapter 10); and finally the limits and exceptions to the application of the Treaties (Chapter 11).

5
Values, Objectives, and Principles Governing the Union Competences

Functional approach. Since the Lisbon Treaty, the Treaties now clearly express the values on which the Union is founded.[1] The introductory title of the TEU (Title I 'Common Provisions') sets out the values of the Union (Article 2 TEU) and provides the Union with a list of objectives (Article 3 TEU). In order to delineate the jurisdiction of the Union, the Treaties first describe the objectives of the Union and then set out the legal rules pursuant to which these objectives are to be pursued (the 'legal basis' for Union action). In addition, the Treaties contain a supplementary legal basis for Union action for which specific provision is not made in the Treaties, but which is necessary to attain one of the objectives set out therein (Article 352 TFEU; Article 203 EAEC). Consequently, Union competence is not so much defined according to subject-matter as it is 'functionally' circumscribed to what is required by the objectives set out in the Treaties (see Article 1, first subpara. TEU). This 'functional' approach also underpins the EAEC Treaty, which contains the legal basis for action of the (only remaining) Community on Atomic Energy (see para. 1-015, *supra*). The exercise of the Union's competence is further subject to compliance with the principles of subsidiarity (where the competence in question is non-exclusive) and proportionality. Other important principles with which Union action has to comply are the principles of sincere cooperation and equal treatment.

5.001

I. Values of the Union

Values common to the Member States. Article 2 TEU proclaims that the Union is founded on the values of respect for human dignity, freedom, democracy, equality, the rule of law, and respect for human rights, including the rights of persons belonging to minorities. It further adds that these values are common to the Member States 'in a society in which pluralism, non-discrimination, tolerance, justice, solidarity and equality between women and men prevail'.

5.002

Mutual trust. Respect of the values set out in Article 2 TEU constitutes, together with a commitment to promote these values, one of the conditions for membership of the Union (Article 49 TEU, see para. 4-010, *supra*). The Member States thus freely and voluntarily

5.003

---

[1] Before the Lisbon Treaty, the Treaty on European Union indicated in Article 6(1) that 'the Union is founded on the principles of liberty, democracy, respect for human rights and fundamental freedoms, and the rule of law, principles which are common to the Member States'. The Lisbon Treaty complemented this clause and elevated it into the introductory articles of the Treaties, while giving its elements as 'values' (instead of 'principles') an additional moral dimension.

committed themselves to these values[2] and must respect them, irrespective of whether they act within the scope of Union law.[3] The fact that each Member State shares this set of common values with all other Member States constitutes a fundamental premise of the Union's legal structure[4] and justifies the existence of mutual trust between the Member States that these values will be recognized and that Union law implementing these values will be respected.[5] Each Member State's respect for fundamental rights[6] and the rule of law as guaranteed by an independent judiciary[7] is the bedrock for the mutual trust between the Member States that is at the heart of countless Union policies, such as the functioning of the internal market and the area of freedom, security, and justice (see para. 8-001, *infra*), but also the protection of the Union's financial interests (see para. 20-009, *infra*). All this explains why the existence of a serious and persistent breach by a Member State of these values may lead the Council to suspend certain of the rights deriving from the application of the Treaties to the Member State in question, including the voting right of that Member State in the Council (Article 7(3) TEU, see para. 4-020, *supra*).

During the debate on the EU Constitution a demand was made, in some quarters of civil society, to emphasize the Christian roots of European civilization in the Treaties, or at least in the preamble to the Treaties.[8] Eventually, it was agreed to have the preamble to the TEU refer to the Contracting Parties 'drawing inspiration from the cultural, religious and humanist inheritance of Europe'.

---

[2] C-621/18, *Wightman and Others*, 2018, para. 63

[3] In this regard, see Martín Rodríguez, 'Poland Before the Court of Justice: Limitless or Limited Case Law on Art. 19 TEU?' (2020) European Papers 331–46. More generally on the significance of the Union's values, see Rossi, 'La valeur juridique des valeurs. L'article 2 TUE: relations avec d'autres dispositions de droit primaire de l'UE et remèdes juridictionnels' (2020) RTDE 639; von Bogdandy, 'Der europäische Rechtsraum. Ein Begriff zur Neuausrichtung des Europarechts und besseren Verteidigung europäischer Werte' (2020) AöR 321–57; Wouters, 'Revisiting Art. 2 TEU: A True Union of Values?' (2020) European Papers 255–77; Potacs, 'Wertkonforme Auslegung des Unionsrechts' (2016) EuR 164; Jacqué, 'Crise des valeurs dans l'Union européenne' (2016) RTDE 213; Constantinesco, 'Les valeurs de l'Union, quelques précisions et mises à jour complémentaires', in Potvin-Solis (ed.), *Les valeurs communes dans l'Union européenne* (Bruylant, 2014), 47; Rideau, 'Les valeurs de l'Union européenne' (2012) RA.E 329; Tomuschat, 'Common Values and the Place of the Charter in Europe' (2002) Rev Eur Dr Public 159; Lenaerts and Desomer, 'Bricks for a Constitutional Treaty of the European Union: Values, Objectives and Means' (2002) ELRev 377.

[4] Opinion 2/13, *Accession of the EU to the ECHR*, 2013, para. 168.

[5] Ibid. See further Lenaerts, 'La vie après l'avis: Exploring the principle of mutual (Yet not Blind) Trust' (2017) CMLRev 805–40; Timmermans, 'How Trustworthy is Mutual Trust? Opinion 2/13 Revisited', in Lenaerts et al. (eds), *An Ever-Changing Union? Perspectives on the Future of EU Law in Honour of Allan Rosas* (Hart Publishing, 2019), 21–34; Ladenburger, 'The Principle of Mutual Trust in the Area of Freedom, Security and Justice. Some Reflections on its Corollaries', in Lenaerts et al. (eds), *An Ever-Changing Union? Perspectives on the Future of EU Law in Honour of Allan Rosas* (Hart Publishing, 2019), 163–76; von Danwitz, 'Der Grundsatz des gegenseitigen Vertrauens zwischen den Mitgliedstaaten der EU. Eine wertebasierte Garantie der Einheit und Wirksamkeit des Unionsrechts' (2020) EuR 61–89. See also Rizcallah, *Le principe de confiance mutuelle en droit de l'Union européenne. Un principe essentiel à l'épreuve d'une crise des valeurs* (Larcier, 2020).

[6] C-404/15 and C-659/15 PPU, *Aranyosi and Căldăraru*, 2016, paras 74–104, with a case note by Hong (2016) EuConst 549–63; C-128/18, *Dorobantu*, 2019, paras 46–69.

[7] C-64/16, *Associação Sindical dos Juízes Portugueses*, 2018, paras 27–52, with a case note by Bonelli and Claes (2018) EuConst 622–43; C-216/18 PPU, *L.M.*, 2018, paras 33–79; Case C-619/18, *Commission v Poland*, 2019, paras 42–59, 71–97 and 108–24; C-192/18, *Commission v Poland*, 2019, paras 98–136; C-585/18, C-624/18, and C-625/18, *A.K.*, 2019, paras 114–70. See Bárd and van Ballegooij, 'Judicial Independence as a Precondition for Mutual Trust? The CJEU in *Minister for Justice and Equality v. LM*' (2018) NJECL 353–65. See the discussion in paras 29-003–29-004, *infra*.

[8] See, e.g., Weiler, 'A Christian Europe? Europe and Christianity: Rules of Commitment' (2007) European View 143–50; Menendez, 'A Pious Europe? Why Europe Should not Define itself as Christian' (2005) ELRev 133–48; Mattera, 'L'européanité est-elle chrétienne?' (2003) RMCUE 325–42.

Fundamental values. The values referred to in Article 2 TEU find concrete expression in rights, principles, and rules of Union law.[9] Thus, human dignity, freedom, equality, and the rights of persons belonging to minorities are protected in Union law, together with various other values mentioned in Article 2 TEU, as fundamental rights.[10] Title I of the TEU expressly provides that the Union recognizes the rights, freedoms, and principles set out in the Charter of Fundamental Rights of the European Union (Article 6(1) TEU); that the Union must accede to the European Convention for the Protection of Human Rights and Fundamental Freedoms (Article 6(2) TEU); and that fundamental rights, as guaranteed by the European Convention for the Protection of Human Rights and Fundamental Freedoms and as they result from the constitutional traditions common to the Member States, shall constitute general principles of the Union's law (Article 6(3) TEU, see para. 25-003 *et seq.*, *infra*). The value of equality finds concrete expression in the equality of the Member States before the Treaties, which the Union has to respect, and in the equality of its citizens, who shall receive equal attention from its institutions, bodies, offices, and agencies (Articles 4(2) and 9 TEU; see para. 5-051 *et seq.*, *infra*). Democracy finds expression in the democratic principles set out it Title II of the TEU (see para. 17-046, *infra*) and the Union citizen's democratic rights protected by the Charter of Fundamental Rights.[11] The value of the rule of law finds its expression in the duty of the Court of Justice of the European Union and Member States' courts and tribunals to provide effective legal protection in the fields covered by Union law (Article 19(1), second subpara. TEU), which has been clarified in recent case law.

5.004

Rule of law. Article 19(1), second subpara. TEU gives concrete expression to the value of the rule of law, entrusting the responsibility for ensuring the full application of Union law in all Member States and judicial protection of individuals under Union law to national courts and tribunals and the Court of Justice of the European Union (see also paras 29-003–29-004). The effective judicial protection that courts and tribunals must provide under the second subpara. of Article 19(1) TEU requires full respect of the fundamental right to an effective remedy and to a fair trial, as laid down in Article 47 of the Charter of Fundamental Rights, for which, as noted above, the independence of the judiciary is essential. In the light of the value of the rule of law, which is a condition for the enjoyment of all of the rights derived from Union law, a Member State cannot amend its legislation in such a way as to bring about a reduction in the protection of the value of the rule of law. The Member States are thus required to ensure that, in the light of that value, any regression of their laws on the organization of justice is prevented, by refraining from adopting rules which would undermine the independence of the judiciary.[12]

5.005

Concerns as regards respect for the rule of law in Poland have prompted the Commission to submit a reasoned proposal under Article 7(1) TEU[13] for the Council to determine a clear

---

[9] The Union is also to uphold and promote its values in its external relations; see Articles 3(4) and 21(1) TEU; see also C-72/15 P, *PJSC Rosneft Oil Company*, 2017, para. 72.
[10] See the rights and principles set out in the Charter of Fundamental Rights, *inter alia*, in Article 1 (Human dignity), in Title II ('Freedoms'), Title III ('Equality'), Title IV ('Solidarity'), and Title VI ('Justice').
[11] C-418/18 P, *Puppinck v Commission*, 2019, para. 64; C-502/19, *Junqueras Vies*, 2019, para. 63; see also Articles 39 and 40 of the Charter of Fundamental Rights.
[12] C-896/19, *Repubblika*, 2021, paras 63-5.
[13] Reasoned Proposal in accordance with Article 7(1) TEU regarding the rule of law in Poland—Proposal of 20 December 2017 for a Council Decision on the determination of a clear risk of a serious breach by the Republic of Poland of the rule of law COM(2017)835 final.

risk of a serious breach by Poland of the rule of law. The European Parliament did the same, invoking breaches by Hungary of several values set out in Article 2 TEU (see para. 4-020, *supra*). Whereas these proceedings have not led to any concrete results, many of the issues raised in that context have also been the object of further judicial proceedings.

On the one hand, the Commission has brought infringement proceedings against Poland and Hungary on several aspects of their legislation that it considered in breach of Union law.[14] Thus, the Commission referred Poland to the Court of Justice for the incompatibility with Union law of Polish reforms of the organization of the judiciary that allegedly threaten judicial independence and thereby the fundamental right to a fair trial as guaranteed by Union law. In some of these cases, the Commission has sought interim relief pending the proceedings, which the Court has granted.[15] On 24 June 2019, the Court of Justice concluded that Poland had failed to fulfil its obligations under the second subpara. of Article 19(1) TEU by lowering the obligatory retirement age of the judges of the Supreme Court and by allowing the Polish President to extend the period of judicial activity of judges of that court beyond the newly fixed retirement age.[16] On 5 November 2019, the Court of Justice found a similar infringement of Article 19(1) TEU as regards the different obligatory retirement age for men and women holding the position of judges in the Polish ordinary courts.[17] In 2021, the Court is to pronounce on further infringement actions brought by the Commission against judicial reforms, in particular regarding the disciplinary regime for judges, in the context of which the Court ordered, on 8 April 2020, the suspension of the activity by a newly set up Disciplinary Chamber of the Supreme Court in disciplinary proceedings against judges.[18]

On the other hand, national courts and tribunals have brought issues to the Court of Justice through preliminary references on the interpretation of Union law. In a preliminary ruling of 19 November 2019, the Court clarified the factors to be applied by the referring Labour Law Chamber of the Polish Supreme Court in order to determine whether the Disciplinary Chamber of the Supreme Court meets the guarantees of independence and impartiality necessary to ensure the effective judicial protection required under Article 19(1) TEU in the light of the circumstances in which it was formed, its characteristics, and the circumstances in which its members are appointed.[19] Meanwhile it is has become clear that the risk of breaches of Union values in one Member State directly endangers the application of Union law, with all due safeguards in terms of fundamental rights, in other Member States. Accordingly, the Court of Justice considered, in cases referred to it by other Member States'

---

[14] See also Torres Perez, 'From Portugal to Poland: The Court of Justice of the European Union as Watchdog of Judicial Independence' (2020) MJECL 105–19; Schmidt and Bogdanowicz, 'The Infringement Procedure in the Rule of Law Crisis: How to Make Effective Use of Article 258 TFEU' (2018) CMLRev 1061–100. As regards the situation in Poland, see more generally Sadurski, 'Poland's Constitutional Breakdown' (2019) ELRev 876–9; Martín Rodriguez, 'Poland Before the Court of Justice: Limitless or Limited Case Law on Art. 19 TEU?' (2020) European Papers 331–46.

[15] See C-619/18 R, *Commission v Poland* (order), 2018.

[16] C-619/18, *Commission v Poland*, 2019.

[17] C-192/18, *Commission v Poland*, 2019.

[18] C-791/19 R, *Commission v Poland* (Order), 2020; see also C-204/21, *Commission v Poland* (pending). As regards concerns on the rule of law in Romania, see C-83/19, C-127/19, C-195/19, C-291/19, C-355/19 and C-397/19, *Asociaţia "Forumul Judecătorilor Din România" and Others*, 2021, paras 186-241.

[19] C-585/18, C-624/18, and C-625/18, *A.K. and Others*, 2019. See also C-558/18 and C-563/18, *Miasto Łowicz*, 2020 (reference held inadmissible); C-824/18, *A.B. and Others*, 2021. On judicial appointments, see further para. 29-004, *infra*.

courts called upon by Polish authorities to execute a European arrest warrant, that such courts must refrain from giving effect to the arrest warrant if they consider, upon an assessment not only of the general deficiencies as regards the rule of law in Poland but also the specific characteristics of the concrete case, that there is a real risk that the individual concerned would suffer a breach of his fundamental right to an independent tribunal and, therefore, of the essence of his fundamental right to a fair trial.[20]

Following challenges to the rule of law in some Member States, the Commission has come up with a European Rule of Law mechanism in order to promote the rule of law and prevent problems from emerging or deepening.[21] A yearly rule of law report assesses relevant developments in all the Member States, referring to requirements under Union law, but also to recommendations and opinions of the Council of Europe, which provide for standards and best practices.[22] In addition, the Union legislature provided for a mechanism protecting the Union budget against breaches of the principles of the rule of law affecting its sound financial management or the protection of the financial interests of the Union.[23]

II. Objectives of the European Union

Specific objectives. Originally, the main objective of the European Community was the establishment of a common market. In essence, the impediments to the free movement of goods, persons, services, and capital had to be removed to create, at the stage of the European Union, an internal market without internal frontiers. Additionally, the Community developed a flanking common policy and common activities. Since then, these objectives have been expanded and supplemented with non-economic objectives, which has led to the long and broad list of Union objectives currently set out in Article 3 TEU.[24]

5.006

The Union's first aim is to promote peace, the Union's values, and the well-being of its peoples (Article 3(1) TEU). Second, the Treaty refers to 'an area of freedom, security and justice without internal frontiers, in which the free movement of persons is ensured in conjunction with appropriate measures with respect to external border controls, asylum, immigration and the prevention and combating of crime' (Article 3(2) TEU). Third, reference is made to the establishment of an internal market[25] to ensure 'the sustainable development of Europe

---

[20] C-216/18 PPU, *LM*, 2018, with note Wendel (2019) CDE 189–15; C-354/20 PPU and C-412/20 PPU, *L and P*, 2020, paras 35–69.

[21] See the Commission's 2020 Rule of Law Report of 30 September 2020—The rule of law situation in the European Union, COM(2020)580 final.

[22] Thus, the first Rule of Law Report, issued in 2020 (see n. 21, *supra*) was accompanied by twenty-seven country reports assessing the justice system, the anti-corruption framework, media pluralism, and other institutional checks and balances, referring, *inter alia*, to reports from the European Commission for Democracy Through Law (the 'Venice Commission') of the Council of Europe.

[23] Regulation (EU, Euratom) 2020/2092 of the European Parliament and of the Council of 16 December 2020 on a general regime of conditionality for the protection of the budget, OJ 2020 L443I/1 (see para. 20-009, *infra*).

[24] See Reimer, 'Ziele und Zuständigkeiten—Die Funktionen der Unionszielbestimmungen' (2003) EuR 992–1012; Larik, 'From Specialty to a Constitutional Sense of Purpose: On the Changing Role of the Objectives of the European Union' (2014) ILCQ 935–62.

[25] At the instigation of French President Nicolas Sarkozy, reference to 'free and undistorted competition' was removed from the final text of the Treaty. However, Protocol (No. 27), annexed to the TEU and TFEU, on the internal market and competition (OJ 2010 C83/309), explicitly states that 'the internal market as set out in Article 3 TEU includes a system ensuring that competition is not distorted'. See C-610/10, *Commission v Spain*, 2012, para. 126.

based on balanced economic growth and price stability, a highly competitive social market economy, aiming at full employment and social progress, and a high level of protection and improvement of the quality of the environment' and the promotion of scientific and technological advance. The internal market is further linked to objectives such as combating social exclusion and discrimination; the promotion of social justice and protection; equality between women and men; solidarity between generations and protection of the rights of the child; the promotion of economic, social, and territorial cohesion and solidarity among Member States; respect for the Union's rich cultural and linguistic diversity; and the safeguarding and enhancement of Europe's cultural heritage (Article 3(3) TEU). Fourth, Article 3(4) TEU refers to the establishment of an economic and monetary union whose currency is the euro.[26] Fifth, the TEU provides the Union with specific objectives as to its external action (Article 3(5) TEU and Article 21(1) TEU).[27] Article 21(2) TEU provides a list of nine objectives that the Union is to pursue in its external action (see para. 10-001, *infra*).

5.007 **Horizontal objectives.** The objectives set out in Article 3 TEU have to be complemented by further objectives laid down in the 'provisions of general application' of Title II of the TFEU, which the Union must take into account in the implementation of its policies (so-called 'overarching' or 'horizontal' objectives). Accordingly, the Union must aim, in all its activities, to eliminate inequalities and to promote equality between men and women (Article 8 TFEU). Furthermore, in defining and implementing its policies and activities, the Union shall take into account requirements linked to the promotion of a high level of employment; the guarantee of adequate social protection; the fight against social exclusion and a high level of education, training, and protection of human health (Article 9 TFEU);[28] and combat discrimination based on sex, racial or ethnic origin, religion or belief, disability, age, or sexual orientation (Article 10 TFEU; see, *infra*, para. 5-051 *et seq.*, *infra*). It must also take into account environmental protection, in particular with a view to promoting sustainable development (Article 11 TFEU)[29] and consumer protection (Article 12 TFEU).[30] In formulating and implementing the Union's agriculture, fisheries, transport, internal market, research, and technological development and space policies, the Union and the Member States must pay full regard to the welfare requirements of animals (as 'sentient beings'), while respecting the legislative or administrative provisions and customs of the Member States relating in particular to religious rites, cultural traditions, and regional heritage (Article 13 TFEU).[31]

---

[26] See also Article 119 TFEU.

[27] For an application of the principle that, pursuant to Article 3(5) TEU, the Union is to contribute to the strict observance of international law, including the principles of the United Nations Charter, see C-363/18, *Organisation juive européenne*, 2019, para. 48. See also Aust, 'Eine völkerrechtsfreundliche Union? Grund und Grenze der Öffnung des Europarechts zum Völkerrecht' (2017) EuR 106–20.

[28] See C-201/15, *AGET Iraklis*, 2016, paras 77–78; C-620/18, *Hungary v European Parliament and Council*, 2020, paras 41–42; C-626/18, *Poland v European Parliament and Council*, 2020, paras 46–7.

[29] Ferraris, 'The Role of the Principle of Environmental Integration (Article 11 TFEU) in Maximising the "Greening" of the Common Agricultural Policy' (2018) ELRev 410–23; Holder and Lee, *Environmental Protection, Law and Policy: Text and Materials* (Cambridge University Press, 2007), chapter 4; Wasmeier, 'The Integration of Environmental Protection as a General Rule for Interpreting Community Law' (2001) CMLRev 159–77; Schumacher, 'The Environmental Integration Clause in Article 6 of the EU Treaty: Prioritising Environmental Protection' (2001) Env L Rev 29–43.

[30] See T-224/10, *Association belge des consommateurs test-achats v Commission*, 2011, para. 43.

[31] This objective was inserted in the Treaties by the Treaty of Lisbon. See, however, already Protocol (No. 33), annexed to the EC Treaty by the Treaty of Amsterdam, on protection and welfare of animals, (OJ 1997 C340/110). Ensuring the welfare of animals did not for all that constitute a general principle of Union law: C-189/01 *Jippes and Others*, 2001, paras 71–79. As far as religious rites are concerned, see C-426/16, *Liga van Moskeeën en Islamitische Organisaties Provincie Antwerpen*, 2018, paras 63–4; C-497/17, *Œuvre d'assistance aux bêtes d'abattoirs*,

Other horizontal objectives are ensuring the provision and good functioning of services of general economic interest (Article 14 TFEU; see para. 9-019, *infra*), the promotion of good governance and ensuring the participation of civil society (Article 15 TFEU), and the protection of personal data (Article 16 TFEU). Finally, Article 17 TFEU states that the Union is to respect the status of churches and religious associations or communities and of philosophical and non-confessional organizations in the Member States.[32]

All these objectives are to be treated on equal footing with the objectives set for the Union in other specific provisions of the Treaties. Indeed, in accordance with Article 7 TFEU, the Union has to ensure consistency between its different policies and activities 'taking all of its objectives into account'.

Legal status of objectives. According to the Court of Justice, the aims on which the establishment of the Union is based cannot have the effect of 'imposing legal obligations on the Member States or of conferring rights on individuals'.[33] They depend, for their implementation, on the policies pursued by the Union and the Member States, with the result that their legal impact is limited to guiding the interpretation of Union law.[34] Thus, Union competence is often inferred from specific Treaty provisions read together with the 'objectives of the Union' or, before the Treaty of Lisbon entered into force, the 'requirements of the common market' enshrined in Article 3 EC.[35] The Court interprets the Treaty provisions in the light of the Union's objectives.[36] It has thus inferred from the objective of ensuring undistorted competition in the internal market (listed in Article 3(g) EC), read in conjunction with Articles 10, 81, and 82 EC [*now Article 4(3) TEU and Articles 101 and 102 TFEU*] an obligation for Member States not to adopt any measures which may render ineffective the competition rules for undertakings set out in Articles 81 and 82 EC [*now Articles 101 and 102 TFEU*].[37] Conversely, an objective such as an 'open market economy with free

5.008

2019, paras 44–52, with a case note by Clerc (2019) RA.E 173–84; C-336/19, *Centraal Israëlitisch Consistorie van België and Others*, 2020, paras 39–81. For the objectives of environmental and animal protection, see Camm and Bowles, 'Animal Welfare and the Treaty of Rome—A Legal Analysis of the Protocol on Animal Welfare and Welfare Standards in the European Union' (2000) J Env L 197–205; Van Calster and Deketelaere, 'Amsterdam, the Intergovernmental Conference and Greening the EU Treaty' (1998) E Env L Rev 17–19. For an overview of the evolution of Union legislation on the matter, see Leone, 'Farm Animal Welfare under Scrutiny: Issues Unsolved by the EU Legislator' (2020) EJLS 47–84; Sowery, 'Sentient Beings and Tradable products: The Curious Constitutional Status of Animals under Union Law' (2018) CMLRev 55–100.

[32] See Article 17(1) and (2) TFEU. Article 17(3) adds: 'Recognising their identity and their specific contribution, the Union shall maintain an open, transparent and regular dialogue with these churches and organisations'. Article 17 thus expresses the neutrality of the European Union towards the organization by the Member States of their relations with churches and religious associations and communities (C-414/16, *Egenberger*, 2018, para. 58; C-68/17, *IR*, C-68/17, para. 48). See Tischbirek, 'A Double Conflict of Laws: The Emergence of an EU "Staatskirchenrecht"?' (2019) GLJ 1066–78; Watson and Oliver, 'Is the Court of Justice of the European Union Finding Its Religion' (2019) Fordham ILJ 847–74.

[33] C-339/89, *Alsthom Atlantique*, 1991, para. 9; C-9/99 *Echirolles Distribution*, 2000, para. 25; C-484/08 *Caja de Ahorros y Monte de Piedad de Madrid*, 2010, paras 46–7. For their legal force, see also Reimer (n. 24, *supra*); Durand, 'Les Principes', in de Cockborne et al. (eds), *Commentaire Mégret—Le droit de la CEE. 1. Préambule. Principes. Libre circulation des marchandises* (Editions de l'Université de Bruxelles, 1992), Nos 12–18, at 13–19; Pescatore, 'Les objectifs de la Communauté européenne comme principes d'interprétation dans la jurisprudence de la Cour de Justice', Ganshof van der Meersch (ed.), *Miscellanea W.J. Ganshof van der Meersch* (Bruylant, 1972), Part II, 325–69.

[34] C-149/96, *Portugal v Council*, 1999, paras 86–7 (objective of economic and social cohesion).

[35] For the common transport policy, see 22/70 *Commission v Council*, 1971, para. 20; for compliance with the conditions of competition, see 97/78, *Schumalla*, 1978, para. 6.

[36] 270/80, *Polydor*, 1982, para. 16.

[37] 311/85 *VVR*, 1987, para. 24; 267/86 *Van Eycke*, 1988, para. 20 (see para. 9-012, *infra*).

competition' (Article 119 TFEU [*ex Article 4 EC*]) must be read in conjunction with the provisions of the Treaty designed to implement it.[38]

III. The Principle of Conferral of Competences

5.009   **Fundamental principles.** The Union may act only within the limits of the competences conferred upon it by the Treaties (the principle of conferral). Furthermore, the exercise by the Union of its competences is governed by the principles of subsidiarity and proportionality. These fundamental principles governing the division of competence between the Union and the Member States are set out in Title I ('Common provisions') of the Treaty on European Union (Articles 4 and 5 TEU). Competences not conferred upon the Union by the Treaties remain with the Member States (Articles 4(1) and 5(2) TEU).

The Treaty on the Functioning of the European Union determines the areas of Union competence, their delimitation, and the arrangements for exercising them (Article 1(1) TFEU). In Title I, the TFEU sets out the categories and areas of competence (Articles 2 to 6 TFEU). Further details about the scope of these competences and the arrangements for exercising them are to be found in the subsequent provisions of the TFEU relating to each area (Article 2(6) TFEU).[39] However, the scope of the common foreign and security policy and the arrangements for exercising this competence are set out in Title V of the TEU.

A. Need for a legal basis

5.010   **Principle of conferral.** Article 5(1) TEU states that the limits of Union competences are governed by the principle of conferral (which is also known as the principle of 'attribution of competence'). Pursuant to that principle 'the Union shall act only within the limits of the competences conferred upon it by the Member States in the Treaties to attain the objectives set out therein' (Article 5(2) TEU). This principle must be respected in both the internal action and the international action of the Union.[40] The choice of the appropriate legal basis

---

[38] C-9/99, *Echirolles Distribution*, 2000, para. 24.
[39] See Part Two ('Non-discrimination and citizenship of the Union'), Part Three ('Union policies and internal actions'), Part Four ('Association of the overseas countries and territories'), and Part Five ('External action by the Union') of the TFEU. For the discussion of the scope of the various Union competences, see Chapters 6 to 9, *infra*, and, for external action, Chapter 10, *infra*.
[40] Opinion 2/94, *Accession by the Communities to the Convention for the Protection of Human Rights and Fundamental Freedoms*, 1996, para. 24; ECJ, Opinion 2/00, *Carthagena Protocol*, 2001, para. 5; Case C-370/07, *Commission v Council*, 2009, para. 46. For legal basis as the precondition for legislative and executive action on the part of the Union, see Krämer, 'Legal Bases for Normative Acts in EU Law'—A Norm-Analytical and Constitutional Study' (2019) Rechtstheorie 1–39; Engel, *The Choice of Legal Basis for Acts of the European Union: Competence Overlaps, Institutional Preferences, and Legal Basis Litigation* (Springer, 2018), 142; Cremona, 'EU External Relations: Unity and Conferral of Powers', in Azoulai (ed.), *The Question of Competence in the European Union* (OUP, 2018), 65–85; Craig, 'Competence: Clarity, Conferral, Containment and Consideration' (2004) ELRev 323–44; Van Ooik, *De keuze van rechtsgrondslag voor besluiten van de Europese Unie* (Kluwer, 1999), 483; Triantafyllou, *Des compétences d'attribution au domaine de la loi. Etude sur les fondements juridiques de l'activité administrative Communautaire* (Bruylant, 1997). See also Lenaerts, *Le juge et la constitution aux Etats-Unis d'Amérique et dans l'ordre juridique européen* (Bruylant, 1988), No. 300, 346–349, and Nos 309–311, 357–62; Emiliou, 'Opening Pandora's Box: The Legal Basis of Community Measures Before the Court of Justice' (1994) ELRev 488–507; Lenaerts and van Ypersele, 'Le principe de subsidiarité et son contexte: étude de l'article 3 B du traité CE' (1994) CDE 13–30 and 35–44; Barents, 'The Internal Market Unlimited: Some Observations on the Legal

has constitutional significance, as the principle of conferral implies that the Union must link the acts it adopts to provisions of the TFEU which actually empower it to adopt such acts.[41] All Union action must be founded upon a legal basis laid down in the Treaties. The legal basis for Union acts may, of course, also be found in another Union act which they are designed to implement. In this latter case, a Union institution or body cannot act unless its action is based on a basic act having a legal basis in the Treaties which (1) defines the Union's competence *ratione materiae* and (2) specifies the means of exercise of that competence, that is to say, the legislative instruments and the decision-making procedure.

(1) Competence *ratione materiae*. In the first place, the legal basis determines the extent of the competence conferred on the Union in a specific field or for the achievement of stated objectives. Most Treaty articles conferring a competence on the Union, at the same time specify the objectives to be pursued by the Union in that field.   **5.011**

The competence *ratione materiae* thus directly affects the 'vertical' division of competence between the Union and the Member States.[42] Some competences conferred on the Union are 'exclusive' (see Article 2(1) TFEU), which means that the Union alone has jurisdiction. However, in most fields both the Union and the Member States are competent to act (see paras. 5-022–5-027). Where the Union is not empowered to act, such action comes within the residual competence of the Member States.[43] This is without prejudice to the use, by the Council (with the consent of the European Parliament), of the 'supplementary' legal basis laid down in Article 352 TFEU.[44]

The conferral of ever more competences to the Union through successive Treaty amendments has given rise to a debate about the most appropriate distribution of competence between the Union and the Member States, which has found expression in the introduction of the principle of subsidiarity in particular (see para. 5-028 *et seq.*, *infra*) and in the call for a more precise delimitation of competences.[45] The Treaty of Lisbon has partially responded to this call in so far as it codifies some of the principles that were to be found only in the case law of the Court of Justice and sets out a limitative list of exclusive competences of the Union (see para. 5-022 *et seq.*, *infra*).

(2) Way competences are exercised. In addition, the legal basis determines the way in which the Union exercises its competence *ratione materiae*, specifying the applicable   **5.012**

Basis of Community Legislation' (1993) CMLRev 85–109; Bradley, 'The European Court and the Legal Basis of Community Legislation' (1988) ELRev 379–402.

[41] C-687/15, *Commission v Council*, 2017, para. 49; Opinion 1/15, *EU-Canada PNR Agreement*, 2017, para. 71.

[42] C-370/07, *Commission v Council*, 2009, para. 49. See von Bogdandy and Bast, 'Die vertikale Kompetenzordnung der Europäischen Union—Rechtsdogmatischer Bestand und verfassungsrechtliche Reformperspektiven' (2001) Eu GRZ 441–58.

[43] This corollary of the principle of conferral is expressly mentioned in Articles 4(1) and 5(2) TEU ('Competences not conferred upon the Union in the Treaties remain with the Member States').

[44] Nevertheless, the Council can use the 'supplementary' legal basis of Article 352 TFEU only if it remains within the limits traced by the Treaties; see para. 5-020, *infra*.

[45] See the call for a wide debate in Declaration (No. 23), annexed to the Treaty of Nice, on the future of the Union, (OJ 2001 C80/85) and the 'Declaration of Laeken' of the European Council of 14 and 15 December 2001. For further discussion of the delimitation of competences as between the Union and the Member States, see Konstadinides, *Division of Powers in European Union Law: The Delimitation of Internal Competence between the EU and the Member States* (Kluwer, 2009); von Bogdandy and Bast, 'The European Union's Vertical Order of Competences: The Current Law and Proposals for its Reform' (2002) CMLRev 227–68.

decision-making procedure and the available legislative instruments. As far as the appropriate legislative instrument is concerned, some Treaty articles restrict action on the part of the Union to 'directives', 'directives or regulations', 'recommendations', or 'incentive measures', whilst others authorize any 'measures' to be taken.[46] As far as the decision-making procedure is concerned, the Treaty articles determine what institutions are to be involved in the adoption of an act and how this is to take place.[47] Accordingly, the choice of legal basis determines whether the ordinary legislative procedure applies, requiring both the European Parliament and the Council (by qualified majority) to approve the proposed act, or rather a special legislative procedure, for instance providing for the Council to decide unanimously without the need for the adoption of the act by the European Parliament. A dispute as to the correct legal basis for an act is not a purely formal one inasmuch as a different decision-making procedure may affect the determination of the content of the act adopted.[48] This will be the case, for example, where a Treaty article requiring the Council to decide by unanimity rather than by qualified majority is wrongly used.[49]

The decision-making procedure and any limitation as to the legislative instruments which may be used determine the horizontal allocation of powers among the Union institutions according to which 'each institution shall act within the limits of the powers conferred on it in the Treaties, and in conformity with the procedures, conditions and objectives set out in them' (Article 13(2) TEU). At the same time, this allocation of powers influences the vertical relationship between the Union and the Member States. Where the decision-making procedure requires there to be a unanimous vote in the Council, each Member State has a right of veto. Where an institution is entitled to adopt a regulation, it may restrict the power of the Member States to a greater degree than where it is empowered only to adopt directives, since, in principle, a directive leaves the Member States with more latitude than a regulation.

5.013 **Choice of legal basis.** Given the consequences of the legal basis in terms of substantive competence, decision-making procedure, and appropriate legislative instruments, the choice of the correct legal basis is of constitutional importance.[50] An institution may not simply choose the Treaty provision it deems most fortuitous in terms of scope or procedure for realizing the objective pursued. The choice of legal basis for an act must be 'based on objective factors which are amenable to judicial review'.[51] In this respect the Court refers systematically to the aim and content of the measure.[52] The mere fact that a Treaty provision

---

[46] See the lists of instruments in Articles 218 and 288 TFEU and the discussion of acts of the institutions and bodies, para. 27-001 *et seq.*, *infra*.
[47] C-370/07, *Commission v Council*, 2009, para. 48, with case note by Heliskoski (2011) CMLRev 555–67; C-244/17, *Commission v Council*, 2018, paras 29–30 and 35–7, with a case note by Van Elsuwege and Van der Loo (2019) CMLRev 1333–54; See the discussion of decision-making in para. 17-003 *et seq.*, *infra*.
[48] See, e.g., 45/86, *Commission v Council*, 1987, para. 12; 68/86, *United Kingdom v Council*, 1988, para. 6; 131/86, *United Kingdom v Council*, 1988, para. 11.
[49] e.g. C-211/01, *Commission v Council*, 2003, para. 52; C-244/17, *Commission v Council*, 2018, paras 34–47.
[50] Opinion 2/00, *Carthagena Protocol*, 2001, para. 5; C-370/07, *Commission v Council*, 2009, paras 46–9; Opinion 1/08, *General Agreement on Trade in Services*, 2009, para. 110.
[51] 45/86, *Commission v Council*, 1987, para. 11; C-263/14, *Parliament v Council*, 2016, para. 43, with a case note by Sánchez-Tabernero (2017) CMLRev 899–920; C-482/17, *Czech Republic v European Parliament and Council*, 2019, para. 31.
[52] C-300/89, *Commission v Council*, 1991, para. 10; C-482/17, *Czech Republic v European Parliament and Council*, 2019, para. 31. For the practical interpretation of the 'objective factors', see Van Nuffel, *De rechtsbescherming van nationale overheden in het Europees recht* (Kluwer, 2000), 180–211.

has already served as the legal basis for a similar act in the past does not imply *ipso facto* that a new act must be based on that same legal basis, as the legal basis is to be determined for each act specifically on the basis of its objective and content.[53] Nevertheless, the legal framework within which new rules are situated may be taken into account, in particular in so far as that framework is capable of shedding light on the purpose of those rules.[54] In the case of an act amending existing rules, it is therefore important to take into account, for the purposes of identifying its legal basis, the existing rules which it amends and, in particular, their objective and content.[55] In an area in which the Union legislature has already coordinated the Member States' laws, it should in any event be able to adapt the existing Union legislation to changes in circumstances or advances in knowledge, having regard to its task of safeguarding the general interests and the overarching objectives of the Union recognized in the TFEU.[56]

Institutions, Member States, and to a lesser extent individuals have often challenged the legal basis of Union acts, with the parties adopting a stance reflecting their differing (political) interests. In such cases, the Court of Justice acts as a constitutional court, reviewing the horizontal and vertical division of powers within the Union.[57] Often the Court will be asked whether the Union legislature has used a correct legal basis. Exceptionally, the question will be whether the Treaties contain at all a sufficient legal basis for adopting a particular act. In this way, it annulled a directive of the European Parliament and the Council on tobacco advertising on the ground that those institutions had adopted a piece of legislation—at the Commission's proposal—which exceeded the bounds set by the Treaties for harmonization.[58]

Applicable legal basis. If a Union act can be based both on a general legal basis and a more specific one, that act must be taken on the basis of the more specific legal basis.[59] Sometimes an act may pursue the objective of a specific Treaty provision, while at the same have an impact on the functioning of the internal market (e.g. an environmental protection measure harmonizing product or production standards, thus facilitating the free movement of goods or undistorted competition). Often an act is composed of several components, regulating separate policy domains (e.g. a measure affecting both agriculture and other sectors). In all those cases where an act pursues a twofold purpose or has a twofold component and where one of those is identifiable as the main or predominant purpose or component whereas the

5.014

---

[53] C-81/13, *United Kingdom v Council*, 2014, para. 36.
[54] C-482/17, *Czech Republic v European Parliament and Council*, 2019, para. 32.
[55] Ibid., para. 42.
[56] C-620/18, *Hungary v European Parliament and Council*, 2020, paras 41–2; C-626/18, *Poland v European Parliament and Council*, 2020, paras 46–7.
[57] Lenaerts (n. 40, *supra*), Nos 309–311, at 357–62. See also De Baere and Van den Sanden, 'Interinstitutional Gravity and Pirates of the Parliament on Stranger Tides: the Continued Constitutional Significance of the Choice of Legal Basis in Post-Lisbon External Action' (2016) EuConst 85–113.
[58] C-376/98, *Germany v European Parliament and Council*, 2000; see commentaries by Mortelmans and van Ooik, 'Het Europese verbod op tabaksreclame: verbetering van de interne markt of verbetering van de volksgezondheid?' (2001) AAe 114–30; Hervey, 'Up in Smoke? Community (Anti-)tobacco Law and Policy' (2001) ELRev 101–25; Cornides, 'Eine Richtlinie löst sich in Rauch auf' (2001) ZfRV 130–5; Usher (2001) CMLRev 1519–43; Gosalbo Bono, 'L'arrêt "tabac" ou l'apport de la Cour de justice au débat sur la délimitation de compétences' (2001) RTDE 790–808; Amtenbrink and Appeldoorn, 'Is er leven na het Tabaksreclamearrest?' (2000) SEW 413–20; Barents, 'De tabaksrichtlijn in rook opgegaan' (2000) NTER 327–31.
[59] C-490/10, *European Parliament v Council*, 2012, para. 44; C-48/14, *European Parliament v Council*, 2015, paras 36–7.

other is merely incidental, the act must be taken on the basis of the Treaty provision that is most closely linked to the main or predominant purpose or component. This is the 'centre of gravity' criterion. For instance, if the harmonization of national legislations is only an incidental effect of an act that primarily pursues a different objective, then this act must be taken on the basis of the Treaty provision that corresponds to the main objective or the predominant component.[60] Conversely, a general Treaty article such as Article 114 TFEU offers a sufficient legal basis for a measure aimed at harmonizing national legislations, even if this measure pursues secondary objectives that are covered by other Treaty provisions.[61] The same applies in respect of the external competences of the Union: international agreements relating to the common commercial policy, development cooperation, or environmental protection all find their legal basis in the Treaty provisions that correspond to the main or predominant objective or component of the agreement.[62]

Before the Treaty of Lisbon, the 'centre of gravity' was also used as the criterion to determine whether a measure had to be taken on the basis of the EC Treaty or rather on the basis of Title V (CFSP) or Title VI (PJSS) of the EU Treaty.[63] In the current Treaties the criterion continues to apply in order to delineate, pursuant to Article 40 TEU, the common foreign and security policy (CFSP) and the other competences of the Union; again, the test is whether the act has as its main objective or predominant component the execution of the CFSP or else relates to other policy domains.[64]

5.015 **Multiple legal bases** If the envisaged Union act pursues at the same time several objectives that are intrinsically linked, without one being secondary to the others, then the act must be based on the different corresponding Treaty provisions taken together.[65] The use of a multiple legal basis is however excluded when the decision-making procedures prescribed by the relevant Treaty provisions are incompatible,[66] and/or when combining the legal bases is liable to undermine the Parliament's rights.[67] If no Treaty provision can be found that supports the act as a whole, the act must be split and the various components must each be adopted separately on the basis of the appropriate Treaty provision.

---

[60] See, for instance, 68/86, *United Kingdom v Council*, 1988, paras 14–16; C-70/88, *European Parliament v Council*, 1991, paras 16–18; C-338/01, *Commission v Council*, 2004, para. 55.
[61] C-377/98, *Netherlands v European Parliament and Council*, 2001, paras 27–8; C-491/01, *British American Tobacco (Investments) and Imperial Tobacco*, 2002, paras 93–4.
[62] Opinion 2/00, *Protocol van Cartagena*, 2001, paras 22–44 (environmental protection); C-377/12, *Commission v. Council*, 2014, para. 34. See Broberg and Holdgaard, 'Demarcating the Union's Development Cooperation Policy after Lisbon: Commission v. Council (Philippines PCFA)' (2015) CMLRev 547; Govaere, 'Multi-faceted Single Legal Personality and a Hidden Horizontal Pillar: EU External Relations Post-Lisbon' (2011) CYELS 87.
[63] See, e.g., C-440/05, *Commission v Council*, 2007, paras 71–3; C-91/05, *Commission v Council*, 2008, paras 73–4.
[64] C-263/14, *Parliament v Council*, 2016, para. 43. See , 'The Choice of Legal Basis and the Principle of Consistency in the Procedure for Conclusion of International Agreements in CFSP Contexts: Parliament v. Council (Pirate-Transfer Agreement with Tanzania)' (2017) CMLRev 899.
[65] 165/87, *Commission v Council*, 1988, para. 11; C-155/07, *Parliament v Council*, 2008, paras 34–6. See, e.g., Opinion 1/15, *Draft agreement between Canada and the European Union on the transfer and processing of Passenger Name Record data*, 2017, paras 95–118.
[66] C-130/10, *European Parliament v Council*, 2012, paras 42–5. See De Baere, 'From "Don't Mention the Titanium Dioxide Judgment" to "I Mentioned it Once, But I Think I Got Away with it All Right": Reflections on the Choice of Legal Basis in EU External Relations after the Legal Basis for Restrictive Measures Judgment"' (2013) CYELS 537.
[67] C-178/03, *Commission v European Parliament and Council*, 2006, paras 57–9, with a case note by Koutrakos (2007) CMLRev 171.

In the 'Titanium Dioxide' judgment, for instance, the Court decided that a Council Directive pertaining to the harmonization of programs aimed at diminishing and ultimately eliminating pollution caused by waste produced by the titanium dioxide industry was, according to its aim and content as they appear from its actual wording, indissociably concerned with both the protection of the environment pursuant to Article 130 S EEC [*now Article 192 TFEU*] and the elimination of disparities in conditions of competition, thus forming a harmonizing measure in the sense of Article 100 A EEC [*now Article 114 TFEU*]. Combining those legal bases was impossible because that would undo the participation rights granted to the European Parliament pursuant to Article 100 A EEC (which at the time provided for decision-making through the cooperation procedure). The Court thus deemed Article 100 A EEC to be the correct legal basis for the entire Directive and gave priority to the legal basis that ensured the greatest right of participation for the European Parliament in the legislative process.[68]

In order to determine whether decision-making procedures in various Treaty provisions are compatible, the Court will first look at the impact the combination of legal bases has on the participation rights of the European Parliament. Accordingly, the Court does accept the use of a dual legal basis when combining the procedural requirements of both Treaty provisions still results in the widest possible participation of the Parliament.[69] Furthermore, the Court considers the requirement of unanimity in the Council incompatible with a procedure that provides for qualified majority in the Council. For this reason Article 114 TFEU, which provides for decision-making by qualified majority, cannot be combined with the Articles 113 TFEU or 115 TFEU, which require unanimity.[70] Likewise, a Treaty provision providing for the use of the ordinary legislative procedure cannot be combined with a Treaty provision imposing unanimity in the Council.[71] The compatibility of the decision-making procedures must, however, not be examined when a specific legal basis in a Treaty provision is to be combined with the supplementary legal basis of Article 352 TFEU.[72]

Sanction. A Union act which has not been based on the correct legal basis is invalid and can be annulled, even when a legal basis is available on the basis of which the act could have been taken. However, an argument contesting the legal basis of an act may have only formal significance where the legal basis argued for does not entail any stricter procedural requirements than the one on which the act is actually founded.[73] If the choice of another legal basis has no effect on the procedure followed for the adoption of the act or its content the dispute will not result in annulment of the act.[74] Moreover, an error as to the legal basis will not affect the validity of the act in question where the persons affected enjoyed all of the procedural guarantees which may have been applicable and the error did not have any adverse

5.016

---

[68] C-300/89, *Commission v Council*, 1991, paras 17–25.
[69] C-491/01, *British American Tobacco (Investments) and Imperial Tobacco*, 2002, paras 103–11; C-178/03, *Commission v European Parliament and Council*, 2006, para. 59.
[70] C-338/01, *Commission v Council*, 2004, para. 58. See Klamert, 'Conflicts of Legal Basis: No Legality and No Basis but a Bright Future under the Lisbon Treaty?' (2010) ELRev 497.
[71] C-130/10, *European Parliament v Council*, 2012, paras 45–8.
[72] C-166/07, *European Parliament v Council*, 2009, para. 69, with a case note by Corthaut, (2011) CMLRev 1271–96.
[73] 165/87, *Commission v Council*, 1988, para. 19; C-268/94, *Portugal v Council*, 1996, para. 79; C-491/01, *British American Tobacco (Investments) and Imperial Tobacco*, 2002, paras 97–8.
[74] e.g. C-184/02 and C-223/02, *Spain and Finland v European Parliament and Council*, 2004, paras 42–4; C-81/13, *United Kingdom v Council*, 2014, paras 65–7.

effect on their legal position.[75] The obligation to state the legal basis not only flows from the duty to state reasons, but is also grounded in the principles of legal certainty and conferral.[76] The failure to mention the legal basis will only be tolerated if the correct legal basis can nevertheless unambiguously be determined on the basis of other elements.[77]

B. Competences distinguished according to the legal basis

5.017 **Distinction depending on legal basis.** In accordance with Article 5(2) TEU, the Union shall only act within the limits of the competences conferred upon it by the Member States in the Treaties to attain the objectives set out therein. The Union exercises the competences conferred upon it, first and foremost, when its action falls, expressly or impliedly, within the scope of one or more specific Treaty provisions. In addition, the Union may act outside the scope of specific Treaty provisions where such action is necessary to attain the 'objectives set out [in the Treaties]'. This refers to the 'flexibility clause' laid down in Article 352 TFEU.

1. Competences conferred expressly or impliedly by the Treaties

5.018 **Specific or general legal basis.** Action by the Union is founded, in principle, on a 'specific' provision of the Treaties which confers the competence to act. Part Three of the TFEU confers competence on the Union to act in various areas such as customs cooperation (Article 33 TFEU); agriculture (Article 38 *et seq.* TFEU); transport (Article 90 TFEU); employment (Article 145 TFEU); education, vocational training, youth, and sport (Article 165 *et seq.* TFEU); culture (Article 167 TFEU); public health (Article 168 TFEU); common commercial policy (Article 206 *et seq.* TFEU). The competence to act is defined by the list of its objectives and the means that may be employed in order to attain them.[78] The objectives and means mentioned act as the demarcation of competence conferred on the Union by the Treaty provision in question. Some Treaty articles delineate the competences they confer on the Union even further, and authorize the Union to act solely to the extent that it respects specific policy prerogatives of the Member States[79] or that there is no harmonization of national laws and regulations.[80]

The Treaties also contain 'general' provisions empowering the Union to adopt the 'measures for the approximation of the provisions laid down by law, regulation, or administrative action in Member States which have, as their object, the establishment and functioning of

---

[75] T-213/00, *CMA CGM and Others v Commission*, 2003, paras 65–103.
[76] C-370/07, *Commission v Council*, 2009, paras 38, 39, and 46.
[77] 45/86, *Commission v Council*, 1987, para. 9; T-70/99, *Alpharma v Council*, 2002, paras 110–21.
[78] cf. 242/87, *Commission v Council*, 1989, paras 6–37.
[79] See, e.g., the areas reserved to the Member States in Article 165(1) (content of teaching and organization of education systems) and Article 166(1) (content and organization of vocational training) TFEU. See in this regard, Van Nuffel (n. 52, *supra*), at 102–21. See also the areas in which the application of certain legal bases is precluded, particularly Article 153(4) (fundamental principles of national social security systems) and (5) (pay, the right of association, the right to strike, and the right to impose lock-outs), and Article 173(3), second subpara. (tax provisions and provisions relating to the rights and interests of employed persons) TFEU.
[80] See Article 19(2) (action to combat discrimination); Article 149 (employment); Article 153(2), first subpara., indent (a) (social policy); Article 165(4) (education); Article 166(3) (vocational training); Article 167(5) (culture); Article 168(5) (public health); Article 173(3) (industry); Article 195(2) (tourism); Article 196(2) (civil protection); and Article 197(2) (administrative cooperation) TFEU. As far as the external powers of the Union are concerned, this is confirmed in Article 207(6) (common commercial policy) TFEU.

the internal market' (Article 114(1) TFEU) or to issue, in any field, 'directives for the approximation of such laws, regulations or administrative provisions of the Member States as directly affect the establishment or functioning of the internal market' (Article 115 TFEU). Such provisions may not, however, be used as a legal basis in order to circumvent an express exclusion of harmonization laid down in specific articles of the Treaties.[81]

Implied competence. Where the Union acts on the basis of a specific or a general Treaty provision, it exercises its powers using the means and the procedure laid down in the Treaty provision concerned. Some Treaty provisions do not expressly provide for all the necessary means in order to attain the objectives of the competence *ratione materiae* in question. In such cases, the Court of Justice has recognized that it is implicit in the Union competence that additional means may be used in order to achieve the objectives. **5.019**

In this way, it fell to the Court to determine whether the Community had the power to negotiate and conclude the European Agreement concerning the work of crews of vehicles engaged in international road transport (AETR).[82] By judgment of 31 March 1971, it held that although the Treaty provisions empowering the Community to take measures within the framework of the common transport policy 'do not expressly confer on the Community authority to enter into international agreements, nevertheless the bringing into force ... of Regulation No 543/69 of the Council on the harmonization of certain social legislation relating to road transport ... necessarily vested in the Community power to enter into any agreements with third countries relating to the subject-matter governed by that regulation'.[83] Whenever the Treaties have conferred on the Union internal competences for the purpose of attaining a specific objective, the Union has authority to enter into the international commitments necessary for the attainment of this objective even in the absence of an express provision concerning the matter.[84]

Because an implied competence goes to the limits of the principle of conferral laid down in Article 5(1) TEU, it must be applied strictly.[85] The Union is entitled to rely on an implied competence only where it is necessary to ensure the practical effect of the Union competence at issue.[86] The close relationship between the implied competence and the express competence that it supplements must be shown by objective evidence which the Court of Justice can review. Thus, the Court considered that the Union's competence to issue legislation in fields such as environmental protection or maritime safety entails the competence to require the Member States to introduce criminal sanctions in order to ensure that the rules that it lays down in that field are fully effective, that is, when the application of effective, proportionate, and dissuasive criminal penalties by the competent national authorities is

---

[81] C-376/98, *Germany v European Parliament and Council*, 2000, para. 79 (for commentaries, see n. 58, *supra*).
[82] 22/70, *Commission v Council*, 1971. The acronym 'AETR' stands for 'Accord européen sur les transport routiers' (European Agreement on Road Transport ('ERTA')).
[83] Ibid., para. 28.
[84] Opinion 1/76, *Draft Agreement establishing a European laying-up fund for inland waterway vessels*, 1977, para. 3. See Chamon, 'Implied Exclusive Powers in the ECJ'S Post-Lisbon Jurisprudence: The Continued Development of the ERTA Doctrine' (2018) CMLRev 1101–41; Conway, 'Conflicts of Competence Norms in EU Law and the Legal Reasoning of the ECJ' (2010) GLJ 966. See also the discussion of the external powers of the Union: para. 10-037, *infra*.
[85] T-496/11, *United Kingdom v ECB*, 2015, para. 105, with a case note by Marjosola (2015) CMLRev 1491.
[86] C-295/90 *European Parliament v Council*, 1992, paras 18–20; T-240/04, *France v Commission*, 2007, para. 37; T-143/06, *MTZ Polyfilms v Council*, 2009, para. 47. See also 9/74, *Casagrande*, 1974, paras 4–6; 281/85, 283/85–285/85, and 287/85, *Germany, France, Netherlands, Denmark and United Kingdom v Commission*, 1987.

an 'essential measure' for combating serious offences.[87] More recently, the General Court did not, however, recognize that the European Central Bank (ECB) had an implicit competence to regulate the activity of securities clearing infrastructures since Article 129(3) TFEU expressly enables the Union legislature to grant that competence to the European Central Bank, which the legislature had not yet done.[88]

The Treaty provision providing for the express competence with which the implied competence is associated determines the decision-making procedure which the Union has to follow in exercising that competence. Accordingly, whenever the Union legislates on the right of residence of students and dependants pursuant to an implied competence contained in Article 18 TFEU, which empowers the Union to adopt rules designed to prohibit any discrimination on grounds of nationality, it has to do so in accordance with the procedure prescribed by the second para. of Article 18 TFEU.[89]

2. Supplementary competence to achieve Union objectives (Article 352 TFEU)

5.020 **Flexibility clause.** Article 352 TFEU establishes a supplementary legal basis for the Union to take the appropriate measures 'if action by the Union should prove necessary, within the framework of the policies defined in the Treaties, to attain one of the objectives set out in the Treaties, and the Treaties have not provided the necessary powers'.[90] Consequently, action pursuant to Article 352 is justified only where no other Treaty provision confers on the Union the necessary express or implied competence.[91] The Union may refer to the supplementary legal basis in combination with other specific Treaty provisions where these provisions do not confer on the Union the necessary powers to attain the objectives pursued.[92]

---

[87] C-176/03, *Commission v Council*, 2005, paras 48–51, with case notes by Tobler (2006) CMLRev 835–54; van Ooik (2006) SEW 78–85 and Apps (2006) ColJEL 625–37. See further White, 'Harmonisation of Criminal Law under the First Pillar' (2006) ELRev 81–92. By contrast, the Court held that the (then) Community was not competent to determine the type and level of the criminal penalties to be applied: C-440/05, *Commission v Council*, 2007, paras 66–70. For an example, see Directive 2008/99/EC of the European Parliament and of the Council of 19 November 2008 on the protection of the environment through criminal law, OJ 2008 L328/28. The Lisbon Treaty has provided for a specific Union competence to establish minimum rules with regard to the definition of criminal offences and sanctions to ensure the effective implementation of Union harmonization measures (see Article 83(2) TFEU). This does not take away that outside the ambit of Article 83(2) TFEU a Union competence may still entail the implied power to require the Member States to introduce criminal sanctions in order to ensure the effective implementation of Union rules.

[88] T-496/11, *United Kingdom v ECB*, 2015, para. 105. See Marjosola, 'Missing Pieces in the Patchwork of EU Financial Stability Regime? The Case of Central Counterparties' (2015) CMLRev 1491.

[89] cf. C-295/90, *European Parliament v Council*, 1992, paras 18–20.

[90] Article 308 EC provided for a legal basis where action should prove necessary 'to attain, in the course of the operation of the common market, one of the objectives of the Community and this Treaty has not provided the necessary powers'.

[91] 45/86, *Commission v Council*, 1987, para. 13; C-436/03, *European Parliament v Council*, 2006, paras 36–46; C-166/07, *European Parliament v Council*, 2009, paras 40–1. See also 242/87, *Commission v Council*, 1989, in which the Court of Justice dismissed an application for annulment of the decision by which the Council had adopted the European Community action scheme for the mobility of university students (Erasmus) on the basis of Articles 128 and 235 EEC (Article 235 EEC being the predecessor of Article 308 EC, itself renumbered into Article 352 TFEU). The Court held that the dual legal basis of Articles 128 and 235 was lawful inasmuch as the decision also concerned scientific research. This fell outside the scope of Article 128, which—as it was worded in the EEC Treaty—authorized the Council to adopt 'a common vocational training policy'. The Council adopted a second Erasmus decision solely on the basis of Article 128 EEC following the omission of the research aspect from the Commission proposal. Cf. C-51/89, C-90/89 and C-94/89, *United Kingdom and Others v Council*, 1991. For the extension of Community competence made possible by Article 308 EC, see Bungenberg, 'Dynamische Integration, Art. 308 und die Forderung nach dem Kompetenzkatalog' (2000) EuR 819–900.

[92] C-402/05 P and C-415/05 P, *Kadi and Al Barakaat International Foundation*, 2008, paras 211-214; C-166/07, *European Parliament v Council*, 2009, para. 69. See Konstadinides, 'Drawing the line between Circumvention and Gap-Filling: An Exploration of the Conceptual Limits of the Treaty's Flexibility Clause' (2012) YEL 227.

However, Article 352 may not be used to supplement a specific Treaty provision that limits Union competence by excluding coverage of certain policy areas or the use of certain instruments. Measures based on Article 352 may therefore not entail harmonization of Member States' laws or regulations in cases where the Treaties exclude such harmonization (see Article 352(3)).

In addition, the action must be necessary to attain one of the objectives set out in the Treaties. This necessity requirement is amenable to judicial review. In a 1996 Opinion the Court of Justice unambiguously held that since the institutional system of the Union is based on the principle of conferral, Article 352 TFEU cannot be used as the legal basis for the adoption of provisions whose effect would, in substance, be to amend the Treaties without following the procedure that the latter provide for that purpose.[93]

Moreover, it is explicitly stated that recourse to Article 352 TFEU is not possible for the purpose of attaining objectives pertaining to the CFSP and that action based on Article 352 must respect the limits on the Union's competence set out in the second para. of Article 40 TEU, that is to say, may not affect the procedures and powers foreseen in the TEU with respect to the CFSP (see Article 352(4)).[94]

Article 352 TFEU creates a supplementary competence and does not contain any obligation for the Union to use it.[95]

Procedure. Article 352 TFEU lays down the precise decision-making procedure which the Union must follow whenever it exercises this supplementary competence. The Council must act unanimously on a proposal from the Commission and after obtaining the consent of the European Parliament (Article 352(1)). Before the entry into force of the Treaty of Lisbon, the European Parliament was only consulted in this connection.[96] Where recourse is made to Article 352 TFEU in combination with other Treaty provisions, the relevant procedural requirements are to be combined. Contrary to its case law relating to the use of a dual legal basis flowing from several specific Treaty provisions, the Court thus allows for the unanimity requirement of Article 352 TFEU to be combined with other procedures—such as the ordinary legislative procedure—that would otherwise provide for qualified majority voting.[97] The reason for this is that the Court applies the principle of conferral strictly, meaning that all provisions of a Union act must find a legal basis in the Treaties, some of

5.021

---

[93] Opinion 2/94, *Accession by the Communities to the Convention for the Protection of Human Rights and Fundamental Freedoms*, 1996, para. 30 (Opinion holding that the accession of the Community to the ECHR would exceed the limits of Article 308 EC [*now Article 352 TFEU*], cf. para. 25-015, *infra*). See also Declaration (No 42), annexed to the Lisbon Treaty, on Article 352 TFEU (OJ 2010 C83/351).

[94] See also Declaration (No. 41), annexed to the Lisbon Treaty, on Article 352 of the TFEU (OJ 2010 C83/350), according to which an action based on Article 352 TFEU can relate to the Union's objectives set out in Article 3(2), 3(3), and—in the framework of non-CFSP external competences—Article 3(5), but cannot only pursue the objectives set out in Article 3(1) TEU ('to promote peace, [the Union's] values and the well-being of its peoples'). In the same Declaration, the Intergovernmental Conference recalls that in accordance with Article 31(1) TEU, no legislative acts may be adopted in the area of CFSP.

[95] 22/70, *Commission v Council*, 1971, para. 95 ('Although Article 235 [*now Article 352 TFEU*] empowers the Council to take any '*appropriate* measures'... it does not create an obligation, but confers on the Council an option, failure to exercise which cannot affect the validity' of a decision); C-370/12, *Pringle*, 2012, para. 67.

[96] See Article 308 EC.

[97] C-166/07, *European Parliament v Council*, 2009, para. 69 (combination of unanimity voting with the co-decision procedure required by Article 159 EC [*now Article 175 TFEU*]). See Corthaut, 'Case C-166/07, European Parliament v. Council of the European Union—Institutional Pragmatism or Constitutional Mayhem?' (2011) CMLRev 1271–96.

them in specific Treaty provisions, others in Article 352 TFEU. This is necessary to safeguard the division of competence between the Union and its Member States, the primary purpose of the legal basis requirement.

In the same way as ex Article 308 EC, Article 352 TFEU does not specify any particular types of legislative measure ('the appropriate measures'), as a result of which all means are possible, and recourse will never have to be made to implied powers. However, the Lisbon Treaty introduced the obligation for the Commission to draw national parliaments' attention to proposals based on Article 352 (Article 352(2)).

C. Exclusive and non-exclusive competence

5.022 **Classification.** Depending on their relationship to the competences of the Member States, the Union's competences are subdivided into exclusive and non-exclusive competences (see Articles 2–4 TFEU). In areas of exclusive competence, only the Union may legislate and adopt legally binding acts. Member States may act only if so empowered by the Union or for the implementation of Union acts (Article 2(1) TFEU). In areas where the Union is not exclusively competent, both the Union and the Member States may act with a view to attaining the objectives of the Treaties. The Treaties distinguish between two types of non-exclusive competence. On the one hand, there are areas in which the Union 'shares' competence with the Member States (Articles 2(2) and 4 TFEU). In areas of 'shared competence' Member States may act to the extent that the Union has not exercised its competence; they lose their competence in so far as the Union actually exercises its own competence (the pre-emption principle; see para. 5-026, *infra*). On the other hand, there are areas in which the Union has competence to carry out actions to support, coordinate, or supplement the actions of Member States (Articles 2(5) and 6 TFEU). Such actions may not supersede the competences of the Member States in these areas.

In this way, the Treaty of Lisbon introduced, for the first time, a clear definition of the different categories of competence in the Treaties (see Article 2 TFEU). Moreover, it added lists of the most important areas of competence by category of competence (Articles 3 to 6 TFEU). Areas not listed fall under the general category of 'shared competence' (Article 4(1) TFEU).

5.023 **Exclusive competences.** Exclusive competences are those which have been definitively and irreversibly forfeited by the Member States by reason of their straightforward transfer to the Union. In that event, Member States may act only if so empowered by the Union or to implement measures adopted by the Union. Article 3 TFEU sums up the areas in which the Union has exclusive competence. These are: (1) the customs union; (2) the establishing of the competition rules necessary for the functioning of the internal market; (3) monetary policy for the Member States whose currency is the euro; (4) the conservation of marine biological resources under the common fisheries policy; and (5) common commercial policy (see Article 3(1) TFEU).

Article 3(1) TFEU confirms in essence the generally accepted exclusive competences of the Union. Before the Treaty of Lisbon introduced this list of exclusive Union competences, the Court of Justice had already established the exclusive nature of the Union's competence in two fields on the basis of the wording and the context of the Treaty provisions concerned. The first was the competence to conduct a common commercial policy vis-à-vis third countries with regard to trade in goods.[98] The second was the Union's competence conferred by Article 102 of the 1972 Act of Accession to determine conditions for fishing with a view to ensuring protection of fishing grounds and the conservation of the biological resources of the sea.[99] In addition, two other areas were generally accepted to be exclusive Union competences, namely the Union's competence for the customs union[100] and the Union's monetary policy as regards the Member States participating in the third stage of Economic and Monetary Union[101] (see para. 9-033 *et seq.*, *infra*). Article 3(1) TFEU now adds the exclusive competence to establish the competition rules necessary for the functioning of the internal market (Article 3(1)(b) TFEU).[102] Moreover, as far as the common commercial policy is concerned, Article 3(1)(e) TFEU makes no distinction between goods and services, which means that, in contrast to the Court's pre-Lisbon case law, both are covered by the exclusive competence.

For its part, Article 3(2) TFEU confirms the case law of the Court of Justice by establishing an 'exclusive competence' for the Union to conclude an international agreement where its conclusion is provided for in a legislative act of the Union or is necessary to enable the Union to exercise its internal competence, or in so far as its conclusion may affect common rules or alter their scope (see para. 10-037, *infra*).

The Treaties preclude Member States from establishing enhanced cooperation between themselves in areas which fall within the exclusive competence of the Union (see Article 329(1) TFEU). Furthermore, the Union cannot transfer a field in which it has exclusive competence back to the Member States because the text of the Treaties itself definitively rules out competence on the part of the Member States.

Authorization. Where the Union has exclusive competence, any action by a Member State in the same field is *a priori* in conflict with the Treaties.

5.024

The fact that a particular competence is exclusive does not preclude the Union from delegating certain means of exercising that competence to the Member States (see Article 2(1) TFEU). In so doing, the Member States may act as agents of the Union pursuant to a 'specific authorization'.[103] In such a case, the Union specifies in what way and according

---

[98] Opinion 1/75, *Draft OECD Understanding on a Local Cost Standard*, 1975, 1363–5 (para. 5-023, *supra*); 41/76, *Donckerwolcke*, 1976, para. 32; Opinion 1/78, *International Agreement on Natural Rubber*,1979, paras 52–60; Opinion 2/91, *Convention No 170 of the International Labour Organisation concerning safety in the use of chemicals at work*, 1993, para. 8; C-347/03, *Regione autonoma Friuli-Venezia Giulia*, 2005, paras 71–83. See Rosas, 'EU External Relations: Exclusive Competence Revisited' (2015) Fordham ILJ 1073.

[99] 3–4/76 and 6/76, *Kramer*, 1976, paras 39–41; 804/79, *Commission v United Kingdom*, 1981, paras 17–18; Opinion 2/91 (n. 98, *supra*), para. 8.

[100] It was generally accepted that, as a result of the introduction of the common customs tariff, Article 26 EC on the customs union precluded any parallel competence on the part of the Member States.

[101] See also, post Lisbon, C-370/12, *Pringle*, 2012, paras 50 and 94, with a case note by De Witte and Beukers (2013) CMLRev 805. See Adam and Parras, 'The European Stability Mechanism through the Legal Meanderings of the Union's Constitutionalism: Comment on Pringle' (2013) ELRev 848.See also C-422/19 and C-423/19, *Dietrich*, 2021, paras 29-58.

[102] The exclusive character of the Union's competence to legislate in this matter does not affect the Member States' competence to implement the Union's rules on competition (see paras 9-014–9-015, *infra*) or to take legislative action themselves with respect to situations that fall outside the 'competition rules necessary for the functioning of the internal market' (thus, Articles 101 and 102 TFEU apply only if trade between Member States is affected: see paras 9-014–9-015, *infra*).

[103] 41/76, *Donckerwolcke*, 1976, para. 32.

96   VALUES, OBJECTIVES, AND PRINCIPLES ON UNION COMPETENCES

to what procedure the Member States are to act.[104] Accordingly, the Court of Justice was prepared in principle to accept Member States taking measures to preserve fish stocks 'as trustees of the common interest' since the Council had not yet formulated any policy following the entry into effect of Article 102 of the 1972 Act of Accession. They had to do so 'as part of a process of collaboration with the Commission and with due regard to the general task of supervision which [was given] to the Commission'.[105] The exclusive character of a Union competence would however be compromised if an 'authorization' were found to exist in an area in which the Union cannot take a position on the envisaged national measures.[106]

5.025   **Shared competences.** By means of a non-exhaustive list,[107] Article 4(2) TFEU enumerates the most important competences that the Union shares with the Member States: (1) internal market; (2) social policy, for the aspects defined in the TFEU;[108] (3) economic, social, and territorial cohesion; (4) agriculture and fisheries, excluding the conservation of marine biological resources; (5) environment; (6) consumer protection; (7) transport; (8) trans-European networks; (9) energy; (10) area of freedom, security, and justice; and (11) common safety concerns in public health matters for the aspects defined in the TFEU. Article 4(3) and (4) TFEU mentions other competences falling within the category of 'shared competences' with respect to which the Treaty expressly provides that the exercise of these competences by the Union 'shall not result in Member States being prevented from exercising theirs'. This applies to the areas of research, technological development, and space (Article 4(3) TFEU) and development cooperation, and humanitarian aid (Article 4(4) TFEU). These competences listed in Article 4(3) and (4) TFEU are also called 'parallel' competences.

Moreover, the Treaty mentions two other policy areas, for which no further classification is given. It concerns the coordination of the economic and employment policies of the Member States (Articles 2(3) and 5(1) and (2) TFEU) and the definition and implementation of a common foreign and security policy, including the progressive framing of a common defence policy (Article 2(4) TFEU). Since all competences outside the areas referred to in Articles 3 and 6 are shared by the Union with the Member States (see Article 4(1) TFEU), these two policy areas can only be classified as falling within the general category of shared competences.

---

[104] Lenaerts, 'Regulating the Regulatory Process: "Delegation of Powers" in the European Community' (1993) ELRev 23–49, in particular, 27–32.
[105] 804/79, *Commission v United Kingdom*, 1981, para. 30.
[106] See Lenaerts, 'Les répercussions des compétences de la Communauté européenne sur les compétences externes des Etats membres et la question de la "preemption"', in Demaret (ed.), *Relations extérieures de la Communauté européenne et marché intérieur: aspects juridiques et fonctionnels* (College of Europe/Story, 1988), 39, 47–54. For the 'specific authorization' by which Union export rules permit Member States to subject dual-use goods to export controls, see paras 10-005–10-006, *infra*. Another example is Council Decision 1999/405/EC of 10 June 1999 authorizing the Kingdom of Spain to accede to the Convention establishing the Inter-American Tropical Tuna Commission on a temporary basis (IATTC), OJ 1999 L155/37. Nevertheless, the Court went far in discovering an authorization in 174/84, *Bulk Oil*, 1986, paras 15–19 and 33 (authorization for the United Kingdom to prohibit oil exports to Israel inferred from the fact that there was no express prohibition of export restrictions in the EEC–Israel Agreement and that oil was excluded from the Council regulation establishing common rules for exports).
[107] Article 4(2) TFEU refers in this respect to 'the following principal areas'.
[108] See also Article 5(3) TFEU, which provides that the Union may take initiatives to ensure coordination of Member States' social policies.

In an area of shared competence, the Union may in principle repeal the Union measure, leaving the Member States in a position to exercise their powers in full again. The repeal must, however, accord with the objectives of the Treaty provision forming the legal basis of the measure and with the principle of subsidiarity (see para. 5-028, *infra*).

Pre-emption. In areas of shared competence the Member States may only exercise their competence to the extent that the Union has not exercised its competence.[109] The Member States may again exercise their competence to the extent that the Union has decided to cease exercising its competence (Article 2(2) TFEU). With this provision, the Lisbon Treaty codified the doctrine of pre-emption, according to which Member States lose their power to enact rules in an area of shared competence to the extent that the Union has exercised its competence.[110]

5.026

Once the Union has exercised its competence, national rules must give way to the Union's provision in so far as there is a conflict between them (primacy of Union law; see para. 23-010, *infra*). In accordance with the pre-emption doctrine, the Union's exercise of its competence in a given field will limit the Member State's competence to act to matters that have not yet been regulated by the Union. In any given case, it is to be determined to what extent Union action still leaves room for the Member States to legislate. Accordingly, the Court of Justice held in the *AETR* case that the Union's exercise of its competence relating to the common transport policy 'excludes the possibility of concurrent powers on the part of the Member States, since any steps taken outside the framework of the [Union] institutions would be incompatible with the unity of the common market and the uniform application of [Union] law'.[111] Depending upon the extent to which the Union exercises its competence to regulate a given matter, that exercise may confer upon it an 'exclusive nature'.[112] However, this does not alter the nature of the competence, which remains shared and is thus not exclusively transferred to the Union within the meaning of Article 2(1) TFEU.[113]

---

[109] For two examples where the Court of Justice upheld the Member States' competence to act in sensitive policy fields, see C-638/16 PPU, *X and X*, 2017, paras 40–4 (visas on humanitarian grounds); C-507/17, *Google*, 2019, paras 61–73 (territorial scope of dereferencing).

[110] Arena, 'The Doctrine of Union preemption in the EU Internal Market: Between Sein and Sollen' (2011) Col JEL 477; Schütze, 'Supremacy Without Pre-emption? The Very Slowly Emergent Doctrine of Community Pre-emption' (2006) CMLRev 1023–48; Cross, 'Pre-emption of Member State Law in the European Economic Community: A Framework for Analysis' (1992) CMLRev 447–72. For comparisons with the pre-emption principle in the constitutional law of the United States, see Lenaerts (n. 40, *supra*), Nos 436–468, at 525–566 (for the doctrine of pre-emption, see Nos 167–174, at 176–85).

[111] 22/70, *Commission v Council*, 1971, para. 31. See also Opinion 1/03, *New Lugano Convention on jurisdiction and the recognition and enforcement of judgments in civil and commercial matters*, 2006, paras 115–32 and the 'open skies' judgments discussed in para. 10-039, *infra*. See Baumé, 'Competence of the Community to Conclude the New Lugano Convention on Jurisdiction and the Recognition and Enforcement of Judgements in Civil and Commercial Matters: Opinion 1/03 of 7 February 2006' (2019) GLJ 681; Mengozzi, 'The EC External Competencies: From the ERTA Case to the Opinion in the Lugano Convention', in Maduro and Azoulai (eds), *The Past and Future of EU Law: The Classics of EU Law Revised on the 50th Anniversary of the Rome Treaty* (Hart Publishing, 2010), 127.

[112] Opinion 2/91, *Convention No 170 of the International Labour Organisation concerning safety in the use of chemicals at work*, 1993, para. 9; see also Opinion 1/94, *Agreement establishing the World Trade Organisation*, 1994, paras 72–105; Opinion 2/92, *Third Revised Decision of the OECD on national treatment*, 1995, paras 31–6 (para. 10-039, *infra*). See Chamon, 'Implied Exclusive Powers in the ECJ's Post-Lisbon Jurisprudence: The Continued Development of the ERTA Doctrine' (2018) CMLRev 1101; Dashwood, 'Mixity in the era of the Treaty of Lisbon', in Hillion and Koutrakos (eds), *Mixed Agreements Revisited: The EU and its Member States in the World* (Hart Publishing, 2010), 351.

[113] C-491/01, *British American Tobacco (Investments) and Imperial Tobacco*, 2002, para. 179 (competence to harmonize under Article 95 EC [*now Article 114 TFEU*] is not exclusive). For these so-called *compétences exclusives par exercice*, see also Lenaerts and van Ypersele (n. 40, *supra*), at 20–8.

So as to limit the instances where the Union's action in a given area would have the effect of excluding the Member States' power to still enact rules in that area, the Lisbon Treaty has specified in a Protocol on the exercise of shared competence that 'when the Union has taken action in a certain area, the scope of this exercise of competence only covers those elements governed by the Union act in question and therefore does not cover the whole area'.[114] Likewise, with respect to the areas of shared competence mentioned in Articles 4(3) and 4(4) TFEU (research, technological development, space, development cooperation, and humanitarian aid), the TFEU provides that 'the exercise of that competence shall not result in Member States being prevented from exercising theirs'.

5.027 **Supporting competences.** Finally, the Treaties mention areas where the Union is competent to 'support, coordinate or complement the actions of the Member States, without thereby superseding their competence in these areas' (Article 2(5) TFEU). The areas in question are: (1) protection and improvement of human health; (2) industry; (3) culture; (4) tourism; (5) education, vocational training, youth, and sport; (6) civil protection; and (7) administrative cooperation (Article 6 TFEU). It follows from Article 4(1) TFEU that these areas are not regarded as 'shared competences' in the sense of Article 2(2) TFEU. Within this distinct category of 'supporting' competences, the Union may take action but its legally binding acts may not entail harmonization of Member States' laws or regulations (Article 2(5) TFEU). The provision according to which the Union's action in these areas shall not supersede Member States' competence indicates that Union measures may generally not restrict the Member States' regulating power in the areas concerned (no application of the pre-emption doctrine). Yet, in accordance with the principles of primacy of Union law and of sincere cooperation, Member States are not to adopt measures putting at risk the uniform application of the acts adopted by the Union in the areas concerned.

IV. The Principle of Subsidiarity

A. Role played by the principle

5.028 **Function.** As set out in Article 5(1) TEU, the exercise of Union competences is governed by the principle of subsidiarity, which is defined in Article 5(3) TEU. That principle arose in a socio-economic context as limiting intervention by the authorities to such matters that the persons or groups concerned could not deal with themselves. Later, it acquired the additional meaning of an obligation for the authorities whenever taking action to weigh up the different levels of authority at which action may be taken.[115] The EU Treaty introduced the principle in this latter meaning into the EC Treaty as a reaction to a degree of dissatisfaction in some Member States about the way in which the Community was exercising its powers.[116]

---

[114] Protocol (No. 25), annexed to the TEU and TFEU, on the exercise of shared competence, OJ 2010 C83/307.
[115] For the origin of the subsidiarity principle, see Craig, 'Subsidiarity: A Political and Legal Analysis' (2012) JCMS 72; Millon-Delsol, *L'Etat subsidiaire. Ingérence et non-ingérence de l'Etat: le principe de subsidiarité aux fondements de l'histoire européenne* (Presses Universitaires de France, 1992); Wilke and Wallace, *Subsidiarity: Approaches to Power-sharing in the European Community* (Royal Institute of International Affairs, 1990); Adonis and Jones, 'Subsidiarity and the European Community's Constitutional Future' (1991) Staatswissenschaft und Staatspraxis 179–96.
[116] Earlier, the Single European Act had introduced a reference to the principle when introducing an express competence for the Community with regard to the environment, in the framework of which Article 130r(4) EEC

Above all, following the extension of qualified majority voting in the Council, there was a growing feeling that the Member States might also be caught unaware by Community action markedly restricting their freedom to frame their own policies in areas not directly targeted by that action. In federal Member States, moreover, the constituent entities felt the loss of 'national' sovereignty as an encroachment of the Community on their powers, whilst they themselves had no say in the matter.

As formulated in Article 5(3) TEU, the principle of subsidiarity acts as a filter between the existence of the Union's competence and the possibility of actually exercising that competence. When the Union is competent, it may exercise that competence only in accordance with the principle of subsidiarity. This principle thus constitutes a guide as to how competence at Union level must be exercised. The implementation of the principle is further specified by a protocol to the Treaties on the application of the principles of subsidiarity and proportionality (the 'Subsidiarity Protocol').[117]

B. The requirements of subsidiarity

Definition. Wherever the Union does not possess exclusive competence, it may take action only '*if* and *in so far* as the objectives of the proposed action cannot be sufficiently achieved by the Member States ... but can rather, by reason of the scale or effects of the proposed action, be better achieved at Union level' (Article 5(3), first subpara. TEU, emphasis added). This definition tests Union action against both a decentralization criterion and an efficiency criterion: the Union acts *only if* the proposed objectives cannot be sufficiently achieved by the Member States and if they can be *better* achieved by the Union. The expression 'in so far' in Article 5(3) TEU imposes a further proportionality requirement (see para. 5-036, *infra*). Union action will conflict with the principle of subsidiarity only where it can be shown that the objective sought can be achieved just as well by the Member States either by individual action or by cooperation between the Member States concerned.[118] In this regard, the ability of the Member States to act 'either at central level or at regional and local level' must be taken into account (Article 5(3), first subpara. TEU).

5.029

In examining whether a (proposed) Union action respects the principle of subsidiarity, the action must be reviewed against the objectives that the Union purports to achieve.

---

laid down the principle that the Community was to take action relating to the environment 'to the extent to which the objectives ... can be attained better at Community level than at the level of the individual Member States'. The EU Treaty deleted this specific mention of the principle of subsidiarity when the principle was set out in general terms in Article 5 EC for all Community competences. With only minor changes, the Treaty of Lisbon retained the definition of the subsidiarity principle in Article 5(3) TEU.

[117] Protocol (No. 2), annexed to the TEU and TFEU, on the application of the principles of subsidiarity and proportionality (OJ 2010 C83/206), inserted by the Lisbon Treaty to replace Protocol (No. 30), annexed to the EC Treaty by the Treaty of Amsterdam, on the application of the principles of subsidiarity and proportionality, OJ 1997 C340/105, which was on its turn based on the 'overall approach to the application by the Council of the subsidiarity principle and Article 3b [*now Article 5(3) TEU*]' (1992) 12 EC Bull. points I.15–I.22, adopted by the European Council held in Edinburgh on 11 and 12 December 1992.

[118] However, the *acquis communautaire* would be affected if the Union had to justify its action against possible intergovernmental action on the part of all Member States: Lenaerts and van Ypersele, 'Le principe de subsidiarité et son contexte: étude de l'article 3 B du traité CE' (1994) CDE 13–30 and 35–44, 45–57; Van Nuffel (see n. 52, *supra*), at 394–6.

The initial Protocol on the application of the principles of subsidiarity and proportionality set out concrete guidelines for applying the principle of subsidiarity.[119] According to that Protocol, the following issues needed to be considered in examining whether the subsidiarity principle was satisfied: (1) whether the issue under consideration had transnational aspects which could not be satisfactorily regulated by action by Member States; (2) whether actions by Member States alone or lack of Community action would conflict with the requirements of the Treaty (such as the need to correct distortions of competition or avoid disguised restrictions on trade or strengthen economic and social cohesion) or would otherwise significantly damage Member States' interests; and (3) whether action at Community level would produce clear benefits by reason of its scale or effects compared with action at the level of the Member States.[120] These guidelines have not been taken over in the Subsidiarity Protocol attached to the Treaties by the Treaty of Lisbon, yet they do describe situations in which Union action will easily meet the subsidiarity requirements. If Union action is tested against objectives such as the achievement of uniform or coherent rules or the equal treatment of EU citizens or legal persons, it is obvious that Union action will be more efficient than individual action by Member States or voluntary coordination of national policies. In such cases, the Court of Justice can but conclude that the objective sought by the Union or the matter dealt with is normally in itself such that national action would inevitably fall short (with the result that Union action is necessarily 'better'; see para. 5-033, *infra*).[121] Since the subsidiarity principle requires that the proposed action can, by reason of its scale or effects, be better achieved at the level of the Union in view of the objectives set by the Union, it is not intended to limit the Union's competence on the basis of the situation of any particular Member State taken individually.[122]

C. Application of the principle of subsidiarity

5.030 **Scope.** Article 5(3), first subpara. TEU requires the Union to comply with the principle of subsidiarity in 'areas which do not fall within its exclusive competence'. This applies equally to the first measure that the Union adopts and to existing measures where they are tightened (e.g. where a recommendation or a communication is replaced by a binding measure). In contrast, where the Union has exclusive competence, it does not have to take account of the principle of subsidiarity set out in Article 5(3), although it does have to comply with the principle of proportionality set out in Article 5(4) (see para. 5.039, *infra*).

5.031 **Institutional implementation.** The application of the principle of subsidiarity falls, in the first place, to the institutions of the Union, which must observe the provisions of the Protocol on the application of the principles of subsidiarity and proportionality (Article

---

[119] Protocol, annexed to the EC Treaty by the Treaty of Amsterdam, on the application of the principles of subsidiarity and proportionality (n. 117, *supra*).
[120] Ibid., point 5, second para. (reiterating the guidelines set out in the European Council's overall approach—n. 116, *supra*—point I.18).
[121] See C-58/08, *Vodafone*, 2010, paras 77–8; C-508/13, *Estonia v European Parliament and Council*, 2015, paras 47–8; C-358/14, *Poland v European Parliament and Council*, 2016, paras 115–22. For an example, see C-539/09, *Commission v Germany*, 2011, para. 84. See further para. 5-033, *infra*.
[122] See C-508/13, *Estonia v European Parliament and Council*, 2015, para. 53; C-358/14, *Poland v European Parliament and Council*, 2016, para. 119.

5(3), second subpara. TEU). In so far as Union legislation is concerned, the principle restricts the action of the European Parliament and the Council. When proposing legislative acts, the Commission must therefore already take into account the regional and local dimension of the action envisaged.[123] Any draft legislative act[124] must be justified with regard to the principles of subsidiarity and proportionality and should, therefore, contain a detailed statement making it possible to appraise compliance with the principles of subsidiarity and proportionality.[125] The Commission is also to report annually on the application of Article 5 TEU.[126]

Control by national parliaments. Since the Treaty of Lisbon, national parliaments are competent to control the application of the subsidiarity principle in accordance with the procedure laid down in the Subsidiarity Protocol (Article 5(3), second subpara. TEU).[127] This 'early warning system' complements parliaments' right to be informed about draft legislative acts pursuant to the Protocol on the role of national parliaments in the European Union (see para. 15-007 *et seq.*, *infra*). 5.032

In view of national parliaments' scrutiny, any Commission proposal or other draft legislative act, as well as any position taken by the European Parliament and the Council in the course of the legislative process, is sent to all national parliaments.[128] If the Commission proposes to base its action on the flexibility clause (Article 352 TFEU), it must specifically draw national parliaments' attention to the proposed use of that article (Article 352(2) TFEU). Within eight weeks of the transmission of a draft legislative act, any national parliament (or any chamber of a national parliament) may send a reasoned opinion to the Presidents of the European Parliament, the Council, and the Commission stating the reasons for which it considers that the draft in question does not comply with the principle of subsidiarity. If the draft legislative act concerns a matter for which, under national law, competence exists

---

[123] Protocol on the application of the principles of subsidiarity and proportionality (n. 117, *supra*), Article 2.

[124] This term not only covers Commission proposals, but also refers to initiatives from a group of Member States, initiatives from the European Parliament, requests from the Court of Justice, recommendations from the European Central Bank, and requests from the European Investment Bank for the adoption of a legislative act (ibid., Article 3).

[125] Ibid., Article 5. Accordingly, the reasons for concluding that a Union objective can be better achieved at Union level must be substantiated by qualitative and, wherever possible, quantitative indicators. (Ibid.).

[126] Ibid., Article 9, which further provides that this report will be forwarded to the Economic and Social Committee and the Committee of the Regions.

[127] See Granat, *The Principle of Subsidiarity and its Enforcement in the EU Legal Order: The Role of National Parliaments in the Early Warning System*, (Hart Publishing, 2018); Öberg, 'National Parliaments and Political Control of EU Competences: A Sufficient Safeguard of Federalism?' (2018) E Pub L 695; Miettinen and Tervo, 'Subsidiarity, Judicial Review and National Parliaments after Lisbon: Theory and Practice' (2017) ERT 15; Fabbrini and Granat, '"Yellow Card, but No Foul": The Role of the National Parliaments under the Subsidiarity Protocol and the Commission Proposal for an EU Regulation on the Right to Strike' (2013) CMLRev 115; Kiiver, *The Early Warning System for the Principle of Subsidiarity: Constitutional Theory and Empirical Reality* (Routledge, 2012); Barrett, 'The King is Dead, Long Live the King: The Recasting by the Treaty of Lisbon of the Provisions of the Constitutional Treaty Concerning National Parliaments' (2008) ELRev 66–84; Kiiver, 'The Treaty of Lisbon, the National Parliaments and the Principle of Subsidiarity' (2008) MJECL 77–83; Tans, 'De oranje kaart: een nieuwe rol voor nationale parlementen?' (2007) RW 442–6; Cooper, 'The Watchdogs of Subsidiarity: National parliaments and the Logic of Arguing in the EU' (2006) JCMS 281–304; Wyatt, 'Could a "Yellow Card" for National Parliaments Strengthen Judicial as well as Political Policing of Subsidiarity?' (2006) CYELP 1–17. For an empirical inquiry into the effect of the Early Warning System on the democratic legitimacy of the EU, see Cooper, 'National Parliaments in the Democratic Politics of the EU: The Subsidiarity Early Warning Mechanism, 2009–2017' (2019) CEP 919. See also Jaroszynski, 'National Parliaments' Scrutiny of the Principle of Subsidiarity: Reasoned Opinions 2014-19' (2020) EuConst 91.

[128] Protocol on the application of the principles of subsidiarity and proportionality (n. 117, *supra*), Article 4. See also Protocol (No. 1) on the role of National Parliaments in the European Union (OJ 2010 C83/203), Article 2.

with regional parliaments with legislative powers, it will be for the national parliament to consult the regional parliaments concerned.[129] In this respect, Belgium has gone further by putting the parliaments of its autonomous regions ('Regions' and 'Communities') on the same level as the chambers of the federal parliament for the application of the Protocol (see para. 15-010, *infra*).

The Commission, the European Parliament, and the Council must take account of the reasoned opinions issued by national parliaments. The draft legislative act must be reviewed where reasoned opinions on non-compliance with the principle of subsidiarity represent at least one-third of all the votes of the national parliaments, whereby every national parliament gets two votes, which are allocated in accordance with the national parliamentary system; the threshold is one-fourth in the case of a Commission proposal or an initiative from a group of Member States related to police cooperation or judicial cooperation in criminal matters.[130] After having reviewed its draft legislative act, the Commission (or another instance from which the draft act originated) may decide to maintain, amend, or withdraw it, while giving the reasons for its decision.[131] This implementation of the 'early warning' procedure has received the name 'yellow card' after the football term for 'warnings' issued by referees. Out of the three instances where national parliaments amassed sufficient opinions to trigger the yellow card procedure, the Commission has once withdrawn its proposal[132] but twice maintained it.[133]

The Lisbon Treaty has not introduced the so-called 'red card' procedure that some had proposed and according to which a two-third majority of the national parliaments would have forced the Commission to amend or even withdraw its proposal. With respect to matters falling under the ordinary legislative procedure, the Subsidiarity Protocol however foresees the possibility of having a legislative proposal rejected immediately, while leaving the final decision to discard such proposal not to the national parliaments but to the Union legislature itself. Under this so-called 'orange card' procedure, the Commission must review a proposal made under the ordinary legislative procedure where reasoned opinions on non-compliance with the principle of subsidiarity represent at least a simple majority of the votes allocated to the national parliaments. Again, the Commission may decide to maintain its

---

[129] Ibid., Article 6 (it is for each national parliament or each chamber of a national parliament to consult regional parliaments 'where appropriate'). For the different modes of application of the early warning mechanisms in the national parliaments, see para. 15-010, *infra*.

[130] Ibid., Article 7(2), first subpara. (refers, for the threshold of 'one-fourth', to Article 76 TFEU).

[131] Ibid., Article 7(2), second subpara.

[132] This concerned the so-called Monti II-proposal of 21 March 2012 for a Council Regulation on the exercice of the right to take collective action within the context of the freedom of establishment and the freedom to provide services, COM(2012) 130, which by 22 May 2012 had received sufficient negative opinions to trigger the 'yellow card'.

[133] See, first, the proposal of 17 July 2013 for a Council Regulation on the establishment of the European Public Prosecutor's Office (COM(2013) 534), which had received a sufficient number of negative opinions by 28 October 2013, but was maintained and eventually led to a legislative act adopted through enhanced cooperation, see Council Regulation (EU) 2017/1939 of 12 October 2017 implementing enhanced cooperation on the establishment of the European Public Prosecutor's Office ('the EPPO') (OJ 2017 L283/1) and, second, the proposal of 8 March 2016 for a Directive of the European Parliament and of the Council amending Directive 96/71/EC of The European Parliament and of the Council of 16 December 1996 concerning the posting of workers in the framework of the provision of services (COM(2016) 128); which had received a sufficient number of negative opinions by 10 May 2016, but was equally maintained and ultimately adopted as Directive (EU) 2018/957 of the European Parliament and of the Council of 28 June 2018 amending Directive 96/71/EC concerning the posting of workers in the framework of the provision of services (OJ 2018 L173/26).

proposal if it justifies this decision in a reasoned opinion, which is to be submitted to the Union legislature. However, if, by a majority of 55 per cent of the members of the Council or a majority of the votes cast in the European Parliament, the legislature is of the opinion that the proposal is not compatible with the principle of subsidiarity, the legislative proposal shall not be given further consideration.[134]

Judicial review. Judicial review of the validity of Union acts extends to compliance with the principle of subsidiarity.[135] The Union Courts examine whether both the substantive requirements laid down in Article 5(3) TEU and the procedural requirements laid down in the Subsidiarity Protocol have been respected.[136] In accordance with the protocol, Member States may bring an action for annulment before the Court of Justice against a legislative act on grounds of infringement of the principle of subsidiarity on behalf of their national parliament or of one of its chambers.[137] The Committee of the Regions may also bring such an action against legislative acts where the TFEU provides that it must be consulted.[138]

5.033

In theory, the principle of subsidiarity may appear to constitute an important limitation where the Union acts aim to achieve broadly framed objectives, such as those already contained in the original EEC Treaty.[139] In practice, however, the limitation placed on Union action by the principle of subsidiarity is not that important whenever it is considered whether such action affords 'clear benefits' or is 'better' than action at national level. This is because Union action is invariably tested against the objectives that the Union purports to achieve. As already mentioned, if Union action is tested against objectives such as the achievement

---

[134] Protocol on the application of the principles of subsidiarity and proportionality (n. 117, *supra*), Article 7(3).

[135] See, e.g., C-377/98, *Netherlands v European Parliament and Council*, 2001, paras 30–3; C-491/01, *British American Tobacco (Investments) and Imperial Tobacco*, 2002, paras 180–3; C-154/04 and C-155/04, *Alliance for Natural Health*, 2005, paras 104–8, with a case note by Vandamme (2006) LIEI 305–18. See Harvey, 'Towards Process-Oriented Proportionality Review In The European Union' (2017) E Pub L 93; Panara, 'The Enforceability of Subsidiarity in the EU and the Ethos of Cooperative Federalism: A Comparative Law Perspective' (2016) E Pub L 305; Horsley, 'Subsidiarity and the European Court of Justice: Missing Pieces in the Subsidiarity Jigsaw?' (2012) JCMS 267; Van Nuffel, 'The Protection of Member States' Regions through the Subsidiarity Principle', in Panara and De Becker (eds), *The Role of the Regions in European Governance* (Springer, 2010); Timmermans, 'Is het subsidiariteitsbeginsel vatbaar voor rechterlijke controle?' (2007) SEW 224–30; Ritzer, 'Die Kontrolle des Subsidiaritätsprinzips: Geltende Rechtlage und Reformperspektiven' (2006) EuR 116–37; Chaltiel, 'Le principe de subsidiarité dix ans après de traité de Maastricht' (2003) RMCUE 365, 368–70. For a discussion concerning the Court's approach towards subsidiarity review, see Moens and Trone, 'The Principle of Subsidiarity in EU Judicial and Legislative Practice: Panacea or Placebo' (2014) J Legis Stud 65; Portuese, 'The Principle of Subsidiarity as a Principle of Economic Efficiency' (2011) Col JEL 231.

[136] C-358/14, *Poland v European Parliament and Council*, 2016, para. 113.

[137] See Protocol on the application of the principles of subsidiarity and proportionality (n. 117, *supra*), Article 8, first para. (refers to an action brought 'in accordance with their legal order').

[138] Ibid., Article 8, second para. (see also para. 13-033, *infra*). This possibility exists irrespective of whether the action is brought to protect the prerogatives of the Committee, in contradistinction to actions brought under Article 263, third para. TFEU. See Panara, 'The "Europe with the Regions" before the Court of Justice' (2019) MJECL 271; Piattoni and Schönlau, *Shaping EU Policy from Below. EU Democracy and the Committee of the Regions* (Edward Elgar Publishing, 2015), 157.

[139] For a possible application in the field of *competition policy*, see Wesseling, 'Subsidiarity in Community Antitrust Law: Setting the Right Agenda?' (1997) ELRev 35–54; Van den Bergh, 'Economic Criteria for Applying the Subsidiarity Principle in the European Community: The Case of Competition Policy' (1996) Int'l Rev Law & Econ 363–83; for *internal-market policy*, see Schmidhuber and Hitzler, 'Binnenmarkt und Subsidiaritätsprinzip' (1993) EuZW 8–10; for a possible application in the field of *social policy*, see Spicker, 'The Principle of Subsidiarity and the Social Policy of the European Community' (1991) J Eur Soc Policy 3–14; for *environmental policy*, see Macrory, *Regulation, Enforcement and Governance in Environmental Law* (Cameron May, 2008), Chapter 21; Lenaerts, 'The Principle of Subsidiarity and the Environment in the European Union: Keeping the Balance of Federalism' (1994) Fordham ILJ 846–895; Wils, 'Subsidiarity and EC Environmental Policy: Taking People's Concerns Seriously' (1994) J Env L 85–91.

of uniform or coherent rules or the equal treatment of EU citizens or legal persons, it is obvious that Union action will be more efficient than individual action by Member States or voluntary coordination of national policies.[140] In such cases, the objective sought by the Union or the matter dealt with is normally in itself such that national action would inevitably fall short (with the result that Union action is necessarily 'better').[141] Moreover, since, when considering Union action, the institutions make a judgement of complex practical and political circumstances, the courts will carry out a marginal review only of that judgement as it is set out in the statement of reasons of the act concerned.[142] Above all, the principle of subsidiarity therefore makes sense in so far as it compels consideration by the Union institutions of the necessity to take action at the stage of formulating proposals or in subsequent stages of the decision-making process. Various Treaty provisions already limit action on the part of the Union to encouraging and 'if necessary' supporting and supplementing action on the part of the Member States.[143]

V. The Principle of Proportionality

A. Role played by the principle

5.034   Role. The principle of proportionality restricts the authorities in the exercise of their powers by requiring a balance to be struck between the means used and the aim pursued (or result to be reached).[144] It is a general principle of law which affects the exercise of powers

---

[140] See Van Nuffel, 'The Protection of Member States' Regions Through the Subsidiarity Principle', in Panara and De Becker (eds), *The Role of Regions in EU Governance* (Springer, 2011), 58.

[141] See, apart from the cases cited in n. 121, *supra*, also C-377/98, *Netherlands v European Parliament and Council*, 2001, para. 32; C-491/01, *British American Tobacco (Investments) and Imperial Tobacco*, 2002, paras 180–3; C-103/01, *Commission v Germany*, 2003, para. 47; C-154/04 and C-155/04, *Alliance for Natural Health*, 2005, paras 104–7, with a case note by Vandamme (2006) LIEI. 305–18; C-58/08 *Vodafone and Others*, 2010, paras 76–8; C-547/14, *Philip Morris Brands*, 2016, paras 221–2. See Delhomme, 'The Ban on Tobacco for Oral Use Upheld by the Court of Justice: On Subsidiarity and Proportionality in EU Lifestyle Risks Policy' (2019) European J Risk Regul 227; Abaquesne de Parfourus, '"Breaking through the Foul and Ugly Mists of Vapours"—Regulation of Alternative Tobacco and Related Products by the New TPD and Exercise of EU Competence' (2018) GLJ 1291; see already Van Nuffel, *De rechtsbescherming van nationale overheden in het Europees recht* (Kluwer, 2000), 364–88.

[142] See C-233/94, *Germany v European Parliament and Council*, 1997, paras 22–9; C-377/98, *Netherlands v European Parliament and Council*, 2001, para. 33; C-508/13, *Estonia v Parliament and Council*, 2015, para. 61; C-547/14 *Philip Morris Brands and Others*, 2016, paras 225–7; subsidiarity was considered summarily in C-84/94, *United Kingdom v Council*, 1996, paras 80–1, with a case note by Van Nuffel (1997) ColJEL 298–309. For an exposition of this duty to provide a statement of reasons, see Lenaerts and van Ypersele (n. 40, *supra*), at 75–80, and Van Nuffel (n. 52, *supra*) at 412–24; for the duty to state grounds in general, see para. 27-007, *infra*. A call for more extensive judicial review is to be found in König and Lorz, 'Stärkung des Subsidiaritätsprinzips' (2003) JZ 167–73. The Court of Justice has also used the principle of subsidiarity as an aid to interpretation; see C-114/01 *AvestaPolarit Chrome Oy*, 2003, paras 56–7.

[143] See, *inter alia*, Articles 147 TFEU (employment); Article 165(1) TFEU (education); Article 167(2) TFEU (culture); and Article 168(2) TFEU (public health); paras 9-046–9-055, *infra*. See Lenaerts, 'Subsidiarity and Community Competence in the Field of Education' (1994/95) Col JEL 1–28.

[144] For general discussions, see Young and de Búrca, 'Proportionality', in Vogenauer and Weatherill (eds), *General Principles of Law—European and Comparative Perspectives* (Hart Publishing, 2017), 418, and the various comparisons to proportionality in various Member States in chapters 9–14 thereof; Harbo, *The Function of Proportionality Analysis in European Law* (Hotei, 2015) 350; Harbo, 'The Function of the Proportionality Principle in EU Law' (2010) ELJ 158–85; Tridimas, *The General Principles of EU Law* (OUP, 2007), Chapters 3–5; Bermann, 'Proportionality and Subsidiarity', in Barnard and Scott (eds), *The Law of the Single European Market*, (Hart Publishing, 2002), 75–100; Kischel, 'Die Kontrolle der Verhältnismässigkeit durch den Europäischen Gerichtshof' (2000) EuR 380–402; Jans, 'Proportionality Revisited' (2000) LIEI 239–65; Emiliou, *The Principle of Proportionality in European Law—A Comparative Study* (Kluwer, 1996); de Búrca, 'The Principle of Proportionality and its Application in EC Law' (1993) YEL 105–50; Jans, 'Evenredigheid: ja, maar waartussen?' (1992) SEW 751–70;

by Member States as well as by the Union. In the case law, the principle of proportionality serves principally to assess the legality of an exercise of power where an admittedly legitimate aim is pursued, but at the same time other objectives or interests deserving of protection are damaged. The exercise of power in such a case will be regarded as lawful only if it is appropriate to attain the intended aim and also necessary in that alternative forms of exercise of power—which would inflict no or less damage on other objectives or interests worthy of protection—would not be capable of achieving the intended aim. The principle is also applied in connection with the imposition of sanctions (see para. 25-023, *infra*).

Applications. All Union action on the basis of the Treaties must be limited to what is appropriate and necessary to achieve the purported objectives. The principle of proportionality is invoked when Union action conflicts with other Union objectives or legitimate interests of private parties or Member States. The principle of proportionality also guides the Court of Justice in resolving possible conflicts between objectives of Union policy, such as between agricultural policy and fundamental rights including the right to property and the freedom of expression,[145] or between several fundamental rights, in order to strike 'a fair balance between them'.[146]

5.035

Member States must also respect the principle of proportionality when implementing Union law. Accordingly, it falls to the Court to assess whether national measures which impede the free movement of goods, persons, or services or the freedom of establishment—central objectives of the internal market—can be justified because they seek to attain legitimate objectives. In this connection, the Court of Justice will in particular have regard to whether the national measures pursue their objectives in a proportional manner.[147] Member States must also respect the principle of proportionality when they apply and enforce Union law, for instance when they impose sanctions.[148]

B. The requirements of proportionality

Requirements. As has already been mentioned, the principle of proportionality requires action to be both 'appropriate' to attain its objectives and not go beyond what is 'necessary' to that effect.[149]

5.036

Van Gerven, 'Principe de proportionnalité, abus de droit et droits fondementaux' (1992) JT 305–9. See, critically, Petursson, *The Proportionality Principle as a Tool for Disintegration in EU law* (Lund University, 2014).

[145] e.g. 44/79, *Hauer*, 1979, para. 23; 265/87, *Schräder*, 1989, para. 15.

[146] e.g. C-752/18, *Deutsche Umwelthilfe*, 2019, para. 50 (balance between the right to effective judicial protection and the right to liberty set out in Article 6 Charter); T-1-4/89 and T-6-15/89, *Rhône-Poulenc and Others v Commission* (order), 1990, para. 22 (balance between conflicting procedural rights, namely respect for business secrets and the adversarial nature of court proceedings).

[147] Paras 7-034 and 7-042 (trade in goods), 7-062, 7-067, and 7-071 (movement of persons), 7-094 (freedom to supply services) and 7-106 (free movement of capital), *infra*.

[148] e.g. C-497/15 and C-498/15, *Euro-Team and Spirál-Gép*, 2017, paras 36–66; C-210/10, *Urbán*, 2012.

[149] C-611/17, *Italy v Council*, 2019, para. 55; C-482/17, *Czech Republic v European Parliament and Council*, 2019, para. 77. The second condition is also referred to as the requirement, when there is a choice between several appropriate measures, to have recourse to the least onerous (the 'less restrictive alternative'). Sometimes, reference is made to a third condition, according to which 'the disadvantages caused must not be disproportionate to the aims pursued'. On that third condition, see para. 5-038, *infra*.

5.037 **Appropriateness.** Action is appropriate where it is capable of attaining the intended aim. The Court of Justice leaves a measure of discretion to the authority concerned[150] and only considers whether it has committed a manifest error of assessment.[151] Thus, the Court does not replace the assessment of the authority concerned by its own *ex post facto* assessment. Where it is asked to assess Union legislation, it often considers that the area concerned involves political, economic, and social choices in which the Union legislature is called upon to undertake complex assessments and where the Union legislature must be allowed broad discretion. However, the Union institutions that adopted the act in question must be able to show before the Court that in adopting the act they actually exercised their discretion, which presupposes the taking into consideration of all the relevant factors and circumstances of the situation the act was intended to regulate.[152] Accordingly, the institutions must at the very least be able to produce and set out clearly and unequivocally the basic facts which had to be taken into account as the basis of the contested measures and on which the exercise of their discretion depended.[153] Only if the measure adopted is manifestly inappropriate in relation to the objective that the competent institutions are seeking to pursue can its lawfulness be affected.[154] In addition, in order to be appropriate, the measure must pursue this objective in a consistent manner.[155] This last requirement has become particularly important in the application of the internal market freedoms.[156]

5.038 **Necessity.** Action is necessary where it cannot be replaced by some alternative form of action which would have equal effectiveness (*effet utile*) having regard to the intended aim and be less detrimental to another objective or interest protected by Union law. An appropriate measure may not entail needless adverse effects.[157] The Court of Justice respects the

---

[150] The EU legislature's broad discretion applies not only to the nature and scope of the measures to be taken but also, to some extent, to the finding of the basic facts, see C-482/17, *Czech Republic v European Parliament and Council*, 2019, para. 77; see also C-5/16, *Poland v European Parliament and Council*, 2018, para. 151; C-62/14, *Gauweiler and Others*, 2015, paras 68–70. See Tridimas and Xanthoulis, 'A legal Analysis of the Gauweiler Case: Between Monetary Policy and Constitutional Conflict' (2016) MJECL 17; Weatherill, 'The Limits of Legislative Harmonization Ten Years after Tobacco Advertising: How the Court's Case Law has become a "Drafting Guide"' (2011) GLJ 827.

[151] 40/72, *Schroeder v Germany*, 1973, para. 14. See also 265/87, *Schräder*, 1989, para. 22; C-133/93, C-300/93, and C-362/93, *Crispoltoni*, 1994, paras 43–8; C-280/93, *Germany v Council*, 1994, paras 89–95; and C-611/17, *Italy v Council*, 2019, paras 56–8.

[152] C-482/17, *Czech Republic v European Parliament and Council*, 2019, para. 81. See also C-62/14, *Gauweiler and Others*, 2015, paras 68–70. This can be achieved through an impact assessment, but the absence thereof does not in and of itself result in a breach of the principle of proportionality, see C-482/17, *Czech Republic v European Parliament and Council*, 2019, paras 83–5. See also Hofmann, 'The Interdependencies between Delegation, Discretion, and the Duty of Care', in Mendes (ed.), *EU Executive Discretion and the Limits of Law* (OUP, 2019), 234; Mendes, 'Discretion, Care and Public Interests in the EU Administration: Probing the Limits of Law' (2016) CMLRev 419.

[153] C-482/17, *Czech Republic v European Parliament and Council*, 2019, para. 81.

[154] C-233/94, *Germany v Parliament and Council*, 1997, paras 55 and 56; C-157/96, *National Farmers' Union and Others*, 1998, para. 61; C-210/03, *Swedish Match*, 2004, para. 48; C-58/08, *Vodafone*, 2010, paras 51–71; C-203/12, *Billerud Karlsborg and Billerud Skärblacka*, 2013, paras 35–7; C-78/16 and C-79/16, *Pesce and Others*, 2016, para. 50; C-643/15 and C-647/15, *Slovakia and Hungary v Council*, 2017, paras 206–24. See Harvey, 'Towards Process-Oriented Proportionality Review in the European Union' (2017) CMLRev 93; Sauter, 'Proportionality in EU Law: A Balancing Act?' (2013) CYELS 439; Tridimas, *The General Principles of EU Law* (OUP, 2006) 138.

[155] C-169/07, *Hartlauer*, 2009, paras 55–63. See Wendland, 'When Good is Not Good Enough: A Comparative Analysis of Underinclusiveness and the Principle of Coherence under Proportionality Review' (2018) MJECL 332–56; Langer and Sauter, 'Het coherentievereiste in het Unierecht' (2018) SEW 138–48.

[156] See also Gormley, 'Inconsistencies and Misconceptions in the Free Movement of Goods' (2015) ELRev 925; Mathisen, 'Consistency and Coherence as Conditions for Justification of Member State Measures Restricting Free Movement' (2010) CMLRev 1021–48.

[157] See, e.g., C-58/08, *Vodafone*, 2010, para. 68; C-453/03, C-11/04, C-12/04, and C-194/04, *ABNA and Others*, 2005, paras 76–88 (measures held to go further than necessary for the protection of public health to the detriment

objective that the authority seeks to achieve through its action and, as a rule, does not take account of other measures which would not achieve it to a sufficient extent, even if such measures would have no or less effect on a protected objective or interest. Consequently, the Court generally does not weigh the detriment done to the objective or interest deserving of protection against the advantages of the action for the objective pursued, that is to say whether, on the whole, the disadvantages caused would be disproportionate to the objectives pursued.[158] If it did so, the Court would be able to allow different objectives to prevail over those that the authority concerned chose.[159] There is nevertheless one area in which the Court takes the view that the objective chosen by the authority may have to yield to a higher value. This is the value of respect for fundamental rights.[160]

C. Application of the principle of proportionality

Protection of legitimate interests. Article 5(4) TEU expresses the principle of proportionality as a limitation on action by the Union, the content and form of which 'shall not exceed what is necessary to achieve the objectives of the Treaties'. However, action founded upon a legal basis afforded by the Treaties can hardly go beyond the objectives *of the Treaties* without at the same time exceeding the confines of the legal basis in question, which would mean that the action would be *ultra vires*. Rather, the principle of proportionality requires a given action not to go beyond what is necessary to achieve the objective *of that action*.[161] In that sense, the principle, as it is expressed in Article 5(4) TEU provides protection for Member States, regional and local authorities, trade and industry, and citizens against Union action involving obligations or burdens which are not proportionate to the objective pursued. Such legal subjects may plead infringement of the principle of proportionality where the Union unreasonably affects their interests. It flows from Article 5(4) TEU that the principle of proportionality restricts not only the substance but also the form of legislative action. The formulation of the principle of proportionality does not detract from its

5.039

---

of economic interests of manufacturers). That condition is also referred to as the requirement to opt for the 'least onerous' or 'less restrictive' alternative. See C-331/88, *Fedesa*, 1990, para. 13.

[158] In cases in which the Court of Justice announces that it may assess whether the disadvantages were disproportionate to the objectives pursued, it often only tests whether the measures were appropriate and necessary and generally confirms the weighing of interests as conducted by the (Union or Member State) authority; see, e.g., C-189/01, *Jippes and Others*, 2001, paras 80–100; C-562/08, *Müller Fleisch*, 2010, paras 43–47; C-58/08, *Vodafone and Others*, 2010, paras 53 and 69. See Van Nuffel (n. 52, *supra*), 311–20. See, however, C-176/09, *Luxemburg v European Parliament and Council*, 2011, paras 68–71; C-547/14, *Philip Morris Brands and Others*, 2016, paras 185–90.

[159] See, with regard to environment protection, Notaro, 'The New Generation Case Law on Trade and Environment' (2000) ELRev 467, 486–7.

[160] 44/79, *Hauer*, 1979, paras 23 and 30; C-379/08 and C-380/08, *Raffinerie Mediterranee (ERG) and Others*, 2010, paras 80 and 86 (para. 25-019, *infra*), see also Article 52(1) Charter of Fundamental rights (see para. 25-019, *infra*). For the problems raised by the overall balancing of interests, see Lenaerts and van Ypersele (n. 40, *supra*), 56–60, and Van Nuffel (n. 52, *supra*), 320–8.

[161] The test to be applied solely concerns the question whether the means chosen for the Union action concerned do not go further than what is necessary to attain the objectives of that action: see C-493/17, *Weiss*, 2018, paras 71–100. This test flows from the wording itself of Article 5(4) TEU, and may not be confused with national understandings of proportionality, as was however done by the German Constitutional Court in BVerfG of 5 May 2020 (2 BvR 859/15, 2 BvR 980/16, 2 BvR 2006/15, and 2 BvR 1651/15). See also X, 'Not Mastering the Treaties: The German Federal Constitutional Court's PSPP Judgment' (2020) CMLRev 969–74.

application as a 'general principle' of Union law, a principle that also applies to the Member States (see para. 25-023, *infra*).

5.040 **Protecting national powers.** The first subpara. of Article 5(3) TEU provides that the Union is to take action only 'in so far as' the objectives of the proposed action cannot be sufficiently achieved by the Member States but can rather, by reason of the scale or effects of the proposed action, be better achieved at Union level. In this manner, that provision embodies a specific application of the principle of proportionality with a view to protecting the residual powers of the Member States (in addition to the more general expression of that principle in Article 5(4) TEU). In accordance with the Protocol on the application of the principles of subsidiarity and proportionality, draft legislative acts must therefore contain an assessment of the proposal's financial impact and, in the case of a directive, of its implications for the rules to be put in place by Member States, including, where necessary, the regional legislation.[162] Draft legislative acts should also take account of the need for any burden, whether financial or administrative, falling upon the Union, national governments, regional or local authorities, economic operators, and citizens, to be minimized and commensurate with the objective to be achieved.[163]

5.041 **Protecting national identity.** Since the Treaty of Lisbon, the Treaties list 'national identity' as a particular interest that the Union must respect. Article 4(2) TEU requires the Union to respect the 'national identities [of the Member States], inherent in their fundamental structures, political and constitutional, inclusive of regional and local self-government'[164] as well as 'their essential State functions, including those for ensuring the territorial integrity of the State, and for maintaining law and order and safeguarding national security'.[165] This clause prevents the Union—as a matter of principle—from taking measures requiring the Member States to adapt their political and constitutional structures or the way in which they organize the essential functions of a State.[166] Article 4(2) TEU does not provide a basis for Member States to derogate from obligations imposed by EU law since that would undermine the primacy and uniform application of EU law, and hence the equality of the Member States before the law also protected in Article 4(2) TEU. Together with the principle of proportionality, Article 4(2) TEU prohibits that provisions of EU law unduly restrict the national constitutional space.[167] The national constitutional space cannot, however, be protected

---

[162] Protocol on the application of the principles of subsidiarity and proportionality (n. 117, *supra*), Article 5.
[163] Ibid. See C-620/18, *Hungary v European Parliament and Council*, 2020, para. 115.
[164] See C-524/14 P, *Commission v Hansestadt Lübeck*, 2016, paras 15–22; C-156/13, *Digibet and Albers*, 2014, para. 34; see already before the Treaty of Lisbon: C-428/07, *Horvath*, 2009, paras 49–53.
[165] Article 4(2) TEU, last sentence, adds that 'In particular, national security remains the sole responsibility of each Member State'; see C-715/17, C-718/17, and C-719/17, *Commission v Poland, Hungary and Czech Republic*, 2020, paras 139–72 and 178–88; C-511/18, C-512/18, and C-520/18, *La Quadrature du Net and Others*, 2020, paras 135–6; C-623/17, *Privacy International*, 2020, paras 30–49 and 74–5.
[166] e.g. C-51/15, *Remondis*, 2016, paras 40–1; C-518/07, *Commission v Germany*, 2010, paras 52–5 (requirement for Member States to ensure that the national supervisory authority with regard to the processing of personal data is free from State scrutiny does not go further than necessary to achieve the objective of independence imposed by the Union legislation). See van der Schyff, 'Exploring Member State and European Union Constitutional Identity' (2016) CMLRev 227.
[167] e.g. C-208/09, *Sayn-Wittgenstein*, 2010, paras 89–94; C-438/14, *Bogendorff von Wolffersdorff*, 2016, paras 64–84 (see para. 6-020, *infra*). See Spieker, 'Framing and Managing Constitutional identity Conflicts: How to Stabilize the Modus Vivendi Between the Court of Justice and National Constitutional Courts' (2020) CMLRev 361; di Federico, 'The Potential of Article 4(2) TEU in the Solution of Constitutional Clashes Based on Alleged Violations of National Identity and the Quest for Adequate (Judicial) Standards' (2019) E Pub L 347; Kaczorowska-Ireland, 'What is the European Union required to Respect under Article 4(2) TEU?: The Uniqueness Approach' (2019) E Pub L 57; Rademacher, 'Die "Verfassungsidentität" als Grenze der Kompetenzübertragung auf die Europäische

when it tends to weaken the values on which the Union is founded.[168] Therefore, whilst it is legitimate for a Member State to encourage the use of its official language or languages, such an objective cannot justify restrictions on the right to free movement that go beyond what is strictly necessary for the achievement of that objective.[169]

Institutional implementation. The institutions of the Union must apply the principle of proportionality in accordance with the aforementioned Protocol on the application of the principles of subsidiarity and proportionality ('Subsidiarity Protocol') (Article 5(3), second subpara. TEU). Each institution must ensure constant respect for the principle of proportionality.[170] It follows that all draft legislative acts must be justified with regard to the principle of proportionality.[171] The Protocol does not, however, install any mechanism of scrutiny by national parliaments on compliance with the principle of proportionality.

5.042

In the case law of the Court of Justice, a breach of the principle of proportionality may lead to the invalidity or annulment of those Union acts which cannot be justified by the purported objective.[172]

VI. The Principle of Sincere Cooperation

A. Role played by the principle

Definition. Pursuant to the principle of sincere cooperation, the Union and the Member States shall, in full mutual respect, assist each other in carrying out tasks which flow from the Treaties (Article 4(3), first subpara. TEU).[173] Article 4(3) TEU requires Member States to 'take any appropriate measure, general or particular, to ensure fulfilment of the obligations

5.043

Union?' (2018) EuR 140–58; Skouris, 'L'identité nationale: qui détermine son contenu et selon quels critères?', in *Liber Amicorum Antonio Tizzano* (Giappichelli, 2018), 912; Van Nuffel, 'De nationale identiteit: bouwsteen of splijtzwam voor het recht van de Europese Unie', (2017) TBP 354; Haratsch, 'Nationale Identität aus europarechtlicher Sicht' (2016) EuR 131–46; Cloots, *National Identity in EU Law* (OUP, 2015); Claes, 'National Identity: Trump Card or Up For Negotiation?', in Arnaiz and Llivinia (eds), *National Constitutional Identity and European Integration* (Intersentia, 2013), 109; Corthaut, *EU ordre public* (Kluwer, 2012); Von Bogdandy and Schill, 'Overcoming Absolute Primacy: Respect for National identity Under the Lisbon Treaty' (2011) CMLRev 1417.

[168] See C-673/16, *Coman*, 2018, paras 42–51; C-715/17, C-718/17, and C-719/17, *Commission v Poland, Hungary and Czech Republic*, 2020, paras 139–72 and 178–88.

[169] C-391/09, *Runevic-Vardyn and Wardyn*, 2011, paras 85–93; C-202/11, *Las*, 2013, paras 25–33, with a case note by Cloots (2014) CMLRev 623; C-15/15, *New Valmar*, 2016, paras 50–6, with a case note by Sibony (2016) RTDE 821. See also para. 9-054, *infra*.

[170] Protocol (No. 2) on the application of the principles of subsidiarity and proportionality (n. 117, *supra*), Article 1.

[171] Ibid., Article 5.

[172] e.g. C-453/03, C-11/04, C-12/04, and C-194/04, *ABNA and Others*, 2005, paras 80–5. See Harbo, 'Introducing Procedural Proportionality Review in European Law' (2017) LJIL 25.

[173] See also Article 192 EAEC. For a general discussion, see Roes, 'Limits to Loyalty: The Relevance of Article 4(3) TEU' (2016) CDE 253–83; Klamert, *The Principle of Loyalty in EU Law* (OUP, 2014), 354; Temple Lang 'Article 10 EC—The Most Important "General Principle" of Community law' and Gormley, 'Some Further Reflections on the Development of General Principles of Law within Article 10 EC', both in Bernitz, Nergelius, and Cardner (eds), *General Principles of EC Law in a Process of Development* (Kluwer Law International, 2008), 75–113 and 303–14, respectively; Temple Lang, 'Developments, Issues and New Remedies—The Duties of National Authorities and Courts under Article 10 of the EC Treaty' (2004) Fordham ILJ 1904–39; Hatje, *Loyalität als Rechtsprinzip in der Europäischen Union* (Nomos, 2001); Blanquet, *L'article 5 du traité CEE. Recherche sur les obligations de fidélité des Etats membres de la Communauté* (Librairie Générale de Droit et de Jurisprudence, 1994).

arising out of the Treaties or resulting from the acts of the institutions of the Union' and to 'facilitate the achievement of the Union's tasks' (second and third subparas) and, at the same time, to 'refrain from any measure which could jeopardise the attainment of the Union's objectives' (third subpara.). The principle of sincere cooperation (sometimes referred to as the duty of loyal cooperation or the duty to cooperate in good faith) is thus formulated in terms of a positive and a negative obligation, to which the Member States are subject in their dealings with the Union and between themselves. Since the principle of sincere cooperation is an expression of Union solidarity,[174] it is not the same as the principle of international law that States are required to implement in good faith the treaties which they conclude.[175] The principle of sincere cooperation is a reflection of the principle of 'federal good faith' which is designed to secure mutual respect of the powers of the legislative, executive, and judicial bodies of different levels of authority within a federal system and readiness to cooperate.[176] Article 4(3) TEU is binding on 'all the authorities of Member States',[177] including, for matters within their jurisdiction, the courts[178] and decentralized authorities.[179]

5.044 Scope. Since it is chiefly the national authorities that have to implement Union law, most of the decided cases involving the principle of sincere cooperation are concerned with the application of the principle to the Member States. Nevertheless, increasing activity on the part of the Union has made it clear that the Union institutions are also subject to the principle of sincere cooperation in their relations both with Member States and with each other.[180] Since the Lisbon Treaty, the Treaties explicitly provide that '[t]he institutions shall practice mutual sincere cooperation' (Article 13(2) TEU). However, the adoption of a legislative measure by the Council cannot constitute a breach of the principle of sincere cooperation attaching to either the Council or the Member States, which defend their interests in that institution.[181]

---

[174] See *Commission v France*, 1969, para. 16.
[175] See Constantinesco, 'L'article 5 CEE, de la bonne foi à la loyauté communautaire', in Capotorti et al. (eds), *Du droit international au droit de l'intégration. Liber amicorum P. Pescatore* (Nomos, 1987), 97–114; for a discussion on the relationship between sincere cooperation in EU law, the principle of international law concerning good faith, and federal good faith, see De Baere and Roes, 'EU Loyalty as Good Faith' (2015) ICLQ 829.
[176] Van Gerven and Gilliams, 'Gemeenschapstrouw: goede trouw in E.G.-verband' (1989-90) RW 1158, 1159. On federal loyalty, see, e.g., Alen and Haljan (eds), *Constitutional Law in Belgium* (Wolters Kluwer, 2020), 358, 180. That does not mean that the Union principle alters the division of powers between the Union and the Member States; see Due, 'Artikel 5 van het EEG-Verdrag. Een bepaling met een federaal karakter?' (1992) SEW 355, 366; see, however, also Neframi, 'Principe de coopération loyale et principe d'attribution dans le cadre de la mise en oeuvre du droit de l'Union' (2016) CDE 221–51. For examples from Belgium, see Verhoeven, 'The Application in Belgium of the Duties of Loyalty and Co-operation' (2000) SEW 328–30.
[177] See, with respect to ex Article 10 EC, 80/86, *Kolpinghuis Nijmegen*, 1987, para. 12.
[178] Ibid. See also the earlier case 14/83, *Von Colson and Kamann*, 1984, para. 26. For Article 86 ECSC, see C-341/94, *Allain*, 1996, para. 25. See Láncos, 'A Hard Core Under the Soft Shell: How Binding Is Union Soft Law for Member States?' (2018) E Pub L 755.
[179] For municipal bye-laws, see 85/85, *Commission v Belgium*, 1985, paras 22–3; C-518/11, *UPC Nederland*, 2013, paras 59–63.
[180] 230/81, *Luxembourg v European Parliament*, 1983, para. 37. See, *inter alia*, 44/84, *Hurd v Jones*, 1986, para. 38, and 52/84 *Commission v Belgium*, 1986, para. 16; C-65/93, *European Parliament v Council*, 1995, para. 23; C-319/97, *Kortas*, 1999, para. 35; C-29/99, *Commission v Council*, 2002, para. 69. See also Declaration (No. 3), annexed to the Treaty of Nice, on Article 10 EC Treaty, OJ 2001 C80/77. See Dimopoulos, 'Taming the Conclusion of Inter Se Agreements between EU Member States: The Role of the Duty of Loyalty' (2015) YEL 286.
[181] C-63/90 and C-67/90, *Portugal and Spain v Council*, 1992, para. 53. See Woodhouse, 'With Great Power, Comes No Responsibility? The 'Political Exception' To Duties of Sincere Cooperation for National Parliaments' (2017) CMLRev 443; den Hertog and Stroß, 'Coherence in EU External Relations: Concepts and Legal Rooting of an Ambiguous Term' (2013) Eur For Aff Rev 373; Horsley, 'Reflections on the Role of the Court of Justice as the 'Motor' of European Integration: Legal Limits To Judicial Lawmaking' (2013) CMLRev 931.

B. The requirements of the principle of sincere cooperation

Twofold duty. Where a provision of Union law contains a specific obligation for Member States, a finding that there has been a failure to fulfil the obligation in question may unquestionably be made without also finding a breach of the principle of sincere cooperation.[182] Where, in contrast, there is no such obligation, a Member State's conduct may nonetheless constitute a breach of the principle of sincere cooperation. This is because the Court of Justice has gradually broadened its interpretation of the 'obligations arising out of the Treaties or resulting from the acts of the institutions of the Union' and of the requirement not to 'jeopardise the attainment of the Union's objectives' (Article 4(3) TEU, equally laid down in ex Article 10 EC). The upshot is: (1) ancillary obligations with which the Member States and the institutions must comply in implementing a specific provision of Union law or even independently of such implementation ('supplementary requirements' of the principle of sincere cooperation);[183] and (2) a prohibition on Member States or institutions to act where acting would constitute a misuse of powers ('derogatory requirements' of the principle of sincere cooperation).[184]

5.045

1. Supplementary requirements

Duty of care. In the first place, Article 4(3), second subpara. TEU puts the Member States under a duty to take all measures necessary to implement provisions of Union law (see para. 18-002 *et seq.*, *infra*). In so doing, they have to lay down the necessary sanctions in so far as the actual Union provisions themselves do not provide for any.[185] In addition, the Member States are under a general duty of care in implementing Union law. They have to take all appropriate measures to guarantee the full scope and effect of Union law. Often, that extends beyond the adoption of legal measures, but may also require concrete action, for instance to fight plant diseases,[186] or to manage forests,[187] or to ensure that public authorities make their payments in time.[188] They must also deal with any irregularities as quickly as possible[189]. The conduct of other Member States or apprehension of internal difficulties cannot justify a failure to apply Union law correctly.[190] Where the implementation of Union law raises special difficulties, the Member States should submit them to the Commission and work together with it in good faith with a view to overcoming the difficulties[191].

5.046

---

[182] See, e.g., C-48/89, *Commission v Italy*, 1990; C-539/09, *Commission v Germany*, 2011, para. 87; C-316/19, *Commission v Slovenia*, 2020, paras 121–2.

[183] Failure to comply with an undertaking to remedy an infringement of the Treaty itself constitutes a breach of the principle: C-374/89, *Commission v Belgium*, 1991, paras 12–15.

[184] cf. Van Gerven and Gilliams (n. 176, *supra*), 1160–2.

[185] For sanctions, see para. 18-004, *infra*.

[186] C-443/18, *Commission v Italy*, 2019, para. 90.

[187] C-441/17, *Commission v Poland*, 2018, para. 268.

[188] C-122/18, *Commission v Italy*, 2020, paras 37–68.

[189] C-34/89, *Italy v Commission*, 1990, para. 12; C-28/89, *Germany v Commission*, 1991, para. 31; C-277/98, *France v Commission*, 2001, para. 40.

[190] C-265/95, *Commission v France*, 1997, paras 55 and 63.

[191] 52/84, *Commission v Belgium*, 1986, para. 16; 94/87, *Commission v Germany*, 1989, para. 9; C-217/88, *Commission v Germany*, 1990, para. 33. C-75/97, *Commission v Belgium*, 1999, para. 88; C-404/97, *Commission v Portugal*, 2000, para. 40; C-261/99, *Commission v France*, 2001, para. 24; C-378/98, *Commission v Belgium*, 2001, para. 31; C-499/99, *Commission v Spain*, 2002, para. 24. Where a Member State notifies difficulties in transposing a directive, no obligation can be inferred from Article 4(3) TEU for the Commission to submit a proposal to amend the directive or to delay bringing an action for failure to fulfil obligations: C-239/99, *Commission v Belgium*, 2000, paras 25–9.

In accordance with the principle of sincere cooperation, the national courts are entrusted with securing the legal protection that citizens derive from the direct effect of provisions of Union law.[192] The courts must also ensure that provisions of Union law not endowed with direct effect are given *effet utile*. This can be done by interpreting national law as far as possible in conformity with Union law (a duty which rests on all governmental bodies).[193] But courts must also refrain from applying national provisions that conflict with Union law (see also the derogatory requirements, para. 5-049, *infra*). As far as Member States' implementation of the legal instruments referred to in Article 288 TFEU is concerned, Article 4(3) TEU constitutes an additional ground for the duty of Member States to repeal national provisions incompatible with a Union regulation[194] and for the direct effect of non-implemented directives which are unconditional and sufficiently precise.[195]

The principle of sincere cooperation moreover obliges all national authorities to remedy any unlawful consequences of an infringement of Union law (see para. 23-019, *infra*). Member States are required to eliminate the unlawful consequences of a breach of Union law,[196] though in exceptional circumstances it may be possible to regularize operations or measures which are unlawful in the light of Union law.[197] Where individuals suffer loss or damage as a result of breaches of Union law for which the State can be held responsible, it is inherent in the 'system of the Treaties' and Article 4(3) TEU that the Member State in question must allow a claim to be made against the public authorities.[198]

5.047 **Duty to cooperate.** Article 4(3) TEU puts each Member State and the Commission under a duty of sincere cooperation with institutions of other Member States responsible for implementing Union law.[199] As a result of the obligation mutually to facilitate the implementation of Union law, Member States must recognize the equivalence of each other's product tests, diplomas, and evidence of professional qualifications in the context of the free movement of goods, persons, and services.[200] The principle of sincere cooperation entails a

---

[192] 33/76, *Rewe*, 1976, para. 5, and 45/76, *Comet*, 1976, para. 12.
[193] C-106/89, *Marleasing*, 1990, para. 8; C-262/97, *Engelbrecht*, 2000, para. 39. See Van Elsuwege, 'The Duty of Sincere Cooperation and Its Implications for Autonomous Member State Action in the Field of External Relations', in Varju (ed.), *Between Compliance and Particularism: Member State Interests and European Union Law* (Springer, 2019), 283–97; Holdgaard, Elkan, and Schaldemose, 'From Cooperation to Collision: The ECJ's AJOS Ruling and the Danish Supreme Court's Refusal To Comply' (2018) CMLRev 17; Leczykiewicz, 'Effectiveness of EU Law before National Courts: Direct Effect, Effective Judicial Protection, and State Liability', in Arnull and Chalmers (eds), *Oxford Handbook of European Union Law* (OUP, 2015), 213; Spaventa, 'Opening Pandora's Box: Some Reflections on the Constitutional Effects of the Decision in *Pupino*' (2007) EuConst 5.
[194] 74/86, *Commission v Germany*, 1988, paras 10–12.
[195] 190/87, *Oberkreisdirektor des Kreises Borken and Others*, 1988, paras 22–4. See Dougan, 'Primacy and the Remedy of Disapplication' (2019) CMLRev 1459; Prechal, 'Direct Effect, Indirect Effect, Supremacy and the Evolving Constitution of the European Union', in Barnard (ed.), *The Fundamentals of EU Law Revisited: Assessing the Impact of the Constitutional Debate* (OUP, 2012), 50; Klamert, 'Judicial Implementation of Directives and Anticipatory Indirect Effect: Connecting the Dots' (2006) CMLRev 1251.
[196] C-395/17, *Commission v Netherlands*, 2019, para. 98. See also C-231/06 to C-233/06, *Jonkman and Others*, 2007, paras 37 and 38; C-196/16 and C-197/16, *Comune di Corridonia and Others*, 2017, para. 35; C-597/17, *Belgisch Syndicaat van Chiropraxie and Others*, 2019, para. 54.
[197] C-261/18, *Commission v Ireland*, 2019, paras 75–6.
[198] C-6/90 and C-9/90, *Francovich and Others*, 1991, paras 33–6; see also para. 23-019, *infra*.
[199] C-251/89, *Athanasopoulos and Others*, 1991, para. 57; C-165/91, *Van Munster*, 1994, para. 32 (see para. 7-079, *infra*); C-202/97, *Fitzwilliam Executive Search*, 2000, paras 51–9; C-178/97, *Banks and Others*, 2000, paras 38–45. Where a bilateral agreement between Member States is liable to impede the application of a provision of Union law, the Member States concerned are under a duty to assist each other in order to facilitate the application of the relevant provision: 235/87, *Matteucci*, 1988, paras 17–19.
[200] See, with regard to the free movement of goods: C-25/88, *Wurmser and Others*, 1989, para. 18 (para. 7-034, *infra*); with regard to the free movement of persons: 71/76 *Thieffry*, 1977, paras 15–19; C-340/89, *Vlassopoulou*,

principle of mutual trust.[201] That does not imply, however, that acts of other Member States cannot be called into question. Therefore, in the context of fighting social fraud by posted workers, it follows from the principle of sincere cooperation not only that any institution of a Member State must carry out a diligent examination of the application of its own social security system, but also that the institutions of the other Member States are entitled to expect the institution of the Member State concerned to fulfil that obligation. Accordingly, a Member State may decide to disregard certain documents issued by another Member State if the authorities of that second Member State have failed to take evidence of fraud into consideration.[202]

In various situations, the principle of sincere cooperation requires Member States' authorities and Union institutions to cooperate closely. This is the case, for example, in case of a breach of the privileges and immunities granted to the institutions, which can often be remedied only by close cooperation between the institution concerned and the national authorities.[203] The institutions are also under a duty to collaborate with the Member States' judicial authorities. In the context of the enforcement of competition rules, national courts and the Commission must cooperate to overcome difficulties arising from an investigation decision adopted by the Commission.[204] As far as the Court of Justice is concerned, that collaboration takes the form of the preliminary ruling procedure provided for in Article 267 TFEU. Furthermore, every Union institution—especially the Commission in view of its duty of ensuring that Union law is applied—must give its active assistance to a national court conducting a preliminary judicial inquiry into breaches of a provision of Union law that makes a request for information concerning potential evidence of such breaches.[205]

The duty to cooperate also puts Member States under an obligation to consult the Union institutions where they propose adopting measures affecting the Staff Regulations of Union officials.[206] Pursuant to the principle of sincere cooperation, the Commission, for its part, has to display the necessary diligence where a Member State notifies the wish to derogate from a harmonization measure under Article 114(4) and (5) TFEU.[207] The duty to cooperate may further oblige institutions to take into account principles laid down in Union

---

1991, para. 14 (self-employed persons), and 222/86, *Unectef v Heylens*, 1987, para. 12 (workers) (para. 7-062, *infra*). For similar rulings concerning free movement of services, see para. 7-094, *infra*. See Janssens, *The Principle of Mutual Recognition in EU Law* (OUP, 2013); Mostl, 'Preconditions and Limits of Mutual Recognition' (2010) CMLRev 405; von Danwitz, 'Der Grundsatz des gegenseitigen Vertrauens zwischen den Mitgliedstaaten der EU. Eine wertebasierte Garantie der Einheit und Wirksamkeit des Unionsrechts' (2020) EuR 22–60.

[201] C-359/16, *Altun*, 2018, para. 40. On mutual trust, see para. 5-003, *supra*; with respect to the area of freedom, security, and justice, see para. 8-001, *infra*.

[202] C-359/16, *Altun*, 2018, para. 61.

[203] C-316/19, *Commission v Slovenia*, 2020, paras 119–29 (failure to cooperate with the ECB to remedy the breach of the inviolability of the ECB archives by unilaterally seizing at the premises of the Central Bank of Slovenia documents connected to the performance of the tasks of the ESCB).

[204] C-94/00, *Roquette Frères*, 2002, paras 91–4.

[205] C-2/88 Imm., *Zwartveld and Others*, 1990, paras 17–22; C-234/89, *Delimitis*, 1991, para. 53. See Rovetta and Gambardella, 'Access to EU Antidumping/Subsidy Confidential Files: The EU Law "Zwartveld Sincere Cooperation Doctrine", Surprise What You Are Looking for Already Exists' (2014) Glob Trade Cust J 338. The Commission may refuse to provide information in order to avoid any interference with the functioning and independence of the Union or to safeguard its interests; see C-275/00, *Frist and Franex*, 2002, para. 49.

[206] 186/85, *Commission v Belgium*, 1987, para. 39.

[207] C-319/97, *Kortas*, 1999, paras 35–6. See Maletić, *The Law and Policy of Harmonisation in Europe's Internal Market* (Edward Elgar Publishing, 2013), 82.

legislation, even where it is, strictly speaking, only applicable to the Member States and not to the institutions.[208]

5.048 **Interinstitutional cooperation.** In principle, the duties of sincere cooperation apply between the institutions of the Union in the same way as they do between these institutions and the Member States.[209] In particular, that is true of decision-making procedures based on interinstitutional dialogue,[210] such as the legislative process.[211] Where the Council is under a duty to consult the European Parliament, it should avail itself of all the openings afforded by the Treaties and the Parliament's Rules of Procedure in order to obtain the Parliament's prior opinion. In turn, the Parliament should comply with a justified request from the Council to deal with a particular proposal urgently (see para. 17-035, *infra*). If the Parliament fails to do so, the Council is entitled to adopt the relevant act without awaiting the Parliament's opinion.[212] Pursuant to the principle of sincere cooperation the Commission may only withdraw a legislative proposal if it disagrees with amendments proposed by the Parliament or the Council after fully taking the concerns of the Parliament or the Council that gave rise to these amendments into account.[213]

2. Derogatory requirements

5.049 **Respect for Union interest.** As has already been mentioned, Article 4(3) TEU prohibits any measure which could jeopardize the attainment of the objectives of the Union. Under that provision, Member States are therefore precluded from reinforcing agreements in restraint of competition concluded by undertakings contrary to Article 101 TFEU.[214] More generally, Member States must allow measures preventing Union rules from having full force and effect (*effet utile*) to be set aside. A national court which has to apply Union law must have jurisdiction to do everything necessary to set aside provisions of (even constitutional) law that might prevent Union rules from having full effect.[215] Furthermore, Member States must make sure that procedural conditions applicable to claims seeking to assert rights derived from Union law are not less favourable than those relating to similar domestic claims

---

[208] F-65/07 *Aayhan*, 2009.
[209] 204/86 *Greece v Council*, 1988, para. 16.
[210] C-65/93, *European Parliament v Council*, 1995, para. 23, with case notes by Heukels (1995) CMLRev 1407–26 and Van Nuffel (1995) Col JEL 504, at 511–15.
[211] C-128/17, *Poland v European Parliament and Council*, 2019, paras 73–5.
[212] Ibid., para. 28.
[213] C-409/13, *Council v Commission*, 2014, paras 83 and 97–106.
[214] See the judgments cited in the discussion of competition in para. 9-012, *infra*. However, such a requirement exists only where there is already a clear Union policy: 229/83, *Leclerc*, 1985, para. 20.
[215] C-213/89 *Factortame and Others* (*Factortame I*), 1990, para. 20 (setting aside the rule of British constitutional law to the effect that a court may not give interim relief against the Crown especially in the form of an order setting aside the application of an act of Parliament). See also the earlier case 106/77, *Simmenthal*, 1978, para. 22, containing no express reference to Article 5 [*later Article 10*] EC (the national court has to refuse to apply any conflicting provision of national law of its own motion and does not have to await a ruling of its national Constitutional Court as required by its national legal system on the constitutionality of the domestic provision). See further the discussion of the primacy of Union law, paras 23-010–23-018. There is no obligation, however, to disapply a national provision where the issue before the national court concerns a situation which lies outside the scope of Union law: C-264/96, *ICI*, 1998, paras 31–5. See Capik, 'Five Decades Since *Van Gend en Loos* and *Costa* Came to Town: Primacy, Direct and Indirect Effect Revisited', in Lazowski and Blockmans (eds), *Research Handbook on EU Institutional Law* (Edward Elgar Publishing, 2016), 403; Claes, 'The Primacy of EU Law in European and National Law', in Chalmers and Arnull (eds), *The Oxford Handbook of European Union Law* (OUP, 2015), 184. Crucially, however, only provisions of Union that have direct effect result in this duty to set conflicting provisions of national law aside; for the other measures national courts are under a duty of consistent interpretation, limited, however, by the requirement not to interpret national law *contra legem*, see C-573/17, *Popławski*, 2019, paras 55–79.

(*principle of equivalence*) and are not such as in practice to make it impossible or excessively difficult to enforce those rights (*principle of effectiveness*).[216] When a judgment of the Court of Justice holds that a national measure is in breach of Union law a Member State cannot adopt rules that could make it more difficult to execute that judgment.[217]

Article 4(3) TEU puts Member States under a duty to respect the division of competences between the Union and the Member States. Where a Union act is adopted, conflicting national measures must be set aside pursuant to the principle of the primacy of Union law, at least in so far as the Union act has direct effect.[218] Member States must not exercise their powers (in particular in the field of international relations) in such a way as to affect the Union act or alter its scope.[219] Likewise, Member States must preserve the negotiation position of the Union before an international agreement is concluded, by refraining from taking unilateral actions that may jeopardize the success of the negotiations in question.[220] During the period for transposition of a directive, Member States must refrain from adopting measures which would jeopardize the achievement of what is provided for in the directive.[221] In situations in which Member States take action because the Union has failed to act in an area of exclusive Union competence, the principle of sincere cooperation requires them to refrain from adopting measures that do not have regard to the common interest.[222]

Respect for institutional balance. Lastly, the principle of sincere cooperation requires Member States to refrain from taking measures which might jeopardize the independence of the Union institutions and hence the institutional balance.[223] A Member State must avoid taking any measures that would result in members or civil servants of the Union institutions directly or indirectly losing the benefit of the privileges and immunities to which they are entitled under the relevant Protocol.[224] Equally, Member States may not exercise their competence in the area of social security systems in such a way that recruitment by Union

5.050

---

[216] 33/76 *Rewe*, 1976, para. 5; 45/76 *Comet*, 1976, paras 13–16; C-234/04 *Kapferer*, 2006, para. 22; C-574/15, *Scialdone*, paras 24–61. See also para. 23-018, *infra*. See Wallerman, 'Towards an EU Law Doctrine on The Exercise of Discretion in National Courts? The Member States' Self-Imposed Limits on national Procedural Autonomy' (2016) CMLRev 339.

[217] C-200/14, *Georgiana Câmpean*, 2016, para. 40.

[218] C-573/17, *Popławski*, 2019, paras 55–79.

[219] 22/70, *Commission v Council*, 1971, para. 22 (*AETR* case); Opinion 1/03, *New Lugano Convention on jurisdiction and the recognition and enforcement of judgments in civil and commercial matters*, 2006, para. 116. See also para. 10-039, *infra*, regarding limitations on the international action of the Member States.

[220] C-246/07, *Commission v Sweden*, 2010, paras 69–105; see also Opinion 1/13, *Lugano Convention on jurisdiction and the recognition and enforcement of judgments in civil and commercial matters*, para. 119; C-266/03, *Commission v Luxembourg*, 2005, paras 58–9, and C-433/03, *Commission v Germany*, 2005, paras 64–5; De Baere, "O, Where is Faith? O, Where is Loyalty?' Some Thoughts on the Duty of Loyal Co-operation and the Union's External Environmental Competences in the light of the PFOS Case' (2011) ELRev 405–19.

[221] C-129/96, *Inter-Environnement Wallonie*, 1997, para. 45; para. 27-020, *infra*; for a general discussion of standstill obligations, see Meyring, 'Europarechtliche Stillhalteverpflichtungen bei der nationalen Gesetzgebung' (2003) EuR 949–59. See also Ross, 'Effectiveness in the European Legal Order(s): Beyond Supremacy to Constitutional Proportionality?' (2006) ELRev 476; Drake, 'Twenty Years after Von Colson: The Impact of 'Indirect Effect' on the Protection of the Individual's Community Rights' (2005) ELRev 329.

[222] This also applies when Member States exceptionally take action in areas that fall within the exclusive competences of the Union: see the judgment on fisheries after the expiry of the transitional period: 804/79 *Commission v United Kingdom*, 1981, para. 30 (see nn. 99 and 105, *supra*, together with the discussion of powers in para. 5-023, *supra*).

[223] 208/80, *Lord Bruce of Donington*, 1981; 230/81 *Luxembourg v European Parliament*, 1983. See also C-345/95, *France v European Parliament*, 1997.

[224] 85/85, *Commission v Belgium*, 1986, paras 22–3; C-502/19, *Junqueras Vies*, 2019, para. 93.

institutions of national officials is impeded or discouraged.[225] Member States are also not entitled to adopt any measures which would result in a charge on the Union budget.[226] Finally, Member State courts must refrain from reviewing preparatory national acts leading to a decision by a Union institution if review of that decision is meant to be exclusively reserved to the Union Courts.[227]

VII. The Principle of Equal Treatment

A. Field of application

5.051 **General principle of law.** The principle of equal treatment requires persons in the same situation to be treated in the same way. In other words, it requires that comparable situations must not be treated differently and that different situations must not be treated in the same way unless such treatment is objectively justified (prohibition of discrimination). It is a general principle of Union law,[228] which is enshrined in the Charter of Fundamental Rights of the European Union.[229] Moreover, it is one of the 'values' on which the Union is founded (Article 2 TEU, added by the Treaty of Lisbon). Among the Union's objectives, the fight against discrimination and the promotion of equality between women and men have a prominent place (Article 3(3) TEU; see also Article 157 TFEU). The principle of equal treatment further finds expression in the Treaties in the form of the general prohibition of discrimination on grounds of nationality (Article 18 TFEU) and in the obligation incumbent on the Union to respect 'the equality of Member States before the Treaties'[230] (Article 4(2) TEU, introduced by the Treaty of Lisbon). Although the EAEC Treaty does not contain any

---

[225] C-647/13, *Melchior*, 2015, paras 25–9 (measure disregarding periods of work completed as a contractual agent in a Union institution in relation to eligibility for unemployment benefit); C-515/14, *Commission v Cyprus*, 2016, para. 52 (age-related criterion deterring workers from taking work in another Member State, or in a Union institution).

[226] See the judgments concerning European Schools, para. 13-048, *infra*. Accordingly, Member States are, on the basis of Article 4(3) TEU, also liable for a loss of own resources, even if that is the result of an error committed by an overseas territory or country listed in Annex II TFEU that is dependent on that Member State, see C-395/17, *Commission v Netherlands*, 2019, paras 71–7; see also C-391/17, *Commission v United Kingdom*, 2019, paras 69–75.

[227] C-219/17, *Berlusconi and Fininvest*, 2018, paras 43–51, with a case note by Brito Bastos (2019) CMLRev 1355; see also C-414/18, *Iccrea Banca*, 2019, paras 40–1.

[228] 117/76 and 16/77, *Ruckdeschel*, 1977, para. 7. For a general discussion, see Rossi and Casolari (eds), *The Principle of Equality in EU Law* (Springer, 2017), 316; Muir, *EU Equality Law: The First Fundamental Rights Policy of the EU* (OUP, 2018) 212; Tobler, 'The Prohibition of Discrimination in the Union's Layered System of Equality Law: From Early Staff Cases to the Mangold Approach', in Court of Justice of the European Union, *The Court of Justice and the Construction of Europe: Analyses and Perspectives on Sixty Years of Case-law* (Springer, 2013), 443–71; Ellis and Watson, *EU Anti-Discrimination Law* (OUP, 2012), 519; Bell, 'The Principle of Equal Treatment: Widening and Deepening', in Craig and De Búrca (eds), *The Evolution of EU Law* (OUP, 2011), 611–38; Tridimas, *The General Principles of EU Law* (OUP, 2013), chapter 2; Ellis, *EU Anti-Discrimination Law* (OUP, 2005), 401; Bell and Waddington, 'Reflecting on Equalities in European Equality Law' (2003) ELRev 349–69; Lenaerts, 'L'égalité de traitement en droit communautaire: un principe unique aux apparences multiples' (1991) CDE 3–41.

[229] Chapter III of the Charter, which deals with equality before the law (Article 20); non-discrimination (Article 21); cultural, religious, and linguistic diversity (Article 22); equality between men and women (Article 23); the rights of the child (Article 24); the rights of the elderly (Article 25); and integration of persons with disabilities (Article 26).

[230] See Lenaerts and Van Nuffel, 'Advanced Integration and the Principle of Equality of Member States within the European Union', in Kaddous and Auer (eds), *Les principes fondamentaux de la Constitution européenne* (Helbing & Lichtenhahn/Bruylant/L.G.D.J., 2006), 245–76; Classen, 'Die Gleichheit der Mitgliedstaaten und ihre Ausformungen im Unionsrecht' (2020) EuR 255–69.

explicit provision which corresponds to Article 18 TFEU, the prohibition of discrimination on grounds of nationality is a general principle which is also applicable under the EAEC Treaty to situations coming within the scope of application of that Treaty[231].

A number of Treaty provisions refer to the obligation to treat market participants in the same way.[232] For instance, the second subpara. of Article 40(2) TFEU provides that the common organization of the agricultural markets shall 'exclude any discrimination between producers or consumers within the Union'.

Scope. The institutions may not adopt any act based on criteria in breach of the principle of equality. The Union institutions are to respect the principle of equal treatment not only in their legislative activity,[233] but also where they conclude international agreements[234] or where they implement Union legislation by adopting implementing acts,[235] or in the treatment of their own staff.[236] Furthermore, all Union acts must be interpreted in accordance with the principle of equal treatment.[237] In addition, the principle of equality within the scope of application of Union law is also binding on the Member States; they must respect the principle when implementing Union acts.[238] When a discrimination in breach of Union law has been found, measures must be taken in order to restore equal treatment. Until this has happened, respect for the principle of equality can only be assured by extending the benefits enjoyed by the advantaged group to the disadvantaged group.[239] Accordingly, every national court must set aside any discriminatory national measure, without having to await or request action by the national legislature to eliminate the discrimination.[240]

5.052

1. Prohibition of discrimination on grounds of the nationality of a Member State

Discrimination on grounds of nationality. The first para. of Article 18 TFEU prohibits any discrimination on grounds of nationality '[w]ithin the scope of application of the Treaties' and 'without prejudice to any special provisions contained therein'.[241] This right is also

5.053

---

[231] C-115/08, ČEZ, 2009, paras 87–98, with a case note by Möstl (2010) CMLRev 1221.

[232] See Article 40(2), second subpara.; Article 101(1)(d); Article 102, second para., indent (c) TFEU.

[233] e.g. 20/71, *Sabbatini v European Parliament*, 1972, para. 13; C-25/02, *Rinke*, 2003, paras 25–28 (prohibition of indirect discrimination on grounds of sex); C-210/03, *Swedish Match*, 2004, paras 70–1 (different treatment of different tobacco products); C-344/04, *IATA and ELFAA*, 2006, paras 93–9 (different treatment of different means of transport); C-127/07, *Arcelor Atlantique et Lorraine and Others*, 2008 (different treatment of different sectors of industry with regard to greenhouse gas emissions). See Voss, 'The Principle of Equality: A Limit to the Commission's Discretion in EU Competition Law Enforcement?' (2013) GAR 149.

[234] C-122/95, *Germany v Council*, 1998, paras 59–72.

[235] e.g. C-221/09, *AJD Tuna*, 2011, paras 86–113.

[236] Accordingly, the Council infringed the principle of equal treatment by applying the Staff Regulations differently with regard to institutions which were in the same situation: T-164/97, *Busaca and Others v Court of Auditors*, 1998, paras 48–61 (upheld on appeal: C-434/98 P, *Council v Busaca and Court of Auditors*, 2000). The European Central Bank was found to have infringed the principle of equal treatment by granting an education allowance only to staff in receipt of expatriation allowance: T-94/01, T-125/01, and T-286/01, *Hirsch and Others v ECB*, 2003, paras 45–72.

[237] C-402/07 and C-432/07, *Sturgeon*, 2009, paras 48–61; C-581/10 and C-629/10, *Nelson and TUI Travel*, 2012, paras 28–40.

[238] C-42/11, *Lopes Da Silva Jorge*, 2012, para. 39; C-401/11, *Soukupová*, 2013, paras 26–8; C-234/12, *Sky Italia*, 2013, paras 15–24, with a case note by van den Bergen, (2014) LIEI 305; C-195/12, *Industrie du bois de Vielsalm & Cie*, 2013, para. 48 *et seq*.

[239] e.g. C-406/15, *Milkova*, 2017, paras 66–8; C-193/17, *Cresco*, 2019, para. 79.

[240] C-406/15, *Milkova*, 2017, para. 67.

[241] See, generally, O'Brien, *Unity in Adversity: EU Citizenship, Social Justice and the Cautionary Tale of the UK* (Hart Publishing, 2017) 33–58, van der Mei, 'The Outer Limits of the Prohibition of Discrimination on Grounds of Nationality: A Look through the Lens of Union Citizenship' (2011) MJ 62; Rossi, 'Das Diskriminierungsverbot nach Art. 12 EGV' (2000) EuR 197–217.

enshrined in Article 21(2) of the Charter of Fundamental Rights, which, as it corresponds to Article 18 TFEU, is interpreted accordingly.[242] In a situation governed by Union law,[243] a Member State must not discriminate, be it in an indirect way, against nationals of other Member States. Thus, a Member State may not make the award of a right subject to the condition that the person concerned is a national of another Member State that has entered into a reciprocal agreement with that Member State.[244] In practice, discrimination is often indirect in nature (see para. 6-018, *infra*), for instance by distinguishing on the basis of the place or duration of residence. Individuals too are subject to the prohibition of discrimination on grounds of nationality, in particular where a group or organization exercises a certain power over individuals and is in a position to impose on them conditions which adversely affect the exercise of the fundamental freedoms guaranteed under the Treaties.[245] Indeed every citizen of the Union has the right not be discriminated against on the basis of nationality within the substantive scope of Union law.[246] In contrast, Article 18 TFEU does not prohibit differences in treatment between nationals of Member States and nationals of third countries,[247] so nationals of third countries cannot succeed by invoking Article 18 TFEU.[248]

In some circumstances, however, a difference in treatment may be objectively justified, for example, an obligation imposed only on non-residents to pay security in respect of infringements as long as no international or Union instruments existed to ensure that a fine may if necessary be enforced in another Member State,[249] or a residence requirement which places a Member State's own nationals at an advantage but is based on objective considerations that are independent of the nationality of the persons concerned and proportionate to the legitimate aim of the national provisions.[250] Just as they cannot justify a barrier to the fundamental principles of free movement,[251] considerations that have been specifically

---

[242] See C-703/17, *Krah*, 2019; para. 18.
[243] Before the Lisbon Treaty entered into force, Article 12 EC applied only 'within the scope of application of this Treaty', i.e. the scope of Community law, excluding the former second and third pillars. Nevertheless, the Court of Justice had already considered that the principle laid down in Article 12 EC was applicable to measures adopted under the former third pillar where they infringed provisions of Community law, in particular the provisions on the freedom of movement and residence of citizens of the Union (C-123/08 *Wolzenburg*, 2009, paras 44–7). For an example of a situation where that condition was not fulfilled, see C-581/18, *RB*, 2020, paras 28–60.
[244] 186/87, *Cowan*, 1989, para. 13.
[245] C-411/98, *Ferlini*, 2000, para. 50; see also C-281/98, *Angonese*, 2000, paras 30–6; C-94/07, *Raccanelli*, 2008, paras 38–48. See Krenn, 'A Missing Piece in the Horizontal Effect 'Jigsaw': Horizontal Direct Effect and the Free Movement of Goods' (2012) CMLRev 177.
[246] C-85/96, *Martínez Sala*, 1998, paras 54–65.
[247] C-22/08 and C-23/08, *Vatsouras and Koupatantze*, 2009, para. 52, with a case note by Damjanovic (2010) CMLRev 847. See Friðriksdóttir, *What Happened to Equality?: The Construction of the Right to Equal Treatment of Third-Country Nationals in European Union Law on Labour Migration* (Brill, 2017), 89–92; Brouwer and de Vries, 'Third-country Nationals and DIscrimination on the Ground of Nationality: Article 18 TFEU in the Context of Article 14 ECHR and EU Migration Law: Time for a New Approach', in van den Brink, Burri, and Goldschmidt (eds), *Equality and Human Rights: Nothing but Trouble? Liber Amicorum Titia Loenen* (Utrecht University, 2015), 123; Hublet, 'The Scope of Article 12 of the European Communities Vis-à-Vis Third-Country Nationals: Evolution at Last?' (2009) ELJ 757.
[248] C-45/12, *Hadj Ahmed*, 2003, para. 38 *et seq.*; C-291/09, *Guarnieri*, 2011, para. 20.
[249] C-224/00, *Commission v Italy*, 2002, paras 20–4. See since that judgment, however, Council Framework Decision 2005/214/JHA of 24 February 2005 on the application of the principle of mutual recognition to financial penalties OJ 2005 L76/16.
[250] See C-138/02, *Collins*, 2004, paras 65–73; C-103/08, *Gottwald*, 2009, paras 31–40. See also C-73/08 *Bressol and Others*, 2010, paras 62–81, with a case note by Garben (2010) CMLRev 1493. See also Verschueren, 'Preventing 'Benefit Tourism' in the EU: A Narrow or Broad Interpretation of the Possibilities Offered by the ECJ in *Dano*?' (2015) CMLRev 363.
[251] See paras 7-039–7-040 (goods), 7-071–7-072 (persons) and 7-091–7-092 (services), *infra*.

addressed in Union harmonization measures or aims of a purely economic nature cannot justify discrimination on grounds of nationality.[252] In addition, a Member State may obviously treat its nationals differently from nationals of other Member States where it enacts legislation for vessels flying the national flag outside its territorial waters, since, under the rules of public international law, it may exercise its jurisdiction beyond territorial sea limits only over vessels flying its flag.[253]

Specific prohibitions. Article 18 TFEU, which lays down the general principle of the prohibition of discrimination on grounds of nationality, applies independently only to situations governed by Union law in respect of which the Treaties lay down no specific prohibition of discrimination.[254] In fact, the words 'special provisions' in Article 18 TFEU refer to other Treaty provisions specifying the principle set forth in that article, such as the Treaty provisions on the free movement of goods, persons, services, and capital which express the basic condition of the internal market, namely that all factors of production, irrespective of the nationality of persons[255] or the origin of goods,[256] services,[257] and capital[258] may participate in the market (see para. 7-011, *infra*). It follows that whenever a situation is covered by one of the Treaty provisions on free movement, that situation must be considered on the basis of that specific provision and not of Article 18 TFEU.[259]

5.054

Combination with citizenship of the Union. As mentioned before, every citizen of the Union has the right not to suffer discrimination on grounds of nationality in all situations falling 'within the scope of application of the Treaties'. Such situations include those involving the exercise of the fundamental freedoms guaranteed by the Treaties, in particular the exercise of the right enjoyed by citizens of the Union to move and reside within the territory of the Member States (see Article 21 TFEU).[260] A person can rely on Article 18 TFEU in combination with Article 21 TFEU if he or she, being a national of a Member State and thus a citizen of the Union, lawfully resides in the territory of another Member State.[261]

5.055

---

[252] See C-115/08, ČEZ, 2009, paras 109 and 110–36 (in the context of the EAEC Treaty); C-628/11, *International Jet Management*, 2014, para. 70. See Tryfonidou, 'The Notions of "Restriction" and "Discrimination" in the Context of the Free Movement of Persons Provisions: From a Relationship of Interdependence to one of (Almost Complete) Independence' (2014) YEL 385.

[253] C-379/92, *Peralta*, 1994, para. 47.

[254] C-193/94, *Skanavi and Chryssanthakopoulos*, 1996, para. 20; C-131/96, *Mora Romero*, 1997, para. 10; C-296/15, *Medisanus*, 2017, para. 62; C-420/15, *U*, 2017, para. 16; C-591/17, *Austria v. Germany*, 2019, paras 39–41, with a case note by Chapuis-Doppler and Delhomme (2019) MJ 849

[255] See Article 37(1); Article 45(2); Article 49, second para.; Article 92 and Article 200 (5) TFEU.

[256] See Article 36, last sentence; Article 95(1); Article 110, first para. TFEU.

[257] See Article 57, third para. and Article 61 TFEU.

[258] See Article 65(3) TFEU.

[259] See, e.g., C-422/01, *Skandia and Ramstedt*, 2003, para. 61; C-387/01, *Weigel and Weigel*, 2004, paras 57-59; C-591/17, *Austria v Germany*, 2019, para. 41; C-581/18, *TÜV Rheinland LGA Products and Allianz IARD*, 2020, para. 31.

[260] C-224/98, *D'Hoop*, 2002, para. 29; C-148/02, *Garcia Avello*, 2003, para. 24; C-224/02, *Pusa*, 2004, para. 17; C-209/03, *Bidar*, 2005, para. 33; C-524/06, *Huber*, 2008, para. 71. For a discussion, see Neuvonen, *Equal Citizenship and Its Limits in EU Law: We the Burden?* (Hart Publishing, 2016), 40–88; Van Nuffel and Cambien, 'De vrijheid van economisch niet-actieve EU-burgers om binnen de EU te reizen, te verblijven en te studeren' (2009) SEW 144–54; Lenaerts, 'Union Citizenship and the Principle of Non-discrimination on Grounds of Nationality', in X (ed.), *Festskrift til Claus Gulmann—Liber Amicorum* (Forlaget Thomson A/S, 2006) 289–309; White, 'Free Movement, Equal Treatment, and Citizenship of the Union' (2005) 54 ICLQ 885–906.

[261] C-85/96, *Martínez Sala*, 1998, para. 61. Lawful residence in the territory of another Member State suffices. It is not required that the citizen concerned has actually moved from one Member State to another: see C-148/02, *Garcia Avello*, 2003, paras 13 and 27; C-200/02, *Zhu and Chen*, 2004, para. 23-006, *infra*); C-11/06, *Morgan and Bucher*, 2007, para. 23; C-523/11, *Prinz and Seeberger*, 2013, para. 25.

Moreover, Article 18 TFEU also applies where a family member of a citizen of the Union has made use of his or her right of free movement (as opposed to the citizen himself or herself), where this results in unequal treatment.[262]

The exercise of the fundamental right to free movement enables citizens of the Union to claim equal treatment in a broad range of areas. For instance, a jobseeker in another Member State may claim equal treatment with regard to the grant of a financial benefit designed to facilitate access to the employment market in that Member State.[263]

The Court of Justice likewise applies Article 18 TFEU to the conditions governing access to education. Consequently, it is contrary to the principle of non-discrimination for a Member State to distinguish, as regards the level of educational fees relating to a vocational training, between students who are its nationals and students who are nationals of other Member States.[264] This case law was subsequently extended to university enrolment fees[265] and aspects related to access to education.[266] Subsequently, after the introduction of citizenship of the Union,[267] the Court has held that assistance given to students for maintenance and for training, such as student grants or subsidised loans,[268] or student discounts on transportation fees,[269] also fall within the scope of the Treaties for the purposes of Article 18 TFEU. Pursuant to Article 24(2) of Directive 2004/38 the equal treatment in granting social assistance does however require that the residence of the Union citizen on the territory of the host Member State meets the requirements of Directive 2004/38 (see para. 6-010, *infra*). Furthermore, in *Cowan* the Court held that tourists coming from other Member States should get access to compensation granted to victims of violent crimes on the same conditions as nationals of the host Member State.[270] The *Petruhhin* judgment makes clear that equal treatment also extends to the protection against extradition.[271] Union citizens

---

[262] C-403/03, *Schempp*, 2005, paras 22–5.
[263] C-138/02, *Collins*, 2004, paras 54–64; C-442/16, *Gusa*, 2017, paras. 26–46; C-483/17, *Tarola*, 2019, paras 43–5. See Coutts, 'The Shifting Geometry of Union Citizenship A Supranational Status from Transnational Rights' (2019) CYEL 318; Kramer, 'Earning Social Citizenship in the European Union: Free Movement and Access to Social Assistance Benefits Reconstructed' (2016) CYEL 270.
[264] 293/83, *Gravier*, 1985, paras 11–26. For an overview on the case law of the Court with regard to Article 18 TFEU, access to education, and the conditions under which the free movement of students is exercised, see Hoogenboom, 'In Search of a Rationale for the EU Citizenship Jurisprudence' (2015) OJLS 301.
[265] 24/86, *Blaizot*, 1988, paras 10–24; C-47/93, *Commission v Belgium*, 1994.
[266] C-357/89, *Raulin*, 1992, paras 35–43 (requirement to have a residence permit in order to be allowed to pursue higher studies); 42/87, *Commission v Belgium*, 1988, paras 7–9 (no State funding of educational establishments for students who are nationals of Member States other than Belgium and Luxembourg); C-65/03, *Commission v Belgium*, 2004, paras 25–9, and C-147/03, *Commission v Austria*, 2005, paras 31–5; C-73/08, *Bressol and Others*, 2010, paras 40–6 (additional university entry requirements for students from other Member States).
[267] Students who move to another Member State to pursue studies make use of the right laid down in Article 18 EC (see para. 1-042, *supra*).
[268] C-209/03, *Bidar*, paras 37–42. The Court thereby overruled earlier case law in which it held that such assistance fell outside the scope of the Treaty (39/86, *Lair*, 1988, paras 11–16; 197/86, *Brown*, 1988, paras 14–19). For a discussion of the *Bidar* case, see Golynker (2006) ELRev 390–401; De Waele (2005) NTER 122–7; Brand (2005) ColJEL 293–304. See also, Hoogenboom, 'Mobility of Students and the Financial Sustainability of Higher Education Systems in the EU: A Union of Harmony Or Irreconcilable Differences?' (2013) CYELP 15; Pennings, 'EU Citizenship: Access to Social Benefits in Other EU Member States' (2012) Int'l J Comp Lab L & Ind Rel 307; Van der Mei, 'Union citizenship and the 'De-nationalisation' of the Territorial Welfare State. Comments on case C-456/02 Trojani and Case C-209/03 Bidar' (2005) EJML 203–11; Armbrecht, 'Ausbildungsförderung für Studenten-Gleicher Zugang für Unionsbürger?' (2005) ZEuS 175–209; Dougan, 'Fees, Grants, Loans and Dole Cheques: Who Covers the Costs of Migrant Education within the EU?' (2005) CMLRev 943–86.
[269] C-75/11, *Commission v Austria*, 2012, para. 42 *et seq.*
[270] 186/87, *Cowan*, 1989, para. 17; see also C-45/93, *Commission v. Spain*, 1994, paras 5–10.
[271] C-182/15, *Petruhhin*, 2016, paras 29–33, with a case note by Böse, (2017) CMLRev 1781; see also C-247/17, *Raugevicius*, 2018, paras 44–5. The Court has extended this reasoning to also encompass EEA nationals who

moreover have a right to be treated like the citizens of the host Member State in respect of the language used in court proceedings.[272]

A difference in treatment can be justified if it is based on objective considerations independent of the nationality of the persons concerned and is proportionate to the legitimate aim of the national provisions.[273] It is thus permissible for a Member State to ensure that the aforementioned grant of social benefits and assistance to cover the maintenance costs of students from other Member States does not become an unreasonable burden that could have consequences for the overall level of assistance which may be granted by that State.[274] A Member State may reserve this assistance to students who have demonstrated a certain degree of integration into the society of that Member State, for example by demanding that the student has resided in that Member State for a sufficiently long period of time.[275] In accordance with the principle of proportionality, a discriminatory measure will however not be justified where non-discriminatory measures could suffice in order to achieve the legitimate objective pursued.[276] In the case of student discounts on transport fees, for example, the Court held that the existence of a real link between the student and the host Member State could effectively be proven on the basis of the mere enrolment of the student in an educational institution recognized or financed by that Member State.[277]

Scope of application of the Treaties. Article 18 TFEU prohibits discrimination on grounds of nationality 'within the scope of application of the Treaties'. The Court interprets that scope of application broadly. First, national legislation adopted in implementation of primary or secondary Union law clearly falls within the scope of application of the Treaties.[278] Second, the ambit of the Treaties also extends to certain international agreements concluded amongst the Member States in connection with the Treaties. These agreements may not be implemented in a way that discriminates against nationals of other Member States.[279]

5.056

It follows from the case law that even when a particular matter falls within the competence of the Member States (e.g. legislation concerning criminal law or the way children are given a name), Union law sets certain limits to the exercise of that competence since national legislative provisions 'may not discriminate against persons to whom Union law gives the

---

have made use of the free movement of services, see C-879/19, *I.N.*, 2020, para. 75. See Weyembergh and Catteau, 'L'extradition des citoyens européens vers des pays tiers: quels enseignements tirer des arrêts Petruhhin et suivants' (2019) CDE 451–83; Pozdnakova, 'Aleksei Petruhhin: Extradition of EU Citizens to Third States' (2017) EP 1; Szaluzzo, 'EU Law and Extradition Agreements of Member States: The Petruhhin Case' (2017) EP 435.

[272] C-274/96, *Bickel and Franz*, 1998, paras 13–31; C-322/13, *Grauel Rüffer*, 2014, paras 19–26.

[273] e.g. C-224/98 *D'Hoop*, 2002, para. 36; C-148/02, *Garcia Avello*, 2003, para. 31; C-209/03, *Bidar*, 2005, para. 54; C-524/06, *Huber*, 2008, para. 75.

[274] C-209/03, *Bidar*, 2005, para. 56; C-359/13, *Martens*, 2015, para. 34; C-438/14, *Bogendorff von Wolffersdorff*, 2016, para. 48

[275] C-158/07, *Förster*, 2008, paras 48–55. This is confirmed by Article 24(2) of Directive 2004/38 (see para. 6-015). See Thym, 'The Elusive Limits of Solidarity: Residence Rights Of and Social Benefits For Economically Inactive Union Citizens' (2015) CMLRev 17.

[276] C-147/03, *Commission v Austria*, 2005, paras 60–6; C-73/08 *Bressol and Others*, 2010, paras 77–81.

[277] C-75/11, *Commission v Austria*, 2012, paras 53–5. See Guild, Peers, and Tomkin (eds), *The EU Citizenship Directive: a Commentary* (OUP, 2019), 243–4.

[278] e.g. C-29/95, *Pastoors and Trans-Cap*, 1997, paras 13–18.

[279] e.g. C-28/04, *Tod's*, 2005, paras 20–7.

right to equal treatment or restrict the fundamental freedoms guaranteed by Union law'.[280] National legislative provisions are subject to the prohibition of discrimination laid down in Article 18 where they fall within the scope of application of the Treaties by reason of their effects on intra-Union trade in goods and services or on free movement of persons, even where they do not as such restrict the free movement of goods, services, or persons.[281] This applies for example in respect of copyrights[282] or the possibility to initiate court proceedings without first having to provide security.[283] Member States must also exercise their tax powers in accordance with Article 18 TFEU. The Court found a violation of Article 18 TFEU in respect of a German infrastructure use charge that was offset for German residents through a corresponding relief from the motor vehicle tax.[284]

As regards matters which fall outside the scope of the Treaties, it is not contrary to Article 18 for persons to be treated differently on grounds of their nationality. This may arise, for example, in civil law matters when the private international law of a Member State takes nationality as the connecting factor for determining the applicable substantive law[285] or in matters of taxation where, in a convention on double taxation concluded between the Member States, the criterion of nationality appears in a provision which is intended to allocate fiscal sovereignty.[286] As regards, by contrast, the exercise of fiscal sovereignty granted by such a provision, the Member State in which that sovereignty is vested must observe the principle of equal treatment.[287]

5.057 **Combating discrimination.** The second para. of Article 18 TFEU empowers the European Parliament and the Council, acting under the ordinary legislative procedure, to adopt 'rules designed to prohibit such discrimination'. This means that the European Parliament and the Council may take the necessary measures to prohibit all forms of discrimination on grounds of nationality. The measures need not be confined to the right to equal treatment flowing from the first paragraph of Article 18, but may also deal with ancillary aspects which ought to be settled in order to secure effective exercise of that right. The Court of Justice has held that Article 18 was the only proper legal basis for a Council directive on students' right of residence on the ground that equal treatment in the matter of access to vocational training requires that students have the right to reside in the Member State where they have been admitted to vocational training.[288]

---

[280] e.g. 186/87, *Cowan*, 1989, para. 19 (right to compensation of a person who is a victim of an offence, which comes under the French law of criminal procedure and, as a result, within the competence of the Member State). See also C-224/02, *Pusa*, 2004, paras 22–35 (rules on enforcement for the recovery of debts).
[281] C-323/95, *Hayes*, 1997, para. 16; C-122/96, *Saldanha and MTS*, 1997, para. 20. However, there are limits to the scope of Union law, see C-291/96, *Grado and Bashir*, 1997, paras 13–14.
[282] C-92/92 and C-326/92, *Phil Collins and Others*, 1993, paras 19–28; C-360/00, *Ricordi & Co. Bühnen- und Musikverlag*, 2002, paras 24–34.
[283] C-43/95, *Data Delecta and Forsberg*, 1996, paras 10–22; C-323/95, *Hayes*, 1997, paras 13–17; C-122/96, *Saldanha en MTS*, 1997, paras 16–24.
[284] C-591/17, *Austria v Germany*, 2019, paras 37–78. However, the difference in treatment resulting from the possibility of requiring offenders using a vehicle registered in a Member State other than Germany to pay a sum as security in order to ensure payment of the fine imposed was not deemed disproportionate to the objective pursued: ibid., paras 91–110.
[285] C-430/97, *Johannes*, 1999, paras 26–9.
[286] C-241/14, *Bukovansky*, 2015, paras 37–8; C-168/19 and C-169/19, *HB and IC*, 2020, paras 18–19.
[287] C-241/14, *Bukovansky*, 2015, para. 38.
[288] C-295/90, *European Parliament v Council*, 1992, paras 15–20.

2. Prohibition of discrimination on grounds of sex/gender

Prohibition of discrimination. An important application of the prohibition of discrimination is the obligation that men and women must be treated equally.[289] Article 3(3) TEU requires the Union to promote in all its action 'the equality between women and men', whereas Article 10 TFEU requires that '[i]n defining and implementing its policies and activities, the Union shall aim to combat discrimination based on sex'. The Court of Justice has referred to equal treatment of men and women as one of the fundamental human rights whose observance it has a duty to ensure.[290] The principle is also enshrined in Article 23 Charter of Fundamental Rights of the European Union.[291] The principle of equal treatment prohibits the Union and the Member States to discriminate on grounds of sex. It is also expressed in the Treaties, in the form of the principle, that male and female workers should receive equal pay for equal work or work of equal value (Article 157(1) TFEU),[292] which encompasses pension rights.[293]

5.058

The principle applies to access to employment and, consequently, in principle also to military occupations.[294] However, Union law does not preclude compulsory military service being reserved to men.[295] The principle further applies to the end of a career and thus precludes different retirement ages for male and female judges.[296] As a result of the prohibition of discrimination on grounds of sex, a worker may not be discriminated against because he or she or his or her partner wishes to undergo a gender-reassignment operation or has undergone such an operation.[297] Similarly, a Member State may not require a person, who

---

[289] See Mulder, *EU Non-Discrimination Law in the Courts: Approaches to Sex and Sexualities Discrimination in EU Law* (Hart Publishing, 2017); Beveridge, 'Gender, the Acquis and Beyond', in Dougan and Currie (eds), *50 Years of the European Treaties: Looking Back and Thinking Forward* (Hart Publishing, 2009) 393–413; Hervey and O'Keeffe (eds), *Sex Equality Law in the European Union* (John Wiley & Sons, 1996); Millns, 'Gender Equality, Citizenship and the EU's Constitutional Future' (2007) ELJ 218–37; Masselot, 'The State of Gender Equality Law in the European Union' (2007) ELJ 152–68; Hervey, 'Thirty Years of EU Sex Equality Law: Looking Backwards, Looking Forwards' (2005) MJECL 307–25; Jacqmain, 'Egalité entre travailleurs féminins et masculins' (2000) JTDE 201–10; Mancini and O'Leary, 'The New Frontiers of Sex Equality Law in the European Union' (1999) ELRev 331–53.

[290] C-43/75, *Defrenne*, 1976, paras 26–30; C-185/97, *Coote*, 1998, para. 23. For a survey of the case law, see Costello and Davies, 'The Case Law of the Court of Justice in the Field of Sex Equality since 2000' (2006) CMLRev 1567–616; Pager, 'Strictness vs. Discretion: The European Court of Justice's Variable Vision of Gender Equality' (2003) AJCL 553–609; Shaw 'Gender and the European Court of Justice', in De Burca and Weiler (eds), *The European Court of Justice* (OUP, 2001) 87–142.

[291] For an application of this provision leading to the partial invalidation of a Directive, see C-263/09, *Association belge des Consommateurs Test-Achats*, 2011, paras 15–34.

[292] See the discussion of indirect discrimination, para. 5-063, *infra*, and the discussion of social policy, para. 9-046, *infra*. For a blatant example, see C-206/00, *Mouflin*, 2001, paras 28–31. Until the Treaty of Amsterdam, Article 119 EC [now Article 157 TFEU] referred only to 'equal work'; however, the principle was already extended to 'the same work' by Council Directive 75/117/EEC of 10 February 1975 on the approximation of the laws of the Member States relating to the application of the principle of equal pay for men and women, OJ 1975 L45/19, now replaced by Directive 2006/54/EC of the European Parliament and of the Council of 5 July 2006 on the implementation of the principle of equal opportunities and equal treatment of men and women in matters of employment and occupation, OJ 2006 L204/23.

[293] C-171/18, *Safeway*, 2019, paras 12–45. See earlier, C-43/75, *Defrenne*, 1976; C-262/88, *Barber*, 1990; C-200/91, *Coloroll Pension Trustees*, 1994; C-408/92, *Avdel Systems*, 1994; C-28/93, *van den Akker*, 1994. For an overview of the application of the principle of equality to pensions, see Ellis and Watson, *EU Anti-Discrimination Law* (OUP, 2012), 180–272.

[294] C-273/97, *Sirdar*, 1999, paras 11–29; C-285/98, *Kreil*, 2000, paras 15–32 (in spite of the constitutional ban on military service for women); the exclusion of women from service in special commando units may, however, be justified on the basis of Directive 76/207/EEC (n. 302, *infra*): *Sirdar*, paras 21–32.

[295] C-186/01, *Dory*, 2003, paras 29–42.

[296] C-192/18, *Commission v Poland*, 2019, paras 58–84.

[297] C-13/94, *P.*, 1996, paras 13–24, with a case note by Brems (1996) ColJEL 339–45; C-117/01, *K.B.*, 2004, paras 30–4; C-423/04, *Richards*, 2006, paras 27–31.

has changed gender, not only to fulfil physical, social, and psychological criteria but also to satisfy the condition of not being married to a person of the gender that he or she has acquired as a result of that change, in order to be able to claim a State retirement pension as from the statutory pensionable age applicable to persons of his or her acquired gender.[298] The Court of Justice considers, however, that discrimination on grounds of sexual orientation does not fall within the prohibition of discrimination on grounds of sex.[299]

In many areas, the Union-law principle of equal treatment of men and women has prompted better protection for women against unjustified discrimination.[300] Equality between men and women with regard to labour market opportunities and treatment at work is also among the objectives of Union social policy (see Article 153(1)(i) TFEU).[301] On the basis of Article 157(3) TFEU the Union has adopted directives to ensure equal treatment for men and women as regards access to employment, vocational training, promotion, and working conditions,[302] and in the field of social security.[303] Outside the context of the labour market, the Union has adopted directives on the basis of Article 19 TFEU, for instance with regard to equal treatment between men and women in access to and supply of goods and services.[304]

5.059 **Positive discrimination.** All this does not mean that the Member States are not entitled to take measures embodying 'positive discrimination'. The guarantee of equal access to employment and of equal promotion opportunities for men and women does not preclude measures to enhance equal opportunity for men and women which are intended, *inter alia*,

---

[298] C-451/16, *MB*, 2018, paras 26–53, with case notes by Hamilton (2019) ILARC 335; Vallet-Pamart (2018) RDEA 365. See Dunne, 'Transgender Rights in Europe: EU and Council of Europe Movements towards Gender Identity Equality', in Ashford and Maine (eds), *Research Handbook on Gender Sexuality and the Law* (Edward Elgar Publishing, 2020), 134–49.

[299] C-249/96, *Grant*, 1998, paras 24–47, with a case note by McInnes (1999) CMLRev 1043–58. See also para. 5-0634, *infra*.

[300] The principle also opposes the discriminatory effects of legislation intended to protect women; see, *inter alia*, the case law rejecting a national ban on night work by women: C-345/89, *Stoeckel*, 1991; C-158/91, *Levy*, 1993; C-203/03, *Commission v Austria*, 2005, paras 42–50 and 69–75. See Foubert, *The Legal Protection of the Pregnant Worker in the European Community: Sex Equality, Thoughts of Social and Economic Policy and Comparative Leaps to the United States of America* (Kluwer, 2002), 389; Caracciolo di Torella and Masselot, 'Pregnancy, Maternity and the Organisation of Family Life: An Attempt to Classify the Case Law of the Court of Justice' (2001) ELRev 239–60; Masselot and Berthou, 'La CJCE, le droit de la maternité et le principe de non-discrimination—vers une clarification?' (2000) CDE 637–56; De Vos, 'Le travail de nuit: La "Realpolitik" de l'égalité!' (1993) JT 1–7.

[301] Article 137 EC took over the wording of Article 2 of the Social Agreement (para. 9-046, *infra*), pursuant to which the Council adopted, on 15 December 1997, Directive 97/80/EC on the burden of proof in cases of discrimination based on sex, OJ 1998 L14/6, now replaced by Directive 2006/54/EC (n. 292, *supra*).

[302] Council Directive 76/207/EEC of 9 February 1976 on the implementation of the principle of equal treatment for men and women as regards access to employment, vocational training and promotion, and working conditions, OJ 1976 L39/40, now replaced by Directive 2006/54/EC (n. 292, *supra*). See also Council Directive 86/613/EEC of 11 December 1986 on the application of the principle of equal treatment between men and women engaged in an activity, including agriculture, in a self-employed capacity, and on the protection of self-employed women during pregnancy and motherhood, OJ 1986 L359/56, now replaced by Directive 2010/41/EU of the European Parliament and of the Council of 7 July 2010 on the application of the principle of equal treatment between men and women engaged in an activity in a self-employed capacity, OJ 2010 L180/1.

[303] Council Directive 79/7/EEC of 19 December 1978 on the progressive implementation of the principle of equal treatment for men and women in matters of social security, OJ 1979 L6/24. See also Council Directive 86/378/EEC of 24 July 1986 on the implementation of the principle of equal treatment for men and women in occupational social security schemes, OJ 1986 L225/40, now replaced by Directive 2006/54/EC (n. 292, *supra*). For a survey of the case law, see Cousins, 'Equal Treatment and Social Security' (1994) ELRev 123–45.

[304] Council Directive 2004/113/EC of 13 December 2004 implementing the principle of equal treatment between men and women in the access to and supply of goods and services, OJ 2004 L373/37. See Krois, 'Directive 2004/113/EC on Sexual Equality in Access to Goods and Services: Progress or Impasse in European Sex discrimination Law?' (2005) Col JEL 323–38.

to eliminate actual instances of inequality which affect women's opportunities.[305] However, this exception does not authorize a Member State to adopt or tolerate measures which guarantee absolute and unconditional priority for women in the matter of promotion or employment. Where both male and female candidates are equally qualified and where there are fewer women than men at the level of the relevant post, priority may be given to the promotion of female candidates if it is not excluded for one or more criteria specific to individual candidates—which may not be such as to discriminate against female candidates—to tilt the balance in favour of some male candidates.[306] Article 157(4) TFEU provides, with a view to ensuring full equality in practice between men and women in working life, that the principle of equal treatment shall not prevent any Member State from maintaining or adopting measures providing for specific advantages in order to make it easier for the under-represented sex to pursue a vocational activity or to prevent or compensate for disadvantages in professional careers.

3. Other prohibited forms of discrimination

Forbidden grounds. In defining and implementing its policies and activities, the Union shall aim to combat discrimination based on sex, racial or ethnic origin, religion or belief, disability, age, or sexual orientation (Article 10 TFEU).[307] Moreover, the Council, acting unanimously in accordance with a special legislative procedure and after obtaining the consent of the European Parliament, may take appropriate action to combat discrimination on these grounds (Article 19 TFEU). The grounds listed in Articles 10 and 19 TFEU do not encompass, however, all the grounds listed in Article 21 of the Charter.[308]

5.060

---

[305] Article 2(4) of Directive 76/207 (n. 302, *supra*). This applied where, in order to tackle the under-representation of women, a ministry, in principle, reserved nursery places for women employees: C-476/99, *Lommers*, 2002, paras 31–50. This was not the case, however, where a measure entitled only female employees with children to a service credit for the purpose of calculating their pensions: C-366/99, *Griesmar*, 2001, paras 62–7 (the measure was in breach of the principle of equal pay and consequently discriminated against men). See Waddington and Bell, 'Exploring the Boundaries of Positive Action Under EU Law: A Search for Conceptual Clarity' (2011) CMLRev 1503; Barmes, 'Navigating Multi-layered Uncertainty: EU, Member State and Organizational Perspectives on Positive action', in Healy, Kirton, and Noon (eds), *Equality, Inequalities and Diversity—Contemporary Challenges and Strategies* (Palgrave MacMillan, 2010), chapter 4; Prechal, 'Equality of Treatment, Non-Discrimination and Social Policy: Achievement in Three Themes' (2004) CMLRev 533.

[306] C-409/95, *Marschall*, 1997, paras 21–35, with a case note by Brems (1998) ColJEL 668–75; C-158/97, *Badeck and Others*, 2000, paras 13–67; C-407/98, *Abrahamsson and Anderson*, 2000, paras 39–65; EFTA Court, E-1/02, *EFTA Surveillance Authority v Norway* (2003) *Reports of the EFTA Court* 1, with note by Tobler (2004) CMLRev 245–60. In *Marschall* the Court qualified an earlier judgment according to which rules giving priority to equally qualified female candidates for promotion or employment in sectors of public employment where they were under-represented were precluded by Directive 76/207/EEC: C-450/93, *Kalanke*, 1995, paras 15–24. That judgment came in for severe criticism, see Brems (1995/96) Col JEL 172–9; De Schutter and Renauld (1996) JTT 125–9; Moore (1996) ELRev 156–61; Charpentier (1996) RTDE 281–303; Prechal (1996) CMLRev 1245–59. See also Croon, 'Comparative Institutional Analysis, the European Court of Justice and the General Principle of Non-Discrimination—or—Alternative Tales on Equality Reasoning' (2013) ELJ 153; Caruso, 'Limits of the Classic Method: Positive Action in the European Union After the New Equality Directives' (2003) Harv ILJ 331–86; Hauquet, ''L'action positive, instrument de l'égalité des chances entre hommes et femmes' (2001) RTDE 305–33; Suhr, 'Grenzen der Gleichbehandlung: Zur Vereinbarkeit von Frauenquoten mit dem Gemeinschaftsrecht' (1998) Eu GRZ 121–8; Barnard, 'The Principle of Equality in the Community Context: *P., Grant, Kalanke* and *Marschall*: Four Uneasy Bedfellows?' (1998) Cambridge LJ 352–73.

[307] In addition, Article 9 TEU proclaims the general principle of the equality of citizens of the Union before the Union's institutions, bodies, offices, and agencies (principle of democratic equality).

[308] Article 21 of the Charter also lists colour, social origin, genetic features, language, political or other opinions, membership of a national minority, property, and birth as prohibited grounds of discrimination. Accordingly, while the Union—and the Member States when implementing Union law—must respect the principle of non-discrimination on those grounds when implementing other policies, the Union does not have the legislative competence to take measures with the sole purpose of combating discrimination on these grounds. On this relationship between Article 19 TFEU and Article 21 of the Charter, see C-223/19, *YS*, AG Kokott Opinion, 2020,

Under Article 19 TFEU, the Council has adopted directives prohibiting discrimination on the basis of racial or ethnic origin[309] and a general framework for equal treatment in employment and occupation.[310] The purpose of the second directive is to combat any form of discrimination on the grounds of religion or belief,[311] disability,[312] age,[313] or sexual

---

point 106. For examples concerning a ground that is not covered by Article 10 TFEU, but fall within the scope of Article 21 of the Charter, see, e.g., C-566/10 P, *Italy v Commission*, 2012, para. 75 (language); C-223/19, *YS*, 2020, paras 82–5 (property).

[309] Council Directive 2000/43/EC of 29 June 2000 implementing the principle of equal treatment between persons irrespective of racial or ethnic origin, OJ 2000 L180/22. For the scope of the notion of 'direct discrimination' employed in Article 2(2) of the Directive, see C-54/07, *Feryn*, 2008, paras 21–8; see further C-668/15, *Jyske Finans*, 2017; C-83/14, *CHEZ Razpredelenie Bulgaria*, 2015, with a case note by Lahuerta (2017) CMLRev 797. See further, in general, Atrey, 'Race Discrimination in EU Law after Jyske Finans' (2018) CMLRev 625; Atrey, 'Redefining Frontiers of EU Discrimination Law' (2017) PL 185; Schiek and Lawson (eds), *European Union Non-Discrimination Law and Intersectionality: Investigating the Triangle of Racial, Gender and Disability Discrimination* (Routledge, 2016); Bell, *Racism and Equality in the European Union* (OUP, 2009); Bell, 'EU Anti-racism Policy; the Leader of the Pack?', in Meenan (ed.), *Equality Law in an Enlarged European Union. Understanding the Article 13 Directives* (Cambridge University Press, 2007) 145–76; Jones, 'The Race Directive: Redefining Protection from Discrimination in EU Law' (2003) EHRLR 515–26; Mahlmann, 'Gleichheitsschutz und Privatautonomie—Probleme und Perspektiven der Umsetzung der Richtline 2000/43/EG gegen Diskriminierungen aufgrund von Rasse und etnischer Herkunft' (2002) ZEuS 407–25; Nickel, 'Handlungsaufträge zur Bekämpfung von ethnischen Diskriminierungen in der neuen Gleichbehandlungsrichtlinie 2000/43/EC' (2001) NJW 2668–72; Sewandono, 'De Rassenrichtlijn en de Algemene Wet gelijke behandeling' (2001) SEW 218–26. For the origins of the Directive, see Tyson, 'The Negotiation of the European Community Directive on Racial Discrimination' (2001) EJML 199–229. Pursuant to Articles 213 and 235 EC [*now Articles 337 and 352 TFEU*], the European Monitoring Centre on Racism and Xenophobia was set up in Vienna, which has been meanwhile converted into the Fundamental Rights Agency (para. 13-046, *infra*). See also the first para. of Article 29 EU (on PJCC) and Council Framework Decision 2008/913/JHA of 28 November 2008 on combating certain forms and expressions of racism and xenophobia by means of criminal law, OJ 2008 L328/55.

[310] Council Directive 2000/78/EC of 27 November 2000 establishing a general framework for equal treatment in employment and occupation, OJ 2000 L303/16. For general considerations, see Bell and Waddington, 'Reflecting on Inequalities in European Equality Law' (2003) ELRev 349–69; Bayart, 'De opmars van het discriminatierecht in de arbeidsverhoudingen' (2002) JTT 309–29; Dollat, 'Vers la reconnaissance généralisée du principe de l'égalité de traitement entre les personnes dans l'Union européenne' (2002) JTDE 57–64; Waddington and Bell, 'More Equal than Others: Distinguishing European Union Equality Directives' (2001) CMLRev 587–611.

[311] e.g. C-157/15, *Achbita*, 2017 and C-188/15, *Bougnaoui*, 2017, with a case note by Cloots (2018) CMLRev 589; C-414/16, *Egenberger*, 2018; C-68/17, *IR*, 2018; C-193/17, *Cresco Investigation*, 2019, paras 76–89. See Ciacchi, 'The Direct Horizontal Effect of EU Fundamental Rights' (2019) EuConst 294; Lourenço, 'Religion, Discrimination and the EU General Principles' Gospel: Egenberger' (2019) CMLRev 193; Steinfeld, 'A Bonfire of Religious Liberties' (2019) Cambridge LJ 28; Busschaert and De Somer, 'You Can Leave Your Hat on, but Not Your Headscarf: No Direct Discrimination on the Basis of Religion' (2017) Int'l J Comp Lab L & Ind Rel 553; Mangold and Payandeh, 'Diskriminierungsschutz und unternehmerische Freiheit im Unionsrecht. Anmerkungen zu den Urteilen des EuGH v. 14.3.2017 in den Rs. C-157/15 (Achbita) und C-188/15 (Bougnaoui)' (2017) EuR 700–24; Pitt, 'Religion or Belief; Aiming at the Right Target?', in Meenan (ed.), *Equality Law in an Enlarged European Union. Understanding the Article 13 Directives* (Cambridge University Press, 2007) 202–29.

[312] See C-303/06, *Coleman*, 2008 (the prohibition of discrimination is not limited to employees who are themselves disabled, but also applies where less favourable treatment of an employee is based on the disability of his or her child); C-363/12, *Z*, 2014, with a case note by Finck and Kas, (2015) CMLRev 281; C-16/19, *VL*, 2021, paras 21-60. See also Favalli and Ferri, 'Defining Disability in the European Union Non-discrimination Legislation: Judicial Activism and Legislative Restraints' (2016) E Pub L 541; Schiek, 'Intersectionality and the Notion of Disability in EU Discrimination Law' (2016) CMLRev 35. For Union competence with regard to the integration of persons with disabilities, see Quinn, 'Disability Discrimination Law in the European Union', in Meenan (ed.), *Equality Law in an Enlarged European Union. Understanding the Article 13 Directives* (Cambridge University Press, 2007) 202–29; Whittle, 'The Framework Directive for Equal Treatment in Employment and Occupation: An Analysis from a Disability Rights Perspective' (2002) ELRev 303–26; Sarapas, 'Les droits des personnes handicappées dans le domaine des transports européens' (2000) RMCUE 395–406. Interestingly, the Union legislature laid down accessibility requirements for products and services which facilitate independent living for persons with disabilities under the internal market legal basis: Directive (EU) 2019/882 of the European Parliament and of the Council of 17 April 2019 on the accessibility requirements for products and services, OJ 2019 L151/70 (based on Article 114 TFEU). See Ferri, The European Accessibility Act and the Shadow of the 'Social Market Economy' (2020) ELRev 660–80.

[313] e.g. C-411/05, *Palacios de la Villa*, 2007, with a case note by Waddington (2008) CMLRev 895, (collective agreements providing for a compulsory retirement age held not to infringe Directive 2000/78); C-88/08, *Hütter*,

orientation[314] as regards employment and occupation. The European Parliament and the Council may adopt, under the ordinary legislative procedure, incentive measures, excluding any harmonization of the laws and regulations of the Member States, to support action taken by the Member States (Article 19(2) TFEU).

Where a person suffers discrimination outside that context, he or she can bring an action on the basis of Article 21(1) of the Charter of Fundamental Rights, which, in addition to the grounds for discrimination mentioned in Article 19 TFEU, prohibits discrimination on grounds of colour, social origin, genetic features, language, political or any other opinion, membership of a national minority, property and birth, and on the basis of the general principle of equal treatment,[315] unless his or her situation contains no link with Union law.[316]

Union law is without prejudice to the competence of the Member States to provide or not for marriage for persons of the same sex.[317] Member States cannot, however, refuse to recognize a right of residence to the same-sex spouse of a Union citizen returning to his Member State, even if that Member State does not itself provide for same-sex marriages.[318] Originally, the Union Courts have not regarded unequal treatment of married couples and homosexual couples as prohibited discrimination. The Courts referred to

---

2009 (national legislation not taking into account professional experience acquired before the age of 18 held to infringe Directive 2000/78); C-555/07, *Kücükdeveci*, 2010 (national legislation on dismissal not taking into account period of employment before the age of 25); C-258/15, *Salaberria Sorondo*, 2016 (recruitment of police officers restricted to candidates under certain age held not to discriminate on grounds of age); F-83/07 *Zangerl-Posselt*, 2009, paras 76–8 (recruitment condition for Union staff members held not to discriminate). See Numhauser-Henning, 'The EU Ban on Age-Discrimination and Older Workers: Potentials and Pitfalls' (2013) Int'l J Comp Lab L & Ind Rel 391; Wiesbrock, 'Mandatory Retirement in the EU and the US: The Scope of Protection against Age Discrimination in Employment' (2013) Int'l J Comp Lab L & Ind Rel 305; Schlachter, 'Mandatory Retirement and Age Discrimination under EU Law' (2011) Int'l J Comp Lab L & Ind Rel 287; Jans, 'The effect in National Legal Systems of the Prohibition of Discrimination on Grounds of Age as a General Principle of Community Law' (2007) LIEI 53–66; Meenan, 'Reflecting on Age Discrimination and Rights of the Elderly in the European Union and the Council of Europe' (2007) MJECL 39–82.

[314] e.g. C-81/12, *Accept*, 2013; C-258/17, *E.B.*, 2019, with a case note by Fines (2020) CMLRev 243, (in the latter case the Court clarified that Member States must correct the ongoing consequences of historic discriminations as of the date of entry into force of Directive 2000/78/EC, namely 3 December 2003); C-507/18, *NH*, 2020, paras 28–58. See Fitzpatrick, 'The "Mainstreaming" of Sexual Orientation into European Equality Law', in Meenan (ed.), *Equality Law in an Enlarged European Union. Understanding the Article 13 Directives* (Cambridge University Press, 2007) 313–41.

[315] See C-144/04 *Mangold*, 2005, paras 74–7 (age); C-13/05, *Chacón Navas*, 2006, paras 55–6 (sickness and disability), with a case note by Waddington (2007) CMLRev 487–99. See further Lenaerts, 'Le respect des droits fondamentaux en tant que principe constitutionnel de l'Union européenne', in Dony and De Walsche (eds), *Mélanges Michel Waelbroeck* (Bruylant, 1999), I, 423–57. See Mazák and Moser, 'Adjudication by Reference to General Principles of EU Law: A Second Look at the Mangold Case Law', in Adams, de Waele, Meeusen, and Straetmans (eds), *Judging Europe's Judges: The Legitimacy of the Case Law of the European Court of Justice* (Hart Publishing, 2013), 61.

[316] C-427/06, *Bartsch*, 2008, paras 16–24. No such link arises from Article 19 TFEU taken on its own, or from Directive 2000/78 before the time-limit for its transposition had expired (C-427/06, *Bartsch*, 2008, paras 16–24). Such a link does, however, arise after the expiry of that time-limit, so that the primary law principle of non-discrimination on the ground of age can be relied upon between private parties, while Directive 2000/78 contributes to filling in the contents of that principle (C-555/07 *Kücükdeveci*, 2010, paras 20–7). See Article 51(1) Charter, and further, generally, Fontanelli, 'Some Reflections on the General Principles of the EU and on Solidarity in the Aftermath of Mangold and Kücükdeveci' (2011) E Pub L 225; Muir, 'Of Ages in—and Edges of – EU Law' (2011) CMLRev 39; De Mol, 'Kücükdeveci: Mangold Revisited— Horizontal Direct Effect of a General Principle of EU Law' (2010) EuConst 293.

[317] C-443/15, *Parris*, 2016, paras 57–9, with a case note by Möschel (2017) CMLRev 1835. See Bell, 'Gender Identity and Sexual Orientation: Alternative Pathways in EU Equality Law' (2012) AJCL 127.

[318] C-673/16, *Coman*, 2018, paras 28–56, with case notes by Belavusau and Kochenov (2020) CMLRev 227; Tryfonidou (2019) ELRev 663; Stehlík (2018) ICLR 85.

the legislature's power to make societal choices connected with the assessment of such discrimination.[319] The Court of Justice did not consider that the situation of a married official was comparable to the same-sex partnerships recognized by some Member States. Later the Court has clarified that Union law prohibits unequal treatment between same-sex partnerships and marriages if such a same-sex partnership has the effect of placing the same-sex partners in a similar position as married couples in respect of their eligibility for certain benefits under national law.[320] The same goes for advantages that are granted to workers on the occasion of their marriage. Those cannot be denied to persons of the same sex who entered into a partnership because they were precluded from marrying and who find themselves in a similar situation as workers who conclude a marriage.[321] According to the Staff Regulations, Union officials in a non-marital relationship recognized by a Member State as a stable partnership who do not have legal access to marriage should be granted the same range of benefits as married couples.[322] For some benefits, this also extends to other kinds of non-marital partnerships recognized by a Member State.[323] Likewise, Union legislation on the right of citizens of the Union and their family members to move and reside freely within the territory of the Member States includes among the 'family member' of a citizen the registered partner if the legislation of the host Member State treats registered partnership as equivalent to marriage.[324] It is also contrary to the principle of equal treatment for the Union institutions to make the grant of an allowance for an official's children who have lost their other parent dependent upon the condition that the official was married to that other parent.[325]

---

[319] C-249/96, *Grant*, 1998, para. 48; T-264/97, *D. v Council*, 1999, para. 32; C-122/99 P and C-125/99 P, *D. v Council*, 2001, paras 47–52; for a critical view, see Berthou and Masselot, 'Le mariage, les partenariats et la CJCE: ménage à trois' (2000) CDE 679–94. See further Zukaite, 'Does the Prohibition of Same-sex Marriages Violate Fundamental Human Rights and Freedoms?' (2005) Int'l J Baltic L 1–23; Weyembergh, 'Les droits des homosexuels devant le juge communautaire' (1998) JTDE 110–13; Guiguet, 'Le droit communautaire et la reconnaissance des partenaires de même sexe' (1999) CDE 537–67; Jessurun d'Oliveira, 'Vrijheid van verkeer voor geregisteerde partners in de Europese Unie' (2001) NJB 205–10.

[320] See also the prohibition of discrimination on the ground of sexual orientation laid down in Article 21(1) of the Charter, which applies between private parties; C-267/06, *Maruko*, 2008, paras 72–3; C-147/08, *Römer*, 2011, paras 37–52.

[321] C-267/12, *Hay*, 2013, paras 37–47. For an overview of the Court's case law on non-discrimination on the ground of sexual orientation, see Zaccaroni, 'Differentiating Equality? The Different Advancements in the Protected Grounds in the Case Law of the European Court of Justice', in Rossi and Casolari (eds), *The Principle of Equality in EU Law* (Springer, 2017), 179–84.

[322] Council Regulation (EC, Euratom) No. 723/2004 of 22 March 2004 amending the Staff Regulations of officials of the European Communities and the Conditions of Employment of other servants of the European Communities, OJ 2004 L124/1) makes certain benefits formerly granted only to married couples available to an official who is registered as a stable non-marital partner, provided that the couple produces a legal document recognized as such by a Member State, or any competent authority of a Member State, acknowledging their status as non-marital partners, neither partner is in a marital relationship or in another non-marital partnership, the partners are not related in specified ways, and the couple has no access to legal marriage in a Member State (Article 1d(1) and Annex VII, Article 1(2)(c)). Cf. C-460/18 P, *HK v Commission*, 2019, paras 66–85 (with regard to the survivor's pension, cohabitants not considered to be in a situation comparable to that of married persons or that of partners who entered into a registered partnership).

[323] See T-58/08 P, *Roodhuijzen*, 2009, paras 68–102 (on medical insurance). See also C-485/08 P *Gualtieri v Commission*, 2010, paras 70–6 (marital status considered relevant factor for determining amount of daily subsistence allowance).

[324] Directive 2004/38/EC of the European Parliament and of the Council of 29 April 2004 on the right of the citizen of the Union and their family members to move and reside freely within the territory of the Member States, OJ 2004 L158/77 (on that Directive, paras 5-055 and 6-015).

[325] T-307/00, *C v Commission*, 2003, paras 48–56.

B. Content

1. Substantive discrimination

Definition. In Union law, the prohibition of discrimination not only requires equal treatment formally to be complied with, but also that no inequality is caused in practice. Where that occurs, there is substantive discrimination. According to the Court of Justice, it is specifically prohibited to treat 'either similar situations differently or different situations identically'.[326] In order to categorize cases as 'similar' or 'different', they must be considered in the light of the aims of the measure in question. Substantive discrimination will be tolerated only if the difference in treatment of similar cases (or, conversely, the undifferentiated treatment in the presence of differing cases) is justified.[327] In order for this to be so, the 'unequal' treatment must be proportionate to the objective sought by the authority.[328] Often, the reason given in justification is considered together with the question as to whether the cases concerned are similar or different.[329]

5.061

2. Direct and indirect discrimination

Definitions. Discrimination is direct where a measure employs a prohibited distinguishing criterion (e.g. nationality) or applies the same rules to differing situations. Indirect discrimination arises where, although not making use of a prohibited distinguishing criterion, a provision has effects coinciding with or approaching those of such a prohibited criterion by using other discerning criteria which are not as such prohibited.[330] Indirect discrimination also arises where an apparently neutral rule has a more burdensome impact on some people protected by a forbidden ground of discrimination.[331] Accordingly, the Court of Justice has held that '[t]he rules regarding equality of treatment ... forbid not only overt discrimination ... but also all covert forms of discrimination which, by the application of other criteria of differentiation, lead in fact to the same result'.[332] Thus, for instance, a criterion of place or duration of residence may in fact produce the same result as discrimination on grounds of nationality.[333] A measure will also be indirectly discriminatory where it distinguishes only formally between different cases, but in reality treats them the same.

5.062

---

[326] 13/63 *Italy v Commission*, 1963, 165; see also 8/82 *Wagner*, 1983, para. 18. For instances in which dissimilar situations required differing measures, see 230/78, *Eridania*, 1979, paras 18–19; T-47/91, *Auzat v Commission*, 1992 and T-75/91, *Scaramuzza v Commission*, 1992.

[327] 117/76 and 16/77 *Ruckdeschel*, 1977, para. 7; C-390/15, *RPO*, 2017, paras 42–51. For a case in which unequal treatment arising out of uniform rules (establishment of a common organization of the market in bananas) laid down for differing situations was justified by the aim of integrating the national markets, see C-280/93, *Germany v Council*, 1994, para. 74; this judgment was criticized in Everling, 'Will Europe Slip on Bananas? The Banana Judgment of the Court of Justice and National Courts' (1996) CMLRev 401, 415–16.

[328] For different treatment which was objectively justified but not proportional, see C-29/95, *Pastoors and Trans-Cap*, 1997, paras 19–26; C-390/15, *RPO*, 2017, para. 53.

[329] See, e.g., 35/80 *Denkavit Nederland*, 1981, paras 16–17. Accordingly, it is possible to find that the principle of equality has been infringed where a difference in treatment does not have regard to the principle of proportionality: see C-323/95, *Hayes*, 1997, paras 24–5.

[330] For a general discussion, see Maliszewska-Nienartowicz, 'Direct and Indirect Discrimination in European Union Law—How to Draw a Dividing Line?' (2014) Int'l J Soc Sci 41; Garronne, 'La discrimination indirecte en droit communautaire: vers une théorie générale' (1994) RTDE 425–49.

[331] For an example of such a disparate impact case, see C-157/15, *Achbita*, 2017, para. 34.

[332] 152/73 *Sotgiu*, 1974, para. 11. See also 41/84, *Pinna*, 1986, para. 23; 33/88 *Allué and Other*, 1989, paras 11–12. For an application under the EAEC Treaty, see C-115/08 *ČEZ*, 2009, paras 95–7.

[333] See, e.g., C-29/95, *Pastoors and Trans-Cap*, 1997, paras 17–18; C-103/08, *Gottwald*, 2009, paras 27–8; C-73/08 *Bressol and Others*, 2010, paras 44–6.

5.063 **Indirect discrimination.** The Court of Justice has repeatedly had to consider cases of indirect sex discrimination, particularly when interpreting the 'principle of equal pay for male and female workers for equal work or work of equal value' enshrined in Article 157 TFEU.[334] Thus, the question arose whether a difference in the level of pay for work carried out part time and the same work carried out full time was capable of constituting discrimination on grounds of sex where the category of part-time workers was exclusively or predominantly comprised of women. The Court held that different treatment was acceptable 'in so far as the difference in pay between part-time work and full-time work is attributable to factors which are objectively justified and are in no way related to any discrimination based on sex'.[335] It is for the national court, which has jurisdiction to make findings of fact and interpret the national legislation, to determine whether a pay policy of a given employer or a statutory provision which in fact affects women more than men can be objectively justified. The measures chosen in the policy or provision must correspond to a real need on the part of the undertaking or a necessary aim of a national social policy and be in proportion to the objective pursued (that is to say, appropriate and necessary in order to attain that objective).[336] In addition, in other circumstances in which a national or a Union measure is couched in neutral terms but women are in fact disadvantaged, it must be examined whether the criterion employed is justified by objective factors independent of any discrimination on grounds of sex.[337]

3. Reverse discrimination

5.064 **Internal situations.** The Union prohibition of discrimination only applies within the scope of application of Union law. This means that in respect of the Treaty provisions relating to the free movement of goods, persons, services, and capital, a person may not rely on the prohibition of discrimination if he or she is in a purely internal situation to which the Treaty provisions do not apply.[338] The same goes for the prohibition of discrimination stated in Article 18 TFEU, which can only be invoked by a Union citizen in combination with the right to travel to and reside in another Member State under Article 21 TFEU.[339] As a result of the increasing range of circumstances in which persons may derive rights from Union law with regard to the Member State of which they are nationals, it has become more difficult to identify a purely internal situation.[340]

---

[334] See also para. 5-062, *supra*. For this and other instances of indirect discrimination, see, for instance, Tobler, *Indirect Discrimination: A Case Study Into the Development of the Legal Concept of Indirect Discrimination Under EC Law* (Intersentia, 2005); Hervey, 'Justification for Indirect Sex Discrimination in Employment: European Community and United Kingdom Law Compared' (1990) ICLQ 807–26; Adinolfi, 'Indirect Discrimination on Grounds of Sex in Collective Labour Agreements' (1992) CMLRev 637–45; Prechal, 'Combating Indirect Discrimination in Community Law Context' (1993) LIEI 81–97.

[335] 96/80, *Jenkins*, 1981, paras 11–12. See Petterson, 'Discrimination against Part-Time and Fixed-Term Workers: A Critical Legal Positivist Analysis' (2015) Int'l J Comp Lab L & Ind Rel 47.

[336] See, e.g., 170/84, *Bilka*, 1986, para. 36 (wages policy of an employer); 171/88, *Rinner Kühn*, 1989, paras 14–15 (national provision). The Court of Justice held that there was a justified national social policy objective in C-229/89, *Commission v Belgium*, 1991, paras 19–26. For the temporal effects of Article 157 TFEU, see para. 23-033, *infra*.

[337] C-25/02, *Rinke*, 2003, paras 36–42; C-123/10, *Brachner*, 2011, para. 56; C-7/12, *Riežniece*, 2013, para. 39.

[338] e.g. C-250/08, *Commission v Belgium*, 2011, paras 40–1; C-268/15, *Ullens de Schooten*, 2016, paras 45–58. See Peeters, 'The Repartition of Tax Powers in Federal States within the Context of the European Union' (2012) EC Tax Rev 124. Compare the stricter requirement for a transborder situation for the application of the provisions on free movement of persons and services (see paras 7-055 and 7-085, *infra*) with the relatively ready acceptance of a transborder factor in applying the provisions on free movement of goods (see para. 7-028, *infra*).

[339] C-212/06, *Gouvernement de la Communauté française and Gouvernement wallon*, 2008, para. 39.

[340] See Iglesias Sánchez, 'Purely Internal Situations and the Limits of EU Law: A Consolidated Case Law or a Notion to be Abandoned?' (2018) EuConst 7–36; De Beys, 'Le droit européen est-il applicable aux situations

In a purely domestic situation falling outside the field of application of Union law, a Member State is not subject to the Union prohibition of discrimination and also not debarred under Union law from exercising 'reverse discrimination' by treating its own subjects or national situations less favourably than nationals of other Member States or than situations stemming from other Member States that fall within the scope of Union law.[341] The unequal treatment this would cause may thus solely be reviewed under the framework of the internal legal system of the State in question.[342] Accordingly, a Member State may well consider such unequal treatment contrary to a national principle of equal treatment. Yet in many instances national law will accept such different treatment because the purely internal situation is deemed to be 'different' compared to the situation falling within the scope of Union law, or because the differentiated treatment is deemed to be justified.[343]

---

purement internes? A propos des discriminations à rebours dans le marché unique' (2001) JTDE 137–44; Papadopoulou, 'Situations purement internes et droit communautaire: un instrument jurisprudentiel à double fonction ou une arme à double tranchant?' (2002) CDE 95–129.

[341] C-379/92, *Peralta*, 1994, para. 27; C-132/93, *Steen*, 1994, paras 8–11. See also Verbist, *Reverse Discrimination in the European Union—A Recurring Balancing Act* (Intersentia, 2017), 358; Croon-Gestefeld, 'Umgekehrte Diskriminierungen nach dem Unionsrecht—Unterschiedliche Konzepte im Umgang mit einem gemeinsamen Problem' (2016) EuR 56–75; Oosterom-Staples, 'To What Extent Has Reverse Discrimination Been Reversed?' (2012) EMIL 151; Hanf, '"Reverse Discrimination" in EU Law: Constitutional Aberration, Constitutional Necessity, or Judicial Choice' (2011) MJECL 29.

[342] C-64/96 and C-65/96, *Uecker and Jacquet*, 1997, para. 23 (which makes it clear that the introduction of citizenship of the Union makes no difference to this position). See also König, 'Das Problem der Inländerdiskriminierung—Abschied von Reinheitsgebot, Nachtbackverbot und Meisterprüfung?' (1993) AöR 591–616.

[343] C-212/06, *Gouvernement de la Communauté française and Gouvernement wallon*, 2008, paras 38–40. See also the Judgment 11/2009 of 21 January 2009 of the Constitutional Court of Belgium (see the discussion by Van Elsuwege and Adam in (2009) EuConst 327–39).

6
Citizenship of the Union

6.001 **Treaty provisions.** Title II of the TFEU ('Provisions on democratic principles') sets out by stressing the principle of the equality of the Union's citizens, mentioning at the same time Union citizenship as additional to national citizenship (Article 9 TEU). In 1992, the Treaty on European Union introduced the idea of citizenship of the Union to make clear that the European Union confers rights not only on persons who are engaged in an economic activity, but to all persons who have the nationality of a Member State. The Lisbon Treaty merged the provisions of the EC Treaty on non-discrimination with the ones on citizenship in Part Two of the TFEU ('Non-discrimination and Citizenship of the Union'), that is, Articles 18 to 25 TFEU.

I. Creation of Citizenship of the Union

6.002 **Steps towards citizenship.** The idea of conferring certain rights on Member State nationals as citizens of the supranational entity grew up in parallel with proposals to bring together the various integration paths into a single European Union (see para. 1-040 *et seq.*, *supra*).[1] At the instigation of the Paris Summit (December 1974), the Tindemans Report on European Union (1975) considered possible ways of strengthening the protection of citizens' rights and of making European solidarity tangible by means of external signs.[2] Also on the instructions of the Paris Summit, the Commission brought out reports on the feasibility of introducing a uniform passport, establishing a passport union and conferring special rights on citizens of the Member States, *inter alia*, so as to allow them to vote and stand as a candidate in municipal and, possibly also, regional elections and to hold public office at those levels.[3]

6.003 **People's Europe.** Citizens did not start to become more involved in the integration process until the first direct elections to the European Parliament in 1979. In 1985, the Adonnino Committee set up by the European Council produced two reports containing further proposals on how to attain a people's Europe.[4] The proposals received a positive reception at the Milan European Council of 28 and 29 June 1985[5] and have since either largely been

---

[1] For a survey, see the Commission's communication to the European Parliament of 24 June 1988 entitled 'A people's Europe' (1988) EC Bull. Suppl 2.
[2] (1976) EC Bull. Suppl. 1, 29–31. For the Paris Summit, see (1974) 12 EC Bull. point 1104, No. 13.
[3] Towards European citizenship, 'A Passport Union' and 'The Granting of Special Rights', reports presented by the Commission in implementation of points 10 and 11, respectively, of the final communiqué issued at the European Summit held in Paris on 9 and 10 December 1974, (1975) EC Bull. Suppl 7.
[4] A People's Europe, Reports from the ad hoc Committee (1985) EC Bull. Suppl 7 (reports of 29–30 March and 28–29 June 1985). For the Committee's terms of reference, see (1984) 6 EC Bull. point 1.1.9.
[5] (1985) 6 EC Bull. point 1.4.8. In the *Erasmus* judgment, the Court of Justice referred to 'achievement of a people's Europe' as one of the Union's general objectives: 242/87, *Commission v Council*, 1989, para. 29.

translated into measures securing free movement of persons and mobility for students—including the famous Erasmus exchange programme—or resulted in the conferral of new competences on the Union in the social and cultural spheres by the Single European Act and the EU Treaty.[6] As the Adonnino Committee had proposed, the Union's image and identity have been strengthened through the adoption of a flag and an anthem, a Union driving licence, and an agreement amongst the Member States on a uniform passport (see para. 14-001, *infra*).

Citizenship of the Union. The threads leading to the grant of political rights to Member State nationals were not woven together until it was decided to give such persons the status of 'citizens of the Union'. At Spain's instigation, the 1990–1991 Intergovernmental Conference decided to introduce citizenship of the Union concurrently with the establishment of the European Union.[7] During the negotiations on the Maastricht Treaty in 1992, which set up the European Union, an agreement was thus reached to create a legal bond between the Union and its citizens.[8] The EU Treaty inserted 'Part Two' of the EC Treaty on 'Citizenship of the Union',[9] now replaced by Part II of the TFEU on 'Non-discrimination and citizenship of the Union'. The introduction of citizenship has provided the justification for the Union, acting under Article 352 TFEU, to foster European citizenship and to improve conditions for civic and democratic participation at Union level by supporting awareness raising and dissemination and cooperation activities (e.g. town-twinning).[10] The Lisbon Treaty also made clear that the members of the European Parliament directly represent the Union's citizens, rather than the 'peoples of the [Member] States' (see para. 12-012, *infra*).

6.004

---

[6] See Schockweiler, 'La dimension humaine et sociale de la Communauté européenne' (1993) 4 RMUE 11–45, especially 14–35.

[7] See Closa, 'The Concept of Citizenship in the Treaty on European Union' (1992) CMLRev 1137, at 1153–57; Solbes Mira, 'La citoyenneté européenne' (1991) RMC 168–70. For the first worked-out proposal, see the text submitted to the Intergovernmental Conference by the Spanish delegation on 24 September 1990, reproduced in Laursen and Vanhoonacker (eds), *The Intergovernmental Conference on Political Union* (European Institute of Public Administration/Martinus Nijhoff, 1992), 328–32.

[8] For an overview of this evolution, see Maas, 'The Origins, Evolution, and Political Objectives of EU Citizenship' (2014) GLJ 797.

[9] For general discussions of citizenship of the Union, see, amongst others, Goudappel, *The Effects of EU Citizenship: Economic, Social and Political Rights in a Time of Constitutional Change* (Cambridge University Press, 2010); Dollat, *La citoyenneté européenne: théorie et statuts* (Bruylant, 2008); Schönberger, *Unionsbürger; Europas föderales Bürgerrecht in vergleichender Sicht* (Tübingen, Mohr Siebeck 2005); O'Leary, *The Evolving Concept of Community Citizenship. From the Free Movement of Persons to Union Citizenship* (Kluwer Law International, 1996); the articles in the 'Special issue: European Citizenship at Center-Stage' (2009) Col JEL 2; Chiti, 'Consequences of Citizenship in Europe—Are New Layers of Complexity Emerging?' (2007) E Rev Priv L 99–123; Calliess, 'Der Unionsbürger: Status, Dogmatik und Dynamik' (2007) EuR 7–42; Dougan, 'The Constitutional Dimension to the Case Law on Union citizenship' (2006) ELRev 613–41; Reich, 'The Constitutional Relevance of Citizenship and Free Movement in an Enlarged Union' (2005) ELJ 675–98; Kostakopoulou, 'Ideas, Norms and European Citizenship: Explaining Institutional Change' (2005) MLR 233–67; Oosterom-Staples and Vazquez Muñoz, 'Burgerschap van de Unie' (2004) SEW 494–506.

[10] See Council Regulation (EU) No. 390/2014 of 14 April 2014 establishing the 'Europe for Citizens' programme for the period 2014–2020 (OJ 2014 L115/3), replacing Council Decision of 26 January 2004 establishing a Community action programme to promote active European citizenship (civic participation) (OJ 2004 L30/6) and itself now succeeded by the Regulation (EU) 2021/692 of the European Parliament and the Council of 28 April 2021 establishing the Citizens, Equality, Rights and Values Programme for the period 2021–2027, which contains a 'citizens' engagement and participation strand' (OJ 2021 L156/1).

II. Granting Citizenship

6.005 **Citizenship of the Union.** Article 20(1) TFEU creates the 'citizenship of the Union'. It concerns a legal bond between the Union and its citizens. The Treaties attach specific rights and obligations to this relationship. Under Article 20(2) TFEU a Union citizen 'shall enjoy the rights and be subject to the duties provided for in the Treaties'. The Court of Justice denotes the citizenship of the Union to be the 'fundamental status of nationals of the Member States'.[11]

6.006 **Nationality of a Member State.** A citizen of the Union is defined as any person holding the nationality of a Member State (Article 9 TEU and Article 20(1) TFEU).[12] Citizenship of the Union is additional to, and does not replace, national citizenship (Article 9 TEU and Article 20(1) TFEU).[13]

Since citizenship depends on a person having the status of a national of a Member State, the Union differs fundamentally from federal States, in which nationality invariably falls within the jurisdiction of the federal authority.[14] Whether a person has the nationality of a Member State is to be determined solely by reference to the nationality rules of the Member State concerned.[15] This is because what underlies the bond of nationality is a 'special relationship of allegiance to the State and reciprocity of rights and duties'.[16] A declaration annexed to the EU Treaty authorized Member States to declare, for information, who were to be considered their nationals for the purpose of application of Union law.[17] The Court of Justice considers

---

[11] C-184/99, *Grzelczyk*, 2001, para. 31; C-82/16, *K.A.*, 2018, para. 47.

[12] The European Parliament used the same definition in its Declaration of fundamental rights and freedoms of 12 April 1989 (OJ 1989 C120/51), Article 25(3) of which states that a Community citizen shall be 'any person possessing the nationality of one of the Member States'. For an overview on the scholarly debate on the effect of the derivative quality of the acquisition of Union citizenship on its essence, see Kochenov, 'The Essence of EU Citizenship Emerging from the Last Ten Years of Academic Debate: Beyond the Cherry Blossoms and the Moon?' (2013) ICLQ 103–7.

[13] The Treaty of Amsterdam added this provision to Article 17 EC so as to make it absolutely clear that Union citizenship is complementary. Its wording ('Citizenship of the Union complements and does not replace national citizenship') was only slightly changed by the Treaty of Lisbon (see Article 20(2) TFEU).

[14] Schönberger, 'European Citizenship as Federal Citizenship. Some Citizenship Lessons of Comparative Federalism' (2007) E Rev Priv L 61–81; Closa, 'Citizenship of the Union and Nationality of Member States' (1995) CMLRev 487; Kovar and Simon, 'La citoyenneté européenne' (1993) CDE 285, 294. For an overview of the difficulties that the link between the possession of the nationality of a Member State and citizenship of the Union entails and the evolution in mitigating these difficulties, see Kostakopoulou, 'When EU Citizens become Foreigners' (2014) EuR 451–5.

[15] This principle of international law was confirmed by Declaration (No. 2), annexed to the EU Treaty -, on nationality of a Member State (OJ 1992 C191/98) and the Decision of the Heads of State or Government, meeting within the European Council on 11 and 12 December 1992, concerning certain problems raised by Denmark on the Treaty on European Union (Section A, 'Citizenship', OJ 1992 C348/2). For Union citizenship influencing national citizenship, see Rostek, 'The Impact of Union Citizenship on National Citizenship Policies' (2007) Tulane E & Civ LF 89–156.

[16] 149/79, *Commission* v *Belgium*, 1980, para. 10.

[17] See Declaration (No. 2)(cited in n. 15, *supra*). Only two Member States made use of this possibility. See the declaration made upon signature of the EEC Treaty by the Government of the Federal Republic of Germany on the definition of the expression 'German national' (mentioned in the final act to the EEC Treaty) and the declaration made on the accession of the United Kingdom by the British Government on the definition of the term 'nationals', OJ 1972 L73/196), replaced by a declaration of 1982, OJ 1983 C23/1 (that declaration was reiterated, in slightly modified form, at the time of signature of the Treaty of Lisbon; see the Declaration (No. 63), annexed to the Lisbon Treaty, by the United Kingdom of Great Britain and Northern Ireland on the definition of the term 'nationals', OJ 2010 C83/358). See also Hailbronner, 'Germany', in Bauböck et al. (eds), *Acquisition and Loss of Nationality: Policies and Trends in 15 European Countries. Volume 2: Country Analyses* (Amsterdam University Press, 2006), 213–51; Simmonds, 'The British Nationality Act 1981 and the Definition of the Term "National" for Community Purposes' (1984) CMLRev 675–86; Bleckmann, 'German Nationality within the Meaning of the EEC Treaty' (1978) CMLRev 435–46.

itself bound by these declarations for the purpose of determining the scope of citizenship of the Union.[18] Where a Member State withdraws from the Union, its national citizenship no longer entails Union citizenship.[19]

At the same time, the Court has held that, when exercising their powers in the sphere of nationality, the Member States must have due regard to Union law.[20] The power of the Member States to lay down the conditions for the acquisition and loss of nationality is amenable to judicial review in so far as it affects the rights conferred by the Union on citizens of the Union.[21] A decision to withdraw nationality that leads to the loss for the person concerned of his or her status of citizen of the Union may be reviewed in the light of the general principles of Union law, in particular the principle of proportionality, taking into account the consequences of that loss for the situation of each person concerned and, if relevant, for that of the members of their family.[22]

Where having the nationality of a Member State is a condition for enjoyment of a Union right, Union law requires Member States to recognize the nationality of another Member State without imposing any other condition (e.g. residence in the territory of the Member State whose nationality is relied on).[23] This means that Member States must unconditionally accept the citizenship of the Union conferred by another Member State (through bestowal of the nationality of that State). In this way, Union law diverges from international law where a State may refuse to recognize the nationality of a person if it was granted contrary to international law and, in the case of a person having plural nationality (of two or more foreign States), may have regard to the 'master' nationality.[24] A Member State cannot

---

[18] C-192/99, *Kaur*, 2001, paras 19–27; T-230/94, *Farrugia v Commission*, 1996, paras 16–31. See Hall, 'Determining the Scope ratione personae of European Citizenship: Customary International Law Prevails for Now' (2001) LIEI 355–60.

[19] For this implication of a Member State's withdrawal from the Union concerning its nationals' Union citizenship, see Van der Mei, 'EU Citizenship and Loss of Member State Nationality' (2018) European Papers 1326–31; More, 'From Union Citizen to Third-Country National: Brexit, the UK Withdrawal Agreement, No-Deal Preparations and Britons Living in the European Union', in Cambien, Kochenov, and Muir (eds), *European Citizenship under Stress: Social Justice, Brexit and Other Challenges* (Brill Nijhoff, 2020), 458–81.

[20] C-369/90, *Micheletti and Others*, 1992, para. 10; C-179/98, *Mesbah*, 1999, para. 29; C-192/99, *Kaur*, 2001, para. 19; C-200/02, *Zhu and Chen*, 2004, para. 37; C-135/08, *Rottmann*, 2010, paras 39–45, with case note by Kochenov (2010) CMLRev 1831.

[21] C-135/08, *Rottmann*, 2010, paras 46–8, with double case note by Jessurun d'Oliveira, de Groot, and Selling (2011) EuConst 138–60. See Dougan, 'Some Comments on Rottmann and the "Personal Circumstances" Assessment in the Union Citizenship Case Law', in Shaw (ed.), *Has the European Court of Justice Challenged Member State Sovereignty in National Law? EUI Working Papers* (RSCAS, 2011) 17–18.

[22] C-135/08 *Rottmann*, 2010, paras 50–9; C-221/17, *Tjebbes*, 2019, paras 27–49. See van Eijken, 'Tjebbes in Wonderland: On European Citizenship, Nationality and Fundamental Rights' (2019) EuConst 714–30; Van der Mei, 'EU Citizenship and Loss of Member State Nationality' (2018) European Papers 1319 – 25; Shaw (ed.), *Has the European Court of Justice Challenged Member State Sovereignty in Nationality Law, EUI Working Papers* (RSCAS, 2011), 43. Other general principles of Union law which Member States must, arguably, respect in this context are the fundamental rights. See, already Hall, 'Loss of Union Citizenship in Breach of Fundamental Rights' (1996) EL Rev 129–43.

[23] C-369/90, *Micheletti and Others*, 1992, paras 10–11 (on freedom of establishment), with critical note by Jessurun d'Oliveira (1993) CMLRev 623–37; C-200/02, *Zhu and Chen*, 2004, para. 39, with case notes by Carlier (2005) CMLRev 1121–31, Tryfonidou (2005) E Pub L 527–41, Hofstötter (2005) ELRev 548–58, Vanvoorden (2005) Col JEL 305–21. See also Kunoy, 'A Union of National Citizens: The Origins of the Court's Lack of Avantgardisme in the Chen Case' (2006) CMLRev 179–90. *Micheletti* does not apply, however, to a worker who has both the nationality of the host Member State and that of a third country with which the Union has concluded an association agreement, for the purpose of invoking that agreement: C-179/98 *Mesbah*, 1999, paras 29–41.

[24] See Zimmermann, 'Europäisches Gemeinschaftsrecht und Staatsangehörigkeit der Mitgliedstaaten unter besonderer Berücksichtigung der Probleme mehrfacher Staatsangehörigkeit' (1995) EuR 54–70. The Court of Justice points out that the Hague Convention of 12 April 1930, on certain questions relating to the conflict of nationality laws (League of Nations Treaty Series, Vol. 179, p. 89), does not impose an obligation but simply provides

therefore preclude the application of Union law by relying, with regard to nationals of another Member State who are residing on their territory—and hence fall within the scope of application of Union law—on the fact that the persons concerned also have the nationality of the Member State of residence.[25]

III. Substance of Citizenship

6.007 **Rights associated with citizenship.** Articles 21 to 24 TFEU list the rights that the Treaties link to the citizenship of the Union (see the discussion in paras 6-008–6-022, *infra*). Those rights are vested in citizens of the Union in their capacity as nationals of a Member State and therefore as Union citizens even if they are not in gainful employment or self-employed. Those articles not only codify rights recognized by Union law before the EU Treaty entered into force (right to move and reside, right of petition), but also create rights of considerable political importance (right to vote and stand as a candidate in European and municipal elections; diplomatic protection; right to apply to the European Ombudsman).[26] In the Charter of Fundamental Rights of the European Union, the rights of citizens of the Union are enshrined in the chapter entitled 'Citizenship'.[27]

The case law of the Court reveals that citizenship of the Union, as the 'primary status' of nationals of the Member States, has a wider scope than the rights that are specifically listed in Articles 21–24 TFEU. On the one hand, the Court has made clear that Article 20 TFEU precludes national measures that deny Union citizens the effective enjoyment of the most important rights attached to the status of citizen of the Union, even when a Union citizen invokes those rights against his or her own Member State (see para. 6-017, *infra*). On the other hand, the right to move and reside (Article 21 TFEU) has developed into a prohibition of any measure a Member State may take to restrict the right to move and reside in another Member State (see paras 6-019, *infra*).

The Council, acting unanimously and after obtaining the consent of the European Parliament, may adopt provisions to strengthen or to add to the rights listed in Article 20(2). Any provisions so adopted can only enter into force after approval by the Member States in accordance with their respective constitutional requirements (Article 25, second para., TFEU; see para. 3-007, *supra*).[28]

---

an option, in the case of dual nationality, for the contracting parties to give priority to their own nationality over any other: C-148/02, *Garcia Avello*, 2003, para. 28.

[25] C-148/02, *Garcia Avello*, 2003, para. 28; for a discussion of the case, see Verlinden (2005) Col JEL 705–16; Iliopoulou (2004) RTDE 559-79.

[26] For a survey, see Kadelbach, 'Union Citizenship', in von Bogdandy and Bast, *Principles of European Constitutional Law* (Hart Publishing, 2010) 443–78; Staeglich, 'Rechte und Pflichten aus der Unionsbürgerschaft' (2004) ZEuS 485–531.

[27] See Articles 39 to 46 of the Charter. For the fact that citizenship confers rights on persons regardless of their economic activity, see C-413/99, *Baumbast and R.*, 2002, paras 81–4.

[28] On this 'double political safeguard of federalism' preventing that the incorporation of fundamental rights into the status of EU citizen would be judicially driven, see Lenaerts, 'Linking EU Citizenship to Democracy' (2016) CYELP XVI–XVII.

A. Free movement and residence rights

Free movement and residence. Citizenship of the Union entails the right 'to move and reside freely within the territory of the Member States, subject to the limitations and conditions laid down in the Treaties and by the measures adopted to give them effect' (Article 21(1) TFEU). Union citizens can rely directly on Article 21(1) TFEU, which is framed sufficiently precisely and unconditionally so as to confer direct effect on the rights in question.[29] The Court considers this a 'fundamental and personal' right that is moreover confirmed by Article 45(1) of the Charter of Fundamental Rights.[30] It follows from Article 21(1) TFEU that a national of a Member State who does not enjoy a right of residence as a result of other provisions of Union law may, simply by virtue of being a citizen of the Union, enjoy a right of residence directly pursuant to that article.[31]

6.008

A national of one Member State who has moved to and resides in another Member State cannot be denied that right merely because he subsequently acquires the nationality of the second Member State in addition to his nationality of origin, otherwise the effectiveness of Article 21(1) TFEU would be undermined.[32] A citizen is deemed to have made use of his right of free movement, as soon as he has travelled to another Member State, even if only in transit.[33] Moreover, a third-country national residing in a Member State who subsequently obtains the nationality of another Member State of the Union is entitled to rely on Article 21(1) TFEU, even if he has never resided in the Member State that granted him its nationality.[34]

Implementing legislation. The European Parliament and the Council may adopt provisions under the ordinary legislative procedure with a view to facilitating the exercise of the right to move and reside freely within the territory of the Member States (Article 21(2) TFEU).[35] Under the same circumstances, the Council may, acting unanimously after consulting the European Parliament, adopt measures concerning social security or social protection (Article 21(3) TFEU) and concerning passports, identity cards, residence permits, or any other such document (Article 77(3) TFEU).

6.009

---

[29] C-413/99, *Baumbast and R.*, 2002, paras 80–6. For the implications of the fact that the right of residence ensues directly from the Treaty, see Dougan and Spaventa, 'Educating Rudy and the (non-)English Patient—A Double-bill on Residency Rights under Article 18 EC' (2003) ELRev 699–712. For an application of Article 18 together with Articles 39 and 42 EC [*now Articles 21, 45, and 48 TFEU*], see C-135/99 *Elsen*, 2000, paras 33–6.

[30] C-162/09, *Lassal*, 2010, para. 29. The exercise of that right of free movement may nevertheless be restricted in accordance with public international law when a Union citizen exercises the functions of Head of State: C-364/10, *Hungary v Slovak Republic*, 2012, paras 44–52. See Wiesbrock, 'The Self-Perpetuation of EU Constitutionalism in the Area of Free Movement of Persons: Virtuous or Vicious Cycle?' (2013) Global Constitutionalism 125; Spaventa 'Seeing the Wood Despite the Trees? On the Scope of Union citizenship and its Constitutional Effects' (2008) CMLRev 13.

[31] See, e.g., C-413/99, *Baumbast and R*, 2002, para. 84, and C-456/02 *Trojani*, 2004, para. 31; C-50/06, *Commission v Netherlands*, 2007, para. 32.

[32] C-165/16, *Lounes*, 2017, para. 53. See De Groot, 'Free Movement of Dual EU Citizens' (2018) European Papers 1075; Oosterom-Staples, 'The Triangular Relationship Between Nationality, EU Citizenship and Migration in EU Law: A Tale of Competing Competences' (2018) NILR 431; Réveillère, 'Family Rights for Naturalized EU Citizens: Lounes' (2018) CMLRev 1866–70.

[33] C-191/16, *Piscotti*, 2018, paras 31–5.

[34] C-398/19, *BY*, 2020, paras 27–34.

[35] Before the Treaty of Lisbon, it was provided that such Union action was not possible for 'provisions on passports, identity cards, residence permits or any other such document' or for 'provisions on social security or social protection' (see Article 18(3) EC). That constraint was removed by the Treaty of Lisbon (see Articles 21(3) and 77(3) TFEU).

6.010 Directive 2004/38. In April 2004, the various earlier Union instruments dealing with the right of residence of citizens of the Union were simplified and merged in Directive 2004/38/EC of the European Parliament and of the Council on the right of citizens of the Union and their family members to move and reside freely within the territory of the Member States.[36] The purpose of the Directive is to facilitate the exercise of the primary and individual right to move and reside freely within the territory of the Member States, which is conferred directly on citizens of the Union by Article 21(1) TFEU, and to strengthen that right.[37] This Directive confers a right of residence on citizens of the Union who are either economically active (as a worker or as a self-employed person) or who, while not economically active, possess sufficient means of existence to prevent them from becoming a burden on the social assistance system of the host Member State. The Directive seeks to avoid that nationals of other Member States become an undue burden on the social assistance systems of the host Member State.[38] The concept of 'social assistance system of the Member State' is a concept that has its own independent meaning in Union law and cannot be defined by reference to concepts of national law.[39] It refers to assistance granted by the public authorities that compensates for a lack of stable, regular, and sufficient resources[40].

Directive 2004/38 provides for three categories of residence rights for Union citizens and their family members (regardless of their nationality): a right of residence of a maximum period of three months (Article 6), a right of residence for a period exceeding three months (Article 7), and a permanent right of residence that is obtained after a continuous legal residence of five years in the host Member State (Article 16). Together with those three categories,[41] the derived rights of family members and the restrictions that can be put on the right of residence of Union citizens and their family members by reason of public policy, public security, or public health are discussed below (6.011 – 6.016). Under Article 5(1) of Directive 2004/38 all citizens of the Union and their family members may enter the territory of another Member State if they hold a valid identity card or a valid passport. A third-country national who is married to a national of a Member State cannot be expelled on the sole ground that he or she does not carry a valid identity card, passport, or visa. The

---

[36] Directive 2004/38/EC of the European Parliament and of the Council of 29 April 2004 on the right of the citizen of the Union and their family members to move and reside freely within the territory of the Member States amending Regulation (EEC) No. 1612/68 and repealing Directives 64/221/EEC, 68/360/EEC, 72/194/EEC, 73/148/EEC, 75/34/EEC, 75/35/EEC, 90/364/EEC, 90/365/EEC, and 93/96/EEC, OJ 2004 L158/77 (adopted on the basis of Articles 12, 18, 40, 44, and 52 EC [*now Articles 18, 21, 46, 52, and 59 TFEU*]). See, generally, Guild, Peers, and Tomkin (eds), *The EU Citizenship Directive: A Commentary* (OUP, 2019).

[37] C-673/16, *Coman*, 2018, para. 18.

[38] C-333/13, *Dano*, 2014, para. 74, with case note by Düsterhaus (2015) EuConst 121. See Kramer, 'Earning Social Citizenship in the European Union: Free Movement and Access to Social Assistance Benefits Reconstructed' (2016) CYEL 270; O'Brien, 'Civis Capitalist Sum: Class As The New Guiding Principle of EU Free Movement Rights' (2016) CMLRev 937; Verschueren, 'Preventing 'Benefit Tourism' in the EU: A Narrow or Broad Interpretation of the Possibilities offered by the ECJ in Dano?' (2015) CMLRev 363; Steiger, 'Freizügigkeit in der EU und Einschränkungen von Sozialleistungen für EU-Ausländer—Vom Verlust der richtigen Balance zwischen den Interessen der Mitgliedstaaten und den Rechten des Einzelnen sowie der Notwendigkeit einer primärrechtskonformen Auslegung der Freizügigkeitsrichtlinie' (2018) EuR 304–38.

[39] See, e.g., in the context of Council Directive 2003/86/EC of 22 September 2003 on the right to family reunification, OJ 2003 L251/12: C-578/08, *Chakroun*, 2010, paras 45–51, case notes by Kunoy and Mortansson (2010) CMLRev 1815 and Wiesbrock (2010) EuConst 462.

[40] Ibid. paras 46 and 49.

[41] In more detail, see Guild, Peers, and Tomkin (eds), *The EU Citizenship Directive: A Commentary* (OUP, 2019), 89–228.

protection of the right to family life requires that such a person be given the opportunity to prove his identity and marital status by other means.[42]

The fact that the right of residence is derived directly from the Treaties has the consequence that all restrictions and conditions imposed by the Member States on that right must be applied having regard to the general principles of Union law, such as the principle of proportionality.[43] Member States may not impose requirements as to the origin of the resources that citizens of the Union must have in order to benefit from a right of residence in order not to unduly restrict that right.[44] The Court of Justice thus held in *Grzelczyk* that the requirement for economically inactive Union citizens to have sufficient resources in order to obtain the right to reside in another Member State cannot be interpreted as meaning that recourse to that Member State's social assistance system automatically entails the loss of this right of residence. The reason is that the right of residence for economically inactive citizens of the Union implies the existence of a certain degree of financial solidarity between nationals of the host Member State and nationals of other Member States.[45] More recently, however, the Court of Justice held in its *Dano* judgment that Member States cannot be expected to grant social assistance to economically inactive Union citizens who exercise their right to freedom of movement with the sole aim of benefitting from such assistance of another Member State although they do not have sufficient resources to invoke a right of residence under Directive 2004/38.[46] In order to determine whether the claim by a national of another Member State constitutes an 'unreasonable' burden[47] on a national social assistance system, it is not contrary to the principle of proportionality that Member States take into account the cumulative effect that similar claims would generate.[48]

Residence up to three months. Directive 2004/38 confers on Union citizens the right of residence on the territory of another Member State for a period of up to three months without any conditions or any formalities other than the requirement to hold a valid identity card or passport (Article 6(1)). Union citizens and their family members enjoy this right as long as they do not become an unreasonable burden on the social assistance system of the

6.011

---

[42] C-459/99, *MRAX*, 2002, paras 53–62; C-68/89, *Commission v Netherlands*, 1991; see also Article 5(4) of Directive 2004/38. With regards to the legal position of unmarried couples in the context of EU migration, see Spalding, 'Where Next After Coman?' (2019) EMIL 117.

[43] C-413/99, *Baumbast and R.*, 2002, paras 85–94; T-66/95, *Kuchlenz-Winter v Commission*, 1997, paras 47–8. As regards the latitude available to Member States in implementing the right of residence for the various categories of beneficiaries (and members of their families), see C-424/98 *Commission v Italy*, 2000, paras 20–48. See Scheuing, 'Freizügigkeit als Unionsbürgerrecht' (2003) EuR 744–92.

[44] C-200/02, *Zhu and Chen*, 2004, paras 29–33; C-408/03, *Commission v Belgium*, 2006, paras 38–52. This encompasses resources made available by third parties, or generated by precarious employment of a person without work permit, see C-93/18, *Bajrati*, 2019, paras 30–8; C-836/18, *RH*, 2020, para. 31.

[45] C-184/99, *Grzelczyk*, 2001, paras 37–46; C-140/12, *Brey*, 2013, para. 72.

[46] C-333/13, *Dano*, 2014, paras 78–80. See Thym, 'The Elusive Limits of Solidarity: Residence Rights of and Social Benefits for Economically Inactive Union Citizens' (2015) CMLRev 17; Shuibhne, 'Limits Rising, Duties Ascending: the Changing Legal Shape of Union Citizenship' (2015) CMLRev 889; Zahn, '"Common Sense" or a Threat to EU Integration? The Court, Economically Inactive EU Citizens and Social Benefits' (2015) ILJ 573.

[47] For a detailed assessment on the meaning of 'unreasonable burden', see Verschueren, 'Free Movement or Benefit Tourism: The Unreasonable Burden of Brey' (2014) EMIL 147.

[48] C-67/14, *Alimanovic*, 2015, paras 61–2; C-299/14, *García Nieto*, 2016, paras 45–50. Mantu and Minderhoud, 'EU Citizenship and Social Solidarity' (2017) MJECL 703; Spaventa, 'Earned Citizenship— Understanding Union Citizenship Throught Its Scope', in Kochenov (ed.), *EU Citizenship and Federalism: The Role of Rights* (Cambridge University Press, 2017), 204; Babayev, 'Re-Shaping the Paradigm of Social Solidarity in the EU: On the UK's Welfare Reforms and Pre- and Post-EU Referendum Developments' (2016) EJ Soc Sec 356; Iliopoulou-Penot, 'Deconstructing the Former Edifice of Union Citizenship? The Alimanovic Judgment' (2016) CMLRev 1007.

host Member State (Article 14(1)). Accordingly, economically non-active Union citizens are not entitled to social assistance during this three-month period (Article 24(2); para. 6-015, *infra*).[49]

6.012 **Residence exceeding three months.** Article 7(1) of the Directive grants the right of residence for a period longer than three months to (a) Union citizens who are workers or self-employed persons in the host Member State, (b) all other Union citizens who have sufficient resources for themselves and their family members not to become a burden on the social assistance system of the host Member State during their period of residence and comprehensive sickness insurance cover in that State, (c) Union citizens following a course of study in the host Member State, if they have comprehensive sickness insurance cover in that State and assure the relevant authority that they have sufficient resources in the above sense, and (d) family members accompanying or joining a Union citizen who satisfy the conditions of Article 7(1)(a), (b) or (c).[50] Member States may impose a registration requirement on Union citizens who reside for longer than three months. A 'residence card' may only be given to family members of a Union citizen who do not have the nationality of a Member State.[51]

The right of residence for a period longer than three months exists as long as the Union citizens and their family members meet the conditions set in Article 7 of the Directive (Article 14(2)). However, in line with the Court's judgment in *Grzelczyk*,[52] an expulsion measure should not be the automatic consequence of recourse to the social assistance system (see Article 14(3)). Before recourse is had to expulsion, the host Member State must examine whether the difficulties are temporary in nature and, in order to determine whether a person becomes an undue burden on the social assistance system, must take into account the duration of the residence, the personal circumstances, and the amount of assistance already provided to the Union citizen.[53] Member States may only verify whether a Union citizen or his or her family members meet the residence requirements if there is a specific reason to doubt whether that is the case (Article 14(2)).[54] A removal measure may only be taken against employed persons, self-employed persons, or jobseekers having a real chance of being recruited for reasons of public order or public security (Article 14(4)). A Member State is, however, not under an obligation to provide social assistance to nationals of other Member States who do not meet the conditions of Article 7.[55]

6.013 **Permanent residence.** Directive 2004/38 confers a right of permanent residence to citizens of the Union who reside continuously on the territory of the host Member State for five

---

[49] C-299/14, *García Nieto*, 2016, paras 43–5.
[50] A Union citizen who is no longer a worker or self-employed person is to retain that status in the circumstances listed in Article 7(3) of the Directive. For an application, see C-67/14, *Alimanovic*, 2015, paras 53–61. With respect to persons meeting the conditions under Article 7(1)(c), Article 7(4) of the Directive limits qualifying 'family members' to the spouse or registered partner and dependent children.
[51] Directive 2004/38, Articles 8 and 9.
[52] C-184/99, *Grzelczyk*, 2001, para. 43.
[53] Recital 16 of the preamble of Directive 2004/38.
[54] C-308/14, *Commission v United Kingdom*, 2016, paras 82–4. See O'Brien, 'The ECJ Sacrifices EU Citizenship in Vain: Commission v. United Kingdom' (2017) CMLRev 209.
[55] C-333/13, *Dano*, 2014, paras 67–84; C-67/14, *Alimanovic*, 2015, paras 48–62. See O'Brien, 'Civis Capitalist Sum: Class As the New Guiding Principle of EU Free Movement Rights' (2016) CMLRev 937; Minderhoud, 'Job-Seekers Have a Right of Residence but No Access to Social Assistance Benefits under Directive 2004/38' (2016) MJECL 342.

years (Article 16).[56] In some instances the right of permanent residence may be obtained sooner, provided the conditions of Article 17, which aim to ensure that the citizen is sufficiently integrated,[57] are fulfilled.

Family members. Directive 2004/38 extends the right of free movement and residence to family members of citizens of the Union, even if they do not have the nationality of a Member State (so-called 'third-country nationals').[58] Article 2(2) of the Directive defines 'family member' as: (a) the spouse; (b) the partner with whom the Union citizen has contracted a registered partnership, on the basis of the legislation of a Member State, if the legislation of the host Member State treats registered partnerships as equivalent to marriage and in accordance with the conditions laid down in the relevant legislation of the host Member State; (c) the direct descendants who are under the age of 21 or are dependants and those of the spouse or partner as defined in point (b); (d) the dependent direct relatives in the ascending line and those of the spouse or partner as defined in point (b).[59] According to the Court of Justice, the status of 'dependent' family member is the result of a factual situation characterized by the fact that *material support* for that family member is provided by the citizen of the Union who has exercised his or her right of free movement or by his or her spouse.[60] The concept of spouse also covers persons who concluded a lawful same-sex marriage in a Member State, even when the host Member State does not allow for same-sex marriages.[61] The category of direct descendants covers any parent–child relationship, whether biological or legal, thus including adopted children.[62] It does not include children who are in the foster care of an adult without the formation of such a relationship.[63] The category of ascendants includes parents of a minor Union citizen who are his or her primary carers, even though they are not 'dependent' on their child but are instead in the opposite situation. For the Court, any other interpretation would deprive the child's right of residence as a Union citizen of its effectiveness.[64]

6.014

---

[56] C-162/09, *Lassal*, 2010, paras 29–40; C-378/12, *Onuekwere*, 2014, with case note by Coutts (2015) CMLRev 531; C-244/13, *Ogieriakhi*, 2014.

[57] C-32/19, *AT*, 2020, paras 40–3.

[58] For a detailed overview of the rights granted to third-country family members by the different Community directives which were replaced by Directive 2004/38, see Barrett, 'Family matters: European Community Law and Third-country Family Members' (2003) CMLRev 369–421; Berneri, *Family Reunification in the EU: The Movement and Residence Rights of Third Country National Family Members of EU Citizens* (Bloomsbury, 2017).

[59] The category of ascendants also includes parents of a minor having the nationality of one of the Member States who are his or her primary carers, even though they are not 'dependent' on their child but are instead in the opposite situation. Any other interpretation would deprive the child's right of residence as a citizen of the Union of effectiveness (C-200/02, *Zhu and Chen*, 2004, paras 44–6).

[60] 316/85, *Lebon*, 1987, para. 22; C-200/02, *Zhu and Chen*, 2004, para. 43. Proof of the need for material support may be adduced by any appropriate means, while a mere undertaking from the Union national or his or her spouse to support the family members concerned need not be regarded as establishing the existence of the family members' situation of real dependence (C-1/05, *Jia*, 2007, para. 43).

[61] C-673/16, *Coman*, 2018, paras 28–51. See Kochenov and Belavusau 'Same-Sex Spouses: More Free Movement, But What About Marriage? Coman' (2020) CMLRev 227; MacLennan and Ward, 'The Constitutional Dimension of Case C-673/16 Coman on the Prohibition of Discrimination on the Basis of Sexual Orientation: The Role of Fundamental Rights in Interpreting EU Citizenship' (2020) Col JEL 36–61; Rijpma, 'You Gotta Let Love Move' (2019) EuConst 324; Tryfonidou, 'The ECJ Recognises the Right of Same-Sex Spouses to Move Freely Between EU Member States: The Coman Ruling' ELRev 663; Stehlik, 'The CJEU Crossing the Rubicon on the Same-Sex Marriages? Commentary on Coman Case' (2018) ICLR 85.

[62] C-129/18, *SM*, 2019, paras 48–54.

[63] Ibid., paras 55–72 (not covering children placed with Union citizens under a legal guardianship system such as Algerian *kafala*; such a child may however be considered as one of the other family members pursuant to Article 3(2)(a) of the Directive, read in the light of Article 7 and Article 24(2) of the Charter). See Strumia, 'The Family in EU Law After the SM Ruling: Variable Geometry and Conditional Deference' (2019) EP 389.

[64] C-200/02, *Zhu and Chen*, 2004, paras 44–6.

The rights conferred by Article 21(1) TFEU and Directive 2004/38 on third-country nationals who are family members of a Union citizen are not 'autonomous' rights but only rights derived from the exercise of the Union citizen of his or her right to free movement.[65] Such derived right of residence is based on the need to ensure that a Union citizen can effectively exercise his or her right to free movement and residence in the Union. Where a Union citizen has never exercised his or her right of free movement and always resided in the Member State of which he or she is a national, Article 21 TFEU and Directive 2004/38 do not apply and cannot therefore be invoked by the Union citizen's family members.[66] However, the right under Article 21(1) TFEU may be wider in that the family members of a Union citizen who exercised his or her right of free movement to another Member State and subsequently obtained the nationality of that Member State without losing his or her original nationality, may not rely on Directive 2004/38 in order to claim a right of residence,[67] but they are eligible for a derived right of residence under Article 21(1) TFEU, on conditions which must not be stricter than those provided for by Directive 2004/38 for the grant of such a right to a third-country national who is a family member of a Union citizen who has exercised his or her right of freedom of movement by settling in a Member State other than the Member State of which he or she is a national.[68] Pursuant to its Article 3(1), Directive 2004/38 only applies to family members who 'accompany' or 'join' a citizen of the Union who moves to or resides in the host Member State.[69] Article 3(1) is given a broad interpretation by the Court holding that it is not required that the family member already had prior legal residence in a Member State.[70] In the case of a spouse of a Union citizen, the marriage need not have taken place before the Union citizen moves to the host Member State.[71] However, as the right of residence of family members to reside is derived of the status of the Union citizen on whom they are dependent, their rights under Directive 2004/38 are 'dynamic', and may thus be lost if the Union citizen no longer lawfully resides in the host Member State, for instance because the Union citizen has left to serve a prison sentence in his or her Member State of origin.[72] Article 13 of Directive 2004/38 lays down the conditions under which family members retain a right of residence in the event of divorce or of dissolution of a registered partnership.[73]

---

[65] C-40/11, *Iida*, 2012, para. 66; C-87/12, *Ymeraga and Ymeraga-Tafarshiku*, 2013, para. 34; C-456/12, *O. and B.*, 2014, para. 36; C-82/16, *K.A.*, 2018, para. 50. See Schoenmakers and Hoogenboom, 'Singh and Carpenter Revisited: Some Progress but No Final Clarity' (2014) MJECL 494; Tryfonidou, '(Further) Signs of a Turn of the Tide in the CJEU's Citizenship Jurisprudence, Case C-40/11 Iida, Judgment of 8 November 2012, Not Yet Reported' (2013) MJECL 302.

[66] C-127/08, *Metock*, 2008, paras 76–9; C-87/12, *Ymeraga and Ymeraga-Tafarshiku*, 2013, paras 24–33. See already earlier: C-64/96 and C-65/96, *Uecker and Jacquet*, 1997, paras 16–21.

[67] C-165/16, *Lounes*, 2017, paras 31–44. See Réveillère, 'Family Rights for Naturalized EU Citizens: Lounes' (2018) CMLRev 1855.

[68] C-165/16, *Lounes*, 2017, paras 45–62.

[69] E.g. C-40/11, *Iida*, 2012, paras 49–65.

[70] C-291/05, *Eind*, 2007, paras 41–4; C-127/08, *Metock*, 2008, paras 48–80. The latter judgment explicitly reversed prior case law: C-109/01, *Akrich*, 2003, paras 50–4 (which did require prior lawful residence in a Member State). See Costello, 'Metock: Free Movement and 'Normal Family Life' in the Union' (2009) CMLRev 587.

[71] C-127/08, *Metock and Others*, 2008, paras 85–93; see case note by Cambien (2009) Col JEL 321–41; C-551/07 *Sahin* (order), 2008, paras 24–33; C-673/16, *Coman*, 2018, paras 39–40.

[72] C-94/18, *Chenchooliah*, 2019, paras 50–67. The loss of beneficiary status in the sense of Article 3(1) of Directive 2004/38 does not mean, however, that the procedural protection in respect of expulsion orders provided for by Article 15 of the Directive would no longer be applicable to any subsequent expulsion of the family member; see C-94/18, *Chenchooliah*, 2019, paras 68–71.

[73] e.g. C-218/14, *Singh*, 2015. See Strumia, 'Divorce Immediately, or Leave. Rights of Third Country Nationals and Family Protection in the Context of EU Citizens' Free Movement: Kuldip Singh and Others' (2016) CMLRev 1373.

Under Article 21(1) TFEU, a family member of a Union citizen also enjoys a derived right of residence in the Member State of which the Union citizen has the nationality, when that Union citizen has actually resided with that family member in another Member State and returns to the Member State of which he or she is a national.[74] An 'actual' residence in another Member State exists where a Union citizen has created or maintained a family life in that Member State in compliance with the conditions set out in Article 7(1) or (2) or Article 16 of Directive 2004/38. The Union citizen would indeed be deterred from leaving the Member State of nationality when he or she is not certain that any family life created or maintained in the host Member State can be continued upon return to the Member State of nationality.[75]

Finally, it must be noted that the children of a national of a Member State who is or has been employed in the territory of another Member State may claim a right of residence in order to pursue their education on the basis of Article 10 of Regulation 492/2011, without having to meet the conditions of Directive 2004/38.[76]

Equal Treatment. Subject to such specific provisions as are expressly provided for in the Treaties and secondary law, all Union citizens and their family members residing on the basis of Directive 2004/38 in the territory of the host Member State are to enjoy equal treatment with the nationals of that Member State within the scope of the Treaties (Article 24(1)). As such, the Directive contains a specific expression of the principle of equal treatment laid down in Article 18 TFEU[77] (see paras 5-053–5-057, *supra*). Nonetheless, Directive 2004/38 does not require a Member State to confer entitlement to social assistance during the first three months of residence[78] (or the longer period during which a citizen continues to seek employment with genuine chances of being hired)[79] nor, prior to the acquisition of the right of permanent residence, to grant maintenance aid for studies consisting of student grants or student loans to persons other than workers, self-employed persons, persons who retain such status, and members of their families (Article 24(2)).[80] Moreover, a Union citizen only

6.015

---

[74] C-456/12, *O. and B.*, 2014, paras 44–9. See also C-673/16, *Coman*, 2018, paras 19–26 (this also applies to the spouses of a same-sex marriage that was lawfully concluded while residing in another Member State, even though the Member State to which the Union citizen returns does not recognize same-sex marriages, C-673/16, *Coman*, 2018, paras 52–6). See Ward and MacLennan, 'Citizenship and Incremental Convergence With Fundamental Rights?' (2019) CLJ 283.

[75] C-456/12, *O. and B.*, 2014para. 54. On the implications of this ruling on the abuse of family reunification in order to circumvent reverse discrimination, see Kroeze, 'Distinguishing between Use and Abuse of EU Free Movement Law: Evaluating Use of the 'Europe-route' for Family Reunification to Overcome Reverse Discrimination' (2018) EP 1209.

[76] C-310/08, *Ibrahim*, 2010, para. 59; C-413/99, *Baubast and R*, 2002, paras 63 and 75; C-480/08, *Teixeira*, 2010, para. 36; C-181/19, *Jobcenter Krefeld—Widerspruchsstelle*, 2020, paras 34–9. See also C-115/15, *NA*, 2016, paras 56–62 (residence rights of the children and of the parent who takes care of them not dependent on the parent still being a migrant worker or still residing in the Member State concerned); C-401/15 and C-403/15, *Depesme and Others*, 2016 (notion of child is the same as in Directive 2004/38, also covering the child of a spouse or registered partner of a worker who supports that child). See further para. 7-060.

[77] For an example of the direct application of Article 18 TFEU in the context of citizenship, see C-22/18, *TopFit*, 2019, paras 26–67.

[78] C-22/08 and C-23/08, *Vatsouras and Koupatantze*, 2009, paras 34–5; C-299/14, *García Nieto*, 2016, paras 43–5. See Shuibhne, '"What I Tell You Three Times is True" Lawful Residence and Equal Treatment after Dano' (2016) MJECL 908.

[79] Benefits of a financial nature which, independently of their status under national law, are intended to facilitate access to the labour market cannot be regarded as constituting 'social assistance' within the meaning of Article 24(2) of Directive 2004/38: C-22/08 and C-23/08, *Vatsouras and Koupatantze*, 2009, paras 44–5, with case note by Damjanovic (2010) CMLRev 847.

[80] See also C-209/03, *Bidar*, 2005, paras 49–63; C-158/07, *Förster*, 2008, paras 45–60.

enjoys a right to equal treatment under Article 24 if his or her residence in the territory of the host Member State complies with the conditions of Directive 2004/38. Consequently, as stated above, Member States have the possibility of refusing to grant social benefits to economically inactive Union citizens who exercise their right to freedom of movement with the sole aim of social assistance benefit in another Member State, although they do not have sufficient resources to claim a right of residence under Directive 2004/38.[81]

6.016 **Public policy.** As Article 21(1) TFEU refers to the 'limitations and conditions laid down in the Treaties', that provision does not preclude Member States from limiting the right to move and to reside on the basis of Article 45(3) TFEU and Articles 52 and 62 TFEU. These provisions allow for restrictions on the free movement of persons and services on grounds of public policy, public security, or public health. Under Article 27 of Directive 2004/38 the right of residence of Union citizens and their family members may thus be limited for reasons of public policy, public security, or public health.[82] Every restriction must respect the principle of proportionality,[83] and be 'based exclusively on the personal conduct of the individual concerned'.[84] Previous criminal convictions are not to constitute grounds for the taking of such measures in themselves;[85] the same applies to alleged war crimes that give rise to the refusal of refugee status of the applicant pursuant to Article 1F of the Geneva Convention or Article 12(2) Directive 2011/95.[86] Accordingly, a Member State may not refuse entry to a third-country national who is the spouse of a Member State national on the ground that alerts for the third-country national were entered in the Schengen Information System, without first verifying whether the presence of this person constitutes a genuine, present, and sufficiently serious threat to one of the fundamental interests of society.[87] Moreover, for a person to be expelled, the 'genuine threat' must in principle remain until the moment of his or her expulsion.[88]

Article 28 of Directive 2004/38 offers protection against removal decisions, with Union citizens and their family members enjoying more protection if they are better integrated in the host Member State.[89] Thus, the enhanced protection provided for in Article 28(3)(a) of the

---

[81] C-333/13, *Dano*, 2014, para. 78, with case note by Peers (2015) CLJ 195.
[82] The Directive replaces Council Directive 64/221/EEC of 25 February 1964 on the coordination of special measures concerning the movement or residence of foreign nationals which are justified on grounds of public policy, public security, or public health, OJ 1963–1964 English Special Edition (I) 117, which already allowed for exceptions on public policy, public security, or public health grounds.
[83] See already C-101/94, *Commission v Italy*, 1996, paras 25–6; C-294/00, *Deutsche Paracelsus Schulen für Naturheilverfahren*, 2002, paras 38–66.
[84] Directive 2004/38 (n. 36, *supra*), Article 27(2), first subpara; see previously Directive 64/221, Article 3(1). See also C-304/14, *CS*, 2016, paras 39–41, with case note by Neuvonen (2017) CMLRev 1201. See further Kostakopoulou and Ferreira, 'Testing Liberal Norms: The Public Policy and Public Security Derogations and the Cracks in European Union Citizenship' (2014) Col JEL 167.
[85] Directive 2004/38 (n. 36, *supra*), Article 27(2), first subpara; see previously Directive 64/221, Article 3(2). Thus, automatic expulsion from the territory is not permitted of nationals of other Member States found guilty on that territory of drug offences: C-348/96, *Calfa*, 1999, paras 16–29; C-482/01 and C-493/01, *Orfanopoulos and Others*, 2004, paras 66–71. cf. C-340/97, *Nazli*, 2000, paras 50–64 (the same applies to workers deriving rights from association agreements); C-441/02, *Commission v Germany*, 2006, para. 33.
[86] C-331/16 and C-366/16, *K and H.F.*, 2018, paras 38–67. See Coutts, 'The Expressive Dimension of the Union Citizenship Expulsion Regime: Joined Cases C-331/16 and C-366/16, K and HF' (2018) EP 833.
[87] C-503/03, *Commission v Spain*, 2006, paras 41–59; C-331/16 and C-366/16, *K and H.F.*, 2018, paras 38–67.
[88] C-482/01 and C-493/01, *Orfanopoulos and Others*, 2004, paras 79 and 82; C-136/03, *Dörr and Ünal*, 2005, paras 41–3.
[89] C-145/09, *Tsakouridis*, 2010, paras 24–38; C-348/09, *P.I.*, 2012, paras 33–4, with case note by Azoulai and Coutts (2013) CMLRev 553; C-400/12, *M.G.*, 2014, paras 30–8; C-316/16 and C-424/16, *B and Vomero*, 2018, paras 40–61, with case note by Carabot (2019) CMLRev 771.

Directive is available to a Union citizen only in so far as he or she first satisfies the eligibility condition for the protection referred to in Article 28(2) of the Directive, namely having a right of permanent residence under Article 16 of the Directive.[90]

Directive 2004/38 also formulates procedural requirements for the exercise of the public policy reservation by Member States.[91] In this way, the Directive restricts the Member State's residual power in the sphere of public policy.[92] The procedural protection offered by Directive 2004/38 extends to any person who at one time was a beneficiary of a right of residence. Hence, the expulsion of a family member of a Union citizen who was left behind when the family member returned to his or her Member State of origin to serve a prison sentence is still governed by Directive 2004/38.[93]

Except in cases where an expulsion order was made on grounds of public policy or public security, it cannot be accompanied by a ban to re-enter the country.[94] Even in the case of an exclusion order on grounds of public policy or public security, the order must be amenable to review after a reasonable period, pursuant to Articles 32 and 33 of Directive 2004/38.

Right of residence of third-country nationals to safeguard the effective enjoyment of Union citizenship. As set out above, a third-country national who is a family member of a Union citizen derives no right of residence from Union secondary law if that Union citizen has not exercised his or her right to free movement. However, the Court of Justice considers that exceptionally a right of residence must be granted to such a third-country national if Union citizenship would otherwise be rendered ineffective. This concerns situations where because of a refusal to grant a right of residence to a third-country national the Union citizen would be deprived of the genuine enjoyment of the substance of the rights which the status of Union citizen confers on him or her.[95] The Court thus held in *Ruiz Zambrano* that a Colombian couple residing in Belgium with young children who had Belgian nationality could not be refused the right to reside and work in that Member State as otherwise their

6.017

---

[90] C-378/12, *Onuekwere*, 2014, para. 27; C-316/16 and C-424/16, *B and Vomero*, 2018, para. 49. A period of detention does not necessarily break that period of residence, C-424/16, *B and Vomero*, 2018, paras 63-83. See also C-331/16 and C-366/16, *K and H.F.*, 2018, paras 68-77. See Coutts, 'The Shifting Geometry of Union Citizenship: A Supranational Status from Transnational Rights' (2019) CYEL 328-30.

[91] Directive 2004/38 (n. 36, *supra*), Articles 30 to 33. See, previously, with respect to the procedural safeguards laid down by Directive 64/221: 36/75, *Rutili*, 1975, paras 33-9; 30/77, *Bouchereau*, 1977, paras 15-30; 131/79, *Santillo*, 1980, paras 11-19; 115 and 116/81, *Adoui and Cornuaille*, 1982, paras 14-19; C-297/88 and C-197/89, *Dzodzi*, 1990, paras 57-69; C-175/94, *Gallagher*, 1995, paras 1-26; C-65/95 and C-111/95, *Shingara and Radiom*, 1997, paras 1-45; C-357/98, *Nana Yaa Konadu Yiadom*, 2000, paras 17-43; C-459/99, *MRAX*, 2002, paras 100-4; C-82/16, *K.A.*, 2018, paras 93-6.

[92] Corthaut, *EU ordre public* (Wolters Kluwer, 2012), 92-110; see also Peers, 'National Security and European Law' (1996) YEL 363-404; Hubeau, 'L'exception d'ordre public et la libre circulation des personnes en droit communautaire' (1981) CDE 207-56. For further consideration of the development of the concept of 'ordre public', see Chaltiel, 'L'ordre public devant la Cour de justice des Communautés européennes' (2003) RMCUE 120-3; Karydis, 'L'ordre public dans l'ordre juridique communautaire: un concept à contenu variable' (2002) RTDE 1-26. However, the Member States enjoy a significant amount of discretion in determining the thresholds mentioned in Article 28(2) of the Directive, see Pistoia, 'The Unbearable Lightness of a Piecemeal Approach. Moving Public Policy or Public Security Offenders in Europe' (2014) E Pub L 750.

[93] C-94/18, *Chenchooliah*, 2019, paras 68-71.

[94] Article 15(3) of Directive 2004/38; C-94/18, *Chenchooliah*, 2019, paras 72-88.

[95] C-34/09, *Ruiz Zambrano*, 2011, paras 43-44; C-256/11, *Dereci*, 2011, paras 66-7. See Thym, 'Family as Link: Explaining the Judicial Change of Direction on Residence Rights of Family Members from Third States', in Verschueren (ed.), *Residence, Employment and Social Rights of Mobile Persons, On How EU Law Defines Where They Belong* (Intersentia, 2016), 11; Raucea, 'Fundamental Rights: The Missing Pieces of European Citizenship?' (2013) GLJ 2021.

Belgian children would have to leave the Union in order to accompany their parents.[96] It follows from subsequent case law that a situation in which a Union citizen would be deprived of the 'genuine enjoyment of the substance of the rights which the status of Union citizen confers upon him' means a situation in which that citizen is in fact obliged to leave the territory of the Union as a whole.[97] The mere fact that it is desirable for a Union citizen to stay with his family members who are not nationals of a Member State is not sufficient to consider that the Union citizen is forced to leave the territory of the Union.[98] Accordingly, where the Union citizen is an adult, a relationship of dependency, capable of justifying the grant to the third-country national concerned of a derived right of residence under Article 20 TFEU, is conceivable only in exceptional cases, where, in the light of all the relevant circumstances, any form of separation of the Union citizen from the member of his family on whom he is dependent is not possible.[99] In the case of minors, however, the assessment of the existence of such a relationship of dependency must be based on consideration, in the best interests of the child,[100] of all the specific circumstances, including the age of the child, the child's physical and emotional development, the extent of child's emotional ties to each of his parents, and the risks that separation from the third-country national parent might entail for that child's equilibrium. The existence of a family link with that third-country national, whether natural or legal, is not sufficient, and cohabitation with that third-country national is not necessary in order to establish such a relationship of dependency.[101] It is immaterial when the relationship of dependency started.[102]

It follows that in those situations where the effective enjoyment of Union citizenship is at stake, the fact that a Union citizen has not exercised his or her right of free movement does not therefore constitute a 'purely internal situation'.[103] The third-country national derives

---

[96] C-34/09, *Ruiz Zambrano*, 2011, paras 43–44, with case note by Lansbergen and Miller (2011) EuConst 287.

[97] C-86/12, *Alokpa and Moudoulou*, 2013, paras 20–36; C-165/14, *Rendon Marín*, 2016, paras 78–9. See also C-82/16, *K.A.*, 2018, paras 47–62 (Article 20 TFEU precludes a practice of a Member State that consists in not examining an application for residence for the purposes of family reunification, submitted on its territory by a third-country national family member of a Union citizen who is a national of that Member State and who has never exercised his or her right to freedom of movement, solely on the ground that that third-country national is the subject of a ban on entering the territory of that Member State, without any examination of whether there exists a relationship of dependency between that Union citizen and that third-country national of such a nature that, in the event of a refusal to grant a derived right of residence to the third-country national, the Union citizen would, in practice, be compelled to leave the territory of the European Union as a whole and thereby be deprived of the genuine enjoyment of the substance of the rights conferred by that status). See also Tryfonidou, 'Redefining the Outer Boundaries of EU Law: The Zambrano, McCarthy and Dereci trilogy' (2012) E Pub L 493; Hinarejos, 'Citizenship of the EU: Clarifying "Genuine Enjoyment of the Substance" of Citizenship Rights' (2012) CLJ 279.

[98] C-434/09, *McCarthy*, 2011, para. 56; C-256/11, *Dereci*, 2011, paras 66–7. See also C-133/15, *Chavez-Vilchez*, 2017, paras 68–71 (if the Union citizen is a child his or her dependency on a parent who is a third-country national determines whether that child will be forced to leave the territory of the Union if a right of residence is denied to that parent, even though another parent is a Union citizen and capable of taking on the daily care of the child), with case note by Kroeze (2017) SEW 482. See Kochenov, 'The Right to Have What Rights? EU Citizenship in Need of Clarification' (2013) ELJ 502; Wiesbrock, 'Union Citizenship and the Redefinition of the 'Internal Situations' Rule: The Implications of Zambrano' (2011) GLJ 2077.

[99] C-82/16, *K.A.*, 2018, para. 76.

[100] The Court refers to Article 24 of the Charter of Fundamental Rights of the European Union, see, e.g., C-82/16, *K.A.*, 2018, para. 71.

[101] C-133/15, *Chavez-Vilchez*, 2017, para. 71; C-82/16, *K.A.*, 2018, para. 76. See van Eijken and Phoa, 'The Scope of Article 20 TFEU Clarified in Chavez-Vilchez: Are the Fundamental Rights of Minor EU Citizens Coming of Age?' (2018) ELRev 949.

[102] C-82/16, *K.A.*, 2018, paras 77–80.

[103] C-434/09, *McCarthy*, 2011, paras 45–50, with case note by Van Elsuwege (2011) EuConst 308; see also Sánchez, 'Purely Internal Situations and the Limits of EU Law: A Consolidated Case Law or a Notion to be Abandoned?' (2018) EuConst 22–4.

his or her right of residence in such situations not from the right to free movement and residence of the Union citizen provided for in Article 21 TFEU, but from the Union citizenship laid down in Article 20 TFEU. Article 20 TFEU is without prejudice to the possibility for the Member States to restrict the residence right of the third-country national on the basis of considerations of public policy and public security under conditions similar to those laid down for the free movement rights in the TFEU.[104]

B. Right to equal treatment and prohibition on obstacles to the right to move and reside

Equal treatment. Among the rights which are associated with the status of Union citizen is the right enshrined in Article 18 TFEU not to be discriminated on grounds of nationality within the scope of application of the Treaties.[105] As discussed above (see para. 5-055, *infra*), the right to equal treatment may be relied upon when a Union citizen exercises his or her economic freedoms guaranteed by the Treaties,[106] and also whenever an economically inactive Union citizen relies on his or her right under Article 21 TFEU to move to another Member State or to reside there. The Court has observed in this regard that 'Union citizenship is destined to be the fundamental status of nationals of the Member States, enabling those who find themselves in the same situation to enjoy the same treatment in law irrespective of their nationality, subject to such exceptions as are expressly provided for'.[107] Article 21 TFEU precludes, in principle, any form of disadvantaging nationals of a Member State on the sole ground that they have exercised their right to move and to reside in another Member State.[108] The Court also gives a wide meaning to the 'right to move and reside freely', and it accepts that this encompasses activities such as pursuing education in another Member State.[109] In parallel with the free movement of economically active persons (see para. 7-044, *infra*), a Union citizen may also invoke Article 21 TFEU where a group or organization exercises a certain power over individuals and is in a position to impose on them conditions that adversely affect the exercise of the fundamental freedoms guaranteed under the Treaty.[110]

6.018

---

[104] C-165/14, *Rendón Marín*, 2016, paras 81–6, and C-304/14, *CS*, 2016, paras 36–49.

[105] e.g. C-85/96, *Martínez Sala*, 1998, para. 62.

[106] e.g. C-138/02, *Collins*, 2004, para. 61 (while exercising the right to seek employment in another Member State).

[107] C-184/99, *Grzelczyk*, 2001, para. 31. See Neuvonen, *Equal Citizenship and Its Limits in EU Law: We The Burden?* (Bloomsbury, 2016); Brinkmann, 'Equal Treatment on the Ground of Nationality for EU Migrant Workers' (2015) EMIL 239.

[108] e.g. C-503/09, *Stewart*, 2011, paras 80–6; C-359/13, *Martens*, 2015, para. 25. See Ksovgaard-Petersen, 'Market Citizenship and Union Citizenship: An "Integrated" Approach? The Martens Judgment' (2015) LIEI 281; Shuibhne, 'Limits Rising, Duties Ascending: the Changing Legal Shape of Union Citizenship' (2015) CMLRev 889.

[109] C-76/05, *Schwarz and Gootjes-Schwarz*, 2007, paras 90–4, with case note by Shuibhne (2008) CMLRev 771; C-11/06 and C-12/06, *Morgan and Bucher*, 2007, paras 23–32. The Court refers to the objectives of the Treaties to promote the mobility of students and teachers (Article 6, sub e TFEU and Article 165(2), second indent TFEU), see, e.g., C-11/06 and C-12/06, *Morgan and Bucher*, 2007, para. 27; C-523/11 and C-585/11, *Prinz and Seeberger*, 2013, para. 29.

[110] C-22/18, *TopFit and Biffi*, 2019, paras 27–40 (Articles 18 and 21 TFEU invoked by amateur athlete against national sports association), see Lindholm and Parrish 'Horizontal Direct Effect of Union Citizenship and the Evolving Sporting Exception: TopFit' (2020) CMLRev 1283–304.

6.019 **Prohibition of obstacles.** Article 21 TFEU prohibits any national legislation likely to dissuade Union citizens from exercising their right to freedom of movement and residence. As in the case of economic freedoms, the right of free movement of a Union citizen is thus not only protected by a prohibition of discrimination (Article 21 in conjunction with Article 18 TFEU), but also by the prohibition of measures which, even though they apply without distinction to nationals of the Member States, contain a restriction of the right to move and reside in another Member State.[111] This applies, in the first place, to measures by which a Member State prohibits its own nationals from leaving its territory in order to enter the territory of another Member State.[112] In addition, other measures dissuading a Union citizen from exercising the right to free movement are prohibited unless such treatment is objectively justified. Thus, Article 21 TFEU prohibits, in principle, a Member State from refusing to recognize a family name that one of its nationals obtained in accordance with the law of another Member State[113] and to register a common family name in the same way as it was registered in the Member State of origin of one of the spouses[114] where such refusal would create serious inconveniences of a professional and personal nature that affect the right to free movement of the Union citizen in question. However, Article 21(1) TFEU does not guarantee that moving to another Member State has no effects at all in terms of taxation[115] or social security.[116]

6.020 **Grounds for justification.** Differences in treatment between Union citizens or other obstacles to their right to free movement are only justified if they are based on objective considerations of public interest that apply independently of the nationality of the persons concerned and are proportionate to the legitimate objective pursued by the national measure.[117] With regard to aid for education abroad, a Member State may, for example, attach conditions to ensure that the aid is granted only to students who have demonstrated a certain degree of integration into the society of that Member State.[118] In that context, however, a Member State may not give undue weight to an element that is not necessarily representative for the degree to which the applicant has a real and effective link with that Member State, to the exclusion of any other representative elements.[119] This is the case with a residence requirement imposed by a Member State for funding of studies abroad that excludes from financing students who did not reside in that Member State immediately

---

[111] e.g. C-152/05, *Commission v Germany*, 2008, paras 20–30.

[112] C-434/10, *Aladzhov*, 2011, paras 24–25, and C-430/10, *Gaydarov*, 2011, paras 24–5.

[113] C-353/06, *Grunkin and Paul*, 2008, paras 21–9; C-208/09, *Sayn-Wittgenstein*, 2010, paras 60–71, with case note by Besselink (2012) CMLRev 671. See Javobi, 'A Furstin by any Other Name—European Citizenship and the Limits of Individual Rights in the E.C.J.' (2011) Col JEL 643.

[114] C-391/09, *Runevic-Vardyn and Wardyn*, 2011, paras 72–8. See Claes and Reestman, 'The Protection of National Constitutional Identity and the Limits of European Integration at the Occasion of the Gauweiler Case' (2015) GLJ 917.

[115] C-365/02, *Lindfors*, 2004, para. 34; C-403/03, *Schempp*, 2005, paras 44–5.

[116] C-208/07, *von Chamier-Glisczinski*, 2009, paras 83–7. See Rennuy, 'The Emergence of a Parallel System of Social Security Coordination' (2013) CMLRev 1221.

[117] C-406/04, *De Cuyper*, 2006, paras 39–40; C-192/05, *Tas-Hagen and Tas*, 2006, paras 30–3; C-499/06, *Nerkowska*, 2008, paras 32–4; C-221/07, *Zablocka-Weyhermüller*, 2008; C-523/11 and C-585/11, *Prinz and Seeberger*, 2013, para. 33; C-359/13, *Martens*, 2015, para. 34. See Koutrakos, Shuibhne, and Syrpis (eds), *Exceptions from EU Free Movement Law: Derogation, Justification and Proportionality* (Hart Publishing, 2016).

[118] C-209/03, *Bidar*, 2005, paras 56–7; C-11/06 and C-12/06, *Morgan and Bucher*, 2007, paras 23–32; C-523/11 and C-585/11, *Prinz and Seeberger*, 2013, para. 36. Neuvonen, 'In Search of (Even) More Substance for the 'Real Link' Test: Comment on Prinz and Seeberger' (2014) ELRev 125.

[119] C-11/06 and C-12/06, *Morgan and Bucher*, 2007, paras 42–6.

prior to the studies abroad but nevertheless demonstrate sufficient links with the society of that Member State.[120] As regards the above-mentioned limits to the registration of certain family names the Court recognized (with reference to the need, under Article 4(2) TEU, to respect the national identities of the Member States) that it is legitimate for a Member State to protect the official national language,[121] or to apply a constitutionally protected right of equal treatment prohibiting the acquisition or possession of nobility titles.[122] Similarly, a Member State may draw a distinction between its own nationals and other Union citizens in applying the constitutional protection against extradition of its own nationals to a third country for the purpose of prosecution.[123] Nevertheless, in accordance with the principle of proportionality, a legitimate objective may justify a restriction of the free movement and equal treatment rights flowing from Union citizenship only in so far as it cannot be attained by less restrictive measures.[124]

C. Political rights

Right to participate in municipal and European elections. Article 22 TFEU proclaims that every citizen of the Union residing in a Member State of which he or she is not a national has the right to vote and to stand as a candidate in municipal and European Parliament elections in the Member State in which he or she resides, under the same conditions as nationals of that State (Article 22(1) and (2) TFEU). Accordingly, the prohibition of discrimination on grounds of nationality is applied in respect of the exercise of political rights fostering the integration of Member State nationals who have made use of their right freely to reside in other Member States.[125] Pursuant to Article 19(2) EC [*now Article 22(2) TFEU*], the Council adopted Directive 93/109[126] and Directive

6.021

---

[120] C-523/11 and C-585/11, *Prinz and Seeberger*, 2013, paras 33–40; C-220/12, *Menenes*, 2013, paras 34–41.
[121] C-391/09, *Runevic-Vardyn and Wardyn*, 2011, paras 85–7.
[122] C-208/09, *Sayn-Wittgenstein*, 2010, paras 89–92; C-438/14, *Bogendorff von Wolffersdorff*, 2016, paras 64–71. See Mohay and Tóth, 'Nobility Titles and Free Movement: Case C-438/14 Nabiel Peter Bogendorff von Wolffersdorff' (2017) Pecs J Int'l & Eur L 30.
[123] C-191/16, *Pisciotti*, 2018, paras 36–56. See also C-182/15, *Petruhhin*, 2016, paras 25–50; C-897/19 PPU, *IN*, 2020, paras 55–75; C-398/19, *BY*, 2020, paras 38–67. The Member State of nationality of the Union citizen must be informed so that it can issue a European Arrest Warrant, if that Member State accepts its jurisdiction to prosecute; if it does not do so, and in order to avoid impunity, the Union citizen can be extradited to the third country (if all other conditions are fulfilled, such as the respect of Article 19 of the Charter). By contrast, where an extradition request has been made by a third country for a Union citizen who has exercised his right to free movement, not for the purpose of prosecution, but for the purpose of enforcing a custodial sentence, the requested Member State, whose national law prohibits the extradition of its own nationals out of the Union for the purpose of enforcing a sentence and makes provision for the possibility that such a sentence pronounced abroad may be served on its territory, is required to ensure that that Union citizen, provided that he resides permanently in its territory, receives the same treatment as that accorded to its own nationals in relation to extradition, see C-247/17, *Raugevicius*, 2018, paras 26–50.
[124] C-208/09, *Sayn-Wittgenstein*, 2010, paras 93–4; C-391/09, *Runevic-Vardyn and Wardyn*, 2011, paras 88–93; C-438/14, *Bogendorff von Wolffersdorff*, 2016, paras 72–83; C-191/16, *Pisciotti*, 2018, paras 48–55.
[125] C-145/04 *Spain v United Kingdom*, 2006, para. 66. At the same time, the direct relationship between the Union and its citizens is powerfully reflected by the fact that any given MEP is not necessarily elected solely by nationals of one particular Member State. This makes it legitimate for MEPs to carry out their mandate independently of their nationality; para. 12-016, *infra*. See also Fabrrini, 'The Political Side of EU Citizenship in the Context of EU Federalism', in Kochenov (ed.), *EU Citizenship and Federalism: the Role of Rights* (OUP, 2015), 271. Pliakos, 'La nature juridique de l'Union européenne' (1993) RTDE 187, 194. See also the interesting points raised by Kochenov, 'Free Movement and Participation in the Parliamentary Elections in the Member State of Nationality: An Ignored Link?' (2009) MJECL 197–223.
[126] Council Directive 93/109/EC of 6 December 1993 laying down detailed arrangements for the exercise of the right to vote and stand as a candidate in elections to the European Parliament for citizens of the Union residing in

94/80[127] which provide for 'detailed arrangements' for the exercise of the right to vote and to stand as a candidate in elections for the European Parliament and in municipal elections. Member States may, however, provide that only their own nationals may hold the office of elected head, deputy, or member of the governing college of the executive of a basic local government (Article 5 of Directive 94/80).

The two directives are designed to make the right to vote independent of nationality and require non-nationals to be subject to the same conditions, if any, as apply to nationals, in particular as regards duration of residence and evidence of residence in the constituency. A voter is entitled to exercise the right to vote if he or she has expressed the wish to do so.[128] If voting is compulsory in the Member State of residence, Union citizens on the electoral roll are also obliged to vote;[129] once their names have been entered on the electoral roll, voters are to remain thereon under the same conditions as voters who are nationals.[130] Both directives provide for derogations for any Member State in which the proportion of Union citizens of voting age who reside in it but are not nationals of it exceeds 20 per cent (this only applied to Luxembourg). In view of the specific features and balances linked to the fact that its Constitution provides for three different languages and a territorial division into regions and communities, Belgium was given the possibility to apply a specific residence condition in respect of voting in municipal elections in a limited number of local government units, the names of which are to be notified in advance. In the end, however, no use was made of this derogation.[131]

The Treaty of Lisbon has given these political rights an even stronger constitutional footing, linking citizenship and democracy as Article 10(3) TEU guarantees the right for every citizen to participate in the democratic life of the Union.[132] As the Court has explained in *Delvigne*,[133] Article 39(1) of the Charter corresponds to the right guaranteed in Article 20(2)(b) TFEU to vote and stand as a candidate at elections to the European Parliament. Article 39(2) of the Charter, which provides that members of the European Parliament shall be elected by direct universal suffrage in a free and secret ballot, corresponds to Article 14(3) TEU; Article 39(2) of the Charter thus takes over the basic principles of the electoral

---

a Member State of which they are not nationals, OJ 1993 L329/34 (see also para. 12-014, *infra*). See the analysis by Shaw, *The Transformation of Citizenship in the European Union: Electoral Rights and the Restructuring of Political Space* (Cambridge University Press, 2007).

[127] Council Directive 94/80/EC of 19 December 1994 laying down detailed arrangements for the exercise of the right to vote and to stand as a candidate in municipal elections by citizens of the Union residing in a Member State of which they are not nationals, OJ 1994 L368/38. In a statement for the minutes, Spain declared that if the United Kingdom decided to extend the application of Directive 94/80 to Gibraltar, such application would be deemed to be without prejudice to Spain's position with regard to Gibraltar.

[128] Directive 93/109, Article 8(1); Directive 94/80, Article 7(1).

[129] Directive 93/109, Article 8(2); Directive 94/80, Article 7(2).

[130] Directive 93/109, Article 9(4); Directive 94/80, Article 8(3).

[131] Directive 94/80, Article 12(2). This is justified by the penultimate recital in the preamble. In a statement for the minutes, Belgium declared that it would apply that derogation only in 'some of the local government units in which the number of [Union] voters [not of Belgian nationality] exceeded 20% of all voters where the Belgian Federal Government regarded the specific situation as justifying an exceptional derogation of that kind', OJ 1994 L368/46. The European Parliament deplored the fact that it was not consulted on this derogation from the right to vote: resolution of 5 April 1995, OJ 1995 C109/40. For the substance of this potential derogation, see Foubert, 'Gemeentekiesrecht voor EU-burgers' (1998) TBP 79–84. Belgium failed to implement the directive within the prescribed period: C-323/97, *Commission v Belgium*, 1998.

[132] Lenaerts, 'Linking EU Citizenship to Democracy' (2016) CYELP VII–XVII.

[133] C-650/13, *Delvigne*, 2015, para. 41.

system in a democratic State.[134] Article 20(2)(b) TFEU only applies the principle of non-discrimination on grounds of nationality to the exercise of the right to vote in elections to the European Parliament, by providing that every citizen of the Union residing in a Member State of which he or she is not a national is to have the right to vote in those elections in the Member State in which he or she resides, under the same conditions as nationals of that State.[135] Hence, Article 39(1) of the Charter does not apply to a Union citizen's right to vote in the Member State of which he is a national.[136] By contrast, Article 39(2) constitutes the expression in the Charter of the right of Union citizens to vote in elections to the European Parliament in accordance with Article 14(3) TEU and Article 1(3) of the 1976 Act,[137] and thus serves as the framework for assessing limitations on that right based on national law.[138]

D. Right to protection

Protections. Citizens of the Union enjoy a number of special protections. In the territory of third countries in which their Member State is not represented, Union citizens are entitled to protection by the diplomatic or consular authorities of any Member State on the same conditions as nationals of that State (Article 23 TFEU). Article 23, first para. TFEU provides that the Member States are to 'adopt the necessary provisions and start the international negotiations required to secure this protection'.[139] The Council, acting in accordance with a special legislative procedure and after consulting the European Parliament, may adopt directives establishing the coordination and cooperation measures necessary to facilitate such protection (Article 23, second para. TFEU).[140]

6.022

Furthermore, the second and third paras of Article 24 TFEU give every Union citizen the right, respectively, to petition the European Parliament in accordance with Article 227 TFEU[141] and to apply to the European Ombudsman established under Article 228 TFEU.[142]

---

[134] See also C-502/19, *Junqueras Vies*, 2019, paras 63–4. On the elections for the European Parliament, see also, *infra*, para. 12-014.
[135] C-145/04, *Spain v United Kingdom*, 2006, para. 66; C-650/13, *Delvigne*, 2015, para. 42.
[136] C-650/13, *Delvigne*, 2015, para. 43.
[137] Act concerning the election of the members of the European Parliament by direct universal suffrage, annexed to Council Decision 76/787/ECSC, EEC, Euratom of 20 September 1976 (OJ 1976 L278/1), as amended by Council Decision 2002/772/EC, Euratom of 25 June 2002 and 23 September 2002 (OJ 2002 L283/1; 'the 1976 Act').
[138] C-650/13, *Delvigne*, 2015, paras 44–5.
[139] For the earlier 'Guidelines for the protection of unrepresented EC nationals by EC missions in third countries', see the Commission's answer of 4 May 1994 to Question No. E-822/94 (Kostopoulos), OJ 1994 C362/50. See also Moraru, 'Protection of EU Citizens Abroad: A Legal Assessment of the EU citizen's Right to Consular and Diplomatic Protection' (2011) Perspectives on Federalism 170.
[140] See Council Directive (EU) 2015/637 of 20 April 2015 on the coordination and cooperation measures to facilitate consular protection for unrepresented citizens of the Union in third countries and repealing Decision 95/553/EC, OJ 2015 L106/1; see Moraru, 'An Analysis of the Consular Protection Directive: Are EU Citizens Now Better Protected in the World?' (2019) CMLRev 417–62. Prior to the introduction of Article 23, second para. TFEU by the Treaty of Lisbon, the Treaty did not provide for any role to be played by Union institutions in this regard. As a result, the implementing rules were based on intergovernmental agreements and on former Titles V and VI of the EU Treaty. See the Decisions of the representatives of the governments of the Member States, meeting within the Council, of 19 December 1995 regarding protection for citizens of the European Union by diplomatic and consular representations (Decision 95/553/EC, OJ 1995 L314/73) and of 25 June 1996 on the establishment of an emergency travel document (Decision 96/409/CFSP, OJ 1996 L168/4, adopted under Title V of the EU Treaty). See Szczekalla, 'Die Pflicht der Gemeinschaft *und* der Mitgliedstaaten zum diplomatischen und konsularischen Schutz' (1999) EuR 325–42.
[141] C-261/13 P, *Schönberger v European Parliament*, 2014. For more on the right to petition see para. 12-011, *infra*.
[142] C-234/02 P, *European Ombudsman v Lamberts*, 2004; C-337/15 P, *European Ombudsman v Staelen*, 2017. On the European Ombudsman, see paras 13-039–13-041, *infra*.

Union citizens are entitled to exercise those rights even if they reside in a third country. The same rights likewise accrue to all other natural or legal persons residing or having their registered office in a Member State (see paras 12-011 and 13-039, *infra*). Finally, the fourth para. of Article 24 TFEU empowers any 'citizen of the Union' to write to any of the institutions, bodies, offices, or agencies in any of the Treaty languages and receive an answer in that language.[143] The Treaty of Lisbon introduced the right for a significant number of citizens to submit an initiative to the Commission (Article 11(4) TEU and Article 24, first para. TFEU; see para. 17-013, *infra*).

---

[143] See para. 14-024, *infra*. Under Declaration (No. 4), annexed to the Treaty of Nice, the institutions of the Union, the European Economic and Social Committee, the Committee of the Regions and the European Ombudsman were to ensure that the reply to any written request by a citizen of the Union was made within a reasonable period.

7
The Internal Market

Internal market. The establishment of an internal market remains one of the principal tasks entrusted to the Union (Article 3(3) TEU). The internal market is defined as 'an area without internal frontiers in which the free movement of goods, persons, services, and capital is ensured in accordance with the provisions of the Treaties' (Article 26(2) TFEU). The functioning of the internal market is to be ensured in the sense that all practices impeding the establishment of the internal market are to be eliminated as far as possible. Before the entry into force of the Lisbon Treaty, the EC Treaty referred in this connection to the establishment of a 'common market', without defining that notion. In 1986, the Single European Act supplemented the task of establishing and ensuring the common market with the aim of progressively establishing an 'internal market' by the end of 1992, defined as an 'area without internal frontiers'. At the same time, the EC Treaty still referred to the 'common market' as a frame of reference for the compatibility of activities assessed under the Treaty provisions on competition and State aid.[1] The Lisbon Treaty has replaced the words 'common market' throughout with 'internal market', which leaves the internal market as the sole expression of the objective of market integration pursued by the Union.   **7.001**

I. The Establishment of the Internal Market

A. Scope of the internal market

Market integration. The establishment of a common market was the most important task entrusted to the Community by the EEC Treaty and, later, the EC Treaty. The scope of the common market could be inferred from the list of tasks and the provisions set out in the EC Treaty. These tasks and provisions have not been substantially changed by the Lisbon Treaty, even though it replaced the term 'common market' with 'internal market'.   **7.002**

Negative integration. The establishment of the internal market includes first the elimination, between Member States, of obstacles to the free movement of goods, persons,[2] services, and capital (Article 26(2) TFEU). Before the introduction in the Treaties of the concept of internal market, the Court of Justice already described the common market as involving 'the elimination of all obstacles to intra-Community trade in order to merge the national   **7.003**

---

[1] See Articles 81 to 82 EC [*now Articles 101 to 102 TFEU*] and 87 to 88 EC [*now Articles 107 to 108 TFEU*], where references to activities being held '(in)compatible with the common market' have been replaced by references on activities being '(in)compatible with the internal market'.

[2] 'Free movement of persons' in this context refers to the free-movement provisions on economically active persons, namely workers and self-employed persons (see para. 7-044 *et seq.*, *infra*). For the right of free movement of persons regardless of economic activity, see para. 6-008 *et seq.*, *supra*.

markets into a single market bringing about conditions as close as possible to those of a genuine internal market'.[3] As in the EC Treaty, the TFEU has broken down the objective of eliminating obstacles to trade into the free movement of goods (Part Three, Title II) and the free movement of persons, services, and capital (Part Three, Title IV). The intention of the relevant provisions is that every market participant should be able to deploy his or her labour and capital, sell or buy goods, and perform or receive services across the Union's 'internal' frontiers without being impeded by national rules maintaining or reintroducing frontiers by means of trade restrictions. That is why within the scope of application of the Treaties any form of discrimination on the grounds of nationality is prohibited (Article 18 TFEU; see para. 5-050 *et seq.*, *supra*). As the Treaty provisions on the free movement of goods, persons, services, and capital come down to the enforcement of prohibitory provisions, they have been termed instruments of 'negative integration'.

Free movement of goods, including the abolition of customs duties between the Member States, led to the introduction of a common customs tariff for goods coming from third countries. From the beginning, the resulting customs union was set within the framework of a common commercial policy (see Article 3(1)(b) EC). Free movement of persons did not directly give rise to any common policy on persons from non-Community countries wishing to enter the territory of the Member States. It was not until the Amsterdam Treaty that the Community was empowered to adopt 'measures concerning the entry and movement of persons' (see Article 3(1)(d) EC), which subsequently developed into a more general competence to ensure the absence of internal frontier checks for persons and to frame a common policy on asylum, immigration, and external border control (see para. 7-010, *infra*).

7.004 **Positive integration.** From the outset, it was clear that in the agricultural and transport sectors the 'common market' could not be attained by abolishing all national restrictions on trade between Member States. In all Member States, governments had taken those sectors outside the mechanism of the free market, *inter alia*, through guaranteed prices for agricultural products, investment in transport infrastructure, and State operation of means of transport. Since the rules on the free movement of goods and services could not be declared to be applicable in full to those sectors,[4] the market could be unified only by bringing national policies into alignment. Therefore, the EC Treaty and, nowadays, the TFEU provide for a common policy in the field of agriculture and fisheries and a common policy in the field of transport. As a result, the TFEU still contains, after the title on free movement of goods, a title on 'agriculture and fisheries' (Title III, Part Three) and, after the title on free movement of persons, services, and capital, a title on 'transport' (Title VI, Part Three). Since these fields have developed into autonomous policy areas for the Union, they will

---

[3] 15/81, *Schul*, 1982, para. 33.

[4] That continues to hold true today, although not for the same reasons. For instance, an intermediation service the purpose of which is to connect, by means of a smartphone application and for remuneration, non-professional drivers using their own vehicle with persons who wish to make urban journeys, must be regarded as being inherently linked to a transport service and, accordingly, must be classified as 'a service in the field of transport' within the meaning of Article 58(1) TFEU that is thus exempt from the normal rules on services, C-434/15, *Asociación Profesional Élite Taxi*, 2017, paras 33–49; C-320/16, *Uber France*, 2018, paras 16–26. See also Hatzopoulos, 'After Uber Spain: the EU's approach on the Sharing Economy in Need of Review?' (2019) ELRev 89–99.

hereinafter be discussed amongst the other Union policies (see paras 9-003–9-011, *infra*).[5] Nonetheless, the fact that the Treaties provided for powers to enact rules in these fields demonstrates that the establishment of the common/internal market does not constitute a purely negative form of integration, that is, the enforcement of prohibitory provisions. It also requires the Union institutions to fulfil their Treaty obligations to act towards laying down common policies (i.e. 'positive integration').[6].

Undistorted competition. A third component of the internal market is constituted by the rules ensuring that competition is not distorted.[7] The EC Treaty expressly referred to a 'system ensuring that competition in the internal market is not distorted' (see Article 3(1)(g) EC). Whereas, for political reasons, this reference no longer features in the Treaties,[8] it is clear from the Protocol on the internal market and competition attached to them by the Lisbon Treaty that the internal market includes a system ensuring that competition is not distorted.[9] An internal market in which internal frontiers no longer impede free trade would not remain intact if the internal frontiers were to be retained or reintroduced by the action of undertakings or Member States. That could arise where an undertaking had a dominant position on a particular market, where undertakings formed cartels or where a Member State itself operated an undertaking or granted aid to its own undertakings. In order to obviate distortions of competition, Title VII of Part Three contains provisions applying to undertakings (Articles 101 to 105 TFEU) and provisions relating to public involvement in undertakings (Article 106 TFEU) and State aid to undertakings (Articles 107–109 TFEU). The rules on competition will be discussed below amongst the Union's other internal policies (see paras 9-014–9-028, *infra*). Indeed, the objective of ensuring that competition is not distorted in the internal market goes beyond the aim of integrating national markets to safeguard more generally the benefits of effective competition in terms of supply, prices, and innovation.[10]

7.005

Approximation of legislation. Lastly, the Treaties foresaw that the common/internal market could not be attained merely by prohibiting trade restrictions, discrimination, and distortions of competition. The unequal position of traders in the market is often ascribable to differences in national legislative or administrative provisions that are not incompatible with the provisions of the Treaty as such. Consequently, the Union's action includes the general task of positive integration (alongside the common agricultural and transport policies), which consists in approximating the laws of the Member States to the extent required for the functioning of the internal market (Articles 113 to 117 TFEU). From the outset, it has also been possible for the Union to take supplementary action (Article 352 TFEU).

7.006

---

[5] For the concept of 'liberalization', that is common to all these policy domains, see Dunne, 'Liberalisation and the Pursuit of the Internal Market' (2018) ELRev 803–36.
[6] For the Council's obligations with regard to the common transport policy, see 13/83 *European Parliament v Council*, 1985, para. 53 and paras 64–71 (see para. 9-010, *infra*).
[7] 32/65, *Italy v Council and Commission*, 1966, 405.
[8] See para. 5-006, *supra*.
[9] Protocol (No. 27), annexed to the TEU and TFEU, on the internal market and competition (OJ 2010 C83/309).
[10] The market integration objective remains however fully relevant to the Union's competition rules; see C-468/06 to C-478/06, *Sot. Lélos kai Sia EE and Others*, 2008, paras 65–6.

B. From common market to internal market

7.007 **Common market.** According to Article 8 EEC, the common market was to be established over a transitional period of twelve years with the result that the transitional period was over on 31 December 1969. Economic growth during the Community's early years produced even quicker results: by means of the so-called 'acceleration decisions' the Member States introduced the customs union earlier than had been anticipated.[11] Nevertheless, the Community did not succeed in achieving the common market in all its component parts before the end of the transitional period. Technical complications and political sensitivities stood in the way of adopting measures to secure the right of establishment and liberalize capital movements. The accession of new Member States, budgetary disagreements, and economic recession produced *euro-sclerosis*, bringing the achievement of the common market to a standstill. Admittedly, the Court of Justice had given a broad interpretation to the provisions on free movement, but residual disparities between national legislation could be harmonized only in so far as they directly affected the establishment or functioning of the common market, and this required a unanimous vote in the Council (Article 100 EEC).

7.008 **White Paper.** At the European Council held in Copenhagen in December 1982, the Commission succeeded in persuading the Heads of State or Government that work had to be carried out on 'priority measures ... to reinforce the internal market'.[12] At the European Council's request, the Commission adopted in June 1985 the White Paper entitled 'Completing the internal market', setting out an extensive programme with a view to eliminating all the remaining barriers.[13] The White Paper classified the barriers in three categories: physical, technical, and fiscal. The physical barriers encompassed frontier checks, which existed principally because of technical and fiscal differences between Member States. According to the White Paper, if those differences disappeared, any frontier check would become superfluous, provided that ancillary measures were taken for the security of citizens, immigration, and the control of drugs. Technical barriers were the result of the differing requirements to which Member States subjected products and services with a view to protecting, for instance, safety, health, or the environment. Rather than harmonizing these requirements, the Commission proposed fostering the equivalence and mutual recognition of national legislation. The Commission regarded the abolition of fiscal barriers as an important part of the internal market, but recognized that this was a controversial question. Consequently, the White Paper confined itself to proposing that efforts should be made towards mutual adjustment of national legislation. The White Paper announced some 300 measures to be adopted in accordance with a detailed timetable by no later than 1992 in order to abolish all these barriers.

---

[11] Decision of 12 May 1960 of the representatives of the Member States of the European Economic Community meeting within the Council on quickening the pace for achieving the objectives of the Treaty, JO 1217/60; Decision of 15 May 1962 of the representatives of the Member States of the European Economic Community meeting within the Council on quickening the pace for achieving the objectives of the Treaty, JO 1284/62; Council Decision 66/532/EEC of 26 July 1966 concerning the abolition of customs duties and the prohibition of quantitative restrictions as between Member States and the application of the common customs tariff duties to products not mentioned in Annex II [*now Annex I*] to the Treaty, JO 2971/66.

[12] (1982) 12 EC Bull. point 1.2.3.

[13] Commission of the European Communities, *Completing the Internal Market: White Paper from the Commission to the European Council (Milan, 28–29 June 1985)*, 14 June 1985, COM(85) 310 final. The Milan European Council broadly welcomed the White Paper (1985) 6 EC Bull. point 1.2.5.

Objective 1992. The Single European Act added Articles 8a, 8b, and 8c to the EEC **7.009**
Treaty, which committed the Union to adopting measures 'with the aim of progressively
establishing the internal market over a period expiring on 31 December 1992'. It introduced
in the EEC Treaty the definition of the 'internal market' as 'an area without internal frontiers
in which the free movement of goods, persons, services, and capital is ensured in accordance with the provisions of the Treaties' (Article 8a EEC, thereafter Article 14(2) EC, now
Article 26(2) TFEU). Moreover, the Single European Act conferred new powers to attain
this goal by laying down harmonization measures. Article 100a EEC (thereafter Article 95
EC, now Article 114 TFEU) empowered the Council to adopt, by a qualified majority and
with the participation of the European Parliament, measures for the 'approximation of the
provisions laid down by law, regulation or administrative action in Member States which
have as their object the establishment and functioning of the internal market' (see paras 7-
112–7-116, *infra*).[14]

From common/internal market to an area of freedom. At the moment of its introduc- **7.010**
tion in the Treaties, the 'internal market' concentrated on ensuring the free movement of
goods, persons, services, and capital between Member States and thus has a more limited
scope than the pre-existing 'common market'.[15] Indeed, the White Paper which launched
the internal market did not cover competition, agricultural, or transport policy. At the same
time, the definition of the internal market as an 'area without internal frontiers' showed
that the intended result was more ambitious than the establishment of a 'common market',
which merely set out to achieve 'open' internal frontiers, but did not affect the relevance of
those frontiers.[16] In contrast, the internal market 'without internal frontiers' requires any
formality imposed upon entry into the territory of a Member State from another Member
State to be abolished. For this purpose, the Union has been given the competence to ensure
the absence of any internal frontier checks for persons and to frame a common policy on
asylum, immigration, and external border control (Articles 67(2) and 77 TFEU: see para.
8.007 *et seq.*, *infra*). Furthermore, through the abolition of internal frontiers, the Treaties
no longer seek to attain merely an open market but an 'area'. The use of this term makes it
clear that integration is not confined to economic factors of production, but extends to the
whole of life in society.[17] The Amsterdam Treaty added the idea of the Union as 'an area of

---

[14] The Single European Act made not only for more flexible decision-making but also for a greater role for
the European Parliament by providing in Article 100a(1) EEC for the (new) procedure of cooperation with the
Parliament. The EU Treaty maintained this trend by replacing the procedure provided for in Article 100a [*later
Article 95*](1) EC by the new co-decision procedure. Article 95(2) EC did, however, preclude the application of
Article 95(1) to fiscal provisions, to those relating to the free movement of persons and to those relating to the
rights and interests of employed persons—which is still the case for Article 114(2) TFEU.
[15] For the debate on the relationship between the common market and the internal market, which has now
become obsolete, see Mortelmans, 'The Common Market, the Internal Market and the Single Market, What's in a
Market' (1998) CMLRev 101–136. For the meaning of the term 'internal market', see also Gormley, 'Competition
and Free Movement: Is the Internal Market the Same as a Common Market?' (2002) E Bus LRev 517–22; Müller-
Graff, 'Die Verdichtung des Binnenmarktsrechts zwischen Handlungsfreiheiten und Sozialgestaltung' (2002) EuR
Beiheft 1, 7–73; Dehousse and Demaret, 'Marché unique, significations multiples' (1992) JT 137–141; Pescatore,
'Some Critical Remarks on the "Single European Act"' (1987) CMLRev 9–18; Ehlermann, 'The Internal Market
Following the Single European Act' (1987) CMLRev 361–404; Forwood and Clough, 'The Single European Act
and Free Movement—Legal Implications of the Provisions for the Completion of the Internal Market' (1986)
ELRev 383–408.
[16] See, e.g., 118/75, *Watson and Belmann*, 1976, para. 17.
[17] See Barents, 'De Europese ruimte: contouren van een nieuw rechtsbegrip', (2018) SEW 248–58.

freedom, security and justice' (Article 2, fourth indent, EU).[18] Article 3(2) TEU now explicitly states that the Union is to offer its citizens an 'area of freedom, security and justice without internal frontiers'. Accordingly, nationals of the Member States now enjoy a general right of free movement and residence, irrespective of any economic activity, as citizens of the Union (see the discussion in para. 6-008 *et seq.*, *supra*).

II. The Treaty Provisions on Free Movement

7.011 **Four freedoms.** The foundations of the internal market are the Treaty provisions on the free movement of goods (Articles 28 to 37 TFEU) and the free movement of persons (workers and self-employed persons), services, and capital (Articles 45 to 66 TFEU). The prohibition on Member States' discriminating against goods, persons, services, and capital from other Member States is intended to secure the ability freely to deploy factors of production across frontiers. The Court of Justice also emphasizes in its interpretation of the 'four freedoms' the consumer's right freely to purchase goods and receive services in other Member States.[19] As far as goods are concerned, the rules on 'free movement' encompass, since the judgment in *Dassonville* (1974), not only the prohibition of discrimination but also a prohibition of other—even potential—barriers to free movement.[20] The Court's case law has gradually extended that broad interpretation to the rules on the supply of services and, subsequently, to the rules on the movement of persons and capital.[21] At the same time, the Court has held, also in respect of the free movement of persons, services, and capital, that a Member State may impose non-discriminatory restrictions on free movement only if they pursue an aim in the general interest and comply with the principle of proportionality. In other words, it has extended the case law on free movement of goods to cover the other freedoms.[22] The provisions on the free movement of services, which are provided cross-border without the provider or the recipient of the services moving, are increasingly being interpreted in parallel with the provisions on free movement of goods.[23] As to the obligations flowing from the Treaties with regard to the treatment of providers of services from other Member States, they frequently match the obligations which apply in regard to employees or self-employed

---

[18] See Lindahl, 'Finding a Place for Freedom, Security and Justice: The European Union's Claim to Territorial Unity', (2004) ELRev 461–84; Labayle, 'Le Traité d'Amsterdam. Un espace de liberté, de sécurité et de justice' (1997) RTDE 813, 824–5.
[19] Paras 7-029 and 7-084, *infra*.
[20] 8/74, *Dassonville*, 1974. On the lasting impact of that case, see also Schütze, '"Re-reading" Dassonville: Meaning and understanding in the history of European law' (2018) ELJ 376–407.
[21] cf. paras 7-029 (goods) and 7-062 (persons), 7-088 (services) and 7-100 (capital), *infra*.
[22] cf. para. 7-037 *et seq.* (goods) and 7-070–7-074 (persons), 7-090–7-094 (services) and para. 7-105 (capital), *infra*. For the convergence of the four freedoms, see Snell, 'And Then There Were Two: Products and Citizens in Community Law', in Tridimas and Nebbia (eds), *European Union Law for the Twenty-First Century*, Vol. II (Hart Publishing, 2004) 49–72; Bernard, 'Fitting the Remaining Pieces into the Goods and Persons Jigsaw?' (2001) ELRev 35–59; Jarass, 'Elemente einer Dogmatik der Grundfreiheiten II' (1995) EuR 202–26 and (2000) EuR 705–23. For the convergence of the four freedoms and competition law, see O'Loughlin, 'EC Competition Rules and Free Movement Rules: An Examination of the Parallels and their Furtherance by the ECJ *Wouters* Decision' (2003) E Comp LRev 62–69; Steinberg, 'Zur Konvergenz der Grundfreiheiten auf der Tatbestands- und Rechtfertigungsebene' (2002) Eu GRZ 13–25; Mortelmans, 'Towards Convergence in the Application of the Rules on Free Movement and on Competition?' (2001) CMLRev 613–49.
[23] For a joint application of trade in goods and trade in services, see C-390/99, *Canal Satélite Digital*, 2002, paras 39–41.

persons from other Member States.[24] In order to promote free movement of goods and services, harmonization of national provisions relating to the production and distribution of goods and services is carried out; the free movement of persons is further assisted by the harmonization and mutual recognition of diplomas and professional rules.[25]

Applicable freedom. In certain situations, a national measure affects multiple freedoms at the same time. In such circumstances it needs to be examined to what extent each of these freedoms is restricted, and whether, in the case at hand, one of the freedoms prevails over the others. If it is clear that, in the circumstances of the case, one of those freedoms is entirely secondary in relation to the other, the Court will, in principle, examine the contested measure in relation to the latter freedom only.[26] For example, the Court decided that a UK law prohibiting the importation of lottery advertisements and tickets was to be considered under the provisions on the freedom to provide services because the importation of these goods could not be considered independently of the lottery to which they related, and the latter was to be considered as a service within the meaning of the Treaties.[27] Similarly, the Court held, as regards legislation limiting the right to acquire, use, or dispose of immovable property in Hungary, that the restriction of the freedom of establishment imposed by that legislation was the direct consequence of the restriction that this legislation imposed on the free movement of capital, so that it must only be examined in the light of the latter freedom.[28] The Court has considered that, for determining the applicable Treaty provision, the purpose of the legislation concerned must be taken into consideration.[29] Thus, national legislation that subjects holdings in undertakings established in other Member States to less favourable tax treatment than holdings in undertakings established in that Member State, may fall within both the provisions on freedom of establishment and on the free movement of capital,[30] unless it is clear that the legislation intends to apply only to holdings that confer a definite influence over the company's decisions and therefore falls within the scope of the provisions on freedom of establishment only.[31]

7.012

---

[24] For the parallel treatment of two freedoms, see C-439/99, *Commission v Italy*, 2002, paras 35–41; C-294/00, *Deutsche Paracelsus Schulen für Naturheilverfahren*, 2002, paras 38–52. To make the supply of services conditional upon the satisfaction of requirements which apply for establishment in a Member State is, however, a denial of the freedom to offer services in a Member State from an establishment in another Member State: para. 7-094, *infra*.

[25] For professional rules and diplomas, see paras 7-075–7-077, *infra*; for harmonization, see also paras 7-108–7-116, *infra*.

[26] e.g C-390/99, *Canal Satélite Digital*, 2002, para. 31; C-71/02, *Karner*, 2004, para. 46; C-36/02, *Omega Spielhallen*, 2004, paras 26–7; C-452/04, *Fidium Finanz*, 2006, paras 34 and 44–9, see case note by O'Brien (2007) CMLRev 1483–99.

[27] C-275/92, *Schindler*, 1994, paras 21–5. See also C-137/09, *Josemans*, 2010, para. 50; C-403/08 and C-429/08, *Football Association Premier League Ltd and Others*, 2011, paras 77–84; C-98/14 *Berlington Hungary Tanácsadó és Szolgáltató and Others*, 2015, paras 30–3.

[28] C-235/17, *Commission v Hungary*, 2019, paras 51–3 (restrictions on the usufruct of agrarian lands). See also C-197/11 and C-203/11 *Libert and Others*, 2013, paras 62–3.

[29] C-446/04, *Test Claimants in the FII Group Litigation*, 2006, para. 90; C-212/09, *Commission v Portugal*, 2011, para. 41; C-385/12, *Hervis Sport- és Divatkereskedelmi*, 2014, para. 22; C-323/18, *Tesco-Global Áruházak*, 2020, para. 52.

[30] C-212/09, *Commission v Portugal*, 2011, para. 434.

[31] C-446/04, *Test Claimants in the FII Group Litigation*, 2006, para. 91; C-196/04, *Cadbury Schweppes*, 2006, paras 31–3; C-524/04, *Test Claimants in the Thin Cap Group Litigation*, 2007, paras 26–35; C-719/18, *Vivendi*, 2020, paras 37–45. Measures (also) applying to non-controlling shareholdings are assessed under the free movement of capital (para. 7-101, *infra*).

A. Free movement of goods

7.013 **Treaty rules.** In principle, the realization of free movement of goods requires Member States to abolish all measures constituting a barrier to trade within the Union.[32] Abolition of restrictive national measures of a fiscal nature is the corollary of the establishment of a customs union, entailing prohibition of duties on imports and exports and any charges having equivalent effect in trade between Member States (Articles 28 and 30 TFEU; see paras 7-015–7-023, *infra*) and the setting-up of the Common Customs Tariff vis-à-vis third countries (Articles 31 and 32 TFEU; see para. 7-024, *infra*).[33] Non-fiscal measures, namely quantitative restrictions on imports and exports and measures having equivalent effect, are prohibited by Articles 34–36 TFEU,[34] which form the basis for a comprehensive body of case law (see paras 7-026–7-043, *infra*). For the sake of completeness, it should be noted that Article 37 TFEU requires Member States to organize any State monopolies of a commercial character so as to preclude any discrimination between Member States' nationals regarding conditions under which goods are procured and marketed.[35]

As all the Treaty provisions laying down prohibitions have direct effect since the end of the transitional period,[36] individuals may enforce the free movement of goods vis-à-vis Member States. Those prohibitions are also binding on the institutions of the Union itself,[37] although the case law allows the Union a degree of discretion in balancing free movement of goods against other legitimate policy objectives.[38] In principle, restrictive measures agreed between individuals are not caught by those prohibitions.[39] Taken in conjunction with Article 4(3) TEU, however, the prohibiting provisions require Member States to take all necessary and appropriate measures to eliminate barriers to free movement of goods the cause of which lies outside the sphere of the State.[40] The Council has specified this obligation in a

---

[32] For an exhaustive discussion of free movement of goods, see Barnard, *The Substantive Law of the EU: the Four Freedoms* (OUP, 2016), Part II; Oliver (ed.), *Oliver on Free Movement of Goods in the European Union* (5th edn, Hart Publishing, 2010); Gormley, *EU Law of Free Movement of Goods and Customs Union* (OUP, 2009); Perišin, *Free Movement of Goods and Limits of Regulatory Autonomy in the EU and WTO* (TMC Asser, 2008); Mayer, 'Die Warenverkehrsfreiheit im Europarecht— Eine Rekonstruktion' (2003) EuR 793–824. See also Commission Notice Guide on Articles 34-36 of the Treaty on the Functioning of the European Union (TFEU), OJ 2021 C100/38.

[33] The Treaty of Amsterdam deleted from the chapter entitled 'The Customs Union' the rules on the progressive abolition of customs duties between the Member States (the former Articles 13 to 17 EC) and on the establishment of the common customs tariff (the former Articles 18 to 27).

[34] The Treaty of Amsterdam amended the title of the chapter 'Elimination of quantitative restrictions between Member States' to 'Prohibition of quantitative restrictions between Member States' and repealed the transitional provisions (the former Articles 31 to 33 and 35 EC).

[35] 59/75, *Manghera*, 1976; C-347/88, *Commission v Greece*, 1990; C-387/93, *Banchero*, 1995; C-189/95, *Franzén*, 1997, paras 30–66; C-438/02, *Hanner*, 2005, paras 32–49; C-170/04, *Rosengren*, 2007, paras 17–26. In the event of an infringement of Article 37 TFEU, it is no longer possible to rely on the exception provided for in Article 36 TFEU; see C-157/94, *Commission v Netherlands*, 1997, para. 24.

[36] See the discussion of the Treaty articles in paras 7-015, 7-016, and 7-026, *infra*.

[37] 80 and 81/77, *Commissionaires Réunis*, 1978, para. 35; C-108/01, *Consorzio del Prosciutto di Parma and Others*, 2003, paras 53–9.

[38] e.g. 37/83 *Rewe-Zentrale*, 1984, para. 20; C-51/93, *Meyhui*, 1994, para. 21; C-233/94 *Germany v European Parliament and Council*, 1997, para. 43. See Mortelmans, 'The Relationship Between the Treaty Rules and Community Measures for the Establishment and Functioning of the Internal Market—Towards a Concordance Rule' (2002) CMLRev 1303–46.

[39] C-159/00, *Sapod Audic*, 2002, para. 74. For the addressees of the prohibitions (and the question whether they may be individuals), see Mortelmans, 'Excepties bij non-tarifaire intracommunautaire belemmeringen: assimilatie in het nieuwe EG-Verdrag?' (1997) SEW 182, 185–6.

[40] C-265/95, *Commission v France*, 1997, paras 30-2 (concerning acts taken by individuals against products from other Member States); C-112/00, *Schmidberger*, 2003, paras 57–64 (individuals blocking traffic on the

regulation, under which the Commission is responsible for monitoring compliance.[41] The prohibitions stemming from the free movement of goods also apply to the activities of private organizations relating to standardization and certification in so far as a Member State considers goods certified by that organization to be in conformity with national law and restricts the trade in products that have not been certified by that organization.[42]

Goods concerned. Free movement of goods applies both to 'products originating in Member States' and to 'products coming from third countries which are in free circulation in Member States' (Article 28(2) TFEU; see also Article 29 TFEU).[43] The Court of Justice has defined 'goods' as 'products which can be valued in money and which are capable, as such, of forming the subject of commercial transactions'.[44] As a result, the rules on free movement of goods are applicable, for example, to articles of artistic, historic, archaeological, or ethnographic value[45] and also to non-recyclable waste.[46]

7.014

1. The customs union

Customs union. The abolition of customs duties between Member States goes against the most-favoured nation clause enshrined in Article I of the General Agreement on Tariffs and Trade (GATT), which puts contracting parties under an obligation to accord any preferential treatment of any product originating in or destined for any other country to the like product originating in or destined for the territories of all other GATT countries. All Member States are contracting parties to GATT and the World Trade Organization (WTO), which replaced the GATT in 1995 and took over the basic rules of the original General Agreement.[47] GATT accepts, however, as an exception to the most-favoured nation clause, the establishment of a customs union, which is defined as an area within which customs duties and other restrictive regulations of commerce are eliminated with respect to substantially all the trade between the constituent territories of the Member States and in which substantially the same duties and other regulations of commerce are applied vis-à-vis third countries (Article XXIV GATT). GATT does impose conditions to the effect that the transitional period for achieving such a customs union must follow a schedule for the formation of the customs union within a reasonable length of time and that the customs union taken

7.015

Brenner motorway). See also Ronkes Agerbeek (2004) ELRev 255–66; Jaeckel, 'The Duty to Protect Fundamental Rights in the European Community' (2003) ELRev 508–27.

[41] Council Regulation (EC) No. 2679/98 of 7 December 1998 on the functioning of the internal market in relation to the free movement of goods among the Member States, OJ 1998 L337/8. See Gimeno Verdejo, 'La réponse communautaire aux blocages des réseaux de transport: application et perspectives d'avenir du règlement n° 2679/98 en vue de la protection du marché intérieur' (2002) CDE 45–93; Mattera, 'Un instrument d'intervention rapide pour sauvegarder l'unicité du Marché intérieur: le règlement 2679/98. De nouveaux pouvoirs pour la "Commission Prodi"' (1999) RMUE 9–33.

[42] C-171/11, *Fra.bo*, 2012, paras 21–32.

[43] 41/76, *Donckerwolcke*, 1976, paras 15–21; 125/88, *Nijman*, 1989, para. 11.

[44] 7/68, *Commission v Italy*, 1968, 428.

[45] Ibid. See Mattera, 'La libre circulation des oeuvres d'art à l'intérieur de la Communauté et la protection des trésors nationaux ayant une valeur artistique, historique ou archéologique' (1993) 2 RMUE 9–31.

[46] C-2/90, *Commission v Belgium*, 1992, paras 23–8, with case note by De Sadeleer (1993) CDE 672-698; see also De Sadeleer, 'La circulation des déchets et le Marché unique européen' (1994) RMUE 71–116.

[47] For the General Agreement on Tariffs and Trade and the World Trade Organization, see para. 10-010 *et seq, infra*.

as a whole must not introduce higher duties for third countries.[48] The EC Treaty set out a timetable for the stage-by-stage introduction of a customs union. Whenever Member States have acceded to the Union, a new transitional period has been laid down for the abolition of customs duties and charges having equivalent effect between Member States. The culmination of the customs union envisaged by the Treaties is the establishment and uniform application of a common customs tariff vis-à-vis third countries[49].

a. Prohibition of customs duties and charges having equivalent effect

7.016 **Customs duties.** In trade in goods between Member States, customs duties on imports and exports and charges having equivalent effect are prohibited. This prohibition also applies to customs duties of a fiscal nature (Article 30 TFEU).[50] It means that charges collected by a Member State where goods cross its border are prohibited. This embraces not only import and export duties, but also transit charges.[51] By Council decision of 26 July 1966 customs duties were completely abolished as from 1 July 1968.[52] The prohibition has had direct effect ever since the end of the transitional period.[53]

7.017 **Charges having equivalent effect.** Articles 28 and 30 TFEU couple the ban on customs duties on imports and exports with a prohibition of charges having equivalent effect. The Court of Justice interprets that expression very broadly:

> any pecuniary charge, however small and whatever its designation and mode of application, which is imposed unilaterally on domestic and foreign goods by reason of the fact that they cross a frontier, and which is not a customs duty in the strict sense, constitutes a charge having equivalent effect ... even if it is not imposed for the benefit of the State, is not discriminatory or protective in effect or if the product on which the charge is imposed is not in competition with any domestic product.[54]

Charges collected on crossing 'regional' borders within a Member State, such as taxes levied in a municipality of a Member State on goods which are transported across the territorial boundaries of that municipality[55] or contributions imposed by the authorities of an overseas territory on exports of goods,[56] are likewise prohibited, even where they are levied on

---

[48] For the significance of Article XXIV of GATT for the customs union within the Union and free trade agreements with third countries, see Cremona, 'Rhetoric and Reticence: EU External Commercial Policy in a Multilateral Context' (2001) CMLRev 359–96.

[49] See also Article 206 TFEU, which stresses the positive contribution of the customs union to world trade. See Witte, *Zollkodex der Union* (Beck, 2018); Starink, 'Veertig jaar EU-douane-unie' (1998) SEW 241–52.

[50] The Amsterdam Treaty repealed the obligation to abolish existing duties (the former Articles 13 and 16 EC) and replaced the ban on the introduction of new duties or the increase of existing duties (stand-still provision) set out in the former Article 12 EC by a straightforward prohibition of customs duties and charges having equivalent effect. For import duties, charges having equivalent effect and permitted charges, see Schön, 'Der freie Warenverkehr, die Steuerhoheit der Mitgliedstaaten und der Systemgedanke im europäischen Steuerrecht' (2001) EuR 216–33 and 341–62.

[51] 266/81, *SIOT*, 1983, paras 16–19.

[52] Council Decision 66/532/EEC of 26 July 1966 abolishing customs duties and prohibiting quantitative restrictions as between Member States and applying the duties of the common customs tariff to products not mentioned in Annex II to the Treaty, JO 2971/66.

[53] 26/62, *Van Gend & Loos*, 1963, at 13. The obligation to abolish existing charges having equivalent effect under the former Article 13(2) EC (33/70, *SACE*, 1970, paras 9–10) and the former Article 16 EC (18/71, *Eunomia*, 1971, paras 6–7) have also been held to have direct effect.

[54] 2 and 3/69, *Sociaal Fonds Diamantarbeiders*, 1969, para. 15/18, 222; see also C-39/17, *Lubrizol France SAS*, 2018, para. 24.

[55] C-72/03, *Carbonati Apuani*, 2004, paras 21–9. See also, C-173/05, *Commission v Italy*, 2007, paras 35–44.

[56] C-293/02, *Jersey Produce Marketing Organisation*, 2005, paras 61–7.

goods coming from or destined for another region of the same Member State.[57] The prohibition of charges having an effect equivalent to customs duties also applies to charges levied by Member States on goods in transit through their territory, including those imported directly from third countries.[58]

The Court has held the following to be contrary to the Treaties: a charge imposed to cover the cost of compiling statistics on movements of goods across frontiers;[59] pecuniary charges imposed on grounds of sanitary inspection of goods when they cross the frontier[60] and charges imposed for compulsory quality controls on exports;[61] pecuniary charges on the importation of excess manure within a region of a Member State[62] and pecuniary charges imposed on electricity exported to another Member State or to a third country solely in cases where the electricity was generated within the national territory.[63] A Member State may not charge traders taking part in intra-Union trade the cost of inspections and administrative formalities carried out by customs offices.[64] Even if such a charge is imposed, not by virtue of a unilateral measure adopted by the authorities, but as a result of a series of private contracts, it will be caught by the prohibition laid down in Articles 28 and 30 TFEU.[65]

b. *Permissible charges*

Three types. The broad interpretation of 'charges having equivalent effect' reduces the number of permissible pecuniary charges on intra-Union trade in goods to such an extent that only three types of charges satisfy the Union-law test.

7.018

(1) Consideration for service rendered. In the first place, Member States may charge for a service provided to the importer or exporter by the authorities ('consideration'). The Court of Justice has limited this possibility by imposing strict conditions. The consideration may not exceed either the value or the cost of the service actually rendered to the importer or exporter and may be charged only in 'special cases'. Administrative activity intended to maintain a system imposed in the general interest (e.g. a phytosanitary or plant-health examination) cannot be regarded as a service rendered to the importer or exporter such as to justify the imposition of a pecuniary charge.[66]

7.019

(2) Charges forming part of Union regulation. Charges imposed for the purposes of implementing a Union regulatory regime constitute a second exception to the extensive prohibition of charges having equivalent effect. For instance, the Court of Justice has held that certain charges imposed in connection with the common agricultural policy[67] and fees

7.020

---

[57] C-163/90, *Legros and Others*, 1992, paras 10–18; C-363/93, C-407/93, C-408/93, C-409/93, C-410/93, and C-411/93, *Lancry and Others*, 1994, paras 25–32 (charge levied on imports); C-485/93 and C-486/93, *Simitzi*, 1995, paras 10–22 (charges levied on imports and exports). See Slotboom, 'L'application du Traité CE au commerce intraétatique? Le cas de l'octroi de mer' (1996) CDE 9–29; Graser, 'Eine Wende im Bereich der Inländerdiskriminierung? Zur Entscheidung des EuGH in der Rechtssache *Lancry*' (1998) EuR 571–9.
[58] C-173/05, *Commission v Italy*, 2007, paras 27–33.
[59] 24/68, *Commission v Italy*, 1969, paras 14–17.
[60] 29/72, *Marimex*, 1972, para. 8; 87/75, *Bresciani*, 1976, paras 4–9.
[61] 63/74, *Cadsky*, 1975, paras 2–8.
[62] C-254/13, *Orgacom*, 2014, paras 21–6.
[63] C-305/17, *FENS*, 2018, paras 29–51.
[64] 340/87, *Commission v Italy*, 1989, para. 17.
[65] C-16/94, *Dubois and Général Cargo Services*, 1995, paras 13–21.
[66] 39/73, *Rewe-Zentralfinanz*, 1973, para. 4.
[67] 106/81, *Kind v EEC*, 1982, para. 21.

charged for inspections required by a Union directive[68] do not constitute charges having an effect equivalent to import or export duties.

7.021 **(3) Internal taxation.** Third, a charge may not be characterized as a charge having equivalent effect if it forms part of a general system of internal taxation applying systematically to categories of products according to objective criteria applied without regard to the origin of the products. In that case the charge will not fall within the scope of Articles 28 and 30 TFEU, but come within the scope of Article 110 TFEU and will, therefore, have to comply with the requirements set by that provision.[69] The prohibition of discrimination applies to internal taxation 'of any kind' (e.g. excise duty, VAT, registration charges, and road fund taxes).[70] As far as internal taxation is concerned, Article 110 TFEU requires Member States not to impose directly or indirectly on products from other Member States any taxation in excess of that imposed on similar domestic products or impose internal taxation of such a nature as to afford protection to other domestic products. The criterion for testing whether a tax is caught by Article 110 TFEU is therefore the discrimination or protection resulting therefrom.[71] The prohibition of discrimination also covers discrimination between national products which are processed and marketed on the domestic market and national products which are exported in an unprocessed state to other Member States.[72] Article 110 TFEU has direct effect.[73]

7.022 **Identification of discrimination.** The application of Article 110 TFEU requires a demarcation of the market for the national products with which the products imported (or to be exported) compete. It must therefore be considered which domestic products are similar or substitutable for the relevant imported products.[74] Then, it needs to be examined to what extent the taxation imposed on the products imported (or to be exported) discriminates against imported products or protects domestic products. The comparison ranges over all aspects of the imposition of the tax (determination of the basis of assessment, determination of rates, methods of collection of amounts due) and extends beyond a formal inquiry to determine whether the taxation measure disadvantages products in practice.[75]

---

[68] 46/76, *Bauhuis*, 1977, para. 31.

[69] C-393/04 and C-41/05, *Air Liquide Industries and Others*, 2006, paras 51 and 56; C-206/06, *Essent Netwerk Noord*, 2008, para. 41; C-221/06, *Stadtgemeinde Frohnleiten and Gemeindebetriebe Frohnleiten*, 2007, paras 30–73; C-198/14, *Visnapuu*, 2015, paras 49–55; C-39/17, *Lubrizol France SAS*, 2018, paras 24–6. See Schön, 'Der freie Warenverkehr, die Steuerhoheit der Mitgliedstaaten und der Systemgedanke im europäischen Steuerrecht' (2001) EuR 341–62. One and the same charge cannot be caught both by the provisions on charges having equivalent effect and by the prohibition of discriminatory internal taxation laid down in Article 110 TFEU: 94/74, *IGAV*, 1975, paras 12–13.

[70] C-402/14, *Viamar*, 2015, paras 33–5.

[71] C-149/91 and C-150/91, *Sanders Adour and Guyomarc'h Orthez Nutrition animale*, 1992, para. 19. Article 110 TFEU does not preclude 'reverse discrimination' arising where a Member State imposes internal taxation on its domestic products which is higher than that imposed on similar products imported from other Member States: 86/78, *Peureux*, 1979, para. 32.

[72] C-234/99, *Nygård*, 2002, para. 20.

[73] For the first para. of Article 110 TFEU, see 57/65, *Lütticke*, 1966, 211; for the second para. of Article 110, see 27/67, *Fink Frucht*, 1968, 232.

[74] See 170/78, *Commission v United Kingdom*, 1980, paras 12–24, and 1983, paras 7–28; 356/85, *Commission v Belgium*, 1987, paras 9–21; C-167/05, *Commission v Sweden*, 2008, paras 42–61 (consideration whether higher taxation on wine promoted the domestic consumption of beer). In the absence of similar or substitutable domestic products, the taxation is not in breach of Article 110 TFEU: 158/82, *Commission v Denmark*, 1983, para. 22; C-383/01, *De Danske Bilimportører*, 2003, paras 38–42.

[75] 112/84, *Humblot*, 1985, para. 15; cf. C-113/94, *Casarin*, 1995, paras 17–26 (new French system of progressive taxation on motor vehicles held to be compatible with Article 110 TFEU); C-421/97, *Tarantik*, 1999, paras 20–32; C-265/99, *Commission v France*, 2001, paras 40–51. See also C-345/93, *Fazenda Pública*, 1995, paras 12–20; C-393/98 *Gomes Valente*, 2001, paras 20–44.

Burden offset or justified. For the purposes of the legal categorization of a tax which is imposed in accordance with the same criteria on domestic products and on products imported (or to be exported), it is necessary to take account of the destination of the proceeds of the taxation. Taxation is incompatible with Article 110 TFEU and therefore prohibited where it discriminates against the product imported (or to be exported). This may be the case where the revenue from such taxation is intended to finance activities from which domestic products primarily benefit as a result of which the fiscal burden on domestic products is neutralized by the advantages that the charge is used to finance whilst the charge on the products imported (or to be exported) constitutes a net burden.[76] If the proceeds of the charge fully offset the burden borne by the domestic products, the burden is in fact borne exclusively by products imported (or to be exported) and the charge must be regarded as a charge having equivalent effect prohibited by the Treaties.[77] Within these limits, a Member State may differentiate a charge on the basis of objective criteria, such as the nature of the raw materials used or the production processes employed, provided that the differentiation pursues policy objectives that are compatible with Union law (e.g. environment protection[78]).

7.023

c. *The Common Customs Tariff*

Customs tariffs. Further to the abolition of customs duties in intra-Union trade in goods, the Council adopted Regulation No. 950/68 on the basis of Articles 28 and 111 EEC, which introduced a Common Customs Tariff for goods from third countries as from 1 July 1968.[79] Article 31 TFEU provides that the Council is to fix Common Customs Tariff duties. In the meantime, major changes have been made in the customs tariff, *inter alia*, as a result of bilateral agreements with third countries and the ratification of agreements reducing tariffs which have arisen in the multilateral trade negotiations under the auspices of the GATT. The legal basis for these 'conventional' alterations to the Common Customs Tariff is to be found in the provisions concerning the common commercial policy (Article 207 TFEU). In pursuance of the Council regulations, the Commission has to draw up the customs tariff in force on the basis of a detailed nomenclature. The Commission has to adopt each year, by means of a regulation, the complete version of the nomenclature, together with the autonomous and conventional rates of duty in force.[80] The Union has exclusive competence with regard to the establishment of the customs union (Article 3(1)(a) TFEU).

7.024

Customs legislation. In order to secure uniform application of the common tariffs, it was necessary to harmonize the Member States' differing customs legislation. The Council has adopted directives and regulations pursuant to other Treaty provisions relating to such matters as determining the origin of goods, customs value, the various customs arrangements (bringing into free circulation, warehousing, inward and outward processing, temporary

7.025

---

[76] 73/79, *Commission v Italy*, 1980, paras 15–16 (discrimination against imported products); C-234/99, *Nygård*, 2002, paras 21–2 (discrimination against products to be exported).

[77] C-78/90-C-83/90, *Compagnie commerciale de l'Ouest and Others*, 1992, para. 27; see also C-254/13, *Orgacom*, 2014, paras 21–33.

[78] C-213/96, *Outokumpu*, 1998, paras 30–41. For the relationship between a discriminatory tax system and State aid incompatible with the common market, see C-234/99, *Nygård*, 2002, paras 50–65.

[79] Regulation No. 950/68 (EEC) of the Council of 28 June 1968 on the Common Customs Tariff, OJ 1968 English Special Edition (I) 275; replaced by Council Regulation (EEC) No. 2658/87 of 23 July 1987 on the tariff and statistical nomenclature and on the Common Customs Tariff, OJ 1987 L256.

[80] Article 12 of Regulation No. 2658/87 (see preceding n.).

import/export, etc.), exemption from customs duties, and payment of customs debt.[81] Custom authorities of the Member States used to cooperate on the basis of intergovernmental agreements and in the context of the police and judicial cooperation in criminal matters (Title VI of the EU Treaty). Since the Lisbon Treaty, the European Parliament and the Council are to take measures in accordance with the ordinary legislative procedure in order to strengthen customs cooperation between the Member States and between the latter and the Commission (Article 33 TFEU).

2. Prohibition of non-tariff restrictions

7.026 **Non-tariff barriers.** The GATT includes non-tariff barriers among the trade restrictions to be abolished in a customs union. In addition to the chapter on the customs union, Title II of Part Three of the Treaty on the Functioning of the European Union includes a chapter on prohibition of quantitative restrictions between Member States. Thus, Article 34 TFEU prohibits 'quantitative restrictions on imports and all measures having equivalent effect' and Article 35 TFEU 'quantitative restrictions on exports and all measures having equivalent effect'. Article 36 TFEU, however, permits such restrictions and measures where they are justified on grounds of public morality, public policy, or public security; the protection of health and life of humans, animals, or plants; the protection of national treasures possessing artistic, historic, or archaeological value; or the protection of industrial and commercial property, provided that they do not constitute a means of arbitrary discrimination or a disguised restriction on trade between Member States.

The provisions prohibiting quantitative restrictions and measures having equivalent effect have direct effect.[82] Article 34 TFEU does not solely prohibit measures emanating from the State which, in themselves, create restrictions on trade between Member States, it may also apply where a Member State abstains from adopting the measures required in order to eliminate or prevent obstacles to the free movement of goods which are created by actions taken by individuals on its territory aimed at products originating in other Member States.[83] In such a case, it has to be considered whether the Member State concerned can rely on the grounds that may be pleaded in justification of trade restrictions under Union law.[84]

The need to invoke these prohibitory provisions diminishes in practice where the national measures which might otherwise hinder trade in goods have been harmonized at Union level and made subject to a system of mutual recognition (see paras 7-108–7-116, *infra*).

---

[81] With effect from 1 January 1994, most of these rules have been replaced by Regulation (EEC) No. 2913/92 of 12 October 1992 establishing the Community Customs Code (OJ 1992 L302/1), which the Council adopted on the basis of Articles 28, 100a, and 113 EC [*now Articles 31, 114, and 207 TFEU*]. See also Lasok, *The Trade and Customs Law of the European Union* (The Hague, Kluwer Law International, 1998). The latest version of the Uniform Customs Code is laid down in Regulation (EU) No. 952/2013 of the European Parliament and of the Council of 9 October 2013 laying down the Union Customs Code (OJ 2013 L269/1).

[82] For Article 34 TFEU, see 74/76 *Iannelli*, 1977, para. 13; for Article 35 TFEU, see 83/78, *Pigs Marketing Board*, 1978, para. 66.

[83] C-265/95 *Commission v France*, 1997, paras 30–2 (which refers to Member States' obligation under the principle of sincere cooperation, now set out in Article 4(3) TFEU), see para. 5-046, *supra*).

[84] Ibid., paras 33–66 (consideration of possible justificatory grounds and of the proportionality of the national measures which were in fact taken).

a. Prohibition of quantitative restrictions and measures having equivalent effect

Quantitative restrictions. The Court of Justice has defined 'quantitative restrictions' as 'measures which amount to a total or partial restraint of, according to the circumstances, imports, exports or goods in transit'.[85] These are measures which introduce a limitation depending upon the quantity or the value of the goods concerned. Since most trade 'quotas' had already been abolished before the EEC Treaty entered into effect under the auspices of the OECD,[86] the prohibition of quantitative restrictions raises only a few problems per se.

7.027

Measures having equivalent effect. However, alongside quantitative restrictions, all measures having equivalent effect are also prohibited. This ancillary prohibition came to have great significance owing to its broad scope. The original interpretation given to that prohibition by the Commission[87] opened the way to a broad interpretation by the Court of Justice.

7.028

Indeed, in the 1974 judgment in *Dassonville*, the Court of Justice held that '[a]ll trading rules enacted by Member States which are capable of hindering, directly or indirectly, actually or potentially, intra-Community trade are to be considered as measures having an effect equivalent to quantitative restrictions'.[88] In that case, the Court categorized, as a measure having equivalent effect, a Belgian provision prohibiting the import of Scotch whisky without a certificate of origin. Importers, such as Dassonville, which obtained the product from another Member State where it was in free circulation, found it less easy to get hold of that certificate than importers who obtained it directly from the country of origin. Thus, the Court of Justice interpreted the concept of measures having equivalent effect in the broadest possible manner. The test was no longer, as the Commission had suggested, the distinction made by the relevant national provision between domestic and imported products, but simply whether the measure directly or indirectly, actually or potentially, hindered the free movement of goods. Accordingly, a measure, even if it has neither the object nor the effect of treating goods coming from other Member States less favourably, falls within the scope of the concept of a 'measure having equivalent effect to quantitative restrictions', within the meaning of Article 34 TFEU, if it hinders access to the market of a Member State of products originating in another Member State.[89] Hence, once any link can be made between a national measure and the import of goods, the application of Article 34 TFEU is not precluded on the sole ground that all the facts of the specific case are confined to a single Member State.[90] Nevertheless, it must be observed that in some cases the Court has held

---

[85] 2/73, *Geddo*, 1973, para. 7.
[86] On 14 January 1955 the Council of Ministers of the Organisation for European Economic Cooperation (now OECD, see para 1-004, *supra*) adopted, pursuant to Article 4 of the OEEC Treaty, a Code with a list of products for which liberalization was required to be achieved.
[87] Commission Directive 70/50/EEC of 22 December 1969 on the abolition of measures which have an effect equivalent to quantitative restrictions on imports and are not covered by other provisions adopted in pursuance of the EEC Treaty, OJ 1970 English Special Edition (I) 17.
[88] 8/74, *Dassonville*, 1974, para. 5. This has been the test ever since; see, e.g., C-385/10, *Elenca*, 2012, para. 22; C-354/14, *Capoda Import-Export*, 2015, para. 39; C-169/17, *Asociación Nacional de Productores de Ganado Porcino*, 2018, para. 21.
[89] See, e.g., C-591/17, *Austria v Germany*, 2019, para. 121.
[90] C-321-C-324/94, *Pistre and Others*, 1997, paras 44–5; C-448/98, *Guimont*, 2000, paras 21–4. Only the application of the measure to imported products is prohibited: *Guimont*, paras 15–21. See De Beys, 'Le droit européen est-il applicable aux situations purement internes? A propos des discriminations à rebours dans le marché unique' (2001) JTDE 137–44; Papadopoulou, 'Situations purement internes et droit communautaire: un instrument jurisprudentiel à double fonction ou une arme à double tranchant?' (2002) CDE 95–129.

that the restrictions on trade in goods were too 'uncertain and indirect' to hinder trade between Member States.[91]

7.029 **The implications of *Dassonville*.** The definition of 'measures having equivalent effect' takes in a complete range of legislative and administrative measures which are applicable without distinction to domestic and imported products, yet have a—sometimes minimal—effect on potential sales of imported products and hence on the free movement of goods. The Court of Justice thus held that an unlawful measure having an effect equivalent to a quantitative restriction was involved in the case of a Belgian provision which, in order to avoid confusing butter and margarine, provided that margarine could be marketed only in cubic form. Although the provision drew no distinction between domestic and imported products, it was nevertheless of such a nature as to render the marketing of imported products 'more difficult or more expensive either by barring them from certain channels of distribution or owing to the additional costs brought about by the necessity to package the products in question in special packs which comply with the requirements in force on the market of their destination'.[92]

In principle, the same touchstone is used to assess national provisions governing, for example, import and export formalities; requirements to be fulfilled by products (such as requirements relating to the name, form, dimensions, weight, composition, presentation, labelling, or packaging);[93] price rules;[94] methods of sale and advertising;[95] conditions for public tenders or intellectual property rights. According to the Court, measures adopted by a Member State are to be regarded as measures having equivalent effect to quantitative restrictions where their object or effect is to treat products originating in other Member States less favourably or where they (otherwise) hinder the access of such products to the market of that Member State.[96] The Court also clarified that the latter is not normally the case for selling arrangements that apply to all traders operating within the national territory and that affect in the same manner, in law and in fact, the marketing of domestic products and of products originating from other Member States.[97] In contrast, requirements to be fulfilled by products lawfully manufactured and marketed in another Member State constitute measures of equivalent effect to quantitative restrictions even if those requirements apply to all products alike.[98] Indeed, such requirements typically hinder the access to the market of the Member State concerned.

A national provision constitutes a measure having equivalent effect to a quantitative restriction where it discriminates against imported products or, at least, hinders the access

---

[91] C-69/88, *Krantz*, 1990, para. 11; C-93/92, *CMC Motorradcenter*, 1993, para. 12; C-379/92, *Peralta*, 1994, para. 24; see to the same effect, 155/80, *Oebel*, 1981, paras 11–21; 75/81, *Blesgen*, 1982, para. 9; 145/85, *Forest*, 1986, para. 19; C-23/89, *Quietlynn and Richards*, 1990, paras 10–11; C-140/94, C-141/94, and C-142/94, *DIP and Others*, 1995, para. 29; C-134/94, *Esso Española*, 1995, para. 24; C-169/17, *Asociación Nacional de Productores de Ganado Porcino*, 2018, paras 21–8.
[92] 261/81, *Rau*, 1982, para. 13.
[93] See the survey in Capelli, 'La libre circulation des produits alimentaires à l'intérieur du marché commun' (1993) RMCUE 790–811.
[94] C-333/14, *Scotch Whisky Association*, 2015, para. 32.
[95] But see para. 7-043, *infra*.
[96] C-110/05, *Commission v Italy*, 2009, para. 37; C-142/05 *Mickelsson and Roos*, 2009, para. 24.
[97] C-267/91 and C-268/91, *Keck and Mithouard*, 1993, para. 17; C-110/05, *Commission v Italy*, 2009, para. 36. See para. 7-043, *infra*.
[98] C-110/05, *Commission v Italy*, 2009, paras 35 and 37; C-142/05, *Mickelsson and Roos*, 2009, para. 24.

to the market of the Member State concerned. This is the case for measures that do not affect trade in products imported or reimported through parallel channels in the same way as trade in products manufactured in the home market or imported into that market by approved distributors.[99] A prohibition on the use of a certain product, even if applicable without distinction as regards its origin, has also been held to constitute a measure having equivalent effect to quantitative restrictions.[100] The Court of Justice considered the prohibition in Italian traffic regulations on using a motorcycle and a trailer together to constitute a measure having equivalent effect to a quantitative restriction to the extent that its effect is to hinder access to the Italian market for trailers which are specially designed for motorcycles and are lawfully produced and marketed in other Member States.[101] Indeed, a prohibition on the use of a product in a Member State has a considerable influence on the behaviour of consumers, which, in its turn, affects the access of that product to the market of that Member State.[102]

Free movement of goods concerns not only traders but also consumers. It requires that consumers resident in one Member State may travel freely to the territory of another Member State to shop under the same conditions as the local population and that businesses may direct advertising to consumers from other Member States.[103]

Export restrictions. Traditionally, in contradistinction to the broad interpretation of the concept of measures having effect equivalent to quantitative restrictions on imports (Article 34 TFEU), the Court of Justice regarded as measures having equivalent effect to quantitative restrictions on exports (Article 35 TFEU) 'national measures which have as their specific object or effect the restriction of patterns of exports and thereby the establishment of a difference in treatment between the domestic trade of a Member State and its export trade in such a way as to provide a particular advantage for national production or for the domestic market of the State in question at the expense of the production or of the trade of other Member States'.[104] An example of such a restriction on exports is where a Member State requires wine protected by a designation of origin to be bottled in the region of production.[105] Measures which are applicable without distinction to domestic and export trade were thus held to fall outside the scope of Article 35 TFEU.[106]

7.030

---

[99] C-240/95, *Schmit*, 1996, paras 16–22.
[100] C-110/05, *Commission v Italy*, 2009, paras 56–7; C-142/05, *Mickelsson and Roos*, 2009, paras 26–8.
[101] C-110/05, *Commission v Italy*, 2009, para. 58.
[102] Ibid., para. 56. See also C-428/12, *Commission v Spain*, 2014, paras 29–30.
[103] C-362/88, *GB-INNO-BM*, 1990, para. 8 (consumers may not be deprived of access to advertising available in the country where purchases are made).
[104] 15/79, *Groenveld*, 1979, para. 7. Since the Treaty provisions on free movement of goods also apply to the Union institutions, Union measures may also constitute measures having equivalent effect: C-469/00, *Ravil and Others*, 2003, paras 40–4, and C-108/01, *Consorzio del Prosciutto di Parma and Others*, 2003, paras 54–9.
[105] C-388/95, *Belgium v Spain*, 2000, paras 36–42. For the justification identified by the Court of Justice in the good reputation of the wine in question, see Bianchi, 'La mise en bouteille obligatoire des vins de qualité dans la région de production' (2001) RMCUE 343–50.
[106] 155/80, *Oebel*, 1981, paras 15–16; 237/82, *Jongeneel Kaas*, 1984, paras 22–7; 15/83, *Denkavit Nederland*, 1984, paras 16–18. For further applications, see C-302/88, *Hennen Olie*, 1990, paras 17–18; C-339/89, *Alsthom Atlantique*, 1991, paras 13–16; C-332/89, *Marchandise and Others*, 1991, paras 16–17; C-47/90, *Delhaize and Le Lion*, 1992, paras 11–27; C-169/17, *Asociación Nacional de Productores de Ganado Porcino*, 2018, paras 29–31. For the distinction between this case law and that on Article 34 TFEU, see Weatherill, 'After *Keck*: Some Thoughts on How to Clarify the Clarification' (1996) CMLRev 885, 902–3; Roth, 'Wettbewerb der Mitgliedstaaten oder Wettbewerb der Hersteller?' (1995) ZHW 78–95;

In later case law, however, the Court of Justice has shown itself prepared to adopt a broad interpretation of export restrictions, similar to the *Dassonville* interpretation of import restrictions. Thus, a Belgian prohibition on requiring from a consumer a deposit or payment before the expiry of a period for withdrawal was held to be contrary to Article 35, even though it was applicable to all traders active in Belgium, since its actual impact was greater on exports than on the marketing of goods on the Belgian domestic market.[107] The same applied within Belgium to a Flemish obligation to draw up all invoices in Dutch, failing which they were null and void; such a measure mainly affected cross-border trade as it is less likely that a buyer established outside Belgium understands Dutch than it is for a Belgian buyer.[108] All the same, in this context, too, a measure will not qualify as a measure having equivalent effect to a quantitative restriction on exports where its effect on exports is too 'uncertain and indirect'.[109]

b. Exceptions

7.031 **Survey.** The *Dassonville* definition of measures having equivalent effect to a quantitative restriction brings within the prohibition set out in Article 34 TFEU a whole series of national provisions which pursue policy objectives in the general interest and thereby restrict trade. In so far as the policy in question cannot be justified on the basis of Article 36 TFEU, strict application of Article 34 TFEU would make it impossible to pursue those objectives. As a result, pending harmonization of such national provisions—which would neutralize their effect of hampering trade—the Court of Justice has accepted in the *Cassis de Dijon* case law an additional exception which allows measures to be reconciled with Article 34 TFEU where they protect legitimate interests in a reasonable manner (the rule of reason). It is for the Member State to prove that its measure that restricts trade (or its failure to prevent a restriction of trade) comes within one of the exceptions provided for in Article 36 TFEU or that it is covered by the rule of reason.[110] In addition, the Court of Justice has, by the judgment in *Keck and Mithouard*, taken all national provisions on methods of sale without discriminatory effects outside the scope of the *Dassonville* definition of measures having equivalent effect.[111]

7.032 **(1) Article 36 TFEU Grounds for justification.** The exceptions provided for in Article 36 TFEU relate to measures of a non-economic nature[112] and are strictly interpreted by the Court of Justice.[113] Only those interests listed in the Treaty article (protection of public morality; public policy; public security; health and life of humans, animals, or plants; national

---

[107] C-205/07, *Gysbrechts*, 2008, paras 42–44.
[108] C-15/15, *New Valmar*, 2016, paras 36–47.
[109] C-412/97, *ED and Fenocchio*, 1999, para. 11 (with a reference to the case law cited in n. 90, *supra*).
[110] But see the view taken in Directive 70/50 (para. 7-028, *supra*) and the *Keck and Mithouard* case law on sales methods (para. 7-043, *infra*), where the burden of proof has to be discharged by the person arguing for protection of the free movement of goods.
[111] The consideration that such provisions have only a minimal impact on intra-Union trade (para. 7-043, *infra*) also underlies the judgments cited in n. 90, *supra*.
[112] 7/61, *Commission v Italy*, 1961, 329; 238/82 *Duphar*, 1984, para. 23; 288/83 *Commission v Ireland*, 1985, para. 28. This does not mean that rules justified by objective circumstances may not also make it possible to achieve additional objectives of an economic nature sought by the Member State: 72/83 *Campus Oil*, 1984, para. 36. See also Oliver, 'When, if Ever, Can Restrictions on Free Movement be Justified on Economic Grounds?' (2016) ELRev 147–75.
[113] 13/68, *Salgoil*, 1968, 463.

treasures possessing artistic, historic, or archaeological value; and industrial and commercial property) are capable of justifying a measure restricting trade.[114]

Absence of harmonization. Article 36 TFEU does not amount to a constitutionally protected core of residual powers of the Member States. A Member State may no longer justify a measure on the basis of Article 36 TFEU where the national legislation intended to protect the specific interest concerned has been harmonized.[115] This explains, for instance, why it was not possible for a Member State to rely on Article 36 in respect of a ban on the export of calves, in view of a Union directive fully harmonizing the measures necessary for the protection of the health of calves.[116]

7.033

Proportionality. In addition, the measure may not constitute 'a means of arbitrary discrimination or a disguised restriction on trade between Member States'. This means that the measure must be proportionate to the pursued objective. The interest may not be capable of being as effectively protected by measures which do not restrict intra-Union trade too much.[117] Hence, Article 36 TFEU cannot be relied on to justify measures containing restrictions which primarily seek to lighten the administration's burden or reduce public expenditure, unless, in the absence of these measures, this burden or expenditure would clearly exceed the limits of what can reasonably be required.[118] Moreover, a restrictive measure can be considered appropriate to achieve the objective pursued only if it genuinely reflects a concern to secure the attainment of that objective in a consistent and systematic manner.[119]

7.034

A Member State is not entitled unnecessarily to subject products to tests where the Member State in which they originated has already carried out tests which satisfy the requirements of health protection and the results are available.[120] In the absence of harmonization, it is for the Member State to decide on the level of protection of human health and life they wish to ensure.[121] In the event that a Member State wishes to rely on Article 36 in order to justify a measure restricting the free movement of goods, it must be able to show that the measure is founded on a detailed assessment of the risk, based on the most recent reliable scientific data available. Where it proves to be impossible to determine with scientific certainty the

---

[114] 113/80, *Commission v Ireland*, 1981, paras 7–8; C-249/07, *Commission v Netherlands*, 2008, paras 38–40; C-148/15, *Deutsche Parkinson Verein*, 2016, paras 28–46. Article 36 TFEU can only be relied upon to justify measures restricting trade, not to justify derogations to secondary Union law (C-197/08, *Commission v France*, 2010, para. 49; C-198/08, *Commission v Austria*, 2010, para. 38; C-221/08, *Commission v Ireland*, 2010, para. 50); C-108/09, *Ker-Optika*, 2010, paras 59–76. See also Alemanno, 'Balancing Free Movement and Public Health: The Case of Minimum Unit Pricing of Alcohol in Scotch Whisky' (2016) CMLRev 1037–64.

[115] 148/78, *Ratti*, 1979, para. 36; C-445/06, *Danske Slagterier*, 2009, para. 25; C-573/12, *Ålands Vindkraft*, 2014, paras 57–63. A harmonizing directive precludes recourse to Article 36 even if the directive itself does not lay down any Union procedure for monitoring compliance or any penalties: C-5/94, *Hedley Lomas*, 1996, paras 18–20, with case note by Van Calster (1996/97) Col JEL 132–45. Where harmonization of national legislation has been carried out pursuant to Article 114 TFEU, account must be taken of Article 114(4) to (7); para. 7-115, *infra*.

[116] C-1/96, *Compassion in World Farming*, 1998, paras 47–64; see Van Calster, 'Export Restrictions—A Watershed for Article 30' (2000) ELRev 335–52.

[117] 104/75, *De Peijper*, 1976, para. 17. For a very flexible application, see C-320/93, *Ortscheit*, 1994, paras 17–20.

[118] C-387/18, *Delfarma*, 2019, para. 30.

[119] C-333/14, *Scotch Whisky Association*, 2015, para. 37.

[120] 272/80, *Frans-Nederlandse Maatschappij voor Biologische Produkten*, 1981, paras 14–15; 25/88, *Wurmser and Others*, 1989, para. 18: 'That rule is a particular application of a more general principle of mutual trust between the authorities of the Member States'. See also C-373/92, *Commission v Belgium*, 1993, paras 8–10; C-293/94, *Brandsma*, 1996, paras 10–13; C-432/03, *Commission v Portugal*, 2005, para. 46.

[121] E.g. C-95/01, *Greenham and Abel*, 2004, para. 37; C-333/08 *Commission v France*, 2010, para. 85; C-333/14, *Scotch Whisky Association*, 2015, para. 52.

existence or extent of the alleged risk to public health, a Member State may take protective measures on the basis of the precautionary principle without having to await full proof that the risk actually exists and is a major one.[122]

7.035 **Discrimination.** In the absence of harmonization and if the national measure does not exceed what is necessary to attain one of the objectives listed in Article 36 TFEU, that article will justify the measure, even if it embodies formal discrimination or has a discriminatory effect.

7.036 **Intellectual property.** The exception provided for in Article 36 TFEU for 'protection of industrial and commercial property' (such as patents, designs, copyrights, and trademarks) has obliged the Court of Justice to strike a balance between the principle of free movement of goods and protection of the rights in question. The Treaties do not affect the existence of exclusive rights recognized under national legislation with regard to industrial and commercial property (see Article 345 TFEU), but do set limitations on the exercise of such rights. Article 36 only admits derogations from free movement of goods to the extent to which they are justified for the purpose of safeguarding rights which constitute the 'specific subject-matter' of such property.[123]

The 'exhaustion' doctrine expounded by the Court of Justice states that the owner of the right cannot rely on his exclusive right in order to prevent the importation and marketing of a product which has been marketed in another Member State by himself, with his consent, or by a person economically or legally dependent on him.[124] Where a patentee is legally bound under national law or Union law to market his or her products in a Member State, he or she cannot be deemed to have given their consent to the marketing of the products concerned. They are therefore entitled to oppose importation and marketing of those products by a third party in the State where they are protected.[125] Putting a product on the market outside the European Economic Area does not entail exhaustion of the right to contest importation without consent.[126]

7.037 **(2) The rule of reason *Cassis de Dijon*.** In the leading *Cassis de Dijon* judgment of 20 February 1979, the Court of Justice opened the door to certain 'reasonable' national

---

[122] C-95/01, *Greenham and Abel*, 2004, paras 39–50; C-333/08, *Commission v France*, 2010, paras 86–93; C-333/14, *Scotch Whisky Association*, 2015, paras 53–9; C-663/18, *BS and CA*, 2020, paras 85–95. For the precautionary principle, see para. 25-023.

[123] For rights related to copyrights, see 78/70, *Deutsche Grammophon*, 1971, paras 11–13; for trademarks, 192/73 *Van Zuylen*, 1974, paras 7–10, reconsidered in C-10/89, *Hag GF*, 1990, paras 10–20; C-9/93, *IHT Internationale Heiztechnik and Danzinger*, 1994, paras 40–6; 16/74, *Centrafarm*, 1974, paras 7–8; C-317/93, *Deutsche Renault*, 1993, paras 30–9; for patents, 15/74 *Centrafarm*, 1974, paras 8–9. For copyrights, see 55 and 57/80, *Musik-Vertrieb membrane*, 1981, paras 11–13 (as regards free movement of services, see previously 62/79, *Coditel*, 1980, paras 12–14); for designations and indications of origin, see *Commission v Germany*, 19757, paras 7–18; C-3/91, *Exportur*, 1992, paras 23–38; C-388/95, *Belgium v Spain*, 2000, paras 47–75; for designs, see 53/87, *CICRA and Maxicar*, 1988, para. 11, and 238/87, *Volvo*, 1988, para. 8.

[124] In addition to the judgments cited in the preceding n., see as regards patents: 187/80, *Merck*, 1981, paras 9–14; as regards trademarks: 119/75, *Terrapin*, 1976, paras 5–8 (also the right to a trade name); 102/77, *Hoffmann-La Roche*, 1978, paras 6–14; 3/78, *Centrafarm*, 1978, paras 7–22; C-427/93, C-429/93, and C-436/93, *Bristol-Myers Squibb and Others*, 1996; C-71/94, C-72/94, and C-73/94 *Eurim-Pharm*, 1996; C-232/94, *MPA Pharma*, 1996; as regards copyrights: 158/86 *Warner Brothers and Others*, 1988, paras 1–19; with regard to designs, see 144/81, *Keurkoop*, 1982, paras 22–29.

[125] 19/84, *Pharmon*, 1985, paras 22–7 (compulsory licence); C-267/95 and C-268/95, *Merck and Beecham*, 1996, paras 26–54.

[126] C-355/96, *Silhouette International Schmied*, 1998, para. 26; C-173/98, *Sebago and Maison Dubois*, 1999, para. 21; C-414/99-C-416/99, *Zino Davidoff and Others*, 2001, paras 30–67; C-479/04 *Laserdisken*, 2006, paras 17–27.

measures in restraint of trade being regarded as compatible with Article 34 TFEU on grounds other than those listed in Article 36 TFEU. The Court had been called upon to rule on a provision of German law requiring various alcoholic beverages to have a minimum alcoholic strength. The requirement for fruit liqueurs to have a minimum of 25 per cent alcohol content prevented *Cassis de Dijon*, which contained only 15 to 20 per cent alcohol and was freely marketed in France, from being imported into Germany. The Court accepted that, in the absence of common rules, it was for Member States to 'regulate all matters relating to the production and marketing of alcohol and alcoholic beverages on their own territory'. The Court went on to state that '[o]bstacles to movement within the Community resulting from disparities between the national laws relating to the marketing of the products in question must be accepted in so far as those provisions may be recognized as being necessary in order to satisfy mandatory requirements relating in particular to the effectiveness of fiscal supervision, the protection of public health, the fairness of commercial transactions, and the defence of the consumer'.[127]

Four conditions. In cases concerning the application of Article 34 TFEU, the Court of Justice requires the given national measure invariably to satisfy four requirements. 7.038

(1) Absence of harmonization. First, a Member State is allowed to apply a measure restricting trade only in so far as there is no legislation at Union level. In fact, the rule of reason constitutes an exception to the prohibition of measures having equivalent effect pending the adoption of Union legislation. Once national legislation has been harmonized, a Member State may, in principle, no longer deviate from the Union rule.[128] 7.039

(2) Mandatory requirements. Next, the measure adopted by the Member State must be justified by a 'mandatory requirement' (*exigence impérative*) recognized or to be recognized by the Court of Justice, such as protection of consumers,[129] fairness of commercial transactions,[130] effectiveness of fiscal supervision,[131] combating fraud,[132] completion of the internal market by establishing statistics on the trading of goods between Member States,[133] protection of public health,[134] protection of the environment[135] including the reduction of greenhouse gas emissions,[136] road 7.040

---

[127] 120/78, *Rewe*, 1979, para. 8. Later the Court of Justice was to refer to that case as follows (in 302/86, *Commission v Denmark*, 1988, para. 6): '[I]n the absence of common rules relating to the marketing of the products in question, obstacles to free movement within the Community resulting from disparities between the national laws must be accepted in so far as such rules, applicable to domestic and imported products without distinction, may be recognised as being necessary in order to satisfy mandatory requirements recognized by Community law. Such rules must also be proportionate to the aim in view. If a Member State has a choice between various measures for achieving the same aim, it should choose the means which least restricts the free movement of goods.' Cf. Article 114 TFEU, which refers to 'major needs'.
[128] e.g. C-221/00, *Commission v Austria*, 2003, para. 42; C-573/12, *Ålands Vindkraft*, 2014, para. 57; C-549/15, *E.ON Biofor Sverige*, 2017, para. 76; C-242/17, *L.E.G.O.*, 2018, para. 52. But see Article 114(4) and (5) TFEU; para. 7-115, *infra*.
[129] 27/80, *Fietje*, 1980, paras 10–11; C-524/14, *Commission v Czech Republic*, 2016, para. 46.
[130] 6/81, *Industrie Diensten Groep*, 1982, paras 7–9.
[131] 823/79, *Carciati*, 1980, para. 9.
[132] See also C-184/96, *Commission v France*, 1998, paras 23–37; C-524/14, *Commission v Czech Republic*, 2016, para. 52.
[133] C-114/96, *Kieffer and Thill*, 1997, paras 29–31.
[134] 120/78, *Rewe*, 1979, paras 8–11.
[135] 302/86, *Commission v Denmark*, 1988, paras 7–9; C-320/03, *Commission v Austria*, 2005, paras 71–84; C-549/15, *E.ON Biofor Sverige*, 2017, para. 84. See Notaro, 'The New Generation Case Law on Trade and Environment' (2000) ELRev 467–91.
[136] C-573/12, *Ålands Vindkraft*, 2014, paras 77-78 and 82; C-242/17, *L.E.G.O.*, 2018, para. 64.

safety,[137] proper functioning of the public telecommunications network,[138] protection of cultural works,[139] including the protection of books as cultural objects,[140] and maintenance of press diversity with a view to safeguarding freedom of expression.[141] This list is not exhaustive, but may be supplemented by other non-economic policy aims in the general interest.[142] A national measure that is taken in pursuance of economic interests may only be justified if it also aims at achieving a non-economic policy interest.[143] Avoiding a major distortion of the financial balance of the social security system does, for example, constitute a mandatory requirement.[144] A restriction of the free movement of goods may also be justified on the ground of the need to protect fundamental rights, such as freedom of expression and freedom of assembly.[145]

7.041 **(3) Application without distinction.** A Member State can comply with 'mandatory requirements' only by means of a measure which is applicable without distinction to domestic and imported products, even if it is indirectly discriminatory,[146] in particular where it will be more difficult for imported products than for domestic products to conform to the measure or where the particular nature of the imported products would have necessitated a derogating measure. In this way, the Court of Justice had to consider whether the Belgian measure of requiring margarine to be packaged in cubes was justified[147] and whether, in *Cassis de Dijon*, the German minimum alcoholic strength requirement, which did not involve foreign products being treated differently from domestic ones, but in practice kept foreign spirits off the German market was justified.[148] Similarly, the Court was asked to rule on the compatibility with EU law of a deposit and return system for packaging of beer and soft drinks laying down the same rules for national producers and producers from other Member States.[149] A measure which makes a distinction between domestic and imported products and so directly discriminates against the latter may be tolerated only if it satisfies Article 36 TFEU. Such a measure ceases to be discriminatory, however, where the distinction is due to particular characteristics of the product. Accordingly, before the harmonization at Union level of the rules concerning shipments of waste, it was possible to justify preferential treatment for domestic, as opposed to imported waste, by the principle that

---

[137] C-314/98, *Snellers Auto's*, 2000, para. 55; C-354/14, *Capoda Import-Export*, 2015, para. 43.
[138] C-388/00 and C-429/00, *Radiosistemi*, 2002, para. 44.
[139] 60-61/84, *Cinéthèque*, 1985, para. 23.
[140] C-531/07, *LIBRO*, 2009, para. 34.
[141] C-368/95, *Familiapress*, 1997, para. 18.
[142] A risk of seriously undermining the financial balance of the social security system may possibly constitute a mandatory requirement: C-120/95, *Decker*, 1998, para. 39; C-322/01, *Deutscher Apothekerverband*, 2003, para. 122, with case note by Lang (2005) CMLRev 189–204.
[143] See, in respect of the free movement of capital, C-105/12 to C-107/12, *Essent*, 2013, para. 52.
[144] C-120/95, *Decker*, 1998, para. 39; C-322/01, *Deutscher Apothekerverband*, 2003, para. 122.
[145] C-112/00, *Schmidberger*, 2003, para. 74.
[146] For this expression, see para. 5-059, *supra*.
[147] 261/81, *Rau*, 1982, paras 16–20 (see also para. 7-029, *supra*).
[148] Para. 7-037, *supra*. Another example is 302/86, *Commission v Denmark*, 1988, where what was at issue was a deposit-and-return system under which containers for beer and soft drinks not approved by a national agency might be used for only a maximum quantity of 3,000 hectolitres a year. Although the system did not distinguish between domestic and foreign producers, it impeded the import of drinks from other Member States in otherwise than approved containers. Cf. C-237/94, *O'Flynn*, 1996, para. 18, in which the Court of Justice held that measures which are applicable without distinction in terms of nationality must be regarded as indirectly discriminatory if they can be more easily satisfied by national workers than by migrant workers or where there is a risk that they may operate to the particular detriment of migrant workers.
[149] C-309/02, *Radlberger Getränkegesellschaft*, 2004, paras 60–9.

environmental damage should as a matter of priority be remedied at source.[150] In such a case, the 'non-discrimination' requirement is satisfied, and the rule of reason may be applied.[151] In a spate of judgments the Court accepted that a national measure aimed at promoting renewable energy was justified on grounds of environmental protection—under the rule of reason—even though it did not treat electricity produced in other Member States in the same manner as locally produced electricity.[152] In this respect the Court emphasized that an increased use of renewable energy sources also serves to protect the health and life of humans, animals, or plants, which are objectives that are listed in Article 36 TFEU.[153]

(4) Proportionality. Lastly, the national measure must be proportionate to the intended aim. If a Member State has a choice between different measures to attain the same objective it should choose the means which least restrict the free movement of goods.[154] A national measure must not only be appropriate in order to achieve an aim in the general interest (which is regarded as a 'mandatory requirement'), but it must also be indispensable in the sense that there are no less restrictive means available for achieving the intended aim.[155] In the *Cassis de Dijon* case, the Court of Justice held that it would go too far to 'regard the mandatory fixing of minimum alcohol requirements as being an essential guarantee of the fairness of commercial transactions, since it is a simple matter to ensure that suitable information is conveyed to the purchaser by requiring the display of an indication of origin and of the alcohol content on the packaging of products'.[156] The Court further referred to reciprocal recognition of national provisions as a particular application of the principle of proportionality when it held that '[t]here is therefore no valid reason why, provided that they have been lawfully produced and marketed in one of the Member States, alcoholic beverages should not be introduced into any other Member State'.[157] A Member State wishing to apply a measure restricting trade must show that the aim pursued by the measure is not already achieved by the legislation in force in the Member State from which the imported product originates. The burden of proof in fact requires the Member State to show why its own situation differs so much from that of other Member States as to necessitate a specific measure.[158] Article 34 TFEU thus precludes a national rule which does not allow a trader to show that an imported product satisfied the prescribed requirements already in its State of

7.042

---

[150] C-2/90, *Commission v Belgium*, 1992, para. 34; Cf. C-221/06, *Stadtgemeinde Frohnleiten and Gemeindebetriebe Frohnleiten*, 2007, paras 60–8.

[151] In some cases, the Court of Justice appears not to rule out a justification on grounds of 'mandatory requirements' even in the case of discriminatory measures, e.g. C-203/96, *Dusseldorp and Others*, 1998, paras 44–50; C-389/96, *Aher-Waggon*, 1998, paras 18–19; C-209/98, *Sydhavnens Sten & Grus*, 2000, paras 48–50 (environmental protection and public health); C-531/07, *Fachverband der Buch- und Medienwirtschaft*, 2009, paras 18–22 and 34 36 (obligation to sell imported books at fixed prices). See Notaro, 'The New Generation Case Law on Trade and Environment' (2000) ELRev 467, at 489.

[152] C-573/12, *Ålands Vindkraft*, 2014, paras 65–82; C-204/12 to C-208/12, *Essent Belgium*, 2014, paras 82–8.

[153] C-573/12, *Ålands Vindkraft*, 2014, para. 80; C-204/12 to C-208/12, *Essent Belgium*, 2014, para. 93. See also C-492/14, *Essent Belgium*, 2016, para. 101.

[154] See, e.g., C-51/94, *Commission v Germany*, 1995, paras 32–7; C-114/96, *Kieffer and Thill*, 1997, paras 31–8.

[155] See para. 7-034, *supra*, and the general discussion of the principle of proportionality in paras 5-033–5-035, *supra*.

[156] 120/78, *Rewe*, 1979, para. 13. The Court has also referred to labelling requirements as a less restrictive means of preventing confusion arising between butter and margarine than cubic packaging: 261/81, *Rau*, 1982, para. 17.

[157] 120/78, *Rewe*, 1979, para. 14.

[158] See Mattera, 'L'article 30 du traité CEE, la jurisprudence "cassis de Dijon" et le principe de la reconnaissance mutuelle' (1992) RMUE 13–71, and 'L'Union européenne assure le respect des identités nationales, régionales et locales, en particulier par l'application et la mise en oeuvre du principe de la reconnaissance mutuelle' (2002) RDUE 217–39.

origin.[159] However, the mere fact that one Member State imposes stricter rules than those applicable in other Member States does not mean that the former are *ipso facto* incompatible with Articles 34 and 36 TFEU.[160] In a few cases concerning national regulation of the electricity market the Court accepted that in certain circumstances it may be necessary to favour national production, in order to promote the production of electricity using sources of renewable energy.[161]

7.043 **(3) Rules governing selling arrangements** *Keck and Mithouard.* The *Dassonville* interpretation of Article 34 TFEU raised questions about the permissibility of national legislation relating to selling arrangements, which, although not intended to regulate trade in goods between Member States, nevertheless affect the volume of sales within the Member State concerned and hence also impede the sale of products from other Member States. In this way, the Court of Justice delivered a number of controversial rulings on Sunday-trading legislation.[162] The question arose as to whether such indirect influence on free movement of goods sufficed in order for the legislation concerned to be regarded as unlawful measures having equivalent effect.[163]

In the judgment of 24 November 1993 in *Keck and Mithouard* the Court introduced, within the class of measures applicable without distinction to domestic and imported products, a distinction between provisions laying down requirements which products have to satisfy and provisions restricting or prohibiting certain selling arrangements. The Court then declared that

> contrary to what has previously been decided, the application to products from other Member States of national provisions restricting or prohibiting certain selling arrangements is not such as to hinder directly or indirectly, actually or potentially, trade between Member States within the meaning of the *Dassonville* judgment ... so long as those provisions apply to all relevant traders operating within the national territory and so long as they affect in the same manner, in law and in fact, the marketing of domestic products and of those from other Member States.[164]

---

[159] e.g. C-388/00 and C-429/00, *Radiosistemi*, 2002, paras 44–6.
[160] C-333/08, *Commission v France*, 2010, para. 105.
[161] C-573/12, *Ålands Vindkraft*, 2014, paras 91–119; C-204/12 to C-208/12, *Essent Belgium*, 2014, paras 97–115; C-492/14, *Essent Belgium*, 2016, paras 104–10.
[162] C-145/88, *Torfaen Borough Council*, 1989; C-312/89, *Conforama and Others*, 1991 and C-332/89, *Marchandise and Others*, 1991; C-169/91, *Council of the City of Stoke-on-Trent and Norwich City Council*, 1992.
[163] Some commentators advocated restricting the concept of 'measures having equivalent effect': Van der Woude, 'The Limits of Free Circulation: The Torfaen Borough Council Case' (1990) Leiden JIL 57–63; Mortelmans, 'Article 30 of the EEC Treaty and Legislation Relating to Market Circumstances: Time to Consider a New Definition?' (1991) CMLRev 115–36; Steiner, 'Drawing the Line: Uses and Abuses of Article 30 EEC' (1992) CMLRev 749–74. Others argued for retaining its broad scope: Gormley, 'Recent Case Law on the Free Movement of Goods: Some Hot Potatoes' (1990) CMLRev 825–57; Arnull, 'What shall we do on Sunday?' (1991) ELRev 112–24. See also the appraisal by Wils, 'The Search for the Rule in Article 30 EEC: Much Ado About Nothing?' (1993) 475–92 and the survey of the debate by Straetmans, *Consument en markt* (Kluwer, 1998), 323–6.
[164] C-267/91 and C-268/91, *Keck and Mithouard*, 1993,para. 16 (in that case the Court considered that Article 34 did not apply to a French provision imposing a blanket ban on resale at a loss; ibid., para. 18). For some commentaries on the judgment, see the contributions by Rosas, Nicolaïdis, Bernard, and Regan, in Maduro and Azoulai (eds), *The Past and Future of EU Law* (Hart Publishing, 2010) 433–73; Kovar, 'Dassonville, Keck et les autres: de la mesure avant toute chose', (2006) RTDE 213–47; González Vaqué, 'La jurisprudencia relativa al artículo 28 CE (antiguo artículo 30 TCE) sobre la libre circulación de mercancías después de *Keck y Mithouard*' (2000) GJ 24–38; Picod, 'La nouvelle approche de la Cour de justice en matière d'entraves aux échanges' (1998) RTDE 169–89; Becker, 'Von "Dassonville" über "Cassis" zu "Keck"—Der Begriff der Maßnahmen gleicher Wirkung in Art. 30 EGV' (1994) EuR 162–74; Chalmers, 'Repackaging the Internal Market: The Ramifications of the *Keck* Judgment' (1994) ELRev 385–403; Mattera, 'De l'arrêt "Dassonville" à l'arrêt "Keck": l'obscure clarté d'une jurisprudence riche en principes novateurs et en contradictions' (1994) RMUE 117–60; Poiares Maduro, '*Keck*: The End? The Beginning of the End? Or Just the End of the Beginning?' (1994) Ir JEL 30–43.

Accordingly, a measure governing selling arrangements which may affect trade between Member States, yet does not discriminate either 'in law' or 'in fact' against traders from other Member States, is no longer regarded as a measure having equivalent effect. In addition to the ban on selling at a loss or for a low margin,[165] the Court of Justice has accepted that 'selling arrangements' cover, for example, the imposition of minimum prices,[166] rules relating to sales outlets,[167] making sales on rounds,[168] shop-opening hours,[169] advertising,[170] and promotions.[171] By contrast, rules on packaging and labelling do not constitute selling arrangements.[172]

Rules on selling arrangements that do not apply to all traders[173] or are liable to affect products from other Member States more than domestic products will not fall within the exception established by *Keck and Mithouard* and are to be considered as measures having equivalent effect within the meaning of Article 34 TFEU.[174] The Court of Justice has held that a discriminatory effect ensues, for example, from a blanket prohibition on the advertising of alcoholic beverages, because such a ban is liable to impede access to the market by products from other Member States more than it impedes access by domestic products, with which consumers are instantly more familiar.[175] If it can be shown that a measure governing selling arrangements has discriminatory effects, it may still be justified in accordance with the *Cassis de Dijon* criteria in so far as it is applicable without distinction to domestic and imported products;[176] a formally discriminatory measure may be retained only under one of the exceptions provided for in Article 36 TFEU.[177]

---

[165] See, in addition to *Keck and Mithouard* (see preceding ns), C-63/94, *Belgapom*, 1995, paras 8–15.

[166] e.g. C-221/15, *Etablissements Fr. Colruyt*, 2016, paras 35–40.

[167] C-391/92, *Commission v Greece*, 1995, paras 9–21; C-387/93, *Banchero*, 1995, paras 32–44; C-189/95, *Franzén*, 1997, paras 69–72 (system of import licences); C-322/01, *Deutscher Apothekerverband*, 2003. paras 68–76 (concerning a ban on mail order sales).

[168] C-254/98, *TK-Heimdienst Sass*, 2000, paras 24–37.

[169] C-401/92 and C-402/92, *Tankstation 't Heuskse and Boermans*, 1994, paras 10–12; C-69/93 and C-258/93, *Punto Casa and PPV*, 1994, paras 12–14; C-418-C-421/93, C-460-C-462/93, C-464/93, C-9-C-11/94, C-14-15/94, C-23-24/94, and C-332/94, *Semeraro Casa Uno and Others*, 1996, paras 9–28.

[170] C-292/92, *Hünermund and Others*, 1993, paras 17–24; C-320/93, *Ortscheit*, 1994, para. 9; C-412/93, *Société d'Importation Leclerc-Siplec*, 1995, paras 18–24; C-34-36/95, *De Agostini and TV Shop*, 1997, paras 40–7; C-405/9, *Gourmet International Products*, 2001, paras 18–25; C-71/02, *Karner*, 2004, paras 38–9. Legislation imposing requirements with regard to the products themselves is not covered, see C-315/92, *Verband Sozialer Wettbewerb*, 1994, paras 17–24; C-470/93, *Mars*, 1995, paras 11–14; C-158/04 and C-159/04, *Alfa Vita Vassilopoulos*, 2006, paras 17–18. See further C-143/06, *Ludwigs—Apotheke*, 2007 (where a prohibition on advertising medicinal products was not assessed as a selling arrangement, presumably because it involved direct discrimintation; see González Vaqué, 'La sentencia "Ludwigs-Apotheke" relativa a la publicidad de los medicamentos: ¿Dónde estás "Keck y Mithouard"?' (2008) Rev EDE 67).

[171] This does not apply to rules relating to sales promotions which are liable to alter the content of the product: C-368/95, *Familiapress*, 1997, paras 11–12, with case note by Ballon (1998) Col JEL 172–8.

[172] e.g. C-12/00, *Commission v Spain*, 2003, para. 76.

[173] C-198/14, *Visnapuu*, 2015, paras 104–7 (retail licences for alcohol reserved to domestic manufacturers).

[174] e.g. C-141/07, *Commission v Germany*, 2008, para. 34–44; C-158/04 and C-159/04, *Alfa Vita Vassilopoulos*, 2006, para. 20; C-110/05, *Commission v Italy*, 2009, paras 35–7; C-142/05 *Mickelsson and Roos*, 2009, para. 24; C-148/15, *Deutsche Parkingson Verein*, 2016, paras 23–6.

[175] C-405/98, *Gourmet International Products*, 2001, paras 19–21. For the importance of 'market access' as a criterion, see the commentary by Straetmans (2002) CMLRev 1407–21. For the notion of 'market access', see Snell, 'The Notion of Market Access: A Concept or a Slogan?' (2010) CMLRev 437–72.

[176] C-34-36/95, *De Agostini and TV Shop*, 1997, paras 44–5; C-441/04, *A-Punkt Schmuckhandel*, 2006, paras 25–9.

[177] See, e.g., C-320/93, *Ortscheidt*, 1994, paras 9–22; C-189/95, *Franzén*, 1997, paras 69–77; C-254/98, *TK-Heimdienst Sass*, 2000, para. 36; C-322/01, *Deutscher Apothekerverband*, 2003, paras 68–76; C-198/14, *Valev Visnapuu*, 2015, paras 97–129.

The concept of 'selling arrangements' covers only provisions of national law that regulate the manner in which goods may be marketed.[178] Rules concerning the manner in which goods may be transported are not within the scope of that concept. The Court thus found that the German infrastructure use charge could not constitute a mere selling arrangement.[179]

B. Free movement of workers and self-employed persons

1. General scope

7.044 **Treaty rules.** The Treaty provisions on free movement of workers and self-employed persons—together referred to as the 'free movement of persons'—seek to attain an optimum allocation of supply and demand in the Union market through complete movement of economic operators.[180] They are therefore intended to 'facilitate the pursuit by Union citizens of occupational activities of all kinds throughout the Union'.[181] The provisions preclude Member States from discriminating against or imposing restrictions on both workers (Article 45 TFEU) and self-employed persons (Article 49 TFEU) who are nationals of another Member State. The Treaties provide for exceptions on grounds of public policy, public security, or public health (Article 45(3) and 52 TFEU) where the Union may adopt implementing regulations (Article 45(3)(d)) or coordinating directives (Article 52(2)), and also as regards employment in the public service (Article 45(4) and 52 TFEU). The provisions of the Treaties laying down prohibitions have direct effect,[182] not only vis-à-vis Member States in respect of action of public authorities, but also vis-à-vis associations or organizations not governed by public law in respect of acts resulting from the exercise of their legal autonomy creating obstacles to free movement of persons.[183] The prohibition of discrimination on grounds of nationality thus applies in cases where a group or organization exercises a certain power over individuals and is in a position to impose on them conditions which adversely affect the exercise of the fundamental freedoms guaranteed under the Treaties.[184] Similarly, Article 49 TFEU can be invoked against a trade union or a group of trade unions initiating collective action against a private undertaking in order to induce that undertaking to enter into a collective agreement, the terms of which are liable to deter it from exercising freedom of establishment.[185] The free movement provisions may also

---

[178] On the limits of this approach, see Schütze, 'Of Types and Tests: Towards a Unitary Doctrinal Framework for Article 34 TFEU?' (2016) ELRev 826–42.
[179] C-591/17, *Austria v Germany*, 2019, paras 128–9.
[180] For general discussions, see Barnard, *The Substantive Law of the EU: The Four Freedoms* (OUP, 2016), part III; Minderhoud en Trimikliniotis (eds), *Rethinking the Free Movement of Workers; the European Challenges Ahead* (Wolf Legal Publishers, 2009); Weiss and Wooldridge, *Free Movement of Persons within the European Community* (Kluwer law international, 2007); Carlier and Guild, *L'avenir de la libre circulation des personnes dans l'UE* (Bruylant, 2006); Rogers and Scannell, *Free Movement of Persons in the Enlarged European Union* (Sweet & Maxwell, 2005); Carrera, 'What Does Free Movement Mean in Theory and Practice in an Enlarged EU?' (2005) ELJ 699–721.
[181] 143/87, *Stanton*, 1988, para. 13, and 154 and 155/87, *Wolf and Microtherm Europe*, 1988, para. 13.
[182] See for Article 45(1) to (3) TFEU, 41/74, *Van Duyn*, 1974, paras 5–7; see for Article 49 TFEU, 2/74, *Reyners*, 1974, para. 30.
[183] 36/74, *Walrave*, 1974, paras 15–23 (para. 21 states in general terms that 'Article 48 [*now Article 45 TFEU*], relating to the abolition of any discrimination based on nationality as regards gainful employment, extends likewise to agreements and rules which do not emanate from public authorities'); C-415/93, *Bosman*, 1995, paras 82–7; C-94/07, *Raccanelli*, 2008, paras 40–6; C-325/08, *Olympique Lyonnais*, 2010, paras 30–2.
[184] C-411/98, *Ferlini*, 2000, para. 50 (concerning Article 12 EC [*now Article 18 TFEU*]).
[185] C-438/05, *International Transport Workers' Federation and Finnish Seamen's Union*, 2007, paras 32–7 and 57–66.

be invoked against collective agreements.[186] The Court of Justice has held that the prohibition of discrimination enshrined in Article 45 TFEU applies to an individual employer.[187] However, it is not certain whether the prohibition of non-discriminatory restrictions can be invoked against private persons.[188]

Legislation. The Treaties give the Union the task of issuing directives or making regulations to facilitate free movement of workers (Article 46) and directives securing freedom of establishment (Article 50(2) TFEU). As far as migrant workers and self-employed persons are concerned, Article 48 TFEU contemplates ancillary measures in the social security field. As regards taking up and pursuing activities as self-employed persons, Article 53 TFEU provides for directives for the mutual recognition of diplomas, certificates, and other evidence of formal qualifications.[189]

7.045

Workers and self-employed persons. As a result, workers and self-employed persons are subject to different Treaty rules. In view of the common objective of the free movement of persons and of the fact that Union legislation frequently confers identical rights on workers and self-employed persons, both sets of rules will be discussed together.[190] Ultimately, these provisions give shape to the 'fundamental right' of citizens to freedom to seek employment, to work, to exercise the right of establishment, and to provide services in any Member State (Article 15(2) of the Charter of Fundamental Rights).

7.046

2. Beneficiaries

Survey. The rules on free movement of workers and the right of establishment, respectively, apply to workers and self-employed persons who are nationals of a Member State and who find themselves in a situation warranting a connection with Union law.

7.047

a. Nationals of a Member State

Nationality. Free movement of workers and the right of establishment apply, in principle, only to nationals of a Member State.[191] Subject to the limitations set by the Treaty provisions relating to citizenship of the Union, each Member State determines the conditions on which a natural person acquires and loses his or her nationality (for companies, see para. 7-065, *infra*).

7.048

Third-country nationals covered. Nevertheless, persons other than workers or self-employed persons having the nationality of a Member State may enjoy the advantages of free movement.[192] Union legislation has extended enjoyment of certain rights to members

7.049

---

[186] C-271/08, *Commission v Germany*, 2010, paras 42–4; C-379/09, *Casteels*, 2011, paras 19–20.
[187] C-281/98, *Angonese*, 2000, paras 30–6; C-94/07, *Raccanelli*, 2008, paras 45–6.
[188] For a critical view on the judgment in *Angonese*, see Körber (2000) EuR 932, 940–52; Stuyck (2001) SEW 112–18; for a less critical view, see Van der Steen (2001) NTER 4–9; Lengauer (2001) Zf.RV 57–65.
[189] The Lisbon Treaty has not altered the rights that workers and self-employed persons may derive from the Treaties. It did however adapt, to a certain extent, the decision-making process by which the institutions are to facilitate free movement pursuant to the relevant Treaty provisions.
[190] See C-107/94, *Asscher*, 1996, para. 29.
[191] See Article 45(2) and Article 49 TFEU: 238/83, *Meade*, 1984, para. 7.
[192] Free movement also applies to workers (regardless of their nationality) of a provider of services established in a Member State, who must be able to move within the Union together with the provider of services: C-113/89, *Rush Portuguesa*, 1990, para. 12; C-43/93, *Van der Elst*, 1994, para. 21; C-244/04, *Commission v Germany*, 2006, paras 30–64.

of the families of employed persons,[193] self-employed persons,[194] and other persons on whom Union law confers a right of residence,[195] regardless of their nationality. The rights of family members are generally limited to the Member State in respect of which the persons they accompany have exercised their right to free movement.[196] Agreements concluded with third countries have also conferred rights on nationals of third countries and members of their families (see para. 8-013, *infra*).

b. Qualifying workers

7.050 **Union definition.** Article 45(2) TFEU prohibits 'any discrimination based on nationality between workers of the Member States'. The concept of 'worker' employed in Articles 45 to 48 TFEU is a concept of Union law with an independent meaning. Indeed, if the definition of that concept could be determined unilaterally by national law, it would be possible for each Member State to eliminate at will the protection afforded by the Treaties to certain categories of persons.[197] In view of the fact that the Treaties do not define the concept of 'worker', the Court of Justice has clarified its scope by taking the view that it defines the field of application of one of the freedoms guaranteed by the Treaties and, as such, may not be interpreted restrictively.[198]

7.051 **The concept of 'worker'.** The Court of Justice bases itself on objective criteria which distinguish the employment relationship by reference to the rights and duties of the persons concerned. The essential feature of an employment relationship is that 'for a certain period of time a person performs services for and under the direction of another person in return for which he receives remuneration'.[199] This encompasses three separate criteria.

First of all, there needs to be the pursuit of real and genuine activity for remuneration, to the exclusion of activities on such a small scale as to be regarded as purely marginal and ancillary. The type of work is irrelevant, provided that an economic—that is, a remunerated—activity is involved.[200] Hence, the activities of professional or semi-professional sportsmen are covered by the provisions on the free movement of workers, with the exception of activities which are of sporting interest only, and therefore not of an economic nature.[201] By the same token, persons undergoing a traineeship will be considered workers if the training period is completed under the conditions of genuine and effective activity as an employed

---

[193] 40/76 *Kermaschek*, 1976, para. 9. See the (old) Directive 68/360 and Regulations Nos 1612/68 and 1251/70; paras 7-057 and 7-060, *infra*. For a discussion, see Ziekow, 'Der gemeinschaftsrechtliche Status der Familienangehörigen von Wanderarbeitnehmer' (1991) DöV 363–70.

[194] See Directives 73/148 and 75/34, since replaced by Directive 2004/38/EC of the European Parliament and of the Council of 29 April 2004 on the right of the citizen of the Union and their family members to move and reside freely within the territory of the Member States amending Regulation (EEC) No. 1612/68, OJ 2004 L158/77.

[195] See para. 11-002.

[196] See, e.g., C-10/05, *Mattern*, 2006, para. 28 (no right for a third country national married to an EU national to take up an activity as an employed person in a Member State other than the one in which his spouse pursues an economic activity).

[197] 75/63, *Hoekstra (née Unger)*, 1964, 184.

[198] 53/81, *Levin*, 1982, para. 13.

[199] 66/85, *Lawrie-Blum*, 1986, para. 17.

[200] 196/87, *Steymann*, 1988, paras 12–14 ((commercial) activities carried out by members of a community based on religion or another form of philosophy); C-456/02, *Trojani*, 2004, paras 17–24 (performing jobs for the Salvation Army in return for board and lodging and some pocket money).

[201] 36/74, *Walrave*, 1974, paras 4–7; professional footballers: 13/76, *Donà*, 1976, para. 12, and C-415/93, *Bosman*, 1995, paras 73–6 (paras 7-059 and 7-062, *infra*).

person.[202] The Court has further held that an official of the European Union (or of another international organization) who is a national of a Member State other than that in which he or she is employed must be regarded as a migrant worker.[203] The duration of the work is not relevant: free movement of workers also covers persons carrying out genuine part-time work.[204]

Second, the person in question must perform services for and under the direction of another person. As it is the case for the application of the first criterion, this must be determined on the basis of all the factors and circumstances characterizing the arrangements between the parties, such as the sharing of the commercial risks of the business and the freedom for a person to choose his or her own working hours and to engage his or her own assistants.[205] It may not always be self-evident to identify the actual employer under whose direction the person in question performs services, in particular in case of workers who concluded an employment contract with one undertaking but are actually at the disposal of another undertaking. In such case, the objective situation of the employed person and all the circumstances of the employment must be taken into account in order to identify the entity that actually exercises authority over the worker, bears in reality the relevant wage costs, and has the actual power to dismiss that worker.[206]

Third, the services must be performed in return for remuneration. Neither the origin of the funds from which the remuneration is paid, nor the limited amount of the remuneration can have any consequence in regard to whether or not the person is a worker for the purposes of Union law.[207] Hence, it is not necessary that the remuneration received in exchange for the work performed should cover the costs of subsistence of the person concerned (and his dependants). Thus, free movement of workers applies to employment relationships where the remuneration provided for genuine work is under the minimum subsistence level laid down in the Member State of employment,[208] even if the person concerned claims a supplementary benefit in the host Member State in order to supplement his or her remuneration.[209]

Link with the labour market. Free movement of workers (especially in connection with unemployment insurance) applies only to persons who have already participated in the labour market by exercising an effective and genuine occupational activity which has conferred on them the status of workers within the Union law meaning of that term.[210] A woman who

7.052

---

[202] 66/85, *Lawrie-Blum*, 1986, para. 19; C-3/90, *Bernini*, 1992, para. 15; C-109/04, *Kranemann*, 2005, paras 13–15.
[203] C-411/98, *Ferlini*, 2000, para. 42 (official European Union); C-233/12, *Gardella*, 2013, paras 24-27 (official European Patent Office).
[204] 53/81, *Levin*, 1982, para. 17; C-22/08 and C-23/08, *Vatsouras and Koupatantze*, 2008, para. 29; C-14/09, *Genc*, 2010, paras 26–8.
[205] C-3/87, *Agegate*, 1989, para. 36. The fact that a person is related by marriage to the director and sole owner of the undertaking does not mean that that person cannot be regarded as being a worker within the meaning of Article 45 TFEU if he or she pursues an effective and genuine activity in a relationship of subordination: C-337/97, *Meeusen*, 1999, paras 14–16.
[206] C-610/18, *AFMB*, 2020, paras 48–80 (interpretation of the notion of 'employer' in the context of Regulation 883/2004 on the coordination of social security systems).
[207] 53/81, *Levin*, 1982, para.16; 344/87, *Bettray*, 1989, paras 15 and 16; and C-188/00, *Kurz*, 2002, para. 32; C-22/08 and C-23/08, *Vatsouras and Koupatantze*, 2008, paras. 27–8.
[208] 53/81, *Levin*, 1982, para. 15.
[209] 139/85, *Kempf*, 1986, para. 14.
[210] C-278/94, *Commission v Belgium*, 1996, para. 40; C-224/98, *D'Hoop*, 2002, para. 18. For the differing position of workers and jobseekers, see C-138/02, *Collins*, 2004, paras 30–1. However, after exercising his or her right of free

temporarily ceases to exercise an occupation due to pregnancy and childbirth does not lose her status as a worker for that reason alone.[211] The protection of free movement extends to job-seekers, but only as long as they are potential participants in the labour market. The principle of free movement of workers only requires that the legislation of a Member State gives the persons concerned a reasonable time in which to apprise themselves, in the territory of the host Member State, of offers of employment corresponding to their occupational qualifications and to take, where appropriate, the necessary steps in order to be hired. Jobseekers may, however, be required to leave the territory of that State if they have not found employment there after six months, unless the persons concerned provide evidence that they are continuing to seek employment and that they have genuine chances of being hired.[212]

Workers employed by an undertaking established in a Member State but 'posted' to another Member State for a certain period in order to carry out work there under a contract concluded by that undertaking with a customer or a linked undertaking, do not fall under the Treaty provisions on free movement of workers.[213] As long as those workers remain in an employment relationship with the undertaking making the posting, their situation continues to be governed by the Treaty provisions on the free movement of services under which their employer provides its services in the host Member State. In order to ensure adequate social protection, the Union legislature has harmonized the conditions under which the host Member State is to make such posted workers subject to the rules on remuneration and working conditions applicable to the workers employed by an undertaking established on its territory (see para. 7-075, *infra*).

7.053 **Other beneficiaries.** The provisions relating to free movement of workers may be relied on by others than the workers employed in another Member State, in particular by employers. In order to be truly effective, the right of workers to be hired and employed without discrimination necessarily entails as a corollary the employer's entitlement to hire them in accordance with the rules governing freedom of movement for workers.[214] The Court of Justice has also held that a private-sector recruitment agency which represents a worker and seeks employment on his or her behalf may, in certain circumstances, rely on the rights directly granted to Union workers by Article 45 TFEU.[215]

---

movement, a jobseeking citizen of the Union may not suffer discrimination on grounds of nationality: *D'Hoop*, paras 27–40 (see para. 5-053).

[211] C-507/12, *Saint-Prix*, 2014, paras 33–47.

[212] C-292/89, *Antonissen*, 1991, paras 16 and 22. Accordingly, a Member State cannot automatically oblige jobseekers to leave their territory after their time has expired: C-344/95, *Commission v Belgium*, 1997, paras 12–18. For the reasonable time enjoyed by a Turkish national in order to seek work under the relevant Association Agreement, see C-171/95, *Tetik*, 1997, paras 27–48.

[213] See C-49/98, *Finalarte*, 2001, paras 22–3. That is because such workers return to their country of origin after the completion of their work without gaining access to the labour market of the host Member State. See already C-113/89, *Rush Portuguesa*, 1990, para. 15; C-43/93, *Van der Elst*, 1994, para. 21.

[214] C-350/96, *Clean Car Autoservice*, 1998, paras 19–20; C-379/11, *Caves Krier*, 2012, paras 28–9; C-202/11, *Las*, 2013, para. 18.

[215] C-208/05, *ITC*, 2007, paras 22–8.

c. Self-employed persons and companies

Establishment. The right of establishment relates to activities in another Member State not carried out by way of gainful employment. This means economic activities carried on by a person outside any relationship of subordination with regard to the conditions of work or remuneration and under his or her own responsibility.[216] 'Establishment' of a natural or legal person within the meaning of the Treaties involves the pursuit of an economic activity in the Member State concerned through a fixed establishment.[217] If an occupational activity is not carried out in a lasting way, it may constitute the supply of a service (see para. 7-082, *infra*). Both natural and legal persons enjoy the right of establishment. The first para. of Article 49 TFEU refers to 'freedom of establishment of nationals of a Member State in the territory of another Member State'. For the purposes of the application of freedom of establishment, Article 54 TFEU equates companies or firms 'formed in accordance with the law of a Member State and having their registered office, central administration or principal place of business within the Union' with natural persons who are nationals of Member States.[218] Article 54 does not apply to 'non-profit-making' companies or firms (see the second para. of that article).

7.054

d. Connection with Union law

Transfrontier situation. A person may rely on the Treaty provisions on free movement of workers or the right of establishment only where his or her situation exhibits a genuine transfrontier factor. These Treaty provisions cannot be applied to situations wholly internal to a Member State.[219] For instance, a transfrontier situation exists where a person works, has worked, or intends to work in the territory of a Member State other than the one in which he or she resides and/or of which he or she is a national.[220] The fact that an employment relationship is potentially of a transfrontier nature is insufficient to cause Union law to apply. When Moser, a German national, argued that the refusal of the *Land* of Baden-Württemberg to let him undertake teacher training on the ground that he was a member of the Communist Party made it impossible for him to apply for teaching posts in another Member State, the Court of Justice held that a purely hypothetical prospect of employment in another Member State did not establish a sufficient connection with Union law to justify the application of Article 45 TFEU.[221]

7.055

A Member State is entitled to impose stricter requirements upon its own nationals than upon nationals of other Member States ('reverse discrimination', see para. 5-061, *supra*). However, a Member State's own nationals may not be disadvantaged simply because they have exercised their right to free movement, for example by studying or

---

[216] C-268/99, *Jany and Others*, 2001, paras 34–50 (definition applied to prostitution).
[217] C-221/89, *Factortame Limited and Others (Factortame II)*, 1991, para. 20; C-357/10 to C-359/10, *Duomo Gpa*, 2012, paras 30–2. See also para. 7-063 *et seq.*, *infra*.
[218] C-106/16, *Polbud—Wykonawstwo*, 2017, para. 32.
[219] 175/78, *Saunders*, 1979, para. 11; C-152/94, *Van Buynder*, 1995, paras 10–12; C-134/94, *Esso Española*, 1995, paras 13–16; C-225-C-227/95, *Kapasakalis and Others*, 1998, para. 22; C-18/95, *Terhoeve*, 1999, para. 26; C-95/99 to C-98/99 and C-180/99, *Khalil*, 2001, para. 69; C-208/05, *ITC*, 2007, para. 29; C-212/06, *Government of the French Community and Walloon Government*, 2008, para. 33; C-139/12, *Caixa d'Estalvis i Pensions de Barcelona*, 2014, para. 42; C-268/15, *Ullens de Schooten*, para. 47. See, with regard to the Union provisions governing the right of residence of nationals of other Member States and their spouses: C-297/88 and C-197/89, *Dzodzi*, 1990, para. 28.
[220] C-336/96, *Gilly*, 1998, para. 21; C-227/03 *van Pommeren-Bourgondiën*, 2005, paras 40–4; C-470/04, *N.*, 2006, para. 28. See also C-378/97, *Wijsenbeek*, 1999, paras 18–23.
[221] 180/83, *Moser*, 1984, para. 18.

working in or by moving to another Member State.[222] When the Dutchman Knoors applied to the Netherlands authorities for an authorization to carry on the trade of a plumber in his own country on the ground of the skills which he had acquired in Belgium, the Netherlands had to recognize those skills. The Court of Justice explained in *Knoors* that a Member State may not discriminate against nationals who, by taking advantage of the facilities existing in the matter of freedom of movement and establishment, are in a situation which may be assimilated to that of any other person enjoying the rights and freedoms guaranteed by the Treaties.[223] Hence, there is no question of a purely internal situation where a national holds a professional diploma issued in another Member State, not even if the diploma is not actually recognized by a provision of Union law.[224] This also applies to nationals wishing to use a diploma that does not afford access to employment or self-employment, but nevertheless affords advantages for the exercise of a profession.[225] Any Union national who, irrespective of his or her place of residence or nationality, has worked in another Member State falls within the scope of free movement of workers or freedom of establishment.[226] In addition, the Court of Justice considered that an Italian who had studied in Austria could rely on the provisions relating to the free movement of workers as against an Italian employer who, as proof of knowledge of German, accepted only a certificate issued locally.[227] Similarly, the provisions on free movement of workers or freedom of establishment can be relied on by persons who move their residence to a Member State other than the one in which they pursue their occupational activity and who are treated less favourably than persons having their residence in the latter Member State.[228]

The applicability of the free movement of workers or the right of establishment is also important for the members of the family of such a worker or self-employed person. A national who makes use of the free movement of workers or the freedom of establishment, has the right to bring along his or her family members, regardless of their nationality (see para. 7-057, *infra*). Upon return to his or her Member State of origin, his or her family members must enjoy at least the same rights of entry and residence there as would be granted to him or her under Union law if the national in question chose to enter and reside in another Member State, even if the family members concerned are not nationals of a Member State.[229]

---

[222] C-224/98, *D'Hoop*, 2002, paras 27–35; C-224/02, *Pusa*, 2004, para. 17; C-520/04, *Turpeinen*, 2006, paras 20–3; C-406/04, *De Cuyper*, 2006, para. 39; C-192/05, *Tas-Hagen and Tas*, 2006, paras 30–2; C-76/05, *Schwarz and Gootjes-Schwarz*, 2007; para. 93; C-11/06 and C-12/06, *Morgan*, 2007, para. 25; C-499/06 *Nerkowska*, 2008, para. 32; C-353/06, *Grunkin and Paul*, 2008, paras 21–8; C-221/07, *Zablocka-Weyhermüller*, 2008, para. 35. See Tryfonidou, 'Reverse Discrimination in Purely Internal Situations: An Incongruity in a Citizens' Europe' (2008) 35 LIEI 43–67; Staples, 'Heeft omgekeerde discriminatie zijn langste tijd gehad?' (2002) NTER 205–9.
[223] 115/78, *Knoors*, 1979, paras 20 and 24.
[224] C-61/89, *Bouchoucha*, 1990, paras 11 and 14. On the concept of a purely internal situation, see Arena, *Le "situazioni puramente interne" nel diritto dell'Unione europea* (Editoriale Scientifica, 2021).
[225] See, for the use of an LLM degree, C-19/92, *Kraus*, 1993, paras 17–18 (para. 7-062, *infra*).
[226] C-419/92, *Scholz*, 1994, para. 9. cf. C-443/93 *Vougioukas*, 1995, para. 38; C-107/94, *Asscher*, 1996, paras 31–4; C-18/95, *Terhoeve*, 1999, paras 27–8.
[227] C-281/98, *Angonese*, 2000. See Stuyck (2001) SEW 112–8, who criticizes the judgment for failing to find that this was a purely internal situation (see also n. 187, *supra*).
[228] C-152/03, *Ritter-Coulais*, 2006, paras 31–2 (workers); C-212/05, *Hartmann*, 2007, paras 15–20 (workers); C-470/04, *N.*, 2006, para. 28 (self-employed persons).
[229] C-370/90, *Surinder Singh*, 1992, paras 21 and 23.

Territorial aspects. An employment relationship must exhibit not only a transfrontier element but also a sufficiently close link with the territory of the Union.[230] A national of a Member State who works for an undertaking of another Member State continues to enjoy the protection of Union law while working temporarily outside the Union, provided that he or she was working on behalf of the undertaking.[231] Union law is also applicable to a national of a Member State working for an embassy of another Member State in a third country as regards those aspects of his or her employment relationship which are governed by the law of the second Member State.[232]

7.056

3. Substance
a. Right to enter, leave, and reside
Entry and residence rights. Effective exercise of the right to obtain employment in another Member State is conditional upon the worker or the jobseeker being able readily to enter or leave the host Member State and reside there. This also applies to persons wishing to engage in self-employed activities in another Member State. The rights enshrined in Articles 45(3)(b), (c) and (d) and 49 TFEU have been enlarged upon in Directive 2004/38,[233] which repeals previous directives on free movement of workers and self-employed persons[234] and replaces them with a uniform set of rules, which also applies to non-economically active citizens of the Union (see para. 6-010 *et seq., supra*).

7.057

The right of residence of a qualifying worker extends to his or her spouse or registered partner and their descendants who are under the age of 21 years or are dependants, as well as to dependent relations in the ascending line of the worker and his or her spouse or registered partner, irrespective of their nationality (Directive 2004/38, Article 2; see para. 6-014, *supra*). Workers and self-employed persons who have been employed in a Member State, and members of their families, are entitled to remain in the territory of that State (Article 45(3)(d) TFEU and Directive 2004/38, Article 17).

b. Prohibition of discriminatory and non-discriminatory obstacles
Content. Article 45(2) TFEU provides that freedom of movement for workers is to entail 'the abolition of any discrimination based on nationality between workers of the Member

7.058

---

[230] See, e.g., C-248/96, *Grahame and Hollanders*, 1997, para. 36 (work in the territory of an overseas territory of a Member State).
[231] 237/83, *Prodest*, 1984, para. 7. See also C-60/93, *Aldewereld*, 1994, paras 14–15 and 20-24; C-544/11, *Petersen and Petersen*, 2013, paras 34–43.
[232] C-214/94, *Boukhalfa*, 1996, paras 15–17. Consequently, the connection is not only with the territory but also with the law of a Member State, see case note by Lhoest (1998) CMLRev 247–67.
[233] See n. 194, *supra*. The Directive was adopted on the basis of Articles 12, 18, 40, 44, and 52 EC [*now Articles 18, 21, 46, 50, and 59 TFEU*].
[234] See in particular, with regard to the free movement of workers: Council Directive 68/360/EEC of 15 October 1968 on the abolition of restrictions on movement and residence for workers of Member States and their families, OJ 1968 English Special Edition (II) 485 (adopted on the basis of Article 40 EC [*now Article 46 TFEU*]). See, with regard to the freedom of establishment, Council Directive 73/148/EEC of 21 May 1973 on the abolition of restrictions on movement and residence within the Community for nationals of Member States with regard to establishment and the provision of services, OJ 1973 L172/14 (adopted on the basis of Article 44 and 52 EC [*now Articles 50 and 59 TFEU*]). See also Regulation (EEC) No. 1251/70 of the Commission of 29 June 1970 on the right of workers to remain in the territory of a Member State after having been employed in that State, OJ 1970 English Special Edition (II) 402; and Council Directive 75/34/EEC of 17 December 1974 concerning the right of nationals of a Member State to remain in the territory of another Member State after having pursued therein an activity in a self-employed category, OJ 1975 L14/10 (adopted on the basis of Article 308 EC [*now Article 352 TFEU*]).

States as regards employment, remuneration and other conditions of work and employment'. In addition, the first para. of Article 49 TFEU states that 'restrictions on the freedom of establishment of nationals of a Member State in the territory of another Member State shall be prohibited'. The Treaties preclude not only any form of discrimination in the exercise of free movement of workers (see paras 7-059–7-060, *infra*) and the right of establishment (see paras 7-061–7-062, *infra*), but also measures that are applicable without distinction to a Member State's own nationals and nationals from other Member States if they treat persons less favourably where they exercise, or want to exercise, their right of free movement or of establishment in a Member State other than their own (see para. 7-063, *infra*).

7.059 **Prohibited discrimination against workers.** Article 45(2) TFEU prohibits all direct or indirect discrimination[235] between nationals of a given Member State and nationals of other Member States.[236]

In some cases, the place of residence is held to be an unjustifiable criterion.[237] The Court of Justice has indeed held in several cases concerning fiscal measures that, although the criterion of permanent residence in a Member State applies irrespective of the nationality of the taxpayer concerned, there is a risk that it will work in particular against taxpayers who are nationals of other Member States as it is often such persons who in the course of the year leave the Member State concerned or take up residence there.[238] Nevertheless, a Member State may, in principle, tax the income of a taxpayer who is employed in that State but has his or her residence elsewhere more heavily than the same income of a resident taxpayer. Generally, this will not involve any discrimination since there are objective differences between resident and non-resident taxpayers justifying a difference in treatment, in particular as to concerns taking account of the taxpayer's personal and family circumstances when making an assessment to tax.[239] This will, however, result in unjustified discrimination, where a non-resident taxpayer receives the major part of their income in the Member State in which they work and insufficient income in the State of their residence to enable their personal and family circumstances to be taken into account there for taxation purposes.[240] Such discrimination may take place both against beneficiaries of free movement of workers and beneficiaries of freedom of establishment.[241]

---

[235] For these terms, see paras 5-059–5-060, *supra*.

[236] 152/73 *Sotgiu*, 1974, paras 10–13; 33/88, *Allué and Others*, 1989, paras 11–12; C-90/96, *Petrie and Others*, 1997, paras 53–6. Use of the criterion of nationality does not invariably constitute prohibited discrimination, see C-336/96, *Gilly*, 1998, paras 30–4 (double taxation of frontier workers).

[237] See, e.g., C-350/96, *Clean Car Autoservice*, 1998, paras 26–43.

[238] See, e.g., C-175/88, *Biehl*, 1990, para. 14; C-111/91, *Commission v Luxembourg*, 1993, paras 9–10 and para. 23; C-151/94, *Commission v Luxembourg*, 1995, paras 12–22. See also C-155/09, *Commission v Greece*, 2011, paras 42–9. See further, in respect of the exclusion of children living outside Luxembourg who are dependent on the worker for child benefits, C-802/18, *Caisse pour l'avenir des enfants*, 2020, para. 65.

[239] C-279/93, *Schumacker*, 1995, paras 30–5; C-336/96, *Gilly*, 1998, paras 47–50; C-391/97, *Gschwind*, 1999, paras 20–32.

[240] C-279/93, *Schumacker*, 1995, paras 36–47.

[241] C-80/94, *Wielockx*, 1995, paras 20–7. See also the (unjustified) indirect discrimination in C-107/94, *Asscher*, 1996, paras 37–49. See Weber, 'In Search of a New Equilibrium between Tax Sovereignty and the Freedom of Movement within the EC' (2007) Intertax 585–616; Wattel, 'Red Herrings in Direct Tax Cases before the ECJ' (2004) LIEI 81–95; Van Thiel, 'Removal of Income Tax Barriers to Market Integration in the European Union: Litigation by the Community Citizen Instead of Harmonisation by the Community legislature?' (2003) EC Tax Rev 4–19; Farmer, 'The Court's Case Law on Taxation: A Castle Built on Shifting Sands?' (2003) EC Tax Rev 75–81; Vanistendael, 'The Compatibility of the Basic Economic Freedoms with the Sovereign National Tax Systems of the Member States' (2003) EC Tax Rev 136–43; Vanistendael, 'The Consequences of *Schumacker* and *Wielockx*: Two Steps Forward in the Tax Procession of Echternach' (1996) CMLRev 255–69; Keeling and Shipwright, 'Some

Since free movement of workers holds good for all forms of gainful employment, discrimination on grounds of nationality is prohibited, in principle, in professional sport. Nevertheless, the Court of Justice has accepted that foreign players may be excluded from certain matches for reasons of a non-economic nature which relate to the particular nature and context of such matches and are thus of sporting interest only, such as matches between national teams from different countries.[242] In *Bosman* the Court made clear that nationality clauses are contrary to Article 45 TFEU for matches between football clubs composed of professional players.[243]

The right to free movement does not guarantee workers that any move to another Member State will be wholly neutral in respect of social security, as such a move may be less or more advantageous due to the differences between the national legislations. This holds true, in particular, in areas where the Member States are free to determine the connecting factors under their legislation, in the absence of harmonization or coordination by the Union. One example concerns the scope of application of national rules governing collective representation of employees in the management and governance bodies of a company, which the Member States are free to limit to employees who work at establishments of that company on their territory.[244]

Equal treatment for migrant workers. The prohibition of discrimination was further specified in Council Regulation No. 1612/68 of 15 October 1968,[245] which has since been replaced by Regulation No. 492/2011 of the European Parliament and of the Council.[246] The latter regulation guarantees equal treatment within a given Member State of national workers and workers who are nationals of other Member States as regards all conditions of employment and work, in particular as regards remuneration, dismissal, and, in the event of unemployment, reinstatement or re-employment (Article 7(1)); social and tax advantages (Article 7(2)); access to vocational training schools and retraining centres (Article 7(3)); membership of trade unions and the exercise of trade-union rights, including the right to vote (Article 8(1)); and housing (Article 9).[247] Union legislation confers on the worker's spouse and dependent children the right to take up any activity as an employed person.[248] In addition, migrant workers' children must be admitted to general educational, apprenticeship, and vocational training courses under the same conditions as nationals of the host

7.060

Taxing Problems concerning Non-Discrimination and the EC Treaty' (1995) ELRev 580–97; for testing tax rules against the right of establishment, see also para. 7-066, *infra*.

[242] 13/76 *Donà*, 1976, paras 14–15.

[243] C-415/93, *Bosman*, 1995, paras 127–37 (for the ruling on transfer fees, see para. 7-062, *infra*). Nationals of countries can also invoke the prohibition of discrimination on the basis of association agreements concluded by the Union with third countries, see C-438/00, *Kolpak*, 2003, paras 24–58 (concerning a Slovakian handball player), and Pautot, 'La liberté de circulation des sportifs professionnels en Europe' (2001) RMCUE 102–5. For the controversial case of *Bosman*, see Defalque (1996) JT 539–46; Hilf and Pache (1996) NJW 1169–77; Weatherill (1996) CMLRev 991–1033; Van Nuffel (1996) Col JEL 345–59, and a number of articles in (1996) RMCUE For sport, see also para. 9-051, *infra*.

[244] C-566/15, *Erzberger*, 2017, paras 34–40.

[245] Regulation (EEC) No. 1612/68 of the Council of 15 October 1968 on freedom of movement for workers within the Community, OJ 1968 English Special Edition (II) 475.

[246] Regulation (EU) No. 492/2011 of the European Parliament and of the Council of 5 April 2011 on freedom of movement for workers within the Union, OJ 2011 L141/1.

[247] These articles were numbered in the same manner in both Regulation 1612/68 and Regulation 492/2011.

[248] Regulation No. 1612/68, Article 11, now replaced by Article 23 of Directive 2004/38 (see para. 7-057, *supra*).

Member State (Article 10 of Regulation 492/2011).[249] This right to access to education goes together with a right of residence for these children and the parent(s) who care for them (see para. 6-014, *supra*) as well as with the right to equal treatment as regards entitlement to the social advantages laid down in Article 7(2) of that regulation, which, like the rights of residence, originally has its source in the status of the parent concerned as a worker but must be maintained after the loss of that status so as to prevent the children's right to equal access to education from being deprived of any practical effect.[250]

The Court of Justice has associated application of the requirement for equal treatment primarily with the expression 'social and tax advantages' (Article 7(2) Regulation 492/2011), defining it very broadly as all advantages 'which, whether or not linked to a contract of employment, are generally granted to national workers primarily because of their objective status of workers or by virtue of the mere fact of their residence on the national territory and the extension of which to workers who are nationals of other Member States therefore seems suitable to facilitate their mobility within the [Union]'.[251] Accordingly, the Court of Justice counted as a social advantage the migrant worker's right to use his or her own language—in proceedings not linked to the employment relationship—before the courts of the Member State in which he or she resided, on the ground that this played 'an important role in the integration of a migrant worker and his [her] family into the host country'.[252] In the same spirit, Article 7(2) of the Regulation puts a Member State that allows its nationals to obtain permission for foreign unmarried companions to reside with them under a duty to afford the same opportunity to nationals of another Member State.[253] The grant of a social advantage may not, in principle, be made dependent on the condition that the worker or members of his or her family dependent upon him or her be resident within the territory of the Member of State of employment.[254] A worker may rely on Article 7(2) if he or she was carrying on an activity as an employed person in his or her host Member State at the time of the accession of his or her Member State of origin to the Union and has continued to carry on such activity after that accession.[255] Still, a Member State may restrict entitlement to certain social benefits to persons resident in its territory where this condition of residence is objectively justified and proportionate to the objective pursued.[256]

7.061 **Prohibited discrimination with respect to establishment.** As far as freedom of establishment is concerned, the Court of Justice held in *Reyners* that the prohibition of discrimination

---

[249] This provision corresponds to Article 12 of Regulation 1612/68.
[250] C-181/19, *Jobcenter Krefeld—Widerspruchsstelle*, 2020, paras 40–55.
[251] 207/78, *Even*, 1979, para. 22. For the concept of 'social advantages', see Ellis, 'Social Advantages: A New Lease of Life?' (2003) CMLRev 639, 642–52. This includes, for example, a maintenance grant for the pursuit of university studies (39/86 *Lair*, 1988, para. 28); a funeral payment (C-237/94, *O'Flynn*, 1996, paras 17–30); unemployment benefits paid to young people who have just completed their studies ('tideover allowances') and are the dependants of workers resident in Belgium (C-278/94, *Commission v Belgium*, 1996, paras 25–31); a benefit conditional on residence (C-57/96, *Meints*, 1997, paras 44–8); the grant of a savings-pension bonus (C-269/07 *Commission v Germany*, 2009, paras 37–47); benefits to cover subsistence costs (C-181/19, *Jobcenter Krefeld—Widerspruchsstelle*, 2020, paras 41–2). See also note by Peers to *O'Flynn* and *Commission v Belgium* (1997) ELRev 157–65.
[252] 137/84 *Mutsch*, 1985, paras 16–17. For the extension of this right to all persons who exercise their right of free movement, see C-274/96, *Bickel and Franz*, 1998, paras 13–31 (see para. 5-055, *supra*).
[253] 59/85 *Reed*, 1986, paras 28–9.
[254] C-337/97, *Meeusen*, 1999, paras 21–5; C-447/18, *UB*, 2019, para. 41. See also C-542/09, *Commission v Netherlands*, 2012, 31–55 (discriminatory residence requirement for funding of studies pursued outside the Netherlands).
[255] C-447/18, *UB*, 2019, para. 42.
[256] C-213/05, *Geven*, 2007, paras 26–30; C-287/05, *Hendrix*, 2007, paras 50–8.

on grounds of nationality laid down in Article 43 EC [*now Article 49 TFEU*] has direct effect.[257] Article 49 TFEU not only prohibits direct discrimination on the grounds of nationality but also prohibits indirect discrimination, such as the refusal of the Paris Bar to admit a Belgian who held a Belgian diploma recognized by a French university as equivalent to the requisite French degree and, in addition, had fulfilled the French vocational training requirements for persons not holding a French diploma.[258] Thus, Article 49 TFEU prohibits any national rule which places nationals of another Member State in a less favourable situation than nationals of the Member State in question in the exercise of a self-employed activity. A Member State restricts the freedom of establishment by giving a permit only to companies who already have their seat or another form of establishment on the territory of that Member State.[259] The Court further held German legislation obliging a Greek hydrotherapist to have his name entered in the registers of civil status in a form modifying its pronunciation and thereby causing potential clients possibly to confuse him with other persons to be contrary to Article 49 TFEU.[260] Freedom of establishment also means that self-employed persons from other Member States enjoy non-discriminatory access to social advantages to which they would be entitled under Regulation No. 492/2011 (see para. 7-060, *supra*) if they were workers.[261]

Since the 'nationality' of companies normally flows from the place of their seat, indirect discrimination will arise where a Member State employs a criterion which is liable to work more particularly to the disadvantage of companies having their seat in other Member States.[262] Hence, the legislation of a Member State may not provide for a difference in treatment between taxpayers on the basis of the place where the company owned by those taxpayers employs a certain number of workers for a certain period of time.[263] However, a progressive turnover tax on retailers is not discriminatory on the sole basis that foreign retail chains are in fact far more likely to fall within the higher tax bands than local supermarkets.[264]

Indirect discrimination also arises where a Member State directly awards a concession to an undertaking established in that Member State, because this works to the detriment of undertakings located in another Member State to which the concession may also be of interest.[265] The prohibition of direct or indirect discrimination on grounds of nationality must also be taken into account in registering vessels. Such a grant of 'nationality' to a vessel is a condition for the exercise of the right of establishment which cannot be made to depend

---

[257] 2/74 *Reyners*, 1974, para. 30.
[258] 71/76, *Thieffry*, 1977, para. 19. For architects, see 11/77, *Patrick*, 1977, para. 18; for employees, see 222/86 *Heylens*, 1987, paras 11–12 (football trainer).
[259] C-338/09, *Yellow Cab Verkehrsbetriebs*, 2010, paras 35–40.
[260] C-168/91, *Konstantinidis*, 1993, para. 17.
[261] C-111/91, *Commission v Luxembourg*, 1993, paras 16–18 and 33. C-337/97, *Meeusen*, 1999, paras 26–30.
[262] C-330/91, *Commerzbank*, 1993, paras 13–15 (residence for tax purposes); C-101/94, *Commission v Italy*, 1996, paras 8–28 (corporate seat); C-311/97, *Royal Bank of Scotland*, 1999, paras 28–31 (discrimination as compared with national companies in a like situation); C-397/98 and C-410/98, *Metallgesellschaft and Others*, 2001, paras 37–76 (discrimination against subsidiaries of foreign companies as compared with subsidiaries of domestic companies).
[263] C-464/05, *Geurts and Vogten*, 2007, paras 18–22; case note by Parisis (2008) JTDE 76–9.
[264] C-323/18, *Tesco-Global Áruházak*, 2020, paras 58–76. See also, for a turnover tax on telecom providers, C-75/18, *Vodafone Magyarország Mobil Távközlési*, 2020, paras 38–56.
[265] C-231/03, *Coname*, 2005, paras 17–20.

190   THE INTERNAL MARKET

on the nationality of the owners or charterers and, in the case of a company, on the nationality of the shareholders or directors, or on their place of residence or domicile.[266]

The Court of Justice has held that it is a 'corollary' of free movement of persons, in particular the right to pursue an employed or self-employed activity in another Member State and to reside there after having pursued such an activity, that there should be access to leisure activities available in that Member State. Therefore, French legislation under which only French nationals could register a leisure craft in France was held not to be compatible with free movement.[267] It clearly emerges from this case law that the Court treats the Treaty provisions on free movement of workers and freedom of establishment as having to be read together in governing free movement of persons.

7.062   **Non-discriminatory obstacles.** The Treaty provisions on free movement of persons also preclude a restriction of the mobility of economic operators if the restriction applies without distinction to a Member State's own nationals and nationals of other Member States. In the 1988 judgment in *Wolf*, the Court of Justice declared incompatible with the principles of free movement of persons a national measure which both in law and in fact was applicable in the same way to nationals of the Member State in question and to nationals of other Member States but nevertheless restricted free movement of persons because it treated *all* Union nationals less favourably where they had been employed in the territory of more than one Member State.[268] The 1993 judgment in *Kraus* took the further step of aligning the effect of the provisions on free movement of persons very closely with that of the provisions on free movement of goods and services. The Court of Justice held that the Treaty provisions on the free movement of persons preclude any national measure which, even though it is applicable without discrimination on grounds of nationality, is liable to hamper or to render less attractive the exercise by a national of any Member State of fundamental freedoms guaranteed by the Treaties.[269] Kraus, a German national, challenged a German provision requiring German nationals (and nationals of other Member States) to apply for authorization in order to use an academic title of Master of Laws (LLM) obtained in another Member State. The Court of Justice held that this would accord with the Treaty provisions on the free movement of persons only in so far as the obligation was proportionate to the aim of protecting the public and intended solely to verify that the title was properly awarded.[270] It follows that these Treaty provisions prohibit all measures that disadvantage nationals of a Member State who exercised their right to free movement through employment or other activities in another Member State or who intend to exercise this right.

---

[266] C-221/89, *Factortame Limited and Others* (*Factortame II*), 1991, paras 22–33; the same form of words is to be found in C-246/89 *Commission v United Kingdom*, 1991, paras 23–31; C-93/89, *Commission v Ireland*, 1991, paras 10–11; C-334/94 *Commission v France*, 1996, paras 12–19; C-62/96, *Commission v Greece*, 1997, paras 17–18. More recently, the Court clarified that even a condition of having the nationality of one of the Member States or EEA States (as opposed to requiring the nationality of one specific Member State) is not compatible with Article 43 EC [*now Article 49 TFEU*] (C-299/02, *Commission v Netherlands*, 2004, paras 19–26).

[267] C-334/94 *Commission v France*, 1996, paras 21–3; C-151/96, *Commission v Ireland*, 1997, paras 11–16; C-62/96, *Commission v Greece*, 1997, paras 19–20.

[268] 154-155/87, *Wolf and Microtherm Europe*, 1988, paras 9–14. See also 143/87 *Stanton*, 1988, paras 9–14, delivered on the same date.

[269] C-19/92, *Kraus*, 1993, para. 32; with case notes by Roth (1993) CMLRev 1251–58, and Denys (1994) C.D.E. 638–62.

[270] C-19/92, *Kraus*, 1993, paras 32–8.

Similarly, the Court considered that a Member State may not, without due justification, make the exercise of a profession dependent on the condition of having previously been established in a region of that Member State because such a condition is unfavourable to persons who have exercised their freedom of establishment by practising that profession in another Member State.[271] Likewise, the Court held that whereas it may be appropriate to require job candidates to prove their bilingualism, such a requirement is disproportionate to the objective pursued if it is impossible to provide proof thereof in any other way than by providing a certificate obtained in that province or that Member State.[272] In addition, the requirement that an activity as an accountant in Belgium requires prior authorization and cannot be combined with any other artisanal, agricultural, or commercial activity, is non-discriminatory to the extent that it applies regardless of the nationality of the accountant, but may still have the effect of discouraging accountants from other Member States, where those restrictions do not apply, from having an establishment in Belgium.[273]

Consequently, provisions which preclude or deter a national of a Member State from leaving the Member State in which he or she is pursuing an economic activity in order to exercise the right to freedom of movement constitute an obstacle to that freedom even if they apply without regard to the nationality of the worker concerned.[274] With regard to free movement of workers, the Court of Justice has held that such an obstacle exists only where such provisions affect access of workers to the labour market.[275] In *Bosman* the Court characterized as an obstacle to free movement of workers the transfer rules adopted by sports associations according to which, at the expiry of his contract, a professional footballer could be taken on by a new club only if it paid his old club a transfer fee.[276] In *Krah* the Court found that rules of an Austrian university that restricted the number of years worked in a particular academic position at another university, whether located in Austria or in another Member State, to be taken into account for determining seniority to be an obstacle to free movement of workers as they could discourage academics abroad to leave their Member State and apply for a post at the Austrian university.[277] With respect to the right of establishment, the Court equally held that a restriction of that right may exist where a national measure has the effect of restricting access to the market of the Member State concerned.[278] That is the case for measures of a Member State that reserve the exercise of a self-employed activity to

---

[271] C-456/05, *Commission v Germany*, 2007.
[272] C-281/98, *Angonese*, 2000, paras 37–46; C-317/14, *Commission v Belgium*, 2015, paras 28–31.
[273] C-384/18, *Commission v Belgium*, 2020, paras 73–81.
[274] C-18/95, *Terhoeve*, 1999, para. 39; C-232/01, *Van Lent*, 2003, para. 16; C-209/01, *Schilling and Fleck-Schilling*, 2003, para. 25; C-464/02, *Commission v Denmark*, 2005, para. 35; C-345/05, *Commission v Portugal*, 2006, para. 16; C-104/06, *Commission v Sweden*, 2007, para. 18; C-522/04, *Commission v Belgium*, 2007, para. 65; C-318/05, *Commission v Germany*, 2007, para. 114.
[275] C-190/98, *Graf*, 2000, para. 23 (if not there would only be a 'too uncertain and indirect' possibility within the meaning of the case law on free movement of goods cited in n. 96, *supra*: ibid., para. 25). See Ranocher, 'Grundfreiheiten und Spürbarkeitstheorie' (2001) ZfRV 95–107.
[276] C-415/93, *Bosman*, 1995, paras 94–104 (for commentaries, see n. 243, *supra*). See also C-325/08, *Olympique Lyonnais*, 2010, paras 27–37 (obligation for a young professional footballer to sign a contract at the end of his training period held to be a restriction on the free movement of workers).
[277] C-703/17, *Krah*, 2019, paras 47–54. Compare with an earlier case, in which it was considered 'too uncertain and indirect' for Austrian rules on seniority in the context of additional paid annual leave to be capable of being regarded as hindering free movement of workers: C-437/17, *Gemeinsamer Betriebsrat EurothermenResort Bad Schallerbach*, 2019, paras 35–41.
[278] C-442/02, *CaixaBank France*, 2004, paras 12–14, with note by Spaventa (2005) CMLRev 1151–68; C-518/06, *Commission v Italy*, 2009, paras 64–71; C-384/08, *Attanasio Group*, 2010, paras 44–5; C-565/08, *Commission v Italy*, 2011, paras 46–53.

certain economic operators, such as allowing only pharmacists to operate pharmacies.[279] The freedom of market access entails the freedom to determine the nature and size of the economic activity that will be developed in the host Member State, and thus also the right to reduce that activity or to divest and terminate the establishment.[280]

Given that Articles 45 and 49 TFEU are applicable to the situation of a national of a Member State who is a worker or self-employed person in a Member State other than the one in which he or she resides, those articles preclude Member States from enacting measures that deter nationals from taking up residence in another Member State, for example by refusing a subsidy for owner-occupied dwellings if the dwelling built or purchased is situated in the territory of another Member State.[281]

By prohibiting discriminatory and non-discriminatory obstacles that limit market access, the case law on the free movement of persons comes close to the Court's holding that a measure of a Member State is an 'obstacle' to the free movement of goods when it treats goods coming from another Member State less favourably by applying measures that are directly or indirectly discriminatory, or by denying access to the market of that Member State in a different manner (see para. 7-028, *supra*).[282] As in the case of the free movement of goods, an obstacle to free movement of persons may be justified by pressing reasons of public interest, provided that it applies without distinction as to nationality, is appropriate, and does not exceed what is necessary to attain its intended objective (see para. 7-070 *et seq.*, *infra*).

c. Primary and secondary right of establishment

7.063 **Definition of establishment.** According to the second para. of Article 49 TFEU, freedom of establishment includes 'the right to take up and pursue activities as self-employed persons and to set up and manage undertakings, in particular companies and firms within the meaning of the second para. of Article 54, under the conditions laid down for its own nationals by the law of the country where such establishment is effected'. The term 'establishment' is broadly construed in the case law so as to allow a Union citizen to participate, on a stable and continuous basis, in the economic life of a Member State other than his or her Member State of origin and to profit therefrom, so as to contribute to economic and social interpenetration within the Union in the sphere of activities of a self-employed person.[283] However, the substance of the freedom of establishment is not the same in the case of natural persons or of companies.

7.064 **Natural persons.** As far as natural persons are concerned, freedom of establishment encompasses, alongside the right to create a first establishment in the territory of another Member State (the primary right of establishment), a secondary right of establishment in order to 'set up and maintain, subject to observance of the professional rules of conduct, more than one place of work within the [Union]'.[284] A self-employed person may open a

---

[279] C-531/06, *Commission v Italy*, 2009, paras 44–5.
[280] C-201/15, *AGET Iraklis*, 2016, para. 53.
[281] C-152/05, *Commission v Germany*, 2008, paras 20–5.
[282] C-456/05, *Commission v Germany*, 2007, paras 51–60.
[283] C-55/94, *Gebhard*, 1995, para. 25, with case notes by Ballon (1996/97) Col JEL 145–51; Goffin (1996) CDE 723–43.
[284] 107/83, *Klopp*, 1984, para. 19.

second office in another Member State or participate in setting up a company.[285] Article 49 TFEU provides that the prohibition of restrictions on the freedom of establishment is also to apply to restrictions on the 'setting-up of agencies, branches or subsidiaries by nationals of any Member State established in the territory of any Member State'.

Companies. Union law recognizes a secondary right of establishment for companies incorporated under the law of a Member State, but not the primary right to move their seat. Unlike natural persons, companies exist only by virtue of the law determining the conditions governing their formation and operation. Member States' legislation differs considerably in terms of the connection required to exist with the national territory when setting up a company under national law and with regard to changing that connection.[286] Hence, Article 54 TFEU recognizes three criteria for conferring the 'nationality' of a Member State on a company: the statutory seat, the place of central management and control, and the place of central administration.

7.065

In the absence of rules laid down by Union legislation or by convention, the Court of Justice has held that Articles 49 and 54 TFEU do not confer on companies incorporated under the laws of a Member State a right to transfer their central management and control and their central administration to another Member State while retaining their status as companies incorporated under the legislation of the first Member State.[287] Indeed, the power of a Member State to define the connecting factor required of a company governed by its law includes the possibility not to permit such a company to retain that status if the company intends to reorganize itself in another Member State by moving its seat to the territory of the latter, thereby breaking the connecting factor required under the national law of the Member State of incorporation.[288] However, the Member State in which a company is incorporated may not, without due justification, prevent that company from converting itself into a company governed by the law of the Member State to which it transfers its central management and control.[289] Likewise, Articles 49 and 54 TFEU preclude requiring a company formed in one Member State to be reincorporated in another Member State in order for it to retain legal capacity in this latter Member State.[290] The freedom of establishment is also applicable to the transfer of the registered office of a company formed in accordance

---

[285] In *Klopp* (see preceding n.), the Court of Justice held that a lawyer was entitled to open a second set of chambers in another Member State. See also C-55/94, *Gebhard*, 1995, para. 24; C-53/95, *Kemmler*, 1996, paras 10–14. See, with regard to auditors, C-106/91, *Ramrath*, 1992, para. 22, and with regard to doctors, dentists, and veterinary surgeons, C-351/90, *Commission v Luxembourg*, 1992, para. 24.

[286] See Halbhuber, 'National Doctrinal Structures and European Company Law' (2001) CMLRev 1385–420.

[287] 81/87, *Daily Mail and General Trust PLC*, 1988, para. 24; C-210/06, *Cartesio*, 2008, para. 124.

[288] C-210/06, *Cartesio*, 2008, paras 110.

[289] C-210/06, *Cartesio*, 2008, paras 111–13.

[290] C-208/00, *Überseering*, 2002, paras 52–94 (a Member State cannot deny a company legal capacity on the basis of the presumption that it has moved its actual centre of administration to its territory). See Engsing Sørensen, 'The Fight against Letterbox Companies in the Internal Market' (2015) CMLRev 85–117; Roth, 'From Centros to Überseering: Free Movement of Companies, Private International Law, and Community Law' (2003) ICLQ 177–208; Jonet, 'Sociétés commerciales—La théorie du siège réel à l'épreuve de la liberté d'établissement' (2003) JTDE 33–7; Rammeloo, 'The Long and Winding Road Towards Freedom of Establishment for Legal Persons in Europe' (2003) MJECL 169–96; Lombardo, 'Conflict of Law Rules in Company Law after *Überseering*: An Economic and Comparative Analysis of the Allocation of Policy Competence in the European Union' (2003) E Bus Org LR 301–36; Ballarino, 'Les règles de conflit sur les sociétés commerciales à l'épreuve du droit communautaire d'établissement' (2003) RCDIP 373–402. For a survey of the constraints which Union law places on the 'emigration' and 'immigration' of companies, see Wymeersch, 'The Transfer of the Company's Seat in European Company Law' (2003) CMLRev 661–95.

with the law of one Member State to the territory of another Member State, for the purposes of its conversion, in accordance with the conditions imposed by the legislation of this other Member State, into a company incorporated under the law of the latter Member State, when there is no change in the location of the real head office of that company.[291] If a Member State allows a company to transfer its seat to another Member state while retaining the status of company under the laws of the first Member State, such a transfer of seat may not result in unjustified disadvantages for that company.[292] In any event, a Member State is precluded from providing that the transfer of the registered office of a company incorporated under the law of that Member State to another Member State, for the purposes of its conversion into a company incorporated under the law of the latter Member State, is subject to the prior liquidation of the company in the first Member State.[293]

7.066 **Secondary right of establishment.** Union law confers a secondary right of establishment on companies incorporated under the laws of a Member State to set up agencies, branches, and subsidiaries in other Member States.[294] In the case of subsidiaries, the right to secondary establishment will often imply shareholdings. However, Article 49 TFEU solely concerns national legislation intended to apply to those shareholdings which enable the holder to exert a definite influence on a company's decisions and to determine its activities.[295]

It is inherent in the exercise of the freedom of establishment that a national of a Member State who wishes to set up a company may choose to form it in the Member State whose rules of company law seem to him or her the least restrictive and then to set up branches in other Member States. The fact that a company is incorporated in a particular Member State in order to take advantage of more favourable legislative rules therefore does not in itself constitute an abuse of the right of establishment.[296] When a company wishes to establish a branch in another Member State, a Member State cannot impose conditions on setting up this branch solely on the ground that the parent company does not conduct any business in the Member State in which it is established and pursues its activities only in the Member State where its branch is established.[297] Moreover, all restrictions imposed on grounds of imperative requirements in the general interest (e.g. in relation to combating fraud or protecting creditors) must satisfy the requirement of proportionality.[298]

---

[291] C-106/16, *Polbud—Wykonawstwo*, 2017, paras 29–44, with note by Benedetti and Van Waeyenberge, (2019) ELRev 416–30; Szydło (2018) CMLRev 1549–72. See also C-66/18, *Commission v Hungary*, 2020, paras 159–63.
[292] C-371/10, *National Grid Indus*, 2011, paras 37–86.
[293] C-106/16, *Polbud—Wykonawstwo*, 2017, paras 46–65.
[294] See Roussos, 'Realising the Free Movement of Companies' (2001) E Bus LRev 7–25; Drury, 'Migrating Companies' (1999) ELRev 354–72.
[295] C-323/18, *Tesco-Global Áruházak*, 2020, para. 52 (see also para. 7-012, *supra*). Measures restricting non-controlling shareholdings are assessed under the free movement of capital (para. 7-101, *infra*).
[296] C-212/97, *Centros*, 1999, paras 18–27; C-167/01, *Inspire Art*, 2003, paras 95–8 and 136–8; C-196/04, *Cadbury Schweppes*, 2006, para. 37. However, in so far as such action does not conflict with freedom of establishment, a Member State is entitled to take measures designed to prevent certain of its nationals from attempting, under cover of the rights created by the Treaty, improperly to circumvent their national legislation: *Centros*, paras 24–5; *Inspire Act*, para. 136; *Cadbury Schweppes*, para. 35.
[297] C-212/97, *Centros*, 1999, para. 29; C-167/01, *Inspire Art*, 2003.
[298] See, e.g., C-212/97, *Centros*, 1999, paras 34–8; C-167/01, *Inspire Art*, 2003, paras 133–4. See Behrens, 'Reactions of Member State Courts to the *Centros* Ruling by the ECJ' (2001) E Bus Org LJ 159–74; Wouters, 'Private International Law and Companies' Freedom of Establishment' (2001) E Bus Org LR 101–39; Forsthoff, 'Niederlassungsrecht für Gesellschaften nach dem *Centros*-Urteil des EuGH: Eine Bilanz' (2000) EuR 167–96; Ebke '*Centros*—Some Realities and Some Mysteries' (2000) AJCL 623–60.

The provisions concerning freedom of establishment prohibit the Member State of origin from hindering the establishment in another Member State of agencies, branches, or subsidiaries of a company incorporated under its legislation.[299] Article 49 TFEU therefore precludes national legislation that confers tax advantages to parent companies whose subsidiaries are established in the same Member State, but not at all, or only under less favourable conditions, to parent companies with subsidiaries in other Member States.[300] The freedom of establishment is equally restricted when a Member State subjects subsidiaries of companies established in another Member State to a less favourable tax regime than subsidiaries of domestic companies.[301] Likewise, Article 49 precludes national legislation which, in the case of companies established in the Member State concerned belonging to a consortium, makes a form of tax relief subject to the requirement that the holding company's business consists wholly or mainly of the holding of shares in subsidiaries established in that Member State.[302] The exercise of the freedom of establishment is equally deterred by national rules that do not allow for the registration of mergers when some of the companies concerned are established in another Member State.[303] In the same vein, it would run counter to Article 49 to make the registration or operation with a view to carrying out an economic activity in a Member State of vessels owned by a legal person conditional on the seat of that legal person being located in that Member State. Such a condition would preclude the operation of such vessels by agencies, branches, or subsidiaries of companies established in another Member State.[304]

4. Permitted restrictions
a. Restrictions on grounds of public policy, public security, and public health

Justificatory grounds. Under Article 45(3) TFEU, Member States may place limitations on the free movement of workers on grounds of public policy (*ordre public*), public security, or public health. In some cases, individuals may also rely on these justificatory grounds.[305] Restrictions may also be imposed on freedom of establishment on the same grounds (Article 52(1) TFEU).

7.067

Just like for the justifications set out in the Treaty for restrictions to the free movement of goods, a Member State may no longer justify a measure on the basis of Articles 45(3) or 52(1) TFEU where the interest in question has been harmonized at Union level. That is the case for administrative requirements with respect to the setting-up or carrying-out of economic activities that fall within the scope of application of Directive 2006/123 (the 'Services

---

[299] C-264/96, *ICI*, 1998, para. 21; C-446/03, *Marks & Spencer*, 2005, para. 31; C-196/04, *Cadbury Schweppes*, 2006, para. 42. See also C-170/05, *Denkavit*, 2006, paras 20–30 (tax emption of dividendes paid to subsidiary conditional on parent company being a resident of the Member State concerned); C-650/16, *A/S Bevola*, 2018, paras 15–20.

[300] C-200/98, *X and Y*, 1999; C-251/98, *Baars*, 2000; C-446/03, *Marks & Spencer*, 2005, paras 30–4.

[301] C-397/98 and C-410/98, *Metallgesellschaft and Others*, 2001, paras 37–76; C-231/05, *Oy AA*, 2007, paras 30–43; C-650/16, *A/S Bevola*, 2018, paras 21–66.

[302] C-264/96, *ICI*, 1998, paras 22–30. See Travers, 'Residence Restraints on the Transferability of Corporate Trading Losses and the Right of Establishment in Community Law' (1999) ELRev 403–25. For other tax rules held to be contrary to Article 43 EC [*now Article 49 TFEU*], see, e.g., C-254/97, *Baxter*, 1999 (tax deductibility of costs of research only if research carried out in the Member State); C-141/99, *AMID*, 2000 (loss not capable of being set off against the profit made during previous years in so far as the profit came from a permanent establishment abroad).

[303] C-411/03, *SEVIC Systems*, 2005, paras 20–3.

[304] C-334/94, *Commission v France*, 1996, paras 16 and 19; see also C-221/89, *Factortame Limited and Others* (*Factortame II*), 1991, para. 35. See, with regard to aircraft, C-203/98, *Commission v Belgium*, 1999.

[305] C-415/93, *Bosman*, 1995, para. 86; C-350/96, *Clean Car Autoservice*, 1998, para. 24.

Directive'), following which Member States may no longer justify, on the basis of primary Union law, any requirement prohibited by Article 14 of that Directive[306] (see para. 7-115, *infra*).

As regards restrictions to residence rights, the justificatory grounds set out in the Treaties are further fleshed out in Directive 2004/38 of the European Parliament and of the Council,[307] which codifies all existing Union legislation on the right of citizens of the Union to reside within the territory of the Member States (see para. 6-016, *supra*). The Directive makes clear that a measure may only be justified on one of those grounds in so far as it is proportional to the aim pursued thereby.[308] The rights associated with citizenship of the Union demand that any such derogation from the principle of free movement be interpreted strictly.[309] By virtue of Article 45(3) TFEU a Member State may refuse to allow a worker who is a national of another Member State or his or her family members, regardless of their nationality, to enter its territory or reside therein only on the ground that his or her presence or conduct constitutes a genuine and sufficiently serious threat to the requirements of public policy,[310] affecting one of the fundamental interests of society.[311] Although Union law does not impose upon the Member States a uniform scale of values, it does not permit a Member State to apply an arbitrary distinction to the detriment of nationals of other Member States. The Court of Justice held, for example, that conduct on the part of nationals of other Member States is not a sufficiently serious threat where similar conduct by nationals of the Member State in question does not give rise to repressive measures or other genuine and effective measures intended to combat such conduct.[312] A genuine and sufficiently serious threat affecting one of the fundamental interests of society is also required where public policy or public security is invoked as justification for limitations on the freedom of establishment or to provide services, such as a rule that the managers of an undertaking or the seat of an undertaking must be established in the Member State in question.[313] Moreover, Directive 2004/38 requires measures taken on grounds of public policy or public security to be 'based exclusively on the personal conduct of the individual concerned' (see para. 6-016, *supra*).[314]

b. Employment in the public service and exercise of public authority

7.068 **Public service.** According to Article 45(4) TFEU, the provisions of that article do not apply to 'employment in the public service'. This exception applies only to posts 'which involve direct or indirect participation in the exercise of powers conferred by public law and duties designed to safeguard the general interests of the State or of other public authorities', since

---

[306] C-593/13, *Rina Services*, 2015, paras 35–41.

[307] Directive 2004/38/EC of the European Parliament and of the Council of 29 April 2004 on the right of the citizen of the Union and their family members to move and reside freely within the territory of the Member States, OJ 2004 L158/77, Article 27(1).

[308] Ibid., Article 27(2). This principle has been developed in the case law of the Court of Justice, see C-101/94, *Commission v Italy*, 1996, paras 25–6; C-294/00, *Deutsche Paracelsus Schulen für Naturheilverfahren*, 2002, paras 38–66.

[309] C-482/01 and C-493/01, *Orfanopoulos and Others*, 2004, para. 65.

[310] 36/75, *Rutili*, 1975, para. 28. See now Directive 2004/38 (n. 194, *supra*), Article 27(2), second subpara. For an application in respect of establishment, see C-66/18, *Commission v Hungary*, 2020, paras 180–3.

[311] 30/77, *Bouchereau*, 1977, para. 35. See now Directive 2004/38 (n. 194, *supra*), Article 27(2), second subpara.

[312] 115 and 116/81, *Adoui and Cornuaille v Belgium*, 1982, para. 8; See also 249/86, *Commission v Germany*, 1989, paras 17–20; C-363/89, *Roux*, 1991, paras 29–31; C-268/99, *Jany and Others*, 2001, paras 55–62; C-100/01, *Oteiza Olazabal*, 2002, paras 27–45.

[313] C-114/97, *Commission v Spain*, 1998, paras 44–7; C-355/98, *Commission v Belgium*, 2000, paras 27–34.

[314] Directive 2004/38 (n. 194, *supra*), Article 27(2), first subpara.; see previously Directive 64/221, Article 3(1).

such posts presume 'the existence of a special relationship of allegiance to the State and reciprocity of rights and duties which form the foundation of the bond of nationality'.[315] Other posts cannot be reserved for a Member State's own nationals, not even for considerations relating to the preservation of national identity.[316] Moreover, once a worker is admitted into the public service of a Member State, Article 45(4) cannot be relied on by that Member State in order to restrict the rights which he or she derives from Article 45(1) to (3) TFEU.[317] A Member State is also precluded from relying on the exception to limit access to a public service for its own nationals in a situation presenting a connection with free movement.[318]

This restrictive interpretation of the expression 'public service' means that a large number of posts that do not involve the exercise of public authority, but where the employer is a public authority, are not taken outside the scope of the Treaties.[319] The legal categorization of the employment relationship between the employee and the administration—that is to say, whether the relationship is governed by private or public law—is irrelevant for this purpose.[320] Accordingly, the Court of Justice has held that civil servants' and public employees' posts in public water, gas, and electricity distribution services;[321] public-sector research; education; health; postal and telecommunications services;[322] radio and television;[323] some seamen's occupations;[324] private security posts;[325] and members of an occupational guild[326] do not fall within the exception. Even where persons are granted powers conferred by public

---

[315] 149/79, *Commission v Belgium*, 1980, para. 10.

[316] C-473/93, *Commission v Luxembourg*, 1996, para. 35 (there are less far-reaching means of protecting that interest recognized by Article 6(3) EU [*see now Article 4(2) TEU*]). For the impact of Union law on national civil-service law, see Kämmerer, 'Europäisierung des öffentlichen Dienstrechts' (2001) EuR 27–48.

[317] 152/73, *Sotgiu*, 1974, para. 4; C-392/05, *Alevizos*, 2007, para. 70.

[318] C-298/14, *Brouillard*, 2015, para. 33.

[319] A number of guidelines were set out in the Commission communication on its action in respect of the application of Article 48(4) EC [*now Article 45(4) TFEU*]: OJ 1988 C72/2; see Guillén and Fuentetaja, 'Free Movement of Workers and Public Administration: The ECJ Doctrine on the Interpretation of the Scope of Article 39(4) EC' (1999) E Rev Priv L 1567–93; Handoll, 'Article 48(4) EEC and Non-National Access to Public Employment' (1988) ELRev 223–41.

[320] 152/73, *Sotgiu*, 1974, paras 5–6. However, Article 45(4) TFEU does not cover employment by a private natural or legal person: C-283/99, *Commission v Italy*, 2001, para. 25.

[321] C-473/93 *Commission v Luxembourg*, 1996, para. 31; *Commission v Belgium*, 1996, para. 17; C-290/94, *Commission v Greece*, 1996, para. 34. For an early case, see 149/79 *Commission v Belgium*, 1982, paras 8–9 (drivers and manual workers employed by railways).

[322] C-473/93 *Commission v Luxembourg*, 1996, para. 31; C-290/94, *Commission v Greece*, 1996, para. 34. According to the Court of Justice, the following do *not* fall within the exception: various manual occupations, crèche nurses and children's nurses employed by local authorities (149/79, *Commission v Belgium*, 1982, paras 8–9; although the exception was held to cover controllers, night watchmen, and local authority architects); nurses in public hospitals (307/84, *Commission v France*, 1986, para. 13); medical specialists working in the public service (C-15/96, *Schöning-Kougebetopoulou*, 1998, para. 13); directors and teachers in institutions specializing in supplementary instruction and music and dancing schools (147/86, *Commission v Greece*, 1988, paras 19–21); foreign-language assistants at universities (33/88, *Allué and Others*, 1989, para. 9); primary school teachers (C-473/93, *Commission v Luxembourg*, 1996, paras 32–4); secondary school teachers (C-4/91, *Bleis*, 1991, para. 7); trainee teachers (66/85, *Lawrie-Blum*, 1986, paras 27–9); and researchers at a national research institution (225/85, *Commission v Italy*, 1987, para. 9; although the exception was held to cover posts involving management duties or advising the State).

[323] C-290/94, *Commission v Greece*, 1996, para. 34 (which also mentions musicians in municipal and local orchestras and opera houses).

[324] C-37/93, *Commission v Belgium*, 1993, paras 1–6. As far as masters and chief mates are concerned, the Court of Justice has since held that their powers conferred by public law were too incidental to warrant application of the exception: C-405/01, *Colegio de Oficiales de la Marina Mercante Española*, 2003, paras 42–5, and C-47/02, *Anker and Others*, 2003, paras 61–4.

[325] C-114/97, *Commission v Spain*, 1998, para. 33; C-355/99, *Commission v Belgium*, 2000, para. 26; C-283/99, *Commission v Italy*, 2001, para. 20.

[326] C-213/90, *ASTI*, 1991, paras 19–20; C-171/01, *Wählergruppe Gemeinsam*, 2003, paras 90–3.

law, it is still necessary that such powers are exercised on a regular basis by their holders and do not represent a very minor part of their activities in order for them to fall within Article 45(4).[327] The concept of 'employment in the public service' does not encompass employment by a private, natural or legal, person, whatever the duties of the employee.[328]

7.069 **Exercise of official authority.** Nationals of a Member State have no right of establishment in another Member State in respect of 'activities which in that State are connected, even occasionally, with the exercise of official authority' (Article 51 TFEU). This exception is also interpreted restrictively by the Court of Justice. It relates only to activities which 'taken on their own, constitute a direct and specific connection with the exercise of official authority' and not the profession as such of which those activities form a part.[329] Consequently, the profession of a lawyer (*avocat*) cannot be reserved to nationals, since the most typical activities of that profession, such as consultation and legal assistance and representation and defence of parties in courts, cannot be regarded as participating in the exercise of official authority.[330] Sitting as a substitute judge could certainly be restricted to nationals.[331] This is not so for other legal professions, such as a notary[332] or a legal trainee completing his or her training at a court as such a person will act in accordance with the instructions and under the supervision of a training principal.[333] The exception of Article 51 TFEU does not apply to activities that do not imply the power to make decisions, the power to exercise force, or the possibility of taking enforcement measures.[334] Moreover, the exception will not apply when the activities connected with the exercise of official authority are separable from the professional activity in question taken as a whole.[335] Likewise, a private body cannot be regarded as participating in the exercise of official authority where it performs functions that are merely auxiliary and preparatory vis-à-vis an entity which itself exercises official authority.[336] Other examples of activities that the Court has considered not to constitute activities that involve exercising official authority include the activities of road accident experts,[337] court-appointed translators,[338] commissioners with insurance undertakings,[339]

---

[327] C-405/01, *Colegio de Oficiales de la Marina Mercante Española*, 2003, para. 44, and C-47/02, *Anker and Others*, 2003, para. 63.
[328] C-109/04, *Kranemann*, 2005, para. 19; C-345/08, *Peśla*, 2009, para. 29.
[329] 2/74, *Reyners*, 1974, paras 45–6. The following activities have been held not to constitute the exercise of public authority: the establishment of institutions for supplementary instruction and vocational training schools and giving private lessons at home (147/86, *Commission v Greece*, 1988, paras 8–10); the design, programming, and operation of data-processing systems (C-3/88, *Commission v Italy*, 1989, para. 13); the activities of experts on traffic accidents (C-306/89, *Commission v Greece*, 1991, para. 7); the post of 'approved commissioner' with Belgian insurance undertakings (C-42/92, *Thijssen*, 1993, paras 16–22); the concession for a lottery computerization system (C-272/91, *Commission v Italy*, 1994, paras 6–13); the activities of private security undertakings and their staff (C-114/97, *Commission v Spain*, 1998; C-355/98, *Commission v Belgium*, 2000, para. 26; C-283/99, *Commission v Italy*, 2001, para. 20); activities of advice and assistance in tax matters (C-451/03, *Servizi Ausiliari Dottori Commercialisti*, 2006, paras 47–9); and the provision of public emergency services (C-160/08 *Commission v Germany*, 2010, paras 80–6).
[330] *Reyners*, cited in the preceding n., para. 52.
[331] This is probably also true of (Bavarian) lay assessors according to the view taken by the Commission in its answer of 5 September 1996 to Question No. E-1580/96 (Sakellariou), OJ 1996 C356/61.
[332] C-47/08, *Commission v Belgium*, 2011 (and the parallel judgments of the same day in cases C-50/08, C-51/08, C-53/08, C-54/08, and C-61/08); C-342/15, *Piringer*, 2017; C-392/15, *Commisson v Hungary*, 2017.
[333] C-345/08, *Peśla*, 2010, paras 30 and 33.
[334] C-47/08, *Commission v Belgium*, 2011, para. 86 and the cases cited therein.
[335] 2/74, *Reyners*, 1974, para. 47.
[336] C-393/05, *Commission v Austria*, 2007, paras 35–49; C-404/05, *Commission v Germany*, 2007, paras 37–48; C-438/08 *Commission v Portugal*, 2009, paras 36–7.
[337] C-306/89, *Commission v Greece*, 1991, para. 7.
[338] C-372/09 and C-373/09, *Peñarroja Fa*, 2011, paras 43–4.
[339] C-42/92, *Thijssen*, 1993, paras 16–22.

tax advisors,[340] certification services without decision-making powers,[341] private security firms,[342] public ambulance services,[343] and chimney sweeps.[344]

c. Restrictions based on the rule of reason

Rule of reason. So long as the requirements for access to a given occupation have not been harmonized, Member States may themselves determine what knowledge and skills are needed in order to exercise it, and require diplomas or a professional qualification. The case law accepts that the obstacles to free movement of persons created by such requirements may be justified by public-interest requirements, provided that the restriction does not go beyond what is appropriate and necessary in order to satisfy those requirements.[345] More generally, the Court of Justice declares—in terms similar to those employed in its case law on the free movement of goods and services—that national measures liable to hinder or render less attractive the exercise of free movement of workers or self-employed persons may be compatible with the freedoms guaranteed by the Treaties if they satisfy the following conditions (rule of reason).[346]   **7.070**

(1) **Absence of harmonization.** Member States can only invoke public-interest requirements to justify restrictions in matters that have not been harmonized at Union level.[347] As set out above, for administrative requirements prohibited by Article 14 Directive 2006/123 (the 'Services Directive'), that means that there can be no justification by invoking legitimate interests recognized in the Court's case law under the right of establishment (see further para. 7-115, *infra*).   **7.071**

(2) **Mandatory requirements.** The measures must be justified by mandatory requirements in the general interest. As regards measures governing the exercise of a professional activity, these may consist of rules relating to organization, qualifications, professional ethics, supervision, and liability[348] and with regard to the knowledge of languages required in order to exercise the professional activity.[349] More generally, however, obstacles to the free movement of persons may be justified to attain policy aims accepted by the case law in the areas of trade in goods and services, such as consumer protection;[350] protection of public health;[351] road traffic   **7.072**

---

[340] C-451/03, *Servizi Ausiliari Dottori Commercialisti*, 2006, paras 47–9.
[341] C-327/12, *SOA Nazionale Costruttori*, 2013, paras 50–4. But see C-142/20, *Analisi G. Caracciolo*, 2021, paras 52–3.
[342] C-355/98, *Commission v Belgium*, 2000, para. 26.
[343] C-160/08, *Commission v Germany*, 2010, paras 80–6.
[344] C-293/14, *Hiebler*, 2015, paras 32–9.
[345] See 96/85, *Commission v France*, 1986, para. 11 (self-employed persons); C-204/90, *Bachmann*, 1992, para. 28 (employees).
[346] For a list of the conditions, see C-55/94, *Gebhard*, 1995, para. 37 (which refers to C-19/92, *Kraus*, 1993, para. 32). See Tesauro, 'The Community's Internal Market in the Light of the Recent Case-Law of the Court of Justice' (1995) YEL 1, 7–10. Naturally, national measures must also comply with the fundamental rights of the persons concerned, see para. 25-011.
[347] C-299/02, *Commission v Netherlands*, 2004, para. 17.
[348] C-55/94, *Gebhard*, 1995, para. 35, following 71/76, *Thieffry*, 1977, para. 12. See also C-340/89, *Vlassopoulou*, 1991, para. 9 (ensuring that a person has the knowledge and skills required in order to pursue a particular occupation); C-106/91, *Ramrath*, 1992, para. 35 (rules relating to the integrity and independence of auditors); C-101/94, *Commission v Italy*, 1996, paras 19–24 (rules for the supervision of securities dealers); C-19/92, *Kraus*, 1993, para. 35 (protection of the public against the unlawful use of academic titles).
[349] C-424/97, *Haim*, 2000, paras 50–61.
[350] C-204/90, *Bachmann*, 1992, para. 16.
[351] 96/85, *Commission v France*, 1986, para. 10. It is for the Member States to determine the level of protection that they wish to afford to public health and the way in which that level is to be achieved. Since the level

safety[352] and the protection of victims of road traffic accidents;[353] effectiveness of fiscal controls;[354] the prevention of tax avoidance[355] and deceptive or abusive practices[356] and the need to preserve the cohesion of the tax system[357] (but not avoiding loss of tax revenue[358] or administrative considerations[359]); the need to avoid the risk of seriously undermining the financial balance of the social security system;[360] overriding requirements relating to the general interest, such as the protection of the interests of creditors, minority shareholders, employees, or the taxation authorities;[361] the social protection of employees and the facilitation of the related administrative controls;[362] the protection of jobs and conditions of employment of the members of a trade union;[363] the encouragement of employment[364] or the maintenance of employment in small and medium-sized undertakings;[365] providing social housing;[366] the objective of achieving successful integration;[367] the protection of an established right, such as the retention of patients following several years of professional activity;[368] maintaining or promoting the use of an official language;[369] preserving or improving the education system;[370] promoting higher education[371] and encouraging student mobility[372] and, in view of the social importance of sport, maintaining a balance between football clubs and supporting the search for talent and the training of young players;[373] respecting fundamental

---

may vary from one Member State to another, Member States must be allowed discretion (C-322/01, *Deutscher Apothekerverband*, 2003, para. 103; C-169/07, *Hartlauer*, 2009, para. 30; C-531/06, *Commission v Italy*, 2009 paras 35 and 44–5; C-171/07 and C-172/07, *Apothekerkammer des Saarlandes and Others*, 2009, para. 19); C-570/07 and C-571/07, *Blanco Pérez and Chao Gómez*, 2010, para. 44.

[352] C-246/00, *Commission v Netherlands*, 2003, para. 67.
[353] C-518/06, *Commission v Italy*, 2009, para. 74.
[354] C-204/90, *Bachmann*, 1992, para. 18 (see also the parallel judgment of the same date, C-300/90, *Commission v Belgium*, 1992, para. 11); C-264/96, *ICI*, 1998, para. 26.
[355] C-446/03, *Marks & Spencer*, 2005, paras 49–56; C-231/05, *Oy AA*, 2007, para. 58. In this context, the Court also referred to the need to safeguard the balanced allocation of the power to impose taxes between the Member States (C-446/03, *Marks & Spencer*, 2005, paras 43–6), a ground of justification which needs to be assessed in conjunction with other grounds, such as the prevention of tax avoidance (see, e.g., C-347/04, *Rewe Zentralfinanz*, 2007, paras 39–44 and C-231/05, *Oy AA*, 2007, paras 51–6).
[356] C-196/04, *Cadbury Schweppes*, 2006, paras 55–6; C-66/18, *Commission v Hungary*, 2020, paras 184–6.
[357] C-204/90, *Bachmann*, 1992, para. 21, and C-300/90, *Commission v Belgium*, 1992, para. 14 (where this ground was accepted as a justification); C-264/96, *ICI*, 1998, para. 29 (where this ground was not accepted as a justification); C-650/16, *A/S Bevola*, 2018, paras. 41–50 (where this ground was accepted as a justification, subject to proportionality).
[358] C-264/96, *ICI*, 1998, para. 28.
[359] C-18/95, *Terhoeve*, 1999, paras 44–5 (the aim of simplifying and coordinating the levying of taxes and contributions is not a justification).
[360] C-158/96, *Kohll*, 1998, para. 41; C-208/05, *ITC*, 2007, para. 43.
[361] C-208/00, *Überseering*, 2002, para. 92.
[362] C-490/04, *Commission v Germany*, 2007, paras 70 and 71; C-202/11, *Las*, 2013, para. 28.
[363] C-438/05, *International Transport Workers' Federation and Finnish Seamen's Union*, 2007, paras 77–89.
[364] C-208/05, *ITC Innovative Technology Center*, 2007, para. 39.
[365] C-464/05, *Geurts and Vogten*, 2007, paras 25–6.
[366] C-197/11 and C-203/11, *Libert* 2013, paras 51–2.
[367] C-561/14, *Genc*, 2016, paras 52–6.
[368] C-456/05, *Commission v Germany*, 2007, para. 63.
[369] C-379/87, *Groener*, 1989, para. 19; C-222/07, *UTECA*, 2009, para. 27.
[370] C-40/05, *Lyyski*, 2007, paras 39–40.
[371] C-20/12, *Giersch*, 2013, para. 53; as for the quality of higher education, see C-66/18, *Commission v Hungary*, 2020, paras 187–9.
[372] C-542/09, *Commission v Netherlands*, 2012, para. 72.
[373] C-415/93, *Bosman*, 1995, paras 106–10 (transfer fees not appropriate for achieving these aims); C-325/08, *Olympique Lyonnais*, 2010, paras 39–48 (compensation for clubs must not go beyond what is necessary to encourage recruitment of young players and to fund those activities).

rights;[374] and preventing criminal offences being committed against persons in prostitution, in particular human trafficking, forced prostitution, and child prostitution.[375] Sometimes, the Court finds a restriction justified in the light of a number of mandatory requirements, taken together.[376] Purely economic reasons cannot justify restrictions that are prohibited by the Treaties,[377] unless a restriction is dictated by reasons of an economic nature in the pursuit of an objective in the public interest.[378] Moreover, a Member State has a legitimate interest in preventing its nationals from abusing the possibilities offered by the Treaties to evade national legislation, for instance in respect of professional know-how.[379]

(3) Application without distinction. The measures must be applied in a non-discriminatory manner from the point of view of nationality (even if they are indirectly discriminatory).[380] **7.073**

(4) Proportionality. Lastly, there is the requirement of proportionality: the measures must be appropriate for attaining the objective pursued and must not exceed what is necessary in order to attain that objective. National measures are appropriate for securing attainment of the objective relied upon only if they genuinely reflect a concern to attain that objective in a consistent and systematic manner.[381] Accordingly, a Member State may impose conditions on the acquisition of immovable property in certain municipalities in order to ensure that persons with low incomes or other socially disadvantaged sections of the population of those municipalities have access to sufficiently wide housing options. The acquisition of a house may, however, not be reserved for inhabitants with a sufficiently close link to those municipalities if conditions used to that effect do not have a real connection to the objective of protection of the low income population.[382] Another example is the case of a Member State that seeks to increase the number of inhabitants that hold a higher education degree and decides to that effect to provide financial assistance on the basis of criteria that make it likely that the beneficiaries will return to that Member State to participate in its labour market. The Court held that requiring prior residence may be disproportionate in this respect if it has the effect of giving an outsize weight to only one factor used to determine whether a genuine link with the national labour market exists, a factor which, in addition, may not even be wholly relevant.[383] In order not to exceed what is necessary to attain the **7.074**

---

[374] C-112/00, *Schmidberger*, 2003, paras 71–4 (the case concerns free movement of goods, but refers generally to 'a fundamental freedom guaranteed by the Treaty'); C-438/05, *International Transport Workers' Federation and Finnish Seamen's Union*, 2007, para. 45.

[375] C-340/14 and C-341/14, *Trijber and Harmsen*, 2015, para. 68; C-230/18, *PI*, 2019, para. 70.

[376] C-446/03, *Marks & Spencer*, 2005, paras 41–51, with case note by Schiller (2006) EuR 275–84; C-231/05, *Oy AA*, 2007, paras 51–60.

[377] C-201/15, *AGET Iraklis*, 2016, paras 72 and 96–7.

[378] C-515/14, *Commission v Cyprus*, 2016, para. 53. Accordingly, the risk of seriously undermining the financial balance of the social security system constitutes an overriding reason in the public interest capable of justifying a restriction to the free movement of workers: ibid. (see also n. 366, *supra*).

[379] 115/78, *Knoors*, 1979, para. 25. This was held to be the case in C-61/89, *Bouchoucha*, 1990.

[380] For this expression, see para. 5-063, *supra* and C-451/03, *Servizi Ausiliari Dottori Commercialisti*, 2006, paras 36–7. Most instances which have arisen before the Court of Justice have been concerned with national measures which, albeit not making any distinction as to nationality, nevertheless place nationals of other Member States indirectly at a disadvantage. Sometimes the Court uses the expression 'indirect discrimination' to denote more specifically the type of measures which cannot be justified in the case at issue, cf. C-237/94, *O'Flynn*, 1996, paras 18–20.

[381] C-106/91, *Ramrath*, 1992, paras 29–31; C-338/04, C-359/04, and C-360/04, *Placanica and Others*, 2007, paras 53 and 58; C-169/07, *Hartlauer*, 2009, para. 55; C-42/07, *Liga Portuguesa de Futebol Profissional*, 2009, para. 61; C-531/06, *Commission v Italy*, 2009, paras 44–5 and para. 66; C-539/11, *Ottica New Line di Accardi Vincenzo*, 2013, paras 47–56.

[382] C-197/11 and C-203/11, *Libert*, 2013, paras 49–60.

[383] C-20/12, *Giersch*, 2013, paras 72–82.

objective set in processing applications for recognition of foreign diplomas and vocational qualifications, the national authorities must inquire into the equivalence of the knowledge and qualifications obtained abroad (see para. 7-077, *infra*). Furthermore, a public body recruiting staff for posts or assessing seniority for personnel that takes account of previous employment in the public service may not make a distinction according to whether such employment was in the public service of the particular Member State or in the public service of another Member State.[384] Likewise, a university may not restrict the number of years worked for another university, whether in the same or in another Member State, to be taken into account for assessing seniority, if the content of the job is identical.[385]

It is up to the Member State which relies on a mandatory requirement to justify a restriction to demonstrate that its rules are appropriate and necessary to attain the legitimate objective being pursued. However, that burden of proof is not so extensive that it requires the Member State to prove, positively, that no other conceivable measure could enable that objective to be attained under the same conditions.[386] Where a Member State subjects an economic activity to certain requirements, the fact that another Member State imposes less strict rules does not automatically mean that the first Member State's rules are disproportionate.[387] Moreover, Member States must be able to achieve objectives of general interest by means of rules the observance of which can be easily enforced and supervised by the competent authorities.[388]

5. Harmonization and recognition of professional rules

7.075 **Harmonization.** Freedom of establishment is made more difficult by rules which differ from one Member State to another and are applicable without distinction to nationals and to subjects of other Member States. Article 50 TFEU makes provision for harmonization of such rules. The Union legislature adopted a series of directives on the harmonization of company law.[389] In 2001, a European form of company, the Societas Europea (SE), was

---

[384] C-419/92, *Scholz*, 1994, paras 11–12; C-15/96, *Schöning-Kougebetopoulou*, 1998, paras 21–8; C-187/96, *Commission v Greece*, 1998, paras 17–23; C-195/98, *Österreichischer Gewerkschaftsbund—Gewerkschaft öffentlicher Dienst*, 2000, paras 33–51; C-224/01, *Köbler*, 2003, paras 70–7; C-514/12, *Zentralbetriebsrat der gemeinnützigen Salzburger Landeskliniken Betriebs*, paras 22–45; C-24/17, *Österreichischer Gewerkschaftsbund, Gewerkschaft Öffentlicher Dienst*, 2019, paras 67–92.

[385] C-703/17, *Krah*, 2019, para. 62 (see para. 7-062, *supra*). However, a restriction is possible in respect of prior experience in a different or more junior position: ibid., para. 63.

[386] C-518/06, *Commission v Italy*, 2009, para. 84.

[387] C-108/96 *Mac Queen and Others*, 2001, paras 33–4; C-294/00, *Deutsche Paracelsus Schulen für Naturheilverfahren*, 2002, paras 44–50. See also the case law on the provision of services, para. 7-094, *infra*.

[388] C-400/08, *Commission v Spain*, 2011, para. 124.

[389] Besides the directives adopted on the basis of Article 44(2)(g) EC [*now Article 50(2)(g) TFEU*] on matters such as formation and alteration of capital, annual accounts and consolidated annual account, mergers and division of companies, auditing, and disclosure requirements of branches of foreign companies and single-member companies, directives were also adopted pursuant to Article 94 EC [*now Article 115 TFEU*], in particular on tax treatment of mergers, divisions, and parent/subsidiary companies. Most of these early directives have since been recast, see, e.g., Directive 2012/30/EU of the European Parliament and of the Council of 25 October 2012 on coordination of safeguards which, for the protection of the interests of members and others, are required by Member States of companies within the meaning of the second para. of Article 54 TFEU, in respect of the formation of public limited liability companies and the maintenance and alteration of their capital, with a view to making such safeguards equivalent (OJ 2012 L315/74) and Directive (EU) 2017/1132 of the European Parliament and of the Council of 14 June 2017 relating to certain aspects of company law (OJ 2017 L169). See, generally, Di Luca, *European Company Law* (Cambridge University Press, 2017).; Dorresteijn, *European Corporate Law* (Kluwer Law International, 2008); Grundmann and Möslein, *European Company Law: Organization, Finance and Capital Markets* (Intersentia, 2007). For a general assessment, see Deakin, 'Reflexive Governance and European Company Law' (2009) 15 ELJ 224–45; Grundmann, 'The Structure of European Company Law: From Crisis to Boom' (2004) E Bus Org LR 601–33; Winter, 'EU Company Law on the Move' (2004) LIEI. 97–114.

introduced under Article 308 EC [*now Article 352 TFEU*] which allows companies incorporated under the laws of different Member States to merge or to set up a holding company or a common subsidiary.[390] In 2003, the Council, acting under the same article of the Treaty, made it possible for natural or legal persons coming under the laws of different Member States to establish a European Cooperative Society (SCE).[391] Under (the predecessor of) Article 50 TFEU, the Union legislature also adopted directives harmonizing the law relating to the stock exchange.[392] After the financial crisis of 2008, the initial coordination of securities markets through a network of national authorities[393] has been replaced—on the basis of Article 114 TFEU—by a European system of financial supervision, run by independent European supervisory authorities, one for the banking sector, one for the securities sector, and one for the insurance and occupational pensions sector.[394]

In order to 'make it easier' for self-employed activities to be taken up and pursued, the Union legislature is empowered to adopt directives for the mutual recognition of diplomas,

---

[390] Council Regulation (EC) No. 2157/2001 of 8 October 2001 on the Statute for a European company (SE), OJ 2001 L294/1, as supplemented by Council Directive 2001/86/EC of 8 October 2001 with regard to the involvement of employees, OJ 2001 L294/22. See McCahery, 'Does the European Company Prevent the "Delaware Effect"' (2005) ELJ 785–801; Edwards, 'The European Company— Essential Tool or Reviscerated Dream?' (2003) CMLRev 443–64; Fouassier, 'Le statut de la "société européenne": Un nouvel instrument juridique au service des entreprises' (2001) RMCUE 85–8; Blanquet, 'Enfin la société européenne' (2001) RDUE 65–109, and 'La société européenne n'est plus un mythe' (2001) R.D.I.D.C. 139–170; Roelvink, 'De Europese vennootschap na Nice' (2001) SEW 162–5; Hopt, 'The European Company (SE) under the Nice Compromise: Major Breakthrough or Small Coin for Europe?' (2000) Euredia 465–75.

[391] Council Regulation (EC) No. 1435/2003 of 22 July 2003 on the Statute for a European Cooperative Society (SCE), OJ 2003 L207/1, as supplemented by Council Directive 2003/72/EC of 22 July 2003 with regard to the involvement of employees, OJ 2003 L207/25. This regulation was validly adopted under Article 308 EC [*now Article 352 TFEU*]: see C-436/03, *European Parliament v Council*, 2006, with case note by Gutman (2006) 13 Col JEL 147–87.

[392] The directives adopted by the Council pursuant to Article 44 EC [*now Article 50 TFEU*] have since been mostly replaced by directives or regulations adopted by the European Parliament and the Council pursuant to Article 95 EC [*now Article 114 TFEU*] (possibly in combination with Article 44 EC [*now Article 50 TFEU*]): Directive 2001/34/EC of 28 May 2001 on the admission of securities to official stock exchange listing and on information to be published on those securities, OJ 2001 L184/1; Regulation (EU) No. 596/2014 of the European Parliament and of the Council of 16 April 2014 on market abuse (market abuse regulation), OJ 2014 L173/1; Regulation (EU) 2017/1129 of the European Parliament and of the Council of 14 June 2017 on the prospectus to be published when securities are offered to the public or admitted to trading on a regulated market, OJ 2017 L168/12 (based on Article 44 EC [*now Article 50 TFEU*]). Further directives have been adopted on the basis of Article 47(2) EC [*now Article 53(1) TFEU*]: Directive 2009/65/EC of the European Parliament and of the Council of 13 July 2009 on the coordination of laws, regulations, and administrative provisions relating to undertakings for collective investment in transferable securities (UCITS), OJ 2009 L302/32; Directive 2013/36/EU of the European Parliament and of the Council of 26 June 2013 on access to the activity of credit institutions and the prudential supervision of credit institutions and investment firms, OJ 2013 L176/338; Directive 2014/65/EU of the European Parliament and of the Council of 15 May 2014 on markets in financial instruments, OJ 2014 L173/349. See Athanassiou, 'Towards a more integrated primary issuance market for securities in the EU: Legal and policy issues', (2020) MJECL 137–57

[393] Initially, coordination of the securities markets occurred through consultation of the competent national authorities in a Committee of European Securities Regulators and a European Securities Committee; see Commission Decisions 2001/527/EC and 2001/528/EC of 6 June 2001 (OJ 2001 L191/43 and L191/45, respectively) and Vaccari, 'Le processus Lamfalussy: une réussite pour la comitologie et un exemple de "bonne gouvernance européenne"' (2005) RDUE 803–21; Janin, "Le premier cas pratique d'approche "Lamfalussy"—Les mesures d'exécution de la directive sur les opérations d'initiés et les manipulations de marché (abus de marché)' (2003) RMCUE 658–69; Moloney, 'New Frontiers in EC Capital Markets Law: From Market Construction to Market Regulation' (2003) CMLRev 809–43; Berger and Altemir Mergelina, 'Un nouveau système de régulation communautaire des marchés de valeurs mobilières dans l'Union européenne' (2001) RMCUE 529–34.

[394] As recommended by the High-Level Group chaired by Jacques de Larosière in 2009, the supervisory framework has been be strengthened to reduce the risk and severity of future financial crises. The European System of Financial Supervisors consists of the European Securities and Markets Authority (ESMA), the European Banking Authority (EBA), and the European Insurance and Occupational Pensions Authority (EIOPA), see para. 13-046, *infra*.

certificates, and other evidence of formal qualifications and for the coordination of provisions concerning the taking-up and pursuit of activities as self-employed persons (Article 53(1) TFEU). Pursuant to Article 62 TFEU, this also applies to the provision of services. The coordination measures adopted on the basis of Article 53(1) TFEU must not only have the objective of making it easier to exercise the freedom of establishment or the freedom to provide services, but also of ensuring, when necessary, the protection of other fundamental interests that may be affected by these freedoms.[395] In the banking and insurance sectors, directives have resulted in a substantial liberalization of the right of establishment (on the basis of the predecessor of Article 53 TFEU) and of the supply of services (on the basis of the predecessor of Article 53 TFEU in conjunction with the predecessor of Article 62 TFEU),[396] which have been largely updated and replaced after the financial crisis.[397] On the basis of (the predecessors of) Articles 53 and 62 TFEU, the Union legislature adopted, on 12 December 2006, the Directive on services in the internal market ('Services Directive'),[398] which has considerably strengthened the legal framework for the internal market by prohibiting a great number of obstacles in the Member States' legal orders that hamper either the freedom of establishment or the freedom to provide services (see paras 7-096–7-099, *infra*). As set out below, unlike the Treaty provisions on free movement, the Services Directive does not require a cross-border element, thereby also removing obstacles for economic activities in internal situations (see para. 7-097, *infra*).

In order to facilitate the provision of services by an undertaking through workers 'posted' to carry out work in another Member State, the Union legislature adopted the Posting of

---

[395] C-620/18, *Hungary v European Parliament and Council*, 2020, paras 44–8; C-626/18, *Poland v European Parliament and Council*, 2020, paras 49–54 (referring to the protection of workers as ensured by the horizontal objective set out in Article 9 TFEU).

[396] As regards the banking sector, see, e.g., Directive 2000/12/EC of the European Parliament and of the Council of 20 March 2000 relating to the taking up and pursuit of the business of credit institutions, OJ 2000 L126/1, codifying a series of earlier directives, Directive 2000/46/EC of the European Parliament and of the Council of 18 September 2000 on the taking up, pursuit of ,and prudential supervision of the business of electronic money institutions, OJ 2000 L275/39, and Directive 94/19/EC of the European Parliament and the Council of 30 May 1994 on deposit-guarantee schemes, OJ 1994 L135/5. See Alpa, 'The Harmonisation of the EC Law of Financial Markets in the Perspective of Consumer Protection' (2002) E Bus LRev 523–40; Moreiro Gonzalez, 'La codification de la réglementation communautaire relative à l'activité des établissements de crédit et son exercice' (2001) RTDE 529–50; Garcia Collados, 'La codification des directives bancaires' (2000) Euredia 313–19. For the liberalization of insurance, the Council adopted successive directives on indemnity insurance and life assurance (the 'first generation' in 1973 and 1979; the 'second generation' in 1988 and 1990, and the 'third generation' directives in 1992); the provisions on life assurance were revised in 2002. The emergence of financial groups offering services and products in various financial sectors led to the need for appropriate supervision, resulting in Directive 2002/87/EC of the European Parliament and of the Council of 16 December 2002 on the supplementary supervision of credit institutions, insurance undertakings, and investment firms in a financial conglomerate, OJ 2003 L35/1. Before the set-up of the European System of Financial Supervision, the banking and insurance sectors were subject to coordination within the Committee of European Banking Supervisors, the Committee of European Insurance and Occupational Pensions Supervisors, the European Banking Committee, and the European Insurance and Occupational Pensions Committee, all of which were set up by Commission Decisions of 5 November 2003 (OJ 2004 L3/28 to L3/36); see also Mogg, 'Regulating Financial Services in Europe: A New Approach' (2002) Fordham ILJ 58–82.

[397] As regards banking, see Directive 2013/36/EU of the European Parliament and of the Council of 26 June 2013 on access to the activity of credit institutions and the prudential supervision of credit institutions and investment firms, OJ 2013 L176/338; Directive 2014/49/EU of the European Parliament and of the Council of 16 April 2014 on deposit guarantee schemes, OJ 2014 L173/149; see also Regulation (EU) No. 575/2013 of the European Parliament and of the Council of 26 June 2013 on prudential requirements for credit institutions and investment firms, OJ 2013 L176/1 (adopted pursuant to Article 114 TFEU). As regards insurances, see Directive 2009/138/EC of the European Parliament and of the Council of 25 November 2009 on the taking-up and pursuit of the business of Insurance and Reinsurance (Solvency II), OJ 2009 L335/1, and Directive (EU) 2016/97 of the European Parliament and of the Council of 20 January 2016 on insurance distribution, OJ 2016 L26/19.

[398] OJ 2006 L376/36.

Workers Directive, which lays down a hard core of mandatory rules protecting the working conditions and health and safety of posted workers.[399] In the interpretation of its provisions, account must be taken both of the need to ensure adequate social protection and the objective of facilitating the internal market by ensuring a level playing field for undertakings providing cross-border services.[400] In 2018, this Directive was revised by strengthening the rights of posted workers in the host Member State so that competition between undertakings posting workers to that Member State and undertakings established in that State could develop on a more level playing field.[401] The revised Directive ensures that the terms and conditions of employment of posted workers are as close as possible to those of workers employed by undertakings established in the host Member State, thereby ensuring that the freedom to provide services can be exercised 'fairly'.[402]

Mutual recognition of diplomas. In some sectors, the Council adopted directives dealing with the mutual recognition of diplomas with a view to access to an occupation (not 'academic' recognition) for both employed and self-employed persons. Article 40 EC [*now Article 46 TFEU*] served as the legal basis for these directives, alongside Article 47(1) EC [*now Article 53(1) TFEU*]. They were aimed at medical and paramedical diplomas[403] and architects' diplomas.[404] Directive 89/48 of 21 December 1988, which introduced a general system for the recognition of higher-education diplomas awarded on completion of at least three years' professional education and training[405] marked the abandonment of the sectoral approach.

7.076

---

[399] Directive 96/71/EC of the European Parliament and of the Council of 16 December 1996 concerning the posting of workers in the framework of the provision of services, OJ 1997, L18/1.

[400] See, e.g., C-341/05 *Laval un Partneri*, 2007, paras 62–111 (wage level agreed by Swedish social partners held not applicable under Directive 96/7 to workers posted in Sweden by an Estonian undertaking for not satisfying the condition of minimum rates of pay being rendered 'universally applicable'). For some commentaries, see Reynolds, 'Explaining the Constitutional Drivers behind a Perceived Judicial Preference for Free Movement over Fundamental Rights' (2016) CMLRev 643–77; Joerges, 'Informal Politics, Formalised Law and the Social Deficit of European Integration: Reflections after the Judgments of the ECJ in Viking and Laval' (2009) ELJ 1–19; Rodière, 'Les arrêts Viking et Laval, le droit de grève et le droit de négociation collective' (2008) RTDE 47–66; Syrpis and Novitz, 'Economic and Social Rights in Conflict: Political and Judicial Approaches to Their Reconciliation', (2008) ELRev 411–26; Barnard, 'Social Dumping or Dumping Socialism?' (2008) Cambridge LJ 262–4; Prechal, 'Viking/Laval en de grondslagen van het internemarktrecht' (2008) SEW 425–40. For less controversial judgments, see C-115/14, *RegioPost*, 2015; C-396/13, *Sähköalojen ammattiliitto*, 2015.

[401] Directive (EU) 2018/957 of the European Parliament and of the Council of 28 June 2018 (OJ 2018 L173/16). See Van Nuffel and Afanasjeva, 'The Posting of Workers Directive Revised: Enhancing the Protection of Workers in the Cross-border Provision of Services' (2018) European Papers 1401–27.

[402] C-620/18, *Hungary v European Parliament and Council*, 2020, paras 49–64; C-626/18, *Poland v European Parliament and Council*, 2020, paras 54–70 (rejecting actions for annulment of Directive 2018/957).

[403] In the case of a number of medical and paramedical diplomas, each directive on mutual recognition was coupled with a directive coordinating the study curricula. Doctors: Directives 75/362/EEC and 75/363/EEC of 16 June 1975, OJ 1975 L167/1 and L167/14, together with Directive 84/457/EEC of 15 September 1986 (training in general medical practice), which were repealed and replaced by (one) Directive 93/16/EEC of 5 April 1993, OJ 1993 L165/1; nurses: Directives 77/452/EEC and 77/453/EEC of 27 June 1977, OJ 1977 L176/1 and L176/8; dental practitioners, Directives 78/686/EEC and 78/687/EEC of 25 July 1978, OJ 1978 L233/1 and L233/10; veterinary surgeons, Directives 78/1026/EEC and 78/1027/EEC of 18 December 1978, OJ 1978 L362/1 and L362/7; midwives, Directives 80/154/EEC and 80/155/EEC of 21 January 1980, OJ 1980 L33/1 and L33/8; pharmacists, Directives 85/432/EEC and 85/433/EEC of 16 September 1985, OJ 1985 L253/34 and L253/37.

[404] Directive 85/384/EEC of 10 June 1985, OJ 1985 L223/15.

[405] Council Directive 89/48/EEC of 21 December 1988 on a general system for the recognition of higher-education diplomas awarded on completion of professional education and training of at least three years' duration, OJ 1989 L19/16, supplemented by Council Directive 92/51/EEC of 18 June 1992 on a second general system for the recognition of professional education and training, OJ 1992 L209/25. For the difference between this and the sectoral approach based on minimum harmonization of training, see C-110/01, *Tennah-Durez*, 2003, paras 29–81. For a survey, see Pertek (ed.), *La reconnaissance des qualifications dans un espace européen des formations et des professions* (Bruylant, 1998); Obwexer and Happacher Brezinka, 'The Recognition of Diplomas within the Internal

Those directives have later been replaced by Directive 2005/36/EC on the recognition of professional qualifications,[406] which applies to nationals of a Member State wishing to pursue a regulated profession in a Member State, including those belonging to the liberal professions, other than that in which they obtained their professional qualifications, on either a self-employed or employed basis (Article 2(1)). The recognition of professional qualifications by the host Member State allows the beneficiary to gain access in that Member State to the same profession for which he or she is qualified in the home Member State and to pursue it in the host Member State under the same conditions as its nationals (Article 4). The Directive proceeds on the basis of the principles of minimum harmonization and mutual recognition. In respect of certain activities related to industry, small craft industries, and trade, it provides for automatic recognition of professional experience as sufficient proof of a professional qualification.[407] In respect of medical and paramedical professions and architects, the Directive provides for harmonized minimum training conditions. Qualifications that satisfy these conditions have to be automatically recognized by other Member States.[408] In respect of other professions, the Directive provides for a general system whereby Member States must recognize professional qualifications obtained in another Member State, but it allows the host Member State to require evidence of professional experience where the duration of the education and training in the other Member State is shorter, or completion of an adaptation period or aptitude test where the education and training received in the other Member State differ substantially in respect of the matters covered.[409] The Directive does not affect the operation of the specific directives concerning the provision of services by, and the establishment of, lawyers[410] because those directives do not concern the recognition of professional qualifications, but rather the recognition of the right to practise.[411] The recognition of professional qualifications for lawyers for the

Market' (2000/01) Eur LF 377–86; Favret, 'Le système général de reconnaissance des diplômes et des formations professionnelles en droit communautaire: l'esprit et la méthode. Règles actuelles et développements futurs' (1996) RTDE 259–80; Pertek, 'Une dynamique de la reconnaissance des diplômes à des fins professionnelles et à des fins académiques: réalisations et nouvelles réflexions' (1996) RMUE 89–176.

[406] Directive 2005/36/EC of the European Parliament and of the Council of 7 September 2005 on the recognition of professional qualifications, OJ 2005 L255/22.

[407] See Title III, Chapter II of the Directive and Annex IV thereto.

[408] See Title III, Chapter III of the Directive and Annex V thereto. Poland brought an unsuccessful action for annulment against a number of these provisions of the Directive (C-460/05, *Poland v European Parliament and Council*, 2007). Since a diploma obtained in a non-member country does not necessarily satisfy the harmonized minimum requirements, a Member State does not automatically have to recognize it—not even if other Member States do: C-154/93, *Tawil-Albertini*, 1994, paras 11–13.

[409] See Title III, Chapter I of the Directive. However, where the fields of activity covered by a profession in a Member State greatly differ from those covered in the host Member State, the latter may be obliged to allow a holder of a diploma awarded in the first Member State partially to take up a profession (i.e. limited to those fields of activity covered in both Member States) without imposing compensatory measures (C-330/03, *Colegio de Ingenieros*, 2006, paras 35–9).

[410] Directive 98/5/EC of the European Parliament and of the Council of 16 February 1998 to facilitate practice of the profession of lawyer on a permanent basis in a Member State other than that in which the qualification was obtained, OJ 1998 L77/36. The Court of Justice upheld the validity of that directive in C-168/98, *Luxembourg v European Parliament and Council*, 2000. See also the earlier Council Directive 77/249/EEC of 22 March 1977 to facilitate the effective exercise by lawyers of freedom to provide services, OJ 1977 L78/17. See Pertek, 'L'Europe des professions d'avocat après la directive 98/5 sur l'exercice permanent dans un autre Etat membre' (2001) RMCUE 106–11; Dal and Defalque, 'La directive "établissement avocats" 98/5/CE du 16 février 1998' (1999) JT 693–5.

[411] Directive 98/5 concerns only lawyers who are fully qualified to practise the profession of a lawyer in their Member State of origin (C-313/01, *Morgenbesser*, 2003, para. 45). It does not concern the subsequent application of rules on professional conduct to these lawyers, C-431/17, *Monachos Eirinaios*, 2019, paras 29–35.

purpose of establishment under the professional title of the host Member State *is* covered by Directive 2005/36/EC.

Comparison of qualifications. The national authorities are generally obliged to examine to what extent the knowledge and qualifications attested by a diploma obtained in another Member State correspond to those required by their own rules.[412]. The obligation to compare abilities already acquired with the knowledge and qualifications required by the national rules also applies with regard to persons in possession of a diploma in an area for which a directive on the mutual recognition of diplomas has been adopted but who, nevertheless, cannot rely on the automatic recognition introduced by the directive in question.[413] If the diplomas correspond only partially, the national authorities in question are entitled to require the person to prove that he or she has acquired the knowledge and qualifications which are lacking.[414] In the case of the profession of lawyer, a Member State may thus carry out a comparative examination of diplomas taking account of the differences identified between the legal system of the Member State of origin and that of the host Member State.[415]

7.077

The mutual-recognition directives ensure admission to the selection and recruitment procedures for a regulated profession, but do not themselves afford any right to be recruited.[416] However, it is contrary to the Treaty provisions on free movement of persons for a recruitment procedure to require a person to pass an examination giving access to training organized by the State where that procedure does not enable account to be taken of qualifications that a candidate has already obtained in another Member State by completing such a training.[417]

6. Social security and the free movement of persons

Coordination of social security systems. Article 48 TFEU requires the Council to adopt such measures in the field of social security as are necessary to provide freedom of movement for employed and self-employed migrant workers and their dependants. The article refers to arrangements to secure for them aggregation of all periods taken into account under the laws of the several Member States for acquiring benefits and payment of benefits to persons resident in the territories of Member States. Such arrangements have been laid down in Regulation No. 1408/71 of 14 June 1971,[418] now replaced by Regulation No. 883/

7.078

---

[412] 222/86, *Heylens*, 1987, paras 10–13 (access to gainful employment, as a football trainer); C-340/89, *Vlassopoulou*, 1991, paras 9–21 (access to self-employment, as a lawyer). See also C-19/92, *Kraus*, 1993, paras 32–8 (authorization required in order to use the title LLM obtained in another Member State, para. 7-062, *supra*).

[413] See C-238/98, *Hocsman*, 2000, para. 23 (diploma obtained in a non-member country); C-31/00, *Dreessen*, 2002, para. 28 (diploma fell outside the scope of the directive); C-313/01, *Morgenbesser*, 2003, paras 54–61 (diploma of *maîtrise en droit* does not give access to the Bar and, therefore, does not constitute a diploma, certificate, or other evidence of formal qualifications within the meaning of Directive 89/48). See also C-232/99, *Commission v Spain*, 2002, paras 18–41.

[414] C-340/89, *Vlassopoulou*, 1991, paras 16–23, in which the Court of Justice applied the principles of Directive 89/48 to facts dating back to before the end of the period prescribed for implementing the directive. See, to the same effect, C-234/97, *Fernández de Bobadilla*, 1999; C-313/01, *Morgenbesser*, 2003, paras 62–72.

[415] C-340/89, *Vlassopoulou*, 1991, para. 18; C-345/08, *Peśla*, 2009, paras 42–8.

[416] The fact that a person has been successful in a recruitment examination in one Member State does not entitle that person to be recruited in another Member State: C-285/01, *Burbaud*, 2003, paras 85–93.

[417] Ibid., paras 94–112.

[418] Regulation (EEC) No. 1408/71 of the Council of 14 June 1971 on the application of social security schemes to employed persons and their families moving within the Community, OJ 1971 English Special Edition (II) 416, and the implementing Council Regulation No. 574/72 of 21 March 1972, OJ 1972 English Special Edition (I) 159.

2004 of 29 April 2004.[419] Article 42 EC only covered migrant workers and their dependants. The Treaty of Lisbon extended the scope of application of the Treaty provisions for 'migrant workers and their dependants' to 'employed and self-employed migrant workers and their dependants'. Regulation No. 883/2004 applies, however, to all nationals of a Member State, stateless persons, and refugees resident in the territory of a Member State who are or have been subject to the social security legislation of one or more Member States, as well as to the members of their families and to their survivors.[420] According to this regulation, these persons retain rights which they have acquired in one Member State, with benefits being paid elsewhere in the Union.[421] The Regulation also entitles them to enjoy the same benefits as nationals of the host Member State (Article 4 Regulation No. 883/2004). Acceptance of an employment relationship in another Member State therefore has no (or only minimal) adverse effect on the social security status of the worker concerned. The Regulation enshrines the principle that a worker is to be subject to the legislation of a single Member State only, and indicates by means of a number of conflict-of-law rules what legislation is to be applicable (Title II of Regulation No. 883/2004). The general principle laid down in Article 11(3)(a) of Regulation No. 883/2004 is that employed persons are subject, with regard to social security matters, to the legislation of the Member State in which they work. In specific situations, however, the unrestricted application of that principle might in fact create, rather than prevent, administrative complications for workers as well as for employers and social security authorities, which could impede the freedom of movement of the persons concerned. For such situations, Title II of Regulation No. 883/2004 sets out specific rules.[422]

[419] Regulation (EC) No. 883/2004 of the European Parliament and the Council of 29 April 2004 on the coordination of social security systems, OJ 2004 L166/1 (republished with *corrigendum*: OJ 2004 L200/1) and the 'Implementing' Regulation (EC) No. 987/2009 of the European Parliament and of the Council of 16 September 2009, OJ 2009 L284/1. See Pennings, *European Social Security Law* (2021, Intersentia); Cornelissen, 'The Protection of Social Rights in a Cross-border Situation within the EU: A Historical Overview', (2019) BTSZ 19–34; Paju, *The European Union and Social Security Law* (Hart Publishing, 2019); Fuchs and Cornelissen, *EU Social Security Law: A Commentary on EU Regulations 883/2004 and 987/2009* (Beck/Hart, 2015); Jorens, *50 Years of Social Security Coordination. Past—Present—Future*, (European Commission, 2010).

[420] As to Regulation No. 1408/71, the Court of Justice held that stateless persons and refugees also fell within that regulation in view of the international obligations incumbent on Member States to treat stateless persons and refugees in the same way as their own nationals for the purposes of social security: C-95/99 to C-98/99 and C-180/99, *Khalil and Others*, 2001, paras 39–58. See Baquero Cruz, 'Khalil e.a.: Les réfugiés et les apatrides face au droit communautaire' (2002) CDE 501–16.

[421] As a sample of the extensive case law on the content of entitlements acquired and the calculation thereof, see, in the early years, 21/75, *Petroni*, 1975, paras 10–21 (pensions); 320/82 *D'Amario*, 1983, paras 4–10, and C-131/96, *Mora Romero*, 1997, paras 27–36 (orphans' benefits); 242/83, *Patteri*, 1984, paras 7–11 (family allowances). See, more recently, C-284/15, *M.*, 2016 (unemployment benefits); C-398/18 and C-428/18, *Torrico and Bode*, 2019 (early retirement pensions). For the situation of a person who was employed by the EU institutions, see C-466/15, *Adrien*, 2016 (pensions); C-651/16, *DW*, 2018 (maternity benefit).

[422] Thus, Article 12(1) of Regulation No. 883/2004 provides that a person who is posted by his employer in a particular Member State to another Member State to perform work on that employer's behalf continues to be subject to the legislation of the first Member State provided that the anticipated duration of such work does not exceed twenty-four months and that he/she is not sent to replace another posted person. It follows from the case law that the certificate issued to attest that the worker concerned is properly registered with the social security system of the Member State in which the undertaking employing him is established, is binding on the competent institution of the Member State to which that worker is posted, see C-620/15, *A-Rosa Flussschiff*, 2017, para. 41. However, if the institution of the Member State to which a worker has been posted informs the institution that issued the certificate concrete evidence suggesting that it was obtained fraudulently, the latter institution must, by virtue of the principle of sincere cooperation, review and, where appropriate, withdraw that certificate. If that institution fails to do so, that evidence may be relied on in judicial proceedings in order to satisfy the court of the Member State to which the workers have been posted that the certificates should be disregarded: C-359/16, *Altun*, 2018, paras 48–60. See Rennuy, 'Posting of Workers: Enforcement, Compliance, and Reform', (2020), EJ Soc Sec 212–34; Verschuren, 'The CJEU's Case Law on the Role of Posting Certificates: A Missed Opportunity to Combat Social Dumping', (2020) MJECL 484–502; Van Zeben and Donders, 'Coordination of Social Security: Developments in the Area of Posting' (2001) EJ Soc Sec 107–16.

Title III of the Regulation sets out specific provisions relating to different sorts of benefits, namely: sickness, maternity, and equivalent paternity benefits, benefits in respect of accidents at work and occupational diseases, death grants, invalidity benefits, old-age and survivors' pensions, unemployment benefits, pre-retirement benefits, family benefits, and special non-contributory cash benefits. The Member States' social security institutions have a duty of mutual information and cooperation to ensure the correct implementation of this Regulation; where necessary, they meet in the context of the Administrative Commission set up by this Regulation in order to agree on the question of the legislation applicable.[423]

Article 48 TFEU requires the European Parliament and the Council to adopt measures in accordance with the ordinary legislative procedure. The Treaty of Lisbon removed in this connection the requirement for the Council to act unanimously throughout the procedure. However, it introduced a safeguard clause according to which any Member State which considers that a draft legislative act would affect important aspects of its social security system or the financial balance of that system, may request that the matter be referred to the European Council (Article 48, second para. TFEU).[424] In that event, the European Council can either refer the draft back to the Council, take no action, or request the Commission to submit a new proposal.

Facilitating free movement. The Court of Justice has held that even if the Union legislature has not carried out any coordination in respect of a social security scheme,[425] Articles 45–48 TFEU require social security benefits to which a worker is entitled under that scheme not to be affected as a result of the fact that work was performed in another Member State (or of the fact that the worker moved his or her residence to another Member State[426]). Where the adverse effects experienced by a worker must be overcome without there being specific Union coordination measures, the national authorities may have to apply the rules of Regulation No. 883/2004 by analogy. This was the case where national legislation provided that only periods of employment completed in national public hospitals were to be recognized as pensionable, because the fact that comparable periods completed in public hospitals of other Member States were not so recognized dissuaded workers from exercising their right to freedom of movement and discriminated against workers who had exercised that right.[427] Where a social security entitlement of a migrant worker falls under two different statutory schemes (e.g. a right to a pension after having been employed in two

7.079

---

[423] See Article 75 of Regulation No. 883/2004 (Advisory Committee comprised of representatives of each Member State's government, trade unions, and employers' organizations). Failing any agreement within the Administrative Commission, the Member State where an employee works may bring infringement proceedings under Article 259 TFEU in order to enable the Court to examine the question of the applicable legislation: C-202/97, *Fitzwilliam Executive Search*, 2000, para. 58; C-620/15, *A-Rosa Flussschiff*, 2017, para. 46.

[424] See also Declaration (No. 23), annexed to the Lisbon Treaty, on the second para. Article 48 TFEU, OJ 2010 C83/346 (recalling that the European Council acts by consensus). This possibility of having the matter referred to the European Council is similar to the 'alarm bell' procedure which applies in the field of judicial cooperation in criminal matters, except for the fact that Article 48 does not provide that, where it is not possible to find agreement on a new draft directive, Member States wishing to proceed with enhanced cooperation on the basis of that draft, will be authorized to do so (see para. 17-033, *infra*).

[425] If a benefit falls within the scope of Regulation No. 833/2004, there is no need to assess restrictions on the basis of Article 48 TFEU; see C-398/18 and C-428/18, *Torrico and Bode*, 2019, paras 21–3.

[426] See, e.g., C-396/05, *Habelt and Others*, 2007, para. 78; C-228/07 *Petersen*, 2008, paras 54–5.

[427] C-443/93, *Vougioukas*, 1995, paras 39–42. For a case in which it was held that the negative consequences of working in another Member State could be overcome only by recourse to coordination measures adopted by the Union legislature, see C-360/97, *Nijhuis*, 1999, paras 28–32.

Member States), the application of one set of national rules to a migrant worker may give rise to unforeseen consequences, hardly compatible with Articles 45 to 48 TFEU. According to the Court of Justice, the national authorities should ascertain whether their legislation can be applied literally to migrant workers, in exactly the same way as to non-migrant workers, without causing migrant workers to lose a social security advantage.[428] In addition, the national court concerned should interpret its own legislation in the light of the aims of those articles and, as far as possible, prevent its interpretation from being such as to discourage a migrant worker from actually exercising his or her right to freedom of movement.[429] Where it is impossible to apply national law in conformity with Union law in this way, the national court must fully apply Union law and refrain from applying any provision which would lead to a result contrary to Union law.[430]

In line with its *Dano* judgment, the Court held, however, that in principle nothing precludes that the grant of social assistance to economically inactive Union citizens is made conditional on the requirement that they are entitled to the right of lawful residence—based on Directive 2004/38—on the territory of the host Member State.[431] The need to protect the public funds of the host Member State justifies that, in accordance with Directive 2004/38, checks are carried out to verify whether a person is a lawful resident of the host Member State.[432]

7.080 **Reimbursement of costs.** Article 48 TFEU retains differences between the Member States' social security systems and hence in the rights of persons working in the Member States. Subject to the limits imposed by free movement of goods, persons, services, and capital, the Member States still have the power to determine the conditions under which a person may become affiliated to a social security scheme and entitled to social security benefits.

It is clear that rules making reimbursement of costs incurred for medical products or medical care in another Member State dependent on prior authorization constitute an obstacle to the free movement of goods or the freedom to provide services, respectively. The Court of Justice has held that such a requirement for prior authorization could not be justified with regard to reimbursement of costs for medical products or non-hospital care.[433] However, with regard to reimbursement of costs for hospital treatment and other treatments requiring heavy equipment, a requirement of prior authorization could, in certain circumstances, be justified by the need to safeguard the financial balance of the social security

---

[428] C-165/91, *Van Munster*, 1994, para. 33; C-202/97, *Fitzwilliam Executive Search*, 2000, paras 51–9; C-178/97, *Banks and Others*, 2000, paras 38–45; C-3/08, *Leyman*, 2009, paras 40–50; C-134/18, *Vester*, 2019, paras 28–49.
[429] C-165/91, *Van Munster*, 1994, para. 34. See also C-548/11, *Mulders*, 2013, paras 45–9; C-589/10, *Wencel*, 2013, paras 65–72.
[430] C-262/97, *Engelbrecht*, 2000, para. 40.
[431] C-308/14, *Commission v United Kingdom*, 2016, para. 68.
[432] Ibid., paras 76–81. See Mantu and Minderhoud, 'Exploring the Links between Residence and Social Rights for Economically Inactive EU Citizens' (2019) EJML, 313–37; O'Brien, 'The ECJ Sacrifices EU Citizenship in Vain: Commission v. United Kingdom' (2017) CMLRev 209–44; Verschueren, 'Economically Inactive Migrant Union Citizens: Only Entitled to Social Benefits if They Enjoy a RIght to Reside in the Host State' (2017) EJ Soc Sec 71–82.
[433] C-120/95, *Decker*, 1998 (medical products); C-158/96, *Kohll*, 1998 (dental treatment as an outpatient); C-385/99, *Müller-Fauré and van Riet*, 2003, paras 93–108 (non-hospital services); C-255/09, *Commission v Portugal*, 2011 (non-hospital services). For *Decker* and *Kohll*, see Van Raepenbusch (1998) CDE 683–97; for *Müller-Fauré*, see Flear (2004) CMLRev 209–33.

system.[434] The principles that the Court developed in its case law have been consolidated in the Patients Directive.[435]

C. Freedom to provide services

Treaty rules. Under Article 56 TFEU, restrictions on freedom to provide services within the Union are prohibited within the framework of the provisions set out in the Treaties.[436] Article 62 TFEU states that Articles 51–54 TFEU are to apply to services. Consequently, free movement of services is subject to the same exceptions as the provisions on free movement of workers and self-employed persons with regard to the exercise of public authority (Article 51 TFEU; see para. 7-069, *supra*) and public policy, public security, and public health (Article 52 TFEU; see para. 7-067, *supra*), and is to be facilitated by the mutual recognition of diplomas, certificates, and other evidence of formal qualifications and by further coordinating directives (Article 53 TFEU; see paras 7-075–7-077, *supra*), in particular the 'Services Directive' (see paras 7-096–7-099, *infra*). Just as in the case of the provisions on free movement of workers and self-employed persons, the provisions on the free movement of services not only apply to the action of public authorities but extend also to associations or organizations not governed by public law where they lay down collective rules in the exercise of their legal autonomy.[437] Where it concerns similar situations, the case law interprets the provisions on free movement of services and free movement of goods in a parallel manner, in particular where services are provided across borders without the provider or the recipient moving.

7.081

---

[434] C-157/99, *Smits and Peerbooms*, 2001 and C-385/99, *Müller-Fauré and van Riet*, 2003, paras 66–92; C-372/04, *Watts*, 2006; C-169/07, *Hartlauer*, 2009, para. 47; and C-444/05, *Stamatelaki*, 2007. However, where an insured person has been authorized to receive hospital treatment in another Member State, the Court of Justice has held that a limitation of reimbursement of that treatment to the lower level applicable in that State is incompatible with freedom to provide services (C-368/98, *Vanbraekel and Others*, 2001). Such a limitation does not have a restrictive effect of the free provision of services where a person received unscheduled hospital treatment during a temporary stay in another Member State: C-211/08, *Commission v Spain*, 2010, paras 55–80 (restrictive effect 'too uncertain and indirect': para. 72). See Cousins, 'Patient Mobility and National Health Systems' (2007) LIEI 183–93; Van Nuffel, 'Patients' Free Movement Rights and Cross-border Access to Healthcare' (2005) MJECL 253–70; Nowak, 'Zur grundfreiheitlichen Inanspruchnahme von Gesundheitsleistungen im europäischen Binnenmarkt' (2003) EuR 644–56; Hatzopoulos, 'Killing National Health and Insurance Systems but Healing Patients? The European Market for Health Care Services after the Judgments of the ECJ in Vanbraekel and Peerbooms' (2002) CMLRev 683–729.

[435] Directive 2011/24/EU of the European Parliament and of the Council of 9 March 2011 on the application of patients' rights in cross-border healthcare, OJ 2011 L88/45. This directive has codified the case law on the freedom to provide services in the field of healthcare, while intending to achieve a more general and effective application of principles developed in that case law; see C-243/19, *A*, 2020, paras 66–85. See, more generally, Berki, *Free movement of patients in the EU—A patient's perspective*, (2018, Intersentia); Peeters, 'Free Movement of Patients: Directive 2011/24 on the Application of Patients' Rights in Cross-border Healthcare' (2012) EJ Health L 56; Slegers and Fonteyn, 'La directive 2011/24/24/UE relative à l'application des droits des patients en matière de soins de santé transfrontaliers: bien plus qu'une codification' (2012) EJ Consumer L 61–79.

[436] Before the simplification carried out by the Amsterdam Treaty, the EC Treaty debarred Member States from introducing any new restrictions (former Article 62 EC) and existing restrictions had to be gradually abolished over a transitional period (former Article 59, first para. EC). Just as in the case of freedom of establishment, the provision of services was to be liberalized on the basis of a general programme and implementing directives (former Article 63, first para. EC).

[437] C-51/96 and C-191/97, *Deliège*, 2000, para. 47 (referring to the judgments in *Walrave* and *Bosman*, see para. 7-044, *supra*); C-519/04 P, *Meca-Medina and Majcen v Commission*, 2006, para. 24; C-341/05 *Laval un Partneri*, 2007, para. 98. See Wernsmann, 'Bindung Privater an Diskriminierungsverbote durch Gemeinschaftsrecht' (2005) JZ 224–33.

1. Definition and beneficiaries

7.082 **Services.** The first para. of Article 57 TFEU regards as 'services' those which are 'normally provided for remuneration, in so far as they are not governed by the provisions relating to freedom of movement for goods, capital and persons'. What is therefore covered is activities, for instance of an industrial or commercial character, of craftsmen or of the professions (see Article 57, second para.), which 'normally' yield an economic consideration or 'remuneration'.[438] Services which are normally remunerated, but sporadically provided free of charge, are thus not excluded. Services do not necessarily have to be paid for by the person for whom they are performed,[439] although they do have to be paid for primarily[440] with private money. Accordingly, teaching provided in an educational institution which is principally funded by the State does not constitute a service within the meaning of the Treaties.[441] However, courses given by educational establishments essentially financed by private funds constitute services within the meaning of Article 57 TFEU, even if the private funding is not provided principally by the pupils or their parents.[442] Medical treatment in or outside a hospital which is paid directly by a sickness insurance fund on a flat-rate basis does constitute a service.[443] The mere fact that the compensation is based on rates determined by the government does not affect the qualification as a service.[444] An activity will be regarded as a service, even if it is strictly regulated or even forbidden in some Member States.[445] Medical termination of pregnancy which is prohibited in one Member State constitutes a service when lawfully carried out in another Member State.[446] National legislation requiring profits

---

[438] C-51/96 and C-191/97, *Deliège*, 2000, paras 49–59 (public and private sponsoring as remuneration for sporting activities). See, similarly, under the Services Directive 2006/123/EC, C-360/15 and C-31/16, *X and Visser*, 2018, paras 84–97, with case note by Snell (2019) CMLRev 1119–35 (retail trade in shoes and clothing are services).

[439] 352/85, *Bond van Adverteerders and Others*, 1988, para. 16; C-179/14, *Commission v Hungary*, 2016, para. 155.

[440] Accordingly, the fact that some services (in casu meal vouchers) are purchased by the national social security system for free distribution to certain underprivileged does not preclude the qualification as a service if the bulk is bought by private employers, see C-179/14, *Commission v Hungary*, 2016, para. 160.

[441] C-109/92, *Wirth*, 1993, paras 15–19.

[442] C-76/05, *Schwarz and Gootjes-Schwarz*, 2007, paras 40–1; C-56/09, *Zanotti*, 2010, paras 30–3.

[443] C-157/99, *Smits and Peerbooms*, 2001, paras 56–9 and the case law cited in n. 434, *supra*; C-372/04, *Watts*, 2006, para. 89.

[444] C-372/09 and C-373/09, *Peñarroja Fa*, 2011, para. 38.

[445] On the status under EU law of sensitive services, such as abortion and gambling, see Corthaut, *EU ordre public* (Kluwer, 2012), 110–29. See also Szydło, 'Continuing the Judicial Gambling Saga in Berlington' (2016) CMLRev 1089–105.

[446] C-159/90, *Society for the Protection of Unborn Children Ireland*, 1991, paras 18–21 (also known as the *Grogan* case). Until 2018, Article 40.3.3. of the Irish Constitution prohibited abortion. In order to safeguard that prohibition, a Protocol (No. 7) was appended to the Treaties, declaring that nothing in the Treaties shall affect the application in Ireland of that provision of its Constitution (OJ 1992 C224/130, see now Protocol (No. 35), OJ 2010 C 83/321). Following the turmoil caused by the application of this prohibition in February 1992, the Irish Government secured the adoption by the Contracting Parties as an annex to the EU Treaty of a Declaration, made in Guimarâes on 1 May 1992, in which they give the following 'legal interpretation' of the Protocol: '[I]t was and is their intention that the Protocol shall not limit freedom to travel between Member States or, in accordance with conditions which may be laid down, in conformity with Community law, by Irish legislation, to obtain or make available in Ireland information relating to services lawfully available in Member States'. As a result of a referendum held on 25 November 1992, Article 40.3.3 of the Constitution was amended by the addition of particulars recognising the freedom to travel to another Member State and to obtain and disseminate information regarding lawful abortion elsewhere. Through a new referendum of 25 May 2018, the above-mentioned constitutional provision was again amended to allow for the regulation of termination of pregnancy. See Murphy, 'Maastricht: Implementation in Ireland' (1994) ELRev 94–104; Curtin, note to the *Grogan* judgment of the Court of Justice (1992) CMLRev 583–603. Meanwhile, Protocol (No. 7) on abortion in Malta, annexed to the 2003 Act of Accession, specifies that nothing in the Treaties shall affect the application in the territory of Malta of national legislation relating to abortion, OJ 2003 L236/947.

from a given activity (e.g. a lottery) to be paid to the State or used for specific ends, does not cause that activity to lose its economic character.[447]

Residual nature. Article 57 TFEU regards as 'services' only activities not falling under the other freedoms. Thus, the transmission of television signals is a service, but the material, sound recordings, films, apparatus, and other products used for the emission of television signals are subject to the rules relating to freedom of movement for goods.[448] Nevertheless, Article 57 does not establish any order of precedence between the freedom to provide services and the other fundamental freedoms: the notion of 'services' covers services which are not governed by other freedoms, in order to ensure that all economic activity falls within the scope of the fundamental freedoms.[449] Moreover, services in the field of transport, are governed by the Title of the TFEU relating to transport.[450] However, services that are ancillary to the actual transportation, such as on-board catering, do fall within the scope of the free movement of services.[451]

7.083

Service providers and recipients. According to Article 56 TFEU, the beneficiaries of free movement of services are 'nationals of Member States who are established in a Member State other than that of the person for whom the services are intended'. The provider of the service (not the recipient) must be a national of a Member State (or a company or firm formed in accordance with the law of a Member State; see Article 55 TFEU in conjunction with Article 62 TFEU) and established in a Member State.[452] Freedom to provide services may be relied upon not only by the provider and recipient of services,[453] but also in certain circumstances by the employees of the service provider.[454]

7.084

Transfrontier element. The transfrontier element mentioned in Article 56 TFEU is that the provider and recipient of the service must be established in different Member States. The Treaty refers only to the situation in which a provider of services 'temporarily pursue[s] his activity in the Member State where the service is provided' (Article 57, third para.). This includes the situation where an undertaking 'posts' its workers to another Member State in order to temporarily carry out work there for a customer or linked undertaking.[455] However, the transfrontier element may, in practice, also manifest itself in other ways. Thus, tourists, persons receiving medical treatment, and persons travelling for the purpose of education or business may invoke freedom to provide services.[456] In this connection, the

7.085

---

[447] C-275/92, *Schindler*, 1994, paras 31–5.
[448] 155/73, *Sacchi*, 1974, paras 6–7.
[449] C-452/04, *Fidium Finanz*, 2006, paras 31–3. For the assessment of whether the Treaty provisions on services or those on free movement of capital apply, see also C-602/10, SC Volksbank România, 2012, paras 68–71; C-625/17, *Vorarlberger Landes- und Hypothekenbank*, 2018, paras 20–6 (banking services); C-375/12, *Bouanich*, 2014, paras 24–31 (dividends from shareholdings).
[450] Article 58(1) TFEU. See, for instance, C-434/15, *Asociación Profesional Élite Taxi*, 2017, paras 33–49; C-320/16, *Uber France*, 2018, paras 16–26.
[451] C-16/18, *Dobersberger*, 2019, paras 24–7.
[452] C-290/04, *Scorpio Konzertproduktionen*, 2006, paras 66–8 (the provisions on the freedom to provide services are not applicable to providers of services who are nationals of non-member countries, even if they are established within the Union and an intra-Union provision of services is concerned).
[453] See, e.g., C-33/17, *Čepelnik*, 2018, para. 38; C-311/19, *BONVER WIN*, 2020, para. 21.
[454] C-317/01 and C-369/01, *Abatay and Others*, 2003, para. 106.
[455] See C-113/89, *Rush Portuguesa*, 1990, para. 12; C-43/93, *Van der Elst*, 1994, para. 21; C-33/17, *Čepelnik*, 2018, paras 37–41 (see also para. 7-052, *supra*). These workers may also encompass third-country nationals, see, e.g., see C-91/13, *Essent Energie Productie*, 2014, paras 36–60.
[456] 286/82 and 26/83, *Luisi and Carbone*, 1984 ., para. 16. As regards tourists, see, 186/87, *Cowan*, 1989, paras 15–17; C-45/93, *Commission v Spain*, 1994, paras 5–10; see further Tichadou, 'Der Schutz des Touristen

provider and the recipient of the service do not necessarily have to be established in different Member States. Where a travel agent takes tourists from its own Member State to another Member State and makes use of a guide who may be established in another Member State or in its own Member State, the rules on freedom to provide services are applicable in either case, since services are being provided in a Member State other than the one in which the provider of the services is established.[457]

In addition, the rules on free movement of services apply where the provider of the service and the recipient remain in the Member States where they are established and only the service crosses the border. Thus, the transmission of television signals across an internal frontier falls under the free movement of services both as regards the service provided by cable network operators relaying television programmes sent out by broadcasters in other Member States and as regards the service provided by the broadcasters transmitting advertisements to the public in another Member State on behalf of advertisers established in that Member State.[458] Another case to which those rules apply is that of a service offered by a service provider over the telephone or the internet to potential recipients in another Member State without the provider leaving the Member State where he or she is established.[459]

However, the Treaty provisions on freedom to provide services cannot be applied to activities which are confined in all respects within a single Member State.[460] Freedom to provide services may be relied upon by an undertaking against the Member State in which it is established if the services are provided for persons established in another Member State.[461] The same applies to intermediaries established in the Member State of the potential recipients of the services who make it easier for a supplier of services to offer his or her services across borders.[462] In that respect, the Court has clarified that the application of the Treaty

---

in der Rechtsprechung des Europäischen Gerichtshofs' (2002) ZEuS 299–319; Van der Woude and Mead, 'Free Movement of the Tourist in Community Law' (1988) CMLRev 117. As regards medical activities, see C-159/90, *Society for the Protection of Unborn Children Ireland*, 1991, para. 18. See also, in the context of the EEA agreement, C-897/19 PPU, *I.N.*, 2020, paras 51–4.

[457] C-154/89, *Commission v France*, 1991, para. 11; C-180/89, *Commission v Italy*, 1991, para. 10; C-198/89, *Commission v Greece*, 1991, para. 11.

[458] 352/85, *Bond van Adverteerders and Others*, 1988, paras 14–15. See also C-34-36/95, *De Agostini and TV Shop*, 1997, para. 29; C-250/06, *United Pan-Europe Communications Belgium*, 2007, para. 28; C-298/17, *France Télévisions*, 2018, para. 29; C-87/19, *TV Play Baltic*, 2019, para. 36. For advertising, see also para. 7-043, *supra*.

[459] C-384/93, *Alpine Investments*, 1995, paras 20–2 (services offered by telephone); C-243/01, *Gambelli and Others*, 2003, paras 53–4 (services offered on the Internet); C-788/18, *Stanleyparma Sas di Cantarelli Pietro & Co.*, 2020, para. 16 (online gambling); C-482/18, *Google Ireland*, 2020, para. 24 (online advertising).

[460] C-29-C-35/94, *Aubertin*, 1995, para. 9; C-111/12, *Ordine degli Ingegneri di Verona e Provincia*, 2013, para. 35; C-342/17, *Memoria*, 2018, para. 23. The provision of services between Gibraltar and the United Kingdom was considered to take place within one Member State, see C-591/15, *Gibraltar Betting and Gaming Association*, 2017, para. 43.

[461] C-384/93, *Alpine Investments*, 1995, paras 29–31; C-224/97, *Ciola*, 1999, paras 10–13; C-60/00, *Carpenter*, 2002, para. 29.

[462] C-243/01, *Gambelli and Others*, 2003, para. 58; C-390/18, *X*, 2019, para. 40 (electronic platform for offering short-term accommodation services); C-788/18, *Stanleyparma Sas di Cantarelli Pietro & Co.*, 2020, para. 16 (online gambling). In respect of online platforms, however, a further distinction must be made as to the applicability of Directive 2000/31/EC of the European Parliament and of the Council of 8 June 2000 on certain legal aspects of information society services, in particular electronic commerce, in the Internal Market ('Directive on electronic commerce') (OJ 2000 L178/1). Although an intermediation service which satisfies all the four cumulative conditions laid down in Article 1(1)(b) of Directive 2015/1535, in principle, constitutes a service distinct from the subsequent service to which it relates and must therefore be classified as an 'information society service', that cannot be the case if it appears that that intermediation service forms an integral part of an overall service whose main component is a service coming under another legal classification (C-434/15, *Asociación Profesional Elite Taxi*, 2017, para. 40; C-390/18, *X*, 2019, para. 50). This distinguishes services such as Uber (platform being an integral part of

provisions on freedom to provide services is not dependent on a quantitative criterion, such as the number of cross-border customers or the volume of the services in question.[463] They may indeed be relied upon both in situations where there is a single recipient of services and in those where there is an uncertain number of recipients of services using an uncertain number of services performed by a provider established in another Member State.[464]

Temporary nature. Where the provider of the service goes to the Member State of the recipient of the service, freedom to provide services differs from freedom of establishment by reason of its temporary nature. Free movement of services cannot be relied upon where a national of a Member State establishes his or her principal residence in another Member State in order to provide or receive services there for an indefinite period.[465] Where a person intends to pursue his or her economic activity by means of a stable arrangement and for an indefinite period, the situation must be examined in the light of freedom of establishment, as defined in Article 49 TFEU.[466] The temporary nature of the activities in question has to be determined in the light, not only of the duration of the provision of the service, but also of its regularity, periodicity, or continuity. A provider of services within the meaning of the Treaties may equip him- or herself with some form of infrastructure in the host Member State (including an office, chambers, or consulting rooms) in so far as such infrastructure is necessary for the purposes of performing the services in question.[467] Services within the meaning of the Treaties may cover services which a business established in a Member State supplies with a greater or lesser degree of frequency or regularity, even over an extended period, to persons established in one or more other Member States, for example the giving of advice or information for remuneration. The Court holds that the Treaties do not afford a means of determining, in an abstract manner, the duration or frequency beyond which the supply of a service in another Member State can no longer be regarded as the provision of services within the meaning of the Treaties.[468]

7.086

2. Substance of the freedom to provide services

Prohibited discrimination. Direct effect attaches to the principle of non-discrimination enshrined in the first para. of Article 56 TFEU and the third para. of Article 57 TFEU 'in so far as they seek to abolish any discrimination against a person providing a service by reason of his nationality or of the fact that he resides in a Member State other than that in which the service is to be provided'.[469] Under these rules, persons providing or receiving

7.087

---

a ride-share service, and thus a transport service—C-434/15) and AirBnB (platform service separate from the service, and thus an information society service—C-390/18). See also C-320, *Uber France*, 2018, paras 15–28.

[463] C-311/19, *BONVER WIN*, 2020, paras 24–9 (rejecting a quantitative criterion as it would jeopardize the uniform application of the Treaty provision on freedom to provide services).

[464] Ibid., para. 28.

[465] 196/87, *Steymann*, 1988, para. 17; C-70/95, *Sodemare and Others*, 1997, paras 38–40.

[466] C-387/10, *Commission v Austria*, 2011, para. 22; C-179/14, *Commission v Hungary*, 2016, paras 148–50; C-342/17, *Memoria*, 2018, para. 44.

[467] C-55/94, *Gebhard*, 1995, para. 27. See, with regard to lawyers, C-145/99, *Commission v Italy*, 2002, paras 22–3. In 1986 the Court still held that an insurance company which maintains a 'permanent presence' in another Member State cannot rely on the freedom to provide services 'even if that presence does not take the form of a branch or agency, but consists merely of an office managed by the undertaking's own staff or by a person who is independent but authorized to act on a permanent basis for the undertaking, as would be the case with an agency': 205/84 *Commission v Germany*, 1986, para. 21.

[468] C-215/01, *Schnitzer*, 2003, paras 30 and 31; C-171/02, *Commission v Portugal*, 2004, paras 26–7.

[469] 33/74, *Van Binsbergen*, 1974, para. 27.

services have a right of residence of equal duration to the period during which the services are provided.[470]

First, the Treaty prohibits all forms of direct discrimination. Accordingly, in *Van Binsbergen*, the Court of Justice held that the Netherlands could not restrict the right to represent parties in legal proceedings to persons established in that Member State. Furthermore, the freedom to provide services prohibits all restrictions, 'which do not apply to persons established within the national territory or which may prevent or otherwise obstruct the activities of the person providing the service'.[471] Thus, the Treaty provisions on freedom to provide services preclude making the supply of services conditional upon obtaining a prior authorization or licence, unless this can be justified objectively (see para. 7-089 *et seq.* , *infra*). An obligation that a particular activity may be carried out only under a contract of employment likewise constitutes a restriction on trade in services, for which the Member State concerned must provide justification.[472] Trade in services is also restricted where a service provider is required to have a particular legal form or status or to conduct his or her business on an exclusive basis and there is a prohibition of pursuing profit.[473] This is because such requirements often discriminate indirectly against service providers from other Member States. In addition, the Court of Justice will investigate whether different tax treatment of residents and non-residents constitutes indirect discrimination against service providers established abroad.[474] Equal treatment of nationals of other Member States wishing to pursue activities other than those of an employed person extends so far that they must have the same right as nationals of the host Member State to purchase or lease housing built or renovated with the help of public funds and to obtain reduced-rate mortgage loans.[475] Providers of services (in the same way as self-employed persons) must be able to take part in legal and economic transactions locally in the same way as nationals of the host Member State, even as regards aspects which are not directly connected with their occupational activities.[476] In addition, recipients of services, such as tourists, may not be discriminated against on the basis of their nationality.[477]

7.088 **Non-discriminatory obstacles.** In more recent case law, the Court of Justice has clarified that freedom to provide services not only requires the abolition of all overt and covert[478] discrimination against the provider of the services by reason of his or her nationality or the place at which he or she is established, 'but also the abolition of any restriction, even if it applies without distinction to national providers of services and to those of other Member

---

[470] See the general system of residence rights for Union citizens laid down in Directive 2004/38/EC (n. 194, *supra*), see para. 6-010, *supra*; previously Article 4(2) of Directive 73/148/EEC.
[471] 33/74, *Van Binsbergen*, 1974, para. 10.
[472] C-398/95, *SETTG*, 1997, paras 14–19.
[473] C-439/99, *Commission v Italy*, 2002, para. 32.
[474] See, e.g., C-234/01, *Gerritse*, 2003, paras 23–55; C-169/08, *Regione Sardegna*, 2009 (see also para. 7-061, *supra*) on the right of establishment. For indirect discrimination in the enforcement of indistinctly applicable tax provisions, see C-482/18, *Google Ireland*, 2020, paras 37–54.
[475] 63/86, *Commission v Italy*, 1988, paras 16–20.
[476] As a result national legislation under which non-resident financial institutions are taxed on the interest income received within the Member State concerned, without the possibility to deduct expenses directly related to the activity in question, whereas resident financial institutions may do so, restricts the freedom to provide services, C-18/15, *Brisal*, 2016, para. 28.
[477] C-897/19 PPU, *I.N.*, 2020, paras 55–8. As this extends to the EEA, an Icelandic national holidaying in Croatia is thus entitled to equal treatment with EU Member States' nationals when the Croatian authorities respond to an extradition request made by a third country.
[478] 62 and 63/81, *Seco*, 1982, para. 8.

States, when it is liable to prohibit or otherwise impede the activities of a provider of services established in another Member State where he [or she] lawfully provides similar services'.[479] In this way, the Court applied *Dassonville*, which was concerned with free movement of goods (see para. 7-028, *supra*), to freedom to provide services.[480] National measures applicable to all market operators are contrary to the freedom to provide services where they restrict market access for undertakings from other Member States.[481] This is the case, for example, with national rules prohibiting in a general and absolute manner advertising for a particular service, rendering it impossible for service providers from other Member States to acquire name recognition with potential customers.[482] By the same token, the Court of Justice held that a municipal tax on satellite dishes was contrary to freedom to supply services because it constituted a charge on the reception of broadcasts from foreign operators and therefore impeded the activities of foreign operators more than those of operators established in the Member State in question.[483] The example of the tax on satellite dishes demonstrates that Article 56 TFEU also precludes legislation which makes it more difficult to *receive* services from service providers established in another Member State. Article 56 TFEU further precludes a Member State from providing for tax relief for schooling costs incurred in private schools established in that Member State, but not for school fees paid to private schools established in other Member States. Such legislation discourages taxpayers resident in the Member State concerned from sending their children to schools established in another Member State, and also hinders the offering of education by these schools to children of taxpayers resident in that Member State.[484]

More generally, national measures which prohibit, impede, or render less attractive the exercise of the freedom to provide services are restrictions on that freedom.[485] Yet, measures which only create additional costs in respect of the service in question and which affect in the same way the provision of services between Member States and such provision within one Member State do not fall within the scope of the prohibition laid down in Article 56 TFEU.[486] That may be the case if local providers bear the same charge in a different manner.[487] However, it is contrary to Article 56 TFEU for a Member State to introduce an infrastructure use charge that is simultaneously offset, through a tax relief from the motor vehicle tax, for the Member State's own residents only.[488]

---

[479] C-76/90, *Säger*, 1991, para. 12. For the prohibition of restrictive conditions imposed on members of staff of a provider of services who are not nationals of a Member State, see the judgments cited in n. 192, *supra*.

[480] See also C-381/93, *Commission v France*, 1994, paras 17–21.

[481] C-518/06, *Commission v Italy*, 2009, paras 64–71.

[482] e.g. C-339/15, *Vanderborght*, 2017, paras 63–4.

[483] C-17/00, *De Coster*, 2001, paras 31–5. See, similarly, C-250/06, *United Pan-Europe Communications Belgium and Others*, 2007, paras 28–38 (obligation for cable operators to broadcast certain domestic broadcasters). See, likewise, C-94/04 and C-202/04, *Cipolla and Others*, 2006, paras 55–70 (prohibition of derogation, by agreement, from the minimum fees set for court services and services reserved to lawyers).

[484] C-76/05, *Schwarz and Gootjes-Schwarz*, 2007, paras 64–7; C-318/05, *Commission v Germany*, 2007, paras 77–81.

[485] C-482/18, *Google Ireland*, 2020, para. 26.

[486] Ibid. See also C-591/17, *Austria v Germany*, 2019, paras 136–7. The same goes for a tax regime that does not differ according to whether the provision of services is executed in the host Member State or in other Member States; see C-788/18, *Stanleyparma Sas di Cantarelli Pietro & Co.*, 2020, para. 22.

[487] C-482/18, *Google Ireland*, 2020, para. 26. An obligation for providers from outside a Member State to make a specific tax declaration does not breach Article 56 TFEU if domestic providers of the same service have a general obligation to make declarations for the whole of their tax liabilities: ibid. para. 36.

[488] C-591/17, *Austria v Germany*, 2019, paras 135–50.

As mentioned above, national legislation which deters persons with social security cover in a Member State from seeking medical treatment from service providers established in another Member State, equally constitutes, both for them and for these providers, a restriction on the freedom to provide services (see para. 7-080, *supra*). In certain cases, however, the possible restrictive effects of national legislation may be too 'uncertain and indirect' to be regarded as hindering the free provision of services.[489]

3. Permitted restrictions on freedom to provide services

a. Restrictions on grounds of Articles 51 and 52 TFEU

7.089 **Justificatory grounds.** A Member State may impose restrictions on freedom to provide services which are dependent on the origin of the service and hence discriminate, only on the basis of the derogating provisions of Article 51 TFEU (public authority; see para. 7-069, *supra*) and Article 52 (public policy, public security, and public health; see paras 7-067, *supra*).[490] Objectives of an economic nature cannot in themselves constitute public policy grounds.[491]

Restrictions must be limited to what is appropriate and necessary in order to protect the interests which they seek to safeguard (principle of proportionality). This was held not to be the case with the general prohibition in the Netherlands on distributing radio and television programmes broadcast from other Member States containing advertisements intended for the public in that Member State or subtitled in Dutch. Although in the final analysis the aim of that prohibition was not to secure for a national public foundation all the revenue from advertising, but to safeguard the non-commercial and, thereby, pluralistic nature of the Netherlands' broadcasting system, that objective could be achieved by means of a less restrictive measure, such as making the advertising restrictions imposed on national broadcasters generally applicable.[492] An example of a restriction which can be justified on grounds of public policy is the German prohibition on the commercial exploitation of games simulating acts of homicide. This prohibition did not go beyond what was necessary for the protection of human dignity guaranteed by the German Constitution.[493]

b. Restrictions based on the rule of reason

7.090 **Rule of reason.** In *Van Binsbergen*, the Court of Justice held that 'taking into account the particular nature of the services to be provided, specific requirements imposed on the person providing the service cannot be considered incompatible with the Treaties where they have as their purpose the application of professional rules justified by the general good—in particular rules relating to organization, qualifications, professional ethics, supervision, and liability—which are binding upon any person established in the State in which the service is provided, where the person providing the service would escape from the ambit of those

---

[489] C-211/08, *Commission v Spain*, 2010, paras 55–80 (see n. 434, *supra*). See the corresponding case law with respect to the free movement of goods (para. 7-028, *supra*) and the free movement of persons (see para.7-062, *supra*); C-483/12, *Pelckmans Turnhout*, 2014, para. 25.

[490] See, for instance, C-484/93, *Svensson and Gustavsson*, 1995, paras 12 and 15; C-341/05, *Laval un Partneri*, 2007, paras 115–19; C-153/08, *Commission v Spain*, 2009, paras 36–7.

[491] C-211/91, *Commission v Belgium*, 1992, paras 9–11; C-17/92, *Distribuidores Cinematográficos*, 1993, paras 16–21; C-224/97, *Ciola*, 1999, paras 15–17; C-388/01, *Commission v Italy*, 2003, paras 18–19.

[492] 352/85, *Bond van Adverteerders and Others*, 1988, paras 34–7. See also C-11/95, *Commission v Belgium*, 1996, para. 92.

[493] C-36/02, *Omega Spielhallen*, 2004, paras 29–39.

rules being established in another Member State'.[494] Following the *Cassis de Dijon* line of cases on free movement of goods (see paras 7-037–7-042, *supra*), the Court has formulated conditions for allowing exceptions in respect of freedom to provide services on the basis of a rule of reason.[495] The distinction drawn in *Keck and Mithouard* with regard to selling arrangements does not apply,[496] particularly where access to the market in services in another Member State is restricted.[497]

(1) **Absence of harmonization.** First, an obstacle to the freedom to provide services created by national rules may only be justified in the absence of Union harmonization measures in the field.[498] Therefore, with regard to services that fall within the scope of Directive 2006/123 (the 'Services Directive'),[499] the Member States' rules must be assessed on their compliance with the stricter requirements set out in that Directive, according to which Member States may not make access to or exercise of a service subject to compliance with any requirements which do not respect the principles of non-discrimination and proportionality and are not justified for reasons of public policy, public security, public health, or the protection of the environment (see para. 7-116, *infra*). **7.091**

(2) **Public-interest requirements.** Second, the restrictions must be justified in the public interest, which does not necessarily relate to the protection of the occupation as such,[500] but can also be designed to secure protection for the recipient of the service;[501] consumer protection;[502] protection of employees[503] (for instance, against possible social dumping[504]); protection of investors' confidence in the domestic financial markets;[505] fair trading;[506] the maintenance of order in society;[507] combatting money-laundering and the financing of terrorism;[508] combating fraud;[509] protection of creditors or safeguarding the sound administration of justice in relation to the provision of litigation services on a professional basis;[510] guaranteeing the proper functioning of the land register system and the legality and legal **7.092**

---

[494] 33/74, *Van Binsbergen*, 1974, para. 12.

[495] 205/84, *Commission v Germany*, 1986, paras 27–9; C-154/89, *Commission v France*, 1991, paras 14–15; C-180/89, *Commission v Italy*, 1991, paras 17–18; C-198/89, *Commission v Greece*, 1991, paras 18–19; C-288/89, *Collectieve Antennevoorziening Gouda*, 1991, paras 13–15; C-353/89, *Commission v Netherlands*, 1991, paras 17–19. See Becker, 'Vorraussetzungen und Grenzen der Dienstleistungsfreiheit' (1996) NJW 179–81.

[496] On the undesirability of a *Keck* exception for services, see C-311/19, *BONVER WIN*, AG Szpunar Opinion, 2020, points 60–76 (in its judgment, the Court does not discuss the *Keck* case law).

[497] C-384/93, *Alpine Investments*, 1995, paras 32–9, with case notes by Hatzopoulos (1995) CMLRev 1427–45 and Straetmans (1995/96) Col JEL 154–64; see also with regard to access to the employment market, C-415/93, *Bosman*, 1995, paras 102–3. As set out above, however, even in the context of the free movement of goods, the specific regime for selling arrangements will normally not allow for measures adopted by a Member State that restrict access to the market: see para. 7-043, *supra*.

[498] C-243/01, *Gambelli and Others*, 2003, paras 64–5; C-429/02, *Bacardi France*, 2004, para. 32.

[499] Directive 2006/123/EC of the European Parliament and of the Council of 12 December 2006 on services in the internal market, OJ 2006 L376/36 (see para. 7-096, *infra*).

[500] e.g. C-339/15, *Vanderborght*, 2017, para. 68 ('protection of the dignity of dentists').

[501] 110-111/78, *Van Wesemael*, 1979, para. 28.

[502] 205/84, *Commission v Germany*, 1986, paras 30–3; C-342/14, *X-Steuerberatungsgesellschaft*, 2015, para. 53.

[503] 279/80, *Webb*, 1981, paras 18–19; 62 and 63/81, *Seco*, 1982, para. 14.

[504] C-341/05, *Laval un Partneri*, 2007, para. 103; C-64/18, C-140/18, C-146/18, and C-148/18, *Maksimovic*, 2019, para. 36.

[505] C-384/93, *Alpine Investments*, 1995, paras 42–44.

[506] C-34-36/95, *De Agostini and TV Shop*, 1997, para. 53.

[507] 15/78, *Société Générale Alsacienne de Banque*, 1978, para. 5; C-275/92, *Schindler*, 1994, paras 57–8. This includes, for example, the prevention of both fraud and incitement to squander on gaming; see C-243/01, *Gambelli and Others*, 2003, para. 67; C-338/04, C-359/04, and C-360/04, *Placanica and Others*, 2007, para. 46.

[508] C-212/11, *Jyske Bank Gibraltar*, 2013, paras 62–4.

[509] C-275/92, *Schindler*, 1994, paras 60–3; C-342/14, *X-Steuerberatungsgesellschaft*, 2015, para. 53.

[510] C-3/95, *Reisebüro Broede*, 1996, para. 36. See also C-99/16, *Lahorgue*, 2017, para. 34.

certainty of documents concluded between individuals;[511] ensuring the effectiveness of the supervision of taxation and cohesion of the tax system[512] and the financial balance of the social security system,[513] including maintaining a balanced medical service open to all;[514] the social protection of workers and combating fraud, particularly social security fraud, and preventing abuse;[515] road safety;[516] combating drugs tourism and the related nuisance;[517] ensuring the provision of reliable medicinal products of good quality;[518] protection of intellectual property;[519] promotion of research and development;[520] conservation of the national historical and artistic heritage;[521] proper appreciation of places and things of historical interest and the widest possible dissemination of knowledge of a country's artistic and cultural heritage;[522] maintaining or promoting the use of an official language;[523] the maintenance of a certain level of (television) programme quality;[524] cultural policy intended to safeguard the freedom of expression of the different social, cultural, religious, philosophical, or linguistic components of a State or region,[525] promoting teaching, research, and development;[526] and respecting fundamental rights generally.[527] 'Maintaining industrial peace' as a means of preventing labour disputes from having any adverse effects on an economic sector is not acceptable as a public-interest ground.[528] Neither can a Member State rely on the need to ensure tax revenue,[529] even though they may seek to combat tax fraud.[530] Aims of a purely economic nature cannot constitute overriding reasons in the general interest.[531] Nevertheless, Member States have an overriding interest in preventing their nationals from abusing the free movement in order to evade the application of national legislation governing a particular activity.[532]

[511] C-342/15, *Piringer*, 2017, para. 57.
[512] C-204/90, *Bachmann*, 1992, para. 33; C-150/04, *Commission v Denmark*, 2007, paras 65–74.
[513] C-204/90, *Kohll*, 1998, para. 41.
[514] This objective may also fall within the public health derogation provided for in Article 52: ibid, paras 50–1; C-157/99, *Smits and Peerbooms*, 2001, paras 73–4; C-444/05, *Stamatelaki*, 2007, para. 31.
[515] C-33/17, *Čepelnik*, 2018, para. 44; C-64/18, C-140/18, C-146/18, and C-148/18, *Maksimovic*, 2019, para. 36.
[516] C-55/93, *Van Schaik*, 1994, para. 19.
[517] C-137/09, *Josemans*, 2010, para. 65.
[518] C-570/07 and C-571/07, *Blanco Pérez and Chao Gómez*, 2010, paras 64–6.
[519] 62/79 *Coditel*, 1980, para. 15.
[520] C-39/04, *Laboratoires Fournier*, 2005, para. 23.
[521] C-180/89, *Commission v Italy*, 1991, para. 20.
[522] C-154/89 *Commission v France*, 1991, para. 17; C-198/89, *Commission v Greece*, 1991, para. 21.
[523] C-222/07, *UTECA*, 2009, para. 27.
[524] C-288/89, *Collectieve Antennevoorziening Gouda*, 1991, para. 27; C-6/98 *ARD*, 1999, para. 50.
[525] C-288/89, *Collectieve Antennevoorziening Gouda*, 1991, paras 22–3; and C-353/89 *Commission v Netherlands*, 1991, para. 30 (both judgments were prompted by the Dutch Media Law; see also C-148/91, *Veronica Omroep Organisatie*, 1993; C-23/93, *TV10*, 1994); C-250/06, *United Pan-Europe Communications Belgium and Others*, 2007, paras 40–2 (with respect to must-carry obligations imposed on Brussels cable operator); C-87/19, *TV Play Baltic*, 2019, paras 39–40 (must-carry obligation for provider of television rebroadcasting over satellite networks in respect of Lithuanian cultural channel).
[526] C-281/06, *Jundt*, 2007, paras 56–8.
[527] C-112/00, *Schmidberger*, 2003, paras 71–4 (the case concerns free movement of goods, but refers generally to 'a fundamental freedom guaranteed by the Treaty'); C-36/02, *Omega Spielhallen*, 2004, paras 32–5, with case note by Bulterman and Kranenborg (2006) EL Rev 93–101. See, on these cases, and more generally on the balancing of free movement and fundamental rights and other public policy concerns, Corthaut, *EU ordre public* (Wolters Kluwer, 2012), 50–60 and 110–29.
[528] C-398/95, *SETTG*, 1997, para. 23 (referring to *Collectieve Antennevoorziening Gouda* (n. 524, *supra*), in which economic aims were held to be incapable of constituting a justificatory ground under Article 46 [*now Article 52 TFEU*]).
[529] e.g. C-243/01, *Gambelli and Others*, 2003, para. 61. See also C-249/15, *Wind 1014*, 2018, paras 48–9.
[530] C-249/15, *Wind 1014*, 2018, para. 50.
[531] C-388/01, *Commission v Italy*, 2003, para. 21; C-552/15, *Commission v Ireland*, 2017, para. 89.
[532] C-148/91, *Veronica Omroep Organisatie*, 1993, paras 12–14; C-23/93, *TV10*, 1994, paras 17–22; C-212/97, *Centros*, 1999, paras 23–30.

(3) **Application without distinction.** Third, the restrictions on trade in services must apply without distinction to all providers of services, regardless of the origin of the services and of the nationality of the service providers or of the Member State in which they are established (even if the restrictions discriminate indirectly).[533] A directly discriminatory restriction to the freedom to provide or receive services can be justified only by the expressly derogatory provisions of Articles 51 and 52 TFEU.[534]

7.093

(4) **Proportionality.** Finally, restrictions placed on freedom to provide services must be 'objectively justified' by the need to comply with such objectives in the public interest, that is, be suitable for securing the attainment of the interest pursued and not go beyond what is necessary in order to attain it.[535] The restrictions must be suitable for achieving those objectives, which implies that they have to genuinely reflect a concern to attain these objectives in a consistent and systematic manner.[536] Accordingly, a Member State may not rely on public policy in order to restrict the organisation of gaming when it is at the same time encouraging consumers to participate in games of chance.[537] In a federal Member State, the fact that one federal entity has imposed a restriction with a particular objective whereas other such entities apply a different legal regime, does not undercut the appropriateness of the objective per se.[538]

7.094

Furthermore, restrictions may be imposed only if the public interest is not already protected by the rules of the Member State of establishment of the provider of services and the same result cannot be obtained by less restrictive rules.[539] The obligation imposed on foreign undertakings employing workers in Germany to have certain documents relating to the employment relationship translated into German and to keep them during the posted workers' stay could be objectively justified according to the Court since, in the absence of these requirements, it would become extremely difficult or even impossible for the competent authorities to carry out the monitoring necessary to ensure compliance with the national provisions regarding worker protection.[540]

For the assessment of proportionality, the same principle of mutual recognition applies as with regard to the other freedoms. Accordingly, social legislation designed to protect an interest which is already similarly protected in the Member State in which the provider of services is established, for instance as a result of the implementation of a directive,[541] conflicts with free movement of services.[542] In the context of road safety, a Member State

---

[533] C-490/04, *Commission v Germany*, 2007, para. 86. In some cases however, the Court seems to require the absence of even indirect discrimination: C-234/03, *Contse*, 2005, paras 37–8.
[534] C-153/08, *Commission v Spain*, 2009, paras 37–8; C-546/07, *Commission v Germany*, 2009, paras 47–8.
[535] 110 and 111/78, *Van Wesemael*, 1979, para. 29.
[536] C-42/07, *Liga Portuguesa de Futebol Profissional and Bwin International Ltd*, 2007, para. 38; C-169/08, *Regione Sardegna*, 2009, para. 42.
[537] C-243/01, *Gambelli and Others*, 2003, paras 67–9.
[538] C-156/13, *Digibet and Albers*, 2014, paras 31–9.
[539] C-154/89, *Commission v France*, 1991, para. 15. See, with regard to the imposition of a minimum wage, C-165/98, *Mazzoleni*, 2001, paras 25–9.
[540] C-490/04, *Commission v Germany*, 2007, paras 69–80.
[541] C-341/05, *Laval un Partneri*, 2007, paras 107–10.
[542] 279/80, *Webb*, 1981, paras 18–20. C-272/94, *Guiot*, 1996, paras 19–21, *infra*; C-369/96 and C-376/96, *Arblade and Others*, 1999, paras 32–80; see also C-49/98, C-50/98 to C-54/98, C-68/98 to C-71/98, *Finalarte Sociedade de Construçao Civil and Others*, 2001, paras 28–83; C-279/00 *Commission v Italy*, 2002, paras 19–25 and 33–5; C-244/04, *Commission v Germany*, 2006, paras 44–51. See Giesen, 'Posting: Social Protection of Workers vs. Fundamental Freedoms?' (2003) CMLRev 143–58. See also C-33/17, *Čepelnik*, 2018, paras 46–9.

may subject a service provider who is already subject to technical inspections in another Member State to additional testing only if the first Member State subjects domestic service providers to the same inspections in the same circumstances.[543] For the same reasons, a Member State may not impose unnecessary requirements when it places restrictions upon the possibility to receive a service in another Member State, for example in connection with the reimbursement of medical treatment received abroad.[544] All the same, in view of the particular characteristics of the sector involving games of chance via the internet, the principle of mutual recognition does not apply automatically.[545] The fact that less strict provisions apply in one Member State than in another does not signify in itself that provisions in force in the latter Member State are disproportionate and hence incompatible with Union law.[546]

A requirement for prior authorization or permission may constitute a justified restriction on freedom to provide services where national rules on the receipt or performance of the relevant services have not (yet) been harmonized. A prior authorization scheme must, in any event, be based on objective, non-discriminatory criteria which are known in advance.[547] Such a prior administrative authorization scheme must likewise be based on a procedural system which is easily accessible and capable of ensuring that a request for authorization will be dealt with objectively and impartially within a reasonable time and refusals to grant authorization must be capable of being challenged in legal proceedings.[548] It is only when such requirement can be objectively justified that a Member State may require service providers to have a particular legal form or status.[549] The requirement to have a permanent establishment in the territory of the Member State where services are provided, is the 'very negation of th[e] freedom' to provide services and would therefore be acceptable only if truly 'indispensable for attaining the objective pursued'.[550]

7.095 **Provision of services and establishment.** A Member State may not make the provision of services in its territory subject to compliance with all the conditions required for establishment. This would deprive the right freely to provide services of all practical effectiveness.[551] The Treaties do not require a provider to offer services in the Member State in which it is established as well.[552] If, however, providers of services direct their activities entirely or principally towards the territory of a neighbouring Member State for the purpose of avoiding its

---

[543] C-451/99, *Cura Anlagen*, 2002, para. 46.
[544] C-158/96, *Kohll*, 1998, para. 35; C-157/99, *Smits and Peerbooms*, 2001, paras 45 and 62–9; C-8/02, *Leichtle*, 2004, paras 27–51; C-444/05 *Stamatelaki*, 2007, paras 26–8 and 34–7.
[545] C-42/07, *Liga Portuguesa de Futebol Profissional and Bwin International Ltd*, 2009, paras 68–72. Accordingly, a Member State may take the view that the fact that an operator of services in this sector is already subject to statutory conditions and control in the Member State in which it is established, cannot be regarded as amounting to a sufficient assurance that national consumers will be protected against the risks of fraud and crime, in the light of the difficulties liable to be encountered in such a context by the authorities of the Member State of establishment in assessing the professional qualities and integrity of operators (ibid.).
[546] C-384/93, *Alpine Investments*, 1995, para. 51; C-3/95, *Reisebüro Broede*, 1996, para. 42.
[547] C-205/99, *Analir and Others*, 2001, para. 38; C-157/99, *Smits and Peerbooms*, 2001, para. 90.
[548] C-157/99, *Smits and Peerbooms*, 2001, para. 90.
[549] For the difficulty for a Member State to demonstrate the necessity of such a requirement, see—albeit under Article 15 of the Services Directive—C-209/18, *Commission v Austria*, 2019, paras 78–106.
[550] 205/84, *Commission v Germany*, 1986, para. 52; C-101/94, *Commission v Italy*, 1996, para. 31; C-439/99, *Commission v Italy*, 2002, para. 30. The Court of Justice accepted a requirement for a permanent establishment in, e.g., C-204/90, *Bachmann*, 1992, paras 32–3.
[551] C-154/89, *Commission v France*, 1999, para. 12; C-76/90, *Säger*, 1991, para. 13.
[552] C-56/96, *VT4*, 1997, para. 22.

professional rules of conduct, that Member State may apply its rules relating to the right of establishment and not to the provision of services.[553] A Member State may further prohibit national undertakings from participating in undertakings established in another Member State from which they provide services which would frustrate national legislation,[554] or subject such providers of services to the same conditions as providers established on its own territory.[555] A Member State may not prohibit altogether the provision of certain services by operators established in other Member States, as that would be tantamount to abolishing the freedom to provide services.[556] However, a domestic prohibition on the provision of particular services may make it necessary to ban the same services provided from other Member States.[557]

4. The Services Directive

Overview. On the basis of (the predecessors of) Articles 53 and 62 TFEU, the European Parliament and the Council adopted Directive 2006/123 of 12 December 2006 on services in the internal market[558] in order to create a framework for strengthening the internal market for services. This 'Services Directive' aims to remove obstacles in the Member States' legal orders that hamper the freedom of establishment or the freedom to provide services. It thus lays down general provisions facilitating the exercise of the freedom of establishment and the free movement of services, while maintaining a high quality of services.[559] For the purpose of the Service Directive, a service is defined as any self-employed economic activity, normally provided for remuneration, as referred to in Article 57 TFEU,[560] whereas establishment means the actual pursuit of an economic activity, as referred to in Article 49 TFEU, for an indefinite period and through a stable infrastructure from where the business of providing services is actually carried out.[561]

7.096

First, Chapter II of the Services Directive contains measures aimed at simplifying national administrative procedures so that it becomes easier to start providing services. Crucial in this respect is the requirement for Member States to create points of single contact that may guide service providers through national procedures and formalities.[562] Second, Chapter III Services Directive contains measures aimed at facilitating the establishment in another Member State of service providers, by ensuring that authorization schemes do not create

---

[553] 33/74, *Van Binsbergen*, 1974, para. 13; see also 115/78, *Knoors*, 1979, para. 25.
[554] C-148/91, *Veronica Omroep Organisatie*, 1993, paras 12–14.
[555] C-23/93, *TV10*, 1994, paras 20–2.
[556] C-211/91, *Commission v Belgium*, 1992, para. 12; C-11/95, *Commission v Belgium*, 1996, para. 65.
[557] C-275/92, *Schindler*, 1994, paras 61–2. See also 15/78, *Société Générale Alsacienne de Banque*, 1978, para. 5.
[558] 2006 OJ L376/36. See Hatzopoulos, *Regulating Services in the European Union* (OUP, 2012); Wiberg, *The EU Services Directive: Law or Simply Policy?* (Asser Press, 2014); Barnard, 'Unravelling the Services Directive', (2008) CMLRev 323; Mulder, 'Aangenomen dienstenrichtlijn: sociale dumping of het dumpen van socialisme?' (2008) SEW 2–9; Peglow, 'La libre prestation de services dans la directive n° 2006/123/CE. Réflexion sur l'insertion de la directive dans le droit communautaire existant' (2008) RTDE 67–118; Drijber, 'Van democratie en bureaucratie: de Dienstenrichtlijn is erdoor' (2007) NTER 1–7; Simon, 'La directive "services": quelle contribution au marché intérieur?' (2007) JTDE 33–43.
[559] Directive 2006/123, Article 1(1).
[560] Directive 2006/123, Article 4(1); C-724/18 and C-727/18, *Cali Appartments SCI*, 2020, para. 33. This includes retail trade in goods (C-360/15 and C-31/16, *X and Visser*, 2018, paras 84–97), including the storage of goods for retail purposes but not the goods themselves (C-393/17, *Kirschstein*, 2019, paras 66–77). It does not matter who pays for the service, see C-351/12, *OSA*, 2014, paras 57–63. It also encompasses higher education services, see C-66/18, *Commission v Hungary*, 2020, para. 195.
[561] Directive 2006/123, Article 4(5).
[562] Directive 2006/123, Article 6.

artificial barriers to entry and by requiring Member States to remove or evaluate a number of substantive requirements that tend to make it exceedingly difficult for service providers to establish themselves in a Member State. Third, Chapter IV of the Services Directive seeks to protect both service providers and the recipients of services. Finally, the Services Directives contains provisions in order to help ensure the quality level of services in cross-border situations (Chapter V).[563] To that end the Services Directive introduces mechanisms for administrative cooperation between Member States to make sure that service providers can primarily be held accountable in their Member State of origin (Chapter VI).

7.097 **Scope.** The Services Directive applies in principle to all service providers established in a Member State (Article 2(1) of Directive 2006/123). This means that its application does not require a cross-border element.[564] Indeed, the Services Directive is based on Articles 53(1) and 62 TFEU, which, unlike Articles 49 and 56 TFEU, do not mention any foreign element, allowing thus the Union legislature to extend the scope of application of harmonizing measures to internal situations.[565]

Article 2(2) of the Services Directive nevertheless excludes a number of sensitive sectors, such as non-economic services of general interest,[566] health services,[567] financial services,[568] services that involve the exercise of public authority,[569] social services,[570] and transport services[571] from its scope of application. Those exceptions must, however, be interpreted narrowly, so that services related to those exceptions, but not as such exempted, remain within the scope of the Services Directive.[572] The Services Directive does not apply in the field of taxation (Article 2(3)), nor when its provisions conflict with a provision of another Union act governing specific aspects of access to, or the exercise of, a service activity

---

[563] This encompasses rules on information on providers and their services (Article 22), the professional liability insurance and guarantees (Article 23), and commerical communications by the regulated professions (Article 24, for a definition thereof, see C-19/15, *Verband Sozialer Wettbewerb*, 2016, para. 27; see also the prohibition on canvassing by regulated professions: C-119/09, *Société fiduciaire nationale d'expertise comptable*, 2011, paras 23–46), restrictions on multidisciplinary services (Article 25; see C-209/18, *Commission v Austria*, 2019, paras 116–25; C-384/18, *Commission v Belgium*, 2020, paras 43–59), policy on quality of services (Article 26) and dispute settlement (Article 27).

[564] C-360/15 and C-31/16, *X and Visser*, 2018, para. 110; C-377/17, *Commission v Germany*, 2019, para. 58; C-393/17, *Kirschstein*, 2019, para. 24; C-724/18 and C-727/18, *Cali Appartments SCI*, 2020, para. 56.

[565] C-360/15 and C-31/16, *X and Visser*, 2018, paras 104–10.

[566] By contrast, for-profit education services are covered, see C-393/17, *Kirschstein*, 2019, paras 54–6.

[567] C-57/12, *Femarbel*, 2013, paras 30–53 (distinguishing various care facilities for the elderly, depending on the role of medical professionals in the care). The exception only applies to health services for human, not for veterinary services, see C-297/16, *Colegiul Medicilor Veterinari din România*, 2018, paras 40–1.

[568] C-581/18, *RB*, 2020, para. 43. Also the mobile payment system is not excluded, see C-171/17, *Commission v Hungary*, 2018, paras 41–5.

[569] The conferral of university degrees does not amount to the exercise of public authority, see C-393/17, *Kirschstein*, 2019, para. 60. In addition, chimney sweeps, even if they have a role in enforcing fire safety regulations, are not excluded for the scope of application, see C-293/14, *Hiebler*, 2015, paras 27–7.

[570] C-197/11 and C-203/11, *Libert*, 2013, paras 103–7 (social housing); C-57/12, *Femarbel*, 2013, paras 30–53 (care facilities).

[571] C-168/14, *Grupo Itevelesa*, 2015, paras 38–54 (roadworthiness tests for vehicles); C-434/15, *Asociación Profesional Élite Taxi*, 2017, paras 33–49 and C-320/16, *Uber France*, 2018, paras 15–28 (mediation services for taxi services); C-563/17, *Associação Peço a Palavra*, 2019, paras 28–33 (air carriers). Compare C-340/14 and C-341/14, *Trijber and Harmsen*, 2015, paras 43–59 (harbour tours for tourists are not transport services).

[572] C-724/18 and C-727/18, *Cali Appartments SCI*, 2020, para. 39. Accordingly, the exception for social housing (Article 2(2)(j) of Directive 2006/123) does not extend to activities consisting in the repeated short-term letting, for remuneration, whether on a professional or non-professional basis, of furnished accommodation to a transient clientele that does not take up residence there.

in specific sectors or for specific professions as laid down in a number of Directives (Article 3(1)).[573] Moreover, Article 1 of the Services Directive excludes certain areas of law from its scope.[574]

Establishment. The Services Directive has a far-ranging impact on national administrative law, not so much through its provisions on administrative simplification, which only have a limited scope,[575] but by significantly restricting the Member State's freedom to apply authorization schemes[576] requiring service providers to obtain authorization from any authority—whether at the national, regional, or local level—prior to setting up their business. Thus, Article 9 of the Services Directive requires Member States to first justify the need for any authorization scheme.[577] If such a scheme is nevertheless put in place, the authorization criteria used must be (a) non-discriminatory; (b) justified by an overriding reason relating to the public interest; (c) proportionate to that public interest objective; (d) clear and unambiguous; (e) objective; (f) made public in advance; and (g) transparent and accessible (Article 10(2) of Directive 2006/123).[578] The Services Directive moreover has special rules on the duration of authorizations,[579] on the selection of candidates if only a limited number of authorizations are available,[580] and on authorization procedures and application fees[581] (Articles 11 to 13 of the Services Directive).

7.098

The Services Directive also restricts the type of substantive requirements[582] that Member States may impose on service providers seeking establishment. In part inspired by the case

---

[573] See, e.g., C-360/15 and C-31/16, *X and Visser*, 2018, paras 54–82 (administrative fees already covered by Directive 2002/20/EC of the European Parliament and of the Council of 7 March 2002 on the authorization of electronic communications networks and services ('Authorization Directive') (OJ 2002 L108/21)); C-390/18, *X*, 2019, paras 41–69: exclusion of services (such as the AirBnB platform) that come within the scope of Directive 2000/31/EC of the European Parliament and of the Council of 8 June 2000 on certain legal aspects of information society services, in particular electronic commerce, in the Internal Market ('Directive on electronic commerce') (OJ 2000 L178/1).

[574] The Services Directive does not apply to the liberalization or financing of services of general economic interest (C-171/17, *Commission v Hungary*, 2018, paras 41–5), the abolition of monopolies on providing services (C-171/17, *Commission v Hungary*, 2018, paras 41–5; C-342/17, *Memoria*, 2018, paras 40–3), measures taken to protect or promote cultural or linguistic diversity or media pluralism, criminal law (C-137/17, *Van Gennip*, 2018, paras 100–2; however, Member States may not restrict the freedom to provide services by applying criminal law provisions which specifically regulate or affect access to or exercise of a service activity in circumvention of the rules laid down in that directive; see C-393/17, *Kirschstein*, 2019, paras 61–3), labour law and social security (see C-33/17, *Čepelnik*, 2018, paras 27–36; C-64/18, C-140/18, C-146/18, and C-148/18, *Maksimovic*, 2019, para. 28), and the exercise of fundamental rights.

[575] C-577/10, *Commission v Belgium*, 2012, para. 50.

[576] For the defintion of an 'authorization scheme', see Article 4(6) of Directive 2006/123 ('any procedure under which a provider or recipient is in effect required to take steps in order to obtain from a competent authority a formal decision, or an implied decision, concerning access to a service activity or the exercise thereof'). See also C-360/15 and C-31/16, *X and Visser*, 2018, paras 112–18 (zoning plan is not an authorization scheme); C-724/18 and C-727/18, *Cali Appartments SCI*, 2020, paras 46–53 (authorization scheme for short-term letting).

[577] For an example of overriding reasons relating to the public interest that could justify the existence of an authorization scheme, see C-724/18 and C-727/18, *Cali Appartments SCI*, 2020, paras 62–75 (avoiding rental shortages). See also C-393/17, *Kirschstein*, 2019, paras 70–3 (ensure a high level of higher education and protect the recipients of services).

[578] On those criteria, see, e.g., C-293/14, *Hiebler*, 2015, paras 48–79; C-340/14 and C-341/14, *Trijber and Harmsen*, 2015, paras 67–77; C-137/17, *Van Gennip and Others*, 2018, paras 78–87; C-724/18 and C-727/18, *Cali Appartments SCI*, 2020, paras 76–108.

[579] C-340/14 and C-341/14, *Trijber and Harmsen*, 2015, paras 60–6.

[580] C-458/14 and C-67/15, *Promoimpresa and Melis*, 2016, paras 37–57.

[581] C-316/15, *Hemming*, 2016, paras 26–34.

[582] For the definition of a 'requirement', see Article 4(7) of Directive 2006/123. See also C-360/15 and C-31/16, *X and Visser*, 2018, paras 119–25.

law of the Court of Justice, it prohibits outright some of the most restrictive requirements making the entry of service providers from other Member States exceedingly difficult (Article 14 of Directive 2006/123).[583] Other, less restrictive requirements may only be imposed if the Member State concerned demonstrates that they do not discriminate and are necessary and proportionate (Article 15).[584] Services of general economic interest are not automatically excluded from this assessment.[585]

Where a restriction of the freedom of establishment falls within the scope of Directive 2006/123, there is no need to also examine it in the light of Article 49 TFEU.[586] Indeed, the Court has held that Articles 9 to 13 of Directive 2006/123 provide for exhaustive harmonization concerning the services falling within their scope.[587]

7.099 **Provision of services.** Article 16(1) of the Services Directive requires that Member States respect the right to provide services in a Member State other than that in which the providers are established, by ensuring free access to, and free exercise of, a service activity within its territory. Member States shall not make access to, or exercise of, a service activity in their territory subject to compliance with any requirements which are discriminatory, not necessary for reasons of public policy, public security, public health, or the protection of the environment (which severely limits the justifications Member States can rely on if compared to Articles 51 and 52 TFEU and the rule of reason), or disproportionate. Moreover, some of the most restrictive requirements are prohibited outright (Article 16(2) of the Services Directive).[588]

---

[583] C-593/13, *Rina Services*, 2015, paras 33–41 (discrimination on basis of place of registered office held contrary to Article 14(1) of Directive 2006/123); C-209/18, *Commission v Austria*, 2019, paras 47–53 (seat requirement held contrary to Article 14(1)(b) of Directive 2006/123).

[584] C-179/14, *Commission v Hungary*, 2016, paras 54–70 (legal form held contrary to Article 15(2)(b) of Directive 2006/123) and 81–95 (reserving access to a service activity to particular providers by virtue of the specific nature of the activity held contrary to Article 15(2)(d) of Directive 2006/123); C-360/15 and C-31/16, *X and Visser*, 2018, paras 126–36 (territorial restriction to be assessed in light of Article 15(2)(a) of Directive 2006/123); C-297/16, *Colegiul Medicilor Veterinari din România*, 2018, paras 50–73 (exclusive right to retail and use organic products, special purpose anti-parasitic products, and veterinary medicinal products for veterinaries allowed under Article 15(2)(d) of Directive 2006/123) and paras 74–89 (restrictions on shareholdings contrary to Article 15(2)(c) of Directive 2006/123); C-171/17, *Commission v Hungary*, 2018, paras 76–87 (reserve access to the mobile payment system to particular providers held contrary to Article 15(2)(d) of Directive 2006/123); C-377/17, *Commission v Germany*, 2019, paras 56–96 (minimum and maximum tariffs for architects held contrary to Article 15(2)(g) of Directive 2006/123); C-473/17 and C-546/17, *Repsol Butano*, 2019, paras 41–5 (maximum prices for liquid gas not contrary to Article 15(2)(g) of Directive 2006/123); C-209/18, *Commission v Austria*, 2019, paras 78–103 (restrictions on legal form and shareholding held contrary to Article 15(2)(b) and (c) of Directive 2006/123); C-729/17, *Commission v Greece*, 2019, paras 52–70 (limiting the legal form of mediator training institutions to non-profit companies that must be jointly formed of at least one Bar association and at least one business chamber in Greece, held contrary to Article 15(2)(b) and (c) and (3) of Directive 2006/123).

[585] Article 15(4) of Directive 2006/123 provides that Article 15(1) to (3) are to apply to legislation in the field of services of general economic interests only to the extent that their application does not obstruct the performance, in law and in fact, of the particular task assigned to them. See C-171/17, *Commission v Hungary*, 2018, para. 62. See also C-293/14, *Hiebler*, 2015, paras 73–8 (enforcing fire safety regulation by chimney sweeps may be a service of general economic interest that can justify certain restrictions).

[586] C-179/14, *Commission v Hungary*, 2016, para. 118; C-360/15 and C-31/16, *X and Visser*, 2018, para. 137; C-729/17, *Commission v Greece*, 2019, para. 54.

[587] C-458/14 and C-67/15, *Promoimpresa and Melis*, 2016, para. 61.

[588] See, e.g., C-179/14, *Commission v Hungary*, 2016, para. 102–17 (requiring foreign service providers to have a seat in the territory where they provide services held contrary to Article 16(2)(a) of Directive 2006/123); C-66/18, *Commission v Hungary*, 2020, paras 203–5 (restrictions on higher education services provided by institutions established in other Member States not justified by the aim of maintaining public order).

D. Free movement of capital and payments

1. Definition and substance

Context. Article 63 TFEU prohibits all restrictions on the movement of capital and payments between Member States and between Member States and third countries. The prohibition of Article 63 TFEU has direct effect.[589]

7.100

Capital movement. Free movement of capital constitutes a necessary support for the freedoms discussed above: a transaction in goods or services or establishment in another Member State will often require investment necessitating a capital movement to another Member State. Nevertheless, the EEC Treaty provided only for the gradual abolition over a transitional period of restrictions on capital movements and of discrimination on grounds of nationality or place of establishment/investment. National policy on capital movements is intermeshed with Member States' economic and monetary policies and could be liberalized only when the economic policy options of the Member States were more attuned to each other. The Council introduced a gradual liberalization of the various categories of capital movements, culminating in the general liberalization requirement laid down by Directive 88/361 of 24 June 1988, which entered into force on 1 July 1990.[590] At the start of the second phase of the economic and monetary union (on 1 January 1994) the original Treaty provisions were replaced with a new Title, which provides for the full liberalization of capital movements. The new Article 56 EC—now Article 63 TFEU—went further than the Directive in that it also liberalized, in principle, capital movements with third countries.[591]

7.101

Although the Treaties do not define the term 'movement of capital', it is settled case law that, inasmuch as Article 63 TFEU substantially reproduces the content of Article 1 Directive 88/361, the nomenclature of capital movements annexed thereto retains an indicative value for the purposes of defining the term 'movement of capital', subject to the qualification, contained in the introduction to the nomenclature, that the list set out therein is not exhaustive.[592] The 'movement of capital' not only covers investments and loans, including the loan of a vehicle for use free of charge,[593] but also inheritances[594] and deduction for tax purposes of gifts in money or in kind.[595]

---

[589] C-163/94, C-165/94, and C-250/94, *Sanz de Lera and Others*, 1995, paras 40–8 (Article 56(1) EC in conjunction with Articles 57 and 58(1)(b) EC [*now Articles 63(1), 64 and 65(1)(b) TFEU*]. For a survey of the case law, see Flynn, 'Coming of Age: The Free Movement of Capital Case Law 1993-2002' (2002) CMLRev 773–805.
[590] Council Directive 88/361/EEC of 24 June 1988 for the implementation of [*the former*] Article 67 of the Treaty, OJ 1988 L178/5. Member States could still adopt protective measures in respect of certain capital movements, but only with the Commission's authorization and for a maximum six-month period (Article 3). The first steps towards liberalization were taken with the First Council Directive of 11 May 1960 for the implementation of [*the former*] Article 67 of the Treaty, OJ 1959–1962 English Special Edition 49, and the Second Council Directive (63/21/EEC) of 18 December 1962 adding to and amending the First Directive for the implementation of [*the former*] Article 67 of the Treaty, [1963–1964] OJ English Special Edition 5. No further steps were taken until the programme for achieving the internal market.
[591] Article 7(1) of Directive 88/361 contained only a commitment on the part of the Member States to endeavour to achieve this end.
[592] e.g. C-222/97, *Trummer and Mayer*, 1999, para. 21; C-515/99, C-519/99 to C-524/99, and C-526/99 to C-540/99, *Reisch and Others*, 2002, para. 30; C-376/03, *D.*, 2005, para. 24; C-513/03, *van Hilten-van der Heijden*, 2006, para. 39.
[593] C-578/10, *Van Putten*, 2012, paras 27–36.
[594] C-513/03, *van Hilten-van der Heijden*, 2006, paras 40–2.
[595] C-318/07, *Persche*, 2009, paras 24–30; C-78/18, *Commission v Hungary*, 2020, para. 51.

The 'restrictions' prohibited by Article 63 TFEU cover, generally, any restriction on movements of capital either between Member States[596] or between Member States and third countries.[597] First of all, Article 63 TFEU prohibits State measures which are discriminatory in nature in that they establish, directly or indirectly, a difference in treatment between domestic and cross-border movements of capital that does not correspond to an objective difference in circumstances[598] and which are therefore liable to deter natural or legal persons from other Member States or third countries from carrying out cross-border movements of capital.[599] The prohibition of restrictions on movement of capital thus aims at more than eliminating discrimination based on nationality on the financial markets and precludes all rules which make free movement of capital illusory by preventing market participants from investing in other Member States or by rendering it difficult for undertakings to raise capital in another Member State.[600] Accordingly, national measures dissuading nationals of the Member State in question from taking out loans or making investments in other Member States[601] or making direct foreign investment dependent on authorization[602] are incompatible with the free movement of capital. Even if such measures apply without distinction to both residents and non-residents, they are prohibited if they are liable to deter investors from making investments in another Member State and, consequently, affect access to the market.[603] As in the case of the free movement of services, the distinction in respect of selling arrangements introduced in respect of the free movement of goods by the *Keck and Mithouard* judgment does not apply. Non-discriminatory restrictions are, in principle, prohibited whenever they impede market access to another Member State.[604]

7.102 **Movement of payments.** Free movement of payments relates to transfers of foreign exchange as consideration for a transaction.[605] Since 1 January 1994, all payments have been liberalized in currencies of Member States, in euros, or in currencies of third countries.

2. Permitted restrictions on the free movement of capital and payments

7.103 **Permitted restrictions.** Restrictions on the free movement of capital may be justified on grounds of general interest, including the grounds for exceptions set out in Article 65 TFEU

---

[596] See, e.g., C-105/12 to C-107/12, *Essent*, 2013, para. 39.
[597] See, e.g., C-45/17, *Jahin*, 2018, paras 19–21; C-135/17, *X*, 2019, para. 26; C-78/18, *Commission v Hungary*, 2020, para. 52.
[598] C-446/04, *Test Claimants in the FII Group Litigation*, 2006, para. 46; C-485/14, *Commission v France*, 2015, paras 25–6.
[599] C-78/18, *Commission v Hungary*, 2020, para. 53.
[600] C-35/98, *Verkooijen*, 2000, paras 34–5.
[601] C-484/93, *Svensson and Gustavsson*, 1995, paras 9–10; C-222/97, *Trummer and Mayer*, 1999, para. 26; C-439/97, *Sandoz*, 1999, para. 19. See also C-478/98, *Commission v Belgium*, 2000, para. 20 (prohibition of acquisition of securities for loans issued abroad); C-367/98, *Commission v Portugal*, 2001, paras 45–6; C-483/99, *Commission v France*, 2002, paras 40–2 ('golden shares'; requirement for approval of the acquisition of holdings in privatized companies); C-98/01, *Commission v United Kingdom*, 2003, paras 38–50; C-282/04 and C-283/04, *Commission v Netherlands*, 2006, paras 18–31 (restriction on the possibility of buying voting shares in a privatized company); C-319/02, *Manninen*, 2004, paras 20–3; C-292/04, *Meilicke and Others*, 2007, paras 20–4 (tax credit not applicable to dividends from companies established in other Member States); C-112/05, *Commission v Germany*, 2007, paras 38–56 ('Volkswagen'; capping of shareholders' voting rights); C-235/17, *Commission v Hungary*, 2019, paras 54-58 (acquiring usufruct over agricultural lands reserved to persons having close family ties with the owner of the land).
[602] C-163/94, C-165/94, and C-250/94, *Sanz de Lera and Others*, 1995, paras 24–5; C-302/97, *Konle*, 1999, paras 23 and 38–9; C-54/99, *Eglise de scientology*, 2000, para. 14.
[603] C-171/08, *Commission v Portugal*, 2010, para. 67 (see, to the same effect, the case law with respect to the free movement of goods and persons: paras 7-029, 7-043, and 7-062, *supra*).
[604] C-212/09, *Commission v Portugal*, 2011, paras 63–5.
[605] 286/82 and 26/83, *Luisi and Carbone*, 1984, para. 21.

and other mandatory requirements.[606] However, a distinction must be drawn between unequal treatment permitted under Article 65(1)(a) TFEU and arbitrary discrimination prohibited under Article 65(3) TFEU.[607] Moreover, in certain circumstances, restrictions may be imposed on capital movements (Articles 64 and 66 TFEU) or on capital movements and payments (Article 75 TFEU) to or from third countries.

Explicit justificatory grounds. Article 65(1) b) TFEU allows the Member States to take 'all requisite measures' (a) to prevent infringements of national law and regulations, in particular in the tax field and in regard to the prudential supervision of financial institutions; (b) to lay down procedures for the declaration of capital movements for the purposes of administrative or statistical information;[608] and (c) to take measures justified on grounds of public policy or public security.[609] Moreover, Article 65(1) a) contains a general exception for provisions of tax law which justifiably 'distinguish between taxpayers who are not in the same situation with regard to their place of residence or with regard to the place where their capital is invested'.[610] However, that article cannot be interpreted as meaning that any tax legislation making a distinction between taxpayers by reference to the place where they invest their capital is automatically compatible with the Treaties.[611] Such distinction may indeed not constitute an arbitrary discrimination prohibited under Article 65(3) TFEU.[612] In order for national tax legislation to be compatible with the Treaty provisions on the free movement of capital, the difference in treatment must concern situations which are not objectively comparable or justified by overriding reasons in the public interest and must not go beyond what is necessary to achieve the objective pursued by the measure at issue.[613] In this respect, the Court of Justice found a Flemish inheritance tax reduction applicable to forests subject to a sustainable management plan to be discriminatory to the extent that it did not extend to forests adjacent to the Flemish territory, but not discriminatory as regards forests located elsewhere outside the Flemish territory, as only the former may be subject to a sustainable management plan in accordance with the Flemish legislation.[614]

7.104

---

[606] Moreover, Protocol (No. 32) annexed to the Treaties on the acquisition of property in Denmark by the EU Treaty (OJ 1992. C224/104, now OJ 2010 C83/318) and Protocol (No. 6), annexed to the 2003 Act of Accession, on the acquisition of secondary residences in Malta, (OJ 2003 L236/947) allow these Member States to maintain in force restrictions on the acquisition and holding of immovable property for secondary residence purposes. In the case of Malta, this applies to nationals of the Member States who have not legally resided in that State for at least five years.

[607] C-679/17, *Huijbrechts*, 2018, para. 20.

[608] C-235/17, *Commission v Hungary*, 2019, paras 102–9.

[609] See C-439/97, *Sandoz*, 1999, paras 24–37; C-54/99, *Eglise de scientology*, 2000, para. 19; C-423/98, *Albore*, 2000, paras 17–25; C-478/98, *Commission v Belgium*, 2000, paras 37–8. For restrictions on capital movements in connection with public security, in particular in order to secure energy supplies in a crisis, cf. C-367/98, *Commission v Portugal*, 2002, paras 52–4, and C-483/99 *Commission v France*, 2002, paras 47–54 (requirement for the approval of the acquisition of holdings in privatized companies held to be in breach of free movement of capital) with C-503/99, *Commission v Belgium*, 2002, paras 46–55 (more specifically defined restriction held not to be in breach of free movement of capital); C-235/17, *Commission v Hungary*, 2019, paras 110–22; C-78/18, *Commission v Hungary*, 2020, paras 88–96 (Hungarian transparency law on NGOs could not be justified on grounds of public policy or public security in the absence of a genuine threat).

[610] Declaration (No. 7), annexed to the EU Treaty, on Article 73d EC [*now Article 65 TFEU*] made it clear that Member States are entitled to apply the derogation in respect of capital movements and payments between Member States only as far as provisions in force at the end of 1993 are concerned.

[611] C-319/02, *Manninen*, 2004, para. 28.

[612] C-679/17, *Huijbrechts*, 2018, para. 20.

[613] C-679/17, *Huijbrechts*, 2018, para. 21. See also C-256/06, *Jäger*, 2008, paras 41–2; C-386/04, *Centro di Musicologia Walter Stauffer*, 2006, para. 32; C-318/07, *Persche*, 2009, para. 41.

[614] C-679/17, *Huijbrechts*, 2018, paras 23–9.

A distinction contained in national tax provisions is thus compatible with Union law only if it concerns situations which are not objectively comparable[615] or if it can be justified by overriding reasons in the general interest, such as those related to the cohesion of the tax system.[616] Accordingly, Member State legislation, designed to prevent double taxation, which provides for a tax benefit in relation to dividends paid to persons subject to income tax in that Member State may not exclude from this benefit dividends paid by companies established in other Member States.[617] Conversely, it is not incompatible with Union law for a Member State to deny non-resident taxpayers who hold the major part of their wealth in the Member State where they are resident entitlement to the allowances which it grants to resident taxpayers.[618] Article 65 also does not preclude a Member State from subjecting dividends from shares in companies established in the territory of that Member State and dividends from shares in companies established in another Member State to the same uniform rate of taxation even in the absence of rules to avoid double taxation.[619]

7.105 **Rule of reason.** The Court of Justice is further prepared to inquire into whether a restriction on capital movements can be justified on grounds of general interest other than those mentioned in Article 65(1) TFEU. Restrictions are held to be permissible provided that they are not applied in a discriminatory manner and do not exceed what is necessary in order to achieve an objective in the general interest (rule of reason),[620] such as the need to preserve the cohesion of the tax system;[621] objectives in connection with town and country planning[622] and public housing policy;[623] objectives connected with the carrying on of the activities of agricultural and forestry holdings and the protection of the rural communities dependent on those activities[624] as well as the preservation of jobs in such holdings in cases of inheritance;[625] the objective of maintaining or promoting the use of an official language;[626] or increasing the transparency of financial support granted to natural or legal persons out of public funds granted by the Union, by means of obligations of declaration and publication.[627] Economic grounds cannot in themselves afford a valid justification.[628]

---

[615] C-279/93, *Schumacker*, 1995.
[616] C-204/90, *Bachmann*, 1992; C-300/90, *Commission v Belgium*, 1992; C-35/98, *Verkooijen*, 2000, para. 43; C-315/02, *Lenz*, 2004, paras 34–9; C-379/05, *Amurta*, 2007, paras 42–56; C-250/08, *Commission v Belgium*, 2011, paras 69–77.
[617] C-319/02, *Manninen*, 2004. See, in the same vein, C-446/04, *Test Claimants in the FII Group Litigation*, 2006; C-292/04, *Meilicke and Others*, 2007.
[618] C-376/03, *D*, 2005, paras 25–43.
[619] C-513/04, *Kerckhaert and Morres*, 2006.
[620] e.g. C-367/98, *Commission v Portugal*, 2002, para. 49; C-483/99, *Commission v France*, 2002, para. 45; and C-503/99, *Commission v Belgium*, 2002, para. 45.
[621] See C-35/98, *Verkooijen*, 2000, para. 43.
[622] See C-302/97, *Konle*, 1999, paras 36–49; C-515/99, C-519-524/99, C-526-540/99, *Reisch and Others*, 2002, para. 34; C-300/01, *Salzmann*, 2003, para. 42. See Glöckner, 'Grundverkehrsbeschränkungen und Europarecht' (2000) EuR 592–622.
[623] C-567/07, *Woningstichting Sint Servatius*, 2009, para. 30 (this aim was not, by contrast, accepted as a public-policy ground within the meaning of Article 65 TFEU: ibid., para. 28); C-197/11 and C-203/11, *Libert and Others*, 2013, paras 51–2 (aim to guarantee sufficient housing for low-income or otherwise disadvantaged sections of the local population).
[624] C-370/05, *Festersen*, 2007, paras 27–8; C-679/17, *Huijbrechts*, 2018, paras 31–42; C-52/16 and C-113/16, *SEGRO and Horvath*, 2018, paras 82–3; C-235/17, *Commission v Hungary*, 2019, paras 91–2.
[625] C-256/06, *Jäger*, 2008, para. 50.
[626] C-222/07, *UTECA*, 2009, para. 27.
[627] C-78/18, *Commission v Hungary*, 2020, para. 78. According to the Court 'that objective is apt to improve the level of information enjoyed by citizens on that subject and to enable them to participate more closely in public debate'. See also, C-92/09 and C-93/09, *Volker und Markus Schecke and Eifert*, 2010, paras 68–71.
[628] C-367/98, *Commission v Portugal*, 2002, para. 52.

Proportionality. A parallel may be drawn with the requirement of proportionality applying **7.106**
to permissible derogations from free movement of goods and services, since the 'measures
and procedures referred to in Article 65(1) and (2) shall not constitute a means of arbitrary discrimination or a disguised restriction on the free movement of capital and payments' (Article 65(3) TFEU; cf. Article 36 TFEU). In order for an unequal treatment of
different categories of capital gains to be justified, the treatment cannot go beyond what is
necessary to achieve the objectives pursued by the national regulation. Thus, France could
not deny foreign companies the benefit of a tax exemption enjoyed by companies established in France on the sole ground that the information needed by the French authorities
effectively to combat tax evasion could not be obtained from the competent authorities of
other Member States involved, since it would have been possible to request that the necessary documentary evidence be provided by the taxpayer himself.[629] Similarly, on grounds
of public policy (e.g. preventing illegal activities such as tax evasion, money laundering,
drug trafficking, or terrorism), a Member State may make the export of foreign currency
conditional on a prior declaration, but not on prior authorization, which would make capital movements conditional upon the consent of the administrative authorities.[630] Prior authorization for foreign investment cannot be regarded as a proportionate measure where
the same objective can be achieved by prior notification and the associated possibilities
for supervision and imposing sanctions.[631] In any event, any authorization system must be
based on objective, non-discriminatory criteria which are known in advance to the undertakings concerned, and all persons affected by a restrictive measure of that type must have a
legal remedy available to them.[632]

Movement to and from third countries. Movement of capital to or from third countries **7.107**
takes place in a different legal context than between Member States. It follows that a Member
State may be able to justify a restriction on the movement of capital to or from third countries for a particular reason in circumstances where that reason would not constitute a valid
justification for a restriction on capital movements between Member States.[633] For instance,
where the legislation of a Member State makes the grant of a tax advantage dependent on
satisfying requirements compliance with which can be verified only by obtaining information from the competent authorities of a third country, it is, in principle, legitimate for that
Member State to refuse to grant that advantage if—in particular, because that third country
is not under any obligation to provide information—it proves impossible to obtain such information from that country.[634]

---

[629] C-451/05, *ELISA*, 2007, paras 94–6; C-318/07, *Persche*, 2009, paras 53–69. For a general discussion of the impact of the provisions on free movement of capital on the competence of the Member States in the field of direct taxation, see Dahlberg, *Direct Taxation in Relation to the Freedom of Establishment and the Free Movement of Capital* (Kluwer Law International, 2005).
[630] C-163/94, C-165/94, and C-250/94, *Sanz de Lera and Others*, 1995, paras 23–30. This was already the case under Directive 88/361: C-358/93 and C-416/93 *Bordessa and Others*, 1995, paras 16–31.
[631] e.g. C-515/99, C-519-524/99, and C-526-540/99, *Reisch and Others*, 2002, paras 35–9.
[632] C-367/98, *Commission v Portugal*, 2002, para. 50; C-483/99 *Commission v France*, 2002, para. 45; and C-503/99, *Commission v Belgium*, 2002, para. 46.
[633] C-446/04, *Test Claimants in the FII Group Litigation*, 2006, para. 171; C-101/05, *A*, 2007, paras 36–7; C-78/18, *Commission v Hungary*, 2020, para. 80. This implies conversely that a Member State that fails to distinguish between capital movements coming from third countries and those coming from other Member States may fail to meet its burden of proof in respect of the latter: paras 81–2.
[634] C-101/05, *A*, 2007, paras 58–63.

As far as capital movements to and from third countries are concerned, restrictions existing on 31 December 1993[635] under national or Union law in respect of direct investment (including investment in real estate), establishment, the provision of financial services, or the admission of securities to capital markets may continue to be applied (Article 64(1) TFEU). In order to secure compliance with such restrictions, Member States are entitled to verify the nature and reality of the transactions and transfers in question by means of a prior declaration.[636] The European Parliament and the Council, acting in accordance with the ordinary legislative procedure, may adopt measures on such capital movements (Article 64(2)). Moreover, the Council may unanimously, and after consulting the European Parliament, adopt measures which constitute new restrictions on such capital movements (Article 64(3) TFEU[637]).

In addition, the Council may take such safeguard measures as are strictly necessary where, 'in exceptional circumstances, movements of capital to or from third countries cause, or threaten to cause, serious difficulties for the operation of economic and monetary union' (Article 66 TFEU). The European Central Bank must be consulted and the measures may not go on for more than six months. Article 75(1) TFEU defines the Union's power to take economic sanctions in the sphere of capital movements and payments for the purpose of preventing and combating terrorism and related activities. The European Parliament and the Council, acting in accordance with the ordinary legislative procedure, are to define a framework for such measures, which is to be implemented by the Council (Article 75 TFEU).[638]

III. Harmonization of National Legislation

7.108   **Legal bases for harmonization.** Specific Treaty provisions empower the Union to bring divergent national laws more in line with each other, even though they are completely compatible with Union law, where the disparities between those laws affect the competitive position of the market participants concerned or inadequately protect other interests, such as those of consumers.[639] Thus, the Treaties supplement the provisions on free movement

---

[635] C-135/17, *X*, 2019, paras 25–51. As far as Bulgaria, Estonia, and Hungary are concerned, the date is 31 December 1999 (see Article 18 of the 2003 Act of Accession and Article 16 of the 2005 Act of Accession. As far as Croatia is concerned, the date is 31 December 2002 (Article 12 of the 2011 Act of Accession).

[636] C-163/94, C-165/94, and C-250/94, *Sanz de Lera and Others*, 1995, paras 37–8. See also Ståhl, 'Free Movement of Capital between Member States and Third Countries' (2004) EC Tax Rev 47–56. For a complete picture of the framework for investments from non-member countries, see Vadcar, 'Un cadre communautaire pour l'investissement?' (2001) RMCUE 332–42.

[637] In the absence of such measures, the Commission or the Council may decide that restrictive tax measures adopted by a Member State concerning one or more third countries are to be considered compatible with the Treaties in so far as they are justified by one of the objectives of the Union and compatible with the proper functioning of the internal market. The Council is to act unanimously on application by a Member State (Article 65(4) TFEU).

[638] For the scope of application of Article 75 TFEU, see C-130/10, *European Parliament v Council*, 2012, para. 54 (scope more limited than earlier Articles 60 and 301 EC as Article 75 TFEU no longer refers to the 'interruption or reduction . . . of economic relations with one or more third countries' but merely refers to the definition, for the purpose of preventing terrorism and related activities, of a framework for administrative measures with regard to capital movements and payments, when this is necessary to achieve the objectives set out in Article 67 TFEU), Accordingly, for measures affecting third countries, recourse must be had to Article 215 TFEU.

[639] Andenas and Andersen (eds), *The Theory and Practice of Harmonisation* (Edward Elgar Publishing, 2012); Slot, 'Harmonisation' (1996) ELRev 378–97; Vignes, 'Le rapprochement des législations', in Calleja, Vignes, and Wägenbaur, *Commentaire Mégret. Le droit de la CEE. 5. Dispositions fiscales. Rapprochement des législations*

of goods, persons, services, and capital by providing a legal basis for harmonization, coordination, approximation, and mutual recognition of national legislation or administrative provisions.[640] In addition, Articles 114–118 TFEU afford general legal bases for the 'approximation of legislation', together with the supplementary legal basis of Article 352 TFEU.[641] The Treaty articles that provide a specific legal basis for the development of Union policies generally also enable the Union to harmonize national legislation whenever necessary for pursuing the Union objectives in the area concerned.[642] Some of the changes that the Treaty of Lisbon introduced in specific policy areas resulted in an extension of the Union's powers to harmonize national law.[643] Moreover, the conferral on the Union of specific competences in the fields of intellectual property, tourism, civil protection, and energy have made it less necessary to have recourse to the 'flexibility clause' of Article 352 TFEU.[644] In addition, the Treaty of Lisbon has enabled the Member States to set up 'open methods of coordination' with the Commission in various policy areas. Where there is an open method of coordination, the Member States are encouraged to submit national policies to periodic monitoring and evaluation against guidelines and indicators established in common.[645] In some cases, this voluntary coordination of national policies can make formal harmonization unnecessary.[646]

A. The impact of Union harmonization measures

Expanding Union law. As a result of the harmonization of national legislation, Union law penetrates into areas which are not expressly mentioned as part of the Union's competence.[647] Thus, the Member States had to adapt their national rules to suit directives

7.109

(Editions de l'Université de Bruxelles, 1993), 299–379; for the political implications, see Dougan, 'Minimum Harmonisation and the Internal Market' (2000) CMLRev 853–85.

[640] With regard to the free movement of goods, see Article 113 TFEU (indirect taxation); as regards free movement of persons and services, see Articles 46 and 48; Article 50, in particular para. 2(g); and Articles 52, 53, and 59 TFEU.

[641] Paras 5-017–5-018, *supra*. Before the Treaty of Lisbon, the Treaties also provided for the possibility for the Member States to conclude agreements between themselves which could lead to the approximation of laws (see Article 293 EC; see also para. 28-018, *infra*). The Lisbon Treaty no longer provides for this possibility.

[642] See, for instance, Articles 40 and 41 TFEU relating to agriculture; Article 91 TFEU relating to transport; Article 121 TFEU for the coordination of Union economic policy; Article 153 TFEU as regards social policy.

[643] See, e.g., the extended powers with respect to coordination of national social security law (see para. 7-078, *supra*), immigration laws (see para. 8-012, *infra*), and criminal law (see paras 8-019 and 8-021, *infra*).

[644] See, with respect to intellectual property rights, Article 118 TFEU (entailing the power to provide uniform protection of intellectual property rights throughout the Union and to set up centralized Union-wide authorization, coordination, and supervision arrangements). See with respect to energy, tourism, civil protection, and administrative cooperation, Articles 194 to 197 TFEU (these articles, however, explicitly exclude harmonization measures).

[645] See Article 156, second para. TFEU (on social policy, see also para. 9-046, *infra*); Article 168(2), second para. TFEU (on public health); Article 173, second para. TFEU (on industrial policy); Article 181, second para. TFEU (on research and technological development). Compare the formal coordination of national economic policies on the basis of *ex Article 99 EC* and of national employment policies on the basis of Article 128 EC (see para. 9-049, *infra*).

[646] For this method, see de Búrca, 'The Constitutional Challenge of new Governance in the European Union' (2003) ELRev 814–39.

[647] See Davies, 'Democracy and Legitimacy in the Shadow of Purposive Competence', (2015) ELJ 2; Garben, 'Confronting the Competence Conundrum: Democratising the European Union through an Expansion of its Legislative Powers' (2014) OJLS 1.

coordinating national procedures for the award of public works contracts[648] and the relevant review procedures[649] in order to guarantee free movement of goods, persons, and services in connection with the award of public contracts.[650] In addition, the Union has adopted rules for the coordination of national law on intellectual property[651] and has introduced Union intellectual property rights.[652] Since the Treaty of Lisbon an explicit legal basis exists in this respect (Article 118 TFEU), on the basis of which the Union legislature has created a unitary patent protection, providing Union status to patents granted by the European

---

[648] See, most recently, Directive 2014/23/EU of the European Parliament and of the Council of 26 February 2014 on the award of concession contracts, OJ 2014 L94/1; Directive 2014/24/EU of the European Parliament and of the Council of 26 February 2014 on public procurement, OJ 2014 L94/65 and Directive 2014/25/EU of the European Parliament and of the Council of 26 February 2014 on procurement by entities operating in the water, energy, transport and postal services sectors, OJ 2014 L94/243.

[649] See the Council directives adopted pursuant to Article 100a EC [*now Article 114 TFEU*]: Directive 89/665/EEC of 21 December 1989 on the application of review procedures to the award of public supply and public works contracts, OJ 1989 L395/33, and, specifically as regards the sectors referred to in the preceding n., Directive 92/13/EEC of 25 February 1992 on the application of Community rules on procurement procedures, OJ 1992 L76/14.

[650] Bovis, 'Developing Public Procurement Regulation: Jurisprudence and its Influence on Law Making' (2006) CMLRev 461–95. Bovis, 'Public Procurement in the European Union: Lessons from the Past and Insights to the Future' (2005) Col JEL 53–123; Bovis, 'The New Public Procurement Regime of the European Union: A Critical Analysis of Policy, Law and Jurisprudence' (2005) ELRev 607–30; Arrowsmith, 'An Assessment of the New Legislative Package on Public Procurement' (2004) CMLRev 1277–325. For the review procedures, see Boyenga-Bofala, 'L'impact des directives-recours sur l'organisation des voies de droit internes et les modalités d'exercice par le juge administratif français de son office' (2002) RTDE 499–525.

[651] Council Directive 87/54/EEC of 16 December 1986 on the legal protection of topographies of semiconductor products, OJ 1987 L24/36; Council Directive 91/250/EEC of 14 May 1991 on the legal protection of computer programs, OJ 1991 L122/42; Council Directive 93/83/EEC of 27 September 1993 on the coordination of certain rules concerning copyright and rights related to copyright applicable to satellite broadcasting and cable retransmission, OJ 1993 L248/15; Directive 96/9/EC of the European Parliament and of the Council of 11 March 1996 on the legal protection of databases, OJ 1996 L77/20; Directive 98/44/EC of the European Parliament and of the Council of 6 July 1998 on the legal protection of biotechnological inventions, OJ 1998 L213/13; Directive 98/71/EC of the European Parliament and of the Council of 13 October 1998 on the legal protection of designs, OJ 1998 L289/28; Directive 2001/29/EC of the European Parliament and of the Council of 22 May 2001 on the harmonization of certain aspects of copyright and related rights in the information society, OJ 2001 L167/10; Directive 2001/84/EC of the European Parliament and of the Council of 27 September 2001 on the resale right for the benefit of the author of an original work of art, OJ 2001 L275/32; Directive 2006/115/EC of the European Parliament and of the Council of 12 December 2006 on rental right and lending right and on certain rights related to copyright in the field of intellectual property, OJ 2006 L376/28 (repealing Directive 92/100); Directive 2006/116/EC of the European Parliament and of the Council of 12 December 2006 on the term of protection of copyright and certain related rights, OJ 2006 L372/12; Directive 2008/95/EC of the European Parliament and of the Council of 22 October 2008 to approximate the laws of the Member States relating to trademarks, OJ 2008 L299/25 (repealing Directive 89/104/EEC); Directive 2009/24/EC of the European Parliament and of the Council of 23 April 2009 on the legal protection of computer programs, OJ 2009 L111/16 (repealing Directive 91/250/EEC); Directive (EU) 2015/2436 of the European Parliament and of the Council of 16 December 2015 to approximate the laws of the Member States relating to trademarks, OJ 2015 L336/1 (repealing Directive 2008/95/EC).

[652] See, pursuant to Article 308 EC [*now Article 352 TFEU*], Council Regulation (EC) 40/94 of 20 December 1993 on the Community trademark (OJ 1994 L11/1), which has since become Regulation (EU) 2017/1001 of the European Parliament and of the Council of 14 June 2017 on the European Union trade mark (OJ 2017 L154/1); Council Regulation (EC) No. 2100/94 of 27 July 1994 on Community plant variety rights (OJ 1994 L227/1) and Council Regulation (EC) No. 6/2002 of 12 December 2001 on Community designs (OJ 2002 L3/1). See also, pursuant to Article 100a EEC [*later Article 95 EC, now Article 114 TFEU*], Council Regulation (EEC) No. 1768/92 of 18 June 1992 concerning the creation of a supplementary protection certificate for medicinal products (OJ 1992 L182/1) (for the Union's competence: C-350/92, *Spain v Council*, 1995, paras 25–41), since replaced by Regulation (EC) No. 469/2009 of the European Parliament and of the Council of 6 May 2009 concerning the supplementary protection certificate for medicinal products, OJ 2009 L152/1; Regulation (EC) No. 1610/96 of the European Parliament and of the Council of 23 July 1996 concerning the creation of a supplementary protection certificate for plant protection products (OJ 1996 L198/30) and Directive 2004/48/EC of the European Parliament and of the Council on the enforcement of intellectual property rights (OJ 2004 L157/45; republished with corrigendum: OJ 2004 L195/16). For further particulars, see Tritton, Davis and St Quintin, *Triton on Intellectual property in Europe* (Sweet & Maxwell, 2018); Pila and Torremans, *European Intellectual Property Law* (OUP, 2016); Leistner, 'Harmonization of Intellectual Property Law in Europe: The European Court of Justice's Trade Mark Case Law 2004-2007' (2008) CMLRev 69–91.

Patent Office.[653] Furthermore, there was harmonization in the fields of tourism and civil protection, even before the Treaties provided for a specific competence in these fields (see now Articles 194 and 196 TFEU).[654] As a result of its action to protect tourists and other consumers, in particular with regard to financial services (see paras 7-054, *supra* and 9-056, *infra*), and its action with respect to cross-border collaboration in civil matters (see para. 8-015, *infra*), the Union is becoming increasingly involved in areas of private law, such as the law of contractual and non-contractual liability and family law.[655]

Because of the primacy of Union law, once legislation has been harmonized, it can no longer be amended or replaced by national rules.[656] In policy areas where this influence on national law is not desired, the Treaties have expressly precluded any power to harmonize on the part of the Union.[657] In view of the political implications of harmonization, disputes often arise with regard to the proper legal basis for the relevant Union legislation, with

---

[653] Regulation (EU) No. 1257/2012 of the European Parliament and of the Council of 17 December 2012 implementing enhanced cooperation in the area of the creation of unitary patent protection, OJ 2012 L361/1. The choice of Article 118, first para. TFEU as legal basis for Regulation (EU) No. 1257/2012 was upheld by the Court in C-146/13, *Spain v European Parliament and Council*, 2015, paras 39–53. Likewise, the choice of Article 118, second para. TFEU as legal basis for Council Regulation (EU) No. 1260/2012 of 17 December 2012 implementing enhanced cooperation in the area of the creation of unitary patent protection with regard to the applicable translation arrangements (OJ 2012 L361/89) was upheld by the Court in C-147/13, *Spain v Council*, 2015, paras 68–75. Earlier Spain and Italy had also unsuccessfully challenged the decision to authorize enhanced cooperation in this field, see C-274/11 and C-295/11, *Spain and Italy v Council*, 2013. By means of an international agreement, the participating states (with the exception of Croatia and Spain) have established a United Patent Court (OJ 2013 C175/1) that will be competent in respect of disputes relating to unitary patent protection (once the agreement obtained sufficient ratifications to enter into force). See Baldan and van Zimmeren, 'The Future Role of the Unified Patent Court in Safeguarding Coherence in the European Patent System' (2015) CML Rev 1529–78. A prior draft of the agreement was held to be in breach of the Treaties by the Court: Opinion 1/09, *Draft agreement on the European and Community Patents Court*, 2011.

[654] See, for instance, the Community action plan to assist tourism, Council Decision 92/421/EEC of 31 July 1992 (OJ 1992 L231/26). The EC Treaty did not confer a specific competence to take action in these fields, although they were mentioned as one of the policy spheres listed in *ex Article 3 EC*. Even before that, the Council adopted on 22 December 1986 a decision (86/664/EEC) establishing a consultation and cooperation procedure in the field of tourism (OJ 1986 L384/52) and resolutions on standardized information in existing hotels (86/665/EEC, OJ 1986 L384/54) and fire safety in existing hotels (86/666/EEC, OJ 1986 L384/60). See Guyot, 'Le droit européen du tourisme' (2008) JTDE 101–11.

[655] See the Communications from the Commission to the Council and the European Parliament on European contract law, OJ 2001 C255/1, and on a more coherent European contract law—An action plan, OJ 2003 C63/1 and the more recent Commission documents available at the Commission's website: http://ec.europa.eu/consumers/rights/contract_law_en.htm. For a selection of the general literature with further citations therein, see Gutman, *The Constitutional Foundations of European Contract Law. A Comparative Analysis* (OUP, 2015); Schulze (ed.), *Common Frame of Reference and Existing EC Contract Law* (Sellier, 2009); Boele-Woelki and Grosheide (eds), *The Future of European Contract Law: Essays in Honour of Ewoud Hondius* (Kluwer law international, 2007); Grundmann and Stuyck (eds), *An Academic Green Paper on European Contract Law* (Kluwer law international, 2002); and, with particular regard to developments concerning EU consumer contract law, Howells and Schulze (eds), *Modernising and Harmonising Consumer Contract Law* (Sellier, 2009). Discussion is under way on the utility of a wider ranging harmonization of private law; for a selection of the general literature, see Micklitz and Cafaggi (eds), *European Private Law after the Common Frame of Reference* (Edward Elgar Publishing, 2010); Cafaggi and Muir Watt (eds), *Making European Private Law: Governance Design* (Edward Elgar Publishing, 2008); Andenas et al. (British Institute of International and Comparative law, 2007); Hartkamp et al. (eds), *Towards a European Civil Code* (Kluwer Law International, 2004). For the influence of the case law on family law, see Lenaerts, 'La portée de la jurisprudence de la Cour de justice des Communautés européennes en matière de droit de la famille et des personnes' (2008) RTDF 637–56.

[656] But this only applies to the extent that the national legislation effectively falls within the scope of the harmonizing measure; see C-528/16, *Confédération paysanne*, 2018, paras 77–82. See also C-431/17, *Monarchos Eirinaios*, 2019, paras 30–1, where a distinction is made between the rules on the registration of a lawyer under his home-country professional title, which is harmonized by Directive 98/5/EC, and the subsequent application of rules on professional conduct that are not harmonized.

[657] See para. 5-018, *supra*.

general legal bases or specific Treaty provisions being argued for, depending on the different voting procedures in the Council or the input of the European Parliament (see paras 5-018–5-020, *supra*).

7.110 **Minimum harmonization.** In some cases, a harmonization measure allows the Member States to adopt or maintain stricter rules in its national legislation than those required by the harmonization itself. Where the harmonization measure does not expressly so provide, it has to be inferred from the wording, purpose, and structure of the measure to what extent complete harmonization is intended (*full or exhaustive harmonization*) or whether it leaves the Member States any margin to deviate from a requirement or a level of protection laid down by the measure (*minimum harmonization*).[658] For instance, the Court held that Directive 2005/29[659] constitutes an exhaustive harmonization at the Union level of the rules on unfair business-to-consumer practices. This implies that Member States are precluded from adopting more restrictive measures than those laid down in the Directive, even if the objective is to ensure a higher level of consumer protection.[660] By contrast, the 'money-laundering directive', Directive 2005/60[661] only provides for minimum harmonization, so that Member States may adopt more restrictive provisions to combat money laundering and the financing of terrorism.[662]

7.111 **Mutual recognition.** Harmonization of national legislation becomes protracted where unanimity has to be achieved on detailed rules. Since the 1980s, a major part of harmonization has taken place following an approach whereby only minimum requirements are harmonized, after which the Member States must recognize each other's legislation. That approach links up with the *Cassis de Dijon* case law, which prohibits Member States, in the absence of harmonization, from imposing restrictions on the marketing of products which are lawfully marketed in another Member State, unless such restrictions are necessary in order to protect 'mandatory [or overriding] requirements' (see para. 7-042, *supra*).

As early as 1985, the Council advocated laying down by directive only the basic safety standards for products and leaving it to other bodies (e.g. standardization institutes) to specify them in technical standards. Every administration would then have to accept that products

---

[658] See, e.g., with regard to liability for defective products: C-52/00, *Commission v France*, 2002, paras 13–24; C-154/00, *Commission v Greece*, 2002, paras 9–20; and C-183/00, *González Sanchez*, 2002, paras 23–34; C-402/03, *Skov*, 2006, paras 22–45; C-470/03, *A.G.M.-COS.MET*, 2007, paras 50–4. See also C-445/06, *Danske Slagterier*, 2009, paras 23–5; with respect to the Directive on unfair commercial practices C-304/08, *Zentrale zur Bekämpfung unlauteren Wettbewerbs*, 2010, para. 41. For the differing intensity of harmonization, see Klamert, 'What We Talk About When We Talk About Harmonisation' (2015) CYES 360; Maletic, *The Law and Policy of Harmonisation in Europe's Internal Market* (Edward Elgar Publishing, 2013); Van Nuffel, 'Minimum Harmonisation and Consumer Law—Choice of Legal Basis', in Terryn, Straetmans and Colaert (eds), *Landmark Cases of EU Consumer Law—In Honour of Jules Stuyck*, (Intersentia, 2013), 173–98; Weatherill, 'Supply of and demand for internal market regulation: strategies, preferences and interpretation', in Nic Shuibhne (ed.), *Regulating the Internal Market* (Edward Elgar Publishing, 2006) 29–60; Rott, 'Minimum Harmonisation for the Completion of the Internal Market? The Example of Consumer Sales Law' (2003) CMLRev 1107–35; Kurcz, 'Harmonisation by Means of Directives—Never-ending Story?' (2001) E Bus LRev 287–307.

[659] Directive 2005/29/EC of the European Parliament and of the Council of 11 May 2005 concerning unfair business-to-consumer commercial practices in the internal market ('Unfair Commercial Practices Directive') OJ 2005 L149/22.

[660] See C-540/08, *Mediaprint Zeitungs- und Zeitschriftenverlag*, 2010, para. 37; C-343/12, *Euronics Belgium*, 2013; C-421/12, *Commission v Belgium*, 2014, paras 54–76.

[661] Directive 2005/60/EC of the European Parliament and of the Council of 26 October 2005 on the prevention of the use of the financial system for the purpose of money laundering and terrorist financing, OJ 2005 L309/15.

[662] See C-235/14, *Safe Interenvíos*, 2016, para. 76.

complying with those technical standards also complied with the basic safety standards.[663] The Union legislature has since followed the 'new strategy put forward by the Commission in its White Paper on completing the internal market', whereby harmonization designed to eliminate technical barriers would be limited to requirements for which the mutual recognition of national legislation alone did not produce a satisfactory result (see also paras 7-075–7-077, *supra*).[664] The Union also seeks to forestall measures restricting trade. Union information procedures require Member States to notify any draft technical regulations and standards to the Commission and to take account of any observations submitted by the Commission or other Member States.[665]

B. Harmonization under Articles 114 and 115 TFEU

Harmonization within the internal market. 'Approximation of laws, regulations and administrative provisions' of the Member States may be based on Article 114(1) TFEU where they 'have as their object the establishment and functioning of the internal market' or on Article 115 TFEU where they 'directly affect the establishment or functioning of the internal market'.[666] The manner in which the decision is taken to effect such approximation of national legislation differs sharply: under Article 114 TFEU, the Council and the European Parliament decide in accordance with the ordinary legislative procedure, which requires only a qualified majority in the Council; under Article 115 TFEU, the Council is to act unanimously after consulting the European Parliament. The legal instruments also differ: only directives may be issued under Article 115 TFEU, whereas Article 114 TFEU authorizes the adoption of any 'measures'. Although preference was to be given to directives under Article 114,[667] the Union could impose harmonization of national legislation by regulation

7.112

---

[663] Council Resolution of 7 May 1985 on a new approach to technical harmonization and standards, OJ 1985 C136/1. The following standardization bodies operate at European level: CEN (European Committee for Standardization), Cenelec (European Committee for the Coordination of Electrical Standards), and ETSI (European Telecommunications Standards Institute); see also the Council resolutions of 28 October 1999 on the role of standardization in Europe and on mutual recognition, OJ 2000 C141/1 and C141/5, respectively. See also Ehricke, 'Dynamische Verweise in EG-Richtlinien auf Regelungen privater Normungsgremien' (2002) EuZW 746–53; Andrieu, 'La normalisation européenne, instrument de cohésion—quelques points de repère' (1992) RMCUE 627–30; MacMillan, 'La "certification", la reconnaisance mutuelle et le marché unique' (1991) RMUE 181–211; Waelbroeck, 'L'harmonisation des règles et normes techniques dans la CEE' (1988) CDE 243–75.

[664] *Completing the internal market: Commission white paper for the European Council* (n. 14, *supra*), 19, section 65.

[665] See Directive (EU) 2015/1535 of the European Parliament and of the Council of 9 September 2015 laying down a procedure for the provision of information in the field of technical regulations and of rules on Information Society services, OJ 2015 L241/1, replacing Directive 98/34/EC of the European Parliament and of the Council of 22 June 1998 laying down a procedure for the provision of information in the field of technical standards and regulations and of rules on Information Society services, OJ 1998 L204/37 (For the inapplicability of non-notified provisions, see para. 23-014, *infra*. For an application, see e.g., C-390/18, *X*, 2019, para. 88; C-320/16, *Uber France*, 2018, paras 26–8; see also, in respect of the 1998 directive, C-299/17, *VG Media*, 2017, para. 39; C-194/94, *CIA Security*, 1996, para. 54.

[666] Before the entry into force of the Lisbon Treaty, Article 94 EC referred, in this connection, to the 'establishment or functioning of the common market', while Article 95(1) EC already referred to the 'establishment or functioning of the internal market'. For this difference in terminology, see para. 7-010, *supra*.

[667] See the declaration annexed to the Single European Act that the Commission shall give preference to the use of the instrument of a directive in its proposals pursuant to Article 95(1) EC [*now Article 114(1) TFEU*] if harmonization involves the amendment of legislative provisions in one or more Member States.

too.⁶⁶⁸ In addition, Article 114—and not Article 115—allows Member States to maintain or introduce national provisions derogating from a Union harmonization measure (see para. 7-115, *infra*).

7.113 **Scope of application of Article 114.** The first para. of Article 114 TFEU applies to measures 'for the achievement of the objectives set out in Article 26' '[s]ave where otherwise provided in the Treaties'. The provision has a broad scope of application as a result of the definition of the internal market set out in Article 26 TFEU (see para. 7-001, *supra*). Nevertheless, it does not confer a general power on the Union to regulate the internal market. The application of Article 114 is not triggered by a mere finding of disparities between national rules.⁶⁶⁹ In the judgment by which the Court of Justice annulled the tobacco advertising directive, it held that the measures referred to in Article 95 EC [*now Article 114 TFEU*] must genuinely have as their object the improvement of the conditions for the establishment and functioning of the internal market.⁶⁷⁰ Where such a measure has the aim of preventing the emergence of future obstacles to trade resulting from multifarious development of national laws, the emergence of such obstacles must be likely and the measure in question must be designed to prevent them.⁶⁷¹ Where a measure adopted on the basis of Article 114 TFEU purports to eliminate a distortion of competition, such distortion must be appreciable.⁶⁷² Article 114 TFEU cannot be used as a legal basis for measures which leave unchanged the different laws of the Member States already in existence and cannot be regarded as aiming to approximate the national laws.⁶⁷³ However, where an act based on Article 114 TFEU has already removed any obstacle to trade in the area that it harmonizes, the Union legislature cannot be denied the possibility of adapting that act to any change in circumstances or development of knowledge having regard to its task of safeguarding the general interests recognized by the Treaty.⁶⁷⁴

A number of Treaty articles explicitly preclude the power to harmonize on the part of the Union, for instance with regard to public health (see Article 168(5) TFEU).⁶⁷⁵ In that case, it is not possible for the Union legislature to use other articles of the Treaty, Article 114 TFEU in particular, as a legal basis in order to circumvent the express exclusion of harmonization. However, provided that the conditions for recourse to Article 114 TFEU as a legal basis

---

⁶⁶⁸ Depending on the harmonizing instrument, Union legislation itself gives rise to obligations on individuals (regulations) or does so only after it has been transposed into national law (directives); see C-91/92, *Faccini Dori*, 1994, para. 24. See para. 27-026, *infra*.

⁶⁶⁹ C-482/17, *Czech Republic v European Parliament and Council*, 2019, para. 34; C-358/14, *Poland v European Parliament and Council*, 2016, para. 32.

⁶⁷⁰ C-376/98 *Germany v European Parliament and Council*, 2000, paras 83–4 (for commentaries, see n. 58 to para. 5-013, *supra*). In the aftermath of the Judgment a new Directive on Tobacco Advertising was adopted, which was more limited in scope. The Court rejected Germany's action for the annulment of that new directive (C-380/03, *Germany v European Parliament and Council*, 2006). See also C-518/07, *Commission v Germany*, 2010, paras 49–51 (independence of supervisory authority for processing of personal data held to contribute to the free movement of data). See further C-482/17, *Czech Republic v European Parliament and Council*, 2019, para. 35.

⁶⁷¹ C-376/98 *Germany v European Parliament and Council*, 2000, para. 86; C-377/98, *Netherlands v European Parliament and Council*, 2001, paras 15–18; C-491/01, *British American Tobacco (Investments) and Imperial Tobacco*, 2002, paras 60–1; C-58/08, *Vodafone and Others*, 2010, paras 33–48.

⁶⁷² C-376/98, *Germany v European Parliament and Council*, 2000, para. 106. For limits on the power to harmonize, see Selmayr, Kamann, and Ahlers, 'Die Binnenmarktkompetenz der Europäischen Gemeinschaft' (2003) EWS 49–61; Möstl, 'Grenzen an der Rechtsangleichung im europäischen Binnenmarkt' (2002) EuR 318–50.

⁶⁷³ C-436/03, *European Parliament v Council*, 2006, paras 40–5.

⁶⁷⁴ C-482/17, *Czech Republic v European Parliament and Council*, 2019, para. 38; C-58/08, *Vodafone*, 2010, para. 34.

⁶⁷⁵ See para. 5-015, *supra*.

are fulfilled, the Union legislature cannot be prevented from relying on that legal basis on the ground that public health—or one of the other general interests listed in Article 114(3) TFEU—is a decisive factor in the choices to be made.[676] Where obstacles to trade are existent or likely to emerge in the future, Article 114 TFEU enables the Union legislature to adopt not only measures requiring the Member States to authorize the marketing of certain products, but also measures that oblige them to subject such an authorization to certain conditions, or even to provisionally or definitively prohibit the marketing of the products concerned.[677] By the expression 'measures for the approximation' Article 114 TFEU confers on the Union legislature a discretion as regards the harmonization technique most appropriate for achieving the desired result, in particular in fields which are characterized by complex technical features.[678] The addressees of the measures adopted on the basis of Article 114 TFEU are not necessarily the individual Member States. The legislature may provide for the establishment of a Union body responsible for contributing to the implementation of a process of harmonization if the tasks conferred on such a body are closely linked to the subject matter of the acts approximating the national laws.[679] A Union body may thus be bestowed with the competence to take measures relating to particular products that are directly addressed to market participants.[680]

Before the Lisbon Treaty, the Court has held that Article 95 EC could not be used as a legal basis for measures which predominantly relate to police and judicial cooperation in criminal matters. The Court therefore annulled a Council decision on the conclusion of an international agreement providing for the processing of passenger name records for public security and law-enforcement purposes, even though the initial collection of those data took place in the course of an activity which fell within the scope of (then) Community law.[681] By contrast, Article 95 EC was held to constitute the appropriate legal basis for a directive on the processing of personal data directed essentially at service providers and not governing the activities of public authorities for law-enforcement purposes.[682]

Scope of application of Article 115. Article 115 TFEU covers first and foremost the three areas which Article 114(2) excludes from the application of Article 114(1) TFEU. However, the practical significance of Article 115 is not so great given that harmonization may be carried out in these areas on the basis of other Treaty articles as well.   7.114

The first category listed in Article 114(2) consists of 'fiscal provisions'. This covers all areas and aspects of taxation, whether substantive rules or procedural rules, including

---

[676] C-376/98, *Germany v European Parliament and Council*, 2000, paras 79 and 88; C-482/17, *Czech Republic v European Parliament and Council*, 2019, para. 36.
[677] C-434/02, *Arnold André*, 2004, paras 34–5; C-210/03, *Swedish Match*, 2004, paras 33–4; C-154/04 and C-155/04, *Alliance for Natural Health*, 2005, paras 32–8.
[678] C-66/04, *United Kingdom v European Parliament and Council*, 2005, paras 45–6, with case note by Gutman (2006) Col JEL 147–87.
[679] C-217/04, *United Kingdom v European Parliament and Council*, 2006, paras 44–5; see the notes by Randazzo (2007) CMLRev 155–69 and Gutman (2006) Col JEL147–87.
[680] C-270/12, *United Kingdom v European Parliament and Council*, 2014, paras 100–17.
[681] C-317/04 and C-318/04, *European Parliament v Commission*, 2006. After the annulment, a new agreement was concluded on the basis of ex Articles 24 and 38 EU; see the Agreement between the European Union and the United States of America on the processing and transfer of Passenger Name Record (PNR) data by air carriers to the United States Department of Homeland Security (DHS) (2007 PNR Agreement), see Council Decision 2007/551/CFSP/JHA of 23 July 2007, OJ 2007 L204/16.
[682] C-301/06 *Ireland v European Parliament and Council*, 2009, paras 56–93.

arrangements for the collection of such taxes.[683] In this field, Article 115 is relevant primarily to harmonization of direct taxation[684] since indirect taxation may be harmonized pursuant to Article 113 TFEU (the procedure is the same as for Article 115 TFEU).[685] Fiscal harmonization thus always requires unanimity in the Council.

The second excluded category listed in Article 114(2) refers to provisions 'relating to the free movement of persons'. This involves, above all, aspects of free movement of economically inactive persons. Indeed, as regards persons coming under the rules on workers, self-employed persons, providers, or recipients of services, national provisions may be harmonized under specific articles of the Treaties.[686]

The third category covers provisions 'relating to the rights and interests of employed persons', in respect of which specific articles likewise permit harmonization in some cases.[687]

7.115 **Authorized derogations.** Harmonization of national legislation by the Union legislature could be perceived as a threat by Member States whose legislation is based on a higher degree of protection than that afforded in most other Member States. Article 114(3) TFEU therefore provides that, in its proposals concerning health, safety, environmental protection, and consumer protection, the Commission is to take as its base a high level of protection, taking into account in particular any new development based on scientific facts.[688] In addition, a harmonizing measure may embody a safeguard clause authorizing Member States to take provisional measures on one or more of the grounds listed in Article 36 TFEU (Article 114(10) TFEU).[689]

Lastly, there are the exceptional provisions set out in Article 114(4) and (5) TFEU, which enable a Member State to apply national provisions when the European Parliament and the Council, the Council, or the Commission have adopted a harmonization measure. In

---

[683] C-338/01, *Commission v Council*, 2004, paras 63–7; C-533/03, *Commission v Council*, 2006, para. 47.

[684] e.g. Council Directive 2011/16/EU of 15 February 2011 on administrative cooperation in the field of taxation, OJ 2011 L64/1 (based on both Articles 113 and 115 TFEU) and Council Directive 2003/48/EC of 3 June 2003 on taxation of savings income in the form of interest payments, OJ 2003 L157/38 (based on Article 115 TFEU, but meanwhile repealed by Council Directive (EU) 2015/2060 of 10 November 2015, OJ 2015 L301/1). See on the latter, Dassesse, 'The EU Directive "On Taxation of Savings": The Provisional End of a Long Journey?' (2004) EC Tax Rev 41–6; Malherbe and Hermand, 'La nouvelle directive du 3 juin 2003 sur la fiscalité de l'épargne: éléments d'actualité' (2004) JT 145–50; Berlin, 'La fiscalité de l'épargne dans l'Union européenne. Histoire d'une harmonisation en voie de disparition' (2003) JTDE 162–168. For the competence to harmonize tax, see Lenaerts, 'Die Entwicklung der Rechtsprechung des Gerichtshofs der Europäischen Gemeinschaften auf dem Gebiet der direkten Besteuerung' (2009) EuR 728–48; Lenaerts, '"United in Diversity": also *In Fiscalibus*?', in Hinnekens and Hinnekens (eds), *A Vision of Taxes within and outside European Borders—Festschrift in honor of Prof. Dr. Frans Vanistendael* (Kluwer Law International, 2008) 617–34; Hrehorovska, 'Tax Harmonisation in the European Union' (2007) Intertax 158–66; Vanistendael, 'Memorandum on the Taxing Powers of the European Union' (2002) EC Tax Rev 120–9.

[685] For an example, see Council Regulation (EC) No. 2073/2004 of 16 November 2004 on administrative cooperation in the field of excise duties, OJ 2004 L359/1.

[686] See n. 640, *supra*.

[687] See Article 153(2) TFEU, para. 9-047, *infra*.

[688] According to Declaration (No. 22) annexed to the Treaty of Amsterdam, account must also be taken of the needs of persons with a disability (OJ 1997 C340/135).

[689] See De Sadeleer, 'Procedures for Derogations from the Principle of Approximation of Laws under Article 95 EC' (2003) CMLRev 889–915 and 'Les clauses de sauvegarde prévues à l'article 95 du traité CE' (2002) RTDE 53, 55–7; Bähr and Albin, 'The "Environmental Guarantee" on the Rise? The Amended Article 95 after the Revision through the Treaty of Amsterdam' (2000) EJ L Ref 119–34. On the relationship between harmonizing measures and the possibility to obtain authorizations, see C-547/14, *Phillip Morris Brands*, 2016, para. 71; T-337/13, *CSF v Commission*, 2015, para. 79; T-339/16, T-352/16, and T-391/16, *Ville de Paris v Commission*, 2018, para. 70.

the first place, a Member State may maintain existing measures which it deems necessary on grounds of major needs referred to in Article 36 TFEU or relating to the protection of the environment or the working environment (Article 114(4) TFEU). A Member State may base an application to maintain its already existing national provisions on an assessment of the risk to public health different from that accepted by the Union legislature when it adopted the harmonization measure from which the national provisions derogate. To that end, it must prove that those national provisions ensure a level of health protection which is higher than the Union harmonization measure and that they do not go beyond what is necessary to attain that objective.[690] Next, on grounds of a problem specific to a Member State arising after the adoption of the harmonization measure, the Member State concerned may apply (new) national provisions based on new scientific evidence relating to the protection of the environment or the working environment (Article 114(5) TFEU). In this particular instance, grounds other than protection of the environment or the working environment cannot justify a derogation.[691] In both instances, the Member State has to notify the Commission of the provisions maintained or introduced and of the grounds for maintaining or introducing them.[692] Within six months of notification, the Commission is to approve or reject the national provisions after having verified whether or not they are a 'means of arbitrary discrimination or a disguised restriction on trade between Member States and whether or not they ... constitute an obstacle to the functioning of the internal market' (Article 114(6)).[693] The Commission is not required to formally hear the notifying Member State before it takes its decision.[694] In the absence of a decision by the Commission, the national provisions in question are deemed to have been approved.[695] Rejection or approval constitutes a Commission decision against which an action will lie (e.g. where the

---

[690] C-3/00, *Denmark v Commission*, 2003, paras 63–5.

[691] For the difference between those two situations see, C-512/99, *Germany v Commission*, 2003, para. 41; C-3/00, *Denmark v Commission*, 2003, paras 57–62.

[692] By analogy with the third sentence of Article 108(3) TFEU (see para. 9-026, *infra*), it follows from Article 114(5) that the Member State is debarred from applying 'proposed measures' which deviate from the harmonization measure. Paras 4 to 9 of ex Article 95 EC [*now Article 114 TFEU*] were added by the Treaty of Amsterdam to specify para. 4 of the former Article 100a EC.

[693] See, e.g., the series of decisions of 26 October 1999 (OJ 1999 L329) by which the Commission approved national provisions on the marketing and use of creosote (notified by the Netherlands, Germany, Sweden, and Denmark) but not national provisions on the use of sulphites, nitrites, and nitrates in foodstuffs (notified by Denmark) and concerning mineral wool (notified by Germany). See Verheyen, 'Article 95 EC Treaty in Practice: The European Commission Decisions on creosote, Sulphite, Nitrates and Nitrites' (2000) RECIEL 71–5. The action brought by Denmark against the decision addressed to that Member State resulted in its partial annulment: C-3/00, *Denmark v Commission*, 2003 (as regards nitrites and nitrates); Germany's action against the decision addressed to that Member State was declared unfounded: C-512/99, *Germany v Commission*, 2003.

[694] C-439/05 P and C-454/05 P, *Land Oberösterreich v Commission*, 2007, paras 28–45.

[695] In the pre-Amsterdam Treaty version, Article 100a EC referred, in general terms, to provisions that a Member State wished to 'apply' and the Commission could 'confirm'. Pursuant thereto, on 2 August 1991 Germany notified the Commission of its decision to apply a stricter ban on pentachlorophenol (PCP) than that embodied in Council Directive 91/713/EEC of 21 March 1991, OJ 1991 L85/34, which Germany had voted against in the Council. On 2 December 1992, the Commission adopted a decision 'confirming' the national provisions, OJ 1992 C334/8. On an application from France, the Court of Justice annulled that decision for failure to satisfy the obligation to state the reasons on which it was based: C-41/93, *France v Commission*, 1994, paras 31–7. By Decision 94/783/EC of 14 September 1994, the Commission reconfirmed the derogation granted to Germany, OJ 1994 L316/43. The former Article 100a(4) EC did not contain any time within which the Commission had to take a decision. Failure by the Commission to react to a notification made by a Member State constituted a breach of the principle of sincere cooperation, but did not affect the applicability of the directive in question: C-319/97, *Kortas*, 1999, paras 33–8.

national provisions confirmed are considered not to be proportionate to the major needs referred to in Article 114(4)).[696]

When a Member State is authorized to maintain or introduce national provisions derogating from a harmonization measure, the Commission is to examine immediately whether to propose an adaptation to that measure (Article 114(7)). In the event that the Commission or a Member State considers that another Member State is making improper use of the powers conferred by Article 114, it may bring the matter directly before the Court of Justice by way of derogation from the procedure laid down in Articles 258 and 259 TFEU (Article 114(9)). Such misuse would be present if a Member State continued to apply the diverging national provisions after the Commission had rejected them or if it went beyond the limits of the approval granted by the Commission.

7.116 **Distortion of trade.** Where a difference between national legislations affects the conditions of competition in such a way as to give rise to a 'distortion', the European Parliament and the Council, acting in accordance with the ordinary legislative procedure, may issue the 'necessary directives' or 'other appropriate measures' pursuant to Article 116 TFEU. In order to avoid an amendment of national legislation giving rise to such a distortion, the Commission is to make recommendations to the Member State concerned (Article 117 TFEU).[697]

In practice, national measures impeding trade in goods in non-harmonized areas often prompt the Commission to bring proceedings before the Court of Justice or national courts to make references for preliminary rulings in connection with the obligations arising under Article 34 TFEU. In order to ensure the removal of unjustified barriers to trade, the Union legislature has enacted rules concerning the application by Member States of the principle of mutual recognition in relation to goods which are lawfully marketed in another Member State.[698] Where a Union measure has carried out an exhaustive harmonization of the grounds on which obstacles to trade may be justified, any national measure relating thereto must be assessed in the light of the provisions of that harmonizing measure and not of Articles 34 and 36 TFEU.[699] The Commission has also facilitated the set-up of a network of national 'SOLVIT' centres, each established within a Member State's administration, which provide a fast and informal means of resolving problems that individuals and businesses may still encounter when exercising their rights in the internal market.[700]

---

[696] However, a mere opinion adopted by the Commission on the scope of a certain harmonization measure does not constitute an action that can be challenged by a Member State: T-234/04, *Netherlands v Commission*, 2007, paras 47–73.

[697] After such distortion has arisen, the Council is not entitled to apply Article 116 to the other Member States in order to require them to amend their own legislation or to apply it in favour of a Member State which has caused distortion detrimental only to itself (Article 117(2)). For a general discussion, see Van Grinsven, 'Het distorsiebegrip bij voortschrijdende Europese integratie' (1991) SEW 173–93.

[698] Regulation (EU) 2019/515 of the European Parliament and of the Council of 19 March 2019 on the mutual recognition of goods lawfully marketed in another Member State, OJ 2019 L91/1 (adopted on the basis of Article 114 TFEU). See also Commission Notice Guidance document for the application of Regulation (EU) 2019/515 of the European Parliament and of the Council on the mutual recognition of goods lawfully marketed in another Member State, OJ 2021 C100/16.

[699] C-221/00, *Commission v Austria*, 2003, para. 42 (see paras 7-039–7-040, *supra*).

[700] Commission Recommendation 2013/461/EU of 17 September 2013 on the principles governing SOLVIT (OJ 2013 L249/10) and https://ec.europa.eu/solvit/index_en.htm. See Kokolia, 'Strengthening the Single Market through Informal Dispute-resolution Mechanisms in the EU: The Case of SOLVIT', (2018) MJECL 108–17; Haket and de Vries, 'Handhaving van het EU-interne-marktrecht door SOLVIT' (2016) SEW 370–82.

8
The Area of Freedom, Security, and Justice

Area of freedom, security, and justice. The Lisbon Treaty has brought together in Title V of Part Three of the TFEU ('Area of freedom, security and justice') all competences of the Union in respect of visa, asylum, immigration, judicial cooperation in civil matters, and police cooperation and judicial cooperation in criminal matters. Through its policy in these fields, the Union legislature is to ensure an 'area of freedom, security and justice with respect for fundamental rights and the different legal systems and traditions of the Member States' (Article 67(1) TFEU). The cooperation between the Member States in the area of freedom, security, and justice is based on mutual trust, on the basis of which every Member State must assume, barring exceptional circumstances, that the other Member States respect Union law and fundamental rights.[1] In order to appreciate the significance of the Union competences in this area, it is necessary to first set out the steps by which the Member States have gradually agreed to have recourse to supranational decision-making in matters such as the entry and residence of third-country nationals, police cooperation, and judicial cooperation in civil and criminal matters.

8.001

I. The Gradual Integration of Member States' Action in Matters of Justice and Home Affairs

Checks at internal and external borders. The establishment of an internal market 'without internal frontiers' required any formality imposed upon entry into the territory of a Member State from another Member State to be abolished (see para. 7-001 *et seq.*, *supra*). From 1 January 1993 checks at internal frontiers in principle disappeared for the movement of goods, but for the movement of persons identity checks continued to exist. The development of measures aimed at liberalizing the free movement of persons was largely left to intergovernmental cooperation, most notably in the framework of the Schengen Agreement (para. 1-037 *et seq.*, *supra*). Some Member States actually disputed whether the Community

8.002

---

[1] See, e.g., C-411/10 and C-493/10, *N. S.*, 2011, paras 78–80; C-399/11, *Melloni*, 2013, paras 37 and 63; Opinion 2/13, *Accession of the European Union to the European Convention for the Protection of Human Rights and Fundamental Freedoms*, 2014, para. 191; C-297/17, C-318/17, C-319/17, and C-438/17, *Ibrahim*, 2019, paras 83–5; C-163/17, *Jawo*, 2019, paras 80–3; C-509/18, *PF*, 2019, para. 22; C-508/18 and C-82/19 PPU, *OG and PI*, 2019, para. 43; C-128/18, *Dorobantu*, 2019, paras 46–69. See in particular paras 8-010 and 8-019, *infra*, and, more generally, paras 5-002–5-006, *supra*. See further Maiani and Migliorini, 'One Principle to Rule Them All? Anatomy of Mutual Trust in the law of the Area of Freedom, Security and Justice' (2020) CMLRev 7–44; Mitsilegas, 'Autonomous Concepts, Diversity Management and Mutual Trust in Europe's Area of Criminal Justice' (2020) CMLRev 45–78; Xanthopoulou, 'Mutual Trust and Rights in EU Criminal and Asylum Law: Three Phases of Evolution and the Uncharted Territory beyond Blind Trust' (2018) CMLRev 489–510; Schwarz, 'Let's Talk About Trust, Baby! Theorizing Trust and Mutual Recognition in the EU's Area of Freedom, Security and Justice' (2018) ELJ 124–41.

244   THE AREA OF FREEDOM, SECURITY, AND JUSTICE

was competent to adopt the necessary measures of in the fields of police cooperation and judicial cooperation to accompany the complete liberalization of movements of persons.[2] The EU Treaty (1992) did not settle the debate with regard to Community competence in this respect, but conferred express Community competence with regard to policy on visas, whilst also bringing police cooperation and judicial cooperation within the ambit of justice and home affairs (JHA cooperation), constituting the former 'third pillar' of the EU (see para. 1-038, *supra*). In the meantime, most Member States applied common rules in the context of the Schengen Convention with regard to controls at the external borders and the grant of visas for extended stays of no more than three months (the Schengen *acquis*; see para. 1-039, *supra*).

The Treaty of Amsterdam brought this discussion to a close. The Community became competent to take measures to permit the abolition of checks at the internal frontiers. Furthermore, using additional competences with respect to visa, asylum, and immigration and other 'policies related to free movement of persons' listed in Title IV of the EC Treaty, the Community could adopt flanking measures with respect to the abolition of controls on persons at the internal frontiers and measures to achieve a Community policy at the external borders with regard to entry into and residence in the territory of the Community for third-country nationals.

8.003   **Police and judicial cooperation.** Until the entry into force of the Lisbon Treaty, police and judicial cooperation in criminal matters between Member States remained regulated outside the Community, in Title VI of the EU Treaty. Originally, this 'third pillar' covered all 'cooperation in the fields of justice and home affairs' (JHA). When the Treaty of Amsterdam made the Community competent for measures with respect to visa, asylum, and immigration as well as judicial cooperation in civil matters,[3] only the areas of police cooperation and judicial cooperation in criminal matters (PJCC) remained covered by Title VI of the EU Treaty.[4] In the framework of the PJCC the decision-making power was vested in the Council. Generally, the Council had to decide by unanimity, at the initiative of the Commission or a Member State. The Council only had to consult the European Parliament.

As a result, the European Union became the pre-eminent forum for bringing Member States' criminal law policy closer together and for making a start with European criminal

---

[2] For this debate, see O'Keeffe, 'The Free Movement of Persons and the Single Market' (1992) ELRev 3–19; Plender, 'Competence, European Community Law and Nationals of Non-Member States' (1990) ICLQ 559–610. For interesting reservations about the link made between migration and security, see Huysmans, 'The European Union and the Securitisation of Migration' (2000) JCMS 751–77.

[3] These matters were also the subject of intergovernmental cooperation between the Member States before the EU Treaty (see paras 1-037-1-038). See Müller-Graff, 'The Legal Base of the Third Pillar and its Position in the Framework of the Union Treaty' (1994) CMLRev 493–503.

[4] The Amsterdam Treaty conferred competence on the Community not only to adopt measures with respect to visas, asylum, immigration, and other areas connected with free movement of persons (Articles 61 to 69 EC), but also as regards customs cooperation (Article 135 EC) and countering fraud (Article 280 EC). Nevertheless, even after the Amsterdam Treaty, the—less precise—abbreviation 'JHA' was used for decisions adopted pursuant to the 'third pillar' (Title VI of the EU Treaty). For a discussion of the PJCC provisions, see Monar, 'Justice and Home Affairs in the Treaty of Amsterdam: Reform at the Price of Fragmentation' (1998) ELR 320–35; Peers, *EU Justice and Home Affairs Law* (OUP, 2016). For the implementation of these provisions in the various legal orders of the Member States, see Moore and Chiavario (eds), *Police and Judicial Co-operation in the European Union* (Cambridge University Press, 2004).

law.[5] Article 35 EU conferred on the Court of Justice jurisdiction to give rulings on the validity and interpretation of framework decisions, decisions and implementing measures, and on the interpretation of conventions in so far as the Member State concerned accepted the Court's jurisdiction.[6]

Incorporation of the Schengen *acquis*. The Amsterdam Treaty provided the Community with competences on the basis of which it could convert the rules that the Member States had adopted in the framework of the Schengen cooperation into Community law; the portion of the Schengen *acquis* that was not covered by Community competences could be transposed into 'Union law' in the framework of the police and judicial cooperation in criminal matters (PJCC, the revised 'third pillar', Title VI of the EU Treaty). The Amsterdam Treaty annexed a Protocol to the EU Treaty and the EC Treaty,[7] which declared the entire Schengen *acquis* applicable from the date of entry into force of the Treaty of Amsterdam (Article 2(1), first subpara. of the Protocol). Pursuant to this Schengen Protocol, the Council determined for each provision or decision of the Schengen *acquis* the (Community or non-Community) legal basis.[8] Agreement on the Treaty of Amsterdam was only possible after it was agreed to annex a separate protocol to the Treaties which gave the United Kingdom the right to continue to conduct controls on persons at its frontiers. On the basis of other protocols attached to the EU Treaty and the EC Treaty the Schengen *acquis* remained inapplicable for the United Kingdom and Ireland (see para. 22-003, *infra*). Those Member States, and Denmark, did not participate, in principle, in Community action on the basis of the above-mentioned Title IV EC Treaty.

8.004

Union competences. The Treaty of Lisbon combined both the competences of the Union in the field of police and judicial cooperation in criminal matters with the competences contained in Title IV EC Treaty under the single new Treaty title 'Area of freedom, security and justice' (Title V of Part Three TFEU). This title covers *all* competences of the Union with regard to border checks, asylum, immigration, judicial cooperation in civil and criminal matters, and police cooperation.

8.005

Article 67 TFEU mentions several fields of action in this connection. First of all, the Union is to ensure the absence of internal border controls for persons and to frame a common

---

[5] See also Barents, 'De denationalisering van het strafrecht' (2006) SEW 358–74; Guild, 'Crime and the EU's Constitutional Future in an Area of Freedom, Security and Justice' (2004) ELJ 218–34; Harding, 'Exploring the Intersection of European Law and National Criminal Law' (2000) ELRev 374–90.

[6] Article 35(1), (2), and (3) EU. Subject to certain conditions, Member States and the Commission could submit a dispute to the Court of Justice and bring before it an application for annulment of PJCC framework decisions and decisions. For the jurisdiction of the Court of Justice in the sphere of PJCC, see para. 13-011, *infra*.

[7] Protocol (No. 2) annexed to the EU Treaty and EC Treaty, integrating the Schengen *acquis* into the framework of the European Union, OJ 1997 C340/93.

[8] Council Decision 1999/436/EC of 20 May 1999 determining, in conformity with the relevant provisions of the Treaty establishing the European Community and the Treaty on European Union, the legal basis for each of the provisions or decisions which constitute the Schengen *acquis*, OJ 1999 L176/17. To this end, the Council had to list the provisions which form part of the Schengen *acquis*; see Council Decision 1999/435/EC of 20 May 1999 concerning the definition of the Schengen *acquis* for the purpose of determining, in conformity with the relevant provisions of the Treaty establishing the European Community and the Treaty on European Union, the legal basis for each of the provisions or decisions which constitute the *acquis*, OJ 1999 L176/1 (it names those provisions for which it is unnecessary or inappropriate to determine a legal basis) and the publication of those provisions in OJ 2000 L239 (corrigendum: OJ 2000 L272/24). See, in this regard, Kuijper, 'Some Legal Problems Associated with the Communitarisation of Policy on Visas, Asylum and Immigration Under the Amsterdam Treaty and Incorporation of the Schengen Acquis' (2000) CMLRev 345, 346–50; Den Boer, 'Not Merely a Matter of Moving House: Police Co-operation from Schengen to the TEU' (2000) SEW 336–57.

policy on asylum, immigration, and external border control, based on solidarity between Member States which is fair towards third-country nationals (Article 67(2) TFEU).[9] Second, the Union is to facilitate access to justice, in particular through the principle of mutual recognition of judicial and extrajudicial decisions in civil matters (Article 67(4) TFEU). Third, the Union endeavours to ensure a high level of security through measures to prevent and combat crime, racism, and xenophobia, and through measures for coordination and cooperation between police and judicial authorities and other competent authorities, as well as through the mutual recognition of judgments in criminal matters and, if necessary, through the approximation of criminal laws (Article 67(3) TFEU).

At the substantive level, the Lisbon Treaty enlarged the competence of the Union as regards policies on border checks, asylum, and immigration.[10] The same is true for judicial cooperation in civil matters. It is noteworthy in that connection that the Union's competence regarding mutual recognition and execution of judgments and decisions in extrajudicial cases is no longer limited to 'civil and commercial cases'.[11] The Lisbon Treaty also significantly extended the Union's power to act in the field of judicial cooperation in criminal matters in so far as it enabled the Union to lay down measures aimed at harmonizing not only the definition of certain types of criminal offences and sanctions, but also aspects of criminal procedure.[12]

In all those areas, legislation is enacted, in principle, under the ordinary legislative procedure, whereas action by the Union and the Member States is fully subject to judicial review by the Court of Justice.[13] Also, as far as police and judicial cooperation in criminal matters is concerned, the specific institutional arrangements of the former third pillar have disappeared. Some sensitive matters, however, are still decided by the Council acting unanimously after consulting the European Parliament or, in some cases, after obtaining the consent of the European Parliament.

8.006 **Further development of the Schengen *acquis*.** Since the Lisbon Treaty, the Schengen *acquis* is further being developed on the basis of the provisions of Title V of Part Three of the TFEU, in accordance with the modified Schengen Protocol attached to the Treaties.[14] The Member States can consult personal data relating to nationals of other States through the central Schengen Information System (SIS).[15] The Council has taken the place of the Executive

---

[9] See also Article 80 TFEU, which specifies that the Union's policies in this connection are to be governed by the principles of solidarity and fair sharing of responsibility (which includes the financial implications) between the Member States (Article 80 TFEU).

[10] For an overview, see Peers, 'Legislative Update: EU Immigration and Asylum Competence and Decision-Making in the Treaty of Lisbon' (2008) EJML 219–47.

[11] Brousse, 'Le Traité de Lisbonne et le droit international privé' (2010) JDI 3–34.

[12] For a discussion, see Peers, 'EU Criminal Law and the Treaty of Lisbon' (2008) ELRev 507–29; Herlin-Karnell, 'The Treaty of Lisbon and the Criminal Law: Anything New Under the Sun?' (2008) EJ L Ref 321–37.

[13] See Hinarejos, 'The Lisbon Treaty Versus Standing Still: A View from the Third Pillar' (2009) EuConst 99–116; Ladenburger, 'Police and Criminal Law in the Treaty of Lisbon. A New Dimension for the Community Method' (2008) EuConst 20–40. Before the Lisbon Treaty, the Court of Justice already played a role of capital importance in the development of the area of freedom, security, and justice, see Lenaerts, 'The Contribution of the European Court of Justice to the Area of Freedom, Security and Justice' (2010) ICLQ 1–47.

[14] Protocol (No. 19), annexed to the TEU and TFEU, integrating the Schengen *acquis* into the framework of the European Union, OJ 2010 C83/290. For an overview, see De Capitani, 'The Schengen System after Lisbon: From Cooperation to Integration' (2014) ERA Forum 101.

[15] This second-generation Schengen Information System is based on the dual EU/EC legal basis of Council Decision 2007/533/JHA of 12 June 2007 on the establishment, operation, and use of the second generation Schengen Information System (SIS II), OJ 2007 L205/63, and Regulation (EC) No. 1987/2006 of the European

Committee set up under the Schengen Convention (Schengen Protocol, Article 2). Denmark is part of the Schengen area, but is, in common with Ireland (and the United Kingdom at the time), in a special position in respect of the Schengen *acquis* (see paras 8-027 and 8-028).

New Member States have to accept the Schengen *acquis* in full as part of the Union *acquis* (Schengen Protocol, Article 7). As a result, the Member States which acceded on 1 May 2004 and afterwards participate in two stages, whereby checks on persons at the internal frontiers are eliminated only when those Member States have implemented the Schengen *acquis* in a sufficient manner.[16] At present, this is so for all the Member States concerned, with the exception of Bulgaria, Croatia, Cyprus, and Romania.[17]

Iceland and Norway, which were associated with Schengen cooperation, continue to be associated with the implementation of the Schengen *acquis* and its further development in accordance with procedures agreed by those States and the Council on 18 May 1999.[18] The same is true on the basis of an international agreement concluded with the Union for Switzerland, to which the Schengen *acquis* has been extended as from 12 December 2008[19] and for Liechtenstein since 19 December 2011.[20]

Parliament and of the Council of 20 December 2006 on the establishment, operation, and use of the second generation Schengen Information System (SIS II), OJ 2006 L381/4. As from a date to be determined, these acts will be replaced by Regulation (EU) 2018/1862 of the European Parliament and of the Council of 28 November 2018 on the establishment, operation, and use of the Schengen Information System (SIS) in the field of police cooperation and judicial cooperation in criminal matters, OJ 2018 L312/56 and Regulation (EU) 2018/1861 of the European Parliament and of the Council of 28 November 2018 on the establishment, operation, and use of the Schengen Information System (SIS) in the field of border checks, and amending the Convention implementing the Schengen Agreement, OJ 2018 L312/4. The SIS is related to a system for the exchange of information between national 'Sirene offices' in accordance with the 'Sirene Manual' established by Commission Implementing Decision (EU) 2017/1528 of 31 August 2017, OJ 20147 L231/6.

[16] See Schengen Protocol (n. 14, *supra*; see also para. 22-003–22-004, *infra*), Article 2, which refers to Article 3 of the 2003 Act of Accession and Article 4 of the 2005 Act of Accession. Articles 3 and 4 of the 2003 Act of Accession and the 2005 Act of Accession, respectively, refer to the acts listed in Annex to the Act; Articles 3(2) and 4(2) of those Acts provide that the provisions not so listed, while binding on the new Member States, shall only apply in a new Member State pursuant to a Council decision to that effect after verification in accordance with the applicable Schengen evaluation procedures that the necessary conditions have been met. See also Article 4(2) of the 2011 Act of Accession.

[17] Council Decision 2007/801/EC of 6 December 2007 on the full application of the provisions of the Schengen *acquis* in the Czech Republic, the Republic of Estonia, the Republic of Latvia, the Republic of Lithuania, the Republic of Hungary, the Republic of Malta, the Republic of Poland, the Republic of Slovenia, and the Slovak Republic, OJ 2007 L323/34.

[18] Agreement with the Republic of Iceland and the Kingdom of Norway concerning the latters' association with the implementation, application, and development of the Schengen *acquis*, OJ 1999 L176/35 (corrigendum for certain language versions in OJ 2000 L58/31). The Council concluded a further agreement with Iceland and Norway on 30 June 1999 on the establishment of rights and obligations between Ireland and the United Kingdom of Great Britain and Northern Ireland, on the one hand, and the Republic of Iceland and the Kingdom of Norway, on the other, in areas of the Schengen *acquis* which apply to these States, OJ 2000 L15/2. See Kuijper, 'Some Legal Problems Associated with the Communitarisation of Policy on Visas, Asylum and Immigration Under the Amsterdam Treaty and Incorporation of the Schengen Acquis' (2000) CMLRev 345, 350–4; Den Boer, 'Not Merely a Matter of Moving House: Police Co-operation from Schengen to the TEU' (2000) SEW 336, 350–51. The Schengen *acquis* entered into effect for the Nordic countries on 25 March 2001: Council Decision 2000/777/EC of 1 December 2000 on the application of the Schengen *acquis* in Denmark, Finland, and Sweden, and in Iceland and Norway, OJ 2000 L309/24.

[19] See Article 15(1) of the Agreement between the European Union, the European Community, and the Swiss Confederation on the Swiss Confederation's association with the implementation, application, and development of the Schengen *acquis*, OJ 2008 L53/52, on the basis of which the Council adopted Council Decision 2008/903/EC of 27 November 2008 on the full application of the provisions of the Schengen *acquis* in the Swiss Confederation, OJ 2008 L327/15.

[20] Protocol between the European Union, the European Community, the Swiss Confederation, and the Principality of Liechtenstein on the accession of the Principality of Liechtenstein to the Agreement between the

The Schengen area thus currently encompasses, on the one hand, all Member States except Bulgaria, Croatia, Cyprus, Ireland, and Romania, and, on the other hand, Iceland, Liechtenstein, Norway, and Switzerland.

II. Policies on Border Checks, Asylum, and Immigration with respect to Third-Country Nationals

A. Border checks and visa policy

8.007 **Border checks and visa policy.** The Member States which have taken over the Schengen *acquis* constitute the Schengen area in which checks at the internal frontiers have in principle been abolished.[21] Pursuant to Article 77(1) TFEU, the Union is to develop a policy with a view to ensuring the absence of any controls on persons, whatever their nationality, when crossing internal frontiers. The necessary measures are laid down by the European Parliament and the Council, acting in accordance with the ordinary legislative procedure (Article 77(1)(a) and (2)(e) TFEU).

As to the external borders of the Union, the European Parliament and the Council, acting in accordance with the ordinary legislative procedure, further adopt measures for carrying out checks on persons and the efficient monitoring of the crossing of external borders (Article 77(1)(b) and (2)(a) to (c) TFEU). Such measures concern the checks to which persons crossing external borders are subject,[22] the common policy on visas and other short-stay residence permits, and the conditions under which nationals of third countries have the freedom to travel within the Union for a short period.[23] This Union competence does not affect, however, the Member States' competence concerning the geographical demarcation of their borders (Article 77(4) TFEU). Union measures concerning short-term visas

European Union, the European Community, and the Swiss Confederation on the Swiss Confederation's association with the implementation, application, and development of the Schengen *acquis*; see Council Decision 2008/261/EC of 28 February 2008 on the signature, on behalf of the European Community, and on the provisional application of certain provisions of this protocol, OJ 2008 L83/3.

[21] For the possibility of introducing temporary border checks, see Jorgensen and Sorenson, 'Internal Border Controls in the European Union' (2012) ELRev 249; Groenendijk, 'Reinstatement of Controls at the Internal Borders of Europe; Why and Against Whom?' (2004) ELJ 150–70.

[22] See, initially, Regulation (EC) No. 562/2006 of the European Parliament and of the Council of 15 March 2006 establishing a Community Code on the rules governing the movement of persons across borders (Schengen Borders Code), OJ 2006 L105/1, since replaced by Regulation (EU) 2016/399 of the European Parliament and of the Council of 9 March 2016 on a Union Code on the rules governing the movement of persons across borders (Schengen Borders Code), OJ 2016 L77/1. A protocol to the Treaties specifies that such measures 'shall be without prejudice to the competence of the Member States to negotiate or conclude agreements with third countries as long as they respect Union law and relevant international agreements' (Protocol (No. 23), annexed to the TEU and TFEU, on external relations of the Member States with regard to the crossing of external borders (OJ 2010 C83/304)). See, e.g., C-606/10, *ANAFE*, 2012, paras 20–83. Also *ad hoc* restrictions have been adopted on this basis, see e.g., in the context of the COVID-19 pandemic, Council Recommendation (EU) 2020/912 of 30 June 2020 on the temporary restriction on non-essential travel into the EU and the possible lifting of such restriction, OJ 2020 L208I/1, as amended by Council Recommendation (EU) 2021/816 20 May 2021 (OJ 2021 L182/1).

[23] See formerly Article 62(2)(b) EC. These rules cover matters for which the Community already had competence under the former Article 100c and d EC (Maastricht version).

include: (a) the list of third countries whose nationals must be in possession of visas when crossing the external borders and those whose nationals are exempt from that requirement;[24] (b) the procedures and conditions for issuing visas by Member States;[25] (c) a uniform format for visas;[26] and (d) rules on a uniform visa. As a result of the integration of the Schengen *acquis*, the criteria agreed for the grant of short-term visas between the Schengen States apply within the Union in this regard.

The Lisbon Treaty introduced the competence for the Council, acting unanimously after consulting the European Parliament, to adopt provisions concerning passports, identity cards, residence permits, or any other such document where necessary to facilitate the right of Union citizens to move and reside freely within the territory of the Member States (e.g. with respect to their family members) (Article 77(3) TFEU).[27] Furthermore, the European Parliament and the Council, acting in accordance with the ordinary legislative procedure, may adopt the necessary measures for the gradual establishment of an integrated management system for external borders (Article 77(1)(c) and (2)(d) TFEU). Even before the Lisbon Treaty, the Council had set up an Agency (Frontex) to facilitate and coordinate cooperation between Member States on the management of their external borders.[28] The tasks of this agency have since been strengthened twice, and the European Border and Coast Guard Agency, as it is now officially called (even though it is still often referred to by the name Frontex), is responsible for the integrated management of the external borders in close cooperation with the national authorities.[29] In addition, the Union legislature

---

[24] See, initially, Council Regulation (EC) No. 539/2001 of 15 March 2001 listing the third countries whose nationals must be in possession of visas when crossing the external borders and those whose nationals are exempt from that requirement, OJ 2001 L81/1, and since replaced by Regulation (EU) 2018/1806 of the European Parliament and of the Council of 14 November 2018 listing the third countries whose nationals must be in possession of visas when crossing the external borders and those whose nationals are exempt from that requirement, OJ 2018 L303/39 (this Regulation, however, does not apply to Ireland). See also Peers, Guild, and Tomkin, *EU Immigration and Asylum Law—Vol. 1: Visas and Border Controls* (Nijhof, 2012); Martenczuk, 'Visa Policy and EU External Relations', in Martenczuk and van Thiel (eds), *Justice, Liberty, Security: New Challenges for the External Relations of the European Union* (VUBpress, 2009), 21–52.

[25] See Regulation (EC) No. 810/2009 of the European Parliament and of the Council of 13 July 2009 establishing a Community Code on Visas (Visa Code), OJ 2009 L243/1 (not binding on Denmark and Ireland). See Peers, 'Legislative Update, EC Immigration and Asylum Law: The New Visa Code' (2010) EJML 105–31. As regards the possibility for Member States to issue visas on humanitarian grounds, see C-638/16 PPU, *X and X*, 2017, paras 38–51. The national courts of a Member State that has refused a visa on the basis of a ban issued by another Member State may not review the substantive reasons for that ban; see C-225/19 and C-226/19, *R.N.N.S. and K.A.*, 2020, paras 32–56.

[26] See Council Regulation (EC) No. 1683/95 of 29 May 1995—adopted under the former Article 100c(1) EC—laying down a uniform format for visas, OJ 1995 L164/1, as subsequently amended, now pursuant to Article 77(2)(a) TFEU (not binding on Ireland).

[27] This provision applies only 'if the Treaties have not provided the necessary powers'.

[28] Council Regulation (EC) No. 2007/2004 of 26 October 2004 establishing a European Agency for the Management of Operational Cooperation at the External Borders of the Member States of the European Union, OJ 2004 L349/1. See Mungianu, 'FRONTEX: Towards a Common Policy on External Border Control' (2013) EJML 359; Fischer-Lescano, 'Europäisches Grenzkontrollregime. Rechtsrahmen der europäischen Grenzschutzagentur FRONTEX' (2007) ZaöRV 1219–76.

[29] Regulation (EU) 2019/1896 of the European Parliament and of the Council of 13 November 2019 on the European Border and Coast Guard, OJ 2019 L295/1, replacing Regulation (EU) 2016/1624 of the European Parliament and of the Council of 14 September 2016 on the European Border and Coast Guard, OJ 2016 L251/1 (which had repealed Council Regulation (EC) No. 2007/2004). In accordance with Article 93(5) of Regulation 2019/1896, Frontex had its seat in Warsaw (Poland); see already earlier Council Decision 2005/358/EC of 26 April 2005, OJ 2005 L114/13. See also Regulation (EU) No. 1052/2013 of the European Parliament and of the Council of 22 October 2013 establishing the European Border Surveillance System (Eurosur), OJ 2013 L295/11.

B. Asylum and other international regimes of protection

8.008 **Common asylum policy.** Under the Amsterdam Treaty the Community had powers only to establish 'minimum standards' with respect to the categorization of refugees and the granting and withdrawal of refugee status. Since the Lisbon Treaty the Union is competent to set up a common European asylum system. Pursuant to Article 78(1) TFEU, the Union is to develop a common policy on asylum, subsidiary protection, and temporary protection with a view to offering appropriate status to any third-country national requiring international protection and ensuring compliance with the principle of *non-refoulement*.[31]

European asylum policy must be in accordance with the Geneva Convention of 28 July 1951 and the Protocol of 31 January 1967 relating to the status of refugees, and other relevant treaties[32] (Article 78(1) TFEU).[33] The right to asylum, together with protection in the event of removal, expulsion, or extradition, is also enshrined in the Charter of Fundamental Rights of the European Union.[34] For all legal and practical purposes in relation to asylum matters, Member States are to be regarded as constituting safe countries of origin; according to a protocol annexed to the Treaties, in principle applications for asylum made by a national of a Member State will be regarded as inadmissible for processing by another Member State or admitted only in expressly stated cases.[35]

---

[30] Regulation (EU) 2018/1726 of the European Parliament and of the Council of 14 November 2018 on the European Union Agency for the Operational Management of Large-Scale IT Systems in the Area of Freedom, Security and Justice (eu-LISA), OJ 2018 L295/99 (managing, *inter alia*, the Schengen Information System (SIS II), the Visa Information System (VIS), Eurodac, and the European Travel Information and Authorisation System (ETIAS)). The headquarters of eu-LISA are in Tallinn, Estonia, whilst its operational centre is in Strasbourg, France.

[31] The principle of *non-refoulement* is a principle of international law according to which no refugee may be expelled or returned to territories where his or her life or freedom would be threatened (see, e.g., Article 33(1) of the Geneva Convention relating to the Status of Refugees, n. 32, *infra*).

[32] Geneva Convention relating to the Status of Refugees, signed on 28 July 1951 (*TS* 39 (1954); Cmd 9171), which has been ratified by all the Member States of the European Union. See C-175/08, C-176/08, C-178/08, and C-179/08, *Salahadin Abdulla and Others*, 2010, paras 51–3 (duty to respect the Geneva Convention). Accordingly, there is a (rebuttable) presumption that the treatment of applicants for international protection in all Member States complies with the requirements of the Charter, the Convention relating to the Status of Refugees, signed in Geneva on 28 July 1951; see C-297/17, C-318/17, C-319/17, and C-438/17, *Ibrahim*, 2019, para. 85; C-163/17, *Jawo*, 2019, para. 82. According to Declaration (No. 17), annexed to the Amsterdam Treaty, on Article 63 of the Treaty establishing the European Community, OJ 1997 C340/134), consultations are to be established with the United Nations High Commissioner for Refugees and other relevant international organizations on matters relating to asylum policy. So as to ensure harmonized application of Article 1 of the Geneva Convention, the Council defined a Joint Position (96/196/JHA) on 4 March 1996 on the definition of the term 'refugee', OJ 1996 L63/2.

[33] See also Article 18 of the Charter; C-391/16, C-77/17, and C-78/17, *M*, 2019, paras 67–75.

[34] Article 18 (referring to the Geneva Convention and the Protocol) and Article 19 of the Charter of Fundamental Rights of the European Union. See Peers, 'Immigration, Asylum and the European Union Charter of Fundamental Rights' (2001) EJML 141–69.

[35] Sole Article of Protocol (No. 24), annexed to the TEU and TFEU, on asylum for nationals of Member States of the European Union, OJ 2010 C83/305 (replacing Protocol (No. 29), annexed to the EC Treaty by the Amsterdam Treaty, OJ 1997 C340/103), which mentions, alongside cases where the Member State avails itself of Article 15 ECHR (derogation in the event of war or other public emergency) and the procedure referred to in Article 7 TEU (see para. 4-020, *supra*), the case in which a Member State so decides 'unilaterally in respect of the application of a national of another Member State', in which event the Council is to be informed and the application 'shall be dealt with on the basis of the presumption that it is manifestly unfounded without affecting in any way, whatever the cases may be, the decision-making power of the Member State'. What prompted this protocol was Spain's

Uniform status of international protection. Pursuant to Article 78(2) TFEU the European Parliament and the Council, acting in accordance with the ordinary legislative procedure, set up the common European asylum system.[36] This encompasses, first of all, a uniform status of asylum for nationals of third countries, valid throughout the Union, and a uniform status of subsidiary protection for such nationals who, without obtaining European asylum, are in need of international protection[37] (Article 78(2)(a) and (b) TFEU). The so-called 'Qualification Directive' sets out common minimum standards to be applied during the assessment of an application for asylum or subsidiary protection, ensuring similar treatment of asylum seekers regardless of the Member State where they make their application. However, in order to ensure a genuine equal treatment of asylum seekers, not only the substantive criteria have been harmonized, but also the procedural framework (Article 78(2)(d) TFEU). Where the Union legislature initially only provided for minimum requirements,[38] the current 'Procedures Directive' provides for common procedures for granting and withdrawing international protection in an effort to discourage forum shopping by asylum seekers.[39] Persons whose application for asylum of subsidiary status is rejected may

8.009

---

unhappiness with Belgium's refusal to surrender suspected Basque terrorists who had asked to be recognized as refugees. According to a declaration (No. 48), annexed to the Amsterdam Treaty, on Protocol (No. 29), the Protocol does not prejudice the right of Member States to take the organizational measures they deem necessary to fulfil their obligations under the Geneva Convention of 28 July 1951 relating to the status of refugees, OJ 1997 C340/141. For the tense relationship between the Protocol and the Geneva Convention, see the Commission's answer of 8 December 1997 to Question No. E-3441/97 (Van Dijk), OJ 1998 C174/58 (the Commission considered it 'unfortunate' that the Protocol was included in the Amsterdam Treaty, but was pleased to note that the Protocol nevertheless sought to respect the objectives of the Geneva Convention) and Bribosia and Weyembergh, 'Le citoyen européen privé du droit d'asile?' (1997) JTDE 204–6. Belgium made a unilateral declaration on the Protocol in which it stated that it would carry out an 'individual examination' of any asylum request made by a national of another Member State, OJ 1997 C340/144.

[36] For an analysis of the substance of policy on asylum, see Chetail, De Bruycker, and Maiani, *Reforming the Common European Asylum System* (Brill Nijhoff, 2016); Cherubini, *Asylum Law in the European Union* (Routledge, 2015); Ferguson Sidorenko, *The Common European Asylum System: Background, Current State of affairs, Future Direction* (TMC Asser Press, 2007); Peers and Rogers (eds), *EU immigration and asylum law: text and commentary* (Martinus Nijfoff, 2006); Lynskey, 'Complementing and Completing the Common European Asylum System: A Legal Analysis of the Emerging Extraterritorial Elements of EU Refugee Protection Policy' (2006) ELRev 230–50; Guild, 'Seeking Asylum: Storm Clouds between International Commitments and EU Legislative Measures' (2004) ELRev 198–218; Harvey, 'The Right to Seek Asylum in the European Union' (2004) EHRLR 17–36. For a critical assessment, see Costello and Mouzourakis, 'The Common European Asylum Policy: Where Did it All Go Wrong?', in Fletcher, Herlin-Karnell, and Matera (eds), *The European Union as an Area of Freedom, Security and Justice* (Routledge, 2019).

[37] Directive 2011/95/EU of the European Parliament and of the Council of 13 December 2011 on standards for the qualification of third-country nationals or stateless persons as beneficiaries of international protection, for a uniform status for refugees or for persons eligible for subsidiary protection, and for the content of the protection granted, OJ 2011 L337/9, replacing Council Directive 2004/83/EC of 29 April 2004, OJ 2004 L304/12 (not applicable in Denmark). See C-443/14 and C-444/14, *Alo*, 2016, paras 22–64; C-585/16, *Alheto*, 2018, paras 82–101; C-391/16, C-77/17, and C-78/17, *M and Others*, 2019, paras 76–112; see also pursuant to Directive 2004/83/EC, C-353/16, *MP*, 2018, paras 27–58.

[38] Council Directive 2005/85/EC of 1 December 2005 on minimum standards on procedures in Member States for granting and withdrawing refugee status, OJ 2005 L326/13.

[39] Directive 2013/32/EU of the European Parliament and the Council of 26 June 2013 on common procedures for granting and withdrawing international protection, OJ 2013 L180/249. See C-585/16, *Alheto*, 2018, paras 67–81 and 102–49; C-297/17, C-318/17, C-319/17, and C-438/17, *Ibrahim*, 2019, paras 56–101; C-556/17, *Torubarov*, 2019, paras 38–78; C-924/19 PPU and C-925/19 PPU, *FMS and Others*, 2020, paras 148–65, 175–203 and 232–48; C-808/18, *Commission v Hungary*, 2020, paras 87–128, 155–226, and 281–314. A proposal by the Commission to further reduce differences between the Member States by replacing Directive 2013/32/EU by a regulation, has not yet been adopted; see Proposal for a Regulation of the European Parliament and the Council establishing a common procedure for international protection in the Union and repealing Directive 2013/32/EU (COM(2016)467 final—2016/0224 (COD)).

be returned to their country of origin, or another safe third country, if they cannot obtain a legal immigration status on other grounds.[40]

8.010 **Dublin Regulation.** The existence of common procedures is crucial, as asylum seekers are not at liberty to lodge their application in any Member State of their choice. In order to determine which State is to be responsible for examining applications for asylum in a given case, the Member States established the Dublin Convention in 1990, which entered into effect in 1997.[41] That convention was later replaced by a regulation which determines the Member State responsible for examining an asylum application lodged in one of the Member States by a third-country national (the Dublin II Regulation, since replaced by the Dublin III Regulation),[42] adopted pursuant to Article 78(2)(e) TFEU. In this respect the Council has also adopted a system for the identification of asylum seekers (Eurodac).[43]

The allocation rules in the Dublin II and Dublin III Regulations, which aim at accelerating the processing of applications for international protection in the interest of both applicants and participating States, are based on the principle of mutual trust and the presumption that the treatment of applicants in all Member States complies with the requirements of the Charter of Fundamental Rights and the Geneva Convention.[44] The Court of Justice has, however, clarified that in an exceptional case where, due to major operational problems in the Member State designated as responsible State under the Dublin Regulation, there are substantial grounds for believing that an applicant for international protection would face a real risk of being subjected to inhuman or degrading treatment, in the sense of Article 4

---

[40] Para. 8-010, *infra*.

[41] Convention determining the State responsible for examining applications for asylum lodged in one of the Member States of the European Communities, OJ 1997 C254/1 (for its entry into effect on 1 September 1997, see OJ 1997 L242/63).

[42] Regulation (EU) No. 604/2013 of the European Parliament and of the Council of 26 June 2013 establishing the criteria and mechanisms for determining the Member State responsible for examining an application for international protection lodged in one of the Member States by a third-country national or a stateless person ('Dublin III Regulation'), OJ 2013 L180/31, replacing Council Regulation (EC) No. 343/2003 of 18 February 2003 establishing the criteria and mechanisms for determining the Member State responsible for examining an asylum application lodged in one of the Member States by a third-country national ('Dublin II Regulation', OJ 2003 L50/1 (both not binding on Denmark, but nevertheless applicable in Denmark by virtue of the Agreement concluded between the European Community and the Kingdom of Denmark extending to Denmark the provisions of Regulation No. 343/2003 and Regulation No. 2725/2000 (see the following n.), approved on behalf of the Community by Council Decision 2006/188/EC of 21 February 2006, OJ 2006 L66/37). For an application of the Dublin III Regulation, see C-646/16, *Jafari*, 2017, clarifying what constitutes the issuing of visas and how illegal border crossings must be understood in the context of the arrival of an unusually large number of third-country nationals seeking transit through a Member State in order to lodge an application for international protection in another Member State. See also C-63/15, *Ghezelbash*, 2016, paras 29–61; C-155/15, *Karim*, 2016, paras 14–27; C-201/16, *Shiri*, 2017, paras 26–46; C-490/16, *A.S.*, 2017, paras 24–60; C-670/16, *Mengesteab*, 2017, paras 41–103; C-47/17 and C-48/17, *X and X*, 2018, paras 56–90; C-163/17, *Jawo*, 2019, paras 50–98; C-582/17 and C-583/17, *H and R*, 2019, paras 37–87; C-194/18, *H.A.*, 2021, paras 25–49.

[43] Regulation (EU) No. 603/2013 of the European Parliament and of the Council of 26 June 2013 on the establishment of 'Eurodac' for the comparison of fingerprints for the effective application of Regulation (EU) No. 604/2013 and on requests for the comparison with Eurodac data by Member States' law enforcement authorities and Europol for law enforcement purposes, OJ 2013 L180/1, replacing Council Regulation (EC) No. 2725/2000 of 11 December 2000, OJ 2000 L316/1 (not binding on Denmark—but nevertheless applicable in Denmark by virtue of the agreement mentioned in the preceding n.). See Bell, 'Mainstreaming Equality Norms into European Union Asylum law' (2001) ELRev 20, 26–8; Peers, 'Key Legislative Developments on Migration in the European Union' (2001) EJML 231, 235–6. See also Regulation (EU) 2019/818 of the European Parliament and of the Council of 20 May 2019 on establishing a framework for interoperability between EU information systems in the field of police and judicial cooperation, asylum, and migration, OJ 2019 L135/85. See, moreover, the arrangement between the Union and Norway, Iceland, Switzerland, and Liechtenstein on their participation in eu-LISA (see n. 30, supra), concluded by Council Decision (EU) 2019/837 of 14 May 2019, OJ 2019 L138/9.

[44] C-411/10 and C-493/10, *N. S. and Others*, 2011, paras 78–80.

of the Charter, when transferred to that Member State, the other Member States, including their national courts, may not transfer the applicant to the Member State designated as responsible for examining the application.[45] Whereas the Dublin III Regulation has codified that case law as regards a situation of systemic flaws in the asylum procedure and the reception conditions of applicants in the responsible Member State,[46] the Court further held that the transfer of an applicant must be ruled out in any situation in which there are substantial grounds for believing that the applicant runs a real risk of inhuman or degrading treatment during his or her transfer or thereafter.[47]

The allocation rules laid down in the Dublin II and Dublin III Regulations, however, imply that Member States at the external borders of the Union are bound to be confronted with the bulk of asylum applications. In order to deal with instances where these Member States risk not being able to handle all applications in an appropriate manner, the Union has also established a common system of temporary protection for displaced persons in the event of a massive inflow[48] on the basis of Article 78(2)(c) TFEU. At the height of the Mediterranean asylum crisis of 2015, the Council,[49] moreover, made use of the possibility offered by Article 78(3) TFEU to deviate from these rules in the event of one or more Member States being confronted by an emergency situation characterized by a sudden inflow of nationals of third countries.[50] In this respect, it should be mentioned that, by virtue of Article 80 TFEU, the Union's policies in the area of border checks, asylum, and immigration are to be governed by the principle of solidarity and fair sharing of responsibility (including the financial implications) between the Member States.[51]

Reception conditions. The European Parliament and the Council must lay down standards concerning the conditions for the reception of applicants for asylum or subsidiary protection (Article 78(2)(f) TFEU). The minimum standards for the reception of asylum seekers are designed to ensure them a dignified standard of living and comparable living conditions

8.011

---

[45] Ibid., paras 75–108. See also para. 25–014, *infra*.
[46] Regulation (EU) No. 604/2013, Article 3(2), second subpara.
[47] C-163/17, *Jawo*, 2019, paras 87–90.
[48] Council Directive 2001/55/EC of 20 July 2001 on minimum standards for giving temporary protection in the event of a mass influx of displaced persons and on measures promoting a balance of efforts between Member States in receiving such persons and bearing the consequences thereof, OJ 2001 L212/12 (this directive does not apply to Denmark or Ireland); Van Selm, 'Temporarily Protecting Displaced Persons or Offering the Possibility to Start a New Life in the European Union' (2001) EJML 23–35. See also Decision No. 537/2007/EC of the European Parliament and of the Council of 23 May 2007 establishing the European Refugee Fund for the period 2008 to 2013 as part of the General programme 'Solidarity and Management of Migration Flows', OJ 2007 L144/1 (Denmark alone did not participate in the Fund). On the relationship between Directive 2001/55 and the Dublin Regulation, see C-411/10 and C-493/10, *N.S.*, 2011, para. 93; C-646/16, *Jafari*, 2017, para. 97.
[49] The Council is to act on a proposal from the Commission, after consulting the European Parliament (Article 78(3) TFEU). Acts taken on this legal basis may deviate—limited to these emergency situations—from legislative instruments adopted pursuant to Article 78(2) TFEU; see C-643/15 and C-647/15, *Slovakia and Hungary v Council*, 2017, paras 57–84.
[50] Council Decision (EU) 2015/1523 of 14 September 2015 establishing provisional measures in the area of international protection for the benefit of Italy and of Greece, OJ 2015 L239/146 and Council Decision (EU) 2015/1601 of 22 September 2015 establishing provisional measures in the area of international protection for the benefit of Italy and Greece, OJ 2015 L248/80. The validity of the latter decision was upheld in C-643/15 and C-647/15, *Slovakia and Hungary v Council*, 2017.
[51] Lenaerts, 'The Court of Justice and the Refugee Crisis', in Lenaerts et al. (eds), *An Ever-Changing Union?—Perspectives on the Future of EU law in Honour of Allan Rosas* (Hart Publishing, 2019), 3–19; Caiola, 'Une base juridique pour la solidarité: l'article 80, seconde phrase, TFUE' (2018) CDE 437–93. See also Berthelet, 'Les conséquences des crises migratoires de 2011 et de 2015, une solidarité européenne encore très imparfaite' (2018) CDE 395–435.

in all Member States.[52] Lastly, the European Parliament and the Council must ensure partnership and cooperation with third countries for the purpose of managing inflows of people applying for asylum or subsidiary or temporary protection (Article 78(2)(g) TFEU).

C. Immigration policy

8.012 **Immigration.** With respect to immigration, the Lisbon Treaty has embedded the previous Community competences in a 'common immigration policy' aimed at ensuring, at all stages, the efficient management of migration flows, fair treatment of third-country nationals residing legally in Member States, and the prevention of, and enhanced measures to combat illegal immigration and trafficking in human beings (Article 79(1) TFEU).[53]

The European Parliament and the Council, acting in accordance with the ordinary legislative procedure, are to adopt measures on conditions of entry and residence and standards for the issue by Member States of long-term visas and residence permits,[54] including those for the purpose of family reunification,[55] and on illegal immigration and unauthorized residence, including removal and repatriation of persons residing without authorization.[56]

---

[52] Directive 2013/33/EU of the European Parliament and of the Council of 26 June 2013 laying down standards for the reception of applicants for international protection, OJ 2013 L180/96, which has replaced Council Directive 2003/9/EC of 27 January 2003 laying down minimum standards for the reception of asylum seekers, OJ 2013 L31/18 (not binding on Denmark and Ireland). See also C-601/15 PPU, *J.N.*, 2016, paras 43–82; C-233/18, *Haqbin*, 2019, paras 31–56; C-924/19 PPU and C-925/19 PPU, *FMS and Others*, 2020, paras 204–31, 238–66, and 282–301; *Commission v Hungary*, 2020, paras 155–226.

[53] For an overview, see Azoulai and De Vries (eds), *EU Migration Law: Legal Complexities and Political Rationales* (OUP, 2014).

[54] Besides Council Directive 2003/109/EC of 25 November 2003 concerning the status of third-country nationals who are long-term residents (n. 59, *infra* and accompanying text), see Council Regulation (EC) No. 1030/2002 of 13 June 2002 laying down a uniform format for residence permits for third-country nationals, OJ 2002 L157/1 (as last amended by Regulation (EU) 2017/1954 of the European Parliament and of the Council of 25 October 2017, OJ 2017 L286/9; not binding on Denmark or Ireland); Directive (EU) 2016/801 of the European Parliament and of the Council of 11 May 2016 on the conditions of entry and residence of third-country nationals for the purposes of research, studies, training, voluntary service, pupil exchange schemes, or educational projects and au pairing, OJ 2016 L132/21 (not binding on Denmark or Ireland); Directive 2014/66/EU of the European Parliament and of the Council of 15 May 2014 on the conditions of entry and residence of third-country nationals in the framework of an intra-corporate transfer, OJ 2014 L157/1 (not binding on Denmark or Ireland); Council Directive 2009/50/EC of 25 May 2009 on the conditions of entry and residence of third-country nationals for the purposes of highly qualified employment, OJ 2009 L155/17 (the so-called 'Blue card' Directive; not binding on Denmark). See Peers, 'Legislative Update: EC Immigration and Asylum Law Attracting and Deterring Labour Migration: The Blue Card and Employer Sanctions Directives' (2009) EJML 387–426.

[55] Council Directive 2003/86/EC of 22 September 2003 on the right to family reunification, OJ 2003 L251/12 (not binding on Denmark or Ireland); see C-540/03, *European Parliament v Council*, 2006 (action for annulment against the Directive rejected; see also para. 12-009, *infra*), with case note by Bultermann (2008) CMLRev 245–59; C-561/14, *Genc*, 2016; C-82/16, *K.A.*, 2018. See further Kostakapoulou and Ripoll Servent, 'The Rule of Life: Family Reunification in EU Mobility and Migration Laws', in Fletcher, Herlin-Karnell, and Matera (eds), *The European Union as an Area of Freedom, Security and Justice* (Routledge, 2019); Peers, 'Family Reunion and Community Law', in Walker (ed.): *Europe's Area of Freedom, Security and Justice* (OUP, 2004), 143–97; Groenendijk, 'Family Reunification as a Right under Community Law' (2006) EJML 215–30; Groenendijk and Guild, 'Converging Criteria: Creating an Area of Security of Residence for Europe's Third Country Nationals' (2001) EJML 37–59.

[56] See Council Directive 2001/40/EC of 28 May 2001 on the mutual recognition of decisions on the expulsion of third-country nationals, OJ 2001 L149/34, and, by way of compensation for the financial imbalances resulting from the application of this directive, Council Decision 2004/19/EC of 23 February 2004, OJ 2004 L60/55 (neither the directive nor the decision applies to Ireland and Denmark); see also Council Directive 2002/90/EC of 28 November 2002 defining the facilitation of unauthorized entry, transit, and residence, OJ 2002 L328/17 (this directive does not apply to Denmark) and Regulation (EU) 2019/1240 of the European Parliament and of the Council of 20 June 2019 on the creation of a European network of immigration liaison officers, OJ 2019 L198/88; Directive 2008/115/EC of the European Parliament and of the Council of 16 December 2008 on common standards and procedures in Member States for returning illegally staying third-country nationals, OJ 2008 L348/98 (not binding

They are also to adopt measures defining the rights of third-country nationals residing legally in a Member State, including the conditions governing freedom of movement and of residence in other Member States[57] and measures for combating trafficking in persons, in particular women and children (Article 79(2) TFEU).[58]

In accordance with Directive 2003/109 a Member State is to grant long-term resident status to third-country nationals who have resided legally and continuously within its territory during the previous five years and have sufficient resources and sickness insurance cover for themselves and their dependants.[59] The status may be refused on grounds of public policy or public security.[60] Stricter conditions apply with respect to the right of a long-term resident to reside in the territory of Member States other than the one which granted him or her the long-term resident status, for a period exceeding three months.[61] Subject to certain conditions, long-term residents are to enjoy equal treatment with nationals of the host Member State as regards access to employment and self-employed activities, conditions of employment and working conditions, education and vocational training, recognition of professional diplomas, certificates and other qualifications, social security, tax benefits, access to goods and services and the supply of goods and services made available to the public, and freedom of association.[62] This also relates to social assistance and social protection, even though Member States may limit equal treatment in those fields to the core benefits.[63]

In addition, the European Parliament and the Council, acting in accordance with the ordinary legislative procedure, may establish measures to provide incentives and support for the action of Member States with a view to promoting the integration of third-country nationals residing legally in their territories, but without carrying out any harmonization of the laws and regulations of Member States (Article 79(4) TFEU). It will be up to the Member States to determine the number of third-country nationals who may be admitted to their territory in order to seek work (Article 79(5) TFEU). Furthermore, the Union may cooperate with third countries for the readmission to their countries of origin or provenance of third-country nationals who do not or who no longer fulfil the conditions for entry,

---

on Denmark or Ireland). See Acosta, 'The Good, the Bad and the Ugly in EU Migration Law: Is the European Parliament Becoming Bad and Ugly? (The Adoption of Directive 2008/15: The Returns Directive)' (2009) EJML 19–39. See also C-47/15, *Affum*, 2016, paras 45–93; C-601/15 PPU, *J.N.*, 2016, paras 65–82; C-82/16, *K.A.*, 2018, paras 42–62, 86, 89, and 98–107; C-181/16, *Gnandi*, 2018, paras 35–67; C-444/17, *Arib*, 2019, 35–67; C-924/19 and C925/19 PPU, *FMS and Others*, 2020, paras 104–47; *Commission v Hungary*, 2020, paras 241–66.

[57] On this basis, the application of Regulation No. 883/2004 (and its predecessor Regulation No. 1408/71) on the coordination of social security systems has been extended to third-country nationals legally residing in the territory of the Member States (see para. 7-078, *supra*).

[58] See Askola, 'Violence against Women, Trafficking and Migration in the European Union' (2007) ELJ 204–17.

[59] Council Directive 2003/109/EC of 25 November 2003 concerning the status of third-country nationals who are long-term residents (OJ 2004 L16/44), Articles 4 and 5. For a critical analysis of the Directive (which is not binding on Denmark or Ireland), see Boelaert-Suominen, 'Non-EU Nationals and Council Directive 2003/109/EC on the Status of Third-country Nationals who are Long-term Residents: Five Paces Forward and Possibly Three Paces Back' (2005) CMLRev 1011–52; for an application, see C-40/11, *Iida*, 2012, with case note by Tryfonidou (2012) SEW 302–20.

[60] Council Directive 2003/109/EC (n. 59, *supra*), Article 6(1).

[61] Ibid., Articles 14 to 23.

[62] Ibid., Article 11(1). According to Article 11(3), Member States may retain restrictions to access to employment or self-employed activities where these activities are reserved to nationals, EU, or EEA citizens.

[63] See C-571/10, *Kamberaj*, 2012, paras 64–93.

presence, or residence in the territory of one of the Member States (Articles 78(2)(g) and 79(3) TFEU).[64]

D. Rights derived from agreements with third countries

8.013 **Agreements with third countries.** Third-country nationals may also obtain certain rights where the Union concludes an agreement with their country which confers rights on them. In this way, the association agreements with the Maghreb countries and some decisions of the EU–Turkey Association Council[65] confer on nationals of those countries who are lawfully employed in the Member States the right to be treated in the same way as their own nationals as regards conditions of employment, remuneration, and social security.[66] However, nationals of the third countries concerned do not, as a result, obtain the right to free movement within the Union.[67] According to the Charter of Fundamental Rights of the European Union, nationals of third countries who are authorized to work in the territories of the Member States are entitled to working conditions equivalent to those of citizens of the Union.[68]

---

[64] For an assessment of these readmission agreements, see Molinari, 'The EU and its Perilous Journey through the Migration Crisis: Informalisation of the EU Return Policy and Rule of Law Concerns' (2019) ELRev 824–40; Billet, 'EC Readmission Agreements: A Prime Instrument of the EU's Fight against Irregular Migration. An Assessment after Ten Years of Practice.' (2010) EJML 46.

[65] For these association agreements and decisions, see para. 10-014 et seq., infra. For a general discussion, see Kellerman, 'The Rights of non-Member State Nationals under the EU Association Agreements' (2008) E For Aff Rev 339–82.; Peers, 'EU Migration Law and Association Agreements', in Martenczuk and van Thiel (n. 24, supra) 53–88.

[66] This also applies to resident family members who qualify for a benefit under the legislation of a Member State: C-18/90, *Kziber*, 1991, para. 28; C-126/95, *Hallouzi-Choho*, 1996, paras 21–40; ECJ, C-179/98, *Mesbah*, 1999, paras 42–48 (Cooperation Agreement with Morocco); C-103/94, *Krid*, 1995, paras 21–4; C-113/97, *Babahenini*, 1998, paras 19–31 (Cooperation Agreement with Algeria). However, the agreement with Morocco embodies more limited rights than the agreement with Turkey, which is supplemented by association decisions: C-416/96, *El-Yassini*, 1999, paras 33–67. For examples of rights arising under Decisions 2/76 and 1/80 of the EEC–Turkey Association Council, see C-192/89, *Sevince*, 1990, paras 27–33; C-237/91, *Kus*, 1994, paras 11–36; C-188/00, *Kurz*, 2002, paras 26–70; C-171/01, *Wählergruppe Gemeinsam*, 2003, paras 68–94. For Decision 3/80, see, e.g., C-277/94, *Taflan-Met*, 1996; C-262/96, *Sürül*, 1999, paras 75–105; C-102/98 and C-211/98, *Kocak and Others*, 2000, paras 32–55; C-275/02, *Ayaz*, 2004, paras 34–48; C-383/03, *Dogan*, 2005; C-337/07, *Altun*, 2008, paras 19–64; C-462/08, *Berkleyen*, 2010, paras 15–45; C-14/09, *Genc*, 2010, paras 15–44; C-300/09 and C-301/09, *Toprak and Oguz*, 2010, paras 30–62; C-303/08, *Bozkurt*, 2010, paras 24–61; C-484/07, *Pehlivan*, 2011, paras 35–67; C-187/10, *Unal*, 2011, paras 27–53; C-378/08, *Ziebell*, 2011, paras 47–86; C-7/10 and C-9/10, *Kahveci and Inan*, 2012, paras 22–41; C-268/11, *Gülbahce*, 2012, paras 31–56; C-451/11, *Dülger*, 2012, paras 27–65; C-225/12, *Demir*, 2013, paras 32–49; C-171/13, *Demirci*, 2015, paras 45–73; C-508/15 and C-509/15, *Ucar and Kilic*, 2016, paras 50–77; C-561/14, *Genc*, 2016, paras 32–67; C-652/15, *Tekdemir*, 2017, paras 23–53; C-123/17, *Yön*, 2018, paras 37–89; C-70/18, *A, B, and P*, 2019, paras 32–70; C-89/18, *A*, 2019, paras 22–47. For Article 41(1) of the Additional Protocol to the agreement with Turkey (on establishment and services), see C-37/98, *Savas*, 2000, paras 56–71; C-317/01 and C-369/01, *Abatay and Others*, 2003, paras 58–117; C-92/07, *Commission v Netherlands*, 2010, paras 43–76; C-256/11, *Dereci*, 2011, paras 80–101; C-221/11, *Demirkan*, 2013, paras 32–63 (notion of 'freedom to provide services' in Article 41(1) of the Additional Protocol does not encompass freedom for Turkish nationals who are the recipients of services to visit a Member State in order to obtain services); C-91/13, *Essent Energie Productie*, 2014, paras 21–35; C-507/15, *Agro Foreign Trade & Agency*, 2017, paras 37–52. With regard to the direct effect of such provisions, see para. 26-004, infra.

[67] e.g. C-179/98, *Mesbah*, 1999, para. 356. See also Stangos, 'La jurisprudence récente de la Cour de justice des Communautés européennes concernant les travailleurs migrants, ressortissants de pays tiers' (2000) RAE 107–17.

[68] Charter of Fundamental Rights of the European Union, Article 15(3). cf. para. 7-046, supra.

III. Judicial Cooperation in Civil Matters

Scope. The Union is to develop judicial cooperation in civil matters having cross-border implications, including the adoption of harmonization measures. Judicial cooperation in civil matters is based on the principle of mutual recognition of judgments and of decisions in extrajudicial cases (Article 81(1) TFEU). The Treaty of Amsterdam introduced this competence with regard to private (international) law, while limiting it to measures 'necessary for the proper functioning of the internal market'.[69] With the Lisbon Treaty, the latter limitation disappeared, although Article 81(2) TFEU specifies that the measures are to be adopted 'particularly when necessary for the proper functioning of the internal market'. Although private law is primarily within the competence of the Member States, the Union adopts measures pursuant to Article 81 TFEU which restrict national policy options and, just as in other Union policy areas, may in some cases preclude any parallel exercise of competence by the Member States.[70]

8.014

The European Parliament and the Council take measures in this matter in accordance with the ordinary legislative procedure, with the exception of aspects relating to family law. For measures concerning family law with cross-border implications, the Council acts by unanimous vote on a proposal from the Commission after consulting the European Parliament (Article 81(3), first subpara. TFEU). However, the Council, acting unanimously on a proposal from the Commission after consulting the European Parliament, may adopt a decision determining those aspects of family law with cross-border implications that may be the subject of acts adopted by the ordinary legislative procedure. National parliaments must be notified of any such proposal. If a national parliament opposes the measure within six months of its notification, it cannot be adopted (Article 81(3), second and third subparas TFEU).

Cross-border actions. What is involved is, first, measures aimed at ensuring the mutual recognition and enforcement between Member States of judgments and of decisions in

8.015

---

[69] See Article 65 EC. See Basedow, 'The Communitarisation of Private International Law' (2009) RabelsZ 455–664; Remien, 'European Private International Law, the European Community and its Emerging Area of Freedom, Security and Justice' (2001) CMLRev 53–86. For the relationship with the Hague Conference on Private International Law and the question whether Article 65 EC [*now Article 81 TFEU*] implies the power to conclude agreements with third countries, see Traest, 'Development of a European Private International Law and the Hague Conference' (2003) YPIL 223–259; Kotuby, 'External Competence of the European Community in the Hague Conference on Private International Law: Community Harmonisation and Worldwide Unification' (2001) NILR 1–30.

[70] Thus, e.g., Regulation No. 1347/2000 (currently Regulation No. 2201/2003) (n. 78, *infra*) and Regulation No. 44/2001 (currently Regulation No. 1215/2012) (n. 75, *infra*) preclude any parallel competence on the part of the Member States within the meaning of the *AETR* case law (see para. 5-026 *supra*), which confers an 'exclusive nature' on the Union in the relevant areas. This means that the Member States may no longer act internationally in the fields covered by these regulations without the authorization of the Union. See also Opinion 1/03 on the Community's exclusive competence to conclude the Lugano Convention (n. 77, *infra*). See therefore Regulation (EC) No. 662/2009 of the European Parliament and of the Council establishing a procedure for the negotiation and conclusion of agreements between Member States and third countries on particular matters concerning the law applicable to contractual and non-contractual obligations, OJ 2009 L200/25, and Council Regulation (EC) No. 664/2009 of 7 July 2009 establishing a procedure for the negotiation and conclusion of agreements between Member States and third countries concerning jurisdiction, recognition, and enforcement of judgments and decisions in matrimonial matters, matters of parental responsibility, and matters relating to maintenance obligations, and the law applicable to matters relating to maintenance obligations, OJ 2009 L200/46. In this respect, see Storskrubb, 'Civil justice: Constitutional and Regulatory Issues Revisited' in Fletcher, Herlin-Karnell, and Matera (eds), *The European Union as an Area of Freedom, Security and Justice* (Routledge, 2019)218.

extrajudicial cases,[71] the cross-border service of judicial and extrajudicial documents, and cooperation in the taking of evidence (Article 81(2)(a), (b) and (d) TFEU). In these areas, the Union legislature has adopted regulations, some of which replace and build upon agreements concluded between the Member States or outside the (then) Community framework which the Court of Justice had jurisdiction to interpret.[72]

As far as cross-border service of documents is concerned, a regulation has replaced the convention concluded by the Member States in the context of cooperation in the fields of justice and home affairs.[73] For the purpose of the taking of evidence in civil and commercial matters, another regulation has introduced a system of cooperation between the courts of the Member States.[74] Moreover, as regards recognition and enforcement of judgments, Regulation No. 1215/2012 (as its predecessor, Regulation No. 44/2001) deals with the recognition and enforcement of judicial decisions in civil and commercial matters while laying down common rules as to jurisdiction.[75] That regime took over from the Brussels Convention (or 'Brussels I'), which the Member States concluded as long ago as 1968 pursuant to Article 220 EEC [*later Article 293 EC*].[76] The arrangements were extended

---

[71] Before the Lisbon Treaty, this competence was limited to 'the recognition and enforcement of decisions in civil and commercial cases, including decisions in extrajudicial cases' (Article 65(a), third indent EC).

[72] See paras 28-018–28-019.

[73] Regulation (EU) 2020/1784 of the European Parliament and of the Council of 25 November 2020 on the service in the Member States of judicial and extrajudicial documents in civil or commercial matters (service of documents) (recast) OJ 2020 L405/40, replacing Regulation (EC) No. 1393/2007 of the European Parliament and of the Council of 13 November 2007 on the service in the Member States of judicial and extrajudicial documents in civil or commercial matters, OJ 2007 L324/79 (itself replacing Council Regulation (EC) No. 1348/2000 of 29 May 2000, OJ 2000 L160/37). The Regulation will also be implemented by Denmark, pursuant to Article 3 of the Agreement between the European Community and the Kingdom of Denmark on the service judicial and extrajudicial documents in civil or commercial matters, concluded by Council Decision 2006/326/EC of 27 April 2006 (OJ 2006 L120/23), see OJ 2021 L19/1. See Ekelmans, 'Le règlement 1348/2000 relatif à la signification et à la notification des actes judiciaires et extrajudiciaires' (2001) JT 481–488; Heß, 'Die Zustellung von Schriftstücken im europäischen Justizraum' (2001) NJW 15–23. See, formerly, the Convention of 26 May 1997 on the service in the Member States of the European Union of judicial and extrajudicial documents in civil or commercial matters, OJ 1997 C261/26 (explanatory report in OJ 1997 C261/26). For applications, see C-325/11, *Alder*, 2012, paras 18–42; C-226/13, C-245/13, C-247/13, and C-578/13, *Fahnenbock*, 2015, paras 33–59; C-519/13, *Alpha Bank Cyprus*, 2015, paras 26–77; C-223/14, *Tecom Mical*, 2015, paras 31–69; C-354/14, *Henderson*, 2017, paras 44–99; C-21/17, *Catlin Europe*, 2018, paras 30–57.

[74] Regulation (EU) 2020/1783 of the European Parliament and of the Council of 25 November 2020 on cooperation between the courts of the Member States in the taking of evidence in civil or commercial matters (taking of evidence) (recast), OJ 2020 L405/1, replacing Council Regulation (EC) No. 1206/2001 of 28 May 2001 on cooperation between the courts of the Member States in the taking of evidence in civil or commercial matters, OJ 2001 L174/1. See Mougenot, 'Le règlement européen sur l'obtention des preuves' (2002) JT 17–21; Berger, 'Die EG-Verordnung über die Zusammenarbeit der Gerichte auf dem Gebiet der Beweisaufnahme in Zivil- und Handelssachen (EuBVO)' (2001) IPRax 522–527. For applications, see C-283/09, *Weryński*, 2011, paras 47–69; C-170/11, *Lippens*, 2012, paras 24–39; C-332/11, *ProRail*, 2013, paras 38–54.

[75] Regulation (EU) No. 1215/2012 of the European Parliament and of the Council of 12 December 2012 on jurisdiction and the recognition and enforcement of judgments in civil and commercial matters, OJ 2012 L351/1, replacing Council Regulation (EC) No. 44/2001 of 22 December 2000 on jurisdiction and the recognition and enforcement of judgments in civil and commercial matters, OJ 2001 L12/1. See Van Calster, *European Private International Law* (Hart, 2021) 25–254; Stradler, 'From the Brussels Convention to Regulation 44/2001: Cornerstones of a European law of Civil Procedure' (2005) CMLRev 1637–61; Piltz, 'Vom EuGVÜ zur Brüssel-I-Verordnung' (2002) NJW 789–94. For recent applications, see, e.g., C-451/18, *Tibor-Trans Fuvarozó és Kereskedelmi*, 2019, paras 22–37; C-464/18, *ZX*, 2019, paras 24–41; C-641/18, *Rina*, 2020, paras 27–60; C-59/19, *Wikingerhof*, 2020, paras 19–38; C-73/19, *Movic*, 2020, paras 26–40; C-343/19, *Verein für Konsumenteninformation*, 2020, paras 21–40.

[76] Brussels Convention of 27 September 1968 on jurisdiction and the enforcement of judgments in civil and commercial matters; see the consolidated text in OJ 1998 C27/1. See Van Houtte and Pertegás Sender (eds), *Europese IPR-verdragen* (Acco, 1997); Briggs and Rees, *Civil Jurisdiction and Judgments* (Lloyd's of London Press, 1997). For its interpretation by the Court of Justice, see para. 28-018, *infra*. Interpretation provided by the Court in

to Iceland, Norway, and Switzerland by virtue of the Lugano Convention.[77] Similar regulations have been adopted on jurisdiction and the recognition and enforcement of judgments in matrimonial matters and in matters of parental responsibility[78] and on jurisdiction, applicable law, and recognition and enforcement of decisions and cooperation in matters relating to maintenance obligations.[79] The former regulation replaced a convention concluded by the Member States in the context of cooperation in the fields of justice and home affairs with regard to judicial decisions in matrimonial matters ('Brussels II').[80] Other regulations have laid down rules on jurisdiction and the applicable law with regard to cross-border insolvency proceedings and the recognition of judgments delivered on the basis of such proceedings;[81] on jurisdiction, applicable law, recognition, and enforcement of decisions and acceptance and enforcement of authentic instruments in matters of succession

respect of the provisions of the Brussels Convention is also valid for those of Regulation No. 44/2001 whenever the provisions of those instruments may be regarded as equivalent (C-533/08, *TNT Express Nederland*, 2010, para. 36).

[77] Convention on jurisdiction and the enforcement of judgments in civil and commercial matters (the Lugano Convention, constituting a *de facto* extension of the territorial scope of the Brussels Convention of 27 September 1968), OJ 1988 L319/9. In 2007 a new, revised Lugano Convention was signed by the European Communities, Denmark, Iceland, and Norway: Convention on jurisdiction and the recognition and enforcement of judgments in civil and commercial matters (OJ 2007 L339/3), which entered into force on 1 January 2010 between the EU, Denmark, and Norway (OJ 2010 L140/1); on 1 January 2011 the agreement entered into force as to the Union and Switzerland and on 1 May 2011 as to the Union and Iceland (OJ 2011 L138/1). Liechtenstein is not a party to the Lugano Convention. For the Community's exclusive competence to conclude that Convention, see ECJ, Opinion 1/03, *Competence of the Community to conclude the new Lugano Convention on jurisdiction and the recognition and enforcement of judgments in civil and commercial matters*, 2006.

[78] Council Regulation (EC) No. 2201/2003 of 27 November 2003 concerning jurisdiction and the recognition and enforcement of judgments in matrimonial matters and the matters of parental responsibility, OJ 2003 L338/1: 'Brussels IIa' or 'Brussels IIbis' Regulation), which replaced Council Regulation (EC) No. 1347/2000 of 29 May 2000 on jurisdiction and the recognition and enforcement of judgments in matrimonial matters and in matters of parental responsibility for children of both spouses, OJ 2000 L160/19; *corrigendum* in OJ 2000 C219/6: 'Brussels II'). See the contributions in Mankowski and Magnus (eds), *Brussels IIbis Regulation* (Munich, Sellier, 2012); Watté and Boularbah, 'Les nouvelles règles de conflits de juridictions en matière de désunion des époux. Le règlement communautaire "Bruxelles II"' (2001) JT 369–78; Kohler, 'Internationales Verfahrensrecht für Ehesachen in der Europäischen Union: Die Verordnung "Brüssel II"' (2001) NJW 10–15; Ancel and Muir Watt, 'La désunion européenne: le Règlement dit "Bruxelles II"' (2001) RCDIP 403–57; McEleavy, 'The Brussels II Regulation: How the European Community has Moved into Family Law' (2002) ICLQ 883–908. For the first case see, C-435/06, *C*, 2007, paras 24–77; for the first case pursuant to the urgent preliminary ruling procedure, see C-195/08 PPU, *Rinau*, 2008, paras 47–110; for recent applications, see, e.g., C-527/17, *HR*, 2018, paras 38–66; C-325/18 PPU and C-375/18 PPU, *C.E. and N.E.*, 2018, paras 45–94; C-393/18 PPU, *UD*, 2018, paras 43–70.

[79] Council Regulation (EC) No. 4/2009 of 18 December 2008 on jurisdiction, applicable law, recognition, and enforcement of decisions and cooperation in matters relating to maintenance obligations, OJ 2009 L7/1. See also Council Decision 2009/941/EC of 30 November 2009 on the conclusion by the European Community of the Hague Protocol of 23 November 2007 on the Law Applicable to Maintenance Obligations, OJ 2009 L331/17. For a commentary, see Beaumont, 'International Family Law in Europe—the Maintenance Project, the Hague Conference and the EC: A Triumph of Reverse Subsidiarity' (2009) RabelsZ 509–46. For the first interpretation by the Court of Justice, see C-400/13 and C-408/13, *Sanders and Verhagen*, 2014, paras 20–47; more recently, see C-468/18, *R*, 2019, paras 28–52; C-41/19, *FX*, 2019, paras 30–51.

[80] Convention of 28 May 1998 on jurisdiction and the recognition and enforcement of judgments in matrimonial matters (Second Brussels Convention, OJ 1998 C221/2). For its interpretation by the Court of Justice, see para. 28-018, *infra*.

[81] Regulation (EU) 2015/848 of the European Parliament and of the Council of 20 May 2015 on insolvency proceedings, OJ 2015 L141/19, replacing Council Regulation (EC) No. 1346/2000 of 29 May 2000, OJ 2000 L160/1 (not applicable to Denmark). See Bariatti, 'Recent Case-Law Concerning Jurisdiction and the Recognition of Judgments under the European Insolvency Rules' (2009) RabelsZ 629–59; Bureau, 'La fin d'un îlot de résistance—Le règlement du Conseil relatif aux procédures d'insolvabilité' (2002) RCDIP 613–79; Bos, 'The European Insolvency Regulation and the Harmonisation of Private International Law in Europe' (2003) NILR 31–57. A convention on insolvency proceedings was adopted on 23 November 1995 but did not enter into force as it was not signed by all Member States. For applications, see C-535/17, *NK*, 2019, paras 23–38; C-253/19, *MH*, 2020, paras 14–31.

(with the creation of a European Certificate of Succession);[82] and on the mutual recognition of protection measures.[83] By means of a regulation, the possibility has been created for a judgment on uncontested claims to be certified as a European Enforcement Order, allowing the judgment to be recognized and enforced in another Member State without any intermediate proceedings needing to be brought in that State.[84] The recognition and enforcement of orders relating to evidence gathering are the subject of arrangements adopted in the context of police and judicial cooperation in criminal matters (see para. 8-020, *infra*). The adoption of arrangements in other areas was possible only through the mechanism of enhanced cooperation of a group of Member States. This is the case for regulations concerning jurisdiction, applicable law, and the recognition and enforcement of decisions in matters of matrimonial property regimes,[85] and in matters of the property consequences of registered partnerships.[86]

None of these regulations, however, apply to Denmark. In order to make Regulation No. 44/2001 applicable in Denmark the Council had recourse to a special technique: in 2005 an international agreement was concluded between the Community and Denmark which provides for the application of the provisions of that regulation and its implementing measures to relations between the Community and Denmark.[87] The same technique was used in order to render the provisions of the regulation on the service of documents and its implementing measures (and the Dublin II Regulation, see para. 8-010, *supra*) applicable in relations between the Community and Denmark.[88] Denmark also signed the new Lugano

---

[82] Regulation (EU) No. 650/2012 of the European Parliament and of the Council of 4 July 2012 on jurisdiction, applicable law, recognition, and enforcement of decisions and acceptance and enforcement of authentic instruments in matters of succession and on the creation of a European Certificate of Succession, OJ 2012 L201/107. For applications, see C-218/16, *Kubicka*, 2017, paras 40–66; C-558/16, *Mahnkopf*, 2018, paras 31–44; C-20/17, *Oberle*, 2018, paras 29–59; C-657/17, *WB*, 2019, paras 31–64 and 66–72; C-102/18, *Brisch*, 2019, paras 21–36.

[83] Regulation (EU) No. 606/2013 of the European Parliament and of the Council of 12 June 2013 on mutual recognition of protection measures in civil matters, OJ 2013 L181/4.

[84] Regulation (EC) No. 805/2004 of the European Parliament and of the Council of 21 April 2004 creating a European Enforcement Order for uncontested claims, OJ 2004 L143/15; for applications see, e.g., C-508/12, *Vapenik*, 2013, paras 22–39; C-300/14, *Imtech Marine Belgium*, 2015, paras 27–50; C-511/14, *Pebros Servizi*, 2016, paras 35–45; C-484/15, *Zulfikarpašić*, 2017, paras 29–59; C-66/17, *Chudás*, 2017, paras 25–35; C-518/18, *RD* 2019, paras 23–30. See also, in this connection, Regulation (EC) No. 1896/2006 of the European Parliament and of the Council of 12 December 2006 creating a European order for payment procedure, OJ 2006 L399/1, for applications, see, e.g., C-119/13 and C-120/13, *eco cosmetics and Raiffeisenbank St. Georgen*, 2014, paras 32–49; C-245/14, *Thomas Cook Belgium*, 2015, paras 26–52; C-453/18 and C-494/18, *Bondora*, 2019, paras 34–54; Regulation (EC) No. 861/2007 of the European Parliament and of the Council of 11 July 2007 establishing a European Small Claims Procedure, OJ 2007 L199/1, for applications see C-627/17, *ZSE Energia*, 2018, paras 21–36; C-554/17, *Jonsson*, 2019, paras 18–29. None of these regulations are applicable to Denmark.

[85] Council Regulation (EU) 2016/1103 of 24 June 2016 implementing enhanced cooperation in the area of jurisdiction, applicable law, and the recognition and enforcement of decisions in matters of matrimonial property regimes, OJ 2016 L183/1.

[86] Council Regulation (EU) 2016/1104 of 24 June 2016 implementing enhanced cooperation in the area of jurisdiction, applicable law, and the recognition and enforcement of decisions in matters of the property consequences of registered partnerships, OJ 2016 L183/30.

[87] Agreement between the European Community and the Kingdom of Denmark on jurisdiction and the recognition and enforcement of judgments in civil and commercial matters, OJ 2005 L299/62, approved on behalf of the Community by Council Decision 2006/325/EC of 27 April 2006, OJ 2006 L120/22 (as amended by Council Decision 2009/943 of 30 November 2009, OJ 2009 L331/26). For its entry into force, see OJ 2007 L94/70. For an overview, see Arnt Nielsen, 'Denmark and EU Civil Cooperation' (2016) ZEuP 300. See also C-49/12, *Sunico*, 2013, 27–44; C-368/16, *Assens Havn*, 2017, paras 27–42.

[88] Agreement between the European Community and the Kingdom of Denmark on the service of judicial and extrajudicial documents in civil or commercial matters, OJ 2005 L300/55, approved on behalf of the Community by Council Decision 2006/326/EC of 27 April 2006, OJ 2006 L120/23 (as amended by Council Decision 2009/942 of 30 November 2009, OJ 2009 L331/24). For its entry into force, see OJ 2007 L94/70.

Convention as an independent contracting party, after taking part in the negotiations as such.[89] Pursuant to the 2005 agreement Denmark has committed to applying the modified regime of Regulation No. 1215/2012 in its relations with the Member States of the Union.[90]

Where the Union has not harmonized a particular area or introduced a system of mutual recognition, the Treaty provisions on free movement of persons may require national authorities to accept certificates and analogous documents relative to personal status issued by the competent authorities of the other Member States, unless their accuracy is seriously undermined by concrete evidence relating to the individual case in question. This will be so, in particular, where workers have to prove facts set out in registers of civil status (in their Member State of origin) in order to assert entitlements to social security benefits in another Member State.[91]

Other aspects. In addition, the European Parliament and the Council, acting in accordance with the ordinary legislative procedure, are to take measures to ensure the compatibility of the rules applicable in the Member States concerning conflict of laws and of jurisdiction (Article 81(2)(c) TFEU). Apart from rules on jurisdiction, this relates to instruments such as the Rome Convention concluded by the Member States in 1980 on the law applicable to contractual obligations.[92] The Rome Convention has since been replaced by a regulation on the law applicable to contractual obligations.[93] Likewise, a regulation has been adopted on the law applicable to non-contractual obligations (Rome II).[94] Pursuant to enhanced cooperation a regulation was adopted in the area of the law applicable to divorce and legal separation ('Rome III').[95] The European Union has acceded to the Hague Conference on

8.016

---

[89] OJ 2007 L339/1.
[90] OJ 2013, L79/4.
[91] C-336/94, *Dafeki*, 1997, paras 8–21.
[92] Rome Convention of 19 June 1980 on the law applicable to contractual obligations OJ 1980 L266/1; see the consolidated version in OJ 2005 C334/1). For this Convention, see Van Houtte and Pertegás Sender (eds), *Europese IPR-verdragen* (Acco, 1997), 189–320; Plender, *The European Contracts Convention* (Sweet & Maxwell, 1991); Martigny, 'Internationales Vertragsrecht im Schatten des Europäischen Gemeinschaftsrechts' (2001) ZEuP 308–66. For the harmonization of the rules of private international law, see also Jayme and Kohler, 'Europäisches Kollisionsrecht 2001: Anerkennungsprinzip statt IPR' (2001) IPRax 501–14; for the extent to which Union law influences the application of national conflicts rules, see Wilderspin and Lewis, 'Les relations entre le droit communautaire et les règles de conflits de lois des Etats membres' (2002) RCDIP 1–37. For applications, see C-133/08, *ICF*, 2009, paras 28–64; C-29/10, *Koelzsch*, 2011, paras 30–50; C-384/10, *Voosgeerd*, 2011, paras 22–65; C-64/12, *Schlecker*, 2013, paras 16–44; C-184/12, *Unamar*, 2013, paras 27–52; C-305/13, *Haeger & Schmidt*, 2014, paras 17–51.
[93] Regulation (EC) No. 593/2008 of the European Parliament and of the Council of 17 June 2008 on the law applicable to contractual obligations (Rome I), OJ 2008 L177/6 (not applicable to Denmark; corrigendum in OJ 2009 L309/87); see, e.g., C-135/15, *Nikiforidis*, 2016, paras 25–55; C-28/18, *Kerr*, 2019, paras 32–42; C-548/18, *BGL BNP Paribas*, 2019, 23–38. See Van Calster, *European Private International Law* (Hart, 2021) 256–91.
[94] Regulation (EC) No. 864/2007 of the European Parliament and of the Council of 11 July 2007 on the law applicable to non-contractual obligations (Rome II), OJ 2007 L199/40 (not applicable to Denmark). See Van Calster, *European Private International Law* (Hart, 2021) 293–330; Kadner Graziano, 'Das auf ausservertragliche Schuldverhältnisse anzuwendbare Recht nach Inkrafttreten der Rom-II-Verordnung' (2009) 73 RabelsZ 1–77; Von Hein, 'Of Older Siblings and Distant Cousins: The Contribution of the Rome II Regulation to the Communitarisation of Private International Law' (2009) RabelsZ 461–508; Francq, 'Le règlement Rome II concernant la loi applicable aux obligations non contractuelles. Entre droit communautaire et droit international privé' (2008) JTDE 289–96. For applications, see, e.g., C-412/10, *Homawoo*, 2011, paras 20–37; C-350/14, *Lazar*, 2015, paras 20–30; C-149/18, *da Silva Martins*, 2019, paras 23–42.
[95] Council Regulation (EU) No. 1259/2010 of 20 December 2010 implementing enhanced cooperation in the area of the law applicable to divorce and legal separation, OJ 2010 L343/10; see also C-372/16, *Sahyouni*, 2017, paras 35–49; C-249/19, *JE*, 2020, paras 21–44.

Private International Law, and hence has become a member of that conference alongside the Member States.[96]

8.017 **Civil procedure.** Lastly, Article 81(2)(f) TFEU provides for measures to eliminate obstacles to the good functioning of civil proceedings, if necessary by promoting the compatibility of the rules on civil procedure applicable in the Member States. Since the Lisbon Treaty, the Union has obtained express competences to enact measures aimed at ensuring effective access to justice and the development of alternative methods of dispute settlement (Article 81(2)(e) and (g) TFEU). Even before, the Union had laid down minimum standards for legal aid in cross-border disputes for persons without sufficient financial means[97] and facilitated the use of mediation as a method of settling disputes in civil and commercial matters.[98]

8.018 **European judicial network.** Pursuant to Article 81(2)(h) TFEU, the Union is to support the training of the judiciary and judicial staff. Even before the Lisbon Treaty added this provision, the Council had already established a European judicial network in civil and commercial matters and other forms of collaboration between legal practitioners on the basis of its competence to eliminate obstacles to judicial cooperation in civil matters.[99] Of note is the European e-justice portal site, which is developed by the Commission.[100]

IV. Judicial Cooperation in Criminal Matters

8.019 **Criminal law.** As in the case of judicial cooperation in civil matters, judicial cooperation in criminal matters is based on the principle of mutual recognition of judgments and judicial decisions (Article 82(1) and, more generally, the mutual trust between the Member States as regards the application of the fundamental rights guaranteed in the Union (see also para. 8-001, *supra*).[101] Whereas the Union itself does not incriminate undesired or prohibited

---

[96] See Council Decision 2006/719/EC of 5 October 2006 on the accession of the Community to the Hague Conference on Private International Law, OJ 2006 L297/1. See Boele-Woelki and van Ooik, 'Exclusieve externe bevoegdheden van de EG inzake het Internationaal Privaatrecht' (2006) NTER 194–201; Traest, 'Harmonisation du droit international privé: relation entre la Communauté européenne et la Conférence de La Haye' (2003) RDUnif 499–507.

[97] Council Directive 2002/8/EC of 27 January 2003 to improve access to justice in cross-border disputes by establishing minimum common rules relating to legal aid for such disputes, OJ 2003 L26/41 (the directive does not apply to Denmark).

[98] Directive 2008/52/EC of the European Parliament and of the Council of 21 May 2008 on certain aspects of mediation in civil and commercial matters, OJ 2008 L136/3 (the directive does not apply to Denmark).

[99] Council Decision 2001/470/EC of 28 May 2001 establishing a European Judicial Network in civil and commercial matters, OJ 2001 L174/25 (adopted on the basis of Article 61(c) and (d) and Article 66 EC; not applicable to Denmark; the decision has been amended by Decision No. 568/2009/EC of the European Parliament and of the Council of 18 June 2009, OJ 2009 L168/35). Council Regulation (EC) No. 743/2002 of 25 April 2002 established a general Community framework of activities to facilitate the implementation of judicial cooperation in civil matters, OJ 2002 L115/1 (not applicable to Denmark). See also the European Judicial Training Network (http://www.ejtn.eu), a non-profit international organization which promotes training programmes with a European dimension for members of the judiciary in Europe.

[100] See http://e-justice.europa.eu.

[101] For a critical view of the principle of mutual recognition in criminal matters, see Armada and Weyembergh, 'The Mutual Recognition in Principle and EU Criminal Law', in Fletcher, Herlin-Karnell, and Matera (eds), *The European Union as an Area of Freedom, Security and Justice* (Routledge, 2019)111–135; Roma Valdes, 'The Mutual Recognition Principle in Criminal Matters: a Review' (2015) ERA Forum, 291; Peers, 'Mutual Recognition and Criminal Law in the European Union: Has the Council Got it Wrong?' (2004) CMLRev 5–36; Alegre and Leaf, 'Mutual Recognition in European Judicial Cooperation: A Step Too Far Too Soon? Case Study—the European Arrest Warrant' (2004) ELJ 200–217.

behaviour directly, it seeks to contribute to the application of the Member States' criminal laws by facilitating criminal procedures, in particular for cross-border aspects, and by laying down minimum rules as regards guarantees for offenders and victims in criminal proceedings and minimum rules concerning the definition of criminal offences and sanctions.[102] Union action thus covers both substantive criminal law and criminal procedure.

The transfer to the Union of competences in criminal matters has been possible only by preserving, for certain aspects specified below, the requirement of unanimity voting in the Council. Moreover, a special 'alarm bell procedure' applies to decision-making under Articles 82(1) and (2) and 83(1) and (2) TFEU where a member of the Council considers that a draft directive on minimum rules on criminal procedure or a directive on the harmonization of substantive criminal law would affect fundamental aspects of its criminal justice system (Articles 82(3) and 83(3) TFEU; see para. 22-010, *infra*).

Aspects of criminal procedure. First of all, the Treaties provide for a legal basis as regards the mutual recognition and approximation of Member States' laws on criminal procedure. Article 82(1) TFEU confers on the Union competence to adopt measures to (a) lay down rules and procedures for ensuring recognition throughout the Union of judgments and judicial decisions; (b) prevent and settle conflicts of jurisdiction between Member States; and (c) facilitate cooperation between national judicial or equivalent authorities in relation to proceedings in criminal matters and the enforcement of decisions (Article 82(1) TFEU). The European Parliament and the Council adopt the necessary measures to that end under the ordinary legislative procedure. Accordingly, a European Investigation Order was created on the basis of which a judge may order investigative measures in order to gather evidence.[103] Likewise, a European Protection Order allows a person to seek protection from the criminal behaviour of another person on the basis of a protection order issued by another Member State.[104] As in the case of judicial cooperation in civil matters, the Union may adopt measures to support the training of the judiciary and judicial staff (Article 82(1), second subpara., sub (c) TFEU).

8.020

Furthermore, Article 82(2) TFEU provides for the possibility of harmonizing national criminal rules. The European Parliament and the Council may adopt directives establishing minimum rules concerning the mutual admissibility of evidence, the rights of individuals in criminal procedure,[105] the rights of victims of

---

[102] See Bogensberger, 'Chapter 4—Judicial Cooperation in Criminal Matters' in Kellerbauer, Klamert, and Tomkin (eds), *The EU Treaties and the Charter on Fundamental Rights* (OUP, 2019), 870; Mitsilegas, *EU Criminal Law after Lisbon: Rights, Trust and the Transformation of Justice in Europe* (Hart Publishing, 2016). See also Öberg, 'The Legal Basis for EU Criminal Law Harmonisation: A Question of Federalism?' (2018) ELRev 366–93; Mitsilegas, 'The Impact of Legislative Harmonisation on Effective Judicial Protection in Europe's Area of Criminal Justice' (2019) REALaw 117–42.

[103] Directive 2014/41/EU of the European Parliament and of the Council of 3 April 2014 regarding the European Investigation Order in criminal matters, OJ 2014 L130/1; see also C-324/17, *Gavanozov*, paras 23–38; C-584/19, *A*, 2020, paras 38–75 (distinguishing between the concept of 'issuing judicial authority' for the purpose of the European arrest warrant, n. 110, *infra*, and the concepts of 'judicial authority' and 'issuing authority' for the purpose of the European Investigation Order).

[104] Directive 2011/99/EU of the European Parliament and of the Council of 13 December 2011 on the European protection order, OJ 2011 L338/2.

[105] See Directive 2010/64/EU of the European Parliament and of the Council of 20 October 2010 on the right to interpretation and translation in criminal proceedings, OJ 2010 L280/1—for applications, see C-216/14, *Covaci*, 2015, paras 25–51; C-25/15, *Balogh*, 2016, paras 36–56; C-278/16, *Sleutjes*, 2017, paras 20–34; Directive 2012/13/EU of the European Parliament and of the Council of 22 May 2012 on the right to information in criminal proceedings, OJ 2012 L142/1—for applications, see C-216/14, *Covaci*, 2015, paras 52–68; C-612/15, *Kolev*, 2018, paras

crime,[106] and such other specific aspects of criminal procedure as are identified in advance by the Council, acting unanimously after obtaining the consent of the European Parliament. Such minimum rules may be adopted only '[t]o the extent necessary to facilitate mutual recognition of judgments and judicial decisions and police and judicial cooperation in criminal matters having a cross-border dimension' and must take into account the differences between the legal traditions and systems of the Member States (Article 82(2) TFEU).[107]

After the Amsterdam Treaty, measures in this field were mainly adopted in the form of framework decisions adopted under Article 31 EU under the 'third pillar'. The framework decision on the European arrest warrant[108] is especially noteworthy in this context, as the first implementation in criminal matters of the principle of mutual recognition, which is the 'cornerstone' of judicial cooperation. It replaced the system of formal extradition between Member States[109] by a system of surrender between judicial authorities of sentenced or suspected persons. When a judicial authority issues a European arrest warrant for the surrender of a person, the judicial authority in the Member State of execution may, in principle, refuse to execute such a warrant only on the grounds for non-execution exhaustively listed by Framework Decision 2002/584 and that execution of the warrant may be made subject only to one of the conditions exhaustively laid down in Article 5 thereof.[110] Nonetheless, the

---

77–100; C-467/18, *EP*, 2019, paras 55–63; Directive 2013/48/EU of the European Parliament and of the Council of 22 October 2013 on the right of access to a lawyer in criminal proceedings and in European arrest warrant proceedings, and on the right to have a third party informed upon deprivation of liberty and to communicate with third persons and with consular authorities while deprived of liberty, OJ 2013 L294/1, see, e.g., C-612/15, *Kolev*, 2018, paras 101–11; C-467/18, *EP*, 2019, paras 35–54; and Directive (EU) 2016/1919 of the European Parliament and of the Council of 26 October 2016 on legal aid for suspects and accused persons in criminal proceedings and for requested persons in European arrest warrant proceedings, OJ 2016 L297/1.

[106] See Directive 2012/29/EU of the European Parliament and of the Council of 25 October 2012 establishing minimum standards on the rights, support, and protection of victims of crime, and replacing Council Framework Decision 2001/220/JHA, OJ 2012 L315/57. For an application of Directive 2012/29/EU, see C-38/18, *Gambino*, 2019, paras 28–59; for a case pertaining to Council Framework Decision 2001/220/JHA, see C-105/03, *Pupino*, 2005.

[107] Article 82(2) TFEU makes it plain that the adoption of such rules does not prevent Member States from maintaining or introducing a higher level of protection for individuals.

[108] Council Framework Decision 2002/584/JHA of 13 June 2002 on the European arrest warrant and the surrender procedures between Member States, OJ 2002 L190/1). See further the agreement between the Union, Iceland, and Norway on the surrender procedure, concluded by Council Decision 2006/697/EC of 27 June 2006, OJ 2006 L292/1 (for an application, see C-897/19 PPU, *I.N.*, 2020, paras 71–4). See Wouters and Naert, 'Of Arrest Warrants, Terrorist Offences and Extradition Deals: An Appraisal of the EU's Main Criminal Law Measures against Terrorism after "11 September"' (2004) CMLRev 909–35. The validity of national measures implementing Framework Decision 2002/584/JHA was contested before a number of national constitutional courts, in particular in Germany, Cyprus, the Czech Republic, and Poland and in some Member States the Constitution was adapted to allow for its implementation; see, e.g., Fichera, 'The European Arrest Warrant and the Sovereign State: a Marriage of convenience' (2009) ELJ 70–97; Deen-Racsmany, 'The European arrest Warrant and the Surrender of nationals revisited: The Lessons of Constitutional Challenges' (2006) EJCCL & CJ 271–306; Monjal, 'La décision-cadre instaurant le mandat d'arrêt européen et l'ordre juridique français: la constitutionnalité du droit dérivé de l'Union européenne sous contrôle du Conseil d'Etat' (2003) RDUE 109–87. For the validity of this framework decision, see C-303/05, *Advocaten voor de Wereld*, 2007. As to the validity of the changes made by Council Framework Decision 2009/299/JHA of 26 February 2009 (OJ 2009 L81/24) in respect of execution of a sentence pronounced *in absentia*, see C-399/11, *Melloni*, 2013, paras 47–54.

[109] See the Convention of 10 March 1995, adopted on the basis of the former Article K.3 of the EU Treaty, on simplified extradition procedure between the Member States of the European Union, OJ 1995 C78/2) and the Convention of 27 September 1996 relating to extradition between the Member States of the European Union, OJ 1996 C313/12 (for the explanatory report, see OJ 1997 C191/13.

[110] The European arrest warrant must be issued by a 'judicial authority' within the meaning of Article 6(1) of the Framework Decision, which implies that the authority concerned acts independently in the execution of the responsibilities inherent in the issuing of a European arrest warrant. See C-508/18 and C-82/19 PPU, *OG and PI*, 2019; C-509/18, *PF*, 2019; C-717/18, *X*, 2020; C-510/19, *AZ*, 2020 (assessing whether public prosecutors' offices

Court of Justice has recognized that other limitations may be placed on the principle of mutual recognition and mutual trust between Member States in exceptional circumstances.[111] This may occur where an executing judicial authority has material indicating that there is a real risk of breach of the fundamental right to a fair trial guaranteed by Article 47 of the Charter on account of systemic or generalized deficiencies affecting the independence of the issuing Member State's judiciary. In such a case, the executing authority must refrain from giving effect to the European arrest warrant if there are substantial grounds for believing that, in the particular circumstances, that person will run such a risk if he or she is surrendered to that Member State.[112] Likewise, the executing judicial authority has an obligation to bring the surrender procedure to an end where, in the particular circumstances of the case, there are substantial grounds for believing that, following his or her surrender, the person will run a real risk of being subject to inhuman or degrading treatment within the meaning of Article 4 of the Charter, because of the conditions of detention in the issuing Member State.[113]

In addition to the European arrest warrant, the Council has adopted framework decisions on the execution of orders freezing property or evidence[114] and on the application of the principle of mutual recognition to financial penalties,[115] criminal judgments imposing custodial sentences,[116] and decisions on supervision measures as an alternative to provisional detention[117] as well as on the exchange of information extracted from the criminal record.[118] In addition, the Council has adopted framework decisions on taking account

---

qualified as 'judicial authority'). The status of 'issuing judicial authority' cannot however be denied to judges or courts of the issuing Member State, which act by their nature entirely independently of the executive: C-354/20 PPU and C-412/20 PPU, *L and P*, 2020, paras 41–50.

[111] C 404/15 and C 659/15 PPU, *Aranyosi and Căldăraru*, 2016, paras 80–104.

[112] C-216/18 PPU, *LM*, 2018, paras 58–79. The executing authority cannot presume that there are substantial grounds for believing that such a risk exists without carrying out a specific and precise verification that takes account of, *inter alia*, his or her personal situation, the nature of the offence in question, and the factual context in which that warrant was issued, such as statements by public authorities which are liable to interfere with how an individual case is handled: C-354/20 PPU and C-412/20 PPU, *L and P*, 2020, paras 53–69.

[113] C 404/15 and C 659/15 PPU, *Aranyosi and Căldăraru*, 2016, paras 80–104; C-128/18, *Dorubantu*, 2019, paras 50–85. The European arrest warrant has given rise to further preliminary rulings, including many Grand Chamber judgments; see C-303/05, *Advocaten voor de Wereld*, 2007; C-66/08 *Kozłowski*, 2008; C-123/08, *Wolzenburg*, 2009; C-261/09, *Mantello*, 2010; C-42/11, *Lopes Da Silva Jorge*, 2012; C-396/11, *Radu*, 2013; C-399/11, *Melloni*, 2013; C-182/15, *Petruhhin*, 2016; C-237/15 PPU, *Lanigan*, 2015; C-367/16, *Piotrowski*, 2018; C-573/17, *Popławski*, 2019 (see also C-579/15, *Popławski*, 2017).

[114] Council Framework Decision 2003/577/JHA of 22 July 2003 on the execution in the European Union of orders freezing property or evidence, OJ 2003 L196/45.

[115] Council Framework Decision 2005/214/JHA of 24 February 2005 on the application of the principle of mutual recognition to financial penalties, OJ 2005 L76/16; for an application, see C-60/12, *Baláž*, 2013, paras 24–49; C-671/18, *ZP*, 2019, paras 26–58; C-183/18, *Bank BGŻ BNP Paribas*, 2020, paras 41–79.

[116] Council Framework Decision 2008/909/JHA of 27 November 2008 on the application of the principle of mutual recognition to judgments in criminal matters imposing custodial sentences or measures involving deprivation of liberty for the purpose of their enforcement in the European Union, OJ 2008 L327/27; for applications, see, e.g., C-582/15, *van Vemde*, 2017, paras 22–33; C-573/17, *Popławski*, 2019, paras 35–49; C-314/18, *SF*, 2020, paras 63–68.

[117] Council Framework Decision 2009/829/JHA of 23 October 2009 on the application, between Member States of the European Union, of the principle of mutual recognition to decisions on supervision measures as an alternative to provisional detention, OJ 2009 L294/20.

[118] Council Framework Decision 2009/315/JHA of 26 February 2009 on the organization and content of the exchange of information extracted from the criminal record between Member States, OJ 2009 L93/23 (replacing Council Decision 2005/876/JHA of 21 November 2005, OJ 2005 L322/33). Further arrangements are laid down in Council Decision 2009/316/JHA of 6 April 2009, OJ 2009 L93/33. See also C-25/15, *Balogh*, 2016, paras 41–56.

of criminal convictions in other Member States,[119] on the application of the principle of mutual recognition to decisions rendered in the absence of the person concerned at the trial,[120] and on prevention and settlement of conflicts of exercise of jurisdiction in criminal proceedings.[121]

8.021 **Definition of criminal offences and sanctions.** Article 83(1), first subpara. TFEU enables the European Parliament and the Council, acting in accordance with the ordinary legislative procedure, to adopt directives establishing minimum rules on the definition of criminal offences and sanctions in the area of 'particularly serious crime with a cross-border dimension resulting from the nature or impact of such offences or from a special need to combat them on a common basis'. The forms of criminality that the Treaty mentions are terrorism; trafficking in human beings and sexual exploitation of women and children; illegal drug trafficking; illegal arms trafficking; money laundering; corruption; counterfeiting of means of payment; computer crime; and organized crime. Other areas of crime may be added by the Council, acting unanimously after obtaining the consent of the European Parliament (Article 83(1), second and third subparas TFEU).

Before the Lisbon Treaty, this competence was more curtailed, as Article 31(1)(e) EU referred to the progressive adoption of measures establishing minimum rules relating to the constituent elements of criminal acts and to penalties in the fields of organized crime, terrorism, and illicit drug trafficking. On that basis, the Council already defined crimes in the areas of fraud and forgery, corruption, trafficking in human beings, sexual exploitation, participation in the activities of a criminal organization, and illicit drug trafficking.[122]

---

[119] Council Framework Decision 2008/675/JHA of 24 July 2008 on taking account of convictions in the Member States of the European Union in the course of new criminal proceedings, OJ 2008 L220/32; see also C-171/16, *Beshkov*, 2017, paras 24–47; C-390/16, *Lada*, 2018, paras 26–48.
[120] Council Framework Decision 2009/299/JHA of 26 February 2009 amending Framework Decisions 2002/584/JHA, 2005/214/JHA, 2006/783/JHA, 2008/909/JHA, and 2008/947/JHA, thereby enhancing the procedural rights of persons and fostering the application of the principle of mutual recognition to decisions rendered in the absence of the person concerned at the trial, OJ 2009 L81/24, see, e.g., C-399/11, *Melloni*, 2013.
[121] Council Framework Decision 2009/948/JHA of 30 November 2009 on prevention and settlement of conflicts of exercise of jurisdiction in criminal proceedings, OJ 2009 L328/42.
[122] See Council Decision 2000/375/JHA of 29 May 2000 to combat child pornography on the Internet, OJ 200 L138/1; Council Framework Decision 2000/383/JHA of 29 May 2000 on increasing protection by criminal penalties and other sanctions against counterfeiting in connection with the introduction of the euro, OJ 2000 L140/1, replaced by Directive 2014/62/EU of the European Parliament and of the Council of 15 May 2014 on the protection of the euro and other currencies against counterfeiting by criminal law, OJ 2014 L151/1; Council Framework Decision 2001/413/JHA of 28 May 2001 combating fraud and counterfeiting of non-cash means of payment, OJ 2001 L149/1, replaced by Directive (EU) 2019/713 of the European Parliament and of the Council of 17 April 2019 on combating fraud and counterfeiting of non-cash means of payment, OJ 2019 L123/18; Council Framework Decision 2001/500/JHA of 26 June 2001 on money laundering, the identification, tracing, freezing, seizing, and confiscation of instrumentalities and the proceeds of crime, OJ 2001 L182/1; Council Framework Decision 2002/629/JHA of 19 July 2002 on combating trafficking in human beings, OJ 2002 L203/1, replaced by Directive 2011/36/EU of the European Parliament and of the Council of 5 April 2011 on preventing and combating trafficking in human beings and protecting its victims, OJ 2011 L101/1; Council Framework Decision 2002/946/JHA of 28 November 2002 on the strengthening of the penal framework to prevent the facilitation of unauthorised entry, transit, and residence, OJ 2002 L328/1; Council Framework Decision 2003/568/JHA of 22 July 2003 on combating corruption in the private sector, OJ 2003 L192/54; Council Framework Decision 2004/68/JHA of 22 December 2003 on combating the sexual exploitation of children and child pornography, OJ 2004 L13/44, replaced by Directive 2011/93/EU of the European Parliament and of the Council of 13 December 2011 on combating the sexual abuse and sexual exploitation of children and child pornography, OJ 2011 L335/1; Council Framework Decision 2004/757/JHA of 25 October 2004 laying down minimum provisions on the constituent elements of criminal acts and penalties in the field of illicit drug trafficking, OJ 2004 L335/8 (for an application, see C-634/18, *JI*, 2020, paras 31–52); Council Framework Decision 2005/222/JHA of 24 February 2005 on attacks against information systems, OJ 2005 L69/67, replaced by Directive 2013/40/EU of the European Parliament and of the Council of 12 August 2013 on attacks against information systems, OJ 2013 L218/8. For commentaries, see

Following the terrorist attacks of 11 September 2001, the Council adopted measures to ensure that any assistance to acts of terrorism would be criminal offences.[123] By now, the European Parliament and the Council have defined a number of other crimes, in respect of human trafficking, sexual exploitation, and cybercrimes, replacing the existing framework decisions by directives.[124]

In addition, the Union is empowered to accompany its harmonization measures by minimum rules with regard to the definition of criminal offences and sanctions in the area concerned. If it proves essential in order to ensure the effective implementation of a Union policy, a directive may be established to this end in accordance with the same procedure as was used to adopt the harmonization measure[125] (Article 83(2) TFEU).[126] Even before that competence was made explicit by the Treaty of Lisbon, the Court of Justice had already held that a Community harmonization measure could require the Member States to introduce effective, proportionate, and dissuasive criminal penalties in order to ensure that the rules which it lays down are fully effective.[127]

Crime prevention. The European Parliament and the Council, acting in accordance with the ordinary legislative procedure, may establish measures to promote and support the action of Member States in the field of crime prevention. These measures may not, however, extend to approximation of Member States' legislative and regulatory provisions (Article 84 TFEU). 8.022

Obokata, 'EU Council Framework Decision on Combating Trafficking in Human Beings: A Critical Appraisal' (2003) CMLRev 917–36. See also, to this effect, the definition of 'fraud' in the Convention on the protection of the European Communities' financial interests, para. 20-013, *infra*, the Convention of 17 June 1998, drawn up on the basis of the former Article K.3 of the EU Treaty, on driving disqualifications, OJ 1998 C216/2, and the Joint Actions adopted by the Council on the basis of the former Article K.3 of the EU Treaty on making it a criminal offence to participate in a criminal organization (98/733/JHA of 21 December 1998, OJ 1998 L351/1) and on corruption in the private sector (98/742/JHA of 22 December 1998, OJ 1998 L358/2).

[123] Council Framework Decision 2002/475/JHA of 13 June 2002 on combating terrorism, OJ 2002 L164/3, which builds on Council Common Position 2001/930/JHA of 27 December 2001 on combating terrorism, OJ 2001 L344/90. See Margue, 'Les initiatives menées par l'Union dans la lutte antiterroriste dans le cadre du troisième pilier (Justice et affaires intérieures)' (2002) RDUE 261–81; Dubois, 'The Attacks of 11 September: EU-US Cooperation against Terrorism in the Field of Justice and Home Affairs' (2000) E For Aff Rev 317–35. Council Framework Decision 2002/475/JHA has since been replaced by Directive (EU) 2017/541 of the European Parliament and of the Council of 15 March 2017 on combating terrorism, OJ 2017 L88/6.

[124] See the directives mentioned in n. 122, *supra*.

[125] See Directive 2014/57/EU of the European Parliament and of the Council of 16 April 2014 on criminal sanctions for market abuse (market abuse directive), OJ 2014 L173/179; Directive (EU) 2017/1371 of the European Parliament and of the Council of 5 July 2017 on the fight against fraud to the Union's financial interests by means of criminal law, OJ 2017 L198/29 (see para. 20-013, *infra*).

[126] However, since such directives fall within the area of PJCC, the parallel right of initiative for the Member States must be taken into account (see Article 76 TFEU, to which Article 83(2) TFEU refers).

[127] C-176/03, *Commission v Council*, 2005, para. 48. Given the availability of a Community legal basis, the Court held that it was contrary to Article 47 EU for the Council to lay down on the basis of Title VI of the EU Treaty the sanctions necessary to enforce infringements of a Community harmonization measure. Hence, the Court annulled Council Framework Decision 2003/80/JHA of 27 January 2003 on the protection of the environment through criminal law, OJ 2003 L29/55. See likewise C-440/05, *Commission v Council*, 2007 (annulment of Council Framework Decision 2005/667/JHA of 12 July 2005 to strengthen the criminal-law framework for the enforcement of the law against ship-source pollution, OJ 2005 L255/164). Following the annulment of those framework decisions, Directive 2008/99/EC of the European Parliament and of the Council of 19 November 2008 on the protection of the environment through criminal law, OJ 2008 L328/28 and Directive 2009/123/EC of the European Parliament and of the Council of 21 October 2009 amending Directive 2005/35/EC on ship-source pollution and on the introduction of penalties for infringements, OJ 2009 L280/52 were adopted on the basis of Articles 175(1) and 80(2) EC Treaty, respectively.

8.023 **Eurojust.** The Union also promotes cooperation between national authorities through Eurojust. Eurojust is a unit composed of prosecutors, magistrates, or police officers seconded from each Member State to facilitate the coordination of national prosecution authorities and support criminal investigations into major crime.[128] It has its seat in The Hague. Article 85(1), first subpara. TFEU states that the mission of Eurojust is to support and strengthen coordination and cooperation between national investigating and prosecuting authorities 'in relation to serious crime affecting two or more Member States or requiring a prosecution on common bases, on the basis of operations conducted and information supplied by the Member States' authorities and by Europol'. Eurojust's structure, operation, field of action, and tasks are now to be determined by the European Parliament and the Council by means of regulations adopted in accordance with the ordinary legislative procedure (Article 85(1), second subpara. TFEU).[129] Eurojust has, in particular, the task of strengthening judicial cooperation, including by resolution of conflicts of jurisdiction and by close cooperation with the European Judicial Network.[130]

8.024 **European Public Prosecutor.** Since the Lisbon Treaty, the Treaties hold out the prospect of setting up a European Public Prosecutor's Office, albeit solely in order to combat crimes affecting the Union's financial interests (Article 86(1) TFEU). The European Public Prosecutor's Office is to be established by the Council, acting unanimously after obtaining the consent of the European Parliament (Article 86(1) TFEU) in order to investigate, prosecute, and bring to judgment the perpetrators of offences against the Union's financial interests and their accomplices (Article 86(2) TFEU). In 2013, the Commission proposed to set up the European Public Prosecutor's Office in the form of a Union organ with a decentralized structure,[131] with a European public prosecutor heading the European Public Prosecutor's Office and European public prosecutors in the Member States investigating and prosecuting crimes under the European public prosecutor's supervision and guidance. As no unanimity was reached on the proposal, the Council decided in 2017 to discuss it in the framework of an enhanced cooperation with those Member States willing to create the European Public Prosecutor's Office.[132] This resulted in the adoption of Council Regulation

---

[128] Regulation (EU) 2018/1727 of the European Parliament and of the Council of 14 November 2018 on the European Union Agency for Criminal Justice Cooperation (Eurojust), OJ 2018 L295/138, replacing Council Decision 2002/187/JHA of 28 February 2002 setting up Eurojust with a view to reinforcing the fight against serious crime, OJ 2002 L63/1. Until Eurojust was set up, a Provisional Judicial Cooperation Unit operated by virtue of Council Decision 2000/799/JHA of 14 December 2000, OJ 2000 L324/2.

[129] These regulations must determine arrangements for involving the European Parliament and national Parliaments in the evaluation of Eurojust's activities (Article 85(1), third subpara. TFEU). See Article 67 of Regulation (EU) 2018/1727 (joint evaluation of Eurojust's activities in the framework of an inter-parliamentary committee meeting at the premises of the European Parliament with participation of members of the competent committees of the European Parliament and of the national parliaments).

[130] See Article 85(1), second subpara., sub (c) TFEU. The European Judicial Network in criminal matters was set up by the Council by Joint Action 98/428/JHA of 29 June 1998, OJ 1998 L191/4, now replaced by Council Decision 2008/976/JHA of 16 December 2008 on the European Judicial Network, OJ 2008 L348/130.

[131] See the Commission proposal of 17 July 2013 (COM(2013)534). Some national parliaments rendered a negative opinion on subsidiarity grounds (see, para. 5-032, *supra*). For the earlier debate on this matter, see Zwiers, *The European Public Prosecutor's Office* (Intersentia, 2011); Fijnaut and Groenhuijsen, 'Een Europees openbaar ministerie: kanttekeningen bij het Groenboek' (2002) NJB 1234–41; Veldt, 'Een Europees Openbaar Ministerie: de oplossing voor de EU-fraude?' (2001) JJB 666–71; Van Gerven, 'Constitutional Conditions for a Public Prosecutor's Office at the European Level' (2000) EJCCL & CJ 296–318.

[132] Article 86(1), second and third subpara. TFEU expressly provides for the use of enhanced cooperation in this respect.

(EU) 2017/1939,[133] by which twenty-two Member States[134] established the European Public Prosecutor's Office (EPPO, see para. 13-045, *infra*), which is to start its operational activities in June 2021. The EPPO, which has its seat in Luxembourg, is responsible for investigating, prosecuting, and bringing to judgment the perpetrators of, and accomplices to, specific criminal offences affecting the financial interests of the Union.[135] In relation to those offences the European Public Prosecutor's Office acts as prosecutor in the competent courts of the Member States (Article 86(2) TFEU). It falls to the European Council to determine whether the powers of the European Prosecutor's Office should be extended to include serious crimes affecting more than one Member State (Article 86(4) TFEU). In this connection, the European Council is to act unanimously after obtaining the consent of the European Parliament and after consulting the Commission (ibid.).

V. Police Cooperation

Police cooperation. Article 87(1) TFEU provides for police cooperation involving all the Member States' competent authorities, including police, customs, and other specialized law enforcement services in relation to the prevention, detection, and investigation of criminal offences, both directly and through the European Police Office (Europol).[136] To that purpose, the European Parliament and the Council, acting in accordance with the ordinary legislative procedure, may establish measures concerning: (a) the collection, storage, processing, analysis, and exchange of relevant information;[137] (b) support for the training of staff, and cooperation on the exchange of staff, equipment, and research into crime-detection; and (c) common investigative techniques in relation to the detection of serious forms of organized crime (Article 87(2) TFEU). National police training institutions work together within the framework of the European Police

8.025

---

[133] Council Regulation (EU) 2017/1939 of 12 October 2017 implementing enhanced cooperation on the establishment of the European Public Prosecutor's Office ('the EPPO'), OJ 2017 L283/1. See Brière, 'Le Parquet européen: analyse critique d'une réussite tempérée par d'importants défis à relever' (2019) CDE 149–88; Conway, 'The Future of a European Public Prosecutor in the Area of Freedom, Security and Justice', Fletcher, Herlin-Karnell, and Matera (eds), *The European Union as an Area of Freedom, Security and Justice* (Routledge, 2019), 176–200; Bachmaier Winter (ed.), *The European Public Prosecutor's Office: The Challenges Ahead* (Springer, 2018).

[134] This includes all Member States, except Denmark, Hungary, Ireland, Poland, and Sweden.

[135] This concerns, in accordance with Article 5 of Regulation (EU) 2017/1939, the offences provided for in Directive (EU) 2017/1371 of the European Parliament and of the Council of 5 July 2017 on the fight against fraud to the Union's financial interests by means of criminal law, OJ 2017 L198/29.

[136] See Guild and Geyer, Security Versus Justice? Police and Judicial Cooperation in the European Union (Routledge, 2016); Peers, *EU Justice and Home Affairs Law* (OUP, 2016), Chapter 2; Heckler, 'Europäisches Verwaltungskooperationsrecht am Beispiel der grenzüberschreitenden polizeilichen Zusammenarbeit' (2001) EuR 826–45.

[137] e.g. Directive (EU) 2016/681 of the European Parliament and of the Council of 27 April 2016 on the use of passenger name record (PNR) data for the prevention, detection, investigation, and prosecution of terrorist offences and serious crime, OJ 2016 L119/132 (based on Articles 82(1) and 87(2)(a) TFEU). Before the Lisbon Treaty, see already Council Decision 2000/261/JHA of 27 March 2000 on the improved exchange of information to combat counterfeit travel documents, OJ 2000 L81/1; Council Decision 2000/642/JHA of 17 October 2000 concerning arrangements for cooperation between financial intelligence units of the Member States in respect of exchanging information, OJ 2000 L271/4; Council Decision 2001/886/JHA of 6 December 2001 on the second-generation Schengen Information System, OJ 2001 L328/1; Council Decision 2002/348/JHA of 25 April 2002 concerning security in connection with football matches with an international dimension, OJ 2002 L121/1.

College (CEPOL), established in Budapest.[138] In addition, the Council, acting unanimously after consulting the European Parliament, may establish measures concerning operational cooperation between the different law enforcement authorities.[139] Special arrangements apply in the case of disagreement between the Member States (Article 87(3) TFEU; see para. 22-010, *infra*).

It is also for the Council, acting unanimously after consulting the European Parliament, to determine the conditions and limitations under which national judicial and law enforcement authorities may operate in the territory of another Member State, in liaison and agreement with the authorities of that State (Article 89 TFEU).

8.026 **Europol.** Europol is the Union's agency for law enforcement cooperation. In the form of a 'European Police Office' it was initially established within the framework of the 'third pillar' by a convention concluded between the Member States,[140] starting operations on 1 July 1999. Nowadays, it acts as the European Union Agency for Law Enforcement Cooperation (Europol) pursuant to a regulation adopted on the basis of Article 88 TFEU.[141] In common with Eurojust, Europol has its seat in The Hague. Its mission is to support and strengthen action by the Member States' police authorities and other law enforcement services and their mutual cooperation in preventing and combating serious crime affecting two or more Member States, terrorism, and forms of crime which affect a common interest covered by a Union policy (Article 88(1) TFEU).[142] Since the Lisbon Treaty, it is for the European Parliament and the Council to adopt the regulations laying down Europol's structure, operation, field of action, and tasks, as well as the specific procedures for scrutiny of Europol's activities by the European Parliament and the national parliaments, in accordance with the ordinary legislative procedure (Article 88(2) TFEU).

Operational actions by Europol are possible solely in liaison and in agreement with the authorities of the Member State concerned. The competent national authorities have the exclusive responsibility of applying coercive measures (Article 88(3) TFEU).

---

[138] Regulation (EU) 2015/2219 of the European Parliament and of the Council of 25 November 2015 on the European Union Agency for Law Enforcement Training (CEPOL) and replacing and repealing Council Decision 2005/681/JHA, OJ 2015 L319/1; earlier CEPOL was established at Bramshill (United Kingdom); see Council Decision 2005/681/JHA of 20 September 2005, OJ 2005 L256/63.

[139] See Council Framework Decision 2002/465/JHA of 13 June 2002 on joint investigation teams, OJ 2002 L162/1, and Council Decision 2002/956/JHA of 28 November 2002 setting up a European Network for the Protection of Public Figures, OJ 2002 L333/1.

[140] Convention of 26 July 1995 on the establishment of a European Police Office (Europol Convention), OJ 1995 C316/1. For the interpretation by the Court of Justice of the Europol Convention, see para. 28-019, *infra*. Europol started work on 1 June 1999; see OJ 1999 C185/1. In anticipation of the establishment of Europol, the Member States set up a Europol Drugs Unit (EDU) in 1993 ((1993) 6 EC Bull. point 1.4.19). Its mandate was laid down by Joint Action 95/73/JHA of 10 March 1995, OJ 1995 L62/1) and extended by Joint Action 96/748/JHA of 16 December 1996, OJ 1996 L342/4. See Subhan, 'L'Union européenne et la lutte contre la drogue' (1999) RMCUE 196–201.

[141] Regulation (EU) 2016/794 of the European Parliament and of the Council of 11 May 2016 on the European Union Agency for Law Enforcement Cooperation (Europol), OJ 2016 L135/53.

[142] For the operation of Europol, see Ellermann, 'Von Sammler zu Jäger—Europol auf dem Weg zu einem "europäischen FBI"?' (2002) ZEuS 561–85; for the relationship between Eurojust and Europol, see Berthelet and Chevallier-Govers, 'Quelle relation entre Europol et Eurojust? Rapport d'égalité ou rapport d'autorité?' (2001) RMCUE 468–74.

VI. Exceptional Status of Denmark and Ireland

Denmark. Denmark is bound by the Schengen *acquis* and so has agreed to the elimination of checks on persons at the internal frontiers and to the arrangements regarding checks at the external borders and entry for a short stay. However, in the negotiations leading up to the Treaty of Amsterdam, it obtained the right—laid down in a separate protocol—not to participate in any measure in the field of visas, asylum, immigration, and judicial cooperation in civil matters. With respect to police and judicial cooperation in criminal matters (where decision-making in the Council still required unanimity), though, Denmark had no specific status.[143] In the negotiations leading up to the Lisbon Treaty, it obtained an extension of its opt-out as set out in Protocol (No. 22) on the position of Denmark.[144] Although Denmark continues to be bound by the Schengen *acquis* and participates in the development thereof, pursuant to the Protocol it does not participate in the adoption of measures in the area of freedom, security, and justice.[145] The only exception is that Denmark participates in the measures determining the third countries whose nationals must be in possession of a visa when crossing the external borders of the Member States, or relating to a uniform format for visas.[146] This means that, apart from this exception, Denmark will not be bound by any of the provisions of Title V of Part Three TFEU nor by measures adopted pursuant to that Title (or by decisions of the Court of Justice interpreting them), and is not to bear the financial consequences ensuing therefrom.[147] It follows that its opt-out now includes measures of police and judicial cooperation in criminal matters. However, Protocol (No. 22) provides that Union acts in the field of police and judicial cooperation in criminal matters adopted before the entry into force of the Treaty of Lisbon that are amended 'shall continue to be binding upon and applicable to Denmark unchanged'.[148] The Council decisions on the further development of the Schengen *acquis*, which Denmark transposes in its national legislation pursuant to Protocol (No. 22) only create 'an obligation under international law'.[149]

8.027

Denmark does not have the right to participate in acts adopted under Title V of Part Three of the TFEU where it wishes to do so. Before the Lisbon Treaty, the Union had concluded

---

[143] Article 3 of the initial Schengen Protocol (see para. 8-004, *supra*) provided that Denmark continued to have the 'same rights and obligations' as the other signatories with regard to those parts of the Schengen *acquis* that were determined to have their legal basis in Title VI of the EU Treaty. This covered, among other things, the judicial review provided for by Article 35 EU.

[144] Protocol (No. 22), annexed to the TEU and TFEU by the Lisbon Treaty on the position of Denmark, OJ 2010 C83/299. Denmark may relinquish its separate status by informing the other Member States: Article 7.

[145] Articles 1 and 2 of Protocol (No. 22). For the applicable decision-making procedures, see para. 22-002 *et seq.*, *infra*.

[146] Article 6 of Protocol (No. 22). See, e.g., the participation of Denmark in the adoption of Regulation (EU) 2018/1806 of the European Parliament and of the Council of 14 November 2018 listing the third countries whose nationals must be in possession of visas when crossing the external borders and those whose nationals are exempt from that requirement, OJ 2018 L303/39 (as well as the preceding Council Regulation (EC) No. 539/2001 of 15 March 2001).

[147] Ibid., Articles 2 and 3. Denmark will also not be bound by the Union's data protection rules with respect to activities of police and judicial cooperation in criminal matters: ibid., Article 2a.

[148] Ibid., Article 2. It should be recalled, moreover, that pursuant to Article 9 of Protocol (No. 36), annexed to the TEU, TFEU, and EAEC Treaty on transitional provisions (OJ 2010 C83/322), the legal effects of Union acts adopted on the basis of the EU Treaty prior to the entry into force of the Lisbon Treaty are to be preserved until those acts are repealed, annulled, or amended in implementation of the current Treaties (see also para. 8-028, *infra*).

[149] Protocol (No. 22), Article 4.

international agreements with Denmark regarding the application of a specific measure between Denmark and the other Member States (see para. 22-004, *infra*).[150] Since the Lisbon Treaty, Denmark has, however, the option of abandoning its general opt-out, either as such[151] or else in favour of a system under which—in common with Ireland—it would have the possibility of notifying the other Member States its intention to participate in one or another proposed measure in the area of freedom, security, and justice.[152] On 3 December 2015 a majority of the Danish population (53 per cent) voted by referendum against the use of this possibility, with the result that Denmark, for now at least, only participates in measures that develop on the Schengen *acquis*.

8.028 **Ireland.** Unlike Denmark, Ireland is, in principle, not bound by the Schengen *acquis*. That was also the position of the United Kingdom before its withdrawal from the Union. Since Ireland and the United Kingdom have arrangements between themselves relating to the movement of persons between their territories ('the Common Travel Area'), reference must be made to the United Kingdom's position in order to explain Ireland's. Under a separate protocol to the Treaties—currently Protocol (No. 20)—the United Kingdom had retained the right to conduct controls on persons at its frontiers in order to verify that persons purportedly having the right to enter the United Kingdom do in fact have such a right and to determine whether or not to grant other persons permission to enter the country.[153] The United Kingdom could only verify whether a person meets the conditions for entering laid down by the Union and was not allowed to impose additional conditions.[154] Due to its Common Travel Area with the United Kingdom, Ireland too retains the right to carry out such controls as long as the Common Travel Area arrangements are maintained,[155] which is still the case after Brexit.[156] The other Member States are entitled to exercise controls on persons seeking to enter their territories from Ireland (or the United Kingdom).

It follows from the Schengen Protocol (see para. 8-006, *supra*) that Ireland may request the Council to take part in specific provisions of the Schengen *acquis*.[157] Ireland is also entitled to take part in the adoption of measures that build upon the Schengen *acquis* if it notifies the Council within a reasonable period of its wish to do so[158] (see para. 22-003, *infra*). Ireland

---

[150] This technique was used, for instance, to allow Denmark to participate in the adoption and application of the regulation which replaces the Dublin Convention and the 'Eurodac' system for the identification of asylum seekers and to allow for its participation in Regulation No. 44/2001 ('Brussels I') and the regulation on service of documents (see the rerefences in paras 8-010 and 8-015, *supra*).

[151] Protocol (No. 22), Article 7.

[152] If it exercises this latter option, all the Schengen *acquis* and measures adopted to build upon this *acquis*, which until then have been binding on Denmark as obligations under international law, 'shall be binding upon Denmark as Union law' six months after the date on which the notification takes effect (Protocol (No. 22), Article 8.

[153] Article 1 of Protocol (No. 20), annexed to the TEU and TFEU, on the application of certain aspects of Article 26 TFEU to the United Kingdom and to Ireland (OJ 2010 C83/293), which states that nothing in Articles 26 and 77 TFEU or in any other Treaty provisions shall prejudice the right of the United Kingdom to adopt or exercise such controls.

[154] C-202/13, *McCarthy and Others*, 2014, para. 64.

[155] Article 2 of Protocol (No. 20). See Ryan, 'The Common Travel Area between Britain and Ireland' (2001) MLR 855–74.

[156] Article 38(2) of the Withdrawal Agreement.

[157] Schengen Protocol (see para. 8-006, *supra*), Article 4. Ireland (like the UK before Brexit) does not have the right to participate in the adoption of measures that build upon specific provisions of the Schengen *acquis* if it is not taking part in the latter provisions (Schengen Protocol, Article 5): C-77/05, *United Kingdom v Council*, 2007, paras 54–68, with case note by Rijpma (2008) CMLRev 835–52; C-137/05, *United Kingdom v Council*, 2007, paras 49–56.

[158] Schengen Protocol, Article 5(1).

thus participates in a number of provisions of the Schengen *acquis*,[159] but not, for example, in respect of external border crossings.[160] The same applied to the United Kingdom before Brexit.

Pursuant to yet another protocol to the Treaties—Protocol (No. 21)—Ireland does not, in principle, take part in the further adoption of measures within the area of freedom, security, and justice (Title V of Part Three of the TFEU); it is not bound by such measures (or by decisions of the Court of Justice relating thereto) and it does not bear the financial consequences of such measures.[161] Before the entry into force of the Lisbon Treaty, that arrangement only concerned measures adopted in the field of visa, asylum, immigration, and judicial cooperation in civil matters; since then it concerns the whole area of freedom, security, and justice, including police and judicial cooperation in criminal matters. If Ireland so wishes, it may, however, notify the President of the Council of its intention to take part in the adoption and application of a proposed measure.[162] The same regime applies to measures pursuant to Title V of Part Three of the TFEU that amends a measure to which Ireland is bound (see para. 22-003, *infra*).[163] The opt-in arrangement does not apply to restrictive measures imposed pursuant to Article 75 TFEU on natural and legal persons, groups, or non-State entities.[164]

Unlike the United Kingdom, Ireland has not also been seeking to limit the supervision of the Commission and the Court of Justice as regards compliance with applicable Union law in the area of freedom, security, and justice. In that respect, it must be recalled, first, that Union acts adopted before the entry into force of the Lisbon Treaty on the basis of the EU Treaty (that is to say, principally, acts of police and judicial cooperation in criminal matters), preserve their legal effects until they are repealed, annulled, or amended under the present Treaties,[165] and that for Union acts adopted in the field of police and judicial cooperation in criminal matters prior to the entry into force of the Lisbon Treaty ('PJCC acts'), the powers of the Commission and the Court of Justice were reduced during a transitional

---

[159] See the acts listed in Council Decision 2002/192/EC of 28 February 2002 concerning Ireland's request to take part in some of the provisions of the Schengen *acquis*, OJ 2002 L64/20. As a result of that decision, a number of Union acts are binding on Ireland, even though it did not take part in their adoption, e.g. Council Regulation (EC) No. 2424/2001 of 6 December 2001 on the Schengen Information System (OJ 2001 L328/4). Since 15 March 2021 Ireland has gained full access to the Schengen Information System (SIS II) (n. 15, *supra*).

[160] For example, Ireland (like the United Kingdom) did not participate in the adoption of, for instance, Council Regulation (EC) No. 539/2001 of 15 March 2001 listing the third countries whose nationals must be in possession of visas when crossing the external borders and those whose nationals are exempt from that requirement (n. 26, *supra*), with the result that it is free to draw up its own lists.

[161] Articles 1, 2, and 5 of Protocol (No. 21), annexed to the TEU and the TFEU, on the position of the United Kingdom and Ireland in respect of the Area of Freedom, Security, and Justice (OJ 2010 C83/295) (replacing Protocol (No. 4), annexed by the Amsterdam Treaty to the EU Treaty and the EC Treaty, OJ 1997 C340/99). The same applied to the United Kingdom before Brexit. Ireland may notify the Council that it no longer wishes to be covered by this Protocol: Protocol (No. 21), Article 8 (the United Kingdom did not have that option).

[162] Protocol (No. 21), Article 3. For example, the notification given by Ireland and the United Kingdom that they would participate in the 'Dublin III' Regulation (EU) No. 604/2013 of the European Parliament and of the Council of 26 June 2013 establishing the criteria and mechanisms for determining the Member State responsible for examining an application for international protection lodged in one of the Member States by a third-country national or a stateless person, OJ 2013 L180/31 (see recital 41 in the preamble thereto). For the decision-making procedure and for the possibility of accepting a measure, even after it has been adopted, under the 'enhanced cooperation' procedure, see para. 22-003, *infra*.

[163] Protocol (No. 21), Article 4a.

[164] Ibid., Article 9.

[165] See Protocol (No. 36), annexed to the TEU, TFEU, and EAEC Treaty, on Transitional Provisions, OJ 2010 C83/322, Article 9 (see para. 2-008, *supra*).

period of five years.[166] In that regard, the United Kingdom obtained the possibility, at the expiry of that transitional period on 1 December 2014, of still not accepting the supervisory powers of the Commission and the Court with respect to pre-Lisbon PJCC acts, in which case all such pre-Lisbon PJCC acts would henceforth cease to apply to it.[167] On 24 July 2014, the United Kingdom made use of this possibility, with the effect that the pre-Lisbon PJCC acts in the field of police and judicial cooperation in criminal matters no longer applied to it from 1 December 2014.[168] However, the United Kingdom immediately made use of the possibility offered, in such a situation, to again participate in a selected number of pre-Lisbon PJCC acts, such as the Framework Decision on the European arrest warrant.[169] The Commission and the Court of Justice thus retained their jurisdiction over the United Kingdom in respect of those acts as long as it was a Member State.

---

[166] Ibid., Article 10(1) (see para. 2-008, *supra*).

[167] However, this did not apply with respect to amended acts which were applicable to the United Kingdom (ibid.).

[168] See the list in OJ 2014 C430/17.

[169] Protocol (No. 36), Article 10(5). See the measures listed in Council Decision 2014/857/EU of 1 December 2014, OJ 2014 L345/1 (provisions of the Schengen *acquis*) and in Commission Decision 2014/858/EU of 1 December 2014, OJ 2014 L345/6 (PJCC acts not part of the Schengen *acquis*).

9
Other Areas of Union Policy

Union policies. Part Three of the TFEU on 'Union policies and internal actions' contains the legal basis for Union action in several areas, which are described below, that have not already been covered in Chapters 6 (citizenship of the Union), 7 (the internal market), and 8 (the area of freedom, security, and justice). Before setting out these various policy areas, this chapter first discusses the protection of personal data enshrined in Article 16 TFEU which, while forming part of the 'provisions having general application' of Part One TFEU, also developed into an important policy field for Union action.

9.001

I. Protection of Personal Data

Data protection. Article 16 TFEU not only confirms everyone's right to the protection of personal data concerning them (Article 16(1)) but also entrusts the European Parliament and the Council, acting in accordance with the ordinary legislative procedure, with the adoption of rules with regard to the processing of personal data by Union institutions, bodies, offices, and agencies, and by the Member States when carrying out activities which fall within the scope of Union law, as well as rules relating to the free movement of such data (Article 16(2), first subpara. TFEU; for CFSP, see Article 39 TEU). Before the Lisbon Treaty, such rules were adopted pursuant to the competence for harmonisation in the internal market.[1] Given the far-reaching effects of these rules for all undertakings providing services in the Union, the Union's protective rules have been setting standards for data protection worldwide.[2]

9.002

The right to the protection of personal data is set out in Article 8 of the Charter of Fundamental Rights, which has given rise to important case law clarifying the requirements for the processing of personal data, the right to access to personal data, and the right to have data rectified.[3] Article 16(2), first subpara. TFEU confirms the requirement for control by

---

[1] See the harmonization of national law effected on the basis of Article 95 EC [*now Article 114 TFEU*] by Directive 95/46/EC of the European Parliament and of the Council of 24 October 1995 on the protection of individuals with regard to the processing of personal data and on the free movement of such data (OJ 1995 L281/31) and Directive 2002/58/EC of the European Parliament and of the Council of 12 July 2002 concerning the processing of personal data and the protection of privacy in the electronic communications sector (Directive on privacy and electronic communications) (OJ 2002 L201/37).

[2] See also Bradford, *The Brussels Effect: How the European Union Rules the World* (OUP, 2020).

[3] See, e.g., as regards the right to be forgotten: C-131/12, *Google Spain and Google*, 2014; as regards data retention in the context of electronic communication services: C-293/12 and C-594/12, *Digital Rights Ireland*, 2014; as regards transfer of data to third countries: C-362/14, *Schrems*, 2015; C-311/18, *Schrems*, 2020; as regards access for reasons of national security: C-511/18, C-512/18, and C-520/18, *La Quadrature du Net and Others*, 2020; C-623/17, *Privacy International*, 2020. See Kranenborg, 'Commentary on Article 8 of the EU Charter of Fundamental Rights', in Peers et al. (eds), *The EU Charter of Fundamental Rights. A Commentary* (Hart Publishing, 2014), 223–65.

an independent authority, also guaranteed in Article 8 of the Charter and Article 39 TEU. With respect to the rules governing the processing of personal data by Union institutions, bodies, offices, and agencies,[4] compliance is ensured by an independent supervisory body, the European Data Protection Supervisor (see para. 13-043, *infra*).

As regards the processing of data by other public authorities and private actors, Article 16(2) TFEU has empowered the Union legislature to adopt the General Data Protection Regulation (GDPR),[5] which applies broadly to the processing of personal data by a person ('controller' or 'processor') established in the Union, whether it takes place in the Union or not, and processing of personal data of data subjects in the Union by a controller or processor not established in the Union whenever related to the offering of goods or services in the Union or to the monitoring of their behaviour within the Union.[6] The GDPR also sets requirements for the Member States' independent supervisory authorities and provides for a cooperation mechanism involving the European Data Protection Board, an independent body composed by the national supervisory authorities, which may issue guidance and, in specific cases of conflicting views amongst these authorities, take binding decisions.[7] In a specific Directive, the Union legislature has laid down the rules applicable to prevention, investigation, detection, or prosecution of criminal offences and execution of criminal penalties, including the safeguarding against and the prevention of threats to public security.[8] Furthermore, special rules apply to the protection of personal data in the field of the CFSP, where it is for the Council to lay down the rules with regard to processing of personal data by the Member States carrying out activities falling within the scope of the CFSP (Article 39 TEU and Article 16(2), second subpara. TFEU).

II. Agriculture and Fisheries

9.003   **Common agricultural policy.** The internal market extends to agriculture, fisheries, and trade in agricultural products and is accompanied by the establishment of a common

---

[4] Regulation (EU) 2018/1725 of the European Parliament and of the Council of 23 October 2018 on the protection of natural persons with regard to the processing of personal data by the Union institutions, bodies, offices, and agencies and on the free movement of such data, OJ 2018 L295/39, replacing Regulation (EC) No. 45/2001 of the European Parliament and the Council of 18 December 2000 on the protection of individuals with regard to the processing of personal data by the Community institutions and bodies and on the free movement of such data, OJ 2001 L8/1.

[5] Regulation (EU) 2016/679 of the European Parliament and of the Council of 27 April 2016 on the protection of natural persons with regard to the processing of personal data and on the free movement of such data, and repealing Directive 95/46/EC (General Data Protection Regulation), OJ 2016 L119/1. See Kuner et al., *The EU General Data Protection Regulation (GDPR)—A Commentary* (OUP, 2020); Rücker and Kugler, *New European General Data Protection Regulation, a Practitioner's Guide: Ensuring Compliant Corporate Practice* (Beck, 2018); Kranenborg en Verhey, *De Algemene Verordening Gegevensbescherming in Europees & Nederlands perspectief* (Wolters Kluwer, 2018); Poullet, *Le règlement général sur la protection des données (RGPD/GDPR): analyse approfondie* (Larcier, 2018); Ehmann and Selmayr (eds), *Datenschutz-Grundverordnung* (C.H. Beck, 2018).

[6] Ibid., Article 3(1) and (2).

[7] Ibid., Chapters VI—Independent supervisory authorities (Articles 51 to 59) and Chapter VII— Cooperation and consistency (Articles 60 to 76).

[8] Directive (EU) 2016/680 of the European Parliament and of the Council of 27 April 2016 on the protection of natural persons with regard to the processing of personal data by competent authorities for the purposes of the prevention, investigation, detection, or prosecution of criminal offences or the execution of criminal penalties, and on the free movement of such data, OJ 2016 L119/89, replacing Council Framework Decision 2008/977/JHA of 27 November 2008 on the protection of personal data processed in the framework of police and judicial cooperation in criminal matters, OJ 2008 L350/60. For an application, see C-505/19, *WS*, 2021, paras 107-121.

agricultural policy (CAP) (Article 38(1) and (4) TFEU).[9] The common agricultural policy relates to 'the products of the soil, of stockfarming and of fisheries and products of first-stage processing directly related to these products', as listed in Annex I to the TFEU (Article 38(1) and (3) TFEU).[10] Article 38(2) TFEU provides that the rules laid down for the establishment of the internal market are to apply to agricultural products, save as otherwise provided in Articles 39–44. Article 42 TFEU thus provides that the rules on competition are to apply to production of, and trade in, agricultural products only to the extent determined by the Council, which made it necessary for the Council to adopt an implementing regulation.[11] Both national organizations of agricultural markets and the common organizations of the markets by which the Union replaces them must be applied in conjunction with the rules on free trade and free competition within the internal market.[12] Additional aid to the agricultural sector is thus subject to the rules on State aid set forth in Articles 107, 108, and 109 TFEU.[13]

Objectives. The objectives of the common agricultural policy are listed in Article 39(1) TFEU: (a) increased agricultural productivity; (b) a fair standard of living of the agricultural community; (c) stable markets; (d) secured supplies; and (e) reasonable prices. Over the years, the emphasis has gradually shifted from helping to make good the shortfall in satisfying the Union's own needs to the concern of maintaining farmers' incomes, overproduction notwithstanding. Together with other policy objectives such as environmental protection and public health,[14] agricultural policy is to take account of the particular nature of agricultural activity, the need to effect the necessary adjustments by degrees, and the close links between the sector and the economy as a whole (Article 39(2) TFEU). Every Union measure cannot invariably take all the objectives into account. Hence, measures adopted under the common agricultural policy must be based on a balance of interests in accordance

9.004

---

[9] For an exhaustive discussion of the CAP, see McMahon, *EU Agricultural Law and Policy* (Edward Elgar Publishing, 2019); Bianchi, *La politique agricole commune (PAC)* (Bruylant, 2013); Danielsen, *EU Agricultural Law* (Kluwer, 2013); Skogstad and Verdun, *The Common Agricultural Policy: Policy Dynamics in a Changing Context (Special Issue of the Journal of European Integration)* (Routledge, 2009); McMahon, *EU agricultural law* (OUP, 2008); Bianchi, *La politique agricole commune (PAC): Toute la PAC, rien d'autre que la PAC!* (Bruylant, 2006); Usher, *EC Agricultural Law* (OUP, 2002); Barents, *The Agricultural Law of the EC* (Kluwer, 1994); Van Rijn, 'De ontwikkelingen in het Europees landbouwrecht' (2009) TAgrR 316–24.

[10] 'Annex II' until the Treaty of Amsterdam.

[11] Council Regulation (EC) No. 1184/2006 of 24 July 2006 applying certain rules of competition to the production of, and trade in, certain agricultural products, OJ 2006 L214/7, as amended and supplemented by Articles 206 to 218 and 222 of Regulation (EU) No. 1308/2013 of the European Parliament and of the Council of 17 December 2013. Council Regulation No. 1184/2006 replaced Council Regulation No. 26 applying certain rules of competition to production of and trade in agricultural products, OJ 1959–1962 English Special Edition 129. For the application of EU competition law, see, e.g., C-319/93, C-40/94, and C-224/94, *Dijkstra and Others*, 1995, paras 15–24; for an application of national competition law, see C-137/00, *Milk Marque Ltd and National Farmers' Union*, 2003, paras 57–67. For the priority enjoyed by agriculture over the objectives in respect of competition, see C-280/93, *Germany v Council*, 1994, paras 59–61.

[12] 48/74, *Charmasson*, 1974, paras 6–20 (national organization of agricultural markets); 80 and 81/77 *Commissionaires Réunis*, 1978, paras 22–38 (common organization of the market).

[13] C-111/10, *Commission v Council*, 2013; C-117/10, *Commission v Council*, 2013; C-118/10, *Commission v Council*, 2013; C-121/10, *Commission v Council*, 2013.

[14] e.g. environmental protection (Article 11 TFEU), public health (Article 168(1), first subpara. TFEU), and economic and social cohesion (Articles 174 and 175, first para. TFEU). See, in this connection, Gencarelli, 'La politique agricole commune et les autres politiques communautaires: la nouvelle frontière' (2001) RDUE 173–88; Bianchi, 'La politique agricole commune au lendemain du traité d'Amsterdam' (2001) RTDE 371–95. For environmental protection, see also Jack, *Agriculture and EU Environmental Law* (Ashgate Publishing, 2009); Rosso Grossman, *Agriculture and the Polluter Pays Principle* (British Institute of International and Comparative Law, 2009); Born, 'La conservation de la biodiversité dans la politique agricole commune' (2001) CDE 341–401.

with the principle of proportionality.[15] The common organizations of the markets in agricultural products are, moreover, not a competition-free zone, so that the applicability of the rules on competition law can only be excluded in limited instances.[16]

9.005 **Instruments.** Since the Lisbon Treaty, the European Parliament and the Council, acting in accordance with the ordinary legislative procedure, establish the common organization of agricultural markets and the other provisions necessary for the pursuit of the objectives of the common agricultural policy and the common fisheries policy (Article 43(2) TFEU).[17]

The common agricultural policy is made up primarily of market intervention through the common organizations of the markets, income guarantees for farmers, general quality standards, and rural development actions. Under Article 40(3) TFEU, the European Agricultural Guarantee Fund (EAGF) and of the European Agricultural Fund for Rural Development (EAFRD), both financed through the general budget of the Union, were set up.[18] Measures on fixing prices, levies, aid, and quantitative limitations, and on the fixing and allocation of fishing opportunities, are adopted by the Council on a proposal from the Commission (Article 43(2) and (3) TFEU). Article 43(2) and (3) TFEU each have a specific sphere of application, without there being a hierarchy between the two. Accordingly, the Council may take measures on the basis of Article 43(3) TFEU when the Union legislature has not yet established a framework for exercising the competences conferred on the Union by Article 43(2) TFEU, but the measures taken on the basis of Article 43(3) TFEU cannot involve making a political choice reserved to the Union legislature.[19]

9.006 **Market intervention and income guarantees.** The Union legislature has adopted a common organization of the market for most agricultural products.[20] The management of the common market organizations is entrusted to the Commission. Every common market organization (CMO) proceeds on the basis of the principles of a unified market (free movement of agricultural products and uniform prices), 'Union preference' (utmost self-sufficiency), and financial solidarity within the Union (the Union manages and distributes agricultural expenditure).

As a high level of prices guarantees producers' income, some of the CMOs have provided for price intervention. In order to eliminate the competitive advantage of producers from non-Union countries, the Union imposes import duties and other import levies to cover

---

[15] For the requisite weighing of interests, see 68/86, *United Kingdom v Council*, 1988, paras 10–14; C-122/94, *Commission v Council*, 1996, paras 23–5; for the necessary proportionality in achieving the objectives, see para. 5-035, *supra*. For a number of case studies, see Barents, 'De commautaire maatregelen ter bestrijding van mond- en klauwzeer' (2001) NTER 169–77; Mortelmans and Van Ooik, 'De Europese aanpak van mond- en klauwzeer en de rechtmatigheid van het preventieve vaccinatieverbod' (2001) AAe 911–27; Dehousse and Lewalle, 'La crise de la dioxine: un révélateur des faiblesses de la réglementation alimentaire nationale' (2000) Stud Dipl 5–27.
[16] C-671/15, *Association des producteurs vendeurs d'endives (APVE)*, 2017, paras 34–67.
[17] Before the Lisbon Treaty, the Council acted after consulting the European Parliament. See Bianchi, 'Une PAC 'dénaturée', 'délaissée' et 'malmenée'? Plaidoyer en faveur d'une politique agricole moderne dans le projet de Constitution européenne' (2004) RTDE 71–95.
[18] Article 3(2) of Regulation (EU) No. 1306/2013 of the European Parliament and of the Council of 17 December 2013 on the financing, management, and monitoring of the common agricultural policy, OJ 2013 L347/549.
[19] C-103/12 and C-165/12, *European Parliament and Commission v Council*, 2014, paras 43–81; C-124/13 and C-125/13, *European Parliament and Commission v Council*, 2015, paras 47–81. See also C-113/14, *Germany v European Parliament and Council*, 2016, paras 53–76.
[20] Regulation (EU) No. 1308/2013 of the European Parliament and of the Council of 17 December 2013 establishing a common organization of the markets in agricultural products, OJ 2013 L347/671. See Mögele and Erlbacher (eds), *Single Common Market Organisation* (Beck, Hart, Nomos, 2011)..

the difference between the world market price and a 'threshold price'. Producers exporting surplus products outside the Union are entitled to additional 'export refunds'. Within the Union market, supply and demand determine the price of a given product, but, at the same time, there is a 'target price' (sometimes known as a 'reference' or 'guide' price). If the market price deviates from the target price to such an extent as to reach the 'intervention price', intervention agencies may or must buy in the product.

As long as the agricultural policy made the income support of farmers depend on the quantities produced, this encouraged structural surpluses (butter, cereals, beef, and wine), constituting a heavy burden on the Union budget, which no longer resulted in increased incomes. Therefore, since the 1990s, reforms of the common agricultural policy were implemented, involving the lowering of farm prices towards world market prices. This is accompanied by an increase in direct income support for farmers, which is no longer calculated on the basis of production and dependent on restrictions on the acreage in use or herd size.

The 2003 and 2014 reforms of the CAP developed a system of direct payments to farmers, under which aid is no longer linked to production ('decoupling'). To receive direct payments, farmers must meet certain standards concerning public, animal, and plant health, the environment, and animal welfare; keep their land in good agricultural and environmental condition; and use adequate farming techniques to sustain biodiversity, soil quality, and, more generally, the environment.[21] Since these reforms of the CAP, the income support of farmers has been transferred from the common market organizations to the new system of direct payments to farmers.

In addition to market intervention and income support, the common agricultural policy makes provision for general quality standards, including the protection of geographical indications and designations of origin[22] and the labelling of organic products,[23] and measures to protect animal welfare.[24]

Rural development. In the measures for rural development, the reformed agricultural policy emphasizes environmental measures, afforestation of agricultural land, and structural improvements through early retirement, while seeking at the same time to improve the safety and quality of foodstuffs. The Union makes a financial contribution to the cost of programmes submitted by Member States and regions.[25]

9.007

---

[21] These are called the 'cross compliance' obligations. For an application, see C-428/07, *Horvath*, 2009.

[22] Council Regulation (EC) No. 510/2006 of 20 March 2006 on the protection of geographical indications and designations of origin for agricultural products and foodstuffs, OJ 2006 L93/12. For an application, see C-478/07, *Budějovický Budvar*, 2009. The regulation has since been replaced by Regulation (EU) No. 1151/2012 of the European Parliament and of the Council of 21 November 2012 on quality schemes for agricultural products and foodstuffs, OJ 2012 L343/1.

[23] Council Regulation (EC) No. 834/2007 of 28 June 2007 on organic production and labelling of organic products and repealing Regulation (EC) No. 2092/91, OJ 2007 L189/1. For an application of the latter regulation, see C-393/05, *Commission v Austria*, 2007 and C-404/05, *Commission v Germany*, 2007. See also C-497/17, *Œuvre d'assistance aux bêtes d'abattoirs (OABA)*, 2019 (animals that have been slaughtered in accordance with religious rites without first being stunned do not qualify for the label).

[24] e.g., Council Directives 2008/119/EC and 2008/120/EC of 18 December 2008 laying down minimum standards for the protection of calves and pigs, respectively (Codified versions), OJ 2009 L10/7 and L47/5.

[25] e.g. Regulation (EU) No. 1305/2013 of the European Parliament and of the Council of 17 December 2013 on support for rural development by the European Agricultural Fund for Rural Development (EAFRD), OJ 2013 L347/487. For an assessment of the rural development policy, see Ferraris, 'The 2021-2027 EU Rural Development Policy: A New Paradigm of Shared Management?' (2019) ELRev 855–72.

9.008 **Fisheries.** Fishery measures form a separate part of the common agricultural policy.[26] The power conferred by Article 102 of the 1972 Act of Accession to determine conditions for fishing with a view to ensuring protection of the fishing grounds and conservation of the biological resources of the sea, falls within the exclusive competence of the Union (see para. 5-023, *supra*). The exclusive competence of the Union over the protection of marine biological resources is, however, limited to instances where this is directly linked to the common fisheries policy, and does not encompass wider conservation measures pertaining to the oceans.[27] In 1983 a common fisheries policy was established, which was repeatedly reformed. The Union legislature enjoys a wide discretionary power in this respect, corresponding to the political responsibilities conferred on it by Articles 40 to 43 TFEU.[28] The most important aim of the common fisheries policy is to preserve fish stocks, for the purpose of which catch quotas and specific preservation measures have been laid down.[29] At the same time, it has to ensure the viability and sustainability of the fishery industry and create a fair standard of living for those who depend on fishing activities. To that effect, fishing quota are established taking into account the principle of relative stability.[30] The European Maritime and Fisheries Fund promotes an ecologically sustainable form of fisheries and aquaculture, and supports coastal communities in diversifying their economy.[31]

III. Transport

9.009 **Common transport policy.** Article 90 TFEU requires Member States to pursue the objectives of the Treaties within the framework of a common transport policy.[32] The provisions of the Title of the TFEU headed 'Transport' apply to transport by rail, road, and inland waterway (Article 100(1) TFEU). This is not automatically so as regards sea and air transport. Under the EC Treaty, the Council had to decide whether, to what extent, and by what procedure appropriate provisions were to be laid down.[33] Since the Lisbon Treaty

---

[26] For an overview, see Churchill and Owen, *The EC Common Fisheries Policy* (OUP, 2010); Markus, *European Fisheries Law—From Promotion to Management* (Europa Law Publishing, 2009). For a critical analysis, see Wakefield, *Reforming the Common Fisheries Policy* (Edward Elgar Publishing, 2016).

[27] C-626/15 and C-659/16, *Commission v Council*, 2018, paras 81–6. Protection of the waters surrounding Antarctica, including in zones where no fishing is allowed, therefore does not fall entirely within the exclusive competence of the Union under Article 3(1)(d) TFEU, but also relates to the shared environmental competences.

[28] C-611/17, *Italy v Council*, 2019, para. 27.

[29] See Regulation (EU) No. 1380/2013 of the European Parliament and of the Council of 11 December 2013 on the Common Fisheries Policy, OJ 2013 L354/22.

[30] That principle reflects a criterion for the allocation between Member States of fishing opportunities in the form of quotas allocated to those States. Thus, that principle does not confer on fishermen any guarantee of a fixed quantity of catches of fish, as the requirement of relative stability must be understood as meaning only that each Member State retains the right to a fixed percentage of that allocation, see C-611/17, *Italy v Council*, 2019, paras 80–91.

[31] Regulation (EU) No. 508/2014 of the European Parliament and of the Council of 15 May 2014 on the European Maritime and Fisheries Fund, OJ 2014 L149/1.

[32] For an exhaustive discussion, see Colangelo and Zeno-Zencovich, *Introduction to European Union Transport Law* (Roma TrE-Press, 2015); Maiani and Bieber, *Droit européen de transports* (Schulthess, 2013); Greaves, *EC Transport Law* (Longman, 2000) and, for air transport, Kassim and Handley, *Air Transport and the European Union: Europeanisation and its Limits* (Palgrave Macmillan, 2010). See also Kaeding, *Better Regulation in the European Union: Lost in Translation or Full Steam Ahead: The Transposition of EU Transport Directives Across Member States* (Amsterdam University Press, 2007).

[33] Article 80(2) EC required the Council to act by qualified majority and in accordance with the general decision-making procedure applicable to transport, which became the co-decision procedure with the Treaty of Amsterdam. For the application of freedom to provide services to maritime transport between Member States and between Member States and third countries, see Council Regulation (EC) No. 4055/86 of 22 December 1986, OJ

the European Parliament and the Council, acting in accordance with the ordinary legislative procedure, have to lay down the appropriate provisions. The Economic and Social Committee and the Committee of the Regions need to be consulted (Article 100(2) TFEU).

Actions in the transport sector come under the general rules of the Treaties, especially the rules on the establishment of the internal market, unless the Treaties provide otherwise.[34] Thus Article 58(1) TFEU provides that freedom to provide services in the field of transport shall be governed by the provisions of the Title relating to transport.[35] This has not prevented freedom to provide services from being introduced for transport between Member States and third countries and within Member States (*cabotage*).[36] The Treaty rules on competition also apply in the transport sector.[37]

Instruments. In the context of the common transport policy, the European Parliament and the Council are empowered to adopt, under the ordinary legislative procedure, any measures which they deem appropriate, *inter alia*, in relation to international transport, the conditions under which non-resident carriers may operate transport services, and transport safety, while taking account of 'the distinctive features of transport' (Article 91(1) TFEU; see also Article 94 TFEU). Interestingly, upon a request from the European Parliament, the Court of Justice considered in 1985 that the Council had neglected its obligations to take action in the fields of international transport and freedom to provide cross-border services.[38] Meanwhile, the Union legislature has phased in a Union licensing system for carriage of persons and goods by road to replace the system of national quotas.[39] Alongside this, there has been a gradual liberalization of domestic goods and passenger transport (*cabotage*).[40]

9.010

1986 L378/1; for maritime transport within Member States (maritime cabotage), see Council Regulation (EC) No. 3577/92 of 7 December 1992, OJ 1992 L364/7. For the application of freedom to supply services in air transport, see most recently Regulation (EC) No. 1008/2008 of the European Parliament and of the Council of 24 September 2008 on common rules for the operation of air services in the Community, OJ 2008 L293/3. For the extent to which Union action places limits on the differential treatment of sea transport to non-Union and Union ports, see C-435/00, *Geha Naftiliaki EPE and Others*, 2002, paras 21–2.

[34] 167/73, *Commission v France*, 1974, paras 24–8.
[35] C-434/15, *Asociación Profesional Élite Taxi*, 2017, paras 33–49; C-320/16, *Uber France*, 2018, paras 16–26.
[36] See also C-382/08, *Neukirchinger*, 2011, paras 21–30.
[37] See 156/77, *Commission v Belgium*, 1978, para. 10 (State aid); 209–213/84 *Asjes and Others*, 1986, paras 35-42 (antitrust). The general rules for the implementation of competition law laid down in Regulation No. 1/2003 (see n. 66, *infra*) also apply to the transport sector, although some specific rules apply to transport by rail, road, and inland waterway, see Council Regulation (EC) No. 169/2009 of 26 February 2009, OJ 2009 L61/1.
[38] 13/83, *European Parliament v Council*, 1985. The Court considered that the Council had failed to fulfil its obligations in the fields of international transport and of the conditions under which non-resident carriers might operate transport services in a Member State, since those obligations were sufficiently well-defined in the Treaty: paras 64-68. At the same time, the Court held that there was not yet a coherent set of rules which might be regarded as a common transport policy, but did not regard this as a failure to act considering that the Council had a discretion to decide, for example, whether action in the transport sector must first deal with relations between the railways and the public authorities or with competition between road and rail. Ibid., paras 46–50.
[39] See Regulation (EC) No. 1072/2009 of the European Parliament and of the Council of 21 October 2009 on common rules for access to the international road haulage market, OJ 2009 L300/72 (goods) and Regulation (EC) No. 1073/2009 of the European Parliament and of the Council of 21 October 2009 on common rules for access to the international market for coach and bus services, OJ 2009 L300/88 (passengers). For the liberalization of inland waterways, see Council Regulation (EC) No. 1356/96 of 8 July 1996, OJ 1996 L175/7; for railway transport, see Directive 2012/34/EU of the European Parliament and of the Council of 21 November 2012 establishing a single European railway area, OJ 2012 L343/3.
[40] For the determination of the conditions under which non-resident carriers may transport goods or passengers by inland waterway in a Member State in which they are not established, see Council Regulation (EC) No.

The achievement of the common transport policy, for sea and air transport too, goes hand in hand with the abolition of frontier controls between Member States and harmonization of technical and social rules. In addition, the Union legislature has laid down rules protecting passenger rights, initially only for air transport,[41] but now also for bus, rail, and maritime transport.[42]

9.011 **Non-discrimination.** Member States may not introduce any provisions which are less favourable for carriers of other Member States (Article 92 TFEU).[43] Accordingly, Germany failed to fulfil its obligations under Article 92 TFEU by introducing the infrastructure use charge and by providing, simultaneously, a relief from motor vehicle tax in an amount at least equivalent to that of the charge paid, to the benefit of the owners of vehicles registered in Germany.[44] The Treaties debar carriers from discriminating on grounds of the country of origin or of destination of the goods transported and empower the Council to introduce checks on the part of the Union (Article 95(1) and (3) TFEU, respectively).[45] The Member States are debarred from imposing rates and conditions involving any element of support or protection in the interest of one or more particular undertakings or industries, unless authorized by the Commission (Article 96(1) TFEU). The Commission may authorize such rates and conditions provided that they comply with Article 96(2) TFEU. For the rest, aid measures are caught by the rules set out in Articles 107, 108, and 109 TFEU (see para. 9-021, *infra*), unless they can be justified under Article 93 TFEU on the ground that they meet the needs of coordination

---

3921/91 of 16 December 1991, OJ 1991 L373/1; the equivalent regulations for road passenger services and road haulage services are Regulation (EC) No. 1073/2009 of the European Parliament and of the Council of 21 October 2009 on common rules for access to the international market for coach and bus services, OJ 2009 L300/88, and Regulation (EC) No. 1072/2009 of the European Parliament and of the Council of 21 October 2009 on common rules for access to the international road haulage market, OJ 2009 L300/72.

[41] Regulation (EC) No. 261/2004 of the European Parliament and of the Council of 11 February 2004 establishing common rules on compensation and assistance to passengers in the event of denied boarding and of cancellation or long delay of flights, OJ 2004 L46/1. There is extensive case law interpreting this regulation, see, e.g., C-549/07, *Wallentin-Hermann*, 2008 (mere technical problem in aircraft not qualifying as extraordinary circumstances in which no compensation is due); C-402/07 and C-432/07, *Sturgeon*, 2009 (long delay also gives rise to compensation under same conditions as flight cancellation).

[42] Regulation (EC) No. 1371/2007 of the European Parliament and of the Council of 23 October 2007 on rail passengers' rights and obligations, OJ 2007 L315/14, to be replaced by Regulation (EU) 2021/782 of the European Parliament and of the Council of 29 April 2021 on rail passengers' rights and obligations, OJ 2021 L172; Regulation (EU) No. 1177/2010 of the European Parliament and of the Council of 24 November 2010 concerning the rights of passengers when travelling by sea and inland waterway, OJ 2010 L334/1; Regulation (EU) No. 181/2011 of the European Parliament and of the Council of 16 February 2011 concerning the rights of passengers in bus and coach transport, OJ 2011 L55/1.

[43] Article 76 EC [*now Article 96 TFEU*] may be relied upon to contest any amendment to national legislative provisions but also any change in an administrative practice which may disadvantage carriers from other Member States: C-184/91 and C-221/91, *Oorburg and van Messem*, 1993, paras 12–15.

[44] C-591/17, *Austria v Germany*, 2019, paras 158-164. See also Barbist and Kröll, 'Deutsche Pkw-Maut nicht mit Unionsrecht vereinbar' (2019) EuZW 688; Jaeger, 'Rolling Pennies on the Road. EU Law Conformity of Road Charges for Light Vehicles' (2015) EJLS 126; Zabel, 'Die geplante Infrastrukturabgabe (Pkw-Maut) im Lichte von Art 92 AEUV' (2015) NVwZ 186.

[45] Regulation No. 11 concerning the abolition of discrimination in transport rates and conditions, in implementation of Article 79 [*later Article 75(3)*] of the Treaty establishing the European Economic Community, OJ 1959–1962 English Special Edition 60.

of transport or they represent reimbursement for the discharge of certain obligations inherent in the concept of a public service.

IV. Competition

Undertakings and Member States. The Union is based on an open market economy with free competition, 'favouring an efficient allocation of resources' (Articles 119(1) and (2), 120, and 127(1) TFEU).[46] The 'rules on competition' comprise rules prohibiting distortion of competition by undertakings (Articles 101–106 TFEU) and rules restricting State aid granted to undertakings (Articles 107, 108, and 109 TFEU). A brief overview of the scope of these rules is set out below.[47]

9.012

Although Articles 101 and 102 TFEU are directed at undertakings, the third subpara. of Article 4(3) TEU requires Member States to abstain from any measure which could detract from the effectiveness of those provisions. This is the case, for example, where a Member State requires or favours the adoption of agreements contrary to Article 101 TFEU or reinforces their effects or deprives its own legislation of its official character by delegating to private traders the responsibility for taking decisions affecting the economic sphere.[48] Consequently, it has been held that a Member State infringed Articles 4(3) TEU and 101 TFEU by obliging the national council of customs agents to set a uniform tariff for all customs agents.[49] In such a case, the national authorities must refrain from applying the provisions conflicting with Article 101 or Article 102 TFEU.[50] If those provisions preclude the possibility of competition, no penalties may be imposed on the undertakings concerned in respect of the period preceding the finding of an infringement of Articles 101 or 102 TFEU. But penalties may be imposed for any future conduct in breach of the competition rules. If, however, the national provisions merely encourage or make it easier for undertakings to

---

[46] Unlike Article 3(g) EC Treaty, the provisions on the objectives and values of the Union in the TEU do not refer to 'a system ensuring that competition in the internal market is not distorted'. However, Protocol (No. 27), annexed to the TEU and TFEU, on the internal market and competition, clearly states that 'the internal market as set out in Article 3 TFEU includes a system ensuring that competition is not distorted' (OJ 2010 C83/309). See Steenbergen, 'Het mededingingsbeleid en het Verdrag van Lissabon' (2008) SEW 136–43.

[47] For further information on EU competition law, see, among other works, Jones and Sufrin, *Jones & Sufrin's EU Competition Law: Text, Cases and Materials* (OUP, 2019); Whish & Bailey, *Competition Law*, (OUP, 2018); Bailey and John (eds), *Bellamy & Child, European Union Law of Competition* (OUP, 2018); Faull and Nikpay, *The EU Law of Competition* (OUP, 2014); Van Bael and Bellis, *Competition Law of the European Community* (Kluwer, 2010); Korah, *An Introductory Guide to EC Competition Law and Practice* (Hart Publishing, 2007). See also, Lenaerts, 'Some Thoughts on Evidence and Procedure in European Community Competition Law' (2007) Fordham ILJ 1463–95.

[48] 13/77, *INNO*, 1977, paras 30–3; 209-213/84, *Asjes*, 1986, paras 70–7; 311/85, *Vereniging van Vlaamse Reisbureaus*, 1987, para. 10; 267/86, *Van Eycke*, 1988, para. 16; C-2/91, *Meng*, 1993, para. 14; C-185/91, *Reiff*, 1993, para. 14; C-245/91, *Ohra*, 1993, para. 10; C-35/99, *Arduino*, 2002, para. 35; C-198/01, *Consorzio Industrie Fiammiferi*, 2003, para. 46; C-94/04 and C-202/04, *Cipolla and Others*, 2006, paras 46–7; C-446/05, *Doulamis*, 2008, paras 19–20; C-184/13 to C-187/13, C-194/13, C-195/13, and C-208/13, *API and Others*, 2014, paras 28–9. See also Joliet, 'National Anti-Competitive Legislation and Community Law' (1988) Fordham ILJ 163–88.

[49] C-35/96, *Commission v Italy*, 1998, paras 33–60. See also Ballarino and Bellodi, 'Contraintes étatiques en matière de concurrence' (2003) RDUE 555–89; Schwarze, 'Der Staat als Adressat des europäischen Wettbewerbsrechts' (2000) EuZW 613–27.

[50] C-198/01, *Consorzio Industrie Fiammiferi*, 2003, paras 48–51.

engage in autonomous anti-competitive conduct, those undertakings have to bear the consequences of the infringement of Articles 101 and 102 TFEU themselves.[51]

9.013 **Concept of an 'undertaking'.** In competition law, the concept of an undertaking encompasses every entity engaged in an economic activity, regardless of the legal status of the entity and the way in which it is financed.[52] The term 'economic activity' refers to any activity that consists of offering goods or services on a particular market. In addition, an entity which offers goods or services without seeking profit must be considered to constitute an 'undertaking' if the offer of that entity is in competition with the offers of other market participants that do seek profit.[53] The same criteria apply to an 'association of undertakings' within the meaning of Article 101(1) TFEU.[54] These criteria are not fulfilled in the case of an institution charged with the management of a social security system on the basis of the principle of solidarity[55] or of an organization entrusted by Member States with the exercise of powers which are typically those of a public authority, such as the control and supervision of air space.[56]

A. Rules for undertakings

1. Article 101 TFEU

9.014 **Prohibited agreements.** Article 101(1) TFEU prohibits 'all agreements between undertakings, decisions by associations of undertakings, and concerted practices which may affect trade between Member States and which have as their object or effect the prevention, restriction, or distortion of competition within the internal market'.[57] The prohibited agreements, decisions, or concerted practices, of which Article 101(1) TFEU lists some examples, cover both horizontal 'agreements' between competitors and vertical 'agreements' between producers, suppliers, and customers. In order to be caught by the prohibition, the agreements must affect trade between Member States.[58] This does not mean that the undertakings

---

[51] Ibid., paras 52–7.
[52] For the definition of the term 'undertaking', see C-41/90, *Höfner and Elser*, 1991, paras 21–2; C-244/94, *Fédération française des sociétés d'assurance and Others*, 1995, paras 14–22; C-343/95, *Diego Calì & Figli*, 1997, paras 16–25; C-205/03 P, *FENIN*, 2006, paras 25–7. For *FENIN*, see Krajewski and Farley, 'Non-economic Activities in Upstream and Downstream Markets and the Scope of Competition Law after FENIN' (2007) ELRev 111–24.
[53] C-49/07, *MOTOE*, 2008, para. 27; C-74/16, *Congregación de Escuelas Pías Provincia Betania*, 2017, paras 41–51. See also T-93/18, *International Skating Union v Commission*, 2020, para. 70.
[54] C-309/99, *Wouters and Others*, 2002, paras 56–71 (where a Bar association was regarded as being an 'association of undertakings').
[55] C-159/91 and C-160/91, *Poucet and Pistre*, 1993, paras 17–20; C-218/00, *Cisal di Battistello Veneziano*, 2002, paras 31–46; C-264/01, C-306/01, C-354/01 and C-355/01, *AOK Bundesverband and Others*, 2004, paras 47–65; see note by Drijber (2005) CMLRev 523–33; C-350/07, *Kattner Stahlbau*, 2009, para. 34; C-437/09, *AG2R Prévoyance*, 2011, paras 40–65. Whether and to what extent the scheme at issue may be considered to be applying the principle of solidarity and whether the activity of insurance bodies organizing such a scheme is subject to State supervision, requires a close factual analysis; see C-262/18 P and C-271/18 P, *Commission v Dôvera zdravotná poisťovňa*, 2020, paras 26–52, setting aside the opposite conclusion reached by the General Court in T-216/15, *Dôvera zdravotná poisťovňa v Commission*, 2018.
[56] C-364/92, *Eurocontrol*, 1994, paras 18–31; C-113/07 P, *SELEX*, 2009, paras 66–80.
[57] On the concept of 'agreement', see Hiu Fai Kwok, 'The Concept of 'Agreement' under Article 101 TFEU: A Question of EU Treaty Interpretation' (2019) ELRev 196–221. For the distinction between 'agreements between undertakings', 'decisions by associations of undertakings', and 'concerted practices', see, *inter alia*, T-1/89, *Rhône-Poulenc v Commission*, 1991, paras 118–28. Cf. Pais Antunes, 'Agreements and Concerted Practices under EEC Competition Law: Is the Distinction Relevant?' (1992) YEL 57–77.
[58] See C-295/04 to C-298/04, *Manfredi*, 2006, paras 40–51; Commission Notice—Guidelines on the effect on trade concept contained in Articles 81 and 82 of the Treaty, OJ 2004 C101/81.

concerned have to operate in different Member States: intra-Union trade may be adversely affected where the agreement is between undertakings from one Member State[59] or even between undertakings from non-Union countries where they implement the agreement in the Union.[60]

Agreements between undertakings or decisions of an association of undertakings fall outside the prohibition laid down in Article 101(1) TFEU where they pursue legitimate objectives—such as rules relating to professional ethics or to the fair conduct of sports—and where the consequential effects restrictive of competition are inherent in the pursuit of those objectives.[61] Agreements concluded in the context of collective negotiations between management and labour to improve conditions of work and employment are not caught by Article 101 TFEU.[62]

Prohibited agreements or decisions are automatically void (Article 101(2) TFEU), which means that they have no validity retroactively or vis-à-vis third parties. Nevertheless, the prohibition is not absolute in that Article 101(3) TFEU affords an opportunity for Article 101(1) TFEU to be declared inapplicable. To that end, that provision requires the agreement, decision, or concerted practice in question to have beneficial effects (it must contribute to improving the production or distribution of goods or promote technical or economic progress, while giving consumers a share of the benefit), not to impose disproportionate restrictions on the undertakings concerned, and to afford some opportunity for competition.[63]

Decentralised enforcement. The prohibition set out in Article 101 TFEU has direct effect and may thus be relied upon before national courts, which are to consider whether an agreement, decision, or concerted practice within the meaning of Article 101(1) TFEU exists and, if so, whether it satisfies the requirements of Article 101(3) TFEU.[64] Compensation may be claimed before the national courts for loss caused by an agreement or behaviour that is in breach of Article 101 TFEU (or Article 102 TFEU).[65] The Treaties also require the Commission and the national competition authorities to supervise compliance with

9.015

---

[59] 8/72, *Cementhandelaren v Commission*, 1972, paras 26–31.
[60] 89, 104, 114, 116–177 and 125–129/85, *Åhlström v Commission*, 1988, paras 16–17.
[61] C-309/99, *Wouters and Others*, 2002, para. 97; C-519/04 P, *Meca-Medina and Majcen v Commission*, 2006, paras 42–7; C-184/13 to C-187/13, C-194/13, C-195/13, and C-208/13, *API*, 2014, paras 47–58.
[62] C-67/96, *Albany*, 1999, paras 53–60 (see also the judgments of the same date in C-115-C-117/97, *Brentjens' Handelsonderneming and Others*, 1999 and C-219/97, *Drijvende Bokken*, 1999); C-222/98, *van der Woude*, 2000, paras 24–7; C-437/09, *AG2R Prévoyance*, 2011, paras 28–39; C-413/13, *FNV Kunsten*, 2014, paras 21–42. However, Article 81 does cover collective agreements between self-employed persons or members of a liberal profession: C-180-C-184/98, *Pavlov and Others*, 2000, paras 67–70 C-309/99, *Wouters and Others*, 2002, paras 44–71. See O'Loughlin, 'EC Competition Rules and Free Movement Rules: An Examination of the Parallels and their Furtherance by the ECJ *Wouters* Decision' (2003) E Comp LRev 62–9; Evju, 'Collective Agreements and Competition Law. The *Albany* Puzzle, and *van der Woude*' (2001) Int'l J Comp Lab L & Ind Rel 165–84; Boni and Manzini, 'National Social Legislation and EC Antitrust Law' (2001) World Comp 239–55; Van den Bergh and Camesasca, 'Irreconcilable Principles? The Court of Justice Exempts Collective Labour Agreements from the Wrath of Antitrust' (2000) ELRev 492–508.
[63] These conditions are clearly not fulfilled with a concerted practice aimed at disseminating misleading information in respect of a medicinal product, C-179/16, *F. Hoffmann-La Roche*, 2018, paras 96–101 (case note by Todino and Colombo (2018) J Eur Comp LP 376–8).
[64] For the direct effect of Article 101(1) TFEU, see 127/73, *BRT*, 1974, para. 16. Articles 1 to 6 of Regulation No. 1/2003 (see n. 66, *infra*) confirm the direct effect of Article 101(3) TFEU, which, before 1 May 2004, was precluded by the fact that the Commission had been granted exclusive competence to apply Article 81(3) (Article 9 of Regulation No. 17/62, OJ Eng. Special Ed., 1959–62, 87–93).
[65] C-453/99, *Courage*, 2001, paras 17–28 (in principle also for a person who was a party to that agreement); C-295/04 to C-298/04, *Manfredi*, 2006. For the potential applicants and defendants in such actions, see C-557/12, *Kone*, 2014, paras 18–37; C-724/17, *Skanska Industrial Solutions*, 2019, paras 23–51; C-435/18, *Otis*, 2019,

the competition rules (Articles 104 and 105 TFEU. That supervision is carried out in accordance with provisions adopted by the Council pursuant to Article 103 TFEU. Of those provisions, Regulation No. 1/2003 is of prime importance because of its general scope.[66] Originally, only the Commission was empowered to apply Article 101(3) TFEU and undertakings had to notify all agreements conflicting with Article 101(1) TFEU to it in order to have the prohibition declared inapplicable or, in the event that this was not possible, to avoid the imposition of a fine. With effect from 1 May 2004, Regulation No. 1/2003 abolished the notification system. Undertakings must henceforth work out for themselves whether their agreements conflict with Article 101 TFEU and the whole of that article (including, as a result, para. 3) may be applied by the national courts and the national competition authorities.[67] Responsibility for supervising compliance with Article 101 TFEU is vested primarily in the national courts and the national competition authorities so that the Commission can concentrate on investigating the most serious infringements.[68] In 2019, the role of the national competition authorities was further strengthened by the so-called ECN+ Directive, which lays down provisions on the independence and the powers of such authorities.[69]

20-34. See also Xiaowen, 'The Overarching Principle of Full Effectiveness in Compensation for Indirect Losses: The Lesson from C-435/18 Otis and Others', E Comp J (2020) 1-17. In order to facilitate private damages actions, the European Parliament and the Council adopted Directive 2014/104/EU of 26 November 2014 on certain rules governing actions for damages under national law for infringements of the competition law provisions of the Member States and of the European Union, OJ 2014 L349/1. For its temporal application, see C-637/17, *Cogeco Communications*, 2019, paras 24-34. See further Nowag and Tarkkila, 'How Much Effectiveness for the EU Damages Directive?: On the EU Damages Directive and Contractual Clauses Hindering Antitrust Damages' (2020) CMLRev 433-74; Rodger, Sousa Ferro and Marcos, 'The Antitrust Damages Directive: Facilitating Private Damages Actions in the EU?' (2019) J Eur Comp LP 129-30; Malinauskaite and Cauffman, 'The Transposition of the Antitrust Damages Directive in the Small Member States of the EU—A Comparative Perspective' (2018) J Eur Comp LP 496-512; Van Nuffel, 'Institutional Report', in Bándi et al. (eds), *Private Enforcement and Collective Redress in European Competition Law, FIDE Congress Proceedings Vol. 2*, (Wolters Kluwer, 2016), 187-258. On the interaction between private damages and public enforcement, see also C-360/09, *Pfleiderer*, 2011, paras 19-32; Wils, 'Private Enforcement of EU Antitrust Law and its Relationship with Public Enforcement: Past, Present and Future' (2017) World Comp 40.

[66] Council Regulation (EC) No. 1/2003 of 16 December 2002 on the implementation of the rules on competition laid down in Articles 81 and 82 of the Treaty, OJ 2003 L1/1. Regulation No. 1/2003 is generally applicable unless a separate implementing regulation has been adopted for a particular sector (see for the transport sector, para. 9-009, *supra*).

[67] See also the Commission Notices on the handling of complaints by the Commission under Articles 81 and 82 EC Treaty, OJ 2004 C101/65. Moreover, where the EU public interest so requires, the Commission, acting on its own initiative, may by decision find that Article 101 TFEU is not applicable to an agreement; see Article 10 of Regulation No.1/2003.

[68] For the tensions caused by the decentralised enforcement, see Brook, 'Struggling with Article 101(3) TFEU: Diverging Approaches of the Commission, EU Courts, and Five Competition Authorities' (2019) CMLRev 121-56. See, more generally, Venit, 'Brave New World: The Modernisation and Decentralisation of Enforcement under Articles 81 and 82 of the EC Treaty' (2003) CMLRev 545-80; Gilliams, 'Modernisation: From Policy to Practice' (2003) ELRev 451-74; Paulis and Gauer, 'La réforme des règles d'application des articles 81 et 82 du Traité' (2003) JTDE 65-73. The debate which culminated in this 'decentralization' started with the White Paper on modernization of the rules implementing Articles 81 and 82 EC Treaty, OJ 1999 C132/1. For the extent to which national authorities continue to have the power to apply national competition law, see Article 3 of Regulation No. 1/2003. For the openings for arbitrators, see Komninos, 'Arbitration and the Modernisation of European Competition Law Enforcement' (2001) World Comp 211-38.

[69] Directive (EU) 2019/1 of the European Parliament and of the Council of 11 December 2018 to empower the competition authorities of the Member States to be more effective enforcers and to ensure the proper functioning of the internal market, OJ 2019 L11/3. See Rizzuto, 'The ECN Plus Directive: The Harmonisation of National Procedural Rules Governing the Parallel Enforcement of EU Competition Law in the Internal Market', (2019) E Comp LR 574-83; Wils, 'Independence of Competition Authorities: The Example of the EU and its Member States' (2019) World Comp 149-70.

The national competition authorities, together with the Commission, form the 'European Network of Competition Authorities' (ECN).[70] They are to inform the Commission of the steps they take in investigating infringements of Article 101 TFEU (and Article 102 TFEU) and exchange information amongst themselves and with the Commission.[71] Once the Commission has initiated a procedure of its own, the national competition authorities are relieved of their competence to apply Articles 101 and 102 TFEU.[72] This does not apply to national courts applying Article 101 or Article 102 TFEU. Where the Commission has initiated a procedure, the national court must, however, avoid taking a decision which would conflict with the decision contemplated by the Commission.[73] The national court may, if necessary, stay proceedings and enter into consultations with the Commission.[74] Where the Commission has taken a decision, the national court may not take a decision conflicting with that of the Commission.[75] Where an action for annulment has been brought against the Commission decision, it is for the national court to decide whether it should stay proceedings until a definitive decision has been given by the Union Courts.[76]

Enforcement by the Commission. In order to track down infringements of Articles 101 and 102 TFEU, Regulation No. 1/2003 confers broad powers of investigation on the Commission, including the power to inspect business premises (Articles 17 to 21). Acting under Regulation No. 1/2003, the Commission may make a finding that there has been an infringement of Articles 101 or 102 TFEU and require the undertakings concerned to bring it to an end (Article 7(1)). The Commission may also impose fines or periodic penalty payments (Articles 23 and 24 Regulation No. 1/2003).[77] During the procedure, hearings of interested parties take place in accordance with Article 27 Regulation No. 1/2003 and

9.016

---

[70] A division of work is set out in the Joint Statement of the Council and the Commission on the functioning of the Network of Competition Authorities, entered in the Council minutes upon the adoption of Regulation No. 1/2003 (document No. 15435/02, available at https://ec.europa.eu/competition/ecn/joint_statement_en.pdf). See also Cengiz, 'Multi-level Governance in Competition Policy: the European Competition Network' (2010) ELRev 660–77; Brammer, 'Concurrent Jurisdiction under Regulation 1/2003 and the Issue of Case Allocation' (2005) CMLRev 1383–424; Smits, 'The European Competition Network: Selected Aspects' (2005) LIEI 175–92.

[71] See Articles 11, 12, and 13 of Regulation No. 1/2003 and the Commission Notice on cooperation within the Network of Competition Authorities, OJ 2004 C101/43 (as modified: OJ 2015 C 256/5). See Dekeyser and De Smijter, 'The Exchange of Evidence within the ECN and How it Contributes to the European Co-operation and Co-ordination in Cartel Cases' (2005) LIEI 161–74. Only where the national competition authority constitutes a 'court or tribunal of a Member State' may it refer a question to the Court of Justice for a preliminary ruling under Article 267 TFEU; see Komninos, 'Article 234 EC and National Competition Authorities in the Era of Decentralisation' (2004) ELRev 106–14.

[72] Regulation No. 1/2003, Article 11(6).

[73] Regulation No. 1/2003, Article 16(1), and the Commission Notice on the cooperation between the Commission and the courts of the EU Member States in the application of Articles 81 and 82 EC, OJ 2004 C101/54. See Lenaerts and Gerard, 'Decentralisation of EC Competition Law Enforcement: Judges in the Frontline' (2004) World Comp 313–350.

[74] C-234/89, *Delimitis*, 1991, paras 43–55. The national court may also make a reference to the Court of Justice for a preliminary ruling: 127/73 BRT, 1974, paras 20–3; C-319/93, C-40/94, and C-224/94, *Dijkstra and Others*, 1995, paras 25–36.

[75] Regulation No. 1/2003, Article 16(1).

[76] C-344/98, *Masterfoods and HB Ice Cream*, 2000, paras 45–60. If it has doubts as to the validity of the Commission decision, the national court may always make a reference for a preliminary ruling to the Court of Justice: ibid., para. 57. See Fierstra (2001) NTER 159-163; O'Keefe (2001) ELRev 301–11; Malferrari (2001) EuR 605–16.

[77] For the setting of fines, see the Commission's guidelines in OJ 2006 C210/2. See Völcker, 'Rough justice? An analysis of the European Commission's New Fining Guidelines' (2007) CMLRev 1285–320; Wils, 'The European Commission's 2006 Guidelines on Antitrust Fines: A Legal and Economic Analysis' (2007) World Comp 197–229. See also the Commission Notice on immunity from fines and reduction of fines in cartel cases, OJ 2006 C298/17.

detailed implementing rules drawn up by the Commission.[78] Article 31 Regulation No. 1/2003 confers on the Court of Justice (the General Court) unlimited jurisdiction to review decisions whereby the Commission has fixed a fine or periodic penalty payment.[79]

The Council empowered the Commission to grant exemptions by regulation in respect of categories of agreements.[80] If an agreement satisfies the requirements for 'block exemption', as it is termed, the undertakings concerned may, under the regulation, rely directly on such an exemption from the prohibition set out in Article 101 TFEU.[81] In order to simplify compliance with Article 101 TFEU, the Commission has clarified, in guidelines, in what circumstances vertical agreements (between producer, supplier, or buyer) and horizontal agreements (between competitors), in its view, do not have an appreciable effect on competition or satisfy the requirements of Article 101(3) TFEU.[82] In addition, the Commission publishes policy statements concerning categories of agreements in respect of which it does not consider it necessary to take action.[83]

2. Article 102 TFEU

9.017 **Abuse of dominant position.** Article 102 TFEU prohibits one or more undertakings from abusing a dominant position within the internal market or in a substantial part of it in so far as it may affect trade between Member States. In common with the prohibition laid down by Article 101 TFEU, the corresponding provision of Article 102 TFEU has direct effect[84] and

---

[78] See Commission Regulation (EC) No. 773/2004 of 7 April 2004 relating to the conduct of proceedings by the Commission pursuant to Articles 81 and 82 EC Treaty, OJ 2004 L123/18. See also Decision of the President of the European Commission of 13 October 2011 on the function and terms of reference of the hearing officer in certain competition proceedings, OJ 2011 L275/29.

[79] See Forrester, 'A Challenge for Europe's Judges: The Review of Fines in Competition Cases' (2011) ELRev 185–207.

[80] For the Council's authorisation, see Regulation No. 19/65/EEC of the Council of 2 March 1965 on application of Article 85(3) of the Treaty [*now Article 101(3) TFEU*] to certain categories of agreements and concerted practices, OJ 1965–1966 English Special Edition 36, as amended by Council Regulation (EC) No. 1215/1999, OJ 1999 L148/1, and Regulation (EC) No. 2821/71 of the Council of 20 December 1971 on application of Article 85(3) of the Treaty [*now Article 101(3) TFEU*] to categories of agreements, decisions, and concerted practices (OJ 1971 English Spec. Ed. (III) 1032). For authorizations for individual sectors, see Council Regulation No. 1534/91 of 31 May 1991 (insurance sector), OJ 1991 L143/1, Council Regulations (EC) Nos 1419/2006 of 25 September 2006 and 246/2009 of 26 February 2006 (sea transport and liner shipping companies, respectively) OJ 2006 L269/1 and OJ 2009 L79/1, and Council Regulation (EC) No. 487/2009 of 25 May 2009 (air transport), OJ 2009 L1481.

[81] The Commission has drawn up block exemptions for agreements in Regulation (EU) No. 330/2010 of 20 April 2010, OJ 2010 L102/1 (vertical agreements in general), Regulation (EU) No. 461/2010 of 27 May 2010, OJ 2010 L129/52 (agreements in the motor vehicle sector), Regulation 1218/2010/EU of 14 December 2010, OJ 2010 L335/43 (specialization agreements), Regulation 1217/2010/EU of 14 December 2010, OJ 2010 L335/36 (research and development agreements), Regulation (EU) No. 267/2010 of 24 March 2010 OJ 2010 L83/1 (insurance), Regulation (EC) No. 906/2009, OJ 2009 L256/31 (liner shipping companies), and Regulation (EU) No. 316/2014 of 21 March 2014 (technology transfer agreements), OJ 2014 L93/17.

[82] See, accompanying the block exemptions listed in the preceding note, the Guidelines on Vertical Restraints (OJ 2010 C130/1) on the applicability of Article 101 TFEU to horizontal cooperation agreements (OJ 2011 C11/1) and to technology transfer agreements (OJ 2014 C89/3). In addition, see the guidelines mentioned in n. 58, *supra*, and the Commission's Notice—Guidelines on the application of Article 81(3) of the Treaty, OJ 2004 C101/97. For the latter, see Bourgeois, 'Guidelines on the Application of Article 81 (3) of the EC Treaty or How to Restrict a Restriction' (2005) LIEI 111–21; Kjølbye, 'The New Commission Guidelines on the Application of Article 81(3): An Economic Approach to Article 81' (2004) E Comp LRev 566–77.

[83] See, for instance, the Commission Notice on agreements of minor importance which do not appreciably restrict competition under Article 101(1) of the Treaty on the Functioning of the European Union (De Minimis Notice), OJ 2014 C291/1. The Notice is however not binding upon national competition authorities or national courts: C-226/11, *Expedia*, 2012, paras 23–31, with note by Vijver (2013) CMLRev 1133–44.

[84] 155/73, *Sacchi*, 1974, para. 18.

is subject to supervision by the national courts, the national competition authorities, and the Commission in accordance with the provisions of Regulation No. 1/2003.

A dominant position is determined by defining the relevant market both from the geographic point of view and from the standpoint of the product and by evaluating the market power (not solely market share) of the undertaking or undertakings.[85] Article 102 TFEU lists some instances of prohibited abuse of a dominant position (including limiting of production, markets, or technological development, or 'tying' the conclusion of contracts to the acceptance by parties of supplementary obligations without necessary connection with the subject of the contracts).[86]

Article 102 TFEU also applies where an undertaking holding a dominant position on a particular market has such freedom of conduct on a neighbouring but separate market compared with the other economic operators on that market that, even without it holding a dominant position there, it bears a special responsibility to maintain genuine undistorted competition.[87]

3. Control of concentrations

Merger control. Ever since 21 September 1990, all concentrations of undertakings with a Union dimension have been subject to the obligatory prior notification and control as governed by Regulation No. 139/2004 since 1 May 2004.[88]

9.018

The Union dimension is determined by means of thresholds in terms of the aggregate worldwide turnover of the undertakings concerned and the aggregate Union-wide turnover of the two largest undertakings concerned (Regulation No. 139/2004, Article 1(2)). The requirement for a Union dimension is also satisfied where a concentration meets—lower—thresholds which have a significant impact in at least three Member States (Regulation No. 139/2004, Article 1(3)).[89] In accordance with these criteria, the concentration regulation may also be applied to undertakings which are not established in a Member State and carry

---

[85] 22/76, *United Brands v Commission*, 1978, paras 10–129; T-51/89, *Tetra Pak v Commission*, 1990. See the Commission notice on the definition of the relevant market for the purposes of Community competition law, OJ 1997 C372/5.

[86] For examples, see T-203/01, *Michelin v Commission*, 2003; T-201/04, *Microsoft v Commission*, 2007; C-413/14 P *Intel v Commission*. See also the Commission's Guidance on its enforcement priorities in applying Article 82 EC to exclusionary conduct by dominant undertakings, OJ 2009 C45/7. See also the application of Article 102 TFEU to patent wars: C-170/13, *Huawei Technologies*, 2015, with note by Körber (2016) CMLRev 1107–20 and to rebates: C-23/14, *Post Danmark*, 2015, with note Rummel (2016) CMLRev 1121–31.

[87] T-83/91, *Tetra Pak v Commission*, 1994, paras 112–22, as upheld by C-333/94 P, *Tetra Pak v Commission*, 1996 (packaging); C-307/18, *Generics (UK)*, 2020, paras 123–40 (generic medicines). See, generally, O'Donoghue and Padilla, *The Law and Economics of Article 102 TFEU* (Hart Publishing, 2020); Ibáñez Colomo, 'Beyond the 'More Economics-based Approach': A legal Perspective on Article 102 TFEU Case Law' (2016) CMLRev 709–39.

[88] Council Regulation (EC) No. 139/2004 of 20 January 2004 on the control of concentrations between undertakings (the EC Merger Regulation), OJ 2004 L24/1. See Van Gerven and Snels, 'The New ECMR: Procedural Improvements' (2005) LIEI 193–208; González Díaz, 'The Reform of European Merger Control: *Quid Novi Sub Sole*?' (2004) World Comp 177–99; Brunet and Girgenson, 'La double réforme du contrôle communautaire des concentrations' (2004) RTDE 1–31. See also, more generally, Tricker and Filippitsch, *EU Merger Control* (Sweet & Maxwell, 2020); Rosenthal and Thomas, *European Merger Control* (Beck/Hart, 2010); Furse, *The Law of Merger Control in the EC and the UK* (Hart Publishing, 2007); Navarro et al., *Merger Control in the European Union* (OUP, 2005).

[89] For the notifications, time-limits, and hearings of parties concerned and third parties, see Commission Regulation (EC) No. 802/2004 of 7 April 2004 implementing Council Regulation (EC) No. 139/2004 on the control of concentrations between undertakings, OJ 2004 L133/1.

out their production activities outside the Union.[90] Following notification, the Commission must reach a decision on the compatibility of the concentration with the internal market within the time-limits fixed by Regulation No. 139/2004. Concentrations which would significantly impede effective competition, in the internal market or in a substantial part of it, in particular as a result of the creation or strengthening of a dominant position, are declared incompatible with the internal market and may not be put into effect.[91]

4. Public undertakings and services of general interest

9.019 **Special or exclusive rights.** Under EU competition law, Member States may establish or operate publicly owned undertakings ('public undertakings') or grant undertakings special or exclusive rights.[92] According to Article 106(1) TFEU, such undertakings have to comply with the rules of the Treaties, including the principle of equality and the competition rules.[93] The establishment or operation of public undertakings carrying out economic activities will therefore be incompatible with the Treaties where the undertakings have exclusive rights such that their exercise must be regarded as the abuse of a dominant position and that abuse is liable to affect trade between Member States.[94] Accordingly, the Court of Justice has held that Article 106(1) is infringed by a Member State which grants a monopoly to public placement offices where those offices are unable to satisfy demand on the employment market, placement of employees by private companies is rendered impossible, and the placement activities in question could extend to the nationals or the territory of other Member States.[95] The creation of a dominant position through the grant of an exclusive right within the meaning of Article 106(1) is not incompatible with Article 102 TFEU as such.[96] A Member State is in breach of the prohibitions set out in those two provisions only if the undertaking in question, merely by exercising the exclusive right granted to it, cannot avoid abusing its dominant position[97] or where the grant of exclusive rights is liable to create a situation in

---

[90] T-102/96, *Gencor v Commission*, 1999, paras 78–88 (concerning the same thresholds in Regulation No. 4064/89). Under international law, it must be foreseeable that a proposed concentration will have an immediate and substantial effect in the Union: ibid., paras 90–101. See, in this regard, Slot (2001) CMLRev 1573–86; Ryngaert, *Jurisdiction over Antitrust Violations in International Law* (Intersentia, 2008).

[91] Regulation No. 139/2004, Article 2(3) and Article 8(3), which still refers to compatibility with the 'common market'. Under Regulation No. 4064/89, only concentrations which created or strengthened a dominant position were incompatible with the common market. See also the Commission's Guidelines on the assessment of horizontal and non-horizontal mergers under the Council Regulation on the control of concentrations between undertakings (OJ 2004 C31/5 and OJ 2008 C265/6, respectively), the consolidated Jurisdictional Notice under Council Regulation (EC) No. 139/2004 (OJ 2008 C95/1), and the Commission notices on acceptable remedies (OJ 2008 C267/1), and on restrictions directly related and necessary to concentrations (OJ 2005 C56/24). As regards the substantive control which the Commission has to carry out in relation to concentrations, see C-68/94 and C-30/95, *France and Others v Commission*, 1998, paras 90–250; C-12/03 P, *Commission v Tetra Laval*, 2005 and C-413/06 P, *Bertelsmann AG and Sony Corporation of America v Impala*, 2008, and case note by Rompuy (2008) E Comp LRev 608–12; C-265/17 P, *Commission v UPS*, 2019; see also Bailey, 'Standard of Proof in EC Merger Proceedings: A Common Law Perspective' (2003) CMLRev 845–88.

[92] For an overview, see Buendía Sierra, 'Article 106—Exclusive Rights and Other Anti-competitive State Measures', in Faull and Nikpay (eds). *The EC Law of Competition* (OUP, 2014), Chapter 6; Szyszczak, *The Regulation of the State in Competitive Markets in the EU* (Hart Publishing, 2007); Weiss, 'Öffentliche Unternehmen und EGV' (2003) EuR 165–90; Buendía Sierra, *Exclusive Rights and State Monopolies under EC Law* (OUP, 1999); Blum and Logue, *State Monopolies under EC Law* (Wiley, 1998); Burgi, 'Die öffentlichen Unternehmen im Gefüge des primären Gemeinschaftsrechts' (1997) EuR 261–90.

[93] Article 106(1) refers to Article 18 TFEU.

[94] An undertaking with a statutory monopoly may be regarded as occupying a dominant position within the meaning of Article 102 TFEU, and the territory of the Member State covered by that monopoly may constitute a substantial part of the internal market: 311/84, *CBEM*, 1985, para. 16.

[95] C-55/96, *Job Centre*, 1997, para. 38.

[96] 311/84, *CBEM*, 1985, para. 17.

[97] C-41/90, *Höfner and Elser*, 1991, para. 29.

which the undertaking concerned is led to infringe Article 102 TFEU.[98] An exclusive right that restricts the freedom of establishment of nationals of another Member State will be contrary to Articles 49 and 106 TFEU where that restriction is not appropriate and necessary to satisfy requirements of overriding public interest.[99]

Derogations from the rules on free trade and competition are possible only on the basis of the exceptions provided for in Article 106(2) TFEU for undertakings entrusted with the operation of services of general economic interest or having the character of a revenue-producing monopoly.[100] Examples arise in the fields of transport, (tele)communications, postal services, energy, and other utilities as well as for certain entities implementing social security schemes. The exceptions apply in so far as the application of the Treaty rules would obstruct the performance, in law or in fact, of the particular tasks assigned to the undertakings in question[101] and to the extent that the development of trade is not affected contrary to the interests of the Union.[102] The national court has to determine whether the conduct of a public undertaking contrary to Treaty provisions may be justified under Article 106(2) TFEU.[103] Consequently, the provisions of Article 106(1) and (2) have direct effect.

The Treaties emphasize the role played by services of general interest, yet without associating this with any limitation on the application of the competition rules. Thus, Article 14 TFEU provides that the Union and the Member States are to take care that such services operate on the basis of principles and conditions which enable them to fulfil their missions '[w]ithout prejudice to Article 4 [TEU] or Articles 93, 106 and 107 [TFEU]', 'given the place occupied by services of general economic interest in the shared values of the Union as well as their role in promoting social and territorial cohesion'.[104] Since the Lisbon Treaty, the European Parliament and the Council, acting by means of regulations in accordance with the ordinary legislative procedure, are competent to establish these principles and set these conditions without prejudice to the competence of Member States to commission and to

---

[98] C-260/89, *ERT*, 1991, paras 37–8; see also C-320/91, *Corbeau*, 1993, paras 9–12, and case note by Hancher (1994) CMLRev 105–22. For the determination of abuse and adverse effects on trade between Member States, see also C-179/90, *Merci convenzionali porto di Genova*, 1991, paras 14–22; C-18/88, *GB-INNO-BM*, 1991, paras 17–27; C-163/96, *Raso and Others*, 1998, paras 25–33.

[99] T-266/97, *VTM v Commission*, 1999, paras 105–23.

[100] 155/73, *Sacchi*, 1974, para. 13; C-265/08, *Federutility and Others*, 2010, paras 27–47 (derogation from the competition rules); C-157/94, *Commission v Netherlands*, 1997, para. 32; C-158/94, *Commission v Italy*, 1997, para. 43; C-159/94, *Commission v France*, 1997, para. 49 (derogation from Article 37 TFEU). See Kovar, 'Droit communautaire et service public: esprit d'orthodoxie ou pensée laïcisée' (1996) RTDE 215–42 and 493–533.

[101] C-320/91, *Corbeau*, 1993, paras 13–20; C-67/96, *Albany*, 1999, paras 53–60; C-340/99, *TNT Traco*, 2001, paras 54–8; C-475/99, *Firma Ambulanz Glöckner*, 2001, paras 55–6.

[102] For a discussion of this exception and its relationship with grounds justifying restrictions on free movement, see Wachsmann and Berrod, 'Les critères de justification des monopoles: un premier bilan après l'affaire *Corbeau*' (1994) RTDE 39–61.

[103] 66/86, *Ahmed Saeed Flugreisen and Others*, 1989, paras 53–6; C-260/89, *ERT*, 1991, para. 34.

[104] Article 93 TFEU is concerned with State aid in respect of transport, Article 107 TFEU with State aid generally (see also para. 9-021 *et seq., infra*). See Wehlander, *Services of General Economic Interest as a Constitutional Concept of EU Law* (TMC Asser, 2016); Sauter, 'Services of General Economic Interest and Universal Service in EU Law' (2008) ELRev 167–93; Napolitano, 'Towards a European Legal Order for Services of General Economic Interest', (2005) E Pub L 565–81; Rojanski, 'L'Union européenne et les services d'intérêt général' (2002) RDUE 735–73; Frenz, 'Dienste von allgemeinem wirtschaftlichen Interesse' (2000) EuR 901–25; Rodrigues, 'Les services publics et le traité d'Amsterdam. Genèse et portée juridique du projet de nouvel article 16 du traité CE' (1998) RMCUE 37–46. See also Lenaerts 'Defining the Concept of "Services of General Interest" In Light of the "Checks And Balances" Set Out in the EU Treaties' (2012) Jurisprudencija 1247–67. Declaration (No. 13), annexed to the Amsterdam Treaty, confirmed that Article 16 was to be implemented with full respect for the jurisprudence of the Court of Justice, *inter alia*, as regards the principles of equality of treatment, quality and continuity of public services (OJ 1997 C340/133). Declaration (No. 37), annexed to the Amsterdam Treaty, was concerned with services of general economic interest provided by public credit institutions existing in Germany (OJ 1997 C340/138).

fund such services (Article 14 TFEU).[105] As far as the public service remit of broadcasting organizations is concerned, a protocol to the Treaties confirms that the Member States have competence to provide for the public funding of public service broadcasting.[106] They enjoy wide discretion in defining the scope and organization of such service, taking particular account of objectives pertaining to their national policy.[107]

9.020 **Liberalization.** Article 106(3) TFEU empowers the Commission to address directives or decisions to the Member States. As a result, the Commission may act individually by decision against public undertakings and Member States (alongside its supervisory powers under Article 258 TFEU),[108] but may also issue general rules specifying the Member States' Treaty obligations by directives.[109] On this basis, the Commission has adopted directives for the liberalization of sectors of the economy which in most Member States were the province of publicly owned corporations or monopoly undertakings, such as telecommunications and energy.[110] In parallel with these liberalization measures, the European Parliament and the Council have adopted harmonization directives pursuant to Article 114 TFEU, which especially emphasize opening up non-discriminatory access to infrastructure, for instance in telecommunications.[111]

B. State aid

9.021 **Prohibited aid.** Free competition in the internal market requires a prohibition, in principle, of aid funded out of the public purse which distorts or threatens to distort competition by

---

[105] See further Protocol (No. 26), annexed to the TEU and TFEU, on Services of General Interest, OJ 2016 C202/307.
[106] Protocol (No. 29), annexed to the TEU and TFEU, on the system of public broadcasting in the Member States, OJ 2016 C202/311. See also the Resolution of the Council and of the representatives of the Governments of the Member States, meeting within the Council, of 25 January 1999 concerning public service broadcasting, OJ 1999 C30/1.
[107] C-445/19, *Viasat Broadcasting UK*, 2020, para. 33.
[108] C-48/90 and C-66/90, *Netherlands and Others v Commission*, 1992, paras 27–37. See also Lenaerts, Gutman, and Nowak, *EU Procedural Law* (OUP, 2022), Chapter 5.
[109] For the Commission's discretion, see C-141/02 P, *Commission v T-Mobile Austria*, 2005, paras 66–9, with case note by Castillo de la Torre (2005) CMLRev 1751–63; T-32/93, *Ladbroke Racing v Commission*, 1994, paras 36, 37, and 38 and 44; for the first application of Article 86(3) EC Treaty [now Article 106 TFEU], see Commission Directive 80/723/EEC of 25 June 1980 on the transparency of financial relations between Member States and public undertakings, OJ 1980 L195/35, now replaced by Commission Directive 2006/111/EC of 16 November 2006 on the transparency of financial relations between Member States and public undertakings as well as on financial transparency within certain undertakings, OJ 2006 L318/17.
[110] See Commission Directive 2002/77/EC of 16 September 2002 on competition in the markets for electronic communications networks and services, OJ 2002 L249/21. The Commission's competence was confirmed by the Court of Justice following actions for annulment brought by Member States: 188–190/80 *France, Italy and United Kingdom v Commission*, 1982; C-202/88 *France v Commission*, 1991, para. 14; C-271/90, C-281/90, and C-289/90 *Spain and Others v Commission*, 1992. See also Hocepied, 'Les directives article 90, paragraphe 3: une espèce juridique en voie de disparition?' (1994) RAE 49–63.
[111] See, e.g., the directives of the European Parliament and of the Council of 7 March 2002 on a common regulatory framework for electronic communications networks and services: Framework Directive 2002/21/EC and Directive 2002/19/EC (access), Directive 2002/20/EC (authorization) and Directive 2002/22/EC (universal service), OJ 2002 L108/7, L108/21, and L108/51, respectively. For 'open network provision' or OPN, see, *inter alia*, Council Directive 90/387/EEC of 28 June 1990, OJ 1990 L192/1, since repealed by Framework Directive 2002/21/EC. See Savin, *EU Telecommunications Law* (Edward Elgar Publishing, 2018); Garzaniti, *Telecommunications, Broadcasting and the Internet: EU Competition Law and Regulation* (Sweet & Maxwell, 2010); Bavasso, 'Electronic Communications: A New Paradigm for European Regulation' (2004) CMLRev 87–118; De Streil, Queck and Vernet, 'Le nouveau cadre réglementaire européen des réseaux et services de communications électroniques (2002) CDE 243–341; Franzius, "Strukturmodelle des europäischen Telekommuikationsrechts" (2002) EuR 660–90; for universal service, see Karayannis, 'Le service universel de télécommunications en droit communautaire: entre intervention publique et concurrence' (2002) CDE 315–75.

favouring certain undertakings or the production of certain goods and adversely affects trade between Member States (Article 107(1) TFEU).[112] By way of exception, the Treaties list three types of aid which are, by operation of law, compatible with the internal market (Article 107(2) TFEU) and refers to other types of aid measures which *may* be compatible with the internal market[113] (Article 107(3) TFEU).[114] Even where aid is compatible with the internal market, it may not be 'misused' (Article 108(2) TFEU). Pursuant to Article 109 TFEU, the Council, acting by a regulation, empowered the Commission to grant exemptions for certain categories of aid.[115] The Commission has thus adopted a general 'block exemption' concerning regional aid, aid to small and medium-sized enterprises (SMEs), and aid aimed at objectives such as environmental protection, research, education, or employment.[116] Moreover, it has declared that aid not exceeding EUR 200,000 over any period of three years does not affect trade between Member States and/or does not distort competition.[117]

Concept of State aid. According to the case law, Article 107(1) lays down four cumulative conditions.[118] First of all, the aid should be granted by a Member State or through State resources. As a result, an economic benefit for an undertaking[119] is in the nature of aid only if it can be imputed to the State and is directly or indirectly paid out of public funds.[120] Consequently, Article 107(1) covers not only aid granted directly by the State, but also aid granted by public or private bodies designated or established by the State.[121] Moreover, in

9.022

---

[112] For further particulars, see Parcu and Monti (Botta ed.), *EU State Aid Law: Emerging Trends at National and EU Level* (Edward Edgar Publishing, 2020).; Hofmann and Micheau, *State Aid Law of the European Union* (OUP, 2016); Quigley, *European State Aid Law and Policy* (Hart Publishing, 2015); Hancher, Ottervanger, and Slot, *EC State Aids* (Sweet & Maxwell, 2012); Biondi, Eeckhout, and Flynn (eds), *The Law of State Aid in the European Union* (OUP, 2004). With regard to the definition of State aid, see, for instance, López and Jorge, *The Concept of State Aid under EU Law: From Internal Market to Competition and Beyond* (OUP, 2015); Bacon, 'The Concept of State Aid: The Developing Jurisprudence in the European and UK Courts' (2003) E Comp LRev 54–61.

[113] This list may be supplemented by the Council on a proposal from the Commission (Article 107(3)(e) TFEU).

[114] On the distinction between Article 107(3)(b) and (c), see C-594/18 P, *Austria v Commission*, 2020, paras 18–26.

[115] Council Regulation (EU) 2015/1588 of 13 July 2015 on the application of Articles 107 and 108 of the Treaty on the Functioning of the European Union to certain categories of horizontal State aid, OJ 2015 L248/1.

[116] Since the Treaty of Lisbon, the Treaty explicitly empowers the Commission to do so (see Article 108(4) TFEU). See Commission Regulation (EU) No. 651/2014 of 17 June 2014 declaring certain categories of aid compatible with the internal market in application of Articles 107 and 108 of the Treaty, OJ 2014 L187/1, replacing Regulation (EC) No. 800/2008 of 6 August 2008, OJ 2008 L214/3 (general block exemption regulation). See also Commission Regulation (EU) No. 702/2014 of 25 June 2014, OJ 2014 L193/1 (aid to SMEs in the agricultural sector).

[117] Commission Regulation (EU) No. 1407/2013 of 18 December 2013 on the application of Articles 107 and 108 of the Treaty on the Functioning of the European Union to *de minimis* aid, OJ 2013 L352/1, replacing Commission Regulation (EC) No. 1998/2006 of 15 December 2006 on the application of Articles 87 and 88 of the Treaty to *de minimis* aid, OJ 2006 L379/5. Different rules apply in the case of *de minimis* aid in the sector of agricultural production (see Commission Regulation (EU) No. 1408/2013 of 18 December 2013, OJ 2013 L352/9) and in the fisheries sector (see Commission Regulation (EU) No. 717/2014 of 27 June 2014, OJ 2014 L190/45.

[118] e.g. C-237/04, *Enirisorse*, 2006, para. 39; C-169/08, *Regione Sardegna*, 2009, para. 55; C-76/15, *Vervloet*, 2016, paras 89–108. See also the Commission communication on the concept of 'state aid', OJ 2016 C262/1.

[119] There is no State aid if the beneficiary is not an undertaking for not being engaged in an economic activity: C-262/18 P and C-271/18 P, *Commission and Slovak Republic v Dôvera zdravotná poisťovňa*, 2020, paras 26–52 (body managing a scheme with a social objective and applying the principle of solidarity under State supervision).

[120] C-345/02, *Pearle and Others*, 2004, para. 35.

[121] See, in particular, C-317/98, *PreussenElektra*, 2001, paras 57–66; C-482/99, *France v Commission*, 2002, paras 50–9; C-262/12, *Vent de Colère*, 2013, paras 14–37; C-706/17, *Achema*, 2019, paras 56–72. For the limits thereto, see C-405/16 P, *Germany v Commission*, 2019, paras 48–87, reversing T-47/15, *Germany v Commission*, 2016; see also C-425/19 P, *Commission v Italy*, 2021, paras 57-85. See also Bouchagiar, 'When Do Funds Become State Resources' (2020) EStALQ 19–28.

order to qualify as State aid, a measure must constitute a burden on State resources, or a sufficiently serious risk of such a burden.[122]

Second, the measure must confer an advantage on the recipient. This must be interpreted in broad terms. The aid concept covers not only positive benefits, such as subsidies, loans, and public shareholdings, but also interventions which, in various forms, mitigate the charges which are normally included in the budget of an undertaking and which, without therefore being subsidies in the strict meaning of the word, are similar in character and have the same effect.[123] Thus, tax advantages, although not involving the transfer of State resources, that place the recipients in a more favourable position than other taxpayers, are capable of procuring a selective advantage for the recipients and, consequently, of constituting State aid.[124] Moreover, a general measure must not be involved, but an economic benefit may constitute state aid if, by displaying a degree of selectivity, it is such as to favour 'certain undertakings or the production of certain goods'.[125] Aid measures adopted by a regional authority of a Member State which are applicable only in the territory of the region concerned will constitute selective measures unless the region has sufficiently autonomous powers so as to constitute the appropriate framework of reference for the assessment of the measures.[126] Where the public authorities intervene as shareholders, creditors, or contractors vis-à-vis an undertaking, that public intervention will constitute State aid only where, in similar circumstances, a private shareholder, creditor, or contractor, would not have so intervened.[127]

---

[122] C-72/91 and C-73/91, *Sloman Neptun*, para. 21; C-345/02, *Pearle and Others*, 2004, para. 36; C-399/10 P and C-401/10 P, *Bouygues and Bouygues Télécom v Commission*, 2013, para. 106.

[123] 30/59, *De Gezamenlijke Steenkolenmijnen in Limburg v High Authority*, 1961, at 40; C-387/92, *Banco Exterior de España*, 1994, para. 13; C-39/94, *SFEI and Others*, 1996, paras 57–62; C-393/04 and C-41/05, *Air Liquide Industries and Others*, 2006, para. 29; C-237/04, *Enirisorse*, 2006, para. 42.

[124] C-374/17, *A-Brauerei*, 2018, para. 21; C-20/15 P, *Commission v World Duty Free Group and Others*, 2015, para. 56, with case note by Giraud and Petit (2017) EStALQ 310–15. The progressivity of the rates of certain turnover taxes was, however, not deemed to constitute a selective advantage, see, C-562/19 P, *Commission v Poland*, 2021, paras 24-47; C-596/16 P, *Commission v Hungary*, 2021, paras 30–57.

[125] e.g. C-143/99, *Adria-Wien Pipeline and Wietersdorfer & Peggauer Zementwerke*, 2001, para. 34; C-409/00, *Spain v Commission*, 2003, para. 47; C-308/01, *GIL Insurance and Others*, 2004, para. 68; C-172/03, *Heiser*, 2005, para. 40; C-524/14 P, *Commission v Hansestadt Lübeck*, 2016, paras 41–65; C-20/15 P, *Commission v World Duty Free Group*, 2016, paras 53–93. See Kurcz, 'Can General Measures be ... Selective? Some Thoughts on the Interpretation of a State Aid Definition' (2007) CMLRev 159–82; Gonen, 'Steun of geen steun, een kwestie van (onder meer) selectiviteit' (2007) NTER 14–22. National measures applicable to all economic operators in the Member State concerned without distinction constitute general measures and are not, therefore, selective: C-374/17, *A-Brauerei*, 2018, para. 23; C-20/15 P, *Commission v World Duty Free Group and Others*, 2015, para. 56. Moreover, objectives inherent in the general tax system concerned could justify an *a priori* selective tax regime: C-374/17, *A-Brauerei*, 2018, para. 49; C-308/01, *GIL Insurance*, 2004, paras 74–6; C-78/08 to C-80/08, *Paint Graphos*, 2011, paras 67–76. See Nicolaides, 'Excessive Widening of the Concept of Selectivity' (2017) EStALQ 62–72; Merola, 'The Rebus of Selectivity in Fiscal Aid: A Nonconformist View on and Beyond Case law' (2016) World Comp 533–556. See also Lenaerts, 'State Aid and Direct Taxation', in Kanninen, Korjus and Rosas (eds), *EU Competition Law in Context: Essays in Honour of Virpi Tiili* (Hart, 2009), 291–306.

[126] C-88/03, *Portugal v Commission*, 2006, paras 52–85 (case note by Winter (2007) CMLRev 183–198); C-428/06, C-429/06, C-430/06, C-431/06, C-432/06, C-433/06, and C-434/06, *Unión General de Trabajadores de la Rioja*, 2008, paras 45–143. See also C-169/08, *Regione Sardegna*, 2009, paras 59–64. Moreno González, 'Taxation and Limits of State Aid: the Case Law of the CJEU on Regional Selectivity and Its Application by Spanish Courts' (2017) EStALQ 340-53. For a discussion, see Lenaerts and Cambien, 'Regions and the European Courts: Giving Shape to the Regional Dimension of Member States' (2010) ELRev 609–35; Greaves, 'Autonomous Regions, taxation and EC State-aid Rules' (2009) ELRev 779–793.

[127] C-124/10 P, *Commission v EDF*, 2012, paras 79–105. See Cyndecka, *The Market Economic Investor Test in EU State Aid Law: Applicability and Application* (Kluwer, 2016). However, the Court has specified, in relation to undertakings entrusted with services of a general economic interest such as the French postal services, that 'in the absence of any possibility of comparing the situation of [such an undertaking] with that of a private group of undertakings not operating in a reserved sector, "normal market conditions", which are necessarily hypothetical, must be assessed by reference to the objective and verifiable elements available' (C-341/06 P and C-342/06 P, *Chronopost*, 2008, para. 148, referring to C-83/01 P, C-93/01 P and C-94/01 P, *Chronopost*, 2003, para. 38). See in

Third, the measure must result in a distortion of competition or threaten to distort competition. This will be the case where the measure enables an undertaking to reduce its costs and therefore strengthens its competitive position compared with other undertakings.[128]

Fourth and lastly, the aid measure must affect intra-Union trade. Intra-Union trade is considered to be affected where the aid strengthens the position of an undertaking compared with other undertakings competing in intra-Union trade.[129]

Services of general economic interest. Compensation for services performed by an undertaking in discharging public-service obligations does not constitute aid within the meaning of Article 107 TFEU.[130] The following conditions apply: (a) the recipient undertaking must actually have clearly defined public-service obligations to discharge; (b) the parameters on the basis of which the compensation is calculated must be established in advance in an objective and transparent manner; (c) the compensation cannot exceed what is necessary to cover all or part of the costs incurred in the discharge of public-service obligations, taking into account the relevant receipts and a reasonable profit for discharging those obligations; and (d) where the undertaking that is to discharge public-service obligations in a specific case is not chosen pursuant to a public procurement procedure which would allow for the selection of the tenderer capable of providing those services at the least cost to the community, the level of compensation needed must be determined on the basis of an analysis of the costs that a typical well run undertaking would have incurred in discharging those obligations.[131] Measures that fulfil these criteria do not constitute State aid, and Member States are not under a duty to notify them. Public-service compensation that does not meet these criteria will constitute State aid if the other conditions of Article 107 TFEU are met. However, the Commission has specified that such aid may still be covered by Article 106(2) TFEU, and will, under certain conditions, be exempt from the duty of notification set out in Article 108(3) TFEU.[132]

9.023

Centralized supervision. All State aid which falls within the prohibition set out in Article 107(1) TFEU is subject to the supervision of the Commission pursuant to Article 108 TFEU in accordance with the procedure codified in Regulation No. 2015/1589.[133] For the purposes

9.024

---

the context of the restructuring of banks following a banking crisis, C-579/16, *Commission v FIH Holding A/S and FIH Erhvervsbank A/S*, 2018, paras 44–75 (case note by Cyndecka (2018) EStALQ 546–552).

[128] 730/79 *Philip Morris v Commission*, 1980, para. 11; 259/85, *France v Commission*, 1987, para. 24.

[129] 730/79, *Philip Morris v Commission*, 1980, para. 11; C-518/13, *Eventech*, 2015, paras 64–71, with case note by de Cecco (2016) ELRev 741–752. See also Mathisen, 'What Effect on Trade? A Balancing Act in Circumscribing the Notion of State Aid' (2019) ELRev 532–47.

[130] C-53/00, *Ferring*, 2001, para. 27; C-280/00, *Altmark Trans and Regierungspräsident Magdeburg*, 2003, para. 87.

[131] C-280/00, *Altmark Trans and Regierungspräsident Magdeburg*, 2003, paras 88–94. For this question, see Bracq (2004) RTDE 33–70; van Marissing (2004) SEW 325–330; Louis and Vallery (2004) World Comp 53–74; Nicolaides (2003) E Comp LRev 561–573; Leibenath (2003) EuR 1052–66.

[132] See Commission Decision 2012/21/EU of 20 December 2011 on the application of Article 106(2) of the Treaty on the Functioning of the European Union to State aid in the form of public service compensation granted to certain undertakings entrusted with the operation of services of general economic interest, OJ 2012 L7/3 (adopted on the basis of Article 106(3) TFEU). The Commission has also fleshed out the conditions under which State aid which does not fall within the scope of that decision, and hence must be notified, can be justified under Article 106(2): see Commission Communication—European Union framework for State aid in the form of public service compensation, OJ 2012 C8/15. For these measures, see Sauter, 'The Altmark package Mark II' (2012) E Comp LRev 307–13; Renzulli, 'Services of General Economic Interest: The Post-Altmark Scenario' (2008) E Pub L 399–431; De Beys, 'Aide d'Etat et financement des services publics. Un bilan après l'adoption du paquet post-Altmark' (2006) JTDE 1–10.

[133] Council Regulation (EU) 2015/1589 of 13 July 2015 laying down detailed rules for the application of Article 108 TFEU, OJ 2015 L248/9, which has replaced Council Regulation (EC) No. 659/1999 of 22 March 1999 laying down detailed rules for the application of Article 93 EC Treaty [*now Article 108 TFEU*], OJ 1999 L83/1.

of the Commission's supervision of State aid, the rules differ depending on whether existing aid or aid which Member States wish to introduce or to alter is concerned.[134] In both cases, it is for the Commission alone to determine whether an aid measure is compatible with the internal market, subject to review by the General Court and the Court of Justice.[135] In this connection, the Commission has a broad discretion and this limits, but does not eliminate, the room for judicial review.[136] Using this discretion, the Commission may issue communications and guidelines laying down criteria on the basis of which it intends to assess the compatibility of an aid measure. Those documents do not create autonomous obligations for the Member States, but formulate conditions which the Commission must take into account when exercising its discretion.[137]

A national court may rule on whether or not action by a public authority constitutes State aid and whether or not it was granted in accordance with the applicable procedural rules, but has no jurisdiction to rule on whether an aid measure is compatible or incompatible with the internal market.[138] Nevertheless, it is for the national courts to safeguard, until the final decision of the Commission, the rights of individuals faced with a possible breach by State authorities of the prohibition on implementation laid down by Article 108(3) TFEU.[139] A later Commission decision finding that aid is compatible with the internal market, does not retrospectively regularize measures which were unlawful because they had been taken in disregard of that prohibition.[140] In such a case, the national courts must order the beneficiary of the aid to pay interest for the period of unlawfulness preceding that decision.[141]

In practice, the centralized enforcement of State aid is, however, to be nuanced due to the importance of the various block exemptions (para 9-021, *supra*). As aid measures that fall within the scope of these exemptions do not require notification, the compatibility thereof is primarily assessed by national authorities, albeit under supervision by the Commission.[142]

9.025 **Existing aid.** Existing systems of aid are kept under constant review by the Commission. In this connection, the Commission is to propose any appropriate measures required by the progressive development or the functioning of the internal market (Article 108(1) TFEU). If the Member State concerned does not accept the proposed modification, the Commission initiates the formal *inter partes* investigation procedure (by notice published in the *Official Journal*)

---

[134] As far as the States are concerned which acceded on 1 May 2004, on 1 January 2007 and on 1 January 2013, 'existing aid' on accession is defined in Annex IV to the 2003 Act of Accession pursuant to Article 22 of that Act (OJ 2003 L236/797), in Annex V to the 2005 Act of Accession pursuant to Article 21 of that Act (OJ 2005 L157/268), and in Annex IV to the 2011 Act of Accession pursuant to Article 16 of that Act (OJ 2012 L112/67), respectively.
[135] 78/76, *Steinike und Weinlig*, 1977, para. 9.
[136] C-66/02, *Italy v Commission*, 2005, para. 135; see also C-594/18 P, *Austria v Commission*, 2020.
[137] C-526/14, *Kotnik*, 2016, paras 37–44.
[138] 78/76, *Steinike & Weinlig*, 1977, paras 10–15; C-44/93, *Namur-Les Assurances du Crédit*, 1994, para. 17. For the distribution of tasks as between the national courts and the Commission, see the Commission Notice on the enforcement of State aid by national courts, OJ 2009 C85/1. See also Buendía Sierra, 'State Aid Assessment: What National Courts Can Do and What They Must Do' (2017) EStALQ 406–15; Köhler, 'Respective Roles of Union Organs and National Courts in State Aid Law: Procedural Implications in National Recovery Proceedings' (2014) EStALQ 165–74.
[139] C-284/12, *Deutsche Lufthansa*, 2013, para. 28; C-323/18, *Tesco-Global Áruházak*, 2020, para. 33; C-75/18, *Vodafone Magyarország Mobil Távközlési*, 2020, para. 21.
[140] C-199/06, *CELF*, 2008, para. 40; C-445/19, *Viasat Broadcasting*, para. 21.
[141] C-445/19, *Viasat Broadcasting*, 2020, paras 24–8. This also applies in cases involving services of general economic interest, ibid., paras 29–44.
[142] On this approach, see Colombo, 'State Aid Control in the Modernisation Era: Moving Towards a Differentiated Administrative Integration?' (2019) ELJ 292–316.

that culminates in a decision by which the Commission determines either that the measure—subject, where appropriate, to certain conditions—is not aid or is compatible with the internal market or that the measure is incompatible with the internal market.[143] If the Commission finds that existing aid is incompatible with the internal market having regard to Article 107 TFEU or that such aid is being misused, it is to decide that the Member State concerned must abolish or alter the aid within such time as the Commission shall determine (Article 108(2), first subpara. TFEU). An action may be brought directly before the Court of Justice, by way of derogation from Articles 258 and 259 TFEU, by the Commission, or any interested Member State against a Member State in breach of that obligation (Article 108(2), second subpara. TFEU).

New aid. There is a procedure for the supervision of new aid whose non-observance inevitably leads to the aid being unlawful. Any plans to grant or alter aid must be notified to the Commission in time for it to submit its comments (Article 108(3) TFEU).[144] If, after an initial examination, the Commission should find that the notified measure is not aid or that no doubts are raised as to its compatibility with the internal market, it adopts a decision to that effect.[145] If, in contrast, the Commission should consider that the measure notified raises doubts as to its compatibility with the internal market, it must initiate without delay the *inter partes* procedure provided for by Article 108(2) TFEU.[146] If it does so, the Member State concerned is debarred under the last sentence of Article 108(3) TFEU from putting its proposed measure into effect until the procedure has resulted in a final decision by which the Commission finds that the measure is not aid or is compatible with the internal market. In assessing the compatibility with the internal market, the Commission must, in principle, apply the rules in force at the time it gives its decision.[147] If the Commission determines, in its final decision, that the measure is aid incompatible with the internal market, the measure may not be put into effect.[148] Pending a final decision, a proposed aid measure may be implemented only if the Commission, after being informed of it, fails to carry out the examination involving interested parties and sufficient time has elapsed for the preliminary examination, provided that the Member State gives the Commission prior notice—after which the aid measure comes under the rules relating to existing aid.[149]

9.026

An aid measure that is put into effect in infringement of the obligations arising from Article 108(3) TFEU is unlawful aid.[150] A Commission decision finding such a measure

---

[143] Regulation No. 2015/1589 (n. 133, *supra*), Article 9 in conjunction with Article 23(2).

[144] The obligation to notify the Commission does not apply to categories of aid covered by a 'block exemption'; see para. 9-021, *supra*. Compulsory notification forms have been laid down in Commission Regulation (EC) No, 794/2004 of 21 April 2004 implementing Council Regulation (EC) No. 659/1999, OJ 2004 L140/1.

[145] Regulation No. 2015/1589 (n. 133, *supra*), Article 4(2) and (3). Such a decision may be challenged by interested parties before the Union Courts (C-367/95 P, *Commission v Sytraval and Brink's France*, 1998, paras 33–49).

[146] Article 108(3) TFEU and Regulation No. 2015/1589, Article 4(4). For that obligation, see, for instance, C-294/90, *British Aerospace and Rover v Commission*, 1992, paras 10–15; C-225/91, *Matra v Commission*, 1993, para. 33.

[147] C-334/07 P, *Commission v Freistaat Sachsen*, 2008, paras 52–54. However, where the legal rules under which a Member State notified proposed aid change before the Commission takes its decision, the Commission must ask the interested parties to express their views on the compatibility of that aid with those rules (ibid., para. 56). See, however, the Commission notice on the determination of the applicable rules for the assessment of unlawful State aid, OJ 2002 C119/22.

[148] Regulation No. 2015/1589, Article 9(5).

[149] 120/73, *Lorenz*, 1973, para. 4. For this first investigation, which the Commission has two months to carry out (Regulation (EU) 2015/1589 (n. 133, *supra*), Article 4(7)), see C-99/98, *Austria v Commission*, 2001, paras 34–7.

[150] Regulation (EU) 2015/1589 (n. 133, *supra*), Article 1 (f). See, e.g., C-266/04 to C-270/04, C-276/04, and C-321/04 to C-325/04, *Distribution Casino France and Others*, 2005, para. 30.

to be compatible with the internal market does not have the effect of regularizing it retroactively.[151]

Since the last sentence of Article 108(3) TFEU has direct effect,[152] the national courts are empowered to determine whether a measure which has not been notified to the Commission nevertheless has to be regarded as a new aid measure which, in the absence of notification, must be considered to be unlawful (even if it subsequently transpires that the aid is compatible with the internal market).[153] By the same token, a national court may consider whether (non-notified) aid falls within the categories of aid measures which are exempted by the Commission. If the measure does not satisfy the requirements for such an exemption, the national court may find only that the duty to notify has been infringed; it cannot itself rule on the compatibility of the aid with the internal market. If the national court entertains doubts about the categorization of the measure at issue it may seek clarification from the Commission or request the Court of Justice for a preliminary ruling on the interpretation of Article 107 TFEU.[154] Since compatible aid alone may be implemented, the implementation of planned aid is to be deferred until the doubts as to its compatibility have been resolved by a Commission decision.[155]

9.027 **Intervention by the Council.** Under the third subpara. of Article 108(2) TFEU, a Member State may apply to the Council, which may declare existing or proposed aid compatible with the internal market by a unanimous vote 'if such a decision is justified by exceptional circumstances'.[156] If the Commission has initiated the *inter partes* procedure, the fact that the Member State concerned has made its application to the Council will have the effect of suspending that procedure for a period of three months (Article 108(2), third and fourth subparas TFEU). Where that period has expired, the Council is no longer competent to adopt a decision in relation to the aid concerned. If the Member State concerned has made no application to the Council before the Commission declares the aid in question incompatible with the internal market and thereby closes the *inter partes* procedure, the Council is no longer authorized to declare such aid compatible with the internal market.[157] In addition, the Council cannot validly declare compatible with the internal market an aid measure allocating to the beneficiaries of unlawful aid which a Commission decision has previously declared incompatible with the internal market, an amount designed to compensate for the

---

[151] C-354/90, *FNCE*, 1991, para. 16; C-261/01 and C-262/01, *van Calster and Others*, 2003, para 63 (case note by Van de Gronden (2004) SEW 341–7); C-368/04, *Transalpine Ölleitung in Österreich*, 2006, paras 40–2 (case note by Retter (2007) EStALQ 129–37); C-387/17, *Fallimento Traghetti del Mediterraneo*, 2019, para 59.

[152] 6/64, *Costa*, 1964, 596.

[153] 78/76, *Steinike und Weinlig*, 1977, para. 14; C-44/93, *Namur-Les Assurances du Crédit*, 1994, para. 16; C-295/97, *Industrie Aeronautique e Meccaniche Rinaldo Piaggio*, 1999, paras 44–50.

[154] C-39/94, *SFEI and Others*, 1996, para. 50–1. See also Commission notice on the enforcement of State aid law by national courts, OJ 2009 C 85/1.

[155] If the national court considers it necessary in order to safeguard the interests of the parties, it may order interim relief, such as suspension of the measures at issue (C-39/94, *SFEI and Others*, 1996, para. 52), order non-notified aid which has already been disbursed to be repaid (ibid., para. 70), or order the placement of the funds on a blocked account so that they do not remain at the disposal of the recipient (C-1/09 CELF ('*CELF II*'), 2010, para. 37). A national court before which an application has been brought for repayment of unlawful aid may not stay the proceedings until the Commission has ruled on the compatibility of the aid: *CELF II*, paras 28–40 (case note by Giraud (2010) EStALQ 671–6).

[156] C-110/02, *Commission v Council*, 2004, para. 24. For the broad discretion of the Council in this connection, see C-122/94, *Commission v Council*, 1996, paras 7–25. See, e.g., Council Decisions 2002/361/EC, 2002/362/EC, and 2002/363/EC of 3 May 2002 on the granting of a national aid in favour of road transport undertakings by the authorities of the Netherlands, Italy, and France, respectively, OJ 2002 L131/12, L131/14, and L131/15.

[157] C-110/02, *Commission v Council*, 2004, paras 28–36; C-399/03, *Commission v Council*, 2006, paras 23–37; C-119/05, *Lucchini*, 2007, paras 59–63.

repayments which they are required to make pursuant to that decision.[158] However, the Council is competent to examine a new aid scheme that is connected, but not indissolubly linked to an aid scheme already assessed by the Commission. This is in particular the case if the Council decision is based on new factors resulting from a substantial change in circumstances that occurred between the Commission decision and the time that the Council assessed the new aid scheme.[159]

Repayment of unlawfully granted aid. The Commission will require unlawfully granted aid to be repaid; the procedures for recovering it are left to national law.[160] Moreover, national authorities are under an obligation pursuant to Article 108(3) TFEU to seek, of their own motion, the repayment of aid that was granted in accordance with an exemption scheme, when afterwards it is discovered that the conditions for granting the exemption were not fulfilled.[161]

9.028

An undertaking to which aid has been granted cannot resist the recovery of aid by claiming that it had a legitimate expectation that it was lawful if the procedure laid down in Article 108 TFEU was not complied with when the aid was granted.[162] Similarly, an undertaking cannot resist recovery by invoking rules of national law precluding the recovery of State aid granted in breach of EU law. Such rules are incompatible with EU law and cannot be applied.[163]

However, where the Commission has adopted a decision declaring the aid to be compatible with the internal market, Union law does not impose an obligation of full recovery of the unlawful aid, even in the absence of exceptional circumstances. In such a situation, pursuant to Union law, the national court must order the aid recipient to pay interest in respect of the period of unlawfulness.[164] Pursuant to its domestic law, it may also order the recovery of the unlawful aid, without prejudice to the Member State's right subsequently to re-implement it. It may also be required to uphold claims for compensation for damage caused by reason of the unlawful nature of the aid.[165]

A Member State and an undertaking in receipt of the aid are entitled to challenge a Commission decision on aid measures in proceedings before the General Court (Article 263 TFEU).[166] Once the time-limit laid down has expired, the validity of the decision may no longer be called into question by the Member State concerned (e.g. in infringement proceedings before the Court of Justice under the second subpara. of Article 108(2)).[167] Nor

---

[158] C-110/02, *Commission v Council*, 2004, paras 37–50.
[159] C-111/10, *Commission v Council*, 2013, paras 60–9.
[160] See the Commission Notice on the recovery of unlawful and incompatible State aid, OJ 2019 C247/1. See Ghazarian, 'Recovery of State Aid' (2016) EStALQ 228–34.
[161] C-349/17, *Eesti Pagar*, 2019, paras 83–97.
[162] C-5/89, *Commission v Germany*, 1990, para. 14; C-169/95, *Spain v Commission*, 1997, paras 51–4; C-24/95, *Alcan Deutschland*, 1997, paras 22–54; C-199/06, *CELF* ('CELF I'), 2008, paras 66–8; C-349/17, *Eesti Pagar*, 2019, paras 96–106. For defences of Member States and recipients of aid, see Montaldo and Medina Palomino, 'Aides d'Etat et moyens de défense des entreprises' (1991) RMCUE 11–48.
[163] C-119/05, *Lucchini*, 2007, paras 59–63.
[164] This obligation applies even if the recipient is an undertaking entrusted with the operation of a service of general economic interest: C-445/19, *Viasat Broadcasting UK*, 2020, para. 43.
[165] C-199/06, *CELF* ('CELF I'), 2008, paras 46 and 52–3; C-384/07, *Wienstrom*, 2008, paras 27–9 (case note by Mamut (2009) EStALQ 343–50); C-445/19, *Viasat Broadcasting UK*, 2020, para. 28. See Adriaanse, 'Effectieve handhaving van het Staatssteunrecht ondermijnd?' (2008) NTER 308–17.
[166] 730/79, *Philip Morris v Commission*, 1980, para. 5. For other interested parties entitled to contest Commission decisions relating to State aid, see C-367/95 P, *Commission v Sytraval and Brink's France*, 1998, paras 33–49; Lenaerts, Gutman, and Nowak, *EU Procedural Law* (OUP, 2022), Chapter 7; Winter, 'The Rights of Complainants in State Aid Cases: Judicial Review of Commission Decisions Adopted under Article 88 EC' (1999) CMLRev 521–68.
[167] 156/77, *Commission v Belgium*, 1978, paras 21–4; C-183/91, *Commission v Greece*, 1993, para. 10.

may it be challenged in the national court by the recipient of the aid who has been notified of the decision by the Member State (e.g. after steps have been taken to recover the unlawful aid).[168]

V. Economic and Monetary Policy

9.029 **EMU.** Article 3(4) TEU proclaims that the Union shall establish an economic and monetary union whose currency is the euro. Article 119 TFEU provides a definition of the economic and monetary union which the Union is to establish.[169] The economic policy is conducted by the Member States alongside the Union and is based on the close coordination of Member States' economic policies on the internal market and on the definition of common objectives. The monetary policy includes 'a single currency, the euro, and the definition and conduct of a single monetary policy and exchange-rate policy the primary objective of both of which shall be to maintain price stability and, without prejudice to this objective, to support the general economic policies in the Union' (Article 119(2) TFEU). Unlike economic policy, monetary policy entails a definitive transfer of competence from the national level to the Union. Article 119(3) TFEU underlines the guiding principles of EMU: stable prices, sound public finances and monetary conditions, and a sustainable balance of payments. Currently, nineteen Member States are participating in full in the EMU, with the euro as its currency.[170]

A. Introduction of the Economic and Monetary Union

9.030 **Coordination of economic and monetary policies.** The economic and monetary policy was originally left to the Member States, which were only expected to coordinate their policies.[171]

In the 1970s, the first plans for enlarging the competence of the Community to conduct economic and monetary policy were proposed. On an intergovernmental basis, the European Monetary System was started by the Member States and, subsequently, the ECU was introduced as the unit of account for the exchange rate mechanism and as a means of settling transactions between the Community and the Member States[172] (see para. 1-034 *et seq.*, *supra*).

---

[168] C-188/92, *TWD Textilwerke Deggendorf*, 1994, paras 17–26; C-135/16, *Georgsmarienhütte*, 2018, paras 12–44.
[169] For an overview, see Amtenbrink, Herrmann, and Repasi, *EU law of Economic and Monetary Union* (OUP, 2020); De Gregorio Merino, 'The Institutional Architecture of Economic Union', in Fabbrini and Ventoruzzo, *Research Handbook on EU Economic Law* (Edward Elgar Publishing, 2019), 11–34; Hinarejos, *The Euro Area Crisis in Constitutional Perspective* (OUP, 2015); Tuori and Tuori, *The Eurozone Crisis: A Constitutional Analysis* (Cambridge University Press, 2014); Lenaerts, 'EMU and the EU's Constitutional Framework' (2014) ELRev 753; Louis, 'The Economic and Monetary Union: Law and Institutions' (2004) CMLRev 575–608. On the need for political integration, see Leino and Saarenheimo, 'Fiscal Stabilisation for EMU: Managing Incompleteness' (2018) ELRev 623–47.
[170] The Member States not (yet) participating are Bulgaria, Croatia, the Czech Republic, Denmark, Hungary, Poland, Romania, and Sweden.
[171] See Articles 12(1), 103(1) EEC and Article 107(1) EEC.
[172] The ECU developed into a parallel currency which was used above all on financial markets for the issue of bonds and gradually introduced itself into banking transactions.

It soon became clear, above all in the course of the implementation of the internal-market programme,[173] that the progressive integration of the markets of the Member States necessitated a greater degree of coordination at Community level of the Member States' economic and monetary policies. The elimination of internal frontiers for movements of goods, persons, services, and capital rendered the economies of the Member States so dependent on each other that any national economic policy decision had a direct cross-frontier effect. Furthermore, the internal market accentuated existing regional and structural disequilibria within the Community. The disequilibria brought strong pressure to bear on Member States' exchange rates.

This prompted further steps to be taken in the coordination of economic and monetary policies. A high degree of coordination of economic policies by the Union was likely to result in uniform growth within the Member States and at the same time might decrease the pressure on Member States' monetary policies. A monetary union would eliminate the economic cost of uncertain exchange rates. Liberalization of capital movements and integration of financial markets would make it impossible for many Member States to pursue an independent monetary policy. It became clear that economic union and monetary union were to be achieved in parallel. On the one hand, a centralized monetary policy could not be pursued in the presence of sharply divergent national economies. On the other hand, monetary policy constituted one of the available instruments for intervening in the economy.

First stage. The Single European Act contained a reference to economic and monetary union and also announced a formal amendment of the Treaty 'in so far as further development in the field of economic and monetary policy necessitates institutional changes'.[174] The European Council held in Hanover on 27 and 28 June 1988 set up a committee under the chairmanship of the President of the Commission, Jacques Delors, which proposed that economic and monetary union should be attained in three stages,[175] resulting in a final stage where the Member States would use a common currency. According to the Committee, a single currency was not strictly necessary to monetary union, but commended itself for its economic, psychological, and political advantages. A single currency would reinforce the irreversible nature of EMU, facilitate Community monetary policy, avoid transaction costs in exchanging currencies, and—provided that stability was ensured—have more weight internationally than the individual currencies of the Member States. As their participation in a monetary union implied that Member States could no longer make use of interest rates and exchange rates to protect their competitiveness, guarantees were necessary to assure that Member States would only participate in the final stage if their economies had sufficiently been aligned. On the basis of the Report of the Delors Committee, the Madrid European Council decided in June 1989 that the first stage of EMU should start on 1 July 1990.[176] The

9.031

---

[173] See VerLoren van Themaat, 'Some Preliminary Observations on the Intergovernmental Conferences: The Relations Between the Concepts of a Common Market, a Monetary Union, an Economic Union, a Political Union and Sovereignty' (1991) CMLRev 291–318; Louis, 'A Monetary Union for Tomorrow?' (1989) CMLRev 301–26.
[174] Article 102a(2) EEC.
[175] Committee for the Study of Economic and Monetary Union, *Report on Economic and Monetary Union in the European Community* (Official Publications Office of the European Communities, 1989) [hereinafter 'Report of the Delors Committee']; also published in *Europe*, doc. 1550/1551, 20 April 1989.
[176] (1989) 6 EC Bull. point 1.1.11.

first stage of EMU comprised, on the economic level, achieving the internal market (free movement of goods, persons, services, and capital); reinforcing the Community's regional and structural policies in order to reduce the economic differences between the regions;[177] and introducing new procedures for supervising national economic policies, incorporating specific rules for coordinating budgetary policy (which were to become binding only in the final stage).[178] On the monetary level, the initial stage required the complete liberalization of capital transactions[179] and all Member States had to join the European Monetary System.[180]

9.032 **Second stage.** The EU Treaty made the necessary changes to the EC Treaty to make the second and third stages of EMU possible. Agreement could only be reached in this respect by offering Denmark and the United Kingdom exceptional status in the EU Treaty, as a result of which Denmark is free to decide whether or not to accede to the third stage of the EMU, as was the United Kingdom before its withdrawal from the Union (see para. 9-035, *infra*). As to all other Member States, it was asserted that they are required to accede to the third stage of the EMU as soon as they fulfil all the conditions laid down in the Treaties. The second stage began on 1 January 1994. The economic policies of the Member States and the Community were made subject to the supervisory procedure and rules laid down in the Treaty, albeit without any binding sanctions as yet.[181] Monetary policy remained for the time being in the hands of the Member States, but the currency composition of the ECU was frozen.[182] The European Monetary Institute (EMI) prepared the instruments for the third stage of EMU. As from 1 June 1998, the EMI was replaced by the European Central Bank, which was set up in anticipation of the third stage.[183] Meanwhile, the European Council of 15–16 December 1995 decided not to call the new currency 'ECU', which was the term used in the EU Treaty, but rather 'euro'.[184]

9.033 **Third stage.** On 1 January 1999 the third stage started between the Member States which satisfied the conditions for the adoption of a single currency,[185] both in respect of the legal

---

[177] See, *inter alia*, the reform of the structural funds effected by Council Regulation (EC) No. 2052/88 of 24 June 1988 on the tasks of the Structural Funds and their effectiveness and on the coordination of their activities between themselves and with the operations of the European Investment Bank and the other existing financial instruments, OJ 1988 L185/9.
[178] Council Decision 90/141/EEC of 12 March 1990 on the attainment of progressive convergence of economic policies and performance during stage one of economic and monetary union, OJ 1990 L78/23.
[179] Council Directive 88/361/EEC of 24 June 1988 for the implementation of [the former] Article 67 of the Treaty, OJ 1988 L178/5; para. 7-101, *supra*.
[180] However, not all Member States were participating in the exchange rate mechanism. At the start of the EMS, all the then Member States, with the exception of the United Kingdom took part. The Spanish peseta was accepted into the exchange rate system in July 1989, the pound sterling in October 1990 and the Portuguese escudo in April 1999. Following financial turbulence in September 1992, the pound sterling and the Italian lira suspended their participation in the mechanism. The Austrian schilling acceded on 9 January 1995, the Finnish markka on 14 October 1996 and the Greek drachma on 16 March 1998; the Italian lira re-entered the exchange rate mechanism on 25 November 1996. The Swedish krona never joined the mechanism. The Member States which did not participate in the exchange rate mechanism had acceded to the agreements with regard to the EMS.
[181] See the Council measures mentioned in paras 9-036, 9-037, and 9-040, *infra*.
[182] See Vissol, 'L'écu dans la phase de transition vers UEM' (1994) RMCUE 425–436.
[183] See Decision 98/345/EC taken by common accord of the Governments of the Member States adopting the single currency at the level of Heads of State or Government of 26 May 1998 appointing the President, the Vice-President, and the other members of the Executive Board of the European Central Bank, OJ 1998 L154/33.
[184] Conclusions of the Presidency (1995) 12 EU Bull. point I.3. An action brought against the Commission for using the term 'euro' where the Treaty referred to ECUs was declared inadmissible on the ground that it was directed against a proposal for legislation: T-175/96, *Berthu v Commission* (order), 1997.
[185] To do this, the Council, meeting in the special composition of the Heads of State or Government, had to decide by a qualified majority by no later than 31 December 1996. In December 1996 the Council found that there

aspects (in particular the independence of their national central banks) and in respect of the convergence criteria relating to their economies (Article 140 TFEU). Before 1 July 1998, the Council had to decide which States fulfilled the conditions for the adoption of a single currency, by applying four convergence criteria, more closely formulated in a Protocol: (1) a rate of inflation not exceeding by more than 1.5 percentage points that of the three best performing Member States in terms of price stability; (2) a deficit which was not excessive within the meaning of Article 104; (3) the normal fluctuation margins of the EMS had to have been complied with for at least the preceding two years; and (4) the average long-term interest rate must not have exceeded by more than 2 percentage points that of the three best performing Member States in terms of price stability.[186]

On 3 May 1998 the Council held by decision that Austria, Belgium, Germany, Finland, France, Ireland, Italy, Luxembourg, the Netherlands, Spain, and Portugal fulfilled the conditions for the adoption of the single currency on 1 January 1999.[187] On 31 December 1998 the Council fixed the conversion rates between the euro and the currencies of the eleven participating Member States.[188] Although the participating currencies were replaced by the euro as of 1 January 1999, the use of the euro was confined to transfer payments. On 19 June 2000, the Council found that Greece also fulfilled the conditions for the adoption of the euro and fixed the conversion rate for the Greek drachma, making Greece the twelfth Member State to adopt the euro, as from 1 January 2001.[189]

From 1 January 2002, euro-denominated banknotes and coins were brought into circulation. National banknotes were completely replaced by the euro in all participating States within six months.[190] In the following years other Member States were found to meet the convergence criteria so that they could participate in the third stage of the EMU: Slovenia

---

was not a majority of Member States which fulfilled the conditions. Under Article 121(4) of the EC Treaty, the third stage was then to start automatically on 1 January 1999 between the Member States fulfilling the conditions, regardless of their number. See Council Decision 96/736/EC of 13 December 1996 in accordance with Article 109j of the Treaty establishing the European Community, on entry into the third stage of economic and monetary union, OJ 1996 L335/48.

[186] First subpara. of Article 140(1) TFEU and Protocol (No. 13), introduced by the EU Treaty and now annexed to the TEU and TFEU, on the convergence criteria (OJ 2016 C202/281).

[187] Article 1 of Council Decision 98/317/EC of 3 May 1998 in accordance with Article 109j (4) of the Treaty, OJ 1998 L139/30, by which the Council, meeting in the composition of the Heads of State or Government, adopted the identically worded recommendation drawn up that weekend and submitted to the European Parliament for its opinion: Council Recommendation 98/316/EC of 1 May 1998 in accordance with Article 109j (2) of the Treaty, OJ 1998 L139/21.

[188] Council Regulation (EC) No. 2866/98 of 31 December 1998 on the conversion rates between the euro and the currencies of the Member States adopting the euro, OJ 1998 L359/1 (for the ECB's opinion of the same date on the Commission's proposal, see OJ 1998 C142/1). Under the regulation, conversion rates (to six significant figures) were adopted as one euro expressed in terms of the national currencies of the participating countries (1 euro = 13.7603 Austrian schillings; 40.3399 Belgian francs; 5.94573 Finnish markkas; 6.55957 French francs; 1.95583 Deutsche Mark; 0.787564 Irish pounds; 1936.27 Italian lira; 40.3399 Luxembourg francs; 2.20371 Dutch guilders; 200.482 Portuguese escudo, and 166.386 Spanish pesetas).

[189] Council Decision 2000/427/EC of 19 June 2000 in accordance with Article 122(2) of the Treaty on the adoption by Greece of the single currency on 1 January 2001, OJ L167/7. For the conversion rate, see Council Regulation (EC) No. 1478/2000 of 19 June 2000, OJ 2000 L167/1 (1 euro = 340,750 Greek drachma).

[190] In accordance with the scenario approved by the European Council in Madrid on 15 and 16 December 1995 ((1995) EU Bull. 12, points I.3 and I.49). For the transitional provisions on the 2002 cash changeover, see Guideline ECB/2001/1 of the ECB of 10 January 2001, OJ 2001 L55/80. For the status of the euro, see Ruiz, 'L'introduction de l'euro et la continuité des contrats sur les obligations pécuniaires' (2000) RTDE 705–726; Block, 'Les incidences du passage à l'euro en procédure civile' (1999) JT 97–105; Usher, 'Legal Background of the Euro' (1999) SEW 12–23; Malferrari, 'Le statut juridique de l'euro dans la perspective du droit allemand, européen et international' (1998) CDE 509–560; Botter et al. 'Invoering van de euro in de verschillende lidstaten' (1998) TVVS 361–7; Sunt, 'Juridische aspecten van de invoering van de euro' (1998–1999) RW 761–78.

(as from 1 January 2007);[191] Cyprus and Malta (as from 1 January 2008);[192] Slovakia (as from 1 January 2009);[193] Estonia (as from 1 January 2011);[194] Latvia (as from 1 January 2014);[195] and Lithuania (as from 1 January 2015).[196] This means that nineteen Member States have adopted the euro as their currency.

As mentioned above Denmark has been given an exception in the Treaties (para. 9-035, *infra*). Sweden does not have a formal exception but refuses to make the necessary legislative changes for participating in the third phase. In this Member State, as in Denmark, the political will to introduce the euro is lacking.[197] Besides Sweden, some of the Member States that have joined the Union since 2004 (Hungary, Czech Republic, Poland, Bulgaria, Romania, and Croatia) also have the status of Member States with a derogation.

9.034   **Derogations.** Member States not fulfilling the requisite conditions for adoption of a single currency fall under a derogating system, conduct their own monetary policies, retain their own currencies, and will not take part in the Council's international monetary action. Major rules in force for the third stage of EMU do not apply to them (see the list in Article 139(2) TFEU). For instance, they cannot have sanctions imposed upon them by the Council on account of excessive budget deficits; they are not subject to decisions of the ECB (and their undertakings are not liable to have fines or periodic penalty payments imposed on them by the ECB). They are not able to vote in the Council or the ECB when decisions are taken in this connection, nor entitled to vote on the appointment of members of the Executive Board of the ECB (see para. 22-005, *infra*). Nevertheless, they must avoid excessive deficits (Article 126(1) TFEU) and submit an annual convergence programme to this end.[198] In order to foster convergence of their economies and to obtain support for their monetary policies, these Member States may voluntarily take part in an exchange rate mechanism ('ERM II' or 'EMS 2'), linking their currencies with the euro.[199] At least every two years, or at the request

---

[191] See Council Decision 2006/495/EC of 11 July 2006 in accordance with Article 122(2) of the Treaty on the adoption by Slovenia of the single currency on 1 January 2007, OJ 2006 L195/25. For the conversion rate, see Council Regulation (EC) No. 1086/2006 of 11 July 2006, OJ 2006 L195/1 (1 euro = 239.640 Slovenian tolars).
[192] See Council Decision 2007/504/EC of 10 July 2007 in accordance with Article 122(2) of the Treaty on the adoption by Malta of the single currency on 1 January 2008, OJ 2007 L186/32 and Council Decision 2007/503/EC of 10 July 2007 in accordance with Article 122(2) of the Treaty on the adoption by Cyprus of the single currency on 1 January 2008, OJ 2007 L186/29. For the conversion rates, see Council Regulation (EC) No. 1134/2007 of 10 July 2007, OJ 2007 L256/1 (1 euro = 0.429300 Maltese liras) and Council Regulation (EC) No. 1135/2007 of 10 July 2007, OJ 2007 L256/2 (1 euro = 0.585274 Cyprus pounds).
[193] Council Decision 2008/608/EC of 8 July 2008 in accordance with Article 122(2) of the Treaty on the adoption by Slovakia of the single currency on 1 January 2009, OJ 2008 L195/24. For the conversion rates, see Council Regulation (EC) No. 694/2008 of 8 July 2008, OJ 2008 L195/3 (1 euro = 30.1260 Slovak korunas).
[194] Council Decision 2010/416/EU of 13 July 2010 in accordance with Article 140(2) of the Treaty on the adoption by Estonia of the euro on 1 January 2011, OJ 2010 L196/24. For the conversion rate, see Council Regulation (EU) No. 671/2010 of 13 July 2010, OJ 2010 L196/4 (1 euro = 15.6466 Estonian kroons).
[195] Council Decision 2013/387/EU of 9 July 2013 on the adoption by Latvia of the euro on 1 January 2014, OJ 2013 L195/24. For the conversion rate see Council Regulation (EU) No. 870/2013 of 9 July 2013, OJ 2013 L243/1 (1 euro = 0,702804 Latvian lats).
[196] Council Decision 2014/509/EU of 23 July 2014 on the adoption by Lithuania of the euro on 1 January 2015, OJ 2014 L228/29. For the conversion rate, see Council Regulation (EU) No. 851/2014 of 23 July 2014, OJ 2014 L233/21 (1 euro = 3,45280 Lithuanian litas).
[197] In a referendum held on 28 September 2000, 53.1 per cent of Danes voted against the introduction of the euro. *Europe*, 30 September 2000, 4. In a referendum held on 14 September 2003, 56.1 per cent of the Swedish people voted against the introduction of the euro ((2003) 9 EU Bull. point 1.3.2).
[198] Para. 9-038, *infra*.
[199] See the Resolution of the Amsterdam European Council of 16 June 1997 on the establishment of an exchange rate mechanism in the third stage of economic and monetary union, OJ 1997 C236/5, as effectuated by the Agreement of 1 September 1998 between the European Central Bank and the national central banks of the

of a Member State with a derogation, the Commission and the ECB are to report to the Council, who decides which Member States with a derogation have fulfilled the necessary conditions in the meantime (Article 140(1) TFEU).[200] In the event that the Council abrogates the derogation of a Member State, it is to adopt, by a unanimous vote of the Member States without a derogation and the Member State concerned, the rate at which the euro is to be substituted for its currency, and the necessary accompanying measures (Article 140(2) and (3) TFEU).

Denmark. Denmark is covered by a special protocol, which continues to apply after the Lisbon Treaty.[201] This Member State is free to decide whether or not it takes part in the third stage of EMU, even if it does fulfil the requisite conditions. That was also the case for the United Kingdom, before its withdrawal from the Union.[202] Denmark enjoys the status of a Member State with a derogation in the third stage. Unlike other Member States with a derogation, the exemption may be abrogated only at Denmark's request, in which case the procedure set out in Article 140 TFEU will be followed.[203]

9.035

B. Economic policy

Coordination of economic policy. According to Article 120 TFEU, the economic policies of the Member States must contribute to the achievement of the objectives of the Union as defined in Article 3 TEU, in accordance with the principles of an open market economy with free competition and the principles laid down in Article 119 TFEU. The Member States' economic policies are to be coordinated by means of multilateral surveillance within the Council, which is also applicable to the Member States that are not taking part in the third stage of EMU (Article 121 TFEU). To this end, the Council is to adopt 'broad guidelines' in accordance with a complex procedure whereby the Council, acting on a recommendation from the Commission, submits draft guidelines to the European Council with a qualified majority vote and subsequently, on the basis of the latter's conclusions, is to adopt

9.036

Member States outside the euro area laying down the operating procedures for an exchange rate mechanism in stage three of Economic and Monetary Union, OJ 1998 C345/6 (amended in view of the accession of ten new Member States by an Agreement of 29 April 2004, OJ 2004 C135/3).

[200] The Council will sit in its normal composition when taking that decision, but it must first consult the European Parliament and have the matter discussed in the European Council. It is to act on a proposal from the Commission after receiving, within six months of that proposal, a recommendation of a qualified majority of those among its members representing Member States whose currency is the euro. Member States with a derogation will take part in the decision, which requires a qualified majority (Article 140(2) TFEU)).

[201] Protocol (No. 16), introduced by the EU Treaty and now annexed to the TEU and TFEU, on certain provisions relating to Denmark (OJ 2016 C202/287). In addition, the United Kingdom was covered by a special protocol, see Protocol (No. 15), introduced by the EU Treaty and thereafter annexed to the TEU and TFEU, on certain provisions relating to the United Kingdom of Great Britain and Northern Ireland, OJ 2010 C83/284. See Vigneron and Mollica, 'La différenciation dans l'union économique et monétaire—Dispositions juridiques et processus décisionnel' (2000) Euredia 197–231.

[202] The United Kingdom enjoyed additional exceptions: it did not have to subscribe to the actual objective of monetary union (Article 119(2) TFEU) nor to accept a number of essential obligations which Member States with a derogation accept completely in the third stage. Accordingly, the United Kingdom only had to 'endeavour' to overcome excessive government deficits, did not have to consult the ECB on draft monetary/economic legislation, and was not bound to remove political control from the Bank of England (although it had in fact done so).

[203] See Protocol (No. 16) on certain provisions relating to Denmark. As a result of Section E of the December 1992 decision, Denmark may 'at any time' inform other Member States that it no longer wishes to avail itself of all or part of that decision, upon which Denmark will 'apply in full all relevant measures then in force taken within the framework of the European Union'.

a recommendation setting out the broad guidelines with a qualified majority vote (Article 121(2) TFEU).[204] The European Parliament and the Council, acting by regulations in accordance with the ordinary legislative procedure, may adopt detailed rules for the multilateral surveillance procedure (Article 121(6) TFEU).

Because excessive government deficits could threaten the financial stability of the monetary union, the Member States are to avoid those deficits (Article 126 TFEU). Following the reference values set out in a Protocol annexed to the Treaties, the planned or actual government deficit may not exceed 3 per cent of gross domestic product and government debt may not exceed 60 per cent of gross domestic product.[205] Article 126(2) TFEU accepts the reference values being exceeded when the deficit or debt has declined substantially and continuously and reached a level that comes close to the reference value. If the Commission considers that there is a risk of an excessive deficit, it is to prepare a report and, where appropriate, address an opinion to the Member State concerned and inform the Council (Article 126(3) to (5)). Upon a proposal from the Commission and after hearing any observations from the Member State concerned, the Council is to decide whether an excessive deficit exists and, if so, upon a recommendation from the Commission, make recommendations to that Member State[206] (Article 126(6)–(7)). If the Member State persists in failing to put into practice the Council's recommendations, the Council may give it notice to take remedial measures within a specified time-limit (Article 126(9)). The Council may, acting unanimously in accordance with a special legislative procedure, replace the provisions set out in the above-mentioned Protocol; it may upon a proposal from the Commission lay down detailed rules and definitions for the application of those provisions (Article 126(14), second and third subpara. TFEU).[207]

Next to that, the Treaties impose specific prohibitions on the ECB and the national central banks to supply credit facilities to the Union institutions or the Member States (prohibition of monetary financing of public debt, Article 123 TFEU) or to take over commitments from Member States contrary to the 'no bail-out' principle (Article 125 TFEU).[208] Nonetheless,

---

[204] See, e.g., the broad guidelines for the economic policies of the Member States and the Union adopted by Council recommendations of 26 June 2003 (OJ 2003 L195/1), 12 July 2005 (OJ 2005 L205/28), 14 May 2008 (OJ 2008 L137/13), 13 July 2010 (OJ 2010 L191/28), and 14 July 2015 (OJ 2015 L192/27). See Leino, 'Sovereignty and Subordination: On the Limits of EU Economic Policy Coordination' (2017) ELRev 166–89; Buzelay, 'De la coordination des politiques économiques nationales au sein de l'Union européenne' (2003) RMCUE 235–41.

[205] Protocol (No. 12), introduced by the EU Treaty and now annexed to the TEU and TFEU, on the excessive deficit procedure, OJ 2016 C202/279.

[206] On 25 November 2003 the Council did not take up the Commission's recommendation to address a recommendation to France and Germany, but evaluated the measures taken by those Member States in 'conclusions', which the Court of Justice annulled: C-27/04, *Commission v Council*, 2004, paras 91–2 (annulment since Council 'conclusions' modified a Council recommendation without a recommendation from the Commission and not in accordance with the voting rules prescribed).

[207] In both cases, the Council is to consult the European Parliament; in the former case also the ECB.

[208] See C-370/12, *Pringle*, 2012, paras 129–47 (ESM not in breach of Article 125 TFEU); C-62/14, *Gauweiler*, 2015, paras 94–121 (ECB programme providing for the purchase of government bonds on the secondary market not contrary to Article 123 TFEU), with notes by Borger (2016) CMLRev 139–96 and Martucci (2015) CDE 493–534; C-493/17, *Weiss*, 2018, 101–51 (public sector asset purchase programme not contrary to Article 123 TFEU), with case note by Dawson and Bobic (2019) CMLRev 1005–40. See also Pliakos and Anagnostaras, 'Adjudicating Economics II: The Quantitative Easing Programme Declared Valid' (2020) ELRev 128–46; Steinbach, 'Effect-based Analysis in the Court's Jurisprudence on the Euro Crisis' (2017) ELRev 254–69; Grund and Grle, 'The European Central Bank's Public Sector Purchase Programme (PSPP), the Prohibition of Monetary Financing and Sovereign Debt Restructuring Scenarios' (2016) ELRev 781–803; Craig and Markakis, 'Gauweiler and the Legality of Outright Monetary Transactions' (2016) ELRev 4–24; Adamski, 'Economic Constitution of the Euro Area after the Gauweiler Preliminary Ruling' (2015) CMLRev 1451–90. See also the various commentaries in (2020) GLJ 944–1127.

the Council can take 'the measures appropriate to the economic situation' and grant Union financial assistance where a Member State is in difficulties or is seriously threatened with severe difficulties caused by natural disasters or exceptional occurrences beyond its control (Article 122 TFEU).[209] On the basis of Article 122 TFEU, in 2020 the Council addressed the economic and social consequences of the COVID-19 pandemic through temporary support for the preservation of employment[210] and setting up a Recovery Instrument to boost the recovery of economic activity[211] as part of a wider agreement on the future budget and additional financial means to emerge from the crisis more resilient (dubbed 'NextGenerationEU'; see para. 14-018, *infra*). Furthermore, the Council may adopt measures specific to the Member States of the eurozone in order to strengthen the coordination and surveillance of their budgetary discipline and set out economic policy guidelines for them (Article 136 TFEU).

Meanwhile, the role of the Union in the economic governance of the EMU has increased considerably since the banking crisis of 2008 and the subsequent debt crisis or euro crisis. Since 2009 multiple Member States of the eurozone (Greece, Portugal, Spain, Ireland, and Cyprus) got into difficulties with regard to the financing of their debts, which in the end not only led to the establishment of stabilization mechanisms to cope with stresses on the markets, but also led to profound changes in the legal framework of the EMU, in which the obligations laid down in Treaty provisions were supplemented both with legislative measures adopted pursuant to Articles 121(6), 126(14), 122, and/or 136 TFEU and with intergovernmental agreements.[212]

Stabilization mechanisms. In the first place, the euro crisis required that Member States with difficulties could be supported financially at short notice. Responding to the international financial crisis and the deterioration of the loan terms for Greece and other Member States, in May 2010 the Council established a European Financial Stability Mechanism on the basis of Article 122 TFEU, financed from the Union budget.[213] At the same time, the Member States of the eurozone established a European Financial Stability Facility outside the framework of the Union, which was financed through a private law mechanism (under Luxembourg law).[214]

9.037

---

[209] For the scope of the measures that can be taken on that basis, see C-589/15 P, *Anagnostakis v Commission*, 2017, paras 69–80.
[210] Council Regulation (EU) 2020/672 of 19 May 2020 on the establishment of a European instrument for temporary support to mitigate unemployment risks in an emergency (SURE) following the COVID-19 outbreak, OJ 2020 L159/1
[211] Council Regulation (EU) 2020/2094 of 14 December 2020 establishing a European Union Recovery Instrument to support the recovery in the aftermath of the COVID-19 crisis, OJ 2020 L433I/23. This instrument will be financed by the amount of up to EUR 750 billion that the Union may borrow pursuant to the Eight Own Resources Decision (see para. 14-015) and will be implemented through existing Union funds and (for the largest part of 672.5 billion) through the newly created Recovery and Resilience Facility, established by Regulation (EU) 2021/241 of the European Parliament and of the Council of 12 February 2021, OJ 2021 L57/17. See De Witte, 'The European Union's COVID-19 Recovery Plan: The Legal Engineering of an Economic Policy Shift' (2021) CMLRev 635.
[212] See Estella, *Legal Foundations of EU Economic Governance* (Cambdrige University Press, 2018), 160–95; Keppenne, 'Fiscal rules', in Fabbrini and Ventoruzzo (eds), *Research Handbook on EU Economic Law* (Edward Elgar Publishing, 2019) 35–80.
[213] Council Regulation (EU) No. 407/2010 of 11 May 2010 establishing a European financial stabilisation mechanism, OJ 2010 L118/1.
[214] See the decision of the representatives of the governments of the Member States of the eurozone and the decision of the representatives of the governments of the 27 EU Member States, adopted in the context of the Council (Ecofin) on 9 May 2010, doc. 9614/10.

In 2012, both temporary constructions were replaced by the European Stability Mechanism (ESM), which was set up by mutual agreement between the Member States of the eurozone in the form of an international organization with its seat in Luxembourg.[215] At the request of an ESM Member State, the Board of Governors of the ESM can award stability support in the form of a financial support facility. The Board of Governors will assign the Commission to negotiate, in consultation with the ECB[216] and the International Monetary Fund (IMF), a Memorandum of Understanding with the Member State concerned on behalf of the ESM in which the conditions connected to the facility are described and to monitor the compliance with these conditions.[217] At the request of Germany, a provision was inserted in advance into the Treaties pursuant to the simplified revision procedure (Article 136(3) TFEU) according to which the Member States whose currency is the euro could establish a stability mechanism which will be activated when necessary to guarantee the stability of the eurozone as a whole.[218] In the *Pringle* judgment, the Court of Justice clarified that this Treaty provision constituted only a confirmation of the competence of the Member States to conclude a mutual agreement—respecting Union law—on the establishment of a stability mechanism. As such, the ESM Treaty could enter into force before this Treaty revision was ratified by all the Member States.[219] The Court also indicated that financial support from the ESM to a Member State did not infringe the exclusive competence of the Union with regard to monetary policy nor did it amount to taking over the debt of a Member State as prohibited by Article 125 TFEU.[220]

9.038 **Stability and growth pact.** In order to guarantee the sustainability of the public finances of the Member States on a long-term basis, the Union legislature significantly strengthened both the above-mentioned multilateral surveillance laid down in Article 121 TFEU and the rules aimed at preventing excessive deficits. Pursuant to a stability and growth pact agreed in 1997 and updated in 2005,[221] the Member States have to show each year by means of stability or convergence programmes that their budgetary situation provides an adequate basis

---

[215] Treaty of 2 February 2012 establishing the European Stability Mechanism (ESM Treaty).
[216] On the role of the ECB, see Lettanie, 'The ECB's Performance under the ESM Treaty on a Sliding Scale of Delegation', (2019) ELJ 317–32.
[217] ESM Treaty, Article 13. Even though the Commission does not undertake itself any obligations, it is to act as guardian of the Treaties: C-8/15 to C-10/15, 2016, *Ledra Advertising*, paras 53–9.
[218] European Council Decision 2011/199/EU of 25 March 2011 amending Article 136 of the Treaty on the Functioning of the European Union with regard to a stability mechanism for Member States whose currency is the euro, OJ 2011 L91/1. See para. 3-006 for the simplified revision procedure (Article 48, lid 6 TEU).
[219] C-370/12, *Pringle*, 2012, paras 72–3 and 183–5. See also De Witte and Beuckers, 'The Court of Justice Approves of the Creation of the European Stability Mechanism out the EU Legal Order: Pringle' (2013) CMLRev 805.
[220] Ibid., paras 94–8. In June 2019, the Eurogroup agreed on a revised text of the ESM Treaty, available at https://www.consilium.europa.eu/media/39772/revised-esm-treaty-2.pdf. On 30 November 2020, the Eurogroup agreed to proceed with the reform and the revised Treaty is due to be signed in January 2021, after which the ratification process will commence.
[221] The stability and growth pact, on which the European Council reached agreement in Dublin as long ago as December 1996 (see (1996) 12 EU Bull. point I.3), was elaborated on by Regulation No. 1466/97 on the strengthening of the surveillance of budgetary positions and the surveillance and coordination of economic policies, OJ 1997 L209/1 (as amended by Council Regulation No. 1055/2005 of 27 June 2005, OJ 2005 L174/1) and Council Regulation (EC) No. 1467/97 of 7 July 1997 on speeding up and clarifying the implementation of the excessive deficit procedure, OJ 1997 L209/6 (as modified by Council Regulation No. 1056/2005 of 27 June 2005, OJ 2005 L174/5) and the Resolution of the Amsterdam European Council of 17 June 1997 on the stability and growth pact, OJ 1997 C236/1. For an assessment, see Louis, 'The Review of the Stability and Growth Pact' (2006) CMLRev 85–106; Amtenbrink and De Haan, 'Reforming the Stability and Growth pact' (2006) ELRev 402–13; Heipertz, 'The Stability and Growth Pact - theorizing a Case in European Integration' (2005) JCMS 985–1008; Amtenbrink and De Haan, 'Economic Governance in the European Union: Fiscal Policy Discipline Versus Flexibility' (2003) CMLRev 1075–106.

for price stability and sustainable growth or that they are taking adjustment measures to that end.[222] In 2011 and 2013 the Union legislature adopted on the basis of Articles 121(6), 121(14), and 136 TFEU the so-called 'six-pack'[223] and 'two-pack',[224] legislative packages in which both the preventive part (multilateral surveillance system) and the correcting part (avoidance of excessive deficits) of the stability and growth pact were strengthened.

European Semester. As far as the preventive part is concerned, the Union legislature introduced a strengthened budget surveillance during the first six months of every year (the European Semester), in which the Council sets up the broad guidelines for the Member States' economic policies and under which the Member States will submit stability or convergence programmes and national reform programmes drafted in accordance with the broad guidelines which will be reviewed by the Council, acting on a recommendation from the Commission.[225] In practice, this European Semester is a full-year process as it requires the Member States to already make public by 15 October their draft budget and submit it to scrutiny by the Commission.[226] In November–December the Commission adopts a package of guidance documents, which are discussed in the Council together with the Commission's opinion on these draft budgets.[227] In Spring, the Commission then analyses the economic situation of Member States by issuing country reports, following which the Member States submit the above-mentioned stability or convergence and national reform programmes. These form the basis of country-specific recommendations issued by the Commission which are to be discussed by the European Parliament and the European Council before they are adopted by the Council.[228] According to Article 121(4) TFEU, in the event that the economic policies of a Member State do not correspond to the broad guidelines or threaten to undermine the proper functioning of the EMU, the Commission can issue a warning to the Member State and the Council can issue recommendations by qualified majority vote (excluding the Member State concerned).[229]

9.039

Corrective measures. When it is established on the basis of the preventive part of the stability and growth pact that a Member State from the eurozone has an excessive government deficit and that Member State does not give effect to the recommendations of the Council to reduce the deficit, the Council can impose the sanctions laid down in Article 126(11) TFEU, namely to require the Member State concerned to publish additional information before issuing bonds and securities, to invite the European Investment Bank to reconsider its lending policy towards

9.040

---

[222] See Council Regulation (EC) No. 1466/97, which requires Member States taking part in EMU to submit a stability programme and the others a convergence programme and to regularly update these programmes. These programmes are examined by the Council, which delivers an opinion (see Article 5 of the regulation).
[223] See Regulations (EU) No. 1173/2011, 1174/2011, 1175/2011 and 1176/2011 of the European Parliament and the Council of 16 November 2011; Regulation (EU) No. 1177/2011 of the Council of 8 November 2011 and Directive 2011/85/EU of the Council of 8 November 2011 (all in OJ 2011 L306). Under Regulation No. 1173/2011, the Council may decide to fine Member States that misrepresent relevant deficit and debt data, see C-521/15, *Spain v Council*, 2017.
[224] Regulations No. 472/2013 and 473/2013 of the European Parliament and the Council of 21 May 2013, OJ 2013 L140/1 and L140/11.
[225] Regulation (EC) No. 1466/97 (as amended), Article 2a.
[226] Regulation 473/2013, Articles 4 to 7.
[227] The 'Autumn package' includes the Annual Sustainable Growth Survey and a draft for the employment report that the Council is to adopt jointly with the Commission under Article 148(1) TFEU (see para. 9-049).
[228] Regulation (EC) No. 1466/97, Article 5(2). The Council adopts the country-specific recommendations by adopting the Commission's recommendation with a brief explanation of its possible changes thereto.
[229] Regulation (EC) No. 1466/97, Articles 6 and 10.

the Member State concerned, to require the Member State concerned to make a non-interest-bearing deposit with the Union until the excessive deficit has been corrected, or to impose fines 'of an appropriate size'. Here, the Union legislature has also adopted rules to strengthen the *effet utile* of the procedure laid down in the Treaties. It has determined that every time the Council decides to impose sanctions on a Member State according to Article 126(11) TFEU, normally a fine will be imposed.[230] In the framework of the preventive part of the stability and growth pact, a Member State that neglects to take measures in response to a recommendation from the Council can also be obliged to pay an interest-bearing deposit with the Commission. In case the Member State still does not put its budget in order, it can subsequently be obliged, in the framework of the corrective part, to pay a non-interest-bearing deposit or a fine. To facilitate the imposition of these sanctions, the Council decision in all these cases is assumed to be taken in accordance with the recommendation from the Commission, unless the Council rejects it with a qualified majority vote (rule of 'reversed qualified majority').[231] According to a similar procedure, the Council can also impose sanctions on a Member State where the Commission determines macroeconomic imbalances and that Member State has not taken corrective actions addressing the recommendations issued by the Council.[232]

9.041 **Stability Treaty.** To structurally strengthen the economic union, multiple Member States insisted on a Treaty revision. Since the British government could not agree to this, the other Member States decided to conclude a treaty outside the framework of the Treaties. This Treaty on Stability, Coordination and Governance in the EMU (TSCG) was signed on 2 March 2012 by all Member States at the time, except the United Kingdom and the Czech Republic, and entered into force on 1 January 2013.[233] In Title III of the TSCG (Fiscal Compact) the participating Member States commit themselves to strive towards a budget in balance and to fix the budget rules of the Treaty preferably in national constitutional provisions.[234] By a voting arrangement between the Member States whose currency is the euro, the TSCG applies the above rule of 'reversed qualified majority' in the whole of the excessive deficit procedure of Article 126 TFEU.[235] In case of a Member State's non-compliance with the obligation to provide for a national correction mechanism as required by Article 3(2) TSCG, any other Member State can bring the case before the Court of Justice, which has received jurisdiction for this dispute settlement and can impose a fine analogous to that provided for in the action laid down in Article 260 TFEU.[236]

9.042 **Banking Union.** In order to strengthen the financial system in the Union, several steps were taken in recent years towards a 'banking union' with uniform rules.[237] In 2010 a European system for financial supervision was established in the form of the European Banking Authority (EBA), a European Securities and Markets Authority (ESMA) and a European Insurance and Occupational Pensions Authority (EIOPA).[238] At the same time the capital

---

[230] Regulation (EC) No. 1467/97, Articles 11 and 12.
[231] Regulation (EU) No. 1173/2011, Articles 4 to 6.
[232] See Regulations (EU) No. 1176/2011 and No. 1174/2011.
[233] Treaty of 2 March 2012 on Stability, Coordination and Governance in the Economic and Monetary Union.
[234] Ibid., Article 3.
[235] Ibid., Article 7.
[236] Ibid., Article 8.
[237] For an overview, see Busch and Ferrarini, *European Banking Union* (OUP, 2020).
[238] See Regulation (EU) No. 1093/2010 of the European Parliament and of the Council (EBA); Regulation (EU) No. 1094/2010 of the European Parliament and of the Council (EIOPA), and Regulation (EU) No. 1095/

requirements for banks and the national deposit guarantee schemes were harmonized.[239] In addition, the Union legislature introduced, from November 2014, a centralized prudential supervision over major banking institutions, entrusted to the ECB, in cooperation with the national central banks which are made competent for the supervision of the other banking institutions (the 'Single Supervisory Mechanism' (SSM)).[240] Moreover, a mechanism for managing the resolution of banks facing insolvency was set up (the Single Resolution Mechanism (SRM)), which, like the SSM, is not limited to the Member States of the eurozone but is also open to other Member States that wish to participate. The resolution of a bank is decided by an independent agency, the Single Resolution Board, albeit with the possibility for the Commission or the Council to make objections to its decisions.[241] The Member States participating in the SRM have mutually agreed how the amounts of money that are collected at Member State level are transferred to a permanent emergency fund (the Single Resolution Fund).[242] The agreement instructs the Single Resolution Board to supervise compliance by the participating Member States, and confers jurisdiction on the Court of Justice over disputes between the Member States.[243]

C. Monetary Policy

Eurosystem Monetary policy in the Member States participating in EMU is fully determined by the European System of Central Banks (ESCB), which consists of the European Central Bank (ECB), which has legal personality by virtue of Article 282 TFEU, and the central banks of the Member States. In respect of decisions relating to the Member States that have adopted the euro as their currency, the ECB acts together with only those Member States as Eurosystem

9.043

2010 of the European Parliament and of the Council (ESMA), OJ 2010 L331. All these Regulations were amended by Regulation (EU) No. 2019/2175 of the European Parliament and of the Council, OJ L334/1. See Howell, 'EU Agencification and the rise of ESMA: Are its Governance Arrangements Fit for Purpose?' (2019) CLJ 324–54; Moloney, *The Age of ESMA: Governing EU Financial Markets* (Hart Publishing, 2018).

[239] Directive 2013/36/EU of the European Parliament and of the Council of 26 June 2013, OJ 2013 L176/338 (capital requirements) and Directive 2014/49/EU of the European Parliament and of the Council of 16 April 2014, OJ 2014 L173/149 (deposit guarantee scheme).

[240] Regulation (EU) No. 1024/2013 of the Council of 15 October 2013, OJ 2013 L287/36, as further developed in Regulation (EU) No. 468/2014 of the ECB of 16 April 2014, OJ 2014 L141/1; Bassani, *The Legal Framework Applicable to the Single Supervisory Mechanism: Tapestry or Patchwork?* (Kluwer, 2019); Pizzolla, 'The role of the European Central Bank in the Single Supervisory Mechanism: a new paradigm for EU governance' (2018) ELRev 3–23; Schammo, 'The European Central Bank's Duty of Care for the Unity and Integrity of the Internal Market' (2017) ELRev 3–26; Alexander, 'The ECB and Banking Supervision: Does Single Supervisory Mechanism Provide an Effective Regulatory Framework?', in Andenas and Deipenbrock (eds), *Regulating and Supervising European Financial Markets* (Springer, 2016), 253–76; see also D'Ambrosio, 'The Single Supervisory Mechanism (SSM): Selected Institutional Aspects and Liability Issues', in ibid, 299–356. For the disputed position of non-euro States in the banking union, see Dumitrescu-Pasecinic, 'International law in the European Banking Union: The Case of non-Euro Periphery' (2019) ELRev 359–82. See also, C-219/17, *Berlusconi and Finninvest*, 2018, paras 40–59 (with case note by Brito Bastos (2019) CMLRev 1355–77).

[241] Regulation (EU) No. 806/2014 of the European Parliament and of the Council of 15 July 2014, OJ 2014 L225/1 (central resolution under supervision by the ECB). See further Directive 2014/59/EU of the European Parliament and of the Council of 15 May 2014, OJ 2014 L173/190 (resolution of banks by the national resolution authorities). See C-414/18, *Iccrea Banca*, 2019. See also, C-584/20 P and C-621/20 P, *Commission v Landesbank Baden-Württemberg and SRB*, AG De La Tour Opinion, 2021.

[242] The Agreement of 21 May 2014 on the transfer and mutualization of contributions to a Single Resolution Fund, see Council document 8457/14.

[243] Ibid., Articles 10 and 14.

(Article 282(1) TFEU). The primary objective of the ESCB is to maintain price stability, but by supporting the general economic policies in the Union it also contributes to the achievement of the objectives of the Union as laid down in Article 3 TEU, in accordance with the principles prescribed for economic policy (Article 127(1) TFEU; see Article 120 TFEU).[244] Pursuant to Article 130 TFEU, both the ECB and the national central banks operate within the ESCB independently from the national or Union political authorities[245] (para. 13-021, *infra*).

9.044 **Monetary policy.** The ESCB's primary task is to define and implement the monetary policy of the Union. It also conducts foreign exchange operations, manages the Member States' official foreign reserves, and promotes the smooth operation of payment systems (Article 127(2) TFEU). The Statute of the ESCB defines the monetary functions and operations of the ESCB.[246] The Treaties do not specify the content of the monetary policy, but only state the objectives of the monetary policy—primarily maintaining price stability—and the instruments that are at the disposal of the ESCB to implement that policy. Accordingly, the delimitation of whether a measure falls within the scope of the Union's monetary policy is mainly made on the basis of its objectives, although the instruments that the measure employs in order to attain those objectives are also relevant.[247] The ECB draws up the necessary guidelines for the conduct of monetary policy, with which the national central banks have to comply.[248]

Furthermore, the ESCB is to support the competent authorities tasked with the prudential supervision of credit institutions and the stability of the financial system (Article 127(5) TFEU). The Council, acting by means of regulations in accordance with a special legislative procedure, may unanimously, and after consulting the European Parliament and the European Central Bank, confer on the ECB specific tasks concerning policies relating to the prudential supervision of credit institutions and other financial institutions (but not insurance undertakings) (Article 127(6) TFEU).

9.045 **Euro.** The Union legislature may lay down rules for the use of the euro as a single currency, but without prejudice to the powers of the ECB (Article 133 TFEU).[249] The ECB has the exclusive right to authorize the issue of banknotes denominated in euro, which may only be issued by the ECB and the national central banks as legal tender (Article 128(1) TFEU).[250] The ECB and the central banks of the participating Member States put banknotes denominated

---

[244] See Herdegen, 'Price Stability and Budgetary Restraints in the Economic and Monetary Union: The Law as Guardian of Economic Wisdom' (1998) CMLRev 9–32.

[245] See also the provisions with regard to the term of office of the Governor of a national central bank (ESCB Statute, Article 14.2), according to which the Court of Justice has jurisdiction to review the validity of decisions by the Member States to remove a governor of a national central bank in order to ensure the independence of the system; see C-202/18 and C-238/18, *Rimšēvičs v Latvia*, 2019, paras 43–63 (case note by Smits (2020) EuConst 120–44).

[246] Protocol (No. 4), introduced by the EU Treaty and now annexed to the TEU and TFEU, on the Statute of the European System of Central Banks and of the European Central Bank (OJ 2010 C83/230), Articles 17 to 24.

[247] C-493/17, *Weiss*, 2018, para. 53; see also C-370/12, *Pringle*, 2012, paras 53 and 55; C-62/14, *Gauweiler*, 2015, para. 43.

[248] ESCB Statute, Article 14.3.

[249] See Regulation (EU) No. 651/2012 of the European Parliament and of the Council of 4 July 2012 on the issuance of euro coins, OJ 2012 L201/135. Pursuant to the third subpara. of Article 123(4) EC, according to which the Council was to take the measures necessary for the introduction of the euro, it adopted the necessary measures to protect the euro against counterfeiting. See Council Regulation (EC) No. 1338/2001 of 28 June 2001, OJ 2001 L181/6, and Council Regulation (EC) No. 1339/2001, adopted on the basis of Article 308 EC to extend its effects to non-Eurozone Member States, OJ 2001 L181/11.

[250] See the Decision ECB/2003/4 of the European Central Bank of 20 March 2003 on the denominations, specifications, reproduction, exchange and withdrawal of euro banknotes, OJ 2003 L78/16, and Decision ECB/2001/15 of the ECB of 6 December 2001 on the issue of euro banknotes, OJ 2001 L337/52.

in euro into circulation from 1 January 2002.[251] Only the Member States are authorized to issue coins, but the volume of coins issued must be approved by the ECB (Article 128(2) TFEU). Pursuant to Article 128(2), the Council has harmonized the denominations and technical specifications of euro coins.[252] All euro coins have one common face and one face with a national design.[253]

As far as the exchange-rate mechanism of the euro vis-à-vis the currency of third countries is concerned, the Council may conclude agreements with third countries, if not on a recommendation made by the ECB, at least after consulting the ECB (and on a recommendation from the Commission) 'in an endeavour to reach a consensus consistent with the objective of price stability' (Article 219(1) TFEU). Pursuant to Article 219(3) TFEU, the Union may conclude agreements concerning monetary or foreign exchange matters with third countries. The Union thus concluded agreements entitling Andorra, Monaco, San Marino, and the Vatican City to use the euro as their currency.[254] Also certain third countries, such as Kosovo and Montenegro, use the euro as currency, without formal agreement with the Union in this respect.

VI. Social Policy and Employment

Social policy. The harmonization of national legislation which the Union has carried out in order to realize the free movement of workers or on the basis of general harmonizing provisions (e.g. in respect of the equal treatment of men and women) has often affected Member States' social policy.[255] Since the Single European Act, the Community, now the Union, has the possibility to pursue its own social policy. Article 151, third para. TFEU expresses the Member States' belief that social progress will ensue 'not only from the functioning of the internal market, which will favour the harmonisation of social systems, but also from the procedures provided for in the Treaties and from the approximation of provisions laid down by law, regulation or administrative action'. The Union's competence for pursuing its own social policy has been widened by the addition of a special 'social' harmonization power (initially Article 118a EEC, now Article 153 TFEU), which allows the Union legislature to set out minimum requirements with a view to improving the working environment and protecting workers' health and safety.

9.046

---

[251] Article 10 of Council Regulation (EC) No. 974/98 of 3 May 1998 on the introduction of the euro, OJ 1998 L139/1. Banknotes are denominated in the range of 5 euros to 500 euros. This provision does not preclude Member States from requiring in specific instances that payments are not made in cash, see C-422/19 and C-423/19, *Dietrich*, 2021, paras 59-78.

[252] Council Regulation (EU) No. 729/2014 of 24 June 2014 on denominations and technical specifications of euro coins intended for circulation, OJ 2014 L194/1, replacing Council Regulation (EC) No. 975/98 of 3 May 1998, OJ 1998 L139/6.

[253] See also Commission Recommendation 2009/23/EC of 19 December 2008 on common guidelines for the national sides and the issuance of euro coins intended for circulation, OJ 2009 L9/52.

[254] See the agreements with Andorra (OJ 2011 C369/11), Monaco (OJ 2012 C310/1), San Marino (OJ 2012 C121/5), and Vatican City (OJ 2010 C28/13), for which the Council had each time authorized the Commission to conclude the agreement on behalf of the Union (e.g. Council Decision 2009/904/EC of 26 November 2009 on the position to be taken by the European Community regarding the renegotiation of the Monetary Agreement with the Republic of San Marino, OJ 2009 L322/12). See also Council Decision of 12 July 2011 on the signing and conclusion of the Monetary Agreement between the European Union and the French Republic on keeping the euro in Saint-Barthélemy following the amendment of its status with regard to the European Union, OJ 2011 L189/1.

[255] See Article 39(1)(b) TFEU (agriculture); Articles 46 and 48 TFEU (free movement of workers); Article 166 TFEU (vocational training).

In this respect, reference must be made, first, to the Charter of Fundamental Social Rights of Workers, which the Heads of State or Government of the then Member States (but without the United Kingdom) concluded in 1989.[256] At the Intergovernmental Conference leading to the EC Treaty (1992), the United Kingdom alone opposed the incorporation into the EC Treaty of broader objectives and instruments for the purpose of giving effect to the Charter. The other Member States agreed on more extensive competence to be exercised using the Community's institutions pursuant to a protocol annexed to the EC Treaty and in accordance with an agreement which they concluded (the 'Social Agreement').[257] A few years later, the United Kingdom agreed in the Treaty of Amsterdam to incorporate the content of the Social Agreement in the EC Treaty. This led to the current Articles 151 to 164 TFEU ('social policy'), inserted after the specific title on 'employment' (Articles 145–150 TFEU). Second, and more recently, the European Pillar of Social Rights has been jointly signed by the European Parliament, the Council, and the Commission on 17 November 2017, at the Social Summit for Fair Jobs and Growth in Gothenburg, Sweden.[258] This document expresses principles and rights that are essential for fair and well-functioning labour markets and social security systems. In chapters on 'Equal opportunities and access to the labour market', 'Fair working conditions', and 'Social protection and inclusion' the pillar formulates rights that are already present in the *acquis* of the Union alongside new principles that respond to societal, technological, and economic developments, such as globalization, the digital revolution, or related changes in work patterns. The European Pillar of Social Rights is not a legally binding human rights catalogue, but a political programme to be implemented by the Union and the Member States, pursuant to their respective competences.

9.047 **Minimum harmonization.** As objectives of the social policy of the Union and the Member States, the first para. of Article 151 TFEU refers to the promotion of employment, the steady improvement of living and working conditions, proper social protection, dialogue between management and labour, the development of human resources, lasting high employment, and the combating of exclusion.[259] The Union and the Member States are to take account of the diverse forms of national practices, in particular in the field of contractual relations, and the need to maintain the competitiveness of the Union economy (Article 151, second para. TFEU).

---

[256] (1989) 12 EC Bull. point 1.1.10; the text may be found in Commission of the European Communities, Social Europe, 1/90; see also Blanpain and Engels, *European Labour Law* (The Hague, Kluwer Law International, 1998), 441–8; Bercusson, 'The European Community's Charter of Fundamental Social Rights of Workers' (1990) MLR 624–42; Hepple, 'The Implementation of the Community Charter of Fundamental Social Rights' (1990) MLR 643–54.

[257] See, generally, Jaspers, Pennings, and Peters, *European Labour Law* (Intersentia, 2019); Watson, *EU Social and Employment Law* (OUP, 2014); Barnard, *EU Employment Law* (OUP, 2012); Blanpain, *European Labour Law* (Kluwer, 2008).

[258] The document is to be found (in the form of a booklet) at https://ec.europa.eu/commission/publications/european-pillar-social-rights-booklet_en. See the Commission proposal of 26 April 2017 for an Interinstitutional Proclamation on the European Pillar of Social Rights, COM(2017)251 def. and the Commission Recommendation (EU) 2017/761 of 26 April 2017 on the European Pillar of Social Rights, OJ 2017 L113/56. See also Garben, 'The European Pillar of Social Rights: An Assessment of its Meaning and Significance' (2019) CYES 101–27; Aranguiz, 'Social Mainstreaming through the European Pillar of Social Rights: Shielding "The Social" from "The Economic" in EU Policymaking' (2019) EJ Soc Sec 341–63; Garben, 'The European Pillar of Social Rights: Effectively Adressing Displacement?' (2018) EuConst 210–30.

[259] Article 151, first para. TFEU. The former Article 117 EC referred only to improving the standard of living and working conditions, although a high level of employment and social protection was already mentioned in the former Article 2 EC Treaty.

In order to support and complement Member States' activities, the European Parliament and the Council are to adopt directives embodying minimum requirements relating to (a) improvement of the working environment (with a view to protecting workers' health and safety); (b) working conditions; (c) social security and social protection of workers; (d) protection of workers where their employment contract is terminated; (e) the information and consultation of workers; (f) representation and collective defence of the interests of workers and employers; (g) conditions of employment for third-country nationals legally residing in Union territory; (h) the integration of persons excluded from the labour marke; and (i) equality between men and women with regard to labour market opportunities and treatment at work (Article 153(1) and (2), first subpara., indent (b) TFEU). On this legal basis, the Union legislature has adopted directives improving employment and working conditions, such as the Working Time Directive[260] and several directives relating to health and safety at work[261] or improving information for and consultation of workers, requiring Union-scale undertakings and groups of undertakings to introduce a European Works Council.[262] In addition, the European Parliament and the Council may adopt measures designed to encourage cooperation between Member States in these areas and with a view to combating social exclusion and modernizing systems of social protection, without proceeding to any harmonization of national laws or regulations (Article 153(2), first subpara. indent (a)).[263] In principle, the European Parliament and the Council adopt the directives and other measures in question under the ordinary legislative procedure, after consulting the Economic and Social Committee and the Committee of the Regions; in cases (c), (d), (f), and (g) the Council has to act in accordance with a special legislative procedure, with unanimity, after consulting the European Parliament and the same committees.

---

[260] Directive 2003/88/EC of the European Parliament and of the Council of 4 November 2003 concerning certain aspects of the organization of working time, OJ 2003 L299/9; for applications see e.g. C-344/19, *D.J.*, 2021, paras 21-66; C-580/19, *RJ*, 2021, paras 23-61. In certain sectors more specific legislation applies, such as Directive 2002/15/EC of the European Parliament and of the Council of 11 March 2002 on the organization of the working time of persons performing mobile road transport activities, OJ 2002 L80/35. See, more recently, Directive (EU) 2019/1152 of the European Parliament and of the Council of 20 June 2019 on transparent and predictable working conditions in the European Union, OJ 2019 L186/105; Directive (EU) 2019/1158 of the European Parliament and of the Council of 20 June 2019 on work-life balance for parents and carers and repealing Council Directive 2010/18/EU, OJ 2019 L188/79; Council Directive 2010/18/EU of 8 March 2010 implementing the revised Framework Agreement on parental leave concluded by BUSINESSEUROPE, UEAPME, CEEP, and ETUC, OJ 2010 L68/13; Directive 2008/104/EC of the European Parliament and of the Council of 19 November 2008 on temporary agency work, OJ 2008 L327/9; Council Directive 97/81/EC of 15 December 1997 concerning the Framework Agreement on part-time work concluded by UNICE, CEEP, and the ETUC, OJ 1998 L14/9.

[261] See Council Directive 89/391/EEC of 12 June 1989 on the introduction of measures to encourage improvements in the safety and health of workers at work, OJ 1989 L183/1 (the 'framework' Directive, supplemented by numerous specific protective directives).

[262] Directive 2009/38/EC of the European Parliament and of the Council of 6 May 2009 on the establishment of a European Works Council or a procedure in Community-scale undertakings and Community-scale groups of undertakings for the purposes of informing and consulting employees, OJ 2009 L122/28); Directive 2002/14/EC of the European Parliament and of the Council of 11 March 2002 establishing a general framework for informing and consulting employees in the European Community, OJ 2002 L80/29. See Blanpain, *European Works councils the European directive 2009/38/EC of 6 May 2009' (Special Issue of the Bulletin of Comparative Labour Relations)* (Kluwer, 2009); Rojot, Le Flanchec, and Voynnet-Fourboul, 'European Collective Bargaining, New Prospects or Much Ado about Little?' (2001) Int'l J Comp Lab L & Ind Rel 345–70.

[263] See Council Conclusions 'Combating Poverty and Social Exclusion: An integrated approach' of 16 June 2016, document 9273/16. Based on Article 292 in conjunction with Articles 153 and 352 TFEU the Council adopted on 8 November 2018 a Recommendation on access to social protection for workers and the self-employed, OJ 2019 C387/1.

Such directives and other measures are not to affect the right of Member States to define the fundamental principles of their social security systems and must not significantly affect the financial equilibrium of those systems.[264] In addition, those measures do not prevent any Member State from maintaining or introducing more stringent protective measures (Article 153(4) TFEU).[265] In some cases, Article 153 TFEU is inapplicable, namely in the case of pay,[266] the right of association, the right to strike, and the right to impose lock-outs (Article 153(5) TFEU). However, the fact that the Union does not have competence to regulate these areas does not mean that they fall outside the scope of the provisions on the four freedoms. Hence, collective action which hinders the exercise of one of those freedoms will only be in accordance with Union law if it can be objectively justified.[267]

The Treaties encourage management and labour to conclude agreements at Union level; they may be charged with the implementation of directives adopted by the Council (see paras 17-043–17-044, *infra*). The Commission is charged with promoting dialogue between management and labour at European level (Article 154(1) TFEU) and encouraging cooperation between the Member States by making studies, delivering opinions, and arranging consultations on a variety of subjects (Article 156 TFEU).[268]

The task of the European Social Fund is to render the employment of workers easier, to increase their geographical and occupational mobility, and to facilitate their adaptation to industrial changes and changes in production systems, in particular through vocational training and retraining (Article 162 TFEU; see also Article 166 TFEU as regards vocational training).[269] The Fund is administered by the Commission and assisted by a committee composed of representatives of governments, trade unions, and employers' associations (Article 163 TFEU).[270] The European Parliament and the Council established the European Globalisation Adjustment Fund for Displaced Workers (EGF) to provide support and show solidarity to workers made redundant as a result of major structural changes in world trade patterns due to globalization.[271]

---

[264] Article 153(4) TFEU. However, that does not preclude the Union from laying down legislation concerning social protection on the basis of Treaty provisions not subject to the restriction that the measures may not significantly affect Member States' social security schemes. See C-343/08, *Commission v Czech Republic*, 2010, paras 65–8.

[265] C-609/17 and C-610/17, *TSN*, 2019, para. 48.

[266] See, however, Commission Proposal for a Directive of the European Parliament and of the Council on adequate minimum wages in the European Union, COM(2020) 682. The proposal does not directly affect the level of pay.

[267] C-438/05, *International Transport Workers' Federation and Finnish Seamen's Union*, 2007, paras 39–41; C-341/05, *Laval un Partneri*, 2007, paras 86–8.

[268] The Council set up, pursuant to Article 235 EC [*now Article 352 TFEU*], a European Foundation for the Improvement of Living and Working Conditions (Council Regulation (EC) No. 1365/75 of 26 May 1975, OJ 1975 L139/1 (since replaced pursuant to Article 153(2)(a) TFEU by Regulation (EU) 2019/127 of the European Parliament and of the Council of 16 January 2019 establishing the European Foundation for the improvement of living and working conditions (Eurofound), and repealing Council Regulation (EEC) No. 1365/75, OJ 2019 L30/74) and a European Agency for Safety and Health at Work (Council Regulation (EC) No. 2062/94 of 18 July 1994, OJ 1994 L216/1 (since replaced pursuant to Article 153(2)(a) TFEU by Regulation (EU) 2019/126 of the European Parliament and of the Council of 16 January 2019 establishing the European Agency for Safety and Health at Work (EU-OSHA), and repealing Council Regulation (EC) No. 2062/94, OJ 2019 L30/58), which principally carry out studies and exchange information between Member States.

[269] Council Decision 83/516/EEC of 17 October 1983 on the tasks of the European Social Fund, OJ 1983 L289/38.

[270] See Regulation (EC) No. 1081/2006 of the European Parliament and of the Council of 5 July 2006 on the European Social Fund OJ 2006 L210/12.

[271] Regulation (EU) 2021/691 of the European Parliament and of the Council of 28 April 2021 on the European Globalisation Adjustment Fund for Displaced Workers (EGF) and repealing Regulation (EU) No 1309/2013, OJ 2021 L153/48.

Equal treatment. Article 157 TFEU puts Member States under a duty to ensure the application of the principle that men and women should receive equal pay for equal work or work of equal value.[272] That principle has direct effect.[273] Through the many questions which national courts have referred for preliminary rulings, the Court of Justice has given a broad interpretation to the term 'pay' and has clarified several instances of direct and indirect discrimination.[274] The Union also pursues a general policy on equal opportunities for women and men (see para. 5-058, *supra*).

9.048

Employment. In order to achieve the objective of a high level of employment, the Member States and the Union are to work towards a coordinated strategy for employment and promoting, particularly, a skilled and adaptable workforce and labour markets responsive to economic change (Article 145 TFEU).[275] The Member States are to regard promoting employment as a matter of common concern 'having regard to national practices related to the responsibilities of management and labour'. Their employment policies are to be consistent with the broad guidelines of their economic policies (see para. 9-036, *supra*) and they are to coordinate their action in this respect within the Council (Article 146(1) and (2) TFEU). To this end, the Council is to draw up separate 'guidelines' each year (Article 148(1) and (2) TFEU).[276] On the basis of annual reports furnished by the Member States, the Council is to carry out an examination of the implementation of national employment policies in the light of the employment guidelines. Initially, this so-called 'open method of coordination' essentially resulted in exposing national policies to peer review with the aim of learning from examples of 'best practices'.[277] Nowadays, however, the coercive force of this process has been strengthened through its integration in the annual review of economic governance ('European Semester', see para. 9-039, *supra*). If the Council considers it appropriate, it may, by a qualified majority, make recommendations to the Member States on the basis of a recommendation from the Commission (Article 148(4) TFEU).[278]

9.049

Union employment policy sets out primarily to complement national policies and encourage cooperation. Article 147(1) TFEU provides that the competences of the Member

---

[272] For an assessment of the Union's policy, see Prechal, 'Equality of Treatment, Non-Discrimination and Social Policy: Achievements in Three Themes' (2004) CMLRev 533–51. See also Directive 2006/54/EC of the European Parliament and of the Council of 5 July 2006 on the implementation of the principle of equal opportunities and equal treatment of men and women in matters of employment and occupation, OJ 2006 L204/23; Directive 2010/41/EU of the European Parliament and of the Council of 7 July 2010 on the application of the principle of equal treatment between men and women engaged in an activity in a self-employed capacity, OJ 2010 L180/1.

[273] 43/75, *Defrenne*, 1976, paras 24 and 40. See the discussion of the principle of equal treatment in paras 5-058 and 5-063, *supra*. In the light of the recognition of the principle of non-discrimination as a fundamental right, the original economic aim pursued by that provision of the Treaty, namely the elimination of distortions of competition between undertakings established in different Member States, is secondary to the social aim pursued by it; see C-50/96, *Schröder*, 2000, paras 53–7, and C-270/97 and C-271/97, *Sievers and Schrage*, 2000, paras 53–7.

[274] Para. 5-064, *supra*. For the temporal effect of Article 141 EC [*now Article 157 TFEU*] following the judgments in *Defrenne* and *Barber*, see para. 28-006, *infra*.

[275] See Kilpatrick, 'New EU Employment Governance and Constitutionalism', in de Burca and Scott (eds), *Law and New Governance in the EU and the US* (Hart Publishing, 2012), 121; Raveaud, 'The European Employment Strategy: Towards More and Better Jobs?' (2007) JCMS 411–34.

[276] See Council Decision (EU) 2020/1512 of 13 October 2020 on guidelines for the employment policies of the Member States, OJ 2020 L344/22.

[277] See Dawson, 'The Origins of an Open Method of Coordination', in Dawson (ed.), *New Governance and the Transformation of European Law* (Cambridge University Press, 2011); Ashiagbor, 'Soft Harmonisation: The "Open Method of Coordination" in the European Employment Strategy' (2004) E Pub L 305–32.

[278] See, e.g., the Council Recommendations of 20 July 2020, OJ 2020 C282/1.

States are to be respected. Article 149 TFEU empowers the European Parliament and the Council, acting under the ordinary legislative procedure, to adopt 'incentive measures' designed to encourage cooperation between Member States and to support their action in the field of employment, but makes no provision for harmonization of national administrative and statutory provisions.[279] In addition, the Union has to take the objective of a high level of employment into consideration in the formulation and implementation of other Union policies and activities (Article 147(2) TFEU).

VII. Education, Vocational Training, Youth, and Sport

9.050   **Education.** Since the EU Treaty (1992) the Union is competent to support the policies of the Member States relating to education and vocational training with its own measures. The Court of Justice paved the way for an actual educational policy for the Community, first by construing the expression 'vocational training' in Article 128 EEC as covering most educational curricula[280] and secondly by regarding Community action programmes requiring cooperation between the Member States as 'an application of a common policy'.[281] Since the Lisbon Treaty, the Union's competence in the fields of education, vocational training, youth, and—now also—sport, is limited to carrying out actions to 'support, coordinate or supplement' Member States' action (see para 5-027, *supra*).

As far as education is concerned, Article 165(1) TFEU refers to the Union contributing to the development of quality education by encouraging cooperation between Member States and supporting and supplementing their action. The preamble to the TFEU also lists access to education and its continuous updating as a means of promoting the highest possible level of knowledge of the peoples of the Union. The list of Union tasks set out in Article 165(2) TFEU in order to develop a 'European dimension in education'[282] mentions primarily language teaching and transfrontier aspects of education and work with young people. The aim of encouraging the mobility of students and teachers was realized by the Erasmus programme, which the Union established on the basis of Article 128 EEC relating to vocational training before the insertion in the Treaties of the specific competence for education.[283] Nowadays the Erasmus+ programme for the 2021–2027 period covers a broad range of education, training, youth and sport activities, building on earlier programmes which covered school education (Comenius), higher

---

[279] See, e.g., Decision No. 573/2014/EU of the European Parliament and of the Council of 15 May 2014 on enhanced cooperation between Public Employment Services (PES), OJ 2014 L159/32.
[280] 293/83, *Gravier*, 1985, paras 19–31; 24/86, *Blaizot*, 1988, paras 15–21; 263/86, *Humbel*, 1988, paras 8–20.
[281] 242/87 *Commission v Council*, 1989. See also the interpretation of the principle of non-discrimination on grounds of nationality in conjunction with Article 128 EEC: 295/90 *European Parliament v Council*, 1992, paras 15–20.
[282] Article 165(2), first indent TFEU. On this concept, and its potential beyond mobility, see Grimonprez, 'The European Dimension in Citizenship Education: Unused Potential of Article 165 TFEU' (2014) ELRev 3–26. See also Grimonprez, *The European Union and Education for Democratic Citizenship* (Nomos, 2020), in particular at 630.
[283] See Council Decision 87/327/EEC of 15 June 1987 adopting the European Community Action Scheme for the Mobility of University Students (Erasmus), OJ 1987 L166/20 adopted on the basis of Articles 128 and 235 EEC and replaced by Decision 89/663/EEC of 14 December 1989, based on Article 128 EEC, OJ 1989 L395/23. See also Pertek and Sleiman, 'Les étudiants et la Communauté: l'esquisse d'un statut de l'étudiant en mobilité' (1998) RMCUE 306–21.

education (Erasmus), international higher education (Erasmus Mundus), professional education and vocational training (Leonardo da Vinci), and adult education (Grundtvig).[284]

The Treaties indicate the boundaries set to Union action. First, the Union has to respect the Member States' responsibility for the content of teaching and the organization of educational systems and their cultural and linguistic diversity (Article 165(1) TFEU; see also para. 5-006, *supra*). This does not do away with the Member States' obligation to comply with Union law, in particular the Treaty provisions on free movement and the principle of non-discrimination on grounds of nationality.[285] Secondly, the Union's action is to consist of (a) 'incentive measures', which the European Parliament and the Council adopt in accordance with the ordinary legislative procedure, 'excluding any harmonisation of the laws and regulations of the Member States',[286] and (b) 'recommendations' adopted by the Council by a qualified majority vote on a proposal from the Commission (Article 165(4) TFEU).[287] It is noteworthy that all of the Member States are now coordinating their higher-education policy pursuant to the Sorbonne and Bologna declarations of intent and hence have agreed on a *de facto* harmonization of their education systems outside the framework of the European Union.[288] With the creation of the 'European Higher Education Area' with three cycles (Bachelor, Master, PhD), the Bologna process builds on experience gained in the framework of the Erasmus programme with respect to the European Credit Transfer and Accumulation System (ECTS). Through its participation in the Bologna process, the Commission ensures coordination with the Union's education policy, in particular with respect to the recognition of qualifications for education and training.[289] In addition, the Union has long been tackling aspects of education in the context of its policy on mutual recognition of diplomas (Article 53 TFEU).[290]

Sport. The Treaty of Lisbon extended the Union's competence under the Title 'education, vocational training and youth' to cover sport.[291] Union action in this field is to aim at developing the European dimension in sport by promoting fairness and openness in sporting

9.051

---

[284] See Regulation (EU) 2021/817 of the European Parliament and of the Council of 20 May 2021 establishing Erasmus+: the Union Programme for education and training, youth and sport, OJ 2021 L189/1, replacing Regulation (EU) No. 1288/2013 of the European Parliament and of the Council of 11 December 2013 establishing 'Erasmus+': the Union programme for education, training, youth, and sport, OJ 2013 L347/50.

[285] See C-11/06 and C-12/06, *Morgan and Bucher*, 2007, para. 24; C-73/08, *Bressol and Others*, 2010, para. 28. Member States must also comply with the GATS: C-66/18, *Commission v Hungary*, 2020.

[286] See, e.g., also Decision (EU) 2018/646 of the European Parliament and of the Council of 18 April 2018 on a common framework for the provision of better services for skills and qualifications (Europass), OJ 2018 L112/42. For the exclusion of harmonization, see Hablitzel, 'Harmonisierungsverbot und Subsidiaritätsprinzip im Europäischen Bildungsrecht' (2002) DöV 407–14.

[287] See Recommendation of the European Parliament and of the Council of 18 December 2006 on key competences for lifelong learning, OJ 2006 L394/10.

[288] See the references to the Bologna process on the website of the European Commission's Directorate-General for Education and Culture. For a detailed discussion, see Garben, *EU Higher Education Law: The Bologna Process and Harmonisation by Stealth* (Kluwer, 2011); Garben, 'The Bologna Process from a European Law Perspective' (2010) ELJ 186–210; Terry, 'The Bologna Process and its Impact in Europe: It's So Much More Than Degree Changes' (2008) VJTL 107–227; Pertek, 'L'action communautaire en matière d'éducation et le processus de Bologne' (2004) JTDE 65–70; Verbruggen, 'De Bolognaverklaring kritisch getoest aan het Europees onderwijsbeleid' (2003) SEW 199–212.

[289] Recommendation of the European Parliament and of the Council of 23 April 2008 on the establishment of the European Qualifications Framework for lifelong learning, OJ 2008 C111/1.

[290] Paras 7-075–7-077, *supra*.

[291] Rangeon, 'Le Traité de Lisbonne: acte de naissance d'une politique européenne du sport?' (2010) RMCUE 302–9.

competitions and cooperation between bodies responsible for sports, and by protecting the physical and moral integrity of sportsmen and sportswomen, especially the youngest sportsmen and sportswomen (Article 165(2), last indent TFEU). In order to achieve those objectives, the Union has at its disposal the same instruments as it has for its education policy (Articles 165(3) and (4) TFEU).[292] While contributing to the promotion of European sporting issues, the Union is to take account of 'the specific nature of sport, its structures based on voluntary activity and its social and educational function' (Article 165(1) TFEU). This does not mean that the sports sector is to be protected from the application of the Treaty rules on free movement and competition.[293]

9.052 **Vocational training.** As far as vocational training is concerned, the Union pursues a policy of its own, although it is designed to support and supplement the action of the Member States, which remain responsible for the content and organization of such training (Article 166(1) TFEU). The European Parliament and the Council adopt measures, 'excluding any harmonization of the laws and regulations of the Member States', in accordance with the ordinary legislative procedure (Article 166(4) TFEU).[294] Under Article 308 EC [*Article 352 TFEU*] the Council set up a European Centre for the Development of Vocational Training (Cedefop) to promote and coordinate vocational training in the Member States;[295] as regards promotion of vocational training in third countries, the European Training Foundation was established.[296]

VIII. Culture

9.053 **Incentive measures.** The Union's competence in the cultural field (introduced by the EU Treaty), like that in the sphere of education, is conceived as supplementary (see also Article 6 TFEU), that is, as contributing to the flowering of the cultures of the Member States, whilst emphasizing the common cultural heritage yet respecting national and regional diversity

---

[292] See the Commision's White Paper on sport of 11 July 2007, COM(2007)391 final.
[293] For the application of the Treaty provisions on the free movement of persons and competition, see paras 7-059 and 7-062 and para. 9-015, *supra*. In assessing the proportionality of arrangements concerning sports, the 'specific characteristics' of sports and the 'social and educational function' mentioned in Article 165(1) TFEU need to be taken into account: C-325/08, *Olympique Lyonnais*, 2010, paras 40–5; C-403/08 and C-429/08, *Football Association Premier League*, 2011, paras 93–125; C-22/18, *TopFit and Biffi*, 2019, para. 33. See also Weatherill, *Principles and Practice in EU Sports Law* (OUP, 2017); Parrish, 'Lex sportiva and EU sports law' (2012) ELRev 716–33; Weatherill, 'EU Sports Law: The Effect of the Lisbon Treaty', in Biondi, Eeckhout, and Ripley (eds), *EU Law after Lisbon* (OUP, 2012); Vermeersch, *Europese spelregels voor sport: overzicht van het Europees sportbeleid in wording en de toepassing van het Europees recht op sport* (Maklu, 2009); Bogusz, Cygan, and Szyszczak (eds), *The Regulation of Sport in the European Union* (Edward Elgar Publishing, 2007); Dubey and Dupont, 'Droit européen et sport: Portrait d'une cohabitation' (2002) JTDE 1–15. Declaration (No. 29), annexed to the Amsterdam Treaty, OJ 1997 C340/136 had already emphasized the 'social significance of sport, in particular its role in forging identity and bringing people together'. The Intergovernmental Conference of 1997 therefore called on the bodies of the European Union to 'listen to' sports associations when important questions affecting sport are at issue (Declaration (No. 29)).
[294] See the 'Leonardo da Vinci' Action Programme established by Council Decision 1999/382/EC of 26 April 1999, OJ 1999 L146/33, which subsequently became part of the Erasmus+ programme. Part of the European Social Fund is also dedicated to vocational training.
[295] Council Regulation (EC) No. 337/75 of 10 February 1975, OJ 1975 L39/1, replaced by Regulation (EU) 2019/128 of the European Parliament and of the Council of 16 January 2019 establishing a European Centre for the Development of Vocational Training (Cedefop), OJ 2018 L30/90 (based on Articles 166(4) and 165(4) TFEU).
[296] Regulation (EC) No. 1339/2008 of the European Parliament and of the Council of 16 December 2008 establishing a European Training Foundation, OJ 2008 L354/82.

(Article 167(1) TFEU).[297] Article 167(2) TFEU enumerates the areas in which the European Parliament and the Council may adopt, under the ordinary legislative procedure, incentive measures, excluding any harmonization of the laws and regulations of the Member States, and the Council may adopt recommendations (Article 167(5) TFEU).[298] Examples of incentive measures include the programme 'Creative Europe' supporting European culture and creative sectors[299] and the setting up of the 'Cultural Capital of Europe' events.[300]

Cultural diversity. Union action in the cultural field is to remain complementary on the ground that each Member State wishes to conduct its own cultural policy with its own emphases. Accordingly, the conferral of clearly defined competences on the Union in regard to both culture and education also operates as a protection under Treaty law of the 'national identities' of the Member States (Article 4(2) TEU).

9.054

For some time now, the Court of Justice has recognized cultural aims as overriding or mandatory requirements in view of which Member States may place reasonable restrictions on the free movement of goods, persons, and services.[301] It has thus accepted the fact that Ireland required a Dutch lecturer to have a certificate of knowledge of Irish in order to teach art full time in Ireland, even though the teaching was conducted essentially in English.[302] This was not precluded by free movement of workers. The Court of Justice held that the EC Treaty 'does not prohibit the adoption of a policy for the protection and promotion of a language of a Member State which is both the national language and the first official language' and recognized the importance of education for the implementation of such a policy 'provided that the level of knowledge required is not disproportionate in relation to the objective pursued'.[303] Likewise, the Court accepted the objective pursued by a Member State to promote its official languages by means of an

---

[297] See de Witte, 'Market Integration and Cultural Diversity in EU Law', in Vadi and de Witte (eds), *Culture and International Economic Law* (Routledge, 2015), 193; Craufurd Smith, 'The Evolution of Cultural Policy in the European Union', in Craig and de Búrca, *The Evolution of EU Law* (OUP, 2011), 869; Ward, *The European Union and the Culture Industries: Regulation and the Public Interest* (Ashgate, 2008); Psychogiopoulou, *The Integration of Cultural Considerations in EU law and Policies* (Nijhoff, 2008); Craufurd Smith (ed.), *Culture and European Union Law* (OUP, 2004); Nettesheim, 'Das Kulturverfassungsrecht der Europäischen Union' (2002) JZ 157–66.

[298] In view of the need for the free expression of culture, the Union's action is not restricted to cultural expressions with a European dimension, see Britz, 'Die Freiheit der Kunst in der europäischen Kulturpolitik' (2004) EuR 1–26.

[299] Regulation (EU) 2021/818 of the European Parliament and of the Council of 20 May 2021 establishing the Creative Europe Programme (2021 to 2027), OJ 2021 L189/34, replacing Regulation (EU) No. 1295/2013 of the European Parliament and of the Council of 11 December 2013 establishing the Creative Europe Programme (2014 to 2020), OJ 2013 L347/221.

[300] Decision No. 445/2014/EU of the European Parliament and of the Council of 16 April 2014 establishing a Union action for the European Capitals of Culture for the years 2020 to 2033, OJ 2014 L132/1. See also (based on Article 352 TFEU) Council Regulation (EU) No. 390/2014 of 14 April 2014 establishing the 'Europe for Citizens' programme for the period 2014–2020, OJ 2014 L115/3, replaced by Regulation (EU) 2021/692 of the European Parliament and of the Council of 28 April 2021 establishing the Citizens, Equality, Rights and Values Programme and repealing Regulation (EU) No 1381/2013 of the European Parliament and of the Council and Council Regulation (EU) No 390/2014, OJ 2021 L156/1.

[301] See, for instance, paras 7-040 (goods), 7-072 (persons), and 7-092 (services), *supra*; de Witte, 'Cultural Policy Justifications', in Koutrakos, Nic Shuibhne, and Syrpis, *Exceptions from EU Free Movement Law: Derogation, Justification and Proportionality* (Hart Publishing, 2016), 131; Karydis, 'Le juge communautaire et la préservation de l'identité culturelle nationale' (1994) RTDE 551–60. However, the Court has clarified that Article 151 EC [*now Article 167 TFEU*] in itself is not to be regarded as a provision inserting into Union law a justification for national measures liable to hinder intra-Union trade (C-531/07, *LIBRO*, 2009, para. 151).

[302] C-379/87, *Groener*, 1989.

[303] Ibid., paras 19–21.

obligation to invest in films in one of these languages, even though such a measure may constitute an advantage for undertakings established in that Member State.[304] But when a Member State relies on the protection of national identity (Article 4(2) TEU) to promote the use of one or more official languages, such an objective does not justify restrictions on the free movement that go further than is necessary for attaining that objective (see para. 6-020, *supra*). The protection of an ethno-cultural minority (such as German-speakers in northern Italy) constitutes a legitimate aim, provided that it is not pursued in a disproportionate manner.[305]

IX. Public Health and Consumer Protection

9.055 Health policy. The provisions on public health introduced by the EU Treaty (and amended by the Treaty of Amsterdam) sees Union action as complementing national policies and as directed towards improving public health, preventing human illness and diseases, and obviating sources of danger to physical and mental health (Article 168(1), second subpara, TFEU).[306] In addition to the fight against major health scourges, such action is to cover promotion of research and health information and education and monitoring, early warning of and combating serious cross-border threats to health.

In the field of public health, the Union has competence only to carry out actions to support, coordinate, or supplement the actions of the Member States (Article 6(a) TFEU). However, the Treaties make an exception for 'common safety concerns in public health matters', which are, for the aspects defined by the TFEU, included within the general category of the Union's shared competences (Art. 4(2)(k) TFEU). Accordingly, the European Parliament and the Council may adopt harmonization measures in a number of fields to meet common safety concerns (Article 168(4) TFEU). This applies to (a) measures setting high standards of quality and safety of organs and substances of human origin, blood, and blood derivatives (although Member States are not precluded from maintaining or introducing more stringent measures); (b) measures in the veterinary and phytosanitary fields which have, as their direct object, the protection of public health; and (c) measures setting high standards of quality and safety for medicinal products and

---

[304] C-222/07, *UTECA*, 2009, paras 25–36.

[305] C-274/96, *Bickel and Franz*, 1998, paras 23–30 (discrimination where nationals of other Member States who do not reside in the Member State concerned are precluded from the right conferred on the minority to use their language in judicial proceedings); C-281/98, *Angonese*, 2000, paras 37–45 (discrimination where proof of bilingualism is conditional upon possession of a language diploma that may be obtained only in the national territory). For the situation of minorities under Union law, see also Ahmed, 'The Treaty of Lisbon and Beyond: The Evolution of the European Union Minority Protection?' (2013) ELRev 30–51; Ahmed, *The Impact of EU Law on Minority Rights* (Hart Publishing, 2011); von Arnauld, 'Minderheitenschutz im Recht der Europäischen Union' (2004) *A. Völkerr.* 111–41.

[306] See Ruijter, *EU Health Law & Policy: The Expansion of EU Power in Public Health and Health Care* (OUP, 2019); Klamert, 'Public Health Policy', in Hoffman, Rowe, and Türk (eds), *Specialized Administrative Law and Policy of the European Union* (OUP, 2018); Hervey and McHale, *European Union Health Law* (Cambridge University Press, 2015); Hancher and Sauter, *EU Competition and Internal Market Law in the Healthcare Sector* (OUP, 2012). See also Abaquesne de Parfourus, 'Breaking through the Foul and Ugly Mists of Vapours: Regulation of Alternative Tobacco and Related Products by the New TPD and Exercise of EU Competence' (2018) GLJ 1291–348; Walus, 'National Healthcare Planning and the Internal Market: A Conceptual View on the Impact of EU Law on Member States' Regulatory Autonomy in the Field of Healthcare' (2015) EJ Soc Sec 52–83; Davies, 'The Community's Internal Market-based Competence to Regulate Healthcare: Scope, Strategies and Consequences' (2007) MJECL 215–38; Sander, 'Europäischer Gesundheitsschutz als primärrechtliche Aufgabe und grundrechtliche Gewährleistung' (2005) ZEuS 253–71; Hatzopoulos, 'Is it Healthy to Have an EU Health Law?' (2005) ELRev 697–710; Hervey, 'Community and National Competence in Health after *Tobacco Advertising*' (2001) CMLRev 1421–46.

devices for medical use.[307] In this way, the Union has harmonized foodstuffs legislation and set up the European Food Safety Authority with the task of providing scientific advice and scientific and technical support for the Union's legislation and policies in all fields which have a direct or indirect impact on food safety.[308] Pursuant to that competence, the Union also established a European Medicines Agency and a European Centre for Disease Prevention and Control.[309] In other fields, the European Parliament and the Council are to adopt 'incentive measures'[310] under the ordinary legislative procedure 'excluding any harmonisation of the laws and regulations of the Member States' (Article 168(5) TFEU). The Council may also adopt recommendations by a qualified majority vote on a proposal from the Commission (Article 168(6) TFEU).[311] These instruments are to be used to coordinate the Member States' response to the COVID-19 pandemic, which has also triggered the Commission to submit proposals to strengthen the Union's general resilience to such health threats (creating a 'European Health Union').[312]

In liaison with the Commission, the Member States are to coordinate among themselves their health policies and programmes. To this effect, the Lisbon Treaty introduced, in the area of public health, an open method of coordination similar to that previously implemented in the area of employment (see para. 9-049, *supra*).

In taking such action, the Union must fully respect the responsibilities of the Member States for the definition of their health policy and for the organization and delivery of health

---

[307] See, e.g., (based on Article 168(4)(b) together with Article 114 TFEU) Regulation (EU) 2019/6 of the European Parliament and of the Council of 11 December 2018 on veterinary medicinal products, OJ 2019 L4/43; (based on Article 168(4)(c) together with Article 114 TFEU) Regulation (EU) 2020/1043 of the European Parliament and of the Council of 15 July 2020 on the conduct of clinical trials with and supply of medicinal products for human use containing or consisting of genetically modified organisms intended to treat or prevent coronavirus disease (COVID-19), OJ 2020 L231/12; Regulation (EU) 2017/745 of the European Parliament and of the Council of 5 April 2017 on medical devices, OJ 2017 L117/1; and Regulation (EU) 2017/746 of the European Parliament and of the Council of 5 April 2017 on in vitro diagnostic medical devices, OJ 2017 L117/176. Measures adopted under 168(4)(a) must not affect national provisions on the donation or medical use of organs and blood (Article 168(7) TFEU).

[308] Regulation (EC) No. 178/2002 of the European Parliament and of the Council of 28 January 2002 laying down the general principles and requirements of food law, establishing the European Food Safety Authority, and laying down procedures in matters of food safety, OJ 2002 L31/1 (adopted on the basis of Articles 37, 95, 133, and 152(4)(b) EC [*now Articles 31, 114, 207, and 168(4)(b) TFEU*]). See Szajkowska, 'The Impact of the Definition of the Precautionary Principle in EU Food Law' (2010) CMLRev 173–93; Beurdeley, 'La sécurité alimentaire au sein de l'Union européenne: un concept en gestation' (2002) RMCUE 89–103; Dehousse, Engelstadt, and Gevers, 'La sécurité alimentaire et le principe de la précaution' (2000) Stud Dipl 95–112. See also Regulation (EU) 2019/1381 of the European Parliament and of the Council of 20 June 2019 on the transparency and sustainability of the EU risk assessment in the food chain, OJ 2019 L231/1.

[309] Regulation (EC) No. 726/2004 of the European Parliament and of the Council of 31 March 2004 laying down Community procedures for the authorisation and supervision of medicinal products for human and veterinary use and establishing a European Medicines Agency, OJ 2004 L136/1; Regulation (EC) No. 851/2004 of the European Parliament and of the Council of 21 April 2004 establishing a European Centre for disease prevention and control, OJ 2004 L142/1.

[310] See, e.g., Regulation (EU) 2021/522 of the European Parliament and of the Council of 24 March 2021 establishing a Programme for the Union's action in the field of health ('EU4Health Programme') for the period 2021-2027, OJ 2021 L107/1, replacing Regulation (EU) No. 282/2014 of the European Parliament and of the Council of 11 March 2014 on the establishment of a third Programme for the Union's action in the field of health (2014–2020), OJ 2014 L86/1.

[311] e.g. Council Recommendation (EU) 2020/1475 of 13 October 2020 on a coordinated approach to the restriction of free movement in response to the COVID-19 pandemic, OJ 2020 L337/3; see also Council Recommendation of 30 November 2009 on smoke-free environments, OJ 2009 C296/4; Council Recommendation of 22 December 2009 on seasonal influenza vaccination, OJ 2009 L348/71.

[312] See the Commisson proposals of 11 November 2020 for a regulation on serious cross-border threats to health ((COM(2020)727) and for a reinforced role of the European Medicines Agency and the European Centre for Disease Prevention and Control.

services and medical care (Article 168(7) TFEU). These responsibilities include both the management of health services and medical care and the allocation of the resources assigned to them (ibid.). However, in the organization of their public health and social security systems, the Member States must comply with Union law, in particular the provisions of the Treaties on the freedoms of movement, which prohibit the Member States from introducing or maintaining unjustified restrictions on the exercise of those freedoms in the healthcare sector.[313] Nonetheless, in assessing whether Member States comply with Union law, account must be taken of the fact that a Member State may determine the level of protection which it wishes to afford to public health and the way in which that level is to be achieved.[314] Since the level of protection may vary from one Member State to another, Member States must be allowed the necessary discretion.[315] In this respect, a Member State may, for social reasons, give precedence to organizations working with volunteers if that contributes to objectives relating to solidarity and cost efficiency.[316]

According to Article 168(1) TFEU, all Union policies and activities are to ensure a high level of protection of human health. The Union may therefore adopt, under Articles 113 and 114 TFEU, measures which are designed to eliminate obstacles to the functioning of the internal market and, at the same time, aim to protect public health[317] (see para. 7-112 *et seq.*, *supra*).

9.056 **Consumer policy.** In order to promote the interests of consumers and to ensure a high level of consumer protection, the Union is to contribute to protecting the health, safety, and economic interests of consumers, as well as to promoting their right to information, education, and to organize themselves in order to safeguard their interests (Article 169(1) TFEU).[318] The means employed are harmonizing measures adopted pursuant to

---

[313] C-372/04, *Watts*, 2006, paras 92 and 146; C-531/06, *Commission v Italy*, 2009, paras 35 and 36.
[314] C-169/07, *Hartlauer*, 2009, para. 30; C-171/07 and C-172/07, *Apothekerkammer des Saarlandes*, 2009, paras 18–19; C-341/08, *Petersen*, 2010, para. 51; C-570/07 and C-571/07, *Blanco Pérez and Chao Gómez*, 2010, paras 43–4.
[315] C-169/07, *Hartlauer*, 2009, para. 30; C-171/07 and C-172/07, *Apothekerkammer des Saarlandes*, 2009, paras 18–19; C-341/08, *Petersen*, 2010, para. 51; C-570/07 and C-571/07, *Blanco Pérez and Chao Gómez*, 2010, paras 43–4.
[316] C-133/13, *Spezzino*, 2014, paras 58–62.
[317] See C-197/08, *Commission v France*, 2010, paras 51–2 (protection of public health taken into account in the adoption of fiscal legislation with respect to tobacco products); C-376/98, *Germany v European Parliament and Council*, 2000, para. 88 (by which, however, a general prohibition of all forms of tobacco advertising and sponsoring, even where the tobacco product was not named, was annulled on the ground that Articles 47(2), 55, and 95 EC did not afford a sufficient legal basis). See Hervey, 'Up in Smoke? Community (Anti-)Tobacco Law and Policy' (2001) ELRev 101–25. Articles 47(2), 55, and 95 EC [*now Articles 53, 62, and 114 TFEU*] were used as the legal basis for an adapted tobacco advertising ban in Directive 2003/33/EC of the European Parliament and the Council of 26 May 2003, OJ 2003 L152/16. The action for annulment brought by Germany against this second directive was dismissed by the Court (C-380/03, *Germany v European Parliament and Council*, 2006). Other examples are Directives 2001/82/EC and 2001/83/EC of the European Parliament and of the Council of 6 November 2001 on the Community code relating to veterinary medicinal products and on the Community code relating to medicinal products for human use (OJ 2001 L311/1 and L311/67, respectively); see also the above-mentioned measures adopted under Article 114 TFEU together with Article 168(4) TFEU.
[318] For general discussions, see, for instance, Howells, Wilhelmsson, and Twigg-Flesner, *Rethinking EU Consumer Law* (Routledge, 2017); Reich, Micklitz, Rott, and Tonner, *European Consumer Law* (Intersentia, 2014); Weatherill, *EU Consumer Law and Policy* (Edward Elgar Publishing, 2013); Stuyck, 'The Transformation of Consumer Law in the EU in the Last 20 Years' (2013) MJECL 385–402; De Witte and Vermeersch, *Europees consumentenrecht* (Maklu, 2004); Howells and Wilhelmsson, 'EC Consumer Law: Has it Come of Age?' (2003) ELRev 370–88. For more topical debates, see, for instance, Efroni, 'Gaps and Opportunities: The Rudimentary Protection for 'Data-paying Consumers' under New EU Consumer Protection Law' (2020) CMLRev 799–830; Helberger, Borgesius, and Reyna, 'The Perfect Match? A Closer Look at the Relationship between EU Consumer Law and Data Protection Law' (2017) CMLRev 1427–65.

Article 114 TFEU[319] and measures supporting, supplementing, and monitoring the policy pursued by the Member States, which the European Parliament and the Council are to adopt under the ordinary legislative procedure (Article 169(2) and (3) TFEU).[320] As far as harmonizing measures are concerned, reference must be made to a series of directives relating to unfair terms in consumer contracts, product liability, misleading and comparative advertising, electronic commerce, and alternative dispute resolution of consumer disputes.[321] As far as 'supporting' measures are concerned, Member States may maintain or introduce more stringent measures, provided that they are compatible with the Treaties and that the Commission is notified of them (Article 169(4) TFEU). However, the same is not necessarily true of measures adopted on the basis of Article 114 or 115 TFEU with respect to which the question whether they lay down full or merely minimum harmonization is to be determined for each individual measure on the basis of its wording, purpose, and structure[322] (see para. 7-112 *et seq.*, *supra*). Consumer protection requirements must be taken into account in defining and implementing other Union policies and activities (Article 12 TFEU).

---

[319] See Directive 2000/31/EC of the European Parliament and of the Council of 8 June 2000 on certain legal aspects of information society services, in particular electronic commerce, in the Internal Market ('Directive on electronic commerce'), OJ 2000 L178/1; Directive 2001/95/EC of the European Parliament and of the Council of 3 December 2001 on general product safety, OJ 2002 L11/4; Directive 2005/29/EC of the European Parliament and of the Council of 11 May 2005 concerning unfair business-to-consumer commercial practices in the internal market ('Unfair Commercial Practices Directive'), OJ 2005 L149/22; Directive 2006/114/EC of the European Parliament and of the Council of 12 December 2006 concerning misleading and comparative advertising, OJ 2006 L376/21; Directive 2008/48/EC of the European Parliament and of the Council of 23 April 2008 on credit agreements for consumers, OJ 2008 L133/66; Directive 2011/83/EU of the European Parliament and of the Council of 25 October 2011 on consumer rights, OJ 2011 L304/64; Directive 2013/11/EU of the European Parliament and of the Council of 21 May 2013 on alternative dispute resolution for consumer disputes ('Directive on consumer ADR'), OJ 2013 L165/63; Directive (EU) 2019/770 of the European Parliament and of the Council of 20 May 2019 on certain aspects concerning contracts for the supply of digital content and digital services, OJ 2019 L136/1; Directive (EU) 2019/771 of the European Parliament and of the Council of 20 May 2019 on certain aspects concerning contracts for the sale of goods, OJ 2019 L136/28; Directive (EU) 2020/1828 of the European Parliament and of the Council of 25 November 2020 on representative actions for the protection of the collective interests of consumers, OJ 2020 L409/1. See also Regulation (EU) No. 524/2013 of the European Parliament and of the Council of 21 May 2013 on online dispute resolution for consumer disputes ('Regulation on consumer ODR'), OJ 2013 L165/1. See also C-434/15, *Asociación Profesional Elite Taxi*, 2017, paras 34–42 (with case note by Finck (2018) CMLRev 1619–39); C-320/16, *Uber France*, 2018, paras 18–26; C-390/18, *Airbnb Ireland*, 2019, paras 42–68. For Directive 2005/29/EC, see Anagnostaras, 'The Unfair Commercial Practices Directive in Context: from Legal Disparity to Legal Complexity?' (2010) CMLRev 147–71. Directives were adopted on the basis of Article 100a EEC even before specific competence was introduced in the matter of consumer protection: see, for instance, Council Directive 93/13/EEC of 5 April 1993 on unfair terms in consumer contracts, OJ 1993, L95/29. See also the directives adopted by the Council pursuant to Article 100 EEC on liability for defective products (Directive 85/374/EEC of 25 July 1985, OJ 1985 L210/29, extended by Directive 1999/34/EC of the European Parliament and of the Council of 10 May 1999, OJ 1999 L141/20) and protection of the consumer in respect of contracts negotiated away from business premises (Directive 85/577/EEC of 20 December 1985, OJ 1985 L372/31).

[320] See Regulation (EU) 2021/690 of the European Parliament and of the Council of 28 April 2021 establishing a programme for the internal market, competitiveness of enterprises, including small and medium-sized enterprises, the area of plants, animals, food and feed, and European statistics (Single Market Programme) and repealing Regulations (EU) No 99/2013, (EU) No 1287/2013, (EU) No 254/2014 and (EU) No 652/2014, OJ 2021 L153/1 replacing Regulation (EU) No. 254/2014 of the European Parliament and of the Council of 26 February 2014 on a multiannual consumer programme for the years 2014–20, OJ 2014 L84/42.

[321] See the directives mentioned in n. 319, *supra*.

[322] See para. 7-110, *supra*.

X. Economic, Social, and Territorial Cohesion and Trans-European Networks

9.057 **Regional policies.** Economic, social, and territorial cohesion[323] aims to reduce disparities between the levels of development of the various regions and the backwardness of the least-favoured regions or islands, including rural areas (Article 174 TFEU). The Single European Act incorporated into the EC Treaty a title on economic and social cohesion; since the EU Treaty, cohesion has constituted an express objective for the Union (Article 3(3) TEU).[324]

The Union grants aid through the European Structural and Investment Funds: the European Agricultural Fund for Rural Development (EAFRD),[325] the European Social Fund (ESF),[326] the European Regional Development Fund (ERDF),[327] the European Investment Bank,[328] and other financial instruments such as the European Maritime and Fisheries Fund (EMFF)[329] (Article 175, first para. TFEU). In addition, the Cohesion Fund[330] provides a financial contribution to projects in the fields of the environment and trans-European networks in the area of transport infrastructure (Article 177, second para. TFEU), but only in Member States fulfilling the criteria set out in a Protocol annexed to the Treaties.[331] The European Parliament and the Council, acting in accordance with the ordinary legislative procedure, are responsible for defining the tasks, priority objectives, and the organization of the European Structural and Investment Funds, which may involve grouping the Funds, and for laying down the general rules for coordinating the Funds with one another and with the other financial instruments (Article 177, first para. TFEU).[332] The programmes

---

[323] Before the Lisbon Treaty, the EC Treaty referred to 'Economic and social cohesion'.
[324] For a survey, see Bachtler, Hardy, and Berkowitz, *EU Cohesion Policy: Reassessing Performance and Direction* (Routledge, 2017); Molle, *European Cohesion Policy* (Routledge, 2007); Bandara, 'La politique de cohésion dans l'union européenne et l'élargissement' (2006) RMCUE 177–88; David, 'Territorialer Zusammenhalt: Kompetenzzuwachs für die Raumordnung auf europäischer Ebene oder neues Kompetenzfeld?' (2003) DöV 146–55; Evans, *The EU Structural Funds* (OUP, 1999). See also Fedeli, *EU Regional and Urban Policy: Innovations and Experiences from the 2014-2020 Programming Period* (Springer, 2020).
[325] Para. 9-005, *supra*.
[326] Para. 9-047, *supra*.
[327] According to Article 176 TFEU, that fund is intended to help redress regional imbalances through participation in the development and structural adjustment of regions whose development is lagging behind and in the conversion of declining industrial regions. The European Parliament and the Council adopt implementing decisions relating to the Fund by the ordinary legislative procedure (Article 178, first para. TFEU). See Regulation (EU) No. 1301/2013 of the European Parliament and of the Council of 17 December 2013 on the European Regional Development Fund and on specific provisions concerning the Investment for growth and jobs goal, OJ 2013 L347/289.
[328] Paras 13-037–13-038, *infra*.
[329] Regulation (EU) No. 508/2014 of the European Parliament and of the Council of 15 May 2014 on the European Maritime and Fisheries Fund, OJ 2014 L149/1.
[330] Regulation (EU) No. 1300/2013 of the European Parliament and of the Council of 17 December 2013 on the Cohesion Fund, OJ 2013 L347/281.
[331] Protocol (No. 28), introduced by the EU Treaty and now annexed to the TEU and TFEU, on economic and social cohesion OJ 2016 C202/309) requires the Member State concerned to have a per capita GNP of less than 90 per cent of the Union average (which, up to 2004, limited qualifying Member States to Greece, Ireland, Portugal and Spain and, at present, to Bulgaria, Croatia, Cyprus, the Czech Republic, Estonia, Greece, Hungary, Latvia, Lithuania, Malta, Poland, Portugal, Romania, Slovakia, and Slovenia) and to have a programme for the fulfilment of the economic convergence criteria set out in Article 126 TFEU.
[332] See Regulation (EU) No. 1303/2013 of the European Parliament and of the Council of 17 December 2013 laying down common provisions on the European Regional Development Fund, the European Social Fund, the Cohesion Fund, the European Agricultural Fund for Rural Development, and the European Maritime and Fisheries Fund and laying down general provisions on the European Regional Development Fund, the European Social Fund, the Cohesion Fund, and the European Maritime and Fisheries Fund, OJ 2013 L347/320.

that are financed by the European Structural and Investment Funds are approved by the Commission and implemented by the Member States and their regions in shared management (see para. 20-008, *infra*). Amongst the conditions for the availability of the Funds is that the Member State concerned takes effective action to correct any excessive deficit or significant macro-economic imbalance determined by the Council in the economic governance process (see para. 9-036, *supra*). The Commission may propose to the Council to suspend either commitments or payments for that Member State, upon which the Council decides, as for other corrective action in the framework of economic governance, by 'reverse qualified majority'.[333]

If 'specific actions' prove necessary outside the Funds, the European Parliament and the Council may adopt them under the ordinary legislative procedure (Article 175, third para. TFEU). In this way, a Solidarity Fund has been set up, which can provide rapid assistance to Member States in the event of a major natural disaster,[334] as well as a European Globalisation Adjustment Fund for Displaced Workers (EGF), assisting Member States through support for workers made redundant and self-employed workers whose activity has ceased as a result of major structural changes due to globalization or a global financial and economic crisis.[335] In order to overcome the obstacles hindering cross-border and inter-regional cooperation, the Union has provided for the creation of 'European groupings of territorial cooperation' (EGTC), invested with legal personality and allowing national, regional and local authorities to carry out specific actions of territorial cooperation.[336] In 2015, the Commission launched an Investment Plan for Europe, encompassing a European Fund for Strategic Investments, which created a new framework for supporting investments by the European Investment Bank, on the basis of an agreement concluded between the Commission and the European Investment Bank.[337] In addition the Structural Reform Support Programme (see para. 9-065, *infra*) contributes to enhancing cohesion.

Trans-European networks. Since the EU Treaty, the Treaty provisions on 'trans-European networks' have supplemented the existing Union competence to promote economic and social cohesion. The Union is to contribute to the development of infrastructure networks in the areas of transport, telecommunications, and energy by promoting the interconnection and 'interoperability' of national networks and access to those networks.[338] Importance is attached to linking island, landlocked, and peripheral regions with the central regions of

9.058

---

[333] Ibid., Article 23(9) and (10). On the 'rule of law' conditionality, see para. 20-009.
[334] See Council Regulation (EC) No. 2012/2002 of 11 November 2002 establishing the European Union Solidarity Fund, OJ 2002 L311/3. This regulation is based on the third para. of Article 159 EC [*now Article 175 TFEU*] and Article 308 EC [*now Article 352 TFEU*] so as to make the regulation also applicable to candidate countries.
[335] Regulation (EU) 2021/691 of the European Parliament and of the Council of 28 April 2021 on the European Globalisation Adjustment Fund for Displaced Workers (EGF) and repealing Regulation (EU) No 1309/2013, OJ 2021 L153/48, replacing Regulation (EU) No. 1309/2013 of the European Parliament and of the Council of 17 December 2013 on the European Globalisation Adjustment Fund (2014–2020), OJ L2013 L34/855.
[336] Regulation (EC) No. 1082/2006 of the European Parliament and of the Council of 5 July 2006 on a European grouping of territorial cooperation (EGTC), OJ 2006 L210/19.
[337] Regulation (EU) 2015/1017 of the European Parliament and of the Council of 25 June 2015 on the European Fund for Strategic Investments, the European Investment Advisory Hub, and the European Investment Project Portal ('European Fund for Strategic Investments') OJ 2015 L169/1.
[338] Roggenkamp, 'Transeuropese netwerken. Op weg naar een communautair infrastructuurbeleid?' (1998) SEW 416–23.

the Union. The intention behind Union action is to help to attain the objectives of the single market and economic and social cohesion in such a way that not only economic operators but also communities and citizens benefit (Article 170 TFEU). Member States are to coordinate their policies among themselves, in liaison with the Commission (Article 171(2) TFEU). The European Parliament and the Council are to adopt guidelines covering the objectives, priorities, and broad lines of measures envisaged, identifying projects of common interest.[339] In addition, the Union is to adopt such (harmonization) measures as may prove necessary to ensure the interoperability of networks (Article 171(1) TFEU). Article 171 TFEU constitutes, together with Article 172 TFEU, the specific legal basis for such measures, even where they also cover objectives pursued by the single market.[340] These measures pertain, for example, to arranging for a '.eu' domain on the internet[341] or ensuring the interoperability of the European rail system.[342] The Union may also support projects of common interest financially supported by Member States and contribute, through the Cohesion Fund (para. 9-057, *supra*), to the financing of specific transport projects (Article 171(1) TFEU).[343] The guidelines and measures are drawn up under the ordinary legislative procedure (Article 172, first para. TFEU). Guidelines and projects of common interest that relate to the territory of a Member State require the approval of the Member State concerned (Article 172, second para. TFEU).

XI. Industry

9.059 **Competitiveness.** Article 173(1) TFEU lists aims for fostering the competitiveness of the Union's industry. The Member States are to consult each other to this effect and, where necessary, to coordinate their action, possibly at the initiative of the Commission (Article 173(2) TFEU). The Lisbon Treaty introduced here as well the 'open method of coordination', according to which the Commission may take initiatives to establish guidelines and indicators, organize the exchange of 'best practices' and prepare for periodic monitoring and evaluation. The Union endeavours to attain the objectives of improving the competitiveness of the Union's industry by means of policies and action based on other provisions of the Treaties.[344] The addition (by the EU Treaty) of a title 'Industry' to the Treaties did

---

[339] See the guidelines for trans-European networks or infrastructure established by Regulation (EU) No. 283/2014 of the European Parliament and of the Council of 11 March 2014, OJ 2014 L86/14 (telecommunications infrastructure); Regulation (EU) No. 347/2013 of the European Parliament and of the Council of 17 April 2013, OJ 2013 L115/39 (energy infrastructure); Regulation (EU) No. 1315/2013 of the European Parliament and of the Council of 11 December 2013, OJ 2013 L348/1 (transport network). The guidelines need not necessarily have been preceded by a separate measure adopted beforehand: C-22/96, *European Parliament v Council*, 1998, para. 34.

[340] C-271/94, *European Parliament v Council*, 1996, paras 13–35 (annulment of a decision based on Article 308 EC [*now Article 352 TFEU*]; the decision was subsequently replaced by a decision based on Article 156 EC, OJ 1996 L327/34).

[341] Regulation (EC) No. 733/2002 of the European Parliament and of the Council of 22 April 2002 on the implementation of the .eu Top Level Domain, OJ 2002 L113/1.

[342] See Directive (EU) 2016/797 of the European Parliament and of the Council of 11 May 2016 on the interoperability of the rail system within the European Union, OJ 2016 L138/44.

[343] For general rules for the granting of Union financial aid in the field of trans-European networks, see Regulation (EU) 2021/1153 of the European Parliament and of the Council of 7 July 2021 establishing the Connecting Europe Facility, OJ 2021 L249/38, replacing Regulation (EU) No. 1316/2013 of the European Parliament and of the Council of 11 December 2013 establishing the Connecting Europe Facility, OJ 2013 L348/129.

[344] See European Commission, *A New Industrial Strategy for Europe* COM(2020) 102. For an overview, see Jansen, *From Policy to Law? Industrial Policy under European Union law* (PhD KU Leuven, 2017); Adamsky, 'Europe's (Misguided) Construction of European Prosperity' (2013) CMLRev 47–85.

not confer on the Union competence to conduct its own industrial policy, but enabled the European Parliament and the Council to adopt, under the ordinary legislative procedure, 'specific measures' in support of action taken by the Member States (Article 173(3), first subpara. TFEU).[345] Union action in this field may not lead to the harmonization of the laws and regulations of the Member States (Article 173(3), first subpara. TFEU). The provisions on industry are thus among the areas where the Union may 'carry out actions to support, coordinate or supplement the actions of the Member States' (Article 6, sub b TFEU) (see para. 5-027, *supra*). Moreover, any Union measure may in no event lead to a distortion of competition or contain tax provisions or provisions relating to the rights and interests of employed persons (Article 157(3), second subpara. TFEU).

XII. Research and Technological Development and Space

Union support. Although the Union has long been providing support for research and technological development, the title 'Research and technological development' was introduced for the first time into the Treaties by the Single European Act. The Treaty of Lisbon supplemented these provisions with a legal basis which allows the Union to draw up a European space policy (Article 189 TFEU).

9.060

Title XIX deals with the Union's activities in this field with the objective of strengthening its scientific and technological bases by achieving a European research area in which researchers, scientific knowledge, and technology circulate freely, and encouraging it to become more competitive, including in its industry, while promoting all the research activities deemed necessary by virtue of other Chapters of the Treaties (Article 179 TFEU).[346] Action by the Union is simply to complement activities undertaken by Member States. It is to cover programmes fostering cooperation between undertakings, research centres, and universities, together with international cooperation, disseminating and optimizing the results of research, and stimulating the training and mobility of researchers (Article 180 TFEU).

The Commission is empowered to take any useful initiative to promote coordination of national policies and Union policy (Article 181 TFEU). Again, the Commission is to encourage peer review amongst Member States through the so-called 'open method of coordination', according to which the Commission may take initiatives to establish guidelines and indicators, organize the exchange of 'best practices' and prepare for periodic monitoring and evaluation (Article 181(2)TFEU)—a coordination now integrated in the European Semester process (see para. 9-039, *supra*). The European Parliament and the Council, acting under the ordinary legislative procedure, are to adopt multiannual framework programmes setting out all the activities of the Union (Article 182(1) TFEU). Currently, the Union is supporting research and innovation through the framework programme 'Horizon

[345] See Regulation (EU) 2021/690 of the European Parliament and of the Council of 28 April 2021 establishing a programme for the internal market, competitiveness of enterprises, including small and medium-sized enterprises, the area of plants, animals, food and feed, and European statistics (Single Market Programme) and repealing Regulations (EU) No 99/2013, (EU) No 1287/2013, (EU) No 254/2014 and (EU) No 652/2014, OJ 2021 L153/1, replacing Regulation (EU) No. 1287/2013 of the European Parliament and of the Council of 11 December 2013 establishing a Programme for the Competitiveness of Enterprises and small and medium-sized enterprises (COSME) (2014–2020), OJ 2013 L347/33; see also the Creative Europe Programme (see para. 9-053, *supra*).
[346] See European Commission, *A New ERA for Research and Innovation* COM(2020) 628.

330   OTHER AREAS OF UNION POLICY

Europe'.[347] The Council, acting in accordance with a special legislative procedure and after consulting the European Parliament, may then adopt specific programmes for the implementation of the framework programmes (Article 182(3) and (4) TFEU).[348] Other procedures apply where implementation is carried out by means of supplementary programmes in which only some Member States take part,[349] Union participation,[350] international cooperation,[351] or the creation of joint undertakings by the Union.[352]

The European Parliament and the Council, acting in accordance with the ordinary legislative procedure, are to establish the necessary measures to draw up a European space policy, which may take the form of a European space programme.[353] The Union's measures are to promote joint initiatives, support research and technological development, and coordinate the efforts needed for the exploration and exploitation of space (Article 189(1) and (2) TFEU).

The Union's competence for research and technological development and space is not included among the areas where the Union may take only 'coordinating, complementary or supporting action'. However, it follows from Article 4(3) TFEU that it was not the intention of the Treaty of Lisbon that the exercise by the Union of its competence should prevent the Member States from pursuing their own policy (see para. 5-026, *supra*). Measures adopted with regard to the establishment of a European space policy may not in any event lead to the harmonization of the laws and regulations of the Member States (Article 189(2) TFEU).

XIII. Environment and Energy

9.061   **Sustainable development.** Ever since the Single European Act, the Union has had specific competences with regard to environment policy under the title of the Treaties headed 'Environment'.[354] The aims of the Union's policy are to preserve, protect, and improve the

---

[347] Regulation (EU) 2021/695 of the European Parliament and of the Council of 28 April 2021 establishing Horizon Europe – the Framework Programme for Research and Innovation, laying down its rules for participation and dissemination, and repealing Regulations (EU) No 1290/2013 and (EU) No 1291/2013, OJ 2021 L170/1.

[348] See Council Decision (EU) 2021/764 of 10 May 2021 establishing the Specific Programme implementing Horizon Europe – the Framework Programme for Research and Innovation, and repealing Decision 2013/743/EU, OJ 2021 L167I/1. See also Council Regulation (Euratom) 2021/765 of 10 May 2021 establishing the Research and Training Programme of the European Atomic Energy Community for the period 2021-2025 complementing Horizon Europe – the Framework Programme for Research and Innovation and repealing Regulation (Euratom) 2018/1563, OJ 2021 L167I/81.

[349] Articles 184 and 188, second para. TFEU.

[350] Articles 185 and 188, second para. TFEU.

[351] Article 186 TFEU (see also para. 10-036, *infra*).

[352] Articles 187 and 188, first para. TFEU (para. 13-044, *infra*).

[353] See, e.g., Regulation (EU) 2021/696 of the European Parliament and of the Council of 28 April 2021 establishing the Union Space Programme and the European Union Agency for the Space Programme and repealing Regulations (EU) No 912/2010, (EU) No 1285/2013 and (EU) No 377/2014 and Decision No 541/2014/EU, OJ 2021 L170/69.

[354] For a discussion of environment policy, see Peeters and Eliantonio (eds), *Research Handbook on EU Environmental Law* (Edward Elgar Publishing, 2020); van Calster and Reins, *EU Environmental Law* (Edward Elgar Publishing, 2017); Krämer, *EU Environmental Law* (Sweet & Maxwell, 2016); Langlet and Mahmoudi, *EU Environmental Law and Policy* (OUP, 2016); Lee, *EU Environmental Law: Challenges, Change and Decision-making* (Hart Publishing, 2014); de Saedeleer, *EU Environmental Law and the Internal Market* (OUP, 2014). For the formal recognition of environmental protection as a Union objective, see para. 5-006, *supra*, and the first action programmes adopted in 1973 (OJ 1973 C112) in the form of a declaration or resolution of the Council and representatives of the Member State governments, meeting in the Council. As early as 2 April 1979, the Council adopted, pursuant to Article 235 EC [*now Article 352 TFEU*], Directive 79/409/EEC on the conservation of wild birds, OJ 1979 L103/1. For the development of Union powers, see Jans, 'Environmental Spill-overs into General Community

quality of the environment; protect human health; ensure prudent and rational use of natural resources; and promote an international approach to regional or worldwide environmental problems, in particular combating climate change (Article 191(1) TFEU). The policy aims at a high level of protection taking account of the diversity of situations in the various regions of the Union (Article 191(2), first subpara. TFEU).[355] The Treaties enumerate the principles on which the Union's environment policy is based: the precautionary principle; the principle of preventive action; environmental damage to be rectified as a priority at source; and 'the polluter should pay'.[356] Environmental requirements must be integrated into Union policies in other areas, in particular with a view to promoting sustainable development (Article 11 TFEU, see para. 5-007, *supra*).

Environment policy. The European Parliament and the Council, acting under the ordinary legislative procedure, are to decide what action is to be taken by the Union in order to achieve the objectives of the environment policy (Article 192(1) TFEU).[357] A powerful example is the scheme for greenhouse gas emission trading set up by the Union to fulfil the commitments of the Union and its Member States under the 1997 Kyoto Protocol to the United Nations Framework Convention on Climate Change, to reduce greenhouse gas emissions.[358] In the case of a number of matters, the Council is to take its decisions

9.062

---

law' (2008) 31 Fordham ILJ 1360–86; Stetter, 'Maastricht, Amsterdam and Nice: the Environmental Lobby and Greening the Treaties' (2001) E Env LRev 150–9; Bär and Klasing, 'Fit for Enlargement? Environmental Policy after Nice' (2001) E Env LRev 212–20; Scheuing, 'Regulierung und Marktfreiheit im Europäischen Umweltrecht' (2001) EuR 1–26; Van Calster and Deketelaere, 'Amsterdam, the Intergovernmental Conference and Greening the EC Treaty' (1998) E Env LRev 12–25; Lenaerts, 'The Principle of Subsidiarity and the Environment in the European Union: Keeping the Balance of Federalism' (1994) Fordham ILJ 846–95.

[355] Under Article 191(3) TFEU, the Union is to take account, *inter alia*, of environmental conditions in the various regions and the balanced development of the regions, together with the economic and social development of the Union as a whole. On the objectives of environmental policy, see, e.g., C-24/19, *A and Others*, 2020, para. 47.

[356] For the principle that environmental damage should be rectified at source and the polluter-pays principle: C-293/97, *Standley, Metson and Others*, 1999, paras 51–53 (testing Union law against these principles); C-175/98 and C-177/98, *Lirussi and Bizzaro*, 1999, para. 51; C-318/98, *Fornasar and Others*, 2000, para. 38; C-188/07, *Commune de Mesquer*, 2008, paras 64–89; C-378/08, *ERG and Others*, 2010, paras 52–70; C-543/13, *Fipa Group and Others*, 2015 (interpretation of Union law in the light of those principles). As established in Article 191 TFEU, the polluter-pays principle is directed at action at Union level and cannot be relied upon in order to exclude the application of national legislation where there is no Union legislation: C-378/08, *ERG and Others*, para. 46. For the precautionary principle, see para. 25-022. Article 191(3) TFEU refers to the process of weighing potential benefits and costs which must take place before the Union takes any decision in this field. See Bleeker, 'Does the Polluter Pay? The Polluter-Pays Principle in the Case Law of the European Court of Justice' (2009) E En Env LRev 289–306; Cheyne, 'The Precautionary Principle in EC and WTO Law: Searching for a Common Understanding' (2006) E Env LRev 257–77; De Sadeleer, *Les principes du pollueur-payeur, de prévention et de précaution* (Bruylant, 1999); Vandekerckhove, 'The Polluter Pays Principle in the European Community' (1993) YEL 201–62.

[357] See, e.g., Regulation (EU) 2021/783 of the European Parliament and of the Council of 29 April 2021 establishing a Programme for the Environment and Climate Action (LIFE), and repealing Regulation (EU) No 1293/2013, OJ 2021 L 172/53, replacing Regulation (EU) No. 1293/2013 of the European Parliament and of the Council of 11 December 2013 on the establishment of a Programme for the Environment and Climate Action (LIFE), OJ 2013 L347/185; Directive 2001/42/EC of the European Parliament and of the Council of 27 June 2001 on the assessment of the effects of certain plans and programmes on the environment, OJ 2001 L197/30; Directive 2004/35/EC of the European Parliament and of the Council of 21 April 2004 on environmental liability with regard to the prevention and remedying of environmental damage, OJ 2004 L143/56. Each successive amendment of the Treaty altered the procedure laid down in Article 175(1). In the version embodied in the EEC Treaty, all environmental measures required a Council decision taken by a unanimous vote after consultation of the European Parliament. After the EU Treaty, the cooperation procedure was applied, which was replaced by the co-decision procedure as a result of the Treaty of Amsterdam.

[358] Directive 2003/87/EC of the European Parliament and of the Council of 13 October 2003 establishing a scheme for greenhouse gas emission allowance trading within the Community, OJ 2003 L275/32. Under the EU Emissions Trading Scheme, Member States are required to draw up national allocation plans for each trading period setting out how many emission rights ('allowances') each installation will receive each year. Companies that keep their emissions below the level of their allowances can sell their excess allowances; those facing difficulty in

unanimously in accordance with a special legislative procedure and after consulting the European Parliament (Article 192(2) TFEU).[359] In addition, the European Parliament and the Council are to adopt general action programmes in accordance with the ordinary legislative procedure (Article 192(3) TFEU).[360] In the context of its policies, the Union cooperates with third countries and international organizations (Article 191(4) TFEU). Thus, the Union has become a party, with its Member States, to the 2015 Paris Agreement replacing the Kyoto Protocol.[361]

In principle, it is for the Member States to finance and implement the environment policy (Article 192(4) TFEU). If a measure based on Article 192(1) TFEU involves disproportionate costs for a given Member State, the Council may apply a temporary derogation or provide for financial support from the Cohesion Fund (Article 192(5) TFEU). Member States wishing to maintain or introduce more stringent measures may do so provided that they are compatible with the Treaties and notified to the Commission (Article 193 TFEU).[362] At the same time, harmonization measures are to include a safeguard clause allowing Member States to take provisional measures for non-economic environmental reasons, subject to a procedure of inspection by the Union (Article 191(2), second subpara. TFEU). Within the Union, the European Environmental Agency collects all useful scientific and technical data, and provides these to the Commission and the Member States.[363]

9.063 **Energy.** In a sense, energy has been a central feature of European integration from the outset: coal in the ECSC Treaty and nuclear energy in the EAEC Treaty.[364] Even where the

---

remaining within their allowance limit can take measures to reduce their emissions and/or buy extra allowances on the market. See on this Directive: C-127/07, *Arcelor Atlantique et Lorraine and Others*, 2008.

[359] These are: (a) provisions primarily of a fiscal nature; (b) measures affecting: town and country planning, quantitative management of water resources or affecting, directly or indirectly, the availability of those resources, land use, with the exception of waste management; (c) measures significantly affecting a Member State's choice between different energy sources and the general structure of its energy supply. The extension of the expression 'quantitative management of water resources' by the Treaty of Nice accords with the way in which the Court of Justice confined the areas under (b) to measures relating to the management of limited resources in its quantitative aspects: C-36/98, *Spain v Council*, 2001, paras 50–3. On the notion under (c) of 'significantly affect[ing] a Member State's choice between different energy sources and the general structure of its energy supply', see C-5/16, *Poland v European Parliament and Council*, 2018, paras 37–62. The Council may define (by a unanimous vote) such of those matters as may be decided on under the ordinary legislative procedure (Article 192(2), second subpara. TFEU). Article 192(2) TFEU applies 'without prejudice to Article 114', which may serve as the legal basis for Union measures intended (in part) to protect the environment (para. 5-018, *supra*).

[360] See the Commission Proposal for a Decision of the European Parliament and of the Council on a General Union Environment Action Programme to 2030, COM(2020)652 final, replacing Decision No. 1386/2013/EU of the European Parliament and of the Council of 20 November 2013 on a General Union Environment Action Programme to 2020 'Living well, within the limits of our planet', OJ 2013 L354/171. The measures necessary for the implementation of general action programmes are to be adopted by the procedure laid down in para. 1 or 2 of Article 192 TFEU, depending on the case (Article 192(3), second subpara. TFEU).

[361] Council Decision (EU) 2016/1841 of 5 October 2016 on the conclusion, on behalf of the European Union, of the Paris Agreement adopted under the United Nations Framework Convention on Climate Change, OJ 2016 L282/1.

[362] For a general discussion of the Member States' discretion, see Somsen, 'Discretion in European Community Environmental Law: An Analysis of ECJ Case Law' (2003) CMLRev 1413–53.

[363] Regulation (EC) No. 401/2009 of the European Parliament and of the Council of 23 April 2009 on the European Environment Agency and the European Environment Information and Observation Network, OJ 2009 L126/13.

[364] For the interaction between the Union's environmental and energy policies with the EAEC Treaty, see C-594/18 P, *Austria v Commission*, 2020, paras 39–43. For the relationship between EC and EAEC powers, see Trüe, 'Legislative Competences of Euratom and the European Community in the Energy Sector: The "Nuclear Package" of the Commission' (2003) ELRev 664–85.

Community did not have any specific competence relating to energy, national energy policies have been affected by numerous Union measures in the fields of agriculture, transport, and the environment and national energy markets have been harmonized and liberalized as part of the establishment of the internal market.[365]

Since the Treaty of Lisbon, the Union is endowed with specific competences in the field of energy. Union action is to ensure the functioning of the energy market and the security of energy supply in the Union;[366] promote energy efficiency and saving and the development of new and renewable forms of energy; and promote the interconnection of energy networks (Article 194(1) TFEU). In order to achieve those objectives, the European Parliament and the Council, acting in accordance with the ordinary legislative procedure, are to establish the necessary measures.[367] Such measures may not, however, affect the Member States' right to determine the conditions for exploiting their energy resources, their choice between different energy sources,[368] or the general structure of their energy supply (Art. 194(2), second subpara. TFEU).

XIV. Tourism and Civil Protection

Tourism and civil protection. Before the Lisbon Treaty, the Treaties referred to measures in the sphere of civil protection and tourism (see Article 3(u) EC) without containing any specific competence to lay down such measures. Nevertheless, various aspects of tourism had been the subject of harmonization measures adopted on the basis of Articles 114 and 352 TFEU (see para. 7-109, *supra*). As for civil protection, the Council had used Article 308 EC as the legal basis for setting up a mechanism for cooperation between the Member States and likewise for civil protection assistance interventions.[369]

9.064

The Treaty of Lisbon conferred on the Union a specific competence to lay down measures with respect to the tourism sector, in particular to promote the competitiveness of undertakings in that sector (Article 195 TFEU). It also created a specific competence for civil protection, which enables the Union to encourage cooperation between the Member States with a view to improving the effectiveness of systems for preventing and protecting against natural or man-made disasters (Article 196 TFEU). It is up to the European Parliament and the Council, acting in accordance with the ordinary legislative procedure, to establish the

---

[365] For this liberalization, see para. 9-020, *supra*. See already Council Decision 1999/21/EC, Euratom of 14 December 1998 adopting a multiannual framework programme for actions in the energy sector (1998–2002) and connected measures, OJ 1999 L7/16, together with specific programmes adopted on the basis of Article 308 EC Treaty [now Article 352 TFEU]. See Cameron, 'The Internal Market in Energy: Harnessing the New Regulatory Regime' (2005) ELRev 631–48.

[366] See Talus, *Introduction to EU Energy Law* (OUP, 2016); Delvaux, *EU Law and the Development of a Sustainable, Competitive and Secure Energy Policy: Opportunities and Shortcomings* (Intersentia 2013); Talus, *EU Energy and Policy: A Critical Account* (OUP, 2013); Johnston and Block, *EU Energy Law* (OUP, 2012) ; Baumann, 'Europe's Way to Energy Security: The Outer Dimension of Energy Security: From Power Politics to Energy Governance' (2010) E For Aff Rev 77–95; Haghigi, 'Energy Security and the Division of Competences Between the European Community and its Member States' (2008) ELJ 461–82.

[367] Where these measures are primarily of a fiscal nature, they are to be adopted by the Council in accordance with a special legislative procedure, that it to say, unanimously after consulting the European Parliament (Art. 194(3)).

[368] See C-594/18 P, *Austria v Commission*, 2020, para. 79.

[369] See Council Decision 1999/847/EC of 9 December 1999 establishing a Community action programme in the field of civil protection, OJ 1999 L327/53.

necessary measures (Articles 195(2) and 196(2) TFEU). In order to support the action by the Member States, and to facilitate the coordination thereof, a Union mechanism for civil protection has been established.[370] In the same way as civil protection, tourism is regarded as an area where the Union is competent to support, coordinate, or supplement the actions of the Member States, with the result that any harmonization of the laws and regulations of the Member States is ruled out (see para. 5-027, *supra*).

XV. Administrative Cooperation

9.065 **Implementing Union law.** Effective implementation of Union law by the Member States is essential for the proper functioning of the Union and is therefore regarded as being a matter of common interest. The Lisbon Treaty introduced a legal basis which enables the Union to support Member States' efforts to improve their administrative capacity to implement Union law (Article 197 TFEU).[371] In this connection, Article 197(2) mentions facilitating the exchange of information and exchanges of civil servants and supporting training schemes. The European Parliament and the Council, acting by means of regulations in accordance with the ordinary legislative procedure, are to establish the necessary measures (Article 197(2) TFEU). Thus, they set up a Structural Reform Support Programme, under which the Union may support Member States in institutional, administrative, and structural reforms in view of strengthening their administrations.[372] Again, this is a competence to support, coordinate, or supplement Member States' action, whereby any harmonization of the laws and regulations of the Member States is excluded (Articles 6(g) and 197(2) TFEU).

XVI. Implementation of the Solidarity Clause

9.066 **Solidarity clause.** In the wake of the terrorist attacks of 11 March 2004 in Madrid, the Heads of State or Government of the Member States adopted a declaration on combating terrorism[373] that referred to the solidarity clause then contained in Article I-43 of the EU Constitution, which was later taken over by Article 222 TFEU. Pursuant to that clause, the Union and the Member States are to act jointly in a spirit of solidarity if a Member State is the victim of a terrorist attack or of a natural or man-made disaster. To that end, the Member States are to coordinate their actions in the Council. The Council may have recourse to the structures developed under the common security and defence policy.[374] The

---

[370] Decision No. 1313/2013/EU of the European Parliament and of the Council of 17 December 2013 on a Union Civil Protection Mechanism, OJ 2013 L347/924, as amended by Regulation (EU) 2021/836 of the European Parliament and of the Council of 20 May 2021, OJ 2021 L185/1.

[371] Lafarge, 'Administrative Cooperation Between Member States and Implementation of EU Law' (2010) EPL 597–616.

[372] Regulation (EU) 2021/240 of the European Parliament and of the Council of 10 February 2021 establishing a Technical Support Instrument, OJ 2021 L 57/1, succeeding Regulation (EU) 2017/825 of the European Parliament and of the Council of 17 May 2017 on the establishment of the Structural Reform Support Programme for the period 2017 to 2020, OJ 2017 L129/1.

[373] See the Declaration annexed to the Conclusions of the European Council held in Brussels on 25 and 26 March 2004 (referring to then Article I-42 of the draft EU Constitution).

[374] Article 222(1) and (2) TFEU.

Union is to mobilize 'all the instruments at its disposal, including the military resources made available by the Member States'.[375] The Council, acting by qualified majority on a joint proposal by the Commission and the High Representative of the Union for Foreign Affairs and Security Policy, is to define the arrangements for the implementation of the solidarity clause.[376] The Lisbon Treaty incorporated Article 222 TFEU on the solidarity clause in Part Five of the TFEU on the Union's external action. However, it is clear that actions taken to prevent terrorist threats, to protect democratic institutions and the civilian population, and to assist a Member State in the event of a terrorist attack or natural or man-made disaster (see Article 222(1) TFEU) also have an 'internal' Union component.

---

[375] Article 222(1) TFEU.
[376] See Council Decision 2014/415/EU of 24 June 2014 on the arrangements for the implementation by the Union of the solidarity clause, OJ 2014 L192/53. Article 222(2) TFEU provides for the European Parliament only to be 'informed'. The Council is to decide unanimously where its decision has defence implications: see Article 222(3), first subpara. TFEU, in conjunction with Article 31(1) TEU.

10
External Action of the Union

I. General Provisions on the Union's External Action

10.001 **Principles and objectives.** The Union's action on the international scene is driven by the objectives set out in Article 3(5) TEU and the principles listed in Article 21(1) TEU: democracy, the rule of law, the universality and indivisibility of human rights and fundamental freedoms, respect for human dignity, the principles of equality and solidarity, and respect for the principles of the United Nations Charter and international law.[1] These principles have inspired the Union's own creation, development, and enlargement and the Union seeks to advance them in the wider world and to develop relations and build partnerships with third countries and international, regional, or global organizations sharing these principles (Article 21(1) TEU). Furthermore, in line with these principles, the Union's external action pursues the objectives listed in Article 21(2) TEU: (a) safeguarding its own values, fundamental interests, security, independence, and integrity;[2] (b) consolidating and supporting democracy, the rule of law,[3] human rights, and the principles of international law;[4] (c) preserving peace, preventing conflicts, and strengthening international security,[5] in accordance with the purposes and principles of the United Nations Charter, with the principles of the Helsinki Final Act, and with the aims of the Charter of Paris, including those relating to external borders;[6] (d) fostering the sustainable economic, social, and environmental development of developing countries, with the primary aim of eradicating poverty;[7] (e) encouraging the integration of all countries into the world economy,[8] including through the progressive abolition of restrictions on international trade; (f) helping develop international measures to preserve and improve the quality of the environment and the sustainable management of global natural resources, in order to ensure sustainable development;[9]

---

[1] e.g. C-72/15, *PJSC Rosneft Oil Company*, 2017, para. 112. See in general, Larik, *Foreign Policy Objectives in European Constitutional Law* (OUP, 2016).

[2] e.g. C-584/10 P, C-593/10 P, and C-595/10 P, *Commission, United Kingdom and Council v Kadi*, 2013, para. 103. More generally on the 'external' objectives, see Lonardo, 'Common Foreign and Security Policy and the EU's External Action Objectives: An Analysis of Article 21 of the Treaty on the European Union' (2018) EuConst 584–608.

[3] See also C-72/15, *PJSC Rosneft Oil Company*, 2017, para. 72, linking the objective in Article 21 TEU to the Union's values under Article 2 TEU. See also C-455/14 P, *H v Council*, 2016, para. 41.

[4] e.g. T-348/14, *Yanukovych v Council*, 2016, paras 88–102, affirmed by C-599/16 P, *Yanukovych v Council*, 2017, paras 58–62; see also C-263/14, *European Parliament v Council*, 2016. See further the principle set out in Article 3(5) TEU to contribute to the strict observance of international law, including the principles of the United Nations Charter, see C-363/18, *Organisation juive européenne*, 2019, para. 48. In that respect, see Aust, 'Eine völkerrechtsfreundliche Union? Grund und Grenze der Öffnung des Europarechts zum Völkerrecht' (2017) EuR 106–20.

[5] e.g. C-123/18 P, *HTTS Hanseatic Trade Trust & Shipping v Council*, 2019, para. 7.

[6] e.g. C-72/15, *PJSC Rosneft Oil Company*, 2017, para. 112.

[7] e.g. T-256/11, *Ezz v Council*, 2014, paras 44–6, affirmed by C-220/14 P, *Ezz v Council*, 2015, paras 41–8; see also C-377/12, *Commission v Council*, 2014, paras 35–7.

[8] e.g. Opinion 1/17, *Comprehensive Economic and Trade Agreement between Canada, of the one part, and the European Union and its Member States, of the other part (CETA)*, 2019, para. 84.

[9] e.g. Opinion 2/15, *Free Trade Agreement between the European Union and the Republic of Singapore*, 2017, paras 139–47: sustainable development forms an integral part of the common commercial policy.

(g) assisting populations, countries, and regions confronting natural or man-made disasters; and (h) promoting an international system based on stronger multilateral cooperation and good global governance.

External competences. The Union is to respect these principles and objectives in the development and implementation of the different areas of external action set out in Title I of the TEU and Part Five of the TFEU, and of the external aspects of its other policies. On the basis of these principles and objectives, the European Council is to identify the strategic interests and objectives of the Union (Article 22(1) TEU). The Council and the Commission, assisted by the High Representative of the Union for Foreign Affairs and Security Policy, have the task of ensuring consistency between the different areas of the Union's external action and between those areas and other Union policies (Article 21(3), second subpara. TEU).

10.002

In Part V of the TFEU relating to 'external action by the Union', the Lisbon Treaty has brought together most of the external competences of the Union. Besides provisions on, *inter alia*, the common commercial policy, development cooperation, and cooperation with third countries and humanitarian aid (Articles 206 to 214 TFEU), Part V contains a legal basis for the adoption of restrictive measures against third countries and non-State entities (Article 215 TFEU) and a solidarity clause (Article 222 TFEU; see para. 9-066, *supra*). However, the TFEU does not contain the provisions relating to the CFSP, which are found in Chapter 2 of Title V of the TEU (Articles 23to 46 TEU). The CFSP does not consist of a list of competences, but rather formulates aims and instruments with a view to pursuing a 'foreign policy' alongside and in conjunction with other external Union action.[10] Furthermore, the European Atomic Energy Community (EAEC) has a general power to conclude international agreements within the confines of the competences conferred on it by the EAEC Treaty (see Article 101, first para. EAEC).

In addition, a Union competence may have external dimensions when it applies to third country nationals or situations that are partly connected to third States. The free movement of goods thus extends to goods originating from third countries that are in circulation in the Union (Articles 28(2) TFEU and 29 TFEU); in the context of the free movement of persons, the Council takes measures vis-à-vis third-country nationals in respect of checks at the external borders, asylum, and immigration (Articles 77 to 80 TFEU). Likewise, the market organizations in the context of the common agricultural policy often contain, next to a regime relating to production, a regime for imports, in order to assure the stability of the market and the marketing of the Union production.[11] Moreover, in other areas, such as research and development or the environment, the Treaties expressly refer to the possibility for the Union to conclude international agreements with third countries and international organizations (Articles 186, second subpara. and 191(4), first subpara. TFEU).

In all these areas, the Union's foreign policy consists, on the one hand, of 'autonomous' acts having effects for third countries and their nationals and, on the other, of treaties and agreements concluded with third countries or international organizations ('conventional' acts). The Union may conclude an agreement with one or more third countries or international

---

[10] See, e.g., Opinion 2/15, *Free Trade Agreement between the European Union and the Republic of Singapore*, 2017, paras 139–47 (sustainable development recognised as an objective of the common commercial policy; Takács, Ott, and Dimopoulos (eds), 'Linking Trade and Non-commercial Interests: the EU as a Global Role Model?', CLEER Working Papers, 2013–2014.

[11] e.g. C-280/93, *Germany v Council*, 1994, para. 55.

organizations where the Treaties so provide or where the conclusion of an agreement is necessary in order to achieve, within the framework of the Union's policies, one of the objectives referred to in the Treaties, or is provided for in a legally binding Union act or is likely to affect common rules or alter their scope (Article 216 TFEU.).

II. The Common Commercial Policy

A. Scope

10.003 **Trade in goods.** Following the abolition of national customs duties and charges of equivalent effect in the early years of the Communities, the Council introduced a Common Customs Tariff and uniform customs rules for goods from, or destined for, third countries which are processed in the Union (see para. 7-025, *supra*). In order to prevent Member States from putting their own undertakings at an advantage or otherwise introducing inequalities in the trade field, the Treaties have provided for the internal market to be underpinned by a common commercial policy (Title II of Part Five of the TFEU). By way of measures required to be based on 'uniform principles', Article 207(1) TFEU mentions both autonomous measures (changes in tariff rates, achievement of uniformity in liberalization measures, export policy, and measures to protect trade) and the conclusion of tariff and trade agreements. This list is not exhaustive and does not rule out other methods of regulating external trade.[12] Article 207 TFEU constitutes the legal basis for autonomous and conventional acts of the Union which specifically relate to international trade, unless they are expressly contemplated by other provisions of the Treaties, such as Article 31 TFEU (customs tariff) or Articles 209 to 211 TFEU (development cooperation). A Union act specifically relates to international trade if it is essentially intended to promote, facilitate, or govern trade and has direct and immediate effects on trade in the products concerned.[13] As the common commercial policy must take the general objectives of the Union's external action into account, it encompasses provisions that make trade dependent on the respect of sustainability requirements (e.g. relating to social protection of workers or environmental protection).[14]

10.004 **Trade in services and intellectual property.** International trade in services is gradually accounting for a greater share than trade in goods. When harmonizing the conditions for the free movement of services and/or the freedom of establishment, the Union often regulates the status of natural and legal persons who are subjects of third countries as well. In addition, the status of subjects of the Union in third countries and the status of the subjects of third countries in the Union is often the subject matter of international agreements concluded by the Union with third countries. The Treaty of Nice expanded

---

[12] Opinion 1/78, *International Agreement on Natural Rubber*, 1979, para. 45.
[13] C-347/03, *Regione autonoma Friuli-Venezia Giulia*, 2005, para. 75; C-411/06, *Commission v European Parliament and Council*, 2009, para. 71.
[14] See, e.g., Opinion 2/15, *Free Trade Agreement between the European Union and the Republic of Singapore*, 2017, paras 139–66. In addition, fundamental rights can be indirectly protected through trade agreements, see Depaigne, ''Protecting Fundamental Rights in Trade Agreements between the EU and Third Countries' (2017) EL Rev 562–76.

the scope of the common commercial policy to agreements in the fields of trade in services and the commercial aspects of intellectual property.[15] Since the Lisbon Treaty, Article 207(1) TFEU confirms that the common commercial policy covers the conclusion of tariff and trade agreements relating to both trade in goods and services, and the commercial aspects of intellectual property,[16] adding the possibility to conclude such agreements relating to 'foreign direct investment'.[17] As the protection of foreign direct investment largely takes the form of various forms of investor–state dispute settlement, the Union is also competent to provide for mechanisms in this field, provided they are compatible with the autonomy of the Union legal order[18] and respect the competences of the Member States in this matter.[19]

According to Article 207(5) TFEU, international agreements relating to services in the transport sector do not come under the common commercial policy, but remain subject to the provisions of the Treaties relating to transport.[20]

Exclusive competence. The delimitation of the common commercial policy is of great importance for the external policy of the Union institutions and the Member States. First, the European Parliament and the Council adopt measures under the common commercial policy in accordance with the ordinary legislative procedure, which implies that the Council decides by qualified majority (Article 207(2) TFEU).[21] Only in respect of agreements in the areas of trade in services, the commercial aspects of intellectual property, and foreign direct investment does Article 207 TFEU provide for exceptions. In those areas the Council decides by unanimity where such agreements include provisions for which unanimity is required for the adoption of internal rules (Article 207(4), second subpara. TFEU)[22].

10.005

---

[15] See Opinion 1/08, *General Agreement on Trade in Services*, 2009, para. 119. See Hermann, 'Common Commercial Policy After Nice: Sisyphus Would Have Done a Better Job' (2002) CMLRev 7–29; Krenzler and Pitschas, 'Progress or Stagnation?: The Common Commercial Policy After Nice' (2001) E For Aff Rev 291–313 (for the German version, see (2001) EuR 442–61); Vincent, 'Les relations entre l'Union européenne et l'Organisation mondiale du commerce: du nouveau pour le praticien?' (2001) JTDE 105–10; Neframi, 'La politique commerciale commune selon le traité de Nice' (2001) CDE 605–46; Grard, 'La condition internationale de l'Union européenne après Nice' (2000) RAE 374–88).

[16] This only concerns arrangements in respect of intellectual property that have a specific link to international trade, such as the TRIPS agreement; see C-414/11, *Daiichi Sankyo*, 2013, paras 52–61; C-389/15, *Commission v Council*, 2017, paras 45–76. See in general, Dimopoulos, 'The Effects of the Lisbon Treaty on the Principles and Objectives of the Common Commercial Policy' (2010) E For Aff Rev 153; Kaddous, 'The Transfomation of the EU Common Commercial Policy', in Eeckhout and López-Escudero (eds), *The European Union's External Action in Times of Crisis* (Hart Publishing, 2016) 429.

[17] This does not cover portfolio investments: Opinion 2/15, *Free Trade Agreement between the European Union and the Republic of Singapore*, 2017, paras 81–4. These fall within the scope of the free movement of capital (Article 63 TFEU), which is not covered by the exclusive competences of the Union: ibid., paras 227–38.

[18] Opinion 1/17, *Comprehensive Economic and Trade Agreement between Canada, of the one part, and the European Union and its Member States, of the other part (CETA)*, 2019, paras 106–19.

[19] Opinion 2/15, *Free Trade Agreement between the European Union and the Republic of Singapore*, 2017, paras 285–304. A regime, which removes disputes from the jurisdiction of the courts of the Member States, cannot be established without the Member States' consent.

[20] Article 207(5) TFEU refers to Title VI of Part Three of the TFEU and Article 218 TFEU. This exception confirms the case law of the Court of Justice in Opinion 1/94: Opinion 1/94, *Agreement establishing the World Trade Organisation*, 1994, paras 48–9. Commercial policy measures may concern transport services if that aspect constitutes a necessary ancillary aspect of those measures (ibid., para. 51) and hence it is not required that the agreement concerned relates exclusively or predominantly to trade in transport services (Opinion 1/08, *General Agreement on Trade in Services*, 2009, para. 163).

[21] Before the Lisbon Treaty, these measures were also adopted by the Council by a qualified majority vote, but without any involvement of the European Parliament (see Article 133(2) TFEU).

[22] A comparison with Article 133(5) EC shows that, since the Lisbon Treaty, unanimity is no longer required solely because the Union seeks to conclude an agreement in an area where it has not yet adopted internal measures

Second, the common commercial policy is vested exclusively in the Union and therefore excludes in principle any national measures from the outset (Article 3(1) TFEU).[23]

Even before the Lisbon Treaty, it was established case law that the common commercial policy—at least as regards goods[24]—constitutes an area of exclusive Union competence.[25] Until the Lisbon Treaty, Union competence in respect of agreements on trade in services and the commercial aspects of intellectual property was not exclusive.[26] The Lisbon Treaty has, however, provided the Union with exclusive competence in respect of trade in goods and services,[27] as well as for the commercial aspects of intellectual property rights.[28] Moreover, it conferred competence on the Union in respect of foreign direct investment, an area in which the Member States used to be very active on the international level.[29] Nevertheless, the Court of Justice has acknowledged that there are situations in which Member States are entitled to take part in the negotiation and conclusion of a trade agreement alongside the Union.[30] The Member States may participate in an agreement where financing constitutes an essential element of the scheme established thereby and is to be borne out of their budgets.[31] Furthermore, national commercial policy measures are permissible by virtue of a 'specific authorization' of the Union (see para. 5-024, *supra*). In its Opinion on the EU–Singapore free trade agreement the Court has clarified that the competence to conclude an agreement is also shared with the Member States when the agreement establishes a dispute settlement mechanism on the basis of which disputes may be subtracted from the jurisdiction of the judiciary of the Member States.[32]

---

or where a 'horizontal' agreement is involved. For the scope of Article 133(5) and (6) EC, see Opinion 1/08, *General Agreement on Trade in Services*, 2009, paras 130–50.

[23] See, e.g., C-305/17, *FENS*, 2018, paras 49–51: Member States do not have any power allowing them unilaterally to introduce charges having an effect equivalent to customs duties on exports to third countries.

[24] This included agreements on cross-border trade in services and protection against the import of counterfeit goods.

[25] Opinion 1/75, *Draft Understanding on a Local Cost Standard drawn up under the auspices of the OECD*, 1975.

[26] Opinion 1/08, *General Agreement on Trade in Services*, 2009.

[27] Opinion 2/15, *Free Trade Agreement with Singapore*, 2017, paras 33–7; C-137/12, *Commission v Council*, 2013, paras 51–77.

[28] C-389/15, *Commission v Council*, 2017, paras 45–77. International commitments concerning intellectual property entered into by the European Union fall within the common commercial policy if they display a specific link with international trade in that they are essentially intended to promote, facilitate, or govern such trade and have direct and immediate effects on it. See also, Opinion 2/15, *Free Trade Agreement with Singapore*, 2017, para. 112; C-414/11, *Daiichi Sankyo*, 2013, paras 49–55. For a measure relating to intellectual property rights that does not fall within the scope of the commercial policy, see Opinion 3/15, *Marrakesh Treaty to Facilitate Access to Published Works for Persons who are Blind, Visually Impaired or Otherwise Print Disabled*, 2017, paras 60–101.

[29] Hence the transitional regime provided for in Regulation (EU) No. 1219/2012 of the European Parliament and of the Council of 12 December 2012 establishing transitional arrangements for bilateral investment agreements between Member States and third countries, OJ 2012 L351/40.

[30] Member States are also entitled to continue negotiations which they started at a time when they still had competence in the relevant field where a new distribution of competences as between the Union and the Member States threatens to jeopardize the successful outcome of the negotiations (22/70, *Commission v Council*, 1971, paras 86–90) or where their participation is required in order to secure the Union's participation in the relevant agreement (3, 4, and 6/76, *Kramer*, 1976, paras 34–44/45).

[31] Opinion 1/78, *International Agreement on Natural Rubber*, 1979, para. 60.

[32] Opinion 2/15, *Free Trade Agreement between the European Union and the Republic of Singapore*, 2017, paras 290–2.

B. Autonomous measures

Import and export regime. Alongside the Common Customs Tariff, the Council has adopted common rules for imports[33] and exports.[34] **10.006**

Initially, the import rules allowed Member States to maintain quantitative restrictions in respect of some products. Since 1994 imports have been liberalized and only the Union may take supervisory and safeguard measures. The general import rules do not apply to textile products from third countries where imports come under a specific import regime.[35] In addition, since 1971 the Council grants by regulation general tariff preferences for certain industrial goods, textile products, and agricultural products originating from developing countries; in this manner the Union seeks to expand the export revenue of those countries.[36] The tariff preferences are made conditional upon respect for human rights.[37] The beneficiary countries have to comply with the principles laid down in human rights and labour rights conventions listed in an annex to the regulation.[38] A special import regime has been introduced in order to allow manufacturers to bring certain key medicines onto the market only in developing countries at prices lower than those in developed countries. Under this regime, the import of such 'tiered priced' products into the Union is prohibited.[39]

The Union export rules provide that, in principle, exports to third countries are free. Therefore, Member States do not have any power allowing them unilaterally to introduce charges having an effect equivalent to customs duties on exports to third countries.[40] However, Union export rules do allow Member States to apply restrictions in their trade relations with third countries in order to protect the interests listed in Article 36 TFEU justifying restrictions on intra-Union trade in goods.[41] Although the Member States have a degree of discretion, for instance in assessing a risk to their national security, such restrictions on freedom of exportation may not exceed what is appropriate and necessary in order to protect the interests in question.[42] A Member State may no longer rely on this exception if

---

[33] See Regulation (EU) 2015/478 of the European Parliament and of the Council of 11 March 2015 on common rules for imports, OJ 2018 L83/16 (replacing Council Regulation (EC) No. 260/2009 of 26 February 2009 on the common rules for imports, OJ 2009 L84/1, itself replacing Council Regulation (EC) No. 3285/94 of 22 December 1994, OJ 1994 L349/53).

[34] See Regulation (EU) 2015/479 of the European Parliament and of the Council of 11 March 2015 on common rules for exports, 2015 OJ L83/34 (replacing Council Regulation (EC) No.1061/2009 of 19 October 2009 establishing common rules for exports, OJ 2009 L291/1, itself replacing Council Regulation (EEC) No. 2603/69 of 20 December 1969 establishing common rules for exports, OJ 1969 English Special Edition (II) 590).

[35] Regulation (EU) 2015/936 of the European Parliament and of the Council of 9 June 2015 on common rules for imports of textile products from certain third countries not covered by bilateral agreements, protocols, or other arrangements, or by other specific Union import rules, OJ 2015 L160/1.

[36] Regulation (EU) No. 978/2012 of the European Parliament and of the Council of 25 October 2012 applying a scheme of generalized tariff preferences, OJ 2012 L303/1.

[37] See, e.g., Council Regulation (EC) No. 552/97 of 24 March 1997 temporarily withdrawing access to generalized tariff preferences from the Union of Myanmar, OJ 1997 L85/8 (on account of the systematic use of forced labour in Myanmar (Burma)), repealed by Regulation (EU) No. 607/2013 of the European Parliament and of the Council of 12 June 2013, OJ L181/13, as reports indicated that the abuses were no longer widespread; Council Regulation (EC) No. 1933/2006 of 21 December 2006 temporarily withdrawing access to the generalized tariff preferences from the Republic of Belarus, OJ 2006 L405/35 (still in force).

[38] See Article 19(1)(a) of Regulation 978/2012. Countries wishing to benefit from the more attractive GSP+ status, must comply with additional conditions.

[39] Regulation (EU) 2016/793 of the European Parliament and of the Council of 11 May 2016 to avoid trade diversion into the European Union of certain key medicines, OJ 2016 L135/39..

[40] C-305/17, *FENS*, 2018, paras 49–51.

[41] Regulation (EU) 2015/478 (n. 33, *supra*), Articles 1 and 24(2).

[42] C-70/94, *Werner*, 1995, paras 8–29; C-83/94, *Leifer*, 1995, paras 7–30 (dual-use goods).

the necessary protection of the interests in question is already ensured by a Union measure (e.g. a measure imposing sanctions).[43] At the same time, Member States must place trust in each other as to export checks made by other Member States and, where necessary, cooperate with other Member States and the Commission.[44] As far as goods which may be used for both civil and military purposes (dual-use goods) are concerned, the Council has adopted Union rules on such export checks.[45]

Turning to agricultural products, account must be taken of the instruments provided for under the common agricultural policy (see para. 9-003 *et seq.*, *supra*).

10.007 **Protective measures.** In accordance with the rules agreed in the context of GATT and of the WTO, the Union legislature has drawn up instruments with a view to taking protective measures in respect of dumped or subsidized imports: products which are imported into the Union for an export price below their normal value (dumping) or whose export is subsidized in the country of origin, may have an anti-dumping or countervailing duty imposed on them where the marketing of the products concerned causes producers in the Union to suffer injury.[46] The Commission investigates whether dumping or subsidies are involved, together with the question of injury, and may impose a provisional duty where the Union interest so requires. Subsequently, the Council may impose a definitive duty within a specific time-limit.[47] If necessary, the Union may also initiate dispute settlement procedures, notably within the framework of the World Trade Organization. In 2019, the Union established a framework for the screening of foreign direct investments into the Union likely to affect security or public order, which includes cooperation between the Member States and the possibility for the Commission to issue an opinion on such investments.[48]

---

[43] C-124/95, *Centro-Com*, 1997, para. 46.

[44] Ibid., paras 49 and 52.

[45] Council Regulation (EC) No. 428/2009 of 5 May 2009 setting up a Community regime for the control of exports, transfer, brokering, and transit of dual-use items, OJ 2009 L134/1, see previously, Council Regulation (EC) No. 1334/2000 of 22 June 2000 setting up a Community regime for the control of exports of dual-use items and technology, OJ 2000 L159/1. See Hohmann, 'Neufassung der Dual-Use Verordnung: Änderung für die Exportwirtschaft und für global agierende Dienstleistungsanbieter' (2002) EWS 70–76; Karpenstein, 'Die neue Dual-Use Verordnung' (2000) EuZW 677–80; Koutrakos, 'The Reform of Common Rules on Exports of Dual-Use Goods under the Law of the European Union' (2000) EJ L Ref 167–89. Previously, there was an 'integrated regime' consisting of a CFSP decision and an EC regulation (see Council Decision 94/942/CFSP of 19 December 1994 on the joint action adopted by the Council concerning the control of exports of dual-use goods, OJ 1994 L367/8 and Council Regulation (EC) No. 3381/94 of 19 December 1994 setting up a Community regime for the control of exports of dual-use goods, OJ 1994 L367/1); before that, such goods came within the general derogation clause of the Union export rules.

[46] Regulation (EU) 2016/1036 of the European Parliament and of the Council of 8 June 2016 on protection against dumped imports from countries not members of the European Union, OJ 2016 L176/21; Regulation (EU) 2016/1037 of the European Parliament and of the Council of 8 June 2016 on protection against subsidized imports from countries not members of the European Union, OJ 2016 L176/55. See, previously, Council Regulation (EC) No. 1225/2009 of 30 November 2009 on protection against dumped imports from countries not members of the European Community, OJ 2009 L343/51 and Council Regulation (EC) No. 597/2009 of 11 June 2009 on protection against subsidized imports from countries not members of the European Community, OJ 2009 L188/93. See Van Bael and Bellis, *EU Anti-dumping and Other Trade Protections* (Kluwer Law International, 2019).

[47] Articles 7 and 9 of Regulation (EU) 2016/1036 (see n. 46, *supra*). Where the import of particular products is unnecessarily restricted by a combination of anti-dumping measures or anti-subsidy measures with safeguard tariff measures which may be imposed under Regulation (EU) 2015/755 of the European Parliament and of the Council of 29 April 2015 on common rules for imports from certain third countries (OJ 2015 L123/33) and Regulation 2015/478 (n. 33, *supra*) in order to obtain protection against sharply increased imports, the Council, acting by simple majority, may adjust the measures in question by virtue of Regulation (EU) 2015/477 of the European Parliament and of the Council of 11 March 2015 on measures that the Union may take in relation to the combined effect of anti-dumping or anti-subsidy measures with safeguard measures, OJ 2015 L83/11.

[48] Regulation (EU) 2019/452 of the European Parliament and of the Council of 19 March 2019 establishing a framework for the screening of foreign direct investments into the Union, OJ 2019 L79I/1.

C. Trade agreements and cooperation agreements

Bilateral agreements. As a major economic power, the Union has trade relations with most countries in the world and makes use, to this end, of the competences conferred on it by Article 207 TFEU as well as Articles 217 and 352 TFEU. A variety of agreements (trade agreements, free-trade agreements, cooperation agreements, association agreements[49]) often give rise to lasting cooperation, which is administered by bilateral cooperative bodies ('joint committees' or 'joint commissions'). Increasingly, 'cooperation agreements' have been concluded, which go beyond commercial cooperation, as they are also designed to secure economic cooperation as well as 'partnership and cooperation agreements', which couple economic issues with political commitments. Since the 1990s, commitments to respect human rights are thus included in free trade agreements or in the political framework agreements to which such trade agreements are linked (see also para. 10-022, *infra*). The Union has concluded trade and cooperation agreements with the Central and Eastern European countries[50] and some republics of the former Soviet Union;[51] with South Africa,[52] Australia, and New Zealand;[53] and with most countries in Asia[54] and Latin

10.008

---

[49] For association agreements concluded pursuant to Article 217 TFEU, see para. 10-014 *et seq.*) For an overview, see Dony, 'Quel Avenir Pour la Politique Commerciale de l'Union Européenne' (2017) RTDE 189; Kuijper, 'Post-CETA: How We Got There and How to Go On' (2017) RTDE 181.

[50] Trade and cooperation agreements were concluded with Hungary (26 September 1988, OJ 1988 L327/2), Poland (19 September 1989, OJ 1989 L339/2), the Soviet Union (19 December 1989, OJ 1990 L68/3), Czechoslovakia (7 May 1990, OJ 1990 L291/29), Bulgaria (8 May 1990, OJ 1990 L291/8), Romania (22 October 1990, OJ 1991 L79/13), Albania (11 May 1992, OJ 1992 L343/1), Estonia (11 May 1992, OJ 1992 L403/2), Latvia (11 May 1992, OJ 1992 L403/11), Lithuania (11 May 1992, OJ 1992 L403/2), and the former Yugoslav Republic of Macedonia (29 April 1997, OJ 1997 L348/2). As from 1991, the agreements with central and south-eastern European countries were replaced by association agreements preparing for Union membership (see para. 10-017, *infra*).

[51] See the partnership and cooperation agreements concluded with Russia (OJ 1997 L327/3), Ukraine (OJ 1998 L49/3), Moldova (OJ 1998 L181/3), Kazakhstan (OJ 1999 L196/3), Kyrgyzstan (OJ 1999 L196/48), Georgia (OJ 1999 L205/3), Uzbekistan (OJ 1999 L229/3), Armenia (OJ 1999 L239/3), Azerbaijan (OJ 1999 L246/3), and Tadjikistan (OJ 2009 L350/3). Agreements with Belarus and Turkmenistan have not yet been ratified by the Union, though an interim agreement is in place with Turkmenistan (OJ 2011 L80/1). With some of these states the original agreement has been replaced by enhanced agreements; see Kazakhstan (OJ 2016 L29/3), or even association agreements as with Georgia, Moldova, and Ukraine (see para. 10-018, *infra*).

[52] Cooperation Agreement with the Republic of South Africa of 10 October 1994, OJ 1994 L341, replaced by the association agreement 'on trade, development and cooperation' of 11 October 1999 (OJ 1999 L311/3), concluded by Council Decision 2004/441/EC of 26 April 2004 (OJ 2004 L127/109). Currently, South Africa has concluded an economic partnership agreement together with other countries of the Southern African Development Community, see para. 10-019, *infra*.

[53] Framework Agreement with Australia of 7 August 2017 (OJ 2017 L237/) and Partnership Agreement on Relations and Cooperation with New Zealand (OJ 2016 L321/1). With each country negotiations have started in view of establishing a free trade agreement.

[54] See the agreements on commercial and economic cooperation of 21 May 1985 with China (OJ 1985 L250/2) (preceded by a 'classical' trade agreement) and of 16 June 1992 with Mongolia (OJ 1993 L41/46); the cooperation agreements of 7 March 1980 with the member countries of the Association of South-East Asian Nations (ASEAN: Indonesia, Malaysia, the Philippines, Singapore, and Thailand), OJ 1980 L144/2; accession of Brunei: OJ 1985 L81/2; extension to Vietnam: OJ 1999 L117/30), of 15 June 1988 with the countries party to the Charter of the Cooperation Council for the Arab States of the Gulf (United Arab Emirates, Bahrein, Saudi Arabia, Oman, Qatar, and Kuwait), OJ 1989 L54/3), of 15 June 1992 with Macao (OJ 1992 L404/27), of 20 December 1993 with India (OJ 1994 L223/24), of 18 July 1994 with Sri Lanka (OJ 1995 L85/33), of 20 November 1995 with Nepal (OJ 1996 L137/15), of 29 April 1997 with Laos (OJ 1997 L334/14) and Cambodia (OJ 1997 C107/7), of 25 November 1997 with Yemen (OJ 1998 L72/18, replacing the agreement of 9 October 1984, OJ 1985 L26/2) and of 24 November 2001 with Pakistan (OJ 2004 L378/22), replacing the agreement of 23 July 1985, OJ 1986 L108/2). See also the free trade agreements with South Korea (OJ 2011 L127/6, following on the framework agreement concluded on 28 October 1996, OJ 2001 L90/45, since succeeded by a new framework agreement, OJ 2013 L20/2), with Singapore (OJ 2019 L294/1), and with Vietnam (OJ 2020 L186/6, replacing the cooperation agreement of 17 July 1995, OJ 1996 L136/29). On 9 November 2009, a Partnership and Cooperation Agreement was signed with Indonesia, OJ 2014 L125/

America.[55] Initially, such agreements were consistently concluded under Articles 133 and 308 EC [*now Articles 207 and 352 TFEU*]. Since the creation of specific legal bases for development cooperation (Article 209 TFEU) and for economic, financial, and technical co-operation (Article 212 TFEU), it became possible also to conclude agreements on those legal bases in combination with the common commercial policy (see para. 10-024, *infra*). A number of other Treaty provisions formed, in conjunction with Article 207 TFEU, the legal basis for the Comprehensive Economic and Trade Agreement (CETA) concluded with Canada.[56]

10.009 **Multilateral agreements.** In addition, the Union has approved various commodity agreements negotiated in the United Nations Conference on Trade and Development (UNCTAD).[57] Multilateral trade and tariff agreements are principally negotiated in the context of the WTO (see paras 10-010–10-011).

D. Participation in GATT and the World Trade Organization

10.010 **GATT and WTO.** All the Member States are party to the 1947 General Agreement on Tariffs and Trade (GATT),[58] under which the signatory States undertake to grant products from the other signatory States 'most-favoured-nation' treatment and to refrain from imposing any non-tariff barriers to trade not included amongst the safeguard measures permitted by GATT. The EU customs union constitutes an exception to the most-favoured-nation clause and is expressly authorized by Article XXIV of GATT (see para. 7-015, *supra*). Though the Community (and later the Union) was not a GATT Contracting Party, from the outset, it has regarded itself as bound by GATT, and it has taken part since the introduction of the

---

17; on 17 July 2017 an Economic Partnership Agreement was concluded with Japan (OJ 2018 L330/3), accompanied by a wider Strategic Partnership Agreement (OJ 2018 L2016/4).

[55] See the framework cooperation agreement concluded on 22 February 1993 with the Republics of Costa Rica, El Salvador, Guatemala, Honduras, Nicaragua, and Panama (OJ 1999 L63/38), replaced by the political dialogue and cooperation agreement with the Republics of Costa Rica, El Salvador, Guatemala, Honduras, Nicaragua, and Panama (OJ 2014 L111); the framework agreement concluded on 23 April 1993 with the Cartagena Agreement *and* its member countries, namely Bolivia, Colombia, Ecuador, Peru, and Venezuela (OJ 1998 L127/10), followed by the trade agreement with Colombia and Peru (OJ 2012 L354/3), to which also Ecuador has acceded (OJ 2016 L356/3); the interregional framework cooperation agreement concluded on 15 December 1995 with the Southern Common Market ('Mercado Común del Sur' or 'Mercosur') and its Party States (Argentina, Brazil, Paraguay, and Uruguay) (OJ 1999 L112/65), followed by the political deal reached on 28 June 2019 between the Union and Mercosur states (Argentina, Brazil Paraguay, and Uruguay) on a new 'ambitious, balanced and comprehensive trade agreement'. An economic partnership, political coordination, and cooperation agreement of 8 December 1997 exists with Mexico (OJ 2000 L276/45) and an association agreement was signed with Chile on 18 November 2002 (OJ 2002 L352/1, following on from the framework cooperation agreement of 21 June 1996, OJ 1999 L42/46).

[56] Council Decision (EU) 2017/37 of 28 October 2016 on the signing on behalf of the European Union of the Comprehensive Economic and Trade Agreement (CETA) between Canada, of the one part, and the European Union and its Member States, of the other part, OJ 2017 L11/1 (on the basis of Articles 43(2), 91, 100(2), 153(2), 192(1), and 207(4), first subpara. TFEU). On these new encompassing trade agreements, see Griller, Obwexer, and Vranes (eds), *Mega-Regional Trade Agreements: CETA, TTIP, and TiSA—New Orientations for EU External Economic Relations* (OUP, 2017).

[57] See, e.g., Council Decision 2008/579/EC of 16 June 2008 on the signing and conclusion on behalf of the European Community of the International Coffee Agreement 2007, OJ 2008 L186/12, and Council Decision 2002/970/EC of 18 November 2002 concerning the conclusion on behalf of the European Community of the International Cocoa Agreement 2001, OJ 2002 L342/1.

[58] The General Agreement on Tariffs and Trade (GATT) was concluded in Geneva on 30 October 1947 by the Protocol of Provisional Application, UNTS, Vol. 55, 194; Cmnd 7258.

Common Customs Tariff in the multilateral negotiating rounds for the gradual liberalization of world trade, in which it is represented by the Commission. In the 1972 *International Fruit* judgment, the Court of Justice held that the role given in this respect by the Member States to the Community at the time had, as its consequence, that not only the Member States but also the Community was bound by the multilateral arrangements made in the framework of the GATT.[59] The World Trade Organization replaced the GATT as a fully fledged international organization. The Union has become a member of the WTO alongside its Member States.[60] The WTO constitutes the framework for the trade relations in all areas that are included in the agreements annexed to the WTO agreement, the principal ones being the amended version of the GATT, the General Agreement on Trade in Services (GATS), the Agreement on the Trade-related Aspects of Intellectual Property Rights (TRIPs), and the rules and procedures pertaining to dispute settlement and trade policy review.

Dispute settlement. As noted before, the Member States and the Union are members of the WTO. Some matters within the scope of the WTO still fall within the competence of the Member States,[61] whilst others fall within the exclusive competence of the Union.[62] When the Union exercises its voting rights within the WTO bodies, it has a number of votes equal to the number of votes held by the Member States that are WTO members; the Member States and the Union cannot, however, have more votes than the number of Member States.[63] The settlement of disputes between WTO members is entrusted to the Dispute Settlement Body (DSB). The DSB may remit a dispute to a Panel of arbiters. Panel reports can be appealed before the Standing Appellate Body. The final decision is binding and entitles a party to impose trade sanctions if the other party to the dispute does not comply with it.[64]

10.011

Within the Union legal order, the Union is at liberty to settle disputes with its trading partners within the framework of the WTO, possibly by negotiation. Consequently, where a report of a Panel or of the Standing Appellate Body finds that there is a conflict between a Union measure and WTO obligations, that report cannot, in principle, be pleaded before the Union Courts in proceedings brought against the Union measure in question (see para. 26-005, *infra*). In anti-dumping or anti-subsidy cases, there exists, however, a simplified

---

[59] Ibid., paras 14–15. For the question as to whether GATT provisions may be pleaded, see para. 26-005, *infra*.
[60] Accordingly, commitments entered into under these agreements fall within the common commercial policy; see Opinion 2/15, *Free Trade Agreement between the European Union and the Republic of Singapore*, 2017, paras 36 and 54; C-66/18, *Commission v Hungary*, 2020, para. 73.
[61] e.g. portfolio investments; see Opinion 2/15, *Free Trade Agreement between the European Union and the Republic of Singapore*, 2017, paras 225–44.
[62] e.g. C-414/11, *Daiichi Sankyo*, 2013, paras 49–61.
[63] Article IX (1) WTO-Agreement.
[64] Understanding on Rules and Procedures Governing the Settlement of Disputes, Annex 2 to the WTO Agreement, OJ 1994 L336/234. See Mitchell, 'Proportionality and Remedies in WTO Disputes' (2007) EJIL 985–1008; Lavranos, 'The Communitarization of WTO Dispute Settlement Reports: An Exception to the Rule of Law' (2005) ELJ 313–38; Rosas, 'Implementation and Enforcement of WTO Dispute Settlement Findings: An EU Perspective' (2001) JIEL 131–44; Cottier, 'Dispute Settlement in the World Trade Organisation: Characteristics and Structural Implications for the European Union' (1998) CMLRev 325–78; Kuijper, 'The New WTO Dispute Settlement System: The Impact on the European Community' (1995) JWT 49–71; Petersmann, 'The Dispute Settlement System of the World Trade Organisation and the Evolution of the GATT Dispute Settlement System since 1948' (1994) CMLRev 1157–244.

procedure which the Commission can use to bring Union measures into line with a report drawn up by the Dispute Settlement Body.[65]

Moreover, in certain circumstances, the review undertaken as part of the WTO's dispute settlement system may result in a legal finding that measures taken by a WTO member are not in conformity with the law of that organization and can, ultimately, give rise to international liability on the part of the Union, a member of the WTO, because of a wrongful act.[66] The Union also provided for a mechanism to ensure an effective and timely exercise of its right to suspend or withdraw concessions or other obligations following the adjudication of trade disputes under the WTO dispute settlement system or other international trade agreements.[67] However, since 11 December 2019, due to the blockage of new appointments to the WTO's Standing Appellate Body, the latter is no longer able to deliver binding resolutions of trade disputes and guarantee the right to appellate review.[68]

Member States and the Union must cooperate closely in applying the WTO Agreement. The duty to cooperate is all the more imperative where the Union or a Member State is authorized to take cross-retaliation measures but can do so effectively only in an area for which the other is competent.[69]

III. Association

10.012 **Association.** The Union is entitled to involve certain countries and territories closely in its operation by means of an 'association'. As regards countries and territories which come under the sovereignty of a Member State but are not part of the Union, Article 203 TFEU empowers the Council to determine the details and procedure of such an association. Furthermore, Article 217 TFEU authorizes the Union to conclude agreements with third countries or international organizations so as to establish an association. Associations allow for the import of goods originating in the third countries concerned into the Union at zero or reduced tariffs. Sometimes a free-trade area is created. Then, rules of origin are necessary to determine the conditions pursuant to which goods originating in the third countries concerned may circulate freely within the free trade area, without being subject to customs duties or quantitative restrictions.

---

[65] Regulation (EU) 2015/476 of the European Parliament and of the Council of 11 March 2015 on the measures that the Union may take following a report adopted by the WTO Dispute Settlement Body concerning anti-dumping and anti-subsidy matters, OJ 2015 L83/6, replacing Council Regulation (EC) No. 1515/2001 of 23 July 2001, OJ 2001 L201/10. See Blanchard, 'L'effet des rapports de l'Organe de règlement des différends de l'OMC à la lumière du règlement (CE) 1515/2001 du Conseil de l'Union européenne' (2003) RMCUE 37–48.

[66] C-66/18, *Commission v Hungary*, 2020, para. 84. Accordingly, the Commission may bring an infringement action against a Member State that is in breach of its obligations under WTO in order to avoid such outcome (ibid., paras 86–93).

[67] Regulation (EU) No. 654/2014 of the European Parliament and of the Council of 15 May 2014 concerning the exercise of the Union's rights for the application and enforcement of international trade rules, OJ 2014 L189/50.

[68] See Regulation (EU) 2021/167 of the European Parliament and of the Council of 10 February 2021 amending Regulation (EU) No 654/2014 concerning the exercise of the Union's rights for the application and enforcement of international trade rules, OJ 2021 L49/1.

[69] Opinion 1/94, *Agreement establishing the World Trade Organisation*, 1994, paras 108–9.

A. Association of overseas countries and territories

Overseas countries and territories. At the time of the signing of the EEC Treaty many countries and territories were still related to a Member State of the Union as colonies. Most of those countries and territories did not join the Community at that time, but were made the subject matter of a specific regime laid down in Part Four of the EEC Treaty, now Part Four of the TFEU (Articles 198 to 204 TFEU).[70] Since most areas colonized by the Member States became independent in the 1960s (e.g. Congo and Suriname), this scheme now applies only to thirteen overseas countries and territories (OCTs) having special relations with Denmark (Greenland), France, and the Netherlands;[71] it also applied to a number of territories with a special relationship to the United Kingdom before Brexit.[72] Those overseas countries and territories—all islands—are not to be confused with the ultra-peripheral regions to which the Treaties do apply in full (see para. 11-007, *infra*).

10.013

The purpose of the OCT association is to 'promote the economic and social development of the countries and territories and to establish close economic relations between them and the Union as a whole' (Article 198, second para. TFEU).[73] To this end, the association establishes a free-trade area between the Union and the overseas countries and territories, whereby the Member States endeavour to apply to their trade with those overseas countries and territories the same treatment as they accord to each other, but the overseas countries and territories determine their trade policy vis-à-vis the Member States themselves, subject to the condition that they treat all the Member States in the same way (see Articles 199, points (1) and (2) and 200 TFEU). All the Member States contribute towards the development of the overseas countries and territories through the European Development Fund set up for that purpose (Article 199, point 3 TFEU). On the basis of Article 203 TFEU the Council, acting unanimously, lays down provisions as regards the content of the association 'on the basis of the experience acquired under the association ... and of the principles set out in the Treaties'. In order to reconcile the aims of the association with the principles underlying the common agricultural policy, the Council has arranged matters so that agricultural

---

[70] See, generally, Murray, *The European Union and Member State Territories: A New Legal Framework Under the EU Treaties* (TMC Asser, 2012); Kochenov (ed.), *EU Law of the Overseas: Outermost Regions, Associated Overseas Countries and Territories, Territories Sui Generis* (Kluwer, 2011) For a recent application, see C-391/17, *Commission v United Kingdom*, 2019 and C-395/17, *Commission v Netherlands*, 2019 (Member States are responsible for the CTO customs fraud relating to their territories).

[71] The countries and territories to which the provisions of Part Four of the TFEU are applicable (listed in Annex II to the Treaties): Greenland, New Caledonia and Dependencies, a number of the French COMs or *collectivités d'outre mer* (French Polynesia, Wallis and Futuna Islands, Saint Pierre and Miquelon, and Saint-Barthélemy), the French Southern and Antarctic Territories, Aruba and the Netherlands Antilles (Bonaire, Curaçao, Saba, Sint Eustatius, and Sint Maarten). For the special status of Greenland, Aruba, and the Netherlands Antilles, see also para. 11-007, *infra*. See, for the competence for monetary emission in New Caledonia, French Polynesia, and Wallis and Futuna, Protocol (No. 18), annexed to the Lisbon Treaty, on France (OJ 2010 C83/289).

[72] Anguilla, Cayman Islands, Falkland Islands, South Georgia and the South Sandwich Islands, Monserrat, Pitcairn, Saint Helena and Dependencies, British Antarctic Territory, British Indian Ocean Territory, Turks and Caicos Islands, British Virgin Islands, and Bermuda. See also Article 3 of the Agreement on the withdrawal of the United Kingdom of Great Britain and Northern Ireland from the European Union and the European Atomic Energy Community, OJ 2020 L29/7.

[73] For the 'advantages' that association confers on those countries and territories, see C-430/92, *Netherlands v Commission*, 1994, para. 22. The association arrangements apply only to products originating in those countries and territories: C-310/95, *Road Air*, 1997, paras 29–36. The application of the association regime does not bring a territory within the sphere of application of the Treaties; see C-181/97, *van der Kooy*, 1999, paras 32–42 (Netherlands Antilles held not to be part of the Union for the application of the VAT Directive).

products from overseas countries and territories are on an equal footing with Union products, but a safeguard clause enables the Union to react, to a limited extent, to difficulties to which free access of products originating in those countries and territories to the Union market may give rise.[74]

The OCT association scheme is now substantively identical to that of the association agreements which the Union has concluded under Article 217 TFEU. Unlike those agreements, however, on account of its 'autonomous' nature, the OCT association does not require any institutions of its own.

B. Association agreements pursuant to Article 217 TFEU

10.014 **Scope.** Article 217 TFEU and Article 206 EAEC provide the legal basis for the Union to 'conclude with one or more States or international organizations agreements establishing an association involving reciprocal rights and obligations, common action and special procedures'. Because association is defined in this way, there is a need for a degree of institutionalization of the international cooperation so as to make it possible for decisions to be taken in common. As the Court of Justice has held, an association agreement creates 'special, privileged links with a third country which must, at least to a certain extent, take part in the [Union] system'[75]. The Union has the power to conclude association agreements relating to any area coming under the Treaties.[76] Thus, an association agreement may cover free movement of workers who are nationals of the third country party to the agreement even though the power to adopt the necessary implementing measures is not vested in the Union.[77] On the Union side, the financing and other arrangements for implementing association agreements are often enshrined in an internal agreement concluded by the representatives of the governments of the Member States, meeting in the Council.[78]

10.015 **Institutional framework.** With a view to its implementation and further development, each association agreement sets up a joint body composed, on the one hand, of members of the national governments or the members of the Council—generally supplemented by members of the Commission—and, on the other, of members of the government of each third country involved. That association council (sometimes called 'council of ministers' or, to

---

[74] Council Decision 2013/755/EU of 25 November 2013 on the association of the overseas countries and territories with the European Union ('Overseas Association Decision'), OJ 2013 L344/4. See previously, Council Decision 2001/822/EC of 27 November 2001 on the association of the overseas countries and territories with the European Community, OJ 2001 L314/1, which replaced Council Decision 91/482/EEC of 25 July 1991, OJ 1991 L263/1. The safeguard clause contained in Decision 91/482/EEC was declared lawful in T-480/93 and T-483/93, *Antillean Rice Mills and Others v Commission*, 1995, paras 81–97, as confirmed on appeal in C-390/95 P, *Antillean Rice Mills v Commission*, 1999. For the validity of Decision 97/803/EEC, see C-17/98, *Emesa Sugar (Free Zone) and Aruba*, 2000, paras 27–67.
[75] 12/86, *Demirel*, 1987, para. 9. 'Reciprocal rights and obligations' does not mean equality of contractual obligations: 87/75, *Besciani*, 1976, para. 22.
[76] For the rights third-country nationals derive from association agreements, see Kellerman, 'The Rights of Non-member State Nationals under the EU Association Agreements' (2008) EJ L Ref 339–82. For a discussion (and a comparison) of the content of association agreements, see Hummer, 'Die räumliche Erweiterung des Binnenmarktrechts' (2002) EuR 75–146; Lenaerts and De Smijter, 'The European Community's Treaty-Making Competence' (1996) YEL 1, 19–47.
[77] 12/86, *Demirel*, 1987, para. 10.
[78] See, for instance, in the case of the ACP–EC Partnership Agreement, n. 96, *infra*.

suit the title of the agreement, the 'cooperation council') takes its decisions by unanimous vote. Preparatory and executive powers may be delegated to the association (or cooperation) committee, which is made up of representatives of the members of the association council. Generally, each association engenders (by virtue of the agreement itself or of a decision of the association council) an advisory parliamentary body, consisting of members of the European Parliament and of the parliament(s) of the third country or countries concerned. Generally, the association council has jurisdiction to rule on any disputes between the Contracting Parties relating to the interpretation or application of the association agreement. If a settlement cannot be reached, it is possible to have recourse to arbitration.[79]

Association agreements. Association agreements play a fundamental role in the Union's external policy. All association agreements simplify access to the Union market for goods from the countries concerned and, at the same time, commit the Union to cooperate with them economically and financially. In most agreements, the Union unilaterally grants a zero tariff or (in the case of 'sensitive' products, such as textiles) a reduced tariff. The third countries undertake, for their part, to grant products from the Union most-favoured-nation status and not to apply any fiscal discrimination.[80] Besides economic considerations, political considerations play an important part in determining whether such agreements are concluded and implemented.[81] Whereas some of these agreements prepare for a possible accession (see para. 10-017, *infra*), others form part of the Union's development policy (see para. 10-018, *infra*). In addition, the agreements on the future relationship with the United Kingdom after its withdrawal from the Union have been adopted on the basis of Article 217 TFEU and Article 206 EAEC (see para. 4-018, *supra*).

10.016

Preparation for accession.[82] The first time the Union made use of the competence to conclude association agreements concerned the agreements it concluded in the 1960s with Greece and Turkey to prepare them for possible accession.[83] These were followed in the 1970s by agreements with Cyprus and Malta.[84] The agreements with Greece, Cyprus, and Malta have lapsed since their accession in 1981 and 2004. Pursuant to the association agreement, Turkey and the Union have constituted a customs union since 1 January 1996.[85] In

10.017

---

[79] For these bodies, see Ntumba, 'Les institutions mixtes de gestion des accords conclus entre la CEE et les pays en voie de développement (PVD)' (1988) RMC 481–486; Lenaerts and De Smijter, 'The European Community's Treaty-Making Competence' (1996) YEL 47–57.

[80] For the content of these preferential agreements and their compatibility with the GATT, see Schoneveld, 'The EEC and Free Trade Agreements: Stretching the Limits of GATT Exceptions to Non-Discriminatory Trade?' (1992) JWT 59–78.

[81] See, for instance, the repudiation of the cooperation agreement with Yugoslavia in 1991: Council Decision 91/602/EEC of 25 November 1991, OJ 1991 L325/23. See Fransen, 'The EEC and the Mediterranean Area: Associations and Cooperation Agreements' (1992) Leiden JIL 215–43.

[82] This paragraph builds on Chapter 23 contributed by De Smijter to Lenaerts and Van Nuffel, *Constitutional Law of the European Union* (Sweet & Maxwell, 2004), 924–35.

[83] Agreement of 12 September 1963 establishing an Association between the EEC and Turkey (JO 1964, 3687; English text published in OJ 1973 C113/1), with an Additional Protocol of 23 November 1970 (OJ 1972 L293/3), as fleshed out by, *inter alia*, (internal) Agreement 64/737/EEC (OJ 1964 3705) and a number of decisions of the Association Council (such as Decisions 2/76 and 1/80 (unpublished) and 3/80, OJ 1983 C110/60); Agreement of 9 July 1961 with Greece (OJ English Special Edition, Second Series, I. External Relations (1), 3).

[84] See Agreement of 5 December 1970 between the EEC and Malta, OJ 1971 L61/1; Agreement between the EEC and Cyprus, OJ 1973 L133/1.

[85] Decision No. 1/95 of the EC-Turkey Association Council of 22 December 1995 on implementing the final phase of the Customs Union, OJ 1996 L35/1.

October 2005 accession negotiations with Turkey were officially opened (see para. 4-014, *supra*).

Shortly after the disintegration of the communist structures in Central and Eastern Europe, the Union began to conclude association agreements with the Central European countries. These so-called 'Europe Agreements' embodied a timeframe for various liberalization measures intended to lead to the creation of a free-trade area in industrial products between the Union and the Central European countries concerned. Moreover, they also contained provisions relating to the liberalization of the movement of workers, establishment and the provision of services,[86] and a chapter on 'approximation of legislation' pursuant to which the associated partner was to endeavour to make its legislation compatible with that of the Union. Consequently, the Europe Agreements represented for both parties the means par excellence for effectively preparing the Central European countries for later membership of the European Union. Accession negotiations began in 1998, which led to the accession of these European countries in 2004 and 2007 (see paras 4-006 and 4-007).

Since 1999, the European Union concluded stabilization and association agreements with Croatia and other countries in the Western Balkans, namely Albania, Bosnia and Herzegovina, Kosovo, Montenegro, Serbia, and North Macedonia (previously the Former Yugoslav Republic of Macedonia).[87] These agreements were the centrepiece of a broader stabilization and association process to prepare these countries for their possible accession and encourage them to engage in regional cooperation.[88] These agreements provide for the gradual establishment of a bilateral free-trade area with the Union. Croatia has since acceded to the Union, whereas Albania, Montenegro, Serbia, and North Macedonia have been recognized as candidate Member States (see para. 4-014, *supra*).

10.018 **Neighbourhood.** Since the 1970s, the Union has concluded agreements, often styled 'co-operation agreements', with virtually every country in the Mediterranean area.[89] The agreements with the Maghreb countries (Algeria, Morocco, Tunisia) and some decisions of the EU–Turkey Association Council require the Member States to treat nationals of those countries who are lawfully on their territory in the same way as their own nationals as regards conditions of employment, remuneration, and social security (see para. 8-013, *supra*).

---

[86] See, e.g., C-327/02 *Panayotova*, 2004 (agreements between the Communities and Bulgaria, Poland, and Slovakia).

[87] See Grabar-Kitarovic, 'The Stabilization and Association Process: The EU's Soft Power as its Best' (2007) E For Aff Rev 121–25; Pippan, 'The Rocky Road to Europe: The EU's Stabilisation and Association Process for the Western Balkans and the Principle of Conditionality' (2004) E For Aff Rev 219–45. See further, Papadimitrou, Petrov and Greicevci, 'To build a State: Europeanization, EU Actorness and State-building in Kosovo' (2007) E For Aff Rev 219–38.

[88] The stabilization and association agreement with the Former Yugoslav Republic of Macedonia was signed on 9 April 2001 and approved by the Union by decision of 23 February 2004, OJ 2004 L84/1—it entered into force on 1 April 2004: OJ 2004 L85/26); the agreement with Croatia was signed on 29 October 2001, approved on behalf of the Union by Decision of 13 December 2004 (OJ 2005 L26/1—it entered into force on 1 February 2005); the agreement with Albania was signed on 12 June 2006 and approved by decision of 26 February 2009 (OJ 2009 L107/165—it entered into force on 1 April 2009: OJ 2009 L104/57); the agreement with Montenegro was signed on 12 October 2007 and approved by decision of 29 March 2010, OJ 2010 L108/1—it entered into force on 1 May 2010; the agreement with Serbia was signed on 29 April 2008 and approved by decision of 22 July 2013 and entered into force on 1 September 2013 (OJ 2013 L278); the agreement with Bosnia and Herzegovina was signed on 16 June 2008, approved by decision of 21 April 2015 and entered into force on 1 June 2015 (OJ 2015 L164); the agreement with Kosovo was signed on 27 June 2015 and approved by decision of 12 February 2016 (OJ 2016 L71/1) and entered into force on 1 April 2016 (OJ 2016 L78/1).

[89] For the first Association Agreements with Cyprus and Malta: see n. 84, *supra*.

Pursuant to undertakings entered into by the Union at the Euro-Mediterranean Conference held in Barcelona on 27 and 28 November 1995,[90] the existing association agreements are gradually replaced by agreements which are eventually to lead to the establishment of a Euro-Mediterranean Free Trade Area[91]. Henceforward, the Palestine Authority is also to be involved,[92] alongside Israel. Since 2004, the so-called Euro-Mediterranean Partnership has become part of a wider European Neighbourhood Policy (see para. 10-025, *infra*). In the framework thereof an 'Eastern Partnership' has, since 2009, also resulted in association agreements with Georgia, Moldova, and Ukraine.[93]

ACP countries. After most of the colonized areas in Africa obtained their independence, the Community concluded association agreements signed at Yaoundé (Cameroon) in 1963 and 1969 with those African States.[94] Following the accession of the United Kingdom, the Community entered into negotiations with a number of States in Africa, the Caribbean, and the Pacific, which culminated in an association agreement being concluded with those 'ACP States'. The ACP–EC Convention was signed at Lomé (Togo) on 28 February 1975, following which it was renewed every five years.[95] A new ACP–EC Agreement was concluded at Cotonou (Benin) on 23 June 2000 by the Community, its Member States, and the ACP States for a twenty-year period starting on 1 March 2000.[96] On 3 December 2020, a political deal was reached on the text for a new Partnership Agreement, on the basis of which a new agreement was initialled on 15 April 2021. Pending its ratification, the Cotonou Agreement has been extended until 30 November 2021, unless the new Agreement enters into force or is provisionally applied before that date.[97] The ACP–EC Partnership Agreement is to

10.019

---

[90] See the Barcelona Declaration and the programme of work (1995) 11 EU Bull. point 2.3.1.

[91] See the Euro-Mediterranean Agreements. The structure for Union financial and technical aid was the Euro-Mediterranean partnership: Council Regulation (EC) No. 1488/96 of 23 July 1996 on financial and technical measures to accompany the reform of economic and social structures in the framework of the Euro-Mediterranean partnership (MEDA), OJ 1996 L189/1, now replaced by Regulation (EC) No. 1638/2006 (see n. 131, *infra*). For a discussion, see the contributions in Osman and Philip (eds), *Le partenariat euro-méditerranéen. Le processus de Barcelone: nouvelles perspectives* (Bruylant, 2003).

[92] See the Euro-Mediterranean Interim Association Agreement of 24 February 1997 on trade and cooperation between the European Community, of the one part, and the Palestine Liberation Organization (PLO) for the benefit of the Palestine Authority of the West Bank and the Gaza Strip, of the other part, OJ 1997 L187/1. See also C-386/08, *Brita*, 2010.

[93] See the association agreements with Georgia (OJ 2014 L261/4, concluded by Council Decision (EU) 2016/838 of 23 May 2016, OJ 2016 L141/26), Moldova (OJ 2014 L269/4), concluded by Council Decision (EU) 2016/839 of 23 May 2016, OJ 2016 L141/28), and Ukraine (OJ 2014 L161/1); see Van der Loo, *The EU-Ukraine Association Agreement and Deep and Comprehensive Free Trade Area: A New Legal Instrument For EU Integration Without Membership?* (Brill, 2016).

[94] JO 1964, 1430 and OJ 1970 L282. English version in OJ 1974 English Special Edition, Second Series I, External Relations.

[95] ACP-EC Convention of 28 February 1975, OJ 1976 L25; Second ACP-EC Convention of 31 October 1979, OJ 1980 L347; Third ACP-EC Convention of 8 December 1984, OJ 1986 L86; Fourth ACP-EC Convention of 15 December 1989, OJ 1991 L229/3 (concluded for ten years and since revised by the Convention of Mauritius of 4 November 1995, OJ 1998 L156/3).

[96] OJ 2000 L317/3, approved by Council Decision 2003/159/EC of 19 December 2002 (OJ 2003 L65/27) and OJ 2005 L209/27 (after amendment by agreement of 25 June 2005, approved by Council Decision 2008/373/EC of 28 April 2008, OJ 2008 L129/44, in accordance with Article 95, which provides that amendments may be made at the end of each five-year period). See Babarinde and Faber, 'From Lomé to Cotonou: Business as Usual?' (2004) E For Aff Rev 27–47; Arts, 'ACP-EU Relations in a New Era: The Cotonou Agreement' (2003) CMLRev 95–116; Vincent, 'L'entrée en vigueur de la convention de Cotonou' (2003) CDE 157–76; Petit, 'Le nouvel accord de partenariat ACP-UE' (2000) RMCUE 215–19.

[97] Article 1 of Decision No. 2/2020 of the ACP-EU Committee of Ambassadors of 4 December 2020 to amend Decision No. 3/2019 of the ACP-EU Committee of Ambassadors to adopt transitional measures pursuant to Article 95(4) of the ACP-EU Partnership Agreement, OJ 2020 L420/32.

promote and expedite the economic, cultural, and social development of the ACP States, with a view to contributing to peace and security and to promoting a stable and democratic political environment (Article 1, first para.). Because the non-reciprocal trade advantages granted by the Lomé Convention were found to be in breach of the norms of the World Trade Organization, the agreement provided for the conclusion of economic partnership agreements with reciprocal advantages. The Union sought to couple these agreements to regional integration[98] and thus to conclude economic partnership agreements with seven regions: the Caribbean, West-Africa, Central-Africa, East- and Southern Africa, the South-African Development Community, the East-African Community, and the island nations in the Pacific Ocean.[99] Since it proved impossible to have these Economic Partnership Agreements (EPAs) concluded between all regional groups of ACP countries and the Union, many ACP countries individually signed EPAs with the EU. In April 2020, the ACP Group of States became an international organisation, the Organisation of African, Caribbean and Pacific States (OACPS).

The new EU/African-Caribbean-Pacific partnership agreement is expected to be signed in the second half of 2021. The Agreement is composed of a common foundation to all countries, which sets out the values and priorities, along with three regional protocols (Africa, Caribbean, Pacific), tailored to each region's needs. The regional protocols will have their own specific governance to organise the relations between the different regions and the EU. The three regional Joint Parliamentary Assemblies (Africa-EU, Caribbean-EU, Pacific-EU) will meet in advance of meetings of the relevant regional Council of Ministers. There will also be an overarching joint OACPS-EU framework, comprising the OACPS-EU Joint Parliamentary Assembly (JPA), which will be composed of members of the three regional parliamentary assemblies.. The new Partnership Agreement will be concluded for an initial period of 20 years.

The majority of the ACP States, moreover, have enjoyed access to the Union markets without quotas or tariffs because of their status as 'least developed country' on the basis of a special regime ('everything but arms') within the system of tariff preferences.[100] In addition to the trade advantages, the Union has been granting administrative, technical, and financial assistance to projects in the ACP States. The ACP–EC Partnership Agreement has not included any provisions on the free movement of workers, but it did oblige the Member States and the ACP countries to accord each other's nationals, who were legally employed in their respective territories, treatment free from any discrimination based on nationality as regards working conditions, remuneration, and dismissal relative to their own nationals.[101]

---

[98] ACP-EC Partnership Agreement, Article 35.
[99] See, e.g., the Economic Partnership Agreement between the European Union and its Member States, of the one part, and the Southern African Development Community (SADC) EPA States, of the other part (OJ 2016 L250/1). The SADC EPA States comprise Botswana, Lesotho, Mozambique, Namibia, Eswatini (formerly Swaziland) and South Africa.
[100] Articles 17 and 18 of Regulation (EU) No. 978/2012 of the European Parliament and of the Council of 25 October 2012 applying a scheme of generalised tariff preferences and repealing Council Regulation (EC) No. 732/2008, OJ 2012 L303/1.
[101] ACP-EC Partnership Agreement, Article 13(3). Article 274 of the Fourth ACP-EC Convention itself prohibited ACP States and EU Member States from discriminating between nationals of different Member States or ACP States without putting them under an obligation to treat nationals of Member States and of ACP States identically: 65/77, *Razanatsimba*, 1977, paras 12–14. A Member State may reserve more favourable treatment to the nationals of a given ACP country in so far as such treatment results from the provisions of an international agreement comprising reciprocal rights and advantages: ibid., para. 19.

Each of the ACP States has undertaken to accept the return and readmission of any of its nationals who are illegally present on the territory of a Member State of the EU.[102] Also the new Partnership Agreement addresses migration and mobility in all of its dimensions, with all partners recognising the need for enhanced cooperation to ensure effective management of migration.

As far as the financing of the ACP cooperation is concerned, the Member States elected to finance the aid from national contributions made available to the European Development Fund, which was separate from the Union budget, but which was administered by the Commission (and which also provided aid to the overseas countries and territories mentioned in Part IV TFEU).[103] The new Partnership Agreement does not include a dedicated fund. For the 2021-2027 period, cooperation with African, Caribbean and Pacific States will be financed under the Union budget. The European Investment Bank may also grant loans and other financial assistance.

EEA Agreement.[104] Another major agreement which was concluded by the Union under Article 217 TFEU [*at that time Article 238 EEC*] is the Agreement on the European Economic Area (EEA Agreement) signed at Oporto on 2 May 1992 and which came into force on 1 January 1994.[105] The EEA Agreement has been concluded between the Community and its Member States, on the one hand, and the EFTA countries (see para. 1-019, *supra*), except for Switzerland, on the other.[106] Following the accession of Austria, Finland, and Sweden to the European Union in 1995, the participating States on the side of the EFTA are Iceland, Liechtenstein, and Norway.

10.020

The EEA Agreement creates a free-trade area (not a customs union) between the Union and the three EFTA states. With the EEA Agreement, the three EFTA States accepted to take over a major part of the Union *acquis*: this concerns the Treaty provisions and secondary Union law with respect to the free movement of goods, persons, services, and capital; the

---

[102] ACP-EC Partnership Agreement, Article 13(5)(c).
[103] C-316/91, *European Parliament v Council*, 1994, paras 34–8; see the Internal Agreement between the Representatives of the Governments of the Member States of the European Union, meeting within the Council, on the financing of European Union aid under the multiannual financial framework for the period 2014 to 2020, in accordance with the ACP-EU Partnership Agreement, and on the allocation of financial assistance for the Overseas Countries and Territories to which Part Four of the Treaty on the Functioning of the European Union applies, OJ 2013 L210/1; see previously, the Internal Agreement between the Representatives of the Governments of the Member States, meeting within the Council, on the Financing of Community Aid under the Multiannual financial framework for the period 2009 to 2013 and on the allocation of financial assistance for the Overseas Countries and Territories, OJ 2006 L247/32.
[104] The paragraphs on the EEA build on Chapter 23 contributed by De Smijter to Lenaerts and Van Nuffel, *Constitutional Law of the European Union* (Sweet & Maxwell, 2004), 924–35.
[105] OJ 1994 L1. For a general commentary, see Arnesen et al. (eds), *Agreement on the European Economic Area: A Commentary* (Nomos, 2018). Signature of the Agreement was possible only after amendments; after an adverse opinion from the Court of Justice on the compatibility of the system of judicial supervision envisaged in the draft EEA Agreement with provisions of the EEC Treaty, the Agreement was adjusted in that respect (ECJ, Opinion 1/91, *Draft Agreement between the Community, on the one hand, and the countries of the European Free Trade Association, on the other, relating to the creation of the European Economic Area*, 1991). In a second opinion, the Court held the revised agreement to be compatible with EC law (ECJ, Opinion 1/92, *Draft Agreement between the Community, on the one hand, and the countries of the European Free Trade Association, on the other, relating to the creation of the European Economic Area*, 1992).
[106] On 6 December 1992, 50.3 per cent of the total population and eighteen of the twenty-six cantons voted against Swiss ratification of the EEA Agreement. The EEA Agreement did not come into effect as regards Liechtenstein until 1 May 1995 after the Principality had taken the necessary measures with regard to its regional union with Switzerland (OJ 1995 L140/30; see Article 7(1) of Decision No. 1/95 of the EEA Council of 10 March 1995, OJ 1995 L86/58).

competition rules; and areas such as research and development, the environment, education, and social policy.

In order to ensure a homogeneous application of the relevant provisions, the EEA Agreement provides for ongoing consultations to take place during the Union legislative process.[107] Moreover, there is a parallel system of supervision and dispute settlement. The powers exercised, one the Union side, by the Commission and the Court of Justice with respect to the monitoring of the application of the provisions of the EEA Agreement by Union institutions, Member States, and persons within their jurisdiction[108] are exercised, as far as the EFTA States are concerned, with respect to those States and persons within their jurisdiction, by the EFTA Surveillance Authority (ESA, based in Brussels)[109] and the EFTA Court (based in Luxembourg).[110] In order to secure homogeneity, provisions of the EEA Agreement which are essentially identical to corresponding rules of primary or secondary Union law are interpreted by the EFTA Surveillance Authority and the EFTA Court in accordance with the case law of the Court of Justice.[111] For its part, the Court of Justice sometimes refers to the case law of the EFTA Court.[112] In the event of a conflict of interpretation between a person coming under the Union legal order, on the one hand, and an EFTA State, on the other, the Union or an EFTA State may bring the dispute before the EEA Joint Committee, which will try to find a solution.[113] If the Joint Committee does not manage to settle the dispute, the matter may be brought before the Court of Justice.[114]

IV. Development Cooperation and Humanitarian Aid

10.021 **Sustainable development.** Although a specific competence for the Community in respect of development cooperation was first incorporated in the EC Treaty by the EU Treaty, the Community had already been pursuing its own development policy for some

---

[107] See, e.g., EEA Agreement, Article 99(1) (in preparing Union legislation, the Commission is to seek advice from experts of the EFTA States) and Article 99(3) (continuous information and consultation process in the EEA Joint Committee).

[108] EEA Agreement, Article 109(1). By this means the Commission carries out its Union supervisory duties (see Article 17(1) TFEU; para. 12-058, *infra*).

[109] Article 109 of the EEA Agreement and Articles 5, 22, and 31 of the Agreement between the EFTA States on the establishment of a Surveillance Authority and a Court of Justice. For the Rules of Procedure of the Surveillance Authority, see OJ 1994 L113/19.

[110] Articles 32 and 34 of the Agreement between the EFTA States on the establishment of a Surveillance Authority and a Court of Justice.

[111] See, e.g., EFTA Court, E-1/94, *Restamark*, 1994, paras 24, 32–3, 46–52, 56, 60, 64–6, and 79–80; EFTA Court, E-9/07 and E-10/07, *L'Oréal*, 2008, paras 27–37 (reversing earlier case law in the light of a recent ECJ judgment); E-10/17, *Nye Kystlink*, 2018, paras 73, 112, and 119; E-8/19, *Scanteam*, 2020, paras 59, 61, and 65–67. For a critical appraisal of the EFTA Court's case law, see Kronenberger, 'Does the EFTA Court interpret the EEA Agreement as if it were the EC Treaty? Some Questions Raised by the *Restamark* Judgment' (1996) ICLQ 198–212. This does not mean, however, that legal instruments have the same value in the national legal order, see Bekkedal, 'Understanding the Nature of the EEA Agreement: On the Direct Applicability of Regulations' (2020) CMLRev 773–98.

[112] e.g. C-13/95 *Süzen*, 1997, para. 10; C-34-36/95, *De Agostini*, 1997, para. 37; C-172/99, *Liikenne*, 2001, para. 2; C-286/02, *Bellio F.lli*, 2004, paras 34 and 57–60; C-375/15, *BAWAG PSK Bank für Arbeit und Wirtschaft und Österreichische Postsparkasse*, 2017, para. 43; C-21/18, *Textilis*, 2019, para 21; C-542/18 RX-II and C-543/18 RX-II, *Simpson v Council*, 2020, para. 80.

[113] EEA Agreement, Article 111(1). Note that only the Union and the EFTA States are entitled to bring a dispute on interpretation before the EEA Joint Committee, not the EU Member States.

[114] See Article 111(3) of the EEA Agreement.

considerable time. Thus, the scheme for overseas countries and territories (Part Four of the EC Treaty; see para. 10-013, *supra*) and the association policy with regard to countries in the Mediterranean area and the ACP States (see paras 10-018–10-019) aimed primarily to promote those countries' economic and social development. In association therewith, various common commercial policy measures displayed development policy aspects without detracting from their commercial policy nature (see para. 10-003, *supra*). The competences conferred on the Union in Articles 208 to 211 TFEU have, as their primary objective, the reduction and, in the long term, the eradication of poverty.

In view of the broad objectives pursued by development cooperation policy,[115] it must be possible for a measure to cover a variety of specific matters. Where a measure contains clauses concerning several specific matters, the Treaty provisions on development cooperation afford a sufficient legal basis, provided that development cooperation is the essential object of the measure and the obligations contained in those clauses are not so extensive as to constitute, in fact, objectives distinct from those of development cooperation.[116] The Court has thus accepted that an agreement based on Article 209 TFEU may also encompass provisions in respect of transport, environment, and the readmission of third-country nationals.[117] The same applies to respect for human rights. Compliance with international human rights standards is a precondition for benefitting from tariff preferences (see para. 10-008, *supra*) and plays an important role in agreements concluded by the Union in pursuance of its trade and development cooperation policy.[118] The Union must take the objectives of development cooperation into account whenever it adopts policies that may have consequences for developing countries (Article 208(1), second subpara. TFEU). Within their respective spheres of competence, the Union and the Member States are to cooperate with third countries and the competent international organizations (Article 211 TFEU) and must comply with the commitments and take account of the objectives they have approved in the context of the United Nations and other competent international organizations (Article 208(2) TFEU). This includes the 2030 Agenda for Sustainable Development adopted by the United Nations in September 2015, which has defined seventeen concrete Sustainable Development Goals, which the Union institutions and Member States committed to in the European Consensus on Development.[119]

---

[115] See also Article 21 TEU (para. 10-001, *supra*).

[116] Case C-268/94, *Portugal v Council*, 1996, para. 39 (by analogy with Opinion 1/78 on the common commercial policy: para. 10-003, *supra*); C-91/05, *Commission v Council*, 2008, paras 64–78 (Treaty provisions on development cooperation do not afford a sufficient legal basis for a measure mainly pursuing CFSP objectives).

[117] C-377/12, *Commission v Council*, 2014, paras 34–62.

[118] See C-268/94, *Portugal v Council*, 1996, paras 23–9 (references to respect for human rights in agreements in the field of development policy may be an important factor in the exercise of the right of the Union—on the basis of international law—to have the agreement suspended or terminated where the third country has violated human rights). See also Dimier, 'Constructing Conditionality: The Bureaucratization of EC Development Aid' (2006) E For Aff Rev 263–80; Delaplace, 'L'Union européenne et la conditionnalité de l'aide au développement' (2001) RTDE 609–26. As regards trade, more generally, see Marín Durán, 'Sustainable Development Chapters in EU Free Trade Agreements: Emerging Compliance Issues' (2020) CMLRev 1031–68; Bronckers and Gruni, 'Taking the Enforcement of Labour Standards in the EU's Free Trade Agreements Seriously' (2019) CMLRev 1591–622; Fierro, 'Legal Basis and Scope of Human Rights Clauses in EC Bilateral Agreements: Any Room for Positive Interpretation?' (2001) ELJ 41–68; Ward, 'Framework for Cooperation between the European Union and Third States: A Viable Matrix for Uniform Human Rights Standards?' (1998) E For Aff Rev 505–36.

[119] Joint statement by the Council and the representatives of the governments of the Member States meeting within the Council, the European Parliament, and the Commission—The New European Consensus on Development 'Our World, Our Dignity, Our Future', OJ 2017 C210/1.

10.022 **Instruments for development cooperation.** Under Article 209(1) TFEU,[120] measures for the implementation of development cooperation policy, including possibly multiannual cooperation programmes with developing countries or programmes with a thematic approach, are adopted by the European Parliament and the Council under the ordinary legislative procedure. Such measures may be financed by the Union[121] and may also receive support for their implementation from the funds of the European Investment Bank.[122] Whereas programmes supported by the Union have, as their primary objective, the reduction and, in the long term, the eradication of poverty, they should also contribute to fostering sustainable economic, social, and environmental development, and consolidating and supporting democracy, the rule of law, good governance, human rights, and the relevant principles of international law.[123] Detailed rules for Union cooperation with third countries and competent international organizations may be incorporated in agreements between the Union and the countries or international organizations in question which are negotiated and concluded in accordance with Article 218 TFEU. This is without prejudice to Member States' competence to negotiate in international bodies and to conclude international agreements on development cooperation themselves (Article 209(2) TFEU). Development cooperation policy therefore does not constitute an exclusive competence of the Union; the Union's development cooperation policy and that of the Member States are to complement and reinforce each other.[124] In order to promote the complementarity and efficiency of their action, the Union and the Member States are to coordinate their policies on development cooperation and consult each other on their aid programmes, including in international organizations and during international conferences. They may undertake joint action and are to contribute if necessary to the implementation of Union aid programmes (Article 210(1) TFEU).[125] The Commission may take any useful initiative to promote the coordination of the policies of the Union and the Member States (Article 210(2) TFEU).

10.023 **Humanitarian aid.** Since the Treaty of Lisbon, the Treaties contain a specific legal basis for Union action in the field of humanitarian aid.[126] The Union's operations in the field of humanitarian aid are intended to provide ad hoc assistance and relief and protection for people in third countries who are victims of natural or man-made disasters, in order to meet the humanitarian needs resulting from these different situations (Article 214(1) TFEU).

---

[120] For a general discussion, see Van den Sanden, *Between Constitutional Structures and Policy Objectives: An Examination of the Legal Framework of EU Development Cooperation* (PhD KU Leuven, 2018); Broberg and Holdgaard, 'EU Development Cooperation Post-Lisbon: Main Constitutional Challenges' (2015) ELRev 349; Mold, *EU Development Policy in a Changing World: Challenges for the 21st Century* (Amsterdam University Press, 2007).

[121] See Regulation (EU) No. 233/2014 of the European Parliament and of the Council of 11 March 2014 establishing a financing instrument for development cooperation for the period 2014-2020, OJ 2014 L77/44, and Regulation (EU) No. 230/2014 of the European Parliament and of the Council of 11 March 2014 establishing an instrument contributing to stability and peace, OJ 2014 L77/1 (the latter based on both the Treaty provisions on development cooperation and on economic, financial, and technical cooperation with third countries, see para. 10-024, *infra*).

[122] Article 209(3) TFEU. The EIB grants such support, e.g., in the context of the ACP-EU Partnership.

[123] See Article 2 of Regulation (EU) No. 233/2014 (mentioned in n. 121, *supra*).

[124] Article 208, first subpara. TFEU; see also C-268/94, *Portugal v Council*, 1996, para. 36.

[125] See also C-316/91, *European Parliament v Council*, 1994, paras 25–7.

[126] For an overview, see Sassoli and Carron, 'EU Law and International Humanitarian Law', in Patterson and Södersten, *A Companion to European Union Law and International Law* (Wiley-Blackwell, 2016), 413–26; Orbie and Versluys, 'European Union Humanitarian Aid: Lifesaver or Political Tool?', in Orbie (ed.), *Europe's Global Role: External Policies of the European Union* (Routledge, 2008), 91.

Union aid in this connection is not restricted to developing countries. The Union's measures and those of the Member States have to complement and reinforce each other (Article 214(1) and (2) TFEU). Union humanitarian aid operations are to be coordinated and consistent with those of international organizations and bodies, in particular those forming part of the United Nations system (Article 214(7) TFEU). The European Parliament and the Council, acting in accordance with the ordinary legislative procedure, establish the measures defining the framework within which the Union's humanitarian aid operations are implemented. In this context, Article 214(5) TFEU provides for the setting up of a European Voluntary Humanitarian Aid Corps.[127] The Union may also conclude agreements with third countries and competent international organizations, such as the Food Assistance Convention.[128] This is without prejudice to the Member States' competence to negotiate in international bodies and to conclude international agreements (Article 214(4) TFEU).

V. Economic, Financial, and Technical Cooperation with Third Countries and Neighbourhood Policy

Cooperation with third countries. The Treaty of Nice introduced a specific provision enabling the Union to adopt measures for economic, financial, and technical cooperation with third countries other than developing countries. Article 212(2) TFEU serves as the legal basis for a whole series of measures which are adopted by the European Parliament and the Council, acting in accordance with the ordinary legislative procedure.[129] However, as far as urgent financial assistance to a third country is concerned, the necessary decisions are taken by the Council, acting by a qualified majority on a proposal from the Commission (Article 213 TFEU). These measures must be consistent with the development policy of the Union. The arrangements for Union cooperation with third countries and international organizations may be the subject of agreements between the Union and the third parties concerned, which are to be negotiated and concluded in accordance with Article 218 TFEU (see para. 21-002 *et seq.*, *infra*). This is without prejudice to the Member States' competence to negotiate in international bodies and to conclude international agreements (Article 212(3), second subpara. TFEU). Policy on economic, financial, and technical cooperation does not therefore constitute an exclusive competence of the Union.

10.024

European Neighbourhood Policy. An example of cooperation with non-developing third countries based on Article 212 TFEU is the European Neighbourhood Policy (ENP). This policy was started with a view to the accessions in 2004 and aims at avoiding new dividing

10.025

---

[127] See Regulation (EU) No. 375/2014 of the European Parliament and of the Council of 3 April 2014 establishing the European Voluntary Humanitarian Aid Corps ('EU Aid Volunteers initiative'), OJ 2014 L122/1.

[128] Council Decision 2012/738/EU of 13 November 2012 on the conclusion, on behalf of the European Union, of the Food Assistance Convention, OJ 2012 L330/1. The Union also cooperates with non-state actors; see also Dalia, 'The European Union's Humanitarian Aid and Cooperation with Partners: The Framework Partnership Agreements', in Cosgrove-Sacks (ed.), *Europe, Diplomacy and Development: New Issues in EU Relations with Developing Countries* (Palgrave, 2011), 166.

[129] Before the Lisbon Treaty, under Article 181a (2) EC, the Council acted by a qualified majority, except where concluding association agreements referred to in Article 310 EC or agreements with candidate Member States for accession to the Union. The European Parliament was consulted. Development cooperation measures, by contrast, were adopted by the European Parliament and the Council under the co-decision procedure (Article 179(1) EC). Accordingly, the involvement of the European Parliament depended on the degree of development of the beneficiary countries. The Lisbon Treaty did away with this anomaly.

lines in Europe by promoting stability and prosperity within and beyond the new borders of the European Union.[130] The Neighbourhood Policy builds, on the one hand, on the partnership and cooperation agreements and association agreements concluded with former Soviet Republics (Armenia, Azerbaijan, Georgia, Moldova, Ukraine, and Belarus) (the 'Eastern Partnership') and, on the other hand, on the association agreements concluded within the framework of the Euro-Mediterranean Partnership (see para. 10-018, *supra*). Existing programmes of Union assistance to these countries were replaced by a European Neighbourhood Instrument.[131]

The Lisbon Treaty inserted into the Treaties a clause enabling the Union to conclude specific agreements with neighbouring States. Article 8(1) TEU provides that the Union 'shall develop a special relationship with neighbouring countries', aiming to establish an area of prosperity and good neighbourliness, founded on the values of the Union and characterized by close and peaceful relations based on cooperation. Article 8(2) TEU adds that, for that purpose, the Union may conclude agreements with the countries concerned which may contain reciprocal rights and obligations as well as the possibility of undertaking activities jointly.

VI. The Common Foreign and Security Policy (CFSP)

10.026 **Separate framework.** The Treaties elaborate the procedures and instruments for the Common Foreign and Security Policy (CFSP), which cover all areas of foreign policy and all security questions facing the Union (Article 24 TFEU).[132] These encompass all 'political' aspects of the external action of the Union, which the Member States at the time of the establishment of the European Union (1992) did not want to confer as a new competence on the Community, and for which separate rules were laid down in Title V of the EU Treaty (the then 'second pillar' of the Union). The CFSP replaced European Political Cooperation (EPC), which formed the framework for coordination of the foreign policy of the Member States before the entry into force of the EU Treaty. The Lisbon Treaty kept the provisions relating to the CFSP in Chapter 2 of Title V of the TEU. The 'specific rules and procedures' for the CFSP mean that the policy is implemented by the European Council and the Council. No legislative acts are adopted in the context of the CFSP; therefore, the role of the

---

[130] See, initially, the Presidency conclusions of the Copenhagen European Council of 12 and 13 December 2002, and, more recently, the Joint Communication of the Commission and the High Representative of the Union for Foreign Affairs and Security Policy of 18 November 2015—Review of the European Neighbourhood Policy, JOIN(2015) 50 final. See Hillion, 'Anatomy of EU Norm Export towards the Neighbourhood: The Impact of Article 8 TEU', in Van Elsuwege and Petrov (eds), *Legislative Approximation and Application of EU Law in the Eastern Neighbourhood of the European Union: Towards a Common Regulatory Space?* (Routledge, 2014); Rhattat, 'Du processus de Barcelone à la politique européenne de voisinage. Le dialogue interculturel dans l'espace euro-méditerranéen entre coexistence et affrontements' (2007) RMCUE 100–107; Kelley, 'New Wine in Old Wineskins: Promoting Political Reforms through the New European Neighbourhood Policy' (2006) JCMS 29–55; Magen, 'The Shadow of Enlargement: Can the European Neighbourhood Policy Achieve Compliance' (2006) Col JEL 383–427.

[131] Regulation (EU) No. 232/2014 of the European Parliament and of the Council of 11 March 2014 establishing a European Neighbourhood Instrument, OJ 2014 L77/27; see previously Regulation (EC) No. 1638/2006 of the European Parliament and of the Council of 24 October 2006 laying down general provisions establishing a European Neighbourhood and Partnership Instrument, OJ 2006 L310/1.

[132] For an in-depth analysis, see Butler, *Constitutional Law of the EU's Common Foreign and Security Policy—Competence and Institutions in External Relations* (Hart Publishing, 2019).

European Parliament is more limited than in other areas (see para. 19-004, *infra*). In addition, the right of initiative of the Commission is more restricted (see para. 19-003, *infra*). The special status of the CFSP further flows from the lack of jurisdiction of the Court of Justice, in principle, over CFSP acts (see para. 13-012, *infra*).

Substantive scope. The introduction of a 'common' foreign and security policy has not prompted the Member States to take joint action on any aspect of foreign and security policy. The CFSP rather affords an institutional framework which facilitates the framing and execution of a common policy in matters on which all of the Member States agree that action must be taken at Union level. The TEU does not lay down any substantive rules with which the Union's common foreign and security policy must comply, except that the CFSP be based on the development of mutual political solidarity among Member States, the identification of questions of general interest, and the achievement of an ever-increasing degree of convergence of Member States' actions (Article 24(2) TEU). The Member States are to judge themselves, in the context of the European Council and the Council, whether a matter should be covered by the common policy.[133] Only questions of security policy are specified in the Treaties (see Article 43 TEU).

10.027

Institutions and instruments. The Treaty provisions do, however, describe the institutional actors responsible for CFSP, the procedures by which the CFSP is given shape, and the type of decisions it may require.

10.028

As regards institutional actors and procedures, the Lisbon Treaty made major changes to the CFSP by creating the 'High Representative of the Union for Foreign Affairs and Security Policy', who now plays a key role in the field of the CFSP. The policy line for the CFSP is still determined by the European Council, which is to define the Union's strategic interests and the CFSP's objectives and general guidelines (Article 26 (1) TEU).[134] The Council is to frame the CFSP and take the decisions necessary for defining and implementing it on the basis of the general guidelines and strategic lines defined by the European Council (Article 26(2) TEU). The High Representative, together with the Member States, is responsible for putting the CFSP into effect (Article 26(3) TEU). In principle, the European Council and the Council take their decisions by a unanimous vote (Article 31(1), first subpara. TEU). However, since the Treaty of Amsterdam, Council decisions can be taken in certain cases by a qualified majority vote (see para. 19-002, *infra*).

As regards the 'decisions' taken in the framework of the CFSP, Article 25(b) distinguishes between decisions defining actions to be undertaken and those defining positions to be taken—together with any decisions arranging for the implementation of those two kinds of decisions. Before the Lisbon Treaty, the former decisions took the form of 'joint actions' and the latter of 'common positions'. Where necessary, the Council may also conclude an agreement with one or more States or international organizations (Article 37 TEU).[135]

---

[133] See Article 26(1) and Article 28(1) TEU. For a survey of matters covered, see Hill, 'Renationalising or Regrouping? EU Foreign Policy Since 11 September 2001' (2004) JCMS 143–63.

[134] Before the Lisbon Treaty, the European Council was to decide on 'common strategies' (Article 13(2) EU). For the first, see Common Strategy 1999/414/CFSP of the European Union of 4 June 1999 on Russia (OJ 1999 L157/1).

[135] See, for instance, Council Decision 2009/820/CFSP of 23 October 2009 on the conclusion on behalf of the European Union of the Agreement on extradition between the European Union and the United States of America and the Agreement on mutual legal assistance between the European Union and the United States of America, OJ 2009 L291/40. See Stessens, 'The EU-US Agreement on Extradition and on Mutual legal Assistance', in Martenczuk and van Thiel (eds), *Justice, Liberty, Security: New Challenges for the External Relations of the European Union*

10.029 **Union positions.** The Union's decisions defining positions in matters of CFSP include those defining the Union's approach to particular matters of a geographical or thematic nature (Article 29 TEU). By means of decisions defining positions—named 'common positions' before the Lisbon Treaty—the Council has been formulating objectives and priorities for Union policy vis-à-vis specific third countries[136] and defining a common stance of the Member States for international conferences (e.g. on disarmament)[137] and for action on the part of the Union in international organizations,[138] such as the International Criminal Court.[139] The Council has also adopted decisions laying down common rules governing control of exports of military technology and equipment.[140] From the outset, 'common positions' have been used to impose economic sanctions against third countries, sometimes pursuant to a superior international obligation, that is to say binding resolutions of the United Nations Security Council. Since the Lisbon Treaty, the Union then adopts both a CFSP decision and an act implementing that CFSP decision on the basis of the TFEU (see para. 10-031, *infra*).

10.030 **Operational decisions.** Other CFSP decisions define actions to be taken by the Union—'joint actions' before the Lisbon Treaty—including operational action (see Article 28(1) TEU). Such Council decisions have afforded a basis for support to the activities of other international organizations (e.g. on disarmament),[141] but also for the Union's own humanitarian aid actions,[142] Union support for the restoration of democracy,[143] or a peace

---

(VUBpress, 2009) 341–66; Sari, 'The Conclusion of International Agreements by the European Union in the Context of the ESDP', (2008) ICLQ 53–86.

[136] See, e.g., Council Decision 2010/128/CFSP of 1 March 2010 amending Common Position 2003/495/CFSP on Iraq, OJ 2010 L51/22 (amending the pre-Lisbon Common Position on Iraq, 2003/495/CFSP of 7 July 2003, OJ 2003 L169/72). Before the Lisbon Treaty, see, e.g., the Common Position on Burma/Myanmar (2003/297/CFSP of 28 April 2003, OJ 2003 L106/36) and Common Position 2005/304/CFSP of 12 April 2005 concerning conflict prevention, management, and resolution in Africa, OJ 2005, L97/57.

[137] See, e.g., Council Decision (CFSP) 2015/2096 of 16 November 2015 on the position of the European Union relating to the Eighth Review Conference of the Convention on the Prohibition of the Development, Production and Stockpiling of Bacteriological (Biological) and Toxin Weapons and on Their Destruction (BTWC), OJ 2015 L303/13; Council Decision 2012/712/CFSP of 19 November 2012 relating to the 2013 Review Conference of the Convention on the Prohibition of the Development, Production, Stockpiling and Use of Chemical Weapons and on their Destruction (CWC), OJ 2012 L321/68.

[138] e.g. Common Position 2007/762/CFSP of 22 November 2007 on participation by the European Union in the Korean Peninsula Energy Development Organisation (KEDO), OJ 2007 L305/62.

[139] Council Decision 2011/168/CFSP of 21 March 2011 on the International Criminal Court and repealing Common Position 2003/444/CFSP, OJ 2011 L76/56.

[140] Council Common Position 2008/944/CFSP of 8 December 2008 defining common rules governing control of exports of military technology and equipment, OJ 2008 L335/99, as subsequently amended by Council Decisions based on Article 29 TEU (see, e.g., Council Decision (CFSP) 2019/1560 of 16 September 2019, OJ 2019 L239/16).

[141] e.g. Council Decision (CFSP) 2019/938 of 6 June 2019 in support of a process of confidence-building leading to the establishment of a zone free of nuclear weapons and all other weapons of mass destruction in the Middle East, OJ 2019 L149/63; Council Decision (CFSP) 2019/538 of 1 April 2019 in support of activities of the Organisation for the Prohibition of Chemical Weapons (OPCW) in the framework of the implementation of the EU Strategy against Proliferation of Weapons of Mass Destruction, OJ 2019 L93/2; Council Decision (CFSP) 2017/2283 of 11 December 2017 in support of a global reporting mechanism on illicit small arms and light weapons and other illicit conventional weapons and ammunition to reduce the risk of their illicit trade, OJ 2017 L328/20.

[142] e.g., support for the conveying of humanitarian aid in Bosnia and Herzegovina (Decision 93/603/CFSP of 8 November 1993, OJ 1993 L286/1).

[143] e.g., the dispatch of a team of observers for the parliamentary elections in the Russian Federation (Decision 93/604/CFSP of 9 November 1993, OJ 1993 L286/3), support for the transition towards a democratic and multiracial South Africa (Decision 93/678/CFSP of 6 December 1993, OJ 1993 L316/45), support for the democratic transition process in the Democratic Republic of Congo (Joint Actions 96/656/CFSP of 11 November 1996, OJ 1996 L300/1, and 97/875/CFSP of 19 December 1997, OJ 1997 L357/1) and support for the democratic process

process[144] in specific third countries or regions (e.g. in South-Africa, Congo, the Middle-East, and Bosnia and Herzegovina) and intervention in crisis-stricken areas (e.g. through the appointment of a Special Representative of the European Union to the Balkans, the Middle-East, Afghanistan, Georgia, and other regions[145]). As long ago as 1994 the Union agreed, in connection with the conflict in Bosnia and Herzegovina, to take over the administration of the city of Mostar for two years.[146] Meanwhile, the Union has established various police missions as well as military missions, first in the Balkans, and later on in Africa, Asia, and the Middle East (see para. 10-032, *infra* on the common security and defence policy). Accordingly, police missions have been established in Afghanistan, Congo, and the Palestinian Territories,[147] as well as border assistance missions (Gaza, Libya, Moldova/Ukraine),[148] missions in support of security sector reform (Guinea-Bissau and Congo, the Horn of Africa, Mali and Niger, Iraq and Ukraine),[149] and monitoring missions

---

in Nigeria (Joint Action 98/735/CFSP of 22 December 1998, OJ 1998 L354/1). See Youngs, 'European Union Democracy Promotion Politics: Ten Years On' (2001) E For Aff Rev 355–73; Weber, 'Die EU-Mission in Kongo: Perspektive einer Europäischen Friedenspolitik' (2006) EuR 879–89.

[144] See, for instance, the support for the implementation of the Lusaka Ceasefire Agreement and the peace process in the Democratic Republic of Congo (Common Position 2003/319/CFSP of 8 May 2003, OJ 2003 L115/87), the support for the OAU peace process between Ethiopia and Eritrea (Council Common Position 2000/420/CFSP of 29 June 2000, OJ 2000 L161/1), the support given to the Middle East peace process (Decision 94/276/CFSP of 19 April 1994, OJ 1994 L119/1, as subsequently supplemented).

[145] See Article 33 TEU. In this way, Special Representatives were appointed for, *inter alia*, the African Great Lakes Region (e.g. Joint Action 2009/128/CFSP of 16 February 2009, OJ 2009 L46/36), for the Middle East peace process (e.g. Council Decision (CFSP) 2020/250 of 25 February 2020, OJ L54I/3), for the Palestinian Authority (Joint Action 97/289/CFSP of 29 April 1997, OJ 1997 L120/2), for Kosovo (e.g. Council Decision (CFSP) 2020/1135 of 30 July 2020, OJ 2020 L247/25, for the Former Yugoslavian Republic of Macedonia (FYROM) (e.g. Joint Action 2009/706/CFSP of 15 September 2009, OJ 2009 L244/25), for Afghanistan and Pakistan (e.g. Joint Action 2009/467/CFSP of 15 June 2009, OJ 2009 L151/41), for Bosnia and Herzegovina (e.g. Joint Action 2009/181/CFSP of 11 March 2009 OJ 2009 L67/88), for the South Caucasus (e.g. Joint Action 2009/133/CFSP of 16 February 2009, OJ 2009 L46/53), for Moldova (Joint Action 2009/132/CFSP of 16 February 2009, OJ 2009 L46/50), for Sudan (e.g. Joint Action 2009/134/CFSP of 16 February 2009, OJ 2009 L46/57), for Central Asia (e.g. Council Decision (CFSP) 2020/252 of 25 February 2020, OJ 2020 L54I/7), for the Sahel (e.g. Council Decision (CFSP) 2020/253 of 25 February 2020, OJ 2020 L54I/9), for the Horn of Africa (e.g. Council Decision (CFSP) 2020/251 of 25 February 2020, OJ L54I/5 for the African Union (OJ 2009 L322/50) and for the crisis in Georgia (e.g. Council Decision (CFSP) 2020/254 of 25 February 2020, OJ 2020 L54I/12).

[146] It did so on the basis of a memorandum of understanding concluded by the EU and the WEU with the local authorities, see, e.g., Council Decision 94/308/CFSP of 16 May 1994, OJ 1994 L134/1, as supplemented); for its phasing out, see Joint Action 96/476/CFSP of 26 July 1996 (OJ 1996 L195/1).

[147] e.g. Council Joint Action 2004/847/CFSP of 9 December 2004 on the EUPM in Kinshasa (Congo) regarding the Integrated Police Unit (EUPOL KINSHASA), OJ 2004 L367/30; Council Joint Action 2005/797/CFSP of 14 November 2005 on the EUPM for the Palestinian Territories (EUPOL COPPS), [2005] L300/65; Council Joint Action 2007/369/CFSP of 30 May 2007 on establishment of the EUPM in Afghanistan (EUPOL AFGHANISTAN), OJ 2007 L139/33.

[148] e.g. Council Joint Action 2005/889/CFSP of 12 December 2005 on establishing a European Union Border Assistance Mission for the Rafah Crossing Point (EU BAM Rafah), OJ 2005 L327/28.

[149] e.g. Council Joint Action 2005/355/CFSP of 2 May 2005 on the European Union mission to provide advice and assistance for security sector reform in the Democratic Republic of the Congo (EUSEC RD Congo), OJ 2005 L112/20, as replaced most recently by Council Decision 2010/329/CFSP of 14 June 2010 on the EUPM undertaken in the framework of reform of the security sector (SSR) and its interface with the system of justice in the Democratic Republic of the Congo (EUPOL RD Congo), OJ 2010 L149/11; Council Joint Action 2008/112/CFSP of 12 February 2008 on the European Union mission in support of security sector reform in the Republic of Guinea-Bissau (EU SSR GUINEA-BISSAU), OJ 2008 L40/11; Council Decision 2014/486/CFSP of 22 July 2014 on the European Union Advisory Mission for Civilian Security Sector Reform Ukraine (EUAM Ukraine), OJ 2014 L217/42; Council Decision (CFSP) 2017/1869 of 16 October 2017 on the European Union Advisory Mission in support of Security Sector Reform in Iraq (EUAM Iraq), OJ 2017 L266/12. See also training missions, such as Council Decision (CFSP) 2016/610 of 19 April 2016 on a European Union CSDP Military Training Mission in the Central African Republic (EUTM RCA), OJ 2016 L104/21.

(Indonesia and Georgia).[150] In addition, missions aimed at strengthening the rule of law have been set up in Iraq, Georgia, and Kosovo.[151]

10.031 **Restrictive measures.** Where the Union wishes to act internationally by adopting sanctions or 'restrictive measures' against third countries, groups, or individuals, both CFSP and other Union competences come into play.[152] Since the entry into force of the EU Treaty (1993), such restrictive measures generally come under the CFSP. On the basis of Article 29 TEU, the Council, acting unanimously, determines the persons and entities that are to be the subject of the restrictive measures that the Union adopts in the field of the CFSP.[153] Article 215 TFEU serves as a bridge between the Union's objectives in matters of the CFSP and Union action falling within the scope of the TFEU.[154] It allows for the adoption of the necessary measures by the Council, acting by a qualified majority on a joint proposal from the High Representative and the Commission, in order to give effect to CFSP decisions imposing restrictive measures, where such necessary measures fall within the scope of the TFEU. By having recourse to regulations, the Council ensures their uniform application in all Member States. In practice, the CFSP decision and the non-CFSP regulation are adopted at the same moment and have a similar content.[155] The Court of Justice has clarified that this does not mean that the CFSP decision is encroaching on the non-CFSP regulation as those two types of act have different functions, one declaring the Union's position with respect to the restrictive measures to be adopted and the other constituting the instrument giving effect to those measures at Union level.[156]

Whereas initially such restrictive measures consisted of general arms embargoes and economic or financial sanctions, more and more 'smart' sanctions are now being taken, such as the freezing of assets of specific persons and entities and restrictions on the admission into the Union of specified third-country nationals (visa or travel bans). Before the Lisbon Treaty, the Treaty provisions only provided for restrictive measures against third States. The Court of Justice held that those provisions could also be invoked as legal basis for restrictive measures vis-à-vis the leaders of such States, as well as against persons and entities that had close ties with them or were under their direct or indirect control,[157] but not for

---

[150] e.g. Council Joint Action 2005/643/CFSP of 9 September 2005 on the European Union Monitoring Mission in Aceh (Indonesia) (Aceh Monitoring Mission—AMM), OJ 2005 L234/13; Council Joint Action 2008/736/CFSP on the European Union Monitoring Mission in Georgia (EUMM Georgia), OJ 2008 L248/26.

[151] The Kosovo Rule of Law Mission is still ongoing; see Council Decision (CFSP) 2020/792 of 11 June 2020 amending Joint Action 2008/124/CFSP on the European Union Rule of Law Mission in Kosovo (EULEX KOSOVO), OJ 2020 L193/9. For Iraq, see Council Decision 2010/330/CFSP of 14 June 2010 on the European Union Integrated Rule of Law Mission for Iraq (EUJUST LEX-IRAQ), OJ L149/12, which ended on 31 December 2013; see also earlier for Georgia: Council Joint Action 2004/523/CFSP of 28 June 2004 on the European Union Rule of Law Mission in Georgia (EUJUST THEMIS), OJ 2004 L228/21.

[152] For an overview, see Camaron (ed.), *EU Sanctions: Law and Policy Issues Concerning Restrictive Measures* (Intersentia, 2013); Beaucillon, *Les mesures restrictives de l'Union européenne* (Bruylant, 2013).

[153] See C-72/15, *PJSC Rosneft Oil Company*, 2017, para. 88 (taking account of the wide scope of the aims and objectives of the CFSP, the Council has a broad discretion in determining such persons and entities).

[154] C-72/15, *PJSC Rosneft Oil Company*, 2017, para. 89; C-130/10, *European Parliament v Council*, 2012, para. 59.

[155] See, e.g., Council Decision (CFSP) 2018/1544 of 15 October 2018 concerning restrictive measures against the proliferation and use of chemical weapons, OJ 2018 L259/25, and Council Regulation (EU) 2018/1542 of 15 October 2018 concerning restrictive measures against the proliferation and use of chemical weapons, OJ 2018 L259/12.

[156] C-72/15, *PJSC Rosneft Oil Company*, 2017, para. 89

[157] C-402/05 P and C-415/05 P, *Kadi and Al Barakaat International Foundation v Council and Commission*, 2008, paras 163–6.

restrictive measures against persons without ties to the ruling regime of a third state.[158] Since the Lisbon Treaty, Article 215(2) TFEU clearly indicates that restrictive measures may also be taken against natural or legal persons, groups, or non-State entities.[159] In December 2020, the Council established an additional framework for targeted restrictive measures to address serious human rights violations and abuses worldwide,[160] allowing for a wide array of sanctions, such as travel bans, freezing of assets of persons responsible for such human rights breaches, or persons supporting them or associated with them.[161]

Sometimes, sanctions agreed under the CFSP may be carried out directly by the Member States.[162] Generally, however, a CFSP sanction has to be implemented by a Union measure in another field of Union competence, such as the common commercial policy or police and judicial cooperation in criminal matters.[163] Article 215(1) TFEU states that where a CFSP decision provides for 'the interruption or reduction, in part or completely, of economic and financial relations with one or more third countries', the Council is to adopt 'the necessary measures'. Where a CFSP decision so provides, the Council may also adopt restrictive measures against natural or legal persons and groups or non-State entities (Article 215(2) TFEU). In either case, the Council acts on a joint proposal from the High Representative and the Commission. Restrictive measures may further entail administrative measures with regard to capital movements and payments, such as the freezing of funds, financial assets, or economic gains. Article 75 TFEU offers a specific legal basis for measures restricting capital movements and payments when necessary to achieve objectives of the Area of Freedom, Security and Justice, most notably in order to combat terrorism and related activities.[164] The framework for such measures is to be defined by the European Parliament and the Council, acting by means of regulations in accordance with the ordinary legislative procedure; the Council, on a proposal from the Commission, adopts the necessary measures to implement the framework.

Before the Lisbon Treaty, the Union Courts reviewed the legality of restrictive measures implemented by Community measures, *inter alia*, as to their compatibility with fundamental rights and procedural safeguards, but did not have jurisdiction to rule on CFSP acts providing for such restrictive measures to be taken in the first place.[165] Since the Lisbon Treaty,

---

[158] Ibid., paras 167–78. Nevertheless, those measures could be adopted if they were also adopted on the basis of Article 308 EC Treaty (*now Article 352 TFEU*), paras 194–236.

[159] See C-130/10, *European Parliament v Council*, 2012, paras 56–65.

[160] Council Decision (CFSP) 2020/1999 of 7 December 2020 concerning restrictive measures against serious human rights violations and abuses, OJ 2020 L410I/13, and Council Regulation (EU) 2020/1998 of 7 December 2020 concerning restrictive measures against serious human rights violations and abuses, OJ 2020 L410I/1.

[161] Ibid., Articles 2 and 3.

[162] See, e.g., sanctions as imposed pursuant to a UN Security Council resolution against Nigeria by Common Positions of 20 November 1995 (95/515/CFSP), OJ 1995 L298/1, and 4 December 1995 (95/544/CFSP), OJ 1995 L309/1 (restrictions on visas for, e.g., members of the government and their families, sports boycott, and arms embargo).

[163] e.g. Council Decision 2003/48/JHA of 19 December 2002 on the implementation of specific measures for police and judicial cooperation to combat terrorism in accordance with Article 4 of Common Position 2001/931/CFSP, OJ 2003 L16/68. See, in this connection, Hörmann, 'Die Befugnis der EG zur Umsetzung von Resolutionen des UN-Sicherheitsrates zur Bekämpfung des internationalen Terrorismus' (2007) EuR 121–33.

[164] This does not prevent restrictive measures adopted pursuant to Article 215(2) TFEU as well as the measures implementing them also to be taken to combat terrorism: C-130/10, *European Parliament v Council*, 2012, paras 63–6.

[165] See, for instance, the judgments in C-584/10 P, C-593/10 P and C-595/10 P, *Commission and United Kingdom v Kadi*, 2013; C-402/05 P and C-415/05 P, *Kadi and Al Barakaat International Foundation v Council and Commission*, 2008; T-341/07 *Sison v Council*, 2009; T-256/07, *People's Mojahedin Organization of Iran v Council*, 2008. See De Hert and Weis, 'Terrorismelijsten en de paradox van de rechtsbescherming' (2009) SEW 336–42;

the Court of Justice of the European Union has jurisdiction to review the legality of CFSP decisions taken in this connection insofar as they provide for restrictive measures against natural or legal persons (Article 275, second para. TFEU; see para. 13-012, *infra*).[166]

10.032 **Common security and defence policy.** Pursuant to Article 24(1) TEU, the CFSP shall cover all areas of foreign policy and all questions relating to the Union's security, including the progressive framing of a common defence policy that might once lead to a common defence.[167]

The common security and defence policy (CSDP) is described in a separate section of Title V of the TEU as forming an integral part of the CFSP.[168] It is to provide the Union with an operational capacity drawing on civilian and military assets to be used on missions outside the Union for peace-keeping, conflict prevention, and strengthening international security (Article 42(1) TEU). The Union's tasks include 'joint disarmament operations, humanitarian and rescue tasks, military advice and assistance tasks, conflict prevention and peace-keeping tasks, tasks of combat forces in crisis management, including peace-making and post-conflict stabilisation' (Article 43(1) TEU).[169] All these tasks are to contribute to the fight against terrorism, *inter alia*, by supporting third countries in combating terrorism in their territories (Article 43(1) TEU). Since 2003 the Union has initiated military operations, first in the Former Yugoslav Republic of Macedonia (now North Macedonia; this operation has since been replaced by an EU police mission)[170] and subsequently in Congo[171] and

---

Almqvist, 'A Human Rights Critique of European Judicial Review: Counter-Terrorism Sanctions' (2008) ICLQ 303–31; Schmahl, 'Effektiver Rechtsschutz gegen "targeted sanctions" des UN-Sicherheitsrats' (2006) EuR 566–76. See further the (abundant) literature on the *Kadi* case referred to in para. 26-015, *infra*.

[166] The Court has interpreted its jurisdiction so that it may review the legality of CFSP decisions providing for restrictive measures against natural or legal persons through both direct actions pursuant to Article 263 TFEU and the preliminary reference procedure (Article 267 TFEU), see C-72/15, *PJSC Rosneft Oil Company*, 2017, paras 50–81.

[167] According to Article 42(2), first subpara. TEU, the progressive framing of a common defence policy will lead to an actual 'common defence' when the European Council, acting unanimously, so decides. In that case, it must recommend to the Member States the adoption of such a decision in accordance with their constitutional requirements.

[168] For a general appraisal, see Koutrakos, *The EU Common Security and Defence Policy* (OUP, 2013); Naert, *International Law Aspects of the EU's Security and Defence Policy* (Intersentia, 2010); Oppermann, 'Public Opinion and the Development of the European Security and Defence Policy' (2007) E For Aff Rev 149–67; Duke and Ojanen, 'Bridging Internal and External Security: Lessons from the European Security and Defence Policy' (2006) JEI 477–94; Dietrich, 'Die rechtlichen Grundlagen der Verteidigungspolitik der Europäischen Union' (2006) ZaöRV 663–97; Graf von Kielsmansegg, 'Die verteidigungspolitischen Kompetenzen der Europäischen Union' (2006) EuR 182–200; Trybus, 'With or without the EU Constitutional Treaty: towards a Common Security and Defence Policy' (2006) ELRev 145–66.

[169] The tasks listed in Article 43(1) TEU are known as the 'Petersberg tasks' following the Petersberg Declaration made by the WEU States on 19 June 1992. They were significantly extended by the Lisbon Treaty (compare Article 17(2) EU with Article 43(1) TEU). See Pagani, 'A New Gear in the CFSP Machinery: Integration of the Petersberg Tasks in the Treaty on European Union' (1998) EJIL 737–49; Graf von Kielmansegg, 'The Meaning of Petersberg: Some Considerations on the legal Scope of ESDP Operations' (2007) CMLRev 629–48.

[170] e.g. Council Joint Action 2003/92/CFSP of 27 January 2003 on the European Union military operation in the Former Yugoslav Republic of Macedonia ('Concordia'), OJ 2003 L34/26, succeeded by Council Joint Action 2003/681/CFSP of 29 September 2003 on the European Union Police Mission in the Former Yugoslav Republic of Macedonia (EUPOL 'Proxima'), OJ 2003 L249/66, and Council Joint Action 2005/826/CFSP of 24 November 2005 on the establishment of an EU Police Advisory Team in the Former Yugoslav Republic of Macedonia (EUPAT), OJ 2005 L307/61.

[171] Council Joint Action 2003/423/CFSP of 5 June 2003 on the European Union military operation in the Democratic Republic of Congo ('ARTEMIS'), OJ 2003 L143/50, launched by Council Decision 2003/432/CFSP of 12 June 2003, OJ 2013 L147/42.

Bosnia and Herzegovina;[172] Chad and the Central-African Republic;[173] Somalia and off the Somali coast (against acts of piracy);[174] Mali;[175] and the southern part of the Mediterranean, as well as mixed civilian-military operations in Sudan, Somalia, and Mali.[176]

The capabilities to carry out the tasks mentioned above are provided by the Member States (Article 42(3) TEU). The operational capacity for the CSDP was originally provided by the Western European Union (WEU; see para. 1-012, *supra*), which is now integrated into the European Union.[177] In connection with its take-over of the WEU structures, the Council has set up an Institute for Security Studies and a Satellite Centre.[178] For the purposes of implementing the CSDP, the EU has its own political and military structures (see para. 19-007, *infra*), which have taken charge of the EU police missions and military operations.[179] The EU can also have recourse to NATO assets and capabilities for its operations[180] and invite non-EU allies to participate in its operations (see para. 10-033, *supra*). Since the Lisbon Treaty, Member States undertake progressively to improve their military capabilities (Article 42(3), second subpara. TEU). To that effect, a European Defence Agency had already been established in July 2004 (see Articles 42(3) TEU and 45 TEU),[181] which is to identify operational requirements, to promote and implement measures strengthening the industrial and technological base of the defence sector, and to participate in defining a European capabilities and armaments policy. It is to assist the Council in evaluating the improvement of military capabilities (Article 42(3), second subpara. TEU). The Lisbon Treaty

---

[172] Council Joint Action 2004/570/CFSP of 12 July 2004 on the European Union military operation in Bosnia and Herzegovina ('ALTHEA'), OJ 2004 L252/11, launched by Council Decision 2004/803/CFSP of 25 November 2004, OJ 2004 L353/21.

[173] Council Decision 2008/101/CFSP of 28 January 2008 on the launching of the European Union military operation in the Republic of Chad and in the Central African Republic (Operation EUFOR Tchad/RCA), OJ 2008 L39.

[174] Council Decision 2008/918/CFSP of 8 December 2008 on the launch of a European Union military operation to contribute to the deterrence, prevention, and repression of acts of piracy and armed robbery off the Somali coast (Atalanta), OJ 2008 L330/19.

[175] Council Decision (CFSP) 2015/76 of 19 January 2015 launching the European Union CSDP mission in Mali (EUCAP Sahel Mali), OJ 2019 L51/29.

[176] See, e.g., Council Joint Action 2005/557/CFSP of 18 July 2005 on the European Union civilian-military supporting action to the African Union mission in the Darfur region of Sudan, OJ 2005 L188/46.

[177] Cammileri, 'Le traité de Nice et la politique européenne de la défense' (2000) RAE 389–97; Duke, 'CESP: Nice's Overtrumped Success?' (2001) E For Aff Rev 155–75. For the former relationship between WEU and EU, see Cahen, 'L'Union de l'Europe occidentale (UEO) et la mise en oeuvre de la future défense commune de l'nion européenne' (1996) RMCUE 21–35.

[178] Council Decision 2014/75/CFSP of 10 February 2014 on the European Union Institute for Security Studies, OJ 2014 L41/13, replacing Council Joint Action 2001/554/CFSP of 20 July 2001, OJ 2001 L200/1; Council Decision 2014/401/CFSP of 26 June 2014 on the European Union Satellite Centre, OJ 2014 L188/73, replacing Council Joint Action 2001/555/CFSP of 20 July 2001, OJ 2001 L200/5.

[179] For a detailed overview, see Naert, *International Law Aspects of the EU's Security and Defence Policy, with a Particular Focus on the Law of Armed Conflict* (Intersentia, 2010), Chapter 3; Stewart, 'Capabilities and Coherence? The Evolution of European Union Conflict Prevention' (2008) E For Aff Rev 229–53; Benoit, 'Le lancement des premières opérations militaires de l'Union européenne' (2004) RMCUE 235–40; Solana, 'Politique européenne de sécurité et de défense: de l'opérationnalité aux opérations' (2003) RMCUE 148–50.

[180] Presidency Report on strengthening of the common European policy on security and defence, Annex III to the Presidency conclusions of the European Council held in Cologne on 3 and 4 June 1999 (1999) 6 EU Bull. point I.62. For the necessary arrangements with NATO, see para. 25-032, *infra*.

[181] Council Decision (CFSP) 2015/1835 of 12 October 2015 defining the statute, seat, and operational rules of the European Defence Agency, OJ 2015 L266/55, originally established by Council Joint Action 2004/551/CFSP of July 12, 2004 on the establishment of the European Defence Agency, OJ 2004 L245/17. The full name of the European Defence Agency is 'Agency in the field of defence capabilities development, research, acquisition and armaments' (Article 42(3), second subpara. TEU). It has its own legal personality and is based in Brussels. See the Agency's website at: http://eda.europa.eu/. Cooperation in the field of armaments has existed since 1996 in the context of the Western European Armament Group.

allows the Council to entrust the execution of a mission of the Union to a group of Member States that are able and willing to carry out such missions (Article 42(5) and 44(1) TEU). Article 42(7) TEU provides that if a Member State is the victim of armed aggression on its territory, the other Member States have an obligation towards it to provide aid and assistance by all the means in their power, in accordance with the United Nations Charter.[182]

10.033   NATO. For those States which are members of NATO, that organization is to remain the foundation of their collective defence and the forum for its implementation (Article 42(7) TEU). The CFSP must respect the obligations of certain Member States under NATO and be compatible with the policy established within that framework (Article 42(2), second subpara. TEU).[183] This means that a CSDP action could not be directed against a Member State of NATO.[184] There are to be permanent and continuing consultations with the non-EU European allies, in particular before decisions are taken on matters affecting their security interests.[185] Non-EU European allies may participate in an operation conducted by the Union for which NATO assets are deployed and are invited to take part in operations conducted by the Union where no NATO assets are to be used.[186] The Union aims to have a strategic partnership with NATO on the basis of which the two organizations may collaborate in crisis management while retaining their independence of decision-making. This collaboration is founded upon 'permanent arrangements' between the Union and NATO.[187] Pursuant to the 'Berlin plus' arrangements the Union is given assured access to NATO's planning and logistics capabilities for its own military operations.[188]

10.034   Non-participation. The policy of the Union must not prejudice the specific character of the security and defence policy of certain Member States (Article 42(2), second subpara. TEU)[189]. At the same time, the CFSP decision-making procedure allows Member States to make a formal declaration that they abstain in a given vote. They will then not be obliged to apply the relevant decision (Article 31(1) TEU, see para. 19-002, *infra*). Ever since

---

[182] Article 42(7) TEU was introduced by the Lisbon Treaty and took over the mutual defence clause of the Treaty establishing the Western European Union (see para. 1-012, *supra*).

[183] For the North Atlantic Treaty (Washington Treaty), see para. 1-012, *supra*. See Kintis, 'NATO-WEU: An Enduring Relationship' (1998) E For Aff Rev 537–62; Österdahl, 'The EU and its Member States, Other States and International Organisations—The Common European Security and Defence Policy After Nice' (2001) Nordic JIL 341–72; McLaren, 'Europe's Efforts to Develop an Autonomous Defense Capability, A Constitution for Europe, and the Implications for NATO' (2005) Col JEL 523–56.

[184] See the conclusions of the European Council held in Brussels on 24 and 25 October 2002 (2002) 10 EU Bull. point I.15, section 2.

[185] Ibid., point I.15, sections 3 to 5.

[186] Ibid., point I.15, sections 11 and 15. Accordingly, third countries have been invited to participate in the military operations of the European Union pursuant to agreements concluded on the basis of Article 24 EU (now Article 37 TFEU), see, e.g., the agreement between the European Union and Croatia on the participation of Croatia in the European Union military operation in the Republic of Chad and in the Central African Republic, concluded by Council Decision 2008/783/CFSP of 15 September 2008, OJ 2008 L268/32, and the agreement between the European Union and the USA on the participation of the USA in the European Union Rule of Law Mission in Kosovo, concluded by Council Decision 2008/814/CFSP of 13 October 2008, OJ 2008 L282/32.

[187] These arrangements are to be found in the joint declaration by the European Union and NATO of 16 December 2002 on the European Security and Defence policy (see NATO Press Release (2002) 142, available on the NATO website). NATO also concluded an agreement with the European Union on the security of information, based on Article 24 EU (approved by Council Decision 2003/211/CFSP of 24 February 2003, OJ 2003 L80/35).

[188] The terms 'Berlin plus' refer to the ministerial meeting of the North Atlantic Council on 3 June 1996 in Berlin where it was agreed that a European Security and Defence Identity should be built within NATO. The European Council welcomed the 'Berlin Plus' arrangements in the conclusions of its meeting held in Thessaloniki on 19 and 20 June 2003 (2003) 6 EU Bull. point I.23, section 60.

[189] For example, in Declaration (No. 35), annexed to the 2003 Act of Accession, Malta emphasizes its neutrality.

the introduction of the CFSP in 1993, Denmark has made clear that it does not participate in the elaboration and implementation of decisions and actions of the Union which have defence implications, in particular the common security and defence policy (CSDP). That position is now laid down in a specific protocol to the Treaties.[190]

Enhanced cooperation. The Treaties allow the Member States to establish enhanced cooperation between them in the field of the CFSP, under a procedure which is slightly different from that applicable in other fields (see para. 22-006, *infra*).[191] Before the Lisbon Treaty, Article 17(4) EU expressly provided for the development of closer cooperation between two or more Member States on a bilateral level, 'in the framework of the WEU and the Atlantic Alliance', provided that such cooperation did not impede cooperation within the Union. In this way, France and the Federal Republic of Germany set up a Franco-German brigade, with headquarters in Strasbourg, as long ago as 12 January 1989. Subsequently, Belgium, Luxembourg, and Spain joined this 'Eurocorps', in which national units are placed under a common command, and a number of other Member States have become associated with the Eurocorps. For the benefit of those Member States whose military capabilities meet strict criteria and who have made commitments in respect of undertaking the most demanding missions, the Lisbon Treaty went as far as organizing a form of enhanced cooperation by setting out the conditions for 'permanent structured cooperation' (PESCO) between Member States (Article 46 TEU). Within this framework the Council adopts decisions and recommendations by unanimity, but taking into account the votes of the representatives of the participating Member States only (Article 46(6) TEU). PESCO is open to Member States which fulfil the criteria and have made the commitments on military capabilities set out in a Protocol annexed to the Treaties.[192] It is for the Council, acting by a qualified majority after consulting the High Representative, to adopt a decision establishing PESCO and determining the list of participating Member States (Article 46(1) and (2) TEU). Thus, PESCO was established in 2017 by twenty-five Member States,[193] subscribing to commitments such as increased defence budgets and defence investment expenditure and developing the interoperability of their forces.[194] If a participating Member State no longer fulfils the criteria or is no longer able to meet the commitments set out in the Protocol, the Council, acting by

10.035

---

[190] Article 5 of Protocol (No. 22), annexed to the TEU and TFEU, on the position of Denmark (OJ 2010 C83/299), replacing the Protocol on the position of Denmark, annexed to the EC Treaty and EU Treaty by the Amsterdam Treaty, which itself confirmed Part C of the Decision of the Heads of State and Government, meeting within the European Council, concerning certain problems raised by Denmark on the Treaty on European Union (OJ 1992 C348/2). See Howarth, 'The Compromise on Denmark and the Treaty on European Union: A Legal and Political Analysis' (1994) CMLRev 765, 776–9.

[191] This was made possible by the Treaty of Nice. However, under Articles 27a to e EU such cooperation was not possible for matters having military or defence implications (see para. 22-007, *infra*).

[192] Protocol (No. 10), annexed to the TEU and TFEU, on permanent structured cooperation established by Article 42 TEU, OJ 2010 C83/275.

[193] Council Decision (CFSP) 2017/2315 of 11 December 2017 establishing permanent structured cooperation (PESCO) and determining the list of participating Member States (OJ 2017 L331/57). Denmark and Malta are not participating because of their traditional neutrality policy in military matters. The United Kingdom did not participate either.

[194] Any Member State who, at a later stage, wishes to participate in the permanent structured cooperation is to notify its intention to the Council and the High Representative. If that Member State fulfils all the criteria, the Council adopts a decision confirming that Member State's participation, by a qualified majority (of the already participating Member States) and after consulting the High Representative (Article 46(3) TEU).

a qualified majority in accordance with Article 238(3)(a) TFEU, may adopt a decision suspending the participation of the Member State concerned (Article 46(4) TEU).[195]

VII. Other External Competences of the Union

10.036 **Explicit treaty-making power.** In the areas of Union external action discussed above, the Treaties expressly empower the Union to conclude international agreements. In addition, there are other policy fields where the Union is expressly empowered to conclude international agreements, namely on the readmission of third-country nationals to their countries of origin or provenance (Article 79(3) TFEU);[196] research and technological development (Article 186, second para. TFEU);[197] the environment (Article 191(4), first subpara. TFEU);[198] and on an exchange-rate system for the euro in relation to non-Union currencies (Article 219(1) TFEU).[199] The Union can exercise these external competences even in respect of matters which are not yet the subject of rules at Union level.[200] Moreover, even when a Treaty provision does not expressly confer on the Union the power to conclude an international agreement in a given area, such power may be provided for in a legally binding Union act (see Article 216(1) TFEU). This is the case whenever a Union act (legislative or non-legislative) confers on Union institutions the power to negotiate arrangements with third countries or international organizations.[201]

10.037 **Implied treaty-making power.** The Union may conclude international agreements not only in those cases where the Treaties or a legally binding Union act so provide, but also 'where the conclusion of an agreement is necessary in order to achieve, within the framework of the Union's policies, one of the objectives referred to in the Treaties ... or is likely to affect

---

[195] Any participating Member State may withdraw from permanent structured cooperation after notifying its intention to the Council, which shall take note that the Member State in question has ceased to participate (Article 46(5) TEU).

[196] This provision was added by the Lisbon Treaty. However, even before the Lisbon Treaty, the Union (then Community) already concluded agreements with third countries on immigration, on the basis of Article 63 EC. See, e.g., the agreements concluded with the Government of the Hong Kong Special Administrative Region of the People's Republic of China (PRC) and the Macao Special Administrative Region of the PRC on the readmission of persons residing without authorisation, approved by Council Decision 2004/80/EC of 17 December 2003 (OJ 2004 L17/23) and 2004/424/EC of 21 April 2004 (OJ 2004 L143/97), respectively; and the Memorandum of Understanding with the National Tourism Administration of the PRC on visa and related issues concerning tourist groups from the PRC (OJ 2004 L83/12).

[197] See, e.g., the Agreement on scientific and technical cooperation concluded with Israel, approved by Council Decision 2004/576/EC of 29 April 2004, OJ 2004 L261/47.

[198] See, e.g., Council Decision 2005/370/EC of 17 February 2005 on the conclusion of the Convention on access to information, public participation in decision-making, and access to justice in environmental matters, OJ 2005 L124/1 (Aarhus Convention), further implemented by Regulation No. 1367/2006 of the European Parliament and of the Council of 6 September 2006, OJ 2006 L264/13; Council Decision 2006/500/EC of 29 May 2006 on the conclusion of the Energy Community Treaty, OJ 2006 L198/15. See Van Eeckhoutte and Corthaut, 'The Participation of the EU and its Member States in Multilateral Environmental Negotiations Post-Lisbon', (2017) YEL 1–61; Thieme, 'European Community External Relations in the Field of the Environment' (2001) E Env L Rev 252–64.

[199] See Herrmann, 'Monetary Sovereignty over the Euro and External Relations of the Euro Area: Competences, Procedures and Practice' (2002) E For Aff Rev 1–24; Weiss, 'Kompetenzverteilung in der Währungspolitik und Aussenvertretung des Euro' (2002) EuR 165–91; Lebullenger, 'La projection externe de la zone euro' (1998) RTDE 459–78. For representation by the ECB, see ESCB Statute, Article 6. For possible arrangements in the framework of the IMF, see Bini Smaghi, 'A Single EU Seat in the International Monetary Fund?', in Jørgensen (ed.), *The European Union and International Organizations* (Taylor & Francis, 2009), 61 *et seq.*

[200] C-459/03, *Commission v Ireland*, 2006, paras 94–5; C-240/09, *Lesoochranárske zoskupenie*, 2011, paras 35–40; C-600/14, *Germany v Council*, 2017, paras 62–9.

[201] Opinion 1/94, *Agreement establishing the World Trade Organisation*, 1994, para. 95.

common rules or alter their scope' (Article 216(1) TFEU). This Treaty provision, which was introduced by the Lisbon Treaty, codifies the external powers which—according to long-standing case law of the Court of Justice—flow implicitly from the Treaties and secondary Union law.[202]

The Court of Justice has indeed held that authority for the Union to enter into international commitments may not only arise from an express attribution by the Treaties, but may also flow implicitly from their provisions, or from provisions which the institutions have adopted pursuant to those provisions. The Court has concluded, in particular, that whenever Union law created for the institutions of the Union powers within its internal system for the purpose of attaining a specific objective, the Union has authority to enter into the international commitments necessary for the attainment of that objective even in the absence of an express provision in that connection.[203]

First, such authority for the Union to enter into international commitments flows by implication from measures adopted by the institutions in so far as it is necessary to secure the effectiveness of those measures.[204] The Court of Justice thus held in the *AETR* judgment that the Union was empowered to accede to an international agreement on working conditions in international road transport on the ground that the Council had adopted a regulation internally on the harmonization of certain social legislation relating to road transport.[205] Hence, the international agreement in question could affect these rules or alter their scope. This corresponds to the last situation mentioned in Article 216(1) TFEU. Second, it is also possible for the Union to be competent to act externally in an area where it has not yet adopted rules.[206] Indeed, where a competence cannot be effectively exercised without involving third countries, the Union is entitled *ipso facto* to act externally, even if the first use made of that competence is to conclude and implement an international agreement.[207] This was the case with an agreement on a European inland-waterways fund which could not be concluded without involving third countries whose vessels used the waterways in question.[208] In such a situation, therefore, the Union has external competence because its

---

[202] For an overview, see Chamon, 'Implied Exclusive Powers in the ECJ's Post-Lisbon Jurisprudence: The Continued Development of the ERTA Doctrine' (2018) CMLRev 1101–42; Dony, 'Retour sur les compétences externes implicites de l'Union' (2018) CDE 109–76.

[203] Opinion 2/91, *Convention No 170 of the International Labour Organisation concerning safety in the use of chemicals at work*, 1993, para. 7; Opinion 2/94, *Accession by the Communities to the Convention for the Protection of Human Rights and Fundamental Freedoms*, 1996, para. 26.

[204] Opinion 2/91 (n. 203, *supra*), para. 7; 3, 4 and 6/76, *Kramer*, 1976, para. 19/20.

[205] See the *AETR* judgment of 31 March 1971, 22/70, *Commission v Council*, 1971, paras 16–29 (quoted in para. 5-019, *supra*). For later examples of international competence implicitly arising out of existing Union legislation, see Opinion 1/92, *Draft Agreement between the Community, on the one hand, and the countries of the European Free Trade Association, on the other, relating to the creation of the European Economic Area*, 1992, paras 39–40; Opinion 1/94, *Agreement establishing the World Trade Organisation*, 1994, para. 77; Opinion 1/03, *Lugano Convention on jurisdiction and the recognition and enforcement of judgments in civil and commercial matters*, 2006, paras 114–73; Opinion 1/13, *Convention on the civil aspects of international child abduction*, 2014, paras 65–90. In so far as the judgments of the Court of Justice of 5 November 2002 on the bilateral 'open skies' agreements hold that Union legislation on air transport confers exclusive external competence in respect of some aspects (fares, booking systems, and slot allocation) (n. 208, *infra*), this also constitutes recognition of external powers arising for the Union out of internal legislation.

[206] C-600/14, *Germany v Council*, 2017, paras 62–9.

[207] Opinion 1/94, *Agreement establishing the World Trade Organisation*, 1994, paras 82–5; Opinion 2/92, *Third Revised Decision of the OECD on national treatment*, 1995, paras 31–2.

[208] See Opinion 1/76, *Draft Agreement establishing a European laying-up fund for inland waterway vessels*, 1977, para. 4. In the judgments of 5 November 2002 on the bilateral 'open skies' agreements, the Court of Justice considered that as regards freedom to provide services in the field of air transport, external competence was not

internal competence may be exercised effectively only together with an external competence. This corresponds with the situation where the conclusion of an international agreement is 'necessary in order to achieve, within the framework of the Union's policies, one of the objectives referred to in the Treaties', as also mentioned in Article 216(1) TFEU.

These two situations already hint at some parallelism between the Union's internal and external powers to act. On the basis of this reasoning, for example, Article 43 TFEU and Article 91 TFEU, respectively, constitute the legal basis for a number of fisheries and transport agreements that the Union has concluded with third countries.[209] Implied treaty-making powers for the Union may also exist in areas where the Treaties do not provide for an express power to conclude international agreements, but recognize the competence of the Union and its Member States to foster cooperation with third countries and competent international organizations, notably in the fields of education (Article 165(3) TFEU), vocational training (Article 166(3) TFEU), culture (Article 167(3) TFEU), and public health (Article 168(3) TFEU). In these cases, international cooperation may take place via the '(incentive) measures' provided for in the articles in question, which are intended to be consonant with the complementary nature of the competences concerned.[210] The Union may further cooperate with third countries in respect of trans-European networks (Article 171(3) TFEU), pursuant to the procedure laid down in Article 172 TFEU. In accordance with Article 216(1) TFEU and the case law referred to above, it is likewise possible to infer a power for the Union to conclude any necessary international agreements in these policy areas.[211]

The *AETR* judgment already underscored that, to the extent to which international action on the part of the Member States is likely to detract from Union legislation, the external competence of the Union arising implicitly from internal legislation is exclusive, in the sense that it precludes any autonomous action on the part of the Member States (see para. 10-039, *infra*). Article 3(2) TFEU confirms the exclusive nature of the Union competence in

---

necessary in order to effectively exercise internal competence: C-467/98, *Commission v Denmark*, 2002, paras 54–64; C-468/98, *Commission v Sweden*, 2002, paras 51–61; C-469/98, *Commission v Finland*, 2002, paras 55–65; C-471/98, *Commission v Belgium*, 2002, paras 65–75; C-472/98, *Commission v Luxembourg*, 2002, paras 59–69; C-475/98, *Commission v Austria*, 2002, paras 65–75; C-476/98, *Commission v Germany*, 2002, paras 80–90 (at the same time the Court of Justice recognized, however, that there was external Union competence on the basis of the *AETR* case law; see n. 205, *supra*. See also Opinion 3/15, *Marrakesh Treaty to Facilitate Access to Published Works for Persons Who Are Blind, Visually Impaired or Otherwise Print Disabled*, 2017, paras 102–30.

[209] For the external competence in the field of judicial cooperation in civil matters, see van Loon and Schulz, 'The European Community and the Hague Conference on Private International Law', in Martenczuk and van Thiel (n. 135, *supra*) 257–301; Kotuby, 'External Competence of the European Community in the Hague Conference on Private International Law: Community Harmonisation and Worldwide Unification' (2001) NILR 1–30. For the lack of external competence as regards social policy, see Novitz, "A Human Face' for the Union or More Cosmetic Surgery? EU Competence in Global Social Governance and Promotion of Core Labour Standards' (2002) MJECL 231–261.

[210] Flaesch-Mougin, 'Le traité de Maastricht et les compétences externes de la Communauté européenne: à la recherche d'une politique externe de l'Union' (1993) CDE 351, 357–8.

[211] See, *e.g.*, the Agreements, concluded by the Community in 1995 on the basis of Articles 149 and 150 EC [*now Articles 165 and 166 TFEU*], with the USA establishing a cooperation programme in higher education and vocational training, renewed by Council Decision 2001/196/EC of 26 February 2001, OJ 2001 L17/7 and Council Decision 2006/910/EC of 4 December 2006, OJ 2006 L346/33. See to this effect, Lenaerts, 'Education in European Community Law after Maastricht' (1994) CMLRev 7, 39.

this situation.[212] When it is not covered by this latter Treaty provision, Union competence is shared with Member States' competence in so far as the conclusion of an international agreement simply contributes to attaining one of the objectives of the Treaties, which do not fall in the ambit of an exclusive Union competence listed in Article 3(1) TFEU.[213]

Article 352 TFEU. Furthermore, the Union has an additional power under the Treaties to conclude international agreements if it takes 'appropriate measures' under Article 352 TFEU where action by the Union proves necessary, within the framework of the policies defined in the Treaties, to attain one of the objectives set out in the Treaties.[214] Article 352 TFEU may, however, be used as a legal basis only if the Treaties have not provided the necessary powers, and hence cannot be employed where the means of acting externally are already present by implication in an internal competence.[215] Moreover, international agreements based on Article 352 TFEU may not lead to the harmonization of the laws of the Member States where the Treaties exclude such harmonization (Article 352(3) TFEU) and recourse to that article is not possible for international agreements relating to the CFSP (Article 352(4) TFEU).

10.038

VIII. Relationship to the Member States' International Powers

Pre-emption of national powers. As some Treaty provisions explicitly recognize,[216] the Union's non-exclusive external competences do not deprive Member States of the power to act externally. The principle of sincere cooperation (Article 4(3) TEU) requires, however, that to the extent to which Union rules are promulgated for the attainment of the objectives of the Treaties, the Member States, outside the framework of the Union institutions, do not assume obligations which affect those rules or alter their scope.[217] The case law following *AETR* implies that Member States retain their powers as long as the Union has not,

10.039

---

[212] Opinion 2/15, *Free Trade Agreement between the European Union and the Republic of Singapore*, 2017, paras 171–2; see also C-240/09, *Lesoochranárske zoskupenie*, 2011, paras 29–38. See further Hervé, 'L'avis 2/15 de la Cour de justice - Et maintenant, que faire du partage des compétences entre l'Union et ses États?' (2017) CDE 693–735.

[213] Opinion 2/15, *Free Trade Agreement between the European Union and the Republic of Singapore*, 2017, para 242. The external competence of the Union is, however, exclusive if the corresponding internal competence cannot be effectively exercised without external action, see ECJ, Opinion 1/03, *New Lugano Convention on jurisdiction and the recognition and enforcement of judgments in civil and commercial matters*, 2006, para. 115.

[214] 22/70, *Commission v Council*, 1971, para. 95. See, e.g. already the seven bilateral agreements on cooperation in the field of education and training under the Erasmus Programme concluded between the EEC and Austria, Finland, Iceland, Norway, Sweden, Switzerland and Liechtenstein, respectively, and approved by Council Decisions 91/611/EEC to 91/617/EEC of 28 October 1991 on the basis of Article 235 EEC [*now Article 352 TFEU*], OJ 1991 L332/1 - L332/71.

[215] See Kovar, 'Les compétences implicites: jurisprudence de la Cour et pratique communautaire', in Demaret (ed.), *Relations extérieures de la Communauté européenne et marché intérieur: aspects juridiques et fonctionnels* (College of Europe/Story, 1988), 15, 22–31; Raux, 'Le recours à l'article 235 du traité CEE en vue de la conclusion d'accords externes', *Etudes de droit des Communautés européennes. Mélanges offerts à P.-H. Teitgen* (Pedone, 1984), 407, 428.

[216] See Article 191(4) TFEU, Article 209(2) TFEU, Article 213(3) TFEU, and Article 219(4) TFEU. See also Declaration (No. 36) to the Treaty of Lisbon on Article 218 of the Treaty on the Functioning of the European Union concerning the negotiation and conclusion of international agreements by Member States relating to the area of freedom, security and justice, OJ 2016 C 202/349.

[217] 22/70, *Commission v Council*, 1971, para. 22. In that judgment, the Court of Justice therefore held not only that Union (then Community) competence *existed* (see para. 10-037, *supra*) but also that the Member States could no longer act in that area and that, as a result, the Union had *exclusive* competence (para. 5-023, *supra*).

or only partially, exercised its (non-exclusive) competences.[218] Where the Union adopts a measure—internally or internationally—the Member States must attune their international action in the light of that measure. Since the Lisbon Treaty, the Treaties enumerate the Union's exclusive competences (see relevant para. 5-023, *supra*). This enumeration includes the cases where previous action on the part of the Union prevents the Member States from acting on their own on the international level. Largely inspired by the case law of the Court of Justice,[219] Article 3(2) TFEU indeed provides that the Union 'shall also have exclusive competence for the conclusion of an international agreement when its conclusion is provided for in a legislative act of the Union or is necessary to enable the Union to exercise its internal competence, or insofar as its conclusion may affect common rules or alter their scope'.

First of all, this provision makes clear that whenever a treaty-making power is laid down in a Union legislative act, that power excludes the Member States' power to start negotiations on the same subject matter.[220] Second, Article 3(2) TFEU refers to the above-mentioned implied treaty-making powers of the Union by indicating that such powers exclude parallel Member State action when the conclusion of an international agreement is 'necessary to enable the Union to exercise its internal competence' or 'may affect common rules or alter their scope' (see para. 10-037, *infra*). It follows from the Court's case law on Union rules liable to be 'affected' or 'altered' that Member States are no longer competent to conclude an international agreement where doing so would affect the uniform and consistent application of Union rules and the proper functioning of the system that they establish.[221] By the same token, a Member State is debarred from submitting a proposal within an international organization which is likely to affect the application of Union legislation in that field.[222] To determine whether Union rules are affected, account must be taken not only of the area covered by the Union rules and by the provisions of the envisaged international agreement or action, but also of the nature and content of those rules and those provisions.[223] For instance, a Member State may not enter into international commitments falling within an area which is already largely covered by Union rules, even if there is no contradiction between those

---

[218] See, for example, Opinion 1/94, *Agreement establishing the World Trade Organisation*, 1994, paras 88–89 and 101–105; see case note by Van Nuffel, (1995) Col JEL 338, 348–51. See also Maubernard, 'L'intensité modulable des compétences externes de la Communauté européenne et de ses Etats membres' (2003) RTDE. 229–46. There is an exception where the internal Union power can only be exercised effectively together with the external power (see para. 10-037).

[219] See C-114/12, *Commission v Council*, 2014, paras 65–7.

[220] See C-114/12, *Commission v Council*, 2014, paras 64–104; C-626/15 and C-659/16, *Commission v Council*, 2018, paras 110–11; C-265/19, *Recorded Artists Actors Performers*, 2020, para. 90. Whereas the Union has treaty-making power whenever such power is conferred upon Union institutions in a legally binding Union act (see Article 216(1) TFEU), that power thus constitutes an exclusive Union power only where it is laid down in a 'legislative' act, that is an act adopted according to a legislative procedure.

[221] C-66/13, *Green Network*, 2014, paras 24–65. This also precludes that a national court applies a provision of national law in lieu of the pre-empted agreement, ibid*em*, paras 68–74.

[222] ECJ, Case C-45/07 *Commission v Greece*, 2009, paras 20–3; C-246/07 *Commission v Sweden*, 2010, paras 92–105.

[223] Opinion 1/03, *New Lugano Convention on jurisdiction and the recognition and enforcement of judgments in civil and commercial matters*, 2006, paras 114–33, with a note by Kruger in (2006) Col.J.E.L. 189–199 and Lavranos in (2006) CMLRev 1087–1100. See also Kuijper, 'The Opinion on the Lugano Convention and the Implied External relations Power of the European Community', in Martenczuk and van Thiel (n. 135, *supra*) 187–210. The criterion of 'affecting' Union law only concerns secondary Union law, and does not apply to provisions of primary Union law (e.g. the Treaty provisions on free movement of capital), see Opinion 2/15, *Free Trade Agreement between the European Union and the Republic of Singapore*, 2017, paras 168–224.

commitments and the Union rules.[224] Accordingly, the Court considered that a number of bilateral agreements relating to access to air transport ('open skies' agreements) between individual Member States on the one hand and the United States on the other hand were concluded in breach of Union law because they were contrary to Union legislation on fares and booking systems.[225] Similarly, the Court concluded that Member States could not negotiate (next to the Union) on an international agreement to protect neighbouring rights of broadcasting organizations, because this concerns an area that is largely covered by Union legislation and the negotiations could affect or alter the scope thereof.[226] To determine whether Member States retain the power to enter into international commitments, account must also be taken of the nature of the Union rules concerned, in particular whether they contain clauses relating to the treatment of nationals of third countries[227] or to the complete harmonization of a particular issue.[228] Union rules will not be affected by action on the part of the Member States where the Union has adopted only minimum requirements in the relevant area.[229] It is necessary to take into account not only the current state of Union law in the area in question but also its future development, insofar as that is foreseeable at the time of analysis.[230] In any event, the mere existence of a Treaty provision, without the further adoption of internal Union acts, is not sufficient for there to be common rules that can be affected by an international agreement. Therefore, the fact that an international agreement may affect the free movement of capital (Article 63 TFEU) is insufficient to conclude that the agreement falls within the exclusive competence of the Union pursuant to Article 3(2) TFEU.[231]

---

[224] Opinion 2/92, *Third Revised Decision of the OECD on national treatment*, 1995, paras 33–6; Opinion 2/00, *Cartagena Protocol*, 2001, paras 45–7.

[225] See the *Open Skies* judgments of 5 November 2002: C-467/98, *Commission v Denmark*, 2002, paras 75–112; C-468/98, *Commission v Sweden*, 2002, paras 71–108; C-469/98, *Commission v Finland*, 2002, paras 75–113; C-471/98, *Commission v Belgium*, 2002, paras 88–126; C-472/98, *Commission v Luxembourg*, 2002, paras 81–118; C-475/98, *Commission v Austria*, 2002, paras 88–126; C-476/98, *Commission v Germany*, 2002, paras 101–37. At the same time, the Court of Justice held that there had been an infringement of Article 43 EC [*now Article 49 TFEU*] concerning establishment in those judgments and in C-466/98, *Commission v United Kingdom*, 2003. See, similarly, the later judgment in C-523/04, *Commission v Netherlands*, 2007, with case note by Lykotrafiti in (2007) E Comp LRev 578–83. For those judgments, see Franklin, 'Flexibility vs. Legal Certainty: Article 307 EC and Other Issues in the Aftermath of the Open Skies Cases', (2005) E For Aff Rev 79–115; Slot and Dutheil de la Rochère (2003) CMLRev 697–713; Heffernan and McAuliffe, 'External Relations in the Air Transport Sector: the Court of Justice and the open Skies Agreements' (2003) ELRev 601–19. Open skies agreements with individual Member States were replaced by an Air Transport Agreement between the European Communities and its Member States, on the one hand, and the USA, on the other hand, OJ 2007 L134/1. See Grard, '"Ciel ouvert" entre l'Union européenne et les États Unis enfin! Déjà? Bientôt …' (2009) RMCUE 145–53; Mendes de Leon, 'De luchtvaart-overeenkomst tussen de EG en de VS van 2008: Les jeux ne sont pas encore faits' (2009) SEW 236–43.

[226] C-114/12, *Commission v Council*, 2014, paras 68–102. In the same vein, Opinion 1/13, *Convention on the civil aspects of international child abduction*, 2014; Opinion 3/15, *Marrakesh Treaty to Facilitate Access to Published Works for Persons Who Are Blind, Visually Impaired or Otherwise Print Disabled*, 2017, paras 102–30. See also See also Arena, 'The ERTA Pre-emption Effects of Minimum and Partial Harmonisation Directives: Insights from Opinion 3/15 on the Competence to Conclude the Marrakesh Treaty' (2018) ELRev 770–779.

[227] C-467/98, *Commission v Denmark*, 2002, para. 83 (and the parallel judgments in the 'open skies' cases). In addition, the Court referred to the situation where the Community expressly conferred on its institutions powers to negotiate with third countries (Ibid.).

[228] Opinion 1/94 (n. 20, *supra*), paras 95–6; C-467/98, *Commission v Denmark*, 2002, para. 84

[229] Opinion 2/91, *Convention No 170 of the International Labour Organisation concerning safety in the use of chemicals at work*, 1993, paras 18–21; case notes by Emiliou (1994) ELRev 76–86 and Timmermans (1994) SEW 622–7.

[230] Opinion 2/91 (n. 229, *supra*), paras 25–6; ECJ, Opinion 1/03 (n. 205, *supra*), para. 126.

[231] Opinion 2/15, *Free Trade Agreement between the European Union and the Republic of Singapore*, 2017, paras 229–36.

The upshot is that the extent of the Member States' international powers depends on whether or not the Union has exercised its internal and external competences exhaustively (principle of *pre-emption*).[232] Crucially, Member States cannot avoid the consequences of the principle of pre-emption by providing for mechanisms to avoid contradictions between Union law and the agreement envisaged; the absence of any conflict between Union rules and the international agreement envisaged does not rule out that Union rules are affected by the agreement, and hence that Member States no longer have competence to conclude it.[233] That may be different only in those areas of shared competence mentioned in Articles 4(3) and 4(4) TFEU (research, technological development, space, development cooperation, and humanitarian aid) for which the TFEU provides that 'the exercise of that competence shall not result in Member States being prevented from exercising theirs'.

10.040 **Transparency.** The allocation of competences between the Union and the Member States in the field of external relations constitutes a purely internal matter as far as the Union is concerned. However, its changing nature makes contracting parties uncertain as to who is assuming the international obligations flowing from a given agreement. Indeed, other parties have made the conclusion of an international agreement on the part of the Union conditional upon its being signed in parallel by the Member States.[234] It is for this reason, too, that multilateral agreements often require signatory international organizations to deposit a declaration as to the situation with regard to the internal division of competences.[235] In such a case, the Union is subject to an obligation of international law requiring it to submit a complete declaration of its competences. Where the Council authorizes the Commission to accede to a convention, the principle of sincere cooperation to which the institutions are subject requires the Council to enable the Commission to comply with international law by submitting a complete declaration of competences.[236]

---

[232] By the same token, Protocol (No. 23), annexed by the Lisbon Treaty to the TEU and TFEU, on external relations of the Member States with regard to the crossing of external borders (OJ 2010 C83/304), which replaces the corresponding Protocol (No. 11), annexed to the EC Treaty by the Amsterdam Treaty), confirms that Member States have competence to conclude agreements with third countries 'as long as they respect Union law and other relevant international agreements'. See also Declaration (No. 36) on Article 218 TFEU (n. 216, *supra*). For the operation of 'pre-emption', see already Lenaerts, 'Les répercussions des compétences de la Communauté européenne sur les compétences externes des Etats membres et la question de la "preemption"', in Demaret (ed.), *Relations extérieures de la Communauté européenne et marché intérieur: aspects juridiques et fonctionnels* (College of Europe/ Story, 1988) 39, 54–62; for 'pre-emption' generally, see para. 5-026, *supra*.

[233] Opinion 1/03 (n. 205, *supra*), paras 129–30.

[234] See Articles 2 and 3 of Annex IX to the United Nations Convention of 10 December 1982 on the Law of the Sea (OJ 1998 L179/113), which stipulated that the majority of the Member States had to accede thereto before the Community could accede. See Stein, 'External Relations of the European Community: Structure and Process', *Collected Courses of the Academy of European Law I*, 1990, 115, 161–2; Simmonds, 'The Community's Participation in the U.N. Law of the Sea Convention', in O'Keeffe and Schermers (eds), *Essays in European Law and Integration* (Kluwer, 1982), 141, 179–95. For the Convention, see para. 11-006, *infra*.

[235] See, e.g., Article 44 of the United Nations Convention of 13 December 2006 on the Rights of Persons with Disabilities, approved by the Community, together with an annexed declaration on (shared) competence, by Council Decision 2010/48/EC of 26 November 2009, OJ 2010 L23/35; Articles 29 and 30 of the Hague Convention on Choice of Court Agreements of 30 June 2005, approved by the Community, together with the annexed declaration on (exclusive) competence, by Council Decision 2009/397/EC of 26 February 2009, OJ 2009 L133/1; Article 5 of Annex IX to the United Nations Convention of 10 December 1982 on the Law of the Sea and the Community's Declaration concerning the competence of the European Community with regard to matters governed by that Convention and the Agreement of 28 July 1994 relating to the implementation of Part XI of the Convention, OJ 1998 L179/129.

[236] C-29/99, *Commission v Council*, 2002, paras 67–71.

11

Limitations and Exceptions to the Application of the Treaties

I. Personal Scope of the Treaties

Personal scope. The scope *ratione personae* of the Treaties covers, generally speaking, all who come under the jurisdiction of the Member States. As far as free movement is concerned, originally the Treaties conferred rights only on Member State nationals who were engaged in an economic activity. However, Union legislation and case law have extended enjoyment of a number of those rights to Member State nationals who are not engaged in an economic activity (and even to nationals of third countries who are dependants of nationals of Member States (see para 7-049)). Moreover, since the introduction of the citizenship of the Union, the Treaties confer residence and other rights on all nationals of the Member States as citizens of the Union (see para. 6-007 *et seq.*, *supra*). More generally, legislative acts adopted by the Union institutions in the various policy areas confer rights and obligations on all natural and legal persons who come within their scope of application, often without any consideration of nationality. Such persons may invoke Union law in domestic courts against other persons or against authorities of their own or another Member State.[1]

11.001

Third-country nationals. Traditionally, nationals of third countries did not enjoy any uniform status under Union law that determined their access to the territory of the Member States, their rights of residence, and the activities they were allowed to carry on there. However, as a result of the abolition of checks carried out on persons at the Union's internal frontiers, the Member States had to agree on uniform rules on third-country nationals entering and residing in their territory. Since the Treaty of Amsterdam, the Union has initiated a common policy in the field of visas, asylum, and immigration pursuant to Title IV of the EC Treaty and, since the Lisbon Treaty, this policy is based on the provisions on the area of freedom, security, and justice of Title V of Part Three of the TFEU (see para. 8-002 *et seq.*, *supra*). In this way, third-country nationals are subject to common rules as to entry and residence in the territories of the Member States. However, some Member States do not take part in the adoption of those rules and are not bound by them.[2] In addition, nationals from third countries may enjoy derived rights of free movement which accrue to them as members of a Union citizen's family.[3] Finally, some nationals of third countries are entitled

11.002

---

[1] However, where a person invokes the Treaty provisions on free movement of persons, he or she may not normally rely on such provisions against authorities in his or her own State (i.e. where there is a 'purely internal situation') unless, in exercising free movement, he or she finds him or herself in a situation equivalent to that of a national of another Member State: para. 5-064, *supra*.

[2] See the special position of Denmark, para. 8-027, *supra*, and the exceptional status of Ireland, para. 8-028, *supra*.

[3] Paras 7-049 and 8-013, *supra*. For the extent to which nationals of third countries might rely on more rights than EU nationals, see Weiss, 'Gibt es eine EU-Inländerdiskriminierung? Zur Kollision von Gemeinschaftsrecht mit Welthandelsrecht und Assoziationsrecht' (1999) EuR 499–516.

to assert rights in these respects by virtue of international agreements concluded between their countries and the Union.

Nationals of third countries may enforce the rights that they derive from Union law before the Court of Justice and the General Court on the same terms as citizens of the Union.[4] Third-country nationals with the right of residence in a Member State are entitled to access to documents of the Union institutions and have the right to petition the European Parliament or to make a complaint to the European Ombudsman (see para. 6-022, *supra*).

II. Temporal Scope of the Treaties

A. Entry into force of the Treaties

11.003 **Entry into force.** Each of the Treaties stipulates the conditions and time of its entry into force. The entry into force of the ECSC, EEC, EAEC, and EU Treaties was conditional upon their ratification by all the Contracting Parties in accordance with their respective constitutional requirements and the deposit of the instruments of ratification.[5] Ratification by all Member States was also a requirement for the entry into force of Treaties amending those Treaties (see para. 3-002, *supra*) and of Treaties governing the accession of new Member States (see para. 4-012, *supra*). Each Treaty specified the exact day following the deposit of the last instrument of ratification on which it is to enter into force.[6] Unless otherwise provided, such a Treaty will apply to the future effects of situations arising prior to the date on which it entered into force.[7] Accordingly, the Court has held that, where the Act concerning

---

[4] Article 263, fourth para. TFEU and Article 265, third para. TFEU refer to 'any natural or legal person'.
[5] Article 99 ECSC; Article 247 EEC; Article 224 EAEC; Single European Act, Article 33; EU Treaty, Article 52; Treaty of Amsterdam, Article 14; Treaty of Nice, Article 12; Treaty of Lisbon, Article 6. The ECSC Treaty provided for the instruments of ratification to be lodged with the French Government; the instruments of ratification of the subsequent Treaties were to be lodged with the Italian Government.
[6] The same day under Article 99 of the ECSC Treaty (namely 23 July 1952); the first day of the following month under Article of the 247 EEC Treaty, Article 224 of the EAEC Treaty (since the Benelux countries last deposited their instruments of ratification on 13 December 1957, this was 1 January 1958) and Article 33 of the Single European Act. The Treaty of Amsterdam entered into force under Article 14 on the first day of the second month following the deposit of the instrument of ratification by the last signatory State (namely 1 May 1999). The same arrangements applied to the Treaty of Nice by virtue of Article 12 thereof (entry into force on 1 February 2003). Article 52(2) of the EU Treaty fixed an earliest date for its entry into force (1 January 1993), failing which it was to enter into force on the first day of the month following the deposit of the instrument of ratification by the last State to do so (this proved to be 1 November 1993). The Treaty of Lisbon adopted the same system in Article 6(2), fixing the earliest date of entry into force as 1 January 2009, failing which it was to enter into force on the first day of the month following the deposit of the last instrument of ratification (which proved to be 1 December 2009). The Accession Treaties also laid down a fixed (earliest) date for their entry into force: 1 January 1973 in the second para. of Article 2 of the Accession Treaty of 22 January 1972 (OJ 1972 English Special Edition (I) (27 March) 5); 1 January 1981 in the second para. of Article 2 of the Accession Treaty of 28 May 1979 (OJ 1979 L291/9); 1 January 1986 in the first subpara. of Article 2(2) of the Accession Treaty of 12 June 1985 (OJ 1985 L302/9); 1 January 1995 in the first subpara. of Article 2(2) of the Accession Treaty of 24 June 1994 (OJ 1994 C241/13); 1 May 2004 in Article 2(2) of the Accession Treaty of 16 April 2003 (OJ 2003 L236/17); 1 January 2007 in Article 4(2) of the Accession Treaty of 25 April 2005 (OJ 2005 L157/11); 1 July 2013 in Article 3(3) of the Accession Treaty of 19 December 2011 (OJ 2012 L112/10). For full references to the Accession Treaties, see paras 4-002–4-008, *supra*.
[7] C-122/96 *Saldanha and MTS*, 1997, para. 14; C-321/97, *Andersson and Andersson*, 1999, paras 35–46; C-512/99, *Germany v Commission*, 2003, para. 46. For the resolution of intermediate temporal problems (in particular in connection with the entry into force of Accession Treaties, see Kaleda, 'Immediate Effects of Community Law in the New Member States: Is There a Place for a Consistent Doctrine?' (2004) ELJ 102–22). For applications in the case law, see C-366/05, *Optimus*, 2007; C-414/07, *Magoora*, 2008; C-256/15, *Nemec*, 2016, paras 24–6; C-235/17, *Commission v Hungary*, 2019, paras 25–7.

the conditions of accession of a Member State contains no specific conditions with regard to the application of a provision of the Treaties, that provision must be regarded as being immediately applicable and binding on that Member State from the date of its accession, with the result that it applies to the future effects of situations arising prior to that new Member State's accession.[8] However, in order to ensure observance of the principles of legal certainty and the protection of legitimate expectations, the substantive rules of Union law must be interpreted as applying to situations existing before their entry into force only in so far as it follows clearly from their terms, objectives, or general scheme that such effect must be given to them.[9] As regards procedural rules, they are generally held to be of immediate application.[10] Where a Treaty (or a protocol thereto) makes it necessary to adopt implementing measures, the principle of good administration requires the preliminary work leading to the adoption of those measures to be started before the entry into force of the Treaty, in order for them to be applicable from a date as close as possible to that of the entry into force of the Treaty.[11]

B. Duration of the Treaties

Limited validity of the ECSC Treaty. Only the ECSC Treaty was concluded for a specific period: it expired on 23 July 2002 (ECSC Treaty, Article 97). This is because the Contracting Parties regarded the ECSC as a provisional first step towards European integration (see para. 1-009, *supra*). Since the tasks of the ECSC could be taken over by the EC, the ECSC Treaty was not extended.[12] As from 24 July 2002, the sectors previously covered by the ECSC Treaty became subject to the EC Treaty (now TFEU).[13] The succession of the legal framework of the EC Treaty (*lex generalis*) to that of the ECSC Treaty (*lex specialis*) was held to be part of the unity and continuity of the Community legal order.[14] The continuity of the Community legal order and the objectives which govern its functioning—notably in the field of competition—thus required that, in so far as the European Community succeeded to the ECSC, it was to ensure compliance with the rights and obligations which applied *eo tempore* to both Member States and individuals under the ECSC Treaty. In conformity with the principles governing the temporal application of the law, situations that were definitively established

11.004

---

[8] C-122/96, *Saldanha and MTS*, 1997, para. 14; C-162/00, *Pokrzeptowicz-Meyer*, 2002, para. 50; C-441/08, *Elektrownia Pątnów*, 2009, para. 32. As regards Accession Treaties, the Court considers that the Act of Accession of a new Member State is based essentially on the general principle that the provisions of Community law apply *ab initio* and *in toto* to that State, derogations being allowed only in so far as they are expressly laid down by transitional provisions: C-420/07, *Apostolides*, 2009, para. 33. The Court however has jurisdiction to interpret the provisions of the Treaties as regards their application in a new Member State only with effect from the date of that State's accession to the Union: C-302/04, *Ynos*, 2006, para. 36; C-96/08, *CIBA*, 2010, para. 14.

[9] C-162/00, *Pokrzeptowicz-Meyer*, 2002, para. 49; C-441/08, *Elektrownia Pątnów*, 2009, para. 33. See also T-348/04, *SIDE v Commission*, 2008, paras 50–6; T-24/07, *ThyssenKrupp Stainless*, 2009, para. 85.

[10] 212/80 to 217/80, *Salumi and Others*, 1981, para. 9; C-61/98, *De Haan*, 1999, para. 13; T-334/07, *Denka International v Commission*, 2009, para. 45; C-17/10, *Toshiba Corporation*, 2012, paras 44–67; C-610/10, *Commission v Spain*, 2012, paras 45–8.

[11] T-164/99, T-37/00, and T-38/00, *Leroy and Others v Council*, 2001, para. 82.

[12] See the Resolution of the Council of the European Union and the representatives of the governments of the Member States, meeting within the Council of 20 July 1998 concerning the expiry of the Treaty establishing the European Coal and Steel Community, OJ 1998 C247/5.

[13] See, e.g., the Communication from the Commission concerning certain aspects of the treatment of competition cases resulting from the expiry of the ECSC Treaty, OJ 2002 C152/5.

[14] Case T-24/07, *ThyssenKrupp Stainless v Commission*, 2009, paras 80–4.

before the expiry of the ECSC Treaty had to be assessed under the substantive provisions of the ECSC Treaty even if, after the expiry of that Treaty, such assessment was to be carried out on the basis of the procedural provisions laid down under the EC Treaty.[15]

11.005 **Unlimited period.** The subsequent Treaties were concluded for an unlimited period (EEC Treaty, Article 240 and EAEC Treaty, Article 208; see also EU Treaty, Article 51 [*now Article 53 TEU*]; Treaty of Amsterdam, Article 13; Treaty of Nice, Article 11; and Treaty of Lisbon, Article 3).[16] The fact that a Union, having its own institutions and powers, was established for an unlimited duration demonstrates that the Member States intended to create a new legal order, which binds both their subjects and themselves.[17] In order to bring about the abrogation of the Treaties and, with them, the Union, the Member States may not rely unconditionally on the rule of international law that a treaty may be terminated if the parties conclude a subsequent treaty between them.[18] It appears to be contrary to Union law for the Member States simply to bring an end to European integration by means of an amendment to the Treaties or in some other manner.[19]

However, Article 50 TEU makes it possible for a Member State to unilaterally withdraw from the European Union. At the end of the period provided for in Article 50(3) TEU the Treaties cease to apply to the State in question.[20]

III. Territorial Scope of the Treaties

11.006 **Jurisdiction of Member States.** The territorial scope of the Treaties is defined by Article 52(1) TEU, which declares the Treaties to be applicable to all of the Member States, which are listed therein.[21] The territorial scope of application of the Treaties is thus constituted by the Member States of the Union. Secondary Union law applies in principle to the same area as the Treaties themselves.[22]

Under international law, the Treaties apply to all areas which are under the sovereignty or within the jurisdiction of the Member States. As far as Union legislation on checks at external borders is concerned, the Treaties expressly confirm that the Union's competence in that area is not to affect the competence of the Member States concerning the geographical demarcation, in accordance with international law, of their borders (Article 77(4) TFEU).[23] The territorial scope of the Treaties is further specified in Article 355 TFEU, which contains

---

[15] Ibid., paras 85–9; see also T-405/06, *ArcelorMittal Luxembourg and Others v Commission*, 2009, paras 59–69.
[16] The TEU and TFEU also expressly state that they are concluded for an unlimited period (see Article 53 TEU and Article 356 TFEU).
[17] 6/64, *Costa*, 1964, at 593 (para. 1-025, *supra*).
[18] For this rule, see Article 54 of the 1969 Vienna Convention (para. 26-013, *infra*).
[19] This question is directly related to the possible substantive limitations on amending the Treaties, para. 3-010, *supra*.
[20] The Treaties thus ceased to apply to the United Kingdom following its withdrawal from the Union on 1 February 2020. See also C-621/18, *Wightman*, 2018, para. 54 and paras 4-016–4-017, *supra*.
[21] Article 52 was introduced by the Treaty of Lisbon. Before that, the EU Treaty did not define its territorial scope, but simply employed the expression 'Member States'. In contrast, Article 299(1) of the EC Treaty (now repealed) declared that the EC Treaty was applicable to all the Member States, which were listed therein. For the EAEC Treaty, see Article 198 EAEC.
[22] C-132/14 to C-136/14, *European Parliament and Commission v Council*, 2015, para. 77.
[23] C-457/18, *Slovenia v Croatia*, 2020, para. 105.

provisions on territories with a special status under Union law, such as the Member States' overseas territories (see also Article 51(2) TEU; see the discussion in para. 10-013, *supra*).[24]

The application of the Treaties extends to the airspace and maritime waters, which come under the sovereignty or within the jurisdiction of the Member States; territorial waters; and, in so far as the Member State concerned lays claim to it, the fishing zone or exclusive economic zone, together with the continental shelf.[25] The Union itself accepted the international rules adopted in 1982 in the Convention on the Law of the Sea.[26] As long as the northern part of the territory of Cyprus is occupied, the Union *acquis* applies, according to a protocol annexed to the 2003 Act of Accession, only to those (southern) areas in which the Government of the Republic of Cyprus exercises effective control.[27]

Within that framework, the Treaties apply to legal relationships which can be located 'within the territory of the Union', by reason of the place where they are entered into or of the place where they take effect[28] or by reason of a sufficiently close link with the law of a Member State and thus the relevant rules of Union law.[29]

---

[24] For a general discussion, see Ziller, 'The European Union and the Territorial Scope of European Territories' (2007) VUWLR 51–62; Ziller, 'Flexibility in the Geographical Scope of EU Law: Diversity and Differentiation in the Application of Substantive Law on Member States' Territories', in De Búrca and Scott (eds), *Constitutional Change in the EU—From Uniformity to Flexibility?* (Hart Publishing, 2000), 113–31; Groux, '"Territorialité" et droit communautaire' (1987) RTDE 5–33.

[25] Most Member States limit their territorial waters to 12 nautical miles from the baseline, except for Greece (6 nautical miles). In accordance with the Council Resolution of 3 November 1976, OJ 1981 C105/1, the Member States concerned have set their fishing zone or an exclusive economic zone in the North Sea and the North Atlantic Ocean at 200 nautical miles. Where a State has exclusive rights over the continental shelf in respect of the exploration and the exploitation of the natural resources of the sea-bed and subsoil of the shelf (see also C-347/10, *Salemink*, 2012, paras 31–5), it also has exclusive fishing rights in an exclusive economic zone (cf. Articles 77–81 and 55–73 of the Convention on the Law of the Sea, see following n.). For the contested general application of Union law to the continental shelf, see Waverijn and Nieuwenhout, 'Swimming in ECJ Case Law: The Rocky Journey to EU Law Applicability in the Continental Shelf and Exclusive Economic Zone' (2019) CMLRev 1623–1648; Michael, 'L'application du droit communautaire au plateau continental des Etats membres et ses conséquences' (1983) RMC 82–90; Van der Mensbrugghe, 'La CEE et le plateau continental des Etats membres', in *Mélanges F. Dehousse* (Nathan/Labor, 1979), Vol. II, 311–317. For the limitations imposed by customary international law on Union competence, see C-286/90, *Poulsen and Diva Navigation*, 1992, paras 21–34; for its competence in respect of the conservation of the fishery resources of the high seas, see *Poulsen*, paras 9–11, and C-405/92 *Mondiet*, 1993, paras 12–15; C-25/94, *Commission v Council*, 1996, para. 44.

[26] United Nations Convention on the Law of the Sea, signed at Montego Bay on 10 December 1982, which was ratified by the Community (together with the Agreement of 28 July 1994 relating to the implementation of Part XI thereof) by Council Decision 98/392/EC of 23 March 1998, OJ 1998 L179/1. See Garzón Clariana, 'L'Union européenne et la Convention de 1982 sur le droit de la mer' (1995) BTIR 36–45. Nonetheless, the nature and the broad logic of the Convention prevent the Court of Justice from being able to assess the validity of a Union measure in the light of that Convention: C-308/06, *Intertanko and Others*, 2008, paras 53–65.

[27] Article 1 of Protocol (No. 10) on Cyprus, annexed to the 2003 Act of Accession, suspends the application of the *acquis* in those areas of the Republic of Cyprus in which the Government of the Republic of Cyprus does not exercise effective control. This does not preclude application of Union rules on the recognition of judgments to those delivered by courts located in the southern area, but concerning land situated in the northern area (C-420/07, *Apostolides*, 2009, paras 32–9). See Skoutaris, 'The Application of the Acquis Communautaire in the Areas not under the Effective Control of the Republic of Cyprus: The Green Line Regulation' (2008) 45 CMLRev 727–55; Bilge, 'La situation juridique de Chypre dans ses deux composantes par rapport au droit communautaire' (2006) RMCUE 586–91; Yakemtchouk, 'Chypre: la réunification avortée' (2004) RMCUE 239–96; Klebes-Pelissier, 'L'adhésion de la République de Chypre à l'Union européenne' (2003) RTDE 441–69: Berramdane, 'Chypre entre adhésion à l'Union européenne et réunification' (2003) RDUE 87–108. See para. 11-008, *infra* for the procedure for bringing this exceptional regime to an end.

[28] See 36/74, *Walrave*, 1974, para. 28; 237/83, *Prodest*, 1984, paras 6–7 (para. 7-056, *supra*); 89, 104, 114, 116–17 and 125–29/85, *Åhlström v Commission*, 1988, paras 16–17 (para. 9-014, *supra*); T-102/96, *Gencor v Commission*, 1999, paras 89–108 (para. 9-018, *supra*).

[29] C-214/94, *Boukhalfa*, 1996, para. 15 (para. 7-056, *supra*). For a definition of the legal subjects of the Union, see also Vanhamme, *Volkenrechtelijke beginselen in het Europees recht* (Europa Law Publishing, 2001), 131–48.

11.007 **Territories with specific status.** The Treaties provide for certain overseas territories to have a special status. As far as the French overseas departments (Guadeloupe, French Guiana, Martinique, Réunion, and since 2011, Mayotte);[30] Saint-Barthélemy and Saint-Martin;[31] the Azores, Madeira, and the Canary Islands[32] are concerned, the provisions of the Treaties apply in principle, although the Council may adopt specific measures making the application of the Treaties subject to certain conditions in view of the structural social and economic situation of those areas (Article 349 and Article 355(1) TFEU). Such measures may concern both the conditions relating to the application of primary Union law and those relating to the application of acts of secondary Union law adopted pursuant to that primary law.[33]

Part Four of the TFEU (Articles 198 to 204 TFEU) contains special association arrangements for the overseas countries and territories (OCTs) listed in Annex II to the Treaties (Article 355(2) TFEU).[34] While the Court has ruled that the general provisions of the Treaties, namely those which are not referred to in Part Four of the TFEU, are not applicable to OCTs in the absence of an express reference,[35] the Member State on which they are dependent may nevertheless incur certain liabilities on the basis of the principle of sincere cooperation (Article 4(3) TEU) in instances where those OCTs commit certain errors in applying the OCT regime resulting in financial losses for the Union due to a loss of own resources.[36] However, most of the countries and territories listed in the original

---

[30] For the change in status of Mayotte, see n. 57, *infra*. The term 'overseas departments' (*départements d'outre-mer* or DOM), which appeared in Article 299(2) of the EC Treaty, no longer appears in Articles 349 and 355(2) TFEU. On these territories (not to be confused with the 'overseas communities' (*collectivités d'outre-mer*), before 2003 'overseas territories' or *territoires d'outre-mer*, TOM), see Murray, *The European Union and Member State Territories: A New Legal Framework Under the EU Treaties* (TMC Asser, 2012); Kochenov (ed.), *EU Law of the Overseas: Outermost Regions, Associated Overseas Countries and Territories, Territories Sui Generis* (Kluwer, 2011); Perrot, 'Les régions ultrapériphériques françaises selon le Traité de Lisbonne' (2009) RTDE 717; Faberon and Ziller, *Droit des collectivités d'outre-mer* (*LGDJ*, 2007); Gautron, 'Le statut communautaire des DOM et des PTOM' (2006) RAE 385–93. Initially, the EC Treaty was to be fully applicable to the French *départements d'outre mer* (DOM) only after two years; see, *inter alia*, 148/77, *Hansen*, 1978, paras 7–10. The third subpara. of the former Article 227(2) EC authorized the Council to determine specific conditions of application without derogating from the Treaty provisions mentioned in the first subpara. of that provision. Consequently, the Council was not empowered to authorize France to collect charges in a DOM —contrary to 'free movement of goods' mentioned in the first subpara.—on products coming from other French departments (C-363/93 and C-407/93 to C-411/93, *Lancry*, 1994, paras 36–8), but this did not prevent the Council from authorizing exemptions from those charges subject to strict conditions (C-212/96, *Chevassus-Marche*, 1998, paras 1–54).

[31] The Lisbon Treaty added Saint Barthelémy and Saint Martin to the territories listed in Article 299(2) EC. Both territories were formerly part of a French overseas department (Guadeloupe), but since 2007 constitute separate overseas communities. However, unlike the other French overseas communities, they are not mentioned in Annex II to the Treaties. Consequently, their status under Union law has not changed with the Lisbon Treaty.

[32] With regard to the Canary Islands, see Council Regulation (EEC) No. 1911/91 of 26 June 1991 on the application of the provisions of Community law to the Canary Islands, OJ 1991 L171/1. For an application, see C-186/07, *Club Náutico de Gran Canaria*, 2008, para. 18 (common system of VAT not applicable to the Canary Islands). The derogation provided for in Article 25 of the 1985 Act of Accession and Protocol (No. 2) thereto applied to the Canary Islands, just as it applied to Ceuta and Melilla. See C-45/94, *Ayuntamiento de Ceuta*, 1995, paras 14–21 and 42.

[33] C-132/14 to C-136/14, *European Parliament and Commission v Council*, 2015, paras 64–79.

[34] For the list of those areas, see para. 10-013, *supra*. For the purposes of the application of certain provisions of Union legislation, work performed in such an area may be equated with work carried out in the territory of the Member State concerned: C-248/96, *Grahame and Hollanders*, 1997, para. 36 (see para. 7-056, *supra*). The second subpara. of Article 355(2) TFEU excludes countries and territories having special relations with the United Kingdom which are not listed in Annex II; this referred only to Hong Kong.

[35] C-384/09, *Prunus and Polonium*, 2011, paras 28–32; C-24/12 and C-27/12, *X and TBG*, 2014, para. 45; C-395/17, *Commission v Netherlands*, 2019, para. 76; see also C-391/17, *Commission v United Kingdom*, 2019, para. 74.

[36] C-395/17, *Commission v Netherlands*, 2019, paras 71–7; see also C-391/17, *Commission v United Kingdom*, 2019, paras 69–75.

annex to the EEC Treaty have since become parties, as independent States, to the ACP–EC Conventions (see para. 10-019, *supra*). In 1984, an amendment to the Treaties caused them not to apply to Greenland as from 1 February 1985,[37] following which Greenland is now also covered by Part Four of the TFEU. In accordance with a Protocol to the EEC Treaty, the Netherlands declared that the EEC Treaty was not applicable to Surinam and the Netherlands Antilles—territories which since have become independent or fall under the association arrangements.[38]

The Treaties are also applicable to European territories for whose external relations a Member State is responsible,[39] which, when the United Kingdom was still a Member State in practice mainly boiled down to Gibraltar, but is still relevant for Andorra.[40] The 1972 Act of Accession provided that major areas of Community law should not apply to Gibraltar,[41] in particular free movement of goods and harmonization measures adopted for that purpose.[42] The other provisions of the Treaties did fully apply,[43] until the withdrawal of the United Kingdom from the Union.[44]

---

[37] Treaty of 13 March 1984 amending, with regard to Greenland, the Treaties establishing the European Communities, OJ 1985 L29/1. In a referendum held on 23 February 1982, the people of Greenland expressed the desire to leave the Community, whereupon the Danish Government applied to have the Treaty amended. However, Greenland remains part of Denmark and therefore falls by virtue of Articles 2, 3, and 4 of that Treaty under the association arrangements provided for in Part Four of the TFEU. For the specific legal regime governing the relationship between the Union and Greenland, see Council Decision 2014/137/EU of 14 March 2014 on relations between the European Union on the one hand, and Greenland and the Kingdom of Denmark on the other, OJ 2014 L76/1. See also the Fisheries Partnership Agreement between the European Community and the Government of Denmark and the Home Rule Government of Greenland, concluded on behalf of the Community by Council Decision 2006/1006/EC of 21 December 2006, OJ 2006 L411/27 (extended by successive protocols), to be replaced by the Sustainable Fisheries Partnership Agreement between the European Union, of the one part, and the Government of Greenland and the Government of Denmark, of the other part, OJ 2021 L175/1.

[38] Surinam, which became independent on 16 June 1976, has acceded to the ACP–EC Convention. The association arrangements provided for in Part Four of the EEC Treaty (now Part Four TFEU) apply to the Netherlands Antilles by virtue of the Convention of 13 November 1962 amending Part Four of the EEC Treaty, OJ 1964 2414 and to Aruba, which became independent from the other Antilles on 1 January 1986 and has—like the Antilles and the Netherlands—the status of an autonomous 'country' within the Kingdom of the Netherlands. See the Rijkswet van 20 juni 1985, houdende vaststelling van enige overgangsbepalingen in verband met het verkrijgen van de hoedanigheid van land in het Koninkrijk door Aruba, *Stb*. 370 (Dutch Act of 20 June 1985 on transitional measures pertaining to Aruba obtaining the status of country within the Kingdom). With respect to voting right for the elections to the European Parliament, see C-300/04, *Eman and Sevinger*, 2006 (see para. 12-015, *infra*).

[39] Article 355(3) TFEU; Article 198, second para. EAEC. Before the entry into force of the Lisbon Treaty, the EU Treaty (in contrast to the EC Treaty) was not stated to be applicable to territories for the foreign relations of which a Member State is responsible. Acts adopted pursuant to the EU Treaty were, therefore, where appropriate, expressly declared to be applicable to Gibraltar. See, e.g., Council Decision 2003/642/JHA of 22 July 2003 concerning the application to Gibraltar of the Convention on the fight against corruption involving officials of the European Communities or officials of Member States of the European Union, OJ 2003 L226/27.

[40] The Treaties expressly exclude other territories, which could qualify (e.g. the Channel Islands and the Isle of Man while the United Kingdom was still a Member State; see n. 48, *infra*). Nor are the Treaties considered to apply to Andorra (for the EC–Andorra Agreement, see para. 10-008, *supra*).

[41] See Article 28 (exclusion of measures relating to certain agricultural products and to the harmonization of turnover tax) and Annex I(I) (customs legislation) of the 1972 Act of Accession. Accordingly, Article 12(2) of Council Directive 91/477/EEC of 18 June 1991 on control of the acquisition and possession of weapons did not apply to Gibraltar; see C-267/16, *Buhagiar*, 2018, paras 61–72.

[42] C-30/01, *Commission v United Kingdom*, 2003, paras 47–59 (this follows from Gibraltar's exclusion from the customs territory of the Union).

[43] C-349/03, *Commission v United Kingdom*, 2005, paras 40–54 (provisions on VAT and excise duties), with case note by Stanley (2007) CMLRev 195-203; CFI, Joined Cases T-195/01 and T-207/01, *Government of Gibraltar v Commission*, 2002, para. 12. With respect to voting right for the elections to the European Parliament, see C-145/04, *Spain v United Kingdom*, 2006 (see para. 12-015, *infra*).

[44] The Treaties ceased to apply to Gibraltar pursuant to Article 3(1)(b) of the Withdrawal Agreement (OJ 2020 L29/10) on the same date as they ceased to apply to the United Kingdom, subject, however, to Article 1 of the Protocol on Gibraltar attached to the Withdrawal Agreement (OJ 2020 L29/153, see Article 185, final para. of the Withdrawal Agreement).

The Treaties exclude the Faroe Islands[45] from their scope and provide for special arrangements for the Åland Islands (located between Sweden and Finland).[46] They also contained special arrangements in respect of the UK Sovereign Base Areas in Cyprus (Akrotiri and Dhekelia),[47] and the Channel Islands and the Isle of Man, which are Crown dependencies, but not part of the United Kingdom.[48]

11.008 **Change in territorial jurisdiction.** Apart from those specific arrangements for particular areas, the application of the Treaties coincides with the territorial jurisdiction of the Member States under international law. Union law is automatically applicable to areas acquired by a Member State as a result of a change in its frontiers and it deals with territories ceded by a Member State in the same way as it would with a third country. Such changes do not require any amendment of the Treaties,[49] but consultation between the Member States is advisable.[50] Accordingly, the European Council decided that it was unnecessary to amend the Treaties when the *Länder* of the former German Democratic Republic acceded to the Federal Republic of Germany on 3 October 1990 and therefore to the Communities.[51] The Council adopted a number of adjusting and transitional measures in the light of German reunification.[52] A similar solution is foreseen for Cyprus in the event that a settlement is found for bringing the factual partition of the island to an end. By means of a protocol annexed to the 2003 Act of Accession, the Council, acting unanimously, is then to decide on

---

[45] Article 355(5)(a) TFEU, and Article 198, fourth para. EAEC, indent (a). The EU Treaty had removed from those articles Denmark's option, which was open to it until the end of 1975 but never exercised, to declare the Treaties applicable to the Faroe Islands.

[46] Article 355(4) TFEU, and Article 198, third para. EAEC, provide that the Treaties are applicable to the Åland Islands in accordance with the provisions of Protocol (No. 2) to the 1994 Act of Accession (see OJ 1995 L75/18).

[47] Article 355(5)(b) TFEU, as amended by Protocol (No. 3) to the 2003 Act of Accession, OJ 2003 L236/940 provides that the Treaty is to apply to the 'United Kingdom Sovereign Base Areas of Akrotiri and Dhekelia in Cyprus' only to the extent necessary to ensure the implementation of the exceptional arrangements set out in that protocol. After Cyprus became independent in 1960, the United Kingdom has continued to maintain two military bases in southern Cyprus; see the Commission's Opinion on Cyprus's application to accede (1993) EC Bull. Suppl 5, 12. After the withdrawal of the United Kingdom from the European Union, a special regime laid down in a Protocol attached to the Withdrawal Agreement applies (OJ 2020 L29/146).

[48] Article 355(5)(c) TFEU and Article 198, fourth para., indent (c) EAEC. The Treaties applied to the Channel Islands and the Isle of Man only to the extent necessary to ensure the implementation of the special arrangements for those islands set out in Protocol (No. 3) to the 1972 Act of Accession. See C-171/96, *Pereira Roque*, 1998, paras 34–58; C-293/02, *Jersey Produce Marketing Organisation*, 2005, paras 35–41. See further Sutton, 'Jersey's Changing Constitutional Relationship with Europe' (2005) Jersey LR 1.

[49] The Community accepted the independence of Algeria in 1962 without amending Article 227(2) EEC, which treated that country as a French overseas department. The EU Treaty deleted the reference to Algeria. The transfer of the Saar to the Federal Republic of Germany necessitated an amendment to the Treaties, since Germany sought a change in the allocation of votes (n. 32 to para. 3-009, *supra*).

[50] For the general obligation to consult other Member States, see Ehlermann, 'Mitgliedschaft in der Europäischen Gemeinschaft—Rechtsproblem der Erweiterung, der Mitgliedschaft und der Verkleinerung' (1984) EuR 113, 118–19.

[51] See the conclusions of the Dublin European Council of 28 April 1990 (1990) 4 EC Bull. point I.5. Under the Protocol annexed to the EEC Treaty on German internal trade and connected problems, the FRG was entitled to regard trade with the GDR as part of German internal trade. Nevertheless, the GDR did not form part of the Community and goods from the GDR were not regarded as originating in the FRG: 14/74, *Norddeutsches Vieh- und Fleischkontor*, 1974, para. 6.

[52] See the package of legislation adopted by the Council on 4 October 1990, OJ 1990 L353; Westlake, 'The Community Express Service: The Rapid Passage of Emergency Legislation on German Unification' (1991) CMLRev 599–614. See also Drobnig, 'Die Eingliederung der ehemaligen DDR in die Europäischen Gemeinschaften' (1991) ZfRV 321–32; Grabitz, 'L'unité allemande et l'intégration européenne' (1991) CDE 423–41; Glaesner, 'Les problèmes de droit communautaire soulevés par l'unification allemande' (1990) RMC 647–54; Jacqué, 'L'unification de l'Allemagne et la Communauté européenne' (1990) RGDIP 997–1018.

the adaptations to the terms concerning the accession of Cyprus with regard to the Turkish Cypriot Community.[53]

The territorial field of application of the Treaties also adjusts itself where a Member State changes the status of a territory under its sovereignty.[54] Nevertheless, in some of these cases the Member States have revised the Treaties.[55] This not only ensures acceptance on the part of the Member States, but also provides a democratic foundation for the acceptance into the Union, or the loss, of what is often a substantial population. To ensure involvement of other Member States in changes in the status of overseas Danish, French, or Netherlands territories, the Treaty of Lisbon has enabled the European Council, on the initiative of the Member State concerned, to adopt a decision amending the status, with regard to the Union, of those countries and territories (Article 355(6) TFEU).[56] In 2011, the European Council thus added Mayotte to the list of overseas territories in Article 355(1) TFEU.[57]

Where a State wishes to join, or rejoin, the Union, this can occur only in accordance with the accession procedure laid down in Article 49 TEU (see para. 4-012, *supra*).

Acts with specific territorial scope. Acts of the Union institutions, in principle, cover the same geographical field of application as the Treaty on which they are based.[58] Member States' extension of their exclusive fishing zones to 200 miles off their North Sea and North Atlantic coasts therefore resulted in a commensurate extension of the field of application of Union measures relating to a structural policy for the fishing industry.[59] Nevertheless, Union legislation sometimes defines its own field of application. For instance, customs law

11.009

---

[53] Protocol (No. 10) on Cyprus, annexed to the 2003 Act of Accession, Article 4. After the rejection of the proposed plan for reunification, on the eve of accession, the Council laid down measures to facilitate trade and other links between the northern and southern areas of the island, whilst ensuring that appropriate standards of protection were maintained as to the security of the European Union with regard to illegal immigration, threats to public order, and public health. See Council Regulation (EC) No. 866/2004 of 29 April 2004 on a regime under Article 2 of Protocol (No. 10) of the Act of Accession, OJ 2004 L161/128 (republished with *corrigendum*: OJ 2004 L206/51; see also Commission Implementing Regulation (EU) 2015/1472 of 26 August 2015 on amending Annex I to Council Regulation (EC) No. 866/2004 on a regime under Article 2 of Protocol (No. 10) to the Act of Accession, OJ 2015 L225/3). For the extraordinary elections of the representatives in the European Parliament to be held in the whole of Cyprus in the event of a settlement of the Cyprus problem, see Council Decision 2004/511/EC of 10 June 2004 concerning the representation of the people of Cyprus in the European Parliament in the case of a settlement of the Cyprus problem, OJ 2004 L211/22. See further, Rumelili, 'Transforming Conflicts on EU Borders: The Case of Greek-Turkish Relations' (2007) JCMS 105–26.

[54] In 1976 France granted Saint-Pierre-et-Miquelon, which were associated with the Community as *territoires d'outre mer* (TOM), the status of *départements d'outre mer* (DOM) by Law No. 76-664 of 19 July 1976. As a result, the islands became part of the Community by virtue of Article 227(2) EEC. Similarly, they left the Community in 1985 when, by Law No. 85-595 of 11 June 1985, the islands resumed the status of TOMs.

[55] See the Convention on the Netherlands Antilles (n. 38, *supra*), by which the Member States sought to introduce in a Protocol to the EEC Treaty special arrangements for imports of petroleum products refined in the Netherlands Antilles (JO 1964, 2416; now Protocol (No. 31) annexed to the TEU and TFEU, OJ 2010 C83/315), and the Treaty on the withdrawal of Greenland (n. 37, *supra*).

[56] This concerns the territories listed in Articles 355(1) and (2). The European Council is to act unanimously after consulting the Commission.

[57] European Council Decision 2012/419/EU of 11 July 2012 amending the status of Mayotte with regard to the European Union, OJ 2012 L204/131 (Mayotte ceasing to be an overseas country or territory, to which the provisions of Part Four of the TFEU apply, and becoming an outermost region of the Union within the meaning of Article 349 TFEU). See also C-132/14 to C-136/14, *European Parliament and Commission v Council*, 2015, paras 64–79 (rejection of action for annulments brought by the European Parliament and the Commission against Council acts taken pursuant to Article 349 TFEU following the state in status of Mayotte).

[58] C-132/14 to C-136/14, *European Parliament and Commission v Council*, 2015, para. 77.

[59] 61/77, *Commission v Ireland*, 1978, paras 45–50. See also 3, 4, and 6/76, *Kramer*, 1976, paras 30–3.

does not apply to certain areas coming under the jurisdiction of a Member State.[60] However, the fact that particular areas have an exceptional status under the Treaties does not mean that the Court of Justice has no jurisdiction to give preliminary rulings on questions referred by courts in those areas, even though Union law is only partially in force there.[61] Conversely, secondary Union law may be applicable in areas which do not belong to the Member States. For instance, Monaco comes within the customs territory of the Union,[62] other Union acts are declared by agreement to be applicable to Monaco,[63] and Union legislation on euro banknotes and coins applies in Monaco, San Marino, the Vatican City, and some other areas which have obtained, by agreement, the right to use the euro as their currency unit.[64] As a result of agreements with third countries, a substantial part of Union law also applies in third countries, in particular the States belonging to the European Economic Area (see para. 10-020, *supra*).

11.010 **Extraterritorial effects.** The application of Union law sometimes depends on factors situated outside the territorial jurisdiction of the Member States. That is generally the case with autonomous or conventional measures of Union commercial policy. Union measures may impose obligations—even on non-Union undertakings—having to be complied with outside the territory of the Union.[65] Union competition policy may be applied to undertakings which are established outside the Union and not incorporated under the laws of one of the Member States but which act in the Union (see paras 9-014 and 9-018).

IV. Exceptions to the Application of the Treaties

11.011 **Internal or external security.** According to Article 4(2) TEU, the Union "shall respect [the Member States'] essential State functions, including ensuring the territorial integrity of the State, maintaining law and order and safeguarding national security". It also provides that "national security remains the sole responsibility of each Member State". Yet, the measures that Member State take in that respect cannot render Union law inapplicable nor exempt the Member States from their obligation to comply with Union law.[66] Nevertheless, Articles

---

[60] For the customs territory of the Union, see Article 4 of Regulation (EU) No. 952/2013 of the European Parliament and of the Council of 9 October 2013 laying down the Union Customs Code, OJ 2013 L269/1 (see para. 7-015, *supra*).

[61] C-100/89 and C-101/89, *Kaefer and Procacci*, 1990, paras 8–10 (Polynesia, a *territoire d'outre mer*); C-355/89, *Barr and Montrose Holdings*, 1991, paras 6–10 (Isle of Man).

[62] Under Article 4(2) of Regulation (EU) No. 952/2013 of the European Parliament and of the Council of 9 October 2013 laying down the Union Customs Code (OJ 2013 L269/1), the Principality of Monaco, as its territory is defined in a bilateral convention signed with France, forms part of the customs territory. Before a customs agreement was signed with the EC (Agreement on Cooperation and Customs Union between the European Economic Community and the Republic of San Marino, OJ 2002 L84/43), San Marino also belonged to the customs territory of the Community. The Vatican City and Andorra do not belong to the customs territory (but see the Cooperation Agreement with the Principality of Andorra, OJ 2005 L135/14).

[63] See the Agreement on the application of certain Community acts on the territory of the Principality of Monaco, approved by Council Decision 2003/885/EC of 17 November 2003, OJ 2003 L332/41.

[64] See para. 9-043, *supra*. On the monetary level, special relations existed between France and Monaco and between Italy and San Marino and the Vatican City. On behalf of the Union, France and Italy conducted the respective negotiations as a result of which those three States obtained the right to use the euro as their currency unit.

[65] See, e.g., C-177/95, *Ebony Maritime and Loten Navigation*, 1997, paras 15–27 (sanction imposed in respect of the conduct of vessels on the high seas—conduct giving good reason to believe that a breach of sanctions imposed on Yugoslavia might result—irrespective of whether the vessels were flying the flag of a Member State).

[66] C-511/18, C-512/18 and C-520/18, *La Quadrature du Net*, 2020, paras 99 and 135-36. See also C-623/17, *Privacy International*, 2020, paras 44 and 74-75.

346 to 348 TFEU allow the Member States to deviate from their general Treaty obligations on grounds of internal or external security.[67] Articles 346 and 347 TFEU authorize a Member State to take unilateral measures where 'the essential interests of its security' are at stake (Article 346(1) TFEU) or 'in the event of serious internal disturbances affecting the maintenance of law and order, in the event of war, serious international tension constituting a threat of war, or in order to carry out obligations entered into by the Member State for the purpose of maintaining peace and international security' (Article 347 TFEU). In such a situation, a Member State may withhold information which it would otherwise be bound to provide (Article 346(1)(a) TFEU) or take such measures as it considers necessary that are connected with the production of, or trade in, weapons, munitions, and war material (Article 346(1)(b) TFEU). In 1958, by a unanimous vote, the Council adopted a list of the products to which Article 346 TFEU applies.[68] One example of the effects of this exceptional provision is that, where a Member State adopts an aid measure in favour of activities relating to products appearing on that list, the Commission cannot initiate an investigation procedure under Article 108 TFEU,[69] because activities falling within the military sphere fall outside the scope of that Treaty.[70]

Just as in the case of the exceptions provided for in the TFEU with regard to the free movement of goods, persons, services, and capital (see Articles 25, 45(3), and (4); 51–52; and 65 TFEU), and the derogation provided for in Article 72 TFEU in the context of the Area of Freedom, Security and Justice with regard to the maintenance of law and order and the safeguarding of internal security,[71] Articles 346 and 347 TFEU must be strictly construed.[72] These articles leave Member States free, to a degree, to estimate themselves whether there is a risk to security and to what extent the risk justifies departing from the obligations laid down by the Treaty. However, a Member State which seeks to rely on those provisions is to furnish evidence that the derogations in question are proportionate to the alleged risk

---

[67] See Lebeck, 'National Security Exceptions to EU Law: European Customs Policies and Beyond' (2010) ELRev 98; Trybus, 'The Limits of European Community Competence for Defence' (2004) E For Aff Rev 189–217 and 'The EC Treaty as an Instrument of European Defence Integration: Judicial Scrutiny of Defence and Security Exceptions' (2002) CMLRev 1347–72; Peers, 'National Security and European Law' (1996) YEL 363, 379–87. However, those provisions do not authorize any derogation from the principles of liberty, democracy, and respect for human rights and fundamental freedoms (C-402/05 P and C-415/05 P, *Kadi and Al Barakaat International Foundation*, 2008, paras 302–3).

[68] The list was published as the Council's answer of 27 September 2001 to question E-1324/01 (Staes), OJ 2001 C364E/85; a detailed list was published in connection with a CFSP Code of Conduct for Weapons Exports; see now the common list of military equipment covered by the European Union code of conduct on arms export, as regularly adopted by the Council, e.g. on 14 March 2016, OJ 2016 C122/1. For an example of the application of Article 346(1)(b) TFEU to public procurement of military equipment, see C-615/10, *Insinööritoimisto InsTiimi*, 2012. See Trybus, 'The Tailor-Made EU Defence and Security Procurement Directive: Limitation, Flexibility, Descriptiveness and Substitution' (2013) ELRev 1; Poell, 'Offsets in Defence Procurement under EU Law' (2013) EuZW 774. The export regime adopted by the Council on 'dual-use goods' (civil and military use) expressly provides that it does not affect Article 296 EC: Article 26 of Regulation No. 428/2009 of 5 May 2009 setting up a Community regime for the control of exports, transfer, brokering, and transit of dual-use items, OJ 2009 L134/1.

[69] See T-26/01, *Fiocchi munizioni*, 2003, paras 58–9.

[70] C-61/03, *Commission v United Kingdom*, 2005, paras 35–45.

[71] C-715/17, C-718/17, and C-719/17, *Commission v Poland, Hungary and Czech Republic*, 2020, para. 144; see also C-643/15 and C-647/15, *Slovak Republic and Hungary v Council*, 2017, paras 306–9.

[72] 13/68, *Salgoil*, 1968, 463; 222/84, *Johnston*, 1986, paras 25–6; C-414/97, *Commission v Spain*, 1999, para. 21; C-337/05, *Commission v Italy*, 2008, paras 42–52; C-157/06, *Commission v Italy*, 2008, paras 22–33; C-284/05 *Commission v Finland*, 2009, para. 46; C-615/10, *Insinööritoimisto InsTiimi*, 2012, para. 35; C-474/12, *Schiebel Aircraft*, 2014, paras 33–4; C-187/16, *Commission v Austria*, 2018, para. 77; C-715/17, C-718/17, and C-719/17, *Commission v Poland, Hungary and Czech Republic*, 2020, paras 144–5.

to security,[73] and that they effectively took action to address the risk.[74] In this connection, the Court has held that the confidentiality obligation by which Union and national officials are bound in the implementation of the Union customs system is capable of protecting the essential security interests of Member States.[75] Article 347 TFEU refers to Member States consulting each other with a view to taking steps together to prevent the functioning of the internal market being affected by a measure which a Member State feels itself called upon to take. The consultation with other Member States may make unilateral national measures unnecessary should the outcome of the consultation be a decision to adopt a Union measure.[76] If the national measures have the effect of distorting the conditions of competition, the Commission, together with the Member State concerned, will examine how these measures can be adjusted to the rules laid down in the Treaty (Article 348, first para. TFEU).[77] In the event that the Member State makes 'improper use' of the powers provided for in Articles 346 and 347 TFEU, the Commission,[78] or any Member State, may bring the matter directly before the Court of Justice by way of derogation from the procedure laid down in Articles 258 and 259 TFEU. The Court is to give its ruling *in camera* (Article 348, second para. TFEU). Pending its decision on the substance, the Court of Justice may make an order prescribing interim measures.[79] In the first, and so far only, application of Article 348 TFEU, the Commission accused Greece of having infringed rules of the common commercial policy without being in one of the situations for which Article 347 TFEU provided for exceptions, by imposing a ban on imports and trade in products from the former Yugoslav Republic of Macedonia (now North Macedonia). The Court of Justice did not have to rule on the case, since the Commission discontinued the proceedings in view of the conclusion of an agreement between Greece and North Macedonia.[80] The procedure provided for in Article 348, second para. TFEU is applicable only where 'improper use' of the powers provided for in Articles 346 and 347 TFEU is alleged, and does not prevent the Commission from bringing an action against a Member State under Article 258 TFEU for failure to fulfil other Treaty obligations.[81]

---

[73] Trybus 'The EC Treaty as an Instrument of European Defence Integration: Judicial Scrutiny of Defence and Security Exceptions' (2002) CMLRev 1347, 1364–69. According to the Court of Justice, the Member State must prove that reliance on Article 346 of the TFEU is necessary to protect the essential interests of its security: C-414/97, *Commission v Spain*, 1999, para. 22; C-284/05, *Commission v Finland*, 2009, paras 47–9.

[74] C-93/17, *Commission v Greece*, 2018, paras 88–90.

[75] C-284/05, *Commission v Finland*, 2009, para. 51; see also the parallel cases of the same date: C-294/05, *Commission v Sweden*, 2009; C-372/05, *Commission v Germany*, 2009; C-387/05, *Commission v Italy*, 2009; C-409/05, *Commission v Greece*, 2009; C-461/05, *Commission v Denmark*, 2009; C-239/06, *Commission v Italy*, 2009, and further, C-38/06, *Commission v Portugal*, 2010.

[76] Koutrakos, 'Is Article 297 EC a "Reserve of Sovereignty"?' (2000) CMLRev 1339–62; see also Corthaut, *EU ordre public* (Wolters Kluwer, 2012), 138–42.

[77] C-246/12 P, *Ellinika Nafpigeia v Commission*, 2013, paras 36–43. This will be the case, for example, where a national aid measure benefits activities connected with products not on the Council's list of 15 April 1958 or having a 'dual use': T-26/01, *Fiocchi munizioni*, 2003, para. 63. For the Commission's powers in this connection, see ibid., paras 74–5.

[78] In this connection, the Commission has to look after the Union's interests, not those of third countries: C-120/94 R, *Commission v Greece* (order), 1994, paras 99–101.

[79] Ibid., paras 38–45 (with case note by Vanhamme (1994/95) Col JEL 134–9).

[80] C-120/94 *Commission v Greece* (order), 1996. Advocate General FG Jacobs took the view that Greece had not abused the then Article 297 EC: C-120/94, *Commission v Greece*, AG Jacobs Opinion, 1995, paras 61–72; see also Peers (n. 66, *supra*), 384–7.

[81] C-372/05, *Commission v Germany*, 2009, paras 28–30.

The derogations laid down in Articles 346–348 TFEU do not take away from the Union any substantive competence to deal with security aspects in a Union act. Moreover, a measure taken by a Member State on grounds of public security does not necessarily fall, in its entirety, outside the scope of Union law. Decisions taken by the Member States with regard to the organization of their armed forces are thus not outside the application of Union law where they raise the question of respecting the principle of equal treatment of men and women in employment relationships, in particular with regard to access to military occupations.[82] Nevertheless, an exception is made for the application of Union law to decisions of Member States relating to military organization whose aim is the defence of their territory or of their essential interests.[83] Where the Union itself has laid down rules, however, it may be hard for a Member State to invoke exceptional circumstances.[84]

Transitional derogations. During the transitional period which was provided for in the EEC Treaty, a Member State could apply to the Commission for authorization to take protective measures if difficulties arose that were serious and liable to persist in any sector of the economy or that could bring about serious deterioration in the economic situation of a given area.[85] Every Accession Treaty provides for a transitional period during which similar protective measures can be taken at the request of an acceding Member State.[86] Furthermore, a specific Treaty provision gives the Commission the power to grant a Member State temporary derogations of its obligations under the Treaties in case that Member State is threatened by serious difficulties as regards its balance of payments (Article 141(1) TFEU).

11.012

---

[82] C-273/97, *Sirdar*, 1999, para. 19, and C-285/98, *Kreil*, 2000, para. 16.

[83] C-186/01, *Dory*, 2003, paras 35–42 (Germany's decision to ensure its defence in part by compulsory military service limited to men is the expression of a choice of military organization to which Union law is not applicable). For critical observations, see Trybus (2003) CMLRev 1269–80; for a somewhat favourable view, see Koutrakos (2003) MLR 759–68; Anagnostaras (2003) ELRev 713–22; Dietrich (2003) DöV 883–9.

[84] See C-124/95, *Centro-Com*, 1997, para. 46 (where exceptions to the Union export regime were relied on; see para. 10-006, *infra*). See also Gilsdorf, 'Les réserves de sécurité du traité CEE, à la lumière du traité sur l'Union européenne' (1994) RMCUE 17, 18–19 and 23–5, where it is argued that a CFSP decision may also raise the hurdles that a Member State must overcome in order to invoke such safeguard clauses.

[85] Article 226(1) EEC; for applications, see 13/63, *Italy v Commission*, 1963, at 175–9; 73 and 74/63, *Handelsvereniging Rotterdam*, 1964, 11–14; 37/70, *Rewe-Zentrale*, 1971, paras 2–19; 72/72, *Einfuhr- und Vorratsstelle Getreide*, 1973, paras 4–20.

[86] See Article 135 of the 1972 Act of Accession; Article 130 of the 1979 Act of Accession; Article 379 of the 1985 Act of Accession; Article 152 of the 1994 Act of Accession; Article 37 of the 2003 Act of Accession; Article 36 of the 2005 Act of Accession; Article 37 of the 2011 Act of Accession. See also Garcia-Duran Huet, 'Le traité d'Athènes, un traité d'adhésion comme les autres?' (2004) RMCUE 290–2; Van Haersolte, 'Het Toetredingsverdrag 2003 (alias het Verdrag van Athene)' (2003) NTDE 301, 308–310.

PART III
INSTITUTIONAL ACTORS OF THE EUROPEAN UNION

The Union is served by a single institutional framework (Article 13(1) TEU), that consists of various institutions and bodies. The Treaties identify seven 'institutions' of the Union: the European Parliament, the European Council, the Council, the European Commission, the Court of Justice of the European Union, the European Central Bank (ECB), and the Court of Auditors (Article13(1) TEU; Article 3(1), first subpara, EAEC).[1] Except for the ECB, which has legal personality in accordance with Article 282(3) TFEU,[2] the Union's institutions do not have legal personality, but act on behalf of the Union.[3] The most important characteristics of every institution—with the exception of the ECB and the Court of Auditors—are set out in Title III TEU. Provisions relating to the ECB and the Court of Auditors and detailed provisions on the other institutions are set out in the TFEU. Each institution is attributed a proper task in order to attain the objectives of the Union. The institutions must act within the limits of the powers conferred on them by the Treaties, and in conformity with the procedures, conditions, and objectives set out therein; in doing so, they are to operate in mutual sincere cooperation (Article 13(2) TEU). This rule must be understood in the light of the institutional balance that is at the heart of the institutional framework of the Union (see para. 16-007 *et seq.*, *infra*).

In addition to its institutions, the Union has a number of consultative committees, bodies, offices, and agencies, established by or pursuant to the Treaties and with or without legal personality. In so far as the Treaties, the statutes annexed to them, or - for some bodies, offices, or agencies - acts of secondary Union law do not regulate their establishment and operation, Union institutions, bodies, offices, and agencies have the power to decide on their internal organization.

Chapter 12 gives an overview of the powers, composition, operation, and internal organization for each of the four 'political institutions' (European Parliament, European Council, Council, and European Commission). Chapter 13 discusses the three other institutions (Court of Justice of the European Union, European Central Bank, and Court of Auditors) and the other bodies, offices, and agencies of the Union. Some elements common to their functioning as organs of the Union are set out in Chapter 14. Chapter 15 discusses the role of the Member States as actors of the Union, whereas Chapter 16 sets out the main principles governing the relationship between the Union's institutional actors.

---

[1] C-176/03, *Commission v Council* (order), 2004, (European Economic and Social Committee does not constitute an 'institution' entitled to be joined in proceedings before the Court of Justice pursuant to Article 40 of the CJ Statute).

[2] See also Article 9.1 of Protocol (No. 4), annexed to the TEU and TFEU, on the Statute of the European System of Central Banks and of the European Central Bank [ESCB Statute], OJ 2010 C83/230.

[3] For the position of the Union in the legal systems of the Member States and at international level, see para. 14-003 *et seq.*, *infra*.

12
The Political Institutions of the Union

I. The European Parliament

Representative assembly. The European Parliament[1] was originally established as the 'Common Assembly' of the ECSC and as the 'Assembly' of the EEC and the EAEC, merged as long ago as 1957 into a single Assembly for the three Communities. It was not long before the Assembly started to refer to itself as the 'European Parliament'.[2] The title 'European Parliament' did not gain general acceptance until the Single European Act provided that the institutions of the European Communities were to be 'henceforth designated as referred to hereafter' (Single European Act, Article 3(1)). In the institutional framework of the ECSC, the European Parliament played a modest role supervising the High Authority.[3] Since the EEC and EAEC, and even more as a result of later amendments and additions to the Treaties, the European Parliament nowadays participates in the decision-making and plays a major role in establishing the Union's budget. The European Parliament embodies, at the Union level, the respect for the democratic principle that 'the peoples should take part in the exercise of power through the intermediary of a representative assembly'.[4] Yet, the European Parliament's role does not lie only in giving political expression to the will of the democratic majority within the Union, it also gives citizens of the Union and other persons affected by action taken by the Union a means of making their views known on the policy which is being conducted.

12.001

A. Powers

1. Nature

Overview. According to Article 14(1) TEU, the European Parliament exercises, jointly with the Council, legislative and budgetary functions and exercises, in addition, functions of political control and consultation as laid down in the Treaties. The discussion hereafter will address the European Parliament's powers (a) to take part in Union decision-making; (b) to adopt the EU budget in cooperation with the Council; and (c) to supervise other institutions and bodies of the Union. Moreover, the European Parliament may advise and adopt resolutions pertaining to societal issues. Even where the power to act lies with other institutions or with national governments, the European Parliament is entitled to 'invite them to act'.[5]

12.002

---

[1] See in general Corbett et al., *The European Parliament* (Harper, 2016); Ripoll Servent, *The European Parliament* (Blackwell's, 2017). For the website of the European Parliament, see http://www.europarl.europa.eu/.
[2] Resolutions of 20 March 1958, JO 6, 20 April 1958 ('European Parliamentary Assembly') and of 30 March 1962, JO 1962, 1045 ('European Parliament').
[3] Article 20 ECSC.
[4] 138/79, *Roquette Frères v. Council*, 1980, para. 33; 139/79, *Maïzena v Council*, 1980, para. 34; C-300/89, *Commission v Council*, 1991, para. 20; C-502/19, *Junqueras Vies*, 2019, paras 63–5.
[5] 230/81, *Luxembourg v European Parliament*, 1983, para. 39.

2. Survey of powers

a. Participation in decision-making

12.003 **Co-legislator.** The Court of Justice has held that participation of the European Parliament in Union decision-making is an essential procedural requirement with which other institutions must comply, failing which the act adopted may be annulled.[6] Since the Lisbon Treaty the European Parliament and the Council act on an equal footing in the context of the ordinary legislative procedure (see para. 17-019, *infra*). Even before the changes brought about by the Lisbon Treaty, the European Parliament had sufficient decision-making and supervisory powers to constitute part of the Union's 'legislature' for the purposes of Article 3 of Protocol (No. 1) to the ECHR.[7]

All the same, the European Parliament still has no right of initiative. The European Parliament may, acting by a majority of its component members, request the Commission to submit any appropriate proposal on matters on which it considers that a Union act is required for the purpose of implementing the Treaties (Article 225 TFEU), but this does not amount to a genuine right to initiate legislation (see para. 17-016, *infra*). Neither does the European Parliament have a decisive say in the ordinary procedure for amending the Treaties; the role of 'constituent assembly' in this connection falls to the Member States.[8]

12.004 **External relations.** The European Parliament also has a role to play in respect of the conclusion of international agreements. It has to give its consent to association agreements, to the agreement whereby the Union is to accede to the ECHR, to international agreements establishing a specific institutional framework or having important budgetary implications for the Union, and to international agreements relating to policy areas where internal legislation is adopted in accordance with the ordinary legislative procedure or a special legislative procedure involving consent of the European Parliament (Article 218(6) TFEU). Consent of the European Parliament, acting by a majority of its component members, is required for the accession of new Member States to the Union (Article 49 TEU).

In addition, the European Parliament is consulted on the conclusion of all other international agreements, with the exception of those coming under the CFSP (Article 218(6) TFEU). In decision-making with regard to the CFSP, the European Parliament has only an (unenforceable) right to be consulted on 'the main aspects and the basic choices' (Article 36, first para. TEU)[9] and the right to address questions and recommendations to the Council and the High Representative (Article 36, second para. TEU). In accordance with Article 218(10) TFEU the European Parliament must, however, be 'immediately and fully informed' about international agreements in the area of the CFSP. This right enables the European Parliament to exercise democratic control over the exercise of the external competences of the Union, including the CFSP, and to verify whether its prerogatives have been respected, a right which is judicially enforceable.[10]

---

[6] 138/79, *Roquette Frères*, 1980 and 139/79, *Maïzena*, 1980 on breaches of the right to be consulted.
[7] Judgment of the European Court of Human Rights of 18 February 1999 in Case No. 24833/94 *Matthews v United Kingdom*.
[8] Article 48(2) to (5) TEU. See para. 3-002 *et seq., supra*.
[9] See Article 36, first para. TEU. Article 225 TFEU does not apply to decision-making in connection with the CFSP (Article 24(1), second subpara. TEU). For the limited role of the European Parliament in PJCC matters before the entry into force of the Lisbon Treaty, see Articles 39(1) EU and 41(1) EU.
[10] See C-658/11, *European Parliament v Council*, 2014, paras 75–86; C-263/14, *European Parliament v Council*, 2016, paras 68–85.

b. Budgetary authority

Finances. The European Parliament and the Council together form the budgetary authority of the Union. The European Parliament has the final say over all categories of expenditure[11] and may also reject the budget in its entirety. The exercise by the Parliament of its budget powers is a fundamental event in the democratic life of the European Union and requires that it holds a public debate in plenary sitting.[12] It has made use of these powers on several occasions in order to assert its views in respect of the most diverse policy matters.

12.005

This power also enables the European Parliament to increase its limited say in decision-making with regard to the CFSP where action of the Union is charged to the EU budget.[13]

The European Parliament's power to give a discharge to the Commission in respect of the implementation of the budget reinforces the European Parliament's supervision of the Commission.

c. Supervision of other institutions and bodies

Supervision of the Commission. Since the EU Treaty entered into force, the European Parliament has to approve the members of the Commission proposed for appointment; since the Lisbon Treaty, the Parliament has first to 'elect' by a majority of its component members the person whom the European Council, acting by a qualified majority, proposes to appoint as President of the Commission, after which the Council may select, in agreement with the President-elect and on the basis of suggestions made by the Member States, the other persons whom it proposes for appointment as members of the Commission (see para. 12-064). The Commission is subject, as a body, to a vote of consent by the European Parliament, after which it is formally 'appointed' by the European Council, acting by a qualified majority (Article 17(7) TEU).

12.006

The Commission is politically answerable to the European Parliament. This is reflected, in the first place, in the European Parliament's right to put oral or written questions to the Commission (Article 230, second para. TFEU).

In addition, the European Parliament has the right to pass a motion of censure on the activities of the Commission (Article 234 TFEU). Such a motion may be submitted by a tenth of its members.[14] However, such a motion may, at the earliest, be voted on three days after it has been submitted. In order for a motion to be carried, it must obtain a two-thirds majority of the votes cast, representing a majority of MEPs. If such a motion is carried, the members of the Commission have to resign as a body. Pending their replacement, they continue to deal with current business only. So far, the European Parliament has held votes on motions of censure several times, but a motion has never been carried.[15] On 14 January

---

[11] Before the Lisbon Treaty, this was true only in respect of non-compulsory expenditure (para. 20-001, *infra*).
[12] See C-237/11 and C-238/11, *France v European Parliament*, 2012, para. 68; C-73/17, *France v European Parliament*, 2017, para. 35.
[13] Para. 19-006, *infra*.
[14] EP Rules of Procedure, Rule 127(1).
[15] See Debates of the European Parliament, 1972, 156/8, and 156/52 (motion withdrawn without being put to a vote); 1976, 204/121 (no majority); 1976, 210/287 (motion withdrawn without being put to a vote); 1977, 215/63 (no majority); 1990, 386/85, and 386/316 (no majority); OJ 1991 C240/167 (no majority); OJ 1993 C21/30 and C21/124 (no majority); OJ 1997 C85/103 (following a report of a committee of inquiry on 'mad cow disease': no majority); OJ 1999 C104/97 (following allegations of fraud, mismanagement, and nepotism made against individual Commissioners of the Santer Commission: no majority); OJ 2005 C85E/18 (no majority on 4 May 2004 following allegations of mismanagement in Eurostat), OJ 2006 C92E/384 (no majority on 8 June 2005 following

1999, the European Parliament failed, by a relatively narrow margin, to obtain the necessary majority to pass a motion of censure against the Santer Commission. The Parliament then proposed that a committee of independent experts be set up to examine the way in which the Commission detected and dealt with fraud, mismanagement, and nepotism. When the committee submitted its first (critical) report, the Santer Commission decided to resign as a body. Following the collective resignation of the Commission, a discussion was initiated as to the possibility of compelling individual Commissioners to resign. In a framework agreement concluded between the Commission and the European Parliament, the Commission accepted that, where the European Parliament expresses a lack of confidence in a member of the Commission, the President of the Commission will either request that member to resign or to explain his or her decision not to do so to the European Parliament.[16] The Treaties now provide that a member of the Commission has to resign if the President so requests (Article 17(6) TEU; see para. 12-068). The possibility of a motion of censure being carried against the Commission, together with the vote of consent in the process of appointment of the Commission, constitutes the cornerstone of the Commission's political accountability to the European Parliament.

12.007 **Relations with the Council and the European Council.** The Treaties do not confer any general power of supervision on the European Parliament as far as the Council is concerned. The reason for this is that members of the Council are accountable to their national parliaments (Article 10(2) TEU). The third para. of Article 230 TFEU merely provides for the Council to be 'heard by the European Parliament in accordance with the conditions laid down by the Council in its Rules of Procedure'.[17] Nevertheless, the Council has committed to answering questions from the European Parliament.[18]

In addition, the Head of Government of the Member State that holds the presidency of the Council comes to provide information to the European Parliament.[19] In CFSP matters, the obligation to inform the European Parliament rests on the High Representative, who has to regularly consult the European Parliament on the main aspects and the basic choices of the CFSP and the common security and defence policy (Article 36, first para. TEU)[20]. The

---

alleged conflict of interests of Commission President Barroso); *Europe*, No. 11206, 28 November 2014 (no majority on 27 November 2014 following allegations of Commission President Juncker's involvement in Luxembourg tax-avoidance rulings); motion of 12 May 2016 concerning alleged inaction on endocrine disruptors (withdrawn without being put to a vote).

[16] Framework Agreement of 26 May 2005 on relations between the European Parliament and the Commission, OJ 2006 C117E/125, point 3, as confirmed by the Framework Agreement of 20 October 2010 on relations between the European Parliament and the Commission, OJ 2010 L304/47, point 5.

[17] See Council Rules of Procedure, Article 26.

[18] See the Solemn Declaration of Stuttgart, 19 June 1983, EC Bull. 1986, point 2.3.3. As regards CFSP, such obligation follows from Article 36, second para. TEU.

[19] The President of the Council reports on multilateral economic surveillance, just as the Commission does, and may be invited to appear before the competent parliamentary committee if the Council has made its recommendations public (Article 121(4) and (5) TFEU). He or she is to inform the Parliament of any decision of the Council taken where a Member State fails to comply with measures for deficit reduction (Article 126(11) TFEU).

[20] See also Rule 119(1) and (2) of the EP Rules of Procedure. Rule 119(4) provides that the High Representative is to be invited to every plenary debate that involves foreign, security, or defence policy. As far as concerns the European Parliament's access to sensitive information in the field of security and defence policy, the rules laid down in the Interinstitutional Agreements between the European Parliament and the Council of 20 November 2002 (OJ 2002 C298/1) and of 12 March 2014 (OJ 2014, C95/1).

President of the European Council has to present a report to the European Parliament after each of the meetings of the European Council (Article 15(6)(d) TEU).

Relations with other institutions and bodies. The supervision exercised indirectly by the European Parliament over other institutions and bodies takes the form of its right to appoint the European Ombudsman and to be consulted on the appointment of members of the Court of Auditors and of the Executive Board of the ECB and of the Director of OLAF.[21] The European Parliament further has the right to obtain information from the Court of Auditors and the ECB.[22]

12.008

Legal proceedings. The European Parliament may bring proceedings before the Court of Justice for the annulment of acts of the European Council, the Council, the Commission, or the ECB (Article 263 TFEU).[23] The Parliament may also bring an action in the Court of Justice for failure to act against the European Council, the Council, the Commission, or the ECB.[24] However, the prerogatives which it exercises in connection with the common foreign and security policy (CFSP) may not be enforced by bringing proceedings in the Court of Justice.[25]

12.009

Inquiries. Lastly, the European Parliament's right of supervision extends to the right to hold inquiries into alleged contraventions of Union law or maladministration in its implementation (Article 226 TFEU). Even the conduct of national authorities in implementing Union law may be the subject of an inquiry by the European Parliament. At the request of a quarter of its members, the European Parliament may set up a temporary committee of inquiry.[26] The right of inquiry does not exist 'where the alleged facts are being examined before a court and while the case is still subject to legal proceedings' (Article 226, first para. TFEU). The exercise of the right of inquiry is governed by an agreement between the Parliament, the Council, and the Commission concluded in 1995.[27] Nonetheless, since the Lisbon Treaty,

12.010

---

[21] See the further discussion of these Union bodies in paras 13-021, 13-026, and 13-043, *infra*. In 1994, the European Parliament had already expressed a wish to be involved in the appointment of members of the Court of Justice and requested arrangements to be made for meeting prospective members of the Court prior to their appointment: resolution of 9 February 1994 (OJ 1994 C61/126). Since the Lisbon Treaty, a panel has to give its opinion on the suitability of the candidate proposed for appointment. That panel includes one member proposed by the European Parliament (see para. 13-014, *infra*).

[22] Articles 284(3), 287(1) and (4), and 319(1) TFEU.

[23] The Nice Treaty abolished the requirement that an action brought by the European Parliament must seek to safeguard its prerogatives. Subject to that condition, the EU Treaty had codified in Article 230 EC [*now Article 263 TFEU*] the European Parliament's right to bring proceedings as recognised by the Court of Justice: see C-70/88 *European Parliament v Council*, 1990, paras 11–31. That right was not embodied in Article 173 EEC and had not been accepted in earlier case law: 302/87 *European Parliament v Council*, 1988, paras 8–28. A first example of an action not brought to safeguard prerogatives was the Parliament's action for partial annulment of Council Directive 2003/86/EC of 22 September 2003 on the right to family reunification (see para. 8-012, *supra*), rejected in C-540/03, *European Parliament v Council*, 2006.

[24] Article 265, first para. TFEU. See 13/83, *European Parliament v Council*, 1985, paras 13–19.

[25] Article 275 TEU. This does not preclude, however, that the European Parliament seeks to enforce its right to be informed under Article 218(10) TFEU; see C-658/11, *European Parliament v Council*, 2014, paras 75–86; C-263/14, *European Parliament v Council*, 2016, paras 68–85.

[26] See also EP Rules of Procedure, Article 208, which governs the operation of such committees of inquiry. See further Syrier, *The Investigative Function of the European Parliament—Holding the EU Executive to account by conducting investigations* (Wolf Legal Publishers, 2013).

[27] Decision 95/167/EC, Euratom, ECSC of the European Parliament, the Council, and the Commission of 19 April 1995 on the detailed provisions governing the exercise of the European Parliament's right of inquiry, OJ 1995 L113/2.

detailed provisions are to be adopted by the European Parliament after obtaining the consent of the Council and the Commission (Article 226, third para. TFEU).

12.011 **Right to petition.** The fact that the European Parliament acts as the voice of the citizens finds a further expression in the right of petition. All citizens of the Union and any natural or legal person residing or having its registered office in a Member State have the right to petition the European Parliament (Articles 24, second para. and 227 TFEU).[28] This right must be seen as part of the citizen's right to participate in the democratic life of the Union, as provided for in Article 10(3) TEU.[29] The Rules of Procedure of the European Parliament lay down further rules for this right of petition.[30]

B. Composition

12.012 **Representatives of the citizens.** Until the Lisbon Treaty, the European Parliament was considered to consist of 'representatives of the peoples of the States brought together in the Community' (Article 189 EC). Now, the European Parliament consists of 'representatives of the Union's citizens' (Article 14(2) TEU). Since 1979, MEPs have been elected by direct universal suffrage. This gives the institution a direct democratic legitimacy which others lack.[31] MEPs are elected for a five-year term by direct universal suffrage (Article 14(3) TEU).[32] Since they represent citizens directly and not their Member States, they form a genuine supranational institution. This means that all MEPs may participate in debates and decision-making even in policy areas in which not all Member States of the Union participate.[33]

12.013 **Number of MEPs.** Article 14(2), first subpara. TEU provides that the representation of citizens is to be degressively proportional to the size of the population of the Member States, with a minimum of six and a maximum of ninety-six members per Member State. The precise composition is to be determined by the European Council, acting unanimously on the initiative of the European Parliament and with its consent (Article 14(2), second subpara. TEU).[34] Currently, there are 705 parliamentary seats.

---

[28] Now also confirmed in Article 44 of the Charter of Fundamental Rights of the European Union. See further Guckelberger, 'Das Petitionsrecht zum Europäischen Parlament sowie das Recht zur Anrufung des Europäischen Bürgerbeauftragten im Europa der Bürger' (2003) DöV 829–38; Maniatis, 'Le règlement des pétitions au Parlement européen' (2002) RDUE 133–45; Marias, 'The Right to Petition the European Parliament after Maastricht' (1994) ELRev 169–83; Pliakos, 'Les conditions d'exercice du droit de pétition' (1993) CDE 317–50. Cf. Article 44 of the Charter of Fundamental Rights; see Holdscheidt, 'Die Ausgestaltung des Petitionsrechts in der EU-Grundrechtecharta' (2002) EuR 441–8. The introduction of Article 194 EC by the EU Treaty transformed a 'custom' into a right of petition protected by the Treaties. See previously the exchanges of letters between the European Parliament, the Council and the Commission of the European Communities of 12 April 1989 on the right to petition, OJ 1989 C120/90.

[29] C-261/13P, *Schönberger v European Parliament*, 2014, paras 14–17; see also C-418/18 P, *Puppinck*, 2019, para. 54.

[30] EP Rules of Procedure, Rules 226 to 229. For the Petitions Web Portal of the European Parliament, see https://petiport.secure.europarl.europa.eu/petitions/en/home.

[31] C-502/19, *Junqueras Vies*, 2019, paras 63–5, where the Court recalls how Article 10(1) TEU, which states that the functioning of the Union shall be founded on representative democracy, is merely the expression of the value of democracy mentioned in Article 2 TEU, and that the quality of being an MEP therefore derives directly from the fact of being directly elected by universal suffrage in a free and secret election.

[32] See in respect of the protection of the right to vote, which is also laid down in Article 39 of the Charter of Fundamental Rights of the European Union: C-650/13, *Delvigne*, 2015, paras 40–58.

[33] Resolution of the European Parliament of 19 January 1994, OJ 1994 C44/88.

[34] See European Council Decision 2013/312/EU of 28 June 2013 establishing the composition of the European Parliament, OJ 2013 L181/5, replaced by European Council Decision (EU) 2018/937 of 28 June 2018 OJ 2018 L165I/2. Article 1 of Decision 2018/937 defines 'degressive proportionality' as follows: 'the ratio between the

Before the Lisbon Treaty, the allocation of parliamentary seats to the various Member States was laid down in the Treaties, and was amended upon each accession of new Member States and following German reunification.[35] In order to ensure the efficient functioning of the European Parliament, the Treaty of Amsterdam fixed the maximum number of MEPs at 700, which the Treaty of Nice however raised again to 732 and the 2003 and 2005 Acts of Accession to 736 and, temporarily, even to 788 members.[36] The Treaty of Lisbon eventually fixed the maximum number of MEPs at 750, plus the President (see Article 14(2) TEU).[37] This maximum number was not immediately applied, and a later Treaty amendment adjusted the transitional regime agreed in the Lisbon Treaty in order to temporarily allow for adding new members beyond the maximum laid down in Article 14(2) TEU. The European Parliament elected in May 2014 was the first to be composed of 751 members pursuant to the decision taken by the European Council in 2013 following the principles laid down in the Lisbon Treaty.[38]

In June 2018, the European Council adopted a new decision introducing a system according to which, before each new election, the seats are distributed among the Member States in an objective and sustainable manner in accordance with the principle of degressive proportionality and taking account of the demographic development of the population of the Member States. For the 2019–2024 parliamentary term, since the withdrawal of the United Kingdom from the Union, Germany has ninety-six representatives; France seventy-nine; Italy seventy-six; Spain fifty-nine; Poland fifty two; Romania thirty three; the Netherlands twenty-nine; Belgium, the Czech Republic, Greece, Hungary, Portugal, and Sweden each twenty-one; Austria nineteen; Bulgaria seventeen; Denmark, Finland, and Slovakia each fourteen; Ireland thirteen; Croatia twelve; Lithuania eleven; Latvia and Slovenia each eight; Estonia seven; and Cyprus, Luxembourg, and Malta each six representatives (together 705 members).[39] At the beginning of the 2019–2024 parliamentary term, when the United Kingdom was still a Member State of the Union, the Parliament had the same composition as in May 2014. Once the United Kingdom's withdrawal became effective on 1 February

---

population and the number of seats of each Member State before rounding to whole numbers is to vary in relation to their respective populations in such a way that each [MEP] from a more populous Member State represents more citizens than each [MEP] from a less populous Member State and, conversely, that the larger the population of a Member State, the greater its entitlement to a large number of seats in the European Parliament'.

[35] Initially, the allocation of seats was laid down in the Act on the direct election of the European Parliament (now repealed), as subsequently amended by the Acts of Accession. The Treaty of Amsterdam incorporated the distribution of seats in Article 190 EC. Note that before the 1994 elections, the new German *Länder* were represented only by eighteen observers. See also C-25/92, *Miethke v European Parliament* 1993.

[36] For the short period between the date of accession and the beginning of the new parliamentary term, the new Member States were represented in the European Parliament by members of their national parliaments (see the 2003 Act of Accession, Article 25).

[37] The European Council of 21 and 22 June 2007 had decided to work on a Treaty reform on the assumption of a composition of 750 members. At the Intergovernmental Conference of 2007, Italy's request to have an additional seat was accommodated by not taking the seat of the Parliament's President into account for calculating the maximum number of 750.

[38] Germany had ninety-six seats; France seventy-four; Italy and the United Kingdom seventy-three each; Spain fifty-four; Poland fifty-one; Romania thirty-two; the Netherlands twenty-six; Belgium, the Czech Republic, Greece, Hungary, and Portugal twenty-one each; Sweden twenty; Bulgaria and Austria eighteen; Denmark, Finland, and Slovakia thirteen each; Ireland, Lithuania, and Croatia eleven each; Latvia and Slovenia eight each; Cyprus, Estonia, Luxembourg, and Malta six each.

[39] Pursuant to Article 3(1) of Decision (EU) 2018/937 (see n. 37, *supra*).

2020, the Parliament's composition changed, with additional members from the other Member States taking up their seats at that moment.[40]

12.014 **Direct elections.** Initially, the European Parliament consisted of delegates designated by the respective national parliaments from among their members.[41] Nevertheless, the EEC Treaty itself looked forward to the direct election of the Parliament in accordance with a uniform procedure in all Member States. The Treaty required the European Parliament to draw up 'proposals' to this end, after which the Council, acting unanimously and—since the EU Treaty—with the assent of the Parliament, which was to act by a majority of its component members, was to lay down the necessary provisions. Those provisions were then to be recommended to the Member States for adoption in accordance with their respective constitutional requirements (Article 190(4) EC Treaty). This is still the procedure set out in Article 223(1) TFEU. Using this procedure, the Council adopted the Decision of 20 September 1976 and the Act annexed thereto concerning the election of the representatives of the Assembly by direct universal suffrage,[42] which laid down certain principles concerning the elections but has not set out a uniform procedure for elections. Since its amendment in 2002,[43] the 1976 Act provides that members of the European Parliament are to be elected on the basis of proportional representation, using the list system or the single transferable vote (Act, Article 1(1)). Member States may opt for a preferential list system (Act, Article 1(2)), may establish constituencies or other subdivisions for elections (Article 2), and may set a minimum threshold for the distribution of seats (Article 3) and ceilings for candidates' election expenses (Article 4). Subject to the provisions of the Act, the electoral procedure is to be governed in each Member State by its national provisions,[44] which, however, may not affect the essentially proportional nature of the voting system.[45] Since the first elections to the European Parliament in June 1979, the elections are held in all Member States in the period starting on a Thursday morning and ending on the following Sunday corresponding to the same period five years before.[46] Within the European

---

[40] Ibid., Article 3(2). See also, Fabbrini and Schmidt, 'The Composition of the European Parliament in Brexit Times: Changes and Challenges' (2019) ELRev 711–725.
[41] Article 138(1) EEC. The choice which Article 21 ECSC left to each Member State to have members of the Assembly directly elected or designated by the national parliaments was abolished when in 1958 the Assembly merged into the Common Assembly of the three Communities, constituted in accordance with Article 138 EEC.
[42] Decision 76/787/ECSC, EEC, Euratom of the representatives of the Member States meeting in the Council relating to the Act concerning the election of the representatives of the Assembly by direct universal suffrage, OJ 1976 L278/1. See Alonso de León, 'Four Decades of the European Electoral Act: A Look Back and a Look Ahead to an Unfulfilled Ambition' (2017) Eur L Rev 353–68; Costa, *The History of European Electoral Reform and the Electoral Act 1976* (European Parliamentary Research Service, 2016).
[43] See Article 3 of Decision 2002/772/EC. Article 14 of the Act (there was a corresponding provision also in the original version) empowers the Council to adopt any necessary implementing measures unanimously, in accordance with an unusual procedure: the Council acts on a proposal from the Parliament, after consulting the Commission, and after endeavouring to reach agreement with the Parliament in a conciliation committee consisting of the Council and representatives of the Parliament. See also the most recent amendment by Council Decision (EU, Euratom) 2018/994 of 13 July 2018, OJ 2018 L178/1 (entering into force after completion of all national ratification procedures), introducing some technical amendments, such as allowing Member States to provide for advance voting, postal voting, and electronic and internet voting, as well as voting by citizens residing in third countries.
[44] C-502/19, *Junqueras Vies*, 2019, para. 69.
[45] Act, Article 8. Voting is compulsory in Belgium, Bulgaria, Cyprus, Greece, and Luxembourg. Usually in other Member States, the turnout for elections to the European Parliament is relatively low, reaching 50.66 per cent in the 2019 elections.
[46] Act, Articles 10 and 11, allowing the Council to determine another electoral period not more than two months before or one month after that period.

Parliament there has been some support for the idea to set up a Union-wide constituency for the election of part of the members of the European Parliament in order to trigger a truly European campaign.[47] When voting on the most recent proposals for revision of the Act, however, the Parliament has not been able to find a majority on introducing such system of 'transnational lists'.[48]

The five main European political parties agreed in 2014 to nominate, before the elections, a 'lead candidate' who would be their candidate for election as President of the Commission following the elections. After the elections, the European Council effectively proposed the lead candidate of the political party obtaining most seats in the Parliament as President of the Commission.[49] This commonly called '*Spitzenkandidaten*' (lead candidates) process is not anchored in law[50] and remains controversial, not in the least because it limits the European Council's prerogative to propose a candidate for President of the Commission. In the 2019 elections to the European Parliament, the main European political parties campaigned again with (one or more) lead candidates, but the European Council proposed to elect another candidate,[51] which the Parliament did.

In line with the provision that the electoral procedure is governed by national law, the European Parliament must 'take note' of the results officially declared by the Member States, although it may review the credentials of members of the European Parliament (Act, Article 12).[52] Once a Member State has declared the final result, the duly elected persons automatically become members of the European Parliament, entitled to the immunities bestowed upon them, even though their mandate only starts at the first session of the Parliament.[53]

Right to participate in elections. Before the Lisbon Treaty, the Court of Justice considered that neither (current)Article 223 TFEU nor the 1976 Act defines expressly and precisely who are to be entitled to vote and to stand as candidates in elections to the European

12.015

---

[47] See resolution of the European Parliament of 15 July 1998, OJ 1998, C292/66 (adopting the Anastassopoulos report), not followed on this issue by Council Decision 2002/772/EC.

[48] The idea appeared in reports adopted in 2009, 2011, and 2012 by the committee on Constitutional Affairs, but failed to be adopted by the Parliament's plenary and has neither been included in Parliament's most recent proposal for a revision of the Act: resolution of 11 November 2015, P8_TA(2015)0395.

[49] Jean-Claude Juncker, lead candidate of the European People's Party.

[50] Article 17(4) TEU requires the European Council to propose a candidate for the Presidency of the Commission '[t]aking into account the elections to the European Parliament' (see para. 12-064, *infra*). On that basis the European Parliament has recalled the 'Spitzenkandidaten process' in its decision of 7 February 2018 on the revision of the Framework Agreement on relations between the European Parliament and the European Commission, OJ 2018, C463/98 (warning in point 4 that it 'would be ready to reject any candidate in the investiture procedure of the President of the Commission who was not appointed as a "Spitzenkandidat" in the run-up to the European elections'). The Framework Agreement itself indicates in point 4, as revised in 2018, that members of the Commission may participate in elections to the European parliament, including as 'Spitzenkandidat' (OJ 2018 L45/46).

[51] German Defence Minister Ursula von der Leyen, belonging to the European People's Party, which had campaigned with her fellow countryman Manfred Weber as lead candidate. See Dawson, 'The lost Spitzenkandidaten and the Future of European Democracy' (2019) MJECL 731–5; 'Editorial—Spitzenkandidaten and the European Union's System of Government' (2019) EuConst 609–18; Péraldi-Leneuf, 'Spitzenkandidaten 2019: la grande illusion?' (2019) JDE 149; Cloos, *Spitzenkandidaten: A Debate about Power and about the Future Development of the EU*, European Policy Brief, September 2019; Goldoni, 'Politicising EU Lawmaking? The Spitzenkandidaten Experiment as a Cautionary Tale' (2016) ELJ 279–95.

[52] This power does not amount to a general power to review the official declaration, but must be given a limited scope (C-393/07 and C-9/08 *Italy and Donnici v European Parliament*, 2009, paras 50–73). See also C-208/03 P, *Le Pen*, 2005, paras 43–58 (duty to 'take note' of a communication from a Member State that a MEP is disqualified as a result of a criminal conviction).

[53] C-502/19, *Junqueras Vies*, 2019, paras 60–95.

Parliament, leaving this to be determined by each Member State in compliance with Union law, and in particular the principle of equal treatment. Member States could thus validly choose to grant the right to vote and to stand as a candidate to certain persons who have close links to them, other than their own nationals or citizens of the Union resident in their territory.[54] However, the Netherlands could not, without infringing the principle of equal treatment, deny the right to vote and to stand as a candidate to Dutch nationals resident in the Netherlands Antilles or Aruba while at the same time granting this right to Dutch nationals resident in a third country.[55]

Article 22 TFEU applies the principle of non-discrimination on grounds of nationality to the exercise of the right to vote and to stand as a candidate in elections to the European Parliament, by providing that every citizen of the Union residing in a Member State of which he or she is not a national is to have this right in the Member State in which he or she resides, under the same conditions as nationals of that State. The detailed arrangements surrounding this right are laid down in Council Directive 93/109/EC of 6 December 1993.[56] A person having the right to vote may exercise it either in the Member State of residence or in his or her home Member State; a person eligible to stand as a candidate may do so in only one Member State (Directive 93/109, Article 4). If a Member State requires candidates to have been nationals for a certain minimum period, Union citizens are deemed to satisfy that condition if they have been nationals of a Member State for that period (Directive 93/109, Article 3). Where nationals of the Member State in question are required to have spent a certain minimum period as a resident in the electoral territory of that State in order to be able to vote or to stand for election, Union citizens satisfy that condition if they have resided for an equivalent period in other Member States. Nevertheless, this does not apply in the case of a Member State that imposes specific conditions as to the length of residence in a given constituency or locality (Directive 93/109, Article 5). Where, in a given Member State, the proportion of Union citizens of voting age who reside in it but are not nationals of it exceeds 20 per cent of the total number of Union citizens residing there who are of voting age, the directive authorizes the Member State in question to restrict non-nationals' right to vote and to stand in elections to those who have been resident in that State for a specified minimum period (Directive 93/109, Article 14).[57] As far as the right to stand for election is

---

[54] C-145/04, *Spain v United Kingdom*, 2006. In response to the ruling of the European Court of Human Rights in *Matthews* (see para. 25-014, *infra*), the United Kingdom gave Commonwealth citizens residing in Gibraltar the right to vote in the 2004 elections for the European Parliament. This discretion is, however, contested by some in the wake of Brexit, see the pending case C-673/20, *Préfet du Gers and Institut National de la Statistique et des Études Économiques*, OJ 2021 C98/5, where the applicants are seeking a continued right to vote for certain UK nationals residing in France after Brexit.

[55] C-300/04, *Eman and Sevinger*, 2006, paras 40–61.

[56] Council Directive 93/109/EC of 6 December 1993 laying down detailed arrangements for the exercise of the right to vote and stand as a candidate in elections to the European Parliament for citizens of the Union residing in a Member State of which they are not nationals, OJ 1993 L329/34. See Fabbrini, 'The Political Side of EU Citizenship in the Context of EU Federalism', in Kochenov (ed.), *EU Citizenship and Federalism* (OUP 2015); Shaw, *The Transformation of Citizenship in the European Union: Electoral Rights and the Restructuring of Political Space* (Cambridge University Press, 2007); Oliver, 'Electoral Rights under Article 8b [later Article 19] of the Treaty of Rome' (1996) CMLRev 473–98.

[57] This allowed Luxembourg to require nationals of other Member States to have previously resided in its territory for at least five of the last six years in order to be able to vote and for at least ten of the last twelve years in order to be able to stand as a candidate: see the law of 28 January 1994, *JO du Grand-Duché de Luxembourg*, 31 January 1994. Meanwhile, the requirement of prior residence has been abolished.

concerned, account must be taken of the restrictions which national criminal law may impose in relation to eligibility.

Conditions for exercise of office. MEPs are to vote on an individual and personal basis, are not bound by any instructions, and do not receive a binding mandate (Act on the Direct Election of the European Parliament, Article 6(1)).[58] The European Parliament is to lay down the regulations and general conditions governing the performance of the duties of its members after consulting the Commission and with the approval of the Council, acting by a qualified majority, except for the tax arrangements for members or former members, for which unanimity is required (Article 223(2) TFEU). This Statute for MEPs emphasizes the 'free and independent' status of the MEPs and specifies their entitlements as to salary and allowances.[59] The Act further provides that the holding of a number of offices as member of the government of a Member State, or member or staff member of another Union institution or body, is incompatible with being an MEP (Act, Article 7(1)).[60] Originally, the Act expressly provided that an MEP might also be a member of a national parliament. However, since 2004, the capacity of MEP is incompatible with the office of member of a national parliament (Act, Article 7(2)). It should be noted that national rules may prescribe other incompatibilities. Pursuant to the Protocol (No. 7) on the privileges and immunities of the European Union, MEPs enjoy privileged free movement and may not be the subject of proceedings in respect of opinions which they express in the performance of their duties.[61] During the session of the European Parliament, MEPs enjoy immunity from any measure of detention and legal proceedings in other Member States than their own and the immunities accorded to members of the national parliament in their own Member State.[62] However, from the moment that a person has been elected as an MEP he or she already enjoys the freedom of movement ensured by Article 9, second para. Protocol (No. 7), most notably to enable the newly elected MEP to attend the first session.[63] This parliamentary immunity may not be claimed if an MEP is found in the act of committing an offence and may be waived by the European Parliament.[64]

12.016

---

[58] See Böttger, 'Die Rechtsstellung des Abgeordneten des Europäischen Parlaments' (2002) EuR 898–916.

[59] Statute for Members of the European Parliament, adopted by Decision (2005/684/EC, Euratom) of the European Parliament of 28 September 2005, OJ 2005 L262/1 and implemented by Decision of the Bureau of 19 May and 9 July 2008, OJ 2008 C159.

[60] Since members of a government of a federated State or of a devolved legislative body may represent that Member State in the Council since the EU Treaty entered into force, holding such an office would also appear to be incompatible with membership of the European Parliament. Moreover, Article 305, third para. TFEU provides that membership of the Committee of the Regions is incompatible with being an MEP.

[61] Protocol (No. 7), annexed to the TEU, TFEU, and EAEC Treaty, on Privileges and Immunities (OJ 2010 C83/266). For the scope of MEPs' privileged free movement under Article 7 of the Protocol, see 208/80, *Bruce of Donington*, 1981, para. 14, and T-345/05, *Mote*, 2008, paras 47–51. For the scope of the immunity for opinions expressed in the performance of their duties, which has to be established on the basis of Union law alone, and the Parliament's right to defend immunity under its Rules of Procedure, see C-200/07 and C-201/07, *Marra*, 2008, paras 24–45; C-163/10, *Patriciello*, 2011, paras 25–35; T-42/06, *Gollnisch v European Parliament*, 2010. It should be noted that, in contradistinction to the immunities conferred by Article 9 of the Protocol, the immunity conferred by Article 8 cannot be waived by the Parliament (see *Marra*, para. 44).

[62] C-502/19, *Junqueras Vies*, 2019, paras 77–78.

[63] Ibid., paras 79–81.

[64] Protocol (No. 7) on Privileges and Immunities, Article 9, and EP Rules of Procedure, Rules 5 to 9. For the possibility of invoking immunity in connection with an investigation carried out by the European Anti-Fraud Office OLAF; see T-17/00, *Rothley and Others v European Parliament*, 2002, as upheld by C-167/02 P, *Rothley and Others v European Parliament*, 2004. For another example, see T-345/05, *Mote*, 2008.

C. Operation

12.017 **Rules of Procedure.** In so far as the Treaties do not provide otherwise, the European Parliament operates in accordance with its Rules of Procedure, adopted by a majority of its members (Article 232, first para. TFEU).[65] Within a parliamentary term—which runs concurrently with the term of office of the members—the Parliament sits in annual 'sessions' until the first meeting of a newly elected Parliament.[66] The annual session includes monthly meetings of committees and political groups and plenary sessions ('part-sessions' that usually take a week, subdivided into daily 'sittings').[67]

The Commission is entitled to attend meetings.[68] Members of the Commission, the Council, and the European Council may make statements to the European Parliament.[69] For its part, the Commission ensures that the responsible Commissioner is present at the plenary session or in committee when the European Parliament requests his or her presence.[70] Debates in the Parliament are public (EP Rules of Procedure, Rule 121(2)).

12.018 **Seat.** Meetings of the European Parliament are held in accordance with the provisions of the Treaties. Pursuant to Article 289 EC [*now Article 341 TFEU*], the governments of the Member States have determined, in the First Decision on the Seats of the Institutions of 12 December 1992, that the European Parliament has its seat in Strasbourg, where the twelve monthly plenary sessions, including the budget session,[71] are to be held. Additional plenary sessions are to be held in Brussels, where the parliamentary committees also meet. The general secretariat and its departments have remained in Luxembourg.[72] By requiring that the European Parliament should meet in principle every month in Strasbourg, the governments endorsed that institution's previous practice. In determining its internal organization, the Parliament must respect the national governments' competence to determine its seat. Only if the European Parliament holds its twelve ordinary part-sessions, including the budgetary part-session, in Strasbourg, may it hold additional part-sessions in Brussels.[73] By incorporating the Decision on the Seats of the Institutions into a Protocol to the Treaty[74]

---

[65] Rules of Procedure of the European Parliament [EP Rules of Procedure], accessible at https://www.europarl.europa.eu/doceo/document/lastrules/TOC_EN.html?redirect.
[66] The newly elected Parliament meets for the first time on the first Tuesday in the month after the end of the election period (Act on the Direct Election of the European Parliament, Article 11(3)). Article 229, first para. TFEU requires the Parliament to meet in any event on the second Tuesday in March.
[67] See EP Rules of Procedure, Rule 153
[68] Article 230, first para. TFEU.
[69] Article 230, second and third para. TFEU and EP Rules of Procedure, Rule 132(1). See also point 47 of the Framework Agreement of 20 October 2010 (n. 19, *supra*), which provides that members of the Commission may be heard at their request.
[70] Points 45 and 48 of the Framework Agreement of 20 October 2010 (n. 19, *supra*).
[71] See C-237/11 and C-238/11, *France v European Parliament*, 2012; see, however, C-73/17, *France v European Parliament*, 2018; C-92/18, *France v European Parliament*, 2020 allowing for a pragmatic calendar, including holding plenary sessions in Brussels, during one of which the final vote on the budget may take place.
[72] Article 1(a) of the First Decision on the Seats of the Institutions of 12 December 1992, para. 14-020, *infra*.
[73] The Court of Justice annulled the European Parliament's vote to hold only eleven part-sessions in Strasbourg in 1996 on the ground that it infringed the First Decision on the Seats of the Institutions: C-345/95, *France v European Parliament*, 1997, paras 13–35. The Court held that the constraints as regards the organization of parliamentary work imposed by the Decision on the Seats of the Institutions did not conflict with the Parliament's power of internal organization (paras 30–2). See also para. 14-020, *infra*. Following the COVID-19 outbreak in March 2020, the Parliament held its plenary sessions until May 2021 only in Brussels.
[74] See now Protocol (No. 6), annexed to the TEU, TFEU, and EAEC Treaty, on the location of the seats of the institutions and of certain bodies, offices, agencies, and departments of the European Union, OJ 2010 C83/265.

(Protocol on Seats, see para. 14-020, *infra*), the Treaty of Amsterdam gave these rules the status of primary Union law.

Proceedings. Before each part-session (i.e. the meeting convened as a rule each month and composed of several daily sittings) the European Parliament draws up its agenda.[75] Save as otherwise provided in the Treaties, the European Parliament acts by an absolute majority of the votes cast (Article 231, first para. TFEU). A number of Treaty articles require it to act by a majority of its component members[76] and/or by two-thirds of the votes cast.[77] The Parliament is quorate when one-third of its component members is present in the Chamber (EP Rules of Procedure, Rule 178(2)). MEPs prepare decisions to be adopted at the plenary session in parliamentary committees.[78] The composition of committees should reflect, as far as possible, the composition of the Parliament.[79] Each responsible committee designates one of its members as the rapporteur for each file, who will prepare a draft resolution, potential amendments, to the legislative proposal at issue, and an explanatory statement.[80] On the basis of the preparatory work by the committees, the plenary will vote on the resolution and any amendments.

12.019

D. Internal organization

Internal bodies. The European Parliament elects a President and a Bureau from among its members (Article 14(4) TEU). The Bureau consists of the President and the Vice-Presidents of Parliament, together with the Quaestors sitting in an advisory capacity (EP Rules of Procedure, Rule 24). The President, Vice-Presidents, and Quaestors are elected in that order by MEPs for a term of office of two and a half years (see EP Rules of Procedure, Rules 15 to 19). The President presides over parliamentary proceedings and represents the Parliament in its relations with the outside world (EP Rules of Procedure, Rule 22). The Rules of Procedure entrust the Bureau with financial, administrative, and organizational tasks (EP Rules of Procedure, Rules 25 and 28). The President of the European Parliament, together with the chairmen of the political groups, form the Conference of Presidents, which decides on the internal organization of the Parliament, the composition and competences of the parliamentary committees, and the relations with other institutions and bodies of the Union (EP Rules of Procedure, Rules 26 and 27). The presidents of all parliamentary committees ('Conference of Committees Chairs') may address recommendations to the

12.020

---

[75] EP Rules of Procedure, Rule 158(1). The draft agenda drawn up by the Conference of Presidents (para. 12-020, *infra*) may be amended at that time at the proposal of a committee, a political group or a number of MEPs (ibid.).

[76] See Articles 223(1), second para.; 225; 229, second para.; 232, first para.; 234, second para.; 294(7)(b) and (c); 314(4)(c) and (7) (b) and (c) TFEU and Articles 17(7), 48(7), fourth subpara. and 49 TEU.

[77] Two-thirds majority of the votes cast, representing a majority of the component members: Article 234, second para. TFEU; Article 354, fourth para. TFEU. Other different majorities are laid down in the EP Rules of Procedure. On the application of the voting rules, see C-650/18, *Hungary v European Parliament*, AG Bobek Opinion, 2020.

[78] Twenty standing committees have been set up pursuant to Rule 206 of the EP Rules of Procedure, as amended. For temporary committees of inquiry, see para. 12-010, *supra*. For the manner of operation of these committees, see Yordanova, *Organising the European Parliament: The Role of Committees and their Legislative Influence* (ECPR Press, 2013); G. McElroy, 'Committee Representation in the European Parliament' (2006) 7 EU Politics 5–29; Mamadouh and Raunio, 'The Committee System: Powers, Appointments and Report Allocation' (2003) JCMS 335–51.

[79] EP Rules of Procedure, Rule 209(2).

[80] Ibid., Rules 51 and 55.

Conference of Presidents pertaining to the work of the committees and the agenda for the meetings (EP Rules of Procedure, Rule 29). The Bureau appoints a Secretary-General to head the Secretariat (EP Rules of Procedure, Rule 234). The Secretariat has a staff of around 7,500 and is divided into a legal service and twelve Directorates-General. In addition, the MEPs have their own staff.

12.021 **Political groups and parties.** Most MEPs belong to political groups; the remainder are referred to as non-attached.[81] A political group must have members from at least one-quarter of the Member States and at least twenty-three members.[82] A political group can only be set up on the basis of political affinity.[83] As indicated above, the chairmen of the political groups exercise certain powers together with the President of the Parliament as the Conference of Presidents.

In some political groups, the members have underpinned their political cooperation by forming a European political party.[84] The European Parliament and the Council, acting in accordance with the ordinary legislative procedure, lay down the regulations governing political parties at European level and, in particular, the rules regarding their funding (Article 224 TFEU).[85] According to the relevant regulation, a political party at European level must be represented, in at least one quarter of the Member States, by members of the European Parliament or members of the national or regional parliaments or must have received, in at least one quarter of the Member States, 3 per cent or more of the votes cast in each of those Member States at the most recent European Parliament elections.[86] In addition, it must have participated in elections to the European Parliament, or have expressed the intention to do so.[87] An independent Authority decides on the registration of European political parties and their compliance with the conditions laid down in the regulations, including on funding.[88] In case of non-compliance, the Authority may impose sanctions.[89] Article 10(4) TEU declares that political parties at European level 'contribute to forming European

---

[81] Ibid., Rules 33 to 36.
[82] Ibid., Rule 33(2).
[83] Ibid., Rule 33. This requirement ensues from social and political circumstances peculiar to parliamentary democracies and from the specific features and responsibilities of the European Parliament: T-222/99, T-327/99, and T-329/99, *Martinez and Others v European Parliament*, 2001, paras 145–8, confirmed on the merits by C-488/01 P, *Martinez v European Parliament*, 2003, and set aside, as to the admissibility of the action brought by a political party, by Case C-486/01 P, *Front National v European Parliament*, 2004. This does not preclude members of a group in their day-to-day conduct from expressing different political opinions on any particular subject: T-222/99, T-327/99, and T-329/99, *Martinez and Others v European Parliament*, 2001, paras 80–94.
[84] See the Party of European Socialists (PES) (established in 1974), the Alliance of Liberals and Democrats for Europe (ALDE, formerly European Liberal Democrat and Reform Party) and the European People's Party (EPP) (both set up in 1976), the European Green Party, European Free Alliance, Party of the European Left and European Democratic Party (all set up in 2004), the EUDemocrats (set up in 2005), the Alliance of European Conservatives and Reformists (AECR, supporting the ECR Group set up in 2009), the European Christian Political Movement (set up in 2002), and the Identity and Democracy Party (set up in 2014).
[85] Regulation (EU, Euratom) No. 1141/2014 of the European Parliament and of the Council of 22 October 2014 on the statute and funding of European political parties and European political foundations, OJ 2014 L317/1, see previously, Regulation (EC) No. 2004/2003 of the European Parliament and of the Council of 4 November 2003 on the regulations governing political parties at European level and the rules regarding their funding, OJ 2003 L297/1. The register of European political parties and foundations is governed by Commission Delegated Regulation (EU, Euratom) 2015/2401 of 2 October 2015, OJ 2015 L333/50. See von Arnim, 'The New EU Party Financing Regulation' (2005) ELRev 273–84.
[86] Regulation (EU, Euratom) No. 1141/2014, Article 3.
[87] Ibid.
[88] Ibid., Article 6 (see para. 13-044, *infra*).
[89] Ibid., Article 27.

political awareness and to expressing the will of citizens of the Union'.[90] However, the existence of European political parties has not, so far, prevented political debate at European level from attracting less attention from public opinion than national political discussions. European elections tend to be dragged too easily in the wake of national issues and it is often hard to regard them as a genuine indication of voters' views on future European policy choices.

II. The European Council

Union institution. The European Council obtained the status of 'institution' only upon the entry into force of the Lisbon Treaty. As long ago as 1974, the Heads of State or Government of the Member States started meeting a few times a year at 'summit conferences' (see para. 1-033, *supra*). Article 2 of the Single European Act enshrined this meeting in the Treaties under the name of the 'European Council'.[91] That new organ was deliberately not given any legal status in the Community Treaties so as to prevent the institutional balance between Community institutions from being upset by an intergovernmental and politically higher-ranking organ. In addition, the European Council obtained some specific tasks, in particular in the context of the CFSP. Whereas the Treaty of Lisbon included the European Council among the 'institutions' of the Union (Article 13(1) TEU), it has been at pains not to involve that institution in the normal course of the legislative proceedings.

12.022

A. Powers

Evolution. When they started to meet in 1974, the Heads of State or Government delicately stated that the arrangements regarding the European Council did not in any way affect the rules and procedures laid down in the Community Treaties.[92] Although the European Council was initially not involved in the Community decision-making process and did not take legally binding decisions, it was clear that, on the political level, the institutionalization of the meetings of the Heads of State or Government did have consequences for the position of the Commission and the Council. The subjects on which the European Council was to confer were initially prepared by national civil servants, rather than by the Commission. The Council's role was also weakened to the extent that crucial decisions, which that institution was empowered to take by a majority vote, were often left to the European Council, which had to find a consensus. The trend became even clearer after 1987 when decision-making in the Council was no longer by consensus, as a result of the 1966 'Luxembourg Compromise'.[93] The European Council was increasingly given more formal tasks.

12.023

---

[90] See also Article 12(2) of the Charter of Fundamental Rights of the European Union. See further Bressanelli, *Europarties After Enlargement—Organization, Ideology and Competition* (Palgrave Macmillan, 2014).
[91] For a detailed discussion, see Foret and Rittelmeyer (eds), *The European Council and European governance. The Commanding Heights of the European Union* (Routledge, 2014); Werts, *The European Council* (Harper, 2008).
[92] Communiqué of the Heads of State or of Government meeting in Paris on 9 and 10 December 1974 (1974) 12 EC Bull., point 1104(3).
[93] See the discussion of the operation of the Council, para. 12-048, *infra*.

The EU Treaty conferred on the European Council the task of providing 'the Union with the necessary impetus for its development' and defining 'the general political guidelines' (Article 4, first para. EU). In addition, the European Council obtained some specific tasks in the context of the Communities' decision-making process[94] and in the context of the CFSP.[95] As regards CFSP, the Treaty of Amsterdam institutionalized the practice of politically sensitive issues being transferred from the Council to the European Council: it provided that a vote was not to be taken if a member of the Council declared that, for important and stated reasons of national policy, it intended to oppose a measure which would otherwise be adopted by a qualified majority; the Council, acting by a qualified majority, would then request that the matter be referred to the European Council for decision by unanimity.[96]

The Lisbon Treaty further developed the European Council's tasks. It is now clear that decisions of the European Council may have binding effects. According to Article 263, first para. TFEU, acts of the European Council intended to produce legal effects vis-à-vis third parties are subject to review by the Court of Justice.[97]

12.024 **High-level steering and conciliation.** According to Article 15(1) TEU, the European Council's tasks remain to provide the Union with the necessary impetus for its development and to define the general political directions and priorities of the Union.

More specifically, the European Council defines the strategic guidelines for legislative and operational planning within the area of freedom, security, and justice (Article 68 TFEU) and adopts conclusions on the broad lines of the economic policies of the Member States and the Union (Article 121(2), second subpara. TFEU) and on the employment situation in the Union (Article 148(1) TFEU).[98] In addition, the European Council is to identify the strategic interests and objectives of the Union's external action (Articles 22(1) and 26(1) TEU). It regularly assesses the threats facing the Union in order to enable the Union and its Member States to take effective action (Article 222(4) TFEU). The CFSP is the only field where the European Council is responsible not only for determining the objectives and defining the general guidelines, but also—together with the Council—for defining and implementing that policy.[99]

In addition, the European Council continues to play the role of political arbitrator in certain fields where the Council has the power to adopt measures by qualified majority and where a member of the Council intends to oppose the adoption of a measure for important

---

[94] It was to discuss a conclusion on the Member States' and the Union's economic policies (Article 99(2) EC) and employment situation (Article 128(1) EC).

[95] The European Council was to define the principles of, and general guidelines for, the CFSP and could decide on the progressive framing of a common defence policy (Articles 13(1)–(2) and 17(1) EU).

[96] Article 23(2), second subpara. EU (CFSP) and Article 27c, second para. (enhanced cooperation in connection with the CFSP).

[97] e.g. C-370/12, *Pringle*, 2012, paras 31–7. Compare T-192/16, *NF v European Council*, 2017 (a European Council declaration deemed not to constitute a legally binding act).

[98] As was the case even before the Lisbon Treaty, the European Council receives reports from the Council on the guidelines of the economic policies of the Member States and of the Union (Article 121 TFEU); the Council and the Commission on the employment situation in the Union and on the implementation of the guidelines for employment (Article 148(1) and (5) TFEU); the European Central Bank on the activities of the European System of Central Banks and monetary policy (Article 284(3), first subpara. TFEU); and from the Commission on the application of Article 5 TEU (Article 9 of Protocol (No. 2), annexed to the TEU and TFEU, on the application of the principles of subsidiarity and proportionality, OJ 2010 C83/206).

[99] See Articles 24(1), 26(1), and 32 TEU.

political reasons or because it would affect fundamental aspects of national systems for social security or criminal justice.[100] In such a case, that member of the Council may request the measure to be referred to the European Council, which will then try to find a consensus on the proposed measure.

There is no intention that the European Council should involve itself with the legislative work carried out by the Council jointly with the European Parliament. To this end, the Treaties stress that the European Council 'shall not exercise legislative functions' (Article 15(1) TEU). In practice, however, the compromises reached by the European Council in sensitive cases may lead to detailed guidelines that do not leave much latitude to the Council and the Parliament if they do not want to upset a political agreement which has been attained.[101] The European Council cannot, however. impose any conditions limiting the Commission's right of initiative or changing the decision-making rules in the Council.[102]

Constituent decisions. On some occasions, the European Council is called upon to take decisions as a 'constituent authority'.

12.025

First, there is the case where the European Council intervenes in the ordinary revision procedure for the amendment of the Treaties provided for by Article 48 TEU (see para. 3-003 *et seq., supra*) or takes decisions under the simplified revision procedure to amend certain provisions of Part Three TFEU (Article 48(6) TEU; see para. 3-006, *supra*). The European Council also acts as a constituent authority in so far as it may decide, in respect of certain provisions of the Treaties, to replace a special legislative procedure by the ordinary legislative procedure and voting by unanimity by qualified majority voting (see, e.g., Articles 31(3) and 48(7) TEU and 312(2) TFEU).[103] In the course of the progressive framing of a Union defence policy, the European Council, acting unanimously, may decide to establish a common defence for the Union. In that event, it is to recommend to the Member States the adoption of the relevant decisions in accordance with their respective constitutional requirements (Article 42(2), first subpara. TEU).

Second, the European Council is to lay down a number of important institutional arrangements to complement the Treaty provisions on the institutions, concerning such matters as the composition of the European Parliament (Article 14(2), second subpara. TEU); the list of Council configurations and their Presidency (Articles 16(6) and (9) TEU and 236 TFEU); and the rotation system for members of the Commission (Articles 17(5) TEU and

---

[100] See Article 31(2), second subpara. TEU (opposition against CFSP decision for 'vital and stated reasons of national policy'); Article 48 TFEU (opposition against a social security measures that would affect 'important aspects of its social security system' or 'the financial balance of that system'); Articles 82(3) and 83(3) TFEU (opposition against certain PJCC measures that would affect or 'fundamental aspects of its criminal justice system'). See also Articless 86(1), second subpara. and 87(3) TFEU (opposition against certain PJCC measures by a group of at least nine Member States).
[101] See Editorial Comments 'An Ever Mighty European Council—Some Recent Institutional Developments' (2009) CMLRev 1383–93.
[102] C-643/15 and C-647/15, *Slovak Republic and Hungary v Council*, 2017, paras 143–9.
[103] The European Council acts unanimously after obtaining the consent of the European Parliament, given by a majority of its component members; no national parliament is to oppose the decision. For another possibility of Treaty amendment by the European Council, see Article 86(4) TFEU (which enables the European Council, acting unanimously after obtaining the consent of the European Parliament and consulting the Commission, to extend the powers of the European Public Prosecutor's Office); see para. 8-024, *supra*.

244 TFEU). The European Council also proposes to the European Parliament a candidate for President of the Commission and appoints the Commission (Article 17(7) TEU) and appoints the High Representative of the Union for Foreign Affairs and Security Policy (Article 18(1) TEU) and the members of the executive board of the ECB (Article 283(2), second subpara. TFEU).[104]

In its role of 'constituent authority', the European Council further determines the conditions for the accession of a Member State (Article 49, first para. TEU) and has to be notified by Member States who wish to withdraw from the Union of their intention to do so (Article 50(2) TEU).[105] Further, the European Council may amend the status under Union law of a Danish, French, or Netherlands overseas territory (Article 355(6) TFEU). Lastly, it is the European Council which is to determine the existence of a serious and persistent breach by a Member State of the values referred to in Article 2 TEU, which may lead to the suspension of certain Treaty rights of the Member State in question (see Article 7(2) TEU).

B. Composition

12.026 **Composition.** The European Council consists of the Heads of State or Government of the Member States, together with its President and the President of the Commission (Article 15(2) TEU). The High Representative of the Union for Foreign Affairs and Security Policy is entitled to take part in the work of the European Council (Article 15(2) TEU). The members of the European Council may decide to be assisted by a Minister or, in the case of the President of the Commission, by a member of the Commission (Article 15(3) TEU). Before the Lisbon Treaty, the European Council consisted of the Heads of State or Government of the Member States and the President of the Commission, assisted by the Ministers of Foreign Affairs of the Member States and a member of the Commission (Article 4, second para. EU).[106]

12.027 **President of the European Council.** Initially, the European Council met under the chairmanship of the Head of State or Government of the Member State which held the Presidency of the Council (Article 4, second para. EU). Since the Lisbon Treaty, the

---

[104] Before the Lisbon Treaty, the President of the Commission was nominated by the Council meeting in the composition of the Heads of State or Government, whereas the President and the other members of the Commission were appointed by the Council (see Article 214(2) EC). The members of the executive board of the ECB were appointed by the governments of the Member States at the level of the Heads of State or Government (Article 112(2)(b) EC).

[105] The Union negotiates and concludes an agreement with the State concerned, setting out the arrangements for its withdrawal, in the light of the guidelines provided by the European Council (Article 50(2) TEU). The Treaties normally cease to apply to the State in question from the date of entry into force of the withdrawal agreement or, failing that, two years after the notification to the European Council of the intention to withdraw, but the European Council, in agreement with the Member State concerned, may decide to extend this period (Article 50(3) TEU) (see also paras 4-015 and 4-016, *supra*).

[106] See the Solemn Declaration of Stuttgart, 19 June 1983 (1983) 6 EC Bull. point 2.1.1 and Article 2 of the Single European Act. It was agreed, however, that the President of the European Council was to invite the Economic and Finance Ministers to participate in European Council meetings when the European Council was discussing matters relating to economic and monetary union (see Declaration (No. 4) of the signatories of the EU Treaty on Part Three, Title VI of the Treaty establishing the European Community).

European Council has a full-time President, who is elected by the European Council, by a qualified majority, for a term of two and a half years,[107] renewable once (Article 15(5) TEU).[108] In the event of an impediment or serious misconduct, the European Council can end the President's term of office in accordance with the same procedure (ibid.). In that event, and in the case of an impediment because of illness and in the event of his or her death, the President of the European Council will be replaced, where necessary, until the election of his or her successor, by the member of the European Council representing the Member State holding the six-monthly Presidency of the Council (European Council, Rules of Procedure, Article 2(4)).

The President of the European Council may not hold a national mandate (Article 15(6) TEU). The President's tasks are to (a) chair the European Council and drive forward its work; (b) ensure the preparation and continuity of the work of the European Council in cooperation with the President of the Commission, and on the basis of the work of the General Affairs Council; (c) endeavour to facilitate cohesion and consensus within the European Council; and (d) present a report to the European Parliament after each of the meetings of the European Council. In addition, the President of the European Council ensures, at his or her level and in that capacity, the external representation of the Union on issues concerning its common foreign and security policy, without prejudice to the powers of the High Representative of the Union for Foreign Affairs and Security Policy (Article 15(6) TEU).

Euro Summit. Following a meeting of the European Council a meeting can be held of the Heads of State or Government of the Member States having the euro as their currency and the President of the European Commission (a 'Euro Summit') as provided for by the Treaty on Stability, Coordination and Governance in the Economic and Monetary Union (see para. 9-041, *supra*).[109] The President of the European Central Bank (ECB) is invited to these meetings, which are not meetings of the European Council. Nevertheless, the President of the Euro Summit is elected at the same time and for the same period as the President of the European Council by the Heads of State or Government of the Member States that have the euro as their currency.[110] Until now this has always been the person holding the office of President of the European Council. The meetings of the Euro Summit are prepared by the Eurogroup, that is, the Member States of the Council that have the euro as their currency (see para. 12-040, *infra*).

12.028

---

[107] See Decision 2009/879/EU of the European Council of 1 December 2009, OJ 2009 L315/48 (election of Herman Van Rompuy as first President of the European Council, later re-elected, see Decision 2012/151/EU, OJ 2012 L77/17); Decisions 2014/638/EU and 2017/444/EU of 30 August 2014 viz. 9 March 2017, OJ 2014 L262/5 and OJ 2017 L67/87 (election and re-election of Donald Tusk) and Decision 2019/1135 of 2 July 2019, OJ 2019 L179/1 (election of Charles Michel).

[108] Declaration (No. 6), annexed to the Lisbon Treaty, states that in choosing the persons called upon to hold the offices of President of the European Council, President of the Commission and High Representative of the Union for Foreign Affairs and Security Policy 'due account is to be taken of the need to respect the geographical and demographic diversity of the Union and its Member States' (Declaration (No. 6) on Article 15(5) and (6), Article 17(6) and (7), and Article 18 of the Treaty on European Union), OJ 2010 C83/338). On the President's role, see Tömmel, 'The Standing President of the European Council: Intergovernmental or Supranational Leadership?' (2017) JEI 175–89.

[109] Treaty on Stability, Coordination and Governance in the Economic and Monetary Union, Article 12(1).

[110] Ibid. This is done by a simple majority of the votes.

C. Operation

12.029 **Rules of procedure.** The European Council operates in accordance with the Rules of Procedure which it adopted pursuant to Article 235(3) TFEU by a simple majority.[111]

12.030 **Meetings.** The European Council meets twice every six months, convened by its President.[112] Special meetings may be convened by the President when the situation so requires (Article 15(3) TEU).

Meetings of the European Council are not public (European Council Rules of Procedure, Article 4(3)). Where the European Council adopts a decision, it may decide, in accordance with the voting arrangement applicable for the adoption of that decision, to make public the results of votes, as well as the statements in its minutes and the items in those minutes relating to the adoption of that decision.[113]

The European Council meets in Brussels. In exceptional circumstances, the President of the European Council, with the agreement of the General Affairs Council or the Committee of Permanent Representatives, acting unanimously, may decide that a meeting of the European Council will be held elsewhere.[114] Before the Lisbon Treaty, the Member State presiding over the Council was responsible for organizing European Council meetings. Each Member State presiding over the Council used to organize meetings of the European Council in its own territory. From 2002 onwards, one European Council meeting per Presidency was to be held in Brussels. As from the accession of new Member States in 2004, all European Council meetings were to be held in Brussels.[115]

12.031 **Decision-making.** The European Council takes its decisions by consensus '[e]xcept where the Treaties provide otherwise' (Article 15(4) TEU).[116] Some Treaty articles require the European Council to take decisions unanimously.[117] Abstentions by members present in person or represented do not prevent the adoption of such decisions (Article 235(1), third subpara. TFEU). In other cases, the European Council may take decisions by a qualified majority.[118] For qualified majority voting, the same arrangements apply as in the Council

---

[111] See European Council Decision 2009/882/EU of 1 December 2009 adopting its Rules of Procedure, OJ 2009 L315/51. For earlier rules of procedure, see Annex I to the Conclusions of the European Council held on 21 and 22 June 2002 in Seville ((2002) 6 EU Bull. point I.27); before then, see the Communiqué of the Heads of State or Government meeting in Paris on 9 and 10 December 1974 (1974) 12 EC Bull. point 1104(3); Decision of the European Council meeting in London (1977) 6 EC Bull. point 2.3.1; Solemn Declaration of Stuttgart of 19 June 1983 (1983) 6 EC Bull., point 1.6.1.

[112] Ordinary meetings of the European Council last for a maximum of two days, unless the European Council or the General Affairs Council, on the initiative of the President of the European Council, decides otherwise (European Council Rules of Procedure, Article 4(1)).

[113] In such case, the explanations of the vote given when the vote was taken are also made public at the request of the member of the European Council concerned, 'with due regard for these Rules of Procedure, legal certainty and the interests of the European Council' (European Council Rules of Procedure, Article 10(1)).

[114] European Council Rules of Procedure, Article 1(2).

[115] See Declaration (No. 22), annexed to the Nice Treaty, on the venue for European Councils (OJ 2001 C80/85), according to which this would be the case 'when the Union comprises 18 members'.

[116] Before the Lisbon Treaty, the European Council invariably took its decisions by consensus.

[117] See, e.g., Article 7(2) TEU; Article 14(2), second subpara. TEU; Article 17(5) TEU; 22(1), third subpara. TEU; 24(1), second subpara. TEU; Article 31(3) TEU; Article 42(2) TEU; Article 48(6), second subpara. TEU; Article 48(7), fourth subpara. TEU; Article 50(3) TEU; Article 86(4) TFEU; 312(2), second subpara. TFEU; Article 355(6) TFEU.

[118] See, e.g., Article 17(7), first and third subparas, TEU; Article 18 TEU and Article 236 TFEU; Article 283(2), second subpara. TFEU.

(Article 235(1), second subpara. TFEU, which refers to Article 16(4) TEU and Article 238(2) TFEU; see para. 12-047 *et seq.*, *infra*). The European Council acts by a simple majority for procedural questions and for the adoption of its Rules of Procedure (Article 235(3) TFEU).[119]

When a vote is held in the European Council, neither its President nor the President of the Commission may vote. Members may vote on behalf of no more than one other member (Article 235(1), first and second subparas, TFEU). The voting procedure is opened by the President, on his or her own initiative. The presence of two-thirds of the members of the European Council is required to enable the European Council to vote. The President of the European Council and the President of the Commission do not count towards the quorum (European Council Rules of Procedure, Article 6(3)).

Decisions of the European Council on an urgent matter may be adopted by a written vote where the President of the European Council proposes to use that procedure. Written votes may be used where all members of the European Council having the right to vote agree to that procedure (European Council Rules of Procedure, Article 7).

Relations with the European Parliament. The President of the European Council has to present a report to the European Parliament after each of the meetings of the European Council (Article 15(6)(d) TEU). The member of the European Council representing the Member State holding the Presidency of the Council presents to the European Parliament the priorities of its Presidency and the results achieved during the six-month period (European Council Rules of Procedure, Article 5). Initially, the European Parliament obtained information about the activities of the European Council only on the occasion of the report which the Minister of Foreign Affairs of the Member State holding the Presidency of the Council and the President of the Commission made before the Parliament at the end of each Presidency. Starting in 1981, the Head of State or Government occupying the Presidency of the European Council came before Parliament to report, initially half-yearly, subsequently after every European Council.[120]

12.032

The European Council has the right to be heard by the European Parliament (Article 230, third subpara. TFEU). It is represented before the European Parliament by its President (European Council Rules of Procedure, Article 5). The President of the European Parliament may be invited to be heard by the European Council (Article 235(2) TFEU).

D. Internal organization

General Secretariat. At the administrative level, the European Council and its President are assisted by the General Secretariat of the Council, under the authority of its Secretary-General (Article 235(4) TFEU and European Council Rules of Procedure, Article 13(1)). The Secretary-General of the Council attends the meetings of the European Council and

12.033

---

[119] For another case of decisions where the European Council decides by a simple majority, see Article 48(3), first and second subparas, TEU (ordinary revision procedure).
[120] Werts (n. 94, *supra*). See also the Solemn Declaration of Stuttgart (n. 114, *supra*), point 2.1.4.

412 THE POLITICAL INSTITUTIONS OF THE UNION

takes all the measures necessary for the organization of proceedings (European Council Rules of Procedure, Article 13(2)).

III. The Council

12.034 **Designation.** As a result of the Merger Treaty, the 'Council of the European Communities' replaced the Special Council of Ministers of the ECSC, the Council of the EEC, and the Council of the EAEC. Following the entry into force of the EU Treaty, the institution[121] decided that henceforth it would be known as the 'Council of the European Union'.[122] Since the Lisbon Treaty, the Treaties refer only to the 'Council' (Article 13(1) TEU).

A. Powers

12.035 **Survey.** According to Article 16(1) TEU, the Council, jointly with the European Parliament, exercises legislative and budgetary functions and carries out policy-making and coordinating functions as laid down in the Treaties. The Council's decision-making power also extends to the Union's external action. It may also exercise implementing powers. Moreover, the Council takes decisions as to the appointment of members of other Union bodies.

1. Decision-making

12.036 **Policy choices.** Union decision-making is carried out virtually always via the Council, which adopts most legislation on the basis of a Commission proposal, together with the European Parliament. Together with the European Parliament the Council makes the policy choices intended to attain the objectives set out in the Treaties. In many cases, the Council has to assess complex economic situations and has a discretion as to what priorities should be given to these policies,[123] the actual aim of any given action, and the suitability of its action in order to achieve that aim;[124] the nature and scope of such action; and, to a certain extent, the determination of basic data.[125] In addition, the Council decides on the general budget of the Union together with the European Parliament (see para. 20-001, *infra*). As far as external action is concerned, the Council concludes international agreements negotiated by the Commission or the High Representative on behalf of the Union. The Council and the Commission, assisted by the High Representative, are responsible for ensuring the consistency between the various areas of the Union's external action and between these and its other policies (Article 21(3), second subpara. TEU). Decision-making in connection with the CFSP falls almost entirely to the Council.

---

[121] See, in general, Westlake and Galloway, *The Council of the European Union* (Harper, 2004). For the Council's website, see http://www.consilium.europa.eu/.
[122] Decision 93/591/EU, Euratom, ECSC, EC of 8 November 1993, OJ 1993 L281/18 (*corrigendum* L285/41). The Merger Treaty was repealed by Article 9 of the Treaty of Amsterdam.
[123] See, e.g., 13/83, *European Parliament v Council*, 1985, para. 50.
[124] Para. 19-002, *infra*.
[125] 138/79, *Roquette Frères v Council*, 1980, paras 25–6.

2. Coordination

Coordination. The Council carries out coordinating functions as laid down in the Treaties (Article 16(1) TEU) and may adopt non-binding measures vis-à-vis the Member States to bring national policies and Union action into line with each other. Articles 121 and 126(9) and (11) TFEU give the Council a specific power to coordinate the Member States' economic policies and it may impose sanctions in this connection. Also, as regards the CFSP, Member States' policies are coordinated in the European Council and the Council (Article 32 TEU).[126]

12.037

3. Implementation

Implementing powers. Implementation of legislative acts falls, in principle, to the Commission. However, in duly justified specific cases, the power to adopt implementing acts may be conferred on the Council (Article 291(2) TFEU; see para. 18-012, *infra*). The Council is also responsible for implementing the CFSP, together with the High Representative.[127] The Treaties confer certain implementing powers expressly on the Council, in particular with regard to economic monitoring (Article 121(3) and Article 126 TFEU).

12.038

4. Relationship to other institutions and bodies

Appointments and other prerogatives. Because it is made up of representatives of the Member States, the Council has a number of prerogatives which enable it to influence, to some extent, the operation of the other institutions, with the exception of the European Parliament.[128] Thus, the Council is to propose candidates for appointment to the Commission and appoints the members of the Court of Auditors,[129] may alter the number of Advocates General at the Court of Justice,[130] and determines the emoluments of most members of the institutions, except for the European Parliament.[131] The Council also appoints members of other bodies or determines their exact composition.[132] Furthermore, the Council must approve the Rules of Procedure of the Court of Justice and the General Court, and the Rules of Procedure of the Court of Auditors; together with the European Parliament it may amend the Statute of the Court of Justice.[133] In addition, for other bodies, it adopts the rules governing their organization.[134] The Council is further entitled to exercise some control over the activities of the Commission: it can ask it to carry out studies and

12.039

---

[126] See also, with regard to PJCC before the entry into force of the Lisbon Treaty, Article 34(1) EU.
[127] Article 291(2) TFEU, which refers to Articless 24 and 26 TEU.
[128] Even though, since the Treaty of Amsterdam, the Council has to approve the 'regulations and general conditions governing the performance of the duties' of the Members of the European Parliament (Article 223(2) TFEU).
[129] Article 17(7) TEU and Article 286(2) TFEU
[130] Article 252 TFEU.
[131] Article 243 TFEU. See, e.g., the Council decisions of 1 December 2009 laying down the conditions of employment of the President of the European Council, of the High Representative of the Union for Foreign Affairs and Security Policy and of the Secretary-General of the Council of the European Union (OJ 2009 L322/35, L322/36, and L322/38). In addition, the Council has to approve amendments to the Statute of the Court of Justice, the Rules of Procedure established by the Court of Justice and the General Court (Article 253, sixth para. TFEU; Article 254, fifth para. TFEU and Article 281, second para., TFEU), and the Rules of Procedure of the Court of Auditors (Article 287(4), fifth subpara. TFEU).
[132] This applies, *inter alia*, to the European Economic and Social Committee (para. 13-031, *infra*) and the Committee of the Regions (para. 13-034, *infra*).
[133] Articles 253, sixth para, 254, fifth para. 281, second para. and 287(4), fifth para. TFEU.
[134] See Article 242 TFEU.

make proposals[135] and participates in controlling the Commission's implementation of the budget.[136] The Council is entitled to consult the Court of Auditors, the European Economic and Social Committee, and the Committee of the Regions.[137] It is also entitled to an annual report from the ECB[138] and may monitor the latter's policy by having its President attend meetings of the ECB's Governing Council[139]

Lastly, the Council has the right to bring actions for annulment or for failure to act in the Court of Justice.[140]

B. Composition

12.040 **Configurations.** The Council consists of a representative of each Member State at ministerial level, who may commit the government of the Member State in question and cast its vote (Article 16(2) TEU). Each Member State itself determines the person of ministerial rank who is to represent it.

Depending on the subject matter under discussion, the Council is to meet in various 'configurations' (Article 16(6) TEU). The list of Council configurations is to be adopted by the European Council by a qualified majority (Article 236(a) TFEU).[141] However, two Council configurations are established by the Treaties themselves: the General Affairs Council and the Foreign Affairs Council (Article 16(6) TEU). The General Affairs Council has the task of ensuring consistency in the work of the different Council configurations and of preparing and ensuring the follow-up to meetings of the European Council, in liaison with the President of the European Council and the Commission (Article 16(6), second subpara. TEU).[142] It is responsible for the overall coordination of policies, institutional and administrative questions, horizontal dossiers, which affect several of the Union's policies, and any dossier entrusted to it by the European Council. The Foreign Affairs Council is to elaborate the Union's external action on the basis of strategic guidelines laid down by the European

---

[135] Article 241 TFEU; Article 122 EAEC (para. 17-018, *infra*).
[136] Para. 17-045, *infra*.
[137] Article 287(4), second subpara. TFEU; Article 304 TFEU; Article 307 TFEU.
[138] Article 284(3) TFEU.
[139] Article 284(1) TFEU. The President of the Council may submit a motion for deliberation, ibid.
[140] Article 263, second para. TFEU; Article 265, first para. TFEU.
[141] See European Council Decision 2010/594/EU of 16 September 2010, OJ 2010 L263/12. Before the Lisbon Treaty, the list of configurations was adopted by the Council itself in its General Affairs and External Relations configuration. This 'practice' was laid down for the first time when the Council Rules of Procedure were amended on 5 June 2000 (OJ 2002 L230/7), and confirmed in the Council Rules of Procedure of 22 July 2002, which reduced the number of configurations (for the earlier more extensive list, see OJ 2000 C174/2) and transformed the long-standing General Affairs Council into the General Affairs and External Relations Council. The Lisbon Treaty split that configuration into separate Council configurations. Article 4 of Protocol (No. 36), annexed to the TEU, the TFEU, and EAEC Treaty, on transitional provisions (OJ 2010 C83/322) provides that, until the entry into force of the European Council decision adopted under Article 16(6), first subpara, TEU, the list of Council configurations, in addition to the General Affairs and the Foreign Affairs Councils, should be established by the General Affairs Council, acting by a simple majority. See Decision of the Council (General Affairs) 2009/878/EU of 1 December 2009 establishing the list of Council configurations in addition to those referred to in the second and third subparas of Article 16(6) of the Treaty on European Union, OJ 2009 L315/46, which adapted the list of Council configurations set out in Annex I to the Council Rules of Procedure, further adapted by European Council Decision 2010/594/EU.
[142] See also Article 3 of European Council Decision 2009/881 (n. 161, *infra*) and Article 2(2) and (4) of the Council's Rules of Procedure.

Council and ensure that the Union's action is consistent (Article 16(6), third subpara. TEU). It is responsible for the whole of the European Union's external action, namely common foreign and security policy, common security and defence policy, common commercial policy, development cooperation, and humanitarian aid (Article 16(6), third subpara. TEU).[143] In the General Affairs Council, each Member State is represented by the Minister or State Secretary of its choice.[144] Sometimes, the General Affairs Council meets together with another configuration (a 'jumbo' Council), or specialized configurations ('Special Councils') meet jointly.

Alongside the General Affairs Council and the Foreign Affairs Council, there are at present eight configurations of the Council: (1) Economic and Financial Affairs (ECOFIN); (2) Justice and Home Affairs; (3) Employment; Social Policy; Health and Consumer Affairs; (4) Competitiveness (Internal Market, Industry, Research, and Space); (5) Transport, Telecommunications, and Energy; (6) Agriculture and Fisheries; (7) Environment; and (8) Education, Youth, Culture, and Sport[145].

Since the EU Treaty, the General Affairs Council has surrendered some of its coordinating influence. This is because, as far as matters relating to Economic and Monetary Union are concerned, the 1991 Intergovernmental Conference put the emphasis on the ECOFIN Council.[146] The ECOFIN Council occasionally meets informally[147] with only representatives of Member States whose currency is the euro;[148] this meeting is called the 'Eurogroup' or 'Euro Council' (see para. 12-028, *supra*). The meetings of the Eurogroup are presided over by a President who is elected for a period of two and a half years by the ministers of the Member States participating in the euro area.[149] In order to improve the Eurogroup's accountability, the Commission has suggested that the Vice-President of the Commission in charge of the Economic and Monetary Union could be appointed as president of the Eurogroup.[150]

Policy coordination increasingly takes place at the level of the Heads of State or Government within the European Council. In the past, the Treaties made use of decisions taken by the

---

[143] See also Article 2(5) of the Council Rules of Procedure.

[144] See Annex I to the Council Rules of Procedure. In practice, it is generally the Member States' Ministers of Foreign Affairs or Ministers or State Secretaries responsible for European Affairs.

[145] See the list in Annex I to the Council Rules of Procedure.

[146] See the declarations adopted when the EU Treaty was signed: Declaration (No. 3) on Part Three, Titles III and VI [*later Titles III and VII*] of the EC Treaty and Declaration (No. 4) on Part Three, Title VI [*later Title VII*] of the EC Treaty. Under Article 2(2) of the Council Rules of Procedure, tasks are to be assigned to the General Affairs Council 'having regard to operating rules for the Economic and Monetary Union'.

[147] C-105/15 P to C-109/15 P, *Mallis v Commission and ECB*, 2016, para. 61 (Eurogroup is an informal meeting, not a Council configuration); C-597/18 P, C-598/18 P, C-603/18 P, and C-604/18 P, *Council v Dr. K. Chrysostomides & Co. and Others*, 2020, paras 86–8 (Eurogroup is not a Union entity established by the Treaties, but an instrument of intergovernmental coordination). On the consequences of this informality for the accountability of the Eurogroup, see Craig, 'The Eurogroup, power and accountability' (2017) ELJ 234–49.

[148] Protocol (No. 14) attached to the TEU and the TFEU on the Euro Group, Article 1. The procedures in the Council are adapted thereto. See Article 16 of the Council Rules of Procedure and the annex thereto. The most recent 'working methods' of the Eurogroup of 26 February 2007 are to be found in doc. ECFIN/CEFCPE(2008)REP/50842 rev 1 of 3 October 2008, available at https://www.consilium.europa.eu/media/21457/08-10-03-eurogroup-working-methods.pdf.

[149] Protocol (No. 14) on the Euro Group, Article 2. See also annex 1 ('Ten measures to improve the governance of the euro area') attached to the statement of the Euro Summit of 26 October 2011.

[150] See the Commission Communication of 6 December 2017 'A European Minister of Economy and Finance', COM(2017) 823 final.

Council in the configuration of the Heads of State or Government. In practice, meetings of this configuration of the Council generally coincided with those of the 'European Council', although legally there was a difference: unlike the European Council, the Council meeting in the composition of the Heads of State or Government had to apply the Council's operating rules and did not include the President of the Commission, even though the latter attended its meetings. The Council met in this composition for some major decisions relating to EMU[151] and constitutional decisions, such as the appointment of the President of the Commission.[152] Since the Lisbon Treaty, these decisions are taken by the European Council (see para. 12-064, *infra*).

12.041   **Representatives at ministerial level.** Before the EU Treaty entered into force, each government had to delegate 'one of its members' to the Council.[153] However, in federal Member States, such as Germany and Belgium, the federal government shares powers with the governments of the federated entities. At the insistence of those Member States, the EU Treaty altered the composition of the Council so as to allow members of government of federated entities to represent their Member State in the Council. Article 16(2) TEU now provides that each Member State is represented by a representative at ministerial level, who may commit the Member State (even though Article 16(2) TEU uses the term 'the *government* of the Member State') in question and cast its vote. Since each Member State has only one representative in the Council, a federal Member State has to determine who is delegated to the Council and how that representative is to defend, as one view in the Council, what may be conflicting views within the Member State.[154] The composition of the Council as it is defined in Article 16(2) TEU also confirms the practice whereby a Member State is represented by junior ministers who under domestic law do not form part of the government, but are nevertheless deemed to be of 'ministerial level'.

12.042   **Presidency of the Council.** Since the Lisbon Treaty, the Council configurations are chaired by representatives of the Member States on the basis of equal rotation,[155] the conditions of which are established by the European Council by a qualified majority (Articles 16(9) TEU and 236(b) TFEU). The only exception is the Foreign Affairs Council, which is chaired by the High Representative for Foreign Affairs and Security Policy (Article 18(3) TEU, see para. 12-065, *infra*).[156] The 2007 Intergovernmental Conference agreed that the Presidency of the Council, with the exception of the Foreign Affairs configuration, would be held by pre-established groups of three Member States for a period of eighteen months.[157] To this

---

[151] See Article 121(2), (3) and (4) EC (decision on entry into the third stage of EMU) and Article 122(2) EC (discussion of which Member States with a derogation may take part in EMU). For the application of these provisions, see Council Decision 96/736/EC of 13 December 1996, OJ 1996 L335/48.

[152] See Article 214(2), first subpara. EC (nomination of the President of the Commission) and Article 7(2) EU (determination of the existence of a serious and persistent breach by a Member State of principles mentioned in Article 6(1) EU). See also Article 40.2 of the ESCB Statute (see para. 13-022, *infra*).

[153] Merger Treaty, Article 2, first para. repealed by Article 50 of the EU Treaty.

[154] Para. 15-016, *infra*. When the Council decides by a qualified majority and each Member State has more than one vote, the number of votes cast is always expressed as a single block. If a single view cannot be reached within a Member State, its representative may abstain. For the various effects of abstention, see para. 12-046, *infra*.

[155] For an overview, see Fuchs, 'Die rotierende EU-Ratspräsidentschaft' (2020) EuR 431–49.

[156] Moreover, the informal meetings of the Eurogroup are chaired by a president elected for a period of two and a half years, see para. 12-040, *supra*.

[157] See Declaration (No. 9), annexed to the Lisbon Treaty, on Article 16(9) of the Treaty on European Union concerning the European Council decision on the exercise of the Presidency of the Council, OJ 2010 C83/341, which set out a Draft European Council Decision in an annex.

purpose, the European Council adopted a Decision,[158] which was further implemented by a Decision of the Council.[159] In order to make up such groups of Member States, account is to be taken of 'their diversity and geographical balance within the Union'.[160] Each member of the group chairs, for a six-month period, all configurations of the Council, with the exception of the Foreign Affairs configuration, while being assisted by the other members of the group. However, members of the group may decide alternative arrangements among themselves.[161] Accordingly, Italy, Latvia, and Luxembourg, each for six months, held the Presidency of the Council in the period from July 2014 to December 2015, and the Netherlands, Slovakia, and Malta in the period from January 2016 to June 2017. On 26 July 2016, the Council decided to change the order of the following Presidencies as the United Kingdom indicated, after the referendum on leaving the Union, that it did not wish to hold the Presidency in the following year and in order to add Croatia to the list.[162] On that basis, Romania, Finland, and Croatia held the Presidency of the Council each for a period of six months between January 2019 and June 2020, with Germany, Portugal, and Slovenia doing the same between July 2020 and December 2021; France, the Czech Republic, and Sweden between January 2022 and June 2023; and Spain, Belgium, and Hungary between July 2023 and December 2024.

Before the Lisbon Treaty, each Member State occupied the Presidency of the Council in rotation for a period of six months.[163] The order was determined by the Council by unanimous vote.[164] In order to ensure continuity in the Council's activities the Presidency was assisted, if needs be, by the next Member State to hold the Presidency.[165] Even before this, there was the practice of the 'troika', whereby the previous and the next President of the Council assisted the holder of the office for the time being.[166] The EU Treaty formally enshrined this practice for the purposes of the external representation of the Union and the

[158] European Council Decision 2009/881/EU of 1 December 2009 on the exercise of the Presidency of the Council, OJ 2009 L315/50, by which the European Council adopted the Decision set out in Annex to Declaration (No. 9) (see n. 160, *supra*).
[159] Council Decision 2009/908/EU of 1 December 2009 laying down measures for the implementation of the European Council Decision on the exercise of the Presidency of the Council, and on the chairmanship of preparatory bodies of the Council, OJ 2009 L322/28 (corrigendum: OJ 2009 L344/56).
[160] Article 1(1) of European Council Decision 2009/881 (n. 161, *supra*) and Article 2 of Council Decision 2009/908 (n. 162, *supra*).
[161] Article 1(2) of European Council Decision 2009/881 (n. 161, *supra*) and Article 20(2) of the Council Rules of Procedure.
[162] Council Decision (EU) 2016/1316 of 26 July 2016 amending Decision 2009/908/EU, laying down measures for the implementation of the European Council Decision on the exercise of the Presidency of the Council, and on the chairmanship of preparatory bodies of the Council, OJ 2016 L208/42 (which lays down the order of the presidencies until the second half of 2030).
[163] See Elgström, 'The Presidency: The Role(s) of the Chair in European Union Negotiations' (2006) HJD 171–95; Hummer and Obwexer, 'Die "EU-Präsidentschaft"' (1999) EuR 401–51.
[164] See the second para. of Article 203 EC (as amended by Article 12 of the 1994 Act of Accession); Council Decision (2007/5/EC, Euratom) of 1 January 2007 determining the order in which the office of President of the Council shall be held, OJ 2007 L1/11, Article 1(1). The Council, acting unanimously on a proposal from the Member State concerned, could decide that a Member State would hold the Presidency during a period other than that resulting from the above order (Article 1(2)). Under a similar provision in the previous Council Decision, the order of the Presidencies of Germany and Finland was reversed for 2006–2007 at their request by Council Decision (2002/105/EC, ECSC, Euratom) of 28 January 2002, OJ 2002 L39/17. Before Article 12 of the 1994 Act of Accession entered into force, Article 203, second para. EC laid down a cycle determined by the alphabetical order of the names of the Member States in their respective languages. In the subsequent cycle, the same list was taken but the order of each pair of Member States on the list was inverted.
[165] Article 18(4) EU.
[166] For the first occurrence of this, see the London report on European Political Cooperation (1981) EC Bull. Suppl. 3, 14-18, especially point 10.

implementation of the CFSP.[167] In order to ensure that the troika had sufficient weight internationally, the order of succession of the Member States was constructed in such a way that the troika virtually always included one 'large' Member State.[168] Since the Lisbon Treaty, it is no longer for the Council's Presidency to represent the Union externally as this task has been conferred both upon the Commission and the High Representative for Foreign Affairs and Security Policy, who also presides the Foreign Affairs Council.

C. Operation

12.043 **Rules of Procedure.** The Council operates in accordance with the provisions of the Treaties and the Rules of Procedure which it adopts pursuant to Article 240(3) TFEU.[169] The Council is not entitled to depart from its Rules of Procedure without formally amending them.[170] The President convenes the Council on his or her own initiative or at the request of one of its members or the Commission (Article 237 TFEU). Dates for meetings of the Council are made known to the Member States seven months before the beginning of each sixth-month period (Council Rules of Procedure, Article 1(2)). Where a rapid decision is required in matters coming under the CFSP, the High Representative may convene an extraordinary Council meeting within forty-eight hours or, in an emergency, at even shorter notice (Article 30(2) TEU). Meetings take place in Brussels, except in April, June, and October, when the Council meets in Luxembourg, or, if the Council so decides by a unanimous vote, elsewhere.[171] The Commission is invited to take part in Council meetings, unless the Council decides by a majority vote to deliberate in its absence. The same applies to the European Central Bank (Council Rules of Procedure, Article 5(2)). Members of the Council and the Commission may be accompanied by civil servants (Council Rules of Procedure, Article 5(3)). Exceptionally, a representative of other bodies may be invited to a meeting concerning matters falling within the remit of the body in question. The Treaties confer this right on the President of the ECB (Article 284(2) TFEU).

12.044 **Public nature of deliberations.** The Council meets in public when it deliberates and votes on a draft legislative act (Article 16(8) TEU and 15(2) TFEU; Council Rules of Procedure, Article 5(1)). In order to make this possible, each Council meeting is divided into two parts, dealing respectively with deliberations on legislative acts and non-legislative activities (Article 16(8) TEU).[172]

---

[167] Article J.5(3) of the original EU Treaty.
[168] See Council Decision 95/2/EC, Euratom, ECSC of 1 January 1995 determining the order in which the office of President of the Council shall be held (OJ 1995 L1/220), as agreed at the European Council held in Brussels on 12 and 13 December 1993 ((1993) 12 EC Bull. point I.18, 17–18), upon entry into force of the 1994 Accession Treaty.
[169] See the current Rules of Procedure, adopted by Council Decision 2009/937/EU of 1 December 2009, OJ 2009 L325/35, replacing the Rules of 15 September 2006, OJ 2006 L285/47, and the previous versions of 22 March 2004 (OJ 2004 L106/22), 22 July 2002 (OJ 2002 L230/7), 5 June 2000 (OJ 2000 L149/21), 31 May 1999 (OJ 1999 L147/13), 6 December 1993 (OJ 1993 L304/1; amended by OJ 1995 L31/14 and OJ 1998 L337/40) and of 24 July 1979 (OJ 1979 L268/1, as amended on 20 July 1987 (OJ 1987 L291/27).
[170] 68/86, *United Kingdom v Council*, 1988, para. 48. Non-compliance with the Rules of Procedure may constitute an infringement of an essential procedural requirement within the meaning of Article 263, second para. TFEU (*United Kingdom v Council*, para. 49).
[171] Sole Article 1, para. (b), of the Protocol on Seats, para. 14-020, *infra*, and Article 1(3) of the Council Rules of Procedure.
[172] Council Rules of Procedure, Articles 3(6) and 7(1).

Legislative deliberations are open to the public, and documents submitted to the Council in relation thereto and the Council minutes relating to legislative deliberations are made public.[173] Moreover, the Council publishes the results of its votes, together with explanations of votes by members of the Council or their representatives on the Conciliation Committee provided for under the ordinary legislative procedure, statements in the minutes, and items relating to the Conciliation Committee meeting (Council Rules of Procedure, Article 7(2) and (4)). Public access is secured by relaying the Council meeting to another room by audiovisual means and by posting a recorded version on the Council's website (Council Rules of Procedure, Article 7(3)).

The Council's first deliberations on important new non-legislative proposals are also open to the public where they relate to the adoption of rules which are legally binding in or for the Member States, by means of regulations, directives, or decisions.[174] The same is true for subsequent Council deliberations on such proposals where the Presidency of the Council so decides, unless the Council or Coreper agree otherwise (Council Rules of Procedure, Article 8(1), second subpara.). In these cases, the Council publishes the results of votes and explanations of votes by Council members, as well as the statements in the Council minutes and the items in those minutes relating to the adoption of such acts (Council Rules of Procedure, Article 9(1)). Policy debates on the Council's or the Commission's operational programme and debates on important issues affecting the interests of the European Union and its citizens are also open to the public (Council Rules of Procedure, Article 8(2) and (3)). At the request of a member of the Council, results of votes, explanations of votes, and the statements in the Council minutes may also be published. When the Council adopts a decision in the field of CFSP this decision must be taken by unanimous vote (Council Rules of Procedure, Article 9(2)(a)).[175]

In all those cases, results of votes and declarations of vote may be consulted on the internet; the minutes are available on the Council's website.[176] The Council adopts the necessary rules on security to cover matters where secrecy is required.[177]

Vote. A valid vote may be held in the Council if a majority of the members of the Council who are, under the Treaties, entitled to vote are present (Council Rules of Procedure, Article 11(4)).[178] Although a Member State may be represented by persons other than ministers (e.g. by its Permanent Representative; see para. 12-051, *infra*), such a representative may not vote. The right to vote may be delegated only to another member of the Council (Article 239 TFEU; Council Rules of Procedure, Article 11(3)). Members of the Council vote in the

12.045

---

[173] On access to these documents, see, para. 14-030 *et seq*, *infra*.

[174] Article 8(1), first subpara. of the Council Rules of Procedure makes an exception for internal measures; administrative or budgetary acts; acts concerning interinstitutional or international relations; or non-binding acts (such as conclusions, recommendations, or resolutions). The Presidency is to identify which new proposals are important and the Council or Coreper may decide otherwise, whenever appropriate (ibid.).

[175] Explanations of votes are made public at the request of the Council members concerned 'with due regard for these Rules of Procedure, legal certainty and the interests of the Council'; a Council decision is also required to make public statements entered in the Council minutes and items in those minutes (Council Rules of Procedure, Article 9(2), second and third subparas).

[176] For the Council website, see n. 124, *supra*.

[177] Article 24 of the Council Rules of Procedure, as implemented by Council Decision 2011/292/EU of 31 March 2011, OJ 2011, L141/17.

[178] Decisions taken under Article 322 TFEU (decisions on expenditure for enhanced cooperation) must, however, be taken by a unanimous vote of all the members.

order in which the Member States hold the Presidency (Council Rules of Procedure, Article 11(2)).

12.046 **Three types of voting requirements.** As far as voting in the Council is concerned, there exist, alongside specific rules, three types of voting requirements which have to be attained depending on the Treaty article serving as the legal basis for the act to be adopted.[179] First, if the legal basis in question does not specify that the Council has to vote by a particular majority, the act has to be adopted by a qualified majority (Article 16(3) TEU).[180] In that case, or where the Treaty article in question expressly requires a qualified majority, a double majority threshold must be met. To attain the qualified majority, a decision must receive the support of at least 55 per cent of the Member States (i.e. currently fifteen Member States); those Member States must, at the same time, represent at least 65 per cent of the total population of the Union (Article 16(4) TEU). Second, where a Treaty article requires the Council to act by a simple majority, it has to act by a majority of its component members (Article 238(1) TFEU). Third, where the Treaty article serving as the legal basis requires the Council to vote unanimously, the act cannot be adopted if any Member State votes against.[181]

There may be no doubt as to the applicable voting requirement for a Council decision. Accordingly, it is not allowed to decide in a single decision on matters that require a qualified majority vote and matters that require a unanimous vote.[182] Furthermore, it must be noted that the effect of abstentions differs depending on whether a decision is to be taken by qualified or simple majority or by unanimity. While abstentions make it more difficult to achieve a qualified or simple majority, they do not prevent a decision from being adopted by unanimous vote, since they are not regarded as votes cast against the proposal where a unanimous vote is required (Article 238(4) TFEU).[183]

12.047 **Qualified majority.** As from 1 November 2014, all decisions taken by a qualified majority require at least 55 per cent of the members of the Council, comprising at least fifteen of them and representing Member States making up at least 65 per cent of the population of the Union (Article 16(4), first subpara. TEU). The threshold of 55 per cent implies that at least fifteen Member States must vote in favour. Decisions that the Council or the European Council are to take by a qualified majority but not on the basis of a proposal from the Commission or from the High Representative of the Union for Foreign Affairs and Security Policy, will need to be approved by at least 72 per cent of the members of the Council (i.e. twenty Member States) representing Member States comprising at least 65 per cent of the population of the Union (Article 238(2) TFEU). In addition, in both instances, a blocking minority is to include at least four members of the Council, failing which the qualified

---

[179] For special requirements as to majorities, see para. 17-007, *infra*, where Union decision-making is discussed. For matters in relation to which not all Member States take part in decision-making, the voting right of the Member State concerned is suspended and the requirement for unanimity or a particular majority vote is amended accordingly; see paras 22-002, 22-005, and 22-011, *infra*.
[180] Before the Lisbon Treaty, Article 205 EC required a simple majority in such a case.
[181] Unanimity is required for numerous Union decisions of a general nature and for some decisions taken at the request of the Court of Justice (Article 252, first para. TFEU) or at the request of the EIB (Article 308, third para. TFEU). In principle, unanimity is required for decisions taken in connection with the CFSP (see Article 31, first subpara. TFEU). The same applied for PJCC prior to the entry into force of the Lisbon Treaty (see Article 34(2) EU).
[182] C-28/12, *Commission v Council*, 2015, paras 51–3.
[183] This is also the rule for votes on matters relating to the CFSP.

majority will be deemed to have been attained (Article 16(4) TEU). In order to apply these conditions, the Council updates annually the population figures for each of the Member States and publishes them in Annex III of the Council Rules of Procedure.[184]

Council decisions are considered to have reached a qualified majority when the above-mentioned thresholds are met. Nevertheless, when the Intergovernmental Conference of 2007 established the current thresholds for a qualified majority, it agreed that, in certain situations, Member States may ask for the vote to be postponed.[185] This has been specified in a Council decision, according to which, if members of the Council representing at least 55 per cent of the population or at least 55 per cent of the number of Member States necessary to constitute a blocking minority, indicate their opposition to the Council adopting an act by a qualified majority, the Council is to 'discuss' the issue.[186] The Council is then required to 'do all in its power' to reach, within a reasonable time and without prejudicing obligatory time-limits, a 'satisfactory solution' to address 'concerns' raised by the members of the Council who indicated their opposition.[187]

Special arrangements apply in areas where not all Member States participate in decision-making.[188] In such cases, a qualified majority will require at least 55 per cent of the members of the Council representing the participating Member States, comprising at least 65 per cent of the population of these States. A blocking minority must include at least the minimum number of Council members representing more than 35 per cent of the population of the participating Member States, plus one member (Article 238(3)(a) TFEU). Decisions which the Council is to take by a qualified majority but not on the basis of a proposal from the Commission or from the High Representative of the Union for Foreign Affairs and Security Policy, will need to be approved by at least 72 per cent of the members

---

[184] Article 2(2), Annex III of the Council Rules of Procedure. Thus, pursuant to Council Decision (EU, Euratom) 2020/2030 of 10 December 2020 amending the Council's Rules of Procedure (OJ 2020 L419/24), the 2021 population figures for each Member State (and the percentage of the total population of the Union) are the following for the period from 1 January 2021 until 31 December 2021: Germany 83 100 961 (18,54 per cent), France 67 098 824 (14,97 per cent), Italy 60 897 891 (13,58 per cent), Spain 47 329 981 (10,56 per cent), Poland 37 958 138 (8,47 per cent), Romania 19 317 984 (4,31 per cent), the Netherlands 17 549 457 (3,91 per cent), Belgium 11 549 888 (2,58 per cent), Greece 10 709 739 (2,39 per cent), the Czech Republic 10 557 001 (2,35 per cent), Sweden 10 330 000 (2,30 per cent), Portugal 10 295 909 (2,30 per cent), Hungary 9 769 526 (2,18 per cent), Austria 8 897 000 (1,98 per cent), Bulgaria 6 951 482 (1,55 per cent), Denmark 5 816 443 (1,30 per cent), Finland 5 521 292 (1,23 per cent), Slovakia 5 457 873 (1,22 per cent), Ireland 4 964 440 (1,11 per cent), Croatia 4 058 165 (0,91 per cent), Lithuania 2 794 090 (0,62 per cent), Slovenia 2 095 861 (0,47 per cent), Latvia 1 907 675 (0,43 %), Estonia 1 328 976 (0,30 per cent), Cyprus 888 005 (0,20 per cent), Luxembourg 623 962 (0,14 per cent) and Malta 514 564 (0,11 per cent). With a total population of the Union of 448 285 127, the 65 per cent threshold represents 291 385 333 inhabitants
[185] Declaration (No. 7) annexed to the Treaty of Lisbon on Article 16(4) TEU and Article 238(2) TFEU.
[186] Council Decision 2009/857/EC of 13 December 2007 relating to the implementation of Article 9C(4) of the TEU and Article 205(2) of the TFEU between 1 November 2014 and 31 March 2017 on the one hand, and as from 1 April 2017 on the other, OJ 2009 L314/73, Article 4.
[187] Council Decision 2009/857/EC (fn. 189), Article 5. It is then up to the President of the Council, with the assistance of the Commission, to undertake any initiative necessary to 'facilitate a wider basis of agreement in the Council': ibid., Article 6.
[188] See the reference to Article 238(3) TFEU in Article 46(3), third subpara. and (4), third subpara, TEU (permanent structured cooperation in the framework of the common security and defence policy); Article 50(4), second subpara. TEU (arrangements relating to the withdrawal of a Member State); Article 121(4), third subpara. TFEU (recommendations to a Member State regarding its economic policy); Article 126(13), third subpara. TFEU (excessive government deficits); Article 136(2), second subpara. TFEU, Article 138(3), second subpara. TFEU, Article 139(4), second subpara. TFEU and Article 140(2), third subpara. TFEU (certain decisions relating to the eurozone); Article 330, third para. (enhanced cooperation); and Article 354, second and third paras TFEU (suspension of Treaty rights).

of the Council representing the participating Member States, comprising at least 65 per cent of the population of these States (Article 238(3)(b) TFEU).

12.048 **Majority voting in practice.** For a long time the rules on (qualified) majority voting laid down in the Treaties did not reflect reality. In July 1965 the Community was struck by a serious crisis when France refused to take part in Council meetings (the 'empty chair' policy) and complained about majority voting on Council decisions bearing on fundamental policy choices, even though the Treaty allowed this to take place with regard to matters such as agricultural policy after the second stage of the transitional period (1 January 1966). In order to break out of the impasse, the Council, meeting on 17 and 18 January and 28 and 29 January 1966 adopted the so-called 'Luxembourg Compromise', in which the Member States declared, *inter alia*, that where—in cases where acts could be adopted by a majority vote on a proposal from the Commission—'very important interests' of one or more of the partners were at stake, the members of the Council would try, within a reasonable time-limit, to find a solution acceptable to all of them 'while respecting their mutual interests and those of the Community, in accordance with Article 2 of the Treaty'.[189] Subsequently, differences of opinion existed as to what had to be done when divergent views could not be fully reconciled. Although the 'Compromise' did not renounce the principle of majority voting, it did find a practice whereby almost all Council acts, with the exception of budgetary measures, were adopted by a unanimous vote. This practice became further entrenched following the accession of the United Kingdom, which attached constitutional importance to the Compromise, since it was partly on the strength of it that Britain joined the Community. Nevertheless, it proved possible from time to time for acts to be adopted against the will of a minority. Thus, in May 1982 the farm prices were determined for the first time by a qualified majority vote.

As a result of the Single European Act, the number of Treaty articles prescribing a vote by qualified majority increased dramatically. It therefore appeared essential to rein in the previous practice. The Council succeeded in so doing by means of an amendment to its Rules of Procedure adopted on 20 July 1987.[190] As a result, the President is required, at the request of a member of the Council or of the Commission, to open a voting procedure, provided that a majority of the Council's members so decides (see Council Rules of Procedure, Article 11(1), second subpara.). This means that negotiations must be continued in the Council only if fourteen Member States object to a vote being held. Once the Commission is persuaded that a given proposal has the support of the required majority, it can call for a vote and get the proposal adopted.

This rule has been maintained, although changes as to the thresholds necessary to attain the qualified majority have remained a reason for some Member States to request that the decision-making process be blocked when important interests are at stake. First, such request led to a political decision taken by the Council on the occasion of the accession of new Member States in 1995, when it determined the weighted votes to be given to the new Member States as from 1 January 1995. This so-called 'Ioannina Compromise' covered the situation where a certain number of Member States, not constituting a blocking minority

---

[189] Luxembourg Compromise, Part B, section 1 (1966) 3 Bull. CE 10.
[190] For that decision, see n. 172, *supra*.

as such, would indicate their intention to oppose the adoption by the Council of a decision by qualified majority.[191] In such a case, the Council would 'do all in its power' to reach an agreed solution which could be adopted by a majority larger than that required for qualified majority voting. Following the changes made to the voting procedure by the Treaty of Nice and the 2003 Act of Accession, this Ioannina Compromise was not adapted and lost its practical effect. Second, as explained above, similar arrangements have been agreed in the negotiations leading to the Lisbon Treaty, allowing a group of Member States that does not constitute a blocking minority to ask for a postponement of the vote (see para. 13-048, *infra*). A declaration annexed to the Lisbon Treaty formulated these arrangements as a 'draft decision' of the Council,[192] which the Council subsequently adopted to be applied from 1 November 2014 onwards.[193] Poland had asked the Intergovernmental Conference of 2007 to include these arrangements in the Treaties themselves. The IGC did not accede to this request but agreed that they would be laid down in a Council decision. At the same time, however, a protocol was added to the Treaties which provides that that decision cannot be amended or abrogated by the Council without a preliminary deliberation in the European Council, acting by consensus[194].

Evolution of the 'qualified majority'. Initially, where the Council was to act by a 'qualified' majority, the Treaties allotted to each Member State a specific number of votes—depending on the Member State's population size, but corrected to give more weight to the smaller Member States[195]—and required a specific number of those votes to be cast in favour.[196] When the Treaty of Nice was approved, agreement was reached on a more complex decision-making system that required differing thresholds to be met in order to attain

12.049

---

[191] Council Decision of 29 March 1994 concerning the taking of a Decision by qualified majority by the Council (OJ 1994 C105/1, adapted because only three new Member States acceded to the Union on 1 January 1995, OJ 1995 C1). For a comparison with the Luxembourg Compromise, see 'Editorial Comments: the Ioannina Compromise—Towards a Wider and Weaker European Union?' (1994) CMLRev 453–57. See also De l'Ecotais, 'La pondération des voix au Conseil de ministres de la Communauté européenne' (1997) RMCUE 324–7. For the significance of a 'right of veto', see also Van Nuffel, *De rechtsbescherming van nationale overheden in het Europees recht* (Kluwer, 2000), 453–8.
[192] Declaration (No. 7) on Article 16(4) TEU and Article 238(2) TFEU (n. 188, *supra*).
[193] Council Decision 2009/857/EG of 13 December 2007 (n. 189, *supra*).
[194] Protocol (No. 9), annexed to the TEU and TFEU, on the decision of the Council relating to the implementation of Article 16(4) TEU and Article 238(2) TFEU between 1 November 2014 and 31 March 2017 on the one hand, and as from 1 April 2017 on the other, OJ 2010 C83/274. See further 'Editorial—Not dead yet. Revisiting the "Luxembourg Veto" and its Foundations' (2017) EuConst 1–12.
[195] The final allocation of votes was not based on objective criteria, but reflected the influence in decision-making which the Member States in fact allow each other: De l'Ecotais, 'La pondération des voix au Conseil de ministres de la Communauté européenne' (1996) RMCUE 388–93 and 617–20 and (1997) RMCUE 324–7.
[196] Before 1 May 2004, France, Germany, Italy, and the United Kingdom each had ten votes; Spain eight; Belgium, Greece, the Netherlands, and Portugal five each; Austria and Sweden four each; Denmark, Finland, and Ireland three each; and Luxembourg two. There was a qualified majority if the Commission proposal received sixty-two out of the eighty-seven weighted votes or 71.26 per cent (hence the blocking minority consisted of twenty-six votes). Where the Council did not vote on a Commission proposal, there was already a dual requirement in order to attain a qualified majority: sixty-two weighted votes in favour out of eighty-seven, which had to be cast by at least ten out of fifteen members. The allocation of votes among the Member States in Article 205(1) EC was adjusted with a view to the accession of ten new Member States by Protocol (No. 10) on the enlargement of the Union annexed to the EC Treaty by the Treaty of Nice (OJ 2001 C80/49), and subsequently by Article 12 of the 2003 Act of Accession and Article 10 of the 2005 Act of Accession. Protocol (No. 10) referred to Declaration (No. 20), annexed to the Nice Treaty, on the enlargement of the European Union (OJ 2001 C80/80), which was adjusted by the European Council held in Brussels on 24 and 25 October 2002 to take account of the fact that Bulgaria and Romania would not be acceding in 2004. See also Declaration (No. 21), annexed to the Nice Treaty, on the qualified majority threshold and the number of votes for a blocking minority in an enlarged Union.

a 'qualified' majority:[197] first, a specific number of votes of the Member States had to be reached; second, a majority of the Member States had to vote in favour; and third, these Member States had to represent at least 60 per cent of the population. With a view to simplification, the 2003 Convention proposed to abandon the method for calculating the qualified majority based on the attainment of a specific number of weighted votes and retain only the two additional conditions introduced by the Treaty of Nice—albeit in a slightly adapted version (that is to say, a majority of the Member States representing 60 per cent of the total population of the Union). Starting from that proposal, the 2003 Intergovernmental Conference laid down, in the Constitution for Europe, a system based on higher majority thresholds (55 per cent of the members of the Council and 65 per cent of the population of the Union). Eventually, that system was preserved in the Lisbon Treaty with entry into force as from 1 November 2014 (Article 16(4) TEU). Until 31 October 2014, the arrangements existing since the Treaty of Nice were kept in place, in accordance with the Protocol on transitional provisions annexed to the Treaties (Article 16(5) TEU).[198] As mentioned above, the Intergovernmental Conference leading to the Lisbon Treaty could not reach consensus as to the new calculation of the qualified majority without agreeing that in some instances where a qualified majority is reached, Member States in the minority may seek postponement of the vote. Until 31 October 2014, the existing arrangements were kept in place; after that date, and until 31 March 2017, a member of the Council could still request that a decision be adopted under the system for qualified majority votes in place until 31 October 2014.[199]

12.050 **'A' and 'B' items.** In practice, the Council does not have to take a formal vote on many acts, since the decision is prepared by the national delegations and the Commission in working parties and in the Committee of Permanent Representatives (Coreper; see para. 12-051, *infra*). All matters on which Coreper has already reached agreement appear on the agenda for Council meetings as 'A' items. The Council approves them without further ado unless a member requests that the particular item be subjected to further discussion (Council Rules of Procedure, Article 3(6) and (8)). In that event, the agenda item in question is generally sent back to Coreper. Matters on which Coreper has not reached agreement but which are nevertheless up for decision may be placed on the agenda as 'B' items by a member of the Council or the Commission. The Council then endeavours to reach agreement or to get a sufficient majority behind the proposal, after which it may be sent back to Coreper to be finalized. It then returns on the agenda for the Council meeting for approval as an 'A' item.

---

[197] Article 3(1) of Protocol (No. 10) on the enlargement of the European Union (n. 199, *supra*) announced that this system would take effect on 1 January 2005. However, that Article was repealed by Article 12(2) of the 2003 Act of Accession, which introduced the system of differing majority thresholds with effect from 1 November 2004.

[198] Protocol (No. 36) on transitional provisions (n. 144, *supra*), Article 3(3). In order to obtain a qualified majority, a particular number of votes had to be obtained and, at the same time, a majority of the Member States representing at least 62 per cent of the population of the Union had to vote in favour. France, Germany, Italy, and the United Kingdom each had twenty-nine votes; Spain and Poland twenty-seven; Romania fourteen; the Netherlands thirteen; Belgium, the Czech Republic, Greece, Hungary, and Portugal twelve each; Austria, Bulgaria, and Sweden ten each; Denmark, Finland, Ireland, Lithuania, and Slovakia seven each; Cyprus, Estonia, Latvia, Luxembourg, and Slovenia four each; and Malta three. A qualified majority was attained where the Commission proposal obtained 255 out of 345 weighted votes (or 73.91 per cent) and, at the same time, the majority of the members of the Council voted in favour. In any case, a member of the Council could request verification that the Member States constituting the qualified majority represented at least 62 per cent of the total population of the Union. If that condition was shown not to have been met, the decision in question was not adopted: Protocol (No. 36), Article 3(3). Where the Council did not vote on a Commission proposal, the 255 out of 345 weighted votes had to be cast by at least two-thirds of the members: ibid.

[199] Protocol (No. 36) on transitional provisions (n. 144, *supra*), Article 3(2).

Urgent matters may be dealt with by a written vote.[200] That procedure is also used for routine matters.[201] The formal vote on an act takes place in the Council, not in the working party or in Coreper. The latter only carry out the preparatory work and determine whether or not there is a consensus or a sufficient majority. If there is no consensus or an insufficient majority, the Council has to cut the Gordian knot.[202]

D. Internal organization

Coreper. The Committee of Permanent Representatives of the Governments of the Member States (Coreper) prepares the work of the Council and carries out tasks assigned to it by that institution (Article 16(7) TEU and Article 240(1) TFEU).[203] Each Member State delegates to it a Permanent Representative, who has the status of an ambassador based in Brussels, together with a Deputy Permanent Representative, who has the diplomatic rank of Minister. The Permanent Representatives head the Member States' Permanent Representations to the European Union, which are in continuous contact with the ministries in their respective Member States. Coreper has two parts, which are not in a hierarchical relationship. Part I consists of the Deputy Permanent Representatives. It deals chiefly with matters concerning the internal market and technical and economic questions. Part II, which comprises the Permanent Representatives themselves, discusses general issues and questions of foreign policy. A special committee discharges Coreper's tasks in the field of agricultural policy.[204]

12.051

Coreper is an auxiliary body and cannot exercise the decision-making powers conferred by the Treaties on the Council.[205] In this context, Coreper is to ensure consistency of the Union's policies and actions and see to it that the principles of legality, subsidiarity, proportionality, and providing reasons for acts are respected, together with the rules establishing the powers of Union institutions, bodies, offices, and agencies; the budgetary provisions; and the rules on procedure, transparency, and the quality of drafting.[206] In the cases

---

[200] The Council or Coreper decides by a unanimous vote whether to take advantage of this possibility; if the President proposes recourse to written votes, such a vote may take place if all Member States agree (Council Rules of Procedure, Article 12(1), first subpara.). The Commission's agreement is required to the use of that procedure where the written vote is on a matter brought before the Council by that institution (Council Rules of Procedure, Article 12(1), second subpara.). For the purposes of implementing the CFSP, there exists a simplified written procedure which makes use of COREU (*correspondance européenne*), a confidential communications network linking the national Foreign Ministries, the Commission, and the Council's General Secretariat (Council Rules of Procedure, Article 12(2)(d)). Under that procedure, a proposal made by the Presidency is deemed adopted if no member of the Council objects within a period laid down by the Presidency.

[201] See further Novak, *La prise de décision au Conseil de l'Union européenne: pratiques du vote et du consensus* (Dalloz, 2011); Hayes-Renshaw, Van Aken, and Wallace, 'When and Why the EU Council of Ministers Votes Explicitly', (2006) JCMS 161–94; De Zwaan, The Permanent Representatives Committee: Its Role in European Decision-making (Elsevier, 1995).

[202] So as to preserve efficient decision-taking with delegations of twenty-five Member States around the table, the Council adopted, on 22 March 2004, 'Working methods for an enlarged Council', OJ 2004 L106/42 (see now Annex V to the Council Rules of Procedure, 'Council working methods'). They call upon delegations to avoid pointless presentations and keep their interventions brief, substantive, and to the point (see points 6-13).

[203] This Committee is known as 'Coreper', an abbreviation of *Comité des représentants permanents*.

[204] Article 5(4) of the Decision of 12 May 1960 of the representatives of the Member States of the European Economic Community meeting within the Council on quickening the pace for achieving the objectives of the Treaty, JO 1960 1217, and the Council Decision of 20 July 1960 setting up the committee (1960) 5 EC Bull. 74–75.

[205] C-25/94, *Commission v Council*, 1996, paras 25–8.

[206] Council Rules of Procedure, Article 19(1).

mentioned in Article 19(7) of the Council's Rules of Procedure, Coreper is entitled to adopt procedural decisions (Article 240(1) TFEU).

12.052 **Working parties.** Various committees and working parties, consisting of national civil servants and representatives of the Commission, operate under the auspices of Coreper.[207] Some working parties are brought together on an *ad hoc* basis, others are permanent. The first discussions of Commission proposals for legislation generally take place within these working parties. They report to Coreper, which in turn refers the matters onto the Council.[208] Member States may choose to delegate representatives of decentralized governments, to the extent that they are competent to represent the Member State.

12.053 **Preparatory committees.** The Treaties expressly entrust a number of committees with the task of preparing the work of the Council, without prejudice to Coreper's general competence. As far as financial and monetary questions are concerned, the Economic and Financial Committee does the preparatory work for the Council (Article 134(2), second indent TFEU; see para. 13-036, *infra*). For the purposes of promoting coordination of employment and social policies, the advisory Employment and Social Protection Committees contribute to the preparation of Council proceedings (Articles 150 and 160 TFEU; see para. 13-036, *infra*). As for the area of freedom, security, and justice, a standing Committee facilitates coordination of the Member States' competent authorities (Article 71 TFEU).[209] For advice on the implementation of the CFSP, the Council has a Political and Security Committee (Article 38, first para. TEU) consisting of the 'Political Directors' from the Member States or their deputies.[210] This committee plays a central role in European security and defence policy, including crisis management. It exercises, under the responsibility of the Council and the High Representative, political control and strategic direction of crisis management operations and may be authorized, for the purpose and for the duration of a crisis management operation, to take the relevant decisions (Article 38, second and third paras TEU; see para. 19-007, *infra*).

---

[207] See, *inter alia*, the '207 Committee' (previously '133 Committee') set up pursuant to Article 207 TFEU; the Committee on Cultural Affairs set up by Resolution of the Council of the Ministers responsible for cultural affairs meeting within the Council of 27 May 1988 (OJ 1988 C197/1); and the Financial Services Committee set up by Council Decision 2003/165/EC of 18 February 2003 (OJ 2003 L67/17).

[208] See Council Rules of Procedure, Articles 19(3) and 21. In the case of agricultural affairs, reports are made to the Special Agriculture Committee.

[209] Council Decision 2010/131/EU of 25 February 2010 on setting up the Standing Committee on operational coordination on internal security, OJ 2010 L52/50. Before the Lisbon Treaty, this 'coordinating committee' dealt with technical aspects of policy relating to PJCC, whilst the broader political and institutional implications were left to Coreper. The original Article K.4 of the EU Treaty created this committee (known as the 'K.4 Committee'). The K.4 Committee replaced the Coordinators' Group (para. 1-038, *supra*), which was wound up after the EU Treaty entered into effect.

[210] Council Decision 2001/78/CFSP of 22 January 2001 setting up the Political and Security Committee, OJ 2001 L27/1. The Political and Security Committee is assisted by the Committee for civilian aspects of crisis management (set up by Council Decision 2000/354/CFSP of 22 May 2000, OJ 2000 L127/1) and by the Military Committee of the European Union (set up by Council Decision 2001/79/CFSP of 22 January 2001, OJ 2001 L127/4). See also para. 19-003, *infra*. For a brief period, there was an Interim Political and Security Committee (Council Decision 2000/143/CFSP of 14 February 2000, OJ 2000 L49/1) and an Interim Military Body (Council Decision 2000/144/CFSP of 14 February 2000, OJ 2000 L49/2). Compare its role pre-Lisbon as set out in Juncos and Reynolds, 'The Political and Security Committee: governing in the shadow' (2007) E For Aff Rev 127–47, with its current role, as set out in Maurer and Wright, 'Still Governing in the Shadows? Member States and the Political & Security Committee in the Post-Lisbon EU Foreign Policy Architecture' (2021) JCMS, https://doi.org/10.1111/jcms.13134.

Presidency of committees and working parties. Since the Lisbon Treaty, Coreper is chaired by the Permanent Representative or the Deputy Permanent Representative of the Member State holding the Presidency of the General Affairs Council; the various committees and working parties are chaired by a delegate of the Member State chairing the relevant Council configuration, unless the Council decides otherwise.[211] The Political and Security Committee and various other preparatory bodies of the Foreign Affairs Configuration are chaired by a representative of the High Representative for Foreign Affairs and Security Policy.[212] Some other Council preparatory bodies are chaired by a fixed, elected chair,[213] or by the General Secretariat of the Council.[214] This complex arrangement for the Presidency of committees and working parties was set up upon the entry into force of the Lisbon Treaty, and replaces the previous system whereby Coreper and all committees and working parties were chaired by representatives of the same Member State, namely the Member State holding the Presidency of all Council configurations for a six-month period. The previous system enabled the Member State holding the Presidency to make an impression on Council policy through its diplomats and civil servants during that period. As explained above, the Lisbon Treaty still requires each Member State to chair, for a six-month period, the Council configurations, except for the Foreign Affairs Council, but organizes this by groups of three Member States that may decide alternative arrangements among themselves on the Presidency of Council configurations. Moreover, the Foreign Affairs Council is now chaired by the High Representative for Foreign Affairs and Security Policy (see para. 12-065, *infra*). With respect to the external affairs of the Union, it is thus no longer for the Member State holding the Presidency to set the political agenda. In all other matters, the Member State holding the Presidency—or, if an arrangement has been made to this end, another Member State from the same group of three Member States—is to take all necessary steps to have work advanced between meetings of Coreper, working parties, or committees, for example, by organizing bilateral consultations and by requesting the delegations of the Member States to take a position on specific proposals for amendment of the documents discussed.[215] Finally, it should be mentioned that the Commission is represented, not only at Council meetings, but also in Coreper and the working parties.[216] As a result, it plays a dynamic role in the legislative process (see para. 17-017, *infra*).

12.054

General Secretariat. The Council's administrative structure is its General Secretariat (Article 240(2) TFEU),[217] which is based in Brussels. The Secretary-General is

12.055

---

[211] See Article 2 of European Council Decision 2009/881/EU of 1 December 2009 on the exercise of the Presidency of the Council (OJ 2009 L315/50), and Article 19(4) of the Council Rules of Procedure of the same date.

[212] Ibid. The list of preparatory bodies chaired either by the six-monthly Presidency (e.g. preparatory bodies in the area of trade and development, such as the '207 Committee') or by a representative of the High Representative (e.g. several CFSP preparatory bodies) is set out in Annex II ('Chairmanship of the preparatory bodies of the Foreign Affairs Council') to Council Decision 2009/908/EU of 1 December 2009 laying down measures for the implementation of the European Council Decision on the exercise of the Presidency of the Council, and on the chairmanship of preparatory bodies of the Council (OJ 2009 L322/28, *corrigendum*: OJ 2009 L344/56).

[213] See Article 5 and Annex III ('Chairpersons of Council preparatory bodies with a fixed chair') of Council Decision 2009/908/EU (see n. 215, *supra*), that mentions, *inter alia*, the Economic and Financial Committee, the Employment Committee and the Social Protection Committee.

[214] Ibid. (mentioning, *inter alia*, the Security Committee and the Working Party on Codification of Legislation). See also the Working Party on the United Kingdom, which like the ad hoc Working Party on Article 50 TEU has been chaired by the General Secretariat: Council Decision (EU) 2020/121 of 28 January 2020, OJ 2020 L23/1.

[215] See also the tasks entrusted to the Presidency in so far as the preparation for meetings is concerned in Annex V of the Council Rules of Procedure ('Council working methods', n. 205, *supra*).

[216] See Ponzano, 'Les relations entre le Coreper et la Commission européenne' (2000)1 DUE 23–38.

[217] See also Council Rules of Procedure, Article 23.

responsible for running the General Secretariat.[218] The General Secretariat is divided into eight Directorates-General (A to I) and a legal service. It employs around 3,000 staff.[219] The General Secretariat organizes meetings of the Council, Coreper, and the working parties; translates and distributes documents; assists the President; and deals with the Council's relations with the other institutions.

IV. The European Commission

12.056 **Designation.** As a result of Article 9 of the Merger Treaty, the 'Commission of the European Communities' replaced the High Authority of the ECSC, the Commission of the EEC, and the Commission of the EAEC. Ever since the entry into force of the EU Treaty, the Commission[220] has referred to itself by the short title of 'European Commission'.[221] Even though that is now the official designation of that institution (see Article 13(1) TEU), the Treaties also use the shorter 'Commission'.

A. Powers

12.057 **Survey.** Article 17(1) TEU unequivocally declares that the Commission is the Union institution which promotes the general interest of the Union and takes appropriate initiatives to that end. It further sets out a detailed description of the roles played by that institution, in particular in monitoring the application of the law and initiating legislation, together with its budgetary powers, executive powers, and powers of representation.[222] The Commission is also responsible for initiating the Union's annual and multiannual programming with a view to achieving interinstitutional agreements. Its supervisory powers, participation in decision-making, and implementing powers are fleshed out in other Treaty articles, together with powers with regard to the Union's external relations policy. As far as CFSP action on the part of the Union is concerned, the Commission has virtually no supervisory power, its participation in decision-making is limited, and apart from the implementation of the budget, has only such tasks of implementation and representation as the Council delegates to it.

1. Supervision

12.058 **Guardian of the Treaties.** The Commission ensures that the provisions of the Treaties and the measures taken pursuant thereto by the institutions are applied (see Article 17(1) TEU). It therefore checks that the other institutions (the Council and the European Parliament), bodies, and agencies, the Member States, and natural and legal persons comply with Union

---

[218] The Secretary-General is appointed by the Council (Article 240(2), first subpara. TFEU). See Council Decision (EU) 2015/654 of 21 April 2015 appointing the Secretary-General of the Council of the European Union for the period from 1 July 2015 to 30 June 2020 (OJ 2015 L107/74).
[219] See https://www.consilium.europa.eu/en/general-secretariat/staff-budget.
[220] See, in general, Nugent and Rhinard, *The European Commission* (Macmillan International, 2015); Spence and Edwards, *The European Commission* (Harper, 2006). For the Commission's website, see http://ec.europa.eu/.
[221] *Europe*, No. 6130, 8/9 November 1993, 7.
[222] Before the Lisbon Treaty, Article 211 EC listed the tasks which the Commission was to carry out 'in order to ensure the proper functioning and development of the common market'.

law.[223] To this end it receives information in the shape of informal or formal complaints and information with which it has to be provided pursuant to specific provisions.[224] Where Union provisions so provide (e.g. with regard to competition law), the Commission is obliged to respond to complaints from natural or legal persons.[225] In the event of failure to comply with Union law on the part of national authorities, citizens may submit a complaint to the Commission.[226] However, there is no formal procedure obliging the Commission to take any action in response to citizens' complaints.[227]

In the event that the Commission finds that other institutions or certain bodies, offices, or agencies have infringed Union law, it may bring an action for annulment or for failure to act in the Court of Justice (Articles 263 and 265 TFEU).[228]

If a Member State fails to fulfil its obligations, the Commission puts it on notice, giving it the opportunity to rectify matters and submit any observations. If necessary, it will then deliver a reasoned opinion, with which the Member State has to comply within a specified period, failing which it can be summoned before the Court of Justice (Article 258 TFEU—see para. 29-043 et seq., infra).[229] If the Court of Justice finds that the Member State has infringed Union law, the Member State is required to take the necessary measures to comply with the Court's judgment, failing which the Commission may bring the case before the Court, after giving the Member State concerned the opportunity to submit its observations, and ask the Court to order payment of a lump sum or a penalty payment (Article 260(1) and (2) TFEU, see para. 29-046, infra). Where the Commission brings an action against a Member State for failure to fulfil its obligation to notify measures transposing a directive adopted under a legislative procedure, the Commission may obtain the imposition of a lump sum[230] or penalty payment[231] when it brings its initial action based on Article 258 TFEU (Article 260(3) TFEU, introduced by the Lisbon Treaty, see para. 29-053, infra).

In certain circumstances, the Commission is entitled to impose fines on natural or legal persons for infringements of competition law (see para. 9-016, supra).

---

[223] For a survey, see Andersen, *The Enforcement of EU Law: The Role of the European Commission* (OUP, 2012); Van Rijn, 'The Investigative and Supervisory Powers of the Commission', in Curtin and Heukels (eds), *Institutional Dynamics of European Integration. Essays in Honour of Henry G. Schermers*, Vol. II (Martinus Nijhoff, 1994) 409–21. For some critical comment, see Palacio Vallelersundi, 'La Commission dans son rôle de gardienne des Traités' (2001) RDUE 901–7.

[224] See the annual reports of the Court of Auditors (Article 287(4), first subpara. TFEU) and of the ECB (Article 284(3) TFEU). See the obligations to provide information imposed on the Member States by, inter alia, Articles 108(3); 114(5) and (8); 121(3), second subpara.; 140(2); 148(3) and 193. As far as natural and legal persons are concerned, see, inter alia, the obligation to notify certain concentrations of undertakings; para. 9-018, supra.

[225] See the complaints relating to breaches of Articles 101 and 102 TFEU under Article 7 of Regulation No. 1/2003 (para. 9-015, supra); as for other formal complaints, there are in particular the questions put by members of the European Parliament (para. 12-006, supra).

[226] A standard form is to be found on the website of the Commission (https://ec.europa.eu/info/about-european-commission/contact/problems-and-complaints/how-make-complaint-eu-level/submit-complaint_en); see also the Administrative procedures for the handling of relations with the complainant regarding the application of European Union law, annexed to the Commission Communication 'EU law: Better results through better application', COM(2016)8600 OJ 2017 C18/10.

[227] See the discussion of the action for failure to fulfil obligations (Article 258 TFEU) in para. 29-040, infra

[228] The Commission can also bring an action against the ECB (Articles 263, third para. and 265, fourth para. TFEU) and against decisions of the Board of Governors and the Board of Directors of the EIB (Article 271(b) and (c) TFEU).

[229] The Treaties preclude such supervision in connection with the obligation (in the third stage of EMU) to avoid excessive government deficits (Article 126(10) TFEU).

[230] C-549/18, *Commission v Romania*, 2020, paras 64–87; C-550/18, *Commission v Ireland*, 2020, paras 74–99.

[231] C-543/17, *Commission v Belgium*, 2019, paras 78–93.

12.059　CFSP. The Treaties do not give the Commission the task of supervising whether the obligations entered into under the CFSP are complied with (see para. 19-006, *infra*).[232]

2. Participation in decision-making

12.060　**Decision-making.** The Commission has a key role in the decision-making process as it has a virtually exclusive right to initiate legislation in all the fields of competence of the Union, except for PJCC, where it shares this right with the Member States, and the CFSP, where it has no right of initiative (see para. 17-012, *infra*). In this connection, the Treaties explicitly state that the Union's legislative acts can be adopted only on the basis of a Commission proposal, except where the Treaties provide otherwise (Article 17(2) TEU).[233] At the same time, it is the Commission which submits the draft EU budget (Article 314(2) TFEU; see para. 20-001, *infra*). In view of its decisive role in the decision-making process, the Commission may take part in sessions of the European Parliament (see para. 12-019, *infra*) and in meetings of the Council (see para. 12-043, *supra*). In some cases, the Commission also has the power to take decisions (Article 17(1) TEU). That decision-making power consists mainly[234] of means whereby the Commission takes steps for the purpose of coordinating Member States' policies (e.g. Article 168(2) TFEU on public health),[235] or, as the guardian of Union law, assesses whether Member States have complied with their Treaty obligations (e.g. State aid). Furthermore, the Treaties empower the Commission to formulate recommendations (Article 292 TFEU) or deliver opinions on various matters dealt with in the Treaties.[236]

Moreover, the Commission draws up numerous reports in pursuance of its duty to keep other institutions informed[237] and on its own initiative,[238] and is entitled to consult the

---

[232] Before the Lisbon Treaty, the same applied to PJCC. The only power that the Commission had in this respect was the right to bring an action for annulment against PJCC framework decisions and decisions of the Council (Article 35(6) EU).

[233] C-409/13, *Council v Commission*, 2015, para. 68.

[234] See, however, the powers to adopt acts of a general nature provided for, *inter alia*, in Articles 45(3)(d) and 106(3) TFEU (para. 9-019, *supra*).

[235] See Articles 1682(2); 171(2); 173(2); 181(2) and 210(2) TFEU. As far as social provisions are concerned, see its task of promoting dialogue between management and labour (Article 154 TFEU) and its power to organize consultations between the Member States (Article 156 TFEU).

[236] See also the recommendations provided for in, *inter alia*, Articles 60, second para.; 97, third para.; 117(1); 143(1), first subpara. TFEU and opinions addressed to Member States (Article 156 TFEU); for recommendations and opinions addressed to the Council, see para. 17-012, *infra*. Before the Lisbon Treaty, Article 211, second indent EC empowered the Commission more generally to formulate recommendations or deliver opinions on matters dealt with in the Treaty if it expressly so provided or if the Commission considered it necessary. For an application, see the Commission Recommendation of 12 July 2004 on the transposition into national law of Directives affecting the internal market, OJ 2005 L98/47.

[237] Alongside the General Report on the Activities of the European Union intended for the European Parliament (Article 249(2) TFEU, see also Article 233 TFEU), the Commission also makes three-yearly reports to the European Parliament, the Council, and the European Economic and Social Committee on non-discrimination and citizenship (Article 23, first para. TFEU) and economic and social cohesion (Article 175, second para. TFEU: the latter report is also to be forwarded to the Committee of the Regions); an annual report to the European Parliament and the Council on social policy (Article 159 TFEU: the latter report is also to be forwarded to the European Economic and Social Committee), on research and technological development (Article 190 TFEU) and on measures taken for countering fraud (Article 325 TFEU); reports to the European Parliament on particular social problems (Articles 159 and 161, second para. TFEU) and on the results of multilateral economic surveillance (Article 121(5) TFEU) and a number of reports to the Council on matters relating to Economic and Monetary Union (Articles 121(3), first subpara.; 126(3), first subpara. and 140(1), first subpara. TFEU; see also former Articles 116(2)(b) and 122(2) EC). See, in addition, the annual report for the European Council, the European Parliament, the Council, and national parliaments on the application of Article 5 TEU (Article 9 of Protocol (No. 2), annexed to the TEU and TFEU, on the application of the principles of subsidiarity and proportionality, OJ 2010 C83/206; that report is also to be sent to the Committee of the Regions and the European Economic and Social Committee). The Commission, together with the Council, also produces an annual report on the employment situation in the Union (Article 148(5) TFEU).

[238] The Commission has committed itself to issuing annual reports on competition policy, the application of Union law, and the completion of the internal market.

Court of Auditors, the European Economic and Social Committee, and the Committee of the Regions.[239]

3. Implementation

Implementing powers. The Commission has extensive powers of implementation. First, it is, in principle, the institution competent for adopting 'implementing acts' where legally binding Union acts need to be implemented under uniform conditions (see Article 291(2) TFEU; see para. 18-012, *infra*). The Commission has to act in accordance with the rules and general principles laid down by the European Parliament and the Council (Article 291(3) TFEU; see para. 18-014, *infra*). Second, the Commission adopts 'delegated acts' where it has been so authorized by a legislative act (see Article 290 TFEU; see para. 18-010, *infra*). In any event, the Commission has the task of implementing the EU budget (Article 317 TFEU; see para. 20-007, *infra*).

12.061

4. Representation

Representation. The Commission represents the Union in legal transactions within each Member State (Article 335 TFEU; see para. 14-004, *infra*) and, as a rule, also in international transactions (Article 17(1) TEU; see para. 14-006, *infra*).[240] However, in areas coming under the CFSP, the Union is represented by the High Representative of the Union for Foreign Affairs and Security Policy, who is to be assisted by the European External Action Service (see para. 14-006, *infra*).

12.062

B. Composition

Number of Commissioners. The present Commission has twenty-seven members (often referred to as 'Commissioners'), including the President and the High Representative of the Union for Foreign Affairs and Security Policy. In the Commission a national of each Member State is a member (Article 17(4) TEU).[241] In the past the idea was regularly floated that the Commission would be more agile if the number of commissioners were more limited. Politically, it has proven virtually impossible to end the rule that each Member State has one of its nationals as a member of the European Commission.

12.063

Before the 2004 accessions, the rule was that the Commission included at least one national of each of the Member States, but could not include more than two nationals of any given Member State. In practice, the five large Member States were entitled to two members each and the other Member States to one.[242] The Council could alter the number of members of the Commission by unanimous vote.[243]

---

[239] Articles 287(4), second subpara.; 304 and 307 TFEU.

[240] C-73/14, *Council v Commission*, 2015, paras 57–9 (Article 335 TFEU extends to representation before international courts and tribunals).

[241] Article 246, third para., TFEU provides for an exception thereto in the event that the Council should decide unanimously not to fill a vacancy.

[242] Originally, the High Authority of the ECSC and the Commission of the EEC had nine Members and the Commission of the EAEC five. With the Merger Treaty, the number of Members of the single Commission came to nine (after a transitional period when it had fourteen Members: Merger Treaty, Article 32). Since then the number of Members has been increased to thirteen (Council Decision of 1 January 1973, OJ 1973 L2/28); to fourteen (1979 Act of Accession, Article 15, OJ 1979 L291); to seventeen (1985 Act of Accession, Article 15, OJ 1985 L302); and to twenty (1994 Act of Accession, Article 16, as amended by Council Decision of 1 January 1995, OJ 1995 L1/4). As a result of Article 42(2)(a) of the 2003 Act of Accession, the Commission has been enlarged by one Member for each new Member State. Between 1 May and 30 October 2004, the Commission had thirty Members.

[243] Article 213(1), third subpara. EC. See, e.g., the Council Decision of 1 January 1973, n. 245, *supra*. See Temple Lang, 'How Much Do the Smaller Member States Need the European Commission? The Role of the Commission in a Changing Europe' (2002) CMLRev 315–35.

The Treaty of Nice introduced the present system while stating that, 'when the Union consists of 27 Member States', a system would be introduced whereby the number of members of the Commission would be smaller than the number of Member States.[244] Accordingly, the 2003 Convention proposed that the Commission would consist of a President, the Union Minister for Foreign Affairs, and thirteen 'European Commissioners' selected on the basis of a system of equal rotation between the Member States. In addition, the Commission would have comprised non-voting 'Commissioners', coming from the Member States that would not have one of their nationals selected as European Commissioner. Several Member States insisted, however, on preserving the right for each Member State to have one of its nationals appointed as a full member of the Commission. The EU Constitution struck a compromise, which has largely been taken over by the Treaty of Lisbon (Article 17(4) and (5) TEU). Under that compromise, the first Commission appointed after the entry into force of the Treaty of Lisbon would still consist of one national of each Member State, but, as from 1 November 2014, the Commission would consist of a number of members, including its President and the High Representative, corresponding to two-thirds of the number of Member States, unless the European Council, acting unanimously, decided to alter this figure. The members of the Commission would be selected on the basis of a system of strictly equal rotation between the Member States as regards the determination of, the sequence of, and the time spent by, their nationals as members of the Commission.[245] Each Commission would have to be so composed as to reflect satisfactorily the demographic and geographical range of all the Member States (Article 17(5) TEU and Article 244 TFEU). The precise arrangements were to be adopted by the European Council, acting unanimously (Article 244 TFEU).

In the end, the European Council decided to preserve the system of one commissioner for each Member State. In order to accommodate the concerns of the Irish people after the 2008 negative referendum on the Lisbon Treaty, the European Council of 11 and 12 December 2008 agreed that, after the entry into force of the Lisbon Treaty, a decision would be taken 'in accordance with the necessary legal procedures' to ensure that the Commission continues to include one national of each Member State (see para. 2-002, *supra*). This decision was adopted by the European Council on 22 May 2013, stating that the Commission consists of a number of members, including the President and the High Representative of the Union for Foreign Affairs and Security Policy, equal to the number of Member States.[246]

12.064 **Appointment.** Commissioners have to be chosen on the ground of their general competence and European commitment from persons whose independence is beyond doubt

---

[244] Article 4 of Protocol (No. 10) on the enlargement of the European Union (n. 199, *supra*), which heralded further amendments to Article 213(1) EC and further provided how the Council had to determine the number of Members of the Commission and the system of rotation. For reservations, see Bradley, 'Institutional Design in the Treaty of Nice' (2001) CMLRev 1095, 1117–19.

[245] Consequently, the difference between the total number of terms of office held by nationals of any given pair of Member States could never be more than one (Article 244(a) TFEU).

[246] European Council Decision 2013/272/EU of 22 May 2013 concerning the number of members of the European Commission, OJ 2013 L165/98. The European Council announced that it would assess the impact of its decision on the functioning of the Commission sufficiently in advance of the appointment of the first Commission following the date of accession of the thirtieth Member State or the appointment of the Commission succeeding that which took office on 1 November 2014, whichever date would be earlier. No document has yet been adopted that contains such assessment.

(Article 17(3), second subpara. TEU). Since the Lisbon Treaty, members of the Commission are appointed by the European Council, acting by a qualified majority. Before, they were appointed by the Member State governments 'by common accord' and, since the Treaty of Nice, by the Council acting by a qualified majority. The European Parliament's say in the appointment of the President and members of the Commission has been gradually increased.[247]

The European Council, acting by a qualified majority, proposes a candidate for the Presidency who then needs to be elected by the European Parliament (Article 17(7), first subpara. TEU).[248] The proposal must take the elections to the European Parliament into account and be adopted after appropriate consultations (ibid.).[249] The main European political parties represented in the European Parliament have interpreted the 'taking into account' of the elections in the sense that the 'lead candidate' of the party obtaining most seats or able to collect sufficient support in the Parliament should be proposed as candidate for the Presidency of the Commission—an understanding not shared by everyone, particularly within the European Council (see para. 12-014, *supra*). Pursuant to its Rules of Procedure, the European Parliament requests the candidate to make a statement and to present his or her political guidelines.[250]

If the Parliament elects the candidate for the Presidency, it is for the Council, acting by a qualified majority and in common accord with the President-elect, to adopt the list of the other persons whom it proposes for appointment as members of the Commission, on the basis of the suggestions made by Member States (Article 17(7), second subpara. TEU). The European Parliament requests the Commissioners-designate to appear before

---

[247] The European Parliament pressed for a say in the appointment of the Commission ever since the early days of the Community: see the resolution of 27 June 1963, JO 1963 1916. As long ago as 1983, the European Council decided, in the Solemn Declaration of Stuttgart (n. 114, *supra*), that, before appointing the President of the Commission, the Member State governments would seek the opinion of the enlarged Bureau of the European Parliament and that, after the members of the Commission had been appointed, the European Parliament would vote on the Commission's proposed programme (point 2.3.5). The EU Treaty added the obligation for the Parliament to be *consulted* on the person whom the governments wished to appoint as President; at the same time, the national governments had to nominate the other persons whom they wished to appoint as members of the Commission *in consultation with* the nominee for President and the appointment of the President and members of the Commission as a body depended on the European Parliament's approval. So, Jacques Santer was nominated in the Decision of the representatives of the Governments of the Member States of 26 July 1994 (OJ 1994 L203/20) which was only adopted after the European Parliament had delivered its opinion on 21 July 1994 (even though the governments had already agreed on the person to be appointed on 15 July 1994 at an extraordinary meeting of the European Council in Brussels). The Treaty of Amsterdam made the appointment of the President depend upon the *approval* of the European Parliament and required the governments to reach *agreement* with the nominee President on the other persons whom they intended to appoint as Commissioners. Lastly, the Nice Treaty introduced a qualified majority vote for the nomination of the President and the appointment of the President and Members of the Commission and replaced 'governments of the Member States' by 'the Council'. As far as the Members from the new Member States appointed on 1 May 2004 were concerned, a simplified procedure was applied whereby the members were appointed by the Council, acting by qualified majority and by common accord with the President of the Commission (2003 Act of Accession, Article 45(2)(a)).

[248] See, most recently, European Council Decision (EU) 2019/1136 of 2 July 2019 proposing to the European Parliament a candidate for President of the European Commission, OJ 2019 L179/1 (proposing Ursula von der Leyen as successor to Jean-Claude Juncker).

[249] Declaration (No. 6), annexed to the Lisbon Treaty (OJ 2010 C83/338), also states that in choosing the persons called upon to hold the office of President of the Commission (and also the persons to be appointed as President of the European Council and High Representative of the Union for Foreign Affairs and Security Policy) 'due account is to be taken of the need to respect the geographical and demographic diversity of the Union and its Member States' (see n. 111, *supra*).

[250] EP Rules of Procedure, Rule 124(1). If the candidate does not obtain the required majority, the President of the Parliament will invite the European Council to propose a new candidate within one month. Ibid., Rule 214(4),

the appropriate committees according to their prospective fields of responsibility. This occurs at public hearings where each Commissioner-designate is invited to make a statement and answer questions.[251] The prospect of a negative vote in Parliament then requires the Council, in accord with the President-elect of the Commission, to adopt a new list of persons proposed for appointment.[252] Next, the President, the High Representative, and the other members of the Commission are submitted collectively to a vote of consent by the European Parliament. On the basis of that consent, the Commission is appointed by the European Council, acting by a qualified majority (Article 17(7), third subpara. TFEU).

The President of the Commission appoints Vice-Presidents, other than the High Representative, from among its members (Article 17(6)(c) TEU).[253]

12.065 **High Representative of the Union.** As was explained earlier, the EU Constitution created the function of 'Union Minister of Foreign Affairs', which was taken over by the 2007 Intergovernmental Conference, under the title 'High Representative of the Union for Foreign Affairs and Security Policy'. The High Representative of the Union for Foreign Affairs and Security Policy is part of the College of Commissioners, as one of the Commission's Vice-Presidents, but his or her status is somewhat singular owing to his or her dual role. On the one hand, the High Representative conducts the Union's common foreign and security policy, including its common security and defence policy, as mandated by the Council. On the other hand, he or she is responsible within the Commission for handling external relations and for coordinating other aspects of the Union's external action (Article 18(2) and (4) TEU). As befits this dual role, the High Representative is appointed by the European Council, acting by a qualified majority, with the agreement of the President of the Commission, and is also submitted, together with the President and the other members of the Commission, to a vote of consent by the European Parliament (Articles 17(7) and 18(1) TEU).[254] This dual role also explains why, as far as the CFSP is concerned, the High Representative is answerable to the European Council, which may

---

[251] Ibid., Rule 125(1)-(2) and Annex VII to the Rules of Procedure on the approval of the Commission and monitoring of commitments made during the hearings. According to that Annex, such hearing may take place only after the committee for legal affairs has confirmed the absence of any conflict of interests. The hearing results in an evaluation letter approving or rejecting the Commissioner-designate or requesting additional hearing and another hearing.

[252] See, most recently, the replacement on 25 November 2019 of the first list adopted by the Council on 10 September 2019 (OJ 2019 L233 I/1) by a new list (OJ 2019 L304/16) in which candidates proposed initially by the Hungarian, Romanian, and French governments were replaced; the first two because of conflict of interests claimed by the Parliament before the hearings, the last because of an investigation on misappropriation of public funds, after having been heard twice. Similarly, as regards the previous Commissions, the Council had to replace the first list of Commissioners-designate on 5 November 2004 to replace the candidates initially proposed by the Italian and the Latvian governments (OJ 2004 L333/12), on 22 January 2010 to replace the candidate initially proposed by the Bulgarian government (OJ 2010 L20/5), and on 15 October 2014 to replace the candidate initially proposed by the Slovenian government (OJ 2014, L299/29).

[253] The Nice Treaty amended Article 217 EC, which, since the EU Treaty, provided that the President could appoint one or two Vice-Presidents. Prior to that, Article 14 of the Merger Treaty provided that the President and six Vice-Presidents were to be appointed by the Member State governments from amongst the Members of the Commission.

[254] In choosing the person called upon to hold the offices of High Representative 'due account is to be taken of the need to respect the geographical and demographic diversity of the Union and its Member States': Declaration (No. 6), annexed to the Lisbon Treaty, see n. 111, *supra*. The first High Representative appointed was Baroness Catherine Ashton of Upholland, initially in the first Barroso Commission for its remaining term (European Council Decision 209/880/EU, OJ 2009 L315/49) and thereafter in the second Barroso Commission (European Council Decision 209/950/EU, OJ 2009 L328/69).

end his or her tenure by the same procedure by which he or she is appointed. In contrast, when the High Representative carries out the tasks entrusted to him or her as a member of the Commission, he or she will be bound by Commission procedures (Article 18(1) and (4) TEU).[255]

Term of office. Since the EU Treaty, the Commissioners' (renewable) term of office is five years (Article 17(3) TEU), like the European Parliament. Before, their term of office was four years. This means that the legislative work is interrupted every five years when the membership of the institutions changes. The association of the term of office of members of the Commission with the election of the European Parliament enables the political outcome of the elections to be reflected, to some extent, in the composition of the Commission. So long as the European Council has not appointed new members to the Commission at the end of the latter's term of office, the old Commission remains in office, but its powers are limited to dealing with current business.[256] This occurred most recently with the Juncker Commission, whose term ended on 31 October 2019 with the von der Leyen Commission only being appointed on 28 November 2019 to take office as from 1 December 2019.[257]

12.066

Independence. In carrying out its responsibilities, the Commission must be completely independent (Article 17(3), third subpara. TEU). This applies, in the first place, to the Commission as an institution, which has to weigh the different interests of groups and Member States against the general interest of the Union. As far as individual members of the Commission are concerned, this means that they may not seek or take instructions from any government or any other institution, body, office, or entity; that they may not, in principle, engage in any other gainful or other occupation; and that they must take care in accepting certain appointments or benefits even after they have ceased to hold office (Articles 17(3), third subpara. TEU and 245, second para. TFEU). The Member States also undertake to respect the independence of members of the Commission (Article 245 TFEU). In point of fact, they are entitled to assert their national interests in the Council.

12.067

Having regard to the importance of the responsibilities assigned to them, it is important that the members of the Commission observe the highest standards of conduct. Hence, it is their duty to ensure that the general interest of the Union takes precedence at all times, not only over national interests, but also over personal interests.[258] When entering upon

---

[255] Article 18(4) TEU provides that the High Representative is bound by Commission procedures 'to the extent that this is consistent with paragraphs 2 and 3'. Likewise, where the President of the Commission requests the High Representative to resign, he or she will have to do so 'in accordance with the procedure set out in Article 18(1)' (Article 17(6) TEU). Where a motion of censure is carried and the Commission is to resign as a body, the High Representative is under a duty only to 'resign from the duties that he or she carries out in the Commission' (Article 17(8) TEU).

[256] This has been the view taken by the Commission's Legal Service, see already *Europe*, No. 6396, 12 January 1995, 6.

[257] Likewise, after the expiry of the term of office of the Prodi Commission on 31 October 2004, that Commission stayed into office until the appointment of the (first) Barroso Commission on 19 November 2004 (OJ 2004 L344/33), which on its turn stayed beyond the end of its term on 31 October 2009 as the appointment of the new Commission was delayed, in view of the pending ratification of the Lisbon Treaty, until 9 February 2010 (OJ 2010 L38/7). Earlier, a similar situation occurred after the expiry of the term of office of the Commission presided over by Jacques Delors on 6 January 1995 because the European Parliament wished to pronounce on the nominated President (Santer) and other Members of the Commission at its first plenary session which MEPs from the Member States which acceded on 1 January 1995 were to attend, which led to their appointment by decision of the representatives of the governments of the Member States of 23 January 1995, OJ 1995 L19/51.

[258] C-432/04, *Commission v Cresson*, 2006, paras 70–1.

their duties, they give a solemn undertaking that they will respect these obligations. This is done at a formal sitting of the Court of Justice. The Commission has specified the duties of independence in a Code of Conduct, including rules on participation in politics and on activities after holding office.[259] In the event of a breach of the obligations following from the Treaties, the Commission itself, and the Council, may apply directly to the Court of Justice (Article 245(2), second subpara. TFEU), after the person concerned has been informed, in sufficient time, of the complaints made against him or her and after he or she has had the opportunity of being heard.[260] If the Court finds that a breach of a certain degree of gravity has been committed, it may impose a penalty, such as compulsory retirement or the deprivation in whole or in part of the right to a pension or other benefits in its stead (Articles 245, second para. and 247 TFEU). This procedure was used for the first time when the Council brought an action against Martin Bangemann, a former member of the Commission who resigned in order to take up an appointment with a company active in the sector for which he had been competent.[261] However, the application was withdrawn after Mr Bangemann gave an assurance that he would not take up any appointment with any undertaking in the sector for a certain period.[262] In contrast, the Court had to give judgment on an application brought against former Commissioner Edith Cresson for appointing a close acquaintance as her 'personal adviser', in dubious circumstances. The Court held that she had acted in breach of the obligations arising from her office as a member of the Commission.[263]

12.068   **Voluntary or compulsory retirement.** Apart from formal replacement, or death, a member of the Commission gives up his or her duties on voluntary or compulsory retirement. Compulsory retirement takes place where the European Parliament decides for political reasons to pass a motion of censure requiring the Commission to resign as a body (Article 234 TFEU; see para. 12-006, *supra*) or where the Court of Justice compulsorily retires a member of the Commission on an application by the Council or the Commission on the ground that he or she no longer fulfils the conditions required for the performance of his or her duties or if he or she has been guilty of serious misconduct (Article 247 TFEU). A member of the Commission also has to resign if the President so requests (Article 17(6), second subpara. TEU).[264] This power has been given to the President in case a member of the Commission would refuse to resign voluntarily at a time when the President has lost confidence in this member and is of the opinion that the continued membership of this member

---

[259] Commission Decision of 31 January 2018 on a Code of Conduct for the Members of the European Commission, OJ 2018 C65/7,
[260] C-432/04, *Commission v Cresson*, 2006, paras 103–9.
[261] See the Council Decision of 9 July 1999 (OJ 1999 L192/55; for the application thereof, see Case C-290/99, *Council v Bangemann*, OJ 1999 C314/2); see also the resolution of the European Parliament of 22 July 1999 (OJ 1999 C301/34).
[262] See the Council Decision of 17 December 1999 on the settlement of the Bangemann case, OJ 2000 L16/73, which was subject to the proviso that Mr Bangemann would withdraw his action against the Council Decision of 9 July 1999 (T-208/99, OJ 1999 C314/14). See also T-227/99 and T-134/00, *Kvaerner Warnow Werft v Commission*, 2002, paras 47–60 (validity of a Commission decision unaffected by the fact that Mr Bangemann had taken leave of absence after his announcement that he had accepted an appointment outside the Commission before the Council's decision not to replace him) and C-334/99, *Germany v Commission*, 2003, paras 17–27 (following the Commission's decision to grant Mr Bangemann 'leave of absence' until the Council decided whether to replace him, the composition of the Commission was lawful, since that decision had no influence on Mr Bangemann's status as Member of the Commission).
[263] C-432/04, *Commission v Cresson*, 2006, paras 70–71.
[264] Before the Lisbon Treaty, Article 217(4) EC required the President to obtain the approval of the College before requesting a member of the Commission to resign.

may jeopardize the public trust in the Commission.[265] As far as the High Representative is concerned, the President's request has to be confirmed by the European Council, acting by a qualified majority (Articles 17(6), second subpara. and Article 18(1) TEU). In each of these cases, the Council, by common accord with the President of the Commission and after consulting the European Parliament,[266] appoints a replacement (a new member of the same nationality) by a qualified majority vote or decides, unanimously on a proposal from the President of the Commission, that the vacancy is not to be filled (Article 246, second and third paras TFEU).[267] However, the High Representative must be replaced by the European Council, acting by a qualified majority and with the agreement of the President of the Commission (Article 18(1) TEU and Article 246, fifth para. TFEU). Where the President has to be replaced, the procedure laid down in Article 17(7) TEU has to be applied (see Article 246, fourth para. TFEU).

In the event that the Commission as a body is made to resign by the European Parliament, the Commission, including the High Representative, remains in office and continues to deal with current business until it is replaced (Article 234 TFEU). The same is true where all members of the Commission voluntarily resign (Article 246, sixth para. TFEU). That was different before the Lisbon Treaty, as the Treaties merely provided that, in the case of voluntary resignation, the resigning members of the Commission remained in office until such time as they were replaced (see Article 215, fourth para. EC).[268] Nevertheless, the members of the Commission who resigned as a body on 16 March 1999 declared that, although under the Treaties their powers were not limited in the circumstances (voluntary resignation), they had decided to exercise their powers in a restrictive manner until such time as they were replaced, that is to say, they would deal with current and urgent business, and comply with their institutional and legal obligations, but not take fresh political initiatives.[269]

---

[265] See T-562/12, *Dalli v Commission*, 2015, paras 136–42. In that case the General Court had to determine whether a member of the Commission had voluntarily resigned on 16 October 2012 without a prior request by President Barroso (confirmed by order of 14 April 2016, C-394/15 P, *Dalli v Commission*, 2016).

[266] In such case, the European Parliament does not have a right to consent. However, under point 6 of the Framework agreement between the European Parliament and the Commission (see n. 19, *supra*), the President of the Commission will 'seriously consider the result of the Parliament's consultation before giving accord to the decision of the Council'.

[267] E.g., if the Commission's term of office is coming to an end, the Council may take a unanimous decision under Article 246, third para. TFEU that there is no need to fill the vacancy. See, e.g., Council Decision 1999/493/EC, ECSC, Euratom of 9 July 1999 on the composition of the Commission, OJ 1999 L192/53. In 2019, the Council did not adopt the proposal by President Juncker not to fill in the vacancies caused by the resignation of two members of the Commission who had been elected to the European Parliament (see doc. C(2019)5151 final). Eventually, however, the Council did not seek to appoint replacements.

[268] Therefore, after their decision of 16 March 1999 to resign as a body, the Commission's powers were not confined to dealing with current business: T-219/99, *British Airways v Commission*, 2003, paras 46–56. In an earlier case, the General Court did not rule on whether or not the Commission's powers were limited after 16 March 1999: T-228/99 and T-233/99, *Westdeutsche Landesbank Girozentrale v Commission*, 2003, paras 94–100 (decision by which the Commission declared State aid incompatible with the common market falls in any event under the heading of 'current business').

[269] Press communiqué of 17 March 1999, doc. IP/99/186. See Rodrigues, 'Quelques réflexions juridiques à propos de la démission de la Commission européenne—de la responsabilité des institutions communautaires comme "manifestation ultime de la démocratie"?' (1999) RMCUE 472-83; Tomkins, 'Responsibility and Resignation in the European Commission' (1999) MLR 744-65.

C. Operation

12.069 **Rules of Procedure.** The Commission has to act collectively in accordance with the Treaties and its Rules of Procedure, adopted pursuant to Article 249(1) TFEU.[270] It works under the political guidance of its President, who is to decide on its internal organization in order to ensure that it acts consistently, efficiently, and as a collegiate body (Article 17(6)(b) TFEU).[271] The President of the Commission convenes the Commission to meet at least once a week (Commission Rules of Procedure, Article 5). Its meetings are not public, and its discussions are confidential (Commission Rules of Procedure, Article 9). The Secretary-General and the President's Head of Cabinet attend its meetings and other persons may be heard (Commission Rules of Procedure, Article 10).

12.070 **Collective responsibility.** The Commission acts by a majority of its members (Article 250, first para. TFEU). It is quorate if a majority of its members is present (Article 250, second para. TFEU and Commission Rules of Procedure, Article 7). However, decisions may be taken by means of a written procedure whereby a proposal made by one or more members is deemed to have been adopted if no member enters a reservation within a specified period or asks that the proposal be discussed at a meeting.[272] The fact that Commissioners participate equally in decision-making is indicative of the collegiate nature of the Commission, which means that 'decisions should be the subject of a collective deliberation and that all the members of the college of Commissioners bear collective responsibility on the political level for all decisions adopted'.[273] In a framework agreement between the European Parliament and the Commission, it is stated, however, that, without prejudice to the principle of Commission collegiality, each member of the Commission is to take political responsibility for action in the field of which he or she is in charge.[274]

Provided that the principle of collective responsibility is fully respected, the Commission may empower one or more of its members to take management or administrative measures on its behalf and subject to such restrictions and conditions as it shall impose.[275]

---

[270] The present Rules of Procedure were adopted by the Commission on 29 November 2000 (OJ 2000 L55/60), and most recently amended on 6 November 2011 (see OJ 2011 L296/58). Previous versions date from 18 September 1999 (OJ 1999 L252/41) and 17 February 1993 (OJ 1993 L230/16, adopted pursuant to Article 16 of the Merger Treaty) and 31 January 1963 (provisionally retained after the Merger Treaty entered into force by decision of 6 July 1967, JO 1967 147/1). Annexed to the Rules of Procedure are, *inter alia*, the Commission provisions on security (Commission Decision of 29 November 2001, OJ 2001 L317/1), the detailed rules on public access to documents (Commission Decision of 5 December 2001, OJ 2001 L345/94), and the provisions on document management (Commission Decision of 23 January 2002, OJ 2002 L21/23).

[271] See Müller, *Political Leadership and the European Commission Presidency* (OUP, 2019); Karagiannis, 'Le Président de la Commission' (2000) CDE 36–55.

[272] Commission Rules of Procedure, Article 12. According to that Article, the procedure in question may be employed only if the departments involved are in agreement and the proposal has been approved by the Commission's Legal Service.

[273] 5/85, *AKZO Chemie v Commission*, 1986, para. 30. For the principle of collegiality, see also Mistò, 'La collégialité de la Commission européenne' (2003) RDUE 189–255.

[274] Framework Agreement on relations between Parliament and the Commission of 20 October 2010 (n. 19, *supra*), point 4.

[275] Commission Rules of Procedure, Article 13(1). According to the Court of Justice, the system of delegation of authority remains within the Commission's power of internal organization since the Commission does not thereby divest itself of powers (the decisions may still be the subject of judicial review as Commission decisions and the Commission may always reserve certain decisions for itself) and the procedure is necessary for the sound functioning of the Commission's decision-making power: 5/85, *AKZO Chemie v Commission*, 1986, paras 35–7; 97–99/87, *Dow Chemica Ibérica and Others v Commission*, 1989, para. 58; T-300/05 and T-316/05, *Cyprus v Commission*,

D. Internal organization

Directorates-General. The President of the Commission decides on its internal organization and lays down guidelines within which the Commission is to work (Article 17(6)(a) and (b) TEU). He or she structures the responsibilities incumbent upon the Commission, allocates them among its members, and may reshuffle the allocation of those responsibilities during the Commission's term of office (Article 248 TFEU). Accordingly, the President assigns to members of the Commission special fields of activity with regard to which they are specifically responsible for the preparation of Commission work and the implementation of its decisions.[276] The President of the Commission is to notify the European Parliament in due time if he or she intends to reshuffle the allocation of responsibilities amongst the members of the Commission.[277] The members of the Commission are to carry out the duties devolved upon them by the President under his or her authority (Article 248 TFEU). The members of the Commission have their own private office ('cabinet') and give policy directions to one or more services. The Commission's administrative services consist of Directorates-General and equivalent departments (Commission Rules of Procedure, Article 21). The Directorates-General (DGs), which are subdivided into directorates, each deal with a specific area of policy under the leadership of a Director-General.[278] Other departments include the Secretariat-General, the Legal Service, and a number of offices.[279]

12.071

2009, paras 211–15 (on the notion of 'management and administrative measures': paras 216–24). See the earlier recognition of the delegation of the power of signature for management and administrative measures: 48/69, *ICI v Commission*, 1972, paras 12–14, and 52/69, *Geigy v Commission*, 1972, para. 5; 8/72, *Cementhandelaren v Commission*, 1972, paras 11–13; 43 and 63/82, *VBVB and VBBB v Commission*, 1984, paras 12–14. No management or administrative measure constitutes a decision finding an infringement of Article 101(1) TFEU in the authentic language: T-79/89, T-84/89, T-85/89, T-86/89, T-89/89, T-91/89, T-92/89, T-94/89, T-96/89, T-98/89, T-102/89, and T-104/89, *BASF and Others v Commission*, 1992, paras 57–9; C-137/92 P, *Commission v BASF and Others*, 1994, paras 62–5; T-80/89, T-81/89, T-83/89, T-87/89, T-88/89, T-90/89, T-93/89, T-95/89, T-97/89, T-99/89, T-100/89, T-101/89, T-103/89, T-105/89, T-107/89, and T-112/89, *BASF and Others v Commission*, 1995, paras 96–102. With regard to State aid, see T-435/93, *ASPEC and Others v Commission*, 1995, paras 100–4 and T-442/93, *AAC and Others v Commission*, 1995, paras 81–95. Neither does a decision to issue a reasoned opinion or to commence infringement proceedings before the Court of Justice constitute a measure of administration or management: C-191/95, *Commission v Germany*, 1998, paras 33–7. Powers conferred by delegation may be subdelegated to the Directors-General and Heads of Department unless this is expressly prohibited in the empowering decision (Commission Rules of Procedure, Article 13(3)).

[276] Commission Rules of Procedure, Article 3(2), second subpara.

[277] Point 7 of the Framework Agreement of 20 October 2011 on relations between the European Parliament and the Commission (n. 19, *supra*).

[278] For internal policy: DG Agriculture and Rural Development (AGRI), DG Climate Action (CLIMA), DG Competition (COMP), DG Communications Networks, Content and Technology (CONNECT), DG Defence Industry and Space (DEFIS), DG Economic and Financial Affairs (ECFIN), DG Education, Youth, Sport and Culture (EAC), DG Employment, Social Affairs and Inclusion (EMPL), DG Energy (ENER), DG Environment (ENV), DG Financial Stability, Financial Services and Capital Markets Union (FISMA), DG Internal Market, Industry, Entrepreneurship and SMEs (GROW), DG Migration and Home Affairs (HOME), DG Justice and Consumers (JUST), DG Maritime Affairs and Fisheries (MARE), DG Mobility and Transport (MOVE), DG for Structural Reform Support (REFORM), DG Regional and Urban Policy (REGIO), DG Research and Innovation (RTD), DG Health and Food Safety (SANTE), and DG Taxation and Customs Union (TAXUD). For external relations: DG European Civil Protection and Humanitarian Aid Operations (ECHO), DG International Partnerships (INTPA), DG European Neighbourhood and Enlargement Negotiations (NEAR), and DG Trade (TRADE). For general services: DG Communication (COMM), DG Budget (BUDG), DG Human Resources and Security (HR), DG Informatics (DIGIT), DG for Interpretation (SCIC), and DG for Translation (DGT). For more information, see the Commission's website: https://ec.europa.eu/info/departments_en.

[279] Such as the Internal Audit Service (IAS); the internal 'think tank' Inspire, Debate, Engage and Accelerate Action (IDEA); the Foreign Policy Instruments (FPI); the Joint Research Centre (JRC); the Offices for infrastructure

The different departments closely cooperate in the preparation and implementation of Commission decisions and must consult each other before submitting a document to the Commission (Commission Rules of Procedure, Article 23(1) to (3)). The Legal Service must, in any event, be consulted on all drafts or proposals for legal instruments and on all documents that may have legal implications (Commission Rules of Procedure, Article 23(4)). The Commission's seat is in Brussels, but a number of its departments are established in Luxembourg.[280] With around 32,000 officials, the Commission constitutes the largest of the institutions.

---

and logistics in Brussels (OIB) and Luxembourg (OIL); the Statistical Office (Eurostat), the European Anti-Fraud Office (OLAF); and the Paymaster Office (PMO). See also, on an interinstitutional basis, the Publications Office (OP) and the European Personnel Selection Office (EPSO) (see para. 13-043, *infra*).

[280] See the sole Article, para. (c), of the Protocol on Seats (para. 14-020, *infra*), which refers, as regards the departments to remain in Luxembourg, to the list in the Decision on Provisional Location of 8 April 1965 (para. 14-019, *infra*). See also C-137/92 P, *Commission v BASF and Others*, 1994, paras 41–2 (for the purpose of the extension of procedural time-limits on account of distance, the Commission has its 'habitual residence' in Brussels).

13
Other Institutions and Bodies of the Union

Institutions, bodies, offices, and agencies. Besides the four political institutions discussed in the previous chapter, the Union has three other 'institutions': the Court of Justice of the European Union, the European Central Bank (ECB), and the Court of Auditors. The institutional framework of the Union consists of a range of other bodies, offices, and agencies, some of which having legal personality. The political institutions are assisted by advisory committees, such as the Economic and Social Committee and the Committee of the Regions (Article 13(4) TFEU). Furthermore, the European Investment Bank fulfils its tasks as an independent legal person. After discussing the European Ombudsman, who also acts independently (Article 288 TFEU), this chapter presents the other Union bodies, offices, and agencies.

13.001

I. The Court of Justice of the European Union

Establishment. The institution known as the Court of Justice of the European Union consists of two independent courts: the Court of Justice and the General Court.[1] Originally, the Court of Justice exercised jurisdiction in accordance with each of the three Community Treaties and the protocols on the Statute appended thereto. By means of a new Protocol on the Statute of the Court of Justice of the European Union, the Treaty of Nice introduced a single Statute for this institution.[2] From 1 September 1989, the Court of Justice consisted of two independent courts, one bearing that name, the other entitled the Court of First Instance.[3] Since the Lisbon Treaty, the full name 'Court of Justice of the European Union' is used to distinguish the institution from the independent court that is called 'Court of Justice', whereas the Court of First Instance was given the name 'General Court'. The Lisbon Treaty also made it possible to establish 'specialised courts' under the aegis of the Court of Justice of the European Union (Article 19(1), first subpara. TEU).

13.002

---

[1] For the website of the Court of Justice of the European Union, see http://curia.europa.eu/.

[2] See now Protocol (No. 3), annexed to the TEU, TFEU, and the EAEC Treaty, on the Statute of the Court of Justice of the European Union, OJ 2010 C83/210, which replaced Protocol (No. 6) on the Statute of the Court of Justice, annexed to the EU Treaty, the EC Treaty, and the EAEC Treaty (OJ 2001 C80/53). The provisions of the Statute have the same normative force as Treaty articles (see Article 51 TEU and Article 207 EAEC), although the European Parliament and the Council, acting in accordance with the ordinary legislative procedure and at the request of the Court of Justice and after consultation of the Commission, or on a proposal from the Commission and after consultation of the Court of Justice, may amend the provisions of the Statute (with the exception of Title I and Article 64: see Article 281 TFEU).

[3] Council Decision 88/591/ECSC, EEC, Euratom of 24 October 1988 establishing a Court of First Instance of the European Communities [hereinafter: CFI Decision], OJ 1988 L319/1, and L241, based on Article 32d ECSC, Article 168a EEC, and Article 140a EAEC. The EU Treaty rooted the existence of the Court of First Instance in the EC Treaty itself (see former Article 225(1) EC).

'Specialized courts' sit as first instance courts and may hear cases in specific areas. To this end, the European Parliament and the Council, acting in accordance with the ordinary legislative procedure, have to adopt a regulation, either on a proposal from the Commission after consultation of the Court of Justice or at the request of the Court of Justice after consultation of the Commission, which lays down the rules on the organization of the specialized court and the extent of the jurisdiction conferred upon it (Article 257, first and second paras, TFEU). To date, only one specialized court was established, namely the European Union Civil Service Tribunal,[4] which, from 2005 until 2016, settled disputes between the European Union and its staff. On 1 September 2016 the European Union Civil Service Tribunal was abolished, and its jurisdiction was transferred to the General Court.[5] This was part of a broader reform in 2015, when it was decided to progressively increase the number of judges at the General Court to better deal with the rising number of cases before the General Court and the long delays in deciding those cases.

Unless the Statute of the Court of Justice of the European Union or the regulation establishing the specialized court provides otherwise, the Treaty provisions relating to the Court of Justice are to apply to the General Court and the specialized courts.[6]

A. Jurisdiction

13.003 **Decentralized enforcement of Union law.** The Court of Justice of the European Union ensures that in the interpretation and application of the Treaties the law is observed (Article 19(1), first subpara. TEU). This does not mean that the Court of Justice and the General Court automatically hear and determine all disputes whose outcome depends on the correct application of Union law. The founders of the Communities and the Union opted for a system under which enforcement of Community and Union law was left, in principle, to the national courts. Since the Lisbon Treaty, the Treaties explicitly state that Member States must provide remedies sufficient to ensure effective legal protection in the fields covered by Union law (Article 19(1), second subpara. TEU). This implies that Member States must ensure the independence and impartiality of the courts that may have to decide on litigation in the fields covered by Union law (see paras 29-003–29-004).[7]

A dispute relating to Union law may be brought before the Court of Justice of the European Union only if this is permitted under one of the procedures prescribed by the Treaties.[8]

---

[4] Council Decision (2004/752/EC, Euratom) of 2 November 2004 establishing the European Union Civil Service Tribunal, OJ 2004 L333/7. See also Declaration (No. 16), annexed to the Nice Treaty, which called upon the Court of Justice and the Commission 'to prepare as swiftly as possible a draft decision establishing a judicial panel which has jurisdiction to deliver judgments at first instance on disputes between the Community and its servants' (OJ 2001 C80/80). For a discussion, see Mahoney, 'The Civil Service Tribunal: The Benefits and Drawbacks of a Specialised Judicial Body' (2011) Human Rights LJ 11; Kraemer, 'The European Union Civil Service Tribunal: A New Community Court Examined After Four Years of Operation' (2009) CMLRev 1873–1913.

[5] Regulation (EU, Euratom) 2016/1192 of the European Parliament and of the Council of 6 July 2016 on the transfer to the General Court of jurisdiction at first instance in disputes between the European Union and its servants, OJ 2016 L200/137.

[6] See Articles 254, sixth para. and 257, sixth para. TFEU.

[7] C-64/16, *Associação Sindical dos Juízes Portugueses*, 2018, paras 27-52; C-216/18 PPU, *LM*, 2018, paras 33-79; C-619/18 *Commission v Poland*, 2019, paras 42–59, 71–97, and 108–24; C-192/18, *Commission v Poland*, 2019, paras 98–136; C-585/18, C-624/18, and C-625/18 *A.K.*, 2019, paras 114–70.

[8] See 66/76, *CFDT v Council*, 1977, para. 8; C-583/11 P, *Inuit Tapiriit Kanatami v European Parliament and Council*, 2013, para. 98.

When interpreting the provisions with respect to these procedures, the Court of Justice has to respect the limits to the jurisdiction conferred on it by the Treaties.[9] The Court of Justice has interpreted its own jurisdiction only exceptionally in a manner exceeding the literal scope of a given procedure, *inter alia*, in order to fill a lacuna in the system of legal protection or to secure the coherence of the Union's legal order.[10]

Dual purpose of remedies. According to Article 19(3) TEU, the Court of Justice of the European Union: (a) rules on actions brought by a Member State, an institution, or a natural or legal person; (b) gives preliminary rulings, at the request of courts or tribunals of the Member States, on the interpretation of Union law or the validity of acts adopted by the institutions; and (c) rules in other cases provided for in the Treaties. As set out in Part VI of this book these procedures serve a dual purpose. On the one hand, they enable the Court, together with the national courts, to see to it that Union law is correctly interpreted and applied in the Member States (see Chapter 29). On the other, they seek to guarantee judicial redress against Union institutions and bodies, agencies, and offices for individuals, Member States, or (other) institutions that are affected by acts of the Union (see Chapter 30). **13.004**

(a) Preliminary references. The Court of Justice decides on preliminary references made by national courts and tribunals as to the interpretation of Treaty provisions or the interpretation or validity of acts of the institutions, bodies, offices, or agencies of the Union (Article 267 TFEU; see also para. 19-015 *et seq.*, *infra*). This procedure serves to assure the uniform application of Union law in the Member States. The procedure enables natural and legal persons to have Union law applied correctly in disputes pending before national courts or tribunals. Observations in preliminary reference procedures may be made by the parties before the national court, but also by the Member States, for example, when the preliminary reference relates to a possible conflict between national law and Union law. The Court of Justice also has jurisdiction to answer preliminary questions referred by national courts on the interpretation of conventions concluded by the Member States and over which they have given the Court jurisdiction to interpret the convention by way of a Protocol (see paras 28-018–28-020). **13.005**

(b) Direct actions against Union acts. In addition, the Court of Justice of the European Union offers judicial protection to natural and legal persons, to Member States, and to institutions, bodies, offices, or agencies of the Union when they bring an action against an (other) institution, body, office, or agency of the Union.[11] This can be done pursuant to **13.006**

---

[9] C-50/00 P, *Unión de Pequeños Agricultores v Council*, 2002, paras 44–5.

[10] See 294/83, *Les Verts v European Parliament*, 1986, paras 23–5, and C-70/88, *European Parliament v Council*, 1990, paras 11–27 (recognition of the fact that the Parliament may be a defendant or an applicant in proceedings, respectively, despite the wording of Article 173 EEC, for the sake of institutional balance; para. 16-010, *infra*); C-2/88, Imm. *Zwartveld and Others* 1990, paras 15–26 (interpretation of the privileges and immunities of the Communities in the light of the duty of sincere cooperation within the meaning of Article 10 EC, para. 5-047, *supra*); 314/85, *Foto-Frost*, 1987, paras 12–17 (where it was held that national courts have no power to declare Community acts invalid in spite of the limitation of the obligation to make references for preliminary rulings to national courts of last instance); C-47/07 P, *Masdar*, 2008, paras 49–50 (interpretation of the Treaty provisions on actions for damages against the Community so as to include also actions for unjust enrichment); C-72/15, *PJSC Rosneft Oil Company*, 2017, paras 58–81 (review of the validity of restrictive measures pursuant to Article 275 TFEU also possible through the preliminary reference procedure). See Lenaerts, 'The Rule of Law and the Coherence of the Judicial System of the European Union' (2007) CMLRev 1–35.

[11] Only in one special case, provided for in Article 14.2 of the Protocol on the Statute of the European System of Central Banks and of the European Central Bank, does the Court of Justice also have jurisdiction to review the validity of a decision taken by national authorities, see C-202/18 and C-238/18, *Rimšēvičs v Latvia*, 2019, paras 43–63.

Article 263 TFEU (action for annulment), Article 265 TFEU (action for failure to act), and Articles 268 TFEU and 340 TFEU (action for damages) (see para. 30-002 *et seq., infra*). Natural or legal persons may only bring an action for annulment pursuant to Article 263(4) TFEU against binding acts of the institutions, bodies, offices, or agencies, that are addressed to them, or which are of direct and individual concern to them, as well as against regulatory acts which are of direct concern to them and do not require further implementing measures.[12] Natural and legal persons who cannot bring a direct action challenging the legality of an act with a general scope of application because of this admissibility requirement, may challenge the validity of such an act in an incidental manner by raising an exception of illegality (Article 277 TFEU) or before the national court, which is not competent to declare such an act invalid,[13] but may be moved to make a preliminary reference as to the validity thereof to the Court of Justice. In this way, the Treaties provide for a complete system of remedies and procedures to review the legality of acts of the institutions, bodies, offices, or agencies of the Union (see para. 30-041 *et seq., infra*).[14] The Court of Justice of the European Union also decides disputes between the Union and its civil servants and other staff members (Article 270 TFEU).

13.007 (c) **Infringement actions.** The Court of Justice further rules on actions brought by the European Commission pursuant to Articles 258 and 260 TFEU against Member States for failure to comply with their obligations under the Treaties (see para. 29-039 *et seq., infra*). A Member State may also bring such a case against another Member State in accordance with Article 259 TFEU.

13.008 (d) **Other procedures.** The Court of Justice of the European Union decides cases that are submitted to it pursuant to an arbitration clause (Article 272 TFEU). In the future the Court may also be given jurisdiction over disputes between private parties relating to European intellectual property rights.[15] Furthermore, Member States may submit a case to the Court of Justice pursuant to an arbitration clause (Article 273 TFEU).[16] In accordance with Article 344 TFEU Member States are under an obligation not to submit a dispute concerning the interpretation or application of the Treaties to any method of settlement other than those provided for therein. This means that the Court of Justice has exclusive jurisdiction over disputes between Member States relating to the interpretation or application of Union law. Accordingly, Member States who oppose each other in respect of an alleged breach of Union law obligations are precluded from submitting such a dispute to an international court.[17] Finally, the Court of Justice gives advisory opinions pursuant to Article 218(11) TFEU in respect of international agreements which the Union purports to conclude.

13.009 **Jurisdiction of Court of Justice and General Court.** Since 31 October 1989, part of the jurisdiction of the Court of Justice of the European Union outlined above has been transferred

---

[12] C-456/13 P, *T & L Sugars v Commission*, 2016, paras 29–51.
[13] 314/85, *Foto-Frost*, 1987, para. 20.
[14] 294/83, *Les Verts v European Parliament*, 1986, para. 23; C-50/00 P, *Unión de Pequeños Agricultores v Council*, 2002, paras 40–2; C-583/11 P, *Inuit Tapiriit Kanatami v European Parliament and Council*, 2013, paras 92–6; C-274/12 P, *Telefónica v Commission*, 2013, para. 57.
[15] This will happen when the Council is to confer jurisdiction pursuant to Article 262 TFEU.
[16] C-370/12, *Pringle*, 2012, paras 170–7; C-648/15, *Austria v Germany*, 2017, paras 19–30.
[17] C-459/03, *Commission v Ireland*, 2006, paras 123–38; see also C-284/16, *Achmea*, paras 31–60.

to the General Court (before the Lisbon Treaty: the Court of First Instance).[18] The General Court was set up in order to alleviate the Court of Justice's case load and to assign specific tasks to each of the two courts, thereby improving the quality of judicial review.[19] This re-ordering of jurisdiction was equally intended to allow the Court of Justice to concentrate on its role as the highest court guaranteeing the unity and consistency of Union law.[20] Initially, the General Court ruled only on some direct actions brought by natural and legal persons against Community institutions and bodies. The Treaty of Nice enlarged the jurisdiction of the General Court.[21] According to Article 256(1) TFEU, the General Court has jurisdiction over all direct actions against institutions, bodies, offices, or agencies with the exception of those assigned to a specialized court and those reserved in the Statute for the Court of Justice. Article 256(3) TFEU adds that the General Court may be given jurisdiction to hear and determine questions referred for a preliminary ruling in specific areas laid down by the Statute.[22] Consequently, the exact jurisdiction of the Court of Justice and of the General Court can only be determined by reference to Article 51 of the Statute of the Court of Justice of the European Union, as last amended in 2019.[23]

At present, only the Court of Justice has jurisdiction to give preliminary rulings, since the Statute does not confer any jurisdiction on the General Court in this regard. Jurisdiction is further reserved to the Court of Justice in respect of actions for annulment, or for failure to act, brought by an institution against a legislative act or an act of the European Parliament, the European Council, the Council, the Commission, or the European Central Bank, or a failure by the institutions concerned to adopt such acts. The Court of Justice also has exclusive jurisdiction over actions for annulment or for failure to act brought by a Member State against a legislative act or an act of the European Parliament, the European Council, or the Council (with the exception of certain Council acts of a clearly executive nature, such as decisions in respect of State aid, trade protection measures, or implementing acts taken by the Council pursuant to Article 291 TFEU[24]), or a failure by the institutions concerned

---

[18] There has been an incremental transfer of jurisdiction, first by Article 3 of the CFI Decision (OJ 1988 L319/1, which came into force on 31 October 1989), as amended by Council Decision 93/350 of 8 June 1993 (OJ 1993 L144/21, which took effect on 1 August 1993), by Council Decision 94/149 of 7 March 1994 (OJ 1994 L66/29, which entered into force on 15 March 1994) and Decision 1999/291/EC, ECSC, Euratom of 26 April 1999 (OJ 1999 L114/52, which entered into force on 16 May 1999). The CFI Decision was repealed on the entry into force on 1 February 2003 of a new CJEU Statute (n. 2, *supra*).
[19] See Forwood, 'The Court of First Instance, its Development and Future Role in the Legal Architecture of the European Union', in Arnull, Eeckhout, and Tridimas (eds), *Continuity and Change in EU Law—Essays in Honour of Sir Francis Jacobs* (OUP, 2008), 34: Lenaerts, 'Le Tribunal de première instance des Communautés européennes: regard sur une décennie d'activités et sur l'apport du double degré d'instance au droit communautaire' (2000) CDE 323–411.
[20] For further discussion of the jurisdiction of the courts, see Lenaerts, Gutman, and Nowak, *EU Procedural Law* (OUP, 2022).
[21] For the changes to the judicial system, see Azizi, 'Opportunities and Limits to the Transfer of Preliminary Reference Proceedings to the Court of First Instance', in Pernice, Kokott, and Saunders (eds), *The Future of the European Judicial System in a Comparative Perspective* (Nomos, 2006), 241; Tizzano, 'La Cour de justice après Nice: le transfert de compétences au Tribunal de première instance' (2002) RDUE 665–85; Craig, 'The Jurisdiction of the Community Courts Reconsidered' (2001) Texas Int'l LJ 555–86; Johnston, 'Judicial Reform and the Treaty of Nice' (2001) CMLRev 499–523; Lenaerts and Desomer, 'Het Verdrag van Nice en het "post-Nice"—debat over de toekomst van de Europese Unie' (2001–2002) RW 73, 78–81.
[22] The article adds, however, that when the General Court considers that the case requires a decision of principle likely to affect the unity or consistency of Union law, it may refer the case to the Court of Justice for a ruling (Article 256(3), second subpara. TFEU).
[23] See Regulation (EU, Euratom) 2019/629 of the European Parliament and of the Council of 17 April 2019 amending Protocol (No. 3) on the Statute of the Court of Justice of the European Union (OJ 2019 L111/1).
[24] CJEU Statute, Article 51, first para. The Council decisions against which actions are not reserved to the Court of Justice are 'decisions taken by the Council under the third subpara. of Article 108(2) TFEU; acts of the Council

to adopt such acts; over an action for annulment against an act of the Commission relating to a failure to comply with a judgment delivered by the Court under the second subpara. of Article 260(2) or (3) TFEU (collection by the Commission of lump sums and penalty payments); and over actions for annulment or for failure to act against an act, or a failure to act by, the Commission under Article 331(1) TFEU (relating to enhanced cooperation). This means that, alongside all actions brought by natural and legal persons against Union institutions, bodies, offices, or agencies, the General Court will hear and determine actions brought by Member States against all acts of, or failures to act by, the Commission (with the two exceptions mentioned); acts of, or failures to act by, the Council in the cases mentioned above; acts of, or failures to act by, other institutions (except for the European Parliament and the European Council; this therefore includes the European Central Bank); and acts of, or failures to act by, any Union body, office, or agency. Actions brought by an institution against acts of, or failures to act by, a Union body, office, or agency will equally be heard and determined by the General Court. Moreover, the General Court has jurisdiction to decide on appeals brought against decisions of the specialized courts (Article 256(2) TFEU).

There is a right of appeal to the Court of Justice against decisions of the General Court on points of law only (Article 256(1), second subpara. TFEU), except where the General Court decides on appeals brought against decisions of specialized courts. In the last case, the General Court's decisions may be subject to review by the Court of Justice only exceptionally, namely where there is a serious risk of the unity or consistency of Union law being affected.[25] This mechanism was in place when the General Court decided on appeals against decisions of the Civil Service Tribunal.[26] Moreover, an appeal against a decision of the General Court concerning a decision from an independent board of appeal of a Union office or agency, mentioned in the Statute, can be brought only if the Court of Justice first allows it to proceed for raising an issue that is significant with respect to the unity, consistency, or development of Union law.[27]

13.010 **Fields of limited jurisdiction.** The Court of Justice of the European Union exercises its powers in respect of disputes which come within the scope of the provisions of the Treaties. This encompasses, in full, matters of police and judicial cooperation in criminal matters (PJCC), over which jurisdiction of the Court of Justice used to be more limited (see para. 13-011, *infra*). By contrast, the Court still has only limited jurisdiction in the fields covered by the common foreign and security policy (CFSP; see para. 13-012, *infra*).

13.011 **Area of freedom, security, and justice.** Before the entry into force of the Lisbon Treaty, the jurisdiction of the Court of Justice of the European Union was limited as regards both matters falling under Title IV, Part Three EC Treaty (visas, asylum, immigration, and other

---

adopted pursuant to a Council regulation concerning measures to protect trade within the meaning of Article 207 TFEU; acts of the Council by which the Council exercises implementing powers in accordance with the second para. of Article 291 TFEU'.

[25] Article 260(2), second subpara. and (3), third subpara. TFEU. This may occur where the First Advocate General puts this proposition to the Court of Justice within one month of delivery of the decision by the General Court: CJEU Statute, Article 62. For an example, see C-197/09, RX-II, *M v EMEA*, 2009.

[26] See, e.g., C-579/12 RX-II, *Commission v Strack*, 2013 (the suffix 'RX' denotes 'réexamen' of 'reconsideration').

[27] CJEU Statute, Article 58a (condition introduced by Regulation 2019/679, n. 23, *supra*).

policies related to free movement of persons, which included judicial cooperation in civil matters) and matters of police and PJCC.[28]

The Court of Justice of the European Union now has full jurisdiction over all matters falling under Title V of Part Three of the TFEU (which incorporates both the provisions previously contained in Title IV of Part Three of the EC Treaty and the Union's competences in the field of PJCC). However, as regards PJCC, the Lisbon Treaty has not done away with the clause according to which the Court of Justice of the European Union has no jurisdiction to review the validity or proportionality of operations carried out by the police or other law-enforcement services of a Member State or the exercise of the responsibilities incumbent upon Member States with regard to the maintenance of law and order and the safeguarding of internal security (Article 276 TFEU).[29] As regards Chapter 4 (judicial cooperation in criminal matters) and Chapter 5 (police cooperation), the jurisdiction of the Court of Justice of the European Union remained subject to limits during a transitional period in respect of PJCC acts adopted before the entry into force of the Lisbon Treaty (see para. 2-008, *supra*).[30] Since the expiry on 30 November 2014 of the transitional period, the Court has obtained full jurisdiction in respect of all PJCC acts.[31]

Jurisdiction in the field of the CFSP. Even after the entry into force of the Lisbon Treaty, the Court of Justice of the European Union has no jurisdiction with respect to the provisions of the Treaties relating to the common foreign and security policy (CFSP) and acts adopted on the basis of those provisions (Article 24(1), second subpara. TEU and Article 275, first para. TFEU). This exclusion of jurisdiction is a derogation from the rule of general jurisdiction which Article 19 TEU confers on the Court to ensure that, in the interpretation and application of the Treaties, the law is observed, and must, therefore, be interpreted narrowly.[32] In this field, the Treaties confer on the Court only jurisdiction to (a) rule on actions for annulment brought by natural or legal persons against decisions of the Council providing for restrictive measures against natural and legal persons[33] and (b) ensure that implementation of the CFSP does not affect the application of Union competence in other areas (Article 275, second para. TFEU and Article 40 TEU).[34]

13.012

---

[28] See Barents, 'The Court of Justice after the Treaty of Lisbon' (2010) CMLRev 709; Lenaerts, 'The Contribution of the European Court of Justice to the Area of Freedom, Security and Justice' (2010) ICLQ 1–47; Fennelly, ' "The Area of Freedom, Security and Justice" and the European Court of Justice—A Personal View' (2000) ICLQ 1, 4–8.

[29] See, previously, Article 35(5) EU. However, there is no trace in the TFEU of Article 68(2) EC, according to which, as regards measures or decisions taken to ensure the absence of controls on persons crossing internal borders, the Court of Justice had no jurisdiction to rule on any measure or decision relating to the maintenance of law and order and the safeguarding of internal security.

[30] Pursuant to Protocol (No. 36) on transitional provisions, the Court retained jurisdiction over these acts under the conditions applicable before the entry into force of the Lisbon Treaty.

[31] However, the United Kingdom used the option provided for in Protocol (No. 36) on transitional provisions to elect that a PJCC act adopted prior to 1 December 2009 applied in the United Kingdom only if that Member State has expressly chosen this to be the case. See Protocol (No. 36), Article 10(4) and (5).

[32] C-439/13P, *Elitaliana v Eulex Kosovo*, 2015, para 42; C-455/14 P, *H v Council, Commission and European Union Police Mission (EUPM) in Bosnia and Herzegovina*, 2016, para. 40 *et seq.*; C-72/15, *PJSC Rosneft Oil Company*, 2017, paras 58–81.

[33] Article 275, second para. TFEU. For the restrictive measures in question, see para. 10-031, *infra*.

[34] See, before the entry into force of the Lisbon Treaty, C-91/05 *Commission v Council*, 2008.

B. Composition

13.013 **Judges and Advocates General.** The Court of Justice consists of one judge for each Member State (since 1 February 2020 twenty-seven in total), assisted by Advocates General and a Registrar (Article 19(2) TEU and Articles 252, first para. and 253, fifth para. TFEU). The Advocates General, 'acting with complete impartiality and independence', assist the Court of Justice by making, in open court, reasoned submissions prior to the Court's deliberations.[35] The number of Advocates General, which is currently fixed at eleven, may be increased by the Council, acting unanimously, if the Court of Justice so requests (Article 252, first para. TFEU)[36]. Currently there is one Advocate General coming from each of the five largest Member States (France, Germany, Italy, Poland, and Spain); the remaining Advocates General originate from the other Member States on the basis of a rotation schedule.[37]

The General Court consists of at least one judge for each Member State and a Registrar. In order to cope with the increasing workload of the General Court, the number of judges has been gradually increased to forty-seven (since 1 September 2016) and ultimately two for each Member State (as of 1 September 2019). No Advocates General are appointed to the General Court, but the Statute may provide for that Court to be assisted by Advocates General (Article 19(2), second subpara. TEU and Article 254, first and fourth paras TFEU).[38]

13.014 **Appointment.** The Judges and Advocates General of the Court of Justice and the Judges of the General Court are appointed by common accord of the governments of the Member States for a six-year term.[39] Membership is partially renewed every three years, although retiring members are eligible for reappointment (Article 19(2), third subpara. TEU and Articles 253 and 254 TFEU).[40] Since the Lisbon Treaty, appointment takes place after

---

[35] Article 252, second para. TFEU. On the role of the Advocate General, see Bobek, 'A Fourth in the Court: Why are there Advocates-General in the Court of Justice?' (2011-2012) CYELS 529; Sharpston, 'The Changing Role of the Advocate-General', in Arnull, Eeckhout, and Tridimas (eds), *Continuity and Change in EU Law—Essays in Honour of Sir Francis Jacobs* (OUP, 2008) 21. The Court of Justice considers that the fact that the parties may not submit observations in response to the Advocate General's opinion is not in conflict with Article 6 ECHR: C-17/98 *Emesa Sugar (Free Zone) and Aruba* (order) 2000, paras 10–18; rightly criticized in Lawson (2000) CMLRev 983–90; Benoît-Rohmer, 'L'affaire *Emesa Sugar*: l'institution de l'avocat general de la Cour de justice des Communautés européennes à l'épreuve de la jurisprudence *Vermeulen* de la Cour européenne des droits de l'homme' (2001) CDE 403–26. Initially, it appeared that the European Court of Human Rights took another view: see the judgment of 7 June 2001 in *Kress v France* (2001) SEW 440–4, with case note by Lawson; (2001) RTDE 809–19, with case note by Benoît-Rohmer. However, when invited to assess the ECJ's system, the European Court of Human Rights did not see any problem as parties have the right to ask for the oral procedure to be reopened: decision of 20 January 2009 in *PO Kokkelvisserij v Netherlands*, No. 13645/05, with case note by Vande Heyning (2009) CMLRev 2117–25.

[36] See Council Decision 2013/336/EU of 25 June 2013 increasing the number of Advocates-General of the Court of Justice of the European Union, OJ 2013 L179/92 (increase up to eleven as from 7 October 2015).

[37] Ibid.

[38] Article 49 of the Statute of the Court of Justice nevertheless retains the existing rule that one of the members of the General Court may be called upon to perform the task of an Advocate General. For the impact of Advocates General, see Ritter, 'A new look at the role and impact of Advocates-General collectively and individually', (2006) Colum JEL 751–74.

[39] See Bobek (ed.), *Selecting Europe's Judges. A Critical Review of the Appointment Procedures to the European Courts* (OUP, 2015); Dumbrovský, Petkova, and van der Sluis, 'Judicial Appointments: The Article 255 TFEU Advisory Panel and Selection Procedures in the Member States' (2014) CMLRev 455. For the fact that such act is not attributable to the Council and also not otherwise subject to judicial review, see C-424/20 P(R), *Representatives of the Governments of the Member States v Sharpston* (order of the Vice-President), 2020, paras 23–8; T-550/20 *Sharpston v Council and Representatives of the Governments of the Member States* (order), 2020, paras 31–8.

[40] See CJEU Statute, Article 9 (for the Court of Justice).

obtaining the opinion of a panel on the suitability of the candidates to perform the duties of Judge or Advocate General. That panel is composed of seven persons chosen from among former members of the Court of Justice and the General Court; members of national supreme courts; and lawyers of recognized competence, one of whom is to be proposed by the European Parliament. To that end, the Council, on the initiative of the President of the Court of Justice, adopts a decision establishing the panel's operating rules and a decision appointing its members (Article 255 TFEU).[41] The panel hears the candidates in private and issues a reasoned opinion, which is forwarded to the governments of the Member States.[42]

Members of the specialized courts are appointed by the Council, acting unanimously (Article 257, fourth para. TFEU).[43]

Conditions for appointment. Judges and Advocates General of the Court of Justice and judges of the General Court as well as judges of the specialized courts are 'chosen from persons whose independence is beyond doubt'. The Treaties further require judges and Advocates General of the Court of Justice to 'possess the qualifications required for appointment to the highest judicial offices in their respective countries' or to be 'jurisconsults of recognised competence' (Article 19(3) TEU and Article 253, first para. TFEU); judges of the General Court must 'possess the ability required for appointment to high judicial office' (Article 19(3) TEU and Article 254, second para. TFEU); judges of specialized courts must 'possess the ability required for appointment to judicial office' (Article 257 TFEU).

13.015

Duties. Before taking up their duties, each judge and Advocate General has to take up an oath in open court to perform his or her duties impartially and conscientiously and to preserve the secrecy of the deliberations of the Court (CJEU Statute, Articles 2 and 8).[44] Members may not hold any political or administrative office and are subject to the same requirements as members of the Commission as regards engaging in any other occupation and the acceptance of appointments and benefits. A judge or Advocate General may be deprived of his or her office only if, in the unanimous opinion of the other judges and Advocates General, he or she no longer fulfils the requisite conditions or meets the obligations arising from his or her office (CJEU Statute, Articles 6 and 8). If the office of judge or Advocate General becomes vacant before the end of the term of office as a result of death or voluntary or compulsory retirement, the successor is appointed for the remainder of his or her predecessor's term of office (CJEU Statute, Article 7).

13.016

---

[41] See Council Decision 2010/124/EU of 25 February 2010 relating to the operating rules of the panel provided for in Article 255 of the TFEU OJ 2010 L50/18. Its members are appointed by taking into account 'a balanced membership of the panel, both in geographical terms and in terms of representation of the legal systems of the Member States'; see Council Decision 2010/125/EU of 25 February 2010 appointing the members of the panel OJ 2010 L50/20.

[42] See Articles 7 and 8 of the operating rules for the panel, as annexed to Council Decision 2010/124/EU. Such a hearing is not held where it is proposed to reappoint a sitting Judge or Advocate General (ibid., Article 7).

[43] Members of the Civil Service Tribunal were appointed by the Council after consulting a committee consisting of former members of the Court of Justice and the Court of First Instance (*now the General Court*) and lawyers of recognized competence (Annex I to the CJEU Statute, Article 3). The operating rules of that committee were laid down by Council Decision 2005/49/EC, Euratom of 18 January 2005, OJ 2005 L21/13.

[44] See also the Code of Conduct for Members and former Members of the Court of Justice of the European Union, OJ 2016 C483/1.

C. Procedure

13.017 **Rules of Procedure.** The Court of Justice operates in accordance with the procedure laid down in the Treaties, the Statute of the Court of Justice of the European Union, and the Rules of Procedure, which the Court itself adopts but has to submit to the Council for its approval.[45] Procedure before the General Court is determined by the Statute of the Court of Justice of the European Union and by the Rules of Procedure, which, under Article 254, fifth para. TFEU, the General Court establishes in agreement with the Court of Justice. Those Rules must be approved by the Council as well.[46] The procedure of the specialized courts is based on the Statute of the Court of Justice of the European Union and on their own Rules of Procedure, which, under Article 257, fifth para. TFEU, they are to establish in agreement with the Court of Justice. Those Rules have to be approved by the Council. In Part VI of this book the preliminary reference procedure (see para. 29-029 *et seq.*, *infra*) and the procedures for direct actions before the Court of Justice and the General Court (see para. 30-026 *et seq.*, *infra*) are discussed.

D. Internal organization

13.018 **Chambers.** Both in the Court of Justice and in the General Court, the judges elect the President and Vice-President from among their number for a term of three years. The President and Vice-President may be re-elected. Both Courts appoint their Registrar and lay down the rules governing his or her service (Articles 253, third and fourth paras, and 254, third and fourth paras, TFEU). The Court of Justice sits in Chambers of three or five judges or in a Grand Chamber (fifteen judges) or, exceptionally, as a Full Court.[47] Cases are sent to the Grand Chamber when a Member State or institution that is party to the proceedings so requests, or whenever the Court considers this to be justified by the difficulty or importance of the case or particular circumstances.[48] Decisions of the Full Court are valid only if seventeen judges are sitting.[49] The General Court sits in Chambers of three or five judges. In certain cases it may sit in a Grand Chamber (fifteen judges) or be constituted by a single judge.[50] The judges and Advocates General are assisted by law clerks, known as legal secretaries or *référendaires*.[51] The Court of Justice of the European Union employs some 2,250

---

[45] Article 253, sixth para. TFEU. The consolidated text of the Rules of Procedure of the Court of Justice (CJ Rules of Procedure) can be found on the website of the Court of Justice of the European Union: http://curia.europa.eu/. For procedure before the Court, see Lenaerts, Gutman, and Nowak, *EU Procedural Law* (OUP, 2022), Chapters 23 to 25.

[46] Article 254, fifth para. TFEU. See Articles 47 to 62b of the CJEU Statute and the consolidated text of the Rules of Procedure of the General Court, which can be found on the Court's website: http://curia.europa.eu/. See Lenaerts, Gutman, and Nowak, *EU Procedural Law* (OUP, 2022), Chapters 23 to 25.

[47] Article 251 TFEU and CJEU Statute, Articles 16 and 17.

[48] CJEU Statute, Article 16, third subpara.; CJ Rules of Procedure, Article 60(1).

[49] CJEU Statute, Article 17, fourth para. The Grand Chamber is presided over by the President of the Court and consists of the Vice-President, three of the Presidents of the Chambers of five Judges, the Judge Rapporteur, and such judges as are necessary to bring the number to fifteen (CJ Rules of Procedure, Article 27).

[50] CJEU Statute, Article 50; GC Rules of Procedure, Articles 13, 15, and 29. Article 50 of the CJEU Statute also provides for the possibility for the General Court to sit as a full court, but no such instances have been provided for in the GC Rules of Procedure.

[51] See Erniquin, 'Les référendaires attachés aux juridictions supérieures' (2003) JT 717–29; Kennedy, 'Beyond Principals and Agents —Seeing Courts as Organizations by Comparing *Référendaires* at the European Court of Justice and Law Clerks at the U.S. Supreme Court' (2000) Comp Polit Stud 593–625. For their recruitment, see also T-406/04 *Bonnet v Court of Justice*, 2006.

staff. When the Court of Justice was established by the ECSC Treaty, its seat was fixed in Luxembourg,[52] which is where both the Court of Justice and the General Court are based.[53]

II. The European Central Bank

Union Institution. The European Central Bank (ECB)[54] is a Union institution with legal personality.[55] It performs its tasks since 1 June 1998 as the linchpin within the European System of Central Banks, which is composed of the ECB and the national central banks of the Member States, whether they have adopted the euro or not. The national central banks are the only shareholders of the ECB.[56] The key for subscription to shares in the ECB takes account of each Member State's share of the population of the Union and of its GDP.[57] The ECB took over the tasks which the EC Treaty had entrusted to the European Monetary Institute (EMI), an independent body with legal personality, since 1 January 1994, the start of the second stage of EMU.[58]

13.019

A. Powers

Tasks The ECB conducts the monetary policy of the Union together with the national central banks of the Member States which adopted the euro as their currency; together they form the 'Eurosystem' (Article 282(1) TFEU). As long as there are EU Member States outside the euro area, the Eurosystem co-exists with the ESCB. Furthermore, the ECB has a

13.020

---

[52] Para. 14-019, *infra*.
[53] Sole Article, para. (d), of the Protocol on Seats (para. 14-020, *infra*). Article 3 of the Decision on Provisional Location of 8 April 1965 (para. 14-019, *infra*) itself provided that existing and future judicial and quasi-judicial bodies set up under the Community Treaties should have their seat in Luxembourg. See also the Declaration to the Decision of 29 October 1993 (para. 14-021, *infra*). In a unilateral declaration by Luxembourg, of which the Conference took note in signing the Nice Treaty (OJ 2001 C80/87), that Member State undertook not to claim the seat of the Boards of Appeal of the Office for Harmonization in the Internal Market (trademarks and designs), even if those Boards were to become judicial panels within the meaning of Article 220 EC.
[54] For the ECB website, see http://www.ecb.int/.
[55] Article 282(2) TFEU. Before the Lisbon Treaty the ECB was not a Union institution, but an independent Community body; see C-11/00 *Commission v European Central Bank*, 2003, paras 89–96. See, in general, Krauskopf and Steven, 'The Institutional Framework of the European System of Central Banks; Legal Issues in the Practice of the First Ten Years of its Existence' (2009) CMLRev 1143; Zilioli and Selmayer, 'The Constitutional Status of the European Central Bank' (2007) CMLRev 335; Zilioli and Selmayer, *The Law of the European Central Bank* (Hart Publishing, 2001).
[56] ESCB Statute, Article 28.2.
[57] Ibid., Article 29.1. For the most recent subscription key, see Decision (EU) 2020/137 of the ECB of 22 January 2020, OJ 2020 L27/4; for the measures necessary for the paying-up of the capital of the ECB, see most recently Decision (EU) 2020/138 of the ECB of 22 January 2020 (OJ 2020 L27/6—for participating Member States) and Decision (EU) 2020/136 of the ECB of 22 January 2020 (OJ 2020 L27/1—for non-participating Member States). For permitted increases in the ECB's capital, see Council Regulation (EC) No. 1009/2000 of 8 May 2000, OJ 2000 L115/1.
[58] Under Article 123(2) EC, the assets and liabilities of the EMI were transferred to the ECB, which liquidated the EMI. The EMI was directed and managed by a Council, consisting of a President and the governors of the national central banks; see Article 117(1), first subpara. EC. Its first president was Baron A Lamfalussy, followed up as from 1 July 1997 by WF Duisenberg until the start of the ECB. The EMI operated in accordance with its Statute; see Article 117(1), third subpara. EC and Protocol (No. 19), annexed to the EC Treaty, on the Statute of the European Monetary Institute, OJ 1992 C224/115. The EMI's seat was established at Frankfurt, The EMI itself had replaced the Committee of Governors of the central banks and the European Monetary Cooperation Fund, See Article 117(1), first subpara. and (2), fifth indent EC.

number of specific tasks relating to the prudential supervision of the credit institutions established in the Member States of the euro area and participating non-euro area Member States (Article 127(6) TFEU), within the Single Supervisory Mechanism.[59]

Under Article 130 TFEU and Article 286(3) TFEU, the ECB—just like the national central banks—exercises its powers and carries out its tasks and duties completely independently of the political authorities of the Union and the Member States or any other body. That independence does not mean that the ECB is separated entirely from the Union but seeks to shield the ECB from political influences in exercising the specific tasks attributed to it.[60] The Statute of the European System of Central Banks (ESCB) governs the financial and administrative independence of the ECB.[61] That statute is set out in a Protocol annexed to the Treaties, together with that of the ECB.[62] The ECB ensures that the ECB itself and the national central banks (of Member States whose currency is the euro) carry out the tasks which the TFEU confers on the ESCB (see para. 9-043 et seq., supra).[63] In order to do so the ECB can adopt regulations and decisions, make recommendations, and give opinions (Article 132(1) TFEU). The ECB is entitled to impose fines and periodic penalty payments on undertakings for failure to comply with obligations imposed by its regulations and decisions (Article 132(3) TFEU).[64] In addition, the ECB supervises the national central banks to make sure that they comply with their obligations and may bring a national central bank before the Court of Justice if it finds that there has been an infringement (Article 271(d) TFEU).[65] The national central bank concerned is under a duty to take the necessary measures to comply with the Court's judgment finding that it has failed to fulfil its obligations, but cannot be fined if it persists in the infringement.[66]

---

[59] See Council Regulation (EU) No. 1024/2013 of 15 October 2013 conferring specific tasks on the European Central Bank concerning policies relating to the prudential supervision of credit institutions, OJ 2013 L287/63.

[60] C-11/00, *Commission v European Central Bank*, 2003, paras 134–5. For the substance of that independence, see ibid., paras 130–2. See also Lavranos, 'The Limited, Functional Independence of the ECB' (2004) ELRev 115–23; Elderson and Weenink, 'The European Central Bank Redefined? A Landmark JUdgment of the European Court of Justice' (2003) Euredia 273–301.

[61] See, *inter alia*, Article 27 (independent audit of accounts), Article 28 (capital of the ECB), and Article 36 (staff) of the ESCB Statute.

[62] Article 129(2) TFEU and Protocol (No. 4), annexed to the TEU and TFEU, on the Statute of the European System of Central Banks and of the European Central Bank [ESCB Statute], OJ 2010 C83/230 (replacing the Protocol annexed to the EC Treaty, OJ 1992 C224/104). Notwithstanding the status of that Protocol as part of the Treaties (Article 51 TEU), some of its articles may be amended by the European Parliament and the Council, acting in accordance with the ordinary legislative procedure. They act either on a recommendation from the ECB and after consulting the Commission or on a proposal from the Commission and after consulting the ECB (Article 129(3) TFEU and ESCB Statute, Article 40). In areas subject to this simplified amendment mechanism it is therefore difficult for the ECB to rely on the existence of an implicit regulatory power, see T-496/11, *United Kingdom v European Central Bank*, 2015, paras 103–10.

[63] ESCB Statute, Article 9.2.

[64] The ECB exercises this power within the limits and under the conditions laid down in Council Regulation (EC) No. 2532/98 of 23 November 1998 concerning the powers of the European Central Bank to impose sanctions, OJ 1998 L318/4. For the applicable infringement procedure, see European Central Bank Regulation (EC) No. 2157/1999 of 23 September 1999, OJ 1999 L264/21. See Fernández Martín and Texieira, 'The Imposition of Sanctions by the European Central Bank' (2000) ELRev 391–407.

[65] Article 271(d) TFEU confers on the Council of the ECB the same powers as are conferred on the Commission by Article 258 TFEU. See also ESCB Statute, Article 35.6 and Gaiser, 'Gerichtliche Kontrolle im Europäischen System der Zentralbanken' (2002) EuR 517, 520–3. Remarkably, Article 14.2 of the ESCB Statute makes provision for proceedings to be brought in the Court of Justice against a decision relieving a governor of a central bank from his or her office by the Governing Council of the ECB or by the governor concerned.

[66] Compare Article 271(d), last sentence TFEU with Article 260 TFEU.

B. Composition

Organization. The decision-making bodies of the ECB govern the ESCB (Article 282(2) TFEU). The Governing Council formulates the Union's monetary policy; the Executive Board implements that policy and gives the necessary directions to the national central banks.[67] The ECB's Governing Council is made up of the governors of the central banks of Member States whose currency is the euro and the members of the ECB's Executive Board. The Executive Board consists of the President, the Vice-President, and four members (Article 283(1) and (2) TFEU).

13.021

The European Council, acting by a qualified majority, appoints the Executive Board for a non-renewable eight-year term on a recommendation from the Council, after consulting the European Parliament and the ECB's Governing Council.[68] Member States outside the euro area have no voting rights.[69] Candidates for office must be nationals of Member States who adopted the euro and be of recognized standing and professional experience in monetary or banking matters (see Articles 139(2)(h) and second subpara. and 283(2) TFEU). Before their appointment, the European Parliament invites the nominees for President, Vice-President, or other Executive Board members of the ECB to make a statement before the committee responsible and answer questions put by MEPs.[70] If the Parliament's opinion on a nominee is negative, it will request the Council to submit a new nomination.[71] Board members perform their duties on a full-time basis and may be compulsorily retired only by the Court of Justice on an application by the Governing Council or the Executive Board.[72]

As long as there are Member States which have not adopted the euro, the governors of the central banks of all the Member States, together with the President and Vice-President of the ECB, will have certain responsibilities as the General Council of the ECB (Article 141(1) TFEU).[73]

The prudential supervision on credit institutions is prepared and implemented by the Supervisory Board, which is made up of a Chair and Vice-Chair (appointed by the Council acting by a qualified majority), four representatives of the ECB, and one representative of each of the national competent authorities from the participating Member States.[74] The

---

[67] ESCB Statute, Article 12.1, first and second subparas. The second subpara. also provides that the Governing Council may delegate powers to the Board.

[68] See the first Decision (98/345/EC) taken by common accord of the governments of the Member States adopting the single currency at the level of Heads of State or Government of 26 May 1998 appointing the President, the Vice-President, and the other members of the Executive Board of the European Central Bank, OJ 1998 L154/33. Willem ('Wim') Duisenberg was appointed President; after he stepped down in 2003, he was replaced by Jean Claude Trichet, succeeded as from 1 November 2011 by Mario Draghi, and as from 1 November 2019 by Christine Lagarde.

[69] See Article 139(2)(h) and (4) TFEU

[70] EP Rules of Procedure, Rule 130(1).

[71] Ibid., Rule 130(4).

[72] ESCB Statute, Articles 11.1 and 11.4. Article 11.4 makes it possible for a Board member to be retired (as in the case of a member of the Commission) if he or she no longer fulfils the conditions required for the performance of his or her duties or if he or she has been guilty of serious misconduct. The Code of Conduct for the members of the Governing Council may be found in OJ 2002 C123/9.

[73] For those responsibilities, see ESCB Statute, Article 46.

[74] Council Regulation (EU) No. 1024/2013 of 15 October 2013 conferring specific tasks on the European Central Bank concerning policies relating to the prudential supervision of credit institutions, OJ 2013 L287/63, Article 26.

454   OTHER INSTITUTIONS AND BODIES OF THE UNION

Chair and Vice-Chair of the Supervisory Board are appointed upon a proposal from the ECB by the Council, after approval from the European Parliament, by way of an implementing decision, adopted by qualified majority without taking into account the vote of the non-participating Member States.[75]

C. Operation

13.022 **Operation.** The seat of the ECB is in Frankfurt.[76] In principle, both the Governing Council and the Executive Board take their decisions by a simple majority vote, although in some cases the Governing Council has to act by a qualified majority of votes weighted according to the national central banks' shares in the ECB's subscribed capital.[77] The European Council, acting unanimously, may adopt a decision amending the voting rules of the Governing Council; that decision must be ratified by the Member States in accordance with their national constitutions.[78] In this way, a system was introduced on the accession of the new Member States in 2004 to the effect that not all governors of national central banks have the same voting rights.[79] That system entered into force on 1 January 2015.[80] Depending on the size of the share of their Member State in the aggregate GDP of the Member States which have adopted the euro and in the total aggregated balance sheet of the monetary financial institutions of those Member States, the national central banks are allocated to groups within which the right to vote rotates.[81] Central banks from Member States ranked first to fifth—currently, Germany, France, Italy, Spain, and the Netherlands—share four voting rights; all others share eleven voting rights. The voting rights take turns on a monthly rotation.

D. Internal organization

13.023 **Rules of Procedure.** The internal organization of the ECB is determined by its Rules of Procedure, adopted by the Governing Council.[82] The proceedings are

---

[75] Ibid., Article 26(3) The Chair is to be chosen on the basis of an open selection procedure from among individuals of recognized standing and experience in banking and financial matters who are not members of the Governing Council; the Vice Chair is be chosen from among the members of the Executive Board of the ECB. Ibid.

[76] Second Decision on the Seats of the Institutions of 29 October 1993, taken over by the Protocol on Seats, Sole Article, para. (i); para. 14-021, *infra*. See ESCB Statute, Article 37 and Heim, 'The European Central Bank: Was it Not Bound to Go to Luxembourg?' (1994) ELRev 48–55.

[77] For the Governing Council, see ESCB Statute, Articles 10.2 and 10.3 (qualified majority); for the Executive Board, see ESCB Statute, Article 11.5.

[78] ESCB Statute, Article 40.2.

[79] Decision 2003/223/EC of the Council meeting in the composition of the Heads of State or Government of 21 March 2003 on an amendment to Article 10.2 of the Statute of the European System of Central Banks and of the European Central Bank, OJ 2003 L83/66.

[80] According to Article 10.2 ESCB Statute, the rotation system was to be implemented as from the date on which the number of members of the Governing Council (i.e. governors of national central banks and members of the Executive Board) exceeded twenty-one (which happened upon the adoption of the euro by Slovakia on 1 January 2009), unless the Governing Council would postpone the start of the rotation system until the number of *governors* in the Governing Council exceeded eighteen (which occurred with the accession of Lithuania to the euro area on 1 January 2015).

[81] ESCB Statute, Article 10(2).

[82] ESCB Statute, Article 12.3 and the ECB's Rules of Procedure adopted pursuant thereto on 19 February 2004 (OJ 2004 L80/33). The Rules of Procedure of the Executive Board of the ECB were adopted by ECB

confidential.[83] The President of the Council and a member of the Commission may take part, without any voting rights, in meetings of the Governing Council; moreover, the President of the Council may submit a motion for deliberation (Article 284(1) TFEU). The ECB employs some 3,500 staff.

III. The European Court of Auditors

Establishment. The Court of Auditors[84] was brought into being in 1975 as an independent supervisory body by the Treaty change that established the present budgetary procedure.[85] The EU Treaty put the Court of Auditors on an equal footing with the other institutions.[86] On 9 December 1993, the Court decided to take the name of 'European Court of Auditors'.[87]

13.024

A. Powers

The European Court of Auditors examines the accounts of all revenue and expenditure of the Union. The external audit of the budget which it carries out results in an annual report which is forwarded to all the institutions and published (Article 287 TFEU; see para. 20-011, *infra*). In addition, the Court may submit observations, particularly in the form of special reports, on specific questions (Article 287(4), second subpara. TFEU). The Court may also deliver opinions at the request of one of the other Union institutions[88] and is consulted on legislation relating to the budget and accounts.[89] The Court further assists the European Parliament and the Council in supervising and implementing the budget (see para. 20-011, *infra*).

13.025

Decision of 12 October 1999 (OJ 1999 L314/34). For the Rules of Procedure of the General Council of the ECB of 17 June 2004, see OJ 2004 L230/61; for the Rules of Procedure of the Supervisory Council, see OJ 2014 L182/56.

[83] ESCB Statute, Article 10.4. Under this provision, the Governing Council may decide, however, to make the outcome of its deliberations public. See C-442/18 P, *ECB v Espírito Santo Financial (Portugal)*, 2019, paras 41–9; C-396/19 P, *ECB v Insolvent Estate of Espírito Santo Financial Group*, 2020, paras 49–54.

[84] For the website of the Court of Auditors, see http://eca.europa.eu/.

[85] Treaty of 22 July 1975 amending certain financial provisions of the Treaties establishing the European Communities and of the Treaty establishing a Single Council and a Single Commission of the European Communities, OJ 1977 L359/1 (para. 20-001, *infra*). The Court of Auditors took over the task that the ECSC Treaty conferred on auditors and the EEC Treaty and the EAEC Treaty on an Audit Board, which the Merger Treaty also made responsible for the ECSC budget,

[86] See Article 7(1) EC [*now Article 13(1) TEU*]. The Court of Auditors was in fact already equated to an institution before as regards the status of its members, officials, and other servants.

[87] (1993) 12 EC Bull. point 1.7.41. For a survey, see O'Keeffe, 'The Court of Auditors', in Curtin and Heukels (eds), *Institutional Dynamics of European Integration. Essays in Honour of Henry G. Schermers* (Martinus Nijhoff, 1994), 177–94; Inghelram, 'The European Court of Auditors: Current Legal Issues' (2000) CMLRev 129–46; Engwirda and Moonen, 'De Europese Rekenkamer: positie, bevoegdheden en toekomstperspectief' (2000) SEW 246–57; Kok, 'The Court of Auditors of the European Communities: "The Other European Court in Luxembourg"' (1989) CMLRev 345–67.

[88] Article 287(4), second subpara. TFEU. Under Article 144(2) of the Financial Regulation, it may publish the opinion after consulting the institution concerned.

[89] Article 322 TFEU.

B. Composition

13.026 **Composition.** The European Court of Auditors consists of one national from each Member State (Article 285, second para. TFEU). Members of the Court are appointed, not by the governments of the Member States or by the European Council, but by the Council by a qualified majority vote (following the Treaty of Nice), after consulting the European Parliament (Article 286(2) TFEU). Prospective members must belong, or have belonged, to external audit bodies or be especially qualified for that office in their respective countries. Their independence must be beyond doubt (Article 286(1) TFEU). Before their appointment, candidates nominated as members are invited by the European Parliament to make a statement before the committee responsible and answer questions put by MEPs.[90] If the Parliament's opinion on an individual nomination is negative, it will request the Council to submit a new nomination.[91] The members are appointed for a renewable six-year term (Article 286(2) TFEU).

13.027 **Independence.** As in the case of Commissioners, members of the European Court of Auditors have to be completely independent in the performance of their duties in the general interests of the Union (Article 285 TFEU). They are subject to the same rules as those applicable to Commissioners with regard to occupations incompatible with their office and with their professional duties as members of the Court of Auditors (see Article 286(3) and (4) TFEU). When they take up office they solemnly undertake to respect those obligations.[92] The independence of the Court of Auditors is made clear by the fact that its members may not be removed before the end of their term of office except at the request of the Court of Auditors itself if the Court of Justice finds that the member concerned no longer fulfils the requisite conditions or meets the obligations arising from his or her office (Article 286(5) and (6) TFEU).[93]

C. Operation

13.028 **Rules of Procedure.** The European Court of Auditors acts collectively in accordance with the Treaties, the Financial Regulation,[94] and its Rules of Procedure, which it draws up subject to the approval of the Council.[95] It may establish internal chambers in order to adopt certain categories of reports or opinions (Article 287(4), third subpara. TFEU). The members of the Court elect a President from among their number to serve a three-year term (Article 286(2), second subpara. TFEU). He or she convenes and chairs meetings of the

---

[90] EP Rules of Procedure, Rule 129(1).
[91] EP Rules of Procedure, Rule 129(4). In practice, a negative opinion on a candidate does not always prevent that candidate from being appointed, but sometimes it prompts a candidate to withdraw his candidacy.
[92] As in the case of members of the Commission, they take an oath, at a solemn sitting of the Court of Justice.
[93] See C-130/19 *Court of Auditors v Pinxten*, AG Hogan Opinion, 2020.
[94] Regulation (EU, Euratom) 2018/1046 of the European Parliament and of the Council of 18 July 2018 on the financial rules applicable to the general budget of the Union, OJ 2018 L193/1; see previously Regulation (EU, Euratom) No. 966/2012 of the European Parliament and of the Council of 25 October 2012 on the financial rules applicable to the general budget of the Union, OJ 2012 L298/1 (para. 20-007, *infra*).
[95] Article 287(4), fifth subpara. TFEU. Before the Nice Treaty added this legal basis to the Treaties, the Court of Auditors used to adopt its Rules of Procedure on the basis of its powers of internal organization. See, at present, the Rules of Procedure of 11 March 2010 OJ 2010 L103/1. For the collective nature of the Court of Auditors, see Article 1 of the Rules.

Court, which are not open to the public.[96] The Court adopts its reports and opinions by a majority of its members.[97] For the purposes of carrying out its auditing duties, the Court has formed Chambers which share out their respective responsibilities and have the task of preparing the deliberations of the Court.[98]

D. Internal organization

Staff. The European Court of Auditors has been based in Luxembourg since it was first set up.[99] A Secretary-General appointed by the Court itself is responsible for its secretariat and for personnel policy and administration.[100] The Court has a staff of around 900, employed in its administrative departments and audit groups.

13.029

IV. Advisory Bodies

A. The European Economic and Social Committee

Advisory tasks. The Treaties make provision for committees advising on Union decision-making in which representative interest groups may make their views known. In this way, the ECSC Treaty set up a Consultative Committee consisting of producers, workers, consumers, and dealers in order to assist the High Authority. The EC and EAEC Treaties created the Economic and Social Committee[101] in order to advise the Council, the Commission, and—since the Lisbon Treaty—the European Parliament (Article 13(4) TEU). This committee consists of representatives of organizations of employers, the employed, and other parties representative of civil society, notably in socio-economic, civic, professional, and cultural areas (Article 300(2) TFEU).[102] The Treaties list the matters in respect of which an opinion has to be sought from the Committee before a decision is taken.[103] In addition to

13.030

---

[96] See Rules of Procedure, Articles 20 and 22.
[97] Ibid., Article 25. The Court of Auditors determines which decisions are to be adopted by a majority of the Members of the Court; other decisions are to be taken by a majority vote of the Members present (Article 25(2) and (3)), possibly by a written procedure (Article 25(5)).
[98] Rules of Procedure, Article 10.
[99] Decision of the Representatives of the Governments of the Member States of 5 April 1977 on the provisional location of the Court of Auditors, OJ 1977 L104/40, as confirmed by the Protocol on Seats, Sole Article, para. (e); para. 14-020, *infra*.
[100] Rules of Procedure, Article 13.
[101] The Treaties refer to the 'Economic and Social Committee' without the adjective 'European'. However, the Committee has consistently used the name 'European Economic and Social Committee' as its official designation. See the website of the European Economic and Social Committee, http://eesc.europa.eu/.
[102] See also Articles 3(2) and Article 165 EAEC. The nature of the composition of the Economic and Social Committee must be reviewed at regular intervals by the Council to take account of economic, social, and demographic developments within the Union. The Council is to adopt decisions to that end on a proposal from the Commission (Article 300(5) TFEU).
[103] See the obligation for the European Parliament and the Council in Articles 43(2); 46; 50; 59(1); 91(1); 95(3), first subpara.; 113; 114(1); 115; 148(2); 149, first para.; 153(2), second subpara.; 156, third para.; 157(3); 164; 165(4); 166(4); 168(4); 169(3); 172, first para.; 173(3), first subpara.; 175, third para.; 177, first para.; 178, first para.; 182(1) and (4); 188, first and second paras; 199(1), (2), and (3) TFEU and Articles 194(2) TFEU. See the obligation in the EAEC Treaty for the Commission to consult laid down in Article 9, first para.; Article 31, first para.; Article 32, first para.; Article 40; Article 41, second para.; Article 96, second para.; and Article 98, second para. See also Panke, 'The Committee of the Regions and the European Economic and Social Committee: How Influential are Consultative Committees in the European Union?', (2013) JCMS 452; Hayder, 'Der Europäische Wirtschafts- und

obligatory consultation, the Commission and the Council may request an opinion if they consider it desirable. The Committee may also deliver opinions on its own initiative (Article 304, first para. TFEU).[104]

13.031 **Composition.** The European Economic and Social Committee may have no more than 350 members (at present 329 members). Since the Lisbon Treaty, the exact composition of the Committee is to be determined by the Council, acting unanimously on a proposal from the Commission (Article 301, second para. TFEU).[105] Members are appointed by the Council by a qualified majority vote on proposals from the Member States (Article 302(1) TFEU). The Council is to consult the Commission and may obtain the opinion of European bodies that are representative of the various economic and social sectors and of civil society to which the Union's activities are of concern (Article 302(2) TFEU). Members are appointed for a renewable five-year term (Article 302(1) TFEU). They are not bound by any mandatory instructions, and in the Union's general interest (Article 300(4) TFEU) they must be completely independent in the performance of their duties.

13.032 **Operation.** The European Economic and Social Committee adopts its own rules of procedure.[106] Twice during their term of office, the members of the Committee are to elect a President and a Bureau, which is required to reflect the sectors represented on the Committee itself.[107] The President convenes the Committee at the request of the European Parliament, the Council, the Commission, or its Bureau.[108] The Committee has set up specialist sections for the principal fields covered by the Treaties.[109] The seat of the European Economic and Social Committee is in Brussels.[110] It has a staff of about 700 officials.

B. The Committee of the Regions

13.033 **Advisory tasks.** Since the entry into force of the EU Treaty, representatives of regional and local bodies also have a right to be consulted in the decision-making process.[111]

Sozialausschuss (EWSA)—eine unterschätzte EU-Institution' (2010) EuZW 171; Ferté and Roncin, 'Quel avenir pour le Comité économique et social européen?' (2001) RMCUE 52–9.

[104] The EU Treaty introduced this possibility in Article 262, first para. EC, although the Committee's Rules of Procedure already provided for it. The Commission submits its three-yearly report on economic and social cohesion to the European Economic and Social Committee (Article 175, second para. TFEU.

[105] See, most recently, Council Decision (EU) 2019/853 of 21 May 2019 determining the composition of the European Economic and Social Committee, OJ 2019 L139/15. Before the Lisbon Treaty, the Treaties allocated each Member State a number of members (Article 258, first and second paras EC, amended upon the accession to the Union of new Member States).

[106] See the Rules of Procedure adopted pursuant to the second para. of Article 303 TFEU (which, since the EU Treaty, no longer have to be approved by the Council); the latest version was adopted on 28 January 2021 (OJ 2021 L46/47), replacing the version adopted on 17 July 2002 (last codified version published in OJ 2019 L 184/23).

[107] Article 303, first para. TFEU and ESC Rules of Procedure, Rule 4.

[108] Article 303, third para. TFEU and ESC Rules of Procedure, Rule 32. Under that article, the Committee may be convened on a proposal from its Bureau, with the approval of the majority of its members.

[109] The Committee sets up its sections at the inaugural session following each renewal (ESC Rules of Procedure, Rule 17).

[110] Sole Article, para. (f), of Protocol (No. 6), annexed to the TEU, TFEU, and EAEC Treaty, on the location of the seats of the institutions and of certain bodies, offices, agencies, and departments of the European Union, OJ 2010 C83/265. The ECSC Consultative Committee was based in Luxembourg.

[111] By Decision of 24 June 1988 (OJ 1988 L247/23), the Commission set up a Consultative Council of Regional and Local Authorities, which was wound up after the Committee of the Regions started its work (Commission Decision of 21 April 1994, OJ 1994 L103/28).

The EU Treaty established a Committee of the Regions,[112] which, in the same way as the European Economic and Social Committee, is entitled to be consulted by the European Parliament, the Council, and the Commission where the Treaties so provide[113] and may issue an opinion on its own initiative where it considers such action appropriate (Article 307, first and fourth paras TFEU). The Committee of the Regions may also be consulted by the European Parliament, the Council, or the Commission in all other cases, in particular those that concern cross-border cooperation, in which one of those institutions considers it appropriate (Article 307, first para. TFEU). The Committee is informed of every request for an opinion made to the European Economic and Social Committee with a view to its delivering an opinion on the matter if it considers that specific regional aspects are involved (Article 307, third para. TFEU).[114]

The Lisbon Treaty conferred on the Committee of the Regions *locus standi* to bring an action for annulment for the purpose of protecting its prerogatives[115] or to denounce an infringement of the principle of subsidiarity.[116]

Composition. The Committee of the Regions may have no more than 350 members (at present 329 members). Since the Lisbon Treaty, the Council is to determine the exact composition of the Committee, using the same procedure as with respect to the European Economic and Social Committee (Article 305, second para. TFEU).[117] Despite its name, the Committee of the Regions is composed not only of representatives of regional authorities but also of representatives of local authorities. The members consist of representatives of regional and local bodies who either hold a regional or local authority electoral mandate or are politically accountable to an elected assembly (Article 300(3) TFEU).[118] The members

13.034

---

[112] Like the European Economic and Social Committee, the Committee of the Regions has taken on the designation 'European Committee of the Regions', although the Treaties still refer to the Committee without the adjective 'European'. See, generally, Martinico, 'History of a (Limited) Success: Five Points on the Representativeness of the Committee of the Regions' (2018) PF96; Van Aken et al., *CoR's Future Role and Institutional Positioning* (Committee of the Regions, 2014); Ricci, 'The Committee of the Regions and the Challenge of European Governance', in Panara and De Becker (eds), *The Role of the Regions in EU Governance* (Springer, 2011), 109; Piattoni, 'The Committee of the Regions: Multi-Level Governance after Enlargement', in Best, Christiansen, and Settembri (eds), *The Institutions of the Enlarged European Union: Continuity and Change* (Edward Elgar Publishing, 2008), 162–82; Domorenok, 'The Committee of the Regions: in Search of Identity' (2009) Regional and Federal Studies, 143–63; Kottmann, 'Europe and the Regions: Sub-National Entity Representation at Community Level' (2001) ELRev 159–76. For the website of the Committee of the Regions, see http://www.cor.europa.eu/.

[113] See Articles 91(1); 148(2); 149, first para.; 153(2), second subpara.; 164; 165(4), first indent; 166(4); 167(5), first indent; 168(4); 172, first and third paras; 175, third para., 161, first and second paras; 178, first para.; 192(1), (2), and (3) TFEU.

[114] Conversely, every act requiring an opinion of the Committee of the Regions is also submitted to the Economic and Social Committee for its opinion (except as regards culture) and to the European Parliament. The Committee of the Regions also receives the three-yearly report on economic and social cohesion provided for in Article 175, second para. TFEU.

[115] Article 263, third para. TFEU.

[116] See Article 263, third para. TFEU and Article 8 of Protocol (No. 2), annexed to the TEU and TFEU, on the application of the principles of subsidiarity and proportionality (OJ 2010 C83/206), by virtue of which the Committee can bring an action under Article 263 TFEU on grounds of infringement of the principle of subsidiarity—irrespective of whether or not such action is intended to protect its prerogatives—in respect of legislative acts for the adoption of which the TFEU provides that it be consulted.

[117] See, most recently, Council Decision (EU) 2019/852 of 21 May 2019 determining the composition of the Committee of the Regions, OJ 2019 L139/13. Before the Lisbon Treaty, Article 263, third para. EC explicitly distributed the members among the Member States in the same way as the members of the European Economic and Social Committee.

[118] The requirement that the proposed members must have an electoral mandate was introduced by the Nice Treaty. Before, each Member State decided whether to put forward (indirectly) elected representatives. The nature of the composition of the Committee must be reviewed at regular intervals by the Council to take account of

of the Committee are appointed by the Council by a qualified majority vote in accordance with the proposals made by each Member State, together with an equal number of alternate members (Article 305, third para. TFEU). Consequently, the Member States themselves decide which domestic levels of administration they wish to have represented on the Committee, one of the reasons for this being that the status and powers of regional and local bodies differ greatly from one Member State to another. As in the case of their counterparts at the European Economic and Social Committee, members of the Committee of the Regions are appointed for a renewable five-year term, may not be bound by any mandatory instructions, and have to be completely independent in the performance of their duties in the Union's general interest (Article 300(4) and 305, second para. TFEU).

13.035 **Operation.** The Committee of the Regions adopts its own rules of procedure.[119] Twice during their term of office, the members are to elect a President, who convenes it on his or her own initiative or at the request of the European Parliament, the Council, or the Commission (Article 306 TFEU).[120] The members also elect a Bureau, taking into account the geographical balance of the Union.[121]

The Committee of the Regions shares certain services with the European Economic and Social Committee. As a result, the Committee of the Regions is also based in Brussels.[122]

C. Other committees

13.036 **Consultative bodies.** In a number of policy areas, the Treaties involve national civil servants, representatives of interest groups, and independent experts in the decision-making process by means of committees created for that purpose. Pursuant to Article 242 TFEU, the Council adopts the rules governing committees provided for in the Treaties (by a simple majority vote) after receiving the opinion of the Commission. Examples are the Advisory Committee on Transport, consisting of experts designated by the national governments, attached to the Commission (Article 99 TFEU), and the Committee of the European Social Fund, composed of representatives of governments, trade unions, and employers' associations and presided over by a member of the Commission, which assists the Commission in administering the Fund (Article 163 TFEU.[123] Likewise, the Treaties set up the Employment Committee[124] and the Social Protection Committee,[125] to which each Member State and

---

economic, social, and demographic developments within the Union. The Council is to adopt decisions to that end, on a proposal from the Commission (Article 300(5) TFEU).

[119] Rules of Procedure adopted by the Committee of the Regions on 31 January 2014, OJ 2014 L65/41, replacing previous versions.

[120] The President has to convene the Plenary Assembly at least once every three months and is under a duty to hold an extraordinary meeting if requested by at least a quarter of the members (Rules of Procedure, Rule 14).

[121] Rules of Procedure, Rule 30,

[122] Sole Article, para. (g), of the Protocol on Seats; para. 14-020, *infra*.

[123] Rules of the Transport Committee, adopted by the Council on 15 September 1958, OJ1952–1958 English Special Edition 72; Rules of the Committee of the European Social Fund, adopted by the Council on 25 August 1960, OJ 1959–1962 English Special Edition 65.

[124] Council Decision (EU) 2015/772 of 11 May 2015 establishing the Employment Committee, OJ 2015 L121/12.

[125] Council Decision (EU) 2015/773 of 11 May 2015 establishing the Social Protection Committee, OJ 2015 L121/16.

the Commission appoint two members (Articles 150 and 160 TFEU). These committees consult management and labour in order to perform their task of formulating opinions and contributing (together with Coreper) to the preparation of Council proceedings (see para. 12-053, *supra*). An important role is played by the Economic and Financial Committee, which keeps the economic and financial situation of the Member States and the Union under review and reports to the Council and the Commission (Article 134(2), second indent TFEU).[126] It prepares (together with Coreper) certain Council proceedings and carries out such other advisory and preparatory tasks as the Council should entrust to it (Article 134(2), third and fourth indents TFEU). The Member States, the Commission, and the ECB each appoint no more than two members of the Committee (Article 134(2), second subpara. TFEU).[127]

A number of Union acts have set up advisory committees, the Council being deemed to have the power to determine their rules by virtue of Article 242 TFEU. This also applies to the committees which supervise the Commission's implementing powers under the various comitology procedures (see para. 18-014, *infra*). Each such committee consists of representatives of the Member States and one representative of the Commission. Just as in the case of committees created by the Treaties, the Commission pays for the costs of these committee meetings out of its budget.

V. The European Investment Bank

Tasks. The European Investment Bank (EIB)[128] is an independent Union body endowed with legal personality.[129] Its task is to finance, by recourse to the capital market and utilizing its own resources, private and public investment projects fostering the balanced and steady development of the Union (Article 309 TFEU). Together with the Structural Funds and other financial instruments, the EIB seeks in this way to promote economic, social, and territorial cohesion within the Union.[130] In addition, as part of the Union's development policy, it may finance projects to be carried out in non-Union countries.[131]

13.037

---

[126] Statutes of the Economic and Financial Committee as revised by Council Decision 2012/245/EU of 26 April 2012, OJ 2012 L121/22. This committee is the successor of the Monetary Committee, which kept under review the monetary and financial situation of the Member States and the Community and advised the Council and the Commission (see Article 114(1) EC).

[127] The two members appointed by the Member States comprise one senior official from the administration and one from the national central bank, which does not attend all meetings; see Article 4 of the Statute of the Economic and Financial Committee.

[128] For the website of the EIB, see http://www.eib.org/.

[129] See Articles 308 and 309 TFEU, and Protocol (No. 5), annexed to the TEU and TFEU, on the Statute of the European Investment Bank (EIB Statute) (codified version of March 2020 available on the Bank's website). For the EIB as a Union body, see 110/75, *Mills v European Investment Bank*, 1976, paras 7–14, C-15/00 *Commission v European Investment Bank*, 2003, para. 75; for the extent of its financial and institutional independence, see 85/86, *Commission v European Investment Bank*, 1988, paras 28–30; C-370/89, *SGEEM v European Investment Bank*, 1992, paras 12–17; C-15/00, *Commission v European Investment Bank*, 2003, paras 101–10. For further details, see Dunnett, 'The European Investment Bank: Autonomous Instrument of Common Policy?' (1994) CMLRev 721–63.

[130] For economic and social cohesion, see Article 175 TFEU (para. 9-057, *supra*); see also Articles 170 and 171 TFEU on Trans-European Networks.

[131] See EIB Statute, Article 16(1).

13.038 **Operation.** The members of the EIB are the Member States (Article 308, second para. TFEU), each subscribing fixed amounts of its capital.[132] General directives for the EIB's credit policy and important decisions such as increases in capital are adopted by the Board of Governors, which consists of ministers designated by the Member States (in practice, the Finance Ministers).[133] Save as otherwise provided in its Statute, the Board of Governors adopts decisions either by majority, whereby a majority must represent at least 50 per cent of the subscribed capital, or by qualified majority, whereby eighteen votes in favour representing 68 per cent of the subscribed capital are required.[134] The Board of Governors approves the Bank's Rules of Procedure[135] and therefore has the power to organize internal matters and ensure the internal operation of the EIB in conformity with the interests of its good administration.[136] The Board of Directors takes the strategic decisions in respect of granting loans and guarantees and raising loans.[137] It also ensures that Member States fulfil their obligations under the EIB Statute.[138] The Board of Directors consists of twenty-eight directors, of whom the Member States and the Commission nominate one each. They are then appointed by the Board of Governors for a five-year term.[139] The Board of Directors generally takes its decisions by at least one-third of the members with voting rights representing at least 50 per cent of the capital; where a qualified majority is required, eighteen votes in favour and 68 per cent of the capital are needed.[140] Responsibility for the current business of the Bank lies with the Management Committee, which consists of a President and eight Vice-Presidents, who are appointed for a six-year term by the Board of Governors on a proposal from the Board of Directors.[141] Members of the Board of Directors and of the Management Committee perform their duties in complete independence and may be dismissed only by the Board of Governors.[142] The European Investment Bank has its seat in Luxembourg.[143]

VI. The European Ombudsman

13.039 **Task.** The European Ombudsman[144] looks into complaints of maladministration in the activities of Union institutions, bodies, offices, or agencies, with the exception of the Court of Justice of the European Union acting in its judicial role (Article 228 TFEU).[145] According

---

[132] Ibid., Articles 4 and 5.
[133] Ibid., Article 7(1) and (2).
[134] Ibid., Article 8.
[135] Ibid., Article 7(3)(h).
[136] C-15/00, *Commission v European Investment Bank*, 2003, paras 67–81.
[137] EIB Statute, Article 9(1).
[138] Article 271(a) TFEU, which gives the Board of Directors the same powers as are enjoyed by the Commission under Article 258 TFEU.
[139] EIB Statute, Article 9(2).
[140] Ibid., Article 10.
[141] Ibid., Article 11.
[142] Ibid., Article 9(2), last subpara. Article 9(3) and Article 11(8). Members of the Management Committee may be retired only on a proposal from the Board of Directors (ibid., Article 11(2)).
[143] Protocol on Seats, Sole Article, para. (h). See Article 5 of the Decision on Provisional Location of 8 April 1965 (see para. 14-019, *infra*).
[144] For the Ombudsman's website, see https://www.ombudsman.europa.eu/.
[145] See, generally, Vogiatzis, *The European Ombudsman and Good Administration in the European Union* (Palgrave Macmillan, 2018); Inglese and Binder, 'The European Ombudsman', in Levi-Faur and van Waarden (eds), *Democratic Empowerment in the European Union* (Edward Elgar Publishing, 2018), 85–107; Hofmann and Ziller

to the Ombudsman, there is 'maladministration' if a public authority fails to observe a rule or principle which is binding on it.[146] The regulations and general conditions governing the performance of the European Ombudsman's duties are laid down by the European Parliament in accordance with a special procedure, under which the Commission delivers an opinion and the Council grants its approval by a qualified majority (Article 228(4) TFEU).[147]

Appointment. The European Parliament elects, after each election of the European Parliament, the European Ombudsman for the duration of its term of office (Article 228(2) TFEU).[148] The Ombudsman may be dismissed by the Court of Justice only at the request of the European Parliament.[149] He or she has to be completely independent in the performance of his or her duties, which are to be carried out on a full-time basis.[150] The Ombudsman is assisted by his or her own secretariat, established at Strasbourg.[151] The Ombudsman's seat is that of the European Parliament.[152]

13.040

Inquiries. The European Ombudsman conducts inquiries into maladministration by Union institutions, bodies, offices, or agencies, either on his or her own initiative or on the basis of complaints submitted to him or her directly or through an MEP.[153] Such a complaint may be made by any citizen of the Union or any natural or legal person residing or having its registered office in a Member State.[154] The Ombudsman will not investigate a complaint if the facts have been known to the complainant for more than two years[155] or if the facts are, or have been, the subject of legal proceedings.[156] This means that a complainant must decide

13.041

(eds), *Accountability in the EU: The Role of the European Ombudsman* (Edward Elgar Publishing, 2017); Tsadiras, 'Unravelling Ariadne's Thread: the European Ombudsman's investigative powers' (2008) CMLRev 757–70.

[146] See the 1997 Annual Report, 22. For the broad interpretation given to this expression in practice, see recent annual reports and Yeng-Seng, 'Premier bilan de l'activité du médiateur européen: d'une politique des petits pas à une pratique consolidée' (2003) RMCUE 326, 329–30.

[147] Decision of the European Parliament of 9 March 1994 on the regulations and general conditions governing the performance of the Ombudsman's duties, OJ 1994 L113/15, as amended by Decision of the European Parliament of 18 June 2008, OJ 2008 L189/25 [Statute Ombudsman]. See also the Implementing Provisions adopted by decision of the European Ombudsman of 20 July 2016, OJ 2016 C321/1.

[148] The Ombudsman thus has a term of office of five years, but his mandate may be renewed by the next European Parliament. The Ombudsman has to be a Union citizen, have full civil and political rights, offer every guarantee of independence, and meet the conditions required for the exercise of the highest judicial office in his or her country or have the acknowledged competence and experience to undertake the duties of Ombudsman (Statute Ombudsman, Article 6(2)). Since the responsible parliamentary committee was unable to reach agreement on the first candidate to be approved by the plenary session, the EP Rules of Procedure were amended so as to enable several nominations to be put forward (see now Rule 231). Nominations must have the support of at least thirty-eight MEPs who are nationals of at least two Member States and may be heard by the responsible parliamentary committee. The plenary session then chooses between them. For the appointment procedure, see T-146/95, *Bernardi v European Parliament*, 1996 (action for annulment held to be unfounded).

[149] The Ombudsman may be dismissed if he or she no longer fulfils the conditions required for the performance of his or her duties or if he or she is guilty of serious misconduct (Article 228(2), second subpara. TFEU).

[150] Article 228(3) TFEU; Statute Ombudsman, Articles 9 and 10(1).

[151] Statute Ombudsman, Article 11(1).

[152] Ibid., Article 13.

[153] Article 228(1), second subpara. TFEU.

[154] Article 228(1), first subpara. TFEU. Naturally, other persons may place facts before the European Ombudsman in order to induce him or her to carry out an inquiry on his or her own initiative. 'How to make a complaint' is set out on the Ombudsman's website.

[155] Statute Ombudsman, Article 2(4).

[156] Article 228(1), second subpara. TFEU. In addition, prior to making a complaint the appropriate administrative approaches must have been made to the institution or body concerned (Statute Ombudsman, Article 2(4)). An official or other servant of the Communities may make a complaint concerning work relationships with a Community institution or body only if all the possibilities for the submission of internal administrative requests

whether to bring judicial proceedings or to bring a complaint before the Ombudsman (which does not cause time for bringing judicial proceedings to stop running).[157] Before making a complaint, a complainant must have followed the appropriate administrative procedures with the institutions or bodies concerned.[158]

The Ombudsman's first task is to try to seek a solution with the institution or body concerned.[159] If the Ombudsman finds that there has been maladministration, he or she informs the institution concerned—which then has three months to inform him or her of its views—and may make recommendations for resolving the matter.[160] At this point, the Ombudsman forwards a report to the European Parliament and to the institution concerned. The Ombudsman keeps the complainant informed of the outcome of the inquiries[161] and reports to the responsible committee of the European Parliament.[162]

Union institutions and bodies must supply any information requested and give access to any documents in their possession, subject to compliance with the security rules of the institution or body concerned.[163] The Ombudsman may not divulge information or documents obtained in the course of inquiries.[164] The national authorities must provide the Ombudsman with any information requested which may help to clarify instances of maladministration by Union institutions or bodies unless provision of the said information is precluded by national law.[165] Provided that he or she complies with the applicable national law, the Ombudsman may cooperate with similar authorities in Member States.[166]

VIII. Other Union Bodies, Offices, and Agencies

13.042 **European External Action Service.** Since the entry into force of the Lisbon Treaty, a European External Action Service (EEAS) assists the High Representative of the Union for Foreign Affairs and Security Policy in his or her various tasks of conducting the CFSP, chairing the Foreign Affairs Council, fulfilling the responsibilities in external relations incumbent on him or her within the Commission, and coordinating the Union's external

---

and complaints under the Staff Regulations have been exhausted and the relevant time-limits have expired (Statute Ombudsman, Article 2(8)).

[157] T-209/00, *Lamberts v European Ombudsman*, paras 65–6, upheld by C-234/02 P, *European Ombudsman v Lamberts*, 2004.
[158] Statute Ombudsman, Article 2(4).
[159] Statute Ombudsman, Article 3(5).
[160] Article 228(1), second subpara. TFEU and Statute Ombudsman, Article 3(6). For the Ombudsman's discretion to close a case or to reach a friendly settlement, see C-234/02 P, *European Ombudsman v Lamberts*, 2004, para. 82, and judgment upheld thereby: T-209/00, *Lamberts v European Ombudsman*, 2002, paras 78–85.
[161] Statute Ombudsman, Article 3(7). See also C-337/15 P, *European Ombudsman v Staelen*, 2017 (Ombudsman condemned to pay damages because of a qualified breach of the duty to act diligently).
[162] EP Rules of Procedure, Rule 232. It is not possible to bring an action for failure to act against the Ombudsman on account of his or her refusal to initiate an inquiry; see T-103/99, *Associazione delle cantine sociali Venete v European Ombudsman and the European Parliament* (order), 2000.
[163] Statute Ombudsman, Article 3(2).
[164] Ibid., Article 4(1). If he or she learns of facts which he or she considers might relate to criminal law, the competent national authorities must be notified. The Ombudsman must inform the institution with authority over the official or other servant and may do so if he or she discovers facts calling into question the conduct of the staff member from the disciplinary point of view (Statute Ombudsman, Article 4(2)).
[165] Ibid., Article 3(3).
[166] Ibid., Article 5.

action (Article 18(2)–(4) TEU). The Council is to determine the organization and functioning of the EEAS, on a proposal from the High Representative after consulting the European Parliament and after obtaining the consent of the Commission (Article 27(3) TEU).[167] Before the Lisbon Treaty, the external action of the Communities relied mainly on the administrative support provided by the relevant Commission's Directorates General, including the delegations established by the Commission in third countries and at international organizations, whereas in CFSP matters the Presidency of the Council was to rely on the General Secretariat of the Council and the diplomatic services of the Member States. Together with the creation of the office of High Representative of the Union for Foreign Affairs and Security Policy, the Lisbon Treaty introduced an integrated external action service with the EEAS, which comprises officials from relevant departments of the General Secretariat of the Council and of the Commission as well as staff seconded from national diplomatic services (Article 27(3) TEU).[168] The EEAS consists of a central administration in Brussels and of the Union delegations in third countries and at international organizations (see para. 14-006, *infra*). The EEAS is a functionally autonomous body, separate from the Commission and the Council's General Secretariat, under the authority of the High Representative.[169] The EEAS is also to assist the Commission and the President of the European Council and may extend appropriate support to the other Union institutions and bodies. Without being conferred any legal personality, the EEAS is endowed 'with the legal capacity necessary to perform its tasks'.[170] The day-to-day administration of the EEAS is ensured by an Executive Secretary-General.[171]

Separate offices. In order to carry out certain tasks effectively, various sectors of the administration have a degree of independence.[172] Examples are, on an interinstitutional footing,[173] the Publications Office of the European Union (OP);[174] the European Personnel Selection Office (EPSO);[175] the European Administrative

13.043

---

[167] See Council Decision 2010/427/EU of 26 July 2010 establishing the organization and the functioning of the European External Action Service, OJ 2010 L201/30. See Morgenstern-Pomorski, *The Contested Diplomacy of the European External Action Service: Inception, Establishment and Consolidation* (Routledge, 2018); Spence and Bátora (eds.), *The European External Action Service—European Diplomacy Post-Westphalia* (Springer, 2015); Blockmans and Hillion (eds), *EEAS 2.0—A Legal Commentary on Council Decision 2010/427/EU Establishing the Organisation and Functioning of the European External Action Service* (SIEPS/CEPS, 2013); Erkelens and Blockmans, 'Setting up the European External Action Service: An act of Institutional Balance' (2012) EuConst 246–79. On the role of the European Parliament in establishing the EEAS, see Raube, 'The European External Action Service and the European Parliament' (2012) HJD 65.

[168] All staff members of the EEAS are covered by the Staff Regulations and the Conditions of Employment of Other Servants and have the same rights and obligations, regardless whether they are officials of the European Union or temporary agents coming from the diplomatic services of the Member States: Council Decision 2010/427/EU (fn. 167), Article 6(7). They are to carry out their duties solely with the interests of the Union in mind and are not to seek or take instructions from any government, authority, organisation or person outside the EEAS or any body or person other than the High Representative: ibid., Article 6(2).

[169] Council Decision 2010/427/EU (fn. 167), Article 1(2).

[170] Council Decision 2010/427/EU (fn. 167).

[171] Council Decision 2010/427/EU (fn. 167), Article 4.

[172] For the legitimacy of such bodies, see Curtin, 'Holding (Quasi-)autonomous EU administrative actors to public account' (2007) ELJ 523–41.

[173] See, generally, Hummer, 'From "Interinstitutional Agreements" to "Interinstitutional Agencies/Offices"' (2007) ELJ 47–74.

[174] Decision 2009/496/EC of the European Parliament, the European Council, the Council, the Commission, the Court of Justice of the European Union, the Court of Auditors, the European Economic and Social Committee, and the Committee of the Regions of 26 June 2009, OJ 2009 L168/41. The Office is based in Luxembourg as a result of Article 8 of the Decision on Provisional Location (para. 14-019, *infra*).

[175] Decision 2002/620/EC of the European Parliament, the Council, the Commission, the Court of Justice, the Court of Auditors, the Economic and Social Committee, the Committee of the Regions, and the European

School;[176] and, for services answerable to the Commission, Eurostat (the statistical authority of the Union);[177] the Office for the administration and payment of individual entitlements;[178] and the Offices for infrastructure and logistics.[179] The European Anti-Fraud Office (OLAF) set up by the Commission carries out powers of investigation in complete independence.[180] The European Data Protection Supervisor, introduced pursuant to Article 286 EC [*now Article 16 TFEU*], also operates completely independently and supervises the application by the institutions of the Union legislation in the field of data protection.[181] The European Data Protection Supervisor is appointed by the European Parliament and the Council by common accord and is to act completely independently, assisted by a secretariat.[182] Article 8 EAEC provides for the establishment by the Commission of a Joint Nuclear Research Centre, which has evolved towards a general research-based organization active in various fields (JRC).[183] Contrary to what their titles might suggest, the Union 'Funds' are not separate bodies, but operate as normal administrative departments of the Commission.[184]

Ombudsman of 25 July 2002, OJ 2002 L197/53; for its operation and internal organization, see Decision 2002/621/EC of the Secretaries-General of those institutions and committees and of the Representative of the European Ombudsman of 25 July 2002, OJ 2002 L197/56.

[176] Decision 2005/118/EC of the European Parliament, the Council, the Commission, the Court of Justice, the Court of Auditors, the European Economic and Social Committee, the Committee of the Regions, and the Ombudsman of 26 January 2005 setting up a European Administrative School, OJ 2005 L37/14.

[177] Based in Luxembourg as a result of Article 9(a) of the Decision on Provisional Location; see now the Protocol on Seats, Sole Article, para. (c) (para. 14-020, *infra*). For its role, see Commission Decision 2012/504/EU of 17 September 2012, OJ 2012, L251/49.

[178] Established by the Commission by decision of 6 November 2002, OJ 2003 L183/30. This 'Paymaster Office' (PMO) is responsible for determining, calculating, and paying pecuniary entitlements of staff of the Union,

[179] The Commission established these offices in Brussels (OIB) and Luxembourg (OIL) by decisions of 6 November 2002, OJ 2003 L183/35 and L183/40, respectively. The Commission's Directorate-General for Health and Food Safety (DG SANTE) has a Directorate on Health and Food Audits and Analysis, previously called the 'Food and Veterinary Office' (FVO), which is based in Grange (Ireland). The Second Decision on the Seats of the Institutions of 29 October 1993 (para. 14-021, *infra*) provided that its seat was to be determined by the Irish Government.

[180] Commission Decision 1999/352/EC, ECSC, Euratom of 28 April 1999 establishing the European Anti-Fraud Office (OLAF), OJ 1999 L136/20). The Director of OLAF is appointed by the Commission, after consulting the European Parliament and the Council: Article 5(1) of Decision 1999/352 and Article 17(2) of Regulation (EU, Euratom) No. 883/2013 of the European Parliament and of the Council of 11 September 2013 concerning investigations conducted by OLAF, OJ 2013 L248/1. The members of OLAF's Supervisory Committee are appointed by common accord of the European Parliament, the Council, and the Commission: Article 15(2) of Regulation 883/2013. See Inghelram, *Legal and Institutional Aspects of the European Anti-Fraud Office (OLAF): An Analysis With a Look Forward to a European Public Prosecutor's Office* (Europa Law Publishing, 2011); Stefanou, White and Xanthaki, *OLAF at the Crossroads—Action against EU fraud* (Hart Publishing, 2011); Xanthaki, 'What is EU Fraud? And Can OLAF Really Combat It?' (2010) JFC 133–51.

[181] Articles 52 *et seq.* of Regulation (EU) 2018/1725 of the European Parliament and of the Council of 23 October 2018 on the protection of natural persons with regard to the processing of personal data by the Union institutions, bodies, offices, and agencies and on the free movement of such data, OJ 2018, L295/39, replacing Regulation (EC) No. 45/2001 of the European Parliament and of the Council of 18 December 2000 on the protection of individuals with regard to the processing of personal data by the Community institutions and bodies and on the free movement of such data, OJ 2001 L8/1. See the obligation to this effect in Article 8 of the Charter of Fundamental Rights of the European Union. For an assessment, see Hijmans, 'The European Data Protection Supervisor: The Institutions of the EC Controlled by an Independent Authority' (2006) CMLRev 1313–42.

[182] The seat of the European Data Protection Supervisor is in Brussels. Its website is http://www.edps.europa.eu/.

[183] See Commission Decision 96/282/Euratom of 10 April 1996 on the reorganization of the Joint Research Centre, OJ 1996 L107/12. The JRC has institutes located in Petten (Netherlands), Karlsruhe (Germany), Ispra (Italy), Seville (Spain), and Geel (Belgium).

[184] e.g., European Social Fund (ESF, see also Article 162 TFEU); European Globalization Adjustment Fund (EGF); and Fund for European Aid to the Most Deprived (FEAD): DG Employment, Social Affairs and Inclusion; European Agricultural Guarantee Fund (EAGF); and European Agricultural Fund for Rural Development

It is worth mentioning at this juncture that a number of international agreements concluded by the Union— especially Association Agreements—have created joint consultative bodies and joint decision-making bodies.[185]

Independent legal persons. Some Union bodies take the form of separate legal persons under the name of agencies, foundations, centres, or offices. A few legal persons have been set up in a specific institutional context, such as the Authority for European political parties and European political foundations, entrusted with the registering, controlling, and imposing of sanctions on European political parties and European political foundations;[186] and the European Data Protection Board, composed of the heads of the Member States' supervisory authorities in data protection and of the European Data Protection Supervisor, which is to ensure the consistent application of the General Data Protection Regulation.[187]

13.044

Most independent agencies, foundations, centres, or offices (hereinafter called 'agencies') are governed by a Management Board composed of representatives of the Member States and the Commission, with an Executive Director being responsible for the agency's daily management. In 2012, the European Parliament, the Council, and the Commission agreed on a 'common approach' with political commitments as to the role, structure, management and operation, and supervision of agencies.[188] These agencies have a measure of independence in regard to their budgets and personnel policies. Their special status does not prevent their acts from being subject, in many cases, to the Commission's administrative supervision and invariably to judicial review (see para. 18-022 *et seq.*, *infra*).

Treaty agencies. Some of these Union agencies are explicitly referred to by the Treaties. The EAEC Treaty established a Supply Agency, which has legal personality and financial autonomy and operates under the Commission's supervision (Articles 52–56 EAEC).[189] In the area of judicial cooperation in criminal matters and police cooperation, Articles 85 and 88 TFEU refer to Eurojust and Europol (see paras 8-023 and 8-025). Both agencies had been set up before the entry into force of the Lisbon Treaty under the non-Community provisions of the EU Treaty. The European Police Office (Europol) was established by a convention concluded between the Member States;[190] it became a genuine Union agency with legal

13.045

(EAFRD): DG Agriculture and Rural Development; European Regional Development Fund (ERDF) and Cohesion Fund: DG Regional Policy.

[185] For further details, see paras 10-008 and 10-015, *infra*. Admittedly, such bodies are not 'Union' bodies as such, but their decisions may sometimes be enforced as part of Union law: see para. 26-004, *infra*.

[186] Article 6 of Regulation (EU, Euratom) No. 1141/2014 of the European Parliament and of the Council of 22 October 2014 on the statute and funding of European political parties and European political foundations, OJ 2014 L317/1 (see para. 12-021, *supra*). The Director of the Authority is appointed for a five-year non-renewable term by the European Parliament, the Council, and the Commission by common accord, on the basis of proposals made by a selection committee composed of the Secretaries-General of those institutions following an open call for candidates. Ibid, Article 6(3). The Authority is located in the European Parliament: ibid., Article 6(5).

[187] Articles 68 to 76 of the Regulation (EU) 2016/679 of the European Parliament and of the Council of 27 April 2016 on the protection of natural persons with regard to the processing of personal data and on the free movement of such data (General Data Protection Regulation), OJ 2016 L119/1. The secretariat of the Board is provided by the European Data Protection Supervisor (ibid., Article 75).

[188] See the Common Approach annexed to the Joint Statement of the European Parliament, the Council, and the Commission of 19 July 2012, available on https://europa.eu/european-union/sites/europaeu/files/docs/body/joint_statement_and_common_approach_2012_en.pdf,

[189] For the statute of the Agency, see Council Decision 2008/114 (EC, Euratom) of 12 February 2008, OJ 2008 L41/15.

[190] Convention of 26 July 1995, based on the former Article K.3 of the Treaty on European Union, on the establishment of a European Police Office (Europol Convention), OJ 1995 C316/2.

personality as from 1 January 2010,[191] now carrying out the tasks provided for in Article 88 TFEU as the European Union Agency for Law Enforcement Cooperation (Europol).[192] Eurojust was set up by the Council as a body with legal personality.[193] It is now officially the European Union Agency for Criminal Justice Cooperation (Eurojust),[194] carrying out the tasks set out in Article 85 TFEU. Eurojust is composed of national members seconded by each Member State in accordance with its legal system, that is, a prosecutor, judge, or officer of equivalent competence. The national members form a college under the chairmanship of a President chosen from amongst their number.[195] Both agencies are established in The Hague.[196]

Since the Lisbon Treaty, Article 86 TFEU envisaged the establishment of a European Public Prosecutor's Office responsible for investigating, prosecuting, and bringing to judgment the perpetrators of offences against the Union's financial interests (see para. 8-024, *supra*). The European Public Prosecutor's Office (EPPO) has been set up as a single Office based in Luxembourg, but operating through a decentralized structure.[197] The general oversight of EPPO and its strategic decisions are in the hands of EPPO's College, consisting of the European Chief Prosecutor, who heads the EPPO, and one European Prosecutor per Member State.[198] EPPO's Permanent Chambers monitor and direct the investigations and prosecutions, which are conducted by the European Delegated Prosecutors, located in the Member States.[199]

Other independent agencies are foreseen in Article 45 EAEC and Article 187 TFEU, which allow for the set-up of joint undertakings for research and development.[200] In addition,

---

[191] Council Decision 2009/371/JHA of 6 April 2009 establishing the European Police Office (Europol), OJ 2009 L121/37.

[192] Currently governed by Regulation (EU) 2016/794 of the European Parliament and of the Council of 11 May 2016 on the European Union Agency for Law Enforcement Cooperation (Europol), OJ 2016 L135/53.

[193] Council Decision 2002/187/JHA of 28 February 2002 setting up Eurojust with a view to reinforcing the fight against serious crime (OJ 2002 L63/1).

[194] Regulation (EU) 2018/1727 of the European Parliament and of the Council of 14 November 2018 on the European Union Agency for Criminal Justice Cooperation (Eurojust), OJ 2018 L295/138.

[195] Ibid., Articles 7–10.

[196] The Second Decision on the Seats of the Institutions of 29 October 1993 provided that Europol was to have its seat at The Hague. See also the Protocol on Seats, Sole Article, para. (j) and Article 1 of Council Decision 2009/371. Thereafter, the Eurojust was also established in The Hague; see Article 1(c) of the Third Decision on Seats (para. 14-021, *infra*). From the outset, it carried out its activities in that city on a provisional basis in accordance with recital 17 in the preamble to the decision establishing Eurojust.

[197] Council Regulation (EU) 2017/1939 of 12 October 2017 implementing enhanced cooperation on the establishment of the European Public Prosecutor's Office ('the EPPO'), OJ 2017 L283/1.

[198] Ibid., Articles 8 to 9 and 11(1). The European Chief Prosecutor is to be appointed by the European Parliament and the Council (acting by simple majority) by common accord for a non-renewable term of seven years from a short-list of candidates selected by an independent selection panel: ibid., Article 14. The European Prosecutors are chosen by the Council (acting by simple majority) for each Member State from a list of three candidates following an opinion by the same selection panel: ibid., Art. 16,

[199] Ibid., Article 10,

[200] See, e.g., the Joint European Torus (JET) joint undertaking set up by Council Decision of 30 May 1978 at Culham, OJ 1978 L151/10. The undertaking's statutes are appended to that decision. Not all members of JET's staff are officials of the EAEC: see 271/83, 15, 36, 113, 158, and 203/84 and 13/85 *Ainsworth v Commission and Council*, 1987, paras 19–23. On the legal status of JET staff members, see further: T-45/01, *Sanders and Others*, 2007; T-144/02, *Eagle and Others*, 2007. See also the Galileo Joint Undertaking (on satellite radio-navigation), currently governed by Regulation (EU) No. 1285/2013 of the European Parliament and of the Council of 11 December 2013, OJ 2013 L347/1, whose tasks have been taken over by the European GNSS Agency (see n. 226, *infra*) and the European Joint Undertaking for ITER and the Development of Fusion Energy (Fusion for Energy), set up by Council Decision 2007/198/Euratom of 27 March 2007 (OJ 2007 L90/8), which has its seat in Barcelona.

OTHER UNION BODIES, OFFICES, AND AGENCIES   469

pursuant to the Protocol on the Statute of the EIB, the EIB's Board of Governors has set up a European Investment Fund.[201]

Other Union agencies. On a more general note, the Union legislature is entitled to set up an independent body whenever this squares with action pursuant to a specific Treaty article or Article 352 TFEU (see para. 18-022 *et seq., infra*).[202] In this way, it has created the European Centre for the Development of Vocational Training (Cedefop),[203] the European Foundation for the Improvement of Living and Working Conditions (EUROFOUND),[204] and the European Agency for Cooperation.[205] A series of bodies were able to start operation once the Member States decided on the location of their seats on 29 October 1993:[206] the European Environmental Agency (EEA);[207] the European Training Foundation (ETF);[208] the European Monitoring Centre for Drugs and Drug Addiction (EMCDDA);[209] the European Medicines Agency (EMA);[210] the European Union Intellectual Property Office (EUIPO),[211] and the European Agency for Safety and Health at Work (EU-

13.046

---

[201] Statutes of the European Investment Fund, adopted on 14 June 1994, as subsequently amended by the general meeting (available on https://www.eif.org/news_centre/publications/statutes.htm). Shareholders in the Fund are the European Union, the European Investment Bank and a group of financial institutions.

[202] On the increased use of these powers, see Chamon, *EU Agencies—Legal and Political Limits to the Transformation of the EU Administration* (OUP, 2016); Weiß, 'Dezentrale Agenturen in der EU-Rechtsetzung' (2016) EuR 631–65; Simoncini, 'Legal Boundaries of European Supervisory Authorities in the Financial Markets: Tensions in the Development of True Regulatory Agencies' (2015) YEL 319–50; Everson, Monda, and Vos (eds), *European Agencies in Between Institutions and Member States* (Kluwer Law International, 2014); Scholten and Rijnsbergen, 'The Limits of Agencification in the European Union', (2014) GLJ 1223–55.

[203] Council Regulation (EEC) No. 337/75 of 10 February 1975, OJ 1975 L39/1 (para. 9-052, *supra*), now replaced by Regulation (EU) 2019/128 of the European Parliament and of the Council of 16 January 2019, OJ 2019 L30/90. For its nature as a Community body, see 16/81 *Alaimo* v *Commission*, 1982, paras 7–12. As agreed when the seats of various new bodies were allocated on 29 October 1993, the Council moved the Centre's seat from Berlin to Thessaloniki: Council Regulation (EC) No. 1131/94 of 16 May 1994, OJ 1994 L127/1.

[204] Council Regulation (EEC) No. 1365/75 of 26 May 1975, OJ 1975 L139/1, now replaced by Regulation (EU) 2019/127 of the European Parliament and of the Council of 16 January 2019, OJ 2019 L30/74 (see n. to para. 9-047, *supra*). Its seat is in Ireland (Article 4(2)), more specifically in Dublin.

[205] Council Regulation (EEC) No. 3245/81 of 26 October 1981, OJ 1981 L328/1. The Agency should deal with personnel policy and recruitment as regards staff which the Community makes available as part of its financial and technical cooperation with developing countries but has never become operational.

[206] By the Second Decision on the Seats of the Institutions of 29 October 1993, para. 14-021, *infra*. The regulations setting up these bodies provided that they were to enter into force on the day following the date on which the competent authorities took a decision as to where they were to be based. They therefore entered into force on 30 October 1993 (see the notice in OJ 1994 L294/29).

[207] Council Regulation (EEC) No. 1210/90 of 7 May 1990, OJ 1990 L120/1, now replaced by Regulation (EC) No. 401/2009 of the European Parliament and of the Council of 23 April 2009, OJ 2009, L126/13. The Agency's seat is in the Copenhagen area.

[208] Council Regulation (EEC) No. 1360/90 of 7 May 1990, OJ 1990 L131/1, now replaced by Regulation (EC) No. 1339/2008 of the European Parliament and of the Council of 16 December 2008, OJ 2008 L354/82 (para. 9-052, *supra*). Its seat is at Turin.

[209] Regulation (EC) No. 1920/2006 of the European Parliament and of the Council of 12 December 2006, OJ 2006 L376/1. The Centre's seat is at Lisbon.

[210] Regulation (EC) No. 726/2004 of the European Parliament and of the Council of 31 March 2004 laying down Community procedures for the authorization and supervision of medicinal products for human and veterinary use and establishing a European Medicines Agency, OJ 2004 L136/1, replacing Council Regulation (EEC) No. 2309/93 of 22 July 1993, OJ 1993 L214/1 (which had established the European Agency for the Evaluation of Medicinal Products, the name of which was changed to European Medicines Agency by Regulation 726/2004). Following the UK's notification to withdraw from the Union, the Agency's seat has been transferred from London to Amsterdam; see Regulation (EU) 2018/1718 of the European Parliament and of the Council of 14 November 2018, OJ 2018 L291/3.

[211] Regulation (EU) 2017/1001 of the European Parliament and of the Council of 14 June 2017 on the European Union trademark, OJ 2017 L154/1. For its predecessor, the Office for Harmonization in the Internal Market (Trade Marks and Designs) (OHIM), see Council Regulation (EC) No. 40/94 of 20 December 1993 on the Community trade mark, OJ 1994 L11/1. The Office is responsible for organizing procedures for applying for and using the Community trademark and the Community design. It has a Board of Appeal, against whose

OSHA).[212] The Council has further set up a Community Plant Variety Office (CPVO);[213] a Translation Centre for Bodies of the European Union (CdT);[214] a European Union Agency for Fundamental Rights (FRA);[215] and the European Agency for Reconstruction.[216] In 2002, the European Parliament and the Council established the European Food Safety Authority (EFSA);[217] the European Maritime Safety Agency (EMSA); the European Aviation Safety Agency (EASA);[218] the European Union Agency for Cybersecurity (ENISA, initially the European Network and Information Security Agency);[219] the

---

decisions an action may be brought in the General Court. The Second Decision on the Seats of the Institutions of 29 October 1993 provided that the Office was to have its seat in Spain. The Spanish Government decided that it was to be located in Alicante. See the declaration of the Council and the Commission annexed to Regulation No. 40/94, OJ 1994 L11/36.

[212] Council Regulation (EC) No. 2062/94 of 18 July 1994, OJ 1994 L216/1, now replaced by Regulation (EU) 2019/126 of the European Parliament and of the Council of 16 January 2019, OJ 2019 L30/58 (see n. to para. 9-047, *supra*). Pursuant to the Second Decision on the Seats of the Institutions of 29 October 1993, the Spanish Government determined that its seat would be at Bilbao: see the declaration of the Council and the Commission annexed to Regulation No. 2062/94.

[213] Council Regulation (EC) No. 2100/94 of 27 July 1994 on Community plant variety rights, OJ 1994 L227/1, as amended, *inter alia*, by Council Regulation (EC) No 2506/95 of 25 October 1995, OJ 1995 L258/3 (introduction of a procedure before the General Court against decisions of Boards of Appeal by analogy with the appeal procedures in respect of the Community trademark). The Office is responsible for organizing procedures relating to applications for and the use of Community plant variety rights. The Office is based in Angers (France): see the Decision taken by common accord of the representatives of the governments of the Member States of 6 December 1996, OJ 1997 C36/1.

[214] Council Regulation (EC) No. 2965/94 of 28 November 1994, OJ 1994 L314/1. The Centre, which is based in Luxembourg, provides translation services for the aforementioned bodies and for institutions and bodies of the Union which have their own translation services should they wish to make use of the Centre's services. For the implementing provisions necessary to ensure the confidentiality of certain activities of the Translation Centre, see OJ 1999 C295/3.

[215] Council Regulation (EC) No. 168/2007 of 15 February 2007 establishing a European Union Agency for Fundamental Rights, OJ 2007 L53/1. The seat of the Agency is in Vienna (Ibid., Article 23 (5)). The Agency was established as the successor to the European Monitoring Centre on Racism and Xenophobia (established by Council Regulation (EC) No. 1035/97 of 2 June 1997, OJ 1997 L151/1), which also had its seat in Vienna. See De Schutter, *Fundamental Rights in the European Union* (OUP, 2013); von Bogdandy and van Bernstoff, 'The EU Fundamental Rights Agency within the European and International Human Rights Architecture: The Legal Framework and Some Unsettled Issues in a New Field of Administrative law' (2009) CMLRev 1035–68; Howard, 'The European Union Agency for Fundamental Rights' (2006) EHRLR 445–55; and the contributions in Alston and De Schutter (eds), *Monitoring Fundamental Rights in the EU. The Contribution of the Fundamental Rights Agency* (Hart Publishing, 2005). See further the Agreement between the European Community and the Council of Europe on cooperation between the European Union Agency for Fundamental Rights and the Council of Europe (OJ 2008 L186/7).

[216] Council Regulation (EC) No. 2454/1999 of 15 November 1999 (OJ 1999 L299/1), as amended by Council Regulation (EC) No. 2667/2000 of 5 December 2000 (OJ 2000 L306/7). The Agency's operational centre was located at Pristina, its seat in Thessaloniki. It was operational until 31 December 2008 in accordance with Council Regulation (EC) No. 1756/2006 of 28 November 2006, OJ 2006 L332/18.

[217] Regulation (EC) No. 178/2002 of the European Parliament and of the Council of 28 January 2002 laying down the general principles and requirements of food law, establishing the European Food Safety Authority and laying down procedures in matters of food safety, OJ 2002 L31/1 (see para. 9-055, *supra*). After operating provisionally in Brussels, the Authority's seat was established in Parma (Italy) by the Third Decision on Seats. See Alemanno and Gabbi (eds), *Foundations of EU Food Law and Policy: Ten Years of the European Food Safety Authority* (Routledge, 2016).

[218] Regulation (EC) No. 1406/2002 of the European Parliament and of the Council of 27 June 2002 establishing a European Maritime Safety Agency, OJ 2002 L208/1, and Regulation (EC) No. 1592/2002 of the European Parliament and of the Council of 15 July 2002 on common rules in the field of civil aviation and establishing a European Aviation Safety Agency, OJ 2002 L240/1, now replaced by Regulation (EU) 2018/1139 of the European Parliament and of the Council of 4 July 2018, OJ 2018 L212/1. The Maritime Safety Agency has its seat in Lisbon, the Aviation Agency in Cologne (see the Third Decision on Seats).

[219] Regulation (EU) 2019/881 of the European Parliament and of the Council of 17 April 2019 on ENISA (the European Union Agency for Cybersecurity) and on information and communications technology cybersecurity certification, OJ 2019 L151/15, replacing Regulation (EC) No. 460/2004 of the European Parliament and of the

European Centre for Disease Prevention and Control (ECDC);[220] and the European Union Agency for Railways (ERA).[221] Bodies that were established more recently include the European Fisheries Control Agency (EFCA);[222] the European Border and Coast Guard Agency (FRONTEX);[223] the European Chemicals Agency (ECHA);[224] the European Institute for Gender Equality (EIGE);[225] the European Global Navigation Satellite System (GNSS) Supervisory Authority (GSA), which is to be transformed into the European Union Agency for the Space Programme;[226] the European Institute of Innovation and Technology (EIT);[227] the European Union Agency for the Cooperation of Energy Regulators (ACER);[228] the Office of the Body of European Regulators for Electronic Communications (BEREC);[229] the European Asylum Support Office (EASO);[230] the three supervisory bodies of the European system for financial supervision, namely the European

---

Council of 10 March 2004 establishing the European Network and Information Security Agency, OJ 2004 L77/1. It is located in Athens, Greece and has a second office in Heraklion, Greece.

[220] Regulation (EC) No. 851/2004 of the European Parliament and of the Council of 21 April 2004, OJ 2004 L142/1. It has its seat in Stockholm (see the Third Decision on Seats).

[221] Regulation (EU) 2016/796 of the European Parliament and of the Council of 11 May 2016, OJ 2016 L138/1, replacing Regulation (EC) No. 881/2004 of the European Parliament and of the Council of 29 April 2004 (establishing a European Railway Agency), OJ 2004 L164/1. It has its seat in Lille-Valenciennes (see the Third Decision on Seats).

[222] Regulation (EU) 2019/473 of the European Parliament and of the Council of 19 March 2019 on the European Fisheries Control Agency, OJ 2019 L83/18, that replaced Council Regulation (EC) No 768/2005 of 26 April 2005 (establishing a Community Fisheries Control Agency), OJ 2005 L128/1. The Agency has its seat in Vigo (Regulation 2019/473, Article 27(4)).

[223] Regulation (EU) 2016/1624 of the European Parliament and of the Council of 14 September 2016, OJ 2016 L251/1; see previously Council Regulation (EC) No. 2007/2004 of 26 October 2004 establishing a European Agency for the Management of Operational Cooperation at the External Borders of the Member States of the European Union, OJ 2004 L349/1 (see para. 8-007, supra). The Agency has its seat in Warsaw (see Council Decision 2005/358/EC of 26 April 2005, OJ 2005 L114/13).

[224] Regulation (EC) No. 1907/2006 of the European Parliament and of the Council of 18 December 2006 concerning the Registration, Evaluation, Authorisation and Restriction of Chemicals (REACH), establishing a European Chemicals Agency, OJ 2006 L396/1. The Agency has its seat in Helsinki (see the Third Decision on Seats).

[225] Regulation (EC) No. 1922/2006 of the European Parliament and of the Council of 20 December 2006, OJ 2006 L403/9. The Institute has its seat in Vilnius (see Decision 2006/966/EC taken by common agreement between the representatives of the Governments of Member States of 11 December 2006, OJ 2006 L403/61), after being provisionally located in Brussels.

[226] Regulation (EU) No 912/2010 of the European Parliament and of the Council of 22 September 2010 (setting up the European GNSS Agency), OJ 2010 L276/11. The agency has its seat in Prague (see Decision of the Representatives of the Governments of the Member States of 10 December 2010, OJ 2010 L342/15). For its transformation, see the Commission Proposal for a Regulation of the European Parliament and the Council establishing the space programme of the Union and the European Union Agency for the Space Programme, COM/2018/447 final.

[227] Regulation (EC) No. 294/2008 of the European Parliament and of the Council of 11 March 2008, OJ 2008 L97/1. The Institute has its seat in Budapest (see Decision 2008/634/EC taken by common agreement between the Representatives of the Governments of the Member States of 18 June 2008, OJ 2008 L206/16).

[228] Regulation (EU) 2019/942 of the European Parliament and of the Council of 5 June 2019, OJ 2019, L158/22. The Agency has its seat in Ljubljana (see Decision 2009/913/EU taken by common agreement between the Representatives of the Governments of the Member States of 7 December 2009 (OJ 2009 L322/39).

[229] Regulation (EU) 2018/1971 of the European Parliament and of the Council of 11 December 2018 establishing the Body of European Regulators for Electronic Communications (BEREC) and the Agency for Support for BEREC (BEREC Office), OJ 2018 L321/1. The Agency has its seat in Riga (see Decision 2010/349/EU taken by common agreement between the Representatives of the Governments of the Member States of 31 May 2010 (OJ 2010 L156/12).

[230] Regulation (EU) No. 439/2010 of the European Parliament and the Council of 19 May 2010 establishing a European Asylum Support Office, OJ 2010 L132/11. The Office is located in Valletta Harbour, Malta (see Decision 2010/762/EU taken by common agreement between the Representatives of the Governments of the Member States of 25 February 2010, OJ 2010 L324/47).

472   OTHER INSTITUTIONS AND BODIES OF THE UNION

Securities and Markets Authority (ESMA);[231] the European Banking Authority (EBA);[232] and the European Insurance and Occupational Pensions Authority (EIOPA);[233] and the Single Resolution Board (SRB).[234] In order to support the initiatives ensuring fair labour mobility, the European Parliament and the Council most recently established the European Labour Authority (ELA).[235]

In the area of police and judicial cooperation in criminal matters, Eurojust and Europol have been joined by the European Union Agency for Law Enforcement Training (CEPOL), taking the place of the European Police College,[236] and the European Agency for the Operational Management of Large-Scale IT Systems in the Area of Freedom, Security and Justice (EU-LISA).[237]

A number of bodies with legal personality have been set up in connection with the CFSP, mostly under the non-Community provisions of the EU Treaty, before the entry into force of the Lisbon Treaty. These include the European Union Institute for Security Studies (EUISS);[238] a European Union Satellite Centre (SATCEN);[239] as well as a European Defence Agency (EDA).[240]

13.047   **Executive agencies.** The above-mentioned Union agencies must be distinguished from the executive agencies with legal personality which the Council—pursuant to Article 352 TFEU—has mandated the Commission to set up.[241]. Under its own control and

---

[231] Regulation (EU) No. 1095/2010 of the European Parliament and of the Council of 24 November 2010 establishing a European Supervisory Authority (European Securities and Markets Authority), OJ 2010 L331/84. The ESMA has its seat in Paris.

[232] Regulation (EU) No. 1093/2010 of the European Parliament and of the Council of 24 November 2010 establishing a European Supervisory Authority (European Banking Authority), OJ 2010 L331/12. Following the UK's notification to withdraw from the Union, the seat from the EBA has been transferred from London to Paris; see Regulation (EU) 2018/1717 of the European Parliament and of the Council of 14 November 2018, OJ 2018 L291/1.

[233] Regulation (EU) No. 1094/2010 of the European Parliament and of the Council of 24 November 2010 establishing a European Supervisory Authority (European Insurance and Occupational Pensions Authority), OJ 2010 L331/43. The EIOPA has its seat in Frankfurt.

[234] Regulation (EU) No. 806/2014 of the European Parliament and of the Council of 15 July 2014 establishing uniform rules and a uniform procedure for the resolution of credit institutions and certain investment firms in the framework of a Single Resolution Mechanism and a Single Resolution Fund, OJ 2014 L225/1. The seat of the SRB is in Brussels.

[235] Regulation (EU) 2019/1149 of the European Parliament and of the Council of 20 June 2019 establishing a European Labour Authority, OJ 2019 L186/21. Provisionally located in Brussels, its seat is to be established in Bratislava; see Decision (EU) 2019/1199 by common accord between the Representatives of the Governments of the Member States of 13 June 2019, OJ 2019 L189/68. See also Van Nuffel, 'De Europese Arbeidsautoriteit: een nieuw agentschap voor eerlijke arbeidsmobiliteit binnen de interne markt', in Verschueren (ed.), *Detachering—Nieuwe ontwikkelingen in het Europees recht vanuit Belgisch en Nederlands perspectief* (Die Keure, 2019), 227–58.

[236] Regulation (EU) 2015/2219 of the European Parliament and of the Council of 25 November 2015 on the European Union Agency for Law Enforcement Training (CEPOL), OJ 2015 L319/1, replacing Council Decision 2005/681/JHA of 20 September 2005 establishing the European Police College (CEPOL), OJ 2005 L256/63 (see para. 8-025, *supra*). CEPOL is established in Budapest.

[237] Regulation (EU) 2018/1726 of the European Parliament and of the Council of 14 November 2018, OJ 2018 L295/99 (see para. 8-007, *supra*). EU-LISA is based in Tallinn.

[238] Council Decision 2014/75/CFSP of 10 February 2014, OJ 2014 L41/13, replacing Council Joint Action 2001/554/CFSP of 20 July 2001, OJ 2001 L200/1. The institute has its seat in Paris.

[239] Council Decision 2014/401/CFSP of 26 June 2014, OJ 2014 L188/73, replacing Council Joint Action 2001/555/CFSP of 20 July 2001, OJ 2001 L200/5 (see para. 10-032, *supra*). The centre is established at Torrejón de Ardoz (Spain). Denmark is not taking part in those activities of the centre that have implications for defence policy.

[240] Council Decision 2011/411/CFSP of 12 July 2011, OJ 2011 L183/16, replacing Council Joint Action 2004/551/CFSP of 12 July 2004, OJ 2004 L245/17 (see para. 10-032, *supra*). The Agency has its seat in Brussels. Denmark is not bound by this Decision.

[241] On the basis of Council Regulation (EC) No. 58/2003 of 19 December 2002 laying down the statute for executive agencies to be entrusted with certain tasks in the management of Community programmes, OJ 2003 L11/1.

responsibility, the Commission may entrust such executive agencies, for a limited time, with certain tasks relating to the management of Union programmes.[242]

Connected bodies. The Member States have, by convention, created a number of bodies which fall outside the framework of the Treaties, yet are closely connected with it. These are the European University Institute in Florence[243] and the various European Schools.[244] The Union is represented in the management of those bodies and the EU budget covers costs not paid by the Member States.[245] As a result of the latter aspect, a Member State which acts in breach of the Statute of the European Schools thereby producing a burden on the EU budget, also infringes Article 4(3) TEU.[246]

13.048

---

[242] See Commission Implementing Decision (EU) 2021/173 of 12 February 2021 establishing the European Climate, Infrastructure and Environment Executive Agency, the European Health and Digital Executive Agency, the European Research Executive Agency, the European Innovation Council and SMEs Executive Agency, the European Research Council Executive Agency, and the European Education and Culture Executive Agency and repealing Implementing Decisions 2013/801/EU, 2013/771/EU, 2013/778/EU, 2013/779/EU, 2013/776/EU and 2013/770/EU, OJ 2021 L50/9..

[243] Convention of 19 April 1972 setting up a European University Institute, OJ 1976 C29/1 [the Convention]. Article 9 EAEC, which provides for the establishment of 'an institution of university status', has never been implemented.

[244] See the establishment of a European School in Luxembourg by the Statute of the European School of 12 April 1957 and in other places of work of institutions and bodies by the Protocol on the establishment of European Schools of 13 April 1962 adopted pursuant to that Statute. The 1962 protocol has been replaced by the Convention of 21 June 1994 defining the Statute of the European Schools, OJ 1994 L212/3 [the Statute] (this convention was concluded between the Member States and the three Communities; it was ratified on behalf of the EC and the EAEC by a Council decision of 17 June 1994 pursuant to Article 235 EC [*now Article 352 TFEU*] and Article 203 EAEC and on behalf of the ECSC by a Commission decision based on the first para. of Article 95 ECSC).

[245] See the representative of the Union on the High Council of the European University Institute (Convention, Article 6(3); the representative does not have voting rights) and the Union representative on the Board of Governors of the European Schools (Statute, Article 8(1); that representative does have the right to vote) and the Union's contribution towards operating costs (provided for in Article 19(2) of the Convention and Article 25(2) of the Statute).

[246] 44/84, *Hurd v Jones*, 1986, paras 36–45; C-6/89, *Commission v Belgium*, 1990. cf. C-132/09, *Commission v Belgium*, 2010.

14
The Union as an International Organization

14.001 **Symbols of the Union.** The European Union is an international organization bestowed with legal personality, which has succeeded to the European Communities. In common with other international organizations the Union possesses rules relating to its financing, seat, language use, staff regulations, transparency, and access to documents, which are discussed in this chapter.

Before the establishment of the European Union, the image and identity of the Communities had already been strengthened through the adoption of the flag and the anthem of the Council of Europe[1] and the introduction of a Union driving licence.[2] The Member States also agreed amongst themselves to introduce a passport of uniform pattern.[3] The flag and the anthem have developed into symbols of the European Union, together with the euro, the motto, 'United in diversity', and 9 May as 'Europe Day'.[4] Next to the introduction of Union citizenship, these symbols reflect a Union that is developing more State-like characteristics. In order not to stress these elements, it was decided during the 2007 Intergovernmental Conference that the Treaties should not contain any explicit reference to these symbols, unlike what was proposed for the EU Constitution, which mentioned the symbols of the Union in Article I-8.[5] From its side, the European Parliament included a reference to the Union's symbols in its Rules of Procedure (Rule 238).

---

[1] The official flag of the Union is rectangular in form and blue in colour and has at its centre a circle of twelve five-pointed gold stars (the number twelve symbolizes perfection and entirety and hence is not linked to the number of Member States; see the Commission's answer of 22 November 1993 to Question No. E-1701/93 (Von Wechmar), OJ 1994 C219/31); its anthem is the music of the Ode to Joy from the fourth movement of Beethoven's Ninth Symphony (both printed in (1986) 4 EC Bull. 52–3). See the request contained in the European Parliament's resolution of 11 April 1983 (OJ 1983 C128/18), the proposal in the report of the Adonnino Committee to attain a people's Europe (1985 EC Bull. Suppl 7), the approval of that proposal by the European Council ((1985) 6 EC Bull. points 1.4.7 and 1.4.8), and the declaration of the Presidents of the Council and the other institutions ((1986) 4 EC Bull. point 2.1.8.1). See also Bieber, 'Die Flagge in der EG', in Fiedler and Ress (eds), *Verfassungsrecht und Völkerrecht. Gedächtnisschrift für Wilhelm Karl Geck* (Heymanns, 1989), 59–77. Further particulars on the flag as the European emblem may be found in T-127/02, *Concept—Anlagen u. Geräte nach 'GMP' für Produktion u. Labor v OHIM*, 2004 (on the prohibition to register trademarks on account of their similarity to the European emblem).

[2] First Council Directive 80/1263/EEC of 4 December 1980 on the introduction of a Community driving licence, OJ 1980 L375/1; Council Directive 91/439/EEC of 29 July 1991 on driving licences, OJ 1991 L237/1.

[3] See the resolutions adopted on 23 June 1981 and 30 June 1982 by the representatives of the governments of the Member States, meeting within the Council (OJ 1981 C241/1 and OJ 1982. C179/1, respectively), confirmed by the European Council at Fontainebleau on 25 and 26 June 1984 (1984) 6 EC Bull. points 1.1.9 and 3.5.1), on 14 July 1986 (OJ 1986 C185/1) and on 10 July 1995 (OJ 1995 C 200/1). See Denza, 'Le passeport européen' (1982) RMC 489–93.

[4] The celebration of 9 May refers to the day in 1950 on which Robert Schuman pronounced the declaration containing the proposal that led to the creation of the ECSC (see para. 1-008, *supra*). For these symbols, see Röttinger, 'Die Hoheitszeichen der Europäischen Union —ein paar vielleicht nicht nur theoretische Rechtsfragen' (2003) EuR 1095–108; Favret, 'L'Union européenne: 'l'unité dans la diversité'—Signification et pertinence d'une devise' (2003) RTDE 657–60. On their impact, see Theiler, *Political Symbolism and European Integration* (Manchester University Press, 2005).

[5] See, however, Declaration (No. 52), annexed to the Lisbon Treaty (OJ 2010 C83/355), in which sixteen of the Member States declare that these symbols will for them continue as symbols to express the sense of community of the people in the European Union and their allegiance to it.

I. Legal Personality and Representation

Legal personality and legal capacity. The Treaties confer legal personality on the Union (Article 47 TEU). Before the Lisbon Treaty, the Treaties conferred legal personality on each of the Communities (Article 281 EC; Article 184 EAEC; see also Article 6 ECSC), but not on the European Union, although the latter was widely considered to have functional legal personality.[6] Under Article 1, third para. TEU, the European Union has replaced and succeeded the European Community. The European Atomic Energy Community continues to exist as a separate entity with its own legal personality (see para. 2-003, *supra*). The fact that the Union has legal personality means, first, that the Union is a subject of international law (see para. 14-005, *infra*).[7] Second, it enjoys the most extensive legal capacity accorded to legal persons governed by public law[8] under the laws of the Member States, in particular to acquire or dispose of property and to be a party to legal proceedings (Article 335 TFEU).[9]

14.002

Position in the domestic legal systems. The fact that the Union has legal capacity and the capacity to enter into transactions in the domestic legal systems means that it may also sue and be sued. Thus, the Union may appear before the national courts, except in disputes which, under the Treaties, have to be brought before the Court of Justice of the European Union. In this way, the Union Courts have exclusive jurisdiction to entertain damages claims for non-contractual liability based on the second para. of Article 340 TFEU.[10] Since the national courts have no jurisdiction to entertain such claims, they are likewise not entitled to prescribe, with regard to one of the institutions, any interim measure or measure of inquiry (e.g. commissioning an expert report) whose purpose is to establish the role of that institution in the events which allegedly caused damage.[11]

14.003

---

[6] See Blokker, 'International Legal Personality of the European Communities and the European Union: Inspirations from Public International Law' (2016) YEL 1; Erlbacher, 'Rechtspersönlichkeit und Rechtsnachfolge', in Hummer and Obwexer (eds), *Der Vertrag von Lissabon* (Nomos, 2009), 123, In view of the considerable autonomy conferred upon the European Union, it was argued that the Union was to be regarded as having legal personality under international law even before this was made explicit; see Österdahl, 'The EU and its Member States, Other States and International Organisations—The Common European Security and Defence Policy After Nice' (2001) Nordic JIL 341–50; Wessel, 'De Europese Unie in de internationale rechtsorde' (T.M.C. Asser Press, 2001) 11–37, more cautiously, see Grard, 'La condition internationale de l'Union européenne après Nice' (2000) RAE 374, 375–8; Tiilikainen, 'To Be or Not to Be? An Analysis of the Legal and Political Elements of Statehood in the EU's External Identity' (2001) E For Aff Rev 223–41.The argument for the Union's legal personality was strengthened in particular after the Treaty of Amsterdam introduced, in Article 24 EU, the power of the Council to conclude agreements with third countries and international organizations. In the agreements concluded by the Council on behalf of the Union before the Lisbon Treaty, the European Union was already indicated as a participating party bound by the agreements.

[7] The flip side of this is that the Union also has international responsibility; see Delgado Casteleiro, *The International Responsibility of the European Union: From Competence to Normative Control* (Cambridge University Press, 2016).

[8] See 43/59, 45/59, and 48/59, *Von Lachmüller and Others v Commission*, 1960, 472; 44/59, *Fiddelaar v Commission*, 1960, 543.

[9] See also Article 185 EAEC. This also encompasses the representation of the European Union before an international court or tribunal; see C-73/14, *Council v Commission*, paras 58–9. Moreover, Article 218(9) TFEU does not apply as to the determination of the content of the Union's position, ibid., paras 63–9. As for representation in national court, see C-199/11, *Otis*, 2012, paras 27–36.

[10] In addition to the jurisdiction of the Court of Justice to entertain claims for damage caused by Union institutions or the ECB or their servants (non-contractual liability: Articles 268 and 340 TFEU), there are also staff disputes (Article 270 TFEU) and disputes brought before the Court pursuant to arbitration clauses (Article 272 TFEU).

[11] C-275/00, *Frist and Franex*, 2002, paras 43–8.

Any other body, office, or agency of the Union with legal personality in its own right takes part in domestic legal transactions in the Member States independently. They may participate in legal proceedings before the competent national courts, provided that the disputes do not come within the jurisdiction of the Court of Justice of the European Union. Thus, disputes based on non-contractual liability are generally governed by the system of liability determined by the second para. of Article 340 TFEU.[12]

14.004 **Representation in the domestic legal systems.** In the domestic legal systems of the Member States, the Union is, in principle, represented by the Commission. However, it may also be represented by each of the institutions, by virtue of their administrative autonomy, in matters relating to their respective operation (Article 335 TFEU[13]). In principle, the Commission is empowered to act before the national courts, but it may authorize another institution to do so.

14.005 **International legal capacity.** Just like the Member States, the Union, as a legal person, has the capacity to exercise rights in international legal transactions and enter into obligations over the whole field of its objectives.[14] This means that the Union may, in principle, conclude agreements with third countries and international organizations, be held liable under international law if it breaches its obligations, and take action itself where its rights are infringed. If a Union institution concludes an agreement, the agreement will be binding on the Union and it will be liable for its performance.[15]

The Union and the EAEC have the capacity to conclude international agreements, including multilateral agreements establishing an international organization.[16] In some cases, the Union may only conclude international agreements together with the Member States (see para. 21-013 *et seq.*, *infra*). It may likewise accede to an international organization, provided that the statutes of the organization permit non-States to join.[17] In some instances, the Union has taken the place of its Member States; generally, it becomes a member alongside the Member States, as in the case of the World Trade Organization (WTO).[18] In the event that the Union becomes a member of an international organization alongside the Member

---

[12] See, e.g., Article 35.3 of the ESCB Statute.
[13] Before the Lisbon Treaty, Article 282 EC stated that the Community was to be represented by the Commission. In practice, however, the other institutions also engaged in domestic legal transactions, in particular pursuant to their power to engage in expenditure authorized under the budget (see para. 20-007, *infra*).
[14] See 22/70, *Commission v Council*, 1971, paras 13–14; 3, 4, and 6/76 *Kramer*, 1976, paras 17–18.
[15] C-327/91, *France v Commission*, 1994, paras 24–5.
[16] Opinion 1/76, *Draft Agreement establishing a European laying-up fund for inland waterway vessels*, 1977, para. 5. For internal limitations on powers in this connection, see para. 18-023, *infra*.
[17] Various international organizations, particularly those established before the Communities, do not allow non-States to be members, but permitted the Communities—and now the Union—to take part in their activities without voting rights as an 'observer' or with some similar status. See, for instance, the Council of Europe (resolution of the Committee of Ministers of May 1951); the UN General Assembly (Resolution 3208 (XXIX) of 11 October 1974); the International Labour Organization (ILO Constitution, Article 12(2)). For representation at the UN, see the Council's answer of 30 November 2000 to Question No. E-2810/00 (Titford), OJ 2001 C113E/181. See also the website of the EU delegation to the UN: http://www.eu-un.europa.eu/. See further, the contributions in Kaddous (ed.), *The European Union in International Organisations and Global Governance—Recent Developments* (Hart Publishing, 2015); Blavoukos and Bourantonis (eds), *The EU Presence in International Organisations* (Routledge, 2011); Wouters, Hoffmeister and Ruys (eds), *The United Nations and the European Union: an ever stronger partnership* (TMC Asser Press, 2006).
[18] See para. 10-010, *infra*. See also Gstöhl, ' "Patchwork Power" Europe: The EU's Representation in International Institutions' (2009) E For Aff Rev 385–403; Hoffmeister, 'Outsider or Frontrunner? Recent Developments under International and European Law on the Status of the European Union in International Organizations and Treaty Bodies' (2007) CMLRev 41–66.

States, that organization has to decide whether the Union should have voting rights of its own or whether it may exercise the Member States' rights on terms to be determined.[19] In the latter case, before any meeting of the organization it will require a declaration to be made indicating whether competence lies with the Union or the Member States in respect of a particular item of the agenda and who is to exercise the right to vote.[20] The Union and the Member States have to coordinate their positions in advance. Where the Union is empowered under Union law to conclude an international agreement in the context of an organization but cannot do so itself under the rules of that organization, it may exercise its external competence through the medium of the Member States acting jointly in the Union's interest.[21]

International representation of the Union. Article 221 TFEU provides for 'Union delegations' which are to represent the Union in third countries and at international organizations.[22] The delegations are placed under the authority of the High Representative of the Union for Foreign Affairs and Security Policy and act in close cooperation with Member States' diplomatic and consular missions (Article 222(2) TFEU). The Union delegations have been integrated into the European External Action Service (EEAS), which comprises officials of the Council and the Commission as well as staff seconded from the diplomatic services of the Member States (see para. 13-042, *supra*). Staff in delegations comprise EEAS staff and, where appropriate for the implementation of the Union budget and Union policies, Commission staff.[23] Each Head of Delegation has authority over all staff in the delegation, whatever their status, and for all its activities.[24] The Head of Delegation receives instructions from the High Representative and the EEAS. In areas where the Commission exercises external powers, that institution may also issue instructions to delegations.[25]

14.006

Since the Lisbon Treaty, the external action of the Union is thus supported by a single diplomatic and administrative apparatus. Yet, outside the framework of the CFSP, the Treaties still do not lay down general rules on the external representation of the Union. In matters coming within the CFSP, the Union is represented by the High Representative of the Union for Foreign Affairs and Security Policy (Article 27(2) TEU)[26] and by the President of the

---

[19] Govaere, Capiau and Vermeersch, 'In-Between Seats: The Participation of the European Union in International Organisations' (2004) E For Aff Rev 155–87; Neuwahl, 'Shared Powers or Combined Incompetence? More on Mixity' (1996) CMLRev 667–87; Sack, 'The European Community's Membership of International Organisations' (1995) CMLRev 1227–56.

[20] C-25/94, *Commission v Council*, 1996.

[21] Opinion 2/91, *Convention No 170 of the International Labour Organisation concerning safety in the use of chemicals at work*, 1993, para. 5.

[22] See Koops and Macaj, *The European Union as a Diplomatic Actor* (IES, 2015); Schmalenbach, 'Die Delegationen der Europäischen Union in Drittländern und bei Internationalen Organisationen' (2012) EuR Beiheft 125. Before the Lisbon Treaty, the Union/Communities did not set up diplomatic missions. Nevertheless, pursuant to its power of internal organization and its power to conduct negotiations on agreements, the Commission had established delegations in more than a hundred and fifty third countries and with international organizations based in Geneva, Paris, Nairobi, New York, Rome, and Vienna. For its part, the General Secretariat of the Council set up liaison offices in Geneva and New York in order to maintain contacts with the international organizations based in those cities.

[23] Council Decision 2010/427/EU of 26 July 2010 establishing the organization and the functioning of the European External Action Service (OJ 2010 L201/30), Article 5(2).

[24] Ibid., Article 5(2).

[25] Ibid., Article 5(3).

[26] Before the Lisbon Treaty, the Union was represented by the Presidency of the Council. The Presidency was assisted by the High Representative for the CFSP and, if needs be, by the next Member State to hold the Presidency; the Commission was to be 'fully associated in [those] tasks' (Article 18(1) to (4) EU).

European Council 'at his or her level and in that capacity' (Article 15(6), second subpara. TEU). The power to represent the Union externally for matters falling outside the CFSP is, however, not attributed by the Lisbon Treaty to a single institution. The way in which the Union manifests itself externally coincides with the powers that each institution has to act externally.

Where international discussions relate to subjects which fall within the competence of the Union, a delegation from the Commission will normally attend (e.g. in respect of trade policy), but when the negotiation and conclusion of an agreement are envisaged, it is for the Council to nominate the Union negotiator or the head of the Union's negotiating team, depending on the subject of the agreement envisaged (Article 218(3) TFEU; see para. 21-003, *infra*). In the event that the discussions also cover subjects within the competence of the Member States, they will generally insist on their own representatives being present. In such a case, 'unity in the international representation of the Union' requires there to be close cooperation between the Member States and the Union institutions, both in the process of negotiating and concluding agreements and in the fulfilment of the obligations entered into.[27] The Member States are invariably represented alongside the Union in international organizations whose sphere of action is more broadly defined than the competences of the Union. The Union and its Member States must then make arrangements as to how their position is to be represented in the organization and how voting rights are to be exercised.[28]

Depending on whether the subject matter largely falls within the scope of the Union's exclusive competences or not, the Commission or the Member State holding the Council Presidency will act. A breach of such an arrangement may result in the annulment of the decision by which the institution concerned determined its action in the organisation in question.[29] The Commission represents the Union when it acts before an international court or tribunal.[30]

II. Privileges and Immunities

14.007 **Scope.** In common with other international organizations, the Union enjoys privileges and immunities with a view to being able to carry out its tasks undisturbed. These privileges and immunities—enshrined in a Protocol appended to the Treaties in accordance with Article 343 TFEU[31]—have a purely functional character: they are intended to avoid any interference with the functioning and independence of the Union.[32]

---

[27] Opinion 2/91, *Convention No 170 of the International Labour Organization concerning safety in the use of chemicals at work*, 1993, para. 36; Opinion 1/94, *Agreement establishing the World Trade Organization*, 1994, para. 108; Opinion 2/00, *Cartagena Protocol*, 2001, para. 18; C-246/07, *Commission v Sweden*, 2010, para. 73. See also Opinion 1/78, *Draft Convention of the International Atomic Energy Agency on the Physical Protection of Nuclear Materials, Facilities and Transports*, 1978, paras 34–6.

[28] Such arrangements may be enshrined in the decision by which the Union concludes the international agreement concerned.

[29] C-25/94, *Commission v Council*, 1996, paras 48–51.

[30] C-73/14, *Council v Commission*, 2015, paras 55–8.

[31] See now Protocol (No. 7), annexed to the TEU, TFEU, and EAEC Treaty, on the Privileges and Immunities of the European Union, OJ 2010 C83/266, which replaced Protocol (No. 36), appended by the Member States to the EC Treaty in accordance with Article 291 EC, on the Privileges and Immunities of the European Communities. Article 291 EC took over the wording of Article 28 of the Merger Treaty as a result of the simplification introduced by the Amsterdam Treaty. See Schmidt, 'Le Protocole sur les privilèges et immunités des Communautés européennes' (1991) CDE 67–99.

[32] C-2/88, Imm., *Zwartveld and Others*, 1990, paras 19–20.

In order to secure their independence, the ECB, the EIB, and other Union bodies with legal personality are also covered by the Protocol on Privileges and Immunities.[33] An agreement concluded between the Member States also grants privileges and immunities to the military and civilian personnel who the Member States make available for CFSP activities of the Union.[34]

Exemption from inquiry and taxation. First, the Protocol provides that the Union's premises, buildings, and archives are inviolable; exempt from search, requisition, confiscation, or appropriation; and not to be the subject of any administrative or legal measure of constraint without the authorization of the Court of Justice (Articles 1 and 2).[35] As far as garnishee orders are concerned, the jurisdiction of the Court of Justice is confined to considering whether such a measure is likely to interfere with the proper functioning and the independence of the European Union.[36] For the rest, the garnishee procedure is governed by the applicable national law. In addition, the Union is exempt from direct taxes (Article 3, first para.) and from customs duties and restrictions on imports and exports (Article 4). Under bilateral arrangements with Member States, appropriate measures are to be taken to remit or refund indirect taxes paid on purchases made by the Union for its official use (see Article 3, second para.). This includes all types of purchase, including obtaining a supply of services, which are necessary for the accomplishment of the Union's task, but it is required that the indirect taxes should be included in the purchase price.[37] This exemption does not apply to direct taxes levied on parties contracting with the Union, even when such taxes are passed on to the Union.[38]

14.008

Staff rights. The Protocol provides for specific rules for officials and other servants of the Union, such as the immunity from prosecution for what they have done, said, or written in their official capacity (Article 11 of the Protocol). Article 12 of the Protocol provides that officials and other servants are to be exempt from national taxes on salaries, wages, and emoluments paid to them by the Union and have to pay a tax for the benefit of the Union on their Union salaries.[39] This tax is intended to secure the independent operation of the Union and to place staff from different Member States on an equal footing.[40] Since those privileges and immunities are conferred on officials solely in the interests of the Union, each

14.009

---

[33] For the EIB and the ECB, see Article 343 TFEU, and Articles 21 and 22 of the Protocol and Article 39 of the ESCB Statute. As far as other bodies and agencies are concerned, see the regulations establishing them referred to in para. 13-044 *et seq., supra*.

[34] See the agreement between the EU Member States of 17 November 2003, OJ 2003 C321/6.

[35] See also C-316/19, *Commission v Slovenia*, 2020, paras 67–110 (breach by Slovenia of the inviolability of the archives of the ECB by unilaterally seizing, at the premises of the Central Bank of Slovenia, documents connected to the performance of the tasks of the ESCB).

[36] 1/87 SA, *Universal Tankship* (order), 1987, para. 3; 1/88 SA, *Générale de Banque v Commission*, 1989, para. 15 (case numbers include the initials 'SA' for the French '*saisie-arrêt*').

[37] C-199/05, *European Community v Belgian State*, 2006, paras 31–44; C-163/14, *Commission v. Belgium*, 2016, paras 38–45.

[38] C-437/04, *Commission v Belgium*, 2007, paras 48–63.

[39] See Regulation (EEC, Euratom, ECSC) No. 260/68 of the Council of 29 February 1968 laying down the conditions and procedure for applying the tax for the benefit of the European Communities, OJ 1968. It does not empower the Union to make freelance interpreters subject to Union tax: T-202/96 and T-204/96, *Von Löwis and Alvarez-Cotera v Commission*, 1998, paras 51–8. This exemption from national tax is to be distinguished from the fiscal immunity enjoyed by the Union itself, under specific conditions: C-437/04, *Commission v Belgium*, 2007, paras 50–9. This does not preclude Member States from being able to grant certain social allowances to staff of the Union institutions having their seat on their territory, see C-62/11, *Feyerbacher*, 2012, paras 32–48.

[40] 85/86, *Commission v European Investment Bank*, 1988, para. 23.

institution is required to waive the immunity of an official or other servant wherever it considers that such waiver is not contrary to the Union's interests (Article 17 of the Protocol). The privileges and immunities provided by the Protocol to officials and other servants of the Union, also apply to the members of the Commission, the Court of Justice of the European Union, the European Central Bank, and the Court of Auditors.[41] Members of advisory bodies enjoy privileges and immunities in the performance of their duties and during their travel to and from the place of meeting.[42]

III. The Budget of the Union

14.010 **General budget.** Each year a general budget of the European Union is drawn up.[43] The European Parliament and the Council work together in establishing the budget, thereby together constituting the 'budgetary authority'. This is done in accordance with the budgetary procedure set out in Article 314 TFEU (see para. 20-001 et seq. , *infra*). The provisions on financial provisions are set out in Title II, Part Six TFEU, as further developed in the Financial Regulation which the Council adopts pursuant to Article 322 TFEU and Article 183 EAEC.[44] As set out below, the budget is predominantly financed from the Union's own resources. Within the limit of those resources, the Multiannual Financial Framework organizes the Union expenditure for a period of several years, currently from 2021 to 2027.

A. General principles

14.011 **Scope of the annual budget.** In principle, all items of revenue and expenditure for each financial year are to be included in estimates and shown in the budget (Article 310 TFEU). Both administrative expenditure and operating expenditure are charged to the general budget.[45] However, in the case of the CFSP the Council may decide, by unanimous vote, that operating expenditure will not be charged to the general budget.[46] Operational expenditure arising from operations having military or defence implications is always borne

---

[41] Protocol on Privileges and Immunities, Articles 19 and 20; ESCB Statute, Articles 22 and 39 and Article 286(8) TFEU.
[42] Protocol on Privileges and Immunities, Article 10, second para.
[43] Ever since 1994 the budget has been entitled the 'general budget of the European Union'. See Article 9(6) of the Amsterdam Treaty which took over Article 20(1) of the Merger Treaty.
[44] Regulation (EU, Euratom) 2018/1046 of the European Parliament and of the Council of 18 July 2018 on the financial rules applicable to the general budget of the Union, OJ 2018 L193/1; see previously Regulation (EU, Euratom) No. 966/2012 of the European Parliament and of the Council of 25 October 2012, OJ 2012 L298/1. For general discussions of this subject, see Zamparini and Villani-Lubelli (eds), *Features and Challenges of the EU Budget* (Edward Elgar Publishing, 2019); Lindner, *Conflict and Change in EU Budgetary Politics* (Routledge, 2006); and European Commission, *European Union—Public Finance*, 2014, freely available on the EU Publications Office's website.
[45] The distinction between these two types of expenditure dates back to the ECSC: since the ECSC financed its expenditure out of levies on the coal and steel sectors, its budget was divided into administrative expenditure, which came under the general budget, and operating expenditure, which was covered by a separate budget.
[46] See Article 41(2) TEU. Administrative expenditure is always charged to the general budget (Article 41(1) TEU). That system already existed before the Lisbon Treaty (see Article 41(3) EU). See also the interinstitutional agreement concluded by the European Parliament, the Council, and the Commission on 16 July 1997 on provisions regarding the financing of the CFSP (1997) 7/8 EU Bull. point 2.3.1. Initially, the EU Treaty determined, as far as the CFSP (and JHA cooperation) was concerned, that operational expenditure could be charged to the EU

by the Member States (Article 41(2), first subpara. TEU). Where expenditure is charged to the Member States, it is allocated in accordance with the GNP scale, unless the Council decides otherwise by a unanimous vote (Article 41(2), second subpara. TEU).[47] Member States which have abstained by formal declaration from CFSP decisions under the second subpara. of Article 31(1) are not obliged to contribute to the financing of operations having military or defence implications (Article 41(2), second subpara. TEU). This applies in any case to Denmark.[48] Furthermore, Member States are only obliged to pay their share of the institutions' administrative costs in some instances in which the Treaties authorize them not to take part in the operations in question.[49]

A further exception to the 'unity' of the budget is loans incurred or made by the Union and the activities of the European Central Bank,[50] the European Investment Bank,[51] and bodies or agencies having legal personality in their own right have their own budgets.

Structure of the budget. In accordance with the annual nature of the budget, it contains the revenue resulting from the amounts collected during the financial year[52] and the expenditure authorized for the financial year in question.[53] The general budget of the Union is published annually in the *Official Journal*. The expenditure of Union institutions is set out in separate sections of the budget.[54] Under the chapters of each section, expenditure is grouped into items according to its nature or purpose and subdivided in accordance with the Financial Regulation.[55] The budget is drawn up in euros.[56]

14.012

The budget is otherwise constructed in accordance with the classical rules governing public finances. Accordingly, the Treaties require the budget to be in balance as to revenue and

---

budget *only if* the Council so decided by unanimous vote. In practice, the Council decided virtually always that it should be so charged with the result that in fact operational expenditure was invariably charged to the budget unless the Council decided otherwise.

[47] Reference is made to the GNP scale in Article 26 of Council Decision (CFSP) 2021/509 of 22 March 2021 establishing a European Peace Facility, and repealing Decision (CFSP) 2015/528 of 27 March 2015 establishing a mechanism to administer the financing of the common costs of European Union operations having military or defence implications (Athena), OJ 2021 L102/14.

[48] Article 5 of the Protocol (No. 22), annexed to the TEU and TFEU, on the position of Denmark, OJ 2010 C83/299. See, e.g., the exception for Denmark in Council Decision 2015/528 of 27 March 2015 (n. 47, *supra*) and as regards the EU Satellite Centre in Council Decision 2014/401/CFSP of 26 June 2014, OJ 2014 L188/73 (allowing Denmark to contribute for expenses without defence implications).

[49] Thus, there is no obligation for Member States to contribute towards the financing of expenditure in respect of enhanced cooperation if they do not participate therein, with the exception of the administrative costs entailed for the institutions, unless the Council, acting unanimously, decides otherwise (Article 332 TFEU). By the same token, Article 5 of Protocol (No. 21), annexed to the TEU and TFEU, on the position of the United Kingdom and Ireland in respect of the Area of Freedom, Security and Justice (OJ 2010 C83/295) provides that a Member State not bound by a measure adopted pursuant to Title V of Part Three of the TFEU is to bear no financial consequences of that measure other than administrative costs entailed for the institutions, unless the Council unanimously decides otherwise.

[50] ESCB Statute, Articles 26 and 27.

[51] See EIB Statute, Articles 7(3)(f) and 12.

[52] Financial Regulation, Article 10(1).

[53] Under the first para. of Article 316 TFEU, the Financial Regulation provides for exceptions for unexpended appropriations.

[54] See Article 316, third para. TFEU, as elaborated in Articles 46 to 53 of the Financial Regulation, which provides for separate sections for all institutions and, by virtue of Article 2(67) of the Financial Regulation, also for the European Economic and Social Committee, the Committee of the Regions, the European Ombudsman, the European Data-Protection Supervisor, and the European External Action Service.

[55] Article 316, second para. TFEU.

[56] Article 320 TFEU; Financial Regulation, Article 19.

expenditure (Article 310(1), third subpara. TFEU and Article 314(10) TFEU). If at the end of the financial year, there is a shortfall or a surplus of revenue over expenditure, the deficit or the surplus is carried over to the subsequent year's budget.[57]

B. Revenue

14.013 **Own resources.** The revenue side of the budget covers the Union's own resources. The ECSC operated from the outset with its own resources, consisting of levies on the production of coal and steel. In common with most international organizations, the EEC and the EAEC initially only had financial contributions from the Member States.[58] A system of own resources eventually resulted from the First Decision on Own Resources of 21 April 1970.[59] Since that system meant that considerable financial resources were taken outside the scope of national supervision, its adoption was coupled with the grant of budgetary powers to the European Parliament. Article 311, second para. TFEU provides that, without prejudice to other revenue, the budget is to be financed wholly from own resources. The decision on the system of own resources is adopted by the Council in accordance with a special legislative procedure, acting unanimously and after consulting the European Parliament; it enters into force only after being approved by the Member States in accordance with their respective constitutional requirements (Article 311, third para. TFEU). For the period from 2014 to 2020, the system was set out in the Seventh Decision on Own Resources of 26 May 2014;[60] it has been significantly changed in 2020 with the adoption of the Eighth Decision on Own Resources applicable as from 1 January 2021 once approved by the national parliaments.[61]

14.014 **Revenue sources.** The Union's own resources consist of four sources of revenue: (1) levies, Common Customs Tariff duties, anti-dumping duties, and other duties established within the framework of trade with third countries; (2) the application of a uniform rate to the total amount of value added tax (VAT) receipts collected divided by the weighted average VAT rate calculated for the relevant year; (3) the application of a uniform rate to the weight of plastic packaging waste generated in each Member State that is not recycled; and (4) the application of a rate to be determined pursuant to the budgetary procedure to the sum of all the Member States' gross national income (GNI).[62]

In addition, there is miscellaneous revenue, such as the proceeds of the Union tax on officials' salaries,[63] the fines imposed by the Commission for infringements of the competition

---

[57] Financial Regulation, Article 18. That budgetary principle is also expressed in Article 7 of the Seventh Decision on Own Resources and Article 8 of the Eighth Decision on Own Resources. See also C-284/90, *Council v European Parliament*, 1992, para. 31; note by Van den Bossche (1994) CMLRev 653–68.
[58] See Article 201 EEC and Article 173 EAEC (old version).
[59] Council Decision 70/243/ECSC/EEC/Euratom of 21 April 1970 on the replacement of financial contributions from Member States by the Communities' own resources, OJ 1970 English Special Edition (I) 224.
[60] Council Decision 2014/335/EU, Euratom of 26 May 2014 on the system of own resources of the European Union, OJ 2014 L168/105.
[61] Council Decision (EU, Euratom) 2020/2053 of 14 December 2020 on the system of own resources of the European Union, OJ 2020 L424/1.
[62] Article 2(1) of the Eighth Decision on Own Resources.
[63] See Article 12 of the Protocol on Privileges and Immunities and Regulation (EEC, Euratom, ECSC) No. 260/68 of the Council of 29 February 1968 laying down the conditions and procedure for applying the tax for the benefit of the European Communities, OJ 1968 L56/8.

rules,[64] and the lump sums and penalty payments which may be imposed on the Member States in application of Article 260 TFEU.

Extension of own resources. The first two sources of revenue are based on fiscal systems resulting from harmonization at Union level. Unlike the first 'traditional' source of income, the second source was not introduced until after the Sixth VAT Directive of 17 May 1977 harmonized the VAT basis of assessment throughout the Community.[65] The VAT assessment basis to be taken into account for each Member State may not exceed 50 per cent of its GNI; the maximum rate applied to the VAT assessment base is currently set at 0.30 per cent.[66] After the United Kingdom repeatedly complained that it was paying much more into the budget than the Communities spent in that country, a hard-won compromise was reached by the European Council meeting at Fontainebleau on 25 and 26 June 1984 whereby the British VAT contribution was reduced and the contributions of other Member States increased, although Germany enjoyed a more advantageous regime as it refused to finance the concession to the United Kingdom in full. The 'correction of budgetary imbalances' was incorporated in the Second Decision on Own Resources (1985), subsequently extended and amended by the Fifth Decision on Own Resources (2001) so as to diminish the share of Union financing, not only for Germany, but also for Austria, the Netherlands, and Sweden. Currently, a correction mechanism benefits Austria, Denmark, Germany, the Netherlands and Sweden.[67]

14.015

The last category of own resources—the uniform rate to the sum of all Member States' GNI—was introduced by the Third Decision on Own Resources in order to cope with rising expenditure on the part of the Union. The rate of the contribution is determined under the budgetary procedure in the light of revenue from all other sources and of the expenditure anticipated in the financial year. The correction mechanism also applies to this category of own resources. The total amount of own resources assigned to the Union was fixed by the Eighth Decision on own resources at 1.46 per cent of the sum of all the Member States' GNIs; in case of significant changes in the GNIs, this ceiling can be recalculated by the Commission in accordance with a formula laid down in the decision.[68]

The third category of own resources—the uniform rate to plastic packaging waste—was only introduced in 2020 with the Eighth Decision on Own Resources. It results from a revision of the revenue system triggered in 2014, when a High Level Group on Own Resources was asked to review the system of own resources. Following up on the 2017 report of that Group,[69] the Commission proposed, in May 2018, a basket of new resources consisting

---

[64] See, *inter alia*, Articles 17 and 18 of Regulation No. 11/60, Articles 23 and 24 of Regulation No. 1/2003 and Articles 14 and 15 of Regulation No. 139/2004 (paras 9-016–9-018, *supra*).
[65] Sixth Council Directive (77/388/EEC) of 17 May 1977 on the harmonization of the laws of the Member States relating to turnover taxes—Common system of value added tax: uniform basis of assessment, OJ 1977 L145/1, now replaced by Council Directive 2006/112/EC of 28 November 2006 on the common system of value added tax, OJ 2006 L347/1.
[66] Eighth Decision on Own Resources, Article 2(1)(b).
[67] Ibid., Article 2(4).
[68] Ibid., Article 3.
[69] See the report on http://ec.europa.eu/budget/mff/hlgor/final-report/index_en.cfm. The Group was composed of representatives of the European Parliament, the Council, and the Commission, under the presidency of former European commissioner Mario Monti. In its report of 17 January 2017, the Group advocated for considering the Union's own resources no longer so much as a transfer of national resources or a national expense, but rather as the financing mechanism for policies with an added value at the European level which the Member States

of a share of taxable profits attributed to each Member State pursuant to Union rules on the Common Consolidated Corporate Tax Base (once the relevant legislation would be adopted), a share of the revenue generated by the allowances auctioned under the European Emissions Trading System, and a national contribution calculated on the amount of non-recycled plastic packaging waste.[70] In order to better respond to the socio-economic impact of the COVID-19 pandemic, the Commission amended its proposal in May 2020 so as to complement the own resources—for the first time—with the possibility for the Union to borrow funds on capital markets to be invested under Union programmes (including the newly created Recovery and Resilience Facility) in accordance with a new EU Recovery Instrument,[71] while also increasing the maximum amount of Member States' contributions to the Union budget under the 2021–2027 Multiannual Financial Framework (MFF; see para. 14-018, *infra*).[72] On 21 July 2020 the European Council found a political agreement on that proposal as part of the overall package agreed on the MFF,[73] which formed the basis of the subsequent negotiations leading to the relevant legal texts.[74] The Eighth Own Resources Decision thus enables the Commission to borrow up to EUR 750 billion on capital markets, the repayment of which is to be borne by the Union budget.[75] It also introduces, as new own resource for the Union as from 1 January 2021, the application of a uniform rate to the weight of plastic packaging waste generated in each Member State that is not recycled.[76]

14.016 **Future development of own resources.** The European Council of 21 July 2020 further agreed on the introduction of new own resources beyond 2021.[77] In a new interinstitutional agreement on budgetary matters, the European Parliament, the Council, and the Commission accordingly agreed that proposals will be put forward on a carbon border adjustment mechanism and on a digital levy and also to have the Union's Emission Trading System reviewed in order to come forward with additional new resources to be introduced by January 2023.[78]

---

cannot conduct on their own. The report offered new ideas for own resources aimed at improving the functioning of the internal market (e.g. a European company tax) and supporting policies in the fields of energy, environment and climate (e.g. taxes on electricity or levies on motor fuel).

[70] Proposal of 2 May 2018 for a Council Decision on the system of Own Resources of the European Union, COM(2018)325 final.

[71] See Council Regulation (EU) 2020/2094 of 14 December 2020 establishing a European Union Recovery Instrument to support the recovery in the aftermath of the COVID-19 crisis, OJ 2020 L433I/23 (based on Article 122 TFEU, see para. 9-036, *supra*). For the Recovery and Resilience Facility, see Regulation (EU) 2021/241 of the European Parliament and of the Council of 12 February 2021, OJ 2021 L57/17. See further De Witte, 'The European Union's COVID-19 Recovery Plan: The Legal Engineering of an Economic Policy Shift' (2021) CMLRev 635.

[72] Amended proposal of 28 May 2020 for a Council Decision on the system of Own Resources of the European Union, COM(2020)445 final.

[73] Conclusions of the European Council of 21 July 2020, EUCO 10/20.

[74] It should be noted that the unanimity required for the Council to adopt the Eighth Decision on Own Resources and the Multiannual Financial Framework could be obtained only after the European Council of 10 and 11 December 2020 agreed on a certain understanding of Regulation (EU, Euratom) 2020/2092 of the European Parliament and of the Council of 16 December 2020 on a general regime of conditionality for the protection of the Union budget, OJ 2020 L433I/1 (see para. 20-009, *infra*), which has been opposed by Hungary and Poland.

[75] Eighth Decision on Own Resources, Article 3.

[76] Ibid., Article 2(1)(c) and (2).

[77] Conclusions of the European Council of 21 July 2020, EUCO 10/20, point 140 *et seq*.

[78] See Annex II ('Interinstitutional cooperation on a roadmap towards the introduction of new own resources') to the Interinstitutional Agreement of 16 December 2020 between the European Parliament, the Council, and the Commission on budgetary discipline, on cooperation in budgetary matters and on sound financial management, as well as on new own resources, including a roadmap towards the introduction of new own resources, OJ 2020 L433I/28 (indicating in point 10 that, as from 2024, further new own resources could be a financial transaction tax and a financial contribution linked to the corporate sector or a new common corporate tax base).

C. Expenditure

Compulsory and non-compulsory expenditure. Before the Lisbon Treaty, the Union's expenditure was divided into compulsory and non-compulsory expenditure. Compulsory expenditure was expenditure necessarily resulting from the Treaties or from acts adopted in accordance therewith. All other expenditure was non-compulsory. The distinction was important in so far as the European Parliament had the last word on non-compulsory expenditure (see Article 272(6) EC; see para. 20-001 *et seq.*, *infra*). Given the political stakes, the Parliament and the Council were often at loggerheads about the classification of expenditure. By way of a series of consecutive interinstitutional agreements, the European Parliament, the Council, and the Commission have been laying down a classification of expenditure and a procedure for reaching agreement on the classification of new budget items. In order to keep expenditure under control, these interinstitutional agreements impose strict budgetary discipline.[79] The constraints resulting from the multiannual financial perspective adopted have made the distinction between compulsory and non-compulsory expenditure less important in practical terms. The Lisbon Treaty has introduced a new procedure for the adoption of the budget, which has given the European Parliament a final say over all expenditure (see para. 20-001, *infra*). Consequently, the distinction between compulsory and non-compulsory expenditure is now only of historical interest.

14.017

Multiannual financial framework. The Treaty of Lisbon replaced the institutional practice by a system of multiannual financial frameworks, established for a period of at least five years (Article 312 TFEU). The Council is to adopt a regulation laying down this financial framework, acting unanimously after obtaining the consent of the European Parliament, which requires a majority of its component members. The Treaties however enable the European Council, acting unanimously, to adopt a decision allowing the Council to lay down the financial framework by a qualified majority (Article 312(2) TFEU), which has not yet occurred. The multiannual financial framework (MMF) determines the amounts of the annual ceilings on commitment appropriations by category of expenditure[80] and the amount of the annual ceiling on payment appropriations. It further lays down any other provisions required for the annual budgetary procedure to run smoothly (Article 312(3) TFEU). For the MMF 2021–2027, the European Council found, on 21 July 2020, a political agreement including a temporary mechanism dubbed 'NextGenerationEU', organizing for the above-mentioned borrowing of up to EUR 750 billion (see para. 14-015, *supra*) to be spent on loans and grants to the Member States through a Recovery Instrument (see para. 9-036, *supra*). Moreover, a number of other Union programmes will be given additional funds to stimulate the recovery of the Union's economy.[81] After obtaining consent from the European Parliament, the Council has adopted the new MFF, which is applicable as from 1

14.018

---

[79] See the Interinstitutional Agreement of 16 December 2020 (n. 78, *supra*). The three institutions adopted, first, the Joint Declaration of 30 June 1982 (OJ 1982 C194/1) and then the successive Interinstitutional Agreements of 29 June 1988 (OJ 1988 L185/33), 29 October 1993 (OJ 1993 C331/1), 6 May 1999 (OJ 1999 C172/1), 7 November 2002 (OJ 2002 C283/1), 17 May 2006 (OJ 2006 C139/1), and 2 December 2013 (OJ 2013 C 373/1).
[80] The categories of expenditure, limited in number, must correspond to the Union's major sectors of activity (Article 312(3) TFEU).
[81] European Council conclusion of 21 July 2020, EUCO 10/20.

January 2021.[82] Furthermore, the European Parliament, the Council, and the Commission are to ensure that the financial means are made available to allow the Union to fulfil its legal obligations in respect of third parties (Article 323 TFEU).

IV. The Seats of the Institutions and Bodies

14.019 **Provisional locations.** Article 341 TFEU puts the national governments under a duty to determine the seat of the institutions of the Union by common accord (see also Article 189 EAEC).[83] However, it was a long time before the definitive locations were determined. When the ECSC Treaty entered into force, the Foreign Ministers agreed that the High Authority and the Court of Justice would start work in Luxembourg and that the Assembly would hold its first session in Strasbourg, where the Council of Europe's Hemicycle was available. The Council met in Luxembourg, where the departments of the institutions, including the secretariat of the Assembly, were located. Following the entry into force of the EEC and EAEC Treaties, the two Commissions held their meetings in Brussels on grounds of convenience. The EEC and EAEC Councils also met in Brussels, followed by the committees of the Assembly, which continued to operate in Strasbourg and Luxembourg.

Concurrently with the establishment by the Merger Treaty of a single Council and a single Commission, the representatives of the national governments adopted the Decision on Provisional Location of 8 April 1965 pursuant to the power conferred by that Treaty to settle 'certain problems peculiar to the Grand Duchy of Luxembourg'.[84] The Decision declared that Luxembourg, Brussels, and Strasbourg were to remain the provisional places of work of the institutions of the Communities (Article 1). As far as the institutions were concerned, the decision provided that during the months of April, June, and October, the Council would hold its sessions in Luxembourg (Article 2), that the Court of Justice would remain in Luxembourg (Article 3), and that the General Secretariat of the Assembly and its departments would remain in Luxembourg (Article 4), together with certain departments of the Commission (Articles 5–9). Since the governments were unable to reach agreement on the seats of the institutions,[85] the institutions remained free to determine their internal organization within the confines of the decision. Thus, the European Parliament was entitled to decide to hold its plenary sessions in Strasbourg, meetings of political groups and parliamentary committees in Brussels—with the gradual transfer of some members of staff required for this purpose,[86] and special or additional plenary sessions in Brussels during

---

[82] See Council Regulation (EU, Euratom) 2020/2093 of 17 December 2020 laying down the multiannual financial framework for the years 2021–2027, OJ 2020 L443I/11, following on Council Regulation (EU, Euratom) No. 1311/2013 of 2 December 2013 laying down the multiannual financial framework for the years 2014–2020, OJ 2013 L347/884.
[83] 230/81, *Luxembourg v European Parliament*, 1983, para. 35.
[84] Decision of the Representatives of the Governments of the Member States on the provisional location of certain institutions and departments of the Communities (*Treaties establishing the European Communities*, 1978, Office for Official Publications, Luxembourg, 837), adopted pursuant to Article 37 of the Merger Treaty.
[85] On 30 June 1981 a Conference of Representatives of the Governments, convened for this purpose in 1980, merely confirmed the Member States' power and maintained the status quo (as agreed at the European Council held in Maastricht on 23 and 24 March 1981; (1981) 3 EC Bull. point 1.1.8).
[86] 230/81, *Luxembourg v European Parliament*, 1983, paras 37–58; C-213/88 and C-39/89, *Luxembourg v European Parliament*, 1991, paras 35–8, 42–4, and 54–8.

the weeks when the political groups and parliamentary committees met.[87] The division of staff must not be such, however, as to mean that the secretariat is no longer based in Luxembourg.[88]

Seats of institutions. By the First Decision on the Seat of the Institutions of 12 December 1992,[89] the national governments at last acted upon Article 289 EC [*now Article 341 TFEU*][90] The decision fixed a seat for each institution without altering the status quo: the European Parliament was to have its seat in Strasbourg, but was to continue to work in Brussels and Luxembourg (see para. 12-018, *supra*); the Council was to have its seat in Brussels, but to continue to hold its meetings in April, June, and October in Luxembourg; the Commission was to have its seat in Brussels, but its departments located in Luxembourg were to remain there; the Court of Justice, the Court of First Instance (now the General Court), and the Court of Auditors were to continue to have their seats in Luxembourg. Consequently, the Union institutions have no common seat and indeed most of them have more than one place of work.[91] Above all, the fact that the European Parliament is obliged to meet in Strasbourg, whilst the institutions with which it collaborates institutionally operate principally in Brussels, makes for needless costs and inconvenience for all those concerned.[92] The Treaty of Amsterdam enshrined those arrangements in a Protocol annexed to the Treaties (the 'Protocol on Seats', which was taken over by the Lisbon Treaty),[93] meaning that they can only be changed through the procedure for amending the Treaties.

14.020

Seats of other bodies. A decision of the national governments was required to fix the seats of the EIB, the EMI, and the ECB. In order to determine the locations of other bodies, the governments of the Member States often had recourse to Article 341 TFEU to fix the seat of the body in question, even though such body is not an 'institution'.[94] Accordingly, by the Decision on Provisional Location of 8 April 1965 the national governments fixed the working places of a number of bodies and departments. By the same token, the Heads of State or Government, acting under Article 289 EC [*now Article 341 TFEU*], fixed the

14.021

---

[87] 358/85 and 51/86, *France v European Parliament*, 1988, paras 29–41.
[88] 108/83, *Luxembourg v European Parliament*, 1984, para. 31. See Neville Brown, 'The Grand Duchy Fights Again: Comment on Joined Cases C-213/88 and C-39/89' (1993) CMLRev 599–611.
[89] Decision of 12 December 1992 taken by common agreement between the Representatives of the Governments of the Member States on the location of the seats of the institutions and of certain bodies and departments of the European Communities, OJ 1992 C341/1.
[90] C-345/95, *France v European Parliament*, 1997, para. 23.
[91] Although the European Parliament argued that this practice was contrary to Articles 10, 199, and 289 EC [*now Articles 4(3) TEU and 232 and 341 TFEU*] (see the position taken by the Parliament on 20 April 1993, OJ 1993 C150/26), the Court of Justice endorsed maintaining several places of work for that institution in C-345/95, *France v European Parliament*, 1997.
[92] See also C-237/11 and C-238/11, *France v European Parliament*, 2012, para. 70; see, however, C-73/17, *France v European Parliament*, 2018; C-92/18, *France v European Parliament*, 2020 allowing for a pragmatic calendar, including holding plenary sessions relating to the budget in Brussels.
[93] Protocol (No. 6), annexed to the TEU, the TFEU, and the EAEC Treaty, on the location of the seats of the institutions and of certain bodies, offices, agencies, and departments of the European Union, OJ 2010 C83/265, which replaces Protocol (No. 8), annexed to the EU Treaty and the Community Treaties, on the location of the seats of the institutions and of certain bodies and departments of the European Communities and Europol, OJ 1997 C 340/112).
[94] See, based on Article 289 EC or Article 341 TFEU, the decisions taken by common agreement between the representatives of the governments of Member States on the location of the seat of various bodies, as mentioned together with the regulation establishing those bodies in ns to para. 13-046, *supra*. However, in determining the seat of the European Monitoring Centre on Racism and Xenophobia, the representatives of the national governments based their decision of 2 June 1997 (OJ 1997 C194/4), not on Article 289 EC, but simply on the regulation establishing that body (see n. to para. 13-046, *supra*).

definitive location of certain bodies and departments by, *inter alia*, the First Decision on the Seat of the Institutions of 12 December 1992,[95] the Second Decision on the Seat of the Institutions of 29 October 1993,[96] and the Third Decision on Seats of 13 December 2003.[97] In other instances, the Union legislature has fixed the seat of a body in the act setting up that body, or in an amending act,[98] even if only to incorporate the location earlier determined by the governments of the Member States.[99] The European Parliament has recently taken issue with Member States determining the location of agencies by reference to Article 341 TFEU.[100]

V. Status of Officials and Other Servants

14.022   Officials and servants. The institutions and bodies of the European Union employ more than 55,000 officials. Under Article 336 TFEU, the European Parliament and the Council, acting by means of regulations in accordance with the ordinary legislative procedure on a proposal from the Commission and after consulting the other institutions concerned, are to lay down the Staff Regulations of officials of the European Union and the Conditions of Employment of other servants of the Union.[101] The latter set of rules consists of special rules applying to staff who do not have the status of Union officials.[102]

---

[95] See n. 89, *supra*. The Decision fixed the seat of the Economic and Social Committee at Brussels and the seats of the Court of Auditors (at that time still not an 'institution') and of the European Investment Bank in Luxembourg (Article 1(e) to (g)).

[96] Decision of 29 October 1993 taken by common agreement between the Representatives of the Governments of the Member States, meeting at Head of State and Government level, on the location of the seats of certain bodies and departments of the European Communities and of Europol, OJ 1993 C323/1. See, for the relevant bodies and departments, para 13-046, *supra*.

[97] Decision 2004/97/EC, Euratom taken by common agreement between the Representatives of the Member States, meeting at Head of State or Government level, of 13 December 2003 on the location of the seats of certain offices and agencies of the European Union, OJ 2004 L29/15. See the bodies and agencies mentioned in para. 13-046, *supra*.

[98] e.g. the regulations—cited in ns to para. 13-046, *supra*—establishing the European Fisheries Control Agency (EFCA), the European Securities and Markets Authority (ESMA), the European Banking Authority (EBA), the European Insurance and Occupational Pensions Authority (EIOPA), the Single Resolution Board (SRB), and the European Agency for the Operational Management of Large-Scale IT Systems in the Area of Freedom, Security and Justice (EU-LISA), and the Council decision amending the Council Regulation establishing the European Border and Coast Guard Agency (FRONTEX).

[99] e.g. the regulations—cited in ns to para. 13-046, *supra*—establishing the European Centre for the Development of Vocational Training (Cedefop), the European Training Foundation (ETF), the European Union Agency for Fundamental Rights (FRA), and the Office of the Body of European Regulators for Electronic Communications (BEREC). See also Regulation (EU) No. 543/2014 of the European Parliament and of the Council of 15 May 2014 amending Council Decision 2005/681/JHA establishing the European Police College (CEPOL), OJ 2014 L163/5.

[100] See C-743/19, *European Parliament v Council* (pending), in which the Parliament requests the annulment of the Decision (EU) 2019/1199 of the Representatives of the Governments of the Member States of 13 June 2019 determining the seat of the European Labour Authority.

[101] Regulation (EEC, Euratom, ECSC) No. 259/68 of the Council of 29 February 1968 laying down the Staff Regulations of Officials and the Conditions of Employment of Other Servants of the European Communities and instituting special measures temporarily applicable to officials of the Commission, OJ 1968 English Special Edition (I) 30 (Staff Regulations; Conditions of Employment of Other Servants).

[102] The Conditions of Employment of Other Servants apply to temporary staff, auxiliary staff, contract staff, local staff, and special advisers. The executive agencies responsible for managing Union programmes operate partly with officials of the institutions and partly with contract staff (Article 17 of Regulation No. 58/2003 (n. to para. 13-047, *supra*). National civil servants seconded to the European External Action Service under Article 27(3) TEU have the status of temporary staff under the conditions set out in Article 6 of Council Decision 2010/427/EU of 26 July 2010 establishing the organization and the functioning of the European External Action Service, OJ 2010 L201/30.

The Staff Regulations and the Conditions of Employment of Other Servants apply to the institutions, and to most other Union bodies, such as Eurojust[103] and Europol. The EIB and the ECB may lay down their own staff regulations.[104]

Status. Formerly, officials' posts were classified in four categories (A (LA in the case of the language service), B, C, D) in descending order of rank (for instance A 1 to A 8).[105] Since 1 May 2004, the established staff are organized in two function groups: administrators (AD), corresponding to administrative, advisory, linguistic, and scientific duties; and assistants (AST), corresponding to executive, technical, and clerical duties.[106] Within each function group, officials are classified in grades in ascending hierarchical order.[107] In this way, a Director-General (AD 16 or AD 15), possibly assisted by a Deputy Director-General, will have, under him or her, Directorates run by Directors (AD 15 or AD 14). In turn, each Directorate is divided into administrative units in which administrators work under Heads of Units (AD 14 to AD 9). Each administration has one or more appointing authorities. In principle, officials are appointed following an open competition.[108] Normally, only nationals of Member States are recruited, the aim being to achieve the broadest possible geographical basis.[109]

14.023

Officials are obliged to carry out their duties and conduct themselves solely with the interests of the Union in mind.[110] Officials must refrain from any unauthorized disclosure of information received in the line of duty, even after they have left the service, unless that information has already been made public or is accessible to the public.[111] Anyone deriving rights from the Staff Regulations (including dependants and persons taking part in open competitions) may bring proceedings in the General Court after submitting a complaint to the appointing authority which has been rejected expressly or by implication.[112]

---

[103] See Article 65 of Regulation (EU) 2018/1727 on the European Union Agency for Criminal Justice Cooperation (Eurojust), OJ 2018 L295/138.
[104] EIB Statute, Article 13(7); ESCB Statute, Article 36(1).
[105] Under the former system, Category A (eight grades) comprised staff engaged in administrative and advisory duties; category B (five grades) executive duties; category C (five grades) clerical duties; category D (five grades) manual or service duties; LA (6 grades) translating and interpreting, and each grade was divided into a number of salary steps. The system of salary steps still applies under the revised Staff Regulations.
[106] See Council Regulation (EC, Euratom) No. 723/2004 of 22 March 2004 amending the Staff Regulations of officials of the European Communities and the Conditions of Employment of other servants of the European Communities, OJ 2004 L124/1.
[107] See Article 5 of the amended Staff Regulations. In order to be recruited in function group AD it is necessary to have a university degree or equivalent professional experience; for function group AST, the requirement is for a diploma of post-secondary education or a diploma of secondary education and at least three years of appropriate professional experience.
[108] Ibid., Article 29(1). A different procedure may be employed for the recruitment of senior officials (Directors-General or their equivalent in grade AD 16 or AD 15 and Directors or their equivalent in grade AD 15 or AD 14) and, in exceptional cases, for recruitment to posts which require special qualifications (Article 29(2)) as well. Recruitment has been entrusted to the European Personnel Selection Office (see para. 13-043, *supra*). See https://epso.europa.eu/.
[109] Ibid., Article 27. Under Article 28(a), an official may be appointed only if 'he is a national of one of the Member States of the Union, unless an exception is authorized by the appointing authority, and enjoys his full rights as a citizen'.
[110] Ibid., Article 11.
[111] Ibid., Article 17; see also Article 339 TFEU.
[112] See Staff Regulations, Article 90 (administrative procedure) and Article 91 (appeal to the Court of Justice of the European Union). For further particulars, see Lenaerts, Arts and Maselis, *Procedural Law of the European Union* (2nd edn, OUP, 2022), Chapter 16.

VI. Rules Governing Languages

14.024 **Treaty languages.** When the EEC and EAEC Treaties were signed, it was provided that the text in each official language of the Contracting Parties was equally authentic (Article 248 EEC; Article 225 EAEC).[113] As a result of the successive accession treaties, authentic Bulgarian, Czech, Croatian, Danish, English, Estonian, Finnish, Greek, Hungarian, Irish, Latvian, Lithuanian, Maltese, Polish, Portuguese, Romanian, Slovak, Slovenian, Spanish, and Swedish texts of the EEC and EAEC Treaties and of the amending and supplementing treaties came into being alongside the Dutch, French, German, and Italian texts.[114] All subsequent amending treaties provide that the text in each Treaty language is equally authentic.[115] As a result, the Treaties on which the Union is based exist in twenty-four authentic languages

14.025 **Official languages of the Union.** Every citizen of the Union may write to the institutions, the European Economic and Social Committee, the Committee of the Regions, and the Ombudsman in one of the Treaty languages, and receive a response in the same language (Article 24, fourth para. TEU). The rules governing the languages of the institutions are determined by the Council, acting unanimously, without prejudice to the Statute of the Court of Justice of the European Union (Article 342 TFEU; Article 190 EAEC). In Article 1 of Regulation No. 1, the Council declares the twenty-four languages to be official languages and working languages of the Union.[116] Irish only obtained that status in 2007, and not all documents need to be translated into that language.[117] A Member State or one of its nationals may write to Union institutions in any Union language and the reply has to be drawn up in the same language (Article 2 of Regulation No. 1).[118] Documents sent by a Union

---

[113] However, the ECSC Treaty was only authentic in the French version (Article 100 ECSC)

[114] Article 55 TEU and Article 225 EAEC, as most recently amended by the second para. of Article 60 of the 2005 Act of Accession. In 1984, Letzeburgisch, which is not a Treaty language, became an official language of the Grand Duchy of Luxembourg (alongside French and German).

[115] See Single European Act, Article 34; EU Treaty, Article 53; Amsterdam Treaty, Article 15; Nice Treaty, Article 13; Lisbon Treaty, Article 7. It is noted that the language regime for intergovernmental conferences is determined by the participating States; see, e.g., the Commission's answer of 20 December 2002 to Question No. P-3442/02 (Dehousse), OJ 2003 C110E/213.

[116] Regulation No. 1 determining the languages to be used by the European Economic Community, OJ 1952–1958 English Special Edition, 59, as amended upon the accession of each new Member State (referring now in Article 1 to languages 'of the Union'). Irish has been included in the list only since 2007 (see Council Regulation (EC) No. 920/2005 of 13 June 2005, OJ 2005 L156/3, which provides for a transitional period during which the institutions are not bound to translate all acts into Irish). See, more generally, Van der Jeught, *EU Language Law* (Europa Law Publishing, 2015); see also Vogiatzis, 'The linguistic policy of the EU institutions and political participation post-Lisbon' (2016) ELRev 176–200; Schilling, 'Beyond Multilingualism: On Different Approaches to the Handling of Diverging Language Versions of a Community Law' (2010) ELJ 47–66; Vanhamme, 'L'équivalence des langues dans le marché intérieur: l'apport de la Cour de justice' (2007) CDE 359–80; Schübel-Pfister, 'Enjeux et perspectives du multilinguisme dans l'Union européenne: après l'élargissement, la "babélisation" ' (2005) RMCUE 325–333; Yvon, 'Sprachenvielfalt und europäische Einheit—Zur Reform des Sprachenregimes der Europäischen Union' (2003) EuR 681–95. The 'language policy' of the European Union should also be concerned with the clarity of the communication; see Aziz, 'Mainstreaming the Duty of Clarity and Transparency as part of the Good Administrative Practice in the EU' (2004) ELJ 282–95.

[117] See Council Regulation (EU, Euratom) 2015/2264 of 3 December 2015 extending and phasing out the temporary derogation measures from Regulation No. 1 of 15 April 1958 determining the languages to be used by the European Economic Community and Regulation No. 1 of 15 April 1958 determining the languages to be used by the European Atomic Energy Community introduced by Regulation (EC) No. 920/2005, OJ 2015 L322/1.

[118] See also Article 24, fourth para. TFEU, proclaiming the right of every citizen of the Union to write to any of the institutions, the European Economic and Social Committee, the Committee of the Regions and the European Ombudsman in one of the Treaty languages and have an answer in the same language.

institution to a Member State or to one of its nationals must be drafted in the official language of that State (Article 3) and, where the Member State has more than one official language, the language to be used is to be governed by the general rules of its law, if the Member State so requests (Article 8). An irregularity in this respect is a ground for annulment only if, were it not for that irregularity, the procedure could have led to a different result,[119] or if the irregularity has negative procedural consequences for the person concerned.[120]

Regulations and other documents of general application must be drafted in all the official languages (Article 4) and the *Official Journal* must be published in all official languages (Article 5).

The language regimes do not, however, reflect a general principle according to which a citizen may demand that any act that may affect his or her interests is always drafted in his or her own language.[121] As demonstrated below, the institutions and bodies of the Union may lay down rules on the use of languages. Yet, in accordance with Regulation No. 1, the principle that all language versions are equally authentic also applies to secondary Union law. In order to secure legal certainty, all existing acts, which are translated into a new official language upon the accession of a Member State, are also authentic in that language as from the date of accession.[122] In principle, all the authentic language versions have the same weight and it makes no difference what proportion of the population of the Union the language in question represents.[123] As a result of the need for uniform interpretation of Union law, texts are not considered in isolation, but in cases of doubt are interpreted and applied in the light of the other authentic language versions.[124] The wording used in one language version of a Union provision can therefore not serve as the sole basis for the interpretation of that provision, or be made to override the other language versions in that regard.[125] In the case of divergence between language versions, the provision in question must be interpreted by reference to the purpose and general scheme of the rules of which it forms a part.[126] Individual

---

[119] C-465/02 and C-466/02, *Germany and Denmark v Commission*, 2005, para. 37; T-219/04 *Spain v Commission*, 2007, para. 35. Where versions of an instrument in other, non-authentic languages are also sent to the person concerned, this does not affect its legality: 40–48, 54–56, 111, 113–114/73, *Suiker Unie and Others v Commission*, 1975, paras 114–15. Whereas procedural documents, such as decisions and statements of objections defining the institution's position must be sent to their addressee in the language of the case, annexes thereto, which do not emanate from the institution, must be regarded as supporting documentation and must be brought to the addressee's attention as they are: T-77/92, *Parker Pen v Commission*, 1994, paras 70–4; T-148/89, *Tréfilunion v Commission*, 1995, paras 19–21.

[120] C-608/13 P, *CEPSA v Commission*, 2016, para. 36.

[121] C-147/13, *Spain v Council*, 2015, para. 31. See in respect of the staff regulations, which fall outside the scope of application of Regulation No. 1, C-621/16 P, *Commission v Italy*, 2019, affirming the judgment in T-353/14 and T-17/15, *Italy v Commission*, 2016; C-377/16, *Spain v European Parliament*, 2019, paras 36–7.

[122] See 1972 Act of Accession, Article 155; 1979 Act of Accession, Article 147; 1985 Act of Accession, Article 397; 1994 Act of Accession, Article 170; 2003 Act of Accession, Article 58, 2005 Act of Accession, Article 58; 2011 Act of Accession, Article 52. Acts which have not been published in the official language of a Member State in the *Official Journal* cannot be enforced against individuals in that Member State (161/06, *Skoma-Lux*, 2007, paras 32–50). See also Lasinki-Sulecki, 'Late Publication of EC Law in Languages of New Member States and its Effects: Obligations on Individuals Following the Court's Judgment in Skoma-Lux' (2008) CMLRev 705–25.

[123] C-296/95, *EMU Tobacco and Others*, 1998, para. 36.

[124] 19/67, *Bestuur van de Sociale Verzekeringsbank*, 1967, 354. For an example, see C-327/91, *France v Commission*, 1994, para. 35; see also the (somewhat amusing) Question No. 1896/92 (McCubbin) and the Commission's answer of 3 September 1993, OJ 1994 C251/1.

[125] C-261/08 and C-348/08, *Zurita García and Choque Cabrera*, 2009, para. 55.

[126] 30/77, *Bouchereau*, 1977, para. 14; see, more recently, C-72/95, *Kraaijeveld*, 1996, paras 28–31; C-267/95 and C-268/95, *Merck and Beecham*, 1996, paras 21–4; C-257/00, *Givane and Others*, 2003, paras 29–50; C-428/02, *Fonden Marselisborg Lystbådehavn*, 2005, paras 41–7; C-187/07, *Endendijk*, 2008, para. 23; C-239/07 *Sabatauskas and Others*, 2008, para. 38; C-340/08, *M and Others*, 2010, paras 38–69; C-230/09 and C-231/09, *Kurt and*

decisions do not necessarily have to be drawn up in all the official languages. Even if an individual decision is published in the *Official Journal* and is translated into all the official languages for the information of citizens, only the language used in the relevant procedure will be authentic and will be used to interpret that decision.[127]

14.026 **Other official languages of the Member States.** In 2005, the Council considered that, as part of the efforts being made to bring the Union closer to all its citizens, the richness of its linguistic diversity had to be taken more into consideration. It was considered that allowing citizens the possibility of using additional languages in their relations with the Union institutions would be an important factor in strengthening their identification with the European Union's political project. Accordingly, since 2005, the Council may authorize the official use of languages other than the languages referred to in Regulation No. 1 whose status is recognized by the Constitution of a Member State on all or part of its territory or the use of which as a national language is authorized by law.[128] For this purpose, Member States are to conclude administrative arrangements with the Council, and possibly other Union institutions and bodies, which will allow a Member State to use one of these other languages in the Council and in other institutions and bodies. The direct or indirect costs associated with implementation of these arrangements are to be borne by the requesting Member State. Furthermore, a Member State can provide for a right of its citizens to communicate with Union institutions or bodies in one of these languages; the Member State in question will then be responsible for translations into or from one of the official languages of the Union. Finally, administrative arrangements may also provide for translation in one of these languages of acts adopted by the European Parliament and the Council under the ordinary legislative procedure. However, such translations will not have the status of law. In an administrative arrangement with the Council, Spain has committed itself to enable the use of Basque, Catalan, and Galician in the aforementioned situations.[129]. Since the entry into force of the Lisbon Treaty, the Treaties explicitly provide that they may be translated into any other languages as determined by Member States among those which, in accordance with their constitutional order, enjoy official status in all or part of their territory[130].

14.027 **Linguistic regime in the Court of Justice.** For the rules on the use of languages before the Court of Justice, Article 7 of Regulation No. 1 refers to the Rules of Procedure.[131] The Rules of Procedure of the Court of Justice and those of the General Court provide that any of the Treaty languages may be used as the language of the case, which is to be chosen by the

---

Thomas Etling and Others, 2011; C-419/10, *Hofmann*, 2012, para. 68; C-604/11, *Genil 48*, 2013, para. 38; C-498/13, *Agrooikosystimata*, 2015, paras 33--8; C-554/16, *EP Agrarhandel*, 2018, paras 36–46. See also Lenaerts and Gutierrez-Fons, *Les méthodes d'interprétation de la Cour de justice de l'Union européenne* (Bruylant, 2020), 15–22.

[127] C-361/01 P, *Kik v Office for Harmonization in the Internal Market*, 2003, para. 87, with case note by Shuibhne (2004) CMLRev 1093–111.

[128] Council Conclusion of 13 June 2005 on the official use of additional languages within the Council and possibly other institutions and bodies of the European Union, OJ 2005 C148/1.

[129] Administrative arrangement between the Kingdom of Spain and the Council of the European Union, OJ 2006 C40/2.

[130] Article 55(2) TEU; Article 358 TFEU.

[131] Following on from Article 342 TFEU, which refers, as regards the rules governing languages, to the Statute of the Court of Justice of the European Union, Article 64 of that Statute states that until the rules governing the language arrangements applicable at the Court of Justice and the General Court have been adopted in the Statute, the provisions of the Rules of Procedure of the Court of Justice and of the General Court governing language arrangements are to continue to apply.

applicant.[132] However, where the defendant is a Member State or a national of a particular Member State, the applicant must opt for the official language (or one of the official languages) of that State.[133] Nevertheless, at the joint request of the parties or at the request of one of the parties (provided that it is not a Union institution), and after the opposite party and the Advocate General have been heard, the Court may authorize an official language other than the language of the case to be used.[134] Questions referred for a preliminary ruling are dealt with in the language of the court that made the reference.[135]

Although, in principle, all documents are translated into the language of the case and the parties plead in that language, the Rules of Procedure provide for exceptions. Member States are entitled to use their official language (at their election) and the President may conduct the hearing in a language other than the language of the case. By the same token, Judges and Advocates General may put questions in another official language and the latter often deliver their Opinions in their native tongue.[136] Witnesses and experts may be authorized to use another language, even a language other than one of the Treaty languages.[137] In order to avoid the internal use of interpreters, the two Courts use French as their working language. Judgments, orders intended for publication, and Opinions (of the Court or Advocates General) are reported in all official languages.[138] The texts of documents drawn up in the language of the case or in any other language authorized by the Court are authentic.[139]

Linguistic regime in other institutions. Article 6 of Regulation No. 1 provides that the Union institutions may stipulate in their rules of procedure which of the official languages are to be used in specific cases. Thus, the European Parliament works on the basis that each MEP is entitled to use his or her official language and provides that documents are to be drawn up in, and speeches interpreted into, all the official languages.[140] Consequently, knowledge of languages is not required in order to stand for election to the European Parliament.[141] Speeches in Parliament may also be interpreted into any other language the Bureau may consider necessary. Interpretation is provided in committee and delegation meetings for the official languages used and requested by the members.[142] An exception to the normal rule on the use of languages is made for committee meetings in urgent cases concerning recommendations on the Union's external policies.[143]

14.028

---

[132] CJ Rules of Procedure, Articles 36 and 37(1); GC Rules of Procedure, Articles 44 and 45(1).

[133] CJ Rules of Procedure, Article 37(1); GC Rules of Procedure, Article 45(1). This situation may arise where the Court of Justice of the European Union adjudicates pursuant to an arbitration clause contained in a contract concluded with Union institutions or bodies (Article 272 TFEU).

[134] CJ Rules of Procedure, Article 37(1); GC Rules of Procedure, Article 45(1)).

[135] CJ Rules of Procedure, Article 37(3).

[136] The Registrar arranges for translation into the language of the case (CJ Rules of Procedure, Article 39; GC Rules of Procedure, Article 47.

[137] CJ Rules of Procedure, Article 38(7); GC Rules of Procedure, Article 46(6).

[138] CJ Rules of Procedure, Article 40; GC Rules of Procedure, Article 48. Since 1 January 1994 an exception has been made for staff cases, where the judgment is generally published only in the language of the case. For a discussion, see Mulders, 'Translation at the Court of Justice of the European Communities', in Prechal and van Roermund (eds), *The Coherence of EU Law* (OUP, 2008), 45–61.

[139] CJ Rules of Procedure, Article 41; GC Rules of Procedure, Article 49.

[140] EP Rules of Procedure, Rule 167; see the Resolution of the European Parliament of 6 May 1994 on the right to use one's own language, OJ 1994 C205/528.

[141] Resolution of the European Parliament of 14 October 1982 on multilingualism of the European Community, OJ 1982 C292/96; see also its Resolution of 24 March 2009 on 'multilingualism: an asset for Europe and a shared commitment', OJ 2010 C117 E/59.

[142] EP Rules of Procedure, Rule 167(3) and (4).

[143] EP Rules of Procedure, Rule 118(4).

In other institutions, it is not practicable for all the official languages to be on an equal footing as working languages. The European Council and the Council deliberate and take decisions 'only on the basis of documents and drafts drawn up in the languages specified in the rules in force governing languages', but may decide otherwise by unanimous vote on grounds of urgency.[144] As far as the CFSP is concerned, meetings at official level and exchanges of information among Member States are conducted in English and French.[145] In practice, English and French are chiefly used for communications within the Council, the exception being meetings of the Council itself. The Commission has to annex instruments adopted by it at a meeting in the authentic language or languages to the minutes of the meeting at which they were adopted.[146] In the case of instruments of general application, this means that translation is required in all the official languages of the Union; in other cases, translation in the language or languages of those to whom they are addressed suffices. In the Court of Auditors, reports, opinions, observations, and statements of assurance must be drafted in all the official languages.[147] Whilst these rules on the use of languages are complied with, in practice French, English, and (to a lesser extent) German are used as working languages within the administration.[148] When recruiting officials, the institutions may impose knowledge of one of these languages in the interest of the service, provided this requirement is justified by objective reasons and the required level is proportionate to the actual needs of the service.[149]

14.029 **Linguistic regime in other bodies.** The Treaties do not contain any provision on the use of languages by other bodies and agencies of the Union, which means that their power of internal organization is not restricted in this respect. The Council has made the rules governing the use of languages by the institutions applicable when setting up certain bodies.[150] Those rules also apply in Europol and Eurojust.[151] In the Regulation establishing the Office for Harmonisation in the Internal Market (trademarks and designs)—which has now become the EU Intellectual Property Office—the Council broke away from the principle that

---

[144] European Council Rules of Procedure, Article 9(1); Council Rules of Procedure, Article 14(1).

[145] See Declaration (No. 29) annexed to the EU Treaty. See also the Council's answer of 8 October 2000 to Question No. E-1212/01 (Marchiani), OJ 2002 C40E/25. The previous EPC practice continues to apply to the simplified written procedure (COREU). This consists of using only English and French as working languages: see the answer of the Presidency of 6 November 1985 to Question No. 1673/84 (Formigoni) (1985) 2 EPC Bulletin doc. 85/242, 140.

[146] Commission Rules of Procedure, Article 17(1). Instruments adopted by the written procedure, the empowerment procedure, the delegation procedure, and by way of subdelegation (para. 12-070, *supra*) are to be attached, in the authentic language or languages, in such a way that they cannot be separated, to a day note recorded in the minutes (Commission Rules of Procedure, Article 17(2)–(5)).

[147] Rules of Procedure of the Court of Auditors, Article 28(1).

[148] For discussions of the language regime, under which English is increasingly obtaining the upper hand, see de Witte, 'Language Law of the European Union: Protecting or Eroding Linguistic Diversity?', in Craufurd Smith (ed.), *Culture and European Union Law* (OUP, 2004) 205–42. Fenet, 'Diversité linguistique et construction européenne' (2001) RTDE 235–69; Oppermann, 'Reform der Sprachenregelung?' (2001) NJW 2663–8.

[149] C-566/10, *Italy v Commission*, 2012, paras 88–97.

[150] See the regulations establishing these bodies mentioned in para. 13-046, *supra*. The regulation establishing the European Training Foundation stipulates that the Governing Board shall determine by unanimity the language regime of the Foundation 'taking into account the need to ensure access to, and participation in, the work of the Foundation by all interested parties' (Article 8(2)).

[151] Article 64 of Regulation (EU) 2016/794 (Europol) and Article 71 of Regulation (EU) 2018/1727 (Eurojust). Spain considered that the corresponding rules in the acts previously governing those bodies had been broken by the establishment of English and French as *de facto* working languages and brought an action against notices of vacancy requiring knowledge of those languages, which was, however, declared inadmissible (C-160/03, *Spain v Eurojust*, 2005).

all the official languages are on an equal footing by providing that only English, French, German, Italian, and Spanish are to be the languages of the Office.[152] The Office arranges for the translation of trademark applications submitted in other official languages of the Union (Regulation 2017/1001, Article 146(3), second subpara). In proceedings before the Office, so long as the applicant is the sole party to proceedings before the Office, the language used for filing the application for registration remains the language of proceedings (Article 146(4)) and all documents necessary for dealing with the application will be drawn up in that language.[153] In opposition, revocation, or invalidity proceedings, the language of the proceedings is such language of the Office as the applicant chooses (Article 146(3), first subpara. and (5)), unless the parties agree to use another official language (Article 146(8)).[154] Applications for the registration of designs are subject to similar rules.[155] The Court of Justice has held that the choice to limit the languages to those which are most widely known in the European Union is an appropriate and proportionate linguistic solution to the difficulties arising where parties with different languages cannot agree on the language to be used. In so far as direct proceedings between the Office and the applicant can be conducted in the language of the applicant, the rules on use of languages in the Office are therefore not in breach of the principle of equal treatment.[156] Likewise, the Court of Justice ruled that the choice made by the Council to only provide for translations into German, English, and French in respect of Union patents—and thus to treat the other official languages differently—is appropriate and proportionate to the legitimate objective of improving access to patent protection by reducing the cost thereof.[157]

VII. Transparency and Access to Documents

Access to documents. The Treaties stress that decisions by the Union are taken 'as openly as possible' (Articles 1, second para. and 10(3) TEU; Article 15(1) TFEU). The debate on the need for the Union to be 'transparent' has resulted in greater openness as regards the operation of, in particular, the Council and the Commission. From a practical perspective the citizens' ability to have access to documents issued by the institutions or in their possession is crucial in this respect.[158] As a result of the Treaty of Amsterdam, access to these

14.030

---

[152] Article 146(2) of Regulation (EU) 2017/1001 on the European Union trademark; OJ 2017 L154/1; previously Article 119(3) of Council Regulation (EC) No. 207/2009 on the European Union trademark (OJ 2009 L78/1), preceded by Article 115(2) of Council Regulation (EC) No. 40/94 on the Community trademark, OJ 1994 L11/1. Cf. the equality of official languages in dealings with the Community Plant Variety Office (Article 34(2) and (3) of Regulation (EC) No. 2100/94). See Gundel, 'Zur Sprachenregelung bei den EG-Agenturen— Abschied auf Raten von der Regel der "Allsprachigkeit" der Gemeinschaft im Verkehr mit dem Bürger?' (2001) EuR 776–83.

[153] T-120/99, *Kik v Office for Harmonisation in the Internal Market*, 2001, para. 61, as upheld by C-361/01 P, *Kik v Office for Harmonisation in the Internal Market*, 2003, paras 44–9.

[154] See also GC Rules of Procedure, Article 45(4), for the language regime applicable to disputes relating to intellectual property rights.

[155] Article 98 of Council Regulation (EC) No. 6/2002 of 12 December 2001 on Community designs, OJ 2002 L3/1.

[156] T-120/99, *Kik v Office for Harmonization in the Internal Market*, 2001, paras 62–3, as upheld by C-361/01 P, *Kik v Office for Harmonization in the Internal Market*, 2003, paras 82–96.

[157] C-147/13, *Spain v Council*, 2015, paras 32–47.

[158] See Declaration (No. 17) to the EU Treaty on the right of access to information and the Birmingham Declaration of 16 October 1992—A Community close to its citizens (1992) 10 EC Bull. point I.8. For a general discussion, see Harden, 'Citizenship and Information' (2001) E Pub L 165–93; Curtin, 'Citizens' Fundamental Right of Access to EU Information: An Evolving Digital *Passepartout*?' (2000) CMLRev 7–41; Bradley, 'La transparence de l'Union européenne: une évidence ou un trompe l'oeil?' (1999) CDE 283–360.

documents was enshrined in Treaty law. At present, Article 15(3) TFEU gives any citizen of the Union and any natural or legal person residing or having its registered office in a Member State a right of access to documents of the Union institutions, bodies, offices, and agencies. That right is also enshrined in Article 42 of the Charter.[159] General principles and limits on grounds of public or private interest governing this right of access are determined in Regulation No. 1049/2001 of the European Parliament and the Council,[160] which applies to the European Parliament, the Council, and the Commission, but is also made applicable to bodies with legal personality established pursuant to the Treaties.[161] Regulation No. 1049/2001 applies to all documents held by an institution, that is to say, documents drawn up or received by it and in its possession, in all areas of activity of the Union.[162] If a document has already been released and is easily accessible, it is sufficient for the institution to inform the applicant how to obtain the requested document.[163] Other documents must, in principle, be disclosed upon request, but the regulation provides for a number of exceptions in this regard (see para. 14-031, *supra*). The regulation requires each institution or body to keep a register and also provides for special treatment for sensitive documents.[164] Each institution, body, office, or agency must elaborate, in its own rules of procedure, specific provisions regarding access to its documents.[165] However, there is no obligation to create

---

[159] On the constitutional value of the right of access to documents, see C-57/16 P, *ClientEarth v Commission*, 2018, paras 73–81.

[160] Regulation (EC) No. 1049/2001 of the European Parliament and of the Council of 30 May 2001 regarding public access to European Parliament, Council and Commission documents, OJ 2001 L145/43. See Kranenborg, 'Access to Documents and Data Protection in the European Union: On the Public Nature of Personal Data' (2008) CMLRev 1079–114; De Leeuw, 'The Regulation on Public Access to European Parliament, Council and Commission Documents in the European Union: Are Citizens Better Off?' (2003) ELRev 324–48; Schram, 'Openbaarheid van Europese bestuursdocumenten' (2003) NJWb 581–92; Bartelt and Zeitler, 'Zugang zu Dokumenten der EU' (2003) EuR 487–503; Schauss, 'L'accès du citoyen aux documents des institutions communautaires' (2003) JTDE 1–8; Wägenbaur, 'Der Zugang zu EU-Dokumenten—Transparenz zum Anfassen' (2001) EuZW 680–85. When the European Parliament, the Council, and the Commission act in pursuance of the EAEC Treaty, they should draw guidance from the regulation; see recital 5 in the preamble to the regulation and Declaration (No. 41), annexed to the Amsterdam Treaty on the provisions relating to transparency, access to documents, and the fight against fraud, OJ 1997 C340/140. For the importance of the right of access to documents, see the earlier case, C-58/94, *Netherlands v Council*, 1996, paras 34–7. Since Article 255 EC [*now Article 15(3) TFEU*] requires further implementing measures, that article does not have direct effect: T-191/99, *Petrie and Others v Commission*, 2001, paras 34–5.

[161] See the amendments made by the Council to this effect on 22 July 2003 in several regulations establishing such bodies (OJ 2003 L245).

[162] Article 2(3) of Regulation No. 1049/2001. Under the former rules, access to a document of which the institution itself was not the originator had to be sought from its author; see T-92/98, *Interporc v Commission*, 1999, paras 65–72, upheld by C-41/00 P, *Interporc v Commission*, 2003, paras 34–59. The public's right of access to documents does not imply a duty on the part of the institution to reply to any request for information from an individual: T-106/99, *Meyer v Commission* (order), 1999, para. 35.

[163] Regulation No. 1049/2001, Article 10(2). See also T-106/99, *Meyer v Commission* (order), 1999, para. 39 (access to documents is not applicable where the documents have already been published in the *Official Journal*).

[164] Article 9 of Regulation No. 1049/2001 provides for the classification of documents as 'top secret', 'secret', or 'confidential'.

[165] See Article 15(3), third subpara. TFEU For the implementation thereof; see also Rule 122 of the EP Rules of Procedure and the Decision of the Bureau of the European Parliament of 28 November 2001 (OJ 2001 C374/1; consolidated version in OJ 2005 C289/6); Council Decision 2001/840/EC adding as Annex III (now Annex II) to the Rules of Procedure specific provisions regarding public access to Council documents (OJ 2001 L313/40); the provisions appended as an annex to the Rules of Procedure adopted by the Commission by Decision of 5 December 2001 (OJ 2001 L345/94); Decision No. 12/2005 of the Court of Auditors of the European Communities of 10 March 2005 regarding public access to Court of Auditors documents, OJ 2009 C67/1; Decision 2003/603/EC of the European Economic and Social Committee of 1 July 2003 (OJ 2003 L205/19), Decision No. 64/2003 of the Committee of the Regions of 11 February 2003 (OJ 2003 L160/96). See Driessen, 'The Council of the European Union and access to documents' (2005) ELRev 675–96.

a document that did not yet exist by retrieving information from a database in order to accede to a request for access.[166]

Refusal of access. Under Regulation No. 1049/2001, a person requesting access to documents is not required to justify his or her request (Article 6(1)) and therefore he or she does not have to demonstrate any interest in having access to the documents.[167]   **14.031**

Regulation No. 1049/2001 provides that the institutions and bodies are to refuse access to a document so as to protect certain interests,[168] namely (a) the public interest as regards public security, defence and military matters, international relations,[169] or the financial, monetary, or economic policy[170] of the Union or a Member State[171] and (b) the privacy and integrity of the individual[172] (Article 4(1)). Unless there is an overriding public interest in disclosure, access to a document is also to be refused where disclosure would undermine the protection of (a) commercial interests of a natural or legal person,[173] including intellectual property; (b) court proceedings[174] and legal advice;[175] or (c) the purpose of

---

[166] C-491/15 P, *Typke v Commission*, 2017, paras 30–50.
[167] T-124/96, *Interporc v Commission*, 1998, para. 48; T-391/03 and T-70/04, *Franchet and Byk v Commission*, 2006, para. 82.
[168] On the exceptions to the right of access to document, see Adamski, 'How Wide is "The Widest Possible"? Judicial Interpretation of the Exceptions to the Right of Access to Official Documents Revisited' (2009) CMLRev 521–49.
[169] C-350/12 P, *Council v in 't Veld*, 2014; T-851/16, *Access Info Europe v Commission*, 2018, paras 24–59 (documents relating to the EU–Turkey negotiations on the migration crisis; see also T-852/16, *Access Info Europe v Commission*, 2018, paras 24–53). There is no requirement that the reports must first be classified as 'TRÈS SECRET/TOP SECRET', 'SECRET', or 'CONFIDENTIEL' before the Council can invoke this exception, see C-576/12 P, *Jurašinović*, 2013, paras 38–48.
[170] T-590/10, *Thesing and Bloomberg Finance v ECB*, 2012, confirmed on appeal by C-28/13 P, *Thesing and Bloomberg Finance v ECB* (order), 2014.
[171] The Union legislature enjoys a broad discretion in applying the public interest exceptions of Article 4(1)(a) (C-266/05 P, *Sison v Council*, 2007, paras 32–6).
[172] See C-28/08 P, *Commission v Bavarian Lager*, 2010 (where access is requested to documents including personal data, application should be made of Regulation No. 45/2001, now replaced by Regulation (EU) 2018/1725; see para. 9-002, *supra*). On this basis the General Court has accepted that the European Parliament may refuse access to information detailing the expenditures by individual MEPs; see T-639/15 to T-666/15, and T-94/16, *Psara v European Parliament*, 2018, paras 41–98.
[173] See T-355/04 and T-446/04, *Co-Frutta v Commission*, 2010, paras 99–107 and 122–40; T-237/05, *Editions Odile Jacob v Commission*, 2010, paras 109–29. Third parties may also object to the release of documents on this ground: C-178/18 P, *MSD Animal Health Innovation v European Medicines Agency*, 2020, affirming T-729/15, *MSD Animal Health Innovation v European Medicines Agency*, 2018.
[174] For access requested to the Commission's pleadings before the Court of Justice, see C-514/07 P, C-528/07 P and C-532/07 P, *Sweden and API v Commission*, 2010; C-213/15 P, *Commission v Breyer*, 2017. The purpose of this exception is to ensure both the protection of work done within an institution and confidentiality and the safeguarding of professional privilege for lawyers: T-92/98, *Interporc v Commission*, 1999, paras 40–2 (holding that the exception for court proceedings cannot enable the Commission to escape from its obligation to disclose documents which were drawn up in connection with a purely administrative matter). In any case, access cannot be precluded generally for documents that have been drawn up by an institution for specific judicial proceedings. Where the Commission has received a request for access to documents which it has supplied to a national court in the context of its cooperation with national courts in applying competition law, it must verify whether their disclosure would constitute an infringement of national law. In the event of doubt, it must consult the national court and refuse access only if that court objects to disclosure of the documents: C-174/98 P and C-189/98 P, *Netherlands and Van der Wal v Commission*, 2000, paras 20–33. See also T-391/03 and T-70/04, *Franchet and Byk v Commission*, 2006, paras 88–103.
[175] This exception protects an institution's interest in seeking legal advice and receiving frank, objective, and comprehensive advice: C-39/05 P and C-52/05 P, *Sweden and Turco v Council*, 2007, paras 42–3. For the protection of internal legal advice in administrative proceedings, see C-506/08, *Sweden v Commission and My Travel v Commission*, 2011 and T-237/05, *Editions Odile Jacob v Commission*, 2010, paras 156–61 (access to opinion of the Commission's legal service may be refused to preserve the freedom of the legal service to express its views and its ability effectively to defend before the Union judicature, on an equal footing with the representatives of other parties, the Commission's definitive position and the internal decision-making process of that institution); T-610/97 R *Carlsen v Council* (order of the President), 1998, paras 43–53 (access may be refused on account of

inspections, investigations, and audits[176] (Regulation No. 1049/2001, Article 4(2)). When access is requested to documents relating to an administrative procedure with specific rules on access to the file, it is presumed that the access to these documents will undermine the protection of the commercial interests of the undertakings concerned and/or the protection of the purpose of the investigation. This presumption applies to documents from administrative procedures in matters of competition[177] and State aid,[178] exchanges with national competition authorities,[179] bids submitted by tenderers,[180] OLAF investigations,[181] and infringement proceedings between the Commission and a Member State.[182]

An institution or body may also refuse access to internal and preparatory documents if disclosure of the document would seriously undermine the institution's decision-making process, unless there is an overriding public interest in disclosure (Regulation No. 1049/2001, Article 4(3)).[183] However, the Commission is not entitled to presume that, for as long as it has not made a decision regarding a potential proposal, disclosure of documents drawn up in the context of an impact assessment could, in principle, seriously undermine

the maintenance of legal certainty and stability of Union law). However, disclosure of documents containing the advice of an institution's legal service on legal questions arising when legislative initiatives are being debated increases the transparency and openness of the legislative process and strengthens the democratic right of European citizens to scrutinize the information which has formed the basis of a legislative act. Consequently, Regulation No. 1049/2001 imposes, in principle, an obligation to disclose the opinions of the Council's legal service relating to a legislative process: C-39/05 P and C-52/05 P, *Sweden and Turco v Council*, 2007, paras 40–68. In addition, legal advice that does not pertain to a particular legislative proposal enjoys protection under this exception; see T-851/16, *Access Info Europe v Commission*, 2018, paras 81–96 (see also T-852/16, *Access Info Europe v Commission*, 2018, paras 75–90).

[176] This exception applies only where disclosure of the documents in question may endanger the completion of inspections, investigations or audits: T-391/03 and T-70/04, *Franchet and Byk v Commission*, 2006, para. 109. Acts of investigation may remain covered by the exception as long as the investigation continues, even if the particular inspection that gave rise to the report to which access is sought is completed: T-20/99, *Denkavit Nederland v Commission*, 2000, para. 48. The definition of 'investigation' is not limited to searches carried out to establish an offence or irregularity and to procedures aiming to collect and verify information with a view to taking a decision but cover every structured and formalized procedure that has the purpose of collecting and analysing information in order to enable the institution to take a position in the exercise of its Treaty powers: C-331/15 P *France v Schlyter*, 2017, paras 43–55, setting aside T-402/12, *Schlyter v Commission*, 2015.

[177] C-404/10 P, *Commission v Éditions Odile Jacob*, 2012 and C-477/10 P, *Commission v Agrofert Holding*, 2012 (merger control); C-365/12 P, *Commission v EnBW Energie Baden-Württemberg*, 2014, paras 56–7 (procedure under Article 101 TFEU).

[178] C-139/07 P, *Commission v Technische Glaswerke Ilmenau*, 2010, paras 55–62.

[179] T-623/13, *Unión de Almacenistas de Hierros de España v Commission*, 2015, para. 64 (documents sent by national competition authorities to the Commission pursuant to Article 11(4) of Council Regulation (EC) No. 1/2003).

[180] T-339/10 and T-532/10, *Cosepuri v EFSA*, 2013, para. 101

[181] T-110/15, *International Management Group v Commission*, 2016, paras 33–7.

[182] C 514/11 P and C 605/11 P, *LPN and Finland v Commission*, 2013 (documents from the pre-litigation stage). This extends to documents relating on EU Pilot procedures, see C-562/14 P, *Sweden v Commission*, 2017, affirming T 306/12, *Spirlea v Commission*, 2014. The General Court held that access to documents relating to the investigation must be refused in order to prevent a breach of confidentiality affecting the proper functioning of such proceedings: T-105/95, *WWF UK v Commission*, 1997, para. 63; T-309/97, *The Bavarian Lager Company v Commission*, 1999, paras 45–6 (refusal during the inspection and investigation stage); T-191/99, *Petrie and Others v Commission*, 2001, paras 67–9 (refusal after institution of proceedings in the Court of Justice). For criticism of the lack of access to the finding of an infringement and the reasoned opinion, see Krämer, 'Access to Letters of Formal Notice and Reasoned Opinions in Environmental Law Matters' (2003) E Env L Rev 197–203.

[183] See T-403/05, *MyTravel v Commission*, 2008, paras 42–68 (disclosure of internal report held to seriously undermine the decision-making freedom of the Commission—set aside on appeal by C-506/08 P, *MyTravel v Commission*, 2011); T-391/03 and T-70/04, *Franchet and Byk v Commission*, 2006, paras 135–9 (the right to a fair hearing invoked by the applicants as an overriding interest is not an overriding public interest justifying disclosure of the requested documents).

its ongoing decision-making process for developing such a proposal.[184] Moreover, an institution cannot refuse to grant access to documents pertaining to its deliberations merely on the basis that they contain information relating to positions taken by representatives of the Member States.[185] Similarly, the Council cannot refuse to disclose documents that show which Member States suggested certain amendments.[186] Those exceptions apply only where the risk of the public interest being undermined is reasonably foreseeable and not purely hypothetical.[187] In any event, exceptions must be applied strictly.[188] Therefore, if it cannot be shown that the decision-making process would be seriously undermined, also documents relating to the trilogue of an ongoing legislative procedure may also not be refused, as there is no presumption that such documents will not be disclosed.[189]

Under the regulation, a Member State may request the Commission or the Council not to disclose a document originating from that Member State without its prior consent.[190] If a Member State makes such a request, it is obliged to state the reasons for that objection by reference to the exceptions mentioned in Regulation No. 1049/2001; where it fails to do so, the institution requested must consider, for its part, whether one of these exceptions applies. If the Member State concerned has reasoned its objection against the disclosure of the documents at stake, the institution requested must refuse disclosure, while setting out the reasons relied on by that Member State.[191]

Where a document includes items of information falling within one of the grounds for refusing access, the principle of proportionality requires the institutions or bodies to consider granting access to the items for which those exceptions do not apply.[192] Within fifteen working days of receipt of a written application, the institution or body must either grant access or refuse it totally or partially. If an application for access is refused or unanswered, the applicant must seek, by means of a confirmatory application, a formal refusal, against

---

[184] C-57/16 P, *ClientEarth v Commission*, 2018, para. 112. This applies regardless of the nature, legislative or otherwise, of the proposal envisaged and the fact that the documents concerned contained environmental information within the meaning of Article 2(1)(d) of Regulation No. 1367/2006.

[185] T-111/00, *British American Tobacco International v Commission*, 2001, paras 52–7.

[186] T-233/09, *Access Info Europe v Council*, 2011, paras 55–85, affirmed on appeal in C-280/11 P, *Council v Access Info Europe*, 2013, paras 27–40 and 53–64.

[187] C-39/05 P and C-52/05 P, *Sweden and Turco v Council*, 2008, paras 40–3; T-211/00, *Kuijer v Council*, 2002, paras 56–70 (adverse reports about human rights in third countries are not necessarily prejudicial to the Union's relations with those countries).

[188] e.g. T-264/04, *WWF European Policy Programme v Council*, 2007, para. 39.

[189] T-540/15, *De Capitani v European Parliament*, 2018, paras 57–114. The fact that the documents were released after the conclusion of the legislative procedure did not affect the *locus standi* of the applicant, who should be able to raise the illegality committed by the European Parliament in not providing access earlier (ibid., paras 26–33).

[190] Regulation No. 1049/2001, Article 4(5).

[191] C-64/05 P, *Sweden v Commission and Others*, 2007. This means that the General Court itself must examine the document concerned in order to assess whether the institution is right to refuse access; see C-135/11 P, *IFAW Internationaler Tierschutz-Fonds v Commission*, 2012, paras 77–9, setting aside T-362/08, *IFAW Internationaler Tierschutz-Fonds v Commission*, 2011.

[192] C-353/99 P, *Council v Hautala*, 2001, paras 21–31, upholding T-14/98, *Hautala v Council*, 1999, paras 75–88, and C-353/01 P, *Mattila v Council and Commission*, 2004, paras 29–32; T-331/11, *Besselink v Council*, 2013, para. 83; T-851/16, *Access Info Europe v Commission*, 2018, paras 114–24. Such partial access under Article 4(6) of Regulation No. 1049/2001 is, however, not always possible, see, e.g., T-852/16, *Access Info Europe v Commission*, 2018, paras 107–16; T-639/15 to T-666/15 and T-94/16, *Psara v European Parliament*, 2018, paras 121–31 (it would be an unreasonable administrative burden for the European Parliament to sift through tens of thousands of individual documents—relating to expenses made by MEPs—to retrieve the ones not covered by the exception for the protection of the individual).

which an action for annulment will lie and/or a complaint may be made to the European Ombudsman.[193]

In principle, the exceptions relating to access to documents apply for a maximum period of thirty years. In the case of documents covered by the exceptions relating to privacy or commercial interests and in the case of sensitive documents, the exceptions may, if necessary, continue to apply after this period.[194] Subject to these limitations, documents of historical or administrative value of the institutions and bodies may be consulted after the expiry of the thirty-year period in the institutions' historical archives.[195]

Finally, other instruments of Union law may also guarantee access to documents beyond what is provided for in Regulation No. 1049/2001. In this respect attention must be drawn to Regulation No. 1367/2006,[196] which guarantees the right of public access to environmental information received or produced by Union institutions or bodies and held by them. Under Article 6(1) of Regulation No. 1367/2006 an overriding public interest in disclosure in the sense of Article 4(2) of Regulation No. 10149/2001 shall be deemed to exist where the information requested relates to emissions into the environment,[197] thus resulting in access to documents despite the existence of other exceptions under Regulation No. 1049/2001.[198] Conversely, other instruments of Union law may provide additional grounds for refusing access to documents, such as in the case of the minutes of the General Council of the ECB, which are confidential pursuant to the Statute of the European System of Central Banks and of the European Central Bank.[199]

---

[193] Regulation No. 1049/2001, Articles 6, 7, and 8. A person may also make a new demand for access relating to documents to which he has previously been denied access. Such an application requires the institution concerned to examine whether the earlier refusal of access remains justified in the light of any change in the legal or factual situation which has taken place in the meantime: C-362/08 P, *Internationaler Hilfsfonds v Commission*, 2010, para. 57.

[194] Regulation No. 1049/2001, Article 4(7).

[195] See Council Regulation (EEC, Euratom) No. 354/83 of 1 February 1983 concerning the opening to the public of the historical archives of the European Economic Community and the European Atomic Energy Community (OJ 1983 L43/1), as amended, most recently, by Council Regulation (EU) 2015/496 of 17 March 2015, OJ 2015 L79/1.

[196] Regulation (EC) No. 1367/2006 of the European Parliament and of the Council of 6 September 2006 on the application of the provisions of the Aarhus Convention on Access to Information, Public Participation in Decision-making and Access to Justice in Environmental Matters to Community institutions and bodies, OJ 2006 L264/13.

[197] On what constitutes 'emissions into the environment', see C-673/13 P, *Commission v* Stichting Greenpeace Nederland and Pesticide Action Network Europe (PAN Europe), 2016, paras 34–83.

[198] T-329/17, *Hautala v European Food Safety Authority*, 2019, paras 43–125. See also C-60/15 P, *Saint-Gobain Glass Deutschland v Commission*, 2017.

[199] C-442/18 P, *ECB v Espírito Santo Financial (Portugal)*, 2019, paras 31–48.

15
The Member States of the Union

National authorities. Within the field of action of the European Union, the national authorities remain continuously involved in the adoption, implementation, and enforcement of decisions, both within the institutions of the Union and through the exercise of their own functions. As explained below, that applies to the parliamentary, executive, and judicial authorities of the Member States, both at national and sub-national level. The Union is to respect the 'fundamental structures, political and constitutional, inclusive of regional and local self-government' as part of the 'national identities' of the Member States (Article 4(2) TEU). In order to emphasize the multiple democratic foundations of the Union, the Treaties refer to the particular role of national parliaments, which 'contribute actively to the good functioning of the Union' (Article 12 TEU). Article 12 TEU specifies a number of ways in which national parliaments make that contribution, either through their participation in constituent decisions of the Union or through their involvement in the Union's decision-making and in the implementation of Union acts.[1]

15.001

I. The Member States as Constituent Authority

Requirement of ratification. The Treaties on which the Union is founded were concluded by representatives of the national governments. In each Member State, the parliament has to approve the Treaties (sometimes after a referendum) before the government can deposit the instrument of ratification. Moreover, amendments to the Treaties are determined by common accord of the representatives of the governments of the Member States or are decided unanimously by the European Council and do not enter into force until they have been ratified by all Member States 'in accordance with their respective constitutional requirements',[2] except for the simplified revision procedure laid down in Article 48(7) TEU

15.002

---

[1] Article 12 TEU refers to national parliaments' contributions (a) through being informed by the institutions of the Union and having draft legislative acts of the Union forwarded to them; (b) by seeing to it that the principle of subsidiarity is respected; (c) by taking part, within the framework of the area of freedom, security, and justice, in the evaluation mechanisms for the implementation of the Union policies in that area; (d) by taking part in the revision procedures of the Treaties; (e) by being notified of applications for accession to the Union; and (f) by taking part in inter-parliamentary cooperation between national parliaments and with the European Parliament. See Barrett, '"The King is Dead, Long Live the King": the Recasting by the Treaty of Lisbon of the Provisions of the Constitutional Treaty Concerning National Parliaments' (2008) ELRev 66–84. For a detailed overview on how different national parliaments exercise their new powers under the Lisbon Treaty, see the Thirteenth Bi-annual Report 'Developments in European Union Procedures and Practices Relevant to Parliamentary Scrutiny' prepared by the COSAC Secretariat in May 2010 (available at www.cosac.eu/relevant-bi-annual-reports).

[2] Article 48(2) to (6) TEU. See the discussion of the entry into effect of the (amending) Treaties (para. 3-005, *supra*) and of the procedure for acceding to the Union (Article 49 TEU; para. 4-012, *supra*). On this role of Member States as 'Masters of the Treaty', see Sowery, 'The Nature and Scope of the Primary Law-making Powers of the European Union: the Member States as the "Masters of the Treaties?"' (2018) ELRev 205–23. See also Albi and Ziller (eds), *The European Constitution and National Constitutions: Ratification and Beyond* (Kluwer, 2006).

under which a national parliament can make known its opposition against a draft amendment initiated by the European Council within six months. The Treaties also prescribe the procedure of ratification in accordance with national constitutional requirements for a number of decisions with 'constitutional' status at Union level.[3] It is thus for each Member State's constitutional order to determine who is to decide on membership of the Union and on the related transfer of national powers.[4]

15.003 **Domestic organization of ratification.** Since the subject matter of the decision to ratify, or not to ratify, is the text resulting from negotiations between the national governments, the decision is confined to approval or rejection of that text and there is no possibility of making any changes to it. If a Member State rejects the text, the latter may be modified only by common accord between the national governments, and whether it will ultimately be adopted depends on its being approved by all the Member States. A Member State is at liberty to frame its constitutional law in such a way that the government has to consult the national parliament before approving the proposed text[5] or—conversely—that certain 'constituent' decisions are deemed to have been already approved by a government act. By the same token, a Member State may make ratification of a Treaty amendment dependent upon its approval by all the federated entities competent to that end.[6] In practice, some Member States hold a referendum which has to have a favourable outcome before Treaty amendments can be ratified.[7] Applicant Member States have, in many cases, held a referendum on the Treaty by which they accede to the Union[8] and some Member States may not be ready to take a major decision with regard to the Union without the express approval of the people.[9]

---

[3] These include the acts on the direct election of the European Parliament and the Union's own resources (see para. 3-007, *supra*).

[4] That determination relates to the question in which (direct or representative) manner, by which (legislative or executive) body and at which (national or possibly decentralized) level the decision is taken. For the question as to whether Union law subjects that ultimate right of decision of the Member States (*Kompetenz-Kompetenz*) to formal and substantive constraints, see paras 3-009–3-010, *supra*.

[5] See Lepka and Terrebus, 'Les ratifications nationales, manifestations d'un projet politique européen—la face cachée du Traité d'Amsterdam' (2003) RTDE 365, 382–6. Generally, the national parliament has, at most, the right to be informed during the negotiations and to have cognizance of the draft Treaty before it is signed. See Article 168 of the Belgian Constitution and the commentary by Ingelaere, 'De Europeesrechtlijke raakvlakken van de nieuwe wetgeving inzake de internationale bevoegdheid van de Belgische Gemeenschappen en Gewesten' (1994) SEW 67, 79–81; Louis and Alen, 'La Constitution et la participation à la Communauté européenne' (1994) BTIR 81, 84.

[6] This was the case in Belgium as regards the ratification of the EU Treaty (para. 1-042, *supra*), the Treaty of Amsterdam (para. 1-050, *supra*), the Treaty of Nice (para. 1-053, *supra*), and the Lisbon Treaty (para. 2-002, *supra*). This does not mean of itself that the regions are part of the 'constituent authority' at Union level. If the national government ratifies a Treaty amendment without awaiting the requisite approvals, the Member State is bound as a party to the Treaty. See also Van Nuffel, 'Does EU Decision-Making Take into Account Regional Interests?', in Cloots, De Baere, and Sottiaux (eds), *Federalism in the European Union* (Hart Publishing, 2012) 191, at 207. For the involvement of decentralized bodies in the negotiations resulting in the Treaty of Nice, see Wiedmann, 'Der Vertrag von Nizza—Genesis einer Reform' (2001) EuR. 185, 196–202.

[7] In this way, referendums were held to approve the Single European Act (para. 1-041, *supra*), the EU Treaty (para. 1-042, *supra*), the Treaty of Amsterdam (para. 1-050, *supra*), the Treaty of Nice (para. 1-053, *supra*), and the Lisbon Treaty (para. 2-002, *supra*). In some cases, the decision to ratify a Treaty was subjected to a referendum; in others, the referendum related to the amendment to the Constitution which was required in order to ratify; see Lepka and Terrebus (n. 5, *supra*), at 378–82.

[8] Paras 4-002–4-007, *supra*.

[9] See the referendum held in Italy on 18 June 1989 on the status of Italian Members of the European Parliament and the referendums held in Denmark on 28 September 2002 and in Sweden on 14 September 2003 on the introduction of the single currency (para. 9-033, *supra*). For a study of the various referendums, see Mendez and Mendez, 'Referendums and European integration: Beyond the Lisbon Vote' (2010) Pub L 223–30; Roberts-Thomson, 'EU Treaty Referendums and the European Union' (2001) JEI 105–37.

France has thus made the future accession of Member States dependent on the positive outcome of a referendum.[10]

The Treaties leave Member States the freedom to organize the involvement of their citizens or national parliaments with constituent decisions, such as Treaty amendments or the accession of new Member States. Nonetheless, Article 48 TEU associates national parliaments with some aspects of the revision procedure[11] and Article 49 TEU requires national parliaments to be notified of applications for membership of the Union. On that basis, Article 12 TEU refers to the national parliaments as 'taking part in the revision procedures of the Treaties' and 'being notified of applications for accession'. As far as the revision procedure is concerned, Article 48(7) TEU provides for the possible opposition by a national parliament against an amendment decision proposed by the European Council 'within six months of the date of [the] notification [of the European Council decision]'. Whereas this provision requires national parliaments to take the initiative to oppose the amendment decision, some Member States require the government to obtain parliamentary consent before supporting that decision of the European Council. This is the case, for example, for the Austrian *Nationalrat*,[12] the German *Bundestag* and *Bundesrat*,[13] the Danish *Folketing*, the Latvian *Saeima*, and the Slovakian *Národná Rada*.[14] In Member States with bicameral parliaments, the opposition under Article 48(7) TEU may come from either one of the chambers[15] or require that both chambers oppose the decision of the European Council.[16] In Germany, if the matter falls within the exclusive competence of the *Bund*, consent must be obtained only from the *Bundestag*. In other cases, either the *Bundestag* or the *Bundesrat* may oppose a European Council decision based on Article 48(7) TEU.[17] Regional parliaments may be involved in Member States with a

---

[10] See Article 88-8 of the French Constitution. However, the holding of a referendum will not be constitutionally mandated where a three-fifths majority in both the *Sénat* and the *Assemblée Nationale* supports accession. In the past, France has already held a referendum for the purposes of enlargement. See the referendum on 23 April 1972 on the accession of Denmark, Ireland, and the UK to the European Communities.

[11] See, apart from the approval by Member States of amending Treaties or European Council amending decisions 'in accordance with their respective constitutional requirements' (Article 48(4) and (6)), the notification to national parliaments of proposals for amendment of the Treaties (Article 48(2)), the participation of representatives of national parliaments in the Convention (Article 48(3)), and the possibility for a national parliament to oppose initiatives taken by the European Council pursuant to Article 48(7) TEU.

[12] In Austria, the *Nationalrat*, after having obtained the consent of the *Bundesrat*, authorizes the motion of the government. The authorization requires a two-thirds majority in each Chamber. See Article 23i of the bill implementing the Lisbon Treaty. See Annex to the COSAC Thirteenth Bi-annual Report (n. 1, *supra*), 30.

[13] In its judgment of 30 June 2009 (see para. 23-029, *supra*), the *Bundesverfassungsgericht* held that the law implementing the Lisbon Treaty (the 'Extending act') was unconstitutional on the ground that the powers of the *Bundestag* and *Bundesrat* needed to be enhanced. It found that Article 48(7) TEU 'is not a sufficient equivalent to the requirement of ratification' and accordingly, the idea of tacit parliamentary consent to adopt a Treaty amendment was rejected. The application of Article 48 (7) TEU requires the passage of a law within the meaning of Article 23(1), second sentence, of the Basic Law. In addition, consent may not be given in an abstract fashion. Therefore, the *Bundesverfassungsgericht* limited the flexibility sought by Article 48(7) TEU. The same applies to the special passarelle clause laid down in Article 88(3) TFEU. See Judgment of 30 June 2009, 2 BvE 2/08, para. 414. See also Annex to the COSAC Thirteenth Bi-annual Report (n.1, *supra*) 183, and Kiiver, 'German Participation in EU Decision-Making after the Lisbon Case: A Comparative View on Domestic Parliamentary Clearance Procedures' (2009) GLJ 1287–96.

[14] See Section 6 of the European Union (Amendment) act 2008.

[15] For example, this is the case for the Belgian, Czech and Irish Parliaments. See the COSAC Thirteenth Bi-annual Report (n. 1, *supra*), 28.

[16] For example, this is the case for France and Spain: ibid. In Slovenia, in the event of conflicting views between the two chambers, the views of the lower chamber prevail: ibid.

[17] See also Annex to the COSAC Thirteenth Bi-annual Report (n. 1, *supra*) 199–200.

federal structure. That raises the question, for example, in Belgium, whether all regional parliaments would have a right to oppose a decision of the European Council based on Article 48(7) TEU.[18]

II. The Member States as Actors in Decision-making

A. The role of the national governments

15.004 **Interaction between administrations.** Decision-making in the context of the Union is based on action by the Member States. The Heads of State or Government of the Member States meet and take decisions in the framework of the European Council. Ministers in national (or regional)[19] governments, in their capacity as members of the Council, take the main decisions in the context of the Union, often together with the European Parliament. National civil servants and Union officials meet in order to carry out preparatory work for decision-making in the Council (see para. 20-051 *et seq.*, *infra*). This gives rise to a relationship which facilitates the subsequent implementation of Union acts. In many cases, the same national civil servants are indeed members of committees which supervise *ex post* the way in which the Commission or other Union bodies implement those acts, or they may prepare the necessary implementing measures themselves. This interaction between national civil servants and Union officials gives the lie to the widespread idea that decision-making is in the hands of 'Eurocrats'.[20]

In the case of some acts, the Treaties make express recourse to the 'governments of the Member States'.[21] Where the Treaties refer to a 'common accord of the governments of the Member States', the representatives of the national governments[22] adopt the act in question, yet in coming together to adopt it they do not constitute a body of the Union. Consequently, such meetings have to be distinguished from the Council, which is a Union institution.[23] Since the Lisbon Treaty, decisions formerly adopted by the Council or the governments of the Member States 'at the level of Heads of State or Government'[24] are adopted by the European Council (see para. 12-022, *supra*).

---

[18] See Declaration (No. 51), annexed to the Lisbon Treaty, by the Kingdom of Belgium on national Parliaments (OJ 2010 C83/355) and the literature referred to in para. 15-010, *infra*.

[19] For the involvement of decentralized authorities, see paras 15-014–15-017, *infra*.

[20] For an assessment from a 'democratic' standpoint, see para. 17-046 *et seq.*, *infra*. See also Curtin, 'Challenging Executive Dominance in European Democracy' (2014) MLR 1–32; Buitendijk and Van Schendelen, 'Brussels Advisory Committees: A Channel for Influence' (1995) ELRev 37–56.

[21] See the references to the 'governments of the Member States' (Article 99 TFEU; Article 127(3) TFEU; Article 130 TFEU; Article 253 TFEU; Article 240(1) TFEU; Article 254 TFEU; Article 255 TFEU; Article 282(3) TFEU; Article 341 TFEU and a 'conference of representatives of the governments of the Member States' (Article 48 TEU).

[22] The representatives of the governments do not have to be members of government. For instance, on 27 April 1994 the governments left it to the Permanent Representatives to appoint a Member of the Commission for the remainder of his predecessor's term of office (Decision 94/282 of 27 April 1994, OJ 1994 L121/41; *corrigendum* L131/26): see *Europe*, No. 6220, 28 April 1994, 5.

[23] See C-424/20 P(R), *Representatives of the Governments of the Member States v Sharpston* (order of the Vice-President), 2020, para. 26.

[24] See the references to the 'governments of the Member States at the level of Heads of State or Government' in Articles 112(2)(b) and 117(1), second subpara. EC.

B. The role of the national parliaments

Indirect involvement. The Lisbon Treaty conferred on the national parliaments the specific role to see to it that the Union legislature respects the principle of subsidiarity (Article 12(b) TEU, which refers to the Protocol on the application of the principles of subsidiarity and proportionality; see para. 15-010, *infra*). The national (or regional) parliaments are not directly involved in the formulation of acts of the Union. In some cases, they do play a role of their own before such acts obtain their full force. This is true of a number of acts having constitutional status (see para. 15-002, *supra*). It is also true in the case of directives, where the choice of the form and methods of attaining the result to be achieved is left to the 'national authorities' (Article 288, third para. TFEU).[25] It often falls to national (or regional) parliaments to transpose a directive into national law (see para. 15-011, *infra*).

15.005

Indirectly, however, members of national parliaments may influence Union decision-making through their contacts with their counterparts in the European Parliament and through influence brought to bear on national ministers sitting in the Council. Article 12 TEU refers to that influence, stating that draft legislative acts are forwarded by the Union institutions to national parliaments in accordance with the Protocol on the role of national parliaments in the European Union (Article 12(a) TEU; see para. 15-007, *infra*) and calling for inter-parliamentary cooperation between national parliaments and the European Parliament (Article 12(f) TEU). This call for inter-parliamentary cooperation is further set out in Protocol (No. 1) on the role of national parliaments in the European Union, mentioning the conferences of Parliamentary Committees for Union Affairs, which have long since been regularly convened under the name of 'the Conference of European Affairs Committees' (COSAC).[26]

Scrutiny of governmental action in the Council. As already observed, national parliaments may influence decision-making at Union level by bringing pressure to bear on members of the Council, who are answerable to them. In practice, the influence of the national parliament varies greatly depending on the Member State considered.[27] Most parliaments have a standing committee to scrutinize 'European' business, such as a committee on European Affairs. In bicameral systems, each of the chambers of parliament may have its own committee[28] or the two chambers may jointly set up a common committee.[29] In other

15.006

---

[25] See para. 27-018 *et seq., infra* PJCC framework decisions, which may no longer be adopted following the entry into force of the Lisbon Treaty, also left the choice of the form and methods of achieving the intended result to the 'national authorities' (Article 34(2)(b) EU).

[26] Article 10 of Protocol (No. 1), annexed to the TEU, TFEU, and EAEC Treaty, on the role of National Parliaments in the European Union (OJ 2010 C83/203). On the relationship between national Parliaments and the European Parliament, see the 21st Bi-annual Report 'Developments in European Union Procedures and Practices Relevant to Parliamentary Scrutiny' prepared by the COSAC Secretariat in June 2014. See also the Guidelines for Interparliamentary Cooperation in the European Union, adopted by the Conference of Speakers of the European Union Parliaments in Lisbon on 21 June 2008.

[27] Information on parliamentary scrutiny can be found in the COSAC's Bi-annual reports, in particular the 27th Bi-annual Report 'Developments in European Union Procedures and Practices Relevant to Parliamentary Scrutiny', prepared by the COSAC Secretariat in May 2017. See also Raunio, 'Holding Governments Accountable in European Affairs: Explaining Cross-national Variation' (2005) J Legis Stud 319–42.

[28] See, for instance, the committees set up in Austria by the *Nationalrat* and the *Bundesrat*, and in France by the *Assemblée nationale* and the *Sénat*, in Germany by the *Bundesrat* and *Bundesrat* (set up in the wake of the discussion about the EU Treaty pursuant to amendments to the Basic Law: Articles 45 and 52(3)(a), respectively).

[29] See, for instance, the committee set up by the two chambers of the Parliament jointly in Belgium, in Ireland, in Romania, and in Spain. In the Netherlands, only the *Tweede Kamer* has created a European affairs committee; see Del Grosso, *Parlement en Europese integratie* (Kluwer, 2000). Furthermore, a standing committee on European

parliaments the normal departmental committees deal with the adoption, transposition and subsequent implementation of acts of the Union.

In any event, parliamentary scrutiny of the role played by the national government in Union decision-making is possible only if (1) the parliament is in possession of the necessary information concerning the activities of the Union; (2) influence may actually be brought to bear on a member of the Council; and (3) that member may be called to account for how he or she voted in the Council. As regards the first issue, recent Treaty amendments have significantly enhanced the national parliaments' right to information. As far as the other two matters are concerned, the impact of a given national parliament will depend on what powers are conferred upon it under domestic law. That said, the parliamentary scrutiny exercised at national level plays a part in determining the democratic character of the operation of the Union (see para. 17-048, *infra*).

15.007 **(1) Right of national parliament to be informed.** The Protocol to the Treaties on the role of national parliaments provides that all Commission consultation documents (green and white papers and communications) are to be forwarded directly by the Commission to (both chambers of) the national parliaments upon publication.[30] In addition, all proposals and other draft legislative acts presented to the European Parliament and to the Council must simultaneously be sent to (both chambers of[31]) the national parliaments.[32] The national parliaments must also be informed in advance if the Commission is to submit a proposal for application of the flexibility clause[33] or if the European Council intends to make use of the possibility to introduce, in a given field, qualified majority voting or the ordinary legislative procedure.[34] They also receive an annual report from the Court of Auditors at the same time as the European Parliament and the Council.[35]

The national parliaments obtained this autonomous right to receive legislative proposals only upon the entry into force of the Lisbon Treaty. Before then, it was merely provided that Commission proposals for legislation were to be made available in good time 'so that

---

affairs has been set up, *inter alia*, by the Danish *Folketing*; by the Finnish, Greek, and Portuguese Parliament; and by the Swedish *Riksdag*.

[30] Article 1 of Protocol (No. 1) on the role of National Parliaments in the European Union (n. 26, *supra*, which replaced Protocol (No. 9), annexed by the Amsterdam Treaty to the EU Treaties and the Community Treaties, OJ 1997 C340/113). Article 1 of the Protocol adds that the Commission must also forward the annual legislative programme as well as any other instrument of legislative planning or policy to national parliaments, at the same time as to the European Parliament and the Council.

[31] See Article 8 of Protocol (No. 1) on the role of National Parliaments in the European Union (n. 26, *supra*). As far as Belgium is concerned, this refers not only to the chambers of the federal parliament, but also to the parliamentary assemblies of the Communities and the Regions (see the Declaration by the Kingdom of Belgium on national Parliaments (n. 18, *supra*).

[32] Article 2 of Protocol (No. 1) on the role of National Parliaments in the European Union (n. 26, *supra*). The protocol defines 'draft legislative act' as proposals from the Commission, initiatives from a group of Member States, initiatives from the European Parliament, requests from the Court of Justice, recommendations from the European Central Bank, and requests from the European Investment Bank for the adoption of a legislative act (Article 2, second subpara).

[33] See Article 352(2) TFEU, which refers to the procedure for monitoring the subsidiarity principle laid down in Protocol (No. 2), annexed to the TEU and TFEU, on the application of the principles of subsidiarity and proportionality (OJ 2010 C83/206); see para. 5-032, *supra*.

[34] Article 6 of Protocol (No. 1) on the role of National Parliaments in the European Union (n. 26, *supra*), which refers to the powers that Article 48(7) TEU confers on the European Council in that respect. National parliaments must be informed of the initiative of the European Council at least six months before any decision is adopted.

[35] Article 7 of Protocol (No. 1) on the role of National Parliaments in the European Union (n. 26, *supra*).

the government of each Member State may ensure that its own national parliament receives them as appropriate'.[36] This did not give the national parliament a Union-law right of information, although in some Member States the government was bound under domestic law to provide the national parliament or the competent parliamentary committee with all Commission proposals[37] and to inform parliament of the stance which it intends to take in the Council. In several of the Member States that acceded to the Union in 2004, the Constitution was amended not only to allow for accession but also to impose on the national government a duty to inform the national parliament in advance on the decisions to be taken at the level of the Union.[38] In any case, the duty to inform the national parliaments results in numerous documents being sent to these parliaments, where the information may be sifted by the general 'European' committee or by the normal departmental committees (which is often more effective).

This information forms the basis for the national parliaments' monitoring of compliance with the principle of subsidiarity (see para. 15-010, *infra*), but also allows national parliaments to exchange views with the Commission in the context of a 'political dialogue'. That goes back to a commitment entered into by the Barroso Commission in May 2006 not only to inform national parliaments on new proposals and consultation documents, but also to invite their reaction so as to improve the process of policy formulation.[39] This allows national parliaments to express their views on the desirability of draft legislative acts, instead of—or in addition to—issuing a 'reasoned opinion' on compliance with the subsidiarity principle. At the same time, the information sent to national parliaments may facilitate the scrutiny of their own government's action in the Council.

(2) **Influence on the national government.** In order to allow enough time for discussion of draft legislative acts, the Protocol on the role of national parliaments requires that there be an eight-week period between the time when a Commission draft is made available in all languages to the European Parliament and the Council and the date on which it is placed on a Council agenda for decision (see para. 17-016, *infra*). As to the influence of parliamentary scrutiny on the position taken by the government, Denmark has organized its governmental structure in such a way that a Minister must defend in the Council the point of view

15.008

---

[36] See Point 2 of Protocol (No. 9) on the role of national parliaments in the European Union (n. 30, *supra*).
[37] In Belgium, the government entered into such an obligation vis-à-vis both chambers of the parliament and the parliaments of the Communities and Regions (Article 92*quater* of the special law of 8 August 1980 on institutional reform; see Louis and Alen, n. 5, *supra*, at 84–5). Commission legislative proposals were also made available, *inter alia*, to the Danish *Folketing*, the German *Bundesrat* (para. 2 of the *Gesetz zur EEA*, BGBl. II, 1986, 1102), the House of Commons and the House of Lords, both Chambers of the Austrian Parliament, the Netherlands *Tweede Kamer*, the French *Sénat* and *Assemblée* (Law of 10 May 1990 and Article 88-4 of the Constitution), the Italian parliament (*Legge-Fabbri* of 16 April 1987), the Portuguese parliament (Law No. 20/94 of 15 June 1994), and the Finnish parliament. In the Netherlands, the government had to publish certain draft decisions to be taken in the area of freedom, security, and justice and submit them to the parliament before they are adopted: Article 3 of the *Rijkswet* of 10 July 2008 ratifying the Lisbon Treaty, *Stb.* 2008, 301 (see previously Articles 3 and 4 of the *Rijkswet* of 19 December 2001 ratifying the Treaty of Nice, *Stb.*, 2001, 617; Article 3(1) of the *Rijkswet* of 17 December 1992 ratifying the EU Treaty, *Stb.*, 1992, 692, and Article 3 of the *Rijkswet* of 24 December 1998 ratifying the Treaty of Amsterdam, *Stb.*, 1998, 737).
[38] See Article 10b of the Czech Constitution, Article 35/A of the Hungarian Constitution, Article 3a of the Slovak Constitution, and Articles 3 and 4 of the Constitutional Act on the Membership of Lithuania in the European Union.
[39] Jančić, 'The Game of Cards: National Parliaments in the EU and the Future of the Early Warning Mechanism and the Political Dialogue', (2015) CMLRev 939–76; Jančić, 'The Barroso Initiative: Window Dressing or Democracy Boost?' (2012) ULR 78–91.

approved by the parliamentary committee on European affairs[40] The Finnish, Estonian, and Swedish Governments are placed under a similar obligation vis-à-vis their national parliaments.[41] In Germany,[42] in the light of the judgment of the *Bundesverfassungsgericht* on the Lisbon Treaty,[43] prior parliamentary assent is required for the simplified revision procedure and other decisions by which the European Council or the Council would decide to render the ordinary legislative procedure or qualified majority voting applicable[44] as well as for other important decisions (even if the Treaty provisions themselves do not provide for the intervention of national parliaments), such as the exercise of the flexibility clause.[45] In addition, in order to defend the interests of the *Länder*, the German *Bundesrat* may commit the Federal Government to follow its opinion in certain circumstances.[46] In Austria, depending on whether the matter comes within the competence of the *Länder* or the federal authorities, the Council member is bound by a common position adopted by the *Länder* or one of the federal legislative chambers.[47] Consent from the Netherlands parliament must be

---

[40] The Minister submits a draft negotiating mandate to the parliamentary committee, in which each Member has the same number of votes as the number of Members of parliament which he or she represents. That mandate constitutes only a political undertaking; see Hagel-Sørensen and Rasmussen, 'The Danish Administration and its Interaction with the Community Administration' (1985) CMLRev 273, 279–86; Rasmussen, 'Über die Durchsetzung des Gemeinschaftsrechts in Dänemark' (1985) EuR 66–74.

[41] Basilien-Gainche, 'Parlements Scandinaves et affaires européennes: Quand le contrôle de l'action gouvernementale devient modèle' (2009) RMCUE 527–31; Bernitz, 'Sweden and the European Union: On Sweden's Implementation and Application of European Law' (2001) CMLRev 903, 915; Aalto, 'Accession of Finland to the European Union: First Remarks' (1995) ELRev 625–26.

[42] See Kiiver (n.13, *supra*), 1289.

[43] Judgment of 30 June 2009, 2 BvE 2/08, paras 315–21 (see n. 13, *supra*).

[44] See Articles 31(3) and 48(7) TEU and Articles 81(3), 153(2), fourth subpara., 192(2), second subpara, 312(2), second subpara., and 333(1) and (2) TFEU.

[45] Article 352 TFEU. See also Articles 82(2), second subpara. and 83(1), third subpara. TFEU.

[46] Depending on whether the Federal State has exclusive competence, whether it has actually exercised a non-exclusive power in respect of matters where the *Länder*, the structure of Land authorities, or Land administrative procedures are primarily affected, or whether, in contrast, the *Länder* have exclusive competence: Article 23(4) and (5) of the Basic Law provide respectively for a simple opinion of the *Bundesrat*, for an opinion with which the Federal Government has to pay the greatest possible respect, or for direct participation of a representative of the *Länder* in the Council proceedings. As far as the second type of opinion is concerned, the implementing law of 12 March 1993 (*Gesetz über die Zusammenarbeit von Bund und Ländern in Angelegenheiten der Europäischen Union*)—modified in 2006 and 2009—provides that, in the event that there continues to be disagreement with the Federal Government, the *Bundesrat* may resolve by a two-thirds majority to confirm the opinion, which render that opinion 'decisive'. Following the Lisbon-judgment of the *Bundesverfassungsgericht*, Article 23 (6) of the Basic Law was also amended. It now lists explicitly 'school education, culture [and] broadcasting' as matters of exclusive competence of the *Länder*. See further Panara, 'Germany: A Cooperative Solution to the Challenge of European Integration', in Panara and De Becker (eds), *The Role of the Regions in EU Governance* (Springer, 2011), 133–56; Suszycka-Jasch and Jasch, 'The Participation of the German Länder in Formulating German EU-Policy' (2009) GLJ 1215–56; Panara, 'The German Länder in the Process of European Integration between Föderalismusreform and Reform Treaty' (2008) E Pub L 585–614.

[47] In matters coming within the legislative competence of the *Länder*, the representative in the Council is bound in principle by a position on which the *Länder* have reached agreement among themselves. That position may be departed from only on compelling grounds relating to foreign policy and integration. A similar obligation exists with regard to positions adopted by the lower house (*Nationalrat*) in matters coming under the legislative competence of the federal authorities and by the upper house (*Bundesrat*) as regards Union measures having to be implemented by a constitutional law. In discussing measures which would result in an amendment to Austrian constitutional provisions, the Austrian Minister may diverge from the position adopted by the national parliament only if the *Nationalrat* does not intimate its opposition within a specified time. See Eberhard, 'Austria: The Role of the "Länder" in a "Centralised Federal State"', in Panara and De Becker (eds), *The Role of the Regions in EU Governance* (Springer, 2011), 215–34; Pollak and Slominski, 'Influencing EU Politics? The Case of the Austrian Parliament' (2003) JCMS 707–29; Egger, 'L'Autriche—Etat membre de l'Union européenne. Les effets institutionnels' (1996) RMCUE 380, 383; Seidl-Hohenveldern, 'Constitutional Problems Involved in Austria's Accession to the EU' (1995) CMLRev 727, 735–6; Griller, 'Verfassungsfragen der österreichischen EU-Mitgliedschaft' (1995) ZfRV 89, 102–7.

obtained in relation to certain acts of the Council to be adopted in the area of freedom, security, and justice that are not subject to the ordinary legislative procedure.[48]

In other Member States, the parliament does not have the power to confer a specific mandate on the national government but has a right to be consulted on certain issues before the government defines its position.[49]

(3) Accountability of the national government. Even if a government is not specifically obliged to take account of the views of the national parliament, the parliament may hold it politically answerable for the positions that it takes up within the Council. In this connection, Article 10(2) TEU recalls that the governments representing the Member States in the European Council and the Council are 'themselves democratically accountable either to their national parliaments, or to their citizens'. To that effect, it is crucial that the Council meet in public when it deliberates and votes on a draft legislative act (Article 16(8) TEU). As a result, national parliaments may see how the members of the Council have acted.[50] In addition, the agendas for and the outcomes of meetings of the Council, including the minutes of meetings where the Council is deliberating on draft legislative acts, are forwarded directly to national parliaments, at the same time as to Member States' governments.[51]

15.009

Subsidiarity scrutiny of Union legislative acts. The Lisbon Treaty vested national parliaments with new powers to check *ex ante* as well as *ex post* whether Union legislative acts comply with the principle of subsidiarity (see para. 5-029, *supra*). Since the Protocol on the application of the principles of subsidiarity and proportionality[52] does not specify the internal procedures that national parliaments must follow in order to exercise these new powers, important differences exist among the national parliaments.[53]

15.010

As to the *ex-ante* control, that is, when considering whether to send the Union institutions a reasoned opinion on whether a draft legislative act complies with the subsidiarity principle (the 'early warning mechanism' set out in Article 6 of the Protocol), one might distinguish different ways in which national parliaments may intervene. First, in some Member States, the plenary of the parliament takes the final decision as to whether a reasoned opinion is issued, regardless of any diverging views expressed by the parliamentary committee(s) in

---

[48] See Article 3(2) of the *Rijkswet* of 10 July 2008 (n. 37, *supra*). On previous systems, see Besselink, 'An Open Constitution and European Integration: The Kingdom of the Netherlands' (1996) SEW 192, 196. For the changes introduced by the Lisbon Treaty, see Besselink and van Mourik, 'The Netherlands—The Roles of the National Parliament and the European Parliament in EU Decision-Making: The Approval of the Lisbon Treaty in the Netherlands' (2009) E Pub L 307–18.

[49] For instance, this is true of the German *Bundestag* (Basic Law, Article 23(3)) and the implementing law of 12 March 1993, as further modified. The former French Prime Minister Balladur entered into a similar undertaking: see *Europe*, No. 6264, 1 July 1994, 4; see now Article 88-4 of the Constituion as further developed in the 'circulaire du Premier ministre du 21 juin 2010 relative à la participation du Parlement au processus décisionnel européen', JORF No. 142, 22 June 2010.

[50] For the limitations to this democratic control, see para. 17-048 *et seq.*, *infra* In this respect, access must be granted to virtually all documents relating to the legislative process, even in respect of ongoing legislative procedures, see C-280/11, *Council v Access Info Europe*, 2013 (documents revealing which Member State has made a particular proposal) and T-540/15, *Di Capitani v European Parliament*, 2018 (information relating to trilogues of ongoing legislative procedure).

[51] Article 5 of Protocol (No. 1) on the role of National Parliaments in the European Union (n. 26, *supra*).

[52] Protocol (No. 2), annexed to the TEU and TFEU, on the application of the principles of subsidiarity and proportionality (OJ 2010 C83/206).

[53] See also the COSAC Thirteenth Bi-annual Report (n. 1, *supra*). For an overview of the application in practice, see Jaroszyński, 'National Parliaments' Scrutiny of the Principle of Subsidiarity: Reasoned Opinions 2014–2019' (2020) EuConst 91–119.

charge of monitoring compliance with the principle of subsidiarity.[54] Second, some national parliaments/chambers have decided that the plenary will only intervene where the parliamentary committee(s) in charge of monitoring compliance with the principle of subsidiarity finds the proposal to be contrary to it.[55] Finally, in some national parliaments, the decision is normally adopted by a committee but the plenary may recall the final vote.[56] By contrast, in some Member States, the plenary does not play any role and has delegated the task of sending reasoned opinions to the Committee on European Affairs.[57] As far as the involvement of regional parliaments is concerned, the Protocol leaves it to the national parliament to consult, where appropriate, regional parliaments with legislative powers.[58] However, Belgium has gone further by putting the parliaments of its federated entities ('Regions' and 'Communities') on the same level as the chambers of the federal parliament for the application of the Protocol. In a declaration attached to the Lisbon Treaty, Belgium has made clear that, in accordance with its constitutional law, the parliamentary assemblies of its autonomous regions act, in terms of the competences exercised by the Union, as components of the 'national parliamentary system'.[59] The parliamentary assemblies concluded a cooperation agreement in order to agree on the conditions under which one or more of them may issue a reasoned opinion and express either one or two of the votes allotted by the Protocol to the national parliaments.[60]

As to the *ex post* control, Article 8 of the Protocol provides that Member States may notify 'in accordance with their legal order' an action for annulment—as provided for by Article 263 TFEU—on grounds of infringement of the principle of subsidiarity on behalf of their national parliaments or a chamber thereof.[61] In most Member States, the decision to bring such action for annulment lies in the province of the national parliament or parliamentary chamber as such.[62] However, the French Government must notify an action for annulment

---

[54] Ibid., 21 (Dutch *Tweede Kamer* and Finnish *Eduskunta*).

[55] Ibid. (Polish *Senat* and Lithuanian *Seimas*).

[56] Ibid. (Spanish *Congreso de los Diputados* and *Senato* and Belgian *Kamer van volksvertegenwoordigers/Chambre des représentants*).

[57] Ibid. (Danish *Folketin*, Italian *Camera dei Diputati*, Bulgarian *Narodno Sabranie*, and Latvian *Saeima*).

[58] Protocol (No. 2) on the application of the principles of subsidiarity and proportionality (n. 33, *supra*) Article 6.

[59] Declaration (No. 51), annexed to the Lisbon Treaty, by the Kingdom of Belgium on national Parliaments (OJ 2010 C83/355). See Vandenbruwaene and Popelier, 'Belgian Parliaments and the Early Warning System', in Jonsson Cornell and Goldoni (eds), *National and Regional Parliaments in the EU-Legislative Procedure Post-Lisbon: The Impact of the Early Warning Mechanism* (Hart Publishing, 2017), 181–98; De Becker, 'Belgium—The State and the Sub-State Entities Are Equal, but is the State sometimes More Equal than the Others?', in Panara and De Becker (eds), *The Role of the Regions in European Governance* (Springer, 2011); Pas, 'The Belgian "National Parliament" from the Perspective of the EU Constitutional Treaty', in Kiiver (ed.), *National and Regional Parliaments in the European Constitutional Order* (Europa Law, 2006), 57–76; Van Looy, 'Het Vlaams Parlement als "nationaal parlement" in de Europese Unie (Ceci n'est pas une fiction)' (2007) TVW 28–49.

[60] See the cooperation agreement of 29 March 2017 on the exercise of the powers allotted by the Treaties to the national Parliaments, *Belgisch Staatsblad/Moniteur belge* 17 July 2018.

[61] This possibility already existed before the entry into force of the Lisbon Treaty in so far as it was up to any Member State to determine the domestic authorities on behalf of which it brought an action before the Court. See Van Nuffel, 'What's in a Member State? Central and Decentralised Authorities before the Community Courts' (2001) CMLRev 871, 879. See also the discussion in Lenaerts and Cambien, 'Regions and the European Courts: Giving Shape to the Regional Dimension of Member States' (2010) ELRev 609–35; Cygan, 'Regional Governance, Subsidiarity and Accountability within the EU's Multi-level Polity' (2013) Eur Pub L 161; Besselink and van Mourik, 'The Parliamentary Legitimacy of the European Union: The Role of the States General within the European Union' (2012) ULR 28.

[62] See the COSAC Thirteenth Bi-annual Report (n. 1, *supra*), at 29. In Luxembourg, the Conference of Presidents of the *Chambre des Deputés* may take the decision to bring an action for annulment where it is not possible to call in the plenary before the expiration of the time-limit set out in Article 263 TFEU (see also the Annex to the COSAC Thirteenth Bi-annual Report, 338).

to the Court of Justice where sixty members of the *Sénat* or of the *Assemblée nationale* support the initiative to bring such action.[63] Likewise, in Germany, the *Bundestag* is bound to bring an action for annulment at the request of one fourth of its members.[64] In addition, while in most cases the Committee on European Affairs drafts a report on the basis of which the plenary casts its vote, in some Member States a certain number of members may call in the plenary to intervene.[65] Where the national parliament votes in favour of bringing an action for annulment, the national government often has no choice but to start (or notify) proceedings before the Court of Justice.[66] However, in the Netherlands, Spain, and Sweden, the request from the national parliament is not legally binding. As far as Belgium is concerned, such action may be brought not only on behalf of the chambers of the federal parliament, but also on behalf of the parliamentary assemblies of the federated entities, each of which may trigger the action.[67]

Scrutiny of implementing acts. The option available to national parliaments of securing influence by controlling their government's position in the Council continues, in practice, to be limited to the legislative activity of the Union. Indeed it appears impossible for national parliaments to monitor the numerous acts by which the Commission or the Council implement Union legislation.[68] To a certain extent, however, such control is being exercised by civil servants from the various national ministerial departments who monitor the Commission's executive activities under the 'comitology' system or sit in the working parties of the Council (see para. 18-014 *et seq.*, *infra*). It is only with respect to the area of freedom, security, and justice that the Treaties now provide for a role to be played by national authorities, in collaboration with the Commission, in the evaluation of the implementation of the Union policies by the Member States (Article 70 TFEU) and that national parliaments, together with the European Parliament, are called upon to evaluate the activities of Eurojust and Europol (Articles 85(2) and 88(2), second subpara. TFEU).[69]

15.011

---

[63] See Article 88-6 of the French Constitution.

[64] See Article 23 (1a) of the Basic Law.

[65] See the COSAC Thirteenth Bi-annual Report (n. 1, *supra*), 29. For example, Section 109d of the Rules of Procedure of the Czech *Poslanecká sněmovna* provides that a group of at least forty-one deputies may call in the plenary to adopt a resolution to bring an action for annulment. The same applies to seventeen Senators of the Czech *Senát*. Likewise, in Spain, two parliamentary groups or a fifth of the members of the *Congreso de los Diputados* or the *Senado* may call in their respective plenary to take a final decision. See the Annex to the COSAC Thirteenth Bi-annual Report, 88 and 465.

[66] Ibid., 29. See, e.g., the Austrian *Nationalrat*, the Czech *Poslanecká sněmovna* and the *Senát*, the French *Assemblée Nationale* and *Sénat*, the German *Bundestat* and *Bundesrat*, the Irish Houses of the *Oireachtas*, the Polish *Sejm*, and the *Senat*.

[67] See the Declaration, annexed to the Lisbon Treaty, by the Kingdom of Belgium on national Parliaments, OJ 2010 C83/355) and Article 7 of the cooperation agreement of 29 March 2017 on the exercise of the powers allotted by the Treaties to the national Parliaments (see n. 60, *supra*).

[68] In a memorandum dated 19 January 1998 from the President of the Council (the United Kingdom having the Presidency at the material time), the UK government considered that the Commission's implementing legislation does not lend itself to detailed scrutiny because it is too voluminous and often technical, administrative, or ephemeral, but that arrangements should be made to maintain an overview of the Commission's delegated legislative role. There could also be more involvement of individual Departmental Select Committees. In its 7th Report, the House of Commons Select Committee on Modernisation considered that scrutiny of Commission legislation was 'fine in principle provided that no excessive burden is imposed' thereby. In practice such scrutiny 'would operate 2 or 3 times a year' (i.e. on a limited scale).

[69] See also Article 12(c) TEU (that refers to 'national parliaments' being involved, even though Article 70 TFEU mentions only evaluation by 'Member States' and speaks of the national parliaments and the European Parliament being informed of the contents and the results of the evaluation).

III. The Member States' Role in Implementing Union Law

15.012 **Implementing Union law.** The Member States are responsible for implementing Union law except where this task has been expressly assigned to a Union institution, body, office, or agency (see para. 18-002, *infra*). Each Member State itself determines which bodies are to implement Union law (including the transposition of directives) and at what level of authority this is to take place (see para. 18-003, *infra*). In many Member States this has resulted in changes in the domestic legal system, affecting both the organization of the national administration and internal constitutional relationships.[70] For instance, in many cases the executive has been entrusted with the task of implementing directives.[71] When new Member States accede to the Union, the task of adjusting national law to Union law is sometimes left to the national government to be carried out by means of subordinate legislation,[72] or national parliaments may put in place a 'fast-track' legislative procedure.[73] Article 4(3) TEU puts the Member States under a duty, not only to take all necessary implementing measures, but also to adjust domestic law so as to ensure the effectiveness (*'effet utile'*) of Union law (see para. 5-046, *supra*). Various public bodies are equally caught by that obligation in view of their close organizational or functional connection with the public authorities.[74] However, at Union level it is only the 'Member State', represented by the national government, which is liable for any breaches of the obligation to implement Union law.

---

[70] See Cloots, De Baere, and Sottiaux (eds), *Federalism in the European Union* (Hart Publishing, 2012); Jans et al., *Europeanisation of Public Law* (Europa Law Publishing, 2007); Knill, *The Europeanisation of National Administrations* (Cambridge University Press, 2001).

[71] Fromage, 'La transposition de directives européennes et ses conséquences sur l'équilibre des pouvoirs exécutif et législatif nationaux. Regards croisés sur l'Allemagne, l'Espagne et l'Italie' (2014) Rev Union européenne, 551–60. Thus in France the incorporation of numerous directives is left to the executive as a result of the narrow interpretation put on the scope of '*lois*' and the broad interpretation given to the scope of '*règlements*' (Constitution, Articles 34 and 37): Laprat, 'Réforme des traités; le risque du double déficit démocratique. Les Parlements nationaux et l'élaboration de la norme communautaire' (1991) RMC 710, 713. Sometimes, too, the national parliament authorizes the government to implement directives. This is the case in Italy, Portugal, and Spain: Laprat, 713. Under the La Pergola law of 9 March 1989, the Italian Parliament passes an annual '*legge comunitaria*' authorizing the government to take the necessary measures in order to transpose Union obligations into national legislation; see Tizzano, 'La nouvelle loi italienne pour l'exécution des obligations communautaires' (1990) RMC 532–40; Zampini, 'L'Italie, en amont du manquement ... Un problème de compétences entre l'exécutif, le parlement et les régions' (1994) RTDE 195–228; Villamena, 'State and Regions Vis-à-Vis European Integration: The "Long (and Slow) March" of the Italian Regional State', in Panara and De Becker (eds), *The Role of the Regions in EU Governance* (Springer, 2011), 157, 173–6.

[72] In Spain, Law No. 47/85 of 27 December 1985 authorized the government to adopt all such '*decretos legislativos*' as were necessary in order to implement Community law; see Arpio Santacruz, 'Spanish Adaptation to Community Law: 1986–1988' (1991) ELRev 149, 150. In Ireland, after the High Court held in *Meagher v Minister for Agriculture and Food and the Attorney General* that s. 3(2) of the European Communities Act 1972 was unconstitutional for empowering the executive to enact subordinate legislation amending or repealing primary legislation in order to implement Community law, the Supreme Court set the decision aside on the basis of Article 29.4.5 of the Constitution, according to which no provisions of the Constitution invalidate laws enacted, acts done, or measures adopted by the State necessitated by membership of the Communities. In some cases, it held, it was proper for Community obligations to be discharged by administrative rather than legislative procedures (*Meagher v Minister for Agriculture and Food and the Attorney General* [1994] 2 CMLR 654–7 and 663–80). See 'Application of Community law by national courts', Annex VI to the Commission's eleventh annual report to the European Parliament on monitoring the application of Community law OJ 1994 C54/176.

[73] For example, this was the case for Cyprus, Poland, and Lithuania. See the relevant sections in Kellermann et al. (eds), *The Impact of EU Accession on the Legal Orders of New EU Member States and (pre-)Candidate Countries: Hopes and Fears* (TMC Asser Press, 2006).

[74] As far as the direct effect of directives is concerned, see para. 27-025, *infra*; for a study of the instrumental approach to the concept of the 'State', see Hecquard-Théron, 'La notion d'Etat en droit communautaire' (1990) RTDE 693–711.

IV. The Member States' Role in Connection with the Judicial Implementation and Enforcement of Union Law

Effective legal protection in fields covered by Union law. The national courts play an essential part in dealing with Union law. They determine, for instance, all disputes arising in each Member State in relation to the application of Union law.[75] As a result of the decentralized enforcement of Union law, each national court is a 'Union court'. Since the Lisbon Treaty, the Treaties expressly state that Member States must provide remedies sufficient to ensure effective legal protection in the fields covered by Union law (Article 19(1), second subpara. TEU). This implies that, in the light of the fundamental importance of judicial review for the rule of law, itself a fundamental value of the Union pursuant to Article 2 TEU, each Member State must ensure the independence and impartiality of the courts that may have to decide on questions in the fields covered by Union law (see para. 29-003–29-004, *infra*).[76]

15.013

When interpreting Union law, national courts have to take account of the characteristics of that law, such as its own terminology and the co-existence of several, equally authentic, linguistic versions (see paras 29-005–29-006). If necessary, national courts may, and in some circumstances, must make a reference for a preliminary ruling to the Court of Justice.[77] If national courts apply national law in a way that is contrary to Union law, this may, in certain circumstances, found an action by the Commission against the Member State in question for infringement of Union law.[78] A sufficiently serious breach of Union law by a national court ruling at last instance may give rise to entitlement to compensation for the damage resulting from that breach (see para. 23-019, *infra*).

As far as former non-Community acts of the Union are concerned, the role played by the national courts depends on the status of those acts in the national legal order (see para. 28-011, *infra*).

V. The Role Played by Decentralized Authorities of the Member States

Decentralization within the Member States. Most Member States have one form or another of geographical decentralization, as a result of which real decision-making powers are vested in regional or local authorities. In those Member States described as 'federal' (Austria, Belgium, Germany) or 'regionalized' (Italy), the Constitution allows the regions to take certain decisions independently with regard to particular policy fields. Some Member

15.014

---

[75] This is because only specific forms of action may be brought before the Court of Justice, the General Court, and the specialized courts, see para. 13-003 *et seq.*, *supra*

[76] C-64/16, *Associação Sindical dos Juízes Portugueses*, 2018, paras 27–52; C-216/18 PPU, *LM*, 2018, paras 33–79; C-619/18 *Commission v Poland*, 2019, paras 42–59, 71–97, and 108–24; C-192/18, *Commission v Poland*, 2019, paras 98–136; C-585/18, C-624/18, and C-625/18 *A.K.*, 2019, paras 114–70.

[77] See Lenaerts, Gutman, and Nowak, *EU Procedural Law of the European Union* (OUP, 2022), Chapter 3. An information note on references by national courts for preliminary rulings may be found on the website of the Court of Justice under 'Court of Justice' and 'Procedure'; see also OJ 2019 C380/1.

[78] See C-129/00, *Commission v Italy*, 2003, paras 29–33; C-154/08, *Commission v Spain*, 2009, paras 125 and 126 (not isolated or numerically insignificant judicial decisions but a widely held judicial construction which has not been disowned by the supreme court, but rather confirmed by it, would be covered).

States confer less extensive powers on their regions (France) or provide for a form of decision-making autonomy for specific parts of the national territory (Finland, Portugal). In yet other Member States (territorial) decentralization is limited to giving powers of their own to local authorities and purely administrative units. Except for Germany, the devolution of powers to a regional level of authority has occurred only in recent decades; moreover, in some Member States the question of devolution is completely off the agenda.[79] In view of the different forms of territorial decentralization in the Member States, it is impossible to define the intermediate level of authority in a uniform way with a view to involving citizens more closely in action taken by the Union.[80] Since the Treaties govern only the relationship between the Member States (and their nationals) and the relationship between the Union and the Member States (and their nationals), regional and local authorities, as 'parts' of the national authority, are subject to the same duty to implement and apply Union law (see para. 5-043, *supra*).[81]

15.015 **Involvement of regional authorities.** The Union's policies are attuned in many instances to the regions. Since the Lisbon Treaty, the Union is under a general obligation to respect the fundamental political and constitutional structures of the Member States as regards 'regional and local self-government' (Article 4(2) TEU).[82] In various areas, the Treaties require the Union to take account of specific regional situations.[83] In addition, the Union grants aid to certain regions as part of its action to strengthen economic and social cohesion (see para. 9-057, *supra*). In so far as the Member States concerned make the necessary internal arrangements to this effect, regional authorities are involved in implementing that aid policy.[84] Furthermore, the Union is increasingly empowered to conduct policies in areas which in federal systems are predominantly dealt with at the regional level of authority (the

---

[79] See Panara and De Becker, 'The Role of the Regions in the European Union: The "Regional Blindness of Both the EU and the Member States"', in Panara and De Becker (eds), *The Role of the Regions in EU Governance* (Springer, 2011), 297–346; Bengoetxea, 'Autonomous Constitutional Regions in a Federated Europe', in Cloots, De Baere, and Sottiaux (eds), *Federalism in the European Union* (Hart Publishing, 2012) 230–48.

[80] This is one of the aims of the TEU: see Article 1, second para. TEU. See Van Nuffel, 'Does EU Decision-Making Take into Account Regional Interests?', in Cloots, De Baere, and Sottiaux (eds), *Federalism in the European Union* (Hart Publishing, 2012) 190–209.

[81] See, in this respect, Declaration by the Kingdom of Belgium on national Parliaments (n. 18, *supra*, in which Belgium makes clear that 'in accordance with its constitutional law, not only the Chamber of Representatives and Senate of the Federal Parliament, but also the parliamentary assemblies of the Communities and the Regions act, in terms of the competences exercised by the Union, as components of the national parliamentary system or chambers of the national Parliament' (see the literature referred to in n. 59, *supra*). See also the Statement by the Kingdom of Belgium on the signing of treaties by the Kingdom of Belgium as a Member State of the European Union (OJ 1998 C351/1), in which that Member State declares that, irrespective whether a Federal, Regional, or Community Minister signs a treaty for Belgium, the Kingdom, as such, will in all cases be bound, in respect of its whole territory, by the provisions of the treaty and that the Kingdom alone, as such, will bear full responsibility for compliance with the obligations entered into in the treaties concerned.

[82] See the discussion of the principle of proportionality, para. 5-041, *supra*; for the extent to which the principle of subsidiarity requires account to be taken of decentralised authorities, see para. 5-029 *et seq.*, *supra* Some commentators infer from Article 4(3) TEU an obligation for the Union to take account of the federal structure of Member States; see Epiney, 'Gemeinschaftsrecht und Föderalismus: "Landes-Blindheit" und Pflicht zur Berücksichtigung innerstaatlicher Verfassungsstrukturen' (1994) EuR 301–24; cf. Van Nuffel, *De rechtsbescherming van nationale overheden in het Europees recht* (Kluwer, 2000), 288–94.

[83] See Article 13 TFEU ('regional heritage'); Article 39(2)(a) TFEU ('structural and natural disparities between the various agricultural regions'); Article 46(d) TFEU ('employment in the various regions'); Article 91(2) TFEU ('standard of living and level of employment in certain regions'); Article 96(2) TFEU ('appropriate regional economic policy'); Article 167(1) TFEU ('regional diversity' of culture); Article 191(2) and (3) TFEU (diversity of situations and environmental situations in the various regions). See Van Nuffel (n. 80, supra), 193–5.

[84] See already Hessel and Mortelmans, 'Decentralised Government and Community Law: Conflicting Institutional Developments' (1993) CMLRev 905, 920–5 and 932–4.

environment and matters affecting people, such as education, culture, and public health). It is then the regions which have to implement the policies. As a result, they are increasingly asking for a say in the formulation of these Union policies, in like manner to members of the national government and national civil servants.[85] However, direct participation of the regions in Union decision-making is difficult to arrange given the great disparities between Member States in this area of the structure of the State.[86]

Participation of regions in Union decision-making. In order to involve the responsible regional ministers in decision-making, Article 16(2) TEU allows them to represent their Member State in the Council, provided that they are authorized to commit the national government and cast its vote (see para. 12-041, *supra*). Regional ministers may avail themselves of this possibility if the national legal system makes provision for such authorization. Such an authorization may be granted to ministers of regional governments for individual Council meetings or by the conferral of a general authority.[87] At the same time, it has to be agreed who is to sit in the Council and how the Member State's votes are to be cast, especially where the regions' views differ.[88] This also applies to the representation of the 'Member State' within the numerous working parties and committees which prepare the Council's work and within the committees which assist the Commission with the implementation of Union law. In this connection, too, a Member State may designate members of regional authorities,

15.016

---

[85] Reich, 'Zum Einfluss des europäischen Gemeinschaftsrechts auf die Kompetenzen der deutschen Bundesländer' (2001) EuGRZ 1–18.

[86] See, for instance, Scherpereel, 'Sub-national Authorities in the EU's Post-Socialist States: Joining the Multi-level Polity?' (2007) JEI 23–46; Magnon, 'Le statut constitutionnel des collectivités infra-étatiques dans l'Union européenne' (2006) RAE 395–404; Nanclares, 'Comunidades autonomas y Union Europea hacia una mejora de la participacion directa de las comunidades autonomas en el proceso decisorio comunitario' (2005) RDCE 759–805; Speer, 'Innerstaatliche Beteiligung in europäischen Angelegenheiten—Der Fall Spanien' (2000) DöV 895–905; Feral, 'Les incidences de l'intégration européenne sur les collectivités territoriales françaises' (1994) RMCUE 53–7; Neßler, 'Die "neue Ländermitwirkung" nach Maastricht' (1994) EuR 216–29; Vaucher, 'Réalité juridique de la notion de région communautaire' (1994) RTDE 525–50; Wuermeling, 'Das Ende der "Länderblindheit": Der Ausschuß der Regionen nach dem neuen EG-Vertrag' (1993) EuR 196–206. For the status of local authorities, see Fleurke and Willemse, 'Effects of the European Union on Sub-national Decision-making: Enhancement or Constriction?' (2007) JEI 69–88; Hobe, Biehl, and Schroeter, 'Der Einfluß des Rechts der Europäischen Gemeinschaften/Europäischen Union auf die Struktur der kommunalen Selbstverwaltung' (2003) DöV 803–12; Schmidt, 'Sind die EG und die EU an die Europäischen Charta der kommunalen Selbstverwaltung gebunden?' (2003) EuR 936–48; Ehlers, 'Kommunalaufsicht und europäisches Gemeinschaftsrecht' (2001) DöV 412–17; Le Mire, 'Les répercussions de la construction européenne sur les collectivités locales' (1991) RMC 785–96.

[87] A general authority is conferred in Belgium by Article 81(6) of the special law of 8 August 1980 on institutional reform, which empowers the governments of the Belgian Communities and Regions to commit the State in the Council where one of their members represents Belgium pursuant to a cooperation agreement. See De Becker, 'Belgium: The State and the Sub-State Entities Are Equal, But Is the State Sometimes More Equal Than the Others?', in Panara and De Becker (eds), *The Role of the Regions in EU Governance* (Springer, 2011), 251–74; Ingelaere, 'De Belgische deelstaten en de Europese Unie', in Geudens and Judo (eds), *Internationale betrekkingen en federalisme: staatsrechtconferentie 2005* (Larcier, 2006), 149–161. As for representing the interests of the German and Austrian *Länder*, see n. 46 and n. 47, *supra*, respectively. For the (not yet realized right of participation of) Spanish *Comunidades autónomas*, see Chicharro Lázaro, 'The Spanish Autonomous Communities in the EU: The Evolution from the Competitive Regionalism to a Cooperative System', in *The Role of the Regions in EU Governance* (*supra*), 185–214; Ross and Salvador Crespo, 'The Effect of devolution on the Implementation of European Community Law in Spain and in the United Kingdom' (2003) ELRev 210–30. In Italy, Article 117(5) of the Constitutional Law of 18 October 2001 provides for the participation of the regions and autonomous provinces in decisions regarding the elaboration of legislative acts at Community level. See Villamena (n. 71, *supra*), 157–83.

[88] In this way, the Belgian federal authority and the Belgian Communities and Regions concluded a cooperation agreement on 8 March 1994 pursuant to Article 92*bis* of the special law of 8 August 1980 on the representation of the Kingdom of Belgium in the Council of Ministers of the European Union, Belgisch Staatsblad/Moniteur belge, 17 November 1994; see Lejeune, 'Le droit fédéral belge des relations internationales' (1994) RGDIP 578, 610–15. For more details on the possibility of participation by decentralized authorities, see Van Nuffel (n. 82, *supra*), at 472–88.

provided that it is understood that those persons represent the Member State as a whole.[89] Likewise, regional delegates may be integrated in permanent representations to the EU.[90] Given that the regions therefore depend in the first instance on whether a compromise can be reached within their Member State, the system of direct representation in the Council and other bodies cannot always be used to defend their interests.[91] Moreover, even if a federal State—with one vote—defends the interests of its regions, the views of Member States of a more centralized persuasion may yet win the day in the Council or the relevant body.[92]

Regional authorities may have their say in decision-making directly through the Committee of the Regions (Articles 300 and 305–307 TFEU; see para. 13-033, *supra*). The Committee's terms of reference are purely advisory, but it may nevertheless bring specific interests of the regions to the attention of the institutions that have a determinative influence on decision-making (Commission, Council, and, sometimes the European Parliament). The Committee also has the right to bring legal proceedings against acts of the institutions for infringement of the principle of subsidiarity (see para. 13-033, *supra*). Despite its title, however, the Committee also has representatives of local authorities among its members and hence its positions take account of their special interests as well.

15.017 **Participation of regions in implementation.** The Member States are at liberty to leave implementation of some aspects of Union law to federated or decentralized entities, provided that that allocation of powers enables the Union measures to be implemented correctly. In such a case, the Member State is responsible for implementing Union norms, even though the matter falls within a domain for which domestically only the regional authorities are competent to act.[93] If a Member State is held liable for a region's conduct or failure to act, it is then not entitled to hide behind the domestic division of powers or federal structure in order to avoid the Court of Justice making a finding of an infringement or to escape its obligation to bring such infringement to an end (see para. 18-005, *infra*). In some Member States, the national authorities may take the place of the region in breach and do what is necessary in order to bring infringements of Union law to an end; sometimes the national authorities are then entitled to recover the costs from the region concerned (see para. 18-005, *infra*). Just as the Commission may bring an infringement action against the national authorities only, these national authorities only may rely upon the remedies which are available to a 'Member State' in order to challenge a Union act.[94]

---

[89] See the Commission's answer of 10 April 2003 to question E-0777/03 (Bautista Ojeda), OJ 2003 C11E/116.
[90] Regions may also be represented by delegations independent from that of the central Member State. However, for the purposes of determining entitlement to an expatriation allowance in accordance with the second indent of Article 4(1)(a) of Annex VII to the Staff Regulations, 'work done for another State' only covers work done for the permanent representation of a Member State and not work done for political subdivisions of that State (C-7/06 P, *Salvador García*, 2007; C-8/06 P, *Herrero Romeu*, 2007; C-9/06 P, *Salazar Brier*, 2007; C-10/06 P, *de Bustamante*, 2007).
[91] The fact that two compromises have to be reached (domestically and within the Council) has, of course, implications for the political control which can be exercised within a given region by the representative assembly over the regional government.
[92] Wiedmann, 'Föderalismus als europäische Utopie. Die Rolle der Regionen aus rechtsvergleichender Sicht. Das Beispiel Deutschlands und Frankreichs' (1992) AöR 46, 47.
[93] 96/81, *Commission v Netherlands*, 1982, para. 12; 227–230/85, *Commission v Belgium*, 1988, paras 9–10 (see also further case law cited in para. 18-005, *infra*).
[94] C-95/97, *Région Wallonne v Commission* (order), 1997, paras 6–8. For this issue, see Van Nuffel, 'What's in a Member State? Central and Decentralised Authorities before the Community Courts' (2001) CMLRev 871–901. For more details, see Lenaerts, Gutman, and Nowak, *EU Procedural Law of the European Union* (OUP, 2022), Chapter 7.

16
The Relationships between the Institutional Actors

Interaction. The European Union constitutes a level of government in its own right: institutions of the Union draw up legislation which has to be implemented and complied with within the Member States. For the sound functioning of the Union, it is important to have clear rules on the normative relationship between acts adopted at Union level, on the one hand, and national law, on the other. From a political point of view, it is equally important to adequately organize the way in which the various interests existing both within the Member States and across borders are being reconciled through the interplay of the actors involved in Union decision-making. In this connection, attention should be paid to the specific interests which are structurally embodied in the various institutions of the Union and to the balance between institutions required by the Treaties.

16.001

I. Relationship between the Institutions of the Union and the Member States

Primacy of Union law. Both the provisions of the Treaties and the secondary legislation based on them have primacy over the rules of national law of each of the Member States. This primacy arises out of the case law of the Court of Justice, according to which the objectives of the Treaties could not be achieved uniformly and effectively if the effect of Union law differed from Member State to Member State on the basis of national law (see para 23-010 et seq.).[1] In order to secure compliance with Union law, the Court of Justice has recognized the right of citizens (and other legal subjects) to rely directly on provisions of Union law as against national authorities and, in some cases, as against other citizens (or other legal subjects) (see para. 23-031 et seq., infra). These principles of 'primacy' and 'direct effect' have now been generally accepted within the national legal systems. They are the ultimate guarantee of the equality of Member States and their citizens before Union law (Article 4(2) TEU and Article 20 Charter of Fundamental Rights of the Union).

16.002

Sincere cooperation. Article 4(3) TEU requires the Member States to do everything necessary to ensure fulfilment of their obligations under Union law and to abstain from any action which might jeopardize the attainment of the objectives of the Union. This principle of sincere cooperation also holds good for the Union institutions, which must cooperate in good faith with the Member States and amongst each other in attaining the objectives of the Union (see Article 13(2), second sentence, TEU; see further paras 5-043–5-052). In

16.003

---

[1] See also Declaration (No. 17), annexed to the Lisbon Treaty, concerning primacy (OJ 2010 C83/344).

addition, the Member States' national policy sphere is protected by the principle of conferral and the principles of subsidiarity and proportionality (Article 5 TEU; see paras 5-010–5-042). In that connection, the Lisbon Treaty requires the Union to respect the Member States' 'national identities, inherent in their fundamental structures, political and constitutional, inclusive of regional and local self-government' as well as 'their essential State functions, including ensuring the territorial integrity of the State, maintaining law and order and safeguarding national security' (Article 4(2) TEU; see para. 5-041, *supra*).

II. Representation of Interests through Institutions and Member States

16.004 **Representation of interests.** The Member States are not only the subject of Union decision-making but, as a result of the involvement of the national (or regional) governments in the Council, also one of the actors involved in that decision-making. Citizens, too, are not only the subjects of Union decision-making, but, in electing the members of the European Parliament, they determine the composition of one of the main actors participating in that decision-making. In contradistinction to traditional intergovernmental organizations, the interests of citizens are defended not only by the action of national authorities contributing to Union decision-making, but also by a directly representative institution—the European Parliament—and by other institutions, bodies, offices, and agencies that carry out their tasks independently of national interests in the general interest of the Union.[2] To that effect, the Union institutions engage in regular dialogue with representative associations and civil society (Article 11(2) TEU), whilst citizens can also take the initiative of inviting the Commission to submit proposals for legislation (Article 11(4) TEU; see para. 17-013, *infra*). In order to ensure the transparency of interest representation and the trust of Union citizens in the legitimacy of the legislative and administrative processes the European Parliament and the Commission have set up a Transparency Register for organizations and self-employed persons seeking to directly or indirectly influence Union policy and decision-making.[3] Registration is voluntary but dependent on the organizations and persons providing financial information relating to the activities covered and respecting a code of conduct. From its side, the Commission allows its members and their Cabinet members as well as its Directors-General to meet only interest representatives that are registered in the Transparency Register. The Parliament, the Council, and the Commission

---

[2] For an outstanding analysis, see already Jacqué, 'Cours général de droit communautaire', Collected Courses of the Academy of European Law I, 1990, 237, 289.

[3] See the Agreement between the European Parliament and the European Commission of 16 April 2014 on the transparency register for organizations and self-employed individuals engaged in EU policy-making and policy implementation, OJ 2014, L277/11, replacing the agreement between the two institutions of 23 June 2011, on its turn following up on earlier initiatives taken by the respective institutions: the Commission's communication 'European Transparency Initiative—A framework for relations with interest representatives' of 27 May 2008, and the European Parliament's code of conduct regarding interest groups (Annex X to the Rules of Procedure, Provisions governing the application of Rule 9(4)—Lobbying in Parliament). See Richez, 'Lobbying européen et lobbying américain: vers une plus grande convergence des pratiques' (2005) RMCUE 601–5; Rideau, 'Les groupes d'intérêt dans le système institutionnnel communautaire' (1993) RAE 49–73; McLaughlin, Jordan, and Maloney, 'Corporate Lobbying in the European Community' (1993) JCMS 191–212. For studies of lobbying in practice, see Coen and Richardson (eds), *Lobbying the European Union: Institutions, Actors, and Issues* (OUP, 2009); Pedler and Van Schendelen (eds), *Lobbying the European Union* (Dartmouth, 1994).

recently agreed on a joint Transparency Register, which provides a framework for members of the European Parliament and the successive Presidencies of the Council to apply similar conditions in their contacts with interest representatives.[4]

Union and national interests. It emerges from the structure of the Treaties that every time action on the part of the Union significantly affects the interests of the Member States, the relevant decision is reserved for the governments in the European Council or the Council. In the case of certain 'constitutive' acts, such as, of course, amendments to the Treaties, the matter is ultimately decided by the national parliaments or even by referendum, where the Treaties refer to the 'constitutional requirements' of each Member State.

16.005

As a counterbalance to the defence of 'national' interests, the Treaties provide for the involvement of the other Union institutions with a view to identifying and defending the 'common' interest. Thus, the Commission takes views on the basis of its independent position and the European Parliament voices the majority views of its directly elected members. The remaining Union institutions likewise perform tasks intended to safeguard particular common interests.[5]

It is no surprise, therefore, that Union decision-making is designed to reconcile 'national' and 'common' interests through interaction between the Council, the Commission, and the European Parliament. Where decisions are taken by intergovernmental procedures, the (European) Council's large degree of independence in reaching a decision results in a compromise being struck between purely 'national' positions. Where the common interest prevails, the Treaties place the power in the hands of an independent Union institution. Accordingly, the Commission acts alone in monitoring compliance with Treaty obligations and, hence, ensuring equality before Union law.

Individual interests. When it comes to the representation of interests specific to citizens of the Union (and other individuals), the Treaties rely, on the one hand, on the ways in which individuals may make their voices heard in their own Member States and, on the other, on the say which individuals and interest groups have at Union level, namely involvement in decision-making via the European Parliament and through administrative and judicial remedies. 'Democratic scrutiny' of Union policy is therefore exercised both at national and at Union level (see paras 20-004–20-021).

16.006

III. Balance between the Institutions

Institutional balance. Since the institutions of the Union respectively reflect national or common interests, the allocation of powers among them is based on a delicate balance between the interests which they represent. The principle of institutional balance thus reflects 'a system for distributing powers among the different [Union] institutions, assigning to each

16.007

---

[4] Agreement between the European Parliament, the Council of the European Union and the European Commission on a mandatory transparency register [politically agreed on 7 December 2020], following on the Commission's proposal of 28 September 2016 for an Interinstitutional Agreement on a mandatory Transparency Register, COM(2016)627 final.
[5] See, for instance, compliance with the law (Court of Justice); due and proper management of the Union's resources (Court of Auditors); maintenance of price stability (ECB).

institution its own role in the institutional structure of the [Union] and the accomplishment of the tasks entrusted to the [Union]'.[6] The rule set out in Article 13(2) TEU that '[e]ach institution shall act within the limits of the powers conferred upon it in the Treaties and in conformity with the procedures, conditions and objectives set out in them' must be read in the light of the principle of institutional balance. Apart from the requirement for each institution to remain within the powers conferred on it, this principle means—as further set out below—that each institution (1) has the necessary independence in exercising its powers; (2) may not unconditionally assign its powers to other institutions, bodies, offices, or agencies; and (3) must pay due regard to the powers of the other institutions.

The Court of Justice enforces respect for the principle of institutional balance. That is why it is prepared to review the institutions' compliance with their powers.[7] The principle of sincere cooperation (Article 4(3) TEU; see para. 5-043 *et seq.*, *supra*) also puts the Member States under a duty to comply with the principle of institutional balance, while, in turn, requiring the institutions to have due regard to the powers of the Member States. The 'balance' that has to be guaranteed does not necessarily mean that the most 'balanced' relationship between the different interests at stake has to be achieved, but reflects the balance of power laid down in the Treaties.[8] In areas which do not fall under the exclusive competence of the Union, the Member States may entrust tasks to the institutions outside the Union's institutional framework, such as the task of coordinating a collective action undertaken by the Member States or managing financial assistance, provided that those tasks do not alter the essential character of the powers conferred on those institutions by the Treaties.[9]

16.008 **(1) Power of internal organization.** First of all, institutional balance presupposes that each institution is empowered to determine its own organization and manner of operation within the limits of the rules laid down in the Treaties.[10] In order to enable it to function smoothly, an institution is entitled to introduce its own internal decision-making procedure and establish procedures for monitoring whether its internal operations are in order. In so doing, an institution must take care to comply with the principles enshrined in the Treaties.[11] Even

---

[6] C-70/88, *European Parliament v Council*, 1990, para. 21. See, more generally, Craig, 'Institutions, Power and Institutional Balance', in Craig and de Burca (eds), *The Evolution of EU Law* (OUP, 2010), 41–83; Barents, 'De post-Lissabon-rechtspraak over het institutioneel evenwicht' (2019) SEW 327–48; Chamon, 'Institutional Balance and Community Method in the Implementation of EU legislation Following the Lisbon Treaty' (2016) CML Rev 1501; Chamon, 'The Institutional Balance, an Ill-Fated Principle of EU Law?' (2015) E Pub L, 371–92; Christiansen, 'The European Union after the Lisbon Treaty: An Elusive Institutional Balance', in Biondi, Eeckhout, and Ripley (eds), *EU Law after Lisbon* (OUP, 2012), 228.

[7] C-70/88, *European Parliament v Council*, 1990, paras 22–3; 294/83, *Les Verts v European Parliament*, 1983, para. 25. See also C-409/13, *Council v Commission*, 2015, para. 77 (annulment can be sought of Commission's decision to withdraw a legislative proposal) as well as the Court's judgments in litigation on the correct legal basis for Union acts (see paras 5-013–5-016, *supra*) or on the extent of powers to adopt implementing acts (see para. 18-021, *infra*).

[8] See Jacqué, 'Cours général de droit communautaire', *Collected Courses of the Academy of European Law I* (1990), 237, 292. See the appraisal of those relationships from the point of view of the separation of powers in paras 16-011–16-013, *infra*, and from the democratic standpoint in para. 17-046 *et seq.*, *infra*.

[9] C-370/12, *Pringle*, 2012, paras 153–77 (see further para. 2-010, *supra*).

[10] This is true even if the act establishing the institution does not make express provision to this effect. The Court of Auditors was a case in point before the addition of the fifth subpara. of Article 248(4) EC [*now Article 287(4) TFEU*] (see para. 13-105, *supra*). However, the Council has to approve the Rules of Procedure of the Court of Justice and of the General Court (Article 253, sixth para. and Article 254, fifth para. TFEU) and, at present, also the Rules of Procedure of the Court of Auditors (Article 287(4), fifth subpara. TFEU). For the extent of this power, see C-58/94, *Netherlands v Council*, 1996, paras 37–3.

[11] With regard to the decision-making procedure, see 5/85, *AKZO Chemie v Commission*, 1986, paras 37 and 40, and the other judgments with regard to the principle of collective responsibility as it affects the Commission; para.

independent Union bodies such as the European Investment Bank must comply with the limits that Union law places on the power of internal organization. According to the Court of Justice, the ECB, and the EIB exceeded those limits by introducing their own systems for combating fraud which precluded the investigatory powers conferred on the independent body OLAF by the Union legislature with regard to all Union institutions and bodies.[12] The institutions' independence is protected by privileges and immunities granted to them and their members (see para. 14-007 et seq., supra). In addition, Article 4(3) TEU requires Member States to abstain from any measure which might interfere with the internal functioning of the Union institutions.[13] That article, together with Article 13(2) TEU, also prescribes a reciprocal duty to cooperate in good faith on the part of the institutions and the Member States. This means, for instance, that in their internal organization the institutions have to take account of the powers of the Member States and of the other institutions. Accordingly, it has been held that in its resolutions on the question of its places of work the European Parliament has to respect the national governments' power to determine the seats of the institutions, together with the existing provisional decisions and the definitive decision on the location of the seats of the institutions.[14] The institutions are not entitled to rely on their privileges and immunities in order to neglect their duty to cooperate with the national authorities in view of the purely functional character of those rights conferred on the Union.[15] Still, national authorities are required to cooperate with the institutions in order to eliminate the unlawful consequences of any violation of their privileges and immunities.[16]

(2) **Limits to the delegation of powers.** An institution may not upset the institutional balance by assigning the powers conferred on it to other bodies. The Court of Justice has explained this principle by reference to Article 3 ECSC, which entrusted the tasks of the ECSC to the 'institutions of the Community ... within the limits of their respective powers, in the common interest'. The Court held that

16.009

> there can be seen in the balance of powers which is characteristic of the institutional structure of the Community a fundamental guarantee granted by the Treaty in particular to the undertakings and associations of undertakings to which it applies. To delegate a discretionary power, by entrusting it to bodies other than those which the Treaty has established to effect and supervise the exercise of such power each within the limits of its own authority, would render that guarantee ineffective.[17]

13-075, *supra*; with regard to monitoring internal operations, see C-15/00, *Commission v European Investment Bank*, 2003, paras 67–8.

[12] C-11/00, *Commission v European Central Bank*, 2003, paras 172–82; C-15/00, *Commission v European Investment Bank*, 2003, paras 67–8.

[13] See 208/80, *Lord Bruce of Donington*, 1981, paras 14 and 19; 230/81, *Luxembourg v European Parliament*, 1983, para. 37. See also C-345/95, *France v European Parliament*, 1997, para. 32; C-73/17, *France v European Parliament*, 2018, para. 43; C-92/18, *France v European Parliament*, 2020, para. 23.

[14] 230/81, *Luxembourg v European Parliament*, 1983, para. 38; C-345/95, *France v European Parliament*, 1997, para. 31. See also 294/83, *Les Verts v European Parliament*, 1986, para. 25 and paras 51–5 (the European Parliament had introduced a scheme for the reimbursement of election campaign expenses unlawfully since the Act on the Direct Election of the European Parliament left such matters to the Member States to determine).

[15] C-2/88 Imm., *Zwartveld and Others*, 1990, para. 21. For the nature of the privileges and immunities, see para. 14-007 et seq., *supra*.

[16] C-316/19, *Commission v Slovenia*, 2020, paras 119–29 (see para. 5-048, *supra*).

[17] 9/56, *Meroni v High Authority*, 1958, 152. See Lenaerts, 'Regulating the Regulatory Process: "Delegation of Powers" in the European Community' (1993) EL Rev 23, 40–9.

This does not preclude an institution from delegating 'implementing' powers to other bodies in circumstances not detracting from the balance between the institutions (see para. 18-008 *et seq., infra*).

16.010 **(3) Respect for each other's independence.** In their relationship with each other and in exercising their powers, the institutions must further take care not to jeopardize each other's independence.[18] The practice adopted by an institution may not have the effect of depriving other institutions of a prerogative granted to them by the Treaties.[19] This is, in particular, true of the European Parliament's power to take part in the Union's legislative process, which constitutes 'an essential factor in the institutional balance intended by the [Treaties]' as 'it reflects at [Union] level the fundamental democratic principle that the peoples should take part in the exercise of power through the intermediary of a representative assembly'.[20] In the framework of the ordinary legislative procedure, in which the European Parliament and the Council jointly exercise the legislative function upon a proposal from the Commission, mutual respect and cooperation between the three institutions is essential. It would be contrary to the principle of institutional balance for the Commission to exercise its right to withdraw a proposal as a right of veto in the conduct of the legislative process.[21] After submitting a proposal, the Commission may therefore withdraw that proposal only in duly justified circumstances and in respect of the principle of sincere cooperation (see para. 17-017, *infra*). In the context of the Union's external competences, the Council and the Commission must respect each other's prerogatives. Thus, the Commission could not, on the basis of its power of external representation, sign an agreement resulting from negotiations conducted with a third country without the Council's prior approval.[22] However, it was entitled to submit legal observations to an international tribunal, as such action does not encroach on the Council's prerogative as regards policy making.[23] From its side, the Council could not exercise its power to address directives to the Commission as negotiator by imposing detailed negotiating positions.[24]

Institutional balance requires a sanction to be able to be brought to bear on any practice by which an institution exercises its powers without due regard for the other institutions' powers. It is therefore for the Court of Justice to review any act said to affect the institutional balance. Yet, before the EC Treaty was amended by the EU Treaty, the European Parliament, according to the wording of Article 173 EEC, had no right to bring an action for annulment against acts of the Council or the Commission in order to safeguard its prerogatives. In a 1990 judgment the Court of Justice held that the absence of such a right 'may constitute a procedural gap, but it cannot prevail over the fundamental interest in the maintenance and observance of the institutional balance laid down in the Treaties establishing the European Communities'.[25] It went on to hold that an action for annulment brought by the Parliament

---

[18] See 25/70, *Köster*, 1970, paras 4 and 8–9; Opinion 1/59, *Procedure for amendment pursuant to the third and fourth paras of Article 95 of the ECSC Treaty*, 1959, 273.

[19] 149/85, *Wybot*, 1986, para. 23.

[20] 138/79, *Roquette Frères v Council*, 1980, para. 33, and 139/79 *Maïzena v Council*, 1980, para. 34. See also Article 10(2) TEU ('[c]itizens are directly represented at Union level in the European Parliament').

[21] C-409/13, *Council v Commission*, 2015, paras 75–83.

[22] C-660/13, *Council v Commission*, 2016, paras 30–6.

[23] C-73/14, *Council v Commission*, 2015, paras 39–77.

[24] C-425/13, *Commission v Council*, 2015, paras 86–92.

[25] C-70/88, *European Parliament v Council*, 1990, para. 26. See also C-106/96, *United Kingdom v Commission*, 1998, paras 21–37 (annulment of a Commission decision implementing expenditure for which the Council had not adopted a basic act on the ground that the Commission had thereby infringed Article 7(1) EC; see also para. 20-007, *supra*).

against an act of the Council or the Commission would be admissible provided that the action sought only to safeguard the Parliament's prerogatives and was founded only on submissions alleging their infringement.[26] Consequently, the need to preserve the institutional balance laid down in the Treaties may exceptionally move the Court to take corrective action by way of an interpretation of the relevant provisions of the Treaties.[27] As far as the judiciary is concerned, institutional balance does not impede the courts from interpreting the Treaties as giving natural and legal persons a general right to compensation from a Member State for damage resulting from its infringement of Union law.[28]

IV. The Allocation of the Classical Functions of a State

Checks and balances. Union decision-making gives rise to both legislative and implementing acts (see para. 18-008, *infra*); additionally, it often requires legislative or implementing action in the Member States (see para. 18-002, *infra*). The judicial resolution of disputes arising in connection with the application of Union law falls, in principle, to the national courts, but in certain clearly defined cases is entrusted to the Court of Justice and the General Court (see para. 29-001 *et seq.*, *infra*). Within the national legal systems, the principle of separation of powers (at least in theory) requires the legislative, executive, and judicial functions to be allocated to different organs of the State in order to avoid citizens having to face an administration which holds all the powers without their exercise being subject to any political or judicial review. It is thus central to upholding the rule of law, which is one of the values common to the Member States (see para. 5-002 *et seq.*, *supra*). The principle of separation of powers does not signify that each function has to be carried out completely independently by a single public authority. Instead it is effectuated through a system of checks and balances designed to ensure that public authorities are required to cooperate with each other or to supervise each other. The question arises as to how that system is constituted in the Union legal order.[29]

16.011

Legislative and executive powers. Union institutions have a legislative function where the Treaties provide a legal basis; sometimes the Treaties also require action on the part of national parliaments (see para. 17-006, *infra*). The European Parliament is generally involved in the Union legislative process, most prominently under the ordinary legislative procedure, in addition to the Council. Implementation of legislation generally falls to the Commission, which can also be authorized to supplement or amend certain non-essential elements of a legislative act (see para. 18-010, *infra*). Given that the power to take legislative decisions virtually always lies with the Council, albeit mostly on an equal footing with the European Parliament, it does not square with the principle of separation of powers that it should also perform executive tasks yet not be subject to effective political supervision. In contrast, the executive function performed by the Commission is completely compatible

16.012

---

[26] C-70/88, *European Parliament v Council*, 1990, para. 27. In this connection the Court reversed its ruling in 302/87, *European Parliament v Council*, 1988, paras 8–28. See the discussion in para. 12-019, *supra*, and the amendments which have since been made to Article 230, third para. EC [*now Article 263, third para. TFEU*].

[27] Jacqué (n. 2, *supra*), 294.

[28] C-46/93 and C-48/93, *Brasserie du Pêcheur and Factortame* (*Factortame IV*), 1996, paras 24–30.

[29] For an analysis of the Union legal order in the light of that principle, see Lenaerts, 'Some Reflections on the Separation of Powers in the European Community' (1991) CMLRev 11–35.

with that institution's role in the legislative process in so far as it consists principally of its right to initiate legislation, a right which in systems characterized by separation of powers is likewise generally vested in the executive. Moreover, the Commission is accountable to the European Parliament as to the manner in which it performs its executive function. Both at Union and Member State level, the principle of democracy indeed requires that the administration be subject to the instructions of the government which is accountable to its parliament (see para. 17-046 *et seq., infra*). Where some independent bodies may have regulatory functions or carry out tasks that must be free from political influence, these authorities must nonetheless be required to comply with the law and their acts must be subject to review by the competent courts.[30]

Where national authorities are involved in the implementation of Union legislative acts, the constitutional rules of each Member State determine whether legislative or executive bodies are responsible for the necessary decision-making. An example is the transposition of directives into national law. When implementing Union law, Member States should duly respect the principle of the separation of powers which characterizes the operation of the rule of law.[31]

16.013 **Judicial powers.** The independence of the judiciary is guaranteed in the Union legal order. The Union's political institutions have no influence on the course of pending proceedings; they are, however, under a duty to cooperate with judicial authorities.[32] In view of the principle of the primacy of Union law, both the Union and national courts have to frequently rule on the compatibility of national law with Union law. When national courts have to make such rulings, Article 4(3) TEU puts them under a duty to set aside legislative measures which are incompatible with Union law even if the court hearing the case normally has no jurisdiction to review whether such measures are constitutional under domestic law. The right to effective judicial protection as set out in Article 47 Charter requires Member States to preserve the independence and impartiality of national courts applying and interpreting Union law (see paras 29-003–29-004). In this context, the principle of the separation of powers requires the independence of the national judiciary to be ensured in relation to the legislature and the executive.[33] Furthermore, the Treaties give natural and legal persons the right to obtain compensation before national courts for damage caused to them by a Member State as a result of breaches of Union law, even if the national legislature was

---

[30] C-518/07, *Commission v Germany*, 2010, paras 41–56.
[31] C-279/09, *DEB Deutsche Energiehandels-und Beratungsgesellschaft*, 2010, para 58.
[32] For the duty to cooperate as far as Union institutions are concerned, see C-2/88 Imm., *Zwartveld and Others*, 1990, paras 21–2.
[33] C-585/18, C-624/18, and C-625/18, *A. K. and Others*, 2019, para. 124. See also C-452/16 PPU, *Poltorak*, 2016, para. 35, and C-477/16 PPU, *Kovalkovas*, 2016, para 36 (the term 'judicial authority' in Council Framework Decision 2002/584/JHA of 13 June 2002 on the European arrest warrant and the surrender procedures between Member States refers to the judiciary which, in accordance with the principle of separation of powers, must be distinguished from the executive). Compare, however, C-627/19 PPU, *ZB*, 2020 (Belgian public prosecutor may act as the judicial authority for EAW for undergoing punishment even if no appeal before a court is possible) with C-508/18 and C-82/19 PPU, *OG and PI*, 2019 (German public prosecutors are not judicial authorities allowed to issue EAW to enable prosecution because of potential influence from the minister of Justice) and C-509/18, *PF*, 2019 (prosecutor-general of Lithuania deemed sufficiently independent to serve as issuing judicial authority for EAW to enable prosecution); C-625/19 PPU, *XD*, 2019 (Swedish public prosecutors are judicial authorities allowed to issue EAW to enable prosecution as an appeal is possible before a court). See further C-566/19 PPU and C-626/19 PPU, *JR and YC*, 2019; C-489/19 PPU, *NJ*, 2019.

responsible for the breach in question.[34] In this way, Union law has an impact on the scope of the separation of powers under the national legal systems.[35]

At Union level, the requirement for adequate legal protection entails that all acts of Union institutions, regardless of whether they are of a legislative or executive nature, must be able to be reviewed for conformity with the Treaties. Since the Union is intended to be a '[Union] based on the rule of law', 'neither its Member States nor its institutions can avoid a review of the question whether the measures adopted by them are in conformity with the basic constitutional charter, the [Treaties]'.[36] The principle of separation of powers does not therefore preclude judicial review of measures adopted by the Union legislature, or of other acts with legal effects adopted by the European Parliament.[37] There are indeed several examples of instances where legislative acts of the Union were found to be invalid in whole or in part by the Court.[38]

---

[34] C-46/93 and C-48/93, *Brasserie du Pêcheur and Factortame (Factortame IV)*, 1996, paras 31–36; C-224/01, *Köbler*, 2003, paras 100–26; C-160/14, *Ferreira da Silva e Brito*, 2015, paras 46–60.

[35] See the discussion of the principle of sincere cooperation in para. 5-046, *supra*.

[36] 294/83, *Les Verts v European Parliament*, 1986, para. 23. For a discussion, see Lenaerts, 'Case 294/83, *Parti écologiste "Les Verts" v European Parliament*, 1986. The Basic Constitutional Charter of a Community Based on the Rule of Law', in Poiares Maduro and Azoulai (eds), *The Past and Future of EU Law. The Classics of EU Law Revisited on the 50th Anniversary of the Rome Treaty* (Hart Publishing, 2009) 295–342.

[37] 294/83, *Les Verts v European Parliament*, 1986, paras 24–5. See, in particular, 230/81, *Luxembourg v European Parliament*, 1983, paras 14, 16, and 19.

[38] See, e.g., C-376/98, *Germany v European Parliament and Council*, 2000; C-92/09 and C-93/09, *Volker und Markus Schecke and Eifert*, 2010; C-236/09, *Association Belge des Consommateurs Test-Achats*, 2011; C-293/12 and C-594/12, *Digital Rights Ireland*, 2014. See also C-362/14, *Schrems*, 2015; C-311/18, *Facebook Ireland and Schrems*, 2020.

PART IV
DECISION-MAKING IN THE EUROPEAN UNION

Decision-making in the European Union is largely based on interaction between the European Parliament, the Council, and the Commission. The Treaties prescribe different decision-making procedures depending on the extent to which the Member States have agreed in each given field that the national governments—represented in the Council—will share their power of decision with the European Parliament and the Commission. In this connection, a distinction should be made between decision-making which leads to the adoption of legislative acts (Chapter 17) and decision-making for the purpose of implementing legislation (Chapter 18). Since the Lisbon Treaty, a uniform system of decision-making exists in all areas of Union competence. Only CFSP decision-making still exhibits particular features and will, therefore, be dealt with separately (Chapter 19). The Treaties also provide for a budget procedure (Chapter 20), and a procedure for the conclusion of international agreements (Chapter 21). In areas of Union competence in which not all Member States participate, decision-making is restricted to the participating Member States (Chapter 22).

17
The Legislative Procedures

I. General Principles

A. Definition of legislation

Traditional position. Within the national legal systems legislative acts can usually be clearly distinguished from executive acts, as they are adopted by separate institutions, namely, the legislative branch as opposed to the executive branch. At the Union level, no such formal distinction existed for a long time. Before the Lisbon Treaty, the Treaties did not define 'legislation' at Union level, nor the Union's 'legislative' process. Nevertheless, it has always been clear that many legally binding acts adopted at Union level were of a legislative nature. Legislative acts were generally to be adopted by the Council on a proposal from the Commission and, usually, with the participation of the European Parliament as well. Since there was no formal legislative process, there were also no specific instruments for legislative action.[1]

17.001

Formal distinction. The Lisbon Treaty introduced a clear distinction between legislative and other acts of the Union with the aim of making decision-making at Union level more democratic and transparent. The Treaties now unambiguously use the term 'legislative act' for acts based on a provision of the Treaties and adopted pursuant to a legislative procedure, that is, under the 'ordinary legislative procedure' or, in specific cases, under a 'special legislative procedure' (Article 289(1) to (3) TFEU; see para. 17-019 *et seq., infra*). Therefore, other legally binding acts of a general nature that are directly based on the Treaties do not qualify as 'legislative acts' in the strict sense of the Treaties,[2] even if some are—from the point of view of their content—of a legislative nature.[3] The qualification of acts to be adopted as 'legislative acts' has direct consequences for the operation of the institutions,[4] the scrutiny exercised by national parliaments of respect for the principle of subsidiarity,[5] the possibility

17.002

---

[1] Therefore, implementing acts of a general nature needed to be distinguished from legislative acts, in the first place, by reason of their legal basis: they constituted 'legislative' acts if they were directly based on a Treaty article and 'implementing acts' if they were based on legislative acts or on earlier implementing acts (see para. 18-008, *infra*).

[2] C-643/15 and C-647/15, *Slovak Republic and Hungary v Council*, 2017, paras 57–84. A measure based on Article 78(3) TFEU is not adopted through a legislative procedure and is thus not a legislative act, even though such an emergency measure may undercut actual legislative acts based on other Treaty provisions.

[3] See para. 17-038, *infra*.

[4] See, e.g., the obligation for the Council to meet in public, which applies only when it deliberates and votes on draft legislative acts (Articles 16(8) TEU and 15(2) TFEU.

[5] The fact that acts adopted pursuant to such procedure are not 'legislative acts' implies that they are not subject to the requirement that draft-legislative acts must be forwarded to national parliaments (Article 2 of Protocol (No. 1) on the role of national parliaments in the European Union; see para. 15-007, *supra*) or to scrutiny of compliance with the principle of subsidiarity (Article 3 of Protocol (No. 2) on the application of the principles of subsidiarity and proportionality; see para. 5-032, *supra*). See C-643/15 and C-647/15, *Slovak Republic and Hungary v Council*, 2017, para. 193.

530   THE LEGISLATIVE PROCEDURES

to delegate powers to the Commission,[6] and judicial review.[7] Besides legislative acts, the Union institutions adopt acts for the implementation of legally binding acts of the Union. These acts encompass delegated acts (Article 290 TFEU) and implementing acts (Article 291 TFEU) and are designated by the specific adjective in their title (see para. 18-008, *infra*). It follows that legislative acts are now formally distinguished from other acts adopted by the institutions of the Union.

The EU Constitution had proposed to go one step further and distinguish between legal instruments to be used for legislative acts and non-legislative acts respectively: legislative acts would take the form of a 'European law', or a 'European framework law'. For non-legislative action, institutions were to use a 'European regulation' or a 'European decision'. The 2007 Intergovernmental Conference decided not to adopt that terminology, as it referred too much to a 'constitutional' order, but the Treaty of Lisbon preserved the clear distinction between legislation and implementation.

The Union may adopt legislative acts in all of the fields for which it is competent,[8] except for the common foreign and security policy where the adoption of 'legislative acts' is expressly ruled out (Articles 24(1), first subpara. and 31(1) TEU).

B. Basic outline of legislative process

17.003 **Legislative procedures.** As mentioned above, the Lisbon Treaty introduced the 'ordinary legislative procedure', which consists in the joint adoption by the European Parliament and the Council of a regulation, directive, or decision on a proposal from the Commission (Article 289(1) TFEU, referring to the procedure laid down in Article 294 TFEU). In specific cases provided for by the Treaties, the adoption of a regulation, directive, or decision by the European Parliament with the participation of the Council, or by the Council with the participation of the European Parliament, is to constitute a 'special legislative procedure' (Article 289(2) TFEU).[9]

The co-existence of the 'ordinary legislative procedure' and various forms of 'special legislative procedures' shows that the Treaties do not prescribe a general procedure for the adoption of all legislative acts.[10] Instead, each Treaty article which provides for action by the Union lays down how that action is to be carried out. This may be done by mere reference to the fact that the action is to be adopted 'in accordance with the ordinary legislative procedure' (set out in Article 294 TFEU) or by setting out the concrete procedural steps

---

[6] Article 290 TFEU (see para. 18-010, *infra*).
[7] Legislative acts are no 'regulatory acts', which under some circumstances can be challenged more easily by private parties by means of an action for annulment (Article 263(4) TFEU; see para. 30-011, *infra*).
[8] The reference in Articles 2(1) TFEU (exclusive competences) and 2(2) TFEU (shared competences) to the Union's competence to 'legislate and adopt legally binding acts' does not seem to rule out the adoption of legislative acts in other areas, such as the areas where the Union is to support, coordinate, or supplement Member States' action (Articles 2(5) and 6 TFEU).
[9] Best, 'Legislative Procedures after Lisbon: Fewer, Simpler, Clearer' (2008) MJECL 85–96. For overviews of the various legislative procedures before the Lisbon Treaty, see Piris, 'After Maastricht, are the Community Institutions More Efficacious, More Democratic and More Transparent?' (1994) ELRev 449–87; Raworth, *The Legislative Process in the European Community* (Kluwer, 1993), 129–49.
[10] In contrast, a general procedure exists for Union participation in international agreements (Article 218 TFEU; see Chapter 21).

to be taken 'in accordance with a special legislative procedure'. The procedure that most commonly applies in all fields of action of the Union, except for the CFSP, is the ordinary legislative procedure (see para. 16-022, *supra*). A few Treaty articles set forth the procedural steps to be taken for the adoption of general acts without qualifying them as a 'legislative procedure' (see para. 17-033, *infra*). As a result, acts adopted under those articles are not 'legislative acts' in the strict sense of the Treaties.[11]

Where a Treaty provision sets out the procedure to be followed for the adoption of a legislative act, the institutions concerned are to act within the limits of the powers conferred upon them by the Treaties. That implies that the institutions may not, in a legislative act, provide for certain aspects to be adopted by them in accordance with a different procedure— whether for the purpose of strengthening or easing the legislative procedure.[12] Rather than creating such a 'secondary legal basis', the institutions should have recourse to implementing or delegated acts (see para. 18-008 *et seq., infra*), or adopt a new legislative act.

It should be noted that the European Council may decide—on its own initiative and by a unanimous vote—that, in some cases where the Treaties provide for legislation to be adopted under a special legislative procedure or where the Treaties provide for the Council to act unanimously in a given area, decisions will in future be taken under the ordinary legislative procedure or by qualified majority vote, as the case may be (Article 48(7) TEU; see para. 3-006, *supra*).

Interaction between the political institutions. It follows that virtually all legislative procedures involve the European Parliament, the Council, and the Commission.[13] The European Parliament and the Council are, as a general rule, entitled to legislate only if the Commission exercises its right of initiative (Article 17(2) TEU; see para. 17-012, *infra*). As far as 'legislative acts' are concerned, the decision-making power is assigned to the European Parliament and the Council.[14] Under the ordinary legislative procedure, the European Parliament and the Council act on the same footing as co-legislators; where a special legislative procedure applies, the European Parliament usually does not have the same degree of involvement, and the Council has the decision-making power. Where the Treaties provide for general rules to be adopted, without qualifying the procedure as 'legislative', the decision-making power is mostly left to the Council, even though the European Parliament may be involved in one way or another in the decision-making process (see para. 17-040 *et seq., infra*). In addition, some Treaty provisions empower the Commission and the European Central Bank[15] to adopt acts of a general nature within the limits of a power conferred on them to

17.004

---

[11] See C-643/15 and C-647/15, *Slovak Republic and Hungary v Council*, 2017, paras 57–84. Conversely, the act declaring the budget to be definitively adopted under Article 314(9) TFEU, even though the outcome of a special legislative procedure, does not, due to the nature of the budget, take the form of a legislative act in the sense of Articles 288 and 289(2) TFEU; see C-77/11, *Council v European Parliament*, 2013, para. 60.

[12] C-133/06, *European Parliament v Council*, 2008, paras 54–61. See also C-540/13, *European Parliament v Council*, 2015, paras 32–40, and C-317/13 and C-679/13, *European Parliament v Council*, 2015, paras 42–50; C-363/14, *European Parliament v Council*, 2015, paras 58–67 (no relaxation of the legislative procedure).

[13] See Hosli, 'Who has Power in the EU? The Commission, Council and Parliament in Legislative Decision-making' (2006) JCMS 391–417.

[14] See Article 289(1)-(2) TFEU. Accordingly, the TEU confers the 'legislative function' on both the European Parliament (see Article 14(1) TEU) and the Council (see Article 16(1) TEU), while ruling out any legislative functions for the European Council (Article 15(1) TEU).

[15] Article 132(1) TFEU.

that end by the Treaty provision at issue.[16] The Treaties further provide for the possibility to conclude interinstitutional agreements concerning relations between the institutions.[17]

17.005 **No duty to legislate.** The power of the Union's institutions to legislate is not associated with a correlative duty to do so. A duty to legislate does arise, however, where the Treaties commit an institution to adopting a particular act.[18] If the substance of the obligation is sufficiently clearly defined in the Treaties, a failure to comply with it will constitute an omission against which an action for failure to act will lie.[19] If neither the Council nor the European Parliament is under a duty to act, those institutions are, in principle, not bound to any time at which they must take a decision on a Commission proposal.[20]

17.006 **Role of Member States.** National authorities do not participate as such in the legislative process, which is reserved for the institutions of the Union. Accordingly, the governments of the Member States participate in the Union legislative process in their capacity as Council members. Exceptionally, the Treaties provide for a direct role for the governments of the Member States, but that does not concern the adoption of legislative acts.[21] Nevertheless, national parliaments do play a role in the legislative process. First, some Union measures tantamount to an amendment of the Treaties must be adopted in accordance with the national constitutional requirements, which in practice usually implies that they have to be approved by the national parliaments as well (see para. 3-007, *supra*). More generally, national parliaments may influence decision-making at Union level by bringing pressure to bear on members of the Council, who are answerable to them (see para. 15-006 *et seq.*, *supra*). As mentioned before, such parliamentary scrutiny is possible only if (a) the parliament is in possession of the necessary information concerning the activities of the Union; (b) influence may actually be brought to bear on a member of the Council; and (c) that member may be called to account for how he or she voted in the Council. In order to facilitate this level of democratic control the Commission must send all legislative proposals to the national parliaments in accordance with the Protocol on the role of national parliaments (see para. 15-007, *supra*). In some Member States, governments may be under an obligation to first consult their national parliament before taking a position in the Council, and to take that position into account. The Council, moreover, publishes the result of its votes, in order to allow a national parliament to hold a member of the government accountable after the vote has taken place. Since the Treaty of Lisbon, national parliaments also have the power to

---

[16] Articles 105(3) and 106(3) TFEU (competition) and Article 108(4) TFEU (State aid). See 188–190/80, *France, Italy and United Kingdom v Commission*, 1982, paras 4–7 (following an application of Article 86(3) EC [*now Article 106(3) TFEU*]; see para. 9-020, *supra*). For the scope of the Commission's power to take decisions, see also para. 12-060, *supra*.

[17] Article 295 TFEU (see para. 17-042, *infra*).

[18] For an obligation to act, see, *inter alia*, Article 215(1) TFEU; para. 10-031, *infra*. Before the Lisbon Treaty, a duty to legislate also arose where a number of Treaty articles committed an institution to adopting a particular act within a specified time (see: Articles 61, 62, and 63 EC and Articles 67 EC; Article 104(14), third subpara. EC; Article 255(2) EC; Article 286(2) EC). The Lisbon Treaty repealed these provisions or deleted the time-limit formerly laid down therein (the same had already happened with Articles 6, 7, and 8 of the Amsterdam Treaty).

[19] For such an obligation on the part of the Council, see 13/83, *European Parliament v Council*, 1985, para. 64 (concerning the obligation arising under Article 71(2) EC; see para. 9-010, *supra*).

[20] See the Commission's answer of 20 November 1998 to Question No. P-3242/98 (Jarembowski), OJ 1999 C297/62. For a commentary, see Schorkopf, 'Die Untätigkeit des Rates der Europäischen Union im Gesetzgebungsverfahren' (2000) EuR 365–79.

[21] e.g. Article 253, first para. TFEU (appointment of Judges and Advocates General to the Court of Justice) and Article 341 TFEU (establishing the seat of the institutions).

review legislative acts of the Union in the light of the principle of subsidiarity, both during the legislative procedure, and also—if needs be—afterwards, by bringing an action for annulment (see paras 5-032–5-033).

C. Decision-making power

1. Participation of the Council

Council. As set out above, under the ordinary legislative procedure, the European Parliament and the Council exercise influence on the same level. When special legislative procedures or non-legislative procedures apply, the decision-making power is, however, still mainly concentrated in the Council. The majority of Treaty articles provide for acts of a general nature to be adopted by the Council either unanimously or by a qualified majority (for details of voting in the Council, see para. 12-046 *et seq., supra*). If a Treaty article does not specify that the Council has to vote by a particular majority, the act has to be adopted by a qualified majority (Article 16(3) TEU).[22] The requirement for the Council to act unanimously generally reflects Member States' concern to preserve the last word in sensitive matters or in areas in which the Union recently obtained competence to act. Accordingly, when the Union was given competence to act in the various fields covered by the area of freedom, security, and justice, the initial provisions of the EU Treaty required the Council to adopt decisions by unanimity. Some Treaty amendments later, the Lisbon Treaty introduced qualified majority voting in many of these fields, while again adding new fields for which the Council is to decide by unanimity (see para. 8-005 *et seq., supra*).

17.007

Impact of voting requirements. Where a Treaty article requires an act of the Council to be adopted unanimously, each Member State has a decisive say in the outcome of the legislative process: either the Council adopts a piece of legislation to which each Member State can reconcile itself, or no text at all. Where, in contrast, the Council takes its decision by a qualified majority vote, the interaction with the Commission and the European Parliament ensures that there is a genuine three-way dialogue. In such a case, the Commission (by means of a proposal)—and possibly the European Parliament (by means of amendments in the ordinary legislative procedure)—is in a position to present to the Council a legislative text which does not necessarily have to meet with the approval of every Member State.

17.008

Consequently, the requirement for a unanimous vote does not only make it more difficult for agreement to be reached between the Member States in the Council, it also deprives the Commission of the room for manoeuvre which its right to make proposals affords in a procedure requiring only a qualified majority vote (see para. 17-017, *infra*).

2. Participation of the European Parliament

Degrees of involvement. Notwithstanding its direct democratic legitimacy, the European Parliament does not always take part in the legislative process. The European Parliament does, however, act as co-legislator on equal footing with the Council under the ordinary legislative procedure, which is the procedure for adopting legislative acts applicable in most

17.009

---

[22] Before the Lisbon Treaty, Article 205 EC required a simple majority in such a case.

fields of competence of the Union. However, in addition to the ordinary legislative procedure, there are special legislative procedures, which provide for different degrees of participation of the European Parliament: consultation and consent (see para. 17-035 *et seq., infra*). Furthermore, there are some Treaty articles that provide for no decision-making input from the Parliament or simply for it to be informed of the measures adopted (see para. 17-039 *et seq., infra*).

17.010 **From consultation to cooperation to co-decision.** It was not until the 1980s that the European Parliament succeeded in increasing its say in Community decision-making.[23] For a long time, the Parliament's only right was to be consulted in certain cases and to deliver a non-binding opinion.[24] Grant of decision-making power in the budgetary procedure in 1970 gave the Parliament a means of blocking other institutions' decisions with financial implications. In the judgments of 29 October 1980 in the isoglucose cases, the Court of Justice held that consultation of the Parliament constituted an essential procedural requirement and annulled a regulation which the Council had adopted without consulting the Parliament.[25]

In 1987 the Single European Act then increased Parliament's say by introducing 'assent' and 'cooperation' procedures and extending majority voting in the Council, which enlarged the Commission's scope for taking over parliamentary amendments.[26] The assent procedure, which gave the European Parliament a veto, was introduced for the accession of new Member States and the conclusion of association agreements (see para. 17-037, *infra*). That procedure still applies in various fields, but since the Lisbon Treaty it has been renamed as 'consent'. The 'cooperation' procedure[27] was introduced to increase the European Parliament's involvement in the Community's legislative process[28] and to make it possible for the Council to act by a qualified majority rather than by a unanimous vote. The move to qualified majority voting brought about the flexibility which was considered necessary in order to adopt the substantial corpus of legislation for achieving the internal market (see para. 7-009, *supra*). The cooperation procedure consisted of two stages. In the first stage, the European Parliament gave its opinion on the Commission proposal, after which the Council adopted a common position. In the second stage, the European Parliament could propose amendments to that common position or reject it. Compared to the procedure of mere 'consultation', the possibility afforded by the cooperation procedure to propose amendments allowed the Parliament to have a real influence on decision-making. The Parliament's say in this procedure, however, was weak in two respects: it could not submit its amendments

---

[23] For a survey of the increasing parliamentary involvement in decision-making, see Corbett, Jacobs, and Shackleton, 'The European Parliament at Fifty: A View from the Inside' (2003) JCMS 353–73.
[24] The ECSC Treaty also required the European Parliament to give its approval in the 'minor amendment' procedure provided for in Article 95.
[25] 138/79, *Roquette Frères v Council*, 1980, paras 33–7, and 139/79, *Maïzena v Council*, 1980, paras 34–8 (see also para. 17-011, *infra*).
[26] In addition to the general commentaries on the Single European Act (para. 1-041, *supra*), see Bieber, 'Legislative Procedure for the Establishment of the Single Market' (1988) CMLRev 711–24; Domestici-Met, 'Les procédures législatives communautaires après l'Acte unique' (1987) RMC 556–71.
[27] Initially, the EEC Treaty provided that in such a case the Council was to act 'by a qualified majority on a proposal from the Commission in cooperation with the European Parliament'. Subsequently, the procedure was set out in Article 252 EC and referred to in that Treaty as the 'procedure laid down in Article 252 of the Treaty'.
[28] C-300/89, *Commission v Council*, 1991, para. 20.

directly to the Council (with a view to their being approved by a qualified majority)[29] and could not prevent an act which it viewed with disfavour from being adopted.[30] In order to give the European Parliament a greater say in precisely those two respects, the EU Treaty introduced the co-decision procedure in 1993.

This co-decision procedure afforded the European Parliament both a right to propose amendments and a right of veto. This is the procedure which the Lisbon Treaty has renamed the 'ordinary legislative procedure', while using the term 'special legislative procedure' for procedures in which the European Parliament is merely consulted or is to give its consent. When it introduced the co-decision procedure, the EU Treaty also reordered the field of application of the various legislative procedures so as to increase parliamentary involvement across the board. In various policy areas, a procedure involving a greater say on the part of the Parliament, sometimes even the new co-decision procedure, replaced a procedure under which the Parliament had no or only a small say. However, the fact that the Parliament's role was increased piecemeal in stages meant that its say in the legislative process differed from case to case, which made it difficult to have a clear insight into its legislative role.[31] Where, in addition, the different aspects of a given policy area were governed by different procedures, there was also a threat to the coherence of the policy concerned.[32] The Treaty of Amsterdam improved matters in this respect by confining the cooperation procedure to aspects of EMU and, for all other matters, largely replacing it by co-decision. The Lisbon Treaty further increased the say of the European Parliament by making the ordinary legislative procedure (co-decision) applicable in most fields of action of the Union, including police and judicial cooperation in criminal matters. That procedure has turned the European Parliament and the Council into the Union's 'co-legislators'. Meanwhile, the Lisbon Treaty has abolished the cooperation procedure and replaced it with the ordinary legislative procedure[33] or by a non-legislative procedure requiring only consultation of the European Parliament.[34]

Essential procedural requirement. In the judgments in the isoglucose cases, the Court of Justice held that the European Parliament's participation in Union rule-making reflects, at Union level, the 'fundamental democratic principle that the peoples should take part in the exercise of power through the intermediary of a representative assembly'. It was on this ground that the Court held that procedures providing for the involvement of the Parliament

17.011

---

[29] In the second stage, the Council had to act unanimously if it wished to diverge from the Commission proposal. Consequently, where the Commission was prepared to take the Parliament's amendments over in an amended version of its proposal, the chance for the Parliament of its amendments being adopted by the Council was higher than when the Commission did not amend its initial proposal. In the latter case, Parliament's amendments could be adopted by the Council only by unanimity, that is to say, only if no Member State opposed them.

[30] If the Commission did not withdraw its proposal, the Council could still adopt, by a unanimous vote, a common position rejected by the Parliament. In the Framework Agreement of 26 May 2005 on relations between the European Parliament and the Commission (OJ 2006 C117E/125) the Commission undertook to withdraw a legislative proposal in that event unless there were important reasons for not doing so. In the first seven cases in which the Parliament rejected a Council common position, the Council adopted three common positions by a unanimous vote; on one occasion, the Commission withdrew its proposal and replaced the original one with new proposals: see the Commission's answer of 5 August 1996 to Question No. E-1861/96 (Schleicher), OJ 1996 C356/106. For a case study, see Earnshaw and Judge, 'The European Parliament and the Sweeteners Directive: From Footnote to Inter-Institutional Conflict' (1993) JCMS 103–16.

[31] See the criticism of Boest, 'Ein langer Weg zur Demokratie in Europa. Die Beteiligungsrechte des Europäischen Parlaments bei Rechtsetzung nach dem Vertrag über die Europäische Union' (1992) EuR 182, 191.

[32] De Gucht (with the collaboration of Keukeleire), *Besluitvorming in de Europese Unie* (Maklu, 1994), 58.

[33] e.g. Article 121(6) TFEU

[34] e.g. Articles 125 and 128(2) TFEU.

were essential procedural requirements for the adoption of legislative acts and that if those procedures were disregarded the acts in question could be declared void.[35] The European Parliament's prerogatives are infringed where an act is wrongly adopted on a legal basis which does not provide for the same involvement of the Parliament as the correct legal basis. If this results in a diminished role for the European Parliament in the decision-making procedure or affects the content of the act, the act may be declared invalid.[36] As more and more Treaty articles require the European Parliament to be involved in decision-making and the various legislative procedures call for different degrees of involvement, the Parliament is keeping an increasingly steady eye on the choice of legal basis made by the Commission and—in the second place—by the Council. In some cases, this has led the Parliament to challenge a legislative act before the Court of Justice on the ground of an allegedly incorrect choice of legal basis.[37]

D. Right of initiative

17.012 **Right of initiative.** Since the Lisbon Treaty, the Treaties expressly provide that Union legislative acts may be adopted only on the basis of a Commission proposal, except where the Treaties provide otherwise; other acts are to be adopted on the basis of a Commission proposal where the Treaties so provide (Article 17(2) TEU). These provisions confirm the system laid down in the initial Community Treaties where generally the Commission was the only institution empowered to submit a proposal for legislation, with the result that the other institutions could not legislate in the absence of a prior proposal from the Commission.[38] Apart from the CFSP,[39] the Commission's right of initiative covers all the fields of competence of the Union. Generally, a formal 'proposal' is needed, as is the case under the ordinary legislative procedure, which applies in most fields of Union action, but sometimes a recommendation[40] suffices.

In specific cases provided for by the Treaties, legislative acts may be adopted on the initiative of a group of Member States or of the European Parliament,[41] on a recommendation from the European Central Bank[42] or at the request of the Court of

---

[35] 138/79, *Roquette Frères v Council*, 1980, para. 33, and 139/79, *Maïzena v Council*, 1980, para. 34; C-300/89, *Commission v Council*, 1991, para. 20.

[36] Compare C-363/14, *European Parliament v Council*, 2015, paras 84–96 with C-316/91, *European Parliament v Council*, 1994, para. 16.

[37] See, for instance, C-14/15 and C-116/15, *European Parliament v Council*, 2016; C-363/14, *European Parliament v Council*, 2015; *European Parliament and Commission v Council*, C-132/14 to C-136/14, 2015; C-48/14, *European Parliament v Council*, 2015.

[38] The ECSC system was different in so far that the Commission was empowered to adopt acts itself, except in exceptional cases where the Council took the decision on a proposal from the Commission: see, for instance, Article 59(2) and (5) ECSC.

[39] For the right of initiative in the CFSP, see the relevant paras of Chapter 18.

[40] See, for authorization to conduct international negotiations: Article 207(3), second subpara. TFEU and Article 218(3) TFEU. See also Article 121(2), first subpara. and (4), first subpara. TFEU; Article 126(7) TFEU; Article 219(1), (2), and (3) TFEU; Article 143(1), second subpara. TFEU; Article 144(2) TFEU (economic and monetary provisions); Article 148(4) TFEU (employment).

[41] See Article 7(1) TEU. See also, for decisions taken on the basis of a proposal from the European Parliament, Article 223(1) TFEU, and Act on the Direct Election of the European Parliament, Article 14.

[42] See Article 129(3) and (4) TFEU (regarding the Statute of the ESCB and of the ECB); Article 219(1) and (2) TFEU (agreements concerning monetary or foreign exchange regime matters). These measures may also be taken at the initiative of the Commission after consulting the ECB (Article 219(1) and (2) TFEU)).

Justice⁴³ or the European Investment Bank.⁴⁴ The right of initiative of a group of Member States mainly applies in the field of PJCC,⁴⁵ where the Commission shares the right of initiative with the Member States, which may submit an initiative provided that it emanates from a group consisting of at least a quarter of the Member States.⁴⁶ As a result, the Commission cannot influence decision-making in that field to the same extent as it can in fields in which it has the exclusive right of initiative and the prerogatives associated with that right (see para. 17-017, *infra*).

In sum, legislative acts of the Union are generally adopted on a proposal from the Commission, although in specific cases the right of initiative falls to a group of Member States, the European Parliament, the European Central Bank, the Court of Justice, or the European Investment Bank.⁴⁷ Only exceptionally may Union acts be adopted by the Council in the absence of any such initiative.⁴⁸

Citizens' initiative. A remarkable innovation introduced by the Lisbon Treaty is the possibility for a group of citizens to invite the Commission to initiate legislation. At the initiative of at least one million citizens coming from a significant number of Member States, the Commission may be invited to submit 'any appropriate proposal' on matters where citizens consider that a legal act of the Union is required for the purpose of implementing the Treaties (Article 11(4) TEU). The right to undertake a citizens' initiative thus constitutes an instrument concerning the right of citizens to participate in the democratic life of the Union, provided for in Article 10(3) TEU.⁴⁹ Pursuant to Article 24 TFEU the procedures and conditions required for such a citizens' initiative are established by the European Parliament and the Council. In accordance with Regulation No. 2019/788, the organizers of a citizens' initiative are required, before starting to collect statements of support from signatories, to have the proposed initiative registered by the Commission,⁵⁰ which may refuse

17.013

---

⁴³ See Article 252, first para. TFEU (decision to increase the number of Advocates General); Article 257, first para. TFEU (establishment of specialized courts); and Article 281, second para. TFEU (amendment of the Statute of the Court of Justice of the European Union). In the last two cases, the measures concerned may also be taken at the initiative of the Commission after consulting the ECJ (Ibid.).
⁴⁴ Article 308, third para. TFEU (amendment of the Statute of the EIB). This measure may also be taken at the initiative of the Commission after consulting the European Parliament and the EIB (Ibid.).
⁴⁵ See, however, also Article 7(1) TEU (on a proposal by one-third of the Member States, the European Parliament, or the Commission) and (2) (on a proposal from one-third of the Member States or the Commission). See also Article 108(2), third subpara. TFEU, which exceptionally provides for the adoption of a measure on application of a Member State. Article 67(1) EC provided for action on a proposal from the Commission or on the initiative of a Member State, but only during a transitional period of five years following the entry into force of the Amsterdam Treaty, after which the Council was invariably to act on a proposal from the Commission; see Article 67(2) EC.
⁴⁶ Article 76 TFEU. Before the Lisbon Treaty, in the field of PJCC, any Member State could submit a proposal on an individual basis (Article 34(2) EU). In connection with JHA cooperation, initiatives often—but not invariably—appeared to stem from the Member State occupying the Presidency; see, for instance, as regards the period 1 July 1996 to 30 June 1997 the Council's answer of 17 November 1997 to Question No. E-2405/97 (Nassauer), OJ 1998 C102/39.
⁴⁷ See, in this connection, the definition of 'draft legislative acts' in Article 2, second subpara. of Protocol (No. 1), annexed to the EU, TFEU, and EAEC Treaty, on the role of National Parliaments in the European Union (OJ 2010 C83/203) and Article 3 of Protocol (No. 2), annexed to the TEU and TFEU, on the application of the principles of subsidiarity and proportionality (OJ 2010 C83/206).
⁴⁸ Articles 160, 243, 286(7), and 301, third para. TFEU. See also Article 354, third para. TFEU and Article 7(3) TEU.
⁴⁹ C-418/18 P, *Puppinck v Commission*, 2019, para. 54.
⁵⁰ Regulation (EU) 2019/788 of the European Parliament and of the Council of 17 April 2019 on the European citizens' initiative, OJ 2019 L130/55, Article 6.

registration if the admissibility criteria are not met.[51] Within twelve months from a chosen date after the registration, organizers can collect statements of support. The one million signatories of a citizens' initiative must come from at least one quarter of the Member States with a minimum number of signatories fixed by the Regulation for each Member State.[52] Where a citizens' initiative fulfils these conditions, the Commission will communicate its legal and political conclusions on the citizens' initiative, indicating the measures it intends to take, if any, and its reasons for doing so.[53] Thus, the provisions pertaining to the citizens' initiative do not oblige the Commission to comply with the request made through the citizens' initiative.[54]

17.014

No right of initiative for the Council or European Parliament. Except for the cases mentioned above, the Commission is the only institution entitled to submit proposals for legislation. Neither the European Parliament nor the Council may force the Commission to submit a proposal; they can only invite the Commission to make a proposal (see para. 17-018, *infra*). The Commission, as an independent expert institution, has the capacity to ensure that every legislative initiative is technically correct and also in the interests of the Union as a whole. No provision is made for a right of initiative on the part of the Council. As such, the Treaties sought to offer a constitutional guarantee aiming to avoid the introduction of legislative initiatives that might take a step backwards in the integration process. After all, measures adopted by the Council are the outcome of negotiations between the Member States, which in any concrete policy context defend their own interests and are not necessarily concerned, in the first place, with the preservation of the achievements of the EU's integration process. The fact that initially the European Parliament was given little or no part to play in the legislative process, meant that it obtained no right of initiative.[55] In view of the democratic legitimacy of the directly elected European Parliament, it would seem justified to confer a right of initiative also on the

---

[51] See, e.g., C-589/15 P, *Anagnostakis v Commission*, 2017 (affirming T-450/12, *Anagnostakis v Commission*, 2015); C-420/16 P, *Izsák and Dabis v Commission*, 2019 (affirming T-529/13, *Izsák and Dabis v Commission*, 2016). See also T-44/14, *Costantini v Commission*, 2016; T-754/14, *Efler and Others v Commission*, 2017 (annulling the refusal to register); T-646/13, *Bürgerausschuss für die Bürgerinitiative Minority SafePack—one million signatures for diversity in Europe v Commision*, 2017 (annulling the refusal to register); T-561/14, *European Citizens' Initiative One of Us v Commission*, 2018. See also Athanasiadou, 'The European Citizens' Initiative: Lost in Admissibility?' (2019) MJECL 251–70; Lupo, 'The Commission's Power to Withdraw Legislative Proposals and its "Parliamentarisation", Between Technical and Political Grounds' (2018) EuConst 311–31; Inglese, 'Recent Trends in European Citizens' Initiatives: The General Court Case Law and the Commission's Practice' (2018) E Pub L 335–361; Karatzia, 'The European Citizens' Initiative in Practice: Legal Admissibility Concerns' (2015) ELRev 509–30.

[52] Regulation (EU) 2019/788, Article 3(1) (the thresholds correspond with the number of MEPs assigned to each Member State, multiplied by 751).

[53] Regulation (EU) 2019/788, Article 15. See also Vogiatzis, 'Between Discretion and Control: Reflections on the Institutional Position of the Commission within the European citizens' Initiative Process' (2017) ELJ 250–71; Braun Binder and Vegh, 'Revidierte Verordnung zur Europäischen Bürgerinitiative: Lehren aus Erfahrungen?' (2019) EuR 302–23. For a Citizens' initiative that has led to a proposal by the Commission addressing at least part of the concerns of the organizers of the citizen's initiative, see the citizens' initiative 'Ban glyphosate and protect people and the environment from toxic pesticides' (ECI(2017)000002), which has led to Regulation (EU) 2019/1381 of the European Parliament and of the Council of 20 June 2019 on the transparency and sustainability of the EU risk assessment in the food chain, OJ 2019 L231/1. Also, the new Drinking Water Directive (Directive (EU) 2020/2184 of the European Parliament and of the Council of 16 December 2020 on the quality of water intended for human consumption (recast), OJ 2020 L435/1), is the result of the first successful citizen's initiative ('the Right2Water initiative').

[54] C-418/18 P, *Puppinck v Commission*, 2019, paras 53–72.

[55] The European Parliament has such a right only under Article 223(2) TFEU (laying down the regulations and general conditions governing the performance of the duties of its Members); Article 226, third para. TFEU (determining the detailed provisions governing the exercise of the right of inquiry); Article 228(4) TFEU (Ombudsman Regulations). See also the discussion of Article 225 TFEU (para. 17-018, *infra*).

European Parliament, possibly combined with a duty to consult the Commission. Meanwhile, the European Parliament makes active use of its right under Article 225 TFEU to invite the Commission to submit any appropriate proposal (see para. 17-018, *infra*). Furthermore, the European Parliament and the Council may express requests for initiatives in the context of the interinstitutional dialogue that takes place before and after the Commission adopts its annual work programme and encompasses exchanges of view on envisaged initiatives.[56]

Formulating proposals. The right to propose legislation means that the Commission can decide whether or not the Union should act and, if so, on what legal basis; in what legal form (if the legal basis permits a choice); and what content and implementing procedures the proposal should embody. Especially where the adoption of a legislative act is characterized by a wide discretion, the Commission itself decides when it is appropriate to formulate and submit legislative proposals.[57]

17.015

As discussed, the Commission submits its initiatives in accordance with its annual working programme drawn up in consultation with the European Parliament and the Council.[58] In response to the demand for democracy and transparency, the Commission has long been issuing consultative documents, 'green papers', in order to encourage political debate. Packages of related proposals for legislation have been published in the form of 'white papers'.[59] In line with the principles of 'better regulation',[60] the Commission consults interest groups affected (the 'stakeholders') and the administrative authorities in the Member States before it adopts any proposal. Representatives of interest groups themselves also regularly contact members of the Commission or its administration (see para. 16-004, *supra*). Since the Lisbon Treaty, the Commission is generally required to 'carry out broad consultations with parties concerned in order to ensure that the Union's actions are coherent and transparent' (Article 11(3) TEU). Indeed, the Protocol on the application of the principles of subsidiarity and proportionality requires the Commission to consult widely before proposing legislation.[61] It must justify the relevance of its proposals with regard to the principle of subsidiarity, and its proposals should contain a detailed statement making it possible to appraise compliance with these principles.[62] In the case of proposals for legislation that may

---

[56] See the Interinstitutional Agreement between the European Parliament, the Council, and the Commission on Better Law-making, OJ 2016 L123/1, points 6–7 (exchanges take place before the submission of a 'letter of intent' from the President of the Commission, following the debate after the President's yearly address to the Parliament on the "State of the Union" and then again after the adotion of the Commission's work programme; eventually the three political institutions are to agree on a 'joint declaration on annual interinstitutional programming').

[57] C-418/18 P, *Puppinck v Commission*, 2019, paras 87–97; T-571/93, *Lefebvre and Others v Commission*, 1995, paras 32–9.

[58] See the Interinstitutional Agreement between the European Parliament, the Council, and the Commission on Better Law-making (OJ 2016 L123/1), that succeeded to the Interinstitutional Agreement between the European Parliament, the Council, and the Commission of 16 December 2003 on Better Law-making, point 3 *et seq*. (OJ 2003 C321/1). As far as the Parliament is concerned, its involvement in legislative planning is governed by Rule 38 of the EP Rules of Procedure.

[59] Thus, the Commission's White Paper on European Governance contained proposals designed to get more people and organizations involved in shaping and delivering Union policy: OJ 2001 C287/1.

[60] See the Commission Communications 'Better Regulation: Delivering Better Results for a Stronger Union', COM(2016)615 final; 'Completing the Better Regulation Agenda: Better Solutions for Better Results', COM(2017)675 final; 'Better Regulation: Taking Stock and Sustaining our Commitment', COM(201)178 final.

[61] Protocol (No. 2), annexed to the TEU and TFEU, on the application of the principles of subsidiarity and proportionality (OJ 2010 C83/206), Article 2 (which makes an exception for 'cases of exceptional urgency').

[62] Ibid., Article 5. The reasons for concluding that a Union objective can be better achieved at Union level are to be substantiated by qualitative and, wherever possible, quantitative indicators. At the same time, the Protocol requires the Commission to take duly into account the need for any burden, whether financial or administrative,

bring about important economic, ecological, or social consequences, the Commission has committed, in its 'better regulation' programme, to carry out a prior impact assessment, which is made public at the end of the legislative process.[63] Such an impact assessment is not binding on either the European Parliament or the Council, which remain free to adopt, in the legislative procedure, measures other than those that were the subject of that impact assessment.[64] Still, where the Union legislature is asked to demonstrate the proportionality of a legislative act, such impact assessment may be instrumental in establishing that it had sufficient information at its disposal to make informed choices on the suitability and necessity of the adopted measures.[65]

17.016 **Publication of initiatives.** The Commission formulates each proposal which it wishes to submit as a text ready to be adopted, and publishes it in the *Official Journal* (part C). Such proposals and other preparatory documents on general matters that have been approved within the Commission are referred to as 'COM documents'. They are usually made available on the Commission's website.[66] Initiatives for the adoption of a PJCC legislative act submitted to the Council by a group of Member States or the Commission are also published in the *Official Journal*.[67]

According to the Protocol on the role of national parliaments in the European Union, all Commission documents (green and white papers and communications) are to be forwarded to national parliaments upon publication.[68] Draft legislative acts must also be forwarded to national parliaments.[69] In order to allow enough time for discussion of the draft legislative act, the Protocol requires that there be an eight-week period between the time when a draft is made available in all languages to the European Parliament and the Council and the date when it is placed on a Council agenda for decision (adoption of an act or of a position under a legislative procedure).[70] Before taking any legislative initiative, the

---

falling upon the Union, national governments, local authorities, economic operators, and citizens to be minimized and commensurate with the objective to be achieved: ibid. (see also the discussion of the principles of subsidiarity and proportionality in paras 5-029–5-031, and 5-039, *supra*).

[63] See the Interinstitutional Agreement between the European Parliament, the Council of the European Union and the European Commission on Better Law-making, OJ 2016 L123/1, points 13 (which also announces impact assessments for non-legislative acts, delegated acts, and implementing acts with similar impact) and 18.

[64] See C-343/09, *Afton Chemical*, 2010, paras 30 and 65; C-477/14, *Pillbox 38*, 2016, para. 65; C-5/16, *Poland v European Parliament and Council*, 2018, para. 159.

[65] See C-482/17, *Czech Republic v European Parliament and Council*, 2019, paras 76–98; C-128/17, *Poland v European Parliament and Council*, 2019, paras 30–47. See also C-58/08, *Vodafone and Others*, 2010, paras 55–8; C-547/14, *Philip Morris Brands and Others*, 2016, para. 189; C-5/16 *Poland v European Parliament and Council*, 2018, paras 150–65; C-616/17, *Blaise*, 2019, paras 41–51. In particular where the Union legislature has a broad discretion since its action involves political, economic, and social choices and it is called upon to undertake complex assessments and evaluations, it must base its choice on objective criteria appropriate to the aim pursued by the legislation in question, taking into account all the facts and the technical and scientific data available at the time of adoption of the act in question, see C-127/07, *Arcelor Atlantique*, 2008, paras 57–8.

[66] Together with documents published by the Commission's general secretariat (SEC documents), COM documents are available from Eur-Lex: http://eur-lex.europa.eu/en/index.htm.

[67] Council Rules of Procedure, Article 17(1)(c). Other initiatives for PJCC acts are published in the *Official Journal*, unless decided otherwise (Council Rules of Procedure, Article 17(2)(a)).

[68] Protocol (No. 1), annexed to the EU, TFEU, and EAEC Treaty, on the role of National Parliaments in the European Union (OJ 2010 C83/203), Article 1. The Commission is also to forward the annual legislative programme, as well as any other instrument of legislative planning or policy, to national parliaments, at the same time as it forwards them to the European Parliament and the Council (ibid.).

[69] Ibid., Article 2.

[70] Ibid., Article 4; see Article 3(3) of the Council Rules of Procedure. The Council may derogate from the eight-week period in cases of urgency.

Commission must always notify the European Parliament.[71] Moreover, in all fields where the European Parliament acts in a legislative capacity it is to be informed, on a par with the Council, at every stage of the legislative process.[72]

Amending or withdrawing a proposal. When the Commission is entitled to submit a formal 'proposal', it has a significant influence over the course of decision-making. So long as the Council has not acted, the Commission is entitled to amend its proposal at any time during the procedure leading to the adoption of a Union act (Article 293(2) TFEU). It may therefore amend its proposal at any time while it is under discussion in the Council (and before that, in the working parties and Coreper) and the European Parliament. In view of the flexibility demanded by the legislative procedure with a view to achieving a convergence of views between the institutions, no formalities have to be complied with towards the other institutions in order to amend a proposal and amendments do not have to be made in writing.[73] Thus, an 'amendment of a proposal' may consist of a member of the Commission approving a compromise proposal put forward by the Presidency of the Council, even if it involves a significant change to the original proposal.[74] Since the right not to submit a proposal is a corollary of the right of initiative, the Commission may, in principle, also withdraw its proposal,[75] except in the ordinary legislative procedure from the second reading onwards. Although this right to withdraw a proposal is not set out in the Treaties, it has been recognized by the Court of Justice.[76] However, the Commission's right to withdraw a proposal does not confer any right of veto in the conduct of the legislative process since that would be contrary to the principles of conferral of powers (Articles 4(1) and 5(2) TEU) and institutional balance (Article 13(2) TEU). The Commission may withdraw its proposal where an amendment planned by the European Parliament and the Council would distort the proposal in a manner which prevents achievement of the objectives pursued by it and would thus deprive the proposal of its *raison d'être*.[77] A proposal may also be withdrawn when it has long been submitted to the legislature without any chance of adoption.[78] The Commission must do so in full respect of the principle of sincere cooperation, in particular by having due regard to the concerns of the European Parliament and the Council and

17.017

---

[71] Framework Agreement of 20 October 2010 on relations between the European Parliament and the European Commission (OJ 2010 L304/47), point 13.

[72] Ibid., points 8 and 12.

[73] C-280/93, *Germany v Council*, 1994, para. 36.

[74] C-445/00, *Austria v Council*, 2003, paras 16–17 and 44–7; C-643/15 and C-647/15, *Slovak Republic and Hungary v Council*, 2017, paras 179–85. Within the Commission, however, such amendment must, however, first have been approved by a majority of the Commissioners within the College. Legislative files are discussed on a weekly basis within the Group on Inter-Institutional Relations (the 'GRI') and, where needed, also by the meeting of Heads of Cabinet (the 'hebdo') ahead of the meeting of the College of Commissioners. See, most recently, the Working Methods of the European Commission, as contained in the Communication of 1 December 2019 from the President to the Commission, 13 (available at https://ec.europa.eu/info/working-methods-von-der-leyen-commission_en).

[75] See already the Commission's answer of 23 January 1987 to Question No. 2422/86 (Herman), OJ 1987 C220/6.

[76] C-409/13, *Council v Commission*, 2015, paras 74–83.

[77] Ibid., para. 83. This case concerned a decision to withdraw that was made (during trilogues) in the first reading of the ordinary legislative procedure.

[78] The Commission has committed to provide detailed explanation in due time before withdrawing any proposal on which Parliament has already expressed a position at first reading of the ordinary legislative procedure and, as regards special legislative procedures on which the Parliament is consulted, to withdraw a legislative proposal that Parliament has rejected, unless it has important reasons to maintain its proposal, which are stated before Parliament. See Framework Agreement of 20 October 2010 on relations between the European Parliament and the European Commission (OJ 2010 L47), points 39 and 40(iv).

by informing the co-legislators in a timely manner of its intention.[79] The decision of the Commission to withdraw a proposal must be reasoned and is an act that can be challenged through an action for annulment.

As has been noted, where the Council has to adopt an act on a proposal from the Commission, it may amend the proposal only by a unanimous vote (Article 293(1) TFEU), except in a few particular cases.[80] Consequently, except in those cases, as soon as one Member State is in agreement with a Commission proposal, the Council has to reach agreement on the proposal that has been submitted and that may be constantly amended by the Commission until it obtains the support of a sufficient majority. If the Council is unanimous in wishing to adopt an act which differs in some fundamental way from the Commission's proposal, the latter may deprive the Council of its power of decision by withdrawing the proposal.[81] The Commission's room for manoeuvre is significantly greater where the Council has to act by a qualified majority than when it is required to take a unanimous decision. In the first case, the Commission will amend its proposal during the negotiations in the Council just sufficiently in order to obtain the number of votes required; in the second case, the Commission has to comply with the wishes of all the Member States, either by amending its proposal itself or by sticking to its proposal and seeing the Council possibly alter it by a unanimous vote. If the Council wishes to depart from the Commission's proposal, it cannot introduce just any provision: its amendments must remain within the scope of the act as defined in the original Commission proposal.[82]

In those policy areas where the Treaties give the Commission the initiative in the form of a recommendation, it does not have the same influence on decision-making. When the Council has received the recommendation, it can still decide by the same majority even if it does not take up the recommendation and the power to take the decision cannot be removed from it.[83]

17.018 **No obligation.** In principle, the Commission cannot be compelled to submit a proposal, although, in some instances, the Treaties require the Commission to examine whether it should submit a proposal.[84] In addition, Article 241 TFEU empowers the Council (acting by a simple majority vote) to 'request the Commission to undertake any studies the Council considers desirable for the attainment of the common objectives, and to submit to it any appropriate proposals', whilst Article 225 TFEU confers on the European Parliament 'acting by a majority of its component members' the right to 'request the Commission to submit any appropriate proposal on matters on which it considers that a Union act is

---

[79] Ibid., paras 83 and 97–106. See also the Interinstitutional Agreement between the European Parliament, the Council of the European Union and the European Commission on Better Law-making, OJ 2016 L123/1, point 9.
[80] Article 293(1) TFEU makes an exception for the cases referred to in Article 294(10) and (13) TFEU (the conciliation phase of the ordinary legislative procedure) and in Articles 310, 312, 314, and Article 315, second para. TFEU (certain budgetary provisions).
[81] C-409/13, *Council v Commission*, 2015, paras 90–5.
[82] C-408/95, *Eurotunnel and Others*, 1997, paras 37–9; see also 355/87, *Commission v Council*, 1987, paras 42–4 (amendments tested against the 'subject-matter' and the 'objective' of the proposal).
[83] C-27/04, *Commission v Council*, 2004, para. 80 (where Commission recommendations—and not proposals—are placed before the Council, it may modify the measure recommended by the majority required for the adoption of that measure). See also ibid., para. 92 (Council decision taken on a recommendation from the Commission cannot be modified without a fresh recommendation from the Commission).
[84] Article 114(7) and (8) TFEU.

required for the purpose of implementing the Treaties'. Because the Commission's right to make proposals is essentially in the nature of a 'power', no general obligation for the Commission to submit proposals at the request of the Council or the Parliament may be inferred from those articles.[85] However, since the Lisbon Treaty, those articles explicitly require the Commission to inform the Council and the European Parliament, respectively, of its reasons if it does not submit a proposal.[86] Even before that, the Commission gave the European Parliament and the Council an undertaking to take account of any requests made and to provide a prompt and sufficiently detailed reply to the parliamentary committees concerned and to the Council's preparatory bodies.[87] In July 2019, the newly elected President of the European Commission, Ursula von der Leyen, committed to respond with a proposal for a legislative act—in full respect of the proportionality, subsidiarity, and better law-making principles—whenever the European Parliament, acting by a majority of its component members, adopts a resolution requesting that the Commission submit legislative proposals.[88]

Similarly, the Commission is not legally obliged to comply with a request addressed to it by Member States wishing to establish enhanced cooperation between themselves. If the Commission fails to submit a proposal to the Council, 'it shall inform the Member States concerned of the reasons for not doing so' (Article 329(1), first subpara. TFEU).[89] By the same token, the Commission is not obliged to comply with a request for a proposal submitted by citizens in accordance with Article 11(4) TEU (para. 17-014, *supra*).

An obligation to submit a proposal does exist in those exceptional cases in which the Treaties impose an obligation to legislate (see para. 17-005, *supra*). In such case, a refusal on the part of the Commission to submit a proposal may be challenged by an action for failure to act (Article 265 TFEU). The Commission is also bound to 'submit its conclusions to the Council without delay' in the event that the Council or a Member State requests it to make a recommendation or a proposal pursuant to Article 135 TFEU in order to enable the Council to legislate on specific matters relating to EMU. Having regard to the cautious wording of that article, it does not require the Commission formally to submit a proposal.

---

[85] See also T-2/04, *Korkmaz v Commission* (order), 2006 (no action for annulment possible against the Commission's refusal to submit to the Council a proposal for an appropriate measure).

[86] Unlike Articles 192 and 208 EC. See also the Interinstitutional Agreement between the European Parliament, the Council and the Commission on Better Law-making, OJ 2016 L123/1, point 10 (Commission will reply to such requests within three months stating the intended follow-up and, where no proposal is envisaged, it will indicate the reasons thereto and possible alternatives); Framework Agreement of 20 October 2010 on relations between the European Parliament and the European Commission (OJ 2010 L47), point 16.

[87] See already point 14 of the framework agreement of 26 May 2005 (n. 71, *supra*), point 9 of the interinstitutional agreement of 16 December 2003 on better law-making (n. 58, *supra*) and point 3.3 of the Code of Conduct agreed between the European Parliament and the Commission on 15 March 1995, OJ 1995 C89/69. For action taken by the Commission on the European Parliament's first four legislative initiatives, see its answer of 1 August 1996 to Question No. E-1859/96 (Schleicher), OJ 1996 C345/110.

[88] von der Leyen, *A Union that strives for more—My agenda for Europe—Political Guidelines for the next European Commission 2019-2020*, available at https://ec.europa.eu/info/strategy/priorities-2019-2024_en#documents.

[89] Similarly, the Commission was not obliged to comply with a request made by a Member State for the Commission to submit a proposal for the implementation of former Title IV of the EC Treaty, as it was merely provided that the Commission 'shall examine' any such request (Article 67(2), first indent EC).

II. The Ordinary Legislative Procedure

17.019 **Ordinary legislative procedure.** The ordinary legislative procedure for the adoption of legislative acts, set out in Article 294 TFEU, makes adoption of acts dependent upon the approval by the European Parliament and the Council—the 'co-legislators'—of a Commission proposal. If the co-legislators reach agreement, the act is adopted as a regulation, directive, or decision of both the European Parliament and the Council, signed by both Presidents (see Article 297(1), first subpara. TFEU).

The ordinary legislative procedure replaces the former 'co-decision' procedure set out in Article 251 EC. The ordinary legislative procedure now applies to virtually all fields of action of the Union where the Council has to decide by qualified majority,[90] including PJCC.[91] However, it does not apply in the context of the CFSP.[92]

17.020 **Trilogues.** As set out in Article 294 TFEU, the ordinary legislative procedure provides for successive positions taken by the European Parliament and the Council in a 'first reading' and 'second reading', with direct negotiations between the co-legislators taking place only at the third reading (conciliation stage) and only if a legislative file has gone through the first and second readings without the institutions agreeing on the text.[93] Very soon after the introduction of the co-decision procedure, it became clear that compromise-building was not efficient if the co-legislators could only enter into direct negotiations at the conciliation stage. Although the Treaties do not expressly provide for it, informal 'trilogue' meetings were organized between representatives of the European Parliament, the Council, and the Commission, initially only to prepare for the conciliation meetings. Presently, the institutions started informal negotiations towards 'early agreements' at the second reading or even, once the Treaty allowed for it, at the first reading.

Nowadays, the 'trilogues' have become standard practice in the ordinary legislative procedure, with the majority of legislative acts adopted in the ordinary legislative procedure resulting from compromises agreed in trilogues. In the parliamentary term 2014–2019, this enabled the co-legislators to adopt a legislative act in 89 per cent of the files in the first reading and 11 per cent in the second reading, with not a single file reaching the conciliation stage.[94] As explained below, the trilogues are organized as 'informal' negotiations taking place before or between the 'formal' procedural steps required by Article 294 TFEU.

Trilogues thus developed as a constitutional practice outside the Treaties,[95] reflecting the 'mutual sincere cooperation' that institutions are to practice in the exercise of their

---

[90] However, in some cases the Council acts by qualified majority under a special legislative procedure (para. 17-034, *infra*); see, e.g., Article 311 TFEU.
[91] See, e.g., Articles 81 to 89 TFEU in conjunction with Article 76 TFEU.
[92] See Article 24(1), second subpara. TEU and 31(1), first subpara. TEU, stating that the adoption of legislative acts under the CFSP shall be excluded.
[93] Initially, such agreement was only possible at the second reading. Since the Amsterdam Treaty (1999), it has become possible to adopt a text at first reading if the Council agrees with the position taken by the Parliament on the Commission proposal.
[94] See the European Parliament's *Activity Report—Development and Trends of the Ordinary Legislative Procedure—1 July 2014–1 July 2019 (8th parliamentary term)*, available at https://www.europarl.europa.eu/ordinary-legislative-procedure/en/home.html.
[95] See Van Nuffel, 'The European Union Co-Legislator in Action: Some Thoughts on Trilogues, Transparency and the Trias Politica', in Leysen et al., (eds), *Semper Perseverans—Liber Amicorum André Alen* (Intersentia, 2020), 917–31; Roederer-Running and Greenwood, 'The European Parliament as a Developing Legislature: Coming of

powers.[96] They are not governed by any constitutional or legislative text, but only received some formalization in 2007 in practical arrangements agreed between the European Parliament, the Council and the Commission,[97] and in the Parliament's Rules of Procedure. Each institution mandates its representatives in the trilogues in accordance with their internal working methods. The European Parliament's negotiating team is presided by the Chair of the parliamentary committee responsible for the matter, but led by the MEP who is acting as rapporteur and further consists of 'shadow rapporteurs' from every other political group that wishes to participate.[98] The Parliament's team acts upon the mandate set out in the report adopted in the responsible parliamentary committee as confirmed, where requested, by a vote in plenary session.[99] On behalf of the Council the negotiations are carried out by representatives of the Member State holding the Presidency on the basis of a provisional Council position referred to as a 'general approach'. On behalf of the Commission it is the competent Commissioner and his or her services that take part in the negotiations.

First reading in Parliament. The ordinary legislative procedure begins with the proposal from the Commission,[100] which is submitted to the co-legislators (see Article 294(2) TFEU). The President of the Parliament refers the matter to the competent parliamentary committee (EP Rules of Procedure, Rule 48). The committee verifies whether the proposed act has the correct legal basis, whether it respects the principles of subsidiarity and proportionality and fundamental rights, and whether sufficient financial resources are provided (EP Rules of Procedure, Rules 39 to 43). Generally, the committee adopts a report comprising any draft amendments, a draft legislative resolution, and an explanatory statement (EP Rules of Procedure, Rule 51), on which the Parliament holds a vote at the plenary session (EP Rules of Procedure, Rule 59).[101] In order for the Parliament to give its opinion more expeditiously, its President, a parliamentary committee, a political group, a certain

17.021

Age in Trilogues?' (2017) JEPP 735–54; Reh, 'Is Informal Politics Undemocratic? Trilogues, Early Agreements and the Selection Model of Representation' (2014) JEPP 822–41; Huber and Shackleton, 'Codecision: A Practitioner's View from Inside the Parliament', (2013) JEPP 1040–55; Rasmussen, 'Twenty Years of Co-decision since Maastricht: Inter-and Intra-institutional Implications' (2012) JEI 735–51.

[96] Article 13(2) TEU, see para. 5-044, *supra*.

[97] See the Joint Declaration of the European Parliament, the Council and the Commission on practical arrangements for the codecision procedure (Article 251 of the EC Treaty), OJ 2007 C145/5. Whereas that declaration refers to the co-decision procedure as applicable at that time, the institutions continue to apply it in the context of the ordinary legislative procedure, taking into account, where appropriate, the amendments made meanwhile to the relevant Treaty provisions.

[98] EP Rules of Procedure, Rule 74(1). See also the Code of Conduct for negotiating in the context of the ordinary legislative procedures, adopted by the Conference of Presidents on 28 September 2017 (published as Annex III to the European Parliament's *Handbook on the Ordinary Legislative Procedure*, November 2017, available at https://www.europarl.europa.eu/ordinary-legislative-procedure/en/home/home.html).

[99] EP Rules of Procedure, Rule 71(2).

[100] For the exceptional cases in which the initiative does not emanate from the Commission, see para. 17-031, *infra*.

[101] Rule 52 of the EP Rules of Procedure sets out two simplified procedures which the chair of a committee may follow provided that no objection is made by a certain number of the members of the responsible committee. First, the chair may move that the committee approve a proposal without amendments (Rule 52(1)). Second, the chair may move that a report be drawn up with amendments, which is deemed to have been adopted if no objection is made. In the latter case, the draft legislative resolution is put to a vote in the plenary session without debate (Rule 52(2)). Furthermore, under Rule 159 any legislative proposal adopted in committee with fewer than one-tenth of the members voting against is placed on the draft agenda of Parliament for a single vote without amendment, unless political groups or a certain number of the members of Parliament have requested in writing that the item be open to amendment. Such items are without debate unless Parliament decides otherwise on a proposal from the Conference of Presidents, or if requested by a political group or a certain number of members.

number of MEPs, the Commission, or the Council may request that a debate on a proposal be treated as urgent. In the event that the Parliament accepts such a request, the consultation is placed on the agenda as a priority item and debate may take place at the plenary session without a (written) report from the responsible committee (EP Rules of Procedure, Rule 163). The Parliament communicates the position it adopts at the first reading to the Council (Article 294(3) TFEU).

17.022 **First reading in Council.** If the Council approves the European Parliament's position, it may adopt the proposed act in the wording that corresponds to the position of the Parliament (Article 294(4) TFEU).[102] As far as the Commission is concerned, this means that, at this stage, it cannot oppose an act on which the Parliament and the Council are in full agreement.[103] However, it must be noted that, in principle, the Council may adopt acts which differ from the proposal from the Commission only by unanimity (Article 293(1) TFEU). Hence, where the Parliament proposes amendments to the Commission proposal and where the Commission does not take over these amendments in an amended proposal, the Council (complying with the applicable voting requirement) must act unanimously. If the Commission does take over the Parliament's amendments in an amended proposal, the Council acts by a qualified majority.

17.023 **Trilogues at the first reading.** Usually the institutions will already hold informal 'trilogues' at the first reading, during which the representatives of the European Parliament will negotiate with the Council Presidency and the Commission on the basis of their respective negotiation mandates. Where the three institutions find an agreement before the Parliament formally adopted a position in plenary, the Council Presidency will communicate to the parliamentary committee that the Council will formally approve the results of the negotiations if they are first confirmed by the plenary of the Parliament.[104] The Commission's agreement with the result of the trilogues implies that it is prepared to amend its proposal along the agreed terms. The Parliament will then adopt (in plenary session) the text on which agreement has been found as its position at the first reading, which will then be approved by the Council by qualified majority (since the Commission amended its proposal in line with Parliament's position). Trilogues may also lead to agreement on a legislative proposal after the Parliament adopted its position in the first reading. In that case, the chair of the committee will inform the Presidency of the Council that if the Council confirms the results of the negotiations in its position in first reading, the Parliament's plenary will be recommended at the start of the second reading to adopt the Council's position without amendments.[105]

---

[102] In that respect, the Treaty of Amsterdam simplified the procedure which, in the version provided for in the original EU Treaty, invariably required both an opinion of the European Parliament and a 'common position' (former Article 189b(2), second subpara. EC). Under that procedure, final approval of the Council was possible only in the second stage, after the Parliament had approved the common position or failed to pronounce upon it in time (former Article 189b(2), third subpara. points (a) and (b), EC).

[103] Once the Council has adopted an act, the Commission of course can no longer withdraw its proposal; see Article 293(2) TFEU.

[104] Joint declaration on practical arrangements for the codecision procedure (Article 251 EC Treaty), OJ 2007 C145/5, point 14.

[105] Ibid., point 18. This is referred to as an 'early' second reading agreement to be distinguished from the second reading agreement reached after Parliament has taken a formal position at second reading.

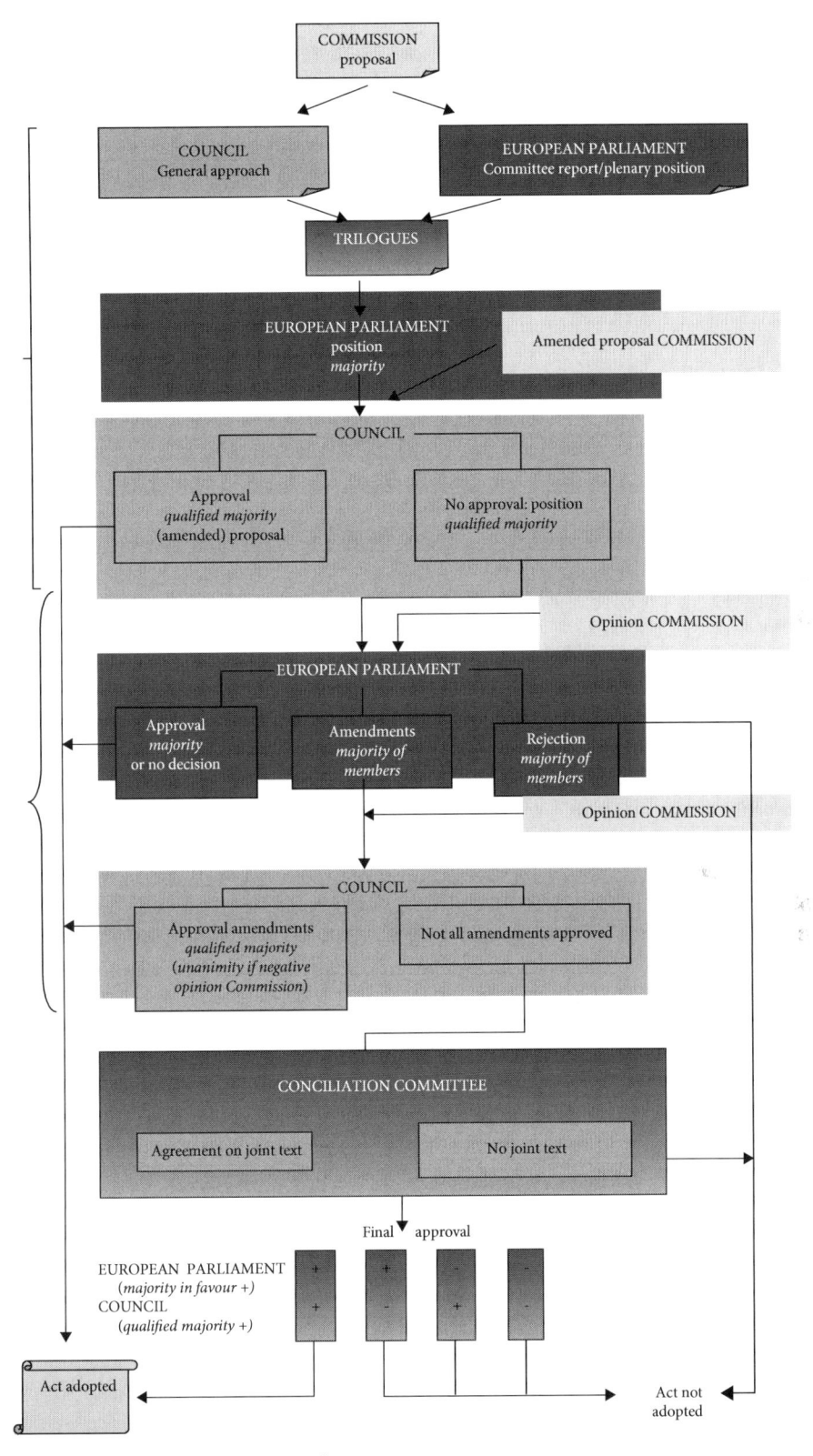

Figure 17.1 Ordinary legislative procedure

17.024 **Initiation of the second reading.** The second reading is opened whenever the Council fails to adopt the position of the European Parliament in the first reading. The Council adopts a position by a qualified majority (Article 294(6) TFEU).[106] The Council is to fully inform the Parliament of the reasons which led it to adopt its position (Article 294(6) TFEU). The Council's position and the statement of reasons are published in the *Official Journal*.[107] The Commission shall fully inform the Parliament of its position (Article 294(6) TFEU). When the President of the Parliament announces the Council's position at the plenary session, it is deemed to have been referred to the committee responsible at the first reading, which draws up a recommendation for the second reading on behalf of the plenary session (EP Rules of Procedure, Rules 63(1) and (2) and 67). The recommendation may propose that the Parliament approve the Council's position, adopt amendments, or reject it.[108]

17.025 **Adoption or rejection by Parliament at the second reading.** If, within three months of the communication of its position by the Council, the European Parliament approves it or has not taken a decision, the act in question is deemed to have been adopted in the wording which corresponds to the Council's position (Article 294(7), point (a) TFEU). Within that period, the Parliament may, however, decide to reject the Council's position. If it does so decide, by a majority of its component members, the proposed act is deemed not to have been adopted (Article 294(7), point (b) TFEU).[109]

17.026 **Amendments by Parliament at the second reading.** Within the same three-month period, the European Parliament may also propose amendments to the Council's position (Article 294 (7), point (c) TFEU). The adoption of amendments requires a majority of the component members of the European Parliament. In its Rules of Procedure, the Parliament has limited its right to move amendments to those which seek (a) to restore wholly or in part the position adopted by the Parliament at its first reading; (b) to reach a compromise between the co-legislators; (c) to amend a part of the text of a Council position which was not included in—or differs in content from—the proposal submitted at the first reading; or (d) to take account of a new fact or legal situation which has arisen since the first reading (EP Rules of Procedure, Rule 68(2)).[110] The Parliament forwards the amended text to the Council and the Commission, whereupon the latter delivers an opinion on the amendments (Article 294 (7), point (c) TFEU).

17.027 **Adoption by Council at the second reading.** If, within three months of the matter being referred to it, the Council, acting by a qualified majority, approves all the European Parliament's amendments, the act in question is deemed to have been adopted (Article 294(8), point (a) TFEU). Since the Council does not decide on a proposal from the Commission in the

---

[106] Before the Lisbon Treaty, the position adopted by the Council in the first reading was called a 'common position' (see Article 251(2) EC).

[107] Council Rules of Procedure, Article 17(1)(b).

[108] A proposal to amend or reject the Council's position may also be made by a political group or by a certain number of MEPs (EP Rules of Procedure, Rules 67(1)).

[109] The Treaty of Amsterdam abolished the possibility for the Council to convene a meeting of the Conciliation Committee in these circumstances. The proposed act was then only deemed not to have been adopted if the European Parliament rejected it again by an absolute majority of its component Members (former Article 189b(2)(c) EC).

[110] The President of Parliament may waive these rules if new elections have taken place since first reading; EP Rules of Procedure, Rule 68(3).

second reading, whether a particular parliamentary amendment succeeds does not depend on whether the Commission is prepared to take it over. Nonetheless, in the second reading the Commission still has a certain influence in that if it delivers a negative opinion, the Council has to act unanimously (Article 294(9) TFEU).[111] Given that the Commission's intervention in the second reading phase is limited to delivering an opinion and that the second reading is centred on the Council's position, it follows from Article 293(2) TFEU that the Commission can no longer amend, let alone withdraw, its proposal.

Trilogues at the second reading. As at the first reading, informal trilogues may take place so as to enable the Council to accept all the European Parliament's second-reading amendments.[112] The negotiators must thereby respect the time-limit of three months for the Parliament and the Council to take their respective positions, which can only be extended by a maximum of one month.[113] If the trilogue results in an agreement before the Parliament has voted, the Presidency of the Council may inform the competent parliamentary committee that the Council will accept the result of the trilogue by way of amendments to its position, provided that the European Parliament will confirm them by a vote in plenary session.[114]

17.028

Conciliation. If the Council, at the second reading, is minded not to adopt all the amendments, the President of the Council, in agreement with the President of the Parliament, convenes within six weeks a Conciliation Committee, composed of the members of the Council or their representatives and an equal number of members representing the Parliament (Article 294(8), point (b), and (10) TFEU).[115] The delegation of the Parliament consists of three members appointed by the political groups as permanent members of the successive Conciliation Committees and other members who are assigned for each separate conciliation, preferentially chosen among the members of the committees concerned.[116] The Conciliation Committee has the task of 'reaching agreement on a joint text' within six weeks of its being convened on the basis of the positions of the co-legislators at the second reading (Article 294(10) TFEU). In order to find a solution, the Committee is to reconcile the points of view of the Parliament and the Council on the basis of examination of all the aspects of the disagreement.[117] Agreement is reached by a qualified majority of members

17.029

---

[111] The Commission undertakes to take the utmost account of parliamentary amendments unless there are important grounds for not doing so, in which case it has to explain its decision: point 37 of the Framework Agreement of 20 October 2010 on relations between the European Parliament and the European Commission (OJ 2010 L47), point 13, reiterating point 31 of the framework agreement of 26 May 2005 (n. 30, *supra*).

[112] See the code of conduct for negotiating in the context of the ordinary legislative procedures, as approved by the Conference of Presidents on 28 September 2017..

[113] Article 294(7), (8) and (14) TFEU. It is also to be noted that at the second reading the Parliament needs the majority of its component members for adopting a legislative text deviating from the Council's common position (Article 294(7)(c) TFEU), whereas any approval at the first reading of the Commission proposal or at the second reading of the Council's first reading position merely requires the usual majority of votes cast.

[114] See Joint declaration on practical arrangements for the co-decision procedure (Article 251 EC Treaty), OJ 2007 C145/5, point 23.

[115] The Conciliation Committee does not constitute a delegation of the Council as an institution but represents the views of the 'members of the Council'. See the Joint declaration of the European Parliament, the Council, and the Commission on practical arrangements for the co-decision procedure, OJ 2007 C145/5.

[116] See EP Rules of Procedure, Article 77(3).

[117] Before the Lisbon Treaty, Article 251(4) EC provided that, in fulfilling the task of reaching agreement on a joint text, the Committee was to address the common position 'on the basis of the amendments proposed by the European Parliament'. For the Court, however, this provision did not limit the wide discretion of the Committee

of the Council or their representatives and a majority of the members representing the Parliament. The Commission takes part in the Conciliation Committee's deliberations and takes all necessary initiatives with a view to reconciling the positions of the Parliament and the Council (Article 294(11) TFEU). This means that the Commission is no longer entitled to withdraw its proposal. If no agreement is reached within the time-limit then the proposal is deemed not to have been adopted (Article 294(12) TFEU).

If the Conciliation Committee approves a joint text, the act has to be finally adopted in a third reading by the Parliament by a majority of the votes cast and by the Council by a qualified majority.[118] If one of the co-legislators fails to approve the proposed act within six weeks of its approval by the Conciliation Committee, it is deemed not to have been adopted (Article 294(13) TFEU).[119] Consequently, neither the Council nor the Parliament can force through an act which has not been approved by the other co-legislator.[120]

17.030 **Time-limits.** As far as the time-limits are concerned, all three-month periods may be extended by a maximum of one month and all six-week periods by no more than two weeks at the initiative of the European Parliament or the Council (Article 294(14) TFEU).

17.031 **Commission acting as broker.** Without acting as co-legislator, the Commission plays a key role in the ordinary legislative procedure, in which it acts as an honest broker.[121] After having submitted its proposal, the Commission may facilitate the compromise-building between the negotiation positions of the co-legislators throughout the procedure. The Commission may also formally determine the course of the procedure if it refuses in the first reading to take over the amendments of the European Parliament in an amended proposal or if it delivers a negative opinion in the second reading on the amendments proposed by the Parliament, hence making the Council's adoption of those amendments conditional upon its approving them by a unanimous vote. Accordingly, the Commission's position will prevail— provisionally—if at least one Member State agrees with it.[122]

---

to reconcile the points of view of the Parliament and the Council on the basis of examination of all the aspects of their disagreement: C-344/04, *IATA and ELFAA*, 2006, paras 57–9. Neither is the Committee, in its negotiations, restricted to what is set out in the Commission's proposal; in order to safeguard the Commission's right of initiative, the joint text should, however, have the same subject matter as the original Commission proposal.

[118] The Council acts by a qualified majority even where the joint text finally adopted diverges from the Commission proposal (see Article 293(1) TFEU, which makes an exception for Article 294(10) and (13) TFEU).

[119] See the negative outcome on 1 March 1995 of the vote in the plenary session of the European Parliament on a joint text of a directive on legal protection of biotechnological inventions on which agreement had already been reached between the European Parliament and Council delegations in the Conciliation Committee, OJ 1995 C68/26, and the negative vote on 4 July 2001 on a joint text of a directive on company law concerning takeover bids, OJ 2002 C65E/57.

[120] Under the first version of the co-decision procedure, the Council was entitled to confirm, by a qualified majority vote, the common position to which it had agreed before the conciliation procedure was initiated, possibly with amendments proposed by the Parliament. In that event, the act was finally adopted unless, within six weeks of the date of confirmation by the Council, the European Parliament rejected the text by an absolute majority of its component Members, in which case the proposed act was deemed not to have been adopted (see former Article 189b(6), second sentence EC). For an example, see the decision of the European Parliament of 19 July 1994 rejecting the text on the application of open network provision (OPN) to voice telephony which the Council had confirmed following conciliation in accordance with Article 189b(6) EC (OJ 1994 C261/13).

[121] See Borras, 'The European Commission as Network Broker' (2007) European Integration (online papers) 1–14.

[122] At the Conciliation Committee stage the Commission opinion no longer has influence on the necessary majorities which need to be mustered in the Council and the Parliament—if the conciliation is successful—in order to adopt the definitive act (see para. 17-029, *supra*).

The Commission plays a more limited role where a legislative act emanates from the initiative of a group of Member States, a recommendation by the European Central Bank, or a request of the Court of Justice. In that event, the Commission does not participate in the first and second readings and it is not obliged to take part in the proceedings of the Conciliation Committee. It may therefore not compel the Council to take its decision unanimously. However, the Commission may give an opinion at the request of the Parliament or the Council or on its own initiative (but without this having any impact on the voting requirements in the Council) and it may take part in the Conciliation Committee if it deems it necessary (Article 294(15) TFEU).

Two legislative chambers. In theory, the European Parliament occupies a strong negotiating position vis-à-vis the Council in that it may bring an end to the decision-making process by rejecting the Council's position. Nevertheless, the Parliament does not exercise its right to reject the Council's position lightly.[123] Rejection requires a majority vote of the Parliament's component members. What is more, it serves no purpose for the Parliament to reject the Council's position when the Parliament would like the Union to legislate in the area concerned: in such a case, the Parliament is obliged to 'co-decide' with the Council. The decisive influence exercised by the Parliament is, in practice, not based on its 'negative' veto,[124] but on the fact that the Council cannot adopt any act which has not been expressly or impliedly approved by the Parliament. All in all, the ordinary legislative procedure has developed into a successful way of striking compromises, in consert with the Commission, between the two chambers of the Union legislature.[125]

17.032

Voting requirements and alarm bell procedure. The ordinary legislative procedure is characterized by the possibility for the Council to agree, by qualified majority, with a position adopted by the European Parliament. It is only at the first and second readings that the Council may be required to act unanimously where the Commission does not take over, or gives a negative opinion on, amendments proposed by the Parliament. Before the Lisbon Treaty, the Council was to act unanimously throughout the co-decision procedure in some instances.[126] In those cases, the Lisbon Treaty has provided for qualified majority in the Council.[127] However, when a legislative act cannot, in all its provisions, be covered by a specific legal basis laid down in the Treaties, it must be based on Article 352 TFEU as well—in order to respect the principle of conferral of competence to the Union—which in turn means that the ordinary legislative procedure foreseen in the specific legal basis must be combined with the unanimity requirement from Article 352 TFEU.[128]

17.033

---

[123] For the first two cases, see ns 119 and 120, *supra*.

[124] This was the case with the procedure laid down in Article 189b EC as introduced by the original EU Treaty; n. 120, *supra*.

[125] In the German federal legislative process, a *Vermittlungsauschuss* (conciliation committee), which negotiates between the directly elected *Bundestag* and the *Bundesrat*, consisting of representatives of the *Länder* governments, operates with some success. The Union conciliation system was modelled on the German system, but is not completely comparable with it since the directly elected *Bundestag* retains the principal legislative powers. See Foster, 'The New Conciliation Committee under Article 189b EC' (1994) ELRev 185–94.

[126] See Article 42 EC (social security); Article 47(2), second sentence EC (access to professions); and Article 151(5) EC (incentive measures in the field of culture). Although this restricted, to a considerable extent, the leeway for reaching agreement between the institutions, it meant that the Treaty did not regard the requirement for unanimity as being incompatible with the co-decision procedure.

[127] See Article 53 TFEU (access to professions) and Article 167(5) TFEU (incentive measures in the field of culture).

[128] C-166/07, *European Parliament v Council*, 2009, with case note by Corthaut (2011) CMLRev 1271–96.

Furthermore, with respect to the coordination of national social security systems (Article 48 TFEU), the Lisbon Treaty has introduced an 'alarm bell procedure' or 'emergency brake',[129] allowing any Member State which considers that a draft legislative act would affect important aspects or the financial balance of its social security system to request that the matter be referred to the European Council. In that event, the ordinary legislative procedure will be suspended for a period of up to four months, during which the European Council may decide (by consensus[130]) either to refer the draft back to the Council to have the ordinary legislative procedure resumed, or not to take action, or to request the Commission to submit a new proposal, in which case the act originally proposed will be deemed not to have been adopted. Likewise, an 'alarm bell procedure' has been introduced for certain harmonization measures with respect to national criminal law that the European Parliament and the Council adopt in accordance with the ordinary legislative procedure (Articles 82(3) and 83(3) TFEU). It enables any Member State which considers that a draft directive would affect fundamental aspects of its criminal justice system to request that the draft directive be referred to the European Council. In that event, the ordinary legislative procedure will likewise be suspended for a period of up to four months, during which time the European Council may decide, by consensus, to refer the draft back to the Council to have the ordinary legislative procedure resumed. Within the same time-frame, in case of disagreement, and if at least nine Member States wish to establish enhanced cooperation on the basis of the draft directive concerned, they are to notify the European Parliament, the Council, and the Commission accordingly. In such a case, the authorization to proceed with enhanced cooperation will be deemed to be granted.[131] In practice, this means that no separate decision of the Council, acting by a qualified majority, on a proposal from the Commission and after obtaining the consent of the European Parliament is needed for the Member States concerned to be authorized to adopt, as Union law applicable to them, the draft directive. The automatic authorization to proceed with enhanced cooperation should constitute a powerful incentive for the European Council to try hard to reach a consensus. If it nevertheless fails to do so, Member States that want to go ahead in this sensitive policy area will not be prevented from doing so.

III. Special Legislative Procedures

A. Participation of the Council

17.034 **Unanimity or qualified majority.** Article 289(2) TFEU regards the instances in which the Council does not decide jointly with the European Parliament as 'special legislative procedures', that is to say those cases in which legislation is to be adopted 'by the European Parliament with the participation of the Council' or 'by the latter with the participation of the European Parliament'. The second option is the more frequent one: in this case the

---

[129] See Dougan, 'The Treaty of Lisbon 2007: Winning Minds, not Hearts' (2008) CMLRev 617–703, 643.
[130] See Declaration (No. 23), annexed to the Lisbon Treaty, on the second para. of Article 48 TFEU (OJ 2010 C83/346), which recalls that in this case, in accordance with Article 15(4) TEU, the European Council acts by consensus.
[131] Article 82(3), second subpara. and 83(3), second subpara. TFEU, which refer to Article 20(2) TEU and 329(1) TFEU. See para. 22-010, *infra*.

Council has the power of decision, acting unanimously or by a qualified majority, whilst the European Parliament is consulted[132] (see para. 17-035, *infra*) or has to give its consent[133] (see para. 17-037, *infra*). It is only in a few cases that the Treaties provide that legislation is to be adopted 'by the European Parliament with the participation of the Council'. In that event, the European Parliament acts 'with the approval of the Council'[134] or 'after obtaining the consent of the Council'.[135]

In the field of PJCC, the Union legislature now acts, in principle, under the ordinary legislative procedure. However, in specific cases, a special legislative procedure applies. The Council is to decide by unanimity, after obtaining the consent of the European Parliament, on some important decisions with respect to judicial cooperation in criminal matters,[136] whilst some sensitive aspects of police cooperation require the Council to decide by unanimity after consulting the European Parliament.[137]

B. Participation of the European Parliament

1. Consultation

Duty to consult. Several Treaty articles require the Council to act in accordance with a special legislative procedure, after consulting the European Parliament.[138] In such a case, the Council requests an opinion, which is adopted in accordance with the procedure for the first reading under the ordinary legislative procedure described above. As long ago as 1980,

17.035

---

[132] See Articles 21(3) (measures concerning social security or social protection); 22(1) and (2) (arrangements concerning participation in municipal elections and elections to the European Parliament); 64(3) (measures constituting a step backwards as regards the liberalization of the movement of capital to or from third countries); 77(3) (provisions concerning passports identity cards, residence permits, or any other such document); 81(3) (measures concerning family law with cross-border implications); 87(3) (operational cooperation between police authorities); 89 (operations of police authorities in other Member States); 113 (harmonization of legislation concerning indirect taxation); 115 (harmonization of rules directly affecting the internal market); 118, second para. (creation of European intellectual property rights); 126(14), second subpara. (provisions replacing the Protocol on excessive deficit procedure); 127(6) (conferral of specific tasks on ECB); 153(2), third subpara. (certain measures on social policy); 192(2), first subpara. (certain measures on environment); 194(3) (certain measures on energy); 203 (association of OCTs); 262 (conferral of jurisdiction in relation to European intellectual property rights); 308, third para. (amendments to Statute of European Investment Bank); and 311, third para. TFEU (provisions on own resources of the Union), where the Council is to decide unanimously, and Art. 23, second para. (measures facilitating diplomatic protection) and 182(4) TFEU (specific programmes implementing multiannual framework programmes) where the Council is to decide by a qualified majority vote.

[133] See Articles 19(1) (combating discrimination); 25 strengthening of or adding to rights of citizens of the union); 82(2)(d) (identification of specific aspects of criminal procedure); 86(1) (establishment of European Public Prosecutor's Office); 311, fourth para. (implementing measures for the Union's own resources system); and 352 TFEU (flexibility clause), where the Council is to decide unanimously and Article 311, fourth para. TFEU, where the Council is to decide by a qualified majority.

[134] See Article 223(2) TFEU (adoption of regulations and general conditions governing the performance of the duties of MEPs) and Article 228(4) TFEU (adoption of Ombudsman regulations). In both cases the European Parliament is to act 'after seeking an opinion from the Commission'.

[135] See Article 226, third para. TFEU (detailed provisions on the right of inquiry), which also requires the European Parliament to obtain the consent of the Commission.

[136] See, e.g., the establishment of a European Public Prosecutor's Office (Article 86(1) TFEU). See also, even though not formally described as 'special legislative procedure', the procedure to be followed for extension of the scope of application of judicial cooperation to aspects of criminal procedure not currently mentioned in the Treaties (Article 82(2)(d) TFEU) and the identification of additional areas of crime in respect of which minimum rules may be established (Article 83(1), third subpara. TFEU).

[137] See, e.g., operational cooperation between police authorities (Article 87(3) TFEU) and operations on the territory of another Member State (Article 89 TFEU).

[138] See n. 132, *supra*.

the Court of Justice held that consultation of the Parliament constitutes an essential procedural requirement[139] (see para. 17-010, *supra*).

The fact that it is compulsory to consult the Parliament means that the Council must exhaust all the possibilities of obtaining its opinion in time.[140] The Court of Justice adverted to the possibility for the Council to request the Parliament to declare the consultation a matter of urgency (see para. 17-021, *supra*) or for a request to be made for the Parliament to meet in extraordinary session (Article 229, second para. TFEU). Before the Parliament has delivered its opinion, the Council may consider the Commission's proposal or attempt to arrive at a common approach or even a common position within the Council provided that it does not adopt its final position before it is apprised of the Parliament's opinion.[141]

For its part, the Parliament is under a duty to cooperate in good faith with the Council. Accordingly, the Parliament was not entitled to challenge the Council for adopting a regulation on 21 December 1992 which had to be adopted for political and technical reasons before the end of 1992, without waiting for the Parliament to give its opinion. The Parliament had decided to deal with the proposal for a regulation as a case of urgency on 18 December 1992, during its last session of the year. However, the Parliament decided to adjourn that session without having debated the proposal and it was impossible to convene an extraordinary session of the Parliament before the end of the year.[142]

The Council is bound to consult the Parliament and to allow it a reasonable time to deliver its opinion, but it is not under any duty to state in what way, if any, it took account of it. It is sufficient that the act adopted by the Council refers to the opinion requested (Article 296, second para. TFEU; see para. 27-007, *infra*).

17.036 **Reconsultation of the Parliament.** If the European Parliament is consulted at an early stage in the legislative process, it is possible that the proposal on which it delivered its opinion will be amended in the course of further discussion in Council working parties and Coreper. Further consultation will then be unnecessary if the amended proposal as a whole essentially corresponds to the original proposal (e.g. amendments made regarding only technical aspects or methods)[143] or where the amendments made essentially modified the proposal in the manner indicated by the Parliament.[144] It cannot be argued, however,

---

[139] 138/79, *Roquette Frères v Council*, 1980, paras 33–7 and 139/79, *Maïzena v Council*, 1980, paras 34–8.
[140] 138/79, *Roquette Frères v Council*, 1980, para. 36 and 139/79, *Maïzena v Council*, 1980, para. 37.
[141] C-417/93, *European Parliament v Council*, 1995, para. 10.
[142] C-65/93, *European Parliament v Council*, 1995, paras 24–8 (in which an action for annulment of Council Regulation No. 3917/92 extending into 1993 the application of generalized tariff preferences in respect of products originating in developing countries, OJ 1992 L396/1, was dismissed); see Van Nuffel (1995) Col JEL 504, 511–15. See also the discussion of the duty to cooperate in good faith in para. 5-048, *supra*.
[143] 41/69, *ACF Chemiefarma v Commission*, 1970, paras 68–70; 817/79, *Buyl v Commission*, 1982, paras 23–4; 828/79, *Adam v Commission*, 1982, paras 24–5; 1253/79, *Battaglia v Commission*, 1982, paras 24–5. See, e.g., C-280/93, *Germany v Council*, 1994, paras 38–42; C-417/93, *European Parliament v Council*, 1995, paras 16–26; C-58/01, *Océ Van der Grinten*, 2003, paras 101–2; see Van Nuffel (n. 142, *supra*), 505–9. A change in the legal form of a measure (directive rather than a regulation) does not constitute in itself a substantial change; see T-125/96 and T-152/96, *Boehringer Ingelheim Vetmedica v Council and Commission*, 1999, para. 133.
[144] C-331/88, *Fedesa and Others*, 1990, para. 39; C-13 to C-16/92, *Driessen and Others*, 1993, paras 23–5; C-408/95, *Eurotunnel and Others*, 1997, paras 46–63. The European Parliament itself has determined that the Council may reconsult it where it substantially amends or intends to substantially amend the draft legally binding act on which Parliament originally delivered its position, except where this is done in order to incorporate Parliament's amendments (EP Rules of Procedure, Rule 84(1), which also refers to Rule 61(1), according to which reconsultation may also be sought 'where the nature of the problem with which the proposal is concerned substantially changes as a

that the amendments were essentially in line with what the Parliament was proposing on the basis of opinions not adopted by the Parliament as a whole but only by parliamentary committees.[145]

Since proper consultation of the European Parliament in the cases provided for by the Treaties constitutes one of the means enabling it to play an effective role in the legislative process of the Union, the Council cannot avoid reconsulting the Parliament on the ground that it was sufficiently informed as to the Parliament's opinion on the essential points at issue.[146] If it could, this would seriously undermine the maintenance of the institutional balance intended by the Treaties and would amount to disregarding the influence that due consultation of the Parliament can have on adoption of the measure in question.[147] If the Council fails to reconsult the Parliament on a proposal after substantial amendment, the act in question will not have been lawfully adopted and may be annulled.[148]

2. Consent

Parliament's veto. Since the Single European Act, a number of Treaty articles have required proposed acts to be given the consent of the European Parliament.[149] This means that the act only comes into being if the Parliament approves it. The Parliament takes its decision on the basis of a report from the responsible parliamentary committee recommending that the proposal as a whole be adopted or rejected (EP Rules of Procedure, Rule 105(1)). Given that no amendments may be proposed, consent constitutes *de facto* a right of veto.

17.037

Consent is only rarely used in a (special) legislative procedure. Initially, consent was required outside the legislative process proper only for the accession of new Member States and the conclusion of association agreements.[150] In that context, the Parliament succeeded occasionally in having a real influence on the Union's external policy by attaching conditions to its consent.[151]

At present, the Parliament's consent is required for the adoption of some legislative acts that are to be adopted in accordance with a special legislative procedure,[152] for the adoption of a number of 'institutional' decisions,[153] and for the adoption of acts under the 'flexibility clause' of Article 352 TFEU. In the latter case, it may happen that an act finds its legal basis in a specific Treaty article, providing for the ordinary legislative procedure combined with

---

result of the passage of time or changes in circumstances' or where 'new elections to Parliament have taken place since it adopted its position, and the Conference of Presidents considers it desirable').

[145] C-388/92, *European Parliament v Council*, 1994, para. 17.

[146] C-21/94, *European Parliament v Council*, 1995, paras 24–6.

[147] Ibid., para. 26; see also C-392/95, *European Parliament v Council*, 1997, para. 22.

[148] e.g. C-65/90, *European Parliament v Council*, 1992, paras 20–1; C-388/92, *European Parliament v Council*, 1994; C-21/94, *European Parliament v Council*, 1995, paras 17–28; C-392/95, *European Parliament v Council*, 1997, paras 14–24. See also T-164/97, *Busaca and Others v Court of Auditors*, 1998, paras 79–102.

[149] Before the Lisbon Treaty, the Treaties consistently required the Council to obtain the 'assent' of the European Parliament.

[150] See Articles 237 and 238 EEC.

[151] See the discussion of the part played by the European Parliament in the procedure for the conclusion of international agreements in para. 21-012, *infra*.

[152] e.g. Articles 19(1) (combating discrimination); 25 (strengthening or complementing the rights of Union citizens); 311, fourth para. (implementing measures for the system of the own resources of the Union) TFEU. There is also a special legislative procedure for the adoption of the budget (Article 314 TFEU).

[153] e.g. Article 14(2), second para. TEU (composition of the European Parliament); Article 17(7), third para. TEU (approval of the Commission as a college); Article 127(6) TFEU (conferral of specific tasks upon the ECB).

Article 352 TFEU, because not all the aspects of the legislative act in question are covered by the specific Treaty article. In such a situation, the Council is to act by unanimity throughout the several stages of the procedure based on Article 294 TFEU, while making sure that the European Parliament gives its 'consent' before the final adoption of the act.[154] Furthermore, the Parliament must give its consent for the adoption of important international agreements (Article 218(6) TFEU),[155] for revisions of the Treaties (Article 48(3), second subpara. and (7), fourth subpara. TEU), for the accession of new Member States (Article 49 TEU), for agreements relating to the withdrawal of a Member State (Article 50(2) TEU), and for the suspension of certain rights of a Member State (Articles 7(1), (2) and (5), TEU and Article 354, fourth para. TFEU). In addition, the Council may only authorize Member States to initiate an enhanced cooperation after obtaining the consent of the European Parliament (Article 329(1), second para. TFEU).

IV. Other Procedures

17.038 **Non-legislative procedures.** Since the Lisbon Treaty, only the ordinary legislative procedure and the special legislative procedures lead to the adoption of 'legislative acts' (see para. 17-002, *supra*). Some Treaty articles set out the procedural steps to be taken for the adoption of acts of a general nature without qualifying these steps as a 'legislative procedure'. Some of those non-legislative procedures do not differ from special legislative procedures.[156] With respect to some Treaty provisions, the acts to be adopted may also be of a similar 'legislative' nature to acts adopted pursuant to legislative procedures.[157] However, given the formal definition applied by the Treaties, those acts are not 'legislative acts' in the strict sense of the Treaties (see para. 17-002, *supra*).[158] Whereas most often the Council is the institution designated to adopt such acts, on a proposal of the Commission, there are some Treaty provisions that directly empower the Commission or the European Central Bank to adopt non-legislative acts of a general nature.[159]

17.039 **Various institutional configurations.** In matters where the Council is to adopt acts outside the ordinary legislative procedure and the special legislative procedures, the involvement of the European Parliament is not always guaranteed (see para. 17-040, *infra*). That will be the case where the Treaties require the political Union institutions to agree amongst themselves

---

[154] See, e.g., C-166/07, *European Parliament v Council*, 2009, with case note by Corthaut (2011) CMLRev 1271–96.
[155] The Parliament has reserved the right to adopt recommendations at any stage of the international negotiations (EP Rules of Procedure, Rule 114(4)).
[156] e.g. Articles 74 and 103 TFEU (Council acts on a Commission proposal, by qualified majority, and after consulting the European Parliament).
[157] e.g. Article 103 TFEU, which forms the legal basis for the adoption of instruments such as Regulation No 1/2003 (see para. 9-015) and Article 155(2) TFEU, pursuant to which the Council may implement agreements concluded at Union level by management and labour (see para. 17-044, *supra*). See also Dougan (n. 129, *supra*), 647.
[158] Compare, e.g., Article 43(2) TFEU (ordinary legislative procedure for common organization of agricultural markets) with Article 43(3) TFEU (non-legislative measures on fixing prices, levies, aid, and quantitative limitations); see C-103/12 and C-165/12, *European Parliament and Commission v Council*, 2014, paras 47–86; C-124/13 and C-125/13, *European Parliament and Commission v Council*, 2015, paras 43–82; C-113/14, *Germany v European Parliament and Council*, 2016, paras 53–78. Compare also Article 78(2) TFEU (ordinary legislative procedure for a common European asylum system) with Article 78(3) TFEU (non-legislative acts in an emergency situation); C-643/15 and C-647/15, *Slovak Republic and Hungary v Council*, 2017, paras 57–84.
[159] See para. 17-004, *supra*.

on certain arrangements (see para. 17-042, *infra*). A different procedure is the possibility for the social partners to conclude collective agreements (see para. 17-043, *infra*). Finally, it is worth looking at the specific input of various other bodies in (legislative or non-legislative) procedures leading to the adoption of Union acts of a general nature (see para. 17-045, *infra*).

A. Other involvement of the European Parliament

Consultation. Some non-legislative procedures require the Council to consult the European Parliament before adopting non-legislative acts of a general nature.[160] Still, other articles in the Treaties provide for no involvement of the European Parliament in the adoption of such acts.[161] In such a case, the Council (or the Commission) may validly act without consulting the Parliament. Nevertheless, the political institutions may still seek its opinion.[162] An institution may even undertake to consult the European Parliament as much as possible.[163]

17.040

Information. A number of provisions on financial and economic matters require the Council (or the Commission) merely to 'inform' the European Parliament of acts adopted.[164] In such cases, the European Parliament is informed only after the measure has been adopted and therefore can have no influence on decision-making. The other political institutions have often committed themselves to keeping the European Parliament informed, in particular in the field of external relations. Accordingly, the Council has undertaken to inform the Parliament about trade agreements (see now Articles 207(3) and 218(10) TFEU).[165] The Commission has undertaken to ensure, within its means, that the European Parliament is kept informed and is fully associated with the preparation, negotiation, and conclusion of international agreements and accession negotiations[166] and the preparation and conduct of international conferences,[167] and to take its views into account in the area of the CFSP.[168]

17.041

B. Interinstitutional agreements

Interinstitutional agreements. In addition, the European Parliament has a claim to be involved in decision-making where other institutions have committed themselves to allowing it to play a part. For a long time, interinstitutional agreements have been concluded between

17.042

---

[160] See Articles 74; 78(3); 81(3); 95(3); 103(1); 109; 125(2); 128(2); 140(2); 150; 160; 188, first para.; 322(2); and 349 TFEU.
[161] See Articles 31; 66; 107(3)(e); 112; 122(1); 126(6) to (9); 143(2); 242; and 243 TFEU. See also all the Treaty articles conferring a power of decision on the Commission (para. 12-060, *supra*).
[162] 165/87, *Commission v Council*, 1988, para. 20.
[163] See already the Commission's communication to the European Parliament of 8 June 1973 ((1973) 6 EC Bull. point 1201) and the Council's answer of 25 May 1984 to Question No. 2277/83 (Lady Elles), OJ 1984 C173/17.
[164] See the obligation for the Council under Article 121(2), third subpara. TFEU and for its President under Article 121(5) TFEU (which also puts the Commission under a duty), Article 122(2) TFEU; Article 126(11), second subpara. TFEU; Article 219(1) TFEU; Article 134(3) TFEU; see also Article 155(2) TFEU.
[165] See the Luns-Westerterp procedures, para. 21-005, *infra*.
[166] Framework Agreement of 20 October 2010 (n. 71, *supra*), points 23–26 and 28 and Annex III ('Negotiation and conclusion of international agreements').
[167] Ibid., point 27.
[168] Ibid., point 10. See further C-658/11, *European Parliament v Council*, 2014, paras 69–87; C-263/14, *European Parliament v Council*, 2016, paras 68–85.

the European Parliament and other institutions, on the basis of specific Treaty provisions.[169] Since the Lisbon Treaty, the Treaties expressly provide for the possibility for the European Parliament, the Council, and the Commission to conclude interinstitutional agreements which may be of a binding nature (Article 295 TFEU; see para. 27-049, *infra*). Also outside those provisions, various interinstitutional agreements have been concluded in which the European Parliament, the Council, and the Commission enter into obligations which are binding upon them in so far as they do not infringe provisions of the Treaties or detract from the institutional balance sought thereby.[170] Such agreements may flesh out decision-making procedures or simplify them.[171]

C. Involvement of the social partners

17.043 **Dialogue between management and labour.** The Union recognizes and promotes, at the level of the Union, the role of the social partners—workers' and employers' representative organizations—taking into account the diversity of national systems and facilitating dialogue between the social partners, while respecting their autonomy (Article 152 TFEU). From the outset, workers' and employers' representatives have had an advisory role in Union decision-making as members of the European Economic and Social Committee (EC/EAEC) and of the ECSC Consultative Committee (see para. 13-030, *supra*). The social partners meet regularly for 'tripartite consultation' with representatives of the Council and the Commission; together with the Presidents of the European Council and the Commission they also meet in the form of a Tripartite Social Summit for Growth and Employment (Article 152 TFEU).[172]

The dialogue between management and labour may potentially lead to 'contractual relations' (Article 155(1) TFEU). Under Article 154 TFEU, when the Commission is minded to submit proposals in the social policy field, it has to consult management and labour twice: the first time, on the possible direction of Union action and, the second time, if it considers Union action advisable, on the content of the envisaged proposal (Article 154(2) and (3) TFEU). On the occasion of such consultation, management and labour may inform the Commission of their wish to deal with the matter by agreement or by other contractual relations. They have nine months to conclude the procedure, although an extension may be decided upon jointly with the Commission (Article 154(4) TFEU). However, the Commission is not obliged to take account of the advice given by management and labour or of their wish to deal with a particular matter amongst themselves.[173]

---

[169] See Article 287(3), third subpara. TFEU; before the Lisbon Treaty, see also Articles 193, third para.; 218(1); 272(9), fifth subpara. EC, which authorized the institutions concerned to determine relations *inter se* by 'common accord' or by agreement.

[170] For references to such agreements, case law implementing them, and doctrinal commentaries, see paras 27-049–27-050.

[171] e.g. the Joint Declaration on the implementation of the new co-decision procedure (see n. 97, *supra*) and the interinstitutional agreement of 13 April 2016 on Better Law-making (OJ 2016 L123/1); see earlier the 'conciliation procedure' laid down in the Joint Declaration of the European Parliament, the Council, and the Commission of 4 March 1975 (OJ 1975 C89/1), points 1 and 2.

[172] The Lisbon Treaty introduced this 'Social Summit' in the Treaties. It is held prior to the spring and autumn sessions of the European Council; see Council Decision (EU) 2016/1859 of 13 October 2016 on the Tripartite Social Summit for Growth and Employment, OJ 2016 L284/27.

[173] Watson, 'Social Policy After Maastricht' (1993) CMLRev 481, 503.

Negotiating agreements. In the event that management and labour wish to negotiate an agreement, the negotiation stage is left solely to them. The Treaties do not determine between which social partners negotiations are to be conducted at Union level.[174] The Commission did decide, however, to set up Sectoral Dialogue Committees (composed of equal numbers of representatives from the two sides of industry) promoting dialogue between the social partners at European level.[175] The Treaties provide that if management and labour conclude an agreement, it may be implemented by the Union or by the Member States.

17.044

The Union is empowered to implement such an agreement if the signatory parties make a joint request to that effect, provided that it relates to matters covered by Article 153 TFEU (Article 155(2), first subpara. TFEU). In that event, the Council is to act by a qualified majority on a proposal from the Commission; if, however, the agreement contains one or more provisions relating to one of the areas for which Article 153(2) TFEU requires unanimity, the Council has to decide by a unanimous vote (Article 155(2), second subpara. TFEU). The Council implemented the first agreements concluded by management and labour by means of directives.[176] As a result, the provisions of the agreements are binding on Member States as regards the result to be achieved, but they retain the power to determine the form and methods.[177] The Commission and the Council are in no case obliged to implement agreements at the request of signatory parties. According to the General Court, the Commission is not required to grant a joint request of the signatory parties seeking the implementation of that agreement at Union level and, to that end, submit a proposal for a decision to the Council as this would undercut the Commission's right of initiative under Article 17(1)

---

[174] T-135/96, *UEAPME v Council*, 1998, paras 75–9.

[175] See Commission Decision of 20 May 1998, OJ 1998 L225/27. As far as the 'tripartite social summit' is concerned, the guidelines on the composition of delegations of workers' and employers' representatives are set out in Article 2(3) of Decision (EU) 2016/1859 (n. 172, *supra*). See also the Commission's Practical Guide for European Social Partner Organisations and their National Affiliates (July 2017), available at https://ec.europa.eu/social/main.jsp?langId=en&catId=329.

[176] At cross-industry level, see Council Directive 2010/18/EU of 8 March 2010 implementing the revised Framework Agreement on parental leave concluded by BUSINESSEUROPE, UEAPME, CEEP, and ETUC, OJ 2010 L68/13 (agreement of 18 June 2009 annexed thereto), replacing Council Directive 96/34/EC of 3 June 1996 on the Framework Agreement on parental leave concluded by UNICE, CEEP, and the ETUC, OJ 1996 L145/4 (agreement of 14 December 1995 annexed thereto) and Council Directive 97/81/EC of 15 December 1997 concerning the Framework Agreement on part-time work concluded by UNICE, CEEP, and the ETUC, OJ 1998 L14/9 (agreement of 6 June 1997 annexed thereto). Whereas the first of those directives is based on Article 155(2) TFEU, the two others were still based on Article 4(2) of the Social Agreement. See also Council Directive 1999/70/EC of 28 June 1999 concerning the framework agreement on fixed-term work concluded by ETUC, UNICE, and CEEP, OJ 1999 L175/43 (agreement of 18 March 1999 appended as an annex), which was based on Article 139(2) of the EC Treaty. The parties to the agreements in question are the umbrella organizations for workers (ETUC) and employers in the private (UNICE, now BUSINESSEUROPE) and public (CEEP) sectors. A number of sectoral instruments were based on Article 139(2) EC, e.g., Council Directive 1999/63/EC of 21 June 1999 concerning the Agreement on the organization of working time of seafarers concluded by the European Community Shipowners' Association (ECSA) and the Federation of Transport Workers' Unions in the European Union (FST), OJ 1999 L167/33 (agreement of 30 September 1998 appended as an annex) and Council Directive 2000/79/EC of 27 November 2000 concerning the European Agreement on the Organisation of Working Time of Mobile Workers in Civil Aviation concluded by the Association of European Airlines (AEA), the European Transport Workers' Federation (ETF), the European Cockpit Association (ECA), the European Regions Airline Association (ERA), and the International Air Carrier Association (IACA), OJ 2000 L302/57 (agreement of 22 March 2000 appended as an annex).

[177] The directives in question provide that the social partners themselves may introduce the necessary implementing measures by agreement (cf. para. 18-006, *infra*).

TEU.[178] However, the Council has no power to amend an agreement concluded between the social partners; it merely decides whether a Union-level agreement is to have legislative status. The European Parliament only has the right to be informed (Article 155(2) TFEU). In the absence of any direct involvement of the European Parliament, the democratic legitimacy of such legislation rests on the role played by the social partners as well as on the necessary approval by the Council of the outcome of the negotiations.[179] In order to secure compliance with the principle of democracy, the Commission and the Council must check the representative nature of the social partners concerned in the light of the content of each agreement.[180]

If the Council does not adopt an implementing decision, the agreement in question is to be implemented in accordance with the procedures and practices specific to management and labour and the Member States (see para. 18-006, *infra*). This was the case with the agreements concluded by the social partners on teleworking, work-related stress and harassment, and violence at work.[181] In the absence of implementation by Union legislation, the legal force of agreements concluded between management and labour at Union level remains uncertain, particularly because the question of the framework for the negotiations leading up to the conclusion of such agreements, including guarantees as to the representative nature of the negotiators for the workers and employers concerned, is not regulated.[182]

D. Involvement of other bodies and groups

17.045 **Dialogue and consultation.** Since the Lisbon Treaty, the Union institutions are required to give citizens and representative associations the opportunity to make known

---

[178] T-310/18, *European Federation of Public Service Unions (EPSU) v Commission*, 2019, paras 83–90 (appeal pending, C-928/19 P, *European Federation of Public Service Unions (EPSU) v Commission*, AG Pikamäe Opinion, 2021, paras 68-s72).

[179] T-135/96, *UEAPME v Council*, 1998, paras 88–9. For a critical view of the democratic legitimacy of management and labour, see Langenbucher, 'Zur Zulässigkeit parlamentersetzender Normgebungsverfahren im Europarecht' (2002) ZEuP 265–286; Betten, 'The Democratic Deficit of Participatory Democracy in Community Social Policy' (1998) ELRev 20–36. Indeed, democratic legitimacy requires the involvement of Union institutions; see Britz and Schmidt, 'Die institutionalisierte Mitwirkung der Sozialpartner an der Rechtsetzung der Europäischen Gemeinschaft—Herausforderung des gemeinschaftsrechtlichen Demokratieprinzips' (1999) EuR 467–98. See EP Rules of Procedure, Rule 84, by which the Parliament seeks to play some role in this procedure.

[180] T-135/96, *UEAPME v Council*, 1998, para. 89. The Commission set out criteria to that effect in its communication on the application of the Agreement on Social Policy of 14 December 1993 (COM(93)600 final), as mentioned in the judgment in *UEAPME v Council*. In that judgment, the Court of First Instance (now the General Court) declared inadmissible an action brought for annulment of Directive 96/34/EC (n. 176, *supra*) by the European Union of Crafts and Small and Medium-sized Enterprises (UEAPME), which was not involved in the negotiations on the framework agreement on parental leave. See Lenaerts, 'Le statut de la négociation collective dans la jurisprudence européenne' (2009) RDS/TSR 3, 16–18.

[181] Framework Agreement of 16 July 2002 concluded by UNICE/UEAPME, the CEEP, and the ETUC on telework; Framework Agreement of 8 October 2004 concluded by UNICE/UEAPME, the CEEP and the ETUC on work-related stress; Framework Agreement of 26 April 2007 concluded by BUSINESSEUROPE/UEAPME, the CEEP, and the ETUC on harassment and violence at work (all available from the website of the Commission's DG for Employment, Social Affairs and Equal Opportunities).

[182] See Vigneau, 'Etude sur l'autonomie collective au niveau communautaire' (2002) RTDE 653–83, and, earlier, the issues adumbrated by Vandamme, 'Quel espace contractuel pour les partenaires sociaux après le traité de Maastricht' (1992) RMCUE.788–92; Nyssen, 'Le rôle des partenaires sociaux dans l'élaboration et la mise en oeuvre du droit communautaire' (1993) Ann Dr Louv 319, 328–31; Watson (n. 173, *supra*), at 506–9; Gadbin, 'L'association des partenaires économiques et sociaux organisés aux procédures de décision en droit communautaire' (2000) RTDE 1–46.

and exchange their views publicly in all areas of Union action (Article 11(1) TEU). The institutions are to 'maintain an open, transparent and regular dialogue with representative associations and civil society' (Article 11(2) TEU, see para. 17-046, *infra*). In various areas, legislative procedures, as well as non-legislative procedures, involve compulsory consultation of especially constituted bodies.[183] In the first place, there are the economic and social interest groups, which can make their views known through the European Economic and Social Committee. Various Treaty articles require the Council or the Commission to consult that committee before adopting an act (see para. 13-030, *supra*). The EU Treaty recognized the specific interests of regional and local authorities and set up the Committee of the Regions, which has to be consulted by the Council on certain matters. These are matters in respect of which policy is conducted in several Member States by federated entities or decentralized authorities pursuant to rules on the devolution of powers (see para. 13-033, *supra*). The opinions of those committees are in no way binding, but may influence decision-making if the views they contain are taken up by other Union institutions that have a say in decision-making on the matters in question.

In addition, the Treaties sometimes require institutions or bodies which are considered to have relevant expertise in the field to be consulted. Accordingly, in some cases where the Council[184] or the European Parliament and the Council[185] do not have to decide on a Commission proposal, they must nonetheless 'consult' the Commission. In economic and monetary matters, some Treaty articles require the Commission or the Council to seek the opinion of the Economic and Financial Committee,[186] whilst other articles oblige the Council[187] or the European Parliament and the Council[188] to consult the ECB. In one case, the opinion of the ECB is so crucial that the consultation has to endeavour to reach a 'consensus' between the Council and the ECB (Article 219, first sentence TFEU). In relation to these matters, however, the Commission does not have its full right to submit proposals and the European Parliament is not always involved in the decision-making process.[189]

---

[183] Obradovic, 'Good Governance Requirements Concerning the Participation of Interest Groups in EU Consultations' (2006) CMLRev 1049–85.

[184] Article 129(4) TFEU; Article 302(2) TFEU; Article 49, first para. TEU; Act on the Direct Election of the European Parliament, Article 14. As far as application of Article 259 EC [*now Article 302 TFEU*] is concerned (appointment of members of the European Economic and Social Committee), the Court of Justice has held that it is sufficient for the Commission to be present at the Coreper meeting at which consensus is reached on a decision submitted to the Council as a Part A item of the agenda: 297/86, *CIDA v Council*, 1988, paras 27–30. A Commission opinion is also required by Article 242 TFEU.

[185] Article 129(3) TFEU; Article 281, second para. TFEU. The European Parliament lays down regulations and general conditions after seeking the 'opinion' of the Commission under Article 223(2) TFEU (performance of MEPs' duties) and Article 228(4) of the EC Treaty (Ombudsman Regulations).

[186] For the Commission, see Article 126(4) TFEU and Article 143(1), second subpara. TFEU; for the Council, see Article 134(3) TFEU and Article 144(3) TFEU.

[187] For the ECB, see the general obligation under Articles 127(4) TFEU and the specific obligations under Articles 66; 126(14), second subpara.; 127(6), 128(2); 129(4); 138; 219(1)to (3); 134(3) TFEU; and Article 48 (3) TEU.

[188] See Article 129(3) TFEU.

[189] See the cases where the Commission makes a 'recommendation' (para. 17-012, *supra*) and the European Parliament is merely 'informed' (para. 17-041, *supra*).

V. Democratic Content of Decision-Making

17.046 **Expressions of democracy.** Democracy is one of the values upon which the Union is founded (Article 2 TEU).[190] The basic premise of democracy is that all public authority emanates from the people. In practice this is operationalized through the election of a representative assembly, which participates in the decision-making, or at the very least controls the decision-making process. The Lisbon Treaty introduced a Title II in the TEU 'Provisions on democratic principles'.[191]

The functioning of the Union is founded on representative democracy (Article 10(1) TEU). Article 10(2) TEU adds that 'Citizens are directly represented at Union level in the European Parliament' and 'Member States are represented in the European Council by their Heads of State or Government and in the Council by their governments, themselves democratically accountable either to their national parliaments, or to their citizens'. These provisions find their origin in the EU Constitution. In the EU Constitution it was stated that the democratic life of the Union relies, not only on the principle of 'representative democracy' (in other words, the participation of the citizens through their representatives in the European Parliament and in the national parliaments), but also on the principle of 'participatory democracy'.[192] In this connection, the Lisbon Treaty requires the Union institutions to give citizens and representative associations the opportunity to make known and exchange their views publicly in all areas of Union action (Article 11(1) TEU). The institutions are to 'maintain an open, transparent and regular dialogue with representative associations and civil society' (Article 11(2) TEU), in particular with the social partners (Article 152 TFEU) and with churches, religious associations, and communities and philosophical and non-confessional organizations (Article 17(3) TFEU). This appeal to dialogue is specifically reflected in the obligation imposed on the Commission to carry out broad consultations with parties concerned and to take note of any initiative put forward by a significant number of citizens (Article 11(3) and (4) TEU; see para. 17-013, *supra*).

17.047 **Parliamentary control at Union level.** According to the Court of Justice, the European Parliament's participation reflects the fundamental democratic principle that the people should take part in the exercise of power through the intermediary of a representative assembly (see para. 17-011, *supra*). The European Parliament has a decisive say in the decision-making when the Union institutions act in accordance with the ordinary legislative procedure. However, it results from the foregoing analysis that the European Parliament may not 'co-decide' with the Council on Union legislation in all cases; in some, the Council

---

[190] See C-518/07, *Commission v Germany*, 2010, para. 41.
[191] See, generally, the contributions in Wouters, Verhey, and Kiiver (eds), *European Constitutionalism beyond Lisbon*, (Intersentia, 2009): van Gerven, 'Wanted: More Democratic Legitimacy for the European Union. Some Suppositions, Propositions, Tests and Observations in Light of the Fate of the European Constitution', 147–83; Lenaerts and Cambien, 'The Democratic Legitimacy of the EU after the Treaty of Lisbon', 185–207; Harlow, 'Transparency in the European Union: Weighing the Public and Private Interest', 209–38); Verhey, 'Fostering Executive Accountability in the EU: A Key Issue', 239–58). See also Piris, *The Lisbon Treaty: A Legal and Political Analysis* (Cambridge University Press, 2010), Chapter 3 and Sieberson, 'The Treaty of Lisbon and its Impact on the European Union's Democratic Deficit' (2008) Col JEL 445–65.
[192] See also Peters, 'European Democracy after the 2003 Convention' (2004) CMLRev 37–85; for modern forms of democratic supervision (e.g. via the internet), see Weiler, 'The European Union belongs to its Citizens: Three Immodest Proposals' (1997) ELRev 150–6; Curtin, *Postnational Democracy. The European Union in Search of a Political Philosophy* (Kluwer Law International, 1997).

can even take a decision against the wishes of the European Parliament (see para. 17-010, *supra*). In these cases, areas that used to be subject to parliamentary control in the Member States were transferred to the Union and made subject to a form of decision-making whereby the decisive say was not given to the European Parliament, but to the national governments in the Council. Fortunately, these cases now constitute the exception. The principle is the application of the ordinary legislative procedure. It follows that legislative acts reflect the will of a directly elected body in all areas that are subject to Article 294 TFEU.

Parliamentary control at national level. When legislative acts are not adopted in accordance with the ordinary legislative procedure so that the European Parliament usually only has an advisory role, they do not emanate from a representative assembly but from members of national governments assembled in the Council. This practice is not necessarily undemocratic if the members of government are subject to effective parliamentary control.[193] Consequently, decision-making will exhibit an absolute democratic deficit only in so far as the Member States themselves do not provide for parliamentary scrutiny of action taken by members of government in the Council.[194] The national legal system must ensure that the national parliament is given the necessary information about the activities of the Council and may, possibly, constrain the responsible national minister to comply with the brief given to him or her by the national parliament (see paras 15-006–15-009). Where the Council acts by a qualified majority, this form of political control does not, however, guarantee that every national parliament's view will be reflected in Union legislative acts. It is only where the Council acts unanimously that ministers may be called to account to their national parliament for every act adopted.

17.048

Democracy in a federal structure. The assessment of the democratic character of decision-making at the Union level is therefore intrinsically linked to the 'federal' nature of the Union. Where the European Parliament co-decides on legislative acts, those acts reflect the will of a directly elected representative assembly at Union level, but, as the ordinary legislative procedure involves qualified majority voting in the Council, not necessarily the will of each national parliament. National parliaments only retain control over Union legislation when the Council decides by unanimity. Unanimity voting, however, makes it rather difficult to reach decisions at Union level, and may result in a democratic majority at Union level being prevented from pursuing its views because of a position taken by a minority. The manner in which Union decision-making in a particular area is subject to parliamentary control thus ultimately depends on the political choice to make the decision in that area dependent on the democratic majority at Union level or the democratic majority within each of the Member States. The voice of the European Parliament therefore only makes the decision-making in the Union democratic to the extent that one accepts that policy choices should be made by a democratic majority at Union level.

17.049

In any event, decision-making is only truly democratic if there are also certain guarantees for minorities at Union level. For instance, the minimal representation of small Member States results in an allocation of the seats in the European Parliament and the votes in the

---

[193] See Auel, 'Democratic Accountability and National Parliaments: Redefining the Impact of Parliamentary Scrutiny in EU Affairs' (2007) ELJ 487–504.
[194] This also applies to regional ministers who act in the Council (by agreement) and have to answer to their representative assemblies.

Council that do not correspond exactly with the share of each Member State in the total population of the Union. In the same vein, the veto right that Member States retain in areas where the Council decides by unanimity is necessary to avoid the decision-making resulting in decisions that are unacceptable for one or more Member States. This is the procedural translation of the obligation resting on the Union to respect the national identity of each Member State (Article 4(2) TEU). In such a 'federal' system judicial review is needed as a means to ensure the conformity of Union decisions with the checks and balances laid down in the Treaties. It is the task of the Court of Justice of the European Union to carry out that review. It enjoys a 'monopoly' in that respect,[195] known in the German literature as the *Verwerfungsmonopol* of Union acts.

17.050 **Dual democratic legitimacy.** The democratic quality of Union decision-making thus ultimately depends on the dual democratic legitimacy of, on the one hand, the directly elected European Parliament, which defends the common interest, and, on the other hand, the national parliaments, which supervise the manner in which governments defend the Member State interests in the Council. In this way, in its judgments of 12 October 1993 (the '*Maastricht Urteil*') and 30 June 2009 (the '*Lissabon Urteil*'), the German *Bundesverfassungsgericht* (Constitutional Court) held that although, as European integration stands, the European Parliament constitutes a supplementary democratic support for the European Union, the Union still obtains its actual democratic legitimacy from the control that the national parliaments exercise over it.[196] In the view of the European Court of Human Rights, however, the European Parliament, which derives democratic legitimation from the direct elections by universal suffrage, must be seen as reflecting concerns as to 'effective political democracy' within the European Union.[197] In any event, the changes to the decision-making process introduced by the Lisbon Treaty build on precisely this idea of the dual democratic legitimacy of the Union.[198] In those cases where the Council decides by a qualified majority vote, the ordinary legislative procedure now normally applies and, therefore, the European Parliament has a decisive say (see para. 17-019 *et seq., supra*). In those cases where the Council decides by unanimity, the ordinary legislative procedure generally does not apply, but the national parliaments are able to exercise decisive control over the position which the national government adopts in the Council. In all cases, the Lisbon Treaty reinforces the mechanisms which facilitate control by national parliaments over the activities of their respective members of government in the Council (see para. 15-006 *et seq., supra*).

---

[195] C-314/85, *Foto-Frost*, 1987, paras 12–20.
[196] See paras 39–45 of the first judgment and para. 276 *et seq.* of the second judgment (for references to the text of the judgment and commentaries, see para. 23-029, *infra*).
[197] European Court of Human Rights, judgment of 18 February 1999, *Matthews v United Kingdom*, No. 24833/94, para. 52.
[198] On the similar changes to the decision-making process introduced by the EU Constitution, see Sommermann, 'Verfassungsperspektiven für die Demokratie in der erweiterten Europäischen Union: Gefahr der Entdemokratisierung oder Fortentwicklung im Rahmen europäischer Supranationalität?' (2003) DöV 1009–17.

18
The Implementation of Union Legislation

Duty to implement. The Treaties did not set up a uniform system for the implementation of Union legislation: where necessary, each act determines its implementation procedures itself; where the act in question does not do so, the principle applies that 'Member States shall take any appropriate measure, general or particular, to ensure fulfilment of the obligations arising out of the Treaties or resulting from the acts of the institutions of the Union' (Article 4(3), second subpara. TEU). Since the Lisbon Treaty, the Treaties state that Member States are to adopt 'all measures of national law necessary to implement legally binding Union acts' (Article 291(1) TFEU). Accordingly, Union law is implemented as a rule by (using the term coined at the time of the European Communities) *administration communautaire indirecte*. Whether a legislative act provides for implementation at Union level (*administration communautaire directe*), or leaves implementation entirely to the Member States, in either case the enforcement of the rules of Union law and the imposition of sanctions for breaches thereof fall primarily to the national administrative and judicial authorities. The Commission is empowered to conduct administrative inquiries itself and to fine individuals only very exceptionally.[1] The following sections discuss, first, implementation by the Member States and, subsequently, implementation by Union institutions, bodies, offices, or agencies.

18.001

I. Implementation by the Member States

Executive federalism. Article 4(3) TEU puts Member States under a duty to implement provisions of Union law so as to ensure fulfilment of the obligations contained therein. Member States are to adopt all measures of national law necessary to implement legally binding Union acts (Article 291(1) TFEU).[2] Where a piece of Union legislation makes no specific provision, its implementation is a matter, in the first place, for the Member States.[3] In this respect the Union exhibits characteristic features of a federal system in which legislative power is assigned to the federation, but executive power is vested in the federated entities (*executive federalism, Vollzugsföderalismus*). The Treaties expressly establish such a system with regard to directives, which, after adoption by the Union legislature, are binding on the Member States as to the result to be achieved, but leave the choice of the form and methods by which they are incorporated into national law to the national authorities (Article 288, third para. TFEU). Although in theory, therefore, directives leave certain

18.002

---

[1] Paras 9-016–9-018, *supra* (competition cases). For the allocation of powers of implementation, see Möllers, 'Durchführung des Gemeinschaftsrechts' (2002) EuR 483–516.
[2] See also Dubey, 'Administration indirecte et fédéralisme d'exécution en Europe' (2003) CDE 87–133.
[3] T-492/93 and T-492/93 R, *Nutral v Commission*, 1993, para. 26, upheld by C-476/93 P, *Nutral v Commission*, 1995, para. 14.

policy choices to the Member States, in practice they are often formulated in such detail that the Member States are left only with the task of implementing them mechanically. The obligation to implement Union legislation also applies where it is cast in a different form (e.g. that of a regulation) but its substance needs specifying or it has to be applied in individual cases in order for it to be effective.[4] In many cases, Member States also have to legislate in order to be able to apply and enforce implementing rules adopted by Union institutions, bodies, offices, or agencies themselves and in order to be able to impose sanctions in the event of their breach.[5]

When implementing acts in the field of police and judicial cooperation in criminal matters, Member States may invoke the responsibilities incumbent upon them with regard to the maintenance of law and order and the safeguarding of internal security (Article 72 TFEU). Since the Lisbon Treaty, the Treaties provide for specific forms of parliamentary control over the Union's policy in the area of freedom, security, and justice. The European Parliament and the national parliaments are to be associated in the objective and impartial evaluation of the implementation of the Union's policies at national level which is to be conducted by the Member States in collaboration with the Commission (Article 70 TFEU).

18.003 **Domestic organization of implementation.** The Member States carry out their task of implementing Union law in accordance with their particular constitutional traditions. Depending on the subject matter, the implementation of a Union provision may fall within the remit of legislative or executive bodies at national or regional level.[6] Each such body is under a duty to amend domestic law so as to make it conform with Union law.[7] The division of powers within a Member State does not preclude a breach of the duty to implement Union legislation from being invariably imputed to the State itself at Union level 'whatever the agency of the State whose action or inaction is the cause of the failure to fulfil its obligations, even in the case of a constitutionally independent institution'.[8]

18.004 **Supervision of correct implementation.** The Commission, as guardian of the Treaties, supervises the ways in which Member States implement Union law. The Commission may bring an action under Article 258 TFEU against a Member State which fails to fulfil its obligations to implement Union law (see para. 29-039 *et seq., infra*). If the Court of Justice finds that the Member State has indeed failed to fulfil its obligations, the State will be required

---

[4] See, e.g., 30/70, *Scheer*, 1970, para. 10; 137/80, *Commission v Belgium*, 1981, paras 3–9 (a Member State is under a duty to adopt the necessary implementing measures so as to apply the regulation establishing the Staff Regulations of Union officials).
[5] See Curtin and Mortelmans, 'Application and Enforcement of Community Law by the Member States: Actors in Search of a Third Generation Script', in Curtin and Heukels (eds), *Institutional Dynamics of European Integration. Essays in Honour of Henry G. Schermers*, Vol. II (Martinus Nijhoff, 1994), 423–66.
[6] 96/81, *Commission v Netherlands*, 1982, para. 12.
[7] See 314-316/81 and 83/82, *Waterkeyn*, 1982, para. 14 (bodies exercising legislative power and the judiciary); C-8/88, *Germany v Commission*, 1990, para. 13 (federated States and other territorial authorities). For judicial bodies, see para. 7-045, *supra*.
[8] 77/69, *Commission v Belgium*, 1970, para. 15; 8/70, *Commission v Italy*, 1970, para. 9. See also 30/72, *Commission v Italy*, 1973, para. 11 (a Member State must take account, in its domestic legal system, of the consequences of its adherence to the Union and, if need be, adapt its budgetary procedures accordingly); C-423/00, *Commission v Belgium*, 2002 (Member State held to be in breach because a cooperation agreement between the federal authority and regional authorities was required for implementation and could not be approved by those entities in time); C-543/17, *Commission v Belgium*, 2019 (Member State in breach because of the failure by one region to implement a directive in a timely manner). For liability on the part of Member States for decentralized/devolved authorities, see para. 18-005, *infra*.

to take the necessary measures to comply with the Court's judgment, failing which the Court may impose a lump sum and/or a penalty payment if second proceedings are brought (Article 260(1) and (2) TFEU).[9] As the Court held in 1963 in *Van Gend & Loos* (see para. 1-026, *supra*), individuals who have a direct interest in the correct implementation of Union law may make sure that Member States fulfil their obligations in respect of the implementation of Union law. This is because, under Article 4(3) TEU, the national courts are under a duty to secure the effectiveness (*effet utile*) of Union law. Individuals deriving rights from that law may have them enforced in a non-discriminatory manner by the courts. Since the 1991 judgment in *Francovich*, they may claim damages from a Member State whose breach of Union law causes them to suffer loss or damage. For the sake of the uniform application of Union law, this holds good irrespective of whether the breach committed within the national legal order is attributable to the legislature, the executive, or the judiciary (see para. 23-019, *infra*).

Participation of regions in implementation. The Member States are at liberty to leave implementation of some aspects of Union law to federated or decentralized entities, provided that that allocation of powers enables the Union measures to be implemented correctly. In 'federal' Member States (Belgium, Germany, and Austria) or 'regionalized' Member States (Italy, Spain) the national constitution confers on regional authorities a degree of decision-making autonomy. In other Member States only some areas have been granted a form of autonomous decision-making (Finland, Portugal). The mere fact that different regional bodies of a Member State lay down different rules for the implementation of Union rules encompassing minimum requirements does not constitute discrimination contrary to Union law.[10]

18.005

Here, too, the rule applies that at Union level only the Member State is responsible for implementing Union norms, even though the matter falls within a domain for which domestically only the regional authorities are competent to act. This can be illustrated by the practice of Belgium, which has been adding a declaration to its Minister's signature of amending Treaties and accession Treaties stating that that signature also binds the Belgian federated entities (regions and communities). That practice is based on a statement whereby Belgium confirms that, regardless whether the Treaty is signed by a minister of the federal, community or regional governments, 'it will in all cases be the Kingdom as such that is bound, in respect of its whole territory, by the provisions of the Treaties which it has concluded', and that 'the Kingdom alone, as such, will bear full responsibility for compliance with the obligations entered into in the Treaties concerned'.[11] Thus, the 'Kingdom of Belgium' has been condemned to pay a lump sum and a penalty payment pursuant to Article 260 TFEU because

---

[9] See para. 29-053, *infra*. e.g. C-533/11, *Commission v Belgium*, 2013, paras 31–4 and 49–74 (lump sum and penalty payment for failure to comply with C-27/03, *Commission v Belgium*, 2004). Where the Commission brings a case before the Court on the ground that the Member State concerned has failed to fulfil its obligation to notify measures transposing a directive, the Court can impose these sanctions without there being a need for the Commission to bring a second action pursuant to Article 260(3) TFEU (see para. 29-052); see C-543/17, *Commission v Belgium*, 2019, paras 47–68 and 78–93 (penalty payment); C-549/18, *Commission v Romania*, 2020, paras 44–56 and 64–87 (lump sum); C-550/18, *Commission v Ireland*, 2020, paras 54–66 and 74–99 (lump sum).

[10] C-428/07, *Horvath*, 2009, paras 47–57. See also C-156/13, *Digibet and Albers*, 2014, paras 33–8 (a difference in domestic legislation between regions within a Member State is not proof as such that this domestic legislation is not appropriately pursuing certain objectives).

[11] Statement by the Kingdom of Belgium on the signing of treaties by the Kingdom of Belgium as a Member State of the European Union, OJ 1998 C351/1.

the Belgian regions failed to provide for adequate urban waste-water treatment facilities in a number of districts.[12]

Where a Member State is held liable for the conduct or failure to act of a decentralized body, it is not entitled to hide behind the domestic division of powers or federal structure either to avoid the Court of Justice making a finding of an infringement[13] or to escape its obligation to bring such infringement to an end.[14] Consequently, a Member State may not rely on the defence that, under national constitutional law, the federal executive has no authority to give instructions to a regional legislative authority which is in breach of its Treaty obligations.[15] By contrast, the fact that a regional legislative authority is sufficiently autonomous under national constitutional law may be relevant for the establishment of a breach of Union law, in particular in the field of State aid.[16] Each Member State must ensure that individuals obtain reparation for damage caused to them by non-compliance with Union law, whichever public authority is responsible for the breach and whichever public authority is, in principle, under the law of the Member State concerned, responsible for making reparation.[17] Each Member State's constitutional system must ensure that Treaty obligations are complied with.

In some Member States, the national authorities may take the place of the region in breach and do what is necessary in order to bring infringements of Union law to an end.[18] Such

---

[12] C-533/11, *Commission v Belgium*, 2013, para. 74 (lump sum and penalty payment under Article 260(2) TFEU for failure by regional authorities to comply with earlier judgment); see also C-543/17, *Commission v Belgium*, 2019, para. 93 (penalty payment under Article 260(3) TFEU for failure by one region to communicate to the Commission its provisions for implementing a directive in a timely manner).

[13] See already 69/81, *Commission v Belgium*, 1982, para. 5. See, more recently, C-274/98, *Commission v Spain*, 2000, para. 20; C-383/00, *Commission v Germany*, 2002, para. 18; C-388/01, *Commission v Italy*, 2003, paras 25–6; C-357/03 *Commission v Austria*, 2004, para. 10; C-358/03 *Commission v Austria*, 2004, para. 13. See also C-46/98, *Carmen Media Group*, 2010, paras 69–70 (federal government and German *Länder* are collectively responsible for ensuring free movement of services), and compare with C-156/13 *Digibet and Albers*, 2014, para. 35 (distinguishing between the vertical relationship and possible duty of coordination between the authorities of the *Land* concerned and the federal authorities, and the horizontal relationship between the *Länder* having their own legislative powers).

[14] 96/81, *Commission v Netherlands*, 1982, para. 12; 227–230/85, *Commission v Belgium*, 1988, paras 9–10.

[15] C-323/96, *Commission v Belgium*, 1998, paras 40–42 (in which judgment was given against Belgium because the Flemish Parliament had infringed Union rules on the award of public contracts).

[16] See C-88/03, *Portugal v Commission*, 2006; C-428/06, C-429/06, C-430/06, C-431/06, C-432/06, C-433/06, and C-434/06, *Unión General de Trabajadores de la Rioja*, 2008 (aid measures adopted by a sufficiently autonomous region could not be held to be selective in that they relate to a particular region only, and hence do not constitute State aid prohibited by Union law); C-524/14 P, *Commission v Hansestadt Lübeck*, 2016, paras 40–66 (aid given by region to a regional airport not deemed selective in the absence of proof that airliners serving other airports of the Member State not receiving the aid were comparable to the airliners serving the regional airport receiving aid); C-236/16 and C-237/16, *Asociación Nacional de Grandes Empresas de Distribución (ANGED)*, 2018, para. 29. See also para. 9-022, *supra*.

[17] C-302/97, *Konle*, 1999, para. 62 (territorially decentralized body may be held liable); C-424/97, *Haim*, 2000, paras 61–2 (functionally decentralized body may be held liable); C-224/01, *Köbler*, 2003, paras 44–7 and 50 (Member State must designate the court competent to determine disputes concerning the reparation of damage resulting from judicial decisions). See Anagnostaras, 'The Allocation of Responsibility in State liability Actions for Breach of Community Law: A Modern Gordian Knot?' (2001) ELRev 139–58. As to calling into account a Belgian region, see Verhoeven, 'The Application in Belgium of the Duties of Loyalty and Cooperation' (2000) SEW 328, 331–2.

[18] Pursuant to Article 169 of the consolidated Belgian Constitution, Article 16(3) of the Special Law of 8 August 1980 on institutional reform provides that the Belgian State may act instead of a Belgian Community or Region where judgment is given against the State by an international or supranational court following a failure on the part of the Community or Region concerned to comply with an international or supranational obligation. For that substitution mechanism, see Ingelaere, 'De Europeesrechtlijke raakvlakken van de nieuwe wetgeving inzake de internationale bevoegdheid van de Belgische Gemeenschappen en Gewesten' (1994) SEW 67, 76–79; Lejeune, 'Le droit fédéral belge des relations internationales' (1994) RGDIP 578, 619–21; for the limits to the federal State's ability to act in the place of the Community or Region, see Louis and Alen, 'La Constitution et la participation à la Communauté européenne' (1994) BTIR 81, 99–103.

mechanism will normally require a prior finding of infringement by the Court of Justice.[19] Furthermore, the national authorities may sometimes recover from the region concerned all costs incurred as a result of the infringement (including any damages which have had to be paid).[20]

Although the Treaties do not impose any obligation to 'rule on the division of competences by the institutional rules proper to each Member State, or on the obligations which may be imposed on federal and [federated] authorities respectively', they do impose requirements with regard to the effectiveness of the domestic arrangements, that is to say, as to 'whether the supervisory and inspection procedures established according to the arrangements within the national legal system are in their entirety sufficiently effective to enable the Union requirements to be correctly applied'.[21] To this end, domestic law often has to be adapted. Thus the requirement to notify the Commission of all implementing measures already adopted puts the Member State under a duty not merely to rely on a general principle of loyalty of the federated entities towards the federation (e.g. the German *Grundsatz des bundesfreundlichen Verhaltens*) but expressly to require the federated entities (e.g. the *Länder*) to notify the measures they take to the federation.[22] Decentralized authorities should apply Union provisions having direct effect even if this means refraining from applying provisions emanating from a superior authority within their Member State.[23]

Implementation by the social partners. In social matters, Member States may leave the implementation of Union provisions to be agreed between management and labour.[24] Article 153(3) TFEU provides that a Member State may entrust management and labour, at their joint request, with the implementation of directives adopted pursuant to that article and of Council decisions implementing, at Union level, agreements between management and labour (see Article 155 TFEU)[25]. In such a case, the Member State is to ensure that management and labour introduce the necessary measures by agreement within the period

18.006

---

[19] See C-357/03, *Commission v Austria*, 2004, para. 8. In Belgium, however, Article 16(4) of the Special Law of 8 August 1980 on institutional reform enables the State, with respect to international or European Union obligations to reduce reduction of greenhouse gases, to act instead of a Belgian Community or Region if the latter does not respond to a reasoned opinion issued by the Commission under Article 258 TFEU (or has been found non-compliant by a body under the UN Framework Convention on Climate Change). See Alen and Haljan (eds), *Constitutional Law in Belgium* (Wolters Kluwer, 2020), 314–15.

[20] It is a matter of national law to determine to what extent a fine can be passed onto the defaulting regional authority. In Belgium, e.g., see Article 5 of the cooperation agreement between the Federal Government, the Communities, the Regions, and the Community commissions pertaining to the implementation of Article 3, § 1 of the Treaty on Stability, Coordination and Governance in the Economic and Monetary Union, *Belgisch Staatsblad/Moniteur belge*, 18 December 2013. For the difficulties this may pose, see Bams and Corthaut, 'De financiering van de Gemeenschappen en de Gewesten na de Zesde Staatshervorming—Responsabilisering in de schaduw van Europa', in Alen et al. (eds), *Het federale België na de Zesde Staatshervorming* (die Keure, 2014), 618. For the substitution of the State and the recovery of costs in Austria, see Schäffer 'Europa und die österreichische Bundesstaatlichkeit' (1994) DöV 181, 192; for Germany, see Härtel, 'Durchsetzbarkeit von Zwangsgeld-Urteilen des EuGH gegen Mitgliedstaaten' (2001) EuR 617, 628–30; for the possibility of substitution (in the broad sense) in Spain and the United Kingdom before its withdrawal, see Ross and Salvador, 'The Effect of Devolution on the Implementation of European Community Law in Spain and in the United Kingdom' (2003) ELRev 210, 218–27.

[21] C-8/88, *Germany v Commission*, 1990, para. 13.

[22] C-237/90, *Commission v Germany*, 1992, paras 23, 25, and 29. See also C-151/12 *Commission v Spain*, 2013, paras 30–8.

[23] 103/88, *Fratelli Costanzo*, 1989, paras 31–3.

[24] See Steyger, 'European Community Law and the Self-Regulatory Capacity of Society' (1993) JCMS 171–90.

[25] As regards agreements concluded at Union level, the Council implementing 'decision' normally takes the form of a 'directive': see para. 17-044, *supra*. On the fact that such 'implementing' decision is constitutive in the legislative process rather than a form of 'implementation', see n. to para. 18-012, *infra*.

prescribed for transposing the directive or decision in question, and must take any necessary measure enabling it at any time to be in a position to guarantee the results imposed by the directive or the decision (Article 153(3), second subpara. TFEU). Accordingly, the national authorities must see to it that workers who do not benefit from the protection of the directive or decision by other means, in particular where they are not members of a trade union, where they are not covered by a collective agreement, or where such an agreement does not fully guarantee the protection in question, are in fact covered.[26] Also, in the case of agreements concluded by management and labour at Union level, if the Council does not adopt an implementing act, such an agreement is to be implemented 'in accordance with the procedures and practices specific to management and labour and the Member States' (Article 155(2), first subpara. TFEU). The Treaties give no indication as to whether or not there is an obligation for the Member States themselves to implement such an agreement. It appears from a declaration on that Treaty provision that this was not the intention of the Contracting Parties.[27]

18.007 **Uniform and full application of Union law.** In the absence of common rules in the matter, the Member States act, when implementing Union law, in accordance with the procedural and substantive rules of their own national law. In so doing, however, they must always pay due regard to the requirements of the uniform application of Union law.[28] The implementation of Union law may not create unequal treatment between persons. The need to ensure that Union law is fully applied requires Member States not only to bring their legislation into conformity with Union law but also to do so by adopting rules of law capable of creating a situation which is sufficiently precise, clear, and transparent to allow individuals to know the full extent of their rights and rely on them before the national authorities.[29] Where national legislation has been the subject of different relevant judicial constructions, some leading to the application of that legislation in compliance with Union law, others leading to the opposite application, it must be held that, at the very least, such legislation is not sufficiently clear to ensure its application in compliance with Union law.[30]

In order to ensure the uniform and full application of Union law, the Union legislature may indicate precisely what implementing measures the Member States must adopt and what sanctions they must provide. In the absence of any provision in the Union rules laying down specific sanctions, the Member States are free to adopt such sanctions as appear to them

---

[26] 143/83, *Commission v Denmark*, 1985, para. 8; C-306/07, *Andersen*, 2008, paras 25–34; C-405/08, *Ingeniørforeningen i Danmark*, 2010, paras 39–45. See Adinolfi, 'The Implementation of Social Policy Directives Through Collective Agreements?' (1988) CMLRev 291–316.

[27] Declaration (No. 27), annexed to the Amsterdam Treaty, on Article 118b *[later Article 139](2)* of the Treaty establishing the European Community [*now Article 155 TFEU*] envisages the 'first' of the arrangements for application of the agreements between management and labour as taking the form of collective bargaining according to the rules of each Member State and involving 'no obligation on the Member States to apply the agreements directly or to work out rules for their transposition, nor any obligation to amend national legislation in force to facilitate their implementation' (OJ 1997 C340/136). This declaration takes over the wording of Declaration (No. 2) on Article 4(2) of the Social Agreement (the wording of which was taken over by Article 139 EC); see in this sense T-310/18, *European Federation of Public Service Unions (EPSU) v Commission*, 2019, para. 63 (appeal pending, C-928/19 P, *European Federation of Public Service Unions (EPSU) v Commission*, AG Pikamäe Opinion, 2021, para. 75.

[28] 205-215/82, *Deutsche Milchkontor*, 1983, para. 17.

[29] C-162/99, *Commission v Italy*, 2001, para. 22; C-313/99, *Mulligan*, 2002, paras 46–54. The obligation to implement has been clarified in the case law principally with regard to directives; para. 27-019, *infra*.

[30] C-129/00, *Commission v Italy*, 2003, para. 33, with annotations by Peerbux-Beaugendre (2004) RTDE 201–15; Mortelmans, van der Gronden (2004) AAe 192–205, and Serena Rossi (2005) CMLRev 829–49.

to be appropriate, including criminal sanctions.[31] In any event, the Member States must ensure that infringements of Union law are penalized under conditions, both procedural and substantive, which are analogous to those applicable to infringements of national law of a similar nature and importance and make the penalty effective, proportionate, and dissuasive.[32] Moreover, the national authorities must proceed, with respect to infringements of Union law, with the same diligence as that which they bring to bear in implementing corresponding national laws.[33] Where national law contains a general principle according to which everyone is presumed to know the law, that principle may also be applied in the case of sanctions for infringements of Union law.[34] Member States must ensure compliance with the general principles of Union law and fundamental rights when implementing Union law.[35]

II. Implementation by Institutions, Bodies, Offices, or Agencies of the Union

A. Relation between legislation and implementation

Legislation and implementation. Acts adopted at Union level include not only rules of a legislative nature but also detailed provisions which make it possible to implement legislative provisions in practice and decisions which apply legislative and other general rules to individual situations. The Court of Justice stated as follows in this connection: 'The concept of implementation ... comprises both the drawing up of implementing rules and the application of rules to specific cases by means of acts of individual application'.[36]

18.008

Traditionally, it was not easy in the Union legal order to make a formal distinction between legislation and implementation of legislation, in the broad sense defined above.[37]

---

[31] 50/76, *Amsterdam Bulb*, 1977, paras 32–33. For a critical view on the usefulness of criminal sanctions in environmental law, see Faure, 'European Environmental Criminal Law: Do We Really Need It?' (2004) E Env LRev 18–29.

[32] 68/88, *Commission v Greece*, 1989, para. 24; C-326/88, *Hansen*, 1990, para. 17. As far as the ECSC was concerned, this followed from Article 86 ECSC: C-341/94, *Allain*, 1996, paras 23–4. See also the requirement for sanctions for unlawful discrimination to be effective and to have a deterrent effect, 14/83, *Von Colson and Kamann*, 1984, paras 23–24. For sanctions based on violations of humanitarian international law and human rights, see C-84/95, *Bosphorus*, 1996, para. 26.

[33] 68/88, *Commission v Greece*, 1989, para. 25.

[34] C-262/99, *Louloudakis*, 2001, paras 76–7. Where determination of the arrangements applicable has given rise to difficulties, however, account must be taken of the good faith of the offender when determining the penalty actually imposed on him: ibid.

[35] e.g. 201 and 202/85, *Klensch*, 1986, para. 8 (principle of non-discrimination); C-36/99, *Idéal tourisme*, 2000, para. 36 (principle of equal treatment); C-387/02, C-391/02, and C-403/02, *Berlusconi*, 2005, para. 76 (non-retroactivity of harsher penalty); C-42/17, *M.A.S*, 2017, paras 29–62 (nuancing the duty to effectively combat fraud against the Union spelled out in C-105/14, *Taricco*, 2015: national legislation must be disapplied only if that does not lead to a breach of the principle that offences and penalties must be defined by law because of the lack of precision of the applicable law or because of the retroactive application of legislation imposing conditions of criminal liability stricter than those in force at the time the infringement was committed).

[36] 16/88, *Commission v Council*, 1989, para. 11. See more recently, C-440/14 P, *National Iranian Oil Company v Council*, 2016, paras 36–41.

[37] The Treaty only distinguished between 'legislative' and other acts in so far as Article 207(3) EC provided that the Council was to define the cases 'in which it is to be regarded as acting in its legislative capacity' with a view to allowing greater public access to documents in those cases.

The Treaties did not set up separate legislative and executive institutions[38] and it was also impossible to classify the acts that those institutions adopt as legislative or implementing acts on the basis of their form. The distinction between legislation and implementation of legislation was therefore determined in the first place by the type of provision which served as the legal basis for the act in question. If the act was based on an article of the Treaties, it could be regarded as a 'legislative act', at least in so far as its content was also formulated in general, abstract terms. In contrast, implementing (or executive) acts were involved where they were based on legislative acts (or on earlier implementing acts).

Since the Lisbon Treaty, a formal distinction is made between legislative acts and other, non-legislative, acts of the Union. For a start, the Treaties now lay down a definition of 'legislative acts' (see para. 17-002, *supra*). In addition, they provide for two specific forms of Union executive acts, that are now also formally distinguishable from the instruments used for the adoption of legislative acts. On the one hand, there are instances where implementation of legislative acts or other binding Union acts is necessary at the Union level. In those cases, the Commission (or, exceptionally, the Council) may adopt 'implementing acts' (Article 291(2) and (4) TFEU). On the other hand, the Treaty of Lisbon has created the possibility for the European Parliament and the Council to delegate the power to supplement or amend the non-essential elements of legislative acts to the Commission acting by means of 'delegated acts' (Article 290 TFEU). Even though delegated acts are, in practice, also used to implement legislative acts—and thus largely meet the criteria set out above in respect of implementation in the broad sense—they are not considered 'implementing acts' in the sense of Article 291 TFEU.[39]

18.009 **General conditions for implementation.** The largest part of the legally binding acts adopted by the Union institutions constitute implementation in the broad sense defined above (including both implementing and delegated acts). Implementation measures are necessary whenever legislative acts or other acts based directly on the Treaties cannot determine every aspect of a particular policy. Where the Union legislature adopts a basic act (a regulation, directive, or decision) pursuant to a Treaty provision and in accordance with a legislative or other Treaty-based procedure, it may thus provide for acts implementing that basic act, whereby the procedure laid down by that Treaty provision no longer plays any role in the adoption of the implementing acts. The institutional balance underlying the Treaty system of power allocation even prohibits the institutions from inserting in a legislative act a 'secondary legal basis' enabling further acts to be adopted in accordance with a less or more stringent procedure than the one laid down in the Treaty (see para. 17-003, *supra*), instead of having recourse to implementing or delegated acts. Both legislative acts and other acts of general application (hereinafter also referred to as 'basic acts') may require implementation at Union level. Where an institution has adopted a basic act that makes provision for implementing powers, it is contrary to the Union's legislative system to apply that act to individual cases with a special procedure that derogates from the rules laid down in the basic act.[40]

---

[38] Indeed, the legislative function is spread over the European Parliament, the Council and the Commission (see para. 17-004, *supra*), whilst the Commission and—exceptionally—the Council also perform executive functions (see para. 18-012, *infra*).

[39] For an overview of the institutional implications of these changes, see Xhaferri, 'Delegated Acts, Implementing Acts, and Institutional Balance Implications Post-Lisbon' (2013) MJECL 557–75.

[40] 113/77, *NTN Toyo Bearing Company v Council*, 1979, para. 21. See also C-313/90, *CIRFS and Others v Commission*, 1993, para. 44 (an individual decision may not impliedly amend a measure of general application); C-246-249/94, *Cooperativa Agricola Zootecnica S. Antonio and Others*, 1996, paras 30–1.

The Court of Justice has ruled that only the Union legislature is competent to lay down the 'essential elements' of a particular subject matter.[41] This is made explicit in Article 290(1) TFEU in respect of delegated acts (see para. 18-010, *infra*). Therefore, provisions that lay down the essential elements of a basic legal regime and whose adoption require political choices falling within the responsibilities of the Union legislature, cannot be adopted in the form of implementing or delegated acts.[42] More generally, a non-legislative act is invalid where it conflicts with the act on the basis of which it was adopted or lays down essential elements of a basic legal regime. The institutions and the Member States, and, in some circumstances, individuals, too, may obtain a court ruling on the legality of an implementing act.[43] The institution empowered to adopt implementing acts must ensure that the implementing act is adopted in the manner prescribed in the basic act and does not go beyond implementation of the principles of the basic act.[44] An implementing act, for example, may not alter the temporal scope of the basic act.[45] An implementing act can only derogate from the provisions of a basic act[46] if such derogation is expressly provided for in the basic act and consistent with its general system and essential elements.[47] Accordingly, an institution may not go against the conditions that that institution itself laid down in a prior act on the basis of which the later act is adopted.[48]

The fact that an implementing act is subordinate to a legislative act forms part of the general hierarchy of Union rules (see para. 23-005, *infra*). In the same way that a constitutional rule of Union law always ranks higher than a legislative act, a legislative act takes precedence over an implementing act.

B. Implementation by the Commission or the Council

1. Delegation to the Commission

Delegated acts. Since the Lisbon Treaty, the Treaties enable the European Parliament and the Council[49] to adopt legislative acts delegating to the Commission the power to adopt 'non-legislative acts of general application' to supplement or amend certain non-essential elements of the legislative act (Article 290(1), first subpara. TFEU). Delegated acts thus involve rules coming within the regulatory framework as defined by the legislative act, but

18.010

---

[41] 25/70, *Köster*, 1970, para. 6; C-240/90, *Germany v Commission*, 1992, paras 36–7.

[42] C-355/10, *European Parliament v Council*, 2012, paras 64–84; C-363/14, *European Parliament v Council*, 2015, paras 46–57; C-540/14 P 16, *DK Recycling und Roheisen v Commission*, 2016, paras 47–56; C-696/15 P, *Czech Republic v Commission*, 2017, paras 75–8.

[43] For some examples, see 22/88, *Vreugdenhil and Others*, 1989, paras 17–25; C-212/91, *Angelopharm*, 1994, paras 31–8; C-244/95, *Moskof*, 1997, paras 27–105; C-106/97, *Dutch Antillian Diary Industry*, 1999, paras 65–6.

[44] 25/70, *Köster*, 1970, paras 6 and 7.

[45] C-93/00, *European Parliament v Council*, 2001, paras 39–43.

[46] 38/70, *Tradax*, 1971, para. 10; C-14/06 and C-295/06, *European Parliament and Denmark v Commission*, 2008, paras 50–3.

[47] 230/78, *Eridania*, 1979, para. 8. See 100/74, *C.A.M. v Commission*, 1975, paras 27–8.

[48] C-393/01, *France v Commission*, 2003, paras 40–60.

[49] Article 290(1) TFEU mentions delegation by 'legislative acts'. It follows that the delegation can also be given by the Council (or by the European Parliament) acting alone where that institution adopts legislation in accordance with a 'special legislative procedure'. See, generally, Bergström and Ritleng (eds), *Rulemaking by the European Commission: The New System for Delegation of Powers* (OUP, 2016); Craig, 'Delegated and Implementing Acts', in Schütze and Tridimas (eds), *Oxford Principles of European Union Law* (OUP, 2018), 716–47; critically of the effects of the Lisbon reform: Tovo, 'Delegation of Legislative Powers in the EU: How EU Institutions Have Eluded the Lisbon Reform' (2017) ELRev 677–705.

which the Union legislature prefers to have adopted by the Commission.[50] These acts of the Commission bear the term 'delegated' in their title (Article 290(3) TFEU). The legislative act must explicitly define the objectives, content, scope, and duration of the delegation of power,[51] which, as discussed above, may not cover the essential elements of an area (Article 290(1) TFEU).[52] The essential elements of basic legislation are those which, in order to be adopted, require political choices falling within the responsibilities of the Union legislature.[53] Moreover, the legislature must specify whether the delegation confers the power to amend the legislative act or to supplement it (in a separate act).[54] It is possible for a delegated regulation to amend a directive, but that practice causes practical difficulties.[55]

The legislative act must explicitly determine the conditions of application to which each delegation is subject.[56] Accordingly, it may provide that a delegated act enters into force only if no objection has been expressed by the European Parliament or by the Council within a given period, and/or that the European Parliament or the Council may revoke the delegation (Article 290(2) TFEU).[57] In the exercise of delegated powers, the Commission is not subject to 'comitology' control by the Member States as mentioned in Article 291 TFEU (see para. 18-014 *et seq., infra*).[58] However, the Commission has announced its intention systematically to consult experts from the Member States' authorities or organize consultations before adopting the delegated act.[59] The delegated act is published and enters into force only after the period for expressing objections has expired. That period is determined in the legislative act on a case by case basis, but should not be less than two months and may be extended at the request of the European Parliament or the Council.[60]

---

[50] C-427/12, *Commission v European Parliament and Council*, 2014, para. 38; C-44/16 P, *Dyson v Commission*, 2017, para. 58.

[51] C-696/15 P, *Czech Republic v Commission*, 2017, paras 45–54. See also Chamon, 'Limits to Delegation under Article 290 TFEU' (2018) MJCEL 231–45.

[52] The definition of delegated acts is very similar to that of acts which, under the Second Comitology Decision, are subject to the regulatory procedure with scrutiny (see para. 18-019, *infra*). It should be noted that, since the entry into force of the Lisbon Treaty and as long as the Second Comitology Decision (see para. 18-014, *infra*) was not replaced by a new Comitology Regulation, the institutions agreed not to have recourse anymore to the regulatory procedure with scrutiny as laid down in the Second Comitology Decision. However, Article 12 of the Comitology Regulation has maintained the regulatory procedure with scrutiny of Article 5a of the Second Comitology Decision for the purposes of existing basic acts still making reference thereto.

[53] C-355/10, *European Parliament v Council*, 2012, para. 65; C-44/16 P, *Dyson v Commission*, 2017, para. 61. Identifying the elements of a matter which must be categorized as essential needs to be based on objective factors amenable to judicial review, and requires account to be taken of the characteristics and particular features of the field concerned, C-44/16 P, *Dyson*, 2017, para. 62 (see also C-363/14, *European Parliament v Council*, 2015, para. 47; C-540/14 P, *DK Recycling und Roheisen v Commission*, 2016, para. 48). See also Ritleng, 'The Reserved Domain of the Legislature', in Bergström and Ritleng (eds), *Rulemaking by the European Commission: The New System for Delegation of Powers* (OUP, 2016), 133–55.

[54] C-286/14, *European Parliament v Commission*, 2016, paras 40–57.

[55] Král, 'On the Practice of Amending or Supplementing EU Directives by EU Delegated Regulations' (2020) ELRev 409–14.

[56] See the Communication of 9 December 2009 from the Commission to the European Parliament and the Council—Implementation of Article 290 of the Treaty on the Functioning of the European Union, COM(2009)673 final.

[57] The European Parliament decides on such an objection or revocation by majority of its component members, and the Council by a qualified majority (Article 290(2), second subpara. TFEU).

[58] As a legally binding act, a delegated act of the Commission may in turn determine the conditions under which it needs further implementation pursuant to Article 291 TFEU.

[59] Point 28 of the Interinstitutional Agreement between the European Parliament, the Council of the European Union and the European Commission of 13 April 2016 on Better Law-Making, OJ 2016 L123/1, as further developed in the Common Understanding between the European Parliament, the Council, and the Commission on Delegated Acts annexed thereto.

[60] Point 18 of the Common Understanding between the European Parliament, the Council and the Commission on Delegated Acts, annexed to the Interinstitutional Agreement between the European Parliament, the Council of the European Union, and the European Commission of 13 April 2016 on Better Law-Making, OJ 2016 L123/1.

Difference with implementing acts. The category of delegated acts did not exist before the Lisbon Treaty, but some basic acts conferred on the Commission the power to adopt measures supplementing or amending non-essential elements of the basic act. When that power was made subject to control by the Member States, the Commission adopted such measures in accordance with the 'comitology' procedure set out below. Since the Lisbon Treaty, such measures fall under the definition of delegated acts of Article 290 TFEU and can no longer be considered implementing acts in the sense of Article 291 TFEU. In the course of the legislative procedure there is often discussion between the European Parliament and the Council as to whether the power that would be conferred in the proposed legislative act to the Commission to develop supplementary rules should be a delegation of powers under Article 290 TFEU or a conferral of implementing powers within the meaning of Article 291 TFEU. According to the Court of Justice, the Union legislature has discretion when it decides to confer on the Commission a delegated power pursuant to Article 290(1) TFEU or an implementing power pursuant to Article 291(2) TFEU.[61] However, when the Commission is given the power to amend the non-essential elements of a legislative act, this always requires a delegated act.[62] In order to facilitate the choice between delegated and implementing acts, the European Parliament, the Council, and the Commission agreed, in 2019, on some non-binding criteria for the application of Articles 290 and 291 TFEU.[63]

18.011

2. Implementation by the Commission (or the Council)
a. *General principles*
Implementing acts. Where legally binding acts of the Union need uniform conditions for their implementation, implementing powers are to be conferred on the Commission or the Council.[64] In principle, in these circumstances, the power of implementation is to be

18.012

---

[61] C-427/12, *Commission v European Parliament and Council*, 2014, paras 24 and 38–39 (the judicial review is limited to the question whether the legislature could reasonably and without clear error arrive at its choice); C-65/13, *European Parliament v Commission*, 2014, paras 45–6; C-88/14, *Commission v European Parliament and Council*, 2015, paras 28–48; C-540/14 P, *DK Recycling und Roheisen v Commission*, 2016, paras 44–55. See also Vosa, 'Delegation or Implementation? The Ambiguous Divide' (2017) ELRev 737–50.

[62] C-88/14, *Commission v European Parliament and Council*, 2015, paras 28–48, see also C-65/13, *European Parliament v Commission*, 2014, para. 45. Nevertheless, after the Lisbon Treaty it is also possible to find implementing acts amending the non-essential elements of legislative acts (e.g. Commission Implementing Directive (EU) 2018/1581 of 19 October 2018 amending Council Directive 2009/119/EC as regards the methods for calculating stockholding obligations, OJ 2018 L263/57). Such acts, however, are adopted under the new comitology framework pursuant to the transitional regime laid down in Article 13 of the Comitology Regulation, whereby acts that used to be adopted using the old regulatory procedure of Article 5 of the Second Comitology Decision, are now adopted pursuant to the examination procedure, even if they involve amending the non-essential elements of legislative acts. Such examples should, however, become ever rarer as the references to the old comitology decisions gradually disappear from Union legislative acts.

[63] Non-binding criteria for the application of Articles 290 and 291 of the TFEU, 18 June 1999, OJ 2019, C223/1.

[64] It should be noted that in agricultural matters the Treaties specify both the power to enact legislation and the power to adopt executive acts in Article 43, paras 2 and 3 TFEU, but the acts adopted under Article 43(3) TEU are not implementing acts in the sense of Article 291(2) TFEU: C-124/13 and C-125/13, *European Parliament and Commission v Council*, 2015, paras 52–4. As regards social policy, Article 155(3) TFEU refers to the possibility for the Council to 'implement' social agreements concluded at Union level. Such a Council 'implementing' decision is not adopted pursuant to a legislative procedure and, hence, does not constitute a legislative act. Nevertheless, because of the general nature of the agreements in question and the fact that such agreements, even if approved by a Council decision, need further 'implementation', such a Council 'implementing' decision can also be considered as constituting a procedural step in the legislative process rather than a form of 'implementation', see also para. 17-038, *supra*.

conferred on the Commission. Union acts may confer implementing powers on the Council only 'in duly justified specific cases'[65] and in the field of the CFSP[66] (Article 291(2) TFEU).[67] Where the Commission exercises implementing powers, it has traditionally been subject to control by the Member States, which consists of the Commission's proposed implementing acts being discussed in committees of representatives of the Member States. This system is known as 'comitology'[68] (see para. 18-014, *infra*). Since the entry into force of the Lisbon Treaty, the word 'implementing' is to be inserted in the title of implementing acts of the Commission or the Council (Article 291(4) TFEU).[69]

18.013 **Wide interpretation of 'implementation'.** An implementing power will be validly conferred only if it is sufficiently specific, in the sense that its bounds must be clearly specified.[70] As stated before, implementing powers encompass both regulatory powers and the power to apply rules to specific cases by means of individual decisions (see para. 18-008, *supra*). Moreover, the term 'implementation' has to be given a wide interpretation. In complex areas, such as the organization of the market in agricultural products, the Union legislature may be forced to confer wide powers of discretion and action on the Commission.[71] More generally, within the framework of its implementing power, the Commission is competent to take all measures that are necessary or appropriate for the implementation of the basic act concerned, provided that these measures are not contrary to it.[72] Even where the Commission has no express power to this effect, its implementing provisions may impose penalties, which, within the context of the policy in question, are designed to secure the proper financial management of Union funds.[73] A measure intended to harmonize national legislation may confer powers on the Commission to compel the Member States to take temporary measures if otherwise the aims of the harmonization would be jeopardised[74].

---

[65] See, for instance, C-440/14 P, *National Iranian Oil Company v Council*, 2016, paras 47–65. See already before the Lisbon Treaty: 16/88, *Commission v Council*, 1989, para. 10; C-257/01, *Commission v Council*, 2005, paras 50–61, with case notes by Drijber (2005) SEW 438–441 and Randazzo (2005) CMLRev 1737–50; C-133/06, *European Parliament v Council*, 2008, paras 45–50.

[66] See Articles 24 and 26 TEU.

[67] Article 291(2) TFEU relates solely to legally binding acts of the Union which lend themselves, in principle, to implementation by the Member States, but which must, for a particular reason, be implemented by the Commission or the Council for the purpose of ensuring that they are applied uniformly within the Union. That is not so for an act establishing a power to impose a fine on a Member State, because such an act does not lend itself to implementation by the Member States themselves as such implementation involves the adoption of an enforcement measure in respect of one of them. See C-521/15, *Spain v Council*, 2017, paras 48–9. See Chamon, 'Fining Member States under the SGP, or how enforcement is different from implementation under Article 291 TFEU: Spain v. Council' (2019) CMLRev 1495–520.

[68] The Court of Justice approved this system as long ago as 25/70, *Köster*, 1970, para. 9. See Bradley, 'Comitology and the Law: Through a Glass, Darkly' (1992) CMLRev 693–721. See also Blumann, 'La Commission, agent d'exécution du droit communautaire. La comitologie', in Louis and Waelbroeck (eds), *La Commission au coeur du système institutionnel des Communautés européennes* (Editions de l'Université de Bruxelles, 1989), 49–77; Blumann, 'Le pouvoir exécutif de la Commission à la lumière de l'Acte unique européen' (1988) RTDE 23–59; Ehlermann, 'Compétences d'exécution conférées à la Commission—La nouvelle décision-cadre du Conseil' (1988) RMC 232–9.

[69] Since 1 December 2009, the Council has thus adopted 'implementing regulations' and 'implementing decisions'; see C-65/13, *European Parliament v Commission*, 2014, para. 41. Implementing acts of the Commission were not qualified by the term 'implementing' as long as the 1999 Comitology Decision had not been replaced by a Comitology Regulation pursuant to Article 291(3) TFEU, which occurred with Regulation (EU) No. 182/2011 of the European Parliament and of the Council (see para. 18-014, *infra*). The term 'implementing' is not added to those acts which are still adopted under the regulatory procedure with scrutiny (see para. 18-019, *infra*).

[70] 291/86, *Central-Import Münster*, 1988, para. 13.

[71] 23/75, *Rey Soda*, 1975, paras 10–11; C-159/96, *Portugal v Commission*, 1998, paras 40–1.

[72] C-78/16 and C-79/16, *Pesce*, 2016, para. 46.

[73] C-240/90, *Germany v Commission*, 1992, paras 35–42. See also the earlier case 25/70, *Köster*, 1970, para. 7.

[74] C-359/92, *Germany v Council*, 1994, paras 30–9.

b. Control over the implementation by the Commission: 'comitology'

Comitology. As already mentioned, in conferring implementing powers on the Commission, the European Parliament, and the Council may subject the Commission to control by committees composed of representatives of the Member States (Article 291(3) TFEU).[75] Before the Lisbon Treaty, the Council had to lay down the 'principles and rules' for this control pursuant to Article 202 EC.[76] Since the Lisbon Treaty, it is up to the European Parliament and the Council, acting in accordance with the ordinary legislative procedure and by means of a regulation, to lay down the rules and general principles for mechanisms for control by Member States of the Commission's exercise of implementing powers (Article 291(3) TFEU). Unlike the delegation of powers pursuant to Article 290 TFEU, which can only be laid down in a legislative act, implementing powers under Article 291 TFEU can be conferred by all 'legally binding Union acts', thus also by acts that have not been adopted in accordance with the ordinary or a special legislative procedure, or by another implementing act. Like a delegation of powers, the power to adopt implementing acts is granted with a view to the adoption of legally binding acts.

18.014

Pursuant to Article 202 TEC, the Council adopted the First Comitology Decision on 13 July 1987, which limited and enumerated the number of implementing procedures (advisory committee, management committee, and regulatory committee).[77] After the introduction of the co-decision procedure, the European Parliament expressed the wish to also exercise control over the implementation of acts adopted by co-decision. The Council responded to this wish when it adopted the Second Comitology Decision on 28 June 1999,[78] especially after the amendments made to that decision on 17 July 2006,[79] which introduced the regulatory procedure with scrutiny (by the Council and the European Parliament). After the entry into force of the Lisbon Treaty, the European Parliament and the Council adopted, pursuant to Article 291(3) TFEU, the current Comitology Regulation.[80]

---

[75] C-183/16 P, *Tilly-SabcoSAS v Commission*, 2017, paras 90–2.

[76] According to the third indent of Article 202 EC—added by the Single European Act—the Council was to 'confer on the Commission, in the acts which the Council adopts, powers for the implementation of the rules which the Council lays down' and 'may impose certain requirements in respect of the exercise of these powers'. The procedures in question had to be 'consonant with principles and rules to be laid down in advance by the Council, acting unanimously on a proposal from the Commission and after obtaining the opinion of the European Parliament'. In this way, the third indent of Article 202 EC confirmed the former practice whereby the Council, acting under Article 211 EC, conferred implementing powers on the Commission to be exercised in accordance with detailed rules laid down by the Council.

[77] Council Decision 87/373/EEC of 13 July 1987 laying down the conditions for the exercise of implementing powers conferred on the Commission, OJ 1987 L197/33. The Council may not introduce any other procedures: 16/88, *Commission v Council*, 1989, para. 14.

[78] Council Decision 1999/468/EC of 28 June 1999 laying down the procedures for the exercise of implementing powers conferred on the Commission, OJ 1999 L184/23. See Jacqué, 'Implementing Powers and Comitology', in Joerges and Vos (eds), *EU Committees: Social Regulation, Law and Politics* (Hart Publishing, 1999), 59–69; Moteira González, 'Änderung des normativen Rahmens der Komitologie' (2003) ZEuS 561–88; Lenaerts and Verhoeven, 'Towards a Legal Framework for Executive Rule-Making in the E.U.? The Contribution of the New Comitology Decision' (2000) CMLRev 645–86.

[79] Council Decision 2006/512/EC of 17 July 2006 amending Decision 1999/468/EC laying down the procedures for the exercise of implementing powers conferred on the Commission, OJ 2006 L200/11 (see the consolidated version of the Second Comitology Decision, published in OJ 2006 C255/4). See also the Statement by the European Parliament, the Council, and the Commission concerning the Council Decision of 17 July 2006, OJ 2006 C255/1. For an assessment, see Szapiro, 'Comitologie: rétrospectives et prospective après la réforme de 2006' (2006) RDUE 545–86; Van der Plas, 'Rol Europees Parlement fors toegenomen door nieuw Comitologiebesluit' (2006) SEW 410–24; Christiansen, 'The 2006 Reform of Comitology: Problem Solved or Dispute Postponed?' (2006) Eipascope 9–17.

[80] Regulation (EU) No. 182/2011 of the European Parliament and of the Council of 16 February 2011 laying down the rules and general principles concerning mechanisms for control by Member States of the Commission's exercise of implementing powers, OJ 2011 L55/13.

The Comitology Regulation sets out the available procedures between which the European Parliament and the Council acting in accordance with the ordinary legislative procedure, or the Council must choose when conferring implementing powers on the Commission. All procedures invariably require the Commission to submit a draft of the envisaged implementing act to a committee made up of representatives of the Member States and chaired by a representative of the Commission, who has no vote.[81] The Commission keeps a register to publish the draft implementing acts submitted to the committees and the outcome of the votes (Comitology Regulation, Article 10).[82] In case of a substantive amendment of the implementing act after the opinion of the committee was given, it is appropriate for the Commission to again seek the opinion of the committee.[83]

18.015   **Two types of procedure.** The Comitology Regulation offers the legislature a choice between two procedures: the advisory procedure and the examination procedure. Both are based on a common procedural framework laid down in Article 3 of the Comitology Regulation.[84] This is a simplification in comparison with the system in place before the Lisbon Treaty, which encompassed three procedures (advisory procedure, management procedure, and regulatory procedure), to which a fourth option (the regulatory procedure with scrutiny) was added in 2006. In the management and regulatory procedures, the Commission had to submit its draft implementing act to the Council whenever the committee delivered a negative opinion. The Comitology Regulation has replaced that system with the possibility for the Commission to submit its draft implementing act to an appeals committee that is also composed of representatives of the Member States. Depending on what sort of procedure the legislature sets up in the basic act, the Member States can control the Commission's implementing role to a greater or lesser extent.

Article 2 of the Comitology Regulation sets out criteria on the basis of which the legislature may choose a committee procedure.[85] The examination procedure is applicable to implementing measures of a general scope and to other implementing measures relating to programmes with substantial implications; the common agricultural and common fisheries policies; the environment, security, and safety, or protection of the health or safety of humans, animals, or plants; the common commercial policy; or taxation. The advisory procedure applies when this is deemed appropriate, and in all other cases. If the Union legislature seeks to depart from these criteria, it must state the reasons for doing so.[86]

---

[81] In areas where at times urgent measures must be taken, the legislature, when adopting the basic act, may make Article 8 of the Comitology Regulation applicable, on the basis of which a Commission implementing act enters into force before it has been submitted to the committee, but must be revoked if the committee delivers a negative opinion.

[82] See also Article 9(2) of the Comitology Regulation, as to access to the documents, as well as T-188/97, *Rothmans v Commission*, 1999 (as far as access to its documents are concerned, a committee comes under the Commission).

[83] See T-240/10, *Hungary v Commission*, 2013, paras 81–7.

[84] See, e.g., as to the time limits of Article 3(3) of the Comitology Regulation, C-183/16 P, *Tilly-SabcoSAS v Commission*, 2017, paras 95–118.

[85] In addition, Article 6 of the Second Comitology Decision describes the procedure which may be applied where the basic instrument confers on the Commission the power to decide on safeguard measures.

[86] The advisory procedure may apply to implementing acts that are normally to be adopted using the examination procedure 'in duly justified cases' (Comitology Regulation, Article 2(3)). As far as the former comitology procedure was concerned, see C-378/00, *Commission v European Parliament and Council*, 2003, paras 43–55 (an unreasoned choice departing from those criteria was declared void); C-122/04, *Commission v European Parliament and Council*, 2006, paras 32–45 (no departure from those criteria found).

Advisory procedure. Where the Union legislature has set up an advisory committee, the Commission must obtain its opinion, but is not bound by it. It must, however, take the utmost account of the conclusions drawn from the discussions within the committee and of the opinion delivered (Comitology Regulation, Article 4).   **18.016**

Examination procedure. If the Union legislature has set up an examination procedure, the Commission must also seek the opinion of the committee, which adopts its position by qualified majority vote, as laid down in the Treaties for acts adopted by the Council on a proposal from the Commission. The outcome of the vote in the committee determines the further procedure.   **18.017**

Where the committee delivers a positive opinion, the Commission shall adopt the draft implementing act (Comitology Regulation, Article 5(2)).

Where the committee delivers a negative opinion, the Commission shall not adopt the draft implementing act. The Commission may, however, either submit an amended version of the draft implementing act to the same committee, or submit the draft implementing act to the appeal committee for further deliberation (Comitology Regulation, Article 5(3)). The appeal committee shall deliver its opinion by the same majority as provided for the committee. Where the appeal committee delivers a positive opinion, the Commission shall adopt the draft implementing act; where the appeal committee delivers a negative opinion, the Commission shall not adopt the draft implementing act. When the appeal committee lacks the required (qualified) majority in favour or against the measure, and thus fails to adopt an opinion, the Commission may adopt the draft implementing act[87] (Comitology Regulation, Article 6(3)).

When already at the level of the committee no qualified majority in favour or against is reached, and the committee thus fails to deliver an opinion, the Commission may adopt the draft implementing act, except where (a) that act concerns taxation, financial services, the protection of the health or safety of humans, animals, or plants, or definitive multilateral safeguard measures; (b) the basic act provides that the draft implementing act may not be adopted where no opinion is delivered; or (c) a simple majority of the component members of the committee opposes it.[88] Where an implementing act is nonetheless deemed to be necessary, the Commission may either submit an amended version of that act to the same committee, or submit the draft implementing act to the appeal committee for further deliberation (Comitology Regulation, Article 5(4)). In the latter case the procedure before the appeal committee proceeds as set out above.

In practice, the procedure does not often produce negative opinions, since the Commission ensures that its implementing function is conducted smoothly by negotiating with the delegations of the Member States on the committee beforehand.

---

[87] In the case of the adoption of definitive multilateral safeguard measures, the Commission shall only adopt the draft implementing act when the appeal committee delivers a positive opinion (Comitology regulation, Article 6(4)).
[88] A special procedure applies for the adoption of draft definitive anti-dumping or countervailing measures, where no opinion is delivered by the committee and a simple majority of its component members opposes the draft implementing act (Comitology Regulation, Article 5(5)).

18.018 **Right of scrutiny for the European Parliament and the Council.** In the committees only representatives of the Member States (in practice, national civil servants) exercise control over the Commission. The Commission must, however, also send the documents that it submits to the committees, to the European Parliament, and the Council (Comitology Regulation, Article 10(4)). Where a basic act is adopted under the ordinary legislative procedure, either the European Parliament or the Council may at any time indicate to the Commission that, in its view, a draft implementing act exceeds the implementing powers provided for in the basic act (Comitology Regulation, Article 11). Unlike the committee composed of the representatives of the Member States, neither the European Parliament nor the Council may prevent the Commission from adopting the implementing act. The Commission must merely review the draft implementing act, taking account of the positions expressed, and inform the European Parliament and the Council whether it intends to maintain, amend, or withdraw the draft implementing act.

18.019 **Previous comitology procedures.** As mentioned before, the comitology system before the Treaty of Lisbon provided for a formal role for the Council in the procedure. Under the management procedure, the Commission had to communicate to the Council any implementing acts which were not given a positive opinion by the committee. In that event, the Commission could defer application of the measures for a few months during which the Council, acting on its own initiative by a qualified majority, could take a different decision.[89] In the regulatory procedure, whenever the committee could not muster a sufficient majority for a favourable opinion, the Commission had to submit the measures envisaged to the Council as a formal proposal.[90] If the Council had neither adopted the proposed implementing act within the time limit set for doing so, nor had mustered a majority to oppose it, the Commission was allowed to adopt the proposed implementing act.[91] These procedures have been abolished by the Comitology Regulation, which has replaced references to the management and regulatory procedures in all basic acts with references to the examination procedure.[92]

By contrast, the Comitology Regulation has left the references to the regulatory procedure with scrutiny in the basic acts unaltered,[93] so that this procedure is still used for now.

Where the Union legislature sets up a regulatory committee with scrutiny, the draft implementing acts of the Commission are scrutinized by both the Council and the European Parliament. If the committee votes by a qualified majority (determined in the same way as in the case of an examination committee) in favour of the measures envisaged,

---

[89] Second Comitology Decision, Article 4.

[90] Where the basic act did not specify precisely the period within which the Commission had to submit a proposal to the Council, the Commission was entitled to seek additional advice before presenting an amended proposal, in particular where it was faced with a measure which is scientifically and politically highly complex and sensitive: C-151/98, P *Pharos v Commission*, 1999, paras 20–7.

[91] Second Comitology Decision, Article 5(6). This procedure is comparable to variant (a) (the '*filet*') under the First Comitology Decision which did not however allow the Council to reject the proposed measures by a qualified majority. Under variant (b) (the '*contrefilet*') provided for in the First Comitology Decision, the Commission was in a weaker position, since it enabled the Council to reject the proposal by a simple majority. For the differences between these variants, see C-417/93, *European Parliament v Council*, 1995, para. 26, and C-417/93, *European Parliament v Council*, 1995, Opinion of Advocate General Léger, point 92. Compare the case note by Van Nuffel (1995) ColJEL 504, 508, with Bradley, 'Institutional Aspects of Comitology: Scenes from the Cutting Room Floor', in Joerges et al. (eds), *EU Committees: Social Regulation, Law and Politics* (Hart Publishing, 1999), 71, 76–79.

[92] Comitology Regulation, Article 13.

[93] Comitology Regulation, Article 12.

they must be submitted for scrutiny to the European Parliament and the Council. Either institution may, within three months from the date of referral to them, oppose the adoption of the draft measure proposed by the Commission, justifying its opposition by indicating that the draft measure exceeds the implementing powers provided for in the basic act or that it is not compatible with the aim or the content of the basic act or does not respect the principles of subsidiarity or proportionality.[94] In that event, the Commission cannot adopt the proposed measure. The Commission may then submit to the committee an amended draft of the measures or present a legislative proposal on the basis of the Treaties to modify the basic act. If, within the said period, neither the European Parliament nor the Council opposes the draft measures, they can be adopted by the Commission.

If the committee does not muster a sufficient majority in order to deliver a positive opinion, or if no opinion is delivered, the Commission has to submit its draft to the Council as a formal proposal and has to forward it to the European Parliament at the same time.[95] Within two months from the date of referral to it, the Council can act on the proposal by qualified majority; within four months of the date of referral to it, the European Parliament may oppose adoption of the act on one of the grounds mentioned above. If the Council opposes the proposed measures, they may not be adopted. In that event, the Commission may submit to the Council an amended proposal or present a legislative proposal on the basis of the Treaties (taking into account possible objections formulated by the European Parliament). If the Council envisages adopting the proposed measures (or if it does not act within the two-month period), the proposed measures are submitted to the European Parliament. If the European Parliament opposes the proposed act, it may not be adopted. In that event, the Commission may submit to the committee an amended draft of the act or present a legislative proposal on the basis of the Treaties. If the European Parliament does not oppose the proposed measures, they may be adopted by the Council.

Consultation of expert committees. In implementing legislation, not only does the Commission need to have regard to the politically sensitive nature of certain measures, but scientific and technical problems also arise. For this reason, various Union measures provide for the involvement of a scientific or technical committee with a view to their implementation. Where such a committee is set up, it must be consulted even if the instrument to be implemented does not say so in so many words, because such consultation constitutes the only guarantee that a Union measure is necessary and adapted to the objective pursued.[96] An infringement of internal procedural rules of such a committee, which are intended to ensure that Member States' representatives have the time necessary to consult the different national administrative authorities, experts, or professional organizations, may constitute an infringement of essential procedural requirements and result in the annulment of the measure concerned.[97]

18.020

Control on implementation by Commission and Council. As stated before, a Union act may confer implementing powers on the Council 'in duly justified specific cases' (Article

18.021

---

[94] Second Comitology Decision, Article 5a (3). The potential grounds for objection are thus broader than those provided for in the examination procedure.
[95] Second Comitology Decision, Article 5a(4).
[96] C-212/91, *Angelopharm*, 1994, paras 31–8.
[97] C-263/95, *Germany v Commission*, 1998, paras 31–2.

291(2) TFEU, see para. 18-012, *supra*). The European Parliament has often claimed that the task of implementation should be entrusted fully to the Commission. The reason is that this would enable both the Council and the European Parliament itself to supervise the Commission by virtue of their constitutional prerogatives. Both institutions should check that the Commission does not exceed the implementing power conferred on it. If it does, the European Parliament and the Council—and also any Member State—can bring an action for annulment of Commission measures in the Court of Justice.[98] In addition, the European Parliament may hold the Commission to account politically for the way in which it fulfils its executive role (see para. 12-006, *supra*). Where, in contrast, the Council itself undertakes implementation, it is not possible for the European Parliament to exercise political control to the same extent. As far as general implementing measures are concerned, there is thus a danger of the Council evading involvement of the European Parliament in the legislative process—under a special legislative procedure in which the Council decides after consulting the Parliament—by adopting a vague piece of legislation and then giving it a completely different scope. Although the Court of Justice may find against such a practice,[99] the European Parliament's political control vis-à-vis the Council is, in practice, confined to the right to ask parliamentary questions (see para. 12-007, *supra*).

It must be stated, however, that this problem has become far less real since the Lisbon Treaty extended the scope of application of the ordinary legislative procedure to most fields of competence of the Union. Consequently, the European Parliament often enjoys a power of co-decision on the substance of the legislative act adopted, including the way in which it will be implemented. Furthermore, since the Lisbon Treaty comitology regulations are also adopted under the ordinary legislative procedure, which gives the European Parliament a decisive say as to the way in which comitology control is organized.

In addition, the Lisbon Treaty, as mentioned before, has created a new category of implementing acts (in the broad sense)—the delegated acts—which are subject to equal control by the European Parliament and the Council (Article 290 TFEU, see para. 18-010, *supra*). When adopting Union legislation, the European Parliament generally prefers giving the Commission the power to adopt delegated acts over the power to adopt implementing acts subject to comitology. Within the Council the preference rather goes to the latter form of implementing power, as it guarantees a more important role for the Member States at the drafting stage of implementing acts than they have in respect of delegated acts. As

---

[98] For cases which were successfully brought by a Member State, see C-366/88, *France v Commission*, 1990, paras 17–25; C-303/90, *France v Commission*, 1991, paras 27–35; C-325/91, *France v Commission*, 1993, paras 14–17; C-159/96, *Portugal v Commission*, 1998, paras 25–50; C-289/96, C-293/96, and C-299/96, *Denmark, Germany and France v Commission*, 1999, paras 53–103; C-89/96, *Portugal v Commission*, 1999, paras 12–14; C-393/01, *France v Commission*, 2003, paras 40–60; C-239/01, *Germany v Commission*, 2003, paras 54–76. The power of implementation was not considered to have been exceeded in C-296/93 and C-307/93, *France and Ireland v Commission*, 1996, paras 11–24; C-9/95, C-23/95, and C-156/95, *Belgium and Germany v Commission*, 1997, paras 21–41; C-285/94, *Italy v Commission*, 1997, paras 20–46. Before the broadening of its right to bring an action for annulment (see para. 12-011, *supra*), the European Parliament could do so where the Commission measure at issue infringed a legislative act adopted under a procedure providing for the involvement of the Parliament. See, e.g., C-156/93, *European Parliament v Commission*, 1995, paras 12–13.

[99] See, e.g., C-303/94, *European Parliament v Council*, 1996, paras 21–33; C-93/00, *European Parliament v Council*, 2001, paras 35–44; C-403/05, *European Parliament v Commission*, 2007, paras 40–68; C-14/06 and C-295/06, *European Parliament and Denmark v Commission*, 2008, paras 50–78 and the inquiry carried out by the Court of Justice 46/86, *Romkes*, 1987, paras 15–20; C-417/93, *European Parliament v Council*, 1995, paras 28–33; C-133/06, *European Parliament v Council*, 2008, paras 52–9.

stated, the Union legislature has some discretionary margin as to whether a delegated or implementing power is conferred on the Commission (see para. 18-011, *supra*).

C. Implementation by other bodies, offices, or agencies

Independent executive bodies, offices, or agencies. In increasing numbers of policy areas, the Union legislature has entrusted executive functions in specific domains to independent bodies, offices, or agencies, that are bestowed with legal personality and are authorized to adopt legally binding acts vis-à-vis natural and legal persons,[100] such as the European Intellectual Property Office; the Community Plant Variety Office; the European Chemicals Agency; the European Medicines Agency; the European Aviation Safety Agency; and the authorities that are part of the European system for financial supervision (the European Banking Authority, the European Insurance and Occupational Pensions Authority, and the European Securities and Markets Authority) (see paras 13-044–13-046). This involves a delegation of powers that does not correspond to the cases described in Articles 290 TFEU and 291 TFEU, but is nonetheless in accordance with the Treaties.[101] Delegation of the management of Union programmes to executive agencies allows the Commission to outsource certain of its own management tasks.[102] In some cases, bodies with legal personality (known as offices, agencies, centres, and foundations) perform executive functions in coordinating or supplementing action taken by the Member States. In that case, they collect and disseminate information, set up the machinery for coordinating action on the part of the competent national authorities, and carry out studies with a view to developing policy further.[103] Generally, what is involved is a genuine amalgam of *administration communautaire directe* and *indirecte*[104] in which Union and national experts administer policy areas in collaboration with interest groups.[105]

18.022

Limits on delegation. The Union legislature may delegate powers to an independent executive body, provided that the delegation is precisely delineated and amenable to judicial review in the light of the objectives established by the legislature.[106] The reason for this is that if the body had discretionary powers, the policy choices would no longer lie with the institutions that have the political responsibility under the Treaties. This would detract from the

18.023

---

[100] See 9/56, *Meroni v High Authority*, 1958, at 146 *et seq.*, and the parallel judgment 10/56 *Meroni v High Authority*, 1958.

[101] C-270/12, *United Kingdom v European Parliament and Council*, 2014, paras 79–86; Chamon, 'Beyond Delegated and Implementing Acts: Where do EU Agencies Fit in the Articles 290 and 291 TFEU Scheme?', in Tauschinsky and Weiß (eds), *The Legislative Choice Between Delegated and Implementing Acts in EU Law: Walking a Labyrinth* (Elgar, 2018), 174–99.

[102] Council Regulation (EC) No. 58/2003 of 19 December 2002 laying down the statute for executive agencies to be entrusted with certain tasks in the management of Community programmes, OJ 2003 L11/1 (see para. 13-147, *supra*).

[103] See the tasks assigned to other Union bodies, offices and agencies with legal personality mentioned in paras 13-045–13-046, *supra*.

[104] Lenaerts, 'Regulating the Regulatory Process: "Delegation of Powers" in the European Community' (1993) ELRev 23, 46–7.

[105] See Chamon, *EU Agencies: Legal and Political Limits to the Transformation of the EU Administration* (OUP, 2016), 389; Chiti, 'The Emergence of a Community Administration: The Case of European Agencies' (2000) CMLRev 309–43; Vos, 'Reforming the European Commission: What Role to Play for EU Agencies?' (2000) CMLRev 1113–34.

[106] C-270/12, *United Kingdom v European Parliament and Council*, 2014, paras 41–53. In that case an independent body may also adopt acts of general application, ibid., para. 65.

institutional balance on which the Union is based (see para. 16-009, *supra*)[107]. Accordingly, the Commission may not delegate the execution of a Union programme to an executive agency where this would involve 'discretionary powers in translating political choices into action'.[108] Also, where the Union delegates tasks to international bodies,[109] it must take into account that the international agreement that delegates these powers may not impede on the competences of the Union and its institutions as set out in the Treaties.[110] An international agreement between the Union and third States may devolve dispute settlement to a specific dispute-resolution system. However, in order to preserve the autonomy of the Union legal order, that dispute-resolution system may not have the effect of binding the Union and its institutions, in the exercise of their internal powers, to a particular interpretation of the rules of Union law.[111]

18.024 **Judicial review.** In addition, an institution may not delegate more powers than it possesses itself. Independent executive bodies are therefore subject to the same obligations with regard to adequate legal protection as the Union institutions. Their decisions must state the reasons on which they are based (Article 296, second para. TFEU) and be brought to the notice of the persons to whom they are addressed (Article 297 TFEU). In addition, decisions which produce legal effects must be amenable to judicial review.[112] The Court of Justice of the European Union has jurisdiction in actions for annulment against acts of bodies, offices, or agencies of the Union intended to produce legal effects vis-à-vis third parties (Article 263, first para. TFEU)[113].

Some legislative acts setting up bodies, offices, or agencies still provide that the legality of an act of the body, office, or agency in question may be reviewed by the Commission. The Commission's express or implied approval or disapproval of the act will then constitute an act amenable to judicial review.[114] As regards agencies empowered to take legally binding

---

[107] 9/56, *Meroni*, 1958, 151 *et seq.* See also 98/80, *Romano*, 1981, para. 20 (a commission set up by the Council does not have the power to adopt acts having the force of law in view of the implementing powers vested in the Commission by the Treaties).

[108] See recitals 4 and 5 in the preamble to Regulation No. 58/2003 and Article 6(1) thereof (n. 102, *supra*). For this constraint on the delegation of executive tasks by the Commission, see Remmert, 'Die Gründung von Einrichtungen der mittelbaren Gemeinschaftsverwaltung' (2003) EuR 134–45; Craig, 'The Constitutionalisation of Community Administration' (2003) ELRev 840, 848–54. A plea for more autonomous executive agencies may be found in Majone, 'Delegation of Regulatory Powers in a Mixed Polity' (2002) ELJ 319–39.

[109] See Lenaerts, 'Regulating the Regulatory Process: "Delegation of Powers" in the European Community' (1993) ELRev 23, 37–40.

[110] See Opinion 1/76, *Draft Agreement establishing a European laying-up fund for inland waterway vessels*, 1977, para. 5 and paras 15–16.

[111] Opinion 1/76, *Draft Agreement establishing a European laying-up fund for inland waterway vessels*, 1977, paras 21–2; Opinion 1/91, *Draft agreement between the Community, on the one hand, and the countries of the European Free Trade Association, on the other, relating to the creation of the European Economic Area*, 1991, paras 37–53; Opinion 1/09, *Draft agreement on the European and Community Patents Court*, 2011, paras 60–89.

[112] 9/56, *Meroni*, 1958, at 149–51. See, e.g., T-148/97, *Keeling v Office for Harmonisation in the Internal Market*, 1998, paras 31–4; T-117/08, *Italy v European Economic and Social Committee*, 2011, paras 29–35; T-411/06, *Sogelma v European Agency for Reconstruction*, 2008, paras 33–57 (review of that agency's decision); T-70/05 *Evropaïki Dynamiki v European Maritime Safety Agency*, 2010, paras 61–75 (annulment of contract awarded by that agency), affirmed by C-252/10 P, *Evropaïki Dynamiki v European Maritime Safety Agency* (order), 2011. For actions for annulment, see para. 30-003 *et seq., infra*.

[113] Similarly, the Court has jurisdiction in actions for a failure to act against bodies, offices, and agencies of the Union (Article 265(1) TFEU).

[114] See, e.g., T-369/94 and T-85/95, *DIR International Film and Others v Commission*, 1998, paras 52–5 (decision of the European Film Distribution Office attributed to the Commission). Following the 2013 agreement on a Common Approach for decentralized agencies, this system has been abandoned for most agencies. See also Article 28 of Regulation (EC) No. 851/2004 establishing the European Centre for Disease Prevention and Control (OJ

decisions, the legislative acts nowadays generally provide that the person concerned must first apply to a board of appeal, against whose decision an appeal will lie to the Union Court.[115] This is, for instance, the case for the decisions taken by the European Intellectual Property Office, the Community Plant Variety Office,[116] the European Chemicals Agency,[117] and certain decisions taken by the three supervising authorities of the European System for financial supervision, for which a joint body of appeals was established,[118] and by the Single Resolution Board.[119] In some cases, acts provide that a direct action will lie in the Union Court against decisions of the body, office, or agency concerned,[120] for instance against decisions rejecting requests for access to their documents.[121] Also, when the act establishing the body, office, or agency does not organize the review of the legality of the acts of the body, office, or agency in question, the Court of Justice will, in any event, have jurisdiction to control the validity of acts intended to have legal effects vis-à-vis third parties (see para. 30-005, *infra*). The same applies where the Union delegates tasks to international bodies.

Delegation of powers in the Treaties. The Treaties themselves have entrusted the performance of certain tasks to independent bodies with discretionary powers. The two most important independent bodies to which tasks have been entrusted are the European Central Bank (ECB) and the European Investment Bank (EIB). Since the Lisbon Treaty, however, only the EIB retains that status, as the ECB is now an institution in the sense of Article 13(1) TEU.

18.025

As an independent body, the European Investment Bank has substantial latitude with regard to policy within the confines of the powers which it derives from the Treaties and the statute appended thereto.[122] This independent status may only be altered by revising the Treaties. Nevertheless, the acts of the EIB are also subject to judicial supervision[123] and the

---

2004, L142/1). See further Article 22 of Regulation No. 58/2003 with regard to executive agencies entrusted with certain tasks in the management of Community programmes (n. 102, *supra*) and Craig (n. 108, *supra*), at 849–51.

[115] See Simoncini, *Administrative Regulation Beyond the Non-delegation Doctrine: A study on EU Agencies* (Hart Publishing, 2018), 157–62; Chamon, 'Les agences décentralisées et le droit procédural de l'UE' (2016) CDE 555–61; Navin-Jones, 'A Legal Review of EU Boards of Appeal in Particular the European Chemicals Agency Board of Appeal' (2015) EPL 143–68; Chirulli and De Lucia, 'Specialised Adjudication in EU Administrative law: The Boards of Appeal of EU Agencies' (2015) ELRev 832–57.

[116] cf. the Board of Appeal of the European Intellectual Property Office (Article 165 of Regulation (EU) No. 2017/1001 of the European Parliament and of the Council of 14 June 2017 on the European Union trade mark, OJ 2017 L154/1) and of the Community Plant Variety Office (Article 45 of the regulation establishing the Office, OJ 1995 L258/3). See also the European Aviation Safety Agency (Articles 105 to 114 of Regulation (EU) 2018/1139 (OJ 2018 L212/1) and the Complaints Board dealing with certain disputes arising under the Convention defining the status of the European Schools, established by Article 27 of the Convention (alongside the exclusive jurisdiction of the Court of Justice over disputes between Contracting Parties relating to the interpretation and application of the Convention: Article 26), OJ 1994 L212/9.

[117] Article 94 of Regulation (EC) No. 1907/2006 (OJ 2006, L396/1).

[118] Article 58 of Regulation (EU) No. 1093/2010, OJ 2010 L331/12. See Chamon, 'De Gemeenschappelijke Bezwaarcommissie van de Europese Toezichthoudende Autoriteit' (2020) SEW 171–84.

[119] Article 86 of Regulation (EU) No. 806/2014 (OJ 2014 L225/1).

[120] e.g. as regards the European Data-Protection Supervisor, see Article 64 of Regulation (EU) 2018/1725 (OJ 2018 L295/39). For another example, see C-515/17 P and C-561/17 P, *Uniwersytet Wrocławski and Republic of Poland v Research Executive Agency*, 2020.

[121] e.g. T-439/08, *Joséphidès v Commission and EACEA*, 2010, paras 33–8; T-407/07, *CMB Maschinenbau & Handels GmbH and J. Christof v Commission*, 2011, paras 58–61; T-716/14 *Tweedale v European Food Safety Authority*, 2019.

[122] See Article 308, third para. TFEU, which refers to the Statute of the European Investment Bank, laid down in Protocol (No. 5), annexed to the TEU and TFEU, OJ 2010 C83/251).

[123] See Article 271(b) and (c) TFEU and C-15/00, *Commission v European Investment Bank*, 2003, para. 75.

EIB must report to political authorities. The Court of Justice has made it clear that the functional independence enjoyed by the European Investment Bank does not have the consequence of separating it entirely from the European Union and exempting it from every rule of Union law.[124] The fact that it is independent does not preclude the Union legislature from adopting legislative acts applying to it, for instance relating to the prevention of fraud.[125]

The Treaties also confer tasks on Eurojust and Europol in the field of judicial cooperation in criminal matters and police cooperation, respectively (see para. 13-046, *supra*). The concrete field of action of these legally independent bodies is to be determined, however, by regulations adopted pursuant to Articles 85 and 88 TFEU. The European Parliament and the Council, by means of regulations adopted in accordance with the ordinary legislative procedure, are to determine arrangements for involving the European Parliament and national parliaments in the evaluation of the activities of Eurojust and Europol (Articles 85(1), third subpara. and 88(2), second subpara. TFEU; see paras 8-023 and 8-026). Another example of a body to which powers are delegated by the Treaties is the Political and Security Committee (Article 38 TEU; see para. 19-007, *infra*), which is, however, not a separate legal person.

---

[124] C-15/00, *Commission v European Investment Bank*, 2003, para. 102. See, similarly, with regard to the ECB: C-11/00, *Commission v European Central Bank*, 2003, para. 135.

[125] C-15/00, *Commission v European Investment Bank*, 2003, paras 103–9. See, similarly, with regard to the ECB: C-11/00, *Commission v European Central Bank*, 2003, paras 136–44.

19
CFSP Decision-making

Specific procedures. Decision-making in respect of the Common Foreign and Security Policy (CFSP) is subject to the 'specific rules and procedures',[1] which are laid down in Chapter 2 of Title V of the TEU. In this field, the Contracting Parties never wished to make the national governments—represented in the Council—share their power of decision with the Commission and the European Parliament in the same way as in other fields of Union action. According to Article 24(1), second subpara. TEU, the CFSP is to be defined and implemented by the European Council and the Council acting unanimously and put into effect by the Member States or the High Representative of the Union for Foreign Affairs and Security Policy. The adoption of legislative acts is excluded (ibid.). Pursuant to the same provision, the 'specific role of the European Parliament and of the Commission in this area is defined by the Treaties'. It is clear from the following analysis that policy-making and implementation with respect to the CFSP still preserves many characteristics of intergovernmental cooperation.[2]

19.001

I. Policy-making under the CFSP

Decision-making. All acts that the Union wishes to adopt under the common foreign and security policy (CFSP; see Chapter 2 of Title V of the TEU) emanate from the European Council and/or the Council.[3] The European Council is responsible for identifying the strategic interests and objectives of the Union for the CFSP and defines the general guidelines for the CFSP (Article 26(1) TEU). The Council defines and frames the CFSP on the basis of general guidelines and strategic lines defined by the European Council (Article 26(2), first subpara. TEU). The Council and the High Representative of the Union for Foreign Affairs and Security Policy ensure the unity, consistency, and effectiveness of action by the Union (Article 26(2), second subpara. TEU).

19.002

In principle, the European Council and the Council have to act unanimously (Article 31(1), first subpara. TEU). As in other fields, abstention does not prevent unanimity from being

---

[1] See Article 24(1), second subpara. TEU.
[2] See also the fact that the Court of Justice has only limited jurisdiction with respect to the CFSP (Article 275 TFEU; see para. 13-012, *supra*).
[3] For a description of decision-making in this area, see Butler, *Constitutional Law of the EU's Common Foreign and Security Policy—Competence and Institutions in External Relations* (Hart Publishing, 2019); Gosalbo-Bono and Naert, 'The Reluctant (Lisbon) Treaty and Its Implementation in the Practice of the Council', in Eeckhout and Lopez-Escudero (eds), *The European Union's External Action in Times of Crisis* (Hart Publishing, 2016), 13–84; Pernice and Thym, 'A New Institutional Balance for European Foreign Policy?' (2003) E For Aff Rev 369, 374–80; Müller-Brandeck-Bocquet, 'The New CFSP and ESDP Decision-Making System of the European Union' (2002) E For Aff Rev 257–82; for a discussion of the early practice, see Keukeleire and MacNaughtan, *The Foreign Policy of the European Union* (Palgrave Macmillan, 2008), Chapter 6.

attained. An abstaining member of the Council may qualify the abstention by making a formal declaration under the second subpara. of Article 31(1) TEU. If it makes such a declaration, the Member State is not obliged to apply the decision in question, but must accept that it binds the Union. This is termed 'constructive abstention'. Article 31(1) TEU provides that, in a spirit of mutual solidarity, the Member State concerned is to refrain from any action likely to conflict with or impede Union action based on the decision in question, and that the other Member States are to respect its position. It is only if the members of the Council qualifying their abstention in this way represent at least one-third of the Member States comprising at least one-third of the population of the Union, that the decision will not be adopted.[4]

The TEU further provides for a limited number of instances where the Council decides by a qualified majority (Article 31(2) TEU). This is so when the Council adopts a decision defining a Union action or position on the basis of a decision of the European Council relating to the Union's strategic interests and objectives[5] or on a proposal from the High Representative following a specific request from the European Council and when adopting decisions implementing such decisions. It also acts by a qualified majority when appointing a special representative (Article 31(2), first subpara. TEU).[6] The qualified majority will be calculated in the same way as in other fields (see para. 12-047 et seq., supra). It follows that the possibility to decide by qualified majority is in fact limited to the technical implementation of measures agreed on by all Member States. Moreover, qualified majority voting could be introduced in the CFSP (by the Amsterdam Treaty) only by also providing for a special 'alarm bell procedure'. If a member of the Council declares that, for vital and stated reasons of national policy, it intends to oppose the adoption of a decision to be taken by a qualified majority, no vote is taken and the Council, acting by a qualified majority, may request that the matter be referred to the European Council for decision by unanimity (Article 31(2), second subpara. TEU). Still, the European Council may unanimously decide that the Council is to act by a qualified majority in other cases (Article 31(3) TEU). However, no decision having military or defence implications may be taken by a qualified majority (Article 31(4) TEU).

The Council takes decisions relating to procedural questions by a simple majority vote (Article 31(5) TEU).

19.003 **Initiative and preparatory tasks.** Any Member State and the High Representative, possibly with the Commission's support,[7] may submit an initiative or proposal to deal with a particular question (Article 30(1) TEU). Whereas in other areas of external action the powers

---

[4] Before the Lisbon Treaty, Article 23(1), first subpara. EU required, in this connection, that the members of the Council qualifying their abstention represented more than one-third of the votes, weighted in accordance with Article 205(2) of the EC Treaty.

[5] Article 23(1) EU stated, in this connection, that the Council was to act by qualified majority 'when adopting joint actions, common positions or taking any other decision on the basis of a common strategy'. See, e.g., Council Joint Action 1999/878/CFSP of 17 December 1999 establishing a European Union Cooperation Programme for Non-proliferation and Disarmament in the Russian Federation, OJ 1999 L331/11, adopted pursuant to Common Strategy 1999/414/CFSP of the European Union of 4 June 1999 on Russia, OJ 1999 L157/1, and on the basis of Articles 14 and 23(2) EU.

[6] See Article 33 TEU.

[7] Before the Lisbon Treaty, the Commission itself could submit proposals in the field of the CFSP (Article 22(1) EU).

of initiative, implementation, and representation are vested in the Commission, acting as a College, the Commission's role in CFSP matters is confined to supporting proposals submitted by the High Representative, who is a member of the College. Accordingly, the Commission itself does not have a right of initiative.[8] In areas concerning both the CFSP and other fields of external action, the Commission and the High Representative may submit joint proposals (Article 22(2) TEU).[9]

The Political and Security Committee (PSC) advises the Council and is the privileged interlocutor of the High Representative.[10] The Political and Security Committee meets at the place where the Council has its seat, one week before the Council meets or, if the Council so requests, together with the Council. The PSC's position also appears on the agenda for Coreper meetings.[11] The Council has accelerated means of decision-making at its disposal. Thus, the PSC monitors the international situation on a permanent basis in areas covered by the CFSP (Article 38, first para. TEU). In military matters the activities of the Council and the PSC are prepared by a Military Committee (EUMC) on which the Chiefs of Defence sit. The EUMC is assisted by the Military Staff (EUMS), which is part of the General Secretariat of the Council.[12] The Military Staff performs early warning, situation assessment, and strategic planning tasks.[13] In addition, the High Representative is entitled, at very short notice, to convene a meeting of the Council either of its own motion or at the request of a Member State (Article 30(2) TEU).[14]

Involvement of European Parliament. The Council is entitled to act as regards the CFSP without seeking the opinion of the European Parliament. However, the High Representative, as President of the Foreign Affairs Council, must regularly consult the Parliament on the

19.004

---

[8] The Commission may take the view, however, that a question falls within another field of competence of the Union and submit a proposal based on the corresponding Treaty article (e.g. for a measure under the common commercial policy or under Union development cooperation policy). In such a case Article 4(3) TEU may well restrict a Member State's options to submit an initiative at the same time under the CFSP: see to that effect, with respect to the situation pre-Lisbon, Heukels and De Zwaan, 'The Configuration of the European Union: Community Dimensions of Institutional Interaction', in Curtin and Heukels (eds), *Institutional Dynamics of European Integration. Essays in Honour of Henry G. Schermers*, Vol. II (Martinus Nijhoff, 1994), 195, 217.

[9] See, e.g., the joint proposals for Council Regulation (EU) No. 1286/2009 of 22 December 2009 amending Regulation (EC) No. 881/2002 imposing certain specific restrictive measures directed against certain persons and entities associated with Usama bin Laden, the Al-Qaida network and the Taliban, OJ 2009 L346/42; Council Regulation (EU) No. 1295/2011 of 13 December 2011 amending Regulation (EU) No. 1284/2009 imposing certain specific restrictive measures in respect of the Republic of Guinea, OJ 2011 L330/1; Council Regulation (EU) No. 401/2013 of 2 May 2013 concerning restrictive measures in respect of Myanmar/Burma and repealing Regulation (EC) No. 194/2008, OJ 2013 L121/1; Council Regulation (EU) 2015/1755 of 1 October 2015 concerning restrictive measures in view of the situation in Burundi, OJ 2015 L257/1; Council Regulation (EU) 2017/2063 of 13 November 2017 concerning restrictive measures in view of the situation in Venezuela, OJ 2017 L295/21.

[10] Article 38, first para. TEU.

[11] See the annex to Council Decision 2001/78/CFSP of 22 January 2001 setting up the Political and Security Committee, OJ 2001 L27/1.

[12] See the manner of operation and organization set out in annexes to Council Decision 2001/79/CFSP of 22 January 2001 setting up the Military Committee of the European Union, OJ 2001 L27/4 and to Council Decision 2001/80/CFSP of 22 January 2001 on the establishment of the Military Staff of the European Union, OJ 2001 L27/7. The Military Staff consists of seconded military personnel headed by a three-star flag officer. The Military Committee is chaired by a four-star flag officer on appointment. See also Council Decision (EU) 2015/1027 of 23 June 2015 concerning the rules applicable to experts on secondment to the General Secretariat of the Council and repealing Decision 2007/829/EC, OJ 2015 L163/40.

[13] See the annex to Council Decision 2001/80/CFSP of 22 January 2001 on the establishment of the Military Staff of the European Union, OJ 2001 L27/7.

[14] The simplified written procedure (COREU) may be used in implementing the CFSP (Council Rules of Procedure, Article 12(2)(d); para. 12-043, *supra*).

main aspects and the basic choices of the CFSP and the common security and defence policy and keep the Parliament informed of how those policies evolve (see Article 36, first para. TEU).[15] In addition, he or she must ensure that the Parliament's views are 'duly taken into consideration'. Agreements have been reached between the European Parliament and the Council on the way in which the Parliament is given access to sensitive information in the field of security and defence policy.[16]

For its part, the Parliament may make recommendations to the Council and the High Representative (Article 36, second para. TEU). The parliamentary committee responsible for the CFSP prepares any recommendations and may be authorized by the President of the Parliament to draw them up using an urgency procedure (EP Rules of Procedure, Rule 118(1) and (2)). The European Parliament may adopt such recommendations relatively quickly, as they do not have to be translated into all the official languages for the committee stage in urgent cases and are deemed to have been adopted at the next plenary session if no objection is made by at least a certain number of the Parliament's component members (EP Rules of Procedure, Rule 118(4) and (6)).

II. Implementation of the CFSP

19.005 **Implementation by Council and Member States.** The implementation of CFSP decisions lies principally in the hands of the Member States and the Council, with the High Representative being responsible for securing their implementation (see Article 26(3) TEU). The European External Action Service (EEAS; see para. 13-042, *supra*) offers assistance with the administrative and financial implementation.[17] In third countries and international conferences, the diplomatic and consular missions of the Member States and the Union delegations are to cooperate in ensuring that the policy adopted by the Council is implemented (Article 35 TEU).

Where the international situation requires operational action by the Union, the Council adopts the necessary decisions.[18] The Council determines the way in which such decisions are to be implemented (Article 28(1) TEU).[19] If the Council does not do this, implementation of the CFSP is left to the Member States, which are to support the CFSP 'actively and unreservedly in a spirit of loyalty and mutual solidarity', to 'comply with the Union's action in this area' and to 'refrain from any action which is contrary to the interests of the

---

[15] Interinstitutional Agreement of 2 December 2013 between the European Parliament, the Council, and the Commission on budgetary discipline, on cooperation in budgetary matters, and on sound financial management, OJ 2013 C373/1, points 23–25. Before the Lisbon Treaty, this was a task for the Member State holding the Presidency of the Council (Article 21 EU), see also the Interinstitutional Agreement of 17 May 2006 between the European Parliament, the Council, and the Commission on budgetary discipline and sound financial management, OJ 2006 C139/1, point 43.

[16] Interinstitutional Agreement of 20 November 2002 between the European Parliament and the Council concerning access by the European Parliament to sensitive information of the Council in the field of security and defence policy, OJ 2002 C298/1, together with the Decision of the European Parliament of 23 October 2002 on the implementation of that agreement, OJ 2002 C298/4.

[17] See Blockmans and Hillion (eds), *EEAS 2.0—A Legal Commentary on Council Decision 2010/427/EU Establishing the Organisation and Functioning of the European External Action Service* (SIEPS/CEPS, 2013).

[18] Before the Lisbon Treaty, such decisions took the form of 'joint actions' (see Article 14(1) EU).

[19] Accordingly, whenever it deems it necessary, the Council may, on a proposal from the High representative, appoint a special representative with a mandate in relation to particular policy issues (Article 33 TEU).

Union or is likely to impair its effectiveness as a cohesive force in international relations' (Article 24(3) TEU). In order to enable prior consultations to take place within the Council, a Member State has to provide prompt information of any plan to adopt a position or to take action pursuant to a Council decision adopted under Article 28(1) TEU, except in the case of measures constituting merely a national transposition of Council decisions. Only in cases of 'imperative need arising from changes in the situation' and where the Council does not itself review its previous position may a Member State take the necessary measures, as a matter of urgency, in the absence of a Council decision and inform the Council immediately afterwards (Article 28(3) and (4) TEU). If a Member State has major difficulties implementing a Council decision adopted under Article 28(1) TEU, it must refer them to the Council. The Council is then to seek appropriate solutions consistent with the objectives of the joint action which do not impair its effectiveness (Article 28(3) TEU).

When the Council has adopted a decision defining the approach of the Union to a particular matter of a geographical or thematic nature,[20] implementation of that decision falls to the Member States, which are to ensure that their national policies conform to the Union positions (Article 29 TEU). They are to uphold the Union's positions in international organizations and at international conferences (Article 34(1) TEU).[21]

Supervision of implementation. The European Parliament, the Commission, and the Court of Justice play a more limited role in the CFSP than in other fields of Union policy.[22] The European Parliament may call the Council to account but may not impose sanctions upon it for the conduct of its policy in view of its limited supervisory powers over that institution. However, under the budgetary procedure, the Parliament is entitled to refuse to charge certain administrative or operational expenditure to the general budget.[23] For this reason, the Council and the Commission came to an understanding with the European Parliament on the financing of the CFSP, which has been laid down in interinstitutional agreements.[24] Each time the Council adopts a decision in the field of the CFSP entailing expenses, the High Representative will immediately communicate an estimate of the costs envisaged (financial statement) to the European Parliament.[25] Since the Court of Justice has only limited jurisdiction with respect to the provisions of the CFSP, it cannot review most acts of the Council or the Member States which are based thereon.[26] In any event, the Commission does not have the power pursuant to Article 258 TFEU to supervise that national implementing measures comply with the obligations imposed on Member States in the field of the CFSP.[27] As a result, parliamentary or judicial supervision of national measures implementing the

19.006

---

[20] Before the Lisbon Treaty, such decisions took the form of 'common positions' (see Article 15 EU).
[21] For the international representation of the Union, see para. 14-006, *infra*.
[22] See the statement in Article 24, second para. TEU.
[23] See para. 20-001, *infra*.
[24] See Interinstitutional Agreement of 2 December 2013 between the European Parliament, the Council, and the Commission on budgetary discipline, on cooperation in budgetary matters, and on sound financial management, OJ 2013 C373/1, points 23–25. See previously the interinstitutional agreements of 16 July 1997 (1997) EU Bull. point 2.3.1; of 6 May 1999, OJ 1999 C172/9, and of 17 May 2006, OJ 2006 C139/1.
[25] Ibid., point 25. The financial statement (*fiche financière*) is to relate, *inter alia*, to the timeframe, staff employed, use of premises and other infrastructure, transport facilities, training requirements, and security arrangements (ibid.).
[26] See para. 13-012, *supra*.
[27] Since the Court of Justice does not, in principle, have jurisdiction with respect to the CFSP (Article 275 TFEU), Article 258 TFEU does not apply to the provisions on the CFSP. Because the Commission has no determinative influence on the CFSP, the European Parliament cannot pass a motion of censure under Article 234 TFEU in respect of its role in this policy.

CFSP takes place primarily in the Member States. At Union level, supervision of the implementation of the CFSP consists chiefly of political supervision by the Council and the High Representative, which have a duty to ensure that the policy is properly implemented by the Member States (Article 24(3), third subpara. TEU). That supervision may also be carried out within the Political and Security Committee (Article 38, first para., *in fine* TEU).

19.007 **Military operations.** As far as security and defence policy is concerned, the Union relies on the operational capacity of Member States to deploy military forces capable of the tasks referred to in Article 43 TEU (Article 42(3) TEU; see para. 10-032, *supra*). In order to formulate and implement Union decisions and measures with implications in the defence sphere, the Union uses the Political and Security Committee (PSC), assisted by the Military Committee and the Military Staff.[28] The PSC exercises political control and strategic direction of crisis management operations (Article 38, second para. TEU). The operations themselves are carried out by units made available by the Member States. In this connection, the European Defence Agency assists the Council in evaluating the improvement of military capabilities (Article 42(3), second subpara. TEU). The Council may confer on a group of Member States, that are willing and capable to do so, the implementation of a task in connection with the common security and defence policy (Article 42(5) TEU). It is then for those Member States, in association with the High Representative, to agree among themselves on the management of the task (Article 44(1) TEU). Where completion of that task entails major consequences or requires amendment of the decision determining the task, the Council is to adopt the necessary decisions (Article 44(2) TEU).

Under the third para. of Article 38 TEU, the Council may authorize the PSC, for the purpose and duration of a crisis management operation, to take the relevant decisions concerning the political control and strategic direction of the operation.[29] In this way, the PSC has, for example, directed military operations of the European Union in the Former Yugoslav Republic of Macedonia (now North Macedonia), Congo, Chad and the Central African Republic,[30] and more recently the Somali coast and the Southern Central Mediterranean.[31] The same applies to police missions of the Union.[32]

---

[28] For their operation and organization, see the annexes to Council Decisions 2001/79/CFSP and 2001/80/CFSP of 22 January 2001 (n. 12, *supra*).

[29] What is involved therefore is a delegation authorized by the Treaty of discretionary powers; see also para. 18-025, *supra*.

[30] See Article 4 of Council Joint Action 2003/92/CFSP of 27 January 2003 on the European Union military operation in the Former Yugoslav Republic of Macedonia, OJ 2003 L34/26; Articles 7 and 10 of Council Joint Action 2003/423/CFSP of 5 June 2003 on the European Union military operation in the Democratic Republic of Congo, OJ 2003 L143/50; and Article 6 of Council Joint Action 2007/677/CFSP of 15 October 2007 on the European Union military operation in the Republic of Chad and in the Central African Republic, OJ 2007 L279/21. Examples of decisions taken by the PSC pursuant to those joint actions are to be found in OJ 2003 L170/15 and L170/19 and OJ 2008 L107/60. For a detailed overview, see Naert, *International Law Aspects of the EU's Security and Defence Policy, with a Particular Focus on the Law of Armed Conflict and Human Rights* (Intersentia, 2010), Chapter 3.

[31] Decisions by the PSC relating to piracy in Somalia (e.g. Political and Security Committee Decision (CFSP) 2020/401 of 12 March 2020, OJ 2020 L79/2), and the Southern Central Mediterranean (Political and Security Committee Decision (CFSP) 2020/289 of 19 February 2020, OJ 2020 L61/4).

[32] For another example, see Article 11(2) of Council Joint Action 2005/797/CFSP of 14 November 2005 on the European Union police mission in the Palestinian Territories, OJ 2006 L331/21, and, for a decision taken pursuant to this joint action, OJ 2006 L331/21. For a recent PSC decision in this respect, see Political and Security Committee Decision (CFSP) 2019/1165 of 2 July 2019 extending the mandate of the Head of Mission of the European Union Police Mission for the Palestinian Territories (EUPOL COPPS) (EUPOL COPPS/1/2019), OJ 2019 L182/43.

The Union's security and defence policy takes account of existing forms of military cooperation and of specific positions of particular Member States (Article 42(2), second subpara. TEU[33]). By virtue of a Protocol to the Treaties, Denmark does not participate in the elaboration and implementation of decisions and actions of the Union that have defence implications.[34] In that Protocol, however, Denmark has undertaken not to prevent the other Member States from further developing their cooperation in this area.

---

[33] Article 42(2), second subpara. TEU refers, in particular, to the obligations of certain Member States in connection with their membership of NATO. Article 17(4) EU also referred to the Western European Union (WEU).

[34] Article 5 of Protocol (No. 22), annexed by the Lisbon Treaty to the TEU and TFEU, on the position of Denmark, OJ 2010 C83/299. Denmark had already adopted this stance upon the introduction of the CFSP in 1993 (see para. 10-034, *infra*).

20
The Budgetary Procedures

I. Adoption of the Budget

20.001 **Procedure.** Article 314 TFEU, introduced by the Lisbon Treaty, governs the procedure for the yearly adoption of the budget. It replaces the unwieldy procedure provided for in Article 272 EC,[1] under which the budget was adopted in stages, with the Council placing drafts before the European Parliament on two occasions. After the first reading by the Parliament, the Council already had the last word on compulsory expenditure. The Parliament took the definitive decision on non-compulsory expenditure in the second reading. Moreover, if the Parliament was dissatisfied with the Council's final decision on compulsory expenditure, it could reject the draft budget and ask for a new draft to be submitted. Owing to the fact that the budget has to be in balance, that decision indeed affected the amount of leeway the Parliament had with regard to non-compulsory expenditure.[2]

The procedure introduced by the Lisbon Treaty is significantly less cumbersome. Under Article 314 TFEU, the draft budget is established by the Commission and then subject to one reading only by the Council and the European Parliament—the two branches of the Union's budgetary authority. Since the procedure for the adoption of the budget no longer distinguishes between compulsory and non-compulsory expenditure, the European Parliament thus has the final say—together with the Council—over all expenditure. However, the budget must remain within the limits of the multiannual financial framework (see para. 14-018, *supra*).

As set out below, the procedure of Article 314 TFEU has recourse to a Conciliation Committee in order to have the European Parliament and the Council agree on a joint text. In the past, interinstitutional agreements already provided for tripartite dialogue ('trilogue') between the Commission, the Parliament, and the Council even before the Commission established the preliminary draft budget and likewise before and after the European Parliament's (first) reading of the budget.[3] Pursuant to Article 324 TFEU, the Presidents of the Parliament, the Council, and the Commission are to take all the necessary steps to promote consultation and the reconciliation of the positions of the institutions.

---

[1] For the origins of this provision, see the Treaty of 22 April 1970 amending Certain Budgetary Provisions of the Treaties establishing the European Communities and of the Treaty establishing a Single Council and a Single Commission of the European Communities [First Treaty on Budgetary Provisions]; and the Treaty of 22 July 1975 amending Certain Budgetary Provisions of the Treaties establishing the European Communities and of the Treaty establishing a Single Council and a Single Commission of the European Communities [Second Treaty on Budgetary Provisions], OJ 1977 L359/1.

[2] The Parliament has used this power on three occasions; see the resolutions of the European Parliament of 13 December 1979 (OJ 1980 C4/37), 16 December 1982 (OJ 1983 C13/67), and 13 December 1984 (OJ 1985 C12/90).

[3] See the interinstitutional cooperation in the budgetary sector provided for in Annex I to the Interinstitutional Agreement of 16 December 2020 between the European Parliament, the Council, and the Commission on budgetary discipline, on cooperation in budgetary matters, and on sound financial management, as well as on new own resources, including a roadmap towards the introduction of new own resources, OJ 2020 L433I/28. For earlier agreements, see para. 14-017, *supra*.

Draft budget. Every year each institution, with the exception of the ECB, draws up estimates of its expenditure for the following year before 1 July.[4] The Commission consolidates these estimates in a draft budget. The draft budget, containing an estimate of revenue and expenditure, must be placed before the European Parliament and the Council no later than 1 September of the year preceding the year in which the budget is to be implemented (Article 314(1) and (2), first subpara. TFEU). At that stage, the Council adopts its position on the draft budget and forwards it, before 1 October of the same year, to the Parliament, informing the latter in full of the reasons which led it to adopt its position. If the Parliament, within forty-two days of this communication, approves the position of the Council or does not take any decision, the budget stands as finally adopted (Article 314(3) and (4)(a) and (b) TFEU).

20.002

If the European Parliament, by a majority of its component members, adopts amendments, the amended draft is forwarded to the Council and the Commission. In that case, the President of the Parliament, in agreement with the President of the Council, must convene a meeting of the Conciliation Committee, except where the Council, within ten days of the draft being forwarded, informs the European Parliament that it has approved all its amendments (Article 314(4)(c) TFEU).

Conciliation Committee. The Conciliation Committee in this context is modelled on the conciliation committee which may be convened in the course of the ordinary legislative procedure (see para. 17-029, *supra*). It is composed of the members of the Council (or their representatives) and an equal number of members representing the European Parliament. The Conciliation Committee attempts to reach agreement on a joint text within twenty-one days of its being convened, on the basis of the positions of the Parliament and the Council. Agreement requires a qualified majority of the members of the Council (or their representatives) and a majority of the representatives of the Parliament. The Commission takes part in the Conciliation Committee's proceedings and takes all the necessary initiatives with a view to reconciling the positions of the Parliament and the Council (Article 314(5) TFEU).

20.003

If, within the fixed deadline of twenty-one days,[5] the Conciliation Committee does not approve a joint text, the Commission is to submit a new draft budget (Article 314(8) TFEU).[6] If it reaches agreement within this deadline, the joint text is to be approved by the European Parliament (acting by a simple majority) and the Council (acting by qualified majority) within a period of fourteen days of that agreement (Article 314(6) TFEU). The Parliament needs a majority of its component members to reject the joint text. The Court has stressed that the exercise by the Parliament of its budgetary powers in plenary sitting constitutes a fundamental event in the democratic life of the European Union.[7] If the Parliament rejects

---

[4] Under Article 39 of Regulation (EU, Euratom) 2018/1046 of the European Parliament and of the Council of 18 July 2018 on the financial rules applicable to the general budget of the Union, OJ 2018 L193/1 ('the Financial Regulation'), the Commission and the budgetary authority may agree to bring forward certain dates in the procedure provided that this does not have the effect of reducing or delaying the periods allowed for considering the relevant texts.

[5] The purpose of the deadlines and time limits laid down in that provision is to ensure that the annual budget of the EU is adopted by the end of the year preceding the financial year in question, as a possible failure to observe them can result in the application of Article 315 TFEU concerning a provisional budget, see C-73/17, *France v European Parliament*, para. 35.

[6] Since the entry into force of the Lisbon Treaty, the Conciliation Committee failed to find an agreement on the budgets for 2011, 2013, 2015, and 2019, which required the Commission to submit a new draft budget every time.

[7] C-73/17, *France v European Parliament*, para. 34.

it, the Commission is to submit a new draft budget. It must also do so where the Council rejects the joint text and the Parliament fails to take a decision (Article 314(7)(b) and (c) TFEU).

If, within the fourteen-day period laid down in Article 314(6) TFEU, there has been no debate and vote in the European Parliament on the joint text on the draft annual budget, the joint text may be adopted by the Council alone, under the conditions laid down in Article 314 (7)(a) TFEU.[8] Also, if both institutions approve the text or fail to take a decision, or if one of the institutions approves the text while the other one fails to take a decision, the budget is definitively adopted in accordance with the joint text (Article 314(7)(a) TFEU).

If the European Parliament approves the joint text whilst the Council rejects it, the Parliament may, within fourteen days from the date of the rejection, and acting by a majority of its component members and three-fifths of the votes cast, decide to confirm all or some of its amendments. If it fails to reach this special majority, the position agreed in the Conciliation Committee on the budget heading which is the subject of the amendment is retained (Article 314(7)(d) TFEU).

20.004 **Constraints.** In exercising their decision-making powers under this procedure, the institutions need to take account of the constraints imposed upon their powers by the Treaties and the acts adopted thereunder. In particular, they have to maintain a balance between expenditure and revenue (Article 314(10) TFEU).[9] The Commission, for its part, may amend the draft budget at all times during the procedure, but only until such time as the Conciliation Committee is convened (Article 314(2), second subpara. TFEU).

20.005 **Adoption of budget.** When the procedure provided for in Article 314 TFEU has been completed, the President of the European Parliament declares that the budget has been definitively adopted (Article 314(9) TFEU).[10] That declaration endows the budget with binding force vis-à-vis the institutions and the Member States.[11]

20.006 **Amending budget.** If, in the event of unavoidable, exceptional, or unforeseen circumstances, expenditure or revenue is not in accordance with the estimates, the Commission may decide whether it is necessary to propose an amending budget.[12] The amending budget is adopted in accordance with the procedure laid down in Article 314 TFEU.

Article 315 TFEU applies when the budget has not yet been voted at the beginning of the financial year. In that event, the Commission may, in principle, undertake monthly expenditure of one-twelfth of the relevant budgetary appropriations for the preceding financial year, provided that the monthly expenditure does not exceed one-twelfth of the appropriations provided for in the draft budget.[13]

---

[8] Ibid., para. 40.
[9] Infringement of the principle that the budget must be in equilibrium constitutes a ground for annulling the act of the President of the Parliament declaring that the budget has been finally adopted. See C-284/90, *Council v European Parliament*, 1992, paras 32–3.
[10] C-77/11, *Council v European Parliament*, 2013, paras 49–72.
[11] Ibid., para. 51; see, previously, 34/86, *Council v European Parliament*, 1986, para. 8.
[12] Financial Regulation, Article 42. Prior to the Financial Regulation of 25 June 2002, there was a formal distinction between amending and supplementary budgets, but this was abolished as it served no practical purpose.
[13] Article 315, first para. TFEU in conjunction with Article 16(2) of the Financial Regulation. The Council may decide to authorize an increase in the 'provisional twelfths'. However, the European Parliament may decide to reduce this expenditure (Article 315, second, third, and fourth paras TFEU).

II. Implementation of the Budget and Audit

Implementation of expenditure. The Commission implements the budget in cooperation with the Member States on its own responsibility and within the limits of the appropriations, having regard to the principles of sound financial management (Article 317, first para. TFEU).[14] Other institutions and bodies may also engage in expenditure as authorized under the budget. The implementation of the budget is framed by the Financial Regulation[15] and any other financial rules adopted by the European Parliament and the Council, acting in accordance with the ordinary legislative procedure and after consulting the Court of Auditors, pursuant to Article 322 TFEU. The Commission's power to implement the budget is separate from its power to implement legislative measures (see para. 18-012 et seq., supra).[16] Consequently, any implementation of expenditure by the Commission presupposes, in addition to the entry of the relevant appropriation in the budget, the prior adoption of a legally binding Union act providing a legal basis for the Union's action, except in cases provided for by the Financial Regulation (Article 310(3) TFEU). Prior adoption of such a 'basic act' is not required where expenditure is implemented for non-significant Union action.[17] The situations where this may occur are defined in the Financial Regulation.[18]

20.007

Shared, direct, and indirect management. The Commission implements the budget under one of the three following modes.

20.008

First, the major part of the budget is implemented under 'shared management' with the Member States,[19] which cooperate with the Commission to ensure that the appropriations are used in accordance with the principles of sound financial management (Article 317, first para. TFEU). Shared management implies that budget implementation is delegated to the Member States. They must take all legislative, regulatory, and administrative measures to protect the financial interests of the Union, namely by ensuring the correct and effective implementation of actions financed from the budget; designating bodies responsible for the management and control of Union funds; preventing, detecting, and correcting irregularities and fraud; and cooperating, in accordance with the Financial Regulation and sector-specific rules, with the Commission, OLAF, and the Court of Auditors.[20] The Commission monitors the management and control systems established in Member States and, where

---

[14] For a good overview, see European Commission, *European Union—Public Finance*, 2014, freely available on the EU Publications Office website.
[15] Regulation (EU, Euratom) 2018/1046 of the European Parliament and of the Council of 18 July 2018 on the financial rules applicable to the general budget of the Union, OJ 2018 L193/1 (see also para. 14-010, *supra*).
[16] 16/88, *Commission v Council*, 1989, paras 16-19; C-106/96, *United Kingdom v Commission*, 1998, para. 22.
[17] See C-239/96 R and C-240/96 R, *United Kingdom v Commission* (order), 1996, paras 41–6; C-106/96, *United Kingdom v Commission*, 1998, paras 21–37 (annulment of a Commission decision to carry out expenditure for which the Council had not adopted a basic act).
[18] Interinstitutional Agreement on legal bases and implementation of the budget (OJ 1998 C344/1; see also (1998) 7/8 EU Bull. point 1.6.1), as taken over in Article 58 of the Financial Regulation. Such expenditure concerns appropriations for pilot schemes, preparatory actions, and specific or indefinite actions carried out by the Commission by virtue of its prerogatives (other than the right of initiative) and appropriations intended for the internal administration of each institution.
[19] See Financial Regulation, Articles 62(1)(b) and 63.
[20] Financial Regulation, Article 63(1). For those Member States participating in enhanced cooperation pursuant to Council Regulation (EU) 2017/1939 (39), this also includes cooperation with the European Public Prosecutor's Office (EPPO).

funds are used in breach of applicable law, may exclude expenditure from Union financing, interrupt payment deadlines, and suspend payments.

Second, the budget may be directly implemented by the Commission's own departments, Union delegations, or the Commission's executive agencies ('direct management').[21] In this case, the budget implementation is subject to the internal control system set out in the Financial Regulation (see para. 20-010, *supra*).

Third, where the basic act so provides,[22] budget implementation tasks may be entrusted to selected persons or entities, such as Union bodies, international organizations, third countries, public law bodies, as well as certain bodies governed by private law that are provided with adequate financial guarantees ('indirect management').[23] In order to ensure an adequate protection of the Union financial interests, it is then for the Commission to assess the systems, rules, and procedures of the persons or entities implementing Union funds and to take appropriate supervisory measures.[24]

The Commission confers the necessary powers to implement their own sections of the budget on the European Economic and Social Committee, the Committee of the Regions, the European Ombudsman, the European Data Protection Supervisor, and the European External Action Service.[25] Nevertheless, it retains responsibility for financial management, even where the implementation of the budget is entrusted to national authorities or to the Union and the Member States jointly. On the basis of the information provided to it by the institutions by 1 March each year, the Commission draws up annual accounts for the Union, with financial statements of assets and liabilities and budget implementation reports, and forwards them to the European Parliament, the Council, and the Court of Auditors.[26]

20.009 **Rule of law conditionality.** In November 2020, the European Parliament and the Council agreed on a general regime of conditionality for the protection of the budget, in a Regulation[27] adopted, pursuant to Article 322 TFEU, after the European Council of 10 and 11 December 2020 issued conclusions in this respect.[28] The Regulation provides for rules protecting the budget in case of breaches of 'the principles of the rule of law in the Member States', which may arise where the independence of the judiciary is endangered; where public authorities fail to prevent, correct, and sanction arbitrary or unlawful decisions or to prevent conflicts of interests; or where legal remedies are unavailable of ineffective.[29] If such

---

[21] Financial Regulation, Article 62(1)(a).
[22] This is also possible, without provision in a basic act, in the cases mentioned in Article 58 of the Financial Regulation (see n. 15, *supra*).
[23] Financial Regulation, Article 62(1)(c).
[24] Ibid., Article 154(3).
[25] Article 317, second para. TFEU; Financial Regulation, Article 59.
[26] Article 318 TFEU; Financial Regulation, Articles 241 to 245.
[27] Regulation (EU, Euratom) 2020/2092 of the European Parliament and of the Council of 16 December 2020 on a general regime of conditionality for the protection of the Union budget, OJ 2020 L433I/1. See Fisicaro, 'Rule of Law Conditionality in EU Funds: The Value of Money in the Crisis of European Values' (2020) European Papers 695–722.
[28] Conclusions of the European Council of 11 December 2020, EUCO 22/20. The European Council indicated, *inter alia*, that the Commission agreed to develop guidelines on its application of the Regulation and that, if an action for annulment is brought against the Regulation, these guidelines will be finalized after the judgment of the Court of Justice, with the Commission not proposing any measures under the Regulation until these guidelines are finalized. It also recalls recital 26 of the Regulation according to which a Member State concerned, which considers that the principles of objectivity and equal treatment of Member States are being seriously breached, may have the matter referred to the European Council.
[29] Regulation 2020/2092 (n. 27, *supra*), Article 3.

breaches affect or seriously risk affecting the sound financial management of the Union budget or the protection of the Union's financial interests in a sufficiently direct way, the Commission may propose to the Council, after prior notification of the Member State concerned, to adopt appropriate measures, such as the suspension of payments or commitments, the early repayment of loans, and the prohibition to conclude new commitments.[30] The Council is to adopt its decision, with a qualified majority, within one month or, in exceptional circumstances, three months. The measures taken are to be lifted if the conditions that justified them are no longer fulfilled.[31]

Internal control. The uptake and utilization of Union funds by the Union institutions is subject to internal and external controls. In accordance with the Financial Regulation, each institution entrusts authorizing officers with implementing revenue and expenditure in accordance with the principles of sound financial management. The authorizing officers are responsible for ensuring that the requirements of legality and regularity are complied with and introduce appropriate procedures for management and internal audit.[32] An internal auditor is charged with verifying the proper operation of budgetary implementation systems and procedures and reporting to his or her institution thereon.[33]

20.010

External audit. The external controls are carried out in the first instance by the Court of Auditors and subsequently by the European Parliament, working together with the Council. The Court of Auditors examines the accounts of all revenue and expenditure of the Union. It examines not only the general budget, but also the accounts of all bodies, offices, or agencies set up by the Union in so far as the relevant constituent instrument does not preclude such examination (Article 287(1), first subpara. TFEU).[34] The purpose of the audit is to establish that all revenue has been received and all expenditure incurred in a lawful and proper manner having regard to financial regulations and the substantive provisions on the basis of which the operations were carried out.[35] The Court of Auditors also verifies that the financial management has been sound[36] and accordingly that resources have been utilized efficiently.[37] In particular, the Court is to report on any cases of irregularity.[38]

20.011

The external audit is carried out after operations have been performed, but does not have to wait until the accounts for the relevant financial year have been closed (Article 287(2) TFEU).

---

[30] Ibid., Articles 4–5.
[31] Ibid., Article 6.
[32] Article 322(b) TFEU; Financial Regulation, Articles 73 and 74.
[33] Financial Regulation, Articles 117 and 118. For the changes in terms of internal audits, see Craig, 'The Constitutionalisation of Community Administration' (2003) ELRev 840, 845–6.
[34] Article 12 of the EIB Statute sets up a special committee to verify the Bank's operations and accounts. However, the Court of Auditors does examine expenditure of Union funds carried out by the EIB on the Commission's instructions. Article 287(3), third subpara. TFEU refers to the Court of Auditors' right of access to information held by the EIB, which is to be governed by an agreement between the Court of Auditors, the EIB, and the Commission.
[35] See Article 287(2) TFEU and Financial Regulation, Article 255(1).
[36] Article 287(2), first subpara. TFEU.
[37] On the Court's assessment criteria, see Brenninkmeijer, Moonen, Debets and Hock, 'Auditing Standards and the Accountability of the European Court of Auditors (ECA)', (2018) ULR 1–17; Stephenson, 'Reconciling Audit and Evaluation? The Shift to Performance and Effectiveness at the European Court of Auditors', (2015) Eur J Risk Regul 79–89.
[38] Article 287(2), first subpara., TFEU.

The Court of Auditors is entitled to have access to all necessary decisions and information, which Union institutions, any bodies managing revenue or expenditure on behalf of the Union, any natural or legal person in receipt of payments from the budget; and national audit bodies or the relevant national departments are under a duty to provide on request. Where necessary, it will carry out its inspections on the spot in Union institutions and on the premises of the aforementioned bodies and natural or legal persons. Where investigations are carried out in Member States, the Court of Auditors works in liaison with national audit bodies or competent departments, provided that they wish to take part in the audit. The Court and the national audit bodies are to cooperate in a spirit of trust while maintaining their independence.[39]

After the close of each financial year, the Court of Auditors draws up an annual report which is forwarded to the other institutions and published, together with their replies to the Court's observations, in the *Official Journal* (Article 248(4), first subpara. TFEU). Persons mentioned in reports have the right to be heard.[40]

20.012 **Discharge.** The European Parliament is empowered to give a discharge to the Commission in respect of the implementation of the budget; it acts on a recommendation from the Council, acting by qualified majority. The Parliament decides by a majority of the votes cast.[41] The Council and the Parliament take their decisions in the light of the accounts and the financial statement and the evaluation report submitted by the Commission[42] the annual report of the Court of Auditors,[43] the statement of the Court of Auditors of assurance as to the reliability of the accounts and the legality and regularity of the underlying transactions,[44] and any relevant special reports of that institution (Article 319(1) TFEU).

Before giving a discharge to that institution, the European Parliament may ask the Commission to give evidence with regard to the execution of expenditure or the operation of financial control systems and to provide any necessary information (Article 319(2) TFEU). As in the case of the Council's recommendation, the decision giving discharge may be accompanied by observations on the implementation of the budget. The Commission has to take all appropriate steps to act on those observations and to report to the Parliament and the Council on measures taken (Article 319(3) TFEU). The discharge is a decision that formally closes the accounts. Although it has no effect on the Commission's legal position, the Parliament's refusal to discharge it in full or in part is a powerful political signal.[45]

---

[39] Article 287(3) TFEU. See, in this connection, Flizot, 'Les rapports entre la Cour des comptes européenne et les institutions supérieures de contrôle des Etats membres. Quelle application du principe du subsidiarité?' (2002) RMCUE 112–21.

[40] See C-315/99 P, *Ismeri Europa v Court of Auditors*, 2001, paras 27–35, and the discussion by Inghelram in (2001) CDE 707–28.

[41] See Article 5 of the Procedure for the consideration and adoption of decisions on the granting of discharge in Annex V to the EP Rules of Procedure.

[42] See Article 318 TFEU.

[43] Article 287(4), first subpara. TFEU.

[44] Article 287(1), second subpara. TFEU. The statement is submitted to the European Parliament and the Council and published in the *Official Journal*.

[45] The European Parliament refused to give the Commission a discharge for the 1982 financial year (OJ 1984 C337/23; subsequently, discharge was given for purposes of closure of the accounts by resolution of 15 March 1985, OJ 1985 C94/153) and the 1996 financial year (resolution of 4 May 1999, OJ 1999 C279/115: the reasons, which were adopted on 17 December 1998, are appended thereto). See Beurdeley, 'Les motifs du refus de décharge relatif au budget général de l'Union européenne' (2000) RMCUE 696–702). It provisionally refused to give a discharge in respect of the 1990 financial year (resolution of 27 October 1993, OJ 1993 C315/89) and for the 1992 financial year (see the resolution of 21 April 1994, OJ 1994 C128/322; discharge was granted by decision of 5 April 1995, OJ 1995

Nevertheless, the Commission may be dismissed only if a motion of censure is passed by the Parliament (see para. 12-006, *supra*).

Combating fraud. More than half of Union resources are utilized by national authorities, for which the Commission has set up control systems in a number of policy areas. Under Article 325 TFEU, the Union, and the Member States are to counter fraud and any other illegal activities affecting the financial interests of the Union through deterrent measures affording effective protection in the Member States and in all the Union's institutions, bodies, offices, and agencies. Article 325(1) TFEU requires the Member States to counter fraud and any other illegal activity affecting the financial interests of the Union through effective and deterrent measures.[46] While they are free to provide for administrative or criminal penalties or a combination of the two, they must nonetheless ensure that cases of serious fraud or any other serious illegal activity affecting the financial interests of the Union in customs matters are punishable by criminal penalties that are effective and dissuasive.[47]

20.013

The investigative duties conferred on the Commission by Union legislation are now performed by the European Anti-Fraud Office (OLAF; see para. 13-043, *supra*), which may undertake both internal investigations in Union institutions and bodies and external investigations in the Member States.[48] Protection of the Union's financial interests indeed means combating fraud and other irregularities at all levels at which those interests are liable to be affected, that is within both the Member States and the Union institutions and bodies.[49] As far as combating fraud at the Union level is concerned, Union bodies may not introduce their own systems to prevent and combat fraud in place of the general power of investigation vested in OLAF by Union legislation.[50]

L141/51; see also OJ 1995 C109/51). The grant of a discharge was also postponed for the 1997 financial year, see the resolution of 4 May 1999, OJ 1999 C279/119 (discharge was granted by decision of 19 January 2000, OJ 2000 L45/36) and for the 1998 financial year, see the resolution of 13 April 2000, OJ 2000 C40/381 (discharge was granted by resolution of 6 July 2000, A5-0190/2000).

[46] C-105/14, *Taricco*, 2015, para. 37; C-42/17 *M.A.S. and M.B.*, 2017, para. 30. On the direct effect of Article 325(1) TFEU, see C-42/17, *M.A.S. and M.B.*, para. 38.

[47] C-42/17 *M.A.S. and M.B.*, 2017, paras 33–5; C-612/15, *Kolev*, 2018, para. 54.

[48] See Regulation (EU, Euratom) No. 883/2013 of the European Parliament and of the Council of 11 September 2013 concerning investigations conducted by the European Anti-Fraud Office (OLAF) (OJ 2013 L248/1), replacing Regulation (EC) No. 1073/1999 of the European Parliament and the Council on 25 May 1999 (OJ 1999 L136/1), and the Interinstitutional Agreement of 25 May 1999 between the European Parliament, the Council and the Commission concerning internal investigations by the European Anti-Fraud Office (OLAF) (OJ 1999 L136/15). For the terms and conditions for internal investigations in relation to the prevention of fraud, corruption, and any illegal activity detrimental to the Union's interests, see amongst others, Council Decision 1999/394/EC, Euratom of 25 May 1999 (OJ 1999 L149/36); the Commission Decision 1999/396/EC, ECSC, Euratom of 2 June 1999 (OJ 1999 L149/57); and the Decision of the European Parliament of 18 November 1999, OJ 2003 L61/112 (see Rule 12 of the EP Rules of Procedure). See Groussot and Popov, 'What's Wrong with OLAF?: Accountability, Due Process and Criminal Justice in European Anti-fraud Policy' (2010) CMLRev 605–43; Trasca, 'La place de l'Office Européen de Lutte Antifraude dans la répression de la fraude au budget communautaire' (2008) CDE 7–82. See also para. 12-016, *supra* with regard to the discussion as to whether Members of the European Parliament may invoke parliamentary immunity in the context of an OLAF investigation.

[49] C-11/00, *Commission v European Central Bank*, 2003, paras 103–4, and C-15/00, *Commission v European Investment Bank*, 2003, paras 134–5.

[50] According to the Court of Justice, the expression 'financial interests of the Community' covers the use by the ECB and the EIB of their own resources, even though they are managed autonomously: C-11/00, *Commission v European Central Bank*, 2003, paras 89–97, and C-15/00, *Commission v European Investment Bank*, 2003, paras 120–36. The fact that these bodies are subject to Union legislation on combating fraud does not detract from their functional independence: see para. 18-025, *supra*. See also Marchegiani, 'La BEI et l'OLAF, un conflit de nature constitutionnelle' (2000) RMCUE 690–5. For a critical analysis, see Goebel, 'Court of Justice Oversight over the

Since the Union has no criminal jurisdiction, the prosecution of financial fraud is left principally to the Member States. The Member States are under a duty to coordinate their action aimed at protecting the Union's financial interests against fraud and to take the same measures to counter fraud affecting those financial interests as they take in respect of their own financial interests (Article 325(2) and (3) TFEU).[51] In order to make combating fraud more effective, common legal rules have been created for all areas covered by Union policies which are applicable to the sanctions provided for by Union law.[52] Under Article 325(4) TFEU, the European Parliament, and the Council are to adopt, in accordance with the ordinary legislative procedure and after consulting the Court of Auditors, the necessary measures in the field of the prevention of and the fight against fraud affecting the Union's financial interests.[53] As has already been mentioned, this covers the fight against fraud at both the Union and the national levels.

Before the Lisbon Treaty, such measures could not concern the application of national criminal law or the national administration of justice.[54] National provisions of criminal law were harmonized through conventions established by the Council pursuant to Title VI of the EU Treaty (PJCC) in which general rules and a common definition of fraud were formulated.[55] Currently, Article 83(2) TFEU allows for the Union legislature to establish minimum rules concerning the definition of criminal offences and sanctions, which it has done in the form of Directive 2017/1731,[56] which has replaced these conventions with effect from 6 July 2019.[57] Furthermore, for those Member States that

European Central Bank: Delimiting the ECB's Constitutional Autonomy and Independence in the Olaf Judgment' (2006) Fordham ILJ 610–54.

[51] C-105/14, *Taricco*, 2015, paras 34–48; C-42/17 *M.A.S. and M.B.*, 2017, 29–43; C-612/15, *Kolev*, 2018, paras 49–76.

[52] Council Regulation (EC, Euratom) No. 2988/95 of 18 December 1995 on the protection of the European Communities' financial interests, OJ 1995 L312/1. See Wolfgang and Ulrich, 'Schutz der finanziellen Interessen der Europäischen Gemeinschaften' (1998) EuR 616–647; Lenaerts, 'Sanktionen der Gemeinschaftsorgane gegenüber natürlichen und juristischen Personen' (1997) EuR 17–46. See also, Directive (EU) 2019/1937 of the European Parliament and of the Council of 23 October 2019 on the protection of persons who report breaches of Union law, OJ 2019 L305/17.

[53] See, e.g., Regulation (EU) 2021/785 of the European Parliament and of the Council of 29 April 2021 establishing the Union Anti-Fraud Programme and repealing Regulation (EU) No 250/2014, OJ 2021 L172/110, replacing Regulation (EU) No 250/2014 of the European Parliament and of the Council of 26 February 2014 establishing a programme to promote activities in the field of the protection of the financial interests of the European Union (Hercule III programme), OJ 2014 L84/6.

[54] Article 280(4) EC. See Veldt Foglia, '(Nog) geen strafrecht in de Eerste Pijler?' (2002) SEW 162–9. See also, on the basis of Articles 113 and 115 TFEU, Council Directive 2010/24/EU of 16 March 2010 concerning mutual assistance for the recovery of claims relating to taxes, duties, and other measures, OJ 2010 L84/1, which may also be used to combat fraud against the Union, as in the case of cigarette smuggling, see, e.g., C-34/17, *Donnellan*, 2018.

[55] Convention of 26 July 1995 on the protection of the Communities' financial interests, OJ 1995 C316/48 (explanatory report in OJ 1997 C191/1). See further the additional protocols to the above Convention of 27 September 1996 (OJ 1996 C313/2; explanatory report in OJ 1998 C11/5) and 19 June 1997 (OJ 1997 C221/11); see also the Convention drawn up on the basis of the former Article K.3 of the EU Treaty on the fight against corruption involving officials of the European Communities or officials of Member States of the European Union (adopted by Council act of 26 May 1997, OJ 1997 C195/1). For the interpretation by the Court of Justice of these conventions and the protocols thereto, see paras 28-018–28-019, *infra*.

[56] Directive (EU) 2017/1371 of the European Parliament and of the Council of 5 July 2017 on the fight against fraud to the Union's financial interests by means of criminal law, OJ 2017 L198/29. See Di Francesco Maesa, 'Directive (EU) 2017/1371 on the Fight Against Fraud to the Union's Financial Interests by Means of Criminal Law: A Missed Goal?' (2018) European Papers, 1455–69; Juszczak and Sason, 'The Directive in the Fight against Fraud to the Union's Financial Interests by Means of Criminal Law (PFI Directive): Laying Down the Foundation for a Better Protection of the Union's Financial Interests?' (2017) Eurcrim 80–7.

[57] Directive 2017/1371, Article 16.

participate in the enhanced cooperation regarding the European Public Prosecutor, the European Public Prosecutor's Office (EPPO) is now responsible for investigating, prosecuting, and bringing to judgment the perpetrators of, and accomplices to, criminal offences affecting the financial interests of the Union as set out in Directive 2017/1371 (see para. 8-024, *supra*).[58]

---

[58] Council Regulation (EU) 2017/1939 of 12 October 2017 implementing enhanced cooperation on the establishment of the European Public Prosecutor's Office ('the EPPO'), OJ 2017 L283/1. For an analysis, see Brière, 'Le Parquet européen: analyse critique d'une réussite tempérée par d'importants défis à relever' (2019) CDE 149–88.

21

The Procedure for Concluding International Agreements

I. Field of Application of the Procedure

21.001 **Article 218 TFEU.** Article 218 TFEU sets out the internal procedure for negotiating and concluding 'agreements between the Union and third countries or international organisations'. That Treaty provision does not itself confer any power on the Union to act internationally, but applies whenever the Union wishes to conclude an agreement. The Union is empowered to do so where the Treaties expressly so provide,[1] where it is necessary in order to achieve one of the objectives of the Union, where it is provided for in a legally binding Union act, or where it is likely to affect common rules or alter their scope (Article 216 TFEU). The term 'agreement' is used here 'in a general sense to indicate any undertaking entered into by entities subject to international law which has binding force, whatever its formal designation'.[2] The decision by which the Union approves a given agreement refers in its preamble not only to the Treaty provision constituting the substantive legal basis, but also to the provision of Article 218 TFEU which sets out the applicable procedure.[3]

This Article 218 TFEU procedure applies in all fields of Union activity, including the CFSP and police and judicial cooperation in criminal matters.[4] Before the Lisbon Treaty, a separate procedure applied for the adoption of agreements in those fields.[5]

---

[1] See Article 8(2) TEU; Article 37 TEU; Article 79(3) TFEU; Article 186, second para. TFEU; Article 191(4), first subpara. TFEU; Article 207(3) TFEU; Article 209(2), first subpara. TFEU; Article 212(3), first subpara. TFEU; Article 214(4), first subpara. TFEU; Article 217 TFEU; Article 219(1) TFEU.

[2] Opinion 1/75, *Draft Understanding on a Local Cost Standard drawn up under the auspices of the OECD*, 1975, 1359–60. Article 218 TFEU does not cover guidelines agreed with a third country which do not constitute a binding agreement: C-233/02, *France v Commission*, 2004; see the case note by Lavranos and van Ooik (2004) SEW 543–7. According to Declaration (No. 5) annexed to the EU Treaty, the expression 'formal agreements' in Article 111(1) EC [*now Article 219(1) TFEU*] did not introduce a new category of international agreement.

[3] For an overview, see Heliskoski, 'The Procedural Law of International Agreements: A Thematic Journey through Article 218 TFEU' (2020) CMLRev 79–118. Articles 101 to 106 EAEC set out detailed rules for the conclusion of agreements by Euratom; no such rules were contained in the ECSC Treaty.

[4] A declaration annexed to the Lisbon Treaty confirms that Member States continue to have the power to negotiate and conclude agreements in this field 'in so far as such agreements comply with Union law' (Declaration (No. 36), annexed to the Lisbon Treaty, on Article 218 TFEU concerning the negotiation and conclusion of international agreements by Member States relating to the area of freedom, security, and justice, OJ 2010 C83/349).

[5] See Article 24 EU, pursuant to which the Council authorized the Presidency of the Council, assisted by the Commission as appropriate, to open negotiations. Agreements were concluded by the Council on a recommendation from the Presidency. Article 24(5) EU provided that no agreement was to be binding on a Member State whose representative in the Council stated that it had to comply with the requirements of its own constitutional procedure. The other members of the Council could then agree that the agreement would nevertheless apply provisionally.

The same procedural requirements apply to amendments of agreements and to additional or implementing protocols concluded together with, or on the basis of, the agreement itself.[6] In principle, the denunciation of an agreement also comes under Article 218 TFEU.[7]

II. Procedure for the Negotiation and Conclusion of Agreements

General outline. Article 218 TFEU constitutes a general provision of 'constitutional' import, since in conferring certain powers on the Union institutions it seeks to establish a balance between the institutions.[8]   21.002

The Council authorizes the opening of negotiations, adopts negotiating directives, authorizes the signing of agreements, and concludes them (Article 218(2) TFEU). The Commission is, in most cases, responsible for conducting the negotiations. The European Parliament, for its part, is consulted or (for certain agreements) has to give its consent. In any event, the European Parliament must be immediately and fully informed at all stages of the procedure (Article 218(10) TFEU). The Treaties provide for a degree of symmetry between the procedure for the adoption of internal Union acts and the procedure for the conclusion of international agreements. In this way, the institutional balance laid down in the Treaties, whereby the European Parliament and the Council exercise in any given field the same competences in the internal and external sphere, is ensured.[9]

Throughout the procedure, the Council acts by a qualified majority. However, the Council has to take its decision by a unanimous vote where the agreement in question covers a field for which, at the internal level, unanimity is required for the adoption of a Union act, and in the case of association agreements and of cooperation agreements with States that are candidates for accession[10] (Article 218(8) TFEU). Unanimity will also be required for the agreement by which the Union is to accede to the European Convention of Human Rights (ibid; see para. 25.016, *infra*).

A. Negotiations

Union negotiator. Negotiations for the conclusion of an international agreement start after the Council adopts a decision authorizing the negotiations. In that decision, the Council is to nominate the Union negotiator (or head of the Union's negotiating team), depending on the subject of the agreement envisaged. The Council acts on recommendations from the Commission, except where the envisaged agreement relates exclusively or principally to the CFSP, in which case recommendations emanate from the High Representative (Article   21.003

---

[6] Accordingly, Rule 114 of the EP Rules of Procedure deals with the 'conclusion, renewal or amendment of an international agreement'.
[7] See, e.g., Council Decision 91/602/EEC of 25 November 1991 denouncing the Cooperation Agreement between the European Economic Community and the Socialist Federal Republic of Yugoslavia, OJ 1991 L325/23, which was adopted in accordance with the procedure set out in Article 238 EEC [*now Article 217 TFEU*].
[8] C-327/91, *France v Commission*, 1994, para. 28.
[9] C-658/11, *European Parliament v Council*, 2014, para. 56.
[10] For such agreements, see Article 212 TFEU.

218(2) and (3) TFEU). Before the Lisbon Treaty, agreements with third countries or international organizations were invariably negotiated by the Commission.[11] Article 218(2) and (3) TFEU leaves more latitude to the Council as far as the nomination of the negotiator is concerned. Negotiations are expressly reserved to the Commission only as regards agreements in the field of the common commercial policy (Article 207(3) TFEU). Nevertheless, it follows from Article 17(1) TEU that, with the exception of the CFSP and other cases provided for in the Treaties,[12] it is for the Commission to ensure the Union's external representation. Accordingly, the intention behind Article 218(2) and (3) TFEU appears to be that negotiations should be conducted, as far as the CFSP is concerned, by the High Representative, whereas, in all other areas, negotiations should normally be conducted by the Commission or, in specific cases (e.g. mixed agreements), by a 'negotiating team' involving the Commission and representatives of the Council or of the Member States.

So as to make effective recommendations to the Council with a view to the adoption of negotiating directives, the Union negotiator is entitled to have exploratory discussions with potential third parties.[13] The Union negotiator conducts the negotiations in consultation with a special committee which may be appointed by the Council and within the framework of such directives as the Council may issue to it (Article 218(4) TFEU).[14] When the Council has designated a special committee, the Commission must provide the special committee with all the information necessary for it to monitor the progress of the negotiations, such as the general aims announced and the positions taken by the other parties throughout the negotiations.[15] Since the Council has to approve the agreement ensuing from the negotiations, it is useful that the Council has access to that information. However, neither the special committee nor the Council may impose on the negotiator binding negotiating positions.[16] The European Parliament, for its part, must be fully informed by the Commission (or the High Representative) of its recommendations and of the progress of international negotiations.[17] The Parliament must, in any event, be immediately and fully informed at all stages of the procedure (Article 218(10) TFEU). This information must enable the Parliament to exercise democratic control over the external action of the Union, in particular by reviewing the choice of legal basis for the international agreement, in order to assess whether its prerogatives have been respected.[18] In its Rules of Procedure, the Parliament has provided that in the case of any international agreement it may request the Council not to authorize the opening of negotiations until the Parliament has stated its position on the proposed negotiating mandate and that it may adopt recommendations to be taken into account before the relevant international agreement is concluded.[19] Such acts adopted by

---

[11] See Article 300(1), first subpara. EC. For the Commission's capacity to negotiate, see Keukeleire and MacNaughtan, *The Foreign Policy of the European Union* (Palgrave Macmillan, 2008), Chapter 6, 86–93.

[12] e.g. Article 219(3) TFEU (see para. 14.006, *supra*).

[13] Flaesch-Mougin, 'Le traité de Maastricht et les compétences externes de la Communauté européenne: à la recherche d'une politique externe de l'Union' (1993) CDE 351, 378.

[14] See, as regards agreements relating to the common commercial policy, Article 207(3), third subpara. TFEU, which provides that the Commission is to regularly report to the special committee and to the European Parliament on the progress of negotiations.

[15] C-425/13, *Commission v Council*, 2015, paras 65–6.

[16] Ibid., paras 67 and 88–92.

[17] EP Rules of Procedure, Rule 114(1) and (2).

[18] C-658/11, *European Parliament v Council*, 2014, para. 79; C-263/14, *European Parliament v Council*, 2016, paras 68–83. In both cases the Council decisions to sign and conclude the agreement were annulled because of the failure to duly inform the European Parliament.

[19] EP Rules of Procedure, Rule 114(3) and (4).

the Parliament are not in any way binding on the Commission or the Council, but are important where the conclusion of the agreement in question is contingent on the Parliament's consent.

Monetary affairs. By way of derogation from Article 218 TFEU, there are special rules on negotiations 'where agreements concerning monetary or foreign exchange regime matters need to be negotiated by the Union with one or more States or international organisations' (Article 219(3) TFEU). In such a case, the Council is to decide on the arrangements for the negotiation and conclusion of the agreement in question by a qualified majority on a recommendation from the Commission and after consulting the European Central Bank. These arrangements are to ensure that the Union expresses a single position (Article 219(3) TFEU). Depending on the formula chosen by the Council, negotiations on these matters need not necessarily be entrusted to the Commission. The Commission is entitled, however, to be fully associated with the negotiations.[20]

21.004

B. Conclusion of agreements

1. Initialling and signature

Division of powers. After the negotiations have closed, the text of the draft agreement is initialled by the negotiators. The power to sign the agreement is vested in the Council, which acts on a proposal from the Union negotiator (Article 218(5) TFEU). At the same time, a decision may be adopted on the provisional application of the agreement before it enters into force (ibid.).[21] Where the agreement is concerned with a matter in respect of which both the Union and the Member States have competence, the Union and the Member States must determine together who has the right of signature. Since that right entails the power to take the final decision as to the content of the agreement and creates an impression in other subjects of international law as to the division of competence between the Union and the Member States, the decision as to who has the right of signature is amenable to judicial review.[22] Under the so-called Luns-Westerterp procedures, the European Parliament was confidentially and informally informed about each initialled association and trade agreement. It now flows from Article 218(10) TFEU that at this stage, too, the Parliament must be immediately and fully informed.

21.005

Unlike in the case of initialling, which is intended only to fix the definitive text of the agreement, obligations ensue from signature for a contracting party, whether or not it signs subject to ratification. Until such time as it makes its intention clear not to become a party, a signatory State or international organization is obliged to refrain from acts which would defeat the object and purpose of the agreement.[23] This international-law principle of good

---

[20] Article 219(3) TFEU. For cases in which negotiating mandates were conferred on the Member States, see, e.g., the monetary agreements concluded by Italy on behalf of the Community with San Marino and the Vatican City, OJ 2001 C209/1, and C299/1, respectively; and by France on behalf of the Community with Monaco, OJ 2002 L142/59. These agreements have since all been replaced by agreements negotiated by the Commission, see n. 254 to 9-045.

[21] See Driessen, 'Provisional Application of International Agreements by the EU' (2020) CMLRev 741–72.

[22] C-25/94, *Commission v Council*, 1996, paras 29–37.

[23] Article 18, point (a), of the Vienna Convention of 21 March 1986 on the Law of Treaties between States and International Organizations or between International Organizations (para. 26.013, *infra*).

faith applies equally after the agreement has been ratified and during the period prior to its entry into force.[24] It applies to the Union institutions when an agreement has been approved by the Union, the date of its entry into force is known, and the Union adopts acts conflicting with provisions of the agreement.[25] Individuals may challenge such acts in reliance on the principle of protection of legitimate expectations in so far as the acts in question conflict with provisions of the agreement which have direct effect for them following the agreement's entry into force.[26]

2. Power to conclude agreements

21.006 **Council.** The Council concludes agreements on a proposal from the Union negotiator. There are different rules in this respect for agreements relating to monetary and exchange-rate matters. In such cases, the Council does not decide on a proposal from the Commission but on a recommendation from the ECB or from the Commission after consulting the ECB (Article 219(1) TFEU). Moreover, the conclusion of such agreements is subject to such arrangements as the Council decides upon pursuant to Article 219(3) TFEU (see para. 21.004, *infra*).

The Council generally 'concludes' an agreement by means of a decision concluding the agreement 'on behalf of the Union'. The fact that the Council adopts a decision (or a regulation) to this end, does not deprive the agreement of its legal force as an international agreement concluded by the Union.[27] An agreement obtains the force of Union law after it has entered into effect internationally.[28] Agreements concluded by the Union are published in the *Official Journal*.[29]

The Council also takes decisions to suspend an agreement, on a proposal from the Commission or the High Representative.[30] The same procedure applies where the Council establishes the positions to be adopted on the Union's behalf in a body set up by an agreement, when that body is called upon to adopt acts having legal effects, with the exception of acts supplementing or amending the institutional framework of the agreement (Article 218(9) TFEU).[31]

---

[24] Ibid., Article 18, point (b).
[25] T-115/94, *Opel Austria v Council*, 1997, paras 90–4.
[26] Ibid., para. 94 (the judgment in the *Opel Austria* case accordingly annulled a regulation imposing duties only a few days before the EEA Agreement prohibiting such duties entered into effect).
[27] See Everling, 'The Law of the External Economic Relations of the European Community', in Hilf, Jacobs, and Petersmann (eds), *The European Community and GATT* (Kluwer, 1986), 85, 96.
[28] C-66/18, *Commission v Hungary*, 2020, para. 69. See also earlier, 181/73, *Haegeman*, 1974, paras 5 and 6; C-366/10, *Air Transport Association of America and Others*, 2011, para. 73; Opinion 1/17, *Comprehensive Economic and Trade Agreement between Canada and the EU*, 2019, para. 117.
[29] Council Rules of Procedure, Article 17(1)(d). This applies to agreements concluded by the Union in the field of the CFSP, unless the Council decides otherwise on the grounds of Articles 4 and 9 of Regulation (EC) No. 1049/2001 of the European Parliament and of the Council of 30 May 2001 regarding public access to European Parliament, Council. and Commission documents (Council Rules of Procedure, Article 17(1)(e)).
[30] The application of an agreement may also be suspended by and in accordance with the procedure for imposing economic sanctions. See the discussion of Article 215 TFEU at para. 10.031, *supra*. Accordingly, the trade concessions under the Cooperation Agreement with Yugoslavia were suspended (Council Regulation (EEC) No. 3300/91 of 11 November 1991, OJ 1991 L315/1) and an embargo was brought in against Haiti by way of derogation from the Fourth ACP-EC Convention (Council Regulation (EEC) No. 1608/93 of 24 June 1993, OJ 1993 L155/2) under Article 133 EC [*now Article 207 TFEU*]. For the validity under international law of the suspension of the Cooperation Agreement with Yugoslavia, see C-162/96, *Racke*, 1998 (see para. 26.013, *infra*).
[31] C-244/17, *Commission v Council*, 2018, paras 20–38. This also holds true for the position to be taken at meetings of bodies that were set up under an agreement to which the Union is not a party; see C-399/12, *Germany v Council*, 2014, paras 48–68. The European Parliament must be 'immediately and fully informed' about any

Commission. The Commission (or the High Representative) is sometimes vested with the power to conclude agreements. This is limited to the conclusion of a small number of administrative agreements.[32]

21.007

Internal Union powers vested in the Commission cannot alter the allocation of powers between the Council and the Commission with regard to the conclusion of international agreements. Consequently, the Commission has no power to conclude an agreement with a third country on the application of the competition rules, even though, internally, it does have the power to adopt individual decisions in that field.[33] Even when agreeing non-binding guidelines with a third country, the Commission must take account of the division of powers and the institutional balance established by the Treaties.[34]

Article 218(7) TFEU allows the Council, when concluding an agreement, to authorize the Union negotiator to approve modifications on behalf of the Union where the agreement provides for them to be adopted by a simplified procedure or by a body set up by the agreement. The Council may attach specific conditions to such authorization.

3. Involvement of the European Parliament

Democratic control. With the exception of agreements that relate exclusively to the CFSP,[35] the Council has at least to consult the European Parliament before concluding the agreement (Article 218(6), second subpara. TFEU; see para. 21.009, *infra*). For five important categories of agreements, the Parliament must give its consent (see para. 21.010, *infra*). In areas where the Parliament does not need to be consulted, such as the CFSP, it nevertheless has the right to be immediately and fully informed about an envisaged agreement 'at all stages of the procedure' (Article 218(10) TFEU). The failure to inform the Parliament is an infringement of an essential procedural requirement, which can result in the invalidity of the decision by which the agreement was approved.[36]

21.008

---

decision taken by the Council in this connection (see Article 218(10) TFEU). For the Commission's undertaking to this effect, see point 23 of the Framework Agreement on relations between the European Parliament and the European Commission (OJ 2010 L304/47). See also Rule 115 of the EP Rules of Procedure. On the legal value of a position adopted pursuant to Article 218(9) TFEU, see C-620/16, *Commission v Germany*, 2019, paras 75–100; see also C-600/14, *Germany v Council*, 2014, paras 69–71.

[32] See Article 220 TFEU (relations with international organisations) and Article 6 of the Protocol on Privileges and Immunities (para. 14.007, *supra*) (agreements for the recognition by third countries of Union *laissez-passer* as valid travel documents).

[33] C-327/91, *France v Commission*, 1994, paras 40–3 (annulling the decision whereby the Commission sought to conclude the Agreement with the United States of America regarding the application of the competition laws of the European Communities and the United States, which was signed and entered into force on 23 September 1991). Agreements on cooperation in the field of competition have since been concluded by the Council pursuant to Article 83 EC [now Article 103 TFEU] and—as far as mergers are concerned—Article 308 EC [now Article 352 TFEU]; the Commission had to conclude such agreements only as far as the ECSC was concerned: see Council and Commission Decision 95/145/EC, ECSC of 10 April 1995, OJ 1995 L95/45 (concluding again the 1991 agreement) and Council and Commission Decision 98/386/EC, ECSC of 29 May 1998, OJ 1998 L173/26 (additional agreement with the United States); Council and Commission Decision 1999/445/EC, ECSC of 29 April 1999, OJ 1999 L175/49 (agreement with Canada); Council Decision 2003/520/EC of 16 June 2003, OJ 2003 L183/11 (agreement with Japan); Council Decision 2009/586/EC of 16 February 2009, OJ 2009 L202/35 (agreement with South Korea).

[34] C-233/02, *France v Commission*, 2004, para. 40.

[35] This refers to cases where the international agreement at issue is based solely on a CFSP legal basis: C-658/11, *European Parliament v Council*, 2014, paras 48–62.

[36] Ibid., paras 80–7; C-263/14, *European Parliament v Council*, 2016, paras 68–83.

a. Consultation

21.009 **Duty to consult.** In matters that do not require the consent of the European Parliament with the international agreement (and except for agreements which relate exclusively to the CFSP), the Council has to consult the European Parliament before concluding the agreement (Article 218(6), second subpara. TFEU). The Parliament has also thus to be consulted where no involvement whatsoever of the Parliament is prescribed for the adoption of internal rules in the matter at issue. The Council has to consult the Parliament before it concludes the agreement in question. If the matter is urgent, the Council may lay down a commensurate time-limit within which the Parliament should deliver its opinion. If the Parliament fails to deliver an opinion within that time-limit, the Council may act (Article 218(6), second subpara. sub (b), TFEU).[37] The Parliament adopts its opinion by a majority of votes cast. The Council is not bound in any way by that opinion. But if the opinion adopted by the Parliament is negative, the President of the Parliament requests the Council not to conclude the agreement in question.[38]

b. Consent

21.010 **Duty to obtain consent.** For five categories of agreements, the Treaties make their conclusion dependent upon the prior consent of the European Parliament (Article 218(6), second subpara. sub (a), TFEU). Before the Lisbon Treaty, the Treaties referred to the 'assent' of the European Parliament (Article 300(3) EC). The Council and the European Parliament may, in an urgent situation, agree upon a time-limit for the consent (Article 218(6), second subpara., sub (a), last sentence TFEU). The Parliament gives its consent by a majority of the votes cast on the basis of a report from the responsible committee which may merely recommend either that the whole of the proposal be accepted or rejected; no amendments may be tabled.[39] If the Parliament decides to withhold its consent, its President informs the Council that the agreement in question cannot be concluded.[40]

21.011 **Five categories of agreements.** The consent procedure applies, in the first place, to association agreements. Second, consent will be required for the agreement by which the Union is to accede to the European Convention of Human Rights. This was introduced by the Lisbon Treaty. Third, consent has to be obtained for other agreements establishing a specific institutional framework by organizing cooperation procedures. Since most 'cooperation agreements' establish bilateral bodies, this provision refers, in all likelihood, to agreements which establish a more complex institutional structure, yet are not concluded as an association agreement.[41] The fourth category of agreements requiring parliamentary consent are those having 'important budgetary implications' for the Union.[42] The final category consists of

---

[37] Accordingly, the agreement between the EC and the USA on the processing and transfer of PNR data by Air Carriers to the United States Department of Homeland Security, Bureau of Customs and Border Protection, was concluded by Council Decision 2004/496/EC of 17 March 2004, OJ 2004 L183/183, the European Parliament not being able to deliver an opinion within the time-limit laid down 'in view of the urgent need to remedy the situation of uncertainty in which airlines and passengers found themselves, as well as to protect the financial interests of those concerned' (see point 3 of the preamble). However, the decision was annulled by the Court because it was adopted under the wrong legal basis (see C-317/04 and C-318/04, *European Parliament v Council and Commission*, 2006).
[38] EP Rules of Procedure, Rule 114(8).
[39] EP Rules of Procedure, Rule 114(7).7. See also EP Rules of Procedure, Rule 105(4).
[40] EP Rules of Procedure, Rule 114(7).
[41] Flaesch-Mougin (n. 13, *supra*), 385–6. A first example is the WTO Agreement, para. 10.010, *supra*.
[42] In order to ascertain whether an agreement has important budgetary implications, account must be taken of whether expenditure under the agreement is spread over several years; of a comparison of the expenditure under

agreements covering fields to which either the ordinary legislative procedure applies or a special legislative procedure under which the Parliament's consent is required. This last category was significantly enlarged by the Lisbon Treaty. Before the Lisbon Treaty, consent was required only for agreements entailing amendment of an act adopted under the co-decision procedure. Accordingly, the Council could not, by means of an international agreement, detract from internal legislation which the Parliament and the Council had adopted under the co-decision procedure. However, so long as no internal act had been adopted, the Council was entitled to conclude international agreements in the field in question after merely consulting the Parliament. Since the Lisbon Treaty, consent is thus required for all matters that require the approval of the Parliament in respect of internal legislation, regardless of whether such legislation has actually been adopted. This means that the consent of the Parliament is required for trade agreements, as the common commercial policy is subject to the ordinary legislative procedure (Article 207 TFEU).

Political impact. The power of consent enables the European Parliament to have a real say in the Union's foreign policy.[43] The Parliament has sometimes withheld its consent to additional protocols to association agreements until the negotiators agreed to provisions complying with the Parliament's wishes regarding, in particular, respect for human rights in the third country concerned.[44] Thus, already in March 1988, the Parliament withheld its consent to additional protocols to the EEC–Israel Agreement until such time as Israel complied with the requirement under a Community regulation to afford agricultural products from the occupied territories direct access to the Community.[45] Consent gives the Parliament a means of applying pressure with a view to its being more closely involved in the drawing up of agreements or of particular clauses therein. By this means, the Parliament may obtain concessions from the Council with regard to the involvement of the Parliament going beyond the specific confines of a particular agreement.[46] More recently, on 11 February 2010, the Parliament withheld its consent to an agreement with the United States on the processing and transfer of Financial Messaging Data from the Union to the United States for purposes of the Terrorist Finance Tracking Program[47] and on 4 July 2012—for the

21.012

---

the agreement with the amount of the appropriations designed to finance the Union's external operations; and, where the agreement relates to a particular sector, of a comparison between the expenditure entailed by the agreement and the whole of the budgetary appropriations for the sector in question, taking the internal and external aspects together. See C-189/97, *European Parliament v Council*, 1999, paras 29–33.

[43] See Thym, 'Parliamentary Involvement in European International Relations', in Cremona and de Witte (eds), *EU Foreign Relations Law. Constitutional Fundamentals* (Hart Publishing, 2008) 201–32; Soriano, 'Analyse de l'évolution de l'action extérieure de l'UE dans le domaine des droits de l'homme, de la démocratie et de l'Etat de droit' (2005) Ann Fac Dr Liège 5–42; Bosse-Platière, 'Le Parlement européen et les relations extérieures de la Communauté européenne après le Traité de Nice' (2002) RTDE 527–53; Hilf and Schorkopf, 'Das Europäische Parlament in den Aussenbeziehungen der Europäischen Union' (1999) EuR 185–202.

[44] See the European Parliament's refusal to give its consent to Protocols with Syria, (OJ 1992 C39/52 and C39/55) and Morocco, (OJ 1992 C39/54). Consent was ultimately given on 28 October 1992 (but not for one of the Protocols with Syria, OJ 1992 C305/64); for the Protocols in question, see OJ 1992 L352/14 (Morocco) and OJ 1992 L352/22 (Syria). On 15 December 1987, the European Parliament deferred giving its consent to two financial protocols annexed to the EEC–Turkey Agreement on similar grounds (OJ 1988 C13/28; it gave its consent thereto on 20 January 1988, OJ 1988 C49/52).

[45] OJ 1988 C94/55 (consent withheld on 9 March 1988; for the political reasons, see (1988) 3 EU Bull. points 2.4.13–15); OJ 1988 C290/60 (consent given on 12 October 1988); Silvestro, 'Les Protocoles financiers CEE-Israël à l'examen du Parlement européen' (1991) RMCUE 462–4.

[46] Flaesch-Mougin (n. 13, *supra*), 385.

[47] European Parliament, resolution P7_TA(2010)0029, OJ 2010 C341E/100.

first time in matters of trade—to the multilateral Anti-Counterfeiting Trade Agreement (ACTA).[48]

III. Mixed Agreements

21.013 **Legal reasons.** External action on the part of the Union often takes the form of a mixed agreement, where both the Union and the Member States are parties.[49] Most multilateral agreements to which the Union is a party and all the present association agreements fall into this category. Close cooperation is required between the Member States and the Union institutions where the subject matter of an agreement appears to fall partly within the competence of the Union and partly within that of the Member States (see paras 10.005 and 14.006). In such a case, the agreement will be concluded both by the Union and by the Member States, unless the agreement does not allow international organizations such as the Union to sign and the Union exercises its external competence through the medium of the Member States.[50] The Court of Justice has further held that the Member States may participate in an agreement where the financing falls to them and constitutes an essential element of the agreement (see para. 10.005, *supra*). Finally, a Member State may participate in an international agreement alongside the Union as the international representative of certain dependent territories which are not part of the sphere of application of Union law.[51]

21.014 **Political reasons.** In practice, mixed agreements also come to the fore in other circumstances for a variety of political reasons in areas not covered by exclusive Union competence.[52] The other contracting parties may ask for the agreement to be concluded as a mixed agreement. In addition, Member States often choose to be party to the agreement. In this way, the conclusion of the agreement is not hampered by any disputes as to the precise limits of Union competence and the Member States remain in a position to take implementing measures themselves. In the case of an agreement which establishes institutions with

---

[48] European Parliament, resolution P7_TA(2012)0287. For a commentary, see Eckes, 'How the European Parliament's Participation in International Relations Affects the Deep Tissue of the EU's Power Structures' (2014) IJCL 904–29.

[49] See, expressly, Article 102 EAEC. For an extensive discussion, see the articles in Hillion and Koutrakos, *Mixed Agreements Revisited: The EU and its Member States in the World* (Hart Publishing, 2010); Eeckhout, *External Relations of the European Union, Legal and Constitutional Foundations* (OUP, 2004), 190–225; O'Keeffe and Schermers (eds), *Mixed Agreements* (Kluwer, 1983); Leal-Arcas, 'The European Community and Mixed Agreements' (2001) E For Aff Rev 483–513. See also, for the practical consequences of mixity on negotiations, Van Eeckhoutte and Corthaut, 'The Participation of the EU and its Member States in Multilateral Negotiations Post-Lisbon' (2017) YEL 1–61; Corthaut and Van Eeckhoutte, 'Legal Aspects of EU Participation in Global Environmental Governance under the UN Umbrella', in Wouters et al. (eds), *The European Union and Multilateral Governance—Assessing EU Participation in United Nations Human Rights and Environmental Fora* (2012, Palgrave Macmillan), 145–70.

[50] 2/91, *Convention No 170 of the International Labour Organisation concerning safety in the use of chemicals at work*, 1993, para. 5.

[51] Opinion 1/78, *International Agreement on Natural Rubber*, 1979, para. 62. The special position of the Member State concerned has no effect on the demarcation of spheres of competence within the Union: Opinion 1/94, *Agreement establishing the World Trade Organisation*, 1994, paras 17–18.

[52] This encompasses both exclusive competence within the meaning of Article 3(1) TFEU (see, e.g., Opinion 2/15, *Free Trade Agreement between the European Union and the Republic of Singapore*, 2017) and Article 3(2) TFEU (see, e.g., Opinion 3/15, *Marrakesh Treaty to Facilitate Access to Published Works for Persons who are Blind, Visually Impaired or Otherwise Print Disabled*, 2017). See also Schroeder, 'Freihandelsabkommen und Demokratieprinzip—Eine Untersuchung zur parlamentarischen Legitimation gemischter Verträge' (2018) EuR 119–39.

powers of decision, the mixed form guarantees that the Member States keep their voting rights in those institutions or that the Union—in the event that the Member States do not exercise their voting rights themselves—has a number of votes equal to the number of Member States.[53] The mere fact that international action of the Union falls within a competence shared between it and the Member States does not preclude the possibility of the required majority being obtained within the Council for the Union to exercise that external competence alone.[54] However, the Court has accepted that the Member States may resort to mixity when there is no possibility of the required majority being obtained within the Council for the Union to be able to exercise alone the external competence that it shares with the Member States in a particular area, but this does not affect the possibility for the Union to act alone in the same area in the future, if such majority can be found.[55] Similarly, in instances where some Member States have a specific role to play in an international organization, it is appropriate that the Union does not act alone, to the exclusion of those Member States.[56]

Consequences. In any event, a mixed agreement does not result in any shift in the respective powers of the Union and the Member States to give effect to the obligations arising for each of them out of the agreement. At most, the conclusion of a mixed agreement may prevent the agreement from being regarded as an exercise of power by the Union which results in a policy area being taken outside the sphere of competence of the Member States.[57]

21.015

IV. Opinion of the Court of Justice

Objective. Any Member State,[58] the European Parliament,[59] the Council, and the Commission may obtain the opinion of the Court of Justice as to whether an envisaged agreement is compatible with the Treaties.[60] Where the Court's opinion is adverse, the agreement may enter into force only after it is amended or after the Treaties have been revised in accordance with one of the procedures provided for by the Treaties (Article 218(11) TFEU).[61] The procedure for obtaining the prior opinion of the Court is intended to avoid

21.016

---

[53] For voting rights and, more generally, participation in such bodies, see Hoffmeister, 'Outsider or Frontrunner? Recent Developments under International and European Law on the Status of the European Union in International Organisations and Treaty Bodies' (2007) CMLRev 41–68; Sack, 'The European Community's Membership of International Organisations' (1995) CMLRev 1227, 1232–56; Neuwahl, 'Shared Powers or Combined Incompetence? More on Mixity' (1996) CMLRev 667, 678–87. See also Van Eeckhoutte and Corthaut (n. 49, *supra*).
[54] C-626/15 and C-659/16, *Commission v Council*, 2018, para. 126.
[55] C-600/14, *Germany v Council*, 2017, paras 66–8.
[56] C-626/15 and C-659/16, *Commission v Council*, 2018, paras 125–33.
[57] For liability in the case of 'mixed' international obligations of the Union and its Member States, see Björklund, 'Responsibility in the EC of Mixed Agreements—Should Non-Member Parties Care?' (2001) Nordic JIL 373–402.
[58] In this way a Member State may also convey the doubts of a regional parliament that, in accordance with the national procedural requirements, must also give its consent to a mixed agreement, see, e.g., Opinion 1/17, *Comprehensive Economic and Trade Agreement between Canada and the EU*, 2019 (initiated by Belgium, following difficulties in the ratification process of the Comprehensive Economic and Trade Agreement (CETA) at the regional level).
[59] The European Parliament was given the right to obtain an opinion by the Treaty of Nice.
[60] Before the Lisbon Treaty, the Court of Justice only had jurisdiction to give an opinion on the compatibility of an agreement with the provisions of the EC Treaty. The EU Treaty did not confer jurisdiction on the Court to rule on the compatibility of CFSP or PJCC agreements with that Treaty. For the CFSP, see however Article 275 TFEU.
[61] For the different revision procedures, see Chapter 3.

complications that would result from a finding made in judicial proceedings that an international agreement which is binding on the Union is incompatible with provisions of the Treaties on account of its content or the procedure by which it was concluded.[62] Such a judicial decision 'could not fail to provoke, not only in a [Union] context but also in that of international relations, serious difficulties and might give rise to adverse consequences for all interested parties, including third countries'.[63] Article 103 EAEC provides for a similar review procedure with regard to agreements which Member States propose concluding with third States.[64] However, the EAEC Treaty does not allow the opinion of the Court of Justice to be sought on agreements concluded with third parties by the Union on the basis of that Treaty.[65]

21.017 **Conditions.** The Court of Justice will accept as an 'envisaged agreement' an agreement whose subject matter is known, even if there is not yet agreement on the full text. Especially as regards a question of competence 'it is clearly in the interests of all the States concerned, including third countries, for such a question to be clarified as soon as any particular negotiations are commenced'.[66] In so far as the subject matter of the envisaged agreement is known, questions of competence may be submitted to the Court of Justice before negotiations have formally begun.[67] No time-limit is prescribed for making a request for an opinion and hence such a request may be made after the negotiations have come to an end[68] and even after the agreement has been signed but before the Union's consent to be bound by the agreement is finally expressed.[69] Once the Union has concluded an international agreement, the Court of Justice no longer has jurisdiction to give an opinion on it.[70] In such proceedings, any issues that potentially cast doubt on the substantive or formal validity of the agreement having regard to the Treaties may be raised. Questions relating to the division of competence to conclude such an agreement as between the Union and the Member States are particularly liable to be raised.[71] Since the answer to such a question depends on the

---

[62] For an overview, see Adam, *La procédure d'avis devant la Cour de justice de l'Union européenne* (Bruylant, 2011).
[63] Opinion 1/75, *Draft Understanding on a Local Cost Standard drawn up under the auspices of the OECD*, 1975, 1361.
[64] See Opinion 1/78, *Draft Convention of the International Atomic Energy Agency on the Physical Protection of Nuclear Materials, Facilities and Transports*, 1978, paras 2–3.
[65] This does not prevent the Court of Justice from ruling, under both the Union Treaties and the EAEC Treaty, on an application for annulment of the decision by which such an agreement is approved (para. 26.006, *infra*): C-29/99, *Commission v Council*, 2002, para. 54.
[66] Opinion 1/78, *International Agreement on Natural Rubber*, 1979, para. 35.
[67] Opinion 2/94, *Accession by the Communities to the Convention for the Protection of Human Rights and Fundamental Freedoms*, 1996, paras 16–18.
[68] Opinion 1/75, *Draft Understanding on a Local Cost Standard drawn up under the auspices of the OECD*, 1975, 1361.
[69] Opinion 1/94, *Agreement establishing the World Trade Organisation*, 1994, para. 12.
[70] Opinion 3/94, *Framework Agreement on Bananas*, 1995, paras 8–23. This does not mean that an action for annulment cannot be brought against the decision by which the Union concluded the agreement: ibid., para. 22; C-122/95, *Germany v Council*, 1998, para. 42 (see para. 26.006, *infra*). See also Karagiannis, 'L'expression "accord envisagé" dans l'article 228 §6 du traité CE' (1998) CDE 105–36.
[71] Opinion 1/75, *Draft Understanding on a Local Cost Standard drawn up under the auspices of the OECD*, 1975, 1360; Opinion 1/78, *Draft Convention of the International Atomic Energy Agency on the Physical Protection of Nuclear Materials, Facilities and Transports*, 1978, para. 5 and para. 30; Opinion 2/91, *Convention No 170 of the International Labour Organisation concerning safety in the use of chemicals at work*, 1993, para. 3; Opinion 2/92, *Third Revised Decision of the OECD on national treatment*, 1995, paras 13–14; Opinion 1/94, *Agreement establishing the World Trade Organisation*, 1994, para. 9; Opinion 1/03, *New Lugano Convention on jurisdiction and the recognition and enforcement of judgments in civil and commercial matters*, 2006; Opinion 2/15, *Free Trade Agreement between the European Union and the Republic of Singapore*, 2017; Opinion 3/15, *Marrakesh Treaty to Facilitate Access to Published Works for Persons who are Blind, Visually Impaired or Otherwise Print Disabled*, 2017. See also Article 196(2) of the CJ Rules of Procedure ('A request for an Opinion may relate both to whether the

scope of Union competence, the Court accepts jurisdiction in these proceedings to rule on the correct legal basis for the Union to use in order to approve the agreement in question.[72] However, the procedure for obtaining an opinion is not intended to solve difficulties associated with implementation of an envisaged agreement which falls within shared Union and Member State competence.[73]

In addition, the procedure of asking an opinion from the Court of Justice also serves the purpose of clarifying major substantive issues of EU constitutional law raised by an envisaged international agreement before the Union binds itself as a matter of international law.[74]

---

envisaged agreement is compatible with the provisions of the Treaties and to whether the European Union or any institution of the European Union has the power to enter into that agreement'). For further details, see Lenaerts, Gutman, and Nowak, *EU Procedural Law* (OUP, 2022), Chapter 12.

[72] Opinion 2/92, *Third Revised Decision of the OECD on national treatment*, 1995, paras 9–14; Opinion 2/00, *Cartagena Protocol*, 2001, paras 5–12; Opinion 1/08, *General Agreement on Trade in Services*, 2009, paras 109–10; for a critical view, see Maubernard, 'L'intensité modulable' des compétences externes de la Communauté européenne et de ses Etats membres' (2003) RTDE 229–64. See also Gattinara, 'La compétence consultative de la Cour de justice après les avis 1/00 et 2/00' (2003) RDUE 687–741.

[73] Opinion 2/00, *Cartagena Protocol*, 2001, para. 17.

[74] Opinion 1/09, *Draft agreement creating a Unified Patent Litigation System*, 2011; Opinion 2/13, *Accession of the European Union to the European Convention for the Protection of Human Rights and Fundamental Freedoms*, 2014; Opinion 1/15, *Draft agreement between Canada and the European Union on the Transfer of Passenger Name Record data from the European Union to Canada*, 2017; Opinion 1/17, *Comprehensive Economic and Trade Agreement between Canada and the EU*, 2019. See also Opinion 1/19, *Istanbul Convention*, AG Hogan Opinion, 2021.

22

Decision-making Restricted to Particular Member States

22.001 **Survey.** In two policy areas, the Treaties formulate a system of decision-making under which not all Member States take part in the adoption of acts: (1) the area of freedom, security, and justice (Title V of Part Three of the TFEU) and (2) Economic and Monetary Union (Title VIII of Part Three of the TFEU). On top of this, the system of enhanced cooperation affords a general opportunity for Union acts to be adopted between a number of Member States only. Whenever decision-making is limited to certain Member States, the Council has to adapt voting requirements accordingly. In principle, the other Union institutions and bodies take part in the decision-making with the same composition and manner of operation as in the case of decision-making involving all the Member States. The *rationale* is that members of the Commission, the European Parliament, and other bodies do not represent particular Member States. The Court of Justice, too, has the same composition when it adjudicates in disputes on the interpretation and application of acts adopted under these systems of decision-making.

I. Area of Freedom, Security, and Justice

22.002 **Adjusted decision-making.** When the Council adopts measures under Title V of Part Three of the TFEU (area of freedom, security, and justice), in principle, the decision-making proceeds without the participation of Denmark and Ireland. These two Member States have been granted special status by Protocol (see paras 8-027 and 8-028). Before its withdrawal from the Union, this also applied to the United Kingdom. The provisions of Title V, the measures adopted pursuant to that title, and the international agreements concluded by the Union under that title, together with the decisions of the Court of Justice interpreting such provisions or measures, are not binding upon, or applicable in, those Member States.[1] Adjusted voting requirements apply in the case of acts adopted by the Council. Unanimous decisions are taken by all members of the Council with the exception of the representatives of the governments of the Member States concerned (Denmark and Ireland); a qualified majority is defined in accordance with Article 238(3) TFEU (see para. 12.047 *et seq.*, *supra*).[2] The composition and operation of the other institutions and bodies remain unchanged. This also applies to measures adopted pursuant to Title V of Part Three of the

---

[1] Article 2 of Protocol (No. 21), annexed to the TEU and TFEU, on the position of the United Kingdom and Ireland in respect of the area of freedom, security, and justice, (OJ 2010 C83/295) and Article 2 of Protocol (No. 22), annexed to the TEU and TFEU, on the position of Denmark, (OJ 2010 C83/299).
[2] Article 1 of the Protocol on the position of the United Kingdom and Ireland in respect of the area of freedom, security, and justice (n. 1, *supra*) and Article 1 of the Protocol on the position of Denmark (n. 1, *supra*).

TFEU which build upon the Schengen *acquis*.³ Before setting out the somewhat different ways in which Denmark and Ireland remain outside Union policy in the area of freedom, security, and justice, it must be noted that both Member States may abandon the special status conferred on them by its Protocol by simple notification.⁴ No such possibility was provided for in the case of the United Kingdom.

Non-participation of Ireland. Because of its special status, Ireland does not participate in the adoption of acts pursuant to Title V of Part Three of the TFEU. Nevertheless, this Member State has the possibility to 'opt-in' with respect to certain acts.⁵ First, the Schengen Protocol allows Ireland to request, at any time, to accept some or all provisions of the Schengen *acquis* (Schengen Protocol, Article 4, first para.). The Council is to decide on this request by unanimity of the Schengen Member States and Ireland.⁶ As regards measures that build upon the Schengen *acquis*, Ireland may also notify its wish to take part (Schengen Protocol, Article 5(1)). The Court of Justice clarified that this right only exists for measures building on provisions of the Schengen *acquis* that this Member State already accepted.⁷ If Ireland does not express such a wish, the other Member States are automatically authorized to apply the rules on 'enhanced cooperation' among themselves.⁸ Furthermore, if Ireland does not wish to take part in the acts building on provisions of the Schengen *acquis* despite having made a notification pursuant to Article 4 of the Schengen Protocol—accepted in a Council decision—as to these provisions, it is to notify the Council within three months, following which the decision-making process is suspended to allow the Council to decide under which conditions Ireland can still be considered to take part in the relevant provisions of the Schengen *acquis*.⁹ The Council will take that decision by qualified majority, whereby it seeks to 'retain the widest possible measure of participation of the Member States concerned without seriously affecting the practical operability of the various parts of the Schengen *acquis*, while respecting their coherence'.¹⁰ If the Council is not able to adopt a decision within four months of having received the Commission proposal, the European Council may take such decision at its next meeting, at the request of any Member State,

22.003

---

³ See Article 5(1), first subpara. of Protocol (No. 19), annexed to the TEU and TFEU, integrating the Schengen *acquis* into the framework of the European Union, OJ 2010 C83/290 ('Schengen Protocol'). For the integration of the Schengen *acquis*, see para. 8-004, *supra*. In the event that Denmark should nevertheless participate in the adoption of measures building upon the Schengen *acquis* pursuant to Title IV, the measures concerned will not constitute 'Union law' as far as Denmark is concerned, but will create an obligation under international law; see Article 3 of the Schengen Protocol and Article 4 of the Protocol on the position of Denmark (n. 1, *supra*).

⁴ Article 7 of the Protocol on the position of Denmark (n. 1, *supra*) (the other Member States have to be informed) and Article 8 of the Protocol on the position of the United Kingdom and Ireland in respect of the area of freedom, security, and justice (n. 1, *supra*) (the Council has to be notified in writing).

⁵ See Fletcher, 'Schengen, the European Court of Justice and Flexibility Under the Lisbon Treaty: Balancing the United Kingdom's "Ins" and "Outs"' (2009) EuConst 71–98; Dougan, 'The Treaty of Lisbon 2007: Winning Minds, not Hearts' (2008) CMLRev 617, 684–7.

⁶ Schengen Protocol, Article 4, second para.

⁷ C-77/05, *United Kingdom v Council*, 2007, paras 62–8; C-137/05, *United Kingdom v Council*, 2007, para. 50, with a case note by Rijpma (2008) CMLRev 835–52. The classification of an act as a proposal or initiative aiming to 'build upon the Schengen *acquis*' is to rest on objective factors which are amenable to judicial review, in particular the aim and the content of the act: C-77/05, *United Kingdom v Council*, 2007, para. 77 and C-137/05, *United Kingdom v Council*, 2007, para. 56. See further C-44/14, *Spain v European Parliament and Council*, 2015, paras 26–60 (the provisions of the Schengen Protocol do not prevent the Council from arranging for limited forms of cooperation with Ireland in the areas concerned).

⁸ Schengen Protocol, Article 5(1), second subpara.

⁹ Dougan qualifies this as a 'de facto "expulsion" mechanism': Dougan (n. 5, *supra*), 684.

¹⁰ Schengen Protocol, Article 5(3).

acting by a qualified majority on a proposal from the Commission.[11] If neither the Council nor the European Council has adopted a decision, the Council is to resume the procedure for adopting the measure building on the Schengen *acquis*. In that case, it is for the Commission to decide on the extent to which Ireland can still be considered taking part in the relevant area of the Schengen *acquis*.[12] A parallel regime applied to the United Kingdom before its withdrawal from the Union.

Second, as regards other measures adopted pursuant to Title V of Part Three of the TFEU, Ireland is entitled to take part if it notifies the President of the Council in writing within three months after a proposal or an initiative has been presented to the Council that it wishes to take part in the adoption and application of the proposed measure.[13] If, after a 'reasonable' period has elapsed, such a measure cannot be adopted with Ireland taking part, the Council may adopt it without its participation.[14] As has already been mentioned, if Ireland does not take part, the Council adopts its measures by an adjusted majority and the resultant measures are not applicable in Ireland. All the same, Ireland may notify its intention to the Council and the Commission that it wishes to accept such a measure at any time; in such case the procedure provided for in the Treaties for Member States wishing to take part in an existing form of enhanced cooperation applies *mutatis mutandis* (see para. 22.012, *infra*).[15] These provisions also apply to measures proposed or adopted pursuant to Title V which amend an existing measure by which Ireland is bound. In such a case, however, where the Council, acting on a proposal from the Commission, determines that the non-participation of Ireland in the amended version of the existing measure makes the application of that measure 'inoperable' for other Member States or the Union, it may urge Ireland to take part in the adoption of the amending measure.[16] If, within two months, Ireland has not notified its intention to do so, the existing measure shall no longer be binding upon or applicable to it.[17] However, the Council may determine that Ireland is to bear the direct financial consequences, if any, 'necessarily and unavoidably incurred' as a result of the cessation of its participation in the existing measure.[18] A parallel regime applied to the United Kingdom before its withdrawal from the Union.

22.004 **Non-participation of Denmark.** Unlike Ireland, Denmark does not have the general possibility to participate in the adoption of acts pursuant to Title V; it participates solely in the adoption of measures relating to the determination of third countries whose nationals require visas when crossing the external borders of the Member States and to the uniform format for visas and measures building on the Schengen *acquis*.[19] Exceptionally, the Union

---

[11] Ibid., Article 5(4).
[12] Ibid., Article 5(5), which leaves it open for the Member State concerned to withdraw its notification that it does not wish to take part in the measure building on the Schengen *acquis*.
[13] Protocol on the position of the United Kingdom and Ireland in respect of the area of freedom, security, and justice (n. 1, *supra*), Article 3(1).
[14] Ibid., Article 3(2).
[15] Ibid., Article 4.
[16] Ibid., Article 4a(2), first subpara.
[17] This is so unless that Member State notifies its intention to accept the measure before the entry into force of the existing measure: ibid., Article 4a(2), second subpara.
[18] Ibid., Article 4a(3).
[19] Protocol on the position of Denmark (n. 1, *supra*), Articles 4 and 6. If Denmark transposes a measure building upon the Schengen *acquis* in its internal legislation, this only constitutes an obligation under international law, ibid., Article 4(1).

has concluded an agreement with Denmark to make certain Union measures applicable to Denmark (see para. 8.015, *supra*). Before the Treaty of Lisbon Denmark did participate in the police and judicial cooperation in criminal matters; as those policy areas are now part of Title V of Part Three of the TFEU, Denmark no longer participates in them. However, with the Treaty of Lisbon Denmark has been given the option to participate more fully in the adoption and application of measures adopted under Title V if it notifies the other Member States of its wish to do so. In that case the Schengen *acquis* will become binding on Denmark as Union law, and Denmark will get the possibility, under arrangements similar to the ones existing at present for Ireland, to take part in the adoption and application of a measure adopted under Title V or to accept an existing measure adopted under Title V.[20] However, as a majority of the Danish electorate voted against that option in a 2015 referendum (see para. 8.027, *supra*), Denmark participates, for now, only in measures determining the third countries whose nationals must be in possession of a visa, measures, relating to a uniform format for visas, and measures that build upon the Schengen *acquis*.

II. Economic and Monetary Union

Adjusted decision-making. As far as Economic and Monetary Union is concerned, the Union has a system of decision-making which is restricted to the Member States whose currency is the euro because they satisfied the conditions laid down to that end (see para. 9.033, *supra*). The voting rights of Member States with a derogation are to be suspended in respect of Council acts based on provisions relating to EMU which do not apply to them (Article 139(2) and (4) TFEU). The number of votes required to attain a qualified majority has been adjusted as a result.[21] A Protocol to the Treaties confirms that the ministers of the States participating in the euro area may meet informally amongst themselves to discuss questions related to their shared specific responsibilities for the single currency.[22] A meeting of the ECOFIN Council comprising only representatives of Member States participating in the euro is known as the 'Eurogroup'[23] (see para. 12.040, *supra*). The Commission takes part in these meetings; the ECB may also be invited to take part. Whenever matters of common interest are concerned, they are to be discussed by ministers of all Member States; however, decisions are to be taken by the Council in accordance with the procedures determined by the Treaties. Member States participating in the euro area convene at the level of the Heads of State or Government at a Euro Summit (see para. 12.028, *supra*).[24]

22.005

---

[20] See Article 8 of the Protocol on the position of Denmark (n. 1, *supra*) and the Annex to that Protocol.
[21] See Article 238(3)(a) TFEU.
[22] See Article 1 of Protocol (No. 14), annexed to the TEU and TFEU, on the Eurogroup, (OJ 2010 C83/283), which was added by the Lisbon Treaty. See, before the Lisbon Treaty, the resolution of the European Council of 13 December 1997 on economic policy coordination in stage 3 of EMU and on Treaty Articles 111 and 113, OJ 1998 C35/1.
[23] The first such meeting was held on 5 June 1998 and was chaired, not by the British Chancellor of the Exchequer (representing the Member State occupying the Presidency of the Council), but by the Austrian Finance Minister (representing the Member State which was to take over the Presidency on 1 July 1998), see *Europe*, No. 7235, 5 June 1998, 6. On 12 October 2008, the financial crisis prompted the Eurogroup to meet for the first time at the level of Heads of State and Government, with the UK Prime Minister also attending. See Editorial Comments in (2009) CMLRev 1383, 1388.
[24] As to the status of the Eurogroup, see also C-597/18 P, C-598/18 P, C-603/18 P, and C-604/18 P, *Council v K. Chrysostomides & Co.*, 2020.

In principle, Member States with a derogation do not take part in decision-making in the ECB. They are not involved in the appointment of members of the ECB's Executive Board, do not have a member on the board, and do not have the Governor of their central bank sit on the Governing Council.[25] Since the ECB carries out some tasks regarding the central banks of Member States with a derogation and is to deliver opinions concerning them,[26] those Member States are nevertheless involved in the decision-making in those respects. It is for this reason that the ECB has a General Council, consisting of the President and Vice-President of the ECB and the Governors of all the national central banks, to take the necessary decisions in this regard.[27] The composition and operation of the other institutions and bodies, including the Economic and Financial Committee, will remain unchanged regardless as to whether the decisions to be taken affect all the Member States or only those without a derogation.

Under a Protocol to the Treaties, introduced by the EU Treaty at the time of the creation of the EMU, Denmark is in a special situation in that it is not under an obligation to take part in the third stage of EMU (see para. 9.035, *supra*). The opt-out granted to Denmark means that it is regarded as a Member State with a derogation in the third stage.[28] Before its withdrawal from the Union, the United Kingdom also had a position according to which it was not obliged to take part in the EMU. Its position was different from that of a Member State with a derogation but had the same implications for decision-making in the Council and the ECB.[29]

III. Enhanced Cooperation between Member States

22.006 **Differentiated integration.** Cooperation between Member States in the area of freedom, security, and justice and in the framework of the EMU are forms of differentiated integration, in that not all Member States are involved, and Member States accede when they deem it appropriate to do so. Such differentiated integration could also be found in intergovernmental forms of cooperation. Examples were the European Monetary System (see para. 1.035, *supra*) and the Schengen Convention (see para. 1.039, *supra*) which acted between the participating Member States as precursors to the relevant Community policies.[30] As far as the CFSP is concerned, a similar form of differentiated integration exists between some of the Member States where a Member State formally abstains from voting and hence does not have to apply the decision concerned (Article 31(1), second subpara. TEU; see para. 19.002, *supra*).

---

[25] Article 283 TFEU in conjunction with Article 139(2) TFEU; ESCB Statute, Articles 10.1 and 11.2 in conjunction with Article 42.
[26] For instance, the authorities of a Member State with a derogation are obliged under Article 127(4) TFEU to consult the ECB on any proposed act in the latter's fields of competence.
[27] ESCB Statute, Articles 44 to 46.
[28] Article 1 of Protocol (No. 16), annexed to the TEU and TFEU, on certain provisions relating to Denmark (OJ 2010 C83/287).
[29] See Articles 6, 7, and 8 of Protocol (No. 15), annexed to the TEU and TFEU, on certain provisions relating to the United Kingdom of Great Britain and Northern Ireland, OJ 2010 C83/284.
[30] See also Benelux cooperation, para. 1-004, *supra*.

Enhanced cooperation. The Treaty of Amsterdam created a general framework for enhanced (formerly 'closer') cooperation between some—but not all—Member States, which is now enshrined in Title IV of the TEU (Article 20 TEU) and Title III of Part Six of the TFEU (Articles 326 to 334 TFEU).[31] It enables Member States to cooperate more closely, under certain conditions, within the framework of the Union's non-exclusive competences, while making use of its institutions, and exercise those competences by applying the relevant provisions of the Treaties. At the request of a number of Member States, the Council or the European Parliament and the Council have thus adopted measures in the framework of enhanced cooperation as regards the law applicable to divorce and legal separation ('Rome III');[32] jurisdiction, applicable law, and the recognition and enforcement of decisions in matters of matrimonial property regime;[33] the property consequences of registered partnership;[34] the creation of unitary patent protection;[35] and the establishment of the European Public Prosecutor's Office.[36] In addition, a number of Member States have been authorized to set up enhanced cooperation in respect of a financial transaction tax,[37] which has, however, not yet resulted in a concrete measure. Enhanced cooperation is not possible in areas of exclusive Union competence. Acts adopted in the framework of enhanced cooperation are binding only on those Member States which participate in such cooperation. They do not form part of the *acquis*, which has to be accepted by candidate States for accession to the Union (Article 20(4) TEU).

22.007

Initially, enhanced cooperation among Member States was made possible for Community matters and for PJCC only. Since the Treaty of Nice, enhanced cooperation among Member States had also been available for the CFSP, albeit subject to additional conditions.[38] However, no recourse was made to the possibility of enhanced cooperation. The Lisbon Treaty made the applicable conditions the same for all policy areas of the Union, although the procedure remains slightly different for enhanced cooperation relating to CFSP matters. In addition, the Lisbon Treaty created a framework for establishing 'permanent structured

---

[31] For an overview of the use of enhanced cooperation, see Kroll and Leuffen, 'Enhanced Cooperation in Practice: An analysis of differentiated integration in EU secondary law' (2014) JEPP 353–73. For commentaries on the Treaty framework, see Ehlermann, 'Differentiation, Flexibility, Closer Co-operation: The New Provisions of the Amsterdam Treaty' (1998) ELJ 246–70; Chaltiel, 'Le traité d'Amsterdam et la coopération renforcée' (1998) RMCUE 289–93; Kortenberg, 'Closer Cooperation in the Treaty of Amsterdam' (1998) CMLRev 833–54; Gaja, 'How Flexible is Flexibility under the Amsterdam Treaty?' (1998) CMLRev 855–70. See also Tuytschaever, 'Nauwere samenwerking volgens het Verdrag van Nice' (2001) SEW 375–87; Bribosia, 'Différenciation et avant-gardes au sein de l'Union européenne' (2000) CDE 57–115.

[32] Council Regulation (EU) No. 1259/2010 of 20 December 2010 implementing enhanced cooperation in the area of the law applicable to divorce and legal separation, OJ 2010 L343/10.

[33] Council Regulation (EU) 2016/1103 of 24 June 2016 implementing enhanced cooperation in the area of jurisdiction, applicable law, and the recognition and enforcement of decisions in matters of matrimonial property regimes, OJ 2016 L183/1.

[34] Council Regulation (EU) 2016/1104 of 24 June 2016 implementing enhanced cooperation in the area of jurisdiction, applicable law, and the recognition and enforcement of decisions in matters of the property consequences of registered partnerships, OJ 2016 L183/30.

[35] Regulation (EU) No. 1257/2012 of the European Parliament and of the Council of 17 December 2012 implementing enhanced cooperation in the area of the creation of unitary patent protection, OJ 2012 L361/1. For the translation regime, see the enhanced cooperation initiated by Council Regulation (EU) No. 1260/2012 of 17 December 2012 implementing enhanced cooperation in the area of the creation of unitary patent protection with regard to the applicable translation arrangements, OJ 2012 L361/89.

[36] Council Regulation (EU) 2017/1939 of 12 October 2017 implementing enhanced cooperation on the establishment of the European Public Prosecutor's Office ('the EPPO'), OJ 2017 L283/1.

[37] Council Decision of 22 January 2013 authorising enhanced cooperation in the area of financial transaction tax, OJ 2013 L22/11.

[38] See Articles 27a to 27e EU.

cooperation' among Member States in the field of the Common Security and Defence Policy (Article 42(6) TEU, see para. 10.035, *supra*).

22.008 **Substantive requirements.** Member States proposing to embark on enhanced cooperation may do so only if the cooperation satisfies the requirements laid down in Articles 326 and 327 TFEU. Substantively, the cooperation must be aimed at furthering the objectives of the Union, at protecting its interests, and at reinforcing its integration process (Article 20(1), second subpara. TEU) and must comply with the Treaties and Union law (Article 326, first para. TFEU). In addition, it must not undermine the internal market or economic, social, and territorial cohesion; must not constitute a barrier to, or discrimination in, trade between Member States; and must not distort competition between them (Article 326, second para. TFEU). At the same time, it must respect the competences, rights, and obligations of those Member States which do not participate in it. Those Member States, in turn, must not impede its implementation by the participating Member States (Article 327 TFEU).[39]

22.009 **Formal requirements.** Enhanced cooperation must concern at least nine Member States[40] and must be authorized by the Council (see para. 22.010, *infra*). The Council is to give its authorization as a last resort only, when it has established that the objectives of such cooperation cannot be attained within a reasonable period by the Union as a whole (Article 20(2) TFEU).[41] Enhanced cooperation may be authorized in policy areas where the Council decides with unanimity; it then serves the purpose of breaking through the deadlock resulting from the persistent opposition to a particular proposal, voiced by one or more Member States.[42] When enhanced cooperation is being established, it shall be open to all Member States, subject to compliance with any conditions of participation laid down by the authorizing decision and, where applicable, with the acts already adopted within that framework (Article 20(1), second para. TEU and Article 328(1), first subpara. TFEU). The Commission and the Member States participating in enhanced cooperation are to ensure that they promote participation by as many Member States as possible (Article 328(1), second subpara. TFEU).

22.010 **Authorization.** Member States intending to establish enhanced cooperation in all fields outside the CFSP are to address a request to the Commission, specifying the scope and objectives of the enhanced cooperation proposed. The Commission may then submit a proposal to the Council (Article 329(1), first subpara. TFEU).[43] If the Commission submits a proposal, the Council takes its decision by a qualified majority, after obtaining the consent of the European Parliament (Article 329(1), first subpara. TFEU)[44].

---

[39] Before the Lisbon Treaty, specific additional substantive requirements applied for enhanced cooperation in the field of the CFSP (see Articles 27a and b EU). In the case of PJCC-related enhanced cooperation, Article 40(1) EU required that the proposed cooperation respect the powers of the Community and the objectives of PJCC and that it had the aim of enabling the Union to develop more rapidly into an area of freedom, security, and justice.

[40] Before the Lisbon Treaty, eight Member States were sufficient in this connection (see Article 43(g) EU).

[41] C-274/11 and C-295/11, *Spain and Italy v Council*, 2013, paras 47–59 (limited review of this assessment in respect of the authorization to set up an enhanced cooperation relating to the unitary patent protection).

[42] Ibid., paras 33–41. It is thus not a misuse of power for the Council to authorize an enhanced cooperation in a field subject to the unanimity requirement, as is the case with Article 118(2) TFEU. For another example, see Council Decision of 22 January 2013 authorizing enhanced cooperation in the area of financial transaction tax, OJ 2013 L22/11.

[43] If the Commission does not submit a proposal, it is to inform the Member States concerned of the reasons for not doing so.

[44] Before the Lisbon Treaty Article 11(2) EC merely required the European Parliament to be consulted, except in areas covered by the co-decision procedure. Article 11(2) EC further stipulated that a member of the Council

The procedure is somewhat different for enhanced cooperation relating to the CFSP.[45] Under Article 329(2) TFEU the Member States make their request directly to the Council. The Council takes its decision acting unanimously after obtaining the opinion of the High Representative and the Commission, in particular on whether the enhanced cooperation proposed is consistent with the CFSP and with other Union policies, respectively.[46] The European Parliament is not consulted; the request is merely forwarded to it for information (Article 329(2) TFEU).

A few Treaty articles on the area of freedom, security, and justice provide for a system of automatic authorization. This is the case, first of all, when Ireland notifies its wish not to take part in measures that build upon the Schengen *acquis* (see para. 8.028, *supra*). Second, the Treaties provide for automatic authorization of enhanced cooperation within the framework of the 'alarm bell' procedure provided for in Articles 82(3) and 83(3) TFEU on the harmonization of procedural or substantive aspects of national criminal law (see para. 8.019, *supra*). This procedure enables any Member State which considers that a draft directive would affect fundamental aspects of its criminal justice system, to request that the draft directive be referred to the European Council. If the European Council does not reach a consensus within the timeframe specified and if at least nine Member States wish to establish enhanced cooperation on the basis of the draft directive concerned, they have to notify the European Parliament, the Council, and the Commission. In such a case, the authorization to proceed with enhanced cooperation will be deemed to be granted.[47] Third, the TFEU provides for enhanced cooperation in certain areas in which the Council is to decide by unanimous vote, namely the establishment of a European Public Prosecutor's Office and operational cooperation between national law enforcement authorities (Articles 86(1) and 87(3) TFEU). If a unanimous vote cannot be achieved in the Council in these areas, a group of at least nine Member States may request that the voting procedure be suspended and that the draft measures be referred to the European Council. In case of disagreement within the European Council, and if at least nine Member States wish to establish enhanced cooperation, the authorization to proceed with enhanced cooperation will be deemed to be granted. This has been the case for the European Public Prosecutor's Office, where the Member States concerned have adopted, within the framework of enhanced cooperation, a Commission proposal on which no unanimity could be reached in the Council (see para. 8.024, *supra*).[48]

---

could request that the matter be referred to the European Council. That possibility was abrogated by the Lisbon Treaty.

[45] Before the Lisbon Treaty, special procedural arrangements also applied to enhanced cooperation relating to PJCC matters (see Article 40(a) EU).

[46] In this connection too, Article 27c EU, provided for the possibility to have the matter referred to the European Council, which would then have to decide by unanimity. That possibility was abrogated by the Lisbon Treaty.

[47] Article 82(3), second subpara. and 83(3), second subpara. TFEU, which refer to Article 20(2) TEU and 329(1) TFEU.

[48] Council Regulation (EU) 2017/1939 of 12 October 2017 implementing enhanced cooperation on the establishment of the European Public Prosecutor's Office ('the EPPO'), OJ 2017 L283/1. The initiative for the enhanced cooperation was taken by Belgium, Bulgaria, Croatia, Cyprus, Czech Republic, Finland, France, Germany, Greece, Lithuania, Luxembourg, Portugal, Romania, Slovakia, Slovenia, and Spain; Latvia, Estonia, Austria, and Italy have later decided to also participate in the enhanced cooperation leading to the adoption of Council Regulation (EU) 2017/1939. Malta and the Netherlands have been authorized to participate in the enhanced cooperation after the adoption of Council Regulation (EU) 2017/1939, which thus now applies to twenty-two Member States.

22.011 **Adjusted decision-making.** The provisions on enhanced cooperation allow Member States to make use of the Union's institutions and exercise its competences by applying the relevant provisions of the Treaties (Article 20(1), first subpara. TEU). This means that the procedure to be followed is that prescribed in the Treaty provision constituting the legal basis. Although all members of the Council may take part in the relevant deliberations, only those representing participating Member States may take part in the vote (Article 20(3) TEU and Article 330, first para. TFEU). Where unanimity is required, this refers to the votes of the representatives of the participating Member States only. In the case of acts requiring to be adopted by a qualified majority, the number of votes required to adopt a decision is calculated in accordance with Article 238(3) TFEU (Article 330, second and third paras TFEU).[49] The Council may decide that in cases where a Treaty article which may be applied in the context of enhanced cooperation provides for the Council to act unanimously, decisions will be taken by qualified majority. To adopt that decision, the Council is to act with the unanimous vote of all participating Member States (Article 333(1) TFEU). Using the same procedure and after consulting the European Parliament, the Council may decide that where a Treaty article requires decisions to be adopted under a special legislative procedure, decisions will be taken under the ordinary legislative procedure (Article 333(2) TFEU; see para. 3.008, *supra*). However, none of these possibilities exist for decisions having military or defence implications (Article 333(3) TFEU). It should be noted that in this way Article 333 TFEU makes it possible for a smaller group of Member States to strengthen the integration process not only by developing the substantive content of Union policy in a particular area, but also by streamlining the decision-making process in that area towards standard Union decision-making concerning legislative acts. An example could be harmonization or coordination of national legislation in the field of direct taxation between nine or more Member States participating in the euro.

22.012 **Participation in existing enhanced cooperation.** Any Member State wishing to become a party to an existing form of enhanced cooperation outside the CFSP is to notify its intention to the Council and the Commission (Article 331(1), first subpara. TFEU). The Commission then decides, within four months of the date of notification, on the participation of the Member State concerned. If it considers that the conditions of participation have been fulfilled, it may adopt any transitional measures necessary with regard to the application of the acts already adopted within the framework of enhanced cooperation (Article 331(1), second subpara. TFEU). Where the Commission considers that the conditions of participation have not been fulfilled, it is to indicate the necessary arrangements to be adopted by a specified deadline. On the expiry of that deadline, it shall re-examine the request. If the Commission still issues a negative opinion, the Member State concerned may refer the matter to the Council, which decides on the request, taking into account the votes of the participating Member States only, and may adopt the necessary transitional measures on a proposal from the Commission (Article 331(1), third subpara. TFEU).

Where a Member State wishes to become a party to an existing form of enhanced CFSP cooperation, it must notify its intention to the Council, the High Representative, and the Commission (Article 331(2), first subpara. TFEU). The Council (namely the Member States

---

[49] See para. 12.047 *et seq.*, *supra*.

taking part in the enhanced cooperation) decides on such request after consulting the High Representative. It may, on a proposal from the High Representative, also adopt any transitional measures necessary with regard to the application of the acts already adopted within the framework of enhanced cooperation. Where the Council considers that the conditions of participation have not been fulfilled, it shall indicate the necessary arrangements to be adopted and set a deadline for re-examining the request for participation (Article 331(2), first subpara. TFEU).

Judicial review. Enhanced cooperation is, with the exception of the CFSP, fully subject to the jurisdiction of the Court of Justice. This means that the Court of Justice may exercise supervision as regards the Council authorization to engage in enhanced cooperation[50] and as regards decisions to allow a Member State to participate in enhanced cooperation after it has been established. The Court of Justice also has jurisdiction over the implementation of enhanced cooperation, which means that it may review the relevant acts adopted in the framework of an authorized enhanced cooperation,[51] and it can enforce the correct application of such acts using the usual Union procedures.[52]

22.013

This is different only for enhanced cooperation in the field of the CFSP, given the limited jurisdiction of the Court in that field.[53] The Court has jurisdiction, however, under Article 40 TEU, to see to it that the implementation of CFSP enhanced cooperation does not affect Union competences in other fields and vice versa (see para. 30-013, *infra*).

---

[50] See C-209/13, *United Kingdom v Council*, 2014, paras 33–40 (authorization to engage in enhanced cooperation on a financial transaction tax); C-274/11 and C-295/11, *Spain and Italy v Council*, 2013 (authorization to engage in enhanced cooperation on unitary patent protection). See also Pistoia, 'Enhanced Cooperation as a Tool to ... enhance integration? Spain and Italy v. Council' (2014) CMLRev 247–60; Lamping, 'Enhanced Cooperation in the Area of Unitary Patent Protection: Testing the Boundaries of the Rule of Law' (2013) MJECL 589–600.

[51] e.g. C-146/13, *Spain v Council*, 2015 (implementation of the enhanced cooperation relating to the unitary patent protection), with case note by Pistoia (2016) ELRev 711–26.

[52] See, e.g., C-372/16, *Sahyouni*, 2017; C-249/19, *JE*, 2020 (interpretation of Council Regulation (EU) No. 1259/2010 of 20 December 2010 implementing enhanced cooperation in the area of the law applicable to divorce and legal separation); C-558/16, *Mahnkopf*, 2018, para. 41 (interpreting Council Regulation (EU) 2016/1103 of 24 June 2016 implementing enhanced cooperation in the area of jurisdiction, applicable law, and the recognition and enforcement of decisions in matters of matrimonial property regimes).

[53] Before the Lisbon Treaty, the Court's jurisdiction was also limited as regards enhanced cooperation relating to PJCC matters (see Articles 40 and 46 EU). See Donner, 'De derde pijler en de Amsterdamse doolhof' (1997) SEW 370.

PART V
SOURCES OF LAW OF THE EUROPEAN UNION

The law of the European Union ('EU law' or 'Union law') consists of the rules enshrined in the Treaties on which the Union is based and acts adopted by the Union institutions pursuant to the Treaties, as applied and interpreted by national courts and the Court of Justice of the European Union. The status of Union law in the national legal systems is a matter of Union law itself. Chapter 23 sets out the various forms of Union law and their internal hierarchy, followed by a discussion of the effects of Union law in the national legal systems, in particular the primacy and the direct effect of Union law. The different sources of Union law are then analysed in turn. Chapter 24 discusses the Treaties as primary Union law. Chapter 25 sets out the status of fundamental rights and general principles of Union law, with a survey of the applicable rights and principles. Chapter 26 presents the status of international law instruments and principles within the Union legal order. Chapter 27 goes into the details of the various acts that may be adopted by Union institutions and bodies, in particular regulations, directives, decisions, recommendations and opinions, as well as other acts. Chapter 28 completes the overview of Union law sources with a discussion of other acts, such as those adopted within the framework of the Union by Member States governments, social partners' agreements and non-Community acts adopted before the entry into force of the Lisbon Treaty, as well as the case law of the Union courts.

23
Union Law and its Effects in the National Legal Systems

I. Forms of Union Law

Union law. 'Union law' consists of the rules enshrined in the Treaties and acts adopted pursuant thereto, as applied and interpreted by the national courts and the Court of Justice. Depending on the origin of the provisions, a distinction may be made between constitutive norms which come into being as a result of action on the part of the Member States themselves (primary Union law), rules created by Union institutions and bodies (secondary or 'derived' Union law), and other rules which have been accepted by case law as being general principles of the Union's legal order. Secondary Union law is constituted by the legislative acts and other acts of the institutions, bodies, offices, or agencies, usually in the form of specific instruments of Union law ('autonomous' acts see, *inter alia*, Article 288 TFEU) as well as the international agreements concluded by the Union ('conventional' acts).

23.001

Primary and secondary law. Union law encompasses rules which arise as a result of action both by the Member States and by Union institutions and bodies. As has already been mentioned, the sources of Union law may therefore be divided into primary and secondary (or derived) Union law, the latter consisting of (conventional and autonomous) acts of institutions and bodies, as supplemented by fundamental rights and the general principles recognized in the Union legal order.[1] The discussion of the forms of Union law will be based upon this distinction, starting with the ranking order of the various types of provisions. Interinstitutional agreements and collective agreements are a particular form of Union law. The same is true for certain acts of the governments of the Member States and for the case law of the Court of Justice and the General Court, which plays an important part in constructing the Union legal order, even though the tasks of the Union Courts are limited to the interpretation and application of each of the other legal sources.

23.002

Since the entry into force of the Lisbon Treaty, the characteristics and legal effects previously attributed to the different forms of Community law now apply, more broadly, to the various forms of Union law (see para. 2.006, *supra*). Acts adopted before the entry into force of the Lisbon Treaty outside the Community framework remain in force, with the specific legal regime surrounding them, until they are repealed or amended.

---

[1] On the relationship between primary and secondary law, see Syrpis, 'The Relationship between Primary and Secondary Law in the EU' (2015) CMLRev 461–87.

II. Sources of Law and their Hierarchy

23.003 **Hierarchy.** Just as is the case for the primacy of Union law, the relationship between the various sources of Union law is not expressly laid down in the Treaties. Nevertheless, the authors of the Treaties always assumed the existence of a hierarchy between them. This emerges from Article 263 TFEU, under which an action may be brought—in the Court of Justice or in the General Court—for the annulment of acts of Union institutions, *inter alia*, on the ground of 'infringement of the Treaties or of any rule of law relating to their application' (see also Article 146 EAEC). Consequently, judicial review extends to examining whether the acts in question are compatible with all superior legal rules.

23.004 **Primary law.** At the top of the hierarchy of norms, there are the provisions of primary Union law (see para. 24.001 *et seq.*, *infra*), including fundamental rights and the general principles of law whose observance the Court of Justice ensures pursuant to Article 19 TEU (see para. 25.002 *et seq.*, *infra*). Since the institutions and bodies have to act within the powers conferred upon them by the Treaties, secondary or derived Union law is subordinate to those primary norms. Fundamental rights and general principles of law play a role in the interpretation and application of Treaty provisions and other rules of Union law. Therefore, in accordance with a general principle of interpretation, an EU measure must be interpreted, as far as possible, in such a way as not to affect its validity and in conformity with primary law as a whole and, in particular, with the provisions of the Charter.[2]

23.005 **Secondary law.** In the field of secondary Union law, it is not the form (regulation, directive, etc.) of a given act, but its nature which determines its place within the legal order. Special priority attaches to international law in the Union legal order. The legal force of international agreements concluded by the Union is superior to that of other 'derived' Union acts (see para. 26.002, *infra*). Some principles of international law enshrined in treaties or having the force of customary law take precedence as general principles of Union law (see para. 26.013, *infra*). Apart from international agreements concluded by the Union, there is no predetermined ranking order of the various forms of act which the institutions may adopt. As already said, their place in the legal order is determined by their nature and not by their form. Thus, legislative acts take precedence over delegated or implementing acts (see para. 18.009, *supra*).[3] Moreover, some acts of the Council stand out as being organic in character. In so far as other acts are based upon such an organic act, they may not depart from it unless the organic act is expressly amended.[4] Agreements concluded between institutions are binding upon the institutions concerned by virtue of the principle that an authority is bound by rules which it has itself adopted (*patere legem quam ipse fecisti*; see para. 27.050, *infra*).

23.006 *Lex posterior* **and** *lex specialis*. In addition, as regards the relationship between equivalent provisions of Union law, the principle applies that a later provision (*lex posterior*) prevails

---

[2] C-540/13 *European Parliament v Council*, 2015, paras 38–40; C-317/13 and C-679/13 *European Parliament v Council*, 2015; C-547/14 *Philip Morris Brands and Others*, 2016, para. 70; C-391/16, C-77/17, and C-78/17, *M*, 2019, para. 77.

[3] However, since the Lisbon Treaty, implementing acts—like delegated acts—are also formally distinguishable from legislative acts by their title (see para. 18-008, *supra*).

[4] e.g. with regard to the Second Comitology Decision: C-378/00, *Commission v European Parliament and Council*, 2003, paras 40–2.

over an earlier one and a specific provision (*lex specialis*) over a more general one (*lex generalis*). However, in order for this to be so, the later or more specific provision must intend to limit or replace the earlier or general provision, respectively.[5]

National law. In each Member State, Union law is applied in conjunction with the applicable rules of national law. As a consequence, the application of Union law relies, in practice, on national legislative and implementing provisions and on the interpretation and application given to Union law by national case law. These national sources of law do not form a source of Union law as such, although they influence the recognition of general principles of Union law (see para. 25.021 *et seq.*, *infra*). In exceptional cases, the Court of Justice and the General Court have to apply national law.[6] This occurs, for example, in disputes brought before the Union Courts pursuant to an arbitration clause (Article 272 TFEU) concerning a contract governed by the law of a particular Member State.[7] In the absence of an express reference to national law, the application of a provision of Union law may necessitate a reference to the laws of the Member States only where the Union Courts cannot identify in Union law, or in the general principles of Union law, criteria enabling them to define the meaning and scope of such a provision by way of independent interpretation.[8]

23.007

III. The Principles of Primacy and Direct Effect of Union Law

Principles. The status of Union law in the national legal systems is a matter of Union law itself.[9] This means that Union law differs from the classical rule of international law that a State determines, apart from the limitations to which it expressly commits itself, the status of international commitments in its legal system. The case law of the Court of Justice relating to the primacy and the possible direct effect of Union law has made it clear that Union law *as such* has effect in the national legal system.[10] Both the Union and the Member States as well as individuals are entitled to enforce the proper application of Union law. On the ground of the need to secure the full effect of Union law, the Court of Justice has developed

23.008

---

[5] See, e.g., C-481/99, *Heininger and Heininger*, 2001, paras 36–9; C-444/00, *Mayer Parry Recycling*, 2003, paras 49–57; C-439/01, *Cipra and Kvasnicka*, 2003, paras 34–40; C-355/12, *Nintendo*, 2014, para. 23; C-263/18, *Nederlandse Uitgeversbond*, 2019, para. 55; C-617/15, *Hummel Holding*, 2017, para. 26; C-41/19, *FX*, 2020, para. 33. See also T-6/99, *ESF Elbe-Stahlwerke Feralpi v Commission*, 2001, para. 102 (ECSC Treaty as a *lex specialis*). See further C-434/15, *Asociación Profesional Elite Taxi*, AG Szpunar Opinion, 2017, points 92–3.

[6] See, e.g., in the context of trademark law, C-263/09 P, *Edwin Co. v OHIM*, 2011, paras 44–58. As the national courts do not have jurisdiction to review the validity of certain preparatory acts in the context of banking supervision, it is inevitable that the Court of Justice and the General Court will have to apply national law in that context as well: see C-219/17, *Berlusconi and Finninvest*, 2018; C-414/18, *Iccrea Banca*, 2019. See also Lenaerts, 'Interlocking Legal Orders in the European Union and Comparative Law' (2003) ICLQ 873–906; Kohler and Knapp, 'Nationales Recht in der Praxis des EuGH' (2002) ZEuP 701–26. See further Prek and Lefèvre, 'The EU Courts as 'National' Courts: National Law in the EU Judicial Process' (2017) CMLRev 369–402.

[7] See Van Nuffel, 'De contractuele aansprakelijkheid van de Europese Gemeenschap: een bevoegdheidskluwen ontward' (2000–2001) AJT 157–62.

[8] See Lenaerts and Gutman, ' "Federal Common Law" in the European Union: A Comparative Perspective from the United States' (2006) AJCL 1–121; Lenaerts and Corthaut, 'Rechtsvinding door het Hof van Justitie' (2006) AAe 581–8. See further T-43/90, *Díaz García v European Parliament*, 1992, para. 36; T-172/01, *M. v Court of Justice*, 2004, para. 71. For a good example, see the concept of 'lawyer' for the purposes of the Statute of the Court of Justice of the European Union and the CJ and GC Rules of Procedure; see C-515/17 P and C-561/17 P, *Uniwersytet Wrocławski v Research Executive Agency*, 2019, paras 57–68.

[9] 26/62 *Van Gend & Loos*, 1963, 10–12.

[10] See paras 1.025–1.027, *supra*.

in its case law other requirements with which the national legal system must comply in order to secure the primacy of Union law in practice, which are set out below.[11] Hereinafter, the requirements flowing from the principles of primacy and full effectiveness of Union law are set out both from the perspective of the Court's case law and from the legal systems of the Member States that are to accommodate these principles.

23.009 **CFSP.** As for legal effects, the Treaties make no distinction between acts adopted within the framework of the CFSP and acts adopted in other areas. The principle of the primacy of Union law therefore applies in full to any Union act, including those adopted within the framework of the CFSP. All the same, the Court of Justice has limited jurisdiction with respect to the provisions of the Treaties relating to the CFSP or with respect to acts adopted on the basis of these provisions (Article 275 TFEU; see para.13.012, *supra*).[12]

A. Requirements flowing from the primacy of Union law

1. The principle of primacy of Union law

23.010 **Precedence of primary and secondary Union law.** In its 1964 judgment in *Costa v ENEL* the Court of Justice first articulated the principle that Community law takes precedence over the domestic law of the Member States. The Court held that 'the law stemming from the Treaty, an independent source of law, could not, because of its special and original nature, be overridden by domestic provisions, however framed, without being deprived of its character as Community law and without the legal basis of the Community itself being called into question'.[13] The Court derived the primacy of Community law from the specific nature of the Community legal order, referring to the danger that, if the effect of Community law could vary from Member State to Member State in deference to subsequent national laws, this would be liable to jeopardize the attainment of the objectives set out in Article 10 EC [*now Article 4(3) TEU*] and give rise to discrimination prohibited by Article 12 EC [*now Article 18 TFEU*] (see para. 1.027, *supra*). The case was concerned with the primacy of a number of provisions of primary Community law. The Court also upheld the primacy of secondary Community law on the same grounds.[14]

---

[11] In addition, the Member States are under a duty to take all necessary measures to implement provisions of Union law; see para. 18-002, *supra*.

[12] This has led some to question whether it is appropriate to extend primacy to those CFSP acts that escape judicial review by the ECJ; see Butler, *Constitutional Law of the EU's Common Foreign and Security Policy* (Hart Publishing, 2019); see also Hinarejos, *Judicial Control in the European Union: Reforming Jurisdiction in the Intergovernmental Pillars* (OUP, 2010), 151–2.

[13] 6/64 *Costa*, 1964, at 594; for the origins of the case, and with it the origins of the doctrine of primacy, see Arena, 'From an Unpaid Electricity Bill to the Primacy of EU Law: Gian Galeazzo Stendardi and the Making of Costa v. ENEL' (2019) EJIL 1017–37; for the further development of the primacy of Community law, see Skouris, 'Der Vorrang des Europäischen Unionsrechts vor dem nationalen Recht. Unionsrecht bricht nationales Recht' (2021) EuR 3–27; Beljin, "Die Zusammenhänge zwischen dem Vorrang, den Instituten der innerstaatlichen Beachtlichkeit und der Durchführung des Gemeinschaftsrechts' (2002) EuR 351–76; De Witte, 'Le retour à *Costa*. La primauté du droit communautaire à la lumière du droit international' (1984) RTDE 425–54. See further, on the primacy of Union law, including the second and third pillar, Lenaerts and Corthaut, 'Of birds and Hedges: The Role of Primacy in Invoking Norms of EU Law' (2006) ELRev 287–315. See as to the third pillar, however, C-573/17, *Popławski*, 2019, paras 50–109.

[14] 14/68, *Wilhelm*, 1969, para. 6; 11/70, *Internationale Handelsgesellschaft*, 1970, para. 3; 249/85 *Albako*, 1987, para. 14.

The case law of the Court of Justice concerned the effects of Community law, that is, the former first pillar of the Union. Since the entry into force of the Lisbon Treaty, the requirements established by the Court of Justice in its case law apply, in principle, to all forms of Union law. Yet, the Treaties contain no express reference to the primacy of Union law, although the framers of the EU Constitution intended to incorporate such a reference. Indeed, the EU Constitution provided in this regard that '[t]he Constitution and law adopted by the institutions of the Union in exercising competences conferred on it shall have primacy over the law of the Member States' (Article I-6). The 2007 Intergovernmental Conference chose, however, not to incorporate such a reference. However, it stated in a declaration annexed to the Lisbon Treaty that '[t]he Conference recalls that, in accordance with well settled case law of the Court of Justice of the European Union, the Treaties and the law adopted by the Union on the basis of the Treaties have primacy over the law of Member States, under the conditions laid down by the said case law'.[15] The declaration further quotes an opinion of the Council's Legal Service on the primacy of EC law, which refers to the Court's case law according to which 'this principle is inherent to the specific nature of the European Community' and states that '[t]he fact that the principle of primacy will not be included in the future treaty shall not in any way change the existence of the principle and the existing case law of the Court of Justice'.[16] All this amounts to a general recognition of the principle of primacy of Union law.

Precedence over any rule of national law. As long ago as *Costa* v. *ENEL*, the Court held that Community law could not be overridden by 'domestic legal provisions, however framed'[17]. It follows that Union law (since the Lisbon Treaty) takes precedence over any rule of domestic law which is at variance with it, including 'principles of a national constitutional structure'.[18] This is because if Union law were only binding on the Member States to the extent that it is consistent with their constitutional structure, a situation would ensue in which the application of Union law would differ from one Member State to another. Moreover, important principles which are common to the constitutional traditions of the Member States (see also Article 2 TEU; para. 5.002, *supra*) are subscribed to by the Union itself, notably respect for democracy (see para. 17.046, *supra*), fundamental rights (see para. 25.001 *et seq.*, *infra*), and the rule of law (see para. 30-001 *et seq.*, *infra*).[19] As far as fundamental rights are concerned, the Charter of Fundamental Rights of the European Union applies to the institutions, bodies, offices, and agencies of the Union, and to the Member States when they are implementing Union law (para. 25-008 *et seq.*, *infra*). When a Union act requires national implementing measures, national authorities and judicial bodies may only apply national fundamental rights protection standards to the extent that this does not put the level of protection of the Charter and the primacy, uniformity, and effectiveness of Union law at risk.[20]

23.011

---

[15] Declaration (No. 17), annexed to the Lisbon Treaty, concerning primacy, OJ 2010 C83/344.
[16] Opinion 11197/07 (JUR 260).
[17] 6/64, *Costa*, 1964, 594.
[18] 11/70, *Internationale Handelsgesellschaft*, 1970, para. 3 (which referred in particular to 'fundamental rights as formulated by the constitution of [the] State', but see Union protection of fundamental rights: para. 25.002 *et seq.*). An example may be found in C-285/98, *Kreil*, 2000. See also 30/72, *Commission v Italy*, 1973, para. 11 (precedence over 'budgetary legislation or practice').
[19] For further details, see De Witte, 'Community Law and National Constitutional Values' (1991) 2 LIEI 1–22. See also Corthaut, *EU ordre public* (Wolters Kluwer, 2012), Chapter 12.
[20] C-399/11, *Melloni*, 2013, paras 53–64.

23.012 **Conflict.** The primacy of Union law means that conflicting national legal rules must give way to provisions of Union law. In order to determine whether such a conflict exists, the aim and purpose of the Union provision must be assessed in the light of what it contains and what—deliberately or not—it does not contain. The national provision continues to be effective solely for those aspects which the Union provision has left unaffected.[21] Often the question arises as to how far a Union act allows the Member States to adopt measures with regard to aspects not dealt with in the Union act. In such a case, it must be inferred from the aims and object of the Union act whether that act governs the area exhaustively or whether it still leaves some latitude for regulation by Member States. If the Union has not exercised a competence which it shares with the Member States, the latter remain free to make their own policy choices in the area covered by that competence.[22] A matter not expressly dealt with by the Union act may be regulated by the Member States provided that their action does not thereby undermine the aims and object of the Union act.[23] In the same way, it has to be determined whether a Union harmonization measure entails 'full' or 'complete' harmonization or whether it allows Member States to deviate from the Union measure (see para. 7-110, *supra*). In some areas, action by the Union may preclude any competence on the part of the Member States (see para. 5-023, *supra*). A national measure is compatible with Union law if it respects both primary and secondary Union law. In the light of the hierarchy of norms of Union law this implies that the mere fact that a national measure is in conformity with a norm of secondary Union law does not in and of itself mean that this measure also complies with primary Union law.[24]

2. The principle of interpretation in conformity with Union law

23.013 **Avoiding conflict.** The primacy of Union law is a conflict rule which applies where a legal relationship is governed by conflicting national and Union rules. Where the application of a national rule is likely to result in a conflict with a Union rule, it must first be determined whether the rules cannot be interpreted and applied in such a way as to avoid a conflict. Naturally, the Union rule must be interpreted in a uniform way in all Member States. As far as the interpretation of national law is concerned, the Court of Justice considers that Article 4(3) TEU places all public authorities,[25] and therefore also judicial authorities, under a duty to interpret the national law that they have to apply as far as possible in conformity with the requirements of Union law.[26] This entails the obligation to change established case law if it is based on an interpretation that is not in conformity with Union law.[27] National courts must therefore consider whether national law (legislation and case law[28]) can be interpreted

---

[21] For examples in the case law, see in particular 40/69, *Bollmann*, 1970, paras 4–5; 50/76, *Amsterdam Bulb*, 1977, paras 9–30; 111/76, *Van den Hazel*, 1977, paras 13–27; 255/86 *Commission v Belgium*, 1988, paras 8–11; 60/86, *Commission v United Kingdom*, 1988, para. 11; 190/87, *Moorman*, 1988, paras 11–13. See also Hwang, 'Anwendungsvorrang statt Geltungsvorrang? Normlogische und institutionelle Überlegungen zum Vorrang des Unionsrechts' (2016) EuR 355–72.

[22] C-566/15, *Erzberger*, 2017, para. 36; C-638/16 PPU, *X and Y*, 2017, paras 40–5; C-507/17, *Google*, 2019, para. 72.

[23] C-355/00, *Freskot AE*, 2003, paras 18–33; C-416/01, *ACOR*, 2003, paras 21–62.

[24] e.g. C-345/09, *van Delft*, 2010, paras 85–6.

[25] C-53/10, *Mücksch*, 2011, paras 21–34 (lower national authorities).

[26] See C-106/98, *Marleasing*, 1990, para. 8; ECJ, C-262/97, *Engelbrecht*, 2000, para. 39; ECJ, C-60/02, *Criminal proceedings against X*, 2004, paras 59–60.

[27] C-441/14, *Dansk Industri*, 2016, paras 33–4; C-55/18, *Federación de Servicios de Comisiones Obreras (CCOO)*, 2019, para. 70.

[28] See C-456/98, *Centrosteel*, 1998, paras 16–17, with case note by Corthaut (2002) Col J Eur L, 293–310.

or applied in such a way that there is no conflict with Union law. This applies to all rules of Union law, including fundamental rights, general principles of Union law, and rules of international law which are applicable in Union law.[29] Where national law is interpreted in conformity with the provisions of a directive, this practice is referred to as interpretation consistent with a directive (see para. 27-029, *infra*).

Interpreting national law in conformity with Union law may enable public authorities to avoid situations in which national rules have to be set aside on account of a conflict with Union law.[30] However, the duty to interpret national law in conformity with Union law is limited by general principles of Union law, such as the principle of legal certainty, the principle of legality, and the prohibition of retroactivity.[31] Accordingly, the principles of legal certainty and non-retroactivity preclude this obligation to interpret national law in conformity with Union law from leading to the criminal liability of individuals being determined or aggravated.[32] Likewise, the principle of interpretation in conformity with Union law cannot serve as the basis for an interpretation of national law *contra legem*.[33]

3. Duty to set aside conflicting national rules

Inapplicability of conflicting national rules. In the 1978 judgment in *Simmenthal* ('*Simmenthal II*'), the Court of Justice held that 'in accordance with the principle of the precedence of Community law, the relationship between provisions of the Treaty and directly applicable measures of the institutions on the one hand and the national law of the Member States on the other is such that those provisions and measures not only by their entry into force, render automatically inapplicable any conflicting provision of current national law but—in so far as they are an integral part of, and take precedence in, the legal order applicable in the territory of each of the Member States—also preclude the valid adoption of new national legislative measures to the extent to which they would be incompatible with Community law.'[34]

23.014

Consequently, Member States are under a duty not only to avoid adopting a measure conflicting with Community law—Union law since the Lisbon Treaty—and to change any existing conflicting measure,[35] but also—so long as the conflicting measure has not been amended—to refrain from applying it.[36] In the judgment in *Simmenthal II*, the Court of Justice held that 'every national court must, in a case within its jurisdiction, apply Community law in its entirety and protect rights which the latter confers on individuals and

---

[29] For the interpretation and application of national law in the light of fundamental rights, see para. 25.002, *infra*; for the interpretation and application of national law in the light of general principles of Union law, see para. 25.020, *infra*; for the interpretation and application of national law in the light of applicable rules of international law, see para. 26.002, *infra*.

[30] Interpretation in conformity with Union law also makes the question of the direct effect of Union law unnecessary (i.e. 'can the provision of Union law be relied upon by the person seeking redress?'). See Betlem, 'The Doctrine of Consistent Interpretation—Managing Legal Uncertainty' (2002) OJLS 397–418.

[31] On the limits of the duty of consistent interpretation, see C-573/17, *Popławski*, 2019, paras 74–6. See also para. 27-016, *infra* (on regulations) and para. 27.030 *et seq*. (on directives).

[32] See C-579/15, *Popławski*, 2017, para. 32; C-554/14, *Ognyanov*, 2016, paras 63–4; C-387/02, C-391/02 and C-403/02, *Berlusconi*, 2005, paras 70–8; C-60/02, *Criminal proceedings against X*, 2004, paras 61–3.

[33] See C 579/15, *Popławski*, 2017, para. 33

[34] 106/77, *Simmenthal*, 1978, para. 17.

[35] See also 159/78, *Commission v Italy*, 1979, para. 22.

[36] See 48/71, *Commission v Italy*, 1972, paras 6–8. *A fortiori*, a Member State is debarred from adopting specific measures to extend a provision found to be contrary to Union law: C-101/91, *Commission v Italy*, 1993, paras 22–3.

must accordingly set aside any provision of national law which may conflict with it, whether prior or subsequent to the Community rule'.[37] As primacy only applies when there is a conflict between a national measure and Union law, the question whether a national measure must be set aside only arises if that measure cannot be interpreted in conformity with Union law.[38] Where a national court is faced with a national provision that is incompatible with Union law, it must decline to apply that provision, without being compelled to make a reference to the Court for a preliminary ruling before doing so.[39] If necessary, a national court must alter established case law that is incompatible with Union law to that effect.[40] Where the incompatibility of a provision of national law with Union law is alleged in proceedings in which the national court is asked to annul that provision, a finding of incompatibility will lead to its annulment. The duty to set aside conflicting rules applies not only to national courts, but also to public bodies, including administrative bodies.[41] In order to comply with that duty, lower administrative authorities, such as local authorities, must refrain of their own motion from applying provisions adopted by a higher authority in breach of Union law.[42] Likewise, national authorities may not apply provisions of agreements concluded between Member States if they conflict with Union law.[43] The incompatibility of national legislation with Union provisions can be definitively remedied only by means of national provisions that are binding and have the same legal force as those that have to be modified.[44] Accordingly, the duty to refrain from applying national rules incompatible with Union law applies even with regard to rules which have been declared unconstitutional by the national constitutional court, but have not yet lost their binding force.[45]

However, in *Popławski II*,[46] the Court has clarified that the principle of the primacy of Union law cannot have the effect of undermining the essential distinction between provisions of Union law which have direct effect and those which do not and, consequently, of creating a single set of rules for the application of all of the provisions of Union law by the national courts. While the national courts are required, under the principle of primacy, to interpret national law in conformity with the requirements of the whole of Union law, their duty to set aside conflicting provisions of national law is restricted to those provisions of Union law that have direct effect (see para. 23-032 *et seq.*, *infra*). Indeed, as an organ of a Member State, any national court has the obligation to refrain from applying any provision of national law which is contrary to a provision of Union law with direct effect in the case pending before it.[47] By contrast, a provision of Union law which does not have direct effect

---

[37] 106/77, *Simmenthal* ('*Simmenthal II*'), 1978, para. 21. See also 249/85, *Albako*, 1987, para. 17; C-262/97, *Engelbrecht*, 2000, para. 40. For directives, see also para. 27-032, *infra*.

[38] C-282/10, *Dominguez*, 2012, para. 23; C-97/11, *Amia*, 2012, paras 27–31; C-752/18, *Deutsche Umwelthilfe*, 2019, paras 40–2.

[39] C-555/07, *Kücükdeveci*, 2010, paras 53–55. In such a case, the national court cannot be prevented from making such reference either: ibid.

[40] C-614/14, *Ognyanov*, 2016, para. 35.

[41] 103/88, *Fratelli Costanzo*, 1989, para. 31. See, e.g., national competition authorities: para. 9.012, *supra*.

[42] 103/88, *Fratelli Costanzo*, 1989, para. 31. See also C-378/17, *The Minister for Justice and Equality and The Commissioner of the Garda Síochána*, 2018, paras 31–52, with note Lazzerini (2019) REALaw 197–208. See also Drake, 'The Principle of Primacy and the Duty of National Bodies Appointed to Enforce EU Law to Disapply Conflicting National Law: An Garda Síochána' (2020) CMLRev 557–68.

[43] C-469/00, *Ravil and Others*, 2003, para. 37.

[44] See C-145/99 *Commission v Italy*, 2002, paras 37–9.

[45] C-314/08 *Filipiak*, 2009, paras 81–5.

[46] C-573/17, *Popławski*, 2019, paras 50–109.

[47] Ibid., para. 61; see also C-409/06, *Winner Wetten*, 2010, para. 55; C-282/10, *Dominguez*, 2012, para. 41; C-569/16 and C-570/16, *Bauer and Willmeroth*, 2018, para. 75; C-824/18, *A.B.*, 2021, paras 140–149; C-30/19, *Braathens Regional Aviation*, 2021, para. 58.

may not be relied on, as such, in a dispute coming under Union law in order to set aside a conflicting provision of national law.[48] If a provision of Union law does not have direct effect, its enforcement in the national legal order can only be triggered by the Commission by bringing an infringement action against the Member State (Articles 258 to 260 TFEU; see para. 29-039, *infra*), or by national courts interpreting national law as far as possible in line with Union law (see para. 23-013, *supra*) or awarding damages because of State liability (see para. 23-019 *et seq.*, *infra*).

A national measure will not only be inapplicable if it is substantively incompatible with a provision of Union law, it may also be inapplicable if it was adopted contrary to a procedure laid down by Union law. This will be the case where a Member State failed to notify technical provisions to the Commission in accordance with a Union procedure for the provision of information.[49] A technical provision which has not been notified to the Commission will be inapplicable only if it constitutes a barrier to trade.[50]

A national court may not decide that a national measure that is contrary to Union law should continue to apply provisionally for reasons of legal certainty.[51] However, when a national measure is in conflict with Union rules aimed at protection of the environment, the Union objective of environmental protection may, in certain circumstances, be better achieved by temporarily maintaining the consequences of the annulled act than by annulling the measure retroactively.[52] Moreover, the disapplication of a national measure is not allowed if it would entail a breach of the principle that offences and penalties must be defined by law, either because of the lack of precision of the applicable law or because of the retroactive application of legislation imposing conditions of criminal liability stricter than those in force at the time the infringement was committed.[53] Similarly, the principle of effectiveness of Union law and respect of the right, guaranteed by Article 47(1) of the Charter, to effective judicial protection do not oblige a national court to set aside a provision of national law if, in so doing, it infringes another fundamental right guaranteed by Union law.[54]

Simmenthal. In *Simmenthal II* the Court of Justice was seized of a question referred to it for a preliminary ruling by an Italian court, which had held that the imposition of certain inspection fees was incompatible with Community law and had therefore ordered the Italian tax authorities to repay them. The tax authorities appealed, relying on case law of the Italian

23.015

---

[48] C-573/17, *Popławski*, 2019, para. 62.
[49] C-194/94, *CIA Security International*, 1996, paras 45–54; C-443/98, *Unilever Italia*, 2000, paras 31–52; C-159/00, *Sapod Audic*, 2002, paras 48–52 (concerning Council Directive 83/189/EEC of 18 March 1993 requiring Member States to notify any draft technical regulations and standards to the Commission, replaced by Directive 98/34 and, subsequently, by Directive 2015/1535; see para. 7.111, *supra*); Voinot, 'Le droit communautaire et l'inopposabilité aux particuliers des règles techniques nationales' (2003) RTDE 91–112; Candela Castillo, 'La confirmation par la Cour du principe de non-opposabilité aux tiers des règles techniques non notifiées dans le cadre de la directive 83/189/CEE: un pas en avant vers l'intégration structurelle des ordres juridiques nationaux et communautaire' (1997) RMCUE 51–9.
[50] C-226/97, *Lemmens*, 1998, para. 35.
[51] C-409/06, *Winner Wetten*, 2010, paras 53–69.
[52] See the special circumstances at issue in C-41/11, *Inter-Environnement Wallonne en Terre wallonne*, 2012, paras 59–62; C-379/15, *Association France Nature Environnement*, 2016, paras 37–42. See also C-411/17, *Inter-Environnement Wallonnie and Bond Beter Leefmilieu Vlaanderen*, 2019, paras 167–82 (maintaining the effects of national law in order to ensure the continuity of electricity supply—see also Belgian Constitutional Court, no. 34/2020 of 5 March 2020, B.26-B.33.4).
[53] C-42/17, *M.A.S and M.B*, 2017, paras 46–62, with case note by Rauchegger (2018) CMLRev 1521–47.
[54] C-752/18, *Deutsche Umwelthilfe*, 2019, para. 43. On the competing considerations that nuance the duty to set conflicting provisions of Union law aside, see also Dougan, 'Primacy and the Remedy of Disapplication' (2019) CMLRev 1459–1508.

Constitutional Court to the effect that a national law which conflicted with Community law was also incompatible with the Italian Constitution. On this view, the national court could not set aside the law in question until such time as it had been declared unlawful by the Constitutional Court. The Court of Justice ruled that a national court which must apply provisions of Community law is 'under a duty to give full effect to those provisions, if necessary refusing of its own motion to apply any conflicting provision of national legislation, even if adopted subsequently, and it is not necessary for the court to request or await the prior setting aside of such provisions by legislative or constitutional means'.[55] In later case law the Court specified that if a national court is under an obligation to submit certain questions first to a national constitutional court with the result that it cannot immediately set aside a provision of national law deemed to be contrary to Union law, the national court must in any event take any necessary measure to ensure the provisional judicial protection of the rights conferred under the Union's legal order and to refrain from applying that conflicting provision after the constitutional court has ruled.[56]

23.016 *Factortame.* The Court of Justice went even further in the 1990 judgment in *Factortame I*, in which the UK House of Lords asked whether an English court had the power, under Community law, to grant an interim injunction against the Crown where a party claimed to be entitled to rights under Community law.[57] The problem had arisen after the Divisional Court of the Queen's Bench Division had applied to the Court of Justice for a preliminary ruling on the compatibility with Community law of nationality requirements imposed by the 1988 Merchant Shipping Act and the 1988 Merchant Shipping (Registration of Fishing Vessels) Regulations in order to put an end to the practice of 'quota hopping' by which foreign vessels without any genuine link with the UK were using its fishing quotas. The House of Lords had to decide whether that court could suspend the relevant provisions by way of interim relief, the Court of Appeal having determined that under common law the courts had no power to suspend the application of Acts of Parliament in that way. Starting out from its judgment in *Simmenthal II* and the principle of sincere cooperation, the Court of Justice ruled that

> the full effectiveness of Community law would be impaired if a rule of national law could prevent a court seized of a dispute governed by Community law from granting interim relief in order to ensure the full effectiveness of the judgment to be given on the existence of the rights claimed under Community law. It follows that a court which in those circumstances would grant interim relief, if it were not for a rule of national law, is obliged to set aside that rule.[58]

By so ruling, the Court safeguarded rights derived by individuals from Union law against action of a public authority, even where it had not been finally determined that the action in question was incompatible with Union law.[59]

---

[55] 106/77, *Simmenthal*, 1978, para. 24.
[56] C-188/10 and C-189/10, *Melki and Abdeli*, 2010, para. 53. See also C-689/13, *PFE*, 2016, paras 39–41.
[57] C-213/89, *Factortame and Others* ('*Factortame I*'), 1990, paras 14–15.
[58] Ibid., para. 21. On 11 October 1990, the House of Lords affirmed the interlocutory injunction against the Secretary of State. See Barav and Simon, 'Le droit communautaire et la suspension provisoire des mesures nationales—Les enjeux de l'affaire *Factortame*' (1990) RMC 591–7.
[59] That the United Kingdom legislation was indeed incompatible with Community law was only determined following the Court's judgment giving a preliminary ruling on questions which had already been referred in

Full effectiveness. In the judgments in *Simmenthal II* and *Factortame I*, the Court of Justice **23.017**
linked the primacy of Union law with the duty of the national court to secure the full effectiveness (*effet utile*) of Union law, even at the expense of the legal tradition of its own Member State. Just as the primacy principle was associated with Article 10 EC [*now Article 4(3) TEU*] in *Costa v ENEL*, that duty on the part of the national court was also derived from the principle of sincere cooperation enshrined in that article (see para. 5-046, *supra*). As a general rule, the full effectiveness of Union law requires Member States to nullify the unlawful consequences of a breach of Union law.[60] Such an obligation is owed by every organ of the Member State concerned within the sphere of its competence,[61] so that the Member State's administrative authorities and courts that are called upon, within the exercise of their respective powers, to apply provisions of Union law are under a duty to give full effect to those provisions.[62] Consequently, in principle any taxes levied in breach of Union law or benefits unduly refused are to be refunded or paid out, respectively. Where consent has been granted without duly complying with a procedure imposed by Union law, the national court must revoke or suspend that consent so that the correct procedure can be followed.[63] Over time, the Court of Justice has gradually specified more precisely the requirements which Article 4(3) TEU imposes on Member States with a view to securing the 'full effectiveness' in the national legal system of rights derived from Union law.[64]

Remedies under national law. The rights conferred by Union law can be enforced before **23.018**
national courts using the rules on jurisdiction and procedure laid down by the Member States for their legal order (principle of national procedural autonomy). In the absence of Union rules governing the matter, it is—in accordance with this principle—for the domestic legal system of each Member State to designate the courts and tribunals having jurisdiction and to lay down the detailed procedural rules governing actions for safeguarding rights which individuals derive from Union law. But the Member States are responsible for ensuring that those rights are effectively protected in each case.[65] As discussed in more depth

---

C-221/89, *Factortame and Others* ('*Factortame II*'), 1991 and the judgment given on an action brought by the Commission under Article 226 EC [*now Article 258 TFEU*], C-246/89, *Commission v United Kingdom*, 1991. In the latter case, the President of the Court had already granted an application from the Commission for an interim order requiring the United Kingdom to suspend the nationality requirements of the legislation at issue: C-246/89 R, *Commission v United Kingdom* (order of the President), 1989. This was followed by the case concerning State liability for the breach of Community law: C-46/93 and C-48/93, *Brasserie du Pêcheur and Factortame* ('*Factortame IV*'), 1996 (para. 23.020, *infra*).

[60] C-6/90 and C-9/90, *Francovich and Others*, 1991, para. 36; see earlier with regard to the corresponding provision of Article 86 ECSC: 6/60, *Humblet*, 1960, 569.
[61] C-8/88, *Germany v Commission*, 1990, para. 13; C-201/02, *Wells*, 2004, para. 64.
[62] C-349/17, *Eesti Pagar*, 2019, para. 91; C-628/15, *The Trustees of the BT Pension Scheme*, 2015, para. 54.
[63] C-201/02, *Wells*, 2004, paras 64–70.
[64] The relevant case law is only discussed in outline in the following sections. For a more exhaustive discussion, see Lenaerts, Gutman, and Nowak, *EU Procedural Law* (OUP, 2022), Chapter 4. Cf. Ortino, 'A Reading of the EU Constitutional Legal System through the Meta-principle of Effectiveness' (2016) CDE 91–114; Wallerman, 'Can Two Walk Together, Except They be Agreed? Preliminary References and (the Erosion of) National Procedural Autonomy' (2019) ELRev 159–77; Ross, 'Effectiveness in the European Legal Order(s): Beyond Supremacy to Constitutional Proportionality?' (2006) ELRev 476–98; Delicostopoulos, 'Towards European Procedural Primacy in National Legal Systems' (2003) ELJ 599–613; Temple Lang, 'The Duties of National Courts under Community Constitutional Law' (1997) ELRev 3–18; Fitzpatrick and Szyszczak, 'Remedies and Effective Judicial Protection in Community Law' (1994) MLR 434–41; Snyder, 'The Effectiveness of European Community Law: Institutions, Processes, Tools and Techniques' (1993) MLR 19, 40–7; Steiner, 'From Direct Effects to Francovich: Shifting Means of Enforcement of Community Law' (1993) ELRev 3–22.
[65] See, e.g., C-268/06 *Impact*, 2008, paras 44 and 45; C-317/08 to C-320/08 *Alassini and Others*, 2010, para. 47; C-30/19, *Braathens Regional Aviation*, 2021, paras 29–59; C-194/19, *H.A.*, 2021, paras 25–49.

in Chapter 29 (see para. 29-009 *et seq.*, *infra*), the principle of full effectiveness of Union law implies that the national rules governing claims by which individuals seek to enforce the rights that they derive from Union law 'must not be less favourable than those relating to similar domestic claims' (principle of equivalence) and must not embody requirements and time-limits 'such as in practice to make it impossible or excessively difficult' to exercise those rights (principle of effectiveness).[66] It appears from *Factortame I* and a number of other judgments that the national court must, where necessary, refrain from applying the national legal rules which govern a particular matter, so as to secure the full effectiveness of Union law.[67] Administrative bodies, too, must set aside conflicting procedural rules in order to give full effect to Union law.[68] However, a national court is not required to extend to infringements of Union law a remedy under national law permitting only in the event of infringement of the ECHR or one of the protocols thereto, the rehearing of criminal proceedings closed by a national decision having the force of *res judicata*.[69] Similarly, while Union law does not preclude a Member State from ordering the coercive detention of officials that are unwilling to comply with an order to implement Union law as a matter of equivalence, such measure may only be taken to the extent that national law provides for a proper legal basis for such a measure.[70]

4. Liability of the Member State for damage arising out of a breach of Union law

23.019 *Francovich.* The Court of Justice held in *Francovich* that '[t]he full effectiveness of Community rules would be impaired and the protection of the rights which they grant would be weakened if individuals were unable to obtain redress when their rights are infringed by a breach of Community law for which a Member State can be held responsible'.[71]

---

[66] 33/76 *Rewe*, 1976, para. 5, and 45/76, *Comet*, 1976, paras 13–16; see also 68/79, *Just*, 1980, paras 25–6; 199/82, *San Giorgio*, 1983, paras 12–17; C-574/15, *Scialdone*, 2018, paras 24–61; C-234/17, *XC*, 2018, paras 25–59. See Girerd, 'Les principes d'équivalence et d'effectivité: encadrement ou désencadrement de l'autonomie procédurale des Etats membres?' (2000) RTDE 75–102.

[67] See, e.g., C-377/89, *Cotter and McDermott*, 1991, paras 20–2 and 26–7 (married women held entitled to benefits/compensatory payments paid to married men in respect of a spouse deemed to be dependent even though this was contrary to a prohibition of unlawful enrichment laid down by Irish law); C-208/90, *Emmott*, 1991, paras 23–4 (Irish authorities held not entitled to rely on procedural rules relating to time-limits for bringing proceedings in an action brought against them by an individual in order to protect rights directly conferred upon him by a Community directive so long as Ireland had not properly transposed the directive into national law); C-271/91, *Marshall* ('*Marshall II*'), 1993, paras 30 and 34–5 (Ms Marshall had succeeded in her claim for unlawful sex discrimination under the equal treatment directive following 152/84 *Marshall* ('*Marshall I*'), 1986; the Court held that the limit imposed on any damages claim which might be awarded by an Industrial Tribunal under the 1975 Sex Discrimination Act was unlawful), see the case note by Curtin (1994) CMLRev 631–52. See Szyszczak, 'Making Europe More Relevant to its Citizens: Effective Judicial Process' (1996) ELRev 351–77; Hoskins, 'Tilting the Balance: Supremacy and National Procedural Rules' (1996) ELRev 365–77. See also para. 29-011, *infra*. For more recent examples, see C-689/13, *PFE*, 2016, paras 37–42; C-585/18, C-624/18 and C-625/18, *A.K.*, 2019, 155–66.

[68] C-118/00, *Larsy*, 2001, paras 50–3.

[69] C-234/17, *XC*, 2018, para. 59.

[70] C-752/18, *Deutsche Umwelthilfe*, 2019, paras 29–56.

[71] C-6/90 and C-9/90, *Francovich and Others*, 1991, para. 33. The principle is therefore intended both to protect the rights of individuals and to maintain the primacy of Community law; see Aboudrar-Ravanel, 'Responsabilité et primauté, ou la question de l'efficience de l'outil' (1999) RMCUE 544–58. Among numerous studies, see Davis, 'Liability in Damages for a Breach of Community Law: Some Reflections on the Question of who to Sue and the Concept of the State' (2006) ELRev 69–80; Tridimas, 'Liability for Breach of Community Law: Growing Up and Mellowing Down?' (2001) CMLRev 301–32; Dantonel-Cor, 'La violation de la norme communautaire et la responsabilité extracontractuelle de l'Etat' (1998) RTDE 75–91; Van Gerven, 'Bridging the Unbridgeable: Community and National Tort Laws after *Francovich* and *Brasserie*' (1996) ICLQ 507–44. Some commentators consider that Union law also puts individuals under a duty to make good damage resulting from a breach of Union law; see Kremer, 'Die Haftung Privater für Verstösse gegen Gemeinschaftsrecht' (2003) EuR 696–705. This is true of competition law; see para. 9.015.

The Court went on to state that 'the principle whereby a State must be liable for loss and damage caused to individuals as a result of breaches of Community law for which the State can be held responsible is inherent in the system of the Treaty' and that a further basis for the obligation of Member States to make good such loss and damage is to be found in the duty of sincere cooperation in Article 4(3) TEU.[72] That principle applies to any case in which a Member State breaches Union law, irrespective of the authority of the Member State whose act or omission was responsible for the breach.[73] It follows that an individual may bring a damages claim in the national courts on account of an act or omission of a legislative organ[74] or on account of decisions of judicial bodies adjudicating at last instance.[75]

Conditions for liability. The conditions under which that liability gives rise to a right to reparation from the State depend on the nature of the breach of Union law giving rise to the loss and damage.[76] The Court of Justice made clear in *Factortame IV* that the conditions under which the State may incur liability for damage caused to individuals by a breach of Union law cannot, in the absence of particular justification, differ from those governing the liability of the Union in like circumstances.[77] With regard to an act or omission of the legislature or executive in breach of Union law, that law confers a right of reparation where three conditions are met: (1) the rule of law infringed must be intended to confer rights on individuals, (2) the breach must be sufficiently serious, and (3) there must be a direct causal link between the breach of the obligation resting on the State and the damage sustained by the injured parties.[78] The same three conditions apply to State liability for damage resulting from the decision of a judicial body adjudicating at last instance.[79] According to the Court of Justice, this does not mean that the State cannot incur liability for acts of the legislature, executive, or the judiciary under less strict conditions on the basis of national law.[80] As to

23.020

---

[72] C-6/90 and C-9/90, *Francovich and Others*, 1991, paras 35–6. See also C-752/18, *Deutsche Umwelthilfe*, 2019, para. 54.

[73] C-224/01, *Köbler*, 2003, para. 31.

[74] C-46/93 and C-48/93, *Brasserie du Pêcheur and Factortame*, 1996, paras 34–6.

[75] C-224/01, *Köbler*, 2003, paras 30–59; C-173/03, *Traghetti del Mediterraneo*, 2006, paras 30–40; C-160/14, *Ferreira da Silva e Brito*, 2015, paras 46–60. See Silveira and Perez Fernandes, 'Preliminary References, Effective Judicial Protection and State Liability. What if the Ferreira da Silva Judgment had not been Delivered?' (2016) Rev EDE 631–66; Ruffert (2007) CMLRev 479–86; Breuer (2004) ELRev 243–54; Wegener (2004) EuR 84–91, and for a somewhat critical view, Wattel (2004) CMLRev 177–90, and Steyger (2004) NTER 18–22. For earlier discussions of this question, see Anagnostaras, 'The Principle of State Liability for Judicial Breaches: The Impact of European Community Law' (2001) E Pub L 281–305; Blanchet, 'L'usage de la théorie de l'acte clair en droit communautaire: une hypothèse de mise en jeu de la responsabilité de l'Etat français du fait de la fonction juridictionnelle?' (2001) RTDE 397–438; for a critical view, see Wegener, 'Staatshaftung für die Verletzung von Gemeinschaftsrecht durch nationale Gerichte?' (2002) EuR 785–800. Apart from state liability, other remedies may also be available in case of violation of Union law by a Member State Court, see Varga, 'National Remedies in the Case of Violation of EU Law by Member State Courts' (2017) CMLRev 51–80.

[76] C-6/90 and C-9/90, *Francovich and Others*, 1991, para. 38.

[77] C-46/93 and C-48/93, *Brasserie du Pêcheur and Factortame*, 1996, paras 40–2.

[78] Ibid., paras 50–1; C-392/93, *British Telecommunications*, 1996, para. 39; C-168/15, *Tomášová*, 2016, paras 22–34. These rules have applied to legislative acts of the Union since 5/71, *Zuckerfabrik Schöppenstedt v Council*, 1971, para. 11: see Lenaerts, Gutman and Nowak, *EU Procedural Law* (OUP, 2022) Chapter 11. For the parallel with the rules on liability applying to the Union, see C-352/98 P, *Laboratoires pharmaceutiques Bergaderm and Goupil v Commission*, 2000, paras 38–44; for breaches of fundamental rights, see Van Gerven, 'Remedies for Infringements of Fundamental Rights' (2004) E Pub L 261–84.

[79] C-224/01, *Köbler*, 2003, paras 51–3; C-173/03, *Traghetti del Mediterraneo*, 2006, paras 42–45.

[80] C-46/93 and C-48/93, *Brasserie du Pêcheur and Factortame*, 1996, para. 66; C-224/01, *Köbler*, 2003, para. 57; C-173/03, *Traghetti del Mediterraneo*, 2006, para. 45. See, e.g., in Belgium with respect to the regulatory activity of the administration: Cass. 14 January 2000, *Arr Cass* 2000, No. 33, referred to in the Eighteenth Annual Report on monitoring Community law, COM(2001)309 fin. According to this 'Evobus' judgment, any ordinary breach of Union law by an administrative authority may constitute a 'fault' for which the State can be held liable. See also Cass 8 December 1994, *Arr Cass* 1994, No. 541 (the second 'Anca' judgment, in which the State was held to be

liability under Union law, it is for the national courts to assess whether those conditions are met, taking into account the guidance that the Court of Justice has given in respect of the three conditions.

23.021 **(1) Provision conferring rights on individuals.** Among the provisions which confer rights on individuals are the Treaty provisions governing the four freedoms.[81] In *Factortame IV*, the Court of Justice ruled that the right of reparation exists whether or not the relevant provision of Union law has direct effect.[82]

23.022 **(2) Sufficiently serious breach.** A breach of Union law will be 'sufficiently serious' if it has persisted despite a judgment of the Court of Justice from which it is clear that the conduct in question constituted an infringement.[83] However, the right of reparation does not depend on the existence of a prior judgment of the Court of Justice.[84] Still, although the national courts have jurisdiction to decide how to characterize the breaches of Union law at issue, the Court of Justice will indicate a number of circumstances which the national courts might take into account,[85] and it will even characterize the breach itself if it has all the information necessary to that end.[86] The national court must take account of the clarity and precision of the rule infringed, whether the infringement and the damage caused was intentional or involuntary, whether any error of law was excusable or inexcusable, and the fact that the position taken by a Union institution may have contributed towards the adoption or maintenance of national measures or practices contrary to Union law.[87] Accordingly, the incorrect transposition of provisions of a directive which are capable of bearing several interpretations and on which neither the Court nor the Commission has given any guidance does not necessarily constitute a sufficiently serious breach (see para. 27-035, *infra*). Where, however, at the time when it committed the infringement, a legislative or administrative organ of the Member State in question was not called upon to make any legislative choices and had only considerably reduced discretion, or even none at all, the mere infringement of Union law may be sufficient to establish the existence of a sufficiently serious breach.[88] The Court already held in *Francovich* that there is a sufficiently serious breach where a Member State fails to take any of the measures necessary to achieve the result prescribed by a directive within the period it lays down.[89] In any event, the existence and scope of the

---

liable for a breach of Community law by a judicial body); see further Weyts, 'Overheidsaansprakelijkheid wegens schending van het EU-recht', in Cariat and Nowak (eds), *Le droit de l'Union européenne et le juge belge/ Het recht van de Europese Unie en de Belgische rechter* (Bruylant, 2015), 397–422.

[81] C-446/04, *Test Claimants in the FII Group Litigation*, 2006, para. 211; C-445/06, *Danske Slagterier*, 2009, paras 21–6.

[82] C-46/93 and C-48/93, *Brasserie du Pêcheur and Factortame*, 1996, paras 18–23, with case notes by Foubert (1996) Col JEL 359–72 and Oliver (1997) CMLRev 635–80.

[83] C-46/93 and C-48/93, *Brasserie du Pêcheur and Factortame*, 1996, para. 57.

[84] Ibid., paras 91–6.

[85] Ibid., paras 56 and 58–64, likewise paras 75–80 (the existence of fault may be taken into account only in order to determine whether the breach is sufficiently serious). For further clarification, see C-94/95 and C-95/95, *Bonfaci and Others and Berto and Others*, 1997.

[86] See C-392/93, *British Telecommunications*, 1996, para. 41; C-118/00, *Larsy*, 2001, paras 40–9; C-224/01, *Köbler*, 2003, paras 101–26; C-452/06, *Synthon*, 2008, paras 36–46.

[87] C-118/00, *Larsy*, 2001, para. 39; C-224/01, *Köbler*, 2003, para. 55.

[88] C-5/94, *Hedley Lomas*, 1996, para. 28 (infringement of Article 29 EC [now Article 35 TFEU], which prohibits quantitative restrictions on exports).

[89] C-178/94, C-179/94, C-188/94, C-189/94, and C-190/94, *Dillenkofer and Others*, 1996, paras 22–6. For failure to transpose a directive, see para. 27.035, *infra*.

discretion available to the Member State must be determined by reference to Union law and not by reference to national law.[90] The mere fact that a national court has deemed it necessary to make a preliminary reference on the interpretation of Union law to the Court of Justice in the course of national proceedings relating to State liability for breach of Union law is not decisive for the determination of the question whether Union law was breached in a sufficiently serious manner by a Member State.[91]

As far as liability for judicial decisions is concerned, the national court must take account of non-compliance by the court adjudicating at last instance with its obligation to make a reference for a preliminary ruling under the third paragraph of Article 267 TFEU.[92] An incorrect application of Union law by a judicial body adjudicating at last instance does not constitute a sufficiently serious breach where the answer to the question is not expressly covered by Union law, not provided by the case law of the Court of Justice, and not obvious.[93]

(3) Direct causal link. Lastly, in order for the State to incur liability, there must be a direct causal link between the breach of the Union obligation resting on the State and the loss or damage sustained by those affected. It is for the national court to assess whether the loss or damage claimed flows sufficiently directly from the breach of Union law to render the State liable to make it good.[94]   23.023

Reparation for loss and damage. Provided that these conditions, prescribed by Union law itself, are met, it is on the basis of the rules of national law on liability that the State must make reparation for the consequences of the loss and damage caused.[95] It is the national legal system which determines against what (central or decentralized) authority the claim must be made (see para. 18-005, *supra*) and which designates the judicial authority competent to determine disputes relating to compensation for damage.[96] Naturally, the formal and substantive conditions laid down by national law must not be less favourable than those relating to similar domestic claims and must not be such as to make it impossible or excessively difficult to obtain compensation, in practice.[97]   23.024

---

[90] C-424/97, *Haim*, 2000, para. 40.
[91] C-244/13, *Ogieriakhi*, 2014, paras 51–5.
[92] C-224/01, *Köbler*, 2003, para. 55; C-173/03, *Traghetti del Mediterraneo*, 2006, paras 32 and 43.
[93] C-224/01, *Köbler*, 2003, paras 121–2. This position is not altered by the fact that the national court should have made a reference for a preliminary ruling: ibid., para. 123. See also C-168/15, *Tomášová*, 2016, paras 25–34.
[94] C-446/04, *Test Claimants in the FII Group Litigation*, 2006, para. 218; C-420/11, *Leth*, 2013, paras 45–7.
[95] C-6/90 and C-9/90, *Francovich and Others*, 1991, paras 42–3.
[96] C-224/01, *Köbler*, 2003, paras 44–7 and 50 (concerning compensation for damage resulting from a judicial decision conflicting with Union law).
[97] See para. 29.012, *infra*, and, for the transposition of directives, para. 27.036, *infra*. Thus, it has been held that the following conditions for State liability should be set aside on the ground that they would impede effective judicial protection: a condition making reparation dependent upon the legislature's act or omission being referable to an individual situation; a condition requiring proof of misfeasance in public office (C-46/93 and C-48/93, *Brasserie du Pêcheur and Factortame*, 1996, paras 67–73); and a rule totally excluding loss of profit as a head of damage (ibid., para. 87). For the national courts' subsequent decisions in the *Brasserie du Pêcheur* and *Factortame* litigation, see the judgment of the *Bundesgerichtshof* of 24 October 1996, III ZR 127/91 (1996) Eu ZW 761 (State held not liable in *Brasserie du Pêcheur* because of the lack of a causal link) and the judgment of the Queen's Bench Division of 31 July 1997 in *R. v Secretary of State for Transport, ex p. Factortame and Others (No. 5)* [1997] TLR 482 and (1998) RTDE 93–5 (State held liable for a serious breach). In determining the loss or damage for which reparation may be granted, the national court may always inquire whether the injured person showed reasonable care so as to avoid the loss or damage or to mitigate it (C-178/94, C-179/94, C-188/94, C-189/94, and C-190/94 *Dillenkofer and Others*, 1996, para. 72; C-524/04, *Test Claimants in the Thin Cap Group Litigation*, 2007, paras 124–6; C-445/06, *Danske Slagterier*, 2009, paras 58–69). See further Emiliou, 'State Liability under Community Law: Shedding More Light on the *Francovich* Principle?' (1996) ELRev 399–411. See also C-66/95, *Sutton*, 1997, paras 28–35; C-90/96, *Petrie and Others*, 1997, para. 31; C-127/95, *Norbrook Laboratories*, 1998, paras 106–12.

B. Incorporation in the Member States' legal systems

23.025 **Monist systems.** The principle of primacy of Union law formulated by the Court of Justice was not automatically applied by each Member State in its domestic legal system. This was possible in the 'monist' Member States, which give international legal norms per se precedence over domestic law. On that ground, those Member States accepted that Union law took precedence in its own right in the domestic legal system.[98]

Accordingly, the primacy of Union law found immediate acceptance in the Netherlands' legal system. This was because it already recognized the principle of the supremacy of international law even before it was codified in the 1953 Constitution. The 1983 Constitution reads as follows: 'Legal provisions valid within the Kingdom shall not be applied if to do so would not be compatible with provisions of treaties and acts of international organisations which are binding on any person' (Article 94). Since Article 12 of the EEC Treaty therefore had precedence in domestic law in so far as it was 'binding on any person', the court hearing *Van Gend & Loos* had only to ascertain, through the preliminary reference to the Court of Justice, whether the provision was capable of having legal effects on individuals (see para. 1-026, *supra*).[99]

Likewise, in Belgium, it had been argued since the early years of the Community that international law, including (then) Community law, took precedence over domestic law. In the judgment of 27 May 1971 in *Franco-Suisse Le Ski*, the Supreme Court (*Hof van Cassatie/Cour de Cassation*) accepted that view in confirming that a law could not prohibit the repayment of charges collected contrary to Article 12 of the EEC Treaty on the ground that:

> where there is a conflict between a domestic provision and a provision of international law which has direct effects in the domestic legal order, the rule laid down by the treaty must prevail; that priority follows from the very nature of international law laid down by treaty; this applies *a fortiori* where, as in this case, the conflict arises between a provision of domestic law and a provision of Community law; this is because the treaties which brought Community law into being established a new legal order by virtue of which the States limited the exercise of their sovereign powers in the areas defined in those treaties;... it follows from the foregoing that the Judge was obliged to refrain from applying the provisions of domestic law which conflict with [Article 12 EEC].[100]

Consequently, both Belgian and Dutch law followed the Court of Justice in deriving the primacy of Community—now Union—law from the very nature of that law.

---

[98] See the discussion in Lenaerts and Van Nuffel (Cambien and Bray, eds), *European Union Law* (Sweet & Maxwell, 2011) of the Benelux countries (paras 21.021 and 21.032–21.033), Austria (para. 21.040), the Baltic States (paras 21.043–21.045), Poland (para. 21.051) and Bulgaria (21.053).
[99] Prechal, 'La primauté du droit communautaire aux Pays-Bas' (1990) RFDA 981–2.
[100] Cass 27 May 1971, *Arr Cass* 959; (1972) SEW 42. On the application of Union law in Belgium, see further Van Meerbeeck, 'Le droit de l'Union européenne devant les juridictions de l'ordre judiciaire', in Cariat and Nowak (eds), *Le droit de l'Union européenne et le juge belge/ Het recht van de Europese Unie en de Belgische rechter*, (Bruylant, 2015), 189–221; Van Nuffel, 'Technieken van doorwerking van EU-recht in het Belgische privaatrecht', in Samoy, Sagaert, and Terryn (eds), *Invloed van het Europese recht op het Belgische privaatrecht* (Intersentia, 2012), 1–40; Wytinck, 'The Application of Community Law in Belgium (1986-1992)' (1993) CMLRev 981–1020; Lenaerts, 'The Application of Community Law in Belgium' (1986) CMLRev 253–86.

Dualist systems. By contrast, in 'dualist' systems, international legal provisions do not form part of the domestic legal system unless and until they have been incorporated therein by a provision of national law. If the principle of primacy of Union law is given no legal force superior to the provision incorporating it, the process of incorporation does not necessarily secure the primacy for Union law.[101] Thus, the legal force of primary and secondary Union law in the United Kingdom was based upon section 2(1) of the 1972 European Communities Act. As far as the relationship with domestic law is concerned, although section 2(4) did not recognize the primacy of Union law as such, it did provide that any enactment passed, or to be passed, shall be construed and have effect subject to the 'foregoing provisions' of that section, which include section 2(1), the effect of which was to incorporate the whole of Union law into the law of the United Kingdom. The European Communities Act thus ranked supreme in the sense that anything in UK substantive law inconsistent with any of rights and obligations flowing from Union law was abrogated or had to be modified to avoid the inconsistency, even if contained in primary legislation.

Generally,[102] it is particularly in Member States that provide for a system of constitutional review that the question arises as to whether Union law must be regarded as being subordinate to the national constitution and whether provisions of Union law may be tested against the national constitution. From the point of view of Union law, it is irrelevant what method a given Member State uses in order to provide a basis for the primacy of Union law within its domestic legal system, provided that that law actually is given precedence over domestic law. This latter outcome must be achieved in spite of the reluctance which some constitutional courts have shown in accepting the primacy of Union law.[103]

Support for primacy in national law. In practice, most national legal systems combine 'monist' and 'dualist' elements. Most Member States have introduced in their constitutions a provision that authorizes the transfer of decision-making powers to the Union in their constitutions. In Belgium the Constitution was amended in 1970 to introduce an Article 25*bis* (now Article 34) which provides that the exercise of certain powers can be transferred to international organizations by way of act of parliament or treaty. A similar clause was inserted in the Dutch Constitution (Article 92) and the German Constitution (Article 24).

23.026

23.027

---

[101] Compare the developments in Ireland with those in Denmark as set out in paras 21.034 and 21.036, respectively, in Lenaerts and Van Nuffel (Cambien and Bray, eds), *European Union Law* (Sweet & Maxwell, 2011). See further the discussion in the same book of the Czech Republic, Slovakia, Hungary, and Malta (paras 21.047 to 21.050). See also the judgment of the Danish Supreme Court (*Højesteret*) of 6 December 2016 in Case No. 15/2014 *Dansk Industri (DI) acting for Ajos A/S vs. The estate left by A*, in response to C-441/14, *Dansk Industri*, 2016; see further Madsen, Palmer Olsen and Šadl, 'Legal Disintegration? The Ruling of the Danish Supreme Court in AJOS', VerfBlog, 2017/1/30, https://verfassungsblog.de/legal-disintegration-the-ruling-of-the-danish-supreme-court-in-ajos/.

[102] For a more extensive survey of the primacy of Union law in the national legal systems, see Łazowski (ed.), *The Application of EU law in the New Member States—Brave New World* (Cambridge University Press, 2010); Kellermann et al. (eds), *The Impact of EU Accession on the Legal Orders of New EU Member States and (Pre) Candidate Countries: Hopes and Fears* (TMC Asser Press, 2006); Henrichs, 'Gemeinschaftsrecht und nationale Verfassungen. Organisations- und verfahrensrechtliche Aspekte einer Konfliktlage' (1990) Eu GRZ 413–23; Bonichot et al., 'L'application du droit communautaire dans les différents Etats membres de la Communauté économique européenne' (1990) RFDA 955–86; Pescatore, 'L'application judiciaire des traités internationaux dans la Communauté européenne et dans ses Etats membres', *Etudes de droit des Communautés européennes. Mélanges offerts à P. H. Teitgen* (Pedone, 1984), 355–406.

[103] See the discussion below of the judgment of 5 May 2020 of the German Constitutional Court (para. 23.029). In addition to the commentators cited above, see Darmon, 'Juridictions constitutionnelles et droit communautaire' (1988) RTDE 217–51; Schermers, 'The Scales in Balance: National Constitutional Courts v. Court of Justice' (1990) CMLRev 97–105.

Both in Germany (Article 23(1)) and France (Article 88) a more specific provision was inserted in the Constitutions before the adoption of the EU Treaty, laying down the conditions under which those States have become Member States of the European Union. Most non-founding Member States have inserted similar provisions in their constitutions.[104] While those provisions do not mention the primacy of Union law, they may nonetheless enable national courts to found the primacy of Union law not only on the specificity of Union law itself, but also on a provision of national constitutional law. Consequently, the French *Conseil constitutionnel* derives the primacy of Union law from Article 88 of the French Constitution.[105] The Belgian Supreme Administrative Court (*Raad van State/ Conseil d'Etat*) in its *Goosse* and *Orfinger* decisions went even further and has held to this effect that Article 34 of the Belgian Constitution does not only afford the constitutional basis for the transfer of powers to the European Union but also for the jurisdiction of the Court of Justice to ensure the uniform interpretation of Union law, even though this limits the legal effects of national constitutional provisions.[106]

From a Union perspective it is irrelevant on what basis a Member State arrives at recognizing the primacy of Union law, as long as Union law is effectively granted primacy over national law. Problematic in this respect was the thesis of the Italian Constitutional Court derived from the fact that Article 11 of the Italian Constitution allows for the transfer of competences to international organizations. According to the Italian Constitutional Court this implied that every national law that is contrary to Union law is automatically also in conflict with the Italian Constitution, with the result that lower courts could not give primacy to Union law over the contrary national law without first referring a question as to the constitutionality of the law to the Italian Constitutional Court (see para. 23-015, *supra*). In 1984 the Italian Constitutional Court abandoned that thesis.[107]

23.028 **Relationship between Union law and the national constitution.** In Member States that provide for a system of constitutional review the question soon arose to what extent the primacy of Union law could be reconciled with the necessity to ensure that all norms that are applied within a Member State are in accordance with the national constitution. In some Member States the constitutional court has taken the position that primacy of Union law is only possible to the extent that Union law respects the limits set by the national constitution to the competences of the Union.[108] Therefore, some scholars have tried to explain the relationship between Union law and national law from a non-hierarchical perspective ('constitutional pluralism').[109] Nonetheless, the reservations expressed by certain constitutional

---

[104] For an overview, see Lenaerts and Van Nuffel (Cambien and Bray, eds.), *European Union Law* (Sweet & Maxwell, 2011), para. 21.034 *et seq*.
[105] Décision No. 2004-505 DC of 19 November 2004.
[106] *Raad van State/Conseil d'Etat*, 5 November 1996, No. 62.621 (*Goosse*) and No. 69.922 (*Orfinger*), discussed in 'Annex VI—Application of Community law by national courts' to the Fourteenth Annual Report on monitoring the application of Community law (1996), OJ 1997 C332/202.
[107] Judgment No. 170/84 of 8 June 1984; for an English translation, see (1994) CMLR 756; see Barav, 'Cour constitutionelle italienne et droit communautaire: le fantôme de *Simmenthal*' (1985) RTDE 313–41. More recently, see Gaja, 'New Developments in a Continuing Story: The Relationship Between EEC Law and Italian Law' (1990) CMLRev 83–95.
[108] The leading example is Germany, discussed hereafter in para. 23.029. See also, e.g., Belgium, discussed, *infra*, at para. 23.030.
[109] See Walker, 'The Idea of Constitutional Pluralism' (2002) MLR 317–59; Poiares Maduro, 'Contrapunctual law: Europe's constitutional pluralism in action', in Walker (ed.) *Sovereignty in Transition* (OUP, 2003), 501–37; Kumm, 'The Jurisprudence of Constitutional Conflict: Constitutional Supremacy in Europe before and after the Constitutional Treaty' (2005) ELJ 262–307; Avbelj and Komárek, 'Four Visions of Constitutional Pluralism' (2008)

courts do not pose a problem from a Union law perspective either, provided that in practice the effective and uniform application of Union law within the Member States concerned is not impeded.[110]

German Constitutional Court. In this respect the *Solange* case law of the *Bundesverfassungsgericht* (German Constitutional Court) has been particularly influential. A (then) Community measure was challenged in a German court on the ground that it violated fundamental rights enshrined in the German Basic Law (*Grundgesetz*). Although the Court of Justice answered a question referred for a preliminary ruling by the court concerned by saying that the measure did not infringe any fundamental right,[111] the national court deemed it necessary to bring the matter before the *Bundesverfassungsgericht* too. That court held that the transfer of sovereignty to the Community made under Article 24 of the Basic Law could not result in Community legislation detracting from the essential structure of the Basic Law. Despite the judgment of the Court of Justice and the primacy of Community law, the *Bundesverfassungsgericht* considered that it was necessary to conduct a second review of the Community legislation in the light of the fundamental rights guaranteed by the Basic Law *so long as* the Community legal order lacked a democratically elected parliament with legislative powers and powers of scrutiny and a codified catalogue of fundamental rights.[112] In order to guarantee the uniform application of Community law, the Court of Justice confirmed, for its part, that observance of fundamental rights formed part of the requirements that Community acts had to satisfy in order to be valid and therefore had to be enforced within the context of Community law itself.[113] In 1986, after considering the case law of the Court of Justice, the *Bundesverfassungsgericht*, referring to the importance that the Community institutions attached to the protection of fundamental rights and democratic decision-making, declared that an additional review of Community legislation in the light of the fundamental rights guaranteed by the Basic Law was no longer necessary *so long as* the case law of the Court of Justice continued to afford the level of protection found.[114]

23.029

The *Solange* case law of the *Bundesverfassungsgericht* has operated as a most valuable impetus for the consolidation of democracy and respect for fundamental rights at the level of the Union, now reflected in Article 2 TEU as well as in Title II of the TEU and the Charter

---

EuConst 524–7; Baquero Cruz, 'The Legacy of the Maastricht-Urteil and the Pluralist Movement' (2008) ELJ 389–422; Barents, 'The Precedence of EU Law from the Perspective of Constitutional Pluralism' (2009) EuConst 421–46; Avbelj and Komárek (eds), *Constitutional Pluralism in the European Union and Beyond* (Hart Publishing, 2012).

[110] See, in this respect, Baquero Cruz, *What's Left of the Law of Integration* (OUP, 2018), Chapter 3 ('Against Constitutional Pluralism').

[111] 11/70, *Internationale Handelsgesellschaft*, 1970, paras 3–20.

[112] The judgment in question is the so-called (first) *Solange* judgment of 29 May 1974, BVerfGE 37, 271; for an English translation, see (1974) 2 CMLR 540; see Ipsen, 'BVerfG versus EuGH re "Grundrechte"' (1975) EuR 1–19.

[113] 44/79 *Hauer*, 1979, paras 13–16 (in which reference is made to the judgments in *Internationale Handelsgesellschaft* and *Nold* and to the fact that the institutions recognized 'that conception' in the Joint Declaration of 5 April 1977; para. 25.003, *infra*).

[114] Judgment of 22 October 1986 (*Solange II*) (1986) BVerfGE 73, 339; for an English translation, see (1987) 3 CMLR 225; see the commentary by Frowein (1988) CMLRev 201–6. The *Bundesverfassungsgericht* referred to the Joint Declaration of 5 April 1977 and the Declaration of the European Council of 7 and 8 April 1978 on democracy (1978) 3 EC Bull. 5. For the ensuing debate, see, among others, Ehlermann, 'Zur Diskussion um einen "Solange III"-Beschluss: Rechtspolitische Perspektiven aus der Sicht des Gemeinschaftsrechts' (1991) EuR 27–38; Everling, 'Brauchen wir "Solange III"?' (1990) EuR 195–227; Tomuschat, 'Aller guten Dinge sind III?' (1990) EuR. 340–61.

of Fundamental Rights of the European Union. In matters fully determined by Union law, the *Bundesverfassungsgericht* now directly enforces the Charter of Fundamental Rights of the European Union rather than the Basic Law—this as a matter of primacy of Union law— when it reviews the conformity with fundamental rights of the relevant German implementation acts.[115]

On the contrary, the *Bundesverfassungsgericht* stated its 'conditional' acceptance of the primacy of Union law on 12 October 1993 when it ruled on the constitutionality of the law ratifying the EU Treaty.[116] It set out that German constitutional law accepted acts of the 'European institutions and bodies' only in so far as they remained within the bounds of the Treaty provisions approved by the ratification law and made it plain that it would itself review whether such acts remained within the bounds of the Union's principles of conferred powers, subsidiarity, and proportionality.[117] In a judgment of 30 June 2009, the *Bundesverfassungsgericht* held the German federal law ratifying the Lisbon Treaty compatible with the Basic Law, while requiring certain amendments to be made to the laws governing the role of the *Bundesrat* and *Bundestag* (chambers of the federal parliament) in the framework of the Union's decision-making process.[118] In this judgment, the *Bundesverfassungsgericht* further clarified that it will review whether Union law runs the risk of depriving the Basic Law's constitutional identity from its core content ('identity review').[119] However, in *Honeywell* the *Bundesverfassungsgericht* later stressed the exceptional nature of this, and held that while it still reserves the right to review Union acts with regard to the Basic Law, the Union could only be deemed to have acted *ultra vires* if the Court of

---

[115] German Constitutional Court, 6 November 2019, 1 BVR 16/13 ('Recht auf Vergessen I'), and, of the same date, 1 BVR 276/17 (Recht auf Vergessen II'). These judgments incorporate the *Åkerberg Fransson* and *Melloni* case law of the Court of Justice (C-617/10, *Åkerberg Fransson*, 2013; C-399/11, *Melloni*, 2013—see, *infra* para. 25.012) and constitute a remarkable completion of the *Solange* jurisprudence wholly consistent with Union law. See also Wendel, 'The two-Faced Guardian—or How One Half of the German Federal Constitutional Court Became a European Fundamental Rights Court' (2020) CMLRev 1383–426; Thym, 'Friendly Takeover, or: the Power of the "First Word"'. The German Constitutional Court Embraces the Charter of Fundamental Rights as a Standard of Domestic Judicial Review' (2020) EuConst 187–212.

[116] The '*Maastricht-Urteil*'; for the text, see (1993) Eu GRZ 429; (1993) EuR 294; (1974) 1 CMLR 57. For the conditional nature of that acceptance, see Zuleeg, 'The European Constitution under Constitutional Constraints: The German Scenario' (1997) ELRev 19–34.

[117] Points C.I.3. and C.II.2., under b, ibid., 89 and 94, respectively. Among the many commentaries on that judgment, see; Hahn, 'La Cour constitutionnelle fédérale d'Allemagne et le Traité de Maastricht' (1994) RGDIP 107–26; Herdegen, 'Maastricht and the German Constitutional Court: Constitutional Restraints for an "Ever Closer Union"' (1994) CMLRev 235–49; Ipsen, 'Zehn Glossen zum Maastricht Urteil' (1994) EuR 1–21; Kokott, 'Deutschland im Rahmen der Europäischen Union—zum Vertrag von Maastricht' (1994) AöR 207–37; Meessen, 'Maastricht nach Karlsruhe' (1994) NJW 549–54; Tomuschat, 'Die Europäische Union unter der Aufsicht des Bundesverfassungsgerichts' (1993) Eu GRZ 489–96. For the role which the Court of Justice could play in this connection by giving preliminary rulings at the request of the German Constitutional Court, see Grimm, 'The European Court of Justice and National Courts: The German Constitutional Perspective after the Maastricht Decision' (1997) Col JEL 229–42.

[118] Judgment of 30 June 2009, 2 BvE 2/08, available in English at: http://www.bundesverfassungsgericht.de/entscheidungen/es20090630_2bve000208en.html. See Ziller, 'The German Constitutional Court's Friendliness towards European Law: On the Judgment of *Bundesverfassungsgericht* over the Ratification of the Treaty of Lisbon' (2010) E Pub L 53–73; Thym, 'In the Name of Sovereign Statehood: A Critical Introduction to the Lisbon Judgment of the German Constitutional Court' (2009) CMLRev 1795–822; Schorkopf, 'The European Union as an Association of Sovereign States: Karlsruhe's Ruling on the Treaty of Lisbon' (2009) GLJ 1219–40; Niedobitek, 'The Lisbon Case of 30 June 2009—A Comment from the European Law Perspective' (2009) GLJ 1267–75. See also Editorial Comments (2009) CMLRev 1023–33; Doukas, 'The Verdict of the German Federal Constitutional Court on the Lisbon Treaty: Not Guilty, But Don't Do It Again!' (2009) ELRev 866–88; Halberstam and Möllers, 'The German Constitutional Court says "Ja zu Deutschland!"' (2009) GLJ 1241–58.

[119] Judgment of 30 June 2009, 2 BvE 2/08 paras 238–41.

Justice—after being properly given the opportunity to address the matter, if need be after a preliminary ruling request from the *Bundesverfassungsgericht* itself—has not rectified what the *Bundesverfassungsgericht* sees as a sufficiently qualified breach of the Union's constitutional framework, thereby committing a 'manifest error' (in the eyes of the *Bundesverfassungsgericht*).[120] The judgment of the Court in *Mangold*[121] as to the horizontal direct effect of general principles of Union law (para 25-020, *infra*) was deemed not to fall foul of that standard.

This form of benevolent vigilance was put under strain in the wake of the crisis of the euro area. When the European Central Bank announced its—never-implemented— plan for Outright Monetary Transactions (OMT),[122] this plan, and the role the *Bundesbank* would have to play in putting it into operation as part of the ESCB, were challenged before the *Bundesverfassungsgericht*. In line with the approach announced in *Honeywell*, the *Bundesverfassungsgericht* submitted a request for a preliminary ruling on the validity of the scheme to the Court of Justice.[123] Following the Court's reply in *Gauweiler*,[124] the *Bundesverfassungsgericht*, while expressing some concern about the impact of the plan, upheld the participation of Germany in the OMT.[125] When a second set of monetary interventions[126] was challenged before the *Bundesverfassungsgericht*, the latter made a new reference for a preliminary ruling[127] setting out its concerns, which the Court of Justice rejected in its judgment in *Weiss*.[128] Consequently, the *Bundesverfassungsgericht* dismissed the Court's assessment of the proportionality of the contested ECB acts as wholly inadequate[129] and thus constituting a 'manifest error' in the sense of *Honeywell*.[130] Yet, the *Bundesverfassungsgericht* stopped short

---

[120] Judgment of 6 July 2010, 2 BvR 2661/06.
[121] C-144/04, *Mangold*, 2005; see also C-427/06, *Bartsch*, 2008 and C-555/07, *Kücükdeveci*, 2010.
[122] Decisions of the Governing Council of the European Central Bank (ECB) of 6 September 2012 on a number of technical features regarding the Eurosystem's outright monetary transactions in secondary sovereign bond markets ('the OMT decisions').
[123] Judgment of 14 January 2014, 2 BvR 2728/13, 2 BvR 2729/13, 2 BvR 2730/13, 2 BvR 2731/13, 2 BvE 13/13.
[124] C-62/14, *Gauweiler*, 2015.
[125] Judgment of 21 June 2016, 2 BvR 2728/13, 2 BvE 13/13, 2 BvR 2731/13, 2 BvR 2730/13, 2 BvR 2729/13, with case note by Classen (2016) EuR 529–43; see further Sauer, 'Der novellierte Kontrollzugriff des Bundesverfassungsgerichts auf das Unionsrecht' (2017) EuR 186–205. See also Tischendorf, 'Europa unter deutscher Supervision. Die Verantwortung der Verfassungsorgane des Bundes für die Geld- und Außenhandelspolitik der Europäischen Union' (2018) EuR 695–723.
[126] Decision (EU) 2015/774 of the European Central Bank of 4 March 2015 on a secondary markets public sector asset purchase programme, OJ 2015 L121/20, since replaced by Decision (EU) 2020/188 of the European Central Bank of 3 February 2020 on a secondary markets public sector asset purchase programme (OJ 2020 L39/12).
[127] Judgment of 18 July 2017, 2 BvR 859/15; 2 BvR 1651/15; 2 BvR 2006/15; 2 BvR 980/16.
[128] C-493/17, *Weiss*, 2018.
[129] Judgment of 5 May 2020, 2 BvR 859/15. The *Bundesverfassungsgericht* simply applied the three-step German understanding of proportionality ('geeignet, erforderlich, angemessen'), whereas the Court of Justice did not go into this third step, as it is not provided for in Article 5(4) TEU, defining the principle of proportionality applicable to acts of Union institutions—also the German version of Article 5(4) TEU only speaks of 'erforderlich', see C-493/17, *Weiss*, 2018, paras 71–100. See also X, 'Not Mastering the Treaties: The German Federal Constitutional Court's PSPP judgment' (2020) CMLRev 969–74; Dermine, 'The Ruling of the Bundesverfassungsgericht in PSPP—An Inquiry into its Repercussions on the Economic and Monetary Union: Bundesverfassungsgericht 5 May 2020, 2 BvR 859/15 and others, PSPP' (2020) EuConst 525–51; Wegener, 'Karlsruher Unheil—Das Urteil des Bundesverfassungsgerichts vom 5. Mai 2020 (2 BvR 859/15) in Sachen Staatsanleihekäufe der Europäischen Zentralbank' (2020) EuR 347–63.
[130] The judgment not only applies the wrong proportionality test, derived from German law but contrary to the wording of Article 5(4) TEU (paras 5.034 *et seq. supra*), it also raises issues concerning the uniform application of Union law, and hence the equality of Member States and their citizens before Union law (Article 4(2) TEU; Article 20 of the Charter of Fundamental Rights of the European Union).

of then declaring these ECB acts to be *ultra vires*, by giving the ECB the opportunity to better explain the proportionality of the measures. The ECB did respond to this, and the *Bundestag* subsequently indicated that these additional arguments sufficed to meet the conditions set by the *Bundesverfassungsgericht*,[131] thus defusing the conflict. Thereafter, the *Bundesverfassungsgericht* held that there were no grounds to consider the response given to its earlier judgment manifestly inadequate and dismissed the applications brought to have that judgment executed.[132]

23.030 **Belgian Constitutional Court.** A good illustration of the influence which the German *Solange* case law still has for other Member States[133] is offered by the case law of the Belgian Constitutional Court (*Grondwettelijk Hof/ Cour constitutionnelle*). As far as the acceptance of primacy of Union law over provisions of constitutional law is concerned, the state of Belgian law has indeed become less clear since the Constitutional Court held that it has jurisdiction to assess the constitutionality of laws ratifying a treaty and of treaties themselves.[134] However, the Constitutional Court did not hold that Union law ranks lower than the Constitution. Moreover, the review of the constitutionality of laws by way of preliminary rulings from the Constitutional Court has been expressly excluded for laws 'ratifying a constituent treaty with respect to the European Union or the European Convention on Human Rights'. The Constitutional Court thus found that it lacked jurisdiction to review whether the national law approving the European Single Act violated the principle of non-discrimination by not providing for compensation for the customs agents that lost activities due to the establishment of the internal market.[135] Nevertheless, according to the Constitutional Court in a more recent judgment, the Belgian Constitution does not allow for the discriminatory abridgement of the identity as enshrined in the political and the constitutional basic structure of the State or the core values of the protection offered by the Constitution to legal subjects.[136]

---

[131] See, first, the Account of the monetary policy meeting of the Governing Council of the European Central Bank held in Frankfurt am Main on Wednesday and Thursday, 3–4 June 2020, https://www.ecb.europa.eu/press/accounts/2020/html/ecb.mg200625~fd97330d5f.en.html, and, second, the Antrag der Fraktionen CDU/CSU, SPD, FDP und BÜNDNIS 90/DIE GRÜNEN (19/20621), as adopted on 2 July 2020.

[132] Decision of 29 April 2021, 2 BvR 1651/15, paras 95–111.

[133] For an overview of the approach in other Member States, see Lenaerts and Van Nuffel (Cambien and Bray, eds), *European Union Law* (3rd edn, Sweet & Maxwell, 2011), para. 21.034 *et seq*.

[134] Judgment of 16 October 1991, No. 26/91, *B.S./M.B.*, 23 November 1991, *A.A.*, 1991, 271; see also judgments of 3 February 1994, No. 12/94, *B.S./M.B*, 11 March 1994, *A.A.*, 1994, 211; and of 26 April 1994, No. 33/94, *B.S./M.B.*, 22 June 1994, *A.A.*, 1994, 419. See the critical commentary by Louis, 'La primauté, une valeur relative?' (1995) CDE 23–8; Popelier, 'Ongrondwettige verdragen: de rechtspraak van het Arbitragehof in een monistisch tijdsperspectief' (1994–1995) RW 1076–80; for an approving commentary, see Brouwers and Simonart, 'Le conflit entre la Constitution et le droit international conventionnel dans la jurisprudence de la Cour d'arbitrage' (1995) CDE 7–22; Melchior and Vandernoot, 'Contrôle de constitutionnalité et droit communautaire dérivé' (1998) RBDC 3–45.

[135] Judgment of 14 January 2004, No. 3/2004, *MB* 9 March 2004.

[136] Judgment of 28 April 2016, No. 62/2016, para. B.8.7. See also the contributions in (2017) TBP 293–372 (special edition *Stabiliteitsverdragarrest Grondwettelijk Hof*); Rosoux, 'L'ambivalence ou la double vocation de l'identité nationale—Réflexions au départ de l'arrêt n° 62/2016 de la Cour constitutionnelle belge' (2019) CDE 91–148; El Berhoumi et al., 'Het Stabiliteitsverdrag-arrest van het Grondwettelijk Hof: een arrest zonder belang?' (2017) CDPK 398–429.

C. The direct effect of Union law

Van Gend & Loos. Ever since the 1963 judgment in *Van Gend & Loos*, it is clear that individuals may derive rights directly from Union (then Community) law[137]. In that judgment, the Court of Justice gave a preliminary ruling on a question raised by the Netherlands *Tariefcommissie* as to whether individuals might derive rights from Article 12 EEC which the courts had to protect. The Court of Justice held that '[t]o ascertain whether the provisions of an international treaty extend so far in their effects it is necessary to consider the spirit, the general scheme and the wording of those provisions'.[138] The Court inferred from the special nature of the Community legal order that Community law is 'intended to confer upon [individuals] rights which become part of their legal heritage' (see para. 1-026, *supra*). The Court stated that '[t]hese rights arise not only where they are expressly granted by the Treaty, but also by reason of obligations which the Treaty imposes in a clearly defined way upon individuals as well as upon the Member States and upon the institutions of the Community'. After inquiring into the substance and wording of Article 12 EEC, the Court held that the prohibition laid down in that article on Member States increasing import duties or charges having equivalent effect which they already applied in their trade with each other had direct effect.[139]

23.031

Conditions for direct effect. Not all of the provisions of Union law have direct effect.[140] The decisive test for determining whether or not a given provision has direct effect is its content. The Court of Justice has consistently held that a provision produces direct effect if it is 'clear and unconditional and not contingent on any discretionary implementing measure'.[141] Although the Court has not always formulated that test in the same way, it refers to a provision which is sufficiently precise ('clear') and requires no further implementation (involving a margin of discretion) by Union or national authorities in order to achieve the effect sought in an effective manner ('unconditional').[142] A provision that is only given concrete scope through the enactment of measures by the institutions or the Member States does not confer any rights on individuals which national courts may enforce.[143] Such is the case, for instance, for a provision which puts an authority under a duty to act, except for those aspects for which the authority has no discretion. A prohibition to act—like the standstill provision of Article 12 EEC—is a plain example of a provision which affords the Member States no discretion, and hence has direct effect.

23.032

A provision has direct effect where the court is able, without the operation of other implementing measures, to reach an interpretation which may be applied to the case at issue, as a result of which individuals may enforce the rights derived from that provision.[144] The judgment in *Van Gend & Loos* already made clear that a provision does not lack sufficient clarity simply on the ground that the national court deemed it necessary to make a

---

[137] 26/62, *Van Gend & Loos*, 1963, 11–13.
[138] Ibid., 12.
[139] Ibid., 12–13.
[140] C-573/17, *Popławski*, 2019, para. 59.
[141] 44/84, *Hurd*, 1986, para. 47.
[142] See C-128/92, *Banks*, 1994, Opinion AG Van Gerven, point 27.
[143] 28/67, *Molkerei-Zentrale Westfalen*, 1968, 153; 13/68, *Salgoil*, 1968, 461.
[144] See, e.g., 12/81, *Garland*, 1982, paras 14–15.

reference to the Court of Justice on the interpretation of the provision in question. In *Van Gend & Loos*, the Court of Justice indicated that 'an illegal increase [of a customs duty] may arise from a rearrangement of the tariff resulting in the classification of the product under a more highly taxed heading and from an actual increase in the rate of customs duty'. That interpretation allowed the Netherlands court to apply the prohibition set out in Article 12 EEC to the benefit of an undertaking.[145] Likewise, Article 45 TFEU (free movement of workers) is not prevented from having direct effect because para. 3 of that article contains a reservation with regard to limitations justified on grounds of public policy, public security, or public health. This is because 'the application of those limitations is ... subject to judicial control'.[146]

23.033 **Direct effect of primary law.** The Court of Justice has repeatedly had to rule on whether provisions of the Treaties have direct effect.[147] Where a Treaty provision is recognized as having direct effect, an individual may rely upon it against Union and national authorities (vertically) and, in some cases, against other individuals (horizontally).[148] The application of the Treaties in the Member States does not depend on whether they have been transposed into the national legal system. When a Treaty provision having horizontal direct effect is invoked against an individual, the fact that the Member States have not enacted any provisions to implement this provision is therefore not such as to exclude its application. Treaty provisions where the horizontal effect has been recognized include Articles 101 and 102 TFEU (see paras 9.015 and 9.017); Article 157 TFEU (see para. 9-048, *supra*); and, vis-à-vis organizations not governed by public law where they lay down collective rules in the exercise of their legal autonomy, the provisions on the free movement of persons, and the freedom to provide services (see paras 7.044 and 7.081; see also para. 6.018, *supra* as regards non-economically active citizens). If a provision has direct effect, such is the case from the time when it entered into force or, as the case may be, from the end of the transitional period. In exceptional cases, however, the Court of Justice may place limitations on the temporal effect of a judgment recognizing the direct effect of a provision (see para. 28.006, *supra*).

The same applies to the Charter of Fundamental Rights of the European Union. The Court has indeed found that several rights enshrined in the Charter have horizontal direct effect, with the result that national courts must apply it between private parties notwithstanding the existence of conflicting provisions of national law.[149] However, a national court is not

---

[145] 26/62, *Van Gend & Loos*, 1963, 14–15.
[146] 41/74, *Van Duyn*, 1974, para. 7. See, with regard to Article 56 EC [*now Article 63 TFEU*] (free movement of capital), C-163/94, C-165/94, and C-250/94, *Sanz de Lera and Others*, 1995, para. 43.
[147] e.g., it has long been established that the following articles of the TFEU have direct effect: Article 18 TFEU; Article 28 TFEU; Article 30 TFEU; Articles 34, 35, and 36 TFEU; Article 37(1) and (2) TFEU; Articles 45 to 62 TFEU in general, and particularly Articles 45, 49, 56, and 57 TFEU; Article 101(1) TFEU; Article 102 TFEU; Article 106(1) and (2) TFEU; Article 108(3), last sentence, TFEU; Article 110, first and second paras TFEU; and Article 157 TFEU. See already the list in Schermers and Waelbroeck, *Judicial Protection in the European Union* (Kluwer, 2001), § 359, 183–5 (with a list of provisions to which the Court of Justice denied direct effect at 185).
[148] See, e.g., 36/74, *Walrave*, 1974, paras 17–25 (Articles 12, 39, and 49 EC [*now Articles 18, 45, and 56 TFEU*]); 43/75, *Defrenne*, 1976, para. 39 (Article 119 EC [*now Article 157 TFEU*]); C-281/98, *Angonese*, 2000, paras 30–6 (Article 48 EC [*now Article 45 TFEU*]); C-555/07, *Kücükdeveci*, 2010, paras 50–6 (granting horizontal effect to the general principle of Union law relating to non-discrimination on grounds of age—Article 21 of the Charter of Fundamental Rights of the European Union) and C-684/16, *Max-Planck-Gesellschaft zur Förderung der Wissenschaften*, 2018 (granting horizontal direct effect to the right to paid annual leave—Article 31(2) of the Charter).
[149] See, e.g., C-176/12, *AMS*, 2014, para. 47; C-414/16, *Egenberger*, 2018, para. 76; C-193/17, *Cresco Investigation*, 2019, paras 76–89 (Article 21 of the Charter); C-684/16, *Max-Planck-Gesellschaft zur Förderung der Wissenschaften*, 2018, para. 79 (Article 31(2) of the Charter); see, *infra*, para. 25.010.

required, solely on the basis of Union law, to refrain from applying a provision of national law which is incompatible with a provision of the Charter of Fundamental Rights of the European Union which, like Article 27, does not have direct effect.[150]

Direct effect of secondary law. Alongside provisions of the Treaties, provisions contained in acts of Union institutions may be invoked by individuals. In principle, whether such provisions have direct effect depends on the same substantive criteria that apply to Treaty provisions.[151] However, depending on the type of act, additional factors may have to be taken into account.[152] As far as international agreements concluded by the Union are concerned, it must always be ascertained whether the possible direct effect of their provisions is consistent with the spirit, the general scheme, and the terms of the agreement.[153] Provisions of autonomous acts of the institutions have direct effect, in principle, if the substantive criteria are fulfilled, but their vertical or horizontal effect further depends on the type of act in which they are laid down. Under Article 288 TFEU, regulations are binding and 'directly applicable' without any need for transposition, on all within the national legal system who are substantively affected thereby. Where a provision of a regulation has direct effect, an individual may rely upon it against other individuals too.[154] There is no such horizontal direct effect in the case of provisions of directives, which, if they satisfy the requirements for direct effect, can embody only obligations for State bodies.[155]

23.034

Direct applicability. In indicating that a provision has 'direct effect', the Court of Justice sometimes uses the expression 'direct applicability'.[156] Some commentators consider that these expressions are not strictly defined and use both of them in referring to the possibility for an individual to rely upon a provision.[157] For a clearer understanding of the effect of Union law, it is nevertheless more illuminating to make a distinction between 'direct applicability' (whether a provision requires implementation *as a legal instrument*) and 'direct effect' (whether the *substance* of a provision may be relied upon in order to make a claim).[158] Where a provision is 'directly applicable', and hence does not require implementation in the national legal system—which is the case for Treaty provisions and regulations—it follows, as explained above, that, where that provision fulfils the substantive conditions for 'direct effect', it cannot only be relied upon against Union and national authorities but, in some cases, also against other individuals.

23.035

---

[150] C-176/12, *Association de médiation sociale*, 2014, paras 44–8; C-573/17, *Popławski*, 2019, para. 63.
[151] See 9/70 *Grad*, 1970, paras 5–6; see also C-486/08, *Zentralberiebsrat der Landeskrankenhäuser Tirols*, 2010, para 21–5 (same conditions apply to agreements concluded between the social partners which are implemented by a directive of the Council). For a survey of the direct effect of various provisions of Union law, see Prinssen and Schrauwen (eds), *Direct Effect. Rethinking a Classic of EC Legal Doctrine* (Europa Law, 2002); Pescatore, 'The Doctrine of "Direct Effect": An Infant Disease of Community Law' (1983) ELRev 155–77.
[152] For an overview discussing the Charter, directives, and framework decisions, see C-573/17, *Popławski*, 2019, paras 63–71.
[153] Para. 26.003, *infra*.
[154] Para. 27.016, *infra*.
[155] Para. 27.022 *et seq.*, *infra*. For decisions, see para. 27.041, *infra*.
[156] C-213/03, *Pêcheurs de l'Étang de Berre*, 2004, para. 39.
[157] See, for instance, Lauwaars and Timmermans, *Europees recht in kort bestek* (Kluwer, 2003), 22–4 and 107–9; Barents and Brinkhorst, *Grondlijnen van Europees recht* (Kluwer, 2003), 52; see also Prechal, 'Does Direct Effect Still Matter?' (2000) CMLRev 1047–69.
[158] See already Winter, 'Direct Applicability and Direct Effect: Two Distinct and Different Concepts in Community Law' (1972) CMLRev 425–38.

24
The Treaties: Primary Union Law

I. Status of Primary Union Law

24.001 **Constitutional law.** Primary Union law consists of those provisions which were adopted directly by the Member States in their capacity as 'constituent authority', meaning, in the first place, the Union Treaties and the Treaties amending or supplementing them, including the Accession Treaties and the annexed Acts of Accession. Together with fundamental rights and the general principles of Union law, these Treaty provisions constitute the 'constitutional' provisions of Union law.[1] This is because they serve as the legal basis for action on the part of the Union and unquestionably take precedence over the law of the Member States.[2] Where Treaty provisions satisfy the test formulated by the Court of Justice for direct effect, they may as such confer rights on individuals (see para. 23.031, *supra*). The Court has also considered fundamental rights and general principles of Union law to be part of the Union's primary law.[3] However, the specific position of fundamental rights and general principles of Union law will be discussed in Chapter 25.

24.002 **Adoption and amendment.** Primary Union law comes into being by mutual agreement between the Member States and may be amended only in accordance with the proper procedure. In the case of the Treaties, that procedure is the amendment procedure prescribed by Article 48 TEU and some simplified procedures, which in any event are based on approval by the Member States in accordance with their respective constitutional requirements.[4] Unless otherwise provided, such a Treaty will apply to the future effects of situations arising prior to the date on which it entered into effect (see para. 11.003, *supra*). At the same time, the provisions of the Acts of Accession and the adjustments of secondary legislation annexed to those Acts themselves and ensuing therefrom constitute provisions of primary law, which, unless otherwise provided, may be amended or repealed only by recourse to the procedures prescribed for amending the original Treaties.[5] In the absence of express authority, provisions of secondary legislation cannot detract from provisions of primary law,

---

[1] See 294/83 *Les Verts v European Parliament*, 1986, para. 23 ('the basic constitutional charter, the Treaty'); C-402/05 P and C-415/05 P, *Kadi and Al Barakaat International Foundation*, 2008, para. 285 ('the constitutional principles of the EC Treaty, which include the principle that all Community acts must respect fundamental rights'); C-621/18, *Wightman*, 2018, para. 44 ('the founding Treaties, which constitute the basic constitutional charter of the European Union').

[2] For the 'constitutional' nature of primary Union law, see Heintzen, 'Hierarchisierungsprozesse innerhalb des Primärrechts der Europäischen Gemeinschaft' (1984) EuR 35, 40, and the commentators cited in para. 1.028, *supra*. For the precedence of primary law over secondary Union law, see, e.g., C-445/00 R, *Austria v Council* (order of the President), 2001, paras 82–93; T-144/99, *Institute of Professional Representatives before the European Patent Office v Commission*, 2001, paras 50–4; T-243/07 *Poland v Commission*, T-247/07 *Slovak Republic v Commission*, T-248/07 *Czech Republic v Commission*, and T-262/07 *Lithuania v Commission*, 2012 (annulment of decisions held incompatible with Act of Accession).

[3] C-402/05 P and C-415/05, P *Kadi and Al Barakaat International Foundation*, 2008, para. 308.

[4] For these procedures, see paras 3.001–3.007, *supra*.

[5] See, e.g., Article 7 of the 2003 and 1994 Acts of Accession, Article 6 of the 1985 Act of Accession, and 31-35/86, *LAISA and Others v Council*, 1988, para. 12.

such as a protocol annexed to an Act of Accession.[6] In exceptional cases only, a rule of primary law provides that it may be amended by the Union institutions acting on their own.[7]

Judicial review. The Court of Justice has no jurisdiction to rule on the validity of primary Union law. Since the Treaties and the amendments thereto do not constitute acts of the institutions within the meaning of Article 13 TEU and Article 263 TFEU, the Court of Justice has no jurisdiction to consider their legality in the framework of an action for annulment.[8] It may merely give preliminary rulings on the interpretation of primary Union law (see Article 267(a) TFEU). This means that provisions constituting an integral part of the Acts of Accession are also not subject to judicial review by the Court of Justice[9]. The Court of Justice is competent, however, to review the validity of decisions of the European Council amending the Treaties pursuant to the simplified Treaty revision procedures laid down in Article 48(6) TEU. While such a decision amends the Treaties, the Court may nevertheless review whether the procedural and substantive requirements laid down in Article 48(6) TEU have been observed.[10]

24.003

II. Survey of the Treaties as Primary Union Law

Union Treaties. Primary Union law comprises, first and foremost, the Union Treaties (the TEU, TFEU; before 23 July 2002 also the ECSC Treaty) and the EAEC Treaty. In principle the broad field of competence of the TEU and TFEU also embraces the atomic energy sector. However, it follows from Article 106a(3) EAEC, as introduced by Protocol to the Lisbon Treaty, that the provisions of the TEU and of the TFEU 'shall not derogate' from the provisions of the EAEC Treaty.[11] Before the entry into force of the Lisbon Treaty, the same rule was formulated in Article 305 EC (now repealed). As far as the nuclear energy sector is concerned, this means that the TEU and TFEU do not apply whenever the EAEC Treaty contains a derogating provision.[12] Where the EAEC Treaty does not lay down rules on a particular matter for the nuclear energy sector, the matter in question falls within the TEU and the TFEU.[13] Thus, the rules on the free movement of workers set out in the TFEU apply

24.004

---

[6] C-445/00, *Austria v Commission*, 2003, paras 57–64.
[7] For the procedures in question, see para. 3.008, *supra*. For an application after the introduction in 1993 of a common organisation of the market in bananas, which was the subject of a special 'protocol on bananas' annexed to the EEC Treaty, see C-280/93, *Germany v Council*, 1994, paras 113–8.
[8] 31-35/86, *LAISA and Others v Council*, 1988, para. 12; T-584/94, *Roujansky v Council* (order), 1994, para. 15, upheld by C-253/94 P *Roujansky v Council* (order), 1995.
[9] 31-35/86, *LAISA and Others v Council*, 1988, paras 13–8; C-572/15 F. *Hoffmann-La Roche*, 2016, paras 29–33 (no judicial review of provisions consolidating provisions earlier inserted in a Union regulation by an Accession Act).
[10] C-370/12, *Pringle*, 2012, paras 30–7.
[11] Protocol (No. 2), annexed to the Lisbon Treaty, amending the Treaty establishing the European Atomic Energy Community, OJ 2007 C306/199; see C-115/08, *ČEZ*, 2009, para. 85.
[12] See Cusack, 'A Tale of Two Treaties: An Assessment of the Euratom Treaty in Relation to the EC Treaty' (2003) CMLRev 117–42. This was also true of the ECSC Treaty as a result of Article 305 EC, which provided that the EC Treaty should 'not affect' the ECSC Treaty: see, e.g., 27 to 29/58, *Compagnie des Hauts Fourneaux et Fonderies de Givors and Others v High Authority*, 1960, 255; 188 to 190/80, *France, Italy and United Kingdom v Commission*, 1982, paras 30–1; 239/84, *Gerlach*, 1985, paras 10–11; C-18/94, *Hopkins and Others*, 1996, paras 11–24.
[13] See, pursuant to Article 305 EC, 188 to 190/80, *France, Italy and United Kingdom v Commission*, 1982, para. 32 (the application of a directive based on Article 86(3) EC to public undertakings in the atomic energy sector does not derogate from the EAEC Treaty); Opinion 1/94, *Agreement establishing the World Trade Organisation*, 1994, para. 24 (in the absence of any EAEC provision relating to external trade, agreements concluded pursuant to Article 133 EC also extend to EAEC products).

to all employees in the nuclear energy sector who are not in 'skilled employment' within the meaning of Article 96 EAEC Treaty. Likewise, in the absence of any rules in this respect in the EAEC Treaty, the rules on State aid and the requirements as regards environmental protection following from the TFEU and Union secondary law, apply to the nuclear energy sector.[14] In this way, Union law adopted pursuant to the TEU and TFEU operates as the *lex generalis*, supplementing, where necessary, the *lex specialis* (EAEC law).

For the sake of the coherence of Union law, the Court of Justice often looked for assistance, when interpreting Treaty provisions, from a comparison of provisions of the other Treaties which resolved the question at issue more clearly[15] or explicitly.[16] The Court of Justice has interpreted the provisions concerning the institutions in the various Treaties in conjunction with each other, and where necessary, reconciling them.[17] Where an institution lays down rules on its internal functioning, it necessarily acts in the field of all the Treaties.[18]

24.005 **Amending Treaties.** In so far as later Treaties (such as the Single European Act, the EU Treaty, the Treaty of Amsterdam, the Treaty of Nice, and the Treaty of Lisbon) amended and supplemented the Union Treaties, their provisions likewise constitute primary Union law.

24.006 **Protocols.** Primary law also includes the protocols annexed to the Treaties, which form 'an integral part' thereof (Article 51 TEU and Article 207 EAEC).[19] It follows that the statutes of the Court of Justice of the European Union, the European Investment Bank, and the European Central Bank, which are contained in protocols, have the same legal status as the Treaties. A protocol may therefore make changes in the Treaties and other provisions of primary law.[20] Where particular Member States are given a special position diverging from the rules of the Treaties, it is often formulated in a protocol. Important examples are, within the framework of the EMU, Protocol (No. 16) on certain provisions

---

[14] C-594/18 P, *Austria v Commission*, 2020, paras 32 and 41–6.

[15] C-61/03, *Commission v UK*, 2005, paras 30–6, and C-65/04, *Commission v UK*, 2006, para. 19 (the fact that, unlike the EC Treaty, the EAEC Treaty lacks derogatory clauses with respect to defence, shows that the EAEC Treaty was not intended to apply to the military use of nuclear energy). See also 13/60, *Geitling v High Authority*, 1962, 102 (interpretation of Article 65 ECSC by analogy with Article 81 EC); 294/83, *Les Verts v European Parliament*, 1986, para. 24 (argument based on Article 38 ECSC in an interpretation of Article 173 EEC recognizing that an action for annulment could be brought against the European Parliament). In *Continental Can*, the Court refused to take account, in interpreting Article 82 EC, of an *a contrario* argument based on the wording of Article 66 ECSC: 6/72, *Europemballage and Continental Can v Commission*, 1973, para. 22.

[16] C-115/08, *ČEZ*, 2009, paras 87–91 (prohibition by the EC Treaty of discrimination on grounds of nationality also held to be applicable within the ambit of the EAEC Treaty); 9/56, *Meroni v High Authority*, 1957 and 1958, 140–1 (reasoning by analogy from Article 241 EC and Article 156 EAEC in interpreting Article 36 ECSC) (see also 10/56, *Meroni v High Authority*, 1957 and 1958, 162–3, and 15/57, *Compagnie des Hauts Fourneaux de Chasse v High Authority*, 1957 and 1958, 224–5, delivered on the same day); 266/82, *Turner v Commission*, 1984, para. 5 (reference to the second para. of Article 34 ECSC in applying Article 233 EC). See also 314/85, *Foto-Frost*, 1987, paras 13–18 (determination of the duty of courts, not being courts of last instance, to make a reference for a preliminary ruling under Article 234 EC by analogy with Article 41 ECSC) and the converse case in C-221/88, *Busseni*, 1990, paras 10–6 (reference made to Article 234 EC and Article 150 EAEC in order to determine the scope of Article 41 ECSC).

[17] 101/63, *Wagner*, 1964, at 200–1.

[18] 230/81, *Luxembourg v European Parliament*, 1983, paras 14–20. For the unity of the Staff Regulations of the various institutions, see T-164/97, *Busaca and Others v Court of Auditors*, 1998, paras 48–61 (upheld on appeal, see C-434/98 P, *Council v Busaca and Court of Auditors*, 2000).

[19] T-164/99, T-37/00, and T-38/00, *Leroy and Others v Council*, 2001, para. 58.

[20] Ibid., para. 67.

relating to Denmark, as well as, with regard to the area of freedom, security, and justice; Protocol (No. 21) on the position of the United Kingdom (then still a Member State) and Ireland in respect of the area of freedom, security, and justice; and Protocol (No. 22) on the position of Denmark. Such protocols may not derogate from basic provisions of the Treaty to which they are annexed.[21] This means that they must always be interpreted in a manner which accords with such basic provisions. In case of doubt, a protocol must be interpreted so as to avoid a conflict with general principles of law, such as the principle of equal treatment.[22]

Accession Treaties. As has already been mentioned, primary Union law encompasses all provisions which have been agreed between the Member States and the acceding State with regard to the conditions of accession and the resultant adjustments to the Treaties, namely the Accession Treaty, the Act of Accession, and provisions forming an integral part thereof.[23] In interpreting those provisions, regard must be had to the foundations and system of the Union, as established by the original Treaties.[24] However, these provisions have the same legal status as the provisions of the original Treaties. 24.007

Declarations. In signing each of the Union Treaties and the Treaties amending them, the Member States, as an 'intergovernmental conference', adopted declarations or took note of unilateral declarations made by Member States, which are annexed to the final act of the intergovernmental conference.[25] Unlike protocols, such declarations are not binding.[26] Declarations which are signed by all the Member States may nevertheless be taken into account by the Court of Justice in interpreting provisions of the Treaties,[27] at least in so far as they do not conflict with those provisions.[28] This also applies to unilateral declarations on the part of the Member States in which they define who is to be considered their nationals for Union purposes (see para. 6.006, *supra*). 24.008

---

[21] C-280/93, *Germany v Council*, 1994, para. 117.

[22] T-333/99, *X v ECB*, 2001, para. 38. For a case in which the protocol itself provides that its application squares with fundamental principles of the internal market and free movement, see C-445/00, *Austria v Council*, 2003, paras 65–75.

[23] C-140/05, *Valeško*, 2006, para. 74. See further C-36/04, *Spain v Council*, 2006 (action to test a regulation against an Act of Accession dismissed).

[24] 231/78, *Commission v United Kingdom*, 1979, para. 12; C-233/97, *KappAhl Oy*, 1998, paras 18–21. See also T-324/05 *Estonia v Commission*, 2009, para. 208, confirmed on appeal: C-535/09 P, *Estonia v Commission*, 2011 (Accession Treaty not to be interpreted in the light of secondary Union law, but rather the other way around).

[25] Such declarations are sometimes made after signature; see, e.g., the Declaration of 1 May 1992 of the High Contracting Parties interpreting Protocol (No. 7) annexed to the EU Treaty and the Community Treaties (n. to para. 7.082, *supra*) and the declarations made by the European Council and the unilateral declarations made by Denmark at the European Council held on 11 and 12 December 1992 on the occasion of the Danish ratification of the EU Treaty (OJ 1992 C348; para. 1.042, *supra*).

[26] Toth, 'The Legal Status of the Declarations Annexed to the Single European Act' (1986) CMLRev 803, 812; see also the Commission's answer of 1 December 1997 to question no. E-3008/97 (Hager), OJ 1998 C134/56.

[27] See Article 31(2)(b) of the Vienna Convention of 23 May 1969 on the law of treaties (see para. 26.013, *infra*), which for the purpose of interpreting a treaty considers its context to be, *inter alia*, any instrument which was made by one or more parties in connection with the conclusion of the treaty and accepted by the other parties as an instrument related to the treaty. See Schermers, 'The Effect of the Date 31 December 1992' (1991) CMLRev 275, 276. For an example, see C-77/05 *United Kingdom v Council*, 2007, para. 67.

[28] See also C-233/97 *KappAhl Oy*, 1998, paras 22–3 (declaration made during the accession negotiations not to be used in interpreting the Act of Accession as it was not reflected in the wording of the Act). Conversely, a declaration to which reference is made in provisions of an Act of Accession must be taken into account when applying those provisions: T-187/99, *Agrana Zucker und Stärke v Commission*, 2001, paras 58–70.

24.009 **Constitutional acts.** Some acts which the European Council or the Council adopt pursuant to the Union Treaties may be regarded as primary Union law because their entry into force depends on their being adopted by the Member States in accordance with their respective constitutional requirements (see para. 3.007, *supra*). Although they may possibly not be subject to judicial review by the Court of Justice,[29] the Court does not shirk from subordinating their provisions to the general principles enshrined in the Treaties.[30]

---

[29] In any event, the European Court of Human Rights assumed in the judgment in *Matthews* that the 1976 Act on the direct election of the European Parliament as 'a treaty within the Community legal order' could not be challenged before the Court of Justice: European Court of Human Rights, 18 February 1999, *Matthews v United Kingdom*, No. 24833/94, para. 33. On the basis of this finding, the United Kingdom was found to have violated Article 3 of the First Protocol to the ECHR by excluding Gibraltar from the election of the European Parliament (see para. 25.014, *infra*).

[30] See, with regard to the Third Decision on Own Resources, C-284/90, *Council v European Parliament*, 1992, para. 31. See, for further particulars, Arnauld, 'Normenhierarchien innerhalb des primären Gemeinschaftsrechts—Gedanken im Prozess der Konstitutionalisierung Europas' (2003) EuR 191–216.

25
Fundamental Rights and General Principles of Union Law

Beyond general principles. According to Article 19(1) TEU, the Court of Justice and the General Court ensure that 'in the interpretation and application of the Treaties the law is observed' (see also Article 136 EAEC). Recognition of 'the law' as a source of Union law has enabled the Court of Justice to have recourse to general principles in interpreting and applying Union law.[1] Ever since 1969 it has been clear that 'fundamental human rights [are] enshrined in the general principles of [Union] law and protected by the Court'.[2] Article 6(3) TEU still refers to the fundamental rights guaranteed by the European Convention for the Protection of Human Rights and Fundamental Freedoms of 4 November 1950 (ECHR) or resulting from the constitutional traditions common to the Member States as 'general principles of the Union's law'. However, since the entry into force of the Lisbon Treaty, the Union also 'recognizes' the rights, freedoms, and principles set out in the Charter of Fundamental Rights of the European Union (Article 6(1) TEU), which has the same legal value as the Treaties. Hence, the Charter constitutes a source of primary Union law.

25.001

I. Fundamental Rights

A. Status of fundamental rights

Constitutional principles. For the Court of Justice, the principle that all Union acts must respect fundamental rights is one of the 'constitutional principles of the [Treaties]'.[3] The Treaties recognize the primary-law value of the Charter of Fundamental Rights of the European Union and also refer to fundamental rights as laid down in the European Convention for the Protection of Human Rights and Fundamental Freedoms and resulting from the constitutional traditions common to the Member States (Article 6(1) and (3) TEU). In addition, the TFEU specifically refers to respect for fundamental rights in the context of the 'area of freedom, security and justice' (Article 67(1) TFEU) and to the 'fundamental social rights' that the Union and the Member States are to 'have in mind' in setting their policies (Article 151 TFEU).[4] The fundamental rights recognized in Union law

25.002

---

[1] Expressly mentioned in C-46/93 and C-48/93, *Brasserie du Pêcheur and Factortame* ('*Factortame IV*'), 1996, paras 24–30. See, generally, Lenaerts and Gutiérrez-Fons, 'The Constitutional Allocation of Powers and General Principles of EU Law' (2010) CMLRev 1629.

[2] 29/69, *Stauder*, 1969, para. 7; see also 11/70, *Internationale Handelsgesellschaft*, 1970, para. 4.

[3] C-402/05 P and C-415/05 P, *Kadi and Al Barakaat International Foundation v Council and Commission*, 2008, para. 285; C-584/10 P, C-593/10 P, and C-595/10 P, *Commission and Others v Kadi*, 2013, para. 67.

[4] The first para. of Article 151 TFEU refers to the fundamental social rights set out in the European Social Charter (n. 15, *infra*).

have to be respected not only by the Union institutions and bodies but also by the Member States where they implement Union law (see para. 25.009, *infra*). Moreover, all provisions of Union law have to be interpreted in the light of these fundamental rights.[5] A serious and persistent breach of fundamental rights on the part of a Member State may result, under the procedure set out in Article 7 TEU, in the suspension of certain of the rights deriving from the application of the Treaties (see para. 4.020, *supra*). In a less strictly legal perspective, the Treaties refer to 'human rights'. That is the case for respect for human rights as one of the values on which the Union is founded (Article 2 TEU)[6] and as an objective to which the Union must contribute in its relations with the wider world (Article 3(5) TEU; see also Article 21(1) and (2)(b) TEU, which refer to the 'universality and indivisibility' of human rights).

1. Fundamental rights as general principles of Union law

25.003 **Increased importance.** The original Treaties made no express mention of fundamental rights, although a fundamental right to equal treatment did underlie the prohibition of discrimination on grounds of nationality (Article 12 EC [*now Article 18 TFEU*]) and the principle of equal pay for men and women for equal work (Article 141 EC [*now Article 157 TFEU*]) (see para. 9.048, *supra*). Initially, the Court of Justice merely held that it could not rule on the compatibility of Community measures with fundamental rights guaranteed by the Constitution of a Member State.[7] In the 1970 judgment in the *Internationale Handelsgesellschaft* case, the Court held, however, that 'respect for fundamental rights formed an integral part of the general principles of law protected by [it]' and that the protection of fundamental rights 'whilst inspired by the constitutional traditions common to the Member States, must be ensured within the framework of the structure and objectives of the Community'.[8] In *Nold* the Court then specified that in safeguarding fundamental rights, the Court would not only draw inspiration from the constitutional traditions common to the Member States, but also from international treaties for the protection of human rights concluded by the Member States.[9] The European Parliament, the Council, and the Commission associated themselves with that case law in a Joint Declaration of 5 April 1977.[10]

The EU Treaty (1992) introduced, for the first time, an express reference to the protection of fundamental rights and provided that the Union was to respect 'fundamental rights, as guaranteed by the European Convention for the Protection of Human Rights and Fundamental Freedoms signed in Rome on 4 November 1950 and as they result from the constitutional traditions common to the Member States, as general principles of Community law' (Article 6(2) EU). The formulation of Community protection for fundamental rights

---

[5] See, e.g., C-305/05, *Ordre des barreaux francophones et germanophone and Others*, 2007, paras 27–37; C-578/08, 2010, *Chakroun*, para. 44; C-579/12 RX-II, *Commission v Strack*, 2013, paras 40 and 45–6; C-129/13 and C-130/13, *Kamino International Logistics and Datema Hellmann Worldwide Logistics*, 2014, paras 69–70; C-131/12, *Google Spain and Google*, 2014, para. 68; C-391/16, C-77/17, and C-78/17, *M*, 2019, para. 77; C-136/17, *GC*, 2019, paras 53–9; C-507/17, *Google*, 2019, para. 60.
[6] See also C-175/08, C-176/08, C-178/08, and C-179/08, *Salahadin Abdulla and Others*, 2010, para. 90 (integrity of the person and individual liberties are part of the 'fundamental values' of the Union).
[7] 1/58, *Stork*, 1959, 26.
[8] 11/70, *Internationale Handelsgesellschaft*, 1970, para. 4.
[9] 4/73, *Nold v Commission*, 1974, para. 13.
[10] Joint Declaration of the European Parliament, the Council and the Commission, OJ 1977 C103/1. See Forman, 'The Joint Declaration on Fundamental Rights' (1977) ELRev 210–15.

was prompted by the constitutional courts of some Member States, especially by the *Bundesverfassungsgericht* (see para. 23.029, *supra*).

Guiding sources. In protecting fundamental rights, the Court of Justice has been guided by the constitutional traditions common to the Member States and by treaties on human rights, most of all the ECHR.[11] The legal position of the Member States with regard to the ECHR is identical inasmuch as they are all bound thereby and by the jurisdiction of the European Court of Human Rights (see para. 1.007, *supra*). In the interpretation and application of Union law the Court of Justice takes into account the provisions of the ECHR and, in so doing, refers regularly to the case law of the European Court of Human Rights.[12] In addition, in a situation in which Union law is not applicable, the Court of Justice sometimes refers to the applicable case law of the European Court of Human Rights.[13] Nevertheless, Union law does not determine the relationship between national law and the ECHR in such a situation.[14]

25.004

In order to determine the precise scope of a Union fundamental right, the Court of Justice also has regard to other conventions adopted under the aegis of the Council of Europe, such as the European Social Charter,[15] the Community Charter of Fundamental Social Rights of Workers,[16] and agreements concluded within the ambit of the United Nations—such as the International Covenant on Civil and Political Rights of 19 December 1966 (ICCPR)[17] and

---

[11] C-415/93, *Bosman*, 1995, para. 79; T-10/93, *A. v Commission*, 1994, paras 48–9; see also the earlier case 222/84, *Johnston*, 1986, para. 18. See further Murray, 'The Influence of the European Convention on Fundamental Rights on Community Law' (2011) Fordham ILJ 1388.

[12] e.g. C-109/01, *Akrich*, 2003, paras 59 and 61; C-105/03, *Pupino*, 2005, para. 60; C-189/02 P, C-202/02 P, C-205/02 P to C-208/02 P, and C-213/02 P, *Dansk Rørindustri and Others v Commission*, 2005, paras 215–19; C-229/05 P, *PKK and KNK v Council*, 2007, paras 75–82; C-402/05 P and C-415/05 P, *Kadi and Al Barakaat International Foundation v Council and Commission*, 2008, paras 311, 344, 360, 363, and 368; C-89/08 P, *Commission v Ireland and Others*, 2009, para. 54; C-45/08, *Spector Photo Group*, 2009, paras 42 and 43; C-518/07 *Commission v Germany*, 2010, para. 21; C-411/10 and C-493/10, *N.S.*, 2011; C-399/11, *Melloni*, 2013, para. 50; C-293/12 and C-594/12, *Digital Rights Ireland*, 2014, paras 47, 54, and 55; C-619/18, *Commission v Republic of Poland*, 2019, para. 71; C-220/18 PPU, *Generalstaatsanwaltschaft*, 2018, para. 99; C-245/19 and C-246/19, *Etat luxembourgeois*, 2020, para. 96; C-511/18, C-512/18, and C-520/18, *La Quadrature du Net and Others*, 2020, paras 125 and 128; T-54/14, *Goldfish and Others v Commission*, 2016, paras 52--4. See Schaefer, 'Die Europäische Menschenrechtskonvention als Faktor der europäischen Integration' (2017) EuR 80–105; Frese and Palmer Olsen, 'Spelling It Out—Convergence and Divergence in the Judicial Dialogue between CJEU and ECtHR' (2019) Nordic JIL 429.

[13] See, *inter alia*, C-109/01, *Akrich*, 2003, paras 58–60 (concerning the right to respect for family life in a situation in which Union law does not confer on a national of a third country who is married to a national of a Member State the right of residence in that Member State); C-71/02 *Herbert Karner Industrie-Auktionen*, 2004, para. 51; C-256/11, *Dereci*, 2011, paras 70–4; C-638/16 PPU, *X and X*, 2017, para. 38.

[14] C-571/10, *Kamberaj*, 2012, paras 62–3.

[15] See 149/77, *Defrenne*, 1978, para. 28; C-438/05, *International Transport Workers' Federation and Finnish Seamen's Union*, 2007, para. 43 and C-341/05, *Laval un Partneri*, 2007, para. 90; C-268/06, *Impact*, 2008, para. 113; C-271/08, *Commision v Germany*, 2010, para.37; C-579/12 RX, *Commission v Strack*, 2013, para. 27; C-306/16, *Maio Marques da Rosa*, 2017, para. 50; C-569/16 and C-570/16, *Bauer*, 2018, paras 52 and 81; C-684/16, *Max-Planck-Gesellschaft zur Förderung der Wissenschaften*, 2018, paras 52 and 70; C-119/19 P and C-126/19 P, *Commission and Council v Carreras Sequeros*, 2020, paras 113–23. The European Social Charter was signed at Turin under the auspices of the Council of Europe on 18 October 1961 (which has been ratified by all the Member States; for the text, see ETS No. 35. It is also available from the Council of Europe website at http://conventions.coe.int/.) See Khaliq, 'The EU and the European Social Charter: Never the Twain Shall Meet?' (2013) CYELS 169. See also C-135/08, *Rottmann*, 2010, paras 52–3 (European Convention on Nationality) and C-511/18, C-512/18, and C-520/18, *La Quadrature du Net and Others*, 2020, para. 162 (European Convention on Cybercrime).

[16] C-268/06, *Impact*, 2008, para. 112; C-116/08, *Meerts*, 2009, para. 37; C-222/14, *Maïstrellis*, 2015, para. 38; C-306/16, *Maio Marques da Rosa*, 2017, para. 50; C-119/19 P and C-126/19 P, *Commission and Council v Carreras Sequeros*, 2020, paras 113–24. For the 1989 Community Charter of the Fundamental Social Rights of Workers, see para. 9.046, *supra*.

[17] 374/87, *Orkem v Commission*, 1989, para. 31; C-297/88 and C-197/89, *Dzodzi*, 1990, para. 68; C-249/96, *Grant*, 1998, paras 43–7; C-540/03, *Parliament v Council*, 2006, para. 37; T-48/96, *Acme Industry v Council*, 1999,

the Convention on the Rights of the Child[18]—or within the framework of the International Labour Organization.[19]

2. The Charter of Fundamental Rights of the European Union

25.005 **Towards a European catalogue of rights.** In order to provide the Union with its own catalogue of fundamental rights, the European Parliament formulated a proposal thereto in its Declaration of fundamental rights and freedoms of 12 April 1989,[20] although it was not followed through to any great extent.

The decisive impetus for a genuine catalogue of fundamental rights of the European Union came from the Cologne European Council of June 1999,[21] which conferred the task of drawing up a Charter of Fundamental Rights to a 'forum' (later called a 'convention'). This convention started work on 1 February 2000 under the presidency of the former German President Roman Herzog with representatives of national governments, the European Parliament, and national parliaments and a representative of the President of the Commission. Representatives of the Court of Justice and the Council of Europe, including the European Court of Human Rights, were present as observers.[22] This unique formula inspired the Convention, which was set up after the Treaty of Nice, to reflect on the future of the Union (see para. 1.057, *supra*). In September 2000 the Convention arrived at a consensus on a draft Charter which was subsequently approved by the European Council, the European Parliament, and the Commission.[23]

25.006 **Charter of Fundamental Rights.** On 7 December 2000 the Charter of Fundamental Rights of the European Union was solemnly proclaimed at Nice by the European Parliament, the Council, and the Commission.[24] The Charter brings together rights which ensue out of

---

para. 30. The International Covenant on Civil and Political Rights of 19 December 1966 (UNTS, Vol. 99, 171) has been ratified by all the Member States.

[18] C-540/03, *European Parliament v Council*, 2006, paras 37 and 57, with case note by Bultermann (2008) CMLRev 245–59; C-244/06, *Dynamic Medien*, 2008, paras 39–40. See also C-135/08, *Rottmann*, 2010, para. 52 (1961 Convention on the Reduction of Statelessness) and para. 53 (Universal Declaration of Human Rights, adopted by the General Assembly of the United Nations on 10 December 1948).

[19] See 149/77, *Defrenne*, 1978, para. 28 (ILO Convention No. 3); C-438/05, *International Transport Workers' Federation and Finnish Seamen's Union*, 2007, para. 43; C-341/05 *Laval un Partneri*, 2007, para. 90 (ILO Convention No. 87); C-214/10, *KHS*, 2011, paras 41–2 (ILO Convention No. 132).

[20] OJ 1989 C120/51; discussed by Weiler et al. (eds), *Au nom des peuples européens/In the name of the peoples of Europe* (Nomos, 1996), 171–364.

[21] Annex IV to the conclusions of the European Council held at Cologne on 3 and 4 June 1999 (1999) 6 EU Bull. point I-64.

[22] The composition and manner of operation of the forum was determined by the European Council held at Tampere on 15 and 16 October 1999 (1999) 10 EU Bull. point I.2. In addition to various governmental and non-governmental organizations, the Committee of the Regions, the Economic and Social Committee, and the European Ombudsman were also heard. For its establishment, see De Búrca, 'The Drafting of the European Union Charter of fundamental Rights' (2001) ELRev 126–38; Desomer, 'Het Handvest van de grondrechten van de Europese Unie' (2001) TBP 671, 671–3.

[23] (2000) 10 EU Bull. point I.2.I and (2000) 11 EU Bull. point I.2.1.

[24] (2000) 12 EU Bull. point I.2.2. Its proclamation preceded the meeting of the European Council held at Nice on 7–9 December 2000 and the conclusion on 10 December 2000 of the Intergovernmental Conference which reached agreement on the Nice Treaty. The text of the Charter was published in OJ 2000 C364/1. For an analysis of the content, see Maus, 'La charte des droits fondamentaux de l'Union Européenne et la protection des droits de l'homme en Europe' (2005) ZöR 297–312; Ashiagbor, 'Economic and Social Rights in the European Charter of Fundamenal Rights' (2004) EHRLR 62–72; Lenaerts and De Smijter, 'A "Bill of Rights" for the European Union' (2001) CMLRev 273–300; Bribosia and De Schutter, 'La Charte des droits fondamentaux de l'Union européenne' (2001) JT 281–93; Goldsmith, 'A Charter of Rights, Freedoms and Principles' (2001) CMLRev 1201–16; Betten, 'The EU Charter of Fundamental Rights: a Trojan Horse or a Mouse?' (2001) Int'l J Comp Lab L & Ind Rel 151–64;

the constitutional traditions and international obligations common to the Member States, the ECHR, the Social Charter, the Charter of Fundamental Social Rights of Workers, the case law of the Court of Justice, and the European Court of Human Rights and Union legislation on data protection and worker participation. On the eve of the signature of the Lisbon Treaty, the Charter of Fundamental Rights was proclaimed again in Strasbourg on 12 December 2007 and published in the *Official Journal*.[25] This second publication of the Charter incorporates the changes proposed by the EU Constitution. In addition to the preamble,[26] the Charter is composed of six titles setting out rights which cut across the traditional division between political and civil rights and economic and social rights (see para. 25.018, *supra*). Apart from some rights connected with citizenship of the Union (see para. 6.007 *et seq*., *supra*), the fundamental rights set forth in the Charter may be invoked in the context of Union law by anyone, including persons who are not nationals of Member States.

Legal status. At the time of the first proclamation of the Charter, the discussion about its legal status was postponed to a subsequent intergovernmental conference.[27] The Charter was therefore not incorporated in the Treaties and its provisions were not expressly given force of law in any other way. Nonetheless, this did not prevent the Charter from being seen as an authoritative catalogue of fundamental rights, having regard to the broad participation in drawing up the text and its subsequent approval by the national governments (within the European Council), the European Parliament, and the Commission. According to many commentators, the institutions and bodies of the Union and likewise the Member States were bound to respect the Charter,[28] as it was confirming the general principles inherent in the rule of law which reflect the constitutional traditions common to the Member States. In this connection, the Union Courts frequently referred to the provisions of the Charter even before the entry into force of the Lisbon Treaty.[29]

25.007

As has already been mentioned, the Lisbon Treaty conferred on the Charter the same legal force as the Treaties.[30] Unlike the EU Constitution, which contained the full text of the

---

Pache, 'Die Europäische Grundrechtscharta—ein Ruckschritt für den Grundrechtsschutz in Europa?' (2001) EuR 475–94.

[25] OJ 2007 C303/1.

[26] See Busse, 'Eine kritische Würdigung der Präambel der Europäischen Grundrechtecharta' (2002) Eu GRZ 559–76.

[27] See the call for a debate on the status of the Charter in Declaration (No. 23), annexed to the Nice Treaty, on the future of the Union, OJ 2001 C80/85 and the Laeken Declaration ((2001) 12 EU Bull. point I.27, where it is stated that 'Thought would also have to be given to whether the Charter of Fundamental Rights should be included in the Basic Treaty' ('and to whether the European Community should accede to the European Convention on Human Rights'); Craig, 'Constitutional Process and Reform in the EU: Nice, Laeken, the Convention and the IGC' (2004) E Pub L 653.

[28] For the view that the Community institutions 'bound themselves' to the European Charter, see Hirsch Ballin, 'Eén wezenlijke maatstaf voor alle actoren in de Gemeenschap' (2001) SEW 330–7; Alber, 'Die Selbstbinding der europäischen Organen an die Europäischen Charta der Grundrechte' (2000) Eu GRZ 349–53. See also the communication from the Commission on the legal nature of the Charter of fundamental rights of the European Union, COM(2000) 644 fin.

[29] See, e.g., C-540/03, *European Parliament v Council*, 2006, paras 38 and 58; C-432/05, *Unibet*, 2007, para. 37. The European Court of Human Rights referred to the Charter in ECtHR, No. 28957/95, *Goodwin v United Kingdom*, 2002, para. 100. See also Toggenburg, 'The EU Charter: Moving from a European Fundamental rights Ornament to a European Fundamental Rights Order', in Palmisano (ed.), *Making the Charter of Fundamental Rights a Living Instrument* (Hotei, 2015), 9; Knook, 'The Court, the Charter, and the Vertical Division of Powers in the European Union' (2005) CMLRev 367–98.

[30] See C-403/09 PPU, *Detiček*, 2009, para. 53; C-555/07, *Kücükdeveci*, 2010, para. 22, with case note by Roes (2010) Col JEL 497–19; C-578/08, *Chakroun*, 2010, para. 44; C-399/11, *Melloni*, 2013, para. 47; C-569/16 and C-570/16, *Bauer*, 2018, para. 51. See, generally, Lenaerts, 'Exploring the Limits of the EU Charter of Fundamental

Charter, the Lisbon Treaty did not incorporate the Charter into the Treaties. Instead, Article 6(1) TEU states that '[t]he Union recognises the rights, freedoms and principles set out in the [Charter], as adapted at Strasbourg, on 12 December 2007, which have the same legal value as the Treaties'. That provision emphasizes that the provisions of the Charter in no way extend the competences of the Union as defined in the Treaties. Moreover, the rights, freedoms, and principles in the Charter 'shall be interpreted in accordance with the general provisions in Title VII of the Charter governing its interpretation and application and with due regard to the explanations referred to in the Charter, that set out the sources of those provisions' (Article 6(1), third subpara. TEU; see para. 25.012, *supra*).[31]

Within the Intergovernmental Conference that negotiated the Lisbon Treaty, it proved impossible to reach consensus with regard to the reference to the Charter as a binding source of law without agreeing on derogatory arrangements for the United Kingdom and Poland, which were laid down in a protocol annexed to the Treaties.[32] According to that protocol, the Charter does not extend the ability of the Court of Justice or any court or tribunal of Poland or of the United Kingdom, to find that national measures or practices of these Member States are inconsistent with the fundamental rights, freedoms, and principles that it reaffirms.[33] It is further stated that the Charter does not create justiciable rights in these Member States except in so far as national law has provided for such rights.[34]

B. Scope of fundamental rights' protection

1. Protection vis-à-vis institutions and bodies of the Union

25.008 **Union institutions and bodies.** The institutions and bodies of the Union have to respect fundamental rights, including the rights, freedoms, and principles set out in the Charter. Since respect for fundamental rights is a condition of the lawfulness of Union acts, the Court of Justice has held that measures incompatible with respect for these rights are 'not acceptable' in the Union.[35] To that effect, judicial remedies are available in the Union Courts against Union acts which violate fundamental rights.[36] If the wording of Union law is open

---

Rights' (2012) EuConst 375; Iglesias Sanchez, 'The Court and the Charter: The Impact of the Entry Into Force of the Lisbon Treaty On the ECJ's Approach to Fundamental Rights' (2012) CMLRev 1565.

[31] Lenaerts and Gutierrez-Fons, *Les méthodes d'interprétation de la Cour de justice de l'Union européenne* (Bruylant, 2020), 107–64, dealing specifically with the interpretation of the Charter. For examples of cases in which the explanations have been referred to, see para. 25.012, *infra*.

[32] Protocol (No. 30), annexed to the TEU and TFEU, on the application of the Charter of Fundamental Rights of the European Union to Poland and to the United Kingdom, OJ 2010 C83/313. See Barnard, 'So Long, Farewell, Auf Wiedersehen, Adieu: Brexit and the Charter of Fundamental Rights' (2019) MLR 350.

[33] See, however, C-411/10 and C-493/10, *N.S.*, 2011, paras 119–20 (protocol does not exempt these Member States from the obligation to comply with the Charter, nor does it prevent courts from ensuring complicance with the Charter). See Faraguna, 'Taking Constitutional Identities Away from the Courts' (2016) Brooklyn JIL 548; Lazzerini, 'The Scope and Effects of the Charter of Fundamental Rights in the Case Law of the European Court of Justice', in Palmisano (ed.), *Making the Charter of Fundamental Rights a Living Instrument* (Hotei, 2015), 51.

[34] Protocol (No. 30), Article 1.

[35] C-402/05 P and C-415/05 P, *Kadi and Al Barakaat International Foundation v Council and Commission*, 2008, para. 284; C-584/10 P, C-593/10 P, and C-595/10 P *Commission and Others v Kadi*, 2013, para. 67. See also Rudolf Mögele, 'Grundrechtswahrung im EU-Normsetzungsprozess' (2020) EuR 3–21.

[36] See, e.g., C-404/92 P, *X. v Commission*, 1994, paras 17–25, with case note by De Smijter (1995) Col JEL 332–8; F-46/09, *V v European Parliament*, 2011, paras 111–27. However, the assessment of the legality of a Union act in the light of fundamental rights cannot be based on claims relating to the consequences of that act in a specific case; see

to more than one interpretation, preference should be given to the interpretation that renders the provision consistent with the fundamental rights protected by the Union legal order (see para. 25.002, *supra*).[37] A provision of a Union act requiring implementation by the Member States may itself violate fundamental rights if it requires, or expressly or impliedly authorizes, the Member States to adopt or retain national legislation not respecting those rights.[38]

Even before the Charter was proclaimed, it followed from the case law of the Court of Justice that institutions and bodies of the Union have to comply with the rights embodied in the ECHR. Consequently, the provisions in the Charter pertaining to the administration of justice and the principles derived from Article 6 ECHR apply to actions brought in the Court of Justice and the General Court.[39] This does not mean, however, that the Commission is regarded as a tribunal within the meaning of Article 47 of the Charter or Article 6 ECHR in procedures imposing sanctions.[40]

The duty to respect fundamental rights also applies when the Union institutions conclude international agreements,[41] or act in the field of the CFSP.[42] However, given the limited jurisdiction of the Court in the latter field (see para. 13.012, *supra*), it cannot always be judicially enforced.[43] The Union institutions must also comply with fundamental rights when they have been given the competence to act outside the legal framework of the Union.[44]

2. Protection vis-à-vis Member States implementing Union law

Implementation of Union law. Fundamental rights are an integral part of the Union legal order. As a result of the primacy of Union law, any action on the part of the Member States taken within the scope of Union law has to comply with the Union requirements with

25.009

C-104/97 P, *Atlanta v European Community*, 1999, para. 43; C-119/19 P and C-126/19 P, *Commission and Council v Carreras Sequeros*, 2020, para. 153.

[37] C-305/05, *Ordre des barreaux francophones and germanophones*, 2007, paras 27–37 (see further case law cited in n. 5).

[38] C-540/03, *European Parliament v Council*, 2006, para. 23.

[39] C-510/11 P, *Kone and Others v Commission*, 2013, paras 20–32 and 45; C-501/11 P, *Schindler Holding v Commission*, 2013, paras 33–8; C-58/12 P, *Groupe Gascogne v Commission*, 2013, paras 32 and 67–96; C-295/12 P, *Telefónica and Telefónica de España v Commission*, 2014, paras 51–7; T-406/10, *Emesa-Trefilería and Industrias Galycas v Commission*, 2015, paras 123 and 127.

[40] 209-215/78 and 218/78, *Van Landewyck v Commission*, 1980, para. 81; T-54/03, *Lafarge v Commission*, 2008, para. 38; T-56/09 and T-73/09, *Saint-Gobain Glass France and Others v Commission*, 2014, para. 77. See Wils, 'Fundamental Procedural Rights and Effective Enforcement of Articles 101 and 102 TFEU in the European Competition Network' World Comp (2020) 5–34; Mickonyté, *Presumption of Innocence in EU Anti-Cartel Enforcement* (Brill, 2018); Zampini, 'Convention européenne des droits de l'homme et droit communautaire de la concurrence' (1999) RMCUE 628–47; Wils, 'La compatibilité des procédures communautaires en matière de concurrence avec la Convention européenne des droits de l'homme' (1996) CDE 329–54.

[41] T-512/12, *Front populaire pour la libération de la saguia-el-hamra et du rio de oro (Front Polisario) v Council of the EU*, 2015, para 228; Opinion 1/17, *Comprehensive Economic and Trade Agreement between Canada, of the one part, and the European Union and its Member States, of the other part (CETA)*, 2019, paras 189–22. See Wouters 'The EU Charter of Fundamental Rights—Some Reflections on its External Dimension' (2001) MJ 3.

[42] C-402/05 P and C-415/05 P, *Kadi and Al Barakaat International Foundation v Council and Commission*, 2008; C-130/10, *European Parliament v Council*, 2012, paras 83–4. See Hillion, 'Decentralised Integration? Fundamental Rights Protection in the EU Common Foreign and Security Policy' (2016) European Papers 55.

[43] This is partially compensated for through the restrictive interpretation given by the Court to this exception to its jurisdiction; see, e.g., C-439/13 P, *Elitaliana v Eulex Kosovo*, 2015, para. 42; C-72/15, *PJSC Rosneft Oil Company*, 2017, paras 58–81.

[44] C-8/15 P to C-10/15 P, *Ledra Advertising v Commission and ECB*, 2016, para. 67.

regard to the protection of fundamental rights.[45] In this respect Article 51(1) of the Charter provides that the rights, freedoms, and principles protected by the Charter are addressed to the Member States 'only when they are implementing Union law'.[46] It follows that when a rule of Union law applies, the fundamental rights protected by the Charter apply as well. As the Court of Justice made clear in *Åkerberg Fransson*, Article 51(1) of the Charter confirms the case law of the Court of Justice, which required already before the proclamation of the Charter that Member State action within the scope of Union law complies with the fundamental rights protected by the Union.[47]

First of all, the Member States implement Union law (or, according to the case law pre-dating the Charter act 'within the scope of Union law') where they apply Treaty provisions[48] or implement Union acts, in particular where applying or implementing regulations[49] or transposing directives into national law.[50] Member States also implement Union law when they are performing their obligations under an international agreement, such as the GATS, that forms part of EU law.[51] To determine whether a national measure is 'implementing Union law' within the meaning of Article 51(1) of the Charter, it must be ascertained, among other things, whether the national measure is intended to implement a provision of Union law; what the character of that measure is and whether it pursues objectives other than those covered by Union law, even if it is capable of indirectly affecting Union law; and whether there are specific rules of Union law on the matter or capable of affecting it.[52] A national measure is thus implementing Union law where the Member State is bound by a specific obligation under Union law to ensure a certain result.[53] The same goes for a national measure that strikes a balance between animal welfare and the freedom to manifest religion, where a Union regulation does not itself effect the necessary reconciliation between animal welfare and the freedom to manifest religion, but provides a framework for the reconciliation

---

[45] 222/84, *Johnston*, 1986, para. 18.
[46] C-617/10, *Åkerberg Fransson*, 2013, paras 21–2. See, generally, Hamulak and Mazak, 'The Charter of Fundamental Rights of the European Union Vis-à-Vis the Member States—Scope of its Application in the View of the CJEU' (2017) CYIL 161; Dougan, 'Judicial Review of Member State Action Under the General Principles and the Charter: Defining the "Scope of Union Law"' (2015) CMLRev 1201; Fontanelli, 'The Implementation of European Union Law by Member States Under Article 51(1) of the Charter of Fundamental Rights' (2014) Col JEL 193; Hancox, 'The Meaning of 'Implementing' EU Law under Article 51(1) of the Charter: Åkerberg Fransson' (2013) CMLRev 1411.
[47] C-617/10, *Åkerberg Fransson*, 2013, paras 18–20. See Rauchegger, 'The Interplay Between the Charter and National Constitutions after Akerberg Fransson and Melloni', in de Vries, Bernitz, and Weatherill (eds), *The EU Charter of Fundamental Rights as a Binding Instrument* (Hart Publishing, 2015) 93; Eeckhout, 'The EU Charter of Fundamental Rights and the Federal Question' (2002) CMLRev 945–94; Van Bockel and Wattel, 'New Wine into Old Wineskins: The Scope of the Charter of Fundamental rights of the EU after Åkerberg Fransson' (2013) ELRev 866.
[48] 222/86, *Heylens*, 1987, paras 14–16 (Article 39 EC [*now Article 45 TFEU*]).
[49] 5/88, *Wachauf*, 1989, paras 16–22; ECJ, C-2/92, *Bostock*, 1994, paras 16–27. Similarly, a Member State issuing or executing a European arrest warrant pursuant to Council Framework Decision 2002/584/JHA of 13 June 2002 on the European arrest warrant and the surrender procedures between Member States (OJ 2002 L190/1), is simply implementing EU law, see, e.g., C-216/18 PPU, *LM*, 2018, para 37.
[50] 222/84, *Johnston*, 1986, paras 13–21; C-465/00, C-138/01, and C-139/01, *Österreichischer Rundfunk and Others*, 2003, paras 68–91; C-20/00 and C-64/00, *Booker Aquaculture and Hydro Seafood GSP*, 2003, paras 88–92. See Fontanelli, 'Implementation of EU Law through Domestic Measures after Fransson: The Court of Justice Buys Time and 'Non-preclusion' Troubles Loom Large' (2014) ELRev 682.
[51] C-66/18, *Commission v Hungary*, 2020, paras 212–16.
[52] C-40/11, *Iida*, 2012, para. 79; C-87/12, *Ymeraga and Others*, 2013, paras 11 and 12; C-206/13, *Siragusa*, 2014, paras 24–6; C-198/13, *Julián Hernández and Others*, 2014, para. 37; C-177/17 and C-178/17, *Demarchi Gino and Garavaldi*, 2017, para. 20; C-540/16, *Spika and Others*, 2018, para. 22.
[53] See C-650/13, *Delvigne*, 2015, paras 31–3.

which Member States must achieve between those two values; in making that choice, as required by Union law, Member States are implementing Union law.[54] Where the provisions of Union law in the area concerned do not govern an aspect of a given situation and do not impose any specific obligation on the Member States with regard thereto, the national rule enacted by a Member State as regards that aspect falls outside the scope of application of the Charter and the situation concerned cannot be assessed in the light of the provisions of the Charter.[55] That is, for instance, the case with the conditions for carrying over annual leave granted by national law beyond the minimum period of four weeks required by Directive 2003/88, to which Article 31(2) of the Charter cannot be applied.[56] A Member State is also 'implementing Union law' where a national measure constitutes a necessary step in the procedure for adoption of a Union measure and the Union institutions have only a limited or non-existent discretion with regard to that measure.[57]

Second, any use by a Member State of exceptions provided for by Union law in order to justify an impediment to a right or freedom guaranteed by the Treaty must be regarded as 'implementing Union law'. This is particularly the case when the measure constitutes an obstacle to the free movement of goods, persons, services, and capital as guaranteed by the Treaties and the Member State concerned invokes overriding reasons of general interest to justify that obstacle.[58] If such a national measure violates a fundamental right, it will not be covered by the justificatory ground relied on and thus constitute a prohibited restriction to free movement.[59] The Court of Justice has further held that respect for fundamental rights may constitute in itself a ground for restricting the freedoms guaranteed by the Treaties.[60] In such a case, the competent authorities enjoy a wide margin of discretion in order to determine whether the restrictions placed upon intra-Union trade are proportionate in the light of the protection of fundamental rights.[61]

The Member States also have to comply with fundamental rights when they implement CFSP acts of the Union.[62] However, as far as action undertaken by the Member States pursuant to the CFSP is concerned, Article 275 TFEU restricts review by the Court of Justice. Protection of fundamental rights in that context therefore rests primarily on the protection afforded by the national legal systems under the supervision of the institutions set up by the ECHR.

---

[54] C-336/19, *Centraal Israëlitisch Consistorie van België and Others*, 2020, paras 47–9.
[55] C-609/17 and C-610/17, *TSN*, 2019, para. 53; see also C-198/13, *Julian Hernández*, 2014, para. 35; C-243/16, *Miravitlles Ciurana*, 2017, para. 34; C-152/17, *Consorzio Italian Management and Catania Multiservizi*, 2018, paras 34–5.
[56] C-609/17 and C-610/17, *TSN*, 2019, para. 41–55.
[57] See C-97/91, *Oleificio Borelli v Commission*, 1992, paras 9–14; C-269/99, *Carl Kühne and Others*, 2001, paras 57–8.
[58] C-260/89, *ERT*, 1991, para. 43; C-235/17, *Commission v Hungary*, 2019, para. 65.
[59] C-390/12, *Pfleger*, 2014, paras 35–6; C-201/15, *AGET Iraklis*, 2016, paras 62–5; see already C-260/89, *ERT*, 1991, para. 43; C-368/95, *Familiapress*, 1997, paras 24–5. See Lenaerts 'The Court of Justice of the European Union and the Protection of Fundamental Rights' (2011) PYIL 79.
[60] C-112/00, *Schmidberger*, 2003, paras 69–94; C-414/16, *Egenberger*, 2018, para. 80; C-555/19, *Fussl Modestraße Mayr*, 2021, para. 55.
[61] C-112/00, *Schmidberger*, 2003, para. 82.
[62] C-354/04 P, *Gestoras Pro Amnistía and Others*, 2007, para. 51; C-355/04 P, *Segi and Others*, 2007, para. 51.

25.010 **Application between private parties.** Article 51(1) does not address the question whether, in addition to Union and Member State authorities, individuals may also be directly required to comply with certain provisions of the Charter. Still, it does not exclude such 'horizontal effect' either.[63] The fact that a Treaty provision is primarily addressed to the Member States does not preclude its application between private parties. Therefore, the Court has accepted that some provisions of the Charter are sufficient in themselves to confer on individuals a right which they may rely on as such in a dispute with another individual.[64] That is, first, the case with the prohibition on discrimination laid down in Article 21(1) of the Charter.[65] That equally applies to the right to paid annual leave recognized in Article 31(2) of the Charter.[66] Moreover, the Court has found that search engine operators are under an obligation to take sufficiently effective measures to ensure the protection of the data subject's fundamental rights enshrined in Articles 7 and 8 of the Charter, including effective de-listing.[67] The Court has also accepted that Article 47 of the Charter has horizontal direct effect.[68]

25.011 **Interpretation by the Court of Justice.** Where national rules fall within the scope of Union law and reference is made to the Court of Justice for a preliminary ruling, the Court considers that it must provide all the criteria of interpretation needed by the national court to determine whether the national rules are compatible with fundamental rights.[69] The Court of Justice refuses to consider the compatibility with fundamental rights of a national measure which lies 'outside the scope of Union law'.[70] Thus, Union law had nothing to say about a deprivation of liberty after a sentence under provisions of national criminal law which were not designed to secure compliance with rules of Union law. Whilst any deprivation of liberty may impede the person concerned from exercising his or her right to free movement, a purely hypothetical prospect of exercising that right does not establish a sufficient connection with Union law.[71]

---

[63] C-684/16, *Max-Planck-Gesellschaft zur Förderung der Wissenschaften*, 2018, para. 76. See Frantziou, *The Horizontal Effect of Fundamental Rights in the European Union: A Constitutional Analysis* (OUP, 2019). See also Prechal, 'Horizontal Direct Effect of the Charter of Fundamental Rights of the EU', (2020) Rev EDE 407–26; Muir, 'The Horizontal Effects of Charter Rights given Expression to in EU Legislation, from Mangold to Bauer' (2019) REALaw 185–215; De Mol, 'De horizontale directe werking van de grondrechten van de Europese Unie' (2016) SEW 458; Leczykiewicz 'Horizontal Application of the Charter of Fundamental Rights' (2013) ELRev 479; Spaventa, 'The Horizontal Application of Fundamental Rights as General Principles of Union Law', in Arnull et al., (eds) *A Constitutional Order of States?: Essays in EU Law in Honour of Alan Dashwood* (Hart Publishing, 2011), 199.
[64] C-176/12, *AMS*, 2014, para. 47; C-414/16, *Egenberger*, 2018, paras 76 and 78; C-569/16 and C-570/16, *Bauer*, 2018, para. 85; C-684/16, *Max-Planck-Gesellschaft zur Förderung der Wissenschaften*, 2018, paras 77–9; C-193/17, *Cresco*, 2019, 76. See Frantziou, '(Most of) the Charter of Fundamental Rights is Horizontally Applicable' (2019) EuConst 306.
[65] C-176/12, *AMS*, 2014, para. 47; C-414/16, *Egenberger*, 2018, para. 76; C-193/17, *Cresco Investigation*, 2019, paras 76–89.
[66] C-684/16, *Max-Planck-Gesellschaft zur Förderung der Wissenschaften*, 2018, para. 79.
[67] C-507/17, *Google*, 2019, para. 70; C-136/17, *GC*, 2019, para. 66 (an operator of a search engine must balance some rights of the data subject with the rights of the users of his service under Article 11 of the Charter (right to access to information).
[68] C-396/13, *Sähköalojen ammattiliitto*, 2015, paras 19–26.
[69] C-260/89, *ERT*, 1991, para. 42; C-159/90, *Society for the Protection of Unborn Children Ireland*, 1991, para. 31; C-2/92, *Bostock*, 1994; C-112/00, *Schmidberger*, 2003, para. 75; C-27/11, *Vinkov*, 2012, para. 58; C-276/12, *Sabou*, 2013, para. 28; C-390/12, *Pfleger and Others*, 2014, paras 25–26.
[70] C-256/11, *Dereci*, 2011, paras 71–2; C-117/14, *Nisttahuz Poclava*, 2015, paras 27–44; C-395/15, *Daouidi*, 2016, paras 60–8; C-638/16 PPU, *X and X*, 2017, paras 38–48; C-609/17 and C-610/17, *Terveys- ja sosiaalialan neuvottelujärjestö*, 2019, paras 41–55; C-469/18 and C-470/18, *IN and JM*, 2019, 17–26.
[71] See C-129/14 PPU, *Spasic*, 2014, para. 55; C-444/15, *Associazione Italia Nostra Onlus*, 2016, para. 62.

3. Limitations to the application of the Charter

Scope and interpretation of rights and principles. Pursuant to Article 6(1), third subpara. TEU, the rights, freedoms, and principles set out in the Charter shall be interpreted 'in accordance with the general provisions in Title VII of the Charter governing its interpretation and application and with due regard to the explanations referred to in the Charter, that sets out the sources of those provisions'. These 'explanations' refer to the explanations prepared under the authority of the Praesidium of the Convention which drafted the Charter in 2000 and updated under the responsibility of the Praesidium of the European Convention, which drafted the EU Constitution.[72]

25.012

In so far as rights recognized by the Charter are based on the Union Treaties, they have to be exercised under the conditions and within the limits defined by those Treaties (Article 52(2))[73]. When the Charter contains rights which correspond to rights guaranteed by the ECHR, the meaning and scope of those rights is the same as those laid down by that convention,[74] but this does not prevent Union law from providing more extensive protection (Article 52(3)).[75] Where a provision of the Charter affords a stronger protection than the ECHR (e.g. the right to marry in Article 9 of the Charter, which, unlike Article 12 of the ECHR, does not refer to the gender of the partners), that provision may lead to a stronger protection under the ECHR as well since the European Court of Human Rights will take this factor into account.[76]

The Court of Justice has further held that the references in the Charter to the Member States' constitutions do not mean that national authorities may invoke the Charter in order to set aside the primacy of Union law. In *Melloni*,[77] the question arose as to whether Spain could make the execution of a European arrest warrant conditional upon observance of a stricter protection of the right to be heard than ensured under the Charter. The Court made clear that national authorities and courts may apply national standards of protection of fundamental rights only to the extent that the level of protection of the Charter, as interpreted

---

[72] See the preamble to the Charter and Article 52(7) thereof. For the explanations relating to the Charter, see OJ 2007 C303/17. See also Jacqué, 'The Explanations Relating to the Charter of Fundamental Rights of the European Union', in Peers et al., *The EU Charter of Fundamental Rights: A Commentary* (Hart Publishing, 2014), 1715. For examples of the explanations being used, see, e.g., C-617/10, *Åkerberg Fransson*, 2013, para. 20; C-129/14 PPU, *Spasic*, 2014, paras 54–5; C-444/15, *Associazione Italia Nostra Onlus*, 2016, para. 62C-569/16 and C-570/16, *Bauer and Willmeroth*, 2018, para. 55; C-688/18, *TX and UW*, 2020, para. 35; C-575/18 P, *Czech Republic v Commission*, 2020, para. 52; C-119/19 P and C-126/19 P, *Commission and Council v Carreras Sequeros*, 2020, paras 112–15.

[73] Eeckhout (n. 47), 979–91.

[74] C-400/10 PPU, *McB.*, 2010, para. 53; C-562/13, *Abdida*, 2014, para. 47; C-235/17, *Commission v Hungary*, 2019, para. 72 (right to property under Article 17 of the Charter and Article 1 of the First Protocol to the ECHR); C-469/17, *Funke Medien NRW*, 2019, para. 73 (freedom of the press under Article 11 of the Charter and Article 10(1) ECHR); C-220/18 PPU, *ML*, 2018, paras 60–70 and C-128/18, *Dorobantu*, 2019, paras 50–6 (detention conditions under Article 3 ECHR and Article 4 of the Charter).

[75] For the relationship between the Charter and the ECHR, see Kokott and Sobotta 'Protection of Fundamental Rights in the European Union: On the Relationship between EU Fundamental Rights, the European Convention and National Standards of Protection' (2015) YEL 60; Bratza, 'The European Convention on Human Rights and the Charter of Fundamental Rights of the European Union: A Process of Mutual Enrichment', in Rosas (ed.), *The Court of Justice and the Construction of Europe: Analyses and Perspectives on Sixty Years of Case-Law* (Asser, 2012) 176; Callewaert, 'Die EMRK und die EU-Grundrechtecharta' (2003) Eu GRZ 198–206; Drzemczewski, 'The Council of Europe's Position with Respect to the EU Charter of Fundamental Rights' (2001) Human Rights LJ 14–32.

[76] For an example, see ECtHR, No. 28957/95, *Goodwin v United Kingdom*, 2002, paras 94–104, more specifically para. 100.

[77] C-399/11, *Melloni*, 2013.

by the Court, and the primacy, unity, and effectiveness of Union law are not compromised.[78] This is relevant for those provisions of the Charter that result from the constitutional traditions common to the Member States, as they must be interpreted 'in harmony with those traditions' (Article 52(4)) and since 'full account' must be taken of national laws and practices as specified in the Charter (Article 52(6)). This also applies to Article 53 of the Charter, according to which the provisions of the Charter may not be interpreted in such a way that they would restrict or adversely affect rights guaranteed, in their respective fields of application, by Union law, international law, international agreements, or Member States' constitutions. According to this provision, in applying the Charter, in principle, the norm applying the highest level of protection should prevail.[79] However, where a Union measure fully determines the action of the Member States and in so doing expresses the will of the Union legislature to set the protection of fundamental rights at a uniform level that is fully compatible with the Charter, the national authorities cannot prevent the application of that measure on the grounds that it restricts or adversely affects fundamental rights guaranteed by the national constitution. They can thus not refuse, contrary to such a measure, to execute a European Arrest Warrant (which was the real issue in *Melloni*). This would indeed undermine the primacy, unity, and effectiveness of Union law—the essential characteristics of the Union legal order.[80] In contrast, as the Court stated in *Åkerberg Fransson*, in a situation where action of the Member States is not entirely determined by Union law, it is possible that the application of national standards of fundamental rights does not compromise the level of protection provided by the Charter nor the primacy, unity, and effectiveness of Union law.[81] A clear articulation of this case law in the context of national constitutional law can be found in the so-called *Recht auf Vergessen I & II* cases of the German *Bundesverfassungsgericht* (Constitutional Court).[82]

Since the transposition of a directive by the Member States is covered, in any event, by the situation referred to in Article 51 of the Charter, in which the Member States are implementing Union law, the level of protection of fundamental rights provided for in the Charter must be achieved in such a transposition, irrespective of the Member States' discretion in transposing the directive.[83] But when a Union act does not seek to achieve

---

[78] Ibid., paras 55–64; see also C-617/10, *Åkerberg Fransson*, 2013, para. 29; C-476/17, *Pelham and others*, 2019, para. 80; C-516/17, *Spiegel Online*, 2019, para. 21; C-128/18, *Dorobantu*, 2019, para. 79; C-469/17, *Funke Medien NRW*, 2019, para. 32. See further Besselink, 'The Parameters of Constitutional Conflict after Melloni' (2014) ELRev 531.

[79] See Alonso Garcia, 'The General Provisions of the Charter of Fundamental Rights of the European Union' (2002) ELJ 492–514.

[80] C-399/11, *Melloni*, 2013, paras 58–62; C-128/18, *Dorobantu*, 2019, para. 79; Pérez, 'Melloni in Three Acts: From Dialogue to Monologue' (2014) EuConst 308.

[81] C-617/10, *Åkerberg Fransson*, 2013, para 29; C-42/17, *M.A.S and M.B*, 2017, paras 40–62 ('Taricco II', as it further develops C-105/14, *Taricco and Others*, 2015). See Maesa, 'Effectiveness and Primacy of EU Law V. Higher National Protection of Fundamental Rights and National Identity: A Look through the Lens of the Taricco II Judgment' (2018) eucrim 50; Viganò, 'Melloni overruled? Considerations on the 'Taricco II' judgment of the Court of Justice' (2018) NJECL 18.

[82] German Constitutional Court, 6 November 2019, 1 BVR 16/13 ('Recht auf Vergessen I'), and, of the same date, 1 BVR 276/17 (Recht auf Vergessen II"). These judgments incorporate the *Åkerberg Fransson* and *Melloni* case law of the Court of Justice. See also para. 23.029, *supra*. See further Wendel, 'The Two-faced Guardian—or How One Half of the German Federal Constitutional Court Became a European fundamental Rights Court' (2020) CMLRev 1383–1426; Thym, 'Friendly Takeover, or: the Power of the "First Word". The German Constitutional Court Embraces the Charter of Fundamental Rights as a Standard of Domestic Judicial Review' (2020) EuConst 187–212.

[83] C-516/17, *Spiegel Online*, 2019, paras 20–1; C-469/17, *Funke Medien NRW*, 2019, paras 31–2.

full harmonization, this has consequences as to the possibility of relying on Article 53 of the Charter without undermining the primacy, unity, and effectiveness of Union law.[84] Similarly, when the territorial scope of Union legislation is limited to the territory of the Union, as is the case for the obligations for search engine operators to dereference certain records, it is possible for national authorities to extend those obligations to the rest of the world on the basis of national constitutional standards.[85]

Finally, to the extent that provisions of the Charter do not embody rights or freedoms but rather 'principles', Article 52(5) restricts judicial enforcement of those provisions to the interpretation and the review of the legality of acts adopted by the institutions, bodies, offices, and agencies of the Union and by the Member States—within the limits of their respective powers—with a view to implementing those principles.[86] This does not mean, however, that acts other than those directly implementing the Charter may not be indirectly reviewed for compliance with the principles enshrined therein.[87]

4. Relationship with the protection offered by the European Convention of Human Rights

Protection against acts of the Union. Article 6(2) TEU provides that the Union 'shall accede' to the ECHR (see para. 25.015, *infra*). Even though the Union has committed itself to respecting fundamental rights, including the ECHR, it is not (yet) a party to that Convention.[88] Therefore, the European Commission of Human Rights (now abolished) considered that a petition would not lie against Community institutions.[89] The European Court of Human Rights confirmed that acts of the Community could not be tested against the ECHR, because the Community was not a party to the Convention.[90] The same indubitably

25.013

---

[84] For a case involving absence of such full harmonization, leading to the applicability of national constitutional standards, see C-42/17, *M.A.S. and M.B.*, 2017, paras 29–62.

[85] C-507/17, *Google*, 2019, para. 72.

[86] C-282/10, *Dominiguez*, 2012, para 16; C-571/10, *Kamberaj*, 2012, para 79; C-356/12, *Wolfgang Glatzel v Freistaat Bayern*, 2014, paras 75–6; C-176/12, *Association de Médiation Sociale*, 2014, para. 49; C-470/12, *Pohotovost'*, 2014, para. 52. See Frantziou, 'The Binding Charter Ten Years on: More than a "Mere Entreaty"?' (2019) YEL 73; Krommendijk, 'Principled Silence or Mere Silence on Principles? The Role of the EU Charter's Principles in the Case Law of the Court of Justice' (2015) EuConst 321; Guðmundsdóttir, 'A Renewed Emphasis on the Charter's Distinction between Rights and Principles: Is a Doctrine of Judicial Restraint More Appropriate?' (2015) CMLRev 685–719. For a summary on the different views regarding the measures that are reviewable in the context of the principles of the Charter see: Lock, 'Rights and Principles in the EU Charter of Fundamental Rights' (2019) CMLRev 1201.

[87] See C-175/08, C-176/08, C-178/08, and C-179/08, *Salahadin Abdulla and Others*, 2010, para. 54 (secondary Union law must be interpreted in a manner which respects the principles recognized by the Charter). See Guðmundsdóttir, 'A Renewed Emphasis on the Charter's Distinction between Rights and Principles: Is a Doctrine of Judicial Restraint more Appropriate?' CMLRev (2015) 685; Lenaerts, 'Exploring the Limits of the EU Charter of Fundamental Rights' (2012) EuConst 375.

[88] See, generally, Popelier, Van de Heyning, and Van Nuffel (eds), *Human Rights Protection in the European Legal Order: The Interaction between the European and the National Courts* (Intersentia, 2011); Lawson, *Het EVRM en de Europese Gemeenschappen* (Kluwer, 1999); Schermers, 'The European Communities Bound by Fundamental Human Rights' (1990) CMLRev 249–58.

[89] ECtHR, No. 8030/77, *CFDT v EEC*, 1987, 231. The European Commission of Human Rights took the view that a complaint made against a Member State which was merely implementing a judgment of the Court of Justice was inadmissible as the Community legal order itself guaranteed respect for the ECHR: European Commission of Human Rights, No. 13258/87, *M. & Co. v Germany*, 1990, 46 (complaint about the implementation by Germany of a judgment given by the Court of Justice under Article 256 EC; declared inadmissible). In another case, however, the implementation by a Member State of a Community agricultural regulation was tested against the ECHR: European Commission of Human Rights, No. 1450/89, *Procola and Others v Luxembourg*, 1993, para. 5.

[90] ECtHR, No. 24833/94, *Matthews v United Kingdom*, 1999, para. 32; ECtHR, No. 13645/05, *Coöperatieve producentenorganisatie van de Nederlandse Kokkelvisserij v Netherlands*, 2009, B.2.; Nanopoulos, 'Killing Two

applies to Union acts in general. However, the European Court of Human Rights has never clarified whether lodging a complaint against all the Member States would make it possible to review Union acts in the light of the ECHR. So far, all complaints brought for this purpose against all the Member States have been dismissed by the European Court of Human Rights without it having ruled on its jurisdiction *ratione personae*.[91]

25.014 **Protection against Member States' implementation of Union law.** According to the European Court of Human Rights, an indirect review may nevertheless be carried out by testing the act by which a Member State gives effect to Union provisions against the Convention.[92] The European Court of Human Rights has held that the fact that the Member States have transferred competence to the Union does not, in principle, release them from their obligations to comply with the ECHR. That Court has declared that it is competent to review acts adopted within the framework of the Union against the ECHR in so far as the Union legal order itself does not afford equivalent protection.[93] In *Matthews v United Kingdom* such protection was clearly not secured since the complaint related to the exclusion of inhabitants of Gibraltar from the direct election of the European Parliament, as laid down in the Act on the direct election of the European Parliament, which, as an act of primary law, could not be reviewed by the Court of Justice.[94]

In *Bosphorus v Ireland*[95] the European Court of Human Rights was asked to rule on an alleged violation of property rights by a decision of a Member State implementing a Union act imposing economic sanctions. The Court held that Member State action taken in compliance with Union obligations is justified as long as the Union is considered to protect fundamental rights, as regards both the substantive guarantees offered and the mechanisms controlling their observance, in a manner which can be considered at least equivalent to that for which the ECHR provides.[96] However, any such presumption can be rebutted if, in the

---

Birds with One Stone? The Court of Justice's Opinion on the EU's Accession to the ECHR' (2015) Cambridge LJ 185.

[91] ECtHR, No. 51717/99, *Guérin Automobiles v Belgium and Others*, 2000; ECtHR, No. 6422/02 and 9916/02, *SEGI and Gestoras Pro-Amnistía v Belgium and Others*, 2002; ECtHR, No. 56672/00, *Senator Lines v Belgium and Others*, 2004. See also Tulkens, 'L'Union européenne devant la Cour européenne des droits de l'homme' (2000) RUDH 50–7. Conversely, the General Court manifestly lacked jurisdiction to entertain an application to annul a decision of the Commission of Human Rights: Order of 16 November 1995, *Zanone v Council of Europe and France*, T-201/95, unreported; appeal rejected by ECJ Order of 23 May 1996, *Zanone v Council of Europe and France*, C-9/96 P, unreported.

[92] ECtHR, No. 17862/91, *Cantoni v France*, 1996, para. 30 (review in the light of the ECHR not precluded by the fact that the national provision was based almost word for word on a Union directive).

[93] ECtHR, No. 24833/94, *Matthews v United Kingdom*, 1999, paras 33–4; ECtHR, No. 45036/98, *Bosphorus v Ireland*, 2005, paras 155–6;

[94] In *Matthews* the United Kingdom was held to have violated the right to free elections enshrined in Article 3 of the First Protocol to the ECHR. For further particulars, see Winkler, 'Der Europäische Gerichtshof für Menschenrechte, das Europäisches Parlament und der Schutz der Konventionsgrundrechte im Europäischen Gemeinschaftsrecht' (2001) Eu GRZ 18–27; De Schutter and L'Hoest, 'La Cour européenne des droits de l'homme juge du droit communautaire: Gibraltar, l'Union européenne et la Convention européenne des droits de l'homme' (2000) CDE 141–214. For the Act, see para. 12.014, *supra*; for the status of provisions of primary law, see paras 24.003–24.009, *supra*. The implementation of the judgment in the United Kingdom was contested by Spain before the Court of Justice, but the application was dismissed, see C-145/04, *Spain v United Kingdom*, 2006.

[95] ECtHR, No. 45036/98, *Bosphorus v Ireland*, 2005; case notes by Jacqué (2005) RTDE 749–67; Douglas-Scott (2006) CMLRev 243–254; Hinarejos Parga (2006) ELRev 251–9; Schohe (2006) EuZW 33–64; Eckes (2007) E Pub L 47–67.

[96] See already *M. & Co.* (see n. 89, *supra*), 145. By 'equivalent' the Court means 'comparable'; any requirement that the organization's protection be 'identical' could run counter to the interest of international cooperation pursued: *Bosphorus v Ireland*, para. 155. The European Court recently affirmed the *Bosphorus* principle in ECtHR, No. 17502/07, *Avotins v Latvia*, 2016, para. 115. See also Cragl, 'An Olive Branch from Strasbourg? Interpreting

circumstances of a particular case, it is considered that the protection of Convention rights was manifestly deficient.[97] In the *Kokkelvisserij* case, the European Court of Human Rights ruled that the presumption also applies to the procedures followed within the European Union, and in particular the procedures of the Court of Justice of the European Union.[98] As regards the question whether the protection of Convention rights was 'manifestly deficient', the European Court of Human Rights held in the *Bosphorus* case that the protection of fundamental rights by Union law could be considered to be—and to have been at the relevant time—'equivalent' to that of the Convention system.[99] Likewise, it considered in the *Kokkelvisserij* case that the applicant had not shown that the protection afforded to it was manifestly deficient.[100]

It follows from the case law of the European Court of Human Rights that the application of the *Bosphorus* presumption is subject to two conditions: first, the absence of any margin of manoeuvre on the part of a Member State's authorities and, second, the deployment of the full potential of the supervisory mechanisms provided for by Union law. When these two conditions are fulfilled, a Member State is presumed to comply with the requirements of the Convention, unless it is demonstrated that, in the particular case, the protection of the Convention rights was manifestly deficient so that the presumption is rebutted. In the latter case, the Member State action will be fully scrutinised on its compliance with the Convention, in the same way as in the case where the presumption does not apply.[101]

When assessing whether the Union's own supervisory mechanism has deployed its full potential - the second condition - the European Court of Human Rights looks into the concrete application of the Union's preliminary reference mechanism, for example, by assessing whether any refusal by a national court to refer to the Court of Justice was justified and/or duly reasoned.[102] As far as the first condition is concerned, the European Court of Human

---

the European Court of Human Rights' Resurrection of Bosphorus and Reaction to Opinion 2/13 in the Avotiņš Case' (2017) EuConst, 551; Glas and Krommendijk 'From Opinion 2/13 to Avotins: Recent Developments in the Relationship between the Luxembourg and Strasbourg Courts' (2017) HRLR 567; Lebeck, 'The European Court of Human Rights on the relation between ECHR and EC-law: The Limits of Constitutionalisation of Public International Law' (2007) ZöR 195–236; Lindner, 'Grundrechtsschutz in Europa—System einer Kollisionsdogmatik' (2007) EuR 160–193; Haratsch, 'Die Solange-Rechtsprechung des Europäischen Gerichtshofs für Menschenrechte. Das Kooperationsverhältnis zwischen EGMR und EuGH' (2006) ZaöRV 927–47; Lavranos, 'Das So-Lange-Prinzip im Verhältnis von EGMR und EuGH—Anmerkung zu dem Urteil der EGMR v 30.06.2005, Rs.450 36/98' (2006) EuR 79–92.

[97] ECtHR, No. 45036/98, *Bosphorus v Ireland*, 2005, para. 156.
[98] ECtHR, No. 13645/05, *Coöperatieve producentenorganisatie van de Nederlandse Kokkelvisserij v Netherlands*, 2009, B.3, with case note by Van de Heyning (2009) CMLRev 2117–25.
[99] ECtHR, No. 45036/98, *Bosphorus v Ireland*, 2005, paras 159–65.
[100] *Coöperatieve producentenorganisatie van de Nederlandse Kokkelvisserij v Netherlands*, B.3. In that case, the European Court of Human Rights was asked to rule on the compatibility with Article 6 ECHR of the fact that, in preliminary proceedings before the Court of Justice, an association involved in the proceedings before the referring Dutch court, did not have the opportunity to respond to the Advocate General's Opinion. In response, the European Court of Human Rights referred to the possibility for the Court of Justice to order the reopening of the oral proceedings after the Advocate General has read out his or her opinion (which the Court had refused to do as the applicant had submitted no precise information which made it appear useful or necessary to do so) and the possibility for the referring national court to submit a further request for a preliminary ruling if it had found itself unable to decide the case on the basis on the first such ruling.
[101] See ECtHR No. 17502/17, *Avotiņš v Latvia*, 2016, paras 105–12; on this case, see also Lenaerts, 'La vie après l'avis: Exploring the Principle of Mutual (Yet Not Blind) Trust' (2017) CMLRev 805–40.
[102] See ECtHR No. 12323/11, *Michaud v France*, 2012, paras 114–5; ECtHR No; 40324/16 and 12623/17, *Bivolaru and Moldovan v France*, 2021, paras 130–1 (presumption not held applicable due to circumstances in which no preliminary reference was submitted to the Court of Justice, but no breach of Convention rights found). Compare

Rights has explained that Member States remain fully responsible under the Convention where they act outside their strict international legal obligations, which is the case where they enjoy a margin of discretion under Union law.[103] In the *M.S.S.* case the European Court of Human Rights held that Belgium had infringed Article 3 ECHR by returning asylum seekers to Greece and thereby exposing them to the risks generated by the systemic deficiencies in the asylum procedure in Greece and to detention and living conditions that constituted degrading treatment. According to the European Court of Human Rights, the provisions of the Dublin Regulation indicating the Member State responsible for the examination of asylum applications gave Belgium the necessary freedom to assess whether or not an asylum seeker should be returned to the responsible Member State.[104] In subsequent case law, the Court of Justice confirmed that interpretation of the Dublin Regulation. The Court of Justice ruled that Member States may not transfer an asylum seeker where they could not have been unaware of the fact that systemic deficiencies in the asylum procedure and in the reception conditions of asylum seekers in that Member State amount to substantial grounds for believing that the asylum seeker would face a real risk of being subjected to inhuman or degrading treatment within the meaning of Article 4 of the Charter.[105]

25.015 **Necessity of accession to the ECHR.** As a complaint cannot (yet) be lodged in the European Court of Human Rights against the Union institutions, the only protection of fundamental rights provided vis-à-vis the Union institutions consists of a review at last instance by the Court of Justice. If the issue raised has not yet been considered by the European Court of Human Rights, it is possible that the Court of Justice will put a different construction on the scope of the ECHR than that Court would have done. For instance, the Court of Justice ruled in its *Hoechst* judgment of 1989 that the inviolability of the home protected by Article 8 ECHR does not extend to business premises, whereas the European Court of Human Rights later ruled otherwise.[106] The Court of Justice has then adjusted its case law to that development.[107]

Where there is conflicting case law of the Court of Justice and the European Court of Human Rights concerning the scope of the ECHR, national (and Union) authorities are liable to be squeezed between the primacy of Union law, on the one hand, and their obligations under the ECHR, on the other.[108]

ECtHR No. 17502/17, *Avotiņš v Latvia*, 2016, paras 109–11; ECtHR No. 40324/16 and 12623/17, *Bivolaru and Moldovan v France*, 2021, paras 112–6 (presumption held to apply, even though no reference had been made).

[103] ECtHR, No. 45036/98, *Bosphorus v Ireland*, 2005, para. 157; ECtHR, No. 30696/09, *M.S.S. v Belgium and Greece*, 2011, para. 338; ECtHR, No. 12323/11, *Michaud v France*, 2012, para. 103; ECtHR, No. 47287/15, *Ilias and Ahmed v Hungary*, 2019.

[104] ECtHR, No. 30696/09, *M.S.S. v Belgium and Greece*, 2011, paras 24–264 (referring to Regulation 343/2003/EC of the Council of 18 February 2003, see para. 8.010).

[105] C-411/10 and C-493/10, *N.S. and M.E.*, 2011, paras 94 and 106; C-4/11, *Puid*, 2013, para. 30; C-394/12, *Abdullahi*, 2013, paras 60–2; C-490/16, *A.S.*, 2017, para. 41; C-646/16, *Jafari*, 2017, para. 101. See also C-163/17, *Jawo*, 2019, paras 76–98; C-297/17, *Ibrahim*, 2019, paras 81–101.

[106] Cf. 46/87 and 227/88, *Hoechst v Commission*, 1989, paras 17–18 (inviolability of the home under Article 8 ECHR held not to extend to business premises) and ECtHR, No. 13710/88, *Niemietz v Germany*, 1992, Series A, Vol. 251-B, 23; ECtHR, No. 37971/97, *Colas Est and Others v France*, 2002 (Article 8 ECHR also applies to business premises).

[107] C-94/00 *Roquette Frères*, 2002, para. 29 (see also n. 191, *infra*).

[108] See further Hirsch, 'Schutz der Grundrechte im 'Bermuda-Dreieck' zwischen Karlsruhe, Strasbourg und Luxemburg' (2006) EuR 7–18; Eaton, 'Reforming the Human Rights Protection System Established by the European Convention on Human Rights' (2005) Human Rights LJ 1–17; Callewaert, 'Het EVRM en het communautair recht: een Europese globalisering?' (2001) NTER 259–67; Krüger and Polakiewicz, 'Vorschläge

FUNDAMENTAL RIGHTS 675

That problem will be resolved when the Union accedes to the ECHR.[109] In that case, individuals will be able to contest alleged violations of fundamental rights by acts of the Union institutions before the European Court of Human Rights.

The concept of accession of the Union to the ECHR was traditionally problematic from the point of view of both the ECHR and (then) Community law. From the perspective of the ECHR, accession by the Union was problematic because the ECHR as it stood was only open to accession by the Member States of the Council of Europe. However, accession of the Union has been made possible by amendments introduced by the Fourteenth Protocol to the ECHR.[110] On the Community side, the Court of Justice declared that accession of the Community to the ECHR would entail a substantial change in the Community's system for the protection of human rights and have fundamental implications for the Community and the Member States. In view of the constitutional significance of such a change, it could be brought about only by way of an amendment of the Treaties.[111] The Lisbon Treaty carried out the necessary Treaty amendments allowing for such accession. Article 6(2) TEU provides that the Union 'shall accede' to the ECHR, whilst making it clear that such accession 'shall not affect the Union's competences as defined in the Treaties'.

Negotiations on Union accession to the ECHR. The accession of the Union requires the conclusion of an agreement that has to determine the Union's participation in the control bodies of the ECHR and ensure that individual applications are correctly addressed to the Union or the Member States.[112] In accordance with Protocol (No. 8) attached to the Treaties, the accession agreement must preserve the specific characteristics of the Union and Union law, and ensure that accession of the Union shall not affect the competences of the Union or the powers of its institutions.[113]

25.016

---

für ein kohärentes System des Menschenrechtesschutzes in Europa: Europäische Menschenrechtskonvention und EU-Grundrechtcharta' (2001) Eu GRZ 92–105.

[109] See, already, the Commission communication of 19 November 1990, SEC(90) 2087 fin, supported by the European Parliament in its resolution of 18 January 1994, OJ 1994 C44/32; see, previously, the Commission's memorandum of 4 April 1979 on the accession of the European Communities to the Convention for the Protection of Human Rights and Fundamental Freedoms (1979) EC Bull. Suppl. 2.

[110] Protocol (No. 14) to the Convention for the Protection of Human Rights and Fundamental Freedoms, amending the control system of the Convention (CETS No. 194). Article 17 of the Protocol provides for the insertion of a new para. 2 in Article 59 of the Convention, which reads: "The European Union may accede to this Convention." Following the ratification by the last member of the Council of Europe to do so (Russia), the Fourteenth Protocol entered into force on 6 June 2010.

[111] Opinion 2/94 *Accession by the Communities to the Convention for the Protection of Human Rights and Fundamental Freedoms,* 1996, paras 34–5, with notes by Bernaerts (1996) Col JEL 372–81 and Gaja (1996) CMLRev 973–89. For (in many respects well-directed) criticism, see De Schutter and Lejeune, 'L'adhésion de la Communauté à la Convention européenne des droits de l'homme. A propos de l'avis 2/94 de la Cour de justice des Communautés' (1996) CDE 555–606; Vedder, 'Die "verfassungsrechtliche Dimension"—die bisher unbekannte Grenze für Gemeinschaftshandeln? Anmerkung zum Gutachten 2/94, EMRK, des EuGH' (1996) EuR 309–19. See also Benoît-Rohmer, 'L'adhésion de l'Union à la Convention européenne des droits de l'homme' (2000) RUDH 57–61; Krüger and Polakiewicz, 'Proposals for a Coherent Human Rights Protection System in Europe' (2001) RUDH 1–14.

[112] See Protocol (No. 8), annexed by the Lisbon Treaty to the TEU and TFEU, relating to Article 6(2) TEU on the accession of the Union to the European Convention on the Protection of Human Rights and Fundamental Freedoms OJ 2010 C83/273, which provides that the agreement relating to the accession of the Union to the ECHR is to make provision for preserving the 'specific characteristics of the Union and Union law', in particular with regard to the Union's participation in the control bodies of the ECHR and the 'mechanisms necessary to ensure that proceedings by non-Member States and individual applications are correctly addressed to the Member States and/or the Union as appropriate'.

[113] Ibid., Articles 1 to 3 (which also requires that nothing in the accession agreement affects Article 344 TFEU).

In 2010 negotiations were opened between the Member States of the Council of Europe in view of an amendment of the Convention, in the framework of which the Commission were acting on behalf of the Union and which resulted in April 2013 in a draft accession agreement. According to the draft agreement, complaints could be lodged against the Union after exhaustion of domestic legal remedies. Member States would be able to act alongside the Union as co-defendants whenever complaints are brought on the compatibility with the ECHR of provisions of primary Union law. The Union would be able to act as co-defendant whenever complaints are brought against Member State measures implementing Union law.

In December 2014, the Court of Justice issued an Opinion in which it made clear that the draft accession agreement was, in several specific respects, incompatible with Article 6(2) TEU and Protocol (No. 8).[114] The Court pointed out that the control system set out in the draft accession agreement would undermine the autonomy of the EU legal system, for example by failing to recognize that as a matter of principle Member States should have faith in the observance of fundamental rights by other Member States, by allowing the European Court of Human Rights in the application of the co-defendant mechanism to rule on the interpretation of Union law and by leaving the final supervision of the compatibility with fundamental rights of CFSP acts—for which the Court of Justice has only limited competence—to a judicial organ outside the Union legal order.[115] The Court of Justice's Opinion required the Member States of the Council of Europe to continue the negotiations in view of achieving consensus on amendments to the draft accession agreement. The accession negotiations were resumed in June 2020.

On behalf of the Union, the agreement governing accession will have to be concluded by the Council, acting unanimously, after obtaining the consent of the European Parliament (Article 218(6)(a)(ii) and (8) TFEU). The decision concluding this agreement enters into force only after it has been approved by the Member States in accordance with their respective constitutional requirements (Article 218(8) TFEU). Of course, this agreement must also be ratified by the other Parties to the ECHR that are not Member States of the European Union.

C. Survey of rights protected

25.017 **Fundamental rights.** As has already been mentioned, fundamental rights enshrined in the Charter of Fundamental Rights of the European Union, the European Convention for the Protection of Human Rights and Fundamental Freedoms (ECHR), the International Covenant on Civil and Political Rights, and other international conventions, or following from the constitutional traditions common to the Member States, may be invoked in the

---

[114] Opinion 2/13, *Accession of the EU to the ECHR*, 2013. See generally, Douglas-Scott, 'The Relationship Between the EU and the ECHR Five Years on from the Treaty of Lisbon', in de Vries, Bernitz, and Weatherill (eds), *The EU Charter of Fundamental Rights as a Binding Instrument* (Hart Publishing, 2015), 21; Eeckhout, 'Opinion 2/13 on EU Accession to the ECHR and Judicial Dialogue: Autonomy or Autarky' (2015) Fordham ILJ 955; Spaventa, 'A Very Fearful Court? The Protection of Fundamental Rights in the European Union after Opinion 2/13' (2015) MJ 35; Storgaard, 'EU Law Autonomy versus European Fundamental Rights Protection—On Opinion 2/13 on EU Accession to the ECHR' (2015) HRLR 485.
[115] Opinion 2/13, *Accession of the EU to the ECHR*, 2013, paras 255–6, under reference to Opinion 1/09, *Agreement on the European and Community Patents Court*, 2011, paras 78, 80, and 89.

context of Union law. As long as the Union is not a party to the ECHR, the ECHR is not formally an act of the Union legal order. Consequently, the fundamental rights review by the Court of Justice is primarily based on the rights protected by the Charter, especially when these implement the protection provided by the ECHR in Union law.[116]

Rights enshrined in the Charter. The Charter of Fundamental Rights of the European Union brings fundamental rights together in a comprehensive document with six titles that recognize both political and civil rights and economic and social rights. Most of these provisions have resulted in an extensive case law of the Court of Justice, which can only be sampled here.

25.018

The first Title 'dignity' reaffirms human dignity (Article 1),[117] the right to life (Article 2), the right to integrity of the person (Article 3), the prohibition of torture and inhuman or degrading treatment or punishment (Article 4),[118] and the prohibition of slavery and forced labour (Article 5).

By way of 'freedoms', Title II sets forth: the right to liberty and security (Article 6);[119] respect for private and family life (Article 7);[120] protection of personal data (Article 8);[121] the right to marry and found a family (Article 9); freedom of thought, conscience, and religion (Article 10);[122] freedom of expression and information (Article 11);[123] freedom of assembly

---

[116] e.g. C-398/13 P, *Inuit Tapiriit Kanatami v Commission*, 2015, paras 45–6; C-601/15 PPU, *N.*, 2016, para. 46; T-770/16, *Korwin-Mikke v Parliament*, 2018, para. 38.

[117] e.g. C-79/13, *Saciri*, 2014, para. 35; C-353/16, *MP*, 2018, para. 36; C-297/17, C-318/17, C-319/17, and C-438/17, *Ibrahim*, 2019, paras 83–5; C-233/18, *Haqbin*, 2019, para. 46.

[118] e.g. C-404/15 and C-659/15 PPU, *Aranyosi and Căldăraru*, 2016, paras 84–8; C-578/16 PPU, *C.K.*, 2017, paras 59–69; C-353/16, *MP*, 2018, paras 36–46; C-297/17, C-318/17, C-319/17, and C-438/17, *Ibrahim*, 2019, paras 83–5; C-163/17, *Jawo*, 2019, paras 80–3; C-391/16, C-77/17, and C-78/17, *M*, 2019, para. 94; C-128/18, *Dorobantu*, 2019, paras 56–85.

[119] e.g. C-601/15 PPU, *J.N.*, 2016 para. 53; C-509/18, *PF*, 2019, para. 46; C-508/18 and C-82/19 PPU, *OG and PI*, 2019, para. 68; C-752/18, *Deutsche Umwelthilfe*, 2019, paras 44–56; C-511/18, C-512/18, and C-520/18, *La Quadrature du Net and Others*, 2020, paras 123–5.

[120] C-540/03 *European Parliament v Council*, 2006, para. 58; C-275/06 *Promusicae*, 2008, para. 64; C-450/06 *Varec*, 2008, para. 48; C-145/09, *Tsakouridis*, 2010, para 52 C-578/08; *Chakroun*, 2010, paras 44 and 63; C-356/11 and C-357/11, *O and S*, 2012, paras 79–80; C-291/12, *Schwarz*, 2013, paras 24–65; C-199/12 to C-201/12, *X, Y and Z*, 2013, paras 54 and 57; C-419/14, *WebMindLicenses*, 2015, paras 70–82; C-362/14, *Schrems*, 2015; Opinion 1/15, *Transfer of Passenger Name Record data from the European Union to Canada*, 2016, paras 150, 181, 203, 211, 215, and 217; C-203/15 and C-698/15, *Tele2 Sverige and Others*, 2016, paras 92–111; C-82/16, *K.A.*, 2018, paras 98–107; C-207/16, *Ministerio Fiscal*, 2018, paras 48–63; C-129/18, *SM*, 2019, paras 65–7; C-136/17, *GC*, 2019, para. 59; C-221/17, *Tjebbes*, 2019, paras 45–8; C-78/18, *Commission v Hungary*, 2020, paras 121–32; C-245/19 and C-246/19, *Etat luxembourgeois*, 2020, para. 96; C-511/18, C-512/18, and C-520/18, *La Quadrature du Net and Others*, 2020; C-623/17, *Privacy International*, 2020; C-746/18, *H.K.*, 2021. See Brkan, 'The Essence of the Fundamental Rights to Privacy and Data Protection: Finding the Way Through the Maze of the CJEU's Constitutional Reasoning' (2019) GLJ 864.

[121] C-92/09 and C-93/09, *Volker und Markus Schecke and Eifert*, 2010, paras 65–86; C-291/12, *Schwarz*, 2013, paras 24–65; C-131/12, *Google Spain and Google*, 2014, paras 53, 58, 68–9, and 74; C-293/12 and C-594/12, *Digital Rights Ireland*, 2014, paras 29–69; C-362/14, *Schrems*, 2015, para 39–40 and 99; Opinion 1/15, *Transfer of Passenger Name Record data from the European Union to Canada*, 2016, paras 150, 181, 203, 211, 215, and 217 C-203/15 and C-698/15, *Tele2 Sverige*, 2016, paras 92–111; C-207/16, *Ministerio Fiscal*, 2018, paras 48–63; C-136/17, *GC*, 2019, para. 59; C-78/18, *Commission v Hungary*, 2020, para. 133; C-245/19 and C-246/19, *Etat luxembourgeois*, 2020, para. 96; C-511/18, C-512/18, and C-520/18, *La Quadrature du Net and Others*, 2020; C-623/17, *Privacy International*, 2020; C-746/18, *H.K.*, 2021.

[122] e.g. C-157/15, *Achbita*, 2017, paras 27–8, and C-188/15, *Bougnaoui*, 2017, paras 29–30; C-426/16, *Liga van Moskeeën*, 2018, paras 38–80; C-25/17, *Jehovan todistajat—uskonnollinen yhdyskunta*, 2018, paras 63–75; C-336/19, *Centraal Israëlitisch Consistorie van België and Others*, 2020, paras 39–81.

[123] e.g. C-468/10 and C-469/10, *ASNEF and FECEMD*, 2011, paras 40–2; C-163/10, *Patriciello*, 2011, para. 31; C-360/10, *SABAM*, 2012, para. 48; C-314/12, *UPC Telekabel Wien*, 2014, paras 49–57; C-157/14, *Neptune Distribution*, 2015, para. 64 *et seq.*; C-203/15 and C-698/15, *Tele2 Sverige and Others*, 2016, para. 92 *et seq.*; C-547/14, *Philip Morris Brands and Others*, 2016, paras 147–56; C-161/17, *Renckhoff*, 2017, para. 41; C-516/17, *Spiegel*

and of association (Article 12);[124] freedom of the arts and sciences (Article 13);[125] the right to education (Article 14);[126] freedom to choose an occupation and the right to engage in work (Article 15);[127] freedom to conduct a business (Article 16);[128] the right to property (Article 17);[129] the right to asylum (Article 18);[130] and protection in the event of removal, expulsion, or extradition (Article 19).[131]

Under the heading 'equality', Title III recognizes: equality before the law (Article 20);[132] non-discrimination (Article 21);[133] cultural, religious, and linguistic diversity (Article 22);[134] equality between men and women (Article 23);[135] the rights of the child (Article 24);[136] the rights of the elderly (Article 25);[137] and integration of persons with disabilities (Article 26).[138]

Online, 2019, paras 40–9; C-469/17, *Funke Medien NRW*, 2019, para. 73; C-136/17, *GC*, 2019, para. 59; C-746/18, *H.K.*, 2021; C-392/19, *VG Bild-Kunst*, 2021, para. 49; C-555/19, *Fussl Modestraße Mayr*, 2021, paras 80–94. See also T-770/16, *Korwin-Mikke v Parliament*, 2018, paras 38–51 and 68.

[124] C-78/18, *Commission v Hungary*, 2020, paras 110–19.

[125] C-476/17, *Pelham*, 2019, para. 35; C-66/18, *Commission v Hungary*, 2020, paras 222–6.

[126] C-161/17, *Renckhoff*, 2017, para. 42; C-830/18, *PF and others*, 2020, para. 41; this also encompasses the freedom to found educational establishments, see C-66/18, *Commission v Hungary*, 2020, paras 229–30.

[127] C-141/11, *Hörnfeldt*, 2012, para. 37; C-544/10, *Deutsches Weintor*, 2012, para. 44; C-233/12, *Gardella*, 2013, para. 39; C-284/15, *M. and M.*, 2016, paras 33–4.

[128] e.g. C-544/10, *Deutsches Weintor*, 2012, para. 54; C-283/11, *Sky Österreich*, 2013, paras 41–67; C-101/12, *Schaible*, 2013, para. 25; C-134/15, *Lidl*, 2013, para. 27 et seq.; C-314/12, *Telekabel Wien*, 2014, para. 49; C-477/14, *Pillbox 38 (UK)*, 2016, paras 155–62; C-201/15, *AGET Iraklis*, 2016, paras 66–8; C-66/18, *Commission v Hungary*, 2020, para. 231; C-223/19, *YS*, 2020, paras 86–9 ; C-28/20, *Airhelp*, 2021, para. 49.

[129] e.g. C-227/10, *Luksan*, 2012, para. 68; C-360/10, *SABAM*, 2012, para. 41; C-12/11, *McDonagh*, 2013, paras 59–65; C-283/11, *Sky Österreich*, 2013, paras 31–40; C-416/10, *Križan and Others*, 2013, paras 113–15; C-314/12, *UPC Telekabel Wien*, 2014, paras 49–63; C-398/13 P, *Inuit Tapiriit Kanatami v Commission*, 2015, paras 60–1; C-8/15 P to C-10/15 P, *Ledra Advertising v Commission and ECB*, 2016, paras 69–74; C-477/14, *Pillbox 38 (UK)*, 2016, paras 163–4; C-161/17, *Renckhoff*, 2017, para. 41; C-258/14, *Florescu and Others*, 2017, paras 51–9; C-220/17, *Planta Tabak-Manufaktur Dr. Manfred Obermann GmbH & Co. KG*, 2019, paras 92–100; C-235/17, *Commission v. Hungary*, 2019, paras 67–89; C-469/17, *Funke Medien NRW*, 2019, para. 72 (intellectual property); C-482/17, *Czech Republic v European Parliament and Council*, 2019, paras 132–8; C-265/19, *Recorded Artists Actors Performers*, 2020, paras 85–8; C-223/19, *YS*, 2020, paras 90–2; C-392/19, *VG Bild-Kunst*, 2021, para. 54. See also C-28/20, *Airhelp*, 2021, para. 49.

[130] e.g. C-411/10 and C-493/10, *N.S.*, 2010, para. 75; C-181/16, *Gnandi*, 2018, para. 53; C-391/16, C-77/17, and C-78/17, *M*, 2019, paras 100 and 107; C-924/19 PPU and C-25/19 PPU, *FMS*, 2020, paras 175–203.

[131] e.g. C-562/13, *Abdida*, 2014, paras 46–50; C-181/16, *Gnandi*, 2018, para. 57; C-391/16, C-77/17 and C-78/17, *M*, 2019, paras 94–5; C-182/15, *Petruhhin*, 2016, paras 51–60; C-247/17, *Raugevicius*, 2018, para. 49; C-897/19 PPU, *I.N.*, 2020, paras 63–70.

[132] See, e.g., C-208/09, *Sayn-Wittgenstein*, 2010, para. 89; C-550/07 P, *Akzo Nobel Chemicals v Commission*, 2010, paras 54–9; C-390/15, *Rzecznik Praw Obywatelskich*, 2017, paras 38–40; C-113/19, *Luxaviation* (order), 2020, paras 36–9; C-634/18, *JI*, 2020, paras 41–6 ; C-555/19, *Fussl Modestraße Mayr*, 2021, paras 95–106.

[133] C-303/05 *Advocaten voor de Wereld*, 2007, para. 46; C-555/07 *Kücükdeveci*, 2010, para. 22; C-236/09, *Test Aankoop*, 2011, para. 17; C-447/09, *Prigge*, 2011, para. 38; C-566/10 P, *Italy v Commission*, 2012, para. 75; C-439/11 P, *Ziegler v Commission*, 2013, para. 132; C-528/13, *Léger*, 2015, paras 52 et seq.; C-414/16, *Egenberger*, 2018, paras 42–82; C-193/17, *Cresco Investigation*, 2018, paras 77–89; C-68/17, *IR*, 2018, paras 35, 38, and 69; C-223/19, *YS*, 2020, paras 82–5; C-336/19, *Centraal Israëlitisch Consistorie van België and Others*, 2020, paras 82–92.

[134] e.g. C-391/09, *Runevic-Vardyn and Wardyn*, 2011, para. 86; C-336/19, *Centraal Israëlitisch Consistorie van België and Others*, 2020, paras 84–94.

[135] C-236/09, *Test Aankoop*, 2011, para. 17.

[136] C-540/03 *European Parliament v Council*, 2006, para. 58; C-244/06 *Dynamic Medien*, 2008, para. 41; C-403/09 PPU, *Detiček*, 2009, paras 53–4 and 58–60; C-211/10 PPU, *Povse*, 2010, para. 64; C-400/10 PPU, *McB.*, 2010, paras 60–2; C-356/11 and C-357/11, *O and S*, 2012, paras 79–80; C-648/11, *MA and Others*, 2013, paras 57–9; C-133/15, *Chavez-Vilchez*, 2017, para. 70; C-376/16, *Piotrowski*, 2018, para. 37; C-82/16, *K.A.*, 2018, paras 98–107; C-129/18, *SM*, 2019, paras 55–72; C-221/17, *Tjebbes*, 2019, paras 45–8; C-233/18, *Haqbin*, 2019, para. 54.

[137] T-560/15 P, *LM v Commission*, para. 15.

[138] C-356/12, *Glatzel*, 2014, paras 74–86.

Under 'solidarity', Title IV covers: workers' right to information and consultation within the undertaking (Article 27);[139] the right of collective bargaining and action (Article 28);[140] the right of access to placement services (Article 29); protection in the event of unjustified dismissal (Article 30); fair and just working conditions (Article 31);[141] prohibition of child labour and protection of young people at work (Article 32);[142] the right to family and professional life (Article 33);[143] the right to social security and social assistance (Article 34);[144] the right to health care (Article 35);[145] the right to access to services of general economic interest (Article 36);[146] the right to environmental protection (Article 37);[147] and the right to consumer protection (Article 38).[148]

Title V 'citizens' rights' enshrines: the right to vote and to stand as a candidate at elections to the European Parliament (Article 39);[149] the right to vote and to stand as a candidate at municipal elections (Article 40); the right to good administration (Article 41), including the right to an impartial and fair treatment of a case by the Union institutions,[150] the right to correspond in an official language,[151] and the right to be heard and have access to a file;[152] the right of access to documents (Article 42);[153] the right to refer cases of maladministration to the European Ombudsman (Article 43);[154] the right to petition the European Parliament

---

[139] e.g. C-176/12, *Association de médiation sociale*, 2014, para. 44.

[140] e.g. C-438/05 *International Transport Workers' Federation and Finnish Seamen's Union*, 2007, paras 43–44; C-341/05 *Laval un Partneri*, 2007, paras 90–1; C-297/10 and C-298/10, *Hennigs*, 2011, para. 67; C-447/09, *Prigge*, 2011, para. 47; C-312/17, *Bedi*, 2017, paras 67–9; C-699/17, *Allianz Vorsorgekasse*, 2019, para. 56; C-28/20, *Airhelp*, 2021, para. 47.

[141] e.g. C-155/10, *Williams and Others*, 2011, para. 18; C-214/10, *KHS*, 2011, para. 37; C-579/12 RX-II, *Commission v Strack*, 2013, paras 26–39 (annual leave); C-12/17, *Dicu*, 2018, para. 25; C-147/17 *Sindicatul Familia Constanța*, 2018, paras 49–88; C-684/16, *Max-Planck-Gesellschaft zur Förderung der Wissenschaften*, 2018, paras 62–81; C-569/16 and C-570/16, *Bauer*, 2018, paras 79–92; C-619/16, *Kreuziger*, 2018, para. 29; C-609/17 and C-610/17, *TSN*, 2019, paras 41–55; C-119/19 P and C-126/19 P, *Commission and Council v Carreras Sequeros*, 2020, paras 109–28 and 132–3; see also C-55/18, *Federación de Servicios de Comisiones Obreras (CCOO)*, 2019, para. 30; C-344/20, *D.J.*, 2021, para. 27 (right of every worker to a limitation of maximum working hours and to daily and weekly rest periods).

[142] T-512/12, *Front Polisario v Council*, 2015, para. 228.

[143] C-222/14, *Maïstrellis*, 2015, para. 39; C-174/16, *H*, 2017, paras 31–2 and 44; C-366/18, *Ortiz Mesonero*, 2019, paras 44–52.

[144] E.g. C-571/10, *Kamberaj*, 2012, paras 80–92.

[145] E.g. C-28/09, *Commission v Austria*, 2011, para. 121; C-544/10, *Deutsches Weintor*, 2012, paras 45 and 55.

[146] C-121/15, *ANODE*, 2016, paras 40 and 51; C-5/19, *Overgas Mrezhi and Balgarska gazova asotsiatsia*, 2020, para. 58.

[147] e.g. C-28/09, *Commission v Austria*, 2011, para. 121; C-444/15, *Associazione Italia Nostra Onlus*, 2016, para. 62.

[148] e.g. C-470/12, *Pohotovosť*, 2014, para. 52; C-568/15, *Zentrale zur Bekämpfung unlauteren Wettbewerbs Frankfurt am Main*, 2017, para. 28; C-105/17, *Kamenova*, 2018, para. 34; C-453/18 and C-494/18, *Bondora*, 2018, paras 40 and 53–4, C-430/17, *Walbusch Walter Busch*, 2019, para. 34; T-224/10, *Test-Achats v Commission*, 2011, para. 43.

[149] C-650/13, *Delvigne*, 2015, paras 42–52; C-502/19, *Junqueras Vies*, 2019, para. 86. See Hardt, 'Fault Lines of the European Parliamentary Mandate: The Immunity of Oriol Junqueras Vies' (2020) EuConst 1–16.

[150] C-385/07 P *Der Grüne Punkt—Duales System Deutschland v Commission*, 2009, para. 179; C-439/11 P, *Ziegler v Commission*, 2013, paras 155–60; T-138/14, *Chart v European External Action Service*, 2015, paras 110–20; T-48/17, *ADDE v European Parliament*, 2019, paras 40–62.

[151] C-377/16, *Spain v European Parliament*, 2019, para. 36.

[152] C-109/10 P, *Solvay v Commission*, 2010, paras 48 and 53; C-27/09 P, *France v Commission*, 2011, para. 66; C-221/09, *AJD Tuna*, 2011, para. 49; C-277/11, *M.M.*, 2012, paras 81-92; C-584/10 P, C-593/10 P, and C-595/10 P, *Commission and Others v Kadi*, 2013, para. 98 *et seq.*; C-129/13 and C-130/13, *Kamino International Logistics and Datema Hellmann Worldwide Logistics*, 2014, para. 29; C-141/12 and C-372/12, *YS*, 2014, paras 66–8; T-314/16 and T-435/16, *VG v. Commission*, 2018, para. 101; T-48/17, *ADDE v European Parliament*, 2019, paras 32–9.

[153] C-57/16 P, *ClientEarth v Commission*, 2018, paras 73–81.

[154] C-337/15 P, *European Ombudsman v Staelen*, 2017, para. 29.

(Article 44);[155] the right to freedom of movement and of residence (Article 45);[156] and the right to diplomatic and consular protection (Article 46).

Under the heading 'justice', Title VI recognizes: the right to an effective remedy;[157] to a fair trial[158] within a reasonable time[159] by an independent and impartial tribunal[160] previously established by law;[161] and to effective legal aid[162] (Article 47),[163] the presumption of innocence,[164] and the right of defence (Article 48);[165] the principles of legality and proportionality of criminal offences and penalties (Article 49);[166] and the right not to be tried

---

[155] C-261/13 P, *Schönberger v European Parliament*, 2014, para. 14.
[156] C-162/09, *Lassal*, 2010, para. 29; C-543/12, *Zeman*, 2014, para. 39.
[157] C-432/05, *Unibet*, 2007, para. 37; C-47/07 P, *Masdar (UK) v Commission*, 2008, para. 50; C-317/08 to C-320/08 *Alassini and Others*, 2010, para. 61; C-69/10, *Samba Diouf*, 2011, paras 48–49; C- 199/11, *Commisson v Otis*, 2012, paras 56–63; C-260/11, *Edwards and Pallikaropoulos*, 2013, para. 33; C-93/12, *ET Agrokonsulting-04-Velko Stoyanov*, 2013, paras 59–60; C-501/11 P, *Schindler*, 2013, paras 33–8; C-418/11, *Texdata Software*, 2013, paras 71–9; C-510/11 P, *Kone v Commission*, 2013, paras 20–32; C-168/13 PPU, *Jeremy F*, 2013, paras 42–7; C-470/12, *Pohotovosť*, 2014, paras 53–4; C-562/13, *Abdida*, 2014, paras 51–2; C-583/13 P, *Deutsche Bahn*, 2015, paras 41–8; C-543/14, *Ordre des barreaux francophones et germanophones*, 2016, paras 27–38; C-439/14 and C-488/14, *SC Star Storage and Others*, 2016, paras 35–63; C-243/15, *LZ*, 2016, paras 54–72; C-201/16, *Shiri*, para. 44; C-682/15, *Berlioz Investment Fund*, 2017, paras 51–9 and 75–101; C-181/16, *Gnandi*, 2018, paras 52–8; C-585/16, *Alheto*, 2018, paras 102–18 and 144–9; C-556/17, *Torubarov*, 2019, paras 48–78; Opinion 1/17, *Comprehensive Economic and Trade Agreement between Canada, of the one part, and the European Union and its Member States, of the other part (CETA)*, 2019, paras 190–201; C-663/17 P, C-665/17 P, and C-669/17 P, *ECB v. Trasta Komercbanka*, 2019, paras 52–79; C-752/18, *Deutsche Umwelthilfe*, 2019, paras 29–56; C-924/19 PPU and C-925/19 PPU, *FMS*, 2020, paras 109–47 and 282–301; C-245/19 and C-246/19, *Etat luxembourgeois*, 2020, paras 54–105; C-225/19 and C-226/19, *R.N.N.S. and K.A.*, 2020, paras 32–56; C-30/19, *Braathens Regional Aviation*, 2021, paras 29–59; C-194/19, *H.A.*, 2021, paras 25.49.
[158] C-402/05 P and C-415/05 P *Kadi and Al Barakaat International Foundation*, 2008, paras 335–53; C-292/10, *G*, 2012, para 47–51; C-619/10 *Trade Agency*, 2012, paras 52–68; C-399/11, *Melloni*, 2013, para. 49; C-584/10 P, C-593/10 P, and C-595/10 P, *Commission and Others v Kadi*, 2013, para. 98 *et seq*.; C-300/11, *ZZ*, 2013, para. 53; C-530/12 P, *OHIM v National Lottery Commission*, 2014, paras 52–9; C-437/13, *Unitrading*, 2014, paras 14–35; C-127/13 P, *Strack v Commission*, 2014, para. 53; C-419/14, *WebMindLicenses*, 2015, paras 86–9; C-614/14, *Ognyanov*, 2016, para. 23; C-38/18, *Gambino and Hyka*, 2019, para. 39; see also T-54/14, *Goldfish and Others v Commission*, 2016. See further the discussion of 'general principles of Union law' in para. 25.025, *infra*.
[159] C-50/12 P, *Kendrion v Commission*, 2013, paras 77–106; C-334/12 RX-II, *Arango Jaramillo and Others v EIB*, 2013, paras 40–5.
[160] C-393/10, *O'Brien*, 2012, paras 47–8; C-64/16, *Associação Sindical dos Juízes Portugueses*, 2018, paras 27–52; C-216/18 PPU, *LM*, 2018, paras 33–79; Opinion 1/17, *Comprehensive Economic and Trade Agreement between Canada, of the one part, and the European Union and its Member States, of the other part (CETA)*, 2019, paras 189–204 and 223–44; C-585/18, C-624/18 and C-625/18, *A.K.*, 2019, paras 114–70; C-896/19, *Reppublika*, 2021, paras 47–73. See also para. 29.004, *infra*.
[161] C-127/13 P, *Strack v Commission*, 2014, paras 48–52; C-542/18 RX-II and C-543/18 RX-II, *Simpson and H.G. v Council and Commission*, 2020, paras 55–8 and 69–83.
[162] C-279/09, *DEB Deutsche Energiehandels-und Beratungsgesellschaft*, 2010, paras 31–6.
[163] On the relationship between Article 47 of the Charter and Article 19(1) TEU, see Prechal, 'Effective Judicial Protection: Some Recent Developments— Moving to the Essence' (2020) REALaw 175–90 (see also para. 29.003, *infra*). The principle of effective judicial protection laid down in Article 47 of the Charter also ensures effective judicial protection for Member States; see C-578/18 P *Czech Republic v Commission*, 2020, paras 46–85.
[164] e.g. C-220/13 P, *Nicolaou v Court of Auditors*, 2014, paras 35–7; C-74/14, *Eturas and Others*, 2016, para. 38; C-614/14, *Ognyanov*, 2016, para. 23; T-474/04 *Pergan Hilfsstoffe für industrielle Prozesse v Commission*, 2007, para. 75. This also encompasses the right to remain silent and protection against self-incrimination, see C-481/19, *Consob*, 2021, paras 34–58.
[165] e.g. C-383/13, *G and R*, 2013, para. 35; C-166/13, *Mukarubega*, 2014, paras 42–3; C-129/13, *Kamino International Logistics*, 2014, paras 28–9; C-399/11, *Melloni*, 2013, paras 47–54; C-612/15, *Kolev*, 2018, paras 101–11; C-216/18 PPU, *LM*, 2018, paras 33–79. See also para. 25.025 as to the general principle of law.
[166] C-303/05 *Advocaten voor de Wereld*, 2007, para. 46; C-105/14, *Taricco and Others*, 2015, paras 54–7; C-650/13, *Delvigne*, 2015, paras 53–7; C-218/15, *Paoletti and Others*, 2016, paras 25–42; C-42/17, *M.A.S and M.B*, 2017, paras 51–61 (clarifying the judgment in C-105/14, therefore also called 'Taricco II'); C-115/17, *Clergeau*, 2017, paras 25–41; C-384/17, *Dooel Uvoz-Izvoz Skopje Link Logistic N&N*, 2018, paras 40–3; C-113/19, *Luxaviation* (order), 2020, para. 41; C-634/18, *JI*, 2020, paras 47–51. See also para. 25.025 as to the general principle of law.

or punished twice in criminal proceedings for the same criminal offence (*ne bis in idem*, Article 50).[167]

Rights elaborated in other instruments. Even before the proclamation of the Charter of Fundamental Rights, the Court of Justice and the General Court ruled on many fundamental rights listed in the Charter,[168] such as: 25.019

- the principle of equal treatment;[169]
- the right to a fair hearing (Article 6 ECHR)[170] including the right to effective judicial control (i.e. existence of a judicial remedy; see also Article 13 ECHR),[171] the right to legal process within a reasonable time,[172] the right to judicial review by an independent and impartial judicial body,[173] the right of reply in adversarial proceedings,[174] the presumption of innocence,[175] the right of access to a lawyer,[176] and the right to call witnesses;[177]
- the principle of legality in relation to crime and punishment (*nullum crimen, nulla poena sine lege*), which implies that a provision of criminal law may not be applied

---

[167] e.g. C-617/10, *Åkerberg Fransson*, 2013, paras 30–3; C-129/14 PPU, *Spasic*, 2014, paras 56–74; C-486/14, *Kossowski*, 2016; C-217/05 and C-350/15, *Orsi and Baldetti*, 2017, paras 16–26; C-524/15, *Menci*, paras 17–64; C-596/16 and C-597/16, *di Puma and Zecca*, 2018, 24–46; C-537/16, *Garlsson Real Estate*, 2018, paras 21–63; C-234/17, *XC*, 2018, paras 20–59; C-505/19, *WS*, 2021, paras 67–106. See also para. 25.025 as to the general principle of law. See further Vervaele, 'The Application of the EU Charter of Fundamental Rights (CFR) and Its Ne bis in idem Principle in the Member States of the EU' (2013) REALaw 113.

[168] Weiler, 'Methods of Protection: Towards a Second and Third Generation of Protection', in Cassese (ed.), *Human Rights and the European Community: Methods of Protection* (Nomos, 1991), 567.

[169] e.g. C-119/19 P and C-126/19 P, *Commission and Council v Carreras Sequeros*, 2020, paras 134–40. See para. 5.051, *supra*.

[170] 98/79, *Pecastaing*, 1980, paras 21–2; T-535/93, *F. v Council*, 1995, paras 32–5. Cf. T-83/96, *Van der Wal v Commission*, 1998, paras 45–7, set aside on appeal by C-174/98 P and C-189/89 P, *Netherlands and Van der Wal v Commission*, 2000, paras 17–18; C-349/07, *Sopropé*, 2008, paras 33–7.

[171] 222/84, *Johnston*, 1986, para. 18; 222/86, *Heylens*, 1987, para. 14; C-97/91, *Oleificio Borelli v Commission*, 1992, paras 13–14; C-269/99, *Carl Kühne and Others*, 2001, paras 57–8; C-185/97, *Coote*, 1998, paras 20–2; C-402/05 P and C-415/05 P, *Kadi and Al Barakaat International Foundation v Council and Commission*, 2008, para. 335; C-501/11 P, *Schindler v Commission*, 2013, paras 33–8. This fundamental right does not require a court to grant interim measures with regard to the right of residence: C-297/88 and C-197/89, *Dzodzi*, 1990, para. 68. See also C-50/00 P, *Unión de Pequeños Agricultores v Council and Commission*, 2002, paras 32–45; C-263/02 P, *Commission v Jégo-Quéré*, 2004 (different approach to the completeness of the Union system of legal remedies and procedures by reference to Articles 6 and 13 ECHR).

[172] See the application (as a general principle of law, but applying Article 6 ECHR by analogy) in T-213/95 and T-18/96, *SCK and FNK v Commission*, 1997, paras 53–64, and the application of the principle of law derived from Article 6 ECHR to proceedings before the Court of First Instance (now General Court) in C-185/95 P, *Baustahlgewebe v Commission*, 1998, paras 20–2 and 26–48; C-238/99 P, C-244/99 P, C-245/99 P, C-247/99 P, C-250-252/99 P, and C-254/99 P, *Limburgse Vinyl Maatschappij NV and Others v Commission*, 2002, paras 164–235; C-341/06 P and C-342/06 P, *Chronopost*, 2008, paras 44–60; C-385/07 P, *Der Grüne Punkt—Duales System Deutschland v Commission*, 2009, paras 177–88.

[173] C-506/04, *Wilson*, 2006, paras 43–61; C-308/07 P, *Gorostiaga Atxalandabaso v European Parliament*, 2009, paras 41–6.

[174] C-17/98, *Emesa Sugar (Free Zone) and Aruba* (order), 2000, paras 10–18 (the fact that a party may not submit observations in response to the Advocate-General's opinion does not conflict with the right to a fair hearing; see para. 13.013, *supra*); C-450/06, *Varec*, 2008, paras 44–54 (adversarial principle).

[175] C-199/92 P, *Hüls v Commission*, 1999, paras 149–50; C-235/92 P, *Montecatini v Commission*, 1999, paras 175–6; C-189/02 P, C-202/02 P, C-205/02 P to C-208/02 P, and C-213/02 P, *Dansk Rørindustri and Others v Commission*, 2005, paras 69–76; C-344/08, *Rubach*, 2009, paras 30–1; C-45/08, *Spector Photo Group*, 2009, para. 43. See also the right not to be compelled to testify against oneself (enshrined as regards criminal matters in Article 14(3)(g) of the ICCPR), which has been enforced also in connection with complying with the rights of the defence; n. 272, *infra*).

[176] C-7/98, *Krombach*, 2000, paras 35–46; C-305/05, *Ordre des barreaux francophones et germanophone and Others*, 2007.

[177] C-189/02 P, C-202/02 P, C-205/02 P to C-208/02 P, and C-213/02 P, *Dansk Rørindustri and Others v Commission*, 2005, paras 68–75.

extensively to the detriment of the defendant[178] and that provisions of criminal law may not have retroactive effect (Article 7 ECHR)[179] and that any detention must be lawful (Article 5);[180]
- retroactive imposition of a lighter penalty (Article 15 ICCPR);[181]
- the principle *ne bis in idem* (Article 4 of the Seventh Protocol to the ECHR);[182]
- the right to human dignity[183] and the prohibition of degrading treatment (Article 3 ECHR);[184]
- respect for private life,[185] family life,[186] the home and correspondence (Article 8 ECHR),[187] in particular respect for a person's physical integrity,[188] the right to keep one's state of health private,[189] medical confidentiality,[190] and the right to inviolability of one's home;[191]
- freedom to manifest one's religion (Article 9 ECHR);[192]
- freedom of expression (Article 10 ECHR);[193]

---

[178] C-74/95 and C-129/95, *Criminal proceedings against X*, 1996, para. 25; C-266/06 P, *Evonik Degussa v Commission*, 2008, paras 38–40.

[179] 63/83, *Kirk*, 1984, para. 22; C-60/02, *Criminal proceedings against X*, 2004, para. 63; C-189/02 P, C-202/02 P, C-205/02 P to C-208/02 P, and C-213/02 P, *Dansk Rørindustri and Others v Commission*, 2005, paras 215–32; C-550/09 *E and F*, 2010, para. 59.

[180] C-752/18, *Deutsche Umwelthilfe*, 2019, para. 46.

[181] C-387/02, C-391/02, and C-403/02, *Berlusconi and Others*, 2005, para. 68.

[182] C-238/99 P, C-244/99 P, C-245/99 P, C-247/99 P, C-250-252/99 P, and C-254/99 P, *Limburgse Vinyl Maatschappij NV and Others v Commission*, 2002, paras 59–63 (see para. 25.024, *infra*); C-17/10, *Toshiba Corporation*, 2012, paras 93–103. See Wasmeier, 'The Development of Ne Bis In Idem into a Transnational Fundamental Right in EU Law: Comments on Recent Developments' (2006) ELRev 565–78.

[183] C-337/98, *Netherlands v European Parliament and Council*, 2001, paras 70–7.

[184] C-220/18 PPU, *ML*, 2018, paras 60–70 and C-128/18, *Dorobantu*, 2019, paras 70–9 (detention conditions).

[185] For the protection of personal data, see C-369/98, *Fisher and Fisher*, 2000, paras 32–8; C-465/00, C-138/01, and C-139/01, *Österreichischer Rundfunk and Others*, 2003, paras 73–90; C-518/07 *Commission v Germany*, 2010, para. 21; for the protection of confidential information and business secrets, see C-450/06, *Varec*, 2008, para. 48; C-136/17, *GC*, 2019, para. 76; C-511/18, C-512/18, and C-520/18, *La Quadrature du Net and Others*, 2020; C-623/17, *Privacy International*, 2020. See also 165/82, *Commission v United Kingdom*, 1983, para. 13, although this judgment makes no reference to the ECHR. See further Van Nuffel, 'Human Rights and Competition law—Do Undertakings Have a "Fundamental Right" of Protection of Confidential Business Information?', in Arts et al. (eds), *Mundi et Europae civis—Liber Amicorum Jacques Steenbergen* (Larcier, 2014), 579–92.

[186] 249/86, *Commission v Germany*, 1989, para. 10. See in particular with regard to family reunification, 12/86, *Demirel*, 1987, para. 28; C-60/00, *Carpenter*, 2002, paras 40–6; C-540/03, *European Parliament v Council*, 2006, para. 52 *et seq.*; C-578/08 *Chakroun*, 2010, paras 44 and 63.

[187] With regard to the Commission's powers to carry out investigations in supervising compliance with the competition rules, see 136/79, *National Panasonic v Commission*, 1980, paras 19–20; 5/85, *AKZO Chemie v Commission*, 1986, paras 25–7.

[188] C-404/92 P, *X. v Commission*, 1994, paras 17–24, in which it was held that the Commission had violated Article 8 ECHR in that, although a would-be official had refused an AIDS test, the Commission had nevertheless had a test performed on him from which the presence of the disease could be inferred; C-377/98, *Netherlands v European Parliament and Council*, 2001, paras 70 and 78–80.

[189] T-176/94, *K. v Commission*, 1995, para. 31, English abstract at I-A-203.

[190] C-62/90, *Commission v Germany*, 1992, para. 23.

[191] 46/87 and 227/88, *Hoechst v Commission*, 1989, paras 17–18 (same form of words in *Dow Benelux v Commission* and *Dow Chemical Ibérica v Commission*, cited in n. 218, *infra*) and C-94/00, *Roquette Frères*, 2002, paras 22–99 (see n. 107, *supra*); C-583/13 P, *Deutsche Bahn v Commission*, 2015, paras 19–36. See Lienemeyer and Waelbroeck (2003) CMLRev 1481–97; Kranenborg, 'Art. 8 EVRM en de verificatiebevoegdheden van de Commissie' (2003) SEW 49–57.

[192] 130/75, *Prais v Council*, 1976, paras 6–19.

[193] 43/82 and 63/82, *VBVB and VBBB v Commission*, 1984, para. 34; 60–61/84, *Cinéthèque*, 1985, paras 25–6; C-159/90, *Society for the Protection of Unborn Children Ireland*, 1991, paras 30–1; C-260/89, *ERT*, 1991, para. 44; C-219/91, *Ter Voort*, 1992, paras 35–8; C-23/93, *TV10*, 1994, paras 23–5; C-368/95, *Familiapress*, 1997, paras 18 and 25–33; C-112/00, *Schmidberger*, 2003, paras 79–80; C-71/01, *Herbert Karner Industrie-Auktionen*, 2004, paras 50–1; C-421/07, *Damgaard*, 2009, paras 25–8. For the relationship with the obligations imposed by the Staff Regulations of officials, see C-150/98 P *Economic and Social Committee v E*, 1999, paras 12–18; C-274/99 P,

- freedom of association (Article 11 ECHR)[194] and freedom of peaceful assembly,[195] in particular the right to be a member of a trade union and to take part in trade union activities;[196]
- rights of ownership or the right to property as protected by constitutional law in all Member States[197] and Article 1 of Protocol No. 1 to the ECHR,[198] including intellectual property rights;[199]
- the right to take collective action, including the right to strike;[200]
- freedom to carry on an economic activity (trade or profession);[201]
- the right of everyone lawfully within the territory of a State to liberty of movement therein and to freely choose his or her place of residence therein (Article 2 of Protocol No. 4 to the ECHR).[202]

Balancing fundamental rights. It appears from the case law that—except for the rights enshrined in Articles 1 to 4 of the Charter[203]—these fundamental rights are not unfettered prerogatives but must be viewed in the light of their social function. The Union may subject the enjoyment of fundamental rights to restrictions, provided that the restrictions 'in fact correspond to objectives of general interest pursued by the Union and that they do not constitute a disproportionate and intolerable interference which infringes upon the very substance of the right guaranteed'.[204] To the same effect, Article 52(1) of the Charter states that any limitation on the exercise of the rights and freedoms recognized therein must be provided for by law and respect the essence of those rights and freedoms and that, subject

25.020

Connolly v Commission, 2001, paras 37–56; C-340/00 P, *Commission v Cwik*, 2001, paras 17–28. See also C-100/88, *Oyowe and Traore v Commission*, 1989, para. 16, which makes no reference to the ECHR.

[194] C-415/93 *Bosman*, 1995, para. 79; T-222/99, T-327/99, and T-329/99, *Martinez and Others v European Parliament*, 2001, paras 230–5 (confirmed on the merits by C-488/01 P, *Martinez v European Parliament* (order), 2003).

[195] C-235/92 P, *Montecatini v Commission*, 1999, para. 137; C-112/00, *Schmidberger*, 2003, paras 79–80. See Mann and Ripke, 'Überlegungen zur Existenz und Reichweite eines Gemeinschaftsgrundrechts der Versammlungsfreiheit' (2004) Eu GRZ. 125–33.

[196] 36/75, *Rutili*, 1975, paras 31–2 (where Articles 8, 9, 10, and 11 ECHR are mentioned in one breath; see also n. 202, *infra*). For officials' freedom of association recognized by the Staff Regulations, as interpreted in the light of 'general principles of labour law' (with no reference to the ECHR), see 175/73, *Union Syndicale v Council*, 1974, paras 14–15; C-193 and C-194/87, *Maurissen v Court of Auditors*, 1990, paras 13–38.

[197] 4/73, *Nold v Commission*, 1974, para. 14.

[198] 44/79, *Hauer*, 1979, paras 17–30; C-347/03, *Regione autonoma Friuli-Venezia Giulia*, 2005, paras 118–33; C-402/05 P and C-415/05 P, *Kadi and Al Barakaat International Foundation*, 2008, paras 356 and 358. For a discussion, see Lenaerts and Vanvoorden, 'The Right to Property in the Case Law of the Court of Justice of the European Communities', in Vandenberghe (ed.), *Propriété et droits de l'homme/Property and Human Rights* (die Keure/La Charte, 2006), 195–240.

[199] C-479/04, *Laserdisken*, 2006, para. 65; C-275/06, *Promusicae*, 2008, para. 62.

[200] C-438/05, *International Transport Workers' Federation and Finnish Seamen's Union*, 2007, paras 43–4; C-341/05, *Laval un Partneri*, 2007, paras 90–1.

[201] 230/78, *Eridania*, 1979, paras 20–2; 240/83, *ADBHU*, 1985, paras 9–13; C-200/96, *Metronome Musik*, 1998, para. 21. This fundamental right has generally been raised before the Court of Justice together with the right to property, in which case the Court has considered them together (see 4/73, *Nold v Commission*, 1974) or considered the right to carry on a trade or profession and the right to property one after another (see 44/79, *Hauer*, 1979, paras 31–2; 265/87, *Schräder*, 1989, para. 18; and C-280/93, *Germany v Council*, 1994, paras 81–7).

[202] 36/75, *Rutili*, 1975, para. 32; C-370/05, *Festersen*, 2007, paras 35–7.

[203] These fundamental rights are absolute, see C-411/10 and C-493/10, *N.S.*, 2011, paras 86 and 94; C-404/15 and C-659/15 PPU, *Aranyosi and Căldăraru*, 2016, paras 85–6. See also Lenaerts, 'Limits on Limitations: The Essence of Fundamental Rights in the EU' (2019) GLJ 779–93.

[204] 265/87, *Schräder*, 1989, para. 15; C-200/96, *Metronome Musik*, 1998, para. 21; see also 44/79, *Hauer*, 1979, paras 23 and 30.

to the principle of proportionality, limitations may be made only if they are necessary and genuinely meet objectives of general interest recognized by the Union or the need to protect the rights and freedoms of others.[205] Any limitation to a fundamental right must thus always respect the essence of that right[206] and remain properly proportionate to the public-interest aim pursued (see also para. 7.033 *et seq.*, *supra*). When several rights guaranteed by the Charter are at stake in a case it is possible that they collide, so that it may be necessary to limit all of them in order to strike a fair balance as to the protection offered by all of them.[207] If the Union legislature has only balanced fundamental rights in respect of the territory of the Union, the territorial effect of legislation affecting fundamental rights should be limited to the Union.[208] Likewise, the ECHR declares that certain fundamental rights are to be subject to no restriction 'except such as is in accordance with the law and is necessary in a democratic society in the interests of national security, public safety or the economic well-being of the country, for the prevention of disorder or crime, for the protection of health or morals, or for the protection of the rights and freedoms of others' (Article 8 § 2 ECHR; see to the same effect Articles 9 § 2, 10 § 2, and 11 § 2 ECHR).[209]

II. General Principles of Union law

A. Status of general principles of Union law

25.021 **General principles of law.** As mentioned above, recognition of 'the law' as a source of Union law (see Article 19(1) TEU) has enabled the Court of Justice to have recourse to general principles in interpreting and applying Union law.[210] These principles form part of the Union legal order and hence infringement of them by Union institutions or bodies constitutes an 'infringement of the Treaties or of any rule of law relating to their application' within

---

[205] e.g. C-92/09 and C-93/09, *Volker und Markus Schecke and Eifert*, 2010, paras 65–86; C-12/11, *McDonagh*, 2013, para. 61; C-416/10, *Krizan and others*, 2013, para. 113; C-129/14 PPU, *Spasic*, 2014, paras 55 and 56; C-293/12 and C-594/12, *Digital Rights Ireland*, 2014, paras 38–69; C-201/15, *AGET Iraklis*, 2016, para. 70; C-528/15, *Al Chodor*, 2017, paras 38 and 40; C-524/15, *Menci*, 2018, para. 40; C-537/16, *Garlsson Real Estate*, 2018, para. 42; C-476/17, *Pelham*, 2019, paras 32–9; C-505/17, *Google*, 2019, paras 60–1; C-136/17, *GC*, 2019, para. 59; C-752/18, *Deutsche Umwelthilfe*, 2019, paras 45–52; C-245/19 and C-246/19, *Etat luxembourgeois*, 2020, para. 51; T-68/08, *FIFA v Commission*, 2011, para. 143.

[206] For examples where the Court of Justice held that the essence of the fundamental right was breached, see C-362/14, *Schrems*, 2015, paras 94–5; C-569/16 and C-570/16, *Bauer and Willmeroth*, 2018, paras 59–62. For an example where the essence of the fundamental right was not breached according to the Court of Justice, see C-28/20, *Airhelp*, 2021, para. 47.

[207] C-245/19 and C-246/19, *Etat luxembourgeois*, 2020, para. 50; see also C-275/06, *Promusicae*, 2008, paras 63–5; C-314/12, *UPC Telekabel Wien*, 2014, para. 46.

[208] C-505/17, *Google*, 2019, paras 60–72.

[209] See 36/75, *Rutili*, 1975, para. 32; 136/79, *National Panasonic v Commission*, 1980, para. 19; C-219/91, *Ter Voort*, 1992, para. 38. Compare C-112/00, *Schmidberger*, 2003, para. 79, and C-71/01, *Herbert Karner Industrie-Auktionen*, 2004, paras 50–1; C-379/08 and C-380/08, *Raffinerie Mediterrannee (ERG) and Others*, 2010, paras 80–91 (balance of interests performed by the Court of Justice having regard to the authority's margin of appreciation) with C-368/95, *Familiapress*, 1997, paras 26–33 (balance of interests left to the national legal system). For limitations of fundamental rights resulting from economic sanctions imposed by the Union, see C-84/95, *Bosphorus*, 1996, paras 21–6; C-402/05 P and C-415/05 P, *Kadi and Al Barakaat International Foundation v Council and Commission*, 2008, paras 355–71. See also the balancing of interests conducted in T-176/94 *K. v Commission*, 1995, paras 33–45.

[210] See Van Malleghem, 'Les principes généraux du droit dans la balance' (2016) CDE 39–63; Lenaerts and Gutiérrez-Fons, 'The Role of General Principles of EU Law', in Arnull et al. (eds), *A Constitutional Order of States: Essays in European Law in Honour of Alan Dashwood* (Hart Publishing, 2011), 179.

the meaning of the second paragraph of Article 263 TFEU.[211] Some general principles afford guidance for the Union's administration where it encounters ambiguities or lacunae in Union legislation which it has to apply. Other general principles are constitutional in nature and the Union institutions must comply with them when adopting legislative acts.[212] In so far as they are applicable, they apply not only to acts of Union institutions or bodies but also to measures adopted by Member States in implementing Union law[213] and at least some may be relied on against private parties and thus have horizontal direct effect.[214] As far as possible, Union acts have to be interpreted in conformity with such general principles.[215] The Court also considers the general principles of international law as forming part of the general principles of Union law (see para. 26.013, *infra*).

Sources. On some occasions, Treaty provisions explicitly refer to general principles. Thus, Article 6(3) TEU states that fundamental rights, as guaranteed by the ECHR and as they result from the constitutional traditions common to the Member States, shall constitute general principles of the Union's law. Article 340 of the TFEU (see also Article 188 EAEC) puts the Union under a duty to make good any damage caused by its institutions or by its servants in the performance of their duties 'in accordance with the general principles common to the laws of the Member States' (this being the Union regime for non-contractual liability). The general principle that an unlawful act or omission gives rise to an obligation to make good the damage caused, includes the obligation for public authorities to make good damage caused in the performance of their duties.[216] The Court of Justice applies general principles which it finds, if not expressly, at least implicitly in the legal traditions of the Member States.[217] A general principle is usually put forward where it is obviously associated with legal concepts applying in the Member States. Where, however, the existence and substance of a general principle and any possible derogations from such a principle are less

25.022

---

[211] 112/77, *Töpfer v Commission*, 1978, para. 19.

[212] C-36/02, *Omega Spielhallen*, 2004, paras 34–35; C-101/08, *Audiolux and Others*, 2009, paras 62–3; C-174/08, *NCC Construction Danmark*, 2009, paras 42 and 45.

[213] See, for instance, 260/89, *ERT*, 1991, paras 41–3; C-144/04, *Mangold*, 2005, para. 78 (principle of non-discrimination in respect of age); C-555/07, *Kücükdeveci*, 2010, paras 53–5 (principle of equal treatment); C-197/91, *FAC*, paras 23–5 (principle of lawfulness of administrative action); C-28/08, *Dokter and Others*, 2006, paras 73–8 (rights of the defence); C-206/13, *Siragusa*, 2014, paras 31, 32, and 35. See Sever, 'General Principles of Law and the Charter of Fundamental Rights' (2016) CDE 167–92; Tridimas, 'Fundamental Rights, General Principles of EU Law, and the Charter' (2014) CYELS 361; Mazak and Moser, 'Adjudication by Reference to General Principles of EU Law: A Second Look at the Mangold Case Law', in Adams et al. (eds), *Judging Europe's Judges: The Legitimacy of the Case Law of the European Court of Justice* (Hart Publishing, 2013), 61; Temple Lang, 'The Sphere in which Member States are obliged to comply with the General Principles of Law and Community Fundamental Rights Principles' (1991) LIEI 23–35.

[214] C-144/04, *Mangold*, 2005, para. 78; C-555/07, *Kücükdeveci*, 2010, paras 53–5. See Van Meerbeeck, 'De la généralité in abstracto des principes généraux à leur effet direct in concreto' (2016) CDE 65–90; Papadopoulos, 'Criticising the Horizontal Direct Effect of the EU General Principle of Equality' (2011) EHRLR 439.

[215] See, e.g., C-402/07 and C-432/07, *Sturgeon*, 2009, para. 48 (principle of equal treatment); C-340/08, *M and Others*, 2010, para. 64 (legal certainty); T-334/07, *Denka International*, 2009, para. 116 (precautionary principle).

[216] C-46/93 and C-48/93, *Brasserie du Pêcheur and Factortame* ('*Factortame IV*'), 1996, paras 28–9. See Lenaerts, 'Interlocking Legal Orders in the European Union and Comparative Law' (2003) ICLQ 873.

[217] See Schwarze, 'Tendances vers un droit administratif commun en Europe' (1993) RTDE 235–45; for an outstanding survey with numerous references to learned articles and textbooks, see Tridimas, *The General Principles of EU Law* (OUP, 2006); Schermers and Waelbroeck, *Judicial Protection in the European Union* (Kluwer, 2001); Bernitz and Nergelius (eds), *General Principles of European Community Law* (Kluwer Law International, 2000). See also Lenaerts, 'Le droit comparé dans le travail du juge communautaire' (2001) RTDE 487–528 and 'Interlocking Legal Orders in the European Union and Comparative Law' (2003) ICLQ 873–906. On the method of discovery of general principles by the ECJ and the objections thereto in *Mangold*, see: Lenaerts and Guitiérrez-Fons, 'The Constitutional Allocation of Powers and General Principles of EU Law' (2010) CMLRev 1654–660.

clear, the Court of Justice makes more exhaustive inquiries into its status in the national legal systems or in treaties that the Member States have signed.[218] This does not prevent the Court from recognizing a principle of law which can be derived neither from the constitutional traditions common to the Member States nor from international agreements. One example is the right of a legal person not to be forced to give evidence against itself in a procedure under competition law. According to the Court, this right is not derived from the constitutional traditions common to the Member States, nor from Article 6 ECHR or Article 14 of the International Covenant on Civil and Political Rights, but arises out of the rights of the defence.[219]

Moreover, several general principles of law are supported by the Charter of Fundamental Rights of the European Union.[220] Thus, the Court refers to the right to be heard, as expressed in Article 41(2) of the Charter—which sets out the right to good administration as applicable before Union institutions and bodies—as a legal principle of general application which must be observed by Member States' authorities implementing Union law.[221]

Some constitutional principles are set out in the Treaties themselves, such as the principle of sincere cooperation (Article 4(3) TEU; see para. 5.043 *et seq.*, *supra*), the principle of conferral (Article 5(2) TEU; see para. 5.010, *supra*), the principle of subsidiarity (Article 5(3) TEU; see para. 5.028 *et seq.*, *supra*), the principle of proportionality (Article 5(4) TEU; see para. 5.034 *et seq.*, *supra*) the principle of non-discrimination (*inter alia*, Article 18 TFEU; see para. 5.051 *et seq.*, *supra*); and the principle of institutional balance (Article 13(2) TEU; see para. 16.007 *et seq.*, *supra*); others are recognized by other provisions of primary or secondary Union law.[222] In one case, the Court of Justice even applied a constitutional principle against the wording of the Treaties itself, namely that of observance of institutional balance.[223] Furthermore, the Treaties provide that the Union is to recognize the rights,

---

[218] See, e.g., 155/79, *AM & S v Commission*, 1982, paras 18–22 (confidentiality of exchange of letters between lawyer and client; para. 25.024, *infra*); 46/87 and 227/88, *Hoechst v Commission*, 1989, paras 17–19, and the parallel judgments 85/87, *Dow Benelux v Commission*, 1989, paras 28–30, and 97–99/87, *Dow Chemical Ibérica v Commission*, 1989, paras 14–16 (the Court of Justice found that the legal systems of all the Member States provided protection against arbitrary or disproportionate intervention by public authorities in the sphere of a natural or legal person's private activities, but it did not extend the fundamental right of inviolability of the home to business premises; para. 25.019, *supra*). See, generally, Besson, 'General Principles and Customary law in the EU Legal Order', in Vogenauer and Weatherill (eds), *General Principles of Law: European and Comparative Perspectives* (Hart Publishing, 2017), 105.

[219] 374/87, *Orkem v Commission*, 1989, paras 32–5, and the parallel judgment 27/88, *Solvay v Commission*, 1989 (n. 272, *supra*). On the difficulty of applying principles known from the context of criminal law to competition law, see Bernardeau and Thomas, 'Principes généraux du droit et contrôle juridictionnel en droit de la concurrence—"M. Jourdain: juge pénal?"' (2016) CDE 365–84.

[220] See C-176/12, *Association de Médiation Sociale*, 2014, para. 47; C-569/16 and C-570/16, *Bauer*, 2018, para. 51; C-68/17, *IR*, 2018, paras 67–9; C-684/16, *Max-Planck-Gesellschaft zur Förderung der Wissenschaften*, 2018, para. 20; C-414/16, *Egenberger*, 2018, para. 76; C-193/17, *Cresco*, 2019, para. 76; T-54/99, *max.mobil.Telekommunikation Service v Commission*, 2002, paras 48 and 57 (concerning the right to sound administration and the right to an effective remedy before a tribunal). See Murphy, 'Using the EU Charter of Fundamental Rights Against Private Parties after Association De Médiation Sociale' (2014) EHRLR 170; Pech, 'Between Judicial Minimalism and Avoidance: The Court of Justice's Sidestepping of Fundamental Constitutional Issues in Römer and Dominguez' (2012) CMLRev 1841; Fontanelli, 'General Principles of the EU and a Glimpse of Solidarity in the Aftermath of Mangold and Kücükdeveci' (2011) E Pub L 225.

[221] See, e.g., in asylum and migration cases, C-277/11, *M.*, 2012, paras 49–50; C-166/13, *Mukarubega*, 2014, paras 41–51; C-249/13, *Boudjlida*, 2014, paras 30–41.

[222] See, e.g., the budgetary principles set out in the Financial Regulation and the Decisions on Own Resources (paras 14.011–14.012, *supra*).

[223] C-70/88, *European Parliament v Council*, 1990, paras 26–7 (discussed in para. 16.010, *supra*). For the principle of democracy, see also para. 17.046, *supra*.

freedoms, and principles set out in the Charter of Fundamental Rights (Article 6(1) TEU) and, as already indicated, proclaim that fundamental rights, as guaranteed by the ECHR and as they result from the constitutional traditions common to the Member States, constitute general principles of the Union's law (Article 6(3) TEU).

B. Survey of general principles of Union law

Principles of sound administration. According to the Charter of Fundamental Rights, every person has the right to have his or her affairs handled impartially, fairly, and within a reasonable time by the institutions and bodies of the Union.[224] In addition, the Member States may invoke the protection of that principle.[225] As set out above, Union principles of good administration may also be invoked before national authorities where the Member State concerned is implementing Union law, which offers a workaround to the fact that Article 41 of the Charter only concerns the Union itself.[226] Among the principles of law classed as 'principles of sound administration',[227] a prominent place is occupied by the principle of legal certainty, according to which legal rules must be clear and their application foreseeable for all interested parties.[228] This means, in the first place, that every Union act intended to have legal effects must be based on a provision of superior law which is expressly stated to be its legal basis (see para. 5.010 *et seq.*, *supra*). Legal certainty also requires certain requirements to be fulfilled, such as the requirement for acts to state the reasons on which they are based (see para. 27.007, *infra*) and to be notified to interested parties in a language which they understand.[229] Every measure of the institutions having legal effects must be clear and precise and must be brought to the notice of the person concerned in such a way that he or she can ascertain exactly the time at which the measure comes into being and starts to have legal effects.[230] Consequently, Union acts imposing obligations on

25.023

---

[224] Charter of Fundamental Rights, Article 41(1). See para. 25.018, *supra*.

[225] C-521/15, *Spain v Council*, 2017, paras 88–9; C-611/17, *Italy v Council*, 2019, 92–5.

[226] C-225/19 and C-226/19, *R.N.N.S and K.A.*, 2020, paras 33–4. See also C-482/10, *Cicala*, 2011, para. 28; C-141/12 and C-372/12, *YS and Others*, 2014, para. 67; and C-166/13, *Mukarubega*, 2014, para. 44.

[227] See in the Charter of Fundamental Rights of the European Union, in particular, the right to good administration (Article 41), the right of access to documents (Article 42), the right to an effective remedy and to a fair trial (Article 47), the presumption of innocence and right of the defence (Article 48), the principles of legality and proportionality of criminal offences (Article 49), and the right not to be punished twice in criminal proceedings for the same offence (Article 50). See Hoffman and Mihaescu, 'The Relation between the Charter's Fundamental Rights and the Unwritten General Principles of EU Law: Good Administration as the Test Case' (2013) EuConst 73; Lenaerts, 'Beginselen van behoorlijk bestuur in de Europese Unie', in Opdebeek and Van Damme, *Beginselen van behoorlijk bestuur* (die Keure, 2006), 67–98; Kanska, 'Towards Administrative Human Rights in the EU—Impact of the Charter of Fundamental Rights' (2004) ELJ 296–326; Lais, 'Das Recht auf eine gute Verwaltung unter besonderer Berücksichtigung der Rechtsprechung des Europäischen Gerichtshofs' (2002) ZEuS 447–82; Popelier, 'Legal Certainty and Principles of Proper Law Making' (2000) EJ L Reform 321–42.

[228] C-325/91, *France v Commission*, 1993, para. 26. For the application of legal rules interpreted by the Court of Justice, see 43/75, *Defrenne*, 1976, paras 71–5; C-143/93, *Van Es Douane Agenten*, 1996, paras 27–33; C-177/96, *Banque Indosuez and Others*, 1997, paras 26–31; C-72/10, *Criminal Proceedings against Costa*, 2012, para. 74; C-362/12, *Test Claimants in the Franked Investment Income Group Litigation*, 2013, para. 44; C-573/12, *Ålands Vindkraft*, 2014, paras 125–31; C-98/14, *Belington Hungary and Others*, 2015, para. 77. See also Van Meerbeeck, 'The Principle of Legal Certainty in the Case Law of the European Court of Justice: From Certainty to Trust' (2016) ELRev 275.

[229] 6/74, *Farrauto*, 1975, para. 6. See Raitio, 'Legal Certainty, Non-Retroactivity and Periods of Limitation in EU Law' (2008) Legisprudence 1–23.

[230] C-470/00 P, *European Parliament v Ripa di Meana and Others*, 2004, paras 65-71; T-115/94, *Opel Austria v Council*, 1997, para. 124.

individuals which are not notified to them—as well as national provisions that impose such obligations by implementing Union law—must be duly published (see para. 27.008, *infra*). Union rules must enable those concerned to know precisely the extent of the obligations which are imposed on them, in particular where they are liable to have financial consequences.[231] Further expressions of the principle of legal certainty include respect for acquired rights,[232] the requirement for measures imposing penalties to have an unambiguous legal basis (*nullum crimen, nulla poena sine lege*),[233] the fact that measures having adverse effects on individuals may not be retroactive,[234] the existence of time-limits for challenging (Union) administrative acts,[235] the importance of not calling into question judicial decisions that have become definitive (*res judicata*),[236] and the limitation period imposed for the imposition of sanctions.[237] In accordance with the principle of legal certainty, Union law, in principle, does not require an administrative body with the *power* to reopen a decision that has become final to do so if that decision was based on an incorrect application of Union law.[238] In the context of the implementation of Union law, particularly with respect to rules entailing financial consequences, legal certainty requires that the rights conferred on individuals by Union law be implemented in a way which is sufficiently precise, clear, and foreseeable to enable the persons concerned to know precisely their rights and their obligations, to take steps accordingly, and to rely on those rights, if necessary, before the national courts.[239] The introduction of a mere practice, which has no binding legal effects with regard to the persons concerned, does not meet these requirements.[240]

Individuals as well as Member States' authorities may further rely on the principle of protection of legitimate expectations. That principle protects any legitimate expectations created by the Union authorities.[241] However, the conduct of a national authority, which is

---

[231] C-158/06, *ROM-projecten*, 2007, paras 23–31; C-501/11 P, *Schindler v Commission*, 2013, paras 56–8; C-482/17, *Czech Republic v European Parliament and Council*, 2019, paras 153–6.

[232] 12/71, *Henck*, 1971, paras 4–5 (where the law is subsequently changed, the provision in question must be interpreted in the light of the law as it was at the time when the provision was applied); 10/78, *Belbouab*, 1978, para. 8.

[233] 117/83, *Könecke*, 1984, para. 11; C-308/06, *Intertanko*, 2008 (see also para. 25.019, *supra*); C-501/11 P, *Schindler Holding and Others v Commission*, 2013, paras 57–8; T-138/07, *Schindler Holding and Others v Commission*, 2011, para. 96.

[234] 63/83, *Kirk*, 1984, para. 22. A new rule may, however, be applied to future effects of situations which arose under earlier rules: 84/78, *Tomadini*, 1979, para. 21. For the retroactive entry into effect of Union measures, see para. 27.009, *infra*.

[235] C-453/00, *Kühne & Heitz*, 2004, para. 24; C-367/09, *SGS Belgium and Others*, 2011, para. 68.

[236] C-2/08, *Fallimento Olimpiclub*, 2009, para. 22; C-526/08, *Commission v Luxembourg*, 2010, paras 26–7; C-352/09, *ThyssenKrupp Nirosta v Commission*, 2011, paras 123–34; C-456/11, *Gothaer Allgemeine Versicherung and Others*, 2012, para. 40; C-539/10 P and C-550/10 P, *Stichting Al Aqsa v Council*, 2012, para. 49; C-213/13, *Impresa Pizzarotti*, 2014, paras 58–64; C-69/14, *Târşia*, paras 30 and 38; C-505/14, *Klausner Holz Niedersachsen*, 2015, para. 38; C-620/17, *Hochtief Solutions AG Magyarországi Fióktelepe*, 2019, paras 54–60.

[237] 48/69, *ICI v Commission*, 1972, para. 49; C-341/13, *Cruz & Companhia*, 2014, paras 42–65.

[238] C-453/00, *Kühne & Heitz*, 2004, paras 20–8.

[239] C-308/06, *Intertanko and Others*, 2008, para. 69.

[240] C-171/18, *Safeway*, 2019, para. 25. This applies in particular when they may have negative consequences on individuals and undertakings. See C-49/16, *Unibet International*, 2017, para. 46; C-167/17, *Klohn*, 2018, para. 50; C-611/17, *Italy v Council*, 2019, para. 111.

[241] 112/77 *Töpfer v Commission*, 1978, paras 18–20; see examples in 120/86, *Mulder*, 1988, 170/86, *von Deetzen*, 1988, and C-526/14, *Kotnik*, 2016, paras 61–9; C-606/10, *ANAFE*, 2012, paras 78–81; C-545/11, *Agrargenossenschaft Neuzelle*, 2013, paras 23–43; T-203/96, *Embassy Limousines & Services v European Parliament*, 1999, paras 73–88; T-347/03, *Branco v Commission*, 2005, para. 102. The principle of protection of legitimate expectations is often relied on in staff cases: T-123/89, *Chomel v Commission*, 1990, paras 25–31; C-119/19 P and C-126/19 P, *Commission and Council v Carreras Sequeros*, 2020, paras 141–6. It may also be invoked by Member States, e.g. C 335/09 P, *Poland v Commission*, 2012, paras 180–1. The principle of good faith is the corollary in public international law of the principle of protection of legitimate expectations: T-115/94, *Opel Austria v Council*, 1997, para. 93 (para. 26.013, *infra*). See Kolb, 'Principles as Sources of International Law (with Special Reference

responsible for applying Union law but is acting in breach of that law, cannot give rise to legitimate expectations on the part of a person of beneficial treatment contrary to Union law.[242] The existence of a mere Commission proposal for a measure[243] or the fact that the Commission remained for a long time without taking any action after delivering a reasoned opinion before bringing an action in the Court under Article 258 TFEU[244] does not create a legitimate expectation. In addition, the mere inclusion into a database of candidates, without guarantee as to employment, does not create legitimate expectations as to the continued use of that database.[245] Neither can a prudent and alert economic operator plead infringement of the principle if he or she is able to foresee that the adoption of a Union measure is likely to affect his or her interests.[246] The principle of protection of legitimate expectations may oblige a Union authority to adopt transitional measures intended to protect the expectations which traders may legitimately have derived from the retention of Union rules.[247] On account of the same principle, a legal measure cannot unconditionally be retroactively withdrawn. The retroactive withdrawal of an unlawful measure is permissible provided that the withdrawal occurs within a reasonable time and that the institution from which it emanates has had sufficient regard to how far the beneficiaries of the measure might have been led to rely on its lawfulness.[248] However, a lawful measure which has conferred individual rights or similar benefits may not be retroactively withdrawn.[249] In any event, by virtue of the principle of protection of legitimate expectations, a Union institution cannot be forced to apply Union rules *contra legem*.[250]

As to impartiality, Union institutions must comply with both components of the requirement of impartiality, which are, first, subjective impartiality, by virtue of which no member of the institution concerned may show bias or personal prejudice, and second, objective impartiality, under which there must be sufficient guarantees to exclude any legitimate doubt as to possible bias on the part of the institution concerned.[251]

---

to Good Faith)' (2006) 53 NILR 1–36. For the principle of protection of legitimate expectations in the context of procedures for State aid, see para. 9.028, *supra*.

[242] C-31/91to C-44/91, *Lageder and Others*, 1993, para. 35; C-568/11, *Agroferm*, 2013, para. 53; C-516/16, *Erzeugerorganisation Tiefkühlgemüse*, 2017, para. 69; C-120/17, *Ministru kabinets*, 2018, para. 52; C-236/18, *GRDF*, 2019, para. 50.

[243] C-13 to C-16/92, *Driessen and Others*, 1993, para. 33; C-369/09 P, *ISD Polska and Others v Commission*, 2011, para. 124.

[244] C-317/92, *Commission v Germany*, 1994, para. 4.

[245] C-377/16, *Spain v European Parliament*, 2019, paras 83–8.

[246] C-194/09 P, *Alcoa Trasformazioni v Commission*, 2011, para. 71; C-221/09, *AJD Tuna*, 2011, paras 71–3; C-585/13 P, *Europäisch-Iranische Handelsbank v Council*, 2015, para. 95; C-611/17, *Italy v Council*, 2019, para. 111.

[247] C-138/95, *Affish*, 1997, para. 57; C-182/03 and C-217/03, *Belgium and Forum 187 v Commission*, 2006, paras 147–67.

[248] 7/56 and 3/57 to 7/57, *Algera and Others v Common Assembly of the ECSC*, 1957, 116; 14/81, *Alpha Steel v Commission*, 1982, para. 10; 15/85, *Consorzio cooperative d'Abruzzo v Commission*, 1987, para. 12; T-251/00, *Lagardère and Canal+ v Commission*, 2002, paras 138–52; T-25/04, *González y Díez*, 2007, paras 94–103.

[249] 7/56 and 3/57 to 7/57, *Algera and Others v Common Assembly of the ECSC*, 1957, 115; 159/82, *Verli-Wallace*, 1983, para. 8; C-107/10, *Enel Maritsa Iztok*, 2011, paras 39–40. See Lübbig, 'Die Aufhebung (Rücknahme und Widerruf) von Verwaltungsakten der Gemeinschaftsorgane' (2003) EuZW 233–6.

[250] T-2/93, *Air France v Commission*, 1994, para. 102.

[251] C-439/11 P, *Ziegler v Commssion*, 2013, paras 154–5; C-521/15, *Spain v Council*, 2017, para. 91. See, e.g., C-680/16 P, *August Wolff and Remedia v Commission*, 2019, paras 27–8; T-783/17, *GE Healthcare v Commission*, 2019, paras 173–5.

The Court has also described the precautionary principle as a general principle of Union law requiring the competent authorities to take appropriate measures to prevent specific potential risks to public health, safety, and the environment by giving precedence to the requirements related to the protection of those interests over economic interests.[252] It follows from the precautionary principle that where there is uncertainty as to the existence or extent of risks to human health, protective measures may be taken without having to wait until the reality and seriousness of those risks become fully apparent.[253] Accordingly, where it proves to be impossible to determine with certainty the existence or extent of the alleged risk because the results of studies conducted are inconclusive, but the likelihood of real harm to public health persists should the risk materialize, the precautionary principle justifies the adoption of restrictive measures.[254] A correct application of that principle presupposes, first, identification of the potentially negative consequences for health of the regulated activity, and, second, a comprehensive assessment of the risk to health based on the most reliable scientific data available and the most recent results of international research.[255]

25.024 **Other general principles.** The Court of Justice has to rule quite frequently on whether institutions and Member States have complied with the principles of equal treatment (see para. 5.051, *supra*) and proportionality (see para. 5.034 *et seq.*, *supra*). The principle of proportionality, too, has several aspects, such as the need for sanctions to be proportional to the seriousness of the infringement found[256] and for no greater burdens to be imposed on individuals than is reasonably necessary to attain the policy aim intended.[257] In the Union

---

[252] T-13/99, *Pfizer Animal Health v Council*, 2003, paras 113–5 and T-70/99, *Alpharma v Council*, 2003, paras 134–6; T-74/00, T-76/00, T-83 to T-85/00, T-132/00, T-137/00, and T-141/00 *Artegodan and Others v Commission*, 2002, paras 182–4 (upheld on appeal: C-39/03 P, *Commission v Ategodan and Others*, 2003). See Szajkowska, 'The Impact of the Definition of the Precautionary Principle in EU Food Law' (2010) CMLRev 173–96; Heyvaert, 'Facing the Consequences of the Precautionary Principle in European Community Law' (2006) 31 ELRev 185–206; Kühn, 'Die Entwicklung des Vorsorgeprinzips im EuR.' (2006) ZEuS 487–520; MacMaoláin, 'Using the Precautionary Principle to Protect Human Health: *Pfizer v Council*' (2003) ELRev 723–34; da Cruz Vilaça, 'The Precautionary Principle in EC Law' (2004) E Pub L 369–406; Icard, 'Le principe de précaution: exception à l'application du droit communautaire?' (2002) RTDE 471–97; Alemanno, 'Le principe de précaution en droit communautaire' (2001) RTDE 917–53; Fisher, 'Is the Precautionary Principle Justiciable?' (2001) J Env L 315–34; De Sadeleer, 'Le statut juridique du principe de précaution en droit communautaire: du slogan à la règle' (2001) CDE 91–132. See also Scott, 'Legal Aspects of the Precautionary Principle', in *Brexit Briefings* (The British Academy, 2018); Ladeur, 'The Introduction of the Precautionary Principle into EU Law: A Pyrrhic Victory for Environmental and Public Health Law? Decision-making under Conditions of Complexity in Multi-level Political Systems' (2003) CMLRev 1455–79.

[253] C-616/17, *Blaise*, 2019, paras 41–3; C-528/16, *Confédération paysanne*, 2018, paras 47–53; C-78/16 and C-79/16, *Pesce*, 2016, para. 60; C-236/01, *Monsanto Agricoltura Italia and Others*, 2003, paras 111–-12, referring to T-13/99 *Pfizer Animal Health v Council*, 2003, paras 113–-15 and T-70/99, *Alpharma v Council*, 2003, paras 134–6; T-74/00, T-76/00, T-83 to T-85/00, T-132/00, T-137/00, and T-141/00, *Artegodan and Others v Commission*, 2002, paras 182–4 (upheld on appeal: C-39/03 P, *Commission v Artegodan and Others*, 2003). See also EFTA Court, E-3/00 *EFTA Surveillance Authority v Norway*, 2000–2001, para. 25, and formerly, in connection with the principle of proportionality, C-180/96, *United Kingdom v Commission*, 1998, paras 99–100; C-180/96, *National Farmers' Union and Others*, 1998, paras 63 76–111 and .

[254] C-616/17, *Blaise*, 2019, para. 43; see earlier, C-77/99, *Gowan Comércio Internacional e Serviços*, 2010, paras 73 and 76; C-477/14, *Pillbox 38 (UK)*, 2015, para. 65; C-157/14, *Neptune Distribution*, 2015, paras 81–2; C-111/16, *Fidenato*, 2017, paras 44 and 50; C-151/17, *Swedish Match*, 2018, para. 38. See Luís da Cruz Vilaça, *EU Law and Integration: Twenty Years of Judicial Application of EU law* (Hart Publishing, 2014), 329–38. However, Union institutions may not adopt decisions on the basis of a 'purely hypothetical risk' or a 'zero-risk', see: T-13/99, *Pfizer Animal Health v Council*, 2003, paras 145 and 152.

[255] C-333/08, *Commission v France*, 2010, para. 92; C-343/09, *Afton Chemical*, 2010, para. 60; C-616/17, *Blaise*, 2019, para. 46.

[256] 240/78, *Atalanta*, 1979, para. 15.

[257] 9/73, *Schlüter*, 1973, para. 22; C-217/07, *Arcelor Atlantique*, 2008, para 47; C-283/11, *Sky Österreich*, 2013, para. 50; Young and De Búrca, 'Proportionality', in Vogenauer and Weatherill (eds), *General Principles of Law: European and Comparative Perspectives* (Hart Publishing, 2017), 133. For a summary on the views of legal theorists

legal order there is also a prohibition of the abuse of law.[258] An advantage granted by Union rules may therefore not be obtained where the conditions laid down for obtaining it are created artificially and it appears, from a combination of objective circumstances that, despite formal observance of the conditions laid down by those rules, the purpose of those rules has not been achieved.[259] The application of Union legislation cannot be extended to cover abusive practices, that is to say, transactions carried out, not in the context of normal commercial operations, but solely for the purpose of wrongfully obtaining advantages provided for by Union law.[260] The Court of Justice also recognizes the principle of unjust enrichment.[261] In addition, it has recognized *force majeure* as an exceptional ground for escaping the legal consequences of failing to fulfil an obligation.[262] In the field of the common agricultural policy, *force majeure* may be relied upon in the case of abnormal and unforeseen circumstances beyond the control of the person concerned, the consequences of which could not have been avoided in spite of the exercise of all due care.[263] More generally, the principle that 'no one is obliged to do the impossible' is among the general principles of Union law.[264] In a number of cases, the Court has taken into account such principles as 'natural justice', 'fairness', and 'equity'.[265] In relations between Union institutions and bodies and their personnel, the Union Courts apply general principles of employment law.[266]

Procedural rights. In areas in which the Union has a wide discretion, the Court of Justice is strict in supervising that procedural requirements designed to ensure that individuals' interests have been duly taken into account have been complied with.[267] Many of the

25.025

---

on the different methods through which this balancing exercise can be conducted: Sauter, 'Proportionality in EU Law: A Balancing Act?' (2013) CYELS 439–66.

[258] C-110/99, *Emsland-Stärke*, 2000, paras 50–4; C-58/13 and C-59/13, *Torresi*, 2014, paras 42–51; C-364/10, *Hungary v Slovak Republic*, 2012, para. 58; C-251/16, *Cussens*, 2017, paras 25–44; C-359/16, *Altun*, 2018, para. 49; C-116/16 and C-117/16, *T Danmark*, 2019, paras 68–95; C-115/16, C-118/16, C-119/16, and C-299/16, *N Luxembourg 1*, 2019, paras 95–145 and 154–80. See Triantafyllou, 'L'interdiction des abus de droit en tant que principe général du droit communautaire' (2002) CDE 611–32; Lagondet, 'L'abus de droit dans la jurisprudence communautaire' (2003) JDE 8–12; Weber (2004) LIEI 43–5.

[259] C-110/99, *Emsland-Stärke*, 2000, para. 53; C-255/02, *Halifax and Others*, 2006, para. 81; C-456/04, *Agip Petroli*, 2006, para. 22; C-359/16, *Altun*, 2018, paras 53–61. For an in-depth analysis of the test, see: Vogenauer, 'The Prohibition of Abuse of Law: An Emerging General Principle of EU law', in de La Ferie and Vogenauer (eds), *Prohibition of Abuse of Law: A New General Principle of EU law?* (Hart Publishing, 2011), 512. See also C-610/18, *AFMB*, 2020, para. 69.

[260] C-255/02, *Halifax and Others*, 2006, paras 68–9; C-321/05, *Kofoed*, 2007, para. 38.

[261] C-47/07 P, *Masdar v Commission*, 2008, paras 44–7; C-398/09, *Lady & Kid*, 2011, paras 16–26. See also Jones, *Restitution and European Community Law* (Mansfield Press, 2000). It is possible to bring an action for damages on the basis of Articles 268 TFEU and 340 TFEU in case of damage due to unjust enrichment by the institutions, see C-575/18 P, *Czech Republic*, 2020, paras 81–2.

[262] 68/77, *IFG v Commission*, 1978, para. 11; C-334/08, *Commission v Italy*, 2010, para. 46; C-533/10, *CIVAD*, 2012, paras 24–34; C-99/12, *Eurofit*, 2013, paras 31–49; C-640/15, *Vilkas*, 2017, paras 53–7.

[263] See C-347/93, *Boterlux*, 1994, para. 34; C-209/01, *Parras Medina*, 2002, para. 19.

[264] C-622/16 P to C-624/16 P, *Scuola Elementare Maria Montessori v Commission*, 2018, para. 79.

[265] For 'fairness' and 'equity', see 31/75, *Costacurta v Commission*, 1975, para. 4; 94/75, *Süddeutsche Zucker v Hauptzollamt Mannheim*, 1976, para. 5; for other principles of law, see Schermers and Waelbroeck (n. 217, *supra*), 103–26.

[266] T-192/99, *Dunnett and Others v European Investment Bank*, 2001, paras 85 and 89–90 (employees' right to be consulted about the withdrawal of a financial advantage).

[267] C-72/15, *PJSC Rosneft Oil Company*, 2017, para. 70–6. See Gutman, 'The Essence of the Fundamental Right to an Effective Remedy and to a Fair Trial in the Case-Law of the Court of Justice of the European Union: The Best is Yet to Come?' (2019) GLJ 884; Ojanen, 'Making the Essence of Fundamental Rights Real: The Court of Justice of the European Union Clarifies the Structure of Fundamental Rights under the Charter' (2016) EuConst 318; Drabek, 'A Fair Hearing Before EC Institutions' (2001) E Rev Priv L 529–63; Lenaerts and Vanhamme, 'Procedural Rights of Private Parties in the Community Administrative Process' (1997) CMLRev 531–69.

requirements flow from fundamental rights enshrined in Article 6 ECHR and/or Article 47 of the Charter of Fundamental Rights (see paras 25.017 and 25.018).

The Court takes the view that in all proceedings in which sanctions, in particular fines or penalty payments, may be imposed, the right to be heard is a fundamental principle of Union law which must be respected even in the absence of any provision relating to the procedure in question.[268] The upshot of this is that when any administrative body adopts a measure which is liable to prejudice the interests of individuals, it is bound to put them in a position to express their point of view.[269] In order to enable them effectively to exercise the right to defend themselves, each of them must, where necessary, be informed clearly and in good time of the objections raised against them.[270] Where prior notification of the evidence adduced against a person and a prior hearing of that person would be liable to jeopardize the effectiveness of measures to be taken for the protection of imperative interests such as safeguarding public health or combating terrorism, the authorities may adopt those measures, even without first obtaining that person's views on the elements on which the measures are based. In such case, however, the evidence adduced against that person is to be notified, in so far as reasonably possible, either concomitantly with or as soon as possible after the adoption of the initial measures.[271]

Also as regards the rights of the defence, the Commission may not compel an undertaking to provide it with answers which might involve an admission on its part of the existence of the infringement which it is incumbent on the Commission to prove.[272] Union law requires that principle also to be respected as regards natural persons involved in national proceedings implementing Union law,[273] but not in proceedings that exclusively concern private relations between individuals and cannot lead directly or indirectly to the imposition of a penalty by a public authority.[274] Letters exchanged between a lawyer and his or her client are confidential if the communications were made for the purposes and in the interests of the client's right of defence and emanate from an 'independent' (that is to say, not an 'in-house') lawyer.[275] The Court further recognizes the 'fundamental legal principle' that an

---

[268] 85/76, *Hoffmann-La Roche v Commission*, 1979, para. 9; see also C-135/92, *Fiskano v Commission*, 1994, para. 39; C-89/08 P, *European Commission v Ireland and Others*, 2009, paras 50–9; C-197/09, RX-II *M v EMEA*, 2009, paras 38–59; C-129/13, *Kamino International Logistics and Datema Hellmann Worldwide Logistics*, 2014, paras 28–82. The principle of the right to a fair hearing, to which the principle of the right to be heard is closely linked, also applies to the Member States, in particular in the context of proceedings brought against them, such as those concerning the review of State aid or the monitoring of Member State conduct as regards public enterprises; see C-3/00 *Denmark v Commission*, 2003, paras 45–6.

[269] 121/76, *Moli v Commission*, 1977, para. 20; 322/81, *Michelin v Commission*, 1983, para. 7; C-300/11, *ZZ*, 2013, para. 53; C-584/10 P, C-593/10 P, and C-595/10 P, *Commission and Others v Kadi*, 2013, para. 100; T-346/94, *France-aviation v Commission*, 1995, paras 28–40; T-42/96, *Eyckeler and Malt v Commission*, 1998, paras 76–88. See also, in matters of asylum and migration, the cases mentioned in n. 221, *supra*.

[270] 17/74, *Transocean Marine Paint v Commission*, 1974, para. 15; see also T-39/92 and T-40/92, *CB and Europay v Commission*, 1994, paras 46–61.

[271] C-28/08, *Dokter and Others*, 2006, paras 73–8; C-402/05 P and C-415/05 P, *Kadi and Al Barakaat International Foundation*, 2008, paras 336–48; C-566/14, *Marchiani v European Parliament*, 2016, para. 51; T-228/02, *Organisation des Modjahedines du peuple d'Iran v Council*, 2006, paras 114–51. See also, in respect of investigations into Member States, C-521/15, *Spain v Council*, 2017, paras 61–84.

[272] 374/87, *Orkem v Commission*, 1989, paras 32–35, and the parallel judgment 27/88 *Solvay v Commission*, 1989 (this right is not derived from the constitutional traditions common to the Member States, from Article 6 ECHR or from Article 14 of the International Covenant on Civil and Political Rights, but arises out of the rights of the defence.

[273] C-481/19, *Consob*, 2020, paras 34–68.

[274] C-60/92, *Otto*, 1993, paras 11–17.

[275] 155/79, *AM & S v Commission*, 1982, paras 18–22; T-30/89, *Hilti v Commission* (order), 1991, paras 13–18; T-125/03 and T-253/03, *Akzo Nobel Chemicals and Akcros Chemicals v Commission*, 2007, paras 117–20 (affirmed on

official against whom disciplinary proceedings have been brought is entitled to be assisted by a lawyer, who must be allowed access to the file[276]. Member States, too, are entitled to see their rights of defence guaranteed when proceedings are brought against them relating to State aid control or to the acts of a Member State vis-à-vis publicly owned companies.[277]

Another principle recognized by Union law is that the Commission has to conclude an administrative procedure within a reasonable time.[278] In the field of competition law, the excessive duration of the investigation phase may compromise the rights of the defence where it would actually impede the establishment of evidence designed to refute the existence of conduct susceptible of rendering the undertakings concerned liable.[279]

The principle *ne bis in idem* means that a person cannot be adjudged or sentenced[280] for something for which he or she was already unappealably acquitted or sentenced and, for example, precludes the Union, in competition matters, from finding an undertaking guilty or bringing proceedings against it a second time on the grounds of anti-competitive conduct in respect of which it has been penalized or declared not liable by a previous unappealable Union decision.[281] Where proceedings at Union level are carried on concurrently with national proceedings with a different aim, two sanctions are not necessarily ruled out, although 'a general requirement of natural justice' demands that any previous punitive decision must be taken into account in determining any sanction which is to be imposed.[282] The *ne bis in idem* principle does not preclude the Union from imposing sanctions on a person for the same facts for which he has already been sentenced or tried outside the Union unless this is precluded by an international agreement.[283] But under the Schengen Agreement

---

appeal, see C-550/07 P, *Akzo Nobel Chemicals and Akcros Chemicals v European Commission*, 2010). See Muheme, Neyrinck and Petit, 'Procedural Rights in EU Antitrust Proceedings', in Cauffman and Hao (eds), *Procedural Rights in Competition Law in the EU and China* (Springer, 2016), 129; Gippini-Fournier, 'Legal Professional Privilege in Competition Proceedings before the European Commission: Beyond the Cursory Glance' (2005) Fordham ILJ 967–1048.

[276] 115/80, *Demont v Commission*, 1981, paras 11–12. For access to the file in competition cases, see T-30/91, *Solvay v Commission*, 1995; T-36/91, *ICI v Commission*, 1995; T-37/91 *ICI v Commission*, 1995; C-110/10 P, *Solvay v Commission*, 2011, paras 48–70.

[277] C-3/00, *Danmark v Commission*, 2003, paras 45–6.

[278] C-385/07 P, *Der Grüne Punkt—Duales System Deutschland v Commission*, 2009, paras 190–6; C-40/12, *Gascogne Sack Deutschland v Commission*, 2013, paras 81–5; T-213/95 and T-18/96, *SCK and FNK v Commission*, 1997, para. 56.

[279] C-105/04 P, *Nederlandse Federatieve Vereniging voor de Groothandel op Elektrotechnisch Gebied v Commission*, 2006, paras 35–62; C-113/04 P, *Technische Unie v Commission*, 2006, paras 40–72.

[280] C-617/10, *Åkerberg Fransson*, 2013, para. 34; C-524/15, *Menci*, 2018, paras 40–62 (limitations to the *ne bis in idem* principle). As a consequence, the *ne bis in idem* principle does not appear to have any place in the context of proceedings brought by the Commission against a Member State on the basis of Article 258 TFEU; however, the *res judicata* principle applies: C-526/08, *Commission v Luxembourg*, 2010, paras 25–37.

[281] T-305/94, T-306/94, T-307/94, T-313/94, T-314/94, T-315/94, T-316/94, T-318/94, T-325/94, T-328/94, T-329/94, and T-335/94, *Limburgse Vinyl Maatschappij NV and Others v Commission* ('PVC II'), 1999, paras 86–97, as upheld on appeal (C-238/99 P, C-244/99 P, C-245/99 P, C-247/99 P, C-250-252/99 P, and C-254/99 P *Limburgse Vinyl Maatschappij NV and Others v Commission*, 2002, paras 59–63). See Rosiak, 'The Ne Bis In Idem Principle in Proceedings Related to Anti-competitive Agreements in EU Competition Law' (2012) YARS 111; Wils, 'The Principle of Ne Bis In Idem in EC Antitrust Enforcement: A Legal and Economic Analysis' (2003) World Comp 131–48. See also 18/65 and 35/65, *Gutmann v Commission*, 1966, 119 (the principle prevents the Union from imposing two disciplinary measures for a single offence and from holding disciplinary proceedings more than once with regard to a single set of facts).

[282] 14/68, *Wilhelm*, 1969, para. 11; C-375/09, *Tele2 Polska*, 2011. See Nazzini, 'Fundamental Rights beyond Legal Positivism: Rethinking the Ne Bis In Idem Principle in EU Competition Law' (2014) J Antitrust Enforc 270.

[283] C-289/04 P, *Showa Denko v Commission*, 2006, paras 50–63; C-308/04 P, *SGL Carbon v Commission*, 2006, paras 26–38.

a person whose case has been finally disposed of in a Member State may not be prosecuted again on the same facts in another Member State.[284]

25.026 **Access to the law.** In connection with the principle of open administration, Union law recognizes an obligation to publish or notify binding acts to the parties concerned (see para. 27.008, *infra*). The right of access to documents held by public authorities, which exists in most Member States in the form of a constitutional or legislative principle, now also exists vis-à-vis the Union institutions and bodies.[285]

---

[284] C-187/01 and C-385/01, *Gözütok and Brügge*, 2003, paras 25.48; C-467/04, *Gasparini and Others*, 2006, paras 22–37; C-150/05, *Van Straaten*, 2006, paras 54–61; C-436/04, *Van Esbroeck*, 2006, paras 18–24; C-469/03, *Miraglia*, 2005, paras 28–35; C-297/07, *Bourquain*, 2008, paras 33–52; C-491/07, *Turanský*, 2008, paras 30–45; C-129/14 PPU, *Spasic*, 2014, paras 51–74 (on the *ne bis in idem* principle laid down in Article 54 of the Convention implementing the Schengen Agreement). See Sharpston and Fernández-Martin, 'Some Reflections on Schengen Free Movement Rights and the Principle of Ne bis In Idem' (2008) CYELS 413–48; Ongena, 'De *ne bis in idem*'—regel en de Schengenlanden' (2003) NJWb 762–8; Fletcher, 'Some Developments to the *Ne Bis In Idem* Principle in the European Union: *Criminal proceedings against Hüseyin Gözütok and Klaus Brügge*' (2003) MLR 769–80.

[285] C-58/94, *Netherlands v Council*, 1996, paras 34–40; C-514/11 P and C-605/11 P, *LPN and Finland v Commission*, 2013, para. 40; C-60/15, *Saint-Gobain Glass Deutschland v Commission*, 2017, para. 63. See Paivi, 'Just a Little Sunshine in the Rain: The 2010 Case Law of the European Court of Justice on Access to Documents' (2011) CMLRev 1215–52. The right of access to documents must be regarded as being a general principle of Union law, see in particular Broberg, 'Access to Documents: A General Principle of Community Law' (2002) ELRev 194–205. For access to documents, see para. 14.030, *supra*.

26
International Law

I. International Agreements Concluded by the Union

A. Legal force and direct effect of international agreements

Binding force. Article 218 TFEU lays down the procedure by which the Union concludes agreements with third countries or international organizations (see para. 21.002 *et seq.*, *supra*). Agreements concluded by the Union are binding on the Union institutions and on Member States (Article 216(2) TFEU). The provisions of such agreements form an integral part of the Union legal order from the moment they enter into force.[1] This is in accordance with the 'monist' approach: agreements concluded by the Union form part of the Union legal order without there being any necessity to transpose them into internal provisions of Union law.[2]

26.001

Exceptionally, agreements not concluded by the Union but by the Member States also have binding force. This is so when the Union has assumed, under the Treaties, the competence previously exercised by the Member State in the field to which the agreement applies.[3] This was the case with the General Agreement on Tariffs and Trade (GATT; see para. 10-010, *supra*), since the competence in connection with the application of that agreement was conferred on the Community by the EC Treaty and the Community itself subsequently took part in the tariff negotiations.[4] An agreement concluded by the Member States is also binding on the Union when the Treaties provide that the Union must exercise its competence in accordance therewith. Examples are provided by the Geneva Convention and the

---

[1] 181/73, *Haegeman*, 1974, para. 5; 104/81, *Kupferberg*, 1982, paras 11–13. For obligations entered into by the Union under international law through mere signature, see para. 21.005, *infra*. As far as the temporal effect of international agreements is concerned, unless otherwise provided, an international agreement applies to the future effects of situations which arose before the agreement entered into force: C-162/00, *Pokrzeptowicz-Meyer*, 2002, paras 48–51.

[2] Although the Court of Justice derives its jurisdiction to review such agreements from their nature as 'acts of institutions', see Rideau, 'Les accords internationaux dans la jurisprudence de la Cour de Justice des Communautés européennes: Réflexions sur les relations entre les ordres juridiques international, communautaire et nationaux' (1990) RGDIP 289, 308–312. For a survey of the status of international law in the Union legal order, see Vanhamme, *Volkenrechtelijke beginselen in het Europees recht* (Europa Law, 2001).

[3] C-379/92, *Peralta*, 1994, para. 16.

[4] 21-24/72, *International Fruit Company*, 1972, paras 10–17 (para. 10.010 *infra*). Likewise, the Community replaced the Member States with respect to commitments arising from the Convention of 15 December 1950 on the Nomenclature for the Classification of Goods in Customs Tariffs and from the Convention of the same date establishing a Customs Cooperation Council: 38/75 *Nederlandse Spoorwegen*, 1975, para. 21. This is also the case for some aspects of copyright law, see C-510/10, *DR and TV2 Danmark*, 2012, paras 29–31. In contrast, the Union has not assumed all the powers previously exercised by the Member States in the field of application of the Convention for the Unification of Certain Rules Relating to International Carriage by Air ('Warsaw Convention'); see C-301/08 *Bogiatzi*, 2009, paras 25–33, nor in the field of application of the International Convention for the Prevention of Pollution from Ships of 1973, as supplemented by the Protocol of 17 February 1978 ('Marpol 73/78'), see C-308/06, *Intertanko*, 2008, para. 48. Those conventions are not, therefore, part of the Union legal order.

Protocol relating to the status of refugees and other relevant treaties, which are binding on the Union in the matter of asylum policy (Article 78(1) TFEU).[5]

26.002 **Precedence over secondary law.** The rules ensuing from international agreements binding on the Union rank higher than acts of the Union institutions. According to the Court, 'those agreements have primacy over secondary [Union] legislation'.[6] As early as 1972, the Court considered itself bound to 'examine whether [the] validity [of acts of the institutions] may be affected by reason of the fact that they are contrary to a rule of international law'.[7] In view of the fact that international agreements concluded by the Union rank higher than provisions of secondary Union law, such provisions must, so far as is possible, be interpreted in a manner that is consistent with those agreements.[8] In its *Kadi* judgment of 2008, however, the Court clarified that international agreements binding on the Union cannot have primacy over provisions of primary Union law, including fundamental rights.[9]

Since international agreements concluded by the Union are binding on the Member States, their provisions also take precedence over national law. The Court of Justice takes the view that '[i]t follows from the [Union] nature of such provisions that their effect in the [Union] may not be allowed to vary according to whether their application is, in practice, the responsibility of the [Union] institutions or of the Member States and, in the latter case, according to the effects in the internal legal order of each Member State which the law of that State assigns to international agreements concluded by it'.[10] Accordingly, the supervision exercised by the Commission in ensuring that Member States comply with Union law also extends to making sure that they comply with international agreements binding on the Union.[11] In the case of mixed agreements, concluded jointly by the Union and the Member States, the same is true for those provisions coming within the scope of Union competence.[12] In giving effect to Union law, the Member States must apply national rules as far as possible in the light of the wording and the purpose of such agreements.[13] In a number of cases the Court of Justice has found that a national provision is incompatible with an international agreement concluded by the Union.[14] Moreover, the General

---

[5] C-175/08, C-176/08, C-178/08, and C-179/08, *Salahadin Abdulla and Others*, 2010, paras 51–53; C-31/09 *Bolbol*, 2010, para. 38; C-57/09 and C-101/09, *B and D*, 2010, paras 76–8; C-443/14 and C-444/14, *Alo and Osso*, 2016, paras 28–37.

[6] C-308/06, *Intertanko*, 2008, para. 42.

[7] 21-24/72, *International Fruit Company*, 1972, para. 6.

[8] C-61/94, *Commission v Germany*, 1996, para. 52; C-284/95, *Safety High Tech*, 1998, para. 22; C-286/02, *Bellio F.lli*, 2004, para. 33; C-335/05, *Řízení*, 2007, paras 14–21; C-228/06, *Soysal and Savatli*, 2009, para. 59; C-63/09, *Walz*, 2010, para. 22; C-115/09 *Bund für Umwelt und Naturschutz Deutschland*, 2011, para. 41; C-335/11, *HK Danmark*, 2013, paras 28–32; C-395/15 *Daouidi*, 2016, paras 40–1; C-174/15, *Vereniging Openbare Bibliotheken*, 2016, paras 31–3; C-641/18 *LG and Others*, 2020, paras 46–9; C-265/19, *Recorded Artists Actors Performers*, 2020, para. 62.

[9] C-402/05 P and C-415/05 P, *Kadi and Al Barakaat International Foundation v Council and Commission*, 2008, paras 285 and 308–9.

[10] 104/81, *Kupferberg*, 1982, para. 14. See also 38/75, *Nederlandse Spoorwegen*, 1975, para. 16.

[11] For an example regarding GATS, see C-66/18, *Commission v Hungary*, 2020, paras 68–93.

[12] C-239/03, *Commission v France*, 2004, paras 23–31; C-459/03, *Commission v Ireland*, 2006, paras 83–6 and 121.

[13] C-53/96, *Hermès International*, 1998, para. 28.

[14] See, e.g., 194 and 241/85, *Commission v Greece*, 1988 (infringement of the Second EEC-ACP Convention); C-469/93, *Chiquita Italia*, 1995, paras 54–63 (infringement of Protocol No. 5 to the Fourth ACP-EEC Convention); C-61/94, *Commission v Germany*, 1996, paras 18–58 (infringement of the International Dairy Arrangement concluded under the GATT); C-465/01, *Commission v Austria*, 2004 (infringement of the EEA Agreement and other association agreements with third countries); C-239/03, *Commission v France*, 2004, paras 33–87 (infringement of the Convention for the protection of the Mediterranean Sea against pollution); C-66/18, *Commission v Hungary*, 2020, paras 94–156 (infringement of GATS). For the failure to fulfil an obligation arising under the EEA

Court has annulled an act of a Union institution as being incompatible with such an agreement.[15]

The precedence of international agreements concluded by the Union also applies in the field of the CFSP. However, it can only rarely be judicially enforced given the limited jurisdiction of the Court in this field (see para. 13-012, *supra*).

Direct effect. In judicial proceedings, individuals may rely on a provision of an international agreement concluded by the Union only if the provision in question has direct effect.[16] The test is whether, 'regard being had to its wording and the purpose and nature of the agreement itself, the provision contains a clear and precise obligation which is not subject, in its implementation or effects, to the adoption of any subsequent measure'.[17] A provision of an international agreement concluded by the Union will thus have direct effect if that provision fulfils the general Union law requirements for direct effect (see para. 23-032, *supra*) and where, in addition, direct effect is compatible with the purpose and nature (sometimes expressed as 'the spirit, the general scheme and the terms'[18]) of the agreement in question. As regards the latter, an agreement itself may contain indications as to the effect its provisions are to have in the internal legal order of the Contracting Parties.[19] As regards the former requirements, a particular provision will have direct effect if it contains a clear and precise obligation that is not subject, in its implementation or effects, to the adoption of any subsequent measure.[20]

26.003

The Court, after examining the purpose and nature of the international agreement at issue, has in many cases held the following to have direct effect: provisions of association agreements,[21]

Agreement to accede to an international convention, see C-13/00, *Commission v Ireland*, 2002, paras 14–23. For the application of this to the area of freedom, security, and justice, see Fahey, 'Joining the Dots: External Norms, AFSJ Directives and the EU's Role in the Global Legal Order' (2016) ELRev 105–21.

[15] See T-115/94, *Opel Austria v Council*, 1997, paras 122–3 (regulation in question annulled because it breached the EEA Agreement, which constituted an infringement of the legitimate expectations of the undertaking concerned, para. 26.013, *infra*).

[16] 21-24/72, *International Fruit Company*, 1972, para. 8. In this connection, see Bonafé, 'Direct Effect of International Agreements in the EU Legal Order: Does It Depend on the Existence of an International Dispute Settlement Mechanism?', in Cannizzaro, Palchetti, and Wessel (eds), *International Law as Law of the European Union* (Brill, 2012), 229–48; Corthaut and Van Eeckhoutte, 'Doorwerking van het internationale recht in de Europese rechtsorde: verplichting en uitdaging voor de Belgische rechter' (2012) RW 402–14; Tornay, 'L'effet direct des traités internationaux dans l'ordre juridique de l'Union européenne' (2006) RDUE 325–68; Vanhamme, 'Inroepbaarheid van verdragen en volkenrechtelijke beginselen voor de Europese rechter: stand van zaken' (2001) SEW 247–56.

[17] 12/86, *Demirel*, 1987, para. 14.

[18] See 21-24/72, *International Fruit Company*, 1972, para. 20; 87/75, *Bresciani*, 1976, para. 16.

[19] 104/81, *Kupferberg*, 1982, para. 17.

[20] C-366/10, *Air Transport Association of America*, 2011, para. 55; C-401/12 P to C-403/12 P, *Council, European Parliament and Commission v Vereniging Milieudefensie and Stichting Stop Luchtverontreiniging (Utrecht)*, 2015, paras 52–5. See also Delile, 'L'invocabilité des accords internationaux devant le juge de la légalité des actes de l'Union européenne. État des lieux à l'occasion des arrêts Vereniging Milieudefensie et Stichting Natuur en Milieu' (2015) CDE 151–78; Corthaut and Van Eeckhoutte, 'Doorwerking van het internationale recht in de Europese rechtsorde: verplichting en uitdaging voor de Belgische rechter' (2012) RW 402–14.

[21] See, e.g., 87/75, *Bresciani*, 1976, paras 16–25 (1963 Yaoundé Convention, Article 2(1)); 17/81, *Papst & Richarz*, 1982, paras 25–7 (Association Agreement concluded with Greece, Article 53(1)); C-432/92, *Anastasiou and Others*, 1994, paras 23–7 (provisions of a Protocol to the Association Agreement concluded with Cyprus); C-469/93, *Chiquita Italia*, 1995, paras 30–6 and 57 (Fourth ACP-EC Convention and Protocol No. 5 thereto); T-115/94, *Opel Austria v Council*, 1997, para. 102 (EEA Agreement, Article 10); C-63/99, *Gloszcuk and Gloszcuk*, 2001, paras 29–38, and C-62/00, *Pokrzeptowicz-Meyer*, 2002, paras 20–30; C-235/99, *Kondova*, 2001, paras 30–9; C-257/99, *Barkoci and Malil*, 2001, paras 30–9; C-438/00, *Kolpak*, 2003, paras 24–30 (articles on establishment in Europe Agreements with Poland, Bulgaria, the Czech Republic, and Slovakia, respectively); C-464/14 *SECIL*, 2016, paras 97–133 (provisions of Association Agreements with Lebanon and Tunisia).

free-trade agreements,[22] cooperation agreements,[23] and some other agreements[24] concluded by the Union. A provision is not prevented from having direct effect on the ground that such effect is recognized unilaterally by the Union, but not by the other party to the agreement.[25] Neither is direct effect ruled out on the ground that the agreement provides for a special institutional framework for consultations and negotiations in relation to the implementation of the agreement or for safeguard clauses enabling the parties to derogate from certain provisions of the agreement in specific circumstances.[26]

Originally, the Court considered that even if an international agreement concluded by the Union contains provisions that do not have direct effect, in the sense that they do not create rights which individuals can rely on directly before courts, that fact does not preclude review by the courts of compliance of Union legislation with the obligations incumbent on the Union as a party to that agreement.[27] However, currently the Court rules that it will review the validity of Union legislation in the light of an international agreement only where the nature and the broad logic of the agreement do not preclude this, and, in addition, the provisions of the agreement appear, as regards their content, to be unconditional and sufficiently precise.[28] Consequently, a provision of an international agreement binding on the Union and the Member States can be invoked to review the validity of Union legislation only where its provisions have direct effect. The Court ruled out such effect with respect to the GATT/WTO Agreement (see para. 1.010, *supra*), the United Nations Convention on the Law of the Sea (Montego Bay Convention),[29] and the Kyoto Protocol on climate change.[30] However, as the Union has concluded these agreements, acts of the institutions must, as far as possible, be interpreted in conformity with them,[31] especially where those acts seek to implement such an agreement.[32]

---

[22] See 104/81 *Kupferberg*, 1982, para. 26 (Agreement concluded with Portugal, Article 21, first para.).

[23] See C-18/90, *Kziber*, 1991, paras 15–23 (Agreement concluded with Morocco, Article 41(1); confirmed by C-58/93, *Yousfi*, 1994, paras 16–19); and C-126/95, *Hallouzi-Choho*, 1996, paras 19–20, and C-416/96, *El-Yassini*, 1999 paras 25–32 (Agreement concluded with Morocco, Article 40); C-103/94, *Krid*, 1995, paras 21–4 (Agreement concluded with Algeria, Article 39(1); upheld in C-113/97, *Babahenini*, 1998, para. 17); C-162/96, *Racke*, 1998, paras 30–6 (Agreement concluded with Yugoslavia, Article 22(4)); C-37/98, *Savas*, 2000, paras 46–55 (Additional Protocol of the Agreement concluded with Turkey, Article 41(1)); C-265/03, *Simutenkov*, 2005 (Agreement concluded with Russia, Article 23(1); see case note by Hillion (2008) CMLRev 815–33.); C-97/05, *Gattoussi*, 2006, paras 24–8 (Agreement concluded with Tunesia, Article 64(1)).

[24] C-366/10, *Air Transport Association of America*, 2011, paras 80–105 (Open Sky Agreement with USA).

[25] See 104/81, *Kupferberg*, 1982, para. 18.

[26] Ibid., paras 20–1; see also C-192/89, *Sevince*, 1990, para. 25; C-469/93, *Chiquita Italia*, 1995, para. 36; C-265/03, *Simutenkov*, 2005, para. 24. For GATT and the WTO, see, however, para. 26-005, *infra*.

[27] C-377/98, *Netherlands v European Parliament and Council*, 2001, para. 54.

[28] C-344/04, *IATA and ELFAA*, 2006, para. 39; C-308/06, *Intertanko*, 2008, para. 45; C-120/06 P and C-121/06 P, *FIAMM v Council and Commission*, 2008, para. 110; C-366/10, *Air Transport Association of America*, 2011, paras 52–4; C-135/10 SCF, 2012, paras 43–8; C-363/12 Z, 2014, paras 84–90; C-543/14, *Ordre des barreaux francophones et germanophone*, 2016, paras 49–54; C-401/12 P to C-403/12 P, *Council, European Parliament and Commission v Vereniging Milieudefensie and Stichting Stop Luchtverontreiniging (Utrecht)*, 2015, paras 52–61.

[29] C-308/06, *Intertanko*, 2008, paras 54–65.

[30] C-366/10, *Air Transport Association of America*, 2011, paras 73–7.

[31] e.g. C-240/09, *Lesoochranárske zoskupenie*, 2011, paras 50–1 (in respect of provisions of the Aarhus Convention not having direct effect); C-641/18 *LG and Others*, 2020, paras 46–9 (interpretation of regulation in light of Montego Bay Convention); C-363/12, *Z*, 2014, paras 71–2 and C-395/15 *Daouidi*, 2016, paras 40–1 (due to the lack of direct effect of the United Nations Convention on the Rights of Persons with Disabilities: paras 85–90).

[32] C-135/10, *SCF*, 2012, paras 51–5 (in light of the lack of direct effect of the TRIPS-agreement and of the WIPO Performances and Phonograms Treaty (WPPT): paras 43–8); see also C-265/19, *Recorded Artists Actors Performers*, 2020, para. 62 (Article 8(2) of Directive 2006/115 is to be interpreted in the light of the requirements of the WPPT).

B. Legal force and direct effect of decisions adopted by organs set up by international agreements

International organs. The Court of Justice has further held that the legal force and possible direct effect of international agreements also apply to decisions adopted by institutions set up by the agreement which are responsible for implementing it. In Opinion 1/91 the Court noted that 'international agreements concluded by means of the procedure set out in [Article 300] of the Treaty [*now Article 218 TFEU*] are binding on the institutions of the Community and its Member States and that, as the Court of Justice has consistently held, the provisions of such agreements and the measures adopted by institutions set up by such agreements become an integral part of the Community legal order when they enter into force'.[33] The Court thereby confirmed that such provisions and measures are directly applicable. The Court had in fact previously held that decisions adopted by an association council set up by an association agreement were directly applicable on the ground that they were 'directly connected with the Association Agreement'.[34] That consideration generally holds good for decisions of institutions set up by any international agreement concluded by the Union, such as decisions of a joint committee established by a trade agreement.[35]

26.004

Provisions of such decisions have direct effect if they satisfy the requirements which provisions of the agreement itself must meet in order to have direct effect.[36] In this way, the Court of Justice has held that a number of provisions of decisions of the Association Council set up by the EEC–Turkey Agreement have direct effect.[37]

An international agreement may further provide for its own system of courts, including a court with jurisdiction to settle disputes between the Contracting Parties to the agreement,

---

[33] Opinion 1/91, *Draft agreement between the Community, on the one hand, and the countries of the European Free Trade Association, on the other, relating to the creation of the European Economic Area*, 1991, para. 37. This applies in principle for new Member States as from the date of accession; see the Council's answer of 13 February 1997 to Question No. E-1794/96 (Balfe), OJ 1997 C105/3.

[34] 30/88, *Greece v Commission*, 1989, para. 13, *in fine*; C-192/89, *Sevince*, 1990, para. 9.

[35] Nevertheless, it is often the practice to transpose into Union law decisions taken by a joint committee set up by an agreement or by a cooperation or association council: see, e.g., Article 1 of Council Regulations (EEC) Nos 2229/91, 2230/91, and 2231/91 of 17 June 1991 on the application of Decisions Nos 1/91, 2/91, and 3/91, respectively, of the EEC–Israel Cooperation Council, OJ 1991 L211: 'Decision No 1/91 [2/91 or 3/91] of the EEC-Israel Cooperation Council shall apply in the Community'. See Gilsdorf, 'Les organes institués par des accords communautaires: effets juridiques de leurs décisions. Observations à propos notamment de l'arrêt de la Cour de justice des Communautés européennes dans l'affaire C-192/89' (1992) RMCUE 328, 331–4. For the EEA Agreement, see para. 10-020, *infra*.

[36] C-192/89, *Sevince*, 1990, para. 14. For acts of bodies set up by multilateral agreements (under which the Union does not always have a right of veto), implementing measures are, however, generally still required: see Gilsdorf (n. 35, *supra*), at 336–7.

[37] Ibid., paras 17–26; C-237/91, *Kus*, 1992, paras 27–36; C-355/93, *Eroglu*, 1994, paras 11 and 17; C-171/01, *Wählergruppe Gemeinsam*, 2003, paras 54–67; C-467/02, *Cetinkaya*, 2004, paras 30–1; C-373/03, *Aydinli*, 2005, paras 24–5; C-374/03, *Gürol*, 2005, paras 19–26; C-325/05, *Derin*, 2007, paras 51–2. In the case of Decision No. 3/80, direct effect was not accepted for those provisions requiring implementing measures: cf. C-227/94, *Taflan-Met*, 1996, paras 23–38, and C-262/96, *Sürül*, 1999, paras 48–74. Likewise, direct effect was not accepted for provisions of Decision No. 1/95 that require implementing measures or merely allow or encourage a Contracting Party to take action: C-372/06, *Asda Stores*, 2007, paras 85–9, but was accepted for others, such as Article 4; see, e.g., C-65/16, *Istanbul Lojistik*, 2016, paras 36–50. See, moreover, as to Article 7 of Decision No. 2/76, C-123/17, *Yön*, 2017, para. 38.

and, as a result, to interpret its provisions.[38] In such a case, the decisions of such a court will be binding on Union institutions, including the Court of Justice.[39]

C. Status of agreements concluded within the framework of the GATT/WTO

26.005 **GATT and WTO.** The superior legal force of international agreements concluded by the Union causes them to fetter the freedom of action of the Union institutions and the Member States. The situation is somewhat different as regards the international rules which arise within the framework of the General Agreement on Tariffs and Trade (GATT) and the World Trade Organization (WTO), which do not have the same effect in the Union legal order.

As far as GATT rules are concerned, the Court has held that 'an obligation to recognise them as rules of international law which are directly applicable in the domestic legal systems of the Contracting Parties cannot be based on the spirit, general scheme or terms of GATT'.[40] The Court further stated that 'GATT, which according to its preamble is based on the principle of negotiations undertaken on the basis of 'reciprocal and mutually advantageous arrangements', is characterized by the great flexibility of its provisions, in particular those conferring the possibility of derogation, the measures to be taken when confronted with exceptional difficulties, and settlement of conflicts between the Contracting Parties'.[41] Because of these special features, the Court has never held any GATT rule to have direct effect.[42] According to the Court, such direct effect is necessary, not only in order to derive rights from the rules, but also to enable individuals to rely on them in order to contest the validity of Union acts or the application of national provisions.[43] Commentators had assumed that Member States and institutions could in fact invoke GATT provisions without direct effect for that purpose.[44] However, the Court of Justice made it clear that the special features of GATT also preclude the Court from taking account of GATT rules in assessing the legality of a regulation in annulment proceedings brought by a Member State under Article 263 TFEU.[45]

---

[38] Opinion 1/91, *Draft agreement between the Community, on the one hand, and the countries of the European Free Trade Association, on the other, relating to the creation of the European Economic Area*, 1991, paras 39–40.
[39] Ibid., para. 39. In that Opinion, the Court held, however, that the system of court machinery provided for in the (first) draft agreement creating the European Economic Area was contrary to Article 220 EC [*see now Article 19 TEU*] and, more generally, to the foundations of the Community; ns to para. 25.029, *infra*. In interpreting a provision of Union law, the Court of Justice will take a lead from the construction put on it by the EFTA Court (where the provision also applies in the EFTA States by virtue of the EEA Agreement): see, e.g., C-13/95, *Süzen*, 1997, para. 10; C-34-36/95, *De Agostini*, 1997, para. 37; C-172/99, *Liikenne*, 2001, para. 2; C-286/02, *Bellio F.lli*, 2004, paras 34 and 57–60; T-115/94, *Opel Austria v Council*, 1997, para. 108; T-13/99, *Pfizer Animal Health v Council*, 2003, paras 115 and 143; and T-70/99, *Alpharma v Council*, 2003, paras 136 and 156. For another example, see the dispute-settlement machinery of the World Trade Organization: para. 10.011, *infra*.
[40] C-280/93, *Germany v Commission*, 1994, para. 110.
[41] Ibid., para. 106; for the first such *dictum*, see 21–24/72, *International Fruit Company*, 1972, para. 21.
[42] 21-24/72, *International Fruit Company*, 1972, paras 19–27; 9/73, *Schlüter*, 1973, paras 29–30; 266/81, *SIOT*, 1983, para. 28; 267–269/81, *SPI and SAMI*, 1983, para. 23.
[43] C-469/93, *Chiquita Italia*, 1995, paras 26–9.
[44] See Hahn and Schuster, 'Zum Verstoss von gemeinschaftlichem Sekundärrecht gegen das GATT—Die gemeinsame Marktorganisation für Bananen vor dem EuGH' (1993) EuR 261, 280–1; Petersmann, 'Application of GATT by the Court of Justice of the European Communities' (1983) CMLRev 397, 415–37.
[45] C-280/93, *Germany v Commission*, 1994, para. 109, with case note by Foubert (1995) Col JEL 312–19. For a critical view, see Petersmann, 'Proposals for a New Constitution for the European Union: Building-Blocks for a

Likewise, the Court of Justice will not review the legality of Union acts in the light of agreements concluded under the auspices of the WTO.[46] Although the WTO Agreement replaced GATT with a more stringent dispute-settlement machinery, the Court of Justice has refused to recognize the agreements concluded under the auspices of the WTO as rules which may be relied upon in order to have it review the legality of acts of Union institutions, so as to allow the latter every latitude to resolve disputes with trading partners within the framework of the WTO, possibly through negotiation.[47] For those reasons, it is also not possible to review Union acts in the light of rulings of the WTO Dispute Settlement Body on the compatibility of the Union acts concerned with WTO obligations.[48]

The Court of Justice considers itself under an obligation to review the legality of a contested Union act in the light of the GATT/WTO rules in two circumstances only.[49] First, it will conduct such a review where the Union intended to implement a particular obligation entered into within the framework of the GATT/WTO, which is the case, for example, with the anti-dumping regulation adopted in order to comply with the international obligations assumed by the Union as a result of Article VI of GATT and the GATT Anti-Dumping Code adopted for the purpose of implementing that article.[50] Second, a Union act will be reviewed in the light of the GATT/WTO rules where it expressly refers to specific GATT/WTO provisions.[51] Accordingly, a measure adopted by the Union in order to comply with reports adopted under the WTO dispute settlement machinery cannot be reviewed in the

---

Constitutional Theory and Constitutional Law of the EU' (1995) CMLRev 1164–70; less critical, see Dony, 'L'affaire des bananes' (1995) CDE 461, 487–91. The Court of Justice does accept that the Commission may bring an action under Article 258 TFEU against a Member State which infringes an agreement concluded in connection with GATT; see C-61/94, *Commission v Germany*, 1996, para. 52, with case note by Eeckhout (1998) CMLRev 557–66.

[46] C-149/96, *Portugal v Council*, 1999, paras 34–52; see also C-300/98 and C-392/98, *Parfums Christian Dior and Others*, 2000, paras 41–4; C-307/99 *OGT Fruchthandelsgesellschaft* (order), 2001, paras 24–8; C-377/98, *Netherlands v European Parliament and Council*, 2001, para. 52; C-27/00 and C-122/00, *Omega Air*, 2002, paras 89–97; T-2/99, *T. Port v Council*, 2001; and T-3/99, *Bananatrading v Council*, 2001, paras 51 and 43, respectively. For a relatively approving view, see Mengozzi, 'Les droits et les intérets des entreprises, le droit de l'OMC et les prérogatives de l'Union européenne: vers une doctrine communautaire des "political questions"' (2005) RDUE 229–38; Kuijper and Bronckers, 'WTO Law in the European Court of Justice' (2005) CMLRev 1313–55; Rosas, (2000) CMLRev 797–816. For a critical view, see De Mey, 'Recent Developments on the Invocability of WTO Law in the EC: A Wave of Mutilation' (2006) E For Aff Rev 63–86; Ott, 'Der EuGH und das WTO Recht: Die Entdeckung der politischen Gegenseitigkeit—altes Phänomen oder neuer Ansatz?' (2003) EuR 504–21. In favour of a possibility of reviewing Union law in the light of WTO provisions, see, in particular, Beneyto, 'The EU and the WTO. Direct Effect of the New Dispute Settlement System?' (1996) EuZW 295–99; for a somewhat more cautious view, see Trachtman, 'Bananas, Direct Effect and Compliance' (1999) EJIL 655–78; Eeckhout, 'The Domestic Legal Status of the WTO Agreement: Interconnecting Legal Systems' (1997) CMLRev 11–58.

[47] C-149/96, *Portugal v Council*, 1999 paras 36–46; C-377/02, *Léon Van Parys*, 2005, paras 38–48.

[48] C-104/97 P, *Atlanta v Council and Commission*, 1999, para. 20; T-254/97, *Fruchthandelsgesellschaft Chemnitz v Commission*, 1999, paras 28–30; T-18/99, *Cordis Obst und Gemüse Großhandel v Commission*, 2001, paras 44–60; T-30/99, *Bocchi Food Trade International v Commission*, 2001, paras 49–65 and T-52/99, *T. Port*, 2001, paras 44–60; T-64/01 and T-65/01, *Afrikanische Frucht-Compagnie and Internationale Fruchtimport Gesellschaft Weichert & Co v Council and Commission*, 2004, paras 139–42. See, in this connection, Lavranos, 'Die Rechtswirkung von WTO panel reports im Europäischen Gemeinschaftsrecht sowie im deutschen Verfassungsrecht' (1999) EuR 289–308; Rosas, 'Implementation and Enforcement of WTO Dispute Settlement Findings: An EU Perspective' (2001) JIEL 131–44; Zonnekeyn, 'The Status of Adopted Panel and Appellate Body Reports in the European Court of Justice and the Court of First Instance' (2000) JWT 93–108.

[49] C-280/93, *Germany v Commission*, 1994, para. 111; C-149/96 *Portugal v Council*, 1999, para. 49.

[50] C-69/89, *Nakajima*, 1991, paras 29–31; C-76/00 P, *Petrotub and Republica v Council*, 2003, paras 52–63; T-162/94, *NMB France and Others v Commission*, 1996, paras 99–107; T-19/01, *Chiquita*, 2005, paras 156–71. See Desmedt, 'L'accès des particuliers aux droits et obligations de l'OMC dans la CE' (2003) TBH 357–72; Zonnekeyn, 'The ECJ's *Petrotub* Judgment: Towards a Revival of the '*Nakajima* Doctrine'?' (2003) LIEI 249–66.

[51] 70/87, *Fediol v Commission*, 1989, paras 18–22 (GATT rules invoked as part of international law with a view to a finding whether conduct constituted an illicit trade practice within the meaning of Union law.

light of those reports if the measure does not refer expressly to specific obligations ensuing from those reports.[52] The same applies with regard to the review of Union rules which are amended in order to bring them in line with a report drawn up by the Dispute Settlement Body by means of a simplified procedure (see para. 10.011, *supra*). Such rules cannot be reviewed in the light of WTO rules if it is clear from the subsequent regulations that the Union did not in any way intend to give effect to a specific obligation assumed in the context of the WTO.[53]

The fact that WTO provisions lack direct effect does not preclude the Court of Justice from having jurisdiction to interpret such provisions for the purpose of responding to the needs of the judicial authorities of the Member States where they are called upon to apply their national rules which fall within the scope of those provisions,[54] nor to rule on an action brought by the Commission against a Member State for alleged infringement of these rules.[55] Furthermore, the general international law principle of respect for contractual commitments (*pacta sunt servanda*), laid down in Article 26 of the Vienna Convention on the Law of Treaties of 23 May 1969 means that the Court must, for the purposes of interpreting and applying the WTO provisions, take account of the Dispute Settlement Body's interpretation of the various provisions of that agreement.[56] It does not release national authorities and courts from their obligation to apply national rules as far as possible in the light of the wording and purpose of those provisions. In fields in which the Union has not yet legislated, Union law does not preclude the legal order of a Member State from granting to individuals the right to rely directly on those provisions or from obliging the courts to apply those provisions of their own motion.[57]

D. Interpretation and reviewing the legality of international agreements

26.006 **Judicial review.** Where the Union acts externally by means of international agreements, that action itself is subject to judicial review. Before it is concluded, the 'agreement envisaged' may be referred to the Court of Justice for its opinion (Article 218(11) TFEU); see paras 21.016–21.017). When the agreement enters into force, it becomes *ipso facto* part of the Union legal order.

---

[52] C-377/02, *Léon Van Parys*, 2005, paras 41–54, see case notes by Egli (2006) AJIL 449–54 and Masson (2006) RMCUE 189–94; C-120/06 P and C-121/06 P, *FIAMM*, 2008, paras 114–24. See Peers, 'WTO Dispute Settlement and Community Law' (2001) ELRev 605–10; Zonnekeyn, 'The Latest on Indirect Effect of WTO Law in the EU Legal Order. The *Nakajima* Case-law Misjudged?' (2001) JIEL 597–608. See also C-207/17, *Rotho Blaas*, 2018, paras 42–57.

[53] C-351/04, *Ikea Wholesale*, 2007, paras 29–35.

[54] e.g. C-245/02, *Anheuser-Busch*, 2004, paras 40–6; C-347/03, *Regione autonoma Friuli-Venezia Giulia*, 2005, paras 103–15.

[55] See C-66/18, *Commission v Hungary*, 2020, paras 68–93.

[56] Ibid., para. 92. In addition, should the DSB not yet have interpreted the provisions concerned, it is for the Court to interpret them in accordance with the customary rules of interpretation of international law that are binding on the Union, while observing the principle, set out in Article 26, that an international agreement should be implemented in good faith (ibid).

[57] C-300/98 and C-392/98, *Parfums Christian Dior and Others*, 2000, paras 45–9; C-98/99, *Schieving-Nijstadt*, 2001, paras 54–73; C-431/05, *Merck Genéricos*, 2007, paras 34–48. For the indirect force of WTO rules in the Union legal order, see Snyder, 'The Gatekeepers: The European Courts and WTO law' (2003) CMLRev 313–67.

As an 'act of the institutions', the agreement comes within the jurisdiction of the Court to give preliminary rulings on its interpretation and validity under Article 267 TFEU.[58] With regard to mixed agreements concluded by the Union and its Member States on the basis of joint competence and without any allocation between them of their respective obligations towards the other contracting parties, the Court has jurisdiction to define the obligations which the Union has thereby assumed and, for that purpose, to interpret the provisions of the agreement.[59] The Court further considers that it has jurisdiction to interpret provisions of mixed agreements, which, in accordance with the internal division of competence between the Union and the Member States, are to be implemented by the Member States in so far as the application of national provisions falling within the scope of Union law is concerned.[60] In any event, in the case of mixed agreements, the interpretative jurisdiction applies only as far as the Union is concerned.[61] As regards the interpretation of agreements concluded by the Union with third States, the Court has stressed that, where such agreement contains provisions which are identical or comparable to provisions of the Treaties, the interpretation given to the Treaty provisions cannot be automatically applied by analogy to the interpretation of the agreement, unless there are express provisions to that effect laid down by the agreement itself.[62]

According to the Court of Justice, it is also possible to bring an action for annulment under Article 263 TFEU against the act whereby the Union institutions sought to conclude an agreement.[63] However, the annulment of such an act does not release the Union from its international obligations. In order to guarantee the rights of the contracting parties, the law of treaties confines the possibilities of annulment to cases in which the Union's consent was expressed in circumstances involving a manifest violation of a rule regarding competence which is of fundamental importance.[64] It is therefore advisable that the Union Court should invariably accompany the annulment of consent to an international agreement with a declaration that its legal effects remain unaffected.[65]

---

[58] For the first instance in the case law, see 181/73, *Haegeman*, 1974, paras 4–6.

[59] C-431/05, *Merck Genéricos*, 2007, paras 31–3.

[60] 12/86, *Demirel*, 1987, paras 8–12; C-53/96, *Hermès International*, 1998, paras 22–9; C-300/98 and C-392/98, *Parfums Christian Dior and Others*, 2000, paras 32–40; C-245/02, *Anheuser-Busch*, 2004, para. 41; C-240/09, *Lesoochranárske zoskupenie*, 2011, paras 31–43. See Lenaerts, Gutman, and Nowak, *EU Procedural Law* (OUP, 2022), Chapter 6 (interpretation) and Chapter 10 (rulings on validity); Koutrakos, 'The Interpretation of Mixed Agreements under the Preliminary Reference Procedure' (2002) E For Aff Rev 25–52; Van Nuffel and Vanovermeire, 'Over de bevoegdheid van het Hof van Justitie tot uitlegging van TRIPs en de directe werking van artikel 50 lid 6 TRIPs' (2001) TBH 445–54; Neframi, 'La compétence de la Cour de justice pour interpréter l'Accord TRIPS selon l'arrêt "Parfums Christian Dior"' (2001) RDUE 491–519; Heliskoski, 'The Jurisdiction of the European Court of Justice to Give Preliminary Rulings on the Interpretation of Mixed Agreements' (2000) Nordic JIL 395–412.

[61] See for the EEA Agreement, C-321/97, *Andersson and Andersson*, 1999, paras 26–33; C-140/97, *Rechberger and Greindl*, 1999, paras 37–8; C-300/01, *Salzmann*, 2003, paras 65–71.

[62] See para. 1-020, *supra*, for more recent applications: C-351/08, *Grimme*, 2009, paras 27–9; C-547/10 P, *Confédération suisse v Commission*, 2013, paras 78–83; see further, as regards the Association Agreement with Turkey: C-221/11 *Demirkan*, 2013; C-371/08 *Ziebell*, 2011, paras 58–74.

[63] C-327/91, *France v Commission*, 1994, paras 14–17; Opinion 3/94, *Framework Agreement on Bananas*, 1995, para. 22; C-360/93, *European Parliament v Council*, 1996; C-122/95, *Germany v Council*, 1998, para. 42; see also the earlier Opinion 1/75, *Draft Understanding on a Local Cost Standard drawn up under the auspices of the OECD*, 1975, 1361.

[64] See Article 46(2) of the Vienna Convention of 21 March 1986 on the Law of Treaties between States and International Organizations or between International Organizations (n. 112, *infra*).

[65] Vanhamme (n. 3, *supra*), at 311–15, and Kapteyn, 'Quelques réflexions sur le contrôle de la constitutionnalité des accords conclus par la Communauté avec des pays tiers', in Rodriguez Iglesias, Due, Schintgen and Elsen (eds),

In order to secure uniform application of Union law, the Court of Justice likewise has jurisdiction to give preliminary rulings on the validity and interpretation of decisions of authorities established by international agreements concluded by the Union.[66]

Since, in principle, the Court of Justice does not have jurisdiction with respect to action taken by the Union within the framework of the CFSP (see para. 13.012, *supra*), international agreements concluded in that field are not subject to the jurisdiction of the Court.

II. International Agreements Concluded by Member States with Third Countries

A. Agreements concluded after the Treaties entered into force

26.007 **Member States' agreements.** The Treaties do not preclude that Member States conclude international agreements in respect of matters which fall outside the exclusive competence of the Union.[67]

Agreements that Member States conclude with third countries or international organizations are not binding on the Union.[68] The Court of Justice has no jurisdiction to give rulings on the interpretation of provisions of international law which are binding on Member States outside the framework of Union law[69] and has no power to determine whether a national provision is compatible with such an agreement.[70] International agreements concluded by Member States are binding on the Union, however, where the Treaties refer to them or where, under the Treaties, the Union has taken over the competence formerly vested in the Member States with regard to the application of such agreements (see para. 26.001, *supra*). In order to ensure that Union law is uniformly applied, the Court may interpret provisions of such agreements with effect from the time at which the Union was substituted for the Member States.[71] Where an agreement is binding upon all the Member States, but not upon the Union, the Court endeavours to interpret Union legislation 'taking into account' the international agreement.[72]

Mélanges en hommage à Fernand Schockweiler (Nomos, 1999), 275–85, who refer in this connection to the possibilities afforded by Article 231 EC [*now Article 264 TFEU*].

[66] C-192/89, *Sevince*, 1990, paras 10–11 (decision of an association council; see also the judgments cited in n. 39, *supra*); C-188/91, *Deutsche Shell*, 1993, paras 17–18 (decision of a joint committee). As regards reviewing the validity of such decisions, see Lenaerts, Gutman, and Nowak, *EU Procedural Law* (OUP, 2022), Chapter 10. In this way, the Court may indirectly be calling into the question the validity of an international agreement; see C-28/04, *Tof's and Tod's France*, 2005, paras 18–36 (country of origin principle under the Berne Convention incompatible with principle of equal treatment (Article 18 TFEU)).
[67] C-370/12, *Pringle*, 2012, paras 68–9.
[68] For a discussion of agreements concluded between Member States, see para. 28.004 *et seq., infra*.
[69] 130/73, *Vandeweghe*, 1973, para. 2; C-457/18 *Slovenia v Croatia*, 2020, para. 91.
[70] C-379/92, *Peralta*, 1994, paras 16–17.
[71] 267-269/81, *SPI and SAMI*, 1983, paras 14–19. See also C-439/01, *Cipra and Kvasnicka*, 2003, paras 23–4 (interpretation given of AETR agreement as it was concluded by the Member States in the interest and on behalf of the Community).
[72] C-308/06, *Intertanko*, 2008, para. 52 (on the basis of 'the customary principle of good faith, which forms part of general international law, and of Article 10 EC [*now Article 4(3) TEU*]'). See also C-537/11, *Manzi and Compagnia Naviera Orchestra*, 2014, paras 45–52 (only when all Member States are bound).

In any event, the principle of sincere cooperation places a Member State under a duty to exercise its international powers without detracting from Union law[73] or from its effectiveness (*effet utile*) (see para. 5.043 *et seq.*, *supra*). Accordingly, a Member State must implement its international obligations with third countries—or with other Member States[74]—in such a way as to take account of the obligation to treat its own nationals and nationals of other Member States in the same way.[75]

B. Agreements concluded before the Treaties entered into force

Pre-existing international obligations. In establishing the Communities, the Member States sought to create reciprocal rights and obligations without detracting from their existing international obligations. For this reason, they assumed that agreements which they had concluded with third countries before the Community Treaties entered into force (1 January 1958), in principle, were not set aside by provisions of the Treaties. The Treaty provisions (now Article 351 TFEU and Articles 105 to 106 EAEC) that were adopted to this end still apply to agreements concluded at an earlier date by which Member States continue to be bound and to agreements which new Member States entered into before accession.[76] Of course, this does not mean that all the advantages which the Treaties confer on the Member States, notably the introduction of a customs union, may be extended to third States as a result of the application of agreements concluded prior to accession (see Article 351, third para. TFEU). Article 350 TFEU allows for preference to be given to agreements connected with the Benelux Economic Union. It is designed to prevent the application of Union law from causing the disintegration of the Benelux Union or from hindering its development. Benelux rules may thus be applied in derogation from Union rules only in so far as the Benelux Union is further advanced than the internal market.[77]

26.008

Precedence of international obligations. Pursuant to the first para. of Article 351 TFEU national courts must ensure that third countries' rights under earlier agreements with Member States are honoured and that the correlative obligations of Member States are fulfilled.[78] Article 351 TFEU allows for derogations from any rule of Union law, including primary law, with the exception of principles that form part of the very foundations of the

26.009

---

[73] See, e.g., C-176/97 and C-177/97, *Commission v Belgium and Luxembourg*, 1998 (agreement held to be contrary to a Community regulation); C-246/07, *Commission v Sweden*, 2010 (proposed amendment to an agreement held contrary to principle of cooperation in good faith).

[74] 235/87, *Matteucci*, 1988, paras 8–23 (bilateral social security treaty); C-376/03, *D.*, 2005, paras 58–63 (bilateral tax treaty). See also De Pauw, 'Zijn bilaterale socialezekerheidsverdragen tussen EU-lidstaten en derde landen auomatisch van toepassing op alle EU-onderdanen?' (2002) JTT 257–61. See also, as to bilateral investment treaties, C-284/16, *Achmea*, 2018, paras 31–60.

[75] C-307/97, *Saint Gobain ZN*, 1999, paras 57–8; C-55/00, *Gottardo*, 2002, paras 33–4; C-546/07 *Commission v Germany*, 2010, paras 40–2. This obligation does not apply where such equal treatment would call into question the balance and reciprocity of the relevant international agreement: *Saint Gobain ZN*, para. 59, and *Gottardo*, para. 36.

[76] See, most recently, Article 6 of the 2003 Act of Accession, of the 2005 Act of Accession, and of the 2012 Act of Accession.

[77] Compare 105/83, *Pakvries*, 1984, para. 11 and C-230/15, *Brite Strike Technologies*, 2016, paras 57–64 (priority given to Benelux customs arrangements, namely the dispute settlement mechanism for Benelux trademarks, drawings, and models) with C-473/93, *Commission v Luxembourg*, 1996, paras 42–3 (priority given to Community law as it was held to 'go further' than the relevant provision of the Benelux Treaty).

[78] 10/61, *Commission v Italy*, 1962, para. 10.

Union legal order.[79] It does not apply to a legal relationship with a third country which was not a party to the international agreement in question before the EC Treaty entered into force[80] or the relevant date of accession. In any event, the international obligations in question must be obligations whose performance may still be required by the third country.[81]

It follows that in the event of a conflict between any provision of Union law and an international obligation originating in a prior agreement concluded between a Member State and a third country, Article 351 TFEU allows for the Member State to ensure that the international obligation is complied with. By the same token, a provision of national law which is necessary in order to ensure the performance by the Member State concerned of such an international obligation may be applied even though it conflicts with a provision of Union law.[82] Where a treaty permits a Member State to take a measure which appears to conflict with Union law, yet does not put it under an obligation to do so, the Member State should refrain from such action.[83] The national court has to determine the extent to which the international obligations of the Member State are compatible with Union law.[84] As far as possible, it must interpret those obligations in a manner compatible with Union law.[85]

The application of Article 351 TFEU is subject, however, to two important limitations. First, a Member State is not entitled to rely on that article in order to derive rights vis-à-vis other Member States, contrary to Union law, from agreements concluded before the EC Treaty entered into force or before the date of accession.[86] In principle, this also holds good for multilateral agreements to which third countries—as well as Member States—are parties.[87] If, however, the multilateral agreement itself does not leave any room for the application of derogating provisions between any States party to it, it may be that application of Union law between Member States will 'jeopardise non-member countries' rights'[88] under the agreement.[89] In such a case, the first para. of Article 351 TFEU may perhaps result in the multilateral agreement being given precedence.[90] Second, Article 351 TFEU does not alter the type

---

[79] C-402/05 P and C-415/05 P, *Kadi and Al Barakaat International Foundation v Council and Commission*, 2008, paras 301–4 (which mentions in this connection the protection of fundamental rights, including the review by the Union judicature of the lawfulness of Union measures in the light of such rights).

[80] C-364/95 and C-365/95, *T Port*, 1998, paras 59–65.

[81] See, e.g., C-264/09, *Commission v Slovak Republic*, 2011, paras 29–52; see also, in the case of a division of a third country, C-216/01, *Budějovický Budvar*, 2003, paras 146–67.

[82] C-158/91, *Levy*, 1993, para. 22.

[83] C-324/93, *Evans Medical Ltd*, 1995, para. 32; C-124/95, *Centro-Com*, 1997, paras 54–60. See also C-277/10, *Luksan*, 2012, paras 61–4.

[84] C-158/91, *Levy*, 1993, para. 21.

[85] De Smijter and Vanhamme, 'Een analyse van het arrest *Levy* en zijn implicaties voor de interpretatie van artikel 234 EG-Verdrag' (1993–1994) RW 1387, 1390.

[86] See, e.g., C-475/93, *Thévenon*, 1995 (Regulation No. 1408/71 held to replace a convention between France and Germany); C-478/07, *Budějovický Budvar*, 2009, para. 99 (bilateral agreements between the Czech Republic and Austria); C-284/16, *Achmea*, 2018, paras 31–60 (bilateral investment treaty between the Netherlands and Slovakia).

[87] 10/61, *Commission v Italy*, 1962, 10 (concerning GATT); 812/79, *Burgoa*, 1980, para. 11; 121/85, *Conegate*, 1986, para. 25; 286/86, *Deserbais*, 1988, paras 17–18; C-473/93, *Commission v Luxembourg*, 1996, paras 39–40; C-301/08, *Bogiatzi*, 2009, para. 19 (Warsaw Convention).

[88] The expression was used by Advocate General J Mischo in C-221/89, *Factortame and Others* ('*Factortame II*'), 1991, AG Mischo Opinion, point 15.

[89] In his Opinion in *Factortame II*, cited in the preceding n., the Advocate General considered whether this was the case, but expressly dismissed this possibility: ibid., point 16, last para.; see also C-158/91, *Levy*, 1993, paras 13–22.

[90] For a discussion of this eventuality, see Lenaerts and De Smijter, 'Some Reflections on the Status of International Agreements in the Community Legal Order', in *Mélanges en hommage à Fernand Schockweiler* (Nomos, 1999), 347, 363.

of rights which arise out of international agreements concluded by Member States.[91] This means that an individual cannot rely on Article 351 TFEU in order to invoke a provision of such an agreement which does not have direct effect.[92]

Obligation to eliminate incompatibilities. To the extent that international agreements concluded by the Member States prior to the entry into force of the EC Treaty or the date of accession are not compatible with the Treaties, the second para. of Article 351 TFEU requires the Member State(s) concerned to take all appropriate steps to eliminate the incompatibility. Such 'incompatibility' exists not only where a prior agreement conflicts with an existing provision of Union law, but also where the agreement may impede the Union institutions from effectively exercising competences such as the power to adopt restrictive measures with respect to third countries.[93] The Member States are to take 'all appropriate steps to eliminate the incompatibilities established' and, where necessary, to 'assist each other to this end' or to 'adopt a common attitude'. Accordingly, the Member State(s) in question must start negotiations with a view to adapting the prior agreement. If such negotiations are unsuccessful, the Member State(s) will have, if possible,[94] to denunciate the agreement.[95] Where several Member States are confronted with the same incompatibility, it is for the Commission to take any steps which may facilitate mutual assistance between the Member States concerned and their adoption of a common attitude.[96] A Member State which fails to take all necessary steps to eliminate incompatibilities will be in breach of its obligations under Union law. Despite this, the application of the prior agreement will continue to be assured under the first para. of Article 351 TFEU since that provision is primarily designed to protect the rights of third countries.[97]

26.010

Impact on Union institutions. After the entry into force of the Community Treaties, international agreements concluded by Member States did not become binding on the Community (or, later, the Union) save where the Treaties referred thereto or, exceptionally, where the Communities (or, later, the Union) substituted themselves for the Member States (see para. 26.001, *supra*). The first para. of Article 351 TFEU refers only to obligations of Member States. Nevertheless, 'it would not achieve its purpose if it did not imply a duty on the part of the institutions of the [Union] not to impede the performance of the obligations of Member States which stem from a prior agreement. However, that duty of the [Union] institutions is directed only to permitting the Member State concerned to perform its obligations under the prior agreement and does not bind the [Union] as regards the third country in question.'[98] Article 351 TFEU does not debar the Union from taking action at variance with those obligations[99]

26.011

---

[91] 812/79, *Burgoa*, 1980, para. 10.
[92] C-307/99 *OGT Fruchthandelsgesellschaft* (order), 2001, paras 29–30.
[93] C-205/06, *Commission v Austria*, 2009, paras 35–40; C-249/06, *Commission v Sweden*, 2009, paras 36–41; C-118/07, *Commission v Finland*, 2009, paras 29–32.
[94] C-203/03, *Commission v Austria*, 2005, paras 61–4.
[95] C-62/98, *Commission v Portugal*, 2000, paras 49–50, and C-84/98, *Commission v Portugal*, 2000, paras 58–9. See Klabbers, 'Moribund on the Fourth of July? The Court of Justice on prior agreements of the Member States' (2001) ELRev 187–97; Manzini, 'The Priority of Pre-Existing Treaties of EC Member States within the Framework of International Law' (2001) EJIL 781–92.
[96] C-205/06, *Commission v Austria*, 2009, para. 44; C-249/06, *Commission v Sweden*, 2009, para. 44; C-118/07, *Commission v Finland*, 2009, para. 35.
[97] C-216/01, *Budějovický Budvar*, 2003, para. 172.
[98] 812/79, *Burgoa*, 1980, para. 9.
[99] Petersmann, 'Artikel 234', in von der Groeben, Thiesing, and Ehlermann (eds), *Kommentar zum EWG-Vertrag* (Nomos, 1991), 5738.

and may even require the termination of the prior bilateral agreement between a Member State and a third country if it flows from a later agreement concluded between the Union and that country that the latter no longer wishes to rely on the rights under the previous agreement and envisages its termination upon entry into force of the agreement with the Union.[100]

III. Other Rules of International Law

26.012 **International law.** It is clear from the provisions of Article 351 TFEU itself that it is the Union's intention to fit in with international law. The Court of Justice has declared that the Union must respect international law in the exercise of its competences[101] and that it may therefore examine whether the validity of Union acts is affected by reason of the fact that they are contrary to 'a rule of international law'.[102] The competences of the Union must also be exercised in observance of the undertakings given in the context of the United Nations and other international organizations.[103] Since the Lisbon Treaty, 'respect for the principles of the United Nations Charter and international law' is one of objectives of the Union's external action (Article 21(1), first para. TEU).

A. Customary international law and general principles of law

26.013 **Principles of international law.** Not only provisions of international agreements binding on the Union act as sources of Union law. Mention has already been made of the general principles of law, among which the Court of Justice includes fundamental rights, *inter alia*, as enshrined in treaties on human rights concluded by the Member States (see para. 25.004, *supra*). In interpreting and applying Union law, the Court of Justice also takes customary international law into account.[104] The Court also applies principles of international law, such as the principle of self-determination,[105] the territoriality principle as limiting the extent of the Union's institutions' powers,[106] the immunity of States from jurisdiction for

---

[100] Opinion 2/15, *Free Trade Agreement between the European Union and the Republic of Singapore*, 2017, paras 253–4.
[101] C-286/90, *Poulsen and Diva Navigation*, 1992, para. 9; C-386/08 *Brita*, 2010, paras 39–41.
[102] 21-24/72, *International Fruit Company*, 1972, para. 6. For a survey, see Meessen, 'The Application of Rules of Public International Law within Community Law' (1976) CMLRev 485–501 and, more recently, Vanhamme (n. 2, *supra*), at 255–330.
[103] C-402/05 P and C-415/05 P, *Kadi and Al Barakaat International Foundation v Council and Commission*, 2008, paras 291–7.
[104] C-286/90, *Poulsen and Diva Navigation*, 1992, paras 10, 13–16, and 25–9 (customary law in the context of the law of the sea); C-104/16 P, *Council v Front Polisario*, 2016, paras 88–93 and 123; C-266/16, *Western Sahara Campaign UK*, 2018, para. 47; C-66/18, *Commission v Hungary*, 2020, para. 88. See also, by implication, C-221/89, *Factortame and Others* ('*Factortame II*'), 1991, paras 15–16. See, generally, Delile, 'Les effets de la coutume internationale dans l'ordre juridique de l'Union européenne' (2017) CDE 159–92; Gianelli, 'International Law Within the EU—Customary International Law in the European Union', in Cannizzaro, Palchetti, and Wessel (eds), *International Law as Law of the European Union* (Brill, 2012), 91–110. See, specifically, as to *jus cogens* norms, Cannizzaro, 'In Defence of Front Polisario: The ECJ as a Global Jus Cogens Maker' (2018) CMLRev 569–87.
[105] C-104/16 P, *Council v Front Polisario*, 2016, paras 88–93 and 123; C-266/16, *Western Sahara Campaign UK*, 2018, paras 47 and 63; C-363/18, *Organisation juive européenne*, 2019, para. 35.
[106] 89, 104, 114, 116–117, and 125–129/85, *Åhlström v Commission*, 1988, para. 18; T-102/96, *Gencor v Commission*, 1999, paras 89–108. For more on the territorial scope of the Treaties, see para. 11-006 *et seq.*, *supra*.

sovereign acts performed *iure imperii*,[107] the fact that a State is precluded from refusing its own nationals the right of entry to its territory,[108] the principle that no one is arbitrarily to be deprived of his or her nationality,[109] and the rules of international humanitarian law.[110]

In considering the scope of obligations arising under international agreements, the Court of Justice complies with the rules of customary international law, a notable example being the rules of the 'law of treaties' codified in the 1969 Vienna Convention on the law of Treaties[111] and the 1986 Vienna Convention on the Law of Treaties between States and International Organizations or between International Organizations.[112] Thus, Union law applies the international-law principle of good faith, which debars a contracting party from taking any measure incompatible with an international agreement after it has been ratified but before it has entered into force,[113] and which the parties must respect when they are executing international agreements;[114] as well as the principles of the temporal and territorial scope of application of international agreements;[115] the principles laid down in the 1969 Vienna Convention pertaining to the applicability of successive international agreements[116] and the interpretation of international agreements;[117] the principle of the relative effect of treaties, according to which treaties do not impose any obligations, or confer any rights, on third States (*pacta tertiis nec nocent nec prosunt*);[118] and the rules concerning the suspension and

---

[107] C-154/11, *Mahamdia*, 2012, paras 49–56. See also the special status of Heads of State under public international law, as a result of which the presence of a Head of State in another Member State is not governed by Union law but by international law: C-364/10, *Hungary v Slovak Republic*, 2012, paras 44–52.

[108] 41/74, *Van Duyn*, 1974, para. 22.

[109] C-135/08, *Rottmann*, 2010, para. 53 (principle confirmed in the Universal Declaration of Human Rights and the European Convention on nationality).

[110] C-363/18, *Organisation juive européenne*, 2019, para. 34.

[111] Vienna Convention of 23 May 1969 on the law of treaties (in force since 27 January 1980). Although this convention has not been ratified by all Member States, it is deemed to be a codification of customary international law. For an application, see C-266/16, *Western Sahara Campaign UK*, 2018, para. 58 (Article 31 on interpretation); C-265/19, *Recorded Artists Actors Performers*, 2020, para. 79 (Article 21 on legal effect of reservations); Opinion 1/91 *Draft agreement between the Community, on the one hand, and the countries of the European Free Trade Association, on the other, relating to the creation of the European Economic Area*, 1991, para. 14; C-432/92, *Anastàsiou and Others*, 1994, paras 43 and 50; C-466/98, *Commission v United Kingdom*, 2002, para. 24; see also C-268/94, *Portugal v Council*, 1996, paras 19 and 27, where it was referred to as 'international law'; for the application of such a rule before codification, see 10/61, *Commission v Italy*, 1962, 10. See Kuijper, 'The Court and the Tribunal of the EC and the Vienna Convention on the Law of Treaties 1969' (1998) LIEI 1–23.

[112] Vienna Convention of 21 March 1986 on the Law of Treaties between States and International Organizations or between International Organizations. This Convention also largely codifies customary international law. See Manin, 'The European Communities and the Vienna Convention on the Law of Treaties between States and International Organisations or between International Organisations' (1987) CMLRev 457–81.

[113] Vienna Convention 1969, Article 18(a) as applied in C-27/96, *Danisco Sugar*, 1997, paras 20 and 31; T-115/94, *Opel Austria v Council*, 1997, paras 90–123 (with regard to an agreement concluded by the Community); see also C-308/06, *Intertanko*, 2008, para. 52; C-203/07 P, *Greece v Commission*, 2008, para. 64.

[114] Vienna Convention 1969, Article 26; see also C-104/16 P, *Council v Front Polisario*, 2016, para. 124.

[115] Vienna Convention 1969, Article 28 (temporal scope), see C-466/11, *Currà and Others*, 2012, paras 22–23; Vienna Convention 1969, Article 29 (territorial scope),see C-104/16 P, *Council v Front Polisario*, 2016, paras 94–9; C-266/16, *Western Sahara Campaign UK*, 2018, paras 57–85. See also, Kassoti, 'The EU and Western Sahara: An Assessment of Recent Developments' (2018) ELRev 751–69; Odermatt, 'Fishing in Troubled Waters' (2018) EuConst 751–66; Mensi, 'The Case Western Sahara Campaign UK and the International and Institutional Coherence of European Union External Action. Opening Pandora's Box?' (2018) Eur For Aff Rev 549–64.

[116] Vienna Convention 1969, Article 30; see C-104/16 P, *Council v Front Polisario*, 2016, paras 110–15.

[117] Vienna Convention 1969, Article 31, see C-410/11, *Espada Sánchez*, 2012, para. 22; C-104/16 P, *Council v Front Polisario*, 2016, paras 81–93 and 120–2.

[118] Vienna Convention 1969, Article 34, applied in C-386/08 *Brita*, 2010, paras 40–53 (with regard to the EC–Israel Association Agreement and its non-application to products originating in the West Bank, which are covered by the EC–PLO Association Agreement).

termination of an international agreement on the ground of a fundamental change of circumstances (*rebus sic stantibus* clause).[119] In connection with a question of the succession of States (following the break-up of Czechoslovakia), the Court of Justice referred to the international practice based on the continuity of treaties.[120] The Court sometimes finds it useful in interpreting provisions of Union law to refer to international agreements concluded by the Member States[121] and decisions of international organizations,[122] although it does not treat them as binding. This is obviously not possible where such an agreement conflicts with a higher principle of Union law.[123]

Unlike international agreements, principles of customary international law may only be relied upon by an individual for examining the validity of an act of the Union in so far as, first, those principles are capable of calling into question the competence of the Union to adopt that act and, second, the act in question is liable to affect rights which the individual derives from Union law or to create obligations under Union law in his regard.[124] Since a principle of customary international law does not have the same degree of precision as a provision of an international agreement, judicial review must necessarily be limited to the question whether, in adopting the act in question, the Union institutions made manifest errors of assessment concerning the conditions for applying those principles.[125]

B. Obligations in connection with the United Nations

26.014 **United Nations.** All Union Member States are members of the United Nations (UN). The United Nations Charter[126] provides that membership is open only to 'States', which precludes the Union from joining.[127] As members of the UN, all the Member States are represented in the General Assembly. In the Security Council, France has permanent membership and the right of veto (UN Charter, Article 27(1) and (3)); other Member States may sit thereon as one of the ten non-permanent members. The Union may accede to an agreement concluded under the auspices of the UN where that agreement so permits.[128] Where

---

[119] Vienna Convention 1969, Article 62, applied in C-162/96, *Racke*, 1998, paras 37–60 (applied by the Council in suspending and denouncing the Cooperation Agreement with Yugoslavia). The Court conducts its review only in the light of provisions which may be regarded as a codification of existing customary law: Racke, 1998, paras 24 and 59; see case notes by Klabbers (1999) CMLRev 179–89 and Berramdane (2000) CDE 253–79.

[120] C-216/01, *Budějovický Budvar*, 2003, paras 150–66.

[121] See 92/71 *Interfood*, 1972, para. 6 (agreements concluded at the 1960 and 1961 Tariff Conferences). In particular, this applies to the international agreements which constituted the inspiration for the common customs tariff; see, e.g., 38/77, *Enka*, 1977, paras 24–9 (Convention of 15 December 1950 on the Valuation of Goods for Customs Purposes). See also 24/86, *Blaizot*, 1988, para. 17 (1961 European Social Charter; see para. 25-004, *supra*).

[122] For provisions of the FAO and the World Health Organisation, see 92/74, *Van den Berg*, 1975, paras 2–9; 178/84, *Commission v Germany*, 1986, paras 44 and 52; for explanatory notes and classification opinions of the International Customs Cooperation Council, see 14/70, *Bakels*, 1970, paras 6–11; for recommendations of the International Commission on Radiological Protection, see C-376/90, *Commission v Belgium*, 1992, paras 21–6.

[123] T-192/96, *Lebedef v Commission*, 1998, para. 77 (ILO Convention).

[124] C-366/10, *Air Transport Association of America*, 2011, para. 107.

[125] Ibid., para. 110.

[126] United Nations Charter, signed at San Francisco on 26 June 1945 (TS 67 (1946); Cmd 7015; United Nations Act 1946).

[127] UN Charter, Articles 3 and 4.

[128] e.g. the Agreement of the United Nations Economic Commission for Europe concerning the adoption of uniform technical prescriptions for wheeled vehicles, equipment, and parts which can be fitted to and/or be used on wheeled vehicles and the conditions for reciprocal recognition of approvals granted on the basis of these prescriptions, approved by Council Decision of 27 November 1997, OJ 1997 L346/78.

Member States have to give effect to obligations arising for them under the UN Charter (e.g. resolutions of the Security Council adopted under Chapter VII of the UN Charter), they cannot avoid those obligations by claiming that certain powers have been transferred to the Union.[129] As far as such cases are concerned, the TFEU not only provides that, in principle, pre-existing international obligations take precedence (Article 351, first para. TFEU; see para. 26.009, *supra*), but it also allows the Member States, after prior consultation, to waive Union obligations so as to enable a Member State to carry out 'obligations it has accepted for the purpose of maintaining peace and international security' (Article 347 TFEU; see para. 11.011, *supra*).

Legal status of UN obligations. Since all EU Member States are bound by the obligations arising under the UN Charter, the question may be asked as to whether the Union itself is so bound.[130] The Union Courts had to deal with that issue in the *Kadi* case, where an individual challenged the lawfulness, in the light of fundamental rights, of the EU regulations ordering the freezing of his funds so as to give effect to a resolution adopted by the UN Security Council under Chapter VII of the UN Charter. The Court of First Instance (now the General Court) held that both international law and Union law required the Union institutions to implement the Security Council resolution, without there being any possibility of judicial review of the lawfulness of such implementing measure in the light of fundamental rights.[131] The Court of Justice set aside this judgment as it considered that the Union Courts have to review the lawfulness of all Union acts in the light of fundamental rights, even acts that are designed to give effect to a Security Council resolution adopted under Chapter VII of the UN Charter.[132] Whereas the Court of Justice did not accept the primacy of the UN Charter over provisions of primary Union law and fundamental rights,[133] it confirmed that

26.015

---

[129] See Article 103 of the UN Charter, which provides that States' obligations under the Charter are to prevail over their obligations under any other international agreement, and Article 48(2) of the Charter, which provides that Members of the UN are to carry out decisions for the maintenance of international peace and security 'directly and through their action in the appropriate international agencies of which they are members'. As far as UN obligations are concerned, the Union cannot be regarded as having been substituted for the Member States; unlike in the case of GATT (para. 26-001, *supra*), all competence in that connection has not been transferred to the Union and the Union does not act as an equal partner within the organization.

[130] According to Article 2(6) of the UN Charter, '[t]he Organisation shall ensure that States which are not Members of the United Nations act in accordance with [the principles set out in that article] so far as may be necessary for the maintenance of international peace and security'.

[131] T-315/01, *Kadi v Council and Commission*, 2005, paras 181–225, see also T-306/01, *Yusuf and Al Barakaat International Foundation v Council and Commission*, 2005, with case note by Tomuschat in (2006) CMLRev 537–51. According to the CFI, it was empowered only to check, indirectly, the lawfulness of the resolutions of the Security Council in question with regard to *jus cogens*: T-315/01, *Kadi v Council and Commission*, 2005, paras 226–91 (the CFI found that there had been no breach of principles of *jus cogens*).

[132] C-402/05 P and C-415/05 P, *Kadi and Al Barakaat International Foundation*, 2008, paras 280–327. For a discussion, see Janssens, 'Het Kadi-arrest van het Hof van Justitie inzake terrorismelijsten' (2009) RW 1410; Halberstam and Stein, 'The United Nations, the European Union, and the King of Sweden: Economic Sanctions and Individual Rights in a Plural World Order' (2009) CMLRev 13–72; Thouvenin, 'Le juge international peut-il contrôler la légalité des sanctions adoptées par le Conseil de sécurité?' (2009) RMCUE 373–9; d'Argent, 'Arrêt "Kadi": le droit communautaire comme droit interne' (2008) JDE 265; Tridimas and Gutiérrez-Fons, 'EU Law, International Law and Economic Sanctions against Terrorism: The Judiciary in Distress?' (2009) Fordham ILJ 660–730; De Burca, 'The EU, the European Court of Justice and the International Legal Order after Kadi' (2009) Harv ILJ 1–49; Hinojosa Martinez, 'The Legislative Role of the Security Council in its Fight against Terrorism: Legal, Political and Practical' (2008) ICLQ 333–59.

[133] According to the Court, 'it is not a consequence of the principles governing the international legal order under the United Nations that any judicial review of the internal lawfulness of the contested regulation in the light of fundamental freedoms is excluded by virtue of the fact that that measure is intended to give effect to a resolution of the Security Council adopted under Chapter VII of the Charter of the United Nations': C-402/05 P and C-415/05 P, *Kadi and Al Barakaat International Foundation*, 2008, para. 299. In carrying out judicial review of the

the powers of the Union have to be exercised in observance of the undertakings given in the context of the United Nations[134] and that in the implementation of a resolution of the UN Security Council due account is to be taken of the terms and objectives of the resolution and of the relevant UN obligations relating to such implementation.[135] Where the Union itself does not act, the Union institutions must, in any event, put the Member States in a position to comply with their pre-existing international obligations (see para. 26.011, *supra*). Where only the Union has the competence to give effect to UN obligations, for instance in order to impose economic sanctions, it should take the necessary steps to that effect.[136] Where the Union decides to implement a binding UN resolution, the damage resulting from the economic sanctions imposed by the resolution cannot be attributed to the Union.[137]

26.016 **Review in the light of UN obligations.** Another question is whether, in interpreting and applying provisions of Union law, the courts may test them against the UN Charter and resolutions adopted pursuant to that instrument. This is the case where a Union measure purports to give effect to a UN obligation (e.g. with a view to implementing sanctions imposed by the Security Council).[138] An individual may invoke obligations contained in provisions having direct effect, such as some Security Council resolutions imposing sanctions.[139] As said, when interpreting acts that aim to implement a UN Security Council resolution due account must be taken of the terms and objectives of the resolution concerned.[140] Furthermore, it would appear that the Court of Justice is prepared to take account of resolutions of the UN General Assembly[141] and of rulings of the International Court of Justice in interpreting Union law.[142]

---

contested regulation, the Court found that the inclusion of individuals on a list of persons whose assets were to be frozen, without any guarantee of the communication of the inculpatory evidence against them or as to their being heard, albeit at a later date, and without any possibility for the Court itself to remedy that infringement, constituted a breach of those individuals' rights of defence, right to effective judicial review and right to property: ibid., paras 333–71.

[134] Ibid., paras 291–7.

[135] Ibid., paras 296–7; C-548/09 P, *Bank Melli Iran v Council*, 2011, paras 100–7. See already C-177/95, *Ebony Martime and Loten Navigation*, 1997, paras 20–1 and 31; C-371/03, *Aulinger*, 2006, para. 30.

[136] Petersmann, 'Internationale Wirtschaftssanktionen als Problem des Völkerrechts und des Europarechts' (1981) ZVglRW. 1, 26–7.

[137] T-184/95, *Dorsch Consult v Council and Commission*, 1998, para. 74.

[138] C-84/95, *Bosphorus*, 1996, paras 13–15. See Canor, '"Can Two Walk Together, Except They Be Agreed?" The Relationship between International Law and European Law: The Incorporation of United Nations Sanctions against Yugoslavia into European Community Law through the Perspective of the European Court of Justice' (1998) CMLRev 137–87. More generally on the compatibility with international law of sanctions adopted by the Union, see Karagiannis, 'Sanctions internationales et droit communautaire' (1999) RTDE 363–94.

[139] See Angelet, 'La mise en oeuvre des mesures coercitives économiques des Nations-Unies dans la Communauté européenne' (1993) BTIR 500, 502–5 and 528.

[140] C-380/09 P, *Melli Bank v. Council*, 2012, paras 52–5; C-573/14, *Lounani*. 2017, paras 45–8.

[141] C-364/11, *El Karem El Kott*, 2012, para. 60; C-104/16 P, *Council v Front Polisario*, 2016, paras 90–1 and 105.

[142] C-432/92, *Anastasiou and Others*, 1994, para. 49; C-162/96, *Racke*, 1998, paras 24 and 50; C-104/16 P, *Council v Front Polisario*, 2016, paras 88 and 104–5. See Higgins, 'The ICJ, the ECJ and the Integrity of International law' (2003) ICLQ 1–20.

27
Acts Adopted by the Institutions and Bodies of the Union

I. Autonomous Measures Adopted by Institutions and Bodies

Range of instruments. The first para. of Article 288 TFEU states that the institutions exercise the Union's competences, by adopting regulations, directives, decisions, recommendations, and opinions. Nevertheless, the institutions of the Union make use of instruments other than those listed in the second to the fifth paras of Article 288 TFEU (see para. 27.044 *et seq.*, *infra*). Moreover, other bodies of the Union are also competent to adopt legal acts.

27.001

The Treaties do not offer much guidance with regard to the possibility for the institutions to choose between those different instruments, although they set out a number of formal requirements to be satisfied by acts of the institutions, some of which—pursuant to general principles of Union law—apply also to acts of other bodies.[1]

A. Formal requirements and status

1. Choice between different instruments

Instruments with different legal effects. Article 288 TFEU defines the instruments available to the institutions: regulations, directives, decisions, recommendations, and opinions.[2] As will be indicated in the survey below, it is clear from the definition of these instruments that they do not have the same legal effects.

27.002

Besides the instruments listed in Article 288 TFEU, some Treaty articles also mention other instruments, like 'guidelines' or 'incentive measures' for instance. In addition to the instruments explicitly mentioned by the Treaties, the institutions also commonly use other instruments, the legal effects of which have to be determined on a case-by-case basis.

---

[1] For a general discussion of acts of the institutions and bodies, see Desomer, *The Reform of the Legal Instruments of the European Union* (PhD KULeuven, 2009), available at https://lirias.kuleuven.be/1853851?limo=0; Bast, *Grundbegriffe der Handlungsformen der EU* (Springer, 2006); Van Raepenbusch 'Les instruments juridiques de l'Union européenne', in Dony and Bribosia (eds), *Commentaire de la Constitution de l'Union européenne* (ULB, 2005), 203–18; von Bogdandy, Arndt, and Bast, *Legal Instruments in European Union Law and Their Reform: A Systematic Approach on an Empirical Basis*, (2004) YEL 91–136, Louis, 'Les actes des institutions', in Louis et al., *Commentaire Mégret—Le droit de la CEE. 10. La Cour de justice. Les actes des institutions* (Editions de l'Université de Bruxelles, 1993), 475–540.

[2] The ECSC used a different terminology. ECSC *decisions* were binding in their entirety (Article 14, second para. ECSC) and could be general or individual in character (see Article 33, second para. ECSC). ECSC general decisions corresponded to EC and EAEC regulations and ECSC individual decisions to EC and EAEC decisions. ECSC *recommendations* were binding as to the aims to be pursued, but left the choice of the appropriate methods of achieving those aims to those to whom the recommendations were addressed (Article 14, third para. ECSC). They could therefore be equated with EC and EAEC directives (except that the latter may be addressed only to Member States). ECSC *opinions* had no binding force (Article 14, fourth para. ECSC) and hence corresponded to EC and EAEC recommendations and opinions.

27.003 **Choice.** The institutions are not always free to choose just any of those instruments when exercising their powers. First, they have to be guided by the article of the Treaty which serves as the legal basis for the action to be taken (see para. 5.012, *infra*). Some Treaty articles restrict action on the part of the Union to one or more specific instruments (e.g. 'directives' or 'directives or regulations'), whilst others authorize any 'measures' or 'provisions' to be adopted[3] (e.g. the supplementary competence of Article 352 TFEU). In the field of the CFSP, the Treaties provide only for decisions to be used, together with general guidelines (see Article 25 TEU).

As far as legislative acts are concerned, the Treaties expressly provide that the European Parliament and the Council must refrain from adopting acts not provided for by the relevant legislative procedure in the area in question (Article 296, third para. TFEU, introduced by the Lisbon Treaty). Furthermore, the institutions and bodies have to consider the legal effects of the instrument which they intend to adopt. In particular, they must decide whether they want to enact directly binding, exhaustive provisions (e.g. by way of a regulation) or rather leave the Member States with certain choices when implementing an act (e.g. by adopting a directive), or whether instead they wish to adopt provisions that are not legally binding (e.g. by means of a recommendation). Since regulations and directives have different legal effects, it is generally not recommended to amend an existing directive by adopting a regulation, nor to amend a regulation by a directive,[4] save with regard to provisions which do not need to be implemented by the Member States.[5] Where the Treaties do not specify the type of act to be adopted, the institutions have to select the appropriate instrument on a case-by-case basis, in compliance with the applicable procedures and with the principle of proportionality (Article 296, first para. TFEU). The principle of proportionality precludes the Union from adopting instruments which restrict the powers of the Member States and other legitimate interests more than is necessary for the achievement of its objectives (see para. 5.039, *supra*). Consequently, in some circumstances, preference should be given to instruments which are not directly applicable, such as directives, or even not binding at all, such as recommendations.

2. Distinction between legislative acts and non-legislative acts

27.004 **Distinguishing between legal instruments.** Regulations, directives, and decisions may be used for legislative acts and non-legislative acts, including for delegated acts and implementing acts. Formerly, the title of an act did not disclose whether it was a legislative act or an implementing act. Since the Lisbon Treaty, however, Union legislative acts are distinguished from non-legislative acts by means of their title. Indeed, all acts of the Council or

---

[3] See C-132/14 to C-136/14, *European Parliament and Commission v Council*, 2015, para. 82.
[4] Unlike directives, which need to be transposed by the Member States into their legal systems, regulations are directly applicable and may therefore not be copied into national law (see para. 27-015). When a directive is amended by a regulation, the directive will have provisions with different effects (since the amending provisions become part of the original act), which may generate complications for the transposition at national level. See in this respect Joint practical guide of the European Parliament, the Council and the Commission for persons involved in the drafting of European Union legislation (Publications Office of the European Union, 2015), para. 18.6. For an illustration of these practical problems, see Belgian Council of State, Opinion 68.803/3 of 3 March 2021, paras 4.1–4.3.
[5] This includes provisions of a directive in reality addressed to the Union institutions, such as those regarding the scope of delegated or implementing acts and the comitology procedure, or containing a reporting obligation or a review clause, as well as provisions on repeal of acts or extending the transposition period of a directive.

the Commission adopted to implement a legally binding Union act will henceforward have the word 'implementing' in their title (Article 291(4) TFEU: e.g. 'implementing regulation',[6] 'implementing directive', or 'implementing decision'). Where a legislative act delegates powers to the Commission, the delegated acts adopted by that institution will be designated as such (Article 290(4) TFEU: e.g. 'delegated regulation', 'delegated directive', or 'delegated decision'). Regulations, directives, and decisions not so designated will constitute legislative acts if they are based on an article in the Treaties and adopted pursuant to a legislative procedure (see para. 17.002, *supra*).[7] A distinct regime applies as far as the CFSP is concerned. As proposed in the EU Constitution, the normal CFSP instrument is the 'decision', which is not a legislative act (Articles 24(1), second subpara. and 31(1), first subpara. TEU).

Classification proposed by the EU Constitution. The distinction made by the Lisbon Treaty between legislative and non-legislative—delegated or implementing—acts, constituted the response to a long-standing claim for a substantive distinction to be made between legislative and implementing acts which should be reflected in distinct legal instruments with an internal hierarchy.[8] In this connection, the European Parliament generally proposed that it and the Council should be empowered to adopt legislative acts and the Commission to adopt implementing acts. The Intergovernmental Conference of 2003 responded—at least to a certain extent—to the call for a transparent system of legislative acts[9] by proposing a new system of legislative instruments in the EU Constitution.

27.005

The EU Constitution defined two instruments for legislative action by the Union: the 'European law', corresponding to the present regulation,[10] and the 'European framework law', corresponding to the present directive.[11] For non-legislative action, institutions were to use a 'European regulation' or a 'European decision'. The former would be an act of general application for the implementation of legislative acts, other acts, and certain specific provisions of the EU Constitution[12] and would either have had legal effects

---

[6] For the first example, see Council implementing Regulation (EU) No. 1202/2009 of 7 December 2009 imposing a definitive anti-dumping duty on imports of furfuryl alcohol originating in the People's Republic of China following an expiry review pursuant to Article 11(2) of Regulation (EC) No. 384/96, OJ 2009 L323/48.

[7] It should be noted by way of exception, that 'implementing regulations' for the European Social Fund and the European Regional Development Fund are to be adopted in accordance with the ordinary legislative procedure, see Articles 164 and 178 TFEU.

[8] For a discussion, see Lenaerts, 'A Unified Set of Instruments' (2005) EuConst 57–61; Lenaerts and Desomer, 'Towards a Hierarchy of Legal Acts in the Union? Simplification of Legal Instruments and Procedures' (2005) ELJ 744–65; Blanchet, 'Les instruments juridiques de l'Union européenne et la rédaction des bases juridiques: situation actuelle et rationalisation dans la Constitution' (2005) RTDE 319–43. See as long ago as 18 April 1991 the resolution of the European Parliament on the nature of Community acts, OJ 1991 C129/136, and the resolution of the European Parliament of 17 December 2002 on the typology of acts and the hierarchy of legislation in the European Union, OJ 2004 C31E/126.

[9] Previous Intergovernmental Conferences did not act upon the request to undertake such a discussion contained in Declaration (No. 16), annexed to the EU Treaty, on the hierarchy of Community acts. See Tizzano, 'La hiérarchie des normes communautaires' (1995) RMUE 219–32; Monjal, 'La Conférence intergouvernementale de 1996 et la hiérarchie des normes communautaires' (1996) RTDE 681–716; Kovar, 'La déclaration No 16 annexée au Traité sur l'Union européenne: chronique d'un échec annoncé?' (1997) CDE 3–11.

[10] Article I-33(1), second subpara. of the EU Constitution defined it as 'a legislative act of general application' that 'shall be binding in its entirety and directly applicable in all Member States'.

[11] Article I-33(1), third subpara. of the EU Constitution defined it as 'a legislative act binding, as to the result to be achieved, upon each Member State to which it is addressed' which was to 'leave to the national authorities the choice of form and methods'.

[12] Article I-33(1), fourth subpara. of the EU Constitution did not expressly provide for European regulations to implement other implementing acts. That could however be inferred from Article I-37(2) (referring in general terms to the implementation of all 'legally binding Union acts').

similar to those of the existing regulation or effects similar to those of a directive.[13] The 'European decision' was defined as an act 'binding in its entirety', which, where specifying the persons to whom it was addressed, would be binding only on them—the same definition introduced by the Lisbon Treaty for 'decisions'.[14] The EU Constitution introduced the idea of calling European regulations and European decisions implementing other legally binding acts, 'implementing regulations' and 'implementing decisions' and of calling European regulations adopted pursuant to a delegation of power from the legislature 'delegated European regulations'. Eventually, the Intergovernmental Conference of 2007 took over only the latter changes, together with the new definition of 'decisions'.

3. Manner in which acts come into being

27.006 **Signature and authentication.** Legislative acts adopted under the ordinary legislative procedure have to be signed by the President of the European Parliament and by the President of the Council; legislative acts adopted under a special legislative procedure have to be signed by the President of the institution which adopted them (Article 297(1) TFEU).[15] Non-legislative acts adopted in the form of regulations, directives, or decisions, when the latter do not specify to whom they are addressed, have to be signed by the President of the institution which adopted them (Article 297(2) TFEU).

Authenticating an act by dating it and appending the requisite signatures confirms that the terms of the authenticated instrument correspond to those of the act adopted and enables the competence of the authority issuing the act to be verified.[16] Authentication renders the instrument enforceable and ensures that it is incorporated into the Union legal order.[17] Thereafter, an act may be amended only in accordance with the rules on competence and procedure, apart from simple corrections of spelling and grammar.[18]

---

[13] Pursuant to Article I-33(1), fourth subpara. of the EU Constitution, such a European regulation would be 'binding in its entirety and directly applicable in all Member States' or 'binding, as to the result to be achieved, upon each Member State to which it is addressed' but leaving 'to the national authorities the choice of form and methods'.

[14] cf. Article I-33(1), fifth subpara. EU Constitution and Article 288, fourth subpara. TFEU; see *infra*, para. 27-037, *infra*. However, the TFEU also allows 'decisions' to be used for legislative action (see Article 289(1) TFEU).

[15] Article 15 of the Council Rules of Procedure provides that the text of acts adopted by the Council and that of the acts adopted by the European Parliament and the Council in accordance with the ordinary legislative procedure is to bear the signatures of the President-in-Office and the Secretary-General of the Council.

[16] T-79/89, T-84/89, T-85/89, T-86/89, T-89/89, T-91/89, T-92/89, T-94/89, T-96/89, T-98/89, T-102/89, and T-104/89 *BASF and Others v Commission*, 1992, para. 75.

[17] Ibid. In that case, the Court of First Instance (now the General Court) considered that the defects of the relevant Commission decision, *inter alia*, on account of failure to comply with the authentication procedure, were so manifest and serious as to render the decision non-existent: ibid., para. 96, II-362. On an appeal brought by the Commission, the Court of Justice held that the irregularity was not of such obvious gravity that the decision had to be treated as legally non-existent; accordingly, the Court of Justice set aside the judgment and annulled the Commission decision at issue for infringement of essential procedural requirements: C-137/92 P, *Commission v BASF and Others*, 1994, paras 48–55 and 75–8. See also T-80/89, T-81/89, T-83/89, T-87/89, T-88/89, T-90/89, T-93/89, T-95/89, T-97/89, T-99/89, T-100/89, T-101/89, T-103/89, T-105/89, T-107/89, and T-112/89, *BASF and Others v Commission*, 1995, paras 108–26; T-32/91 *Solvay v Commission*, 1995, paras 49–54; T-37/91, *ICI v Commission*, 1995, paras 88–93 (as confirmed in C-286/95 P *Commission v ICI*, 2000).

[18] T-79/89, T-84/89, T-85/89, T-86/89, T-89/89, T-91/89, T-92/89, T-94/89, T-96/89, T-98/89, T-102/89, and T-104/89, *BASF and Others v Commission*, 1992, para. 35; see also 131/86, *United Kingdom v Council*, 1988, paras 34–9.

The specific authentication procedures laid down in the rules of procedure of the institutions may be regarded as essential procedural requirements within the meaning of the second para. of Article 263 TFEU, which, if infringed, may give rise to an action for annulment.[19]

4. Statement of reasons

Obligation to state reasons. Legal acts must state the reasons on which they are based and refer to any proposals, initiatives, recommendations, requests, or opinions required by the Treaties (Article 296, second para. TFEU). The duty to state reasons constitutes an essential procedural requirement within the meaning of the second para. of Article 263 TFEU and may be raised by the Court of Justice or the General Court of its own motion.[20] If the Court finds the statement of reasons to be inadequate, it will annul the contested act.[21] The Court of Justice has held that the duty to state the reasons on which acts are based does not take 'merely formal considerations into account but seeks to give an opportunity to the parties of defending their rights, to the Court of exercising its supervisory functions and to Member States and to all interested nationals of ascertaining the circumstances in which the [institution] has applied the Treaty'.[22] To this end, the statement of reasons must 'disclose in a clear and unequivocal fashion the reasoning followed by the [Union] authority which adopted the measure in question'.[23]

27.007

Although where a given decision follows a well-established line of decisions, the reasons on which it is based may be given in a summary manner, the Union authority must give an explicit account of its reasoning if the decision goes appreciably further than previous decisions.[24] Where the Union institutions have discretion (power of appraisal), sufficient reasoning is of even more fundamental importance in order to enable the Court to verify whether the factual and legal matters upon which the exercise of the power of appraisal depended were present.[25] The extent of the requirement to state reasons is also influenced by the type of instrument employed by the institution.[26] In the case of an act of general application, the statement of reasons may be confined to indicating the general situation which led to its adoption and the general objectives which it is intended to achieve.[27] If the contested act clearly discloses the essential objective pursued by the institution, it is deemed excessive to require a specific statement of reasons for the various technical choices made.[28] The

---

[19] C-137/92 P, *Commission v BASF and Others*, 1994, para. 76; C-107/99, *Italy v Commission*, 2002, paras 47–8 (breach of requirement for authentication laid down in the Commission's Rules of Procedure). See Lenaerts, Gutman, and Nowak, *EU Procedural Law* (OUP, 2022), Chapter 7. See also T-323/16, *Banco Cooperativo Español v Single Resolution Board*, 2019, paras 74–95 (lack of authentication considered breach of an essential procedural requirement, irrespective of the internal rules of procedure).

[20] 18/57, *Nold v High Authority*, 1959, 51–2. See Lenaerts, Gutman, and Nowak, *EU Procedural Law* (OUP, 2022), Chapter 7.

[21] See, e.g., T-38/92, *AWS Benelux BV v Commission*, 1994, paras 26–36. However, the inadequacy of the statement of reasons for an act is not, in itself, such as to give rise to non-contractual liability of the Union; C-123/18 P, *HTTS Hanseatic Trade Trust & Shipping v Council*, 2019, para. 103; see also C76/01 P, *Eurocoton and Others v Council*, 2003, para. 98.

[22] 24/62, *Germany v Commission*, 1963, 69.

[23] C-350/88, *Delacre and Others v Commission*, 1990, para. 15. See also, C-611/17, *Italy v Council*, 2019, para. 40.

[24] C-350/88, *Delacre and Others v Commission*, 1990, para. 15.

[25] C-269/90, *Technische Universität München*, 1991, paras 14 and 27.

[26] For regulations, see, for instance, 5/67 *Beus*, 1968, 95; for decisions, see 16/65 *Schwarze*, 1965, 888, and C-350/88, *Delacre and Others v Commission*, 1990, para. 16.

[27] C-168/98, *Luxembourg v European Parliament and Council*, 2000, paras 62–8; C-493/17, *Weiss*, 2018, paras 31–2.

[28] C-611/17, *Italy v Council*, 2019, para. 42.

question whether the duty to state reasons has been satisfied must, moreover, be assessed by reference not only to the wording of the act but also to its context and to the whole body of legal rules governing the matter.[29] However, it is a requirement of the principle of subsidiarity that an institution must state its grounds for considering that the objectives of its action cannot be sufficiently achieved by the Member States (Article 5(3) TEU). Likewise, the indication of the legal basis in all Union acts that produce legal effects is essential in the light of the obligation to state reasons.[30]

In order to make it clear that an act was produced in accordance with the procedure prescribed for the adoption of acts of the type in question, Article 296, second para. of the TFEU provides that it must refer to any proposals, initiatives, recommendations, requests, or opinions required by the Treaties. There is no need to mention whether and why a given proposal or opinion was or was not followed.[31] In regulations, directives, and decisions, the Council cites proposals submitted and 'opinions obtained', which it does not restrict to opinions it was required to obtain. Article 296 TFEU does not require acts to refer to any subsequent amendment of the Commission proposal, unless the Commission withdrew its original proposal and replaced it with a new one.[32]

5. Publication or notification—entry into effect

27.008 **Publication and notification.** Article 297 TFEU provides that legislative acts have to be published in the *Official Journal of the European Union*, together with regulations and directives which are addressed to all Member States, as well as decisions that do not specify to whom they are addressed.[33] Those acts are printed in Part L (Legislation) of the *Official Journal*.[34] Other directives, decisions which specify to whom they are addressed, and recommendations have to be notified to their addressees.[35] Unless the Council or Coreper decides otherwise, they are published in the *Official Journal*.[36] The same applies to opinions.[37] The Council or Coreper decides, on a case-by-case basis, whether to publish other Council acts, such as conclusions or resolutions.[38] The European Central Bank may decide to publish its decisions, recommendations, and opinions.[39] It has in fact opted to publish these and

---

[29] C-493/17, *Weiss*, 2018, para. 33. If Member States complain of the statement of reasons, the Court also takes into account whether the Member States have been closely associated with the process of drafting the contested act and are thus aware of the reasons underlying that act; see C-611/17, *Italy v Council*, 2019, para. 41.

[30] C-687/15, *Commission v Council*, 2017, para. 52.

[31] 4/54, *ISA v High Authority*, 1955, 100 (concerning Article 15 ECSC); C-62/88, *Greece v Council*, 1990, para. 29 (concerning Article 190 [*later Article 253*] EC [*now Article 296 TFEU*]).

[32] See Council Rules of Procedure, Annex VI, 'Provisions concerning the forms of acts'. C-280/93 *Germany v Council*, 1994, para. 37. Neither is there a requirement for a summary of the facts establishing that each of the institutions involved in the legislative procedure observed its procedural rules: C-377/98, *Netherlands v European Parliament and Council*, 2001, paras 86–7.

[33] See, with regard to European Council Decisions, Article 12(1) of the European Council Rules of Procedure. The obligation to publish does not however cover decisions taken by a Union institution or body which are only intended to have legal effects within that institution or body, such as decisions on the structure of the services or decisions to launch a study.

[34] Before the amendment made by the EU Treaty to Article 254 EC, directives did not have to be published. In practice, they were published in the *Official Journal*, Part L, under the heading 'acts whose publication is not obligatory'. Likewise, PJCC acts were published under Declaration (No. 9) on Article K.6 [*later Article 34*](2) EU (OJ 1997 C340/133). ECSC acts were also published in this way pursuant to Article 15 ECSC.

[35] Article 297(2), third subpara. TFEU; Council Rules of Procedure, Article 18(1) and (2)(a).

[36] The only exceptions are CFSP decisions: the Council or Coreper decides whether these should be published on a case-by-case basis (Council Rules of Procedure, Article 17(3); see also Article 17(4)).

[37] Council Rules of Procedure, Article 17(2)(b).

[38] Ibid., Article 17(4)(c).

[39] Article 132(2) TFEU.

other legal instruments (guidelines and decisions) in the *Official Journal*.[40] As far as bodies set up by agreements concluded between the Union and third countries are concerned, the Council decides, when such an agreement is concluded, whether their decisions should be published in the *Official Journal*.[41]

The Court of Justice has held that it is a fundamental principle of the Union legal order that an act adopted by the public authorities shall not be applicable to those concerned before they have the opportunity to make themselves acquainted with it.[42] This means that proceedings cannot be brought against individuals for breach of an obligation arising under a regulation where it was not adequately brought to their attention.[43] Union acts which have to be published in the *Official Journal* cannot be enforced in a Member State if they have not yet been published in the *Official Journal* in the official language of that Member State. It is not, in the absence of any rules in that regard in Union law, sufficient that the act in question is available in that language on the internet or that the persons concerned could have learned of the act by other means.[44] However, where a Member State has implemented under national law provisions of a Union act which was not published in the official language of that Member State, those provisions can be enforced against individuals.[45] The principle of legal certainty precludes reliance on a decision addressed to a Member State—which does not have to be published in the *Official Journal*—against individuals, if its content was not made known to them.[46] A rule which complements a Union act without however being stated in that act may be relied on against individuals where they may be deemed to have been aware of it in the light of the circumstances, for instance because it was stated in national legislation.[47]

Entry into force and application. Acts which have to be published in the *Official Journal* pursuant to Article 297(1) and (2) TFEU enter into force on the date specified therein or, in the absence of such date, on the twentieth day following that of their publication. Other directives and decisions take effect upon notification (Article 297(2), third subpara. TFEU). The unity and uniform application of Union law require that, save as otherwise expressly provided, a regulation should enter into force on the same date in all the Member States, regardless of any delays in the distribution of the *Official Journal*. In the absence of evidence to the contrary, a regulation is to be regarded as having been published throughout the Union on the date borne by the issue of the *Official Journal* containing the text of that regulation.[48] If an institution deliberately backdates an act, it infringes the principle of legal certainty.[49]

27.009

---

[40] See the preamble to the Decision of the ECB of 10 November 2000 on the publication of certain legal acts and instruments of the ECB, OJ 2001 L55/68.
[41] Council Rules of Procedure, Article 17(5).
[42] 98/78, *Racke*, 1979, para. 15; see also the parallel judgment of the same date in 99/78, *Decker*, 1979.
[43] C-469/00, *Ravil*, 2003, paras 91 to 100, and C-108/01, *Consorzio del Prosciutto di Parma*, 2003, paras 88–96; C-345/06, *Heinrich*, 2009, paras 41–63 (annex to a regulation which had not been published held to have no binding force vis-à-vis individuals).
[44] C-161/06, *Skoma-Lux*, 2007, paras 15–51; C-140/08, *Rakvere Lihakombinaat*, 2009, paras 31–2; C-146/11, *AS Pimix*, 2012, paras 33–47. See, however, C-410/09, *Polska Telefonia Cyfrowa*, 2011, paras 34–9 (in respect of non-binding guidelines).
[45] C-560/07, *Balbiino*, 2009, paras 31–2; C-140/08, *Rakvere Lihakombinaat*, 2009, paras 33–4.
[46] C-158/06, *ROM-projecten*, 2007, paras 23–31.
[47] C-469/00, *Ravil*, 2003, paras 101–3.
[48] 98/78, *Racke*, 1979, paras 16–17.
[49] T-115/94, *Opel Austria v Council*, 1997, paras 127–32.

The date from which an act takes effect is not necessarily the date from which its provisions apply, as the act may specify a different date for the applicability of its provisions, or some of them. In general, the principle of legal certainty precludes a Union act from taking effect from a point in time before its publication; exceptionally, an act may so take effect on the dual condition that the purpose so demands and the legitimate expectations of those concerned are duly respected.[50] In accordance with the principles of legal certainty and protection of legitimate expectations, new rules apply immediately to the future effects of a situation which arose under the old rules;[51] they can apply to situations existing before their entry into force only in so far as it clearly follows from their terms, objectives, or general scheme that such effect must be given to them.[52] In contrast, procedural rules are generally held to apply to all disputes pending at the time they enter into force.[53] The same principles hold good for the application of the Treaties (see para. 11.003, *supra*) and for international agreements concluded by the Union (see para. 26.001, *supra*).

6. Enforcement

27.010 **Enforcement.** The Union is not competent itself to enforce compliance with its acts. However, acts of the Council, the Commission, or the European Central Bank which impose a pecuniary obligation on natural or legal persons, with the exception of States, are enforceable by virtue of the first para. of Article 299 TFEU. The same is true of judgments of the Court of Justice or the General Court, which Article 280 TFEU declares enforceable under the conditions laid down in Article 299 TFEU.[54] The national authority designated for this purpose by each Member State must append an order for enforcement without any formality other than verification of the authenticity of the act. Enforcement then takes place in accordance with the applicable national rules of civil procedure (Article 299, second para. TFEU). Enforcement may be suspended only by an order of the Court of Justice or the General Court. However, supervising the manner of enforcement falls to the national courts (Article 299, fourth para. TFEU).

7. Judicial review

27.011 **Judicial review.** The legality of a Union act which produces legal effects may be reviewed by the Court of Justice or the General Court when a direct action for annulment is brought against it (Article 263 TFEU), where an objection of illegality is raised (Article 277 TFEU), or where a national court makes a reference to the Court of Justice for a preliminary ruling on its validity (Article 267, first para., indent (b) TFEU). In addition, the Court of Justice may rule on the interpretation of any 'act of the institutions' (ibid.)[55]. However, the Court has only limited jurisdiction in the field of the CFSP (see para. 13.012, *supra*).

---

[50] 98/78, *Racke*, 1979 para. 20; C-110/97, *Netherlands v Council*, 2001, paras 151–7; C-611/17, *Italy v Council*, 2019, para. 106.

[51] 270/84, *Licata v Economic and Social Committee*, 1986, para. 31; C-160/00, *Pokrzeptowicz-Meyer*, 2002, para. 50.

[52] 21/81, *Bout*, 1982, para. 13; C-34/92, *GruSA Fleisch*, 1993, para. 22. For further details, see Kaleda, 'Immediate Effects of Community Law in the New Member States: Is there a Place for a Consistent Doctrine?' (2004) ELJ 102–22.

[53] See 212/80 to 217/80, *Meridionale Industria Salumi and Others*, 1981, para. 9; C-61/98, *De Haan*, 1999, para. 13; C-201/04, *Molenbergnatie*, 2006, para. 31; T-334/07, *Denka International v Commission*, 2009, para. 45.

[54] See also Articles 164 and 159, respectively, EAEC.

[55] For the system of legal redress, see 294/83 *Les Verts v European Parliament*, 1986, para. 23 *et seq.*, and the detailed discussion in Lenaerts, Gutman, and Nowak, *EU Procedural Law* (OUP, 2022), of actions for annulment

B. Regulations

Definition. A regulation has general application and is binding in its entirety and directly applicable in all the Member States (Article 288, second para. TFEU). Sometimes the Union may act only by way of regulations,[56] whereas other Treaty articles provide for the possible use of regulations, alongside other instruments.[57]

27.012

General application. The fact that a regulation has general application means that it is 'applicable to objectively determined situations and involves legal consequences for categories of persons viewed in a general and abstract manner'.[58] The field of application of a regulation is not tailored to specific individuals or situations. A measure does not lose its 'character as a regulation simply because it may be possible to ascertain with a greater or lesser degree of accuracy the number or even the identity of the persons to whom it applies at any given time as long as there is no doubt that the measure is applicable as the result of an objective situation of law or of fact which it specifies and which is in harmony with its ultimate objective'.[59] The general scope of a regulation differentiates it from a decision, which may have individual scope (see para. 27.039, *infra*). Whether a given act has general or individual scope determines whether a natural or legal person may bring an action for its annulment pursuant to the fourth para. of Article 263 TFEU. This is because, according to that provision, an action for annulment may be brought by any natural or legal person, on the one hand, against acts having individual scope or similar effects ('against an act addressed to that person or which is of direct and individual concern to them') and, on the other, against acts of general application provided that the action is brought against a 'regulatory act which is of direct concern to them and does not entail implementing measures'.[60]

27.013

Binding in its entirety. A regulation is binding in its entirety, which means that, unlike a directive, it is intended to subject a situation to rules which are all-embracing and, where necessary, precise. Where a regulation is adopted under the Treaties as a legislative act, it sometimes remains deliberately vague in conferring executive tasks (expressly) on the Union institutions or (implicitly or expressly) on the Member States. Implementing acts are generally adopted in the form of a regulation in areas in which Union legislation imposes extensive administrative tasks on the Union, such as the common agricultural policy. It is only with a regulation that the Union may impose, in a general and abstract manner, obligations upon individuals with immediate effect.[61]

27.014

Direct applicability. Regulations are directly applicable in all Member States. A regulation automatically forms part of a Member State's legal system without it being necessary

27.015

(Chapter 7), the objection of illegality (Chapter 9), and the preliminary ruling procedure (Chapter 6—interpretation—and Chapter 10—review of validity).

[56] For legislative action, see, e.g., Articles 14, 15, 24, 75, 85(1), 86(1), 88(2), 118, second subpara. 121(6), 127(6), 177, 197(2), 207(2), 214(5), 224, 226, 228(4), 257, 291(3), 298(2), 311, fourth subpara. 312(2), 322(1), 336, 349, 352(1) TFEU; for implementing acts, e.g. Articles 45(3)(d), 109 and 132(1), first indent TFEU.

[57] For legislative action, see, e.g., Article 46 TFEU; for other action, see, e.g., Article 103(1) and 132(1) TFEU.

[58] 6/68, *Zuckerfabrik Watenstedt v Council*, 1968, 415.

[59] Ibid.; 101/76, *Koninklijke Scholten Honig v Commission*, 1977, para. 23.

[60] See the discussion in Lenaerts, Gutman, and Nowak, *EU Procedural Law* (OUP, 2022), Chapter 7; Lenaerts, 'Le traité de Lisbonne et la protection juridictionnelle des particuliers en droit de l'Union' (2009) CDE 711, 717–28.

[61] C-573/17, *Popławski*, 2019, para. 66.

to transpose it in any way.[62] Indeed, formal incorporation of provisions of a regulation into the national legal system is regarded as impermissible on the ground that it would bring into doubt 'both the legal nature of the applicable provisions and the date of their coming into force'.[63] Nevertheless, the direct applicability of regulations does not preclude a power on the part of the Member States to take the necessary implementing measures[64] Member States may adopt such measures if they do not obstruct the direct applicability of the regulation, do not conceal its Union nature, and specify that a discretion granted under that regulation is being exercised.[65] National implementing measures may even be necessary in respect of some provisions of regulations.[66]

27.016 **Direct effect.** Individuals are entitled to rely on a regulation before the national courts with a view to having national law which is incompatible therewith disapplied. In accordance with the *Popławski* case law (see para. 23.014, *supra*), that is the case for provisions of a regulation that have direct effect. The Court of Justice has held that 'by reason of their nature and their function in the system of the sources of Community law, regulations have direct effect and are, as such, capable of creating individual rights which national courts must protect'.[67]

The case law does not always draw a distinction between direct applicability of a regulation and the direct effect of its provisions. Nevertheless, it may be taken that a provision of a regulation will have *direct effect* only if it satisfies the same requirements as apply to Treaty articles; in other words, it must be 'clear and precise' and must not 'leave any margin of discretion to the authorities'.[68] The fact that a regulation is *directly applicable* means that it is applied 'in favour of or against those subject to it' without having been transposed into national law.[69] This means that a regulation may not only entail rights for individuals, but also directly impose obligations upon them. Consequently, where a provision of a regulation has *direct effect*, individuals may derive rights from it against both national authorities and other individuals.[70] Even where, on account of its content, a regulation does not have direct effect, national provisions must nevertheless be interpreted as far as possible in the light of its wording and objectives.[71] This principle of consistent interpretation is limited, however, by the general principles of Union law, such as the principle of legal certainty,

---

[62] e.g. C-4/10 and C-27/10, *Bureau national interprofessionel du Cognac*, 2011, para. 66. Given the direct application of a regulation, its entry into force and its application are independent of any transposition into national law, except where a regulation leaves it to the Member States themselves to adopt the necessary legislative, regulatory, administrative, and financial measures to ensure the application of its provisions: C-146/13 *Spain v European Parliament and Council*, 2015, 105–6.

[63] 39/72, *Commission v Italy*, 1973, paras 16–17; see also 34/73, *Variola*, 1973, para. 11; 50/76, *Amsterdam Bulb*, 1977, paras 4–7.

[64] 230/78, *Eridania*, 1979, para. 35; C-403/98, *Azienda Agricola Monte Arcosu*, 2001, para. 26; C-278/02, *Handlbauer*, 2004, paras 25–6.

[65] C-316/10, *Danske Svineproducenter*, 2011, paras 40–1; C-592/11, *Ketelä*, 2012, paras 35–6.

[66] e.g. C-42/10, C-45/10 and C-57/10, *Vlaamse Dierenartsvereniging and Janssens*, 2010, paras 47–50; C-509/11, *ÖBB-Personenverkehr*, 2013, paras 57–62.

[67] 43/71, *Politi*, 1971, para. 9; 93/71, *Leonesio*, 1972, para. 5; see also paras 22–3.

[68] 9/73, *Schlüter*, 1973, para. 32; C-403/98, *Azienda Agricola Monte Arcosu*, 2001, paras 26–8. See Bleckmann, 'L'applicabilité directe du droit communautaire', in *Les recours des individus devant les instances nationales en cas de violation du droit européen: Communautés européennes et Convention des droits de l'homme* (Larcier, 1978), 85, 110; Easson, 'The "Direct Effect" of EEC Directives' (1979) ICLQ 319, 321–2.

[69] 34/73, *Variola*, 1973, para. 10.

[70] See C-253/00, *Muñoz and Superior Fruiticola*, 2002, paras 27–32, with case note by Biondi (2003) CMLRev 1243–50.

[71] See Kronenberger in a case note to C-403/98, *Azienda Agricola Monte Arcosu*, 2001 in (2001) CMLRev 1545–56.

the principle of legality, and the prohibition of retroactivity. Where a regulation empowers Member States to impose sanctions for infringements of the regulation, it cannot, of itself and independently of a national law adopted by a Member State for its implementation, have the effect of determining or aggravating the liability in criminal law of persons who act in contravention of the provisions of that regulation.[72] Moreover, a provision may be relied on against individuals only if they were capable of knowing about it.[73]

C. Directives

Definition. A directive is binding, as to the result to be achieved, upon each Member State[74] to which it is addressed, but leaves to the national authorities the choice of form and methods (Article 288, third para. TFEU).[75] Normally, directives are addressed to all Member States. However, a directive may also be addressed to only one Member State.[76] By leaving the Member States themselves free to determine the way in which the intended result is to be achieved within the national legal system, directives reflect the idea of subsidiarity.[77] It follows that directives are an appropriate means of introducing Union rules that call for existing national provisions to be amended or fleshed out before the Union rules can be applied.[78]

27.017

1. The transposition of directives into national law

Implementation. Unlike regulations, directives are not directly applicable in Member States' domestic legal systems. They obtain their full legislative status only after they have been implemented in national law.[79] Union legislative practice shows a wide variety of

27.018

---

[72] C-60/02, *Criminal proceedings against X*, 2004, paras 61–3; C-573/17, *Popławski*, 2019, paras 74–9.

[73] Para. 25-022, *supra*.

[74] As directives are addressed to the Member States, they do not create obligations for the Union institutions as such, in particular vis-à-vis their staff. In T-518/16, *Carreras Sequeros v Commission*, 2018, paras 60–1, the General Court has however identified three situations in which a directive nevertheless has consequences for the institutions. First, rules or principles laid down in a directive could be relied upon against the institutions where they appear to be merely the specific expression of fundamental Treaty rules and general principles directly applicable to the institutions. Second, a directive could be binding where an institution, within the scope of its organizational autonomy and within the limits of the Staff Regulations, has sought to carry out a specific obligation laid down by that directive or where an internal measure of general application expressly refers to measures laid down by the Union legislature. Third, the institutions must, in their conduct as employer and in accordance with their duty to cooperate in good faith, take account of legislative provisions adopted at Union level. On appeal, the Court has side-stepped whether these three situations are accurately identified by the General Court; see C-119/19 P and C-126/19 P, *Commission and Council v Carreras Sequeros*, 2020, paras 87–94.

[75] The legal force of a directive is equivalent to that of a recommendation made pursuant to the ECSC Treaty: C-221/88, *Busseni*, 1990, para. 21; C-18/94, *Hopkins and Others*, 1996, paras 25–29. However, such a recommendation could be addressed to persons other than Member States (see Article 14, third para. ECSC).

[76] See, e.g., Council Directive 79/174/EEC of 6 February 1979 concerning the flood protection programme in the Hérault Valley, OJ 1979 L38/18 (addressed only to France).

[77] For the directive as a possible instrument amenable to Member States, see Van Nuffel, *De rechtsbescherming van nationale overheden in het Europees recht* (Kluwer, 2000), 246–64. See further Prechal, *Directives in European Community Law. A Study on EC Directives and their Enforcement by National Courts. A Study of Directives and Their Enforcement in National Courts* (OUP, 2005). (which explains all aspects of directives).

[78] The Treaties require directives to be used, *inter alia*, in Articles 23; 50(1); 52(2); 53(1); 59(1); 82(2); 83(1) and (2); 115; 116, second para.; 153(2), first subpara., indent (b) TFEU. Alongside other Treaty articles that do not prescribe the use of any particular legislative instrument (para. 22-103, *infra*), the following are among the articles of the TFEU which provide for the possible use of directives: Articles 46; 103(1); 106(3); 143(2).

[79] 102/79, *Commission v Belgium*, 1980, para. 12. See also Král, 'On the Choice of Methods of Transposition of EU Directives' (2016) ELRev 220–42.

results to be achieved pursuant to a directive. Some directives require legislative measures to be adopted at national level and compliance with those measures to be the subject of judicial or administrative review. Other directives provide that the Member States are to take the necessary measures to ensure that certain objectives formulated in general and unquantifiable terms are attained, whilst leaving the Member States some discretion as to the nature of the measures to be taken. Other directives still require the Member States to obtain very precise and specific results within a specified period.[80]

27.019 **Requirements of legal certainty.** The concrete scope of the obligations imposed by a directive depends on the nature of the provisions of the directive. In any event, the provisions of directives must be implemented with unquestionable binding force, and the specificity, precision, and clarity necessary to satisfy the requirements of legal certainty.[81] In order to secure the full application of directives in law and not only in fact, Member States must make sure that there is a clear legal framework for the area in question, even where there is no practice in the Member State which is incompatible with the directive in question[82] or an activity referred to in a directive does not (yet) exist in a Member State.[83] Indeed, given the fact that situations may change at a given point in time, all natural and legal persons in the Union, including those in the Member State concerned, need to know, with clarity and precision, what are, in all circumstances, their rights and obligations.[84] It is only where transposition of a directive is pointless for reasons of geography that it is not mandatory.[85]

For the purpose of considering whether a directive has been correctly implemented, the scope of national laws, rules, or administrative provisions must be assessed in the light of the interpretation given to them by national courts.[86] Still, in order to achieve the clarity and precision needed to meet the requirement of legal certainty, it may not be sufficient that the settled case law of a Member State interprets the provisions of national law in a manner deemed to satisfy the requirements of a directive.[87] In any event, the legal framework will not be considered clear enough where the case law is not sufficiently settled.[88] Nor is it sufficient to make a general reference to the applicable Union provisions and to the primacy of Union law.[89] Furthermore, a Member State does not fulfil its obligations by maintaining an administrative practice which, albeit consonant with the directive, may be changed as and when the authorities please and is not sufficiently publicized.[90] The principle of legal

---

[80] C-60/00, *Commission v France*, 2002, paras 25–8; C-32/05, *Commission v Luxemburg*, 2006, paras 37–40. This may be problematic in cases where directives are subsequently amended by (delegated) regulations; see Král, 'On the Practice of Amending or Supplementing EU Directives by EU Delegated Regulations' (2020) ELRev 409–14 (see also para. 27-003, *supra*).

[81] This is settled case law of the Court of Justice; see, e.g., C-159/99, *Commission v Italy*, 2001, para. 32. See also Sales, 'La transposition des directives communautaires: une exigence de valeur constitutionnelle sous réserve de constitutionnalité' (2005) RTDE 597–621. For the implementation of directives by collective agreements concluded by management and labour, see para. 17-002, *supra*.

[82] C-339/87, *Commission v Netherlands*, 1990, para. 25 (which refers to a 'specific legal framework').

[83] C-372/00, *Commission v Ireland*, 2001, para. 11; C-441/00, *Commission v United Kingdom*, 2002, para. 15.

[84] C-343/08, *Commission v Czech Republic*, 2010, para. 41.

[85] C-372/00, *Commission v Ireland*, 2001, para. 13; C-441/00, *Commission v United Kingdom*, 2002, para. 17.

[86] C-382/92, *Commission v United Kingdom*, 1994, para. 36: C-300/95, *Commission v United Kingdom*, 1997, para. 37.

[87] C-144/99, *Commission v Netherlands*, 2001, paras 20–1; C-292/07, *Commission v Belgium*, 2009, para. 122; C-530/11, *Commission v United Kingdom*, 2014, paras 33–7.

[88] See, e.g., C-372/99, *Commission v Italy*, 2002, paras 20–8.

[89] C-96/95, *Commission v Germany*, 1997, paras 32–41.

[90] 102/79, *Commission v Belgium*, 1980, para. 11; C-102/08, *SALIX*, 2009, para. 43. See Curtin, 'Directives: The Effectiveness of Judicial Protection of Individual Rights' (1990) CMLRev 709–39, especially 716–18.

certainty requires appropriate publicity for the national implementing measures in such a way as to enable the persons concerned by such measures to ascertain the scope of their rights and obligations in the particular area governed by Union law.[91]

Nevertheless, transposition of a directive into national law does not necessarily require that 'its provisions be incorporated formally and verbatim in express, specific legislation'; sometimes 'a general legal context may, depending on the content of the directive, be adequate for the purpose provided that it does indeed guarantee the full application of the directive in a sufficiently clear and precise manner so that, where the directive is intended to create rights for individuals, the persons concerned can ascertain the full extent of their rights and, where appropriate, rely on them before the national courts'.[92] Accordingly, the existence of general principles of constitutional or administrative law may, exceptionally, make transposition by means of statutory or administrative measures unnecessary.[93] This is also the case for an established judicial practice that meets the above-mentioned requirements as to precision and clarity.[94] As said before, the nature of the provisions of a directive determines the concrete scope of the obligations that are imposed by it. The Court has, for instance, held that a provision which concerns only the relations between the Member States and the Commission does not, in principle, have to be transposed.[95]

Time-limit for implementation. Generally, a directive will not only specify the date by which it enters into effect, but it will also lay down a time-limit within which the Member States must adopt the necessary measures and put them into effect in order to reach the result envisaged by the directive. The institutions will ensure that all directives include a binding time-limit for transposition that is as short as possible and generally does not exceed two years.[96] As a result, a directive imposes an 'obligation to achieve a result' (*obligation de résultat*), which must be fulfilled before the end of the period laid down by the directive.[97] The fact that a directive is belatedly transposed into national law may not cause the date by which the obligations imposed by the directive have to be fulfilled, to be postponed.[98]

27.020

A Member State cannot rely upon domestic difficulties or provisions of its national legal system, even those of its Constitution, for the purpose of justifying a failure to comply with obligations and time-limits resulting from directives.[99] This is because the governments of

---

[91] C-415/01, *Commission v Belgium*, 2003, paras 21–26 (duty to publish maps demarcating special protection areas in order to implement the directive on protection of birds).

[92] 363/85, *Commission v Italy*, 1987, para. 7; C-131/88, *Commission v Germany*, 1991, para. 6; C-361/88, *Commission v Germany*, 1991, para. 15. Recent examples are afforded by C-478/99, *Commission v Sweden*, 2002, paras 10–24; C-233/00, *Commission v France*, 2003, paras 75–87; and C-388/07, *Age Concern England*, 2009, paras 41–52.

[93] 29/84, *Commission v Germany*, 1985, para. 23; for an application, see 248/83, *Commission v Germany*, 1985, paras 18–19 and 30 (equal treatment sufficiently ensured); C-151/12, *Commission v Spain*, 2013, paras 30–8 (constitutional principle deemed insufficient). See Siems, 'Effektivität und Legitimität einer Richtlinienumsetzung durch Generalklauseln' (2002) ZEuP 747–53.

[94] C-530/11, *Commission v United Kingdom*, 2014, paras 33–7.

[95] C-32/05, *Commission v Luxemburg*, 2006, para. 35. The Court added, however, that, given that the Member States are obliged to ensure that Union law is fully complied with, it is open to the Commission to demonstrate that compliance with a provision of a directive governing those relations requires the adoption of specific transposing measures in national law (ibid.).

[96] Point 42 of the Interinstitutional Agreement between the European Parliament, the Council, and the Commission of 13 April 2016 on better law-making, OJ 2016 L123/1.

[97] 8/81, *Becker*, 1982, para. 18.

[98] C-396/92, *Bund Naturschutz in Bayern and Others*, 1994, paras 18–19; see also C-208/90, *Emmott*, 1991, paras 23–4.

[99] 100/77, *Commission v Italy*, 1978, para. 21.

the Member States participate in the preparatory work for directives and must therefore be in a position to prepare, within the period prescribed, the legislative provisions necessary for their implementation.[100] If the period for transposition proves to be too short, a Member State may only seek to convince the institutions to grant an extension.[101] That provisions of a given directive qualify for direct effect does not release the Member State to which it is addressed from the obligation to adopt implementing measures satisfying the purpose of the directive in good time.[102] A Member State does not fulfil its obligation to implement a directive by merely relying on the duty of national courts to set aside conflicting national provisions.[103]

27.021 **Obligations during the period prescribed for implementation.** Before the period prescribed for implementing a directive has expired, there is no obligation for Member States to adopt transposition measures. However, as a result of Article 4(3) TEU, they must, during the period for transposition, refrain from taking any measures which might seriously compromise attainment of the objective pursued by the directive after that period has expired. It is for the national court to assess whether that is the case by considering, in particular, the effects, in practice, of applying the incompatible provisions and of their duration in time.[104] The same applies where a directive provides for a transitional period, during which it does not yet need to be fully transposed.[105]

If the provisions in issue are intended to constitute full and definitive transposition of the directive, their incompatibility might give rise to the presumption that the result prescribed by the directive will not be achieved within the period prescribed if it is impossible to amend them in time.[106] Incompatibility of national measures or non-transposition of certain provisions will not necessarily compromise the result required where a Member State adopts transitional implementing provisions or implements the directive in stages.[107] However, a provision of national law can compromise the result prescribed by a directive, regardless of whether it is concerned with the transposition of the directive or not.[108] This holds true even for constitutional amendments[109].

The obligation not to take any measures which may seriously compromise the aims of a directive even before its transposition applies to national public authorities, but not to

---

[100] 301/81, *Commission v Belgium*, 1983, para. 11; C-319/99, *Commission v France*, 2000, para. 10. If the prescribed period proves too short, all that a Member State can do is take the appropriate initiatives at Union level with the responsible institutions in order to obtain the necessary extension of the period: 52/75, *Commission v Italy*, 1976, para. 12–13.
[101] 52/75, *Commission v Italy*, 1976, para. 12.
[102] 102/79, *Commission v Belgium*, 1980, para. 12.
[103] C-197/96, *Commission v France*, 1997, paras 13–16; C-207/96 *Commission v Italy*, 1997, paras 26–7.
[104] C-129/96, *Inter-Environnement Wallonie*, 1997, paras 45–7; C-14/02, *ATRAL*, 2003, paras 58–60. See Prechal (n. 77 supra), 24–6; Gilliaux, *Les directives européennes et le droit belge* (Bruylant, 1997), 142–5; Klamert, 'Judicial Implementation of Directives and Anticipatory Indirect Effect: Connecting the Dots' (2006) CMLRev 1251–75.
[105] C-316/04, *Stichting Zuid-Hollandse Milieufederatie*, 2005, para. 42; C-138/05, *Stichting Zuid-Hollandse Milieufederatie*, 2006, paras 42–4; C-165/09 to C-167/09, *Stichting Natuur en Milieu*, 2011, paras 79–80.
[106] C-129/96, *Inter-Environnement Wallonie*, 1997, para. 48; C-422/05, *Commission v Belgium*, 2007, paras 62–8.
[107] C-129/96, *Inter-Environnement Wallonie*, 1997, para. 49. See also C-599/12, *Jetair and Travel4you*, 2014, paras 35–7.
[108] C-14/02, *ATRAL*, 2003, paras 58–59; C-144/04, *Mangold*, 2005, paras 66–72; for a discussion of the latter case, see Bauer (2006) NJW 6-12; Foubert (2006) SEW 247–251; Masson (2007) E Pub L 587–93; Riesenhuber (2007) ERCL 63–71.
[109] C-378/07 to C-380/07, *Angelidaki and Others*, 2009, paras 206–7.

individuals.[110] If such measures are nevertheless adopted, they may be set aside by the national courts. These courts are not obliged to do so, however, in procedures brought by individuals in reliance on the direct effect of a directive if the period prescribed for transposition of that directive has not yet expired.[111] In any event, measures adopted before the period for transposition has expired in order to implement a directive must be interpreted as far as possible in a way that is not liable to compromise the result prescribed by the directive (see para. 27.029, *infra*).

2. The direct effect of provisions of an unimplemented or incorrectly implemented directive

Conditions for direct effect. Since directives leave the choice of 'form and methods' to the Member States, they leave, in principle, the competent national authorities some discretion. All the same, they often contain clear, unconditional provisions necessitating no further implementation entailing any policy choices. Still, if a Member State fails to transpose a directive into national law or fails to transpose it properly, an individual may derive rights from those of its provisions which have direct effect, that is the provisions of the directive which are 'unconditional and sufficiently precise' (see para. 23.032, *supra*).[112] According to the Court of Justice, directives must be capable of having direct effect in relations between individuals and Member States because 'the effectiveness [*effet utile*] of such a measure would be weakened if nationals of that State could not invoke it in the courts and if the national courts could not take it into consideration as part of Community law'.[113] In this way, a credit negotiator was entitled to rely, against the German tax authorities, on a tax exemption provided for in the Sixth VAT Directive even though the directive had not yet been implemented in Germany.[114] Whereas the Court initially based this case law on the need to preserve the *effet utile* of directives, more recent case law tends to emphasize the fact that a Member State which has not (correctly) implemented a directive within the prescribed period may not rely on its own failure to perform the obligations which the directive entails (i.e. on the basis of the principle *nemo auditur*) (see para. 27.024, *infra*).[115] In order for a provision of a directive to have direct effect, the Court has held that, in addition to the aforementioned substantive requirements, the following two conditions must be satisfied: (a) the period prescribed for implementing the directive must have expired and (b) the individual must rely upon the relevant provisions against a State body.

27.022

a. Expiry of the time-limit

Expiry of the time-limit. A directive cannot have any direct effect until the period prescribed for implementing it in the national legal system has expired. Direct effect arises

27.023

---

[110] T-172/98, T-175/98 to T-176/98, *Salamander and Others v European Parliament and Council*, 2000, para. 57.
[111] C-157/02, *Rieser Internationale Transporte and Asfinag*, 2004, para. 67.
[112] 8/81, *Becker*, 1982, para. 25; 152/84, *Marshall* ('*Marshall I*'), 1986, para. 46; 103/88, *Fratelli Costanzo*, 1989, para. 29; C-585/16, *Alheto*, 2018, paras 98–9; C-573/17, *Popławski*, 2019, para. 64. For an example of provisions of a directive held not to be sufficiently precise, see C-471/07, *AGIM and Others*, 2010, paras 26–9.
[113] 41/74, *Van Duyn*, 1974, para. 12. For the first cases in which the Court found that directives, in common with regulations, could have direct effects for individuals, see 9/70, *Grad*, 1970, para. 5, and 33/70, *SACE*, 1970, para. 15.
[114] 8/81, *Becker*, 1982, para. 49.
[115] See Emmert and Pereira de Azevedo, 'L'effet horizontal des directives. La jurisprudence de la CJCE: un bateau ivre?' (1993) RTDE 503, 506–17. For examples, see C-388/00 and C-429/00, *Radiosistemi*, 2002, paras 49–66; C-465/00, C-138/01 and C-139/01, *Österreichischer Rundfunk and Others*, 2003, paras 99–100; C-157/02, *Rieser Internationale Transporte and Asfinag*, 2004, para. 67.

only at the end of the prescribed period, provided that the Member State is then in breach of its obligation to transpose the directive.[116] Sometimes a directive prescribes not only a date by which Member States must amend their national provisions, but also a date as from which the amended provisions must be applied. In such a case, the directive cannot produce any effects enforceable by the national courts before the second date has gone by.[117] As soon as a Member State has implemented the directive, its effects reach individuals through the intermediary of the national implementing measures, and there is no need to rely directly on its provisions,[118] unless the implementing measures are incorrect or inadequate.[119] Individuals are also entitled to rely directly on the provisions of a directive where national measures correctly implementing the directive are not being applied in such a way as to achieve the result sought by it.[120]

b. Direct effect only against a Member State

27.024 **Effects against a Member State.** An individual may invoke directly effective provisions of a directive only against a Member State which either failed to implement the directive within the prescribed period or implemented it incorrectly. The Court of Justice has held that 'a Member State which has not adopted the implementing measures required by the directive in the prescribed period may not rely, against individuals, on its own failure to perform the obligations which the directive entails'.[121] The direct effect of directives protects individuals against Member States in breach of their obligation to implement them in the national legal system, with the aim to 'prevent the State from taking advantage of its own failure to comply with [Union] law'[122] and therefore reflects the civil law principle *nemo auditur turpitudinem suam allegans* and the common law doctrine of estoppel.[123]

27.025 **Broad interpretation of the term 'Member State'.** In its judgment in *Marshall I*, the Court of Justice held that 'where a person involved in legal proceedings is able to rely on a directive against the State he may do so regardless of the capacity in which the latter is acting, whether employer or public authority. In either case it is necessary to prevent the State from taking advantage of its own failure to comply with [Union] law'.[124] By putting a broad construction on the term 'State', the Court considerably extended the situations in which an individual may rely on a directly effective provision of a directive. An individual may so rely against 'organisations or bodies which were subject to the authority or control of the State or had special powers beyond those which result from the normal rules applicable to relations between individuals'.[125] This has been held to include not only central authorities,

---

[116] 148/78, *Ratti*, 1979, paras 43–4; see also C-140/91, C-141/91, C-278/91, and C-279/91, *Suffriti and Others*, 1992, paras 11–13.
[117] C-316/93, *Vaneetveld*, 1994, paras 18–19.
[118] 270/81, *Felicitas*, 1982, paras 24–6.
[119] C-253/96 to C-258/96, *Kampelmann and Others*, 1997, paras 42–5.
[120] C-62/00, *Marks & Spencer*, 2002, para. 27.
[121] 148/78, *Ratti*, 1979, para. 22.
[122] 152/84, *Marshall* ('*Marshall I*'), 1986, para. 49; C-91/92, *Faccini Dori*, 1994, para. 22.
[123] See Van Gerven, 'The Horizontal Effect of Directive Provisions Revisited: The Reality of Catchwords', in Curtin and Heukels (eds), *Institutional Dynamics of European Integration. Essays in Honour of Henry G. Schermers*, Vol. II (Martinus Nijhoff, 1994) 335, 343–5.
[124] 152/84, *Marshall I*, 1986, para. 49; see also C-425/12, *Portgás*, 2013, paras 23 and 36.
[125] C-188/89, *Foster and Others*, 1990, para. 18. The Court has clarified that provisions of a directive capable of having direct effect may be relied on against a body that does not display all the characteristics listed in para. 20 of *Foster and Others* read together with those mentioned in para. 18 of that judgment; see C-413/15, *Farrell*, 2017, paras 22–9. See Gijsen, 'Uitleg van het begrip overheidsorgaan van een lidstaat: enkele bespiegelingen van

such as tax authorities,[126] but also geographically decentralized authorities, such as local and regional authorities,[127] and functionally decentralized authorities.[128] Furthermore, it includes bodies, whatever their legal form, which have been made responsible, pursuant to a measure adopted by the State, for providing a public service under the control of the State and have for that purpose special powers beyond those that result from the normal rules applicable in relations between individuals.[129] It appears, therefore, that an individual (or a different governmental body[130]) may derive rights from a directive to be relied on against such bodies regardless of the capacity of the body concerned or whether that body was entrusted with the implementation of the directive in national law.

No horizontal direct effect. Also in *Marshall I*, the Court of Justice held that 'a directive may not of itself impose obligations on an individual and that a provision of a directive may not be relied upon against such a person'.[131] A directive may therefore have vertical but not horizontal direct effect. The Court based its view on the binding nature conferred by Article 249 EC [*now Article 288 TFEU*] on a directive only in relation to 'each Member State to which it is addressed'.[132] Furthermore, the Court of Justice explained in *Faccini Dori* that '[t]he effect of extending that case law [on the direct effect of directives] to the sphere of relations between individuals would be to recognise a power in the Community to enact obligations for individuals with immediate effect, whereas it has competence to do so only where it is empowered to adopt regulations'.[133] In *Faccini Dori*, the Court was faced with the fact that Italy had failed to transpose Directive 85/577 to protect the consumer in respect of contracts negotiated away from business premises. The Court held that a consumer could not rely upon her right to cancel a contract within seven days against the trader with whom she had concluded it in Italy, even though the directive conferred that right unconditionally and sufficiently precisely.[134] It follows that a directly effective provision of a directive cannot be enforced by an individual against another individual and, *a fortiori*, not by a public authority against an individual.[135]

27.026

---

het arrest Farrell/Whitty' (2018) NTER 171–5; Palanco, 'Effet direct oblique et identification des "émanations de l'Etat": l'obscure clarification de la jurisprudence Foster' (2017) RAE 695–704.

[126] 8/81, *Becker*, 1982, para. 49, and C-221/88, *Busseni*, 1990, para. 30

[127] 103/88, *Fratelli Costanzo*, 1989, paras 31–2; C-253/96 to C-258/96, *Kampelmann and Others*, 1997, paras 36–47.

[128] e.g. a constitutionally independent public authority charged with the maintenance of public order and safety (222/84, *Johnston*, 1986, paras 56–7) or a public body responsible for the provision of health care (152/84, *Marshall I*, 1986, paras 49–50).

[129] C-188/89, *Foster and Others*, 1990, para. 20; C-157/02, *Rieser Internationale Transporte and Asfinag*, 2004, paras 22–9; C-356/05, *Farrell*, 2007, para. 40; C-425/12, *Portgás*, 2013, paras 17–31; C-614/11, *Kuso*, 2013, para. 32; C-413/15, *Farrell*, 2017, paras 30–42. For a discussion of the criterion 'public body', see the note to the judgment in *Foster* by Szyszczak (1990) CMLRev 868–71; Prechal, 'Remedies after *Marshall*' (1990) CMLRev 451, 457–462; Curtin, 'The Province of Government: Delimiting the Direct Effect of Directives in the Common Law Context' (1990) ELRev 195–223.

[130] C-425/12, *Portgás*, 2013, paras 32–8.

[131] 152/84, *Marshall I*, 1986, para. 48.

[132] Ibid.

[133] C-91/92, *Faccini Dori*, 1994, para. 24.

[134] Ibid., paras 18 and 30; see also C-192/94, *El Corte Inglés*, 1996, paras 15–21.

[135] 372-374/85, *Traen*, 1987, para. 24; 14/86, *Pretore de Salò*, 1987, paras 19–20; 80/86, *Kolpinghuis Nijmegen*, 1987, paras 9–10; C-168/95, *Arcaro*, 1996, paras 33–8; C-18/00 *Perino* (order), 2001, paras 22–6; C-122/17, *Smith*, 2018, paras 43–4; C-573/17, *Popławski*, 2019, para. 66.

In addition, an individual may not rely on a directly effective provision of a directive against a public authority where this would directly lead to the directive imposing obligations on another individual.[136] Accordingly, the Court held in *Wells* that an individual may not rely on a directive against a Member State where it is a matter of a State obligation directly linked to the performance of an obligation falling, pursuant to that directive, on a third party.[137] Yet, mere adverse repercussions on the rights of third parties, even if the repercussions are certain, do not justify preventing an individual from invoking the provisions of a directive against the Member State concerned.[138] In *Wells*, an individual challenged the decision by which national authorities had given permission for mining operations at a quarry without the environmental impact assessment laid down by a Community directive having first been carried out. The Court considered that the adjoining landowner could invoke the directive even if the fact that mining operations had to be halted to await the results of that assessment was a consequence of the belated performance of the State's obligation. It held that the obligation on the Member State to ensure that the competent authorities carried out the environmental impact assessment was not directly linked to the performance of any obligation which would fall on the quarry owners. It is thus generally possible to rely on a directive in triangular situations, whereby the applicant seeks judicial review of national administrative acts granting an advantage to a private actor.[139]

27.027 **Directives versus regulations.** The fact that the rights enshrined in a directive can be enforced only if the directive has been transposed or, in the absence of (correct) transposition, only against a public body hampers the uniform application throughout the Union of legislation adopted in the form of a directive. Whereas an individual can rely unconditionally against another individual on rights conferred by a regulation, this is possible in the case of a directive only if the directive has been correctly implemented in the Member State in question. This means that individuals in Member States which have not transposed the directive correctly do not enjoy the same rights as individuals in the rest of the Union.[140] Moreover, failure to transpose a directive may mean that it is applied to similar situations differently within a Member State, for instance where certain individuals may assert their rights by making a claim against a public authority (e.g. public-sector employees) whilst others may not enforce the same rights in a private legal relationship (e.g. private-sector employees).[141]

---

[136] C-97/96, *Daihatsu Deutschland*, 1997, paras 24–5. See also (with regard to an ECSC recommendation) C-221/88, *Busseni*, 1990, paras 23–6, in which the ECSC was equated with an individual for the purposes of invoking a provision according preferential treatment in proving certain debts owed to it by an insolvent undertaking. The Court noted that the ECSC's claim for preferential treatment would affect the rights of all other creditors of the undertaking whose debts did not enjoy the same preferential status and therefore ruled that the ECSC's preferential status was not to prejudice the rights of creditors other than the State.

[137] C-201/02, *Wells*, 2004, paras 56 and 58.

[138] Ibid., paras 57–8. See also C-152/07 to C-154/07, *Arcor and Others*, 2008, paras 34–43; C-244/12, *Salzburger Flughafen*, 2013, paras 44–7.

[139] C-508/14, *Český telekomunikační*, 2015, paras 47–8; C-236/18, *GRDF*, 2019, para. 35.

[140] This explains the 'severity' of the Court's case law in relation to Article 260(3) TFEU: the lump sum which may be imposed on a Member State having failed to notify the measures implementing a directive is calculated as from the date set in the directive for its implementation into national law, even if the Commission launches the infringement procedure against the Member State concerned only later, see C-549/18, *Commission v Romania*, 2020, para. 79; C-550/18, *Commission v Ireland*, 2020, para. 90.

[141] The Court of Justice accepted that consequence in 152/84, *Marshall I*, 1986, para. 51. The prohibition of discrimination laid down *in the Treaties* may well apply in relations between individuals because that prohibition has direct effect and, as a Treaty provision, is applicable without further qualification in the national legal systems: 36/74, *Walrave*, 1974, para. 18 *et seq.*

Some commentators consider that it is necessary, in the interest of uniform, equal application of Union law, that an individual should be able to rely against other individuals on clear and unconditional provisions of a directive which has not been (properly) implemented.[142] However, it appears from *Faccini Dori* that a directive does not acquire the same legal force as a regulation after the period prescribed for implementing it has run out.[143]

3. Other effects of an unimplemented or incorrectly implemented directive

Principles ensuring effectiveness. Where a provision of a directive has not been (correctly) implemented, the absence of direct effect does not exclude this provision from having certain 'effects' on the legal position of the authorities or individuals concerned. To that end, the case law has formulated a number of Union-law principles.[144] Thus, the national courts must, provided that the conditions laid down in the case law are fulfilled,[145] (1) construe national law as far as possible in a way which is consistent with the directive and (2) in principle, give the directive in question precedence over conflicting rules of national law. (3) Where, in spite of this, the result required to be obtained by the directive cannot be attained, the Member State will be required to make good the damage caused to individuals as a result of its failure to transpose the directive, provided that certain conditions are fulfilled. Where necessary, the national courts may refer to the Court of Justice for a preliminary ruling on the interpretation of the directive (Article 267 TFEU), without being either compelled to make, or prevented from making, a reference before taking one of the steps mentioned above.[146]

27.028

a. Interpretation in conformity with the directive

Interpretation in conformity with the directive. In the first place, national courts must make use of the methods of interpretation available to them under national law so as to interpret national law as far as possible in conformity with the directive. The Court of Justice has held that 'the Member States' obligation arising from a directive to achieve the result envisaged by the directive and their duty under [Article 4(3) TEU] to take all appropriate measures, whether general or particular, to ensure fulfilment of that obligation, is binding on all the authorities of Member States including, for matters within their jurisdiction, the

27.029

---

[142] See C-271/91, *Marshall*, 1993, AG Van Gerven Opinion, point 12; C-316/93, *Vaneetveld*, 1994, AG Jacobs Opinion, point 18 *et seq.*, and C-91/92, *Faccini Dori*, 1994, AG Lenz Opinion, points 43 *et seq.*; see also Corthaut, note under C-240/98 to C-244/98, *Océano Grupo Editorial*, 2000; C-215/97, *Bellone*, 1998; and C-456/98, *Centrosteel*, 2000, (2002) Col JEL 293–310; Emmert and Pereira de Azevedo (n. 115, *supra*), and Barents, 'Some Remarks on the "Horizontal" Effects of Directives', in O'Keeffe and Schermers (eds), *Essays in European Law and Integration*, (Kluwer, 1982), 97–104; Wyatt, 'The Direct Effect of Community Social Law—Not Forgetting Directives' (1983) ELRev 241–48; for the contrary view, see Timmermans, 'Directives: Their Effect within the National Legal Systems' (1979) CMLRev 533, 541–4; for arguments for and against, see Easson, 'Can Directives Impose Obligations on Individuals' (1979) ELRev 67–79.

[143] For a commentary on this judgment, see Tridimas, 'Horizontal Effect of Directives: A Missed Opportunity' (1994) ELRev 621–36, and the note by Robinson (1995) CMLRev 629–39. Even though this case law was confirmed, the academic debate continued; see Betlem, 'Medium Hard Law—Still No Horizontal Direct Effect of European Community Directives After *Faccini Dori*' (1995) Col JEL 469–96; Emmert and Pereira de Azevedo, 'Les jeux sont faits: rien ne va plus ou une occasion perdue par la CJCE' (1995) RTDE 11–21.

[144] See von Danwitz, 'Rechtswirkungen von Richtlinien in der neueren Rechtsprechung des EuGH' (2007) JZ 697–706; Plaza Martin, 'Furthering the Effectiveness of EC Directives and the Judicial Protection of Individual Rights Thereunder' (1994) ICLQ 26–54; Schockweiler, 'Les effets des directives dans les ordres juridiques nationaux' (1995) RMUE 9–26; Lenz, Sif Tynes, and Young, 'Horizontal What? Back to Basics' (2000) ELRev 509–22.

[145] See in particular, C-573/17, *Popławski*, 2019, paras 50–109.

[146] C-555/07, *Kücükdeveci*, 2010, paras 53–5.

courts. It follows that, in applying the national law ... national courts are required to interpret their national law in the light of the wording and the purpose of the directive in order to achieve the result referred to in the third paragraph of [Article 288 TFEU]'.[147] This holds true not only in applying 'the provisions of a national law specifically introduced in order to implement' the directive,[148] but also 'whether the provisions in question were adopted before or after the directive'.[149] National courts are required to consider national law as a whole in order to assess to what extent it may be applied so as not to produce a result contrary to that sought by the directive.[150]

The general obligation incumbent upon national courts to interpret national law in conformity with the directive exists only once the period for its transposition has expired. However, before that date, national courts are under a duty, in accordance with *Inter-Environnement Wallonie* (see para. 27.021, *supra*), to refrain as far as possible from interpreting national law in a manner which might seriously compromise the attainment of the objective pursued by the directive after the period for transposition has expired.[151]

After the expiry of the time-limit for implementation, the national court is also under a duty to interpret, in the light of the directive, rules of law not adopted specifically in order to transpose the directive at least with respect to facts which occurred after the expiry of that time-limit.[152] Pursuant to a principle of national law according to which more favourable provisions of criminal law have retroactive effect, national courts may set aside domestic provisions which conflict with a directive (whether transposed or not) in respect of offences that occurred before the period prescribed for transposition had expired.[153]

27.030 **Possibility of interpretation in conformity with the directive.** The national court must interpret national law 'as far as possible' in conformity with the directive.[154] The relevant provision of national law must, however, be amenable to such interpretation.[155] The national court is indeed not obliged to make an interpretation *contra legem*.[156] The obligation to interpret national law in conformity with a directive is also 'limited by the general principles of law which form part of [Union] law and in particular the principles of legal certainty and non-retroactivity'.[157] However, within these limits, national courts must, where necessary,

---

[147] 14/83, *Von Colson and Kamann*, 1984, para. 26; 79/83, *Harz*, 1984, para. 26.
[148] Ibid.
[149] C-106/89, *Marleasing*, 1990, para. 8; C-188/07, *Commune de Mesquer*, 2008, paras 80–5.
[150] C-131/97, *Carbonari and Others*, 1999, paras 49 and 50; C-397/01 to C-403/01, *Pfeiffer*, 2004, para. 115; C-12/08, *Mono Car Styling*, 2009, para. 62; C-282/10, *Dominguez*, 2012, paras 27–31; C-42/11, *Lopes Da Silva Jorge*, 2012, para. 56; C-573/17, *Popławski*, 2019, paras 77–9.
[151] C-212/04, *Adeneler*, 2006, para. 113–23; C-364/07, *Vassilakis and Others* (order), 2008, paras 53–71; C-378/07 to C-380/07, *Angelidaki and Others*, 2009, paras 197–201; C-304/08, *Plus Warenhandelsgesellschaft*, 2010, para. 29. Where the directive provides for the application of certain provisions from the date of its entry into force, national provisions that fall within the scope of that directive may have to be interpreted in conformity therewith: C-81/05, *Cordero Alonso*, 2006, paras 27–34.
[152] C-456/98, *Centrosteel*, 1998, para. 17, with note by Corthaut (2002) Col JEL 293–310; C-397/01 to C-403/01, *Pfeiffer*, 2004, para. 117.
[153] C-230/97, *Awoyemi*, 1998, paras 32–45.
[154] C-106/89, *Marleasing*, 1990, para. 8.
[155] C-334/92, *Wagner Miret*, 1993, para. 22.
[156] C-212/04, *Adeneler*, 2006, para. 110; C-176/12, *Association de médiation sociale*, 2014, paras 38–9; C-122/17, *Smith*, 2018, para. 40.
[157] 80/86, *Kolpinghuis Nijmegen*, 1987, para. 13; for an application, see 14/86, *Pretore de Salò*, 1987, para. 20; C-74/95 and C-129/95, *Criminal proceedings against X*, 1996, paras 25 and 31; C-122/17, *Smith*, 2018, para. 40. For the limits which national law may place on the ability to interpret national law in conformity with a directive, see

adjust the existing case law. They must do whatever lies within their jurisdiction to ensure a result which is consistent with the directive.[158] For the same reason, national courts may be required, in certain circumstances, to set aside rules of national law that conflict with the provisions of the directive in question (see para. 27.032, *supra*).

Consequences for individuals. The obligation to interpret national law in conformity with directives holds good irrespective of whether their provisions have direct effect. As a result of such an interpretation of national law, the provisions of the directive in question may also be effective vis-à-vis individuals, who may be subject to certain obligations or forced to drop certain claims vis-à-vis another individual or a public body.[159] In such case, there is no question of a non-implemented directive imposing obligations on individuals as any obligation falling on individuals would be based on the provisions of national law.[160] The duty to interpret national law in conformity with Union law comes up against a limitation, however, where such an interpretation would have the effect of determining or aggravating, on the basis of a directive (in the absence of national legislation adopted for its implementation), the liability in criminal law of persons acting in contravention of the directive's provisions.[161] Even where criminal liability arises under national legislation adopted for the specific purpose of implementing a directive, the national court must take account of the principle that criminal proceedings may not be brought in respect of conduct which is not clearly defined as culpable by law.[162] **27.031**

In proceedings between individuals, it is up to the national court to determine whether, in the absence of direct effect, the provisions of national law can be interpreted to achieve the result claimed by the applicant,[163] if necessary by disapplying conflicting rules of national law.[164] In *Pfeiffer*, which concerned a dispute between employees and their private employer, the Court held that if the application of interpretative methods recognized by national law enables a provision of domestic law to be construed in such a way as to avoid conflict with another rule of domestic law or the scope of that provision to be restricted to that end by applying it only in so far as it is compatible with the rule concerned, the national court is bound to use those methods in order to achieve the result sought by the directive.[165]

Roth, 'Die richtlinienkonforme Auslegung' (2005) EWS 385–96; Schürnbrand, 'Die Grenzen richtlinienkonformer Rechtsfortbildung im Privatrecht' (2007) JZ 910–18.

[158] C-397/01 to C-403/01, *Pfeiffer*, 2004, paras 116–18. See also C-177/10, *Rosado Santana*, 2011, paras 51–61 (also when there is contrary case law from the constitutional court); C-122/17, *Smith*, 2018, para. 39.

[159] Interpreting national law in the light of the directive may result in an individual being held to comply with certain obligations under national law or in that individual being precluded from effectuating claims against another individual. See C-106/89, *Marleasing*, 1990, paras 6–9; C-421/92, *Habermann-Beltermann*, 1994, paras 8–10; C-472/93, *Spano and Others*, 1995, paras 17–18; C-129/94, *Ruiz Bernáldez*, 1996, paras 1–26; C-240/98 to C-244/98, *Océano Grupo Editorial and Others*, 2000, paras 20–32; C-456/98 *Centrosteel*, 2000, paras 13–18, the last two with note by Corthaut (2002) Col JEL 293–310. See further C-53/10, *Mücksch*, 2011, paras 21–34 (directive invoked by a public body against a private party).

[160] C-321/05, *Kofoed*, 2007, para. 45; C-53/10, *Mücksch*, 2011, para. 34.

[161] 14/86, *Pretore di Salò*, 1987, para. 20; 80/86, *Kolpinghuis Nijmegen*, 1987, paras 13–14; C-168/95, *Arcaro*, 1996, para. 42.

[162] C-74/95 and C-129/95, *Criminal proceedings against X*, 1996, para. 25 (which refers to Article 7 ECHR); C-387/02, C-391/02, and C-403/02, *Berlusconi and Others*, 2005, paras 74–7.

[163] See, e.g., C-343/98, *Collino and Chiaperro*, 2000, paras 20–4.

[164] See, e.g., C-456/98, *Centrosteel*, 2000, para. 17

[165] C-397/01 to C-403/01, *Pfeiffer*, 2004, para. 116; C-12/08, *Mono Car Styling*, 2009, para. 63.

b. Disapplication of conflicting national law.

27.032 **Disapplication.** Second, it follows from the primacy of Union law that the provisions of a directive must enjoy precedence over conflicting rules of national law. The question whether a rule of national law must be set aside in so far as it conflicts with a directive arises, however, only if no interpretation of that rule in conformity with that directive proves possible.[166] The directive needs to be sufficiently clear in order to serve as a yardstick.[167] This applies in the first place to measures taken specifically with a view to implementing a directive. The national court must consider 'whether the competent national authorities, in exercising the choice which is left to them as to the form and the methods of implementing the directive, have kept within the limits as to their discretion set out in the directive'.[168] If national law confers on courts and tribunals discretion to apply mandatory rules of law of their own motion, they must examine *ex proprio motu* whether the national authorities remained within the limits of their discretion under the directive.[169] But the review of national law in the light of the directive extends further than measures taken to implement it; it covers all rules governing the application of the directive in the national legal system, including rules that already applied before the directive was adopted.[170] In this connection, a national court may be obliged to refrain from applying national procedural or jurisdictional rules which would impede the protection of rights contained in the directive (see para. 29.008 *et seq.*, *infra*). In principle, the obligation to set aside conflicting rules of national law exists only after the deadline for implementing the directive has expired.[171]

Public authorities other than the courts must also refrain from applying national rules that conflict with a directive. For instance, a local authority has been held to be under a duty to refrain from applying conflicting provisions of a national law.[172] Similarly, a national body established to ensure enforcement of Union law in a particular area must be able to disapply a rule of national law that is contrary to Union law.[173] Moreover, all the authorities of a Member State must take, according to their respective powers, all the general and particular measures necessary to ensure that the result sought by the directive is achieved.[174]

27.033 **Consequences for private parties.** The Court of Justice has clarified the obligation to disapply conflicting rules of national law in a number of cases where provisions of an unimplemented or incorrectly implemented directive have been invoked against a public authority. In such a 'vertical' context, the disapplication of conflicting rules of national law may indirectly have repercussions on the legal position of private parties who draw rights

---

[166] C-122/17, *Smith*, 2018, para. 41; see also C-282/10, *Dominguez*, 2012, 23; C-97/11, *Amia*, 2012, paras 27–41.
[167] See C-72/95, *Kraaijeveld and Others*, 1996, paras 59–61; C-435/97, *World Wildlife Fund*, 1999, paras 69–71; C-287/98, *Linster and Others*, 2000, paras 31–9; C-573/17, *Popławski*, 2019, para. 64.
[168] 51/76, *Verbond van Nederlandse Ondernemingen*, 1977, paras 22–4; 38/77, *Enka*, 1977, paras 10 and 17–18. This is also true of individual decisions: 36/75, *Rutili*, 1975, paras 17–20. See also C-573/17, *Popławski*, 2019, para. 69.
[169] C-72/95, *Kraaijeveld and Others*, 1996, paras 57–8.
[170] 21/78, *Delkvist*, 1978, paras 13–16. For the inapplicability of rules adopted contrary to a duty of notification laid down by a directive, see n. 177, *infra*.
[171] C-157/02, *Rieser Internationale Transporte and Asfinag*, 2004, paras 67–8. For the situation during the period for implementation, see para. 27-021, *supra*.
[172] 103/88, *Fratelli Costanzo*, 1989 para. 33.
[173] e.g. the Irish Workplace Relations Commission, tasked with the enforcement of Council Directive 2000/78/EC of 27 November 2000 establishing a general framework for equal treatment in employment and occupation; see C-378/17, *Minister for Justice and Equality*, 2018, paras 31–52.
[174] C-72/95, *Kraaijeveld and Others*, 1996, para. 61; C-435/97, *World Wildlife Fund*, 1999, para. 70.

from these rules or are exempted under these rules from certain obligations. This will be the case, for example, where a private party challenges the legality of decisions (on grounds of incompatibility with a Union directive) by which national authorities approve private projects having an effect on the environment[175] or grant a marketing authorization to a competitor.[176] The same will be true where national rules are disapplied because they were adopted contrary to a duty of notification imposed by a Union directive.[177] However, in the light of the absence of horizontal direct effect of directives, these cases involving procedural obligations resting on the State must be distinguished from cases where the substantive content of a provision from a directive is invoked in order to set aside conflicting national legislation in a dispute between private parties.[178]

Where a national court is confronted with conflicting rules of national law in litigation between private parties and decides to ask the Court of Justice for a preliminary ruling, it may be prompted by the Court's answer to set aside the conflicting rules of national law.[179] Union law, combined with national standards of interpretation, may also require a national court to set aside conflicting rules of national law where an individual invokes provisions of an unimplemented or incorrectly implemented directive against another individual.[180] However, in such a dispute between private parties, even if the applicable national rules are contrary to provisions of a directive satisfying the conditions required to produce direct effect, a national court which finds that it is unable to interpret those national rules in a manner that is compatible with the directive, is not obliged, solely on the basis of Union law, to set aside those conflicting rules of national law.[181]

Nevertheless, the Court confirmed in *Kücükdevici*—in proceedings between an employee and her former (private) employer—that the principle of non-discrimination on grounds of age, as a general principle of Union law recognized in Article 21 of the Charter of Fundamental Rights of the European Union and given further expression in Directive 2000/78, requires the national court to disapply any contrary provision of national law.[182] Thus, the disapplication of the conflicting national provision—the prohibition on taking into account in calculating the period of notice for dismissals any period of employment completed by the employee before reaching the age of 25—led to the imposition on the employer of the obligation not to discriminate on grounds of age, as expressed both in a general principle of Union law and in Directive 2000/78. This ruling of the Court shows that

---

[175] e.g. the cases cited in n. 174; see also C-201/02, *Wells*, 2004, cited in para. 27-026, *supra*); C-41/11, *Inter-Environnement Wallonie and Terre wallonne*, 2012; C-24/19, *A and Others*, 2020.

[176] e.g C-201/94, *Smith & Nephew and Primecrown*, 1996, paras 35–9.

[177] C-194/94, *CIA Security International*, 1996, paras 32–55; C-443/98, *Unilever Italia*, 2000, paras 45–51; C-390/18, *Airbnb Ireland*, 2019, paras 95–9. See Weatherill, 'Breach of Directives and Breach of Contract' (2001) ELRev 177–86.

[178] C-122/17, *Smith*, 2018, para. 53.

[179] See, e.g., C-85/94 *Piageme and Others*, 1995, paras 1–31; C-441/93, *Pafitis and Others*, 1996, paras 1–70; C-180/95, *Draehmpaehl*, 1997, paras 16–43; C-215/97, *Bellone*, paras 9–18.

[180] See C-397/01 to C-403/01, *Pfeiffer*, 2004, para. 116 (litigation between employees and private employer). The Court considered disapplication of conflicting provisions of national law as an 'interpretative method' to be used by national courts in order to achieve the result sought by the directive where such a method is recognized by national law (ibid.).

[181] C-122/17, *Smith*, 2018, paras 34–57; C-569/16 and C-570/16, *Bauer*, 2018, paras 76–8. See also Wildemeersch, 'Primauté, vous avez dit primauté? Sur l'invocabilité des directives dans les litiges entre particuliers' (2018) RAE 541–53.

[182] C-555/07, *Kücükdeveci*, 2010, paras 51–5. See also C-476/11, *HK Danmark*, 2013, paras 17–32.

to the extent that directives are giving concrete content to a general principle of Union law enshrined in the Charter and that principle lends itself to application between private parties, the horizontal effect of that principle, as understood on the basis of the directive, may lead to disapplication of contrary national provisions.[183] This requires, however, that the principle enshrined in the Charter suffices to confer on individuals a right which they may invoke as such. That is, for instance, the case for the right to an annual period of paid leave set out in Article 31(2) of the Charter[184] but not for Article 27 of the Charter on the information for and consultation of employees within enterprises.[185]

As such the situation in *Kücükdeveci* is also to be distinguished from that in which the disapplication of national provisions would lead to the imposition on an individual, without any basis in national law, of an obligation laid down solely by a directive which had not been (correctly) implemented.[186] In a setting of that kind, disapplication of national provisions is not required by Union law, nor may it have the effect of determining or aggravating, on the basis of the directive and in the absence of a national law enacted for its implementation, the liability in criminal law of persons who act in contravention of that directive's provisions.[187]

c. State liability for damages

27.034 **State liability.** An individual may obtain redress for loss or damage sustained as the result of the non-transposition of a directive by bringing a damages claim against the Member State. The fate of the claim does not depend on the extent to which national law recognizes that the State may be liable for legislative action or inaction. Following the judgment in *Francovich* (see para. 23.019, *supra*), it has become clear that liability for loss or damage caused by a breach of Union law constitutes a general principle of Union law, as 'the full effectiveness of EU rules would be impaired and the protection of the rights which they grant would be weakened if individuals were unable to obtain reparation when their rights are infringed by a breach of EU law for which a Member State can be held responsible'.[188] The Court of Justice has indicated that it would be possible to bring a damages claim where an individual could not rely on the provisions of a non-implemented directive on the ground that such provisions required additional implementing measures and hence could not have direct effect,[189] that the national law could not be interpreted in conformity with the directive,[190] or

---

[183] See also C-441/14, *Dansk Industri*, 2016, paras 30–42; C-414/16, *Egenberger*, 2018, paras 70–82; C-68/17, *IR*, 2018, paras 62–71; C-193/17, *Cresco Investigation*, 2018, paras 77–89.
[184] C-684/16, *Max-Planck-Gesellschaft zur Förderung der Wissenschaften*, 2018, paras 62–81; C-569/16 and C-570/16, *Bauer*, 2018, paras 79–92.
[185] C-176/12, *Association de médiation sociale*, 2014, paras 46–9.
[186] C-233/01, *Riunione Adriatica di Securtà* (order), 2002, paras 20–1 (interpretation cannot enable the national court to give judgment against an individual for the payment of a debt which the Court held not to be based on national law). See also Lenaerts and Corthaut, 'Towards an Internally Consistent Doctrine on Invoking Norms of EU Law', in Prechal and Van Roermund (eds), *The Coherence of EU Law. The Search for Unity in Divergent Concepts* (OUP, 2008), 495–515; A[rnull], 'Editorial: The Incidental Effect of Directives' (1999) ELRev 1–2; Lackhoff and Nyssens, 'Direct Effect of Directives in Triangular Situations' (1998) ELRev.397.
[187] C-168/95, *Arcaro*, 1996, paras 39–43; C-387/02, C-391/02, and C-403/02, *Berlusconi and Others*, 2005, paras 71–8. See Gelter, 'Judicial Federalism in the ECJ's Berlusconi Case: Toward More Credible Corporate Governance and Financial Reporting' (2005) Harv ILJ 487–505.
[188] C-573/17, *Popławski*, 2019, para. 56; see earlier, C-6/90 and C-9/90, *Francovich and Others*, 1991, para. 33.
[189] C-6/90 and C-9/90, *Francovich and Others*, 1991, paras 26–7.
[190] C-334/92, *Wagner Miret*, 1993, para. 22; C-111/97, *Evobus Austria*, 1998, paras 14–21.

that the provisions—albeit satisfying the substantive requirements for direct effect—were invoked against another individual.[191] This does not mean that there is also no right to damages where a provision having direct effect is infringed.

Conditions. In *Francovich* the Court set out the conditions under which Member States are bound under Union law to make good loss or damage suffered by individuals as a result of a failure to transpose a directive.[192] In later case law, the Court extended these conditions to all breaches of Union law. As a result, in the case of directives that were not or incorrectly implemented, State liability will exist under the same three conditions that apply for breaches of Union law in general: (1) the rule of law infringed must be intended to confer rights on individuals, (2) the breach must be sufficiently serious, and (3) there must be a direct causal link between the breach of the obligation resting on the State and the damage sustained by the injured parties[193] (see para. 23.020 *et seq., supra*).

27.035

The first condition depends solely on the content of the directive that the Member State has breached. A directive that contains rights and corresponding obligations aimed at protecting individuals that can be identified by reference to the provisions of the directive alone, will thus be seen as conferring rights on individuals;[194] by contrast, obligations that are owed to the public in general may not meet the test.[195]

As to the second condition, the decisive criterion for a breach of Union law to be regarded as sufficiently serious is whether the Member State has manifestly and gravely disregarded the limits of its discretion.[196] Where a Member State fails to take any of the measures necessary to achieve the result prescribed by the directive within the period it lays down, this in itself will constitute a sufficiently serious breach of Union law.[197] In the case of an incorrectly implemented directive, the breach will be 'sufficiently serious' where the Member State manifestly and gravely disregarded the limits on the exercise of its discretion.[198] Factors which the competent court may take into consideration include, in particular, the clarity and precision of the rule breached and the scope of

---

[191] C-91/92, *Faccini Dori*, 1994, para. 25; C-192/94, *El Corte Inglés*, 1996, para. 22; C-282/10, *Dominguez*, 2012, para. 43. Compare C-97/96, *Daihatsu Deutschland*, 1997, paras 24–6 (where, with regard to a dispute between private legal persons, the Court of Justice did not consider it necessary to inquire into the direct effect of the directive and merely referred to the possibility of a damages claim) with C-253/96 to C-258/96, *Kampelmann and Others*, 1997, para. 46 (where, with regard to disputes between individuals and public undertakings, the Court inquired into direct effect and did not discuss the damages claim).
[192] C-6/90 and C-9/90, *Francovich and Others*, 1991, paras 39–41; C-91/92, *Faccini Dori*, 1994, para. 27.
[193] C-6/90 and C-9/90, *Francovich and Others*, 1991, paras 40–1; C-392/93, *British Telecommunications*, 1996, para. 39; C-501/12 to C-506/12, C-540/12, and C-541/12, *Specht*, 2014, para. 99. These rules have applied to legislative acts of the Union since 5/71, *Zuckerfabrik Schöppenstedt v Council*, 1971, para. 11: see Lenaerts, Gutman, and Nowak, *EU Procedural Law* (OUP, 2022), Chapter 11. For the parallel with the rules on liability applying to the Union, see C-352/98 P, *Laboratoires pharmaceutiques Bergaderm and Goupil*, 2000, paras 38–44; for breaches of fundamental rights, see Van Gerven, 'Remedies for Infringements of Fundamental Rights' (2004) E Pub L 261–84.
[194] C-91/92, *Faccini Dori*, 1994, para. 28; C-17/17, *Hampshire*, paras 57–60.
[195] For an example, see C-222/02, *Paul*, 2004, paras 24–51, where it was held that the duty of a Member State to provide for effective prudential supervision did not confer rights on individuals; by contrast the obligation to set up a deposit guarantee scheme does confer a right on individuals to have their deposits protected up to the limit.
[196] C-470/03, *A.G.M.-COS.MET*, 2007, para. 80, see case note by Bouhier (2007) RTDE 693–719.
[197] C-178/94, C-179/94, C-188/94, C-189/94, and C-190/94, *Dillenkofer and Others*, 1996, para. 26; C-150/99, *Stockholm Lindöpark*, 2001, paras 36–41.
[198] C-392/93, *British Telecommunications*, 1996, paras 39–45

the discretion left to the national authorities.[199] Where, however, at the time when it committed the infringement, a Member State was not called upon to make any legislative choices and had only considerably reduced discretion, or even none at all, the mere infringement of Union law may be sufficient to establish the existence of a sufficiently serious breach.[200] Such a breach of Union law may exist on the basis of the wrong transposition of only one sufficiently clear provision of a directive.[201] Where a directive leaves a degree of discretion to Member States, resulting in their having to make choices when legislating to transpose the directive, the national court hearing a damages claim must take account of all the factors which characterize the situation put before it. Those factors include, in particular, in addition to the clarity and precision of the rule infringed and the measure of discretion left by that rule to the national authorities, whether the infringement or the damage caused was intentional or involuntary, whether any error of law was excusable or inexcusable, and the fact that the position taken by a Union institution may have contributed towards the adoption or maintenance of national measures or practices contrary to Union law.[202] Accordingly, the incorrect transposition of provisions of a directive capable of bearing several interpretations on which neither the Court of Justice nor the Commission have given a ruling does not constitute a sufficiently serious breach.[203]

There is no need for the existence of intentional fault or negligence on the part of the organ of the State for the breach to entail a right to damages, provided that the aforementioned three conditions are satisfied.[204] Nor is reparation dependent on a prior finding by the Court of Justice of an infringement of Union law attributable to the State.[205]

27.036 **Reparation of damage.** Retroactive application in full of the measures implementing the directive constitutes proper reparation, unless the beneficiaries establish the existence of a complementary loss resulting from failure to implement the directive in time, in which case such loss must also be made good.[206] Bringing a claim for damages may be made subject to a reasonable limitation period (such as one year commencing from the entry into force of the measure transposing the directive), provided that such procedural rule is not less favourable than those relating to similar domestic claims.[207] The formal and substantive conditions laid down by national law must indeed not be less favourable than those relating to similar domestic claims and must not be such as to make it impossible or excessively difficult to obtain compensation in practice (see para. 29.012, *infra*).

---

[199] C-318/13, *X*, 2014, para. 42.
[200] C-5/94, *Hedley Lomas*, 1996, para. 28; C-452/06, *Synthon*, 2008, paras 36–45.
[201] C-140/97, *Rechberger and Greindl*, 1999, paras 51–3.
[202] C-278/05, *Robins and Others*, 2007, paras 77–81.
[203] Ibid., paras 42–6; see also C-283/94, C-291/94, and C-292/94, *Denkavit and Others*, 1996, paras 50–3; C-319/96 *Brinkmann Tabakfabriken*, 1998, paras 30–1; C-168/15, *Tomášová*, 2016, paras 27–33. Compare C-318/13, *X*, 2014, paras 46–50, where the assessment is nevertheless left to the national court.
[204] For lack of a direct causal link between the infringement of Union law and the damage, see C-319/96, *Brinkmann Tabakfabriken*, 1998, para. 29.
[205] C-178/94, C-179/94, C-188/94, C-189/94, and C-190/94, *Dillenkofer and Others*, 1996, paras 27–8; C-445/06, *Danske Slagterier*, 2009, paras 37–8.
[206] C-94-95/95, *Bonifaci and Others and Berto and Others*, 1997, paras 51–4; C-373/95, *Maso and Others*, 1997, paras 39–42; C-616/16 and C-617/16, *Pantuso*, 2018, para. 50; C-129/19, *BV*, 2020, para. 29.
[207] C-261/95, *Palmisani*, 1997, paras 28–40.

D. Decisions

Definition. A decision is 'binding in its entirety'. A decision 'which specifies those to whom it is addressed' is 'binding only on them' (Article 288, fourth para. TFEU). It follows that a decision is not necessarily addressed to specific persons and can be general in scope. 27.037

'*Sui generis*' decisions. This definition, introduced by the Lisbon Treaty, is wider in scope than the one contained in Article 249, fourth para. EC, which provided that 'a decision shall be binding in its entirety upon those to whom it is addressed'. Accordingly, a decision in the sense of Article 249 EC necessarily had specific addressees. 27.038
All the same, the institutions often used 'decisions' for binding acts which did not satisfy this definition. These 'decisions' were sometimes referred to as '*sui generis* decisions' (termed in Dutch a *besluit* and in German a *Beschluss* and hence differing from the terms *beschikking* and *Entscheidung* used in Article 249 EC). Contrary to other decisions these '*sui generis* decisions' were acts with a general scope of application, by which the institutions used to adopt binding measures.[208] Since the Lisbon Treaty, such '*sui generis* decisions' are also adopted as decisions under the fourth para. of Article 288 TFEU. Where a Treaty provision provides for the adoption of a decision, another instrument may not be adopted, as this creates uncertainty as to the legal nature and scope of that act.[209]

Individual or general scope. It is clear from the definition in Article 288 TFEU that a decision will often, but not necessarily, be a measure of individual scope. As a measure of individual scope, a decision is an appropriate instrument for implementing acts of the institutions. Thus, when supervising compliance with the competition rules, the Commission addresses decisions to the undertakings and Member States concerned.[210] With regard to Article 106(3) TFEU—which entitles the Commission to adopt both directives and decisions—the Court of Justice has explained that directives enable the Commission to specify in general terms the obligations arising for Member States under the Treaties, while the possibility of adopting decisions empowers the Commission to determine that a given State measure is incompatible with the rules of the Treaties and to indicate what measures the State concerned must adopt in order to comply with its obligations under Union law.[211] 27.039

A decision may be addressed to individuals and Member States alike. A decision addressed to all the Member States may constitute an act of a legislative nature.[212] An innominate act addressed by an institution to a particular person may constitute a decision only if it is intended to produce legal effects.[213]

---

[208] Accordingly, the institutions have been using such 'decisons' when adopting acts on the basis of Treaty provisions that do not require the use of a particular legal instrument (such as Article 308 EC [*now Article 352 TFEU*]), to conclude international agreements or for their internal organization.
[209] C-687/15, *Commission v Council*, 2017, para. 44.
[210] Articles 105(2) and 106(3) TFEU. See also the Treaty articles requiring the Commission to use a decision as a normative instrument: Articles 95(4) and 96(2), second subpara. TFEU.
[211] See C-48/90 and C-66/90, *Netherlands and Others v Commission*, 1992, paras 26–7.
[212] See, e.g., Council Decision 98/415/EC of 29 June 1998 on the consultation of the European Central Bank by the national authorities on draft legislative provisions, OJ 1998 L189/42 (adopted pursuant to Article 105(4) EC [*now Article 127(4) TFEU*] and Article 4 of the ESCB Statute). For decisions addressed to the Member States, see Mager, 'Die staatengerichtete Entscheidung als supranationale Handlungsform' (2001) EuR 661–81.
[213] See Lenaerts, Gutman, and Nowak, *EU Procedural Law* (OUP, 2022), Chapter 7.

27.040 **Binding force.** A decision is binding in its entirety.[214] Decisions addressed to the Member States are binding on all institutions of the State concerned, including the judiciary. Accordingly, they are under a duty, by virtue of the primacy of Union law, to refrain from applying any national provisions which would be likely to hinder the implementation of a decision.[215] Decisions with specific addressees are binding only on the latter.[216] The principle of legal certainty precludes reliance on a decision addressed to a Member State against the beneficiary of that decision, if the decision was not published and its content not made known to the beneficiary.[217] Nevertheless, a public authority may take a particular decision addressed to a specific addressee—such as the refusal by the Commission to grant an authorization for placing a novel product on the market—into account when applying the relevant general obligations.[218]

27.041 **Direct effect.** In certain circumstances the provisions of a decision may have direct effect in the sense that an individual may rely on them in a dispute with a public authority.[219] The Court of Justice has held that '[p]articularly in cases where, for example, the Community authorities by means of a decision have imposed an obligation on a Member State or all the Member States to act in a certain way, the effectiveness (*effet utile*) of such a measure would be weakened if the nationals of that State could not invoke it in the courts and the national courts could not take it into consideration as part of Community law'.[220] The Court added that 'in each particular case, it must be ascertained whether the nature, background and wording of the provision in question are capable of producing direct effects in the legal relationship between the addressee of the act and third parties'.[221] In the same way as provisions of a directive, provisions of a decision may have direct effect only if they are precise and unconditional and the period, if any, within which a Member State had to comply with it has expired.[222] In common with directives, decisions addressed to one or more Member States do not have 'horizontal direct effect'. Decisions which have the Member States as their sole addressees, and hence are binding only upon the Member States, cannot be relied upon by an individual in the context of legal proceedings against another individual.[223]

---

[214] e.g. C-42/10, C-45/10, and C-57/10, *Vlaamse Dierenartsvereniging and Janssens*, 2010, paras 60–5 (mandatory nature of a model document annexed to the decision). See also C-584/18, *D.Z.*, 2020, paras 50–51.

[215] 249/85, *Albako*, 1987, para. 17; also C-584/18, *D.Z.*, 2020, paras 49–63. But see C-362/14, *Schrems*, 2015, para. 65 (a national data protection authority that considers a Commission decision on the 'adequacy' of the level of protection of personal data in a third country to be invalid, is nevertheless bound by that decision, until the Court of Justice has found it invalid following a preliminary reference by a national court in a procedure initiated to that effect by the national data protection authority) as well as the procedure leading to C-311/18, *Facebook Ireland and Schrems*, 2020.

[216] T-173/09 R, *Z v Commission* (order of the President), 2009, paras 28–31.

[217] C-158/06, *ROM-projecten*, 2007, paras 23–31.

[218] C-327/09, *Mensch und Natur*, 2010, paras 25–36.

[219] 249/85, *Albako*, 1987, para. 10. See Verhoeven, 'De rechtstreekse werking van de communautaire beschikking' (2008) AAe 214–16.

[220] 9/70, *Grad*, 1970, para. 5.

[221] Ibid., para. 6. See also the parallel judgments 20/70, *Lesage*, 1970, paras 5–6, 23/70, *Haselhorst*, 1970, paras 5–6.

[222] C-156/91, *Hansa Fleisch Ernst Mundt*, 1992, paras 15–20. See also also C-584/18, *D.Z.*, 2020, paras 64–69.

[223] C-80/06, *Carp*, 2007, paras 20–2.

E. Recommendations and opinions

No binding force. According to the fifth para. of Article 288 TFEU, recommendations and opinions have no binding force.[224] **27.042**

Recommendations are adopted by the Council or, in the specific cases provided for in the Treaties, by the Commission or the European Central Bank (Article 292 TFEU).[225] Where the Council adopts recommendations, it must act on a proposal from the Commission in all cases where the Treaties provide that it shall adopt acts on a proposal from the Commission. In those areas in which unanimity is required for the adoption of a Union act, it must act unanimously (Article 292 TFEU). The Court of Justice has held that recommendations are 'measures which, even as regards the persons to whom they are addressed, are not intended to produce binding effects', and 'generally adopted by the institutions of the [Union] when they do not have the power under the [Treaties] to adopt binding measures or when they consider that it is not appropriate to adopt more mandatory rules'.[226] They do not create rights upon which individuals may rely before a national court.[227] Due to their lack of binding effect it is not possible to challenge the validity of recommendations in a direct action pursuant to Article 263 TFEU.[228]

Union legislation may leave certain decisions to national authorities while allowing the Commission to express an opinion. Such an opinion has no legal effects and is not binding upon the national authorities.[229]

Some legal effect. Nevertheless, a recommendation may not be regarded as having no legal effect at all. The Court of Justice has observed that '[t]he national courts are bound to take recommendations into consideration in order to decide disputes submitted to them, in particular when they cast light on the interpretation of national measures adopted in order to implement them or where they are designed to supplement binding [Union] provisions'.[230] Where several interpretations of national or Union provisions are possible, it would appear that the principle of sincere cooperation (Article 4(3) TEU) requires the national courts to adopt the interpretation which best corresponds to the aim of the recommendation. Thus, **27.043**

---

[224] This was also true of ECSC opinions (Article 14, fourth para. EC), but not of ECSC recommendations (see n. 75, *supra*).
[225] As regards the Council, see, *inter alia*, Articles 121(2), third subpara. and (4), first subpara.; 148(4); 165(4), second indent; 167(5), second indent; 168(6); 319(1) TFEU; as a stage in a supervisory procedure: see Article 126(7) TFEU; as regards the Commission: see para. 12-060, *supra* (participation in decision-making) and para. 17-015, *supra* (right of initiative); as regards the ECB, see Article 129(3) and (4) TFEU; Article 219(1) and (2) TFEU; and Article 289(4) TFEU.
[226] C-322/88, *Grimaldi*, 1989, paras 13 and 16.
[227] Ibid., para. 16.
[228] C-16/16 P, *Belgium v Commission*, 2018, paras 25–45.
[229] 133/79, *Sucrimex and Westzucker*, 1980, para. 16; 151/88 *Italy v Commission* (order), 1989, para. 22; C-593/15 P and C-594/15 P, *Slovak Republic v Commission*, 2017, para. 60. As a result, it also not possible to bring an action for annulment against such an opinion; see C-575/18 P, *Czech Republic v Commission*, 2020, paras 46–4.
[230] C-322/88, *Grimaldi*, 1989, para. 18; C-317/08 to C-320/08, *Alassini and Others*, 2010, para. 40. Accordingly, while it is not possible to challenge the validity of a recommendation through a direct action pursuant to Article 263 TFEU, Article 267 TFEU confers on the Court jurisdiction to deliver a preliminary ruling on the validity and interpretation of all acts of the Union institutions without exception, including recommendations; see C-16/16 P, *Belgium v Commission*, 2018, para. 44.

the Court has found a recommendation to be invalid in a preliminary reference procedure (Article 267 TFEU).[231]

F. Other acts

27.044   **Atypical instruments.** The list of instruments in Article 288 TFEU does not prevent the Union institutions from producing legal effects by means of other instruments.[232] The institutions often have recourse to 'resolutions', 'declarations', 'conclusions', and other atypical instruments, which are not always intended to have legal effects.[233] Some Treaty provisions refer to 'general orientations',[234] 'guidelines',[235] or 'incentive measures'.[236] The latter take the form, in practice, of decisions and action programmes (see paras 9.050 and 9.053, *supra*), whereas guidelines often take the form of recommendations and decisions (see paras 9.036 and 9.049, *supra*). The European Council is to define the 'general guidelines' for the CFSP[237] and the strategic guidelines for legislative and operational planning within the area of freedom, security, and justice.[238] Pursuant to its Statute, the ECB also has the power to issue 'decisions', 'guidelines', and 'instructions' for national central banks.[239] The Commission, for its part, is increasingly using 'communications', 'guidelines', and 'codes of conduct' in which it sets out the way in which it intends to exercise its power of decision in particular sectors.[240] In certain circumstances, including in the context of the financial crisis, the institutions have adopted 'memoranda of understanding'.[241]

---

[231] C-501/18, *BT*, 2021. In that case, the Court held that a national court must take into consideration a recommendation adopted by the European Banking Authority on the basis of its founding Regulation, in the context of an action before it and that individuals harmed by a breach of Union law established by such a recommendation, even if they are not its addressees, must be able to rely on it as a basis for establishing the Member State's liability for the breach of Union law in question (see para. 81). Still, the Court considered the recommendation partially invalid (see paras 82–101). For other legal effects which may arise out of non-binding acts, see para. 27.045, *infra*.

[232] See 22/70, *Commission v Council*, 1971, paras 41–2.

[233] For the function of such informal acts, see Senden, 'Reguleringsintensiteit en regelgevingsinstrumentarium in het Europees Gemeenschapsrecht. Over de relatie tussen wetgeving, soft law en de open methode van coördinatie' (2008) SEW 43–57; Rubio, 'Les instruments de soft law dans les politiques communautaires: vecteur d'une meilleure articulation entre la politique de la concurrence et la politique de cohésion economique et sociale' (2007) RTDE 597–608; Lefèvre, *Les actes communautaires atypiques* (Bruylant, 2006),; Everling, 'Zur rechtlichen Wirkung von Beschlüssen, Entschliessungen, Erklärungen und Vereinbarungen des Rates oder der Mitgliedstaaten der Europäischen Gemeinschaft', in Lüke, Ress, and Will (eds), *Rechtsvergleichung, Europarecht und Staatenintegration. Gedächtnisschrift für L.-J. Constantinesco* (Heymann, 1983), 133, 144–7; Klabbers, 'Informal Instruments before the European Court of Justice' (1994) CMLRev 997, 1003–4. For their status in the national legal systems, see, e.g., Gautier, 'Le Conseil d'Etat français et les actes "hors nomenclature" de la Communauté européenne' (1995) RTDE 23–37.

[234] Article 219(2) TFEU.

[235] See, *inter alia*, Articles 5; 26(3); 68 TFEU and Articles 121(2); 148(2); 171(1), first indent TFEU.

[236] Articles 19(2); 149; 165(4), first indent; 167(5), first indent; 168(5) TFEU.

[237] Articles 25(a) and 26(1) TEU.

[238] Article 68 TFEU.

[239] ECB Statute, Article 12(1).

[240] e.g., with regard to competition policy, see paras 9.016, 9.018 and 9.020, *supra*; see Cosma and Whish, 'Soft Law in the Field of EU Competition Policy' (2003) EBus LRev 25–56. See also the European Parliament's resolution of 4 September 2007 on institutional and legal implications of the use of 'soft law' instruments (P6_TA(2007)0366).

[241] On this novelty, see Karatzia and Konstadinides, 'The Legal Nature and Character of Memoranda of Understanding as Instruments Used by the European Central Bank' (2019) E.L.Rev. 447–467. Compare the memorandum of understanding as an instrument of Union law, based on Article 143 TFEU, at issue in C-258/14, *Florescu*, 2017, with the same instrument used outside Union law in C-8/15 P, *Ledra Advertising v Commission and ECB*, 2016.

Legal effects. The precise legal effects of an 'atypical' act must be determined in the light of its content. Accordingly, the Court held in the *AETR* judgment that the Council's 'proceedings' of 20 March 1970 regarding the stance to be adopted by the national governments in negotiations on an international transport agreement 'could not have been simply the expression or the recognition of a voluntary coordination, but were designed to lay down a course of action binding on both the institutions and the Member States'.[242] Many atypical instruments indicate themselves whether the institution which issued them intended to adopt legally binding norms.[243] It follows from Article 12(1) of the Statute of the ECB that the 'guidelines' and 'instructions' issued by it may contain legally binding provisions.[244]

27.045

In addition, such 'atypical' acts from institutions have legal effects if they create in individuals a legitimate expectation that the institution concerned will adhere to a stated policy line.[245] This also applies in the relationship between institutions and Member States. The Commission is therefore bound by the guidelines and notices that it issues in the area of supervision of State aid where they do not depart from the rules in the Treaty and are accepted by the Member States.[246] In addition, a non-binding act by which an institution regards itself as being bound must be viewed as a rule of conduct from which the institution may diverge only if it gives reasons for doing so, on account of the principle of protection of legitimate expectations[247] and the principle of equal treatment.[248] This does not mean, however, that such an act becomes binding on Member States or other interested parties.[249]

In some cases, an institution is not empowered to adopt acts embodying obligations. Where it nevertheless adopts an act with legal effects, the Court of Justice may declare it void.[250] If an atypical act which has no legal basis either in the Treaties or in any legal act adopted under them is at variance with the provisions of a regulation, the latter take precedence.[251]

---

[242] 22/70, *Commission v Council*, 1971, para. 53.
[243] e.g. C-258/14, *Florescu*, 2017, paras 29–42. See the survey produced by Stefan et al., 'EU Soft Law in the EU Legal Order: A Literature Review' (2019) King's College London Law School Research Paper 1–46; see further Trubek, Cottrell and Nance, ' "Soft Law", "Hard Law", and EU Integration', in de Búrca and Scott (eds), *Law and New Governance in the EU and the US* (Hart Publishing, 2006), 65. Klabbers argues that there is a presumption that even 'informal' instruments are binding (n. 233, *supra*), at 1019–23.
[244] Gaiser, 'Gerichtliche Kontrolle im Europäischen System der Zentralbanken' (2002) EuR 517, 521–2 and 533–4. According to Article 14.3 of the Statute of the European System of Central Banks, the national central banks 'shall act in accordance with the guidelines and instructions of the ECB'.
[245] C-313/90, *CIRFS v Commission*, 1990, paras 34 and 36; T-380/94, *AIUFFASS and AKT v Commission*, 1996, para. 57; T-105/95, *WWF UK v Commission*, 1997, paras 53–5; T-149/95, *Ducros and Others v Commission*, 1997, paras 61–2; C-189/02 P, C-202/02 P, C-205/02 P to C-208/02 P, and C-213/02 P, *Dansk Rørindustri and Others v Commission*, 2005, paras 62–5. See Tournepiche, 'Les communications: instruments privilégiés de l'action administrative de la Commission européenne' (2002) RMCUE 55–62.
[246] C-288/96, *Germany v Commission*, 2000, paras 62–5; C-409/00, *Spain v Commission*, 2003, para. 95; C-91/01, *Italy v Commission*, 2004, para. 45; see also C-594/18 P, *Austria v Commission*, 2020, para. 24.
[247] 81/72, *Commission v Council*, 1973, paras 10–11.
[248] 148/73, *Louwage v Commission*, 1974, para. 12 (internal directive of the Commission); *A. v Commission*, 1994, para. 60 (conclusions of the Council and the Ministers for Health); T-374/04, *Germany v Comission*, 2007, paras 109–11 (guidance contained in a communication of the Commission); T-248/19 *Bilde v European Parliament*, 2020, para. 24 (notice to MEPs from the Parliament's Committee on Legal Affairs with principles on immunity cases).
[249] See, e.g., C-410/09, *Polska Telefonia Cyfrowa*, 2011, paras 31–5; C-526/14, *Kotnik*, 2016, paras 40–5.
[250] See C-303/90, *France v Commission*, 1991, paras 15–35 (annulment of a Commission code of conduct); C-325/91, *France v Commission*, 1993, paras 14–30 (annulment of a Commission communication on the ground that it did not state the legal basis from which it derived legal force); C-57/95, *France v Commission*, 1997 (annulment of a communication by which the Commission purported to impose obligations not already contained in the EC Treaty).
[251] C-110/03, *Belgium v Commission*, 2005, para. 33.

27.046 **Resolutions and conclusions.** A 'resolution' generally contains a statement of intention with regard to a policy programme which an institution wishes to have achieved.[252] In several cases, the Court of Justice has held that a given 'Council resolution' had no binding force[253] or that 'Council conclusions' did not produce any legal effect that could be relied upon before it.[254] All the same, even non-binding 'resolutions' or 'conclusions' can have some legal effects. For one thing, they may be useful for the purposes of interpreting Treaty provisions and binding acts of Union law,[255] although they cannot alter such provisions or acts.[256] Thus, the Court of Justice has had regard to Council resolutions in determining what matters are covered by a policy area assigned to the Union by the Treaties.[257] It is for this reason that, traditionally, whenever they wish to avoid a resolution or a conclusion having effects on the way in which the allocation of powers between the Union and the Member States is interpreted, the members of the Council adopt the relevant act in the form of a 'resolution of the Council and the representatives of the Governments of the Member States, meeting within the Council'.[258] Only on one occasion has the Court of Justice held a Council resolution to have binding force, when it found that it was an application of the duty of sincere cooperation imposed by Article 4(3) TEU. The resolution in fact determined the procedure whereby Member States wished to take the necessary conservation measures in respect of fishery resources in the North Sea.[259] In that case, the resolution contributed to the legitimacy of the temporary measures which the Member States were authorized to take in the absence of a common fisheries policy.[260] Moreover, the Council may not adopt conclusions, where the Treaties explicitly provide for the adoption of a decision, as this creates uncertainty as to the legal nature and scope of that act.[261]

27.047 **Unilateral declarations.** The non-binding acts discussed above must be distinguished from declarations made in the minutes of meetings by institutions or Member States on the

---

[252] See, e.g., the environment action programmes, such as the one provided for in a resolution of 1 February 1993 of the Council of the European Communities and of the representatives of the governments of the Member States, meeting in the Council, OJ 1993 C138/1. The Court of Justice held that this action programme 'does not lay down rules of a mandatory nature': C-142/95 P, *Associazione Agricoltori della Provincia di Rovigo and Others*, 1996, paras 29–32.

[253] See 90–91/63, *Commission v Luxembourg and Belgium*, 1964, 631; 9/73 *Schlüter*, 1973, para. 40; 59/75, *Manghera*, 1976, para. 21.

[254] See C-182/03 and C-217/03, *Belgium and Forum 187 v Commission*, 2006, para. 151.

[255] See e.g., C-91/05, *Commission v Council*, 2008, para. 69 (Council conclusions); C-57/12, *Fédération des maisons de repos privées de Belgique*, 2013, paras 45–7 (communication of the Commission and resolution of the European Parliament); C-5/16, *Commission v Poland*, 2018, paras 76–91 (European Council conclusions); Everling, 'Probleme atypischer Rechts- und Handlungsformen bei der Auslegung des europäischen Gemeinschaftsrechts', in Bieber and Ress (eds), *Die Dynamik des Europäischen Gemeinschaftsrechts/The Dynamics of EC-Law* (Nomos, 1987), 417–33.

[256] 59/75, *Manghera*, 1976, para. 21.

[257] See 293/83, *Gravier*, 1985, para. 22 (access to vocational training); 281/85, 283–285/85 and 287/85, *Germany, France, Denmark and United Kingdom v Commission*, 1987, para. 17 (migration policy).

[258] e.g. the Resolution of the Council and the Representatives of the Governments of the Member States, meeting within the Council of 20 November 2008 on the health and well-being of young people and the Conclusions of the Council and of the Representatives of the Governments of the Member States, meeting within the Council of 21 November 2008 on preparing young people for the 21st century: an agenda for European cooperation on schools (OJ 2008 C319/1 and C319/20, respectively).

[259] What was at issue was the Hague Resolution of 3 November 1976; see 141/78, *France v United Kingdom*, 1979, paras 8–11; 32/79, *Commission v United Kingdom*, 1980, para. 11 ('It is not contested that this resolution is binding on the Member States'); 804/79, *Commission v United Kingdom*, 1981, paras 23–31.

[260] See also 61/77, *Commission v Ireland*, 1978, para. 66.

[261] C-687/1, *Commission v Council*, 2017, paras 44–5 (decision pursuant to Article 218(9) TFEU cannot be replaced by Council conclusions).

occasion of the adoption of Union acts. No reliance may be placed on a unilateral declaration of a Member State for the purposes of interpreting a Union act on the ground that 'the objective scope of rules laid down by the common institutions cannot be modified by reservations or objections which Member States may have made at the time the rules were being formulated'.[262] A declaration made by Member States, acting together, or by the institutions concerned, cannot have any bearing on the objective scope of a Union act.[263] Such a declaration may be used to interpret such an act only where reference is made to its content in the wording of that act,[264] since those affected by an act must be able to rely on what it contains.[265] The Court of Justice may have regard to a joint declaration to a Union act in order to 'confirm' the interpretation that should be given to that Union act.[266] Individual declarations of one or more Member States may have factual importance, in particular where they contain details of the manner in which the adoption of an act was discussed in the Council. In that event, the Court of Justice and the General Court may take the declarations into account in order to determine the content of that discussion and then to review it.[267]

Institutional practice. As far as the institutions' practice is concerned, the Court has plainly stated that '[a] mere practice on the part of the Council cannot derogate from the rules laid down in the Treaty. Such a practice cannot therefore create a precedent binding on Union institutions with regard to the correct legal basis.'[268] Under certain circumstances a constant practice—for instance based on a non-binding act by which an institution regards itself as being bound—must be viewed as a rule of conduct from which the institution may diverge only if it gives reasons for doing so, on account of the principle of protection of legitimate expectations and the principle of equal treatment (see para. 27.045, *supra*).

27.048

II. Interinstitutional Agreements

Agreements between institutions. The institutions have long determined relations *inter se* by way of interinstitutional agreements, on the basis of specific Treaty provisions, for instance in respect of the access of the Court of Auditors to documents of the European Investment Bank.[269] The Lisbon Treaty introduced an express legal basis for the European Parliament, the Council, and the Commission to conclude interinstitutional agreements which may be

27.049

---

[262] 143/83, *Commission v Denmark*, 1985, para. 13; see also 38/69, *Commission v Italy*, 1970, para. 12. For their use in interpreting Union acts, see Schønberg and Frick, 'Finishing, Refining, Polishing: On the Use of *Travaux Préparatoires* as an Aid to the Interpretation of Community Legislation' (2003) ELRev 149–71.
[263] 237/84, *Commission v Belgium*, 1986, para. 17.
[264] See C-292/89, *Antonissen*, 1991, para. 18; C-245/02, *Anheuser-Busch*, 2004, paras 78–80; C-545/11, *Agrargenossenschaft Neuzelle*, 2013, paras 51–2. See also C-368/96, *Generics*, 1998, paras 26–35 (general concept used in a directive interpreted in accordance with criteria set out in minutes of the Council).
[265] C-283/94, C-291/94, and C-292/94, *Denkavit and Others*, 1996, para. 29.
[266] 136/78, *Auer*, 1979, para. 25 (declaration of the Council); C-310/90, *Egle*, 1992, para. 12 (joint declaration by the Commission and the Council). See also 324/82, *Commission v Belgium*, 1984, para. 33.
[267] T-194/94, *Carvel and Guardian Newspapers v Council*, 1995, paras 74–7.
[268] 68/86, *United Kingdom v Council*, 1988, para. 24; 131/86, *United Kingdom v Council*, 1988, para. 29.
[269] See Article 287(3), third subpara. TFEU, implemented by the Tripartite agreement between the European Commission, the European Court of Auditors, and the European Investment Bank of 7 October 2011, available at http://www.eib.org/infocentre/publications/all/tripartite-agreement.htm. See Articles 193, third para.; 218(1); 248(3), third subpara.; 272(9), fifth subpara. EC Treaty which authorized the institutions concerned to determine relations *inter se* by 'common accord' or by agreement.

of a binding nature (Article 295 TFEU).[270] The European Parliament, the Council, and the Commission are increasingly concluding agreements, initially mainly to improve the flow of information to the Parliament and to increase its participation in decision-making.[271] In the meantime, agreements have been reached on other matters, institutional and otherwise.[272] Recent agreements aim at improving the quality and transparency of the legislative process, such as the interinstitutional agreement of 13 April 2016 on better law-making.[273]

The first agreements sometimes took the form of an exchange of letters between the institutions concerned; subsequently, they have normally been officially published. When these agreements concern the relations between the institutions, they are generally concluded by the European Parliament, the Council, and the Commission. However, interinstitutional agreements have also been concluded between institutions and other bodies in varying constellations,[274] in particular between the European Parliament and the Commission, such as the successive Framework Agreements on the relationship between both institutions[275]

---

[270] For general commentaries, see Tournepiche, *Les accords interinstitutionnels dans l'Union européenne* (Bruylant, 2011); Driessen, *Interinstitutional Conventions in EU Law* (Cameron May, 2007); Reich, 'La mise en oeuvre du Traité sur l'Union européenne par les accords interinstitutionnels' (1994) RMCUE 81–5; Monar, 'Interinstitutional Agreements: The Phenomenon and Its New Dynamics After Maastricht' (1994) CMLRev 693–719.

[271] For the relationship between the Council and the European Parliament, see the (never officially published) Luns procedure of 1964 and the 1973 Westerterp procedure (para. 21-005, *infra*) and the Interinstitutional Agreement of 20 November 2002 concerning access by the European Parliament to sensitive information of the Council in the field of security and defence policy (see para. 19-004, *supra*). The following, in particular, have arisen between the European Parliament, the Council, and the Commission: the Joint Declaration of 4 March 1975, OJ 1975 C89/1 (on the consultation procedure, para. 17-042, *supra*); the Joint Declaration of 30 June 1982 and the Interinstitutional Agreements of 29 June 1988, 29 October 1993, 6 May 1999, 7 November 2002, 17 May 2006, 2 December 2013, and 16 December 2020 on budgetary matters (see para. 14-017, *supra*); the Joint Declaration on the implementation of the new co-decision procedure (para. 17-020, *supra*); the Joint Declaration on the Socrates decision of 4 March 1995 (OJ 1995 L132/18); the Interinstitutional Agreement of 16 July 1997 on the financing of the CFSP (1997) 7/8 EU Bull. point 2.3.1); and the Interinstitutional Agreement on legal bases and implementation of the budget (OJ 1998 C344/1). Between the European Parliament and the Commission codes of conduct were concluded in 1990 ((1990) 4 EC Bull. I.6.1) and on 15 March 1995 (OJ 1995 C89/69); furthermore an agreement on procedures for implementing Council Decision 1999/468/EC of 28 June 1999 laying down the procedures for the exercise of implementing powers conferred on the Commission (OJ 2000 L256/19) was concludes, as wells as a framework agreement on relations between the European Parliament and the Commission on 5 July 2000 (OJ 2001 C121/122), 26 May 2005 (OJ 2006 C117E/125) and 20 October 2010 (OJ 2010 L304/47).

[272] See the Joint Declaration of the European Parliament, the Council, and the Commission of 5 April 1977 on fundamental rights (see para. 25-003, *supra*); the Joint Declaration against racism and xenophobia of the European Parliament, the Council, the representatives of the Member States, meeting in the Council, and the Commission of 11 June 1986, OJ 1986 C158) and (as agreed between the European Parliament, the Council, and the Commission) the Interinstitutional agreement on procedures for implementing the principle of subsidiarity (OJ 1993 C329/135) and the Interinstitutional Declaration of 25 October 1993 on democracy, transparency, and subsidiarity (OJ 1993 C329/133); the Interinstitutional Agreement of 25 May 1999 concerning internal investigations by the European Anti-fraud Office (OLAF), OJ 1999 L136/15); the Interinstitutional Agreement of 28 February 2002 on the financing of the Convention on the future of the European Union (OJ 2002 C54/1; extended by Interinstitutional Agreement of 12 December 2002, OJ 2002 C320/1) and the Interinstitutional Agreement of 16 December 2003 on better law-making (OJ 2003 C321/1). As between the Commission and the Council, see the Code of Conduct of 6 December 1993 on public access to documents (OJ 1993 L340/41).

[273] OJ 2016 L123/1. See further the Interinstitutional Agreement of 20 December 1994 on the official codification of legislative texts (OJ 1996 C102/2); the Interinstitutional Agreement of 22 December 1998 on common guidelines for the quality of drafting of Community legislation (OJ 1999 C73/1), the Interinstitutional Agreement of 28 November 2001 on a more structured use of the recasting technique for legal acts (OJ 2002 C77/1), and the Joint Political Declaration of 27 October 2011 on explanatory documents (OJ 2011 C369/15).

[274] e.g. the agreement of 13 December 2001 between the ECB and Europol on combating counterfeiting, OJ 2002 C23/9 and, for the same purpose, the cooperation agreement of 29 March 2004 between the ECB and the International Criminal Police Organisation (Interpol), OJ 2004 C134/9 and the agreement of 9 June 2004 between Europol and Eurojust on information exchange (*Europe*, No. 8722, 10 June 2004, 10).

[275] See the references in n. 271, *supra*.

and the interinstitutional agreement on the transparency register for organizations and self-employed individuals engaged in EU policy-making and policy implementation,[276] which is now being replaced by an agreement between the three institutions.[277] At times, the Member States have spoken out against the practice of the European Parliament and the Commission concluding agreements between themselves, that is to say without involving the Council in the agreement.[278]

Legal force. The institutions can use an interinstitutional agreement to simplify the implementation of procedures laid down in the Treaties, without actually amending those procedures or altering the balance between the institutions.[279] Where the Treaties do not expressly provide for an agreement to be reached, the legal force of an agreement will depend on whether the institutions intended it to be binding.[280] The institutions may merely have intended to coordinate their positions as a first step towards the adoption of subsequent binding acts.[281] An indication is afforded, in the first place, by the title chosen by the institutions: declaration, *modus vivendi*, code of conduct, or agreement (which is stricter). In addition, the legal force of an agreement may be derived from its content. Thus, the fact that the content of an interinstitutional agreement is purely political may preclude its being binding.[282] In contrast, other agreements appear to lay down binding rules of conduct. For instance, the interinstitutional agreement of 2 December 2013 on budgetary discipline, on cooperation in budgetary matters states that it 'is binding on all the institutions for as long as it is in force'.[283] This applies *a fortiori* to the agreement between the ECB and Europol of 13 December 2001, since it provides for dispute resolution by arbitration.[284] There are indications in decided cases that the Court of Justice accepts in principle that interinstitutional

27.050

---

[276] Agreement between the European Parliament and the Commission of 16 April 2014 (OJ 2014 L277/11), replacing the agreement of 23 June 2011 (OJ 2011 L191/29).
[277] See 16-004.
[278] According to Declaration (No. 3), annexed to the Nice Treaty, on Article 10 EC Treaty (OJ 2001 C80/77), interinstitutional agreements 'may be concluded only with the agreement of these three institutions'. Still, this declaration has not been taken over in the list of (existing) declarations annexed to the Lisbon Treaty.
[279] Para. 17-042, *supra*; see also Declaration (No. 3), annexed to the Nice Treaty (n. 278, *supra*), which stated expressly that '[s]uch agreements may not amend or supplement the provisions of the Treaty'. This reflected a lack of trust on the part of the Member States in connection with the agreement concluded between the European Parliament and the Commission on 5 July 2000 (see n. 271, *supra*). According to that declaration, such an agreement should not be possible in the future, since it stated that agreements 'may be concluded only with the agreement of these three institutions'. This would have given the Council a veto.
[280] Monar, 'Interinstitutional Agreements: The Phenomenon and its New Dynamics after Maastricht' (1994) CMLRev 693, 697–703. The Interinstitutional Agreement of 22 December 1998 on common guidelines for the quality of drafting of Community legislation (n. 273, *supra*) expressly provides that the guidelines set out therein 'are not legally binding'.
[281] C-58/94, *Netherlands v Council*, 1996, paras 23–7 (on the Code of Conduct concerning public access to Council and Commission documents; see n. 272, *supra*). However, an institution is bound by a code of conduct vis-à-vis third parties where it adopted the code by decision and thereby voluntarily assumed a series of obligations for itself (*patere legem quam ipse fecisti*); see T-105/95, *WWF UK v Commission*, 1997, paras 53–5.
[282] See the assessment of the Joint Declaration on fundamental rights in the Commission's answer of 1 June 1977 to Question No. 170/77 (Maigaard), OJ 1977 C180/18 and the Council's answer of 23 September 1977 to Question No. 128/77 (Dondelinger), OJ 1977 C259/4, to the effect that, more generally, joint declarations are 'political undertakings' and 'in the final instance it would be for the Court of Justice to assess their legal implications' (see also the answer of the same date to Question No. 169/77 (Maigaard, ibid., concerning the conciliation procedure).
[283] Point 2 of the Interinstitutional Agreement of 2 December 2013 between the European Parliament, the Council, and the Commission on budgetary discipline, on cooperation in budgetary matters, and on sound financial management, OJ 2013 C373/1.
[284] Article 10 of the agreement of 13 December 2001 between the ECB and Europol on combating counterfeiting, OJ 2002 C23/9

agreements have binding force.[285] Sometimes such an agreement is referred to in order to confirm the Court's interpretation of Union law.[286] Moreover, an interinstitutional agreement can be binding in so far as it is an expression of the principle of sincere cooperation enshrined in Article 4(3) TEU.[287] On that basis, the Court of Justice has recognized the binding nature of arrangements concluded between the Commission and the Council to decide on the participation of the Union and the Member States in international organizations where, in areas of shared competences, the Union and the Member States have to agree on the exercise of the voting rights.[288]

---

[285] See 211/80, *Advernier v Commission*, 1984, para. 22 (reference to the Joint Declaration of 4 March 1975); 34/86, *Council v European Parliament*, 1986, para. 50 (reference to the Joint Declaration of 30 June 1982).

[286] 44/79, *Hauer*, 1979, para. 15 (Joint Declaration on fundamental rights); T-194/94, *Carvel and Guardian Newspapers v Council*, 1995, para. 66 (Code of Conduct on public access to documents); C-73/17, *France v European Parliament*, 2018, para. 57 (interinstitutional agreement on budgetary discipline); C-128/17, *Poland v European Parliament and Council*, 2019, paras 30–47, and C-482/17, *Czech Republic v European Parliament and Council*, 2019, para. 82 (impact assessment under interinstitutional agreement on better law-making).

[287] Hilf, 'Die rechtliche Bedeutung des Verfassungsprinzips der parlamentarischen Demokratie für den europäischen Integrationsprozess' (1984) EuR 9, 24–5; Monar (n. 270, *supra*), 700; Bieber, 'The Settlement of Institutional Conflicts on the Basis of Article 4 of the EEC Treaty' (1984) CMLRev 505, 520–1.

[288] C-25/94, *Commission v Council*, 1996, paras 48–9.

28
Other Sources of Union Law

Acts with a Union basis. The instruments referred to in the Treaties include acts that are not formally adopted by Union institutions, such as decisions of the Member States' governments, which nevertheless have a close link with Union law. That also goes for some conventions agreed amongst the Member States in connection with the Union's activities (see paras 28.002–28.004). These instruments are set out below, together with other sources of Union law such as collective agreements between social partners (para. 28.005, *infra*) and, importantly, the case law of the Court of Justice of the European Union (para. 28.006, *infra*). Finally, this chapter explains the ongoing effects of acts adopted before the entry into force of the Lisbon Treaty in areas outside the pre-Lisbon 'Community' framework, that is to say the pre-Lisbon common foreign and security policy and the area of police and judicial cooperation in criminal matters as well as some other conventions agreed between the Member States (see paras 28.007–28.020, *infra*).

28.001

I. Acts of Member State Governments and Conventions between the Member States

Acts of Member States' governments. In some cases, the Member States act in order to carry out a task expressly conferred on the national governments by the Treaties. Alongside amendment of the Treaties, which is the task of a 'conference of representatives of the governments of the Member States' (Article 48(4) TEU), decisions of the 'governments of the Member States' are used chiefly to appoint members of the Court of Justice and the General Court[1] and to fix the seats of institutions.[2] In view of the fact that such acts have their legal basis in the Treaties and are essentially connected with the functioning of the Union, they must be regarded as being Union law. However, given the fact that these are acts of the governments of the Member States and not of the Council, they are probably not amenable to judicial review by the Court of Justice.[3]

28.002

---

[1] See Article 19(2), third subpara. TEU and Articles 253 and 254 TFEU (see para. 13-014, *supra*).
[2] Article 341 TFEU (see para. 14-019 *et seq.*, *supra*).
[3] See already C-424/20 P(R), *Representatives of the Governments of the Member States v Sharpston* (order of the Vice-President), 2020, paras 23–8; T-180/20, *Sharpston v Council and Conference of representatives of the governments of the Member States* (order), 2020, paras 29–35, and T-550/20, *Sharpston v Council and Representatives of the Governments of the Member States* (order), 2020, paras 31–8 (acts of the Conference of representatives of the governments of the Member States cannot be challenged pursuant to Article 263(4) TFEU). See further C-59/18, *Italy v Council* (pending, OJ 2018 C94/15) and C-182/18, *Comune di Milano v Council* (pending, interim measures rejected, see C-182/18 R, *Comune di Milano v Council* (order of the Vice-President), 2018), challenging the press statement on the decision of the representatives of twenty-seven Member States to transfer the seat of the European Medicines Agency from London to Amsterdam due to Brexit, as well as C-743/19, *European Parliament v Council* (pending, OJ 2019 C399/35), challenging the decision of the representatives of the Member States to fix the seat of the European Labour Authority in Bratislava.

28.003 **Member State governments meeting within the Council or the European Council.** Ever since the early years of the Communities, the Member States' governments have concluded agreements among themselves which are not based on the Treaties and which they do not wish to cast as a formal international agreement. The Ministers take such decisions at normal meetings of the Council as 'representatives of the Governments of the Member States meeting within the Council'.[4] Those decisions have sometimes been taken at the level of the Heads of State or Government within the European Council.[5] Such decisions are often closely related to decisions taken by the Council pursuant to the Treaties and intended to achieve uniformity in areas of European integration for which the Union is not competent. When the representatives of the Member States act, not as members of the Council, but as representatives of the governments collectively exercising the competences of the Member States, their acts will evade judicial review on the basis of Article 263 TFEU.[6] However, it does not suffice that a decision is labelled a decision 'of the representatives of the governments of the Member States' to escape judicial review. First it must be established whether an act, given its content and the circumstances surrounding its adoption, truly is an act of the Member States or of the Council or European Council.[7] In matters falling partly within the jurisdiction of the Member States and partly within the jurisdiction of the Union (or in which no consensus could be reached as to whom jurisdiction lay with), decisions have taken the hybrid form of 'decisions of the Council and of the representatives of the Governments of the Member States, meeting within the Council'.[8] These decisions do, however, constitute acts of the Council that are amenable to judicial review by the Court of Justice.[9] Where subsequent Treaty amendments brought a matter within the scope of the Union's competences, earlier resolutions of the representatives of the Governments of the Member States meeting within the Council could, if necessary, be turned into binding Union law.

Decisions taken by the Member States' governments meeting in the Council take various forms (acts, declarations, resolutions, findings), from which it is often clear that the Member States' intention is to adopt a non-binding act.[10] The purpose and content of these acts

---

[4] One of the earliest instances of this was the adoption of the so-called 'acceleration decisions' of 12 May 1960 and 15 May 1962, para. 7-007, *supra*. On such decisions in general, see Mortelmans, 'The Extramural Meetings of the Ministers of the Member States of the Community' (1974) CMLRev 62–91. For a study of their legal force, see Schermers, 'Besluiten van de Vertegenwoordigers der Lid-Staten: Gemeenschapsrecht?' (1966) SEW 545–79; Pescatore, 'Remarques sur la nature juridique des "décisions des représentants des Etats membres réunis au sein du Conseil"' (1966) SEW 579–86; Everling, 'Zur rechtlichen Wirkung von Beschlüssen, Entschliessungen, Erklärungen und Vereinbarungen des Rates oder der Mitgliedstaaten der Europäischen Gemeinschaft', in Lüke, Ress, and Will (eds), *Rechtsvergleichung, Europarecht und Staatenintegration. Gedächtnisschrift für L.-J. Constantinesco* (Heymann, 1983), 133, 147–56; Borchardt and Wellens, 'Soft law in het Gemeenschapsrecht' (1987) SEW 663–727.

[5] See also the circumstances surrounding the 'EU-Turkey statement' of 18 March 2016, as set out in T-192/16, *NF v European Council*, 2017, paras 1–9.

[6] C-181/91 and C-248/91, *European Parliament v Council and Commission*, 1993, para. 12.

[7] Ibid., paras 13–14. See also T-192/16, *NF v European Council*, T-193/16, *NG v European Council* and T-257/16, *NM v European Council*, 2017 (appeal dismissed: C-208/17 to C-210/17, *NF, NG and NM v European Council*, 2018).

[8] e.g. Resolution of the Council and of the representatives of the Governments of the Member States, meeting within the Council, of 20 May 2014 on the overview of the structured dialogue process including social inclusion of young people, OJ 2014 C183/1.

[9] C-28/12, *Commission v Council*, 2015, paras 14–17.

[10] See, e.g., the Declaration by the Council and the representatives of the Governments of the Member States, meeting within the Council, of 16 December 1997 on respecting diversity and combating racism and xenophobia, OJ 1998 C1/14.

determine whether—and if so, what—legal effects ensue from such acts. The fact that new Member States accede by means of the Act of Accession to ' decisions and agreements of the Heads of State or Government of the Member States meeting within the European Council' as well as 'decisions and agreements adopted by the representatives of the Governments of the Member States meeting within the Council'[11] does not confer any additional legal effects on such acts.[12] Nevertheless, the Member States may lay down agreements in such acts which are binding under international law. In such a case, each Member State decides for itself whether the agreements in question are subject to the same ratification procedure as treaties and what legal force is to be given them under national law.[13] This is also true of acts adopted by the national governments at the level of the Heads of State or Government, whether meeting within the European Council[14] or as the European Council.[15]

The obligations that the Member States assume in decisions taken 'within the (European) Council' may not be enforced as such by the Court of Justice. In common with joint declarations made in the Council, however, such acts do have interpretative value in 'confirming' obligations arising for the Member States under Union law (see para. 27.047, *supra*), although the acts in question cannot detract in any way from Treaty provisions.[16]

Conventions and agreements between Member States. In matters coming within their competence, Member States may exercise their powers individually or collectively;[17] in so doing they may therefore conclude agreements amongst themselves.[18] Those agreements must, however, be compatible with Union law and not restrict the autonomy of Union law. Accordingly, they may not have the effect of limiting the jurisdiction of the Court of Justice.[19] Certain of these conventions are so closely related to the objectives of the Treaties that new Member States must pledge to accede to them upon their accession to the Union.[20]

28.004

---

[11] Article 3(1)–(2) of the 2012 Act of Accession; see previously (not yet mentioning acts adopted within the European Council) Article 3(1) of the 2005 Act of Accession; Article 5(1) of the 2003 Act of Accession; Article 4(1) of the 1994 Act of Accession.

[12] For the opposite view, see Schermers and Waelbroeck, *Judicial Protection in the European Union* (Kluwer, 2001), §§ 670–1, 330 (who took the view that since the Act of Accession refers to those decisions, it recognizes them as being Community law).

[13] See Everling (n. 4, *supra*), 136. For the Netherlands, see Besselink, 'An Open Constitution and European Integration: The Kingdom of the Netherlands' (1996) SEW 192, 205.

[14] Decision of the Heads of State and Government, meeting within the European Council, concerning certain problems raised by Denmark on the Treaty on European Union, OJ 1992 C348/2.

[15] Article 3(3) of the 2012 Act of Accession; Article 5(2) of the 2005 Act of Accession, Article 5(3) of the 2003 Act of Accession, and Article 4(3) of the 1994 Act of Accession place 'declarations or resolutions of, or other positions taken up by' the European Council on the same footing as those of the Council. For a commentary dealing specifically with the legal force of resolutions of the European Council, see Martenczuk, 'Der Europäische Rat und die Wirtschafts- und Währungsunion' (1998) EuR 151, 155–7.

[16] 43/75, *Defrenne*, 1976, para. 57, 478 (concerning a resolution of a conference of the Member States). In this way, the Court of Justice may also interpret the actual provisions of such acts.

[17] C-181/91 and C-248/91, *European Parliament v Council*, 1993, para. 16 (concerning humanitarian aid); C-370/12, *Pringle*, 2012, para. 8 (ESM Treaty).

[18] e.g. C-648/15, *Austria v Germany*, 2017 (double taxation treaty, granting jurisdiction to the Court pursuant to Article 273 TFEU); De Witte and Martinelli, 'Treaties between EU Member States as Quasi-Instruments of EU Law', in Cremona and Kilpatrick (eds), *EU Legal Acts—Challenges and Transformations* (OUP, 2018), 157–88.

[19] That is in particular problematic for investor-state arbitration provided for in bilateral investment treaties entered into by the Member States; see C-284/16, *Achmea*, 2018, paras 31–60, with case note by Contartese and Andenas (2019) CMLRev 157–92. See also Hindelang, 'Conceptualisation and Application of the Principle of Autonomy of EU Law—the CJEU's Judgment in Achmea put in Perspective' (2019) ELRev 383–400. In response to that judgment the Member States have concluded the Agreement for the termination of Bilateral Investment Treaties between the Member States of the European Union (OJ 2020 L169/1).

[20] e.g. 2011 Act of Accession, Article 3(4) (see para. 28-018, *infra*).

New Member States also have to accede to international agreements which the Union and the Member States conclude jointly and to 'internal' agreements which the Member States have concluded with each other for the purposes of implementing such international agreements.[21] Before the entry into force of the Lisbon Treaty, the Treaties referred to conventions of the Member States, particularly in the field of police and judicial cooperation in criminal matters (see paras 28.018 and 28.019). Since the entry into force of the Lisbon Treaty, the Treaties no longer mention conventions between Member States as a policy instrument of the Union. Still, existing conventions preserve their legal force (see para. 28.020, *supra*). Moreover, the Member States have continued to conclude conventions amongst themselves in areas that are related to the activities of the Union, but are not based on the Treaties. This includes genuine 'treaties' concluded in the context of the Economic and Monetary Union, such as the ESM Treaty and the Treaty on Stability, Coordination and Governance in the Economic and Monetary Union (see para. 2.010, *supra*). If such agreements do not have a basis in the Treaties, they do not form part of Union law and cannot be interpreted by the Court of Justice.[22] Nevertheless, some of these agreements have made the Court of Justice competent to interpret the agreement.[23]

II. Collective Agreements

28.005 **Collective agreements.** Article 155 TFEU refers to an instrument which does not emanate from a Union body. Under paragraph 1 of that article, should management and labour so desire, the dialogue between them at Union level may lead to contractual relations, including agreements. At present, collective agreements do not have the same legal force throughout the Union in relation to the parties thereto, let alone third parties. In the absence of Union provisions relating to this matter, the legal force of any collective agreements concluded as such at Union level remains unclear (see para. 17.044, *supra*). That is different where such agreements are implemented by Union acts. Before the Treaty of Lisbon, the agreements were implemented by means of directives which made those agreements binding on Member States as regards the result to be achieved, even though they retained the power to determine the form and methods (see para. 27.017 *et seq.*, *supra*). The provisions of such agreement then have direct effect under the same conditions as directives.[24] Likewise, national courts are bound to interpret domestic law, so far as possible, in the light of the wording and the purpose of such agreement.[25] Since the Treaty of Lisbon, Article 155(2) TFEU provides for implementation by Council decision (see para. 17.044, *supra*).

---

[21] See Article 6(2) to (5) and (10) of the 2011 Act of Accession; Article 6(2) to (6) and (11) of the 2005 Act of Accession; Article 6(2) to (6) and (11) of the 2003 Act of Accession; Article 5(2) and (3) of the 1994 Act of Accession.

[22] C-457/18, *Slovenia v Croatia*, 2020, para. 91. Moreover, the action for failure to fulfil obligations is unavailable: C-132/09, *Commission v Belgium* 2010, paras 43–5.

[23] C-370/12, *Pringle*, 2012, paras 170–7 (Court is only competent in respect of ESM Treaty on the basis of Article 273 TFEU, no other actions available).

[24] C-268/06, *Impact*, 2008, para. 58; C-378/07 to C-380/07 *Angelidaki and Others*, 2009, para. 195; C-486/08, *Zentralbetriebsrat der Landeskrankenhäuser Tirols*, 2010, paras 21–5.

[25] C-98/09 *Sorge*, 2010, paras 51–3.

III. The Case Law of the Union Courts

Source of law. In the Union legal order, the case law of the Court of Justice and the General Court constitutes an important source of law. Although they play a crucial role in developing the law, their task is formally limited to interpreting and applying each of the other sources of law discussed above.

28.006

The interpretation that the Union Courts give to a rule of Union law defines the meaning and scope of that rule as it must be or ought to have been understood and applied from the time of its coming into force.[26] It follows that a rule of Union law interpreted in this way must be applied to legal relationships which arose or were formed before the Court gave its ruling on the question on interpretation.[27] In practice, however, such an interpretation may have unexpected effects. A judicial ruling holding that a provision has direct effect may, for instance, impose considerable burdens where authorities or individuals are faced with unforeseen claims from individuals. Accordingly, in exceptional cases, the Court of Justice will impose restrictions on grounds of legal certainty on the *ex tunc* effect of its preliminary rulings on Union law.[28] The Court may thus restrict the direct effect of a provision to claims relating to periods starting on the date on which its judgment was given.[29] Similarly, it may authorize the referring court to maintain the legal effects of certain administrative acts taken in contravention of Union law in order to safeguard overriding interests of legal certainty or energy security until they can be replaced by acts taken in accordance with the proper procedures.[30] Such a restriction may be allowed only in the actual judgment of the Court ruling upon the interpretation sought.[31] It is clear from this alone that the interpretation which the Union Courts give to rules of Union law is not always merely declaratory, but contributes in real terms to the development of that law.[32]

---

[26] C-347/00, *Barreira Pérez*, 2002, para. 44; C-453/02 and C-462/02, *Linneweber and Akritidis*, 2005, para. 41; C-292/04, *Meilicke and Others*, 2007, para. 34. See also, Lenaerts, Gutman, and Nowak, *EU Procedural Law* (OUP, 2022), Chapter 6.

[27] C-453/00, *Kühne & Heitz*, 2004, paras 21–2; with case note by Caranta (2005) CMLRev 179–88.

[28] e.g., C-25/14 and C-26/14, *UNIS and Others*, 2015, paras 47–53. See Bribosia and Rorive, 'Le droit transitoire jurisprudentiel des juridictions européennes' (2002) RDULB 125–52.

[29] See, e.g., in connection with the direct effect of the interpretation given by the Court of Justice to Article 141 EC [*now Article 157 TFEU*], 43/75, *Defrenne*, 1976, paras 71–5. cf. C-262/88, *Barber*, 1990, paras 40–5, in which the Court restricted its interpretation that pensions paid by contracted-out occupational pension schemes constituted 'pay' within the meaning of Article 141 to future pensions as well as to pensions in respect of which legal proceedings had been brought, or an equivalent claim had been made, before the date of the judgment. The EC Treaty was subsequently supplemented by a Protocol (No. 17) concerning Article 119 [*later Article 141*] of the Treaty establishing the European Community (OJ 1992 C224/104), which imposes a particular interpretation of the effects *ratione temporis* of the judgment in *Barber*. According to the Protocol, pensions so interpreted cover only benefits attributable to periods of employment after that date, except where claims have been made within the meaning of the judgment. For judgments delivered before the Protocol entered into force, see C-109/91, *Ten Oever*, 1993, para. 19; and thereafter C-152/91, *Neath*, 1993, paras 13–18; C-200/91, *Coloroll Pension Trustees*, 1994; C-57/93, *Vroege*, 1994, paras 35–43; C-128/93, *Fisscher*, 1994, paras 47–50; C-147/95, *Evrenopoulos*, 1997, paras 30–40 (clarification of the Protocol). For a critical view of the technique whereby the Member States sought to 'correct' the case law of the Court of Justice by means of a protocol, see Curti Gialdino, 'Some Reflections on the *Acquis Communautaire*' (1995) CMLRev 1089, 1117–20. The limitation of the possibility of relying on the direct effect of Article 141 EC did not prevent claimants from relying on national provisions laying down a principle of equal treatment; see C-50/96, *Schröder*, 2000, paras 46–50; C-234/96 and C-235/96, *Vick and Conze*, 2000, paras 46–50, and C-270/97 and C-271/97, *Sievers and Schrage*, 2000, paras 48–52.

[30] C-24/19, *A and Others*, 2020, paras 80–95; C-411/17, *Inter-Environnement Wallonie and Bond Beter Leefmilieu Vlaanderen*, 2019, paras 167–82.

[31] C-437/97, *EKW and Wein & Co.*, 2000, para. 57; C-292/04, *Meilicke and Others*, 2007, para. 36.

[32] For an account of case law as a source of law, see Schermers and Waelbroeck, *Judicial Protection in the European Union* (Kluwer, 2001), §§ 260–6, 133–7.

IV. Non-Community Acts Adopted before the Entry into Force of the Lisbon Treaty

28.007 **Survey.** Before the entry into force of the Lisbon Treaty (1 December 2009), a distinction was made between Community law, which referred to the Community Treaties and the acts adopted pursuant thereto, and non-Community law, which meant legal provisions adopted outside the Community framework. Non-Community law referred, in the first place, to the 'intergovernmental' provisions of the EU Treaty (in particular, Titles V and VI on the common foreign and security policy and on police and judicial cooperation in criminal matters, respectively) and measures adopted pursuant to those provisions. Those CFSP and PJCC measures took the form of particular legal instruments that were not used within the Community framework. Conventions concluded between the Member States pursuant to a number of provisions of the EC Treaty, Article 293 EC in particular, were also to be classified as acts of non-Community law, since those conventions were not Community acts. Since the entry into force of the Lisbon Treaty, the Union's action in each of its fields of competence now gives rise to measures of 'Union law' (see para. 2.006, *supra*). However, pursuant to Article 9 of the Protocol on transitional provisions, acts adopted before 1 December 2009 on the basis of the EU Treaty remain in force and their legal effects are preserved until those acts are repealed, annulled, or amended in implementation of the present Treaties (see para. 2.008, *supra*). The same applies to international agreements concluded by the Member States on the basis of the former Articles 24 and 38 EU. Where appropriate, the prefix 'pre-Lisbon' will be used to distinguish acts adopted before 1 December 2009 from acts adopted after the entry into force of the Lisbon Treaty. Until 1 December 2014 Protocol No. 36 imposed limits on the jurisdiction of the Court of Justice and the Commission over these pre-Lisbon acts,[33] but those have now lapsed.

A. Distinguishing non-Community from Community law

28.008 **Non-Community acts.** The acts adopted by the Union institutions pursuant to the provisions of Title V (common foreign and security policy, CFSP) and Title VI (police and judicial cooperation in criminal matters, PJCC) of the EU Treaty, did not normally have the same legal force as acts of Community law. The most important difference is that, for Community acts, the legal status could be clearly inferred from the case law of the Court of Justice, which has recognized the primacy and the possible direct effect of provisions of Community law. This did not happen in the case of non-Community acts, given the limited jurisdiction of the Court of Justice with regard to them. The legal effects attached to non-Community acts falling outside the Court's jurisdiction—which nowadays only encompass CFSP acts—depend on the form, the content, and the purpose of each act and have to be further appraised in the light of international law.[34]

---

[33] Protocol (No. 36) on transitional provisions, Article 10(1) to (3) (see para. 2.008, *supra*).
[34] Accordingly, Member States could, in principle, refer disputes relating to such acts to the International Court of Justice where they have no connection with pre-Lisbon Community law or (present) Union law. According to Article 292 EC, this was not possible in the case of 'a dispute concerning the interpretation or application of this Treaty' (see, e.g., C-459/03, *Commission v Ireland*, 2006); the same is currently true under Article 344 TFEU of any dispute concerning the interpretation or application of 'the Treaties'.

B. Acts of the European Council and the Council pursuant to the CFSP and PJCC

Specific instruments. For areas coming under the common foreign and security policy (CFSP), Title V of the EU Treaty prescribed specific instruments. Besides 'principles', 'general guidelines', and 'common strategies' decided on by the European Council (Article 13(1) and (2) EU),[35] what was involved was mainly 'joint actions' and 'common positions' (Articles 14 and 15 EU) adopted by the Council, as well as agreements concluded by the Council at international level (Articles 24 and 38 EU). What was formerly adopted in the form of common positions and joint actions now takes the form of a decision determining the actions to be undertaken or positions to be taken by the Union; acts adopted for their implementation also take the form of decisions (Article 25(3)(b) TEU).

28.009

Title VI of the EU Treaty set out the specific instruments to be used for action in the context of PJCC, namely 'common positions', 'framework decisions', and 'decisions', alongside agreements concluded by the Council at international level (see para. 28-017, *infra*) and the PJCC conventions that Member States concluded amongst themselves (see para. 28-019, *infra*)[36]. Since the EU Treaty did not establish any ranking order between these different instruments, the Council had a choice between several instruments for the purpose of regulating a subject matter, subject to the limits imposed by the nature of the instrument selected. Therefore, the fact that a matter was regulated by conventions between the Member States did not prevent the Council from adopting a framework decision to replace the relevant provisions of those conventions.[37]

In addition, the European Council and the Council often adopted declarations or positions containing merely a political assessment or a declaration of intent. Some resolutions or recommendations of the Council, however, set out detailed agreements.[38]

Formal requirements. With the exception of conventions and agreements, which were concluded between the Member States, pre-Lisbon CFSP and PJCC instruments were not subject to any special procedure of approval and ratification by the Member States.[39] They obtained their legal force from their approval by the Council (or the European Council). They constituted instruments of international law, which, in principle, had to be applied by

28.010

---

[35] But a 'common strategy' did have consequences as regards the procedure to be followed by the Council; see para. 19.002, *supra*. For that instrument, see Spencer, 'The EU and Common Strategies: The Revealing Case of the Mediterranean' (2001) E For Aff Rev 31–51. For a survey of CFSP instruments, see Dashwood, 'External Relations Provisions of the Amsterdam Treaty' (1998) CMLRev 1019, 1030–3.

[36] See Van den Brink, 'Besluiten in de tweede en derde pijler van de Europese Unie: van eigenheid naar eenvormigheid?' (2003) Themis 243–53. Initially, both Title V (CFSP) and Title VI (JHA cooperation) of the EU Treaty referred to both common (or joint) positions (former Articles J.2 and K.2) and joint action (former Articles J.3 and K.3). The Treaty of Amsterdam replaced joint action in Title VI (henceforth PJCC) by framework decisions and decisions (see Article 34(2) EU).

[37] C-303/05, *Advocaten voor de Wereld*, 2007, paras 37–42.

[38] See, e.g., in the context of JHA cooperation, the recommendation concerning transit for the purposes of expulsion and the addendum thereto, both of which antedated the entry into force of the EU Treaty, but were published as annexes to the Council recommendation of 22 December 1995 on concerted action and cooperation in carrying out expulsion measures, OJ 1996 C5/3.

[39] See also Article 2 of the 1994 and 2003 Acts of Accession: 'From the date of accession, the provisions of the original Treaties and the acts adopted by the institutions and the European Central Bank before accession shall be binding on the new Member States and shall apply in those States under the conditions laid down in those Treaties and in this Act' (see, similarly, Article 2 of the 2005 Act of Accession).

each Member State as from their entry into force (for framework decisions, however, see para. 28-014, *infra*). Whenever the Council adopted such acts, it could decide by unanimous vote to publish them in the *Official Journal*.[40] PJCC instruments were to be published in the *Official Journal* in any event.[41] In some cases, pre-Lisbon PJCC instruments must also be implemented after the entry into force of the Treaty of Lisbon. The principle of the preservation of the pre-Lisbon legal effects laid down in Protocol No. 36 implies that these implementing measures must still be adopted in accordance with the pre-Lisbon procedure.[42]

28.011 **Effects within the national legal order.** The Member States determine the status and legal effects of pre-Lisbon non-Community acts within their domestic legal systems,[43] although they have to take account what was determined by the EU Treaty itself with respect to the legal effects of these acts and by the case law of the Court of Justice. This was true, in particular, of pre-Lisbon PJCC acts, given the—until 30 November 2014—limited jurisdiction of the Court of Justice in respect of the PJCC according to which it could give preliminary rulings on the interpretation of such a PJCC framework decision, decision, or an implementing measure[44] (Article 35(1) EU), only if the Member State in question had accepted the Court's jurisdiction in this regard (Article 35(3) EU; see para. 13-011, *supra*).[45] All this has enabled the Court to clarify the legal effects of some of these legal instruments within the legal order of the Member States. The Court has also made it clear that, since Article 6 EU provides that the Union respects fundamental rights, Union acts adopted under Titles V and VI of the EU Treaty have to be interpreted in conformity with fundamental rights.[46]

Any further legal effects that might be attached to pre-Lisbon non-Community acts in the domestic legal system of the Member States were to be determined by the Member States themselves. In 'monist' Member States (such as Belgium and the Netherlands), binding pre-Lisbon CFSP and PJCC acts may take precedence over domestic law as acts governed by international law. If their provisions have direct effect (under national law), they can be relied upon by individuals before domestic courts.[47] It was precisely in order to avoid this that Article 34(2)(b) and (c) EU declared that PJCC framework decisions and decisions did not entail direct effect. Nevertheless, the Court of Justice clarified that this does not preclude

---

[40] See Article 17(3) and (4). The decisions were published in Part L of the *Official Journal*.
[41] See Article 17(1)(d) and (e) of the previous version of the Council Rules of Procedure, adopted by Council Decision of 22 March 2004 (OJ 2004 L106/22) (publication of framework decisions, decisions, and agreements).
[42] C-317/13 and C-679/13, *European Parliament v Council*, 2015, paras 51–7; C-595/14, *European Parliament v Council*, 2015, para. 39.
[43] For the former 'third pillar', see Griller, 'Die Unterscheidung von Unionsrecht und Gemeinschaftsrecht nach Amsterdam' (1999) EuR Beiheft 1 45, 64–8; Müller-Graff, 'The Legal Bases of the Third Pillar and its Position in the Framework of the Union Treaty' (1994) CMLRev 493, 508–9.
[44] See, e.g., C-404/07, *Katz*, 2008, paras 10 and 27; C-66/08, *Kozłowski*, 2008, paras 12 and 29. Article 35(1) EU did not mention PJCC common positions, which were also excluded from judicial review under Article 35(6) EU, but could be the subject of a ruling on their interpretation or application under Article 35(7) EU, first sentence.
[45] However, the Court had no jurisdiction to review the validity or the proportionality of operations carried out by the police or other law enforcement services of a Member State or the exercise of the responsibilities incumbent upon Member States with regard to the maintenance of law and order and the safeguarding of internal security: Article 35(5) EU.
[46] C-105/03, *Pupino*, 2005, paras 58–9; C-354/04 P, *Gestoras Pro Amnistía and Others v Council*, 2007, para. 51; C-355/04 P, *Segi and Others v Council*, 2007, para. 51; C-404/07, *Katz*, 2008, paras 48–9.
[47] For similar observations concerning the German legal system, see Meyring, 'Intergovernmentalism and Supranationality: Two Stereotypes for a Complex Reality' (1997) ELRev 221, 238–42.

interested parties from invoking them before national courts as otherwise the jurisdiction of the Court to give preliminary rulings under Article 35 EU would be deprived of most of its effectiveness (see para. 28-014, *infra*). Since 1 December 2014 national courts may refer preliminary questions to the Court of Justice as to the interpretation and the validity of pre-Lisbon PJCC acts.

Common position. Common positions defined the approach of the Union to a particular matter (Articles 15 and 34(2)(a) EU). In the case of the CFSP, the matter was referred to as being 'of a geographical or thematic nature' (Article 15 EU).[48] According to the Court of Justice, a common position required the compliance of the Member States by virtue of the principle of sincere cooperation, which means in particular that Member States were to take all appropriate measures, whether general or particular, to ensure fulfilment of their obligations under Union law.[49] The EU Treaty specified that Member States were to ensure that their national policies conformed to common positions (Article 15 EU).[50] In this connection, Member States were to 'uphold' and 'defend' common positions in international organizations and at international conferences (Articles 19(1)[51] and 37, first para. EU, respectively). However, a common position was not supposed to produce legal effects of itself in relation to third parties.[52] That explains why, under the system established by Title VI of the EU Treaty, common positions—in contradistinction to framework decisions and decisions—could not be the subject of an action for annulment before the Court of Justice and why the Court's jurisdiction to give preliminary rulings did not include rulings on the validity and interpretation of common positions, unlike other pre-Lisbon PJCC acts. However, national courts could ask the Court of Justice to give a preliminary ruling on a common position where the latter, because of its content, has a scope going beyond that assigned by the EU Treaty to that kind of act. It then fell to the Court to find, where appropriate, that the common position was intended to produce legal effects in relation to third parties, to give it its proper categorization, and to give a preliminary ruling.[53] On the basis of Protocol No. 36 on transitional provisions pre-Lisbon, common positions continue to have legal effects. When the Council has taken restrictive measures by way of a CFSP common position, this common position is deemed to correspond with the 'decision adopted in accordance with Chapter 2 of Title V, of the TEU' referred to in Article 215 TFEU.[54]

28.012

Joint action. Joint actions, as part of the CFSP, addressed specific situations where operational action of the Union was deemed to be required. They committed the Member States in the positions they adopted and in the conduct of their activity (Article 14(3) EU).[55] Even if there was a change in circumstances having a substantial effect on a question subject to

28.013

---

[48] See the present Article 29 TEU.
[49] C-354/04 P, *Gestoras Pro Amnistía and Others v Council*, 2007, para. 52; C-355/04 P, *Segi and Others v Council*, 2007, para. 52.
[50] See the present Article 29 TEU.
[51] See the present Article 34(1) TEU.
[52] C-354/04 P, *Gestoras Pro Amnistía and Others v Council*, 2007, para. 52; C-355/04 P, *Segi and Others v Council*, 2007, para. 52.
[53] Ibid., paras 35–43.
[54] C-130/10, *European Parliament v Council*, 2012, paras 106–10.
[55] See the present Article 28(2) TEU. See Dashwood, 'The Law and Practice of CFSP Joint Actions', in Cremona and De Witte (eds), *EU Foreign Relations Law—Constitutional Fundamentals* (Hart Publishing, 2008) 53–77; Münch, 'Die gemeinsame Aktion im Rahmen des GASP: Inhalt, Rechtsnatur und Reformbedürftigkeit' (1996) EuR 415–33.

a joint action, the action was to stand until such time as the Council decided to review its principles and objectives (Article 14(2)).[56] All this did not preclude joint actions from having legal effects vis-à-vis third parties.

28.014 **Framework decision.** A framework decision was a PJCC instrument for the approximation of the laws and regulations of the Member States (Article 34(2)(b) EU). Framework decisions were binding upon Member States as to the result to be achieved but left the choice of form and methods to the national authorities.[57] Article 34(2)(b) EU further provided that framework decisions did not entail direct effect. The Court of Justice held that it followed from the fact that the wording of Article 34(2)(b) EU was identical to that of Article 249 EC, third para., EC, that framework decisions were binding in nature. The binding character of framework decisions places on national authorities, and particularly national courts, an obligation to interpret national law as far as possible in the light of the wording and purpose of the framework decision in order to attain the pursued result.[58] This duty derives from the principle of sincere cooperation, which, according to the Court, also applied within the framework of the pre-Lisbon PJCC. Moreover, the jurisdiction of the Court to give preliminary rulings under Article 35 EU would be deprived of most of its effectiveness if individuals were not entitled to invoke framework decisions in order to obtain a conforming interpretation of national law before the courts of the Member States.[59] As in the case of directives, the obligation on the national court to interpret national law in conformity with a framework decision is limited by general principles of Union law, in particular those of legal certainty and non-retroactivity, and cannot serve as the basis for an interpretation of national law *contra legem*.[60] Also in the case of framework decisions, national courts must take into consideration the whole body of rules of national law and interpret them, so far as possible, in accordance with framework decisions, in order to achieve the result sought by these framework decisions, and if necessary disapply conflicting case law that is not compatible with Union law.[61] However, while national courts are thus required to interpret their national law, to the greatest extent possible, in conformity with Union law, which enables them to ensure an outcome that is compatible with the objective pursued by the framework decision concerned, the primacy of Union law does not require a national court to disapply a provision of national law which is incompatible with the provisions of a framework decision.[62]

28.015 **Decision.** As far as PJCC was concerned, the EU Treaty empowered the Council to adopt 'decisions' for any other purpose consistent with the objectives of Title VI, excluding any approximation of the laws and regulations of the Member States (Article 34(2)(c) EU).[63]

---

[56] See the present Article 28(1), second subpara. TEU.
[57] An analogy could be drawn with the description of directives (para. 27.029, *supra*). For an appraisal of this instrument, see Monjal, 'Le droit dérivé de l'Union européenne en quête d'identité' (2001) RTDE 335–69; Borgers, 'Implementing Framework Decisions' (2007) CMLRev 1361–86.
[58] C-105/03, *Pupino*, 2005, paras 33–4 and 43.
[59] Ibid., paras 35–43. See Monjal, 'La décision-cadre instaurant le mandat d'arrêt européen et l'ordre juridique français: la constitutionnalité du droit dérivé de l'Union européenne sous contrôle du Conseil d'Etat' (2003) RDUE 109, 178–87.
[60] C-105/03, *Pupino*, 2005, paras 44–7; C-42/11, *Lopes Da Silva Jorge*, 2012, para. 55.
[61] C-554/14, *Ognyanov*, 2016, paras 56–70.
[62] C-573/17, *Popławski*, 2019, paras 50–109.
[63] The EU Treaty did not mention decisions amongst the CFSP instruments. The Member States, however, adopted familiar forms of act such as a 'decision of the representatives of the Governments of the Member States';

Such decisions were binding and did not entail direct effect (ibid.). Again, the fact that decisions were binding on the Member States did not preclude them from having legal effects vis-à-vis third parties. The fact that the Court of Justice was competent, under certain circumstances, to determine their interpretation and validity under the preliminary ruling procedure, implied that individuals were entitled to invoke PJCC decisions before the courts of the Member States.

Other acts. Among the various PJCC instruments, Article 34 EU mentioned conventions concluded between the Member States (see para. 28-019, *infra*). In addition, Article 34 EU referred to measures adopted by the Council to implement PJCC decisions and PJCC conventions.[64] The content of such measures determined whether they had legal effects not just vis-à-vis the Member States, but also vis-à-vis third parties. As far as pre-Lisbon CFSP instruments are concerned, legal effects vis-à-vis third parties seemed to have been excluded in the case of 'principles', 'general guidelines', and 'common strategies' adopted by the European Council (Article 13(1) and (2) EU). As a rule, recommendations, resolutions, or declarations adopted by the Council in the pre-Lisbon framework of the CFSP or PJCC were not intended to have legal effects.[65] **28.016**

Article 46 EU did not exclude the jurisdiction of the Court of Justice to ensure, under Article 47 EU, that no provision in Title V or Title VI of the EU Treaty detracted from the Community Treaties. As a result, the Court still had the power to pronounce an action by the institutions which was alleged to constitute an infringement of Community law even if the action was undertaken pursuant to the CFSP or PJCC. Accordingly, the Court had jurisdiction under Article 47 EU to examine whether an act of the Council, which was formally based on Title V or VI of the EU Treaty, but related to a matter coming within the Community's competence, should not instead have been adopted on the basis of a provision of the Community Treaties and in accordance with the procedure prescribed thereby.[66]

C. International agreements concluded by the Union in connection with the CFSP and PJCC

Agreements concluded by the Union. In accordance with Article 24 and Article 38 EU, the Council concluded international agreements with one or more States or international organizations in connection with the CFSP and PJCC. All agreements which the Council concluded on behalf of the EU referred to the European Union[67] as one of the contracting **28.017**

---

see Decision (96/409/CFSP) of the representatives of the Governments of the Member States, meeting within the Council, of 25 June 1996 on the establishment of a temporary travel document OJ 1996 L168/4.

[64] Article 34(2)(c) and (d), second para. EU, respectively. These measures were adopted by the Council by a qualified majority of votes or by a majority of two-thirds of the contracting parties, respectively (ibid.).

[65] For an example, see Council Decision 2005/876/JHA of 21 November 2005 on the exchange of information extracted from the criminal record, OJ 2005 L322/33.

[66] C-170/96, *Commission v Council*, 1998; C-176/03, *Commission v Council*, 2005; C-440/05, *Commission v Council*, 2007; C-91/05, *Commission v Council*, 2008.

[67] See, e.g., the Agreement between the European Union and the North Atlantic Treaty Organization on the security of information, approved by Council Decision 2003/211/CFSP of 24 February 2003, OJ 2003 L80/35; the Agreements between the European Union and the United States of America on extradition and mutual legal assistance in criminal matters, approved by Council Decision 2003/516/EC of 6 June 2003, OJ 2003 L181/25 and concluded on behalf of the Union by Council Decision 2009/820/CFSP of 23 October 2009, OJ 2009 L291/40; and the

parties, which suggests that, internationally, not only were the Member States severally bound, but also the Union as such. Agreements concluded in accordance with Article 24 EU were binding on the institutions of the Union (Article 24(6) EU).[68] Still, Article 24 EU provided that no agreement 'shall be binding on a Member State whose representative in the Council states that it has to comply with the requirements of its own constitutional procedure'.[69] In such a case, the other members of the Council could nevertheless agree that the agreement was to apply provisionally to them (Article 24(5) EU). Agreements concluded under Article 24 EU were published in the *Official Journal*, unless the Council decided otherwise.[70] Under Article 46 EU, the Court of Justice had no jurisdiction to rule on the validity or interpretation of such agreements.[71]

D. Conventions concluded between the Member States

28.018 **Conventions connected with Community law.** Article 293 EC invited the Member States to 'enter into negotiations with each other' with a view to laying down arrangements in matters such as the abolition of double taxation, the mutual recognition of companies, and the reciprocal recognition and enforcement of national judgments. In these areas, but also in other fields, the Member States have concluded conventions amongst themselves with a connection to fields of Community competence, but without their constituting Community law. Conventions concluded in this way were not acts of the institutions, but remained agreements governed by international law to which Article 234 EC [*now Article 267 TFEU*] did not apply.[72]

However, the Member States could provide, in the convention itself or in a protocol thereto, for the Court of Justice to have jurisdiction to interpret its provisions, as was the case with

---

Agreement between the European Union and the Republic of Iceland and the Kingdom of Norway on the application of certain provisions of the Convention of 29 May 2000 on Mutual Assistance in Criminal Matters between the Member States of the European Union and the 2001 Protocol thereto, approved by Council Decision 2004/79/EC of 17 December 2003, OJ 2004 L26/1. See Mitsilegas, 'The External Dimension of EU Action in Criminal Matters' (2007) E For Aff Rev 457–97; Georgopoulos, 'What Kind of Treaty-Making Power for the EU? Constitutional Problems Related to the Conclusion of the EU-US Agreements on Extradition and Mutual Legal Assistance' (2005) ELRev 190–208. See also the Agreement between the European Union and the United States of America on the processing and transfer of Passenger Name Record (PNR) data by air carriers to the United States Department of Homeland Security (DHS), which provisionally applies as of the date of its signature (see Council Decision 2007/551/CFSP/JHA of 23 July 2007, OJ 2007 L204/16). That agreement replaces an earlier agreement between the EC and the USA, concluded under Article 95 EC [*now Article 114 TFEU*], which was denounced by the EC (see OJ 2006 C219/1) after the Court of Justice ruled that it could not have validly been adopted under the first pillar (see C-317/04 and C-318/04, *European Parliament v Commission*, 2006, para. 7.113, *supra*).

[68] However, the Agreement between the European Union and NATO on the Security of Information restricts its application as far as the EU is concerned to the Council of the European Union, the Secretary-General/High Representative, and the General Secretariat of the Council and the Commission (Agreement, Article 3; n. 67, *supra*).

[69] Such a declaration was made, for example, by twelve Member States with regard to the agreements with the USA on extradition and mutual legal assistance in criminal matters (n. 67, *supra*). See Genson, 'Les accords d'extradition et d'entraide judiciaire signés le 25 juin 2003 à Washington entre l'Union européenne et les Etats-Unis d'Amérique' (2003) RMCUE 427–32.

[70] Article 17(1)(h) of the previous version of the Council Rules of Procedure, adopted by Council Decision of 22 March 2004 (OJ 2004 L106/22).

[71] Since the provisions of Article 24 EU applied to such agreements in the sphere of PJCC, the Court of Justice also had no jurisdiction in regard to them.

[72] 56/84, *Von Gallera*, 1984, para. 4.

the 1968 Brussels Convention on jurisdiction and enforcement of judgments in civil and commercial matters, which was concluded pursuant to Article 293 EC.[73] According to the Court of Justice, provisions of a convention concluded on the basis of that article and within the framework defined by it were 'linked to the E[E]C Treaty'.[74] As a result, the Court of Justice reviewed a national provision of procedural law forming part of the provisions to which the Brussels Convention referred in the light of the prohibition of discrimination laid down in Article 12 EC [*now Article 18 TFEU*] and found that the provision in question was contrary thereto.[75]

Although they were not part of Community law, conventions contemplated by Article 293 EC and those that were 'inseparable from the attainment of the objectives of the EC Treaty' as well as 'the protocols on the interpretation of those conventions by the Court of Justice, signed by the present Member States of the Community' constituted part of the *acquis communautaire*.[76] New Member States undertook, in the Act of Accession, to accede to such conventions and to enter into negotiations with the other Member States in order to make the necessary adjustments thereto.[77] Most of these conventions have since been replaced by Union regulations, including the 1980 Rome Convention on the law applicable to contractual obligations, which the Member States concluded outside the framework of Article 293 EC and for which they conferred jurisdiction on the Court of Justice to interpret it.[78] Still relevant is the 1990 Convention on the elimination of double taxation in connection with the adjustment of profits of associated enterprises.[79]

PJCC conventions. Under Article 34(2)(d) EU, the Council was competent to establish conventions in the field of police and judicial cooperation in criminal matters (PJCC), which it recommended to the Member States for adoption in accordance with their respective

28.019

---

[73] Brussels Convention of 27 September 1968 on jurisdiction and the enforcement of judgments in civil and commercial matters (the Brussels Convention, often referred to as the Judgments Convention, now replaced by Regulation (EC) No. 44/2001 and its successor regulation; see para. 8.015, *supra*). Questions on the interpretation and application of the Convention could be referred to the Court of Justice for a preliminary ruling pursuant to the Luxembourg Protocol of 3 June 1971 on its interpretation (OJ 1978 L304/36). Provision was also made for the Court of Justice to interpret the Brussels Convention of 29 February 1968 on the mutual recognition of companies and bodies corporate (see (1969) EC Bull. Suppl. 2) under a protocol of 3 June 1971 appended thereto, which however, like the Convention itself, never entered into force. The Court of Justice has no such jurisdiction in respect of the third convention adopted pursuant to Article 293 EC: Brussels Convention of 23 July 1990 on the elimination of double taxation in connection with the adjustment of profits of associated enterprises, OJ 1990 L225/10.

[74] C-398/92, *Mund & Fester*, 1994, para. 12.

[75] Ibid., paras 13–22.

[76] 2003 Act of Accession, Article 5(2) and 1994 Act of Accession, Article 4(2). Article 3(4) of the 2011 Act of Accession and Article 3(4) of the 2005 Act of Accession limited themselves to listing (by reference to an Annex) the conventions to which the new Member States had to accede. The 1972 and 1979 Acts of Accession only mentioned the Article 293 [EC] conventions, whilst Article 3(2) of the 1985 Act of Accession also referred to conventions which 'are inseparable from the attainment of the objectives of that Treaty and thus linked to the Community legal order' (for the references of the Acts of Accession, see paras 4-002–4-008, *supra*).

[77] 2005 Act of Accession, Article 3(3); 2003 Act of Accession, Article 5(2); 1994 Act of Accession, Article 4(2).

[78] Rome Convention of 19 June 1980 on the law applicable to contractual obligations (see para. 8.016, *supra*; now replaced by Regulation (EC) No. 593/2008), the First Protocol of 19 December 1988 on interpretation of the Convention by the Court of Justice, OJ 1989 L48/1, and the Second Protocol of 19 December 1988 conferring on the Court of Justice of the European Communities certain powers to interpret the Convention, OJ 1989 L48/17; on the jurisdiction of the Court, see C-133/08, *Intercontainer Interfrigo*, 2009, paras 20–1. See also the powers conferred on the Court by Articles 5 and 73 of the Luxembourg Convention for the European patent for the common market (Community Patent Convention), OJ 1976 L17/1, which never collected sufficient ratifications in order to enter into force.

[79] See n. 73, *supra*.

constitutional requirements.[80] Unless they provided otherwise, such conventions, once adopted by at least half of the Member States, entered into force for those Member States (Article 34(2)(d) EU). Within the Member States which are party to them, PJCC conventions have the same legal force as other international conventions, except that the Court of Justice may have jurisdiction to rule on their interpretation. Also, before 1 December 2014, if the Member State concerned had accepted the jurisdiction of the Court of Justice, that court could give preliminary rulings on the interpretation of such conventions (Article 35(1) EU).

Even before the introduction (by the Treaty of Amsterdam) of Article 35 EU, the Member States concluded conventions in the sphere of justice and home affairs (JHA), in respect of which, under the former Article K.3 of the EU Treaty, the Council conferred jurisdiction on the Court of Justice to interpret provisions of conventions and to rule on any disputes regarding their application.[81]

28.020 **Legal effects post-Lisbon.** Since the entry into force of the Lisbon Treaty, the Treaties no longer mention conventions between Member States as a policy instrument of the Union. This does not prevent existing conventions from preserving their legal force, including any interpretative jurisdiction conferred on the Court of Justice.

---

[80] See also Article 3 of the 1994 Act of Accession. See the Convention of 29 May 2000 on Mutual Assistance in Criminal Matters between the Member States of the European Union, established in accordance with Article 34 of the EU Treaty by Council Act of 29 May 2000, OJ 2000 C197/1.

[81] See the Convention of 26 July 1995 on the protection of the European Communities' financial interests (OJ 1995 C316/49) and the Protocol of 29 November 1996, on the interpretation, by way of preliminary rulings, by the Court of Justice of that Convention (OJ 1997 C151/2), both drawn up on the basis of Article K.3 of the Treaty on European Union.

PART VI
JUDICIAL PROTECTION IN THE EUROPEAN UNION

Union law *as such* is part of the national legal systems. A dispute concerning the application of Union law may therefore be brought before a national court, in accordance with the national rules governing jurisdiction and procedure. In that sense, any national court applying Union law is a 'Union court'. In addition, the TEU confers on the Court of Justice of the European Union the task to ensure that in the interpretation and application of the Treaties the law is observed (Article 19, first para. TEU). Where the Treaties confer jurisdiction on the Court of Justice of the European Union to decide a dispute, that dispute is excluded from the jurisdiction of other courts. There is formal cooperation between the Court of Justice and national courts within the framework of the preliminary reference procedure (Article 267 TFEU). This Part discusses the dual system of judicial protection in the Union, involving both the national courts and the Court of Justice of the European Union.[1] On the one hand, they ensure the correct interpretation and application of Union law in the Member States, thereby providing judicial protection against the actions of national authorities and individuals (Chapter 29). On the other hand, they seek to guarantee judicial protection of all those affected by the Union's own actions (Chapter 30).

---

[1] This Part offers a succinct overview of the mechanisms for ensuring effective judicial protection in the Union. For an in-depth analysis and further references to case law and doctrinal articles, see Lenaerts, Gutman, and Nowak, *EU Procedural Law* (OUP, 2022).

29
Judicial Protection Vis-á-Vis Member States and Private Parties

Two paths. Article 19(1) TEU, which gives concrete expression to the value of the rule of law affirmed in Article 2 TEU (see para. 5.005, *supra*), entrusts national courts together with the Court of Justice with the responsibility for ensuring the full application of Union law in the Member States and the judicial protection that individuals derive from Union law. When a dispute involving the application of Union law arises in a Member State, it is for the national courts to apply and enforce that law. If necessary, these courts may refer a question to the Court of Justice for a preliminary ruling on the interpretation of Union law. If a Member State's authority fails to apply Union law correctly, there is also the possibility of raising the issue with the Commission. The Commission may start proceedings against the Member State in question under Article 258 TFEU and may ask the Court of Justice to rule that the Member State has failed to fulfil its obligations under Union law. However, as explained below, national courts do not have the same possibility to cooperate with the Court of Justice with regard to Union action in the field of the common foreign and security policy (CFSP). In this field, no action may be brought against a Member State for failure to comply with Union law.

29.001

I. Enforcement of Union Law in the National Courts

Enforcement of Union law. It is the responsibility of all national authorities to ensure that Union law is applied correctly. Where rights derived from Union law are not being respected or obligations are not complied with within a Member State, it is for the national courts to ensure that the relevant rules of Union law are applied and to impose the necessary sanctions in the event of infringement of those rules. In so doing, the national courts give effect to the requirement for each Member State to ensure effective legal protection within the fields covered by Union law (Article 19(1), second subpara. TEU).

29.002

A. Guarantees for ensuring effective legal protection

Effective legal protection. Although the organization of justice in the Member States falls within the competence of those Member States, they are required to exercise that competence in compliance with the obligations deriving from Union law and, in particular, the obligation stated in the second subpara. of Article 19(1) TEU for the Member States to 'provide remedies sufficient to ensure effective legal protection in the fields covered

29.003

by Union law'. This obligation implies that every Member State must ensure that the national courts which are liable to rule on the application or interpretation of Union law, meet the requirements of effective judicial protection.[1] In this respect, maintaining the independence of national courts is essential, as confirmed by the second para. of Article 47 of the Charter of Fundamental Rights, which refers to access to an 'independent' tribunal as one of the requirements linked to the fundamental right to an effective remedy.[2] In the light of the fundamental importance of judicial review for the rule of law, itself a value on which the Union is founded pursuant to Article 2 TEU, each Member State must ensure the independence and impartiality of all courts that may have to decide on legal issues pertaining to the fields covered by Union law.[3] This obligation is independent from the obligations weighing on the Member States under Article 47 of the Charter. Indeed, the scope of application of Article 19(1) TEU extends to 'the fields covered by Union law', which is wider than the implementation of Union law by Member States laid down in Article 51(1) of the Charter that determines the applicability of Article 47 of the Charter (see para. 25.009, *supra*).[4] The independence of national courts is also essential to the proper operation of the judicial cooperation system embodied by the preliminary ruling mechanism under Article 267 TFEU, which may be activated only by a court or tribunal responsible for applying Union law that satisfies, *inter alia*, that criterion of independence (see para. 29.015, *infra*). Given the fundamental importance of the rule of law for the application of Union law, the Member States are required to ensure that, in the light of that value, any regression of their laws on the organization of justice is prevented, in particular by refraining from adopting rules which would undermine the independence of the judiciary (see para. 5.005, *supra*).

29.004 **Judicial independence.** The Court of Justice has ruled on the requirements of judicial independence in various cases brought before it as regards concerns about judicial reforms possibly undermining the independence of the judiciary, and hence the rule of law, in particular in Poland (see para. 5.005, *supra*). The Court has clarified that the requirement that courts be independent has two aspects to it.[5] The first aspect, which is external in nature, requires that the court concerned exercise its functions wholly autonomously, without being subject to any hierarchical constraint or subordinated to any other body and without taking orders or instructions from any source whatsoever, thus being protected against external interventions or pressure liable to impair the independent judgment of its members and to influence their decisions. The second aspect, which is internal in nature, is linked to impartiality and seeks to ensure that an equal distance is maintained from the parties to the proceedings and their respective interests with regard to the subject matter of those proceedings. That aspect

---

[1] C-64/16, *Associação Sindical dos Juízes Portugueses*, 2018, paras 32–40; C-619/18 *Commission v Poland*, 2019, paras 50–1.

[2] C-64/16, *Associação Sindical dos Juízes Portugueses*, 2018, para. 41.

[3] C-619/18, *Commission v Poland*, 2019, paras 42–59; C-192/18, *Commission v Poland*, 2019, paras 98–106; C-585/18, C-624/18, and C-625/18 *A.K.*, 2019, paras 115–19 and 167–9.

[4] See C-619/18, *Commission v Poland*, 2019, paras 48–54. This also means that under Article 19(1) TEU the restrictions on the applicability of the Charter, including Protocol (No. 30) do not apply: ibid., para. 53. On the relationship between Article 47 of the Charter and Article 19(1) TEU, see Prechal, 'Effective Judicial Protection: Some Recent Developments—Moving to the Essence' (2020) REALaw 175–90.

[5] See, on both elements, C-216/18 PPU, *LM*, 2018, paras 63–5; C-619/18, *Commission v Poland*, 2019, paras 71–3.

requires objectivity and the absence of any interest in the outcome of the proceedings apart from the strict application of the rule of law.

Those guarantees of independence and impartiality require rules, particularly as regards the composition of the body and the appointment, length of service, and grounds for abstention, rejection, and dismissal of its members, in order to dispel any reasonable doubt in the minds of individuals as to the imperviousness of that body to external factors and its neutrality with respect to the interests before it.[6] As regards judicial appointments, it must be noted that the mere fact that judges are appointed by a political organ, such as the President of the Republic, does not give rise to a relationship of subordination of the former to the latter or to doubts as to the former's impartiality, if, once appointed, they are free from influence or pressure when carrying out their role. However, it is still necessary to ensure that the substantive conditions and detailed procedural rules governing appointment decisions are such that they cannot give rise to reasonable doubts as to the independence and impartiality of the judges concerned, once appointed as judge.[7] Those who have the task of adjudicating must receive a level of remuneration commensurate with the importance of their judicial functions.[8] Furthermore, the judges' freedom from all external intervention or pressure requires guarantees protecting them against removal from office.[9] This principle of 'irremovability' requires, in particular, that judges may remain in post, provided that they have not reached the obligatory retirement age or until the expiry of their mandate, where that mandate is for a fixed term. While that principle is not wholly absolute, there can be no exceptions to it unless warranted by legitimate and compelling grounds, subject to the principle of proportionality.[10] The requirement of independence also means that the rules governing the disciplinary regime for judges and, accordingly, any dismissal of judges must provide the necessary guarantees in order to prevent any risk of such regime being used as a system of political control of the content of judicial decisions. These guarantees include rules which define, in particular, both conduct amounting to disciplinary offences and the penalties actually applicable, which provide for the involvement of an independent body in accordance with a procedure which fully safeguards the rights enshrined in Articles 47 and 48 of the Charter, in particular rights of defence, and which include the possibility of bringing legal proceedings against the disciplinary bodies' decisions.[11] In accordance with the principle of the separation of powers that characterizes the operation of the rule of law, the independence of the judiciary must be ensured, in particular, in relation to the legislature and the executive. In order to protect judges from external intervention or pressure liable to jeopardize their independence, the Member State's law must be such as to preclude not only any direct influence, in the form of instructions, but also types of influence

---

[6] C-216/18 PPU, *LM*, 2018, para. 66; C-619/18, *Commission v Poland*, 2019, para. 74.

[7] C-585/18, C-624/18, and C-625/18 *A.K.*, 2019, paras 133–4. See also, as regards judicial appointments in Poland, C-824/18, *A.B. and Others*, , 2021; and pending cases C-487/19, *W.Z.*, AG Tanchev Opinion, 2021; C-508/19, *Prokurator Generalny*, AG Tanchev Opinion, 2021; as regards judicial appointments in Malta, C-896/19, *Repubblika*, 2021.

[8] C-64/16, *Associação Sindical dos Juízes Portugueses*, 2018, para. 45; C-216/18 PPU, *LM*, 2018, para. 64.

[9] C-216/18 PPU, *LM*, 2018, para. 64; C-619/18, *Commission v Poland*, 2019, para. 75.

[10] C-619/18, *Commission v Poland*, 2019, paras 78–97 and 108–22; C-192/18, *Commission v Poland*, 2019, paras 116–36;

[11] C-216/18 PPU, *LM*, 2018, para. 67; C-619/18, *Commission v Poland*, 2019, para. 77. See also pending Case C-791/19, *Commission v Poland*, OJ 2019 C413/36. See also C-83/19, C-127/19, C-195/19, C-291/19, C-355/19 and C-397/19, *Asociaţia "Forumul Judecătorilor Din România" and Others*, 2021, paras 186–241.

which are more indirect and which are liable to have an effect on the decisions of the judges concerned.[12]

B. Interpretation and application of Union law by national courts

29.005 **Specific characteristics of Union law.** When applying Union law, it is first and foremost the national court itself which has to interpret the provisions of Union law that it deems to be applicable to the case at hand. A national court interpreting provisions of Union law has to take account of the fact that Union law uses its own terminology and that legal concepts do not necessarily have the same meaning in Union law and in the various national legal systems,[13] or in Union law and international law.[14] Moreover, Union law texts are drafted in several languages, which are equally authentic and must be given uniform interpretation and application in all Member States.[15] The need for a uniform application of Union law and the principle of equality require that the terms of a provision of Union law which makes no express reference to the law of the Member states for the purpose of determining its meaning and scope must be given an independent and uniform interpretation throughout the Union.[16]

29.006 **Interpretation methods.** Often, a national court cannot confine itself to giving a literal or grammatical interpretation of a provision of Union law.[17] This will be the case, first of all, where different language versions of a provision diverge.[18] In such a case, the provision in question must be interpreted by reference to the objective and general scheme of the Union act in which it is included (see para. 14.025, *supra*).[19] In other cases too, it may be useful for the interpretation of a provision of Union law to consider the legal framework of which that provision forms part (systematic or contextual interpretation) and the objectives pursued by it (teleological or functional interpretation).[20] According to the Court of Justice, any provision of Union law must be placed in its context and interpreted in the light of the provisions of Union law as a whole, its objectives, and its state of evolution at the date on which the provision in question is to be applied.[21] In *Van Gend & Loos* the Court already

---

[12] C-619/18 *Commission v Poland*, 2019, para. 12; C-585/18, C-624/18, and C-625/18 *A.K.*, 2019, paras 124–5.

[13] See, e.g., the distinct meaning of the Union law principle of proportionality laid down in Article 5(4) TEU and the German concept of proportionality—a distinction lost sight of by the German Constitutional Court in its judgment of 5 May 2020 (2 BvR 859/15, para. 1-237), where it applied the German concept of proportionality rather than the concept contained in Article 5(4) TEU, applied by the Court of Justice in C-493/17, *Weiss*, 2018, paras 71–100, which is common to all Member States. This latter concept does not necessarily correspond to the precise understanding of the identically named concept in any of these States.

[14] See, e.g., C-316/19, *Commission v Slovenia*, 2020, paras 68–75 (notion of Union 'archives').

[15] 283/81, *Cilfit*, 1982, paras 18–19.

[16] e.g. C-510/10, *DR and TV2 Danmark*, 2012, paras 33–7.

[17] For an overview of interpretation techniques, see Lenaerts and Gutiérrez-Fons, 'To say What the Law of the EU is: Methods of Interpretation and the European Court of Justice' (2013–2014) Colum JEL 3–61; Lenaerts and Gutiérrez-Fons, *Les méthodes d'interprétation de la Cour de justice de l'Union européenne* (Bruylant, 2020).

[18] Since all the official languages of the Union are the authentic languages of the acts in which they are drafted, all these language versions must, as a matter of principle, be recognized as having the same value for the interpretation of a Union act. Accordingly, the mere fact that most language versions use a particular term, cannot as such be conclusive; see C-24/19, *A and Others*, 2020, paras 38–40; C-412/10, *Homawoo*, 2011, para. 28 and C-16/16 P, *Belgium v Commission*, 2018, para. 49.

[19] C-24/19, *A and Others*, 2020, para. 37.

[20] C-414/16, *Egenberger*, 2018, para. 44; C-511/18, C-512/18, and C-520/18, *La Quadrature du Net and Others*, 2020, para. 105.

[21] 283/81, *Cilfit and Others*, 1982, para. 20; C-24/19, *A and others*, 2020, para. 42.

considered that, for the interpretation of the Treaties, it was necessary to take account of 'the spirit, the general scheme and the wording' of the Treaties (see para. 1.025, *supra*). The Court applies the same methods of interpretation to provisions of secondary Union law. The scope of acts of the institutions must therefore also be determined in the light of their wording, their general scheme, and their objectives.[22] Lastly, if the wording of a provision of Union law is open to more than one interpretation, preference should be given to the interpretation which renders the provision consistent with higher ranking norms such as the Treaties, fundamental rights, other principles of Union law, and international law (see also paras 25.008 and 26.002).[23] Moreover, where a provision of Union law is open to several interpretations, preference must be given to that interpretation which ensures that the provision retains its effectiveness (*effet utile*).[24]

Interpretation tools. To situate a provision of a Union act in its context and to determine its objectives, it is standard practice to consider the preamble to that act and the recitals contained therein, as they often clarify its content. However, since the preamble to a Union act has no binding legal force, it cannot be relied on either as a ground for derogating from the actual provisions of the act in question or for interpreting those provisions in a manner clearly contrary to their wording.[25] For the interpretation of provisions of secondary Union law, useful indications can sometimes be found in the legislative history[26] or preparatory works, such as Commission proposals[27] or opinions or amendments from other institutions and bodies,[28] which may explain why a provision has been included in the final text of the act[29] or was left out.[30] For the interpretation of the Treaties, it is less easy to refer to preparatory acts, as the intergovernmental negotiations on the Treaties have not always been conducted on the basis of documents available to the public.[31]

29.007

Application of Union law. It is for the national court to ensure that Union law acquires its 'full effect'. As is clear from para. 23.010 *et seq.*, *supra*, this means that the court must interpret its national law as far as possible in accordance with the requirements of Union law. Where a conflict between national provisions and Union law cannot be avoided, priority should be given to Union law. An administrative court before which the annulment of provisions contrary to Union law is sought must therefore annul those provisions in the event of a conflict. As a general rule, the national court must set aside all national provisions contrary to Union law and recognize the rights that a party derives from rules of Union law having direct effect.[32]

29.008

---

[22] e.g. C-212/91, *Angelopharm*, 1994, paras 26–38; C-280/04, *Jyske Finans*, 2005, paras 31–44.
[23] e.g. C-305/05, *Ordre des barreaux francophones et germanophone*, 2007, para. 28; C-402/07 and C-432/07 *Sturgeon*, 2009; C-581/10 and C-629/10, *Nelson*, 2012; C-547/14, *Philip Morris Brands*, 2016, para. 70.
[24] e.g. 187/87, *Saarland and Other*, 1988, para. 19; C-434/97, *Commission v France*, 2000, para. 21.
[25] e.g. C-136/04, *Deutsches Milch-Kontor*, 2005, para. 32; C-290/12, *Della Rocca*, 2013, paras 36–9.
[26] e.g. C-267/11 P, *Commission v Latvia*, 2013, para. 54; C-24/19, *A and Others*, 2020, para. 41.
[27] C-89/12, *Bark*, 2013, paras 42 and 45; C-601/15 PPU, *J.N.*, 2016, para. 63; C-115/15, *NA*, 2016, paras 46–7.
[28] e.g. C-190/11, *Mühlleitner*, 2012, para. 40; C-487/11, *Laimonis Treimanis*, 2012, para. 26.
[29] e.g. C-402/03, *Skov*, 2006, paras 27–9; C-310/08, *Ibrahim*, 2010, para. 47; C-58/08, *Vodafone and Others*, 2010, paras 39–59.
[30] e.g. C-215/97, *Bellone*, 1998, paras 11 and 16; C-266/05 P, *Sison v Council*, 2007, paras 36–8; C-443/11, *Jeltes*, 2013, paras 34–5.
[31] See, however, C-370/12, *Pringle*, 2012, paras 134–5; C-538/11P, *Inuit Tapiriit Kanatami v European Parliament and Council*, 2013, para. 49; C-62/14, *Gauweiler*, 2015, para. 100.
[32] C-573/17, *Popławski*, 2019, paras 58–62.

29.009 **Jurisdiction and rules of procedure.** It is for the national legal system of each Member State to designate the courts and tribunals having jurisdiction and to determine the procedural conditions governing actions at law intended to ensure the protection of rights which individuals derive from Union law. The qualification of legal situations based on Union law is a matter for the national court. However, Union law imposes two requirements on jurisdiction and procedural rules in order to ensure the 'full effect' of Union law. These rules should not be less favourable than those relating to similar actions of a domestic nature (principle of equivalence) and should not contain conditions and time-limits that would make it impossible in practice to exercise the rights which the national courts are obliged to protect (principle of effectiveness).[33] To meet this double requirement, the court must, if necessary, set aside a normally applicable procedural rule. In doing so, the court must take into account the role of that provision in the procedure, its progress, and its special features, viewed as a whole, before the various national instances. In the light of that analysis the basic principles of the domestic judicial system, such as protection of the rights of the defence, the principle of legal certainty, and the proper conduct of the procedure, must, where appropriate, be taken into consideration.[34] Hence, the full effect of Union law may, in exceptional circumstances, also include requirements relating to the jurisdiction of a court. For instance, where a directive imposes the obligation to provide an adequate right of appeal and a provision of national law would prevent a court from protecting the rights resulting from this directive because it excludes its jurisdiction in this specific respect, that court would have to disregard that provision of national law.[35]

29.010 **Principle of equivalence.** It follows from the first of the two requirements mentioned that claims based on Union law should be treated equally at procedural level as similar domestic claims.[36] This applies, for example, to rules of evidence and rules on time-limits for appeals and prescription.[37] Thus, Union law does not preclude a Member State from failing to repay charges levied in breach of Union law in circumstances which would lead to an unjust enrichment of the rightholders, if a similar rule applies for the repayment of charges levied in breach of national law. Unjust enrichment may occur, for example, if the person who paid tax, has actually been able to pass it on to third parties and if, moreover, it is certain that he or she would unjustifiably enrich himself or herself if it were to be repaid.[38] According to the Court, the principle of equivalence has not been infringed if the applicable provision of Union law does not occupy a position similar to that of provisions of national law whose infringement may be relied on by the court of its own motion.[39]

29.011 **Principle of effectiveness.** Even if they comply with this first requirement, national procedural rules may still give rise to problems if they make the exercise of rights derived from

---

[33] 33/76, *Rewe*, 1976, para. 5, and 45/76, *Comet*, 1976, paras 13–16.
[34] C-312/93, *Peterbroeck*, 1995, para. 14, and C-430/93 and C-431/93, *van Schijndel and van Veen*, 1995, para. 19; C-222/05 to C-225/05, *van der Weerd*, 2007.
[35] C-462/99, *Connect Austria*, 2003, paras 35–42; C-378/17, *Minister for Justice and Equality*, 2018, paras 36–8 and 50; see also C-317/08 to C-320/08, *Alassini*, 2010.
[36] e.g. C-392/04 and C-422/04, *i-21 Germany and Arcor*, 2006, paras 62–72.
[37] e.g. C-118/08, *Transportes Urbanos y Servicios Generales*, 2010, paras 33–48; C-542/08, *Barth*, 2010; C-246/09, *Bulicke*, 2010.
[38] e.g. C-147/01, *Weber's Wine World*, 2003, paras 103–18; C-398/09, *Lady & Kid*, 2011, paras 16–27.
[39] C-222/05 to C-225/05, *van der Weerd*, 2007, paras 29–38.

Union law practically impossible or excessively difficult.[40] In the event of recovery of undue payments, this applies, for example, to presumptions or rules of evidence which place the burden of proof on the taxpayer that the taxes unduly paid have not been passed on to others, or to particular restrictions as to the proof to be adduced, such as the exclusion of all means of proof other than in writing.[41] The exercise of rights derived from Union law is also precluded if national authorities can refuse to reimburse duties levied in breach of Union law by relying on the principle of excusable error.[42]

However, the principle of effectiveness does not preclude, in the interests of legal certainty, to lay down reasonable time-limits to bring an appeal, even on pain of forfeiture of rights.[43] Thus, where an individual claims a right to which he or she is entitled under a directive, a Member State may, in principle, rely on the expiry of a national limitation period which began to run from the date on which the right in question became due, even if that directive had not yet been correctly transposed at that time. In such a case, the principle of effectiveness does not preclude a limitation period from limiting the retroactive effect of the claim; however, recourse to a limitation period would be contrary to the principle of effectiveness if an individual has no possibility at all of asserting the right conferred upon him or her by the directive.[44] A procedural rule which requires a rejected asylum seeker to submit an application for subsidiary protection status within a time-limit of fifteen working days from the rejection of his or her application for refugee status is incompatible with the principle of effectiveness.[45]

In order to ensure the stability of the law and legal relations and the proper administration of justice, it is important that judicial decisions that have become final after the available remedies have been exhausted or after the time-limits laid down for these remedies have expired, should not be subject to further challenge (principle of *res judicata*).[46] However, the principle of *res judicata* in national law cannot be applied in such a way that an interpretation by a national court which infringes Union law can no longer be called into question in a new dispute between the same parties on a similar issue, since that would infringe the principle of effectiveness.[47]

Compensation for damages. When an action is brought against a Member State for damages caused by a national authority infringing Union law, the national court has to order the Member State concerned to pay damages if the three conditions of the *Brasserie du Pêcheur* case law are met (see para. 23.019 *et seq., supra*). Of course, the conditions laid down by national law must not be less favourable than those applicable to similar national claims and must not make it virtually impossible or excessively difficult to obtain compensation. For example, State liability cannot be made conditional on providing proof either of misuse of

29.012

---

[40] C-430/93 and C-431/93, *Van Schijndel and Van Veen*, 1995, para. 17; C-360/09, *Pfleiderer*, 2011, para. 30; C-835/18, *SC Terracault*, 2020, para. 32. For an example relating to the organization of the court system, see C-268/06, *Impact*, 2008, paras 37–55.
[41] 199/82, *San Giorgio*, 1983, para. 14.
[42] C-188/95, *Fantask*, 1997, paras 35–41.
[43] e.g. C-343/96, *Dilexport*, 1999, paras 23–8.
[44] e.g. C-338/91, *Steenhorst-Neerings*, 1993, paras 17–24; C-410/92, *Johnson*, 1994, paras 22–36; C-188/95, *Fantask*, 1997, paras 42–52; see also C-246/96, *Magorrian and Cunningham*, 1997, paras 36–47; C-62/00, *Marks & Spencer*, 2002, paras 33–47; C-314/09, *Strabag*, 2010; C-640/13, *Commission v United Kingdom*, 2014, paras 32–4.
[45] C-429/15, *Danqua*, 2016, paras 42–9.
[46] C-224/01, *Köbler*, 2003, para. 38; C-234/04, *Kapferer*, 2006, para. 20; compare C-213/13, *Impresa Pizzarotti*, 2014, paras 53–64.
[47] C-2/08, *Fallimento Olimpiclub*, 2009, paras 20–32.

powers in the exercise of a public function[48] or of the intention of the national authority in question to cause the harm.[49] As regards the liability for a breach of Union law by a court of last instance, it is contrary to the principle of effectiveness to make it a condition that the decision of that court should be set aside first.[50]

The conditions that must be satisfied for a Member State to incur liability as a result of a breach of Union law for which it is responsible include that relating to the existence of a direct causal link between the breach and the loss or damage sustained. Nevertheless, where, in a Member State, the existence of an indirect causal link between a breach of national law by that Member State and the damage sustained is regarded as sufficient to incur State liability, an indirect causal link between a breach of Union law and the damage sustained must also, in accordance with the principle of equivalence, be regarded as sufficient for the purposes of rendering that Member State liable for that breach.[51]

In order to determine the damage eligible for compensation, the national court may inquire whether the injured person has made reasonable efforts to prevent the damage or to limit its extent.[52] However, national law may not limit the damage eligible for compensation to the damage caused to certain individual goods, to the exclusion of profit foregone by private individuals. Particularly in disputes of an economic or commercial nature, a complete exclusion of the loss of profit makes compensation for the damage suffered practically impossible.[53]

29.013 **Applying Union law *ex officio*.** The principle of the full effectiveness of Union law does not require the national court to raise, of its own motion, pleas in law and arguments based on Union law in all circumstances. According to the Court of Justice, such an obligation does exist with regard to mandatory rules of Union law where national law requires a national court to raise, of its own motion, internal rules of a mandatory nature.[54] Where national law does not expressly allow the court to apply Union law of its own motion, it is necessary, on the basis of the principles of equivalence and effectiveness, to examine whether Union law requires the national court to do so. In that regard, the Court of Justice has made it clear that the principle of effectiveness does not preclude national procedural rules that prevent a court from raising a plea based on Union law, even at last instance, where, in order to examine it, that court would have to go beyond the bounds of the legal dispute defined by the parties and rely on facts and circumstances other than those relied on by the parties.[55] This would be different, however, if parties did not have a genuine opportunity to raise a plea in fact or in law that would bring about the application of Union law.[56] Moreover, a

---

[48] C-46/93 and C-48/93, *Brasserie du Pêcheur and Factortame*, 1996, paras 69–73.
[49] C-571/16, *Kantarev*, 2018, para. 126.
[50] C-160/14, *Ferreira da Silva e Brito*, 2015, paras 51–9; C-571/16, *Kantarev*, 2018, paras 139–46.
[51] C-417/18, *AW and Others*, 2019, paras 38–40.
[52] e.g. C-524/04, *Test Claimants in the Thin Cap Group Litigation*, 2007, paras 124–7.
[53] e.g. C-46/93 and C-48/93, *Brasserie du Pêcheur and Factortame*, 1996, paras 87–90; C-470/03, *A.G.M.-COS. MET*, 2007, paras 89–96.
[54] C-430/93 and C-431/93, *van Schijndel and van Veen*, 1995, paras 13–14 (Court also considering that where national law allows the national court to invoke of its own motion mandatory rules of national law, it would have to do so). In this regard, see Nowak, *Ambtshalve toepassing van EU-recht door de Belgische burgerlijke rechter* (PhD KU Leuven, 2020); Corthaut, *EU Ordre Public* (Kluwer, 2012), 200–18.
[55] C-430/93 and C-431/93, *van Schijndel and van Veen*, 1995, paras 16–22.
[56] C-222/05 to C-225/05, *van der Weerd*, 2007, para. 36. The judgment then goes on to explain cases where the Court did accept that national courts may be under an obligation to raise claims of Union law of their own motion in terms of equivalence, the existence of a real impossibility to raise a claim of Union law, or because of a

national court must always have the power to raise, of its own motion, a rule of Union law when applicable to the dispute as defined by the parties.[57] Conversely, the principle of effectiveness does not require a national court to apply, of its own motion, a provision of Union law which would run counter to a rule of national law according to which the appellant may not be placed in a less favourable position than that in which he or she would have been had he or she not brought the action (prohibition of *reformatio in peius*).[58]

An exceptional regime exists in the area of consumer law, where the Court requires the national court to go beyond the ambit of the dispute defined by the parties in order to ensure the protection that consumers derive from a number of consumer law directives.[59] In the context of the Unfair Contract Terms Directive, a national court is even obliged to take measures of inquiry of its own motion in order to complete the factual and legal elements necessary to verify whether a contract term is unfair.[60] Such an exceptional regime does not exist in competition law. While the Court has qualified Articles 101 and 102 TFEU as Union rules of public policy,[61] this has not led to a self-standing Union law obligation for national judges to go beyond the ambit of the dispute in order to apply Union competition law *ex officio*. That being said, a national judge may still be obliged to do so on the basis of the principle of equivalence if national procedural law obliges the judge to apply rules of public order beyond the ambit of the dispute defined by the parties.

C. Questions for a preliminary ruling on the interpretation of Union law

Preliminary reference. In order to ensure the uniform application of Union law, Article 267 TFEU establishes a mechanism of judicial cooperation between the Court of Justice and national courts. By means of a reference for a preliminary ruling, a national court may obtain from the Court of Justice, before ruling (i.e. preliminary), the necessary guidance as to the interpretation which it must give to Union law in the proceedings before it ('the main proceedings'), for example, in order to know what action to take in respect of a plea against a provision of national law as being contrary to Union law. The rules governing the preliminary ruling procedure can be found in the Statute and the Rules of Procedure of the Court of Justice (see paras 13.002 and 13.017); practical guidance for national courts and parties can also be found on the Court's website.[62]

29.014

---

directive requiring that judges act *ex officio* in order to ensure the *effet utile* of the directive; ibid., paras 39–40. See also C-312/93, *Peterbroeck*, 1995, paras 14–21 (where it was held that the national court's refusal to entertain pleas not already raised before the tax authorities was contrary to Union law); see further Prechal, 'Community Law in National Courts: The Lessons from Van Schijndel' (1998) CMLRev 681–706.

[57] C-312/93, *Peterbroeck*, 1995.
[58] C-455/06, *Heemskerk and Schaap*, 2008, paras 46–7.
[59] C-243/08, *Pannon*, 2009 (Council Directive 93/13/EEC of 5 April 1993 on unfair terms in consumer contracts, OJ 1993 L95/29); C-227/08, *Martín Martín*, 2009 (Council Directive 85/577/EEC of 20 December 1985 to protect the consumer in respect of contracts negotiated away from business premises, OJ 1985 L372/31); C-377/14, *Radlinger*, 2016 (Directive 2008/48/EC of the European Parliament and of the Council of 23 April 2008 on credit agreements for consumers, OJ 1987 L133/66).
[60] C-137/08, *VB Pénzügyi Lízing*, 2010, paras 45–56; C-511/17, *Lintner*, 2020, para. 38.
[61] C-126/97, *Eco Swiss*, 1999, paras 36 and 39; C-295/04 to C-298/04, *Manfredi and Others*, 2006, paras 31 and 39; C-8/08, *T-Mobile*, 2009, para. 49.
[62] See 'Court of Justice' under 'Procedure' Recommendations to national courts and tribunals in relation to the initiation of preliminary ruling proceedings (OJ 2019 C380/1) and the Practice Directions to Parties concerning cases brought before the Court (OJ 2020 L42I/1).

1. Possibility and obligation to refer questions for a preliminary ruling

a. Courts that may refer questions

29.015 **Court or tribunal.** A reference for a preliminary ruling may be made by any court or tribunal which is called upon to give a ruling in proceedings leading to a judicial decision. Bodies acting as administrative rather than judicial authorities do not meet the definition of 'court or tribunal of a Member State'. In case of doubt, the Court of Justice takes into account a number of factors, including the legal basis of the body, its permanence, its compulsory jurisdiction, its ruling after any adversary procedure, its application of rules of law, and its composition and independence.[63] For example, the Court ruled that the Collège juridictionnel de la Région de Bruxelles-Capitale should be considered as a 'court or tribunal' when it rules in disputes regarding the legality of municipal taxes,[64] but it found that the Greek competition authority was not a clearly distinct third party in relation to the State body acting in the course of competition proceedings.[65] Similarly, the Spanish Central Tax Tribunal was deemed not to be independent given the insufficient guarantee as to the irremovability of the judges and the lack of equal distance to the parties.[66] In this respect, the Court determines the ability to make a reference pursuant to the same standards applied for the assessment of the independence of the judiciary under Article 191(1) TEU and Article 47 of the Charter of Fundamental rights (see para. 29.005, *supra*).[67] An arbitration body set up by agreement is not a court or tribunal within the meaning of Article 267 TFEU if there is no obligation, either in law or in fact, for the contracting parties to refer their disputes to that arbitration tribunal and if the public authorities are neither involved in the decision to go ahead with the arbitration procedure nor have the possibility of intervening of their own motion in the course of the proceedings before the arbitrator.[68] Therefore, the Court of Justice is not competent to rule on questions raised, for example, by the Belgian Collège d'arbitrage de la Commission de Litiges Voyages.[69] International courts are not a 'court or tribunal of a Member State',[70] with the exception of the Benelux Court of Justice when it has to interpret provisions of Union law.[71]

b. Possibility to ask questions

29.016 **Initiative.** Any court or tribunal within the meaning of Article 267 TFEU has the right to make a reference for a preliminary ruling. National procedural law should therefore not create obstacles to the possibility for any court or tribunal to refer questions for a preliminary ruling of its own motion if necessary.[72] For example, a national court must always be

---

[63] 61/65, *Vaassen-Göbbels*, 1966, 273; C-54/96, *Dorsch Consult*, 1997, para. 23; C-274/14, *Banco de Santander*, 2020, paras 51–80.
[64] C-17/00, *De Coster*, 2001, paras 9–22.
[65] C-53/03, *Syfait*, 2005, paras 29–37.
[66] C-274/14, *Banco de Santander*, 2020, paras 51–80.
[67] See C-64/16, *Associação Sindical dos Juízes Portugueses*, 2018, paras 38 and 43; C-272/19, *Land Hessen*, 2020, para. 45–61 (see also paras 29.004 and 29.005, *supra*).
[68] 102/81, *Nordsee*, 1982, paras 10–12. On the contrary, where the conditions are met, an arbitration body qualifies as a court or tribunal within the meaning of Article 267 TFEU; see C-377/13, *Ascendi Beiras Litoral e Alta, Auto Estradas das Beiras Litoral e Alta*, 2014, paras 22–35.
[69] C-125/04, *Denuit and Cordenier*, 2005, paras 11–17.
[70] C-196/09, *Miles*, 2011, paras 37–46 (Complaints Board of the European Schools is not a court or tribunal of the Member States).
[71] C-337/95, *Parfums Christian Dior*, 1997, paras 19–23. This is because the Benelux Court of Justice is a court common to three Member States and, as such, part of their jurisdictional system; see Opinion 1/09, *European and Community Patents Court*, 2011, para. 82.
[72] 166/73, *Rheinmühlen I*, 1974, para. 2.

free to refer a question to the Court of Justice for a preliminary ruling, even in cases where national law would oblige that court to refer certain questions to the national constitutional court or to the plenary assembly of the court concerned.[73] The initiative to ask the question must always come from the court itself,[74] even if the latter usually takes this decision at the request of one of the parties to the proceedings.

Optional questions. Under the second para. of Article 267 TFEU, a court or tribunal of a Member State may request the Court of Justice to give a ruling on questions relating to the interpretation of Union law. A preliminary reference must therefore be *possible* in any procedure in which that authority exercises a judicial function, including in the context of an inquiry procedure or an interlocutory procedure.[75] Within the context of a case, the court or tribunal may freely determine the stage in the proceedings at which the question for a preliminary ruling should be asked. In the light of the requirement for an interpretation of Union law which is useful to the national court, it is necessary for that court to define the factual and legal framework within which the questions raised must be asked, or at least to set out the facts on which those questions are based.[76] In any event, it is required that the court 'considers a decision on the question necessary to enable it to give judgment' (relevance of the question, see para. 29.025, *infra*).[77] The Court of Justice cannot therefore reply if the proceedings before the referring court have already been concluded at the time when the reference for a preliminary ruling is made.[78]

29.017

c. Obligation to ask questions

Duty to refer. The possibility of referring a question for a preliminary ruling becomes an obligation if the question emanates from a court or tribunal falling under the third para. of Article 267 TFEU. That provision requires 'courts or tribunals against whose decisions there is no judicial remedy under national law' to refer a question of interpretation of a provision of Union law to the Court of Justice where such a question is raised in a pending case. The purpose of that rule is to prevent the development of the highest level of case law in a Member State, in breach of Union law, thereby threatening to lead other courts in that Member State to rule in the same way. The third para. of Article 267 TFEU thus targets judgments against which there is no legal remedy to re-evaluate the legal question raised. This provision should therefore be understood as meaning that it covers decisions of the highest courts and other decisions which cannot be appealed in cassation.[79] Judgments in interim relief proceedings do not fall under this category if the question provisionally decided in an interlocutory procedure can be re-examined in an ordinary procedure on the merits.[80] By way of example, in the Belgian legal system, there is an obligation to ask a question for a preliminary ruling for the Supreme Court, the Constitutional Court, the highest

29.018

---

[73] 106/77, *Simmenthal*, 1978, para. 24; C-188/10 and C-189/10, *Melki and Abdeli*, 2010, paras 40–57; C-5/14, *Kernkraftwerke Lippe-Ems*, 2015, paras 32–9; C-689/13, *PFE*, 2016, paras 31–6.
[74] e.g. C-136/12, *Consiglio Nazionale dei Geologi*, 2013, paras 29–31.
[75] e.g. C-60/02, *X*, 2000, paras 25–9.
[76] C-268/15, *Ullens de Schooten*, 2016, paras 50–8; C-614/14, *Ognyanov*, 2016, paras 18–25; C-924/19 PPU and C-25/19 PPU, *FMS*, 2020, paras 166–74.
[77] C-558/18 and C-563/18, *Miasto Łowicz*, 2020, paras 38–60.
[78] 338/85, *Pardini*, 1988, para. 11; see para. 29.028, *infra*.
[79] C-99/00, *Lyckeskog*, 2002, paras 10–19, C-3/16, *Aquino*, 2017, paras 34–6.
[80] 35–36/82, *Morson and Jhanjan*, 1982, paras 8–9.

Administrative Court (Council of State), the Benelux Court of Justice, and any other courts or tribunals against whose decision there is no possibility of an appeal in cassation.[81]

29.019 **Exceptions to the duty to refer.** It follows from the relationship between the second and the third paras of Article 267 TFEU that the third para. requires a court or tribunal to refer a question of interpretation of Union law to the Court of Justice only if it considers that a decision on the question is necessary to enable it to give judgment (requirement of relevance). In addition, in the *CILFIT* judgment, the Court identified two circumstances in which a court referred to in the third para. is not required to submit a—relevant—question.[82] First, this is the case where the court has established that the Union provision in question has already been interpreted by the Court, either in a preliminary ruling in response to a similar question, or in the context of a preliminary ruling or other proceedings in which the Court has ruled on an almost identical question. In such situations, the court is always free to ask the Court, by way of a preliminary question, to amend, nuance, or limit its case law. Second, the obligation to refer lapses if the correct application of Union law is 'so obvious as to leave no scope for any reasonable doubt'.[83] In the *CILFIT* judgment, the Court immediately added that, in order to assess the existence of that second situation, the national court must, however, take account of the characteristic features of Union law and the particular difficulties to which its interpretation gives rise (see para. 29.005, *supra*) and of the risk of divergent case law within the European Union. This second exception to the duty to refer is known as the '*acte clair*' doctrine; the first exception is sometimes referred to as the situation of the '*acte éclairé*'.

2. Subject matter of questions referred for a preliminary ruling

29.020 **Union law.** The first para. of Article 267 TFEU provides that the Court of Justice has jurisdiction to give preliminary rulings on questions concerning the interpretation of the Treaties and of the acts of the institutions, bodies, offices, and agencies of the Union. By virtue of this Treaty provision, the Court interprets all the provisions of primary and secondary Union law referred to in Part V (see paras 24.004 and 27.012 *et seq.*), including international agreements concluded by the Union and decisions of bodies set up by such agreements (see paras 26.001 and 26.004, *supra*). This power is only limited for CFSP acts (see para. 29.023, *infra*). In addition, a number of agreements concluded by the Member States which are connected to Union law have given the Court of Justice the power to give preliminary rulings on the interpretation of their provisions (see para. 28.018, *supra*). The Court interprets fundamental rights and general principles of law when invited to do so in the context of a dispute falling within the scope of Union law, for example when questions arise as to the compatibility with fundamental rights of acts of Union law or of acts adopted by the Member States when implementing Union law (see paras 25.008, 25.009, and 25.020). This means that the Court cannot, for example, rule on questions of interpretation of the European Convention on Human Rights when the subject matter of the dispute before the national court is not

---

[81] For an infringement of Union law based, *inter alia*, on the breach of the duty to refer a question for a preliminary ruling under the third para. of Article 267 TFEU, see C-467/17, *Commission v France*, 2018, paras 105–14.
[82] 283/81, *CILFIT*, 1982, paras 13–21.
[83] See also C-495/03, *Intermodal Transports*, 2005, paras 33–45; C-72/14, *X and van Dijk*, 2015, paras 52–63; C-160/14, *Ferreira da Silva e Brito*, 2015, paras 36–45.

connected in any way with Union law and the applicable national provisions are outside the scope Union law.[84]

The Court does not have jurisdiction to interpret national law unless in the specific case where that law refers to Union law in order to resolve a purely internal situation in accordance with the solutions adopted by Union law, for example, when national competition law provides that it must be interpreted on the basis of the principles of Union competition law.[85]

Furthermore, the Court interprets provisions of Union law only if they apply *ratione loci* and *ratione temporis* in the main proceedings, for example, in the case of a newly acceded Member State, only if the facts date from after the accession.[86]

Interpretation. The Court of Justice has jurisdiction only to interpret Union law and not to apply it to the particular case in the main proceedings. Nor can the Court give a preliminary ruling on the compatibility of national law with Union law.[87] However, where a national court asks whether a national provision is compatible with a provision of Union law, the question can generally be understood—and is reformulated to that effect by the Court—as a question of interpretation of the relevant provision of Union law. It is then for the referring court to draw from the Court's ruling the consequences for the national provision in question.

29.021

Validity of Union acts. According to Article 267 TFEU, the Court of Justice also rules on questions referred for a preliminary ruling concerning the validity of acts of the institutions, bodies, offices, or agencies of the Union. This competence is part of the judicial protection offered by the Court against unlawful acts of the Union (see para. 30-031 *et seq., infra*).

29.022

CFSP. The Court of Justice has no jurisdiction with respect to CFSP provisions nor with respect to acts adopted on the basis of those provisions (Article 24(1), second subpara. TEU and Article 275(1) TFEU), unless the interpretation of Article 40 TEU or the validity of restrictive measures against natural or legal persons adopted by the Council on the basis of Chapter 2 of Title V of the TEU is at issue.[88] Therefore, national courts cannot obtain from the Court of Justice any guidance as to the meaning and scope of CFSP actions. In the event of an infringement of CFSP acts, it is for the national court to determine the precise consequences thereof in the national legal system. It can thus ensure that a public body respects the content of CFSP acts and refrain from applying national provisions which are incompatible with CFSP acts.

29.023

Police and judicial cooperation in criminal matters. Since the Lisbon Treaty, the Court of Justice has ordinary jurisdiction in matters covered by Title V of Part Three of the TFEU on

29.024

---

[84] e.g. C-328/04, *Vajnai* (order), 2005, paras 12–14.
[85] C-297/88 and C-197/89, *Dzodzi*, 1990, paras 36–42; C-280/06, *Autorità Garante della Concorrenza e del Mercato*, 2007, paras 19–29.
[86] e.g. C-302/04, *Ynos*, 2006, paras 35–8.
[87] Moreover, with regard to measures pertaining to police and judicial cooperation in criminal matters, the Court of Justice has no jurisdiction to review the validity or proportionality of operations carried out by the police or other law-enforcement services of a Member State or the exercise of the responsibilities incumbent upon Member States with regard to the maintenance of law and order and the safeguarding of internal security (Article 276 TFEU).
[88] C-72/15, *Rosneft*, 2017, paras 48–81.

the area of freedom, security, and justice (border controls, asylum and immigration, judicial and police cooperation). As regards policies on border controls, asylum, and immigration (Chapter 2) and judicial cooperation in civil matters (Chapter 3), the Lisbon Treaty has thus removed the restriction of former Article 68(1) EC, which limited the Court's jurisdiction in these matters to give preliminary rulings only on questions referred by a national court or tribunal adjudicating at last instance.

Until 30 November 2014, the Court's jurisdiction to give preliminary rulings on PJCC measures adopted on the basis of the EU Treaty prior to the entry into force of the Lisbon Treaty (1 December 2009) was limited. On the basis of the Protocol (No. 36) on transitional provisions, the Court retained, for a transitional period, the limited jurisdiction it held over these measures prior to the Lisbon Treaty, on the basis of former Article 35 EU.[89] For example, the Court had jurisdiction to rule on the interpretation of PJCC framework decisions and decisions, conventions, and implementing measures only to the extent that a Member State had accepted that jurisdiction.[90] However, as soon as a PJCC act adopted before 1 December 2009 was amended, the Court was given full jurisdiction over that act for the Member States to which the amended act applies.[91] In any case, the transitional measures did not apply to PJCC acts adopted after 1 December 2009. After this transitional period (from 1 December 2014 onwards), the Court has acquired full jurisdiction over all PJCC acts. However, the United Kingdom had opted for the possibility laid down in the same Protocol, that from 1 December 2014, the PJCC acts adopted before 1 December 2009 would only apply to the United Kingdom if that Member State expressly so chose.[92]

29.025 **Requirement of relevance.** As stated above, a national court may only ask a question on the interpretation or validity of Union law if a decision on that question is necessary to deliver a judgment. The national courts, which are the only courts having direct knowledge of the facts of the case, are best placed to assess both the need for a preliminary ruling in order to give judgment and the relevance of the questions which they refer to the Court. However, sometimes the Court of Justice has to examine the circumstances in which a question was raised in order to avoid giving an interpretation of Union law that is unrelated to a real dispute or to the subject matter of the main proceedings. In the preliminary ruling procedure, the Court's duty is to assist in the administration of justice in the Member States and not to deliver advisory opinions on general or hypothetical questions.[93]

3. Procedure for asking and answering questions referred for a preliminary ruling
   a. *Formulation of the reference for a preliminary ruling*

29.026 **Form and content of the order for reference.** A national court or tribunal may refer a question for a preliminary ruling in the form and in the language prescribed by national

---

[89] Protocol (No. 36) to the TEU and the TFEU on transitional provisions, Article 10, para. 1.
[90] In doing so, Member States had to indicate whether only national courts of the Member State whose decisions were not subject to appeal under national law could refer questions to the Court of Justice for a preliminary ruling, or whether any national court of that Member State could do so (former Article 35(3) EU). In accordance with former Article 35 EU, the Commission could not refer the Member State concerned to the Court of Justice for failure to comply with PJCC measures. In addition, the legality of PJCC measures could only be reviewed by the Court when a Member State or the Commission brought an action for annulment.
[91] Protocol (No. 36) on transitional provisions, Article 10, para. 2.
[92] Ibid., Article 10, paras 4 and 5.
[93] 244/80, *Foglia*, 1981, paras 18–19; C-83/91, *Meilicke*, 1992, paras 21–34; C-558/18 and C-563/18, *Miasto Łowicz*, 2020, paras 38–60; C-505/19, *WS*, 2021, paras 42–66.

procedural law. Usually, the so-called 'order for reference' takes the form of a judgment. The order for reference must contain all the information necessary for a proper understanding of the factual and legal framework of the main proceedings. In order to indicate the need for a preliminary ruling and the relevance of the question raised, the order for reference must first contain a summary of the subject matter of the dispute and the relevant findings of fact as determined by the referring court or tribunal, or, at least, an account of the facts on which the questions are based.[94] For example, a court referring a question with regard to the interpretation of the prohibition on the abuse of a dominant position (Article 102 TFEU) must state on which relevant market and in what way the undertaking concerned by the main proceedings would hold a dominant position.[95] In addition, the order for reference must set out the tenor of any national provisions applicable in the case and, where appropriate, the relevant national case law.[96] Furthermore, the order for reference must contain a statement of the reasons which prompted the referring court or tribunal to inquire about the interpretation of certain provisions of Union law, and the relationship between those provisions and the national legislation applicable to the main proceedings.[97] For example, questions by means of which a court seeks guidance on the compatibility of national legislation with the Treaty provisions on the free movement of goods, persons, services, or capital require the referring court to indicate which aspects of that legislation would be covered by the Treaty provisions that the court mentions in its question and for what reasons.[98]

If the order for reference does not meet those requirements, the Court may feel obliged to declare the reference for a preliminary ruling inadmissible. The order for reference must not only enable the Court to give helpful answers, but also enable the governments of the Member States and other interested parties to submit observations to the Court on the basis of the order for reference alone.[99] Moreover, since the order for reference has to be translated, the Court recommends a simple, clear, and precise wording, without any unnecessary digressions. The Court also asks that the order for reference briefly sets out the main arguments of the parties to the main proceedings, at least those relating to the subject matter of the reference for a preliminary ruling. Finally, the Court of Justice invites the referring court to briefly state its view on the answer to be given to the questions referred for a preliminary ruling. For the sake of clarity, it is best to include the actual questions referred to the Court for a preliminary ruling in a separate and clearly identified section of the order for reference, preferably at the beginning or at the end of it.[100]

National procedure. A reference for a preliminary ruling suspends the national procedure until the Court of Justice has given its ruling. However, the national court remains competent to adopt interim measures. It is for the referring court to send the order for reference, together with the case file (or a copy thereof), directly to the Court of Justice.[101]

29.027

---

[94] CJ Rules of Procedure, Article 94 (a).
[95] e.g. C-250/06, *United Pan-European Communications Belgium*, 2007, paras 19–23.
[96] CJ Rules of Procedure, Article 94 (b).
[97] CJ Rules of Procedure, Article 94 (c).
[98] See C-268/15, *Ullens de Schooten*, 2016, paras 50–8.
[99] e.g. C-167/94, *Grau Gomis* (order), 1995, paras 8–10.
[100] Recommendations to national courts and tribunals in relation to the initiation of preliminary ruling proceedings (see n. 62, *supra*), paras 17–19.
[101] Address: Court of Justice of the European Union, Registry of the Court, Rue du Fort Niedergrünewald, L-2925 Luxembourg (tel. + 352 43031). Email: ECJ.Registry@curia.europa.eu.

29.028 **Judicial remedies against order for reference.** Union law does not preclude the possibility, under national law, of an appeal against a judgment making a reference for a preliminary ruling. If the referring judgment has been set aside by a higher court and the case is remanded to the first court, that court is free to (again) refer a question to the Court of Justice under Article 267 TFEU, irrespective of the fact that it is bound on points of law by the higher court's ruling.[102] In such a situation, it is for the referring court itself to draw the conclusions from the appeal ruling in order to maintain, amend, or withdraw its reference for a preliminary ruling.[103]

In principle, the reference for a preliminary ruling remains before the Court of Justice as long as it has not been withdrawn by the referring court or overturned by a higher court following an appeal. Where the Court is informed by one of the courts or tribunals concerned that an appeal has been brought against the judgment making a reference for a preliminary ruling and where that appeal has the effect of suspending that judgment, the Court stays the proceedings until such time it is notified that the national court has ruled on the appeal, provided that the appeal does not relate solely to the decision taken by the referring court to ask preliminary questions to the Court of Justice.[104] It is possible that the appeal will result in the case in the main proceedings no longer being pending before the referring court (the court *a quo*), but entirely before the appellate court which has to rule on that case. Where the Court of Justice is informed by one of the courts or tribunals concerned of such 'devolutive effect', it will remove the question referred for a preliminary ruling from its register,[105] except if it cannot be ruled out that the appellate court may still refer the case back to the referring court. If the case can no longer be referred back, the appellate court itself has to decide whether to ask a question for a preliminary ruling, which may be—if necessary—the same question. In any event, the Court shall order that the case be removed from its register as soon as the order for reference is set aside.[106]

b. Consideration by the Court of Justice

29.029 **Submitting observations.** Each order for reference is published in the *Official Journal*. The Registry of the Court of Justice also sends a copy of the order for reference to all the parties to the main proceedings, to all the Member States (with a translation into the/an official language of the Member State), and to the Commission. They may submit written observations to the Court within two months of receipt of this notification, extended by a fixed period of ten days to take account of geographical distance.[107] The order for reference is also notified, with the possibility of submitting observations, to the Union institution, body, office, or agency which adopted the act that is the subject of the reference for a preliminary ruling and to the other States which are parties to the EEA Agreement and also to the EFTA Surveillance Authority, where one of the fields of application of the EEA Agreement is concerned.[108] Other parties may not intervene before the Court unless the national court accepts their intervention in the main proceedings. As regards the representation and

---

[102] C-210/06, *Cartesio*, 2008, para. 94; C-173/09, *Elchinov*, 2010, para. 27.
[103] C-210/06, *Cartesio*, 2008, para. 96.
[104] Ibid., paras 96–7.
[105] C-525/06, *Nationale Loterij* (order), 2009, paras 4–12.
[106] e.g. order in 31/68, *Chanel*, 1970; C-180/12, *Stoilov*, 2013.
[107] Statute of Court of Justice, Article 23 and CJ Rules of Procedure, Article 96.
[108] Statute of Court of Justice, Article 23.

appearance of parties, the Court has regard to the procedural rules in force in the court that made the reference for a preliminary ruling.[109] For example, if these rules do not provide for any representation, a party may itself submit written and oral observations. Parties and other interested parties are not entitled to respond to the written observations submitted except orally at the hearing. A hearing must be requested within three weeks of the written observations being served on all parties and interested parties.[110]

Translations. The preliminary ruling procedure requires not only that the order for reference be translated into all the official languages, but also that written observations not in the language of the case, be translated into that language. Moreover, as the Court of Justice has French as its internal working language, all written observations are translated into that language. The oral procedure is conducted in the language of the case, with the Member States being authorized to use (one of) their own national language(s) (para. 14.027, *supra*).   **29.030**

Internal assignment of a case. The President of the Court of Justice designates a judge to act as Rapporteur for each case in which a document initiating proceedings has been lodged. The First Advocate-General assigns each case to an Advocate-General. After the written observations have been submitted, the Judge-Rapporteur presents a preliminary report to the general meeting of the Court, which meets on a weekly basis with all the Judges, the Advocates-General and the Registrar. In this report, which is not public, the Judge-Rapporteur makes proposals concerning the formation of the Court to which the case is to be referred, that is, a Chamber of five or three Judges, the Grand Chamber or, in exceptional cases, the Full Court (see para. 13.018, *supra*), and addresses the question whether an oral hearing and/or opinion of the Advocate-General is needed. The general meeting determines the formation of the Court and may order measures of inquiry. It also decides that a case which does not raise a new point of law shall be determined without an opinion of the Advocate-General. In addition, if none of the parties makes an application setting out the reasons why they wish to be heard, the general meeting may decide that the case will be considered without a hearing.[111] Similarly, the Court may decide not to hold a hearing if it considers, after the written stage of the procedure, that it has sufficient information to give a ruling.[112] Moreover, the Court may decide to answer the question referred for a preliminary ruling by reasoned order, without a prior hearing, where that question is identical to a question on which the Court has already ruled, where the answer to the question can be clearly deduced from existing case law, or where the answer to the question referred for a preliminary ruling 'admits of no reasonable doubt'.[113] The Judge-Rapporteur and the Advocate-General may at any time request further information from the parties; the general meeting may request further clarification from the referring court.[114]   **29.031**

Oral procedure. The oral procedure is open to all parties and interested parties mentioned in Article 23 of the Statute of the Court, even to those who did not submit written observations to the Court. Since oral submissions are being interpreted, it is essential to speak   **29.032**

---

[109] CJ Rules of Procedure, Article 97(3).
[110] Ibid., Article 76(1).
[111] Ibid., Articles 59 and 60.
[112] Ibid., Article 76(2).
[113] Ibid., Article 99.
[114] Ibid., Articles 62 (1) and 101.

slowly and clearly; in order to help the interpreters, a text of notes for the oral submissions or an outline of the arguments can be sent to the interpretation directorate in advance or delivered to the messenger just before the hearing.[115] Questions may be put to counsel by the President, the other judges, and the Advocate-General both during and after the pleadings. A few weeks after the hearing, the Advocate-General delivers his or her Opinion, which is published on the Court's website the same day. The public reading of the operative part of the Opinion closes the oral procedure. There is no right for the parties to submit observations in response to the Opinion.[116] However, the Court, after hearing the Advocate-General may, of its own motion, acting upon application by the parties, reopen the oral procedure. The Court does so if it considers that it has not been sufficiently informed or that the case must be settled on the basis of an argument that has not been discussed between the parties.[117]

29.033 **Deliberation.** The Court of Justice deliberates in closed session without the presence of the Advocate-General, the Registrar, other servants, or interpreters. Only those judges who were present during the oral procedure take part in the deliberations.[118] An uneven number of judges takes part in the deliberations in order to enable, where necessary, a majority to decide against a minority.

29.034 **Preliminary ruling.** The parties are summoned to the public hearing at which the judgment of the Court of Justice is delivered. On the day of the judgment, the judgment is published on the Court's website and—except for less significant judgments—also published on the EUR-Lex website and in the European Court Reports. The preliminary ruling is also sent to the referring court. The Court appreciates it if the referring court could indicate how it applied the preliminary ruling in the main proceedings, for example by sending a copy of its final decision to the Court.[119] Although the judgments and some orders are published in the various official languages, they are only authentic in the language of the case (see para. 14.027, *supra*).

29.035 **Expedited and urgent procedure.** The average duration of preliminary ruling proceedings before the Court of Justice is currently around fifteen months. In exceptional cases, the President of the Court may, at the request of the referring court, decide to deal with a reference for a preliminary ruling under an expedited procedure.[120] The date of the hearing and the period within which the parties to the main proceedings and other interested parties may lodge written observations are then immediately fixed.[121] In matters relating to the area of freedom, security, and justice (Title V, Part Three TFEU), there is an urgent preliminary ruling procedure under which only the parties to the main proceedings, the Union

---

[115] See the Practice Directions to parties concerning cases brought before the Court (n. 62, *supra*), paras 55–64.
[116] C-17/98, *Emesa Sugar* (order), 2000; C-525/14, *Commission v Czech Republic*, 2016, para. 8.
[117] C-309/02, *Radlberger Getränkegesellschaft and Spitz*, 2004, para. 22; C-584/10 P, C-593/10 P, and C-595/10 P, *Commission v Kadi*, 2013, paras 55–8; C-525/14, *Commission v Czech Republic*, 2016, paras 9–10; C-188/15, *Bougnaoui*, 2017, paras 20–4; C-25/17, *Jehovan todistajat—uskonnollinen yhdyskunta*, 2018, paras 25–9; C-186/19, *Supreme Site Services*, 2020, paras 35–40.
[118] CJ Rules of Procedure, Article 32(1) and (2).
[119] Recommendations to national courts and tribunals on referrals for preliminary rulings (see n. 62, *supra*), para. 29.
[120] CJ Rules of Procedure, Article 105.
[121] e.g. C-189/01, *Jippes and Others*, 2001 (judgment given within three months of the reference for a preliminary ruling); C-370/12, *Pringle*, 2012 (judgment given in Full Court within four months of the reference).

institutions, and the Member State of the referring court may submit written observations and, in cases of extreme urgency, the written procedure may even be dispensed with.[122] It is for the national court applying for the expedited procedure and the urgent procedure, respectively, to set out the circumstances demonstrating urgency.[123] The expedited procedure may also be applied by the Court of its own motion.[124] A reference for a preliminary ruling under the urgent procedure is dealt with by a Chamber of the Court appointed for that purpose, but may be referred to the Grand Chamber.[125] References for a preliminary ruling under an expedited procedure have even been sent to the Full Court.[126]

Costs. The preliminary ruling procedure before the Court of Justice is free of charge; it is for the national court to decide on the costs that it entails for the parties to the main proceedings. If a party has insufficient means and national procedural law so permits, the referring court may grant that party legal aid to cover the costs of the proceedings before the Court. The Court itself may also provide legal assistance.[127]   **29.036**

4. Consequences of preliminary rulings

Binding force for courts. A preliminary ruling is binding on the referring court and on any other court or tribunal hearing the main proceedings.[128] This does not prevent any of those courts encountering difficulties in applying the preliminary ruling from, if necessary, referring a new question to the Court of Justice for a preliminary ruling.[129] Although preliminary rulings themselves contribute to the further development of Union law, the role of the Court is formally limited to explaining and specifying the meaning and scope of rules of Union law as they should always have been understood and applied. Therefore, a preliminary ruling is also binding on all other courts of the Member States dealing with cases affected by the questions answered in the judgment, subject to the possibility for those courts to refer a new question to the Court. For the same reason, a preliminary ruling has retroactive effect, except in cases where the Court limits the temporal scope of its ruling (see para. 28.006, *supra*).   **29.037**

Binding force for administrative authorities. A reference for a preliminary ruling from the Court of Justice also constitutes a binding interpretation of Union law as it must be understood and applied by other national and Union bodies—and by individuals. Following a preliminary ruling that national legislation is incompatible with Union law, the authorities of the Member State concerned must ensure that national law is brought into line with Union law as soon as possible.[130] This does not mean that decisions of national authorities which have become final after the expiry of time limits for appeal or after all legal remedies have been exhausted should be reviewed if it appears that they are based on an interpretation of Union law which a subsequent reference for a preliminary ruling shows to be incorrect. However, an administrative body which has the power under national law to revoke   **29.038**

---

[122] CJ Rules of Procedure, Articles 107 to 114.
[123] See, e.g., C-439/16 PPU, *Milev*, 2016.
[124] e.g. C-370/12, *Pringle*, 2012.
[125] e.g. C-216/18 PPU, *LM*, 2018; C-897/19 PPU, *I.N.*, 2020.
[126] e.g. C-370/12, *Pringle*, 2012; C-621/18, *Wightman*, 2018.
[127] CJ Rules of Procedure, Articles 115 to 118.
[128] C-689/13, *PFE*, 2016, para. 38.
[129] 29/68, *Milch-, Fett-, und Eierkontor*, 1969, paras 2–3.
[130] C-201/02, *Wells*, 2004, paras 65–6.

a decision that has become final may be obliged to do so under Union law. That obligation exists only in respect of a decision which has become final following a judgment of a court or tribunal of last instance which, without first asking the Court of Justice for a preliminary ruling, has given an interpretation of Union law that, according to subsequent case law of the Court of Justice, is incorrect, and then only if the person concerned has referred the matter to the administrative body immediately after becoming aware of that case law.[131]

II. Action for Failure by a Member State to Fulfil its Obligations

29.039 **Infringement by Member States.** If a Member State's conduct is contrary to Union law, the Commission may bring an action against that Member State for failure to fulfil its obligations under the Treaties (Articles 258 to 260 TFEU), meaning all kinds of failure to comply with any rule of Union law which is binding on the Member States.[132] Only CFSP rules are not subject to this action, since the Commission cannot exercise supervision over the Member States in this policy area (Article 275 TFEU; see para. 29.023, *supra*). A failure to comply with Union law may result from both the actions and omissions of a Member State. Before bringing a case before the Court of Justice, the Commission must allow the Member State to defend itself or to put an end to the alleged infringement ('pre-litigation' stage). Only in certain areas can the Commission bring an alleged infringement directly before the Court of Justice, for example, in the area of State aid (Article 108(2) TFEU).[133] At the end of the pre-litigation stage, the defendant Member State may be sued before the Court, which may find that there has been an infringement of Union law and, if it so finds and the Member State concerned fails to comply with the Court's judgment, the Court may impose a lump sum or a penalty payment (Article 260(2) TFEU).

A. Initiative

29.040 **Commission's discretion.** Only the Commission—under Article 258 TFEU—may initiate infringement proceedings against a Member State whenever it considers it appropriate as 'guardian of the Treaties'.[134] Individuals and public authorities may submit a complaint to the Commission against a Member State which they consider to be in breach of Union law. However, the Commission is not obliged to initiate the procedure laid down in Article 258 TFEU in respect of each alleged infringement. It decides whether to start the procedure and, if so, at what time. If the Commission rejects a complaint, this decision cannot be challenged by an action for annulment, since the Commission does not adopt any binding legal acts in the context of this procedure.[135] If the Commission leaves a complaint unanswered,

---

[131] C-453/00, *Kühne & Heitz*, 2004, paras 25–8.
[132] This also encompasses international agreements that are part of Union law; see C-66/18, *Commission v Hungary*, 2020, paras 68–93.
[133] See also Article 114(9) TFEU and Article 348(2) TFEU.
[134] See Commission Communication of 19 January 2017 'EU law: Better results through better application', OJ 2017 C18/10. See also Banks and von Rintelen, 'Infringement Procedures and the Juncker Commission' (2020) ELRev 619–38.
[135] 48/65, *Lütticke v Commission*, 1966; C-575/18 P *Czech Republic v Commission*, 2020, paras 64–5 and 77–8.

it cannot be challenged by an action for failure to act or an action for damages, as it is not in breach of its duty to act.[136]

Member State as defendant. The infringement procedure can only be initiated against a 'Member State'. It is therefore the Member State as such that is addressed, irrespective of the authority which, by its actions or omissions, causes the breach of Union law, even if it is a constitutionally independent institution.[137] Indeed, the internal organization of a Member State should not constitute an obstacle to the correct application of Union law. This means that a Member State can also be held liable for the actions or omissions of its legislature or for actions or omissions of the legislative or administrative authorities of constitutionally autonomous federated entities (see para. 18.005, *supra*). The Member State can also be held in breach because of national case law which is contrary to Union law, at least where it appears that the laws, regulations, or administrative provisions of a Member State were insufficiently clear to ensure an application compatible with Union law.[138] The infringement procedure may not be initiated in respect of acts committed by legal persons governed by private law, unless they can be imputed to the public authorities of a Member State.[139]

29.041

Member State against another Member State. Article 259 TFEU gives a Member State the right to bring an action before the Court of Justice if it considers that another Member State has failed to fulfil an obligation under Union law. However, the Member State must first submit its complaint to the Commission. The Commission must then go through the pre-litigation stage and deliver a reasoned opinion setting out its view as to whether or not there has been a breach of obligations under Union law. If it wishes, the Commission may itself bring the matter before the Court under Article 258 TFEU. If the Commission has not delivered an opinion within three months of the lodging of the complaint, the complaining Member State may bring the complaint before the Court on the basis of Article 259 TFEU. This procedure has only been used exceptionally and has only led to six judgments.[140]

29.042

B. Procedure

Pre-litigation stage. In accordance with Article 258 TFEU, if the Commission considers that a Member State has failed to fulfil an obligation under Union law, it must deliver a reasoned opinion after giving the Member State concerned the opportunity to submit its observations. The 'pre-litigation stage' has a double purpose.[141] On the one hand, it is intended to allow the Member State to fulfil its obligations under Union law before bringing a case before the Court. It is also possible that the Commission and the Member State reach an agreement, which would make further legal action unnecessary. On the other hand, this

29.043

---

[136] C-72/90, *Asia Motor France v Commission* (order), 1990, para. 13; T-117/96, *Intertronic v Commission* (order), 1997, para. 32.
[137] 77/69, *Commission v Belgium*, 1970, para. 15; C-416/17, *Commission v France*, 2018, para. 106.
[138] C-129/00, *Commission v Italy*, 2003, paras 32–3.
[139] e.g. 249/81, *Commission v Ireland*, 1982, paras 10–15.
[140] 141/78, *France v United Kingdom*, 1979; C-388/95, *Belgium v Spain*, 2000; C-145/04, *Spain v United Kingdom*, 2006; C-364/10, *Hungary v Slovak Republic*, 2012; C-591/17, *Austria v Germany*, 2019; and C-457/18, *Slovenia v Croatia*, 2020. The action in the last case was, however, deemed inadmissible as the issues of EU law were incidental to a dispute under international law over which the Court has no jurisdiction.
[141] 74/82, *Commission v Ireland*, 1984, para. 13.

stage allows the Member State concerned to defend itself against the grievances expressed by the Commission. The pre-litigation stage thus guarantees the protection of the rights of the Member State concerned and at the same time defines the subject matter of the proceedings with a view to a possible procedure before the Court.[142]

29.044 **Letter of formal notice.** The pre-litigation procedure starts with the Commission's letter of formal notice. With this letter of formal notice, the Member State is in default. In most cases, this letter is preceded by informal contacts during which the Commission seeks information from the Member State on the problem identified to it. The purpose of the letter of formal notice is to determine the subject matter of the dispute and to provide the Member State invited to submit its observations with the information necessary to prepare its defence.[143] The Member State should be allowed a reasonable period within which to submit its observations.

29.045 **Reasoned opinion.** If the alleged infringement is not being remedied, the Commission may issue a reasoned opinion. The reasoned opinion must set out, in a coherent and detailed manner, the reasons which have led the Commission to believe that the Member State concerned has failed to fulfil its obligations.[144] In the reasoned opinion, the Commission must specify a reasonable time-limit within which the Member State must comply with the opinion.[145]

29.046 **Litigation stage.** After the expiry of that period, the Commission has the possibility—not the obligation—to bring an action before the Court. In so far as the rights of defence of the Member State are not affected, the Commission is not bound by any time-limit.[146] The infringement must exist at the end of the time-limit laid down in the reasoned opinion. Therefore, even if the alleged infringement has been remedied after the expiry of the time-limit laid down in this opinion, the action remains admissible. A finding by the Court of Justice of a Member State's failure to fulfil obligations may in fact be relevant in determining that Member State's liability towards those who suffered damage as a result of their failure to fulfil obligations.[147]

29.047 **Subject matter of the dispute.** The subject matter of the dispute is determined by the pre-litigation procedure and the application with which the Commission lodges the action. The application may not be based on grounds and pleas in law other than those contained in the reasoned opinion. A grievance which was not raised in the pre-litigation procedure is therefore inadmissible.[148] Thus, in an action for failure to transpose a directive, the Commission cannot at the same time accuse the Member State of not complying with that directive, in practice, if the latter aspect has not been dealt with during the pre-litigation stage.[149] However, the wording of the subject matter of the dispute in the application may differ from that in the reasoned opinion where the subject matter

---

[142] e.g. C-463/01, *Commission v Germany*, 2004, para. 25.
[143] 274/83, *Commission v Italy*, 1985, para. 19.
[144] C-347/88, *Commission v Greece*, 1990, para. 24.
[145] C-66/18, *Commission v Hungary*, 2020, paras 45–57.
[146] C-523/04, *Commission v Netherlands*, 2007, paras 27–30.
[147] 39/72, *Commission v Italy*, 1973, para. 11.
[148] e.g. C-234/91, *Commission v Denmark*, 1993, para. 16.
[149] e.g. C-237/90, *Commission v Germany*, 1992, paras 21–2.

of the dispute has not been broadened or changed but, on the contrary, has only been limited.[150]

Burden of proof. The Commission bears the burden of proving the alleged infringement. The existence of an infringement must be assessed at the time of expiry of the time-limit laid down in the reasoned opinion and only at that time.[151] The Commission is required to establish the facts and circumstances necessary to establish the existence of an infringement and cannot rely on any presumption. If the Commission alleges an infringement resulting from the application, in practice, of a national provision, it must provide more specific evidence than in the case of an action directed solely against the content of a national provision. The failure to fulfil obligations can then only be demonstrated by sufficiently detailed and documented evidence of the practice imputed to the national administrative and/or judicial authorities.[152] An administrative practice contrary to Union law only exists where that practice is, to a certain extent, constant and general.[153] A slightly different scenario is a general and persistent infringement in the form of a Member State's authorities generally not complying with the relevant provisions of Union law, as illustrated by a significant number of particular situations.[154]

29.048

Defences. The procedure for failure to fulfil obligations is based on an objective determination of a Member State's failure to fulfil its obligations under the Treaties or an act of secondary legislation. In its assessment of the failure to fulfil obligations, the Court of Justice does not take account of subjective elements, such as the circumstances capable of explaining the Member State's failure to fulfil obligations or of mitigating their actual harmful effects.[155] According to settled case law, a Member State may not rely on provisions, practices, or situations in its national legal order to justify a failure to comply with obligations and time-limits laid down by Union law.[156] Nor do difficulties encountered in the implementation of a Union act entitle a Member State to consider itself unilaterally released from its obligations.[157] Moreover, a Member State cannot invoke the fact that other Member States are not fulfilling their obligations either.[158] In the legal order established by the Treaties, the implementation of Union law by the Member States cannot be made subject to a condition of reciprocity.[159] Finally, a Member State may not rely on the alleged unlawfulness of a Union act addressed to it in proceedings for failure to comply with such act.

29.049

---

[150] C-279/94, *Commission v Italy*, 1997, para. 25; C-601/14, *Commission v Italy*, 2016, paras 29–32; C-590/16, *Commission v Greece*, 2018, paras 36–8; C-626/16, *Commission v Slovak Republic*, 2018, paras 22–35; C-97/17, *Commission v Bulgaria*, 2018, paras 18–22.

[151] 48/71, *Commission v Italy*, 1972, paras 10–14; C-610/10, *Commission v Spain*, 2012, para. 67; C-241/11 *Commission v Czech Republic*, 2013, para. 23; C-261/18, *Commission v Ireland*, 2019, para. 84.

[152] C-287/03, *Commission v Belgium*, 2005, para. 28.

[153] C-441/02, *Commission v Germany*, 2006, para. 50.

[154] C-494/01, *Commission v Ireland*, 2001, para. 136; C-135/05, *Commission v Italy*, 2007, paras 24–32. In such a case, the Commission may adduce, in the litigation stage, examples to demonstrate that the infringement amounts to a general and persistent failure by the Member State concerned to fulfil its obligations under Union law.

[155] 95/77, *Commission v Netherlands*, 1978, para.13; C-644/18, *Commission v Italy*, 2020, para. 87.

[156] e.g. C-236/99, *Commission v Belgium*, 2000, para. 23; C-378/13, *Commission v Greece*, 2014, para. 29; C-261/18, *Commission v Ireland*, 2019, para. 89.

[157] e.g. C-45/91, *Commission v Greece*, 1992, para. 21. See also *Commission v Italy*, 2020, para. 152 (objections based on structural difficulties arising from the socio-economic and budgetary implications of large-scale investments that need to be carried out rejected).

[158] This is settled case law going back to 90/63 and 91/63, *Commission v Luxembourg and Belgium*, 1964 (see para. 1.024, *supra*). For a recent application, see C-715/17, C-718/17, and C-719/17, *Commission v Poland, Hungary and Czech Republic*, 2020, paras 164–8.

[159] C-146/89, *Commission v United Kingdom*, 1991, para. 41.

Indeed, the Treaties have established separate legal remedies for assessing that a Member State has failed to fulfil its obligations (Articles 258 to 260 TFEU) and for reviewing the legality of actions or omissions by the Union institutions (Articles 263 and 265 TFEU).[160] Conversely, the Commission cannot accuse a Member State of infringing a Treaty provision if the Member State confines itself to maintaining a measure adopted on the basis of, and in conformity with, a directive.[161]

C. Consequences of a finding of non-compliance

29.050 **Obligation to execute a judgment.** In its judgment, the Court of Justice either finds that there has been a failure to fulfil obligations or dismisses the action. A finding of failure to fulfil obligations is declaratory in the sense that the failure to fulfil obligations existed before it was established by the Court. If the Court finds that there has been an infringement of Union law, the Member State must take all necessary measures to comply with the judgment (Article 260(1) TFEU). Within their respective spheres of competence, all bodies of the Member State concerned are obliged to ensure the implementation of the judgment. If a judgment finds that certain provisions laid down by law, regulation, or administrative action of a Member State are incompatible with Union law, the bodies participating in the legislative or executive power are therefore obliged to bring those provisions into line with that law. For their part, the courts of the Member State concerned are required to ensure compliance with the judgment in the exercise of their functions, for example by refraining from applying the conflicting provisions.[162] Article 260 TFEU does not lay down a time-limit for compliance with a judgment. However, because of the importance of immediate and uniform application of Union law, the implementation of the judgment should start without delay and be completed as soon as possible.[163]

29.051 **Failure to implement a judgment.** If a Member State fails to take the necessary measures to comply with a judgment of non-compliance, the Commission may relaunch a pre-litigation procedure and then refer the Member State concerned to the Court a second time (Article 260(2) TFEU). In doing so, the Commission is not required to issue a new reasoned opinion but can confine itself to a letter of formal notice (Article 260(2) TFEU). If the Member State concerned has not taken the necessary measures within the time-limit laid down by the Commission, the latter may bring the matter before the Court of Justice again. On that occasion, it may request the payment of a lump sum (fine) or a penalty payment (Article 260(2), second subpara. TFEU).

29.052 **Absence of notification of measures transposing directives.** If Member States fail to fulfil their obligation to notify measures taken to transpose a directive adopted under a legislative procedure, the Commission does not have to wait for the Member State to be referred to the Court a second time to request the payment of a lump sum or penalty payment. Article 260(3) TFEU authorizes it to request such a payment immediately after the (first)

---

[160] 156/77, *Commission v Belgium*, 1978, paras 21–4; C-74/91, *Commission v Germany*, 1992, paras 10–11; C-601/14, *Commission v Italy*, 2016, para. 33; C-620/16, *Commission v Germany*, 2019, paras 85–90. See also, for decisions, C-177/06, *Commission v Spain*, 2007, paras 30–8.
[161] C-475/01, *Commission v Greece*, 2004, paras 15–25.
[162] 314–316/81 and 83/82, *Waterkeyn*, 1982, para. 14.
[163] 131/84, *Commission v Italy*, 1982, para. 7.

pre-litigation procedure has been completed. In order to avoid the application of Article 260(3) TFEU Member States must provide sufficiently clear and precise information on the measures transposing a directive. To that effect they are required to state, for each provision of the directive, the national provision or provisions ensuring its transposition, and this throughout the whole of their territory (possibly accompanied by a correlation table). Thereafter, it is for the Commission to establish, for the purposes of seeking the financial sanction to be imposed on the Member State in question laid down in Article 260(3) TFEU, whether certain transposing measures are clearly lacking or do not cover all of the territory of the Member State in question, bearing in mind that it is not for the Court, in proceedings brought under Article 260(3) TFEU, to examine whether the national measures notified to the Commission ensure a correct transposition of the provisions of the directive in question.[164] The amount of the lump sum is calculated taking into account the time that has elapsed since the expiry of the time-limit set in the directive for its transposition[165]; a penalty starts to run from the date of the Court's judgment or another date set in that judgment till the full transposition of the directive in the national legal order.[166]

Lump sum and penalty payment. The imposition of a lump sum or penalty payment is intended to induce a defaulting Member State to comply with a non-compliance judgment or with the obligation to transpose in full a directive within the time limit, and thus to ensure the effective application of Union law. Whether a lump sum or penalty payment is imposed, or both, depends on the circumstances of the case. The imposition of a lump sum is based on an assessment of the consequences of the failure of the Member State concerned to fulfil its obligations for private and public interests, in particular where the failure to fulfil obligations has persisted long after delivery of the judgment in which it was originally established,[167] or where the transposition in full of a directive went well beyond the time-limit set in that directive.[168] The imposition of a penalty payment is particularly appropriate in order to induce a Member State to put an end, as soon as possible, to an infringement which might persist in the absence of such a measure.[169] A penalty payment can therefore only be imposed if the failure to fulfil obligations persists at the time when the facts are examined by the Court of Justice.[170] The Commission has adopted guidelines on the basis of which it determines the amount of the financial sanction claimed.[171] Although that amount is a 'useful point of reference', it does not bind the Court.[172] Under Article 260(3) TFEU the Court of

29.053

---

[164] C-543/17, *Commission v Belgium*, 2019, para. 59, with note by Gundel (2020) EuR 332–40.
[165] C-549/18, *Commission v Romania*, 2020, para. 79; C-550/18, *Commission v Ireland*, 2020, para. 86. Accordingly, also the period between the the expiry of the time-limit set in the directive for its transposition and the end of the reasoned opinion is taken into account, resulting in a higher amount.
[166] C-543/17, *Commission v Belgium*, 2019, para. 88.
[167] C-241/11, *Commission v Czech Republic*, 2013, para. 40; see also in the case of Article 260(3) TFEU, C-543/17, *Commission v Belgium*, 2019, para. 78.
[168] C-549/18, *Commission v Romania*, 2020, para. 66; C-550/18, *Commission v Ireland*, 2020, para. 76.
[169] C-304/02, *Commission v France*, 2005, paras 80–2.
[170] C-119/04, *Commission v Italy*, 2006, paras 33–46; C-543/17, *Commission v Belgium*, 2019, para. 79.
[171] Communication of 13 December 2005 on the implementation of Article 228 EC (SEC(2005)1658), as complemented by the Communication of 11 November 2010 on the implementation of Article 260(3) TFEU (SEC(2010)1371). According to a Communication of 20 July 2010 (SEC(2010)923), the data used for the calculation of lump sums and periodic penalty payments are adjusted annually; see last, Communication from the Commission on the Adjustment of the calculation for lump sum and penalty payments proposed by the Commission in infringement proceedings before the Court of Justice of the European Union, following the withdrawal of the United Kingdom, OJ 2021 C129/1.
[172] C-387/97, *Commission v Greece*, 2000, para. 89.

Justice is, however, bound by the request of the Commission, which means that contrary to Article 260(2) TFEU, it can only impose the type of financial sanction requested by the Commission, and this within the limits of the amount proposed.[173] According to the Court, the basic criteria to be taken into account in order to ensure the coercive force of a financial sanction are, in principle, the duration of the infringement, its degree of seriousness, and the ability of the Member State to pay. In applying those criteria, regard should be had, in particular, to the effects of failure to comply on private and public interests and to the urgency of getting the Member State concerned to fulfil its obligations.[174] The frequency, the fixed or degressive nature, and the exact calculation of the amount of the penalty payment should be determined on a case-by-case basis.[175] The lump sums and penalty payments due are entered in the budget as revenue of the Union (see para. 14.014, *supra*).

---

[173] C-549/18, *Commission v Romania*, 2020, para. 72; C-550/18, *Commission v Ireland*, 2020, para. 81.
[174] C-550/18, *Commission v Ireland*, 2020, para. 82.
[175] C-278/01, *Commission v Spain,* 2003, paras 42–61; C-70/06, *Commission v Portugal,* 2008, paras 39–54; C-557/14, *Commission v Portugal,* 2016, paras 61–82; C-626/16, *Commission v Slovak Republic,* 2018, paras 82–93; C-93/17, *Commission v Greece,* 2018, paras 107–48. For an example of a penalty payment that is adjusted over time as the Member State gradually starts to comply; see C-378/13, *Commission v Greece,* 2014, paras 47–67.

30
Judicial Protection Vis-à-Vis the Institutions and Bodies of the Union

Rule of law. Union law rules must be upheld and applied not only within the Member States but also by the institutions and bodies of the Union itself. The Court of Justice stated in *Les Verts* that the Community, as it then was, was 'a Community based on the rule of law, in as much as neither its Member States nor its institutions can avoid a review of the question whether the measures adopted by them are in conformity with the basic constitutional charter, the Treaty'.[1] The same applies to the Union.[2] To this end, the Treaties have established 'a complete system of legal remedies and procedures designed to permit the Court of Justice to review the legality of measures adopted by the institutions'.[3] Due to the requirement of equality of the Member States before Union law (Article 4(2) TEU), the legality of the actions of the institutions and bodies of the Union may be assessed only by the Court of Justice in accordance with Union law.[4] In order to ensure that Union law is respected by the institutions and bodies of the Union, the Treaties provide for procedures whereby the Court of Justice may review the legality of their acts directly. Only for CFSP acts is judicial review of the conformity of Union acts with the Treaties not ensured in full. In addition to these 'direct actions', there is the possibility for national courts and tribunals to ask the Court of Justice to give preliminary rulings on the validity of acts of the institutions and bodies. Again, CFSP measures are an exception. A brief description of these two forms of legal protection is followed by an assessment as to how the combination of the two forms constitutes a comprehensive system of legal protection.

30.001

I. Legal Remedies before the Court of Justice

Direct actions. The TFEU provides for specific courses of action directly aiming to have the Court of Justice review the legality of acts, or failures to act, of the institutions and bodies of the Union or deal with their extracontractual liability: actions for annulment (Article 263 TFEU), actions for failure to act (Article 265 TFEU), and actions for damages (Article 268 TFEU). The main conditions for bringing these three actions before the Court of Justice are set out below. Specific procedures such as actions open to officials and other servants of the institutions and bodies are not addressed (see para. 14.022, *supra*). The following overview refers to the 'Court of Justice' as an institution (in the Treaties: 'Court of Justice of the European Union'), regardless of the competent court (Court of Justice or General Court). However, depending on the identity of the applicant and the characteristics of the act challenged, an action must be brought before the Court of Justice itself or before the General Court (see para. 13.009, *supra*).

30.002

---

[1] 294/83, *Les Verts v European Parliament*, 1986, para. 23.
[2] C-583/11 P, *Inuit Tapiriit Kanatami v European Parliament and Council*, 2013, para. 91.
[3] 294/83, *Les Verts v European Parliament*, 1986, para. 23; C-583/11 P, *Inuit Tapiriit Kanatami v European Parliament and Council*, 2013, para. 92.
[4] 314/85, *Foto-Frost*, 1987, paras 15–20.

A. Action for annulment

30.003 **Article 263 TFEU.** Where acts of Union institutions or bodies infringe a rule of Union law, they may be annulled on the basis of Article 263 TFEU. Through this action for annulment, the Court of Justice monitors the 'legality' of the actions of Union institutions and bodies within the scope of the Treaties. However, the Court has no jurisdiction to review the legality of provisions of primary Union law (see para. 24.003, *supra*), nor can it rule on the legality of the actions of Member States or individuals on the basis of an action for annulment. At the same time, the Court can only verify, to a limited extent, the legality of measures adopted in the framework of the CFSP (see para. 30.013, *infra*).

1. Possible defendants

30.004 **Institutions.** The annulment may be sought of legislative acts (of the European Parliament and/or of the Council), acts of the Council, of the Commission, and of the European Central Bank—in so far as they are not recommendations or opinions—and acts of the European Parliament and of the European Council intended to produce legal effects vis-à-vis third parties (first sentence of the first para. of Article 263 TFEU). The addition of the European Parliament is a codification of the ruling of the Court of Justice in *Les Verts*, which recognized that a political party has the right to seek the annulment of a decision of the Bureau of the Parliament which produces legal effects vis-à-vis that party, even though the then Article 173 EEC Treaty merely cited the Council and the Commission as possible defendants in the action for annulment.[5]

30.005 **Other bodies of the Union.** Since the Union constitutes a 'Union based on the rule of law', the Court of Justice may also review the legality of acts of other bodies, offices, or agencies of the Union intended to produce legal effects vis-à-vis third parties (second sentence of the first para. of Article 263 TFEU).[6] This provision was added by the Treaty of Lisbon and confirms the assertion that where an aggrieved individual is not given legal protection in any other way, an action for annulment should be available against acts of bodies, offices, and agencies of the Union which, under the Treaties, are entrusted with the application of Union law.[7] The Court of Justice has no jurisdiction to rule on actions for annulment of acts of national bodies.[8] It also has no jurisdiction over acts of the Representatives of the governments of the Member States.[9]

---

[5] 294/83, *Les Verts v European Parliament*, 1986, paras 24–5.

[6] In accordance with the fifth para. of Article 263 TFEU, special conditions governing appeals against acts of bodies, offices, and agencies of the Union may be laid down in the constituent acts of such bodies, offices, and agencies. See para. 18.024, *supra*.

[7] See 9/56, *Meroni*, 1958, at 149–51; C-160/03, *Spain v Eurojust*, 2005, paras 41–3. For further examples, see para. 18.024, *supra*.

[8] Nevertheless, pursuant to Article 14.2 of the Protocol on the Statute of the European System of Central Banks and of the European Central Bank the Court has jurisdiction to review the validity of national acts pertaining to the appointment and removal of directors of the national central banks; see C-202/18 and C-238/18, *Rimšēvičs and ECB v Latvia*, 2019, paras 43–63. By contrast, the involvement of national authorities in the course of the procedure leading up to an act by bodies, offices, or agencies of the Union cannot affect their classification as Union acts, where the acts of the national authorities constitute a stage of a procedure in which a Union body, office, or agency exercises, alone, the final decision-making power without being bound by the preparatory acts or the proposals of the national authorities; see C-219/17, *Berlusconi and Fininvest*, 2018, para. 43; C-414/18, *Iccrea Banca*, 2019, para. 38.

[9] C-424/20 P(R), *Representatives of the Governments of the Member States v Sharpston* (order of the Vice-President), 2020, paras 23–8 (decision on the appointment of an Advocate-General).

2. Possible applicants

a. Institutions and Member States

Privileged and other applicants. The European Parliament, the Council, the Commission, and the Member States may bring an action for annulment (Article 263(2) TFEU) without having to prove any procedural interest.[10] That right shall be independent of the position adopted by a Member State or an institution at the time of the adoption of an act. Thus, there is no obstacle to a Member State seeking the annulment of an act which it has approved in the Council.[11] There is no such unrestricted right to bring an action for annulment for the Court of Auditors, the European Central Bank, and since the Lisbon Treaty, the Committee of the Regions. Indeed, these applicants may only bring such an action when they seek to preserve their prerogatives (Article 263(3) TFEU).[12] It was with this latter restriction that in 1990 the Court of Justice granted the European Parliament the right to bring an action for annulment, even though the then EEC Treaty granted this right only to the Council and the Commission. In order to ensure that the institutional balance laid down in the Community Treaties would be respected, the Court considered it necessary for the Parliament to be able to subject the respect of its prerogatives by the other institutions to judicial review.[13] The EU Treaty incorporated this right for the Parliament into the former Article 230 EC; subsequently, the Nice Treaty transformed it into an unconditional right to bring an action for annulment. Other Union bodies are not entitled to bring an action for annulment.

30.006

As far as the Member States are concerned, the right to bring an action for annulment is exercised by the national government; federated entities or decentralized authorities of a Member State may bring an action for annulment only under the conditions which apply to 'natural and legal persons'.[14] The latter also applies to third countries.[15]

b. Natural and legal persons

Conditional right to bring an action. The fourth para. of Article 263 TFEU limits the possibility for natural and legal persons ('individuals') to bring an action for annulment before the Court of Justice (in practice, before the General Court). Any natural or legal person may bring such an action only 'against an act addressed to that person or which is of direct and individual concern to them or against a regulatory act which is of direct concern to them and does not entail implementing measures'. Under the fourth para. of Article 263 TFEU, any natural or legal person may thus bring an action against any act addressed to that person. However, acts addressed to other persons (e.g. acts addressed to Member States) or acts of general application which do not constitute a 'regulatory act', such as legislative acts, can only be contested by way of an action for annulment brought by an individual who is directly and individually concerned by the act in question. These are cumulative conditions. Since the Lisbon Treaty, regulatory acts which do not involve implementing measures are

30.007

---

[10] 45/86, *Commission v Council*, 1987, para. 3.
[11] 166/78, *Italy v Council*, 1979, paras 5–6.
[12] Article 8 of the Protocol (No. 2) on the application of the principles of subsidiarity and proportionality also allows the Committee of the Regions to bring an action for infringement of the subsidiarity principle against legislative acts which require it to give an opinion, even if the action does not seek to safeguard its prerogatives (see para. 5.033, *supra*).
[13] C-70/88, *European Parliament v Council*, 1990, paras 11–27.
[14] C-95/97, *Walloon Region v Commission*, 1997, paras 6–8.
[15] cf. T-319/05, *Switzerland v Commission*, 2010 (action dismissed without ruling on admissibility).

subject only to the condition that the natural or legal person must be directly concerned by these acts (para. 30.011, *infra*). Before addressing the conditions of 'direct' and 'individual' concern and the category of 'regulatory acts', it should be stated that the nationality of a natural person or the location of the seat of a legal person is irrelevant for the admissibility of an action for annulment, which is therefore open to legal persons established outside the Union.[16]

30.008 **(1) Direct concern   Quality of the act.** An applicant is *directly* concerned by an act where that act all by itself affects his or her legal position.[17] This is not the case where the act leaves a certain margin of discretion to the Union or national authorities responsible for its implementation. For that reason, it is difficult for an applicant to be directly concerned by a directive, which leaves to the national authorities the choice of form and methods for achieving the result sought by the directive. On the contrary, an applicant is directly concerned by an act of the Union which does not leave any discretion to the authorities responsible for its implementation, since that implementation can be carried out purely automatically on the basis of that act without any further policy choices having to be made. This applied, for example, to Spanish fishermen challenging the legality of the act by which the Commission approved the list of vessels authorized to carry out fishing activities during a transitional period after Spain's accession. The contested Commission act did not leave that Member State any discretion as to which vessels could carry out their activities.[18] Also where the Commission addresses a decision to a Member State prohibiting or ordering the recovery of a planned aid measure, the Member State has no discretion in the matter and the recipient undertaking is thus directly concerned by that decision.[19] This is not necessarily the case when the Commission approves an aid measure proposed by a Member State and a competitor of the beneficiary company wishes to challenge that decision. Indeed, this competitor is only directly concerned by this decision if there is no doubt as to the will of the Member State to actually grant the aid.[20]

30.009 **(2) Individual concern   Quality of the applicant.** According to the criterion developed by the Court of Justice in the *Plaumann* judgment, natural or legal persons are *individually* concerned by an act if it affects them 'by reason of certain attributes which are peculiar to them or by reason of circumstances in which they are differentiated from all other persons and by virtue of these factors distinguishes them individually just as in the case of the person addressed [by that act]'.[21] In the *Plaumann* case, the Commission's refusal to grant Germany derogations on the charges applicable to imports of clementines from third countries could therefore not be challenged by an individual who, in his capacity as an importer, was affected by the contested act, because he was affected in the same way by that act as other economic operators.

---

[16] e.g. C-583/11 P, *Inuit Tapiriit Kanatami v European Parliament and Council*, 2013.
[17] C-386/96 P, *Dreyfus v Commission*, 1998, para. 43.
[18] 207/86, *Apesco v Commission*, 1988, para. 12.
[19] 730/79, *Philip Morris v Commission*, 1980.
[20] e.g. T-435/93, *ASPEC and Others v Commission*, 1995, paras 60–1. For an example where the competitive relationship was nevertheless sufficiently proven so as to make the approval by the Commission of a State aid scheme of direct concern to the applicant, see C-622/16 P to C-624/16 P, *Scuola Elementare Maria Montessori v Commission*, 2018, paras 42–55.
[21] 25/62, *Plaumann v Commission*, 1963, 205.

Case law. The *Plaumann* formula does not in itself give enough clues to immediately know **30.010** whether a natural or legal person is sufficiently individualized by a general act or any other act not addressed to him. The application of the conditions of admissibility by the Court of Justice has therefore led to case law that is difficult to summarize. Very often, the Court of Justice has to declare an action brought by individuals against an act of the Union which is not addressed to them inadmissible. Typical cases are, for example, undertakings or their professional associations challenging Union rules which affect them only in their objective capacity as economic operators. For this reason, a fishing company could not seek the annulment of a Commission regulation prohibiting the use of certain types of fishing nets. Even if such a regulation directly affected the legal position of the undertakings concerned, a fishing undertaking working with those nets was affected by that act in the same way as any other operator actually or potentially in an identical situation.[22] In the meantime, some of the rulings of the Court of Justice have lost their relevance as they concern acts which, since the entry into force of the Lisbon Treaty, are to be seen as 'regulatory acts which do not entail an implementing measure', to which the condition of individual concern no longer applies.

Examples of general acts which nevertheless sufficiently individualize a natural or legal person are, first of all, regulations imposing quotas on named undertakings[23] or establishing fishing rights in respect of named fishing vessels.[24] For the same reason, a decision addressed to a Member State prohibiting or reducing individual aid granted by a Member State affects in a sufficiently individual manner either the undertaking that would benefit from the national aid[25] or the private individual to whom Union aid was granted.[26]

A second set of cases in which individuals are deemed to be individually concerned are those in which the Union institution which adopted the contested act was required by a rule of Union law, when adopting that act, to take account of the situation of a specific group of individuals. For example, an importer could challenge a regulation by which the Commission allowed a Member State to restrict imports of a product from third countries because the Commission, when adopting this regulation, was obliged to take into account the situation of importers with goods in transit.[27]

A third group includes actions brought by private individuals who have procedural rights in the context of certain Union procedures, such as the Commission's monitoring of compliance with competition rules, and who are affected by the contested act in the exercise of those rights. In the context of State aid control, this concerns, for example, the right of interested parties to submit comments if the Commission decides to open the formal investigation procedure (see paras 9.024–9.026). Thus, any interested party may ask the annulment of the Commission's decision that a notified measure does not constitute State aid

---

[22] e.g. C-263/02 P, *Commission v Jégo-Quéré*, 2004, paras 46–8, rejecting the more liberal approach advocated by the Court of First Instance at the time; see T-177/01, *Jégo-Quéré v Commission*, 2002. See also C-50/00 P, *Unión de Pequeños Agricultores v Council*, 2002, paras 32–47, rejecting the alternative proposed by AG Jacobs in his Opinion of 21 March 2002 in that case. See also, para. 30.041 et seq., *infra*.
[23] e.g. 138/79, *Roquette Frères v Council*, 1980, para. 16.
[24] e.g. 207/86, *Apesco v Commission*, 1988, paras 11–12.
[25] e.g. 730/79, *Philip Morris v Commission*, 1980.
[26] e.g. 291/89, *Interhotel v Commission*, 1991, para. 13.
[27] C-152/88, *Sofrimport v Commission*, 1990, paras 10–13.

or that there is no doubt as to its compatibility with the internal market.[28] Such a decision has indeed the effect of not opening the formal investigation procedure under which interested parties may submit comments. However, such an interested party is not necessarily also individually concerned by the decision by which the Commission—at the end of this procedure—declares the aid measure compatible with the internal market: for example, a competing undertaking must demonstrate that it has participated in the formal investigation procedure and that its market position is substantially affected by the aid.[29]

Finally, in some cases, the Court of Justice ruled that an undertaking affected by the contested act in its objective capacity as an economic operator was sufficiently individualized because of special circumstances. Thus, a Catalan producer of sparkling wine entitled 'Gran Cremant' could bring an action for annulment of the Council Regulation which reserved the term 'crémant' for French and Luxembourg sparkling wines. A special circumstance was the fact that the producer had already registered this indication as a trademark for a long time and was prevented by the Regulation from using his trademark.[30] The producer could thus protect his commercial property right.

30.011 **(3) Regulatory acts** Regulatory acts. In order to—slightly—relax the conditions under which natural and legal persons may bring an action for annulment, the Lisbon Treaty, in the fourth para. of Article 263 TFEU, introduced the possibility for a natural or legal person to bring an action for annulment against 'a regulatory act which is of direct concern to him and which does not entail implementing measures'. Regulatory acts are acts of general application having binding legal effects which do not constitute legislative acts.[31] They are therefore delegated acts (Article 290(1) TFEU), implementing acts within the meaning of Article 291(2) TFEU and other non-legislative acts of general application.[32] A natural or legal person may seek the annulment of such a regulatory act if this act does not entail implementing measures in respect of the applicant, irrespective of whether it entails implementing measures for other persons or not.[33] All of this means that an act of general application which does not constitute a legislative act and which does not entail an implementing measure for the applicant (e.g. a Commission regulation directly prohibiting the use of certain fishing nets) may be challenged by any individual directly concerned by that act, even if he or she does not fulfil the condition of being individually concerned.[34] In contrast, where such a regulatory act has been implemented within the Member States or at Union level, or where that act will at a later point entail such implementation vis-à-vis the applicant, even if purely mechanical, an individual may challenge that act only under the conditions of 'direct' and 'individual' concern set out above.[35] In such a case,

---

[28] C-198/91, *Cook v Commission*, 1993, paras 13–26; C-367/95 P, *Commission v Sytraval and Brink's France*, 1998, paras 47–8.
[29] 169/84, *Cofaz v Commission*, 1986, paras 22–5.
[30] C-309/89, *Codorníu v Council*, 1994, paras 14–22.
[31] C-583/11 P, *Inuit Tapiriit Kanatami v European Parliament and Council*, 2013, paras 50–62.
[32] e.g. the measures provided for in Article 43(3) TFEU (agriculture).
[33] C-274/12 P, *Telefónica v Commission*, 2013, paras 30–1.
[34] This means that Jégo-Quéré, as an applicant, would now (and contrary to what was held at the time in C-263/02 P, *Commission v Jégo-Quéré*, 2004) be admitted to bring an action for annulment of what was in effect an 'implementing act' of the Commission.
[35] e.g. C-244/16 P, *Industrias Químicas del Vallés v Commission*, 2018, paras 39–77 (implementation at EU level will follow); C-384/16 P, *European Union Copper Task Force v Commission*, 2018, paras 32–71 (implementation at national level will follow).

the condition of individual concern may constitute an obstacle to bringing a direct action against the regulatory act. In general, however, judicial review of the measure giving effect to that regulatory act will be possible, either at national level, where the regulatory act is implemented by national authorities, or before the General Court, where the regulatory act is implemented by an act of a Union institution or body addressed to the individual concerned or that directly and individually concerns that individual.

3. Reviewable acts

Binding acts. Article 263 TFEU excludes actions for annulment of recommendations and opinions, which shows that such actions can only be brought against binding acts.[36] It concerns all acts adopted by institutions or bodies of the Union, whatever their form or nature, which represent the final position of an institution or body and are intended to produce legal effects.[37] Thus, where an act is adopted as part of a multi-stage procedure, only the final act and not the preparatory acts can be contested by way of an action for annulment. In competition cases, for example, an undertaking cannot bring an action for annulment of decisions of the Commission to open proceedings against an undertaking for an alleged infringement of Articles 101 or 102 TFEU or to send it a 'statement of objections'.[38] In State aid cases, the opening of the formal investigation procedure may in itself produce legal effects—and thus be challenged—if it concerns a new aid measure which cannot be put into effect after the opening of this procedure (see para. 9.026, *supra*).[39]

30.012

CFSP acts. The jurisdiction of the Court of Justice remains largely excluded with regard to CFSP acts (Articles 24(1) TEU and 275 TFEU). Under the second para. of Article 275 TFEU, since the Lisbon Treaty, the Court of Justice (the General Court) has jurisdiction to hear and determine actions for annulment brought by individuals against CFSP decisions of the Council which constitute restrictive measures against natural or legal persons. It concerns a review of the legality of decisions of an individual nature.[40] The same Treaty provision also empowers the Court to ensure, in accordance with Article 40 TEU, that the implementation of the CFSP by the institutions does not affect—either in procedural terms or in terms of the extent of competences—the exercise of the Union's other competences.[41] In the same sense, before the entry into force of the Lisbon Treaty, the Court already examined whether a CFSP act of the Council (relying on the then Title V of the EU Treaty) should not rather have been adopted on the basis of the EC Treaty and in accordance with the procedure laid down therein.[42] According to Article 40 TEU, this competence now also exists in the reverse sense, that is, to prevent the exercise of the Union's other competences from affecting the Union's competences relating to the CFSP. The Court of Justice has indicated that the exclusion of CFSP from its jurisdiction constitutes a derogation from the Court's general jurisdiction to ensure that the law is observed in the interpretation and application

30.013

---

[36] C-16/16 P, *Belgium v Commission*, 2018, paras 25–45. That does not preclude that recommendations may produce some legal effects and could be reviewed in the framework of a reference for a preliminary ruling, ibid., para. 44.
[37] 60/81, *IBM v Commission*, 1981, paras 8–10.
[38] Ibid., para. 21.
[39] C-312/90, *Spain v Commission*, 1992, paras 14–20.
[40] C-72/15, *Rosneft*, 2017, paras 98–103.
[41] See also the second subpara. of Article 24(1) TEU.
[42] C-91/05, *Commission v Council*, 2008.

of the Treaties (Article 19 TEU) and must therefore be interpreted restrictively.[43] Similarly, the Court held that it may examine the validity of international agreements relating exclusively to the CFSP where they have been adopted in breach of the procedure for the conclusion of international agreements laid down in Article 218 TFEU.[44] On the merits, it found that a CFSP decision relating to the signing and conclusion of such an agreement was invalid because the European Parliament had not been fully informed of the conclusion of that agreement in accordance with Article 218(10) TFEU.[45]

30.014 **PJCC measures.** Since the Lisbon Treaty, acts relating to police and judicial cooperation in criminal matters may be the subject of an action for annulment. For PJCC acts adopted before 1 December 2009, until 30 November 2014 the jurisdiction of the Court was still limited to that which it exercised before that date on the basis of ex-Article 35 EU.[46] The latter provision granted the Court jurisdiction only to review the legality of PJCC framework decisions and PJCC decisions in an action brought by a Member State or the Commission.[47] During this transitional period, the legality of PJCC provisions adopted before 1 December 2009 could not be challenged directly before the Court of Justice by institutions other than the Commission, nor by natural or legal persons. As of 1 December 2014, the Court exercises its full jurisdiction in respect of all PJCC acts.

4. Grounds for annulment

30.015 **Possible pleas.** Under Article 263 TFEU, an act may be annulled for (a) lack of competence; (b) infringement of an essential procedural requirement; (c) infringement of the Treaties or of any rule of law relating to their application; or (d) misuse of powers. The third ground of annulment actually includes the first two grounds, since the rules on competence and the essential procedural requirements (e.g. rules relating to decision-making and the requirement to state reasons) form part of the rules laid down in the Treaties or adopted on the basis thereof. The grounds of lack of competence and infringement of essential procedural requirements are nevertheless specific as they may be examined by the Court of its own motion.[48]

5. Time-limit

30.016 **Two months.** An action for annulment must be brought within two months of the date of publication of the act or of its notification to the applicant or, failing that, of the date on which the applicant took note of the act (Article 263(6) TFEU).[49]

---

[43] C-455/14 P, *Council, Commission and European Union Police Mission (EUPM) in Bosnia and Herzegovina*, 2016, para. 40 *et seq*. (Court oversees CFSP decisions in the area of personnel management); C-439/13 P, *Elitaliana v Eulex Kosovo*, 2015, paras 42–9 (Court oversees budget implementation in the case of a CFSP mission).
[44] C-658/11, *Parliament v Council*, 2014, paras 69–74.
[45] Ibid, para. 86.
[46] Protocol (No. 36) to the TEU and the TFEU on transitional provisions, Article 10.
[47] Although former Article 35(6) EU only refers to framework decisions and decisions, this appeal was open against all PJCC provisions adopted by the Council which are intended to produce legal effects on third parties: C-354/04 P *Gestoras Pro Amnistía and Others v Council*, 2007, paras 53–5.
[48] e.g. C-166/95 P *Daffix v Commission*, 1997, para. 24.
[49] See also CJ Rules of Procedure, Articles 50 to 51 and GC Rules of Procedure, Articles 59 to 60.

6. Effect of annulment

Ex tunc and erga omnes. If an action for annulment is well founded, the contested act must be annulled. This means that the act disappears from the Union legal order, with retroactive effect from the moment it was adopted (*ex tunc*) and with regard to everyone (*erga omnes*). However, for reasons of legal certainty, the Court may (provisionally) maintain the effects of an act which has been annulled (Article 264(2) TFEU), for example until such time as a new act is adopted. Furthermore, the institution whose act has been annulled is obliged to take the measures necessary to comply with the judgment (Article 266 TFEU).

30.017

B. Action for failure to act

Article 265 TFEU. In order to provide judicial protection in circumstances where a person seeking justice is not confronted with an act of a Union institution but with the latter's failure to act, Article 265 TFEU provides for an action for failure to act 'in infringement of the Treaties'. A failure by an institution to act constitutes an 'infringement of the Treaties' if the institution concerned is actually required to take an act that produces legal effects. This is the case, for example, where the Commission fails to deal with a complaint that a competitor of an undertaking to which non-notified State aid has been granted, has lodged with the Commission against such aid.[50]

30.018

Defendant and applicant. The action for failure to act may be directed at the European Parliament, the European Council, the Council, the Commission, or the ECB and—since the Treaty of Lisbon—other bodies, offices, and agencies of the Union (Article 265(1) TFEU). It may be brought by the Member States and all Union institutions. The action may also be brought by any natural or legal person in the case of a failure to 'address to that person any act other than a recommendation or an opinion in its regard', which means a failure to adopt a binding act. In order not to provide different legal protection to a natural or legal person depending on whether an act or inaction of an institution or body is involved, the requirement that that act should have been 'addressed to that person' is interpreted, by analogy with the conditions of admissibility laid down in Article 263 TFEU, as meaning that it must be an act addressed to the applicant or which would concern the applicant directly and individually[51] or, since the Treaty of Lisbon, a regulatory act which would concern the applicant directly and would not entail any implementing measures.

30.019

Procedure and effect. An action for failure to act is admissible only if the institution concerned has first been called upon to act and if, two months after being so called upon, it has not defined its position. A position adopted by an institution—whatever its form—terminates the failure to act and, at the same time, the possibility of bringing an action for failure to act. If an institution has adopted a position and that position constitutes a binding act, it may be the subject of an action for annulment. If an institution has not defined its position within the aforementioned two-month period, the action for failure to act may be brought within a further period of two months. If the action is well founded, the Court finds that the institution concerned has failed to act in breach of the Treaties. The

30.020

---

[50] T-95/96, *Gestevisión Telecinco v Commission*, 1998. See also para. 17.005.
[51] C-68/95, *T.Port*, 1996, paras 58–9.

C. Action for damages

30.021 **Article 268 TFEU.** Pursuant to Article 268 TFEU, the Court of Justice of the European Union has exclusive jurisdiction to determine the non-contractual liability of the Union. This concerns liability of the Union for damage caused by its institutions or by its servants in the performance of their duties (second para. of Article 340 TFEU). The action for damages should be brought before the General Court.[52] It is an autonomous action, which is available without there being a need to lodge first an action for annulment or for failure to act, or else when these latter actions are inadmissible.[53] However, it should not be used as an improper action for annulment, for example to circumvent the expiry of the time-limit for bringing an action for annulment.[54] An action for damages is often brought at the same time as an action for annulment.

30.022 **Defendant and applicant.** As the institutions—except for the European Central Bank—do not have legal personality, it is the Union that can be held liable. It is the institution concerned which is the defendant, as representative of the Union.[55] The institutions that may trigger the liability of the Union are not only the 'institutions' referred to in Article 13(1) TEU, but also any other body set up pursuant to the Treaties, such as the European Investment Bank or the European Ombudsman.[56] An action for damages may be brought by any natural or legal person claiming to have suffered damage as a result of acts or conduct of a Union institution or its servants.[57] The Treaties do not exclude the possibility for a Member State to bring such an action, but this has not been done so far.

30.023 **Grounds for liability.** As with the liability of a Member State for an infringement of Union law, the Union's liability is subject to the existence of a right to compensation where three conditions are met: (1) the rule of law infringed is intended to confer rights on individuals; (2) there is a sufficiently serious breach; and (3) there is a direct causal link between the breach of Union law and the damage suffered by the injured parties.[58] Thus, the protection of the rights which individuals derive from Union law does not differ according to whether the damage was caused by a national or a Union body.[59] A breach of Union law is sufficiently serious if it involves a manifest and serious disregard by an institution of the limits of its

---

[52] The first para. of Article 256 TFEU and Article 51 of the Statute of the Court of Justice.
[53] C-8/15 P to C-10/15 P, *Ledra Advertising v Commission*, 2016; C-134/19 P, *Bank Refah Kargaran v Council*, 2020, paras 23–52.
[54] 175/84, *Krohn v Commission*, 1986, paras 32–4.
[55] See 63-69/72, *Werhahn v Council*, 1973, para. 7; T-577/14, *Gascogne Sack Deutschland and Gascogne v Commission* (order), 2015.
[56] e.g. C-370/89, *SGEEM and Etroy v EIB*, para. 16; T-209/00, *Lamberts v European Ombudsman*, 2002 (confirmed by C-234/02 P, *European Ombudsman v Lamberts*, 2004). See, however, in respect of the Euro Group, C-597/18 P, C-598/18 P, C-603/18 P, and C-604/18 P, *Council v Dr. K. Chrysostomides & Co. and Others*, 2020, paras 78–98 and 212–13 (action for damages inadmissible against the Euro Group as it is not a Union entity established by the Treaties).
[57] 118/83, *CMC v Commission*, 1985, para. 31.
[58] C-352/98 P, *Bergaderm and Goupil v Commission*, 2000, para. 42.
[59] C-46/93 and C-48/93, *Brasserie du Pêcheur and Factortame*, 1996, para. 41.

discretion. Where the institution concerned has only a very limited margin of discretion, or no margin at all, the mere infringement of Union law may be sufficient to establish a sufficiently serious breach.[60] A mere breach of the duty to state reasons cannot lead to Union liability.[61] In any event, the Union does not incur liability without fault.[62] The Court did, however, accept that a claim for unjust enrichment may be brought against the Union, even though such a claim is not specifically provided for in Articles 268 and 340 TFEU.[63]

Limitation period. The action against the Union in respect of non-contractual liability shall be subject to a limitation period of five years from the event giving rise to the action,[64] that is to say, five years from the occurrence of the damage. The limitation period is interrupted either by an action brought in the Court of Justice or by an earlier application lodged with the institution concerned, which was followed by such an action.[65]

30.024

D. Plea of illegality

Article 277 TFEU. In order to complete judicial protection against acts of the Union, the Treaties provide for an additional means by which a party to proceedings may obtain, in the context of direct action proceedings, the inapplicability of an act of general application which that party was unable to challenge by means of a direct action. This 'plea of illegality' is not an autonomous legal procedure and can only be raised following a direct action brought in the Court of Justice or the General Court (usually an action for annulment). Accordingly, a party to the proceedings may not rely on Article 277 TFEU to challenge the legality of an act addressed to it in respect of which it could have claimed annulment under Article 263 TFEU. The requirement that it must be an act 'at issue' indicates that there must be a direct legal link between the act against which the action for annulment is brought and the general act covered by the plea of illegality.[66] Thus, in an action for annulment of a decision imposing a fine for infringement of the competition rules, an undertaking may invoke the illegality of the guidelines in which the Commission determined the method of calculation of those fines.[67] Since Article 277 TFEU opens the plea of illegality to 'any party', it may also be raised by a Member State or an institution against a legislative act,[68] even though Member States and institutions do have the right to obtain the annulment of such an act directly.[69]

30.025

---

[60] C-352/98 P, *Bergaderm and Goupil v Commission*, 2000, paras 43–4. See also C-337/15 P, *European Ombudsman v Staelen*, 2017, paras 37–45.
[61] 106/81, *Kind v EEC*, 1982, para. 14; C-76/01 P, *Eurocoton v Council*, 2003, para. 98; C-134/19 P, *Bank Refah Kargaran v Council*, 2020, paras 59–65.
[62] C-120/06 P and C-121/06 P, *FIAMM and FIAMM Technologies v Council and Commission*, 2008.
[63] C-578/18 P *Czech Republic v Commission*, 2020, para. 82. See also C-47/07 P *Masdar (UK) v Commission*, 2008, paras 44 and 46–50.
[64] Statute of the Court of Justice, Article 46.
[65] Ibid.
[66] C-119/19 P and C-126/19 P, *Commission v Carreras Sequeros and Others*, 2020, paras 69–70.
[67] C-189/02 P, C-202/02 P, and C-205-208/02 P, *Dansk Rørindustri and Others v Commission*, 2005, paras 212–13.
[68] C-11/00, *Commission v ECB*, 2003, paras 76–8.
[69] For this reason a Member State may, however, only rely on the invalidity of the legislative act in the course of an action under Article 258 TFEU if the act in question contained such particularly serious and manifest defects that it could be categorized as a non-existent act: C-601/14, *Commission v Italy*, 2016, para. 33.

E. Procedure for direct actions

30.026 **Written and oral proceedings.** The procedure before the Court of Justice and the General Court consists of a written part and an oral part.[70] With the exception of the Member States and the institutions, the parties must be represented by a lawyer authorized to practise before a court of a Member State (or EEA State) during the proceedings.[71] An action has to be brought by the transmission of an application to the Registrar. In principle, the applicant chooses the language of the case.[72] The defendant is allowed a period of two months from service of the application to lodge a defence.[73] The application and the defence may be supplemented by a reply from the applicant and a rejoinder from the defendant within a period prescribed by the President of the Court of Justice or the General Court.[74] However, in proceedings before the General Court, the General Court may decide that a second exchange of pleadings is not necessary.[75] The Member States and institutions may intervene in cases before these Courts; the same applies to any other person claiming to have an interest in the decision of the Court of Justice or the General Court.[76]

When the written procedure has been concluded, the Judge-Rapporteur submits his or her preliminary report. In the Court of Justice, the case is then assigned to a Chamber (see para. 13.018, *supra*); in the General Court, the case was already assigned to a Chamber immediately upon its being brought before that court, but it may be assigned, after the submission of the preliminary report, to a Chamber composed of a different number of judges. The hearing then takes place with the oral submissions of the parties and any interveners. In certain circumstances, the hearing may be dispensed with.[77] Unless the Court decides otherwise, the oral procedure is concluded with the Opinion of the Advocate-General (see para. 29.032, *supra*). In the General Court, a judge may be designated as Advocate-General; however, this possibility is not currently used, which means that the oral procedure is closed at the end of the hearing. The closure of the procedure is followed by the deliberation (see para. 29.033, *supra*). The judgment is delivered in the language of the case, published on the website of the Court of Justice and, with the exception of less important judgments, in all the official languages, on the EUR-Lex website and in the *European Court Reports*.

30.027 **Expedited procedure.** The average duration of the procedure for a direct action is currently around nineteen months before the Court of Justice and (depending on the area) fifteen to twenty-seven months before the General Court. At the request of the applicant or the defendant, the Court of Justice or the General Court may in exceptional cases, having regard to the urgency of the case, decide that a case is to be dealt with under an expedited

---

[70] Article 20 *et seq.* of the Statute of the Court of Justice, as elaborated in the Rules of Procedure of the Court of Justice and the Rules of Procedure of the General Court. Practical guidance for parties to the proceedings can also be found on the website of the Court of Justice for both the Court of Justice and the General Court, in each case under the heading 'Procedure'.

[71] Statute of the Court of Justice, Article 19; see C-515/17 P and C-561/17 P, *Uniwersytet Wrocławski v Research Executive Agency*, 2020, paras 55–69.

[72] CJ Rules of Procedure, Article 37; GC Rules of Procedure, Article 45.

[73] CJ Rules of Procedure, Article 124; GC Rules of Procedure, Article 81.

[74] CJ Rules of Procedure, Article 126; GC Rules of Procedure, Article 83.

[75] GC Rules of Procedure, Article 83.

[76] Statute of the Court of Justice, Article 40.

[77] CJ Rules of Procedure, Article 76 and GC Rules of Procedure, Article 106.

procedure. In that event, the parties may not, in principle, submit a reply, rejoinder, or statement in intervention, but may supplement their arguments in the oral procedure.[78]

Interim measures. Actions brought before the Court of Justice or the General Court do not suspend the effect of the act that is being challenged. However, in order to provide legal protection in the course of proceedings, the Court of Justice or the General Court may, if it considers that circumstances so require, order a stay of execution of the contested measure or any other interim measure (Articles 278 and 279 TFEU). These 'interim measures' require that an action has already been brought before the same Union Court (the main proceedings). The granting of provisional measures is subject to three cumulative conditions: (1) the application for interim measures must appear justified, *prima facie*, which means that the action in the main proceedings has a certain likelihood of success (*fumus boni juris*); (2) the application must be urgent, which means that failure to rule on the main action threatens to cause serious and irreparable harm to the applicant's interests; and (3) the interest of the applicant in ordering interim measures must prevail over the other interests involved in the proceedings.[79] The (Vice-)President of the Court of Justice or the President of the General Court orders interim relief by way of summary procedure, but they may leave that decision to the Court itself.[80] The interim measures are laid down in a decision and remain in force until judgment has been given in the main proceedings or until such time as is specified in the decision.[81] Their enforcement may be ensured through the imposition of a periodic penalty payment.[82]

30.028

Appeal. An appeal on points of law may only be brought before the Court of Justice against judgments and orders of the General Court (second subpara. of Article 256(1) TFEU). The appeal therefore does not constitute a second instance in which a case is submitted to another court for assessment in law and in fact, but is comparable to an appeal in cassation. An appeal may be brought by any party which has been unsuccessful, in whole or in part, in its submissions. An application must be made within two months of service of the contested decision.[83] If the appeal is well founded, the Court of Justice shall quash the contested decision of the General Court. It may then give final judgment in the matter itself, where the state of the proceedings so permits, for example if no additional or renewed findings of fact are necessary.[84] Alternatively, the Court may refer the case back to the General Court for judgment.[85]

30.029

Review. Where specialized courts are set up, the General Court shall have jurisdiction to decide on appeals from their decisions.[86] In exceptional cases, such a decision of the General Court may give rise to a review by the Court of Justice, that is, if there is a serious risk of the

30.030

---

[78] CJ Rules of Procedure, Articles 133 to 135; GC Rules of Procedure, Articles 151 to 155.
[79] For the first two conditions, see CJ Rules of Procedure, Article 160(3) and GC Rules of Procedure, Article 156(4); the third condition was developed in case law.
[80] CJ Rules of Procedure, Article 161(1); see, e.g., C-619/18 R, *Commission v Poland* (order), 2018, para. 5; C-791/19 R, *Commission v Poland* (order), 2020, para. 4.
[81] CJ Rules of Procedure, Article 162; GC Rules of Procedure, Article 158.
[82] C-441/17 R, *Commission v Poland* (order), 2017, paras 89–119.
[83] Statute of the Court of Justice, Article 56.
[84] e.g. C-119/19 P and C-126/19 P, *Commission v Carreras Sequeros and Others*, 2020, paras 129–55.
[85] Statute of the Court of Justice, Article 61. e.g. C-742/18 P, *Czech Republic v Commission*, 2020, paras 136–41.
[86] Annex to the Statute of the Court of Justice, Article 9.

unity or consistency of Union law being affected (Article 256(2) TFEU). This procedure applied as long as the Civil Service Tribunal existed.[87]

II. Judicial Protection through National Courts

30.031   **Ruling on validity.** Where an act of Union law is relevant to the resolution of a dispute pending before a national court or tribunal, that court or tribunal may, pursuant to Article 267 TFEU, refer a question to the Court of Justice for a preliminary ruling as to the validity of that act. The Court of Justice has jurisdiction to give preliminary rulings on the validity of acts of the institutions, bodies, offices, or agencies of the Union (first para. of Article 267 TFEU). There is no limitation of the grounds on which the validity of a Union act can be examined. Union acts against which natural or legal persons cannot bring an action for annulment in the General Court may be the subject of an examination of their validity by the Court of Justice, after a challenge by these persons in the competent national court of the national implementation of these Union acts.

A. Possibility and Obligation to Ask a Question for a Preliminary Ruling on Validity

30.032   **Duty to refer.** According to the second para. of Article 267 TFEU, a national court or tribunal which does not give judgment at final instance *may* refer a question to the Court of Justice for a preliminary ruling on the validity of a Union act. However, if such a national court or tribunal finds that a Union act is invalid, that court or tribunal is *obliged* to refer the matter to the Court for a preliminary ruling.[88] If this were not so, the validity of Union acts could be assessed differently in the Member States. This does not mean that the national court should refer the question of validity to the Court as soon as a party raises a question of validity of a provision of Union law. The national court may itself examine the validity of a Union act and, if it considers that the grounds of invalidity raised are unfounded, dismiss them by finding that the act is valid.[89] It is only where a national court considers that one or more of the grounds of invalidity raised by the parties—or a ground of invalidity raised of its own motion—are well founded that it must stay the proceedings and ask the Court to assess these grounds.[90] In any event, a national court adjudicating at last instance ('a court or tribunal against whose decisions there is no judicial remedy under national law', see para. 29.017, *supra*), is obliged under the third para. of Article 267 TFEU to make a reference for a preliminary ruling as soon as a question concerning the validity of a Union act is raised and the national court considers that a ruling thereon is necessary to enable it to give its decision. Since the *CILFIT* case law (see para. 29.019, *supra*) is not applicable here, a court of last instance must, for example, refer a question to the Court of Justice for a preliminary

---

[87] e.g. C-579/12 RX-II, *Commission v Strack*, 2013; C-542/18 RX-II and C-543/18 RX-II, *Simpson v Council*, 2020.
[88] 314/85, *Foto-Frost*, 1987, paras 12–20.
[89] Ibid., para. 14.
[90] C-344/04, *IATA and ELFAA*, 2006, paras 27–32.

ruling on the validity of a Union act, even if the Court has already declared corresponding provisions of a similar act invalid.[91]

Limitation to the possibility to refer. It should be noted that a party to proceedings cannot plead the illegality of a Union act before a national court if it could undoubtedly have challenged that act under Article 263 TFEU and failed to do so within the prescribed time-limit.[92] Indeed the preliminary ruling procedure does not permit a party to circumvent the irrevocable nature of that act vis-à-vis that party after the expiry of the time-limit for bringing an action. For example, where a Commission decision orders the recovery of unlawful aid, the beneficiary of such aid can no longer challenge the validity of that decision in proceedings before the national court relating to such recovery.[93] Since the Union act is to be regarded as valid as regards the party that could have brought a direct action, there is no point in referring a question of validity to the Court for a preliminary ruling,[94] unless another party to the main proceedings—or the court of its own motion—raises the question of validity. Furthermore, the possibility to refer for a preliminary ruling on the validity of CFSP acts is limited (see para. 30.036, *infra*).

30.033

Comparison with direct action. Unlike an action for annulment, where a party to the proceedings submits its arguments concerning the alleged unlawfulness of an act directly to the Court, a preliminary question on validity of a Union act is formulated by a national court, which cannot be compelled by the parties to put such a question to the Court of Justice. While the legality of a Union act may be challenged through an action for annulment within a limited period of time only, there is no time-limit within which a preliminary question may be raised as to the validity of that act.

30.034

B. Subject Matter of the Question Referred for a Preliminary Ruling on Validity

Secondary Union law. With the exception of CFSP acts, all acts of the institutions, whatever their form or binding effect, are subject to preliminary review of their validity.[95] This therefore also applies to acts adopted by the European Council under the simplified revision procedure (Article 48(6) TEU).[96] Also included are international agreements concluded by the Union and decisions of bodies set up by such agreements (see paras 26.001 and 26.004). Given the need to provide 'complete' judicial protection against Union action, the validity of acts of other bodies set up under the Treaties can also be reviewed. The Treaties themselves

30.035

---

[91] C-461/03, *Gaston Schul Douane-expediteur*, 2005, paras 15–25.
[92] C-239/99, *Nachi Europe*, 2001, paras 28–41.
[93] C-188/92, *TWD Textilwerke Deggendorf*, 1994, paras 17–26. See, however, in the case of recovery of aid granted in the context of an aid scheme of which the beneficiary may not even have been aware that they could fall within its scope, C-212/19, *Compagnie des pêches de Saint-Malo*, 2020. See also C-135/16, *Georgsmarienhütte*, 2020, paras 12–44, in which the Court clarified that an action for annulment of the Commission decision must always be brought in the General Court, even if national proceedings have been launched before the expiry of the time-limit set in Article 263(6) TFEU, because that court has the normal jurisdictional competence to deal with such actions in the area of State aid, subject to an appeal on points of law to the Court of Justice.
[94] e.g. C-119/05, *Lucchini*, 2007, paras 59–63; C-667/13, *Banco Privado Português*, 2015, paras 27–31; see also C-158/14, *A and others*, 2017, paras 67–75; C-414/18, *Iccrea Banca*, 2019, paras 31–575.
[95] C-322/88, *Grimaldi*, 1989, para. 8.
[96] C-370/12, *Pringle*, 2012, paras 30–7.

and other provisions of primary Union law cannot be the subject of preliminary review of their validity (see para. 24.003, *supra*).

30.036 **CFSP acts.** Since the Court of Justice of the European Union has no general jurisdiction in respect of the Treaty provisions on the CFSP or acts adopted under them (see para. 29.023, *supra*), it cannot, in principle, answer questions referred for a preliminary ruling concerning the validity of CFSP acts. The Court may, however, give preliminary rulings on the validity of CFSP acts which provide for restrictive measures against natural or legal persons, and monitor compliance with Article 40 TEU, namely in order to verify that a CFSP act does not affect the exercise of the Union's other competences[97] (see also para. 30.013, *supra*).

30.037 **PJCC acts.** For acts adopted before 1 December 2009 (on the basis of the EU Treaty) in the field of police and judicial cooperation in criminal matters, the jurisdiction of the Court remained, until 30 November 2014, the jurisdiction it exercised on the basis of Article 35 EU. Under former Article 35(1) EU, the Court had jurisdiction to give preliminary rulings only on the validity of framework decisions, decisions, and implementing measures and only in relation to questions referred for a preliminary ruling by courts or tribunals of a Member State which had expressly accepted this jurisdiction (see para. 29.004, *supra*). A first application of this was the judgment by which the Court, at the request of the Belgian Constitutional Court, ruled on the validity of the Council Framework Decision on the European arrest warrant.[98] At present, the Court may give preliminary rulings concerning the validity of all PJCC acts, including those adopted by the Union before 1 December 2009.

C. Consideration of the Question for a Preliminary Ruling on Validity

30.038 **Procedure before national courts.** For the formulation of a preliminary question on validity, the same rules apply as for a preliminary question on interpretation (see para. 29.026 *et seq.*, *supra*). Where the national court questions the validity of a Union act in order to assess the legality of national provisions based on that act, it may order a stay of execution of those national provisions. In order to ensure the uniform application of Union law in the national legal systems, the national court may exercise that power only in compliance with conditions of Union law which ensure parallelism with the conditions under which the Court of Justice orders the suspension of enforcement of contested Union acts. The national court may do so if: (a) it has serious doubts as to the validity of the Union act and, where the question of the validity of that act has not yet been referred to the Court of Justice, it refers that question to the Court of Justice itself; (b) the matter is urgent and threatens to cause serious and irreparable harm to the applicant; (c) the court takes due account of the Union interest; and (d) when assessing all those conditions, it respects the rulings of the Court of Justice or the General Court on the legality of the Union act, or an order for interim measures involving similar interim measures at the level of the Union.[99]

---

[97] C-72/15, *Rosneft*, 2017, paras 61–81 and 85–107.
[98] C-303/05, *Advocaten voor de Wereld*, 2007.
[99] C-143/88 and C-92/89, *Zuckerfabrik Süderdithmarschen and Zuckerfabrik Soest*, 1991, paras 14–33; C-465/93, *Atlanta Fruchthandelsgesellschaft and Others*, 1995.

Procedure before the Court of Justice. The consideration of a preliminary question on validity by the Court of Justice is subject to the same rules as those applicable to a question for a preliminary ruling on interpretation. The institution from which the act in question emanates may, in the proceedings before the Court, submit observations in order to defend the validity of that act.[100]

30.039

Effect of preliminary ruling. Where the Court of Justice declares the Union act concerned to be invalid, the referring court may no longer apply that act. For reasons of legal certainty and uniform application of Union law, any other court should also regard that act as invalid.[101] Like a judgment of annulment, a preliminary ruling establishing invalidity applies not only *erga omnes*, but also has retroactive effect.[102] Where the Court finds that the act in question should not be declared invalid, it does not declare that act to be 'valid', but merely finds that examination of the question has disclosed no factor of such a kind as to affect its validity.[103]

30.040

III. Complete System of Judicial Protection?

Complete system of legal remedies. In *Les Verts*, the Court of Justice described the judicial protection offered by the then EEC Treaty against the action of the former Community as a 'complete system of legal remedies and procedures' designed to permit the Community judiciary to review the measures adopted by the institutions (see para. 30.001, *supra*). Like the Community, the Union is founded on the principle of the rule of law. It is clear from the previous discussion that Member States and institutions may turn directly to the Court of Justice to seek the annulment of a Union act, including a measure of general application. Individuals may bring an action for annulment in the General Court only in respect of acts addressed to them, other acts directly and individually concerning them, and—since the Treaty of Lisbon—regulatory acts which are of direct concern to them and which do not entail implementing measures. However, as the Court of Justice pointed out in *Les Verts*, the Treaties also offer individuals protection against Union measures of general application being applied to their situation where, by virtue of the strict conditions of admissibility laid down in the fourth para. of Article 263 TFEU, those measures cannot be challenged directly in the Union Courts. Indeed, where the Union institutions are entrusted with the administrative implementation of a Union measure of general application, individuals may bring an action for annulment in the General Court against implementing acts of that measure which are addressed to them or which directly and individually concern them, and against implementing acts which directly concern them as regulatory acts (and which do not themselves require further implementing measures). In the context of this action, they may then rely on Article 277 TFEU to plead the illegality of the general measure. In the case of a Union measure that needs to be implemented by the national authorities, those individuals may invoke the invalidity of the measure while challenging the national authorities' action before the competent national court, which may then refer questions on the validity of the

30.041

---

[100] Statute of the Court of Justice, Article 23.
[101] 66/80, *International Chemical Corporation*, 1981, paras 13–14.
[102] C-228/92, *Roquette Frères*, 1994, para. 17.
[103] e.g. C-441/05, *Roquette Frères*, 2007, para. 60.

Union measure to the Court of Justice for a preliminary ruling on the basis of Article 267 TFEU.[104]

30.042 **Potential gaps in the system.** Generally speaking, this system provides adequate protection against unlawful acts emanating from Union institutions. Nevertheless, legal doctrine has pointed to gaps in the system, in that individuals who do not meet the strict admissibility requirements of Article 263 TFEU may not always be able to challenge a Union act that affects their legal position, or may do so only in circumstances where optimal legal protection is not provided.[105] For example, before the amendment of the conditions of admissibility by the Treaty of Lisbon, the system outlined above provided judicial protection against a Union act of general application which was not to be implemented by acts of the institutions, only in limited circumstances. The Court was only able to review the validity of such an act, if the individual was able to provoke a reference for a preliminary ruling on the validity of this act in proceedings before the national court.. In order to find him or herself in this situation, an individual sometimes had to breach national rules that implement the Union measure, only to invoke the invalidity of that measure in the proceedings brought against him or her by a national authority. In the case of a Union measure of general application which is immediately enforceable and does not require national implementation, it was even possible that there was no national means of redress available to trigger a preliminary ruling on validity. The Lisbon Treaty has, in any case, broadened the judicial protection of individuals against Union acts that can be considered as regulatory acts and which directly affect them. But in all cases where the judicial protection of individuals is hinging on a preliminary ruling on validity, there is still the disadvantage that, as a party to national proceedings, that individual cannot compel the competent court to refer a question for a preliminary ruling and, if that court refuses to refer a question, does not have the possibility of having the legality of the Union measure at issue reviewed. In such a case, the Union's system of legal protection does not deploy its full potential, which may trigger the relevant Member State's liability under Union law as well as, as far as respect for fundamental rights is concerned, under the European Convention of Human Rights (see para. 25.014, *supra*).

30.043 **Access to the Union Courts.** In order to meet these concerns to some extent, it has been suggested in the past that the conditions under which individuals can bring an action for annulment in the Union Courts should be interpreted less strictly. In the *UPA* case, for example, following an action brought by a farmers' organization against a Council Regulation amending the common organization of the olive oil market, Advocate-General Jacobs concluded that an individual should be deemed to be individually concerned by a Union act where, 'by reason of his particular circumstances, the measure has, or is liable to have, a substantial adverse effect on his interests'.[106] In the *Jégo-Quéré* case, the then Court of First Instance (now the General Court) found—in an action brought by a French fishing company against a Commission regulation prohibiting certain towed nets—that this was the case where a provision of a Union act of general application 'affects the applicant's legal position in a manner which is both definite and immediate, by restricting his rights or by

---

[104] 294/83, *European Parliament v Les Verts*, para. 23.
[105] See, e.g., Corthaut and Vanneste, 'Waves between Strasbourg and Luxembourg—The Right of Access to a Court to Contest the Validity of Legislative or Administrative Measures' (2006) YEL 475–514.
[106] C-50/00, *Unión de Pequeños Agricultores v Council*, AG Jacobs Opinion, 2002, point 60.

imposing obligations on him'.[107] However, the Court of Justice did not follow these positions in order to avoid the condition of 'individual' concern enshrined in Article 263 TFEU becoming a dead letter.[108] As already indicated, the Lisbon Treaty has partially addressed the concerns by dropping the condition of being 'individually' concerned for actions brought against non-legislative acts of general application—regulatory acts—which do not entail further implementing measures.

Access to national courts. In the *UPA* judgment, the Court of Justice did, however, state that Member States must provide for a system of legal remedies and procedures capable of ensuring respect for the right to effective judicial protection. This judgment is echoed in the rule introduced by the Lisbon Treaty that Member States must provide the necessary legal remedies to ensure effective judicial protection in the fields covered by Union law (Article 19(1), second subpara. TEU). To that end, national courts must, as far as possible, interpret and apply national procedural rules in a way that enables natural and legal personsto challenge before the courts the legality of any national measure relative to the application to them a Union act of general application, by raising the invalidity of that Union act.[109] In order to ensure effective judicial protection, it is not sufficient for a national legal system to provide for a legal remedy which presupposes that, with a view to being able to ask a court to refer a preliminary question on validity, an individual must be subject to administrative or criminal proceedings and to the penalties resulting therefrom.[110]

30.044

Access to courts in CFSP. Although the Union succeeded to the former Community as a 'community governed by the rule of law', the Treaties do not guarantee access to justice in CFSP matters.[111] In the framework of the CFSP, the Court of Justice only has jurisdiction—in addition to the supervision stemming from Article 40 TEU—to hear actions for annulment brought by individuals against Council decisions imposing restrictive measures on natural or legal persons (see para. 30.013, *supra*). In the *Rosneft* judgment, the Court referred to the principles of the rule of law and of effective judicial protection (Article 47 Charter) in order to conclude that, throughout the entire system of judicial remedies and procedures of the Union, it must be possible not only to bring an action for annulment of such CFSP decisions but also, in the context of an action brought in a national court, to call into question the legality of such CFSP decisions in order to induce that court to refer a preliminary question on their validity to the Court of Justice.[112] Furthermore, the Court held that it has jurisdiction to rule on an action for damages brought against the Union in respect of restrictive measures contained in CFSP decisions.[113]

30.045

---

[107] T-177/01, *Jégo-Quéré v Commission*, 2002, para. 51.
[108] C-50/00, *Unión de Pequeños Agricultores v Council*, 2002, para. 44; C-263/02 P, *Commission v Jégo-Quéré*, 2004 (annulment of judgment of the Court of First Instance).
[109] C-50/00, *Unión de Pequeños Agricultores v Council*, 2002, paras 41–2.
[110] See the judgments in C-432/05, *Unibet*, 2007, para. 64 and C-583/11 P, *Inuit Tapiriit Kanatami v European Parliament and Council*, 2013, para. 104, which make clear that having to break the law first and thus having to risk a sanction before the legality of an act can be challenged does not constitute effective judicial protection.
[111] Opinion 2/13, *Accession of the European Union to the European Convention for the Protection of Human Rights and Fundamental Freedoms*, 2014, paras 249–57.
[112] C-72/15, *Rosneft*, 2017, paras 66–77.
[113] C-134/19 P, *Bank Refah Kargaran v Council*, 2020, paras 23–52.

The Authors

Koen Lenaerts
Koen Lenaerts is President of the Court of Justice of the European Union (since October 2015); Professor of European law (part time) at KU Leuven (since 1983). He obtained his law degrees at KU Leuven (lic. iuris, PhD) and Harvard University (LLM, Master in Public Administration). He has been Visiting Professor at Harvard Law School (1989); Legal Secretary (*référendaire*) at the Court of Justice (1984–1985); Professor at the College of Europe, Bruges (1984–1989); member of the Brussels Bar (1986–1989); Judge at the Court of First Instance of the European Communities (1989–2003); Judge at the Court of Justice (since 2003); Vice-President of the Court of Justice (2012–2015).

Piet Van Nuffel
Piet Van Nuffel is a Senior Expert at the Legal Service of the European Commission (since 2009); Professor of European law (part time) at KU Leuven (since 2008). He obtained his law degrees at KU Leuven (lic. juris, PhD) and Harvard Law School (LLM). He has been Visiting Professor at the College of Europe, Natolin (2004–2015); Legal Secretary (*référendaire*) at the Court of First Instance of the European Communities (1999–2001); Administrator in DG Competition of the European Commission (2001–2003); Legal Secretary at the Court of Justice (2003–2009); member of the Cabinet of Marianne Thyssen, Commissioner for Employment, Social Affairs, Skills and Labour Mobility (2016–2019).

The Editor

Tim Corthaut
Tim Corthaut is Auditor at the Belgian Council of State (since 2011); Associate Professor of Public Law (part time) at Vrije Universiteit Brussel (VUB) (since 2014) and Visiting Professor of European Law at Universität Wien (since 2019). He obtained his law degrees at KU Leuven (lic. juris, PhD) and Harvard Law School (LLM). He has been Visiting Professor of European Law at KU Leuven (2015–2018).

Index

For the benefit of digital users, indexed terms that span two pages (e.g., 52–53) may, on occasion, appear on only one of those pages.

abuse of dominant position 9.017, 9.019
abuse of law 25.024
access to documents right 14.030–14.031, 25.026
accession of EU to ECHR 3.007, 5.004, 21.002, 21.011, 25.013, 25.015–25.016
accession to EU 4.009, 11.008
   accession treaties (and acts of accession) 4.013, 11.012, 24.002, 24.003, 24.007
   association agreements with candidates 10.017
   conditions 4.010–4.011
   EU law application to accession states 11.003
      international agreements 28.004
   European Parliament, consent requirement 12.004
   Member States' approval requirement 15.003
   pending applications 4.014
   pre-existing international obligations 26.008–26.011
   procedure 4.012–4.013
   waves of EU enlargement 4.001–4.008
   see also Member States
ACP (African, Caribbean, Pacific)-EC Partnership Agreement 2000 2.010, 10.019, 11.007
acquis communautaire **term** 4.011, 28.018; *see also* EU law
acquisitions, control of 9.018
acte éclairé **and** *acte clair* **doctrines** 29.019
actions for annulment 12.058, 13.006, 13.009, 27.011, 29.022, 30.002–30.003
   applicants 30.006
      European Parliament 12.009, 16.010, 30.006
      natural or legal persons 13.006, 27.013, 30.007–30.011, 30.041–30.043
   defendants 18.024, 30.004–30.005
   effects of annulment 30.017
   grounds for annulment 30.015
      fundamental rights infringement 25.008, 26.002, 26.015
      incorrect legal basis 5.013, 5.015, 5.020
      subsidiarity principle infringement 5.029, 5.033, 15.010
   plea of illegality following 30.025, 30.033
   procedure 30.026–30.030
   reviewable acts 30.012
      CFSP acts 30.013
      international agreements, acts concluding 26.006
      PJCC acts 8.003, 13.011, 30.014
      regulatory acts 30.011
   time-limits for 30.016
actions for damages 13.006, 30.002, 30.021–30.024

actions for failure to act 12.009, 12.058, 13.006, 13.009, 17.005, 30.002, 30.018–30.020
administration of EU law:
   access to documents right 14.030–14.031, 25.026
   administrative cooperation measures 9.065
   civil servants and officials, *see* civil servants and officials
   due process rights 25.008, 25.018, 25.022, 25.025
   good administration right 25.022, 25.023
   maladministration
      European Ombudsman 6.022, 12.008, 13.039–13.041, 20.008
      European Parliamentary inquiries into 12.010
   publication and notification of decisions 25.026, 27.008, 27.040
advertising:
   consumer protection 9.056
   cross-border 7.029, 7.043, 7.085, 7.088, 7.089
   tobacco advertising 5.013, 7.113
advisory bodies:
   Committee of the Regions 5.033, 9.009, 9.047, 12.039, 13.033–13.035, 15.016, 17.045, 20.008
   consultative bodies 13.036
   Economic and Social Committee 9.009, 9.047, 12.039, 13.030–13.032, 17.043, 17.045, 20.008
   staff privileges and immunities 14.007
   see also executive bodies
Advocates General and judges at Court of Justice 1.054, 13.013–13.016, 13.018, 28.002
African, Caribbean, Pacific (ACP)-EC Partnership Agreement 2000 2.010, 10.019, 11.007
AFSJ (area of freedom, security and justice) 5.006, 8.001
   Court of Justice jurisdiction to review acts 13.011
   Denmark and Ireland, special status 8.027–8.028, 22.002–22.004
   immigration and asylum policy, *see* immigration and asylum policy
   judicial cooperation in civil matters 1.037, 1.038, 8.005, 8.014–8.018, 22.007
   Lisbon Treaty reforms 2.003, 8.005, 8.007
   origin of initiative 1.037–1.038, 7.010
   PJCC, *see* PJCC (police and judicial cooperation in criminal matters)
   pre-Lisbon era 1.047, 1.048, 1.049, 1.051, 8.002–8.004
age discrimination prohibition 5.060, 27.033

agencies 13.044–13.046
　AFSJ field 8.007, 13.046
　CFSP field 10.032, 13.046
　decision-making by, *see* decision-making
　executive agencies 13.047
　implementation of EU law 18.022–18.025
　language rules 14.029
　PJCC field
　　Eurojust 8.023, 13.045, 15.011, 18.025
　　Europol 8.025–8.026, 13.045, 15.011, 18.025
　public health field 9.055, 13.046
　seats 13.046, 14.021
　see also executive bodies
Agreement on the European Economic Area 1992 4.005
agricultural policy 7.004, 9.003–9.007, 10.002, 25.024
Åland Islands 11.007
'alarm bell' procedures 8.019, 17.033, 19.002
amendment of Treaties, *see* Treaties, amendment
Amsterdam Treaty 1997 1.017, 1.018, 1.038, 1.039, 1.044, 1.050, 24.005
　amendments to Treaties 1.051, 4.020, 7.010, 8.002–8.004, 17.010
　closer cooperation mechanisms 1.052
　free movement of persons principle 7.003, 8.002
anthem of EU 1.060, 2.004, 6.003, 14.001
anti-competitive agreements 9.014
anti-dumping measures 10.007, 26.005
application of EU law by national courts 29.008–29.013
area of freedom, security and justice, *see* AFSJ (area of freedom, security and justice)
arrest warrants, European 5.005, 8.020, 25.012
asset freezing measures 7.107, 10.031
association policies 10.012
　association agreements 4.003, 8.013, 10.014–10.020, 13.043, 21.011, 26.003
　Cotonou Agreement 2000 2.010, 10.019, 11.007
　EEA Agreement 1992 4.005, 10.020
　European Neighbourhood Policy 10.018, 10.025
　overseas countries and territories 10.013, 11.006, 11.007, 11.008
asylum policy 8.008–8.011, 25.014; *see also* immigration and asylum policy
Austria, parliamentary influence on legislative acts 15.008

banking union 9.042
Barnier, Michel 4.016
Belgium:
　Benelux Union 1.004, 1.039, 26.008, 29.015
　Brussels, seats of institutions and executive bodies in 12.018, 12.030, 12.043, 12.055, 12.071, 13.032, 13.035, 13.042, 14.019–14.020
　Constitutional Court 23.030, 29.018
　primacy of EU law, incorporation in legal system 23.025, 23.027, 23.030
　regional authorities, status of 5.032, 12.041, 15.003, 15.010, 18.005
　Supreme Court 23.025, 29.018, 23.020

belief discrimination prohibition 5.060
benefits, *see* social assistance
Benelux Union 1.004, 1.039, 26.008, 29.015
better regulation programme 17.015
bilateral trade and cooperation agreements 10.008, 21.011, 26.003
block exemptions from competition law 9.016, 9.021, 9.024
bodies, *see* executive bodies
Bologna process 9.050
border checks and visa policy 8.007, 11.006
Brasserie du Pêcheur and Factortame IV **rulings (C-46/93 and C-48/93)** 23.020–23.021, 29.012
Brexit 2.004, 4.016–4.017, 11.007
Brussels Convention on jurisdiction and the enforcement of judgments in civil and commercial matters 1968 1.037, 8.015, 28.018
Brussels I Regulation, Recast (1215/2012/EU) 8.015
Brussels II Convention on jurisdiction and the recognition and enforcement of judgments in matrimonial matters 1998 1.038, 8.015
Brussels, seats of institutions and executive bodies in 12.018, 12.030, 12.043, 12.055, 12.071, 13.032, 13.035, 13.042, 14.019–14.020
Brussels Treaty 1948 1.004, 1.012
budget of EU 1.048, 12.005, 14.010
　adoption procedure 12.060, 20.001–20.006
　audit of 13.025, 20.010–20.011
　fraud control 20.013
　implementation 12.061, 20.007–20.009, 20.012
　Member States
　　budgetary contributions 14.015
　　sincere cooperation duty 5.050, 20.008
　scope 14.011
　structure 14.012
　　expenditure 14.017–14.018
　　revenue 14.013–14.016
Bulgaria, accession to EU 4.007
Bundesverfassungsgericht (German Constitutional Court) 25.003
　Lisbon Treaty judgment 2.002, 15.003, 15.008, 17.050, 23.029
　proportionality test 5.039, 29.005
　Recht auf Vergessen I & II cases 23.029, 25.012
　Solange cases 23.029
Bureau of the European Parliament 12.020

candidates for EU accession 4.010, 4.014, 10.017
capital, free movement of, *see* free movement of capital and payments
case law of Court of Justice 28.006, 29.037–29.038
　EFTA states' alignment with 10.020
Cassis de Dijon **rule ('reasonable' restraints of trade)** 7.037–7.042
CFSP (common foreign and security policy) 1.032
　actors 10.028
　　agencies 10.032, 13.046
　　Commission 12.057, 12.059, 19.003, 19.006

Council 10.028, 12.036, 12.038, 19.002, 19.005
European Council 12.023, 12.024, 19.002, 27.044
European Parliament 12.004, 19.004, 19.006
High Representative, *see* High Representative of the Union for Foreign Affairs and Security Policy
Political and Security Committee 12.053, 12.054, 18.025, 19.003, 19.006, 19.007
Court of Justice's jurisdiction excluded 1.049, 2.008, 10.026, 12.009, 13.010, 19.006, 25.008, 26.006, 30.045
exceptions 12.009, 13.012, 25.008, 30.013, 30.036, 30.045
infringement proceedings unavailable 29.001, 29.023, 29.039
CSDP (common security and defence policy) 2.004, 3.007, 5.025, 10.032–10.034, 12.025, 19.007
decision-making 19.001, 27.004
decision types 10.028–10.031
on EU's participation in international organizations 10.029
implementation of decisions 12.038, 19.005–19.006
initiative and preparatory tasks 19.003
on military operations 19.007
pre-Lisbon era 28.007–28.013, 28.016–28.017
voting rules 3.008, 19.002
enhanced cooperation mechanisms 1.054, 10.035, 22.007, 22.010, 22.012
expenditure, budgetary arrangements 14.011
fundamental rights protection duty 25.008, 25.009
implementing acts in CFSP field 18.012
international agreements in CFSP field 21.003
language rules 14.028
legal basis for acts under 5.014, 10.002
Lisbon Treaty reforms 2.003, 2.008, 10.026
personal data processing in CFSP field 9.002
pre-Lisbon era 1.046, 1.048, 1.051, 10.026
pre-Lisbon acts still in force 28.007–28.013, 28.016–28.017
primacy of EU law, CFSP application 23.009
scope 10.027
as shared competence 5.025
see also external action
Channel Islands 11.007
Charter of Fundamental Rights of the European Union 1.001, 1.060, 5.004, 25.006
adoption of 1.055, 25.005–25.006
citizenship rights, *see* citizenship of EU
derogations for Poland and UK 2.001, 2.004, 25.007
direct effect 23.033, 25.010
equal treatment principle, *see* equal treatment principle
implementation of EU law in compliance with 25.009, 25.012
limitations to application 25.012, 25.020
rights enshrined in 25.017–25.018

status in EU constitutional order 2.004, 23.004, 23.011, 25.001–25.002, 25.007
see also fundamental rights
Charter of Fundamental Social Rights of Workers 1989 9.046
checks and balances system 16.011
children:
family reunification rights 6.014, 6.017
nationality-based discrimination prohibition 7.060
Churchill, Winston 1.004
citizenship of EU 6.001, 6.005
amendments to citizenship rights 3.007
legislative proposals by citizens 16.004, 17.013
Member State nationality, link to 6.006, 7.048
origin of EU citizenship 6.002–6.004
rights associated with 6.007, 25.018
access to documents 14.030–14.031, 25.026
diplomatic or consular protection 6.022
European Ombudsman, right of application to 6.022, 13.039–13.041
European Parliament, right to petition 6.022, 12.011, 16.004
free movement and residence, *see* free movement of persons
language rights, *see* language rights of EU citizens
political rights 6.021, 12.015
see also nationality-based discrimination prohibition
civil protection measures 9.064
civil servants and officials:
of EU
bodies supporting institutions 13.043
disputes, Court of Justice jurisdiction 13.002, 13.006, 14.023
privileges and immunities 5.050, 14.009
Staff Regulations 5.047, 5.060, 14.022
status 14.023
of Member States 7.068, 9.065, 15.004
CJEU, *see* Court of Justice of the European Union
climate change 9.061–9.062, 26.003
closer cooperation, *see* enhanced cooperation mechanisms
co-decision procedure, *see* ordinary legislative procedure
Cohesion Fund 9.057, 9.058
collective action by trade unions 9.047
collective agreements 28.005
comitology procedures, *see* implementing acts, comitology procedures
commercial policy, *see* common commercial policy
Commission, *see* European Commission
Committee of Permanent Representatives (Coreper) 12.044, 12.050–12.054, 17.017
Committee of the Regions 5.033, 9.009, 9.047, 12.039, 13.033–13.035, 15.016, 17.045, 20.008
common agricultural policy 7.004, 9.003–9.007, 10.002, 25.024

816 INDEX

common asylum policy 8.008–8.011, 25.014; see also immigration and asylum policy
common commercial policy:
  CFSP sanctions implementation under 10.031
  as EU exclusive competence 5.023, 10.005
  foreign direct investment 10.004, 10.005, 10.007
  trade and cooperation agreements 10.008–10.009, 21.011, 26.003
  trade in goods
    Common Customs Tariff 7.024–7.025, 10.003, 10.010
    import and export regime 10.006, 10.029
    protective measures 10.007
  trade in services and intellectual property 10.004
  World Trade Organization participation 10.009–10.011, 14.005, 26.001, 26.003, 26.005
Common Customs Tariff for goods from third countries 7.024–7.025, 10.003, 10.010
common fisheries policy 5.023, 5.024, 7.004, 9.008, 11.009
common foreign and security policy, see CFSP (common foreign and security policy)
common market, see internal market
common positions under CFSP and PJCC 28.012
common security and defence policy (CSDP) 2.004, 3.007, 5.025, 10.032–10.034, 12.025, 19.007
common transport policy 7.004, 9.009–9.011
Community law, see EU law
Community method 1.018, 2.010
companies, freedom of establishment, see freedom of establishment
competences system:
  conferral principle 5.009–5.010, 5.016, 5.017, 16.003
  exclusive competences 5.022–5.024, 5.030
    treaty-making 5.023, 10.002, 10.005, 10.039
  external action, competences for 10.002
  functional approach 5.001
  implied competence 5.019
  legal basis, see legal basis for EU acts
  Lisbon Treaty reforms 2.004, 2.010
  shared competences 5.022, 5.025–5.026, 23.012
    mixed agreements 21.013–21.015, 26.006
  sincere cooperation duty towards 5.049
  subsidiarity principle, see subsidiarity principle
  supplementary competences
    to achieve EU objectives (under flexibility clause (TFEU Art. 352)) 5.017, 5.020–5.021, 5.032, 7.108, 15.007, 15.008, 17.037
    to support, coordinate, or supplement Member State acts 5.022, 5.027, 9.059
competition law and policy 9.012
  abuse of dominant position 9.017, 9.019
  anti-competitive agreements 9.014
  competitiveness of industry, policies to support 9.059
  enforcement
    by Commission 9.015, 9.016, 12.058
    by national courts and competition authorities 9.015, 9.024, 9.026, 29.013
  as EU exclusive competence 5.023
  as EU objective 2.004, 5.006, 5.008, 7.005
  merger control 9.018
  public undertakings 9.019–9.020
  sports sector application 9.051
  state aid, see state aid
  transport sector application 9.009
  'undertaking' concept 9.013
concentrations, control of 9.018
Conciliation Committee:
  budgetary role 20.001, 20.002–20.003
  ordinary legislative procedure role 12.044, 17.029, 17.031
Conference on the Future of Europe 2.011
conferral of competences principle 5.009–5.010, 5.016, 5.017, 16.003; see also competences system
Congress of Europe (1948) 1.005
constitution of EU 1.028
  constitutional principles 25.022
  constitutional symbols 1.060, 2.004, 6.003, 14.002
  Constitutional Treaty (draft), see Treaty establishing a Constitution for Europe (draft)
  constitutional values 4.010, 4.020, 5.002–5.005, 10.001, 25.002, 26.012
  direct effect of EU law, see direct effect of EU law
  Lisbon Treaty, constitutional innovations 2.004
  primacy of EU law, see primacy of EU law
  primary EU law 23.003–23.004, 24.001–24.003; see also Charter of Fundamental Rights of the European Union; Treaties
  see also EU as international organization
constitutional acts by Council or European Council 24.009
Constitutional Courts 2.002, 23.028–23.030, 25.003, 29.016
  Belgium 23.030, 29.018
  Court of Justice of the European Union as 1.028, 5.013
  effective protection of EU law duty, see national courts, effective protection of EU law duty
  Germany, see Bundesverfassungsgericht (German Constitutional Court)
  Italy 23.015, 23.027
constitutional law of Member States 1.028, 23.011, 23.015, 23.026, 23.028–23.030
consular or diplomatic protection rights of EU citizens 6.022
consumer policy 9.056, 29.013
Convention on the Future of Europe 1.057
cooperation agreements 10.008, 10.018, 21.011, 26.003
Copenhagen criteria for EU accession 4.010
Coreper (Committee of Permanent Representatives) 12.044, 12.050–12.054, 17.017
Costa v ENEL (6/64) 1.025, 1.027, 23.010–23.011, 23.017
Cotonou Agreement 2000 2.010, 10.019, 11.007

INDEX 817

Council of Europe 1.006, 25.004
  ECHR, *see* European Convention on Human
    Rights 1950
  police and judicial cooperation agreements 1.037
Council of the European Union 1.022, 12.034–12.035
  accession of Member States, role respecting 4.012
  budgetary powers, *see* budget of EU
  configurations 12.040, 12.054
    Foreign Affairs Council 2.004, 12.040,
      12.042, 12.054
    General Affairs Council 12.027, 12.030, 12.040
  constitutional acts by 24.009
  Coreper (Committee of Permanent
    Representatives) 12.044, 12.050–
    12.054, 17.017
  economic policy coordination role 9.036, 9.039–
    9.040, 12.040
  enhanced cooperation, authorization for 22.010–22.011
  external action role 10.002, 12.040
    CFSP 10.028, 12.036, 12.038, 19.002, 19.005
    international agreements, negotiation
      and conclusion 12.036, 21.002–21.006,
      21.009–21.010
  implementing acts
    comitology procedures, *see* implementing acts,
      comitology procedures
    power to adopt 12.038, 18.012, 18.021
  interinstitutional relations 12.039
    Commission 12.043, 16.010
    Court of Auditors 12.039
    European Central Bank 12.039, 12.043, 17.045
    European Council 12.033, 12.040
    European Parliament 12.007, 12.017, 17.004,
      17.035–17.036, 17.039–17.042
    interinstitutional agreements 27.049–27.050
  language rules 14.028
  legislative powers, *see* legislative acts,
    Council powers
  Member States' decisions made within 28.003
  ministerial representatives at 12.041
  national parliamentary influence on ministers
    in 15.008–15.009, 17.006, 17.048
  non-legislative procedures, role in 17.038–17.042
  pre-Lisbon powers 1.048
  presidency of 2.005, 12.042
  publication of acts and decisions 27.008
  resolutions and conclusions 27.008, 27.044, 27.046
  Rules of Procedure 12.043
  Secretary-General 12.033, 12.055
  state aid proceedings, intervention in 9.027
  Treaty amendment proposals
    consultation duties 3.003
    power to adopt under simplified
      procedures 3.007, 3.008
  voting in 12.045–12.046, 17.007–17.008,
    17.033, 17.049
    qualified majority voting, *see* qualified majority
      voting in Council
  see also institutions

countervailing duties 10.007
Court of Auditors 1.022, 13.024, 20.011
  appointments to 12.008, 12.039, 13.026
  independence 13.027
  language rules 14.028
  powers 13.025
  Rules of Procedure 13.028
  staff 13.029
  see also institutions
Court of Justice of the European
    Union 1.022, 13.002
  appeals against General Court decisions 13.009
  case law 28.006, 29.037–29.038
    EFTA states' alignment with 10.020
  as constitutional court 1.028, 5.013
  direct actions to
    for annulment, *see* actions for annulment
    for damages 13.006, 30.002, 30.021–30.024
    for failure to act 12.009, 12.058, 13.006, 13.009,
      17.005, 30.002, 30.018–30.020
    plea of illegality 30.025, 30.033
    procedure 30.026–30.030
  domestic law interpretation and application
    by 23.007, 29.020–29.021
  enforcement of Court's judgments and
    orders 27.010
  European Stability Mechanism role 2.010
  failure to fulfil obligations claims, *see* infringement
    proceedings against Member States
  fundamental rights review 25.001, 25.003–25.004,
    25.008, 25.009, 25.010–25.011, 25.015
  infringement proceedings, *see* infringement
    proceedings against Member States
  international agreements, opinions on 21.016–
    21.017, 25.008, 26.006
  international law application by 25.004, 26.005,
    26.007, 26.012–26.013, 26.016
  judges and Advocates General 1.054, 13.013–
    13.016, 13.018, 28.002
  jurisdiction, *see* jurisdiction of Court of Justice
  language rules 14.027, 29.030, 29.034
  legislative acts, right of initiative 17.012
  preliminary references to, *see* preliminary references
    to Court of Justice
  Rules of Procedure 12.039, 13.017
  seat 13.018, 14.019
  see also institutions
courts of Member States, *see* national courts
COVID-19 pandemic 9.036, 14.015
criminal matters, police and judicial cooperation,
    see PJCC (police and judicial cooperation in
    criminal matters)
Croatia, accession to EU 4.008, 10.017
CSDP (common security and defence
    policy) 2.004, 3.007, 5.025, 10.032–10.034,
    12.025, 19.007
cultural policy 9.053–9.054
  language rights, *see* language rights of EU citizens
customary international law 26.013

customs union 7.003, 7.015, 10.010
  Common Customs Tariff for goods from third countries 7.024–7.025, 10.003, 10.010
  customs duties and charges having equivalent effect, prohibition of 7.016–7.017
  as EU exclusive competence 5.023
  permissible charges 7.018–7.023
  UK's withdrawal from 4.016, 4.018
  see also free movement of goods
Cyprus:
  accession to EU 4.006, 10.017
  EU law application in 11.006, 11.008
  sovereign debt crisis 9.036
Czech Republic, Charter derogations for 2.002

damages actions against EU 13.006, 30.002, 30.021–30.024
Dassonville **ruling (8/74)** 7.011, 7.028–7.029, 7.031, 7.043, 7.088
data protection policy 9.002, 13.043, 13.044
de Gaulle, Charles 1.030, 4.002
decentralised authorities 15.014–15.017, 18.005, 29.041
  in Belgium 5.032, 12.041, 15.003, 15.010, 18.005
decision-making:
  budgetary decisions, *see* budget of EU
  CFSP decision-making, *see* CFSP (common foreign and security policy), decision-making
  decisions of organs set up by international agreements 26.004
  democratic values 17.046–17.050
    European Parliament's role, *see* European Parliament
    national parliamentary scrutiny of legislative acts 2.004, 5.031–5.032, 15.005–15.011, 17.006, 17.016, 17.048
  incentive measures 5.012, 9.049, 9.050, 9.053, 9.055, 27.044–27.045
  institutional practice 27.048
  interinstitutional agreements 23.005, 27.049–27.050
  international agreements, *see* international agreements concluded by EU
  legislative acts, *see* legislative acts; secondary EU law
  legislative procedures, *see* ordinary legislative procedure; special legislative procedures
  Member States' decisions on EU affairs 28.002–28.003
    interstate conventions and agreements 28.004, 28.018–28.020
  non-legislative measures 27.002, 27.004–27.005
  non-legislative procedures 17.038
    dialogue and consultation duties 17.045
    interinstitutional relations 17.039–17.042
    social partners, role in 17.043–17.044
  publication and notification duty 25.026, 27.008, 27.040
  recommendations and opinions, *see* recommendations and opinions
  resolutions and conclusions 27.008, 27.044, 27.046
  restricted to particular Member States 22.001, 22.006
  AFSJ, special status of Denmark and Ireland 8.027–8.028, 22.002–22.004
  enhanced cooperation, *see* enhanced cooperation mechanisms
  Eurozone states, *see* Eurozone
  statements of reasons 27.007
  unilateral declarations 24.008, 27.044–27.045, 27.047
decisions (secondary law instruments) 27.037–27.041
  CFSP decisions, *see* CFSP (common foreign and security policy), decision-making
declarations annexed to Treaties 24.008
declarations, unilateral 24.008, 27.044–27.045, 27.047
defence and security policy 2.004, 3.007, 5.025, 10.032–10.034, 12.025
defence cooperation proposals 1.011
delegated acts 12.061, 18.008, 18.010, 18.021
  actions to annul 30.011
  implementing acts distinguished 18.011, 27.004–27.005
  restrictions on use 18.009
  see also implementing acts; secondary EU law
Delors, Jacques 9.031
democracy 5.004, 16.006
  accession to EU, democracy conditionality 4.010
  elections
    to European Parliament 3.007, 6.021, 12.012, 12.014
    political rights of EU citizens 6.021, 12.015
  EU decision-making, democratic values 17.046–17.050
    European Parliament's role, *see* European Parliament
    national parliamentary scrutiny of legislative acts 2.004, 5.031–5.032, 15.005–15.011, 17.006, 17.016, 17.048
  serious and persistent breach of Treaties procedure 4.019–4.021, 5.003
Denmark:
  accession to EU 4.002
  AFSJ, special status 8.027, 22.002, 22.004
  CSDP, non-participation 10.034, 14.011, 19.007
  economic and monetary union, special status 9.032, 9.033, 9.035, 22.005
  Faroe Islands 11.007
  Greenland 11.007
  judicial cooperation in civil matters, special status 8.015
  parliamentary influence on legislative acts 15.008
  Schengen *acquis*, special status 1.052, 8.004, 8.006, 8.027, 22.004
derogations from EU law 4.011, 5.041, 5.047, 7.115
  Charter derogations for Poland and UK 2.001, 2.004, 25.007

security-based exceptions to Treaty
    obligations 11.011
transitional derogations from Treaties 11.012
development cooperation policy:
    Cotonou Agreement 2000 2.010, 10.019, 11.007
    European Development Fund 10.013, 10.019
    humanitarian aid 10.023, 10.030
    instruments 10.022
    sustainable development 9.061, 10.021
devolved authorities, *see* decentralised authorities
diplomas, mutual recognition of, *see* professional
    qualifications recognition
diplomatic or consular protection rights of EU
    citizens 6.022
direct actions to Court of Justice:
    for annulment, *see* actions for annulment
    for damages 13.006, 30.002, 30.021–30.024
    for failure to act 12.009, 12.058, 13.006, 13.009,
        17.005, 30.002, 30.018–30.020
    plea of illegality 30.025, 30.033
    procedure 30.026–30.030
direct and individual concern 13.006, 27.013,
    30.007–30.010, 30.019, 30.041–30.043
direct applicability 23.035, 27.015–27.016
direct discrimination 5.062
direct effect of EU law 5.046, 16.002, 23.008
    conditions for 23.032
    Court of Justice determinations on 28.006
    decisions of organs set up by international
        agreements 26.004
    direct applicability distinguished 23.035, 27.016
    EU objectives not directly effective 5.008
    Francovich liability 18.004, 23.019–23.024, 27.034–
        27.036, 29.012
    international agreements concluded by EU 26.003
    primacy of EU law, relationship with 5.049, 23.014
    of primary law 23.033, 25.010
    of secondary law 23.034, 27.016, 27.022–
        27.027, 27.041
    Van Gend & Loos ruling (26/62) 1.025–1.026,
        18.004, 23.025, 23.031, 29.006
    see also primacy of EU law
Directives 27.017
    implementation 27.018
        legal certainty, requirements of 27.019
        Member State duties during transposition
            period 27.021
        time-limits for 27.020, 27.023
    unimplemented or incorrectly implemented
        Directives 27.028
        direct effect 27.022–27.027
        domestic law interpretation in conformity
            with 27.029–27.031
        duty to set aside conflicting laws 27.032–27.033
        fines for 29.052–29.053
        Francovich liability for 18.004, 23.019–23.024,
            27.034–27.036, 29.012
    see also implementation of EU law;
        secondary EU law

disability discrimination prohibition 5.060
disasters:
    civil protection measures 9.064
    COVID-19 pandemic 9.036, 14.015
    financial assistance to Member States 9.036, 9.057
    solidarity clause of TFEU 9.066
    third countries, humanitarian aid 10.023, 10.030
discharge of EU budget 20.012
discrimination prohibition, *see* equal treatment
    principle
domestic law of Member States:
    competition law application 9.012
    constitutional provisions 1.028, 23.011, 23.015,
        23.026, 23.028–23.030
    Court of Justice interpretation and application
        of 23.007, 29.020–29.021
    harmonization of, *see* harmonization of
        national laws
    implementing EU law, *see* implementation
        of EU law
    mutual recognition of 7.111
    national court applications, *see* national courts
    nationality-based discrimination
        prohibition 5.056, 5.064
    precedence of international agreements concluded
        by EU 26.002
    primacy of EU law over, *see* primacy of EU law
    proportionality principle protecting 5.041
    public interest/policy objectives, *see* public interest/
        policy restrictions
    unimplemented EU law, conflicts with 27.021,
        27.029–27.033
dominant market position, abuse of 9.017, 9.019
driving licence, EU 6.003, 14.001
drug trafficking control 1.047, 7.106, 8.021
Dublin Convention 1990 (and Dublin regime) 1.038,
    8.010, 25.014
due process rights 25.008, 25.018, 25.022, 25.025
duration of Treaties 11.004–11.005

EAEC (European Atomic Energy
    Community) 1.002, 1.015, 1.017, 1.059, 2.003,
    2.006, 10.002, 24.004
Eastern enlargement 4.006–4.007, 10.017
Eastern Partnership 10.018, 10.025
EC (European Communities) 1.002, 1.041
ECB, *see* European Central Bank
ECHR, *see* European Convention on Human
    Rights 1950
ECOFIN (Economic and Financial Affairs
    Council) 12.040, 22.005
economic and monetary union 9.029
    accession to EU, market economy condition 4.010
    agencies 13.046
    banking union policies 9.042
    Denmark, special status 9.032, 9.033, 9.035, 22.005
    development
        origin of initiative 1.034–1.036, 1.045, 9.030
        three stages 9.031–9.033

820   INDEX

economic and monetary union (*cont.*)
  ECB, *see* European Central Bank
  ECOFIN (Economic and Financial Affairs
    Council) 12.040, 22.005
  economic policy coordination 9.036
  Fiscal Stability Treaty 2012 2.010, 9.041
  free movement of capital and payments, *see* free
    movement of capital and payments
  monetary policy coordination 9.043–9.044
  single currency 9.029, 9.031, 9.033, 9.045
    accession states, *see* Eurozone
    derogating states 9.034, 22.005
  stability and growth pact 9.038–9.040
Economic and Social Committee 9.009,
  9.047, 12.039, 13.030–13.032, 17.043,
  17.045, 20.008
economic, financial, and technical cooperation with
  third countries 10.024–10.025
economic sanctions 7.107, 10.029, 10.031, 25.014
  Kadi ruling (C-402/05 P and
    C-415/05 P) 26.002, 26.015
economic, social, and territorial cohesion
    policies 9.057
  trans-European networks 9.058, 10.037
economically inactive persons, free movement
    rights 6.010, 6.011, 6.015, 6.018, 7.079, 11.001
ECSC (European Coal and Steel Community) 1.002,
  1.008–1.011, 1.017, 3.009, 11.004
education policy 9.050
EEA Agreement 1992 4.005, 10.020
EEAS (European External Action Service) 12.062,
  13.042, 14.006, 19.005, 20.008
EEC (European Economic Community) 1.002,
  1.014, 1.016–1.018
effectiveness (*effet utile*) principle 5.049, 23.014,
  23.018, 29.006, 29.011
  direct effect of EU law, *see* direct effect of EU law
  national courts' effective protection duty, *see*
    national courts, effective protection of EU
    law duty
EFTA (European Free Trade Association) 1.019,
  4.005, 10.020
EGF (European Globalization Adjustment Fund for
  Displaced Workers) 9.057
ELA (European Labour Authority) 13.046
elections:
  to European Parliament 3.007, 6.021,
    12.012, 12.014
  political rights of EU citizens 6.021, 12.015
emergencies, *see* disasters
emissions trading scheme 9.062
employers' representatives:
  collective agreements 28.005
  implementation of EU law 18.006
  non-legislative procedures, role in 17.043–17.044
employment and social policy 9.046–9.049
  equal treatment of men and women, *see* gender-
    based discrimination prohibition
EMU, *see* economic and monetary union

energy policy 9.063
  liberalization of energy sector 9.020
  renewable energy, national measures restricting EU
    trade 7.041, 7.042
  trans-European networks 9.058, 10.037
enhanced cooperation mechanisms 1.054, 22.007
  authorization procedure 22.010–22.011
  CFSP mechanisms 1.054, 10.035, 22.007,
    22.010, 22.012
  Court of Justice supervision of 22.013
  judicial cooperation mechanisms 8.015, 8.016,
    8.024, 22.007
  participation requests 22.012
  restrictions on 5.023
  substantive and formal
    requirements 22.008–22.009
  unitary patent protection 7.109, 22.007
environmental policy:
  access to environmental information right 14.031
  climate change 9.061–9.062, 26.003
  marine biological resources conservation 5.023,
    5.024, 9.008
  national measures conflicting with EU law 23.014
  plastic packaging waste, uniform rate
    on 14.014, 14.015
  renewable energy, national measures restricting EU
    trade 7.041, 7.042
  sustainable development 9.061, 10.021
equal pay right 5.058, 5.063, 9.048
equal treatment principle 5.051, 6.001, 25.018
  age discrimination 5.060, 27.033
  disability discrimination 5.060
  discrimination concept 5.061
    direct and indirect forms 5.062–5.063
    reverse discrimination 5.064
  gender-based discrimination 5.058
    equal pay right 5.058, 5.063
    positive discrimination 5.059
  nationality-based discrimination, *see* nationality-
    based discrimination prohibition
  race discrimination 5.060
  religious discrimination 5.060
  scope 5.052
  sexual orientation discrimination 5.058,
    5.060, 6.014
  transgender persons 5.058
  uniform and full application of EU law duty 18.007
equivalence principle 5.049, 23.018, 29.010, 29.009
Erasmus programme 9.050
Estonia, parliamentary influence on legislative
    acts 15.008
EU as international organization 1.020
  budget, *see* budget of EU
  civil servants and officials, *see* civil servants and
    officials
  language rules, *see* language rights of EU citizens
  legal personality and capacity 1.025, 14.002–
    14.005, 30.022
    external representation 12.042, 12.062, 14.006

INDEX

privileges and immunities
  of EU civil servants 5.050, 14.009
  of institutions 5.047, 12.016, 14.007–14.008, 16.008
seats of institutions and executive bodies 12.018, 12.071, 13.018, 13.022, 13.046, 14.019–14.021, 16.008, 28.002
supranational character of EU law 1.020–1.028, 2.007
symbols of EU 1.060, 2.004, 6.003, 14.002

EU citizens, *see* citizenship of EU

EU law 23.001–23.002
  accession states, application to 11.003
  acquis communautaire term 4.011, 28.018
  administration of, *see* administration of EU law
  case law of Court of Justice 28.006, 29.037–29.038
    EFTA states' alignment with 10.020
  derogations, *see* derogations from EU law
  direct effect, *see* direct effect of EU law
  general principles of, *see* general principles of EU law
  harmonization measures, *see* harmonization of national laws
  implementation, *see* implementation of EU law
  interpretation and application of 29.005–29.013
  lex posterior and *lex specialis* doctrines 23.006
  Lisbon Treaty reforms 2.006–2.008, 17.002, 18.008, 23.002, 27.004–27.005, 28.007
  national courts' effective protection duty, *see* national courts, effective protection of EU law duty
  pre-Lisbon acts still in force 28.007–28.017
  primacy of, *see* primacy of EU law
  primary law, *see* primary EU law
  secondary law, *see* secondary EU law
  supranational character 1.020–1.028, 2.007
  see also decision-making; legislative acts

EU liability in damages 13.006, 30.002, 30.021–30.024

eu-LISA agency 8.007

EU Treaty, *see* Treaty on European Union (TEU)

Euratom (European Atomic Energy Community) 1.002, 1.015, 1.017, 1.059, 2.003, 2.006, 10.002

euro currency 9.029, 9.031, 9.033, 9.045
  accession states, *see* Eurozone
  derogating states 9.034, 22.005
  see also economic and monetary union

Euro-Mediterranean Partnership 10.018, 10.025

Euro Summit meetings 12.028, 22.005

Eurocorps 10.025

Eurojust 8.023, 13.045, 15.011, 18.025

Europe Day (9th May) 1.060, 2.004, 14.001

European Administrative School 13.043

European Agricultural Fund for Rural Development 9.057

European Anti-Fraud Office (OLAF) 12.008, 13.043, 16.008, 20.013

European arrest warrants 5.005, 8.020, 25.012

European Atomic Energy Community (Euratom or EAEC) 1.002, 1.015, 1.017, 1.059, 2.003, 2.006, 10.002, 24.004

European Banking Authority 9.042

European Central Bank 13.020
  establishment 9.032, 13.019
  euro banknote issuance 9.045
  and European System of Central Banks 9.043–9.044, 13.020
  expenditure, budgetary arrangements 14.011
  guidelines and instructions to national central banks 27.044–27.045
  interinstitutional relations
    Council 12.039, 12.043, 17.045
    European Council 12.025, 13.021, 13.022
    European Parliament 12.008, 13.021, 17.045
  legislative powers 17.004, 17.012
  'no bail-out' principle 9.036
  organization and operation 13.021–13.022, 22.005
  publication of acts and decisions 27.008
  Rules of Procedure 13.023
  seat 13.022, 14.021
  securities clearing regulation, no implied competence 5.019
  Single Supervisory and Single Resolution Mechanisms 9.042
  Treaty amendment proposals
    consultation on 3.003
    on ECB's powers 3.008
  see also institutions

European Coal and Steel Community (ECSC) 1.002, 1.008–1.011, 1.017, 3.009, 11.004

European Commission 1.022, 12.056–12.057
  accession of Member States, role respecting 4.012, 4.014
  budgetary powers, *see* budget of EU
  college of Commissioners 2.005, 12.006, 12.063
    appointment 12.064
    collective responsibility 12.070
    High Representative, *see* High Representative of the Union for Foreign Affairs and Security Policy
    independence 12.067
    retirement from 12.068
    term of office 12.066
  competition law and policy role
    antitrust enforcement 9.015, 9.016, 12.058
    merger control 9.018
    state aid control 9.024–9.026
  Directorates-General 12.071
  economic policy coordination role
    European Semester 9.039
    European Stability Mechanism 2.010, 9.037
  European Rule of Law mechanism 5.005
  external action role 10.002
    CFSP 12.057, 12.059, 19.003, 19.006
    external representation of EU 12.042, 12.062, 14.006
    international agreements, negotiation and conclusion 21.002–21.003, 21.007
  Funds for economic, social, and territorial cohesion 9.057, 13.043

822   INDEX

European Commission (*cont.*)
  guardian of Treaties role 12.058, 12.060, 18.004, 29.040
  infringement proceedings, *see* infringement proceedings against Member States
  interinstitutional relations
    Council 12.043, 16.010
    European Council 12.064
    European Parliament 12.005–12.006, 12.017, 12.064, 16.012, 17.016
    interinstitutional agreements 27.049–27.050
  legislative implementation by, *see* delegated acts; implementing acts
  legislative proposals 12.060, 16.012, 17.012, 17.014–17.018
    citizen proposals 16.004, 17.013
    Coreper deliberations on 12.050–12.054, 17.017
    institutional consultation on 17.045
    national parliaments, right to be informed 15.007, 17.016
    subsidiary principle compliance duty 5.031–5.032, 15.005, 15.010, 17.006, 17.015
  membership 1.054
  non-legislative procedures, role in 17.038–17.042
  ordinary legislative procedure, role in 17.020, 17.023, 17.028, 17.031
  pre-Lisbon powers 1.048
  Presidential appointments 1.054, 12.006, 12.014, 12.025, 12.064
  representation of EU 12.057, 14.004
    external representation 12.042, 12.062, 14.006
  Rules of Procedure 12.069
  seat 12.071
  Treaty amendment proposals
    consultation on 3.003–3.004
    EU interests protection 16.005
    power to make 3.003, 3.006
  Vice-President 2.004, 12.040; *see also* High Representative of the Union for Foreign Affairs and Security Policy
  see also institutions
European Communities (EC) 1.002, 1.041
European Convention on Human Rights 1950 1.007, 25.001, 25.002, 25.004, 25.020
  Charter rights corresponding to ECHR rights 25.012, 25.019
  EU accession to 3.007, 5.004, 21.002, 21.011, 25.013, 25.015–25.016
  review of EU law applying ECHR rights 25.013–25.014
European Cooperative Society 7.075
European Council 1.022, 1.033, 12.022, 15.004
  composition 12.026
  constituent decision-making role 12.025
  constitutional acts by 24.009
  Euro Summit meetings 12.028, 22.005
  external action role 10.002, 10.028, 12.023–12.024
    CFSP 12.023, 12.024, 19.002, 27.044
    common defence policy proposals 3.007, 12.025
  high-level steering and conciliation role 12.024
  interinstitutional relations 12.025, 12.026
    Commission 12.064
    Council 12.033, 12.040
    European Central Bank 12.025, 13.021, 13.022
    European Parliament 12.007, 12.017, 12.032
  language rules 14.028
  Lisbon Treaty reforms 2.005
  meetings and decision-making 12.030–12.031
  Member States' decisions made within 28.003
  ordinary legislative procedure
    power to order use 3.006, 3.008, 12.025, 17.003
    role in 17.033
  pre-Lisbon powers 1.048.12.023
  President 12.027
  Rules of Procedure 12.029
  suspension of Membership decisions 4.020, 12.025
  Treaty amendment proposals, consultation duties 3.003–3.004, 3.006
  see also institutions
European Court of Auditors, *see* Court of Auditors
European Court of Human Rights 1.007, 25.004, 25.013–25.015
European Court of Justice, *see* Court of Justice of the European Union
European Data Protection Supervisor 9.002, 13.043, 13.044, 20.008
European Defence Agency 10.032, 13.046
European Defence Community proposal 1.011
European Development Fund 10.013, 10.019
European Economic and Social Committee 9.009, 9.047, 12.039, 13.030–13.032, 17.043, 17.045, 20.008
European Economic Area (EEA) Agreement 1992 4.005, 10.020
European Economic Community (EEC) 1.002, 1.014, 1.016–1.018
European External Action Service (EEAS) 12.062, 13.042, 14.006, 19.005, 20.008
European Free Trade Association (EFTA) 1.019, 4.005, 10.020
European Globalization Adjustment Fund for Displaced Workers (EGF) 9.057
European groupings of territorial cooperation 9.057
European Insurance and Occupational Pensions Authority 9.042
European Investment Bank 9.040, 9.057, 10.019, 10.022, 14.011
  European Investment Fund 13.045
  legislative acts
    implementation 18.025
    right of initiative 17.012
  limits on power of internal organization 16.008
  operation 13.038
  tasks 13.037
European judicial network 8.018, 8.023
European Labour Authority (ELA) 13.046
European Maritime and Fisheries Fund 9.057

European monetary cooperation 1.034–1.036; see also economic and monetary union
European Neighbourhood Policy 10.018, 10.025
European Ombudsman 6.022, 12.008, 13.039–13.041, 20.008
European Parliament 1.022, 12.001–12.002, 17.047
  budgetary powers, see budget of EU
  citizen petitions to 6.022, 12.011, 16.004
  comitology procedures, see implementing acts, comitology procedures
  composition 2.005, 12.012–12.013
  European Ombudsman appointments by 13.040
  external action role 12.004, 19.004, 19.006, 21.002, 21.003, 21.008–21.012
  interinstitutional relations 12.007–12.009
    actions for annulment by 12.009, 16.010, 30.006
    Commission 12.005–12.006, 12.017, 12.064, 16.012, 17.016
    Council 12.007, 12.017, 17.004, 17.035–17.036, 17.039–17.042
    Court of Auditors 12.008
    European Central Bank 12.008, 13.021, 17.045
    European Council 12.007, 12.017, 12.032
    interinstitutional agreements 27.049–27.050
  internal organization 12.020
  language rules 14.028
  legislative powers 12.003, 16.010, 16.012, 17.012, 17.014
    in ordinary legislative procedure, see ordinary legislative procedure
    in special legislative procedures 17.035–17.037
  Lisbon Treaty reforms 2.005, 2.009, 6.004, 12.013
  maladministration inquiries by 12.010
  Members
    conditions for exercise of office 12.016
    election of 3.007, 6.021, 12.012, 12.014
    political groups and parties 12.021
    seat allocations 2.005, 12.013, 17.049
  national parliaments, cooperation with 15.005
  non-legislative procedures, role in 17.039–17.042
  pre-Lisbon powers 1.045, 1.048
  proceedings 12.019
  Rules of Procedure 12.017
  seat 12.018, 14.020
  Treaty amendment proposals
    consultation on 3.003–3.004
    Council amendments, consent requirement 3.007
    EU interests protection 16.005
    power to make 3.003, 3.006
  see also institutions
European Personnel Selection Office 13.043
European political cooperation 1.030–1.033, 1.041
European Public Prosecutor's Office 8.024, 13.045, 20.013, 22.007
European Regional Development Fund 9.057
European Rule of Law mechanism 5.005
European Securities and Markets Authority 9.042
European Semester 9.039, 9.049, 9.060
European Social Fund 9.047, 9.057
European Stability Mechanism 2.010, 9.037, 28.004
European Structural and Investment Funds 9.057
European System of Central Banks 9.043–9.044, 13.020
European Training Foundation 9.052
Europol 8.025–8.026, 13.045, 15.011, 18.025
Eurostat 13.043
Eurozone:
  accessions to 9.033
  derogating states 9.034, 22.005
  ECB, see European Central Bank
  Euro Summit meetings 12.028, 22.005
  Eurogroup meetings 12.040, 22.005
  European Stability Mechanism 2.010, 9.037, 28.004
  monetary policy coordination 5.023, 9.043–9.045
  sanctions for excessive deficits 9.040
  sovereign debt crisis 9.036
  third countries using euro 9.045, 11.009
  see also economic and monetary union
exclusive EU competences 5.022–5.024, 5.030
  treaty-making 5.023, 10.002, 10.005, 10.039
executive agencies 13.047
executive bodies:
  advisory bodies, see advisory bodies
  agencies, see agencies
  connected with EU 13.048
  decision-making by, see decision-making
  fundamental rights protection duties 25.008
  implementation of EU law 18.022–18.025
  language rules 14.029
  seats 13.046, 14.021
  supporting work of institutions 13.042–13.044
  see also institutions
expenditure of EU 14.017–14.018
exports:
  free movement, see free movement of goods
  to third countries 10.006, 10.029
expulsion of EU citizens or their family members 6.010, 6.012, 6.016
external action 2.004
  association agreements 4.003, 8.013, 10.014–10.020, 13.043, 21.011, 26.003
  CFSP, see CFSP (common foreign and security policy)
  common security and defence policy (CSDP) 2.004, 3.007, 5.025, 10.032–10.034, 12.025, 19.007
  competences and legal basis 5.014, 10.002
  Cotonou Agreement 2000 2.010, 10.019, 11.007
  development cooperation policy, see development cooperation policy
  economic, financial, and technical cooperation with third countries 10.024–10.025
  EEA Agreement 1992 4.005, 10.020
  European External Action Service (EEAS) 12.062, 13.042, 14.006, 19.005, 20.008
  European Neighbourhood Policy 10.018, 10.025

external action (*cont.*)
 external representation of EU 12.042, 12.062, 14.006
 Foreign Affairs Council 2.004, 12.040, 12.042, 12.054
 institutional roles
  Commission, *see* European Commission, external action role
  Council, *see* Council of the European Union, external action role
  European Council, *see* European Council, external action role
  European Parliament 12.004, 19.004, 19.006, 21.002, 21.003, 21.008–21.012
  High Representative, *see* High Representative of the Union for Foreign Affairs and Security Policy
 international agreements, *see* international agreements concluded by EU
 international trade, *see* common commercial policy
 overseas countries and territories 10.013, 11.006, 11.007, 11.008
 principles and objectives 5.006, 10.001, 26.012
extradition:
 European arrest warrants 5.005, 8.020, 25.012
 nationality-based discrimination prohibition 5.055, 6.020
extraterritorial effects of Treaties 11.010

Factortame I **ruling (C-213/89)** 23.016–23.017, 23.018
Factortame IV **and** *Brasserie du Pêcheur* **rulings (C-48/93 and C-46/93)** 23.020–23.021, 29.012
failure to act claims 12.009, 12.058, 13.006, 13.009, 17.005, 30.002, 30.018–30.020
failure to fulfil obligations claims, *see* infringement proceedings against Member States
family law matters:
 EU law measures 3.008, 7.109
 judicial cooperation 1.038, 8.014, 22.007
 same-sex marriage recognition 5.060, 25.012
family reunification 5.060, 6.012, 6.014, 6.017, 7.055, 8.012, 11.002
Faroe Islands 11.007
fines, *see* sanctions
Finland, parliamentary influence on legislative acts 15.008
Fiscal Stability Treaty 2012 2.010, 9.041
fisheries policy 5.023, 5.024, 7.004, 9.008, 11.009
flag of EU 1.060, 2.004, 6.003, 14.001
flexibility clause (TFEU Art. 352) 5.017, 5.020–5.021, 5.032, 7.108, 15.007, 15.008, 17.037
food quality standards 9.006
food safety 9.055, 13.046
force majeure 25.024
Foreign Affairs Council 2.004, 12.040, 12.042, 12.054
foreign direct investment policy 10.004, 10.005, 10.007

forerunners of EU, *see* origin of EU
Fouchet Plan 1.030
framework decisions under PJCC 28.014
France:
 accessions to EU, referendum requirement 15.003
 primacy of EU law, incorporation in legal system 23.027
 Strasbourg, seats of institutions and executive bodies in 12.018, 13.040, 14.019, 14.020
 UN Security Council permanent membership 26.014
Francovich **liability** 18.004, 23.019–23.024, 27.034–27.036, 29.012
fraud control by OLAF (European Anti-Fraud Office) 12.008, 13.043, 16.008, 20.013
free movement of capital and payments 7.100–7.102
 public interest/policy restrictions 7.103–7.104
 rule of reason-based restrictions 7.105–7.106
 third countries, capital movements and restrictions 7.107, 10.031
free movement of goods:
 customs union, *see* customs union
 exceptions 7.031
  rule of reason (*Cassis de Dijon* rule) 7.037–7.042
  selling arrangements, rules governing 7.043
  TFEU Article 36 grounds 7.032–7.036
 'goods' concept 7.014, 7.083
 measures against trade-distorting national rules 7.116
 non-tariff barriers prohibition 7.026
  export restrictions 7.030
  quantitative restrictions and measures having equivalent effect 7.027–7.029
 Treaty rules 7.013
free movement of persons 1.038, 6.008
 economically inactive persons 6.010, 6.011, 6.015, 6.018, 7.079, 11.001
 family members of EU citizens
  family reunification 5.060, 6.012, 6.014, 6.017, 7.055, 8.012, 11.002
  spouses, expulsion protection 6.010
 implementing legislation 6.009–6.010
 jobseekers 5.055, 7.052
 nationality-based discrimination prohibition 5.019, 5.055, 6.015, 6.018, 6.020
 obstacles to 6.019–6.020
 political rights in state of residence 12.015
 public interest/policy restrictions 6.016, 6.017
 residence rights
  exceeding three months 6.012
  permanent residence 6.013
  up to three months 6.011, 6.015
 Schengen system, *see* Schengen system
 social assistance provision
  differences between Member States' rules permitted 6.019
  undue burden rules 6.010, 6.012, 6.015
  workers and self-employed persons 7.078–7.080
 students 5.019, 5.055, 6.015, 6.020, 9.050

free movement of workers and self-employed
    persons 7.003
  beneficiaries 7.047
    companies, *see* freedom of establishment
    employers 7.053
    jobseekers 5.055, 7.052
    Member State nationals 7.048
    posted workers 5.047, 7.052, 7.075, 7.078, 7.094
    professional sportspersons 7.051, 7.059, 7.062
    self-employed persons 7.054, 7.063–7.064
    third-country nationals 7.049, 7.055,
      8.013, 10.018
    'worker' concept 7.050–7.052
  expulsion orders 6.012
  nationality-based discrimination
    prohibition 7.058–7.062
  professional qualifications recognition, *see*
    professional qualifications recognition
  public interest/policy restrictions 7.067, 7.072
  public service or official authority
    appointments 7.068–7.069
  right to enter, leave, and reside 7.057
  rule of reason-based restrictions 7.070–7.074
  social assistance provision 7.078–7.080
  territorial link requirement 7.056
  transfrontier situation requirement 7.055
  Treaty rules 7.044–7.046
freedom of establishment:
  of companies 7.065
    harmonized rules 7.075
    nationality-based discrimination
      prohibition 7.061
    secondary right of establishment 7.066
    trade union action restricting 7.044
  'establishment' concept 7.054, 7.063
  freedom to provide services distinguished
    from 7.086, 7.095
  public interest/policy restrictions 7.067
  of self-employed persons, *see* free movement of
    workers and self-employed persons
freedom to provide services:
  freedom of establishment distinguished
    from 7.086, 7.095
  harmonized rules 7.075
  nationality-based discrimination
    prohibition 7.087–7.088
  professional qualifications recognition, *see*
    professional qualifications recognition
  public interest/policy restrictions 7.089, 7.092
  rule of reason-based restrictions 7.090–7.094
  service providers and recipients 7.084
  'services' concept 7.082–7.083, 7.096
  Services Directive (2006/123/EC) 7.067, 7.071,
    7.075, 7.091, 7.096–7.099
  temporary nature requirement 7.086
  transfrontier situation requirement 7.085
  transport services 9.009–9.011
  Treaty rules 7.081
Frontex 8.007, 13.046

fundamental freedoms of internal market 7.003,
    7.011–7.012; *see also* free movement of capital
    and payments; free movement of goods; free
    movement of workers and self-employed
    persons; freedom of establishment; freedom to
    provide services
fundamental rights 25.001, 25.017–25.019
  actions for annulment on fundamental rights
    grounds 25.008, 26.002, 26.015
  balancing rights 25.020
  Charter, *see* Charter of Fundamental Rights of the
    European Union
  due process rights 25.008, 25.018, 25.022, 25.025
  equal treatment, *see* equal treatment principle
  as EU value 5.004, 5.038, 25.002
  as general principles of EU law 25.003–
    25.004, 25.022
  implementation of EU law in compliance
    with 25.009, 25.012
  institutions and executive bodies, protection
    duties 25.008
  see also human rights
**Funds for economic, social, and territorial
    cohesion** 9.057, 13.043
future EU reforms 2.011
Future of Europe Conference 2.011

GATT/WTO participation 10.009–10.011, 14.005,
    26.001, 26.003, 26.005
Gaulle, Charles de 1.030, 4.002
**gender-based discrimination
    prohibition** 5.058, 9.048
  equal pay right 5.058, 5.063, 9.048
  military occupations 5.058, 11.011
  positive discrimination 5.059
General Affairs Council 12.027, 12.030, 12.040
General Court, *see* Court of Justice of the
    European Union
**General Data Protection Regulation (2016/679/
    EU)** 9.002, 13.044
general principles of EU law 25.021, 25.024, 26.013
  due process rights 25.008, 25.018, 25.022, 25.025
  fundamental rights as 25.003–25.004, 25.022
  good administration right 25.022, 25.023
  open administration right 14.030–14.031, 25.026
  proportionality principle, *see* proportionality
    principle
  sources 25.022
Germany:
  Constitutional Court, *see* Bundesverfassungsgericht
    (German Constitutional Court)
  East Germany, extension of EU law on
    reunification 11.008
  NATO accession (1954) 1.012
  parliamentary influence on legislative acts 15.008
  primacy of EU law, incorporation in legal
    system 23.027, 23.029
Gibraltar 11.007
Giscard d'Estaing, Valéry 1.057

good administration right 25.022, 25.023
goods, free movement of, *see* free movement of goods
Greece:
  accession to EU 4.003, 10.017
  accession to Eurozone 9.033
  common commercial policy infringement
    claim 11.011
  sovereign debt crisis 9.036
Greenland 11.007
guardian of Treaties, Commission's role 12.058,
    12.060, 18.004, 29.040
**guidelines of institutions and executive
    bodies** 27.002, 27.044–27.045

harmonization of national laws:
  on criminal procedure 8.020, 17.033, 20.013
  derogations from 5.047, 7.115
  and free movement of goods 7.033, 7.039
  and freedom of establishment 7.075
  full or partial harmonization 23.012
  impact on national law-making 7.109
  legal bases for 5.014, 7.108
    TFEU Articles 114 and 115 7.112–7.116
  minimum harmonization measures 7.110, 9.047
  mutual recognition as alternative to, *see* mutual
    recognition principle
health and safety at work 9.047
health care:
  freedom of movement to receive 7.085, 7.088
    costs reimbursement 7.080, 7.094
  public health policy 9.055, 13.046
  as 'service' 7.082
Herzog, Roman 25.005
**High Representative of the Union for Foreign Affairs
    and Security Policy:**
  appointment 12.025, 12.065
  consultation duties 12.007, 19.004
  European External Action Service support
    for 13.042
  international agreements, role respecting 21.003,
    21.006, 21.007
  joint proposals with Commission 9.066, 10.031
  retirement 12.068
  role 10.002, 10.028, 12.026, 12.036, 12.065,
    19.003
    Chair of Foreign Affairs Council 2.004, 12.042,
      12.043, 12.054, 19.004
    external representation of EU 12.042,
      12.062, 14.006
    as Vice-President of Commission 2.004, 12.040
higher education policy 9.050
history of EU, *see* origin of EU
Horizon 2020 9.060
horizontal direct effect of EU law 23.029,
    23.033, 23.034
  of Charter 23.033, 25.010
  unimplemented or incorrectly implemented
    Directives 27.026
  see also direct effect of EU law

horizontal objectives of EU 5.007
human dignity right 4.010, 4.020, 5.002, 5.004, 7.089,
    10.001, 25.018, 25.019
human rights 25.002
  accession to EU, human rights conditionality 4.010
  ECHR, *see* European Convention on Human
    Rights 1950
  EU's external promotion of
    in development policy measures 10.021
    with sanctions 10.031
    in trade and cooperation agreements 10.008
  fundamental rights of EU, *see* fundamental rights
  serious and persistent breach of Treaties
    procedure 4.019–4.021, 5.003
human trafficking measures 8.012, 8.021
humanitarian aid 10.023, 10.030
Hungary:
  Commission infringement proceedings
    against 5.005
  serious breach of Treaties decision against 4.020,
    4.021, 5.005

Iceland:
  EFTA (European Free Trade Association) 1.019,
    4.005, 10.020
  EU accession proposal rejected 4.014
  judicial cooperation in civil matters 8.015
  Schengen *acquis* implementation 8.006
illegality plea 30.025, 30.033
immigration and asylum policy 1.038, 8.012, 11.002
  asylum policy 8.008–8.011, 25.014
  border checks and visas 8.007, 11.006
  expulsion of EU citizens or their family
    members 6.010, 6.012, 6.016
  family reunification 5.060, 6.012, 6.014, 6.017,
    7.055, 8.012, 11.002
  legal basis 10.002
  Schengen system, *see* Schengen system
immunities, *see* privileges and immunities
implementation of EU law 15.012, 16.012, 18.001–
    18.003, 23.007, 27.018
  administrative support for 9.065
  Commission supervision of, *see* infringement
    proceedings against Member States
  delegated acts, *see* delegated acts
  delegation to executive bodies 18.022–18.025
  ECHR rights applied to 25.014
  on free movement of persons 6.009–6.010
  fundamental rights protection duty 25.009, 25.012
  implementing acts, *see* implementing acts
  legal certainty, requirements of 27.019
  Member State duties during transposition
    period 27.021
  regional parliaments' role 15.017, 18.005
  by social partners 18.006
  time-limits for 27.020, 27.023
  uniform and full application duty 18.007
implementing acts 12.061, 18.008, 18.012
  actions to annul 30.011

INDEX 827

comitology procedures 13.036, 15.011, 18.012, 18.014–18.015
  advisory procedure 18.016
  examination procedure 18.017
  pre-Lisbon era 18.019
  scrutiny right of Council and European Parliament 18.018, 18.019
  Council's power to adopt 12.038, 18.012, 18.021
  delegated acts distinguished 18.011, 27.004–27.005
  expert consultation on 18.020
  national parliamentary scrutiny 15.011
  restrictions on use 18.009
  scope 18.013
  see also delegated acts; secondary EU law
implied EU competence 5.019
imports:
  free movement, *see* free movement of goods
  from third countries 10.006
incentive measures 5.012, 9.049, 9.050, 9.053, 9.055, 27.044–27.045
indirect discrimination 5.062–5.063
industrial policy 9.059
infringement proceedings against Member States 3.011, 4.019, 13.007, 18.004, 29.001, 29.039
  CFSP matters excluded 29.001, 29.023, 29.039
  Francovich liability 18.004, 23.019–23.024, 27.034–27.036, 29.012
  infringement finding, consequences 12.058, 14.014, 18.004, 29.050–29.053
  procedure
    pre-litigation stage 29.043–29.045
    litigation stage 29.046–29.049
  regional parliaments' infringements 18.005, 29.041
  right of initiative 12.058, 29.040–29.042
  rule of law infringements 4.021, 5.005
  sincere cooperation duty infringements, *see* sincere cooperation principle
institutional balance principle 5.050, 16.007–16.010, 17.004, 17.017, 21.002, 25.022
institutions 13.001, 16.001
  advisers to, *see* advisory bodies
  agreements between 23.005, 27.049–27.050
  bodies supporting work of 13.042–13.044
  citizens, engagement with 16.004, 17.013
  decision-making by, *see* decision-making
  external action roles
    Commission, *see* European Commission, external action role
    Council, *see* Council of the European Union, external action role
    European Council, *see* European Council, external action role
    European Parliament 12.004, 19.004, 19.006, 21.002, 21.003, 21.008–21.012
    High Representative, *see* High Representative of the Union for Foreign Affairs and Security Policy
  fundamental rights protection duties 25.008
  institutional balance principle 5.050, 16.007–16.010, 17.004, 17.017, 21.002, 25.022
  institutions set up by international agreements 26.004
  language rules 6.022, 14.025–14.028, 29.030
  legislative acts by, *see* legislative acts
  Lisbon Treaty reforms 2.005, 2.009, 6.004
  Member States, relations with 16.002–16.003
  privileges and immunities 5.047, 12.016, 14.007–14.008, 16.008
  proportionality principle implementation 5.042
  seats 12.018, 12.071, 13.018, 13.022, 14.019–14.021, 16.008, 28.002
  separation of powers 16.011–16.012
  sincere cooperation duties 5.044, 5.047, 5.048
  subsidiarity principle implementation 5.031
  Treaty amendments, EU interests protection 16.005
  see also Council of the European Union; Court of Auditors; Court of Justice of the European Union; European Central Bank; European Commission; European Council; European Parliament; executive bodies
intellectual property rights:
  and free movement of goods 7.036
  international trade context 10.004
  language rules of IP bodies 14.029
  unitary patent protection 7.109, 22.007
intergovernmental cooperation mechanisms 1.029
  CFSP, *see* CFSP (common foreign and security policy)
  defence cooperation proposals 1.011
  enhanced cooperation, *see* enhanced cooperation mechanisms
  justice and home affairs cooperation 1.044
  Lisbon Treaty reforms 2.010
  monetary cooperation, *see* economic and monetary union
  PJCC, *see* PJCC (police and judicial cooperation in criminal matters)
  political cooperation 1.030–1.033, 1.041
internal market:
  accession states in 4.011
  competition law and policy to protect, *see* competition law and policy
  establishment 1.041, 7.001
    common market, transition from 7.007–7.010
    market integration, scope of 7.002–7.006
  as EU objective 2.004, 5.006, 5.008, 7.005
  fundamental freedoms 7.003, 7.011–7.012; *see also* free movement of capital and payments; free movement of goods; free movement of workers and self-employed persons; freedom of establishment; freedom to provide services
  harmonization measures affecting 7.112–7.116
  nationality-based discrimination prohibition, *see* nationality-based discrimination prohibition
  permitted restrictions, *see* public interest/policy restrictions; rule of reason-based restraints of free movement

828 INDEX

international agreements concluded by EU 2.004
  accession states, duty to join 28.004
  amendment of 3.009
  association agreements 4.003, 8.013, 10.014–10.020, 13.043, 21.011, 26.003
  binding force 26.001
  conclusion of
    consent procedure 21.010–21.012
    consultation duty 21.009
    institutional roles 21.005–21.008
  Cotonou Agreement 2000 2.010, 10.019, 11.007
  Court of Justice opinions on 21.016–21.017, 25.008, 26.006
  decisions of organs set up by agreements 26.004
  direct effect of 23.034, 26.003
  entry into force and application 27.009
  European Neighbourhood Policy agreements 10.018, 10.025
  EU's powers to negotiate and conclude 14.005, 21.001
    declaration of competences duty 10.040
    as exclusive competence 5.023, 10.002, 10.005, 10.039
    express and implied 10.036–10.037
    under TFEU Article 352 10.038
  mixed agreements 21.013–21.015, 26.006
  negotiations 21.002–21.003
    Member States' sincere cooperation duty 5.049, 10.039
    on monetary affairs 21.004
  pre-Lisbon era (under CFSP and PJCC) 28.017
  secondary EU law, precedence over 26.002
  trade and cooperation agreements 10.008–10.009, 21.011, 26.003
  see also external action; international law
international agreements concluded by Member States 26.007
  before Treaties entered into force or EU accession 26.008–26.011, 28.007, 28.017
international law:
  binding force 26.001
  concluded by EU, *see* international agreements concluded by EU
  concluded by Member States 26.007
    before Treaties entered into force or EU accession 26.008–26.011, 28.007, 28.017
  Court of Justice's application of 25.004, 26.005, 26.007, 26.012–26.013, 26.016
  customary international law 26.013
  EU law distinguished from 1.021–1.025
  EU relations with third countries governed by 1.020
  European Stability Mechanism governed by 2.010
  international environmental law 9.062, 26.003
  law of the sea 11.006, 26.003
international organizations:
  EU's participation in, CFSP decisions on 10.029
  EU's status as, *see* EU as international organization
  NATO participation 10.032–10.033
  United Nations participation, *see* United Nations
  World Trade Organization participation 10.009–10.011, 14.005, 26.001, 26.003, 26.006
international trade, *see* common commercial policy
interpretation of EU law by national courts 29.005–29.007
invalidity of acts:
  actions for annulment, *see* actions for annulment
  plea of illegality 30.025, 30.033
  preliminary reference questions on 30.031–30.040
investor-state dispute settlement 10.004
Ireland:
  accession to EU 4.002
  AFSJ, special status 8.028, 22.002–22.003
  Irish language 14.025
  Northern Irish border arrangements 4.016
  Schengen *acquis,* non-application 1.039, 1.052, 8.004, 8.006, 8.028, 22.003
  sovereign debt crisis 9.036
  Supreme Court 1.041
Isle of Man 11.007
Italian Constitutional Court 23.015, 23.027

JHA (justice and home affairs) cooperation 1.044, 1.047, 8.002; *see also* PJCC (police and judicial cooperation in criminal matters)
jobseekers, free movement rights 5.055, 7.052
Johnson, Boris 4.016
joint actions under CFSP and PJCC 28.013
Joint Nuclear Research Centre 13.043
judges and Advocates General at Court of Justice 1.054, 13.013–13.016, 13.018, 28.002
judicial cooperation:
  in civil matters 1.037, 1.038, 8.005, 8.014–8.018, 22.007
  in criminal matters, *see* PJCC (police and judicial cooperation in criminal matters)
judicial independence 4.021, 5.003, 5.005, 16.013, 29.003–29.004
jurisdiction of Court of Justice 13.003–13.004, 13.008–13.010, 16.013, 27.011
  arbitration clauses, disputes referred under 13.008, 23.007
  CFSP acts excluded 1.049, 2.008, 10.026, 12.009, 13.010, 19.006, 25.008, 26.006, 30.045
    exceptions 12.009, 13.012, 25.008, 30.013, 30.036, 30.045
    infringement proceedings unavailable 29.001, 29.023, 29.039
  civil service disputes 13.002, 13.006, 14.023
  PJCC acts 2.008, 8.003, 13.010, 13.011, 29.024, 30.014, 30.037
  pre-Lisbon era 1.049, 13.002
  preliminary rulings, scope of jurisdiction 11.009, 25.011, 26.006
  primary law excluded 24.003

INDEX 829

privileges and immunities, *see* privileges and immunities
Treaty amendments 3.011
jurisdiction of Member States 11.006
jurisprudence of Court of Justice 28.006, 29.037–29.038
EFTA states' alignment with 10.020
justice and home affairs cooperation 1.044, 1.047, 8.002; *see also* PJCC (police and judicial cooperation in criminal matters)

Kadi ruling (C-402/05 P and C-415/05 P) 26.002, 26.015
Keck and Mithouard ruling (C-267/91 and C-268/91) 7.031, 7.043, 7.090

Laeken Declaration on the Future of Europe 2001 1.056
language rights of EU citizens:
 in communications with institutions and executive bodies 6.022, 14.025–14.026, 25.023
 in court proceedings 5.055, 7.060, 14.027
 discrimination prohibition 5.060
 language rules of institutions and executive bodies 14.027–14.029, 29.030
 restrictions, proportionality requirement 5.041, 6.020, 7.062, 9.054
 Treaty languages 14.024, 29.005
law of the sea 11.006, 26.003
lawyers, free movement rights 7.064, 7.069, 7.076, 7.077, 7.087
legal basis for EU acts 5.010
 choice of 5.013–5.014
 competence *ratione materiae* determinedy 5.011
 exercise of competences determined by 5.012
 flexibility clause (TFEU Art. 352) 5.017, 5.020–5.021, 5.032, 7.108, 15.007, 15.008, 17.037
 harmonization measures 5.014, 7.108
  TFEU Articles 114 and 115 7.112–7.116
 incorrect basis, effect of 5.016
 legislative procedure determined by 5.012, 17.003
 multiple bases 5.015
 specific or general 5.018
 statement of 27.007
 see also competences system
legal certainty principle 2.007, 5.016, 25.023, 27.009, 27.019
legal personality and capacity of EU 1.025, 14.002–14.005, 30.022
 external representation 12.042, 12.062, 14.006
legal professionals, free movement rights 7.064, 7.069, 7.076, 7.077, 7.087
legislative acts 2.004, 5.031
 actions to annul, *see* actions for annulment
 choice of instrument 27.003
 Commission proposals 12.060, 16.012, 17.012, 17.014–17.018

 citizen proposals 16.004, 17.013
 Coreper deliberations on 12.050–12.054, 17.017
 institutional consultation on 17.045
 national parliaments, right to be informed 15.007, 17.016
 subsidiary principle compliance duty 5.031–5.032, 15.005, 15.010, 17.006
 Council powers 12.036–12.038
  'A' and 'B' items 12.050
  amendment of Commission proposals 17.017
  no right of initiative 17.014
  in ordinary legislative procedure, *see* ordinary legislative procedure
  public deliberations 12.044
  in special legislative procedures, *see* special legislative procedures
 definition 17.001–17.002, 17.038, 18.008
 duties to legislate 17.005, 17.018
 entry into force and application 27.009
 European Central Bank powers 17.004, 17.012
 European Council powers 12.025
 European Parliament's powers 12.003, 16.010, 16.012, 17.012, 17.014
  in ordinary legislative procedure, *see* ordinary legislative procedure
  in special legislative procedures 17.035–17.037
 implementation, *see* implementation of EU law
 institutional balance in legislative proceedings 16.010, 17.004, 17.017
 legal basis, *see* legal basis for EU acts
 national parliamentary scrutiny of 2.004, 5.031–5.032, 15.005–15.011, 17.006, 17.016, 17.048
 nationality-based discrimination, rules to combat 5.057
 ordinary legislative procedure, *see* ordinary legislative procedure
 publication and notification duty 25.026, 27.008
 right of initiative 17.012
 signature and authentication 27.006
 sincere cooperation in legislative proceedings 5.048
 special legislative procedures, *see* special legislative procedures
 statements of reasons 27.007
 see also decision-making; secondary EU law
legislative procedures, *see* ordinary legislative procedure; special legislative procedures
legitimate expectations principle 2.007, 25.023, 27.009, 27.045
Les Verts ruling (294/83) 30.001, 30.004, 30.041
lex posterior and *lex specialis* doctrines 23.006
Leyen, Ursula von der 2.011, 17.018
Liechtenstein:
 EFTA (European Free Trade Association) 1.019, 4.005, 10.020
 Schengen *acquis* implementation 8.006

INDEX

Lisbon Treaty 2007 1.002, 1.018, 1.028, 24.005
  competences system reforms, *see* competences system
  constitutional innovations 2.004
    Charter afforded primary law status 2.004, 25.001, 25.007
  EU law reforms 2.006–2.008, 17.002, 18.008, 23.002, 27.004–27.005, 28.007
  institutional reforms 2.005, 2.009, 6.004, 17.010
  intergovernmental cooperation reforms 2.010
  negotiation and ratification 2.001–2.002
  pillar system abolition 1.032, 1.038, 2.003, 8.005
  Treaty system reforms 2.003, 3.005–3.006
Lisbon Treaty judgment (German Bundesverfassungsgericht) 2.002, 15.003, 15.008, 17.050, 23.029
loyal cooperation principle, *see* sincere cooperation principle
Lugano Convention on jurisdiction and the enforcement of judgments in civil and commercial matters 2007 8.015
Luxembourg:
  Benelux Union 1.004, 1.039, 26.008, 29.015
  European Stability Mechanism seated in 9.037
  seats of institutions and executive bodies in 8.024, 12.018, 12.071, 13.018, 13.029, 13.038, 13.045, 14.019–14.020
'Luxembourg Compromise' 12.023, 12.048

Maastricht Treaty 1992 1.038, 1.042–1.043, 24.005
  amendments to Treaties 1.045
  EU citizenship introduction 6.004
  fundamental rights protection 25.003
  pillar system 1.044, 1.046–1.047, 1.049
  single institutional framework 1.048
  see also Treaty on European Union (TEU)
maladministration:
  European Ombudsman 6.022, 12.008, 13.039–13.041, 20.008
  European Parliamentary inquiries into 12.010
Malta, accession to EU 4.001, 10.017
marine biological resources conservation 5.023, 5.024, 9.008
market dominance, abuse of 9.017, 9.019
marriage, same-sex 5.060, 25.012
May, Theresa 4.016
measures equivalent to quantitative restrictions 7.028–7.029
medical care, *see* health care
Member States:
  accession, *see* accession to EU
  actions for annulment by 30.006
  budgetary contributions 14.015
  CFSP decisions, implementation by 19.005
  civil servants of 7.068, 9.065, 15.004
  competences shared with EU 5.022, 5.025–5.026, 23.012
    mixed agreements 21.013–21.015, 26.006
  courts of, *see* national courts
  decision-making on EU affairs 28.002–28.003
    interstate conventions and agreements 28.004, 28.018–28.020
  domestic law of, *see* domestic law of Member States
  economic policy coordination 9.036
  enhanced cooperation between, *see* enhanced cooperation mechanisms
  EU law implementation, *see* implementation of EU law
  European Parliament, seat allocations 2.005, 12.013, 17.049
  Eurozone states, *see* Eurozone
  infringement proceedings against, *see* infringement proceedings against Member States
  intergovernmental cooperation, *see* intergovernmental cooperation mechanisms
  international agreements concluded by 26.007
    before Treaties entered into force or EU accession 26.008–26.011, 28.007, 28.017
  jurisdiction of 11.006
  legislative acts, right of initiative 12.060, 17.012
  list of 4.001
  ministerial representatives at Council 12.041
  mutual recognition principle, *see* mutual recognition principle
  mutual trust principle 5.003, 5.047, 8.020
  national competition authorities 9.015
  national identities of 5.041, 16.003
  nationality and EU citizenship link 6.006, 7.048
  parliaments of, *see* national parliaments
  presidency of Council 2.005, 12.042
  ratification of Treaties by 3.005, 3.008, 11.003, 15.002–15.003, 23.029–23.030
  sincere cooperation duty, *see* sincere cooperation principle
  state aid, *see* state aid
  subsidiarity principle, *see* subsidiarity principle
  suspension of Membership 4.019–4.021, 5.003
  Treaty amendment proposals
    power to make 3.003, 3.006
      ratification/approval requirement 3.005, 3.007, 3.008, 15.003, 16.005, 17.006
    unilateral declarations by 24.008, 27.044–27.045, 27.047
  veto power 5.012
  withdrawal from EU, *see* withdrawal from EU
Members of European Parliament, *see* European Parliament, Members
merger control 9.018
Merkel, Angela 2.001
military operations 19.007
minimum harmonization measures 7.110, 9.047
mixed agreements 21.013–21.015, 26.006
Monaco, EU law application in 11.009
monetary policy cooperation 5.023, 9.043–9.045; *see also* economic and monetary union
money laundering control 7.092, 7.106, 7.110, 8.021
Monnet, Jean 1.008
Morocco, application to accede to EU 4.010

motto of EU 1.060, 2.004, 14.001
multiannual financial framework 14.018
multiple legal bases 5.015
mutual recognition principle 7.111
  judicial and extrajudicial decisions in civil matters 1.037, 1.038, 8.005, 8.014–8.018, 22.007
  PJCC, *see* PJCC (police and judicial cooperation in criminal matters)
  professional qualifications, *see* professional qualifications recognition
  rule of reason-based restraints, *see* rule of reason-based restraints of free movement
mutual trust principle 5.003, 5.047, 8.020

national competition authorities 9.015
national courts:
  competition law enforcement 9.015, 9.024, 9.026, 29.013
  Constitutional Courts 2.002, 23.028–23.030, 25.003, 29.016
    Belgium 23.030, 29.018
    Germany, *see* Bundesverfassungsgericht (German Constitutional Court)
    Italy 23.015, 23.027
  effective protection of EU law duty 5.005, 5.046, 5.049, 15.013, 18.004, 27.028, 29.002–29.003, 30.044
  duty to set aside conflicting laws 5.049, 16.013, 23.014–23.018, 27.032–27.033, 29.008
  enforcement claims 23.018
  Francovich liability 18.004, 23.019–23.024, 27.034–27.036, 29.012
  interpretation and application of EU law 29.005–29.013
  interpretation of domestic law in conformity with EU law 23.013, 27.029–27.031
  preliminary references, *see* preliminary references to Court of Justice
  EU as party before 14.003
  EU institutions, cooperation with 5.047
  judicial independence 4.021, 5.003, 5.005, 16.013, 29.003–29.004
  Supreme Courts
    Belgium 23.025, 29.018
    Ireland 1.041
    Poland 5.005
national identities of Member States 5.041, 16.003
national laws, *see* domestic law of Member States
national parliaments 15.001
  European Parliament, cooperation with 15.005
  legislative acts, scrutiny of 2.004, 5.031–5.032, 15.005–15.011, 17.006, 17.016, 17.048
  ratification of Treaties by 3.005, 3.008, 11.003, 15.002–15.003, 23.029–23.030
  regional parliaments 15.014–15.017, 18.005, 29.041
    in Belgium 5.032, 12.041, 15.003, 15.010, 18.005
  Treaty amendment proposals

  approval requirement 3.005, 3.008, 15.003, 16.005, 17.006
  consultation on 3.003–3.004, 3.006
nationality-based discrimination prohibition 5.053, 7.003
  and free movement of persons 5.019, 5.055, 6.015, 6.018, 6.020
  workers and self-employed persons 7.058–7.062
  and freedom to provide services 7.087–7.088
  nationality conferrals by other Member States, recognition of 6.006, 6.008
  reverse discrimination 5.064
  rules to combat, adoption of 5.057
  specific prohibitions 5.054
  tax rules, *see* tax discrimination
  third-country nationals with long-term residence status 8.012
  'within the scope of application of the Treaties' 5.056
  see also citizenship of EU; equal treatment principle
NATO (North Atlantic Treaty Organization) 1.004
  EU participation in 10.032–10.033
  Germany's accession (1954) 1.012
natural justice 25.024
***ne bis in idem* principle** 25.025
necessity assessments 5.038, 5.039, 27.003; *see also* proportionality principle
Netherlands:
  Benelux Union 1.004, 1.039, 26.008, 29.015
  parliamentary influence on legislative acts 15.008
  primacy of EU law, incorporation in legal system 23.025, 23.027
Nice Treaty 2001 1.018, 1.053, 24.005
  amendments to Treaties 1.054, 4.020
non-discrimination, *see* equal treatment principle
non-legislative decisions, *see* decision-making
Norway:
  EFTA (European Free Trade Association) 1.019, 4.005, 10.020
  EU accession proposals rejected 4.005, 4.014
  judicial cooperation in civil matters 8.015
  Schengen *acquis* implementation 8.006
notification of EU decisions 25.026, 27.008

objectives of EU 2.004, 5.006–5.008, 10.001, 26.012
OEEC (Organization for European Economic Cooperation) 1.004
offices, *see* executive bodies
officials, *see* civil servants and officials
OLAF (European Anti-Fraud Office) 12.008, 13.043, 16.008, 20.013
open administration right 14.030–14.031, 25.026, 27.008
open method of coordination 7.108, 9.049, 9.055, 9.059, 9.060
operational decisions under CFSP 10.030

INDEX

ordinary legislative procedure 17.1f, 17.019
   'alarm bell' procedure 17.033
   Council and European Parliament as co-
      legislators 1.045, 2.004, 16.010, 17.004, 17.049
      Commission's 'honest broker' role 17.031
      Parliamentary role 17.009–17.011,
         17.032, 18.021
      trilogues (with Commission) 17.020
   European Council provision for 3.006, 3.008,
      12.025, 17.003
   first reading stage
      in Council 17.022
      in European Parliament 17.021
      trilogues at 17.023
   legal basis determining use 5.012, 17.003
   qualified majority voting, *see* qualified majority
      voting in Council
   second reading stage 17.024
      adoption by Council at 17.027
      adoption or rejection by Parliament at 17.025
      amendments by Parliament at 17.026
      conciliation process 17.029
      trilogues at 17.028
   signature and authentication 27.006
   time-limits 17.030
   unanimous voting 5.021, 17.007–17.008,
      17.033, 17.049
   see also legislative acts
ordinary Treaty revision procedure 3.002–3.005
Organization for European Economic Cooperation
      (OEEC) 1.004
organized crime 8.021, 8.025
origin of EU 1.002, 1.040, 1.043
   defence cooperation proposals 1.011
   economic and monetary union, *see* economic and
      monetary union, development
   EU citizenship, origin of 6.002–6.004
   European Atomic Energy Community (Euratom or
      EAEC) 1.002, 1.015, 1.017, 1.059, 2.003, 2.006,
      10.002, 24.004
   European Coal and Steel Community
      (ECSC) 1.002, 1.008–1.011, 1.017,
      3.009, 11.004
   European Communities (EC) 1.002, 1.041
   European Economic Community (EEC) 1.002,
      1.014, 1.016–1.018
   internal market, *see* internal market, establishment
   Lisbon Treaty, *see* Lisbon Treaty 2007
   post-war initiatives for European
      integration 1.003–1.007
   pre-Lisbon form, *see* Amsterdam Treaty 1997;
      Maastricht Treaty 1992; Nice Treaty 2001;
      Single European Act
overseas countries and territories 10.013, 11.006,
   11.007, 11.008
own resources of EU 14.013–14.016

parent companies, freedom of establishment 7.066
Parliament, *see* European Parliament
part-time workers 5.063, 7.051
partnership and cooperation agreements 10.008,
   10.018, 21.011, 26.003
payments, free movement of, *see* free movement of
   capital and payments
penalties, *see* sanctions
permanent residence rights 6.013
permanent structured cooperation
   (PESCO) 10.025, 22.007
personal data protection policy 9.002, 13.043, 13.044
personal scope of Treaties 11.001–11.002
PESCO (permanent structured
   cooperation) 10.025, 22.007
pillar system 1.044, 1.046–1.047, 1.049, 1.051
   abolition 1.032, 1.038, 2.003
PJCC (police and judicial cooperation in criminal
   matters) 8.019
   CFSP sanctions implementation 10.031
   Court of Justice jurisdiction to review acts 2.008,
      8.003, 13.010, 13.011, 29.024, 30.014, 30.037
   crime prevention 8.022
   criminal offences and sanctions 8.021
   criminal procedure 8.020
   enlargement of scope 3.008
   Eurojust 8.023, 13.045, 15.011, 18.025
   European arrest warrants 5.005, 8.020, 25.012
   European Public Prosecutor's Office 8.024, 13.045,
      20.013, 22.007
   Europol 8.025–8.026, 13.045, 15.011, 18.025
   harmonization measures 7.113, 20.013
   legislative acts in PJCC field 17.034
   Lisbon Treaty reforms 2.003, 2.008, 8.005
   pre-Lisbon era 1.044, 1.047, 1.048, 1.049,
      1.051, 8.003
      pre-Lisbon acts still in force 28.007–
         28.017, 28.019
   Schengen Information System 1.039, 6.016, 8.006
   see also AFSJ (area of freedom, security and justice)
plastic packaging waste, uniform rate
   on 14.014, 14.015
plea of illegality 30.025, 30.033
Plevin, René 1.011
Poland:
   Charter derogations for 2.001, 2.004, 25.007
   Commission infringement proceedings
      against 5.005
   serious breach of Treaties decision against 4.020,
      4.021, 5.005
   Supreme Court 5.005
police and judicial cooperation in criminal matters,
   see PJCC (police and judicial cooperation in
   criminal matters)
police missions 19.007
Political and Security Committee 12.053, 12.054,
   18.025, 19.003, 19.006, 19.007
political cooperation 1.030–1.033, 1.041
political groups and parties in European
   Parliament 12.021
political rights of EU citizens 6.021, 12.015

polluter-pays principle 9.061
Popławski II ruling (C-573/17) 23.014, 27.016
Portugal:
  accession to EU 4.004
  sovereign debt crisis 9.036
positive discrimination 5.059
posted workers 5.047, 7.052, 7.075, 7.078, 7.094
potential candidates for EU accession 4.014, 10.017
pre-emption doctrine 5.026
precautionary principle 9.061, 25.023
preliminary references to Court of Justice 5.005,
    5.047, 13.005, 13.009, 15.013, 27.011,
    29.001, 29.014
  and *Francovich* liability 23.022
  jurisdiction for 29.015–29.016
  language rules 14.027, 29.030, 29.034
  obligatory questions 29.018, 30.032
    exceptions to duty to refer 23.014, 29.019
  optional questions 29.017
  preliminary rulings
    binding force 29.037–29.038, 30.040
    ex tunc effect, restrictions on 28.006, 29.037
    scope of Court's jurisdiction 11.009,
      25.011, 26.006
  procedure
    'order for reference' submissions 29.026–
      29.028, 30.038
    observations process 29.029–29.030, 30.039
    internal assignment of case 29.031
    oral procedure 29.032
    deliberations 29.033
    preliminary ruling delivery 29.034
    expedited and urgent procedure 29.035
    costs 29.036
  subject matter of questions 29.020–29.022
    CFSP matters 28.012, 29.023, 30.036
    PJCC matters 28.011, 28.014, 28.019,
      29.024, 30.037
    relevance requirement 29.025
    unimplemented or incorrectly implemented
      Directives 27.028
    validity of acts 30.031–30.040
presidency of Council 2.005, 12.042
President of Commission appointments 1.054,
    12.006, 12.014, 12.025, 12.064
President of European Council 12.027
preventive action principle 9.061
primacy of EU law 2.004, 2.007, 5.049, 7.109,
    16.002, 23.008
  CFSP acts 23.009
  Charter rights, relationship with 25.012
  Costa v ENEL (6/64) on 1.025, 1.027, 23.010–
    23.011, 23.017
  incorporation in Member States 23.027
    constitutional provisions, application to 23.011,
      23.026, 23.028–23.030
    dualist legal systems 23.026
    monist legal systems 23.025
    scope of domestic law-making, effect on 23.012

  national courts' enforcement duty, *see* national
    courts, effective protection of EU law duty
  see also direct effect of EU law
primary EU law 23.003–23.004, 24.001–24.003
  Charter, *see* Charter of Fundamental Rights of the
    European Union
  direct effect of 23.033, 25.010
  precedence over international agreements
    concluded by EU 26.002
  Treaties, *see* Treaties
  see also secondary EU law
principle of effectiveness *(effet utile)* 5.049, 23.014,
    23.018, 29.006, 29.011
  direct effect of EU law, *see* direct effect of EU law
  national courts' effective protection duty, *see*
    national courts, effective protection of EU
    law duty
principle of equivalence 5.049, 23.018,
    29.009, 29.010
privileges and immunities:
  of EU civil servants 5.050, 14.009
  of institutions 5.047, 12.016, 14.007–14.008, 16.008
procedural rights 25.008, 25.018, 25.022, 25.025
product liability 9.056
professional qualifications recognition 5.047,
    7.011, 7.045
  Bologna process 9.050
  harmonized rules 7.075–7.077
  home state use of qualifications obtained in another
    Member State 7.055
  indirect discrimination prohibition 7.061
  restrictions, proportionality requirement 7.074
  see also free movement of workers and self-
    employed persons; freedom to provide services
proportionality principle:
  applications 5.035
    for legitimate interests protection 5.039, 27.003
    for national identity protection 5.041, 16.003
    for national powers protection 5.040
  exercises of EU's exclusive competence,
    proportionality requirement 5.030
  free movement restrictions, proportionality
    requirement
    free movement of capital and payments 7.106
    free movement of goods 7.034, 7.042
    free movement of persons 6.010, 6.016, 6.020
    free movement of workers and self-employed
      persons 7.074, 9.054
    freedom to provide services 7.094
  as general principle of EU law 25.024
  institutional implementation 5.042, 17.015
  proportionality concept 5.036–5.038
  role 5.034
  subsidiarity principle, relationship with 5.009,
    5.029, 5.040
**Protocol No. 36 to Lisbon Treaty on transitional
  provisions** 2.008–2.009
Protocol (No. 11) to the ECHR 1.007
Protocols annexed to Treaties 25.006

public health policy 9.055, 13.046
public interest/policy restrictions:
  on free movement of capital and
    payments 7.103–7.104
  on free movement of goods, *see* free movement of
    goods, exceptions
  on free movement of persons 6.016, 6.017
    workers and self-employed persons 7.067, 7.072
  on freedom to provide services 7.089, 7.092
  on long-term residence status of third-country
    nationals 8.012
  security-based exceptions to Treaty
    obligations 11.011
public service obligations (services of general
    economic interest) 7.098, 9.019, 9.023
public undertakings 9.019–9.020
  employees, free movement rights 7.068
publication of acts and decisions 25.026,
  27.008, 27.040
Publications Office 13.043

qualifications, mutual recognition, *see* professional
    qualifications recognition
qualified majority voting in Council 1.045, 12.046–
  12.048, 17.007–17.008, 17.033
  on advisory body appointments 13.031, 13.034
  calculation of qualified majority 1.054, 2.005,
    12.049
  on CFSP acts 3.008, 19.002
  democracy-based concerns 17.049
  enhanced cooperation, authorization
    decisions 22.010–22.011
  on international agreements 21.003
  on Member State withdrawal agreements 4.015
  on President of Commission appointments 1.054
  on suspension of Member States 4.020
  on Treaty amendments under simplified
    procedures 3.006
quantitative restrictions and measures having
    equivalent effect 7.027–7.029

race discrimination prohibition 5.060
ratification of Treaties 3.005, 3.008, 11.003, 15.002–
  15.003, 23.029–23.030
ratione personae scope of Treaties 11.001–11.002
reasoned decision-making duty 27.007
reception conditions for asylum
    seekers 8.011, 25.014
Recht auf Vergessen I & II cases (German
    Bundesverfassungsgericht) 23.029, 25.012
recommendations and opinions 5.012,
  27.042–27.043
  on economic policy 9.036, 9.039–9.040, 9.049
  on education policy 9.050
  on health policy 9.055
  on rule of law adherence 4.021, 5.005
  on trade-distorting measures 7.116
  see also decision-making
recovery of state aid 9.028

regional aid measures 9.022, 15.015
regional authorities 15.014–15.017, 18.005, 29.041
  in Belgium 5.032, 12.041, 15.003, 15.010, 18.005
regional development policies 9.057
Regulations 27.012–27.016
regulatory acts 30.011
regulatory impact assessments 17.015
religious discrimination prohibition 5.060
renewable energy, national measures restricting EU
    trade 7.041, 7.042
research and technological development policy 9.060
residence rights, *see* free movement of persons
resolutions and conclusions 27.008, 27.044, 27.046
restrictive measures decisions under
    CFSP 7.107, 10.031
revenue of EU 14.013–14.016
reverse discrimination 5.064
right to strike 9.047
rights of due process 25.008, 25.018, 25.022, 25.025
Romania, accession to EU 4.007
Rome Conventions on applicable law 8.016, 28.018
Rome Treaty 1957 (EEC Treaty) 1.014, 1.016–1.018,
  1.020, 1.026
rule of law 5.004–5.005, 30.001
  accession, rule of law conditionality 4.010
  budget, rule of law conditionality 20.009
  European Rule of Law mechanism 5.005
  judicial independence 4.021, 5.003, 5.005, 16.013,
    29.003–29.004
  separation of powers at EU institutional
    level 16.011–16.012
  serious and persistent breach of Treaties
    procedure 4.019–4.021, 5.003
rule of reason-based restraints of free movement:
  free movement of capital and
    payments 7.105–7.106
  free movement of goods (*Cassis de Dijon*
    rule) 7.037–7.042
  free movement of workers and self-employed
    persons 7.070–7.074
  freedom to provide services 7.090–7.094
rural development policy 9.007, 9.057

same-sex marriage recognition 5.060, 25.012
sanctions:
  for competition law infringements 9.016, 14.014
  economic sanctions 7.107, 10.029, 10.031, 25.014
    Kadi ruling (C-402/05 P and
      C-415/05 P) 26.002, 26.015
  for failures to fulfil obligations 12.058, 14.014,
    18.004, 29.052–29.053
  for monetary policy failures 9.040, 13.020
  and right to be heard 25.024
Schengen system 1.039, 1.047, 1.052, 8.002
  Schengen *acquis* 8.006
    Denmark, special status 1.052, 8.004, 8.006,
      8.027, 22.004
    UK and Ireland, non-application 1.039, 1.052,
      8.004, 8.006, 8.028, 22.002–22.003

Schengen Information System 1.039, 6.016, 8.006
short-term visas between Schengen states 8.007
Schuman, Robert (and Schuman Report) 1.008
seats of institutions and executive bodies 12.018, 12.071, 13.018, 13.022, 13.046, 14.019–14.020, 16.008, 28.002
secondary EU law 23.005, 27.001–27.002
  choice of instrument 27.003
  decisions 27.037–27.041
    CFSP decisions, *see* CFSP (common foreign and security policy), decision-making
  direct effect of 23.034, 27.016, 27.022–27.027, 27.041
  Directives, *see* Directives
  for implementation of EU law, *see* delegated acts; implementing acts
  interpretation tools 29.007
  non-legislative measures distinguished 27.004–27.005
  precedence of international agreements concluded by EU 26.002
  procedure for adoption, *see* legislative acts
  Regulations 27.012–27.016
  see also decision-making; primary EU law
Secretary-General of the Council 12.033, 12.055
security and defence policy 2.004, 3.007, 5.025, 10.032–10.034, 12.025
security-based exceptions to Treaty obligations 11.011
self-employed persons, free movement of, *see* free movement of workers and self-employed persons
selling arrangements, restrictive rules governing 7.043
separation of powers at EU institutional level 16.011–16.012
serious and persistent breach of Treaties procedure 4.019–4.021, 5.003, 12.025
Services Directive (2006/123/EC) 7.067, 7.071, 7.075, 7.091, 7.096–7.099
services of general economic interest 7.098, 9.019, 9.023
services provision, *see* freedom to provide services
sex-based discrimination prohibition, *see* gender-based discrimination prohibition
sexual orientation discrimination prohibition 5.058, 5.060, 6.014
shared EU and Member State competences 5.022, 5.025–5.026, 23.012
  mixed agreements 21.013–21.015, 26.006
ship registration 7.061
Simmenthal II **ruling (106/77)** 23.014–23.015, 23.017
simplified Treaty revision procedures 3.006–3.008, 3.011, 24.003
sincere cooperation principle 5.043–5.044, 16.003
  budget, application to 5.050, 20.008
  institutional balance, application to 5.050, 16.007
  international obligations, application to 26.007, 26.010
  requirements of sincere cooperation 5.045
    derogatory requirements (misuse of powers) 5.049–5.050
    supplementary requirements 5.046–5.048
  treaty negotiations, application to 5.049, 10.039
single currency 9.029, 9.031, 9.033, 9.045
  accession states, *see* Eurozone
  derogating states 9.034, 22.005
  see also economic and monetary union
Single European Act 1.041, 12.048, 24.005
  on economic and monetary union 9.031
  on economic, social, and territorial cohesion 9.057
  on EU institutions 1.033, 12.001, 17.010
  on European political cooperation 1.032, 1.041
  internal market provisions 1.041, 7.001, 7.009
single market, *see* internal market
Single Supervisory and Resolution Mechanisms 9.042
social and employment policy 9.046–9.049
  equal treatment of men and women, *see* gender-based discrimination prohibition
social assistance:
  'alarm bell' procedure for legislative acts 17.033
  and free movement of persons
    differences between Member States' rules permitted 6.019, 7.059
    undue burden rules 6.010, 6.012, 6.015
    workers and self-employed persons 7.078–7.080
  as Member State competence 9.047
social partners:
  implementation of EU law 18.006
  non-legislative procedures, role in 17.043–17.044
Social Protocol 1.052
Societas Europea company form 7.075
Solange **cases (German** *Bundesverfassungsgericht*) 23.029
solidarity clause of TFEU 9.066
Solidarity Fund 9.057
sound administration right 25.022, 25.023
sovereign debt crisis in Eurozone 9.036
Spaak, Paul-Henri (and Spaak Report) 1.013, 1.014
space programme 9.060
Spain:
  accession to EU 4.004
  official languages 14.026
  sovereign debt crisis 9.036
special legislative procedures 17.034
  Council's duty to consult European Parliament 17.035–17.036
  European Council, power to override requirement to use 3.006, 3.008, 12.025, 17.003
  European Parliament's right of veto 17.037
  legal basis determining use 5.012, 17.003
  signature and authentication 27.006
  see also legislative acts
Spitzenkandidaten **(lead candidates) process** 12.014, 12.064
sport policy 9.051

sportspersons, professional 7.051, 7.059, 7.062
stability and growth pact 9.038–9.040
staff, official, *see* civil servants and officials
state aid 9.021
   Commission supervision 9.024–9.026
   concept 9.022
   Council intervention 9.027
   recovery of unlawful aid 9.028
   services of general economic interest 7.098, 9.019, 9.023
   see also competition law and policy
statements of reasons 27.007
Strasbourg, seats of institutions and executive bodies in 12.018, 13.040, 14.019, 14.020
strike action 9.047
Structural Reform Support Programme 9.065
students, free movement rights 5.019, 5.055, 6.015, 6.020, 9.050
subsidiarity principle 5.029, 16.003, 27.017
   function 5.028
   institutional implementation 5.031, 17.015
   judicial review of compliance 5.029, 5.033
   national parliaments' role in upholding 2.004, 5.031–5.032, 15.005, 15.010, 17.006
   proportionality principle, relationship with 5.009, 5.029, 5.040
   scope 5.030
   see also competences system
subsidiary companies, freedom of establishment 7.066
succession law 8.015
sui generis **decisions** 27.038
Sunday-trading rules 7.043
supplementary competences:
   to achieve EU objectives (under flexibility clause (TFEU Art. 352)) 5.017, 5.020–5.021, 5.032, 7.108, 15.007, 15.008, 17.037
   to support, coordinate, or supplement Member State acts 5.022, 5.027, 9.059
supranational character of EU law 1.020–1.028, 2.007
supremacy of EU law, *see* primacy of EU law
Supreme Courts:
   Belgium 23.025, 29.018
   Ireland 1.041
   Poland 5.005
suspension of Treaty rights and obligations 4.019–4.021, 5.003
sustainable development 9.061, 10.021
Sweden:
   parliamentary influence on legislative acts 15.008
   refusal to adopt euro currency 9.033
Switzerland:
   judicial cooperation in civil matters 8.015
   relationship with EU 4.014
   Schengen *acquis* implementation 8.006
symbols of EU 1.060, 2.004, 6.003, 14.002

tax discrimination:
   free movement of goods context 7.021–7.023
   free movement of workers and self-employed persons context 7.059
   freedom of establishment context 7.061, 7.066
   freedom to provide services context 7.087, 7.088
   public policy/interest restrictions 7.072, 7.104, 7.106
   as state aid 9.022
technological development policy 9.060
telecommunications sector:
   liberalization 9.020
   trans-European networks 9.058, 10.037
temporal scope of Treaties:
   duration 11.004–11.005
   entry into force 11.003
territorial scope of Treaties, *see* Treaties, territorial scope
terrorism:
   EU sanctions to combat 7.107, 10.031
   PJCC policies on 1.047, 8.021
   solidarity clause of TFEU 9.066
   support for third countries combating 10.032
   terrorist financing control 7.092, 7.110, 21.012
   Trevi Group meetings on 1.037
   see also PJCC (police and judicial cooperation in criminal matters)
TEU, *see* Treaty on European Union (TEU)
TFEU, *see* Treaty on the Functioning of the European Union (TFEU)
third countries:
   actions for annulment by 30.006
   association agreements with 4.003, 8.013, 10.014–10.020, 13.043, 21.011, 26.003
   candidates for EU accession 4.010, 4.014, 10.017
   capital movements and restrictions 7.107, 10.031
   CFSP decisions respecting 10.028–10.031
   cooperation agreements with 10.008, 10.018, 21.011, 26.003
   development policy respecting, *see* development cooperation policy
   economic, financial, and technical cooperation with 10.024–10.025
   EU external border controls 8.007, 11.006
   euro currency states 9.045, 11.009
   Member States' agreements with 26.007
      concluded before Treaties entered into force or EU accession 26.008–26.011, 28.007, 28.017
   Schengen *acquis* implementation 8.006
   trade with, *see* common commercial policy
   transport to and from EU 9.009, 10.004, 10.037
   UK's future relationship with EU 4.018, 10.016
third-country nationals:
   asylum seekers 8.008–8.011, 25.014
   family members of EU citizens
      family reunification 5.060, 6.012, 6.014, 6.017, 7.055, 8.012, 11.002
      spouses, expulsion protection 6.010
   long-term visas and residence permits for 8.012
   sanctions against 7.107, 10.029, 10.031
   short-term visas for 8.007

INDEX

Treaty rights of 11.002
workers and self-employed persons 7.049, 8.013, 10.018
Tindemans, Leo 1.040
tobacco advertising 5.013, 7.113
tourism 7.109, 9.064
tourists, free movement rights 5.055, 7.085, 7.087
trade, international, *see* common commercial policy
trade unions:
collective action 9.047
collective agreements 28.005
freedom of establishment, actions restricting 7.044
non-legislative procedures, role in 17.043–17.044
trafficking in human beings, measures against 8.012, 8.021
trans-European networks 9.058, 10.037
transgender status, discrimination prohibition 5.058
Transparency Register 16.004, 27.049
transport policy 7.004, 9.009–9.011
external transport 9.009, 10.004, 10.037
trans-European networks 9.058, 10.037
transposition of Directives, *see* implementation of EU law
Treaties 23.004, 24.001, 24.004–24.005
accession treaties (and acts of accession) 4.013, 11.012, 24.002, 24.003, 24.007
amendment 2.004, 3.001, 11.008, 24.002
limitations 3.009–3.011
Member State ratification/approval requirement 3.005, 3.007, 3.008, 15.003, 16.005, 17.006
ordinary revision procedure 3.002–3.005
simplified procedures 3.006–3.008, 3.011, 24.003
Commission's guardianship role 12.058, 12.060, 18.004, 29.040
conferral of competences principle 5.009–5.010, 5.016, 5.017, 16.003; *see also* competences system
constitutional acts adopted pursuant to 24.009
declarations annexed to 24.008
direct effect of 23.033
entry into force and application 27.009
exceptions to application
security-based exceptions 11.011
transitional derogations 11.012
languages of 14.024, 29.005
personal scope 11.001–11.002
preambles 29.007
Protocols annexed to 25.006
ratification of 3.005, 3.008, 11.003, 15.002–15.003, 23.029–23.030
serious and persistent breach of 4.019–4.021, 5.003
temporal scope
duration 11.004–11.005
entry into force 11.003
territorial scope 11.006
acts with specific territorial scope 11.009
change in territorial jurisdiction 11.008
extraterritorial effects 11.010

overseas countries and territories 10.013, 11.006, 11.007, 11.008
TEU, *see* Treaty on European Union (TEU)
TFEU, *see* Treaty on the Functioning of the European Union (TFEU)
see also EU law
treaties (international), *see* international agreements concluded by EU
Treaty establishing a Constitution for Europe (draft) 1.028
background to 1.056–1.058
contents 1.059–1.060, 2.003, 2.004, 2.005, 25.007
ratification failure 1.061, 3.005
treaty interpretation rules 26.013
Treaty of Amsterdam 1997, *see* Amsterdam Treaty 1997
Treaty of Lisbon 2007, *see* Lisbon Treaty 2007
Treaty of Maastricht 1992, *see* Maastricht Treaty 1992
Treaty of Nice 2001 1.018, 1.053, 24.005
amendments to Treaties 1.054, 4.020
Treaty of Rome 1957 (EEC Treaty) 1.014, 1.016–1.018, 1.020, 1.026
Treaty on European Union (TEU) 1.001, 1.002, 2.003, 2.007, 24.004
amendment procedure, *see* Treaties, amendment
Article 2 values 4.010, 4.020, 5.002–5.004, 25.002
Article 7 suspension procedure 4.019–4.021, 5.003
Article 49, *see* accession to EU
Article 50, *see* withdrawal from EU
pre-Lisbon form, *see* Amsterdam Treaty 1997; Maastricht Treaty 1992; Nice Treaty 2001
preamble 5.003
Treaty on Stability, Coordination and Governance in the Economic and Monetary Union 2012 2.010, 9.041, 28.004
Treaty on the Functioning of the European Union (TFEU) 1.001, 1.002, 2.003, 2.007, 24.004
amendment procedure, *see* Treaties, amendment
competences system, *see* competences system
competition law chapter, *see* competition law and policy
free movement of goods rules 7.013
free movement of workers and self-employed persons rules 7.044–7.046
freedom to provide services rules 7.081
harmonization measures under Articles 114 and 115 7.112–7.116
international agreement rules, *see* international agreements concluded by EU
non-discrimination and citizenship rules, *see* citizenship of EU; equal treatment principle
solidarity clause 9.066
Turkey:
candidacy for EU accession 4.014, 10.017
Turkish workers, free movement rights 8.013, 10.018

'undertaking' concept (competition law and policy) 9.013

unfair terms in consumer contracts 9.056, 29.013
unilateral declarations 24.008, 27.044–27.045, 27.047
Union courts, *see* Court of Justice of the European Union; national courts
Union law, *see* EU law
unitary patent protection 7.109, 22.007
United Kingdom:
  Crown dependencies 11.007
  as EU Member State
    accession 1.030, 4.002, 12.048
    Charter derogations for 2.001, 2.004, 25.007
    economic and monetary union, special status 9.032, 9.035, 22.005
    PJCC, special status 2.003, 2.008, 8.028, 29.024
    primacy of EU law, incorporation in legal system 23.026
    Schengen *acquis,* non-application 1.039, 1.052, 8.004, 8.006, 8.028, 22.002
    withdrawal (Brexit) 2.004, 4.016–4.017, 11.007
  future relationship with EU 4.018, 10.016
United Nations 26.014
  judicial review in light of UN obligations 26.016
  sanctions, implementation of 10.029, 25.014
    Kadi ruling (C-402/05 P and C-415/05 P) 26.002, 26.015
'United States of Europe' initiative (Churchill) 1.004
unjust enrichment 25.024, 29.010

validity of acts, challenges against:
  actions for annulment, *see* actions for annulment
  plea of illegality 30.025, 30.033
  preliminary reference questions on 30.031–30.040
values of EU 4.010, 4.020, 5.002–5.005, 10.001, 25.002, 26.012
Van Gend & Loos **ruling (26/62)** 1.025–1.026, 18.004, 23.025, 23.031, 29.006
VAT regime 14.014, 14.015
veto power of Member States 5.012
visas and border checks policy 8.007, 11.006
vocational training policy 9.050, 9.052
voting in Council 12.045–12.046, 17.007–17.008, 17.033, 17.049
  qualified majority voting, *see* qualified majority voting in Council
voting rights of EU citizens 6.021, 12.015

welfare benefits, *see* social assistance
Western European Union 1.012
withdrawal from EU 2.004, 4.015, 11.005
  Brexit 2.004, 4.016–4.017, 11.007
  EU citizenship, effect on 6.006
workers, free movement of, *see* free movement of workers and self-employed persons
working time rules 9.047
World Trade Organization 10.009–10.011, 14.005, 26.001, 26.003, 26.005

Printed and bound by CPI Group (UK) Ltd, Croydon, CR0 4YY